Nineteenth-Century Literature Criticism

Topics Volume

Guide to Gale Literary Criticism Series

For criticism on	Consult these Gale series
Authors now living or who died after December 31, 1999	*CONTEMPORARY LITERARY CRITICISM (CLC)*
Authors who died between 1900 and 1999	*TWENTIETH-CENTURY LITERARY CRITICISM (TCLC)*
Authors who died between 1800 and 1899	*NINETEENTH-CENTURY LITERATURE CRITICISM (NCLC)*
Authors who died between 1400 and 1799	*LITERATURE CRITICISM FROM 1400 TO 1800 (LC)* *SHAKESPEAREAN CRITICISM (SC)*
Authors who died before 1400	*CLASSICAL AND MEDIEVAL LITERATURE CRITICISM (CMLC)*
Authors of books for children and young adults	*CHILDREN'S LITERATURE REVIEW (CLR)*
Dramatists	*DRAMA CRITICISM (DC)*
Poets	*POETRY CRITICISM (PC)*
Short story writers	*SHORT STORY CRITICISM (SSC)*
Literary topics and movements	*HARLEM RENAISSANCE: A GALE CRITICAL COMPANION (HR)* *THE BEAT GENERATION: A GALE CRITICAL COMPANION (BG)*
Asian American writers of the last two hundred years	*ASIAN AMERICAN LITERATURE (AAL)*
Black writers of the past two hundred years	*BLACK LITERATURE CRITICISM (BLC)* *BLACK LITERATURE CRITICISM SUPPLEMENT (BLCS)*
Hispanic writers of the late nineteenth and twentieth centuries	*HISPANIC LITERATURE CRITICISM (HLC)* *HISPANIC LITERATURE CRITICISM SUPPLEMENT (HLCS)*
Native North American writers and orators of the eighteenth, nineteenth, and twentieth centuries	*NATIVE NORTH AMERICAN LITERATURE (NNAL)*
Major authors from the Renaissance to the present	*WORLD LITERATURE CRITICISM, 1500 TO THE PRESENT (WLC)* *WORLD LITERATURE CRITICISM SUPPLEMENT (WLCS)*

ISSN 0732-1864

Volume 172

Nineteenth-Century Literature Criticism

Topics Volume

Criticism of Various
Topics in Nineteenth-Century Literature,
including Literary and Critical Movements,
Prominent Themes and Genres, Anniversary
Celebrations, and Surveys of National Literatures

Jessica Bomarito
Russel Whitaker
Project Editors

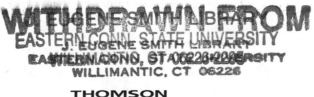
THOMSON
―――――――
GALE

Detroit • New York • San Francisco • New Haven, Conn. • Waterville, Maine • London

Nineteenth-Century Literature Criticism, Vol. 172

Project Editors
Jessica Bomarito and Russel Whitaker

Editorial
Kathy D. Darrow, Jeffrey W. Hunter, Jelena O. Krstović, Michelle Lee, Thomas J. Schoenberg, Noah Schusterbauer, Lawrence J. Trudeau

Data Capture
Frances Monroe, Gwen Tucker

Rights and Acquisitions
Margaret Abendroth, Kim Smilay, Andrew Sprecht

Imaging and Multimedia
Dean Dauphinais, Robert Duncan, Leitha Etheridge-Sims, Lezlie Light, Michael Logusz, Dan Newell, Kelly A. Quin, Denay Wilding

Composition and Electronic Capture
Tracey L. Matthews

Manufacturing
Rhonda Dover

Associate Product Manager
Marc Cormier

LIBRARY OF CONGRESS CATALOG CARD NUMBER 84-643008

ISBN-13: 978-0-7876-8656-7

ISBN-10: 0-7876-8656-5
ISSN 0732-1864

Printed in the United States of America
10 9 8 7 6 5 4 3 2 1

Contents

Preface vii

Acknowledgments xi

Literary Criticism Series Advisory Board xiii

Childhood in Nineteenth-Century Literature
Introduction .. 1
Representative Works .. 1
Overviews .. 2
Romanticism and Childhood .. 20
Childhood in the Works of William Wordsworth .. 46
Childhood in the Works of Charles Dickens .. 72
Childhood in the Works of Leo Tolstoy .. 106
Childhood in the Works of Emily Dickinson .. 129
Further Reading .. 139

Exile in Nineteenth-Century European and American Literature
Introduction .. 141
Representative Works .. 141
Overview .. 143
Exile in French Literature .. 151
Exile in British Literature .. 181
Exile in American Literature .. 202
Women and Exile .. 227
Further Reading .. 247

Urban Life in Nineteenth-Century Literature
Introduction .. 249
Representative Works .. 249
Overviews .. 250
Urban Poetry .. 277
Urban Life and Individual Identity .. 304
Further Reading .. 334

Literary Criticism Series Cumulative Author Index 337

Literary Criticism Series Cumulative Topic Index 443

NCLC Cumulative Nationality Index 457

Preface

Since its inception in 1981, *Nineteeth-Century Literature Criticism* (*NCLC*) has been a valuable resource for students and librarians seeking critical commentary on writers of this transitional period in world history. Designated an "Outstanding Reference Source" by the American Library Association with the publication of is first volume, *NCLC* has since been purchased by over 6,000 school, public, and university libraries. The series has covered more than 450 authors representing 33 nationalities and over 17,000 titles. No other reference source has surveyed the critical reaction to nineteenth-century authors and literature as thoroughly as *NCLC*.

Scope of the Series

NCLC is designed to introduce students and advanced readers to the authors of the nineteenth century and to the most significant interpretations of these authors' works. The great poets, novelists, short story writers, playwrights, and philosophers of this period are frequently studied in high school and college literature courses. By organizing and reprinting commentary written on these authors, *NCLC* helps students develop valuable insight into literary history, promotes a better understanding of the texts, and sparks ideas for papers and assignments. Each entry in *NCLC* presents a comprehensive survey of an author's career or an individual work of literature and provides the user with a multiplicity of interpretations and assessments. Such variety allows students to pursue their own interests; furthermore, it fosters an awareness that literature is dynamic and responsive to many different opinions.

Every fourth volume of *NCLC* is devoted to literary topics that cannot be covered under the author approach used in the rest of the series. Such topics include literary movements, prominent themes in nineteenth-century literature, literary reaction to political and historical events, significant eras in literary history, prominent literary anniversaries, and the literatures of cultures that are often overlooked by English-speaking readers.

NCLC continues the survey of criticism of world literature begun by Thomson Gale's *Contemporary Literary Criticism* (*CLC*) and *Twentieth-Century Literary Criticism* (*TCLC*).

Organization of the Book

An *NCLC* entry consists of the following elements:

- The **Author Heading** cites the name under which the author most commonly wrote, followed by birth and death dates. Also located here are any name variations under which an author wrote, including transliterated forms for authors whose native languages use nonroman alphabets. If the author wrote consistently under a pseudonym, the pseudonym will be listed in the author heading and the author's actual name given in parenthesis on the first line of the biographical and critical information. Uncertain birth or death dates are indicated by question marks. Single-work entries are preceded by a heading that consists of the most common form of the title in English translation (if applicable) and the original date of composition.

- The **Introduction** contains background information that introduces the reader to the author, work, or topic that is the subject of the entry.

- The list of **Principal Works** is ordered chronologically by date of first publication and lists the most important works by the author. The genre and publication date of each work is given. In the case of foreign authors whose works have been translated into English, the list will focus primarily on twentieth-century translations, selecting those works most commonly considered the best by critics. Unless otherwise indicated, dramas are dated by first performance, not first publication. Lists of **Representative Works** by different authors appear with topic entries.

- Reprinted **Criticism** is arranged chronologically in each entry to provide a useful perspective on changes in critical evaluation over time. The critic's name and the date of composition or publication of the critical work are given at the beginning of each piece of criticism. Unsigned criticism is preceded by the title of the source in which it appeared. All titles by the author featured in the text are printed in boldface type. Footnotes are reprinted at the end of each essay or excerpt. In the case of excerpted criticism, only those footnotes that pertain to the excerpted texts are included. Criticism in topic entries is arranged chronologically under a variety of subheadings to facilitate the study of different aspects of the topic.

- A complete **Bibliographical Citation** of the original essay or book precedes each piece of criticism.

- Critical essays are prefaced by brief **Annotations** explicating each piece.

- An annotated bibliography of **Further Reading** appears at the end of each entry and suggests resources for additional study. In some cases, significant essays for which the editors could not obtain reprint rights are included here. Boxed material following the further reading list provides references to other biographical and critical sources on the author in series published by Thomson Gale.

Indexes

Each volume of *NCLC* contains a **Cumulative Author Index** listing all authors who have appeared in a wide variety of reference sources published by Thomson Gale, including *NCLC*. A complete list of these sources is found facing the first page of the Author Index. The index also includes birth and death dates and cross references between pseudonyms and actual names.

A **Cumulative Nationality Index** lists all authors featured in *NCLC* by nationality, followed by the number of the *NCLC* volume in which their entry appears.

A **Cumulative Topic Index** lists the literary themes and topics treated in the series as well as in *Classical and Medieval Literature Criticism, Literature Criticism from 1400 to 1800, Twentieth-Century Literary Criticism,* and the *Contemporary Literary Criticism* Yearbook, which was discontinued in 1998.

An alphabetical **Title Index** accompanies each volume of *NCLC*, with the exception of the Topics volumes. Listings of titles by authors covered in the given volume are followed by the author's name and the corresponding page numbers where the titles are discussed. English translations of foreign titles and variations of titles are cross-referenced to the title under which a work was originally published. Titles of novels, dramas, nonfiction books, and poetry, short story, or essay collections are printed in italics, while individual poems, short stories, and essays are printed in roman type within quotation marks.

In response to numerous suggestions from librarians, Thomson Gale also produces an annual paperbound edition of the *NCLC* cumulative title index. This annual cumulation, which alphabetically lists all titles reviewed in the series, is available to all customers. Additional copies of this index are available upon request. Librarians and patrons will welcome this separate index; it saves shelf space, is easy to use, and is recyclable upon receipt of the next edition.

Citing *Nineteenth-Century Literature Criticism*

When citing criticism reprinted in the Literary Criticism Series, students should provide complete bibliographic information so that the cited essay can be located in the original print or electronic source. Students who quote directly from reprinted criticism may use any accepted bibliographic format, such as University of Chicago Press style or Modern Language Association style.

The examples below follow recommendations for preparing a bibliography set forth in *The Chicago Manual of Style,* 14th ed. (Chicago: The University of Chicago Press, 1993); the first example pertains to material drawn from periodicals, the second to material reprinted from books:

Franklin, J. Jeffrey. "The Victorian Discourse of Gambling: Speculations on *Middlemarch* and *The Duke's Children.*" *ELH* 61, no. 4 (winter 1994): 899-921. Reprinted in *Nineteenth-Century Literature Criticism.* Vol. 168, edited by Jessica Bomarito and Russel Whitaker, 39-51. Detroit: Thomson Gale, 2006.

Frank, Joseph. *"The Gambler*: A Study in Ethnopsychology." In *Freedom and Responsibility in Russian Literature: Essays in Honor of Robert Louis Jackson,* edited by Elizabeth Cheresh Allen and Gary Saul Morson, 69-85. Evanston, Ill.: Northwestern University Press, 1995. Reprinted in *Nineteenth-Century Literature Criticism.* Vol. 168, edited by Jessica Bomarito and Russel Whitaker, 75-84. Detroit: Thomson Gale, 2006.

The examples below follow recommendations for preparing a works cited list set forth in the *MLA Handbook for Writers of Research Papers,* 6th ed. (New York: The Modern Language Association of America, 2003); the first example pertains to material drawn from periodicals, the second to material reprinted from books:

Franklin, J. Jeffrey. "The Victorian Discourse of Gambling: Speculations on *Middlemarch* and *The Duke's Children.*" *ELH* 61.4 (Winter 1994): 899-921. Reprinted in *Nineteenth-Century Literature Criticism.* Eds. Jessica Bomarito and Russel Whitaker. Vol. 168. Detroit: Thomson Gale, 2006. 39-51.

Frank, Joseph. *"The Gambler*: A Study in Ethnopsychology." *Freedom and Responsibility in Russian Literature: Essays in Honor of Robert Louis Jackson.* Eds. Elizabeth Cheresh Allen and Gary Saul Morson. Evanston, Ill.: Northwestern University Press, 1995. 69-85. Reprinted in *Nineteenth-Century Literature Criticism.* Eds. Jessica Bomarito and Russel Whitaker. Vol. 168. Detroit: Thomson Gale, 2006. 75-84.

Suggestions are Welcome

Readers who wish to suggest new features, topics, or authors to appear in future volumes, or who have other suggestions or comments are cordially invited to call, write, or fax the Associate Product Manager:

Associate Product Manager, Literary Criticism Series
Thomson Gale
27500 Drake Road
Farmington Hills, MI 48331-3535
1-800-347-4253 (GALE)
Fax: 248-699-8054

Acknowledgments

The editors wish to thank the copyright holders of the criticism included in this volume and the permissions managers of many book and magazine publishing companies for assisting us in securing reproduction rights. Following is a list of the copyright holders who have granted us permission to reproduce material in this volume of *NCLC*. Every effort has been made to trace copyright, but if omissions have been made, please let us know.

COPYRIGHTED MATERIAL IN *NCLC*, VOLUME 172, WAS REPRODUCED FROM THE FOLLOWING PERIODICALS:

American Transcendental Quarterly, v. 44, fall, 1979. Copyright © 1979 by The University of Rhode Island. Reproduced by permission.—*The Arnoldian,* v. 11, spring, 1984. Reproduced by permission.—*Cahiers Victoriens et Edouardiens,* April, 2000. Reproduced by permission.—*The Charles Lamb Bulletin,* October, 1996; October, 2000. Copyright © The Charles Lamb Society and the contributors 1996, 2000. All rights reserved. All reproduced by permission.—*Comparative Literature,* v. 30, spring, 1978 for "City Life and the Novel: Hugo, Ainsworth, Dickens" by Richard Maxwell. Copyright © 1978 by University of Oregon. Reproduced by permission of the author.—*The Critical Review,* 1981. Reproduced by permission.—*Dickens Studies Annual,* v. 16, 1987. Copyright © 1987 by AMS Press, Inc. All rights reserved. Reproduced by permission.—*Dickinson Studies,* June, 1984 for "The Adult Voice in Dickinson's Child Poems" by David Lloyd. Copyright © 1984 David Lloyd. Reproduced by permission of the author.—*differences: A Journal of Feminist Cultural Studies,* v. 7, summer, 1995. Copyright, 1995, Brown University and *differences: A Journal of Feminist Cultural Studies.* All rights reserved. Used by permission of the publisher.—*ELH,* v. 37, September, 1970. Copyright © 1970 The Johns Hopkins University Press. Reproduced by permission.—*English Studies,* v. 64, 1983. Copyright © 1983, Swets & Zeitlinger. Reproduced by permission.—*Essays in Literature,* v. 16, fall, 1989. Copyright 1989 by Western Illinois University. Reproduced by permission.—*The French Review,* v. 51, December, 1977. Copyright © 1977 by the American Association of Teachers of French. Reproduced by permission.—*History of European Ideas,* v. 17, July, 1993. Copyright © 1993 Pergamon Press Ltd. Reproduced with permission from Elsevier.—*Interpretation: A Journal of Political Philosophy,* v. 22, fall, 1994 for "The Wisdom of Exile: Edward Everett Hale's 'The Man without a Country'" by Colin D. Pearce. Copyright © 1994 *Interpretation.* Reproduced by permission of the publisher and the author.—*Legacy: A Journal of American Women Writers,* v. 3, fall, 1986. Copyright © 1987 by Legacy, A Journal, Inc. All rights reserved. Reproduced by permission of the University of Nebraska Press.—*Nineteenth-Century Contexts,* v. 21, 1999 for "Romanticism and the End of Childhood" by Alan Richardson. Copyright © 1999 OPA (Overseas Publishers Association) N.V. Reproduced by permission of Taylor & Francis, Ltd., http//:www.tandf.co.uk/journals, and the author.—*Nineteenth-Century French Studies,* v. 22, fall-winter, 1993-94. Copyright © 1993 by *Nineteenth-Century French Studies.* Reproduced by permission.—*Prose Studies,* v. 3, December, 1980 for "Nineteenth-Century Urban Sketches: Thresholds of Fiction" by Carol L. Bernstein. Reproduced by permission of Taylor & Francis, Ltd., http//:www.tandf.co.uk/journals, and the author.—*Stanford French Review,* v. 9, spring, 1985 for "Urban Mallarmé" by Robert Greer Cohn. Copyright © 1985 by ANMA Libri and Department of French & Italian, Stanford University. All rights reserved. Reproduced by permission of the publisher and the author.—*Studies in English Literature, 1500-1900,* v. 18, 1968; v. 41, autumn, 2001. Copyright © 1968, 2001 The Johns Hopkins University Press. All reproduced by permission.—*Studies in Romanticism,* v. 42, spring, 2003. Copyright 2003 by the Trustees of Boston University. Reproduced by permission.—*Tennessee Studies in Literature,* v. 27, 1984 for "On the Enrichment of Poor Monkeys by Myth and Dream; or, How Dickens Rousseauisticized and Pre-Freudianized Victorian Views of Childhood" by Mark Spilka. Reproduced by permission of the Literary Estate of the author.—*Victorian Poetry,* v. 22, spring, 1984 for "Learning to Read The City" by William Sharpe. Copyright © West Virginia University, 1982. Reproduced by permission of the author.—*Yearbook of English Studies,* v. 32, 2002. Copyright © Modern Humanities Research Association 2002. Reproduced by permission of the publisher.

COPYRIGHTED MATERIAL IN *NCLC,* VOLUME 172, WAS REPRODUCED FROM THE FOLLOWING BOOKS:

Andrews, Malcolm. From "The Idea of Childhood: A Genealogy," in *Dickens and the Grown-up Child.* University of Iowa Press, 1994. Copyright © 1994 by Malcolm Andrews. All rights reserved. Reproduced by permission of the author.—Crispin, Lucy. From "Living in Exile: Self-Image, Social Role and the Problem of Identity," in *A Garland for Gissing.* Ed-

Thomson Gale Literature Product Advisory Board

The members of the Thomson Gale Literature Product Advisory Board—reference librarians from public and academic library systems—represent a cross-section of our customer base and offer a variety of informed perspectives on both the presentation and content of our literature products. Advisory board members assess and define such quality issues as the relevance, currency, and usefulness of the author coverage, critical content, and literary topics included in our series; evaluate the layout, presentation, and general quality of our printed volumes; provide feedback on the criteria used for selecting authors and topics covered in our series; provide suggestions for potential enhancements to our series; identify any gaps in our coverage of authors or literary topics, recommending authors or topics for inclusion; analyze the appropriateness of our content and presentation for various user audiences, such as high school students, undergraduates, graduate students, librarians, and educators; and offer feedback on any proposed changes/enhancements to our series. We wish to thank the following advisors for their advice throughout the year.

Childhood in Nineteenth-Century Literature

The following entry contains critical commentary on the treatment of childhood in nineteenth-century literature.

INTRODUCTION

The novel *Émile* (1762), an educational treatise written by French Enlightenment scholar Jean-Jacques Rousseau, holds that the goal of education should be to preserve a child's "natural," perfect state. This work was widely read by important German and English Romantic writers who applied these same principles to their own writings and exerted a profound influence on Victorian conceptions of childhood and education. In various works, including Maria Edgeworth's *Moral Tales for Young People* (1801), Charlotte Brontë's *Jane Eyre* (1847), William Wordsworth's *The Prelude* (1850), and Thomas Hughes's *Tom Brown's School Days* (1857), childhood is represented as an ideal state of being. Such works reject the ideas advanced by evangelical writers such as Sarah Trimmer, Mary Margaret Sherwood, and Hannah More, who maintained that children require constant, strict guidance and moral training informed by the Bible and religious traditions. Children are instead viewed as possessing a uniquely informed, accurate view of the world that adults would do well to understand, and as practitioners of an approach to life that adults should emulate. Numerous nineteenth-century writers draw favorable comparisons between adherents of such artistic and political movements as Romanticism and the French Revolution and children possessed of truths about the meaning of life. Many critics have examined Charles Dickens's treatment of childhood in his works, noting how the writer both remarks and expands upon the views offered by Rousseau and Wordsworth and anticipates the work of Sigmund Freud. Leo Tolstoy's works have been similarly analyzed by commentators, who have explored how the author's representation of children and childhood in his works was affected by his personal experiences, as well as by the aesthetics and scholarship of his time. Tolstoy's novel *Detstvo* (1852; *Childhood*) describes a young boy's emotional growing pains, inner conflicts, and his relationships with adults around him. In the novel, which was praised in Russian literary circles, Tolstoy offers support for Rousseau's educational ideas, asserting that children already possess the truth about life and sense what is important, but that their senses can be distorted easily by education and society. Critics have noted

Emily Dickinson's portrayals of children in her poetry as innovative in that the author presents child narrators with adult sensibilities, capable of expressing the wisdom of which children are believed to be uniquely possessed. In general, commentators have maintained that the Victorian literary preoccupation with the concept of idealized childhood, like the use of the imagery of the beauty and virtue of the natural world lost to the blight and evil brought by industrial and urban expansion, is part of the larger nineteenth-century quest to define humanity and morality within a rapidly changing world.

REPRESENTATIVE WORKS

Charlotte Brontë
Jane Eyre. An Autobiography [as Currer Bell] (novel) 1847

Thomas Day
The History of Sandford and Merton: A Work Intended for the Use of Children. 3 vols. (short stories) 1783-89

Charles Dickens
Sketches by Boz, Illustrative of Every-Day Life and Every-Day People [as Boz] (sketches and short stories) 1836
Posthumous Papers of the Pickwick Club [as Boz] (novel) 1837
Oliver Twist (novel) 1838
The Old Curiosity Shop (novel) 1841
A Christmas Carol in Prose (short story) 1843
Dealings with the Firm of Dombey and Son (novel) 1848
The Personal History of David Copperfield (novel) 1850
Hard Times for These Times (novel) 1854
Little Dorrit (novel) 1857
Great Expectations (novel) 1861
The Uncommercial Traveller (sketches and short stories) 1861

Maria Edgeworth
Practical Education [with Richard Lovell Edgeworth] (essays) 1798; also published as *Essays on Education,* 1815
Moral Tales for Young People (short stories) 1801

George Eliot
The Mill on the Floss (novel) 1860

Thomas Hughes
Tom Brown's School Days [published anonymously]
(short stories) 1857; also published as *Schooldays at
Rugby*, 1857

Charles Kingsley
The Water-Babies: A Fairy Tale for a Land-Baby (novel)
1863

Hannah More
Strictures on the Modern System of Female Education.
2 vols. (essays) 1799

Jean-Jacques Rousseau
Émile, ou de l'education. 4 vols. [*Émile, or On Educa-
tion*] (novel) 1762

Mary Margaret Sherwood
†*The History of the Fairchild Family; or, The Child's
Manual: Being a Collection of Stories Calculated to
Shew the Importance and Effects of a Religious Edu-
cation* (short stories) 1818, 1842, and 1847

Catherine Sinclair
Holiday House; a Series of Tales (short stories) 1839;
also published as *Holiday House: A Book for the
Young*

Leo Tolstoy
Detstvo [*Childhood*] (novel) 1852; first published in the
journal *Sovremennik*
Voini i mir. 6 vols. [*War and Peace*] (novel) 1863-69

Sarah Trimmer
*The Guardian of Education, a Periodical Work; Con-
sisting of a Practical Essay on Christian Education,
Founded Immediately in the Scriptures, and the Sa-
cred Offices of the Church of England: Memoirs of
Modern Philosophers, and Extracts from Their writ-
ings; Extracts from Sermons and other Books Relat-
ing to Religious Education and a Copious Examina-
tion of Modern Systems of Education* [founder and
editor] (periodical) 1802-06

Mark Twain
The Adventures of Huckleberry Finn (novel) 1884

William Wordsworth
The White Doe of Rylstone; or, The Fate of the Nortons
(poetry) 1815
*The Prelude; or, Growth of a Poet's Mind, An Autobio-
graphical Poem* (poetry) 1850
The Recluse (unfinished poem) 1888

*All of Dickens's novels were originally published serially in magazines,
usually over periods of one to two years.

†This collection was published in three parts.

OVERVIEWS

Roselee Robison (essay date 1983)

SOURCE: Robison, Roselee. "Victorians, Children, and
Play." *English Studies* 64, no. 4 (1983): 318-29.

[*In the following essay, Robison surveys Victorian con-
ceptions—derived from the educational theories of the
Enlightenment—of childhood, education, and play.*]

> 'I am tired,' said Miss Havisham. 'I want diversion,
> and I have done with men and women. Play.'
>
> I think it will be conceded by my most disputatious
> reader that she could hardly have directed an unfortu-
> nate boy to do anything in the wide world more diffi-
> cult to be done under the circumstances.
>
> (*Great Expectations*, Ch. 8)

Miss Havisham's command might well have bewildered
a stronger head than Pip's. Generations of educational
theorists, from Rousseau and the Edgeworths to Froebel
and Piaget, have attempted to define play and its role in
the child's emotional, intellectual, and social develop-
ment. Pip's inability to oblige Miss Havisham—'I can't
play just now'—suggests the mysterious character of
this activity. An elusive amalgam of spontaneity and de-
light, play is like creativity in that it can neither be
willed nor precisely defined. The kinds of play in which
Victorian children were permitted (or not permitted) to
indulge is not only a fascinating study in itself, but it il-
luminates the ambivalence and inconsistency which
marked the thinking of the age.

Victorian ideas regarding children, learning, and play
were grounded in the educational theories which
emerged in connection with the Enlightenment. As his-
torians have shown, both leisure and education during
the early stages of the Industrial Revolution were deter-
mined by class, with the result that innumerable chil-
dren were untouched by the theorizing of which child-
hood was the subject. Against the hypothetical children
of the educational treatises must be set the masses of
'crooked alphabets' fabricated by the industrial system.[1]
On paper, however, the eighteenth-century child was a
favoured being, his needs, wants, and propensities the
subject of painstaking deliberation. In England, this
philosophical inquiry into the nature and purpose of
education was advanced by four theorists whose influ-
ence was to persist well into the Victorian period: Rich-

ard and Maria Edgeworth; Thomas Day; and Wordsworth. Each of these was in turn profoundly influenced by the most famous of all educational treatises, Rousseau's *Emile.*

Emile (1762) is based upon the revolutionary premise that a child cannot be inoculated with knowledge; he will genuinely learn only what he himself experiences. 'Let him know something not because you told it to him but because he has understood it himself'.[2] Rousseau's model pupil is intellectually a miniature Robinson Crusoe, accepting nothing on hearsay; guided but never coerced by his judicious tutor. It was this aspect of Rousseau's thought, rather than his insistence upon the child's primordial innocence, which the Edgeworths found so attractive. In both their formal educational treatise, *Practical Education* (1798) and the stories which Maria wrote to illustrate it, play is one of the chief means by which Rousseau's empirical approach to learning is implemented. Long before the advent of Froebel and his kindergarten, the Edgeworths had grasped the paradox that play to a child is often deeply serious. Far from being frivolous, his toys and pastimes are thus potent agents of instruction. One of Maria's *Moral Tales for Young People* (1801), 'The Good French Governess', contains a remarkable anticipation of Froebel's concept of educational playthings. In this story, the wise and gentle Madame de Rosier takes her English pupils to a 'rational toyshop'. Upon entering the store, the children are disappointed because they see none of the toys to which they have been accustomed—whips, coaches and horses, dolls, soldiers and drums. Under the tactful guidance of Madame de Rosier, however, they find themselves intrigued by toys which present challenges (Maria Edgeworth's word is 'difficulties')—miniature gardening-tools, a tiny printing-press, an inflatable silk globe, a replica of Priestley's biographical chart, a box of model furniture, kits containing materials for weaving baskets and ribbons. So absorbed do the children become in these purchases that they even engage the interest of their indolent and frivolous mother. Young Herbert in particular benefits from this novel mode of instruction: heretofore almost illiterate, he learns to read so that he may operate his printing-press. Because playing with such toys draws upon the same energies as are exacted by learning, work and play become indistinguishable. In the Edgeworths' educational philosophy, play is 'nothing but a change of employment',[3] a continual succession of challenges and discoveries.[4]

Thomas Day was the friend and colleague of Richard Edgeworth; and in *The History of Sandford and Merton* (1783-9), he dramatizes an educational method which closely resembles that advanced in *Practical Education* and its attendant stories. Guided by their tutor, the intrepid Mr. Barlow, Tommy Merton and Harry Sandford, like the Harcourt children of 'The Good French

Governess', learn a great deal while they are ostensibly playing or being amused. In planting and tending a garden, they learn the principles of agriculture; a conjurer's manipulation of a toy swan introduces them to astronomy; and in building a house, they discover the concept of leverage. This latter activity, which 'fill[s] Tommy's heart with pleasure', is particularly illustrative of the manner in which play can abet instruction. But in Day's philosophy of education, no activity, however pleasurable, can be an end in itself. Mr. Barlow's gratingly didactic voice is never silenced. With ruthless precision, he explains that the will-o'the-wisp is a gaseous emanation; the conjurer's innocent swan, nothing more than a magnetized needle in a lump of wax. This unrelenting purposiveness, later to be deplored by Dickens, reveals the limitations of 'practical education'.

In certain respects, the pragmatists of the Enlightenment were not without insight into the child's needs and capabilities. Acknowledging that both memory and the attention span are necessarily undeveloped in children, the Edgeworths condemn the contemporary practice of forcing them to recite by rote facts of which they have no comprehension. Moreover, unlike the Victorians, who felt that children should be seen and not heard, the Edgeworths believed that children should be encouraged to 'partake of the pleasures of society', expressing their ideas and opinions without fear of ridicule. ('. . . Nor should they be condemned to sit stock still, holding up their heads and letting their feet dangle from chairs that are too high for them'.)[5] But the Edgeworths' ideal of social intercourse, with children and grownups engaged in a mutually civilizing dialogue, rests upon the assumption that a child is a fundamentally rational being. From their point of view, neither sentiment nor the imagination has any place in the process of learning. Any penchant for reverie or 'castle-building' must be checked by rigorous application to some 'novel employment'. To the Edgeworths, a toy is always an educational tool; it is never perceived as the focus of emotions and associations. In their enthronement of reason, they took no account of the feelings which can disrupt the course of learning.

Emile underlies Romantic as well as pragmatic beliefs concerning education and the nature of the child. Of Rousseau's two designated masters of human nature, 'experience and sentiment',[6] the pragmatists emphasized the first, Wordsworth the second. *The Prelude,* which he began to compose in 1799, can be read as educational philosophy as well as a study of the poetic imagination. Like the Edgeworths and Thomas Day, Wordsworth was intrigued by the relationship between play and the growth of the child's mental and moral nature. The opening books of *The Prelude* contain numerous vivid recollections of the poet's games and diversions in childhood: beginning with the vignette of the 'five years' child' bathing in the Derwent, Wordsworth

recalls ice-skating in the moonlight; flying a kite; playing card games or tic-tac-toe by the fire; picnicking on 'the cool green ground'.[7] For Wordsworth as for the Edgeworths, none of the child's pastimes are trivial. But for the pragmatists, such diversions are significant only because they are potential vehicles of instruction. 'It is surprising how much children may learn from their playthings . . . and when the habit of reflection and observation is associated with the ideas of amusement and happiness'.[8] To Wordsworth, on the other hand, the pastimes of his childhood are memorable solely for themselves; each is a manifestation of the mysterious 'joy' which reverberates throughout *The Prelude* and which contrasts so sharply with the Edgeworths' rational delight. Moreover, in the education of the poet, a tutor is conspicuously absent. No governess or Mr. Barlow, however well-intentioned, can reduce the poet's universe to an inflatable globe or an astronomical chart.

The Victorians were no less preoccupied than the Romantics and the theorists of the Enlightenment with the nature of childhood and the child's place in the social order. Their concern, however, took the form of social legislation rather than philosophical inquiry. In certain respects, the social position of the child underwent a major improvement during the course of the nineteenth century. If children were not, in Blake's phrase, 'born for joy', at least they were not born to be maimed by the abuses of industrialism and subsequently punished for their deformity. Lord Shaftesbury's reforms, which restricted both the age at which a child could be set to work and the number of hours which could be exacted of him, were followed, albeit much later, by judicial decisions establishing special procedures for juvenile offenders.[9] Its social consequences apart, such legislation acknowledged that the capabilities and impulses of children differ radically from those of adults. This awareness was also marked by the production of inexpensive toys (a working-class child could have purchased nothing in Maria Edgeworth's 'rational toyshop') and of a literature designed specifically for children. In *Practical Education*, the Edgeworths complain that one of their greatest impediments as teachers is the dearth of books 'fit for children to read'.[10] The abundance of children's books which emerged during the nineteenth century remedied this deficiency; and although most of them were overtly didactic (prompting Charles Lamb's outburst against 'the cursed Barbauld crew'[11]), their mere existence was a tacit admission that children and adults could not be entertained in the same manner. Yet none of these innovations appear to have altered the fundamentally unimaginative view of children which the Victorians inherited from writers such as Day and the Edgeworths. Late in the nineteenth century, Alice Meynell, herself a parent and an educator, remarked that no one in her generation really cared what children thought. How was it, she asked, that people so morbidly sensi-

tive to the opinions of others 'should care nothing for the opinion of children because it was disguised in the manners they were compelled to wear?'[12]

As Mrs. Meynell's query suggests, the Victorians, like the eighteenth-century pragmatists, tended to visualize children as miniature adults. Alison Mager's innovative *Children of the Past,* a collection of 165 photographic portraits of Victorian children, is a gallery of wooden little beings, their stiffness no less the result of their down-scaled adult attire than of the limitations of nineteenth-century photography. One hapless three-year-old is even posed with a pipe and pince-nez, his feet dangling incongruously above the rungs of the chair in which he is 'reading' a newspaper.[13] If such portraits inadvertently parody adult behaviour, they also demonstrate the contemporary indifference to genuinely childish postures and gestures. In Victorian literature, this grotesque vision of children as tiny adults is nowhere better exemplified than in Dickens' Christmas story for 1853, 'The Holly Tree'. Later adapted for one of his most popular readings, 'Boots at the Holly-Tree Inn', this story describes the elopement of two young cousins, Norah and Harry Walmers. The children are finally retrieved by their guardians, but not before their solemn game of being affianced lovers has delighted all the adults privileged to witness it ('They was seven deep at the key-hole'.) In running away to Gretna Green, however, Norah and Harry are not really playing the immemorial children's game of 'Let's pretend we're married', any more than the children in Mager's collection are playing dress-up. Rather, they are enacting roles which the adult world, not they themselves, finds entertaining. Dickens' studies in genuine 'premature maturity'— children whom poverty has forced into adulthood—bear no resemblance to the little lovers of 'The Holly Tree'.

From their eighteenth-century predecessors, the Victorians inherited not only the tendency to view children as miniature adults, but a profound abhorrence of the spoilt or petted child. *Sandford and Merton* opens with a memorable picture of the unregenerate young Harry Sandford: '. . . When his father and mother were sitting at the tea-table with their friends, instead of waiting till they were at leisure to attend him, he would scramble upon the table, seize the cake and bread and butter, and frequently overset the teacups . . .'[14] In Victorian eyes, an unhappy or even a sick child was preferable to such a monstrosity.[15] The fears underlying this attitude are complex. Not only did the spoilt child reverse the appropriate relationship between grown-ups and children, but he disrupted the smooth flow of the amenities. Perhaps most significantly, the spoilt child, 'capricious, tyrannical, passionate, peevish, sullen, and selfish',[16] was irrefutable evidence of man's fallen nature.

Even as Wordsworth and the Romantics were proclaiming the child's kinship with the beauty and innocence of

the natural world, the evangelicals[17] were insisting that children no less than adults were the heirs of original sin. In her widely-read *Strictures on the Modern System of Female Education* (1799), Mrs. Hannah More declared that those who believed in 'the innocence and dignity of man' were deceiving themselves.[18] As Ian Bradley has pointed out, one of the most influential ideological developments of the nineteenth century, occurring near its beginning, was this resurgence of the puritan spirit.[19] Leaving untouched almost no aspect of Victorian life, the evangelicals exerted a particularly decisive effect upon education and play. In the first instance, their preoccupation with the imminence of man's latter end engendered an obsession with time. Discounting Rousseau's contention that the happy child does not take clock-making seriously,[20] eighteenth-century educators had devoted considerable attention to the role played by time in the process of learning. For theorists such as the Edgeworths', the waste of time was an evil primarily because it led to ennui and thence unhappiness. Maria Edgeworth's 'Lazy Lawrence' is a bored and wretched child rather than a delinquent. For the evangelicals, on the other hand, the waste of time was a sin, wilful disobedience to God's express commands. Notably absent in the educational writings of the Edgeworths are those dreary school time-tables which specify the hours to be devoted to study, meals, rest, and play.[21] As we have seen, the Edgeworths' made no sharp distinction between work and play; for them, the two forms of activity were corollaries rather than opposites. To the evangelicals, however, one was the antithesis of the other. 'Yes!' exclaims Mrs. More, 'it is a few short but keen and lively intervals of animated pleasure, snatched from between the successive labours and duties of a busy day . . . which, both to men and to children, yield the truest portion of enjoyment . . .'[22]

What did the evangelicals comprehend by the morsels of pleasure which could thus profitably be sandwiched between stints of labour and effort? Their primary criteria were that such pleasures be 'simple' and that they enhance, no matter how tenuously, the knowledge of God's will. Diversions which were exotic or contrived could only exacerbate man's innate depravity, awakening sensibilities better left dormant and stirring up 'hidden fires'.[23] These standards disqualified not only the Edgeworths' creative playthings, but almost any activity contingent upon the exercise of the imagination: hence, works of fiction and most games. As a means of recreating children fatigued by the long Sabbath, Mrs. More suggests that they be set to selecting and concatenating biblical texts illustrative of specified prayers. Even such dubious diversions required rigorous supervision. In their belief that the corruption of children was as virulent and contagious as measles, evangelical parents often isolated them from one another, hand-picking their companions and engaging suitably pious tutors rather than sending them to public school.[24] The

modern belief that children learn to understand both themselves and other people through play would have struck the evangelical mind as preposterous. As the abundance of autobiographies and memoirs produced during the period shows, what determined the character of the Victorian child's play was less the social and intellectual standing of his family than its religious bias.

Autobiography in the service of cultural history is subject to certain limitations. The experiences and events which it records are necessarily distorted, not only by the writer's distance from his past, but by the conventions exacted by a literary form no less sophisticated than the novel. The themes of unhappiness, loneliness, and privation are among the most persistent of these conventions.[25] Nonetheless, the difference between the experiences of autobiographers who fell under the evangelical aegis and those who did not is arresting. This difference in the very tone of the writing suggests that evangelicals had more difficulty than most Victorians in perceiving any relationship between learning and play and in appreciating the role of play in a child's emotional and social development.

Augustus J. C. Hare's *The Story of My Life* (1896-1900), Ruskin's *Praeterita* (1885-89), and Edmund Gosse's *Father and Son* (1907) all portray the antipathy between evangelical thought and the spontaneity, imaginative vitality, and sense of personal worth which lie at the heart of play. When Hare was five years old, his adoptive mother perceived in him the not uncommon infantile traits of 'reference of everything to himself, [and] greediness of pleasures'.[26] Determined to root out this nascent individualism, she relegated his toys to the attic. With similar intentions, Hare's odious Aunt Esther wanted to remove some of the drawers from a favourite little bookcase so that the boy might 'never have the feeling that the cabinet was wholly mine'.[27] Often forbidden to do '*anything*', a dispensation strangely at odds with the evangelicals' professed abhorrence of idleness, Hare nevertheless cultivated both his imagination and his sense of self by diversions which his mentors did not recognize as such. He talked with the flowers in the garden; drew on every scrap of paper he could find; pored over the 'enchanting woodcuts' in his grandmother's travel-books. The Edgeworthian harmony between learning and pleasure was shattered, Hare snatching his amusements only when he was not 'undergoing education of some kind, and generally of an unwelcome kind'.[28]

Ruskin and Gosse were subjected to a similarly harsh regime, and they resisted the starkness of their lives in a similar manner, by devising amusements so subtle that they went unnoticed. Margaret Ruskin's immediate confiscation of the Punch-and-Judy presented to her son on his birthday is one of the best-known parental outrages in Victorian literature. Prohibiting even the wish

for 'such things as one saw in toy shops', she allowed him a bunch of keys, a ball, a cart, and two boxes of wooden bricks, a spartan collection even by the Edgeworths' standards. When these resources failed him, Ruskin learnt to amuse himself by comparing the colours in his carpet; counting the knot-holes in the floor; and later, producing tiny imitations of his favourite books, drawing type 'as other children draw dogs and horses'.[29] The spirit of levity was even more sternly outlawed in the Gosse household than in the rectory of Hare's uncle Julius and the cloistered garden at Herne Hill. By the terms of his parents' rigorous Plymouth Brethren code, Gosse was forbidden not only toys—the 'drums and flutes and kites and coloured balls' vended in the streets of his Devonshire village—but all books which were not strictly factual. His sole diversions as a small boy were watching the fauna in his father's aquaria and reading the Penny Cyclopedia. Almost stupefied with ennui, he devised for himself a highly creative form of educational play, writing imitations of Philip Gosse's scientific monographs and illustrating them with brightly-coloured creatures of his own invention.[30] When this absorbing pursuit attracted the elder Gosse's notice, it was transformed from play into drudgery. Beneath his father's attempt to teach him to draw, Edmund's joy in his efforts vanished. 'In deep depression of spirits', he could produce nothing but a laboured facsimile of the exquisite drawing given him as a model.

By inventing playthings and diversions for themselves, Hare, Ruskin, and Gosse ironically fostered the very imaginative vitality which their parents sought to suppress. In supplying the components of what modern educators call 'socio-dramatic play'—the games and fantasies which develop the social sense as well as the imagination—they were less successful. The tonal sombreness which broods over *The Story of My Life, Praeterita,* and *Father and Son* arises less from the authors' lack of playthings than of playmates. Young Hare's timid request to play with the neighbourhood children was 'so punished that I never dared to express a wish to play with any child again'. At the same time, he was compelled to play with his cousin Marcus, a malicious child whom he detested. The parents of Ruskin and of Gosse were equally unrelenting in preserving their sons from the contamination of the unregenerate. Dimly aware of John's desolation within the cherished family circle, Mr. and Mrs. Ruskin carefully selected a playmate for him, a decorous boy who exemplified the 'proprieties, true religions, and useful learnings' of their own home.[31] At the age of ten, Edmund Gosse was at last allowed to associate with another child of his own age. But this unexpected indulgence proved less gratifying than might have been expected. Given the run of the garden, Gosse and his new companion walked about, shook the bushes, and climbed along the wall—'that was almost all we ever did do'.[32] Their inertness is revealing. Having been forbidden to play as small chil-

dren, Hare, Ruskin and Gosse found themselves largely incapable of diversion as they approached adolescence. Devoid of the self-confidence which play helps to develop, Ruskin could not acquire the skills and graces of polite society. At the parlour-game, 'La Toilette de Madame', he could only blunder.[33] Hare's capacity for social diversion was similarly impaired. When he went to Harrow, the loneliness of his life at the rectory was for a time unabated: '. . . In playtime I go here, there, and everywhere, but with no one and doing nothing'.[34]

The aura of loneliness and frustration which pervades the recollections of Hare, Ruskin, and Gosse is markedly absent from a group of autobiographies written by women who were born during the second half of the nineteenth century and who escaped the rigours of the evangelical home: Elizabeth Haldane's *From One Century to Another* (1937); Ethel Smyth's *Impressions That Remained* (1919); Gwen Raverat's *Period Piece* (1952); and Flora Thompson's *Lark Rise to Candleford* (1945). In the eyes of the autobiographer, the past can be an idyl no less than a nightmare; one distortion is the obverse of the other. But if these works are free of the muted sense of outrage which dominates the earlier autobiographies, neither are they bathed in a sentimental glow.[35] Even in the untrammelled household of George Darwin and his American wife, children could be treated as though their sensibilities were imperfectly developed. Gwen Raverat (Darwin's granddaughter) recalls the disgust with which she confronted her daily breakfast of salted porridge. Elizabeth Haldane reflects with similar poignancy upon the contemporary belief that children had no aesthetic sense. Everything ugly or outworn in her home was sent to the nursery. She cannot forget the 'disagreeable smell of the . . . brown cardboard slabs' on which the atlases rested.[36] Flora Thompson, a working-class child raised in the Oxfordshire village of Juniper Hill, might easily have depicted her upbringing as a pastoral interlude. What makes her autobiographical trilogy a uniquely valuable document is not only her humble origin, but the honesty and balance with which she recalls her confrontation with adults often embittered by poverty. When she and her brother ask too many questions, they are sent about their business; if they do not do as they are told, their bottoms are 'soundly smacked'.[37]

Parents at the close of the century were ostensibly no less autocratic than the evangelical mentors of Hare, Ruskin, and Gosse. Underlying their severities, however, was a new incertitude respecting the government of their children. The parents of Ethel Smyth, for example, alternately permitted her to chatter and snubbed her for being forward. Punishment could still be disproportionately severe, as when Ethel was flogged with a knitting needle for stealing barley sugar. But it could also be inflicted with a nonchalance unthinkable for such martinets as Hare's mother or his aunt Esther.

Locked in her father's dressing-room for misbehaving, Ethel and her sister ransacked Mr. Smyth's wardrobe and constructed 'a complete effigy of him lying on his back on the floor in full hunting costume'. As a finishing touch, they pricked out an inscription on the pincushion and laid it on the effigy's breast: 'For dear Papa'.[38] This mockery of both their punishment and the adult world which inflicted it apparently elicited no reprimand.

A wave of child-raising theories—'fads and foolishnesses'—emerged during the 1880's. '. . . There were some children who might not ride bicycles, and others who were forbidden to go in boats; some who were forced to play the violin; and others who always had to wear mufflers; some who might not eat currant buns; and others who were obliged to have cold baths . . .'[39] Considered in the aggregate, these theories are negative; they either force or forbid. Nonetheless, towards the close of the century, children began to gain a modicum of independence. Elizabeth Haldane, who was particularly sensitive to the child's sub-ordinate position within the Victorian family, found the changes in methods of child-rearing 'very marked'. In an unwitting return to the fundamental premise of *Emile,* educators began to realize that children were not mere extensions of their parents' wills and desires and that they must be taught to think and act for themselves.

One of the principal signs of this new liberalism, the causes of which remain elusive, was a *laissez-faire* attitude towards play. The small children in Flora Thompson's village were summarily bundled out of doors and told to 'go play' while their mothers did the household chores.[40] Gwen Raverat even regretted that her mother did not exercise a more active surveillance over her children's vigorous games, one of which entailed jumping from a nine-foot wall into the garden. In Elizabeth Haldane's much more sedate household, a similar forbearance prevailed. She and her brothers were left to play their small stock of games by themselves, 'and were not overset by interfering grown-ups . . .'[41] The latitude thus afforded the child's imagination facilitated access to the special realm of fantasy whose precise nature continues to intrigue—and to baffle—modern educators. The close relationship between this mysterious world and play is suggested by the highly personalized games and fantasies of Laura and Edward, the autobiographical protagonists of *Lark Rise to Candleford.* In the eyes of the emancipated children, nature assumes a private significance. They pretend that the scabious which lines the brookside falls in a shower from the sky and that a clump of white violets, of which they are the appointed guardians, is their 'holy secret'.[42] One of the attributes of the child's private world is precisely this clandestine aura. For all their resilience, neither Hare, Ruskin, nor Gosse dared to possess such a world.

Through its connection with childhood and the child's point of view, play is one of the central themes of Dickens' work. But whereas the Victorian autobiographers viewed play only in relation to children, Dickens also perceived its bearing upon the lives of adults. Sleary's famous exhortation near the close of *Hard Times* is meant for Mr. Gradgrind no less than for his maimed children: 'People mutht be amuthed. They can't be alwayth a-learning, nor yet they can't be alwayth a-working, they an't made for it.'[43] Dickens' insight into the child's distinctive mode of perceiving has been analyzed and extolled at length, but what most writers on the subject do not recognise is that the child's feelings and needs are often viewed in relation to the adult sensibilities into which they will presently develop. For Dickens, an adult who does not know how to play is little less pitiable than a child. Despite his comic *grotesquerie, Dombey*'s Mr. feeder, B. A. shares the melancholy which surrounds his morose little charges at Doctor Blimber's. His room is full of playthings which he cannot allow himself to enjoy: a fishing-rod, a pair of boxing-gloves, a chess set, a Spanish grammar, and 'a beautiful little curly second-hand key bugle'.[44] Feeder is not an evangelical, but he has been touched by the evangelical obsession with time. His enjoyment is reserved for a future which will never come.

Even religiously moderate Victorians were tempted to extract some moral or intellectual profit from their diversions.[45] To Dickens, this contemporary endorsement of 'rational recreation' was no less distasteful than the stringent code of the evangelicals. In one of the essays in *The Uncommercial Traveller,* he traces the Victorian zeal for intellectual improvement back to its fountainhead in Thomas Day's Mr. Barlow. The Traveller becomes acquainted with *Sandford and Merton* 'at an unusually early age',[46] and its relentless pragmatism continues to haunt him. The spirit of the officious tutor spoils the child's first visit to the pantomime: as the curtain rises—'click click, ting ting, bang bang, weedle weedle weedle, bang!'—he is suffused with shame at the thought of Barlow's probable reaction. As the remainder of the essay shows, the Victorians could tolerate frivolity only if it were an excuse for edification. The same purposiveness which reduces the conjurer's swan to a lump of wax presides over the Victorian recreations patronized by the Traveller. At the conclusion of 'an uncompromising pantomime', the female impersonator incongruously delivers 'a random eulogium on the virtues'. The world of illusion for which Dickens prized the theatre and which he himself revelled in creating[47] is irreconcilable with both Day's empiricism and its latter-day counterpart, the 'rational recreation' of the Victorians.

Despite his comic annoyance with Mr. Barlow, Dickens was not wholly averse to the tradition which combined learning with pleasure. In 'Mrs. Lirriper's Lodgings',

Major Jackman teaches his young ward arithmetic by means of a delightful game in which the usual mundane commodities are replaced by a hodgepodge assembled from the landlady's kitchen: 'We have here a toasting-fork, a potato in its natural state, two potlids, one egg-cup, a wooden spoon, and two skewers . . .' Nonetheless, Dickens' concept of play differs fundamentally from both that of the eighteenth-century pragmatists and his own contemporaries. For Dickens, play is neither a continual change of employment nor a camouflage for learning. Rather, it is an end in itself, one of the privileges of careworn humanity. It releases the participant from the burden of the mundane, enlarges his sensibilities, and enables him to return to his obligations with a sense of refreshment. Wemmick's 'innocent cheerful playful ways' at Walworth are in part responsible for the equanimity with which he sustains his entanglement in the dark world of Little Britain.[48] In its liberating and regenerating power, play in Dickens' writing is closely allied with the imagination. Fully developed in *Hard Times,* this affinity is established at the outset of his career. In a passage of extraordinary shrewdness, he points out that some degree of imagination, no matter how tenuous, is the psychological basis of play. Reflecting upon the inertia of the urban poor, he observes that people do not automatically begin to play when they leave off work. 'We know that the effect of prolonged and arduous labour is to produce, when a period of rest does arrive, a sensation of lassitude which it requires the application of some stimulus to overcome . . .'[49] Imagination provides this stimulus, without which leisure is nothing but another name for ennui.

In his review of Peter Bailey's *Leisure and Class in Victorian England,* John R. Gillis remarks that 'the precise role of play in the development of individual and collective consciousness still awaits treatment'.[50] This essay makes no pretence of being an exhaustive or detailed investigation of the subject; on the contrary, it has necessarily omitted much relevant material, notably the enormous body of children's literature which began to emerge during the Victorian period. Hopefully, however, it has suggested that a society's attitude towards leisure and play is inseparable from its view of children. In devising the curriculum for Kingswood school, John Wesley forbade the children to play games, maintaining that 'a child who played when he was young would play when he was a man'.[51] He could not have reflected more accurately upon the link between the child's and the adult's capacity for pleasure. In play as in the growth of the imagination and the sensibilities, the child is father of the man. As the lives of Ruskin and Hare—and in fiction, of Tom and Louisa Gradgrind—demonstrate, those who are forbidden to play as children cannot play as men.

Notes

1. Ivy Pinchbeck and Margery Hewitt, *Children in English Society,* II (London, 1973), 403.

2. Jean-Jacques Rousseau, *Emile,* translated by Allen Bloom (New York, 1979), 168.

3. Richard and Maria Edgeworth, *Practical Education* (New York, 1974), 95.

4. The educational theories embodied in 'The Good French Governess' are seemingly at odds with the assertion which Maria Edgeworth makes in the Preface to *Moral Tales*: '. . . We have disclaimed and reprehended all attempts to teach in play'. But the principles advanced in *Practical Education* and dramatized in the stories are not really contradictory. Play as understood by the Edgeworths is a protean activity. As soon as it engrosses the child's attention, it is transformed into learning. '. . . From the moment the attention is fixed, no matter, on what, children are no longer at idle play, they are at active work' (*Practical Education,* I, 55).

5. *Practical Education,* I, 147.

6. *Emile,* Bk. III.

7. William Wordsworth, *The Prelude,* ed. by Carlos Baker (New York, 1965), Bk. I, lines 287; 430; 494; 510; Bk. II, line 89.

8. *Practical Education,* I, 18.

9. Pinchbeck, 488-9. Cf. Margaret May, 'Innocence and Experience: the Evolution of the Concept of Juvenile Delinquency in the Mid-Nineteenth Century', *VS* [*Victorian Studies*], 17 (1973), 13; and Deborah Gorham, '"The Maiden Tribute of Modern Babylon" Re-Examined: Child Prostitution and the Idea of Childhood in Late Victorian England', *VS,* 21 (1978), 253-79.

10. *Practical Education,* I, 343.

11. Percy Fitzgerald, ed., *The Life, Letters, and Writings of Charles Lamb,* I (London, 1886), Letter XLIV.

12. Alice Meynell, *Childhood* (London, Toronto, 1913), 49.

13. Alison Mager, *Children of the Past* (New York, 1978).

14. Thomas Day, *The History of Sandford and Merton* (New York, n.d.), 10.

15. Luann Walther, 'The Invention of Childhood in Victorian Autobiography', in *Approaches to Victorian Autobiography,* ed. by George P. Landow (Athens, 1979), 72.

16. *Practical Education,* I, 159.

17. Throughout this essay, I have used the word 'evangelical' at it is used by Ian Bradley in *The Call to Seriousness: The Evangelical Impact on the Victorians*: not in reference to a particular religious group or sect, but as designating a puritanical cast of thought.

18. Hannah More, *Strictures on the Modern System of Female Education* (Salem, 1809), 109.

19. Ian Bradley, *The Call to Seriousness: The Evangelical Impact on the Victorians* (New York, 1976), 14-15.

20. *Emile*, Bk. III.

21. Pinchbeck, 423.

22. More, 69.

23. *Ibid.*, 56-7.

24. Bradley, 181.

25. Landow, xxxviii.

26. Augustus J. C. Hare, *The Story of My Life* (New York, 1896), 70.

27. *Ibid.*, 150-1.

28. *Ibid.*, 81.

29. John Ruskin, *Praeterita*, I (London, 1907), 13, 17.

30. Edmund Gosse, *Father and Son*, (Boston, 1965), 121ff.

31. *Praeterita*, I, 206.

32. *Father and Son*, 112.

33. *Praeterita*, I, 54, 257.

34. *The Story of My Life*, 172.

35. Landow, xxxviii.

36. Elizabeth S. Haldane, *From One Century to Another* (London, 1937), 93.

37. Flora Thompson, *Lark Rise to Candleford* (London, 1945), 35.

38. Ethel Smyth, *Impressions That Remained* (New York, 1946), 16.

39. Gwen Raverat, *Period Piece* (New York, 1952), 47-8.

40. *Lark Rise to Candleford*, 29.

41. *From One Century to Another*, 25.

42. *Lark Rise to Candleford*, 35.

43. *Hard Times* (London, n.d.), III, 8.

44. *Dombey and Son* (London, n.d.), Ch. 14.

45. Robert Malcolmson, *Popular Recreations in English Society, 1700-1850* (Cambridge, 1979), 168.

46. *The Uncommercial Traveller*, 'Mr. Barlow' (London, n.d.).

47. Jane Welsh Carlyle gave a vivid account of Dickens' skill as a conjurer: '. . . Only think of that excellent Dickens playing the *conjurer* for one whole hour—the best conjurer I ever saw—(and I have paid money to see several) . . . This part of the entertainment concluded with a plum pudding made out of raw flour, raw eggs—all the usual raw ingredients—boiled in a gentleman's hat—and tumbled out reeking—all in one minute before the eyes of the astonished children and astonished grown people!' (Alan and Mary McQueen Simpson, *I Too Am Here: Selections from the Letters of Jane Welsh Carlyle* (Cambridge, 1977, 60-1).

48. *Great Expectations* (London, n.d.), Ch. 51.

49. 'Sunday Under Three Heads' (London, n.d.).

50. *VS*, 23 (1979), 110.

51. Pinchbeck, 351.

Karin Lesnik-Oberstein (essay date 2002)

SOURCE: Lesnik-Oberstein, Karin. "*Holiday House*: Grist to *The Mill on the Floss*, or Childhood as Text." *The Yearbook of English Studies* 32 (2002): 77-94.

[*In the following essay, Lesnik-Oberstein provides an introduction to a series of essays on children in literature that appeared in the 2002* Yearbook of English Studies, *and examines the idea of childhood as a "construction of identity" in literary theory.*]

In his 1814 review of Wordsworth's 'The Excursion', Charles Lamb wrote: '[Wordsworth's] verses shall be censured as infantile by critics who confound poetry "having children for its subject" with poetry that is "childish"',[1] and almost two hundred years later attitudes of this kind, overt or implicit, can still widely be found both in literary criticism in general and in children's literature criticism. This volume of the *Yearbook of English Studies* aims to challenge that view of childhood as either an isolated, special topic within literary studies, of little relevance to wider issues of critical approach or established areas of study about texts, or as simply too obvious and self-evident to write about at any length or with much complexity. The articles in this volume, whether on children's literature or 'adult' literature, differ in their focus and method, but they are similar in that they all argue and demonstrate ways in which considerations of childhood are complex in and

of themselves, and also how they raise, or join in with, challenges to a whole range of much wider critical assumptions and practices.

At issue here is the way childhood has hardly been conceived of in the humanities as a construction of identity.[2] There are already available in other areas critical approaches hinging on theories of identity (feminist, post-colonial, and queer theory) which are not just widely circulated, but are, to a greater or less extent, seen as having a relevance to questions and issues beyond any narrow concept of 'special interest' groups. As Eve Kosofsky Sedgwick suggests with regard to her use of queer theory, 'modern homo/heterosexual definition has become so exacerbated a cultural site because of an enduring incoherence about whether it is to be thought of as an issue only for a minority of (distinctly lesbian or gay) individuals, or instead as an issue that cuts across every locus of agency and subjectivity in the culture'.[3] Sandra Kemp and Judith Squires, similarly, argue with reference to developments in feminist theory: 'The categories of "man" and "woman" (in all their complexity and multiplicity) currently remain constitutive of our identities, and in hierarchically inscribed ways. [. . .] It would seem unlikely that any disciplinary division between "feminism" (which excludes men) and "gender" (which does not) will be sustainable.'[4]

Even if, then, these theories of identity are seen to raise general problems around, for instance, cultural meanings, hierarchies and consciousness, perspectives and politics, childhood, meanwhile, as Charles Lamb feared, usually remains a field regarded with anything from mild amusement to derision, judged either too simple to be serious, or too pure to be touched. The studies that have been devoted to it have equally been seen, and often see themselves, as strictly specialized and local, if not positively marginal. Children's literature criticism is hardly related, and hardly relates itself, to 'adult' literary criticism or theory,[5] and children or childhood are largely written of as a 'separate' focus or topic among a more encompassing 'adult' literary thematics.[6] In fact, childhood seems in many ways not to be registered as a 'subject' as such at all: it may be noted as an instance of this that 'childhood' or the 'child' are rarely included as a 'topic' or 'subject' in indices, even when discussed in some way in a text.

I want here to look further at the dynamics and implications of several of the claims I have sketched above concerning both a separate status of the 'child' in literary studies, and some of the fundamental challenges this area may be argued as raising, in defiance of its critical marginalization or isolation. In order to do this I will turn to discussing the 'childhood' sections of George Eliot's 1860 novel *The Mill on the Floss*.[7] For if there is anything critics seem to agree on, and that therefore directs much of the criticism of these sections of the novel, it is that Eliot, in *The Mill on the Floss*, was preeminently successful in describing childhood, the girl Maggie Tulliver and her relationship with her brother Tom, and that this success moreover is the result of these episodes being autobiographical and of intense personal significance to George Eliot herself.

To begin with, all Eliot's biographers concur in this respect: from John W. Cross in 1885[8] to Kathryn Hughes in 1998[9] the childhood sections of *The Mill on the Floss* are described as being, as Leslie Stephen writes, '[without] doubt [. . .] substantially autobiographical, not, of course, a statement of facts, but as a vivid embodiment of early impressions and the first stages of spiritual development'.[10] The biographers, furthermore, elaborate this 'vivid embodiment of early impressions' to include versions of what Hughes writes:

> Just like little Maggie, she too had run away to join the gypsies, had cried away her whole unhappiness in the wormeaten attic, had felt her mother's disappointment in her plainness. Most crucially, she had known what it was to devote herself to an older brother who did not want her, who meted out stern punishments for minor mistakes, who preferred riding his pony to playing with a little girl. No writer has ever given a better account of the relationship between brother and sister. Tom and Maggie bicker over jam puffs, fishing rods and pocket money. Maggie's spark and cleverness is constantly checked by Tom's need to rule and punish.

(pp. 319-20)

The biographers, then, construct a narrative of a life, and together with that a theory of creativity linking authorship and works in some way: these two aspects are inextricably linked, as a particular kind of narrative is required for certain ideas of what produces both an 'author' and then their works. As Frederick Karl writes in praise of Ruby Redinger's biography, pertinently entitled *George Eliot: The Emergent Self,* 'more than [Gordon] Haight planned to do, she integrated the work with the life'.[11] This 'integration' is produced around ideas of knowledge and experience. The fiction is read as sourced either from other texts of which the 'author' had knowledge, and for which their 'author' status constitutes a transformative force, or from an 'experience'. But what is this 'experience'? As in the quotations from Stephen and Hughes, it is assumed as primary, original, unlearned and spontaneous, self-formulating, claimed as learned through the senses, or associated with any idea of unanalysable and unselfconscious emotion.

Moreover, to the biographers childhood is ultimately such an 'experience', the source for its own representation in the text: an 'embodiment', as Stephen puts it. Experience here must further mean something like a spontaneous process of development which is both unique and specific ('George Eliot'/'Maggie Tulliver') and general ('childhood'; the best 'account of the rela-

tionship between brother and sister'), and which is anterior to the text, which it feeds and fills. 'Embodiment' seems to mean here, paradoxically, something prior to text—apparently a child's body (senses) and 'impressions'—becoming text, a life becoming a story: a 'disembodiment', in fact, if you like. But that transferral of what is constituted as 'life' to text in this case apparently succeeds in resisting any intervening transformation, ensuring the text's own 'lifeness'. As John Rignall writes:

> Her fullest portrayal of childhood, in the first two books of *The Mill on the Floss* [. . .goes] beyond the simple appearance of naturalness to examine the often painful emotional and social reality of the child's world. Eliot was drawing here on her own early experience [. . .]. [Her] ability to enter into the child's mental processes [. . .] can be seen in her grasp of the complex mechanisms of Maggie's reaction to this unhappiness [. . .]. This psychological insight into unconscious mechanisms of defence and compensation is accompanied by an understanding of how childhood is shaped by the pressures and prejudices of the adult world it anticipates.[12]

In other words, this text about childhood is judged to be successful because it is seen as being true to life (judgements again relying on a particular 'author's life' narrative), and this in terms of particular notions of emotion, society, and psychology. And the truth to life establishes childhood as a thing that can be simply itself, recognizable and inevitable: a childhood that 'goes beyond the simple appearance of naturalness' to the 'reality', and this because Eliot as 'author' has the ability to remember, retrieve, re-live, or 'grasp' this childhood in a unique way. Her 'own early experience' guarantees a profundity of knowledge ('ability to enter [. . .] mental processes', 'insight', 'understanding') that prevails over a 'simple appearance', even if that 'appearance' is of 'naturalness'.

This view of George Eliot's ability to re-live or retrieve her childhood, moreover, famously also takes as its endorsement Eliot's partner George Lewes's reports that during the writing of *The Mill on the Floss,* 'Mrs. Lewes is getting her eyes redder and *swollener* every morning as she lives through her tragic story',[13] and Frederick Karl concludes that Eliot 'had reentered some highly sensitive and intimate areas of her life; and her presentation of these conflicts had not alleviated the pain, but intensified it' (p. 330). Eliot's tears and reddened eyes are the physical testament to uncontrollable, spontaneous emotion, both producing, and produced by, the novel. Here memory gushes as the tears do, and opens the well-spring for the text.

Most of the literary critics take the same view as the biographers:[14] as Barbara Hardy writes, 'I take it that *The Mill on the Floss* is the novel most visibly close to

George Eliot's life',[15] while R. P. Draper claims that 'most readers feel that Maggie's childhood experiences are so intensely realised that they must reflect some of the author's own [. . .]. [These] early chapters [are] by common consent regarded as the fullest and most resonant of the novel'.[16] F. R. Leavis famously simply pronounced, 'That Maggie Tulliver is essentially identical with the young Mary Ann Evans we all know.'[17] Childhood in the novel is here also read as sourced from an authorial experience that is anterior to the text, spontaneous, self-defining, and developmental: George Eliot did not have to write this part of the text, she *is* the text, and the text is she. Kathryn Hughes also makes this assumption while seeming to re-evaluate the claim to 'autobiography': '[Eliot] actually left very little direct information about her own early years. [. . .] To bulk out his first chapter [Cross] leaned heavily on the account of Maggie Tulliver's early years in *The Mill on the Floss,* introducing distortions which biographers spent the next one hundred years consolidating into "fact"' (p. 18). But this apparent qualification never for Hughes alters the 'fact' that this section of the novel is about Eliot's own childhood, and her relationship with her brother, and Hughes muses that 'frustratingly, we do not know what Isaac thought about Marian's next book, [. . .] which so obviously draws on their shared childhood' (p. 301-02). *The Mill on the Floss* is, here, the source for Eliot whose childhood is the source for the text, and the circularity itself, some minor 'distortions' aside, remains unexamined. The result of these assumptions overall is that many critics seem to find it hard to conclude anything else about these passages; accounting for their source in this way formulates a childhood which is its own account, and bears no analysis or further explanation: it is enough that it *is,* bearing witness to itself, to its self-evident 'truth' and 'vivid[ness]'. As a reviewer in the *Spectator* of 1860 writes,

> George Eliot seems to us [. . .] to possess in the highest degree the gift of knowing the child-soul in those things which are common to all children [. . .]. [She] describes Maggie Tulliver from her childhood upwards, and traces the influence of all the home associations on the youngs girl's mind. Her active mind, her spirit sensitive to all things, her heart with a hunger and thirst to be loved, are analyzed with a wondrous instinctive knowledge of the inner workings of a child's mind.[18]

If Eliot's childhood is the self-generating well-spring that creates the text as 'life', then several critics make even more specific what this might involve. Gordon Haight provides the precedent for Hughes's musings over Isaac Evans's potential response to *The Mill on the Floss* when he writes: 'One would give a good deal to know what he [Isaac Evans] thought of *The Mill,* which is full of things about *him*. The dead rabbits, the new fishlines, the jagged cropping of Maggie's unruly hair are too real to have been invented'.[19] This 'too realness'

repeats the idea that childhood *is* the self-generating reality anterior to the novel, providing the source for it, thus at one and the same time both defeating fiction and guaranteeing fiction's highest achievement as fiction, and Frederick Karl agrees:

> It is not the books she might have read, however, that reveals the ambiguities of Mary Anne's childhood, but the hair-cutting scene in *Mill* [. . .]. We move circumspectly, aware of the dangers of reading back from fiction to life, but the episode so establishes isolation, strangeness, and difference that it calls out to be linked to Eliot's own development.
>
> (p. 20)

Why is the hair-cutting scene singled out as particularly defining of 'Mary Anne', or of the 'real' that defies 'invention'? And what happens to these claims if I can argue that there is a textual source for this passage?[20]

The passage I am going to suggest may form a source for the hair-cutting passage comes from a children's book: Catherine Sinclair's 1839 novel *Holiday House*.[21] What this first of all alerts us to is one pragmatic outcome of literary criticisms that rest on judgements of value and hierarchical orderings of texts: they have ensured, largely, the separation of children's literature studies (and non-literary texts in general) from adult literary studies (of 'literature'). Therefore, remarkably little has yet been written about any influence of children's books on literature in general.[22] This is apparent especially in such a case as that of *Holiday House* which, although out of print, is well-known and much mentioned amongst historians of children's literature as '"the first example of modern nursery scepticism" [and] the first example of real laughter and a free conscience',[23] and so is not easy to overlook. There is also even (should you wish to use the terms of biographical narrative) at least a hint that Eliot knew of Catherine Sinclair and her work, for she discusses a quote from a cover-blurb written by 'Miss Sinclair' in her well-known essay 'Silly Novels by Lady Novelists'.[24]

Holiday House is about a brother, Harry, and sister, Laura, who live with their older brother Frank, uncle David and grandmother Lady Harriet after the death of their mother, while their father is travelling abroad for his health. Laura, like Maggie Tulliver, has trouble with her hair: while Mrs Tulliver moans that Maggie's 'hair won't curl all I can do with it, and she's so franzy about having it put i' paper, and I've such work as never was to make her stand and have it pinched with th' irons' (p. 12), Laura has to suffer,

> among her many other torments, Mrs Crabtree [the nurse] roll[ing] up Laura's hair every night on all sides of her head, in large stiff curl-papers, till they were as round and hard as walnuts, after which she tied on a

night-cap, as tightly as possible above all, saying this would curl the hair still better. Laura could not lay any part of her head on the pillow, without suffering so much pain, that, night after night, she sat up in bed [. . .] and quietly took the cruel papers out, although she was punished so severely for doing so, that she obeyed orders at last, and lay wide awake half the night with torture [. . .]. 'You may laugh, Frank, for it is fun to you, and death to me,' answered poor Laura, gravely shaking her curls at him. 'I wish we were all bald, like uncle David!'

(pp. 11-13)

Both Maggie and Laura seize the opportunity to remove what to them both are the 'teasing' locks (*Mill*, p. 55, *Holiday House*, p. 39): while Maggie famously 'took out a large pair of scissors' (p. 54) from a drawer in her mother's room, Laura 'unluckily perceived on the table near where they sat, a pair of Mrs Crabtree's best scissors, which she had been positively forbid to touch' (p. 39). Maggie, after 'seizing her front locks [. . .] cutting them straight across the middle of her forehead [. . .]. Snip! went the great scissors again while Tom was speaking', enlists Tom, who 'couldn't help feeling it was rather good fun' to complete the haircut, while Laura

> thought what a good opportunity this might be to shorten them a very little, not above an inch or two; and without considering a moment longer, [. . .] she began snipping off the ends of her hair. Laura was much diverted to see it showering down upon the floor, so she cut and cut on, while the curls fell thicker and faster, till at last the whole floor was covered with them, and scarcely a hair left upon her head.

Once Laura has arrived at this state,

> Harry went into fits of laughing when he perceived what a ridiculous figure Laura had made of herself, and he turned her round and round to see the havoc she had made, saying, 'You should give all this hair to Mr Mills the upholsterer, to stuff grandmama's arm-chair with! At any rate, Laura, if Mrs Crabtree is ever so angry, she can hardly pull you by the hair of the head again! What a sound sleep you will have to-night, with no hard curl-papers to torment you!'
>
> (pp. 39-40)

While once Maggie 'stood cropped in a jagged, uneven manner' (p. 55), '"O, Maggie," said Tom, jumping round her, and slapping his knees as he laughed, "O, my buttons, what a queer thing you look! Look at yourself in the glass—you look like the idiot we throw our nut-shells to at school."'

Where the hair-cutting for both the girls is a liberation from the painful demands to conform to an aesthetics of femininity which they both resist in several similar other ways also, the laughter and ridicule of their brothers and, later, further family, formulates the price of their action. Laura's grandmother pretends not to recognize her:

When Laura entered, [. . .] with her well-cropped head, she uttered an exclamation of perfect amazement. 'Why! who on earth is that? Laura, my dear child! What has become of your hair? Were your curls burned off in the fire? or did the fright make you grow bald? What is the meaning of all this?' [. . .] 'Well, child! speak out!' said Lady Harriet, impatiently, 'Did some hairdresser come to the house and rob you?'

(p. 45)

Similarly, uncle Glegg joshes Maggie with his 'Hey-day! What little gell's this—why I don't know her. Is it some little gell you've picked up in the road, Kezia?' (p. 58).

Further humiliation follows for Laura from her uncle David who teases her by asking 'Or, are you like the ladies of Carthage, who gave their long hair for bows and arrows? [. . .] I never saw such a little fright in my life as you look now' (pp. 45-46), while Maggie must endure a version of this, shorn of the classical allusion, in uncle Pullet's observing 'Why, little miss, you've made yourself look very funny' (p. 58). Both families concur in their half-amused, half-exasperated, condemnation: 'Did you ever know such a little hussy as it is?' asks Mr Tulliver, 'laughing with much enjoyment' (p. 58), where uncle David exclaims, 'hardly able to keep laughing', 'Did any mortal ever hear of two such little torments! [. . .] I wonder if anybody else in the world has two such mischievous children!' (p. 46).

The effect of this on Laura and Maggie is markedly similar too: 'Laura turned perfectly crimson with shame and distress' (p. 45), while 'Maggie's cheeks and ears began to burn [. . .]. Her first flush came from anger' (p. 58), although Laura immediately feels 'convinced of her own great misconduct' (p. 45) and confesses her deed, where as Maggie's anger initially 'gave her a transient power of defiance' which then, however, 'left her in an instant' (p. 58). Maggie subsequently 'burst out into loud sobbing' (p. 58) and Laura confesses 'while the tears came into her eyes'.

The grief and distress of the girls is seen in both cases as their ultimate punishment, beyond even the chastisement or ridicule of their family: Maggie is described as being left to

> that bitter sense of the irrevocable which was almost an everday experience of her small soul. She could see clearly enough, now the thing was done, that it was very foolish, and that she should have to hear and think more about her hair than ever; for Maggie rushed to her deeds with passionate impulse, and then saw not only their consequences, but what would have happened if they had not been done, with all the detail and exaggerated circumstance of an active imagination.

(p. 55)

Laura too acts, throughout *Holiday House*, impulsively, 'without consideration', and in the case of her hair-cutting it is left to Lady Harriet to point out to her what Maggie is made to realize for herself:

I have some thoughts of excusing Laura this time, because she always tells me the truth, without attempting to conceal any foolish thing she does. It will be very long before she has any hair to cut off again, so I hope she may be older and wiser by that time, especially considering that every looking-glass she sees for six months will make her feel ashamed of herself.

(p. 47)

The 'foolish' deed of the hair-cutting will be reflected back to Laura in 'every looking-glass' or when Maggie 'looked in the glass' (p. 55), and this will make the issue of the hair more present to them both, according to the texts, than it ever was in all its tormenting physicality. A pedagogics of experience is thus formulated in both *Holiday House* and *The Mill on the Floss* as converting these attempts at liberation back into a lesson in the inescapableness of the constitution of Laura and Maggie's femininity. Furthermore, this pedagogics of experience must overall transform a childhood constructed in both texts as impetuosity, thoughtlessness, spontaneity, and boundless physical movement, into an adulthood of self-reflection, mental and physical restraint and control, and an awareness of possible consequences.

Finally, Maggie's father and Laura's stand-in father, uncle David, provide comfort to the girls: Mr Tulliver 'took her part' (p. 58), and Laura seeing her uncle 'put on one of his funny looks [. . .] almost forgot her former fright' (p. 46). The episodes end with Maggie finding 'entire deliverance', 'with the dessert' of 'nuts and wine' (p. 59) which the children are allowed to have outside in the summerhouse, while Lady Harriet, in the case of Laura, prepares a 'coach-wheel', slices of bread used as 'spokes' covered in different kinds of jam and honey, as a treat.

Having attempted to illustrate similarities between the hair-cutting episodes in *Holiday House* and *The Mill on the Floss,* I might be asked, however, as already indicated above, what this claim to the existence of a prior textual source might be about: am I mitigating Eliot's putative originality in the formulation of this event, pointing to *Holiday House* as the true original? Am I reformulating the author-narrative created as Eliot by the biographers I quoted above, by suggesting that perhaps this hair-cutting never happened to Eliot herself as a child because it can be shown as existing in *Holiday House*? These ideas involve the replacement of one idea of source ('life' or 'experience') by another (text, in this case *Holiday House*), as they also rest on the establishment of sources as origins as simultaneously motivated by and producing the valuing of that origin as a prized originality. In other words, my claim to a source might be read, according to the biographical criticism I have been describing, as diminishing Eliot's originality and, therefore, her portrayal of a childhood not now,

apparently, her own, not deeply felt or understood as her own spontaneous, involuntary experience: her own memory or knowledge of herself.

On the other hand, this language of sources, origins, and childhoods is, in terms of criticism, redeemable through a process of regression back to an ultimate real child. The originality of Eliot may be recouped, even if routed via Catherine Sinclair, because at the root of any depiction of childhood critics may, and usually do, discover *someone's* memory or experience of their own childhood. And, again, that own childhood is conceived of as both directly (re-)lived and as (therefore) resulting in a unique ability to discern or know childhood generally as such. This regression 'through' any text back to a real childhood can be read in F. J. Harvey Darton's discussion of Catherine Sinclair and, in this type of narrative *therefore,* her works:

> It is evident that she was a genuine 'best-seller'. It is likewise evident that she knew and understood real children, and that children liked her books, and that in her own mind—which was transparently honest, even naïve, whatever she wrote—she reconciled her staid primness in adult conduct with her complete abandonment of all constraint for the young. [. . .] Catherine Sinclair was the first to rollick.
>
> (p. 221)

This return to the real child, come what may, persists as the necessary strategy, overtly or inadvertently, of children's literature criticism up to the present day, defining itself as it does as a criticism for the good of children: children which it must therefore know and define in some way.[25] Daniel Vitaglione and Patricia Thomson equally illustrate the need to refer back to at least someone's real childhood as a guarantor of originality or authenticity when Vitaglione joins with Thomson in 'argu[ing] that [George] Sand's autobiography stood behind the portrait of Maggie Tulliver'.[26]

This return to an originative real child, who is itself an ultimate source without a source, also permits several other critical narratives about the relationship I set up between *Holiday House* and *The Mill on the Floss*: am I, for instance, suggesting not that George Eliot deliberately used the episode from *Holiday House*, but that this book is part of the author's knowledge of her own childhood, in that she read the text when young and that it then became part of her memory of her own childhood?[27] This idea might be partially disrupted by the practical consideration that Eliot would have been twenty years old when *Holiday House* was published in 1839, but it could be rescued by presupposing in turn an earlier source shared by both texts. And, in fact, such a speculative earlier source is, in critical terms, always available again as another step in the regression to the real child, as a real childhood experience shared by many children. In this instance the argument would be that *Holiday House* is not the source for the hair-cutting sections of *The Mill on the Floss,* but that long hair and its painful regulation would have been a common experience for many young girls on their way to being coerced into femininity in the nineteenth century. Thus 'experience' is reconfirmed as the ultimate source for either text, and both Eliot and Sinclair might have struggled with this themselves, or known of girls who did. A. S. Byatt, writing an introduction to *The Mill on the Floss,* also demonstrates on several levels how autobiographies are written of as produced by, as well as producers of, this common experience:

> Lewes praises *Werther* for Goethe's selection and presentation of true 'real' details. (*Werther,* like the *Mill,* has a more than usual autobiographical content and quality.) Lewes wrote: 'Goethe's art is truth. He is so great an artist that the simplest realities have to him significance. Charlotte cutting bread and butter for the children [. . .] the children clinging around Werther for sugar, and pictures of that kind, betray so little inventive power that they have excited the ridicule of some English critics to whom poetry is a thing of pomp, not the beautiful vesture of reality.' Some such illumination of simple realities inspired, I believe, George Eliot's depiction of Tom and Maggie's fishing-rods and jam-puffs.[28]

These critical shifts to the real child and real experience that I have been tracking, do, however, throw up several further problems: there is, first of all, the question of where the idea of controlling girls' hair itself (or the relevance of fishing-rods and jam-puffs to childhood, frequently mentioned by critics) comes from. If this was indeed a common experience for girls, and even if hair might be argued still to be part of constructions of femininity, this 'experience' must in turn have come from somewhere. How did the regulation of hair come to 'mean' something to do with 'femininity'? Or fishing-rods and jam-puffs with 'childhood'? A notion of 'history' or 'culture' is employed in this case to be the supply for the 'experience', thus assuming a history and culture that are themselves unsourced: now more primary, spontaneous, and self-formulating than experience.

Furthermore, childhood is often itself also situated within this view of a primacy of history and culture when it is in turn conceded to be changeable, subject to different conceptions and formulations according to shifts in history or culture.[29] In the case of *Holiday House* and *The Mill on the Floss* this argument leads most frequently to references to the influence with regard to childhood of Jean-Jacques Rousseau's *Émile* in the case of *Holiday House,* and of William Wordsworth's poetry, particularly 'The Prelude' (with Rousseau in turn an influence on that) in the case of *The Mill on the Floss.* Once these references are more closely examined, however, it becomes apparent that this is the regression to the real child in another guise.

For these texts are not read in the end as narratives of childhood, produced as shifting and variable discourses. In these references, instead, Rousseau and Wordsworth are pointed to as the discoverers of the real childhood that had hitherto been overlooked or misunderstood; as Frederick Karl writes: 'The morning [Tom takes Maggie fishing] becomes idyllic, and it becomes one of those "spots of time" Wordsworth referred to, when love of the earth enters into us and helps shape us' (p. 19). Jean Perrot, similarly, writes with regard to children's literature that 'this power of images, which is crucial to holding children's attention, was to be taken into account in the revolutionary system of Jean-Jacques Rousseau, which is based on a realistic observation of play and the behaviour of real children'.[30] Thus Rousseau, initially labelled, for instance, by one children's literature critic the producer of an 'ideology' of childhood, ends up, after all, enabling through this 'ideology [. . .] one of the first attempts [in Thomas Day's *Sandford and Merton* (1783-89)] to depict recognisably real boys exploring a friendship through active incident'.[31] Here even ideology is reality when it comes to childhood.[32]

Even when a view of Wordsworth's poetry as the truth about childhood is criticized, another true childhood is brought in to replace it, as in Margaret Homans's consideration of 'Eliot, Wordsworth, and the Scenes of the Sisters' Instruction', where the childhood of Maggie is seen to be a feminist critique of 'the Wordsworthian myth' of childhood,

> presenting us with a version of childhood far more literal than Wordsworth's. [. . .] A literal recapitulation of childhood could hardly be further from Wordsworth's aim for himself as a poet. [. . .] For Maggie, literalization leads to her death, but it leads for Eliot to something definitively her own—her identity as a novelist of real life and of female experience.[33]

Similarly, Gillian Avery finds the little Fairchilds, from Mrs Sherwood's *The History of the Fairchild Family* (published in several volumes from 1818 to 1847),

> with their squabbles and attempts to resist authority, [. . .] in fact more lifelike than the two children in [. . .] *Holiday House,* a book expressly written to show 'that species of noisy, frolicsome, mischievous children, now almost extinct'. Harry and Laura are boisterous tearaways, but they are more like engines of destruction than children.[34]

And these arguments point again to a crucial difficulty with the return to a 'real' which is supposed to be both the reason for, and measure of, fictional texts: critics read the 'real', including the real 'child', *differently.* Neither claims for a supposed proof from a supposed 'biology' or 'psychology', nor back-up from memories and observations of childhood, can stabilize this real to be more singular, repetitive, or consistent than fiction,

in all its apparently fickle multiplicity.[35] And that is what I am actually suggesting in this analysis of the hunting of origins and sources, be it for the child as such, or for the fictions in which it is taken to dwell: that the child and the real, whether as object, identity, (auto)biography, culture, or history, are as much text (textual) as fiction; as much about interpretation and multiplicity; moreover, and crucially, that this is not a point merely to be claimed or announced as a principle of approach or theory (which some critics do), but that its implications and consequences pervade and must be considered throughout critical analyses and argument.

What, finally, then, can be done critically with *Holiday House* and *The Mill on the Floss,* once childhood is thought of as constructed or discursive? Having dismantled the idea that there is a childhood that can simply speak for itself, our attention may be much more drawn to *how* the texts construct their specific childhoods (and, therefore, adulthoods). Narration is a key consideration here, and one that is significantly little mentioned critically when it comes to childhood, overwhelmed as the criticism apparently is by a supposed accuracy of portrayal of a thing in itself. *Holiday House* constructs a narration that shifts perspectives from self-appointed adult comment and judgement to Laura and Harry's perceptions and consciousnesses, as in the following passage, just before Laura's hair-cutting:

> Harry sat in his chair, and might have been painted as the very picture of a good boy during nearly twenty minutes after Mrs Crabtree [their nurse] departed; and Laura placed herself opposite to him, trying to follow so excellent an example. [. . .] Any one who had observed Harry and Laura at that time, would have wondered to see two such quiet, excellent, respectable children, and wished that all little boys and girls were made upon the same pattern; but presently they began to think that probably Lady Harriet was not so very ill, as no more bells had rung during several minutes, and Harry ventured to look about for some better amusement than sitting still.
>
> (pp. 38-39)

A separation is played out here between unnatural children of art ('painted as the very picture of a good boy', a 'pattern') who would be 'wondered' at by 'any' observer, and the 'natural' Harry and Laura, who have good intentions, but even whose love for their grandmother cannot overcome their inability to sit still for more than 'nearly twenty minutes' and their need 'presently' after 'several minutes' for 'better amusement'. Throughout the text this 'naturalness' is, as I already pointed out in relation to Laura's hair-cutting, constituted by this physical and mental impetuosity ('heedless, frolicsome' (p. 5), 'mischievous', 'lively' (p. 6), is how they are repeatedly described) and the need for 'enjoy[ment]' (p. 37), 'amus[ement] (p. 16), and 'laughing and running' (p. 21). This text there-

fore claims for itself its childhood as 'natural', against a childhood of art, and this is reduplicated in criticism that accepts the text's own claims to 'life', reading itself as the observing 'any one' the text identifies.

The preface to *Holiday House* also constructs this natural child in opposition to a child of art:

> The minds of young people are now manufactured like webs of linen, all alike, and nothing left to nature. From the hour when children can speak, till they come to years of discretion or of indiscretion, they are carefully prompted what to say, and what to think, and how to look, and how to feel; while in most school-rooms Nature has been turned out of doors with obloquy, and Art has entirely supplanted her. [. . .] If Art and Nature could yet be made to go hand in hand towards the formation of character and principle, a graceful and beautiful superstructure might be reared, on the solid foundation of Christian faith and sound morality.
>
> (p. v)

The weaving of the 'minds of young people' as 'webs of linen' is what this text purports not to partake in, as those webs and linen are the deathly traps of 'Art'. It is, therefore, not to 'prompt' children how to say, think, look, or feel, so that this natural child is to be entirely self-generated, except, it then appears, for that 'formation' which is the building of a 'superstructure'. This struggle between bad weaving and good formation or building (formulations here of the 'natural' together with 'art') are elaborated further:

> so that while many natural weeds would be eradicated, and many wild flowers pruned and carefully trained, some lovely blossoms that spring spontaneously in the uncultivated soil, might still be cherished into strength and beauty, far excelling what can be planted or reared by art. [. . .] Books written for young persons are generally a mere dry record of facts, unenlivened by any appeal to the heart, or any excitement to the fancy [. . .] nothing [f]or the habits or ways of thinking, natural and suitable to the taste of children; therefore, while such works are delightful to the parents and teachers who select them, the younger community are fed with strong meat instead of milk [. . .]. In these pages the author has endeavoured to paint that species of noisy, frolicsome, mischievous children, now almost extinct, wishing to preserve a sort of fabulous remembrance of days long past, when young people were like wild horses on the prairies, rather than like well-broken hacks on the road.
>
> (pp. v-vii)

The child as growing plants necessitates further discriminations of plants into 'weeds', which are wholly undesirable, 'wild flowers' which need 'pruning' and 'training', and 'lovely blossoms' which will be 'cherished'. All this gardening of 'eradication' and 'pruning' is not here, however, apparently, the same 'art', as that 'art' which is 'far excell[ed]' by the 'spontaneous' blossoms.[36] The problem pervading this

passage is that of how to write a child which is not being written according to the text itself: this is what is at stake with the 'child' in all texts that make this type of claim, with the paradox at its height in children's literature, produced as it is by adults for children.

There is further the problem of a text that writes itself as speaking to the child which is already there, but which it must also form, albeit according to itself not by 'stuff[ing] the memory' (p. vi), or by giving 'a mere dry record of facts', but by 'appeal[ing] to the heart', or giving 'excitement to the fancy'. The text therefore prescribes for itself this capacity, which is based on an ability not to be like those 'parents and teachers' who 'select' the 'strong meat' misguidedly. And yet, as we saw in the previous quotation, apparently 'any one' as observer can identify Harry and Laura as unnatural when they are behaving as the pattern children of art. The initial division of adults into those who recognize the natural child, amongst whom is included the narrator, and those who do not, leading 'almost' to the 'extinction' of the natural child, is in the text subsequently overcome by a, (for the text) necessary capacity on the part of any implied reader to identify that natural child *as* natural. At the same time the narrator remains hopelessly entrapped in art: she is 'endeavour[ing]' here to 'paint' the natural child, as she is indeed writing it. Furthermore, she wants to 'preserve a sort of fabulous remembrance', situating the text in an already written future after the extinction when this text will be 'fabulous': being writing in a future, if preferably not in its own present.

Constructing its own narration as based on a privileged capacity not to be a certain sort of 'art', also leads to the narrator figuring herself as a storyteller:

> Those who wish to be remembered for ever in the world [. . .] will find no monument more permanent, than the affectionate remembrance of any children they have treated with kindness; [. . .] above all, we never forget those who good-humouredly complied with the constantly-recurring petition of all young people in every generation, and in every house, 'Will you tell me a story?' In answer to such a request [. . .] the author has from year to year delighted in seeing herself surrounded by a circle of joyous eager faces [. . .] smiling at the frolics of Harry and Laura. [. . .] Some friends, aware of their popularity, [. . .] took the trouble of copying them in manuscript for their own young friends.
>
> (p. x)

The text predicts its own eternal popularity because of the now eternal nature of children in this sense: that stories are above all requested and loved. The previously nearly extinct child here is redeemed by its own persistent demand for the stories which are seen to be generated by its own demand. The author-narrator is in-

creasingly knowledgeable about the natural child, and increasingly withdrawn from any production or contamination of all this naturalness: starting out as a gardener, she is now merely a responder to the solicitations of children, and didn't even initially write down the stories herself, leaving this to 'some friends, aware of their popularity'. Moreover, narrator, children loving stories, and 'parents and teachers' are now finally all united as 'we' who 'never forget' the storytellers: all are now children, whether past, present, or future.

The Mill on the Floss is involved in the same issues as *Holiday House*: how to deny a writing of the child once that writing is figured as contaminating, while retaining admissions of a knowledge of itself as written, and how to cope with a narration that writes itself as having a privileged knowledge of that natural child, but which also constructs a readership that shares that privilege, but only as or while readers of this text itself. In a passage in this hair-cutting episode the shifts in narration negotiate this writing of childhood:

> What could [Maggie] do but sob? She sat as helpless and despairing among her black locks as Ajax among the slaughtered sheep. Very trivial, perhaps, this anguish seems to weather-worn mortals who have to think of Christmas bills, dead loves, and broken friendships; but it was not less bitter to Maggie—perhaps it was even more bitter—than what we are fond of calling antithetically the real troubles of mature life. 'Ah, my child, you will have real troubles to fret about by-and-by,' is the consolation we have almost all of us had administered to us in our childhood, and have repeated to other children since we have been grown up.
>
> (p. 56)

Here 'weather-worn mortals' are like those 'parents and teachers' who threatened the natural child with extinction in *Holiday House*. And although the narrator here is clearly not one of the 'weather-worn' mortals, it is initially only 'perhaps' the case that it will claim that privileged knowledge of Maggie's state of anguish. But there is a direct indication that the 'real troubles' of 'adult life' are only 'real' as 'antithetically' defined, and this after all immediately claims a narrator who is in possession of both perspectives: that of the 'child' and the 'adult' together, defining one another 'antithetically'. Furthermore, the apparently 'adult' perspective is therefore one that the narrator stands apart from too: it can pronounce on what 'we' think and do, but by doing so it has to be able to identify that as object. In other words, the narrator can diagnose itself as external to a process of antithetical definition to which it itself initially seemed to be subject. The maintenance of this triple perspective pervades this whole passage, in that the narrator is absolutely privileged in knowing not only what others cannot know, but even in knowing what it itself cannot know:

> We have all of us sobbed so piteously, standing with tiny bare legs above our little socks, when we lost sight

of our mother or nurse in some strange place; but we can no longer recall the poignancy of that moment and weep over it, as we do over the remembered sufferings of five or ten years ago. Every one of those keen moments has left its trace, and lives in us still, but such traces have blent themselves irrecoverably with the firmer texture of our youth and manhood.

> (p. 56)

'We' all have had the same experience, but 'we' can no longer recall this, although this narrator can recall what 'we' can not recall, while not being able to recall it either. And yet it recalls it in this passage. The 'keen' moments are so keen that they leave traces (writing), but are also 'irrecoverabl[e]'. This childhood, then, *is* writable *as* that which is unrecallable and irrecoverable. This forgetting which is not a forgetting is elaborated further:

> and so it comes that we can look on at the troubles of our children with a smiling disbelief in the reality of their pain. Is there any one who can recover the experience of his childhood, not merely with a memory of what he did and what happened to him, [. . .] but with an intimate penetration, a revived consciousness of what he felt then—when it was so long from one Midsummer to another? what he felt when his schoolfellows shut him out of their game because he would pitch the ball wrong out of mere wilfulness; or on a rainy day in the holidays, when he didn't know how to amuse himself, and fell from idleness into mischief, from mischief into defiance, and from defiance into sulkiness; or when his mother absolutely refused to let him have a tailed coat that 'half,' although every other boy of his age had gone into tails already? Surely if we could recall that early bitterness, and the dim guesses, the strangely perspectiveless conception of life that gave the bitterness its intensity, we should not poohpooh the griefs of our children.

> (pp. 56-57)

The enactment of constructing the unrememberable as both rememberable *as* unrememberable and as writable surely is producing much more than simply, as F. R. Leavis, for instance, would have it, 'the experience of a sensitive child in this [. . .] role among insensitive adults [which] is evoked with great poignancy: George Eliot had only to remember' (p. 484). Instead, that apparent 'only . . . remembering' is construed here (as it is in *Holiday House*) as a privileged achievement that yet diagnoses itself as only reaching for that which is unreachable, but produced here after all. The perspective of narration shifts almost from word to word: 'we' 'can look on' 'with a smiling disbelief', but this narrator is now no part of 'we', since it equally knows of the 'smiling disbelief' and 'the reality' of, however, 'their pain': neither 'we' nor 'they', the 'we' none the less has 'legs' and 'socks' that are 'tiny' and 'little', but to whom? Not to the child at the moment of its sobbing, surely, but to the narrator constructing a scene of pathos it then looks upon itself. Its own creation is, as it were, admired for its poignancy.

Similarly, the question of whether there is 'any one who can recover the experience of his childhood?' is on the one hand necessarily rhetorical, for the narration appears to proceed to enact such a recovery, but with a range of perspectives: several types of 'memory' are proposed as 'merely' memories of action and event, but what is desired here is not that kind of memory, but 'intimate penetration', 'revived consciousness of what he felt then'. It is claimed that a time divided as a now of 'mature life' and a then must be merged even while the division is constructed and upheld by the text itself. This is 'memory' defined as itself: a division of two times, 'now' and 'then', nevertheless bridged, albeit under several conditions. And that memory of feeling is immediately provided: 'when it was so long from one Midsummer to another?', a question filling in already that which it appeared to elicit as an unachievable answer. The consequence, on the other hand then, is that this passage of time divided constructs a past which must be there in order for the present of the passage to be there to pose the question 'Is there any one who can recover the experience of his childhood?'. The 'present' and 'past' put each other into question, and are constructed as standing in a relation of mutual definition. The past is written as the 'irretrievable' that poses questions not only about itself, but about whether there can be a present in which these things will ever be known again, while the present poses questions about both itself and that past upon which it in turn depends.[37]

The past and present then, are both recalled and not recalled, and they therefore leave as untouched the conclusion that 'surely if we could recall that early bitterness [. . .] we should not pooh-pooh the grief of our children': has the present of the text recalled 'that early bitterness' or not? As a present it has not, suspended under question, but the text as present to itself *has* written this past, as well as the present that depends on it. Finally, this leaves the question of what the 'dim guesses' are that are apparently part of this present-past, and what is that 'strangely perspectiveless conception of life that gave the bitterness its intensity'. The 'perspectiveless conception' is again relational and comparative: known, but 'strange', and not known because dependent on whether there is a present that can know it ('Surely if we could recall . . .'). The 'dim guesses' also seem to defeat the very 'perspectiveless[ness]': they are intimations of the present which this text figures as itself, and therefore a perspective in their own right, albeit 'dim'. Still, the 'dimness' also repeats the 'under question' status of this present. In this sense the 'intensity' of the 'bitterness' is indeed undecidable in the terms the passage first indicated in its 'perhaps': 'but it was not the less bitter to Maggie—perhaps it was even more bitter'. This 'perhaps', it can now be argued, suspends any hierarchy of past and present here: both are equally present and not present in this passage.

What now seems more clear, however, is that the way *Holiday House* and *The Mill on the Floss* write childhood largely generates a critical response that believes the texts only in terms of their own claims to absolute success: the remarkable thing to most critics, as we have seen from their writings, is that these texts retrieve so wonderfully what the texts themselves diagnose as unretrievable. And yet to the critics the value of a remarkable overcoming of what they see as the hurdle of autobiographical memory, apparently by means of Goethe's and Eliot's great artistry, or Catherine Sinclair's ground-breaking perspicacity about the true nature of children, lies in an unquestioned and unquestionable ability on their own part to instantly recognize and identify what the texts construct as, I am suggesting, impossibility. It must be noted that, by definition and paradoxically, the critics themselves must also, overtly or inadvertently, be claiming to possess a unique capacity for retrieval or observation of childhood in order to make these judgements of the truthfulness or accuracy of these novels. In this way the criticism reinstates a 'real' past and childhood for a novel, *The Mill on the Floss,* which writes a past and a present both as constructed in relation to one another. Similarly, the criticism reads *Holiday House* as one of the discoverers of the real, natural child, while I have read it here as formulating and reformulating the paradoxes of writing a natural child it wishes to preserve as beyond the reach of writing. As long as critics, and not just critics, but any commentators on childhood or, in fact, any text, whether it be labelled as fictional or as autobiography, biography, history or persons pertaining to the identity in question, insist on the regression to the 'real', the claim to authority will triumph over that very reverence for the text this criticism wants to see itself as demonstrating.

Notes

My thanks to Dr Stephen Thomson, Dr Daniela Caselli, and Professor John Pilling for reading and commenting on drafts of this piece. Thanks also to Stephen Thomson for suggesting the title.

1. *Quarterly Review* (October 1814), repr. in: *Contemporary Reviews of Romantic Poetry,* ed. by John Wain (London: Harrap, 1953), pp. 68-70 (p. 69).

2. With sociology in particular the case is different: it has done much work in analysing childhood as a contingent, constructed identity; see for instance, Martin Barker, *Comics, Power, Ideology, and the Critics* (Manchester: Manchester University Press, 1989); *The Sociology of Childhood, Essential Readings,* ed. by Chris Jenks (London: Batsford, 1982); Chris Jenks, *Childhood* (London: Routledge, 1996); *Constructing and Reconstructing Childhood, Contemporary Issues in the Sociologi-*

cal Study of Childhood, ed. by Allison James and Alan Prout (London: Falmer Press, 1990, repr. 1997); *Thatcher's Children? Politics, Childhood and Society in the 1980s and 1990s,* ed. by Jane Pilcher and Stephen Wagg (London: Falmer Press, 1996); Allison James, Alan Prout, and Chris Jenks, *Theorizing Childhood* (London: Falmer Press, 1997); Rex and Wendy Stainton Rogers, *Stories of Childhood: Shifting Agendas of Child Concern* (Hemel Hempstead: Harvester Wheatsheaf, 1992).

3. *Tendencies* (London: Routledge, 1994), p. xii.

4. Introduction to *Feminisms,* ed. by Sandra Kemp and Judith Squires (Oxford and New York: Oxford University Press, 1997), pp. 3-12 (p. 12).

5. There are children's literature critics who do claim an engagement with, and adoption of, 'adult' literary theories and approaches, but see my chapter 'Childhood and Textuality: Culture, History, Literature', in *Children in Culture: Approaches to Childhood,* ed. by Karín Lesnik-Oberstein (London: Macmillan, and New York: St Martin's Press, 1998), pp. 1-28, for an extensive analysis of the problems with these claims. The issue of how 'children's literature' and 'adult' literature might be defined and differentiated is itself part of ongoing debates.

6. See for a more extensive discussion of this issue my article '*Oliver Twist*: The Narrator's Tale', *Textual Practice,* 15.1 (March 2001), 87-100.

7. All references are to George Eliot, *The Mill on the Floss,* ed. by Carol T. Christ (New York and London: Norton, 1994).

8. *George Eliot's Life* (Edinburgh: Blackwood, 1885).

9. *George Eliot: The Last Victorian* (London: Fourth Estate, 1998).

10. *George Eliot* (London: Macmillan, 1902), p. 5.

11. Frederick Karl, *George Eliot: A Biography* (London: HarperCollins, 1995), p. ix, referring to Ruby Redinger, *George Eliot: The Emergent Self* (New York: Knopf, 1975).

12. 'Portrayal of Childhood', in *The Oxford Reader's Companion to George Eliot,* ed. by John Rignall (Oxford: Oxford University Press, 2000), p. 52.

13. Letter from George Henry Lewes to John Blackwood, 5 March 1860, quoted in *The Mill on the Floss,* ed. by Carol T. Christ, p. 429.

14. For examples of the few critics who do not link the childhood episodes in *The Mill on the Floss* to Eliot's 'life' see: R. H. Lee, 'The Unity of *The Mill on the Floss*' (1964), in *George Eliot: The Mill on the Floss and Silas Marner,* Casebook series, ed. by R. P. Draper (London: Macmillan, 1977), pp. 140-59; Sally Shuttleworth, *George Eliot and Nineteenth Century Science: The Make-Believe of a Beginning* (Cambridge: Cambridge University Press, 1984). My arguments in this article have, however, to do with different issues from those mentioned by Lee and Shuttleworth.

15. *Particularities: Readings in George Eliot* (London: Owen, 1982), p. 58.

16. 'The Fictional Perspective: *The Mill on the Floss* and *Silas Marner*', in *George Eliot: The Mill on the Floss and Silas Marner,* pp. 234-51 (pp. 234, 236).

17. *The Great Tradition* (London, Chatto & Windus, 1948), pp. 18-24, repr. in *The Mill on the Floss,* ed. Carol T. Christ, pp. 483-88 (p. 483).

18. Unsigned review of *The Mill on the Floss, Spectator,* 7 April 1860, repr. in *The Mill on the Floss,* ed. Carol T. Christ, pp. 441-44 (p. 441).

19. Gordon S. Haight, *George Eliot's Originals and Contemporaries: Essays in Victorian Literary History and Biography,* ed. by Hugh Witemeyer (London: Macmillan, 1992), p. 14.

20. For one of the few other discussions I have been able to find on textual sources for a childhood section of *The Mill on the Floss* and subsequent implications, see Lila Harper, 'An Astonishing Change in Metaphor: Tom's Education and the Shrew-Mouse', *George Eliot-George Henry Lewes Studies,* 38-39 (September 2000), 76-79. My thanks to Dr Harper for letting me know of her work and making a copy of the article available to me.

21. All references are to Catherine Sinclair, *Holiday House: A Book for the Young* (London: Ward Lock & Bowden, n.d.).

22. There are more studies of the influence of 'adult' literature on children's literature. For one example see, Ulf Boëthius, '"Us is near bein' wild things ourselves": Procreation and Sexuality in *The Secret Garden*', *Children's Literature Association Quarterly,* 22.4 (Winter 1997-98), 188-95.

23. F. J. Harvey Darton, *Children's Books in England: Five Centuries of Social Life,* (1932), 3rd edn, rev. by Brian Alderson (Cambridge: Cambridge University Press, 1982), p. 220.

24. George Eliot, *Selected Critical Writings,* ed. by Rosemary Ashton (Oxford: Oxford University Press, 1992), p. 318.

25. For a more extensive argument of this claim, see my article 'The Psychopathology of Everyday

Children's Literature Criticism', *Cultural Critique,* 45 (Spring 2000), 222-42.

26. Daniel Vitaglione, *George Eliot and George Sand* (New York: Lang, 1993), p. 7, referring to Patricia Thomson, *George Sand and the Victorians* (London: Macmillan, 1977).

27. With thanks to my colleague Phillipa Hardman for suggesting this idea to me, as she related the idea of inserting a text into a memory of an own childhood to claims of not being able to remember whether a memory derives from a photograph or from 'real life'.

28. *The Mill on the Floss,* ed. by A. S. Byatt (London: Penguin, 1979), p. 31, quoting George Henry Lewes, *Life and Works of Goethe* (1855), Book III, Chapter 5 (London: Dent, n.d.), p. 154.

29. The most important text to have analysed childhood as a historically shifting and changing category is Philippe Ariès, *Centuries of Childhood: A Social History of Family Life* (1959), trans. by Robert Baldick (London: Cape, 1962).

30. 'The World of Children's Literature: France', in *The International Companion Encyclopedia of Children's Literature,* ed. by Peter Hunt (London and New York: Routledge, 1996), pp. 717-25 (p. 720).

31. Margaret Kinnell, 'Early Texts Used by Children', in *The International Companion Encyclopedia of Children's Literature,* pp. 141-51 (p. 149).

32. For more extensive analyses of Jean-Jacques Rousseau and John Locke as not the 'discoverers' but the 'inventors' of 'childhood', see Jacqueline Rose, *The Case of Peter Pan or: The Impossibility of Children's Literature* (London: Macmillan, 1984); Karín Lesnik-Oberstein, *Children's Literature: Criticism and the Fictional Child* (Oxford: Clarendon Press, 1994) especially Chapter 3, 'On Knowing the Child: Stories of Origin and the Education-Amusement Divide', pp. 69-99.

33. In *The Mill on the Floss,* ed. by Carol T. Christ, pp. 584-85.

34. 'The Family Story', in *The International Companion Encyclopedia of Children's Literature,* pp. 338-47 (p. 339).

35. My formulations here refer to Jean-François Lyotard's critique of the real in, for instance, *The Postmodern Explained to Children. Correspondence 1982-1985* (1986), trans. by Julian Pefanis and Morgan Thomas (London: Turnaround, 1992).

36. For a more extensive analysis of constructions of ideas of 'nature' with regard to childhood in both criticism and fiction, see Stephen Thomson, 'Substitute Communities, Authentic Voices: The Organic Writing of the Child', in *Children in Culture: Approaches to Childhood,* pp. 248-73.

37. With thanks to Dr Stephen Thomson for providing me with this formulation of a past putting the present into question.

ROMANTICISM AND CHILDHOOD

Samuel Pickering, Jr. (essay date spring 1984)

SOURCE: Pickering, Samuel, Jr. "The 'Race of Real Children' and Beyond in *Tom Brown's School Days.*" *The Arnoldian* 11, no. 2 (spring 1984): 36-46.

[*In the following essay, Pickering compares the Romantic ideas on education and childhood expressed in Thomas Hughes's* Tom Brown's School Days, *William Wordsworth's* Prelude, *and Charlotte Brontë's* Jane Eyre.]

According to Thomas Hughes, Wordsworth was a "learned and venerable poet" whose works people admired and discussed but rarely read. Hughes himself read Wordsworth and at the beginning of *Tom Brown's School Days* cited Wordsworth's statement that the child was the father of the man as an apologia for his own focus on childhood. If Wordsworth were correct, he noted, then the child "must be father to the boy." Wordsworth and Hughes were Lockeans, believing that impressions made upon "tender Infancies" had lasting consequences, and in their major writings both stressed the crucial importance of childhood experience. *The Prelude* was published in 1850, and *Tom Brown's School Days* seven years later. Although the passages which described Wordsworth's childhood had, for the most part, been written before 1805, Tom Brown was cut from the same formative and instructional cloth as Wordsworth's young poet. Many of the educational concerns to which Wordsworth addressed himself in the first books of *The Prelude* were similar to those which Hughes focused on in the initial chapters of *Tom Brown's School Days.* As a child Tom grew up as one of Wordsworth's "race of real children." The Wordsworthian childhood with its high spirits and developing imagination served Tom well until he reached adolescence. Then it was necessary, Hughes thought, to temper Tom's character. To this end he used religion, much as Charlotte Bronte depended upon religion to control Jane Eyre's imagination. A comparison of Hughes's and Wordsworth's treatment of childhood, and to a

lesser extent that of Charlotte Bronte, not only sheds light on Hughes's educational ideas but also prevents the *School Days* from being quickly labelled and inadequately considered, as has often been done, an effusion of Muscular Christianity or just "a cheery, hearty, rattling record of an average boy's lot in the world of one of our great schools."[1]

In the first book of *The Prelude,* Wordsworth stated that he had been "much favoured" by both his birthplace and that "beloved vale" (Esthwaite) to which he moved as a small child. Tom Brown was also favored by his birthplace. He, too, had grown up in a beloved vale, the Vale of White Horse. Apart from the fret of modern life, Tom's birthplace belonged more in the eighteenth than the nineteenth century. "It is not every one who has had the good fortune," Fitzjames Stephens observed in the *Edinburgh Review* (1858), "to be born in a country village with its quaint customs and primitive simplicity." In *The Prelude* Wordsworth recalled the old wives' and fairy tales which he had read as a child and lamented the fact that educators had excluded chapbooks from the nursery. "Oh," he wrote, "give us once again" Robin Hood, Sabra in the forest with St. George, the wishing cap of Fortunatus, and the invisible coat of Jack the Giant-killer, Such stories, Wordsworth thought, expanded children's imaginations, broadened their sensibilities, and thereby indirectly prepared them for life's many mental and moral challenges. Thus the dead man with the "ghastly face" rising "bolt upright" out of Esthwaite's Lake did not frighten him when he was young because, Wordsworth explained, he had seen such sights before in romances and in fairy land. For Hughes the Vale of White Horse was almost an emblematic volume of stories, containing Jack's invisible coat and Fortunatus' cap. Legends associated with Wayland Smith's Cave, the Dragon's Hill, the Giant's Stairs, the Manger, and the Ridgeway appealed like old wives' and fairy tales to a child's imagination. Like Wordsworth Hughes lamented the neglect which was now the lot of such stories. This neglect, he thought, undermined not simply individual character but also love of home and concomitantly the strength of the nation.[2]

In *The Prelude* Wordsworth accused those he called "mighty workmen of our later age" of banishing fairy tales from childhood. These workmen, contemporary educators like Sarah Trimmer, Anna Barbauld, Hannah More, and Jane West, believed that children should be taught useful and moral knowledge almost exclusively. From Locke they, too, had learned the importance of childhood experience. Education, they believed, shaped both the moral and economic man, and they worked, Wordsworth wrote, "to manage books and things" in order to make them act "on infant minds." Fairy tales, they argued, vitiated children's "tastes" and filled their minds with "fantastic visions." Instead of feeding upon dangerous "sweetmeats," children, they stressed, should

imbibe "useful knowledge." From Wordsworth's point of view, and later from that of Hughes, what they taught was not so much useful as it was morally and imaginatively debilitating.[3]

In the fifth book of *The Prelude,* Wordsworth said he was thankful he had been reared "safe from an evil" which was "laid" upon contemporary children and which he thought might have dried him up "body and soul." Born in a freer educational time, he escaped the mighty workmen. Instead "in the season of unperilous choice," he recounted, he ranged at will across the "open ground of Fancy." In contrast, he continued, contemporary educators confined children "like engines," and in trying to control impressions made upon tender infancies manufactured an artificial "model of a child," rather than a real child. "Generous as a fountain," "never quarrelsome," "a miracle of scientific lore," the child at first appeared an exemplar of moral and intellectual virtues. Unfortunately first appearances deceived, and the child lived only to grow "wiser every day." The artificial, bookish education which he received had so limited him that wonder was driven from his soul, and he was trapped within "the pinfold of his own conceit." In contrast the child who roamed across the open ground of fancy, even if only through fairy tales, and not across "woodland beds" and along "river sides," reaped at least "one precious gain": he forgot himself.[4]

Hughes was not so wonderfully articulate as Wordsworth and did not dwell so directly on the abuses of contemporary education. His opinions on education and his metaphoric way of expressing them were similar, however. With its "country legends" and "stories of the old gable-ended farmhouses," the Vale of White Horse was Hughes's open ground of fancy. Like Wordsworth he believed contemporary education separated the mind from the heart and imagination. Although "young England" could "patter" French and German, held opinions about "high art," and was "chock-full of science," it neglected Wordsworth's woodland beds and river sides. Not one young person in twenty, Hughes claims, knew "where to find the wood-sorrel, or bee-orchis" which grew in the next wood or on the down three miles away. Roaming the Vale brought true knowledge and expanded the imagination more than covering "a couple of thousand miles of ground" in, as he called his age, "these railway times." Like Wordsworth Hughes was certain that education confined children's imaginations; although the railway covered more ground than Wordsworth's engine, it still moved mechanically and the results were much the same. Although Wordsworth's "model of a child" appeared selfless, he was actually unbendingly selfish and single-mindedly devoted to personal success. The moral platitudes he repeated were bloodless abstractions, and he felt little sympathy for others. In *Tom Brown,* Hughes also criticized abstract morality and pejoratively called the age "the day of

large views and glorious humanity." Behind such grandiloquent phrases parroted from school or a philosophic primer lay, he thought, little real concern for one's fellow man.[5]

In addition to Wordsworth's educational concerns, Hughes often shared Dickens's views. In *Hard Times* (1854), Dickens contrasted two educational worlds: the world of fairies and imagination, embodied by Sleary's Circus, and the world of utilitarian educational fact, embodied by M'Choakumchild's classroom and Mr. Gradgrind's Stone Lodge. With its penny peep-shows, pink-eyed ladies, dwarfs, wild Indians, boa constrictors, and Irish giant, the Veast was the Sleary's Circus of the *School Days.* In opposition to Hughes's version of utilitarian fact, "new fangled comprehensive plans," and "philanthropic intellectualism," the Veast was another representation of an educational open ground of fancy. Like Dickens and Wordsworth, Hughes emphasized that education of "working boys and young men" should include an equivalent of "the country 'veast.'" At the Veast as in fairy tales, children forgot themselves. Their imaginations wandered freely, expanding their sensibilities and enabling them to sympathize more readily with the lots of others and to meet the challenges of life with less anxiety. The Veast was not, Hughes stressed, a "class amusement." Rigorous determination of which amusements were proper to each class, he believed, constricted children's imaginations, and thereby limited their capacities for understanding and sympathy. Trapped by propriety and false dignity, Wordsworth's model of a child was "never known to mix in quarrels" and would not have enjoyed the Veast and the jingling match.[6]

Shepherds, Wordsworth recounted, were the men that pleased him first. Not so much an emblem of the harmony that could exist between man and nature as a male "old wife," Benjy acted as Tom's shepherd, entertaining him with tale-like accounts of "the doings of deceased Browns" and escorting him to the Veast. Educational workmen would most certainly have disapproved of Benjy. But Tom, like the young poet, was from Wordsworth's "race of real children." Wrestling with Harry Winburn, playing with Jacob Doodlecalf, interrupting lessons in the village school, and throwing rocks at the swallows nesting under the wheelwright's eaves, Tom like Wordsworth's real children was not too wise, learned, or good. Instead like them, he was "wanton, fresh" and "fierce, moody, patient, venturous, modest, shy." "Through doing wrong and suffering," Tom, although his punishments were gentle slaps on the wrist, purchased that "knowledge" beyond books which did not stifle his imagination or his capacity to escape the selfishness which imprisoned children within their own conceits.[7]

Squire Brown's neighbors, the equivalent of Wordsworth's educational workmen, criticized him for letting his son "run wild with all the dirty village boys." Whenever they saw Tom in the middle of a group of boys, loaded with bundles "of cowslip and meadow sweet, or young starlings or magpies," they shrugged their shoulders and muttered that "no good" would come of Tom. In allowing his son to roam across the open ground of fancy, physically and mentally Squire Brown resembled Wordsworth's mother. Arguing that nine men out of ten were made good or evil, useful or not, by their educations, Locke convinced most parents and educators in the eighteenth century that they could determine not only the kinds of adults children became but also the social and economic success they would enjoy. In contrast to such parents and educators, Wordsworth's mother was old-fashioned, "fetching her goodness rather from times past." She, too, knew the importance of early educational experiences, but instead of believing she could shape her children "for times to come," she trusted that God who provided mothers with milk would, through Nature itself, correct and control the development of her children. As a result she was not "puffed up by false unnatural hopes" or "selfish with unnecessary cares." Like Wordsworth's mother, Squire Brown trusted nature. Moreover he did not entertain extravagant hopes for his son or worry unnecessarily about impressions made upon young Tom. Fantastic visions of Tom's future, incited by educators, did not enter his mind, and being as old-fashioned as Wordsworth's mother, he only wanted Tom to "turn out a brave, helpful, truth-telling Englishman, and a gentleman and a Christian.[8]

According to Hughes, the object of schools was "not to ram Latin and Greek into boys" but to make "good future citizens." The most important part of this work was done, he stressed, "out of school hours." At Rugby, Tom's studies were not rigorous, and at first he continued to be "bandied up and down" with real children, characters like East, "frank, hearty, and good-natured, well-satisfied with himself and his position, and chock full of life and spirits." During his first years at Rugby Tom remained mischievous, getting in trouble, for example, with Velveteens the game keeper, much as he had with the wheelwright at home. Along with continuing the spirit of Tom's early informal education, Rugby also tested the value of that education. The years Tom spent roaming the open ground of fancy, at the Veast or playing with the village boys, affected his imagination positively and gave him the capacity to tolerate and appreciate diversity. In contrast to others, he became the friend of those students at Rugby who did not fit in, Martin and Diggs for example.[9]

As Wordsworth believed that fairy tales foreshadowed many of the difficulties children would face and indirectly prepared them for life's trials, so football, Hughes believed, prepared children for life. At Rugby "real children" played football in the right spirit, and like the

reader of fairy tales were unconsciously prepared to meet the "ghastly" things which would rise, not necessarily from Esthwaite's Lake, but from the depths of the self. In a chapter entitled "The War of Independence," Tom and East fought and overcame the bully Flashman. In *Jane Eyre* (1847), young Jane spent much time at the Reeds' house poring over imaginative literature. Books like the *Arabian Nights* and particularly Goldsmith's *History of Rome* served her as fairy tales served Wordsworth's real children and as the Veast served Tom. They appealed to her imagination and in the process so expanded it that they became dragon-slayers, preparing Jane for the evils she would struggle against as a child. As Jane's reading enabled her to recognize John Reed as a Caligula and accordingly helped her to deal with his persecution, so Tom's childhood in the Vale and his experiences in games like football helped him overcome Flashman. On one level Flashman, cruelly enforcing the fagging system and sadistically torturing young boys, "cooking" Tom in fact until he fainted, was simply an ogre. On another level he was that selfish part of a person's character which the model child never overcame. When not controlled, selfishness threatened all children's moral development. Only those, both Hughes and Wordsworth taught, who had wandered through imaginative vales "rich with indigenous produce" could triumph over it when it inevitably began to undermine moral growth.[10]

In his first years at Rugby, Tom was distinguished, Hughes wrote, only for his "excess of boyishness; by which I mean animal life in its fullest measure, good nature and honest impulses, hatred of injustice and meanness, and thoughtlessness enough to sink a three-decker." This boyishness or animal life initially benefitted Tom at Rugby. After he had thrashed Flashman, however, it threatened to impede his development. After the fight Tom's growth did not follow the pattern of Wordsworth's real children. Instead he began to resemble Jane Eyre, before she left Gateshead for Lowood and just after she successfully bearded her aunt, accusing her of being deceitful and hard-hearted. As Mrs. Reed collapsed under Jane's accusations, Jane said her soul began to exult with a sense "of triumph." This exultation was short-lived, however, as Jane recounted that she soon felt poisoned. In hopes of changing her mood, she turned to the dragon-slayer of her early childhood, literature which appealed to the imagination, specifically the *Arabian Nights*. Unlike the earlier occasion in which imaginative literature had helped her overcome John Reed, literature failed her this time, and she wandered dejectedly outside whispering "What shall I do?" Both Charlotte Bronte and Thomas Hughes recognized the formative importance of the child's wandering across the ground of fancy, either imaginatively through books or actually as one of the race of real children. But, unlike Wordsworth, they also recognized the necessity of tempering the imagination and the

spirit. Jane's question about her future should be emended to "What shall I do to be saved?" For Charlotte Bronte right religion provided the answer. Although Tom's victory over Flashman did not lead him to a Jane Eyre-like dejection, the triumph did not provide Tom with substantial or lasting rewards. Instead Tom became something of an outlaw, forever getting into scrapes, so many that "it was a toss-up" whether he would "turn out well or ill." As religion curtailed the abuses of the imagination in *Jane Eyre* and prevented Jane from giving in to her animal impulses and becoming Rochester's mistress, and eventually another Bertha Mason, so it also saved Tom by disciplining his excess of "animal life."[11]

At this juncture in the narrative, a journalist wrote in the *Eclectic Review* (1858), "A delicate little boy appears upon the stage, who is assigned as a chum to Tom Brown, with a view of softening his stoic virtues, and relieving him of a portion of wild oats which threaten to cover his too-neglected field." Metaphorically George Arthur and Tom Brown were two aspects of a child's character, Tom being the healthy physical aspect without which the spirit could not thrive and George being the spiritual aspect without which the body would go astray. In part Hughes used the relationship between Harry Sandford and Tommy Merton in Thomas Day's *Sandford and Merton* (1783-1789) as a model. In recalling the composition of *Tom Brown*, J. M. Ludlow, the friend with whom Hughes shared a library at Copse Hall, wrote in the *Economic Review* (1896) that Hughes said "he had often thought that good might be done by a real novel for boys," one, he continued, which was not so didactic as *Sandford and Merton* but which was "written in a right spirit." When Ludlow agreed with him, Hughes showed him what he had written of *Tom Brown*. Although Hughes wanted to avoid what he saw as the unrelenting preaching of *Sandford and Merton,* Day's novel was on his mind when he composed *Tom Brown*. And despite his disclaimer to Ludlow, the latter half of *Tom Brown,* after George Arthur appeared, was extremely didactic. Mr. Barlow, the minister who educated Sandford and Merton, anticipated the Doctor at Rugby. Like the Doctor, Mr. Barlow believed that the spirit of Christianity formed the basis of right education. Moreover although George Arthur had little except a weak body in common with priggish Master Merton, Tom Brown and Harry Sandford shared a wealth of honest, animal impulses. In Day's novel although Sandford strongly influenced Merton for the better, Merton himself exerted little positive influence upon Sandford. In contrast George and Arthur influenced each other a great deal, so much so that by the conclusion of the book they become almost the same person, metaphorically representing that successful union of body and spirit, which Hughes, like Squire Brown, believed right education should produce.[12]

What his first biographer called "the seductive eloquence of *Rousseau*" influenced Thomas Day's writings. Although the education received by Tommy Sandford differed in particulars from that advocated by Rousseau in *Emilius and Sophia* (1762-1763), "in general the things taught and methods used" resembled those in *Emilius*. In a similar manner, Rousseau, or the educational suggestions which he made and which had percolated through English society, influenced Thomas Hughes, most strongly his attitude towards teaching religion. Rousseau urged delaying religious education until children were young adults. At fifteen, he said, Emilius would not know whether or not he had a soul. Even at that comparatively late age, a child, he thought, was not capable of believing in God and he wrote that if he were "to design a picture of the most deplorable stupidity" it would be "a pedant teaching children their catechism." Ideally for Rousseau, religious education would begin at eighteen. For this stance on religious education, those mighty workmen whom Wordsworth described, assailed Rousseau. In attacking *Emilius* in the *Guardian of Education* (1802), Mrs. Trimmer wrote that *"The expediency of deferring religious instruction beyond the stages of infancy and childhood"* had caused "inconceivable" mischief and was part, she argued, of *"a conspiracy against* CHRISTIANITY *and all* SOCIAL ORDER." In her popular *Letters Addressed to a Young Man* (1801), Mrs. Jane West said she believed that "an intelligent child of seven" could "conceive enough of Christianity to be in reality a Christian." It was "Rousseau's design," she argued, to turn Emilius into a deist. A person who reached eighteen without knowing that God existed, she wrote, would "never be in *much* danger of becoming a Christian."[13]

As Squire Brown rejected the criticisms made by his neighbors of Tom's playing with the village boys, so Hughes ignored the educational workmen who urged the necessity of early religious education. In following Rousseau's footsteps, Hughes did, however, modify the suggestion that religious instruction be deferred until children were eighteen. When Tom and Arthur first shared a study, Arthur was thirteen and Tom fourteen, that age when animal spirits, if not disciplined, could turn into animal passions. Almost immediately the boys exerted a good influence upon each other. When Arthur prayed, risking his schoolmates' ridicule, Tom came to his aid. Soon afterward Tom began praying. Within a short time, Hughes wrote, "Tom was becoming a new boy," fighting a "hard battle" as every boy must "when he finds himself for the first time consciously at grips with self and the devil." For his part, Tom introduced Arthur to health-producing activities: swimming, cricket, and bird-nesting. As Arthur's religion now protected the susceptible adolescent from moral decay, so Tom's animal impulses protected him from physical illness. When fever broke out at Rugby, Arthur was "still frail and delicate, with more spirit than body." He now

had body enough, however, to overcome the fever, something he would not have been able to do had he not met Tom.[14]

As Charlotte Bronte used Bertha Mason as an instructive example of passions undisciplined by religion, so Hughes used East to illustrate the dangers of untempered high spirits. Not sharing a study with Arthur and thereby being apart from spiritual things, East remained adolescent "with a constant fund of animal health and spirits which he did not feel bound to curb in any way." Although East was scrupulously honest, he soon found himself alone. His dislike of the false kept corrupt characters away from him while steady boys avoided him as one with whom "it would be dangerous to be intimate." East's being out of step with the good part of his schoolmates was emblematic of the disorder that untempered animal spirits inflicted upon his character. For Hughes the remedy was religion, and once East was confirmed, all was well.[15]

By the end of the novel, Tom was captain of cricket. In the final game Arthur was a member of the eleven. Although slight, he was "well knit and active"; and when put into the Marylebone match, he performed adequately. He resembled Tom himself, as well as should have, for Tom was now an integral part of his nature. Similarly in the last chapter when Tom returned to Rugby after the Doctor's death, Arthur did not appear. His appearance was unnecessary because he was present as part of Tom, as part of the union of body and spirit which Hughes thought good education should effect. "Cloth of frieze" took hugely, as the writer in the *Eclectic Review* stated, "to cloth of gold," so much so that they became indistinguishable.[16]

Notes

1. Thomas Hughes, *Tom Brown's School Days* (New York: Airmont, 1968), p. 31. This is a readily available paperback edition. James L. Axtell, ed., *The Educational Writings of John Locke* (Cambridge: Cambridge University Press, 1968), p. 114. J. C. Maxwell, ed., *William Wordsworth: The Prelude. A Parallel Text* (New York: Penguin Books, 1978), p. 193, line 411. *Eclectic Review,* series six, 3 (1858), 422.

2. Wordsworth, p. 51, lines 301-04; 189, lines 341-63; 195, lines 444-59. *Edinburgh Review,* 107 (1858), 173. Hughes, pp. 23-24.

3. Wordsworth, p. 189, line 347. Maria Edgeworth, *The Parent's Assistant; or, Stories for Children* (London, 1796), second edition, part one, xi-xii. Mrs. Jane West, *The Advantages of Education; or, The History of Maria Williams* (London, 1803), second edition, I, 3. Hannah More, "The Two Wealthy Farmers," *Cheap Repository Tracts* (London, 1795), part one. 18-20.

4. Wordsworth, pp. 181, lines 224-245; 185, lines 299-314; 187, lines 329-340.

5. Hughes, pp. 20-21.

6. Hughes, pp. 37, 46-47. Wordsworth, p. 185, lines 299-300.

7. Hughes, p. 35. Wordsworth, pp. 193, lines 407-425; 307, line 128.

8. Hughes, pp. 59, 68. Axtell, p. 114. Wordsworth, p. 183, lines 267-85.

9. Hughes, pp. 61, 81. Wordsworth, p. 193, lines 411-13.

10. Hughes, p. 130. Wordsworth, p. 181, lines 236.

11. Hughes, pp. 119, 159. Richard J. Dunn, ed., *Jane Eyre* (New York: Norton, 1971), p. 33.

12. *Eclectic Review,* p. 430. *Economic Review,* 6 (1896), 306-307.

13. James Keir, *An Account of the Life and Writings of Thomas Day, Esq.* (London, 1791), pp. 25-26. George Warren Gignilliat, Jr., *The Author of Sandford and Merton* (New York: Columbia University Press, 1932), p. 293. J. J. Rousseau, *Emilius and Sophia; or, A New System of Education* (London, 1762-1763), II, 257-258. This is the first English translation of *Emilius. Guardian of Education,* 1 (1802), 2, 10-11. Mrs. Jane West, *Letters Addressed to a Young Man, On His First Entrance Into Life* (London, 1801), III, 355-56.

14. Hughes, pp. 198, 232.

15. Hughes, pp. 254-255.

16. Hughes, p. 268. *Eclectic Review,* p. 430.

Alan Richardson (essay date 1999)

SOURCE: Richardson, Alan. "Romanticism and the End of Childhood." *Nineteenth-Century Contexts* 21, no. 2 (1999): 169-89.

[*In the following essay, Richardson argues that the Romantic conception of childhood has declined in popularity during the last centuries and discusses the reasons for this decline as well as its potential and observed consequences.*]

Adolescents regularly bring weapons to school, and the daily violence occasionally erupts into knife-fights; a thirteen-year-old beats another student to death at a prestigious academy. Less affluent urban children spend more time on the streets than at school and drift unthinkingly into criminal activity, and an anxious public allows children to be prosecuted and sentenced as adults. Gangs of inner-city children battle one another for turf, so economically desperate that they fight over scavenging rights to the scrap metal at burnt-out building sites. Teenage pregnancy is epidemic; alarmingly large numbers of unplanned, unwanted infants stand at severe risk of undernourishment, neglect, and abuse. In rural areas, impoverished children of casual agricultural laborers—who more often than not lack literacy skills and political rights—are shamefully and openly exploited, working alongside their parents beginning at ages as young as six or seven.

This list—which could easily be extended—sounds all too familiar, and might have been culled from a month's reading of any major urban newspaper in the U.S. It provides ample evidence (if any further evidence is needed) of the "fall," "disappearance," or "erosion" of childhood which sociologists, social historians, and educationalists have been warning us about for the past dozen years or so (Sommerville; Postman; Suransky). Yet all of these examples are taken from accounts of late-eighteenth- and early-nineteenth-century England, a period during which the modern notion of childhood as a discrete, protected, innocent state devoted to schooling and recreation rather than productive labor was first being widely disseminated across class lines (Chandos 133-54; Pinchbeck and Hewitt 2: 351-53; Place; Liu 251-66). Ironically, as the Romantic ideal of childhood loses its social purchase, the condition of contemporary children begins to resemble more and more that of the majority of their real Romantic-era counterparts. A "Romantic" childhood may soon again become an elite experience, mainly limited to middle- and upper-class families with the economic and cultural capital to afford it—as it was until our own century. In its threatened dissolution, childhood brings us up against the limits of certain canonical forms of Romanticism even in registering their cultural force. It may equally, however, raise questions regarding both the limits of a postmodern devaluation of Romantic values, and the potential for finding something to recuperate in a discourse that, as it recedes from us in time, throws our own cultural practices into sharper outline.

Not everyone would agree, of course, that the demise of the Romantic child is anything to lament. Before considering the case against cultural nostalgia (if not exactly for social complacency), however, I should be more specific about why I use the adjective "Romantic," a notoriously vexed term which recently has again come under assault (Perkins 85-119). After all, an extended childhood considered as a unique period of life, intimately bound up with schooling and other forms of intellectual and moral development, can be traced back to Renaissance humanism or even earlier, and had already succeeded in generating a "new world" of children's toys, books, games, and clothing in eighteenth-century England (Aries; Plumb). This notion of

childhood, perhaps best called "educative," was still, however, an avant-garde ideal largely confined to a social elite (the upper and—especially—the "middling" classes) at the beginning of the Romantic era. What was it that enabled and propelled the democratization of this ideal, particularly at a time when, because of industrialization, children's labor was becoming more rather than less economically valuable (Zelizer)? In his recent and important study *The Children of the Poor*, Hugh Cunningham suggests that the extension to all children (in theory if not always in practice) of the rights and enjoyments previously associated with the children of the dominant group was inextricably bound up with a "change in the representation of childhood" (7) in the early nineteenth century. More specifically, it was the emergence of a "romantic concept of the child" and a "sensibility and rhetoric" among social reformers "unquestionably informed by an internalized acquaintance with the Romantic poets" that made this unprecedented and (in crudely economic terms) unlikely extension of the educative ideal viable (51, 90).

What was novel about the representation of childhood in canonical Romantic writing? In many ways, nothing. The literary "sentimentalization" of childhood—which may have been a necessary condition for taking children out of the workforce (Zelizer 6-12)—can be found throughout eighteenth-century poetry before Wordsworth; even the image of the transcendentalized infant, which Wordsworth seems single-handedly to have revived from the works of such (then) obscure seventeenth-century Anglican writers as Vaughan and Earle, turns out to have been anticipated by several eighteenth-century women poets whose works have only recently been recovered (Babenroth, Cunningham 48). But the Romantics, particularly Wordsworth, Coleridge, Lamb, and De Quincey, succeeded at popularizing an image of the child which was no less powerful for being somewhat incoherent, intermingling the sentimentalism of eighteenth-century verse, the transcendentalism of Vaughan, a Lockean emphasis on the child's malleability, and a Rousseauvian faith in original innocence and "natural" principles of growth. Barbara Garlitz has shown in compelling detail that a single poem by Wordsworth—the "Immortality" ode, with its image of the child as "Best Philosopher," fresh from a heavenly pre-existence and "trailing clouds of glory"—functioned throughout nineteenth-century British culture as at once synecdoche and authority for the new conception of childhood, appearing via citation, quotation, or allusion not only throughout poetry but also in sermons, journal articles, polemics for children's rights, and the writings of pioneering social workers like Mary Carpenter and Thomas Barnardo (see also Cunningham 145). Wordsworth's powerful and eminently memorable articulation of the child's "heaven-born freedom" could be readily deployed within progressive and egalitarian tendencies in British nineteenth-century social thought (Garlitz 649). According to Neil Postman, the "Romantic vision of childhood" similarly facilitated the beginnings of the progressive education movement in the U.S., as well as inspiring "America's greatest book," *The Adventures of Huckleberry Finn* (60-61).

Postman's citation of Twain reminds us that works of children's literature perform no less important cultural work—geared as they are to aid, however directly or indirectly, in the formation of certain kinds of subjectivities—than do the sermons, polemics, and poems for adults surveyed by Garlitz. And nineteenth-century children's literature, both in Britain and America, is pervasively indebted to canonical Romanticism. Here too the "Immortality" ode alone had an extensive influence, and is cited prominently in works as diverse as Kingsley's *Water Babies* (19: 50) and Hughes's *Tom Brown's Schooldays* (33), not to mention its importance for George MacDonald (McGillis). Wordsworth's "child of nature," a Rousseauvian cousin to his "Best Philosopher," becomes an important and recurring figure throughout Victorian children's fiction, as well as crucially shaping "adult" fiction about childhood (Knoepflmacher). The Romantic construction of the child, in its various permutations, was relied upon and further varied throughout nineteenth-century children's literature both in Britain and America (McGavran, MacLeod). As a result, the popular image of the child has long manifested, at least within the Anglo-American tradition, a distinctly Romantic cast.

The culturally dominant construction of childhood, one that becomes more visible as its dominance begins to recede and its inevitability is called into question, can usefully be termed a "Romantic" phenomenon. Though its various features can mostly be found in works written prior to or outside of what we ordinarily call Romanticism—in seventeenth- and eighteenth-century British poetry, in Evangelical children's fiction, in Rousseau, in some facets of Enlightenment education theory—the constellation of those features, and the popularization of the resulting overdetermined construction, belong to the mainstream Romantic tradition (Plotz; Richardson, "Childhood"). The Romantic child may owe its "freedom" to heaven or to a benevolent nature; its growth may be guided by a providentially arranged natural environment or by innate principles of growth (or both); its innocence may have supernatural origins or may instead proceed from its apparent lack of socialization. Either way, the Romantic child makes a strong claim upon us. If we guarantee it a sufficiently benign environment and then, aside from continuing to provide it with ample physical and emotional nurture, we pretty much leave it alone, the child will flourish, may well come to surpass us in its intellectual, ethical, and creative development. If we interfere too extensively and too self-confidently with its growth we risk producing, as Wordsworth will have it in Book V of

The Prelude, a "monster." If, on the other hand, we simply abandon it to the streets, or to early immersion in the workforce, or to inadequate institutions, we have blighted the image of God or of our own best selves. In the wake of Romanticism, the arguments for state-supported, progressive education, for social legislation to assure child welfare, and for the curtailment of child labor could rest on that simple, and that powerful, a foundation.

For all its visceral force, however, did the Romantic image of the child really provide an adequate foundation for social discourses aimed at improving the child's status? Did it elide—or even help to create—conditions as pernicious as those which, armed with Romantic rhetoric, social and educational reformers set out to remedy? Recent work on children's literature and the social construction of childhood, as well as recent critiques (particularly from new historicist and feminist perspectives) of Romanticism, suggests that we should think hard about these questions before we celebrate, with Geoffrey Summerfield and a host of critics before him, the Romantic "defense" of the child. Perhaps most fundamentally, Jacqueline Rose has unmasked the fiction of childhood innocence as a function of "adult desire": an imaginary space for enacting our denial of the "anxieties we have about our psychic, sexual and social being in the world" (xii, xvii). The sentimental construction of childhood innocence codified and endorsed by Romantic authors (here working in conjunction with their un-Romantic contemporaries, from Thomas Day and Anna Barbauld to Leigh Richmond and Sarah Trimmer) can be seen as yet another "burden" which children are forced to take up, one that added to their "repression" even as it diminished their economic exploitation (Sommerville xv, 255). Children, in this reading, were freed from productive labor only to play a different, perhaps no less demanding, role within the capitalist economy as bearers of moral and religious value and as obligatorily blithe denizens of a domestic sphere in which economic man could find respite and emotional renewal (Cunningham 152). Cut off from the productive sphere and expected to enact an impossible fiction, the "innocent" child experiences a kind of social death, as Wordsworth himself seems to acknowledge with his profusion of dead or spectral children: Lucy, Lucy Gray, the Danish Boy, the Boy of Winander (Spiegelman 50-82).

If the domestic and "private" role enjoined upon children during the Romantic era (and since) links them with women within bourgeois ideology, however, Romantic childhood remains, as Mitzi Myers has insisted, as "male-determined" as it is influential ("Little Girls Lost" 135). Canonical Romanticism is a notoriously "masculine" phenomenon, and our cultural enshrinement of the Romantic child has ignored a number of "women's alternative romanticisms" (not to mention alternatives to Romanticism) which might route us past the dead-end that one repeatedly runs up against in Wordsworth's lyrics of childhood, in Lamb's essays, or in De Quincey's fantasies of dead angelic girls (Myers, "Little Girls Lost"). In its distance from the social world, its seeming immateriality, in a word its transcendence, the Romantic child seems deliberately formed to underwrite the wishful autonomy, the privileging of consciousness, and the devaluation of bodily experience for which feminist critics like Marlon Ross and Meena Alexander have disparaged male Romanticism. In this sense, the Romantic child is indeed father of the man.

That canonical Romanticism relies upon and disseminates an illusion of autonomous individuality and an equally wishful evasion of the social and material world lies, of course, at the heart of Marxist and new historicist critiques of what Jerome McGann influentially christened the "Romantic ideology." Deftly and remorselessly working a hermeneutic of suspicion, such analyses suggest that behind the illusion of disinterested transcendence lurks one or more "interested" agendas, from the occlusion of "real" social and economic life to the support of capitalist and imperialist forms of domination. In relation to the historical transformation of childhood in the late eighteenth and early nineteenth centuries, the Romantic construction of childhood as a discrete, unique, critical phase of life has been linked to the programs of discipline, surveillance, and normatization which Foucault delineates in *Discipline and Punish.* Its very susceptibility to "democratic" applications meant that the Romantic ideal could be readily enlisted in ambitious and unprecedented programs to "embrace and regulate" *all* children, not just those of the bourgeoisie (Sommerville 224). As Clifford Siskin has argued in his Foucauldian study of Romantic discourse, the Romantic emphasis on growth and on the self as a "mind that grows" participated in a larger cultural enterprise to place individuals within developmental schemas subject to internalized observation and self-regulation (3). Thus the Romantic cult of childhood can be linked with its apparent contrary, the rationalist and progressive "child-centered" discourse which insures the reproduction of "self-regulated, rational and autonomous subjects" required for the self-perpetuation of modern capitalist economies (Walkerdine 212).

Perhaps, then, the recent spate of jeremiads over the "end of childhood," over the demise, that is, of an identifiably Romantic construction of the child, are misguided. Should we not instead be breathing a collective sigh of relief, trusting (as Rose seems to) that the twilight of the Romantic child may prove the dawn of "other, freer sexualities" and a "more radical social critique" which the myth of Innocence has helped to keep in check (xvii)? Or would this simply constitute an updated, more theoretically sophisticated exercise in construing childhood along the lines of adult desire, now

raised to a millennial pitch?[1] In any case, before altogether consigning childhood to some ideological landfill, we might pause to weigh the social costs of a world without children in the Romantic sense—or, more troubling, a world with only affluent children. If the case can no longer credibly be made for a Romantic childhood in all its Wordsworthian obscurity and splendor, is there nevertheless something valuable, perhaps invaluable, to be salvaged from the Romantic model?

In a critique of the socially debilitating "self-isolation" of canonical Romanticism, Terry Eagleton notes as well the "revolutionary force" of the Romantic sympathetic imagination, the "production of a powerful yet decentred human subject which cannot be formalized within the protocols of rational exchange" (41). If a residue inheres within Romantic representations of childhood that manages to evade the subordination to social discipline that critics like Siskin have analyzed so trenchantly, it lies in moments of decentered subjectivity that have few if any contemporary analogues outside Romanticism: the suspension of habitual consciousness which has struck readers so forcibly in the "Boy of Winander" passage of *The Prelude*; the insistence of Wordsworth and Coleridge that the child sometimes "forget itself" in play or imaginative reading; the sense, shared by Wordsworth and De Quincey, of childhood as at once discontinuous and continuous with the adult self. Latent within the Romantic representation of childhood remains a "radical ideal" (Cunningham 96) that has historically served to counter its implication in disciplinary programs and its utter subordination to adult wishes for a pristine origin and a sacrosanct private sphere. We have noted already how, even in a popularized and somewhat saccharine form, this ideal could help to advance liberal democratic reforms in relation to child labor and welfare. It may be helpful to recall that, contrary to its current bad eminence in Marxist and new historicist circles, Romantic poetry was valued by radical reformers as well; writers in the Chartist press, for example, celebrated the "politics" of poets like Wordsworth, Coleridge, Shelley, and Byron as akin to their own (Shaaban). That Romantic representations of childhood have continued to be read for their radical implications has recently been attested to by Edgar Freidenberg, a veteran of the alternative schools movement who, though sharing Eagleton's negative assessment of Romantic individualism, like Eagleton registers its oppositional force as well.

It might also be worth recalling just how harsh pre-Romantic childhood could be and usually was, particularly for lower-class children—that is, by far the majority of children (Pinchbeck and Hewittz: 387-413). The sheer amount of work, often under dismally abusive conditions, loaded upon children (at least in the "Western" world) throughout much of the past, in preindustrial periods as well as in the high era of industrializa-

tion, is practically unthinkable now, and helps explain why a social historian like Lloyd de Mause can persuasively describe the history of childhood, in contrast to Phillipe Aries's pessimistic, retrograde account, as a progressive and optimistic one (Stone). If a protected, educative childhood is all too easily sentimentalized, so, apparently, is a childhood of labor, as when Valerie Suransky laments the passing of the household as a "productive unit" and criticizes compulsory schooling for "denying the child the right to participate in meaningful labor" (19). In fact, home labor was often *more* arduous than factory work, since, especially in the case of "cottage" industries like spinning, it could expand to fill nearly every waking moment (Pinchbeck and Hewitt 2: 403)—and why should we expect otherwise of the "electronic cottage" industries that Alvin Toffler hopes will redeem children from their "nonproductive" social roles (220)? "Paradoxically," Suransky declares, "in a capitalist society, education is separated from work while ostensibly training the child for work" (20): a paradox noted long ago by Bernard Mandeville, who recommended accordingly that the "children of the poor" be kept out of Charity schools and inured to hard labor and coarse living as early as possible (311). Although, as Suransky notes, the English working class sometimes "defended child labor" this was not "precisely" because it helped preserve "traditional" parent-child bonds (19), but more commonly out of sheer economic necessity, as Sommerville points out (197) and as the most superficial reading of nineteenth-century working-class polemical and autobiographical writings would amply evidence. Cunningham demonstrates that working-class parents often *resisted* the new demands placed on child laborers in the early industrial era, making common cause with liberal reformers (226).

Fantasies of "liberated" children achieving economic independence as free agents in the marketplace can as quickly be dispelled by a few pages of the *Memoir* of Robert Blincoe, who begged to be taken as a chimney sweep and could barely wait (at around the age of seven) to begin work at a cotton factory, credulously believing the recruiters' promises that "they were all, when they arrived at the cotton-mill, to be transformed into ladies and gentlemen: that they would be fed on roast beef and plum-pudding, be allowed to ride their masters' horses, and have silver watches, and plenty of cash in their pockets" (Brown 17). Any argument that, noting the historical infantilization of women, slaves, the working classes, racial minorities, or colonized peoples within modern social discourses, attempts uncritically to portray children themselves as a colonized group (Nodelman), which child-centered discourses "infantilize" (Suransky 8), loses sight of the undeniable fact that children, unlike the various adult groups oppressed in their name, *are* in legitimate need of protection and guidance, though just when their period of dependence ends can vary (within limits) from one culture

and historical era to another.[2] It is altogether too easy for adults to trick, cajole, seduce, or simply beat children into doing what they want, whether such exploitation is masked by a contract "freely" entered into or not. That exploitation has historically and does currently take place within the family is, of course, undeniable. That there would be much more, rather than less, exploitation of children without the protection of the family and of family-oriented legislation is strongly suggested by the history of industrialization under the rising star of laissez-faire capitalism. If child labor laws are relaxed, this will much more likely proceed from a resurgent laissez-faire ideology (already claiming massive de-unionization and the scaling back of social welfare programs among its trophies) than out of legitimate support for "children's rights."[3] And it will again be predominately working-class children who will be "liberated" in this way.

In framing her notorious and still provocative vision of a world without patriarchal oppression—and without childhood—in *The Dialectic of Sex,* Shulamith Firestone avoids the problem of child labor by doing away with the need for labor altogether through something called "cybernetic socialism." It is instructive, then, that her vision of a postchildhood society nevertheless remains, as Suransky puts it, "adultist" (189), grossly underestimating the physical, emotional, and cognitive needs of children, whose long period of dependence on parents (now unequally delegated to mothers) would magically give way to a "greatly shortened dependence on a small group of others in general" (Firestone 11).[4] Her vision of licensed child sexuality similarly (and more creepily) proceeds from wishful adult projection: "Relations with children would include as much genital sex as the child was capable of—probably considerably more than we now believe" (240). Firestone's dehumanizing, technocratic fantasy (she also looks forward to the replacement of childbirth by "artificial reproduction" [230]) is easy enough to dismiss (Suransky 9-11), but her feminist critique of the repressive, patriarchal character of the bourgeois family strikes closer to, well, home. Even some of her more extreme positions have found echoes among more careful feminist thinkers: Juliet Mitchell, for example, similarly (though less directly) heralds the breakup of the nuclear family and the repeal of the incest taboo, with the nurture of children apparently to be taken over by mass institutions (406-16). The dilemma remains, however, that no alternative to the family (however precisely it is constituted) has yet proved viable on a large scale for the rearing of children in modern industrialized societies. Between the lack of alternatives and the steadily increasing number of children who live in single-parent households and are therefore inordinately condemned to beginning their lives in poverty, the "problem now," as Sommerville remarks, is to provide children with "*any* kind of family situation" (264)—configured along traditional lines or otherwise—that will allow them a fair start.[5]

Given that, whether desirable or not, the "cultural revolution" called for by Mitchell seems still farther off now than it did in 1974, how will we protect children for the duration? For children are at risk, not from overt "Down With Childhood" slogans such as Firestone's, but from the tacit, remorseless logic of late capitalism, whose agents have grudgingly welcomed women back into the workforce (as they had been enlisted during the early industrial era) but resist providing truly adequate daycare, extended parental leave, and reliable healthcare; whose adherents will not only agree to employ both members of a couple but will lower wages until two-career families are all but mandatory, blanching, however, at the shorter hours and flexible work schedules which would make humane child-rearing more viable under such conditions, and crying out against the social welfare programs necessary to foster the children of those deemed unemployable. Yet capitalism, like the nuclear family, has proved easier to criticize than to replace. For the present, a sufficiently powerful rhetoric is required if we are to resist the full demands of a triumphant capitalism on behalf of the children who are increasingly regarded as expendable.[6] And, if we don't wish to see an extended, protected childhood again become an elitist preserve, available only to those who can pay an increasingly high price for it, this rhetoric will have to include a democratic appeal.

Those who are presently attempting to frame such a rhetoric have relied, self-consciously or not, on the distinctively Romantic construction of childhood, which facilitated the democratization of an extended, educative childhood in the first place. Postman, who openly values the Romantics, unabashedly adopts their vision of childhood "spontaneity, purity, strength, and joy," and sets out to defend children's "charm, malleability, innocence, and curiosity" (59, xiii). Sommerville, who can be critical of the "sentimentalization" of childhood, nevertheless attributes to (modern) children a power of "imagination" superior to that of adults (160) and asks us to feel intimations of "immortality in fostering the young" (160, 296). Suransky, in a familiar (and no less persuasive) Romantic move, asks whether "any 'theory' can adequately explain such complex and nonoperationally defined experiences as love, attachment, bonding, clinging, and warmth," drawing on recent child development theory to argue that children require the "*irrational* involvement of one or more adults" over and above basic care and instruction (200). These writers are not arguing as conservative apologists for the patriarchal family or seeking to roll back the gains of the women's movement, but rather are asking important and disturbing questions about the status of childhood within a late capitalist order which more "radical"

analyses tend to evade. Far from discrediting them (in Mitchell's terms) as "romantics of the family and of the intimate and of the private" (411), I would ask whether their reliance on Romantic discourse says more about the staying power of the Romantic construction of childhood than it does about the limitations of liberal thought.

Still, one must acknowledge that the Romantic rhetoric of childhood has historically proved no less problematic than the "Romantic ideology" as a whole. It is not simply that, as social historians like Sommerville (200) and Cunningham (96) point out, what is most radically democratic in the Romantic vision has readily become "hackneyed" and inertly nostalgic in later adaptations. Rather, there is a blind-spot in the Romantic approach to childhood that allowed the canonical Romantics themselves to support repressive practices and institutions (the "Madras" system of Andrew Bell is a particularly stark example) even as they opposed the increasing brutalization and "progressive" indoctrination of children in an era of industrialization, burgeoning nationalism, and agricultural "improvement."[7] I would locate this blindness specifically in the transcendental element of the Romantic construction of childhood, one which had significant cultural uses but could also serve to obscure the child's implication in a social and material world, one moreover that seems to have lost whatever force it once had. But if Wordsworth's "Mighty Prophet" and Lamb's "child angel" have lost their valence, other tendencies within the Romantic representation of childhood, as the work of Postman, Sommerville, Suransky, and others attest, remain vital, perhaps even indispensable.

Attending to writers on the periphery of Romanticism may help in framing a post-Romantic approach to childhood which avoids transcendentalism but provides an alternative to exclusively self-regarding ("adultist") or narrowly instrumental views of the child. Blake—canonized only in the twentieth century and notoriously difficult to fit into period definitions—criticizes more consistently and more trenchantly than Wordsworth or Coleridge the child's implication in a social net of oppressive discourses. Yet he also, in songs of Innocence like "Holy Thursday," "The Chimney Sweeper," and "The Little Black Boy," implies that the child's very naiveté can provide it with a potentially saving distance, enabling it to probe ingenuously the various and competing discourses that define its conceptual horizons for rifts and contradictions, playfully deranging them in search of less constricting alternatives.[8] Mary Shelley, in *Frankenstein,* portrays the "construction" of childhood within a masculinist society quite graphically and yet no less subtly for that. Her monster-child's unnatural physical autonomy (he learns to feed himself in a few hours, and can soon find fuel and shelter on his own) only underscores his need for the "irrational" nurture which, as an abandoned infant, he is denied, eventually falling victim to a intense and compulsive hatred which inversely mirrors the love and sympathy that he has desperately and unsuccessfully pursued. Shelley's father, William Godwin, argues in *The Enquirer* that without transcendentalizing the child ("I do not say that a child is the image of God") or abstracting it from the adult world ("Let us never forget that our child is a being of the same nature with ourselves"), one can nevertheless affirm its uniqueness—the peculiarity and excess acknowledged by even so die-hard a social constructionist as Godwin—and oppose the "despotism" of authoritarian education on that basis (60, 87, 142). And, as Mitzi Myers has argued to great effect, even Maria Edgeworth, many of whose works seem so antithetical to Romanticism, develops in certain of her tales (particularly those, like "Lazy Lawrence" and "Simple Susan," concerned with lower-class children) a representation of childhood which achieves "affective power" through unsettling the "binaries of adult and child, agency and communion, logic and love" that Blake, Shelley, and Godwin all put into question as well ("Romancing" 102, 105).

Godwin was mocked in his time for, among other reasons, theorizing that scientific progress and better living conditions could eventually render death a thing of the past. Now quite recent advances in the medical sciences (particularly in human genetics) have led some biologists to believe that Godwin may indeed have been right. Apparently, a number of species (sea anemones and bivalve mollusks among them) suffer nothing comparable to our built-in senescence; they don't die unless something kills them. Human death could prove to have been merely an "artifact" of evolution, and rearranging a strand of genetic code here or there might grant human beings the prospect of immortality. No less eminent a scholar than Hans Jonas has argued that it is already time to begin contemplating the effects of so mind-numbing a development, particularly the possibility that childhood, not simply as a social but as a biological category, might become obsolete, preservation of the self taking precedence over reproduction of the species. His ethical case for continuing to bear children (and therefore, to avoid overcrowding, continuing to accept a maximum human life span of familiar dimensions) is, not surprisingly, steeped in Romanticism, beginning with his stipulation of feeling as the "mother-value of all values" (36) and his Romantic (and democratic) affirmation of the "different and unique" (39).[9] Jonas's argument for maintaining the system of mortality and "natality" depends on our acknowledging the importance of each generation "seeing things for the first time," challenging "habit" with "wonder," bringing a spirit of "eagerness and questioning" to human affairs (39)—ideals that seem "natural" to us because they make up part of a distinctively post-Romantic culture.

These, as Jonas remarks, are "weird fantasies" (40), and perhaps it is best to conclude by returning to children's literature and its active role in the history of childhood. In a review of several "end of childhood" books published in *Children's Literature* several years ago, Janice Alberghene asked whether "children's books help create childhood for us, not the other way around" (193). I think it is obvious that they do stand in a productive and not simply reflective relation to the constructed aspects of childhood and that, moreover, the Romantic heritage of much nineteenth- and twentieth-century writing for children has played and continues to play a key role in this process. But in many cases children's books modify their Romantic legacy, and not always in a watered-down or "hackneyed" manner. Some children's writers who seem to owe most to Romanticism—Maurice Sendak and Eric Carle especially come to mind—do not limit themselves to the purely "imaginative" and securely "innocent" matter endorsed by Coleridge, Wordsworth, and Lamb, and best exemplified by the traditional fairy tale. They also acknowledge, in a manner more reminiscent of Barbauld or Edgeworth, the cognitive needs of child readers, their more than understandable desire for discursive maps and conceptual grids as they work through the arduous and lengthy process of piecing out the densely coded world of adult discourse. It was the canonical Romantics' signal failure in relation to children's reading not to register these needs as well, or to see how traditional children's matter—hornbooks and counting rhymes, bestiaries and illustrated alphabets, riddles and other exercises in building linguistic competence—had long met them in a lively, imaginative manner.

Perhaps here the Romantics might have forged common ground with their more sensible female contemporaries, the group of innovative writers Lamb all too memorably termed the "cursed Barbauld crew" (2: 82)—who might themselves have better learned to appreciate traditional children's culture.[10] Sendak, Carle, and others writing in the latter half of this century—which may well be recorded as the "golden age" of writing for younger children—reassert the rational dame's feel and compassion for the child's cognitive demands in playful, fantastic formats and tonalities which owe more to a distinctly Romantic mode of children's writing. And yet they also understand that, as the Romantics enjoyed pointing out, children do not need to understand everything they read; that children need, on the contrary, to sometimes have their capacities stretched and their expectations broken, to proceed on occasion from words of one syllable to words of five syllables, to fail to quite comprehend why the bestiary features a hippogriff and one of the riddles has no answer. The child needs, in a phrase, the odd "gentle shock of mild surprise." But this need is secondary to the material, affective, and more basic cognitive needs which, as I have been suggesting, the Romantic construction of childhood made it

harder than before to ignore, or to see in one group of children and not another, or to make light of or simply shrug off. If the ingenuous, questing, unique, emotive, dynamic child of the Romantics has lost its power to move us, we may well have lost more in terms of cultural power than we have gained in terms of critical sophistication.

Notes

1. James Kincaid, in a recent book (*Child-Loving*) which rehearses in diluted form some of Rose's arguments—yet, oddly, makes no mention of her work—hopes similarly that by "deconstructing" childhood as it has been constituted since the early nineteenth century, "we can . . . act strategically and politically, act to devise ever more flexible, subversive, even liberating modes of perceiving and acting" (7). For a trenchant critique of "postmodern" attitudes toward childhood, and the way they implicitly favor the needs of adults over those of children, see Elkind.

2. Shahar's compelling statement of this point is worth quoting at length: "Although it cannot be valid to discuss childraising and parent-child relations purely in terms of instinct and natural conduct, there are certainly immutable factors involved. A considerable part of the developmental process is biologically determined, and the continued existence of a society is impossible without the acknowledgement (and conduct attuned to this acknowledgement) that, up to a certain stage in its life, the child has need of nurturing and protection in order to survive. No society could physically survive without a tradition of child-nurturing. And no society with any awareness of its own essence and aims could endure as a society without ways of transmitting knowledge and cultural traditions during the late stages of childhood, and without an effort on the part of those entrusted with the task of socialization of the young generation" (1).

3. Coleridge, ardently supporting legislation to curb at least the worst excesses of child factory labor, recognized the irony—and the implicit collusion with laissez-faire ideology—in considering children "free agents" in a supposedly "voluntary labour" market at the outset of the *first* great era of unfettered capitalism: "Now, nobody will deny that these children are free agents, capable of judging, whether their labour be commensurate with their strength, and whether or no the term of their employment be prejudicial to their health and comfort. Undoubtedly they are free agents; and as they have neither individually, nor collectively, petitioned Parliament to step forward for their protection, we have a right fairly to conclude, that they are well satisfied with their present condi-

tion." Coleridge's ironic laissez-faire apologist also disparages the "tearful" reformers of the "age of sensibilities" who would "open the door to legislative interference" in "cases of free labour" (*Essays* 2: 485-88). His most powerful argument for supporting the legislation lies in a Romantic injunction to "individualize the suffering, which it is the object of this Bill to remedy: follow up the detail in some one case with a human sympathy" (*Shorter Works* 1: 722).

4. That Firestone's speculations owe as much allegiance to futurist as to feminist discourse is suggested by the close parallels in Toffler's *Third Wave,* which similarly finds child-labor laws "anachronistic," heralds a "Child-Free Culture," and advocates a "shorter childhood and youth but a more responsible and productive one" (213, 220, 384). The complicity of such thinking with resurgent laissez-faire ideology is made overt in Newt Gingrich's well-known championing of Toffler's "third wave" vision.

5. My skepticism regarding alternatives to the family should not be taken to imply any opposition to "nontraditional" families—adoptive, variously extended, headed by same-sex parents, etc.—which, to the contrary, seem more needed now than ever. It is heartening to learn that the "principle of the best interest of the child" is being cited in legal decisions that give adoption rights to nontraditional parents such as the domestic partners of lesbian birth-mothers (Moskowitz).

6. For a recent assessment, see the Children's Defense Fund's 1995 year-book. One figure that speaks for many is that the federal government currently spends eleven dollars (per capita) on Americans over the age of sixty-five for every dollar it spends on Americans under the age of eighteen (Miller 242). For a global perspective, and an important articulation of the child's "right to develop normally in mind and body," see the UNICEF report for 1995.

7. On these issues, see Richardson (*Literature, Education, and Romanticism* 91-108).

8. For readings of Blake along these lines, see Larissy; and Richardson (*Literature* 153-66).

9. Jonas's insistence on the value of human difference brings out the potential totalitarian implications of the widespread institution of "artificial reproduction" called for by Firestone: "Such is the working of sexual reproduction that none of its outcome is, in genetic makeup, the replica of any before and none will ever be replicated after. (This is one reason humans should never be 'cloned')" (39). Mary Shelley, who seems to have shared her

father's prophetic gift in regard to the biological sciences, suggests throughout *Frankenstein* that the fantasy, now becoming a reality, of artificially creating life out of dead matter is rooted in the same masculinist desires for autonomy and depreciation of the body and the feminine that feminist critics have located within canonical Romanticism.

10. For a groundbreaking, sympathetic survey of this important group of women writers for children, see Myers, "Impeccable Governesses."

Works Cited

Alberghene, Janice M. "Childhood's End?" *Children's Literature* 13 (1985): 188-93.

Alexander, Meena. *Women in Romanticism: Mary Wollstonecraft, Dorothy Wordsworth and Mary Shelley.* London: MacMillan, 1989.

Aries, Phillippe. *Centuries of Childhood: A Social History of Family Life.* Trans. Robert Baldick. New York: Vintage, 1962.

Babenroth, A. Charles. *English Childhood: Wordsworth's Treatment of Childhood in Light of English Poetry from Prior to Crabbe.* New York: Columbia UP, 1922.

Brown, John. *A Memoir of Robert Blincoe.* Firle, Sussex: Caliban Books, 1977.

Chandos, John. *Boys Together: English Public Schools 1800-1864.* New Haven: Yale UP, 1984.

Children's Defense Fund. *The State of America's Children Yearbook 1995.* Washington: Children's Defense Fund, 1995.

Coleridge, Samuel Taylor. *Essays on His Times in The Morning Post and The Courier.* Ed. David V. Erdman. 3 vols. Princeton: Princeton UP, 1978.

———. *Shorter Works and Fragments.* Edited by H. J. Jackson and J. R. de J. Jackson. 2 vols. Princeton: Princeton UP, 1995.

Cunningham, Hugh. *The Children of the Poor: Representations of Childhood since the Seventeenth Century.* Oxford: Blackwell, 1991.

Eagleton, Terry. *The Function of Criticism: From the Spectator to Post-Structuralism.* London: Verso, 1984.

Elkind, David. *Ties that Stress: The New Family Imbalance.* Cambridge: Harvard UP, 1994.

Firestone, Shulamith. *The Dialectic of Sex: The Case for Feminist Revolution.* New York: Bantam, 1971.

Foucault, Michel. *Discipline and Punish: The Birth of the Prison.* Trans. Alan Sheridan. New York: Vintage, 1979.

Freidenberg, Edgar Z. "Romanticism and Alternatives in Schooling." *The Educational Legacies of Romanticism.* Ed. John Willinsky. Calgary: Wilfrid Laurier UP, 1990.

Garlitz, Barbara. "The Immortality Ode: Its Cultural Progeny." *Studies in English Literature* 6 (1966): 639-49.

Godwin, William. *The Enquirer: Reflections on Education, Manners and Literature.* New York: Augustus M. Kelley, 1965.

Hughes, Thomas. *Tom Brown's School Days.* New York: New American Library, 1986.

Jonas, Hans. "The Burden and Blessing of Mortality." *Hastings Center Report.* (January-February 1992). 34-40.

Kincaid, James R. *Child-Loving: The Erotic Child and Victorian Culture.* New York: Routledge, 1992.

Kingsley, Charles. *The Water-Babies: A Fairy Tale for a Land-Baby. The Life and Works of Charles Kingsley.* 19 vols. London: MacMillan, 1901-3. 19: 1-202.

Knoepflmacher, U. C. "Mutations of the Wordsworthian Child of Nature." *Nature and the Victorian Imagination.* Ed. U. C. Knoepflmacher and G. B. Tennyson. Berkeley: U of California P, 1977. 391-425.

Lamb, Charles, and Mary Lamb. *The Letters of Charles and Mary Lamb.* Ed. Edwin A. Marrs, Jr. 3 vols. to date. Ithaca: Cornell UP, 1975-.

Larissy, Edward. *William Blake.* Oxford: Blackwell, 1985.

Liu, Alan. *Wordsworth: The Sense of History.* Stanford: Stanford UP, 1989.

MacLeod, Anne Scott. "From Rational to Romantic: The Children of Children's Literature in the Nineteenth Century." *Poetics Today* 13 (1992): 141-54.

Mandeville, Bernard. *The Fable of the Bees: Or, Private Vices, Publick Benefits.* Ed. F. B. Kaye, 2 vols. Oxford: Clarendon P, 1924.

McGann, Jerome J. *The Romantic Ideology: A Critical Investigation.* Chicago: U of Chicago P, 1983.

McGavran, James Holt, ed. *Romanticism and Children's Literature in Nineteenth-Century England.* Athens: U of Georgia P, 1991.

Miller, Ken. "Fixing the Capitalist Road." *The Nation* 21 Feb. 1994: 242-44.

Mitchell, Juliet. *Psychoanalysis and Feminism: Freud, Reich, Laing and Women.* New York: Vintage, 1975.

Moskowitz, Ellen. "Two Mothers." *Hastings Center Report.* (March-April 1995). 42.

Myers, Mitzi. "Impeccable Governesses, Rational Dames, and Moral Mothers: Mary Wollstonecraft and the Female Tradition in Georgian Children's Books." *Children's Literature* 14 (1986): 31-59.

———. "Little Girls Lost: Rewriting Romantic Childhood, Righting Gender and Genre." *Teaching Children's Literature: Issues, Pedagogy, Resources.* Ed. Glenn Edward Sadler. New York: Modern Language Association of America, 1992. 131-42.

———. "Romancing the Moral Tale: Maria Edgeworth and the Problematics of Pedagogy." McGavran 96-128.

Nodelman, Perry. "The Other: Orientalism, Colonialism, and Children's Literature." *Children's Literature Association Quarterly* 17 (1992): 29-35.

Perkins, David. *Is Literary History Possible?* Baltimore: Johns Hopkins UP, 1992.

Pinchbeck, Ivy, and Margaret Hewitt. *Children in English Society.* 2 vols. London: Routledge and Kegan Paul, 1969-73.

Place, Francis. *The Autobiography of Francis Place.* Ed. Mary Thrale. Cambridge: Cambridge UP, 1972.

Plotz, Judith. "The Perpetual Messiah: Romanticism, Childhood, and the Paradoxes of Human Development." *Regulated Children/Liberated Children: Education in Psychohistorical Perspective.* Ed. Barbara Finkelstein. New York: Psychohistory P, 1979.

Plumb, J. H. "The New World of Children in Eighteenth-Century England." *Past and Present* 67 (1975): 64-93.

Postman, Neil. *The Disappearance of Childhood.* New York: Delacorte P, 1982.

Richardson, Alan. "Childhood and Romanticism." *Teaching Children's Literature: Issues, Pedagogy, Resources.* Ed. Glenn Edward Sadler. New York: Modern Language Association of America, 1992. 121-30.

———. *Literature, Education, and Romanticism: Reading as Social Practice, 1780-1832.* Cambridge: Cambridge UP, 1994.

Rose, Jacqueline. *The Case of Peter Pan, or The Impossibility of Children's Fiction.* 2nd rev. ed. London: MacMillan, 1993.

Ross, Marlon B. *The Contours of Masculine Desire: Romanticism and the Rise of Women's Poetry.* New York: Oxford UP, 1989.

Shaaban, Bouthaina. "The Romantics in the Chartist Press." *Keats-Shelley Journal* 38 (1989): 26-29.

Shahar, Shulamith. *Childhood in the Middle Ages.* London: Routledge, 1990.

Siskin, Clifford L. *The Historicity of Romantic Discourse.* New York: Oxford UP, 1988.

Sommerville, C. John. *The Rise and Fall of Childhood.* New York: Vintage, 1990.

Spiegelman, Willard. *Wordsworth's Heroes.* Berkeley: U of California P, 1985.

Stone, Lawrence. "The Massacre of the Innocents." *New York Review of Books* 14 Nov. 1974: 25-31.

Summerfield, Geoffrey. *Fantasy and Reason: Children's Literature in the Eighteenth Century.* Athens: U of Georgia P, 1984.

Suransky, Valerie Polakow. *The Erosion of Childhood.* Chicago: U of Chicago P, 1982.

Toffler, Alvin. *The Third Wave.* New York: Bantam, 1981.

UNICEF. *The State of the World's Children 1995.* New York: Oxford UP, 1995.

Walkerdine, Valerie. "On the Regulation of Speaking and Silence: Subjectivity, Class, and Gender in Contemporary Schooling." *Language, Gender and Childhood.* Ed. Carolyn Steedman, Cathy Urwin and Valerie Walkerdine. London: Routledge & Kegan Paul, 1985.

Zelizer, Viviana A. *Pricing the Priceless Child: The Changing Social Value of Children.* New York: Basic Books, 1985.

Linda M. Austin (essay date spring 2003)

SOURCE: Austin, Linda M. "Children of Childhood: Nostalgia and the Romantic Legacy." *Studies in Romanticism* 42, no. 1 (spring 2003): 75-98.

[*In the following essay, Austin concentrates on the presentation of idealized childhood as nostalgic recollection in various nineteenth-century works.*]

At the break of the nineteenth century, that most Romantic desire, the longing for childhood, produced one of the most romantic images, the innocent child of nature. Emotion and image were manifestations of a yearning for the past which we have since called nostalgia. It, too, is a romantic phenomenon (although the word was not widely used until the twentieth century), appearing first in England in medical reports of 1787 about a Welsh soldier suffering from homesickness.[1] We also think of "childhood" as a romantic invention, if only because of historical coincidence; for by the last years of the eighteenth century, children were viewed as autonomous beings rather than mere extensions of a patriarchal family. This change may have been relatively recent, if one accepts the theories of Philippe Ariès and Laurence Stone; or it may have been far more gradual, if one believes their opponents.[2] A more compelling or immediate reason for considering childhood an English romantic phenomenon is Wordsworth: in early poems like "We are Seven," and "Lucy Gray," he portrayed the essential autonomy of an innocent or mythic child whose lineage stretched back to Pelagius.[3] Yet this child of nature became in Wordsworth's translation a retrospective phenomenon, one from whom the subject felt sadly distant. The "Ode: Intimations of Immortality . . ." in which the poet speaks directly about longing for a lost childhood, and "Lucy Gray," in which the figure of childhood disappears, both convey the wonder and desire adults invested in trying to remember their past, unsocialized selves.[4]

During the nineteenth century, the concept of childhood was often the subjective product of individual narration, of a particular life history. Whether an infinitely recessive object of nostalgia, as it is in George Eliot's *The Mill on the Floss* (1860), or a *locus* created for a discarded self, as it is in Mary and Charles Lamb's *Mrs. Leicester's School* (1809), childhood was a construction—immediate and temporary, an extension of present circumstances. For this reason, the image of the child in texts about childhood was a memorative device often working in the absence of conscious remembering. Wordsworth, for instance, in "The Pet-lamb" (1800), channeled nostalgia through the prevailing view of the child as a developing and imperfect being, one I shall call the "imitative child" because in light-hearted visual and verbal representations drawing from this belief, he or she usually appeared in the act of rehearsing adult behavior. Unlike the child of nature with which the poet is usually associated, this child was primarily a social entity. If it returned the viewer to childhood (and I believe it could), it did so through emotional attachment. But so, indeed, does the elusive child of nature in the famous "Lucy Gray" (1799). Indeed both "Lucy Gray" and "The Pet-lamb" employ a pre-romantic iconology of the child for sentimental effects—a practice later writers like Tennyson and Dickens would adopt. Both poems dramatize, furthermore, a nostalgia involving dramatic forms of identification which have little to do with experienced interiority or private memory, with organic form or autonomy—all elements of the self so intertwined, in theory, with the new concept of childhood.

THE TERMS OF CHILDHOOD

In the nineteenth century, nostalgia for childhood usually referred to condition rather than duration; in doing so it rendered an already unstable concept even more fluid. By "child" or "childhood," writers might have meant any period from infancy through young adulthood. Definitions tended to emerge from contexts, betraying confusion and creativity. John Ruskin, at 69 hoping to marry 21-year-old Kathleen Olander, was not "quite clear," he complained to her, "whether you are a child . . .—a pretty girl—or a clever—woman!" Calling her "my dearest child," he adds, anxiously, "Do you

really like *me* to call you that—though you won't answer for anything more?"[5] One might argue that in this example "child" is an intentional figure of speech and that even today "child" and "childhood" often appear as metaphors. Yet Ruskin's disregard of any chronological limits to childhood is symptomatic of its uncertain duration in nineteenth-century social practices. Our modern precision about age, established through law and reinforced through medical regulation, makes the nineteenth-century terms of childhood appear almost arbitrary in comparison. In his recent book on Victorian childhood, James Kincaid announces, "My 'child' . . . is not defined or controlled by age limits since it seems to me that anyone between the ages of one day and 25 years or beyond might, in different contexts play that role" (5). In her study of the same period Carolyn Steedman writes helpfully, "Childhood was a category of dependence, a term that defined certain relationships of powerlessness, submission and bodily inferiority or weakness, before it became descriptive of chronological age" (7).[6] The freedom to set the bounds of childhood—one's own or others'—is a result of different and sometimes disjunctive definitions that also have varied with class and through time.

The term of childhood was hard to fix in part because until 1836 the public registration of birth was not standardized, and because even after this date it was often difficult to discover a person's exact age.[7] The demarcation between childhood and adulthood did change, as Kincaid states, with context; but although various understandings of the periods of life had existed in each era since antiquity, terminology rarely clarified the duration of childhood. If "manhood" in the classical definition began at 28, did childhood encompass "boyhood" (as well as "girlhood") or, an alternative designation, "youth," which lasted through secondary school? Did childhood include "infancy," which traditionally could range from birth to 14 years, or according to Thomas Jameson's reclassification of 1811, only to age seven, after which puberty begins? (Steedman 65). Various answers have been offered. In *Émile* (English translation, 1762), Rousseau marks the end of infancy and the beginning of childhood with the acquisition of language (reminding us that "infans" means "unable to speak"), but otherwise views the years between birth and 15 as a relatively blissful period, during which desire does not exceed physical strength. Puberty ends this happy equilibrium.[8] But often biology did not corroborate legal definitions of childhood. Presumably the age at which a girl and boy could legally marry should have marked the definitive limit of childhood. But in the seventeenth and eighteenth centuries the age of marriageability, which was 14 for boys and 12 for girls, did not necessarily coincide with the age of sexual readiness or with the age of consent.[9] A rise in the legal age of consent through the nineteenth century (from 10 before 1861 to 16 in 1885) suggested a longer official understanding of

childhood, as Kincaid argues; but it also raised the possibility of marriage, contracted and consensual, between persons who were adults in a biological but not a legal sense. Would persons by law denied autonomy but able to marry, either by the arrangements of their parents or by elopement (prompted by sexual readiness), be considered children? If so, what did it mean to be a child in such circumstances?

The eligible age of employment to mark the end of childhood is likewise unhelpful in setting the terms of childhood, not least because it varied among occupations and pertained chiefly to the working classes. Because of the use of child labor in industrializing countries, the protraction of legal childhood occurred largely among the middle classes and reached laboring and rural society much later. Ariès suggests that in France the demand for labor in the textile mills curtailed childhood in the perception of the working classes (376). In the public outrage over "child labor" in England during the first half of the nineteenth century, we may, however, detect a rudimentary notion of childhood, a sense of a social violation of a biological category even though, as E. P. Thompson has shown, working children had been integral to the family economy long before they became a topic of controversy in the 1830s.[10] "Childhood" may have emerged as an issue of industrialization, these facts suggest. Yet we cannot fix periods of childhood when speaking generally of the lower classes. Whereas in the forties children under eight were barred from working in factories, and those under ten from laboring in mines, the minimum age (7) of theatrical employment was not set until 1889 (Steedman 136-37). Moreover, in the campaigns to shorten work hours, children were grouped with women. In these legal and social contexts, children and childhood had no inherent qualities, apart from size, separating them from adult dependents.

In Linda Pollock's judicious reasoning, the concept of childhood was more likely "elaborated" through the centuries than suddenly "born" (94). But the growing awareness of childhood through the nineteenth century did not bring a stable, shared definition of the phase, only a sense that it differed somehow from adult life and lasted longer than it had centuries before. Alice Meynell, writing in the 1890s, treated childhood as a late romantic phenomenon and defined it as a period separate from youth, which was the age of sexual readiness or at least accepted eligibility for marriage. The "fashion of hurrying childhood" persisted, she declares, through the first two decades of the nineteenth century (through Keats, she declares). Joseph Addison, she relates, thought of a 14 year-old child as a young woman in an attempt to prolong youth at the expense of "the bloom of . . . childhood."[11] John Evelyn describes Mrs. Godolphin, Maid of Honour to the Queen in the court of Charles II, as a paragon of wit at age 13. *Quattro-*

cento art "abolished little girls," Meynell writes; they are missing from religious painting, except for an "education of the virgin" or girl saints refusing suitors (256). Likewise the literary tradition of *carpe diem* scanted childhood for the richer subject of youth. Meynell—who under the influence of Ruskin's "Fairy Land" (1883) would write *Children of the Old Masters* in 1903, a study of the few examples in Italian painting that depict children as childlike—thought boys, too, were rushed through childhood. The finding of the boy Christ in the temple might have furnished a model of the precocious child for proud and bereaved fathers such as John Evelyn who, when eulogizing his five-year old son, listed his accomplishments by age two and one-half.[12]

In this confusion, nineteenth-century narratives set the boundaries of childhood by individual experiences. In a retrospective narrative, often a traumatic familial event such as the loss of a parent, a move, or a pronounced change in the organization of the family identifies childhood by its close. In Mary and Charles Lamb's *Mrs. Leicester's School* (1809), the storytellers are all prepubescent, but each girl defines her childhood as a period of her past in which a younger, less competent self coped with sudden change and dislocation. In the parodic second book of Carlyle's *Sartor Resartus* (1833-34), Teufelsdröckh separates his idyllic childhood ("waited on by the four golden Seasons") from his "boyhood," which begins with his formal education at the Entepfuhl Gymnasium. ("Over his Gymnasic and Academic years the Professor by no means lingers so lyrical and joyful as over his childhood.") "There, ended childhood," announces Aurora Leigh, in Elizabeth Barrett Browning's novel-poem of 1856, after describing the death of her father; at the time she is 13, but the loss of her one remaining parent, not her adolescence, marks for her the close in a phase that precedes a crucial dislocation from Italy to England.[13] In George Eliot's *The Mill on the Floss* (1860), "the golden gates of childhood" close in the final lines of the second book, "School-Time," when the family's fortunes reverse and Tom must leave Mr. Stelling's. The traumatic event spurs Tom to seek paid employment and thereby makes him an adult in one definition of the word.

Similarly, for all of the girls in *Mrs. Leicester's School*, disruption of the household marks the border of a peaceful, early stage of childhood and initiates the child's progress toward an understanding of the larger world. The end of childhood does not occur in these stories as internal, organic growth, however; the girls mature through successful adaptation to what many of them delicately call their "circumstances"—the money that establishes and fixes relations (330).[14] Both Emily Barton and Charlotte Wilmot suffer traumatic changes of physical and social place when their fathers lose money: Charlotte's parents flee England and leave her behind,

yet her story emphasizes the shame of forfeiting all her dresses and toys to creditors and of lodging with her father's former clerk. The backwardness of Susan Yates is the fault of poor, rather than cold, parents. Once her father's fortunes change, she moves to one of the "great towns" and learns, she tells her schoolmates, "to distinguish between what is essential in religion, and what is merely formal or ornamental" (330). Her awakening to abstraction is portrayed as a social, not an intellectual, advance made possible by financial comfort. For Maggie Tulliver as well, the "new life of sorrow," which separates childhood from maturity, begins with her father's bankruptcy (168).[15] The noticeable difference between Maggie's girlhood impetuosity in the first and second books and the subdued, penitential nature which both Philip Wakem and Stephen Guest later deplore, between the energetic child and the passive, though still earnest, young woman, coincides with her gradual sexual awakening. But the material trauma, the bankruptcy and auction of the Tullivers' household goods, marks the arbitrary end of her childhood.

The childhoods of the Lambs' stories and George Eliot's novel, written half a century apart, are unstable narrative constructs—phenomena of plotting, in other words—subject to no stringent social, legal, or biological definitions. They raise difficulties for the task of what Frances Ferguson has called "romantic memory," the defining and maintaining of an individual self.[16] This maintenance requires negotiations between the perceptions of a present self and its interpretation of the past. The term of Maggie's childhood is defined in retrospect, as it is by all of Mrs. Leicester's pupils; but the operation and effect of memory in each text differs. The advance out of childhood for the Lambs' children is an ethical move in which remembrances of actions and states of mind are actually re-evaluations of the past based on present and superior knowledge (acquired from "circumstances"). Maggie Tulliver's conception of her own childhood involves evaluations too, but they evince no such awareness of growth, moral or emotional. Instead Maggie feels loss as she physically matures. Her awareness of childhood felicity shifts; she views her own past with envy, and her incessant pining—whether it be for the days she sat on her father's knee or the days with Philip in the Red Deeps—exemplifies how fluid and personal the idea of childhood could be. At sixteen, loved by Philip, she has, she believes, fallen away from her childhood self and values him chiefly for the happiness she has not felt, she says, "since I was a little girl—the days Tom was good to me" (295). Maggie deflects Philip's declarations of love out of loyalty to her brother, but only a few years later she will remember this period with heartsick longing. "Oh Philip, Philip, I wish we were together again—so quietly—in the Red Deeps," she cries to herself, frightened by her sexual passion for Stephen Guest (358). Maggie's own ethical dilemma, which will compel her

to renounce Stephen for a prior commitment to Philip, is really an infinitely recessive nostalgia that has already forced her to suppress this attachment in order to honor an earlier bond with Tom. As Margaret Homans has shown, Maggie's is a most un-Wordsworthian attitude toward childhood (128); yet the novel owes much to the idea of spots-of-time and the re-envisioning of static scenes, particularly in the idyllic opening, which reveals brother and sister playing at the river.[17] There is a difference in the novel between Maggie's memory and the narrator's: the latter summarily ends childhood by hurrying the girl and boy from Mr. Stelling's like a miniature Adam and Eve ushered out of Eden while Maggie tends to protract her childhood by clinging to her earliest attachments, extending and enhancing their felt power. If the narrator summons for us the pleasures of memory as re-emplacement, Maggie's example shows the dangers of attempting to retrieve from a remembered space its emotional contents and denying their loss. Her nostalgia recalls its original, romantic form as illness.

Despite their differences, the Lambs' collection of stories and George Eliot's novel both suggest that in the matter of childhood, memory does not negotiate effectively among spatio-temporal selves. For the decidedly un-nostalgic pupils of Mrs. Leicester's school, the end of childhood marks a disruption in self: something occurs which demands an altered response. In its aftermath, the child appears as another being altogether from the adult. And in no case does any character *initiate* the end of childhood. Childhood is what is remembered as childhood; but it always emerges from the gap created by something that has happened *to* someone. In the meliorative stories the pupils at Mrs. Leicester's tell, memory creates a sense of self through a metamorphosis of external conditions. Maggie Tulliver also confirms the circumstantial rupture between childhood and adulthood, though she resists it. Her remembering attempts to forge a continuity between present and past selves, but it does so through a ruinous reenactment of familial bonds. Her "self," in other words, is the fragile product of a retrogressive memory bent on extending her childhood to a recent point in her ever-receding history.

Maggie's fate—death by drowning, entwined with her brother—is a symbolic manifestation of the doom awaiting any relentless nostalgiac who tries to prolong the past by bringing it to bear on the present, and an unwitting confirmation of Wordsworth's belief in the unrecoverability of the condition of childhood. This belief was expressed most memorably for Victorians in "Ode: Intimations of Immortality" (1807), which treats the loss, awe, and estrangement framing the adult's sense of childhood as features of a common psychological profile. The "Ode" evokes a shared sense among adults of inevitable forgetting, of the remoteness of the condition of childhood. In addition, it conveys the extraordinariness of the ordinary childhood, one contained in the adult's perceptual and memorative field and best summarized as a lost sense of potential. A decade before Wordsworth wrote the poem, Schiller had coined a word, *Bestimmbarkeit,* for this retrospective quality, this condition of infinite possibility in childhood embodied for the adult in the figure of the child.[18] The "Ode," unlike the later, finished *Prelude,* exalts childhood as a condition of vivid and at times visionary perception which fades with age and severs the being of the child from that of the adult. Viewed retrospectively, childhood becomes the one period in which everyone's genius seems to have glimmered. Almost certainly it is only genius or unlimited possibility discovered in hindsight; nonetheless, the childhood of the "Ode" is every man's and woman's memory of endless potential and emotional spontaneity, the latter a favored form of simplicity in the nineteenth century, but a state from which all mature minds feel estranged.[19]

The "Ode," then, depicts childhood as a casualty of normal development. To the poet resurrecting his youth in the two-part *Prelude* of 1799, "so wide appears / the vacancy between me and those days, / . . . That sometimes when I think of them I seem / Two consciousnesses—conscious of myself, / And of some other being" (2.26-31).[20] How much further this time must seem from the ordinary adult being! For him or her, the vanishing of youth means not just the waning of individual potential and a range of possibilities—Schiller's *Bestimmbarkeit*—but a diminished ability to respond to the world. In the "Ode" the *quality* or *affect* of early experiences does not much matter: "be they what they may," they become "a master-light of all our seeing," the poet writes ("Ode" 154, 156), a statement that seems ominous in light of Maggie Tulliver's end. In the "Ode," the passing of infancy and early childhood brings a loss of extraordinariness; even a prosaic existence mourns this passing because, as the poem implies, the existence of *everyone* beyond such a childhood is prosaic. Thus the "Ode" illustrates the sort of unromantic memory which nostalgia typifies: inorganic, unconducive to maintaining a sense of self, and impersonal despite its significant private application. When it made the cut in Palgrave's *Golden Treasury* of 1861, one of the most popular anthologies ever compiled, the "Ode" became the "central reference point" for remembrances of childhood in Britain during that time (Steedman 11).[21] The poem was long and philosophical, attributes out of favor among most critics then; but for these very reasons, and because it described the condition of childhood in general, the poem carried great authority in the eyes of Victorian readers.

CHILDREN OF A WORDSWORTHIAN CHILDHOOD

By 1850, the "Immortality Ode" already had figured in a number of poems, some chosen by Wordsworth him-

self, that had established the poet's image of the child and his understanding of the condition of childhood.[22] Besides the "Ode," the list included pieces from *Lyrical Ballads* of 1798 and 1800 and a handful of early compositions gathered under the subheading "Poems Referring to the Period of Childhood" for the Collected Edition of 1815. Wordsworth himself first conceived of the headings. His exclusions from this category can appear arbitrary, but they give us some idea of his conception of childhood.[23] In "Characteristics of a Child Three Years Old" (1815), the poet describes his daughter Catharine as a "happy Creature of herself . . . all-sufficient" (11-12).[24] Her responses are "[u]nthoughtof" (17), her attention and sense of reality undeveloped; the last lines describe her "chasing wantonly / The many-coloured images imprest / Upon the bosom of a placid lake" (19-21). Hartley Coleridge, whom he addresses in "To H. C. Six Years Old" (1807) has no command of language as yet: the "breeze-like motion and the self-born carol" (4) are "fittest to unutterable thought" (3). Looking at this "faery voyager" (5), the poet is filled with foreboding "[f]or what may be thy lot in future years. . . . Thou are so exquisitely wild" (14, 12). The child, when quintessentially childlike, was pre-social and pre-linguistic (and there is no difference in the poems above between the little girl and the little boy); the child resembled Wordsworth's peasants before external conditions desolated them or age turned their simplicity into clownishness. The child had a marvelous physical vitality, which Wordsworth captured best in the magnificent "Influence of Natural Objects in calling forth and strengthening the imagination in Boyhood and Early Youth" (published separately in 1809 from *The Prelude* of 1799 [1.130-185] and worked into *The Prelude* of 1850 [1.401-63]).

To an adult, the astounding physical energy of the child was usually inextricable from an even more enviable mnemonic vacancy. Childhood was movement without memory because the early years are the one time of life when there is not enough of a past to remember. The "Ode" envisions this state most radically; other poems offer gradations of it. From his seat in a boat on Coniston Lake the extraordinary youth in *The Prelude* of 1799 vows to remember the "beauteous sight before me" (2.162) when he dies (2.161-68). The nostalgic representation of childhood paradoxically seeks through memory to slough off the burden of memory. "[B]ut oh, what happiness to live / When every hour brings palpable access / Of knowledge, when all knowledge is delight, / And sorrow is not there" (*The Prelude* [1850] 2.285-88). In these examples, childhood is a spatio-temporal condition looking forward, not backward. Even the poet of *The Prelude,* who mined his moral and imaginative growth on memory's stores, occasionally longed to be free from their abundance, to relive the time before experience had become the object of reflection. The child devoid of memory could function,

partly because of this mental vacuity, as a memorative device. One famous carrier is Goethe's Mignon from *Wilhelm Meister's Apprenticeship* (1795-96 [trans. Carlyle 1824]) who was, wrote Albrecht Erlenmeyer late in the nineteenth century, "an immortal representation of home-sickness."[25] The innocent child of nature—"concocted," Kincaid has observed, by late Victorians (72-73)—likewise signified the adult's past, her "antiquity," as Alice Meynell wrote in one of her regular columns on children in the 1890s.[26] The repertory of images from which an adult could choose to represent a personal past included nonhuman figures like fairies and animals; children themselves were commonly referred to as pets, lambs, and flowers throughout the eighteenth and nineteenth centuries (Pollock 111). The particular past these diminutive creatures evoked in the beholder's imagination was usually undelineated; the figure mediated an inchoate nostalgia, the *experience* of memory rather than its content.

The child had long been an egocentric construction, enlisted to mediate the adult's preoccupation with childhood. In Georgian "dynastic portraits," children indicated the line of inheritance, and the smallest child attested to a flourishing family. Painting and description obviously favored toddlers and infants as the privileged signifiers of this vitality. According to Ariès, by the end of the eighteenth century, the child's presence had become associated with "ce besoin, autrefois inconnu d'intimité, de vie familière, sinon encore précisement familiale" (382) ["with a hitherto unknown desire of homeliness, for familiar if not yet precisely 'family life'" (343)]. A sense of family even among the middle and lower classes had become connected to autonomy of space, and the presence of the child indicated a claim on this space as the territory of an expanding unit. But well into the nineteenth century, in England as well as in France, the image of the child continued to appear as a marker of family expansion. It was a function that implied (if it did not reflect) a certain replaceability about actual children (as well as one that potentially undermines Ariès' argument for a late eighteenth-century invention of childhood). The romantic phenomenon of the child of nature with which Wordsworth is usually linked was a reaction to this figure and to the social structures it had been impressed to serve. Yet the children he created and chose to represent childhood were not always receptacles of lost potential or remote consciousness. At times they retained something of the emblematic purpose children had served long before the cult of the child signaled a new emotional attachment to children. When these sorts of child-figures evoked childhood, they conveyed shared or public meanings with oblique, personal applications.

Among the early works included in Wordsworth's section reserved for poems about childhood were "The Pet-lamb" and "Lucy Gray"—both from the *Lyrical*

Ballads of 1800. Each poem employs the traditional social iconography of the child to designate the family. The first, however, borrows chiefly from a related and equally traditional figure, that of the imitative child; the second presents a memorable version of a recent invention, the child of nature. Each helps register a slightly different nostalgic tone and aim: the speaker of "The Pet-lamb" displays a complacency and general satisfaction with an adult world and its power structures. In contrast, the narrator of "Lucy Gray" reveals a wistful fantasy of escape from both the civilized world and from the patriarchal tyranny of the family. Despite these ideological differences, both children are memorative objects, images of adult recollection and desire for childhood, and both poems conjure a presocial, prelinguistic childhood through diminutive nonhuman or preternatural figures.[27]

The subtitle of "The Pet-lamb," "A Pastoral," illustrates the condition of this recently domesticated mode at the turn of the nineteenth century. The poem is a verbal analogue of the "pastoral portrait" (a relation of the "dynastic portrait"), which used children frolicking outdoors or caring for animals to convey their parents' ownership of the land (Steward 19). The central scene of the poem, in which a young girl chides an unappreciative lamb her father has rescued from the mountainside, is even framed: the beholder's role is filled by a grown eavesdropper who narrates the entire poem. Although he hears the girl say nothing more than "'Drink, pretty creature, drink'" (2), and although the lamb appears to enjoy its meal, shaking its tail "with pleasure" (10), the child's parting look inspires him to create and sentimentalize a dynastic portrait for vaguely personal ends. As he relates the action, he emphasizes his own emotional response, and his language suggests a male perception. The story he invents for the lamb and the child, whom he calls with romantic paternalism "the little Maiden" (7), is a drama of familial relations in which she plays mother, father, and sibling toward a restive and mysterious "child."

Noticing the lamb straining at his cord, the beholder imagines the girl attributing the animal's discontent to homesickness and the trauma of separation from the mother. In his fancy, she admits that this previous life may be beyond her knowledge. "'Poor creature, can it be / That 'tis thy mother's heart which is working so in thee? / Things that I know not of belike to thee are dear'" (49-51). But her ignorance of an existence beyond human ministrations and concerns brings her back to a catalogue of creature comforts: a soft bed of "tender grass" (7), peerless corn and flowers, a "faithful nurse" in her (39)—she comes daily with water from the brook and new, warm milk—safety in the form of her father's cottage "hard by" (58). She reminds the animal of its lucky escape from the "fearful winds and darkness" (54) of the treacherous mountain, where

"[m]any flocks were on the hills, but thou wert owned by none, / And thy mother from thy side for evermore was gone" (35-36). In this former precarious state, the lamb had neither mother nor owner. The girl fulfills both offices. As nurse she substitutes for the dead mother, and as minion—the darling *(mignon)* on whom her father has bestowed his mountain plunder—she represents him and his rights of ownership. There is, to her, no difference between her nurture and that of the natural mother. The "dam that did thee yean / Upon the mountain-tops no kinder could have been" (39-40) than this little girl who promises to make the lamb her "playmate" (47) when his limbs develop. "Then I'll yoke thee to my cart like a pony in the plough . . . and when the wind is cold / Our hearth shall be thy bed, our house shall be thy fold" (46-48). With her toy beast of burden, the child rehearses the roles of mother/nurse and father/owner. In doing so, she assumes, like many child sitters in pastoral portraits, the *gravitas* of the adult pose (Steward 90).

Yet if the child misunderstands her future and that of the lamb, she speaks only what the imaginative observer improvises for her. Because the narrator reveals nothing about himself other than his identification with the girl, her charm for him must lie in her inadvertent skill at representing roles with which he is familiar. According to most historians of childhood, the droll imitative behavior of children had long been a source of delight to parents, as well as theatergoers. But the kind of approval children's mimicry generally inspired was self-satisfied and distant, hardly the spontaneous sympathy this child excites. "'Nay,' said I, 'more than half [of the song] to the damsel must belong, / For she looked with such a look, and she spake with such a tone, / That I almost received her heart into my own'" (66-68). With the word "received," the poet implies an intense sympathy with the girl that borders on identification. The passivity of the word also suggests a response to a supplicant, as though the child has somehow appealed to him for empathy. It is her frustration with the restless creature that moves the narrator to speak for her and to declare his fabrication or song at least "half" a reality. Her inability to refrain from anthropomorphizing the lamb and her assumptions of authority are, the observer implies, extensions of his own qualities.

In the pastoral portrait, children and animals could be interchangeable; either could represent a sentimental, as well as a legal, attachment to the land (Steward 185-86). The spell under which the eavesdropper immediately falls might originate in the sight of a girl rehearsing responsible stewardship of property through her pet. As in the melodramas that were popular throughout the century, children often were most diverting when they were not playing children at all—but adults, animals, plants, various "stage props"—so too in this poem the

child charms by her enactment of an adult role.[28] She is, in his own fashioning, no child of nature. Rather, she exemplifies the child as "Actor" whom Wordsworth described in his "Ode," performing the roles of mother and father "[a]s if his whole vocation / Were endless imitation" (107-8). The lamb, in comparison, has assumed the role of the child—the primordial child. A creaturely rather than a domestic being whose radical innocence and simplicity we cannot fathom, it assumes the coveted position of the baby in the triad.

It is, in this context, significant that in creating the lamb Wordsworth elided a real girl who figured, at least marginally, in the inspiration of the poem. In calling his "child of beauty rare," "little Barbara Lewthwaite" (13), Wordsworth borrowed the name of an actual girl from Ambleside who, as he revealed in the notes he dictated to Isabella Fenwick in 1843, was one of "two most lovely Sisters," but not the child he overheard talking to her pet lamb.[29] In the poem the "snow-white mountain-lamb" (4) completes the "lovely pair" (14) he remembers—replaces, that is, the other Lewthwaite sister. And, indeed, because the Maiden speaks to the lamb as if it were human, the absent sister assumes a disguised presence, as though she had passed into a lower form like some elusive object of desire from Ovid. The lamb occupies the spaces between the domestic and the wild; it represents innocence and malleability but also recalcitrance and instinct. It can be a pet while it retains a bond with the herd and the untamable forces of nature. In comparison, the child Barbara has grown beyond such originary innocence. When Wordsworth revealed in 1843 that the name he gave his little girl belonged to a living woman who, he notes, was then "much changed as to beauty," he turned the poem into a public souvenir of a real child of the past.[30] So however spontaneous and emotional the projections are, and however tempting it is at first to see the girl's care of the lamb as an instance of the child's close and loving link to nature, the speaker seems moved more by a sense of the fundamental remoteness of the nonhuman world, especially as the adult knows it.

The Maiden in this light replicates the position of the observer and tries to repair loss and distance with forged attachments; but the sympathy that stirs her to anthropomorphize the lamb also prompts her to tether it to a stone. The two acts of bonding and bondage are parallel: while Barbara imagines her lamb as a baby, the narrator moves his "maiden" (a word that indicates her virginity as it manages to suggest the opposite) much closer to a woman than a child. She is not overtly croticized, however, though the complex of experience and emotion invested in her may imply sexual feelings. She and her lamb are more discernibly the objects and vehicles of regressive yearning for that life which is earlier, more primitive, least comprehensible, smallest, and the impulse to appropriate and bond with it: the lamb

bleats for its mother, the girl for the lamb, the observer for the girl. In this sense the poem anticipates the theoretical decline from childhood Wordsworth would articulate in his "Ode" of 1807. The girl and the lamb each embody successive stages of childhood as they recede into the past until they reach the dream state from which our birth is "but a . . . forgetting" ("Ode" 58). The remnant of this state is the severed bond with the mountain landscape and the animal's mother. Both are absent (and the girl does not mention her own mother), and the ties that substitute for them, in comparison, must be forged. They are not "natural," in the sense of original, but re-enactments. The observer likewise fabricates this scenario instead of revealing its parallels with his own past. The girl repeats what the observer does and cannot remember. She amuses and gratifies him with her mimicry, but this behavior barely covers the sense of loss that first impels him to watch and to invent. The beholder's nostalgia is, then, sentimental and impersonal. His ready identification with the scene betrays his own susceptibility to primal affections without revealing to us anything from his own past. While the girl enacts an adult role, the lamb represents the remote Wordsworthian child—recalcitrant, exotic, and unknowable. The figures demonstrate, respectively, the tendency of nostalgic longing to repeat early domestic relations and the far more ambivalent desire for the unfamiliar realm of the "natural" or instinctive.

"Lucy Gray or, Solitude" (1799) similarly illustrates the strangeness of the Wordsworthian child of nature to an adult narrator who portrays her through the normative views of his small rural society and his fantasies of escape. The poem's appearance in the volume of 1815 under "Poems Referring to the Period of Childhood" suggests that Wordsworth viewed "Lucy Gray" as somehow typical of that phase. Lucy herself combines phases of childhood that exist in separate images in "The Pet-lamb": in the course of the poem she regresses from the imitative daughter to the primordial child of nature, an ungendered, empty figure of pure motion. As we know, the poem originated in a story Dorothy Wordsworth heard when she was living with her brother in Goslar. A little girl from Halifax (in Yorkshire) vanished while walking through a snowstorm; searchers were able to track her footprints until they stopped abruptly on the bridge of a canal. The story came to a logical and gruesome ending when the body of the child was dragged from the water. From this sensational event Wordsworth fashioned a kind of ghost story. As he commented later, his poem "spiritualiz[es] the character" of this common girl in part by setting her disappearance in an empty landscape of white marked only by vanishing snow-prints (Curtis 1).

As in "The Pet-lamb," the metamorphosis of Lucy Gray the daughter to Lucy the Wordsworthian child of nature is the fancy of an older mind. The narrator of the

poem—presumably an adult, as he refers to Lucy as a "child"—is curious but relatively detached, showing no sign of the sympathy that excited the inventive narrator of "The Pet-lamb." A conveyer of regional news and superstition, he seems to speak for the community, and although he betrays a tendency to enrich rumor with details, especially as he conjures the child's movements in the poem's last lines, generally his eyes are those of the conventional rural world.[31] They cannot quite bring Lucy into focus: in their light she has the qualities of the domestic and the primordial child. "Oft I had heard of Lucy Gray," he begins, hinting that even before her ecrie end she was considered an anomaly—"[t]he solitary child" (4). In revealing that he "chanced to see" (3) her at dawn, he implies that Lucy is more talked of than seen. He associates her with animals, but small, tractable ones, as though she too once skirted the line between the domestic and the wild:

> You yet may spy the fawn at play,
> The hare upon the green;
> But the sweet face of Lucy Gray
> Will never more be seen.
>
> (9-12)

As he titillates the reader with the end of her story, she becomes not simply an oddity, but an absence. Yet this focus of gossip is also recalled as the "sweetest thing that ever grew / Beside a human door!" (7-8). Lucy again is not so much defined as located—placed near ("by") human territory. Geoffrey Hartman has called her, aptly, "a boundary being."[32] As a "thing" she is too unformed to be recognizable as a boy or girl; her name genders a figure that the eye cannot. Yet as the speaker goes on to assure us, she is human; or she is associated with the human by her physical adjacency to the door, although she grows on the border between the inside of the house which, presumably, contains her and her parents and the outside, the place of "the wild" (2) and the green. The tracking of Lucy's humanness through physical contiguity will reverse when at the end of the story the metonyms that tied Lucy with the human disappear into the nonhumanness of the snowy landscape.

Just as "The Pet-lamb" can be seen as a seemingly conventional piece about the denial of and desire for the remoteness of childhood, so conversely, "Lucy Gray," the romantic poem, may be read as a sinister take on the dynastic child. With her "sweet face" Lucy is for awhile a tractable daughter, and she dies doing a service for her mother at the bidding of her father. Told to "'light / [her] mother through the snow'" with a lantern (15-16), Lucy readily agrees. Events at this point are disjointed and equivocal—a result, most likely, of Wordsworth's efforts to keep to the austerity of fact and so heighten the "spiritualizing" effect of the ballad. Her father does not explicitly contradict her wish, but he "raise[s] his hook" (21), a threat that dissolves as he re-sumes his work in the next line and snaps a faggot. The gesture shows that he is a severe man, and Lucy takes the lantern. When the "wretched parents" (33) begin to search for her later, we wonder just why the mother required Lucy's light to find her way home especially when her sharp eyes "sp[y] / The print of Lucy's feet" (43-44) only a furlong—an eighth of a mile—from the house. We note too that the speaker does not characterize her disappearance as an accident, remembering the equivocal movement of the father's hook. The family of Lucy Gray is hardly a dynasty, but in escaping the father's then uncontestable custody over his children, she empties the household of its most significant metonym of power.

While the lurid imagination of the speaker offers hints of crime, punishment, and the preternatural, his elliptical account also invites us to read "Lucy Gray" as a poem about refusing to grow and about the failure of memory.[33] The daughter, who wants to be self-sufficient and light her own way, dutifully takes the lamp, but she walks carelessly. "Not blither is the mountain roe," the narrator remarks (25), lapsing into the present as he pictures the scene. Her feet are "wanton" (26); and as the storm descends she wanders away through "powdery snow, / That rises up like smoke" (27-28). It is a disappearance, some have remarked, befitting a pastoral elegy: having first been absorbed into the natural world and then, in the poem, returned to the landscape, Lucy is metamorphosed into the doubtful figure of legend.[34] Now untraceable and burdened by no memory or regret, she "never looks behind" and "sings a solitary song" carried by the wind (62-63). (That the song "whistles" in the wind suggests a naturalized Lucy beyond language.) In this way, "Lucy Gray" reverses the narrative direction of "The Pet-lamb" by freeing the child from the cord of familial dependency and the hint of paternal threat. She cludes tracking and passes from the domestic to the creaturely. In her apotheosis as a "living child" (58) roaming the landscape, Lucy embodies the gossipmonger's fantasy of childhood, just as Barbara Lewthwaite manifested the eavesdropper's. But Lucy remembered is permanently foreign to the social world (though portrayed from its perspective). Whereas Barbara's actions mimic those of an adult and encourage a sentimental reaction, Lucy's elicit a longing for childhood as an escape into the pre-social. Whereas Barbara, through her imitative behavior, renders childhood familiar (albeit with force), the figure who appears at the end of "Lucy Gray" keeps it estranged. She embodies its psychological mystery: self-absorbed, empty, without reflection, an embodiment of physical motion only. So although Lucy walks the countryside in the guise of a little girl, she really belongs to the realm of the pretenatural, of superstition; or, she undergoes the profound alteration into trope, as the alternative title of the poem ("Solitude") indicates. Like the pet lamb, she becomes the nonhuman figure that symbolizes the

inaccessibility in memory of the psychological and social condition of childhood.

"LITTLE" AND THE TWO TRADITIONS

Whereas the nostalgia of "Lucy Gray" is subtle and rooted in loss, the sentimentality of "The Pet-lamb" results from a vicarious recovery or, more accurately, from an appropriation of childhood. Hence the diminutive size of the two figures suggests an expressionistic quality to the grown viewer's memory, or a longing for the small figures which, as metonyms, have replaced the contents of his own memory. In many nostalgic representations of childhood, smallness was a crucial element, and the verbal counterpart to the baby in the dynastic portrait was the "little" being. In portraits of large families, like those in the seventeenth-century Dutch painting Ariès observes, "le plus petit enfant," is the affective center of "le sentiment de l'enfance," as well as the family's strength (403). Of the compelling quality of the word "little," Steedman remarks, "Sometimes, during the course of writing [*Strange Dislocations*], I thought that what I was describing here was not 'childhood,' nor 'the child' . . . but *littleness* itself, and the complex register of affect that has been invested in the word 'little'" (9). Littleness came to have a powerful sentimental effect for Victorians, according to Steedman, because it evoked a "visceral sense of the smallness of the self that lies inside" (9). Later, between 1895 and 1920, "long established associations between littleness and interiority and between history and childhood were theorised in emergent psychoanalysis" (77). Yet in nostalgic representation, the miniature had (and has) a value that did not require an elaborate concept of memory or self. In its littleness, a child was (and is) a living souvenir, something reproduced or carried into the present.[35] Dickens once wrote of a man who, having returned to the village of his birth, could not recognize in the middle-aged wife of an acquaintance his first sweetheart and constant playmate of the hayfields. For she "was fat, and if all the hay in the world had been heaped upon her, it could scarcely have altered her face more than Time had altered it from my remembrance. . . . But when her youngest child came in after dinner . . . I saw again, in that little daughter, the little face of the hayfield, unchanged, and it quite touched my heart."[36] A miniature version of an old love, Dickens' little girl accomplishes for the grown man what memory by itself cannot. In a reversal of the organic figure, the child—rather than being father to the man or woman and in effect containing the germ of the adult—becomes a figure of a past shrunk and encapsulated, a grotesque embodiment of an adult seen from vastly far away. Schiller's *Bestimmbarkeit* is gone. Even the child's dynastic function is residual; the figure operates chiefly as a token of the adult's past—his "antiquity," as Alice Meynell would write.

Writers after Wordsworth would use the child to objectify personal memory in place of remembering and all the while retain its social function as a specific object or motive of nostalgia. My illustrative text here is Tennyson's popular "Enoch Arden" (1864). In it, the traditional, dynastic role of the child has assumed the personal, memorative function it has in Dickens' text. Diminutive images of the child function as metonyms of two families, one that dissolves after the disappearance of the father and another that re-forms after his wife's remarriage. The Arden children include an older boy and girl, but an ailing infant bears the impact of the family's financial distress and conveys its pathos. Indeed the infant becomes a sign of the family's moribund state when he dies shortly after the father, Enoch, sails for China in a merchant ship. As the years pass and Enoch does not return, his wife Annie struggles as a small tradeswoman and faces penury even though an old suitor stands ready to marry her and support her children. They respond to his help, but long after both have begun calling him "Father Philip," Annie cannot accept his love. After her marriage to him she still hesitates when entering her new home—until she has a baby: "Then her new child was as herself renewed, / Then the new mother came about her heart, / Then her good Philip was her all-in-all, / And that mysterious instinct wholly died" (519-22).[37] The ekphrastic passage that reveals the new family to Enoch, who has returned after years as a castaway, likewise signals the newly constituted family through the smallest child. What Enoch sees is a middle-class version of the "dynastic portrait": the central figure of this dynasty, framed by the window through which Enoch peers unseen, is the pudgy baby (with "creasy arms" [747]) perched on his father's knee, and he draws frequent glances from his mother on the opposite side of the hearth as he grabs at a ring his older sister dangles from the end of a ribbon, to the laughter of all.

The new baby embodies the "littleness" that excited sentimental reactions to children in part because it emphasized the magnitude of the father's stature. In "Enoch Arden," both babies are male to indicate, respectively, a line of succession in Philip's family and the end of Enoch's. By his very presence, this infant indicates the family's well-being as clearly as do the "cups and silver on the burnished board" (738). In addition to providing the source of distraction for the relaxed family, he signifies Enoch's eclipse as sexual partner. The baby's health and, fundamentally, his existence drive Enoch away to an anonymous death. The poem's window scene thus reflects the traditional public role of the child—a role Enoch, the outside observer, obviously grasps, for it moves him to the private recollection of his own lost infant. In his final moment Enoch—holding the remnant of his own dead "babe in bliss" (894), the lock of hair—mourns his lost "dynasty" and irrevocable past. And in bequeathing his

dead infant's curl to Annie, he reminds her, somewhat reprovingly, of the first family that the new infant has nullified. Although the poem illustrates the seminal role of the husband in creating and sustaining the family, Enoch's choice not to assert parental rights over his surviving children secures readers' sympathy for the lost rights of the natural father. Composed after the most recent statutory intervention diminishing the absolute power of the father over his children in cases of divorce—the Matrimonial Causes Act of 1857 (see Pinchbeck and Hewitt 2: 376-78)—the poem and its enthusiastic reception hint at a public nostalgia for weakening patriarchal privileges.

I have chosen Tennyson's piece and the passage from "The Uncommercial Traveller" for brief discussion to suggest that the imitative child like Barbara Lewthwaite employed for sentimentalized ideological purposes had far more descendants than the mythic child of nature, however compelling it was.[38] Wordsworth's Lucy, particularly the figure of "A Slumber Did My Spirit Seal," permeated Victorian consciousness: the poet Emily Brontë and the painter Alfred William Hunt were haunted by her and her possible death. Her nostalgic effect—based in her significance as an antisocial desire for unreflection—was unsentimental and subtle, compared with that of the imitative child, who provided a more realistic model for narrative poetry and fiction.[39] The miniature often did seem artificial, sometimes because a writer had attempted unsuccessfully to cross the two types and inject a creation of social-realism with a Wordsworthian wisdom (Paul Dombey is an example). As I have shown, even a mythic child of innocence like Lucy or the lamb derived some of its qualities and meaning from a pre-romantic iconology.

Indeed, two concepts of childhood often coexisted. In *The Mill on the Floss*, George Eliot shows the allure of the child of nature through both the narrator's idyllic scenes and Maggie's nostalgia. In contrast, she creates the model "imitative child" in Lucy Deane, whom her cousin Maggie Tulliver envies for her "neatest little rosebud mouth . . . her little round neck with the row of coral beads, her little straight nose . . . her little clear eyebrows." In her spotless dresses, Lucy is diminutive and doll-like. The Dodson clan regards Lucy as a perfect child because "everything about her was neat." Maggie, who is tall for her age, is particularly attracted to Lucy's littleness: "She was fond of fancying a world where the people never got any larger than children of their own age, and she made the queen of it just like Lucy, with a little crown on her head, and a little sceptre in her hand . . . only the girl was Maggie herself in Lucy's form" (53, 54). Maggie's fantasy highlights the ludic quality in Lucy's proper behavior and fussy dresses; she is costumed and exhibited as a miniature woman and is made to play at being a lady. When naughty Maggie pushes Lucy in the mud, she is soiling the family's display item and treating the cousin she normally likes as a doll. That Maggie imagines herself as Lucy in the passage above, yet later longs vaguely for her own childhood, indicates the recessive and forgetful nature of her nostalgia. The conjunction of Maggie and Lucy exemplifies the odd yoking in the nostalgic imagination of an individual conception of one's childhood, albeit shifting and vague, and the highly conventional figures that simultaneously could signify its qualities. Maggie's envy of Lucy is a desire for approval and an instance of the widespread sentimental appeal of miniatures like Lucy Deane for middle-class adults like the Dodsons. She represents the child as family possession, a function that explains her ersatz quality, and she functions as a marker of the family's prosperity by confirming the superior taste and conduct of the adult world. At the same time, she can be sentimentalized as a souvenir of a past beyond detailed recall. The Barbara Lewthwaites and Lucy Deanes were inventions of adults who wanted a concrete and standardized reminder of childhood, a static and uncerebral form of material "re-collection."

Both the imitative and mythic child confirm Mark Pattison's point that childhood "served no purpose" in representation without a "corresponding adulthood to recall it" (61) even after its so-called invention. In "The Pet-lamb," we glimpse the early refashioning of the dynastic object for emotional purposes. The child becomes a memorative object to watch and in this way possess without giving up one's position (in every sense of the word) in the present time and place. The story of Lucy Gray, in contrast, arouses a nostalgia akin to mourning for what one has *not* done—escape growing up—the consequences of which are depressingly apparent in the "Immortality Ode." The appeal of Barbara Lewthwaite and Lucy Deane lives on among the collectors of dolls, miniatures, and other souvenirs which "remember" *for* their possessors. The cultural legacies of the tradition Lucy Gray represents are, in comparison, a matter of some irony. The ambiguous and remote Lucy is a prefiguring of the fallible "living child" or "thing"—*das Es*—which Freud would find and luridly describe. At the same time, the idea of congenital innocence Lucy suggests survived in certain Christian sects and led eventually to the neo-romantic and secular notion of a perennial childhood contained in one's "inner child." These un-Wordsworthian uses of the innocent child are also un-nostalgic. Tellingly, they rely on separate but equally strong ideas of an inner self and, in the case of Freudian psychology, on a complex form of memory and a retrospective idea of the organic being. Hence the Lucy Deanes, not the Lucy Grays, came more regularly to typify childhood in the nostalgic and unromantic memory of Victorians.

Notes

1. In Europe the disease had been known since the seventeenth century. The earliest full discussion occurs in 1688 in Johannes Hofer's "Medical Dissertation on Nostalgia," trans. Carolyn Kiser Anspach, in *Bulletin of the Institute of the History of Medicine* 2 (1934): 376-91; the Welsh case reported by Robert Hamilton is discussed briefly in Richard Hunter and Ida Macalpine, *Three Hundred Years of Psychiatry, 1535-1860* (London: Oxford UP, 1963) 499-500.

2. Philippe Ariès, *L'Enfant et La Vie Familiale sous l'ancien régime* (Paris: Librairie Plon, 1960); the English translation, which I've included when needed, comes from *Centuries of Childhood,* trans. Robert Baldick (New York: Knopf, 1962). Laurence Stone, *The Family, Sex, and Marriage in England, 1500-1800* (London: Weidenfeld & Nicolson, 1977); the opposition is represented most notably by Linda Pollock, *Forgotten Children: Parent-child Relations from 1500 to 1900* (Cambridge: Cambridge UP, 1983) 1-32. Her book usefully summarizes the "Ariès thesis" and its variants. Despite her argument that he and others, including Stone, who make the interest in children sudden and recent (for Stone, between 1540 and 1660, for Ariès in the mid-eighteenth century), and despite her persuasive attacks on their choice and use of evidence, my argument supports a romantic invention of childhood, though I rethink the way this memory works. My discussion of children as products of remembering, in its various forms, reflects the history of childhood, a study of attitudes; it has little to do with the history of children, a study of lived relations: James Christen Steward makes this valuable distinction when observing that each side of the controversy over the invention of childhood does not distinguish the lived life from the attitude. Often, of course, it is a difficult distinction to maintain. See his *The New Child: British Art and the Origins of Modern Childhood, 1730-1830* (Berkeley: University Art Museum and Pacific Film Archive, 1995) 81-82.

3. Some older criticism usefully covers traditions of viewing the child. For a comparison of the two traditions of viewing the child as innocent and as fallen, see Robert Pattison, *The Child Figure in English Literature* (Athens: U of Georgia P, 1978) 49-52. Covering a shorter historical period, Peter Coveney treats the romantic child as a creature of the conflict between Enlightenment and the cult of sensibility in *The Image of Childhood: the Individual and Society: a Study of a Theme in English Literature* (Baltimore: Penguin, 1967) 37-51. Reinhard Kuhn's *Corruption in Paradise: The Child in Western Literature* (Hanover and London: UP of New England, 1982) 32-64 is a satisfying archetypal treatment of the child in English and continental literature.

4. See, for instance, U. C. Knoepflmacher, "Mutations of the Wordsworthian Child of Nature," *Nature and the Victorian Imagination,* ed. U. C. Knoepflmacher and G. B. Tennyson (Berkeley: U of California P, 1977) 394; and Coveney's discussion of the Wordsworthian child of nature (30-51).

5. John Ruskin, *The Gulf of Years: Letters from John Ruskin to Kathleen Olander* (1953; Westport: Greenwood, 1978) 65.

6. James Kincaid, *Child-Loving: The Erotic Child in Victorian Culture* (New York and London: Routledge, 1992); Carolyn Steedman, *Strange Dislocations: Childhood and the Idea of Human Interiority, 1780-1930* (Cambridge MA: Harvard UP, 1995). Kuhn likewise refuses to establish age limits for his study of the child and at the same time distinguishes childhood from boyhood (5-6).

7. Ivy Pinchbeck and Margaret Hewitt, *Children in English Society,* 2 vols. (Toronto: U of Toronto P, 1969) 1: 7.

8. Jean Jacques Rousseau, *Émile ou de l'Éducation* (Paris: Flammarion, 1966) 89, 211-12. To Rousseau a child's strength surpasses his needs *(besoins),* rather than his desires, for a brief period around the ages of 12 and 13. The task of the tutor and parent is to control desires until puberty, after which such a task becomes increasingly difficult. But Rousseau maintains that keeping a child from reading, the company of others, and the idleness of town life may preserve "l'ignorance des désires et la pureté des sens" to age 20 (415). Hence Rousseau imagines a childhood that extends beyond sexual readiness as long as it excludes sexual intercourse.

9. Kincaid's assertion that the gradual rise of the legal (as opposed to the canonical) age of consent as one index of the extension of childhood is somewhat complicated by the fact that the age had been set as high as 21 in the Revised Canonical Laws of 1603 (70).

10. E. P. Thompson, *The Making of the English Working Class* (London: Penguin, 1980) 366-84.

11. Alice Meynell, "That Pretty Person," *Essays* (Westminster, MD: Newman Bookshop, 1947) 256-57.

12. One reason for the focus on the Christ child, according to Meynell, was that he did not have the "transitoriness" of the child in the popular conception. He was a "permanent mystery" (Alice Mey-

nell, *Children of the Old Masters* [New York: Dutton, 1903] 5). Meynell discusses Evelyn's son ("That Pretty Person" 253) as a typical case; but as Pollock points out, Evelyn clearly regarded his son as an extraordinary child (100).

13. Thomas Carlyle, *Sartor Resartus,* ed. Kerry McSweeney and Peter Sabor (Oxford: Oxford UP, 1987) 75, 80. This edition reproduces the text as it appeared in installments in *Fraser's* (1833-34). Elizabeth Barrett Browning, *Aurora Leigh,* ed. Margaret Reynolds (New York: Norton, 1996) 1: 215.

14. *Mrs. Leicester's School,* vol. 3 of *The Works of Charles and Mary Lamb,* ed. E. V. Lucas, 7 vols. (1903; New York: AMS, 1968).

15. George Eliot, *The Mill on the Floss,* ed. Gordon Haight (Oxford: Clarendon, 1980).

16. More specifically, Ferguson describes "romantic memory" as a "characteristic modern way of identifying the stakes of memory in relation to the individual" ("Romantic Memory," *SiR* 35 [1996]: 515).

17. Margaret Homans' superb discussion of the failure of Maggie's Wordsworthian attachment to nature and her past is in *Bearing the Word* (U of Chicago P, 1986) 120-52.

18. Friedrich von Schiller, "Naive and Sentimental Poetry," trans. Julius A. Elias, *Two Essays* (New York: Ungar, 1966). Elias translates *Bestimmbarkeit* as "unlimited *determinacy*" (87) to refer to the "range of those possibilities as potentialities that may still be realized" (216, no. 4). In their edition of *On the Aesthetic Education of Man* (Oxford: Clarendon, 1967) Elizabeth M. Wilkinson and L. A. Willoughby suggest "a state of unlimited potentiality, of pure determinability." The difference in the two translations suggests a fine distinction between the "presence of contending determinations of equal force . . . a state of perfect equilibrium" evoked in nostalgic understandings of childhood (hinted at by Elias' language, but explained here by Wilkinson and Willoughby), and the open significance associated with the figure of the child (i.e., the "entire absence of determination" in Wilkinson and Willoughby [305]).

19. See Bryan S. Turner on nostalgia as a "fundamental condition of human estrangement" in "A Note on Nostalgia" in *Theory, Culture, and Society* 4 (1987): 151. Coveney observes of Wordsworth, "concern with his own childhood became the means of establishing general truths about childhood itself" (31). Marjorie Levinson expands this notion in her study of the personal and political occasion of the composition of the Ode in *Wordsworth's Great Period Poems* (Cambridge: Cambridge UP, 1986) 84-90. Although her focus on the rhetoric of the poem challenges the popular understanding of the poem on which I base my comments, Levinson's important argument exemplifies the periodic connection between nostalgic expression and libertarian discourse, in particular prognostications for Golden Ages to come.

20. William Wordsworth, *The Prelude 1799, 1805, 1850,* ed. Jonathan Wordsworth, M. H. Abrams, and Stephen Gill (New York: Norton, 1979), cited in the text by book and line number.

21. For an account of the anthologized Wordsworth and the popular selections of his poetry in the nineteenth century see Stephen Gill, *Wordsworth and the Victorians* (Oxford: Clarendon, 1998) 102-9.

22. See Gill (10-39) for a survey of the changing nature of Wordsworth's reputation and in particular (30) for his characterization of the Victorian reception of Wordsworth by 1850: see also Fred Kaplan, *Sacred Tears: Sentimentality in Victorian Literature* (Princeton: Princeton UP, 1987) 41-48.

23. For example, of two poems entitled "To a Butterfly," both published in 1807, both referring to the poet's sister and the lost days of childhood, only one appears in this category. The other is included under "Poems Founded on the Affections."

24. William Wordsworth, *Poetical Works,* ed. Thomas Hutchinson and Ernest de Selincourt (Oxford: Oxford UP, 1969). All of Wordsworth's poetry, except for *The Prelude,* will hereafter be cited in the text by line from this edition.

25. D. Hack Tuke, ed. *A Dictionary of Psychological Medicine,* 2 vols. (London, 1892) 2: 858.

26. Alice Meynell, "The Illusion of Historic Time," first published in *Pall Mall Gazette* 13 March 1896; rpt. in *Essays* 264.

27. Steedman traces efforts during the nineteenth century to make the *unheimlich* child familiar through sentimental depictions (21-42, 161-74).

28. It is noteworthy that in the nineteenth-century theater few children played child-parts; most were, as Steedman remarks, "animated stage props" such as elves, sprites, and animals (143).

29. Jared Curtis, *The Fempick Notes of William Wordsworth* (London: Bristol Classical, 1993) 5.

30. Coincidentally, Barbara Lewthwaite saw her name in this volume while she was at school and, to Wordsworth's annoyance, claimed to remember the scene recounted in the poem and what the speaker, whom she identified with Wordsworth, said to her (Curtis 5).

31. Most recently, Pamela Woof has emphasized the role of "hearsay" in the poem ("The 'Lucy' Po-

ems: Poetry of Mourning," *The Wordsworth Circle* 30.1 [1999]: 29-30).

32. Geoffrey Hartman, *Wordsworth's Poetry* (New Haven: Yale UP, 1964) 158.

33. Discussing the Lucy poems in general, Yasunari Takahashi has stressed the connection between the girl and the death of childhood—but as an important milestone in the growth of the poetic imagination; here Lucy is the exceptional and symbolic child. See "Who is Lucy?—On the Structure of Wordsworthian Imagination," *English Criticism in Japan,* ed. Earl Miner (Princeton: Princeton UP, 1972) 174, 177.

34. Woof's examination of the Lucy figures (28-38) follows that of Herbert Hartman ("Wordsworth's Lucy Poems," *PMLA* 49 [1934]: 142), who treats her as an "eighteenth-century elegiac fixture" and a neo-Arcadian commonplace."

35. My use of the miniature as souvenir is indebted to Susan Stewart's *On Longing* (Baltimore: Johns Hopkins UP, 1984).

36. [Charles Dickens], "The Uncommercial Traveller," *All the Year Round* 3 (30 June 1860): 278.

37. All quotations from "Enoch Arden" are cited by line from *Poems of Tennyson,* ed. Christopher Ricks, 3 vols. (London: Longmans, Green, 1969) 2: 625-49.

38. Kincaid corroborates this (72-73); the innocent child may even be a "modern imposition" on Victorian images (73).

39. In, for example, allusions to "She dwelt among the untrodden ways" in two poems of 1838, "How still, how happy!" and "The bluebell is the sweetest flower," in *The Poems of Emily Brontë,* ed. Derek Roper with Edward Chitham (Oxford: Clarendon, 1995); Alfred William Hunt, "Modern English Landscape Painting," *The Nineteenth Century* 7 (1880): 788, in which the dead Lucy of "A Slumber" becomes a metaphor of an emotional involvement in nature that makes a "view" or "prospect" impossible and undesirable.

CHILDHOOD IN THE WORKS OF WILLIAM WORDSWORTH

Mary R. Wedd (essay date October 1996)

SOURCE: Wedd, Mary R. "The Magic of Childhood in the *Two-Part Prelude.*" *The Charles Lamb Bulletin,* no. 96 (October 1996): 142-56.

[*In the following essay, Wedd highlights Wordsworth's depiction of the adult's remembrance and recollection of childhood as idealized and magical in* The Prelude.]

I think it was at the second Wordsworth Summer Conference I attended, in 1972, that I inadvertently got into a fierce argument with a certain learned gentleman. Making polite conversation about Wordsworth, I had let fall what I thought was a truism, that we all know in childhood a particular vividness of perception and intensity of experience, whether of good or ill. I was taken by surprise not only by my companion's categorical denial of this but also by the aggression with which he made it, which has fixed this conversation in my memory. I had the idea that if, as Lamb says, 'lawyers, I suppose, were children once', so too were learned professors. I tried to bring supportive evidence by referring to the exceptional brilliance which many fine writers show when describing their early years in autobiographical or fictional form, but I soon saw that I had better change the subject. I could see what he was thinking about me and I, for my part, was thinking, 'Oh dear! *Poor* little boy!' Perhaps I am wrong but I still tend to the opinion that most people, asked to describe their childhood, pour it out freely and in a much more imaginative way than in their usual communications. When they do not wish to remember, it is for some catastrophic reason and even then, as with Dickens and the blacking-factory, it is liable to erupt.

If one sits down and clears the mind, just allowing things to come, out of the mysterious realm of childhood, even quite ordinary people such as we are will find we have written with a beauty and poignancy quite alien to our workaday selves. If you have not already done so, try it. You may surprise yourself. How much more must this be so where a great poet is concerned, 'a chosen son'. For this was what Wordsworth was doing, letting memories spill out in an inspired stream in the manuscripts that went to make the *Two-Part Prelude.* I do not mean, as we shall see, that he did not use all his poet's art in the process but the inspiration from the childhood memories is undoubted. Later he was to disperse some of the incidents throughout the longer poem but in this early draft we have many of them concentrated together, and, though in the main I do not regret the rearrangement or the extension of the poem to thirteen or fourteen books, there is no denying that we have here a treasure-trove beyond compare.

For each of us there are certain writers whom we read with a sort of self-discovery—'Goodness! I didn't know anyone else felt like that!' What first made me fall in love with Wordsworth's poetry when I read it at school was that recognition of a familiar inner landscape, particularly of childhood, and I am sure that I am not alone.

> Ah! is there one who ever has been young
> And needs a monitory voice to tame
> The pride of virtue and of intellect,
> And is there one, the wisest and the best
> Of all mankind, who does not sometimes wish
> For things which cannot be, who would not give,

If so he might, to duty and to truth
The eagerness of infantine desire?

(*Two-Part Prelude* ii 17-24)[1]

But, of course, try as we may, we cannot recapture in its pristine state the experience of childhood, for it has inevitably become modified by our subsequent development, by adult ways of seeing, by memory. For example, the tiny boy who 'Made one long bathing of a summer's day' or 'stood alone / A naked savage in the thunder-shower' is seen from outside, as in those photographs we are all so shamed by which show a bare baby on a rug. Or, in the woodcock incident, we recognize resonances from *Macbeth* in the words 'when the deed was done' which bring an alien sophistication to the childish sense of guilt. Even a particular memory, vivid though it is, may be inaccurate. My sister and I, relating the same early event, can rarely agree about its details. So it is not an exact recreation of his youthful history that Wordsworth has presented to us. It is something much more complicated and interesting. Certainly he is recalling particular occasions and places which contain for him that vividness, that intensity, that magic which characterize childhood experience and generally they are associated with real remembered locations. In 1805 he adds to his account of the Derwent that it was in 'A little mill-race severed from his stream' that he bathed. It is covered now by concrete but its course on the far side of the river opposite Wordsworth House was still shown on the Ordnance Survey map First Series. In 1974 I followed its hidden course to the old mill with its wheel, still there, though then about to be converted. On the other hand, often there is a conflation of several elements, as in the case of the gibbet which he did *not* see near Penrith, where he rode as a small boy, and the one near Priest Pot at Hawkshead, which he must often have passed later, the remains of which were unearthed during draining operations within living memory. Wordsworth recognizes the situation, both the magic of the recollection and the adult's separation from it.

A tranquillizing spirit presses now
On my corporeal frame, so wide appears
The vacancy between me and those days,
Which yet have such self-presence in my heart
That sometimes when I think of them I seem
Two consciounesses, conscious of myself
And of some other being.

(ibid. ii 25-31)

The adult poet, looking back, provides also a delightful touch, here and there, of the mockheroic, which juxtaposes the crude fairy-tale nature of the child's conscious imagination at that stage with his deeper supernatural experience. When he is kitted out with a bundle of snares at his back, he sees himself as an armed warrior out for slaughter.

That time, my shoulder all with springes hung,
I was a fell destroyer.

(ibid. i 34-5)

Is a pun intended? 'Fell' meaning 'fierce, destructive' and 'Fell' meaning on the fells? I wouldn't put it past Wordsworth. But when he had stolen a bird from someone else's trap,

I heard among the solitary hills
Low breathings coming after me, and sounds
Of undistinguishable motion, steps
Almost as silent as the turf they trod.

(ibid. i 46-9)

There is a pleasant Cumbrian tale, which I always associate with Coleridge's stanza,

Like one, that on a lonesome road
Doth walk in fear and dread,
And having once turned round walks on,
And turns no more his head;
Because he knows, a fearful fiend
Doth close behind him tread.

(*The Ancient Mariner* 446-51)

It is very irreverent of me because really that passage probably relates to Dante's *Inferno*,[2] but the story, which applies even better to Wordsworth's lines, is of a countryman walking home at night over the high fells. To his horror he heard a swishing movement behind him and was convinced that he was being followed. When he stopped the phantom stopped and when he continued walking so did it. At last he plucked up courage to look behind him. There was nothing there. After a while it dawned on him that what he was hearing was the rubbing of one of his trouser-legs against the other.

I don't offer this insight into superstition in order to diminish Wordsworth's experience. When I was very small an evil creature lived behind a curtain that hung on a landing which I had always to pass when I went to bed. Our house had no gas or electricity, only oil-lamps and candles. Perhaps we don't remember sufficiently the primitive conditions in which people used to live and the effect this had on their perception of the world; walking home from work across the fells, for example, or children trudging ten miles to school and back across a Welsh mountain. Anyway, I had no more doubt of the existence of the phantom behind the curtain than I had of my own.

What is remarkable is the way Wordsworth conveys the terrors of childhood and compels us to participate in them, by what Jonathan Wordsworth calls 'deliberate imprecision'.[3] It is uncertainty about what the fearful thing is that is its chief menace. 'Low breathings'— whose? 'Sounds / Of undistinguishable motion'—what can they be? And 'steps / Almost as silent as the turf

they trod'—what does he mean, 'Almost'? Soon one's flesh begins to creep. Yet we are left, as the child was, with a sense that we are on the edge of another kind of reality.

Similarly, when he describes taking the stolen boat, Wordsworth at first regards his younger self with affectionate humour. In his childish imagination based on fairy-tales his boat is 'an elfin pinnace' and, proud of his rowing, he sees her 'heaving through the water like a swan' as he fixes his eye on 'the bound of the horizon'. But his heroic fantasies are doomed to shocked deflation, as behind the 'rocky steep' a 'huge cliff', behaving like a giant with a will of its own, 'Uprear'd its head', 'Rose up between me and the stars' and 'like a living thing / Strode after me.' The word 'Strode' is terrifying. In the passage that follows how brilliantly Wordsworth conjures up that frightening state of disorientation in which nothing seems to be what it is or when the identity of common objects that we take for granted suddenly seems to be in doubt.

> and after I had seen
> That spectacle, for many days my brain
> Worked with a dim and undetermined sense
> Of unknown modes of being: in my thoughts
> There was a darkness, call it solitude,
> Or blank desertion; no familiar shapes
> Of hourly objects, images of trees,
> Of sea or sky, no colours of green fields:
> But huge and mighty forms, that do not live
> Like living men, moved slowly through my mind
> By day, and were the trouble of my dreams.
>
> *(Two-Part Prelude* i 119-29)

As adults, at least for most of the time, we know that dreams are dreams: as children we are not so sure. Those events—of the ghostly footsteps or the ogre cliff—which take place mainly in the mind, are no less real or shocking than the actual horrific sight of the drowned man who, by contrast with the surrounding 'beauteous scene',

> bolt upright
> Rose with his ghastly face.
>
> (ibid. i 278-9)

Such 'tragic facts / Of rural history', Wordsworth says, are 'archetypes', which both persist in their original impact and also provide a nucleus to which 'Far other feelings were attached', the whole constellation having permanence in memory. For example, the 'ordinary sight' at Penrith Beacon was so coloured for the young boy by tales he had heard about the murderer who had been hanged nearby that, combined with the desolate landscape and his temporary separation from the reassuring company of his grandparents' servant, it became imbued with a 'visionary dreariness' impossible to paint in 'colours' or 'words'. He had most of his facts wrong

but 'a long green ridge of turf / whose shape was like a grave' was quite enough. Similarly, the unpromising ingredients for nightmare of a sheep, a tree and a wall were always associated in his memory with the subsequent death of his father. These experiences are given permanence by the strong charge of emotion attached to them and, though grievous, such memories are cherished for the power they exercise. Even when the sense of the supernatural is based on misconception it nevertheless does give an inkling that there is another dimension to existence.

Not all these intimations, however, are related to those severer interventions which correspond to Burke's 'sublime', though Wordsworth says, 'Of their school was I'. In the ravens'-nesting incident, though his object was 'mean' and 'inglorious'—he hoped to extend his pocket-money by claiming destruction of predators—the outcome was not ignoble' (ibid. i 55-7). There *is* an element of fear, indeed. It was physically dangerous and, on another level, there is strangeness and mystery in the transformed world that he experiences, but the fear is not paramount. The wonderful use of 'deliberate imprecision' here conveys, rather, a brief communion with another state of being, uplifting and inspiring.

> Oh, when I have hung
> Above the raven's nest, by knots of grass,
> Or half-inch fissures in the slipp'ry rock,
> But ill sustained, and almost, as it seemed,
> Suspended by the blast which blew amain,
> Shouldering the naked crag, oh at that time,
> While on the perilous ridge I hung alone,
> With what strange utterance did the loud dry wind
> Blow through my ears! the sky seemed not a sky
> Of earth, and with what motion moved the clouds!
>
> (ibid. i 57-66)

Wordsworth is confident that the juxtaposition of the child's developing human emotions 'with high objects, with eternal things' (ibid. i 136), rather than with everyday man-made objects, provides a privileged upbringing.

> purifying thus
> The elements of feeling and of thought,
> And sanctifying by such discipline
> Both pain and fear, until we recognise
> A grandeur in the beatings of the heart.
>
> (ibid. i 137-41)

But the boy, thank goodness, is a real boy. He is of 'A race of real children, not too wise, / Too learned, or too good'.[4] He is proud of his physical prowess and by no means a goody-goody. Equally he rejoices in being in the warm kitchen on a winter's day, playing noughts and crosses or games with grubby playing-cards, or, with his friends he makes a frightful row, staying out

late when he ought to be back home, and showing off like nobody's business his skill at skating. Wordsworth uses all his adult poetic expertise to conjure up this scene. First comes the noise and the vigorous physical activity.

> I wheeled about
> Proud and exulting like an untired horse
> That cares not for its home.
>
> (*Two-Part Prelude* i 154-6)

I am old enough to remember when cars in our country village were a rarity. In fact, in my early childhood I don't remember ever seeing one. In general, if one wanted to get from one place to another, one walked. But if we went some distance—for a picnic say—we were conveyed in a pony-trap with my mother driving. When we children did at last go for our first ride in a car, we were bitterly disappointed because it did not make the glorious echoing noise that the horse's hoofs did under bridges. On the outward journey the pony was frisky and eager to be moving. On the return trip, though one could have left him to find his own way home because he so much wished to be there, his place was slower and if we went up a steep hill we all got out except the driver and walked, 'to spare the horse', as the saying then was. To young Wordsworth in the days when all travel was by horses or on foot this was a simile from everyday life.

Instead of Tennyson's 'murmuring of innumerable bees', which always used to be given in textbooks as an example of onomatopoeia, one could equally well cite

> All shod with steel
> We hissed along the polished ice . . .
>
> (ibid. i 156-7)

An economical illustration this would be, too, as it includes alliteration and assonance as well. Or

> the precipices rang aloud,
> The leafless trees and every icy crag
> Tinkled like iron . . .
>
> (ibid i 163-5)

Wordsworth calls on all his arts to make the experience vivid.

The description then modulates from one key to another.

> while the distant hills
> Into the tumult sent an alien sound
> Of melancholy not unnoticed . . .
>
> (ibid. i 165-7)

That typically Wordsworthan double negative suggests an almost subconscious picking up of the message sent by the quiet landscape.

> while the stars,
> Eastward, were sparkling clear, and in the west
> The orange sky of evening died away.
>
> (ibid. i 167-9)

Even to the child, in the midst of his 'glad animal movements' and surrounded by the 'din', comes a hint of human transience against the permanence of the everlasting hills.

In this changed mood he seeks solitude.

> Not seldom from the uproar I retired
> Into a silent bay, or sportively
> Glanced sideway leaving the tumultuous throng
> To cut across the shadow of a star
> That gleamed upon the ice . . .
>
> (ibid. i 170-4)

There follows a kind of recapitulation in another shape, of the previous first and second subjects. The boys were all whizzing along in joyous abandonment.

> When we had given our bodies to the wind
> And all the shadowy banks on either side
> Came sweeping through the darkness, spinning still
> The rapid line of motion . . .
>
> (ibid. i 175-8)

then Wordsworth suddenly checked his consciously propelled move forward, though he was still carried on by the former momentum.

> . . . then at once
> Have I, reclining back upon my heels,
> Stopped short; yet still the solitary cliffs
> Wheeled by me, even as if the earth had rolled
> With visible motion her diurnal round . . .
>
> (ibid. i 178-82)

It was as if he could see the world turning on its axis in front of his eyes, as the 'solitary cliffs' whizzed by.

> Behind me did they stretch in solemn train
> Feebler and feebler, and I stood and watched
> Till all was tranquil as a summer sea.
>
> (ibid. i 183-5)

He has felt an intimation of 'the peace that passes all understanding'. He has been in touch with what the American Indians call 'the Great Spirit'.

It seems a come-down, then, when in the following passage he addresses what seem to be separate Greek-style nature spirits.

> Ye Powers of earth! ye Genii of the springs!
> And ye that have your voices in the clouds
> And ye that are Familiars of the lakes
> And of the standing pools . . .
>
> (ibid. i 186-9)

They seem to be the adult equivalent of the child's giants and ghosts. He makes them slightly more acceptable in the *Thirteen-Book Prelude,* where he calls them 'presences', 'visions' and 'souls', but I am still uneasy with them. Jonathan Wordsworth says 'they have very much the air of supernatural machinery added later like the sylphs of *The Rape of the Lock'* but, as he points out, they were not an afterthought but were in MS JJ.[5] I remember at an early Wordsworth Summer Conference William Empson asserting vigorously that both Coleridge and Wordsworth believed in such spirits. But I think Wordsworth perhaps did not try to pin down too exactly the presence that he felt. Whether he 'saw one life and felt that it was joy' (ibid. ii 460), or whether tutelary spirits formed him, or he was 'With God and Nature communing' (ibid. i 476), he was alike affirming that there is a transcendental power of which the child is aware in his visionary moments. Whatever it was that was educating him, he says,

> I may not think
> A vulgar hope was yours when ye employed
> Such ministry . . .

> (ibid. i 189-91)

The word 'vulgar' here is not used in the full pejorative sense it has now, but simply means 'ordinary' or 'commonplace'. Wordsworth felt that he was singled out

> . . . when ye through many a year
> Thus by the agency of boyish sports
> On caves and trees, upon the woods and hills,
> Impressed upon all forms the characters
> Of danger or desire, and thus did make
> The surface of the universal earth
> With meanings of delight, of hope and fear,
> Work like a sea.

> (ibid. i 191-8)

It is as though the nature-spirits had used the child's unthinking physical activity as a vehicle whereby they could inscribe on everything round him the characteristic handwriting of the sublime and the beautiful—'danger or desire', 'hope and fear', which being translated became 'meanings of delight'. Thus the whole earth became so full of varied impressions that it was like a fermenting wine or an ever restless sea. When one considers the immense amount a child learns just in the first months one can understand this well.

To a very young child everything is new. Nothing can be taken for granted. One has only to observe a baby discovering its own fingers. Recently I gave some wooden bricks to my great-grandson for his first birthday. You could see him thinking, 'Now, what have we here? What do I do with this?' This process continues with increasing sophistication until at my age I have to learn the function of computer-buttons. But that early

wonder is a precious gift that cannot be entirely preserved once the subsequent body of associations has built up which, in memory, modify the original experience. One does not need to be steeped in the philosophy of Hartley, as Wordsworth and Coleridge were at this time, to recognize in a more general and pragmatic way the importance to us all of the accretion of associations. But occasionally one recaptures something of the freshness, even as an adult. At the age of ten, looking at the sea, Wordsworth felt that original newness.

> How I have stood to images like these
> A stranger, linking with the spectacle
> No body of associated forms . . .

> (ibid. i 403-5)

Nor did he bring with him any 'peculiar sense / Of quietness or peace',

> . . . yet I have stood
> Even while my eye has moved o'er three long leagues
> Of shining water, gathering, as it seemed,
> Through the wide surface of that field of light
> New pleasure, like a bee among the flowers.

> (ibid. i 407-12)

He is living predominantly in the world of his senses but 'even then',

> A Child, I held unconscious intercourse
> With the eternal Beauty . . .

> (ibid. i 394-5)

By some miracle, Wordsworth manages to convey the child's sense of everything being new, nothing being taken as read, despite the intervening years in which the freshness has been obliterated by habit. In recapturing that pristine state of opening the self up to incoming sights and sounds with a kind of surprised discovery, Wordsworth recognizes that, unbeknownst, that receptiveness has allowed the entry also of spiritual visions, 'Gleams like the flashing of a shield' (ibid. i 418), which bring with them calmness and peace.

Not that habit or accumulated associations have no place in the creation of a soul. The pristine wonder of the very young child is replaced by the love that is engendered by familiarity.

> —And if the vulgar joy by its own weight
> Wearied itself out of the memory,
> The scenes which were a witness of that joy
> Remained . . .

and

> . . . did at length
> Become habitually dear, and all
> Their hues and forms were by invisible links
> Allied to the affections.

> (ibid. i 427-30, 439-42)

In Part II, which, as Stephen Parrish says, was 'taken over almost intact into Book II of 1805',[6] it is the turn of Beauty rather than Fear, and perhaps it is particularly in this Part that the last lines of Part I are most vividly exemplified.

> Those recollected hours that have the charm
> Of visionary things, and lovely forms
> And sweet sensations that throw back our life
> And make our infancy a visible scene
> On which the sun is shining.
>
> (ibid. i 460-4)

The Second Part begins by showing how 'the passion' for Nature at first 'came unsought' as concomitant to the 'round of tumult' of the children's games, which were

> Prolonged in summer till the daylight failed;
> No chair remained before the doors, the bench
> And threshold steps were empty, fast asleep
> The labourer and the old man who had sate
> A later lingerer . . .
>
> (ibid. ii 8-12)

These lines are very evocative to me. My grandmother was a needlewoman whose embroidery was so intricate that when she left a piece unfinished at her death no one could be found capable of completing it. One of my earliest memories is of her moving to the window, as evening came, to catch the last of the daylight. Just so might the spinning-wheel be moved in Wordsworth's time and even taken outside. I hope you will forgive me if Wordsworth's reminiscences seem to be touching off mine: it is part of their function for the reader. Also some living *Old* Historicism can sometimes help us to feel ourselves back into the young poet's world. One day in the 1970s I had walked over Claife Heights to Belle Grange in a heatwave. On my way back, passing through Colthouse, I saw an old lady sitting on the wall opposite one of the Beckside cottages which are on the other side of the road from where Wordsworth lodged. She told me that the sun never penetrated inside those houses, so that in summer she came out for warmth. So what with the search for light and the search for heat, it must have been night indeed if the 'threshold steps were empty'.

Every crowd of children needs a headquarters and

> A grey stone
> Of native rock, left midway in the square
> Of our small market-village, was the home
> And centre of these joys . . .
>
> (ibid. ii 31-4)

As emerges later, in the Furness Abbey passage, it was their equivalent of a tuck-shop. It was known as 'Nanny's stone' after 'that old dame / From whom the stone

was named', as T. W. Thompson tells us;[7] and she was Nanny Holme. As Carl Ketcham suggests the word scribbled in the margin of MS A which Miss Darbishire read as 'Rowe' is probably 'power', the old lady's 'counter' being a rocking-stone which folklore endowed with magic qualities.[8] These lines must have been written after Wordsworth had revisited Hawkshead with Coleridge and John in November 1799, when the atrocity of the Assembly Room first outraged their sights. Wordsworth says of this visit in a sonnet of 1802, 'So narrow seemed the brooks, the fields so small'. Like all of us when returning to childhood haunts in later years, William and John doubtless found that everything had shrunk. Everything, that is, except the 'smart assembly-room that perked and flared'. There had been a building of sorts erected about 1650 but it was an unpretentious affair, an upper storey with a shambles underneath, and it left plenty of room where Nanny's stone stood. The new Market House, built in 1790 increased in size so much that the stone had to be removed to make room for it. It perks and flares even more now, having been 'considerably enlarged in 1887', as Cowper tells us.[9]

In the summer more ambitious activities became possible for the schoolboys, 'calmer pleasures' such as rowing among the islands on Windermere or the adventure of riding, for a greater distance than they let on to the landlord of the Red Lion from whom they probably hired the horses. After the roundabout journey they took to and from Furness Abbey, there would certainly not be among them 'an untired horse / That cares not for its home'. In talking of 'Sabine fare' Wordsworth is a bit unjust both to Ann Tyson's housekeeping and to the amount of pocket-money the boys received, as we know from her account-book, which Mrs Heelis (Beatrix Potter) found one day mouldering in an outhouse. In his last year at school Wordsworth received sixpence a week. In the depression of the 1930s the National Assistance allowance for a child's keep was two shillings a week. As Cecil Day Lewis put it,

> Two shillings a week is
> The price of a soul.[10]

In case you have forgotten, there were only four sixpences in two shillings. So I cannot think the Hawkshead schoolboys were deprived, though William, as the eldest then still at school received more than his brothers. But pocket-money always seems a mere pittance to children and it is true that their meals were a bit few and far between. However, when

> to school
> Returned from the half-yearly holidays,
> We came with purses more profusely filled,
>
> (ibid. ii 84-6)

things were different. In January 1796 William received fifteen shillings and the following year a whole guinea, that is one pound one shilling or 105p. With such a sum

they could afford more expensive dainties than Nanny's wares, though I expect their pockets were well stocked up with these as well, when they indulged in the welcome extravagance of hiring horses.

The glorious exuberance of the ride is vividly conjured up, with again a touch of the mock-heroic, as they delighted 'To feel the motion of the galloping steed'. 'With whip and spur we by the Chantry flew' or

> Through the walls we flew
> And down the valley, and, a circuit made
> In wantonness of heart, through rough and smooth
> We scampered homeward.
>
> (ibid. ii 130-3)

Notice that they did to a degree 'spare the horses' 'when, with slackened step, we breathed / Along the sides of the steep hills'. But more typical of their mode is the onomatopoeic line which in the 1805 *Prelude* Wordsworth repeats with such effect in Book X: 'We beat with thundering hoofs the level sand.' However, alongside the pleasure in 'a boisterous race', the presence of Furness Abbey itself is deeply felt, 'A holy scene'.

> in more than inland peace
> Left by the winds that overpass the vale
> In that sequestered ruin trees and towers
> Both silent, and both motionless alike,
> Hear all day long the murmuring sea that beats
> Incessantly upon a craggy shore.
>
> (ibid. ii 112-17)

In Wordsworth's *Unpublished Tour* he leads the reader into the Lake District across the sands and says, 'When the Traveller has reached Ulverston, he may be inclined to visit Furness Abbey'.[11] He praises 'the situation of this Monastery' in its fertile valley 'in a remote corner of the Island & backed by the sea', safe from invasion by the Scots and well suited to meditation and self-discipline. Wordsworth imagines a 'Meditative Monk' retiring to the neighbouring Beacon, which must have 'contributed to devotional feeling by a display of the sublimest works of the Creator'.[12] Alas! if he were to do so today he might get rather a shock, for, as Norman Nicholson pointed out, the Abbey is now 'almost enclosed in Barrow suburbs' . . . 'Yet before the Industrial Revolution Barrow did not exist'.[13]

Once again the children's physical activity is juxtaposed to a contemplative peace.

> Our steeds remounted, and the summons given,
> With whip and spur we by the Chantry flew
> In uncouth race, and left the cross-legged Knight
> And the stone Abbot, and that single wren
> Which one day sang so sweetly in the nave
> Of the old church that, though from recent showers
> The earth was comfortless, and touched by faint

> Internal breezes from the roofless walls
> The shuddering ivy dripped large drops, yet still
> So sweetly 'mid the gloom the invisible bird
> Sang to itself that there I could have made
> My dwelling-place, and lived for ever there
> To hear such music.
>
> (ibid. ii 118-30)

At the risk of breaking the mood, since I am talking about the magic of childhood in more than one of its manifestations, I can't resist a story Wordsworth tells which he would certainly have known in boyhood. Cowper speaks of an underground passage which was reputed to run from Furness Abbey to Hawkshead Hall, where the Monastery administered its very considerable property.[14] Wordsworth does not mention this but outdoes it when he says of the Abbey's quarters,

> Among these gloomy cells is one more terrible than the rest where the wealth of the Abbey is reported to lie hid. Many Persons, as the tradition goes, have attempted to grope their way along the blind passage, which leads to this treasure house, but in vain—lizards, vipers, adders, huge toads, & monsters casting out flames from their wide jaws force them to relinquish their purpose, & madness & death have been the consequence of their fears.[15]

So don't go looking for it tomorrow, whatever you do!

The episode of the boat on Coniston is most interesting, both as to Wordsworth's developing working methods and to the greater or lesser success of them. In *The Vale of Esthwaite,* written in his last year at school, 1787, there is a passage beginning

> Yet if Heaven bear me far away
> To end the evening of my day . . .

and ends

> My soul shall cast the wistful view
> The longing look alone on you.
> As Phoebus, when he sinks to rest
> Far on the mountains in the west,
> While all the vale is dark between
> Ungilded by his golden sheen,
> A lingering lustre softly throws
> On the dear hills where first he rose.[16]

He is writing in the eighteenth-century mode which influenced him at this early time, heroic couplets and some slightly poetic-y language, the sun being called Phoebus, for example, but the lovely simile is essentially there. Just as the sun when sinking in the west throws a reflected light on the eastern hills, so the boy imagines that on his deathbed he would think of the scenes endeared to him in youth. In 1815 he published a reworked version of this—with no Phoebus this time, just the sun—under the category of 'Juvenile Pieces'. In neither poem does he connect the thought with the

boat on Coniston, though in the Fenwick note years later he does associate 'The beautiful image' with that occasion. He says, 'The Poem of which it was the con- clusion was of many hundred lines, and contained thoughts and images most of which have been dispersed through my other writings.'[17]

The first fact that emerges is that Wordsworth com- posed what Stephen Parrish calls 'detached pieces writ- ten to be inserted into it'[18]—the *Two-Part Prelude*—and also utilized passages from other poems such as *The Vale of Esthwaite* and *The Pedlar,* already written, in a kind of patchwork. Some of the 'detached pieces', such as 'Nutting', eventually were not included, and in 1805 neither was the boat on Coniston passage. In 1850 an abbreviated version of it was restored but relegated to Book VIII. In 1799, on the other hand, we are given all the delightful details which, for me, bring the whole thing to life.

> There was a row of ancient trees, since fallen,
> That on the margin of a jutting land
> Stood near the lake of Coniston and made
> With its long boughs above the water stretched
> A gloom through which a boat might sail along
> As in a cloister. An old Hall was near,
> Grotesque and beautiful, its gavel end
> And huge round chimneys to the top o'ergrown
> With fields of ivy. Thither we repaired
> 'Twas even a custom with us, to the shore
> And to that cool piazza. They who dwelt
> In the neglected mansion-house supplied
> Fresh butter, tea-kettle, and earthen-ware,
> And chafing-dish with smoking coals, and so
> Beneath the trees we sate in our small boat
> And in the covert eat our delicate meal
> Upon the calm smooth lake.
>
> (*Two-Part Prelude* ii 140-56)

It is all so solid, the tunnel of trees, the distinctive an- cient building, the domestic implements borrowed from the caretakers so that the boys could cook their catch of fish. Then, as in the skating episode, there is a most mi- raculous, yet natural, modulation into another key.

> It was a joy
> Worthy the heart of one who is full grown
> To rest beneath those horizontal boughs
> And mark the radiance of the setting sun,
> Himself unseen, reposing on the top
> Of the high eastern hills.
>
> (ibid. ii 156-61)

He tells us he was in his fourteenth summer and, as his reference to 'the heart of one who is full grown' has al- ready indicated, he fears we may doubt such an unboy- ish thought at this time and he hastens to reassure us. I rather wish he had not, as it is an interruption.

> And there I said,
> That beauteous sight before me, there I said

> (Then first beginning in my thoughts to mark
> That sense of dim similitude which links
> Our moral feelings with external forms)
> That in whatever region I should close
> My mortal life I would remember you,
> Fair scenes! that dying I would think on you,
> My soul would send a longing look to you:
> Even as that setting sun while all the vale
> Could nowhere catch one faint memorial gleam
> Yet with the last remains of his last light
> Still lingered, and a farewell lustre threw
> On the dear mountain-tops where first he rose.
>
> (ibid. ii 161-74)

The 'sentiment', he tells us, 'far outran the habit of my mind'. Despite, perhaps, protesting a bit too much, Wordsworth has with great skill incorporated the simile from *The Vale of Esthwaite* as the consummation of the vivid childhood scene. Compare this, at your leisure, with the abbreviated version in 1850. Wordsworth calls it a 'beautiful image' and so it is, but is it strong enough to stand on its own, marooned in Book VIII (lines 458- 75)? It must be acknowledged that the apostrophe itself, starting 'Dear native Region', has been tightened up and is an improvement on the rather repetitive passage in 1799, but—oh dear!—I do miss the picnic!

For the second question that the successive changes in this episode raise is that of the relation between the down-to-earth everyday experiences of boyhood and the deeper reflections they give rise to. Coleridge criticized Wordsworth for 'clinging to the palpable' but I think he knew his own business best. The matter-of-factness pro- vides both an anchor and a springboard, if for once I may mix metaphors, and is absolutely essential.

The passages of commentary, which are often most memorable in themselves and provide some of the best loved lines in the poem, are interdependent on the first- hand experiences to which they are attached and inte- gral to the whole. Similarly, the glimpses of a spiritual world, as we have seen, often though not always, fol- low on from intense physical activity. One is reminded of Wordsworth's words to De Quincey on Dunmail Raise.

> At the instant when the organs of attention were all at once relaxing from their tension, the bright star hang- ing in the air above those outlines of massy blackness fell suddenly upon my eye and penetrated my capacity of apprehension with a pathos and a sense of the infi- nite that would not have arrested me under other cir- cumstances.[19]

A wonderful example of this relaxation after tension oc- curs at the end of the passage I call 'strawberries and cream', a favourite of mine. Their pockets flush after the midsummer break, the boys felt that they could af- ford something 'posh' for once. So they rowed across Windermere to Bowness and the White Lion, renamed

the Royal after a visit of Queen Adelaide in 1840. This was no village pub but 'a splendid place, the door beset / With chaises, grooms and liveries'. You could even get a glass of Sir Patrick Spens' 'blood-red wine'. Wordsworth pretends he would have liked it better when it was a more modest inn before the building of the round house on Belle Isle had brought more gentry-trade, but the schoolboy obviously gloried in the 'foolish pomp'. There on the bowling-green they played, making as usual a great noise. I wonder the snooty guests did not complain! But perhaps the children's purchase of strawberries and cream entitled them to commandeer the garden;

> the shouts we sent
> Made all the mountains ring.

(*Two-Part Prelude* ii 203-4)

But after all the excitement and exertion comes the peace and 'a sense of the infinite'.

> But ere the fall
> Of night, when in our pinnace we returned
> Over the dusky lake, and to the beach
> Of some small island steered our course with one,
> The minstrel of our troop, and left him there
> And rowed off gently while he blew his flute
> Alone upon a rock—oh then the calm
> And dead still water lay upon my mind
> Even with a weight of pleasure, and the sky,
> Never before so beautiful, sank down
> Into my heart and held me like a dream.

(ibid. ii 204-14)

Wordsworth goes on to show how Nature, which had seemed to be only incidental to his boyish activities, 'now at length was sought / For her own sake'. He is trying to trace his development but what a difficult exercise it is: 'Hard task to analyse a soul.' Of course, the first introduction to life and learning comes through the mother, to whom Wordsworth pays tribute in the 'infant babe' passage. Fortunately she was there, a beneficent presence, during his crucial earliest years and, surely, as he himself recognized and, in 1805 Book IV, acknowledged, he was most blessed too in lodging with Ann Tyson, 'my old dame, so motherly and good' who 'perused me with a parent's pride' when he returned to her after his first year at Cambridge. She provided him with the security he needed during his years at Hawkshead, while allowing him the equally necessary freedom, for those walks round Esthwaite before breakfast, for example, either alone or with his friend John Fleming of Rayrigg. As school began at 6 or 6.30 in summer and 7 or 7.30 in winter, they must have been out very early indeed. On his solitary dawn expeditions when he 'sate / Alone upon some jutting eminence', the borders between the worlds dissolved, so that he did not know which was which.

> Oft in those moments such a holy calm
> Did overspread my soul that I forgot
> The agency of sight, and what I saw
> Appeared like something in myself—a dream,
> A prospect in my mind.

(ibid. ii 397-401)

Wordsworth is in doubt whether he is indulging in a subjective activity of projection or whether he is really penetrating the veil and entering into another dimension. Either way, this seeming sensitivity to a spiritual world was characterized by a temporary abdication of the physical sense of sight and sound.

> wonder not
> If such my transports were, for in all things
> I saw one life and felt that it was joy.
> One song they sang, and it was audible,
> Most audible then when the fleshly ear,
> O'ercome by grosser prelude of that strain,
> Forgot its functions, and slept undisturbed.

(ibid. ii 458-64)

I don't think that Wordsworth was a theoretician in the sense that Coleridge was. He speaks of 'a toil / Than analytic industry to me / More pleasing' (ibid. ii 427-9). He *felt* the unity of apparently disparate things, and 'Saw blessings spread around me like a sea'. So when along came Coleridge with a theory of 'the One Life' that seemed to fit his experience like a glove, he happily, for the moment, adopted it, as this passage demonstrates. He ends the *Two-Part Prelude* with an apostrophe to Coleridge, calling him, after their wonderful year together in Somerset, 'In many things my brother'.

So Wordsworth completes his record of the magic of childhood. But, apart from the pleasures of nostalgia, what is the point of it? Well, you will have been very much aware that I have missed out so far that famous passage from part I that we all know so well,

> There are in our existence spots of time
> Which with distinct pre-eminence retain
> A fructifying virtue, whence, depressed
> By trivial occupations and the round
> Of ordinary intercourse, our minds
> (Especially the imaginative power)
> Are nourished, and invisibly repaired.
> Such moments chiefly seem to have their date
> In our first childhood.

(ibid. i 288-96)

So childhood has a magic not just for itself but also to nourish, repair and make fruitful the adult mind and imagination, and, as we started by asserting, so it does, particularly when mediated through the art of a great poet, who assures us of the continued existence of a higher realm to which we then seemed to have the key.

Notes

1. All quotations from the *Two-Part Prelude* are taken from William Wordsworth, *The Prelude,*

1798-1799 ed. Stephen Parrish (Ithaca, NY, 1977) (hereafter Parrish).

2. Canto 21; 25-30. See John Livingstone Lowes, *The Road to Xanadu* (London, 1955), pp. 480-1.

3. Jonathan Wordsworth, *The Borders of Vision* (Oxford, 1982) (hereafter *Borders of Vision*), p. 17.

4. *Thirteen-Book Prelude* v 436-7. All quotations from this poem are from *The Thirteen-Book Prelude* ed. Mark L. Reed (2 vols., Ithaca, NY, 1991).

5. *Borders of Vision* 38.

6. Parrish 26.

7. T. W. Thompson, *Wordsworth's Hawkshead* ed. Robert Woof (Oxford, 1970), pp. 251-6.

8. Carl H. Ketcham, "'That 'Stone of Rowe'": *Prelude* (1805) II: 33-47', *Wordsworth Circle* 13 (1982) 174-5. See also *The Fourteen-Book Prelude* ed. W. J. B. Owen (Ithaca, NY, 1985), p. 48.

9. H. S. Cowper, *Hawkshead* (London and Derby, 1899) (hereafter Cowper), p. 29.

10. Carol (c. 1935).

11. *The Prose Works of William Wordsworth* ed. W. J. B. Owen and Jane Worthington Smyser (3 vols., Oxford, 1974) (hereafter *Prose Works*), ii. 293.

12. *Prose Works* ii 296-7.

13. Norman Nicholson, *Greater Lakeland* (London, 1969), p. 134.

14. Cowper 337-8.

15. *Prose Works* ii. 295.

16. Lines 498-513; text from *The Poetical Works of William Wordsworth* ed. Ernest de Selincourt and Helen Darbishire (5 vols., Oxford, 1940-9) (hereafter *PW*), i. 281.

17. *PW* i. 317-18.

18. Parrish 8.

19. Thomas De Quincey, *Recollections of the Lakes and the Lake Poets* ed. David Wright (Harmondsworth, 1970), p. 160.

John Powell Ward (essay date October 2000)

SOURCE: Ward, John Powell. "Earthly Freight: Wordsworth's Poetry of Childhood, 1804-1812." *The Charles Lamb Bulletin*, no. 112 (October 2000): 169-82.

[*In the following essay, Ward addresses Wordsworth's treatment of childhood as a means of offering insights into the poet's personal and literary development.*]

William Wordsworth is the key Romantic poet of childhood, and arguably childhood's major poet in the English language. His main poetry of childhood was written in the six years spring 1798 to spring 1804. That period produced 'Nutting', 'The Idiot Boy', 'We Are Seven', 'Anecdote For Fathers', the description of the Pedlar's early years (*The Excursion* I 108-96), 'The Winander Boy', the Lucy poems, the sonnet 'It is a beauteous evening', 'Gathering Flowers', 'The Pet Lamb', 'The Idle Shepherd-Boys', 'Alice Fell', 'Lucy Gray', all the childhood 'spots of time' in *The Prelude*, and, right at the period's end, the *Immortality Ode* and a few further *Prelude* childhood passages.[1]

Then, suddenly, the poetry of childhood more or less ceases. It becomes highly infrequent and seemingly random for eight years, until he completes the small group of grief-stricken poems resulting from the deaths of his two infant children, Catherine and Thomas, in 1812. Furthermore, as to the writing of childhood, the early spring of 1804 was a high-intensity moment rather than the end of a slow denouement. The completion—in fact the major writing—of the *Immortality Ode* coincided with the writing of *Prelude* Book V, which, as it then stood, dwelt much on formal education and the child's contrasting responses to nature. This fifth book of the autobiographical poem was to conclude the work. It contained the damning description of the over-educated infant prodigy, the 'dwarf man' of 'monstrous birth' (*Prelude* 1805 V 290-369), which was then, at once, contrasted by the refreshing picture of the Winander Boy imitating the hoots of owls and, after their response, seeing the lake in the ensuing silence. Thus was nature infused into the boy's senses of ear and eye. And near the book's end were the two major 'spots of time' passages from the 1799 version—the murderer's gibbet and the waiting-for-the-horses (*Prelude* 1805 XI 278-327; 344-88)—which revealed the impact of scenes on the child's growing mind as hauntingly as any other passages of the entire period.

Much has been written about this sudden change in Wordsworth's inspiration. My rather different question, in this article, is to consider what happened to the poet who had so powerfully treated this subject. His belief in childhood didn't decline, even if the genius by which he evoked it seemed to have left him. Surely he would have made at least some attempt to continue on this path; I believe it can be shown that he did; and, even though the results are not as impressive as the earlier work, they are at lowest interesting, and on occasion rise to something memorable enough. Perhaps more important, they tell us much about his later development, and how it emerged most in a couple of later milestones, most obviously *The White Doe of Rylstone* in 1807 and the group of elegiac poems of 1812, mentioned above.

However, to consider this we must briefly go back to the starting-point. The *Immortality Ode* may have troubled Wordsworth for nearly two years. In spring 1802 he wrote the first four stanzas. But his sister Dorothy records him as writing '*part of* an ode' (my emphasis) at that time.[2] So perhaps he had already intended to continue it later. When he did resume in March 1804, what are usually held to be the rather obscure middle stanzas, v-vii, were followed by the huge climax of the final four stanzas, viii-xi, where the child born 'trailing clouds of glory' is seen as 'Eye among the blind', 'Mighty Prophet! Seer blest!' The child already holds truths 'which we are toiling all our lives to find', yet which remain as 'master light of all our seeing' in our later lives. Despite, even at its close, its foreboding that time is passing, still the 'primal sympathy / Which having been must ever be' will stay with us 'in the faith that looks through death'. That is to say, the end of human existence is faced, even as its beginning is extolled. The near-desperate depression Wordsworth had felt in spring 1802 gets some kind of resolution through growth of the renewed optimism that can grow with maturity. By general critical agreement,[3] the poem mourns and perhaps triumphs over, not the loss of poetic power, but the loss of childhood and youth.

Doubtless there seemed little to add to this majestic effusion and vision. And, almost immediately, as he had in March 1804, Wordsworth also changes his mind about *The Prelude*. It becomes a much longer work, stretching well into early manhood, university, city, travel and first adult political experience. Book V, seen by Mary Moorman as 'a poetic essay on education', remains in that position even while the whole poem grows to well over twice the five-book length. The 'spots of time' certainly go forward to nearly the end (Book xi) of that longer version, but that too is all in place by mid-1805. Reasons for the change of strategy may be clear enough.[4] But a new, key and much-quoted passage was written at the same time. It may be clue to Wordsworth's state of mind on the matter for some time previously:

> Oh mystery of man, from what a depth
> Proceed thy honours! I am lost, but see
> In simple childhood something of the base
> On which thy greatness stands—but this I feel,
> That from thyself it is that thou must give,
> Else never canst receive. The days gone by
> Come back upon me from the dawn almost
> Of life; the hiding-places of my power
> Seem open, I approach, and then they close;
> I see by glimpses now, when age comes on
> May scarcely see at all; and I would give
> While yet we may, as far as words can give,
> A substance and a life to what I feel:
> I would enshrine the spirit of the past
> For future restoration . . .

(*Prelude* 1805 XI 328-42)

These seem profoundly telling lines. It is highly important that they were written almost certainly *after* the great Ode of childhood was completed.[5] Otherwise, we might have thought the expressed wish (to 'give . . . a substance and a life to what I feel') was then achieved by the Ode itself; equally that his feeling of being 'lost' had been alleviated. Instead, the characteristic Wordsworthian contrast between elusive 'depth' and firmer 'honours', and the urgent psychological detail—' . . . the hiding-places of my power / Seem open, I approach, and then they close'—suggests that the matter is still unresolved. The lines were placed in *The Prelude* as a bridging passage between the two major 'spots of time' alluded to already. And it all leads us to ask the wider question, of how a poet carries on when, in such perplexity, just as Wordsworth in the Ode himself asks how humans carry on as childhood slips away, 'farther from the east' and finally into 'the light of common day'. Despite his supposed decline in the mid-1800s, Wordsworth's tropes, images, turns of elusive phrase and tentative aspiration or lost longing, remain with him all his life. His problem in 1804 was, I think, a huge dilemma. How could the vision of childhood simply depart; yet how, if we must all grow up, could it continue?

To discover Wordsworth's answer to this difficulty, we need then to consider how Wordsworth continued, as far as childhood is concerned, and with what results. About a hundred and thirty poems, long and short and on all subjects, were written between March 1804 and June 1812, when the four-year-old Catherine died. A careful reading of all 130 poems turns out to be revealing. Only fourteen of these make any allusion whatever to children or childhood, and only six of that fourteen could be said to make the topic central. This tally omits the last two books of *The Excursion* (VIII and IX) written in 1811, but, in those, Wordsworth turns fully toward the older child, factory labour, and the need for universal education as a political matter. The fourteen poems are: 'Address to My Infant Daughter, Dora' (September 1804), 'Vaudracour and Julia' (probably autumn 1804), 'The Kitten and Falling Leaves' (autumn-winter 1804-5 or winter 1805-6), 'The Blind Highland Boy' (between spring 1804 and spring 1806), 'The Waggoner' (January 1806), 'To the Sons of Burns' (first draft autumn-winter 1805-6), 'Home at Grasmere' (passages added summer 1806), 'Song at the Feast of Brougham Castle' (between October 1806 and April 1807), 'The Force of Prayer' (September 1807), *The White Doe of Rylstone* (mainly autumn 1807), 'Elegiac Stanzas Composed in the Churchyard of Grasmere' (April 1808), the two sonnets 'In due observance of an ancient rite' and 'Feelings of a Noble Biscayan . . .' (both probably 1810), and the 'Epistle to Sir George Howland Beaumont, Bart' (August 1811). The list is deliberately exhaustive. There are no others.

Furthermore, four of the six poems, *directly* on childhood, were the first four of the whole fourteen to be written (the other two are the 1810 sonnets, discussed below). This might suggest that at first Wordsworth wanted to go on writing about childhood or that the habit had become ingrained, to fade away rather quickly. Either way, all these early four have features which divert them from that continuity. The first was 'Address to My Infant Daughter, Dora, on Being Reminded That She Was a Month Old That Day, September 16'.[6] The unwieldy title prefigures the poem. The poem—nearly eighty lines of pentameters—seems committed to giving the subject the closest attention, yet this leads the poet into curious uncertainties. He is first relieved that she has even survived (lines 1 and 6) for one 'life' of the moon's monthly cycle, and that comparison continues through the whole poem. But for twenty lines there is another comparison, with an imagined Indian babe of the same age; and that double comparison, with both moon and Indian babe, prevents the poem ever taking off as a single effusion. The Indian babe picture—'maternal sympathy' but 'a joyless tie / Of naked instinct' (lines 36-8), seems artificially drawn from Wordsworth's always frequent travel reading,[7] and halfway through the poem, he drops it.

But the comparison with the moon, which lasts throughout, is sought overtly too; 'resemblances, or contrasts, that connect, / Within the region of a father's thoughts, / Thee and thy mate and sister of the sky' (lines 43-5). The poetic and prosaic intermingle. 'Fair are ye both, and both are free from stain', yet the moon's cycle is 'renovation without end' while Dora has an evolving lifetime of uncertainty ahead. This, too, provokes only difficulty. At first the response is merely 'Alas!' Quickly, however, Dora's 'smile forbids the thought'—but then again the poet wonders 'shall those smiles be called / Feelers of love . . . ?' with a final uncertain hovering between 'strait passage intricate and dim' and a rather formal 'Joy' to end on. This pervading vacillation may well have led to the distancing sub-title, 'on Being Reminded . . .'. But there is also a note on the poem in the Preface to *Poems (1815)*. Wordsworth states there why, in that edition, the poem was placed right at the end of the section on Fancy, so as to lead easily to that of Imagination.[8] It seems more likely that he was not sure which it belonged to, and my argument here is that he did not know where it stood as a childhood poem, more generally.

The second poem of the four here considered was 'The Kitten and Falling Leaves'. In this poem, the poet and his infant daughter smile at a kitten at play. The poet can only hope that something of her innocent delight 'laughing in my arms' will carry over to himself, despite the inevitable sadnesses of adulthood. The autumnal setting gives a marked contrast to the springtime of the *Immortality Ode*. But the Ode's despair, renewal, and huge final surge are also replaced entirely here by, surely, an echo of the more formal Joy-Melancholy balancing of *L'Allegro* and *Il Penseroso*. The eight-foot rhyming couplets, the comparable length (Milton's pair only a little longer), terms like 'blithe' and 'mirth', and the frequent tendency to avoiding end-stopping too sharply—all these features evoke the Miltonic sound:

> And I will have my careless season
> Spite of melancholy reason,
> Will walk through life in such a way
> That, when time brings on decay,
> Now and then I may possess
> Hours of perfect gladsomeness.

(111-116)[9]

The poem's main passages, the dance of the kitten among the autumn leaves, make the poet merely a wistful spectator.

Thirdly we have 'The Blind Highland Boy', a lyrical ballad somewhat recalling 'The Idiot Boy' in tone and type of story. The blind boy uses a prized turtle-shell as a kind of coracle and floats out on to the lake near his home. A rescue party takes a boat out, grabs him unawares, and brings him back to shore and his distraught mother. The result, that 'though his fancies had been wild, / Yet he was pleased and reconciled / To live in peace on shore' (243-5), leaves his romantic sally into the unknown a qualified one. But our question has to be what appealed to Wordsworth in this story.[10] The child, in the Ode 'thou Eye among the blind', is himself now blind. Physical blindness could place greater emphasis on vision as spiritual; yet, here it seems rather to place the Highland boy's imagination in the sadder light of rash inexperience.

And a key factor here is the poem's date, perhaps as late as spring 1806. For, in February 1805, the poet's mariner brother John was drowned at sea, immersing William and Dorothy in a grief that darkened their lives for years to come. One outcome was an overt absorption with mortality later in the decade but before the deaths of his own infant children in 1812; and the *Essays Upon Epitaphs,* all written in 1810, show Wordsworth having attended to the subject with his whole mind for a long period. A couplet in 'The Blind Highland Boy' strikes one as a brief backward glimpse of his brother's fate:

> Woe to the poor blind Mariner!
> For death will be his doom.

(104-5)

If the poem was written before February 1805, this is coincidence. But 'will', in the context, seems pronounced. Whatever the truth here, the fact that the poem may have been intended simply to entertain the children[11] suggests that Wordsworth is subduing distressing

thoughts, whether of his brother's death or as to childhood itself. Yet, again, the great majestic vision of children, so strong from 1798 to 1804, seems modified, and replaced by bewilderment.

In the remaining early poem focusing directly on childhood, 'Vaudracour and Julia', childhood provides the situation on which the story turns. A Romeo-and-Juliet couple in France (Shakespeare's play is cited at line 91) are forced to elope when an infant is conceived. But when the mother retires to a convent, the illegitimate babe dies 'by some mistake / Or indiscretion of the Father' (279-80), a far cry indeed from the Ode-child's birth trailing clouds of glory. The hapless father becomes a recluse of 'imbecile mind' (306), where the poem ends. Of course, it was written, in autumn 1804, as part of the 1805 *Prelude* (though quickly withdrawn from it), and this may well have been, as often said, to quieten Wordsworth's own mind as to his own illegitimate daughter in France. But is this not a straight inversion of the facts, namely, that Caroline Vallon was *born* through 'some mistake / Or indiscretion of the Father'? It is notable that the other three early poems, just discussed, all refer to Indians ('Address to My Infant Daughter, Dora' 8-38; 'The Kitten and Falling Leaves' 30-32; 'The Blind Highland Boy' 107). Is Wordsworth half-recalling the Forsaken Indian Woman and her hapless babe, one of the 'abandoned women' poems of the early 1790s, which Emile Legouis was so certain spoke of Annette Vallon?[12]

We now move on to the poems where childhood is mentioned only marginally. Certainly, after John Wordsworth's death most reference to childhood in the poems is brief. Commonly, too, the poems' children are growing older. At Canto I 180-204 of *The Waggoner,* there is a hint of the Winander Boy's experience of nature's loud sounds; but it stands alone, and the poem is nearly nine hundred lines long. 'To the Sons of Burns' grew out of a visit to that poet's grave, which for Dorothy Wordsworth only recalled the loss of her brother. Wordsworth could be thinking as much of his own infant son John as of Burns's sons, in his warning that even honest men 'of your Father's name will make / A snare for you'. At the close Burns's sons are 'admonished' (that recurring Wordsworthian term) to 'think, and fear!' Again childhood is now exposed to the relentless real world. In summer 1806, *Home at Grasmere,* mainly drafted in 1800, was taken up again. This was a renewed assault on *The Recluse,* and we recall that that project was the subject of Wordsworth's anxious attention the very moment the childhood poems of spring 1804 were finished.[13] The added passages of 1806 do retain such childhood motif as *Home at Grasmere* possesses, but they force it sideways. If, as Kenneth Johnson says,[14] the idyllic perfection of Grasmere village and lake in 1800 had already turned out to lack something—symbolized no doubt by the oft-cited two

swans gone missing (322-57)—then, Wordsworth may have felt the rapturous beginning of the poem in 1800 needed qualifying, too. There, the boy, Wordsworth himself, aged about eleven, had exclaimed, 'What happy fortune were it here to live!' on seeing the beautiful and peaceful valley of Grasmere below. But in 1806 there is a modifying addition:

> While yet an innocent little-one, a heart
> That doubtless wanted not its tender moods,
> I breathed (for this I better recollect)
> Among wild appetites and blind desires,
> Motions of savage instinct, my delight
> And exaltation.

> *(Home at Grasmere* 910-15)

These 'appetites' included some disobedience, and imagining ships in battle 'matched in deadly fight' (930). It is as though, if fleetingly, his lost mariner brother jostles his own unhealthy compulsions in disconcerting coalition. Childhood seems less fully admirable than it had previously. The 'mighty prophet, seer blest' of the 1804 *Immortality Ode* is now admitted to harbour disturbing instincts. In another passage inserted in 1806 (533-606, esp. 546, 598) a responsible-eldest-daughter figure—though still a child—precurses the unmentioned daughter of the 'Elegiac Stanzas Composed in the Churchyard of Grasmere' (also one of our fourteen poems and to which we will come in due course). But this girl in *Home at Grasmere* embodies just one aspect of the rural community families, appearing here, which were to figure so strongly in *The Excursion.* As both Johnson and Beer point out, *The Recluse* foundered because Wordsworth could seldom generalize beyond his own experience of these small communities. His philosophizing always brought him back there, as *The Excursion* showed, to Coleridge's regret.[15]

* * *

Then, in 1807, there is a change. We come next to what might be termed the *White Doe* group. These are 'Song at the Feast of Brougham Castle', 'The Force of Prayer' and *The White Doe of Rylstone* itself. The young are present in all three, but again they are now older. The poems are newly notable for their castle and abbey settings, as though Wordsworth is beginning to tie nature into human history. The most ancient artifacts sink into their surroundings, but in such a way as to force nature into an arena of large-scale human conflict. Trips with Dorothy in June and Mary in August and September 1807 took Wordsworth to Bolton Abbey, Brougham Castle near Penrith, Lowther Castle, and Egremont Castle near Whitehaven.[16] Internal references to characters and places tie the three resulting poems together, though all can be read independently.

In 'Song at the Feast of Brougham Castle', a minstrel celebrates the restoration of the young Lord Clifford to his lands at the end of the Wars of the Roses. He had

been raised as a shepherd-boy in the hills, taken there by his mother to escape the Yorkists. His father had murdered one of their number in battle and retribution seemed certain. The minstrel proclaims that now, twenty-four years later, Clifford will return to war on the wider national scene and defeat both Scots and French (Hayden II 1022). But the minstrel is wrong: Clifford's Pedlar-like upbringing has attuned him to the softening influences of books and nature, making him a peace-loving leader, for which his people are grateful. The minstrel's confident cry, that Clifford 'hath thrown aside his crook / And hath buried deep his book' (140-1) is premature. The poem works because, to show quietly what really happened to the young man, Wordsworth switches near the end from the eight-foot line to pentameter quatrains recalling Gray's *Elegy*:

> Love had he found in huts where poor men lie;
> His daily teachers had been woods and rills,
> The silence that is in the starry sky,
> The sleep that is among the lonely hills.
>
> In him the savage virtue of the Race,
> Revenge, and all ferocious thoughts were dead:
> Nor did he change; but kept in lofty place
> The wisdom which adversity had bred.
>
> (161-8)

In particular, here, the second stanza has the timbre of Gray's poem.[17] The elegiac sense is general, broadening across all life, to what child and youth alike will eventually face in the course of things. From the point of view of childhood, the other Doe-group poem 'The Force of Prayer' is even more adventitious. Young Romilly's age is unclear (both 'boy' and about to be married; lines 33, 45), but he dies, an event which tradition ties to the founding of Bolton Priory itself, where much of *The White Doe of Rylstone* is set.

And so we turn to *The White Doe of Rylstone,* in which, it seems to me, Wordsworth consciously, or otherwise, faces all that has been happening to his childhood vision, and all that has so deepened, aged, and shaken it. This poem, I suggest, is Wordsworth's attempt to preserve what he can of childhood as a near-transcendental feature of human life but at the cost of inevitably laying his earlier originary optimism to rest. Certain patterns of symbol and imagery work out to achieve this. The poem is far the longest of the period under discussion; it seems like a new start (the 1807 *Poems, in Two Volumes* had been published in April), and Wordsworth saw it, in conception at least, as the highest work he ever produced.[18]

The bald narrative can be summarized. Father and eight young sons of the Norton family go to join the Catholic Rising of the North against Elizabeth in 1569. But the ninth and eldest son, the Clifford-like Francis, resists, and stays at Rylstone Hall (the family seat) with his sister Emily, the only daughter. Herself a Protestant, by persuasion, if not by upbringing, Emily has also been forced by her father to embroider a banner showing the five wounds of Christ. Francis then partly changes his mind, joins his fighting family, and is rejected by his father, but remains near the action. After mixed events, the eight sons and their father are killed. Francis retrieves the banner and escapes, but on his way home is also overtaken and killed, and is buried by neighbours in Bolton Priory. Emily has heard the main news from an old messenger. Now left alone in the world, she is rejoined by a white doe which she had befriended over the years and which now leaves its herd on recognizing her in her roaming. They wander the countryside together for many years until Emily's own death, when she is buried in Rylstone churchyard. The white doe has come to Bolton Priory every Sabbath day since. It becomes legend, it appears in Thomas Whitaker's *History and Antiquities of the Deanery of Craven* (1805), and that is where Wordsworth found it.

But the Doe's own story takes up nearly a third of the poem. It occupies the first and last of the seven cantos, and six hundred lines out of nineteen hundred. The poem's most widely-remembered passage evokes the animal's weekly appearance to the Priory's congregation at the end of divine service; that is to say, when all the poem's main events are long over. The passage comes near the start. What matters is the animal itself:

> When soft!—the dusky trees between,
> And down the path through the open green,
> Where is no living thing to be seen;
> And through yon gateway, where is found,
> Beneath the arch with ivy bound,
> Free entrance to the church-yard ground—
> Comes gliding in with lovely gleam,
> Comes gliding in serene and slow,
> Soft and silent as a dream,
> A solitary Doe!
> White she is as lily of June,
> And beauteous as the silver moon
> When out of sight the clouds are driven
> And she is left alone in heaven;
> Or like a ship some gentle day
> In sunshine sailing far away,
> A glittering ship, that hath the plain
> Of ocean for her own domain.
>
> (I 49-66)

Thereafter, we never quite forget this milky whiteness of the Doe. The contrasting dark foliage of 'dusky trees' and 'ivy' outline it, and its liquid movement (55-58) and the allegorical similes following leave no everyday objects of comparison which can share its world. The rest of the poem is flashback. The Doe appears fleetingly to Emily and Francis in the forest during the main story of the Rising, and then in the long last cantos it accompanies Emily's lonely wanderings. This lovely 'milk-white' Doe (202-972) joins a line of pure-white

literary creatures: Dryden's 'milk-white hind' in *The Hind and the Panther,* Una's 'milk-white lamb' in Spenser's *Faerie Queene* alluded to by Wordsworth in his poem 'Personal Talk', and, of course, his own 'milk-white swans' in *Home at Grasmere* (323), which we have already mentioned. And so the question here is of what this white doe meant to Wordsworth, and how she so stirred his imagination.

The *White Doe* has never been greatly popular. Few critics stay long with it today. At the time, Lamb said that the principal characters 'do nothing', while, for Coleridge, the two aspects of the Doe and the rebellion itself (the 'business parts' as Coleridge called the latter), were too separate. Wordsworth himself came to accept Coleridge's point. As he himself said, 'the mere physical action was all unsuccessful; but the true action of the poem was spiritual'. But his answer to Lamb was that 'gross and visible action' was inappropriate, where 'the Poet is to be predominant over the Dramatist'. That is to say, the entire poem is really about the Doe; in Wordsworth's terms again, 'everything tends to account for the weekly pilgrimage of the Doe'.[19] And the beautiful creature impressed at least some influential readers. In 1841 Tennyson walked the river by the Priory with his mind 'inflamed' by the poem, while in the 1880s the Duke of Devonshire, owner of the estate in which the ruin stands, attempted to introduce a real white doe as a tourist attraction. J. W. Inchbold's painting of the White Doe hangs in the Leeds City Art Gallery.[20]

In his comment on the poem, Geoffrey Hartman suggests that Wordsworth was, in effect, looking for a Protestant imagination to stand in for the iconic forms and signs of Catholicism.[21] The Norton family are an ancestral line of the church's tradition while Francis and Emily are nearer to their individual consciences. Hartman can therefore bring out how the Doe softens Emily's spiritual state in her desolation at the end of the story. Certainly the contrast between the Doe and the Banner as symbols is deliberate. But Hartman also sees the whole poem as marking the end of Wordsworth's fruitful years, just as in autumn 1798 'Nutting' began them (Hartman is as exact as that).[22] And my own feeling is, that by presenting his most melting and luminous extended symbol since the Ode-child 'trailing clouds of glory', Wordsworth effectively and finally marks, too, the end of his long absorption with the newborn child. That child, in the Ode, was itself an embryo-image which seems precursor to this 'milk-white Doe' that moves ethereally through the trees under the moonlight.

John Beer, if less explicitly, seems to be suggesting something similar. What Beer calls the Doe's 'intimations of sublimity'—a clear echo of the Ode's title—raises the matter of just what the Doe stands for. Wordsworth saw her as 'the Apotheosis of the Animal', as

though she rises to the human state. But Beer's view seems preferable, namely, that she is not only human but humans at their highest; indeed, she is more than human, 'an emblem of the finer tone which can be glimpsed from time to time in humanity itself'.[23] So the Doe's innocence, its heavenly provenance, appear intuitively close to that of the Ode-child; her sway and presence move in the same 'celestial light'. Yet there is a difference. For the child must change, it must eventually go forward into 'common day'; but the Doe can 'to her peaceful woods / Return . . . be in heart and soul the same / She was before she hither came' (560-63). And it is moonlight, rather than sunshine or 'the light of common day', the moon hanging over Bolton Priory (938-61), so like the Doe's unblemished and unchanging whiteness, which most suggests this permanence.

There is a kind of embalming, furthermore, of the Doe, as symbol, which communicates itself to the poem's other main symbols. These are the Moon, the Banner, and the Priory. In the Ode, the frequently used images were never repeated. The 'tabor's sound', 'single Field', 'Pansy', 'prison-house', 'imperial palace', 'frost', 'embers', 'Children sport(ing) on the shore', 'race', 'palms' and the rest, appear and are gone in a forward-moving surge. In *The White Doe of Rylstone,* the four main items, deliberately countering each other, are frequently and statically repeated. They set an allegorical scene that is four-square and timeless. The Doe is to Emily what the Banner is to the family, with the Moon and the Priory underpinning each respectively. That is to say—and if this doesn't sound too fanciful—they amount to a kind of mausoleum in which the story functions. And the poem's conclusion points, I suggest, to what this most deeply implies and which holds the key to the poem's place as a marker for where Wordsworth's poetry of childhood has gone to. For, in his final two lines, Wordsworth makes a rather desperate attempt, it seems, to align Emily with the Ode-child:

> 'Thou, thou are not a Child of Time,
> But Daughter of the Eternal Prime!'
>
> (1909-10)[24]

This 'Eternal Prime' clearly evokes the 'primal sympathy / Which having been must ever be' near the Ode's close too. But Emily is *dead.* Whiteness is milky, but also like moonlight and 'the lily in June'; it becomes sepulchral. In short, there has been a displacement symbolically, poetically, and it is the ethereal, other-worldly White Doe that is left central. Near the start of the poem, when we are shown the tourists visiting the churchyard to see the Doe, a mother points it out to her small boy. Seeing it he 'blushed for joy, / A shame-faced blush of glowing red!' (I 182-3).[25] The Doe has all the attention, leaving the child who was life's very origin in the Ode now a mere spectator.

* * *

As far as childhood is concerned, then, I take *The White Doe of Rylstone* to mark the end, however subliminally, of Wordsworth's birth-obsession. From here, until the deaths of the infants in 1812, he will mainly write countless sonnets and make one last desperate attempt at *The Recluse* in 'The Tuft of Primroses'. Time is moving on; he has been a family man for half a decade and is now nearly forty. His brother's death still hung heavy, as many letters show. But there were other events. Soon to follow—art maybe anticipating life—were the near-fatal illnesses of his son John and of Sara Hutchinson in spring 1808. Coleridge's own health was commonly poor, and Wordsworth increasingly felt he should help him with the journal *The Friend,* edited from Allan Bank in 1809. Coleridge's own sons were growing up. Taken up to Keswick as playmates for the Wordsworth children, they naturally enough began to reveal the un-Ode-like rumbustuous tendencies that Molly Lefebure's no-nonsense accounts vividly recount for us. Too, the 1807 Poems achieved a poor press, and this perhaps fuelled the turn toward prose at the same time.[26] There were most obviously the book-length 'pamphlet' on the Convention of Cintra and the *Essays Upon Epitaphs.* But this last-named is the next step in these years' events, and we note the total change of emphasis, in terms of attention to human life, that has taken place. The *Immortality Ode,* culminating the childhood poems of 1798-1804, is about birth. The *Essays Upon Epitaphs* are about life's close.

Certainly, we have to be guarded. Wordsworth had been aware of mortality, for child and adult alike, all his life, including through the great period, as many poems show: the Winander Boy in *The Prelude,* 'We are Seven', 'Lucy Gray', 'The Brothers', 'The Ruined Cottage', 'The Sailor's Mother' and others. But the *Essays Upon Epitaphs* still imply a major shift away from the Ode's first premise. Their immediate occasion was Wordsworth's reading and translations of the epitaphs of the Italian poet Gabriello Chiabrera in the winter of 1809-1810.[27] The first sentence of the opening essay focuses tightly on the topic: 'It need scarcely be said, that an Epitaph presupposes a Monument, upon which it is to be engraven'. But there immediately, and rather surprisingly, follows a brief subtext from the *Immortality Ode,* only to disappear just as quickly. Wordsworth opens by adducing the common 'intimation' which stems from early childhood, that 'some part of our nature is imperishable' (p. 50). He has more than once previously tied this sentiment to both the Ode and 'We Are Seven', two poems he was known always to associate with each other.[28] He then points to the 'early, obstinate, and unappeasable inquisitiveness of children upon the subject of origination' (p. 51). This anticipates Freud's view that a high degree of such inquisitiveness in a small child is a reliable sign of intelligence—a 'best philosopher' perhaps. Finally, this tendency valuably counterbalances the thought of death, for without

its 'genial warmth, a frost could chill the spirit' (p. 52)—evoking the Ode's eighth stanza, 'Heavy as frost, and deep almost as life!' Yet these clustered echoes of the Ode depart at once, and in all three essays Wordsworth then scrupulously analyses the epitaph as cultural trope in close detail. Epitaphs are about mortality but, by their permanence, touch on immortality; are not too exact on individual character; can speak in the dead's own voice; give praise, but as to humility, piety, and faith, rather than worldly achievement; and touch on the deceased's good and bad life-fortune.

The marked echoes of the Ode in the first two pages of the *Essays Upon Epitaphs,* and then its equally total disappearance from them, again imply that the Ode's mythology in Wordsworth's own intellectual frame has now been settled. Perhaps he was briefly trying to reactivate it, or was conveniently resorting to familiar material. Whatever the truth of that, from our point of view, there is an important outcome. We said at the start, that of the fourteen poems of the 1804-1812 period that touch on childhood, only six do so centrally or directly, and we have discussed the early four of these already. The remaining two now follow quite soon after the *Essays Upon Epitaphs.* And they too are now about death. Doubtless from his reading on Cintra, Wordsworth wrote a handful of sonnets on Spain and Portugal: here is the crucial one:

> In due observance of an ancient rite,
> The rude Biscayans, when their children lie
> Dead in the sinless time of infancy,
> Attire the peaceful corse in vestments white;
> And, in like sign of cloudless triumph bright,
> They bind the unoffending creature's brows
> With happy garlands of the pure white rose:
> Then do a festal company unite
> In choral song; and, while the uplifted cross
> Of Jesus goes before, the child is borne
> Uncovered to his grave: 'tis closed,—her loss
> The Mother *then* mourns, as she needs must mourn;
> But soon, through Christian faith, is grief subdued:
> And joy returns, to brighten fortitude.[29]

Not only has the infant's 'glorious birth' vanished; this sonnet's child is dead before the poem even starts. (Is there an unknowing pun here—'the child is *borne* / Uncovered to his grave . . .'? It's possible.) The pair-sonnet which follows ('Feelings of a Noble Biscayan') is more politically partisan on the same matter, taking the 'awful light of heavenly innocence' nearer the world's power-centres. Both poems are little read.[30] But if this first one is rather moving, it is surely in the calm reportage and (*pace* the orthodox concluding credits) neutral acceptance of a tiny life ended so soon that it scarcely has characteristics. 'Sinless' and 'vestments white' are spiritual and physical aspects of the one feature. That whiteness again, 'vestments white' and 'pure white rose', points to the death-rite, cognate with the Essay's concern with epitaphs; and childhood itself, al-

though it remains the focus, is hollowed out. After the triumph of life's beginning in the Ode, here at least childhood is associated with mortality.

It seems, then, that of the six poems of the whole 1804-1812 period to dwell on childhood centrally and directly, four were written quite soon after the Ode itself, and the other two, much later, are solely about infant mortality. Of the rest of our whole starting list of fourteen poems, only two remain to consider. Early in 1808 a Grasmere couple, George and Sarah Green, died crossing the fells in a blizzard. For a day and two nights, their six frightened children awaited their return, unaware of what had happened. The eldest—another potential Wordsworthian 'responsible eldest daughter'—heroically consoled her siblings and portioned out sparse food. The Wordsworths became leaders in raising a fund to help these orphans and took one of them into service themselves; Dorothy even wrote a pamphlet on the story. Yet Wordsworth's resulting poem, 'Elegiac Stanzas Composed in the Churchyard of Grasmere' barely mentions the children at all. He is stirred by the new churchyard grave and the bond between the parents, and his now current concern is with the marriage-bond—his own clearly behind this—which lasts until death in a lifetime companionship. One can only reflect on how differently Wordsworth would have seen this subject if he had written the poem ten years earlier. The 'Epistle to Sir George Rowland Beaumont, Bart', written in August 1811, is a seemingly light-hearted poem in heroic couplets about a family journey to the Cumbrian coast. But they went there because of the increasingly worrying health of little Catherine and Thomas, 'those Infants dear, / A Pair who smilingly sat side by side', and the poet's levity may well be a deflection.[31] In nearly three hundred lines, only eight (112-119) touch the pair at all. The children now aren't even dead; they scarcely enter the picture, even when they seem most relevant to it. And this is the very last of these sparse poems of childhood, in whole or part, before those works that followed the sad events of 1812.

* * *

When Catherine and Thomas died in June and November 1812, aged three and six, respectively, Wordsworth experienced a brief but real resurgence of poetic power. It is now elegiac; yet it came from more than the appalling grief that shook the family. Of course he felt that shatteringly, as his correspondence shows.[32] But he was now poetically prepared, in ways not overtly sought, for any such sad purpose. The result was at least one major poem, the sonnet 'Surprised By Joy', and a group of most moving other pieces with it. The turn to prose, the growing family, his enlarging public eminence,[33] and the near-terminal quarrel with Coleridge, all had taken him gradually further from any pressing sense of childhood innocence as his chief po-

etic matter. The deaths of his children finally swung his poetic thrust into a channel for which he had, unwittingly, long been prepared.

We can offer only a few remarks on these elegiac poems here. They share an indirection, as though to stave off the jagged contrast between slow reflection on mortality and then its terrible immediacy in the event. 'Surprised By Joy' earns its place in the English literary memory by rendering its shock askance. The poet's surprise—'I turned to share the transport—Oh! with whom / But Thee . . .'—comes not from the death itself but at recalling it when thinking of something wonderful. 'Maternal Grief' has lines matching 'The Ruined Cottage' for poignant microscopic detail; but it is the poet's own wife and infant son that he is looking at. 'Characteristics of a Three-Year Old Child' recalls the fluent wandering of 'Three years she grew', with the addition that Catherine, though dead when the poem was written, seems to be still living. And in one untitled poem, sadly almost never read now, the poet turns right away from his grief into calm contemplation of the sky above his lakeland home as night falls. The opening phrase, 'Come ye that are disturbed', suggests what nature is being called upon finally to tranquillize. The day settles, in an allegory of what Wordsworth most needs. The motionless close ends, with a last image of the poet himself still resisting death's total silence:

> Cloud follows cloud
> As thought succeeds to thought, but now ensues
> A pause—the long procession seems to end,
> No straggler left behind—not one appears.
> The breeze that was in heaven hath died away,
> And all things are immoveably composed
> Save here and there an uncomplying Star
> That twinkles in its station self-disturbed.[34]

The fifth line of this excerpt, 'the breeze that was in heaven hath died away', surely recalls, and gently and with some finality, puts aside, the optimistic opening of *The Prelude*; the 'gentle breeze' that 'seems half conscious of the joy it brings', one now so reversed in the direction of its energies.

We are left wondering what is the right inference as to the outcome of the first childhood vision. Perhaps it is this: if all births are, in one sense, the same, yet all the lives that ensue are different and quite unpredictable, then there can *be* no standard follow-up to the childhood vision. Child-death certainly, but also blindness, 'appetites', growing up, fighting in battle, getting pregnant in your teens, losing your own parents, poverty, and indeed young Clifford's 'wisdom' too—all these are the 'earthly freight' the young child must look forward to; and each may spring unawares at any place, any time. The one changeless item is the *Immortality Ode*, surviving two centuries later. The sad irony for Wordsworth was that the deaths of his own infants im-

posed a kind of artificial end-point for this story. Yet the poetic resolution was (I have argued) *The White Doe of Rylstone,* and Wordsworth's increasing sense, thereafter, of mortality in general, already in place, left him ready to cope with its sudden and arbitrary intervention in his own home in 1812 with unique new power.

Notes

1. Unless otherwise noted, all quotations from Wordsworth's poetry in this article come from *William Wordsworth: The Poems* ed., John O. Hayden (Harmondsworth: Penguin, 1977); *The Prelude 1799, 1805, 1850.* Ed. Jonathan Wordsworth, M. H. Abrams and Stephen Gill (London: Norton, 1979; *Home at Grasmere.* Ed. Beth Darlington (Ithaca: Cornell UP, 1977).

2. There is no record in Dorothy's journal of William continuing the poem in the next three weeks, even though she commonly names poems of the time he is working on. *Journals of Dorothy Wordsworth* Ed. Mary Moorman (Oxford UP, 1971) p. 106. Jared Curtis believes the Ode may have been continued in part in June the same year. *Poems, in Two Volumes.* Ed., Jared Curtis (Ithaca: Cornell UP, 1983) p. 271.

3. For example, Lionel Trilling, 'The Immortality Ode' in *The Liberal Imagination: Essays on Literature and Society* (Harmondsworth: Penguin, 1970) pp. 136-65; Thomas McFarland, 'Wordsworth's Best Philosopher' in *The Wordsworth Circle,* Vol. XIII No 2, Spring 1982, pp. 59-67.

4. Cf. Jonathan Wordsworth, *The Borders of Vision* (Oxford: Clarendon, 1982) pp. 246-7.

5. Cf. *The Prelude 1799, 1805, 1850* p. 434 n.; Mary Moorman, *William Wordsworth: A Biography: The Later Years 1803-1850* (Oxford: Clarendon, 1965) p. 20.

6. Dora was born on 16 August 1804. *The Letters of William and Dorothy Wordsworth: The Early Years, 1787-1805,* arranged and edited by Ernest de Selincourt; second edition revised and edited by Chester L. Shaver (Oxford: Clarendon, 1967) p. 496.

7. Cf. Alan Bewell, *Wordsworth and the Enlightenment* (New Haven: Yale UP, 1989) pp. 17-41.

8. *The Prose Works of William Wordsworth* in 3 vols. Ed. W. J. B. Owen and Jane Worthington Smyser (Oxford: Clarendon, 1974) III 37, note.

9. William Wordsworth, *Poems, in Two Volumes, and Other Poems, 1800-1807.* Ed. Jared Curtis (Ithaca: Cornell UP, 1983).

10. Wordsworth recorded later that he first heard the story from an eye-witness of the event. *The Fen-*

wick Notes of William Wordsworth. Ed. Jared Curtis (London: Bristol Classical Press, 1993) p. 27.

11. Moorman, *Biography: The Later Years,* p. 97.

12. Emile Legouis, *William Wordsworth and Annette Vallon* (Archon Books/J. M. Dent & Sons Ltd, 1967) pp. 58-61.

13. Seeking much-needed advice and support, Wordsworth wrote desperately to Coleridge just before the latter left for Malta at the end of March. *Letters: Early Years,* p. 452, 6 March 1804.

14. Kenneth R. Johnson, *Wordsworth and The Recluse* (New Haven: Yale UP, 1984) chapter 6, esp. pp. 217, 231.

15. Johnson ibid. p. 219; John Beer, *Wordsworth and the Human Heart* (London: Macmillan, 1978) p. 170; *Collected Letters of Samuel Taylor Coleridge* in 6 vols. Ed. E. L. Griggs (Oxford UP, 1956-71) IV 574-5.

16. *Letters: Middle Years I 1806-1811,* arranged and edited by Ernest de Selincourt; second edition revised by Mary Moorman (Oxford: Clarendon, 1969) pp. 158, 164; Moorman, *Biography: The Later Years,* pp. 108-110.

17. Dorothy had been reading Gray's *Life and Letters* the previous autumn. The Wordsworth's reading was commonly shared, even if sometimes only in discussion. Gray's *Elegy* was one of Wordsworth's favourite poems. *Letters: Middle Years I,* p. 101.

18. Quoted in Moorman, *Biography: The Later Years,* p. 113.

19. *Letters: Middle Years I,* pp. 221-2, 19 April 1808; *Coleridge Letters* III 98; Moorman, *Biography: The Later Years,* p. 113

20. Stephen Gill, *Wordsworth and the Victorians* (Oxford: Clarendon, 1998) p. 1. Inchbold's painting adorns the cover of Gill's book.

21. Geoffrey H. Hartman, *Wordsworth's Poetry 1787-1814* (New Haven: Yale UP, 1964) pp. 326-329.

22. Hartman ibid 324-31.

23. Beer op. cit. pp. 174, 172.

24. In fact it is not entirely clear whether 'thou' is Emily or the Doe. The Doe's weekly visits are to Bolton Priory (I 1, 58, 169) but Emily is buried in Rylstone churchyard, seven miles away (VII 1869-70). Yet it is clearly Emily's actual grave that the Doe seeks out (1898); it would hardly seek that of Francis, who was buried at Bolton Priory (1540-7). Either Wordsworth made a simple mistake of detail, or he intends a spiritual fusion between woman and animal.

25. One might well ask why the boy should be 'shame-faced'. I take this to be Wordsworth's young son John, then four-and-a-half, and for years ahead distressingly shy himself.

26. *Letters: Middle Years I*, pp. 213-5, 18 April 1808; Molly Lefebure, *The Bondage of Love* (London: Gollancz, 1986) p. 193; Stephen Gill, *William Wordsworth: A Life* (Oxford: Clarendon, 1989) p. 266.

27. The *Essays Upon Epitaphs* appear in *Wordsworth: Prose Works* II 43-119. The editors question what led Wordsworth to Chiabrera in the first place (p. 45). In fact, Wordsworth had been conversant with Italian since Cambridge days; that familiarity, plus the events just listed seems, the answer.

28. *Letters: Middle Years I*, p. 334, 5 May 1809; *Letters*, Middle *Years II 1812-1820*, arranged and edited by Ernest de Selincourt; second edition revised by Mary Moorman and Alan G. Hill (Oxford: Clarendon, 1970) p. 189; Fenwick Notes op. cit. p. 61.

29. William Wordsworth, *Shorter Poems, 1807-1820*. Ed. Carl H. Ketcham (Ithaca: Cornell UP, 1989) pp. 69-70.

30. But the hymnwriter Arthur Baring-Gould may well have, if a couplet in his much-sung 'Onward Christian Soldiers' echoes the lines 'while the uplifted cross / Of Jesus goes before' as it seems to. The couplet is 'With the cross of Jesus / Going on before'.

31. *Letters: Middle Years I*, p. 507, 28 August 1811. For Dorothy Wordsworth's pamphlet, cf. Robert Gittings and Jo Manton, *Dorothy Wordsworth* (Oxford: Clarendon, 1985) p. 168.

32. 'For myself dear Southey I dare not say in what state of mind I am; I loved the Boy with the utmost love of which my soul is capable, and he is taken from me—yet in the agony of my spirit in surrendering such a treasure I feel a thousand times richer than if I had never possessed it. God comfort and save you and all our friends and us all from a repetition of such trials—O Southey feel for me'. *Letters: Middle Years II*, p. 51, 1 December 1812.

33. There was some political difficulty, too. Pressure to explain his retreat from radicalism was compounded with attacks from the other side; unpopularity, perhaps mild risk, from the conservative establishment.

34. These are lines that, in part, de Selincourt states, 'form the basis of' *Excursion* Book IV, 1158-87; see *Wordsworth's Poetical Works*. Ed. Ernest de Selincourt, 5 vols. (Oxford: Clarendon, 1940-49) V: pp. 429-30.

Ann Wierda Rowland (essay date autumn 2001)

SOURCE: Rowland, Ann Wierda. "Wordsworth's Children of the Revolution." *Studies in English Literature, 1500-1900* 41, no. 4 (autumn 2001): 677-94.

[*In the following essay, Rowland outlines Wordsworth's use of children and violence in his writings, as well as the author's recollections of his own childhood, "in order to discover why Wordsworth implicates children in his understanding of revolutionary violence and to thus extend our understanding of how and why he associates France with childhood and youth."*]

William Wordsworth associates France and the revolution with images of childhood and youth. However, because the relationships he suggests are often complex as well as uneasy, the vigor and specificity of such associations have been debated.[1] In book 5 of the 1805 *Prelude*, Wordsworth assigns to childhood, "Our simple childhood," "more power than all the elements"; but it is a power whose political figure seems uncertain.[2] Our simple childhood, he writes, "sits upon a throne" (5:532), and yet its power arises out of an unwillingness "To endure this state of meagre vassalage" which is adult existence, a refusal to "confess" or "submit" (5:542-3). Adding to the question of whether these powers of childhood are monarchal or democratic is the fact that this passage arises from Wordsworth's recollection of "Returning at the holidays" "to my father's house" (5:501-2). There, his "golden store of books" (5:503)— romances, legends, fictions, Arabian tales—awaits him, "lawless tales" (5:548) which collude with children in resisting the grown-up state of "stinted powers" (5:541). Like the "throne" of childhood which enables such resistance, the republican camaraderie that Wordsworth experiences with books as a boy ("oh, then we feel, we feel, / We know, when we have friends . . . then we feel / With what, and how great might ye are in league" [5:546-51]) has a significant, authorizing context in his return to the father's house.

Wordsworth introduces his time in France in book 6 as another recollection of a summer holiday; this holiday, however, is not a return to his father's house, but a "scheme" undertaken "without concern for those / To whom my worldly interests were dear," (6:343-5) perhaps causing discomfort to his family.[3] The long hours spent with his "golden store of books" as a child are now found in France which in 1790 is "standing on the top of golden hours" (6:353), sharing the elevation as well as power of Wordsworth's "simple childhood." Indeed, France promises to extend childhood's resistance to humanity's "meagre vassalage" into a complete revolution or renovation. "Human nature seeming born again" (6:355) is how Wordsworth describes France at this time, suggesting, among other things, that humanity has been returned to a state of infancy or childhood.

This sort of return for Wordsworth again carries ambivalence about diffuse and revolutionary powers. Thus Wordsworth proclaims that "Nature then was sovereign in my heart" (6:346), but adds that the "mighty forms" of Nature had "given a charter to irregular hopes" (6:347-8). At this point, perhaps the best we can say is that the irregular hopes and powers of childhood as well as revolutionary France require the house or "charter" of a legitimating authority, either that of the father, of nature, or of England, the home of the Magna Charta.

Wordsworth's strong urge to return to his father's house sets up the crisis of illegitimacy which France will become for him. Critics who have identified Wordsworth's fears of illegitimacy in the 1805 account of France have rightly pointed to his illegitimate daughter, Caroline, as an unacknowledged yet haunting figure of infancy who forges another connection between France and childhood.[4] Falling on 15 December 1792, in the wake of the September massacres and as the execution of Louis XVI was being debated, the birth of Wordsworth's first child must have seemed a troubling sign that the correspondence between himself and the world—evoked most famously as "Bliss was it in that dawn to be alive, / But to be young was very heaven!"—was at an end (10:692-3).

The termination of such heavenly correspondence does not, however, mean the end of associations between France and youth. Wordsworth continues to turn to images of children and childhood in his descriptions of the violence that ensued as France turned to terror and war. Books 9 and 10 contain troubling images of violent as well as wounded children which explore a disturbing contiguity between innocence and violence, and suggest that Wordsworth understood the violence of revolution through a kind of violence he associated with childhood. Indeed, close attention to the images of these books uncovers textual echoes—"blast," "amain," "trace," "bliss," "bless"—of earlier childhood images and reveals that in writing books 9 and 10, Wordsworth repeatedly returned to memories of his own childhood and, more specifically, to images of the first two books of *The Prelude* written in 1799.

In this essay I want to explore these images of children and violence, as well as their gestures of return to earlier childhood images, in order to discover why Wordsworth implicates children in his understanding of revolutionary violence and to thus extend our understanding of how and why he associates France with childhood and youth. These questions gather particular urgency in the story of Vaudracour and Julia, a tale that Wordsworth offers in the 1805 *Prelude* as a means of narrating or accounting for revolution. "Vaudracour and Julia" narrates a crisis of violence committed by and against children which culminates in the mysterious death of Vaudracour's illegitimate son, a death that I understand

as an obscured scene of infanticide. Rather than an attempt by Wordsworth to deny or dispose of his own illegitimate child, the infanticide in "Vaudracour and Julia" establishes the wounded child as the central image of Wordsworth's personal and political narrative of France and the French Revolution.

The image of the child carries an imperative of return in Wordsworth's poetry. Before turning to the 1805 *Prelude,* I would, therefore, like to offer a model for how to read and understand the repetitions and returns at work in the child images of books 9 and 10. Wordsworth himself provides this model in an earlier poem, *Adventures on Salisbury Plain,* in the scene between the sailor and the beaten child. After stopping an enraged father from beating his son, a child "not five years old" (line 626), the sailor attempts to comfort the boy. He

> stroked the child, outstretch'd
> His face to earth, and as the boy turn'd round
> His batter'd head, a groan the Sailor fetch'd.
> The head with streaming blood had dy'd the ground,
> Flow'd from the spot where he that deadly wound
> Had fix'd on him he murder'd. Through his brain
> At once the griding iron passage found;
> Deluge of tender thoughts then rush'd amain
> Nor could his aged eyes from very tears abstain.[5]

As the child "turn'd round / His batter'd head" to face the man, he displays a wound in the same place where the sailor had fatally wounded another man earlier in the poem. In the 1841 version of this poem, *Guilt and Sorrow,* Wordsworth revises these lines and describes the child's wound as a "Strange repetition of the deadly wound / He had himself inflicted."[6] What is meant to be a face-to-face encounter between the sailor and the child is effaced by this wound as it effectually replaces the child's face and causes a self-splitting wound in the sailor: "through his brain / At once the griding iron passage found." The child's returned gaze thus witnesses both his father's and the sailor's crime not by seeing it but by bearing its wound. Furthermore, the gaze the child returns is, arguably, not the sailor's but the battered face of the murdered man whom the child mirrors through the face of the sailor. The violent blow to the sailor is a blow "through" him, the movement of past violence into the present of the text.

This encounter between the sailor and the child is an encounter between a man and a child as well as an encounter between textual sites of violence. The child's beating recalls and strangely repeats the murder of the traveler. The complexity of this encounter is enacted in the returns and repetitions of the child images in books 9 and 10 of the 1805 *Prelude.* As these images restore us to earlier childhood images, the act of turning and returning to the figure of a child produces troubling moments of self-reflection that, as in the case of the sailor in the passage above, reveal the self to be wounded by

the violence and crimes of the past or of an other. An experience of the self as other, struck through by the force of history, is the experience that Wordsworth confronts and replicates in his poetry of the French Revolution.

I

Confronting the task of describing the revolution's turn to terror, Wordsworth turns to the image of a child at play in a passage that has been slighted or overlooked by most Wordsworthian scholars. In describing the "domestic carnage" of the Terror (10:329), Wordsworth writes with significant equivocation:

> Head after head, and never heads enough
> For those who bade them fall. They found their joy,
> They made it, ever thirsty, as a child—
> If light desires of innocent little ones
> May with such heinous appetites be matched—
> Having a toy, a windmill, though the air
> Do of itself blow fresh and makes the vane
> Spin in his eyesight, he is not content,
> But with the plaything at arm's length he sets
> His front against the blast, and runs amain
> To make it whirl the faster.

(10:335-45)

If this image presents the Terror as child's play, it also suggests a terror in child's play. The child who "sets / His front against the blast, and runs amain"—runs violently, with all his might—matches violence with violence, full force with full force. The image thus suggests a natural violence that is met and countered by a human violence, either the violence of a child at play or the violence of men in revolution. While Wordsworth qualifies the one as "light desires of innocent little ones" and the other as "heinous appetites," the danger, it would seem, of matching them is that they infect each other: violence takes on shades of innocence, and innocence takes on shades of violence.

That said, it is worth pausing a while longer on Wordsworth's qualification of his image—"If light desires of innocent little ones / May with such heinous appetites be matched." The phrase seems almost fastidious, a polite apology for the incongruity of the image to follow. It marks a caution that seems odd given that elsewhere Wordsworth matches violence with children's innocence with little hesitation. For instance, in his 1797 essay, "On the Character of Rivers," written as a preface to *The Borderers,* Wordsworth, in discussing the appeal of vice over virtue, comments that "Power is much more easily manifested in destroying than in creating. A child, Rousseau has observed, will tear in pieces fifty toys before he will think of making one."[7] Wordsworth is quite blunt in this essay in asserting that power associated with childhood can mean the power to destroy, and that such propensities in children can indeed be compared to the bad actions of bad men.

Indeed, the passage from Jean Jacques Rousseau's *Emilius and Sophia* that most likely prompted Wordsworth's reference extends this notion of how innocence can be violent. Rousseau writes: "A child will often put things into disorder, will break every thing it comes near, will grasp a sparrow, as it would a stone, and kill it, without knowing what it is doing. And why? . . . Whether it makes or mars, it is all one to a child, provided the situation of things be changed; as every change necessarily implies action."[8] Rousseau explains his violent child by attributing to children a desire to change the "situation of things," a desire that necessarily implies a desire to act. He also suggests that children act with a severely qualified degree of agency: a child can kill "without knowing what it is doing." Such a child presents a troubling version of innocence, one constituted not by the inexperience of violence, but rather by an experience that is unknowing. This idea of innocence surely informs Wordsworth's choice of a child to image the violence of the revolution. In the figure of a child, an "innocent little one," Wordsworth sees the possibility of a violence that in some way does not know what it does.

For Wordsworth, in the 1790s, the desire to act or change the situation of things, and the possibility of not fully knowing one's actions, are sites of profound anxiety and concern. Indeed, his early poetry displays a persistent fear that acting in the world will somehow be violent, a worry most often manifested in incidents of crime and violent deeds. The description of Rivers's history in "On the Character of Rivers" provides a powerfully compact narrative of the criminal action that most haunts Wordsworth's early poetry: "He goes into the world and is betrayed into a great crime."[9] In this statement, betrayal and crime follow from a departure "into the world," and they follow so immediately as to become "almost coterminous," as Geoffrey Hartman has noted.[10] At the moment of venture one has already been betrayed into crime. Late notes to *The Borderers* and the *Salisbury Plain* poems map the narrative of "He goes into the world and is betrayed into a great crime" as travel to France and being a "witness" to the events of the revolution, suggesting that the particular world that causes Wordsworth such anxiety about action is one of revolution. The desire to change the situation of things, described by Rousseau in the figure of the child, is, for Wordsworth in the 1790s, a revolutionary desire and, given the course of the revolution in France, one that quite possibly leads to violence.

Wordsworth's equivocation in book 10 of *The Prelude*—"If light desires of innocent little ones / May with such heinous appetites be matched"—therefore should not be read as a sign of fastidiousness, but rather as a sign of his continued preoccupation with the question of how innocent desire ends as violent action. The phrase functions as a question—can such things be

matched?—which Wordsworth goes on to answer in the affirmative through the images that follow. Wordsworth calls attention to this image of "light desires" to insist that one problem of revolution lies in this connection between innocence and violence and in the nature of action that turns innocent desire into an experience of violence. For him, the child is a figure of unknowing violence that nevertheless has a claim to innocence. Turning to this child to represent the Terror, Wordsworth suggests that a similar kind of innocent or unknowing self may be found in the crimes and violence of men. In the poems of the 1790s, such as the *Salisbury Plain* poems and *The Borderers,* Wordsworth accounts for what we call an innocent violence through a narrative of "betrayal." In book 10 of the 1805 *Prelude,* however, the image of the child at play as a figure of revolution dispenses with that explanation and returns Wordsworth to earlier images and memories of childhood.

This image thus carries significance for the meaning of revolution and violence in Wordsworth's poetry as well as for the meaning of the child and the innocence of childhood. One might speculate that Wordsworth turns to the image of a child because he saw something in the violence of revolution that reminded him of childhood. Indeed, the violent child of book 10 recalls the earliest childhood episodes of *The Prelude* and reveals that, in the attempt to represent the violence of revolution, Wordsworth is returning to memories of childhood and, more specifically, to images of childhood written seven years earlier. In particular, we should recall the "fell destroyer" and the "plunderer" (1:318, 336) of book 1 who anticipate the child of book 10 in the violence of their play and desire as well as, quite simply, their *rush.* The child who runs to make his toy "whirl the faster" recalls the anxious hurry of the child Wordsworth "Scudding away from snare to snare . . . hurrying on, / Still hurrying, hurrying onward" (1:319-21). This earlier child makes evident two aspects of the revolutionary child otherwise more submerged. First, his designation, "fell destroyer," is another instance, much like Wordsworth's use of Rousseau's violent child, in which the poet makes clear his understanding of children as capable of violence and destruction. This child trapping woodcocks is "alone" and seems a "trouble to the peace" (1:322-3); his sport is both disruption and transgression. The child with the windmill also troubles peace to the extent that he is "not content" with the "air" alone that "makes the vane / Spin in his eyesight" but rather seeks the "blast" and runs against it. Second, the "strong desire" that "o'erpowered [the] better reason" (1:325-6) of the woodcock child casts doubt on any easy assumptions about the "light desires of innocent little ones" (10:338). While the object of the revolutionary child's desire, the spinning of a toy windmill, may be "light," the force of that desire is quite violent. The shock of this passage is the force of desire, the

quality of being "ever thirsty" that in one line describes the men of the Terror as well as the child with a toy. The desires that cause the child to "[set] His front against the blast, and [run] amain" and the people of Paris to demand "head after head" are the same, and they recall the strong and overpowering desire experienced by the "fell destroyer" child.

If the "fell destroyer" and the "innocent little one" share a similar rush of desire, the image of the boy "plunderer," on the other hand, is primarily one of pause:

> Oh, when I have hung
> Above the raven's nest . . .
> But ill sustained, and almost, as it seemed,
> Suspended by the *blast* which blew *amain.*
>
> (1:341-5, emphasis added)

It is no coincidence that the child with the windmill "sets his front against the *blast* and runs *amain.*" The verbal echoes are significant of Wordsworth's repeated returns to an earlier image of childhood. Both children have set themselves against the "blast." In the first passage, however, it is the wind that blows "amain" and poorly suspends the boy in his pause; whereas in the later passage it is the child who runs "amain." The difference between these children is one of age and agency. The child with the windmill, the "innocent little one," is a younger child than the boy "plunderer" who is old enough to hunt and trap on his own. In the pause of this older, preadolescent child, we see a degree of self-consciousness that cannot be found in the younger child who runs violently but unknowingly against the wind. The plunderer's pause of self-reflection yields only a limited self-knowledge, however—the boy knows himself to be "alone" but is buffeted by the wind's "strange utterance" out of any sure knowledge of the world and his place in it: "the sky seemed not a sky / Of earth" (1:348-50). This is a dim self-awareness experienced more as alienation and isolation than as integrity or sufficiency. It is closely tied to the rather limited and troubled sense of agency that both the "fell destroyer" and the "plunderer" experience in these passages.

If Rousseau's child and Wordsworth's innocent at play are unknowing in their violence, how these older children understand their violence—how they know themselves and their deeds—is also at question. It is as if these older children stand at the moment in which they first begin to know their violence but, significantly, they know it as other to themselves, as "a strong desire" that "o'erpowered my better reason," as "Low breathings coming after me, and sounds / Of undistinguishable motion" (1:330-1), as "strange utterance" (1:348). The pause of self-reflection described in the "plunderer" episode thus grants not simply a limited knowledge of the self but a knowledge of something other in the self.

This is the pause that we find repeated and revised in the child image of book 10. However, it is not the

young, unknowing child who pauses in the blast, but the poet who fronts the blast of desire that he finds in the French Revolution and confronts the image of a child. His pause before that image is the qualification that interrupts it—"If light desires of innocent little ones / May with such heinous appetites be matched." The image of the child and the question it provokes in the mind of the poet returns Wordsworth to memories of his own childhood and, specifically, to the images of book 1. In that act of return Wordsworth discovers the desire that fuels the Terror in his own self, in the image of himself as a child. In pausing before the image of his innocent but violent child, Wordsworth confronts not simply an image of his own self, but an image of what is other to his self in himself.

II

Book 10 contains another significant revision of Wordsworth's early childhood images. The description of himself at the time of the revolution, the passage in book 10 that begins: "Bliss was it in that dawn to be alive, / But to be young was very heaven," recalls and significantly revises the passage from book 2, "Blessed the infant babe," one of the central texts of Wordsworth's representations of childhood. Wordsworth introduces the blessed infant babe of book 2 with the explanation:

> Blessed the infant babe—
> For with my best conjectures I would *trace*
> The progress of our being.
>
> (2:237-9, emphasis added)

His project is to "trace" at this point not only because of the element of conjecture that necessarily comes in at the moment of describing infancy, but also because he is, to some extent, engaged in tracing the form and figure of mother and child, of the babe in the mother's arms. Thus he continues:

> blest the babe
> Nursed in his mother's arms, the babe who sleeps
> Upon his mother's breast.
>
> (2:239-41)

Wordsworth also understands the project of the books on France and the French Revolution as a "tracing": the word is significant in this context of his own evolution in political consciousness, from a blissful and blessed naïveté to a wounded, illegitimate knowledge. In looking back over book 10 toward its conclusion, Wordsworth writes:

> Thus, O friend,
> Through times of honour, and through times of shame,
> Have I descended, *tracing* faithfully
> The workings of a youthful mind, beneath
> The breath of great events.
>
> (10:940-4)

Here "tracing" also evokes the maternal figure outlined in book 2. As these lines place the youth "beneath the breath of great events," they recall the infant beneath the breath of the mother.

Earlier in book 10 Wordsworth glosses these "great events" as the movements of "Nature," providing an analysis of the revolution as embodying "nature" and following a natural course. He writes:

> Youth maintains, I knew,
> In all conditions of society
> Communion more direct and intimate
> With Nature, and the inner strength she has—
> And hence, ofttimes, no less with reason too—
> Than age, or manhood even. To Nature then,
> Power had reverted: habit, custom, law,
> Had left an interregnum's open space
> For her to stir about in, uncontrolled.
>
> (10:604-12)

In the "interregnum's open space" which is revolution, nature acts "uncontrolled." Her movements and actions are those of the "youth" who are her intimates. The most important part of this passage is the relationship imagined between "youth" and "Nature": a "Communion more direct and intimate." Intimate communion is an idea that Wordsworth elsewhere uses to describe the relationship between mother and child; in "The Thorn," it is a "sad case" of "communion with a stirring child";[11] in the "Blessed the infant babe" passage of book 2, a "more exact / And intimate communion" is learned from the mother and maintained with "objects which already are beloved" (2:299-302). In these passages of book 10, Wordsworth begins to describe a relationship between youth and "Nature" in the time of revolution which is essentially that of a mother and child.

The blessings of the infant babe in book 2 are the blessings of a unified and corresponding relationship to the mother and, by extension, to the world. The mother is a "beloved presence" from whom emanates a "virtue which irradiates and exalts / All objects through all intercourse of sense" (2:255-60). The infant is thus connected to the world in a "filial bond of Nature." Wordsworth explicitly recalls this model when he evokes his own feelings in the early days of the revolution: "Bliss was it in that dawn to be alive, / But to be young was very heaven!" The passage describes the bliss of many different tempered youths and then turns to Wordsworth's confession of his own sentiment: "Why should I not confess that earth was then / To me what an inheritance new-fallen seems" (10:728-9). In the lines which follow, Wordsworth declares himself at this time to be "a child of Nature." He "moved among mankind" (10:738) as

> In brief, a child of Nature, as at first,
> Diffusing only those affections wider

That from the cradle had grown up with me,
And losing, in no other way than light
Is lost in light, the weak in the more strong.

(10:752-6)

As a young man during the revolution, Wordsworth's movements in the world and feelings for that world are a fluid extension of the infant's. The revolutionary world is simply a wider maternal embrace. The possible loss in moving from the mother to the world is here understood instead as augmentation and combination—light into light, weak into strong—both habits of association and perception learned in the mother's arms, habits which

combine
In one appearance all the elements
And parts of the same object, else detached
And loath to coalesce.

(2:247-50)

Hence Wordsworth's "bliss" to be alive and, more importantly, young at the dawn of revolution, a "bliss" that deliberately chimes the "blessed" state of the infant babe. To be young at a time of "dawn," in other words, when time itself is young, is to experience a correspondence between oneself and the world that is "heaven." In the "bliss" of book 10, Wordsworth claims that the historical coincidence of being young at the time of revolution is no coincidence at all, but instead a state of full significance that re-creates the blessed state of the infant in the mother's arms.

What then happens to this "child of Nature" who moves about the world as the infant moves in its mother's arms? The child's promise of growth without loss, of unity and correspondence with the external world is short-lived. This, Wordsworth continues, "Was my condition, till with open war / Britain opposed the Liberties of France" (10:758-9). The child of Nature receives a "blow." England's declaration of war against France, Wordsworth recounts,

threw me first out of the pale of love,
Soured and corrupted upwards to the source,
My sentiments; was not, as hitherto,
A swallowing up of lesser things in great,
But change of them into their opposites,
And thus a way was opened for mistakes
And false conclusions of the intellect,
As gross in their degree, and in their kind
Far, far more dangerous. What had been a pride
Was now a shame, my likings and my loves
Ran in new channels, leaving old ones dry;
And thus a blow, which in maturer age
Would but have touched the judgement, struck more
 deep
Into sensations near the heart.

(10:760-73)

Wordsworth insists that England's declaration of war is a blow felt all the more deeply because of his youth. In this passage the "child of Nature" has been dealt a blow which not only "Soured and corrupted" his sentiments but "struck more deep" to his very habits of feeling. What had been "A swallowing up of lesser things in great" becomes a "change of them into their opposites." The blow to the child is that which casts him out of the mother's arms and into a relationship with the world that is oppositional and estranged.

This "blow" to the Wordsworthian child also has implications for what we might call his "legitimacy" or his place in the world. In describing the moment of England's declaration of war on France earlier in book 10, Wordsworth represents it as violence against the youth of England, exclaiming:

Oh, much have they to account for, who could
 tear
By violence at one decisive rent
From the best youth in England their dear pride,
Their joy, in England.

(10:275-8)

In this "decisive rent" the relationship between England and its youth is violently altered. For Wordsworth, this is felt as a "shock," indeed the only moment that "might be named / A revolution" for him (10:233, 236-7). The scene that follows is well known: Wordsworth sits in a village church while the congregation offers prayers "To their great Father," and he, "like an uninvited guest / Whom no one owned, sate silent" (10:269, 272-3). This is a scene of Wordsworth's illegitimacy; he sits silent, unowned by any one or by the "Father." The "shock" of this passage and the "blow" to the "child of Nature" is that which casts the Wordsworthian child into illegitimacy.

In the passage of book 10 that begins "Bliss was it in that dawn," Wordsworth returns to the "Blessed the infant babe" passage of book 2 and creates an encounter between the youth of revolution and the infant in the mother's arms, making these figures, as it were, turn to face each other. While Wordsworth employs the maternal imagery and the "blest" status of the infant to describe the youth of revolution, he also insists on the historical vulnerability of that blissful state as the youth is quickly thrown "out of the pale of love." Self-knowledge becomes a knowledge of the self as "alone" (the Wordsworthian boys of book 2) or "uninvited" (the Wordsworthian youth in the village church). Indeed all the children we have examined thus far could be described as "not belonging," a phrase which speaks both to their historical contingency and their knowledge of themselves. This is why the blessed infant babe is so important to Wordsworth: it stands as a figure of perfect and clear belonging, a myth of origin that precedes history or self-knowledge. It is a myth, however, that does not survive the act of return or encounter with the youth of

book 10. For if we turn back from book 10 to the infant passage in book 2, we find an odd anticipation of the blow to come. In Wordsworth's description of the unity and correspondence between mother and child there is a curious, negative assertion about this child: "No outcast he, bewildered and depressed" (2:261). Even as the passage insists the child is *not* an outcast, the moment when the child will be cast out (of the mother's arms, of his legitimate relationship to England) is anticipated. Read as an image recalled and returned to from that of the youth in book 10, this line functions almost as a strange *repetition*; the blow to the youth is read back into the image of the infant. In the encounter between youth and infant, the outcast other is discovered to be present and part of the very origin of the self.

III

Finally, we can turn to the story of Vaudracour and Julia which enacts another encounter between a youth and an infant. In this tale, the problem of an unknowing violence is mapped onto an intergenerational conflict between father and son. Wordsworth offers the story as an alternative means of recounting the revolution from the "public acts / And public persons," the "record and report" otherwise employed (9:546-7, 549). This story of familial conflict is thus introduced as a narrative of revolution much in the same way that allegories of parricide, of sons rebelling against fathers, are so often used as a way to tell or explain the violence of revolution.

As a story of revolution, however, the Vaudracour and Julia episode is precisely not the story of a son's violent uprising against a father. As critics have often noted (and complained), Vaudracour is a character made only more passive and feminized by his repeated encounters with paternal authority; he repeatedly gives himself over to his father, begs forgiveness, and gradually sinks into a melancholic inactivity. Indeed, he is infantilized over the course of the narrative, most often seen

> Propping a pale and melancholy face
> Upon the mother's bosom, resting thus
> His head upon one breast, while from the other
> The babe was drawing in its quiet food
>
> (9:812-5)

and ultimately ending his days *infans,* without speech.[12] Vaudracour is, in fact, a child who *refuses* to rebel against his father. When the more rebellious Julia "coupled with his father's name some words / Of vehement indignation," "the youth / Checked her, nor would he hear of this, for thought / Unfilial, or unkind, had never once / Found harbour in his breast" (9:713-7). Far from being a story of youth rebelling against paternal authority, this story is instead a tale of paternal abuse. Vaudracour's father either locks his son up at

home or denies him entrance there, repeatedly arrests and imprisons him, and throughout forbids him to marry where his affections lie.

The most troubling instance of harm done to a child, however, is found at the end of the story and involves Vaudracour's illegitimate son. Retreating to the country, Vaudracour takes on the role of nursemaid to his child, an occupation meant to console him in his early retirement at the age of twenty-four. The consolation, however, is temporary, as we see in some of the most enigmatic lines Wordsworth ever wrote:

> It consoled him here
> To attend upon the orphan and perform
> The office of a nurse to his young child,
> Which, after a short time, by some mistake
> Or indiscretion of the father, died.
> The tale I follow to its last recess
> Of suffering or of peace, I know not which—
> Theirs be the blame who caused the woe, not mine.
>
> (9:904-11)[13]

Perhaps these lines are so difficult because they insist on Vaudracour's role in the death of his son while at the same time rendering it unavailable to full knowledge. In this way, they function in much the same way as Vaudracour's subsequent silence—"From that time forth he never uttered word / To any living" (9:912-3)—which suggests, in the tradition of Iago and *The Borderers*'s Mortimer, that he is guilty of a crime but refuses to explain or name its nature. Or perhaps these lines mark another experience of violence that is unknowing; "mistake or indiscretion" suggests a destructive act like that of Rousseau's child who kills "without knowing what it is doing." If so, it would seem that the condition of not fully knowing what has been done here spreads to Wordsworth who, in another reflexive moment provoked by the troubling image of a child, oddly asserts that he does not know what happened and therefore cannot be blamed.

I believe that the silence and strangeness of these lines point to the crime of infanticide, that the tale which Wordsworth follows "to its last recess / Of suffering or of peace" is one which traces violence against the child from one generation to the next.[14] Vaudracour is the central child figure of this narrative, an uneasy combination of childlike innocence and criminal violence that reaches a crisis in these lines. As such, he corresponds remarkably to Romantic conventions of representing infanticidal mothers, women who are usually presented as childlike, innocent, if not excessively naïve, and the victims of prior violence and betrayal.[15] As with the death of this child, infanticide complicates the distinction between criminal agency and innocence because of the continuum it suggests between neglect, mistake—the most common forms of infanticide are exposure, suffocation, and shaking—and the deliberate action of murder.

Perhaps the most disturbing aspect of Vaudracour's violence, however, is not its innocent and childlike quality, but rather its repetition of earlier acts and crimes of violence committed against him by his father. To read Vaudracour's involvement in the death of his infant son as infanticide is to understand that act as registering and repeating prior crimes not his own. The primary reason that Vaudracour is such an uneasy combination of innocence and violence, a version of self that is "unknowing" of the violence it commits, is because his self is shown to be wounded if not *founded* by the violence of his father. As a narrative of revolution, therefore, the 1805 story of Vaudracour and Julia inverts the traditional allegory of parricide into one of infanticide, replacing the rebellious youth with the wounded child as an image of history's violence. The crime of infanticide becomes relevant to a narrative of revolution not simply as a figure of revolution's problematic conjunction of innocence and violence; infanticide also provides a way of understanding the self as wounded by the violent crimes of an other, a self which reproduces actions not fully its own. In the figure of the wounded child—in this narrative, both Vaudracour and his illegitimate son—Wordsworth represents history as a violent blow to the self, a blow that casts one into an estranged relationship with the world and reveals the deeds and crimes of others to be inescapably part of the self.

We began this essay with the scene from *Adventures on Salisbury Plain* as a model for how to understand the encounter with an image of a child in Wordsworth's poetry. Through the acts of return required by these images—whether a return to an earlier version of self, or the return of past violence into the present self—Wordsworth constructs an understanding of the self in history, one which acknowledges the extent to which the crimes of others and of the past are part of the self, reproduced in and through the self. This is the work the returned gaze of the wounded child performs in *Adventures on Salisbury Plain,* but it is work that carries risk. The sailor experiences a blow to his self; immediately after, a "Deluge of tender thoughts then *rush'd amain.*"[16] It is significant that the sailor's tender thoughts and tears partake of the violent rush we have seen in various images in *The Prelude.* Here the force is therapeutic, but it is certainly a rush to fill the gap, to heal the "passage" through the brain caused by the child's gaze.

Vaudracour, on the other hand, is not allowed any therapeutic tears. The relationship between him and his illegitimate son collapses into violence and imbecility. A rustic hermit "Cut off from all intelligence with man," Vaudracour is also cut off from his "personal memory," and his retreat becomes a place of self-deterioration: "His days he wasted, an imbecile mind" (9:929-35). Vaudracour's silence and "savage outside" do not gain him the privileged position that many of Wordsworth's marginal characters hold (9:927). In this respect he is like Martha Ray, another possibly infanticidal parent of Wordsworth's poetry, whose monosyllabic insanity seems to signify a self-destruction. Like Martha Ray, Vaudracour has faced the violence of history and not survived the blast.

Notes

1. Alan Richardson, for instance, objects to Laurence Goldstein's and Ronald Paulson's discussions of how William Wordsworth associates the revolution with childhood and youth as "over-literal" and "somewhat forced" (*Literature, Education, and Romanticism* [Cambridge: Cambridge Univ. Press, 1994], pp. 35-6). More recently, however, David Bromwich has repeated these associations (*Disowned by Memory: Wordsworth's Poetry of the 1790s* [Chicago: Univ. of Chicago Press, 1998], p. 2).

2. Wordsworth, *The Prelude: 1799, 1805, 1850,* ed. Jonathan Wordsworth, M. H. Abrams, and Stephen Gill (New York: W. W. Norton, 1979), 5:532-3. All subsequent references will be to this edition and will appear parenthetically in the text according to book and line number. All shortened references to "Wordsworth" indicate William rather than Jonathan Wordsworth.

3. Wordsworth worries about his uncle's displeasure in a letter to his sister Dorothy (*The Early Letters of William and Dorothy Wordsworth, 1787-1805,* ed. Ernest de Selincourt [Oxford: Clarendon Press, 1935], p. 37).

4. See Mary Jacobus, *Romanticism, Writing, and Sexual Difference: Essays on "The Prelude"* (Oxford: Clarendon Press, 1989), pp. 187-205; and Gayatri Chakravorty Spivak, *In Other Worlds: Essays in Cultural Politics* (New York: Routledge, 1988), pp. 47-57.

5. Wordsworth, *Adventures on Salisbury Plain,* in *The Salisbury Plain Poems of William Wordsworth,* ed. Gill (Ithaca: Cornell Univ. Press, 1975), p. 149, lines 640-8.

6. Wordsworth, *Guilt and Sorrow,* in *The Salisbury Plain Poems of William Wordsworth,* p. 261, lines 491-2.

7. Wordsworth, "On the Character of Rivers," in *The Borderers,* ed. Robert Osborn (Ithaca: Cornell Univ. Press, 1982), p. 63.

8. Jean Jacques Rousseau, quoted in Wordsworth, "Rivers," p. 63.

9. Wordsworth, "Rivers," p. 62.

10. Geoffrey Hartman, *Wordsworth's Poetry, 1787-1814* (Cambridge MA: Harvard Univ. Press, 1964, rprt. 1987), p. 134.

11. Wordsworth, *Lyrical Ballads, and Other Poems, 1797-1800,* ed. James Butler and Karen Green (Ithaca: Cornell Univ. Press, 1991), p. 81.

12. See Jacobus, p. 200.

13. These lines and the story as a whole have drawn many complaints. See, for example, de Selincourt's note in his edition of Wordsworth's *The Prelude: Or, Growth of a Poet's Mind,* 2d edn., rev. Helen Darbishire (Oxford: Clarendon Press, 1959), pp. 592-3.

14. Jacobus speculates parenthetically that this might be infanticide, displaced suicide, or mercy killing; otherwise I have found no explanation for these lines (p. 200).

15. See Susanne Kord, "Women as Children, Women as Childkillers: Poetic Images of Infanticide in Eighteenth-Century Germany," *ECS* 26, 3 (Spring 1993): 449-66.

16. Wordsworth, *Adventures,* p. 149, line 647, emphasis added.

CHILDHOOD IN THE WORKS OF CHARLES DICKENS

Vereen M. Bell (essay date fall 1968)

SOURCE: Bell, Vereen M. "The Emotional Matrix of *David Copperfield." Studies in English Literature, 1500-1900* 8, no. 4 (fall 1968): 633-49.

[*In the following essay, Bell applies Sigmund Freud's theory that the writing of fiction is a means of wish fulfillment to Charles Dickens and his work, particularly* David Copperfield.]

Freud's theory that fiction-making is a form of wish fulfillment helps in defining the nature and appeal of Dickens's novels. Dickens was frustrated by the realities of his mature life, and yet he never abandoned the faith that an Edenic existence was still possible. The affair with Ellen Ternan was an expression of this faith, but it merely epitomized the earlier similar child-like infatuations. It was this pursuit of "idealities" that complicated his involvement in *David Copperfield.* The novel is about losses and it culminated in David's learning that the innocence of childhood is inaccessible in the mature life. David's unhappy infatuations with child-women teach him that those creatures are not fit for this world. He must therefore settle for Agnes—the embodiment of mature virtues. However, the emotional growth that David's marriage to Agnes symbolizes was not a growth Dickens himself achieved. Whatever his mind may have known his heart lived in Dingley Dell—in a static world with static people, and his hatred of the iron-cold new order was simply a function of his belief in simpler and happier life. Dickens moved perpetually between real and ideal worlds, and the experience of both his life and work is archetypal.

In the realm of fiction there are two kinds of illusions, the kind that the writer has, and the kind that he creates; and the writer's representation of reality is dependant upon the accuracy and the maturity of his apprehension of it. "Every child at play," says Freud, "behaves like an imaginative writer, in that he creates a world of his own or, more truly, he rearranges the things in his world and orders it in a new way that pleases him better. . . . Now the writer does the same as the child at play; he creates a world of phantasy which he takes very seriously; that is, he creates it with a great deal of affect, while separating it from reality." Freud's reductive generalization may be classically oversimplified, but it does provide a basis for critical evaluation, the basis that we use when we employ the term *sentimentality.* I do not of course mean sentimentality in its conventional sense—equated with contrived pathos in particular and with emotional excess in general, both of which are merely symptoms of sentimentality. Sentimentality is more usefully thought of as the failure of insight in an artist that permits him to portray certain aspects of life more as he wishes them to be than as they are—to create "a world of his own"; to define it negatively, it is an absence of tough-mindedness. Intellectually, to sentimentalize life is to become a victim of one's illusions. It is one of the functions of criticism to distinguish between truth and phantasy in art, to keep separate the two senses (the aesthetic and the psychological) of the word illusion, and to determine the relationship between the two in the act of creation.

Judging from the criticism of the last twenty-five years (since the "the Two Scrooges"), it is difficult not to think of Dickens in this context. Dickens seems to fit Freud's pattern so precisely it is hard to avoid pursuing possibilities in an effort to discover more, through the agency of Freud's major premise, about the relationship between the writer and his work. The purpose of this essay is to offer dome more guarded speculation on the nature of this relationship—between, say, the psyche and creative imagination—by way of explaining in part Dickens's continued hold upon even the most sophisticated critical sensibility. I am thinking of Dickens's work in general, particularly the early novels, but I have tried to focus upon *David Copperfield* because from all the evidence that novel seems to have been the one that Dickens is most deeply involved emotionally. Describing and evaluation Dickens's achievement is a baffling enterprise, but it may be possible to explain

what Dickens's novels mean to us by first understanding what they meant to him.

For Freud, the obvious impulse of phantasy creation was maladjustment. "We can begin by saying that happy people never make phantasies, only unhappy ones. Unsatisfied wishes are the divining power behind phantasies; every separate phantasy contains the fulfilment of a wish, and improves on unsatisfactory reality."[1] Professor Johnson's Dickens appears to have been just such a complex individual, a man with staggering energy, a good portion of which was dedicated to evading or escaping the anxieties and the insistent realities of his mature life. Intellectually he was frustrated by the complacency of England's social conscience; emotionally her was disappointed by the marriage he had made, and yet Kate continued to bear children with depressing regularity. As more children came along, more money was needed to support them. He wrote feverishly, he delivered lectures, he presented readings, he edited journals, he produces plays, he supervised charitable projects. The pattern of Dickens's mature years suggests a man who deliberately contrived to crowd his life with critical and demanding labor. Work killed him probably, but it simplified his existence, and made it endurable. So long as he had something to do—something tangible to be accomplished—he did not have to think about himself, about Kate, and about the emotional needs that he could not fulfill. And, to his credit, Dickens recognized this compulsion in himself as well as anyone has since:

> I am the modern embodiment of the old Enchanters, whose Familiars tore them to pieces. I weary of rest, and have no satisfaction but in fatigue. Realities and idealities are always comparing themselves before me, and I don't like the Realities except when they are unattainable—*then,* I like them of all things. I wish I had been born in the days of Ogres and Dragon-guarded Castles. I wish an Ogre with seven heads . . . had taken the Princess whom I adore—you have no idea how intensely I love her!—to his stronghold on the top of a high series of mountains, and there tied her up by the hair. Nothing would suit me half so well this day, as climbing after her, sword in hand, and either winning her or being killed—*There's* a frame of mind for you in 1857.[2]

A frame of mind indeed for a man forty-five years old—married for twenty-one years and with ten children.

Like his friend Collins, Sickens had found life—that is *his* life—a disappointment. As he grew older and saw it running out on him he began grasping at possibilities. Unlike Collins he had a great streak of optimism—the sense that life somewhere is good and happy—which kept him from giving up, and which in effect merely intensified his despair. The Eden existed for him; he had merely missed it, by some accident or by some fatal choice. The separation from Kate and the affair with Helen Ternan suggest that Dickens considered the fatal

choice to have been his marriage; now, thirteen years before he was to die, he was starting over.

Ellen, of course, was merely the main figure, the culmination of a consistently romantic emotional pattern. Except for Mary Boyle and Mme. de la Rue, all of Dickens's infatuations involved young girls, and all were to have some sort of incarnation in his work. It is hardly necessary to add that these episodes seem to us trite and immature, the phantasies of a man who spent a good portion of his life pursuing his own lost innocence. Certainly Kate was no partner for Eden; and the others, one suspects, were mainly invented. That is to say, Maria Beadnell, Mary Hogarth, Christiana Weller, and finally Ellen were, in their own way, as much creatures of Dickens's imagination as Dora, Little Emily, Little Nell, and Esther Summerson. It is difficult at least to conceive of them as being anything like what Dickens believed them to be; and in the cases of Maria and Christiana Weller, and possibly even Ellen, Dickens himself much have some to some realization of his error. The only image to survive untarnished was Mary's and she died at seventeen. Dickens intended to be buried with her in the same grave, and might have been had not Mary's grandmother supplanted him; he did wear Mary's ring next to his own, and for years after her death he had visitations from her in his dreams. "I solemnly believe," he wrote to his friend Tom Beard, "that so perfect a creature never breathed. I knew her inmost heart, and her real worth and value. She had not a fault."

The experience with Maria Beadnell was typical in another way and all the more remarkable because of the span of time it covered: it began before Dickens had met the Hogarth sisters and was never finally resolved until almost twenty years after his marriage to Kate. When his first love recognized herself in *David Copperfield* and sought Dickens out, he responded with almost precisely the sentimental extravagance of Dickens at seventeen. Her letter, he wrote, had restored him to "the most ardent, and the most disinterested days of my life" which "had you for their Sun"—when "the Dream I lived in . . . refined my heart."[3]

> You are always the same in my remembrance. When you say you are "toothless, fat, old, and ugly" (which I don't believe), I fly away to the house in Lombard Street, which is pulled down, as if it were necessary that the very bricks and mortar should go the way of my airy castles, and see you in a sort of raspberry colored dress with a little black fur trimming at the top. . . . And I have gone over that ground within these twelve months hoping it is not ungrateful to consider whether any reputation the world can bestow is repayment to a man for the loss of such a vision of his youth as mine.
>
> (*Letters,* II, 634)

Professor Johnson writes that "Dickens must have known that at forty-four Maria could hardly be the same

ethereal vision he remembered." The fact is that this seems never to have occurred to him. His mind was contemplating phantasy and he made a characteristic leap outside of time into a realm where things and people do not change. When the fat and silly Maria of the flesh actually appeared, the shock was severe.

The letter (quoted earlier) about being one of "the old Enchanters" was written two years after this disillusioning experience with Maria, and one would think that by that time he might have learned better. At any rate, the passage there about "idealities" and "Realities" that "are unattainable" is an interesting one. One wonders if Dickens ever truly recognized a difference. "Why is it," he writes to Forster, "that as with poor David [Copperfield], a sense comes always crushing on me now when I fall into low spirits, as of one happiness I have missed in life, and one friend and one companion I have never made?" (*Letters*, II, 620-21).

When we consider it as part of the pattern of his life, Dickens's famous preference for *David Copperfield* seems to have involved more than simply a wistful recollection of his childhood. It is true that *David Copperfield,* of all his novels, was most concerned with the events of his own past; but the fact that Dickens should deliberately compare himself at forty-three with David at around twenty suggests that the novel was concerned with a kind of personal mental life as well—with wishes and conflicts that had not changed. It is my feeling that he was moved and involved by David's narrative to the point that David became an extension of his own identity—his present identity. "I am within three pages of the shore," he wrote to Forster, "and am strangely divided, as usual in such cases, between sorrow and joy. Oh, my dear Forster, if I were to say half of what Copperfield makes me feel to-night, how strangely, even to you, I should be turned inside out! I seem to be sending some part of myself into the Shadowy World" (*Letters,* II, 240). The phrasing here implies that he regarded this novel as self-exposure—an autobiography of the present as well as the past.

As its opening passage seems to foreshadow, *David Copperfield* is a novel concerned with loss. David was born with a caul, "which was advertised for sale, in the newspapers, at the low price of fifteen guineas." The advertisement is unsuccessful, "and ten years afterwards the caul was put up in a raffle down in our part of the country . . . I was present myself, and I remember to have felt quite uncomfortable and confused, at a part of myself being disposed of in that way."[4] Intentional or not, an eerie relevance informs this comic conceit. One of the patterns in *David Copperfield* is the young hero's search to find in the world the uterine innocence of his childhood. Wisdom begins for him when he discovers that it is not there, at least not in the form he expected. On one level the conflict is David's, on

the other it is Dickens's own; for both David and Dickens the experience of *David Copperfield* was an exercise in self-instruction. The lesson that David learns is the final stage of maturation; with Dickens, as we have seen, the lesson somehow fails to take. Perhaps I should say with Dickens the man; for Dickens the artist *David Copperfield* was very clearly a turning point. From this point on his vision is tougher, more realistic; his sense of life is less fanciful and optimistic; his imagination is less sentimental and self-indulgent. In effect, Dickens the artist has turned his back on Dingley Dell. Dickens the man, however, has not, and apparently never does. We therefore have in *David Copperfield* the peculiar circumstance of a fictional character, David, who has learned more from his experience than his creator. David learns to mistrust "the first mistaken impulse of an undisciplined heart"; Dickens pursues and cherishes such impulses until his death. David learns what Dickens is intellectually aware of but cannot emotionally accept: that there is no womb after birth itself, no faery realms uncorrupted. Perhaps this is what Dickens meant by sending only "some *part* of myself into the Shadowy World."

David Copperfield's development is usually traced through the unsteady course of his infatuations and love affairs; and the children and women whom he ultimately comes to understand, as well as love, are all too clearly phantasy love affairs of Dickens's own. David has a child mother; Emily is a childhood sweetheart; ultimately he takes a child bride. Some disaster overtakes all three; they are not fit for the world. The world should be a place where they can live but it is not. David's and Dickens's grief is only partly for the personal loss; they must also grieve the loss or the corruption of the childish innocence that Clara, Emily, and Dora symbolize.

David's childhood with his beautiful mother is blissful because his mother is a child like himself; for David there is no essential difference between them, between what they both know and expect of life. They have nothing to do but choose among simple pleasures.

> Now I am in the garden that the back . . . —a very preserve for butterflies, as I remember it, with a high fence, and a gate and padlock; where the fruit clusters on the trees, riper and richer than fruit has ever been since, in any other garden, and where my mother gathers some in a basket, while I stand by, bolting furtive gooseberries, and trying to look unmoved. A great wind rises, and the summer is gone in a moment. We are playing in the winter twilight, dancing about the parlour. When my mother is out of breath and rests herself in an elbow-chair, I watch her winding her bright curls round her fingers, and straightening her waist, and nobody knows better than I do that she likes to look so well, and is proud of being so pretty.

(pp. 15-16)

Their emotions, like their pleasures, are uncomplicated; feeling and tender affection are free and open. Aunt Betsey calls David's mother a "loving baby."

When the Murdstones come they destroy David's and Clara's Eden simply by destroying feeling. "Now, Clara my dear," Murdstone warns, "recollect! control yourself, always control yourself!" For the Murdstone the true mark of maturity is discipline, understood as the power to suppress all emotion—including love. Their creed, as David says, is firmness; and Murdstone himself admits to marrying Clara—"an inexperienced and artless person"—with an aim toward "forming her character, and infusing into it some amount of the firmness and decision of which is stood in need." As Clara languishes under the Murdstones' regimen, and finally dies, a portions of childhood vanishes; the other grimmer world has had its way. What the Murdstones murder is not so much an individual as an idea which that individual, Clara, is inseparably identified with. This is why they carry throughout the first half of the novel such a consistently symbolic weight.

Significantly it is the world, the Murdstones, and not Death that robs David of his child mother. The operation and influence of the Murdstone discipline has destroyed the "loving baby" long before she dies in reality. The result of her death, in fact, is that the child Clara is resurrected to live as she once was in David's imagination; in effect she must die so that the fact of what she has become, has been made into by the Murdstones, will not be there to contradict the recollection of what she was. "Can I say of her innocent and girlish beauty, that it faded, and was no more, when its breath falls on my cheek now, as it fell that night? Can I say she ever changed, when my remembrance brings her back to life, thus only; and, truer to its loving youth than I have been . . . ?" When Peggotty finally completes the narration of Clara's death "the idea of her as she had been of late had vanished from me. I remembered her from that instant, only as the young mother of my earliest impressions . . . In her death she winged her way back to her calm, untroubled youth, and cancelled all the rest" (p. 133). With this image of Clara as she was, David's infancy and childhood are restored to him and preserved in the static world of memory—memory for David, phantasy and imagination for Dickens.

The pattern of David's experience with Emily is essentially the same, except that Clara has been changed from without, while Emily is changed from within. As with his mother, however, David idealizes Emily in retrospect because the memory symbolizes for him a state of existence that is passed. "I am sure I loved that baby quite as truly, quite as tenderly, with greater purity and more disinterestedness, then can enter into the best love of a later time of life, high and ennobling as it is. I am

sure my fancy raised up something round that blue-eyed mite of a child which etherealised, and made a very angel of her" (p. 37). As they grow older David visualizes their happiness as a perpetual sexual childhood. "What happiness (I thought) if we were married, and were going away anywhere to live among the trees and in the fields, never growing older, never growing wiser, children ever, rambling hand in hand through sunshine among flowery meadows, laying down our heads on moss at night, in a sweet sleep of purity and peace . . ." (p. 147). Even Emily herself, an unconvincing part of her, wants to be remembered in this way. In what amounts to a suicide note she leaves behind when Steerforth takes her away, she write to Ham: "Oh, don't remember how affectionate and kind you have all been to me—don't remember you were ever to be married—but try to think of me as if I died when I was little, and was buried somewhere." And when she writes to Ham for the last time, she prays that "In another world, I am forgiven, I may wake a child and come to you."

After Emily has fled with Steerforth we never see her again first-hand. David does not turn his back on her: he grieves for her misery and for the misery she brings down upon the Peggottys; but he never goes to her when she returns, never talks with her. It is as though, as she herself said. she has ceased to exist. The illusion and the dream, again, must not be violated by the fact.

It is typical of David (as it was of Dickens) that when he finds his old illusions crumbling about him he turns to his new one, Dora, for escape—innocent Dora, who is as clearly as may be a reincarnation of his child mother from the pre-Murdstone past. "All this time"—the time immediately following Emily's flight and the discovery of it—"I had gone on loving Dora harder than ever. Her idea was my refuge in disappointment and distress, and made some amends to me even for the loss of my friend . . . The greater the accumulation of deceit and trouble in the world, the brighter and purer shone the star of Dora high above the world" (p. 474). Here are the bright curls again; and the garden (behind Dora's house, where David and Dora are alone together—"but I was wandering in a garden of Eden all the while . . ."). Marriage with Dora is as close as David comes to realizing in his maturity the "calm, untroubled" times of his childhood—"a party-supper-table kind of life," Aunt Betsey calls it.

This time, however, it is David who changes; Dora, the child, does not; and the mindless bliss of their courtship therefore ends in disappointment and guilty regret. Conceivably their happiness, in effect their childhood, might have been sustained had fate cooperated. However, upon Aunt Betsey's losing her fortune and Mr. Spenlow's dying without one, David is thrown back entirely upon his own resources. David then becomes serious and stu-

dious as Dora grows even more frightened and helpless. Through the conspiracy of circumstances David simultaneously realizes his dream and discovers precisely what it is worth.

It is Dora who invents the name "child-wife," and she asks David to call her that in his mind so that he will not come to expect her to be more than she truly is. "I don't mean, you silly fellow, that you should use this name instead of Dora. I only mean that you should think of me that way. When you are going to be angry with me, say to yourself 'it's only my child-wife!' When I am disappointing, say, 'I knew, a long time ago, that she would make but a child-wife!'" (p. 644). Just before she dies she states very plainly the fact that has broader implications than either she or David realizes: "I am afraid it would have been better, if we had only loved each other as a boy and girl, and forgotten it." The context of this passage suggests that she is dying almost as an act of will.

David's reflections on the same subject have been ambiguous in a significant way, tangled in the conflicting claims of emotion and better judgement. In the chapter entitled "Out Housekeeping" David writes:

> The old unhappy loss or want of something had, I am conscious, some place in my heart; but not to the embitterment of my life. When I walked alone in the fine weather, and thought of the summer days when all the air had been filled with my boyish enchantment, I did miss something of the realisation of my dreams; but I thought it was a softened glory of the Past, which nothing could have thrown upon the present time.
>
> (p. 646)

And then four chapters later he writes again:

> What I missed I still regarded—I always regarded—as something that had been a dream of my youthful fancy; that was incapable of realisation; that I was now discovering to be so, with some natural pain, as all men did. But that it would have been better for me if my wife could have helped me more, and shared the many thoughts in which I had no partner; and that this might have been; I knew.
>
> Between these two irreconcilable conclusions: the one, that what I felt was general and unavoidable; the other, that it was particular to me, and might have been different: I balanced curiously, with no distinct sense of their opposition to each other. When I thought of the airy dreams of youth that are incapable of realisation, I thought of the better state preceding manhood that I had outgrown.
>
> (p. 695)

If we judge from both the tone and the sense of these passages, it is inexact, I believe, to say simply that the something that David "missed" or "wanted" was Agnes, and all that she represents. Dickens has not been very clear—perhaps he could not be clear on this subject—but the suggestion is that David has discovered a conflict between what he wants and what he needs. He wants Dora, and he needs Agnes. By extension he wants a world where the simplicity and the innocence of childhood—"the *better* state preceding manhood"—are perpetual; instead, he must settle for the world as it is, and in this world he needs not a loving baby, a fairy sprite, or a child-bride, but a sober counsellor, a guide, an intellectual companion; in short, things being what they are, he must settle for Agnes.

I am aware that in saying "settle for" I am misrepresenting the spirit in which David and Agnes are united. David *says* in the end that he has loved her all his life, and that now "with a better knowledge" of himself he realizes that in marrying Dora he made their childhood together in Canterbury—probably to sanction the faintly illicit character of their love. When David returns from Switzerland, Agnes has kept everything at the old house as it used to be when they were children—"For we were very happy then, I think." But of course just as Dora never becomes a woman Agnes has never truly been a child. David's love for Agnes is therefore represented as more noble and selfless—"founded on a rock"; her love guides him out of the phantasy world of childhood; always pointing upward, Agnes is ever leading him to "something better; ever directing me to higher things." David's marriage to Agnes we are to take as a symbol of his emotional and intellectual growth.

All the same, Agnes—being chiefly a symbol—is not very convincing as a character. She is not only unrealistic in the conventional sense; unlike Dora, say, she does not seem to have much personal identity even in Dickens's imagination. She seems to exist in her creator's mind more as a set of values and virtues than as an animated and substantial being. She is boring to us, in other words, because in truth she is boring to Dickens; she is to Dickens, fittingly enough, something like what *Paradise Lost* was to Dr. Johnson, more a duty than a pleasure. One therefore has the impression that Dickens has made David feel in fact what he is intellectually aware that he himself *should* feel, but does not. His heart lies with the Claras, and the Emilys, and the Doras; and if we doubt this we need only compare the *brio* and warmth of feeling that goes into their characterizations with the contrived and studied sobriety of those embarrassing last chapters devoted to Agnes.

To put this another way, David, if we are to believe what he says, would have known better than to go chasing after a nonexistent Maria Beadnell, or to try and set up housekeeping with an Ellen Ternan; what is more important, he would not have *wanted* to, quite regardless of what might have been possible. Whatever Maria and Ellen were, judging from what we know of them, they decidedly were got Agneses. No doubt after four-

teen years with Kate, Dickens sometimes felt the want of an Agnes of his own, and one supposes that Georgina, or perhaps Miss Burdett-Coutts, might have filled something of this function; but her seems never to have sought out an Agnes in the times when he was the most desperately dissatisfied.

The world that Dickens most wanted, and probably that most people remember and return to in his works, was a cliché which Dickens somehow manages to make fresh and convincing. Most plainly epitomized in Dingley Dell, it is a world in which the normal order of reason is adjourned, a world set apart from time and society, where people, for good or ill, are always what one imagines them to be and rarely change. Static characters have a special appeal, for they convey the illusion of being rooted in a static world. Dear Peggotty is always there for David to go back to; her face and arms are still red and rough, and she still sticks needles into them; her buttons still fly off; in the end, when she has aged a little, she in still carrying in her pocket the enchanted Crocodile-Book. This imaginary world in Dickens's early novels is populated with child men as well as with child women, ranging from amiable incompetents like Mr. Pickwick (and practically everyone else in that novel) to cheerfully senile encumbrances like Aged Parent and outright lunatics like Mr. Nickleby's suitor, whose idea of courtship is invisibly hurling cucumbers and onions over the garden wall ("He's a deal pleasanter without his senses than with 'em," says his keeper). Many of them are quite literally demented; the rest of them, like the Pickwick entourage or the Cheeryble brothers, simply never had much of a mind to begin with, and never cared to. Most of them are agreeably comic characters, but even the sadder cases, like Barnaby Rudge or Dr. Manette, or more complex ones, like Harold Skimpole, Dickens treats with a strangely envious affection. Each of them has a custodian of some kind, a Sam Weller or a Wemmick, and so in the circumstances most of them do very well; and the context even leaves us wondering sometimes whether they are not happier the way they are: Who after all is better off, Jaggers or Aged P.?

Certainly David's friend Mr. Dick is more than merely eccentric; benevolent and loyal as he is, he is also quite as mad as David first surmises him to be. At the same time, however, he is one of the few good people in the novel whom some misfortune does not befall. He is impervious to the evil of the world for the simple reason that for him the real world is irrelevant. The only troubles he knows are imaginary, and being imaginary they are easily dispatched with by a kind word from Aunt Betsey or David or by an afternoon of kite-flying. For Mr. Dick and the other eccentrics like him there is no difference between things as they are and things as they should be. Intellectually they are children, and the world exists for them almost wholly as a state of mind.

The physical and domestic worlds that Mr. Dick and Aunt Betsey inhabit at Dover might be described as a state of mind of a different order, one that Dickens's own—one of his typical imaginary oases, a refuge from both evil and anxiety. Not knowing what he will find, David flees to Dover from the desolate nightmare of Murdstone and Grimby's. Along his way he learns what the rest of the world is like: a bullying carter steals his bag, shopkeepers in effect steal his money, a sinister tinker threatens his life, the boatmen at Dover ridicule his desperation. When he arrives, grimy and threadbare from his journey, he quite simply cleansed: "'Why, if I was you,' said Mr. Dick, considering and looking vacantly at me . . . 'I should wash him!'" Aunt Betsey's little world is literally and figuratively pristine and neat, and David has been literally and figuratively contaminated. As if this were not obvious enough, we also have the comically symbolic ritual with the donkeys, through which the rest of the outer world is continually kept at bay; and when the Murdstones enter to trespass, on donkeys, they are reduced to stammering straight men and driven off by the righteous outrage of David's eccentric fairy god-mother, the mistress of an enchanted estate.

Serious or comic, contrived or convincing, realistic or fanatic, such Edens recur in Dickens's work with compulsive regularity; and the protagonists are continuously passing through them to and from the stony realities of the outside world. From Dingley Dell to the prison is Pickwick's passage from innocence to experience. There is Oliver Twist's rural retreat and the sordid underworld of Fagin's London. There is the warm austere counting-house of Scrooge. There is Bleak House itself and the Chancery, Joe Gargery's forge and Barnard's Inn. In *David Copperfield* again there is the Rookery of David's childhood; the magical boathouse with its kindly father-figure, Mr. Peggotty; Aunt Betsey's cottage at Dover. In *David Copperfield* each of the retreats is finally destroyed, in effect, by forces from the outside, and David matures, reluctantly, as each one is left behind.

In *Great Expectations* this image is given even greater thematic relevance, When Dickens writes of Wemmick and his two personalities and the two distinct environments in which they have life, Walworth and Little Britain, his description is a consciously contrived parable of a man's compromise with necessity. Wemmick at Little Britain is hard, business-like, and unfeeling; Wemmick at Walworth is carefree, open-hearted, and affectionate, and even romantic. In effect Wemmick leads one half of his life as a man and the other half as a child. It is implies that both the suffering which he is a daily witness to and the moral ambiguities of his trading upon it, both norms in the urban civilization, are an

intolerable psychic burden. He therefore contrives an alternative, a better and simpler world of his own imagination. Its appeal is precisely that it is fantastic, that is, unreal.

If Professor Johnson and the others are right about the way the affair with Ellen went (the evidence is still not very substantial) and about the "establishment" at Peckham, Dickens in his last years seems to have managed a real double life of his own, less bizarre than Wemmick's but conceivably not much different in purpose and effect. Kate was gone for good; Georgina had remained behind, efficiently managing the household and tending the four children that were left; there at Gad's Hill Dickens was the responsible public man, dutifully rendering to the world the labor and commitment that it demands. At Windsor Lodge—"a villa with a large garden—were the other world and the other self, hopefully a domestic paradise and in any case a retreat isolated by anonymity; here lived the innocent girl whom he had fallen in love with when she was eighteen, twenty-seven years his junior. We do not know whether Dickens was happy with what he had done; probably he was not. His intentions, however, seem clear. Each of his existences embodied one half of his ambivalent emotional impulses, and with Ellen he was trying to give life, in the real world, to an illusion, an illusion that could become fact rather than remain simply a projection of his unhappy imagination.

I have ranged this far from *David Copperfield* and into other novels in an effort to substantiate my judgment that Dickens *was* David Copperfield at heart not only as a child but from his childhood until he died; and that ironically unlike David he was in a sense a static character himself which never ceased to envision the possibility of a static world. At first glance this would seem a peculiar affliction to find in a novelist who not long ago was made out to be a political radical. One normally expects revolutionaries to be more tough-minded. Clearly, though, what has been misrepresented as his revolutionary fervor was in fact an effect of the more sentimental side of his nature. His fear and hatred of the bleak new order was a function of his naive and stubborn belief in the possibilities of a simpler and happier life. The two feelings were inseparable in him and the intense bitterness was simply the measure of his intense romantic faith.

Toward the end of his biography John Forster has a telling comment upon the firm purpose with which Dickens has pursued his hopes. He is writing about the final failure of Dickens's marriage, and incidentally the passage hints both at the existence of Ellen and the course the affair with her ultimately took.

> Not his genius only, but his whole nature, was too exclusively made up of sympathy for, and with, the real in its most intense form, to be sufficiently provided against failure in the realities around him. There was for him no "city of the mind" against outward ills, for inner consolation and shelter. It was in and from the actual he still stretched forward to find the freedom and satisfactions of an ideal, and by his very attempts to escape the world he was driven back into the thick of it. But what he would have sought there, it supplies to none; and to get the infinite out of anything so finite, has broken many a stout heart.[5]

To those who have followed the biographies of this century—epitomized by Professor Johnson's—Forster's judgment of Dickens the man will seem remarkably accurate. But he is almost surely wrong about the "city of the mind," for it is there manifestly in the novels, particularly in the early ones, even though it apparently did not offer the consolation and shelter Dickens sought.

All of this is now practically commonplace of Dickens criticism, but the subject can be confused by concentrating exclusively on single aspects. For example, to regard the young heroines simply as neurotic projections of a sexual anxiety is to ignore the imaginary context in which they exist. They are only one, perhaps the most conspicuous, feature in a complicated imaginary landscape. That landscape in itself is a fragile and sequestered inner world, and it is populated by a dozen varieties of child-like adults and children pure and simple who are perpetually menaced by time and by the encroachment of the world outside. It was not moral innocence that Dickens sought, but intellectual innocence; and he was motivated not so much by biology and childhood trauma as by an elusive conspiracy of influences that drove him to withdraw from the frustrations of trying to be a sane and happy man in a complex and maddened industrial society.

Dickens knew what his audience wanted because he was his audience. He was at once everyman and a genius endowed with a gift for incarnating the fictions of his imagination in such a way that they became mythic realities. Because his needs were commonplace, and perhaps as embarrassing to him in her last days as they are to us now, in symbolizing them her was also symbolizing our own. What was true of his effect in his own day is true, perhaps in a different way, of ours: "His readers felt in his work, not only the consolations of a lost Eden, . . . but also the pang of loss, the imagery of all the fears they felt in a world not understood, a world busily bent on excluding them from all satisfactions of love and peace."[6] To take up one of these novels now, David Copperfield without Agnes, is still to turn with Dickens into a vivid and haunted city of the mind.

Notes

1. "The Poet in Relation to Day-dreaming," *Collected Papers,* trans. Joan Riviere (London, 1953), LV, 176.

2. Quoted in Edgar Johnson, *Charles Dickens: His Tragedy and Triumph* (New York, 1952), II, 911.

3. *The Letters of Charles Dickens,* ed. Walter Dexter (London, 1937-38), II, 629. Henceforth cited in text as *Letters.*

4. *David Copperfield,* The New Oxford Illustrated Dickens (London and New York, 1960). All quotations from Dickens's novels are from this edition; page numbers henceforth cited in text.

5. *The Life of Charles Dickens,* ed. J. W. T. Ley (New York, 1928), p. 641.

6. Jack Lindsay, *Charles Dickens* (London, 1950), p. 413.

Dirk Den Hartog (essay date 1981)

SOURCE: Hartog, Dirk Den. "*Little Dorrit*: Dickens's Dialogue with Wordsworth." *The Critical Review,* no. 23 (1981): 3-19.

[*In the following essay, Hartog maintains that through his characters in* Little Dorrit *Dickens engages in a debate with William Wordsworth's contention that childhood experiences play an integral role in the formation of an individual's psyche.*]

Recent scholarship has given us a much more detailed picture of the influence of the English Romantics upon Victorian culture; it has also touched on the contribution to novelistic psychology of the Romantics' view of the relationship between childhood and adulthood—the originating and major instance being, of course, Wordsworth's exploration of the ways in which "the Child is Father to the Man", and of the necessary and desirable continuity between early and later selves. For Wordsworth (and his contemporary followers), the childhood past is not simply a determining force in the psyche, to be acknowledged and negotiated with. Because of the normally benign emotional and imaginative influences of primal relationships, childhood is a crucial source of vitality and moral feeling. The self-in-time is conceived in terms of a metaphor of organic plant-growth ("Fair seed-time had my soul"), with the implication by analogy that to lose touch with one's personal past is to invite spiritual malnutrition. Hence the almost religious duty not just of confronting one's past, but of maintaining fidelity to it, of positively embracing it. Hence, too, the deeply conservative implications of this way of thinking about the self: a rediscovery of the "hiding-places of . . . power" in the personal past goes hand in hand with the renunciation of "impatient or fallacious" political hopes, and the desire of "throwing off the incumbrances" of social life. As the nineteenth century proceeded, that emphasis loomed large in the Victorian

novel, which can be seen as seeking, through the Wordsworthian conception of the self, for a spiritual authority sufficiently persuasive to constrain those restlessly expansive energies which contemporary society could not respectably accommodate. But as with all models of Man, of course, the Wordsworthian one is a mixture of disinterested perception and ideological imposition.

For both Wordsworth and George Eliot, early life and adult temperament were such as to make the organic continuity of the self plausible and appealing. Dickens's early life, by contrast, was notoriously different, and it seems reasonable to connect that fact with his very un-Wordsworthian adult nature. It is not altogether true, however, that his response to the past was simply the obverse of Wordsworth's and Eliot's, as several recent critics have suggested. Surprisingly, given the nature of what he had to remember, his writings attempt to work within the Wordsworthian framework. What we find is rather a conflict in him between a natural resentment of his past—issuing, as biographical accounts of his rise to fame show, in a fierce resolve to free himself from it—and a Wordsworthian acknowledgement of dependence on it as a source of emotional nourishment and stability.

David Copperfield is a case in point. It explores David's (Dickens's) past in a spirit of genial acceptance—but it can do so mainly because David, being amiable, boyish, unaggressive, is a purified, or rather, emasculated version of his creator. Purged of Dickens's own self-assertive readiness to resent the past, and thus by nature disposed idealistically to gloss over his mother's shortcomings (and being somewhat helped to do so by the details of the fictional plot), David is able to bask in the glow of nostalgia. In *Little Dorrit*, Amy is an even more extreme case of someone who by her mildness sustains a single-mindedly faithful attitude towards her exploitation-ridden past; she embodies something that Dickens himself, drawn to Wordsworthian psychology perhaps by his very restlessness, would dearly have liked to have had. On the other hand, it is remarkable that such fidelity to the past can be sustained in the un-Wordsworthian social world of *Little Dorrit* only by someone so extraordinary and so unlike Dickens as Amy. For the more one looks at her, the more ambiguous and uncertain a figure she seems, the more unresolved Dickens finally seems to be about what really to make of her. (The same goes for Tattycoram too, Amy's opposite.) Dickens seems to be at once paying his tribute to the Wordsworthian truths in canonizing Amy, while at the same time expressing a reserve about the cost of such an allegiance in an underlying scepticism about this valuation. It is this that makes *Little Dorrit* for me finally a richer and more probing novel of memory than the more charming *David Copperfield*. Where the latter simply concurs with Wordsworthian psychology, and gains its special beauty of tone by a self-suppression on Dickens's part, *Little Dorrit* is a

free-ranging dialogue with it. Which is why his own angry and sarcastic voice in the later novel so readily turns the narrator's role into the novel's main dramatic presence, recurrently threatening to upstage the fictional hero and heroine. To approach the novel like this, though, is to reduce it too much to biographical terms, and to neglect the pretty thorough impersonalization it achieves, the extent to which private tensions are seen as representative social phenomena. We need to give full acknowledgement to the various contexts of social depiction and debate into which the portrait of Amy Dorrit is inserted.

The first of these is the marvellous study—centred upon William Dorrit and radiating outwards to the Gowans and Barnacles—of the dynamics of genteel hegemony, or, as the novel sees it, the social creation of unreality. It's perhaps the most obvious sign of how far the mature Dickens had moved away from the eighteenth-century tradition of static and self-contained characters, towards seeing both protagonists *and* social worlds in terms of processes by which identities are shaped into merely provisional and contingent solidity. Where in the earlier novels comic characters had performed themselves as spontaneous emanations of their being, here performance is a crucial element in the self's continuation. This is certainly the case with Dorrit's chosen identity of lordly gentleman, which requires the continual assumption of the patronizing role. The performance requires the active compliance of others, a willingness in them to assume complementary parts in the "drama" the main character is initiating.

Dickens delights in parodying the language of Dorrit's performances, yet in contrast to the vital if ludicrous linguistic extravagance of earlier types (of whom Flora Finching in this novel is a survivor) is the pleasure we are invited to take in picking our way through the evasions of Dorrit's maze to arrive at its empty centre. This is a sign of the other most interesting trait of his performances, which is their brittleness. For along with Pip, and to some extent David Copperfield, Dorrit is a major study in that kind of insecurity we might call social vertigo—a sensed fragility of the assumed identity. (It is perhaps Dickens's negative version of the Wordsworthian continuity: the liability of the past to implode destructively upon the present.) This nervousness is seen to derive from the tenuousness of the whole system of interlocking roles of which Dorrit is the jittery centre. His psychology touches on something in all of us, perhaps, but he also has a specific social typicality: he represents, partly by analogy, Dickens's deepening interpretation of the psychic condition of the socially mobile person, a condition he seems to have been the first to treat compassionately from the inside. (It was also, of course, Dickens's own state; which suggests why his problematic relationship to memory also has its own socially representative aspect. Was the transition

from *Little Dorrit* to *Great Expectations* not a realization that the attempt to achieve gentility, even in the face of a vertiginous sense of its "unnaturalness", could not be judged in the simply negative way required by Dorrit's case?) All this may well seem to be taking me far from my point, but I hope it is clear enough just how this rather un-Wordsworthian focus on urban social reality nevertheless brings into play Wordsworthian notions about present and past selves. Since the cause of Dorrit's insecurity is largely his denial of his past, his case points to a consideration of the Wordsworthian prerequisites for psychic stability. Interest in Amy Dorrit, who (as a heroine of fidelity) has a contrastingly solid and permanent identity, grows inevitably out of this.

The second social issue in the novel to which Amy is relevant is its running argument with itself about what one might call the moral status of discontent. A number of commentators have seen this, or something like it, as one of *Little Dorrit*'s main concerns, taking Amy as one "answer" in the contest between the appeals of passionate rebellion and Christian resignation. Lionel Trilling's essay in *The Opposing Self* is especially useful. It locates the novel in the context of a post-French Revolutionary, post-Romantic debate about the possibilities of liberation; and it demonstrates the novel's complexity of moral attitude, its awareness of imprisonment both as a remediable social ill and as an inevitable human condition. This sort of complexity can be seen in many aspects of the novel that Trilling doesn't mention. Arthur Clennam, for instance, soon chnges from a man who has good qualities despite his Nonconformist upbringing to one in whom they are paradoxically inseparable from it. Dickens insists on a gentleness in his earnestness, but it is not *just* gentleness that is shown to drive Clennam in the tenacity of conscience with which he pursues his suspicions; it is a sternness that seems the unqualified consequence of his mother's code:

> It was in vain that he tried to control his attention by directing it to any business occupation or train of thought; it rode at anchor by the haunting topic, and would hold to no other idea. As though a criminal should be chained in a stationary boat on a deep clear river, condemned, whatever countless leagues of water flowed past him, always to see the body of the fellow-creature he had drowned lying at the bottom, immovable, and unchangeable, except as the eddies made it broad or long, now expanding, now contracting its terrible lineaments; so Arthur, below the shifting current of transparent thoughts and fancies which were gone and succeeded by others as soon as come, saw, steady and dark, and not to be stirred from its place, the one subject that he endeavoured with all his might to rid himself of, and that he could not fly from.
>
> (p. 742, Penguin edition)

"Criminal", "condemned": the sensibility here directly recalls that Nonconformity which in the opening chapters was merely the object of satire, and the sermonic

eloquence of the narrative is quite at ease in evoking the awesomeness of the inflexible moral imperative. Dickens shows a range of sympathies here not usually accorded to him, reaching beyond his habitual assumptions to recognize something undeniably impressive in Clennam's dour toughness. Later, in a kind of subsidiary echo of this (one that seems to have been quite overlooked by the novel's critics), Mrs Clennam herself is allowed to break free from our normally comic-diagnostic image of her to achieve a telling dignity in her final confrontation with Blandois.

The cumulative effect of such cases as these is to qualify the novel's powerful wish to believe in, and proclaim, the possibilities of liberation. For Arthur, to win complete freedom from his repressive background would be to become, Dickens sees, so much the lesser man. He also sees that simply to dismiss Chivery as a *petit-bourgeois* dupe would be to opt for moral stupidity in the interests of political convenience. Hence the fact that the pervasive social anger of the novel finds fictional gratification only in the minor and comic uprisings of Affery and Pancks, while the central thrust of the plot *seems* to affirm the quietist resignation of Amy, in whom the conservative implications of the Wordsworthian ideal are strongly marked.

Even to a comparatively quick glance, then, *Little Dorrit* must appear as an exploratory novel, which reveals a passion for change and liberation, and yet radically ponders the validity of such hopes. In this it exemplifies the awareness of difficulty and complexity which is the hallmark of the specifically liberal intelligence (Trilling has written finely on this point in *The Liberal Imagination*). Such values are of course very much under attack today by the literary-critical *avant-garde*, who argue that post-Arnoldian criticism has used them as ideology under the guise of a proclaimed disinterestedness. Terence Hawkes, for instance, claims that the pre-eminence accorded to complexity has legitimized the evasion of political commitment. In this context, *Little Dorrit* can help us make the crucial discrimination as to where such a charge is true and where it isn't. For far from ministering to an underlying complacency, the kind of recognition of complexity and difficulty we get here strikes me as something won very much *against* the work's emotional temper, which boils fervently for simplicity and action. For this reason it seems to me that the novel's liberalism is genuinely disinterested, as the play of intelligence that yields the inclusiveness of vision is visibly free of determining pressures. Actually, much of what has traditionally struck some critics as Dickens's ungentlemanly rawness is an oddly admirable dissonance of feeling and perception.

Dickens's treatment of Amy has a genuine complexity. She emerges, I think, as neither a "solution" to the dilemmas of discontent, nor, as other critics would have

it, an evasion of them. Being conceived very much in terms of the Wordsworthian ideal of continuity, she is nevertheless placed—almost experimentally—in a situation radically different from any Wordsworthian norm; and, as part of the flexibility I've been claiming for Dickens, that ideal of continuity is both considered as an answer to this situation and in turn tested by it. One can begin to get at the Wordsworthian import of Amy by considering her family's charge that she is a "complete prison-child" (p. 419) for her inability to join in their pretensions. They are in a sense right, though in this they are mainly paying her an unwitting compliment. What they uncomprehendingly register, in fact, is the quality of spirit that links her closely to Wordsworth's feminine ideal. Her spontaneous, unwilled contentment with the restrictions of her life is close to the philosophy of the Wordsworth who, "moderated and composed", regained health and sanity at Grasmere under the influence of a sister who "Welcomed what was given, and craved no more . . .". This ideal reconciled active domestic responsibility with the essentially Wordsworthian value of the mind's self-possessed repose. The major locale for, and physical analogue of, such repose in the poetry is the scene of contained space, felt not as constriction but as refuge, "a fixed centre of a troubled world". A minor sonnet, undistinguished but representative in outlook, suggests a transition to Amy:

> Nuns fret not at their convent's narrow room;
> And hermits are contented with their cells;
> And students with their pensive citadels;
> Maids at the wheel, the weaver at his loom,
> Sit blithe and happy; bees that soar for bloom,
> High as the highest Peak of Furness-fells,
> Will murmur by the hour in foxglove bells:
> *In truth, the prison, into which we doom*
> *Ourselves, no prison is . . .*

> [my italics]

The vacuous collocation here ("Nuns . . . weavers . . . bees") already expresses a smugly High Tory vision of social harmony as a pastoral idyll (the poem appeared in 1807). Amy Dorrit, on the other hand, might be said to represent Dickens's inquiry into the validity of such an ideal, under the complicating pressures of life as typified by the Marshalsea rather than Grasmere. For her "the prison . . . which . . . no prison is" is a prison indeed, although she apparently bears it without sign of struggle.

It could of course be argued that such parallels reveal merely a common allegiance to general post-Romantic assumptions about the nature of goodness. Yet there are, I think, more specific connections: Amy's affectionate relationship with the grim Marshalsea itself, for instance, as "her birthplace and home". This seems very like a variation on Wordsworth's major theme—that the spiritually healthy self has to be rooted in a particular place, or places, hallowed by memory. True, there can

be nothing of that imaginative resonance of the memory which, in Wordsworth, is at once rooted in the immediacies of time and place, and yet opens out, through these, towards recognition of the "beyondness" of the immanent Spirit. In Dickens (as in George Eliot) this is secularized, as it were; it provides an interesting and plausible psychological explanation of how Amy's extraordinariness arises, and it enables the conservative implications of the continuity idea to be brought within the range of common life, where resignation is bound to be a grimmer business. Nevertheless, the key to Amy's spontaneous goodness is clearly her unresisting fidelity to her childhood affections, either as invested in place, or situated directly in people. Wordsworth's point, of course, was that the two are inseparable; and indeed Amy's self-definitive gesture of kissing the prison bars, and her feeling the gate to be a companion, are acts of filial piety. Moreover, she does have something to be faithful to. Her upbringing in the unwholesome Dorrit family *has* made available a kind of affection and given her a subsequent sense of security. The primary bonds of feeling have been freely implanted in her innermost being, and her relationship with the immediate world, which is interfused with these bonds, is consequently one of affectionate belonging, by virtue of which the sordid and dreary nature of this world is redeemed, "irradiated" if not "exalted". In one sense she has even been the favourite of the family, "by far the best loved of the three", as her father puts it with a kind of honesty (p. 275). Wryly enough, his lethargic conceit and hidden infantile dependence (perceptively allowed to surface only in his breakdown) are themselves shown to contribute to her emotional stability. As he has never rejected her ministering attention in prison, she has consequently never felt unwanted. The novel is never simple-minded about the play of feeling within the family, and never just re-writes Cinderella. Fanny's embrace, for instance, is "a really fond one" (p. 666).

The crucial deviation of Amy's case from the Wordsworthian norm is that with "love" she has absorbed massive does of exploitation and condescension. This brings up the ambiguity in Dickens's own feelings towards his past, and the reflection of this in a certain irresolution in the depiction of Amy, or an ambiguity in the way we are meant to see her.

Several critics in the last few years have moved away from the old debate about Amy's reality as a heroine, to questioning whether she really is given to us as a heroine at all. Instead of "the Paraclete in human form" (Trilling's unfortunate phrase) or "miraculously intervening goodness" (Raymond Williams's), Amy has been seen as a conscious or semi-conscious study in neurotic self-denial. This view of her does underline a lot of things previous discussions have missed, and it does, I think, make the traditional view untenable. But it also tends to assume that the inadequacies in Amy are in

fact recognized as such by the author—which leaves it a puzzle why Dickens proclaims Amy so explicitly *as* a heroine pure and simple (something he never does with Esther Summerson). This view of the novel, in fact, makes no real sense of the novel's disunity; at best, it recognizes the fact of division, but tends to explain it, rather too patly, as a surface commitment in Dickens to a conventional Victorian ideal of feminine selflessness masking an underlying scepticism. In fact, Dickens seems at different points of the novel to be deeply committed to both heroizing and diagnostic explanations: to explain away the former as superficial seems quite wilful. This ambiguity may illustrate the way he both is and is not a typical middle-class Victorian, but to understand it here, I think we need to notice the novel's curiously unsteady attitude towards Amy's relationship with her past, which for *her* flows evenly into the present.

One example of this is the handling of the first focal issue in Amy's case: her burdensome role as the mainstay of a family of spongers. The way she is introduced to us suggests that the Paraclete in human form may well be what Dickens has in mind:

> . . . how much, or how little of the wretched truth it pleased God to make visible to her . . . lies hidden with many mysteries. It is enough that she was inspired to be something which was not what the rest were, and to be that something, different and laborious, for the sake of the rest. Inspired? Yes.
>
> (p. 111)

This hovers between a realistic and an allegorical-moralistic mode, inclining towards "miraculously intervening goodness". The mood continues as the résumé of her early years proceeds into her childhood:

> No matter through what mistakes and encouragements. . . . She took the place of the eldest of the three, in all things but precedence; was the head of the fallen family; and bore, in her own heart, its anxieties and shames.
>
> (pp. 111-2)

The first passage concedes, in its high-toned way, that Amy as a young child may well have been happily ignorant of much of her family's moral squalor. The second seems to be saying, or implying at least, that later years brought full knowledge. This is not an unbelievable claim, and it is consonant with the lofty conception of her Dickens seems to be unfolding. Nevertheless, the next chapter, when she first meets Clennam, would seem to qualify this:

> Her look at her father, half admiring him and proud of him, half-ashamed for him, all devoted and loving, went to his inmost heart.
>
> (p. 122)

There's nothing openly critical here, but one does wonder why, if she is bearing the family shame in quite the way the earlier passage suggests, she could be shown as even half admiring her father. One understands how she *needs* to do this, and the next dozen or so chapters go on to develop a poignant and well-observed picture of her struggle to believe in her father's illusions. In a painful first interview with Clennam, she rationalizes Dorrit's behaviour by explaining it as the consequence of his being in prison, and as a just exaction of the tribute due to his gentlemanly superiority; she then hopefully tries to convince Clennam that it is simply her father's "anxiety" about his children which makes her hide the fact that she and Fanny go out to work (pp. 137-9). Later, she even develops a theory that it is not really Dorrit's "true" self that Clennam is seeing—she's a great believer in his illusion of a nobler past self (which is quietly placed in anticipation by our own first image of him in chapter six). I don't think, either, that all this can be seen as a mere keeping up of appearances; her "innocent", "boastful" "pride" in speaking of her father's manners hardly suggests this. Rather, her protestations to Clennam seem to be a way of sustaining a faith by declaring it, though her faith is understandably fragile, and her "boasting" is soon followed by the admission that "people might not think so well of him outside as they do in prison". Dickens's explicit authorial commentary persists with a purely ennobling interpretation of such faith (see p. 138), but against this, a somewhat different image begins to emerge: not of the moral or psychological cripple some critics seem to find in her, but of a human being with a human propensity towards self-protective illusion, who has not yet achieved the difficult maturity of laying this aside.

This doubleness is related, I think, to Dickens's own double attitude to his past. If he overtly indulges her tendency to evade those perceptions which would most challenge her fidelity, this obviously goes with an impulse to celebrate her in Wordsworthian terms. On the other hand, his own incapacity for Amy's kind of single-minded acceptance, much as he would like to have it (his *Autobiographical Fragment* is very revealing about this), is surely behind his capacity to show Amy's heroic devotion as dependent in her on what we must finally call a weakness, albeit tolerantly so. If weakness sounds too moralistic, it is certainly an absence in her of a clear-sightedness that could hardly be deemed immoral, though it makes Christian resignation more difficult for those people who possess it, like Tattycoram (to some extent), or Dickens himself (though his temporarily harmonious reconciliation with his past in *David Copperfield* might be said to represent a conscious version of Amy's evasiveness).

A similar pattern is suggested by the way the Dorrit family treats Amy. Exploitation and injustice certainly figure prominently here; indeed, this is one main focus of the novel's general engagement with these things as the prevailing conditions of its world, and of its inquiry into how people ought to live in such circumstances. This latter question is raised explicitly in Meagles's comic-serious disagreement with Miss Wade in the second chapter about whether or not a prisoner forgives his prison. Despite the balanced sympathies invited by this exchange, Amy's ostensible moral heroism would seem to bring the novel down firmly on one side, for her achievement is precisely that of forgiving her (very real) prison. Nevertheless, one can't but wonder what exactly she has to forgive, as she never seems quite to face the fact that she is being treated unjustly. One major cause of this is a (somewhat convenient) failure to discriminate between genuine kindness in others and the odiously patronizing benevolence that her father goes in for. Thus, when attacked by him and Fanny for walking arm-in-arm with Nandy, she protests that if she hadn't known of his kindness to the old man, she wouldn't have done it (p. 420). Since she is not her wittier and more agile sister, one must take her as speaking in all innocence, and take this as a clue to how much of the truth about her family's behaviour towards her she does comprehend. It's interesting, however, that one needs clues on this score, for Dickens is curiously reserved about exactly how she does see things at times. Where his earlier reticence about probing the mysteries of a young child's consciousness is quite proper, with the elder Amy he seems to be choosing rather deviously how much to know about her knowledge. The narrative reveals her thoughts neither immediately after this scene, nor after a similar one later where she is charged with unfeelingly resurrecting the past; and the one explicit comment on her reaction to Fanny's condescension towards her is teasingly ambiguous about whether she is habituated to putting up with something she sees, or inured to simply not noticing it (see p. 557). It is almost as if Dickens himself is a bit embarrassed about the implications of admitting her to be so unseeing, for while such perceptions are acute about the kind of mystification of the innocent that a family like the Dorrits could well accomplish, they do threaten Amy's status as moral heroine by suggesting the relative ease of the moral life to her. It is a threat that at this stage of the work Dickens will allow into the novel, but not explicitly confront—hence his attempt (p. 557) to pass off Amy's self-protective naivety as superior Romantic innocence.

We seem to have a case here, then, of the novel's explicit judgment actively obscuring what the presented facts of the portrait imply, which is someone in whom the difficulty of the moral life is alleviated to the point where one can only accept her as a moral heroine in a special or qualified sense. Dickens's awareness of what he's doing on this score is problematic in the first half of the novel, but by Part Two, and Amy's travels, it seems to me more certain that we are being given an

analysis of someone whose exemplary fidelity derives not from moral virtue pure and simple but from a dominating need, sympathetically but dispassionately seen. In Venice, for example, which clearly has a beautiful but disconcerting charm for her but where she is bereft of the familiar things of her life, it is as if the very solidity of her identity—that which makes her a touchstone of value when set against the unreality of many of the others in her world—is in danger of dissolution. She goes about with a "quiet, scared, lost manner"; she "only asked leave to be left alone" (p. 519). As her sense of her own reality has been built on servitude to her family, so, the implication clearly goes, its removal and the consequent freedom for her is too fearful to be borne. Her work is not something that she does from pure asceticism, for it is only *through* that that she derives any secure sense of self at all. Similarly, when Arthur first tells her of her family's change of fortune, her realization that soon "all the familiar experiences would have vanished away" makes her look not sad but "frightened" (p. 467)—a fear that has nothing to do with any premonition of family *vanitas*. The depression she reports in her letters to Clennam has less to do with moral concern than with the newly-acquired servants leaving her "quite lost by her task being done".

During the course of the novel, Dickens seems somehow to have developed the assurance to look at Amy from a consciously psychological perspective, rather than a directly moralizing one. We are still shown her loving concern for her father, for example, but there is a new candour about admitting her gratification in it (see p. 668). Few of Dickens's critics have remarked on this change of tone; but it registers, I think, a new detachment, a more certain recognition that Amy's kind of unproblematic fidelity is not necessarily to be seen as a moral ideal standing intimidatingly against the more divided spirit of others. Dickens now seems free to see it as the product of a special kind of temperament—one in which, for no intrinsically moral reason, the need for security predominates over the need for self-assertion. One example is a passage from the Venice chapters, a masterly rendering of consciousness from within:

> Such people were not realities to the little figure of the English girl; such people were all unknown to her. She would watch the sunset, in its long low lines of purple and red, and its burning flush high up into the sky: so glowing on the buildings, and so lightening their structure, that it made them look as if their strong walls were transparent, and they shone from within. She would watch those glories expire; and then, after looking at the black gondolas underneath, taking guests to music and dancing, would raise her eyes to the shining stars. Was there no party of her own, in other times, on which the stars had shone? To think of that old gate now!
>
> She would think of that old gate, and of herself sitting at it in the dead of night, pillowing Maggy's head; and of other places and of other scenes associated with

those different times. And then she would lean upon her balcony, and look over at the water, as though they all lay underneath it. When she got to that, she would musingly watch it running, as if, in the general vision, it might run dry, and show her the prison again, and herself, and the old room, and the old inmates, and the old visitors: all lasting realities that had never changed.

<div align="right">(p. 520)</div>

The *cost* of her integrity is enforced here with a new severity. "Continuity . . . in self-consciousness" is exemplified in the instinctive play of her thought and imagination, and this instinctiveness suggests that the past is not just the core of her present being, which the self is free to reject (though at a price), but an almost inflexible prison of it. She reacts to the memories with a sense of relief, regaining by them her natural sense of gravity, her "real" self we are tempted to say. She needs them. Yet inseparably interfused with this is an uncompromising sense of the comparative bleakness of that self. We feel the harsh force of "run dry", placed as it is against the dream-like vagueness of the town-scape; the repetition of "old" brings together both reassuring familiarity and monotony—a monotony that the novel at this point couldn't at all see as "sweet". Indeed, the pathos here seems to me to be directed not, as we might expect, at Amy as the virtuous victim of others, but at that, implanted in her by others, by which she is virtuous. The firmness with which the theory of continuity was used to show goodness as necessarily deriving from "deep immovable roots", to use George Eliot's phrase, becomes here a pressure to interpret that "goodness" as something else, something not unambiguously desirable.

I hope it is now clear what I mean by saying that, through Amy Dorrit, Dickens is not so much echoing the tenets of Wordsworthian moral psychology as entering into an exploratory dialogue with them. Moreover, he is interested in an element in Amy that actually contradicts the submissiveness and backward-looking fidelity I have so far been accepting as her defining traits, whatever the understanding and valuation of them may be. On the surface, the tale of her love for Clennam and its eventual fulfilment may only seem a matter of the final, just discovery of the hidden violet. In fact, as with Clennam, it is also seen to involve a liberation of the self from a perverse self-denial, and even, in the proposal scene, to involve too a touch of demure self-assertion:

> He might have released the light little hand after fervently kissing it again; but that, with a very gentle lingering where it was, it seemed to court being retained. He took it in both of his, and it lay softly on his breast.

<div align="right">(p. 884)</div>

It's much too exquisite a gesture to be called a "pass", but it does disclose a quiet sexuality—a womanliness— that finally triumphs over the mutually reinforcing self-

doubt and reticence in which their undeclared love has been poignantly imprisoned. For her to be able to make such a gesture is an achievement, the culminating point in a struggle for self-transcendence that has been carefully traced throughout. Her vision of the de-realizing radiance of Venice, which so suggestively conveys her isolation from social life, had also hinted at this more valuable kind of "reality" and expansive liberation, even though the remoteness and impalpability of the visual scene matched a remote and vaguely indeterminate quality in the desire. There is, in fact, a whole series of scenes to do with her pensive brooding over water, looking out of her window, and the illusory play of sunlight upon prison-bars, which has been woven into the narrative since her earlier visits to the Iron Bridge, all of which represent a contrary movement of feeling *away* from the terms in which her character has been chiefly established, a tender shoot of fresh growth towards a fuller self. Arthur Clennam is the (at this stage) distant focus of these hopes; but one of the purposes of introducing the comic infatuation of John Chivery is to reassure us of her sexual eligibility, and of a will in her to defend her self from the claims of others—a will that qualifies the idea of her as someone who always gives. As her secret love gathers, she uncharacteristically seeks out the solitude in her room; there is, we realize, a subjectivity beyond the Little Mother persona—a persona that even she can at times feel as an imposition.

What all this suggests is that the received notion of Amy as a static character is mistaken. Beyond the overtly given personality, Dickens presents a developing interaction between it and an impulse towards a more inclusive self. Amy is no Jane Eyre, of course, and the interaction is consequently a matter of quiet struggle, easily missed beneath her surface calm. But we can see it in the novel's use of Amy's imputed likeness to a child. Here, we seem to have the same awareness as is presented in Esther Summerson and her nicknames, of how naming at once discloses and confines identity. Clennam's calling her "my child" is natural enough, given her physique and manner, and Victorian conventions; but his role of chivalrous and fatherly protector soon comes to be a means of hiding from himself his true feelings. Amy, in turn, generally accepts the name; it seems a convenient description of what she mainly is. Before long, however, she shows unease about it ("A slight shade of distress fell upon her, at his so often calling her a child" (p. 209)), which is a discomfort with the non-sexual role into which Clennam has cast her. True, the emergent self that feels the discomfort is as fragile as her physique; it's characteristic that her "distress" doesn't articulate itself in words, being left to the sensitive Clennam to notice if not to understand. It's also vulnerable, and she is prone to disavow it under the pressure of embarrassment and anxiety, as when her subsequent letters from Italy show her actually asking Clennam to think of her as his "poor child". It is left to Arthur at the end to come to think of her "not as the poor child . . . but as a woman" (p. 829). Her struggle towards growth is as much with herself as with others. Her meekness is also reinforced by the way in which retreat so plausibly presents itself as loyalty—as when, upset by her family's begging-letters to Clennam, she finally justifies her hasty departure from him in these terms:

> But I had better go home! It was but the other day that my sister told me I had become so used to the prison that I had its tone and character. It must be so. I am sure it must be when I see these things. My place is there. I am better there. It is unfeeling in me to be here, when I can do the least thing there. Good-bye. I had far better stay at home!
>
> (p. 308)

The cruel irony of this is that her best feelings are engaged in it: it looks like a declaration of fidelity and is felt by her as such. In one sense it is, of course, in that it's an abiding by those "lasting realities" in which her self is founded. Yet while these are indeed at the core of her being, they are not her complete self: the kind of antithesis between "true self" and "false self" that her words imply is clearly too simple. The possibilities represented by the Iron Bridge and Clennam, which she seeks to renounce here, are not unreal in the pejorative sense that her father's world is, but only in that, tender growths as they are, they have not been solidified by custom. But as with all people caught in a nostalgia for origins, she understandably can't see that what seems to be integrity is in fact a form of self-betrayal. The same, too, goes for the homesickness with which she reacts to Italy: with her source of security gone, her psyche withdraws upon the past at the sacrifice of its tentative yearnings towards the future. Hence, whereas being called a child by Clennam had previously been a bit cramping, she now welcomes it as a needful reassurance that she is still *somebody's* child. The eventual marriage is so felicitous because, by at once echoing and transforming her original situation, it acknowledges both realities of her being, the old and the new.

In Tattycoram we can see a further consideration of the issues raised by Amy's case. Her situation is clearly a variation on Amy's, though one where all the terms that link them are deliberately altered, as in a formal experiment. Thus, while it contains the same elements of inequality, condescension and kindness, the kindness in her case would seem to be more disinterested, the inequality perhaps more justifiable, and the condescension possibly merely imagined; though the difficulty of making such discriminations with any confidence is partly the point of the comparison. Tattycoram's nature, too, is a mirror-opposite of Amy's: her "lustrous dark hair and eyes" (p. 55) signal a passionateness that contrasts with Amy, and this connects with her opposite

way of reading and reacting to her circumstances—her "full red lips" (p. 240) are significantly noticeable when she is being defiant. Again, in contrast to Amy's heroism of memory, Tatty's flight from her home is in one sense a revolt against her personal past; in obvious contrast to Amy's dependence on her family, part of Miss Wade's appeal to Tatty is in her superficial appearance of complete autonomy. Explicit comparison of the two is also invited by their quaint, identity-conferring names, their differing reactions to which are also significant. And they are finally brought together in overt comparison at the end of the novel by Meagles's would-be edifying sermon on Duty.

All this, however, merely underlines another kind of similarity: it is equally difficult to decide how we are finally meant to judge Tattycoram. Does she represent a persuasive challenge to Amy's overt status as moral heroine, a dramatized proof in her restless vitality that Amy can only be so good because of some deficiency? Does she, that is, represent a revolt of Dickens's whole turbulent being against his sentimental longing to envisage an unproblematic relationship with an embittering past, to imagine someone who *can* forgive his prison? Or does her "unfortunate temper" simply throw Amy into even more exemplary relief, as Meagles thinks it does? Dickens generally seems to be doing his best to keep this question open. Even simple bodily signs partake of ambiguity: Tatty's "lustrous dark hair and eyes" and "full red lips" could be taken to express positive vitality, as similar traits do in Sissy Jupe; but they are also close enough to conventional Victorian insignia of the "dark lady", as seen in their pure form in Miss Wade, to have an air of duplicity about them.

It's not surprising, therefore, that critics have gauged the novel's sympathies on this score so differently, either veering selectively towards extremes—one critic has recently declared Meagles's conduct to be "without exception exemplary", while another finds that "Miss Wade's analysis of [Meagles's] oppressive paternalism rings true"—or hovering vaguely in the middle. Yet the novel's double stance towards its chief rebel seems to me to have been inescapable, for it is part of that dialogue with Wordsworth which is also conducted through the novel's ostensible Wordsworthian saint.

To start with, what is the motive of Tattycoram's revolt? Inequality, surely. This would seem to be the point of our being introduced to her at Marseilles, the Revolutionary connotations of which are enforced by Meagles's amiable but obtuse views about the French and about forgiving one's prison, upon which Tattycoram confronts Meagles with a form of "allonging and marshonging" within his own family circle. Similar ideological overtones also mark Tatty's relations with Miss Wade, and it is the egalitarian nature of Tatty's resentment that Miss Wade plays upon so skilfully in their

opening encounter. In fact Tatty is a nicely-observed cameo of the troubled relations between feeling and language, her initial state stemming from the clash of her impulse to rebel and her internalization of Meagles's dismissal of this as "temper". Miss Wade's first role towards her is thus that of the liberating revolutionary intellectual, providing the repressed feelings with a legitimating analysis.

But there is another explanation of Tatty's conduct than this strictly political one. Meagles persistently explains her to himself in terms of the unhappy temper produced by her orphan background, and this—conveniently for him—dissolves the political question of the inequities of her situation with his family into something that can be indulgently allowed for without cost to his self-esteem. This looks like an intelligent stroke on Dickens's part: Meagles's classic self-protective manoeuvre enhances our sense of his complacency. That Dickens gives Tatty an actually deprived early life makes the necessary anti-simplistic point: even Meagleses need seductive plausibilities to hang their rationalizations upon. Yet for all that, we are given no objective evidence that Meagles's account *is* the wrong one. Self-interested explanations may be suspect, but they are not necessarily false. His report on Tatty's departing accusation, for instance, allows one to infer egalitarian righteousness or neurotic jealousy as governing motives, according to one's own ideological fancy:

> . . . she was determined to go away. She was younger than her young mistress, and would she remain to see *her* always held up as the only creature who was young and interesting, and to be cherished and loved? No. She wouldn't, she wouldn't, she wouldn't! What did we think she, Tattycoram, might have been if she had been caressed and cared for in her childhood, like her young mistress? As good as her? Ah! Perhaps fifty times as good.
>
> (p. 371)

It's only realistic to acknowledge that motives are always mixed; but to leave the question quite so wide open seems to be more a matter of hedging bets. To have taken Tatty firmly at her revolutionary face-value would have presented a clear choice between either endorsing her at the expense of Amy's status in our eyes, or clearly rejecting the egalitarian values she ostensibly stands for, at least when they conflict with the loyalties of memory and dependence. In leaving open the possibility that her revolt may be unjustified because determined by ulterior motives, Dickens is side-stepping this decision, which in fact is a further way of maintaining his irresolution about Amy. If we're inclined to a radical interpretation we can take such things as the "playful" name as a prime cause of Tatty's revolt, as signs of a failure to take her seriously as a person. An equally plausible account, however, would be that the name is simply a tactless exacerbation of an earlier, deeper-

rooted leaning towards discontent. Similarly, Meagles's niceness can be seen as a way of making either the radical point—that it is inequality itself which breeds strain in spirited subordinates, and not the personality of the superior—or alternatively, the point that only someone whose motives derive from circumstances external to the present situation could come to hate such a benevolent employer. What, then, of Tatty's own explanation of her revolt?

> "Oh! I have been so wretched," cried Tattycoram, weeping much more, "always so unhappy, and so repentant! I was afraid of her from the first time I saw her. I knew she had got a power over me through understanding what was bad in me so well. It was a madness in me, and she could raise it whenever she liked. I used to think, when I got into that state, that people were all against me because of my first beginning; and the kinder they were to me, the worse fault I found in them. I made it out that they triumphed above me, and that they wanted to make me envy them, when I know—when I even knew then—that they never thought of such a thing."

(p. 880)

The novel's perceptiveness here first claims our attention. The attribution of a conscious malice has been, of course, sheer paranoia—whatever the Meagles's failings, we are never shown anything to vindicate this. But Dickens is acute to show Tatty thinking in this way: the angry mind does fantasize a malign intentionality in order to validate its feelings. All the same, the phrasing of Tatty's account leaves unresolved whether her paranoia was a cause of her anger, which suits the pro-bourgeois case, or a later consequence of it, the psychologically displaced result of an accurate analysis of her situation, which supports the radical reading by leaving its grounds intact. The same irresolution applies to Tatty's final repentance. If her discontent is seen not as a response to her situation but a "badness" and "madness", then her following admission that she has been deluded about her guardians' malice would then seem to signify a happy ending: cured of her paranoia, which she now knows clearly for what it is, she is now in a position to commit herself confidently to a future of firmly repressing whatever rebellious tendencies have not yet been exorcized. Yet if we see her story as pointing a radical moral, then her *volte-face* is still not necessarily at odds with it: her confidence here will seem no more than an illusion, her "glow and rapture" merely one form of an energy that is still liable to revert back into anger, since she is still left with the real problems of her basically unchanged circumstances, there being no guarantee that these can be satisfactorily dealt with by her newly mystified faith in Meagles's theory plus will-power.

The ambiguity remains, but on one last point—Meagles's all-too-predictable sermon on Duty, with Amy Dorrit as exemplum—the novel *is* of one mind. Here, one can agree with Q. D. Leavis that behind what superficially looks an easily digestible moral, given from a (perhaps admirable) tact as a decoy for the conventionally bourgeois reader, there is a disquieting warning. The complexity of Tatty's struggle has been simply another foreign language to Meagles, and his sermon is the last flourish of that moral stupidity with which his good-heartedness is so compatible; even the enthusiastic amens with which the converted Tatty punctuates his eulogy to Amy cease when he enjoins her to follow in her path. It's as if even in her present state she senses something inappropriate in being asked to emulate someone to whose idiosyncratic moral life the word Duty, with its implications of self-discipline, is hardly applicable.

In contrast to all this, the one character where Wordsworth seems to have been a *straightforward* influence on Dickens is Clennam. It is clearly on Wordsworthian premises about the life of the affections that Dickens diagnoses and explores in him the "tenderness taboo" at the heart of the severer manifestations of Nonconformity and its business and work ethic. He is *par excellence* the Wordsworthian "outcast . . . bewildered and depressed", in whom the absence of affectionate bonds between himself and his parents, and their discouragement in him of anything like the sense of beauty and instinctive empathy that Wordsworth saw as derived from such bonds, has resulted in a feeling of alienation from life, of not being at home in the world. "I am such a waif and stray everywhere", as Clennam puts it. Consequently, though a good man, dutifully grinding in deference to the "respect" for his mother that has been in her upbringing the alternative to love, he is without "will, purpose, hope", the emphatic life of the Wordsworthian norm. And contrary to received critical opinion, the mystery plot in which he and his mother figure is not extraneous, but works to sustain this initial analysis. Clennam experiences his return home as a return to childhood, and his vain attempts to glean information from his mother to answer to his intuition of some misdeed in the family past dramatizes their original lack of communication. Clennam's psychology is not understood in completely Wordsworthian terms: there are also several windy outbursts of Carlylean moral gusto, used to explain why, despite deterministic expectations, he has still remained "a dreamer, after all" (p. 80). But his eventual union with Amy parallels Wordsworth's own recovery from alienation in the later books of *The Prelude*. For just as Clennam is, as her husband and father-figure, both in keeping with the integrity of her experience and a surpassing of it, so she revives and concentrates in him all those fugitive memories that have hitherto composed a kind of half-created soul of his moral being:

> Yet Clennam, listening to the voice as it read to him, heard in it all that great Nature was doing, heard in it all the soothing songs she sings to man. At no Moth-

er's knee but hers had he ever dwelt in his youth on hopeful promises, on playful fancies, on the harvests of tenderness and humility that lie hidden in the early-fostered seeds of the imagination; on the oaks of retreat from blighting winds, that have the germs of their strong roots in nursery acorns. But, in the tones of the voice that read to him, there were memories of an old feeling of such things, and echoes of every merciful and loving whisper that had ever stolen to him in his life.

(pp. 883-4)

Amy anchors within Clennam all those intimations of the "gravitation" and "filial bond" that have survived the Nonconformist ethos. Dickens may in the novel as a whole be unresolved about what Amy actually *is,* but he certainly is at one with Clennam here in the whole-heartedness of his yearning for what she signifies, the serene and restoring tenderness of Wordsworth's saving Mystery, evoked not so much in her speeches as in the poetic creation of that "healthy autumn day" with which she is now associated. In its subtle fusion of autumnal dignity and quiet with spring-like freshness and anima-tion, this description is almost proof in itself that for a man who, as Forster said of him, had "no 'city of the mind' against outward ills, for inner consolation and shelter", the appeal of such a demure embodiment of the "oaks of retreat from blighting winds" could not but have been deep precisely to the degree that Amy's ap-parently direct and unproblematical relationship with her "roots" was a fascination. Nevertheless, it was one that, to his credit, Dickens also displayed a good deal of intelligence in resisting.

Mark Spilka (essay date 1984)

SOURCE: Spilka, Mark. "On the Enrichment of Poor Monkeys by Myth and Dream; or, How Dickens Rous-seauisticized and Pre-Freudianized Victorian Views of Childhood." *Tennessee Studies in Literature* 27 (1984): 161-79.

[*In the following essay, Spilka outlines the theme of childhood in nineteenth-century literature, particularly in the works of Dickens, who, Spilka argues, incorpo-rated the work of Jean-Jacques Rousseau and antici-pated the work of Sigmund Freud in his treatment of childhood.*]

Poor Monkey was the original title of Peter Coveney's book, *The Image of Childhood,* which covers that liter-ary theme from Rousseau to Freud in a manner still un-surpassed. In revising his book for a new edition in 1967 Coveney had chosen his second title for its ex-planatory value, but his first and more poetic title had been chosen a decade earlier for its happy union of Shakespeare with Henry James.[1] Let me begin my own pondering of the childhood theme with some comments on that extraordinary if obscure conjunction.

"Now God help thee, poor monkey!" says Lady Macduff to her son in *Macbeth* (IV, ii), just before the slaughtering of that innocent and vulnerable family by Macbeth's bloody henchmen. In the prologue to Henry James's novel of 1897, *What Maisie Knew,* a concerned lady similarly responds to Maisie's role as a shuttlecock for divorcing parents: "'Poor little monkey!' she at last exclaimed; and the words were an epitaph for the tomb of Maisie's childhood." Shakespeare's wise and witty child is, of course, literally entombed. After a brief ex-change with his mother on his father's apparent deser-tion of his family, and some apt remarks on the buying and selling of new husbands, he defies his intruding murderers and is quickly slain. But James's ultimately wiser child, waiting as it were in the wings, now moves to the dramatic foreground as the point of view and re-flector on her own figurative entombment, which be-comes in turn the novel's central agon. Let us take that useful contrast as our paradigm for the enrichment of poor monkeys in the nineteenth century, when child-hood first emerged as a major literary theme, thanks largely to the genius, not of Henry James, but of Shakespeare's true Victorian heir, the Inimitable—and therefore highly imitable—Charles Dickens.

I

The innocence and vulnerability of children like Maisie and young Macduff are defining aspects of their role in literature; yet curiously they do not even begin to play that role in any dominant or important way until the late eighteenth and early nineteenth centuries. There are few children, and none of them in leading roles, in the plays of Shakespeare and his contemporaries. There are of course those tragic adolescents, Romeo and Juliet, whom Shakespeare saw as young adults; but even when the adolescent quality of their lovers' world is height-ened, as was beautifully the case in the Zeffirelli film of 1968, the point about childhood in that world is that it quickly moves to young adulthood, that the bridge to adulthood is short and swift and may indeed end in early death.

Perhaps the relative brevity of childhood and adoles-cence is one reason for their delayed entrance as impor-tant literary themes. The prolongation of adolescence, the lengthening and complication of the journey into adulthood, are comparatively recent phenomena. If a boy can become a man at thirteen in the old Jewish tra-dition, if a girl can marry at fourteen in Shakespeare's time, then there is nothing especially problematic about childhood; no great gulf separates children from adults, and the center of life, interest, and significant conflict remains the adult world. Hamlet may question the va-lidity and value of that world and may die in the at-tempt to cleanse it; but it is an adult world he lives and

dies in. So too with Juliet and Romeo; and Lady Macduff's "poor monkey" only heightens the horror of that world with a moment's pathos through his sudden death.

The point in cultural history when childhood and adulthood become separate and opposing worlds is clearly the late eighteenth century, when the industrial revolution begins and the political and social revolutions in France, England, and elsewhere mark the emergence of modern society—an urban, mercantile, and democratic society in which the middle class rises while the upper class falls and the poor shift to the city in great numbers. It is of course the middle class in particular which fosters late marriages; which insists on the extension of educational opportunities for its children; and which keeps them children accordingly for longer periods of time, preparing them—ostensibly—for the increasing complexities of the adult world through a curious and perhaps necessary process of prolonged insulation and isolation from it. On the one hand, then, there is the long, insulated journey toward adulthood, and on the other, increasing complexities and difficulties, confusions and alarums, oppressive levelings and assorted blights, in the adult world itself. The opposition which the French philosopher Rousseau had formulated in theory in the eighteenth century has become more and more a fact of modern society, and has in fact been reformulated in our time by the American maverick Paul Goodman as an opposition which makes for "growing up absurd."[2]

But if the adult world now seems—by all reports—absurd, it had seemed rational enough in the eighteenth century, where all such judgments begin, and its denizens had even been deemed innately benevolent by some observers. The notion of innate benevolence, along with others like it, had been generated by those changing philosophical perspectives on the acquisition of knowledge and identity which Ian Watt discusses in *The Rise of the Novel*.[3] Thus, in that leveling age when kings and bishops toppled off high perches, the already fallen creatures below them were no longer conceived as receivers of given places in a fixed vertical hierarchy, and of given rules for living; they were conceived rather as individual perceivers—born free, equal, and by some lights benevolent—who in learning how to live might shape their own identities and futures in a relatively open and largely horizontal world. The search for new Edens in America and elsewhere, new fortunes in trade, new places in the social sun, and the renewal also in social, economic, political, and religious spheres of the Renaissance emphasis on individualism, contributed to this optimistic view of personal happiness and its rightful pursuit. *Robinson Crusoe* was one eighteenth-century celebration of the individual's athletic capacities for pursuing happiness. *Moll Flanders* and *Pamela, Joseph Andrews* and *Tom Jones*, spoke

similarly to the resilient powers of thriving individuals. But the notion that such thriving free-born souls were also born benevolent, and thus willing and vigorously able to share their hardwon happiness with less fortunate strivers, was soon questioned.

In *Virtue in Distress* R. F. Brissenden argues that the sentimental eighteenth-century notion of Benevolent Man was quickly undermined by the glaring contradiction of inequities and injustices in a society composed, supposedly, of amiable free-born persons, and that the originally positive meaning of words like "sentimental" was similarly undermined. Worse yet, the sentimental person, the man or woman of feeling or sensibility, was soon recognized as a weak, vulnerable, essentially shortsighted person, rather than a thriving soul, and therefore as fair game for satire or savaging by such as Jane Austen in England and the Marquis de Sade in France.[4] That adverse reaction was, however, almost equally shortlived. As Brissenden fails to note, words like benevolence, sentimentality, and sensibility would regain their positive currency by mid-nineteenth century, particularly in England, where the delayed impact of Rousseau's concept of Original Innocence would be most strongly felt and where the essential features of his outlook would be most thoroughly domesticated.

Rousseau had developed his seminal views in mid-eighteenth century. He believed in the uncorrupted child of Nature, born in a state of innocence and threatened by the corruption of the adult social world. He further associated Nature with innate human qualities like Feeling, Sensibility, and Imagination. Reason had been aligned with such qualities by the original notion of sensibility, but had become divorced from them as the inadequacies of the benevolent view of man became increasingly—indeed, embarrassingly—evident. It was at that point, in what is now more often called an Age of Reason than an Age of Sensibility, that the conflict between sense and sensibility began, and the failure of the age to cure its social ills was attributed by the advocates of sensibility to reason, and by the advocates of reason to sensibility. Our present placard notions of the Romantic opposition to the Age of Reason as the century turned—the opposition, that is, of Nature-Feeling-Innocence-Childhood, on the one hand, to Society-Reason-Corruption-Adulthood, on the other—derive from that conflict, and so obscure Rousseau's actual belief in the rational cultivation of those naturally benevolent aspects of childhood which might eventually offset social ills—a belief so radical, I might add, that it would eventually displace innately Benevolent Man with his much more plausible successor, the Benevolent Child in need of loving nurture, who as Wordsworth early saw, and as Dostoevsky later insisted, was the only possible Father of Benevolent Man.

Consider in this light Rousseau's emphasis on the child as a being important in itself—not a diminutive adult,

not a passive creature or a tabula rasa to be shaped wholly by training and experience, as in certain eighteenth-century theories—but a self-active soul endowed with natural tendencies to virtue which needed careful nourishment. Or consider the departure here from still older theories: instead of training a child out of its active ills, its childish or animalistic or innately sinful ways, through reason, the originally benevolent nature of the child was to be more fully developed and drawn out by rational procedures: its natural or spontaneous capacity for feeling, what might be called its *affective* innocence, was to be cultivated, much in the manner of current progressive educational systems. The reversal here of eighteenth-century theories was a reversal also of the severe Christian doctrine of Original Sin, the fallen state of natural vice from which children were to be rescued by rational virtue. Rousseau had replaced this older view, surviving from the Middle Ages, with another Christian doctrine, that of Original Innocence or natural virtue, as evinced in the attitude of Christ himself toward little children. In the nineteenth century, when the Evangelical view of childhood flourished, these doctrines would often exist side by side, in modified forms, as applied to different aspects of sensibility—the sinful passions and the innocent affections. But for the moment the important fact to note is the enormous secular influence of the new doctrine of childhood innocence.

The English Romantic poets, notably Blake, Wordsworth, and Coleridge, transposed this doctrine into poetry quite effectively, and, in the process, gave the childhood theme its first important literary utterance. The appeal of the child in a state of nature to these advocates of feeling, spontaneity, and imagination seems obvious enough. Blake stressed the joys of infancy, expanded them even to the joys of innocent sexuality in later life—an expansion his own culture would reject, but which would be advanced in our time by such neo-Romantics as D. H. Lawrence and Norman O. Brown to a more receptive age. Wordsworth, especially in the Immortality Ode, set a pattern of approach to childhood for future decades in his regret for lost innocence and lost religious vision, in his awareness too of the closing shades of the social prison, and in his adult solace through the "philosophic mind" with its fuller grasp of human sorrow. Coleridge stressed the intuitive, imaginative quality of the child's soul and the need to develop that quality further in adulthood by cultivating the child's capacity for wonder, joy, and spontaneity. Again these placard views are more pliant and complex than I have indicated. The important point is that they flourished among Nature poets, cultivators of solitude and communion with nature and with natural types like peasants and children; and that the Victorian novelists, who are essentially urban, social, or immersed in social and civic conflict, transposed them from that source.

The chief transposition was made by Dickens in novels like *Oliver Twist, Dombey and Son, David Copperfield, Bleak House,* and *Great Expectations*—novels in which the infantile perspective is directly or indirectly employed as the dominant point of view. It was Dickens who made the child the emotional, the *affective* center of fiction and used him or her as his validating touchstone for human worth. It was Dickens too who gave symbolic order to the social disorders of his day, especially in later works where the shades of the social prison, legal maze, or dustheap become controlling metaphors. These two devices of Romantic poetry, the use of the child as affective center and the use of controlling metaphors, were applied by Dickens to urban and industrial culture and its many problems. The full force of his achievement may be seen by comparing his best novels with those of other early Victorians who also record the ravages of industrialism in terms of its toll on childhood. Disraeli, Mrs. Gaskell, and Kingsley, in their social novels, depict hunger, starvation, and death among little children; but none of them is able to convey those afflictions from the child's perspective or to give them focus and concentration through symbolic order; nor are they able to command the emotional and attitudinal range which Dickens brought to his subject. For Dickens was working closer to the emotional heart of the problem—the quality of life, not among the suffering poor, but in the Victorian middle-class home, from which cultural center the nature of Victorian life, its values and aspirations, its tone and direction, were manifestly shaped. It is from this environment that Dickens' children are usually drawn and then subjected to lower class ordeals, as Dickens himself was in childhood. We must turn to the Victorian home, then, as incidentally Peter Coveney does not, for our most important clues to the nature of the childhood theme and of the several curious splits in sensibility that theme entails.

II

Sociologists speak of the modern home as fragmented, a mere meeting ground and point of departure for its busy inhabitants, a kind of domestic freeway. But in the Victorian age middle-class homes were conceived as proverbial castles, places of refuge and sanctity, bulwarks against an increasingly commercial and urban culture characterized by ruthless economic practices, by the blight of slums and factories where the poor and their children labored for long hours, and by the blight also of prostitution and crime. In Dickens' *Great Expectations* a criminal lawyer's aide named Wemmick wears two faces expressing the split between domestic and urban culture: one face, hard and wooden, with a postal slit for a mouth, he wears in the city; the other face, genial and relaxed, humane and sensitive, he wears in his home, which he literally calls his castle and models along castle lines, with artificial moat and draw-

bridge and tiny cannons at the entrance. One face is designed to meet the corrupt dehumanizing commercialization of city life; the other the beneficent and genial aspects of domestic life, to which narrow pound the now two-faced Benevolent Man of the eighteenth century has obviously retreated, as indeed he had often retreated in his own time—after long exposure to worldly ills—to more pastoral environs.

As these last thoughts imply, the Victorian home was also conceived as a pastoral retreat. "In the recoil from the City," writes Walter Houghton in *The Victorian Frame of Mind,* "the home was irradiated by the light of a pastoral imagination. It could seem a country of peace and innocence where life was kind and duty natural." "A tent pitch'd in a world not right," said Victorian poet Coventry Patmore; "a bright, serene, restful, joyful nook of heaven in an unheavenly world," said moralist Brockden Brown. Whether urban or suburban, then, the Victorian home continued the pastoral and romantic tradition of the country refuge. But since it was not in fact a country refuge, its pastoral advantages were peculiarly confined and intensified:

> In the home so conceived [writes Houghton], man could recover the humanity he seemed to be losing. Under the intense pressure of competitive life, he felt more and more like a money-making machine, or a cog in the vast mechanism of modern business. . . . But in the home he might escape from this inhuman world. . . . He might feel his heart beating again in the atmosphere of domestic affection and the binding companionship of the family. . . . Small wonder the Victorian home was sentimentalized [adds Houghton]. In the reaction from a heartless world the domestic emotions were released too strongly and indulged too eagerly. Indeed, it may be only by the unabashed display of feeling that one can prove unmistakably to all the world, himself included, that he has a heart.[5]

Thus Houghton explains how and why the eighteenth-century cult of sensibility was domesticated in Victorian times. The result of that process was, I think, a hothouse atmosphere of intense domestic feeling—an atmosphere, moreover, in which certain curiously heightened values flourished.

The damaging blows to religion from the advances of science and the growth of hardheaded materialism had created a moral and religious crisis in the culture at large. The Evangelical movement as it spread through all religious sects may be taken as exemplary of the vigorous response to that dilemma; and yet whatever its enthusiasms, and however commendable its philanthropic aims, it tended to confuse respectability and diligence with spiritual grace and so gave sanction to the new commercial ethos. In that already sacred refuge, the home, moreover, where its chief impact was felt, it further intensified the hothouse atmosphere by sanctifying domestic roles and relations. Thus, under

the new Evangelical aegis, women took on moral and religious roles formerly assigned to churchly figures: mother and sisters were seen as saints and angels, vessels of spiritual perfection, guardians of religious and moral certitudes which flourished nowhere else. Little children too, under the combined aegis of Rousseau and the evangelists, were considered pure and untainted, girls more especially than boys since they seemed daintier and cleaner and had more stake in remaining virginal until marriage. Even fathers, through their exposure to urban ills, took on religious functions: for when not overindulging their affections they served as severe disciplinarians of their children and as patriarchal protectors from encroaching evils. By the end of the century this parental combination of pious affection and grim correction would seem confusing to many observers, who read its double message in highly critical terms. But in fact new evils did exist outside Victorian homes, and the Evangelical stress on the domestic affections, on the one hand, and on strict obedience and harsh punishment on the other, was designed to meet them. In an age of moral and religious crisis, affection and correction were, I think, survival strategies, ways of insulating children from a godless heartless world. They were, moreover, effective strategies, producing a nation which still prizes obedience, especially in its children (as Margaret Thatcher had occasion recently to remind us), and which in its queues and courtesies and unarmed civic order is still one of the wonders of the western world. The Victorians managed well, then, in insulating their children from the new commercial ethos—which they also managed to promote. But they were less successful in coping with the chief evil of their day, sexual depravity, which they tended to see as the only evil, or as representative of all others, since it was in fact the last fixed vertical prohibition to survive the fall of kings and bishops in the eighteenth century.

In dealing with Richardson's novels, Ian Watt speaks of that "tremendous narrowing of the ethical scale" in the eighteenth century by which virtue was redefined "in primarily sexual terms," and "chastity, instead of being only one virtue among many, tended to become the supreme one."[6] That narrowing process—the work essentially of the Puritan middle class—would take on the cast of a major fixation in the nineteenth century, and with ample cause. What we now call Victorian prudery was an attitude toward sexuality which developed partly in reaction to aristocratic excesses in the Regency period (1811-1820), but also to the spread of scandalous French novels and the free-love doctrines they promoted, and to the more tangible spread of sexual license and venereal disease. Adultery, seduction, and prostitution were decidedly on the increase. As Walter Houghton notes, some 42,000 illegitimate children were born in one year in England and Wales; 8,000 prostitutes flourished in London alone, 50,000 in England and Scotland, due to starvation wages for women among

the urban poor, the maintenance of large armed forces, and the postponement of marriage until young middle-class sons could afford to live like gentlemen.[7] In marriage itself widespread ignorance and lack of birth control devices made sex extremely hazardous in its consequences—large families for men to support, early deaths for women from too much childrearing and childbearing. The prudery was founded then on real fears, on real conditions. But whatever its many justifications, the attitude was there as part of the mixture of feeling in the domestic hothouse. On the one hand, domestic affections were cooked up to a high pitch; on the other, sexual feeling was severely repressed and talk about sex forbidden, the whole matter kept under strict taboo, hidden as it were beneath or behind the voluminous skirts and heavy draperies then in fashion. In the meantime, in the cities, prostitution continued to flourish briskly and openly, and prurient interest in sexuality was evidently widespread, as the lively trade in pornography attests.[8]

These domestic conditions of intensely insulated affection for members of the family, especially those of the opposite sex, and of severe censure for sexual expression of any kind, were just about perfect for producing sexual neurosis in Victorian children. Whether they were diffused or merely diversified by the presence of nannies, cooks, and governesses, numerous siblings and dependents, is hard to determine. It seems evident, however, that whatever normal guilt a child might feel for forbidden feelings, under the Freudian dispensation, would be enormously heightened in such homes, and the chances for later resolution enormously lessened. Married love must have been hell, in any case, in a culture which held that no decent woman should experience sexual feeling, and that a man's sexual responses to his wife were a form of desecration. The frequent appearance of the madonnaprostitute syndrome in nineteenth-century fiction, as in the novels of Thackeray, Dickens, Eliot, and Dostoevsky, or the peculiar love for little girls expressed in the lives and works of Dickens, Eliot, Ruskin, Dowson, Dodgson, Barrie, and James, suggests the depths to which the domestic split between sex and affection had carried. It seems clear that childhood itself had become a problematic and conflictual realm in the nineteenth century; and if writers and readers alike turned to that realm from the commercial harshness and ungodliness of the adult world, and from the unbearably conscious guilts and tensions of marriage, seeking relief in childhood innocence, what they found there—along with the emotional freshness they sought—were childhood versions of the problems from which they fled. In facing and expressing those problems as honestly and effectively as they often did, these writers were mapping out new contours of emotional experience, new aspects of sensibility, new ways also of looking at adult inequities, from which the contemporary world still benefits.

III

Suppose we consider first the most obvious benefit, the precocious childhood view of adult inequities, whether social or domestic. It was Dickens who first identified with the childhood victims of social injustice, and who presented from their point of view, and with the emotional honesty, the innocent directness, the touching vulnerability which can be expressed through that perspective, the absurdities, tyrannies, and obtusenesses of the adult social world. Oliver Twist's workhouse request for more gruel is perhaps the most famous instance: the outrageous request of a sensitive middle-class child that the children of the poor should also be decently fed, a request which still carries its outrageous edge, as our jeopardized school lunch programs today attest. By couching that request in middle-class accents, by placing it on the lips of a genteel orphan boy deprived at birth of his rightful status, Dickens seduced his original class-conscious readers into putting their own children, if not themselves, in Oliver's place—as well they might in an age when social slippage was so common that societies were often formed against it. Consider, among Evangelical societies with railroad titles like "The Ladies Association for the Benefit of Gentlewomen of Good Family, Reduced in Fortune Below the State of Comfort To Which They Have Been Accustomed," and "The Friendly Female Society, for the Relief of Poor, Infirm, Aged Widows, and Single Women, of Good Character, Who Have Seen Better Days," the relevant listing also of "The London Orphan Asylum, for the Reception and Education of Destitute Orphans, Particularly Those Descended from Respectable Parents."[9] In the light of such listings, Arnold Kettle's view that we care in the gruel scene "not because it is Oliver and we are close to Oliver (though that of course enters into it), but because every starved orphan in the world, and indeed everyone who is poor and oppressed and hungry is involved," will not do.[10] Even today it is our middle-class selves, or our middle-class children, as mediated through Oliver, for whom we care first and foremost, as we extend our awakened sympathies to those starved orphans in Dickens' novels, who are not themselves responsible for their dead parents' failure—that is to say, *our* failure—to provide for them whether in worse or better days. Our position, in this respect, is much like that of the Benevolent Man from the eighteenth century, who continues to exist in Dickens' novels, but whose exemplary function—after Pickwick—is to assist, rescue, and above all bear witness to this new center of attention and worth, this new and finer gauge of social gravity, the Benevolent Child.

Oliver's later exposure to London crime, Little Nell's trek through industrial phantasmagorias, Esther Summerson's childhood view of Chancery, that "grown boy" Nicholas Nickleby's view of Dotheboys Hall, suggest further the new way of gauging social conditions. Even

with Little Jo, the London sweep with whom Dickens openly asks his more fortunate readers to identify, we interpret the situation of the poor through childlike middle-class eyes. In making us use such eyes, moreover, Dickens exploits our middle-class stake in the domestic affections so as to change our Evangelical, commercial, or utilitarian minds. He uses Rousseau, as it were, as his entering wedge in that assault on our *other* middle-class predilections. Thus Obedience and Forbearance, Diligence and Factuality, are often challenged by his childhood victims of adult inequities. When offered poor nutrition or unrewarding labor or the impoverished abstractions of utilitarian science, these self-active claimants of Rousseauistic rights win our assent by demanding richer fare.

Dickens is often credited with affecting reformist sentiment in his own and future generations through such persuasive fictional assaults. But one historic consequence has gone unremarked. By converting his childhood victims into fledgling rebels, he seems to have set in motion that long historic process whereby a whole generation of self-active children would rebel against our own adult absurdities in the 1960s. Let us call them the Benevolent Generation, in keeping with the Benevolent Man and the Benevolent Child from whence they sprang; but let us add at once that Dickens himself was not quite so Rousseauistic as his rebellious progeny. By mid-career he seems to have discovered that indignant children, however confident of their own innocence and integrity, can behave absurdly too.

Consider in this light his assault on the adult reader's clashing values in *David Copperfield*. With his childish mother and maternal nurse young David enjoys the domestic affections, as that novel opens, which seem proper to his innocent birthright; but when the Evangelical Murdstones control the household, that birthright is usurped and David becomes in their eyes a disobedient criminal to be trained by discipline and punishment out of his innately sinful ways. We rejoice, certainly, when David later escapes these punitive parents and makes his marvellously scary dreamlike way to a more comic domestic sanctuary; but when we learn that he suffers thereafter from an undisciplined heart it may well give us pause. The problem of the undisciplined heart is one that Dickens seems to leave unsolved, unless we grant him the implicit notion that every child has a right to learn about human fallibility from his or her mistakes, and that we as mature and experienced readers may indulge that right, as Dickens himself does so effectively in parts of *Copperfield* and from start to original finish in *Great Expectations*. In doing so, moreover, he credibly expands the infantile perspective, extends it into young adulthood by bringing his childhood victims into situations which not only repeat and amplify their original ordeals, but which now even expose them to their own imperfections.

It is one of the brilliant strokes of *Copperfield* that the harsh stepfather Murdstone is also one of the owners of the wine warehouse at which David later works, and that Murdstone's frightening spinster sister reappears as governess of the girl whom David later wants to marry, the doll-like daughter of another employer like Murdstone, and thus another version of David's unreachable mother. It is one of the nicely educative things about Dickens' novels that parental figures always appear or reappear in positions of social dominance or favor which can then be assessed by domestic tensions and emotions from the childhood period. Thus we twice meet Jaggers and Magwitch as the legal and criminal fathers, respectively, in *Great Expectations*; thus Bounderby, the bully of humility in *Hard Times,* becomes the commercial and marital extension of the utilitarian father Gradgrind; or Krook and the Lord High Chancellor preside as absurdly grotesque fathers over the legal maze in which the orphaned wards mature in *Bleak House.* By keeping alive and sensitive the emotions of maturing middle-class children, as extended to adult inequities of every kind, Dickens domesticates the social scene, retrieves it from dispassionate remoteness, and so develops in us that passionate sense of injustice, and that glimmering or appalling sense of fallibility, we first felt in childhood. He has given social satire a dimension of compassion, pathos, indignation, and indulgent humor which it lacked before he wrote; he has taken it beyond the easy warmth and shrewdness of Fielding, his most obvious eighteenth-century influence, and the intelligent wryness of Swift and other Augustan critics of social follies and personal imperfections.

Let us move on to the advances in psychological fiction, which today seem more spectacular than those in social satire, and which bring us even closer to private imperfections. Though firmly committed to the Romantic cult of childhood innocence, Victorian novelists were too deeply involved with their own childhood experience, and too honest in most of their efforts to evoke it, to rest content with its idyllic aspects. They have given us a number of powerful evocations of the emotional conflicts of childhood, its guilts and fears and psychic damages, for which there is simply no precedent in previous literature. The most important novel in this respect is again *David Copperfield,* where in the first fourteen chapters Dickens moves his hero through a series of surface events which reflect inner problems. An obvious case in point, which I have developed more fully elsewhere,[11] is David's response to the gravestone beneath which his father lies in the churchyard by his childhood home. David feels childish compassion for it "lying out alone there in the dark night" by itself; but when his mother later reads to him in the cold Sunday parlor where his father's funeral was held "how Lazarus was raised up from the dead," David becomes frightened and has to be reassured that the dead are still at rest in their churchyard graves. Still later, when David

is a few years older, his mother marries the mysterious Murdstone while David is safely off with his nurse's family in Yarmouth. When he returns home Nurse Peggotty tries to explain what has happened in his absence: "What do you think?" she begins, "You have a Pa!" David's response to this news is astonishingly revealing: "I trembled and turned white. Something—I don't know what or how—connected with the grave in the churchyard, and the raising of the dead, seemed to strike me like an unwholesome wind." Peggotty further explains that it is a *new* father, not the old one risen from the dead; but when David enters the house he finds Murdstone in the Sunday parlor where his father's funeral took place, sitting beside his mother by the fire; and when he later roams outside into the yard he finds that an empty dog-kennel has been filled up "with a great dog—deep-mouthed and black-haired like Him—and he was very angry at the sight of me, and sprang out to get at me."

Let me say again what I have said elsewhere, that this is brilliant psychological fiction. The harsh Evangelist Murdstone has become the risen and revengeful father whom David once viewed with such benevolent compassion. As his name half-consciously attests, he is the murdered man, and thus the vengeful murderer, who comes from beneath the gravestone to punish David and separate him from the loving mother he has so far unquestioningly possessed. His powers—as we learn from earlier scenes—involve those mysteries of sexual attraction which pull the mother out of David's range. In the meantime the boy's hostility and fear suffuse the outward scene. The projective artistry here extends throughout these early chapters, and lends a psychological dimension to David's Evangelical ordeals which makes them unforgettable. Indeed, they constitute a dreamlike sequence of real events which has influenced writers for the last century. Among the many novelists who have followed Dickens' precedent and have given us close accounts of psycho-sexual conflict extending from early childhood into young adulthood, let me mention only George Eliot, Fyodor Dostoevsky, and Henry James in the nineteenth century, and, in our own time, Kafka, Lawrence, Joyce, and Thomas Wolfe. Let me note also that all these probers of the childhood theme proceed on moral and social as well as psychological grounds; all are moved by the desire to find values to mature by in a culture which has lost its hold on moral, social, and religious certainties. As James would argue in "The Art of Fiction" in 1885, and would go on to demonstrate in *What Maisie Knew,* "the development of the moral consciousness of a child" is a psychological "adventure" worthy of adult pursuit.[12] The ground rules for that adventure were set, I think, in *David Copperfield.*

IV

So far I have implied two basic motives for the intense preoccupation with childhood in nineteenth-century fiction. The one which we can honor most today is the desire, just noted, to come to grips with the terms of childhood conflict so as to renew the grounds for value and for selfhood. The other motive, which rests more unthinkingly on the cult of childhood innocence, is nostalgia: the desire to return to a period of conscious innocence, to find relief from adult conflicts by escaping into what seemed, by selective memory, an idyllic realm, and remaining there—preferring it, in fact, to adulthood. There are, I think, a number of valid aspects to such nostalgia, among which is the spirit of pleasurable fun which we associate with childhood and which makes us appreciate the humor of Dickens or Mark Twain or Lewis Carroll. Such pleasure is after all a way of renewing one's sense of well-being and may be another way of affirming selfhood. But there is another aspect of nostalgia which no longer works so well for us, though it led Victorians by the thousands to shed copious tears, and to a second age when the word "sentimental" acquired positive meaning.

In a sense we too experienced a brief revival of sentimentality in the 1960s; but it differed from that of the nineteenth century in its willingness, as the saying then went, to "let it all hang out," in its free and open traffic, for instance, with sexuality and affection, and in its perhaps too easy fusion of those feelings in such popular refrains as "All You Need Is Love"—for as we now know, you also need some way to deal with the repressed hostility behind all that easy love. Victorian sentimentality was by contrast more uniformly repressive in nature, and its expression and reception in the nineteenth century were, I believe, neurotic phenomena. Dickens is again, unhappily, the most influential exemplar. His early novel, *The Old Curiosity Shop,* derives from popular Evangelical tracts on an unlikely subject, the exemplary piety of dying children.[13] It tells the story, accordingly, of the long delicious journey toward death of an incredibly selfless heroine, Little Nell, who is best described as a "domestic saint writ small."[14] The novel itself was one of the most popular fictions of the age, and easily the most influential. To this book we owe George Eliot's Eppie in *Silas Marner,* Dostoevsky's Nellie in *The Insulted and Injured,* Lewis Carroll's Alice, Harriet Beecher Stowe's Little Eva in *Uncle Tom's Cabin,* Johanna Speyri's *Heidi,* Sir James Barrie's Wendy in *Peter Pan,* James's Maisie, and such modern extensions of the type as Shirley Temple in 1930s films like *The Littlest Rebel,* Carson McCullers' Mick Kelly in the 1940s, Salinger's Phoebe and Esme in the 1950s, and, still more recently, Erich Segal's Jennifer Cavilleri, the young woman whose exemplary death in *Love Story* is worked for all its tearful worth. The supposed rever-

sal of the type in Vladimir Nabokov's *Lolita* (1955) and in recent sexually exploitive films like *The Exorcist* must also be mentioned, since my own tale is one of changing tastes and attitudes and reversed taboos which are really forms of cultural continuity.

It should be said at once that most of the above "imitations" are improvements on the original. Eppie is unruly; Nellie is moody and precociously romantic; Alice pouts and gets angry; Shirley sings and dances; Jennifer sasses; Lolita chews bubble-gum. Nell's counterpart in the subplot of *The Old Curiosity Shop,* the Marchioness, a domestic slavey capable of comically muted resentment of her lot, should stand perhaps at the head of this list as an example of what Dickens himself could do when he was not under the compulsion to confer domestic sainthood on children. Indeed, the Marchioness may well have initiated all such saving graces. But from beginning to end Nell herself is characterized by abstract traits—youth, goodness, beauty, long-suffering unselfishness, untiring patience, maternal wisdom, religious serenity—at least some of which no creature her age ever possessed or should possess; and as Aldous Huxley has shown, her death—when we finally get to it—is presented through a threnody of blank-verse rhythms which blot out actuality in idealized praise.[15] Within recent years some of our more resourceful scholars have come to the defense of Dickens' portrait of Nell, but since the turn of the century there has been a general critical consensus that Nell is a sentimental textual blur, and among psychological critics at least, a general attribution of that textual failure to Dickens' personal involvement with Nell's prototype, his wife's young sister Mary Hogarth, who died in his arms after a sudden illness. At this late date in the history of Dickens criticism I need not rehearse the details of the textual proof of sentimentality, of the biographical proof of its neurotic origins in Dickens' life, or of the modern view of sentimentality—as an effusion of one kind of feeling which inhibits or represses another kind—on which these proofs are based.[16] It seems more important, at this point, to speculate on those cultural attitudes toward the end of childhood innocence which I think we still share with the Victorians, for all our modern reversals, and for which Dickens created the still prevalent mythos.

Victorian preoccupation with the deaths of children was founded, of course, in the very real problem of high mortality rates among them in all classes, but especially among the poor, and with the religious and indeed existential problem of what to make of it. According to one recent theory, what they made of it was a pleasurable social occasion, a radical violation of subjectivity having occurred which dissolved individual limits into funereal communion, or "sacralized intimacy with mankind in general."[17] Thus, thanks to Dickens and the dying Nell, the Victorians in their copious grief enjoyed

transcendant communal unity of a kind we no longer share. It troubles me, I must confess, that they enjoyed it through "an erotic movement toward annihilation," the agent of which was a pubescent girl. Why not a grown woman? If the unifying feeling was erotic, as our resourceful theorist argues, surely a sexually mature woman would have provided a greater death-kick, as Richardson's Clarissa did, for instance, for the preceding century, or Segal's Jennifer for our own. The clue to this peculiar reaction lies, I think, in the hothouse nature of the Victorian home, and in the tensions and repressions experienced there, which Dickens shared with and recreated for his readers, and from which he released them through what I would call neurotic rather than erotic violation. How else can we explain such related phenomena as the cult called Love of Little Girls, by which young men at Oxford in the 1880s invited little girls, as opposed to big ones, to their rooms for tea; or the increased popularity of child-prostitutes by that decade, to the point where grown prostitutes began to dress like them to recapture trade;[18] or the odd desire to marry girls of twelve and thirteen exhibited by Victorians like Ruskin and Ernest Dowson or by the hero of Henry James's first novel, *Watch and Ward*; or the even odder desire in Dickens himself to be buried beside his wife's sister, young Mary Hogarth, as if to possess her spiritually in a final post-carnal embrace which would forever preserve their mutual innocence? Indeed, it was that final vicarious possession through death which Dickens gave to thousands of weeping readers as compensation for their own lost childhoods.

However bizarre such innocent necrophilia seems today, the myth that Dickens created for it is still very much with us. In Vladimir Nabokov's *Lolita,* for instance, there is the same regressive flight through the countryside, ending in deathly tribute to childhood innocence, as in *The Old Curiosity Shop*; and behind that flight there is the same old fear of sexual and emotional personhood in adult women, about which our current feminists have much to say. The chief difference between old and new versions of this regressive myth is that Nabokov's narrator denies the little girl's affective innocence, if not his own, until the final pages, and meanwhile ecstatically reveres her precocious sexuality. And even here his sexual apotheosis of her charms, like his ultimate retreat into that modern version of erotic self-annihilation, aesthetic bliss, is merely the obverse—not the opposite—of Dickens' spiritual apotheosis of the dying Nell in blank-verse threnodies. It is, I think, a form of reverse sentimentality, an effusion of one kind of feeling in the narrator so as to deny another in his supposedly tough beloved. Indeed, Lolita's missing affections—or perhaps I should say her short-shrifted affections—are scarcely relevant to his regressive nostalgia, which—like Grandfather Trent's gambling mania in Dickens' novel—needs only the sacred image of the little mother to sanctify the game. As both Dickens and

Nabokov seem to have recognized, moreover, it is a deadly and disequal game, and not even the attempt to purge the power lust behind it by killing off those comic scapegoats, Quilp and Quilty, can save its necessary victims.[19]

It takes real as opposed to parodic genius, I would argue, to create a reversible sentimental myth like this one, which has enthralled regressive souls for more than a century, and to go on from there—as Dickens did—to create dreamlike visions of growing up absurd which have enthralled what I am going to call emotionally *progressive* souls over the same two centuries. Are there any connecting links, historically, between these two oddly opposing lines? Certainly *one* link *seems* to have disappeared. The little victim of yesteryear, the little mother whom Dickens more or less invented, is no longer with us in her original saintly form. Along with her older saintly sisters, she was knocked off her pedestal by the feminist movement in the 1890s, by the increased freedom also of sexual expression in serious fiction and—after the first World War—in revolutionary fact, and by the breakup finally of the domestic hothouse itself through these and other social changes. The most paradoxical of these changes, for our purposes, was the increased awareness of the conflictual nature of childhood emotional experience which Dickens initiated in dreamlike form in *David Copperfield*.[20] For as that awareness ran to its modern excesses in recent decades, lo and behold, the little domestic saint returned in modern guise as the little nymphet we now exploit so knowingly in novels, films, and advertisements! It is high time, I hope you will agree, that we get rid of that little incubus—or at least knock her off of her sexual pedestal—by retracing our crazy steps. With Dickens, for instance, it was necessary to work through the regressive myth in order to reach his dreamlike vision of growing up absurd; with us, it seems necessary to reverse the process, to work back through our greater knowledge of sexuality and its unconscious powers to a healthier possession of those tender feelings we now tend to repress, as the Victorians repressed sexuality before us.

To do this we will have to reformulate or perhaps reinvent Sigmund Freud, whose appearance at the end of the last century signalled the return of a doctrine rather like that of Original Sin: the doctrine, that is, of the sexual nature of childhood experience in its unconscious aspects, and of the neurotic nature of family experience in its rivalries and tensions and repressive romances. It was a doctrine with considerable relevance for nineteenth-century culture and the kind of neurotic disturbances it produced, and for those modern cultural analogues like the Jewish home in *The Metamorphosis* and *Portnoy's Complaint* or the Southern home in *The Sound and the Fury* and *Look Homeward, Angel* which preserve hothouse ways. It was a doctrine, moreover, toward which novelists themselves were clearly working even before it was formulated, as Freud himself acknowledged. But having worked with that conscious formulation over the past eighty years, and having suffered from its many excesses in recent decades, it seems necessary now to reexamine the unconscious powers of the repressed affections in our domestic freeways. And for this the achievements of nineteenth-century pioneers like Dickens and Dostoevsky, George Eliot and Henry James, may serve as useful models since they tried, with some success, to preserve the domestic affections while giving us our first honest expressions of early sexual conflict. Indeed, if poor monkeys are a richer fictional breed today, innately loving yet at the same time innately jealous, hostile, vengeful creatures who in learning to cope with their own conflictual natures, along with ours, might well grow up to be something other than regressive or absurd, it is novelists like these—Dickens foremost among them—whom we have to thank for that dreamlike, if not altogether mythical, prospect.

Notes

1. See Peter Coveney, *Poor Monkey: The Child in Literature* (London: Rockliff, 1957); revised and reissued, with an introduction by F. R. Leavis, as *The Image of Childhood: The Individual and Society: a Study of the Theme in English Literature* (Baltimore: Peregrine, 1967).

2. Paul Goodman, *Growing Up Absurd: Problems of Youth in the Organized System* (New York: Random House, 1960).

3. Ian Watt, *The Rise of the Novel: Studies in Defoe, Richardson and Fielding* (Berkeley: Univ. of California Press, 1959). See especially ch. 1, on philosophical realism.

4. R. F. Brissenden, *Virtue in Distress: Studies in the Novel of Sentiment from Richardson to Sade* (London: Macmillan, 1974). See especially ch. 2, on the definition of "sentimentalism."

5. Walter E. Houghton, *The Victorian Frame of Mind, 1830-1870* (New Haven: Yale Univ. Press, 1957), pp. 344-46.

6. Watt, *Rise of the Novel*, pp. 156-57.

7. Houghton, *Victorian Frame of Mind*, p. 366.

8. See Kellow Chesney, *The Anti-Society: An Account of the Victorian Underworld* (Boston: Gambit, 1970), pp. 16, 307-64; published in Britain as *The Victorian Underworld* by Maurice Temple Smith Ltd. (1972).

9. See Richard D. Altick, *Victorian People and Ideas* (New York: Norton, 1973), pp. 180-81, for these and other Evangelical society titles.

10. Arnold Kettle, *An Introduction to the English Novel* (New York: Harper, 1960), II, 125.

11. See Mark Spilka, *Dickens and Kafka: A Mutual Interpretation* (Bloomington: Indiana Univ. Press, 1963), pp. 177-82.

12. See *Theory of Fiction: Henry James,* ed. James E. Miller, Jr. (Lincoln: Univ. of Nebraska Press, 1972), pp. 41-42. For James's childhood reaction to a reading of the crucial early chapters of *Copperfield* (the "ply then taken was ineffaceable"), see Leon Edel, "The Dickens Imprint," in *Henry James: The Untried Years, 1843-1870* (New York: Avon, 1978), pp. 98-99.

13. See Samuel Pickering, Jr., *The Moral Tradition in English Fiction: 1785-1850* (Hanover, N.H.: Univ. Press of New England, 1976), pp. 107-22. Pickering focuses here on Legh Richmond's Evangelical tracts, *The Dairyman's Daughter* and *The Young Cottager.*

14. I discuss Nell's domestic saintliness more fully in "Little Nell Revisited," *Papers of the Michigan Academy of Science, Arts, and Letters,* 45 (1960), 427-37; see especially p. 435.

15. Aldous Huxley, *Vulgarity in Literature* (London: Chatto and Windus, 1930), pp. 54-59.

16. See my essay, "Little Nell Revisited," cited in note 14; and see also I. A. Richards' chapter on sentimentality and inhibition in *Practical Criticism: A Study of Literary Judgment* (New York: Harvest, 1929).

17. John Kucich, "Death Worship among the Victorians: *The Old Curiosity Shop,*" *PMLA,* 95 (Jan. 1980), 58-72; my quotations are from pp. 69-70.

18. Chesney, *The Anti-Society,* p. 326.

19. I refer here to the narrator's confession, at the end of the novel, that he has robbed Lolita of her childhood and that she has sobbed nightly after each of their motel couplings. Though he still loves her, even in her bedraggled pregnancy, it is still a deadly and disequal love, as she herself recognizes when she tells him she would sooner go back to his comic double, the honest pervert Quilty, than run off with him again. His vengeful attempt to exorcise the power-lust behind such love by killing Quilty, as Dickens had killed off Nell's nasty sexual pursuer, Quilp, a century before, seems by design a grotesquely comic appeasement of his own guilty conscience; and his subsequent retreat into that modern version of erotic self-annihilation, aesthetic bliss, simply continues that regression in service of the id which has always characterized his celebration of Lolita's erotic charms. I would argue, then, that Nabokov's sophisticated and parodic art is as nostalgically neurotic here as the Victorian sentimental tradition it ostensibly parodies.

20. By 1848, two years before *Copperfield,* Dostoevsky had arrived at an independent view of infantile sexuality in the unpublished fragment, *Netochka Nezvanova*; but it was not until his return from Siberia, after he had absorbed Dickens' precedent, that he was able to develop his richer view of childhood conflict in novels and tales like *The Insulted and Injured, A Raw Youth,* "A Little Hero," and *The Brothers Karamazov.*

Malcolm Andrews (essay date 1994)

SOURCE: Andrews, Malcolm. "The Idea of Childhood: A Genealogy." In *Dickens and the Grown-up Child,* pp. 9-26. Iowa City: University of Iowa Press, 1994.

[*In the following essay, Andrews discusses the historical context and literary traditions that inform Dickens's "treatment of childhood and maturity in a range of his writings."*]

Angus Wilson, in his essay in *Dickens 1970,* draws attention to the eighteenth-century debate on primitivism in its two main forms—the Golden Age and the Noble Savage. Wilson argued, rightly I think, that Dickens renounced these more 'conventional' primitivisms, but 'fell victim to a large extent to the primitivism of childhood as a pre-Adamite Eden'. We are familiar with this fairly habitual perspective on childhood in Dickens: 'these little people . . . who are so fresh from God' (*OCS*,i,4), reflects the elderly narrator in *The Old Curiosity Shop,* as he wonders about Nell. In similar manner the narrator of *A Christmas Carol* apostrophises Tiny Tim: 'Spirit of Tiny Tim, thy childish essence was from God!' (*CB*,69). Children in Dickens's fiction are often presented as little newcomers from a pre-lapsarian world, bewildered as they try to make their way through the streets of Victorian London. It was precisely the perception of this stark incongruity which gave Dickens the germ for *The Old Curiosity Shop.* Wilson is right, I think, in distinguishing between the relevant primitivisms; but at certain points it becomes peculiarly difficult to separate the more 'conventional' from the childhood-as-Eden primitivisms. In fact what Dickens inherited were the contradictions and confusions within the whole cult of primitivism, out of which evolved his own conception of childhood and maturity with all the anomalies implied in the concept of the 'grown-up child'. It is these contradictions that I want to highlight in the following discussion of that debate on primitivism.

That Dickens's ideas about childhood owe something to eighteenth-century primitivism, mediated through the writings of the early Romantics, is a familiar proposition. 'Dickens is the central figure in the transference of the romantic child into the Victorian novel',[1] declared

Peter Coveney in his classic study *The Image of Childhood,* which traced a line of descent from Rousseau and late eighteenth-century 'sensibility' through Blake and Wordsworth to Dickens's treatment of childhood. There have been a few valuable, exploratory studies more recently, but by and large it remains a relatively neglected quarry.[2] There are several problems with the conventional genealogy. One arises from the habitual tendency to underestimate the extent to which Dickens did actually absorb these ideas. It is a largely unchallenged commonplace that Dickens was not himself an 'intellectual' (the usual comparison is with George Eliot), from which it is to be inferred that he did not seriously address abstract ideas in such a way as to suggest he was fully conscious of his intellectual inheritance. Hence, in great measure, the habit in critics of resorting to his childhood experiences for an understanding of his treatment of childhood; they find little evidence of any other particularly fruitful source for his ideas. Another problem is the tendency to oversimplify what he *did* inherit. Coveney credits Dickens with transferring 'the romantic child' into the Victorian novel. But this figure is far from being a coherent entity and internally consistent, issuing as it does from a longstanding and complicated debate about the ideas of primitivism and progress. I wish, therefore, to review certain aspects of eighteenth-century primitivism and its legacy in early nineteenth-century culture.[3] I then want to consider Dickens's response to it as a way of contextualising his treatment of innocence and immaturity.

* * *

Primitivism is the belief that man's greatest happiness and moral nobility was to be found in his original state, the 'state of nature', and that his subsequent history—the history of advancing civilisation—has been one of gradual moral degeneration. In the second half of the eighteenth century this ancient belief was revitalised and at the same time complicated by two factors: the proliferation of first-hand accounts of primitive societies (the American Indians, the South Sea Islanders) and the ascendancy of ideas of progress, particularly those concerning the evolutionary refinement of the species and the political realisation of the natural rights of man. The relation between the two, between the regressivist stimulus of the pictures of the paradisal South Seas communities, and the progressivist impulse in evolutionary speculation and political radicalism seems in principle simply oppositional; but in practice the two were, in many ways, complementary. As Bernard Smith has demonstrated,[4] the figure of the Noble Savage could be manipulated both to satisfy Edenic longings and to provide proof of the base animal nature from which hard-won civilisation had rescued us. It represented the state of natural innocence from which we were misguidedly seduced; and it represented a helpless susceptibility to barbarous impulses which we had learned to control through the exercise of reason. As the locus of incompatible impulses within a culture, the Savage was, in effect, a picturesque prototype of the complicated, contradictory conception of childhood with which the nineteenth century was so preoccupied.

That very thorough historian of the cult of the Noble Savage, H. N. Fairchild, has argued that the two versions of the Noble Savage outlined above were historically separable:

> [the Noble Savage of popular opinion in the 1770s and 1780s] represented a desire to withdraw from civilization, not a desire to reform the world. The Noble Savage of the revolutionary period, on the other hand, becomes a symbol of perfectibilitarianism.[5]

I doubt that the two versions were ever mutually exclusive in the popular imagination. It was, if anything, the first which survived the revolutionary period to linger in the romantic imagination of the early Victorian middle-class. In Fairchild's view the cult of the Noble Savage hardly lasted beyond the Regency age: 'I have a strong impression that the Noble Savage was dead as a philosophically significant figure by 1810, and practically dead as a literary fad by 1820'.[6] Nonetheless, the Savage was *commercially* very much alive still by the mid-century, in the various exhibition Halls in London and the larger cities, where Red Indians and Zulus were frequently put on display. Whether or not one accepts Fairchild's obituary dates for the 'philosophical' and 'literary' vitality of the Savage myth, the more important point is that, in the dying cult of the Savage, it is only the *Savage* who dies. The cultural anxieties that promoted the Noble Savage survived the Savage's demise and persisted in a search for a more sophisticated replacement for the Savage, one which would function both as the focus for sentimental primitivism but also as a diagnostic instrument in any critique of society. Those potent myths, associated with the Savage, about our primitive past and our utopian potential find their new embodiment in the Child.[7] The philosophical and literary vogue of the Noble Savage, in all its complexity, is culturally metamorphosed, naturalised and domesticated for English consumption in the figure of the Child.

Let me retrace some of the more prominent characteristics of the manipulation of the Noble Savage cult. It is extraordinary that the myth survived as long as it did in the face of so much evidence from eighteenth-century travellers of the barbaric practices customary among some of these primitive societies. Its persistence testifies to the strength of that will to believe in primitive nobility. Its survival was helped by some careful editing and sentimentalising of many of these original accounts by the travellers. The most celebrated example of this is *Hawkesworth's Voyages* (1773), in which John Hawkes-

worth, a director of the East India Company, published a compilation of accounts from Captain Cook, Joseph Banks and others, which he modified to ensure their appeal for an English audience highly susceptible to the Noble Savage myth. Through fanciful written accounts and popular prints, images of the Noble Savage were paraded in Europe both as curiosities and as a rebuke to a vitiated culture. On occasions, as mentioned above, they were literally paraded: Indians and South Sea Islanders were brought back to England and put on display in order to confront civilised manners with natural nobility.

The diagnostic function of the Noble Savage in the last quarter of the eighteenth century was particularly conspicuous in the growing attack on 'luxury', where 'luxury' had that special sense of a threat to the moral health of a nation from the acquisition of superfluous wealth. Here is a representative statement of the opposition to 'luxury' and the accompanying invocation of imaginary early societies from Lord Kames' *Sketches of the History of Man* (1788):

> In all times luxury has been the ruin of every state where it prevailed. Nations originally are poor and virtuous. They advance to industry, commerce, and perhaps to conquest and empire. But this State is never permanent: great opulence opens a wide door to indolence, sensuality, corruption, prostitution, perdition.[8]

The anonymous author of an essay 'On Avarice and Luxury, and their influence on the Happiness of Trading People' in 1779 counsels the reader to observe the admirable example of the 'brute creation' whose wishes are limited to the satisfaction of their immediate needs. Unlike man, they are not corrupted by the pressure to acquire a surplus of goods. The writer surmises:

> it must have been a considerable time before [avarice] was known amongst mankind: artless, innocent nature must have been, for many ages, and is, to this day, in some remote corners of the earth, an utter stranger to this unnatural inmate. . . . The love of money and luxury has been so long connived at, in order to promote the interest of trade, that, by becoming merchants we have forgot to be men, and by becoming rich, we have forgot that it is our duty to be honest.[9]

The recognition of the dehumanising and socially disruptive effects of wealth in an advanced civilisation prompts the question of how we are to recover our humanity. Both progressivist and primitivist solutions were to hand, the latter sometimes preparing the ground for the former, as in Rousseau's *Discourse on Inequality* (1754). The radical progressivist might argue that we could recover our natural humanity in a politically sanctioned redistribution of wealth and power, through the exercise of reason in reforming what Thomas Paine referred to as the 'barbarism of the present old governments'. The primitivist recommendation might

be to return to a state of nature; or to reconstruct it imaginatively so as to be able to offer a model of the social harmony and moral integrity consequent on frugality. Thus primitivist and progressivist lines of approach merge: the chief object is either to retrieve or to reconstitute that natural humanity suffocating somewhere beneath the layers of civilisation which increasing affluence has accumulated.

In the 1790s there developed an affinity between the cult of the Noble Savage and the young European radical with his championing of unprejudiced reason. The eponymous hero of Robert Bage's novel *Hermsprong, or Man As He Is Not* (1796) grew up among the Red Indians. This upbringing is responsible for his calmly reasonable and balanced attitudes towards the French Revolution and Paine's *The Rights of Man,* when as a young man he is drawn into an English society riddled with bigotry and paranoia. The not dissimilar character, Frank Henley, from Thomas Holcroft's novel *Anna St. Ives* (1792) in his generous-spirited and rational radicalism feels an affinity with the American Indians: 'I think of sailing for America, where I may aid the struggles of liberty . . . and at the same time may form a society of savages, who seem in consequence of their very ignorance to be less liable to repel truth than those whose information is more multifarious'.[10] Both these exemplary young radical heroes, by no means themselves Noble Savages, have a respect for the primitive infancy of the human race, when poverty, simplicity and ignorance constitute a sounder basis for moral and political judgements. It was part of the glamour of the Noble Savage myth that examples of the survival of this early state could, at the end of the eighteenth century, still be seen 'in some remote corners of the earth'. Less exotically, this early state could also be seen in something nearer to hand—the child. The affinity between the child, the savage and the animal world was already established as self-evident, according to the anthropologist, Lord Monboddo, in 1773:

> Wherever there is progress, there must be a beginning; and the beginning in this case can be no other than the mere animal . . . that common nature which connects us with the rest of the animal creation. From savage men we are naturally led to consider the condition of the brutes; between whom and the savages there is such a resemblance, that there are many who will hardly admit of any difference; and even betwixt us and them at the time of our birth, and for some considerable time after, there is not any material difference.[11]

The association between the Savage and the free-spirited child was made by Wordsworth on several occasions. In the *Prelude* he speculates:

> as if I had been born
> On Indian Plains, and from my Mother's hut
> Had run abroad in wantonness, to sport,
> A naked Savage, in the thunder shower

In some manuscript versions of the poem 'Savage' is replaced by 'Infant'.[12]

The attack on luxury, for which the Savage was enlisted, involved a reappraisal of the state of poverty. 'Nations originally are poor and virtuous', Lord Kames had asserted in 1788. Virtue and poverty become almost synonymous moral assets. 'No one can be reckoned virtuous who has not learned to bear poverty',[13] observed Mary Wollstonecraft in one of her *Original Stories* (1796). Thus alongside the cult of the Noble Savage, and precipitated by the attack on 'luxury', comes the cult of poverty. Poverty here is not abject destitution, which would only brutalise, but a condition of life within a subsistence economy:

> Poverty, that is to say, a state of labour and frequent self-denial, is the state of man—it is the state of all in the happiest and most equal governments, the state of nearly all in every country:—it is a state in which all the faculties both of body and mind are always found to develop themselves with the most advantage, and in which the moral feelings have generally the greatest influence.[14]

This hymn to noble poverty was written by Thomas Day, disciple of Rousseau and author of *Sandford and Merton* (1783-9), the children's book that became a classic for the next hundred years. The book was written in the heyday of the cult of the Noble Savage and can be numbered among the many contemporary attacks on 'luxury'. Its extraordinary popularity for subsequent generations living in very different cultural climates was due partly to its appropriation and modification of many of the values associated with the tenacious primitivist cult. It naturalised and domesticated the exotic myth of the Noble Savage, processing it into a genteel moralistic confrontation, on home ground, between virtuous poverty flourishing in a natural environment and the corrupting effects of an affluence generated by trade. After listening to his tutor's stories of exemplary Laplanders and Greenlanders, young Tommy Merton, the rich man's son, reflects: 'it seems as if those nations, that have little or nothing, are more good-natured, and better, and braver, than those that have a great deal'.[15] Such sentiments are, in effect, an amplification of the statement quoted earlier: 'by becoming merchants we have forgot to be men'. The importance of this text as a part of Dickens's intellectual inheritance and as an influence on his conception of childhood and maturity will be discussed in the next chapter. The point to be underlined here is that this particular critique of luxury relegates its Noble Savage material to intermittent, exemplary illustrations: it is now two English *children* who occupy the foreground and whose contrasted upbringings precipitate this new version of the old debate.

Affection and admiration for the Noble Savage and the virtuous poor were intensified by what might be called a psychological primitivism, the cult of sensibility. This arose from the belief that feeling should be the authentic guide to value judgements. First impressions, intuitive judgements, uncomplicated by rational reflection, were the firmest foundation for morality—the 'culture of the heart' as Lord Kames expressed it.[16] Hannah More's poem *Sensibility* (1782) contains many enthusiastic apostrophes to this fashionable new concept:

> Sweet Sensibility! thou keen delight!
> Thou hasty moral! sudden sense of sight!
> Thou untaught goodness! Virtue's precious seed . . .
> . . . Reason's radiant morn,
> Which dawns soft light before Reflexion's born.[17]

However, the idea of sensibility generates the same complications as those identified within the primitivist-progressivist debate. From one point of view sensibility is a peculiarly primitive virtue—'*untaught* goodness'. It is a natural impulse which must be protected, as the novelist Frances Brooke counselled in 1769:

> I cannot help observing here, that the great aim of modern education seems to be, to eradicate the best impulses of the human heart, love, friendship, compassion, benevolence; . . . if my ideas of things are right, the human mind is naturally virtuous; the business of education is therefore less to give us good impressions, which we have from nature, than to guard us against bad ones, which are generally acquired.[18]

But from another point of view, sensibility is the hallmark of civilised refinement. J. M. S. Tompkins, in her study *The Popular Novel in England,* comments that sensibility 'enshrined the idea of the progress of the human race . . . the heroic and tremendous virtues might be dying out . . . but modern security, leisure and education had evolved a delicacy of sensation, a refinement of virtue, which the age found even more beautiful'.[19] Thus the progressivist version of sensibility sees it as an acquisition, a refinement of feelings exclusive to the educated, high-born classes. But the primitivist version sees it as innate, fragile and vulnerable to the influence of civilisation and the exercise of reason.

One way of resolving this apparent contradiction was to posit a third stage of cultural evolution in which the benefits, without the disadvantages, of the first two stages (primitivism and 'luxury') are combined. This argument was advanced by Hugh Murray, the co-author of the *Encyclopaedia of Geography* (1834), in his *Enquiries Historical and Moral Respecting the Character of Nations and the Progress of Society* (1808). He accepts the familiar primitivist premise to begin with: 'as nations advance in wealth and prosperity, their morals are corrupted instead of being improved'. Primitive nations have 'a certain rude simplicity and native innocence, which, when contrasted with the numerous vices and disorders that spring up in a more advanced stage, merit a decided preference'. But then Murray proposes

a third stage in the evolution of societies. From the state of moral corruption engendered by luxury, 'a gradual refinement takes place; arts, sciences, and philosophy rear their head' until eventually they 'raise the human race to a condition much superior to that crude simplicity from which they had emerged'.[20] According to this account of evolution the hard-won, sophisticated nobility of civilisation is ultimately superior to the nobility of the savage.

It is now time to examine how the terms of the primitivist-progressivist debate were translated from the discourse of Noble Savagery, Virtuous Poverty and Sensibility into the growing cult of Childhood. Most historians of childhood who have touched on this identify the end of the century as the period when childhood began to assimilate these qualities.

A pivotal concept in this period is that intermediary between Noble Savagery and idealised childhood, the child of nature. The type is recognisable in a number of turn-of-century texts: for example Wordsworth's 'Lucy' poems (1799) and in William Godwin's novel *Fleetwood: or, the New Man of Feeling* (1805) (the subtitle signals the continuity and renovation of the older tradition of sensibility). Fairchild devotes a chapter to the study of these fictional children and concludes that the two conceptions (child of nature and Noble Savage) are 'harmoniously related':

> Several of the children of nature whose virtues have been set forth are savages. Conversely, the influence of scenery sometimes operates upon the savage as it does upon the child. Moreover, boys and girls who, in poetry or in actual life, grow up among natural objects, are frequently likened to little savages. . . . We may at least say, then, that the Noble Savage gives something to the child of nature, and that the child of nature gives something to the Noble Savage.[21]

William Godwin's Fleetwood grows up among the Welsh hills, later describing his childhood self as 'the savage of Merionethshire'. At a later point in the novel the child of nature is compared favourably with the poor, stunted child victims of the new industrial age:

> The children were uncouth and ill-grown in every limb, and were stiff and decrepit in their carriage, so as to seem like old men. . . . This is the case in no state of society, but in manufacturing towns. The children of gypsies and savages have ruddy cheeks and a sturdy form, can run like lapwings, and climb trees with the squirrel.[22]

This is an early glimpse of the deformity of childhood under the pressures of the new age: the factory children are like old men, whereas the untrammelled children of nature retain their original freshness and vigour. This is a line of thought promoted in Rousseau's *Emile*, where he frequently cites the children of the rural poor as models of physical vigour and resilience. But these turn-of-the century fictional children of nature are presented with considerable ambivalence. The gypsy children with their natural athleticism are not proposed as models of humanity, even by those who most strongly regret the effects of a highly developed civilisation. Wordsworth, for example, in 'Tintern Abbey', refers to 'The coarser pleasures of my boyish days, And their glad animal movements' as if they represent a crude early stage in his evolution towards the refined spiritual wisdom which it is the main task of the poem to celebrate. Again, *The Prelude* is the account of the '*Growth of a Poet's Mind*'. His Lakeland childhood is presented as the 'seedtime' of his 'soul', a matrix for development, not a rural asylum for preserving the primitive simplicity of the child. Growth, development, evolution—these are his central concerns and they can be easily obscured or even contradicted by presenting him as the great celebrant of the 'romantic child' or 'child of nature'. It is precisely by oversimplifying such issues that we are led to oversimplify Dickens's intellectual inheritance.

The transference of the complex of primitivist/progressivist values from the Savage to the child, partly via the child of nature, was promoted—indeed, it was accelerated—by two factors in this period, which it is now time to consider. The first was the discrediting of the cult of the Noble Savage. The second was the drastic change of attitude towards that other beneficiary of the attack on 'luxury', the Virtuous Poor.

The cult of the Noble Savage withered under attack from several potent anti-primitivist ideologies. One of the more formidable of these was the promulgation of the Aryan myth, itself a product of the idea of polygenism. In *Man and the Natural World* the historian Keith Thomas discussed the terms in which many writers in the late eighteenth century perceived the narrowing gap between man and the animal world, and he relates this to polygenism and racialism:

> as the difference between men and animals ceased to appear an absolute one, polygenism became increasingly attractive. It preserved the superiority of the European by showing that it was 'the lowest rank of men', which, as Tyson put it, was closest to 'the higher kind of animals'. . . . As the notion spread, the effect was to pull down the negro until he was very near the level which the new belief in animal capacity had created for the beasts. . . . By 1799 English racialism was well developed.[23]

For those who accepted this line of argument it was inconsistent also to maintain the nobility of the coloured Savage. At the same time there were unlikely to be any white European Savages to take on the mantle of natural nobility. The case of the Wild Boy of Aveyron initially raised hopes of the existence of such a phenom-

enon. This apparently authentic child of nature, who appeared in Paris in 1800, had grown up in the wild. About 12 years old, he had a mental age of about twelve months. He was subjected to an examination over several weeks by a committee of the Society of Observers of Man, who came to the conclusion that the child was little more than an idiot, impervious to any kind of cultivation: a savage, but devoid of any nobility.

The concept of the Noble Savage was further undermined by the rise of missionary evangelicalism. This movement, while in some respects benign towards the Savage, reinforced the sense of the racial and intellectual superiority of the Christian European with the added conviction of his spiritual superiority, in his claim to bring light to the children of darkness.

In addition to the discrediting of Noble Savagery, there were difficulties in sustaining other forms of primitivism. The sentimental cult of the Virtuous Poor by the genteel middle and upper classes never fully recovered from the impact on England of the French Revolution and the rise of popular radicalism in the 1790s. Once it was perceived that the poor could become politicised and were able to combine in order to exert pressure for political reform and a greater share in political power, they forfeited those qualities of natural innocence, docility and vulnerability which had been sentimentally attributed to them by late eighteenth-century tastes. This was evident in both the political and cultural contexts. While the government in this decade introduced repressive legislation to try to curb radical activity, others were working in subtler ways to influence and control the attitudes of the poor. Hannah More's *Cheap Repository* (1795-8) was concerned to inculcate the benefits of upper-class patronage to those poor people who showed themselves to be respectable and God-fearing. She and her evangelical associates attempted, through their writings and active ministrations, 'to infiltrate and subvert, rather than legislate and overtly control, the day-to-day lives and culture of the poor'.[24]

With the discrediting of these two cult figures, the Virtuous Poor and the Noble Savage, at the beginning of the nineteenth century, by developments in English racialist, evangelical, ethnological and political thinking, most of the moral virtues originally associated with them were bequeathed to that most obvious embodiment of the infancy of the race, the child. The European child, who had for some time been the innocent custodian and exemplar of many of the values embodied in the Virtuous Poor and the Noble Savage, now had, in addition, the great advantages of being politically innocuous—and white.

* * *

In reviewing the primitivist-progressivist debate thus far, it becomes clear that what is at issue is not simply the clash of antithetical positions. Primitivism does not necessarily exclude a progressivist programme: the Romantic 'child of nature' is not an intractable savage but a free spirit with all the latent potential for the growth of reason and spiritual wisdom. The now familiar contention that, in Walter Houghton's words, 'Rousseau and Wesley can be thought of as the immediate fountainheads of the two great streams of Victorian morality',[25] can obscure this issue, in so far as it suggests a polarisation of influence: from Rousseau the unambiguous belief in natural virtue and the corrupting effects of civilisation; from Wesley the puritanical concern to wean the child from its natural tendency towards depravity and inculcate rationality and piety. But, as we have seen, primitivism has its own built-in tensions between a retrogressive and a progressive ideology. One doesn't have to subscribe to Wesleyan Evangelicalism to affirm the progressive developmental line. One can, indeed, be hostile to it and still reasonably endorse a progressivist line that is intimately related to a lingering primitivism. This, it seems to me, is often Dickens's position, so aptly highlighted in the inconsistency noted by John Carey. He did indeed inherit the terms of the old debate about childhood, as Angus Wilson argued: and that debate had never resolved the inconsistencies within the primitivist position. Dickens also worked with the completed metamorphosis of the Savage into the Child, and found himself in the position of reopening the debate in the new terms generated by a changing culture. These new terms are now to be considered.

The child may have inherited the imagined virtues of the primitive condition, but his cultural ascendancy in the early nineteenth century brought a new range of problems. He came to occupy a status equivalent to that assigned to the poor and women—politically disenfranchised, economically dependent on the good will of his superiors, possessed of a dangerously undisciplined emotionalism, and demonstrating an instinctive affinity with the folk culture of the poor. Middle-class children, therefore, had to be weaned from too close an affinity with the culture and status of the poor; and *male* children of the middle class had also to be weaned from the culture and status of women. This twin process is nowhere better dramatised than in *Dombey and Son* and *David Copperfield,* which I will be discussing in detail later.

So the middle-class, male child had what seemed to be wholly incompatible cultural roles to fulfil. He had to be the embodiment of innocence, spontaneity, romance and imagination; but he also had to be a respectable little citizen, wholly differentiated from his juvenile kin in the lower classes, especially the children of the very poor, who were in many instances reverting to a savage state. Dickens, as I shall show in the next chapter, vigorously repudiates the Noble Savage myth, but at the same time repudiates those forces—evangelical, ratio-

nalist, utilitarian—most active in developing and consolidating the new middle-class ideal of childhood and maturity. The grown-up child, the young-at-heart adult—these oxymoronic figures so familiar in Dickens's work are the progeny of the unresolved complexities in the long debate on primitivism. These figures are also partly shaped by newer cultural developments, some of which can be introduced here.

Over the same period as the Child was assuming the values of the Savage, there was a sense of a growing distance between the world of the child and the world of the adult. This polarisation has not really received the attention it deserves in all the discussions of Victorian family structures. Mark Spilka, who is one of the few to have made it something of a special study, argues that 'the point in cultural history when childhood and adulthood became separate and opposing worlds is clearly the late eighteenth century, when the industrial revolution begins and the political and social revolutions in France, England and elsewhere mark the emergence of modern society'.[26]

How did this polarisation come about? Most historians of childhood, however much they disagree on when and how a distinct concept of childhood (as a condition quite separate from adulthood) arose in Europe, agree that by the later eighteenth century, in middle and upper-class English society, childhood was an object of singular attention. Toyshops began to proliferate, as did children's books. Informal family portraits began to show parents frolicking with their children. Gainsborough's paintings of soulful cottage girls were very popular. The commercial and artistic worlds were exploiting a new enthusiasm. These were, however, symptoms of change, not causes. The causes remain elusive. Linda Pollock summarises the main theories about the ascendancy of childhood as follows:[27] the emergence of an education system that institutionalises distinctions between adults and children; changes in the family structure; the rise of capitalism and the wish of the bourgeoisie to have their sons educated in a particular way to enable them to challenge the power of the aristocracy; the increasing maturity of parents; the emergence of a spirit of benevolence. To these might be added a few more. For example, much can be attributed to the rise of Evangelicalism with its emphasis on the sanctity of the home and family and its attention to the spiritual predicament of childhood. Pulling in a slightly contrary direction was the influence of John Locke's ideas on education, which loosened the repressive, disciplinarian approach that characterised seventeenth-century Puritanism, and stressed the importance of the right environment for developing in the initially amoral mind of the child a sense of right and wrong.[28] Related to these movements of thought was the influence of Rousseau's *Emile* and its emphatic belief in the importance of respecting the early natural impulses of the child. This in turn ben-

efited from those more general shifts of attitude in the later eighteenth century that we have already noted in the discussion of primitivism and the special appeal of the *uncultivated,* of frankness, intuitive impressions, and spontaneous emotional expression.

Everything combined to give childhood a special value in this period and an enhanced definition. The more clearly defined it was the more it was distinguished from adulthood. The division between the two worlds can be seen in the way in which childhood itself becomes a Golden Age to which adults long to return, but know that they cannot. Linda Pollock's study of parent-child relations from 1500-1900, based on diaries and autobiographies, finds as a distinctive feature of the nineteenth-century texts the appearance of nostalgia for childhood. She suggests that 'perhaps the wish to retain childhood was linked to the wish to revert back to a predominantly rural society rather than live in an urban, technological one?'[29] This correlation of childhood with a pre-industrial pastoralism, implied also in Mark Spilka's account, is reinforced by the pet names habitually used for children, as summarised by Linda Pollock:

> In the 16th century children were referred to as my son or daughter or . . . 'the child'. When a more abstract term was employed, this was either 'comfort', 'benefit', or 'blessing'. In the next century children were still 'comforts' and 'blessings' and also 'plants', 'birds', 'lambs', 'flowers' and 'pledges'. In the 18th century children were 'buds', 'fruit', 'joys', 'delights', 'pleasures', 'stimulants', 'cares' and 'incumbrances' in addition to 'flowers', 'blessings', 'lambs' and 'plants'. In the 19th century children were referred to as 'lambs' and as 'balls of love', 'blossoms', 'chicks', 'gifts', 'pets', 'treasures', 'froglike', 'a plague' and 'trying'.[30]

Increasingly the natural world provides the sentimental pet-names. It is worth noting that in the eighteenth and nineteenth centuries the natural objects chosen become younger and younger—lambs, blossoms, chicks, pets. The inference is that the adult world feels itself becoming older and older, and at the same time more remote from its natural origins. Increasing longevity in the middle classes made childhood an increasingly small proportion of one's life span, and it therefore, paradoxically, assumed an enhanced significance.[31] It is in this context that the child can be perceived to be akin to the Noble Savage: both are seen to share experience of the dawn of humanity.

The new distance between child and adult was not just a matter of degree. The two were not just increasingly separated points on a long developmental continuum: they were felt to be different *in kind.* A writer in the *Quarterly Review* in 1844, reflecting on children's literature, insists on this basic difference in kind:

> The truth is, though seldom apprehended by juvenile book-writers, that children are distinguished from ourselves less by an *inferiority* than by a *difference* in ca-

pacity—that the barriers between manhood and childhood are marked less by the progress of every power than by the exchange of many.[32]

Properly to acknowledge this 'difference in capacity' would entail a significant shift in perception, as the writer observes: 'A genuine child's book is as little like a book for grown people cut down, as the child himself is like a little old man'. In emphasizing 'exchange' of powers as the child develops into the adult, rather than 'progress' from a condition of 'inferiority', the writer lucidly illustrates the new mysterious status of childhood: it has equal claims to cultural attention because, for a while, it possesses powers that will be lost with maturity. Adults may reach back for those lost powers, but they are irretrievable. Ruskin observed, in *Modern Painters,* 'childhood often holds a truth with its feeble fingers, which the grasp of manhood cannot retain, which it is the pride of utmost age to recover'.[33] Thus the child acquires a kind of spiritual authority unavailable to the adult. As the historian John Somerville remarked of changes in the tenor of children's literature in the nineteenth century:

> The nineteenth century had begun with high-minded authors who taught children the evils of pride in wealth and social status. But as the century wore on, the child characters themselves were increasingly placed in the position of teachers. It was not they who needed redemption but their elders.[34]

This idea of a generic difference between the child and the adult, of 'exchanging' rather than developing special powers, compounds the difficulty of assimilating the child into Victorian culture, or, in other words, of tracing its growth and maturity into an adult. Because, whatever the gains of adulthood—for example its access to the power structures of that society—there are important losses. The idea of the grown-up child emerges as this incompatibility is recognised. The ideal mature human would be one in whom the childlike virtues and powers coexist harmoniously with the adult's strengths, not one in which the grown person has wholly outgrown his childhood. The grown-up child, therefore, is a means of reconciling the primitivist and progressivist polarity as well as the adult-child polarity that emerges in the nineteenth century.

The cult of childhood, like the cult of the Noble Savage, arose largely out of the self-questionings and self-denigration of a refined civilisation. The child became, in the Victorian period, an unwitting beacon as the adult sensed a loss of moral direction. Rapid technological sophistication, increasing specialisation, growing complexity in the power structure, social confusion in the large, packed cities: it is no wonder that people felt the impulse to retreat imaginatively to what they vaguely remembered as the simplicity of childhood or to sentimental pastoralism, neither of which had ever properly caught up with the great age of progress in the nineteenth century. Wordsworth, at the start of the century, distressed by what he felt in his day to be the degeneration of the human mind to a 'savage torpor', sought to regenerate it by going back to 'the primary laws of our nature . . . the essential passions . . . the elementary feelings'.[35] These were to be found in humble and rustic life and in childhood.

The challenge to which, in their different ways, both Wordsworth and Dickens rose was not to encourage the adult to retreat to nature or regress to childhood as an end in itself, but to reintegrate what had been forced apart. They saw this as a programme of cultural reform. Coleridge observed this as the distinguishing mark of Wordsworth's poetry, which was to achieve this reintegration by a course of sustained defamiliarisation:

> To carry on the feelings of childhood into the powers of manhood, to combine the child's sense of wonder and novelty with the appearances, which every day for perhaps forty years had rendered familiar.[36]

This sustaining of the feelings of childhood into adulthood entails reuniting the adult and child within each mature individual. It means therefore a redefinition of maturity which sees it not as that condition which has finally eliminated all immaturity. Rather the reverse: full maturity involves a new respect for immaturity. It means the renascence of the child in the adult.

* * *

The aim of this [essay] has been to sketch out a context for the subsequent discussion of Dickens's treatment of childhood and maturity in a range of his writings. Thus when we encounter the various forms of the grown-up child in his work—the childish old men, the prematurely old children, the cases of arrested development and so on—we are aware that Dickens, no doubt confused himself, is also addressing deep confusions in his own culture about the status of childhood, ideas of original and congenital innocence, and the promotion of natural virtues in the struggle to reform a flawed culture and the corrosion of social relations. This confusion is due both to the inherited paradoxes of the primitive-progressive debate, and also to radical social changes over the first half of the nineteenth century, particularly in the ideas about what constitutes masculine maturity. We do Dickens an injustice to attribute his own confusion, and the gallery of child-adult deformities presented in his fiction, solely or even chiefly to his inability to come to terms with his own childhood experiences.

Notes

1. Peter Coveney, *The Image of Childhood* (Penguin, 1967), p. 110.

2. One of the most penetrating studies of this kind is Dirk Den Hartog's *Dickens and Romantic Psychology* (Macmillan, 1987). My later discussion of *Dombey & Son* owes much to the stimulus of Den Hartog's chapter on that novel. Another important contribution to this debate is Mark Spilka's essay, 'On the Enrichment of Poor Monkeys by Myth and Dream' (see below, note 26).

3. For much of the following discussion of primitivism I am indebted to Louis Whitney's *Primitivism and the Idea of Progress* (New York: Octagon Books, 1965).

4. Bernard Smith, *The European Vision and the South Pacific* (1959; 2nd ed. Yale University Press, 1985).

5. H. N. Fairchild, *The Noble Savage: A Study in Romantic Naturalism* (New York: Russell & Russell, 1928), p. 338.

6. Ibid., p. 299.

7. Rod Edmond's studies of the European interest in the South Pacific lead him to suggest that the Savage myth persisted throughout the nineteenth century and that it coexisted with, rather than was replaced by the cult of childhood.

8. Lord Kames, *Sketches of the History of Man* (Edinburgh, 1788), II, 153-4. Quoted in Whitney, op. cit., pp. 277-8: see her Chapter 2 for an extended discussion of the debate on 'luxury'.

9. Anon., 'On Avarice and Luxury, and their Influence on the Happiness of a Trading People', *London Magazine,* vol. 48 (1779), pp. 538, 554.

10. Thomas Holcroft, *Anna St. Ives* (1792): quoted in Fairchild, p. 163.

11. Lord Monboddo, *The Origin and Progress of Language* (1773: 2nd ed., 1774), I, 147 (quoted in Whitney, pp. 42-3).

12. William Wordsworth, *The Prelude,* Book I (1805-6), ll.301-4: from the edition by E. de Selincourt (2nd ed. revised by H. Darbishire: Oxford University Press, 1959), p. 18 and see fn to l.304. All quotations from Wordsworth's poetry are from this edition, unless otherwise stated.

13. Mary Wollstonecraft, *Original Stories* (1796), Ch. 11.

14. Thomas Day, *Letters of Marius: or Reflections upon the Peace and the East India Bill, and the Present Crisis* (3rd ed., 1784), I, 21-2 (quoted in Whitney, p. 135).

15. Thomas Day, *The History of Sandford and Merton* (Nelson, 1887), p. 310.

16. Lord Kames, *Loose Hints upon Education* (Edinburgh, 1781), p. 232: 'In planning the present work, I had chiefly in view the culture of the heart; prompted by two motives, first, its superior importance in the conduct of life; next, its being in a great measure overlooked by writers upon education'.

17. Hannah More, 'Sensibility', in *Sacred Dramas* (1782), p. 282.

18. Frances Brooke, *The History of Emily Montague* (1769), III, 32-3 (quoted in Whitney, pp. 123-4).

19. J. M. S. Tompkins, *The Popular Novel in England 1770-1800* (University of Nebraska Press, 1961), pp. 92-3.

20. Hugh Murray, *Enquiries Historical and Moral Respecting the Character of Nations and the Progress of Society* (1808), pp. 18-20 (quoted in Whitney, p. 290).

21. Fairchild, pp. 384-5.

22. William Godwin, *Fleetwood: or the New Man of Feeling* (1805: Bentley, 1830), p. 99.

23. Keith Thomas, *Man and the Natural World* (Penguin, 1983), p. 136. The reference is to Edward Tyson, author of *Orang-Outang, sive Homo Sylvestris* (1699).

24. See S. Pedersen, 'Hannah More meets Simple Simon', *Journal of British Studies,* vol. 25 (1986), pp. 84-113.

25. Walter Houghton, *The Victorian Frame of Mind* (Yale University Press, 1957), p. 267.

26. Mark Spilka, 'On the Enrichment of Poor Monkeys by Myth and Dream; or, How Dickens Rousseauisticized and Pre-Freudianized Victorian Views of Childhood', in Don Richard Cox (ed.), *Sexuality and Victorian Literature* (Tennessee University Press, 1984), p. 162.

27. Linda Pollock, *Forgotten Children: Parent-Child Relations from 1500-1900* (Cambridge University Press, 1983), pp. 52-65.

28. For example, 'of all the Men we meet with, Nine parts of Ten are what they are, Good or Evil, useful or not, by their Education': John Locke, *Some Thoughts Concerning Education,* edited by J. Axtell (Cambridge University Press, 1986), p. 114.

29. Linda Pollock, p. 110.

30. Ibid., pp. 110-11.

31. A point suggested to me by Rod Edmond.

32. Anon., 'Children's Books', *Quarterly Review,* vol. 74 (1844), p. 16.

33. John Ruskin, 'Preface to the Second Edition' (1844) of *Modern Painters* ('Popular Edition', 1906), I, xxxi-xxxii.

34. John Somerville, *The Rise and Fall of Childhood* (Sage Publications, 1982), p. 173.

35. Wordsworth, 'Preface' to the 2nd ed. (1802) of *Lyrical Ballads*.

36. S. T. Coleridge, *Biographia Literaria* (1817), Chapter 4.

Abbreviations

All references to Dickens's writings, unless otherwise stated, are to the *Oxford Illustrated Dickens* (Oxford University Press, 1947-58).

BH: *Bleak House*

BR: *Barnaby Rudge*

CB: *Christmas Books*

CS: *Christmas Stories*

DC: *David Copperfield*

DS: *Dombey and Son*

HT: *Hard Times*

LD: *Little Dorrit*

MC: *Martin Chuzzlewit*

MED: *The Mystery of Edwin Drood*

MHC & CHE: *Master Humphrey's Clock and A Child's History of England*

NN: *Nicholas Nickleby*

OCS: *The Old Curiosity Shop*

OMF: *Our Mutual Friend*

PP: *Pickwick Papers*

SB: *Sketches by Boz*

TTC: *A Tale of Two Cities*

UT & RP: *The Uncommercial Traveller and Reprinted Pieces*

Letters: Pilgrim Edition of *The Letters of Charles Dickens* (Oxford University Press, 1965-)

Forster, *Life*: John Forster's *The Life of Charles Dickens*, edited J. W. T. Ley (Palmer, 1928)

CHILDHOOD IN THE WORKS OF LEO TOLSTOY

Andrew Baruch Wachtel (essay date 1990)

SOURCE: Wachtel, Andrew Baruch. "L. N. Tolstoy and His *Childhood*." In *The Battle for Childhood: Creation of a Russian Myth*, pp. 7-57. Stanford, Calif.: Stanford University Press, 1990.

[*In the following excerpt, Wachtel traces Tolstoy's motivation for writing the "pseudo-autobiography"* Child- hood, *and delineates the author's depiction of childhood in the work.*]

In the summer of 1851, when Tolstoy began writing the work that was to become *Childhood,* he was not quite 23 years old. Although he had harbored vague literary plans for years, there was as yet no sign that he would become a professional writer.[1] Since turning eighteen, he had tried his hand at a number of occupations and had, in his own estimation and in that of his family, failed miserably at all of them. He had not gotten a university degree, his efforts to reorganize the family estate had produced no results, he had accumulated gambling debts, and, finally, he had gone off to join his brother as an officer in the Russian Army of the Caucasus. Throughout this period he recorded his thoughts and activities in a remarkably precocious journal. As soon as this journal became available to scholars, it was apparent that it constituted a kind of experimental laboratory, a testing ground on which the young Tolstoy could try out some of the narrative strategies that he used so effectively in his later work.[2] Nevertheless, although Tolstoy the journal writer had already mastered a number of crucial techniques, the transition from diary writer to published author was an arduous one. This transition occurred during the year in which he wrote *Childhood.*

In the final version of *Childhood,* two conflicting impulses are held in delicate equipoise; very generally, they might be called the autobiographical and the novelistic. Throughout his life, Tolstoy was troubled by the tension caused by his desire to speak generally as the teacher of mankind and his talent as an observer of the particular details of the individual life (his own and others). It was this tension, resolved for a time in favor of the general, that after 1877 led to his rejection of almost his entire literary oeuvre. In the 1850's, however, Tolstoy saw the matter somewhat differently. At this stage, he evidently identified autobiography with the specific, while fiction was equated with the general. *Childhood* was something of a synthesis of these two impulses. On the one hand, the narrative is particular and individualized; the autobiographer Irten'ev recounts experiences that relate to him and to him alone. On the other hand, the lyrical tone that pervades the whole, coupled with the fact that Irten'ev is a fictional creation, lend it a feeling of generality; it seems as if Irten'ev's childhood could have belonged to anyone. This balance seems entirely effortless in the published version, but Tolstoy's comments on his work as it was developing indicate that finding a middle ground between the particular and the general, between the autobiographical and the novelistic, was both his most important concern and a source of much difficulty.

It took Tolstoy some time and a number of false starts before he arrived at his ultimate formal conception of *Childhood* in particular and the trilogy in general.[3] Originally, he thought the work would be in four parts and intended to call it *The Four Epochs of Develop-*

ment. Although the plot of the initial version of the section on childhood is similar to that of the final one, there are significant differences as well. For one thing, the original version is less autobiographical.[4] For another, the first version covers a much larger span of time; some of the scenes included would later be incorporated into *Boyhood* and even into *Youth*. Far more important, the complicated relationship between author, narrator, and protagonist still remained to be clarified. The story is told in the first person by an anonymous narrator. However, at the beginning of the first surviving draft there is a small section signed "G. L. N." (that is, Count [in Russian, "Graf"] Lev Nikolaevich). It is in the form of a letter addressed to an unnamed (and quite possibly nonexistent) correspondent and, despite containing a number of conventional formulas, it provides clues to the evolution of Tolstoy's thoughts on the relationship of author to text:

> I wrote them [the "notes," as he calls them, A.W.] for myself, never thinking that there would be a time when I would wish to let anyone read them—Why did I write them? I cannot give you any definite account. I found it pleasant to jot down scenes that illustrate childhood memories so poetically. I found it interesting to examine my development and, most important, I wanted to find some kind of single source in the outline of my life—an aspiration that could guide me.[5]

Since, presumably, this paragraph was destined for publication, the first sentence should be seen as a bow to literary convention. By pretending to have written the "notes" only for himself (even as he is publishing them), Tolstoy attempts to remove the stamp of literariness from them. This device makes them seem more personal, more spontaneous. After the opening disclaimer, however, the introduction becomes more suggestive. It was "pleasant" to "illustrate childhood memories so poetically." The absence of a possessive pronoun attached to childhood (the possessive is, of course, emphatically present in the two sentences that follow) hints at a certain generalizing tendency in the proposed work; a suggestion to take what follows as a depiction not merely of the childhood of G. L. N., but of childhood as such.

The next two sentences, on the other hand, link the work and G. L. N. very closely. He claims that it was interesting "to examine *my development*" and "to find a single source in the outline of *my life*" (italics mine). Despite the fact that the life described in *The Four Epochs of Development* was not Tolstoy's own, he felt (or, at least, pretended to feel) that the patterns of thought and development in it belonged to him. One hesitates, however, to draw sweeping conclusions from this introduction, because it is difficult to see exactly how it was to have been connected to the text that follows. The narrator of the first redaction is never named, so it is possible that Tolstoy originally intended to present the work as an autobiography. It is also conceivable that the introduction was never intended for publication. Either way, the introduction marks a false start; Tolstoy would never identify himself so closely with his text again. Nevertheless, this aborted beginning is important because it suggests that from the very outset, in June or July of 1851, Tolstoy saw his work both as an outlet for the expression of autobiographical material and as a description of childhood in general. A tension between autobiography and fiction, between Tolstoy's presence as an author and as a narrator, was part of the trilogy from its inception.[6]

In January 1852 Tolstoy finished a second draft of *Childhood*. By this time, the work had taken on a fairly coherent shape. The story was told by a narrator who was differentiated from the author by name, and a system of chapters (absent in the first draft) had been introduced. Many of the scenes that would appear in the fourth and final version were already included, as was the idea of presenting a few crucial days in the life of the young boy (instead of attempting a full chronology of the child's life, as had been envisioned in the first version). At the end of the new manuscript, Tolstoy appended two short chapters entitled "To the Readers" and "To Those Esteemed Critics Who Wish to Take This Personally." In the former, Tolstoy made the following programmatic statement: "In my opinion the persona of the author, the writer (creator) is an antipoetical persona. Since I wrote in the form of an autobiography and wanted to interest you in my hero as much as possible, I wished him to have no imprint of authorship and, therefore, I avoided all authorial devices—learned expressions and constructions" (1: 208-9).

In the first version of the introduction, Tolstoy had emphasized the connection between himself and the narrator. Now, however, he underscores the nonautobiographical nature of his work. He disassociates himself from his main character and reminds the reader that this is a work of fiction. The phrase "I wrote in the form of an autobiography" (as opposed to having written a true autobiography) and the words "my hero" are crucial for defining Tolstoy's attitude toward the text here. Yet at the same time, a direct address to the reader is nothing if not the kind of "authorial device" that Tolstoy claims to have avoided. It is not clear what he means by "scholarly expressions and constructions." Perhaps he has in mind didactic generalizations à la Rousseau. Whatever the case, this entire afterword is a clear example of the author's voice intruding on his text to make didactic comments (the following chapter addressed to the critics does the same thing to an even greater extent). As such it flatly contradicts the avowed purpose of the book. It would seem that Tolstoy came to understand the problem himself, for this type of heavy-handed authorial intrusion was eliminated in the third and fourth redactions.[7]

Tolstoy's discomfort with the mix of autobiography and fiction in *Childhood* did not disappear even when he had finished the story. After the final version of *Childhood* had been accepted for publication by *The Contemporary* in the September 1852 issue, Tolstoy wrote a letter to N. A. Nekrasov in response to the latter's request for a sequel: "The autobiographical form that I chose and the obligatory link between the following parts and the preceding one so constrain me that I often feel the desire to abandon them and leave the 1st part without a continuation" (1: 330). This was, in effect, the first "public" statement that Tolstoy made about his work. He continued to emphasize the fictive element ("autobiographical form") just as he had in the abandoned afterword to the second redaction. It is worth noting, however, that Tolstoy might well have felt constrained to play up the fictive here because, as a beginning author, he wanted to emphasize the literariness of his work. In this period prose fiction was the most prestigious type of writing, and Tolstoy naturally wanted to make a career as a writer of belles lettres, not as a memoirist. Like most journals, *The Contemporary* did not tend to publish autobiographies by beginning authors, so the unknown writer might have simply been trying to make an impression on the editor-in-chief. Even so, his complaint that the form of the work was "constraining" bears investigation.

All of Tolstoy's early published works employ first-person narrators; as a beginning writer he clearly found it easier to speak in the first person. This preference is probably a legacy from his early literary laboratory: the diary. However, while a first-person narrator can both analyze himself and pronounce general judgments, those judgments are fated to seem subjective. They obviously emanate from a single viewpoint and express the opinions of an individual. Although Tolstoy's favorite eighteenth-century writers, Rousseau and Laurence Sterne, reveled in subjectivity, by the mid-nineteenth century the expectations of writers and readers had changed radically. In England, France, and Russia novelists were attempting to erase their overt presence from the text insofar as possible. As it turned out, this kind of realism never suited Tolstoy; he needed and wanted direct authorial presence. Later in his career, particularly in *War and Peace* and *Anna Karenina,* he succeeded in creating forms that combined seemingly objective narration with a strong authorial presence. In 1852, however, Tolstoy evidently found it expedient to compromise with the expectations of the public and the critics. Nevertheless, despite severely limiting his direct presence in *Childhood,* he never entirely excised the authorial voice. After the success of *Childhood,* Tolstoy could worry less about pleasing his readers. In *Boyhood* and *Youth* he made increasing use of generalizing statements, and the first-person narrator became more and more constraining.

The tension between the autobiographical and the fictional boiled over in comically naive fashion when Tolstoy saw *Childhood* in print for the first time. It turned out that Nekrasov had, for some unknown reason, published it under the title *The Story of My Childhood.* Tolstoy was furious and dashed off a letter to Nekrasov (although he never mailed it) in which he said, "The very title *The Story of My Childhood* contradicts the sense of the work. Who cares about *my* childhood" (1: 332). Of course, the complaint is illogical, since a reader who believed that the narrator wrote the whole work could just as easily be expected to think that the narrator had written the title as well. Nevertheless, Tolstoy's complaint is telling; immediately, and rather childishly, he connected the word "my" in the title to the author and not to the narrator, thus indicating that he himself did not believe in the illusion he had created. Although this incident might appear simply as an example of bruised authorial self-esteem, it also illustrates the extent to which fiction and autobiography were intertwined for Tolstoy when he was writing *Childhood.*

Perhaps the best formulation of the dual nature of the project can be seen in a diary entry for November 30, 1852: "The 4 Epochs of Life constitutes *my* novel before Tiflis. I can write about him because he is so distant from me" (46: 150-51). Since many of the facts of Irten'ev's life do not coincide with those of Tolstoy's, in what sense could Tolstoy call the work "*my* novel"? It is significant, of course, that he did not say "my life." The italicized "my" indicates that Tolstoy closely identified himself with his work and its hero. At the same time, the words "novel" and "him" indicate that Tolstoy was able to distance himself from his story, to accept it as a fictional construct. The obvious internal contradiction here is one that Tolstoy was evidently never able to solve.

The second sentence deserves special consideration, especially in connection with a diary entry from a slightly earlier period:

> Everyone describes human weaknesses and the humorous side of people by transferring them to invented personages, sometimes successfully, if the author is talented, but more often unnaturally. Why? Because we know mankind's weaknesses in ourselves and in order to show them faithfully we must show them in ourselves, because a particular weakness is appropriate only for a particular person. Very few people have the strength to do this. We try to distort the personage on whom we project our weaknesses as much as possible in order not to recognize ourselves.
>
> (46: 76)

Tolstoy berates others for cowardice and insincerity, yet at this time he himself was not able to write without the help of a mediating character. After all, who was Irten'ev if not an "invented personage" who could stand

for his creator? At this point in his career, Tolstoy could only write about someone who "was distant." In fact, his greatest challenge as a beginning writer lay in creating a literary form that would have the effect of an autobiography, the ring of truth that only unmediated authorial presence can produce, while allowing him to retain a certain narrative distance. Later in life, when Tolstoy talked about the trilogy, it was precisely the presence of a fictitious narrator and the mix of *Dichtung* and *Wahrheit* that he felt called upon to criticize:

> In order not to repeat myself in the depiction of childhood I reread what I had written under that title and regretted that I had written it: it is so bad, so literary, so insincerely written. It could not have been otherwise, first of all because my idea was to write the story not of my childhood but of that of my friends and so the result was a clumsy mix of their childhood and mine, and, second, because at the time of writing I was not at all independent in terms of expression and was under the influence of two writers who strongly affected me then: Sterne (his *Sentimental Journey*) and Töpffer (*Bibliothèque de mon oncle*).
>
> I particularly don't like the last two parts—Boyhood and Youth—. . . I hope that what I write now will be better and, more important, more useful for other people.

> (34: 348-49)

This passage comes from the "Memoirs" (1903) that P. I. Biriukov requested in order to fill out the writer's childhood biography. By then Tolstoy had either forgotten or chosen to ignore the literary and personal reasons that had caused him to write his trilogy in its original form. Why is it that *Childhood* still does not utterly displease its author, as do the two later parts? Probably because even in 1903 Tolstoy retained nostalgic feelings for early childhood. If anything those feelings deepened as he compared them with the following periods of his life.[8] Later in "Memoirs," when describing the basic chronology of his life, he calls the early years "the joyful, poetic period of childhood until the age of 14." The events described in *Boyhood* and *Youth,* on the other hand, are part of "a horrible 20-year period of coarse dissipation" (34: 347). It was, in part, Irten'ev's relatively unjudgmental stance toward the events of his boyhood and youth that bothered the older Tolstoy.

Of course, the very fact that Tolstoy was outraged by Irten'ev's comparatively lenient attitude suggests the degree to which he felt a personal connection to the actions described in the trilogy. Had Irten'ev been a wholly fictional creation, Tolstoy could not have feared that he might "repeat himself" when describing his own childhood. Although he correctly remembers that his "idea" had been to write a work of fiction, the older Tolstoy now judges his work as an autobiography (albeit an untrue and poorly written one). It is bad because it fails to tell the truth about Tolstoy (an intent that did

not exist in 1852). The presence of *Dichtung* and *Wahrheit* is still recognized in the trilogy, but these categories are interpreted in a new context, as falsehood and truth, respectively. It is not the extent to which a section is factual that counts, however (for the second two parts of the trilogy are factually closer to Tolstoy's life than is the first); what is crucial is the interpretation of those facts. *Childhood* depicts a period of innocence in a way that the older Tolstoy sees as ideologically proper; it is therefore not all bad. Although *Boyhood* and *Youth* are more autobiographical, they do not emphasize the horrors of these periods sufficiently; consequently they are insincere and bad.

To sum up Tolstoy's attitude toward the trilogy, I would say that he always regarded it as a group of texts through which he could express extremely personal material in a mediated literary form. Neither purely factual nor purely fictional, the trilogy was a kind of compromise. Sometimes, while writing the work and especially in later life, Tolstoy found such compromises distasteful, but it is clear that for the young writer they were necessary if he was to turn his already well developed self-analytic ability into a literary work.

.

CHILDHOOD IN *CHILDHOOD*

If there is a single overarching message in *Childhood,* it is that childhood is an essentially happy period. This does not exclude unhappy moments, of course, but the overall impression is and—Tolstoy implies—should be one of joyous innocence. While it is perhaps unnecessary to point out that Tolstoy borrowed his theoretical conception of childhood from Rousseau, it is noteworthy that Tolstoy applied this concept more extensively than did its inventor. Although Rousseau may well have had a happy childhood, he devoted less than twenty pages of *Confessions* (a work of approximately 600 pages) to a description of it. When Tolstoy provided Irten'ev with a happy childhood, he clearly was making a conscious choice. The author's own childhood could not have been a happy one, at least in any conventional sense. His mother died before he was two, and, in his own words: "I don't remember my mother at all" (34: 349). His father died when Tolstoy was eight, and thereafter he was shuttled between the homes of grandmothers and aunts. Nevertheless, despite personal experience (or, perhaps, because of it), Tolstoy both considered childhood the happiest time of life in theory and provided Irten'ev with a lyrically joyful version. Through Irten'ev he was finally able to have the childhood he had probably always wanted. Incidentally, Tolstoy's selective use of autobiographical material in *Childhood* illustrates one of the advantages of the pseudo-autobiography. Had he claimed to be writing an autobiography, he might have found it difficult to rewrite his childhood memories so radically.

The perception of childhood as time in paradise is expressed at various points in the work. It is in chapter 15, however, that this theme receives its most elaborate treatment. It is not difficult to discern that this chapter is the key one for the entire story. For one thing, it bears the same name as the title of the book; for another, it is placed between the descriptions of the two days in Irten'ev's life around which the entire narrative is structured. Finally, it lies at the physical midpoint of the work: preceded by fourteen chapters and followed by thirteen.

The chapter begins with two sentences in the author's voice: "Happy, happy irretrievable time of childhood! How can one not love, not cherish its memories?" (1: 43). For the Russian cultural mind, these may have been the most unforgettable sentences Tolstoy ever wrote. For the next 80 years, practically every first-person description of childhood in Russia, whether in fictional or in nonfictional form, was oriented to them. As is typical of authorial statements throughout *Childhood*, these lines are unmotivated by anything preceding them. They are not modified by a personal pronoun or a time marker. Instead, they are simply meant to express the abstract, universal truth about childhood.

The author's statement is followed by one sentence in the voice of the narrator: "Those memories freshen, exalt my soul, and are a source of great enjoyment for me." This sentence defines Irten'ev's personal reasons for writing about childhood. Through recollections of childhood happiness, he hopes to recapture a part of himself that has, evidently, been lost in the process of growing up. His soul in the present needs to be "freshened" through reminiscence. He perceives the world of childhood as an idyllic one, fundamentally different from the world in which he now lives. It is not the case that things simply got steadily worse in the course of Irten'ev's life. He experiences moments of happiness in *Youth* and even in *Boyhood*, but childhood is the only period that he sees as happy in and of itself, regardless of what he may have experienced at a given instant. Of course, it would be a mistake to assert that every moment of Irten'ev's childhood is happy. Tolstoy did not provide Irten'ev with a saccharine childhood. Nevertheless, moments of unhappiness, or even of personal tragedy, do not prevent Irten'ev from recalling his childhood as a golden age, just as moments of happiness in later life do not modify the essentially unfortunate character of boyhood or youth.[9] Tolstoy's model, in which childhood is perceived as a golden age, the highpoint of a person's life, dominated Russian autobiographical conceptions of childhood until well into the twentieth century.

Having characterized childhood from the point of view of author and narrator, Tolstoy proceeds to an extended recreation of a childhood scene from the perspective of Irten'ev the child. The scene described (the child falling asleep at evening tea) seems unremarkable in terms of content. Nothing dramatic happens here, and there is no obvious reason why this particular scene should have impressed itself indelibly on the child's mind. However, the choice of a scene of uneventful domestic bliss is quite logical. It emphasizes Tolstoy's eschewal of traditional plotting techniques and forces the reader to concentrate solely on the mood induced by the recollection:

> Having had your fill of running around, it would happen that you would be sitting at the tea table on your high chair; it's already late and sleep weighs down your eyes, but you don't move from your place, you sit and listen. And how could you not listen? Maman is talking to someone and the sounds of her voice are so sweet, so welcoming. How much those sounds say to my heart! I look at her face with eyes clouded over by sleepiness and suddenly she has become all itsy-bitsy—her face is no bigger than a button.

(1: 43)

The iterative "it would happen" indicates that the scene is a composite, but, with this exception, the rest of the paragraph (indeed, practically the rest of the chapter) stays entirely in the voice of the child.[10] This is by far the most extended section narrated from the child's point of view in *Childhood*. In fact, the successful narrative recreation of such a large chunk of childhood material would almost seem to belie the author's characterization of childhood as an "irretrievable time."

The recreated state of childhood happiness cannot last, however. It is destroyed by the same mind that resurrected it, as soon as that mind begins to question and analyze its own recollections. As the second and third parts of the trilogy will show, childhood innocence was lost under the twin onslaught of civilization and sexuality; the adult narrator's hope that he can recreate it disappears as soon as time and space intrude on the narrative. For the child, only the here and now exist. The narrator, on the other hand, is conscious of the spatial and temporal abyss separating him from his past self. As soon as the consciousness of the reminiscing narrator enters the text, the illusion that the past can be permanently recaptured is destroyed. Thus, at the end of chapter 15, the narrator asks himself: "Will the freshness, the insouciance, the need for love and the strength of belief that one possesses in childhood ever return?" (1: 45). The answer, of course, is that those things cannot return. The chapter, which began on such an ecstatic note, ends in a minor key with the narrator's realization that the "irretrievable time of childhood" is just that: "Is it possible that life has really left such deep scars in my heart that those tears and joys have gone forever? Do only memories remain?" (1: 45). The desire and ability to summon up a past, happy world, coupled with the realization that the world thus recreated is only an illusion, lies at the very core of *Childhood*.

As a number of critics have noticed, *Childhood* has no plot in the normal sense of the word.[11] In fact, for all intents and purposes, nothing really happens in the course of the narrative.[12] The structure of a typical nineteenth-century novel can be likened to that of a motion picture: individual sections are linked in a continuous flow of narrative. The structure of *Childhood,* in contrast, is that of an album of still photographs. Each page contains a certain number of moments captured in time, but, between these moments, there are unavoidable gaps. Each chapter presents a new set of images, but there is no reason to expect that these images should be connected to the ones in the previous chapter in anything but the most general way.[13] The success of *Childhood* was due, most of all, to Tolstoy's ability to use these loosely connected scenes in order to open up the minds of his protagonist and his narrator. The technique he employed—what N. G. Chernyshevsky, in his famous 1856 essay on *Childhood,* called the "dialectic of the soul"—was effective precisely because the absence of a conventional plot ensured that the reader's attention would be focused almost entirely on the younger Irten'ev's perceptions of the world and on the older Irten'ev's analysis of his past self. In order to strengthen the motivation for this powerful psychological presentation of the world, Tolstoy endowed Irten'ev with a prodigious capacity for reminiscence.

In a previous section I quoted the child's description of his feelings when he heard his mother play the piano. "That feeling resembled memories; but memories of what? It seemed you were recalling things that never happened" (1: 31). The image of a young child desperately searching for memories of an even earlier time would play an important role in subsequent Russian accounts of childhood. Most Russian gentry autobiographers recall having been sensitive, precocious children, a perception that this image of the preternaturally responsive Irten'ev certainly helped to form. Nor is this the only instance in which the child evinces a precocious tendency to reminiscence. For example, having just left home for the first time, Irten'ev sits in the carriage and thinks about his mother: "Every reminiscence led me to think about her. I remembered the mushroom that I found the day before in the birch walk, I remembered how Liubochka and Katen'ka argued over who should pick it, and I remembered how they cried saying goodbye to us." He does not remember his mother directly. Instead, he brings her to mind through a string of associative memories.[14] Indeed, it would seem that even as a child Irten'ev had a tendency to convert every experience into a "memory."

Earlier, I characterized the structure of *Childhood* in terms of a photo album. In view of the interlocking memories that hold the narrative together, a different and perhaps more appropriate metaphor suggests itself: one could say that *Childhood* is structured like the wooden "matreshka" dolls with which all Russian children play. The younger Irten'ev remembers something that happened to him; the adult narrator remembers the child remembering; finally, if the scene is autobiographical, one can imagine Tolstoy himself remembering it before placing it in the narrative.

Excluding Irten'ev himself, the central figure in *Childhood* is that of the mother. She is present on the very first page (in the form of a picture that Karl Ivanych hits with a fly swatter), and it is her death that marks the end of Irten'ev's childhood. It is not surprising, therefore, that she should be the only person, other than the child himself, to appear in the chapter called "Childhood." Her character is fully developed in chapter 2, which is entitled "Maman." As with the work as a whole, what is striking about this chapter is its total lack of conventional narrative interest. Instead of being organized around a specific event or events, material is presented in a series of static portraits: mother pouring tea, mother giving a piano lesson to Nikolai's sister, mother smiling, mother asking Nikolai how he slept. The series of portraits is, of course, a particularly effective way to evoke the child's perception of the world. For the child, scenes like this are repeated every day; there is no expectation that they will cease some time in the future, nor any remembrance of a time before they began. In this sense the child's perception of time is cyclical; there are but a limited number of possible events, and these are constantly repeated. The child's apprehension of the world is implicitly opposed by the narrator's. The older Irten'ev is always aware of just how fragile the child's world really is.

The attributes with which Tolstoy endows Irten'ev's mother were destined to be repeated in scores of Russian autobiographies and pseudo-autobiographies. Some of these attributes were part and parcel of a gentry upbringing. These include the ability to play the piano, to embroider, and to speak fluent French and German. Other qualities could not have been inculcated solely through education, but they too became de rigueur for the Russian autobiographical mother. Her eyes express "kindness and love" (1: 8). Her smile makes everyone who sees it happier. She is deeply religious but not fanatically so. She pities and helps the poor and religious pilgrims. She is scrupulously fair and is always good to her serfs. Indeed, in chapter 13, the narrator flashes back to the time before he was born and describes how his mother tried to free her nanny, Natal'ia Savishna. When Natal'ia Savishna refused to accept and expressed a desire to remain with the family, she became the unofficial nanny of all her mistress's children and the majordomo of the household.

Most important of all for the subsequent development of Russian accounts of childhood, Tolstoy emphasizes the close bond connecting mother and son—clearly the

closest bond that ever existed for Irten'ev. The narrator describes the scene of parting from her as follows: "It is strange that, while I vividly remember all the faces of the servants . . . I am completely unable to recall Maman's face or her position: maybe this is because for all of that time I couldn't work up the courage to look at her. It seemed to me that had I done so, my and her grief would have certainly reached impossible proportions" (1: 41). In these few pages of description and commentary, Tolstoy was able to create the pattern for almost all the mothers of Russian autobiography. This is all the more remarkable if we recall that, unlike much else in *Childhood,* the relationship of mother and child was entirely fictional.

While Irten'ev's mother is portrayed quite simply as "an angel," his father is a more complicated figure. In large measure this is due to the fact that the narrator knows his father better. His mother died before he was old enough to judge her or even to remember her very well. The father, on the other hand, is present from time to time throughout the trilogy, and the narrator has evidently had the chance to recognize his father's faults and his virtues. There are two separate chapters in *Childhood* devoted to a description of Irten'ev's father (chapter 3, "Papa," and chapter 10, "What Kind of Man Was My Father?"). The latter begins with a straightforward characterization that captures most of the father's important traits: "He was a man of the previous century and had the elusive combination of character traits typical of the youth of that century: chivalry, resourcefulness, self-confidence, amiability, and love of debauch [*razgul*]. . . . His two great passions were cards and women (1: 28-29).

The most important trait that Tolstoy gives Irten'ev's father is *razgul,* a kind of devil-may-care insouciance coupled with the ability to do nothing at all. In the course of the entire trilogy we never see the father do anything. He does not work and he never did (he was formerly an army officer). He manages his estates but, as we see in chapter 3, he has little control over what is actually done; all his arrangements are altered by his estate manager. Although it seems that Irten'ev feels close to his father, he does allow himself to judge him. Thus, he finishes his characterization as follows: "God only knows, whether he had any moral convictions. His life was so full of various enthusiasms that he never had the time to form any for himself. What is more, his life was so happy that he did not see any need for them" (1: 30). As was the case with the traits that Tolstoy gave Irten'ev's mother, his description of the father was destined to be repeated in many Russian autobiographies and pseudo-autobiographies.

The fact that the portraits of Irten'ev's mother and father are not based primarily on Tolstoy's own memories inevitably leads to the question: In what sense is *Child-hood* autobiographical? To some extent, this question can be answered by examining the development of the work in the course of four drafts. Overall, the first draft of *The Four Epochs of Development* is less autobiographical than the trilogy as we know it. It is in two parts: the first describes childhood, and the second deals with the periods of boyhood and youth, although there are no divisions into defined periods as such. The description of childhood contains, in a rather condensed form, much of the material that would later go into *Childhood.* There are, however, some crucial differences. Irten'ev was to be an illegitimate child (his mother had left her husband to live with her lover, Irten'ev's father), and much of the work's plot as well as the child's reactions to it hinged upon the difficulties inherent in the position of an illegitimate child in Russia. This situation clearly draws on the story of the Islenev family, neighbors of the Tolstoys and relations of his wife-to-be. Even more important, the second part of this first version has almost nothing to do with the remaining parts of the trilogy as it eventually came to be written. In the first draft, the children were brought to Moscow to be educated at a "commercial school." After the death of the mother, the father changes his plans and enrolls them in a "gymnasium." They live in the house of a professor of physiology who is an old acquaintance of the father's. Their life at his house and the problems of being poor and illegitimate form the central thread of the second part of the proposed text. Of the secondary characters present in the trilogy, we see only Karl Ivanych and Grisha. The French tutor is absent, as is the grandmother. Natal'ia Savishna is mentioned, but her character is not developed at all. In short, the life of the narrator of the proposed novel *The Four Epochs of Development* had little in common with Tolstoy's own.

As Tolstoy revised the novel, he began to eliminate some scenes that had nothing to do with his life and to add new scenes (or develop previously existing ones) with an autobiographical resonance. The description of life with Karl Ivanych is lengthened, and, in *Boyhood,* three entire chapters are devoted to his biography. In his *Memoirs,* Tolstoy was later to write: "In *Childhood* I described the German, our teacher Fed. Iv. Rössel, in as much detail as I could under the name of Karl Ivanych" (34: 370). The French *gouverneur* St. Jerome (St. Thomas in real life) appears. So does the grandmother, and, although she is made the mother's mother and not the father's, many of her characteristics are those which Tolstoy describes in his *Memoirs* more than 50 years later. I mention these examples merely to show that, in the course of writing, the trilogy became increasingly autobiographical.[15]

Nevertheless, even in the final version of *Childhood,* it would seem that there are not enough points of contact between the lives of Irten'ev and Tolstoy to justify call-

ing the work a fictionalized autobiography. Rather, it is a hybrid work, a true pseudo-autobiography, which liberally mixes facts from Tolstoy's life with invented situations. This free mixture has prompted Ginzburg to say that the trilogy is composed of "works that are more auto-psychological than autobiographical."[16] Nevertheless, there is evidence showing that the final version of *Childhood* contained enough autobiographical material for Tolstoy's immediate family to recognize themselves. A. V. Goldenveizer describes the moment of recognition quite dramatically. It seems that I. S. Turgenev read *Childhood* aloud to Tolstoy's sister and brother before the identity of the author had been revealed: "From the very first lines Mariia Nikolaevna and Sergei Nikolaevich were stunned: 'But that's us he described! Who is this?' 'At first we just couldn't think about Levochka,' continued Mariia Nikolaevna. 'He had gotten into debt and been taken off to the Caucasus. In all probability we thought about brother Nikolai.'"[17]

There was only one other feature of the content of *Childhood* that was as important for the future development of Russian autobiography and pseudo-autobiography as Irten'ev's portrait gallery. This was the child's attitude toward the physical world around him. The estate on which Irten'ev is depicted as growing up was, in many respects, typical for the estates of the middle rank of Russian gentry. Its most important single trait is self-sufficiency. For the child Irten'ev, the world of the estate is the entire world. It is a telling fact that, on the way to Moscow at the beginning of *Boyhood,* the young Irten'ev finds it hard to believe that there are people who do not know who he and his family are. On the estate, as the child of the master, Irten'ev is the center of the universe. He lives in the midst of the natural world, and the landscapes of rural central Russia have a special meaning for him. Much of the action of *Childhood* (and of the trilogy as a whole) takes place in the city, but the cityscape never makes a positive mark on the boy's consciousness. It is the countryside that resonates within the boy's soul, and Irten'ev's special relationship to nature plays an important role in determining the "plot" of the trilogy.

The natural world is perceived as a sphere of goodness standing against both social evils and personal problems. It is here that the influence of Rousseau on the young Tolstoy is felt most strongly. The idea that childhood innocence is a paradise lost that can best be recaptured through reminiscences of the natural world is repeated from time to time throughout the trilogy.[18] It is not only that nature opposes the baneful influence of civilization. For Tolstoy, nature defies time and space; its beauty, which changes at every season but always returns, recalls a time before the child understood the meaning of death and decay. Of course, since for both Tolstoy and Irten'ev this natural world was connected to a context of a Russian gentry estate, the experience

of the golden age is expressed by reference to the specifics of what a Soviet critic might call the "feudal-patriarchal order." The intense nostalgia evoked by memories of nature on the estate is not merely personal. By the early 1850's it was already clear that an era was drawing to an end; thus, not only would Tolstoy not experience his childhood again, but no one would ever grow up as he had. The system that had been operative at least since the days of Catherine the Great was passing. It is the combination of personal and collective loss that lends the nature scenes such a powerful resonance in the trilogy.

Irten'ev describes himself in the natural world for the first time when he recalls the hunt on the day before his departure for Moscow. If Irten'ev's ability to recall the tiniest details of long-past events seemed amazing when he described people, then his photographic recall of the scene before the hunt is completely beyond the realm of the possible. The description is meant to be in the voice of the child, but it is so hyperrealistic that it cannot possibly be read as a remembered moment. At moments like these, Tolstoy's realism of description ends up contradicting his psychological realism: "There were swarms of ants swarming over the uncovered roots of the oak tree under which I was sitting. They went over the dry gray earth, through the dried oak leaves and the acorns, the desiccated, moss-covered twigs, the yellow-green moss, and the rare thin blades of green grass" (1: 25).

It is not merely the detail with which Irten'ev is able to recall the scene that is unusual. Even more surprising is his conviction that he can commune with nature in a personal way. He looks at a butterfly and notes: "I don't know whether the sun had warmed her up, or whether she had taken the juice from that little grass, but it was clear that she was feeling fine" (1: 25). Nor is Irten'ev's ability confined merely to understanding the moods of lower animals. Nature speaks directly to him. For example, at the beginning of *Boyhood,* when the grieving family is returning to Moscow after Irten'ev's mother's funeral, they are overtaken by a thunderstorm. Naturally, the thunder and lightning scare the boy, but what he feels is not merely a child's normal fear of thunder. He interprets the storm as an apocalyptic moment: "Troubling feelings of anguish and fear grew in me as the storm strengthened, but when the grandiose moment of silence arrived—the moment which usually precedes the outbreak of a thunderstorm—those feelings increased so much that if this state had lasted another quarter of an hour I am sure I would have died of agitation" (2: 10). But nature, which has the power to bring the boy to the point of death, also has the power to change his mood almost immediately. The thunderstorm passes and, with it, so does the boy's anxiety. Indeed, the state of his soul is directly connected to that of the external world: "I experience that inexpressibly

joyful feeling of hope in life, which quickly replaces the heavy feeling of fear. My soul is smiling, just like refreshed and newly merry nature" (2: 11-12).

In addition to being powerfully affected by the actual experience of the natural world, Irten'ev (both the child and the adult) can be moved by the mere recollection of the scenery of his childhood paradise. In *Childhood,* after Irten'ev has embarrassed himself by dancing incorrectly at his grandmother's, he consoles himself with intertwined memories of his mother and of the estate's natural surroundings. The whole passage is in the voice of the child:

> For if Maman had been here, she would not have blushed for her Nikolen'ka . . . and my imagination floated far beyond that dear image. I recalled the meadow in front of the house, the tall lindens in the garden, the clean pond which the swallows soar over, the blue sky in which white transparent clouds stand still, the aromatic stacks of fresh hay, and many other peaceful and joyful memories floated through my roiled imagination.

(1: 72)

The link between memories of the mother and those of the unspoiled land is a symbolically logical one. In later Russian autobiography the mother figure (who can also be a grandmother or a nanny) frequently takes on the overt characteristics of a pagan mother-earth goddess combined with those of an angel in human form.[19] The perfection of the mother and the healing power of nature will become two of the central myths of gentry childhood.

Nor is it only the child who is capable of feeling the refreshing power of nature. In the chapter entitled "Youth," the older Irten'ev senses it as well. He says, "That summer I was young, innocent, free and, therefore, almost happy" (2: 175). Then he begins to reminisce. He looks at the birches, which "hiding behind one another retreated from me into the distance of the pure forest," and he enjoys "exactly the same fresh young strength of life which nature breathed all around me." The chapter ends with the statement: "At that time it seemed as if nature and the moon and I, that we were all one and the same thing" (2: 180).

In a number of important respects, the relationship between Irten'ev and nature corresponds to that which is characteristic for what Bakhtin calls the idyll: "Finally the third characteristic of an idyll . . . is the combination of human life with the life of nature, the unity of their rhythm, a common language for natural phenomena and events of human life."[20] If the trilogy is to be considered an idyll, however, it is an idyll of a specific type: the paradise lost. The narrator has grown up and has left the estate. He can recapture its charm only through memory. In this sense, the estate and childhood are analogous. Memories of one are inextricably linked to memories of the other, and both types of memories "freshen and exalt the soul."

In *Childhood,* Tolstoy presented Russian literature with a model for writing about childhood and proposed an interpretation of the meaning and purpose of this stage of life. From the first, he had hoped that his work would be read as a general statement, not simply as a fictionalized version of his own early years. He must have been gratified when most early reviewers singled out the universality of his portrayal for praise. He would probably have been even more gratified had he known the extent to which his literary method and his myths of childhood permeated Russian autobiographies and pseudo-autobiographies for the next 70 years.[21]

As I noted earlier, in a discussion of *Childhood* in *Diary of a Writer,* Dostoevsky called Tolstoy the poet and historian of the upper-middle gentry class.[22] We are now in a better position to see just how perceptive this statement was. It is true that the kinds of experiences Irten'ev describes were typical of a gentry childhood. In this sense Tolstoy was a kind of historian. But these kinds of experiences had not been expressed in Russia previously, nor (and this is even more important) had they been given a general interpretation. In his overall conception, in his descriptions and interpretation of Irten'ev's surroundings, of his parents, and of Irten'ev himself, Tolstoy invented a Russian gentry attitude toward childhood. In time, his personal myths of childhood became the foundation on which practically all future Russian works on the subject were constructed. In this sense he was not the historian of gentry childhood, but rather its creator, a poet first and foremost.

Notes

1. Eikhenbaum shows that vague literary strivings of this kind were typical of young men of Tolstoy's age and position: "Why did literary projects appear in Tolstoy's programs for 1851? At that time, literature had become a typical occupation for a man of the world" (*Lev Tolstoy,* p. 30).

2. Eikhenbaum was among the first to point out the importance of Tolstoy's journal for his development as a writer. See *Lev Tolstoy,* pp. 33-37.

3. For a more complete account of the development of *Childhood,* see M. A. Tsiavlovsky, "Komentarii k 'Detstvu,'" Tolstoy, *Polnoe sobranie sochinenii,* vol. 1, pp. 303-28.

4. Describing this first version, Tsiavlovsky says: "The story of a family of the Tolstoys' close friends, the Islavins, forms the basis of the narrative" (ibid., p. 305). The final version is not, of course, completely autobiographical either, but it is more autobiographical than this initial version.

For a more comprehensive discussion of the auto-biographicalization of *Childhood,* see pp. 51-53 in this volume.

5. Tolstoy, *Polnoe sobranie sochinenii,* 1: 103. All further citations from the writings of Tolstoy will be made in the text by reference to volume and page number from this edition.

6. In this respect the trilogy differs from the diaries and "A History of Yesterday," even as it grows out of them. In the diaries Tolstoy speaks to himself. He is the implied reader of his own text, as it were. In the latter work the narrator speaks about himself directly to the reader. There is no interaction between author and narrator and (because almost no time has elapsed between narrated event and its narration) no possibility for interaction between the narrator and his past incarnation.

7. Still, it is clear that *Childhood* has a didactic component and that Tolstoy the moralist was already present in his first published work. He says as much in a diary entry for November 30, 1852: "Since it is a novel about an intelligent, sensitive man who has lost his way, it will be instructive" (46: 151).

8. Tolstoy evidently retained a sentimental attachment to childhood and to his first work to the very end of his life. In 1910 he told V. Bulgakov: "When I was writing *Childhood,* it seemed to me that prior to me no one had ever felt or expressed all the poetry and wonder of childhood" (quoted in Ostrovsky, p. 158).

9. Tolstoy's concept of the golden age is rather different from the traditional one. In the idylls of earlier generations there were no moments of unhappiness: nothing interrupted the bliss of those who dwelt in the ideal land. Tolstoy was too much a realist to write an idyll of this sort. He recognized that tragedy and unhappiness are potentially present at any time of life. However, he seems to have felt that moments of tragedy are essentially irrelevant to childhood's ultimate happiness, because the child's innate purity allows him to soar above the details of everyday life.

10. One could claim that the sentence, "How much those sounds say to my heart!" is in the narrator's voice. Although this interpretation is possible, it is not obligatory, since there is no information present in it that the child could not have known, no emotion that he could not have felt.

11. As usual, Eikhenbaum seems to have been the first to make this discovery: "The lack of a plot and his interest in details caused the movement of the novella to become organized not in terms of years or even of days, but of hours. . . . In fact, the composition of *Childhood* is organized around the juxtaposition of separate scenes that are linked by lyric commentary and 'generalizations'" (*Lev Tolstoy,* p. 87).

12. There is, of course, one important event in *Childhood* (the death of Nikolai's mother), but even this moment of action is treated in a peculiarly unnovelistic fashion. At one moment she is alive, bidding farewell to her husband and children, at the next they receive a letter informing them she is ill, and, finally, they arive home just before she dies. The death itself takes place offstage and is included not out of any narrative necessity (there is no need for a death to move the plot forward) but as a point around which a number of set scenes can be arranged, and as a convenient end point for the book.

13. One could also compare the structure of *Childhood* to that of a lyric poem rather than to that of a novel. As in a poem, the connections between sections are linked more to the mood of the text than to the inexorable forward motion of a plot line.

14. Recall also the passage I discuss earlier in which the child thinks of Sonechka in terms of "sweet dreams and memories."

15. The trilogy is not the only example in Tolstoy's oeuvre of a work that became more autobiographical as it was being written. The most famous case is, of course, *Anna Karenina.* The autobiographically based Levin does not even appear in the early drafts. In the course of writing he became more and more central until, in the final version, he is as important as Anna herself.

16. Ginzburg, p. 299.

17. Goldenveizer, p. 175.

18. Indeed, as Markovitch has noted, it runs through Tolstoy's entire oeuvre: "Like Rousseau, Tolstoy believes in the possibility of a 'return to nature,' and in the happy consequences for humankind that would result from it. In order to be good and happy, a person must quit society and its prejudices, must draw closer to the solitude of the fields, the natural life, must become a wild man in the manner of Rousseau" (p. 208).

19. According to Hubbs, this connection is not unique to Russian autobiography, but rather reflects an enduring mythological pattern in Russian culture: "The desire for a woman savior is expressed in a constant adulation of the ethical strengths of the good woman and the refusal to consider the virtues of male heroism" (pp. 230-31). Heldt notes some of these same tendencies in Russian fiction:

"The Russian heroine is generally taken as a marvelous given of nature, a being in whom not only her own and her family's future, but the future hope of Russia resides" (p. 12). For my discussion of how such mother myths were translated into gentry autobiographies, see Chapter 3, pp. 96-99.

20. Bakhtin, p. 259.

21. To some extent, of course, Tolstoy was aware of his influence, both in the realm of fiction and in that of autobiography. A. P. Beliaev, for example, sent his (Tolstoy-influenced) memoirs to the master for comments, and notes that Tolstoy encouraged him to publish them. Tolstoy also read the memoirs of A. K. Chertkova. In his diary for 1909, he characterized the work (which, among other Tolstoyan moments, begins with an epigraph from *Childhood*) as "very good."

22. Dostoevsky, 25: 32.

Bibliography

Works preceded by an asterisk (*) are autobiographical sources and have been annotated by the author.

Aksakov, S. T. "Pis'ma k M. A. Maksimovichu." *Kievskaia starina,* 1893, no. 4: 829-40.

————. "Pis'ma S. T., K. S., i I. S. Aksakovykh k I. S. Turgenevu." *Russkoe obozrenie,* 1894, no. 8: 460-84; no. 9: 5-38; no. 10: 478-501; no. 11: 7-30; no. 12: 599-601.

————. *Sobranie sochinenii v piati tomakh.* 5 vols. Moscow, 1966.

*Aksakova, V. S. *Dnevnik, 1854-55.* St. Petersburg, 1913. Not about the author's childhood.

Alexandrov, Vladimir. *Andrey Bely: The Major Symbolist Fiction.* Cambridge, Mass., 1985.

————. "Kotik Lctaev, The Baptized Chinaman, and Notes of an Eccentric." In John E. Malmsted, ed., *Andrey Bely: Spirit of Symbolism.* Ithaca, N.Y., 1987.

*Almedingen, E. M. *Fanny.* New York, 1970. Based on the first-person notes of the author's aunt, Francine Hermione de Poltoratzky. Original notes written 1913. Positive memories of childhood.

Anikst, M. A., and V. S. Turchin, eds. . . . *v okrestnostiakh Moskvy: Iz istorii russkoi usadebnoi kul'tury XVII-XIX vekov.* Moscow, 1979.

*Anonymous. "Iz nedavnogo proshlogo." *Russkaia starina,* 1910, vol. 143, no. 8: 246-66; no. 9: 441-59. Author born in mid-1850's. Positive memories of childhood.

Ariès, Philippe. *L'enfant et la vie familiale sous l'ancien régime.* Paris, 1973.

Arndt, Walter. *Pushkin Threefold.* New York, 1972.

Avdeenko, A. *la liubliu.* Moscow, 1967.

Averin, B. V. "Iz tvorcheskoi istorii romana I. A. Bunina 'Zhizn' Arsen'eva.'" *Buninskii sbornik.* Orel, 1974.

Axthelm, Peter M. *The Modern Confessional Novel.* New Haven, 1967.

*B—n, S. "Vospominaniia." *Russkaia shkola,* 1911, no. 4: 155-76; no. 5/6: 127-59; no. 7/8: 163-92; no. 9: 79-95. "My dear, irretrievable childhood" (5: 159).

Baboreko, A. *I. A. Bunin: Materialy dlia biografii.* Moscow, 1967.

Bakhtin, M. M. *Literaturno-kriticheskie stat'i.* Moscow, 1986.

Banfield, Ann. *Unspeakable Sentences: Narration and Representation in the Language of Fiction.* Boston, 1982.

Barthes, Roland. *Mythologies.* Tr. Annette Lavers. New York, 1972.

Becker, Seymour. *Nobility and Privilege in Late Imperial Russia.* Dekalb, Ill., 1985.

*Beketova, M. A. "Shakhmatova. Semeinaia khronika." In *Literaturnoe nasledstvo, Aleksandr Blok,* 1982, no. 92, 4 vols. Vol. 3. Not about the author's childhood. Discusses the material and personal surroundings that helped form Blok's character.

*Beliaev, A. P. "Perezhitoe i peredumannoe s 1803 goda." *Russkaia starina,* 1880, vol. 29, no. 9: 1-42. Author born in 1803. Grew up on country estate. "Carefree and happy childhood" (p. 10).

Belyi, A. "Formy iskusstva." *Mir iskusstva,* 1902, no. 12.

————. *Kotik Letaev.* Munich, 1964.

————. *Kreshchenyi kitaets.* Munich, 1969.

————. *Na rubezhe dvukh stoletii.* Letchworth, Hertfordshire, 1966.

————. *Simvolizm.* Moscow, 1910.

*Benois, Alexandre. *Memoirs.* Tr. Moura Budberg. London, 1960. Author born in 1870. A city childhood that is not discussed in depth.

Bilinkis, Ia. S. *O tvorchestve L. N. Tolstogo.* Leningrad, 1959.

Blok, A. A. "Vozmezdie." In *Stikhotvoreniia.* Leningrad, 1955.

Blum, Jerome. *Lord and Peasant in Russia from the Ninth to the Nineteenth Century.* New York, 1969.

Bocharov, S. "L. Tolstoy i novoe ponimanie cheloveka. 'Dialektika dushi.'" In *Literatura i novyi chelovek.* Moscow, 1963.

*Bolotov, A. T. *Zapiski*. St. Petersburg, 1871. Author born in 1738. Almost no description of childhood.

*Bolotov, A. V. *Sviatye i greshnye: Vospominaniia byvshego cheloveka*. Paris, 1924. Author born in 1866. Childhood takes place on family estates in Orel and Tula provinces. "All of this is dear, but distant legend; an irretrievable, good, old, carefree time, insouciant childhood" (p. 11).

Borras, F. M. *Maxim Gorky: The Writer*. Oxford, 1967.

Brochier, Hubert. "Psychoanalyse et désir d'autobiographie." In Claudette Delhez-Sariet and Maurizio Catani, eds., *Individualisme et autobiographie en Occident*. Brussels, 1983.

Brokgaus, F. A., and I. A. Efron, eds. *Entsiklopedicheskii slovar'*. 82 vols. St. Petersburg, 1890-1904.

Bruss, Elizabeth. *Autobiographical Acts: The Changing Situation of a Literary Genre*. Baltimore, 1976.

Bunin, I. A. *Literaturnoe nasledstvo*. Eds. A. N. Dubovnikov and S. A. Makashin. No. 84, 2 vols. Moscow, 1973.

———. *Sobranie sochinenii*. 9 vols. Moscow, 1965-67.

———. *Ustami Buninykh*. Ed. Militsia Green. 3 vols. Frankfurt am Main, 1977.

———. *Vospominaniia*. Paris, 1981.

Chateaubriand, Vicomte de. *René*. In *Oeuvres complètes,* vol. 3. 12 vols. Paris, 1861.

Chekhov, A. P. *Sobranie sochinenii v dvenadtsati tomakh*. 12 vols. Moscow, 1960-64.

Chernyshevsky, N. G. "Detstvo i otrochestvo. Sochinenie Grafa L. N. Tolstogo. Voennye rasskazy Grafa L. N. Tolstogo." In S. P. Bychkov, ed., *L. N. Tolstoy v russkoi kritike*. 2d ed. Moscow, 1952.

*Chertkova, A. K. *Iz moego detstva*. Moscow, 1911. Author born in early 1860's. Childhood takes place in the country on the upper Volga. Chertkova was the wife of one of Tolstoy's chief disciples, V. G. Chertkov. Her happy memories are clearly modeled on Tolstoy's *Childhood.*

Chombart de Lauwe, Marie Jose. *Un monde autre: l'enfance*. Paris, 1971.

Christian, R. F. *Tolstoy: A Critical Introduction*. Cambridge, Eng., 1969.

Chuprina, I. V. *Trilogiia L. Tolstogo 'Detstvo,' 'Otrochestvo,' 'Iunost'.'* Saratov, 1961.

Coe, Richard N. "Mother Russia and the Russian Mother." *Proceedings of the Leeds Philosophical and Literary Society, Literary and Historical Section*. Vol. 19, pt. 6. December 1984, pp. 44-67.

———. *When the Grass Was Taller: Autobiography and the Experience of Childhood*. New Haven, 1984.

Cohen, Elliot. "The Genre of the Autobiographical Account of Childhood—Three Test Cases: The Trilogies of Tolstoy, Aksakov, and Gorky." Ph.D. diss., Yale University, 1973.

Cohn, Dorrit. *Transparent Minds: Narrative Modes for Presenting Consciousness in Fiction*. Princeton, 1978.

Connolly, Julian W. *Ivan Bunin*. Boston, 1982.

Constant, Benjamin. *Adolphe*. Paris, 1867.

*Davydov, N. V. "Iz pomeshchich'ei zhizni proshlogo stoletiia." *Golos minuvshego,* 1916, no. 2: 164-200. This account is primarily about the author's parents. Few details about own childhood.

*Davydov, V. N. *Rasskaz o proshlom*. Moscow, 1931. Author born in 1849. Childhood passed in small town in Kherson province. "My childhood was happy, joyful" (p. 77).

Dieckmann, Eberhard. *Erzählformen im Frühwerk L. N. Tolstojs, 1851-1857*. Berlin, 1969.

*Dmitriev, I. I. *Vzgliad na moiu zhizn'*. Moscow, 1866. Author born in 1760. Memoir written in 1823. Almost nothing about childhood.

Dobychin, L. *Gorod En*. Moscow, 1935.

Dostoevsky, F. M. *Polnoe sobranie sochinenii v tridtsati tomakh*. 30 vols. Leningrad, 1972-.

Drobat, L. S. "O trilogii Tolstogo." In *Iasnopolianskii sbornik, 1980*. Tula, 1981.

Dunn, Patrick P. "'That Enemy Is the Baby': Childhood in Imperial Russia." In Lloyd deMause, ed., *The History of Childhood*. New York, 1974.

Durkin, Andrew. *Sergey Aksakov and Russian Pastoral*. New Brunswick, N.J., 1983.

*Durova, Nadezhda. *Kavalerist-devitsa*. Leningrad, 1985. First published 1836. Author born in 1783. Childhood unhappy. Durova's tomboyish tendencies were suppressed by her mother.

Eagleton, Terry. *Criticism and Ideology*. London, 1976.

Eikhenbaum, B. M. *Lev Tolstoy: Kniga pervaia, piatidesiatye gody*. Leningrad, 1928.

———. *Molodoi Tolstoy*. Berlin, 1922.

Elsworth, J. D. *Andrey Bely: A Critical Study of the Novels*. Cambridge, Eng., 1983.

Emerson, Caryl. *Boris Godunov: Transpositions of a Russian Theme*. Bloomington, Ind., 1986.

Emmons, Terence. *The Russian Landed Gentry and the Peasant Emancipation of 1861*. Cambridge, Mass., 1968.

Evseeva, T. I. "Psikhologiia rebenka v trilogii L. N. Tolstogo 'Detstvo. Otrochestvo. Iunost'.'" In *L. N. Tolstoy kak pedagog*, vol. 2. Tula, 1969.

*Fet, A. A. *Vospominaniia*. Moscow, 1983. Author born in 1820. Childhood passed in Orel province. Ambivalent memories of childhood.

Foster, Liudmila A. *Bibliography of Russian Emigré Literature, 1918-1968*. 2 vols. Boston, 1970.

Fowler, Alistair. *Kinds of Literature: An Introduction to the Theory of Genres and Modes*. Cambridge, Mass., 1982.

Gavrilov, A. I., et al., eds. *Buninskii sbornik*. Orel, 1974.

Gazdanov, Gaito. *Vecher u Klèr*. Ann Arbor, 1979.

Geertz, Clifford. *The Interpretation of Cultures*. New York, 1973.

Genette, Gérard. *Figures III*. Paris, 1972.

Ginzburg, L. Ia. *O psikhologicheskoi proze*. Leningrad, 1977.

Girard, Alain. *Le journal intime*. Paris, 1963.

Gladkov, F. V. *Povest' o detstve*. Moscow, 1980.

*Glinsky, B. B. "Iz letopisi usad'by Sergeevki." *Istoricheskii vestnik*, 1894, vol. 58, no. 10: 57-85. Author born in late 1850's or early 1860's. Happy childhood takes place on country estate in "T" province (probably Tula).

Gogol, N. V. *Polnoe sobranie sochinenii*. 14 vols. Moscow, 1940-52.

Goldenveizer, A. V. *Vblizi Tolstogo*. Moscow, 1959.

Goncharov, I. A. *Oblomov*. Leningrad, 1978.

Gorky, M. *Polnoe sobranie sochinenii v tridtsati piati tomakh*. Ed. M. L. Leonov et al. 35 vols. Moscow, 1968-82.

Greenwood, E. B. *Tolstoy: The Comprehensive Vision*. London, 1975.

*Grot, N. P. *Iz semeinoi khroniki*. St. Petersburg, 1900. Author born in 1825. Childhood takes place on estate in Riazan' province. "We were the happiest of children" (p. 17).

Guillen, Claudio. *Literature as a System: Essays Toward the Theory of Literary History*. Princeton, 1971.

Gunn, Janet. *Autobiography: Toward a Poetics of Experience*. Philadelphia, 1982.

Gusdorf, Georges. "Conditions et limites de l'autobiographie." In *Formen der Selbstdarstellung*. Berlin, 1956.

Gusev, N. N. *Lev Nikolaevich Tolstoy: Materialy k biografii s 1828 po 1855 god*. Moscow, 1954.

Gusev, N. N., et al., eds. *L. N. Tolstoy v vospominaniiakh sovremennikov*. 2 vols. Moscow, 1960.

Gustafson, Richard. *Leo Tolstoy, Resident and Stranger: A Study in Fiction and Theology*. Princeton, 1986.

Hamburger, Käte. *The Logic of Literature*. Tr. Marilynn J. Rose. Bloomington, Ind., 1973.

Heldt, Barbara. *Terrible Perfection: Women and Russian Literature*. Bloomington, Ind., 1987.

*Herzen, A. I. *Byloe i dumy*. In *Sochineniia v deviati tomakh*, vols. 4-5. Moscow, 1956. Most of this famous autobiography is devoted to Herzen's adult years. In English exile he fondly recalled memories of summers on his father's country estates, although, overall, his memories of childhood were ambivalent.

Hobsbawm, Eric. "Introduction. Inventing Traditions." In Eric Hobsbawm and Terence Ranger, eds., *The Invention of Tradition*. New York, 1983.

Hubbs, Joanna. *Mother Russia: The Feminine Myth in Russian Culture*. Bloomington, Ind., 1988.

Iablokov, M. T., ed. *Rod dvorian Arsen'evykh 1389-1901*. Tula, 1903.

Iokar, L. N. "Gorky za chteniem knig o L. Tolstom." *Russkaia literatura*, 1973, no. 3: 151-61.

Iser, Wolfgang. *The Implied Reader: Patterns of Communication in Prose Fiction from Bunyan to Beckett*. Baltimore, 1974.

Ivanov, V. I. "Mladenchestvo." In *Sobranie sochinenii*, vol. 1. Brussels, 1971.

Jauss, Hans Robert. *Toward an Aesthetic of Reception*. Tr. Timothy Bahti. Minneapolis, 1982.

*Kamensky, S. *Vek minuvshii*. Paris, 1958. Author born in 1883. Generally happy childhood in the town of Tambov.

*Karpinskaia, Iu. N. "Iz semeinoi khroniki." *Istoricheskii vestnik*, 1897, vol. 70, no. 12: 853-70. This account is about estate life in general and does not really deal with the author's childhood.

Kassil', Lev. *Konduit i Shvambraniia*. Moscow, 1959.

Kataev, V. P. "Trava zabven'ia." In *Almaznyi moi venets: Povesti*. Moscow, 1981.

*Khvostova, E. A. *Zapiski*. Moscow, 1869. Written in 1836-37. Does not deal with childhood.

Koblitz, Ann Hibner. *A Convergence of Lives*. Boston, 1983.

*Kornilova, O. I. *Byl' iz vremen krepostnichestva*. St. Petersburg, 1890. Author born in 1840's. Childhood on country estate south of Moscow. "I have retained the most joyous memories of my childhood" (p. 8).

Korolenko, V. G. *Istoriia moego sovremennika.* In *Sobranie sochinenii v desiati tomakh,* vols. 5-7. Moscow, 1954-56.

*Kovalevskaia, S. V. *Vospominaniia detstva.* Moscow, 1960. Author born in 1850. Childhood on various country estates. Negative memories.

Kozlik, Frédéric C. *L'influence de l'anthroposophie sur l'oeuvre d'Andréi Biélyi.* 3 vols. Frankfurt, 1981.

Krasnov, G. B. "M. Gorky i literaturnaia traditsiia L. Tolstogo." In *M. Gorky i russkaia literatura.* Gorky, 1970.

*Kropotkin, P. A. *Zapiski revoliutsionera.* Moscow, 1966. Author born in 1842. Childhood spent in Moscow with summers in the country. Ambivalent memories of childhood.

Kuhn, Reinhard. *Corruption in Paradise: The Child in Western Literature.* Hanover, N.H., 1982.

*Kuzminskaia, T. A. *Moia zhizn' doma i v Iasnoi Poliane.* Tula, 1959. Not primarily about the author's childhood.

Kuz'mychev, Ivan. "'Detstvo' i ego literaturnaia predystoriia." *Volga,* 1978, no. 8: 171-87.

*Labzina, A. E. *Vospominaniia.* 2d ed. St. Petersburg, 1914. Memoir written in 1810. Describes period of 1760's and 1770's. No childhood description.

Larrain, Jorge. *The Concept of Ideology.* Athens, Ga., 1979.

Lejeune, Philippe. *Le pacte autobiographique.* Paris, 1975.

*Lelong, A. K. "Vospominaniia." *Russkii arkhiv,* 1913, bk. 2, no. 6: 778-808; no. 7: 52-103; 1914, bk. 2, no. 6/7: 370-407; no. 8: 535-56. Author born in 1841. Childhood on country estate in Riazan' province. "My dear, quiet childhood" (1913, bk. 2, no. 7: 103). This is one of the most extensive and best accounts of childhood available.

Leont'ev, Konstantin. *Egipetsky golub'.* New York, 1954.

Levin, Dan. *Stormy Petrel: The Life and Work of Maxim Gorky.* New York, 1965.

Levitov, A. I. "Moia familiia." In *Sochineniia v odnom tome.* Moscow, 1956.

Lidin, VI., ed. *Literaturnaia Rossiia: Sbornik sovremennoi prozy.* Moscow, 1924.

Likhachov, D. S. *Poeziia sadov.* Leningrad, 1982.

Lotman, Iu. M. *Roman A. S. Pushkina "Evgenii Onegin": Kommentarii.* Leningrad, 1980.

———. "Tema kart i kartochnoi igry v russkoi literature nachala XIX v." In *Trudy po znakovym sistemam,* vol. 7. Tartu, 1975.

Lotman, Iu. M., and B. A. Uspensky. *The Semiotics of Russian Culture.* Ed. Ann Shukman. Ann Arbor, 1984.

*L'vova, E. V. "Davno minuvshee." *Russkii vestnik,* 1901, vol. 275, no. 10: 399-416; vol. 276, no. 11: 76-89. Author born in early 1850's. A rare unhappy childhood as a result of the death of her father and subsequent family impoverishment.

Makashin, S. *Saltykov-Shchedrin.* 2 vols. Moscow, 1951.

Mandel'shtam, O. E. "Shum vremeni." In *Sobranie sochinenii v trekh tomakh.* Ed. G. P. Struve and B. A. Fillipov. 3 vols. Washington, D.C., 1967.

Manning, Roberta Thompson. *The Crisis of the Old Order in Russia: Gentry and Government.* Princeton, 1982.

Markovitch, Milan I. *Jean-Jacques Rousseau et Tolstoï.* Geneva, 1975.

Mashinsky, S. *S. T. Aksakov: Zhizn' i tvorchestvo.* Moscow, 1973.

Medvedev, N., ed. *M. Gorky o detskoi literature.* Moscow, 1952.

*Mengden, E. "Iz dnevnika vnuchki." *Russkaia starina,* 1913, vol. 153, no. 1: 103-31. Author born in 1825. Childhood on country estate. "The sunny days of my childhood" (p. 109).

*Mengden, S. V. "Otryvki iz semeinoi khroniki." *Russkaia starina,* 1908, vol. 134, no. 4: 97-116; no. 5: 325-48. Author born in mid-1860's. Childhood on estate in Tula province. "My happy childhood" (5: 327).

Mikhailovsky, B. V. "Avtobiograficheskaia trilogiia M. Gor'kogo." In *Literatura i novyi chelovek.* Moscow, 1963.

Morson, Gary Saul. *The Boundaries of Genre.* Austin, 1981.

———. *Hidden in Plain View: Narrative and Creative Potentials in 'War and Peace.'* Stanford, 1987.

Muramtseva-Bunina, V. N. *Zhizn' Bunina, 1870-1906.* Paris, 1958.

Muratova, K. D. *M. Gorky: Seminarii.* Moscow, 1981.

Musset, Alfred de. *La confession d'un enfant du siècle.* Paris, 1859.

Nabokov, Vladimir. *The Gift.* New York, 1963.

———. *Look at the Harlequins!* New York, 1974.

*———. *Speak, Memory.* New York, 1947. Author born in 1899. Idyllic childhood in Petersburg and on family estate near that city.

*Obolensky, L. E. "Kartiny proshlogo." *Istoricheskii vestnik,* 1906, vol. 105, no. 9: 771-89; vol. 106, no. 10:

104-32. Author born in early 1850's. Childhood takes place in the country. "Dear, distant childhood" (9: 773).

*Obolensky, V. A. *Ocherki minuvshego*. Belgrade, 1931. Author born in early 1870's. Childhood takes place in Petersburg and on family estate near Smolensk. Positive memories.

Okenfuss, Max J. *The Discovery of Childhood in Russia: The Evidence of the Slavic Primer.* Newtonville, Mass., 1980.

*Osorgin, M. *Vremena*. Paris, 1955. Author born in late 1880's. Childhood spent north of Moscow on the Volga. A strong and lyrical nostalgia for childhood permeates this account.

Ostrovsky, A., ed. *Molodoi Tolstoy v zapisiax sovremennikov*. Leningrad, 1929.

Panaev, I. I. *Literaturnye vospominaniia*. Moscow, 1950.

Panaeva, Avdot'ia. *Semeistvo Tal'nikovykh*. Leningrad, 1928.

Paperno, Irina. *Chernyshevsky and the Age of Realism: A Study in the Semiotics of Behavior.* Stanford, 1988.

Pascal, Roy. "The Autobiographical Novel and the Autobiography." *Essays in Criticism,* 1959, vol. 9, no. 2: 134-50.

———. *Design and Truth in Autobiography.* London, 1960.

*Passek, T. P. *Iz dal'nikh let.* 2 vols. Moscow, 1963. Author born in 1810. Childhood in countryside. She has mixed memories of childhood. Says that writing down childhood memories helped "bring her back to life" during a tragic period of her life (1: 76).

Pasternak, B. L. "Okhrannaia gramota." In *Vozdushnye puti.* Moscow, 1982.

Paterson, Janet M. "L'autoreprésentation: Formes et discours." *Texte,* 1982, no. 1: 177-94.

Pavel, Thomas G. *Fictional Worlds.* Cambridge, Mass., 1986.

Pfeiffer, John Richard. "The Child in Nineteenth-Century British Fiction and Thought: A Typology." Ph.D. diss., University of Kentucky, 1969.

Piksanov, N. K. "Tolstoy i Gorky: Lichnye, ideinye, i tvorcheskie vstrechi." In *Tolstoy i russkaia literatura.* Gorky, 1961.

Pokrovskaia, A. K., and N. V. Chekhov, eds. *Materialy po istorii russkoi detskoi literatury (1750-1855).* Series 1, vol. 1. Moscow, 1927.

Pokrovsky, V. I., ed. *Sergei Timofeevich Aksakov, ego zhizn' i sochineniia: Sbornik istoriko-literaturnykh statei.* 2d ed. Moscow, 1912.

Pomialovsky, N. G. "Meshchanskoe schast'e." In *Sochineniia.* Moscow, 1951.

Raeff, Marc. *Origins of the Russian Intelligentsia: The Eighteenth-Century Nobility.* New York, 1966.

Reshetnikov, F. M. *Mezhdu liud'mi.* In *Sochineniia F. M. Reshetnikova v dvukh tomakh,* vol. 1. St. Petersburg, 1890.

Robinson, Geroid Tanquary. *Rural Russia Under the Old Regime.* Berkeley, 1972.

Romberg, Bertil. *Studies in the Narrative Technique of the First-Person Novel.* Stockholm, 1962.

Rousseau, Jean-Jacques. *Les Confessions.* Paris, 1841.

Rynikov, N. A. *Avtobiografii rabochikh i ikh izuchenie.* Moscow, 1930.

*Sabaneeva, E. A. *Vospominaniia o bylom.* St. Petersburg, 1914. Author born in the 1830's. Childhood takes place on estate in Kaluga province. She sees childhood and its natural surroundings as the foundation of her entire "moral being" (p. 2).

Salaman, Esther. *The Great Confession.* London, 1973.

*Salov, A. I. "Umchavshiesia gody." *Russkaia mysl',* 1897, bk. 7: 1-27; bk. 8: 1-25; bk. 9: 56-81. Author born in 1834. Childhood on father's estate in Penza province. Childhood is "a happy time" (8: 16).

Saltykov-Shchedrin, M. E. *Poshekhonskaia starina.* In *Sobraniia sochinenii v dvadtsati tomakh,* vol. 17. Moscow, 1975.

*Semenov-Tian-Shansky, P. P. *Detstvo i iunost'.* 7th ed. Petrograd, 1917. Author born in 1827. Childhood takes place on estate in Riazan' province. "Happy childhood" (p. 103).

*Shatilov, N. I. "Iz nedavnogo proshlogo." *Golos minuvshego,* 1916, no. 1: 165-201; no. 4: 205-25; no. 7/8: 171-87; no. 9: 21-39; no. 10: 45-71; no. 12: 119-39. Author born in 1850's. Childhood takes place on estates in the Crimea and in Tula province. Generally positive memories of childhood.

*Shestov, I. A. "Vospominaniia: Polveka obyknovennoi zhizni." *Russkii arkhiv,* 1873, no. 2: 166-200. Author born in 1820. Childhood takes place on estate in Smolensk province. Positive memories.

*Skariätina, Irina. *A World Can End.* New York, 1931. Author born in 1890's. Childhood in Petersburg and on estate in Orel province. Very positive memories of childhood.

*Slavutinsky, S. T. "Rodnye mesta." *Russkii vestnik,* 1880, no. 5: 198-240. Positive memories of childhood permeate author's being (p. 240).

*Sokhanskaia, Nadezhda. "Avtobiografiia." *Russkoe obozrenie,* 1896, nos. 6-12. Author born in 1823. Mem-

oir written in 1848. Childhood on isolated country estate in the Ukraine. Childhood generally happy. "We had so much love, so many kisses and caresses!" (6: 483).

Spacks, Patricia Meyer. *Imagining a Self: Autobiography and Novel in Eighteenth-Century England.* Cambridge, Mass., 1976.

Spengemann, William C. *The Forms of Autobiography: Episodes in the History of a Literary Genre.* New Haven, 1980.

Steinberg, Ada. *Word and Music in the Novels of Andrey Bely.* Cambridge, Eng., 1982.

Stolitsa i usad'ba. St. Petersburg, 1913-17.

Stone, Lawrence. *The Family, Sex, and Marriage in England, 1500-1800.* New York, 1977.

Tal'ma, F. J. "Zapiski." *Panteon,* 1851, nos. 1-4.

*Taneev, V. I. *Detstvo i shkola.* Moscow, 1959. Author born in 1840's. Grew up to be important social democrat. Childhood takes place in Vladimir. Ambivalent memories.

Todorov, Tzvetan. *Les genres du discours.* Paris, 1976.

Tolstoy, L. N. *Polnoe sobranie sochinenii.* Ed. V. G. Chertkov et al. 90 vols. Moscow, 1928-58.

*Tolycheva, T. "Semeinye zapiski." *Russkii vestnik,* 1862, vol. 41: 665-705. Not primarily about the author's childhood.

Töpffer, Rodolphe. *La bibliotèque de mon oncle.* New York, 1898.

Tovrov, Jessica. "Mother-Child Relationships Among the Russian Nobility." In David L. Ransel, ed., *The Family in Imperial Russia.* Urbana, Ill., 1978.

*Trotsky, Leon. *My Life.* New York, 1930. Author born in 1879. Childhood takes place in poverty in Kherson province. Unhappy childhood.

*Trubetskoy, E. *Iz proshlogo.* Vienna, no date given, but based on internal evidence the book was published sometime between 1920 and 1923. Author born in 1863. Childhood takes place on country estate near Moscow. Extremely positive memories.

Tur, Evgeniia. *Plemianitsa.* Moscow, 1851.

Tynianov, Iu. N. *Arkhaisty i novatory.* Ann Arbor, 1985.

———. *Poètika, istoriia literatury, kino.* Moscow, 1977.

*Tyrkova-Vil'iams, Ariadna. *To, chego bol'she ne budet.* Paris, 1954. Author born in late 1870's. Childhood spent in Petersburg and on estate in Novgorod province. Happy childhood.

Uspensky, B. A. *Iz istorii russkogo literaturnogo iazyka XVIII-nachala XIX veka.* Moscow, 1985.

*Vereshchagin, A. V. *Doma i na voine.* St. Petersburg, 1885. Author born in mid-1850's. Childhood takes place in Novgorod province. Positive memories.

*Vigel', F. F. *Zapiski.* 2 vols. Moscow, 1928. Author born in 1787. Does not describe childhood.

*Vodovozova, E. N. *Na zare zhizni i drugie vospominaniia.* 2 vols. Moscow, 1934. Author born in 1844. Childhood spent in the Ukraine. Vodovozova was a member of the Petersburg populist intelligentsia. She found all aspects of gentry life, including her own childhood, to be disgusting.

Vonliarliarsky. "Vospominaniia o Zakhare Ivanyche." *Sovremennik,* 1851, vol. 27.

*Vonliarovsky, V. *Moi vospominaniia.* Berlin, 1939. Author born in 1852. Childhood spent on estate in Smolensk province. Positive memories of childhood.

*Von-Ritter, A. A. *Otzvuki minuvshego.* Moscow, 1892. Author born in late 1830's. "Happy childhood" takes place in countryside (p. 107).

Voronov, M. A. "Detstvo i iunost'." In *Povesti i rasskazy.* Moscow, 1961.

Vrangel', N. "Pomeshchich'ia Rossiia." *Starye gody,* July-September 1910, pp. 5-79.

Wasiolek, Edward. *Tolstoy's Major Fiction.* Chicago, 1978.

Wolfe, Humbert. *Now a Stranger.* London, 1933.

Wolohan, Sheila, "The *Bezprizorniki* in Soviet Culture." Unpublished paper, 1988.

Woodward, James A. *Ivan Bunin: A Study of his Fiction.* Chapel Hill, N.C., 1980.

Zaionchkovsky, P. A., ed. *Istoriia dorevoliutsionnoi Rossii v dnevnikakh i vospominaniiakh.* 4 vols. Moscow, 1976-86.

Zirin, Mary. "Forgotten Beginnings. Early Depictions of Russian Girlhood: Nadezhda Durova, Avdot'ia Panaeva, and Nadezhda Sokhanskaia." Unpublished, 1989.

Zweers, Alexander F. *Grown-up Narrator and Childlike Hero: An Analysis of the Literary Devices Employed in Tolstoy's Trilogy Childhood, Boyhood, and Youth.* The Hague, 1971.

Claudia Moscovici (essay date July 1993)

SOURCE: Moscovici, Claudia. "The Unifying Role of Tolstoy's Conception of Childhood." *History of European Ideas* 17, no. 4 (July 1993): 503-15.

[*In the following essay, Moscovici considers "some of the personal, artistic and intellectual forces which play*

a role in Tolstoy's idealisation of childhood," which she views as the author's "effort to find a unifying force for his diverging opinions about the 'ideal' individual and society."]

In his fictionalised autobiography entitled *Childhood,* as well as throughout his more purely fictional writings, Tolstoy expresses a sense of nostalgia for the childhood years. In many of his works, the author presents the state of childhood as being far preferable to adulthood, and especially to 'civilised' adulthood. The following quote, taken from *The Death of Ivan Ilych,* is emblematic of this sentiment:

> 'But strange to say none of those best moments of his pleasant life now seemed at all what they had then seemed—none of them except the first recollections of childhood. There, in childhood, there had been something really pleasant with which it would be possible to live if it could return.'[1]

The purpose of this essay is to explore some of the personal, artistic and intellectual forces which play a role in Tolstoy's idealisation of childhood by focussing primarily upon his positive yet problematic depiction of children and childlike adults in *War and Peace.* Tolstoy's vision of childhood in this text, supported by similar representations in some of his other works, will be interpreted as his partly successful effort to find a unifying force for his diverging opinions about the 'ideal' individual and society.

On the personal level, Tolstoy's idealisation of childhood reveals his artistic need to reshape his own less than happy early years. Andrew Baruch Wachtel provides an accurate description of Tolstoy's real childhood by stating that 'The author's own childhood could not have been a happy one, at least in any conventional sense. His mother died before he was two. . . . His father died when Tolstoy was eight, and thereafter he was shuttled between the homes of grandmothers and aunts.'[2] Tolstoy chooses an optimistic focus upon childhood in particular, because as a point of origin, of maximal potential and of greatest flexibility, childhood offers the artist the greatest opportunity to improve the individual and by extension, society at large, according to the leanings of his imagination. No less importantly, this absolute creative freedom enables Tolstoy to grasp the elusive immortality he sought with particular fervor while he was working on *War and Peace*: 'I reel and reel under the load of death and barely feel strength in myself to put a stop to it,' he wrote in his diary. 'But I don't want death, I want and love immortality. There's no point in choosing. The choice was made long ago. Literature, art, pedagogy and the family.'[3]

Tolstoy frequently begins his refashioning of society negatively, by specifying what his alternative society excludes. For the most part the author eliminates, not without some reservations and contradictions, all the elements of (mostly aristocratic) civilisation which generate, prescribe and perpetuate conventions that, by civilisation which generate, prescribe and perpetuate conventions that, by definition, run contrary to spontaneous, natural life. Thus we may state that partly because the author generally attributes his personal unhappiness to the 'corruptive' conventions of civilised society, he attempts to induce a restorative, childlike state in himself, his readers and more generally, in society as a whole.

For example, during the time he was working on *Childhood,* Tolstoy expressed his dissatisfaction with the idle existence of the Russian gentry:

> 'Oh, my God, my God, what difficult, sad days there sometimes can be! And why are you so sad? No, the consciousness that you are sad and do not know why you are sad, is not so much sorrowful, but rather painful. [. . .] I lived for the third winter in Moscow, a very irregular life, without job, without occupations, without aim [. . .] I say: of a young man who combines several conditions; namely education, a good name and an income of some 10 or 20 thousand. The life of a young man who combines these conditions is most pleasant and completely carefree, if he does not work, but is simply around and loves to be lazy. All salons are open for him, he has the right to have an eye to every potential bride; there is no young man standing higher than he in the esteem of society.'[4]

Through his idealisation of childhood Tolstoy attempts nothing short of a historical deconstruction—and then reconstruction—of individual and collective human identity by retracing the steps of civilisation backwards, towards its putative infancy. As argued by Patricia Carden, this movement backward towards a collective origin retrieved and preserved by the power of our memories—and especially of our memories of childhood—can lead to a movement forward by safeguarding 'the continuity of human experience against the dissolution imposed by temporal flux, which separates our every movement of experience from every other.'[5] In many of Tolstoy's works the recuperative—and unifying—powers of memory usually discover and express timeless truths through an intuitive, infantile perspective as simple as Natasha's when she states 'You know, I think . . . that when you remember, remember everything, you remember all the way back to what was earlier, before you were on the earth.'[6]

Thus, children assume a privileged role in Tolstoy's works both because the author believes that they offer the clearest vision of our spiritual continuity, and because they help resolve his ambivalence about primitive vs certain civilised modes of existence by eluding, and in a sense preceding, both social categories. Tolstoy's idealised fictional children can hardly be labelled either 'civilised'—though their milieu is usually aristo-

cratic—or 'primitive'—though they behave naturally and spontaneously. Rather, their personalities harmoniously combine socialised influences and natural tendencies, such that they provide a sharp contrast to the artificial behaviour of most of the aristocratic adults around them, but usually know quite well how to integrate into their social environment.

Before illustrating how Tolstoy's exemplary children partly reconcile his ambivalence concerning nature vs civilisation, it would be useful to briefly examine the nature of his misgivings. It is generally known that throughout his life Tolstoy oscillated between his identification with a largely Westernised Russian aristocracy and his longing for a 'natural' and particularly Slavic lifestyle, such as that of the Russian peasantry. Caught between these two poles, which are themselves ramified,[7] he alternatively praised and criticised both the 'civilised' and 'uncivilised' ways of life. On the one hand, a pervasive theme in Tolstoy's writings is the early-romantic belief that peasants live in harmony with the 'purity' of nature, whereas 'civilised' society leads a 'spoilt' and superficial existence, centred around absurd conventions which discourage some of the most valuable human qualities: spirituality, sincere emotion and undistorted communication. Tolstoy borrows this general romantic ideology from Rousseau, repeatedly acknowledging his intellectual debt: 'Since I was fifteen, Rousseau has been my teacher. Rousseau and the Gospels have been the two great and benevolent influences on my life.'[8]

Supporting and elaborating this claim, Bakhtin traces Tolstoy's literary development to the idyll, and in particular to Rousseau's novelistic version of the 'sentimental' idyll:

> 'In novels of the Rousseauan type, the major protagonists are the author's contemporaries, people who had already succeeded in isolating individual life-sequences, people with an interior perspective. They heal themselves through contact with nature and the life of the simple people, learning from them the wisdom of life and death.'[9]

One certainly identifies here some of the major Tolstoian motifs. For example, Tolstoy focusses on 'unique' and introspective protagonists, such as Prince Andrei, Levin and Pierre. These types of characters attempt to 'heal' themselves through contact with nature and with 'natural' people, such as the ingenuous women Natasha and Lisa, or the peasants Karatayev and Gerasim. One of the most notable examples of Tolstoy's appreciation of simplicity vs civilisation can be found in *The Death of Ivan Ilych*. In this short story the protagonist realises, partly through contact with his ingenuous son and with the peasant Gerasim, that

> 'Everything progressed and progressed and approached the ideal he had set himself. . . . He saw what a refined and elegant character free from vulgarity, it would

all have when it was ready (p. 265). [. . .] And the further he departed from childhood and the nearer he came to the present the more worthless and doubtful were the joys.'

(p. 295)

As Bakhtin describes it, Tolstoy's protagonists feel disappointed with the progressive chronotope (or temporal and spatial makeup) of their contemporaneous civilisation and turn towards the regressive chronotype of the early-romantic idyll.[10] This movement backwards usually manifests itself temporally as a nostalgia for childhood or for 'primitive' ways of life, and spatially through the idealisation of the human contact with nature.[11] The effect desired by Tolstoy is similar to the one proposed by Rousseau in *Le Contrat Social*: namely, that the reversion of each individual to a 'simple' state of being collectively engenders an harmonious society of such authentic individuals.

Although the importance of the romantic influence on Tolstoy cannot be overestimated, we should take into consideration some of the notable differences between the Rousseauistic and Tolstoian outlooks. The main difference concerns different modes of presentation, or styles, which reflect the widely divergent attitudes of the authors. As Boris Eikhenbaum points out,[12] even though Tolstoy often expresses romantic themes, he presents them in a particularly 'prosaic'[13] manner which deromanticises their content. Instead of focussing almost exclusively upon the moral and emotional turbulances of a few faultless characters—like Rousseau does in his paradigmatic romantic novel, *La Novelle Héloïse*—Tolstoy follows and contributes to the realistic tradition of describing the peripheral, mundane, and seemingly insignificant aspects of life. In his works we witness a great number of dinner parties, of trivial conversations, of absurd military ventures, and of events which have no apparent relevance to the whole of the novel. Even Tolstoy's endorsed protagonists remain relatively inidealised, presented with many unendorsed flaws by the implied author. For example, in *War and Peace*, Pierre is mocked for his repeated 'spiritual revelations' and is taken seriously only when he stops looking for 'grand', 'unifying' principles. Similarly, upon dying, Prince Andrei discovers an unsensationalised 'truth', described through details which are deprived of universal significance:

> 'The first time he had felt it was when the shell had spun like a top in front of him, and he had looked at the stubble field, at the bushes, at the sky, and knew that he was face to face with death.'

(p. 1173)

In several of Tolstoy's writings death itself loses some of its tragic impact when conveyed as a completely natural and spiritual experience. The character of Ivan

Ilych, who experiences this type of 'prosaic' death, is surprised by the simple serenity of the end he had anticipated with such anguish:

'How good and how simple!' he thought. 'And the pain?' he asked himself. [. . .] He sought his former fear of death and did not find it. 'Where is it? What death?' There was no fear because there was no death.

(p. 302)

Similarly, in some of his descriptions of the peasantry Tolstoy refrains from exaltation. The depiction of Karatayev, particularly in the scene in which the peasant relates his personal and family history, illustrates the implied author's unidealising perspective:

'Well, dear man', and a smile changed the tone of his voice, 'we thought it was a misfortune, but it turned out to be a blessing! If it had not been for my sin, my brother would have had to go. And he, my younger brother, has five little ones, while I, don't you see, left only a wife behind.'

(p. 1159)

This scene proves unidealised in several ways. Stylistically, it imitates the simple style of peasant language without inflating it or rendering it more 'poetic'. Tolstoy's description of Karatayev's circumstances betrays an even more telling critical stance. When Karatayev mentions his 'misfortune', he is referring to the fact that he was flogged and conscripted for stealing wood in order to warm his family. This constitutes a less than ideal representation of the Rousseauistic 'harmonious interaction' between the gentry and the peasantry. In his characterisation of Karatayev himself, the author manifests some misgivings. Although he presents the peasant as a man of emulable simplicity, he also discloses—perhaps involuntarily—the limitations of this simplicity. For instance, Karatayev's remark that he left 'only a wife behind' can be construed as lacking sensitivity and emotional depth. Contrasted with characters such as Pierre, Prince Andrei, Anna, Levin, or even Natasha, Nikolai and Lisa, the peasant appears too well-adjusted to life to be able to experience it deeply.

This somewhat critical depiction of Karatayev may be viewed as a matter of the reader's interpretation. However, Tolstoy's diary notes make his ambivalence, towards both 'civilisation' and 'noncivilisation', much more explicit. For example, when working on *War and Peace,* the author responded to the critics' charge that he focussed almost exclusively on a Frenchified Russian gentry by unabashedly asserting that the aristocracy interests him, whereas the peasantry does not:

'The life of clerks, merchants, seminarists and peasants is uninteresting and half unintelligible to me; the life of the aristocrats of that time, thanks to documents of that period and for other reasons, is intelligible, interesting, and dear to me.'[14]

On the other hand, as we have already seen, in many other diary notes as well as throughout his fiction, Tolstoy harshly criticises the 'frivolous' and 'artificial' lifestyle of the Russian aristocracy. One can hardly hold Tolstoy to any of his extreme claims, since as a complex human being and writer he holds a number of different, often contradictory, and changing beliefs. The variations and contradictions we have been examining are significant not because they call for conclusive resolutions, but precisely because they illuminate the author's inherently ambivalent perspective. As Renato Poggioli points out, Tolstoy places too much emphasis upon the uniqueness of each individual to be a populist, but expresses too much attraction for primitive society to be an uncritical aristocrat.[15]

Despite their irreducible polarity, these vacillations provoke the search for tentative correlation of Tolstoy's social perspectives in order to arrive at some lucid, though necessarily incomplete, understanding of the author's conceptions of nature and civilisation. The theme of childhood provides a relatively stable point of departure: one of the author's more consistent tenets—which he espoused up to his latest and almost exclusively religious writings—is his preference for the childlike point of view. The reversion to childhood, as previously suggested, reveals Tolstoy's attempt to eliminate some of the difficulties he has with existent modes of society and to stimulate a collective spirituality. This project is facilitated by the author's own imaginative regression to a less critical, purifying childlike perspective when engaged in descriptions of childhood. However, this explanation does not address the objection of why the artistic 'infection' with an even less critical, peasant optic does not always achieve similar results.

We have proposed that this discrepancy occurs because Tolstoy applies different standards to children and adults. He judges adults according to contradictory criteria. Sometimes he wishes them to be simple and uneducated like peasants or Tartars (*The Cossacks*); at other times he displays more authorial sympathy if they are well-educated and contemplative, like Prince Andrei, Pierre and Levin. Only children evade these dualities, since only they can combine the simplicity of 'primitivism' and the sophistication of 'culture' without incurring the criticisms applicable to either of these two categories. In children simplicity is disassociated from limitations, and intelligence is disassociated from the artificiality and unhappiness which Tolstoy attributes to culture. Thus, through his conception of childhood Tolstoy hopes to unify his preference for simplicity with his aristocratic sensibilities. It is worth examining in more detail the nature and success of Tolstoy's attempt to present childhood as a unifying 'solution'.

When reading *War and Peace,* we are struck by the fact that the characters described in the most favourable light are either children, childlike adults or parents de-

voted to their children. Tolstoy's Rousseauistic perception of children as naturally good is axiomatic. Although it can be challenged by alternative conceptions of human nature—such as the Freudian model—for the purposes of this essay we will accept Tolstoy's premise.

Natasha provides one of the most clear examples of Tolstoy's conception of a childlike character. She is described as girlish, impulsive and affectionate. Her feminine instincts enable her to integrate naturally in society, without abiding by its aristocratic conventions. For example, in the scene in which we are introduced to her, Natasha bursts into the guest room in the middle of her parents' party, unheeding the codes of propriety applicable even to children:

> 'Escaping from her father's embrace, she ran to her mother and, not paying the least attention to her severe remark, hid her flushed face in her mother's lace collar and broke into laughter. . . . She sank onto her mother's lap and went off into such peals of laughter that even the decorous visitor could not help joining in.'
>
> (p. 69)

Despite this obvious lack of propriety, Natasha behaves so naturally and good-naturedly that even the most decorous adults are not offended by her lack of restraint. On the contrary, her spontaneous entrance and childlike laughter add a hint of freshness to the drawing room without disrupting its atmosphere. Natasha seems to have an intuitive grasp of how to integrate into different settings, of how to behave in different circumstances while still remaining true to herself. Unlike the more awkward Pierre, she naturally combines unconventionality and decorum.

The adults' receptivity to Natasha's girlish charm reveals not only her intuitive adaptability, but also the adaptability of adults, who despite their conventionalism respond to her in a positive, accepting manner. The aristocrats' relative malleability can be attributed to Tolstoy's belief that adults can empathise with the naturalness of children despite their multiple layers of 'culture'. Once again this conviction—or hope—relies upon the early-romantic premise that although corrupted by civilisation, human nature is not completely destroyed by it; that its latent natural elements can be recovered and developed. It is this premise which lies at the foundation of Tolstoy's efforts to reform adult society by inducing a childlike perspective.

Nevertheless, it is also important to note the distinctions drawn by the author between acceptable childlike characteristics in children and in adults. To some extent the criteria remain the same. For example, even as an adult Natasha captivates people with her unaltered infantile charm. Although she appears to live in an extended present chronotope, we could hardly call her

static. On the contrary, her life in the present is energetic and elastic, since like all the Rostovs, Natasha is aware of the present's many possibilities. By continuing to characterise her favourably, Tolstoy indicates that, at least in part, childlikeness is desirable in adults.

However, as we will later see, the childlike belief that 'everything is possible' is admired by Tolstoy for its energy in children but criticised for its lack of responsibility in adults. Natasha the girl is allowed to run carefree, whereas Natasha the young woman has to pay for the lack of judgement she exhibits in her involvement with Anatol. It becomes apparent that in Tolstoy 'childlikeness' must assume somewhat different shapes in children and adults. An examination of their common characteristics would help elucidate the author's concept of a childlike adult society.

Natasha's effect on the adult Prince Andrei points to the common features of the adult and childlike worlds. I have described Prince Andrei as 'adult' because in many ways he provides a foil for Natasha: he is highly educated, cosmopolitan, disciplined and already cynical, not only about aristocratic society, but also about what life in general has to offer. Nevertheless, he too is affected by Natasha's contagious appetite for life:

> 'In Natasha Prince Andrei was conscious of a special world pervaded with unknown joys and wholly alien to him—a strange world which even in the avenue at Otradnoe and at the window on that moonlit night had begun to tantalise him (p. 564). [Infected by her energy he decides] I must make the most of my liberty while I feel such youth and vitality in me. . . . Pierre was right when he said one must believe in the possibility of happiness in order to be happy, and now I do believe in it. Let the dead bury their dead; while one has life one must live and be happy!'
>
> (p. 565)

I would suggest that this description of a rejuvenated Andrei offers us an example of Tolstoy's image of the 'ideal' childlike adult: intelligent, sensitive and refined yet also authentic and eager to enjoy the simple pleasures in life. We are moved to question how Natasha succeeded in provoking such a radical shift in Andrei's attitude towards life: and more generally, what process is involved in the restorative transformation of adults by childlike personalities. For some answers we can begin by looking in greater detail at the character of Natasha.

In *War and Peace* Natasha is depicted as a highly 'restorative' character. She both literally and figuratively rejuvenates people, infecting them with her youthful ability to see the rich potential of life. I used the term 'infecting' deliberately, because it is the term employed by Tolstoy to describe the means of artistic transfer. In *What is Art?* the author specifies that the aes-

thetic function of art should be subordinated to its moral function, namely, to 'infecting' a correct moral attitude. Characteristically, Tolstoy defines art mostly in a negative fashion, by establishing what it is not:

'Art is not, as the metaphysicians say, the manifestation of some mysterious Idea of beauty or God; . . . it is not the production of pleasing objects; and, above all, it is not pleasure; but it is a means of union among men, joining them together in the same feelings, and indispensable for the life and progress toward well-being of individuals and of humanity.'[16]

Since Tolstoy intends for the process of infection to occur both intertextually and extratextually, it is important to examine not only how Natasha's personality infects the other characters in the novel, but also how her childlike optic is transferred to the readers, and hence to society in general. In part the infection of the readers corresponds to the infection of the characters: Natasha's appealing and vibrant personality, her generous impulses and her natural spontaneity endear her to characters and readers alike. Nevertheless, because readers are extratextual beings, we can be infected by literary techniques to which fictive characters have no access. For example, we can listen to the author's authoritative descriptions of his heroine, which are almost always positive. We also have access to all of Natasha's thoughts and actions, which allows us to perceive her in a more three-dimensional fashion than the characters who temporally and spatially interact with her on the same textual plane.

The Russian Formalist Victor Shklovsky has provided an insightful analysis of a central technique employed by Tolstoy to convey the desirable childlike optic. According to Shklovsky, the technique which enables art to provide us with this fresh perspective is precisely the optic Tolstoy presented through Natasha's eyes—the unfamiliarised, or to use Shklovsky's terminology, the 'defamiliarised' perspective.[17] This perspective enables us not only to notice things we otherwise omit by force of habit, but also to see them in an artistic fashion:

'The purpose of art is to impart the sensation of things as they are perceived and not as they are known. The technique of art is to make objects 'unfamiliar', to make forms difficult, to increase the difficulty and length of perception because the process of perception is an aesthetic end in itself and must be prolonged.'[18]

However, while Shklovsky views defamiliarisation as an artistic end, Tolstoy uses the technique merely as an artistic means. As we have already noted, for Tolstoy the purpose of art was primarily moral, not aesthetic as for the Formalists. In the following scene, Natasha's uninitiated view of the convention of the opera is supposed to infect the readers with a childlike perspective which is morally critical of cultural conventions.

'The stage consisted of smooth planks in the centre, with some painted cardboard representing trees at the sides, and a canvas stretched over boards in the back.

Girls in red bodices and white petticoats sat in the middle of the state. . . . They were all singing. When they had finished their song the girl in white advanced to the prompter's box, and a man with stout legs encased in silk tights, with a plume and a dagger, began singing and waving his arms about.'

(p. 678)

Let us follow Natasha's 'naive' optic. First she focusses on the centre stage and notices the decorations as artificial, rather than mentally bypassing their visual aspect and seeing them as the setting they are supposed to symbolise. Then she notices the singers, once again taking no mental shortcuts. What naturally catches her eye is their visual reality—their gender and the bright colours of their dresses—rather than their intended representation. Next she observes their action: namely, that they are singing. Once again, she remains ignorant of what the singing is supposed to signify. Finally, she observes the comical and seemingly irrational nature of the opera, as manifested by the incongruous outfit and gestures of the singer.

Throughout her entire telescoping vision, Natasha assesses the opera as it is, rather than as it is supposed to be interpreted. Seeing it without having had any previous knowledge of its meaning and conventions, she notices the nonrepresentational reality which more experienced viewers are conditioned to overlook. The readers are compelled by the narrative structure to go along with Natasha's process of discovery, which is implicitly critical of convention. This criticism becomes more explicit when Natasha emulates 'society' and assumes their uncritical view of the opera. Since for Tolstoy artistic and moral spheres are inextricably tied, Natasha's acceptance of artistic operatic conventions is immediately followed by her acceptance of 'immoral' conventions, as illustrated by her infatuation with Anatol.

Tolstoy uses similar defamiliarisation techniques to convey the childlike personalities of Pierre and Nikolai. Like Rousseau, Tolstoy draws a 'natural' distinction between feminine and masculine childlike behaviour. For example, Nikolai matches his sister's spontaneity, but adds to it a particularly 'masculine' independence and idealism. His brotherly and generous sentiments towards his fellow soldiers, his idealised love for the Tsar, and his distance yet affection for his family reveal his boyishness. Nevertheless, both sexes share the most fundamental element of Tolstoy's conception of the childlike personality: namely, the intuitive detachment from artificial conventions. Just as Natasha had involuntarily questioned artistic conventions, Nikolai, although a valiant soldier, questions the conventions of war when he is faced with having to kill an 'enemy' soldier as innocent-looking and youthful as himself. As with Natasha, this form of naive questioning of what society offers as 'given' is appropriately conveyed through a defamiliarised point of view:

'Rostov reined in his horse, and his eyes sought his foe to see what sort of man he had vanquished. The French dragoon officer was hopping along the ground on one foot, the other being caught in the stirrup. He looked up at Rostov, his eyes narrowed with fear, and flinched as if expecting another blow at any moment. His pale, mud-spattered face—fair, boyish, with light blue eyes and a dimple in the chin—was not at all hostile or suited to the battlefield, but the most simple, familiar kind of face. . . . Rostov, riding with the rest, was conscious of feeling strangely heavyhearted. Something vague and confused that he could not account for had come over him with the capture of that prisoner and the blow he had dealt him.'

(pp. 787-788)

Tolstoy describes here a rudimentary and, for this reason, authentic morality. Rostov's instinctive sense of compassion exceeds and subverts the ethics of war. Noticing not the abstract notion of an 'enemy' but the reality of a fellow man, he is struck by the adversary's fearful gaze and childlike features, which reveal a 'fair, boyish' young man, 'with light blue eyes and a dimple in the chin'. The soldier's ordinary looks and natural emotions underline the similarity of the two men, and, symbolically, of human beings in general.

We have noted that the differences in sex between Natasha and Nikolai were bridged by their underlying similarity of temperament. However, Tolstoy's concept of 'childlikeness' becomes increasingly confusing when we examine the personality differences between the central male childlike characters, Nikolai and Pierre. Nikolai's instinctive moral qualms provide a foil for Pierre's metaphysical considerations. On the level of plot, Tolstoy indicates a preference for Nikolai's simple morality over Pierre's unnecessarily complicated one. Nikolai's instincts enable him to manage his estate efficiently and charitably, whereas Pierre's idealism thwarts his good intentions to help the serfs. Nevertheless, Tolstoy betrays his characteristic ambivalence towards simplicity vs complexity in his juxtaposition of Nikolai and Pierre. It is not altogether clear which childlike personality he sets up as a role-model.

In many ways, Pierre is presented as a more appealing character than any of the Rostovs. He complements their natural detachment from conventions with an admirable mental astuteness and a penchant for introspection. Although he is somewhat contaminated by the stultifying education of an aristocrat—an education which, as for Tolstoy himself, proves to be his most difficult burden—Pierre retains childlike characteristics until he himself is ready to be a father. For example, it is Pierre's authenticity and outspoken honesty which threatens Anna Pavlovna's *soirée,* his way of talking about things as he sees them. The following description of Pierre's unfamiliarised optic when faced with the formalities of inheritance illustrates the young man's artlessness and lack of materialism:

'Anna Mikhailnovna, with a meek, sorrowful, all-forgiving expression, stood near the door with the unknown lady. Prince Vasily was on the other side of the door close to the invalid chair. . . . He held a taper in his left hand and was crossing himself with his right, turning his eyes upward each time he touched his forehead. His face wore a look of serene piety and resignation to the will of God. 'If you do not understand these sentiments', it seemed to say, 'so much the worse for you.'

(p. 116)

We see through Pierre's eyes a portrait of greed and expectation as the entire family awaits to profit from the old count's death. The artificiality of these people is so unfamiliar to Pierre that he is not even aware of it.

However, this defamiliarised optic is only partially Pierre's. The young man perceives the situation through an objective prism which refracts external reality—in this case conventions—into their minute components. Tolstoy complements this vision by adding moral indictments, through an internal depiction of the characters' subjectivities, to his character's uncritical perspective. In turn, Pierre's innocent point of view enhances Tolstoy's condemnations of artifice by providing a sharp contrast to the surrounding self-interested perspectives.

The author's sympathetic treatment of Pierre, despite the character's education and contemplativeness, once again introduces the problematic issue of Tolstoy's ambivalence towards 'civilisation'. It is likely that Tolstoy's sympathetic portrayal of this protagonist reveals less his image of the ideal civilisation than an identification with the created personality. In part, Pierre represents an autobiographical characterisation. The similarity between the author's and his character's self-deprecating and moralising diary notes reveals their resemblance. Nevertheless, in elucidating this issue it is helpful to draw a distinction between Tolstoy's identification with a character and his moral precepts. As the author's diary notes reveal, these two factors are often at odds. Like Pierre, Tolstoy repeatedly expresses his desire to be a less contemplative and thus happier personality, perhaps a Nikolai. Nonetheless, Tolstoy appreciates the cultivated intelligence and introspectiveness of Pierre. I would suggest that the author's reconciliation of these two opposing tendencies can be found in the post-war characterisation of Pierre.

After experiencing the trials of war and learning to appreciate life in its most basic manifestations, Pierre is able to combine simple enjoyment of life with intellectual preoccupations. This harmony is illustrated by his simultaneous involvement in family life and revolutionary politics. Although the war taints his childlike naiveté, this quality is perpetuated and preserved through the education of his children. Hence in adults 'childlikeness' manifests itself through the enjoyment of

interacting with children, especially when this interaction 'infects' adults with children's authentic modes of thought, emotion and action. For this reason family life plays a very important role in Tolstoy's chronotope of regression to childhood. The benefits of the parent-child communication are reciprocal: the process of educating children rejuvenates adults and encourages a healthy moral development in children.

The three childlike characters we discussed are a part of Tolstoy's representation of the family, most obviously illustrated by the Rostovs. The Rostov's familial orientation, manifested by their almost exclusive focus on nurturing their children, is depicted by Tolstoy as an exemplary lifestyle. When the Count and Countess are not childlike themselves in their carefree enjoyment of life, they are facilitating their own children's happiness by providing an affectionate and unrestraining domestic atmosphere. Nevertheless, Tolstoy also indicates that this warm family life proves too indiscrimate with respect to the moment's many potentialities. The older Rostovs lack a sense of duty and stability because they are too involved in enjoying the many satisfactions potentially offered by life. In the end they pay for their lack of adult responsibility with the loss of their estate and their happiness.

However, the positive elements of the older Rostovs' mode of life are preserved and improved by the new generation of families: namely, Natasha and Pierre, and Maria and Nikolai. Unlike their parents, these young couples have been matured by the hardship of war and have learned to combine family happiness with a sense of responsibility. They continue to reinforce the value of childhood not through their former childlikeness, but by becoming model parents. Natasha changes into a big, matronly figure whose life revolves around her husband and children. Tolstoy presents Natasha's transformation from a girl to a mother as exemplary, in terms which resonate with Rousseau's delimiting conception of women's roles:

> 'The subject that wholly absorbed Natasha's attention was her family, that is, her husband, whom she had to keep so that he should belong entirely to her and to the home, and the children, whom she had to bear, give birth to, nurse and rear'

(p. 1383)

Pierre becomes her perfect complement, assuming the nineteenth-century male responsibility of providing a functional societal link for his enclosed family by concerning himself with business and politics, while still remaining devoted to the family nucleus. The particular manner in which this couple educates their children is not elaborated; only its Rousseauistic emphasis upon the 'natural' is specified:

> 'Their way of life and place of residence, their friends and ties, Natasha's occupations, the children's upbringing, were all determined not only by Pierre's expressed

wishes, but by what Natasha surmised them to be from things he mentioned in conversation. . . . Pierre one day told her of Rousseau's views, with which he was in complete agreement, that to have wet-nurses was unnatural and harmful. When their next baby was born, [. . . Natasha] insisted on having her own way, and from that time nursed all of her children herself.

(p. 1385)

It is the second family, the new Rostovs, who fill in the gaps of vagueness concerning children's education. With the systematic determination characteristic of the Bolkonskys, Princess Maria devotes herself not to nurturing but to educating her children. She observes and checks their behaviour by keeping a diary account of it, fulfilling her maternal functions with the rigour required by a scientific study. Much more so than Natasha, she retains significant elements of her former personality—such as her intelligence, aescetic spirituality, education, aristocratic poise and self-discipline—which are now focussed upon her children in her role as mother and educator. Princess Maria and Nikolai gradually form a successful, interdependent couple: he relies upon her spiritual guidance and mental strength, while she benefits from the energetic common sense he exhibits in effectively managing their estate and amending his parents' losses. Through both couples Tolstoy not only illustrates the benefits of family life, but also delineates its ideal organisation, which is structured, in a traditional fashion, around the complementarity of gender roles.

Because of the author's changing and diverse beliefs, it is difficult to wholistically assess the success of Tolstoy's attempt to reconcile his contradictory opinions of culture and simplicity through positive depictions of childhood. This achievement is particularly difficult to measure because of Tolstoy's prosaic approach, which presents all characters in an unidealised fashion. However, what emerges from the author's nostalgia for childhood is a *process* which does contribute to the creation of an integrated self. This process operates through multiple artistic chronotopes: the author's reversion to memories of his own childhood in the creation of childlike characters; the intratextual interaction of children or childlike characters 'infecting' other characters with this optic; and the readers' infection by the author's and his characters' mnemonic regression to childhood, which reveals the coherence of the self and offers a glimpse of the immortality of the soul. The continuity of this multiple process is ensured by the readers' interest in Tolstoy's instructive depictions of childhood and of the cycles of family life.

Notes

1. Leo Tolstoy, 'Death of Ivan Ilych', taken from *Great Short Works of Leo Tolstoy,* trans. Louise and Alymer Maude (New York: Harper & Row, 1967), p. 294.

2. Andrew Baruch Wachtel, *The Battle for Childhood: Creation of a Russian Myth* (CA: Stanford University Press, 1990), p. 44.

3. Quote taken from Patricia Carden's article, 'The Recuperative Powers of Memory', found in *The Russian Novel from Pushkin to Pasternak* (New Haven: Yale University Press, 1983), p. 81.

4. Quote taken from *Grown-Up Narrator and Childlike Hero* by Alexander Zweers (Paris: Mouton, 1971), pp. 36-38.

5. Patricia Carden, 'The Recuperative Powers of Memory', p. 83.

6. *Ibid.*, p. 85.

7. I am referring not only to the differences between the Slavophiles and Westernisers but also to the diverging points of view within these two main groups.

8. Quote taken from *The Battle for Childhood*, p. 38.

9. M. M. Bakhtin, *The Dialogic Imagination,* trans. Caryl Emerson and Michael Holquist (Austin: University of Texas Press, 1981), pp. 228-230.

10. Bakhtin uses the concept of the 'chronotope' to explore the interconnected temporal and spatial dimensions of a text. In the *Dialogic Imagination* he provides the following explanation of this concept: 'We will give the name chronotope (literally, "time space") to the intrinsic connectedness of temporal and spatial relationships that are artistically expressed in literature. . . . We understand the chronotope as a formally constitutive category of literature. . . . In the literary artistic chronotope, spatial and temporal indicators are fused into one carefully thought-out, concrete whole' (p. 84).

11. In describing Tolstoy's chronotope as 'regressive', I use the term in a non-normative sense to denote a temporal and spatial movement backwards to a former individual or societal state.

12. Boris Eikhenbaum, *The Young Tolstoi* (translation), Gary Kern (ed.) (Ann Arbor: Ardis, 1972).

13. The term 'prosaic' is used here in the senses attributed to Bakhtin by Gary Saul Morson and Caryl Emerson in *Mikhail Bakhtin: Creation of a Prosaics,* (1990): 'Prosaics encompasses two related, but distinct, concepts. First, as opposed to "poetics", prosaics designates a theory of literature that privileges prose in general and the novel in particular over the poetic genres. Prosaics in the second sense is far broader than theory of literature: it is a form of thinking that presumes the importance of the everyday, the ordinary, the prosaic' (p. 17).

14. Leo Tolstoy, *War and Peace,* 'Drafts for an Introduction', trans. Ann Dunnigan (Signet Classics, 1968), p. 1365.

15. Renato Poggioli, 'Tolstoy as Man and Artist', *Tolstoy: a Collection of Critical Essays,* Ralph E. Matlaw (ed.) (NJ: Prentice-Hall, 1967).

16. Leo Tolstoy, *What is Art?,* trans. Alymer Maude (Indianapolis: Bobbs Merrill, 1981), p. 52.

17. Victor Shklovsky, 'Art as Technique', Lemon and Reis, *Russian Formalist Criticism: Four Essays* (Lincoln: University of Nebraska Press, 1965).

18. *Ibid.*, p. 12.

CHILDHOOD IN THE WORKS OF EMILY DICKINSON

David Lloyd (essay date June 1984)

SOURCE: Lloyd, David. "The Adult Voice in Dickinson's Child Poems." *Dickinson Studies,* no. 49 (June 1984): 22-31.

[*In the following essay, Lloyd illustrates how Dickinson represents complex conceptions of reality in her poetry by endowing her child narrators with adult powers of perceptions and communication skills.*]

Numerous critics maintain that Emily Dickinson excels at portraying intense, highly realized, internal states of consciousness. Richard Wilbur writes that "her truthfulness lay in her insistence on discovering the facts of her inner experience. She was a Linnaeus to the phenomena of her own consciousness.'" Similarly, Allen Tate states that Dickinson's "poetry is a magnificent personal confession. . . ."[2] In a remarkable essay touching on numerous aspects of Dickinson's poetry, Adrienne Rich writes, "Dickinson is THE American poet whose work consisted in exploring states of psychic extremity."[3]

In the process of exploring and presenting these internal states, Dickinson often chooses not to speak unequivocally in her own voice; instead, she relies on various personae or stances. These stances serve as an important means by which she presents and tests complex dimensions of her inner life. When taking on different voices for different poems, Dickinson might speak as a lover, a wife, a sentimentalist, a Calvinist, a suffering adult, an innocent child, or even as a creature of the natural world (as in poem 1035, where the speaker ostensibly is a fly[4]). In some of her most interesting po-

ems, Dickinson actually merges two or more of these voices. The central voice of many of her most powerful child poems, for instance, fuses elements of a child's consciousness with elements of an adult's perspective.

Of the various personae Dickinson employs, the child's voice is one of the most difficult to use successfully. When writing in the voice of a child, Dickinson faces two crucial problems. First, she must discover how to make best use of those elements of the sentimental apprehension of childhood which suit her purposes while avoiding the kind of easy sentimentality which is largely foreign to her method. As Rich notes, Dickinson does occasionally succumb to sentimentality, such as that evidenced in poem 919: "If I can stop one Heart from breaking."[5] Second, she must take the child poems—which necessarily deal with virtues such as simplicity and innocence—profound and complex enough to satisfy the high standards she has set for, and achieved in, the vast majority of her work. One way Dickinson overcomes these difficulties is by creating a complex speaker: the dominant child's voice becomes strangely and subtly charged with an adult consciousness of the tragic dimensions of human life.

Before one can examine specific poems which reveal the workings of this child/adult voice, a context for Dickinson's perception of childhood must be established. She makes use of many generally accepted nineteenth-century notions of child-like qualities, such as a child's innocence, dependency, curiosity, spontaneity, and inexperience.[6] Her complex use of the child voice finds an additional, perhaps more important, source in her own experience of childhood. Perhaps a study of the child/adult voice can best be begun by a brief look at aspects of her early life.

The poet's biographers generally agree that the adult ED [Emily Dickinson] yearned after and revered the child-like state as an Edenic time of her life. Cody tells that

> Emily Dickinson wished to remain a child, but inevitably one reaches an age when this role becomes incongruous. The innocent humorousness, childlike spontaneity, precocious wisdom, and sexual undifferentiation of her girlhood personality could not have survived her twenties without becoming grotesque. These qualities, fixed features of ED until she was well into her twenties, were, for all this deceptive charm, evidence of an arrest in psychological growth.[7]

Cody also quotes numerous letters demonstrating Dickinson's repeated yearnings for a lost childhood.[8] Somewhat less insistently, Whicher writes of this same tendency:

> Most satisfyingly of all were the children that played in the Dickinson's yard, a band including a niece from the house next door and the minister's children from the parsonage across the street. Emily stimulated their enterprises with childlike zest, for the child's heart in her had never fully yielded.[9]

Clark Griffith, in his critical study of Dickinson, *The Long Shadow,* focuses on this same aspect when he states: "There is the retreat backward into childhood, which is the crucial fact about Emily Dickinson."[10]

Despite her yearning after a lost youth, Dickinson certainly did not lead an ideal childhood of the kind extolled by the great William Wordsworth—one of freedom, carelessness and self-indulgence. Her father was strict, her mother something of a nonentity, and the school she attended (Mount Holyoke Female Seminary) rigid and oppressively religious.[11] Thus, altho Dickinson idealized childhood, she did so from a distinctly adult perspective. She idealized childhood because the blissful ignorance of that state contrasts so markedly with the adult awareness of loss, alienation and death. For Dickinson, the child's ignorance of death and the adult's contrasting sensitivity to death (or, in the adult ED's case, hyper-sensitivity) is especially important as can be seen in poem 1149, "I noticed People disappeared.

Dickinson's sense of childhood is certainly not sentimental in the way that nineteenth century New England culture typically portrayed children. Rather than focussing on the condition of childhood itself, Dickinson glorifies that state specifically in terms of her reaction to an unsatisfactory adult life: her attachment to childhood finds its source in the unfulfilled, intense needs of her adult life. If her life after adolescence had been one of conformity—of social mobility, marriage and family—Dickinson would certainly not have viewed her own childhood in such idealistic terms.

Clark Griffith, in an excellent chapter on Dickinson's child poetry, maintains that the poet uses the child voice in order to mask her attacks on, or probings into, a tragic and unfair universe:"[In her child poems, Dickinson] makes herself completely safe from reprisal; whereupon she is free to cope with—to castigate, or to put on trial, or to laugh up her sleeve at—a universe that is contaminated to the core."[12] Griffith believes that "in the child poems, the dominant motive is that of self-preservation."[13] Certainly the child persona does function in this way, but in stressing the element of "self-preservation," Griffith draws the reader uncomfortably far from the complex way the child voice actually works. Griffiths rightly stresses the tragic aspect of the child poems; but to understand fully the poems, one must closely examine the voices she constructs.

Dickinson approaches childhood from many different angles. Sometimes she speaks as an adult observing or reflecting on specific children who come into her realm of experience (as in poem 1185, most likely concerning

her sister-in-law Susan's children). Sometimes she speaks clearly as an adult reflecting on her own childhood experiences (in poems such as 454, 576, and 600). Sometimes she uses the rhythm, diction, and point of view which signify a child's voice while not making references which define that voice as a child's (see poem 1035, written in a little girl voice tho the obstensible speaker is not a child). Often the central voice of a poem is clearly presented as a speaking child (413, 425 and 467). In this study, Dickinson's child/adult voice will be examined as evidenced in two poems from the last category.

Poem 413 gives no specific information (references to age, to playmates, to parents, etc.) which unequivocally identify the speaker as a child. However, the diction, rhythm and point of view expressed clearly point to a child speaker. For this speaker, the child-like love of recess—a time of play—is of paramount concern when she contemplates "life-after-death." In wishing that God "could make a visit" or take "a Nap," the speaker reveals a childish conception of God as a kind of superstrict, super-vigilant father. Of course, if all this poem does is present the somewhat humorous but inconsequential objections this child makes to imagined conditions of paradise, it would be a cute but forgettable sort of poem. But when contemplating the poem after several readings, one experiences a lingering feeling of dread and senses in the poem an undertone of uneasiness that is certainly not cute or easily forgettable. A closer examination of the diction and prosody reveals certain subtleties and complexities of the voice which cause unconfortable feelings to arise from this somewhat deceptive poem.

The opening stanza immediately strikes a disquieting note, since it presents a homeless, alienated child, one who "never felt at Home" on earth and who imagines she won't feel at home in heaven:

> I never felt at Home—Below—
> And in the Handsome Skies
> I shall not feel at Home—I know—
> I don't like Paradise—

This initially disturbing, plaintive note is submerged in, but never fully eradicated by, the next stanza and a half. In those lines, the speaker gives her seemingly childish reasons for not being comfortable with her received notions of "Paradise": she feels she'll miss recess and will be lonely, since this heaven seems to contain only her and no playmates.

Up to the middle of the third stanza, the child's voice is convincing in its diction and rhythm, even down to the contractions Dickinson uses and the child-like syntax—simple clauses often linked with coordinating conjunctions, an appropriate syntax for a child speaker:

> I don't like Paradise—
>
> Because it's Sunday—all the time—
> And Recess—never comes—
> And Eden'll be so lonesome
> Bright Wednesday Afternoons—

Until this stanza, the abab/cdcd rime scheme—composed of full and half rimes and using a simple diction and regular rhythm—create a sing-song effect. But in the middle of the third stanza, when the speaker objects to God's omnipresent vision, the voice becomes less convincingly childlike:

> If God could make a visit—
> Or ever took a Nap—
> So not to see us—but they say
> Himself—a Telescope

This shift in tone and point of view occuring in the third stanza is first indicated in the non-rime of "say" and "visit"—according to the rime scheme, those words should rime. After noting this disquieting irregularity—a sort of dead space in the rime scheme—the reader next experiences an odd twisting of syntax. Tho Dickinson does not use periods to conclude sentences in this poem, her syntax in the early lines is still quite clear and one can easily mark off beginnings and endings of her "sentences." The sentence which begins stanza three, however, becomes quite complex and sophisticated.

By beginning with "If God could make a visit— / Or even take a Nap," the speaker leads us to believe that we will now hear some cute childish thoughts on the God figure as a father. But after these lines, the sentence changes course, taking off at the idea of God having a nap, "So not to see us—." Whereas the syntax of earlier sentences can be instantly comprehended, it takes the reader a while to absorb and analyze this sentence. To communicate her sense of God's omnipresence, the speaker uses distinctly adult speech patterns beginning with a sophisticated (and frightening) metaphor: God imagined as a telescope focussing from a great distance on each of his creatures: "Himself—a Telescope / Perennial beholds us—." Polysyllabic words—"telescope" and "perennial," the second of which at least is quite out of place in a poem spoken in a child's voice—reinforce the sophistication of this image. The speaker then concludes with a very adult sort of injunction, warning against the wrath of God at "Judgment Day." Thus, in the third and fourth stanzas, there is an adult note creeping into the child's voice.

These subtle shifts in diction, rhythm and rime point to a gathering complexity in point of view. The child's point of view becomes charged with specifically adult notions: of exile from heaven and earth, of tremendous distance and alienation from God, and of God's great

wrath at Judgment Day. In fashioning a child's voice which can express complex adult preoccupations, Dickinson performs a difficult balancing act. If the adult elements were too far submerged for the reader to detect, the poem could seem to be simply portraying a child's perspective—uninformed and therefore irrelevant to adult concerns. If, on the other hand, the adult voice is too insistent, Dickinson will be unable to make her poem capitalize on certain child-like qualities important to the poem's purposes: the innocence and guiltlessness of her child voice allows Dickinson to take a fresh, clear look at the Calvinist vision of Paradise.

Like poem 413, the second poem to be examined— 467—centers on the contrast between the child's and the adult's sense of death. In this poem also, a close reading will reveal an adult dimension to the child's voice, tho Dickinson's method radically differs from the method examined in poem 413.

Poem 467, like 413, begins with a disquieting, somewhat surprising, note, asserting (spoken by a child who also speaks for her playmates) that "We do not play on Graves—," leading the reader to expect the next line to name whatever reasons—superstitious fears, religious scruples, etc.—might cause these children to dislike playing on graves. Instead, the next seven lines list reasons which are wholly self-centered and quite peripheral to the fact of death: the speaker complains about lack of room to play; the slanting of the ground; and the annoying habits of interrupting, sad-faced mourners. Nowhere in these lines does the child speaker show the least consciousness that the dimensions of a dead human body account for the small size of the grave and that the (possibly newly buried) body creates the slant or curve of the ground. The children in general appear not to realize that graves contain bodies; this total ignorance and self-absorption, even in young children, is far too complete for a reader to accept without wonder and some disquiet.

In poem 467 there is again a childish diction, sing-song rhythm and point of view which define the speaking voice as that of a child. As in poem 413, the opening undertone of uneasiness is briefly submerged but picked up later in the poem—this time in stanza two, where the speaker comments on the grief of the mourners with a strange mixture of abstract and concrete language. She fears that the mourners "Hearts"—a cliched metaphor for the feeling element of humans—

> will drop—
> And crush our pretty play—
>
> And so we move as far
> As Enemies—away.

The "Heart" metaphor is, however, saved from being a cliche because of the barely suppressed violence of the extended image—it is a leaden, heavy, physically threatening heart the children fear.

The second stanza causes the reader to wonder if children can indeed be so self-centered and seemingly complacent in the face of powerful, crushing emotion. They move away, in a sort of revulsion from adult displays of intense loss and grief. Yet can they be oblivious to, and unconcerned with, the cause of that sense of loss and grief? These questions about the nature and quality of the children's awareness of death take on added significance because they come to mind at the place in the poem where the language toughens and achieves a stridency more adult than child-like. This change of tone forces one to read "pretty play" as a deprecatory, ironic comment: "We're fearing that their Hearts will drop— / And crush our pretty play—."

It is not until the final stanza that the reader can begin to answer questions concerning the central voice of the poem. Three words in the last stanza seem especially charged with significance and relevant to our examination of the persona. First, one notes that the word "far" is repeated in the space of two lines, a repetition particularly emphasized since the word occurs as a rime:

> And so we move as far
> As Enemies—away—
> Just looking round to see how far
> It is—Occasionally—

The next word which seems to stand out and demand attention is the pronoun "It"—apparently referring to the grave, since "they are" would be the correct construction if the reference is to the mourners, the only other possible referent. Thus, after moving away, the children pause to look back at the grave, to measure the distance. For the first time in the poem, these children are betraying an adult awareness of death: they gauge the distance—how "far" it is (surely in terms of time, not yards)—to the grave.

"Occasionally"—the final word of special significance—concludes the poem. This word indicates that the children's concern with measuring distance to the grave is a continuing concern—and of course that concern will continue thruout their lives, intensifying as they approach old age. "Just looking round" suggests a feigned unconcern, a calualness which reinforces the seeming casualness of "Occasionally." But this unconcern is actually rooted in fear: people don't stare baldly at what they most fear; they glance now and then to measure the distance and ensure their safety.

In sum, the final stanza presents two nonexclusive readings of the poem's voice and point of view. The first reading sees the children's extreme ignorance of death presented in the opening stanzas as a portrayal of sup-

pression and inhibition: because they are too young to emotionally deal with the terror and grief brought on by death they suppress any budding awareness of that reality. The final stanza then serves to show how this suppressed awareness lurks in the children's subconscious mind, breaking thru only in furtive, occasional glances to measure, perhaps unwittingly, "how far / It is" to death.

A second reading brings this poem more clearly in line with poem 413: Dickinson uses the final lines to introduce a specifically adult consciousness into the child's voice. Young children are generally not in the habit of measuring their distance from death. Thus, Dickinson begins the poem by presenting a consciousness too IN-SENSITIVE to death and mourners, even for a child's consciousness. She then ends the poem by introducing a point of view far too CONSCIOUS of the reality of death to be readily attributable to a childish point of view. One extreme throws the other into stark relief, yet they also cohere by working to make the reader examine his own responses to death.

When taken together, these readings show how Dickinson, thru her manipulation of childish and adult perceptions of death, generates an impressive number of possible responses to that reality. There is denial and suppression; fear; real ignorance or feigned ignorance; a practical measuring of distance; and even, one might argue, an acceptance of death (present in the childish attitude of the opening stanzas). These responses are generated for the reader—and for Dickinson—to recognize, examine, and test.

Peter Coveney, when discussing how writers use the material of childhood, notes that especially towards the latter decades of the nineteenth century they increasingly portrayed childhood as a means of escape from the cares of adult life. These sentimentalists

> draw on the general sympathy for childhood that has been diffused; but, for patently subjective reasons, their interest in childhood serves not to integrate childhood and adult experience, but to create a varrier of nostalgia and regret between childhood and the potential responses of adult life. The child indeed becomes a means of escape from the pressures of adult adjustment, a means of regression towards the irresponsibility of youth, childhood, infancy, and ultimately nescience itself.[14]

Dickinson makes quite different use of childhood materials from the patently sentimentalizing use described above. Rather than creating a "barrier of nostalgia," she uses childhood materials as a means of confronting specifically adult concerns. In this sense her perceptions of childhood is more romantic than sentimental or Victorian, if one accepts the definition of the romantic image of the child provided by Coveney:

> The purpose and strength of the romantic image of the child had been above all to establish a relation between childhood and adult consciousness, to assert the continuity of human experience. . . . For Blake, Wordsworth, and, for the most part, Dickens, the image of the child endows their writing with a sense of life, and the same is true of Mark Twain in *Huckleberry Finn.* In writing of the child, their interest was continuously adult; their children function within their total response to adult experience.[15]

It is in presenting adult states of consciousness such as religious doubt, fear of death, and cultural alienation that Dickinson excels. Her consummate use of the adult voice in the child poems contributes to her intense and complex portrayal of those internal state of consciousness.

Notes

This is formal notice that the Johnson number method for identifying Emily Dickinson poems will not be insisted on any longer. Simply the word poem before the number seems adequate at present, or without the word POEM in a series of explications. If R. W. Franklin or another scholar establishes a new numbering scheme, then things may be altered.—Editor.

1. Richard Wilbur, "Sumptuous Destitution" in *Emily Dickinson: A Collection of Critical Essays,* ed., R. B. Sewell (Englewood Cliffs, NJ: Prentice-Hall Inc., 1963), p. 127.

2. Allen Tate, "Emily Dickinson" in ED: a collection of critical essays, p. 27 See also Archibald MacLeish, "The Private World of ED," in *ED: A Collection of Critical Essays*, ESP pp. 154-55.

3. Adrienne Rich, "Vesuvius at Home" in *On Lies, Secrets and Silence* (NY: W. W. Norton and Co., 1979), p. 176.

4. Thomas Johnson, ed., *Collected Poems of ED,* 1960. All subsequent poems by Dickinson will be referred to by Johnson's numbering and quoted from his edition.

5. Rich, pp. 163-64.

6. See Peter Slater, *Children in the New England Mind* (Hamden, CT: Archon Books, 1977) for a full discussion of the nineteenth century sentimental view of children.

7. John Cody, *After Green Pain* (Harvard, 1971), p. 261.

8. Cody, pp. 111, 113, 120, and 216.

9. G. F. Whicher. *This Was a Poet* (Ann Arbor, MI: Univ. of Mich. Press, 1957), pp. 147-48. See also R. B. Sewall, LIFE, vol. II (NY: Farrar, Straus and Giroux, 1974), pp. 331-332.

10. Clark Griffith, *The Long Shadow* (Princeton U.P., 1964), p. 283.

11. Cody, pp. 17-18, 39-101.

12. Griffith, p. 31

13. Griffith, p. 41.

14. Peter Coveney, *The Image of Childhood* (Baltimore, MD Penguin Books, 1967), p. 240.

15. Coveney, p. 240.

Vivian R. Pollak (essay date 1984)

SOURCE: Pollak, Vivian R. "The Second Act: Emily Dickinson's Orphaned Persona." In *Nineteenth-Century Women Writers of the English-Speaking World,* edited by Rhoda B. Nathan, pp. 159-69. Westport, Conn.: Greenwood, 1986.

[*In the following essay, originally delivered at the Nineteenth-Century Women Writers' International Conference in 1980, and updated and published in* Dickinson: The Anxiety of Gender *in 1984, Pollak investigates the treatment and role of childhood in Dickinson's works, particularly as it relates to themes of innocence and death.*]

"Oh Austin . . . I wish we were children now. I wish we were always children, how to grow up I dont know," (Letter 115) Dickinson wrote to her brother in 1853, shortly after he became engaged to her closest friend, Susan Gilbert.[1] Her girlhood was over, but no marriage loomed on the horizon for her, distanced as it was by her vision of union with otherness as the abdication of selfhood. Thus at the age of twenty-two she had already begun to stave off her fears of a desolate future by clinging to an idealized past. In the following year, when she rejected an invitation to visit her pious friend Abiah Root (Abiah was shortly to become a minister's wife), she called herself "your quaint, old fashioned friend." The letter reads,

My Dear Child,

Thank you for that sweet note, which came so long ago, and thank you for asking me to come and visit you, and thank you for loving me, long ago, and today, and too for all the sweetness, and all the gentleness, and all the tenderness with which you remember me—your quaint, old fashioned friend. . . . You asked me to come and see you—I must speak of that. I thank you Abiah, but I dont go from home, unless emergency leads me by the hand, and then I do it obstinately, and draw back if I can. Should I ever leave home, which is improbable, I will with much delight, accept your invitation; till then, my dear Abiah, my warmest thanks are your's, but dont expect me. I'm so old fashioned, Darling, that all your friends would stare.

(*L* 166)

And still later, in 1862, addressing Thomas Wentworth Higginson, the literary critic who advised her to "'delay' to publish" as her "Preceptor," signing herself his "Scholar," she asked, "Could you tell me how to grow—or is it unconveyed—like Melody—or Witchcraft?" "I went to school—but in your manner of the phrase—had no education" (*L* 261). Visiting the thirty-nine-year-old poet in Amherst in 1870, it was this impression of a vulnerable, childlike persona which Higginson carried away as his dominant impression. Writing to his invalid neurasthenic wife, he described his encounter with a saintly simpleton or wise fool:

A step like a pattering child's in entry & in glided a little plain woman with two smooth bands of reddish hair & a face a little like Belle Dove's; not plainer—with no good feature—in a very plain & exquisitely clean white pique & a blue net worsted shawl. She came to me with two day lilies which she put in a sort of childlike way into my hand & said "These are my introduction" in a soft, frightened breathless childlike voice—& added under her breath Forgive me if I am frightened; I never see strangers & hardly know what I say—but she talked soon & thenceforward continuously—& deferentially—sometimes stopping to ask me to talk instead to her—but readily recommencing. Manner between Angie Tilton & Mr. Alcott—but thoroughly ingenuous & simple which they are not & saying many things which you would have thought foolish & I wise—.[2]

(*L* 342a)

"'Oh why do the insane so cling to you,'" his wife inquired not long thereafter.[3] Finally, on her deathbed, just before she lapsed into unconsciousness in May 1886, writing to those same orphaned Norcross cousins some sixteen years her junior to whom she had signed herself "Uncle Emily," whom she had called "Poor Plover," "Dear Peacock," "Dear Children," "Dear little solid gold girl (*s*)," Dickinson concluded, "Little Cousins, Called back," but whether to plenitude or void she did not say (*L* 1046).

Childhood—quintessential romantic metaphor of purified beginnings, edenic freedom, unfallen organic union between self and world, self and nature, self and God; metaphor, in short, of the undivided, uncorrupted, aboriginal self—fascinated Dickinson both as woman and poet, as a number of her critics have been quick to observe.[4] Yet the conclusions they have drawn in their quest for a central idea which would unify Dickinson's boldly disparate images of childhood have differed widely, in part because of their desire to establish a context for this child persona in the obsessions of the poet's life. I too followed this richly suggestive biographical path in my article "Thirst and Starvation in Emily Dickinson's Poetry," where I examined some of the psychosexual causes of the discontinuous cycle of privation, self-privation and qualified self-reliance Dickinson's artistic universe delineates.[5] Her letters of the

1850's establish that her fascination with deliberately shrunken appetites and willfully stunted growth emerged as a defensive posture against the repressive mid-Victorian cult of "True Womanhood."[6] Adopting the style of the pre-pubescent child, she was intent on besting an infantilizing society whose patriarchal sexual politics were writ large in her own "home sweet home" by exaggerating its latent identification of femininity and unselfconsciousness. But what emerges even in her letters is a highly self-conscious parodic stance, best understood as a mode of passive aggression initially directed outward and intended to liberate her "free spirit" from the conformist pressures that she chronicles throughout the correspondence of the formative years before 1858 when she emerges suddenly, abruptly, elliptically as the poet whose voice we recognize.[7] A combatant posing as a noncombatant, Dickinson sought to distance "these problems of the flesh" through the renunciation of the appearance, although not the inner reality, of autonomous selfhood. But even willfully chosen roles are adopted against the heft of socially appointed fates. Masks have a way of fusing with and devouring the reality they are designed to conceal. Hence Dickinson confined to a kind of lifelong house arrest within her father's house and ground, her sexuality shrouded by the virginal white gown of the self-designated, incorporeal bride. However, the figure with whom I shall be concerned in this essay is not the biographical self who lived out a defensive strategy, at once self-protective and self-destructive, which was endemic to the female sensibility of the nineteenth century, as Ann Douglas, Elaine Showalter, Sandra Gilbert, Susan Gubar, Nancy Cott, and others have demonstrated.[8] Rather, I wish to consider the artist who worked "for Immortality" (406) in order to address the following questions. How does childhood function in Dickinson's art and why does she characteristically represent innocence as a value which collapses as soon as it is tested? What are the consequences of this vision of beginnings as subject to abrupt and wholly inexplicable interruption for her poetics, and what is the relationship between childhood and death she imagines most compellingly so that we, like the unwitting Wedding Guest, cannot choose but hear?

Charting the disruptive progressions of the human life cycle, Dickinson often declares that "Finding is the first Act / The second, loss" (870). Most poems of her child group are organized by these absolutes: faith and despair, aspiration and frustration, originating victory and terminal defeat. There is a parthenogenic moment when consciousness is uncontaminated by bereavement and an equally contextless moment when bereavement is unassuaged by the memory of an earlier bliss. Childhood in its pure or archetypal form is the moment before death—in either its ultimate or prefiguring types—violates the persona's faith in a deathless, pain-free universe. Thus I shall be speaking here both of poems

in which Dickinson explicitly names herself "child," "little girl" or, more rarely, "boy," and more generally of those poems which explore crucial turning points from innocence to experience. In many poems, these turning points are inconclusive. In still others, Dickinson measures the unalterable distance between her helpless child persona's ideal of original freedom and the secondary reality of her grotesque psychic bondage. In the following poem, for example, appetites she can neither eliminate nor gratify paralyze her absolutely:

> It would have starved a Gnat—
> To live so small as I—
> And yet I was a living Child—
> With Food's necessity
>
> Upon me—like a Claw—
> I could no more remove
> Than I could coax a Leech away—
> Or make a Dragon—move—
>
> Nor like the Gnat—had I—
> The privilege to fly
> And seek a Dinner for myself—
> How mightier He—than I—
>
> Nor like Himself—the Art
> Upon the Window Pane
> To gad my little Being out—
> And not begin—again—

(612)

Although the romantic ideal of childhood seldom commands her sustained attention, Joanne Feit Diehl's assertion that "Dickinson writes only songs of experience" and that "she does not recall the 'visionary gleam' lost in the process of growth, for it has never been hers" oversimplifies this poet's relationship both to her own personal past and to what R. W. B. Lewis in *The American Adam* has called "the party of hope."[9] Without some individual and cultural memory of this "visionary gleam," which, it could be argued, is encoded by her subverted hymn meters themselves, her vehement protests against the loss of faith she associates with childhood, "earth's confiding time," could never have been written. It is precisely the distance between the romantic archetype and the reality of her deviant experience around which many of her poems are structured. Because Dickinson is a steadfast adherent to neither the "party of hope" nor of "memory," her American Eve has not one but two faces. Indeed, the most characteristic poems of her child group testify to the impossibility of their temporal fusion. The Dickinsonian "I," having lost a coherent vision of its past, never solves the mystery of its origins. The primary function of her victimized child persona is not, as Clark Griffith has asserted, to reveal a universe "contaminated to the core," but rather to insist on the instability of consciousness.[10]

Exposing the vulnerability of mere unaided innocence, Dickinson is concerned with protecting her orphan-exiles both from the suicidal despair of the starvation poem just quoted and from the incurable hopefulness which the dark forces of the universe and the unconscious are compelled to destroy. This latter enterprise is complicated by her child persona's strategic withdrawals from nature and human society and from the aggressive impulses she projects onto others—masculinity, God, "heaven," nature, convention, the world—intent on her destruction. This "I-He," "I-It," "I-They" structure makes her a perfect victim, and a perfect sexual victim at that. The association between femininity and vulnerability these poems emphasize is too widespread to be missed. But such a structure also forecloses any final resolution to the psychological problem with which these poems wrestle: how to live in the world without being imprisoned by it, how to conceive a self in a landscape of absence. As Griffith implies, these strategic retreats are essential to the survival of her voice. When she takes her power in her hand and assaults the world frontally, she is invariably defeated. Poet of strong beginnings, she often concludes with a question mark. Moreover, the economy of her style enables her to pretend to more certainty about her psychological ambitions than she commands:

> I took my Power in my Hand—
> And went against the World—
> 'Twas not so much as David—had—
> But I—was twice as bold—
>
> I aimed my Pebble—but Myself
> Was all the one that fell—
> Was it Goliah—was too large—
> Or was myself—too small?

(540)

Out of this self-critical dialogue between arrogance and humility, a third voice emerges: the voice of the poet mediating this conflict through language which calls attention to the instability of its ironic mode. Dickinson's ironic child persona perpetuates her profoundly ambivalent contract with the rage she tends to represent as unintegrated otherness, but the question she poses in the poem just quoted ("Was it Goliah—was too large—/ Or was myself—too small?") is unanswerable. As bard, with no strong line of female "Great Progenitor(s)" to gird her for combat, she forges an uneasy alliance with her David. As a woman, Dickinson was too shrewd a social observer not to note the equally powerful alliance between the "Soft—Cherubic Creatures—," the "Gentlewomen" against whose "Dimity Convictions—" she protested, and the world which preferred her "'still.'" Thus we find a poem such as the following where the speaker's aggression is partially controlled by a series of startling metamorphoses. "Little Girl," "Bird," "Himself," "Star," she attempts to will herself into a condition of liberated orphanage. A boasting poem which

fails to live up to the promise of its strong beginning, "They Shut Me Up in Prose" illustrates the tension between the romantic myth of childhood freedom and the reality of the Dickinsonian persona's powerlessness. Identifying imaginative play with childhood, play which is still accessible to the adult consciousness, the speaker brags of the ease with which she escaped from a society that wishes to immobilize her. The argument ends, however, with an unconvincing assertion of total freedom. The divorce between the speaker and her environment leaves her with no place to go. Laughing down at those others against whom she defines her strength, purging herself of any conceivable human identity, Dickinson's terminal phrase "No more have I" ends her angry *apologia* with a prosaic, skewed rhyme without resolving the conflict between feelings of helplessness and power the poem describes:

> They shut me up in Prose—
> As when a little Girl
> They put me in the Closet—
> Because they liked me "still"—
>
> Still! Could themself have peeped—
> And seen my Brain—go round—
> They might as wise have lodged a Bird
> For Treason—in the Pound—
>
> Himself has but to will
> And easy as a Star
> Look down upon Captivity—
> And laugh—No more have I—

(613)

In poem after poem the fall which precipitates her child persona out of the paradisiacal garden has also left her stranded in empty space. The continuous relationships that would enable her to move beyond illusory comedy, pathos, or tragedy to maturity—to a successful accommodation between herself and her world—are ruthlessly eliminated by a nature she can neither understand nor command. Consequently, she finds herself trapped in the prison of an alien self; her memory of the liberty she knew "When Memory was a Boy" is "Avoided—like a Dream— / Too wide for any Night but Heaven— / If That—indeed—redeem—" (652).

Bereft of mentors, human or divine, Dickinson is forced to birth herself. Rhetorically, this generational compression begets irony, but her compulsion to enact all the roles in her family romance frustrates her attempts to find the enabling experiences that she associates with mature power. Representing speakers who have lost their childhood in its purely joyous form, who have been prematurely initiated into the anxieties of adulthood, a significant number of these statements are determined to provide her orphan-exiles with a second childhood after some extreme form of separation has isolated the persona from a human environment intent

on killing off her "Real Me." Not surprisingly, given the evangelical religious rhetoric that informs her style (Karl Keller aptly describes her as stamping her foot "at what she stands on"), one of her orphaned persona's stock responses to privation is to imagine that she has a father in heaven who has a new home prepared for her in the sky.[11] When Dickinson's born-again tropes describe "Gates Ajar" family reunions, indulgent Victorian patriarchs, nicely naughty little girls, or any of the other domestic appurtenances of the cottage-style heaven popularized by her contemporary Elizabeth Stuart Phelps in a series of enormously successful spiritualist novels,[12] they generate that disquieting archness for which she has been so roundly spanked by critical hands over the years.

However, this hopeful Christian-derived mythology, when more thoroughly misread, also informs one of the most esthetically harmonious poems of Dickinson's child group, "A loss of something ever felt I—" (959). The sometimes distracting emphasis on other characters, whether as antagonists or allies, has been jettisoned; the speaker's isolated consciousness is the locus of conflict. Disciplined by its resistance to easy resolutions magically enacted, in this orphan's lament the persona cannot adequately name her "Missing All." The poem's theme is the relationship between self-knowledge and lost access to experience. Calling herself "the only Prince cast out," bemoaning a lost "Dominion" that she identifies with maleness, she permits the emphasis to fall on an uncertain quest which is associated with particular places ("Delinquent Palaces," "the site of the Kingdom of Heaven") that her finite vision prevents her from fully repossessing. The speaker's uncertainty about the nature of her lost paradise, perhaps the androgynous consciousness whose presence is experienced as an absence, generalizes the theme well beyond the specific autobiographical sexual context that the poem both incorporates and masters:

> A loss of something ever felt I—
> The first that I could recollect
> Bereft I was—of what I knew not
> Too young that any should suspect
>
> A Mourner walked among the children
> I notwithstanding went about
> As one bemoaning a Dominion
> Itself the only Prince cast out—
>
> Elder, Today, a session wiser
> And fainter, too, as Wiseness is—
> I find myself still softly searching
> For my Delinquent Palaces—
>
> And a Suspicion, like a Finger
> Touches my Forehead now and then
> That I am looking oppositely
> For the site of the Kingdom of Heaven—

To retain her faith in an original harmony between self and nature, self and God, Dickinson's bereaved child persona must effect some compromise between her need for sustaining temporal relationships and her need to free herself of their constricted reality. Space limitations prevent me from considering here those love poems in which an orphaned female persona is abruptly transformed into an uncourted, unhusbanded bride, married to her own phoenixlike imagination of invulnerable identity. Therefore, I should like to conclude this discussion of the two faces of Eve, looking forward toward paradise and backward toward paradise lost, with a transitional poem where the child persona's immersion in nature is delineated with greater narrative particularity than in any of the poems previously discussed:

> I started Early—Took my Dog—
> And visited the Sea—
> The Mermaids in the Basement
> Came out to look at me—
>
> And Frigates—in the Upper Floor
> Extended Hempen Hands—
> Presuming Me to be a Mouse—
> Aground—upon the Sands—
>
> But no Man moved Me—till the Tide
> Went past my simple Shoe—
> And past my Apron—and my Belt
> And past my Boddice—too—
>
> And made as He would eat me up—
> As wholly as a Dew
> Upon a Dandelion's Sleeve—
> And then—I started—too—
>
> And He—He followed—close behind—
> I felt his Silver Heel
> Upon my Ancle—Then my Shoes
> Would overflow with Pearl—
>
> Until We met the Solid Town—
> No One He seemed to know—
> And bowing—with a Mighty look—
> At me—The Sea withdrew—

(520)

Although the "simple" persona's death into disillusion is narrowly avoided, in opting for the "solid town" and in resisting the sea's erotic embrace, she also loses the opportunity to clarify the moral ambiguity of her anesthetized emotional response. As Robert Weisbuch has remarked, the persona aborts a passionate dramatic contest with "experiential unknowns" and "denied irrational urges," but his formulation of this deceptively fragmented soulscape must be particularized somewhat further.[13] At the heart of the poem's insight into the complex relationship between risk and maturation lies a thanatized vision of love and an eroticized vision of death, a blinding vision of powerful mystery which the speaker cannot simultaneously experience and tell. In the end, whether the sea represents the persona's re-

pressed sexual aggression projected onto a lascivious male universe or whether the sea is genuinely shaped as male otherness matters little. What is important here is that these "experiential unknowns" are not wholly unknown. Encountering the "man of noon," the sun god in his watery habitat, Dickinson shapes a contest her childlike persona has no chance of winning in frontal combat. Given this shrewdly politicized sensibility of unequal sexual odds, the pattern of physical advance and retreat is not accompanied by any growth in the persona's consciousness, nor can it be. Designing a drama between male-identified aggression and female-identified passivity, Dickinson is caught between self-preservation and ego-annihilating adventure. "The shore is safer . . . but I love to buffet the sea," (*L* 39) she had written to a friend in her nineteenth year. But by 1862, when she composed her seascape, she had been further schooled in the need for renunciation, that "piercing Virtue," lest the "Wild Nights" of which she dreamed drown her voice in pearly silence.

Notes

This article was written in 1980 and reflects my views at that time. I have updated some of this article in *Dickinson: The Anxiety of Gender* (Ithaca, N. Y.: Cornell University Press, 1984), especially in chapters 1 and 4.

1. All texts for Dickinson's letters are from Thomas H. Johnson and Theodora Ward, eds., *The Letters of Emily Dickinson,* 3 vols. (Cambridge, Mass.: Harvard University Press, 1958). The letter *L* precedes such citations to differentiate letters from poems. All texts for Dickinson's poems are from Thomas H. Johnson, ed., *The Poems of Emily Dickinson,* 3 vols. (Cambridge, Mass.: Harvard University Press, 1955). The parenthetical numbers correspond to the relative chronological numbering in this work.

2. Neither "Belle Dove" nor "Angie Tilton" has been identified. "Mr. Alcott" is Bronson, transcendental seer and father of Louisa May.

3. As quoted in Jay Leyda, *The Years and Hours of Emily Dickinson* (New Haven: Yale University Press, 1960), II, p. 213.

4. Adrienne Rich, for example, writes that "Most of us, unfortunately, have been exposed in the schoolroom to Dickinson's 'little-girl' poems, her kittenish tones. . . . One critic—Richard Chase—has noted that in the 19th century 'one of the careers open to women was perpetual childhood.' A strain in Dickinson's letters and some—though by far a minority—of her poems was a self-diminutization, almost as if to offset and deny—or even disguise—her actual dimensions as she must have experienced them. And this emphasis on her own 'littleness,' along with the deliberate strangeness

of her tactics of seclusion, have been, until recently, accepted as the prevailing character of the poet." "Vesuvius at Home: The Power of Emily Dickinson," *Parnassus,* V (Fall / Winter 1976), p. 58.

5. Vivian R. Pollak, "Thirst and Starvation in Emily Dickinson's Poetry," *American Literature,* VI, no. 1 (March, 1979), 33-49.

6. Three recent works defining nineteenth-century American attitudes toward women are Nancy R. Cott, *The Bonds of Womanhood: "Woman's Sphere" in New England, 1780-1835* (New Haven, Conn.: Yale University Press, 1977); Ann Douglas, *The Feminization of American Culture* (New York: Alfred A. Knopf, 1977); and Barbara Welter, *Dimity Convictions: The American Woman in the Nineteenth Century* (Athens: Ohio University Press, 1976).

7. Only five poems have been identified as having been written before 1858. For discussions of the difficulties of Dickinson chronology, see Johnson, *Poems,* I, pp. xvii-lxvii; and R. W. Franklin, *The Editing of Emily Dickinson: A Reconsideration* (Madison: University of Wisconsin Press, 1967).

8. Douglas, *The Feminization of American Culture,* and "The 'Scribbling Women' and Fanny Fern: Why Women Wrote," *American Quarterly,* XXVII (Spring 1971), 3-24; Elaine Showalter, *A Literature of Their Own: British Women Novelists from Brontë to Lessing* (Princeton: Princeton University Press, 1977); Sandra Gilbert and Susan Gubar, *The Madwoman in the Attic: The Woman Writer and the Nineteenth-Century Literary Imagination* (New Haven, Conn.: Yale University Press, 1979); Nancy Cott, *The Bonds of Womanhood,* and idem, "Passionlessness: An Interpretation of Victorian Sexual Ideology, 1790-1850," *Signs,* IV, no. 2 (Winter, 1978), 219-36.

9. Feit Diehl, "'Come Slowly—Eden': An Exploration of Women Poets and Their Muse," *Signs,* III, no. 3 (Spring, 1978), 574; R. W. B. Lewis, *The American Adam: Innocence Tragedy and Tradition in the Nineteenth Century* (Chicago: University of Chicago Press, 1955). Lewis argues that "a culture achieves identity not so much through the ascendancy of one particular set of convictions as through the emergence of its peculiar and distinctive dialogue," invoking the terms "party of hope" and "party of memory" to describe the ideological extremes from which the seminal dialogue about the nature of the American self emerged.

10. Clarke Griffith, *The Long Shadow: Emily Dickinson's Tragic Poetry* (Princeton: Princeton University Press, 1964), p. 31. Despite my quarrel with

Griffith's basic assumption that Dickinson's child persona functions primarily as an ironic mask behind which she is free to attack a hostile universe, his chapter "The Post-Romantic Child" is indispensable reading on this subject. Evidently, there is some truth in his assertion that "To lie low in order to gain the freedom for striking back—here, surely, is the essence of the child poetry," p. 39. But it is ironic that, in a book which purports to emphasize tragic vision, Griffith views the Dickinsonian child as an essentially comic mask, and has her laughing "up her sleeve" at the malice and hostility of "Nature and God." Dickinson's poetry is genuinely tragic when consciousness itself is death-ridden and those others against whom she defines her strength, including Nature and God, have disappeared from view.

11. Perhaps the most interesting of these poems is "We don't cry—Tim and I" (196), where the persona also furnishes herself with a boyish alter ego. The poem is, as Rebecca Patterson argues in "Emily Dickinson's 'Double' Tim: Masculine Identification," *American Imago,* XXVII (winter, 1971), 330-62, a compelling revelation of the poet's sexual anxieties, as are all those utterances where her flight from femininity propels her into a male persona. However, Albert Gelpi's attempt to assert its artistic merit, in *The Tenth Muse: The Psyche of the American Poet* (Cambridge, Mass.: Harvard University Press, 1975), p. 249, seems to me not to withstand close scrutiny. He writes:

> This early poem contains many of the motifs scattered throughout the love poems: a passion linked to religion, withdrawn into exclusive association, resistant to the death it is doomed to, uncertain of the eternity which offers the only chance for genuine union. The seriousness of the poem is no more betrayed by the witty playfulness than it would be in a poem of Robert Frost or John Crowe Ransom. The poet is employing the resources of the little-girl persona to distract us at first from what she is revealing, but the nursery-rhyme quality, the singsong rhythms, the repetitions and refrains . . . all lead up to the last lines, spaced out with dashes to heighten the recognition. How can we, Tim and I, arrange for simultaneous death? Because we are one and the same person? "I—'Tim'—and Me!"

Gelpi's eloquence almost succeeds in rewriting the poem, but his assertion that it is "resistant to the death it is doomed to" calls for a howl of protest. If Tim and I have any passion at all, it is to quit this vale of tears for the storybook heaven

they can see only if they shut their brown eye to those divisions of desire which Tim may have signified in the author's unconscious, but which he is not made to symbolize in the poem.

12. Barton Levi St. Armand's "Paradise Deferred: The Image of Heaven in the Work of Emily Dickinson and Elizabeth Stuart Phelps," *American Quarterly,* XXIX (Spring, 1977), 55-78 explores significant parallels in the work of these two writers. He argues that "*The Gates Ajar* and Dickinson's poems on spiritual marriage are products of that more pervasive common source: the rebellion against the tyrannical Father-God of New England orthodoxy" (p. 56).

13. Robert Weisbuch, *Emily Dickinson's Poetry* (Chicago: University of Chicago Press, 1975), p. 55.

FURTHER READING

Criticism

Armitt, Lucie. "Haunted Childhood in Charlotte Brontë's *Villette*." *Yearbook of English Studies* 32 (2002): 217-28.

> Examines *Villette* to determine, within the context of the novel, "what it is, precisely, that constitutes childhood and what makes children uncanny."

Ashe, Frederick L. "*Jane Eyre*: The Quest for Optimism." *Studies in the Novel* 20, no. 2 (summer 1988): 121-30.

> Views Brontë's depiction of the eponymous heroine of *Jane Eyre* as a representation of Brontë's own psyche and childhood experience within a framework that allows Jane to achieve the happiness that eluded Brontë in her own life.

Horne, Jackie C. "Punishment as Performance in Catherine Sinclair's *Holiday House*." *Children's Literature Association Quarterly* 26, no. 1 (spring 2001): 22-32.

> Explores the connection between punishment and "the construction of the Romantic child" in Catherine Sinclair's *Holiday House*.

Plotz, Judith. "Childhood Lost, Childhood Regained: Hartley Coleridge's Fable of Defeat." *Children's Literature* 14 (1986): 133-61.

> Provides a reading of "Adolf and Annette" and contends that this fairy tale is an allegory for growing up in general and of Coleridge's own "romantic rearing in particular."

————. "'One Shape, One Feature, and One Size': Romanticism and The Quintessential Child." In *Romanticism and the Vocation of Childhood,* pp. 1-40. New York: Palgrave, 2001.

Delineates the genesis and literary expression of the Romantic childhood ideal during the nineteenth century.

Richardson, Alan. "The Politics of Childhood: Wordsworth, Blake, and Catechistic Method." *ELH* 56, no. 4 (winter 1989): 853-68.

Analyzes the treatment of education in Wordsworth's *Lyrical Ballads* and in Blake's "The Lamb" in relation to traditional methods of religious instruction.

Schefski, Harold K. "Childhood on a Pedestal: Tolstoy's Oasis from Nihilism." *San José Studies* 15, no. 3 (fall 1989): 48-61.

Studies the significance of Tolstoy's representation of children as morally superior to adults in his works.

Smith, Matthew Wilson. "*The Wild Duck*: A Play of Play." *Modern Drama* 45, no. 1 (spring 2002): 9-22.

Explores the treatment of play and its relationship to childhood and adulthood in Henrik Ibsen's play, *Vildanden* (*The Wild Duck*).

Wachtel, Andrew. "Narrating the Past: The Role of Childhood and History in Russian Literary Culture." In *Infant Tongues: The Voice of the Child in Literature,* edited by Elizabeth Goodenough, Mark A. Heberle, and Naomi Sokoloff, pp. 110-22. Detroit, Mich.: Wayne State University Press, 1994.

Observes "the dialogic interaction of different narrative perspectives" in Russian literature, and the connection between this narrative, history, and childhood.

Exile in Nineteenth-Century European and American Literature

The following entry provides critical commentary on the treatment of the theme of exile in nineteenth-century European and American literature.

INTRODUCTION

Nineteenth-century European and American literature includes a broad range of approaches to the treatment of exile. Expatriate writers such as Henry James and Joseph Conrad, according to critic Carola Kaplan, comment on the society, politics, and culture of their home countries and their adopted countries, offering a unique perspective on differences and similarities between nations, as well as on the effects of these realities on the nature of individual identity. French authors, including Honoré de Balzac, François-René de Chateaubriand, and Alfred de Musset, communicate their thoughts and observations on political exile through characters possessed of artistic sensibilities and personal beliefs that isolate them from the rest of society. Victorian Scottish authors express their alienation from their home country and their impressions of the foreign cultures they encountered during their travels in Africa and North America, and these narratives informed subsequent Scottish fiction. Critics have noted how Charles Dickens draws upon his personal life and the political and social climate of his time to provide a thematic representation of exile as an important rite of passage in *A Tale of Two Cities* (1859). Commentator Daniel Marder argues that themes of displacement and isolation in works by such authors as James Fenimore Cooper, Nathaniel Hawthorne, Herman Melville, Mark Twain, Edgar Allan Poe, and Emily Dickinson are illustrative of an American "literature of exile," characterized by a sense of loss of national cultures, a heightened sense of individualism, and a desire to establish structure and order out of unstable and treacherous wilderness. Critic Colin D. Pearce maintains that American writer Edward Everett Hale's "The Man without a Country" (1863) comments on the differences between the political and moral lessons learned by a person who is subject to involuntary exile versus those learned by an individual who is actively engaged in the exercise of his civic responsibility. Numerous critics have studied how the obstacles encountered by women and people of color during the nineteenth century are framed in tales of exile that highlight their struggles for self actualization and personal fulfillment within the confines of the laws and norms of Victorian society. Critic Kari Weil views exile

and melancholy in psychological and political terms, asserting that Claire de Duras and Chateaubriand use these broad themes to explore issues of gender and race, and other commentators have illustrated how works by George Eliot and Constance Fenimore Woolson depict Victorian women's unique experience of exile.

REPRESENTATIVE WORKS

R. M. Ballantyne

Snowflakes and Sunbeams; or, The Young Fur Traders (novel) 1856; also published as *The Young Fur Traders,* 1950

Ungava: A Tale of Esquimaux Land (novel) 1857

The Coral Island: A Tale of the Pacific Ocean (novel) 1858

Honoré de Balzac

Eugénie Grandet [*Eugenia Grandet; or, The Miser's Daughter: A Tale of Everyday Life in the Nineteenth Century*] (novel) 1834; published in *Études de moeurs au XIXe siècle*

La Comédie humaine. 20 vols. [*The Human Comedy*] (novels, novellas, and short stories) vols. 1-16, 1842-46; vol. 17, 1848; vols. 18-20, 1855

François de Barbé-Marbois

Journal d'un déporté non jugé, ou déportation en violation des lois, décrétéde 18 fructidor an V (journal) 1835

Charles Baudelaire

Les fleurs du mal [*The Flowers of Evil*] (poetry) 1857; enlarged editions published in 1861 and 1868

Oeuvres completes de Charles Baudelaire. 19 vols. (poetry, criticism, essays, novel, letters, journals, autobiography, and translations) 1922-63

James Bruce

Travels to Discover the Source of the Nile, in the Years 1768, 1769, 1770, 1771, 1772, and 1773. 6 vols. (travel essays) 1790

Lady Maria Callcott

Journal of a Residence in India [as Maria Graham] (journal) 1812

François-René de Chateaubriand
René ou les effets de la passion [*René*] (novel) 1805

Joseph Conrad
Under Western Eyes (novel) 1911

James Fenimore Cooper
The Pioneers. 2 vols. [published anonymously] (novel) 1823

Charles Dickens
**A Tale of Two Cities* (novel) 1859
**Great Expectations* (novel) 1861

Claire de Duras
Ourika [published anonymously] (novel) 1823

Emily Eden
The Semi-Detached House (novel) 1860
The Semi-Attached Couple (novel) 1861
"Up the Country": Letters Written to Her Sister from the Upper Provinces of India (letters) 1866

George Eliot
Middlemarch: A Study of Provincial Life (novel) 1871-72
Daniel Deronda (novel) 1876

Montstuart Elphinstone
An Account of the Kingdom of Caubul (nonfiction) 1815
The History of India. 2 vols. (history) 1841

John Galt
Voyages and Travels in the Years 1809, 1810, and 1811; Containing Statistical, Commercial, and Miscellaneous Observations on Gibraltar, Sardinia, Sicily, Malta, Serigo, and Turkey (travel essays) 1812
Annals of the Parish; or, The Chronicle of Dalmailing (novel) 1821
The Last of the Lairds; or, The Life and Opinions of Malachi Mailings, Esq. of Auldbiggings (novel) 1826
Lawrie Todd; or, The Settlers in the Woods (novel) 1830
Bogle Corbet; or, The Emigrants (novel) 1831

George Gissing
New Grub Street (novel) 1891
Born in Exile (novel) 1892
The Private Papers of Henry Ryecroft (novel) 1903

James Augustus Grant
A Walk across Africa; or, Domestic Scenes from My Nile Journal (travel essays) 1864

Edward Everett Hale
"The Man without a Country" (short story) 1863; published in the journal *Atlantic Monthly*; published in book form, 1865

Thomas Hardy
Jude the Obscure (novel) 1895

Washington Irving
The Sketch Book of Geoffrey Crayon, Gent. [as Geoffrey Crayon] (short stories) 1819-20

Henry James
Roderick Hudson (novel) 1876
The American (novel) 1877
The Europeans (novel) 1878
Daisy Miller (novel) 1879
The Portrait of a Lady (novel) 1881
The Siege of London. Madame de Mauves (novellas) 1883
The Bostonians (novel) 1886
The Princess Casamassima (novel) 1886
The Ambassadors (novel) 1903
English Hours (travel essays) 1905
The American Scene (travel essays) 1907
"The Jolly Corner" (short story) 1908; first published in the journal *The English Review*
The Ivory Tower (unfinished novel) 1917

David Livingstone
Missionary Travels and Researches in South Africa (travel essays) 1857; abridged edition published as *A Popular Account of Missionary Travels and Researches in South Africa*, 1861
Narrative of an Expedition to the Zambesi and Its Tributaries and of the Discovery of the Lakes Shirwa and Nyssa 1858-1864 [with Charles Livingstone] (travel essays) 1865
The Last Journals of David Livingstone, in Central Africa, from 1865 to His Death. 2 vols. [edited by Horace Waller] (journals) 1874; also published as *The Last Journals of David Livingstone, in Central Africa, from Eighteen Hundred and Sixty-five to His Death*, 1875

Alexander Mackenzie
Voyages from Montreal, on the River St. Laurence, through the Continent of North America, to the Frozen and Pacific Oceans; in the Years 1789 and 1793 [edited by William Combe] (journals) 1801

Sir John Malcolm
The Political History of India, from 1784 to 1823. 2 vols. (history) 1826
Sketches of Persia, from the Journals of a Traveller in the East. 2 vols. (sketches) 1827

Alfred de Musset
La Loi sur la presse (poem) 1835; published in the journal *Revue des Deux Mondes*

Mungo Park
Travels in the Interior of Africa, in the Years 1795, 1796, & 1797 (travel essays) 1799

Michael Scott
Tom Cringle's Log (novel) 1842

Sir Walter Scott
†*Chronicles of the Canongate* (short stories) 1827

Robert Louis Stevenson
The Strange Case of Dr. Jekyll and Mr. Hyde (novella) 1886
The Ebb-Tide: A Trio and Quartette [with Lloyd Osbourne] (novel) 1894

John McDouall Stuart
Explorations in Australia: The Journals of John McDouall Stuart (journals) 1864

Joseph Thomson
To the Central African Lakes and Back: The Narrative of the Royal Geographical Society's East African Expedition, 1878-80 (travel essays) 1881

Constance Fenimore Woolson
Castle Nowhere: Lake-Country Sketches (sketches) 1875
Rodman the Keeper: Southern Sketches (sketches) 1880
The Front Yard and Other Italian Stories (short stories) 1895
Dorothy and Other Italian Stories (short stories) 1896

*All of Dickens's novels were originally published serially in magazines, usually over periods of one to two years.

†This collection contains the short stories "The Highland Widow," "The Surgeon's Daughter," and "The Two Drovers."

OVERVIEW

Carola Kaplan (essay date 1990)

SOURCE: Kaplan, Carola. "The Spectre of Nationality in Henry James' *The Bostonians* and in Joseph Conrad's *Under Western Eyes*." In *Literature and Exile*, edited by David Bevan, pp. 37-54. Atlanta, Ga. and Amsterdam, Netherlands: Rodopi, 1990.

[*In the following essay, Kaplan analyzes Henry James's* The Bostonians *and Joseph Conrad's* Under Western Eyes *to illustrate how each of these expatriate writers express the intractability of social traditions in certain societies, the inevitability of political involvement, and the destructive qualities of their home countries.*]

Shortly after receiving the 1987 Nobel Prize for Literature, Joseph Brodsky, an *émigré* from the Soviet Union, made this comment about the condition of the writer in exile:

A writer in exile is by and large a retrospective and retroactive being. . . . Like the false prophets of Dante's Inferno, his head is forever turned backward and his tears, or saliva, are running down between his shoulder blades. This . . . retrospective machinery is constantly in motion in an exiled writer, nearly always unbeknown to him. Whether pleasant or dismal, the past is always a safe territory, if only because it is already experienced; and the species' capacity to revert, to run backward—especially in its thoughts or dreams . . . is extremely strong in all of us, quite irrespective of the reality we are facing.[1]

On first consideration, this statement does not seem particularly apt for considering the works of the writers Henry James and Joseph Conrad. Both left their respective homelands, America and Poland, for England; and both seem to have adopted British customs and traditions with the peculiar intensity of religious converts.

Yet, although James and Conrad turned their backs on their native countries to assume an adopted British nationality, both remained somewhat ambivalent and unresolved about this decision. Having adopted allegiances and traditions foreign, even opposed, to those of their country of origin, both expatriates faced the task of explaining and justifying in both their lives and in their fiction their apparent desertion of homeland. Both felt, moreover, the need to reply to the unvoiced reproach that they should have remained at home to try to correct the faults of the societies they left behind. Both writers, in middle age, attempted in fictional form to resolve these issues of nationality—Henry James in his novel of 1886, *The Bostonians*,[2] and Joseph Conrad in his 1911 novel, *Under Western Eyes*.[3] In each of these works, the "exiled writer's eyes", in Brodsky's words, are "firmly trained on his past".

Both these novels, *The Bostonians* and *Under Western Eyes,* which are set on native soil (albeit, for Conrad, on Russian-occupied native soil), centre on native reformers and revolutionaries in such a way as to maintain the impossibility of social change. Without exception, James' American reformers are neurotic and egotistical and Conrad's Russian revolutionaries are either ineffectual dreamers or cynical manipulators. Also without exception, the talented and the virtuous are stifled or destroyed: James' figure of the artist, Verena Tarrant, is a voice without anything to say, who is exploited and at last finally suppressed by the power-hungry; Conrad's idealistic revolutionary, Haldin, is killed and the apparently neutral innocent, Razumov, corrupted and maimed.

Both novels attempt to demonstrate not only that social change is impossible in the societies that they present, but that neutrality or abstention from political involvement is impossible as well. For the young and talented, the consequence of living in a corrupt culture is that

their lives are controlled and therefore determined by it. Thus, James and Conrad attempt to demonstrate through their fiction that the decision to stay in their native countries would have destroyed them both as men and as artists.

This is not to suggest that the issue of expatriation is quite the same for Conrad as for James. The decision to leave his native country was a more difficult if perhaps a more pressing one for Conrad than for James since he, in a sense, did not have a nation to leave behind. His choice of exile signifies not mere scepticism about social change in his native land, as it did for James, but despair of the possibility of re-establishing Poland as a separate nation state.

The reason that neutrality is impossible in both James' America and in Conrad's Russia is that the individual is constantly under surveillance. These novels reflect what the French philosopher Michel Foucault would later call the "panoptic" society of the modern world.[4] Since the eighteenth century, as Foucault observes, technological advances have enabled government and other institutions to intrude increasingly on private life. Consequently, for the native of a culture, locked into its grid pattern, placed, scrutinised, and labelled, there is no possibility of privacy or absence from the public arena, of anonymity or private moral choice. Both James and Conrad were centrally aware of these problems.

The model for the panoptic society, as Foucault notes, is the prison. Apparently a humane institution, concerned about the well-being of its inmates, the panopticon is actually designed to obtain maximum control over its inhabitants, to render them harmless, useful, and interchangeable. Ostensibly created to obtain information about its inmates, with a view to ensuring their welfare, it in fact creates information about them, thus in effect producing their individuality or identity. By making use of this knowledge or information about its prisoners, it can proceed to "normalise" them, to place them in their proper positions on the social grid.[5]

What James and Conrad hoped to achieve by leaving their native lands was to extricate themselves from the social grid of the native culture, to confound the all-seeing eyes of their prison of origin. By a literal dislocation, they hoped to slip through the grids of cultural placement, to achieve anonymity in a strange land. In this way, they could, as writers, reverse the process of surveillance, to become the eyes that see rather than the object seen. Analogously, Foucault called his own enterprise as a writer:

> . . . a labyrinth into which I can venture, in which I can move my discourse, opening up underground passages (. . .) in which I can lose myself and appear at last to eyes that I will never have to meet again. I am no doubt not the only one who writes in order to have no face.[6]

This practice describes as well the enterprise of James and Conrad.

This enterprise does however suggest the disturbing possibility that for the author to obtain this privileged vantage point is to become fully complicit with the carceral system he has attempted to escape. In fact, this idea is suggested—although it is not explored—in Foucault's influential essay "What is an Author?" In this essay, Foucault maintains that the author's name functions not as a proper name but rather assumes "a classificatory function (. . .) it establishes a relationship among texts."[7] Linking the "author function" with the type of ownership which is subject to "penal appropriation", Foucault suggests that the author may become the object/victim of such appropriation: "Texts, books, and discourses really began to have authors (. . .) to the extent that authors became subject to punishment, that is, to the extent that discourses could be transgressive."[8] Although he acknowledges that "the author function is linked to the juridical and institutional system that encompasses, determines, and articulates the universe of discourses",[9] he does not directly link the author function with the panopticism of the societies in which the author's discourse operates. Yet he maintains:

> The author is (. . .) a certain functional principle by which, in our culture, one limits, excludes, and chooses; in short, by which one impedes the free circulation, the free manipulation, the free composition, decomposition, and recomposition of fiction.[10]

If this is indeed the function of the author, then the same movement of containment which developed the vast carceral apparatus to define and confine the delinquent, and which founded the asylum to contain the "insane", has also implicated the author. For this reason, the author may be not merely a victim, but also an agent of oppression, and his narrative strategies may also function as strategies of containment and normalisation. Accordingly, the narrative techniques of James and Conrad—or, more precisely, of what Foucault calls the "author function" of James and Conrad—may indeed partake of the panopticism of the societies in which their discourse operates.

This phenomenon does indeed seem to characterise the fictional treatment of women in both *The Bostonians* and *Under Western Eyes*. Both novels consider in order unequivocally to reject the idea of radical social transformation brought about by the efforts of women. James described the subject of *The Bostonians* in this way: "I asked myself what was the most salient and peculiar point in our social life. The answer was: the situation of women, the decline of the sentiment of sex, the agitation on their behalf."[11] The novel *The Bostonians* presents this movement as misguided and futile and its exponents as deluded or self-serving. Thus the narrative serves as a containment strategy against potentially great social disruption.

Under Western Eyes, as well, proposes a radical reconsideration of the roles of women only to undermine any change in their roles or status. The advocacy of a position of leadership for women is put in the mouth of Peter Ivanovich, a charlatan and a buffoon, who himself abuses and exploits those women he does not foolishly idealise. Thus, his point of view is made to appear both ludicrous and untenable. Throughout, the narrative suggests that the worst choice the heroine Natalia might make is a role of political activism. In addition, the original manuscript of the novel contained a scene, which Conrad ultimately omitted, in which the narrator praises Natalia through a disparaging contrast of her with his niece, who writes for a newspaper, who works for political causes, and who undertakes a contractual, egalitarian marriage—all activities of which he strongly disapproves.[12]

In *The Bostonians,* James makes his case for the defeat of the artist and the futility of social movements by centring his narrative on a gifted young woman who, like many of James' gifted young women (Isabel Archer, for example), is an alter-ego. In the course of the narrative, she is exploited, dominated, and defeated. This can be seen as James' first consideration of the question: "What would have happened to me if I had remained in America?"—a premise which continued to haunt him in nightmarish forms, and which he finally exorcised in his most explicit justification of his emigration, the 1906 horror story "The Jolly Corner".[13]

In *The Bostonians,* James determined "to write a very American tale, a tale very characteristic of our social conditions", "as local, as American, as possible, and as full of Boston."[14] He planned to centre the conflict in the mind of a talented young woman orator, who is torn between her loyalty to the movement as well as to her stern New England benefactress, Olive Chancellor, and her love for her impoverished and reactionary southern suitor, Basil Ransom, who proposes to marry her and rescue her from a career and a cause he adamantly opposes.

In the course of writing the novel, which was originally entitled *Verena,*[15] James centred the conflict more and more on the struggle between Olive and Ransom; and he left mainly undisclosed the conflicts in Verena's mind. The effect of this shift in emphasis is that Verena, the most attractive, intelligent, and talented figure in the book, seems passive, weak, and helpless. In short, James makes Verena the vehicle of his thesis that American society suppresses and destroys the young and talented.

To urge his thesis, James carefully changed, in the novel, the facts about the women's movement so as to demonstrate the repressive atmosphere of American society, even within—or especially within—its ranks of would-be reformers. Not only does James move the centre of the movement from New York to Boston, but he changes the very nature of the Boston branch of the movement. Whereas historically the Boston branch was a good deal less militant and more conciliatory than the New York wing and contained substantial numbers of men as well as women,[16] in James' version, the Boston contingent is extremely shrill, militant, hostile toward and exclusive of men. In addition, James goes to some lengths to discredit the participants in the movement, reducing them to cranks, weirdos, faddists, and opportunists. In order to do so, he inserts into the narrative as caricatures some of the great, old-time reformers, who were instrumental in the movement, including former abolitionists and leading figures in Boston society. Perhaps his most scathing portrait is that of Miss Birdseye, whom James based on Miss Elizabeth Peabody,[17] a well-known and esteemed Boston reformer. He describes her as "a confused, entangled, inconsequent, discursive old woman whose charity began at home and ended nowhere".[18]

Behind this satiric portrait of the former abolitionist turned women's rights reformer lie James' unresolved feelings about his own lack of participation in the abolitionist movement or the Civil War. Unlike his father, who had voiced his strong anti-slavery feelings, and his two younger brothers who had fought in the Civil War on the Union side, James had abstained from the War, an abstention that anticipated his departure altogether from American life.[19] The dismissive portrait of the elderly Miss Birdseye's indiscriminate participation in the women's movement serves in the novel to discredit the abolitionist movement as well—or, at the very least, to question the motives of its participants: "Since the Civil War much of her occupation was gone (. . .). It would have been a nice question whether, in her heart of hearts, (. . .) she did not sometimes wish the blacks back in bondage."[20]

In the physical portrait of Miss Birdseye, we can see James' fear of the loss of individuality in a life devoted to causes and centred on the needs of others. Thus, her face "looked as if it had been soaked, blurred, and made vague by exposure to some slow dissolvent. The long practice of philanthropy had not given accent to her features; it had rubbed out their transitions, their meanings."[21] If a life committed to good works robs the doer of the individuality and discrimination essential to a writer, then James has found a way to justify his earlier refusal to join the ranks of the abolitionists or the Union army.

This loss of individuality to the requirements of a public or philanthropic life was to James the symptom of an even more pervasive danger of American life—the total loss of privacy. James decried "the detestable tendency toward the complete effacement of privacy in life and thought everywhere so rampant with us nowadays."[22]

The constrictions of New England society—its distrust of pleasure, its rigid practices, its moralistic vigilance—enmesh all its inmates in its panoptic devices: everyone watches everyone else. Yet the public nature of Verena's life, itself an imprisonment, singles her out for more than usual exploitation. Verena's talent as a speaker makes her a ready victim for promoters and opportunists because she is constantly on view. Her very appearance suggests that she is being vampirised.[23] When Verena first speaks in Boston, Dr Prance notes that she looks anaemic. As Verena's father places his hands on her head to "start her up",[24] there is the suggestion that the old "mesmeric healer" has been draining her blood for his own sustenance. In general, she is a strangely passive speaker—less an orator than a receiver and transmitter. Repeatedly, she insists that she is not the author of her own eloquence: "It was some power outside—it seemed to flow through her (. . .) it wasn't her—she had nothing to do with it".[25] Indeed Verena's course does seem to be determined by outside powers or the power of those outside her—her parents, her friends, her suitors, her fans. There is similarly the suggestion that her ideas come from outside powers as well, from the powerful shapers of ideas in her society—newspapers, public figures, popular opinion, current fashion. In consequence, for all her intelligence, Verena never becomes an artist or speaker in her own right, but remains merely a parrot or a ventriloquist's dummy.

Throughout the narrative, people treat Verena as an object on display. In some, she evokes admiration: in this way, Ransom sees her as a "moving statue"[26] and Henry Burrage, another suitor, wishes to collect her because she is "so peculiar and delicate: he liked her for the same reason that he liked old enamels and old embroideries".[27] Others see her as an object to be used for financial gain: the newspaperman Matthias Pardon wants to manage her lecture tours and suggests to Olive Chancellor, "Couldn't they run Miss Verena together?"[28]

Others want to appropriate her entirely. Olive Chancellor would have her "renounce" life, promise not to marry, and cultivate her own freedom, provided that she uses it to think exactly the way Olive does. Ransom, recently stripped of his slaves, would enslave Verena. He wishes to still her voice and to immure her in the bedroom and nursery of his home. Ready to employ brutal tactics to do so, he reflects: "(. . .) however she might turn and twist in his grasp he held her fast".[29] Thus, Verena, who is always on view as a desirable object, is an inevitable victim: reified and fetishised, she is finally appropriated.

Thus James demonstrates that a Verena Tarrant in American society can only be a voice with nothing to say, or a voice that is silenced. Indeed the narrative strongly suggests that, more than friends or suitors, it is Verena's voice or use of her voice that ultimately betrays her. By attempting to present her ideas through speech, so as to vouch for them, she merely renders them ever more tentative and unpersuasive—even to herself. She is enmeshed in what Jacques Derrida terms "phonocentrism": the attempt to evade "the concealment within speech itself, in the mirage of its immediacy." Presented through speech, her words are particularly unsatisfactory, for, as Derrida notes: "In the spoken address, presence is at once promised and refused (. . .). We are dispossessed of the longed-for presence in the gesture of language by which we attempt to seize it."[30]

The desire or longing for presence is what motivates Verena to speak and her audience to listen. But the fact that Verena must stand in for the presence her words lack constitutes the strongest argument against taking them seriously. Her need to declaim her ideas suggests their insubstantiality. As living metaphor for these ideas, Verena herself seems to lose presence or reality as well. Ironically, she might be better known both to her audience and to herself if she were to disappear, to retreat into the labyrinth of writing, where, if her audience were to follow, they would be not mere spectators but active participants in the play or supplementarity of language. For Verena to be more than performer and her words more than spectacle, she would have to escape as James had done, armed with a writer's weapons: silence, exile, and cunning.

As James shapes it, the disappearing or fading narrative of Verena implicitly makes a persuasive argument for exile, but it makes a dull novel, one that is dry and overdetermined. James does not allow his characters the inner life that distinguishes the characters in most of his other works—Verena is too vacuous and unknown and Olive, until near the end, remains in the background, a distant if formidable foe to Ransom. In no other novel does James so consistently seek to control the reader's reactions with a heavy-handed, satiric authorial voice. In James' account of the Boston meeting of the Women's Movement, for example, the action of the novel stands still for six chapters which describe, "place", and satirically sum up each leader of the movement. Thus, the speaker Mrs Farrinder "at almost any time, had the air of being introduced by a few remarks".[31] Miss Birdseye "was heroic, she was sublime, the whole moral history of Boston was reflected in her displaced spectacles".[32] And Olive Chancellor "had long been preoccupied with the romance of the people. She had an immense desire to know intimately some *very* poor girl".[33] Thus, in describing a society in which all are on view and continually judged, James' method is panoptic as well. James partakes of and is complicit with the carceral technology of the society *The Bostonians* describes.

In *Under Western Eyes,* Conrad reworks the facts of his childhood—his birth into a poor but noble Polish family in Russian-occupied Poland; the visionary patriotism and doomed revolutionary activity of his parents, Apollo and Ewa, which brought them imprisonment and early death; the isolation of his orphaned upbringing; his adolescent distrust of politics, fostered by his adoptive uncle, which engendered in him a conservatism his parents would have deplored, one which would lead him to abandon as a lost cause the fight for Polish nationhood and to emigrate to the west. In *Under Western Eyes,* Conrad recasts his conservative self into the young Russian student, Razumov, and brings him into confrontation with a fictional version of his father, Apollo, in the revolutionary student, Haldin, who bursts into his room and asks his help in escaping after he has assassinated a cruel government official. Razumov betrays Haldin to the police in order to save himself. But he cannot erase their suspicion or free himself from the guilt of his betrayal. Clearly, in this emotionally charged scenario, Conrad deals with his own feelings of having abandoned his homeland and betrayed the revolutionary convictions and activities of his parents, Ewa and Apollo Korzeniowski. Through the figure of Razumov, who no more chooses to be plunged into revolutionary involvement when Haldin invades his room than Conrad himself chose to have revolutionary parents, Conrad explores the implications of the fact that the course of one's life is largely determined from without, although the individual is held accountable for his actions or, more precisely, reactions.

Yet this is not the entirety of the dilemma which the text explores. In centring his narrative on Russian rather than Polish subjects, Conrad is entering not merely alien but enemy territory. Although Haldin's revolutionary activities, like Apollo Korzeniowski's, are in opposition to Russian autocracy, Haldin is the subject of a state which Conrad's father—and Conrad himself—never ceased to regard as the invader.[34] Thus, Haldin's violent fanaticism is more extreme and more unreasonable than Apollo Korzeniowski's participation in a nationalist movement aimed at driving the usurper from native soil. As portrayed by Conrad, Haldin's rebellion is of a fanatical pitch which is uniquely Russian or Dostoevskian. Through Haldin, Conrad is able to portray sympathetically the impulse to rebel against Russian autocracy, yet demonstrate the folly and destructiveness of the anarchistic extremism this despotic government provokes in many of its opponents. In characterising his revolutionaries as Russian, Conrad has displaced his ambivalence about his own revolutionary inheritance onto the territory governed by the enemy who had killed his father.[35]

In fact, Conrad's sympathetic presentation of both Haldin and Razumov is an attempt to occupy in fiction an enemy territory, that of the late nineteenth-century Russian novel. That is, just as Russia had occupied his homeland of Poland, Conrad counter-attacks by invading the fictional territory of Tolstoy and Dostoevsky and by attempting to displace them. Thus, in the figure of Peter Ivanovich, a satiric portrait of Tolstoy,[36] Conrad dismisses Tolstoian idealism as pretentious sham; and, through the appropriation of Dostoevskian techniques for exploring extreme psychic states, he attempts the contradictory task of besting Dostoevsky at his own game, while at the same time demonstrating the madness and impenetrability of these peculiarly Russian characters. That Conrad knew that he was not entirely successful in his attempt at fictional occupation is suggested by the fact that, one third of the way through the novel, he retreated from the enemy territory of Russia to the neutral ground of Geneva.

In actuality, Conrad's text gains power through literary borrowings from more remote fictional sources, ones which provoked less ambivalence in Conrad. The presentation of Razumov's dilemma reverberates with echoes of two other narratives, those of Oedipus and Hamlet. On a psychological level, the text re-enacts Conrad's personal version of the Oedipal drama.[37] Through Razumov's betrayal of Haldin, a character modelled on Conrad's revolutionary father Apollo, and in his falling in love with Haldin's sister, Natalia, based on his mother Ewa, Conrad re-creates his own family romance. In fact, the text, which is filled with imagery of spectres and ghostly visitations is haunted by the much more overtly Oedipal tale that Conrad originally planned to write. After finishing the first part of the novel, in which Razumov betrays Haldin and leaves Russia, Conrad confided his plans for the remaining sections of the novel to his friend Galsworthy:

> The student Razumov meeting abroad the mother and sister of Haldin falls in love with that last, marries her and after a time confesses to her the part he played in the arrest of Haldin and death of her brother.
>
> The psychological developments leading to Razumov's betrayal of Haldin, to his confession of the fact to his wife and to the death of these people (brought about mainly by the resemblance of their child to the late Haldin) form the real subject of the story.[38]

The fact that Conrad never wrote the last part of the novel in this way, although he considers it "the real subject of the story", indicates that he found himself unable to deal so overtly with this material and accounts in part for the loss of interest and power in the watered-down version that Conrad actually wrote. Even in this more oblique version, Razumov's guilt is so great that, like Oedipus, he brings about his own maiming. Only after that is he able to re-enter the human community. In the last part of the novel, which strikingly recalls *Oedipus at Colonus*, Razumov, attended by a devoted woman, Tekla (like Oedipus attended by

Antigone), makes peace with his former enemies, the revolutionaries, who have come to regard him as a sage. Like Oedipus, he has achieved wisdom through suffering, and the narrative promises him a peaceful death off-stage.

On a political level, Razumov's dilemma resembles Hamlet's. Politically, Hamlet's dilemma is that the loyalty his father asks of him requires him to commit the heinous crime of regicide and thus undermine the very hierarchy of power and authority which exacts filial obedience. In the same way, Conrad was torn between loyalty to his memories of a virtuous but revolutionary father and his obligation to the conservative uncle who raised him. So too is Razumov torn between Haldin's claims of virtue and friendship and his own duty to preserve the order of the state, however despotic and unjust.

Clearly, both psychological and political guilt contribute to the overwrought Dostoevskian atmosphere of Conrad's narrative. In turn, the narrative projects this guilt, in the form of constant surveillance, onto the society it depicts. If James' novel is about the panopticism of modern society, and even to some extent makes narrative use of its tactics, Conrad's *Under Western Eyes* is relentlessly panoptic in its method as well as in its subject matter. In this novel, surveillance is the essential condition of human life: life in society is that which is interpreted, categorised, judged, and manipulated through observation. The ambiguity of the title is fitting: the reader never learns under whose Western eyes the tale unfolds—those of the *émigré* Conrad, those of the reader, or those of the dull language teacher, the first-person narrator of Razumov's story. In keeping with the panoptic scene of writing of the text, this first-person narrator is the unauthorised reader and reporter of Razumov's diary, a frequent eavesdropper, and the constant observer of lives in which he does not participate, those of the community of Russian *émigrés* in Geneva.

The world Conrad depicts is claustrophobic. In the Russia presented in the beginning of the novel, one is necessarily a victim of autocratic tyranny or revolutionary tyranny. In the West, one is necessarily a victim of democratic tyranny. If anything, the Western version of panopticism represented by the seemingly neutral language professor who assembles and presents Razumov's interesting "case study", is more insidious and therefore more threatening than the more straightforward and clearly hostile interest of the Russian state. Throughout the narrative, Razumov is under a double surveillance, that of Russia—the combined eyes of the autocratic regime and of the fanatical revolutionaries—and that of the West, as represented by the solicitous, apparently benevolent professor who, in observing, commenting on, and classifying Razumov's actions, acts as one of the agents of normalisation of the Western carceral system.

Clearly, there is no escape from surveillance. Because anonymity is impossible, one cannot be neutral. At first Razumov believes he can hold himself aloof—that he can go about his own quiet, rational existence, whatever evils exist in his society. The narrative demonstrates that he cannot—that he shares the fate of all Russian subjects, of all society, of all humankind.

The reader first comes upon Razumov in the confines of his room. Although that very morning, the minister Mr de P——— had been assassinated, Razumov is not perturbed: "Razumov was one of those men who, living in a period of mental and political unrest, keep an instinctive hold on normal, practical, everyday life. (. . .) his main concern was his work, his studies, and with his own future".[39] What we soon discover is that his room is really a womb: Razumov is not merely uninvolved—he is unformed. The illegitimate son of a priest's daughter and a nobleman, neither of whom has he ever known, Razumov feels utterly alone in the world. He longs for the parents he has never had and substitutes for them a vision of Russia as his mother and of a strong leader as his father, who will run the country and direct his life.[40] Ironically, Haldin's entry gives him the opportunity to be born into society and into selfhood.

In the terms of the neo-Freudian psychoanalyst and philosopher Jacques Lacan, at the beginning of the novel Razumov is still living in the imaginary state of early childhood,[41] diffuse and undifferentiated, fused with his vast and featureless mother, Russia. Although he perceives that "the hard ground of Russia" is "inanimate, cold, inert, like a sullen and tragic mother hiding her face under a winding-sheet—his native soil! his very own—without a fireside, without a heart!" he responds with "readiness" to this land whose snow levels "everything under its uniform whiteness, like a monstrous blank page awaiting the record of an inconceivable history".[42] This imagery suggests that to cling to a cold mother Russia who has never nurtured him is to enfold himself in her winding-sheet, to succumb to death. Rather, he must extricate himself from her oceanic vastness to write on the blank page of his own history.

Razumov has been immobilised as well by the abandonment of his aristocratic father, Prince K., who has given him an allowance without contact or encouragement. In consequence, he idealises this father whom he does not know and who refuses to know him, referring to him in his mind as "He!".[43] Hoping to attain some distinction with which to gain acknowledgment from his father, he sits in his room, in what he will later

come to describe as a state of "suspended animation",[44] fantasising that he will first gain his father's recognition by winning the silver medal at the university for writing the best essay, then go on to a distinguished academic career. In this fantasy, he sees himself as an elderly and celebrated professor.[45] What is missing is any conception of what his adulthood will be like—the years between school prizes and retirement, in which he must make his own way in life. What this fantasy indicates is that he has as yet taken no steps to enter into what Lacan refers to as the symbolic order.[46] In order to do so, he must confront the father, establish his relation to and distinction from him, and take his own place in the world.[47] His opportunity to do so comes with the entrance of Haldin (a father-substitute making claims upon him) into his enclosed existence. Perplexed by what to do, Razumov for the only time in his life calls upon Prince K., receives his limited help and approval, and makes his own assessment of his progenitor as a weak and timid man. When Razumov assures the Prince that he will not embarrass him by calling upon him again, and parts from him with "indulgent contempt",[48] he has come a long way towards establishing his own separate identity.

As he is described at the beginning of the novel, formlessness is Razumov's most distinguishing feature:

> His good looks would have been unquestionable if it had not been for a peculiar lack of fineness in the features. It was as if a face modelled vigorously in wax (. . .) had been held close to a fire till all sharpness of line had been lost in the softening of the material.

He speaks very little and in discussion he is "easily swayed by argument and authority".[49] Because he is "an inscrutable listener",[50] the revolutionist Haldin mistakes him for a sympathiser. Ironically, Razumov, as much as Verena, is the victim of phonocentrism. By having listened quietly to Haldin's ideas, he appears to have lent his presence and therefore his approval to political doctrines he abhors. Razumov finds to his dismay that others have imposed a text upon his silence. In time, Razumov learns to write his own text.

Since, as Lacan notes, language or discourse proceeds from the father,[51] it is questionable, at the beginning of the novel, whether this "young man of no parentage"[52] has anything to express in his talk or in his essay. The first example of Razumov's own authentic discourse is the diary or journal that he keeps, in which, over the course of a year, he comes to define and to claim his own identity. At the end of this extensive piece of writing, he seeks out the revolutionaries for the first time, not to listen to or overhear them, but to speak himself. His discourse is his confession, a narrative of his unique journey. This diary is Razumov's greatest achievement for in it he does succeed in writing his own "inconceiv-

able history". Curiously, this apparently sollipsistic narrative is one through which Razumov, originally known to no-one including himself, becomes knowable to a potentially limitless audience through a process of infinite dissemination—first to Natalia, then to the language professor, and then to countless readers. In written form, Razumov's inscrutability reflects not mere personal eccentricity and alienation but the indeterminacy of language itself.

When, at the beginning of his journey, Razumov leaves the safety of his room—his womb with no views—ostensibly to aid Haldin but actually to turn him in and so clear himself, he first becomes aware of the panoptic nature of his society. For, no matter what he says or does, he finds that there is no way that he can clear himself: he remains "a suspect", "under the merciless suspicion of despotism".[53] Indeed, the text demonstrates that the curiosity of the carceral system and its agents, both East and West, is both infinite and unappeasable. Finally, Razumov learns that in the eyes of society, there are no innocent men, only suspects and criminals. He—like everyone else—is utterly vulnerable. Thus, the narrative points out that Mikulin, Razumov's inquisitor, will soon fall from power into disgrace.

Once aware of his vulnerability, Razumov comes to be haunted by the threat of imprisonment, by the thought that "General T. was perfectly capable of shutting him up in the fortress for an indefinite time".[54] He has a "daymare" in which "he beheld his own brain suffering on the rack—a long, pale figure drawn asunder horizontally with terrific force in the darkness of a vault, whose face he failed to see".[55] Indeed, his fears are confirmed by the many stories of torture and imprisonment that abound in the narrative.

To decrease his own vulnerability, Razumov turns spy himself. Yet as the watched becomes watcher of others, he comes under the further surveillance of his own visual hallucinations, projections of his fear and guilt: repeatedly, he sees Victor Haldin looking at him, and he sees the eyes of General T. and Mikulin simultaneously fixed on him.

Thus, the most terrible realisation the text presents is that Razumov, as well as the Russian revolutionaries, brings his prison with him. There are no borders to the panoptic world, neither without nor within. There is no escape even in the apparent safety of Western society, not even in placid and dull Geneva. In Geneva, Razumov, the "puppet of his past", thinks of himself as a prisoner.[56] And the teacher of languages observes that when Russians go abroad "the shadow of autocracy is with them".[57] That there is really no escape is the point of the last three quarters of the book, which are all set in Switzerland. When at the end of Book I, Razumov tells Mikulin that he plans to retire, Mikulin asks,

"Where to?" Parts two, three, and four demonstrate that this is a rhetorical question. Not surprisingly, by the end of the book, all the Russians have returned to Russia. In a sense, this narrative turn constitutes Conrad's final tactic in his strategy of containment: his rout of the Russian invaders of the West, the fictional equivalent of the Russian invaders of his native Poland, back into the vast confines of Russia.

On the whole, *Under Western Eyes* holds out little hope for the future, for it reveals the lack of freedom in all societies, East and West. Conrad finds in all human structures the claustrophobia that James sees as the peculiar condition of New England. This relentless view makes *Under Western Eyes* a more powerful, if much more terrible, book than *The Bostonians*. The text suggests that the condition of exile gives to people, especially writers, merely a heightened awareness of the fact that there is no refuge.

In sum, both novels depict cultures which are stifling, imprisoning, and impervious to change. Yet if they present a grim picture, they also serve an important purpose. In fact, according to Joseph Brodsky, they fulfill the most important function of the exiled writer in the modern world: they "serve as a warning to any thinking man toying with the idea of an ideal society."[58]

Notes

1. Joseph Brodsky, "The Condition We Call Exile", *The New York Review of Books*, XXXIV, 21 and 22 (January 21, 1988), pp. 16, 18.

2. Henry James, *The Bostonians*, ed. Alfred Habegger, Indianapolis: Bobbs-Merrill, 1976. Subsequent references will be to this edition.

3. Joseph Conrad, *Under Western Eyes*, Harmondsworth: Penguin, 1985. Subsequent references will be to this edition.

4. *Vide* Michel Foucault, *Discipline and Punish*, New York: Vintage Books, 1979, pp. 195-228.

5. Foucault, p. 184.

6. Michel Foucault, *The Archaeology of Knowledge*, trans. A. M. Sheridan Smith, New York: Pantheon, 1982, p. 17.

7. *The Foucault Reader*, ed. Paul Rabinow, New York: Pantheon, 1984, p. 107.

8. *Ibid.*, p. 108.

9. *Ibid.*, p. 113.

10. *Ibid.*, p. 119.

11. *The Complete Notebooks of Henry James*, ed. Leon Edel and Lyall H. Powers, New York: Oxford U. P., 1987, pp. 46-47.

12. *Vide* David Leon Higdon and Robert F. Sheard, "Conrad's 'Unkindest Cut': The Canceled Scenes in *Under Western Eyes*," *Conradiana*, Vol. 19, No. 3, pp. 177-8.

13. James' ambivalence over his abandonment of America emerges repeatedly as a theme in both his fiction and non-fiction; most notably, in his pervasively critical *The American Scene*. See also his short stories "The Point of View", "Pandora", and "Julia Bride".

14. James, *The Complete Notebooks of Henry James*, pp. 19-20.

15. *Ibid.*, p. 30.

16. *Vide* Alfred Habegger, "Introduction", *The Bostonians*, p. xviii.

17. *Vide* Leon Edel, *Henry James: A Life*, New York: Harper & Row, 1985, p. 313.

18. *The Bostonians*, p. 26.

19. Although James cited an "obscure hurt", which has since generated much controversy and speculation, as the reason for his abstention, it was more probably James' distaste for violence and temperamental unsuitability for soldiering that were the primary reasons for his staying out of the war. *Vide* Edel, pp. 57-59.

20. *The Bostonians*, p. 27.

21. *Ibid.*, p. 25.

22. Quoted by Habegger, p. xvi.

23. James' recurrent "vampire fantasy", which surfaces in a number of his works, is noted by Edel, who connects it with James' fear "that self-assertion can bring a loss of love" (p. 82). Indeed, Verena's extreme pliability and desire to please may in fact result from her own fear of losing the love of others, a fear that may predispose her to victimisation.

24. *The Bostonians*, p. 51.

25. *Ibid.*, p. 53.

26. *Ibid.*, p. 57.

27. *Ibid.*, p. 140.

28. *Ibid.*, p. 135.

29. *Ibid.*, p. 382.

30. Jacques Derrida, *Of Grammatology*, trans. Gayatri Spivak, Baltimore: Johns Hopkins U. P., 1974, p. 141.

31. *The Bostonians*, p. 29.

32. *Ibid.*, p. 33.

33. *Ibid.*

34. Conrad's consistency on this point is documented by Jean Aubry, Gustav Morf, Frederick Karl, and Czeslaw Milosz. As late as 1920, Conrad expressed satisfaction at united Polish resistance to the Russian state: "I confess to some little gratification at the thought that the unbroken Polish front keeps Bolshevism off and that apparently the reborn state has one heart and one soul, one indomitable will, from the poorest peasant to the highest magnate." Quoted by Gustav Morf, *The Polish Heritage of Joseph Conrad,* London: Sampson Low, Marston & Co., 1930, pp. 180-1.

35. For many of these ideas on Conrad's revolutionary inheritance, I am indebted to the suggestions of my former graduate student, Michael Mageean, now a doctoral candidate at the University of California at Irvine.

36. Eloise Knapp Hay, *The Political Novels of Joseph Conrad,* Chicago: Chicago U. P., 1961, pp. 283-4.

37. In this story, Frederick Karl observes, Conrad came "very close to deep divisions within him, even to an imaginative re-creation of parricide." *Vide Joseph Conrad: The Three Lives,* New York: Farrar, Strauss, & Giroux, 1979, p. 34.

38. *Ibid.,* p. 636.

39. *Under Western Eyes,* pp. 60-61.

40. *Ibid.,* pp. 78-80.

41. Jacques Lacan, *Ecrits: A Selection,* trans. Alan Sheridan, New York: W. W. Norton & Co., 1977, p. 35.

42. *Under Western Eyes,* p. 78.

43. *Ibid.,* p. 62.

44. *Ibid.,* p. 107.

45. *Ibid.,* p. 63.

46. Lacan, *Ecrits,* p. 37.

47. For an article which makes a similar but more extended case for the necessary confrontation of the protagonist with his father, in order to establish his own identity, see Carola Kaplan, "Absent Father, Passive Son: The Dilemma of Rickie Elliott in Forster's *The Longest Journey*", *Twentieth Century Literature,* Vol. 33, No. 2, pp. 196-210.

48. *Under Western Eyes,* p. 93.

49. *Ibid.,* p. 57.

50. *Ibid.*

51. Lacan's ideas on this subject are neatly summarised by Robert Con Davis, "Critical Introduction: The Discourse of the Father", *The Fictional Father,* ed. Robert Con Davis, Amherst: University of Massachusetts Press, 1981, pp. 21-23.

52. *Under Western Eyes,* p. 61.

53. *Ibid.,* p. 90.

54. *Ibid.,* p. 119.

55. *Ibid.,* p. 121.

56. *Ibid.,* p. 247.

57. *Ibid.,* p. 137.

58. Brodsky, p. 20.

EXILE IN FRENCH LITERATURE

James L. Shepherd, III (essay date January 1958)

SOURCE: Shepherd, James L., III. "The Contribution of a Directoire Exile to a Poem of Alfred de Musset." *Modern Language Notes* 73, no. 1 (January 1958): 39-45.

[*In the following essay, Shepherd relates how Alfred de Musset's commentary on exile in his* La Loi sur la presse *is informed by the details and opinions offered by François de Barbé-Marbois in his* Journal d'un déporté no-jugé.]

In the summer of 1835, Alfred de Musset interrupted for a few days his work on the *Confession d'un enfant du siècle* in order to compose hastily a long poem, the literary merit of which is questionable. Musset was usually loath to treat issues of current politics in his poetical works, but for once he decided to versify his stand on a hotly debated question of national policy. *La Loi sur la presse* appeared in the *Revue des Deux Mondes* in the issue of September 1, 1835. Thereafter, this *pièce de circonstance* was systematically excluded by Musset from all collections of his works that were published during his lifetime. Obviously the poet himself attached little value to it. Surely, if it had been signed by a lesser name than his, it would long since have passed into oblivion.

Since it is by Musset, however, it is included in all recent editions of his complete works, and these editions usually contain notes to explain the references to the contemporary events which occasioned the poem.[1] The most detailed comments are to be found in an article by Jean Giraud, which thoroughly explores the political scene of the day—Fieschi's attempted murder of the

king during a parade to celebrate the fifth anniversary of the July Revolution; the miraculous escape from death of all members of the royal family who were taking part in this ceremony and who were under the regicide's fire; the special mass of thanksgiving held in Notre-Dame Cathedral to celebrate the sparing of their lives; the seizure by the government of this moment as the opportune time to present before the Assembly a censorship bill designed to quench all republican, Bonapartist, legitimist, or other opposition to Louis-Philippe, either in the press or in the theater.[2] All these matters, together with Musset's opposition to the censorship bill, form the subject of the first twenty-seven stanzas of the poem *La Loi sur la presse.* We are not concerned with them here.

At the end of the twenty-seventh stanza, however, Musset states that one of the most serious consequences of the proposed bill is the deportation of all offenders. Aristophanes is represented as addressing the people of France as he says: "Pendant que vous dormez, on bâillonne la presse / Et la chambre en travail enfante une prison." This *prison* is the penal colony which Musset imagines being devised to receive the poor dreamers who dare voice their grievances against the citizen-king's regime. The specter of this new type of imprisonment continues to haunt the poet throughout the remaining seven stanzas. We shall attempt here to trace the source of his ideas on deportation.

Such a punishment was never applied during the Napoleonic and Restoration periods. Mont-Saint-Michel was used as a prison in those days, and French prisoners were never sent farther from their homeland than that island fortress so close to the shores of Normandy and Brittany. At the end of January, 1835, a royal decree stipulated that persons sentenced to deportation and confinement were to be imprisoned in the fort of Doullens, in the *département* of the Somme.[3]

We must go back to the days of the Directoire to find a precedent for the establishment of such a prison colony as Musset visualizes. In the *coup d'état* of 18 Fructidor, Year V of the revolutionary calendar, various duly elected members of the government were arrested on the vague and generally unfounded charge of fomenting revolution. These politicians were sentenced to be deported to Guiana. Many were able to escape, but sixteen underwent deportation. Quickly following the first wave of sentences, various newspapermen, the *chansonnier* Louis-Ange Pitou, and a large number of Catholic priests were similarly arrested and sentenced without trial. Liberty of the press was effectively suppressed.

Any attentive student of French politics in 1835 might have been struck by the similarity between the impending censorship laws, accompanied by the threat of deportation, and the events of Fructidor. Indeed, in reading the debates on the issue, we are not surprised to find Fructidor evoked by the deputy Salverte in a speech, the text of which was printed on August 15, 1835, in the *Journal des Débats.* It is likely that Musset read this speech; his published correspondence reveals that he was a reader of the *Débats* at this time.[4]

There had been published ever since 1799 a series of accounts of the Fructidor deportation by various participants and victims. Musset might have known any of those works, those of Jeannet, Ramel, Pitou, Aymé, La Rue, or Dutertre.[5] After an examination of these we have become convinced that instead Musset was indebted to a much more recently published one: the *Journal d'un déporté non-jugé,* by François de Barbé-Marbois.[6]

In the form of a diary written at the time of the events described, Barbé-Marbois's work was not published until many years later, in fact until a few months previous to the appearance of Musset's poem. After a limited first edition, the *Journal* appeared on the commercial market early in 1835.[7] A publisher's announcement of it was published in the *Journal des Débats* on January 16 of that year. The similarity between certain details treated in this work and those of Musset's poem gives us evidence to believe that the latter's diatribe against deportation was derived from the former. Let us examine the points in common.

Only Barbé-Marbois, among those who wrote down their experiences during the Fructidor episode, dwells on the fact that this particular form of exile was brand-new in the history of the world. Throughout his concluding stanzas Musset too stresses this aspect of the question. He echoes poetically the prose of chapter IV, Volume II of Barbé-Marbois's work. A few quotations here from that chapter will show how close in thought the two writers are on this point. Incidentally, the fact that Barbé-Marbois quotes from Plutarch and compares his deportation to the forms of exile inflicted in Greece and Rome makes an interesting parallel, because all the stanzas we are here concerned with in Musset, that is, XXVII through XXXIV, are also quotations from an observer from antiquity, Aristophanes, whom Musset imagines as coming back to life in order to declare his horror at this new mode of punishment.[8] "Les rigueurs du banissement, de l'exil, de l'ostracisme n'ont rien qui égale celles qu'on nous fait éprouver. . . . Plutarque, adressant des consolations à un banni, lui dit: On n'a pas limité les lieux destinés à ton séjour. On ne t'en interdit qu'un seul. En t'excluant d'une ville, on t'a ouvert toutes les autres. . . . Chez les Grecs . . . on ne savait ce que c'était d'emprisonner et de tourmenter l'exilé jusque dans son banissement. Il avait le choix du lieu de son séjour" (II, 72-74). Compare this with Aristophanes' statement in stanza XXVIII:

On banissait jadis, au temps de barbarie;
Si l'exil était pire ou mieux que l'échafaud,
Je ne sais; mais, du moins, sur les mere de la vie
On laissait l'exilé devenir matelot.
Cela semblait assez de perdre sa patrie.
Maintenant avec l'homme on bannit le cachot.

In each stanza following the one just quoted, the unprecedented nature of this punishment—exile combined with imprisonment—continues to receive emphasis. In stanza XXIX, it is the metaphor of the *plante inouïe;* in stanza XXX, "c'est la première fois qu'on lance une prison"; in stanza XXXI, the phrase *un supplice nouveau.* The last line of stanza XXXII implies the same notion of novelty in punishment: "car le génie humain a fait pis que la mort."

After Barbé-Marbois makes the point that his deportation is a more severe punishment than other forms of exile inflicted formerly, he mentions another novelty connected with his punishment: the fact that it was imposed upon such a large number of men of several walks of life, whereas in antiquity exile was very rare, being inflicted upon only the most outstanding members of the opposition to a regime. "Jusqu'au temps d'Alcibiade l'ostracisme n'avait frappé que des citoyens considérables" (II, 76). After the case of Alcibiades, he continues, ostracism was abolished entirely. Under the Directoire, on the other hand, such punishment is applied much more indiscriminately: "Aujourd'hui . . . on déportera l'écrivain dont la plume, l'orateur dont l'éloquence alarmeront des ministres corrompus" (II, 79).

The same point is made in Musset's poem. The following lines in particular suggest that the punishment is too severe for the crime, since those punished are not the leaders of a revolution or heresy, but mere writers stating their minds:

Qu'ont-ils fait, direz-vous, pour un pareil supplice?
Ont-ils tué leurs rois, ou renversé leurs dieux?
Non; ils ont comparé deux esclaves entr'eux;
Ils ont dit que Solon comprenait la justice
Autrement qu'à Paris les préfets de police,
Et qu'autrefois en Grèce il fut un peuple heureux.

Pauvres gens! c'est leur crime; ils aiment leur pensée,
Tous ces pâles rêveurs au langage inconstant.

Another detail common to both works is the theme of leave-taking. Barbé-Marbois had married a Philadelphia woman, whom he had met during his period of assignment in the United States. In his book he describes the farewell visit that his wife paid him, and her visit with the other prisoners, shortly before they were put aboard the vessel that was to take them from Paris to South America. She had been in Metz at the time of the arrest and had not been able to join her husband until he was already en route to his port of embarkation, Rochefort.

The prisoners' guards allowed Madame de Barbé-Marbois a scant half-hour or less to visit and comfort her husband, a meager reward indeed for the long and tedious journey she had made under such heartbreaking circumstances (I, 123-127).

The concluding stanzas of *La Loi sur la presse* also picture a scene of leave-taking. Those being deported are about to be put aboard the ship which is to transport them to their prison colony, as we learn from the verses: "Voyez-vous ces forçats que de cette machine / On tire deux à deux pour les descendre à bord?" This scene is being witnessed by the citizens of America who have come to the port in order to say farewell to their liberty-loving French friends who are now paying the price for having dared to speak their minds: "Regardez, peuples du nouveau monde! . . . Enfants de l'Amérique, accourez au rivage!" These *enfants de l'Amérique* are most probably Philadelphians who have come down to their port where the French ship has put in to call before its final voyage southwards to Guiana. Philadelphia is mentioned by name in stanza XXIX:

Mais nous, notre océan porte à Philadelphie
Une rare merveille, une plante inouïe,
Que nous ferons germer sur le sol étranger.

The etymology of the name was doubtless significant for Musset. The liberty and brotherly love of the Americans is thus contrasted with the censorship and harsh restrictions of France. Barbé-Marbois too points out the contrast between the freedom of the press in Philadelphia, which he mentions specifically, and the censorship of the Directoire regime.[9]

So, when Musset calls on the Americans, as the symbol of freedom, to come down to the prison ship to commune with the departing Frenchmen:

Passez, Américains, passez tête baissée;
Et que la liberté, leur triste fiancée,
Chez vous du moins au front les baise en arrivant!

it seems that the poet was musing upon several passages from Barbé-Marbois's work, especially the scene of separation from his Philadelphia wife.

The last piece of evidence that we find for our contention that the *Journal d'un déporté non-jugé* played a part in the composition of *La Loi sur la presse* is the use in stanza XXXII of the vague word *machine*: "Voyez-vous ces forçats que de cette machine / On tire deux à deux pour les descendre à bord?" What sort of a machine is it? Musset does not tell us, but since the ship is standing in the waters of a port of call and is soon to depart for the prison colony, we must assume that, during the period of time that it was docked there, the prisoners had been put ashore and had been held in some sort of machine in lieu of a jail, up to the time of departure.

If we consult Barbé-Marbois's work once more, we find that he used the word *machine* in a very similar connection. He was describing the vehicles in which he and fifteen others condemned to deportation were being transported from Paris to Rochefort at the time that his wife was finally able to join them. These were, said the prisoner, large uncomfortable iron cages on wheels: "de grandes cages de fer lourdes et non-suspendues, ayant une seule porte verrouillée et cadenassée" (I, 111). As many as six prisoners were crowded into one of the three horse-drawn cages, during the entire ten days which the trip lasted. Upon their arrival at Rochefort they were transported directly from the cages into the ship's boat. It is probable that Musset's stanza XXXII is a reminiscence of Barbé-Marbois's description of leaving the cages at the time of embarkation: "Une multitude d'habitants de Rochefort et des environs couvrait les remparts et les glacis. Nous descendîmes de nos cages, et, après avoir été comptés et signalés à terre pour la dernière fois, nous fûmes enlevés de cette France où réside tout ce qui m'est cher" (I, 136). Among the various descriptions of the cages Musset might have read, that by Barbé-Marbois is the only one to use the word *machine*.[10]

That Musset is thinking of such a cage when he says *machine* becomes completely clear if we consider that in the stanza immediately preceding this one he says to the Americans:

> Vos monstres quelquefois nous arrivent en cages;
> Venez, c'est votre tour, et que l'homme sauvage
> Fixe ses yeux ardents sur l'homme apprivoisé.

Barbé-Marbois's *Journal* shares with Musset's poem several significant features: insistence upon the novelty of the punishment of deportation, together with allusions to the relative humanity of exile in antiquity; the argument that exile should be confined to a very few important people; sharp contrast between Philadelphia and France, between free Americans and enslaved Frenchmen; and the description of convicts being brought forth from a machine in order to be put aboard a prison ship. Therefore we venture to say that the Directoire exile's book was in part responsible for Musset's angry protest against the impending laws. The forceful way in which Barbé-Marbois represented the horrors of deportation made such an impression on the poet that he was determined to fight against a possible repetition of them in his own day. He wrote *La Loi sur la presse*; he wrote it in such haste that it contains a number of imperfections. In particular, the uninitiated reader cannot be sure where the scene of leave-taking at the end of the poem takes place, nor from what machine the prisoners are being drawn during this scene. The source which we advance furnishes the answers to these questions and thus brings the poem into sharper focus.

Notes

1. *Poésies,* ed. Jean Le Maire (Paris, 1949), pp. 376-77; *Poésies complètes,* ed. Maurice Allem (Paris, 1951), pp. 680-82.

2. *Revue Bleue,* 14 septembre 1912, pp. 327-30.

3. Louis André in *La Grande Encyclopédie,* s. v. "Déportation."

4. *Correspondance (1827-1857),* (Paris, 1907), p. 12.

5. J.-J. Aymé, *Déportation et Naufrage* (Paris, 1800); Georges-Nicolas Jean-net-Oudin, *Notes sur quelques passages du "Mémoire" de Ramel* (Paris, 1799); Jean-Pierre Ramel, *Journal* (Londres, 1799); Dutertre, *Départ du Temple pour Cayenne, des déportés des 17 et 18 fructidor, an V* (Paris, 1800); La Rue, *Histoire du 18 fructidor* (Paris, 1821); Louis-Ange Pitou, *Voyage à Cayenne* (Paris, 1805); L.-A. Pitou, *Analyse de mes malheurs* (Paris, 1816). For a discussion of the contents and relative merits of the first-hand accounts of the episode, see Victor Pierre, "La Déportation à la Guyane après fructidor," *Revue des Questions Historiques,* avril 1882, pp. 441-442.

6. References to Barbé-Marbois's *Journal* in this paper use the pagination of the first edition.

7. On Barbé-Marbois, see E. Wilson Lyon, *The Man Who Sold Louisiana* (University of Oklahoma Press, 1942).

8. This is true of the original printing in the *Revue des Deux Mondes.* Editions published since Musset's death have needlessly changed the poet's punctuation to make Aristophanes' speech consist of stanza XXVII alone, instead of allowing it to continue to the end of the poem.

9. "C'est par l'*Advertiser,* qui m'est adressé de Philadelphie, que j'apprends. . . . C'est en imprimer à Philadelphie plus qu'on n'oserait à Paris. Interdire à un opprimé de recourir aux presses et aux journaux pour repousser une injustice est un acte de tyrannie. . . . C'est à Philadelphie que l'anecdote m'a été racontée," etc. (II, 185).

10. "Les cages de fer ont une origine fort ancienne. On trouve, à l'occasion de ces machines, le passage suivant . . ." (I, 112).

Edward J. Ahearn (essay date December 1977)

SOURCE: Ahearn, Edward J. "Black Woman, White Poet: Exile and Exploitation in Baudelaire's Jeanne Duval Poems." *The French Review* 51, no. 2 (December 1977): 212-20.

[*In the following essay, Ahearn traces Charles Baudelaire's treatment of exile in his poetry, particularly in works inspired by his lover, Jeanne Duval.*]

The satisfactions afforded by poetry are at times rooted in cultural and psychological realities which we may be reluctant to confront. Such is the poetry of Baudelaire associated with his mulatto mistress, Jeanne Duval. This is not to ignore the element of literary convention (the exiled poet, the exotic voyage, the *mulâtresse*) in these texts. Rather it is to suggest that Baudelaire's artistry in part consists of expressing powerfully the human drama which such motifs contain. For the impact of the Jeanne Duval poems is inescapably related to interactions involving self and other, male and female, black[1] and white. In this case at least, the esthetic fulfillment of poetry is revelatory of interpersonal and racial themes which remain at issue in our culture.

To understand this fully we need to review rapidly the role of solitude, love, and exploitation in Baudelaire's esthetic. In his private journal he wrote: "Sentiment de *solitude,* dès mon enfance."[2] Some of his most powerful *spleen* poems (e.g., "La Cloche fêlée" and "Quand le ciel bas et lourd") express an overwhelming personal solitude. Elsewhere too, he is attracted to figures of terrible loneliness—the "homme énigmatique," lacking family, friends and country, in "L'Étranger," the aged women in "Les Petites Vieilles" and "Les Veuves," the rejected artist figure in "Le Vieux Saltimbanque," the child in "Les Vocations" who from birth is "un *incompris.*" "Bénédiction" and "L'Albatros" stress the isolation of the artist, which in "Les Petites Vieilles" and "Le Cygne" deepens into a universal sense of human exile.

This painful isolation has a positive function for Baudelaire, in whom creativity is related to a dialectic of solitude and communion.[3] In the prose poems "A une heure du matin," "Le Crépuscule du soir," "La Solitude," and "Les Foules," isolation liberates the poet from relations with others and is the condition of creativity. In these texts Baudelaire makes solitude a positive value, criticizing normal human interactions and arguing that the artist has the gift of converting his loneliness into a multiplicity and richness of experience, which he derives from the life of others. He takes "un bain de multitude," drawing "une singulière ivresse" from the rest of humanity. Paradoxically this stance is not merely self-aggrandizing; from it there comes a moving poetry of comprehension and love. Thus the essay "Le Peintre de la vie moderne" emphasizes not only solitude but also curiosity, a childlike acuteness of perception, the artist's capacity for observation, the gift of being an "amateur de la vie" who creats a family for himself from the world of others (*Œuvres complètes,* p. 889). Similarly, in "Les Petites Vieilles," the speaker follows grotesquely aged women through the city, clandestinely enriching his own existence by imagining their past lives, only to finish by adopting toward them a loving and protective attitude ("moi qui de loin tendrement vous surveille"), and by expressing a moving sense of community in suffering ("Ruines! ma famille! ô cerveaux congénères!"). It is not far from this to the sympathetic comprehension and somber celebration of the courageous human collectivity in "Le Crépuscule du soir" and "Le Crépuscule du matin."

It is only fair to recognize these positive aspects of Baudelaire's esthetic of solitude.[4] But how can we not be troubled by its negative implications? In 1846 Baudelaire hoped for a literature capable of reaching the majority ("Aux Bourgeois," *Salon de 1846*). But by the late prose poem "Les Fenêtres" (in which he prefers to gaze at a *closed* window in order to enrich his own existence), he is led to ask the devastating question: "Qu'importe ce que peut être la réalité placée hors de moi, si elle m'a aidé à vivre, à sentir que je suis et cc que je suis?"

The ambivalent and negative features of Baudelairean solitude appear in heightened form in his love poetry, in which mingled disgust and idealization characterize the relationship between the poet and the objects of his desire. In *Les Fleurs du mal,* the cycles of poems associated with Jeanne Duval, Madame Sabatier, and Marie Daubrun contain praise and celebration, revelations of beauty, grandeur and even innocence. But these qualities are counterbalanced by the aggression and sadism of poems such as "À celle qui est trop gaie," "Le Flacon," and "À une Madonne," by the universal condemnation of relations between men and women in the concluding poem of the book, "Le Voyage," by the oppressive accumulation of poems in the *Fleurs du mal* section which insist on the destructiveness and degradation of love—especially "La Fontaine de sang," where the speaker's blood is drunk by cruel women, "La Béatrice," in which the muse mocks the poet and joins the devils in a "sale caresse," and "Un Voyage à Cythère," where Baudelaire's journey to the isle of Venus leads to the recognition of his own image as a "ridicule pendu," castrated and crucified to expiate the "infâmes cultes" of love.

Even more negative, and unrelieved by the beauty of some of the love poems, are some of the notes on women, sex, and love in *Mon Cœur mis à nu.* There Baudelaire asserts that "la femme est *naturelle,* c'est-à-dire abominable" (V); that women should not be allowed in church, inasmuch as Venus is "une des formes séduisantes du Diable" (XLIX); that the physical location of the genital organs is "un signe du péché originel. De fait, nous ne pouvons faire l'amour qu'avec des organes excrémentiels" (XXX). Expressing self-disgust as well as hatred of women, the products of a tortured psychology,[5] these notes need to be linked to the larger alienation of self and other which I first discussed. Another note from *Mon Cœur mis à nu* makes this link in characteristically brutal form: "Foutre, c'est aspirer à entrer dans un autre, et l'artiste ne sort jamais de lui-

même" (LXXI). Art and other-directed sexuality are firmly opposed, the goal of the artist being radically subjective and isolated, avoiding intimate contact with the other. This is an especially forceful version of a view of women in relation to art which Baudelaire expressed in more elegant, but still lucidly exploitative terms, in the chapters on women and make-up in "Le Peintre de la vie moderne." Woman is there presented as a *"bel animal,"* lacking intelligence, an idol, but a stupid one. Despite this attack, her beauty is recognized as not only animal but also as artistic. Her use of make-up and other embellishments constitutes her as a work of art, embodying a statue-like superiority to the imperfect world of nature. That is, she is valued in so far as she approximates art, or the artist himself. Indeed, she is the *instrument* of the artist's creation, "l'être . . . *par qui* les artistes et les poètes composent leurs plus délicats bijoux."[6] Behind these delicate poetic jewels, in Baudelaire's virulent version of a Western poetic commonplace, lie the disgust and aggression of the love poems and *Mon Cœur mis à nu.*

These negative features, coexisting with Baudelaire's capacity for ecstasy, are also present in the Jeanne Duval poems. If on the one hand the woman evoked in these texts is powerfully sensual, she is also cold, cruel, and hateful. Despite her "majesté native" and "noble corps," she is the "reine des cruelles," "femme stérile," "femme impure," "bête implacable et cruelle" whom he nonetheless adores, "infâme" vampire whom he curses. In "Remords posthume" he takes vengeance against her by imagining her death; in "Duellum" he pictures himself wrestling with this "amazone inhumaine" in order to "éterniser l'ardeur de notre haine!"; in "Le Possédé" he has come to adore her but views her as wholly destructive, even demonic: *"O mon cher Belzébuth, je t'adore!"*

The ambiguous dialectic between poet and woman-muse is also involved.[7] In "Tu mettrais l'univers entier dans ta ruelle" he views her as a "vil animal," unaware that she has been chosen by nature to form his genius,[8] and in "Une Charogne" he plays especially grotesque variations on the theme of her mortality as opposed to the superiority of his art. But in "Le Balcon," "Un Fantôme," and "Je te donne ces vers," he praises Jeanne movingly, recognizes that she saves him from his horrible solitude, identifies with her in a community of two against the rest of mankind, and celebrates her even in the midst of despair—"Statue aux yeux de jais, grand ange au front d'airain!"

The tensions in the relation of self-other, male-female and artist-muse are therefore evident in the Jeanne Duval poems. Another feature, the element of race, also plays a role. Jeanne is portrayed as a black woman, as one who embodies and who opens up to the poet another world—exotic, far removed from nineteenth-century urban civilization, a world glimpsed through the literary tradition and Baudelaire's own brief travels, a world of great value to the poet and perhaps to the reader—but one which raises disquieting questions as well.

The racial element is sometimes deft, sometimes heavily stereotyped. The woman's body in "Les Bijoux" and "Le Léthé" is "fauve et brun," "poli comme le cuivre." In both poems, she is called a tiger, and together with the imagery of snakes, cats, and other animals,[9] this motif evokes a strongly animal sensuality. There are suggestions of an eroticism mingling innocence, animality, and lubricity—a stereotype of black sexuality in the white mind that is by now well known. Thus in "Parfum exotique" the speaker imagines South Sea women "dont l'œil par sa franchise étonne," and the woman in "Les Bijoux" excites him by uniting "la candeur . . . à la lubricité." A troubling interaction of sexual submission-dominance in relation to race is also present, again in "Les Bijoux," in which the woman has "l'air vainqueur / Qu'ont dans leurs jours heureux les esclaves des Mores"—lines in which race, sex, and control over the other are inseparable. The reversibility of this erotic power is of course evident, in that here the slaves are the conquerors, and this element is apparent as well in "Sed non satiata," in which the black woman becomes a "démon sans pitié" whom the speaker cannot satisfy sexually.

The first stanza of this same text also contains an amazing accumulation of racial and exotic motifs that reveal a cultural stereotype of imposing proportions:

> Bizarre déité, brune comme les nuits,
> Au parfum mélangé de musc et de havane,
> Œuvre de quelque obi, le Faust de la savane,
> Sorcière au flanc d'ébène, enfant des noirs minuits.

The woman's color is evoked not once but three times in these lines ("brune," "ébène," "noirs") and is associated with mysterious and magical forces ("les nuits," "minuits," "obi," "sorcière"). Rare words ("bizarre," "déité" instead of the more usual "déesse," "obi"—an African priest) insist on her exotic, non-European quality. So do the references to tropical nature ("havane," "savane")[10] and to her perfume, through which she is present as an insistently sensual force.

And then there is the allusion to Faust. With what ease the experience of the black woman is translated into a stock formula of the post-romantic period! This reminds us that the interest in the exotic, non-white woman is itself almost a literary and cultural cliché by Baudelaire's time, though lived out and given personal content in his relations with Jeanne Duval. In this connection we must examine the two opening poems of the Jeanne Duval cycle, "Parfum exotique" and "La Chevelure," which I think reveal the fascination that the exotic voyage still holds for the modern reader.

These poems are too rich to be given exhaustive commentary in a short discussion. But several points are relevant to my argument. There is the voyage motif through which, using the woman as inspiration and instrument, the speaker achieves an enriched sense of existence. The poems begin with the poet alone with the woman; he breathes her perfume and thus begins his imaginative journey toward fulfillment. Both poems emphasize the *progression* toward this goal. Thus in "La Chevelure" the second stanza introduces the motifs of voyage and swimming; stanza three reveals the "éblouissant rêve" which Jeanne's hair *contains*; the succeeding three stanzas respectively present a world of heightened sensation, plunge the poet directly *into* this world, and emphasize that in it he has rediscovered an inebriating sense of *total* existence. Similarly, the sonnet form of "Parfum exotique" emphasizes first the beginning of the voyage in the quatrains and then the arrival at and possession of the vision in the tercets. Guided by the woman's perfume, the speaker reaches a port, and attains an exhilarating and sensuous experience:

> Pendant que le parfum des verts tamariniers,
> Qui circule dans l'air et m'enfle la narine,
> Se mêle dans mon âme au chant des mariniers.

This is the second point that I want to make about these texts. They allow a special kind of intuition, inebriating and ecstatic. In "La Chevelure" the speaker says he will plunge his head, which is "amoureuse d'ivresse," into the hair of the woman, and later his thirst for drunkenness is satisfied as he inhales the perfumes of her hair and of the world which it evokes: "Je m'enivre ardemment des senteurs confondues / De l'huile de coco, du musc et du goudron." Similarly, in the conclusion of "Parfum exotique" quoted above, tropical nature is evoked by the perfume of the "verts tamariniers"; an experience of intensity, fusion, and expansion is created by the language ("circule dans l'air et m'enfle la narine"; "se mêle dans mon âme"); there is a sense of identification with the sailors and their communal song through which the isolated speaker attains an augmented sense of sexual power and creativity.

The essential significance of these poems, then, resides in the movement toward a state of intensified being, perhaps having communal overtones, certainly involving an enrichment of the experience of the self, and deriving its value from its participation in an abundant, non-European nature. To the extent that these texts appeal to us, one must feel that they have a similar function, evoking a state of ease, gratification, and innocent physical perfection:

> Une île paresseuse où la nature donne
> Des arbres singuliers et des fruits savoureux;
> Des hommes dont le corps est mince et vigoureux,
> Et des femmes dont l'œil par sa franchise étonne.

This is an idealized vision projecting the needs of European industrial man, the unhappy human being portrayed throughout Baudelaire's work—city-bound, separated from nature, ill at ease with his body, troubled by anguish, guilt, and an obsessive sense of time, submitted to alienating labor. (See the *Tableaux parisiens,* including the substitution of artificial for natural motifs in "Paysage" and "Rêve parisien," and the depiction of suffering and horror in "Le Cygne," "Les Sept Vieillards," "Les Petites Vieilles," and the two "Crépuscules." There is also the contrast between pagan beauty and the "pauvres corps tordus, maigres, ventrus ou flasques" of modern times in "J'aime le souvenir de ces époques nues," as well as the disgust for the poet's body, again in contrast with an idealized view of Greek physical beauty and sexual experience, in "Un Voyage à Cythère." The poems entitled "Spleen," and also "Au Lecteur," and the powerful group of texts at the end of *Spleen et idéal,* portray the anguished condition of modern man. And Baudelaire's awareness of alienated labor is attested by the depiction of the fatigue of "le savant obstiné," "l'ouvrier courbé," and "les débauchés . . . brisés par leurs travaux" in the two "Crépuscules," as well as by the anguish of the poet before the necessity of work in "La Muse vénale," the correspondence, and prose poems such as "La Chambre double" and "À une heure du matin.")

In contrast to all of that, in the island evoked in "Parfum exotique" man is in harmony with nature and is free from work (consider "île paresseuse," "la nature donne"), and bodily pleasure without guilt abounds ("fruits savoureux," "corps . . . mince et vigoureux," "des femmes dont l'œil par sa franchise étonne"). The relevance of this idealized tropical vision (and the significance of the black woman) for the psychic life of nineteenth-century European man are recognized clearly in the second stanza of "La Chevelure":

> La langoureuse Asie et la brûlante Afrique,
> Tout un monde lointain, absent, presque défunt,
> Vit dans tes profondeurs, forêt aromatique!

Here it is clear that the memories evoked by *la chevelure* are not merely personal, but ultimately "racial," that this poem too concerns the situation of modern man, for whom nature in its full power has become distant, absent, almost dead. This lost world seems to live on only in the hair and body of the black woman whom the poet loves, and it is she alone who allows him to be united, or rather reunited, with it, as is apparent in the use of the verbs *retrouver* and *rendre* in the climactic stanzas of the poem:

> Et mon esprit subtil que le roulis caresse
> Saura vous retrouver, ô féconde paresse!
> Infinis bercements du loisir embaumé!
>
> Cheveux bleus, pavillon de ténèbres tendues,
> Vous me rendez l'azur du ciel immense et rond.

Féconde paresse, loisir embaumé, the totality of the *ciel immense et rond*—these are the gifts afforded, through the evolution of the poem, by Jeanne. She serves a *function,* then, not only as other and as woman, but as black—as one learns in teaching these texts to non-whites and women. The last stanza of "La Chevelure," with its determination to sow jewels in her hair, so that she will never refuse the poet's desire, lucidly emphasizes this use to which the poet puts her. The verb *sèmera,* with its suggestions of fertility and productiveness, and the image of the jewels, nuance somewhat the sexual and emotional prostitution that this implies. But the woman retains her essential function in the poet's imaginative activity and his happiness: "N'es-tu pas l'oasis où je rêve, et la gourde / Où je hume à longs traits le vin du souvenir?" As we have seen, that function has to do with the coming to consciousness of, and the search to overcome, a sense of unhappiness and exile which transcends the individual, which is rooted in the contradictions of an entire culture.

The "love poems" of the Jeanne Duval cycle are so powerful, then, because they involve the basic causes of unhappiness in an alienated and highly unnatural society—the poems reveal this meaning when seen against the backdrop of all of *Les Fleurs du mal.* In this connection the *Tableaux parisiens* are especially important, and in particular "Le Cygne," which provides an ultimate perspective on the themes of exile, exploitation, and race. In this text we see the poet, alone and situated precisely in time and space: traversing Paris, he is saddened by the changes being wrought in the city under the Second Empire ("Comme je traversais le nouveau Carrousel"). But from within his solitude, through personal (and also literary and mythic) memory he generates relationships and a moving statement about man's perennial fate as well as the poet's effort to comprehend and transcend it.[11] Thus, the poem is dedicated to Victor Hugo, in voluntary exile in protest against the Emperor. It is enlarged by literary allusions—to Virgil's Andromache and the exiled Ovid. And from personal memory it attains the universal. From a particular image of exile from nature which the speaker had once seen—a captive swan, escaped from its cage, searching for its "beau lac natal"—it moves to an enumeration which by the end of the poem includes all mankind: not only the swan and Andromache, but also orphans and shipwrecked sailors, and finally "quiconque a perdu ce qui ne se retrouve / Jamais, jamais!"—"captifs . . . vaincus . . . bien d'autres encor!"

Thus the poem views all men as in some way "exilés, ridicule[s] et sublime[s], / Et rongé[s] d'un désir sans trêve!" But the generalizing tendency does not reduce the importance of the text's precise historical and cultural statement. The ultimate place of solitude is the city, the urban civilization of nineteenth-century Europe which destroys men and women in the ways described

in the rest of the *Tableaux parisiens.*[12] This is brought home powerfully, and with specially poignant meaning in relation to Jeanne Duval, by an earlier stanza of "Le Cygne" which I have not yet mentioned:

> Je pense à la négresse, amaigrie et phthisique,
> Piétinant dans la boue, et cherchant, l'œil hagard,
> Les cocotiers absents de la superbe Afrique
> Derrière la muraille immense du brouillard.

These lines are disturbing in indicating that the black woman who, like Jeanne Duval, could embody a sense of integral existence, is now herself trapped by the conditions of Western industrial reality. Sick, imprisoned in the same oppressive climate that haunts Baudelaire in the *spleen* poems, she can no longer rediscover "la superbe Afrique" of her origins. She joins the poet in a condition of exile which is perhaps more excruciating for her than for him.

In this stanza, therefore, I think we can read Baudelaire's most convincing comment on the themes that I have been tracing. In his work the alienation of the artist, his need for contact with others and his tendency to exploit them to enrich his existence, even in the intimate realm of love, seem finally to involve the cultural exile of European industrial man. In the exotic voyage poems, "Parfum exotique" and "La Chevelure," the poet manages to transcend imaginatively his unhappy state; together with the speaker in those poems the reader may achieve an ecstatic intuition of being. The rest of the poems in Jeanne's cycle express the poet's complex attitude toward her, including the hatred which somehow cannot wipe out completely the gratitude for the gift which she bestows in the voyage poems. In "Le Cygne," the feeling of exile closes in again with special horror, because in the lines on the black woman lost in Paris we glimpse the movement of an urban, industrial, and colonizing civilization, incapable of returning to the sources of happiness, destroying the being who seemed to hold out the promise of a healthier and more joyful life.

Notes

I am grateful for helpful suggestions on this article to Reinhard Kuhn and Michèle Greenlaw of Brown University.

1. For conflicting statements by contemporaries on Jeanne's physical appearance, see Albert Feuillerat, "L'Architecture des *Fleurs du mal,*" in *Studies by Members of the Yale French Department,* ed. A. Feuillerat (New Haven and London: Yale Univ. Press, 1941), p. 240, n. 50. I refer to Jeanne as black for the sake of concision but also to underscore the racial element, so important in these poems.

2. *Mon Cœur mis à nu,* XII. *Œuvres complètes de Baudelaire,* ed. Y.-G. Le Dantec, Bibliothèque de

la Pléiade (Paris: Gallimard, 1954), p. 1210. All quotations from Baudelaire are from this edition. The sentence quoted in my text is followed by: "Malgré la famille,—et au milieu des camarades, surtout,—sentiment de destinée éternellement solitaire. Cependant, goût très-vif de la vie et du plaisir."

3. Cf. *Mon Cœur mis à nu,* I: "De la vaporisation et de la centralisation du *Moi.* Tout est là." Cf. also J.-P. Richard's reading of the end of "Le Guignon," in which solitude is seen as the condition of poetic creation ("Profondeur de Baudelaire," in *Poésie et profondeur* [Paris: Seuil, 1955], esp. pp. 93-95).

4. See my article, "The Search for Community: The City in Hölderlin, Wordsworth and Baudelaire," *Texas Studies in Literature and Language,* 13 (Spring 1971), esp. 83-89.

5. See Charles Mauron, *Des Métaphores obsédantes au mythe personnel* (Paris: J. Corti, 1963), ch. III, VIII.

6. *Œuvres complètes,* pp. 909-14. On the relations between sexuality and poetic creation in Baudelaire and others I have been helped by Albert Sonnenfeld's illuminating "Onan and the Muses: Vision, Permanence and the Poet," delivered at the French 7 (French Literature of the Twentieth Century) meeting of the Modern Language Association, 27 December 1968, and generously communicated to me in written form by Professor Sonnenfeld.

7. Consult P. M. Pasinetti, "The 'Jeanne Duval' Poems in the *Fleurs du mal,"* in *Baudelaire, A Collection of Critical Essays,* ed. Henri Peyre, Twentieth Century Views (Englewood Cliffs, N. J.: Prentice-Hall, 1962), pp. 86-93 (reprinted from *Yale French Studies,* 1, 2, Fall-Winter 1948); and Michel Deguy, "Le Corps de Jeanne (Remarques sur le corps poétique des *Fleurs du mal),"* *Poétique,* 3 (1970), 334-47.

8. This text illustrates the complexity of the poet's attitude. On one level it is an attack on Jeanne's unintelligence, her lack of awareness of the role she plays in forming the poet; she is a "machine aveugle et sourde," used by nature "pour pétrir un génie." But the sexual implication of "pétrir" (cf. also "ta ruelle," "pour exercer tes dents," "buveur du sang," "fangeuse grandeur") indicates that the poem is also an overt evocation of an intense sexual relationship, marked simultaneously by fascination, gratification, and disgust.

9. Cf. "Le Chat," "Avec ses vêtements," and "Le Serpent qui danse" (not only cats and snakes but "la mollesse / D'un jeune éléphant"), the dog in "Une Charogne," the motifs *toison, moutonnant, encolure, crinière* ("La Chevelure," also "Le Léthé"), and "la grâce enfantine du singe" ("Le Cadre," the third poem in "Un Fantôme"). There is a question as to whether "Les Bijoux," which (like "Le Léthé") was one of the poems censored in 1857, belongs to the Jeanne Duval cycle. See Antoine Adam's edition of *Les Fleurs du Mal* (Paris: Garnier, 1961), p. 432; Albert Feuillerat on the contrary puts the poem with the Jeanne Duval cycle, as do I. See "L'Architecture des *Fleurs du Mal,"* in *Studies by Members of the Yale French Department,* pp. 240-41. In any event, the racial element of the poem is unmistakable, it affects the relationship between woman and speaker significantly, and it therefore has to be included.

10. These words are picked up later in the poem by "pavane" and "caravane," it being said that these four rhyming words in -*avane* are the only such words in the French language.

11. On historical reality and mythic transformation in "Le Cygne," see Henri Lefebvre, *La Révolution urbaine,* Collection Idées (Paris: Gallimard, 1970), pp. 144-46; Lowry Nelson, Jr., "Baudelaire and Virgil: A Reading of 'Le Cygne,'" *Comparative Literature,* 13, 4 (Winter 1961), 332 ff.; and Keith H. MacFarlane, "*Le Cygne* de Baudelaire: 'falsi Simoentis ad undam,'" *L'Information Littéraire,* 27ᵉ année, no. 3 (mai-juin 1975), 139-44.

12. See Walter Benjamin, "On Some Motifs in Baudelaire," in *Illuminations* (New York: Schocken Books, 1969), pp. 155-200; and Victor Brombert, "Baudelaire: City Images and the 'Dream of Stone,'" *Yale French Studies,* 32 (Oct. 1964), 100-05.

Alexander Fischler (essay date fall 1989)

SOURCE: Fischler, Alexander. "Eugénie Grandet's Career as Heavenly Exile." *Essays in Literature* 16, no. 2 (fall 1989): 271-80.

[*In the following essay, Fischler maintains that the characterization of the eponymous heroine in Honoré de Balzac's* Eugénie Grandet *as an exile "not only provided a pretext for a close look at the place of confinement, but allowed careful distinctions between types and degrees of removal."*]

Balzac liked to suggest to his readers that some of the exceptional men and women of *La Comédie humaine* were exiles, more suited for a realm where categories and gradation are irrelevant than for cramped quarters "ici-bas." The argument was a romantic commonplace.

He was able to vitalize it, however, by adding consistently a very literal dimension to exile as metaphor, by suggesting, as he did in *Eugénie Grandet,* that removal from one's habitual environment or sphere of influence is a reality whose effects can be observed,[1] or by arguing, as he did in some of the *Etudes philosophiques,* that the sense of separation from an extraterrestrial sphere is a significant response to a cosmic order perceived by faith and described by theologians and mystics. As illustrated by Eugénie Grandet's career, the assertion that a protagonist is an exile not only provided a pretext for a close look at the place of confinement, but allowed careful distinctions between types and degrees of removal.

Though he used the twin themes of confinement and exile to structure *Eugénie Grandet* from the start, Balzac had some difficulty in positioning his heroine so as to insure that her home, at the top of the "ancienne Grand-Rue," be seen in perspective with a heavenly abode. Part of the positioning problem was due to the author's desire to suggest a very special affinity between the heroine and two of his mistresses, Mme Hanska and Maria du Fresnay. Most of it, however, can be shown to have resulted from concern that Eugénie's necessarily limited perception precluded a sense of exile and from the fact that Balzac realized, as evidenced by his revisions, that an ambiguous connection with the world around ultimately served her characterization better than exile from the world beyond.

The novel was written and published in 1833. In the Edition Béchet, which appeared after serial publication the same year but was dated 1834, it was the first of the "Scènes de la Vie de Province" and was allegedly intended to illustrate the fact that great values (material as well as moral) are to be found in the provinces, far from the madding crowds of Paris. The *Tourangeau,* Balzac, was obviously delighted to confront the connoisseurs of value of both realms and to demonstrate from the start that myopia prevails among them. Here was also an opportunity to show that social exile is a condition both assumed and imposed: while Charles, decked out in finery carefully chosen to dazzle his hosts, is compared by the author to a peacock plumetted into an obscure chicken yard (1054), the *Provinciaux,* united for once in their distaste for fashion and their distrust of the *Parisiens,* scrutinize him mockingly as if he were an exotic giraffe (1058). But the impressions of another observer, the innocent Eugénie, are recorded as well: for her, the young man is a seraph come down from heaven, a phoenix among cousins (1058-59). Charles himself is uneasy in the new setting. By the end of the evening, as he sets out to ascend with the rest of the household, the stairwell does indeed look to him like a chicken roost (1069).

Thus, as exile fosters the defensive responses of contempt and conceit, confinement is shown to foster the naïve worship of a creature who, being more attuned to heaven than to earth, sublimates what she sees. This naïve response of the innocent is what Balzac chose to set at the heart of his novel, for through Eugénie, appearing as an exile from an extraterrestrial sphere, he could invoke an ultimate metaphysical scale to evaluate action whose course would otherwise seem determined by worldly considerations alone.

The Grandet household is presented as a cloistered realm within a provincial world insulated in time from modern reality. Twice removed from common affairs and ruled by its own tyrannical and earth-bound god, "le Dieu Argent," the money god, the Maison Grandet could easily become a testing ground, a station on the way to a higher reality in a spiritual realm. Certainly the three women in the house were to appear in transit, accepting their grim lot on earth while praying for happiness beyond.

Dealing with the generally submissive and retiring Eugénie, Balzac showed that true character would not emerge out of sheer contrast with those who surround her. Hence he compared her repeatedly to the Virgin Mary and then drew freely on the many roles the comparison suggested. With much less effect on characterization, he also compared her to a noble statue, specifically the Venus of Milo, to Penelope, Faust's Marguerite, a linnet, a rare bird, the pure lamb with a golden fleece, and the prey of the pack. In early editions of the novel the author involved himself openly and extensively in the presentation of his Virgin and assumed for this purpose the two complementary roles of artist-creator and worshiper of woman perfected in Mary. The presentation was thus quite formal and clumsy, relying both on the text of the novel and on an external framework which consisted of a "Préambule" and "Epilogue" (deleted after 1843) to which a dedication, "A Maria," was added in the Edition Charpentier of 1839.

The fact that the central character was to be viewed as an exile from a higher sphere was established in the preamble of the early editions. After defending his choice of seemingly plain subjects set against a country background, the author calls attention to the moralities ("mythes" in the manuscript) that can be found in country traditions:

> . . . aujourd'hui le pauvre artiste n'a saisi qu'un de ces fils blancs promenés dans les airs par la brise, et dont s'amusent les enfants, les jeunes filles, les poètes; dont les savants ne se soucient guère; mais que, dit-on, laisse tomber, de sa quenouille, une céleste fileuse. Prenez garde! Il y a des *moralités* dans cette tradition champêtre! Aussi l'auteur en fait-il son épigraphe. Il vous montrera comment, durant la belle saison de la vie, certaines illusions, de blanches espérances, des fils argentés descendent des cieux et y retournent sans avoir touché terre.

(1026)

[. . . today, the poor artist caught only one of these white strands that wander with the breeze, playthings for children, young maidens and poets, which concern not the learned, but which, according to rumor, are dropped from the distaff of a heavenly spinner. Take heed! *Moralities* may be found in this folk tradition. As a result, the author takes it for his epigraph. He will show you how, during life's beautiful season, certain illusions, white hopes, silvery threads descend from heaven and return there without having touched ground.]

Gossamer, in French, is "fil de la Vierge," the Virgin's thread. The folk tradition, which assigns to it a divine origin and a heavenly destination, suggests that one does not pluck it out of the air in vain. Eugénie, we thus learn, is a temporary exile from heaven, drifting untainted through the world and recalling, as the text will tell us repeatedly, a model above.

The epilogue fulfills the promise of the preamble and brings together the Marian strands, relating the portrait drawn in the book to those offered by earlier artists in tribute to the Virgin. The author expresses proper humility in his task (in the manuscript he even slights himself by comparison with the great Madonna painters, asserting he is not one of them, "ni Raphaël, ni Rembrandt, ni Poussin"):

> Peut-être a-t-il trop chargé d'or le contour de la tête de sa Maria; peut-être n'a-t-il pas distribué la lumière suivant les règles de l'art; enfin, peut-être a-t-il trop rembruni les teintes déjà noires de son vieillard, image toute matérielle. Mais ne refusez pas votre indulgence au moine patient, vivant au fond de sa cellule, humble adorateur de la *Rosa mundi,* de Marie, belle image de tout le sexe, la femme du moine, la seconde Eva des chrétiens.
>
> (1201)

[Perhaps he surrounded the head of his Maria with too much gold; failed to distribute light according to the rules of art; or drew too darkly his already dark old man, a wholly material image. Still, do not refuse your indulgence to the patient monk who lives in the depth of his cell, a humble worshiper of the *Rosa mundi,* of Mary, fair image of the entire sex, the monk's spouse, the Christian's second Eve.]

The manuscript ended with an assertion of Eugénie's celestial nature; in the published version of the epilogue, however, she is compared instead with a noble statue taken from Greece that falls into the sea in midpassage and remains forever unknown. Comparison with Mary did not necessarily always support Balzac's argument; when he revised the text for publication, he chose the image of lost treasure in preference to the image of celestial exile, thus stressing in the end, as he had done in the beginning, the theme of the beauty that fades unseen, a more earth-bound cliché. The revisions shift emphasis from celestial origins and destiny to terrestrial confinement.

The third and last item, added to the novel's external frame in 1839, was the dedication "A Maria." Originally it complemented the preamble and epilogue, dedicating the work to woman epitomized in the Virgin Mary and drawing attention to the presentation of Eugénie as exile from heaven. Four years later, when Balzac revised his works again in preparation for the 1843 Edition Furne, he minimized his interpretative involvement and retained only this dedication from the cumbersome external frame of the novel. As a result, despite obviously religious overtones in its wording, the dedication no longer seemed to invoke the Virgin as model for Eugénie, but to address itself to a contemporary:

> A Maria
>
> Que votre nom, vous dont le portrait est le plus bel ornement de cet ouvrage, soit ici comme une brache de buis bénit, prise on ne sait à quel arbre, mais certainement sanctifiée par la religion et renouvelée, toujours verte, par des mains pieuses, pour protéger la maison.
>
> De Balzac
>
> (1027)

> [To Maria
>
> May your name, you whose portrait is the most beautiful ornament of this work, be here like a blessed branch of boxwood, taken from one knows not which tree, but certainly sanctified by religion and always green, renewed by pious hands, to protect the house.
>
> De Balzac]

The contemporary Maria, we now know, was Maria Du Fresnay, née Daminois, Balzac's mistress, whose daughter, Marie, born in 1834, he recognized as his own. André Chancerel and Roger Pierrot, who are responsible for the identification, argued that Maria du Fresnay was the actual model for Eugénie.[2] More recent editors, however, doubt the possibility of such identification. They also point out that in the dedication, the preamble and the epilogue, Balzac not only offered a tribute to Maria Du Fresnay and "the entire [fair] sex," but also to Mme Hanska whom he gave the manuscript as a Christmas present.[3] The holy branch, he could argue, was the boxwood over her portrait, and the conventional Maria-Eva association was, as she knew, one of his favorites. Interestingly enough, however, in a letter dated October 12, 1833 (i.e., while still working on the novel), Balzac announces to his sister, Laure, that he has fathered a child and describes Maria Du Fresnay in terms that recall Eugénie and gossamer from the distaff of the Virgin: "une gentille personne, la plus naïve créature qui soit, tombée comme une fleur du ciel" (1648) [a gentle person, the most naive of creatures, come down from heaven like a flower].

Balzac allowed himself considerable margin when he said in his 1839 dedication that the branch, "taken one knows not from what tree," was renewable; in settling

details of the novel's framing text, he could settle domestic accounts as well. Nonetheless, the Madonna worship and the discussion in the epilogue of woman's place in the creation nearer to the angel than man represented genuine concerns going far beyond the little games he might have been playing with his mistresses.[4] Association with the Virgin Mary was his most expedient device for indicating the superiority of a female protagonist on the grounds of heavenly affinities. As a matter of fact, the manuscript variants indicate that during the composition of the novel Balzac was so taken with this device that he even allowed Charles Grandet to join in the Mary cult midway through the farewell letter to his Parisian mistress, Annette:

> Tu auras du moins embelli ma belle jeunesse, orné mon âme des nobles délicatesses de la femme, je ne pourrai jamais voir les madones de Raphaël sans penser à toi qui as coloré ma seconde enfance des feux de ton visage céleste, qui as sanctifié par ton amour la vie désordonnée à laquelle les jeunes gens se livrent, qui as ennobli les passions mauvaises de ton amant en jettant tes douces voluptés dans mon âme. Si je suis bon, si je vaux quelque chose, c'est par toi.
>
> (1704)

> [You will at least have embellished my beautiful youth, adorned my soul with woman's noble delicacies; I will never be able to look at Raphael's madonnas without recalling you who lent hue to my second childhood with the flames of your heavenly face, who hallowed with love the unruly life that the young espouse, who made noble a lover's foul passions by filling my soul with your exquisite delight. If I am good, if I am worth anything, it is through you.]

These lines to Annette, however, detracted from the theme of celestial virtue in the country and gave Charles a sensitivity that was in direct opposition to the aridity Balzac wanted him to represent. So he changed the text to eliminate this *Ave Annette* and, in the same revision, introduced into the letter a hint at the possibility of marriage between Charles and Eugénie and followed it with a comment on the coldness of tone manifest in the writing: the naïve country girl who reads the letter is unaware of this coldness, but the author marks it as a characteristic of the spoiled, big-city child. Such revisions indicate Balzac's growing awareness of the scale he had adopted by comparing Eugénie to the Virgin—in the final version, only she was to be allowed a hallowing love: "La candeur d'Eugénie avait momentanément sanctifié l'amour de Charles" (1141) [The guilelessness of Eugénie had momentarily sanctified the love of Charles]. Associations with the Madonna were much better suited for her, and, if there were to be extensions to the other virtuous women in the novel, Balzac could handle them just as effectively by reference to feminine angelism and to physical manifestations of the soul's transcendence (notably, in the transfiguration of Mme Grandet before her death). There is only one exception

to the rule, an early reference to Nanon, "plus chaste que ne l'était la Vierge Marie elle-même" (1043) [more chaste than the Virgin Mary herself].

Despite her many virtues, however, Nanon is no exile from heaven. What distinguishes her, as the last line of the novel tells us, is that she does not have wits enough to understand the corruption of the world. Eugénie, on the other hand, overcomes her initial naïveté, learns to assess those about her at their worth, and follows her confessor's advice by coming to terms with the world, albeit uneasily. Her heavenly antecedents and destiny, which may have been clichés at the outset, allow evaluation of her career in the world and explain the nature of her compromise with it, notably in her insistence on remaining a virgin.

Balzac's attempt to insure a metaphysical perspective for his heroine is well illustrated in the famous portrait of Eugénie *à sa toilette*, offered early in the novel (1073-76). This scene, set against the melancholy background of the garden on the morning after Charles's arrival, provided an excuse for a detailed physical description enhanced by the author's own estimate of her beauty and some suggestive analogies. Viewing herself in the mirror after discovering the "mystérieuses beautés particulières aux endroits solitaires ou à la nature inclute" (1074) [the mysterious beauties that are particular to solitary places or untamed nature] which had hitherto seemed ordinary to her, Eugénie concludes that she is unworthy of her cousin. But the author, claiming she is unfair to herself, compares her to the recently discovered Venus of Milo, adding that her beauty is actually "ennoblie par cette suavité du sentiment chrétien qui purifie la femme et lui donne une distinction inconnue aux sculpteurs anciens" (1075) [ennobled by that softness of Christian sentiment which purifies woman and gives her a distinction unknown to ancient sculptors]. Such a description supports the theme of the hidden grandeur and offers a parallel to the lost statue at the end of the epilogue. The associations may appear incongruous when we read the description of the rather homely Eugénie which follows immediately, but Balzac was evidently serious: almost in the same breath he went on to compare his heroine's broad forehead with that of the Jupiter of Phidias.

We are told by Pierrot and Chancerel that consideration of the model, Maria du Fresnay, might have been involved here (448). But, more important, we have evidence of Balzac's desire to anchor Eugénie in more than one world: she must represent enduring beauty, celestial beauty in particular, yet remain of this world, and the reference to slight blemishes in her physical makeup, such as the smallpox which ruined her complexion, achieved the secularization and convey the fact of exile. Balzac adds:

> Le peintre qui cherche ici-bas un type à la céleste pureté de Marie, qui demande à toute la nature ces yeux

modestement fiers devinés par Raphaël, ces lignes vier-
ges souvent dûes au hasards de la conception mais
qu'une vie chrétienne et pudique peut seule conserver
ou faire acquérir; ce peintre, amoureux d'un si rare
modèle, eût trouvé tout à coup dans le visage d'Eugénie
la noblesse innée qui s'ignore; il eût vu sous un front
calme un monde d'amour; et dans la coupe des yeux,
dans l'habitude des paupières, le je ne sais quoi divin.

(1076)

[The painter who seeks in this world a type for the ce-
lestial purity of Mary and asks throughout nature for
those modestly proud eyes that Raphael knew, for those
virgin lines that may often be due to chance at concep-
tion but that are preserved or acquired only by means
of a chaste, Christian life; such a painter, enamored of
so rare a model, would have discovered on Eugénie's
face nobility that is innate but unaware of itself; he
would have seen a world of love under a peaceful brow
and discovered the divine *je ne sais quoi* in the shape
of the eyes, the form of the lids.]

Before dismissing sublimation of Eugénie on the
grounds that it catered to the worst of contemporary
taste, it is useful to note that hackneyed analogies in
this novel, as shown by Ruth Amossy and Elisheva
Rosen in *Les Discours du cliché,* far from being reas-
suring, call attention to departure from convention and
result in a multi-layered narrative structure. Amossy
and Rosen examine, for instance, the repeated conven-
tional references to birds and show how they allow sys-
tematic juxtaposition of aerial and terrestrial, of aspira-
tion and reality, and suggest in the end a heroine who is
"un oiseau qui n'aura guère eu l'occasion de déployer
son vol" [a bird who will never have had a chance to
soar]. They conclude: "la logique du mélodrame se
trouve battue en brèche tout au long d'une intrigue qui
ne feint de s'y soumettre que pour mieux la démystifi-
fier—comme en témoigne un dénouement férocement
ironique où sombre toute possibilité de *happy end*" [the
logic of melodrama is upset throughout a narrative
which pretends to conform to it only to undermine it
the better—witness a ferociously ironic dénouement
where every chance of a happy ending is lost].[5] Amossy
and Rosen feel that the conventional association of Eu-
génie with the Virgin is intended primarily to show her
as a model of feminine virtue. However, if one consid-
ers the association as a means of insuring that the hero-
ine has an ultimate stage beyond the terrestrial, where
the irony of situation and the irony of fate do not apply,
then a happy ending is in fact indicated. There is actu-
ally no good reason to read irony into Balzac's conclu-
sion that "Eugénie marche au ciel accompagnée d'un
cortège de bienfaits" (1198). [Eugénie strides toward
heaven accompanied by a procession of good deeds.]

Although he used her indeed as a model of feminine
virtue, Balzac wanted to evoke more than purity by as-
sociating his heroine with Mary. Until her brief con-
frontation with Grandet and afterwards, she is also, like

the Virgin, a model of submissiveness and obedience,
and long before suffering elevates her, she serves as
guiding spirit. Balzac even suggested that her love for
Charles brings her a fulfillment that lasts long after his
departure. Instead of contaminating her, love conse-
crates her:

Avant la venue de son cousin, Eugénie pouvait être
comparée à la Vierge avant la conception; quand il fut
parti elle ressemblait à la Vierge mère: elle avait conçu
l'amour. Ces deux Maries, si différentes et si bien
représentées par quelques peintres espagnols constitu-
ent l'une des plus brillantes figures qui abondent dans
le christianisme.

(1147)

[Before the arrival of her cousin, Eugénie could be
compared to the Virgin before conception; once he had
left, she resembled the Virgin Mother: she had con-
ceived love. These two Marys, so different and so well
represented by some Spanish painters, constitute one of
the most brilliant figures that abound in Christianity.]

Eugénie follows her lover on a map and communicates
with him via the lovers' star of which Charles had
taught her the beauty and the uses. She can continue in
her main role since Christianity had substituted Mary
for Venus and made the lovers' star into the *stella matu-
tina* or the *maris stella* which guides to the port of
heaven. We learn considerably later that during the first
voyage she had indeed accompanied him "comme cette
image de la Vierge que mettent sur leur vaisseau les
marins espagnols" (1181) [like the image of the Virgin
which Spanish sailors use to decorate their ship].

Did Balzac realize that Eugénie's association with Mary
would, in the end, assume an ironic edge? Clearly she
finds no real fulfillment, and her insistence on being al-
lowed to retain her virginity as precondition for interac-
tion with the world only underscores the contrast be-
tween her sterile lot and that of the Madonna. All her
charity does not compensate for the fact that in the
preservation of her purity she mostly recalls her father,
the hoarder. Balzac, who had noted the manner in which
gold was reflected even in the physiognomy of his mi-
ser, notes in his final portrait of Eugénie that wealth
came to her at the expense of warmth: "L'argent devait
communiquer ses teintes froides à cette vie céleste, et
donner de la défiance pour les sentiments à une femme
qui était tout sentiment" (1197). [Money was to com-
municate its cold tints to this heavenly life and make
emotions seem suspect to a woman who was all emo-
tion.] Her selflessness may contrast with the selfishness
that motivates the world around her, but her purity has
worrisome implications betrayed by her appearance.

Balzac knew that purity was so far out of place in the
world that it might justifiably seem unnatural: in *La
Cousine Bette* he would eventually explore even its

monstrous side, like Racine in *Phèdre.* But in the case of Eugénie, he chose merely to concentrate on the manner in which whiteness contrasts with surrounding gold and grey, the colors most notably associated with her father. She remains pure to the end: "Son visage est blanc, reposé, calme. Sa voix est douce et recueillie, ses manières sont simples. Elle a toutes les noblesses de la douleur, la sainteté d'une personne qui n'a pas souillé son âme au contact du monde [ms. qui n'a pas vécu], mais aussi la roideur de la vieille fille et les habitudes mesquines que donne l'existence étroite de la province" (1198). [Her face is white, rested, calm. Her voice is soft, composed, her manner is simple. She has all the nobility of suffering, the saintliness of a person who has not soiled her soul through contact with the world (ms. who has not lived), but also the stiffness of the old maid and the petty mannerisms that come with the restrictions of provincial existence.]

Philippe Bertault has noted that Balzac was subject to the common confusion of the Immaculate Conception of Mary with the Virgin Birth.[6] This is not the case in *Eugénie Grandet,* whose heroine is to appear immaculately conceived, that is, free from the taint of original sin, and whose name, Eugénie, the well-born, suggests this explicitly. Association with gossamer from Mary's distaff remains fundamental in her presentation even after the metaphor itself disappeared with the deletion of the preamble and epilogue; summarized on the last page of the novel, her story is "l'histoire de cette femme qui n'est pas du monde au milieu du monde" [the story of a woman who is in the world though not of the world].[7] But one finds here, as one does throughout the *Comédie humaine,* from *La Peau de Chagrin* to *La Cousine Bette,* that Balzac wants his reader to view characters who have made a conscious decision to remain intact in the world with a sense of awe, that is, with a mixture of admiration and fear.

Bertault documents Balzac's particular interest in virginity as a form of strength or, more precisely, as conserved energy; he cites the discussion of virginity in *La Cousine Bette* which concludes: "cette grandiose et terrible exception mérite tous les honneurs que lui décerne l'Eglise catholique" (7:152) [this grandiose and terrible exception deserves all the honors it is granted by the Catholic church]. Peter W. Lock in his study of Balzac's hoarders and spendthrifts, describes the virgin's place among the hoarders and cites the same passage as well as another a few lines earlier in the text: "La vie, dont les forces sont économisées, a pris chez l'individu vierge une qualité de résistance et de durée incalculable." [Life, whose energy is spared, assumes in the virginal individual an incalculable quality of resistance and duration.][8] Eugénie's virginity suits her both symbolically and physically to become first a match and foil for Grandet and, eventually, a successor. At the same time, however, considered from the point of view of Balza-

cian hygiene and morality, her virginity and chastity explain also the ironic situation in which we last see her in the novel; for what conserves Eugénie among the living prolongs also her terrestrial exile and underlines the sense of waste which is increasingly associated with her. In the end, she has not only assumed her father's miserly ways and given ground to evil rumor, to the *médisants* who claim she is turning yellow, but, "faite pour être magnifiquement épouse et mère" (1199) [created to be mother and spouse magnificently], she has become an embodiment of wasted vitality and thwarted fruition, justifying the priest's assertion that in denying life she might be guilty of lack of charity. It is interesting to note that the rumor about Eugénie's "yellowing" and the author's expression of a sense of waste, not included in the manuscript, were added in the first edition. Thus, very early, Balzac turned Eugénie's survival into an irony of fate: not only at the expense of the scheming Cruchot de Bonfons, but at her own expense. At best, survival is for her the fulfillment of a religious obligation. Assumption into heaven is indeed to be hoped for her.

The external framework through which Balzac offered his identification of Eugénie with Mary had become cumbersome by the time he was preparing the 1843 Edition Furne. By then, Balzac had also decided to rely within the novel on the more complex and ambiguous aspects of Eugénie's virginity which—instead of bringing out the "je ne sais quoi divin" in her eyes or her heavenly affinities—served to explain the strength of her character and the tragic element in her fate, the sense of waste. It is indeed possible to argue that he was insuring a more complex characterization when, with the 1843 edition, he eliminated the preamble and epilogue, in which he had insisted on comparing the presentation of his heroine with myth-making (in the manuscript) or with illumination and madonna painting. For in the epilogue, even as he apologized for gilding Eugénie's halo excessively, he was still stressing her heavenly nature. In the preamble, on the other hand, in the Félix Davin preface to the *Etudes de moeurs* (1835), and in the novel itself, he had insisted on a secular design, proving that the ordinary and the seemingly trivial were fit subjects for serious dramatization. By 1843 Balzac found that an excessively Christian emphasis not only detracted from the secular design but could preclude tragedy altogether. Preamble and epilogue were thus dismissed, but the readers' reactions were not much affected.

Balzac became annoyed with the preeminence the public gave this novel among his works.[9] It continues to rank among the most popular, and the reasons have not improved: readers still place Grandet at the center of the story and, ignoring all of Balzac's careful juxtapositions, single Eugénie out for worship. Unfortunately, the pure and saintly Eugénie is doomed to seem less

and less tolerable to modern readers unless they can be made to realize that Balzac himself demurred at her canonization and exile in the novel, that he allowed for ambiguity in his final estimate of her position on earth, and that in his design for the novel she represented only one limited touchstone for the reality of Saumur.

Notes

1. After speculating about the glory Grandet might have found if he had exercised his gifts in a larger realm, Balzac notes that he might also have amounted to nothing beyond Saumur: "Peut-être en est-il des esprits comme de certains animaux, qui n'engendrent plus transplantés hors des climats où ils naissent" (1110). [Minds may share the fate of certain animals who stop engendering when transplanted out of the region in which they are born.] All translations are my own, and all page references are to the new Pléiade edition of *Eugénie Grandet*, ed. Nicole Mozet in *La Comédie Humaine*, ed. Pierre-Georges Castex, et al. (Paris: Gallimard, 1976) 3:989-1202, 1644-1748. References to other works by Balzac are to the same edition.

2. "La Véritable Eugénie Grandet," *Revue des Sciences Humaines,* ns 80 (1955): 437-58; cf. Mozet's introduction in the Pléiade edition.

3. Cf. Mozet's introduction in the Pléiade edition. See also Castex's note in the "Classiques Garnier" edition of *Eugénie Grandet* (Paris: Garnier, 1965) 266 and Pierrot's note in Balzac, *Letters à Madame Hanska* (Paris: Bibliophiles de l'originale, 1968) 2:193.

4. In 1833, Balzac is in the midst of a period of intense illuminist concern; see: Lucienne Frappier-Mazur, "Balzac et les images 'reparaissantes': Lumière et flamme dans *La Comédie humaine,*" *Revue des Sciences Humaines,* ns 121 (1966): 45-80. Editors usually call attention to Balzac's enthusiasm during this time for the Virgin and angels of the sculptor Bra, to which he himself attributes the inspiration for *Séraphita*; see the letter to Mme Hanska of November 20 and December 1, 1833, the latter being the date on which he sent her the manuscript of *Eugénie Grandet.*

5. *Les Discours du cliché* (Paris: Société d'édition d'enseignement supérieur, 1982) 62-63, 65.

6. *Balzac et la religion* (Paris: Boivin, 1942) 82n.

7. Naomi Schor offers an excellent feminist/Freudian analysis of Eugénie's compromise with the world as a melancholic solution in *Breaking the Chain: Women, Theory, and French Realist Fiction* (New York: Columbia UP, 1985), 90-107. She unfortunately offers only in a note and does not develop

her claim that the dedication "A Maria" places the novel "under the sign of Mariolatry" and "serves as a matrix, a master signifier of the fiction" (176 n 18).

8. "Hoarders and Spendthrifts in 'La Comédie Humaine,'" *Modern Language Review* 61 (1966): 33.

9. See the Castex "Introduction" xx.

Nicolae Babuts (essay date fall-winter 1993-94)

SOURCE: Babuts, Nicolae. "Baudelaire in the Circle of Exiles: A Study of 'Le Cygne.'" *Nineteenth-Century French Studies* 22, nos. 1 & 2 (fall-winter 1993-94): 123-38.

[*In the following essay, Babuts concentrates on the allegorical representation of exile in Charles Baudelaire's poem, "Le Cygne," asserting that this mode of representation "cannot be confined to the rhetorical level" and is "best understood in the context of its mnemonic origins."*]

Despite various approaches that explore different facets of the poem and several formulas for defining its theme,[1] there is a broad critical consensus that "Le Cygne" is about a form of exile. This circumstance in itself appears to be encouraging, since even implicit agreements of this kind are hard to come by. However, within the general interpretive harmony, to the extent that it exists, many questions about the constitution and significance of the poem's exile remain. In looking at the poem from a cognitive point of view, I argue that the nature of allegory and the manner in which it comes into existence are indifferent neither to the poet's conception of exile nor to the built-in perspective of loss. I indicate in what sense the allegorical mode of exile cannot be confined to the rhetorical level and why it would be best understood in the context of its mnemonic origins.

"Le Cygne" takes shape and substance through a series of dynamic patterns or allegories, each of which illustrates and defines in its own way, the dominant idea of exile. The poem begins and ends within the anaphoric structure erected by "je pense à," "acting," as Leakey so aptly puts it, "as the hinge on which all else turns" (44). And of course, in dedicating the work to Hugo, using, in his letter of dedication, the same terms, "en pensant à vous,"[2] Baudelaire has placed his allegory under the tutelage of the older poet, who, by 1859 in the eyes of Baudelaire's contemporaries, must have appeared as the epitome of exile. Hugo is present in the world of the poem as an ex-officio consultant.[3]

In addition to their status as exiles, and in a more subtle way, what the main figures of the poem have in common is their refusal to submit to the new reality that op-

presses them and distorts their aspirations. The fact that in the poet's state of mind, his melancholy, nothing has changed points to an unwillingness to accept the new circumstances. This stubborn resistance appears at once as a gift, a capacity to transform everything into allegory, and as a tragic flaw, a source of inadaptability and suffering. Indeed the exiles are surrounded by a fatal ambiguity of perspective. Love of their native land, dedication to the past, and consciousness of predetermination are proof of their essential and unique nobility—a concept that, like "la noblesse unique" of "Bénédiction," draws its prestige from the vast well of romantic sensibility.[4] But caught up in the struggle against the unyielding material reality, they turn awkward and foolish. While the oneness of their aspirations brings them to the point of ultimate longing and spiritual ecstasy, the tension of the struggle distorts them, rendering them physically convulsive and, as Christine Crow says about the swan, "half-deranged."[5]

This ambiguity of perspective also produces an irony of illusion. In speaking about the role of the "Simoïs menteur" in the poem, Hampton has accurately seen that the connotation of deception in 'falsi,' only tangential to Virgil, becomes the central concern in Baudelaire" (442). The irony is that the gestures of the exiles continue to be appropriate to a reality that, though having a hypnotic grip on their mental outlook, though dominating their entire metaphoric field, is no longer "present" in the outside world. The idea of "absences" has led Hubert to conclude: "Il s'opère ainsi un renversement de toutes les valeurs. Le néant, l'absence deviennent la réalité suprême. . . ."[6] Yet such is the paradox of literary forms that it would be misleading to equate the lake, the empty tomb, and Africa with "nothingness" because they are images of real entities, forms that the communion with the past takes. As images of absent things or beings they cannot and must not be confused with the existential face of emptiness. The image of an absence is not the same as that absence itself. The perspective has to be defined. Thus from the reader's point of view a description of a loss is not a loss. Even from Baudelaire's or Andromache's point of view, the concept of absence is not wholly negative, for we have no way of dealing with reality except through the perceptual and mnemonic relations established in our brain circuitry. As soon as we engage reality, as soon as we perform an act of cognition or thought, the amount of energy channeled into cerebral action transforms absence and the pain of absence into a plenitude of images and dynamic patterns. Not that the pain disappears; but metaphoric thought emerges as a presence that is at the opposite pole of the void. A true existential void can only occur in the absence of images. As such, it is unstable, because as soon as the mind is aware of it, it becomes not a void but a knowledge of a void.

In spite of this essential cognitive factor, the idea of allegory "as a void" appears to have held its ground. Following Benjamin whose definition he quotes, de Man sees "allegory as a void 'that signifies precisely the non-being of what it represents.'"[7] Their view situates the problem of interpreting the allegories that are at the core of the poem's identity on epistemological grounds. It involves not only our understanding of the operation of allegory but also our whole approach to the production or creation of meaning. Allegory as a formal category has acquired, with time, a wide range of definitions, from the old idea of a prolonged metaphor to the latest postmodernist attempts to see it in opposition to the symbol. Owens identifies it "as the domain of the arbitrary, the conventional, the unmotivated";[8] and Wing offers this succinct definition: Allegory "relays meaning from one semantic level to another, within a limited polyvalence."[9] While aware that allegory has been unfairly discredited by clumsy painters ("Le Poème du hachisch," 1: 430), Baudelaire nevertheless holds it in high esteem. And in describing the possible effects of hashish on an ideal subject, in "Le Poème du hachisch" (1: 430-31), he makes no formal distinction between allegory and symbol.

From the point of view adopted here allegory is simply a subspecies of metaphoric thought and of literary forms in general. And it appears that de Man sees it in the same light, for the attributes he assigns to allegory are simply the virtues of all literature raised to a higher intensity or power. He defines literature in terms that are similar to his definition of allegory: "Poetic language names this void [Rousseau's "unexplainable void"] with ever-renewed understanding, and, like Rousseau's longing, it never tires of naming it again. This persistent naming is what we call literature" (*Blindness* 18). Moreover, "literature bears little resemblance to perception" and "originates in the void that separates intent from reality" (*Blindness* 34). The differences, then, center around the issue of the historical dimension of literary forms and the epistemological choice between two categorially opposed understandings: Does the synchronic moment that constitutes the final form of an allegory or poem have an origin in a mnemonic experience or does it appear from the void in an arbitrary movement of self-reflexiveness? Our interpretation of the text will not be unaffected by our answer.

De Man maintains that there should be a divorce between reality and literature, between the existential project and the depth of allegory.[10] He believes that in saying "tout pour moi devient allégorie," Baudelaire describes "the loss of reality that marks the beginning of poetic states of mind" (*Blindness* 35). Yet the poet does not say that the old Parisian landscape has been lost *for him,* but that he sees it in his mind only: "je ne vois qu'en esprit. . . ." The images of new palaces and old suburbs, once formulated, are not lost, do not symbol-

ize a void, but become effective functional entities within the structural pattern of the poem itself. The allegories that follow do not erase their function. Instead of being displaced, reality becomes origin and background.

The realistic details, the "prosaisms" of the third stanza, which may surprise some critics, are necessary to the authenticity of the allegorical experience. Neither allegory nor literature in general can function without a link to the *perception* of reality. The power to refer and the capacity to draw perceptual elements within its precincts are the sign's most fundamental attributes. The allegorical figures themselves avoid becoming symbols of nothingness and poetic absence through their high degree of perceptual clarity. The swan, who "was vigorously bathing his wings in the dust," is at once, on the dynamic and the visual level, stylized, refined, symbolic, but also strikingly realistic. It is almost as if the dust of the dry gutter has been transformed by the alchemy of language into a medium other than water, but a medium capable of recalling water and everything that water represents. The perceptual clarity of poetic vision is not peripheral but central to the creation of meaning. For although the reader can grasp the irony of the swan's gesture even without a great deal of perceptual information, a knowledge of the behavior of some birds—a sparrow bathing in the dust, for example—enhances the communicative effectiveness of the image. The whole thrust of the allegory of the swan is achieved only when its dynamic pattern is perceptually re-created in memory. Cognition and communication are geared to the interaction between language and perception. Denying the value of this interaction can only lead to an artificial alienation from our cognitive capacities.[11] Baudelaire has taken precautions, a number of indispensable realistic details, like "webbed feet," and "tramping in the mud," in order to show that allegory rises from the bed of everyday reality. And the power of Baudelaire's poem comes, in part, from the tension between the material and visionary realities. It comes not from allegory alone but precisely from the manner in which allegory begins to differentiate itself from reality and to oppose it.

Other texts show that allegory cannot function without the support of reality or of the perception of reality. Figure and ontological background are inextricably linked and one detaches itself from the other not simply as a newly created form contrasting with the primordial chaos but rather as a fully armed figure pointing to the placenta of the real. The fact that an intimate association and exchange of values between allegory and reality are inevitable may explain the affinity that exists between "Le Cygne" and Saint-Amant's poem, "Les Visions," in which the seventeenth-century poet recounts a predicament similar to Baudelaire's:

Le coeur plein d'amertume et l'ame ensevelie
Dans la plus sombre humeur de la melancolie. . . .[12]

Saint-Amant explains that the beauty of the Tuileries Gardens only increases his "cruel tourment" (87). His state of mind and the correspondences involved in it function in a way that is comparable to Baudelaire's poem. The sight of the Tuileries feeds Saint-Amant's anguish just as the sight of the Carrousel and the urban changes stimulate Baudelaire's melancholy. Above all, both poets have the dangerous gift of transforming the everyday, the present, reality into the allegorical forces of the world of imagination. Baudelaire writes:

Paris change! mais rien dans ma mélancolie
N'a bougé! palais neufs, échafaudages, blocs,
Vieux faubourgs, tout pour moi devient allégorie,
Et mes chers souvenirs sont plus lourds que des rocs.

Aussi devant ce Louvre une image m'opprime:
Je pense à mon grand cygne, avec ses gestes fous,
Comme les exilés, ridicule et sublime,
Et rongé d'un désir sans trêve! et puis à vous,

Andromaque. . . .

And Saint-Amant before him:

Si j'y rencontre un cerf, ma triste fantaisie
De la mort d'Actéon est tout soudain saisie;
Les cygnes qu'on y void dans un paisible estang
Me semblent des corbeaux qui nagent dans du sang;
.

Le Louvre, dont l'éclat se fait si bien parestre,
N'est à mes yeux troublez qu'un chasteau de Bicestre;
Le fleuve qui le borde est à moy l'Acheron. . . .
.

O belle Polixene! amante infortunée!

Each poet has a feeling that his imagination has been taken over by a certain melancholy whose influence cannot be shaken off. The effect of this uncontrollable force is to set in motion an interaction between the creative principle and everyday reality whose very familiarity has suddenly become a source of unexpected allegories and revelations. What is striking is that in Saint-Amant's poem the process by which reality is transformed into vision is univocal and therefore more evident. In "Le Cygne" the transition between the two perceptual moments, the initial stimulus and the immediate, almost synesthetic transformation, being elaborated in a post-perceptual moment in memory is more complex and at times imperceptible. But the possibility of this elaboration is prepared by memory's awareness that the transition is already subsumed in Saint-Amant and therefore in tradition. In this sense Baudelaire benefited from his familiarity with the dynamics of the metaphoric field in "Les Visions." The fact that both poems contain references to the Louvre and to swans

indicates that these images may have constituted part of Baudelaire's mnemonic potentials. The two women, Polyxena and Andromache, are sisters-in-law and sisters in misfortune. The first, daughter of Priam and Hecuba, was unlucky in love, having been sacrificed to appease the ghost of Achilles, who had loved her, and unfortunate in her posthumous fame, since François de Molière, the man who celebrated her life, was assassinated apparently before the completion of his romance.[13] The second, Hector's wife, lost her husband, was carried into captivity by Pyrrhus, and eventually had to marry Helenus, himself a slave. What is significant from the point of view of memory is not this logical parallelism, but the fact that both heroines belong to a legendary past, one that had already been glorified by other writers, François de Molière and Virgil respectively. The functional similarity of the apostrophes to the two legendary women implies that memory favors certain rhetorical paths. My claim is not that there is a similarity between two wholes, since Saint-Amant's long, diffuse and sometimes rambling visions differ in impact from Baudelaire's rich, highly condensed, and polyvalent allegories. The concept of the poet's identification with the allegorical figures, fundamental in "Le Cygne," is lacking in "Les Visions." Instead of operating on a symbolic level, Saint-Amant's pity for François de Molière assumes an overt form. And his sympathy for Polyxena does not appear to play a central role. What I am saying is that somewhat in the manner of Lévi-Strauss's handyman ("bricoleur"), tinkerer or maker of myths, memory accumulates appealing images, materials that can then be reshaped and used again.

Far from being symbols for the nothingness or loss of reality that are supposed to have preceded the creative enterprise, the images in the newly founded order of poetry represent a remarkable concentration of spiritual energy. As critics have shown and as Baudelaire himself has acknowledged, many of these images come from various literary sources.[14] A study of possible influences confirms what at this point most people will be willing to grant, namely, that a Baudelaire poem is not a simple recording of a remembrance but a vast synthesis of elements derived from both real life and literary sources. Regardless of their origin, they have been re-created in memory, often stylized, and brought together in a fertile proximity, where each could gain value from the other, each interact and transform the other in the unity of their meaning. They are neither raw elements of the outside reality nor pure rhetorical constructs but rather patterns of a mnemonic reality and as such fit Baudelaire's definition of *"toute la nature"* (*Salon de 1859*, 2: 620). They become correspondences not between an actual swan and the historic Andromache, but between two dynamic patterns in memory, two echoes that answer each other in the clarity of the poem.

Thus the formal order may not reflect the sequence of events that led from the first impulse to the actual writing of the poem. For once the correspondences are within the tension of the metaphoric field, the poet has it in his power to present them in any order he wishes. The resistance that the poem offers to any attempt to decipher its point of departure has not escaped notice. Chambers rightly believes that all three candidates, the new Carrousel, Andromache, and the swan, have equal claim to be considered point of origin, and that the beginning of the poem skillfully mixes them.[15] Houston astutely points out that the "complexity of these relations between Carrousel Square, the swan, and Andromache depends on the order in which they are introduced."[16] Baudelaire begins with an apostrophe to Andromache and indicates that the thought of the illusory stream filled with her tears suddenly impregnated his memory. However, at first unaware of the real link between the new Carrousel and Andromache, a reader remains in suspense. The title itself is not an explanation. It is only in the second stanza of the second part that the poet openly specifies, what appears to be, the chronological sequence of correspondences: Louvre (Carrousel Square)—the swan—Andromache. Yet there is no decisive proof: This sequence could be valid only for a second crossing of the Carrousel Square. Moreover, as we have seen, literary sources, Virgil and Saint-Amant in particular, have at least a partial claim to be called point of departure. And since Andromache is well known to readers, the best justification for the initial reference to her is not chronological but strategic: It is part of a formal order designed to control the opening of the readers' mnemonic potentials.

The central critical issue remains: What is the identity and the dominant urgency of the poem's metaphoric field? We have seen that one of the characteristics that binds the exiled figures is their refusal to submit without protest to a brutal reality. They keep searching for their lost heritage, the native lake, the native river, the native land and trees, the nourishing breast. In time, the past of those in exile grows and fills their present. From a cognitive point of view, the swan cannot bring itself to trade the exalted knowledge of the past for the harsh reality of the present, for the simple reason that the vision of the native lake is now part of its mnemonic potentials and rejecting it would be tantamount to a mutilation of its faculty of seeing. The black woman is no less eloquent in her refusal to submit to the exigencies of her new situation. Knowing well that the Parisian fog cannot contain her native Africa, she lets the palm-trees she carries in memory fill her haggard eyes. Through this act she reaffirms her refusal to submit to a reality that would condition her to deny the past state of grace. Normal vision has to integrate mnemonic potentials and outside stimuli; but the difficulty here is that the values imprinted in the mnemonic potential sequences clash with the afferent signals. This conflict,

which is characteristic of the state of exile, has thus brought about two related consequences: suffering and a heightening of the plenitude of memory. Those who suffer are portrayed as sucking the she-wolf Sorrow, and by that act are transformed into demi-gods. Distress and overstrength of memory lead to the dawn of allegory and myth.

The poet's affinity with those who are exiled, who have lost husband and country, who have lost their life sustaining substance, goes beyond mere sympathy for the underdog, for the defeated. For when he writes, "Ainsi dans la forêt où mon esprit s'exile," the poet places himself in the circle of his characters. He becomes one of them. So much so that in a passage of remarkable perspicuity, Mauron can state: "Ainsi les trois «pauvres» du *Cygne,* avec la foule des exilés, participent du même égocentrisme. Ils ne sont pas Baudelaire, mais mêlés à lui, en une confusion du moi et du non-moi. . . ."[17]

Baudelaire has secured this right not because his inheritance had been taken away from his direct control, though biographical factors undoubtedly played their role, but because he saw himself, in "Bénédiction" and "L'Albatros" for example, as a poet and consequently as a marked man. A marked man and, in a figurative way, a widowed woman. For Baudelaire, as a figural representation of the androgynous poet, does tend to acquire a feminine aura, the majesty of Andromache in mourning. The same alchemy reverses the flow of attributes and endows Andromache with the moral grandeur of an epic hero.[18] It is no accident that Baudelaire had praised Emma Bovary for the fact that, in creating her, Flaubert had to become woman and at the same time had to infuse "un sang viril dans les veines de sa créature" ("Critique littéraire," 2: 81). If Andromache had willingly consented to marry Pyrrhus or Helenus, she would have lost the capacity for covalent bonding characteristic of the circle of exiles. In refusing to give her full assent, she moves toward the opposite pole of a "natural" woman and becomes the ancient equivalent of the Baudelairian dandy.

Because they have literary origins, the exiles can facilitate his entry into the land of his true heritage, the domain of poetry and myth. And the desire to find them and identify them as tutelary fellow sufferers is unending and is reflected in other poems and passages. Thus certain ideal couples emerge: Faust and Marguerite in "Sonnet d'automne," Oreste and Électre in "Le Voyage," and in the dedication of "Les Paradis artificiels." It is clear that to join this aristocracy of sorrow, the poet has to pay a price, involving a period of initiation through suffering and degradation, and a perilous stage of bewilderment. The latter is more evident in the swan's frantic gestures and in the black woman's disorientation. Andromache herself, though not moving, is

"en extase courbée," and has lost her perception of time and place. Those who suck the she-wolf sorrow suggest the legendary twins, whose mother was imprisoned and who had to survive the stage of being set adrift on the Tiber. Although the legend itself is not fully actualized in the poem, the she-wolf image is strong enough to prepare the image of the forest that follows.[19]

In a sense then "Le Cygne" is a parable for the poet's spiritual ascent to the world of memory and a parallel to the dynamics of the creative act. The exiles themselves are engaged in a ritual that consecrates the mnemonic values of myth. The creation of a mythical world is at once the means that enables the poet to transcend everyday misery, humiliation, and suffering, and a goal, the finding of his rightful place and the founding of a new city for a category of beings to which he can belong. Although he believes that in "Le Cygne" the act of thought cannot stop "en un point quelconque où se ferait enfin *le* sens," Chambers has clearly seen that there is a struggle to construct meaning and that the space where it occurs is "ce domaine des signes auquel s'identifie 'je'" ("'Je' dans les 'Tableaux parisiens,'" 65 and 62). It is the ultimate search for meaning.

Most critics would probably agree with this assessment. The disagreement appears to center on the inference one can draw from it. In a remarkably well-written book, Wing looks at "Le Cygne" and concludes: "Each allegorical figure reiterates the impossibility of retrieving a lost origin; the loss which is allegorized here is that which is always already absent. The object ('ce qui ne se retrouve jamais . . .'), moreover, is not easily compensated for by the language that figures its displacement, for language is here powerless to restore the plenitude of an original presence" (*The Limits,* 15). In his major premise Wing accurately describes the predicament of the allegorical figures: They cannot retrieve their native lake or country. Yet although their displacement and suffering are central, what is allegorized is not so much the absent object itself but a dynamic and moral stance, a profession of fierce dedication to the memory of one's own myth, a nostalgic counterinsurgency to forestall the outside reality's subversion of the mnemonic potentials, and a reaffirmation of the inalienable right to claim the endowment of one's origin. Therein lies the plenitude of the allegorical mode. Even critics who see allegory, in contradistinction to symbolic language, as "decentered" writing, willingly recognize the positive aspect of loss. In speaking about Baudelaire's women in mourning and about Andromache in particular, Stamelman writes: "All of their being is concentrated so perfectly, so intently, and so totally on the death, which has given them their identity as widows, that this loss appears as fullness."[20] Indeed it is uncertain that "le beau lac natal" and "la superbe Afrique," though unarguably real, were ever as fraught with meaning as they are now in the perspective of

loss. Signification arises at the crest of the backward look; the quality and value of the past are determined in the act of creating it anew.

The allegory of the swan encompasses several perspectives and becomes a model of the dynamics of observation. First, the poet becomes narrator and introduces himself in the textual relations. As narrator he invites the reader to adopt his point of view; but it is obvious from the variety of readings that the latter does not always fully comply. One has thus a poet observing a swan and the reader observing the observer. And just as Baudelaire, in interpreting the swan's longing for its native lake, reads into the image his own thirst for an edenic beauty and harmony with his environment, so too readers will read into the poet's statement their own desires and needs.

The complexity of the relations of the central dynamic pattern to the various points of view makes it imperative to specify the perspective of loss. For a fundamental difference arises between a loss I myself experience and a loss I witness or hear about. In projecting his own moral exile into the allegorical dimension, Baudelaire shifts the point of view and transfers the burden of meaning from an outright confession to the dynamics of the projection itself. This strategy is designed not only, and not primarily, to communicate a loss but also, and more importantly, to enable the poet to identify himself with other beings who suffer on a stage that has now become universal. This capacity radiates in the depth of his involvement, in the tenderness of his loyalty, and in the solemnity of his tone. The poem bears the marks of a powerful catharsis at work. Interpreting Baudelaire's allegory as a void goes not only against Aristotle's insight but also against every indication we have about the way an individual responds to the report of a loss. The emotions characteristic of the theater and of art in general are modulated by both a distancing, a separation from the suffering individual, and a bond that unites spectator and tragic hero or heroine in a realization of their kinship. On the one hand, through separation, pity, fear and their allied responses are purified of the raw violence that accompanies a direct loss; and on the other hand, through kinship recognition, they are strengthened and endowed with the capacity for spiritual renewal. It is worth noting that distancing plays a role in Andromache's illusion. The scene of her mourning before an empty tomb can be defined in terms of a contrast with a possible scene of mourning before Hector's real grave (Homer speaks of such a grave at the end of the Iliad). From the reader's point of view the fact that the grave itself is not "real" can be a source of irony and pity. But Andromache may welcome the mock ritual as a way, far less painful because of the distance from a real lamentation, to attain the level of the cathartic process, a relief of the weight of memory, and thus a state of "extase."

In a fine comparison between Hugo's allegorical narrative and Baudelaire's allegory in "Le Cygne," Nash speaks of "the swan's or Andromaque's nostalgic dreaming" and adds: "Poetic language with its dizzying, infinitely allusive character signifies for Baudelaire man's state of permanent exile within the pure temporality of impermanence."[21] And there is little doubt that Baudelaire viewed exile as a permanent state. Yet in the perspective of the Baudelairian venture, exile, though indeed a fall, is a condition which confers upon the poet his exalted moral character. It is through exile that Hugo, Andromache, and the swan gained their unmatched prestige. And some form of exile, whether it be physical or moral, is a *sine qua non* of the path to transcendence. However, from a critical standpoint the path is linked to the conviction that language has referential power. For transcendence is conceivable only in a world in which language flows beyond its self-reflexive level. A valuable testimony comes from a contemporary French poet, Bonnefoy, who stresses the consequence of the referential function in the poem: "Baudelaire ne crée pas cette Andromaque, il «pense» à elle, et cela signifie qu'il y a de l'être hors de la conscience. . . ."[22] Andromache is both a dynamic pattern within the metaphoric field of the poem and a figure in referential space, that is to say, one that represents each reader's potential for a legendary Andromache. The appeal of Baudelaire's heroine comes in part from the tension between the two potentialities.

The possibility of transcendence is also linked to the redemptive power of language. There is no explicit statement in the poem to clarify Baudelaire's beliefs. Elsewhere, however, notably in the "Hygiène" fragments, he extolled the therapeutic value of work, that is to say, of writing. But even without that evidence, it would be difficult to conceive a poet who dedicates his life to the creation of literary forms and yet who labors under the impression that their worth in themselves is not also worth to him and to the reader. I am reminded here of Dylan Thomas's note to his poems: "I read somewhere," he writes, "of a shepherd who, when asked why he made, from within fairy rings, ritual observances to the moon to protect his flocks, replied: 'I'd be a damn' fool if I didn't!'" and then adds: "These poems, with all their crudities, doubts, and confusions, are written for the love of Man and in praise of God, and I'd be a damn' fool if they weren't."[23]

In one way it is possible to call the allegory of the swan an attempt to find a moral hygiene that would be effective in blunting the obsession of a poetic undertaking constantly subverted by the forces of "spleen" or to consider it an aesthetic door to salvation. In another way, it is the putting into practice of a formula Baudelaire already held, when he declared: "Dans certains états de l'âme presque surnaturels, la profondeur de la vie se révèle tout entière dans le spectacle, si ordinaire

qu'il soit, qu'on a sous les yeux. Il en devient le symbole" ("Fusées," 1: 659). This passage, expressing one of the most significant of Baudelaire's theoretical beliefs, asserts not only that the mind has the capacity to create a symbolic plenitude in the midst of the ordinariness of the outside reality, but also that meaning offers itself to the intuitive grasp in an epiphanic moment. A symbol or an allegory thus becomes an open manifestation within the heart of reality not apart from it. It does not point indirectly to a value, and much less to a void; rather, it is itself meaning and value. The swan does not stand as a screen between the reader and a hidden or mysterious exile; it is itself the painful face of exile emerging from the shadow of ordinariness into the full light of dynamic equilibrium and visual clarity.

The ending of the poem makes it evident that the formula "je pense à" performs a scrolling function of memory. It allows the poet to focus his attention on each window of a long, potentially endless, series of representative figures. However, once he enters the level of allegory, the image of the swan begins to oppress him ("une image m'opprime") and he is unable to shake off its existential implications. He becomes subject to a tension between the desire for meaning that exacts closure and the kinetic energy of the allegorical mode. The relentless forward movement of allegories cannot be easily arrested. Wing speaks of "the possibilities of language to add new, ultimately endless symbols of humans' displacement from both world and language" ("Exile from Within," 742), and Chambers concurs in describing the process as a drift from equivalence to equivalence ("'Je' dans les 'Tableaux,'" 65). This drift in the paradigmatic mode of exile leads from the urban setting to the forest with the potential for a multiplicity of symbols. In the face of such a potential, Baudelaire's formal ending may turn out to be not "un manque de souffle," as Proust suggests,[24] but, rather surprisingly, a form of yielding in the face of abundance, not poverty, but necessity of restraint, the giddying fear of being overwhelmed by the momentum of the onward scrolling movement of memory.

"Le Cygne" represents one of Baudelaire's most ambitious attempts to explore his condition and define his identity. By the seriousness of its tone and almost religious solemnity of its development, the poem recalls "Bénédiction." In the latter, Baudelaire has analyzed the poet's destiny in direct terms, terms that are commensurate with the traditional romantic (Balzacian in particular) conception of the malediction of the poet, while in "Le Cygne" he turns to the allegorical mode. In both poems the dangerous gift of poetry or allegory comes with the milk of suffering. In both, it is suffering that sets the poet apart. It is, however, significant that in the later poem, at a distance of several years, the distress of the exiles has intensified. The clarity of vision has replaced the poet's moral serenity. It is also clear

that the exiles do not seek to escape their plight by adaptation, but direct their efforts toward reliving the dream of the past, turning their faces to the dawn of memory. Yet it would be inexact to say that they have chosen their destinies. In "Bénédiction," where the poet is "L'Enfant déshérité," there is no hint of a choice. And certainly the condition of exile, in which the swan, Andromache, and the black woman find themselves, is not a reflection of their freedom. Their refusal to submit to the new order is the extent of their action and the mnemonic mode is the measure of their freedom. In the world of exile, if action is not sister to the dream, memory is.

Notes

1. Critics define the theme in a variety of ways. For Lowry Nelson, Jr. "It is *the* memory the poem is about. . . ." "Baudelaire and Virgil: A Reading of 'Le Cygne,'" *Comparative Literature* 13 (Fall 1961): 344. Bernard Weinberg supposes "that the central emotion to be aroused within the poem is one of sorrow." *The Limits of Symbolism: Studies of Five Modern French Poets* (Chicago: University of Chicago Press, 1966) 32. Victor Brombert sees in the larger sense of the poem "le drame de la culture elle-même, drame fondé sur la dialectique de la dissolution et de la continuité." "'Le Cygne' de Baudelaire: Douleur, Souvenir, Travail," in *Études Baudelairiennes* 3, Hommage à W. T. Bandy (Neuchatel: À la Baconnière, 1973) 261. F. W. Leakey describes the theme in terms of exile, "irrecoverable loss," and alienation. "The Originality of Baudelaire's 'Le Cygne': Genesis as Structure and Theme," in *Order and Adventure in Post-Romantic French Poetry,* Essays presented to C. A. Hackett, ed. E. M. Beaumont, J. M. Cocking, and J. Cruickshank (New York: Barnes & Nobles, 1973) 47. Ross Chambers distinguishes three motifs, which come together to define the theme of exile: "motifs du 'souvenir,' de la 'mélancolie,' enfin du 'désir.'" "'Je' dans les 'Tableaux Parisiens' de Baudelaire," *Nineteenth-Century French Studies* 9 (Fall-Winter 1980-81): 63. Timothy Hampton believes that Baudelaire's opposition to Virgil, on a historical level, is reflected in the poem's tendency toward "rhetorical decentralization and myth." "Virgil, Baudelaire and Mallarmé at the Sign of the Swan: Poetic Translation and Historical Allegory," *Romantic Review* 73 (Nov. 1982): 446. Nathaniel Wing defines the poem's allegories of exile as "endless symbols of humans' displacement from both world and language." "Exile from Within, Exile from Without," in *A New History of French Literature,* ed. Denis Hollier (Cambridge, MA: Harvard UP, 1989) 742. And Richard Burton explains: "Beneath its manifest theme of exile, ['Le Cygne'] is a poem about the making, unmaking and re mak-

ing of cities—Troy, Rome, Paris—and the parallel making of a poetic text: itself." Calling it "an anti-*Aeneid,*" he adds: "it portrays History not as an ascending curve but as a relentless downward spiral with cities following one upon the other in endless sequence, each imitating its predecessor in a de based, parodic manner. . . ." *Baudelaire in 1859: A Study in the Sources of Poetic Creativity* (Cambridge: Cambridge UP, 1988) 149-50 and 152.

2. Charles Baudelaire, *Œuvres complètes,* ed. Claude Pichois, Pléiade, 2 vols (Paris: Gallimard, 1975-1976) 1: 1007. All Baudelaire quotations are from this edition.

3. Others have been impressed by the dedication. Burton describes it as a gesture of humility: "It is, therefore, as an absent tutelary deity or spiritual father-figure that Baudelaire, a neophyte seeking initiation into the fraternity of au thentic poets, invokes the name of Victor Hugo at the beginning of 'Le Cygne.'" Richard D. Burton, *The Context of Baudelaire's* Le Cygne (Kendal, Eng.: University of Durham, 1980) 18. Wing, on the other hand, interprets it as an act of daring: "In dedicating 'Le Cygne' to Hugo, Baudelaire is addressing poetry itself," and "is in one sense daring to rival Hugo on his own ground." And the effect is remarkable: "In dedicating three of these texts [in "Tableaux parisiens"] to Hugo, Baudelaire produces complex ambiguities that dramatically underscore the collision between the dominant poetic tradition, represented by Hugo, and the 'new shock' ('le frisson nouveau') produced by *Les fleurs*" ("Exile from Within," 742).

4. Vast but also more specific. Crépet and Blin's edition of *Les Fleurs du mal* (Paris: Corti, 1942), and Antoine Adam's edition of *Les Fleurs du mal* (Paris: Garnier Frères, 1961) offer several "rapprochements" between "Bénédiction" and two Balzac novels *L'Enfant maudit* and *Séraphîta,* which stress, respectively, the ideas of malediction and apotheosis. The two works contain images and seminal ideas that influenced, profoundly I believe, the development of the metaphoric field of "Bénédiction."

5. Christine Crow, "'Le silence au vol de cygne': Baudelaire, Mallarmé, Valéry and the Flight of the Swan," in *Baudelaire, Mallarmé, Valéry: New Essays in Honour of Lloyd Austin,* ed. Malcolm Bowie, Alison Fairlie, and Alison Finch (Cambridge, Eng.: Cambridge UP, 1982) 2.

6. Judd D. Hubert, *L'Esthétique des* Fleurs du mal: *Essai sur l'ambiguïté poétique* (Geneva: Cailler, 1953) 100.

7. Paul de Man, *Blindness and Insight: Essays in the Rhetoric of Contemporary Criticism* (New York:

Oxford UP, 1971) 35. For a discussion of the function of allegory see de Man, "Pascal's Allegory of Persuasion," in *Allegory and Representation: Selected Papers from the English Institute, 1979-80,* ed. Stephen J. Greenblatt (Baltimore: Johns Hopkins UP, 1981), and in the same volume Greenblatt's preface, pp. vii-viii and Joel Fineman's "The Structure of Allegorical Desire," 26-60.

8. Craig Owens, "The Allegorical Impulse: Toward a Theory of Postmodernism," *October* 12 (Spring 1980): 83.

9. Nathaniel Wing, *The Limits of Narrative: Essays on Baudelaire, Flaubert, Rimbaud and Mallarmé* (Cambridge, Eng.: Cambridge UP, 1986) 9.

10. *Blindness,* 35. Elsewhere de Man insists that "the referential function of language is not being denied." *The Resistance to Theory,* vol. 33 of *Theory and History of Literature* (Minneapolis: Univ. of Minnesota Press, 1986) 11. He acknowledges that Mallarmé's key symbols "never entirely lose contact with the concrete reality from which they spring." "Intentional Structure of the Romantic Image," *The Rhetoric of Romanticism* (New York: Columbia UP, 1984) 9. Yet this recognition comes in an attempt to show the existence of two kinds of imaginations. Otherwise, seeing no inconsistency, he wastes no occasion to relegate the referential function of language to the domain of the irrelevant. In her analysis of de Man's dispute with Derrida, Suzanne Gearhart confirms this tendency: "Thus, according to de Man, Rousseau's conception of metaphor of necessity implies a critique of the notion that language is in essence referential and of the correlative notion that language has an origin." "Philosophy Before Literature: Deconstruction, Historicity, and the Work of Paul de Man," *Diacritics* 13 (Winter 1983): 76.

11. For a critique of the "purely verbal view of language," see Robert Scholes, *Textual Power: Literary Theory and the Teaching of English* (New Haven: Yale UP, 1985) 109. Alexander Gelley, while still under de Man's influence, while somewhat overemphasizing "the systematic disjunction between pictorial and semantic modes in the apprehension of texts," is nevertheless able, in the following sentence, to underscore the fundamental role of perceptual data: "It should not be overlooked that we ourselves, as readers of fiction, have to a considerable extent been fashioned by a mimetic representational system, a system that is bound up with an ocular model of reception." *Narrative Crossings: Theory and Pragmatics of Prose Fiction* (Baltimore: Johns Hopkins UP, 1987) 18. George Lakoff and Mark Johnson feel "*that no metaphor can ever be comprehended or even adequately represented independently of its experien-*

tial basis." *Metaphors We Live By* (Chicago: University of Chicago Press, 1980) 19. And Mark Turner writes: "The losses that accompany not knowing the connections between thought, knowledge, and language are too great for literary critical traditions to continue to sustain." *Death is the Mother of Beauty: Mind, Metaphor, and Criticism* (Chicago: University of Chicago Press, 1987) 9.

12. Antoine-Girard de Saint-Amant, *Œuvres complètes,* ed. Ch.-L. Livet, vol. (tome) 1 (Paris: Jannet, 1855) 83.

13. Livet explains in a note that François de Molière, sieur d'Essartine was assassinated in 1628, and that his work *Polyxene,* which came out in 1622, appears to have been completed. See Saint-Amant, 90, note 1.

14. Knowledge of Baudelaire's sources is necessarily imperfect and to a certain extent conjectural. But it would be a mistake to reject it out of hand. Accepting the relative value of intertextual evidence is already the beginning of an interpretation. With the reference to "l'homme d'Ovide," invoking, appropriately enough, a poet who was himself an exile, Baudelaire appears to sanction such a step. He also acknowledges his debt to Virgil in a note "sur les plagiats": "Virgile (tout le morceau d'*Andromaque*)" ("Projets de préface," 1: 184). For other possible reminiscences, see Jacques Crépet and Georges Blin, ed., *Les Fleurs du mal* (Paris: Corti, 1942) 449; Antoine Adam, ed., *Les Fleurs du mal* (Paris: Garnier Frères, 1961) 381-2; Pichois's Pléiade edition of *Oeuvres complètes* already cited; and Théophile Gautier, "Fantaisies d'hiver," *Poésies nouvelles* (Paris: Charpentier, 1863) 87. I have indicated in what way Baudelaire may have benefited from "Les Visions" by Saint-Amant. For an understanding of Baudelaire's relation to Virgil, Nelson's and Hampton's articles are a must. Andrew Bush maintains that "Baudelaire's unacknowledged and unpaid debt has been to Racine." "'Le Cygne' or 'El cisne': The History of a Misreading," *Comparative Literature Studies* 17 (Dec. 1980): 422. For a study of De Quincey's influence and for a view of the dynamic aspect of the "three central figures" in Baudelaire's poem, see John E. Gale, "De Quincey, Baudelaire, and 'Le Cygne,'" *Nineteenth-Century French Studies* 5 (Spring-Summer 1977): 296-307. Additional influences have been suggested. Robert Cargo believes that the image of the forgotten sailors may "have been borrowed from Hugo's *Oceano Nox.*" "A Further Look at Baudelaire's 'Le Cygne,'" *Romance Notes* 10 (1969): 277. And Weinberg thinks that the image of the horn may be "an allusion to Vigny's poem on Roland at Roncevaux" (12).

15. See Ross Chambers, "Mémoire et mélancolie," *Mélancolie et opposition: Les débuts du modernisme en France* (Paris: José Corti, 1987) 167-68.

16. John Porter Houston, *The Demonic Imagination: Style and Theme in French Romantic Poetry* (Baton Rouge: Louisiana State UP, 1969) 101. Keith H. Macfarlane explains: "Il faudra l'impulsion produite par l'éloquence du Simoïs menteur pour mettre en marche le processus mnémonique." "*Le Cygne* de Baudelaire: 'falsi simonentis ad undam,'" *L'Information Littéraire* 27 (1975): 142. Chambers specifies further: "C'est parce que le «je» sujet est désormais exilé dans le temps que le souvenir conjoint d'Andromaque et du cygne lui vient" ("Mémoire et mélancolie," 178). Houston speaks of "an elaborate tangle of unexpected analogies" (100). And P. Mansell Jones assumes "as model, a form of musical composition which is not characterized by common logic." *The Assault on French Literature and Other Essays* (1963; Westport, CT: Greenwood Press, 1976) 130.

17. Charles Mauron, *Le Dernier Baudelaire* (Paris: Corti, 1966) 81. Mauron demonstrates here greater flexibility (greater than in *Des Métaphores obsédantes au mythe personnel,* 1963) in his analysis of the relation between the poet and the main figures in "Le Cygne." He has been able to reach valuable insights, see especially 79-81.

18. Kaplan points out another resemblance between Baudelaire and Andromache: "Andromache herself appears as an artist who has constructed an emblem of her exile, the artificial Simois which reminds her nostalgically of fallen Troy." Edward K. Kaplan, "Baudelaire's Portrait of the Poet as Widow: Three Poëmes en Prose and 'Le Cygne,'" *Symposium* 34 (Fall 1980): 244.

19. For a fine assessment of the forest and horn call images see Leakey, 48-49.

20. Richard Stamelman, "The Shroud of Allegory: Death, Mourning, and Melancholy in Baudelaire's Work," *Texas Studies in Literature and Language* 25 (Fall 1983): 395.

21. Suzanne Nash, Les Contemplations *of Victor* Hugo: An Allegory of the Creative Process (Princeton, NJ: Princeton UP, 1976) 30.

22. Yves Bonnefoy, *L'Improbable* (Paris: Mercure de France, 1959) 160-61.

23. Dylan Thomas, *Collected Poems 1934-1952* (London: J. M. Dent, 1952) vii.

24. Following Proust, some critics have felt compelled to refer to the last line of the poem in disparaging terms. Hubert, one of the earliest, describes it as

"volontairement faible" (101). P. Mansell Jones calls the last phrase "casual," and adds: "One wonders whether a good poem has ever finished so effectively on so feeble a note—*à bien d'autres encor!*" (*Assault on French Literature,* 128). These opinions should be read in the light of Proust's belief that the ending of "Le Voyage," like that of "Le Cygne," "tourne court, tombe presque à plat." Proust adds: "C'est peut-être voulu, ces fins si simples. Il semble malgré tout qu'il y ait là quelque chose d'écourté, un manque de souffle." Marcel Proust, *Contre Sainte-Beuve,* ed. P. Clarac, Pléiade (Paris: Gallimard, 1971) 624. Proust's impression is no doubt authentic. Yet there are critics who view the ending in a different light. In affirming its power, Leakey writes: "There is certainly no 'feebleness' here, no 'fading away' or 'dying fall' . . . The final phrase, in short, compels attention, challenges and haunts the imagination; no other ending is imaginable, and none could serve to associate the reader more fully with the creative experience . . . (Leakey, 49-50). For another favorable interpretation of the last hemistich, see Macfarlane's article (cited in note 15), 144.

Kari Weil (essay date summer 1995)

SOURCE: Weil, Kari. "Romantic Exile and the Melancholia of Identification." *differences: A Journal of Feminist Cultural Studies* 7, no. 2 (summer 1995): 111-26.

[*In the following essay, Weil examines themes of melancholia and exile—both psychological and political—in Claire de Duras's* Ourika *and François-René Chateaubriand's* Réné.]

Alienation, marginality, exile—these are familiar topoi of Romantic literature in France. From the narrator of Rousseau's *Rêveries,* who finds both solace and a symbol for his alienation in the isolated island of Saint Pierre, to Baudelaire's "Le Cygne," whose captive otherness signifies both the psychic and semiotic struggle of the domestic exile of Paris's dispossessed, we find a persistent figuring of the margins as a place from which to consider and to attempt to negotiate the social, political, and psychological boundaries between self and other.

Contemporary theory too, under the influence of feminist and postcolonial inquiry, has focused much attention on marginalized voices in order to analyze, deconstruct, and decenter representations of the relations of power, and also to investigate the effects of marginalization and exile on identity and on the processes of identification. Recently, much attention has been paid to

what appears to be a shift in contemporary patterns of identification given the fact that conventionally undesirable subject positions have joined a widening range of objects of imitation. Theorists of performance have noted that the phenomenon of "passing" increasingly takes place in a new direction of the dominant passing as the dominated—white as persons of color, straight as gay or lesbian (Phelan 96). For many people, especially in academia, the "margins" may appear to be a popular place from which to speak. But clearly, not all margins are constructed or occupied in the same way. The question of why certain marginalized identities are desirable, today or in the Romantic period, should not be separated from the question of who gets to choose to "pass," for whatever physical, psychological or political reasons. It must be remembered, for instance, that the Romantic privileging of certain forms of marginality nevertheless resulted in a politics of assimilation that affirmed the superiority of the European center. This is perhaps because Romanticism, like marginality, was considered to be a stage to pass through, thereby reifying the opposition between those who occupied the margins by choice and those who occupied them by force.

In this paper, I would like to examine how certain positions of marginality are privileged over others, why exile empowers some to speak and to fashion an identity for themselves that enables them to live, while it silences others, or brings them to narrate a life story that hastens their death. The answer to these questions will be related to the gendering of melancholia, an illness that is often constructed in Romantic texts as the psychological counterpart to exile and that makes the frustrated processes of (self-)identification symptomatic. I will be looking at two short novels by authors who were first introduced to each other as émigrés after the French Revolution and who maintained a difficult friendship throughout their efforts at repatriation in a very changed homeland. For both these authors, not surprisingly, exile was a matter of national politics. Political exile, furthermore, is imbricated with questions of gender and race in such a way as to reconstruct the notion of nation or fatherland (*patrie*) in relation to an excluded or abjected subject.

In the much acclaimed and imitated *René* (1802) by Chateaubriand, exile is figured as a young, white French male of a particular melancholic temperament that carries him away from France until he finally settles in the "New World" with an "adopted" family of Indians. In the highly praised but soon forgotten novel *Ourika* (1824) by Mme de Duras, the ahistorical and pastoral setting of *René* is replaced by an aristocratic, Parisian household. It is here that Ourika, a Senegalese girl rescued from slavery at the age of two and brought as a gift to the Maréchale de B., will grow up in the years following the Revolution and through the Terror. Writ-

ten when *René* had reached the height of its popularity, and when René's so-called "mal du siècle" had begun to be a desirable and imitated sickness, Duras's novel can be read as a commentary on that move. Ourika is one of very few female characters, and probably the only non-white, to share some of the symptoms of this French disease but, as we shall see, for different causes and with different effects from those of her white and male counterparts. For René is able to cure himself and relinquish ties to his birthplace by assimilating his self-fashioned otherness into a family of Indians; Ourika's illness and her otherness prove fatal. The similarity of Ourika's death to that of René's sister, Amélie, calls attention to Chateaubriand's privileging of a chosen, esthetic exile at the expense of an imposed and existential one. Duras's text thus exposes the racial and gender ideology of French imperialism abroad and its effects for the definition of Frenchness at home.

The gender politics underlying the "mal du siècle" have been documented in the groundbreaking work of Margaret Waller. Here I wish to build on her findings by focusing more closely on the links between that malady and melancholia, a disease which, according to Théophile Gautier, was "invented" in its modern form in *René* (4). Indeed, René's symptoms are very similar to those described by Freud in the well-known 1917 essay wherein he distinguishes between melancholia, which he sees as a "pathological disposition" (243), and mourning, which he describes as a normal emotion of grief. Both, he explains, are reactions to a lost past and specifically the loss of a loved object, whether a person or "some abstraction which has taken the place of one, such as fatherland, liberty, an ideal, and so on" (243). Both are "painful" kinds of work by which the ego deals with that loss. But where melancholia differs from mourning, Freud suggests, is in the fact that melancholics are not aware of what they have lost. "This, indeed," he writes, "might be so even if the patient is aware of the loss which has given rise to his melancholia, but only in the sense that he knows *whom* he has lost but not *what* he has lost in him" (245).

For both René and Ourika geographical exile thus has its psychological counterpart in melancholia—an uncertain and ambivalent relationship to one's past. But whereas René is able to cure himself of his disease, Ourika remains mired in its pain and accompanying illusion. For him, recovery is a process of changing his relation to his "others," in the first place "othering" his sister, through whom he has maintained his ties to his biological past and its inheritance, and secondly, transferring identification to the Indians to whom he finally tells his story. It is in fact over the dead body of his sister that René is able to produce the narrative that will allow him to mourn his past and bind him to his chosen future. For Ourika, there is no such "progression." If she is unable to mourn, it is because she has no identi-

fiable past and no other that she can claim to have lost. The ability to accommodate loss and leave the past behind is linked to the possibility for performing new identifications and concurrently for disidentifying with former positions. "Passing away" is a part of passing, but the strategies for mourning what has passed are gendered and racialized. Who one gets to pass to, that is to say, is necessarily a function of who one has been perceived as being and of the authority granted that prior position.

Mourning, and specifically, mourning dead women in a poetic lament, is indeed a popular activity among men in the works of early Romanticism. Barbara Johnson has questioned whether Romantic poetry may in fact be dependent on a woman's death, and whether, for example, Lamartine's *Le Lac* were written "not out of a desire to restore the woman to life, but rather out of a desire to write her into death . . . as though his pen were just waiting for a real death to mourn" (629). Johnson reads the satisfaction gained from the woman's death as a sign of the poet's ambivalence towards the reality of his beloved and her power. At the center of *René* is also the death of a woman, Amélie, and the letter that René receives describing her last moments is the catalyst that brings him to tell his story. Here, however, ambivalence toward woman, while certainly a factor, is an insufficient cause of the fulfillment brought by her loss. René's melancholia has at its core a confusion of sexual difference. The work of mourning that Amélie's death excites offers a cure for René's debilitating illness by enabling him to establish a clearer sexual identity and to integrate into the world of men. Already in his prefatory remarks Chateaubriand calls attention to the way in which symptoms of this disease are acquired in "the society of women." In the modern world, Chateaubriand explains, women:

> still have an influence on all the other feelings. They have a certain abandon in their being that they pass on to ours; they make our manly character less definite; and our passions, softened by being mixed with theirs, take on both a quality of uncertainty and of tenderness.[1]
>
> (*Préface de René* 112)

Despite the real losses of his mother (who died in childbirth), his father and his homeland, this quality of "uncertainty," coded as feminine, characterizes René's grief and prevents any resolution of his relation to the past, as it translates into an aimless future. As he relates:

> I lacked something to fill the emptiness of my existence: I went down into the valley, I climbed the mountain calling with all the force of my desires to the ideal object of a future passion; I kissed it in the winds . . . everything became that imaginary phantom. . . .
>
> (128-29)

This objectless longing is coupled both with a disgust for life and a certain pleasure, "quelques charmes" (129) that he takes in displaying his lack. For René as for Freud's patients, a conflict of ambivalence to the lost object appears to be one of the "conditioning factors" in melancholia. This conflict, furthermore, is manifested in his relation to his dead mother and the past she represented, a past with which he identifies and that he desires but that he has been complicitous in destroying—having "cost his mother her life in being born" (119).

Within his story, we see this combination of identification and desire cathected onto his sister. Amélie "was the only person on earth whom I had ever loved . . . all my feelings were mixed up in her, along with the sweetness of my childhood memories. . . . She was almost a mother" (131-32). In Amélie, René falls in love with the image of his own melancholy, that vague longing that, he surmises, both have inherited from their mother: "for we had both a bit of sadness at the bottom of our heart: we got it from God or from our mother"(120). The conflict of incest is exacerbated by this confusion of erotic attraction and identification that is, according to Freud, particular to melancholia, and that allows the loved relation to be preserved while the ego is simultaneously punished for maintaining that love.[2]

In *The Ego and the Id,* Freud elaborates on his previous discussion of melancholy to suggest that such identifications with abandoned object cathexes are the very material of character formation. Drawing on Freud, Judith Butler points out their role in gender formation as well. "Because identifications substitute for object relations," she writes, "and identifications are the consequence of loss, gender identification is a kind of melancholia in which the sex of the prohibited object is internalized as a prohibition" (*Gender* 63). Here we find a different root for the "insidious feminization" of the romantic hero that Waller illustrates. The ambivalent combination of egotism and self-hatred characteristic of mal-du-siècle heroes is an effect not only of the inconstancy of affections, but of the inconstancy of gender and sexual orientation, particularly as it comes into conflict with the growing sexual dimorphism of nineteenth-century French society. The mal du siècle is a symptomatic unrepressing or unforgetting of gender taboos, incorporating a pre-Oedipal gender confusion into the confused class structures and shifting political alliances of postrevolutionary society.

If the modern form of melancholia is constructed as a psychological disease in a particular historical moment, it is nevertheless more universally depicted as a stage that a man must outgrow in order to enter the social contract and find his place within it. Mourning is the ideological process by which the hero's melancholy of gender undergoes its socialization by reversing the process of unrepressing and reestablishing the taboo. I use the masculine deliberately since, as "melancholic doubles," René and Amélie do not negotiate this passage on equal terms. As in the case of Balzac's Eugénie Grandet, paired to her melancholiac cousin, here too the daughter pays the higher price, clinging to her torment while the son successfully moves from melancholia through the work of mourning. Indeed, it is Amélie's death that enables René to cure himself of his melancholia and begin the work of mourning. Her death to this world, symbolically enacted when she takes her vows, is thus propitious for René, providing him with a conscious object for his pain, just as her admission of incestuous desires towards her brother provides him with a clear source of guilt and, consequently, an object more worthy of punishment than himself.

> Oh my friends. I knew then what it was to shed tears for a pain that was not imaginary. My passions, which had been for so long without direction, precipitated on that first prey with fury. I even found a sort of unexpected satisfaction in the plenitude of my sorrow, and I became aware with a secret stirring of joy, that sorrow is not an affection that one expends like pleasure. Moreover (strange thing!) I no longer had the desire to die from the moment I became truly unhappy.
>
> (141)

Amélie's death is proof that the internalized, prohibited object has been abjected and along with it the femininity that confused the nature and direction of René's passions.

Writing on *Eugénie Grandet,* Naomi Schor suggests that the female protagonist's melancholic "retreat into narcissism may in fact be the only form of autonomy available to her in a society where woman's assigned function in the Symbolic is to guarantee the transmission of the phallus" (106). Amélie's retreat, manifested in her entrance into the convent, is, by contrast, the very means by which she fulfills that assigned function since it is at the ceremony of her "sacrifice" that René steps in to assume his paternal role (139). Amélie's "secret," which in the narrative displaces and substitutes for René's own desires, "buried in an eternal oblivion," allows him to excise and lay to rest the femininity he had interiorized as a prohibition, and to take up his proper position within the Symbolic.

René's story, which he finally relates in the "New World" to his "adopted" fathers, is evidence that the work of mourning has achieved its goal, freeing him from his past enough to make his memories tellable. The story, moreover, becomes the vehicle for his insertion into his new family and into a history where he can renounce the "commerce of men," which is to say into a history where women's role in the exchange of the phallus is effaced (117). Relation through narrative takes the place of relation by birth, creation for procreation.

This is the moment where the imbrication of gender identification with geopolitics and culture is most significant.[3] On a symbolic level, it is through his disidentification with the bodies of his mother and sister, and adoption of a new family of fathers, that René disconnects with his past, and perhaps more specifically with the ancien régime (a system founded on "biological" ties of blood), moving towards acceptance of the contractual model of the constitutional monarchy if not also the republic.

It is important to note, however, that in terms of his cultural assimilation, René's relation to the "New World" and his new, chosen past, repeats his contradictory relation to his mother and sister. For him, as for many European travelers, the Indians represent a state of innocence and even nobility that had been a part of, but was now lost to, the European past. As Harry Liebersohn writes,

> once the French Revolution had destroyed nobility as a legal order in France, noble souls yearning for the real thing had to look elsewhere for it—to the Middle Ages or Brahmin India, or tribal warriors. Native American and Oceanic elites were good candidates for ur-nobility, indeed, more authentic and original than compromised European title-bearers.
>
> (758)

Not racially but temporally other, René's identification with the "savages" is a projection of his desire to return to a prerevolutionary, even pre-ancien régime, and pre-melancholic state.

> Happy savages! Oh, would that I could enjoy the peace that forever accompanies you! . . . Your reason was only your needs, and you arrived at the results of wisdom better than I, like a child, between games and sleep.
>
> (125)

Yet the consolation that he finds among the Indians is achieved, as Eric Gans claims for Chateaubriand, "by associating himself with a pre-civilized stability that he is nonetheless aware his presence is contributing to destroy" (572). Indeed in Chactas's blindness we see not only the increasing difficulty for the "civilized savage" to "find his own way," ("*cherch[er] sa route*") (146), but also his dependence on René, the European, for remembering and knowing his own past. Living, "only through [his] memory," it is of France and Louis XIV that Chactas asks René to remind him. In this substitution of the European past for that of the Indian, we see not only what Gans calls the "counter-revolutionary's unavowable complicity with the historical dynamic of the Revolution" (572), but also the European exile's complicity with the spread of French imperialism and the destruction of France's cultural others.

This ambivalent but ultimately destructive relation between France and its others is foregrounded in *Ourika,* a story told from the point of view of the exile who has

no other. On one level then, the confessional frame of *René* is here reversed: rather than the Frenchman recounting the reason behind his chosen exile to the Indians, it is the Senegalese "Négresse" telling the story of her imposed exile in France to a Parisian doctor—the voice of French authority, rationality and, indeed, national health. Most recent readings of this novel have analyzed its representation of Duras's own emotional life—on the one hand, her unrestrained and unrequited love for Chateaubriand and on the other hand, her sense of exclusion from French restoration society not for political reasons (her husband having remained on the list of proscribed persons under the Empire, became a favorite of the restored monarchy), but for physical ones—her prolonged illness and her presumed lack of beauty.[4] But while Ourika and Duras may share this sense of physical exclusion from French society, the representation of racial difference is not simply metaphorical.

Duras's novel sets in play two opposed racial ideologies. The beginning of Ourika's story reads like support for the policy of assimilation that justified French expansion into Senegal in the beginning of the century and that, while promoting belief in the superiority of French culture, also claimed that education was all that separated France from its others—savages can be civilized, as we saw with Chactas.[5] And yet, whereas Africans and Indians might both be savages, it would appear that only the latter could also be "noble," only with the latter could European aristocrats find affinity (Liebersohn 756-57). Duras's novel exposes the differential racism of her society from the viewpoint of one of its victims.

For Duras, Ourika's difference is, like the oriental dress she wears, only a matter of surface. With no memory nor even knowledge of her origins, Ourika's earliest experiences in Mme de B.'s household gave her no sense of her difference: ". . . nothing warned me that this (being black) was a disadvantage . . . and my black color did not stop me from loving myself" (33). Her upbringing, her complete education, and the guidance of Mme de B. directing her taste and judgment, made her into the perfect protégé of her mistress. Next to her, Ourika says, "one was the best one could be . . . and maybe even better, because she lent something of herself to her friends without knowing it: seeing her, hearing her, one believed one resembled her" (32). This identification with Mme de B. is transferred also onto her son Charles who, Ourika says, resembled her in such a way as to be "what Mme de B. must have been" (46). Their relationship is not unlike that of René and Amélie, particularly in its merging of identification and desire.

> He had counted on me for so long, that my friendship was like his life to him; he enjoyed it without feeling

it, neither asking for my interest nor my attention; he knew well that in speaking to me about himself, he told me about me, and that I was more him than himself.

(47-48)

Ourika's near-perfect assimilation, her admired "elegance" and "grace" thus distinguish her from the more popular European depiction of the Negro as physically "deviant,"[6] but also form the basis of what she will painfully come to see as her "blindness" and "error."[7] "Without even being aware," she admits, "I adopted a great disdain for all that was not this world where I passed my life" (32), and this disdain will inevitably turn inward as she becomes the abject of this world, not like Amélie for the purpose of preserving the individual male ego, but rather for the preservation of the "natural order" of white, French society. Ourika's fall is not only into sexuality, but into a racialized sexuality whose difference is clearly shown to be ideologically constructed. The issue of race, that is to say, is integral to Ourika's access to subjectivity that is otherwise achieved according to what has become a somewhat familiar psychoanalytic model. Speaking with the authority of the "fatherland," the Marquise's "no" to miscegenation awakens Ourika out of her dyadic relationship to Mme de B.(with whom she identified to the point of making Ourika confuse her growing fondness for Mme de B's son with maternal love) as she forces her to see her assimilation as a crime against the "order of nature" (37). "Who," the Marquise asks Mme de B.,

> would ever want to marry a Negress? And if, for money, you find someone who would consent to have black children, it would be a man of inferior status with whom she would be unhappy. She can only want those who would not want her . . . Ourika has not fulfilled her destiny: she has placed herself in society without its permission; society will avenge itself.

(36-37)

Overhearing these words from behind a lacquer screen that signals her abjection, her physical and linguistic separation from the other women, Ourika's reaction is an instantaneous recognition of the ideological significance of blackness:

> lightning is not quicker; I saw everything; I saw myself a Negress, dependent, scorned, without future, without support, without a being like me to whom I could unite my fate, until now a toy, an amusement for my benefactor, soon to be rejected by a world in which I am not fit to be admired.

(36)

The Marquise's words force Ourika to disidentify with the only family and culture she had ever known but provide no alternate possibilities for identification. In total isolation, she appears without the means to construct a viable identity.

What is particularly interesting about this scene is the way that sexual difference is displaced in order to draw attention to the racializing interpellations of the social order and the fact that the assumption of sexed subjectivity is in no way prior to the assumption of race.[8] On the contrary, sexual and racial prohibitions function together to guard against miscegenation. Thus, Ourika must take up her proper side not only on the sexual divide, but also on the racial divide between black and white. Melancholia is, for her as for René, the symptom, if not the result, of her inability to accept such distinctions and assume the "proper" side. Whereas René's sickness leads him to seek out new cultural identifications, perhaps as a means to avoid certain sexual and political ones (though the latter are never explicit), Ourika's leads her not to seek but to hide, "deceiving herself," as she admits to her confessor, by putting away all the mirrors in her room and covering all sight of her skin beneath long-sleeved, high-necked clothes, gloves, and a hat with a veil. The "disdain" for other cultures that she had unknowingly learned as a child now turns inward, bringing her to hate herself as the Other, but also preventing her from finding affinity with other oppressed groups. As the events in Santo Domingo, giving rise to widespread debates over the question of freedom for the Negro, attract Ourika's attention, she has "the illusion," she says:

> that elsewhere, at least, there were people like me: since they were unhappy, I believed they were good, and I concerned myself with their destiny. Alas! I was promptly deceived. The massacres of Santo Domingo gave me a new, excruciating pain: until now I had grieved over belonging to an exiled race, now I was ashamed to belong to a race of barbarians and assassins.

(43)

Whereas René resides in what the French thought of as a historical vacuum, Ourika's imagination nourishes itself on the tales of the Revolution, in which she finds a political counterpart, and hence, consolation to her own alienated state: "I envisioned that in this grand disorder, I would be able to find my place; that all the reversed fortunes, all the confused ranks, all the abandoned prejudices would perhaps lead to a state of things where I would be less foreign" (41). Told that she must identify with blacks, but unable to step outside her cultural affiliation that designates blacks as her other as well, Ourika finds instead a strengthening of her identification to Mme de B., in part through her growing love for the latter's son Charles:

> It was in Charles's heart that I sought shelter . . . before, I thought I had loved as a brother; but ever since I felt myself constantly in suffering, I seemed to have aged and my tenderness for him resembled more that of a mother. Only a mother could feel this passionate desire for his happiness, his success. . . .

(50)

Charles is, of course, representative of all that Ourika's blackness denies to her—family, future, and a desire that was perceived as wholly within the "natural order"—"almost nothing in him was involuntary, and yet everything was natural" (47). Ourika's desire for and identification with Charles can be explained by what Butler posits as the need to "institute a disidentification with a position that seems too saturated with injury or aggression, one that might, as a consequence, be occupiable only by the loss of viable identity all together" (*Bodies* 100). But as the only black woman in a world of white aristocrats, there is no viable identity for Ourika, none that is not injurious. As Charles becomes engaged to a woman of his society, she is denied the one identity readily open to women—that of wife and mother—and as a black woman she is condemned, indeed rendered criminal, for desiring that identity. With no outlet for her desire, Ourika, like Amélie and so many French heroines, retreats to a convent, there to preserve her prohibited illusions and thus her melancholia. "Let me go Charles," she demands, "to the only place where I am permitted to think about you forever."[9]

Ourika's interminable "illness" may be read as the affliction imposed by a social order that denies her a place, but perhaps also as a heroic refusal to submit to an order that abjects otherness and negates its loss. Such negation is effected through the work of mourning, understood as a healthier relation to loss, although effected through a less open relation to alterity.[10] Inscribed in René's passage from melancholy to mourning, as we have seen, is a narrative of how one moves from savage to civilized through a move from mother to father. Civilization is born with the effort to construct and preserve one's own story or history.[11] The record of that birth, however, is to be had only through the coincident denial of its maternal origins, and more generally, through the denial of the feminine. At one point in the text, René's melancholy brings him to return to the place of his birth. There, he acknowledges the painful loss of those origins, severed by dissemination:

> The family of man lasts but a day; the breath of God scatters it like smoke. The son hardly knows his father, the father his son, the brother his sister, the sister her brother! The oak tree sees its acorns germinate around it; it is not so with the children of men.
>
> (137)

The image of the oak tree as a metaphor for a continuity between past and present also appears in the opening frame of the text when Chactas encourages René to relate his story and tell his memories. But it is a very different image, no longer contrasted to the lack of organicity in the generations of men:

> My child, I now live only through my memory. An old man with his memories is like a decrepit oak of our woods: the oak no longer adorns itself with its own foliage, but covers its nudity with foreign plants that vegetated on its ancient limbs.
>
> (126)

For Chactas, memory is neither perishable nor painful, but instead is life-sustaining because the effort to retrieve origins has been abandoned. Chactas, the "civilized savage," has learned what René learns upon closing the door to his birthplace, that memories can establish social and aesthetic connections to the past which substitute for generational ones; that they, perhaps like femininity, can be borrowed—the means by which men cover over and protect their nudity, repress their bodily origins, and "pass" as souls. "According to the opinion of the savages," Chateaubriand writes in the *Voyage en Amérique,* "it is the father who creates the soul of the child, the mother only engenders the body" (758). Memories can allow one to forget or to mourn, both of which are "civilizing" functions, propitious for the recreation of patriarchal culture after the Revolution.

Ourika, however, is never allowed to forget her bodily origins, even though she never actually remembers them. Whereas René and Chactas compare themselves to the oak tree, Ourika is seen to die "with the last autumn leaves" (64)—germination and generation as well as any meaningful connection to the past or the future denied to her. Not only can the doctor *not* cure her, the concept of "reason" he represents is an instrument of the racism that oppresses her. Even before she begins to tell her story to the doctor she warns him that he too may find it "*déraisonnable,*" and that this would exclude the possibility of his sympathy. Indeed, it is reason that legitimates Ourika's blackness as other and, consequently, her desire as unreasonable, "*insensée*"(60), in the words of the Marquise, even criminal, outside France, nature, health. Reason is what forced her to silence herself before Charles, to tell him (who tells her everything) nothing of her torment for fear that he would not understand it and therefore would find it unfounded.

> One evening, the conversation turned to the idea of pity, and we wondered whether sorrows inspired more interest because of their effects or their causes. Charles announced himself for cause; he thus thought that all sorrows must be reasonable. But who can say what is reason? is it the same for everyone? do all hearts have the same needs? isn't unhappiness the heart's deprivation of what it needs?
>
> (48)

Ourika knows that neither reason nor pain are universal and that an act of pity that extends only to a pain it finds reasonable is inadequate, especially as it delegitimizes those sorrows and, by extension, those desires that it cannot understand.

A reasonable story about pain, the texts of Chateaubriand and Duras illustrate, is one that gets rid of difference—a kind of story that René can tell, even as exile, but not Ourika. He need never question that he will be understood or pitied (even Souel's harsh words at the end mask a "sympathetic [*compatissant*] heart" (144). On the contrary, his torment becomes an aesthetic privilege, granting special status to the rock where he would sit at sunset and inspiring future writers and artists to imitate his melancholy pose. Not only does Ourika have no one with whom to identify, in the universe of the novel no one would want to identify with this protagonist. Perhaps it is for this reason that Mme de Duras preferred not even to publish her story, saying that her writing "liked solitude."[12]

Over the past twenty years feminist criticism has done much to break the isolation surrounding stories like Ourika's, promoting the rediscovery of older versions, encouraging the publication of new ones, and showing that women like her need not be isolated or alone. And whereas earlier stages of feminist criticism might have read Ourika's story as exemplary of the oppression of woman, black and third world feminists have provided a necessary corrective to this practice by showing the dangers of assimilating all women and their oppression together and of failing to recognize, like Charles, different sufferings and different needs. Pointing to categories of race, ethnicity, religion, class (to name only a few) that differentially divide and oppress women, identity politics has sought to form communities around these categories in order to foster support, lobby for reform, and, more theoretically, to fight against the assumption of a homogeneous subjectivity. But if Ourika's story can be appropriated for feminists today, it is not only because Duras calls our attention to the importance of race in the negotiations of identity (and hence not only to what distinguishes Ourika's exile from that of René, but also from that of Amélie), but because she does not say what sort of identity her race engenders. Moreover, if readers were to claim that Ourika is an inauthentic black because she is created by a white author, they would fall into the trap of seeing racial identity as stable and singular. Duras thus offers an important corrective to the potential dangers of an identity politics that would assume that to be black, for instance, necessarily binds one to a particular subjectivity and to a particular past. This assumption forecloses the possibilities for identification that allow one to put one's past behind—whether that past be read or remembered.

Notes

1. Unless otherwise noted, this and all subsequent translations are my own.

2. "If the love for the object—a love which cannot be given up though the object itself is given up—takes refuge in narcissistic identification, then the hate comes into operation on this substitutive object, abusing it, debasing it, making it suffer and deriving sadistic satisfaction from its suffering" (Freud, "Mourning" 251).

3. I say culture and not race for reasons that will become apparent.

4. See, for instance, Claudine Hermann's introduction to the "édition feministe" of *Ourika*. Future references to this edition will be cited in the text. All translations are my own.

5. For a discussion of French politics in Senegal at this time see Madubuike.

6. On the representation of blackness see Gilman, Hoffman, and JanMohamed.

7. In France, one would have to acknowledge her and her black children as French—the nationality of women and children being determined by their husband or father.

8. I borrow the term "racializing interpellations" from Butler, *Bodies* 18.

9. "The identifications consequent to melancholia" explains Butler, "are modes of preserving unresolved object relations." Butler, *Gender* 63.

10. Julia Kristeva makes similar distinctions between melancholia and mourning, stressing that melancholics exhibit a persistent, if psychotic, engagement with and openness to (feminine) alterity: "Melancholy persons are foreigners in their maternal tongue. They have lost meaning—the value—of their mother tongue—for want of losing the mother. The dead language they speak . . . conceals a Thing buried alive. The latter will not be translated in order that it not be betrayed" (53). Those who mourn, by contrast, deny the loss of the (feminine/maternal) alterity by finding the means to symbolize it. See also the extremely insightful and interesting article concerning the ethics of mourning by Ziarek.

11. Only "civilized peoples have, in order to conserve the memories of their fatherland, monuments, letters and arts . . . the savages have none of all that . . . There is thus, for the tribes of the new world, only one monument, the tomb." *Voyage* 761.

12. "*Dites à lady Glingall que je n'imprime rien. Mes livres aiment la solitude.*" Pailhès 290.

Works Cited

Butler, Judith. *Bodies That Matter*. New York: Routledge, 1993.

———. *Gender Trouble*. New York: Routledge, 1990.

Chateaubriand, François-René de. *Oeuvres romanesques et voyages.* Ed. Maurice Regard. Vol. 1. Paris: Gallimard, 1969. 2 vols.

Duras, Madame de. *Ourika.* Intro. Claudine Hermann. Paris: des femmes, 1979.

Freud, Sigmund. *The Ego and the Id.* 1923. *The Standard Edition of the Complete Psychological Works of Sigmund Freud.* Trans. and ed. James Strachey. Vol. 19. London: Hogarth, 1961. 3-66. 24 vols. 1953-74.

———. "Mourning and Melancholia." 1917. *The Standard Edition.* Vol. 14. 239-60.

Gans, Eric. "Maistre and Chateaubriand: Counter-Revolution and Anthropology." *Studies in Romanticism* 28 (1989): 559-575.

Gates, Henry Louis Jr., ed. *"Race," Writing, and Difference.* Chicago: U of Chicago P, 1985.

Gautier, Théophile. *Histoire du romantisme.* Paris: Charpentier, 1927.

Gilman, Sander. "Black Bodies, White Bodies: Toward an Iconography of Female Sexuality in Late Nineteenth-Century Art, Medicine, and Literature." Gates 223-61.

Hoffman, Léon-François. *Le Nègre romantique.* Paris: Payot, 1973.

JanMohamed, Abdul R. "The Economy of Manichean Allegory: The Function of Racial Difference in Colonialist Literature." Gates 78-106.

Johnson, Barbara. "The Lady in the Lake." *A New History of French Literature.* Ed. Dennis Hollier. Cambridge: Harvard UP, 1989.

Kristeva, Julia. *Black Sun: Depression and Melancholia.* Trans. Léon S. Roudiez. New York: Columbia UP, 1989.

Liebersohn, Harry. "Discovering Indigenous Nobility: Tocqueville, Chamisso, and Romantic Travel Writing." *The American Historical Review* 99.3 (1994): 746-66.

Madubuike, Ihechukwu. *The Senegalese Novel: A Sociological Study of the Impact of the Politics of Assimilation.* Washington D.C.: Three Continents Press, 1983.

Pailhès, G. *La Duchesse de Duras et Chateaubriand d'après des documents inédits.* Paris: Librairie Académique, 1910.

Phelan, Peggy. *Unmarked: The Politics of Performance.* New York: Routledge, 1993.

Schor, Naomi. *Breaking the Chain.* New York: Columbia UP, 1985.

Waller, Margaret. *The Male Malady.* New Brunswick: Rutgers UP, 1993.

Ziarek, Ewa. "Kristeva and Levinas: Mourning, Ethics, and the Feminine." *Ethics, Politics, and Difference in Julia Kristeva's Writing.* Ed. Kelly Oliver. New York: Routledge, 1993.

EXILE IN BRITISH LITERATURE

Alan MacGillivray (essay date 1988)

SOURCE: MacGillivray, Alan. "Exile and Empire." In *The History of Scottish Literature, Volume 3: Nineteenth Century,* edited by Douglas Gifford, pp. 411-27. Aberdeen, Scotland: Aberdeen University Press, 1988.

[*In the following essay, MacGillivray studies nineteenth-century works in which Scottish men and women relate their experiences and impressions of other cultures while travelling abroad, and indicates how these narratives influenced later Scottish fiction.*]

In his short and admittedly inferior novel, *The Surgeon's Daughter* (1827), Sir Walter Scott makes his anti-hero Richard Middlemas exclaim upon the allure of India for an ambitious young man.

> 'Oh, Delhi! oh, Golconda! have your names no power to conjure down idle recollections?—India, where gold is won by steel; where a brave man cannot pitch his desire of fame and wealth so high, but that he may realize it, if he have fortune to his friend?'[1]

These sentiments were felt by many Scotsmen from the middle of the eighteenth century onwards. Like Middlemas, they realised that their proving years 'had better be spent in India, where much may be done in a little while, than here, where nothing can be done save just enough to get salt to our broth, or broth to our salt.' Where was the attraction of spending 'years in this infernal wilderness, cruizing after crowns and half-crowns, when worse men are making lacs and crores of rupees'?[2]

It would no doubt be wrong to ascribe base motives of financial greed to all the young Scotsmen on the make in the later eighteenth century as they took ship for India or North America or the West Indies. Yet those were the days before the more complex nineteenth-century motivations of imperial government service or missionary zeal or scientific knowledge had emerged with their recognised channels of entry through the armed and civil services and the various sponsoring societies. It was the major trading companies like the East India Company or the Hudson's Bay Company and its rival the North-West Fur Company, along with a multitude of lesser trading houses, that drew the lairds' sons and the lads o' pairts and education in the greatest numbers

overseas with the hope of the fortune, at least in Scottish terms, that would enable them to return in middle life to their own land and a secure comfortable position in society. Menie Gray, the surgeon's daughter herself in Scott's novel, returns to her native village and 'appeared to find her only pleasure in acts of benevolence which seemed to exceed the extent of her fortune, had not her very retired life been taken into consideration.'[3]

Undoubtedly Scotland as a whole, and local communities in particular, benefited from the infusion of fresh capital and the dissemination of knowledge about the wider world that attended the return of these voluntary exiles to their poor and isolated homeland. John Galt treats this in two of his novels. Mr Cayenne in *Annals of the Parish* (1821), a loyalist planter from Virginia, brings great benefit to the district of Ayrshire in which he comes to rest in peppery middle age. Galt treats him kindly, and through the eyes of the Reverend Micah Balwhidder we can see that this eighteenth-century 'nabob' is an instrument of social change for the better within the context of an Ayrshire parish. However, when we meet Mr Rupees in Galt's later and more ironical novel, *Last of the Lairds* (1826), we find that the new wealth is being used for the baser purposes of ostentation and the accumulation of a great estate at the expense of poorer neighbours. The Laird of Auldbiggings exclaims bitterly against this practice:

> 'Ye see, when Mr Rupees the Nawbub came hame frae Indy, and bought the Arunthrough property frae the Glaikies, who, like sae mony ithers o' the right stock o' legitimate gentry, hae been smothered out o' sight by the weed and nettle overgrowths o' merchandise and cotton-weavry, he would fain hae bought Auldbiggings likewise, and sent that gett o' the de'il and the law, Caption, to make me an offer; but I was neither a prodigal son nor an Esau, to sell my patrimony for a mess o' pottage, so I gied him a flea in his lug, and bade him tell the Nawbub to chew the cud o' the sin o' covetousness, the whilk is disappointment.'[4]

The Biblical references here very clearly indicate the nature of the tensions that must have afflicted many a Scottish community at that time: the resentment of the traditional landowners, the legitimate stock, against the incomers of dubious origin, alien tares among the home-grown corn; the fear of natural parochial hairy Esau that a sophisticated far-travelled smooth Jacob will unfairly buy out his birthright; the annoyance of the stay-at-home son that the world-wandering ne'er-do-weel ultimately gains a higher reward and more favour in the eyes of the nation. Mr Rupees, on the other hand, for all his self-flattering stories and boring anecdotes of India, puts his side of the matter very pungently:

> '(The people of Scotland) are quite as well disposed to esteem those who, by their own merits, have made their own fortunes, and have brought home from other countries the means of improving their native land. I

have myself spent more money here, Dr Lounlans, on Nawaubpore, than all that the Mailings, since the Ragman's Roll, have had to spend, whether got by thieving in days of yore, or by rack-rents and borrowing in our own time.'

He is savagely contemptuous of the stay-at-home Scots:

> '. . . the daft and the imbecile . . . constitute the majority of the nation at large; for, you know, that every man of sense and talent seeks his fortune abroad, and leaves only the incapable and those who are conscious of their deficiencies at home—'[5]

This, of course, takes us back to the sentiments of Middlemas in *The Surgeon's Daughter*, but with the emphasis more on the poor-spiritedness of the Scottish people than on the poverty of the Scottish environment. Mr Rupees does not speak for his creator, but the alacrity with which Galt again and again set out from Scotland on one commercial or literary venture after another suggests that the main attraction, the zest and adventure of life, lay furth of Scotland.

It is the setting out that is the decisive act, not the returning, nor even the writing about the experience. Leaving aside those transported against their will in the convict ships, the (sadly) much larger number of the guiltless and the exploited who emptied the glens and filled the emigrant ships, and the high proportion of the male population of Scotland who enlisted and put on a red uniform to fight for the Queen, there still remains a significant element, men 'of sense and talent' certainly, educated and articulate equally certainly, moved by ambition or idealism, who voluntarily undertook Scotland's nineteenth-century quest. Many of them chose at some point during or after that quest to write about it. Whether or not what most of them wrote was literature in the accepted sense is arguable; what is certain is that they found a wide readership among the nation's loyal subjects, proud and avid to hear about the strange world being opened up by English enterprise. Scotland's quest, whatever it was, unfolded within that English imperial enterprise; and, although to twentieth-century Scottish sensibilities that seems deplorable, the wandering Scots who undertook it do not seem to have cared a jot. As they left their village schools or their academies or the English schools to which their prosperous parents had sent them, the important thing was to be off and away, into the East India Company service or the trading house in Canada or Jamaica, and out into the wider world that Scots had been attracted towards since the Middle Ages.

In the case of Alexander Mackenzie, however, the trip from Stornoway to the Hudson's Bay Company was interrupted by some formative years in New York and Montreal. For this survey he marks the starting-point, since, although his great journey was made in 1793, it

was 1801 before Scotland could read his *Voyages from Montreal, on the River St Lawrence, through the Continent of North America, to the Frozen and Pacific Oceans.* This crossing of the continent, several years before the American expedition of Lewis and Clark, was described by him in a concise narrative which reveals his genuine interest in the Indians he encountered and at times tried to help. Another interest comes through in the lists of words in two Indian languages which he includes in the account. Yet, while he writes in the main tradition of nineteenth-century exploration with his clear descriptions of people and places and vivid recounting of the events of the journey, he has a rather appealing vagueness about his position at times. The moment of his actual entry into the Pacific Ocean is attended by no expressions of elation:

> At about eight we got out of the river, which discharges itself by various channels into an arm of the sea. The tide was out, and had left a large space covered with sea-weed. The surrounding hills were involved in fog. The wind was at West, which was ahead of us, and very strong; the bay appearing to be from one to three miles in breadth. As we advanced along the land we saw a great number of sea-otters. We fired several shots at them, but without any success, from the rapidity with which they plunged under the water. We also saw many small porpoises or divers. The white-headed eagle, which is common in the interior parts; some small gulls, a dark bird which is inferior in size to the gull, and a few small ducks, were all the birds which presented themselves to our view.

This interest in wild life was not entirely scientific, as he reveals slightly later:

> I had flattered myself with the hope of getting a distance of the moon and stars, but the cloud of weather continually disappointed me, and I began to fear that I should fail in this important object, particularly as our provisions were at a very low ebb, and we had as yet no reason to expect any assistance from the natives. Our stock was, at this time, reduced to twenty pounds weight of pemmican, fifteen pounds of rice, and six pounds of flour, among ten half-starved men in a leaky vessel, and on a barbarous coast. Our course from the river was about West-South-West, distance ten miles.[6]

How often, as the century proceeds, do we find the leaders of expeditions expressing similar gloomy sentiments about their situation, even at a moment of success, and juxtaposing them with the routine details of directions and distances?

Perhaps it is a Scottish characteristic to speak or write reductively about success, even one's own, and to be conscious of the supposedly crowning moment being undermined by drawbacks and tainted by contradictory elements, even by absurdity. When John Galt set out to found the new town of Guelph in the Huron Tract of Upper Canada in 1827, even before misfortune fell upon his Canada Company operation, he was aware of how close the solemnity bordered upon the ridiculous:

> . . . after endeavouring to dry ourselves, and having recourse to the store-basket, I proposed to go to the spot chosen for the town. By this time the sun was set, and Dr Dunlop, with his characteristic drollery, having doffed his wet garb, and dressed himself, Indian fashion, in blankets, we proceeded with Mr Prior, attended by two woodmen with their axes.

> It was consistent with my plan to invest our ceremony with a little mystery, the better to make it be remembered. So intimating that the main body of the men were not to come, we walked to the brow of the neighbouring rising ground, and Mr Prior having shown the site selected for the town, a large maple tree was chosen; on which, taking an axe from one of the woodmen, I struck the first stroke. To me at least the moment was impressive,—and the silence of the woods, that echoed to the sound, was as the sigh of the solemn genius of the wilderness departing for ever.

> The doctor followed me, then, if I recollect correctly, Mr Prior, and the woodmen finished the work. The tree fell with a crash of accumulating thunder, as if ancient Nature were alarmed at the entrance of social man into her innocent solitudes with his sorrows, his follies, and his crimes.

> . . . After the solemnity, for though the ceremony was simple, it may be so denominated, we returned to the shanty, and the rain, which had been suspended during the performance, began again to pour.[7]

Mackenzie the explorer and entrepreneur chose to write only incidentally to his main business, whereas Galt, for us today, is mainly a literary man whose business ventures smack almost of the irrelevant. Yet, objectively, both were important in the development of Canada as a nation and the writing that came of that major involvement has its own significance as documentation of real experience aimed at informing and motivating the reader. Galt's two Canadian novels, *Lawrie Todd, or The Settlers in the Woods* (1830) and *Bogle Corbet, or The Emigrants* (1831), may not be rated along with his *Tales of the West,* the 'theoretical histories' of Ayrshire, but they have a detailed realism that commended them to many readers. This realism and immediacy coming out of personal experience of exciting faraway places was a major factor also in the initial success of another venturer into the Canadian wilderness. R M (Robert Michael) Ballantyne spent a number of years as a clerk in the Red River Settlement for the Hudson's Bay Company and out of this came *The Young Fur Traders* (1856), *Ungava* (1858) and a major share for the author in the development of the comparatively new genre of boys' adventure story. His best-known book, *The Coral Island* (1858) signalled the expansion of his literary territory into a wider empire. In his stories the pervading message to the reader is of the romance and attraction of the wider world; they are advertisements to the young of the Old Country that there is a New World for them to enter and possess; and they will enter it not as exiles but as first citizens. To the writer of the 'Canadian Boat Song', it was indeed a sad separation:

Fair these broad meads—these hoary woods are grand;
But we are exiles from our fathers' land.
. . . Yet still the blood is strong, the heart is High-
 land,
And we in dreams behold the Hebrides.[8]

In the Nova Scotia and Red River settlements many a Highland heart did 'beat heavily beyond the Atlantic roar', but for these others we are considering, the dreams of Scotland were not allowed to figure very large in a generally outgoing and unreflective involvement in new experience.

The most extreme exponent of this attitude wrote not about Canada but about the West Indies. Michael Scott, a Glasgow man, whirls the reader away in the breathless pell-mell narrative of *Tom Cringle's Log* (1836), a succession of sea-fights, violent deaths, drinking parties, farcical situations, vivid descriptions and sentimental asides very reminiscent of Smollett's picaresque novels. There is no time to stop and think, hardly a moment to register new characters before they are whisked off to their fates or dropped out of sight. Through all this roisters the young naval officer hero, cruising the Caribbean on the King's business, making jokes about the Irish and other foreigners, delivering himself of unthinking racist comments about negroes and Hebrews, admiring the ladies of all colours, declaring himself frequently to be true blue English. Paradoxically, however, he is prone to larding his colloquial narrative with a multitude of Scots words, with the occasional qualification, 'as we say in Scotland'. He meets up with several Scots characters, reminding us that many a transported felon or rebel ended up in the West Indies as an indentured servant and worked himself into freedom and some prosperity. Tom Cringle even encounters a 'negro Scotchman . . . the spirit of Nicol Jarvie conjured into a blackamoor's skin!'—who turns out to have been born in the 'good town of Port Glasgow'.[9] Cringle's friend, Aaron Bang, becomes progressively more Scots in speech as he philosophises; and Tom himself, developing a mental allegory about how his Conscience is beset by personified temptations, creates the moral figure of Mistress Adversity,

a wee outspoken—sour—crabbit—gizzened anatomy of an old woman—'you ne'erdoweel, Tam' quoth she, 'is it no enough that you consort with that scarlet limmer, who has just yescaped thorough the winday, but ye maun smoor my first-born, puir Conscience, atween ye? Whare hae ye stowed him, man—tell me that.'[10]

At first sight this contradictory Scots element sitting uneasily within an English frame of reference could be either Michael Scott pandering to the tastes of his Scots readers (*Tom Cringle's Log* was first published in instalments in *Blackwood's Magazine* between 1829 and 1833) or an authorial confusion between himself and his English hero. However, what may be more likely is that this reflects an attitude born of more than a hundred years of Union; the idea that, although you may have been born in Scotland and have Scots speech and feelings, when you have put on an English uniform or have undertaken English imperial business, you have in fact become an Englishman. It is not even necessary to insist, as twentieth-century Scots defiantly do, that you are British; the assimilation is complete, and you may commit the ultimate treason of making stereotyped gibes at your own countrymen—In *Tom Cringle's Log* a parasitical growth strangling the life out of a magnificent cedar tree is blithely described as 'the Scotchman hugging the Creole'.[11] A minor character, Don Ricardo, is revealed as being Scottish by birth and upbringing but Spanish in his identification with society in Cuba; yet, 'in his mountain retreat, sole master, his slaves in attendance on him, he was once more an Englishman, in externals, as he always was at heart, and Richie Cloche, from the Lang Toon of Kirkaldy, shone forth in all his glory as the kind-hearted landlord.'[12] This is Tom Cringle the Scoto-English naval officer speaking, but he articulates an attitude which is probably central to the understanding of Scotland's 'literature of Empire', the desire to identify with the imperial English drive—the Scotchman hugging the Englishman, not to draw out the life but to add to it and to be assimilated into it.

Nowhere did this happen more clearly and more triumphantly than in India. The smallness of the ruling group of Europeans and their need to show a united front to the multitudes that they governed; the code of loyalty, first to the East India Company, and later to the Government service; the military tradition within which so many of the expatriates worked: all these considerations must have had a strong bearing upon the tendency of the Scot in India to conform to English expectations, to seek assimilation. Especially so when a fair number of the Scots entering the Indian service appear to have been of elevated, even aristocratic, birth and breeding. At the highest level, the appointments were political: early in the century, Gilbert Elliot, the first Earl of Minto, was Governor-General; in the middle years, the tenth Earl of Dalhousie; and, just outside our period, in the first decade of the twentieth century, another Minto, the fourth Earl, ruled as Viceroy. The Border Elliots had come far. Under the first Earl of Minto, other Scots rose to prominence, becoming Governors of Madras and Bombay: Sir Thomas Munro, Sir John Malcolm and Mountstuart Elphinstone. All of these men wrote extensively, even copiously. What they wrote arose mainly out of their official responsibilities: letters, memos, reports in all cases, but much more than that in the cases of Malcolm and Elphinstone, who sought a wider readership with their histories and accounts of diplomatic missions. The achievements of Munro, Malcolm and Elphinstone in the establishment and government of British India were immense and would need whole books to describe and assess; their writings show

that they were not solely men of action but were also thoughtful, observant and far-sighted.

Thomas Munro is the closest of the three to our image of the young Scot bent on self-advancement abroad, if only because it was the failure of his father's business in Glasgow after the confiscation of family properties in Virginia that led directly to his sailing to India as a cadet in the East India Company. After his Glasgow University studies in mathematics and chemistry, his reading of literature and his learning of Spanish, this was a picaresque turn in his fortunes reminiscent of Smollett's hero Roderick Random, whose adventures he so much enjoyed. It led him to active military service and administration of a district in South India; to an awareness that the real people of India, the peasants, deserved proper justice and would best receive it on a direct local level; to the Governorship of Madras and to death from cholera. As a writer he was a man of minutes and memos and letters, but in their clear observation of Indian life and society and their direct expression they have a literary merit. He also diagnosed the English imperial disease that is still with us:

> Our Government will always be respected from the influence of our military power; but it will never be popular while it offers no employment to the natives that can stimulate the ambition of the better class of them. Foreign conquerors have treated the natives with violence, and often with great cruelty, but none has treated them with so much scorn as we; none has stigmatized the whole people as unworthy of trust, as incapable of honesty, and as fit to be employed only where we cannot do without them. It seems to be not only ungenerous but impolitic, to debase the character of a people fallen under our dominion; and nothing can more certainly produce this effect than our avowing our want of confidence in them, and, on that account, excluding them as much as possible from every office of importance.[13]

The administrative world of India at the start of the century was a small one and Munro made friends with his fellow Scots, John Malcolm and Mountstuart Elphinstone. Sir John Malcolm seems to have been everybody's friend and was even well known to the Nabob, Mr Rupees, in John Galt's *Last of the Lairds*: 'Canning, I'm told, calls my friend Sir John, Bahaddar Jaw . . .'[14] He well deserved the title 'Bahadur Jah' bestowed on him for his military valour by his Indian admirers, and also the nickname 'Boy Malcolm' for his boyish enthusiasm in all that he undertook. 'What would you do', he was asked as a twelve-year-old candidate for the East India Company service, 'if you met Hyder Ali?' 'I would draw ma sword and cut aff his heid', was the reply that gained him acceptance. The drive and energy this Eskdale man brought both to soldiering and to politics and administration was matched by his application to writing. The pun in Canning's reference to 'Bahaddar Jaw' is to his loquacity of speech, but there is a

similar bulk of writing; Malcolm himself makes fun of this, referring in his initially anonymous *Sketches of Persia* (1828) to 'Sir John Malcolm's ponderous quartos' already written on the subject. Malcolm had been sent on a first diplomatic mission to the Shah of Persia by the Marquis of Wellesley (Wellington's older brother); on the way he had made a treaty with the ruler of Oman, and he had been a great success at the Persian Court. From this, and from his second mission to Persia, entrusted to him in 1808 by Gibby Elliot of Minto, came the 'ponderous quartos', *A History of Persia* (1815), and the *Sketches,* a lively entertaining account of his travels and observations in a land little known by Europeans, interspersed with Persian traditional stories and other anecdotes to make a pleasing narrative for the general reader.

The conversations he reports having with the Shah of Persia illustrate this well. At times there is an echo of Swift's Gulliver explaining Europe to the King of Brobdingnag. Malcolm himself is the Elchee, or Envoy.

> The visit was at its commencement very formal, but the king, evidently desirous to give it another character, said to the Elchee, 'I have heard a report which I cannot believe, that your king has only one wife.' 'No Christian prince can have more,' said the Elchee. 'O, I know that, but he may have a little lady.' 'Our gracious king, George the Third,' replied the Envoy, 'is an example to his subjects of attention to morality and religion in this respect as in every other.' 'This may all be very proper,' concluded his majesty of Persia, laughing, 'but I certainly should not like to be king of such a country.'[15]

Malcolm was popular with the Peacock Throne and was granted a special Order of the Lion and the Sun. Some of this popularity no doubt came from the ability to pay a subtle compliment, such as this from a soldier to the follower of the Prophet:

> After a number of questions on the mines of South America and the arts and manufactures of Europe, the king said, 'All this is astonishing! Persia has nothing but steel.' 'Steel, well managed', said the Elchee, 'has, from the beginning of the world to the present day, commanded all other riches.'[16]

In his long and fruitful life, Malcolm also found time to write a fair amount of not very good poetry, a life of Lord Clive and *Sketch of the Political History of India*. Politics, however, brought him some bitterness. Because Malcolm had been associated in earlier years with the Marquis of Wellesley, distrusted in London for his lofty and extravagant manner and policies, he was denied a Governorship, first in Central India and then in Bombay, until his more junior colleague Elphinstone had retired. However, he at last received his reward and ended his long Indian career as Governor of Bombay.

There are interesting parallels and contrasts to be drawn between the lives and careers of John Malcolm and Mountstuart Elphinstone. Malcolm was much more the

soldier, yet the civilian Elphinstone fought a victorious battle against the Marathas. Elphinstone was the more scholarly, yet it was Malcolm who wrote the more assiduously. Both could see clearly what the present situation demanded and could deal decisively with it, yet Elphinstone had the clearer vision of what it was all about in the long run. He believed in and promoted education for the Indians at a time when the English imperial purpose had scarcely been identified, and wrote while in Bombay:

> . . . it may not be too visionary to suppose a period at which (the natives) might bear to the English nearly the relation which the Chinese do to the Tartars, the Europeans retaining the government and the military power, while the natives filled a large proportion of the civil stations and many of the subordinate employments in the army.[17]

A century later that had come to pass. Some years earlier, Elphinstone had been even more prophetic:

> The most desirable death for us (the British in India) to die of should be the improvement of the natives reaching such a pitch as would render it impossible for a foreign nation to retain the government[18]

The main literary productions of Elphinstone are a *History of India* and his description of Afghanistan as perceived by him on his mission there in 1808, the parallel undertaking to Malcolm's second mission to Persia. These two diplomatic initiatives, along with Charles Metcalfe's embassy to the Sikhs in the Punjab, were Lord Minto's response to the alliance between Napoleon and Czar Alexander of Russia. The intention of each envoy was to win friends and extend British influence in a sensitive area between British and Russian territory. Elphinstone's visit to Afghanistan did not produce significant political results but his book, *An Account of the Kingdom of Caubul and its Dependencies* (1815), remained the authoritative source for many years. The emphasis of the book is firmly on information: there is only a comparatively brief introduction dealing with Elphinstone's own mission before we are taken into a geographical description and sections on the inhabitants, the tribes and the royal government, and appendices on the history, language and other matters. It is clearly and interestingly written without any striving for literary effect, and, to a generation exposed to sensational journalism and television images of strife in Afghanistan, it comes as a relief to read quiet facts which go below the surface and, even after one hundred and seventy years, tell us more about the land and its people than the modern media.

There is a massive literature on India written by Scots of many ranks and professions, as a 1986 exhibition at the National Library of Scotland made clear.[19] Some of the most perceptive and entertaining accounts of the de-

veloping British Raj were naturally written by women. Maria Graham, in her *Journal of a Residence in India*, cast a shrewd and critical eye over the scene in the early years of the century; later came Emily Eden and Charlotte Canning.

One of the most praised books by a female observer was Emily Eden's *Up The Country: Letters written to her Sister from the Upper Provinces of India* (1866). In this journal of the Governor-General's progresses between 1837 and 1840, life's variety is looked at from the standpoint of the First Lady of British India. Emily Eden was half-Scottish; her mother was Eleanor Elliot, sister of the first Lord Minto, who married into the Eden family. George Eden, Emily's bachelor brother, became Governor-General in 1835 and his unmarried sister accompanied him to Calcutta as his hostess and wrote a series of letters home about her experiences.

Perhaps it is the epistolary style of *Up The Country* that makes it so successful. The letters are vivid, chatty and amusing, written in a colloquial sisterly tone, as much concerned with trivia as with great occasions. She describes dinners, dances, tiger-shoots, meetings with Indian princes, sketching and painting excursions (she was quite a talented artist), the luxuries and inconveniences of public life—all with a sharp eye for detail and a ready wit. Frequently her personal feelings come through strongly, as when she is moved by the sights of famine and poverty; she actually bought two orphan girls who were being badly treated and deposited them in a Calcutta orphanage for a kinder upbringing. The two clearest impressions that come across from her letters are of the massive ridiculous lumbering apparatus of the Governor-General's retinue—12,000 attendants, plus camels, elephants, horses, tents and baggage, to be uprooted and shifted a few miles further along the road every day—and the almost desperate concern of the English expatriates to maintain their links with home and create the illusion of an English social life—eagerly awaiting the latest volumes of Lamb or Dickens to come in the packets and flinging themselves into balls, dramatic evenings and receptions during the Simla season. It is an English world that Emily Eden describes, and, although she can quote from *Annals of the Parish,* hers is an English viewpoint. Nevertheless, like Munro and Elphinstone, she has a wider and longer perspective. One is tempted to wonder if perhaps a Scottish cast of thought enabled them to see the imperial institutions rather differently from the majority of the English around them. Emily Eden expresses both a sense of the merit of the Indians and a regret for the manners of the English towards them. She recognises the plight of the Anglo-Indian community, and she has a vision of the future reversal of English fortunes in India. Over all, she comes across as a sensible, warm and entertaining woman and writer. In later years, with India behind her, she enjoyed a little success as a novelist. Of her two

novels, *The Semi-Attached Couple* (1860) and *The Semi-Detached House* (1859), the first was in fact written but not published before she went to India. The characters are Border Eskdales and Douglases, but the spirit and style are totally English.

At first sight, Charlotte Canning's Journal[20] looks like a more superficial view of life at the top in India. Of Scottish origins on both sides of her family, Charlotte Stuart had married the up-and-coming Charles Canning, who was appointed Governor-General in 1856 in succession to Lord Dalhousie. Her Journal of their time in India begins with the trivial social round of the Governor-General's wife, occasions of the kind that Emily Eden could describe sardonically. If this were all that her Journal contained, it would not be worthy of note. However, within a few months of her arrival in Calcutta, Charlotte is describing the events of the Indian Mutiny as if from the Royal Box. Her record of that great assault upon English power and complacency, from the first stirrings of discontent among the sepoys, the early rumours and the initial false official optimism through the catalogue of disasters and the desperate search for reinforcements to the successful outcome in which her husband showed himself to be generous and statesmanlike, makes fascinating reading and vindicates the Journal as a significant document. Nothing later in her writing matched up to it, and indeed tragedy followed close upon the heels of the Cannings' success. Three years later, with Canning now a Viscount and the first Viceroy of India, Charlotte died suddenly of fever, and her grief-stricken husband survived her by only a few months.

It would require much research to prove the soundness of the idea that articulate homegrown Scots became less significant in the official life of the Empire as the century wore on. It was probably true of India with, first of all, the growing reliance of the East India Company upon the products of the East India College at Haileybury and, later, the way in which the examinations for the Indian Civil Service favoured the classically trained products of the English public schools and the Universities of Oxford and Cambridge, as has been suggested by George Davie in *The Democratic Intellect*. The lads o' pairts were perhaps most successful when the Empire was still to a large degree a freelance commercial undertaking; when it became a bureaucratic machine, the job specifications were devised to secure employment for the owners' offspring. Yet, in commerce and the army, in exploration, in the missionary fields, in a host of practical and executive areas, the Scots were still to the fore; fewer of them, however, come to our notice as able to write interestingly for the general reader.

The explorers are exceptions to this trend. They write the great continuing saga of discovery for the avid reading public. From Alexander Mackenzie in Canada, as we have seen, James Bruce, with his *Travels to Discover the Source of the Nile in the Years 1768-73,* and Mungo Park, with *Travels in the Interior of Africa* (1799), the habit is established of the journals that had been kept under circumstances of sometimes incredible hardship and suffering being edited for general publication. Mostly they are of great scientific and geographical interest; at their best they are also personal records of vital human experience, revealing some wit and style. Africa is the stage for much of the movement. Hugh Clapperton followed Mungo Park to West Africa in the 1820s. James Augustus Grant went with Speke to discover the source of the White Nile in Lake Victoria, but unselfishly let his leader reach it alone, similarly playing second fiddle in his book, *A Walk Across Africa* (1864)—'You have had a long walk, Captain Grant', said the Prime Minister, Lord Palmerston, thus inspiring the title. Joseph Thomson pioneered a direct route across Kenya to Uganda, later publishing *To The Central African Lakes and Back* (1881).

Above all, it is David Livingstone who must be given precedence in Africa among the Wandering Scots. He was truly a wanderer. It has been written of him (by Alan Moorehead) that, unlike the other explorers, who proceeded in a straight line to fulfil a purpose or object and then return home, Livingstone travelled in circles, with his mission beginning and ending in Africa. This made him more part of Africa than any others of his generation, so that when he wrote his great accounts of his missionary travels and explorations, the readers sensed his passion and sympathy reaching out to stir their feelings and arouse them to involvement. The evil of the slave trade in Africa was one of his major concerns. It runs like a bloodstained black thread through his three journals, *Missionary Travels* (1857), *Expedition to the Zambesi and its Tributaries* (1865) and *Last Journals* (posthumously in 1874), with one violent episode or encounter after another, and harrowing scenes in abundance.

> When endeavouring to give some account of the slave trade of East Africa, it was necessary to keep far within the truth, in order not to be thought guilty of exaggeration; but in sober seriousness the subject does not admit of exaggeration. To overdraw its evils is a simple impossibility. The sights I have seen, though common incidents of the traffic, are so nauseous that I always strive to drive them from memory. In the case of most disagreeable recollections, I can succeed, in time, in consigning them to oblivion, but the slaving scenes come back unbidden, and make me start up at dead of night horrified by their vividness.[21]

The theme of *Heart of Darkness* is visible in Livingstone's narrative decades before the horrors of the Congo appalled the European conscience. Another foreshadowing of a later issue of guilt occurs in his first journal from Africa. Early in his labours, when he was

still principally a missionary and teacher, Livingstone had had a prickly relationship with the Boers in Southern Africa and diagnosed their condition long before the rest of the white world:

> I attempted to benefit the tribes among the Boers of Magaliesberg by placing native teachers at different points. 'You must teach the blacks', said Mr Hendrick Potgeiter, the commandant in chief, 'that they are not equal to us.' Other Boers told me, 'I might as well teach the baboons on the rocks as the Africans', but declined the test which I proposed, namely, to examine whether they or my native attendants could read best.'[22]

The nineteenth-century involvement of Scots in Australia, as recorded in their writings, is as marked as their achievements in Canada, India or Africa, although there may be a contrast in scale. Lachlan MacQuarie, Governor of New South Wales, did keep his diaries of tours in his territory, including Van Diemen's Land, between 1810 and 1822, but they found their readers only in the columns of the *Sydney Gazette*. Like Galt in Canada, he was concerned to found new towns for settlers but he was as likely to be admonishing the settlers who were already there on the need to pay more attention to their own personal cleanliness and comfort and to build better houses to live in, to be lecturing convicts and to be organising the setting up of street signs. Compared with the Nabobs in India, his daily round was one of mundane normality, doing a dull necessary job with efficiency; similarly, his writing is concise and factual with the bare minimum of conventional literary touches. The best stories from Australia did not receive proper literary treatment. One wishes that Angus McMillan from Skye had continued his *Journal of a Cruise from Greenock to New Holland* (1837) to deal more fully with his exploration of new territories in New South Wales, to articulate clearly the dream of a 'Caledonia Australis', a new Scotland of the South, that would accommodate the flood of emigrants from the Scottish Highlands, and to reveal how this dream crumbled before the prosaic absurdity of the English bureauractic foundation of Gippsland (named after a Governor). What he did write was contained only in a letter.[23]

We have to turn to *The Journals of John McDouall Stuart* (1864) for something resembling a heroic story. Stuart tried over a period of five years to make a crossing of the Australian continent from south to north. After one or two failures, he made it, despite shortages of food and water, weakness of both men and horses, a severe fall from his horse, sufferings from scurvy which nearly blinded him, and the suspicion and hostility of aborigines. On the way he observed birds, collected plants, examined rocks for gold, fixed the centre of the continent, named many landmarks and kept his eloquent journal. His style is factual and detailed but his sufferings are exposed clearly and feelingly. Yet there is time for humour, as when he describes meeting an ab-

origine who greets him with a Masonic sign, which he is able to return.

The tidewash of Scottish emigration was worldwide during the nineteenth century. No continent, no ocean was without its flotsam and jetsam from the wreck of Scotland's failure to provide a harmonious and prosperous community for all her people. The blame was not totally to be laid at the door of the Scottish people themselves, but in a large measure it was their fault, for reasons that lie outside the scope of this essay. The human jetsam cast up on the empty continents of the world found a permanent lodgement there; when the settlers or their children found a writing voice, their work became part of the new literatures of Canada, the United States, Australia or New Zealand. The flotsam, whom we have basically been considering, tended to bob around the world for a few years and then return with the currents—old age, retirement, official posting, the sense of a mission completed—either to their starting point or, frequently, to a more congenial English locality. Their writings are part of their official memorials.

We have already touched on some of the characteristics of this writing. It was the direct expression of people looking outward on the world, not inward to their own mental processes. It was not 'literary' in an aesthetic sense but it was designed to communicate significant matters to a reader of middlebrow tastes and accordingly used some basic literary modes and conventions to facilitate the communication. We can see a reliance on journals, histories, sketches, accounts; there is interesting narrative, detailed and vivid description, commentary frequently of a moral or sympathetic kind, flashes of humour or self-deflating near-mockery, and a personal first-person voice to give authenticity to the tone. The emphasis is firmly on content rather than on technique, for it is a basic premise of the writer that the subject matters to the reader as it does to the writer. It is assumed that the reader wants to 'know', more so than to be merely diverted. Many of the writers are conscious that they were significant actors in the events they are describing, yet there are very few egos on display. It is as if there is an acceptance of a duty to be fulfilled: to enlarge the store of human knowledge and to educate the reader. It is felt that knowledge is power, and by 'knowledge' is meant the accumulation of facts about the real world. The reader's mental map of that world must have its blank spaces filled in with names and features and coloured with confident understanding just as the tantalising empty areas in the atlases were acquiring the lines of rivers, the shapes of great lakes and a proud wash of protective red coloration. Perhaps this duty is an aspect of Scottishness in the writers, a legacy of the education many of them had experienced in their own burgh or village school classroom from dominies trained in a harder discipline than the study of Latin and Greek classics. On the other hand, we can

find that many of those we have been examining here had upbringings that were not typically Scottish in the educational sense. This is not really a contradiction, for the nineteenth century was a time when the official ethos of society, to which most of our subjects subscribed, was particularly close to the Scottish Calvinist ethic promoted in schools and churches.

Finally, as we have seen, the writing, though Scottish in attitude and purpose, contained no awareness of Scottishness as anything more than a continuing aberration within an English pattern of culture and nationality. Even David Livingstone could speak of 'my principles as an Englishman'. No doubt this is to be deplored, but it is a fact that cannot be argued around. There may be an argument that Scots today might wish to develop, that in some way this separation of self from national or cultural roots vitiated the expression, diminished the writing, produced the same visible malaise as can be perceived in the writings of the Kailyard. If there is evidence of this, it in no way diminishes the actual achievement of these writers, which was to have performed with honour in the world of action and to have transmitted this real experience effectively either as fact or as fiction to an interested circle of typical readers.

It has not been the purpose of this essay to consider that other group of articulate Scots who, for one reason or other—ill health, commercial necessity, a sense of alienation—chose to live and work for much of their adult lives beyond Scotland.[24] The writer or artist in exile is a romantic figure in most Western societies. His is a different and more diverse psychology from that of the servant of empire. The motivating impulses behind Thomas Carlyle or James Thomson or George Douglas Brown or George MacDonald deserve and have received fuller treatment elsewhere. However, it would be fitting to end this essay with reference to that most far-flung of Scottish exiles, Robert Louis Stevenson.

While Scotland's 'literature of Empire' moves beyond the optimism and enthusiasm of the early century into a serious and businesslike mood that is sutained throughout the heyday of Victorian and Edwardian imperial complacency, Stevenson strikes a more pessimistic *fin de siècle* note. His writings from the Pacific, *In The South Seas* (1900) and *Vailima Letters* (1895), have much to say about the effect of Western man upon weak and vulnerable societies. The fatal impact was already producing its destructive results, and not only upon the original inhabitants. The opening words of *The Ebb-Tide,* which Stevenson wrote with Lloyd Osbourne, stress the Western intrusion:

> Throughout the island world of the Pacific, scattered men of many European races and from almost every grade of society carry activity and disseminate disease.[25]

But the emphasis in this short and powerful novel is upon the corruption that takes hold of Western man, even in apparent Paradise. The images of disease, drunkenness, degradation and homicidal greed that pervade the story of Herrick and his companions sailing to and invading Attwater's Island take on a universal and allegorical significance beyond their seeming localisation in place and time. If we think back to Richard Middlemas and his lustful visions of limitless wealth won by violence, we can see that they are not really separated by a century of years and a hemisphere of distance from the South Seas. They are the same, and, in Scott's novel, Middlemas undergoes the same debasement.

Stevenson's gloomy vision seems to put Scotland's nineteenth-century imperial writers into a bleaker context. However much good many of them did in their own spheres, however free most of them remained from the corruption of wealth and power, they were all ultimately shipped together on a doomed vessel bound on a tainted and dubious quest. They performed nobly all the tasks required of them and wrote up the log clearly and efficiently before they took their severance and departed. Yet because of the destination and fate of the great ship of Empire, these worthy crew members now carry a degree of apparent blame and their reputation has suffered. Herrick in *The Ebb-Tide* had an insight into his fate:

> He had complied with the ebb-tide in man's affairs, and the tide had carried him away; he heard already the roaring of the maelstrom that must hurry him under.[26]

The ebb-tide of history and political opinion has carried most of the writers dealt with here away from the consciousness of modern Scotland. It may be time that a new flow of thinking about their lives and writings should bring them back.

Notes

1. Sir Walter Scott, *The Surgeon's Daughter,* Melrose Edition (Edinburgh, 1898), Ch. IV, p 42.

2. Ibid., Ch. IV, p 43.

3. Ibid., Ch. XIV, p 131.

4. John Galt, *The Last of the Lairds* (Edinburgh, 1976), Ch. VI, pp 25-6.

5. Ibid., Ch. XVII, p 73.

6. Alexander Mackenzie, *Voyages from Montreal, etc.,* in Walter Sheppe, *First Man West* (California, 1962), pp 231-3.

7. John Galt, *Autobiography* (London, 1833), vol 2 (Epoch Sixth), Ch. IX, pp 58-60.

8. 'Canadian Boat Song', Anonymous (but sometimes attributed to John Galt), in R L Mackie (ed), *A Book of Scottish Verse* (London, 1967).

9. Michael Scott, *Tom Cringle's Log* (London, 1969), Ch. V, p 108.

10. Ibid., Ch. XII, p 263.

11. Ibid., Ch. XIV, p 337.

12. Ibid., Ch. XIV, p 339.

13. Sir Thomas Munro, Letter to Lord Hastings, 12 November 1818, given in Rev G R Gleig, *Life of Sir Thomas Munro* (London, 1830), vol 1, pp 519-20.

14. John Galt, *The Last of the Lairds* (Edinburgh, 1976), Ch. XVII, p 74.

15. Sir John Malcolm, *Sketches of Persia,* vol 2, Ch. XVIII, p 132.

16. Ibid., Ch. XVIII, p 135.

17. Mountstuart Elphinstone, Letter to Governor-General, 1823, quoted in Philip Woodruff, *The Men Who Ruled India,* vol I (London, 1953), p 243.

18. Mountstuart Elphinstone, Letter to Sir James Mackintosh, op. cit., p 221.

19. Scotland and India: Exhibition 7 June-21 September, 1986, National Library of Scotland, Edinburgh.

20. Charlotte Canning, Journal Letters, given in Augustus Hare, *The Story of Two Noble Lives* (London, 1893).

21. David Livingstone, *The Last Journals of David Livingstone in Central Africa* (London, 1880), vol 2, Ch. VIII, p 212.

22. David Livingstone, *Missionary Travels and Researches in South Africa* (London, 1857), Ch. II, pp 37-8.

23. Angus McMillan, in T F Bride, *Letters from Victorian Pioneers* (Melbourne, 1898).

24. Equally it has not been considered appropriate to deal with the significant figure of the Scottish soldier in the nineteenth century. From the Napoleonic Wars at the beginning of the century through the colonial campaigns, the Indian Mutiny and the Crimea down to the second South African War at the end of the century, a host of Scots of all ranks from private to general experienced war at first hand, and some wrote about it. A collection of these writings has still to be made. The soldier stands at the edge of exile, separated from his home and family but probably less affected by his strange surroundings than the administrator, the explorer or the missionary, since he is an instrument of policy rather than an independent agent and it is in the interests of this policy that he should be unreflective about his area of action and its inhabitants.

25. Robert Louis Stevenson and Lloyd Osbourne, *The Ebb-Tide,* Works of Robert Louis Stevenson, Vailima Edition, vol XVIII (London, 1922), Ch. I, p 5.

26. Ibid., Ch. VIII, p 141.

Further Reading

Bumsted, J M, *The People's Clearance 1770-1815* (Edinburgh, 1982).

Calder, Jenni (ed), *The Enterprising Scot* (Edinburgh, 1986).

Donaldson, Gordon, *The Scots Overseas* (London, 1966).

Galbraith, J K, *The Non-Potable Scotch* (London, 1964).

Gibb, Andrew Dewar, *Scottish Empire* (London, 1937).

Hill, Douglas, *The Scots to Canada* (London, 1972).

Mackay, Donald, *Scotland Farewell—The People of the 'Hector'* (Edinburgh, 1980).

Macmillan, David S, *Scotland and Australia 1788-1850* (London, 1967).

Moorehead, Alan, *The White Nile* (London, 1960).

Royle, Trevor, *Death Before Dishonour—The True Story of Fighting Mac: Major-General Sir Hector Macdonald* (Edinburgh, 1982).

Smailes, Helen, *Scottish Empire* (Edinburgh, 1981).

Watson, Don, *Caledonia Australis—Scottish Highlanders on the frontier of Australia* (Sydney, 1984).

Woodruff, Philip, *The Men Who Ruled India,* vol I (London, 1953).

Michael Hollington (essay date April 2000)

SOURCE: Hollington, Michael. "The Losing Game: Exile and Threshold in *A Tale of Two Cities*." *Cahiers Victoriens et Edouardiens,* no. 51 (April 2000): 189-205.

[*In the following essay, Hollington traces Charles Dickens's thematic use of exile to highlight the importance of "rituals of passage" in* A Tale of Two Cities, *and the biographical, literary, and historical context that shaped his treatment.*]

Three contexts may be helpful in introducing the theme of exile in *A Tale of Two Cities.* The first is classical, for the notion of exile that held sway in middle-class

Victorian culture of course drew inspiration from the classics—in particular, from Homer. In ancient Greece, as Moses Finley emphasises, exile was regarded as a kind of death: ". . . banishment was deemed the bitterest of fates. The exile was stripped of all ties that meant life itself; it made no difference in this regard whether one had been compelled to flee or gone from home in the search for land by free choice." (Finley 68) Conversely, too, on the basis of the Descent into Hades in Book XI of *The Odyssey,* and Achilles' lament that it is

> Better, I say, to break sod as a farm hand
> for some poor country man, on iron rations
> than lord it over all the exhausted dead,
>
> (Fitzgerald 201)

one might say that death for the Greeks may have invited comparison with exile.

At any rate, the single most powerful Victorian image of impending exile, Ford Madox Brown's 1855 painting *The Last of England* (a response to bidding farewell to his friend and fellow-artist Thomas Woolner departing for the Australian goldfields in 1852—see Osborne 165 & 1220) can perhaps be read afresh in such perspectives. Here we may see, at the appropriately named port of Gravesend, what appears like a representation, in the male figure at least, of a crossing of the Styx. Woolner's face is ashen-hued, or even black, against the bright colours that surround him, as he stares with spectral and apparently accusing eyes—at us philistines, it would seem, who have driven him from the paradise of England and home by failing to buy his work. Not only is he himself associated with death, but his backward glance also seems malevolent and fatal—like that of Orpheus, perhaps, as he condemns Eurydice to death as he turns around to regard her.

I shall leave to one side for the moment the particular fact that Woolner was nonetheless able to return from Australia in 1854 (never to look back again, so to speak, in his pursuit of a successful career in England), or the more general reflection that artists in modern times have often made great imaginative capital out of exile, in order to introduce a second contextual dimension, which is chiefly political. Here I am thinking not only of the tragic regular mass human shipments away from the British Isles in Dickens's lifetime—the two million emigrants from Ireland between 1845 and 1855, for instance, in the aftermath of the Famine (see Lyons 44)—but also, conversely and ironically, yet of more direct relevance to *A Tale of Two Cities,* of Victorian England's rôle as a refuge for numerous political exiles from Europe. Especially after 1848, Dickens was unusually sympathetic to their plight, and active on their behalf. Unlike George Eliot, he did not meet Marx, but their respective paths came close to crossing once or twice, most interestingly for our purposes when *House-*

hold Words championed Gottfried Kinkel, a member of the circle of German revolutionary exiles, whom Marx and Engels in fact regarded as a fraud. But Dickens was taken in, apparently, by Kinkel's tearjerking stories of the harsh conditions of his imprisonment in Germany.

The conclusion one might tentatively draw from this incident, that he was receptive almost to a fault to the pathos of exile, is strengthened by the reflection that he had earlier been duped by a street-beggar who claimed to know Mazzini, with whom, via the Carlyles (Jane apparently half in love with the handsome Italian), Dickens was indeed in frequent contact—as he was in fact with many Italian dissidents. "I have known Mazzini and Gallenga," he wrote in 1860, to censure Chorley's negative representation of Italy in his novel *Roccabella;* "Manin was tutor to my daughters in Paris." (Letters, IX, 207). Indeed, as he worked on *A Tale of Two Cities* (its completion only just preceding the onset of Garibaldi's successful campaign of national unification), he was again an active member of a committee to help political exiles from Naples. Characteristically he took time off from the rendering of the tribulations of Manette's imprisonment and exile to urge its chairman, Antonio Panizzi, to write an account of their "Ten years trial" for his new journal *All the Year Round.* (Letters, IX, xi & 38)

But such intensities of sympathetic understanding of the trauma of exile are as nothing compared to the extraordinary amount of emotional energy, psychological involvement and personal identification with its characters, that Dickens invested in *A Tale of Two Cities,* which constitutes a third contextual dimension, to be dealt with here at rather greater length. This is the first novel to be written after the painful separation from his wife that took place in 1858, which can be seen for our purposes, quite clearly as a key moment of personal transition, and perhaps more specifically as a kind of voluntary self-exile, or banishment into exile, or both. Relinquishing at the same moment his journal *Household Words,* and replacing it with a new title in which the new novel appeared, Dickens tacitly acknowledged that he could no longer credibly identify himself with the imagery of stable domesticity. Metaphorically at least he had become a version of the figure we find imprinted at the heart of *A Tale of Two Cities,* a wanderer and exile from felicity.

The idea for the new novel had come to him before the separation however—in September 1857, as he acted out a death in a play written in 1856 for amateur domestic theatricals, chiefly by Wilkie Collins, but with a great deal of input (including the initial germ or core idea) from himself. It is significant, perhaps, that for the family hearth Collins and Dickens should choose to write a play about a form of ultimate dual exile: at any rate, *The Frozen Deep* takes us to the furthest ends of

the earth, on a journey to the Arctic, and there has us witness the death of Richard Wardour, a disappointed suitor who saves and sacrifices himself for his rival. Dickens acted the rôle of Wardour in what became an erotically charged atmosphere: in the later, public performances, his leading lady was Maria Ternan, the sister of his mistress-to-be, whom he also met in the course of these theatricals.[1] Using a psychologically curious but proleptic third person narrative form, he describes this "prettily simple and unaffected" girl so spontaneously overcome by emotion at the pathos of the dramatic situation that she discharges her tears over his body on stage in a pretty intimate form of *Liebestod*: "when she had to kneel over Wardour dying, and be taken leave of, the tears streamed out of her eyes into his mouth, down his beard, all over his rags—down his arms as he held her by the hair." The strangeness of the account of this veritably orgasmic shower-bath is heightened by the fact that it is contained in a letter to the philanthropist Angela Burdett Coutts—his "resurrectionist" collaborator in the Urania Cottage scheme for prostitutes and fallen women, which aimed to rehabilitate them by sending them into exile in Australia—a kind of connoisseur in such matters, perhaps.

In the same letter he describes how, at the climax of these tear-floods, the idea of the future novel came to him: "Sometimes of late, when I have been very much excited by the crying of two thousand people over the grave of Richard Wardour, new ideas for a story have come into my head as I lay on the ground, with surprising force and brilliancy." (Letters, VIII, 432) Thus the core idea of *A Tale of Two Cities* can be seen as that of passage from one state to another; it situates itself on a margin or at a threshold, particularly of course that between life and death, for which exile seems to stand as an important figure. We may be reminded here, too, of the historical context of the novel, which treats the French Revolution as a crucial moment of passage between tradition and modernity, and thence too of Walter Benjamin's profound remarks (in the *Passagen-Werk*, itself about threshold experience) on the poverty of modern *rites de passage*:

> this is the name in folklore for ceremonies that accompany death, birth, weddings, puberty, etc. In modern life these transitions have become less and less clearly marked and experienced. We have become very impoverished in threshold experiences. Falling asleep is perhaps the only one left to us. (But there is waking up too).

> *(PW V, i, 617; my translation)*

Seen from this perspective, *A Tale of Two Cities* can be seen as an attempt to reassert, again in part through the figure of exile, the significance of rituals of passage.

At any rate, Dickens felt so stirred by the idea of it that he began writing, in an allegedly spontaneous and unconscious way, on a special personal, transitional day—

the day on which both he and David Copperfield were born: "it is a most astonishing coincidence that I have never . . . begun a book, or begun anything of interest to me, or done anything of importance to me, but it was on a Friday." (Letters, VIII, 432-3) Work on the novel was then interrupted for over a year by the traumas of 1858. Yet when resumed in earnest, it retains unusual marks of self-identification with the novel's twin central male characters, Charles Darnay—who renames himself thus in exile, forsaking his father's name and adopting his mother's, and so providing himself with Dickens's initials—and his double, Sydney Carton. When the novel was finished, he writes again in December 1859 as if he were still acting the part he first assumed almost three years earlier: "I must say that I like my Carton. And I have a faint idea sometimes, that if I had acted him, I could have done something with his life and death." (Letters IX, 177) The character is significantly *my* Carton.

Moreover in 1856 he had bought the "dream house" of his childhood, the residence of a former mayor of Rochester at Gad's Hill, and settled at a strategic point on the path to exile, the London to Dover Road. *A Tale of Two Cities* opens—not surprisingly, on a Friday—at this precise place, at a moment of danger, on a dark November night when highwaymen threaten to dispatch unwary or foolhardy travellers over the border between life and death.

At this point we may leave autobiography momentarily behind, and turn to allegory, which is particularly strongly at work in *A Tale of Two Cities,* transforming this particular road into a general figure of the passage of human life from birth to death from the very earliest pages of the novel. The first chapter, entitled "The Period", simply introduces some general historical reflections on the year 1775, and ends with a panoramic overview of the passing of time, which carries great and small alike, "the creatures of this chronicle among the rest—along the roads that lay before them." (TOTC I, i, 37) Later, the same figure is adapted to convey all that is wrong with high society in Paris at this time, with its abundance of people "unconnected with anything that was real, or with lives passed in travelling by any straight road to any true earthly end." (II, vi, 137) Their indifference has the inevitable historical consequences we witness in the novel: the allegorical road-mender, for instance, one of the Jacques who prepare the revolution (in which he converts, significantly again, to woodsawyer), as the Defarges recognise: "although it is a long time on the road, it is on the road and coming." (II, xvi, 208)

Yet allegory acts to subsume autobiography in *A Tale of Two Cities,* with its phenomenological encoding of the anxieties of middle-aged exile. The particular traveller on the London to Dover road is Lorry, a bachelor in his

sixties forced to take up locomotion again after a lapse of fifteen years since the initial crossing of the Channel Rubicon, the passing of Lucy into exile in his arms at the age of two. Throughout the novel we will see him inevitably travelling towards *his* death, between two vaults, the bank and the grave—sometimes almost wilfully so, as when he is attracted like the mariner in *The Arabian Nights* to the magnetic loadstone rock of death and destruction that is Paris in the era of the Terror. Here at the very beginning, though, all this is embedded in solid realist specification, as we experience the phenomenal *minutiae* of coach travel, and learn that it is uncomfortable as well as dangerous. Lorry has to hang on to a leathern strap to avoid bumping into his fellow travellers, and thus his sleep is fitful and disturbed by dreams and reveries, a mere temporary opiate relief from pain.

"Ainsi vous voyagez toujours?", asks Marthe of Mephistopheles in Gounod's *Faust,* another product of 1859. It was the opera that touched Dickens more profoundly than any other, in part because of the sublime singing of his friend Pauline Viardot, to whom in Paris in the winter of 1855-6 he sent the parts of *Little Dorrit* as they appeared in print. Johnson and Tomalin and others are surely correct in their surmise that it held iconic significance for him as an allegory of his relationship with Ellen Ternan, when, in January 1863, he wept buckets at a performance at the Opéra in Paris: "I couldn't bear it, and gave in completely." (Johnson 502; Tomalin 140) "Dure nécéssité, madame! Sans ami, sans parents! . . . sans femme"; Mephistopheles' ironically seductive reply may have resonated for Dickens with somewhat deeper notes, in which the figure of personal exile lay beneath the banalities of modern travel.

But solitary middle-class journeying by coach is nothing, in *A Tale of Two Cities,* compared with walking in clogged feet, as the peasant revolutionaries do, their arrival witnessed by the mender of roads: "grim, rough, swart, steeped in the mud and dust of many highways." (II, xxiii, 257) The novel reformulates, in a number of profoundly recessed codes, the primary biographical trauma of Dickens's life, its emphasis on travel on foot elaborating a cardinal image of exiled tramping towards death and destruction. Work in a shoe polish factory becomes Manette's shoemaking: "it ought to have been finished long ago," he says of a young lady's walking shoe, making significant dual reference to the novelist and to himself. (II, xviii, 221) "Blacksmith's work" is how Lorry refers to it in code, unconsciously pushing it further in the direction of the revelation of the Dickensian secret. But fortunately Manette is less paranoid than Pip in the next novel *Great Expectations,* where Herbert Pocket's thoroughly complimentary nickname "Handel" is perceived as sadistic insulting reference,

via the Harmonious Blacksmith variations, to his origins—"in a blacking warehouse", so to speak, if we wish to decode the deep confessional stratum of the writing.

It is evident, though, that *A Tale of Two Cities* is devoted to finding a parable language for the healing of personal trauma—to suggest in fact that the pilgrim's progress need not be vain. "My Carton" is its evident vehicle, and two allegorical gestures that he performs towards the end of the novel may serve as examples of the way in which it works. They both concern feet coming and going across an abyss. In the first, in an evident epiphany of the salvation of the two Lucies, he ferries a mother and daughter across the Styx of Lutetia—that is to say, Paris, the quintessential home of mud, with all its possible symbolic connotations of impurity and moral degradation:

> At one of the theatre doors, there was a little girl with a mother, looking for a way across the street through the mud.
>
> He carried the child over, and before the timid arm was loosed from his neck asked her for a kiss.
>
> (III, ix, 343)

The second, more brilliant example translates the black of the warehouse dedicated to the polished shining of boots into a resplendent but ambiguous white:

> He wore the white riding-coat and top-boots, then in vogue, and the light of the fire touching their light surfaces made him look very pale, with his long brown hair, all untrimmed, hanging loose about him. His indifference to fire was sufficiently remarkable to elicit a word of remonstrance from Mr. Lorry; his boot was still upon the hot embers of the flaming log, when it had broken under the weight of his foot.
>
> 'I forgot it,' he said.
>
> (III, ix, 338-9)

Sydney Carton's white topboots of course make his appearance ghostly. The version of Gothic associated with Manette is now transposed, the ghost a mediating salamander who can pass to and fro amongst the fires. The forgetting is salutary, obviously—the shoe, so to speak, now thoroughly finished, its wearer's exile is nearly at an end.

For "my Carton" has clearly functioned hitherto in the text as the apotheosis of what has happened in modernity to rituals of passage and voyage—that is to say, how these have devolved into the aimless and restless locomotion of the inhabitants of modern cities. In this respect, the prominence of the concept of "restlessness" in *A Tale of Two Cities* is a very clear sign of the author's emotional involvement in this text, for it is a favourite term used in connection with his own psycho-

logical crises, his sleeplessness, his prodigious city and country walking, and boundless appetite for travel and distraction. Most significantly, though, it is his regular code-word for the state in which he would "give birth" to a new novel. Regularly at such times he would contemplate some ultimate exile—in the mountaintops of Switzerland, in Siberia, or, most commonly, in Australia. In 1850, for instance, he writes to Mrs. Watson: "I think of flying to Australia and taking to the Bush." Between June and December 1862 he uses the word itself as he actively contemplates a reading tour and new travel book, and describes to Beard how, "constantly disturbed and dazzled by the great chance that seems to be waiting over there, I am restless." The moment of the birth of *A Tale of Two Cities* is a cardinal instance of such a mood, for Dickens describes himself "in the grim despair and restlessness from excitement" (Letters VIII, 423) after the frenzied climax of *The Frozen Deep*.

Thus in *A Tale of Two Cities* we have numerous pointed reflections of such "restlessness". An obvious example is the onomastic Stryver, who elicits Carton's punning ironic commentary: "you were always driving and shouldering and pressing, to that restless degree that I had no chance for my life but in rust and repose." (II, v, 120-1). But the concept is not merely to be aligned with bullying self-promotion and aggrandizement, as with Stryver; it is also of relevance to the far more sympathetic case of Manette's "restlessness":

> Sometimes he gets up in the dead of the night, and will be heard, by us overhead there, walking up and down, walking up and down, in his room. Ladybird has learnt to know then that his mind is walking up and down, in his old prison. She hurries to him, and they go on together, walking up and down, walking up and down, until he is composed. But he never says a word of the true reason of his restlessness to her, and she finds it best not to hint at it to him.

> (II, vi, 128)

In this revealing example of the strong therapeutic urge and concentration of *A Tale of Two Cities* we may note a double movement. The first is inward—the walking up and down has been translated into a purely mental activity (as likewise in Dickens's Prologue to *The Frozen Deep,* which refers to "the secrets of the vast Profound within us" or "the region of the ice-bound soul"— see Johnson 440). But then, in a reverse movement, language is exteriorised or even altogether replaced by mime and gesture or "acting out", again in memory of the play, or equally appositely, of what Dickens in the mid-1850s had felt and experienced as one of the most positive things about France: the expressive, performative theatricality of everyday life. In this movement of return, the talking cure has become here, so to speak, the walking cure.

It will be no surprise, then, that the word 'restless' is used yet more pointedly of the twin central reflections in the novel of Dickens himself—of Charles Darnay in

the case of such urges as his eagerness to be in Paris when he hears of Lorry's Tellson commission ("I wish I were going myself, said Darnay, somewhat restlessly"— II, xxiv, 265), but, above all, and continuously, of Carton. "You know my vagabond and restless habits", he reminds Lorry at the novel's end of what has been emphasised throughout, announcing his intention yet once more to "prowl about the streets a long time." (III, ix, 340) He is the novel's essential *flâneur,* of course, having served an early apprenticeship to the art in Paris (where else?), when he and Stryver "were fellow-students in the Student-Quarter." (II, v, 120) But whilst Stryver graduates to more aggressive and violent modes of walking ("anybody who had seen him projecting himself into Soho while he was yet on Saint Dunstan's side of Temple Bar, bursting in his full-blown way along the pavement, to the jostlement of all weaker people, might have seen how safe and strong he was"—II, xii, 172), Carton remains an unreconstructed Bohemian "lounger", marooned under "the cloud of caring for nothing." (II, xiii, 179)

One cannot of course accuse Dickens himself of "caring for nothing"—however much, as Forster tells us, he feared as a young man a propensity to turn out as a vagabond (especially after the early disappointments of his acting career). What one certainly can see, surrounding the writing of *A Tale of Two Cities,* and its themes of restless locomotion and exile, is the commencement of a more or less obsessive compulsion to hit the road, of which the exhausting public reading tours are the most familiar and startling expressions. They are born in the aftermath of the separation of 1858, and the road they set in motion leads pretty directly to Dickens's death at the early age of 58. I shall spare the full list of the novelist's "Mephisphelean" travels during the period immediately prior to the commencement of writing the novel, that is to say during the "First provincial reading tour" between August 2nd and November 13th 1858, a period of 103 days in which there were 85 readings in more than 40 towns throughout England, Scotland and Ireland, which Dickens then visited for the first time. But there is a kind of rather melancholy litany about the itinerary from which a few representative lyric sequences may be selected: Clifton-Exeter-Plymouth-Clifton at the outset, Liverpool-Dublin-Belfast-Cork or Limerick-Huddersfield-Wakefield-York in the middle, or Manchester-Birmingham-Nottingham-Derby-Manchester towards the end. The moment he set down his pen again after the novel's completion, the "Second provincial reading tour" began, taking in another 14 readings in 19 days between October 8 and 27 in towns such as Cambridge and Ipswich or Bradford and Cheltenham.

These were railway journeys of course, and the Dickensian "restlessness" may well have something to do with the constant new experience of motion at a speed far

exceeding that of a galloping horse (the fastest speed at which, two thousand years, anyone had been able to travel). In *A Tale of Two Cities,* as a premonition of such modernity, there is the aristocratic habit of reckless driving, knocking down children and killing them, or decisively and fatally interrupting Manette's leisurely stroll by the banks of the Seine: "I was walking on a retired part of the quay for the refreshment of the frosty air, at an hour's distance from my place of residence in the Street of the School of Medicine, when a carriage came along beside me, driven very fast." (III, x, 349)[2] Always death is an essential resonance in such rides, in a novel that cites Bürger's *Leonore* (II, ix, 159) to signal its conscious adoption of the German romantic musical and poetic *leitmotif* connecting louder and faster stepping or galloping and ever-approaching death. Dickens had made it early on in a comic mode in the sketch 'Hackney Coaches' in *Sketches by Boz,* traces of which remain in the ironic comparison of the Old Bailey to "a kind of deadly innyard, from which pale travellers set out continually in cabs and coaches, on a violent passage into the other world." (II, ii, 90)

Yet *A Tale of Two Cities* is emphatically not about one-way passage. In fact, at the Old Bailey trial we witness, that at which Charles Darnay is almost condemned to eternal banishment, the indictment is read out, and appears to accuse him, essentially, of the crime of "coming and going"—that is to say, "between the dominions of our . . . serene, illustrious, excellent, and so forth, and those of the said French Lewis", (II, ii, 93)—no bad evocation of the structure and technique of the novel itself, with its constant movement from London to Paris and back. From the beginning in Dickens's writing, exiles, transportees, emigrants and the like are programmed, like Woolner, to return. His characteristic Odyssean emphasis on the *nostos* or homecoming is laid down in "The Convict's Return," in *Pickwick Papers,* which reworks the parable of the prodigal son, who returns from Australia "truly contrite, penitent, and humbled, if ever man was." Micawber's comic redemption and metamorphosis through settled work in exile in Port Middlebay downunder, "that theer bald head of his, a perspiring in the sun," earns him a final return appearance in England in the last pages of *David Copperfield,* and Magwitch in *Great Expectations* finds, like Achilles, that being king of the underworld palls ("it come flat to be there, for all I was growing rich"), and so returns to face with stoic calm an inexorable final further transition: "he was the least anxious of any of us", Pip records, at the novel's end.

Thus in *A Tale of Two Cities* everyone returns from exile—or, more fundamentally, walks down as well as up. The rhythm is irresistible: at the beginning Lorry takes Lucie back to France, having taken her from there to begin with, and her brow expresses the faint memory of the initial crossing. Thereafter she herself, of course,

becomes the novel's 'golden thread', the Ariadne who permits her Theseus to return from the Minotaur's labyrinth. Nothing is forgotten or lost in this text; in terms of her identity, even in exile, she never loses her Frenchness[3]: "although the Doctor's daughter had known nothing of her birth, she appeared to have innately derived from it that ability to make much of little means, which is one of its most useful and agreeable characteristics." (II, vi, 124)

Darnay's exile is similar in kind. It is imaged as a kind of rebirth, albeit of a peculiarly grotesque and ignominious kind: a breeches rebirth, we might call it, as he is compared to those aristocrats who escape the revolution "legs uppermost and half suffocated, in a load of hay". (II, xxiv, 268) "This property and France are lost to me . . . I renounce them" (II, ix, 155) he declares to his uncle. But he too reworks the prodigal theme in two returns to France in which he takes up unfinished business. "You have been a long time coming", (II, ix, 151), the marquis protests, but his sense of feudal obligation survives the surface humiliation of his translation to England. Identity appears deeper and stronger than name, and action, once more, than language: "do you not see me here in France, of my own will?" (III, i, 277), he declares to his captors, in what is intended as a performative rebuttal of their suspicions.

For, unlike the Greeks in Finley's account, Dickens does set great store by the voluntarism of the exiles of *A Tale of Two Cities*: Darnay seeks and gains Manette's trust and approval by presenting himself as "like you, a voluntary exile." (II, x, 164) The apparent physical humiliation of his supposed entry into England is translated into a fixed humility and determination to succeed through lowly and ill-paid work: Darnay is like Micawber in Australia in his willingness to roll up his sleeves, and unlike Pip in having no "great expectations" ("he had expected neither to walk on pavements of gold, nor to lie on a bed of roses"). He willingly eschews the classics and earns his living from teaching French at Cambridge, which Dickens, with his misgivings about Oxbridge, which he did not attend, ironically represents as a kind of moonlighting, not totally dissimilar to Jerry Cruncher's illegal "trade" of digging up corpses for medical students: "he read with undergraduates as a sort of tolerated smuggler who drove a contraband trade in European languages." (II, x, 160) All this willing acceptance of his humble "road" will reach its ontological climax in his acceptance of imprisonment in La Force, the Parisian debtor's prison that is the equivalent of London's Marshalsea. In autobiographical code, Darnay's willing assumption of self-responsibility signifies a therapeutic facing-up to the reality of the cards he's been dealt—an overcoming of "restlessness", perhaps.

And so finally to the return of the arch-wanderer, "my Carton." His trauma, like Dickens's, has deep roots: "I am like one who died young" (II, xiii, 180), and he

projects the failures of his life as a consequence of an obscure secret wound: "I am a disappointed drudge, sir. I care for no man on earth, and no man cares for me" (II, iv, 115) He is the "famished traveller, wearied out by lonely wandering in a wilderness" first conceptualised in connection with Manette's voice at I, vi, 70—or, as he describes himself later, a "forlorn wanderer . . . pacing the dark streets." (II, xx, 239).

But if Carton is Dickens's Melmoth, the novel can be seen a kind of *Melmoth reconcilié* in which passage and transition regain lost significances. Presented as a pre-modern foil to Stryver and his 'striving', his anti-progressive absence of intentionality turns out in the end to be a means of redeeming progress and intentionality from the Faustian transformations it undergoes in the era of revolution.[4] At the end of the novel, returning to the place where he first learnt *flânerie,* he takes once more to the mud of Paris like a duck to water, this time in a paradoxically purposive way "traversing with the decided step of one who remembered the way well, several dark and dirty streets—much dirtier than usual, for the best public throughfare remained uncleansed in those times of terror." (III, ix, 341-2). For everything that Carton does at the end of the novel is actually a kind of gamble—as the two succeeding chapter titles, "A Hand at Cards" and "The Game Made", make plain—and thus not simply to be equated with the bourgeois 'striving' virtues of his aristocratic double.

The figure of the gambler once more recalls Benjamin's *Passagen-Werk,* which can be used to elucidate a particular nexus of motifs evoked in Sydney Carton. His fundamental alienated voluntary exile from life as it is lived by the majority of the characters of the novel is above all a kind of boredom—and Benjamin very suggestively links boredom with gamblers and other seekers of narcotic sensation in the modern city. "It threatens the gambler, the drug user, the flâneur, and the dandy", writes Susan Buck-Morss in her commentary on Benjamin's great project (Buck-Morss 104-5), the first three figures clearly represented in Carton, the fourth in Dickens himself.

But Carton's version of gambling at the end of the novel is of course a very distinctive one. He plays paradoxically, not in order to win, but in order to lose. "Let the Doctor play the winning game; I will play the losing one", he announces to Mr. Lorry (III, 8, 329), accompanying the placing of his bet with a gestural renunciation of his pet drug ("Sydney Carton filled another glass with brandy, poured it slowly out upon the hearth, and watched it as it dropped"-335). More essentially still, he seems to enact a renunciation of *flânerie* in the magnificent white boots passage quoted in part earlier, which begins with him asking Lorry about Lucy's appearance and state of mind:

'How does she look?'

'Anxious and unhappy, but very beautiful.'

'Ah!'

It was a long, grieving sound, like a sigh—almost like a sob. It attracted Mr. Lorry's eyes to Carton's face, which was turned to the fire. A light, or a shade (the old gentleman could not have told which), passed from it as swiftly as a change will sweep over a hill-side on a wild bright day, and he lifted his foot to put back one of the little flaming logs, which was tumbling forward.

(III, ix, 338)

This foot no longer trudges in alienated search of sensation[5]—it puts itself voluntarily into a refining fire that will lead to an awakening from boredom as "participation in the collective sleep." (Buck-Morss 105)

But what is perhaps most beautiful here is the imaging of the moment of transition in Carton's personal evolution through a swift passage of light across landscape which is recognizably English. If I am tempted to suggest that *A Tale of Two Cities* is a novel which combines responsiveness to the motif of exile and travel with a distinctive preoccupation with seasons and weather and the cosmos, it is again, I must confess, partly in order to provide some further fleshing out of the Benjamin nexus. "Nothing bores the average man more than the cosmos. Hence the most intimate connection for him between boredom and the weather," writes Benjamin (Buck-Morss 407), and in this novel we have frequent meteorological ruminations, both upon the divorce of modern civilization from the cosmos, and upon the possibility of reconnection to it.

It begins of course on a dreadful November night of a kind that had been for Dickens, since the very start of his writing career, the most compelling icon of the English experience of the cosmos. "But the streets of London, to be beheld in the very height of their glory, should be seen on a dark, dull, murky winter's night" had been the prescription of *Sketches by Boz,* (SB 53) and a heightened paradoxical 'inverse sublimity' (in Wolfgang Kayser's phrase) is at work in the powerful evocation in the opening pages of "a steaming mist in all the hollows . . . [which] . . . had roamed in its forlornness up the hill, like an evil spirit, seeking rest and finding none." (I, ii, 38) The striking personification here both anticipates Sydney's habitual restless, haunted wanderings, and lends coherence to the initial evocation, in the novel, of a supremely indifferent cosmos, "that arch of unmoved and eternal lights . . . some, so remote from this little earth that the learned tell us it is doubtful whether their rays have even yet discovered it, as a point in space where anything is suffered or done" (I, vi, 81) In such an alienated world, no wonder, then, that Carton languishes for so long under "the cloud of caring for nothing."

But the novel's ending, announced in the image of the hillside illumination, shows us—in anticipation of D. H. Lawrence, perhaps—a Carton reconnected with the cosmos. The play of forces shifts radically—it is now the universe that moves, rather than the man. On his last night-walk he enjoys a privileged perception of all the grand forces of nature that now put his own road in place in relation to them:

> 'There is nothing more to do', said he, glancing upward at the moon, 'until tomorrow. I can't sleep.'
>
> It was not a reckless manner, the manner in which he said these words aloud under the fast-sailing clouds, nor was it more expressive of negligence than defiance. It was the settled manner of a tired man, who had wandered and struggled and got lost, but who at length struck into his road and saw its end.

> (III, ix, 342)

Thus it is that when the Darnays flee from Paris, accompanied by the narrator in 'eternal' present-tense narrative, they are accompanied by the dynamic and strangely protective forces of cosmic energy rather than by any benign or hostile human agency: "the wind is rushing after us, and the clouds are flying after us, and the moon is plunging after us, and the whole wild night is in pursuit of us; but, so far we are pursued by nothing else." (III, xiii, 387)

One might conclude in this cosmic context by returning in a little more detail to another way in which *A Tale of Two Cities* reflects the extraordinary set of transitions that Dickens was attempting to negotiate as he wrote it. As mentioned earlier, It was first published in weekly parts as a kind of booster rocket for the new periodical *All the Year Round,* whose title reworks a quotation from *Othello*—"the story of my life, from year to year." That title and its resonances can be felt in the weather images of the novel, not only as an invitation to biographical reading, but as a signal, both of the novel's interest in the passing of historical time, and of its focus upon the transition of seasons and years into each other. Lucie's 'year-round' appearances outside La Force, the French equivalent of the Marshalsea, for instance—"in all weathers, in the snow and frost of winter, in the bitter winds of spring, in the hot sunshine of summer, in the rains of autumn, and again in the snow and frost of winter" (III, v, 306)—might be seen as an allegorical encoding of the imagination's necessities, of its duty of constancy to the prison trauma which lies at the base of all its metamorphoses. The renewed fulfilment of that duty in this novel seems to provide the assurance that at the end of the novel Sydney's memory will survive "all the year round" and "from year to year", transmitted to succeeding generations in the narrative of the younger Lucie. His life ends up immortalised in a tale told by the daughter of exiles, and the story she hands on serves to redeem and resurrect him from the place of permanent exile.

Notes

1. It is noteworthy how, as with his marriage to Catherine Hogarth, Dickens seems to have fallen indiscriminately for a "job lot" of sisters. To begin with, he seems to have been equally infatuated with Maria and Ellen Ternan, before settling this time for the youngest (the equivalent of Mary Hogarth).

2. Dickens got the detail of aristocratic driving at speed from Mercier's *Tableau de Paris,* as he acknowledges in a letter to Bulwer Lytton of June (Letters IX, 259; Sanders 153).

3. It may be worth saying, perhaps, in this context that though her name may sound like the English Lucy, this is a case of *faux amis.* Her name is really the equivalent of the altogether rarer English 'Lucia', from which it could be deduced that Dickens's aim was to stress that she is quintessentially French.

4. For a suggestive if impressionistic exploration of the significance of Goethe's *Faust* for the era of modernity, see Marshall Berman's *All That Is Solid Melts Into Air* (Berman).

5. For Benjamin, the gambler-flâneur goes in search of his ideal of destiny or good luck in the possibility that his sexual number might turn up amongst the passers-by on the streets or in the arcades: "does he not transform the arcades into a Casino, a gambling hall where he places the red, blue, and yellow chips of emotion on women, on a face that appears suddenly—will it return his gaze?—on a silent mouth—will it speak to him? That which looks out at the gambler from ever number on the green cloth—happiness—here winks to him out of ever woman's body, as the chimera of sexuality: as his type." (Buck-Morss 103)

Bibliography

Benjamin, Walter. *Das Passagen-Werk.* Frankfurt am Main: Suhrkamp Verlag, 1983. (*PW*)

Berman, Marshall. *All That Is Solid Melts Into Air.* London: Verso, 1983. First published 1982. (Berman).

Buck-Morss, Susan. *The Dialectics of Seeing.* Cambridge, MA: MIT Press, 1989.

Dickens, Charles. *Sketches by Boz,* introd. Thea Holme. London: Oxford University Press, 1957 (SB).

———. *A Tale of Two Cities,* ed. George Woodcock, Harmondsworth: Penguin Books, 1970. (TOTC)

———. *The Letters of Charles Dickens.* Pilgrim Edition: Volume 8, eds. Graham Storey and Kathleen Tillo-

tson. Oxford: Clarendon Press, 1995. Volume 9, ed. Graham Storey, 1997. (Letters)

Finley, M. I., *The World of Odysseus.* Harmondsworth: Penguin Books, 1962. First edition 1954. (Finley)

Homer. *The Odyssey,* transl. Robert Fitzgerald. New York: Anchor Books (Doubleday), 1963. First edition 1961. (Fitzgerald)

Johnson, Edgar. *Charles Dickens: His Tragedy and Triumph,* revised and abridged edition. London: Allen Lane, 1977. First edition 1952. (Johnson)

Lyons, F. S. L. *Ireland Since the Famine.* London: Fontana/Collins, 1973. First edition 1971. (Lyons)

Osborne, Charles ed., *The Oxford Companion to Art.* London: Oxford University Press, 1970. (Osborne)

Sanders, Andrew. 'Monsieur heretofore the Marquis: Dickens's St. Evrémonde', *The Dickensian* 81,3 (Autumn 1985), 148-156. (Sanders)

Tomalin, Claire. *The Invisible Woman: The Story of Nell Ternan and Charles Dickens.* London: Viking/Penguin, 1990. (Tomalin)

Lucy Crispin (essay date 2001)

SOURCE: Crispin, Lucy. "Living in Exile: Self-Image, Social Role and the Problem of Identity." In *A Garland for Gissing,* edited by Bouwe Postmus, pp. 41-9. New York and Amsterdam, Netherlands: Rodopi, 2001.

[*In the following essay, Crispin details George Gissing's exploration of psychological and physical exile, as well as social and personal identity in his works. The critic also assesses how his treatment of exile relates to that of other, earlier Victorian writers.*]

"There is the man apart from his necessities."[1] So says Jasper Milvain to Marian Yule, the woman whom he loves but whom he also betrays, in Gissing's *New Grub Street,* published in 1891. Twelve years later, Henry Ryecroft reflects:

> Even in its normal condition (if I can determine what that is) my mind is obviously the slave of trivial accidents. . . . I know just as little about myself as I do about the Eternal Essence, and I have a haunting suspicion that I may be a mere automaton, my every thought and act due to some power which uses and deceives me.[2]

Milvain believes, whatever shabby deed his career-mindedness moves him to, that there is still some persisting, essential "him"—the man *apart* from his necessities. Ryecroft, embracing his delivery from Grub Street, retreats to Devon only to find that self-knowledge and understanding elude him: "I know just as little about

myself as I do about the Eternal Essence." These are very different perspectives on an issue which preoccupied Gissing: the issue of identity, of what constitutes the self, and how far self-knowledge is possible, let alone communicable. What makes an individual who he is? Is there some constant, the man apart from his necessities, or is identity always and entirely conditional?

The individual seeking to know himself, and to live and act from that sense of identity, is a familiar Victorian figure: the individual plotting his own life without the assurance of the Divine blueprint. If the eighteenth century novelist writes from the assumption that "character does not change: it solidifies",[3] the nineteenth-century novelist writes with the understanding that both nature *and* nurture combine to shape an essentially-mutable self. Your social circumstance; what happens to you; what you choose or choose against: all these things matter. And for the mutable self, the road chosen implies a road *not* taken: the self must be plotted, not as a line, but as a tree diagram.

And so many characters in Victorian fiction live with the consciousness of the "*What if?*" story—they see an alternative life they might have had. Dickens's Pip, for example, comments on his first visit to Satis House:

> That was a memorable day to me, for it made great changes in me. But, it is the same with any life. Imagine one selected day struck out of it, and think how different its course would have been.[4]

Eliot's Gwendolen Harleth attempts to rationalize her discontent:

> She often pursued the comparison between what might have been, if she had not married Grandcourt, and what actually was, trying to persuade herself that life generally was barren of satisfaction, and that if she had chosen differently she might now have been looking back with a regret as bitter as the feeling she was trying to argue away.[5]

But Dickens's novels shape out a fundamentally Christian paradigm of gain-through-loss (though some characters are unredeemed), while Eliot, consciously at least, reaches towards a preferred state of existence beyond what she terms "moral stupidity".[6] The alternative life for these writers is something better than actual existence. In Trollope, too, characters visualize alternatives and learn about themselves in the process of choice; what is different is an explicit questioning of assumptions—the loss of commonly-agreed values. Hardy's man also searches for absolutes to shape a preferred alternative: the young Jude wants "something to anchor on, to cling to . . . some place which he could call admirable".[7]

Here I can only nod towards the story of the alternative life in the Victorian novel; I offer this sketch not on its own merits but, rather, to emphasize the fact that Giss-

ing comes at the end of a line of writers who conceive of their characters, consciously and otherwise, living *actual* life in the shadow of an *alternative*. They assume the tree-diagram model of the self. And in the multiplot novel, as the novelist moves in and out of different characters' consciousnesses—to borrow Eliot's term, writes from different "centres of self"—the individual is seen from the inside *and* the outside: the central character of his *auto*biography, yes, but maybe only a walk-on in others' stories. The multiplot novel sees the individual as he exists in time and in the community of selves—in society, that is, which itself is undergoing rapid change.

The question of what to call admirable becomes urgent during the Century of Progress; and what we hold dear helps define who we are. Charles Taylor has shown that:

> It is a form of self-delusion to think that we do not speak from a moral orientation which we take to be right. This is a condition of being a functioning self, not a metaphysical view we can put on or off.[8]

It is only by orienting ourselves in relation to what we hold good that we exist as functioning selves: our identity is fundamentally connected with, a function of, our "goods". And the Victorian period is in large part defined by the erosion of one commonly-agreed value structure; as Ryecroft has it, "our philosophy sees no longer a supreme sanction, and no longer hears a harmony of the universe" (*HR*, 115). Social structures, too, are changing, and self-help has as its corollary a "social vertigo"[9] such as Dickens's Pip experiences. No longer underpinned by common assumptions and values, or by familiar social structures, identity cannot be a matter of instinct: the self must become self-conscious. Little wonder, then, that so many of Gissing's characters in the novels of the '90s are confused about who they are and what they want. Rhoda Nunn's response to Barfoot's proposal makes her feel "she ha[s] to learn herself anew".[10] Godwin Peak seethes with the pride of "an aristocrat of nature's own making".[11] Edwin Reardon, alone in his lodgings, endures "the sensations of an outraged exile" (*NGS*, 336). The self's own self-image may be very different from the social role the individual inhabits.

Gissing noted in his *Commonplace Book*:

> A pollarded tree reminds me of a capable man forbidden to develope [*sic*] naturally and shooting off into slender activities.[12]

"Naturally" is always a loaded word in Gissing: man is distorted from his "natural" development. Like Hardy's, Gissing's man is subject to dreams of an alternative life, but either unable to realize that dream, or the victim of disappointment if the dream *does* become a real-

ity. David Grylls has demonstrated how "the pervasive presence in Gissing of alternatives *all* of which are hopeless confirms the fact that his work is pessimistic in structure as well as in incident".[13] Unlike Peak, Hardy's Jude never made it into a Christminster college; but this disappointment shielded him from the larger awareness which both narrative and reader bear—that nothing in Jude's text seems worth the candle of his ardour. By contrast, Gissing in *The Whirlpool* (1897) allows Alma Rolfe repeatedly to arrive at a kind of life to which she has looked forward with idealistic delight, only to find that it cannot after all satisfy her. In Gissing, the alternative life may be present to the individual mind as reflex response to uncongenial existence, but the formulation of a possible, desirable, or fulfilling alternative is becoming problematic.

In *New Grub Street,* for instance, Reardon is increasingly crippled by his larger ambition, bankrupted by the image of the "serious" writer. *New Grub Street*'s fear is that the image of the writer who aims to make a contribution to literature—who sides *with* culture *against* anarchy—is now lost in the dominance of an uneducated market. The older view of the status of the book survives in the minds of a few men as an alternative object for their lives—but an alternative which has already been rendered obsolete. And Reardon's wife married this future, alternative self. Reardon asks her how she can love him; she replies "'You will be a great man'" (*NGS*, 65). As their marriage falls apart, Reardon pleads, "'Don't you think of me apart from all that I may do or may not do?'" (*NGS*, 196) She does not—she cannot. In her eyes—the eyes of a society where "life was a battle. [One] must either crush or be crushed" (*NGS*, 236)—Reardon is defined by his defeat. By contrast, Amy is "*gloriously* strong" (*NGS*, 65; my italics), ready to revel in the struggle; and in this she belongs with Milvain. Absolute value has disappeared, and we see the nightmare tautology of Social Darwinism: survivors survive. You're a winner if you win. The ducking stool meets Catch Twenty-Two . . .

New Grub Street offers us demonstrations enough that money allows people to inhabit their "better selves"; though Arnold's absolute term has become a relative one. Milvain himself confidently refers Marian to "the man apart from his necessities". But despite his claims there is more to him than his shrewd investment of his personality, this is the major part Gissing offers the reader. In *New Grub Street,* and across the novels of the '90s, Gissing sets his characters in poverty and relative wealth to explore the way that circumstance dictates which *elements* of the character come to the fore: a functional, or functio*ning* identity is determined by external conditions. But this identity may not be congruent with the self's self-image.

Reardon ends his life in exile; Godwin Peak is born there. To be born in exile is to suffer an involuntary de-

barment from a birthright. Peak is offered to us as a man born not himself, already living a life alternative to the one he should. His career is a striving for the lost identity of which the facts of his birth have deprived him. And so the youth who recoiled violently from the possibility of cheating in an exam, becomes the man who undertakes a full-scale, long term deception: he has to distort himself to become himself. John Halperin has noted:

> For Gissing, one's financial and social position determines one's class—not necessarily one's natural class (the class in which one ought to be) but rather the class in which one happened to find oneself.[14]

"Natural" again: Halperin identifies but then sidesteps the problem of what exactly constitutes the imperative: "the class in which one *ought* to be." After all, in what sense is Peak a "natural" aristocrat? He is working class; and yet the violence of his revulsion from "the promiscuity of the vulgar" is undeniable (*BIE,* 103). Where he lives, who he belongs with, feel wrong, whatever the "facts" of the matter are. The word "natural", then, functions to signal an alienation; a disparity between private experience and public appearance—how identity *feels* from the inside versus the shape offered from outside.

Peak's situation has been read as simply a division between true and false self.[15] But this is to clarify the clouded situation Gissing sets up in the novel. For Peak's imposture founders not just on society's forms but also on his own convictions—that good breeding cannot be simulated. And if the article expresses his fastidiousness in one way, his desire to be a clergyman satisfies both his social dilemma and his intellectual desire for moral stabilities. Is Peak what he does—the man *of* his necessities? If so, no wonder his outbursts of self-disgust: in the gentlemen's society to which he aspires his offences against honour are worse, perhaps, than outright crime. Or is he the man disgusted by his own behaviour—the man *apart* from his necessities and recoiling from them? In fact, he must understand himself as both. Peak's speech about the Canon's sermon is described as a "remarkable effort . . . of mind—one might say, of *character*". Reflecting on it later Peak reviews "the *character* he had played" (*BIE,* 128, 146; my italics). Not the part he had played, or the role, but the character. Gissing chooses his word with care: the implication is that there can be no simple or evident division between what is assumed and what is "really" Peak. Gissing's noting of Peak's contradictory impulses is something akin to Tennyson's record, in *In Memoriam,* of the shifting moods of the grieving process: in both cases, what seems so disparate is acknowledged to be part of a single whole. In the end, Peak settles for an incomplete self-definition offered by his legacy—he be-

comes the "independent Englishman, with so and so much a year" (*BIE,* 396). Sidwell also accepts the less-than-inclusive self-definition offered by social class. Rhoda Nunn, in the face of a real emotional response to Barfoot, opts for the partial identity offered by "oddness". Making real to us feelings, or elements of self, which his characters cannot realize in their lives, Gissing writes large the disparity between the functioning self which appears in "real life", and an alternative identity which can be conceived, felt, but not inhabited. Peak dies, as he has lived, in exile.

And for the born exile, home is not a definition but a destination. So many characters in these novels live rootless lives, shifting from lodging to lodging in a fruitless attempt to belong. Alma Rolfe repeatedly changes her life and occupation, each time driven by the belief that she is at last "on her way home". Philip Larkin, whose disillusioned Romanticism is a descendant of Gissing's, gives us a sense of what home represents:

> Lonely in Ireland, since it was not home,
> Strangeness made sense. . . .
> Living in England has no such excuse:
> These are my customs and establishments
> It would be much more serious to refuse.
> Here no elsewhere underwrites my existence.[16]

Home is where you don't feel "strange"; where you know who you are and what you should do: where you find your "shape". But to call anywhere home is to imply an eradication of alternatives; and Alma is only at home in the restless spinning of alternatives: constructing herself, never being herself.

Reardon, Peak, Sidwell, Rhoda Nunn, Alma and Harvey Rolfe: increasingly Gissing's characters struggle less with circumstance than with their own, contradictory, needs and convictions. And in *Ryecroft* Gissing takes this movement to its logical conclusion, putting his protagonist in a situation where circumstance can no longer trouble him. And the removal of external problems functions only to make internal division and confusion more evident. GG, the Editor, feels Ryecroft "was soon thoroughly at home" (*HR,* 6) and assumes his happiness. Ryecroft himself, meanwhile, fears that "the very I . . . consists but with a certain balance of my physical elements, which we call health" (*HR,* 116). Gissing uses the frame text to great effect: it opens up a fresh perspective on the main text, allowing Gissing to register the disparity between GG's perception of the closing years of Ryecroft's life, and Ryecroft's own experience. Indeed, frame and main text, *Ryecroft* as a whole, enact this disparity.

I do not want to claim that Ryecroft has no moments of content, pleasure and satisfaction with his lot, but rather to emphasize the fact that the comfortable nature of his

life is itself confusing: the end of his life was not implied in its beginning. Worse: after only a few days in an alternative idyll so many Gissing characters might envy, Ryecroft is disoriented. "For more than a week my pen has lain untouched" (*HR,* 11). He is disconnected from the action which defines him: what he is, has always been what he does, the man of his necessities—and yet he does it no longer. What, then, is he? The continuity implied in the very fact of a unifying, recording consciousness is brought up against the felt discontinuities between past and present self. A flower, music, a church service, the smell of a book: all these can be the madeleine for Ryecroft, immersing him completely in a past experience even as they reveal the present, experiencing self to be something different. Relishing the sunshine one morning he recalls a walk when "the sun, still pouring on me with its noontide radiance, seemed to fill my veins with life". Now "the sun keeps me alive, but cannot, as in the old days, renew my being" (*HR,* 65, 66). He feels the same but different. Ryecroft's narrative is deliberately created by Gissing as a miscellany because in this it shows Ryecroft's life to have been a series of presents. Adrian Poole described *Ryecroft* as a "comfortable tapestry of self" (Poole, 206); but for Ryecroft his self is less this than a pointillist painting viewed from too small a remove. He can't make sense of his life, can't see the shape: it is a "piece of biography" (*HR,* 177), not an autobiography. Ryecroft the man is only witnessed by, and realized in, *Ryecroft* the text: he can be fully alive only after his death.

Gissing advised his brother to "[deal] with episodes instead of writing biographies"[17]: to undermine the narrator's omniscience is to emphasize the mutability and obscurity of the self. Stevenson's Jekyll, looking at Hyde in the mirror, recognized that "this, too, was myself";[18] but the problem of identity in Gissing is more than the painful acknowledgement of "the dark side"; more, too, than a simple mismatch of aspiration and circumstance. For Gissing's man lives with desires and impulses which are strong but sometimes contradictory; with shifting and uncertain values; and with no models, no instinctive or definitive sense of which of his alternatives is to be preferred. He is never "at home"; and that, of course, is what it is to live in exile. Only the novels constitute Larkin's "elsewhere" for the characters they describe—the elsewhere which confirms in full the confusions of the isolated, individual and recognizably-modern consciousness.

Notes

1. George Gissing, *New Grub Street,* ed. John Goode (Oxford: OUP, 1993), 184; hereafter cited as *NGS.*

2. George Gissing, *The Private Papers of Henry Ryecroft,* ed. Mark Storey (Oxford: OUP, 1987), 118; hereafter cited as *HR.*

3. Patricia M. Spacks, *Imagining a Self: Autobiography and Novel in Eighteenth-Century England* (Cambridge, Mass. and London: Harvard University Press, 1976), 280.

4. Charles Dickens, *Great Expectations,* 1860-61, ed. Angus Calder (Penguin edn, 1985), 101.

5. George Eliot, *Daniel Deronda,* 1876, ed. Barbara Hardy (Penguin edn, 1988), 483.

6. George Eliot, *Middlemarch,* 1871-2, ed. W. J. Harvey (Penguin edn, 1987), 243.

7. Thomas Hardy, *Jude the Obscure,* 1896, ed. C. H. Sisson (Penguin edn, 1985), 65.

8. Charles Taylor, *Sources of the Self: The Making of the Modern Identity* (Cambridge: CUP, 1996), 99.

9. Dirk den Hartog, *Dickens and Romantic Psychology: The Self in Time in Nineteenth-Century Literature* (Basingstoke and London: Macmillan, 1987), 17.

10. George Gissing, *The Odd Women,* intro. Elaine Showalter (1893; Penguin edn, 1993), 167.

11. George Gissing, *Born in Exile,* 1892, ed. David Grylls (Everyman edn, 1993), 30; hereafter cited as *BIE.*

12. George Gissing, *Commonplace Book,* ed. Jacob Korg (New York: New York Public Library, 1962), 63.

13. David Grylls, *The Paradox of Gissing* (London: Allen and Unwin, 1986), 5.

14. John Halperin, *Gissing: A Life in Books* (Oxford: OUP, 1982), 4.

15. See, for instance, Adrian Poole, *Gissing in Context* (Basingstoke and London: Macmillan, 1975), 172.

16. Philip Larkin, "The Importance of Elsewhere", in *Collected Poems,* ed. Anthony Thwaite (London: Faber and Faber, 1988), 104, ll. 1-2, 9-12.

17. Letter to his brother Algernon, 1885, quoted in John Goode, *George Gissing: Ideology and Fiction,* (London: Vision Press, 1978), 18-19.

18. Robert Louis Stevenson, *The Strange Case of Dr Jekyll and Mr Hyde,* 1886, in *The Strange Case of Dr Jekyll and Mr Hyde and Other Stories,* ed. Claire Harmon (Everyman edn, 1996), 144.

EXILE IN AMERICAN LITERATURE

Daniel Marder (essay date 1984)

SOURCE: Marder, Daniel. "Exile and American Tradition." In *Exiles at Home: A Story of Literature in Nineteenth Century America,* pp. 1-21. Lanham, Md., and London: University Press of America, 1984.

[*In the following essay, Marder surveys how themes of displacement and isolation in works by such authors as James Fenimore Cooper, Nathaniel Hawthorne, Herman Melville, Mark Twain, Edgar Allan Poe, and Emily Dickinson are illustrative of an American "literature of exile."*]

> . . . the Wanderer, weary of exile,
>
> * * *
>
> Homeless and hapless, since the days of old,
> When the dark earth covered my dear lord's face,
> And I sailed away with sorrowful heart,
> Over wintry seas, seeking a gold-lord,
> If far or near lived one to befriend me . . .[1]

If the old English *Wanderer* should ever find a "gold lord" to befriend and comfort him, he will be less an exile than refugee. There may remain the nostalgia, the memory, distorted through years of dreaming and idealizing. But those who have regained home values—comfort, acceptance, belonging, love—are no longer exiles. In the exodus from Egypt the Jews were a moving society seeking a refuge where they could replant the culture they carried with them. The pilgrims of Plymouth readily compared themselves with the Hebrews. Both had a far greater sense of gain than loss. It was not the outcast condition that pained them, as with the exile, but the present suffering of migration and settlement in strange places; their temporary pains were soothed with great hopes for the future.

In *Exile's Return,* Malcolm Cowley recognizes the distinction between refugee and exile:

> —a whole world of people with and without talent but sharing the same ideals happily deserted the homeland. Each year some of them returned while others crowded into their places: the migration continued at a swifter rate. But after the middle of the decade the motives behind it underwent an impeccable but real change in emphasis. The earlier exiles had been driven abroad by a hatred of American dullness and puritanism, yet primarily they had traveled *in search* of something—leisure, freedom, knowledge, some quality that was offered by the old culture. Their successors felt the same desires, but felt them less strongly. Instead of being drawn ahead, they were propelled from behind, pushed eastward by the need of *getting away from* something. They are not so much exiles as refugees.[2]

But Cowley has reversed the roles as we ordinarily understand them. Being driven out, all are exiles, but the first group, like the old English wanderer and Bradford's pilgrims, still hope and seek refuge, while the second are beyond hope, not seeking, and so are condemned to remain in the state of exile. The earlier group included Stein, Josephson, Cummings, Pound, Eliot, Hemingway, Fitzgerald, Hart Crane, all seeking and to various extent, finding cultural refuge. "With a greater frequency than ever," wrote Matthew Josephson, "our illuminati buy tickets for a more possible world, for a more breathable air."[3] These Americans were exiles, not in Europe, but in America. *Exile's Return* should have applied not to the American homecoming from abroad, but to the European return, to the search for a lost culture.

We are accustomed to envision the European return as a movement occurring mainly in the early twentieth century. It was then, Hugh Kenner notes in *A Home Made World,* that the "threat and fascination of Europe hung over cautious minds like a menacing cloud."[4] American vastness in itself contributed to the individual's sense of isolation from the main stream of human community. These American minds conceived of European society as the homeland, while the actual home seemed a place of futility and anarchy. In abandoning the American wasteland for the refuge of European cosmopolitanism, the exile of the twentieth century was actually following American literary tradition.

Nostalgia for the European home had been a strain in the American literature from its inception. Puritan poetry was written with one eye, perhaps both, on England. Anne Bradstreet was referred to as *The Tenth Muse Lately Sprung Up In America* (1650). During the Revolution, the nostalgia curled into the form of protest, the movement for American literary independence. In the Preface to the *United States Magazine* (1779), Hugh Henry Brackenridge boasted:

> The British officers . . . have been forced to acknowledge, not without chagrin, that the rebels, as they are pleased to call us, had some damn'd good writers on their side of the question, and that we had fought them no less successfully with the pen than the sword. We hope to convince them yet more fully that we are able to cultivate the belles letters, even disconnected with Great Britain.[5]

But the sources of his *topoi,* as with other European colonials, were rooted still in the civilization born on the Mediterranean shores, Greek, Roman, Jewish.

In the nineteenth century, one by one, American authors returned—Irving, Cooper, Emerson, Hawthorne, James, Howells, Twain, Crane. By the time of Gertrude Stein's lost generation, the European sojourn had been established as something of a ritualistic requirement for men

and women of American letters. Those who found the old country to be their "gold-lord" stayed on, no longer exiles. To Henry Adams, Europe was rotten to the core, England crassly materialistic and France hopelessly corrupt, yet he stayed. Gertrude Stein was fond of saying that America was her country but Paris was her hometown. The old world provided an acceptable milieu, a refuge of artistic commonality. In Europe the American artist could join others in the Byronic tradition of rejecting a handed-down society and of questing for individual enlightenment and expression. There was a community for the artist who preferred the life of the inner self to externalities, who distrusted official modes of social organization and who needed to create a system of his own to avoid enslavement. Within an artistic community, the writer could feel a unity between moral and social structure; individual conceptions of virtue were not separate from social roles.

Even the European developments in science and philosophy at the turn of the century served, not to distinguish the American exiles of the twentieth century from those of the nineteenth, but rather to buttress their traditional insistence on the life of the inner self. Theories of relativity and indeterminacy, the notion that matter itself was not always matter but process, reinforced the idea of reality as a matter of individual perception. These new developments, however, provided a refuge for the early twentieth century exile which was not available to the nineteenth century counterpart. Along with the Bloomsbury group—fostering post-impressionism, literary interiority and circumstantial morality—were the imagists with Ezra Pound in their midst, eschewing literary statements and insisting upon image clusters alone to evoke experience. For Pound, experience was a radiant cluster of ideas rushing into, through and out of a stable shape of movement, a vortex of a culture and a tradition.[6]

Such a vortex was the cultural refuge the American exile at home envisioned in the nineteenth century. For him there were no moveable feasts. He was not "one of us." He could not share in the feeling, "however ill-grounded," as Cowley put it, that "made them regard other members of their own age group, whether artists are athletes or businessmen, as belonging to a sort of secret order . . . leagued in rebellion against the stuffy people who were misruling the world."[7] Exiles at home in nineteenth century America could not share morality or sensitivity to art and its theories, nor could they share in the ritual of escape, the orgies of bizarre behavior that followed rather established patterns.

It was when the party broke up, when the refuge dissipated, that the lost generation really got lost, and exile began for the twentieth century American abroad. Robert McAlmon's *Being Geniuses Together* (1938) was no longer possible. Hart Crane jumped off the stern of a steamer returning him from Mexico. He was only one more contemporary who "had begun to disappear into the dark maw of violence," as Scott Fitzgerald observed.[8] Crane had won a prize with *The Bridge* (1930), seen as a hopeful Whitmanesque response to Eliot's abandonment of modern society in *The Waste Land* (1922). Apparently Crane found that the currents flowing beneath *The Bridge* led not to social cohesion (the history he cites is "tortured") but to an eternal return for the exile: "No embrace opens but the stinging seas."[9] Eliot, of course, found another means of return in the rituals of monarchy and religion. After McAlmon died bitter and lonely in an El Paso hotel, a condition he always managed to escape in the elan of impeccably bad behavior, William Carlos Williams recalled that his magazine, *Contact,* implied all the young man had most on his mind. By then the European sense of being absurd together had alleviated the exile's sensitivity.

The notion that a sense of exile is man's modern feeling, results apparently from our persistent focus on only one or two aspects of the condition—isolation or alienation.[10] Loss, the most essential characteristic, is mostly ignored in our tendency to equate the state of exile with isolation or alienation and to attribute the condition to the intellectual and industrial changes that began after the Civil War. The isolated individual is outside of society while the alienated is hostile as well as outside. Jamesian devotion to living in art rather than life can account for the isolated, and disillusionment with American promise can account for the alienated, but neither are sufficient to account for the exile, who has lost what was once possessed. He has abandoned home because he could not abide it or it could not abide him, yet he yearns to belong as a divorced person might yearn for binding.

In time the pain of loss attenuates. The American sense of cultural loss was most acute after the political severing of the Revolution at the end of the eighteenth century. At the beginning of that century there appears to be little sense of divorce from England. William Byrd, for example, was educated in England as custom dictated and then divided his mature years between Virginia and England as if they were one culture. In spite of Benjamin Franklin's image as typical American, he considered himself thoroughly English until the Revolution. New world literary effort customarily followed British styles and fashions. It was after the Revolution that the American writer became aware of the cultural losses and conscientiously attempted literary independence by focusing on American scene and character. From Brackenridge onward, however, they displayed a common aversion to American licentiousness as contrasted with the disciplined manners and learning of the lost culture. The essential feature that distinguished Cooper's American village culture from Britain's was the threat of self-aggrandizement at the expense of the

community. It is the absence of European cultural constraints that drives Leatherstocking from his place, first on the edge of the settlement and finally from the plains of the West.

When Leatherstocking's story is echoed in the twentieth century by William Faulkner's Ike McCaslin, the licentiousness and greed have come to dominate American society and the remnants of English cultural values are seen almost as relics. The balance between nature and human civilization, disturbed in Cooper's first Leatherstocking tale, *The Pioneers* (1823), can be envisioned later only as an imagined past, one that is pristinely American, not a memory of another culture. It was during the nineteenth century, between the severences of the political revolution at the beginning and the scientific revolution at the end, that American writers freshly and most painfully suffered the sense of exile at home.

I

The condition of exile in America results from excessive individuality, another American tradition. It is more encompassing than the familiar "rugged individualism," a term usually confined to economic exploitation and acquisition. American literature follows this American tradition. Without a shared body of inherited habits, attitudes, and institutions to mediate between the individual and the state, Tocqueville observed, "Each man is forever thrown back on himself alone, and there is great danger that he may be shut up in the solitude of his own heart."[11] To Emerson and Thoreau, the private vision that solitude yields was sacrosanct; joining the common denominators of society was yielding individuality. But society, for Emerson at least, did not comprise a conspiracy, as Tony Tanner sees it in today's American literature, "plotting to shape individual consciousness to suit its own ends."[12] Yet the threat of depersonalization to Chief Broom in *One Flew Over The Cuckoo's Nest,* where community is a combine that controls all the cogs through a gigantic machine, is much the same as the threat to Hawthorne's "Wakefield," who found stepping aside, outside the system, is stepping into a void.

The void in our current literature is sometimes seen as a prelinguistic consciousness while society is an entity composed of linguistic structures. Without societal imposition of language there is no identifiable self, only an amoeba-like immediacy in the flow of existence. But with this imposition, this enculturing, there is behavioral control. The essential paradox, nevertheless, is the same one we find in Hawthorne and Melville, that identity depends upon societal recognition but societal recognition tends to erase the individuality of the identified. Those who accept this situation become performers, fabricating a variety of identities for a variety of occa-sions, like Melville's confidence man and Hawthorne's masks. The self is thus an accumulation of identities as perceived by others, concerned basically with convincing postures rather than integral truths or morals.[13] Within however, twentieth century individuals seek mediation, not between self and culture or community as in the previous century, but only between the world of things identified in language and the internal self. Tony Tanner envisions such struggles taking place in his *City of Words* and in Richard Poirier's *A World Elsewhere.* These are places of refuge from the threats of pure autonomy on the one hand and total enslavement on the other, that is, of disappearance into the self or diffusion into the world's uses.

Although the exile at home in the nineteenth century also perceived this struggle—Melville continuously fought the impress of written forms and his Ahab tragically confused the language with the referent, while Hawthorne's Hester could not escape the identity imprinted on her by the scarlet 'A'—they were more centrally absorbed with an external elsewhere, upon the face of the earth or beyond it. They were still close in time to the European culture and could look upon it as the potential refuge, just as their European forebears had looked upon America. They could either submit to the patterns of Europe, however displaced and transfigured in the American environment, or forego identity. Even if the exile posed as an Emersonian scholar who would think his own thoughts, the pose itself was patterned by a European language. American culture was a displaced culture. Freedom from that culture was shapelessness, licentiousness, myriad private realities without agreements or communications. Even those who thought positively of the American spirit surrendered to the spiritual comfort of the old world: "I find myself in my element in European life," Margaret Fuller wrote home in 1846, "Encumberances are cleared away that used to weary me in America."[14]

Common views of nineteenth century America emphasize not the lost home but the enthusiasms for the fresh culture aborning, the American spirit of progress, achievement of human destiny, and transcendental connections, although notes of doubt occur frequently, even in the positive elevations of Emerson and the celebrations of Whitman. The enthusiasm, of course, serves the disillusionment which is then found to follow in the next century. But the ambience of this American enthusiasm contributed in itself to a sense of exile in the writers of nineteenth century America. Although some—Cooper, Hawthorne, Melville, Twain—sought moments of physical refuge elsewhere, together with those who did not leave home—Poe and Dickinson[15]—they developed a fundamental core of meaning through the formative years of American literature. They produced, we might say, a literature of exile.

II

One of Poe's protagonists in an unfinished novel goes West but not for hunting and trapping as pretended; Julius Rodman rather was "urged by a desire to seek in the bosom of the wilderness that peace" he could not find among men. He "fled to the desert as to a friend." Of course, if Rodman would find peace in the desert of the American West, he would not be an exile, but his search is as much fated as Leatherstocking's. Rodman represents the American tradition of excessive individuality. He is fleeing society not so much because of its American peculiarities and certainly not in preference for another, but essentially because of its inacceptability as society *per se,* realized rather than dreamt.

Unrestricted adherence to an inner reality is the basis of America's individual excessiveness, or the American romance, as Lionel Trilling sees it: "The fact is that American writers of genius have not turned their minds to society . . . the reality they sought was only tangential to society."[16] Henry James is the only exception that Trilling allows. He might also have excepted Washington Irving at the other end of the nineteenth century. Although both acted upon a sense of exile, neither became exiles in America. Washington Irving lived in Europe for seventeen years, essentially as a tourist, and when he returned to America, accommodated himself to its society. James was raised in European schools and eventually settled in London although he never quite relinquished American possibility, not even in his late assessment, *The American Scene* (1907). James' possibility is a vision of European culture reinvigorated by fresh American virtues. The anticipated synthesis occurs in Europe with consequent corruption or destruction of the American character, the energetic innocent, or rejection of the old world society as corrupt. In England, however, he imagined the old world culture thriving without the decadence of the continent. There he found his home. Irving and James, at the beginning and ending of the century, may serve to frame our story of American exiles at home, although the case of James is far more complex.

Introducing the *Sketch Book* in 1819, Irving confesses his essential nature as tourist: "I was always fond of visiting new scenes, and observing strange characters and manners. Even when a mere child I began my travels, and made many tours of discovery into foreign parts and unknown regions of my native city." American attraction was in her sublime scenery while Europe's was in the refinements of a cultivated society. His longing was not to find a home, to belong, but "to escape, in short, from the commonplace realities of the present, and lose myself among the shadowy grandeurs of the past."[17] One commonplace reality he sought to escape was management of the family paint business, a real spectre that haunted him in America. Unlike T. S.

Eliot, who also departed from middle class America for rather specific reasons a century later, Irving sought abroad "the accumulated treasures of age" rather than the authority sanctioned by the past.

During his seventeen year tour (1815-1832) he endeavored to "see the world in as pleasant a light as circumstances will permit." Nothing he discovers convinces him that Europe is "all that it has been represented by sneering cynics and whining poses."[18] Whenever he finds it so, he will abuse it also. Had he stayed at home, the good-natured satire may indeed have grown sneering and cynical, not only because of his distaste for the middle class life of a businessman, but also because of his fundamental aversion to popular movements, to democracy and to its serious tones. New Englanders were unacceptable to Irving somewhat because of their vulgar religions—transcendentalism, unitarianism, evangelicalism—but even more because they lacked congeniality.

Occasionally in the *Sketch Book* Irving expresses a feeling of loneliness but throughout Irving's work we can find only one candidate for the lonely exile—Rip Van Winkle, who awakes in post-Revolutionary America. The "village inn" is now the "union hotel" run by Jonathan Doolittle who lives up to his name. His place is run down, "rickety." A liberty pole replaces the great tree that had sheltered the old inn. King George on the inn sign is now George Washington, and the "very character of the people had changed . . . a busy bustling, disputatious tone . . . instead of the accustomed phlegm and drowsy tranquility . . . haranging vehemently about the rights of citizens . . . a perfect Babylonish jargon to the bewildered Van Winkle." But Rip's confusion is not sustained; it is transformed into pleasure upon learning that the demise of his carping wife is among the changes. His good nature restored, he rejoins society, whatever its altered condition. He had appeased the new democrats with stories of his long absence which they accepted without believing, so now he can assume a social role as a "chronicle of the old times before the War." He represents a preservation of culture, a more or less ridiculous parallel with George Lucacs' description of the post revolutionary individual and artist who is engaged not in "concocting something 'radically new' but . . . of assimilating all that is valuable in previous development and adapting it," although Rip Van Winkle does not really adapt in the way Lucacs would have it.[19]

Irving's notebook describes his discomfort in the uncertainty and transcience of post-Revolutionary America. He was more attuned to the inhabitants of Sleepy Hollow enjoying their drowsy tranquility and resenting the new American spirit, represented by Ichabod Crane, the man with an "anaconda" appetite. As Ichabod rolled his great green eyes over the fat meadow lands of Katrina's father, "his heart yearned after the damsel . . . and his

imagination expanded with the idea, how they might be readily turned into cash and the money invested. . . ." Fortunately for the "country bumpkins" whom he disdainfully ignored, Ichabod's appetite extended to everything: "No tale was too gross or monstrous for his capacious swallow." He had developed a gusto for ghostly lore from his "perfect master," Cotton Mather. Thus, the New England slicker is easy prey for Brom Bones' headless horseman. Katrina is left to this country bumpkin, who is nevertheless something of an aristocrat of the soil with a "degree of rough chivalry in his nature." When Brom's trumped-up ghost frightens Ichabod out of sleepy old America, he flees, we presume, to start up the noisy machinery of Jacksonian America. And in the Hollow of the tranquil past, Irving wishfully concludes, Crane's schoolhouse is allowed to decay after his mysterious disappearance.

Irving admitted that his essential activity had been reverie, daydream, out of which came his spectral and whimsical stories, his extensive reading in German folktales notwithstanding. These stories, like his earlier satires, are of the past itself, not a sense of the past in the present, which would be akin to Lukacs' notion of adapting the past. Instead, Irving engages in pleasurable rearrangements of history. There was little he wanted in the present and though it threatened—"deliver me from all the pervading commonplace which is the curse of our country"[20]—he managed to defeat it, like Brom Bones, in his tales and reveries. In effect he never left home. When he returned from Europe he returned from the European past to the American past.

III

Henry James was eminently a man of the present. But his was a very selective present that continued the civilized past. Quite the opposite of Washington Irving, James was given over to the "actual scene." The concept of his realism, of creating the impression of the actual, stirred in his mind from the beginning, long before it was technically worked out in the Prefaces to the New York editions (1907-1917). At twenty, already a veteran of European schooling, he wrote of "the subtlest influences—birth, education, association—" that prejudice the imagination.[21] At twenty-six, on his first tour of Europe as a mature man, James speculated on the largeness of mind in the Venetian artists, the result of distance that dwarfed prejudice. Veronese "seems to have had in his head a perfect realization of a world in which all things are interfused . . . undramatic and 'impersonal' . . . not a whit of struggle, nor fever, nor longing for the unattainable, simply a glorious sense of the looks of things"[22] In Tinteretto, the "actual scene" is conceived as a "great fragment wrenched out of life and history with all its natural details clinging to it and testifying to its reality."[23] It is the testimony that renders the appearances of reality and neutralizes the artist's prejudices. Here is James' artistic view of civilized society. The only excess it allows is art itself, homeless in America.

"We're the disinherited of Art," declares the narrator in "Madonna of the Future" (1873), "excluded from the magic circle . . . as void of all that nourishes and prompts and inspires the artist as my sad heart is void of bitterness in saying so! We poor aspirants must live in exile."[24] James, therefore, took his American—ignorant of the delicate amenities of civilization but also untainted by its sordid corruptions—to the "actual scene." In the old world, the "spiritual lightness and vigour" of the American, "looking to see something original and beautiful [could] disengage . . . from our ceaseless fermentation and turmoil."[25] American energy could invigorate the European conventions, forms, and manners, drained of their vitality through the centuries of usage. In James' first story of American confrontation with civilization, however, "The Passionate Pilgrim" (1871) is destroyed by his egoistic prejudices. His romantic cloud allows him to see nothing English except the landscape. The culture denies him and he is akin to the man James describes in his Preface to *The American* (1908) whose balloon of experience is cut free from reality. Yet, in dying, the pilgrim reinforces James' hope for the heroic strain in these young imaginations of the West, their promise to re-invigorate civilization.

Roderick Hudson (1876), however, is corrupted in the confrontation. Rather than observe and imaginatively recreate, this American sculptor plunges into the life of Rome. Characteristically undisciplined, he exhibits the uncultured freedom implicit in excessive American individuality. *Daisy Miller* (1878) is another undisciplined American innocent. Insisting on her freedoms, she violates the rules of propriety in Rome and dies as an indirect result. When the over-active American ego is neither corrupted nor destroyed in the confrontation, it is reinforced. Christopher Newman, *The American* (1877), knows exactly what he is after, the best wife possible. Rejection by the decadent nobility strengthens the resolve of his commercial ego which causes the rejection. Back in America, Newman can clearly see the distinction between right and wrong once more and renounce the opportunity for revenge; his dull American sense of decency triumphs over European corruption.

For all his enchantment with the continent, James moved from Paris to London in 1875. England was a place of civilized society rather than the unreachable culture Newman had found. "I feel how Europe keeps holding one at arm's length," James wrote home, "and condemning one to a meagre scraping of the surface."[26] England was an alternative to America. He felt the same uneasiness there as in Cambridge and New York, but in London the lonely state of the exile was easier to endure than at home. It was infused with culture: "I like

feeling in the midst of the English world, however lost in it I may be."[27]

In *Portrait of a Lady* (1881), written just before he returned to America, James appears to be summing up, synthesizing, and refining what he had wrought in his first extended sojourn. Through this vigorous, unfettered American girl, James brings the three worlds of his experience together; America, unrealized potential; Europe, the finest culture but morally corrupt; and England, the 'reserve' that he first deprecates and then comes to appreciate as the basis for civilization because it respects privacy while continuing the culture of the past. Isabel rejects Casper Goodwood, the uncultivated American whose name describes him, and she also rejects the orderly and civilized world of Lord Warburton. It is the illusory world of enchanting culture she chooses, as represented by the Europeanized American, Gilbert Osmond. Osmond is a later-day Roderick Hudson whose life has become a series of dilettantish postures. Isabel's choice is itself a sign that European culture has begun its corruption of the fresh American. When she recognizes the falseness of the world she has chosen, Isabel determines nevertheless to maintain social convention, the appearances of her marriage, which is the defeat of her need for freedom and of her honesty.

James returned to England in 1882, despondent over the deaths of his parents, his sister's poor health, and quarrels with brother William. Perhaps equally debilitating was his lack of American popularity as compared with Twain and Howells. He began to feel "orphaned" rather than cosmopolitan, and his opinion of the American innocent's high moral quality and energetic potential declined. After devoting *The Bostonians* (1886) to his native audience, James turned away from the American character, dropped the international theme, and focused exclusively on the British, a choice which inevitably invited American ghosts. He was also dissatisfied with the results of his artistic method and scope, which had produced only representational relationships, he thought, rather than individual ones, and the scale was limited. With others of his time, James was drawn to the experimentation of Daudet, Goncourt, and Zola, "in spite of their ferocious pessimism and handling of unclean things, they are at least serious and honest."[28] But *The Princess Casamassima* (1886), focused on London's mean streets as well as on its society of wealth and culture, was no improvement. Nor did it contribute to his popularity. Now James questioned his sacrifices of life to art, the passion of the passions. His doubt is rendered in the equivocal response of the disciple in "The Lesson of the Master" (1888) when he learns his mentor has married his girl. It is his nature, the disciple dubiously reasons, which dedicates him to intellectual rather than personal passion, which exiles him from the lived life for the sake of art.

In the nineties, James reached out for living response, which "the usual imbecility of the novel" could not provide, "the reader never touches the subject, and the subject never touches the reader."[29] His efforts at stage drama were haunted by his ghosts, not only of his American past but of the abandoned life together. Even his art of fiction, neglected in his new pursuit of audience, had become a ghost; for example, the artist who prefers the model to the genuine article in "The Real Thing" (1892), and Lord Mellifont, a "style" in "The Private Life" (1893) who ceases to exist when he does not appear before others. Having stooped to the abyss of "vulgarity and platitude" in the theater,[30] and failing, James sought to confront the ghosts directly by returning to the novel, and finally, at the turn of the century, to the international theme. In the unfinished *Sense of the Past,* the protagonist is a ghost of his former self, but "it is not easy to concoct a 'ghost' of any freshness"[31] he discovers before giving up the manuscript. Unlike Cooper and Hawthorne before him or Twain and Faulkner after him, James was not attempting to retreat into another time. His difficulty was simply being trapped in his own past, of repeating what he had already written. The solution of the problem, he told Howells, was to do "a neat little human—and not the less international novel."[32] He deliberately set out, that is, to penetrate the representations that resulted from prejudiced patterns of seeing the social atmosphere and to arrive at a real sense of individual personality.

In *The Ambassadors* (1903), a middle aged American still innocent but less energetic than Christopher Newman, is able to strip away American prejudices and adapt to the pleasures of living in the old world, pleasures alien to his native New England. Yet Strether has the discipline to control his aroused spirit. When he dutifully returns home to Mrs. Newsome, a representative American, he returns to a spiritual exile, to lead also a representative life. In *The Golden Bowl* (1903) Maggie Verver is an advance even over Strether. She also recalls the ghost of the commercial Newman, referring to her royal fiance as a rarity to be obtained only in Europe. But she is also aware of European potential for corruption, unlike her predecessor in *The Portrait of a Lady,* and wants to be "called in," like the Europeanized American, Charlotte, who marries her father. Unlike either Newman or Archer, Maggie knows what she is doing.

Working to deepen American character by immersing it in "civilization," James ironically became nostalgic for New England smells and even sounds. His nostalgia had been increasing at least since the death of Victoria, an event he speculated would mark the end of British civilization. The nostalgia culminated in the trip of 1905 and his reaction in *The American Scene,* where the narrator's gratification with a few remnants of the older America is overwhelmed by the repellent sights of

the newer America. In England again, he entertained a new set of ghosts; the returned ex-patriot of "The Jolly Corner" (1908) who is appalled at the image of the dreadful business type he might have become in America, and the ex-patriot of the unfinished *Ivory Tower* (1917) who finds his old memory of Newport unrecognizably distorted with the vulgar structures of the dehumanized American rich.

More and more James accepted "the essential loneliness" he had described when the British stage turned him away. The loneliness was "deeper than my 'genius', deeper than my 'discipline' . . . deeper, above all, than the deep counterminings of art."[33] Henry James found his "lord" in his art but art was not a "gold lord"; it excluded him from the very life that his fiction proclaimed. He was an exile at home, but not an American home.

IV

Both Irving and James eschewed the American idea of freedom. It was uncivilized. For them people are free in the way D. H. Lawrence defines freedom, "not when they are straying and breaking away [but] when they belong to a living, organic, believing community . . . freest when they are most unconscious of freedom."[34] The freedoms within a society, controlled by society, were abused in the American tradition of excessive individuality. The exiles at home, following this American tradition, sacrifice whatever spiritual comforts societies proffer in order to continue their individualistic searches for an ideal alliance, societal or beyond, which would accommodate the demands of the self.

To the Adamic such as Whitman and Thoreau, the question of identity was an invitation to create a single, separate self. But for the exile at home the question was a painful ambiguity, the self had to be defined in terms of society but also in terms independent of it. Long before the Southern Agrarians proclaimed *I'll Take My Stand* (1930), the nineteenth century exile knew that the stance of unencumbered and direct relationships (rather than societal arrangements) was a lonely and empty one. Without community, freedom was irresponsible and selfish. The integrity of a self to be defined without community was abhorrent.

Actually it was so from the beginning of American independence. "Whichever way I look nothing but the most frightful precipices present themselves to my view," Crèvecoeur writes in his last letter, "what is man when no longer connected to society?"[35] By 1800, Americans had no more moral purpose, Henry Adams decided, than the beavers they drove away; scum were rising to the surface. For all his hope of *Democracy in America* (1835), Tocqueville feared the danger of breaking the chain which aristocracy had forged from peasant to king. These apprehensions were reflected in the novels of James Fenimore Cooper. To cultivate the beautiful in America, Charles Dickens noted in 1841, makes one an outcast, which is the destiny of the typical narrator in Edgar Allan Poe and Hawthorne's "Artist of the Beautiful." Writing *Society and Solitude* (1870) in his later years, Emerson saw that a person needed to be clothed with society or would suffer bareness and poverty. Thus, Melville's sailor orphans in the end swim for the boat, however dismal they know the captain and crew to be. The process of democracy consummated its promise and resulted in those "plated people" whom Emily Dickinson excluded from her imaginary domain. *The Machine in the Garden,* abetted the process, as Leo Marx has demonstrated. It was the last of the exiling factors. Europe, impeded by its traditions, slowly made room for the industrial revolution while America immediately grasped the machine and adapted to its greedy pace. But the railroad of progress goes nowhere in Hawthorne's *House of the Seven Gables,* and the steamboat crashes through the idyll of Huck's raft.

Exiles at Home traces the process of exiling as it develops through six American writers into a major theme of American literature. It is not only the presentation of the exiled attitude but the story of that attitude, how it manifested itself in America, a continuation of an old world habit of vision. Nostalgia for the European past in particular was abetted of course by the democratic dust kicked up in the licentious scramble for material things. Yet, with the celebrators of American opportunity, these exiles at home took pride in their immediate ancestor's rebellion against this past. The nostalgia for it was highly selective, and can be viewed as a retreat to a familiar image, an alleviating interlude in the continuous search for the metaphysical idealization of mankind, often seen as Eden.

The story that begins with Cooper, ends with Twain, who reflects all the others. Cooper, and Hawthorne also, sought and then condemned European society for its aristocratic postures. Although they did not look upon American pretences and opportunists as European parodies, Cooper and Hawthorne were equally pained by "parvenues" overtaking America, their self-serving ambitions hidden in masks of social reform. Shades of Poe are evident in Twain's later loathing of the flesh of man and of the moral sensibility it embodies. Dickinson's evanescent Awe, occasionally perceived in a slant of light from the universe beyond her sentient circumference, is the wonder of existence that Twain reduces to mere thought or dream. Like Melville's *Confidence-Man,* Twain's *Mysterious Stranger* exposes the forlorn state of the human being in an empty eternity, suggesting the existential and absurdist universe that overcame American writers after World War II.

Notes

1. Charles M. Kennedy, trans. *An Anthology of Old English Poetry* (New York: Oxford University Press, 1960), p. 5.

2. (New York: Viking Press, 1951), p. 240.

3. *Portrait of the Artist as American* (New York: Harcourt Brace, 1930), p. 294.

4. *A Home-Made World: The American Modernist Writer* (New York: Knopf, 1975), p. 18.

5. *A Hugh Henry Brackenridge Reader,* ed. Daniel Marder (Pittsburgh: University of Pittsburgh Press, 1970). pp. 70-71.

6. For account of Pound's vorticism and its relation to the vorticism of Wyndom Lewis, see Hugh Kenner, *The Pound Era* (Berkeley: University of California Press, 1971), pp. 232-247.

7. *Exile's Return,* p. 8.

8. Quoted by Cowley, *Exile's Return,* p. 244.

9. "The River," *Collected Poems,* ed. Waldo Frank (New York: Liveright, 1933), p. 18.

10. For example, see Alfred Kazin, Preface, *On Native Grounds* (New York: Harcourt Brace, 1942, rpt, Doubleday Anchor, 1956).

11. Alexis de Tocqueville, *Democracy in America,* trans. George Lawrence, eds. J. P. Mayer and Max Lerner (1835 rpt. New York: Harper and Row, 1966), p. 12.

12. *City of Words: American Fiction 1950-1970* (New York: Harper and Row, 1971), p. 427.

13. For elaboration, see Irving Goffman, *The Presentation of Self in Everyday Life* (New York: Doubleday Anchor, 1959); Manfred Putz, *The Story of Identity: American Fiction of the Sixties* (Stutgart: J. B. Metzler, 1979); Richard Poirer, *The Performing Self* (New York: Oxford University Press, 1971).

14. Cited by James R. Mellow, *Nathaniel Hawthorne in His Times* (Boston: Houghton Mifflin, 1980), p. 326.

15. Actually Poe attended school in England the five years his foster parents lived there.

16. *The Liberal Imagination* (New York: Viking, 1940, rpt. Doubleday Anchor 1950), p. 206.

17. "The Author's Account of Himself", *The Sketch Book,* ed. Haskell Springer (Boston: Twayne, 1978), pp. 8-9.

18. "The Author," *Braceridge Hall,* ed. Herbert F. Smith (Boston: Twayne, 1977), pp. 6-7.

19. *The Historical Novel,* trans. Hannah and Stanley Mitchell (London: Penguin Books, 1969), pp. 13-14.

20. Cited by Margaret Denny and William Gilman, eds. *The American Writer and the European Tradition* (Minneapolis: University of Minnesota Press, 1950), p. 45.

21. Edel, *Letters,* I (1974). p. 45.

22. Edel, *Letters,* I, pp. 138-9.

23. Edel, *Letters,* I, p. 140.

24. *The Reverberator* (London: Macmillan, 1921-3), pp. 397-8.

25. Edel, *Letters,* I, p. 77.

26. Edel, *Letters,* I, p. 428.

27. Edel, *Letters,* II, p. 86.

28. *The Letters of Henry James,* ed. Percy Lubbock (London: Macmillan, 1920), I, p. 105.

29. Lubbock, *Letters,* I, p. 168.

30. Quoted by Leon Edel, *Henry James: The Treacherous Years* (New York: Lippincott, 1969), p. 107.

31. Lubbock, *Letters,* I, p. 363.

32. Lubbock, *Letters,* I, p. 365.

33. Quoted by Edel, *The Treacherous Years,* p. 350.

34. *Studies in Classical American Literature* (1923 rpt. New York: Viking Press, 1951), p. 6.

35. Hector St. John de Crèvecoeur, *Letters from an American Farmer* (New York: E. P. Dutton, 1912), pp. 198-9.

Colin D. Pearce (essay date fall 1994)

SOURCE: Pearce, Colin D. "The Wisdom of Exile: Edward Everett Hale's 'The Man without a Country.'" *Interpretation: A Journal of Political Philosophy* 22, no. 1 (fall 1994): 91-109.

[*In the following essay, Pearce discusses the transformation that exile has on the main character in Edward Everett Hale's "The Man without a Country," and the lessons that can be extracted from that transformation.*]

> When someone reproached Diogenes with his exile, he replied, "Nay, it was through that, you miserable fellow, that I came to be a philosopher."
>
> Diogenes Laertius, *Lives of the Philosophers*

INTRODUCTION

No man was a greater American patriot than Edward Everett Hale, a figure who concerned himself with the formation of American citizens and who exercised a

broad influence from his pulpit in Boston and via his voluminous writings. His short story "The Man Without a Country" is universally regarded as an American classic. Within a year of its publication in the *Atlantic Monthly* in 1863, it had sold a half a million copies. As John R. Adams notes, "Almost at once Philip Nolan, the remorseful exile, became as clearly defined a figure as Washington Irving's Rip Van Winkle or Ichabod Crane; and he was more recognizable as an American character than the protagonists or the antagonists of Hawthorne's or Poe's tales."[1]

One might think that this short story which was so successful in civics textbooks would go the way of most of the patriotic writings of the Civil War period and be forgotten almost as soon as the cannons were silenced.[2] But the tale's enduring relevance is attested to by its continued success.[3] In Francis R. Gemme's view, Hale's story, if approached in the tradition of Aristotle and Donne, remains "highly relevant in this modern age in which questions of legal and moral dissent abound."[4]

Briefly, the tale is narrated by a certain Ingham, who had known Nolan as a young officer in the navy. He was moved to tell his story by reading Nolan's obituary notice in the newspaper in 1863. If Nolan "was near eighty when he died,"[5] we can conclude that he must have been born during the Articles of Confederation period in the early 1780's. Nolan would have been about ten years old when the United States Constitution came into effect in 1791. Nolan's life was thus roughly parallel to the birth of the "New Nation" in the American Revolution and its "death" in the American Civil War in the early 1860's.

The decisive event in Nolan's life was his involvement in the Aaron Burr conspiracy. He met Burr in Louisiana in 1805 and was court-martialled in 1807 in the remote western outpost of Fort Adams for his connection to the Burr scheme. Nolan was "guilty enough" as far as the court was concerned, but when the judge asked him at the close of the proceedings "whether he wished to say anything to show that he had always been faithful to the United States he cried out, in a fit of frenzy: 'Damn the United States! I wish I may never hear of the United States again!'" (p. 11).

The indignant president of the court, "Old Morgan," then decided to give Nolan, like Midas before him, everything he wished. He sentenced the young man to be taken away and, "subject to the approval of the President," arrangements would be made "that you never hear the name United States again." Nolan was then taken onto a Navy ship and for the remainder of his life cruised the oceans on United States vessels under the care of officers and crew who were forbidden to mention, speak or convey any fact, information or detail relevant to the United States whatsoever. "From that mo-

ment, September 23, 1807, till the day he died, May 11, 1863, he never heard her name again. For that half century and more he was a man without a country" (p. 12).

Ingham explains the improbable story of an American seaborne outcast by or in terms of the indifference, secrecy and cowardice of the United States government. It was certain that President Jefferson approved of the sentence if we may "believe the men who say they have seen his signature" (p. 14). The Secretary of the Navy also signed off on the orders for Nolan's "mild custody" (p. 16). In later life, during the 1830's, when he thought he had "some influence in Washington," Ingham tried to "move heaven and earth" to free Nolan, but "it was like trying to get a ghost out of prison. They pretended there was no such man, and never was such a man. . . . It will not be the first thing in the service of which the Department knows nothing!" (p. 36) The conduct of the government in his own case would appear to justify to some extent the young Nolan's initial attitude of contempt for the United States.

> [A]fter 1817, the position of every officer who had Nolan in charge was one of the greatest delicacy. The government had failed to renew the order of 1807 regarding him. What was a man to do? What then, if he were called to account by the Department for violating the order of 1807? Should he keep him? What then if Nolan should be liberated some day, and should bring an action for false imprisonment or kidnapping against every man who had him in charge? . . . the Secretary always said, as they so often do at Washington, that there were no special orders to give, and that we must act on our own judgment. That means, "If you succeed, you will be sustained; if you fail, you will be disavowed."

> (Pp. 40-41)

When he was a young soldier the adventurer Aaron Burr won Nolan over by showing the kind of interest in his particular case which his own government completely failed to show once he had become an aging exile. Whatever the patriotic intention of Hale's story, and its lesson that the United States is wholly worthy of the loyalty of its citizens, the story also shows us that the government of the country is surely capable of unconstitutional behavior, cowardice and incompetence. Loyalty to the United States does not imply unlimited trust in its government.

THE EDUCATION OF AN OUTCAST

The circumstances of Philip Nolan's upbringing were singular. He had grown up in the West during the 1780's and 90's. This "gay, dashing, bright young fellow" was immediately captivated by Aaron Burr when they met, "as the Devil would have it . . . at some dinner party." He "wrote and rewrote and copied . . . long, high worded and stilted letters" to Burr but received no reply. "The other boys in the garrison sneered at him be-

cause he sacrificed in this unrequited affection for a politician the time which they devoted to Monongohela, sledge, and high-low jack" (p. 10). When Burr returned to "seduce him," he was "enlisted body and soul" in the conspiracy. We see then from the start that Nolan was a character whose guiding passion was ambition and honor, things which he associated with the "dashing expedition" of Burr.

Nolan's "formal" education had been irregular and "un-American," if we may speak anachronistically.

> He had been educated on a plantation, where the finest company was a Spanish officer or a French merchant from Orleans. His education, such as it was, had been perfected in commercial expeditions to Vera Cruz, and I think he told me his father once hired an Englishman to be private tutor for a winter on the plantation. He had spent half his youth with an older brother, hunting horses in Texas.
>
> (Pp. 11-12)

Nolan seems to have grown up in the West more like a wild cavalier of aristocratic Europe than a steady citizen of a democratic republic.[6] "[I]n a word, to him, 'United States' was scarcely a reality." And yet when he joined the army as a young man he had sworn "on his faith as a Christian to be true to the 'United States'" (p. 12). Aaron Burr's dream of a new empire in the southwest fired Nolan's imagination and called forth a "flesh and blood" commitment in a way that his situation in the forces of the United States did not.

Nolan then was of a more spirited and daring type than the usual time-servers in the services. But at the same time, as a man of high ambition and great daring, he was dependent on society more than his more average or contented comrades. He needed it as a "playing field" for his virtues in a way they did not.[7] Exile with its permanent obscurity or privacy must therefore be all the more difficult to bear for someone of Nolan's type. The pain he goes through during his banishment bears this out.

NOLAN'S NEED FOR SOCIETY

Nolan's exile meant that he could never satisfy whatever desire he had to know and understand the political developments as they were unfolding in his own country. "No mess liked to have him permanently, because his presence cut off all talk of home or of the prospect of return, of politics, or letters, of peace or of war,—cut off more than half the talk men like to have at sea." Hence Nolan "ate and drank alone" (p. 16). Conversations Nolan did have, but never on matters to do with his own country.

But as we learn at the end of the tale, Nolan had all along been "living for" the United States. His room was decorated with the symbols of American life—map, flag and so on—and his concern to know how his country was developing, to know of the new states, "of emigration, and the means of it,—of steamboats, and railroads, and telegraphs,—of inventions, and books, and literature,—of the Colleges, and West Point, and the Naval School," was great (p. 45). His interest in the fate of country was in inverse proportion to his ability to be a part of it. He was deprived of the thing he came to hunger after most. Only on his deathbed does Ingham's friend Danforth convey to the old man some of the details of American history from 1807 to 1863. But Danforth explains that he "could not make up my mouth to tell him a word about this infernal rebellion" (p. 46).

Thus we are left with the unmistakable impression that Hale wishes to teach through his story the human need for community and membership in a larger group of human beings joined together by mutual trust and a common discourse, or, in his words, to provide "a warning to the young Nolans and Vallandighams and Tatnals of to-day of what it is to throw away a country" (p. 40).

The harshness of Nolan's fate indicates clearly Hale's point in describing the life of a "man without a country," which is to say the individual outside the pale of civic life. Hale is implicitly addressing the liberal doctrines of the State of Nature or making an excursion into "social contract theory." But the fact that Hale gives us a story of exile rather than of man alone in the wilderness shows his basic standpoint.[8] While Hale would allow that the individual can be separated from the community to some degree, the idea of human existence without civil community where Hobbes said his life must be "solitary, poor, nasty, brutish and short" is unthinkable to him.[9] In the State-of-Nature doctrine the individual antedates the social contract, but in the thought of Hale the community is prior to or coeval with the individual.[10]

Thus, in comparing Hale's description of "The Man Without a Country" with Hobbes's State of Nature, we notice some basic differences. Nolan has food and lodging supplied, his jailers are basically well disposed towards him, he leads a highly civilized life in some respects, and he lives to the ripe old age of eighty. Nolan on his ship has all that Hobbesian man desires. He has security of body and possessions as well as private liberty. And yet he is not a happy man. His loss of the "fellowship" of others is a great catastrophe for him.[11]

We are not surprised to learn then that Hale disagrees with Hobbes, who said that nature "dissociates" human beings. For Hale man is a "gregarious animal." "[A]ny one who separates himself from the race of which he is an organic part, at that moment death begins. 'The human race is the individual of which men and women are so many separate cells, or organs.'"[12] Hale makes these remarks in likening the human race to the bees,

who cannot live apart from the hive. He presents man as a higher bee. He thus implicitly takes issue with Hobbes, who allowed that "It is true, that certain living creatures, as Bees, and Ants, live sociably one with another, (which are therefore by Aristotle numbered amongst Political creatures;)" but who insisted that "Mankind cannot do the same."[13]

Thus it appears from a certain angle that Hale takes the side of Aristotle over against the "first liberal," Hobbes.[14] In some sense this is true, as Hale implicitly denies the State of Nature as a starting point for reflections on the human condition. But as we shall see, it is not that simple. Aristotle's case for the naturalness of the city hinged on the highest end of the city, which is philosophy, which is to say the fulfilment of human nature in a self-sufficient, self-absorbed, purely truth-seeking, apolitical way of life. Hale does not believe in the desirability or even the possibility of this justifying "telos" of human community.

To appreciate this aspect of Hale's thought we need to look at his more general statements of principle. In particular we should look at his thoughts on politics and the "life of the mind."

EDWARD EVERETT HALE'S PURE AMERICANISM

In an address entitled "Democracy and Liberal Education," delivered in 1887, Hale attacked the then President of Princeton University, the distinguished Scottish academic James McCosh, for his remarks in a lecture to the Exeter Academy.[15] Hale argued, in effect, that McCosh was "un-American" in his pedagogical purposes because he defended the idea of liberal education as creating "a separate class of men,—sort of a book-made aristocracy . . . to supply our lack of a political body of noblemen by an aristocracy founded on letters and learning." In so doing, Hale explained, McCosh was drawing on analogies "as old as Plato." "They are analogies which come most naturally to a man trained among well-defined classes in social order. But they ought not to be long sustained among people who have been trained in the social order of a democratic republic" ("Democracy and a Liberal Education," p. 43).

For Hale the idea of liberal education should have no "elitist" or exclusivist overtones. Liberal education does not seek "to make any class of scholars." Indeed, "a true republic expects, in the end, to give a liberal education to all its people . . . the republic regards a liberal education not as the good fortune of a governing class, but as the privilege, if you please, the necessity of all" (ibid., pp. 44-45). In the final analysis Hale blurs the line between civic and liberal education completely. Moreover, he defines liberal education in Tocqueville's sense as incompatible with the American regime and American conditions.[16]

Hale's particular concern is the corruptive effect on society of "intellectuals" or, in the older terminology, "sophists." These he defines as those to whom one might send "at ten o'clock to-night, and bid him before two to write up for you Bulgaria. . . . One thousand words, two thousand, ten thousand words, as you have demanded and are willing to pay for." But these modern equivalents of the Athenian sophists ultimately have nothing to say. "And for any uplifting of mankind, for guiding life, for helping society, what is written has not the worth of the money paid for the ink with which it was done!" ("Democracy and a Liberal Education," p. 48).

Philosophy or liberal education, as Hale defines it, uplifts mankind and helps society, not as an ancillary consequence of its pursuit of truth, but as its primary object. "[T]rue literature and true philosophy need to be fed, in every hour, by the tides of the people's life . . . on the other hand, the people's life quickens, enlarges, and with a new dignity controls history and nature, as it is fed by the daily food which it receives from Science, Literature, and Philosophy."[17] In other words philosophy both springs from the people and helps the people to attain its ends. It is not fundamentally at odds with society. Hale makes no mention in his lectures of the execution of Socrates.

Hale therefore has very much an "enlightenment" conception of liberal education's relationship to society. Liberal education illuminates the social world in order that all its members may see and live better. It "lets in the light; it stains the panes; it paints the frescoes on the walls, while it gives its strength and symmetry to the whole." There are no dangerous truths for Hale. All that can be known should be available for all to see. "In all true literature and science, there are no secret medicines or private paths. Everything is really patent. 'Noblesse oblige' and what a man discovers, he discovers: he opens it for universal good" (ibid., p. 50). Moreover,

> The man best fitted by his education to do the manly and godly service expected of an American citizen is not, by that fortune, in any jot separated from the people. The people can lead him quite as much as his books can lead the people . . . The men of letters, the men of liberal education, are not to hold themselves in any sort as parted from other workmen of the country or superior to them . . . Distrust the dainty advice, uttered no matter how gracefully, that you study science for herself, truth for itself, or literature, or philosophy. You study each and all, whatever you learn for mankind.
>
> (Ibid., pp. 61-64)

Hale is, to be sure, careful to add a warning against the "quack or the demagogue who tries to make science or literature popular, by making either of them superficial, petty, or in any jot small" (ibid., p. 65). But in saying

this he does not imply that the political world is inherently problematic from the point of view of liberal education. Hale stays within the framework of politics altogether when discussing the requirements of education.

EDUCATION: CIVIC AND LIBERAL

Part of Hale's concern is to make sure that education in America is, unlike that which the young Nolan received, truly "American education." Hale's starting point is the fact that "there is such a reality as American thought, [and] there are certain principles which belong to the American Government, [and] certain feelings which are experienced by none but an American."[18] America is a "pure democracy" and "is a nation different from any other" (ibid., pp. 71-72). The term "The People" in America designates the "We" in the Constitution. This "We" "is not a class; it is the whole, and this whole is sovereign." Hence "with us any language which speaks contemptuously of this People is treason against the sovereign" (ibid., p. 72). Thus for Hale the "trenchant satires upon democracy . . . of almost all the European schools" derive from their lack of appreciation that the people is the community not the rabble (ibid.).

For Hale American education cannot be European in nature because of a "difference of principle." "We educate all the people with one motive; they educate a part of their people with another" (ibid., p. 81). In discussing what he sees as a needed reform in American college education, which is for some public-spirited soul of wealth and benevolence to endow "one special professorship" in every first-class college "which should be the professorship of America," Hale reveals the thought behind his conceit of having the young Nolan educated by a Spanish officer, a French merchant and an English tutor. The training of American youth should no longer be skewed by its confinement to "English newspapers, French novels, German philosophy, and, lately, Prussian religion" (ibid., p. 82). An "accomplished man in each college" could "show young men and women that the Fathers of a century ago had the greatest genius for government which has ever been seen at one time, in one company of men" and that "the morals of Zola, and the dreams of Tolstoi and of Turgenef, do not fit in with American character and surroundings" (ibid., p. 83).

In what then is the intellect of the American sovereign, which is to say the people, to be trained? It will be trained firstly in the history of the people itself, in the understanding of its government and administration, in the capacity to recognize genius when it crops up in its midst and in "the great lessons of mutual help and tolerance." This training "will not try to make [the pupil] merely a student of language or indeed of any one science. There will be philologists enough, and men of science enough. We shall not crowd him, as a prince with Latin and Greek, or Sanskrit."[19] The American

model shall be George Washington, who "had no knowledge of any language but his own" but who "gained—by a training quite unlike that of the colleges—a strong and easy style of writing" (ibid., p. 114). All this is to happen through such agencies as reading circles, Chautauqua and university extension—"adult education," we might say today.[20]

We can say that Hale saw very clearly the tension between the principles of the American republic and the implicit effects of liberal education;[21] but he resolves this tension in favor of the democratic or civic side of liberal education rather than in the direction of its philosophic ends. While Tocqueville argues that the "threat" to liberty and civilization is no longer from the old order which was dying, but from the new democratic system which was gathering strength, Hale still speaks as though there is a danger from "feudalism" or "caste consciousness."[22]

CHRISTIAN LIBERALISM VERSUS PAGAN ETHICS

We understand more clearly now Hale's vantage point on the American civic condition and his concept of American citizenship. In his interpretation of American republicanism there is no room for a lofty distance from the popular concerns and democratic purposes of the American regime. We observe then that Hale's republicanism is not to be confused with the tradition of aristocratic republicanism emanating out of Greece and Rome. This difference is at the root of Hale's moral and political views. To understand Hale's fundamental standpoint we must, above all, take into account his interpretation of Christianity and what it meant for the political world.

For Hale, Christianity is the fundamental event which divides the republican tradition of the United States from its antecedent in the classical world. In short, for Hale, the advent of Christianity reconciled once and for all vulgar and true virtue, or had the effect of bringing together the sphere of public life with the sphere of genuine truth. Whatever Hale takes to be the precise character of American republicanism, it is to be part of the "New Civilization" of Christianity rather than the "Old Civilization" of "paganism."[23] This is made most apparent in his little essay entitled "The Old and the New Face to Face: A Thumb-Nail Sketch." The scene Hale wants us to envisage here is the "culminating moment" of the old pre-Christian order.[24] At this "moment" we see the faith, courage and morality of St. Paul, side by side with "the moral results of the ancient civilization" represented by Seneca (ibid., p. 74).

Hale says of Seneca's "system" that it indeed represented "the best of Roman morality and Greek philosophy, [but] still it was mean. His daring was the bravest of the men of the old civilization . . . Seneca dared say

no more to Nero, to venture more with him, than did any other man" (ibid., p. 80). Ancient philosophy was cowardly at its heart.

> [A]ll that Seneca's daring could venture was to seduce the baby-tyrant into the least injurious of tyrannies. From the plunder of a province he would divert him by the carnage of the circus. From the murder of a senator he could lure him by some new lust at home. From the ruin of the Empire, he could seduce him by diverting him with the ruin of a noble family. And Seneca did this with the best of motives. He said he used all the power in his hands, and he thought he did. He was one of those men of whom all times have their share. The bravest of his time, he satisfied himself with alluring the beardless Emperor by petty crime from public wrong; he could flatter him to the expedient. He dared not order him to the right.
>
> (Ibid., pp. 80-81)

Hale dismisses the whole philosophic tradition of advising tyrants.[25] He does not consider it an extenuating circumstance that Seneca could have been trying to moderate and improve a horrible regime by "working on" the tyrant, that Seneca might have been concerned to do what he could to improve a tyrannical order rather than simply to occupy the moral high ground. The morality of the philosopher is a low-stakes morality to Hale. It implies an exceedingly dim view of the world and of the prospects for improvement. Moreover, it may imply a certain sympathy with the tyrannical regime as being preferable to a democracy under the best circumstances. For Hale the first order of priority is to smite the tyrant hip and thigh with moral thunder, and damn the consequences. Seneca was concerned only to moderate the excesses of tyranny, whereas St. Paul was concerned to condemn the tyrant to his face.[26] Hale tries to articulate what he suspects might have been Seneca's thoughts on hearing St. Paul's address to the Emperor, which is to say his bearing witness to the encounter of "Faith on one side, before expediency and cruelty on the other!"[27]

> This wild Easterner has rebuked the Emperor as I have so often wanted to rebuke him. He stood there, as I have wanted to stand, a man before a brute. He said what I have thought, and have been afraid to say. Downright, straightforward, he told the Emperor truths as to Rome, as to man, and as to his vices, which I have longed to tell him. He has done what I am afraid to do. He has dared this, which I have dallied with, and left undone. What is the mystery of his power?"[28]

In Hale's hands the tyrant and the philosopher both come to sight as pure "individualists." The tyrant will have the city with its people and its goods all to himself, while the philosopher seeks self-preservation in a cowardly calculating way. Only the Christian teaching can show the way beyond such "egoism" in the direction of true morality. It can give reasons why one should surrender all for the sake of justice here and now. The Christian proves the genuineness of his philanthropy by

brooking no compromise where justice and humanity are concerned.[29]

Given what we have seen of Hale's fundamental position above, it might appear that little more need be said. Hale preaches the individual's sociality because he is a Christian philanthropist, and human beings in all their need for justice and humanity are first to be found in one's own community. "[T]here is no success for a man if he try to live for himself, in himself, and by himself. He must live in the common life or he dies. He must enjoy with the joy of others; he must sorrow in their sorrow."[30]

But if we go deeper into the experience of Hale's Nolan, we find that Hale has created a more complicated picture. It would seem that despite or because of his best efforts to make the case for the essential need of the individual for his community, and for the morality of noble self-sacrifice, Hale ends up making a very strong case for the ennobling effects on the individual of exclusion from full membership in the community or for freedom from the demands of civic life.

NOLAN'S RE-EDUCATION

Nolan's isolation necessarily had the unintended effect of "educating" or more precisely, re-educating him. It turns out that during his exile Nolan became a great reader. A "system was adopted from the first about his books and other reading . . . everybody was permitted to lend him books, if they were not published in America and made no allusion to it" (*The Man Without a Country*, p. 18). Any "American content" had to be cut out of the material he could see. Such a proviso hardly resulted in the exclusion of the largest part of the Western literary tradition. But "[t]his was a little cruel sometimes, when the back of what was cut out might be as innocent as Hesiod" (p. 18) and "Philips swore old Shaw had cut out the *Tempest* from Shakespeare before he let Nolan have it, because he said 'the Bermudas ought to be ours, and by Jove, should be one day'" (p. 19). As it happened, Nolan had "quite a windfall" in the form of "a lot of English books" which an English Admiral had lent to officer Philips at the Cape of Good Hope. Amongst Nolan's main readings then were the Bible, Shakespeare, Walter Scott, Flechier's "Sermons" and the reports in the "foreign papers" of Napoleon's battles and Canning's speeches.

Thus as a man without a country Nolan made a life for himself in which "reading his notes were his profession." His life on board ship became as "methodical" as it had been chaotic back in the western states.

> He said it did not do for anyone to try to read all the time, more than to do anything else all the time; but that he read just five hours a day. "Then," he said, "I keep up my notebooks, writing in them at such and

such hours from what I have been reading; and I in-
clude them in my scrap books." Those were very curi-
ous indeed. He had six or eight, of different subjects.
There was one of History, one of Natural Science, one
which he called "Odds and Ends."

(P. 29)

Nolan's reading and note-taking "took five hours and
two hours respectively of each day," and for "diver-
sion" he would turn to his "Natural History," which
would take "two hours a day more." "These nine hours
made Nolan's regular daily 'occupation.'" Sometimes
the men would bring Nolan birds and fish to study, "but
on a long cruise he had to satisfy himself with centi-
pedes and cockroaches and such small game. He was
the only naturalist I ever met who knew anything about
the habits of the house-fly and mosquito."[31]

Nolan's formal exclusion from civic life left him with
no other option but to cultivate his mind. Thus he be-
came in his life on the high seas a litterateur, a scien-
tist, somewhat of a physician and a kind of poet-priest.
But at the same time he did not lose his old "aristo-
cratic" virtue of courage,[32] and for all the pain of his ex-
ile it seems evident that he grew in his humanity and
dignity.[33] His exile made of him an excellent citizen "in
absentia," as it were. Nolan becomes a better citizen de-
spite or because of the fact that the rule of his "re-
education" was that it be free from all content apper-
taining to his country.

PREACHING PATRIOTISM WHILE LIVING APART

At one point Nolan has occasion to play the role of an
interpreter to a group of slaves liberated by his ship be-
cause he is the only man available who understands
Portuguese. The slaves' emotional response to his ex-
plaining that they were to be taken back to their homes
moves Nolan to give a little sermon to his young friend
Ingham on the relationship of the individual to his coun-
try.

> Youngster, let that show you what it is to be without a
> family, without a home and without a country. And if
> you are ever tempted to say a word or do something
> that shall put a bar between you and your family, your
> home and your country, pray God in His mercy to take
> you that instant home to His own heaven. Stick by
> your family, boy; forget you have a self, while you do
> everything for them.

(P. 35)

Thus Nolan seems to be recommending to the young
boy to seek the opposite situation to his own, in which
he can have no other concern or focus for his life than
himself. Uncompromising dedication to family and
country is to be preferred to a self-absorbed existence
where the other human beings encountered are merely
means to the basic necessities of existence such as food

and shelter. It seems that Nolan's own intellectual
progress and his appreciation of the human costs of be-
ing stateless or "without a country" advance in tandem.
The more learned he becomes, the more emphatic he is
that the citizen should view his country as his mother.
In other words Nolan recommends the virtues of civic
dedication in inverse proportion to his own connection
to such a life.

But there is a fundamental disjunction between Nolan's
own virtues and the virtues he preaches to the boy. No-
where in his little sermon on love of country do the
words "mind," "knowledge" or "intelligence" appear.
Nowhere in it does he allude to the years of study he
has pursued as result of his being exiled. The contradic-
tion between Nolan's little sermon and his actual deal-
ings with Ingham is apparent in the role Nolan played
in Ingham's "formal" education. Ingham explains that
Nolan taught him "a great deal of my mathematics . . .
lent me books, and helped me about my reading" (p.
36). This had a lifelong impact, as indicated by the fact
that we first meet Ingham "devouring to the very stubble
all the current literature [he] could get hold of" (p. 7).
How could Nolan have played this role if he had not
been absorbed with his researches and studies, which is
to say preoccupied solely with his own interests, for all
those years? Would he have been a competent teacher if
he had not blurted out his shocking statement at the
court martial and thereby had remained a "full citizen?"

But if Nolan has palpably improved in all the virtues as
a result of the strange twist of fate that placed him out-
side the pale of political or civic life, why does he not
encourage his young friend or anybody else to try to
maneuver himself into a position, certainly not of exile,
but reminiscent of his own in that the "life of the mind"
and the study of natural phenomena are the major pre-
occupations?

In answer to this question we must recall that Nolan's
"liberation" from the demands of his society was forced
on him in the sense that his life situation was not some-
thing that he chose directly for himself. It was not by
natural inclination that he came to lead his life in pur-
suit of knowledge but by force of circumstance.[34] His
new-found virtues went "against the grain" of his ear-
lier, "freer" life where he had other options, such as
soldier or adventurer, to choose from. Thus the attain-
ment of his new virtue was at the cost of certain basic
natural inclinations that would have had free play back
"on land." We might say that on land the lower and
more naturally powerful of Nolan's inclinations would
have submerged the higher, while this situation was re-
versed in his unique or "artificial" situation at sea.

INDIVIDUAL AND SOCIETY

Despite his early conduct Nolan must have had a good
nature underneath all his youthful wildness, somewhat
like Prince Hal in *Henry IV,* who would later become

the all-conquering Henry V. Otherwise he would not have gone so far in the acquisition of knowledge and the development of his character while floating on the oceans of the world. In the case of Nolan we are dealing not with the pure philosopher nor with a totally undistinguished and ungifted type. Rather we are dealing with the kind of individual who, although perhaps not originally destined to lead the purely philosophical life, is nevertheless well enough endowed by nature to be capable of capitalizing on a situation where the acquisition of learning and the pursuit of the sciences is the only path left open to his mind.

Nolan then is of a type that is susceptible to both the call of his intellect and the call of his community. As such he is neither a total solitary who is by nature fitted for life alone, nor is he simply the citizen and nothing more, who receives full human satisfaction simply by virtue of belonging to, and participating in, the life of the community. To the extent then that Nolan is a "hybrid," which is to say not totally satisfied or fulfilled by his pursuit of knowledge or totally overcoming all the natural inclinations which tended to link him to the life of the community, we can appreciate how drastic a punishment he had received.[35]

Nolan's agonies in exile serve to show just how "superior" as a human type (to use Aristotle's terminology), he would have to have been in order for him to be truly indifferent to the fact of his exile, which is to say truly free from all possible concern or attachment to the land of his birth, to his family and to his "past," so to speak.[36] But being "neither beast nor god" as Aristotle says the man without a city must be, Nolan must endure the costs, even as he takes advantage of the benefits, of his isolated position.[37]

The life of philosophy or science is only a possibility opened up by human society, and is no more the explicit purpose of that society's coming into existence than it is the explicit purpose of the United States Navy to provide the conditions for the flourishing of such a fine human being as Philip Nolan. The community as such does not philosophize and has other concerns than the perfection of the intellect. It must first absorb itself with external security and internal order. It must then pay heed to producing a citizen body that will assume the responsibilities that accompany the end of perpetuating the community's existence. Citizens are expected to obey the law, participate in government, serve in the defense forces, etc. And nobody seriously claims that these requirements on the part of the community are unreasonable.

But it is clear that these reasonable demands are at odds with the ultimate requirements of philosophy or intellectual virtue. Nolan becomes who he is because he found peace and extended periods of "uninterrupted"

time aboard ship. Although Nolan is a kind of prisoner, he is at permanent leisure, while his keepers or supervisors are obliged to work and to fulfil their naval responsibilities.[38] He could do what he did precisely because he is not part of the ship's crew and therefore has none of the demanding responsibilities of a crew member. Nolan's experience is a paradigm of the relation of intellectual to simply civic virtue.

Nolan's strange case serves to remind us of the ambiguity of human nature insofar as it includes both individualist and communitarian tendencies. His becoming a somewhat outstanding human being in exile reminds us that we must expect to feel and appear different from the community norm if we would pursue "self-improvement," to use John Stuart Mill's phrase for our highest individual obligation. The approach to true virtue involves a kind of transformation or conversion, such as Nolan seems to have experienced, from an earlier, inadequate, civic or social stage, into a later, more fully human, individual stage. But the fact that Nolan's achievement of a high degree of human excellence is not accompanied by the fullest personal happiness also reminds us of the tension between the full development of individual potential and simple or ordinary happiness or contentment. The case of "The Man Without a Country" shows us that the situation of those individuals who by whatever means come to cultivate virtues not strictly required or even appreciated by the civic order is ambiguous from the point of view of happiness.

Nolan's nobility seems to consist in the way he accepts the situation in which his imprudence as a youth placed him. He "repented of his folly, and then like a man submitted to the fate he had asked for."[39] In his acceptance of his fate or situation Nolan approaches the life of the philosopher who above all does not complain about the dominion of chance over human life. He accepts his lot by recognizing that some things are forever outside one's control, especially one's past errors and the consequences that flow from them.

CONCLUSION

We must conclude from a study of Hale's great story in the light of his general political principles that while it may make a dramatic plea for patriotism it fails to persuade us of the ultimate sociality of mankind. Hale's story seems, on the surface at least, to demonstrate his claim that the "human race is the individual of which men and women are so many separate cells, or organs." His account of Nolan's "re-education" in exile seems to describe the reintegration of the unfortunate man into the community, to the principles of which he had not been properly educated, but from which he had been expelled. In the course of the story Hale necessarily reveals the interdependence of this reeducation and Nolan's basic condition of alienation from the community.

But if, in his very description of the human need for society, Hale is forced to show that, in the decisive respect of the acquisition of wisdom or knowledge, man cannot be a fully social being, has he not conceded the point that the individual is ultimately of higher dignity than the community and is therefore not simply social?

Hale's case for the community and against "individualism" may work for all the ordinary purposes of showing how "no man is an island." Hale would certainly say that his defense of human sociality is at the same time a case for the fuller development of the individual. But in the final analysis his suggestion that dedication to the community or philanthropical benevolence should be our determining principle cannot be the last word. This is because of the fact that the development of Nolan's natural potential is connected to his loss of full membership in the community. Nolan's "self-realization" is a double-edged sword. On the one hand it involves a fuller appreciation of his fundamental dependence on the community, and on the other hand it involves his transcending the level of community "consciousness" through the cultivation of his reason and his intellect. This fuller intellectual development may not ultimately be an adequate compensation for the pain of his exiled condition, but this simply shows not that man is by nature social, but that "the virtues of our composite nature are human . . . [and] the excellence of reason is a thing apart."[40]

Notes

1. John R. Adams, *Edward Everett Hale* (Boston: Twayne Publishers, 1977), p. 27.

2. Hale himself gave a detailed account of the circumstances surrounding his story's composition. He explains that he was influenced by the careers of Vallandigham, who was expelled from Ohio for opposing the Union cause, and of Napoleon, who suffered his exile on St. Helena. He notes that at a time when it was thought "that the United States *are* a confederacy" (emphasis Hale's), "any lesson was well received by persons of conscience which showed, either positively or negatively, what the word 'Patriotism' means,—or what one's Country is" ("Author's Note to Edition of 1897," in Edward Everett Hale, *The Man Without a Country and Other Stories* [Boston: Little, Brown and Company, 1899], pp. 3-4).

3. Adams summarizes the story's commercial career as follows: "How many anthologies included *The Man Without a Country* is mere speculation, as is also the number of translations. In addition to the printed trade editions, it appeared in Pitman, Graham, and Gregg shorthand; in braille; and as a comic paperback. Numerous inexpensive school editions with suitably educational introductions are accompanied by a patriotic edition sponsored by the Veterans of Foreign Wars and an expensive illustrated volume for the Limited Editions Club (1936) with an introduction by Carl Van Doren. It has been recited on phonograph records; and it has been rewritten for radio programs and, as late as 1973, for a national television network. Although it has been staged as a one act play, it has also been published by Samuel French as a play in three acts, prologue, and epilogue. A commercial moving picture was made in Hollywood, and an operatic version was composed by Walter Damrosch and was sung at the Metropolitan Opera" (*Edward Everett Hale,* p. 35).

4. Francis R. Gemme, *The Man Without a Country and Other Stories* (New York: Delta, 1969), pp. 4, 7.

5. Edward Everett Hale, *The Man Without a Country and Other Tales* (New York: Magnum Books, 1968), p. 28. All page references not otherwise identified are to this edition.

6. John R. Adams says that Nolan's "irregular education, pieced together from private British tutors and by association with foreign commercial interests, had lacked the moral discipline to temper the swagger of an impatient aristocratic youth" (*Edward Everett Hale,* p. 28).

7. "The liberal man will need money for the doing of his liberal deeds, and the just man too for the returning of services . . . and the brave man will need power if he is to accomplish any of the acts that correspond to his virtue, and the temperate man will need opportunity; for how else is either he or any of the others to be recognized? . . . for deeds many things are needed, and more, the greater and nobler the deeds are" (Aristotle, *Nicomachean Ethics,* 1178a30-38).

8. Nolan's situation is akin to that of Defoe's Robinson Crusoe, in that he has been born and reared in society and subsequently cast out. But in Crusoe's case it was the blind forces of nature combined with his proneness to take risks that ushered him to a life without society. In the case of Nolan it was "politics" that forced the change, or more precisely the political climate combined with youthful rashness. Moreover, Nolan is not devoid of all human company whatsoever, as was Robinson, as he is aboard ship and not on a desert island. But ultimately this situation only serves to make Nolan's fate all the more painful. He is within range of "society" but cannot really participate in it. And of course he never again saw his homeland, while Robinson served only twenty-seven years on his island. Defoe is obviously an intellectual source for Hale. More generally Hale

seems to have been under the influence of Fichte, Tolstoi, Dickens, Bunyan, Scott and others.

9. Thomas Hobbes, *Leviathan* (Harmondsworth: Penguin, 1968), chap. xiii, p. 186.

10. In the eighteenth century Montesquieu had said that "where we find man we find him together with others," and following this lead philosophers such as Hume, Paley and Bentham rejected the idea of the State of Nature as a "philosophical fiction" (See Henry D. Aiken, ed., *Hume's Moral and Political Philosophy* [New York: Hafner, 1972], p. 189). Thus British liberalism became "utilitarian liberalism," with its "greatest happiness of the greatest number" principle, while American liberalism continued to talk in terms of the "rights of man." Hale the American patriot would seem to want to keep the rights but abandon the "fiction" out of which they grew.

11. Nolan's life on naval vessels was of course without the distraction of female company. Once at a ball at Naples he had a chance to dance with a southern beauty, but when the topic of "home" arose, she "left poor Nolan alone, as he always was." Nolan "did not dance again" (p. 25). Because he is truly without regular relations to the general membership of any political community, he must perforce spend his days without prospect of family life.

12. Edward Everett Hale, "Democracy and a Liberal Education," in *Addresses and Essays on Subjects of History Education and Government* (Boston: Little Brown, 1900), p. 48.

13. Hobbes supplied six reasons why Hale must be wrong. Firstly man is in competition for honor and dignity; he constantly compares himself to others; he "thinks himself wiser and able to govern the Publique, better than the rest"; he can make judgments of good and evil, "discontenting men, and troubling their peace"; he is "most troublesome when he is at ease"; and his agreement "is by Covenant only, which is Artificiall" (*Leviathan*, chap. xvii, pp. 225-26).

14. Unlike Hale Aristotle draws a very clear distinction between man and the bees, in that "man is much more a political animal than any kind of bee or any herd animal . . . [because] man alone among the animals has speech . . . [and] speech serves to reveal the advantageous and the harmful, and hence also the just and the unjust" (*Politics*, 1253a10). Aristotle then, does not say that man is more "social" in the sense of naturally more in harmony than the bees. Man is more political than the bees, but this means that his capacity to speak about the just and the unjust, the good and the

bad, the advantageous and the disadvantageous makes him more likely to be in conflict, making his community more tenuous and his "socialization" crucial.

15. McCosh was Professor at Queen's University, Belfast, before moving to Princeton. McCosh agrees with Hale that American education has danced to European music and that this is unfortunate. But the issue for McCosh is whether "America has arrived at a stage at which there is a body of men and women who have leisure and taste to cultivate the liberal arts and advance the higher forms of civilization" ("General Introduction: What an American Philosophy Should Be," in *Realistic Philosophy Defended in a Philosophic Series*. 2 vols. [New York: Charles Scribner's Sons, 1887], 1:1). According to McCosh, America is ready. "The time has come, I believe, for America to declare her independence in philosophy . . . she should require that her philosophy have a character of its own." According to McCosh, "Yankees are distinguished from most others by their practical observation and invention . . . The American philosophy will therefore be a REALISM, opposed to IDEALISM on the one hand and to AGNOSTICISM on the other" (ibid., pp. 2-3). In a word, while acknowledging the merits of the thought of Locke, Berkeley, Leibnitz, Hume, Kant, Fichte, Mill and Spencer, McCosh explains that America must "naturalize" these "imports." "[A]s with the emigrants who land on her shores, in regard to whom she insists that they speak her language and conform to her laws; so she should require that her philosophy have a character of its own" (ibid. p. 3).

16. Tocqueville allowed with Hale that it would be dangerous to have the older education given to individuals who must face a society grounded on entirely different principles and requiring entirely other skills. "It is evident that in democratic communities the interest of individuals as well as the security of the commonwealth demands that the education of the greater number should be scientific, commercial, and industrial rather than literary . . . Greek and Latin should not be taught in all the schools." But at a certain point Tocqueville decisively parts company with Hale. He insists on the importance to American life of the "few," the "true scholars," the "elite." "It is important that those who, by their natural disposition or their fortune, are destined to cultivate letters or prepared to relish them should find schools where a complete knowledge of ancient literature may be acquired and where the true scholar may be formed" (Alexis de Tocqueville, *Democracy in America*. 2 vols. [New York: Vintage Books, 1945], 2:66).

17. Ibid., p. 46. One could say on Hale's behalf that he is arguing that philosophy must root itself in the real "flesh and blood" issues of life lest it become simple star-gazing, like the natural philosopher Socrates in Aristophanes' *Clouds*. Philosophy should return to "the cave" from time to time in order not to lose its human bearings. But in the authentically philosophical tradition there is always an "outside" of the cave, and the prime concern is that a few should be able to make their escape into the light or to turn their back on the life of the city. Hale holds back from such thoughts.

18. "The Professor in America," in *Addresses and Essays*, p. 66.

19. "The Education of a Prince," in *Addresses and Essays*, p. 117.

20. According to Hale, "the feudal critics, the people who believe in government by caste" fail to see the importance for education and democracy of the distinction between labor and work. Labor is simple brute effort, and it is the lot of only about 10 per cent of the American population, while work, which "is labor inspired by the Holy Spirit," is the lot of about 90 per cent. According to Hale, the overwhelming majority of this overwhelming majority "are to receive a liberal education" (ibid. p. 124).

21. Hale was worried that the kind of liberal education that McCosh and Tocqueville recommended to the best colleges might have some "un-American" effects. Hale complained about the "Eurocentrism" of college education in his day, meaning that it was not focussed enough on the requirements of American life. Today Hale's own Americanized education would fall under the label of "Eurocentrism," since for all Hale's concern about cleansing American education of its Europeanizing influences, he still conceived of America in terms of the Western experience. Although the term might not be used, the implicit meaning of today's campaign for "political correctness" is also that liberal education is "un-American." Paradoxically, however, the view that such high-quality liberal arts training is not right for America is expressed in precisely those institutions to which McCosh and Tocqueville looked as its home.

22. Tocqueville describes *the* American danger in the following terms: "I know of no country in which there is so little independence of mind and real freedom of discussion as in America . . . there the body is left free, and the soul is enslaved . . . The majority lives in the perpetual utterance of self applause, and there are certain truths which the Americans can learn only from strangers or from experience" (*Democracy in America*, 1:274-

75). "The public, therefore, among a democratic people, has a singular power, which aristocratic nations cannot conceive; for it does not persuade others to its beliefs, but it imposes them, and makes them permeate the thinking of everyone by a sort of enormous pressure of the mind of all upon the individual intelligence" (ibid., 2:11).

23. Hale then is manifestly not a classic, eighteenth-century enlightenment liberal like Edward Gibbon. In Gibbon's hands historical Christianity always has the color of intolerance about it, while paganism is portrayed as tolerance itself. "Such was the mild spirit of antiquity, that the nations were less attentive to the differences than to the resemblances of their religious worship" (*The Decline and Fall of the Roman Empire* [New York: Dell, 1963], p. 44).

24. "The Old and the New Face to Face: A Thumbnail Sketch," in *The Man Without a Country and Other Tales*, p. 77.

25. In Book V of the *Politics* Aristotle does not refrain from showing how a tyrant may be preserved in his position by transforming himself into "the manager of the city" or becoming a competent ruler (*Politics*, 1314b7). References to the classical thinkers' openness to advising tyrants how better to do their job may of course be multiplied.

26. Whatever one may say about the adequacy of Hale's treatment of Seneca, it should be observed that it has the merit of not minimizing the distance between Seneca's famous Stoicism and Christianity. Hale is not influenced by what W. E. H. Lecky describes as the "many curious coincidences of phraseology . . . between the writings of Seneca and the epistles of St. Paul." According to Lecky, "[To] suppose that his [Seneca's] system of morals is in any degree formed after the model, or under the influence of Christianity, is to be blind to the most obvious characteristics of both Christianity and Stoicism; for no other moralist could be so aptly selected as representing their extreme divergence. . . . Of [the essential characteristics of Christianity] all the teaching of Seneca is the direct antithesis. Careless of the future world, and profoundly convinced of the supreme majesty of man, he labored to emancipate his disciples 'from every fear of God and man;' and the proud language in which he claimed for the sage an equality with the gods, represents, perhaps, the highest point to which philosophic arrogance has been carried" (W. E. H. Lecky, *History of European Morals*. 2 vols., (New York: D. Appleton, 1875], 1:363-64).

27. "The Old and the New Face to Face," p. 81.

28. Ibid., p. 83. Hale in criticizing Seneca makes no mention of the most salient features of his life. He

does not mention the fact that Seneca was banished by the Emperor Claudius, that he was accused of complicity in Piso's conspiracy against Nero and was ordered by the tyrant to end his life, which he did in a manner more or less identical to that of Socrates in the *Phaedo*. Thus Hale does not detail the ultimate cost of crossing swords with tyrants, as indeed Seneca, as well as the Christian Paul, was guilty of doing. His purpose is rather to associate pagan philosophy with cowardice and Christianity with moral courage, regardless of historical fact.

29. Hale's Christianity may be called "Lockean" Christianity, but it is obviously held more genuinely or "literally" than it was by Locke. Before the advent of Christianity, Locke says, "Those just measures of right and wrong, which necessity had anywhere introduced, the civil laws prescribed, or philosophy recommended, stood on their true foundations. They were looked on as bonds of society, and conveniences of common life, and laudable practices. But where was it that their obligation was thoroughly known and allowed, and they received as precepts of law; of the highest law, the law of nature?" But Jesus Christ has "changed the nature of things in the world and given the advantage to piety over all that could tempt or deter men from it" by bringing "life and immortality to light" and opening humanity's eyes "upon the endless, unspeakable joys of another life" (*The Reasonableness of Christianity* [London: Rivington et al., 1824], secs. 243-45).

30. "Democracy and Liberal Education," p. 50. Compare John Stuart Mill: "In the Republic, which has [the definition of Justice] for its express purpose, and travels through the whole process of constructing an ideal commonwealth to arrive at it, the result is brought out that Justice is synonymous with the complete supremacy of Reason in the soul . . . [but resolving] justice, preeminently the social virtue . . . into the supremacy of reason within our own minds [involves] a disregard of the fact that the idea and sentiment of virtue have their foundation not exclusively in the self-regarding, but also, and even more directly, in the social feelings: a truth first fully accepted by the Stoics, who have the glory of being the earliest thinkers who grounded the obligation of morals on the brotherhood of the whole human race" ("Grote's Plato," *Edinburgh Review* [April, 1866], p. 171). It is worth noting here that while Mill praises the Stoics for the "glory" of their ethical conceptions, which included the brotherhood of man, Hale describes the great Stoic Seneca as a morally bankrupt symbol of the depravity of ancient morals.

31. Like that other character who in Aristophanes' *Clouds* lived outside the bounds of his political community—the philosopher Socrates—Nolan spent his time in the study of nature, in particular in the study of household insects. In the humorous presentation by Aristophanes it was the study of the digestive system of gnats which absorbed Socrates' attention. The individual may independently become entirely indifferent to the political or social realm, as in the case of the Aristophanic Socrates, or he may be expelled and exiled from this realm, as in the case of Nolan. But the cause of this condition in the case of Socrates is the same as the effect of it in the case of Nolan, i.e., the study of the natural world, or, more generally, a fascination with the natural order. It seems that, potentially at least, the individual, whether somehow innately indifferent to, or expelled from civic membership, finds his home in nature. He substitutes the order of nature for the political order as the fundamental "world" in which he lives and breathes.

32. In one of "the great frigate duels with the English in which the navy was really baptized," Nolan took over a cannon crew and, using the artillery skills he acquired in his youth in the army, led them through the battle. After this episode the Commodore said, "[W]e are all very grateful to you today; you are one of us today; you will be named in the dispatches" (*The Man Without a Country*, p. 27).

33. "He always kept up his exercise and I never heard that he was ill. If any other man was ill, he was the kindest nurse in the world; and he knew more than half the surgeons do. Then if anybody was sick or died, or if the captain wanted him to on any other occasion, he was always ready to read prayers. I have remarked that he read beautifully" (ibid., p. 30).

34. Nolan's situation in some respects reminds us of Rousseau. "The most sociable and the most loving of humans has been proscribed from society by unanimous agreement . . . I would have loved men in spite of themselves." Rousseau's being forced out of the fellowship of human beings and thereby being excluded from the pleasures and happinesses it can bring, although it was ultimately liberating from all cares, was at the same time also a terrible fate. (See *The Reveries of a Solitary Walker*, trans. Charles E. Butterworth [New York: Harper and Row, 1979], pp. 1-5.)

35. Socrates, it would appear, did not want his ultimate rejection of the final authority of the political community on questions of the just and the unjust, or the best way of life for man, to be taken simply for a cold indifference to his "home and

hearth" and to his fellow citizens. In his *Apology to the Jury* he says to his fellow countrymen: "I, men of Athens, salute you and love you," even as he says he will defy the City's commands and "not stop philosophizing"(29d2-4), And later in the trial, just before the vote to convict (34d3-5), he says to the jury, "I, best of men, surely do have some family; for this is also just what Homer says: not even I have grown up 'from an oak or a rock,' but from human beings." Thus the philosopher in his alienation from, and indeed fatal opposition to the City, must try to impress upon his fellow citizens that he is very much like them, and that they should not take him for some sort of freak of nature devoid of all human sentiments.

36. "But such a life [contemplating the truth] would be too high for man; for it is not in so far as he is man that he will live so, but in so far as something divine is present in him; and by so much as this is superior to our composite nature is its activity superior to that which is the exercise of the other [practical] kind of virtue. If reason is divine, then in comparison with man, the life according to it is divine in comparison with human life" (*Nicomachean Ethics*, 1177a25-1178a5).

37. "He who is without a city through nature rather than chance is either a mean sort or superior to man. . . . One who is incapable of participating or who is in need of nothing through being self-sufficient is no part of a city, and so is either beast or god" (*Politics*, 1253a1-5; 27-28).

38. "And happiness is thought to depend on leisure; for we are busy that we may have leisure . . . and the self-sufficiency, leisureliness, unweariedness (so far as this is possible for man) . . . are evidently . . . connected with the activity of reason which is contemplative" (*Nicomachean Ethics*, 1177b5-250).

39. "Finally, feeling that all my efforts were useless and that I was tormenting myself to no avail, I took the only course which remained—that of submitting to my fate without railing against necessity any longer. I have found compensation for all my hurts in this resignation through the tranquility it provides me . . ." (Rousseau, *Reveries*, p. 2).

40. *Nicomachean Ethics*, 1178a20-22.

Anny Brooksbank Jones (essay date 2000)

SOURCE: Jones, Anny Brooksbank. "Strange Meetings: Henry James and *The Siege of London*." In *Questioning the Master: Gender and Sexuality in Henry James's Writing,* edited by Peggy McCormack, pp. 54-67. Newark, Del., and London: University of Delaware Press and Associated University Presses, 2000.

[*In the following essay, Jones offers a feminist reading of Henry James's treatment of alienation, exile, and "strangeness" in* The Siege of London.]

This essay concerns Henry James and his novella *The Siege of London*. It starts, however, in a way that might seem rather alien to a British reader, with a word about me.

I'm an English academic, and a reasonably competent user of my own language. Include my work in an American collection, however, and immediately its language seems slightly quaint or alien, even wrong. The language of the essay that follows attempts no compromise between American and British academic English: not for reasons of national arrogance, nor (entirely) from personal stubbornness. Instead the scene is being set for an examination of strangeness in James's novella, and of what it means for a woman to be—or to make herself—"at home".

The novella's opening pages set out its theme even more theatrically. It's September in Paris, and the city is full of foreign visitors. Among them, in the audience at the Comédie-Française, are the story's four main characters—one Englishman and three Americans surrounded by "persons of provincial or nomadic appearance."[1] Rupert Waterville is an American in Paris for the first time. He finds the evening's "antiquated play" a bore and is more interested in scanning the audience for pretty women (103). George Littlemore is more at home with "European civilization" than his compatriot, and fancies the "French capital could have no more surprises for him" (104). He too finds the play tedious: *L'Aventurière* has "no pretension to novelty" and is acted by doublures or understudies (103). It is not until Waterville spies Nancy Headway that the "historic cobwebs" and "the new-looking curtain," and all the other strange and familiar details of the opening scene, come into focus (103/4).

The familiar "drama of transatlantic relations" is under way. Its cast includes a selection of James's best-known characters: Headway is the headstrong American social climber, Littlemore the sympathetic but neutral narrator, Sir Arthur Demesne the reticent English aristocrat, and Waterville the naive young American observer. The recognition and misrecognition of characters is a key element in the novella. When Waterville makes Mrs Headway's acquaintance at the theatre he cannot make out what kind of woman she is. Littlemore knows her of old but is in two minds whether to acknowledge her.

His reply to Waterville's "'[d]o you know her?'" simultaneously denies and betrays a previous acquaintance: "'[n]o. she's not respectable'" (105). The next 86 pages will turn on this ambiguity, for it seems that without Littlemore's unequivocal endorsement of her good character the American divorcee cannot achieve her ambition to marry the aristocratic young Englishman, Demesne.

Little has been written about *The Siege of London* since its publication in 1883. In the preface to the New York edition James himself pleads "a blank of memory as to the origin of the tale"[2]. He does, however, record a visit to the Comédie-Française six years earlier to see *Le Demi-monde* by the younger Dumas and his irritation at Olivier de Jalin's denunciation of his ex-mistress, Mme. d'Ange, which forms "the main hinge of the action"[3]. What is at stake for James is whether "a gentleman 'tells' on a lady"[4]. The sense of déjà vu is palpable: De Jalin and Mme d'Ange are the originals of Littlemore and Mrs Headway, who watch as their story is acted out by doublures: Littlemore encounters a familiar play and an over-familiar woman, and Mrs Headway meets a ghost from her past (103). The original theatre-goer now directs the action. Those of us who know the story in advance will be more concerned with the relationship between this aventurier, living on his wits in self-imposed exile, and his leading lady.

It is by no means clear that Mrs Headway is a lady, however. She may not even be an exile. Only Littlemore—himself a "man of the world", equally at home in New York, Paris or London—is empowered to say whether she left, absconded or was effectively expelled from the US (117). He met and became friendly with Mrs Headway in California, when she was still a young provincial, "very pretty, good-natured and clever" and with few social pretensions (113). In his account—we have no other of her early years—she was also "ignorant, audacious, crude, . . . full of pluck and spirit, of natural intelligence, and of a certain intermittent, haphazard good taste" (113). She subsequently married several times ("mainly editors"), became "exceedingly divorced" and, as a result, exceedingly wealthy (112). What preoccupies Waterville, Littlemore's sister (Mrs Dolphin), Demesne, and his mother is whether Mrs Headway acted improperly in the acquiring of that wealth and the divesting of those husbands. Since Littlemore is presented as the only authoritative source of information on Mrs Headway, his testimony will be enough to block or enable his old friend's marriage to her aristocrat. There are, apparently, no doubts as to the probity of the informant who shared her piazza and her society in those early years.

Other exiles enjoy a less ambiguous status. As Secretary to the US Legation in London Waterville can mix business with pleasure by keeping an eye on pretty women and Americans. With the licence and affected inscrutability of the immigration officer he polices the border zone, ensuring that any "beauty" he sees is fit to be looked at by people (like him) of irreproachable character. In such circumstances the identification of "unusual" women is essential (104). Experienced though he is in classifying desirable aliens, Waterville too relies heavily on Littlemore's judgement. "You stare at them all alike" Littlemore observes "except when I tell you that they are not respectable—then your attention acquires a fixedness" (104/5).

Mrs Headway will be subjected to more fascinated stares, penetrating glances and averted eyes before efforts to identify her reach their conclusion. It's not simply the facts of her past that her investigators are trying to establish. They want to know how those facts were viewed, and how she must be viewed as a result: like Waterville, they need a representation of her on which to base their own identification.

Unsurprisingly, critics are also keen to identify Mrs Headway. I have already suggested a link between the author/director and his leading 'lady', but James's tendency to make women the focus of his narratives has a wider resonance. Feminists such as Rosi Braidotti have noted a tendency among contemporary male philosophers to ally themselves with "the feminine"[5]. For Braidotti, this is symptomatic of a loss of faith in the all-knowing philosophical subject, which leads Jacques Derrida and others to turn instead to the philosophical 'unconscious' in search of what the history of philosophy and its binary logic have hitherto repressed. Since no philosophical name is available for what they find, they call it "unrepresentable" or "undecidable", "the other", or "the feminine". Identifying Mrs Headway's place in *The Siege of London* may go some way to illustrate the workings of this "repressed" term in James's narrative.

Stare at her as we might, we don't know what Mrs Headway sees. There is a convention that foreigners have special insight into life in their adoptive home. In Mrs Headway's case this insight is crucial, for, like James, she wants to get to the heart of "English society" (141). She wants to originate there, to become well-bred, and once again this involves doublures: like a voodooist with a doll, she'd "like to have" a little girl and "make her" the "nice woman . . . in another style" that she herself longs to become (126). This self-begetting involves cutting the old umbilical cord. By fleeing from America she hopes to avoid determination by her previous husbands and take revenge on the New Yorkers who humiliated her.

Even in England, however, Mrs Headway has the greatest difficulty cutting her "editors" from her autobiography (112). Reflected in her final questionable success is

James's ambivalence towards "English society", and both are linked to the insecurity that another "theorist of exile", Julia Kristeva, a Bulgarian-born linguist working in France, sees as characteristic of the foreigner. In *Strangers to Ourselves,* she describes the "incomprehensible speech [and] inappropriate behaviour" that underlies the exile's insecurity and marginalization[6]. "Your speech, fascinating as it might be on account of its very strangeness, will be of no consequence . . . One will listen to you only in absent-minded, amused fashion, and one will forget you in order to go on with serious matters"[7]. Resonating here is not only the treatment Mrs Headway receives at the hand of her aristocratic acquaintance but also an echo of the way men have always listened to women. Something similar underlies James's concern that his own "conquest of social as well as literary London had been achieved not on the ground of intrinsic charm or literary talent, but because he was yet another freak of nature"[8]. Yet the outsider remains fascinated by exclusive clubs, by their "community of ideas, of traditions [. . . and the members who] understand each others' accents, even each others' variations" (156).

"English society" would not entertain outsiders, however, if it were as self-sufficient as this quotation suggests. In fact its exclusiveness depends on admiring outsiders. Less clear is why outsiders should risk insecurity and humiliation by shoring up what James presents as aristocratic decadence. Kristeva offers one explanation for his ambivalence on this point:

> [the exile] readily bears a kind of admiration for those who have welcomed him [sic], for he rates them more often than not above himself, be it financially, politically or socially. At the same time he is quite ready to consider them somewhat narrow-minded, blind. For his scornful hosts lack the perspective he himself has in order to see himself and to see them. [This detachment] gives him the lofty sense not so much of holding the truth but of making it and himself relative while others fall victim to the ruts of monovalency . . . In the eyes of the foreigner those who are not foreign have no life at all: barely do they exist, haughty or mediocre, but out of the running and thus almost already cadaverized.[9]

Though small, recognizable differences seem to pose no threat to these communities, Mrs Headway's variation is of a completely different order. In the company of its members she is at once amusing and unsettling; she "looked foreign, exaggerated . . . She might have been engaged for the evening" (156). Since "civilization begins at home", an exile with a shady past is destined to remain a "freak of nature" or a "barbarian" in this community (144, 170). And like all communities that recognize only the paternal genealogy, this one allows a woman entry only on fulfilment of certain conditions: she has to alienate herself, take the male name and part, pursue his interests in place of her own and guarantee

the continuity of his line. The condition of Lady Demesne's inclusion—apart, that is, from the elevated entrance fee paid by her banker father—is that she look "for her own happiness in the cultivation of duty and in extreme constancy to two or three objects of devotion chosen once for all" (167). When her husband died she didn't take up the first of the relict's traditional options and "clear out" of the family home (161). Instead she devoted her abilities to the advancement of the son who now inherited her services. "She never admitted, even to herself, that [Sir Arthur] was not the cleverest of men; but it took all her own cleverness, which was much greater than his, to maintain this appearance" (132).

Wealth alone won't entitle Mrs Headway to exchange an obscure patronym for that of "a fine old race" (181). She waits at the border of a motherland she has abandoned and a fatherland that's not ready to accept her, aware that her physical and financial assets are starting to depreciate. Sir Arthur will never need to protest his identity: he has "the blood of a score of Warwickshire squires in his veins: mingled in the last instance with the somewhat paler fluid" of his mother (132). Money of course can darken what would otherwise be beyond the pale, and the greater the difference between the aspiring lady's "fluid" and the patriarchal blue "blood" the greater the sum required. But the ladies will always screen out the red-blooded outsider, however wealthy, who has no patronym to speak of.

For Lady Demesne and Mrs Dolphin, contaminated blood is a life-or-death affair. While men find Mrs Headway "attractive but dangerous", the ladies find her unequivocally "displeasing and dangerous" (135, 167). Lady Demesne's distrust of the "horrible" interloper is restrained in comparison with Mrs Dolphin's phobia for the "dreadful, disreputable, vulgar little woman": "I was afraid she would know who I was and come and speak to me. I was so frightened that I went away" (180/1). James attributes this to the drawbridge effect: the desire that "the class to which she [now] belonged should close its ranks and carry its standard high" (180). "She deeply desired . . . that Mrs Headway's triumphant career should be checked" and with it further claims on the social sphere Mrs Dolphin had made her own (180).

Yet it is precisely the ladies that Mrs Headway is concerned to win over. As long as she can fascinate every man she meets, "men don't count" (143). Being a beautiful object is not enough: she wants a certain social status and knows that the guardians of that status are female. The French psychoanalyst Luce Irigaray has noted that "the circulation of women among men is what establishes the operations of . . . patriarchal society"[10]. Within a society that denies them the status of subject, it is women who watch over the property to

which they are themselves unentitled. They must there-fore distinguish themselves unequivocally from the in-terloper who threatens the value of their investment. They fear her because they cannot identify her or iden-tify with her, and no lady can. "[F]emale relations . . . mother . . . sisters", all refuse to countenance her (143).

Yet Mrs Headway never loses sight of her goal: she wants to be brilliant rather than obscure, and to be seen for what she is or will be, rather than for what she was or might have been. She acknowledges, however, that self-begetting is an ambiguous pleasure. "None of my people are here: and I'm terribly alone in the world" (186). As Kristeva puts it,

> . . . the exile has fled from that origin—family, blood, soil—and, even though it keeps pestering, enriching, hindering, exciting him, or giving him pain . . . the foreigner is its courageous and melancholy betrayer. His origin certainly haunts him, for better or for worse, but it is . . . elsewhere that he has set his hopes, that his struggles take place.[11]

The Siege of London narrates Mrs Headway's struggle to reject her origins; in the process it questions the ways in which we relate to ourselves and to each other. By structuring his novella around the interplay of home and exile, the familiar and the foreign, the superficial and the secret, James is being precociously suggestive. Two years after the publication of *The Siege of London* in the *Cornhill Magazine* in 1883, Sigmund Freud too was in exile, as a student of Jean-Martin Charcot in Paris. His later interest in the interplay of the strange and the familiar in his discussions of 'Das Unheimlich' (the un-home-ly, or uncanny) are crucial for Kristeva's study. Foreigners, she notes, make us uncomfortable: we simultaneously identify with them and reject them. Using Freud's work on the uncanny, she relates this discomfort to an analogous division within ourselves. Following Freud, she describes how uncanny effects arise when the individual attempts unsuccessfully to re-press familiar dangers—whatever does not contribute to pleasure and self-preservation, for example—causing them to erupt in an unfamiliar form. The "narcissistic self . . . projects out of itself what it experiences as dangerous or unpleasant in itself, making of it an alien double"[12]. These uncanny effects are linked to the com-pulsive "recurrence of the same thing—the repetition of the same features or character-traits or vicissitudes, of the same crimes, or even the same names"[13].

It could be argued that compulsive recurrence is a fea-ture of *The Siege of London,* as characters bring the most detailed and persistent scrutiny to bear on a secret they cannot or will not reveal. The theme recurs, of course, in other works. Talking of his *In the Cage,* for example, which turns on the reluctance of the anony-mous heroine to expose a scandalous secret, James de-clares that he neither knows nor wishes to know what

that scandal involves. He is similarly blank when asked to describe the genesis of *The Siege of London*. It's not surprising that some of James's best critics have en-joyed speculating on his own repressed secrets. One of the earliest to do so, James's biographer Leon Edel, has drawn attention to the "gubernatorial" mother and the weighty but rather foolish father; the exceptionally gifted older brother who thought his adoring sibling "vainer and shallower than himself"; the "skeletons in the closets" of James's old US homes, that made the prospect of a return strike him in later years with "a su-perstitious terror of seeing them . . . stretch out strange inevitable tentacles to draw me back and destroy me"[14].

These secrets, which have been explored more recently and in some detail by others, will not detain us here[15]. In order to say something about James's women, we need to turn from secret relations with Oedipal stock-characters to the structure of secrets themselves. In the preamble to his paper on the uncanny, Freud notes that "the German word 'unheimlich' is obviously the oppo-site of 'heimlich' . . . [that is,] the opposite of what is familiar; and we are tempted to conclude that what is 'uncanny' is frightening precisely because it is not known and familiar". We would be wrong, of course. An investigation of the terms and their uses reveals that 'heimlich' moves "in the direction of ambivalence" from "mystical" through "inaccessible to knowledge" to "hidden and dangerous"—at which point "it finally co-incides with its opposite": 'unheimlich'[16].

Irigaray would find this process oddly familiar: in her view there is no possibility of genuine difference within Freud's system. She illustrates this point with reference to his description of the moment when the little girl be-comes aware of her anatomical difference from her male companion.

> At the "sight of the genitals of the other sex," girls "notice the [sexual?] difference" and, it must be admit-ted, its significance too. They feel seriously wronged, often declare that they want to "have something like it too" . . . and fall victim to "envy for the penis" which will leave ineradicable traces on their development and the formation of their character[17].

Her ironic asides and inserted emphases make Iriga-ray's distance from Freud clear. What concerns her about this account, and about Freud's work in general, is that the male is taken as a norm in relation to which the female is seen as deviant or lacking. Freud's little girl is not a little girl at all but a defective boy, a "dis-advantaged little man . . . [w]hose needs are less ca-tered for by nature and who will yet have a lesser share of culture . . . A little man who would have no other desire than to be, or remain, a little man"[18]. For Irigaray the inauguration of heterosexual relations is simply an-other moment in the drama of homosexual relations. The little girl is not different, she is a doublure, an un-

canny, defective version of the male. For Irigaray, the implications of Freud's scenario are clear: with that first envious gaze women acknowledge their inferiority, and assume their role as the mirrors and magnifiers of men.

Freud links women and uncanny secrets explicitly when he registers the "connections which the 'double' has with reflections in mirrors" and the uncanny effects that result when the subject identifies himself with someone else[19]. In Irigaray's terms, the male subject always "identifies himself" with someone else, and that someone is always a woman. In this one-way system, however, she can count on no such affirmation herself. With no-one to reflect back her own image, she remains the exclusive and indispensable object of the self-regarding male. James seems indirectly to acknowledge this when he observes in a discussion of George Sand that "[i]t is the ladies . . . who have lately done most to remind us of man's relations with himself, that is with woman"[20].

One effect of specular relations with men is to rule out the possibility of genuine dialogue. Women who refuse to play the game will find intelligibility itself at risk. When her compatriots conspire to prevent her entry into society Mrs Headway is unable to speak in her own defence. Instead she is "always appealing or accusing, demanding explanations and pledges" (128) or, as Margaret Whitford puts it, seeking "proofs of affection or validation of her existence from the male subject" (128)[21]. Waterville and Littlemore seem to agree that Mrs Headway talks obsessively and "her motives, her impulses, her desires [are] absolutely glaring" (141). And yet they fail to grasp her meaning. When she insists, Littlemore laughs and withdraws: when she tries to present her own account of herself in opposition to his, he can't see it. "You don't know me" she tells him, "you don't understand me. You think you do, but you don't" (184). Her protestations are neutralized and she is defined, once again, in a word. It is his word, "[t]he last word of all": she is a "nuisance, an embarrassment, from the moment anything more than contemplation should be expected of him" (124/5). That point has now been reached: she is a danger to the community, and doesn't "deserve to be spared" (184).

As this exchange demonstrates, there is no safe haven for aliens who are trying to cross borders without security or precedents. Instead Mrs Headway shifts between the new and the old, between unintelligible self-assertion and pleas for male validation. What results is an aura of dislocation and vital unpredictability that those around her find exciting, exasperating, and unsettling. Their interest does little to advance her case however. When (as in the exchange cited) she is too unsettling, her ally is revealed as a neglectful adversary. While she remains more exciting than unsettling there is no reason why Littlemore—"[a]verse" as he is "to active pleasures"—or any other man should help her

(106). Like the aristocratic society she yearns for, her male admirers find a degree of novelty attractive. For them she is a "child of nature" seeking women's conventional status as social object, and she'll remain desirable only as long as she stays in the no-man's land between the two: as long as she's "not respectable", her male companions will find her "adorable" (129, 105, 128). "If she wished to get into society" Littlemore reflects "there was no reason why her bachelor visitors should wish to see her there; for it was the absence of the usual social incumbrances which made her drawing-room attractive" (129). For him, Mrs Headway's "salvation" lies in accepting her place as a marginal, desirable object. Her refusal to accept this role appears, quite understandably, "to irritate him" (129).

Mrs Headway has had enough of male company in no-man's land. She wants a home now, even if it's someone else's, and she wants female relations of her own, even if it means burying her past in a man's. In a genealogy that excludes women with pasts in order to make male futures more secure, this might prove difficult. One reason why this genealogy "is in a rather bad way", however, may be that its obsession is also its blind spot (124). Irigaray characterizes the male genealogy as conflating woman and mother in a "maternal feminine", a "female identity" that men use to symbolize their own lost origins, leaving women with no way of representing theirs[22]. Mrs Headway can reveal "everything" "fifty times over" without giving herself away (119, 177). In a domain that doesn't recognize non-male origins she can talk compulsively about the past she wants to obscure and it will not be identified. It seems that only a man can give her away.

Mrs Headway doesn't want to give her past away, of course, or to have it "identified" by others. There is no attempt to help Lady Demesne's solicitor to assemble data on it for presentation as a more or less respectable history. As Littlemore notes, his compatriot will never be more than "half-right" as long as she's determined "to be different" (128, 120). She wants to specify the headings and the detail, of her past in her own language, and to edit them on her own terms. Yet the language and the symbols available to her all play into the hands of Lady Demesne's solicitor. What the uncomprehending Littlemore witnesses—the "inspiration", the "anxiety and egotism", the excitement, the "flushed face" as she becomes "violent . . . angry . . . passionate . . . incoherent" by turns—is indistinguishable from hysteria (184-86). It could equally be frustration, however, symptomatic of the difficulty women have "in speaking and hearing as women. Excluded and denied by the patriarchal linguistic order they cannot speak in a judicious, coherent way"[23].

Mrs Headway may prefer the regard of women to admiring men, but she knows neither is dispensable. "I don't want to escape notice", she exclaims: what she

wants is "different ways of being looked at" (124). If that includes admiring male glances she'll play along with them, in order to catch the eye of the ladies who have refused to countenance her and to be recognized by them. She continues to shift between wanting to please herself and wanting to please: the "joints and seams" of her negotiations, "where the old and the new [have] been pieced together", are "all of them very visible" (139). For her this is a transitional stage: "[i]f I once get there" she asserts "I shall be perfect"! (144). Littlemore sees things differently: people may change "their desires, their ideal, their effort" but they "don't change their nature" (185). Mrs Headway puts her faith in herself. Littlemore puts his in a transcendental vision of human nature: his vision of her nature. He overrules her once again with a lofty phrase: she won't be perfect but "she won't know when she's wrong, so it doesn't signify" (128).

Littlemore isn't going to be allowed the last word on women's nature nor on men's relation to nature. It is an axiom of feminism that all human functions are not deemed to be present in each individual, but have conventionally been distributed according to sex. Irigaray notes that this "double syntax" enables men to identify themselves with culture, society, reason, and order, for example, and to identify women with "nature", the irrational and the disordered, whatever escapes the categories of culture and the social. Critical though she is of this process, she doesn't deny it a certain self-fulfilling truth, since in her view the paternal genealogy is structured in such a way that no woman can enter it without accepting these definitions. A woman can enter patriarchy, that is, "so long as she is not a'subject', so long as she cannot disrupt through her speech, her desire, her pleasure, the operation of the language that lays down the law, the prevailing organization of power"[24].

As Mrs Headway recognizes, you can enter the paternal genealogy if you are prepared to speak its language. By shifting between unintelligibility and role playing she may be able to "recuperate some element of desire"[25]. An exile "multiplying masks and 'false selves' [she] is never completely true nor completely false"[26]. This "masquerade of femininity" will permit her to become what Freud termed a "normal" woman, by giving her "entry into a system of value that is not hers, and in which she can 'appear' and circulate only when enveloped in the needs/desires/fantasies of others"[27].

It may be James's interest in "the feminine sensibility" that leads him to confront this repressed aspect of patriarchy, its structural alienation of women. There is always ambivalence, however, something compulsive about his pleasure in the sight of women struggling, and his loss of interest when they meet their inevitably bad ends. If loss of interest equates with loss of pleasure we can, as suggested, read the close of *The Siege*

of London as an abandoning of the 'unheimlich' figure when it becomes too insistent. Until this point Waterville and Sir Arthur Demesne can't see enough of her; Lady Demesne and Mrs Dolphin can't stop talking about her; and Littlemore, like James, neglects to resolve the question for as long as "the spectacle might be entertaining" (124).

Reading James one might think there was something inevitable about this displacement of male anxiety onto a female doublure. There are however, as Mrs Headway insists, different ways of looking of looking at women. *The Siege of London* offers a range of models, and underlying each is the question of how we are to deal not only with uncanny strangers, but with the uncanny within ourselves. We could:

- speculate on her obsessively from a distance, interrogate and spy on her, so as expose her (Waterville);

- invite her into our home, inspect her on our own terms and quiz others about her (Sir Arthur and Lady Demesne);

- defame her, refuse to face her, turn away (Mrs Dolphin);

- wait for her to make herself known, casually and unobsessively enjoy her presence, exploit her and, when the time comes, abandon her (Littlemore).

This list may look exhaustive, but there is one notable omission: there is no model for coming to terms with difference—not in order to smooth it over and assimilate it, but in order to recognize and value it. Mrs Headway, the alienated subject, takes the only course available to her: act out what you can, and illuminate in fitful flashes what you can't. The end result is only marginally more promising: Littlemore's final "I don't think Mrs Headway respectable" comes too late to prevent her from marrying Sir Arthur, but ensures that her new life will be defined according to one (male) account of her old one (190).

Unless we acknowledge and come to terms with strangeness there will be no living with ourselves or each other. This is a political point, addressing the alienation of women in patriarchy and of all marginalized groups, at a time when communities are being conceived in global terms and we are increasingly among strangers. As *The Siege of London* indicates, books can participate in this process by helping us to recognize and analyze our symptoms. Those of us who choose this form of feminist critique, however, need to be sure that we're not complicitous with texts' tendency to neutralize uncanny effects by making them more pleasurable than dangerous.

My reading suggests that James will have derived considerably more pleasure than danger from the writing of *The Siege of London,* but that need not necessarily in-

fluence whether we recuperate him for feminism or whether we reject him. My own view is that it really doesn't matter which we do. James will never be more than half right, but that might be enough: it rather depends on what we want from him. There's no reason why we shouldn't play around with him if it suits us: we can exploit him as Littlemore exploits Mrs Headway, speculate on him as long as it's "entertaining", and then abandon him. But though rhetorical revenge is unquestionably sweet, it is not enough. Re-reading James, however sceptically, can only advance the causes of feminism if in the process we come to recognize each other and acknowledge our differences. Only then will there be any possibility of genuine exchange between us.

Notes

1. Henry James, *The Siege of London,* in *"In the Cage" and Other Stories,* (Harmondsworth, England: Penguin, Harmondsworth, England, 1972, 103-91, 103. Hereafter page numbers will be given in parentheses in the body of the text.

2. *The Complete Tales of Henry James,* vol. 14, (New York: Charles Scribner's Sons, 1936), xvi.

3. Ibid.

4. *The Complete Tales of Henry James,* ed. Leon Edel, vol. 5, 1883-84 (London: Rupert Hart Davis, 1965), 10.

5. For the development of this argument see Braidotti's *Patterns of Dissonance: A Study of Women in Contemporary Philosophy,* trans. E. Guild (Cambridge: Polity Press, 1991), 278-84. Margaret Whitford reinforces this point in her *Luce Irigaray: Philosophy in the Feminine* (London: Routledge, 1991), 29-31.

6. Julia Kristeva, *Strangers to Ourselves,* trans. L. Roudiez, (Hemel Hempstead, England: Harvester Wheatsheaf, 1991), 6.

7. Ibid., 20-21.

8. Edel, *Complete Tales,* 9.

9. Kristeva, *Strangers,* 6-7.

10. Luce Irigaray, *This Sex Which is Not One,* trans. C. Porter with C. Burke (Ithaca: Cornell University Press, 1985), 184.

11. Kristeva, *Strangers,* 29.

12. Ibid., 183.

13. Sigmund Freud, "The 'Uncanny,'" in *The Standard Edition of the Complete Psychological Works of Sigmund Freud,* vol. 17, *An Infantile Neurosis and Other Works,* trans. J. Strachey, A. Freud, A.

Strachey, A. Tyson (London: Hogarth Press and the Institute of Psycho-Analysis, 1973), 217-56, 234.

14. Leon Edel, "The James Family," *Henry James Review,* 10, no. 2 (spring 1989): 90-94.

15. See in particular Alfred Habegger's compelling study *Henry James and the 'Woman Business',* (Cambridge: Cambridge University Press, 1989).

16. Freud, "The Uncanny," 220, 226.

17. Luce Irigaray, *Speculum of the Other Woman,* trans. G. C. Gill (Ithaca: Cornell University Press, 1985) 55.

18. Ibid., 26.

19. Freud, "The Uncanny," 234-35.

20. Henry James, *Notes on Novelists with Some Other Notes* (London: Dent, 1914), 237.

21. Whitford, *Luce Irigaray,* 44.

22. Irigaray, *Speculum of the Other Woman,* 71-72.

23. Irigaray, *Je, Tu, Nous* (Paris: Grasset, 1990), 23. Translation my own.

24. Irigaray, *This Sex Which is Not One,* 95.

25. Ibid., 133.

26. Kristeva, *Strangers,* 8.

27. Irigaray, *This Sex Which is Not One,* 134.

WOMEN AND EXILE

Jean Sudrann (essay date September 1970)

SOURCE: Sudrann, Jean. "*Daniel Deronda* and the Landscape of Exile." *ELH* 37, no. 3 (September 1970): 433-55.

[*In the following essay, Sudrann considers George Eliot's expression of her own isolation from society in Daniel Deronda as an arduous path toward ultimate self-actualization.*]

In January 1876, while she was struggling to complete *Daniel Deronda,* George Eliot defined her need of "some human figure and individual experience" through which that "set of experiments in life"—her novels—might fulfill her "endeavour to see what our thought and belief may be capable of."[1] This emphasis on experiment and the indivisibility of idea from lived expe-

rience coupled with her later assertion that she "meant everything in the book to be related to everything else there"[2] is central to any understanding of the structure of George Eliot's last novel. For in *Daniel Deronda*, she does "experiment" to give expression to that "individual" and major "experience" which had been tested on the very pulses of her own life: her complex and long continued isolation from society.

For modern readers to "cut the book into scraps and talk of nothing in it but Gwendolen"[3] reflects a failure to recognize that which should be most recognizable: the way in which the double plot creates for the novel its central definition of isolation in terms which make its relationship to twentieth century treatments of alienation most vivid. I would like to suggest that George Eliot felt her own alienation in terms more "modern" than Victorian, that she sought to define that experience by making it the central subject of her last novel, the only one to have a contemporary setting, and that she then had to bend to new uses the conventional forms of the novel to express the new subject matter.

Attempts to describe the personal experience begin as early as 1848 when Mary Ann Evans addresses an extraordinary outcry to Sara Sophia Hennell:

> Alas for the fate of poor mortals which condemns them to wake up some fine morning and find all the poetry in which their world was bathed only the evening before utterly gone—the hard angular world of chairs and tables and looking glasses staring at them in all its naked prose. It is so in all the stages of life—the poetry of girlhood goes—the poetry of love and marriage—the poetry of maternity—and at last the very poetry of duty forsakes us for a season and we see ourselves and all about us as nothing more than miserable agglomerations of atoms—poor tentative efforts of the Natur Princip to mould a personality. This is the state of prostration. . . .
>
> I feel a sort of madness growing upon me—just the opposite of the delirium which makes people fancy that their bodies are filling the room. It seems to me as if I were shrinking into that mathematical abstraction, a point—so entirely am I destitute of contact that I am unconscious of length or breadth. . . .[4]

Sufficient background for this outburst can be seen in the very physical circumstances of Mary Ann Evans's life during this summer of her twenty-ninth year. She was laboring, with increasing distaste, over the translation of Strauss' *Leben Jesu* at the same time that she was serving as housekeeper, nurse and companion for her ailing father. But neither the demands of the translation nor of the invalid—or not just those demands alone—account for the paradoxically passionate description of non-being.

The story of Mary Ann Evans's wholly characteristic Victorian revolt needs no rehearsal. The price she paid for her intellectual and emotional honesty—the loss of

the communities of family and church and society—created an experience of utter isolation for the author of *Daniel Deronda*. Her letter to Sara Hennell suggests something of the meaning of that experience in its earliest stages, for it begins to define biographically the profound consequences to the sense of self. Full artistic formulation had to wait until the pattern of isolation was broken by an almost complete measure of social acceptance. By 1874, George Eliot was sufficiently able to understand the "sort of madness" she endured in 1848;[5] then she could use that experience of alienation as the effective center of action for her new novel, *Daniel Deronda*.

To do this, she created from her earlier vision of the "naked prose" of a world in which the self is undefinable, a landscape more familiar to the twentieth than to the nineteenth century. The modern reader who comes back to a re-reading of *Daniel Deronda* after he has read, for example, *La Nausée,* can hardly escape noting the extent to which the Eliot novel explores the human condition in terms that would not be wholly foreign to Sartre. Gwendolen Harleth's "world-nausea"[6] and her creator's personal vision of reality reduced to a "miserable agglomeration of atoms" suggest areas of similarity. But Iris Murdoch's description of the determining bias that makes Sartre's Roquentin, the protagonist of *La Nausée,* an "existentialist doubter" reveals the fundamental link between the two worlds. Miss Murdoch asserts that Roquentin is seized by "an old and familiar" metaphysical doubt which he treats in a contemporary fashion because

> . . . he himself is in the picture: what most distresses him is that his own individual being is invaded by the senseless flux; what most interests him is his aspiration to *be* in a different way.[7]

It is possible to define the mode of *Daniel Deronda* as "descriptive brooding upon the doubt situation," springing from the same metaphysical problem Sartre's Roquentin encounters. Unlike so characteristic a Victorian figure of alienation as Carlyle's Herr Teufelsdröckh, George Eliot's characters cannot solve the crisis of separation simply by pitting the everlasting Yea of their own heart beats against the barren mechanism of a clock-work universe. It is precisely their own heart beats which are in question. Gwendolen Harleth's "own individual being is invaded by the senseless flux; what most interests [her] is [her] aspiration to *be* in a different way." Iris Murdoch's description of Roquentin fits George Eliot's heroine as well.

To make the subject of her novel the self's awareness of the self's dissolution and its subsequent struggle to re-form an identity was truly for George Eliot to embark on a major experiment. The formal implementation of that experiment is worked out largely through

the double plot and the series of melodramatic episodes which so startlingly disturb the novel's realistic texture. These are the major technical devices definitive of the novel's scope and complexity; through these, the central relevance of its treatment of illusion and will, of terror, self and the world against an echoing background of legend is made apparent.

Early in *Daniel Deronda*, George Eliot offers to the reader a general comment which, while it helps initially to define the curve of the action, nevertheless resounds throughout the novel with an increasingly ironic ring.

> A human life, I think, should be well rooted in some spot of a native land, where it may get the love of tender kinship for the face of earth, for the labours men go forth to, for the sounds and accents that haunt it, for whatever will give that early home a familiar unmistakable difference amidst the future widening of knowledge: a spot where the definiteness of early memories may be inwrought with affection, and kindly acquaintance with all neighbors, even to the dogs and donkeys, may spread not by sentimental effort and reflection, but as a sweet habit of the blood. . . . The best introduction to astronomy is to think of the nightly heavens as a little lot of stars belonging to one's own homestead.
>
> (3, 50)

To a striking degree, *Daniel Deronda* is a novel of rootless human lives, lives lacking "homestead," "native land," and a family relation to the heavens. Yet to read this passage as the promise of a story of the exile's return can lead only to the familiar critical lament over the novel's fragmented conclusion; for this glimpse of the poetry of a universe where all things are at home and where each is bound to each is a genuine point of departure, not a prophecy of arrival. Deliberately reminiscent of Romantic expressions of the dynamic relatedness of all aspects of the various universe,[8] the passage serves as the measure of what it means "to wake up some fine morning and find all the poetry in which [the] world was bathed only the evening before utterly gone."[9] It evokes the poetry of loss so that the "naked prose" of the novel itself may more adequately deal with the landscape of exile which is the real stage of *Daniel Deronda*.

The complex irony of the title of the first book, "The Spoiled Child," is characteristic of George Eliot's method in creating that stage for her novel. Is the pampered and wilful Gwendolen "spoiled" because the rod has been spared, or does the adjective suggest other, darker abuses deriving from the failure to establish the "sweet habit of the blood" which creates "the poetry of existence"? The ironic emphasis of the title emerges largely through the treatment in the early chapters of Gwendolen's uncle, the Reverend Mr. Gascoigne, as well as from the reader's introduction to Gwendolen herself. The clerical uncle's generous ease and shrewd

benevolence operate so smoothly that his very tone makes the "world in general seem a very manageable place of residence" (3, 63). Yet as the light of George Eliot's irony, affectionate and tolerant though it be, colors this portrait, the reader becomes slowly aware of the extent to which he has been lulled into sharing the Rector's comfortable illusions. These illusions manifest themselves dramatically in his manoeuvres to catch a good husband for his lively young niece, but they are based on vast and wide assumptions. The "world in general" is a comfortable home for the Rector just because he has never lost his early confidence in "the nightly heavens as a little lot of stars belonging to one's own homestead." Gwendolen is "a girl likely to make a brilliant marriage" (4, 67-68) and the match with Grandcourt is "a sort of public affair . . . which . . . might even strengthen the Establishment"; it is "to be accepted on broad general grounds national and ecclesiastical" (13, 176-77). Gascoigne's linking of the particulars of Gwendolen and Grandcourt to the astronomy of the Establishment is a beautiful example of his easy assurance of the validity of his knowledge of that world in which he is so thoroughly and so successfully at home. He takes pride in his "daylight" religion and his lack of "mischevious impracticableness" (3, 60). The daylight practicality of those beliefs is epitomized by his attitude toward Grandcourt: "He held it futile, even if it had been becoming, to show any curiosity as to the past of a young man whose birth, wealth, and consequent leisure made many habits venial which under other circumstances would have been inexcusable" (9, 125). The first phrase of the sentence defines Gascoigne's daylight practicality as a full acknowledgment of the necessary limitations of a middle class clergyman who wishes to maintain his illusions. Actions which would, in any case, be unavailing are unbecoming. The wholly appropriate style for a successful clergyman is to further the *possible* action with the proper decorum.

That style, as well as the assumptions on which it is based, is thoroughly exposed in the interview in which Mr. Gascoigne undertakes to point out to Gwendolen that both her duty and her pleasure lie in her acceptance of a marriage with Grandcourt. With clerical and avuncular heartiness and goodwill, he instructs his niece in the follies of coquetry and the advantages of the match. Gwendolen's response is all obedience: "'I know that I must be married some time—before it is too late. And I don't see how I could do better than marry Mr. Grandcourt. I mean to accept him, if possible.'" Yet the Rector is "a little startled by so bare a version of his own meaning from those young lips. . . . He wished his niece parks, carriages, a title—everything that would make this world a pleasant abode; but he wished her not to be cynical—to be, on the contrary, religiously dutiful, and have warm domestic affections" (13, 179-80). Nothing could make clearer what Sartre would call the "bad faith" of the Rector's advice. Gwendolen's re-

sponse, while it promises the effective action, lacks the operative illusion. Because she hopes to do the right thing for the wrong reason, Gwendolen casts—perhaps even momentarily for the Rector himself—a darkening shadow over his daylight vision of the world as a manageable place of residence. As the bourgeoisie of Roquentin's world are sustained by their illusion of morality, so Gascoigne is sustained by a rectitude easily shown to be simply a private illusion.

A different but equally illusory concept governs Gwendolen in the early stages of the novel. She is not, as her uncle so mistakenly judges, cynical about "parks, carriages, a title"; Gwendolen has a healthy respect for these appurtenances nor does it seem unlikely to her that they form the basis of "warm domestic affections." After all, from the opening pages of the novel, she sees herself as "a princess in exile" whose life should abound in those perquisites essential for residence in the world by "so exceptional a person as herself" (3, 52-53). Yet that is not at all what George Eliot means by "exile"; and Gwendolen, who is "not without romantic conjectures" (21, 275), must undergo a transformation from the fairy-tale princess to the less easily romantic "lost sheep" (36, 494) before her exile is truly accomplished. From the beginning, then, the novel's ironies match the illusory homeland of the Rector with the equally illusory exile of his niece as prologue to the unillusioned and terrible drama of alienation.

Central to the dispelling of these romantic and sentimental illusions of Gwendolen and her uncle is George Eliot's decision to entangle the silly young English girl's life with those of the Jewish characters, archetypal aliens. Not only do these figures elevate and define Gwendolen's dilemma but they create the novel's ultimate import by giving the widest possible significance to the nature of Gwendolen Harleth's life crisis. Alone, at the novel's end, Gwendolen is poised in a solitude quite other than that which surrounds her at the novel's beginning. For at the end, she is aware that she is alone; through that awareness she has been transformed into a true "princess in exile." The novel, then, is concerned not so much with the wanderer's return as it is with the harsh exigencies of how "to be" in exile.

The great variety of "aliens" peopling the world of *Daniel Deronda* define the outer conditions of exile and create the texture essential to establish the work's focus. In addition to the more central figures of Deronda and Mirah, the musician Klesmer, the consumptive prophet Mordecai, and the prima-donna Princess Halm-Eberstein help to establish the nature of the fact as well as the variety of human response to its existence. For each of these aliens, the simple social truth that they are all Jews in a Gentile world marks only the beginning and not the extent of their separateness. Klesmer and the Princess are also artists among Philistines; Mor-

decai, a seer among the blind—a dying man in the midst of the living. The separateness of Gwendolen is also clear from the beginning of the novel. The only child of the twice-widowed Mrs. Davilow's first marriage, she has been robbed of the rightful heritage of all children: a spot of native land. Moreover, the financial uncertainties of her mother's second marriage have deprived her of the easy means of maintaining the place in society to which her birth entitles her. Acutely conscious of her family's existence in "a border territory of rank," she is deeply anxious that "so exceptional a person as herself" (3, 51-52) be appropriately situated. Coupled with the family disintegration is her own lack of sympathy with them which confirms her alienation from even that heritage of birth. She has deliberately, we are told, cut herself off from any knowledge of her father, and one of her first actions in the novel is to pawn the necklace made from a chain which had once been his to cover her losses at roulette.

While Deronda must live in ignorance of his family, and Mirah Cohen has forcibly been separated from hers, Gwendolen, like the Princess Halm-Eberstein, chooses to reject her heritage. These are the given facts of external exile with which the story begins. And Deronda's first action in relation to Gwendolen, the restoration to her of the pawned necklace, immediately links the two characters to the novel's central issue by creating a dramatic metaphor of the subsequent story: the attempted restoration of a proper heritage.

That Gwendolen's family has lost its money and status is, like the Judaism of the other characters, simply the social fact to mark the beginning and not the meaning of her exile. It is the pressure of this outer fact on Gwendolen's sense of her self which is crucial. Again the supporting cast throws into vivid relief the importance of Gwendolen's reaction. There are many ways "to be" in exile, and each of the postures assumed helps to define the dilemma. Klesmer, who calls himself "the wandering Jew" and values himself as musician to be "on level benches with legislators" (22, 284), knows precisely who he is. Mordecai, recognizing that he is "exiled in the rarity of [his] own mind" (43, 605), longs for a more effective identity to implement his lonely dream: "hence it was that his imagination had constructed another man . . . to help out the insufficient first. . . . And as the more beautiful, the stronger, the more executive self took shape in his mind, he loved it beforehand with an affection half identifying, half contemplative and grateful" (38, 530). The Princess attempts, with a terrible energy of will, simply to reject any identity that will interfere with her desires to appear to the world first as the great singer Alcharisi and then as the Russian aristocrat. In each case it is clear not only that the self must be named but also that the creation of that name is ultimately dependent on some established relationship between self and world.

By exploring Gwendolen's need for this established relationship, George Eliot first exposes the pitiful narrowness of the girl's egoism and then defines the dissolution of her "personality" as she shrinks to "that mathematical abstraction, a point . . . entirely destitute of contact."[10] From the beginning, it is clear that the whole pressure of Gwendolen's will is "to do what is pleasant to herself in a striking manner." Yet her knowledge of that pleasure has no other gauge than the reactions of the world. Pleasure for her, then, becomes "whatever she could do so as to strike others with admiration and get in that reflected way a more ardent sense of living" (4, 69). Thus the very world itself becomes a mirror to create pleasure as it reflects the desired image. This relationship with the world suggests that Gwendolen, like her uncle Gascoigne, begins by finding herself in easy command of that which lies outside the self and creates yet another link between the matching illusions of uncle and niece. What Gwendolen sees in that mirror is the vision of herself as "the princess in exile, who in time of famine was to have her breakfast-roll made of the finest-bolted flour from the seven thin ears of wheat, and in a general decampment was to have her silver fork kept out of the baggage" (4, 71). Only as Gwendolen slowly becomes aware of the implications of Mrs. Davilow's complete financial ruin is that self-image shattered.

The sheer amount of space George Eliot devotes to the description of the destruction of the image is sufficient measure of the importance she attaches to the process itself. Of chief interest is the artistry by which the destruction of what Gwendolen believes to be the world and the destruction of her idea of self are shown to be not two separate actions but a single stroke. The news of the loss of her mother's fortune comes in a letter appealing for her return home which Gwendolen receives after an evening of ill-fortune at a continental roulette table.[11] The night is spent getting ready to meet that summons, and just before dawn, Gwendolen turns to look at herself:

> She had a *naive* delight in her fortunate self, which any but the harshest saintliness will have some indulgence for in a girl who had every day seen a pleasant reflection of that self in her friends' flattery as well as in the looking-glass. And even in this beginning of her troubles, while . . . she sat gazing at her image in the growing light, her face gathered a complacency gradual as the cheerfulness of the morning . . . till at last she took off her hat, leaned forward and kissed the cold glass which had looked so warm.
>
> (2, 47)

The mirror of the world as well as the mirror on the wall testify to the justice of Gwendolen's claim that her "silver fork" be "kept out of the baggage." The caress she bestows on her own reflected image is a proper measure of the harmony of Gwendolen's solipsistic world as the novel opens. In subsequent references to this moment, as well as in an elaborate sequence of mirror scenes, George Eliot continues the story of the annihilation of the image of self.

At its simplest, Gwendolen's response to the immediate crisis of financial and social deprivation can be described as her conscious knowledge of the loss of her superiority in the mirror of the world, the giving-up of the sense that the world must necessarily value her as she values herself. Nor is it surprising that her next step is to accept the world's valuation and reject herself: "the self-delight with which she had kissed her image in the glass had faded before the sense of futility in being anything whatever—charming, clever, resolute— what was the good of it all?" (21, 270). All desire to create an image for the mirror is leaving her; how useless it is "to be" any identity at all.

The brilliant scene in which Gwendolen confronts Klesmer with her vulgar artistic ambitions as an avenue to the restoration of the family fortunes through the world's applause is bracketed by two further mirror views. Before Klesmer's arrival, Gwendolen, buoyant with expectancy, watches herself in the drawing room mirror: "seeing her image slowly advancing, she thought, 'I am beautiful'—not exultingly, but with grave decision" (23, 294). Klesmer's full and sure knowledge of his own identity as an artist is added to Gwendolen's self-exposure in this scene to evoke the sense of shame with which she meets Klesmer's final judgment: "'you will hardly achieve more than mediocrity'" (23, 303). Yet the full effect of that interview on Gwendolen is not clear until Klesmer leaves. The noonday light at Offendene then brings "into more dreary clearness the absence of interest from her life. All memories, all objects, the pieces of music displayed, the open piano— the very reflection of herself in the glass—seemed no better than the packed-up shows of a departing fair" (23, 306). Explicitly, at this point, the ruin of the relation between self and the world is linked to the disintegration of that self: the image in the mirror is simply disappearing along with the very chairs and tables of the drawing room.

Only once again in the novel does Gwendolen look at herself in the mirror with any pleasure. Just before Grandcourt comes to make his marriage proposal, both Gwendolen and her mother admire "the reflection in the glass" before which the girl is seated and Mrs. Davilow thinks her daughter "is quite herself again" (27, 340-41). After her marriage, Gwendolen no longer feels "inclined to kiss her fortunate image in the glass" (35, 477). As the new mistress of Ryelands, she is surrounded by images of herself but is either unable to "see the reflections of herself" (31, 407) or, seeing them, "not recognizing herself in the glass panels" (48, 651). The last time in the novel that she looks at herself is

while she waits for Deronda to call before the Grand-courts leave on their yachting expedition. This time, she is conscious of her own beauty but it is profoundly disturbing to her, and she seeks to disguise her image by throwing a black lace shawl over her head and neck.

Now that Gwendolen can once again see an image in the glass, her impulse is toward an activity that will alter that image. The novelist's record of the gesture signals not only the return of some sensation of self but also a reviving will toward self-determination. For if George Eliot links self-recognition to the self's relation to the world, she is equally certain of the dependence of the sense of self on the operation of will. Early in the novel she makes that dependency clear when she describes Gwendolen's "usual world" as one "in which her will was of some avail" (6, 95). The "world nausea" and "sick motivelessness" (24, 317-18) Gwendolen suffers as the Davilows attempt to readjust to narrowed lives is defined as that paralysis of will which marks one aspect of Gwendolen's crisis. Indeed, her experience of alienation is completed only with that utter subjugation of her "peremptory will" (2, 46) which results from her marriage to Grandcourt. The collapse of Gwendolen's "belief in her own power of dominating" (35, 477) comes as the climax of the vivid drama of conflicting wills which is the courtship and marriage. By the destruction of his wife's will, Grandcourt has completed the dissolution of Gwendolen's sense of self, leaving her in a waste space, a "vastness . . . in which she seemed an exile" (6, 95).

The importance of this clash of wills and the skill with which George Eliot handles it can perhaps best be illustrated by her easy movement from episode to metaphor in the use of horses and riding scenes as she dramatizes Gwendolen's movement from mastery to servitude. The sequence begins quietly enough with Gwendolen's teasing to be permitted to have her own horse in the days when the family fortune, though small, seems secure. Her uncle's indulgence of this desire is a further measure of the "daylight practicality" of his match-making for his niece. In Gwendolen's triumph at the Wessex Hunt, matched by her cousin Rex's fiasco, the image becomes a vehicle for the conclusion of that romance even while it is being reinvested with all of its metaphoric sexual power as a prelude to the courtship of Gwendolen and Grandcourt most of which takes place on horseback or, at least, with Gwendolen dressed in her riding habit while a pair of horses is being walked by the groom someplace in the background.

With the firm establishment of the metaphoric richness of the image, George Eliot is able to move it out of the literal narrative into the mental landscape of the novel. Gwendolen has her vision of marriage as a chariot she will mount "and drive the plunging horses herself, with a spouse by her side who would fold his arms and give

her his countenance without looking ridiculous" (13, 173). Grandcourt, too, has his vision of their marriage: "she had been brought to accept him in spite of everything—brought to kneel down like a horse under training for the arena" (28, 365). Even before the marriage takes place, Gwendolen's image has to be adjusted: she begins to feel "as if she had consented to mount a chariot where another held the reins" (29, 373) and where "the horses in the chariot she had mounted were going at full speed" (29, 381). On the wedding day, her image coalesces with Grandcourt's vision: "The cord which united her with this lover and which she had hitherto held by the hand was now being flung over her neck" (31, 401-02). After that, the image belongs to Grandcourt, who notes how "she answered to the rein" (35, 482), while Gwendolen endures "submission to a yoke drawn on her by an action she was ashamed of" (45, 617). In that last exercise of Grandcourt's will, the ensuring that Gwendolen accompany him in the boat, he acts out of his perfect satisfaction "that he held his wife with bit and bridle" (54, 744).

Although necessarily reductive of the full richness of *Daniel Deronda*, the preceding sketch of the mirror and riding sequences, which function to establish the dramatic development of Gwendolen's crisis, does suggest the importance of the language of metaphor in the organization of the novel. Even more central to the novel's theme is the strand of legendary allusion which permeates the diction to support the parallel in story and motive which George Eliot continually draws between the Jewish figures and the characters from English society. By creating a relationship even closer than that of parallel situation and interacting plot, George Eliot seeks to establish the world of *Daniel Deronda* as one world, its figures all actors in the same fundamental human drama, all joined in a common destiny. As she herself says, it is only "fellowship with human travail, both near and afar," that will keep man from "scanning any deep experience lightly" (41, 569). This fellowship with human travail—this link between the "near" Davilows and the Cohens "afar"—is surely what lies behind her insistence that "everything in the book" is "related to everything else there."[12]

The legend which joins these characters into a single world is after all, as Deronda says, "a very ancient story, that of the lost sheep"—and a story of complex motive and infinite ramification, for it speaks not only of the sheep lost in the wilderness but also of the squandered birthright, the exile in a foreign land, and the exultant return home.[13] Recognition of how variously the story may be told helps in the achievement of the "fellowship with human travail." Whether it is Deronda's likeness to the "youthful heroes going to seek the hidden tokens of their birth and its inheritance of tasks" (41, 573), or Mordecai's resemblance to the Ancient Mariner "on the lookout for the man who must hear"

(41, 568) the tale of his dark voyage, or the story of Grandcourt as "a new kind of Jason" caught "between two fiery women" (36, 487) which naturally arouses Deronda's sympathies for "the Hagars and Ishmaels" (36, 489) disinherited and sent into the desert, the language of the novel keeps reminding us that all of the characters are indeed re-enacting the "very ancient story" of the cast-off and the exiled. No wonder, then, that when Deronda returns to London with full knowledge of his name and in full possession of that "precious chest" which is the token of his family and racial heritage, George Eliot describes him as in a "classical, romantic, world-historic position . . . bringing as it were from its hiding place his hereditary armour" (63, 815). Gwendolen, in the climactic stages of her own journey in search of these "hidden tokens" is possessed by a hatred so intense that it can only be described as issuing in "something like the hidden rites of vengeance with which the persecuted have made a dark vent for their rage" (54, 737). "The persecuted" and their "rites of vengeance" link through language the inner turmoil of the English girl to other legends of loss and of "great recognitions" as of "the offspring of Agamemnon," (43, 604) that archetypal prelude to vengeance and the letting loose of the Furies. Gwendolen Harleth's story, then, is equally as resonant with the authority of racial experience as is Deronda's outward quest for visible tokens of identity.

As Deronda moves to reveal the just discovered "hereditary armour," George Eliot reluctantly acknowledges that "it has to be admitted that . . . he wore . . . the summer costume of his contemporaries." This rueful admission points toward a major difficulty: how to convey through these "summer costumes" of the 1860's, through the furnishings of a Victorian world, that "great deal of unmapped country within us which [has] to be taken into account" (24, 321) if the novel is to be a fresh embodiment of those old legends. For George Eliot knows that however she moves her nineteenth century protagonists—from London to Genoa, or simply from Park Lane to Brompton—their real journey is the descent into the self, the dark groping through the "unmapped country within." Her problem is to find an adequate form through which the stages of this journey can be marked so that the Victorian summer costume can be seen as armour indeed. E. S. Gombrich has pointed out that "even the greatest artist—and he more than others—needs an idiom to work in. Only tradition, such as he finds it, can provide him with the raw material of imagery which he needs to represent an event or a 'fragment of nature.'"[14] This need for an idiom and its dependency on the tradition available to the artist at a given moment of time is as real for the writer as it is for the visual artist of whom Gombrich speaks. Twentieth century psychologists have given twentieth century

novelists their own vocabulary by which to describe the descent into the self. George Eliot uses the idiom available to her, the idiom of melodrama.

Discussions of *Daniel Deronda* tend to overlook how often the story erupts into such melodramatic episode as the attempted suicide and rescue of Mirah, the recognition scene between Mordecai and Deronda at Blackfriars Bridge, the curse laid on the Grandcourt diamonds, and the panel which slides back to reveal the dead face and the fleeing figure. Yet each such episode is directly pointed toward the unfolding of the inner adventures of the characters. In the meeting of Mordecai and Deronda at Blackfriars Bridge, George Eliot makes this abundantly clear. The episode is not, in terms of the novel's dramatic movement, particularly successful. But in its very failure, the novelist's intention is laid bare. The scene is set in a glory of sunset light. Deronda, enfolded in an Inverness cape, drifts down the Thames out of that western sky to be greeted by Mordecai as "the prefigured friend [who] had come from the golden background, and had signalled to him." He tells Deronda, "I expected you to come down the river. I have been waiting for you these five years." For Mordecai, the Bridge is "a meeting place for the spiritual messengers" and Deronda, coming out of the sunset sky, comes as Mordecai's "new life—my new self." He comes as that other man, constructed by Mordecai's imagination from the exile of his own mind. Deronda's sympathetic response issues from a nature "too large, too ready to conceive regions beyond his own experience, to rest at once in the easy explanation, 'madness.'" He is capable of recognizing the possibility that in Mordecai there may be "that preternatural guide seen in the universal legend, who suddenly drops his mean disguise and stands a manifest Power" (40, 549-51). The relation of the episode to the legendary quest needs no comment. What should also be clear is that George Eliot is telling us quite explicitly here that she has used the melodramatic props of the cloaked figure in the sunset and the raised white hand of greeting to express the regions beyond those of practical daylight experience, regions that belong to "the un-mapped country within."

Melodrama functions in *Daniel Deronda* not only as a means of giving outward shape to inner drama but also as a way of evoking horror and dread, essential responses to the necessary terror of the descent into the self, the only avenue to the hiding place of the name and the heritage. George Eliot makes explicit the initial connection between fear and the sense of exile in her analysis of another of these moments, one in the finely conceived and richly used sequence of episodes which concern "the picture of an upturned dead face, from which an obscure figure seemed to be fleeing with outstretched arms" (3, 56). The locked panel in the Offendene drawing room inexplicably springs open to reveal the picture at the climax of Gwendolen's success with

her home charades. She has been showing herself off as Shakespeare's Hermione but is startled by the incident out of her role into a primitive display of terror. The narrator explains Gwendolen's excessive response by describing it as:

> that liability of hers to fits of spiritual dread, though this fountain of awe within her had not found its way into connection with the religion taught her or with any human relations. She was ashamed and frightened, as at what might happen again, in remembering her tremor on suddenly feeling herself alone, when, for example, she was walking without companionship and there came some rapid change in the light. Solitude in any wide scene impressed her with an undefined feeling of immeasurable existence aloof from her, in the midst of which she was helplessly incapable of asserting herself. The little astronomy taught her at school used sometimes to set her imagination at work in a way that made her tremble: but always when some one joined her she recovered her indifference to the vastness in which she seemed an exile: she found again her usual world in which her will was of some avail. . . .
>
> (6, 94-5)

The explicit naming of Gwendolen's state as that of "exile" and the recurrence of the astronomical image makes the passage a counterpart of the earlier definition of the home in the universe which is the inheritance of all who are rooted in a native land.[15] This tremor of fear which comes with a knowledge of the self lost in an uncharted immensity is interwoven through the novel with the sense of alienation, the urgency of the quest. Mirah's "terror of the world" (20, 263), which drives her into the attempted Thames suicide, springs from the same source as the terrible fear which drives the Princess Halm-Eberstein to summon her son to Genoa. Even though Deronda's receptivity to enlarged horizons is set in deliberate contrast to Gwendolen's terror of a widened vista, he is by no means without fear: "It was the habit of his mind to connect dread with unknown parentage" (19, 247). In each case dramatized into melodramatic episode, this fear both creates the action (as in Mirah's suicide attempt) and the response to the action (as in Gwendolen's terror of the dead face and the fleeing figure). The dual function suggests the underlying paradox George Eliot explores in her full depiction of Gwendolen's journey where the negative emotion of fear becomes the positive—and only—means of achieving the necessary courage. Fear can paralyze but it can also release. Thus, the novel's evocation of terrors through melodramatic episode enables the novelist to define the emotional fabric of the experience of alienation and to dramatize the inner activity by which the exile learns the terms on which some new relationship between self and world can be established.

As Grandcourt's courtship of Gwendolen proceeds, George Eliot builds up a rich texture of fears for the young girl. In part, the terror is a terror of self; more

accurately, a terror at the failure of knowledge in the face of a newly released self. Just after Gwendolen uses her riding whip to evade once more Grandcourt's proposal, George Eliot tells us that Gwendolen herself does not know what—once the proposal is actually made—her response will be.

> This subjection to a possible self, a self not to be absolutely predicted about, caused her some astonishment and terror: her favorite key of life—doing as she liked—seemed to fail her, and she could not foresee what at a given moment she might like to do.
>
> (13, 173)

The fears mount as the pressures on that unknown self become more complex: the interview with Lydia Glasher, Grandcourt's mistress and mother of his children; Grandcourt's return as her suitor unaffected by the reversal of her family fortunes. With the renewal of the courtship, Gwendolen is strangely poised between triumph and terror; she exults in the renewal of the power of choice and is terror-stricken by the problem of the use of that power.

> Here came the terror. Quick, quick, like pictures in a book beaten open with a sense of hurry, came back vividly, yet in fragments, all that she had gone through in relation to Grandcourt. . . .
>
> (26, 337)

This terror of self and the world, released by the beginnings of her new knowledge of both, can neither be controlled nor used. It can only be repressed, shoved underneath, made to merge back into the darkness of self and world from which it has sprung. From this moment until the moment three months later, when Grandcourt brings his bride in her carriage through the park gates of Ryelands, Gwendolen's whole energy seems to be an energy of repression which reaches its climax on her wedding day when the "mingling of dimly understood facts with vague but deep impressions, and with images half real, half fantastic, [which] had been disturbing her during the weeks of her engagement" is "surmounted and thrust down with a sort of exulting defiance" (31, 402). Yet everything that has been thrust down, mounts to the surface to add its note to the hysterical shrieks with which Gwendolen greets her husband after the message which accompanies Lydia Glasher's restoration of the Grandcourt diamonds has spread its venom: a poison of remembrance.

A subject in "her husband's empire of fear," (35, 479) Gwendolen is momentarily held captive by the fear that paralyzes. Yet at the same time the fear of herself—ignored not conquered during the feverish activities of engagement and marriage—burgeons in the inner darkness. Not until that terror is recognized and, finally, objectified will Gwendolen be released into an understanding of her true heritage. At first she cannot

distinguish between her growing fear of the cold force of her husband's will and the equally potent terror of her self's response. She describes the very vagueness of her dread to Deronda: "'I am frightened at everything. I am frightened at myself. When my blood is fired I can do daring things—take any leap; but that makes me frightened at myself.'" His advice, to make use of this fear, to employ this sensibility "'as if it were a faculty, like vision'" defines a means of restoration through the reawakened will. By suggesting that Gwendolen direct her fears toward "'the idea of increasing that remorse which is so bitter to you,'" Deronda does sound rather a prig. Yet the nightmare of her fear spreads to him in terms that violently couple his past rescue of Mirah with her future failure to save Grandcourt: "It was as if he saw her drowning while his limbs were bound" (36, 508-09). And his advice rings, not in the words of the conventional preacher who exhorts the better self to triumph over the worse, but rather with a full sense of the terrible energy of being: let the evil itself bring to birth the good.

The swift ending of Gwendolen's story concentrates on the manner in which her fear is made to function for her release. The contrasting account of Daniel Deronda's mother, who wills herself to a rejection of her fears and a subsequent return to her chosen exile, expands and intensifies the novel's exploration of the inherent dangers of the terror misunderstood and misused. As Jew, the Princess has rejected her Judaism so that she may be free "'from the pelting contempt that pursues Jewish separateness'" (51, 698); as artist, she has rejected her son, so that she may "'live out the life that was in [her], and not . . . be hampered with other lives'" (51, 688). The same energy of will makes possible the ultimate resignation of her life as the great singer Alcharisi when she is poised at the very height of her career: "'I made believe that I preferred being the wife of a Russian noble to being the greatest lyric actress of Europe; I made believe—I acted that part. It was because I felt my greatness sinking away from me . . .'" (51, 703). The Princess Halm-Eberstein is truly a "princess in exile" in contrast to Gwendolen's childish day-dream of dispossessed royalty. A terrible figure of loss, Deronda's mother is filled with "a great horror" which in itself motivates her summons to her son and her bitter acknowledgement that, instead of mastering the circumstances of alienation by her self-willed rejection of name and family and race, she has made herself forever an exile.

"... it is as if all the life I have chosen to live, all thoughts, all will, forsook me and left me alone in spots of memory, and I can't get away. . . . My childhood—my girlhood—the day of my marriage—the day of my father's death—there seems to be nothing since. Then a great horror comes over me: what do I know of life or death? and what my father called 'right' may be a power that is laying hold of me. . . . Often when I

am at ease it all fades away; my whole self comes quite back; but I know it will sink away again, and the other will come—the poor, solitary forsaken remains of self, that can resist nothing. It was my nature to resist, and say, 'I have a right to resist.' Well, I say so still when I have any strength in me. . . . [But] it is beginning to make ghosts upon the daylight."

(51, 699)

This passage, closely linked to the analysis of Gwendolen's "fits of spiritual dread," also explores the conditions of self-knowledge and contrasts the certainties of a "life well rooted in some spot of native land" with the blankness of a life cut off from kinship. The "spots of memory," with its echo of Wordsworthian "spots of time," are an ironic reminder of a pastoral unity of being which the Princess herself utterly rejects. For her, the self which in its terror resurrects the family concept of "right" is only an ill and fragmented self. Yet the whole novel points precisely toward that self as the only even potentially valid one. The Princess should, as Deronda points out to Gwendolen, have made full use of the resurrection through terror. Even the partial use she has made of it, the summoning of her son, has had its positive value for it has provided the son with the necessary "native land."

Even while the Princess is making this confession, Gwendolen is undergoing her ultimate crisis of fear as she sails with Grandcourt under the blue Mediterranean sky. Through the very melodrama of this climactic episode, George Eliot magnificently manifests her full control over the immensely varied materials from which she has wrought the account of Gwendolen's perilous journey. The description of "the model couple in high life" at home on the "elegant toy" served by a "picturesque crew" as they sail "southward . . . where one may float between blue and blue in an open-eyed dream that the world has done with sorrow" (54, 733), completes the image of exile. Grandcourt's satisfaction in this excursion, which "gave their life on a small scale a royal representation and publicity" (54, 736) is matched by Gwendolen's knowledge that she is separated from the world by the whole sea, isolated "on the tiny plank-island of a yacht" (54, 733), and fully aware of her own helplessness, her inability to assert herself. Her fancy no longer creates for herself the role of princess-in-exile, however royal the progress in Grandcourt's vision. Gwendolen acknowledges the outer adventure as an ironic metaphor:

"It came over me that when I was a child I used to fancy sailing away into a world where people were not forced to live with anyone they did not like. . . . And now, I thought, just the opposite had come to me. I had stept into a boat, and my life was a sailing and sailing away—gliding on and no help—always into solitude with *him,* away from deliverance."

(56, 760)

But for George Eliot fully to express the meaning of this journey requires something other than the conventional technique of making the outer action an image of the inner experience. Somehow the terrors of that inner experience must be objectified into outer reality for the reader to see, even as he has earlier seen—in an unforgettable image—Mrs. Grandcourt magnificently decked in the family diamonds while "the words of the bad dream crawled about the diamonds still" (35, 482). The carefully constructed, superbly paced action which climaxes in Grandcourt's drowning is the novelist's solution to the problem: a lurid and complex objectification of Gwendolen's nightmare life which does also, and necessarily, work beautifully as story.

The simple events are these: Grandcourt takes Gwendolen out sailing in a small boat from the Genoa port. As he puts about, a sudden gust of wind fills the sail; Grandcourt goes overboard. Gwendolen hesitates to throw out to him the life rope. Grandcourt drowns. In Gwendolen's description of the events to Deronda, the only description the reader is given, the entire action becomes simply the final vision of her long sustained desire for Grandcourt's death. Yet Grandcourt is *really* dead. The inner activity has not only taken shape as outer action, but there has been a coalescence of the reality that is the story with the reality that is Gwendolen's inner life. Here, if no place else in the novel, George Eliot has successfully used the idiom available to her, the idiom of melodrama, as the form through which to present an event which must be made to express both the inner and outer lives of her characters, both the events and the meaning of the events.

As the last manifestation of the haunting image of the dead face and the fleeing figure, the episode turns what has been Gothic decoration, used to display the heroine's fine sensibilities, into an anguish of lived terror. More important, it makes the final revelation of the function of that terror.[16] When the Davilows first arrived at Offendene and the youngest of the "inconvenient sisters" unlocked the panel to reveal the picture, Gwendolen's whole energy was concentrated on locking the picture up again and retreating to her room to look at herself in the mirror. The decisiveness of this action prefigures the same febrile energy of repression with which she will thrust down, out of sight and thought, the rising fears which assail her during Grandcourt's wooing and the early days of her marriage. In Genoa, Gwendolen's energies are directed not toward repression but confession; and although she cannot explain the sequence of events, she can identify the image: "'I don't know how it was—he was turning the sail—there was a gust—he was struck—I know nothing—I only know that I saw my wish outside me'" (56, 761). In its own way, this identification of the painting marks the

completion of Gwendolen's journey: it demonstrates a self-knowledge based on understanding and acceptance of desire and its consequences.

After this coalescence of inner and outer life, image and action, into the climactic dramatic moment, the novelist makes of the final chapters a new sounding of the old themes to sketch the outlines of her heroine's new identity. Gwendolen's early flight to the continent is matched by her journey home from Genoa. Just as Daniel Deronda parts from his mother knowing that "he beheld the world changed for him by the certitude of ties . . . as if under cover of the night he had joined the wrong band of wanderers, and found with the rise of morning that the tents of his kindred were grouped far off" (55, 747), so Gwendolen goes from Genoa with her mother and uncle on a journey that is no longer a "sailing out" but a return home, a new vision of

> Offendene and Pennicote under their cooler lights. She saw the grey shoulders of the downs, the cattle-specked fields, the shadowy plantations with rutted lanes where the barked timber lay for a wayside seat, the neatly-clipped hedges on the road from the parsonage to Offendene, the avenue where she was gradually discerned from the windows, the hall-door opening, and her mother or one of the troublesome sisters coming out to meet her. All that brief experience of a quiet home which had once seemed a dulness to be fled from, now came back to her as a restful escape, a station where she found the breath of morning and the unreproaching voice of birds, after following a lure through a long Satanic masquerade, which she had entered on with an intoxicated belief in its disguises, and had seen the end of in shrieking fear lest she herself had become one of the evil spirits who were dropping their human mummery and hissing around her with serpent tongues.
>
> (56, 831)

In that final sentence, the Gothic vocabulary of the inner journey is matched by the Wordsworthian poetry of the harmonious domesticated universe to suggest that the new knowledge, born of Gwendolen's terror, is a knowledge of the necessity of "some spot of a native land." In Genoa, on the railway journey, at Park Lane, what remains of Gwendolen's energy is directed toward the re-establishment of the earlier home. Yet Deronda's final lesson to her demonstrates the vanity of that desire and the necessity of continuing the inner journey.

The revelation Deronda makes of his own past heritage and future plans testifies to the impossibility of the sentimental return and reminds the reader that the function of the homestead is simply as a defining focus for "the future widening of knowledge." Gwendolen's horizon is no longer "that of the genteel romance" (6, 83). Instead, she is now "for the first time feeling the pressure of a vast mysterious movement, for the first time being dislodged from her supremacy in her own world, and getting a sense that her horizon was but a dipping on-

ward of an existence with which her own was revolving" (69, 876). Solitary, certainly, and aware of "immeasurable existence aloof from her," Gwendolen can no longer be indifferent "to the vastness" (6, 95). Her kindly parting from Deronda, releasing him from responsibility, shows a new—if feeble—action of will in "asserting herself" in the immensity. And Gwendolen's story stops with all the "naked prose" of a morning world. After a day and half a night of hysterical shrieking, "after all, she slept." And when she wakens, she knows: "'I shall live. I shall be better'" (69, 879). Stripped of the support of "parks, carriages, a title," in full awareness that she is not "so exceptional a person" who must be accorded what is pleasant to her, and knowing that "the new existence" which "seemed inseparable from Deronda" (65, 840) must be her own responsibility, Gwendolen Harleth has learned "how to be" in exile. Like her creator, she has passed through a crisis of alienation so that she may possess her self. More than a quarter of a century after her confession to Sara Hennell, George Eliot made the terrors of her own crisis the subject of her final novel. In November of 1876, two months after the completed publication of that novel, George Eliot writes again to Sara Hennell:

> It is remarkable to me that I have entirely lost my *personal* melancholy. I often, of course, have melancholy thoughts about the destinies of my fellow-creatures, but I am never in that *mood* of sadness which used to be my frequent visitant even in the midst of external happiness. And this, notwithstanding a very vivid sense that life is declining and death close at hand.[17]

By her own full acceptance of all the "naked prose," George Eliot has created the "poetry" of *Daniel Deronda.*

Notes

1. *The George Eliot Letters,* ed. Gordon S. Haight (New Haven, 1954-56), VI, 216-17. Hereafter cited as *GEL.*

2. *GEL,* VI, 290.

3. *GEL,* VI, 290.

4. *GEL,* I, 264.

5. Earlier and tentative treatments begin with her first fiction, *Scenes of Clerical Life,* and such figures as Maggie Tulliver and Silas Marner broach some of the same problems of exile.

6. George Eliot, *Daniel Deronda,* ed. Barbara Hardy, Penguin English Library (London, 1967), ch. 24, p. 316. Mrs. Hardy's readily available edition is based on that of the Cabinet edition of 1878. All future references to the novel will be to this edition and will be cited by chapter and page in the text.

7. *Sartre: Romantic Rationalist,* Studies in Modern European Thought and Literature (New Haven, 1953), p. 13.

8. See, e. g., *The Prelude,* II. 233-255; *The Rime of the Ancient Mariner,* gloss to lines 263-66. References to both Wordsworth and Coleridge are frequent throughout the novel, e. g.: 17, 225; 20, 250; 24, 309; 40, 548; 41, 568; 56, 751; 69, 864.

9. *GEL,* I, 264; see above, p. 434.

10. *Loc. cit.*

11. See *GEL,* V, 314 for a description of the gambling scene at the Kursaal in Hamburg witnessed by George Eliot. It is worth noting here that the young lady the Lewes' were watching was the grand-niece of Byron, the century's prototypal exile.

12. *GEL,* VI, 290. See above, p. 433.

13. 36, 494. Cf. Luke 15: 4-32.

14. *Meditations on a Hobby Horse* (London, 1965), p. 126.

15. See above, p. 436.

16. See Laurence Lerner, *The Truth Tellers* (London, 1967), pp. 56-57 for an account of Gwendolen's "therapeutic hysteria" which is the only description I have seen of the importance to Gwendolen's story of her self-recognition in this scene.

17. *GEL,* VI, 310. Gordon Haight, in his splendid biography, *George Eliot* (Oxford, 1968), traces with great tact the importance of her ostracism from society and the gradual and hard-won acceptance which became general by December of 1871: "She was now often invited to dinner. In December 1871 she dined with Frederick and Lady Charlotte Locker; besides their daughter Eleanor Locker and her governess, the only other guests were the Dean of Westminster, Arthur Stanley, and his wife Lady Augusta" (p. 452).

Joan Myers Weimer (essay date fall 1986)

SOURCE: Weimer, Joan Myers. "Women Artists as Exiles in the Fiction of Constance Fenimore Woolson." *Legacy: A Journal of American Women Writers* 3, no. 2 (fall 1986): 3-15.

[*In the following essay, Weimer explains how exiled women characters in the works of Constance Fenimore Woolson offer a revealing glimpse into the obstacles and dilemmas faced by nineteenth-century women writers and artists.*]

American women starting to write just after the Civil War found themselves standing on uneven new ground. Not because it was an act of daring for women to

present themselves as professional writers: women novelists of the previous generation had broken that ground, and some, like Susan Warner and Maria Cummins, had written best sellers. These "literary domestics," however, had atoned for their presumption in departing from women's sphere; they made domesticity their subject matter, and justified their work by its moral uplift (Kelley 335, 329).

But among this new generation of women, many writers, like Mary E. Wilkins Freeman, Sarah Orne Jewett, Kate Chopin, and Constance Fenimore Woolson, made no excuses for themselves. They rejected the commitment to moral uplift along with the domestic ideology of the literary domestics. Irony, not sentimentality, characterized the realistic fiction they rooted in the regions they knew best. Labelling them as "regionalists" and "local colorists" has trivialized their work and obscured its universality and artistry. For they were the first American women writers of fiction who saw themselves not just as professionals but as artists, and who saw themselves competing with male writers not just for readers but for laurels.

One of these writers has left a remarkable record of a woman artist's struggle to place herself in relation to the literary domestics, to the male and female giants of literature, to her material, her society, and her sexuality. Constance Fenimore Woolson (1840-1894) published five novels and four volumes of short stories, as well as numerous reviews, sketches and poems, in her short life. Her work deserves to be better known for its complexity, ambiguity, irony, and wit; for its close observation of people and their environments; for its keen analysis of unacknowledged motives; and for the range of voices and tones its style accommodates.[1]

Woolson is of particular interest in women's literary history because she was acutely conscious of her situation as a woman writer. She could hardly be anything else, as the great-niece of James Fenimore Cooper, whose name she bore, and as the "extremely intimate" friend of Henry James (Edel 160), who wrote an admiring essay about her work which he included with his 1888 *Partial Portraits* of Turgenev and George Eliot. These connections forced her to compare herself with major male writers, and raised urgent questions about women and art which she dramatized in a group of short stories.

If a woman wants passionately to be an artist, but lacks talent, what kind of life can she make for herself in the shadow of great art and criticism by men? Or in the shadow of a woman genius of another age? If a woman writer has enormous power, would her work be perceived as being so flawed by the anomaly of genius in woman that it would fail to find an audience? Would her genius be so deforming that it would deprive her of

men's love as well as success? If she is drawn to women but loses them to male rivals, would not her loveless state limit her as an artist? If she allows herself to love a man, won't she become an ordinary woman whose words have no weight with men?

In working out these chilling questions, Woolson's fiction presents only once a character who is successful both as woman and as artist. She is a figure of fantasy who materializes on a Florida beach sitting on a tiger skin, wearing purple velvet, and singing operatic arias ("Miss Elizabetha," *Rodman the Keeper*). When Woolson presents women artists realistically, rather than fantastically, she envisions them as she does most of her women characters—as exiles. And she furthers her exploration of alienation by presenting their proper subject matter as other exiles.

Some of Woolson's female characters begin as voluntary exiles, leaving their homes in order to become painters or preachers, only to find themselves involuntarily exiled from love and self-respect. Some are exiles from their own painful feelings of inadequacy; some from self-knowledge; some from relationships whose loss leads to such devastation that solitude is preferable. The women artists, whether mediocre or brilliant, are ultimately exiled from their own art.

Woolson felt herself an exile for much of her life, her wanderings associated with bereavements. When three of her five older sisters died of scarlet fever in Woolson's first month of life, her parents left their home in New Hampshire with its unbearable memories and moved to Cleveland.[2] When Woolson was 12, her oldest sister contracted tuberculosis from her husband of a few months and died. The next year, her remaining older sister died in childbirth. She learned to be cautious of all attachments, and wary of marriage; by her early twenties she declared herself a spinster. When her father died in her twenty-ninth year, Woolson gave up an independent life in New York to begin a decade of wandering with her mother in the South. Although she found excellent material for fiction in the post-Reconstruction South, she complained to the poet Paul Hamilton Hayne that "a trunk is all the home I have had," and that "I am so eager to go north that I can scarcely wait; an 'exile longing for home.' I like the South; no Yankee-born northerner ever liked it better; but, the years away from home! I have no real home, however" (Hubbell 720, 731).

That nomadic period ended with her mother's death, which destroyed even the fragile home they had built out of their trunks. Abruptly on her own at 39, Woolson was devastated. To bring her out of her depression, her one surviving sister took her to Europe—a removal which turned out to be a permanent exile. While there, she wrote to her fellow expatriate Henry James, who

became her first close friend in Europe, that his writings "are my true country, my real home. And nothing else ever fully is—try as I may to think so" (Edel 93).

At the same time that Woolson was describing herself as a rather pathetic, homeless creature, she was developing her phenomenal powers of observation of people and places and learning to transform this raw material into fiction which brought her recognition and an independent income. Her women characters reflect Woolson's sense of exile but not her success. A remarkable distance exists between Woolson's authorial voice—assured, ironic, in control—and the debilitated lives she assigns to women artists, or to women whose intense interest in human feeling, behavior and motivation identifies them with the writer. These characters' situations seem to reflect her deepest feelings about women and art, convictions which persist from her earliest stories despite the improvement in her own circumstances.

Woolson set many of her early stories in the American equivalents of desert islands: Fort Mackinac on Lake Michigan; a closed community of Zoarites in Ohio; a mining camp on an island in Lake Superior; a solitary house in a salt marsh on Lake Huron; an abandoned cotton plantation after Sherman's march. These isolated settings justify the intensity of the relationships among the castaways who meet there, and function as metaphors for women's various forms of exile. Several stories that are not explicitly about women artists probe the limits of subject matter available to women writers. They present the woman writer as an outsider among outsiders, driven by her own isolation to prey on, even cannibalize, the lives and passions of other women.[3]

The narrator of "Jeannette" (1874) is the widowed aunt of a young lieutenant at Fort Mackinac, where she fills some lonely hours trying to teach a beautiful half-breed woman to read, and encouraging a cold young surgeon to fall in love with her protégée. She seems to expect the doctor to seduce and abandon the girl, so that she can enjoy vicariously the thrill of romantic heart-break. Instead, the surgeon becomes obsessed with the girl and decides to lower himself to marry this "ignorant half-breed" (*Castle Nowhere* 171). The girl escapes his condescension and the woman's manipulation by refusing to marry the doctor. But if the narrator has missed the opportunity to enjoy the girl's broken heart, she still has the pleasure of feeding on the doctor's pain and passion, wondering "how long the feeling lived,—the feeling that swept me along in its train down to the beach-cottage that wild night" (175). She admits no responsibility for the doctor's suffering, nor any inclination to imagine Jeannette's pain had her plot turned out more predictably. She believes she has fallen "into the habit of studying persons very closely" (154), but Woolson's irony shows clearly that she has failed to include herself in her scrutiny.

Despite this distance from her narrator, Woolson seems also to share her fascination with a woman who is everything she and the narrator are not—beautiful, gay, proud, vital, daring—and who therefore attracts and experiences violent romantic passions. Woolson's interest in such women recurs in other stories. It is a complex mixture of envy and attraction, which never evolves into romantic friendship or into the love between kindred spirits which many nineteenth-century women freely enjoyed (Faderman 161, 205). No doubt the deaths of her five sisters made Woolson fearful of devastating loss following intimacy with women. Through women narrators who distance themselves from both men and women, she explores the fictive possibilities and psychological risks in the position of the solitary outsider, the literal or emotional exile.

The narrator of a weak but revealing early tale, "Wilhemena" (1874), is like the narrator of "Jeannette" in her unsettling mixture of manipulation and vicarious romantic involvement, although, unlike the lonely widow, she is a "romantic wife" whose "heart went out to all lovers" (*Castle Nowhere* 273). She tells herself that her interest in Wilhemena is to help her leave her closed Zoarite community to marry her beloved Gustav, who will have none of the community's restrictions now that the Civil War has shown him more of the world. When she runs to tell Wilhemena the news of Gustav's arrival, however, it is in order to experience both the girl's passions and those of her lover: "Her emotion resembled the intensest fire of fever, and yet it seemed natural . . . her slender form throbbed, and pulses were beating under my hands wherever I touched her" (285).

Like the narrator of "Jeannette," this woman is strongly attracted to the woman whose life she manipulates. When Gustav predictably leaves without her, and the girl cries out after him, the woman "drew her head down on my shoulder to stifle the sound; it was better the soldier should not hear it, and its anguish thrilled my own heart also (300). In reserving for herself the cry meant for Wilhemena's lover, the narrator plays his role. Because she admits to none of her real motives, she is driven to practice a rather chilling form of possession of both lovers, trying like the narrator of "Jeannette" to expropriate the passions—even the painful ones—that are absent from her own life.

In a fine early tale, "In the Cotton Country" (1876), the passion preyed upon is not love, but the despair of a woman who has lost everything and everyone in the Civil War. The predatory narrator is a Northern woman whose own life is so empty that she spends much of it as a "solitary pedestrian," and whose own sense of homelessness is so great that she follows a flock of crows, thinking, "The crows at home—that would be something worth seeing" (*Rodman the Keeper* 179). They lead her not to their home but to a "solemn, lonely

old house" whose wretched isolation fascinates her: "Now if there had been two, I should not have gone on. . . . Two houses are sociable and commonplace; but one all alone on a desolate waste like that inspired me with—let us call it interest, and I went forward" (181).

What else might one call it? Certainly a compulsive fascination with solitude perhaps greater than her own, as well as a need to feel someone else's pain. This narrator excuses her own prying into the Southern woman's tragic story by telling herself she is a "Sister of Charity . . . bearing balm and wine and oil for those who suffer" (184). But in fact, she is testing her own tendency toward solitude, wondering how great a deprivation could be endured.

Ann Douglas Wood finds in this "superb story" the narrator's "almost uncontrollable need to . . . get at some stifled part of herself, mysteriously locked in the other woman's past and capable not only of pain but of creativity" (30). Wood is certainly right about the narrator's deprivation and need: she is so fascinated with the other woman's "dry, still eyes of immovable, helpless grief" that she admits, "I used to wait impatiently for the hour when I could enter into the presence of her great silence," even though the other woman's eyes ask, "'By what right are you here?'" (*Rodman the Keeper* 182). But while Woolson can find powerful material in the Southern woman's tragedy, her narrator finds only confirmation of her unstated beliefs that human connection cannot last but can only betray, and that the best protection against such loss is accepting homelessness and habitual solitude. She allows herself only the tenuous, temporary connection that a woman exiled from herself can make with other such exiles.

These narrators, along with their vicarious experience of women's passions, obviously reveal an author in search of material. But they also reveal a guilty awareness that such "material" is the experience of other human beings who cannot be intimately observed without damaging their lives and the observer's own integrity. This was the dilemma Hawthorne had dramatized in tales like "Ethan Brand," "The Birthmark," "Rappaccini's Daughter," and in *The Scarlet Letter*. Since Woolson said that Hawthorne was "always" one of her "gods" (Moore 23), she must have studied eagerly and apprehensively his uneasy "burrowing" into the secret caverns of human nature (Hawthorne 590).[4] She would have recognized her own anxiety in his. But she would have seen too that as a single woman artist she ran risks that Hawthorne did not. He felt rescued from the worst of his isolation, if not from his guilt, by love and marriage. For Woolson, however, love of women threatened devastating disappointment, while love of men, if it didn't kill women outright, could be a trap for the woman who wanted to be an artist.

This dilemma is dramatized in "The Lady of Little Fishing" (1874), one of Woolson's most admired and most misread tales. Here, the central character is a Scottish woman missionary whose power over language links her with the woman artist; her words have such immense authority that they transform the behavior of a group of brutal hunters camped on an island in Lake Superior. The men, awed by her pale, nun-like beauty, call her "Our Lady" (*Castle Nowhere* 359) and treat her like the Madonna. But the moment they discover that she has fallen in love with one of them, her influence is destroyed.

Critics who admire the story tend to take as its theme one character's observation that women perversely care only for the men who care nothing for them: "'O woman! woman! the same the world over!'" (383). But the story is ultimately not about love or women's choices of love objects, but about the perception that a woman's words have weight just so long as she is seen as an angel, a madonna, a sexless, wholly spiritual being. Then she is safe among wolfish men, who will even cook for her, nurse her when she's ill, build a meeting-house for her to conduct services, and build themselves new houses to hold their new, clean, orderly selves. For this mother, sibyl, or angel, men become good children, docile, domestic, and sexless. They are spellbound by "that spotless woman standing alone in the glare of the fire" (361), whose severe words hold back not "one grain of denunciation, one iota of future punishment" (360).

This powerful figure is barely recognizable after she falls in love. Once the men see that she is "common flesh and blood" (379), she is "our Lady no longer; only a woman like any other,—weak and fickle" (392). The Madonna has become Eve, and powerless. The change is not only in the men's perception of her, but in herself, most dramatically in her language. Her "steady voice" becomes "softer, the words at times faltering" (374). When she throws herself at the feet of the man who does not love her, her rhetorical degradation is as great as her personal fall: "Oh, take me with you! Let me be your servant—your slave—anything—anything, so that I am not parted from you, my lord and master, my only, only love" (384). Love is a terrible affliction of which people die—in this case, I think, of shame.

Love leads the Lady not only to the loss of her dignity and verbal power, but to a devastating revelation. She learns that she was deluded in thinking of herself as God's instrument in the wilderness of America and of men's hearts. Since the men reform only out of their idolatrous adoration of her, their reform ends when she falls from her niche. The story thus comments on the contemporary ideology of womanhood and on the strategy of the literary domestics who excused their unlady-

like entry into man's public sphere by claiming to be God's instruments called to save souls (Kelley 295). Woolson suggests not only that God's instruments may be deluded, but that they can retain their power only by sacrificing their capacity for passionate love.

The story also subverts the nineteenth-century belief that a woman's selfless love of one man gives her power over him, and through him, in the world. Instead, love robs a woman of her integrity and power. The story even undercuts the ideology of "the angel of the house." Despite her silvery paleness, her devotion to religion, her strenuous efforts to redeem fallen men, this angel is confined to no home, but takes the whole American wilderness as her sphere. Her role is not to sacrifice herself for men, but to save them by her preaching. They in fact sacrifice for her, giving up their liquor, fights, and dirt, giving her their food and labor. They do give her worshipful love and a home in the wilderness. But Woolson's point is that women's words have power only as long as they are indifferent to these traditional sources of women's power. The lovelessness and home-lessness that torment the narrators of "In the Cotton Country," "Jeannette," and "Wilhemena" here have at least the potential for artistic success.

Another early story, however, which deals explicitly with a woman artist, finds lovelessness as disabling as love. Catherine, the narrator of "Felipa" (1876), has never known the success and power of the Lady of Little Fishing. She describes herself as "an artist, poor and painstaking" (*Rodman the Keeper* 199) who lives a "poor gray life" (218). Her obvious foil is her beautiful friend Christine, whose arrogant power over her lover Edward makes Catherine say to herself, "Fate, in the next world make me one of those long, lithe, light-haired women, will you? I want to see how it feels" (216). But Catherine has a true alter-ego in Felipa, the Minorcan child they meet in Florida. She shares the sexual ambiguity implied by Felipa's name and made explicit by the child's passionate attachment to *both* Christine and Edward—an attachment which amuses and puzzles the adults, but which in fact expresses Catherine's own unacknowledged feelings.

Perhaps because of this repression of her passions, Catherine lacks Felipa's Orpheus-like power over nature. The child dances in circles of pine cones and knows the trees listen when she talks to them. Felipa's artistic powers are still developing, but she worships them in the form of a goddess she has made of saw palmetto pieces and crowned with flowers, and to whom she offers food and other treasures. Catherine does not acknowledge Felipa's artistic gifts, but tries systematically to socialize the child into a properly repressed female like herself who is "gentle," "quiet and good" (209), giving her a "respectable, orderly doll" (217) to replace the palmetto goddess. For such efforts, Cathe-

rine wins exactly nothing—"I was forgotten as usual" (210)—and turns to her painting to escape her pain and anger at being rejected by both children and adults. She sanitizes these emotions as "cynicism" which she calls "a small brass field-piece that eventually bursts and kills the artilleryman. I knew this, having blown up myself more than once; so I went back to my painting and forgot the world" (211). We might also identify these explosives as sexual longings, directed toward women as well as men, which Catherine uses art to evade rather than to express, understand, or transform.

When Christine finally accepts Edward's proposal, Catherine tells herself that she is "glad that the old simple-hearted love was not entirely gone from our tired metallic world" (218). But Felipa recognizes and deals directly with the self-hatred and rage they both feel. She eats the "poison things" (219) in Catherine's paint box, grasping what the woman artist does not—that art can poison when it is used to repress rather than to express honest feeling. Seriously ill, Felipa responds to Edward's attempts to comfort her by stabbing his arm with Catherine's little dagger.

Catherine tells the child's grandfather that since Felipa loved Edward and Christine "both alike," her love "is nothing; she does not know." The old man agrees that Felipa doesn't know the meaning of her attachments, "but *I* know. It was two loves, and the stronger thrust the knife" (220). The stronger love was the one for Christine; the attack was on the man who chose her instead of Felipa, and who also took away the woman she loved. Catherine truly "does not know" what she feels.[5] Using art to deny unfulfillable longings, Catherine finds her attempts to capture on canvas Felipa's complex character or the subtleties of the salt-marsh are "hopeless efforts" (296). Denial of her complicated feelings dooms her as woman and as artist.

Two years after writing "Felipa," Woolson drew attention to the power of women's love for each other in a review she wrote for *The Atlantic* of *Esther Pennefather*. She called the novel a ridiculous book but one with an original subject: "The singular power one woman sometimes has over another. . . . I myself have seen tears of joy, the uttermost faith, and deepest devotion, in mature, well-educated and cultivated women, for some other woman whom they adored" (503). Although Woolson says that as soon as an agreeable man appears, "the whole cloud structure topples over, its battlements dissolve" (503), she does not quite present women's love for each other as "a rehearsal in girlhood of the great drama of woman's life," as Longfellow did in his 1849 novel *Kavanaugh* (Faderman 170). Instead, Woolson describes such women lovers as thinking after marriage "of that old adoration which was so intense

and so pure, so self-sacrificing and so far away" (503). But her imagery of cloud castles indicates what her stories dramatize, that women who love women lose them to men.

The troubled relationship between love and art became even more urgent for Woolson when she moved to Europe in 1879 and developed an intense friendship with Henry James[6]. Three stories she wrote in the next three years place an American woman artist in Europe, and in the shadow of a successful male writer or critic who resembles James. Although her Continental scenes offer women more options than the American desert islands of her earlier fiction, none of these women find success in art or love. This, despite the warmth of James's friendship and her own success as a writer. Her first novel *Anne* came out during her first year abroad, and was one of Harper's best-sellers. But Woolson apparently mistrusted her success. When she imagined a woman writer of real genius, she called her "Miss Grief" and made her work incomprehensible to the reading public. Her other women artists attract the love of masterful men who insist they give up art. Their decisions to marry these men are presented as a "great downfall" (*Dorothy* 193).

Ettie Macks, the heroine of "The Street of the Hyacinth" (1882) has a complexly developed consciousness that shows James's influence on Woolson's work.[7] At the same time, this heroine has important resemblances to the shadowy, mythic Lady of Woolson's earlier tale. Like the Lady, out of place among the savage hunters of Lake Superior, Ettie Macks is an exile in Rome. She has rented the family farm in her tiny Western town of Tuscolee Falls so she can come with her mother to live on the dirty, narrow street of the Hyacinth in the shadow of the Pantheon, to study male masterpieces as part of her education as an artist. In this dedication to her goal, and in her impersonal indifference to the men around her except as they can help her to reach it, Ettie is again like the Lady. Like her too, Ettie has seriously overestimated her own powers. She is finally persuaded by a series of male mentors that she has not a shred of talent.

Although Ettie resembles the Lady in loving a man who doesn't love her, she retains more of her self-respect and dignity than the woman missionary did. When the James-like Raymond Noel, an aloof and successful art critic, proposes marriage not because he loves her but because he is eager to receive her ardent love, Ettie refuses him. Admitting she loves him, she tells Noel she's ashamed to love a man she can't respect or admire, and will learn to overcome her feeling for him. Ettie's honesty and pride shock Noel into realizing he does indeed love this remarkable woman. She agrees to marry him only when she is persuaded she cannot be an artist, and is worn down by his persistence

and her mother's, by her strenuous labors to support herself and her mother by teaching, and by her own reluctant love of Noel. Rayburn Moore concludes that Ettie has found "fulfillment in a marriage to her mentor" (67). But Noel's ironic remark that in marrying him Ettie has suffered "a great downfall" from her "superhuman" heights of integrity (193) is closer to the truth. The imagery of hyacinths makes Woolson's intention clear.

Ettie's "downfall" is linked with the demolition of the Street of the Hyacinth, which "experienced a great downfall, also" (193), pulled down so it would no longer "disfigure" the Pantheon, "the magnificent old Pagan temple" (191) it adjoined. In "Pagan" mythology, Hyacinthus suffered a downfall worse than Ettie's at the hands of his loving mentor, Apollo, who accidentally killed him while teaching him to throw the discus. The street where Ettie came to live is named for the doomed Hyacinthus because Ettie's mentor has slain his beloved's faith in herself as artist and woman. Such female self-assertion would evidently "disfigure" the monumental principles of male culture which Noel upholds both as art critic and as suitor. When Ettie marries him, her integrity, which had survived her admission that she had no talent as an artist, suffers a genuine "downfall."

Woolson imagined another male mentor persuading a woman to give up her artistic ambitions, not because her writing is bad—Woolson never reveals its quality—but because he believes that genius in women is a disfigurement or a delusion. In "At The Chateau of Corinne" (1880), Katherine Winthrop has to choose between her literary ambitions, symbolized by Madame de Staël, whose home on Lake Lehman provides the setting and title of the story, and marriage to John Ford, who cannot abide Madame de Staël or any other literary woman. Ford offers marriage on condition that Katherine cultivate the "simple and retiring womanly graces" and "write no more" (*Dorothy* 263, 285). Katherine's acquiescence, like Ettie's, is a "downfall."

Ford loathes Madame de Staël. His stated objections are personal: she wore a turban, forced her guests to discuss the subject she was writing about, made egotistical demands for sympathy. But his serious, unspoken objections are to de Staël and her heroine Corinne as models of female greatness. Woolson's admiration of them was shared by contemporaries as different as Elizabeth Cady Stanton and Harriet Beecher Stowe (Parker 13, 37). Margaret Fuller, another "martyr to her own uniqueness" (Welter 78), was known as "the American Corinne." But a real cultural ambivalence about these female geniuses emerges in the warning in a popular magazine that while women with minds "equal to any human undertaking" exist, "happily these giants of their kind are rare" (*Young Lady's Companion*

qtd. in Welter 76). Such women have unsexed themselves. By going beyond male-defined limitations, they have become monsters, not women at all.

Ford would emphatically have agreed. He responds to Katherine's defense of Madame de Staël as "a woman of genius" by exclaiming, "'A woman of genius! And what is the very term but a stigma? No woman is so proclaimed by the great brazen tongue of the Public unless she has thrown away her birthright of womanly seclusion for the miserable mess of pottage called "fame."' 'The seclusion of a convent? or a prison?'" asks Katherine (263). This exchange is a fair example of her witty defense of women and Ford's bombastic severity. Yet she masochistically chooses Ford to tell her "the truth, your real opinion" (265) of the volume of poetry she has written and published anonymously. Ford responds with a remarkable outburst of misogyny which seeks to disguise itself as a generous masculine desire to save women from themselves:

> We do not expect great poems from women any more than we expect great pictures; we do not expect strong logic any more than we expect brawny muscle. A woman's poetry is subjective. But what cannot be forgiven—at least in my opinion—is . . . a certain sort of daring. This is its essential, unpardonable sin . . . because it comes . . . from the lips of a woman. For a woman should not dare in that way. Thinking to soar, she invariably descends . . . And to see her leave [her sphere], and come in all her white purity, which must inevitably be soiled, to the garish arena where men are contending, where the dust is rising, and the air is tainted and heavy—this is indeed a painful sight. Every honest man feels like going to her, poor mistaken sibyl that she is, closing her lips with gentle hand, and leading her away to some far spot among the quiet fields, where she can learn her error, and begin her life anew.
>
> (268)

Remarkable words from a man who devotes himself to exposing other people's posturing, and prides himself on male logic.

Ford's misogyny is so overwhelming that it suggests a tangle of motives. Perhaps he wants to punish Katherine for making him a "victim" of her charms while she is engaged to someone else. Perhaps he wants to offend her so as to put distance between himself and a woman whose independence frightens him. Perhaps he wants to set the terms under which he would feel safe enough to marry her. In any case, the violence of his opinions and the space Woolson gives to them indicate that she believed opinions like his were a real obstacle to women writers. The overblown rhetoric she assigns him is a clear sign of her disapproval of this stereotypical masculinity, just as the Lady's romantic effusions signalled the demise of her integrity

When she loses her fiancé and her fortune and decides she must marry Ford, Katherine agrees without much of a struggle to his conditions that she "write no more"

(285). Her greater conflict is over losing the independence which wealth had given her, and which Ford saw as an equally serious obstacle to their marriage. He prefers her impoverished, so that she will "in a measure be dependent upon your husband, and that is very sweet to a self-willed man like myself. Perhaps in time I can even make it sweet to you" (281).

Katherine is not so sure. She tells him, "You are narrow, prejudiced; you do not believe in progress of any kind. You would keep women down with an iron hand" (284). It seems she is right. After their marriage Ford keeps in his study a complete set of Madame de Staël's works as a kind of trophy of what he took from his wife: her independence of mind, her literary aspirations.

The structure of the story indicates Woolson's regret that modern women lack the genius and the independence of Madame de Staël. The story is built on four visits to Coppet, each of which marks a decline in de Staël's prestige and Katherine's independence. In the first, Katherine's fiancé praises Madame de Staël's genius. In the second, Ford savages Katherine's poem. In the third, Katherine has been jilted. And in the fourth, which takes place on a comfortless, wet, cold day, Katherine has lost her fortune, her fiancé, and her hopes for herself as a writer, and accepts Ford's proposal. Katherine's story, worked out in the shadow of a great woman's place of exile, has the same outcome as Ettie's, in the shadow of the Pantheon and the galleries of great male painters. Neither male nor female models of greatness seem of much help to women who would be artists, but who are persuaded that they have no talent and that their only recourse is marriage to men unable to accept independence or talent in women.

By taking Ford's misogynistic, manipulative opinions as Woolson's own, her literary biographer Rayburn Moore mistakenly concludes that she shared his "entire disbelief in the possibility of true fiery genius in women" (157, n. 35).[8] Evidence that Woolson believed in and was inspired by women of genius is found both inside and outside the story. She made her own pilgrimage to Coppet "to stand there just for its association with [Madame de Staël]" (Benedict 226), and placed Charlotte Brontë and George Eliot among her literary luminaries. And in her journal, Woolson objected to the critic Edmund C. Stedman for his condescension to Elizabeth Barrett Browning: "Mr. Stedman does not really believe in woman's genius. His disbelief peeps through every line of the criticism below, whose essence is—'She did wonderfully well for a woman'" (Benedict 93). Since Stedman was her own first literary mentor, she must herself have felt the sting of his condescension. "At the Chateau of Corinne" should be read as a critique of men who belittle women writers.

Woolson wrote one tale about a woman writer of genius. Although "Miss Grief" (1880) is generally consid-

ered Woolson's best story, Harper and Brothers did not include it in the two anthologies of her stories they issued shortly after her death, which included every other story she had published since the last collection of her short fiction in 1880. Since the story depicts a woman genius whose tragic failure is the fault of her society and not of herself, perhaps the publishers felt that like Miss Grief's own work, Woolson's account would not be acceptable to the public.

"Miss Grief" is narrated by a male writer who is everything the woman writer is not: "Young, well and strong, passably good-looking, with some money that one has inherited and more that one has earned," the narrator admits that he takes a "deep, although of course carefully concealed, satisfaction in my own little fame" (574), and in his popularity in the superficial American and English society in Rome. The woman who seeks his help in getting her work published is not young, though younger at 43 than she looks. (Woolson was then 40.) Miss Aaronna Crief, whose name the narrator misreads as "Grief," is not good-looking or well dressed, because she is poor and suffering from hunger and cold. For these reasons, the narrator repeatedly refuses to see her, smugly telling himself that "Grief has not so far visited me here . . . and she shall not now" (574). He assumes she wants to sell him something, and when he learns she is a writer, exclaims, "An authoress! This is worse than old lace" (576).

When the narrator is finally shamed into reading her play, he recognizes that it is "inspired," full of earnestness, passion and "power" which "thrill" him as evidence that she has the "divine spark of genius" (578). But he finds her work deeply flawed "by some fault or lack which seemed wilful perversity, like the work of an evil sprite. It was like a case of jeweller's wares set before you, with each ring unfinished, each bracelet too large or too small for its purpose, each breastpin without its fastening, each necklace purposely broken" (581). This view of the work's fatal flaws is supported by male publishers to whom the narrator sends it. It is never clear whether this judgment is a fair one or whether the woman genius is writing in a way that the men cannot comprehend.

When the narrator overcomes Miss Grief's proud refusal to let him change so much as a "comma," and tries to correct these faults, he finds the flaws inseparable from the genius. It is like "taking out one especial figure in a carpet: that is impossible unless you unravel the whole" (583). As Leon Edel has observed, Henry James took Woolson's metaphor of the "figure in a carpet" for the title of his own tale about the elusive nature of genius. But James's male genius, Hugh Vereker, had fame and disciples. Miss Grief has neither, because in a woman genius is perceived as deforming. An imagination that is "unrestrained, large, vast, like the skies or the wind" (583) makes her too eccentric to communicate with the public she needs.

While the narrator sends out her work to publishers, Miss Grief lies dying. He discovers this through an accidental meeting with her aunt, for he has forgotten all about her. Recognizing her deathbed not only as a scene of desperate poverty but as a sacred shrine, he brings wine, flowers, and candles, and tells himself that lying to her about the fate of her drama is one of his "few good deeds" (584). Believing it is to be published, she says, "I have never known what it was . . . to be fully happy until now . . . Yes, I am happy," (584) she tells herself in amazement.

But it is the narrator's turn for grief, although he tells himself that the reason he has kept her rejected drama in a locked case, and reads it over "once in a while," is that it is a "memento of my own good fortune, for which I should continually give thanks. The want of one grain made all her work void, and that one grain was given to me. She, with the greater power, failed—I with the less, succeeded" (585). Thus he admits the truth of Miss Grief's dying words: "You had success—but I had the greater power" (585).

If successful mediocrity is better than unsuccessful greatness, then he is indeed fortunate. He has married a trivial, narrow-minded society woman, and written trivial, popular books. But secretly, he has made the greater writer "my . . . Miss Grief" (585), has taken into himself the grief of recognizing like Henry James's failed "master" what it means to have everything but "the great thing . . . the sense of having done the best" (James 135).

Woolson herself made no compromises with "the best" she could do. She put her work ahead of everything else, working long days and revising tirelessly. Her considerable success as a writer, however, did not prevent grief from being her regular companion. She struggled all her life with bouts of acute depression which she thought she inherited from her father. She wrote in her journal, "When she woke in the morning not haunted by care or trouble or grief or pain, it was a new sensation, it was a relief. Still it made her feel strange—*old*, strangely indifferent. 'I wonder if I am going to die soon?' she thought" (Benedict 147). Haunted by grief and probably guilt at having survived five of her sisters, securing less of Henry James's time and attention than she wanted, lonely and vulnerable to depressions during a second bout of influenza, she may have committed suicide. Delirious with fever, she either fell or leapt from her balcony in Venice in January of 1894.

But it would be a mistake to see her death as a mark of professional despair. Although her stories show that both genius and mediocrity, love and lovelessness, dis-

able women artists, she herself managed not to be disabled but to remain productive and successful by making art out of those dilemmas. And it would be equally wrong to dismiss her analysis of the excruciating dilemmas of women artists as merely a symptom of her own depressions. Several of her women contemporaries depicted those struggles as equally harrowing.

Both Rebecca Harding Davis and Elizabeth Stuart Phelps portray talented women artists who find they cannot combine art with love and the responsibilities of marriage. While Davis affirms the struggle of an impoverished male artist, Hugh Wolfe in *Life in the Iron Mills* (1861), to express his tragic vision, in "The Wife's Story" (1864) she rejects a woman's attempts to fulfill her artistic potential, even though—or perhaps because—she has a chance to succeed. The story concludes instead that "a woman has no better work in life than . . . to make herself a visible Providence to her husband and child" (19). While the story supports the prevailing domestic ideology that women who stray outside the domestic sphere bring misery to themselves and others, it also testifies eloquently to the agony of having to choose between art and love.[9]

Elizabeth Stuart Phelps's *The Story of Avis* (1877) differs from "The Wife's Tale" in affirming its talented heroine's right to pursue a life of art, but concurs that women cannot combine art with family life. If they want to be artists, they should not marry. At the same time, Phelps insists that the often painful experiences of marriage and motherhood enlarge the sympathies that are the basis of great art—even while they consume a woman's time and energy and prevent her from producing that art. Evidently, this bind ensures that we cannot have the best work of which women are capable.

Unmarried women devoted to art appear in Mary E. Wilkins Freeman's stories, but these women are distinguished by their devotion to art rather than by their talent. The women in "A Village Singer" and "A Poetess" (1891) find their reason for living in their passion for singing and writing. When their work is rejected, the process is not enough to sustain them, and despite their rugged independence, they die.

Although these authors are better known than Woolson, none of their fictions about women artists is more powerful or complex than hers. While she displays strong anxiety that solitary observers may become predators of the lives of others, lacking the self-knowledge that is an indispensable ingredient of great art, she also shows how women who would be artists are coerced by the male-established and male-maintained canon, and punished for the distance between their own vision and male-defined taste. Woolson's fiction shows that withdrawal into voluntary exile from such painful contradictions can become an involuntary separation from oneself, while insisting at the same time that the more pernicious isolation is from one's art, an exile in which all society conspires.

Nevertheless, Woolson believed that women were capable of distinctive greatness in art. She wrote a remarkable sonnet "To George Eliot" (1876) which insists that a woman genius combines the "colossal" power of a Michelangelo with the "finely traced" beauty created by "woman-hands":

> O wondrous woman! shaping with thy pen
> As Michael Angelo did shape from stone,
> Colossal forms of clear-cut outline, when
> We dwell upon thy pages, not alone
> The beauty of thy rose we see, as finely traced
> As roses drawn by other woman-hands
> Who spend their lives in shaping them, but faced
> We find ourselves with giant's work, that stands
> Above us as a mountain lifts its brow,
> Grand, unapproachable, yet clear in view
> To lowliest eyes that upward look. O, how
> Hast thou shed radiance as thy finger drew
> Its shapes! A myriad women light have seen,
> And courage taken, because *thou* hast been![10]

This mixture of power and tenderness is what she hoped her own legacy would be. A month before her death, she thought again of the "giant's work" that a woman could do, and wrote, "I should like to turn into a peak when I die, to be a beautiful purple mountain, which would please the tired, sad eyes of thousands of human beings for ages" (Benedict xvi). Woolson's mountain is metaphorically further from Shelley's Mont Blanc, which embodies the male poet's verbal and sexual power, than her grave is from his in the beautiful Protestant Cemetery in Rome, where she rests a few feet lower than he on the bank that slopes down from the ancient wall. Woolson's purple mountain is instead like her conception of George Eliot's genius, both maternal and phallic. It suggests that at the end of her life she saw the tensions surrounding love and gender identity dramatized in her early fiction as possible sources of distinctive female artistry. Her courage and skill in exploring these and other conflicts faced by the first generation of American women artists should recommend her to modern readers who seek to understand the conditions under which nineteenth-century women wrote.

Notes

My thanks to Doris Faber for generously sharing with me her unpublished biography on Woolson, and to David Weimer and my colleagues at Drew University who commented on an earlier version of this article: Janet Burstein, Terry Kohn, Wendy Kolmar, and John Warner.

1. I am editing a volume of Woolson's short fiction for the American Women Writers series published

by Rutgers University Press. It is scheduled to appear in 1988.

2. All biographical information is from Rayburn S. Moore, Clare Benedict, and Jay B. Hubbell's published work, as well as Doris Faber's unpublished biography.

3. Ann Douglas Wood finds a pattern among the women local colorists of "spying or even preying upon their subject matter" (29).

4. Woolson's "Castle Nowhere" is an elaborate reworking of Hawthorne's "Rappaccini's Daughter." Like Hawthorne, she also gives her preachers characteristics of artists; see "The Lady of Little Fishing" and "Peter the Parson," both in *Rodman the Keeper.*

5. A similar unacknowledged attraction exists between the women in Woolson's "A Florentine Experiment" (1880), *Dorothy and Other Italian Stories.*

6. Leon Edel gives extensive but negatively biased consideration to Woolson's relationship with Henry James in Volume III of his biography of James.

7. Two articles consider the influence of James and Woolson on each other's work: Rayburn S. Moore, "The Strange Irregular Rhythm of Life: James's Late Tales and Constance Woolson." *South Atlantic Bulletin* 41 (1976): 86-93; and Sharon Dean, "Constance Fenimore Woolson and Henry James: The Literary Relationship." *Massachusetts Studies in English* 71.3 (1980): 1-9.

8. Moore finds "little room to question the views expressed here concerning the literary amateur and the limitations of certain types of female writers" (74). He ignores the fact that Ford here rejects *all* types of female writers.

9. Although Davis's heroine is happiest when her husband calls her "Hetty," a name which signifies her contentment with domestic affection, her real name, Hester, points to Hawthorne's Hester Prynne, another woman with an artistic talent and temperament, blighted and warped by the harsh Puritanical attitudes that condemned her sexuality and forced her to use her artistic needlework as her only link to the society that rejected her. Davis saves her Hetty from the agonies—and the stature—of a Hester Prynne.

10. Woolson was clearly aware that this view of woman's genius was not going to suit traditional sensibilities. She published it not in *Harper's, Appel-* ton's, Lippincott's, or the *Atlantic,* her usual outlets, but in *The New Century for Woman.*

Works Cited

Benedict, Clare, ed. *Constance Fenimore Woolson.* London: Ellis, 1929. Vol. II of *Five Generations (1785-1923).*

Davis, Rebecca Harding. "The Wife's Story." *Atlantic Monthly* (July 1864): 1-19.

Edel, Leon. *Henry James.* Vol. III. New York: J. P. Lippincott, 1962, 1964.

Faderman, Lillian. *Surpassing the Love of Men: Romantic Friendship and Love between Women from the Renaissance to the Present.* New York: Morrow, 1981.

Freeman, Mary E. Wilkins. *A New England Nun and Other Stories.* New York: Harper and Bros., 1891.

Hawthorne, Nathaniel. Preface. *The Snow Image and Other Twice-Told Tales. Nathaniel Hawthorne: Selected Tales and Sketches.* Ed. Hyatt Waggoner. New York: Holt, Rinehart, and Winston, 1970.

Hubbell, Jay B. "Some New Letters of Constance Fenimore Woolson." *New England Quarterly* XIV (December 1941): 715-35.

James, Henry. "The Lesson of the Master." 1888. *Henry James: Stories of Writers and Artists.* Ed. F. O. Matthiessen. New York: New Directions, n.d.

Kelley, Mary. *Private Woman, Public Stage: Literary Domesticity in Nineteenth-Century America.* New York: Oxford Univ. Press, 1984.

Moore, Rayburn S. *Constance Fenimore Woolson.* New York: Twayne, 1963.

Parker, Gail, ed. *The Oven Birds: American Women on Womanhood 1820-1920.* New York: Doubleday, 1972.

Phelps, Elizabeth Stuart. *The Story of Avis.* 1877. New Brunswick: Rutgers Univ. Press, 1985.

Welter, Barbara. "Anti-Intellectualism and the American Woman 1800-1860." *Dimity Convictions: The American Woman in the Nineteenth Century.* Athens: Ohio Univ. Press, 1976.

Wood, Ann Douglas. "The Literature of Impoverishment: the Women Local Colorists in America 1865-1914." *Women's Studies* I (1972): 3-45.

Woolson, Constance Fenimore. *Castle Nowhere: Lake-Country Sketches.* Boston: J. R. Osgood & Co., 1875.

———. *Dorothy and Other Italian Stories.* New York: Harper and Bros., 1896, 1899.

Rev. of *Esther Pennefather,* by Constance Fenimore Woolson. *The Atlantic* (October 1878): 503.

———. *The Front Yard and Other Italian Stories.* New York: Harper and Bros., 1895.

———. "Miss Grief." *Lippincott's Magazine* (May 1880): 574-585.

———. *Rodman the Keeper: Southern Sketches.* New York: D. Appleton and Co., 1880; New York: Harper and Bros., 1886, 1899.

———. "To George Eliot." *The New Century for Woman.* 2 (May 20, 1876): 1.

FURTHER READING

Criticism

Briker, Olga. "The Traveler-Exile in Karolina Pavlova's *Phantasmagoria.*" In *Essays on Karolina Pavlova,* edited by Susanne Fusso and Alexander Lehrman, pp. 135-54. Evanston, Ill.: Northwestern University Press, 2001.

> Discusses the unique effect of travel and exile on both subject and personal expression in Karolina Pavlova's *Phantasmagoria.*

Civantos, Christina. "Exile Inside (And) Out: Woman, Nation, and the Exiled Intellectual in José Mármol's *Amalia.*" *Latin American Literary Review* 30, no. 59 (January-June 2002): 55-78.

> Maintains that "not only is exile—every bit as much as nation—at the center of [José Mármol's novel *Amalia*], but that exile in the novel is primarily filtered through the female protagonist Amalia."

Coleman, Patrick. "Exile and Narrative Voice in *Corinne.*" *Eighteenth-Century Culture* 24 (1995): 91-105.

> Contends that the influential narrative voice of *Corinne* is traceable "to [Germaine de] Staël's own experience with exile and other political expressions."

Conner, Wayne. "*L'Esule* (1832-1834): Literature and 'Home Thoughts from Abroad.'" *Italica* 40, no. 4 (December 1963): 297-305.

> Delineates the history of *L'Esule,* a periodical produced from 1832 to 1834 by Italian writers living in exile.

Cooksey, Thomas L. "Rossetti's *intellegenza nova*: Perception, Poetry and Vision in *Dante at Verona.*" *The Victorian Newsletter,* no. 66 (fall 1984): 10-13.

> Investigates Dante Gabriel Rossetti's use of Dante Alighieri's historical experience of exile to represent the alienation and artistic vision of the Victorian-era Romantic poet.

Grieve, James. "Intimations of Mortality: Another of the Meanings of Maupassant's *Pierre et Jean.*" *Australian Journal of French Studies* 19, no. 2 (May-August 1982): 133-47.

> Focuses on the theme of alienation in Guy de Maupassant's *Pierre et Jean.*

Kadish, Doris Y. "Symbolism of Exile: The Opening Description in *Atala.*" *The French Review* 55, no. 3 (February 1982): 358-66.

> Interprets the nature symbolism in the beginning of François René de Chateaubriand's *Atala* as an expression of the author's "exile following the Revolution and his resulting search to resolve the conflicts between his past and his present and his individual and collective consciousness."

Lougy, Robert E. "The Dynamics of Exile and Desire: Narrative Form and Meaning in Thackeray's *Notes of a Journey from Cornhill to Grand Cairo.*" *Modern Language Quarterly* 50, no. 3 (September 1989): 227-47.

> Examines the belief and impulses underlying William Makepeace Thackeray's depictions of foreign people and places in his *Notes of a Journey from Cornhill to Grand Cairo.*

Lowrie, Joyce O. "Motifs of Kingdom and Exile in *Atala.*" *The French Review* 43, no. 5 (April 1970): 755-64.

> Asserts that the themes of exile and kingdom are unifying components in François René de Chateaubriand's *Atala* and that the work presents the Romantic estranged hero as separated from Divine Unity.

Perlinska, Agnieszka. "An Epistolary Triangle: Love, Friendship and Exile in Cyprian Norwid's Private Letters." *Polish Review* 42, no. 2 (1997): 201-14.

> Discusses how, in his letters, Cyprian Norwid relates "a story of a lonely exile who searches for self-realization and recognition despite the profound absence of love, friendship and homeland in his life."

Porter, Carolyn. "Call Me Ishmael; Or, How To Make Double-Talk Speak." In *New Essays on Moby-Dick,* edited by Richard H. Brodhead, pp. 73-108. New York and London: Cambridge University Press, 1986.

> Outlines how Herman Melville's narrative strategy evokes the mood and experience of exile in *Moby Dick.*

Rasmussen, Barbara. "Alice James and the Question of Women's Exile." *Renaissance and Modern Studies* 34 (1991): 45-63.

 Offers commentary on feminist interpretations of women as exiles from their own desires as expressed by Alice James in her diaries.

Saunders, Rebecca. "Gender, Colonialism, and Exile: Flora Annie Steel and Sara Jeannette Duncan in India."

In *Women's Writing in Exile,* edited by Mary Lynn Broe and Angela Ingram, pp. 303-24. Chapel Hill, N.C.: University of North Carolina Press, 1989.

 Regards works by British women writers Flora Annie Steel and Sara Jeannette Duncan in which they chronicle their travels in India and explores how the authors' gender affords them a unique perspective on exile and the experiences of both the colonizers and the colonized.

Urban Life in Nineteenth-Century Literature

The following entry provides critical commentary on literary treatment of urban life during the nineteenth century.

INTRODUCTION

The urbanization that took place during the nineteenth century was accompanied by rapid social and economic changes, all of which had a profound effect on the everyday lives of those who lived and worked in urban areas. During a relatively short period of time, increasingly greater portions of the populace in the United States and Europe went from living in rural farming communities to living in industrialized urban centers that were often overcrowded, unsanitary, and unsafe. The relative proximity of impoverished peoples to the wealthy members of society led to an increased awareness of the problems of the working-class poor, and a great many sociologists, philanthropists, and artists dedicated themselves to exposing and ameliorating the urban ills of poverty, disease, poor sanitation, and substandard housing. The rapidity with which these drastic changes took place created a sense of unease in Victorian society, and authors and artists attempted to capture this emotional and metaphysical air of foreboding in their narratives, in which the depictions of urban settings as gritty and stifling reflect the experiences and sometimes the behaviors of the characters. Victor Hugo's scrutiny of urban spaces in his novel *Notre-Dame de Paris* (1831; *The Hunchback of Notre-Dame*), according to Richard Maxwell, originates an urban gothic narrative approach that was adapted by such authors as W. H. Ainsworth and Charles Dickens. In their "urban sketches," asserts Carol L. Bernstein, nineteenth-century writers develop an innovative approach to representing simultaneously the physical and metaphysical aspects of urban life, imbuing concrete locales and imagery with moral and spiritual significance. Various authors, including poets Walt Whitman, James Thomson, and Stéphane Mallarmé, and prose writers Edgar Allan Poe, George Eliot, and Dickens, approached urban life as symbolic of the human condition. While their approaches differ in tone and style, these authors commonly address issues of individual identity relative to—and within the context of—modern urban life.

REPRESENTATIVE WORKS

W. H. Ainsworth
The Tower of London (novel) 1840

Old Saint Paul's (novel) 1841

Charles Baudelaire
†*Les fleurs du mal* [*The Flowers of Evil*] (poetry) 1857; enlarged editions published in 1861 and 1868
Petits poèmes en prose, Les Paradis artificiels [*Poems in Prose from Charles Baudelaire*] (prose poetry) 1869; also published as *Le Spleen de Paris, petits poèmes en prose*, 1917; also translated as *Paris Spleen*, 1947; and *The Parisian Prowler*, 1989

Charles Booth
‡*Life and Labour of the People in London.* 17 vols. (sociology) 1902-03

William Booth
In Darkest England, and the Way Out (journalism) 1890

John Corry
A Satirical View of London at the Commencement of the Nineteenth Century (satire) 1801

Charles Dickens
Sketches by Boz, Illustrative of Every-Day Life and Every-Day People [as Boz] (sketches and short stories) 1836
Posthumous Papers of the Pickwick Club [as Boz] (novel) 1837
Oliver Twist (novel) 1838
Barnaby Rudge (novel) 1841
The Old Curiosity Shop (novel) 1841
The Life and Adventures of Martin Chuzzlewit (novel) 1844
Bleak House (novel) 1853

Pierce Egan
Life in London; or, The Day and Night Scenes of Jerry Hawthorne, Esq. and his Elegant Friend, Corinthian Tom, Accompanied by Bob Logic, the Oxonian, in their Rambles and Sprees through the Metropolis (novel) 1869

Friedrich Engels
Die Lage der arbeitenden Klasse in England [*The Condition of the Working Class in England in 1844*] (essay) 1845

George Gissing
Workers in the Dawn (novel) 1880
The Nether World (novel) 1889

James Grant
Sketches in London. 2 vols. (sketches) 1839

Margaret Harkness

A City Girl: A Realistic Story [as John Law] (novel) 1887

Tempted London: Young Men [as Law] (novel) 1888

Toilers in London; or, Inquiries Concerning Female Labour in the Metropolis [as Law] (novel) 1889

Victor Hugo

Notre-Dame de Paris [*The Hunchback of Notre-Dame*] (novel) 1831

Les misérables (novel) 1862

Washington Irving

The Sketch Book of Geoffrey Crayon, Gent. [as Geoffrey Crayon] (short stories) 1819-20

Henry James

Washington Square (novel) 1881

The Siege of London. Madame de Mauves (novellas) 1883

A Little Tour in France (travel essays) 1885

The Bostonians (novel) 1886

The Princess Casamassima (novel) 1886

Stéphane Mallarmé

Un coup de dés jamais n'abolira le hasard, poème (prose) 1914

Henry Mayhew

London Labour and the London Poor, Nos. 1-63. 4 vols. (journalism) 1851-62

Andrew Mearns

#*The Bitter Cry of Outcast London* (pamphlet) 1883

G. W. M. Reynolds

The Mysteries of London. 4 vols. (novel) 1845-48

George Augustus Sala

Gaslight and Daylight, with Some London Scenes They Shine upon (sketches) 1859

Twice 'Round the Clock; or, The Hours of the Day and Night in London (sketches) 1859

George R. Sims

How the Poor Live; and, Horrible London (sketches) 1889

James Thomson

The City of Dreadful Night and Other Poems (poetry) 1880

Walt Whitman

Leaves of Grass (poetry) 1855

William Wordsworth

||*The Prelude; or, Growth of a Poet's Mind, An Autobiographical Poem* (poetry) 1850

*These works were originally published serially in periodicals, usually over periods of one to two years.

†*Tableaux parisiens* was first published in the expanded edition of *Les fleurs du mal* published in 1861.

‡Various sections of this work were first published, under various titles, including *Labour and Life of the People in London,* between 1889 and 1892.

#This work has also been attributed to William C. Preston.

||This work was written between 1799 and 1805.

OVERVIEWS

Richard Maxwell (essay date spring 1978)

SOURCE: Maxwell, Richard. "City Life and the Novel: Hugo, Ainsworth, Dickens." *Comparative Literature* 30, no. 2 (spring 1978): 157-71.

[*In the following essay, Maxwell traces the creation of urban gothic by Victor Hugo and the adaptation of that literary approach by William Harrison Ainsworth and Charles Dickens.*]

In 1842, Elizabeth Barrett wrote to her friend Miss Mitford: "And have you observed what I have observed . . . that Charles Dickens has meditated deeply and not without advantage upon Victor Hugo,—and that some of his very finest things . . . are taken from Victor Hugo."[1] The insight is valuable. Hugo was already, I shall suggest, the source for a few important passages in Boz; moreover, he was soon to become a key figure behind the most popular English literature of the forties. I want to illustrate these continuities and examine their implications, first by looking at two novels by W. H. Ainsworth, then by comparing a passage from Hugo with one from Dickens. The texts are few; their significance is that they reveal an attitude toward city life which was soon to be expressed by many European and American novelists. From Hugo to Ainsworth and Dickens, one can trace the genesis of urban Gothic as a standard fictional mode.

Elizabeth Barrett, in the letter just quoted, singles out one of Hugo's novels for special praise: "Is not Notre Dame a more wonderful work, a more sublime *poem*, than anything which our Scott ever performed or imagined, or saw in a dream when he rested from his Ivanhoe? Can you hesitate—can you *not* say *Yes*?" *Nôtre-Dame de Paris* had been published in 1831 and was soon after translated into English. Its impact on both sides of the channel was sensational. As a historical novel it owed a debt to Scott; Hugo, however, made something new of the form, piling innovations and cli-

chés upon each other with fine abandon. No wonder Miss Barrett wrote with such enthusiasm. The book was at once a grand melodrama, whose villain bested even Matthew Lewis' monk and whose intrigues reached from king to beggar; a sweeping treatise advancing a theory of historical change; and an essay on medieval Paris with both archaeological and aesthetic pretensions. *Nôtre-Dame* brought together a feeling for the grotesque, a sense of history, and an obsession with a city. Thus a tradition was born.

One of the first writers in England to work with the pattern established by *Nôtre-Dame* was William Harrison Ainsworth. In 1841, Ainsworth published *Old Saint Paul's,* which is like a marginal gloss on the earlier book. Writing for the popular and respectable *Sunday Times,* he simplified Hugo's plot and ideas, sometimes to the point of absurdity. Frollo and Quasimodo, both essential to *Nôtre-Dame,* disappear completely. Instead of one heroine there are two, so that the conflicting erotic energies which converge on Hugo's Esmeralda are broken up and dissipated. Most important, Hugo's elaborate theory of history, which I shall discuss later, is reduced to a hymn in praise of the rising middle classes (as opposed to wicked courtiers). What remains of the French novel is a picked-over skeleton; the reader may recognize certain structures, but the flesh, the meaning, is largely gone.

Old Saint Paul's embodies Ainsworth's preoccupations at the zenith of his career. He looks to French fiction, Hugo especially, for models. He does not, as yet, display any special understanding of these models. In fact, the only evidence that he ever understood them is a serial he began work on a few years later which he called *Revelations of London.*

Several times during the 1830s, Ainsworth had attempted to interest Dickens in collaborating on a project he called *The Lions of London. The Lions* would have appeared in monthly parts, combining scenes of past and present city life. Dickens stalled, probably refusing the offer outright, but Ainsworth was not discouraged permanently.[2] By 1846 he was making another attempt to write an extended city novel in a past and present format. The title is now *Revelations of London.* Different historical periods are related not by simple juxtaposition but through the device of the man who lives forever. Ainsworth has found a plot which allows him to write about 1599 and then about 1830, with occasional retrospections.

The immediate stimulus for this final version of an old project has yet to be mentioned. *The Lions of London* would have been, by its nature, a pseudo-Dickensian undertaking.[3] *Revelations* retains certain Dickensian overtones but Ainsworth's fascination with French fiction reasserts itself. This time not Hugo but his most effective imitator provides the stimulus.

The relationship between Hugo and Eugène Sue has often been noted.[4] For the moment, only a few continuities between *Nôtre-Dame* and *Les Mystères de Paris* need mention. Sue's trashy, enormously popular serial takes over the earlier novel's sensationalism as well as its focus on the geography and social economy of a great city. Sue's goal, like Hugo's, is to explore the labyrinthine corridors of Paris, penetrating intrigues which link the most diverse people. His main innovation is to dispense with the chronological distancing used by his predecessor. *Les Mystères,* which began to appear in 1842, tells a story which begins in 1838. However melodramatic, the serial is committed to a description of Paris in the late 1830s or early 1840s: the city Sue and his contemporaries lived in.

Novelists on the other side of the channel soon took a professional interest in Sue's new production. In particular, Ainsworth's *Revelations,* despite its long gestation period, is conspicuously an imitation. English revelations are set against French mysteries; the fascinations which produced *Old Saint Paul's* have taken another and perhaps more promising form.

The opening chapter of *Revelations* fulfills this promise. A pair of criminals prowls through some sinister riverfront areas of London. Like Sue's malefactors, these two have more or less colorful nicknames: the Sandman and the Tinker. Also as in the French tradition, they are soon to become involved with a dandified young man who is involved in intrigues all over the city. A third striking feature is the landscape itself. The Sandman and the Tinker arrive finally in an abandoned and ruinous neighborhood, an area off Vauxhall Road which has been used as a dumping ground by riverside industry, including a shipbreaking yard. What is important here is a combination of fantasy and precise topographical description. While the landscape is no doubt authentic, it is being used for a special purpose. The novelist delights in mixing past and present, the debris of myth and technology heaped together with political and pastoral icons:

> Looking around, he beheld huge mill-stones, enormous waterwheels, boilers of steam-engines, iron vats, cylinders, cranes, iron pumps of the strangest fashion, a gigantic pair of wooden scales, old iron safes, old boilers, old gas pipes, old water pipes, cracked old bells, old birdcages, old plates of iron, old pulleys, ropes, and rusty chains, huddled and heaped together in the most fantastic disorder.

> In the midst of the chaotic mass frowned the bearded and colossal head of Neptune, which had once decorated the fore part of a man-of-war. Above it, on a sort of framework, lay the prostrate statue of a nymph, together with a bust of Fox, the nose of the latter being partly demolished, and the eyes knocked in. Above these, three wooden figures from a summer-house,—an old gentleman and two ladies,—laid their heads amica-

bly together. On the left stood a tall Grecian divinity, or warrior, but minus the head and right hand. The whole was surmounted by an immense ventilator, stuck on the end of an iron rod, ascending, like a lightning-conductor, from the steam-engine pump.[5]

Given the vigor of passages like this, one must regret that Ainsworth did not succeed with *Revelations.* Only a year later G. M. Reynolds' *Mysteries of London* became the most read work of fiction in Britain, its popularity, as with Sue, due largely to the lower classes. Ainsworth never quite reached that mass audience; he was too respectable. (Reynolds, by contrast, stooped to shocking political and sexual depths in his fiction.) Furthermore, he was simply not able to finish the book. That initial picture embodies one plight of the modern city whose past is being swept away while its present and future seem to lack coherent form. When Ainsworth tries to develop this theme in terms of plot, he reaches a point of deadlock. His hero, Auriol, gets into increasingly difficult straits, chasing about London attempting to deal with Satan and a group of subsidiary villains. The heroine is harder pressed—she is eventually murdered and her soul captured for Hell. A few minor characters wander about in catacombs underneath the city, but not to much effect. Ainsworth—and this is a unique incident in his career—has written himself into a corner. Many years later (1865) he completed the tale in a few hasty chapters so that it might be issued in book form. But the ending, as it stands, resolves nothing.

Auriol, having made a mess of his nineteenth-century existence, is seemingly transported back to 1599:

> "What can this mean?" he cried. "Have I endured a long and troubled dream, during which I have fancied myself living through more than two centuries?"
>
> "How else, if I were not mad, could I have believed that I had swallowed the fabled elixir vitae? And yet, is it a fable? for I am puzzled still. Methinks I am old—old—old—though I feel young, and look young. All this is madness. Yet how clear and distinct it seems! I can call to mind events in Charles the Second's time. Ha!—who told me of Charles the Second? How know I there was such a king? The reigning sovereign should be James, and yet I fancy it is George the Fourth. Oh! I am mad—clean mad!"
>
> (II, ii)

As this soliloquy progresses, some unknown person makes diabolical comments which imply that Auriol is the victim of a hoax. The novel ends on a note of uncertainty: "He persuaded himself, also, that he could distinguish through the gloom the venerable Gothic pile of Saint Paul's Cathedral on the other side of the water . . . he returned from the window, and said to his supposed grandsire, 'I am satisfied. I have lived centuries in a few nights'" (II, vi). The tentative language implies that the protagonist is the victim of a hoax but one

never learns what could motivate such a deception. All that can be deduced is that Auriol's sense of time has collapsed, leaving his mind in the state of that house on Vauxhall Road. Past and present are inextricably mixed, as they are in the rubble heap.

Neither protagonist nor author can resolve the dialectic of past and present as it bears on the life of the city. Indeed, after 1845 Ainsworth himself became increasingly a relic from the past. His attempt to come to terms with romantic French fiction (Hugo and then Sue) had been a failure. He was more and more looked on as a hopeless hack grinding out lifeless historical novels, an aimless eccentric without a place in the modern world: "I recall a pleasant dinner at Frederick Chapman's [wrote Percy Fitzgerald] . . . where were Forster and Browning. When the latter said casually, 'I met a strange, shabby creature to-day, which on examination resolved itself into Ainsworth,' Forster merely said in his most casual way, 'No, really, did you? God bless me!' and added nothing more."[6]

The notion of London's collapse, with which *Revelations* begins, embodies not only the personal dilemma of a minor Victorian writer but what was for Hugo, and others as well, a dilemma of modern consciousness: how does one *see* the nineteenth-century city? A passage in *Nôtre-Dame* approaches this problem through a description of medieval Paris:

> The spectator, on arriving, out of breath, upon this summit, was at first dazzled by the confusion of roofs, chimneys, streets, bridges, squares, spires, steeples . . . The gaze for some time was utterly bewildered by this labyrinth, in which everything had its particular originality, its reason, its genius, its beauty, everything had proceeded from art, from the most inconsiderable carved and painted house-front, with external timbers, low doorway, and stories projecting each above the other, to the royal Louvre itself, which, at that time, had a colonnade of towers. But here are the principal masses which were distinguished once the eye became accustomed to this tumult of structures.[7]

The pattern of this paragraph is repeated many times in the pages that follow. Hugo's hypothetical viewer is dazzled by the variety of the scene below, "yet that sea of harmony is no chaos." The appearance of chaos stems from the uniqueness of every element, the "particular originality" which calls from all sides for attention. Thus Hugo's description seems always on the point of breaking down, of disintegrating into a catalog which the mind cannot handle. But this never quite happens. The "geometry" of the city always reasserts itself so that one can understand this medieval metropolis as a whole, can see every element in its place.

In the process of thought I have just described, the mind maintains a perilous equilibrium. An important event in *Nôtre-Dame* is the breakdown of this equilib-

rium for Claude Frollo. An alchemist-priest, Frollo fills his cell with "all the rubbish of science." Even the walls are crowded with spells and calculations: "In Gothic, Hebrew, Greek, and Roman letters mixed together, inscriptions overflowed at random, one upon the other, the more recent effacing the more ancient, and all were entangled with each other, like the branches of a bush, or pikes in a melee. It was, indeed, a confused mingling of all philosophies, all human reveries, all human knowledge" (VII, iv). The alchemist's quest after universal knowledge has broken down; he is left sitting among the fragments of his labors, which no longer cohere. Soon Hugo reveals why. "One fixed idea possesses me and tortures my brain like a fire-iron" (VII, iv). The fixed idea is Esmeralda, with whom he has fallen in love.

It is typical of this novel that erotic obsession can be expressed topographically. Midway through *Nôtre-Dame* Frollo stands on the tower of the cathedral: "At his feet was all Paris with her thousand spires and her circular horizon . . . Yet in all that city, the archdeacon saw but one spot on its pavement—the Place du Parvis; in all that crowd, but one figure—the gypsy girl" (VII, ii). Hugo teaches his readers to perceive the geometry of Paris. But Frollo's obsession with Esmeralda blocks his ability to think and see this way. Whether he surveys the city or attempts to achieve absolute knowledge, her influence prevents his mind from functioning properly. "Do you know, young girl, what I always see between the book and me? It is you" (VIII, iv).

Occasionally Frollo is thrown from one extreme to the other; wandering the streets in a "state of hallucination," he perceives only "a chaos of undetermined objects all melting into each other" (IX, i). Paris, in this scene, becomes like the wall of the alchemist's cell. However, these two contrasting states of mind are ultimately symptoms of the same problem. Whether he sees too much or too little, Frollo has lost his ability to perceive the harmony of the world—particularly the human world of the city.

Frollo's moral disintegration is rapid. Esmeralda does not yield to him, and by the last chapter of the novel the priest has sent her to the gallows for her resistance. He watches from his tower as she is hanged, and Hugo again insists on the topography of Frollo's obsession: "In all that immense horizon, spreading around him so many different points of interest, his gaze was fixed only on one spot" (XI, ii). Completely wrapped up in the grisly scene below, Frollo fails to notice Quasimodo, who in a few moments will push him to his death.

The description of medieval Paris, with its subsequent echoes and variations, is one of the memorable passages in *Nôtre-Dame*. Ainsworth included a similar description of London in *Old Saint Paul's* but in comparison it is flat.[8] The writer who wanted to top Hugo's topographical vision would have to try a different kind of companion piece. What does the nineteenth-century city—London or Paris—look like in comparison with its medieval predecessor? This is the question Ainsworth begins to answer in *Revelations* but can never confront comprehensively.

Dickens had more success. After *Old Saint Paul's* and before *Revelations,* he constructed a worthy modern counterpart to Hugo's vista. In *Martin Chuzzlewit* Dickens takes his readers to the roof of Todgers' boarding house. As in medieval Paris the spectator is "dazzled by the confusion of roofs, chimneys, streets, bridges, squares, spires, steeples," so in Victorian London he is overwhelmed with "steeples, towers, belfries, shining vanes, and masts of ships." And the two vistas have a further similarity: every element in the landscape demands special attention. In the medieval scene, however, these conflicting bids for attention stem from the aesthetic integrity of each architectural detail. From Todgers' one perceives a mysterious jumble whose laws—aesthetic, moral, topographical—are unfathomable:

> After the first glance, there were slight features in the midst of this crowd of objects, which sprung out from the mass without any reason, as it were, and took hold of the attention whether the spectator would or no . . . The man who was mending a pen at an upper window over the way, became of paramount importance in the scene, and made a blank in it, ridiculously disproportionate in its extent, when he retired . . . Yet even while the looker-on felt angry with himself for this, and wondered how it was, the tumult swelled into a roar; the hosts of objects seemed to thicken and expand a hundredfold; and after gazing round him quite scared, he turned into Todgers's again, much more rapidly than he came out; and ten to one he told M. Todgers afterwards that if he hadn't done so, he would certainly have come into the street by the shortest cut: that is to say, headforemost.[9]

In *Nôtre-Dame* only Frollo is plagued with such visions, irrational obsession alternating with chaos. Dickens' onlooker, however, is not a distraught Gothic villain; he is nobody in particular and so sees what anyone would see. It appears, then, that Frollo's hallucinations have become the stuff of common life. Instead of a harmonious whole, the city is pandemonium. The final passage of Hugo's Parisian topography evokes the tremendous articulate symphony created by the bells of the medieval city. In modern London the tumult swells into a roar. Under this aural and visual assault, anyone can fall from the roof of Todgers'. A push from Quasimodo or a burden of guilt is not necessary.

The interplay between the view from Todgers' and Hugo's "Bird's-eye view of Paris" is elaborate. Not that these panoramas are unusual as such; the notion of see-

ing a city from the air was popular in the Victorian era.[10] But neither Hugo nor Dickens is concerned with bigness alone. Both are mainly interested in describing an act of seeing—an attempt to comprehend the complexity of an urban vista. Hugo would agree with Dickens that this is much more difficult in modern cities than in medieval ones. Paris, unlike London, had not grown overwhelmingly since medieval times, but it, too, had become a confusing and deceptive place, not merely containing pockets of chaos, like the old city, but living on that chaos and constantly remodeling itself according to principles obscure at best. For Hugo, modern Paris is salvageable only as one of those palimpsests in which the antiquary wanders and attempts to reconstruct an image of lost unity: "Project distinctly upon an azure horizon the Gothic profile of that old Paris; make its outline float in a wintry mist clinging to its innumerable chimneys; plunge it into deep night, and observe the fantastic display of the lights against the darkness of that gloomy labyrinth of buildings" (III, ii). This wonderful landscape cannot be recovered for more than a few instants, at least by the wanderer through the streets. What the modern age offers in place of architecture is books. If Frollo cannot integrate his thoughts because his mind is filled with a vision of Esmeralda, history is also working against him, as Hugo explains in the second edition of *Nôtre-Dame*.

This later edition contains a chapter not previously published (V, ii, "This Will Kill That") which sets forth explicitly a theory of civilization, of cultural transition. According to the theory, the late fifteenth century—when the events of *Nôtre-Dame* take place—is a turning-point of western culture. In these decades, building gives way to print as man's basic way of embodying his aspirations. Knowledge is no longer to be ordered by the communal authority and solidarity of cathedrals. Taking the form of print rather than stone, it explodes into a hundred diverse forms. Architecture, having ceased to be the master art, imitates this anarchy of inquiry and so the harmonies of Gothic Paris disintegrate into the eclecticism of the modern city. Paris, then, becomes a mere shadow of the "metropolis of universal thought," that "second tower of Babel" created by the printing press and by writing as an embodiment of culture.

This theory contributes to a debate that is still alive; compare Marshall McLuhan's speculations on literacy. It contributes also to *Nôtre-Dame* in particular, providing a framework for events and characters. An example is the opening scene of the novel, which takes place in the old Palace of Justice. The palace, Hugo notes, was to be destroyed in 1618 by a political intrigue:

> It is certain that if Ravaillac had not assassinated Henry IV, there would have been no documents about the trial of Ravaillac recorded in the registry of the Palace of

Justice, no accomplices interested in causing the disappearance of said documents, consequently no incendiaries obliged, for want of any better expedient, to burn the registry in order to burn the documents, and to burn the Palace of Justice in order to burn the registry—in short, no fire of 1618. The old palace would still be standing with its Great Hall, and I could say to the reader, "Go see it," and thus we would both be spared trouble—myself the trouble of writing, and him that of perusing, such a description. All of which proves this very novel truth—that great events have incalculable consequences.

(I, ii)

The destruction of the palace embodies in several ways Hugo's sense of the movements of history. The building is annihilated in a battle over written evidence, evidence generated by an assassination which had resulted from the rivalries between Catholic and Protestant. All this, Hugo says, points toward the modern world. The king, the palace, the unique documents (much more vulnerable than printed material) are each lost (III, i; V, ii). What remains, finally, is Hugo's lengthy and painstakingly antiquarian set piece. The words replace the palace, as the novelist observes with irony and delight. And what the first chapter does for this single lost building, *Nôtre-Dame* does for late medieval Paris. If the Book in some sense killed that city, this particular book can replace it, though only as one of many visions of Paris created by the artistic and historic imagination.

The dialectic of "This Will Kill That" stands behind many other passages in the novel. None are more central than those which describe Frollo's state of mind. The priest is troubled and ultimately destructive because he can live in neither the medieval nor the modern world. Caught at a turning point in history, he is too sensitive not to embody the contradictions of his age. For certain other characters this dilemma is quite distant. Quasimodo loves Nôtre-Dame "for the harmonies dwelling in the magnificent whole" and is thus able to use the cathedral as a field for heroic action (rescuing Esmeralda). Frollo, who is specifically contrasted with his foster child, attempts to grasp Nôtre-Dame as a form of knowledge—to *read* it—and this signals his fragmented, explosive consciousness of Paris and of other people:

> He had often been seen stealing along the Rue des Lombards, and furtively entering a small house at the corner of the two streets, Rue des Ecrivains and Rue Marivaux. This was the house Nicolas Flamel had built . . . which . . . was beginning to fall into ruin, so much had the hermetics and alchemists of all countries worn away its walls by simply carving their names on them. It was supposed that Flamel had buried the philosopher's stone in these cellars. Hence the alchemists for two centuries, from Magistri down to Father Pacifique, never ceased to turn the soil over until the house itself, so thoroughly ransacked, had at last crumbled into dust under their feet.

It is certain, too, that the archdeacon had been seized with a most singular passion for the symbolical doorway of Nôtre-Dame, that page of magic written in Stone by Bishop Guillaume de Paris, who has undoubtedly been damned for attaching so infernal a frontispiece to the sacred poem eternally sung by the rest of the structure . . . But what everyone might have remarked was the interminable hours Dom Claude would often spend . . . calculating the angle of vision of that crow which clings to the left side of the doorway, casting its eye upon a mysterious point within the church, where the philosopher's stone is surely hidden, if it be not in Nicolas Flamel's cellar.

(IV, v)

Frollo, Hugo implies, belongs to the occult tradition of late medieval Europe: a subversive tradition presaging the exploits of Faust. For the priest, then, Nôtre-Dame is no longer a coherent microcosm of the universe; it is an enigma to be understood fragmentarily if at all, by a heroic and yet twisted act of will. What knowledge Frollo acquires he would use as a means to political and financial power in a world ruled by men, not God (V, i). In his role as priest, he fears the Book. All the same, he searches eagerly for the philosopher's stone, both in Flamel's rapidly disintegrating house and in the cathedral itself. The latter structure, he discovers, is less delicate than the former. Not only do the secrets of alchemy elude him; he is destroyed by his erotic-alchemical quest and by the creature of a monument to the collective authority of the Church. This failure is absolute; Frollo is Faust too early.

The past-present opposition is much less explicit in *Martin Chuzzlewit*. But Dickens, without Hugo's concern for ideas, develops contrasts that feel similar to those governing *Nôtre-Dame*.

Among the narrow thoroughfares at hand, there lingered, here and there, an ancient doorway of carved oak, from which, of old, the sounds of revelry and feasting often came; but now these mansions, only used for storehouses, were dark and dull, and, being filled with wool, and cotton, and the like—such heavy merchandise as stifles sound and stops the throat of echo—had an air of palpable deadness about them.

To tell of half the queer old taverns that had a drowsy and secret existence near Todgers's, would fill a goodly book; while a second volume no less capacious might be devoted to an account of the quaint old guests who frequented their dimly-lighted parlours . . . These gentry were much opposed to steam and all new-fangled ways, and held ballooning to be sinful, and deplored the degeneracy of the times . . .

As to Todgers's itself . . . it was worthy to stand where it did. There was one staircase window in it: at the side of the house, on the ground-floor: which tradition said had not been opened for a hundred years at least, and which, abutting on an always dirty lane, was so begrimed and coated with a century's mud, that no one pane of glass could possibly fall out, though all were cracked and broken twenty times. But the grand mystery of Todgers's was the cellarage . . .

(Ch. ix)

One could mine from these passages a catalog of antiquarian motifs. The neighborhood is like Irving's Little Britain before its lapse into modernity.[11] Actually, in this case the lapse has already taken place, for behind the ancient doorways lurk warehouses. Change and antiquity live together in comfortable symbiosis; both are cryptic to the wandering stranger and perhaps to the inhabitants too.

Then—immediately following the passages just quoted—one goes upstairs and is met by the chaos of the rooftop. To a large extent this vista consists of the streets and buildings that from below seemed so comfortable. Comfort is now beside the point. The peculiar logic of accepting everything on its own terms because everything is cryptic emerges in an extreme form. No element in the landscape cooperates with any other. London explodes.

This explosion is not, precisely, the fragmentation of knowledge through the power of writing—especially print—which determines in *Nôtre-Dame* the form of the modern city. Hugo's theme is approached, however; first in Dickens' observation that "the man who was mending a pen at an upper window over the way, became of paramount importance in the scene, and made a blank in it, ridiculously disproportionate in its extent, when he retired," later in many other incidents: in the curious paradox of Pecksniff, the architect who can build only with words, despite his professions to the contrary ("My friends . . . My duty is to build, not speak . . . to deal with marble, stone, and brick: not language," Ch. xxxv); in the parallel saga of the Anglo-Bengalee Assurance Company, "with a 'branch' in a first floor over a tailor's at the west-end of the town, and main offices in a new street in the City . . . Anglo-Bengalee Disinterested Loan and Life Assurance Company . . . painted on the very coal-scuttles . . . repeated at every turn until the eyes are dazzled with it, and the head is giddy" (Ch. xxvii); in the city of Eden, which proves to exist mainly as a set of architectural plans; in Tom Pinch's bewildering introduction to London as it is embodied in the advertising columns of a newspaper ("Even those letters of the alphabet, who are always running away from their friends and being entreated at the top of columns to come back, never do come back," Ch. xxxvi); in Jonas' association between newspapers, guilt, and the dynamic of rumors and secrets in London life, first when he is procuring poison ("He was reading a newspaper when I went in . . . While he was speaking to me he still read the newspaper . . . All this time he still read the newspaper," Ch. xlviii) and later when he is on the verge of being caught for the murder of Montague Tigg:

He stopped at the window to think. An opposite shop was lighted up; and the tradesman and a customer were reading some printed bill together across the counter . . . Jonas looked out of the window again. They were still reading the printed paper in the shop opposite, and a third man had joined in the perusal . . . one of the three, who had been glancing over the shoulder of another, stepped back to explain or illustrate some action by his gestures.

Horror! How like the blow he had struck in the wood!

(Ch. li)

All of these scenes hint at a relationship between London and the explosive propagation of words, particularly printed words. That relationship is never stated as Hugo states it and never, one suspects, thought out. Such an effort would have to wait until later in Dickens' career. In one respect, though, Dickens is a step ahead of the author of *Nôtre-Dame*. If *Chuzzlewit* intuits the nature of the modern city, it also builds formally on that intuition. The view from Todgers' is like the experience of reading *Chuzzlewit,* or as Dickens himself says:

If a man habituated to a narrow circle of cares and pleasures, out of which he seldom travels, step beyond it, though for never so brief a space, his departure from the monotonous scene on which he has been an actor of importance, would seem to be the signal for instant confusion. As if, in the gap he had left, the wedge of change were driven to the head, rending what was a solid mass to fragments, things cemented and held together by the usages of years, burst asunder in as many weeks.

(Ch. xviii)

From Todgers' one views a scene at once interdependent (every part counts, though it cannot be said just how or why) and chaotic ("the hosts of objects seemed to thicken and expand a hundredfold"). This simultaneous impression of impenetrable unity and sudden fragmentation, of sharp focus amid an explosion of facts, can be transformed into a principle of plot, a principle with which Dickens has begun to experiment. For example, he takes great care to set contrasting milieux, then proceeds to make connections between them; the "Chuzzlewit—Pecksniff—Todgers—Gamp—Anglo-Bengalee inter-relation" becomes ever tighter, ever more complex until a series of revelations (old Chuzzlewit's impersonation, Jonas' plot, the Anglo-Bengalee fraud) brings the novel to an end.[12]

In what sense is *Martin Chuzzlewit* a response to *Nôtre-Dame*? Two possibilities suggest themselves. The novels may relate to each other by way of that nebulous entity, a climate of opinion. Many people, certainly, were concerned in the early nineteenth century with the growth of the city and with an alarming increase in the complexity of human institutions. Given this general interest, Hugo and Dickens might have been independently inspired to their bird's-eye views of Paris and London.

On the other hand, one can be bolder and argue for the possibility of a direct influence. In 1847 Dickens visited Hugo's home in Paris and observed that the great man's family "made a most romantic show [looking] like a chapter out of one of his own books."[13] The backdrop of this show ("grim old chairs and tables, and old canopies of state from old palaces") makes it likely that Boz was thinking of *Nôtre-Dame,* or at least had it in the back of his mind. The novel had been published in English as early as 1834; the translator was William Hazlitt, Jr., one of Dickens' colleagues on the *Morning Chronicle.* Perhaps Dickens read it then; there was a considerable fuss about the book, partly on irrelevant political grounds.[14] A few years later, some of Hugo's ideas and motifs began turning up in Dickens' novels. For Elizabeth Barrett, in 1842, a good example of the Frenchman's influence was the chapter in *Oliver Twist* describing Fagin's last hours—a steal, she felt, from *Les Derniers Jours d'un Condamné.* Shortly after, in *The Old Curiosity Shop,* Quilp is a malevolent version of Quasimodo (threatening Nell where his French counterpart protects Esmeralda) and the parallel is underlined by a sculptural metaphor applied to both.[15] Ainsworth, meanwhile, had been milking *Nôtre-Dame* for all it was worth. After *The Old Curiosity Shop,* and while Dickens was writing *Barnaby Rudge,* he published *Old Saint Paul's.* Dickens is likely to have looked into the serial, for like his own it featured a group of extreme Protestants intent on burning down London. *Old Saint Paul's* also featured a villainous partnership between an undertaker and a hard-drinking nurse, perhaps ancestors of Mrs. Gamp and Mr. Mould. Not that Dickens was merely pilfering from Ainsworth; if he used *Old Saint Paul's* at all, he converted its melodrama into mordant comedy.

Todgers', in the context of these other conjectured relationships, might have been another carry-over from Ainsworth. Or rather, *Old Saint Paul's* might have served as a reminder, a spark to bring back Hugo's great vista with its crowd of spires, its symphony of bells, its falling priest: elements brilliantly refocused in a few pages of *Martin Chuzzlewit.* This theory seems to me plausible, though I lack the evidence to prove it in any conclusive way.

Martin Chuzzlewit may derive directly from *Nôtre-Dame;* it certainly belongs to a tradition of the city novel which begins with the tale of Quasimodo. The first and perhaps the only person to acknowledge this continuity is Ruskin, in his comments on *Bleak House:* "But the effectual head of the whole cretinous school is the renowned novel in which the hunch-backed lover watches the execution of his mistress from the tower of Nôtre-Dame."[16] Ruskin's insight is brilliant yet a bit askew. He wants to link Dickens and Hugo in terms of shared morbidity—the novel of the city is the novel of death—but this is to ignore some essential aspects of

both authors. Hugo is writing about a preindustrial city and in spite of the extraordinary amount of suffering that occurs in his novel, Gothic Paris is presented as a good place to be—assuming, always, that one's mind functions in the proper way. Quasimodo's does, as I have suggested; Frollo's does not, and this is the source of his downfall.

Dickens, writing about a much later age, is faced with a different problem, though here again morbidity is largely beside the point. From Todgers' one loses one's sense of the way a landscape fits together but one gains the possibility of apprehending things never noticed before, of confronting the explosiveness and confusion of modern life through innovations in novelistic form. *Martin Chuzzlewit* promises this achievement; later novels fulfill it.

One can take exception to Ruskin's vituperative tone. There remains his perception of a link that really does exist, forged from one novel to another, one country to another, over the course of three decades. *Nôtre-Dame* fosters Eugène Sue's serial, which in its turn fosters replies from Hugo (*Les Misérables*) and Balzac (*Splendeurs et Misères des Courtisanes*) as well as a spate of English imitations. Two of Ainsworth's tries have been discussed in detail; shortly after *Revelations* came *The Mysteries of London* by G. M. Reynolds, previously a specialist in imitating Dickens. Lastly, Dickens made his own contribution to the genre, first with the tentative and partial experiments of *Martin Chuzzlewit,* later and much more thoroughly with *Bleak House,* which sums up this literature better than any other book, defining the physical experience of city life while exploring the base of writing on which it is built.

Notes

1. *Elizabeth Barrett to Miss Mitford,* ed. Betty Miller (London, 1954), p. 147.

2. *The Letters of Charles Dickens,* ed. Madeline House and Graham Storey, The Pilgrim Edition, I (Oxford, 1965), 358. For Ainsworth's offer, see n. 5 on the same page.

3. Ainsworth seems to have been thinking both of Pierce Egan's novels and of *Pickwick.* In the early forties Dickens did try, in *Master Humphrey's Clock,* something like the *Lions* formula. The attempt was a failure.

4. For a good, brief account of this relationship see Albert Thibaudet, *French Literature from 1795 to the Present* (New York, 1967), pp. 218, 222-23. For a good essay on Sue which curiously ignores Hugo, see Leslie Fiedler's introduction to *The Monks of Monks Hall* (New York, 1970). See also n. 16 below.

5. *Auriol or the Elixir of Life,* Author's Copyright Edition (London, n.d.), Bk. I, Ch. i. My references are to the book version of the magazine serial *Revelations of London,* since it contains a few extra chapters (see below). Hereafter cited in the text by book and chapter.

6. *Memories of Charles Dickens* (Bristol, 1913), p. 284.

7. *The Hunchback of Nôtre-Dame,* trans. Walter J. Cobb with an afterword by André Maurois, Signet Classics (New York, 1965), Bk. III, Ch. ii. Further references to this edition will appear in parentheses in the text.

8. Quite literally flat. "The whole of the city of London [writes Ainsworth] was spread out like a map before him" (Bk. II, Ch. vi). Hugo worked from maps also, yet was much better at describing the actual experience of looking down on a city.

9. *Martin Chuzzlewit,* ed. and introd. P. N. Furbank (Harmondsworth, England, 1968), Ch. ix. Further references to this edition will appear in parentheses in the text.

10. A few examples: [Robert Mudie], *Babylon the Great: A Dissection of Men and Things in the British Capital* (London, 1825), p. 11; David Masson, "Dead Men Whom I Have Known; or, Recollections of Three Cities: London from the Top of St. Paul's. Part I," *MacMillan's Magazine,* 12 (1865), 275-76; Henry Mayhew, "A View from St. Paul's," *Morning Chronicle,* Letters 1 and 57; *The Unknown Mayhew,* ed. Eileen Yeo and E. P. Thompson (New York, 1971), pp. 97-102; Henry Mayhew, "A Balloon View of London," *The Criminal Prisons of London and Scenes of Prison Life* (London, n.d.), pp. 7-10; "London at Night: Seen From the Summit of St. Paul's" (poem), *Ainsworth's Magazine,* 8 (July 1845), 86-89; "All Round St. Paul's," *All the Year Round,* 19 (April 4, 1868), 392. For a reference to Dickens' viewing of London "from the highest pinnacle of St. Paul's," see Edmund Yates, "London by Night," *The Train,* 2 (1856), 371. For some corresponding views of Paris from Nôtre-Dame, see Walter Benjamin, *Charles Baudelaire: A Lyric Poet in the Era of High Capitalism,* tr. Harry Zohn (London, 1973), pp. 84-86. For the most part (Mayhew is a partial exception), it was natural for Victorians to use St. Paul's as the place for a view over London; when Dickens chooses Todgers', there is—perhaps—a leap from sacred to secular.

11. Washington Irving, "Little Britain," in *The Sketch Book of Geoffrey Crayon, Gent.,* with an afterword by Perry Miller (New York, 1961). This essay, which anticipates some of the *Sketches by Boz,* comments with some cynicism on Irving's search for Olde England.

12. See Furbank's introduction to *Chuzzlewit* (especially p. 17) for an excellent discussion.

13. *The Nonesuch Dickens,* ed. A. Waugh, H. Walpole, W. Dexter, and T. Hatton, 23 vols., XII (Bloomsbury, 1937-38), 6 (*Letters* 2).

14. Kenneth Hooker, *The Fortunes of Victor Hugo in England* (New York, 1938), pp. 32-33.

15. Cf. *Nôtre-Dame,* Bk. VIII, Ch. vi with *The Old Curiosity Shop,* Ch. xxvii. In both cases a strange and deformed creature (Quilp/Quasimodo) seems to be a statue come to life.

16. "Fiction Fair and Foul-I," *The Works of John Ruskin,* ed. E. T. Cook and Alexander Wedderburn, 39 vols. (London, 1908), XXXIV, 277. This essay—first published in 1880 in *Nineteenth Century*—also mentions Eugène Sue.

Carol L. Bernstein (essay date December 1980)

SOURCE: Bernstein, Carol L. "Nineteenth-Century Urban Sketches: Thresholds of Fiction." *Prose Studies* 3, no. 3 (December 1980): 217-40.

[*In the following essay, Bernstein studies the dual nature of the nineteenth-century urban sketch as a literary form in which both the concrete and the conceptual visions of urban life are represented.*]

Writing about the city, especially since 1800, has been as heterogeneous as the city itself. On the one hand, there is an urban space which offers itself to the observer's gaze: that space is replete with objects, houses, crowds, vehicles, types of people, monuments of culture. Beyond the visible hover the abstractions—among them profession, disease, poverty, wealth—which constitute the urban ambiance. The presence of the material world, striking in daylight, may solicit attention even more in a nocturnal atmosphere, when those phenomena may also be veiled. On the other hand, the city may be the site of an encounter between mind and world. Engagement with the city seems to involve an act of reading or of 're-presentation,' even when the gaze is directed outward.[1] The city can be the locus for an act of self-recognition, as in Wordsworth's well-known encounter with the blind Beggar the *The Prelude,* or as in James's *The Princess Casamassima,* where London and Paris are most prominent because of the conflicting cultural claims they exert upon the mind of Hyacinth Robinson during his quest for identity.

Urban sketches share this heterogeneity. They include the polemical outcry against urban misery on the one hand, and the more dispassionate, sociologically oriented journalism—of a Mayhew, for example—on the other. Intersecting this plane of social orientation are the sketches apparently meant for entertainment, the products of a curious flâneur or wanderer about the city, the journalistic work of a Sala or the more imaginative pieces of Dickens. These are not two utterly distinct traditions, for each impinges upon the other: the image of society is apt to be a rhetorical product, shaped by the demands of language and form. Conversely, the fictional sketch is not immune to claims that it represents the actual city, that it reveals hidden or unknown aspects of the urban milieu, or that it expresses a certain ideology. The sketch offers a formal or thematic ground, as much as an historical or cultural one, for the encounter with the city. Its concern with particularity or locale memorializes an urban scene or scenario. But its very form tends to make its space abstract or conceptual. As in Foucault an "operating table" is both a real table and a *"tabula,* that enables thought to operate upon the entities of our world . . . the table upon which, since the beginning of time, language has intersected space," so the sketch, as the space for representing the experience of the city, looks towards both the concrete and the conceptual.[2] It is at once the locus of memory and the attempt to fix in the memory; it is the site of the picturesque and the ground for social outcry; it is the place of illusion and the loss of illusion; it marks the mysterious, unknown, and even uncanny aspects of the city and yet it reassures by externalizing one's anxieties about the city; it evokes a world of bourgeois materialism, and yet it gives free play to the imagination.[3] It seems to prefigure the novel, and yet its relation to the novel is characterized by displacement; as the materials of the sketch enter the larger world of the novel, for example, they often become peripheral. In a more general sense they offer figures for narrativity itself, texts in which the artist inscribes himself and appropriates the city. Any such exchange, however, must be predicated upon a form of representation, and it is in this area that the most basic problem of the sketch emerges.

I

Straightforward mimetic models for representing the city are in bad repute these days, and, as we shall see, there is good reason for considering nonfictional sketches as suspect as fictional sketches. As J. Hillis Miller has shown, if mimesis survives at all in Dickens's *Sketches by Boz,* it is only as imitation of what is itself inauthentic, so that "society" is not real but rather a series of repetitions of forms of behaviour, dress, and even "lives" which are always based on prior models which are fictive or conventional rather than historically grounded.[4] The city becomes, from this perspective, a text. The problematic for the writer then shifts: instead of "rendering" the materiality, the object-ness, the resistance of the city, the writer must read the signs, metaphors, representations-as-maps which the city offers. If it is strange or different, it is not because it contains

new or unknown aspects of reality but because it is, in effect, in a continual process of representing itself. Reading the city-as-text might bring one in touch with the material reality of the city—though there is some question whether this is even a desideratum for such an approach—but it is just as likely to involve one in a continual reading of signs which would never bring one to the true city, the 'true' point of origin. There is still another possibility, one which would involve a passage through mimesis, where the material objects, the 'flora and fauna' of the city, can be described, but must then be interpreted in terms which are in some way non-material or transcendent.[5] Whatever the representational strategy, it must be concerned with the choice of language. This precedes the additional problem of rendering the city culturally intelligible.

We can approach this problem of representation by examining a series of texts about London's slums. One way of regarding writing about the city has been to divide it into two traditions: serious description, especially of the poor and the slums, is opposed to a genre of low-life writing which originated considerably before the nineteenth century and which appears in such works as Pierce Egan's *Life in London* (1821) as well as in a number of books by such writers as G. H. A. Sala.[6] The phrase 'serious description' implies a high degree of representational accuracy, a subordination of the writer to the materials he must render in words. The low-life tradition, intended to entertain, would presumably allow more verbal freedom. Such a division depends in part upon motivation; the rhetorical differences are not so clearly antithetical. The fact that the material conditions of the poor beg to be recognized is also of some relevance.

P. J. Keating applies the term "social explorers" to the writers who investigated England's slums; many of the documents they produced focus on London.[7] For those who lived outside the slums, especially those of the East End, the slums were unknown territory, their inhabitants cast out from civilization. Andrew Mearns's *The Bitter Cry of Outcast London,* a pamphlet published in 1883, describes the conditions of the poor:

> Every room in these rotten and reeking tenements houses a family, often two. In one cellar a sanitary inspector reports finding a father, mother, three children, and four pigs! In another room a missionary found a man ill with small-pox, his wife just recovering from her eighth confinement, and the children running about half-naked and covered with dirt. Here are seven people living in one underground kitchen and a little dead child lying in the same room. Elsewhere is a poor widow, her three children, and a child who had been dead thirteen days. Her husband, who was a cabman, had shortly before committed suicide. Here lives a widow and her six children, including one daughter of 29, another of 21, and a son of 27. Another apartment contains father, mother and six children, two of whom

are ill with scarlet fever. In another nine brothers and sisters, from 29 years of age downwards, live, eat and sleep together. Here is a mother who turns her children into the street in the early evening because she lets her room for immoral purposes until long after midnight, when the poor little wretches creep back again if they have not found some miserable shelter elsewhere. Where there are beds they are simply heaps of dirty rags, shavings or straw, but for the most part these miserable beings find rest only upon the filthy boards. The tenant of this room is a widow who herself occupies the only bed, and lets the floor to a married couple for 2s 6d per week. In many cases matters are made worse by the unhealthy occupations followed by those who dwell in these habitations. Here you are choked as you enter by the air laden with particles of the superfluous fur pulled from the skins of rabbits, rats, dogs and other animals in their preparation for the furrier. Here the smell of paste and of drying match-boxes, mingling with other sickly odours, overpowers you; or it may be the fragrance of stale fish or vegetables, not sold on the previous day, and kept in the room overnight. Even when it is possible to do so the people seldom open their windows, but if they did it is questionable whether much would be gained for the external air is scarcely less heavily charged with poison than the atmosphere within.[8]

A passage like this one presents its horrors straightforwardly enough. The catalogue amasses its representative horrors, not overly visual in its detail, but strongly anchored to the visual and the present by the localizing repetition of "Here." The judgmental words are few, and of a similar cast: "miserable," "immoral," "poison." In fact, their proximity to such terms as "unhealthy" and "sickly," themselves coming after words denoting actual sickness, suggests that judgment and fact are closely interrelated. Moral and physical pestilence become virtually indistinguishable; even description may be fully understood within the framing metaphors of corruption and exploration.

The image of travel and exploration of the city has both cultural and literary antecedents, although the interpretive possibilities vary. Sidonia's advice to Coningsby to travel not to the ancient world but to Manchester places that city among the wonders of the world.[9] Wilderness and sea as metaphors for the city may be more ambiguous—they appear in Balzac—insofar as they are outside the pale of moral civilization.[10] But when a part of the city, a part that is literally adjacent to the world of the explorers, becomes the unknown, there are further and even more serious implications. Thus in *The Bitter Cry of Outcast London* Andrew Mearns writes, "the churches are making the discovery that seething in the very centre of our great cities, concealed by the thinnest crust of civilization and decency, is a vast mass of moral corruption, of heart-breaking misery and absolute godlessness, and that scarcely anything has been done to take into this awful slough the only influences that can purify or remove it" (92). The heart of darkness lies not in

the Congo, but in London. Yet there is a "gulf" between the lowest classes and civilization, and a "TERRIBLE FLOOD OF SIN AND MISERY" threatens to engulf those who are on the side of decency and civilization and religion (92). Such figures are, on the one hand, enabling: they mark the space of exploration in a new way and suggest, at the very least, an altered focus. If, in addition, urban objects do signify beyond their materiality, Mearns has provided the allegorical figure which will interpret the scenes of misery he describes. An urban pilgrim, he comes upon the Slough of Despond. The flood, a literary as well as a Biblical figure of engulfment, threatens to destroy the city. Mearns reveals his interpretive strategy at the beginning of the pamphlet: it moves any perspective on the city beyond the visual—and it is the visual that Mearns finds difficult to convey. What might be a gentler mode of expression in other contexts becomes a comment on the inadequacy of representation: "The misery and sin caused by drink in these districts have often been told, but these horrors can never be set forth either by pen or artist's pencil" (98).[11] The reader may be shocked by all the instances he names; nevertheless, Mearns has "sketched only in faintest outline." Truth requires, paradoxically, the artistic heightening that the writer cannot supply.

> Far more vivid must be our colours, deeper and darker far the shades, if we are to present a truth picture of 'Outcast London'; and so far as we have been able to go we are prepared with evidence, not only to prove every statement, but to show that these statements represent the general conditions of thousands upon thousands in this metropolis.

> (105)

The writer's predicament is analogous to that of the workers in the slums, where "the misery they actually see suggests to them the certain existence of so much more which no human eye discovers" (102). Such metonymies stand in danger of being overwhelmed by the untold horrors they signify, as those horrors threaten to overwhelm workers and writer alike; all three become mediating figures for the deluge that threatens civilization itself. Such bleak allegories become limiting and demonic instances of an urban sublime.

In this precarious situation, language stands outside the series of the deluge: released from the constraints of mimesis, or of metonymy, it is a bulwark against the flood. Mearns finds that he can describe the "human rookeries," the "lower depths" to readers who have no prior conceptions of such misery only by approaching the horrors through other forms of figurative language. Slum conditions are worse than the lair of a wild animal, more like "the middle passage of the slave ship" (94). Language itself can only be a form of displacement. "What goes by the name of a window" has no adequate signifier in civilized discourse. If "putrifying

carcases of dead cats or birds" can be named, the "viler abominations" that surpass them are blanketed in abstraction. Paratactical phrasing emphasizes the ubiquity of filth: "it is exuding through cracks in the boards overhead; it is running down the walls; it is everywhere" (95). The "sickly air" is the prelude to a grim fantasy: "The buildings are in such miserable repair as to suggest the thought that if the wind could only reach them they would soon be toppling about the heads of their occupants" (95). Figurative or rhetorical strategies like these allow Mearns to present the "facts" which compose a "revolting spectacle," a "ghastly reality" which transcends any meretricious drama which "spectacle" might imply.[12] In fact, many of the essays of the social explorers stress the necessity for spectators, for the lives of the poor must be seen, indeed confronted, as appalling spectacles. But Mearns's writing, at least, suggests a puzzling inference: the language of representation can only exist in oblique relation to that which it represents; that very obliquity, however, enables Mearns to find meaning in the visual, to escape an apparent impasse. Thus Mearns ends by denying the primacy of ocular vision in favour of a vision of God. One's eyes can convince one that there is nothing illusory about the condition of the poor. But since such sights can only be signs of a more general situation, the imagination must reach out as the heart must be moved. This is a step towards the still higher vision of a compassionate God.

Thus Mearns's progress through the slums is framed by the threat of apocalypse on the one hand and the reassuring vision of God on the other. This vision of sin blames slumlords, drink and poverty itself—not atypically—though from a contemporary perspective, temperance and religion will seem like somewhat naive and even indirect solutions. (Only one passage in *The Bitter Cry of Outcast London* treats the necessity for the state to institute reforms.) Indeed, there seems to be a somewhat paradoxical thrust to Mearns's pamphlet. On the one hand, it attempts to make accessible, for purposes of social reform, what is vile and unknown—in ways that may shock but not alienate the nineteenth-century reader. On the other hand, the very metaphorical frame that displaces the visual has some startling implications. The distinction between "civilization" and "slough" or "wild animal's lair" or "middle passage of a slaveship," is double-edged, for instead of focussing on a common humanity, it seems rather to emphasize the division between civilization and savagery, 'we' and 'they.'[13] Reform may be tantamount to 'purification' or 'conversion.' It appears, therefore, that the only place to rescue the savages is into the very system that 'produced' them: there is no interrogation of the premises of that civilized system. If that initial image of Mearns suggested something like a volcano, "seething" beneath "the thinnest crust of civilization," and raised the possibility of revolution, that possibility has been avoided by an alternative metaphor.[14]

Even the most factual representation of the city—and there are many essays like Mearns's on outcast London—is apt to be embedded in an ideology. That it should often be Christian should not be surprising.[15] Social reform is conceived of in the context of religious responsibility—of rescuing the heathen; but since the language of such reforming tracts distributes sin indifferently among the poor and, say, their landlords, or among gin and its imbibers, it becomes that much more difficult to identify, in order to eradicate, the evils of the East End. If "Babylon" was so widespread as to be virtually a dead metaphor for London, it was also a blanket metaphor. Yet Mearns's confession that language is inadequate to describe what he has seen could be a sign of a different cultural predicament. There is the concern for the sensibilities of readers who have no prior acquaintance with the dark vision of the slums: thus the attempt to cross boundaries gradually in order to allow for a type of recognition that violence could only thwart. But to cross boundaries gradually can be reduced to a variant of extending the bounds of civilization; there seems to be an underlying desire for cultural preservation, a desire to show the adequacy of traditional ways of thinking about society. Reform goes hand in hand with charity; in both enterprises, Christian sympathy can recognize proximity and at the same time preserve a certain distance.

A similar admixture of horror and 'conservatism' appears in the language of a classic piece of occasional journalism by James Greenwood, "A Night in a Workhouse."[16] Greenwood has himself admitted to the Lambeth workhouse one wintry night in the guise of a pauper come to seek a night's shelter. His identity is known neither to the staff nor to the paupers. Greenwood observes himself along with the paupers: he must eat the meagre food and spend the night on a mattress in an unheated shelter that is not entirely closed in. But his language places him at a more distanced point of judgment; the inmates are divided into the "decent poor" and the "blackguards"; those who will not turn the wheel in the morning to mill flour for their food and lodging are condemned as "lazy." There are, in addition, certain "unnamed horrors" which he cannot mention to his middle-class readers. Nevertheless, two "quiet elderly gentlemen" are received back into thinking humanity by virtue of their discussion on "the merits of the English language" (52). Yet Greenwood is as sensitive as Mearns to "outcast humanity," here "lying around you like covered corpses in a railway shed." His catalogue of the coughs he hears while he lies on his mattress can surely be read as an ironic commentary on the finer urban discriminations.[17]

Greenwood's account of his experience relies upon an order of fact, but at the same time that experience becomes meaningful in the light of certain conventional attitudes. The division into good and evil is less absolute than socially determined: Greenwood's terms invite a Nietzschean reading.[18] (It is possible to claim, for example, that society owes its paupers food and shelter, rather than that the paupers must pay for them with their own labour; ironically, the term "outcast" places the paupers in the position of victims.) It is Greenwood who makes certain acts and language unnameable except in the category of the unnameable: "I have avoided the detail of horrors infinitely more revolting than anything that appears in these papers" (54). By making the world of the outcast unspeakable, or by 'speaking' it in certain figures, Greenwood affirms the very distance that he intends to diminish. The possibility arises, then, that figurative language in non-fictional contexts becomes a form of displacement. The language which ought to convey the concrete or to affirm the real becomes locked into a social contract. Perhaps no forms of language can neutrally represent a world that contains the 'Other' which is the object of exploration. But the tendency to exclude ("I had seen the show—gladly I escaped into the open streets") or to divide (into missionaries and heathen, for example), or to employ terms which have an unexpected ironic resonance ("outcast" London) results in a paradox within the very figures of social exploration. The word "outcast," for example, is extremely appropriate for a group which is barred from the benefits of nineteenth-century "progress"; those who use it demand that society take responsibility for those who are cast out, but not for having cast them out. There is a certain process of creating victims, to which society is blind. In a sense, moving forward into the unknown results in an impasse, for the reader has certain limited choices. He may (1) imagine the unnamed horrors of the slums; (2) accept the report on trust without necessarily imagining greater horrors; (3) or meditate on the necessary gap between language and representation. One might say that it is only if one assumes a mode of linear argument, one which allows for 'pure' motives and straightforward reforms, that such problems arise. What the novels and sketches attest to in their very language is the complexity and ambivalence of societal self-knowledge on the one hand, and of knowledge of society on the other. It is because of this that allegorical or quasi-allegorical models for urban representation in the nineteenth century often seem both powerful and inadequate at the same time.

One might argue that reforming intentions, simply because they point to action, would always demand an interpretive stance towards the city in order to make it intelligible. An attempt merely to exhibit the city might bring us closer to pure representation. A sketch of St. Giles, a notorious rookery or slum, by George Henry Augustus Sala, is in this category. A number of Sala's books—*Twice Round the Clock, Gaslight and Daylight, London Up to Date*—have the ostensible purpose of recording London life. Sala's exploratory stance is, on the surface, less selective and more rudimentary; in a sense

he does not need to explore because he is assailed by the sights, sounds, and objects of St. Giles.

> Where the long lane from St. Giles's to the Strand divides the many-branching slums; where flares the gas over coarse scraps of meat in cheap butchers' shops; where brokers pile up motley heaps of second-hand wares—from fishing-rods and bird-cages to flat-irons and blankets; from cornet-à-pistons and 'Family Encyclopaedias' to corkscrews and fowling-pieces; where linen-drapers are invaded by poorly-clad women and girls, demanding penn'orths of needles, ha'porths of buttons, and farthing-worths of thread; where jean stays flap against door jamps, and 'men's stout hose' gleam gaunt in the shop-windows; where grimy dames sit in coal and potato-sheds, and Jew clothesmen wrestle for the custom of passengers who don't want to buy anything; where little dens, with reminders of à-la-mode beef and hot eel soup, offer suppers, cheap and nasty, to the poor in pocket; where, in low coffee-shops, newspapers a fortnight old, with coffee-cup rings on them, suggest an intellectual pabulum, combined with bodily refreshment; where gaping public-houses receive or disgorge their crowds of tattered topers; where 'general shops' are packed to overflowing with heterogenous odds and ends—soap, candles, Bath brick, tobacco, Dutch cheese, red herrings, firewood, black lead, streaky bacon, brown sugar, birch brooms, lucifer matches, tops, marbles, hoops, brandy balls, pockets of cocoa, steel pens, cheap periodicals, Everton toffy, and penny canes; where on each side, peeping down each narrow thoroughfare, you see a repetition only of these scenes of poverty and misery; where you have to elbow and jostle your way through a teeming, ragged, ill-favoured, shrieking, fighting population—by oyster-stalls and costermongers' barrows—by orange-women and organ-grinders—by flower-girls and match-sellers—by hulking labourers and brandy-faced viragos, squabbling at tavern-doors—by innumerable children in every phase of weazened, hungry, semi-nakedness, who pullulate at every corner, and seem cast up on the pavement like pebbles on the sea-shore. Here, at last, we find the hostelry of the three golden balls, where the capitalist, whom men familiarly term 'my uncle,' lends money.[19]

Syntactic structure virtually recedes before the onslaught of language in this passage. There is, to be sure, some structure: the broader catalogue has its subdivisions, as the supper dens, coffee-shops, and public-houses, each with its separate list of characteristics; or there are the antitheses, somewhat spurious in this context, of the oyster-stalls and costermongers' barrows, orange-women and organ-grinders. All phrases are subordinate to 'where,' which offers only a temporary closure to the sheer crowdedness of the scene; that 'where' will be repeated in all the side streets. The real 'closure,' which can promise only a deferral of misery, lies in the pawn-broker's shop, that place to which, it is implied, all objects will go. The very 'structure' of the passage makes the point for Sala: the catalogue, indiscriminately mingling people and objects, makes him passive, almost an object. He is, in fact, inundated with language. Words and objects are held in uneasy suspen-

sion, on the edge of linguistic and social chaos. What the passage points to, then, is the sheer difficulty of any pure representation of the city; here the assumption is that the city is a collection of objects and rituals: the objects exist as spatial adjuncts to the activities, repeated nightly, of wrestling, demanding, squabbling, etc. This vision of the surface is itself a dubious key to adequate representation; to assume that each object and each action must be represented by a specific word is to put oneself in the power of an endless cascade of language. Even if one were to posit some sort of closure by the representation of a segment of the city, more or less homogeneous and ordered, there remains the possibility of a continuing series of segments, limited only by the totality of objects and actions, of further conceivable series, in the city itself. (Mayhew's massive *London Labour and the London Poor* indicates something about the length of such representation-by-segment, especially if one adds, to the descriptions of each class of worker in those four volumes, the additional essays by Mayhew on the life of the poor.)[20] A completed project in these terms is, of course, inconceivable. We might, therefore, seek another motivation for such a complex catalogue. One possibility is that the catalogue represents the sheer heterogeneity of the raw materials that the writer must then order.[21] It becomes in this way a figure for representation itself. Catalogues, especially in prose, seem to occupy a space between recording what is and offering somewhat rudimentary figures for order. Yet Sala's catalogue suggests still another possibility. The lane along which Sala walks contains a type of life which is to be found in all the side streets: it thus stands in a metonymic relation to the area. It represents the repetition of the vitality as well as the forms of tension that are to be found in St. Giles. If children are like pebbles cast up by the tide, they will also be dragged by the tide to those side streets of repeated, though unseen, existence. Beyond the initial disorder, therefore, the passage makes the lane into a focal point for the slum life that surrounds it. Sala's own position is, however, a curious and self-effacing one, aside from the reference to having to "elbow and jostle." That very phrase, along with the allusion to the tide, carries us back to the theme of inundation; it threatens the neutrality of the observer. No more than Greenwood or Mearns is he immune from some atmospheric contagion, albeit in a less 'cosmic' context. Here the stakes involve autonomy and linguistic control: the writer is in danger of being displaced from the scene.

How, then, can one assert one's presence and control? One way is to invoke what is absent; Sala tries this method in a passage about third-class railway passengers:

> The seven o'clock trainbands are not exactly of the class who drink sherry and play cards; they are more given to selling walnuts than to eating them. They are,

for the most part, hard-faced, hard-handed, poorly-clad creatures; men in patched, time-worn garments; women in pinched bonnets and coarse shawls, carrying a plenitude of baskets and bundles, but very slightly troubled with trunks or portmanteaus. You might count a hundred heads and not one hat box; of two hundred crowding round the pay-place to purchase their third-class tickets for Manchester, or Liverpool, or even further north, you would have to look again, and perhaps vainly after all, for the possessor of a railway rug, or even an extra overcoat. Umbrellas, indeed, are somewhat plentiful; but they are not the slim, aristocratic trifles with ivory handles and varnished covers—enchanter's wands to ward off the spells of St. Swithin, which moustached dandies daintily insert between the roof and the hat-straps of first-class carriages. Third-class umbrellas are dubious in colour, frequently patched, bulgy in the body, broken in the ribs, once much given to absence from the nozzle. Swarming about the pay-place, which their parents are anxiously investing, thirteen-and-fourpence or sixteen-and-ninepence in hand, are crowds of third-class children. I am constrained to acknowledge that the majority of these juvenile travellers cannot be called handsome children, well-dressed children, even tolerably good-looking children. Poor little wan faces you see here, overshadowed by mis-shapen caps, and bonnets nine bauble square; poor little thin hands, feebly clutching the scant gowns of their mothers; weazened little bodies, shrunken little limbs, distorted often by early hardship, by the penury which pounced on them—not in their cradles—they never had any—but in the baker's jacket in which they were wrapped when they were born, and which will keep by them, their only faithful friend, until they die, and are buried by the parish—poor ailing little children are these, and among them who shall tell how many hungry little bellies! Ah! judges of Amontillado sherry; crushers of walnuts with silver nut-crackers; connoisseurs who prefer French to Spanish olives, and are curious about the yellow seal; gay riders in padded chariots; proud cavaliers of blood-horses, you don't know how painfully and slowly, almost agonisingly, the poor have to scrape, and save, and deny themselves the necessaries of life, to gather together the penny-a-mile fare.

(61-2)

This passage contains more figurative and rhetorical developments than the previous one. The railway journey allows Sala to envisage the journey of life; the evocation of an absent upper class provides the contrasting elements for a rigid social system which closes out the possibility of another fate for the poor. The imagining of what is absent cancels out, in effect, the depiction of the scene in merely picturesque terms. The social conscience of the railway passage, however sentimental, is prominent compared with the virtually parenthetical conscience in the description of St. Giles, where poverty and misery are items in a catalogue. In the passage on the slum, Sala's world of surfaces, of plenitude become congestion, of a variety so intense that it is on the verge of collapsing back into sameness, disallows the dominance of any ideational system. The very materiality of the city blocks other forms of awareness in a moment of a strange urban anti-sublime. Like Greenwood, Sala has crossed a threshold into an unknown part of the city; but where Greenwood maintains his sense of identity by adhering to convention, Sala suspends overt interpretation: reduced to a figure elbowing his way through the crowd, he becomes, in some minimal way, his own double.[22]

Sala's description of St. Giles demonstrates the dangers and seductions of objectivity, as it leads the narrating consciousness close to self-effacement. But self-effacement can, in the end, be a figure of concealment which calls attention to itself. Even the non-fictional representation of the city, therefore, is likely to implicate the figure of a narrator who traverses the scene, more or less obscured. While it may be threatened, his stance is always privileged, in the simple sense that he possesses a mobility, a difference, a capacity to withdraw and enter at will. Thus the figures of disguise, the protean narrative personae, are so appropriate for the urban artist. Sala, moreover, places himself in an explicit relation to fiction; *Twice Round the Clock* is dedicated to Augustus Mayhew, whose novel, *Paved with Gold,* incorporates episodes which are "picturesque but eminently faithful photographs of fact."[23] Some of those "photographs" had first appeared as Mayhew's contributions to his brother Henry's documentary *Life and Labour of the London Poor.* The descriptions of a rat fight; of the life of chimney sweeps, into whose society the protagonist enters for a time; of the watercress trade, a marginal occupation which becomes symbolic of the threshold between a life of crime and a life of honest poverty (crime becomes, on this scale, a limiting economic condition)—all are incorporated nearly verbatim into the text of the novel.[24] It is not irrelevant that Sala himself had connections with Dickens's circle, for in parts of his books he abandons the perspective of the journalist to adopt a more comic or fanciful mode that is apparently derived from the *Sketches by Boz.* Sala, who casts himself as Asmodeus, peering through the rooftops of London, assumes a persona which appears in a number of contemporaneous novels.[25] The writer thus places himself in a border zone between fiction and fact.

The impetus towards narrative or fiction appears to be, in the sketches, nearly irresistible. Some of James Grant's begging-letter writers in *Sketches of London* are master fiction-makers, proto-novelists.[26] In other sketches in that book, the workhouse and the debtors' prisons turn into the sites not only of biography but also of romance. All of these instances would support the familiar thesis that writers were finding in the city an ever-widening range of raw materials, and that in that urban setting the presumably superior claims of truth could accommodate themselves to the felicities of romance. Nevertheless, such work embodies a problematic which seems to oppose the possibilities of narra-

tive. The very materiality of the city, especially as Sala conveys it in his sketches, suggests something close to a fixation upon objects. To represent the city in all its object-ness could become an exercise in description, a survey of urban objects whose only meaning lies in their plenitude. There is no necessary connection between description and narrative, as Lukács argues so persuasively; it is the novelist's task to endow the object world with some authentic human signification which in turn enables narrative to develop.[27] But to write truthfully about the city seems to entail a commitment to the visible—at whatever cost to narrative relevance—or to that which is most striking about the city: monuments, theatres, distinct professions. Thus the writer would be as much threatened by, as supported with, an endless progression of observed details, whether they appear as catalogues or as more sophisticated descriptions of street markets, slums, railway stations, lawyers. The street elevation, which appears in certain nineteenth-century documents, is from this perspective a more complex and abstract form of the catalogue or the outside view.[28] Significantly, it appears in early parts of the *Sketches by Boz,* as an image for the external and proprietary interest in the city; then later it is transformed, in "Shops and their Tenants," into a metaphor for the imaginative history of the city. But this is to anticipate. In the various forms of the catalogue, the city is observed from a spatial and synchronic perspective. The urban carnival of objects and signs, to which the recurring descriptions of fairs and theatres in urban sketches testify, presents that challenge to narrative which Wordsworth at the very least anticipated in the seventh book of *The Prelude.*

Thus Sala, despite his professed allegiance to an ideal which blends fact with romance, stands on a threshold which would resist his crossing. The passage on St. Giles reveals, we remember, a certain lack of discrimination not only in the catalogues, but in the lack of syntactical closure. As the figure who elbows his way through the crowd, Sala quite literally lacks the perspective which would enable him to organize his notations into more than a tableau. Lukács' comments on the novel which employs the descriptive mode are applicable to Sala, for whom the "contemporaneity of description transforms the novel into a kaleidoscopic chaos."[29] But the alternative contained in the railway station passage is only a shade more promising. There the interplay between presence and absence, the modified antithesis between high life and low life, and the allusion to narrativity, seem to organize the chaotic matter of the city, to present an ethical stance, and to give meaning to the life of the crowd. Certain great Victorian paintings of crowds, including those of Frith, embody the principle that Sala seems on the verge of actualizing, that of the individual destiny emerging from the undifferentiated mass.[30]

Yet the obstructions to narrative in Sala are equally great. One is the sheer dominance of convention. We can see this indirectly by a glance at one of the most popular texts of the nineteenth century, Pierce Egan's *Life in London,* first published in 1821. Egan's book recounts the 'adventures' in London of the country cousin, Jerry, who comes to visit his city cousin, Tom. But although it has been called the archetypal urban novel of the early nineteenth century, the adventures are little more than excuses for the copious descriptions of the language and rituals of high life and low life in London.[31] For example, a chapter on Almack's, that exclusive weekly assembly to which only the most favoured received invitations from a committee of controlling matrons, is followed by one on All-Max, the site of a riotous gathering at the other end of town—and of the social scale. Entertaining as it was—and still is—the dominant structure of the book is spatial. Its art excludes the middle: a middle line of narrative as well as the middle class. If every place evokes its opposite, or the present poor suggest the absent rich, then the city becomes a closed system. While the contrasts are not so stark, Sala's sketches imply a similar order. Even the 'typical' narrative, exemplified in the life of the poor child, becomes, despite its gesture towards temporality, part of that system. Thus the concern for representing the city in its various aspects, for finding some principle of order, for displaying the typical, can be as much a threat to fictionality as the apparently undifferentiated kaleidoscopic 'presence' of the city. If any text on the city must inevitably move away from the neutral point of absolute imitation, then some directions might be less propitious for fiction than others. If conventions like the antithesis between high life and low life are to work, it may be that some different mode of representation is necessary.

II

While this brief survey of non-fictional sketches does not call into question their documentary status, it should be clear that even writing with the strongest referential motives and leanings finds a 'purely' descriptive language impossible and slips inevitably towards figure. There are, of course, major consequences for an understanding of the novel, since the documents used to measure the novel's historical veracity or the fictional departures from history now appear themselves to be displaced from absolute fact. Previously, one might have said that the description of Jacob's Island in *Oliver Twist,* measured against Mayhew's journalistic report on that notorious slum, or Dickens's description of Tom-all-Alone's in *Bleak House,* compared to a documentary rendering by Mearns or Sims or Booth of any East End slum, would make Dickens's rhetoric, now referentially anchored, seem less exaggerated.[32] The procedures for determining a level of rhetoric or fictionality which distinguishes the novel from non-fiction

still have some value, but one would also have to consider the alternative possibility of a common resort to figural representation. At the same time, the sketches reveal ideological assumptions which endow the urban scene with meanings which are both comprehensive and yet disputable from the perspective of the reader.

These remarks indicate how easily the city may come to be regarded as a storehouse of images for the novelist. This is, to be sure, no peculiar distinction of the city. Nevertheless, it is a matter of history that the nineteenth-century novel gradually extended its scope to include urban scenes and characters that had been beyond its notice previously. But as soon as those images appear in the sketches they become, in effect, prior texts. In its first appearance in written discourse the city becomes, as it were, textualized. But merely to say this is to repeat a commonplace and to ignore the problems that arise from this heap of available images. These are the heterogeneity and the conventions we have already observed: one pole represents chaos, the other a closed system. From neither pole does the transition to temporality seem easily negotiated. The collections of nineteenth-century sketches offer a view of the city as more or less fixed in its rituals, endlessly amassing objects. The spatial spread of the city becomes one more perverse figure for the spatiality of urban representation, fixed in maps as in all other conventional notations. The form of the sketch might revel in its distinctiveness; but it might also seem doomed to the wilderness, forever in sight of the promised land of fiction but forever barred from it. Such an Arnoldian perspective overlooks the possibility that Dickens realizes in the *Sketches by Boz*. One might want to claim that since most of the urban sketches were written later than those of Dickens, they are regressive rather than problematic from the perspective of fiction. But insofar as the problem of representation is not necessarily temporal in itself, we can think of the sketches as forming a play of forces that generates illuminating contrasts.

Suppose we look at the issue in another way. It might seem as if the discussion thus far has served not only to call into question the innocence of the non-fictional sketch, but also to assert its pre-fictional qualities, or, at the very least, its compatibility with more overtly fictional modes of representation. We would thus be on some linear course where the differences among urban sketches would be a matter of degree: all of them would be more or less ideologically motivated, more or less metaphorical, more or less systematic in their presentation of urban matters. But it is precisely at this point that we would be justified in doing a double-take, in breaking the line. For instead of an easy slide into fiction, we encounter a problematic of fiction, a by-product, as it were, of the perspective from the fictional end. One need not discard the metaphors and catalogues, or the exuberance and latent violence of the material

crowding or linguistic plenitude: all of these are elements in fiction. Nevertheless, neither the strict observance of convention, or metaphor-become-convention, nor the sheer giving of oneself to the matter of the city, promises an easy transition to narrative. Rather they would seem to result in some rigid antithesis, some perpetual stand-still between self and the city-as-Other, or an obliteration of self within an urban milieu. What we need is some breaking of the figure, some swerve into an alternative stance towards the city. And this is what we find in Dickens. His sketches project the forms of displacement in two senses. First, those very factors on the original line which seemed to be precursors of fiction now appear, but in a somewhat oblique fashion; metaphor has a different quality, and conventions, like illusions, are as often as not played with or violated. But this is still to note what we might find, so to speak, on the surface of the text. If we think of the sketches as embodying some tendency towards narrative about the city, then a second form of displacement appears when we move from the urban explorers and journalists to Dickens. Here the terms of interpretation change, and with them the relation of narrator, or Boz, to the city. In this second form of interpretation, this second swerve, we find the emblem of a genuine urban narrative.

It should be apparent that the theme of urban exploration is implicated with a thematics of the maze: Mearns's repeated "Here," which serves in one way to dislocate, Sala's repetitive side-streets, and even Greenwood's sense of relief at leaving the workhouse with its unfamiliar topography—all testify to the experiences of dislocation, disorientation or entrapment for which the maze is the emblem. Dickens's "Seven Dials" makes explicit those balancing motifs:

> Look at the construction of the place. The gordian knot was all very well in its way: so was the maze of Hampton Court: so is the maze at the Beulah Spa: so were the ties of stiff white neckcloths, when the difficulty of getting one on was only to be equalled by the apparent impossibility of ever getting it off again. But what involutions can compare with those of Seven Dials? Where is there such another maze of streets, courts, lanes, and alleys. . . . The stranger who finds himself in 'The Dials' for the first time, and stands Belzoni-like, at the entrance of seven obscure passages, uncertain which to take, will see enough around him to keep his curiosity and attention awake for no inconsiderable time. From the irregular square into which he has plunged, the streets and courts dart in all directions, until they are lost in the unwholesome vapour which hangs over the house-tops, and renders the dirty perspective uncertain and confined; and lounging at every corner, as if they came there to take a few gasps of such fresh air as has found its way so far, but is too much exhausted already, to be enabled to force itself into the narrow alleys around, are groups of people, whose appearance and dwellings would fill any mind but a regular Londoner's with astonishment.

· · · · ·

The peculiar character of these streets, and the close resemblance each one bears to its neighbour, by no means tends to decrease the bewilderment in which the unexperienced wayfarer through 'the Dials' finds himself involved. He traverses streets of dirty, straggling houses, with now and then an unexpected court composed of buildings as ill-proportioned and deformed as the half-naked children that wallow in the kennels.[33]

The fact that the Seven Dials is a slum emerges only after a meditation on mazes and a comment on the uncertainty and astonishment experienced by the stranger who confronts this maze and is unable to interpret it. The series to which the Seven Dials belongs—gordian knots, Hampton Court, neckcloths—demands the placing of this new member. At the same time, the stranger, himself a slight enigma, seems almost to displace the unwholesome vapours, to find his way into the labyrinth along with the fresh air. These two movements anterior to the description of the world of the slum mark the first steps over the threshold into fiction. The first is a siting in a context which is primarily cultural, although it may also be memorial; this siting transcends the immediately visible not so much through a "totalizing" metaphor (as one finds in Mearns) as through a "horizontal" series of figures which open up a space for speculative exploration.[34] The very doubleness of the figural direction is crucial: it is not just the thematics of the maze but the incongruity of neck-cloths and buildings, palace and slum, which are nevertheless yoked together, that is central. There is a similar movement in "Gin-Shops." The opening evinces an ostensible concern with a "madness" which has appeared in trade, a madness concerned with display and ostentation in shops, which began "among the linen-drapers and haberdashers" and spread to other trades, including the publicans, "with unprecedented rapidity." What is essentially a 'disease' of trade, of the middle class, spreads to the slums of London:

> Although places of this description are to be met with in every second street, they are invariably numerous and splendid in precise proportion to the dirt and poverty of the surrounding neighbourhood. The gin-shops in and near Drury Lane, Holborn, St. Giles's, Covent Garden, and Clare Market, are the handsomest in town. There is more of filth and squalid misery near those great thoroughfares than in any part of this mighty city.[35]

It is only after this introduction that there is a paragraph on the misery of the slums, followed by a more complete sketch of the gin-shop. Here too, then, we find incongruity in the adjacency of "splendid mansions" to "wretched houses with broken windows patched with rags and paper" (184), but there is a hidden incongruity in the metonymic series for madness which links haberdashers and gin-shops. What Dickens seems to be presenting are figures for culture, but presenting them in such a way that at least one aspect of the figure is hidden or covert. At the same time, culture itself is no longer that which is immediately observable or visible (which might then be tantamount to 'Nature' in some abstract scheme), but that which partakes in the figural. The very terms for representation then stand in need of radical alteration. The accompanying enigmas or paradoxes also open up the space for exploration, for a quest for some hidden secret. And to do so is to suggest the possibility of narration, for whether it be the "stranger," or Boz, or some other narrative voice, his quest will be the traversal of this cultural space.

If we return to "Seven Dials," we can see that the single figure of the labyrinth joins a series of images drawn from theatre, art, language, and writing. An observed scuffle "became general, and terminates, in minor play-bill phraseology, with 'arrival of the policeman, interior of the station-house, and impressive *dénouement.*'" (71).[36] A long descriptive catalogue of the street completes a "'still life' of the subject" (72). The language of the sketch thus hovers between apparent referentiality (now at least a partial fiction) and representation, the latter fully conscious of the artifice and the models which it employs. The same dubious series appears in minor catalogues: "dirty men, filthy women, squalid children, fluttering shuttlecocks, noisy battledores, reeking pipes, bad fruit, more than doubtful oysters, attenuated cats, depressed dogs, and anatomical fowls, are its cheerful accompaniments" (72). Not only the order of the catalogue but the choice of adjectives indicates that this is the meeting place of language and space. A deeper knowledge contradicts the evidence of the eye:

> Now anybody who passed through the Dials on a hot summer's evening, and saw the different women of the houses gossiping on the steps, would be apt to think that all was harmony among them, and that a more primitive set of people than the native Diallers could not be imagined. Alas! the man in the shop ill-treats his family; the carpet-beater extends his professional pursuits to his wife. . . . Animosities spring up between floor and floor; the very cellar asserts his equality.

(72-3)

Houses and people share bad proportions; houses or parts of them act as signs to betray their inhabitants. Reading these signs, however, as the end of the sketch suggests, is often an oblique or deceptive process.[37] The evidence of the eye may feed statistics, but it ought to baffle the interpreter. What he *can* discover is the ways in which the slum and its inhabitants represent themselves; among those ways are the figurative displacements. The process of figuration here is a move not towards abstraction or distancing—as it was in Mearns—but a move towards humanizing, towards recognizing an active volition among the poor.

The interpreter's own moves to place himself within the scene constitute the second step towards realizing the possibility of narration. If his initial entry into the maze

seems to be a form of displacement, the further displacements he effects are an act of inscribing himself upon the city. Here the surrogate figure of the literary man is crucial:

> The second floor front, and the rest of the lodgers, are just a second edition of the people below, except a shabby-genteel man in the back attic. . . . The shabby-genteel man is an object of some mystery, but as he leads a life of seclusion, and never was known to buy anything beyond an occasional pen, except half-pints of coffee, penny loaves, and ha'porths of ink, his fellow-lodgers very naturally suppose him to be an author; and rumours are current in the Dials, that he writes poems for Mr. Warren.
>
> (72)

Somewhat withdrawn and mysterious, the shabby-genteel man, an author only by dint of surmise, of rumour, seems to stand for the difficulties inherent in representation itself: he is a sign for an indeterminate signified, his ink no more than a possible metonymy for authorship. The mystery that surrounds him argues a limit to representation itself. And yet, could not his very indeterminacy be an emblem of the presence of the author in the urban milieu? No art can identify him as more than he appears, as the city for its part declares its unalterable yet mysterious presence. Yet that very mystery generates interpretation of the city. It is as if by entering the Seven Dials, and even by making that shabby-genteel man a signature figure for the artist, Boz has prepared a linguistic ground for urban fiction. If one of the figures in Cruikshank's illustration for "Public Dinners" represents Dickens, one might also say that Boz, also a representation of Dickens, appears in a still further displacement in the shabby-genteel man. In other words, Boz has figuratively displaced the self-representing figures of the Seven Dials to become an authorial figure for that area.

That process of self-inscription, of coming to terms with the otherness of the city in such a way that it is held in a delicate balance with the self, appears even more clearly and paradigmatically in the "Meditations in Monmouth Street." As in "Seven Dials," what is apt to impress readers most is not the presence of the narrator so much as the speculations (a recurring word in the *Sketches*) on an observed locale. Thus the description of second-hand clothes develops into a fantasy about their history or the histories of the wearers, or with the way in which a pair of boots, surmised to be the former possession of a jovial market-gardener, enters into a courtship pantomime with a pair of Denmark satin shoes which once adorned the feet of a servant girl. A more elegant pair of grey cloth boots becomes the property of a smart female; the boots then mime a dialogue with a gallant gentleman in list shoes, to the amusement of an imagined young fellow in long-quartered pumps. High life and low life meet in Monmouth Street, and in Boz's

imagination the scene develops, thanks to all the second-hand shoes, into a dance, replete with corps de ballet.

Such lively meditations occupy a good part of the sketch; they indicate, as Miller has suggested, the way in which even the inferences as to history and causality which one may ascribe to a realistic mode recede before the pressures of the exuberant imagination.[38] But the passages which frame the central part of the sketch are puzzling simply because they have little apparent relation to that centre. Here is the second paragraph:

> The inhabitants of Monmouth Street are a distinct class; a peaceable and retiring race, who immure themselves for the most part in deep cellars, or small back parlours, and who seldom come forth into the world, except in the dusk and coolness of the evening, when they may be seen seated, in chairs on the pavement, smoking their pipes, or watching the gambols of their engaging children as they revel in the gutter, a happy troop of infantine scavengers. Their countenances bear a thoughtful and a dirty cast, certain indications of their love of traffic; and their habitations are distinguished by that disregard of outward appearance and neglect of personal comfort, so common among people who are constantly immersed in profound speculations, and deeply engaged in sedentary pursuits.[39]

One might regard these people as a species of urban mole; what is more important, however, is the quality of their withdrawal, their peaceful and sedentary ways, their profound "speculations." The fantasy-provoking old clothes are more prominent than the shop-owners, whose recessiveness appears in their retiring (rather than attiring) qualities, and whose "disregard of outward appearance" contrasts with the clothes that are all appearance. The clothes take the place of the proprietors, who then give themselves to their mysterious profundities. Of course, not all connections are effaced: "thoughtfulness" may retain a trace of its disinterested connotation, but it is also a sign of a "love of [commercial] traffic"; "speculations" has a double meaning in this context; even "pursuits" must sacrifice some of its innocence to the pun. Yet these signs of proprietary interest are by and large supplanted by the presence of the clothes, which are in turn displaced by the conjuring imagination of Boz. That this series is not strained may appear from the final paragraph, where Boz alludes to the "depths of his meditations," which have in fact so eclipsed the visual that "we might have been rudely staring at [an] old lady for half an hour without knowing it" (80). Proprietorship—a term not explicitly used—passes from the shopowners to the author, as their "profound speculations" traverse the dusk of the street to the twilight zone of writing. Indeed, Boz's final "flight" to become "immersed in the deepest obscurity of the adjacent 'Dials'" (80) has imaginative implications. The form of immersion and self-revelation of the Monmouth street inhabitants has now been assumed

by the narrator. The presence of the narrator, at first recessive in its encounter with the visual, eventually signifies a deepening of the inner gaze: the artist comes to master all speculation, all imaginative traffic. The sketch offers, then, a figure for the activity of writing itself, where the clothes constitute the pre-text.

The clothes contain still another hidden figure. The one life which Boz does infer from a series of outfits (metonymically placed side by side, in such a way that Boz's narrative imagination may supply the continuities) takes a downward course from respectability to crime and poverty. The more cheerful antidote involves incipient narrative which bursts out into a miniature carnival of dance, pantomime, ritual. But there is a tension with the actual emptiness of the shoes, or with the subsequent flight of the imagined occupants when the barrel-organ stops playing. The hidden figure may thus be that of the *Totentanz,* or, more ambiguously, the attempt to ward off death.[40] The interplay between presence and absence, life and death, artifact and nature, gaiety and despair, implies that the sketch is a determined effort—if not desperate then not merely genial—to assert the power of the self. At the same time, the city on its part is threatened with a form of death, as the clothes-as-artifacts may testify to a vanished life or civilization. The image of the necropolis does not appear in strength until the later Dickens novels, but even in *Sketches by Boz* Dickens reckons the ways of discerning life in a still city.[41] "Meditations on Monmouth Street," with its transferences and displacements, its recessive and emergent figures, its dialectic of writer or self and city, becomes a signature piece for the Dickensian mode of writing.

III

If we return to the point of origin, that of representation of the city, we are now in a position to note more fully the problematic which this involves. In the first place, there is the issue of culture (and ideology), which is perceivable in comprehensive metaphors, in serial metaphors which chart a hidden relation among parts of the city, in allusions to a vanishing past, and in certain central episodes which resemble the encounter between two cultures. In the second place, the presence of the observer on the scene of cultural encounter becomes translated into the confrontation of self and other. That presence, as much as any other factor, generates questions about the possibilities of narrative. While the formal problem common to Dickens and the writers of the nonfictional sketches arises from the impact of the visible and the consequent ways of containing or transcending it, the social problem has to do with the preservation of a culture. If the most obvious signs of urban blight, for example, are conveyed in religious, moral, or other conventional terms, then the cure is one prescribed by that very terminology. Various forms of the sketch

embody, therefore, modes of acculturation, whether that of the externally directed colonial explorer or missionary, or that of the internally motivated flâneur who seeks, through the act of strolling itself, to establish the continuities and connections of the city, to re-incorporate the outcast 'other' into the knowable city.[42] But the problem of making the city known can set up false directives, turn the city into a museum containing collections of objects which are neatly classifiable, or from which one might reasonably infer histories or meanings. It is here that the novelist might want to part with the journalist, the sociologist, or the statistician, insofar as the latter three share in an enterprise of collecting and classifying on the one hand, and of reassuring the public about the possibility of knowledge on the other.[43]

Literature of the city seems prone to execute a double movement: the intense observation and exploration of the unknown is followed by a swerve into a metaphor or a systemic pattern which is meant to account for the visible. At the very least, this move towards interpretation constitutes a displacement from the observable scene, so that the final image of the city may appear as a palimpsest. Missionaries and heathens, Vanity Fair, the world threatened by the flood, or high and low, East End and West End, West End and City, even light and dark, are central terms for ways of regarding the city which are as significant for their exclusions as for their inclusions. Moreover, certain metaphors, when examined carefully, indicate a disruption or discontinuity in those comprehensive views of the city. The fear of violence and the continuing awareness of the otherness of parts of the city, tend to undermine that very system of comprehension. That the city is as ultimately knowable as these first explorers assumed now becomes questionable: thus it is the ambiguities rather than the availability of cultural metaphors or schemas that allow the turn towards narrative.

With the possible exception of the labyrinth, urban metaphors may be most efficacious for narrative when they abjure the comprehensive or the systematic. Some of the major metaphors for the city are 'horizontal': the madness for decoration which spreads over the city in "Gin-Shops" is noticeably spatial. By the eventual figure of juxtaposition with the slums, which lies at the heart of the sketch, it allows one to view the gin palaces as dream palaces, fantasies where one can drink gin as an alternative to the waters of Lethe—much as gambling is a fantasy about fate.[44] Such figures are more modest in their claims than the totalizing metaphors: they are provisional figures for culture, and they permit the exchange, transgression, and discontinuity that set a Dickensian narrative in motion. But a more casual stroll or a simple excursion can also connote a move towards the figurative. The move of the Tuggses to Ramsgate,

Mr. Minns's trip to the suburbs, Mr. Dumps's trip to Bloomsbury in "A Bloomsbury Christening"—all journeys which cross boundaries—are steps towards narrative.

Many of the urban sketches contain the presence—implicit or explicit—of an observer on the scene. The roles in which these observers cast themselves are significant. Sala is Asmodeus, the invisible figure who sees everything that goes on beneath the rooftops; he is also a night-watchman, one who is familiar with the secrets of the night and at the same time a guardian of order, a source of reassurance. As excavator—still another persona—he will unearth the artifacts of the city and construct from them an intelligible picture of urban life. Even if he were to depict only the publicly observable life of the city, like the flâneur, he would, as Benjamin notes, turn the exteriors into interiors, impart to them a degree of intimacy and make all forms of external urban life potentially available.[45] All of these personae are observers whose very strategies maintain some separation from the scene. In many of the non-narrative sketches, on the other hand, Dickens—or Boz—inscribes himself on the scene, translates a cultural encounter into a meeting of self and other: thus his "speculations" constitute that act of transgression or exchange which marks out the scene as a space for narrative.[46] While this is by no means necessary—it does not happen in all of the *Sketches*—it marks one way of going beyond the impasses created by the systems and antitheses, as well as the catalogues, which close around the scenes of urban life. This merging into the scene, like the figures for transgression and discontinuity—the beggar woman singing with her baby who breaks the fabric of the night street scene, the mysterious figure in Scotland Yard who represents the persistence of memory as well as the distance from all conventional history—becomes a figure for narrativity.[47]

If urban culture is to be preserved, then it would seem necessary to do so by taking some cognizance of the very ruptures which threaten culture. But if culture is seen not only as the phenomenon of the present but also as that which is continuous with the past, then preservation is a still more precarious enterprise, if it is possible at all. Leigh Hunt strolls about London, meditating on the histories of certain houses, and thus incorporating those histories into the facade of the present.[48] In *Twice Round the Clock*, Sala's evocation of Regent Street—changed considerably between its beginnings in the Regency and the mid-century at which Sala writes—is charged with the *ubi sunt* motif: even as the mores of the street are changing, the figures who would formerly have inspired Thackeray's novels are nowhere to be seen. In fact, the historical consciousness becomes an awareness of decline: it is not only the loss of illusion that Dickens's "Vauxhall by Day" chronicles, but also the decline of the pleasure garden itself from its

eighteenth-century heyday. The decay of small houses—an implicit counterpart to the decay of greater houses—is chronicled in "Shops and their Tenants." But in several sketches, the very notion of history is questioned. In "The First of May," the pastoral glory of May Day acquires the status of a dream of childhood, even as it metamorphoses into the urban celebration of the chimney-sweeps and then into a somewhat motley ceremony. Boz ends his sketch of Scotland Yard by observing that no ordinary history will help the antiquarian of the future to locate the landmarks of that area. The consciousness of what is transitory must, therefore, be caught in the sketch; the newspaper account of the balloon race in "Vauxhall by Day" is emblematic of the process. If writing about the city becomes a sign, as Benjamin suggests, for externalized memory, then the sketch becomes the site for a collector of objects that represent both the cultural past and individual memory.[49]

But this returns us to the mode of textuality. For that vanishing of a certain form of urban life can be conceived of as a source of narrative. It is, to be sure, oblique. For example, buses and coaches in nineteenth-century novels are more or less thematic or peripheral, symbols, but not actual materials, of narrative. The "Lads of the Village," an errant omnibus in "The Bloomsbury Christening," is exemplary: its wayward progress over the space of the city might be a figure for urban narrative.[50] The city, of course, has no exclusive rights over literary vehicles: the stagecoaches of *The Heart of Midlothian* and *Felix Holt*, symbols of a more leisurely past, of a different conception of temporality as well as entrées into narrative, are sufficient evidence. Nevertheless, the plenitude of vehicles in *Sketches by Boz* is linked to a receding past which can only be halted or transfixed within a text. The not entirely nominal metamorphosis or corruption of William Barker into "Bill Boorker" and then "Aggerawatin Bill" in "The Last Cab-Driver, and the First Omnibus Cad" offers a human counterpart. His early life is obscure, his "restlessness of purpose" evident: his "feverish attachment to change and variety nothing could repress" (147). Thus, as a cab-driver symbolizes the shifting of self into assumed characters that seems so much a part of an urban poetics, so non-linearity of narrative is symbolized in the movement of the buses, which constantly change their origins and destinations.[51] Like the social madness in "Gin-Shops" or the speculative exuberance in "Meditations in Monmouth Street," which ends with Boz fleeing from his own imaginative violence, there is a certain apprehension of things getting out of hand, of unpredictability and madness.

Dickens's sketches, then, tend to break away from the taxonomy, articulation, and system which govern so many of the non-fictional sketches and instead regard the city as a more mysterious text. The non-fictional sketches are more closely related in other ways: in their

oblique comments on language—the implication that London is a city of words, whether they are spoken by lawyers (Sala's sketch of the legal profession in *Twice Round the Clock* focuses on legal diction and rhetoric) or written in begging letters; in the containment of a problematic of fiction, as in the comments on the relation of romance to reality; in the use of figures which in one way or another remove the sketch from the scene of representation. The city may be the common ground of encounter, but it also contains an underworld of representation. Wordsworth's reading of the city as a chaos of signs was in one sense entirely accurate; but the city was also a destructive element in which he refused to immerse himself. That immersion, as Sala's own moment of impasse suggests, is no guarantee of a successful emergence and appropriation of the city. But one liberating recognition, which goes beyond the materiality of the city, was that of new correspondences between urban and verbal creation on the one hand, and of the artist's capacity to insert himself into a city now conceived of as a text. That immersion, that tolerance of mystery, that recognition of language's displaced relation to the object-world of the city, might be seen as the very factors which allowed the urban novel to come into being.

Notes

1. See Steven Marcus, "Reading the Illegible," in *The Victorian City,* ed. H. J. Dyos and Michael Wolff, 2 vols. (London and Boston: Routledge and Kegan Paul, 1973) l, 257-76; and Philip Fisher, "City Matters: City Minds," in *The Worlds of Victorian Fiction,* ed. Jerome H. Buckley, Harvard English Studies 6 (Cambridge, Mass. and London: Harvard U.P., 1975), pp. 371-89.

2. Michel Foucault, *The Order of Things* (London: Tavistock Publications, 1970), p. xvii.

3. Cf. Walter Benjamin's *Baudelaire; A Lyric Poet in the Era of High Capitalism,* trans. Harry Zohn (London: New Left Books, 1973), for a discussion of similar functions of the physiologies in nineteenth century Paris.

4. J. Hillis Miller, "The Fiction of Realism: *Sketches by Boz, Oliver Twist,* and Cruikshank's Illustrations," in *Dickens Centennial Essays,* ed. Ada Nisbet and Blake Nevius (Berkeley, Los Angeles and London: U. of California Press, 1971), pp. 85-153. Miller's essay is seminal reading in this area, and this essay is indebted to it at several points.

5. Cf. Peter Brooks, "Romantic Antipastoral and Urban Allegories," *The Yale Review* n.s. 64 (1974), 11-26.

6. See Eileen Yeo, "Mayhew as a Social Investigator," in *The Unknown Mayhew,* ed. E. P. Thompson and Eileen Yeo (London: Merlin Press, 1971), pp. 66-8, for this view of the tradition.

7. *Into Unknown England, 1866-1913: Selections from the Social Explorers* ed. P. J. Keating (London: Fontana, 1976).

8. Andrew Mearns, *The Bitter Cry of Outcast London,* (1883), rptd. in *Into Unknown England,* pp. 95-6.

9. Benjamin Disraeli, *Coningsby* (New York: Century, 1904), p. 107.

10. The following passages are representative:

 "But Paris is an ocean. Throw in the plummet, you will never reach bottom" (p. 37).

 "Paris, you see, is like a forest in the New World where a score of savage tribes, the Illinois, the Hurons, struggle for existence; each group lives on what it can get by hunting throughout society" (p. 133). Honoré de Balzac, *Old Goriot,* trans. Marion Aytoun Crawford (Baltimore: Penguin Books, 1969).

11. One might call this the convention of the indescribable, through which whatever offends or horrifies may be signified but neither named nor described. Dickens and other novelists, as well as the writers of non-fiction, employ it. But while it may authenticate their claims not to step outside the bounds of civilized discourse, no matter how uncivilized the subject, it may also place that subject beyond the limits of representational language. For a different perspective on this problem, see Steven Marcus, "Reading the Illegible," p. 265. Marcus finds a "saving function" in language that "refuse[s] to domesticate these actualities with syntax and imagery."

12. "We shall not wonder if some, shuddering at the revolting spectacle, try to persuade themselves that such things cannot be in Christian England, and that what they have looked upon is some dark vision conjured by a morbid pity and a responding faith. To such we can only say, Will you venture to come with us and see for yourselves the ghastly reality?" (p. 111).

13. The fact—and the irony—of a common humanity is, however, a concern of other social explorers. Mearns's own pity and horror at the plight of the poor are apparent, though they should not cancel out the implications of his choice of language.

14. The image of the volcano had been linked with the idea of social upheaval earlier in the century. See G. M. Matthews, "A Volcano's Voice in Shelley," *ELH,* 24 (1957), 191-228.

15. Two representative pamphlets are Thomas Beames's *The Rookeries of London,* 1850 (rptd. Cass, 1970), and Bishop Roden Noel's *The Spiritual State of the Metropolis,* 1836.

16. James Greenwood, "A Night in a Workhouse" (1866), rptd. in *Into Unknown England*, pp. 33-54.

17. "as for the coughing, to lie on the flagstones in what was nothing better than an open shed, and listen to that, hour after hour, chilled one's very heart with pity. Every variety of cough that I ever heard was to be heard there: the hollow cough; the short cough; the hysterical cough; the bark that comes at regular intervals, like the quarter-chime of a clock, as if to mark off the progress of decay; coughing from vast hollow chests, coughing from little narrow ones—now one, now another, now two or three together" (pp. 45-6).

18. See F. Nietzsche, *The Genealogy of Morals*.

19. George Henry Augustus Sala, *Twice Round the Clock; or the Hours of the Day And Night in London* (London: Houlston and Wright, 1859), pp. 264-66.

20. Henry Mayhew, *London Labour and the London Poor,* 4 vols. (1861 rptd. Cass, 1967); *The Unknown Mayhew* adds a selection of pieces Mayhew wrote for *The Morning Chronicle* in 1849 and 1850.

21. Cf. J. Hillis Miller, "The Fiction of Realism," p. 94.

22. Cf. Walter Benjamin's discussion of Poe's "The Man of the Crowd" in "On Some Motifs in Baudelaire" in *Illuminations* (New York: Harcourt, Brace and World, 1968) pp. 172-5. The 'force' of the crowd in Sala, however, is virtually equated with the force of words.

23. *Twice Round the Clock,* p. vi.

24. Augustus Mayhew, *Paved with Gold, or The Romance and Reality of the London Streets* (London: Chapman and Hall, 1858; rptd. Cass, 1971).

25. For a discussion of the use of Asmodeus figures in the nineteenth century see Jonathan Arac, *Commissioned Spirits* (New Brunswick, New Jersey: Rutgers U.P., 1979). Tom Eaves in Thackeray's *Vanity Fair* is a kindred spirit.

26. James Grant, *Sketches in London* (London, 1840).

27. George Lukacs, "Narrate or Describe," in *Writer and Critic and other essays,* ed. and trans. Arthur Kahn (London: Merlin Press, 1970), pp. 110-48.

28. See, for example, *John Tallis's London Street Views, 1838-1840* (London: Nattali and Maurice, 1969). Each of Tallis' plates has a map, a view, and an elevation of a particular building or street. Since the prints are concerned mainly with commercial establishments, that aspect of middle-class London is dominant in the collection.

29. "Narrate or Describe," p. 133.

30. A number of Frith's paintings, among them "The Railway Station" and "Derby Day," imply this tension between the individual and the crowd. Jem Wilson's heroic rescue of his father and another worker from the burning factory in *Mary Barton* offers a fictional analogue, since Jem separates himself from the watching crowd and then, as if to underscore this process of individuation, emerges twice from the fire.

31. See P. J. Keating, *The Working Classes in Victorian Fiction* (New York: Barnes and Noble, 1971), p. 13.

32. Mayhew's description was printed in *The Morning Chronicle,* 24 September 1849. See also George R. Sims, *How the Poor Live* (1883) and William Booth, *Darkest England and the Way Out* (1890).

33. Charles Dickens, "Seven Dials," in *Sketches by Boz* (London: Oxford U.P. 1969), pp. 69-70,71.

34. For a discussion of totalizing metaphors in nineteenth-century novels, see J. Hillis Miller, "Optic and Semiotic in *Middlemarch,*" in *The Worlds of Victorian Fiction*, pp. 125-45.

35. "Gin-Shops," in *Sketches by Boz,* p. 184.

36. Cf. "The Fiction of Realism," pp. 117-18, for a discussion of the conventions of drama, art, and literature as sources for the *Sketches by Boz.*

37. The ultimate discrepancy appears in Arthur Clennam's perception of Casby in Dickens's *Little Dorrit* (London: Oxford U.P., 1967), p. 149: "He was aware of motes and specks of suspicion, in the atmosphere of that time; seen through which medium, Christopher Casby was a mere Inn sign-post without any Inn—an invitation to rest and be thankful, when there was no place to put up at, and nothing whatever to be thankful for."

38. Cf. "The Fiction of Realism," pp. 96-8.

39. "Meditations in Monmouth Street," in *Sketches by Boz,* p. 74.

40. Cf. Tzvetan Todorov's discussion of the relations between narrative and life, and absence of narrative and death, in "Narrative-Men," in *The Poetics of Prose,* trans. Richard Howard (Ithaca, New York: Cornell U.P., 1977), pp. 66-79.

41. For a discussion of London as a city of death in Dickens's novels see Alexander Welsh, *The City of Dickens* (Oxford: Clarendon Press, 1971).

42. See Benjamin's description of the Parisian flâneur in *Charles Baudelaire: A Lyric Poet in the Era of High Capitalism.*

43. In the book on Baudelaire, Benjamin notes that the French physiologies—in some respects a counterpart to the English sketches—helped to reassure those readers who felt threatened by the uncanny and secret aspects of the big city: "The more uncanny a big city becomes, the more knowledge of human nature . . . it takes to operate in it" (p. 40).

44. Cf. Benjamin's comments on the gambler's "phantasmagoria of time," which corresponds to the flâneur's "phantasmagoria of space," in *Charles Baudelaire: A Lyric Poet in the Era of High Capitalism,* p. 174.

45. See *Charles Baudelaire: A Lyric Poet in the Era of High Capitalism,* pp. 36-7.

46. On the relation of transgression to narrative, see Roland Barthes, *S/Z,* trans. Richard Miller (New York: Hill and Wang, 1974).

47. See "The Streets—Night" in *Sketches by Boz,* pp. 55-6 and "Scotland Yard," in *Sketches by Boz,* pp. 67-8.

48. See Leigh Hunt, *Political and Occasional Essays,* ed. Lawrence Huston Houtchens and Carolyn Washburn Houtchens (New York and London: Columbia University Press, 1962).

49. The idea is central in Benjamin's writings about the city. One version appears in "A Berlin Chronicle," in *Reflections,* trans. Edmund Jephcott (New York and London: Harcourt Brace Jovanovich, 1978), pp. 3-60.

50. Cf. Patricia Parker's exploration of the idea of errancy in narrative in *Inescapable Romance* (Princeton, Princeton U.P., 1979).

51. The importance of masquerades (and of theatricality in general) in an urban poetics is in part an outgrowth of somewhat earlier satirical views of the city. John Corry's *A Satirical View of London at the Commencement of the Nineteenth Century* (London: pr. for G. Kearsley, T. Hurst, 1801) is representative: "The two most powerful motives that keep this vast community in continual agitation, like the undulations of the ocean, are the love of pleasure and the love of gain. Venus and her auxilliary, Bacchus, reign in the fashionable circles. Masquerades, balls, fêtes, public and private theatres, and all the luxurious delights that fancy can devise, minister to the passions and appetites of those sons and daughters of pride" (p. 7).

Deborah Epstein Nord (essay date 1983)

SOURCE: Nord, Deborah Epstein. "The Social Explorer as Anthropologist: Victorian Travellers among the Urban Poor." In *Visions of the Modern City: Essays in History, Art, and Literature,* edited by William Sharpe and Leonard Wallock. 1983. Reprint, pp. 122-34. Baltimore, Md.: The Johns Hopkins University Press, 1987.

[In the following essay, originally published in 1983, Nord discusses the underlying impetus for nineteenth-century writers' comparisons between impoverished city dwellers and native peoples of Africa and other non-European nations.]

Western peoples have often looked to images of non-Western cultures to describe themselves or to evoke aspects of their own culture.[1] In this tradition urban explorers of the nineteenth century developed the habit of comparing the English inhabitants of Victorian slums to Aborigines, South Sea Islanders and, most frequently, to African tribes. It seems that those English writers who reported back to the middle class on their travels into the unknown and uncharted areas of Manchester, Birmingham, and London could not resist making use of the almost obligatory analogy between the urban poor and the "uncivilized" peoples of truly foreign lands. Once the reader of that vast nineteenth-century literature of urban exploration notices the use of such analogies, she or he begins to see them everywhere, to realize that they constitute a virtual literary convention of that genre of writing. It also becomes apparent that the analogy takes on different meanings in different parts of the century and, indeed, as various writers exploited it.

I intend here to offer some speculations about why such a literary convention was used and needed by those social observers who wrote about the "denizens" of the slums. Was this anthropological analogy merely a rhetorical flourish to rouse the interest of readers, to get beyond their normally apathetic or antagonistic responses to the subject of urban poverty? Was the use of this literary convention a simple expression of Victorian racialism, of the earnest conviction that just as black Africans were a race apart from middle-class Englishmen, so too were slum-dwellers, street-laborers, and the unemployed? Or did this way of referring to the underclass help reformers, journalists, and social investigators to communicate something of significance to their readers that they otherwise might have found difficult to convey? I will begin to try to answer these questions by looking at the literature of urban exploration produced at the end of the century and work my way back to mid-century, ending with Henry Mayhew, in many ways the most important urban explorer of his time.

The English/Africa analogy appeared most prevalently in writings of the 1880s and 1890s, those late-Victorian decades in which poverty was "rediscovered" as a national issue and in which numerous middle-class explorers traveled into the *terra incognita* of urban slums, particularly those of the East End of London. A serious

economic depression had hit England—and the rest of Western Europe—at the end of the 1870s; and throughout the 1880s unemployment, labor unrest, sporadic working-class violence, and the birth of the "new unionism" (the organization of unskilled workers) fed middle-class fears of social upheaval and prompted what was called the "socialist revival." Socialist groups like the Social Democratic Federation and the Fabians sought to analyze the causes of poverty; reform-minded professionals like Charles Booth mounted inquiries into the actual extent of poverty in English society; and journalists like W. T. Stead of the *Pall Mall Gazette* published exposés of slum housing, sweat shops, and the white slave trade.

Just as Manchester had been the focus for national interest in the ugly urban results of industrialization in the 1840s and 1850s, so the East End became the chief symbolic example of urban decay in the 1880s and 1890s. In 1845 Disraeli warned that England had become divided into two nations, "rich and poor," and in 1891 Margaret Harkness, chronicler of working-class life in London slums, echoed and amended Disraeli by identifying "two nations, *East* and *West*."[2] What had long been an actual physical contrast between the prosperous West End and the more solidly working-class East End was, in these last decades of the century, turned into what Raymond Williams calls an "interpretive image": the West represented all that was bright, open, dazzling, and enlightened; the East all that was dark, labyrinthine, threatening, and benighted.[3]

The dichotomy of West and East doubled, of course, for England and its Empire.[4] The era of the "rediscovery" of poverty was also the heyday of British Imperialism. The Great Depression at home and competition from Germany and the United States abroad gave Britain the impetus to expand trade and investment in its colonies; and the search for new markets in Africa and Asia brought in its wake missionaries, explorers, anthropologists, and travelers. They penetrated the "dark" continents in an effort to learn, conquer, and convert; and they captured the imaginations of an audience at home, eager for tales of exotic and torturous journeys, wild tribes, and miraculous conversions.

The literature of *urban* exploration depended in fact on this heightened interest in the Empire for much of its language, its form, its legitimacy, and its moral authority. In *How the Poor Live* George Sims, one of the better known popular social investigators of the 1880s, began a section on slum dwellings in this way:

> In these pages I propose to record the result of a journey into a region which lies at our own doors—into a dark continent that is within easy walking distance of the General Post Office. This continent will, I hope, be found as interesting as any of those newly-explored

lands which engage the attention of the Royal Geographical Society—the wild races who inhabit it will, I trust, gain public sympathy as easily as those savage tribes for whose benefit Missionary Societies never cease to appeal for funds.[5]

If you can summon interest in and sympathy for "wild races" far away, Sims seems to be saying, then you can at least read what I have to say about those neglected people in your very midst. Sims is clearly using a rhetorical device to capture the attention of his readers, to enhance the exotic and even sensational quality of his squalid researches, but he is also admonishing the English public for its wilful ignorance of Whitechapel and Bethnal Green and for its facile enthusiasm for alien cultures.

A decade or so later Jack London expressed a similar sentiment with a somewhat sharper ironic edge in his *People of the Abyss.* "O Cook, O Thomas Cook & Son," he apostrophized,

> path-finders and trail-clearers, living sign-posts to all the world, and bestowers of first aid to bewildered travellers—unhesitatingly and instantly, with ease and celerity, could you send me to Darkest Africa or Innermost Tibet, but to the East End of London, barely a stone's throw distant from Ludgate Circus, you know not the way![6]

While England gloried in its expanding Empire and spread "civilization" throughout the world, it forgot or never knew the hungry, unemployed, and poorly-housed denizens of its own cities. Jack London reminded his readers what and where the East End was: if the Empire never saw the setting of the sun, he quipped, the East End was that place over which the sun seldom rose.

The domestic social reformer who made his dependence on the African example most explicit was General William Booth, founder of the Salvation Army. In the summer of 1890 an explorer named Stanley—of Stanley and Livingstone fame—had published *In Darkest Africa,* an account of his journey across the "Lost Continent." Later that same year General Booth came out with a book outlining his plan for the alleviation of poverty in Great Britain: he called it *In Darkest England and the Way Out.* Booth begins this work with an account of Stanley's heroic entry into the "almost impenetrable" tropical forests of the Congo and his discovery of its predatory and godless population, and then interrupts his narrative to ask the inevitable question: "As there is a darkest Africa is there not also a darkest England? . . . May we not find a parallel at our own doors, and discover within a stone's throw of our cathedrals and palaces similar horrors to those which Stanley has found existing in the great Equatorial forest?"[7]

He introduces the already familiar analogy much as George Sims and Jack London did, but he takes it a step further by equating the Arab ivory raiders who exploit African forest dwellers with those Englishmen (he singles out pub-owners) who prey on the vulnerabilities of slum dwellers and unwittingly reduce them to criminals, drunkards, and layabouts. Booth suggests that the Englishman's guilt goes beyond mere *ignorance* of his poorer neighbors: he causes eternal misery, "brooding sullenness" and "dull despair"; he is a slave-driver and an agent of godlessness.

It is clear from these examples of the 1880s and 1890s that the language of domestic social investigation cannot be fully understood without an appreciation of England's place in the constellation of world politics, that England's national concerns—and the way they were discussed—were inseparable from its international ones. London had become the center of an empire, the docks of East London the conduit through which the Empire entered Britain; and the capital took on an aura of new and literal—not just metaphorical—internationalism in these decades. Waves of immigrants gravitated to London's central districts while native Londoners tended to spread out into the new suburbs and outlying areas. The "distant tribes" had more than an analogous relationship to Londoners: they had become Londoners, as London came to reproduce in miniature the world of the Empire. When Margaret Harkness wrote a novel about the Salvation Army, she quite appropriately followed the lead of General Booth by calling her book *In Darkest London,* further narrowing the focus of Booth's own title from benighted nation to benighted city. She opened the novel with a description of Whitechapel Road on a Saturday night:

> There one sees all nationalities. A grinning Hottentot elbows his way through a crowd of long-legged Jewesses. An Algerian merchant walks arm-in-arm with a native of Calcutta. A little Italian plays pitch-and-toss with a small Russian. A Polish Jew enjoys sauer-kraut with a German Gentile. And among the foreigners lounges the East End loafer, monarch of all he surveys, lord of the premises.[8]

The East End thoroughfare has become a Babel, a world in microcosm. The Jew, the Eastern European, or the Mediterranean is as alien to the Englishman as the Hottentot or the Pygmy; and each nationality is perceived as a cluster of stereotypical traits, each individual foreigner a caricature. The Empire brought with it into England the ironic coupling of great riches and great poverty; in this way it reproduced the dichotomy of West End luxury and East End squalor.

The literary convention of comparing the urban poor of England with Africans or other non-Western peoples was not, however, a new one in the 1880s. To be sure, it was widely exploited in the last decades of the century because of the particular political and social circumstances of the period, but it was by then an already available and well-established convention. We have to look to earlier examples of this practice, therefore, for a fuller understanding of its various meanings. We remember, of course, the "Telescopic Philanthropy" chapter in Dickens' *Bleak House*: Mrs. Jellyby devotes herself to the natives of Borioboola-Gha on the left bank of the Niger, as well as to the cultivation of the coffee berry and the settlement of 200 "superfluous" British families there, while her own children fall down stairs, get their heads stuck between iron railings, and generally suffer neglect and misery at their mother's hands. Mrs. Jellyby, now often seen as Dickens' belittling parody of the socially engaged female, functions primarily as Dickens' indictment of the insensitive, myopic philanthropist. Her children represent not only the proper sphere of womanhood but the proper sphere of the reforming middle class: the poor of England.[9] Some eight years before Dickens began *Bleak House,* Friedrich Engels cited the remarks of an East End clergyman in his *Condition of the Working Class*: "'I believe,'" recorded the Reverend G. Alston in the *Weekly Dispatch,* "'that till the Bishop of London called the attention of the public to the state of Bethnal-green, about as little was known at the West-end of this most destitute parish as the wilds of Australia or the islands of the South Seas.'"[10] As early as 1844, then, the division of East and West and the veil of ignorance that presumably separated one part of London from the other were acknowledged by writers on urban poverty as social realities.

Both Dickens and Engels anticipated the later writers I have mentioned by admonishing their readers for ignoring what existed under their noses, for shutting out the misery around the corner while sentimentalizing the plight of those oceans away. But the real master of the particular analogy I have been discussing in the mid-Victorian decades was Henry Mayhew, the author of *London Labour and the London Poor.* It is his work that contains the most sustained and, I believe, the most purposeful use of the analogy. He not only employed the rhetorical strategies I have already discussed, but he chose to adopt the persona of the anthropologist.

Mayhew, a satirist, journalist, amateur actor, and member of the literary bohemia of the 1830s and 1840s (of which Dickens and George Cruikshank were also a part), was asked to undertake a series of articles on the conditions of the London working poor for the *Morning Chronicle* in 1849. The *Chronicle* appointed a number of journalists to cover various industrial cities throughout England, and Mayhew was made "Special Correspondent from the Metropolis."[11] The paper, which had liberal, reformist leanings, responded to the growing middle-class interest in problems of poverty and urban life in general. The cholera epidemic of 1849, which

claimed the lives of the urban poor in far greater numbers than the rest of the population, served to focus even greater attention on the social issues already brought to public consciousness by the Depression of the early 1840s, by the Chartist Movement, and by the publication in 1842 of Edwin Chadwick's Poor Law Commission report on the sanitary conditions affecting the urban poor. The middle class reacted to these phenomenon of the decade with fear of social unrest, with some measure of repugnance, and with an often hesitant desire for reform.

Mayhew continued to publish his "letters" from the Metropolis in the *Chronicle* for just over a year until, in December of 1850, he broke with the paper and began to issue articles from an office of his own in twopenny weekly parts. In 1851-52 the pieces were bound together for publication as *London Labour and the London Poor,* and a four-volume edition was re-issued in 1861-62. In the Preface to the bound volumes Mayhew identified himself as a "traveller in the undiscovered country of the poor," who will supply information "concerning a large body of persons of whom the public had less knowledge than of the most distant tribes of the earth."[12] These remarks, as should by now be obvious, are not unusual and do not distinguish Mayhew from the other "travellers" who wished to capture the imaginations and sympathies of their readers. But, as we shall see, Mayhew was after more than sympathy: he wanted to alter the conventional judgments of his audience by forcing it to see the working poor through the lens of moral science.

On the first page of this first volume, devoted to detailed accounts of London "street-folk"—sellers, buyers, finders, performers, artisans, pedlars, and laborers—Mayhew places himself among the "ethnologists."[13] He introduces the work of Dr. James Prichard on "wandering tribes," those groups of people who are neither pure nomads nor settlers but a "race" in between that attaches itself to various "civilized" tribes all over the globe. Such wanderers, according to Dr. Prichard in his *Natural History of Man,* have languages, physical characteristics, customs, and moral systems *distinct* from those of the settled tribes with whom they intermingle.

James Cowles Prichard, the ethnologist Mayhew mentions, was a leading member of the London Ethnological Society, founded in 1843, and the most influential British theorist of "monogenesis." Prichard and fellow-members of the Society believed, that is, in the "'cherished unity of mankind'": all of humanity was the product of a *single seed,* although various groups—or tribes—were to be found at different stages of development in the same evolutionary process.[14] There is essentially one race, and all variations among humankind can be attributed to *differences in external conditions* and to the different influences that derive from these conditions:

That so great differences in external conditions, by the double influence of their physical and moral agency, should have effected during a long series of ages remarkable changes in the tribes of human beings subject to their operation,—changes which have rendered these several tribes fitted in a peculiar manner for their respective abodes,—is by no means an improbable conjecture. . . .[15]

Wandering tribes, then, would share the same characteristics—physical as well as "moral"—because they exist as nomads, under the same general conditions. Mankind is one but different, all of it moving toward a single point but at a varying pace.[16]

"It is curious," Mayhew concludes after establishing Prichard's theories, "that no one has yet applied the above facts to *the explanation of certain anomalies in the present state of society among ourselves.* That we, like the Kaffirs, Fellahs and Finns, are surrounded by wandering hordes—the 'sonquas' and the 'fingoes' of this country—paupers, beggars and outcasts. . . ."[17] Mayhew will, of course, go on to be the one to do just that, to treat the street-folk of London as an ethnologist observing foreign tribes. Using categories determined by the perception of street-folk as a separate culture, he catalogues their histories, dress, food, religion, language, politics, earnings, amusements, and education. The culture of the streets is not, however, monolithic in Mayhew's view: costermongers, prostitutes, pickpockets, watermen, and street-ballad sellers all have different ways of thinking and behaving, as well as working. In a section devoted to the "backwards slang" of costermongers Mayhew maintains the ethnologist's pose when he remarks that "in my present chapter the language has, I believe, been reduced to *orthography* for the first time."[18] The costers' slang, Mayhew explains, is the result of their desire to "shield their bargainings at market, or their conversation . . . from the knowledge of any Irish or uninitiated fellow-traders."[19] What appears a humorous or frivolous habit of speech to the "traveller" among the poor actually has its origins in the structure and customs of labor.

Mayhew takes an anthropologist's interest in the rules and mores that govern conjugal behavior among the street-folk. Costermen resemble North American Indians, he asserts, in their conduct toward their wives: they regard their women as "inexperienced servants" and punish female "disobedience" with physical abuse.[20] Among certain street-sellers matrimony is regarded as a waste of time and money: only one-tenth of all coster couples are legally married, and fidelity is as common among the unwed as among the wed.[21] But Mayhew wishes to emphasize that financial prohibitions make wedlock an undesirable choice. In Clerkenwell, he adds by way of evidence, as many as one-fifth of all coster couples do marry, quite simply because the incumbent of the parish marries them free of charge at Advent and

Easter. If notions of morality among these people "agree strongly . . . with those of many savage tribes," if these "Nomades of England neither know nor care for the enjoyments of home," Mayhew argues, it is because "*we* are the culpable parties."[22] If the "wandering tribes" of the London streets are improvident, ignorant in matters of religion, and careless of the rules of private property, it is because of the circumstances in which they live and because of our neglect of those circumstances. We deny them both a moral education and the means to make our own morality an expedient alternative to theirs.

What, finally, is the meaning of Mayhew's "ethnological" stance, and what does it add to our understanding of the oft-repeated analogy between the urban poor and the "uncivilized" tribes of foreign lands? Other critics of Mayhew's work have tended to dismiss or regret what Anne Humpherys has called his "weak anthropological analogy."[23] Humpherys herself treats the "wandering tribes" passages of *London Labour and the London Poor* as a lapse in Mayhew's writing and interprets quite literally his statements that the street-folk of London constituted a separate—and inferior—race of people. Further, she sees this lapse as evidence of the belief in "innate qualities" to which Mayhew was drawn periodically during the course of his study.[24]

Gertrude Himmelfarb contends that Mayhew succeeded only in "making 'foreigners,' aliens, out of the 'labouring population.'"[25] Mayhew represented the poor "less as a class in the Marxist sense," she remarks, "than a species in the Darwinian sense."[26] According to Himmelfarb, it is Mayhew and other reformers of his ilk that were responsible for creating the destructive notion of a "culture" of poverty. Both of these critics read Mayhew too literally, and yet neither takes what is quite obviously a conscious literary pose seriously enough.

There is no question that at the beginning of his first volume Mayhew sought to dramatize, even to sensationalize, his subject or that his rhetoric contained elements of crude, racialist thinking; but, more importantly, he sought a new vocabulary and a new perspective for the unimpassioned discussion of urban poverty. In his opening pages Mayhew was groping toward a new way of seeing and of writing about human behavior and of accounting for the disquieting variations in that behavior. He did not abandon this perspective after the first few dramatic pages, but continued to employ it throughout his analysis of the culture of the street-folk.

The language of early, even primitive, anthropology provided writers like Mayhew with the metaphor they needed to describe a new class, the inhabitants of a new kind of neighborhood in a new kind of city. Where would the language come from to discuss with some degree of seriousness the *lumpenproletariat* that dwelled in the slums of the industrial cities of the nineteenth century? If a writer wished to evoke the social scene neither as a pure entertainer nor as a rigidly censorious moralizer, if he or she wished to make an attempt at "scientific" objectivity, what tone and what attitude were available and acceptable?

In the 1830s and 1840s the British nation first attempted to come to terms with the facts of urban-industrial life, and a number of different methods of writing about the urban poor were or became available during these decades. Men like Peter Gaskell and Edwin Chadwick used statistical studies to examine infant mortality, birth rates, sanitation, and the spread of disease in slums; early socialists and revolutionaries developed a critique of industrial capitalism; hidebound moralists preached that slum-dwellers were an inherently inferior lot and deserved their squalid fates; popular writers described the high jinks of upper-class "slummers" in low-life settings; and novelists like Dickens, Disraeli, and Elizabeth Gaskell used fiction to evoke sympathy for the poor and bring about reconciliation between classes.

Social investigators like Mayhew represented yet another tradition; Mayhew was a *reformer* who wished to report in nonfictional form on the human conditions that statisticians represented numerically. He wished to impress upon his audience that the circumstances of slum life produced certain kinds of individuals and, by implication, to suggest that conditions would have to be transformed before individuals could be redeemed or "civilized." He had to convince his public that the people of whom he wrote were *of* English society though separate from it, *related* to the middle class but a "race" apart from it, fellow inhabitants of the same city but members of a different "tribe." Ethnologists seemed to have solved the problem of considering "uncivilized" races abroad: they could embrace non-Western peoples on the grounds of the essential unity of mankind and yet they could explain apparently disturbing differences in customs and beliefs by theories of social evolution and of adaptive behavior. If this feat could be accomplished in regard to South Sea Islanders and African tribes, then surely there was a way to approach the urban slum-dweller as an object of study and not merely as an object of disapprobation, revulsion, or amusement.

Notes

1. This paper was first presented as part of a multi-disciplinary panel on Western views of non-Western cultures at the Society of Fellows in the Humanities, Columbia University, April 1981.

2. Margaret Harkness ("John Law"), *In Darkest London: A Story of the Salvation Army* (London, 1891), pp. 67-68.

3. Raymond Williams, *The Country and the City* (London, 1973), p. 220.

4. See Peter Keating's introductory essay in *Into Unknown England: Selections from the Social Explorers* (Manchester, 1976). I am indebted to Keating's collection of the writings of social explorers and to his *The Working Classes in Victorian Fiction* (New York, 1971).

5. George Sims, *How the Poor Live* (1883), excerpted in Keating's *Into Unknown England,* pp. 5-6.

6. Jack London, *The People of the Abyss* (1903), excerpted in Keating, p. 224.

7. William Booth, *In Darkest England and the Way Out* (1890), excerpted in Keating, p. 145.

8. Harkness, p. 3.

9. See Charles Dickens' *Bleak House* (1852-3), Ch. IV.

10. Friedrich Engels, *The Condition of the Working Class in England,* trans. W. O. Henderson and W. H. Chaloner (Stanford, 1958), pp. 35-36.

11. See E. P. Thompson's introductory essay, "Mayhew and the *Morning Chronicle,*" in *The Unknown Mayhew,* ed. E. P. Thompson and Eileen Yeo (Harmondsworth, Middlesex, 1971).

12. Henry Mayhew, *London Labour and the London Poor* (London, 1851), I, iii.

13. Mayhew, I, 1.

14. See J. W. Burrow, *Evolution and Society* (Cambridge, England, 1970), pp. 98-99, 120-24.

15. James Cowles Prichard, *The Natural History of Man* (London, 1843), p. 4.

16. Burrow argues that this and other Victorian evolutionary theories *avoided* "the unpleasantly relativist implications of a world in which many of the old certainties were disappearing" (p. 99). Mankind was *not* "everywhere the same," at least not at any given moment.

17. Mayhew, I, 2.

18. Mayhew, I, 23.

19. Mayhew, I, 24.

20. Mayhew, I, 43.

21. Mayhew, I, 20.

22. Mayhew, I, 43.

23. Anne Humpherys, *Travels into the Poor Man's Country: The Work of Henry Mayhew* (Athens, Georgia, 1977), p. 71.

24. Humpherys, pp. 71-72.

25. Gertrude Himmelfarb, "The Culture of Poverty," in *The Victorian City,* ed. H. J. Dyos and Michael Wolff (Boston, 1973), II, 719. Anne Humpherys concedes that Mayhew's assertions about the "wandering tribes" do indeed "support Gertrude Himmelfarb's charge that Mayhew contributed to the idea that the poor were a class apart." She defends Mayhew, however, by saying that the general introductory section on street-life was "less important than the rest of his work; it occupied only two pages out of all his volumes . . ." (Humpherys, p. 72). Rather than offering another interpretation of the passages in question, Humpherys simply minimizes their importance.

26. Himmelfarb, p. 711.

URBAN POETRY

William Sharpe (essay date spring 1984)

SOURCE: Sharpe, William. "Learning to Read *The City.*" *Victorian Poetry* 22, no. 1 (spring 1984): 65-84.

[*In the following essay, Sharpe maintains that James Thomson's poem* The City of Dreadful Night *offers an optimistic vision of faith in humanity and community.*]

He was wandering lost in thought through London one night, James Thomson writes, when "a girl's pleasant laugh aroused me. . . . But I was startled as I grew conscious of the immense abyss across which my mind perceived her. Her dress had brushed mine a moment back, yet the star glittering above the house in front of me was not more remote than she."[1] If for Whitman or Baudelaire the chance encounter with the mysterious, exciting *passante* was charged with all the tremendous human potential of the crowded metropolis, Thomson's brush with an unknown passer-by only reconfirmed for the Scottish poet the relentless isolation of city life. Orphaned in London in 1842 at the age of eight, Thomson spent most of his often lonely life in that city, boarding first at school, then with friends, and finally lodging, from 1866 until his death in 1882, in a succession of ever more shabby rooming houses. Ordinarily a witty, cheerful, and industrious man capable of living by his pen, Thomson was afflicted throughout his life by increasingly violent and protracted bouts with chronic alcoholism, insomnia, and depression. At such times he incessantly walked the nighttime streets of London, trying to exhaust himself, but all the while unable to es-

cape sights and thoughts that only deepened his melancholy. Countless such experiences must have contributed to the nightmare of alienation and misery permeating Thomson's masterpiece, *The City of Dreadful Night* (1874), a poem Raymond Williams has called a horrifying "vision of the city as the condition of human life."[2] As the chief Victorian ancestor of *The Waste Land* (1922), *The City* continues to strike readers as "the most faithful and magnificent expression of the spirit of despair in all modern poetry."[3]

But few students of the work notice that the poem also attempts to overcome the very isolation and despair it so vividly conveys.[4] The "Laureate of Pessimism," as Thomson has come to be called, in fact employs many of the traditional doctrines of Stoicism to resist the typically Victorian sense of estrangement and disorientation evoked by the city. What makes this work remarkable among Victorian poems about the city is that it offers a solution to the familiar catalogue of urban complaints and fears, a way of dealing and living with the urban despair to which it at first appears to succumb.

Like *Idylls of the King, The City* relies on a monumental use of the city metaphor for its structure, so that the "City of Night" becomes not only a trope for the disintegration of the self, the darkest hour of an individual soul, but also a figure for the human condition in the modern world—a city, a country, a civilization in decline where "all things good . . . have been . . . strangled by that City's curse" (IX. 20-21).[5] Confronting the image of the city in its largest implications, Thomson utilizes the formal qualities of the episodic long poem to modify step by step the attitude of his audience toward the city. By learning to "read" *The City,* both as poem and place, the poet and his audience can come to terms with their shared plight of living in a world without hope or faith. The act of reading the poem reenacts the poet's process of self-education and discovery, gradually mapping and reordering the urban landscape of fractured identity and bitter disillusion. The narrator of the poem participates in the dreamlike scenes of the even-numbered episodes (II-XX), then later composes and intersperses the odd-numbered commentaries (I-XXI) which attempt to elucidate them. Finally, he writes the Proem that introduces the work. Forced to retrace his steps and relive his nightmare in order to explain it, the poet finds himself in a labyrinth paralleling the urban one he wishes to explore.

I

As the narrator acknowledges in the Proem, both he and his readers travel "the same wild paths though out of sight" (l. 35) of each other and can therefore break out of the isolation of their lonely journeys through the recognition that they are not alone. By addressing and thus capturing the attention of the *passante,* the poet

turns strangers into readers, overcoming their division and connecting all men to himself. The poem itself is the means to accomplish this, the poet's desperate attempt to reach a "sad Fraternity" (l. 36) of fellow sufferers whom his words will have the power to rouse to self-consciousness, if not to transform:

> Yes, here and there some weary wanderer
> In that same city of tremendous night,
> Will understand the speech, and feel a stir
> Of fellowship in all-disastrous fight.
>
> (ll. 29-32)

This never-quite-frustrated sense of community and collective consciousness growing out of the personal isolation enforced by the city is Thomson's most important theme. As early as 1857 he was brooding on it in "The Doom of a City," and by 1864 his formulation of the idea closely resembles the basic plan of *The City*:

> And I wandered about the City, the vast Metropolis which was become as a vast Necropolis. . . . [E]ver and anon, here and there, in wan haggard faces, in wrinkled brows, in thin compressed lips, in drooping frames, in tremulous gestures, in glassy hopeless eyes, I detected the tokens of brotherhood, I recognized my brethren in the great Freemasonry of Sorrow.[6]

Making human identification his keynote, the city poet entices the reader to admit his own inescapable involvement in the relentless landscape of suffering the poem elaborates. His readers are his subject, "Brothers of sad lives" (XIV. 79). Thus the overt and covert connections between men, as regulated by the unique and potent form of their collectivity, the city, become the Victorian city poet's chief concern. As *The Waste Land* later shows even more explicitly, Baudelaire's *hypocrite lecteur* must cross the Channel. There is no true city poetry without him.

Through its reliance on the participation of the reader, the poem paradoxically functions as a map or thread, the key to itself, as well as a skein of despair wherein the self may be lost. As the emphasis in the Proem on serving its special audience makes clear, the poet takes seriously the task of aiding the lost and weary. Therefore, although read first, the Proem calls attention to its having been written last, as an impassioned final word directly addressing its readers, an inviting open-ended coda that contrasts with the austere impersonality of the actual ending of the poem.[7] Through this apostrophe the work comments on its own legibility; it is written specifically for urban "initiates" who share the poet's sense of alienation and loss:

> no secret can be told
> To any who divined it not before:
> None uninitiate by many a presage
> Will comprehend the language of the message,
> Although proclaimed aloud for evermore.
>
> (ll. 38-42)

Yet Thomson does not plan merely to reiterate the familiar; rather, he intends that by threading the labyrinth of the poem itself the members of his "Freemasonry" will learn more about the City and each other. Thus the entry from his notebook describing his sudden encounter with the *passante* calls attention to his greatest obstacle: the remoteness yet closeness of human contact. The insulating quality of urban experience compels each individual obliquely to pick out his own way to consciousness, unaware of fellow seekers whose paths may cross his continually. Not until 1870, at the age of thirty-six, had Thomson become convinced that each man was spiritually alone in the universe, and among other reasons he wrote *The City* to share that discovery, wishing to draw his *semblables* closer together in the knowledge of their common condition.

But instead of proffering any consolation so crude as hope or even resignation, *The City* attempts to alleviate suffering through the presentation of a truth that should make each man's life more his own, and less vulnerable to the indifferent cruelties of existence. The poet writes

> Because a cold rage seizes one at whiles
> To show the bitter old and wrinkled truth
> Stripped naked of all vesture that beguiles,
> False dreams, false hopes, false masks and modes
> of youth;
> Because it gives some sense of power and passion
> In helpless impotence to try to fashion
> Our woe in living words howe'er uncouth.
>
> (ll. 8-14)

The controlled anger that engenders the poem consistently opposes the sleep, suicide, and death which the work at first seems to praise. Rather, the poet's harsh honesty acts like cold water dashed over the heads of the drugged and weary automatons the City creates. Ruthlessly exposing the "false masks" of Victorian complacency, he will instead produce "power and passion" through the potency of his indictment. Insisting on the power of poetry to keep the denizens of his city wide awake, the poet argues that the only responsible attitude toward life lies in the conscious experience of it, in the process of speaking the truth and refusing to accept the mind-forged manacles which shackle the poor and rebellious in the benighted streets of Britain.

Indeed, it is possible to see Thomson's poem in the context of the "discovery of poverty" in the East End that had been begun by Henry Mayhew a decade earlier and which culminated during the eighties and nineties. For although *The City* is as much a psychological as a physical construct,[8] it bears an important kinship to that literature of "exotic" travel through English slums which titillated and shocked the genteel bourgeois of the time. The pestilent gloom that Charles and William Booth, George Gissing, and Andrew Mearns saw emanating from "darkest London" was no less noxious than that

which clouds the pages of *The City*.[9] One can even see in Thomson's insistence on truth and self-awareness the same awakening class-consciousness depicted by Friedrich Engels in *The Condition of the Working Class in England* (1843). By converting his isolated wanderers to members of a secret fraternity of urban oppressed, Thomson invites the reader to discover a growing class identity which may ultimately overcome the reified state of the City's listless inhabitants.

But if Marxist formulations can be read into Thomson's poem, the author did not consciously see his work in a political light. A dedicated champion of freethinking for the poor, Thomson would have nothing to do with programs of social amelioration because of the purposelessness he saw in all human life. In 1865, five years before he began *The City*, Thomson had expressed his aim distinctly:

> Though no word of mine will ever convert any one from being himself into being another Me, my words may bring cheer and comfort and self-knowledge to others who are more or less like myself, and who may have thought themselves peculiar and outcast; it may be to them a friendly voice revealing that they have a brother in the world.[10]

Despite its forbidding atmosphere, in *The City of Dreadful Night* one can discover the solace Thomson intended his poetry to furnish: he uncovers the links, however hidden or perverted by city life, between all men living there and brings them to "self-knowledge" and identity, changing dispirited phantoms into unflinching endurers of urban emptiness. In this project, Thomson has much in common with traditional Stoic teaching. The apparently conflicting ideals of trying to achieve a brotherhood of man while at the same time seeking detachment from the miseries of the external world are both Stoic, as are the goals toward which Thomson applies them: self-awareness and survival. Therefore the conventional concept of "stoic endurance," the Victorian poet's response to a godless universe, gains a more precise meaning when played against the framework of a classical system of belief.[11] For Thomson, the path toward self-possession begins with a gradual rejection of the many misleading avenues of action.

II

As William Schaefer was the first to point out, some of the difficulties of *The City* may be due to Thomson's intermingling the first eleven sections he wrote in 1870 with a second, very different eleven he composed in 1873.[12] The inhabitants of the 1870 City are withdrawn, isolated victims of mental disorder brought on by personal misfortune, while their counterparts in 1873 instead form an articulate community of atheists who seem to condone suicide as a means of escaping the whims of an indifferent universe.

But instead of viewing the work as an imperfect merging of two "vastly different" poems (Schaefer, p. 615), it may be seen rather as a dialectic which teaches one to deal with life in the City. The earlier sections do concentrate on individual despair, but in the completed poem they function more strongly as demonstrations of weak or misguided responses to the City. The later portions reject these responses in favor of a more courageous communal action of self-conscious defiance, exemplified by the Melancholia of the final section.

By 1873 Thomson was a more confident and mature artist, carefully placing the first three sections he had written (II, XVIII, XX) in strategic positions where they would serve, as remnants of his own false search begun in 1870, to indicate the misdirections his urban Everyman should avoid. Vicariously tracing the wrong route through these episodes, the reader learns where not to look for consolation. By the time he reaches the emotionless exemplum of successful adaptation to the City, the reader is ready to accept its solution: the stern impassivity of the Sphinx in section XX.

Section II, the first Thomson wrote, begins the narrative sequence of the poem with streetwandering, an urban experience familiar to the insomniac author. Because the night wanderers are not only projections of Thomson himself but also, as the Proem tells us, of the actual persons of his audience, the poet trails the reader's shadow along with his own, looking for answers:

> Because he seemed to walk with an intent
> I followed him; who, shadowlike and frail,
> Unswervingly though slowly onward went,
> Regardless, wrapt in thought as in a veil:
> Thus step for step with lonely sounding feet
> We travelled many a long dim silent street.
>
> (ll. 1-6)

Evocative of Wordsworth's Cumberland soldier in *The Prelude,* the specter also reminds one of the "familiar compound ghost" with whom Eliot "trod the pavement in a dead patrol" in "Little Gidding." But here the encounter is a barren one, the figure's promising "intent" only a deception. He mechanically leads the narrator to three different sites in the City where, he says, Faith, Hope, and Love have died. Frustrated and disappointed by "this drear pilgrimage to ruined shrines" (l. 28), the narrator asks how life can continue in this condition. The shade compares his own existence to a clock without face or hands: life goes on, purposeless, until it runs down. Then the ghostly figure returns to his three-stop round, circling as the clockworks do, a walking symbol of a symbol.

In section XVIII, written soon afterwards, Thomson uses the harshest language of the poem to describe another ritual of futile motion, this time a man become utterly degenerate through his mad quest to find "the long-lost broken golden thread / Which reunites my present with my past" (ll. 50-51):

> coming level with it I discerned
> That it had been a man; for at my tread
> It stopped in its sore travail and half-turned,
> Leaning upon its right, and raised its head,
> And with the left hand twitched back as in ire
> Long grey unreverend locks befouled with mire.
>
> (ll. 19-24)

A grotesque example of human devolution, this "it" hopes to recover the innocence of youth, becoming again oblivious to life's misery. The thread it seeks

> leads me back
> From this accursed night without a morn,
> And through the deserts which have else no track,
> And through vast wastes of horror-haunted time,
> To Eden innocence in Eden's clime:
>
> And I become a nursling soft and pure,
> An infant cradled on its mother's knee,
> Without a past, love-cherished and secure;
> Which if it saw this loathsome present Me,
> Would plunge its face into the pillowing breast,
> And scream abhorrence hard to lull to rest.
>
> (ll. 56-66)

Usually sympathetic to the plight of the City's inhabitants, the narrator has only unreserved scorn for this compulsive retreat from the burden of experience. Although the Blakean notion of recapturing lost innocence had once sustained him, Thomson now saw any such hopes as a morally degrading deception which had victimized him and many others.[13] As Stoic doctrine points out, a "man is part of the world and should cooperate to serve the world's purposes."[14] The man who gropes for his own life-thread pursues only a solipsistic "solution" which would turn men even more inward, away from the camaraderie they unknowingly share. Moreover, he also brandishes a poisoned dagger and phials of acid, making him the only figure in the poem who threatens the life of another. Thus, this crazed regressor exemplifies the worst of all unmanly deviations, a backward withdrawal from consciousness and maturity which moves in the opposite direction from the narrator's existential search for his own as yet unformed identity. Though perhaps originally written as an isolated account of the mental disorder the city produces, the section is transformed into an instructive episode of misdirection through Thomson's deliberate placing of it as the last of the narrator's encounters with men "each wrapt in his own doom" (I. 54).

Ridiculing this obsession with the womb when the other oblivion, death, is so near, the narrator turns his attention in the following section (XIX) to the River of Suicides (1873). Although usually regarded as a sincere

expression of Thomson's pessimistic philosophy in which he endorses suicide as escape, the River of Suicides represents instead yet another false step away from maturity and self-knowledge. Recognition of one's personal power to gain "secure oblivion" is an important blow for individual freedom. But like many Stoics, Thomson seems to argue that the act itself may be yet another form of weakness or childish withdrawal.[15] In the concluding stanza, a parody of Tennyson's "Lotus Eaters," it is with irony that the poet lullabies his potential suicides to sleep:

> Yet it is but for one night after all:
> What matters one brief night of dreary pain?
> When after it the weary eyelids fall
> Upon the weary eyes and wasted brain;
> And all sad scenes and thoughts and feelings vanish
> In that sweet sleep no power can ever banish,
> That one best sleep which never wakes again.
>
> (ll. 29-35)

That "one best sleep" beckons strongly at the beginning of the poem, but by this point bravely facing the "one brief night" of pain seems preferable to the numbing loss of awareness. As this and the following episode confirm, the nightmare of the City insists on being experienced: neither poem nor poet can lose consciousness in the face of the horror of the City.

Although the confrontation between the Angel and the Sphinx is only the third section Thomson wrote, he later assigned it the important penultimate position in the poem. It sums up all inadequate responses to the City and offers in their place the only tenable alternative: impassive resistance. The scene opens with the weary narrator resting before the moonlit bulk of the cathedral, "a wave-worn rock" before which

> Two figures faced each other, large, austere;
> A couchant sphinx in shadow to the breast,
> An angel standing in the moonlight clear;
> So mighty by magnificence of form,
> They were not dwarfed beneath that mass enorm.
>
> (ll. 8-12)

While the reader may at first identify with the Angel who vigilantly raises his sword toward the impassive Sphinx of life, in the Angel's subsequent three-stage defeat—fallen wings, shattered sword, broken body—one comes to see the Sphinx's greater fitness for existence in a godless universe:

> The moon had circled westward full and bright,
> And made the temple-front a mystic dream,
> And bathed the whole enclosure with its light,
> The sworded angel's wrecks, the sphinx supreme:
> I pondered long that cold majestic face
> Whose vision seemed of infinite void space.
>
> (ll. 43-48)

All the ineffectual illusions of religion are manifest in the Angel's fall. The Sphinx with its vision of "infinite void space" triumphs over the active, idealistic Angel, whose associations with the Christian hereafter and blissful reward (a "mystic dream" it mocks. Even the rich moonlight which traditionally represents the poet's imagination seems chilled by the "vast abyss" which the Sphinx contemplates. As long as men do not fall prey to such false consolations along the way, the solemn regard of the Sphinx (and of Melancholia, whose "undaunted gaze" at life it previews) enables them to endure their existence in the City.

Other early sections of the poem function similarly in the final work, as episodes of misdirection. Sections IV and X, written later on in 1870, also show the personal response to be inadequate, this time by chronicling the City's devastating effects on love. In one of the most powerful scenes of the poem, the narrator comes upon a wild-looking figure who stands alone in a public square, declaiming the story of his journey across a fantastic primeval landscape. While traversing all sorts of natural and cosmic disasters, reminiscent of John Martin's giant cataclysmic canvases, he remains undaunted. But as soon as he sees the specter of the dead woman he had loved, he says, "I was twain, / Two selves distinct that cannot join again" (IV. 71-72).[16] The ghost embraces the part of him that had died with her, and both are swept away forever on the tide of an indifferent sea. Despite his original refrain, "No hope could have no fear," the traveller has given way to the false hopes of love, thus exposing himself to the bereavement which has shattered his identity. The weakness of having hope, Thomson implies, leads to an irrecoverable loss of self.

The day after Thomson completed this vivid parable he reinforced it by beginning a second portrayal of doomed love and the natural but misguided response to it.[17] In section X the narrator enters a brightly lit but silent mansion whose every room features a shrine centered around the portrait of a young woman. Finally penetrating an oratory decorated entirely in black, he discovers the lady of the shrines in funeral repose. A young man kneels beside the bed, resolving to stay by her in death as in life. This mourner's paralysis is the opposite of the previous lover's frenzy, but both wrongly allow their grief to render them helpless.[18]

In subsequent sections (VI and III), the last written in 1870, Thomson begins to chart a painful progress from self-pity and solipsism to eventual stoic self-control. The final success is only achieved in the 1873 portion; nevertheless, by retaining unaltered the earlier expressions of futile woe, Thomson is able to give greater weight and conviction to the more practical stoicism that supersedes them. He transforms his first disoriented

attempts to come to terms with the City by placing them in the context of the final poem, effectively integrating his "two poems" into a dialectically instructive whole.

III

Though the sections which expound Thomson's philosophy are often examined in isolation, they are seldom seen as a gradual progression of alternatives into which the episodes of despair logically fit. The last two sections Thomson wrote in 1870 begin a process of recognition, culminating in the cathedral scene (1873), that through fraternity men can achieve some measure of relief. In section VI the narrator, walking by the river, overhears one phantom tell another how he was ready to go even to hell to escape the City. He

> would have passed in, gratified to gain
> That positive eternity of pain,
> Instead of this insufferable inane.
>
> (ll. 22-24)

But as a resident of the City he was denied entrance: he had no hope to abandon. His companion's response, however, brings a revolutionary idea into the atomized, solitary world of *The City*:

> The other sighed back, Yea; but if we grope
> With care through all this Limbo's dreary scope,
> We yet may pick up some minute lost hope;
>
> And, *sharing it between us,* entrance win,
> In spite of fiends so jealous for gross sin:
> Let us without delay our search begin.
>
> (ll. 58-63, my italics)

Such deluded quests may be fruitless, yet in this episode Thomson begins to hint at the major theme of the poem: by sharing, though not necessarily in conventional consolations like hope, men can eventually forge identity through unflinching consciousness of their situation. The idea arises naturally out of the City's desolation, since values based on human commiseration are alone possible. Thomson is groping toward an answer which his later lines will make explicit: collective action, or at the least dialogue, helps men to combat "the insufferable inane."

The four stanzas of section III, the last which Thomson wrote in 1870, indicate that although he had inklings of how to resolve the problems he had set himself, he was too uncertain and weary of this intensely personal project to proceed. Struggling for a way out of the City's wasteland of grief, helplessness, and utter disillusion, the poet at first boldly asserts, "And soon the eye a strange new vision learns" (l. 8). But unable to see his way clear of "the gloom intense" (l. 14), he gives up and prefaces what was to be a two-and-a-half year hiatus in the composition of the poem with these lines:

> Crushed impotent beneath this reign of terror,
> Dazed with such mysteries of woe and error,
> The soul is too outworn for wondering.
>
> (ll. 26-28)

The breaking point is significant, because in May, 1873, when he took up the poem again, Thomson had formulated that "new vision" which makes the latter portions so forceful. With "renewed assurance" and a clearer sense of the whole, he confidently resumes at the same point where he had left off, the riverside (section VIII). Another man complains that destiny has singled him out for punishment, but his companion argues instead for "the supreme indifference of Fate":

> "The world rolls round for ever like a mill;
> It grinds out death and life and good and ill;
> It has no purpose, heart or mind or will."
>
> (ll. 36-38)

In the monosyllables of these lines one hears the pounding of Blake's Satanic mills, and recalls the opening pages of *Hard Times*. By insisting on the mindless mechanical functioning of the universe, Thomson readjusts traditional Stoic fatalism to suit life in a godless industrial era. The Stoics had held that man should strive for harmony with nature because all its laws and actions inevitably stem from the directing intelligence of the first cause, God. But Thomson substitutes blind Necessity for a divine Fate, thereby describing what man in the city has been reduced to in the most effective terms possible—those of the ubiquitous industrial process. Here Thomson anticipates Eliot's lifeless parade down King William Street: Life and Death are as mechanical as that "automatic hand" of the typist in "The Fire Sermon."

Yet *The City of Dreadful Night* offers an insight into the minds of the "so many" that Eliot's more exterior view omits. This is the radical difference between the two poets and the chief contribution of the 1873 sections. Still, we should be aware that the germ of the later sections is present even in section XI, written in 1870. Truly concerned about the masses, Thomson relentlessly examines the crowd until he can fathom "What men are they who haunt these fatal glooms?" (l. 1). Penetrating the superficialities, he finds in all a common delusion and fate: "rational and yet insane," they foresee their ruin but refuse to acknowledge it. This is what the poem must change, and the narrator, grasping this universal problem, makes the most important discovery in the poem, that whatever their roles in life, all men share the same condition: "these and those are brothers, / The saddest and the weariest men on earth" (ll. 27-28). Only the camaraderie of weariness and freedom from delusion can somehow make their plight bearable.

In 1873 Thomson articulated this intuition more fully in the explicit question which opens section XII. What if

"Our isolated units could be brought / To act together for some common end?" (ll. 1-2) he inquires. Prompted by the sight of a long line of the City's residents, "each silent with his thought" (l. 3), winding slowly toward the cathedral, the poet searches for a way out of the shackles of non-communication. The poem subtly shifts from thinking of the prison to "thinking of the key."

The long procession they form on the way up to the cathedral indicates the power of the City to transform any life it touches.[19] It is actually antiprocessional, exposing how the modern city produces individual alienation while still enforcing outward forms of the old social order. One of the chief representations and strengths of the community of the medieval city, writes Lewis Mumford in *The Culture of Cities,* is the church procession.[20] It offers the key to the peripatetic and social perception of the city, for through the winding streets the group collectively explores the expanding and contracting masses of architecture and space, noting the changes in silhouette, light, and shadow. The procession expresses the variety and fluidity of community life as it makes its way to the embodiment of constancy in change, the sum of their collective perception, the cathedral. Processions are participatory, and there are few spectators. The procession does for all what the modern city poet must do for himself.

However by the mid-nineteenth century the "non-plan of the non-city," resulting from the indiscriminate construction and demolition of the Industrial Revolution, fractured what little communal interaction survived from the Middle Ages (Mumford, p. 183). Yet as Thomson's inverted procession of isolation toward a cathedral of atheism demonstrates, the more men realize their separation, the more they can see in each other a common despair or, worse, the consequences of their own seemingly isolated actions. Thomson's procession serves an authentic purpose finally, beneath its silent, dissociative demeanor and godless destination, for it requires total participation and a renunciation of individual identity for the common acceptance of "this real night." This becomes the advantage of this community over the residents of Eliot's "unreal city"—their awareness of each other.

At the door of the cathedral a porter asks each man what he did before he came to the City. Significantly, the first is a social reformer just come from pleading "for some scant justice to our countless hordes / Who toil half-starved with scarce a human right" (ll. 14-15). He represents the younger, more idealistic Thomson who in *The Doom of a City* (1867) made the ameliorating possibilities of the brotherhood of men his theme.[21]

However, his own urban experience later compelled Thomson to surrender hope of any material aid. Like the Stoic Epictetus, Thomson comes to believe in a human

fellowship that does not depend on the futile hope of doing anything to improve men's physical well-being. Given the grim indifference of life, philosophical enlightenment and increased self-awareness are the only consolations he feels he can legitimately offer. A kind of fatalistic nobility, later to be embodied in Melancholia's "indomitable will," allows his fellow victims to confront their fate. Thus the reformer must admit that his efforts were useless: "I wake from daydreams to this real night" (l. 16). The recognition of this painful reality marks the turning point in the poem, and soon others join the reformer in his confession. An opium smoker, a clown, a monk, a poet with the vain Miltonic intent to "justify the ways of God to man," even a revolutionary—all concede the reality of this night, and enter the cathedral. Finally the narrator also acquiesces and follows after them.

The next episode, XIV, is the intellectual focal point of the poem, as sections XV and XVI are its emotional ones. Here in the cathedral the men of the City enter into a perverse communion, as they did in the procession. Their preacher unites the themes of desolation and fraternity in his first, Miltonic words: "O melancholy Brothers, dark, dark, dark!" (l. 25). Confiding that "Your woe hath been my anguish" (l. 32), the preacher stands in the same relation to the crowd as the poet does to his readers, and he tells them how he has searched the universe for some news to ease their suffering:

> Good tidings of great joy for you, for all:
> There is no God; no Fiend with names divine
> Made us and tortures us; if we must pine
> It is to satiate no Being's gall.
>
> (ll. 39-42)

Rather than merely shocking his readers, Thomson wishes to convince them that these ideas can be liberating as well. As the preacher concludes, "you are free to end it when you will, / Without the fear of waking after death" (ll. 83-84). The key word "free" suggests why everyone has not leapt into the River of Suicides. Though they take suicide very seriously, its real value, as poet and preacher realize in *The City,* is as an emancipating concept, not as an act of defiance or desperate escape.[22]

The fifteenth and shortest section of the poem celebrates the congregation's new-found self-awareness and freedom to act. In a ritual expression of collective suffering it recognizes that only human activity and belief can create value and meaning in an impersonal universe. Revising Christ's words implying spiritual immanence, "Where two or three are gathered together in my name, there am I" (Matthew 18.20), the poet asserts that only Man is there: "Wherever men are gathered, all the air / Is charged with human feeling, human thought" (ll. 1-2). The air is "with our life fraught and overfraught," so that no man breathes alone,

But nourishes warm life or hastens death
 With joys and sorrows, health and foul disease,
Wisdom and folly, good and evil labours,
Incessant of his multitudinous neighbours;
 He in his turn affecting all of these.

(ll. 10-14)

In a few lines Thomson sketches the vast entanglement of social and moral activity that is a vital part of city literature from Blake's "London" to *Bleak House.* Like Blake and Dickens, Thomson insists on the almost endless repercussions of each man's deeds.

The rest of the poem acts as a response to the powerful climax of the cathedral scene.[23] In section XVI, for example, a member of the "shadowy congregation" seconds the preacher's revelation. He complains that he had only one opportunity in all eternity for a happy life with a wife and children, "And this sole chance was frustrate from my birth, / A mockery, a delusion" (ll. 31-32). Encapsulating what is apparently the poet's view, he proclaims, "Our life's a cheat, our death a black abyss" (l. 41).[24] Thomson's decision not to end the scene here indicates his willingness to sacrifice dramatic effect to the larger didactic purpose of the poem. The preacher concludes the section instead on a more positive note: "I ponder these thoughts and they comfort me" (l. 54). The poet appears convinced that they will comfort his readers, too.

In fact, even the ending—usually viewed as a resounding anthem of pessimism—seems to undermine the supposed edifice of unremitting despair of *The City.* In the center of a park that overlooks the city from the north sits the "stupendous superhuman" image of Dürer's *Melancholia.* After describing her in detail (from the engraving, of which Thomson owned a copy) the narrator admits he derives solace from her stoic self-possession. Moreover, he admires her almost transcendent endurance in the face of the terrible fact that "all is vanity and hopelessness":

Unvanquished in defeat and desolation,
Undaunted in the hopeless conflagration
 Of the day setting on her baffled prime.

Baffled and beaten back she works on still,
 Weary and sick of soul she works the more,
Sustained by her indomitable will.

(ll. 47-52)

Despite the characteristically gloomy philosophy, here Thomson sounds surprisingly like William Ernest Henley in "Invictus," that anti-decadent paean to perserverance written about this time (1875). Indeed, the last lines of *The City* suggest that the poet's final intention is to fortify his readers, not, as is usually assumed, to dismay them further:

Her subjects often gaze up to her there:
The strong to drink new strength of iron endurance,

The weak new terrors; all, renewed assurance
And confirmation of the old despair.

(ll. 81-84)

The distinction between the fates of weak and strong is not a casual one; rather, the entire poem illustrates the differing value of their responses, which are summed up here. Perhaps intending to make the division even more marked, for "iron endurance" Thomson had originally written "stern defiance" (Ridler, p. 274). A subtle combination of masochistic pride and the Victorian work-ethic have crept into the poem. Thomson periodically insists that clearsightedness, brotherhood, and a sense of common suffering do not in any significant way combat "the old despair"—even though they may momentarily soften it—but like the Proem the ending of the poem implies otherwise. The syntactic ambiguity that enables "renewed assurance" to form its own unit free of "confirmation of the old despair" seems especially telling. Moreover, anything proposed as a symbol of the City's unity in the face of the void must inevitably take on positive overtones for those it strengthens. By concluding his poem with Dürer's arresting emblem of emotional stamina, Thomson freezes, glorifies, and mythologizes its final moment into a monument of "indomitable will."

IV

The narrator in *The City,* then, is searching for a way to come to terms with the meaninglessness of a universe ruled by blind Necessity. His journey gradually uncovers the hidden connections between the isolated members of his suffering fraternity, eventually showing that freedom and comfort can be achieved through a shared stoic confrontation of the City. Seen in this light, the poem functions like the sacred texts it parodies, bringing "cheer" to those who participate in the bleak routine of the Necropolis. Though an anti-pilgrimage toward a Cathedral of Despair, the poem has much in common with the literature which guides the wanderer toward the Heavenly City.

One of the original epigraphs to *The City,* often overlooked, further elucidates the structure of journey, test, and successful renunciation on the road to enlightened atheism. When Herman Melville called the poem "the modern Book of Job,"[25] he cannot have known that Thomson had originally headed his final draft of the poem with these words: "A land of darkness, as darkness itself, and of the shadow of death; without any order, and where the light is as darkness" (Job 10.22).[26] Thomson must have felt that these lines perfectly expressed the urban and psychological landscapes he wished to portray, for he had used them twice before, word for word, in "A Lady of Sorrow" (1864). That impassioned prose poem forms an hypnotic incantation of the elements which would later become *The City*: a vast city of Night,

swarming multitudes trapped in hopeless lives, the narrator's pained realization that these "*are* my fellow-creatures," even a female "image colossal" who dominates the metropolis as Melancholia does later.[27] Any glance at the earlier work gives ample evidence of the continuity of Thomson's thought, but few connections are more striking than his selecting the quotation from Job to be the last words of "A Lady" and the first of *The City*. Preoccupied with tormented wanderers who seek insight in a "land of darkness," Thomson was fond of thinking of himself as a Job, an Ishmael, an outcast. Like the narrator of Melville's *Moby Dick* he felt that his existence entailed motion, and he used the language of Job to describe it: "I believe I should never have a home, but be always going to and fro on the earth, and walking up and down in it, like him [the devil] of whom I am one of the children."[28]

The shadow of death, so much a part of Job's land of darkness, also suggests both the Twenty-third Psalm and another literary model—*The Pilgrim's Progress*. Like Christian, Thomson's narrator must wrestle with temptation in the valley of shadow, though the fiend he must overthrow is religion itself. But Job more completely exhibits the central psychological struggle in *The City* to define self and existence. Thomson's poem is less the physical, allegorical journey of Bunyan's tale than the Biblical inward search for enlightenment and self-acceptance. In Thomson's anti-religious quest both reader and narrator become Jobs themselves, striving to find a meaning or reason behind the disasters that have befallen them in the City. And as Job comes to terms with his situation through discourse and suffering, refusing to renounce God, so Thomson and his audience have to make their peace with the universe by acknowledging its godless emptiness and purposeless motion, firmly rejecting any religious consolation. The consciousness that there are no answers is the only salvation.

Thomson's metropolis is a true anti-city to the City of God—not an infernal city, which is still theological, but rather a construct with no meaning except what human action assigns. Therefore, Dante lies behind the poem only indirectly, and the references in the poem to the Inferno as a desirable place underline this. Thomson makes it explicit that, despite its torments, the City is not Hell, for his poem is a Book of Job without God in it.

Once we understand the peculiar relation of *The City* to the Bible, the reasons for its radical difference from most other Victorian city poems also become clear. Framed by Blake's "London" (1794) and *The Waste Land* (1922), the tradition of city poetry in nineteenth-century England is largely a search for a transcendent value that the city can no longer provide. In Wordsworth's *Prelude*, Clough's *Dipsychus*, or Arnold's "Kensington Gardens" the city conforms to archetypal notions extending back past Blake and Pope to John the Evangelist and earlier: it is an earthly version of the New Jerusalem which has fallen, producing lust and alienation, disorder and immorality. Only outside the city, in the presence of Nature's restorative powers and away from corrupting urban forces, can salvation be achieved or even attempted.

The poet whose search for meaning in the city streets most closely parallels Thomson's is also the one who seems ultimately furthest from him. In *In Memoriam*, Tennyson's spiritual nadir occurs just before dawn, in the empty street facing his dead friend Hallam's house (section VII). Like Thomson, Tennyson uses Biblical words ironically to indicate the failure of religious consolation: "He is not here," he says, giving the angel's words at Christ's tomb (Luke 24.6) an implication of irreparable loss rather than resurrection. The desolate conclusion of the section typifies an age which equated city experience with spiritual failure: "on the bald street breaks the blank day." Just as Thomson's despairing narrator circles through the city of his poem in search of answer, the bereaved Tennyson also returns to the "dark house" near the end of his work (section CXIX). There, however, the imagined pressure of Hallam's hand enables him to hold fast to his shaken faith, with Nature characteristically presiding at the moment of transformation: "I smell the meadow in the street," the poet rejoices.

Thomson largely banishes nature from his secular, artificial city, and one reason why *The City* steadfastly refuses to fall in with the typical Victorian notion of city as earthly reflection of heaven or hell is simply that these terms have no personal meaning for him. The "trackless wilderness" surrounding the City provides no Wordsworthian mirror of eternity, for Thomson starts from an antithetic premise: he sees the City as a permanent condition. The cities of Blake or Tennyson represent otherworldly destinations, but the horror of Thomson's City derives from there being nothing beyond it: it is a nightmare from which one cannot wake. In the ongoing misery of a life spent in darkened streets, one finds "a certain seeming order" whose grim logic insists that "where this ranges / We count things real" (I. 20-21).

Yet it is not only the physical reality of the City that mingles with allegory here. Rather it is the reality of the experience of life in any city—as an atmosphere, a climate, and even a cause—that the poem presents. The feeling of what it might be like to live in the City becomes far more concrete than any specific urban geography. In a world "Shut out alike from Heaven and Earth and Hell" (VI. 57), the nightmare terrain magnifies the worst characteristics of the nineteenth-century industrial city. Through the intensity of the poet's vi-

sion, the hyper-real and the dreamlike exist side by side. From this context Thomson makes it apparent that a major effect of the "real" city is hallucination. Yet, as in the great city visions of Eliot and Baudelaire, what seems to be apparitional keeps turning out to be brick and stone; one's experience of the city is undoubtedly tangible. The more we know of it the more "real" it becomes to both reader and inhabitants—until, in the central section of the poem, it seems far more concrete than anything that can occur outside of it. Closer to Baudelaire than to any English writer, Thomson shares the anguish of that poet's "Obsession" (1861), where even the darkest starless night swarms with the multiplying shapes of tormenting crowds.

But, the pressures of unceasing "thought and consciousness" evolve from the "strain" of section I to assume heroic dimensions in the figure of Melancholia. *The City of Dreadful Night* becomes both more livable and more legible as the poet and reader "wake up" to the necessity of confronting "this real night," making the bold effort to deal with it fully, not as sleepwalker or hallucinator, false tracers of its intricate text, but as stoic stern endurers, like the wide-eyed Melancholia. What the City does to its inhabitants—implacably eroding love, hope, communication, sanity—must be resisted through self-awareness, fellowship, and sober contemplation. The Victorian victim of the city must fight back with the weapons of the modern urban artist. Out of his "great expression of the spirit of despair," Thomson fashions a persuasive program for collective identity and defiant self-consciousness, which each weary wanderer can achieve through learning to read *The City*.

Notes

1. See Henry S. Salt, "Some Extracts from James Thomson's Note-books," *Scottish Art Review,* 2 (August 1889), 91.

2. *The Country and the City* (Oxford Univ. Press, 1973), p. 236.

3. G. H. Gerould, Introduction to *Poems of James Thomson* (New York, 1927); quoted in *Poetry of the Victorian Period,* Jerome H. Buckley and George B. Woods, eds. (Chicago, 1965), p. 997.

4. A notable exception is Peter C. Noel-Bentley, "'Fronting the Dreadful Mysteries of Time': Dürer's *Melancolia* in Thomson's *City of Dreadful Night*," *VP,* 12 (1974), 193-203. Noel-Bentley correctly assesses the importance for the narrator of Melancolia's "affirmation of endurance"; but his essay does not take up the equally essential role of human fellowship in the poem, which is the main emphasis of this paper.

5. The text cited is from Anne Ridler, *Poems and Some Letters of James Thomson* (Southern Illinois Univ. Press, 1963). Quotes from *The City* will be identified by line and, if necessary, section number.

6. "A Lady of Sorrow" (1864), *Essays and Phantasies* (London, 1881), p. 17.

7. Thomson had originally planned to end with the Proem's appeal, according to ms notations (Ridler, p. 270).

8. Ever since the poem first appeared, readers have consistently referred to it as a nightmare vision, a terrifying mental landscape where the poet's worst miseries are given an allegorical, urban form. Thomson himself suggests this point of view, both in the abstractions of the poem ("The City is of Night") and in his other writings. In "A Lady of Sorrow" (1864), for example, the primary antecedent to *The City,* he speaks of "the streets of the great city, that vast crowded encampment of what you call Life" (p. 39). But we should not overlook the mimetic aspect of Thomson's masterpiece, the relation of the poem to a physical exploration of the city, as well as a psychological one. In the case of "A Lady," where Thomson first explores most of the themes of *The City,* that "city of Life" is London. "I lived in London, and alone" reads the first sentence of the work, and subsequent pages dwell upon "the huge city and all its inhabitants . . . their thoughts, passions, labours, struggles, victories, defeats" (p. 5) which condition the poet's tormented vision. *The City,* I would suggest, is not solely metaphoric in either conception or actuality.

9. See Charles Booth's *Life and Labour of the People in London* (1889-91), William Booth's *In Darkest England, and the Way Out* (1890), Gissing's *Workers in the Dawn* (1880) and *The Nether World* (1889), and Mearns' *The Bitter Cry of Outcast London* (1883), co-authored with W. C. Preston.

10. "Sayings of Sigvat" (1865), *Essays and Phantasies,* p. 214.

11. I am indebted to Professor Carl Woodring of Columbia University, who first pointed out to me the parallels between Thomson and the Stoics.

12. "The Two Cities of Dreadful Night," *PMLA,* 77 (1962), 609-616. Professor Schaefer's essay contains a valuable chart showing the exact date of composition for each section of *The City*: II, XVIII, XX, I, V, XI, VII, IV, X, VI, and III were written in that order between January and October, 1870; VIII, XIX, IX, Proem, XII, XIV, XVII, XV, XIII, XVI, and XXI all followed between May and October, 1873.

13. See William Schaefer, *James Thomson (B. V.): Beyond "The City"* (Univ. of California Press,

1965), p. 74, and George M. Harper, "Blake's *Nebuchadnezzar* in 'The City of Dreadful Night'," *SP,* 50 (1953), 68-80. According to Harper, the groveling figure can be seen as Thomson's version of Blake's *Nebuchadnezzar,* and the entire episode as Thomson's repudiation of Blake, who had exerted an important influence on him for almost twenty years: "Canto XVIII reveals, in Thomson's examination and rejection of Blake's 'Golden String' as a means of escape from the dark night of his dreadful city, an irreconcilable difference" between the two poets (p. 80).

14. F. H. Sandbach, *The Stoics* (New York, 1975), p. 36. Just at the time that he broke off writing *The City* in 1870, Thomson was reading and writing about Stoic philosophy. Reviewing George Long's translation, *The Thoughts of Marcus Aurelius Antoninus* (1870), Thomson contributed three articles on Marcus Aurelius to the *National Review,* October 23 and 30 and November 6, 1870. Thomson also later reviewed Long's translation of Epictetus. See Charles Vachot, *James Thomson (1834-1882)* (Paris, 1964), pp. 303-305.

15. Stoic views on suicide were mixed, Seneca equating it with freedom, Cicero, Zeno, and many others cautioning against it as a quick solution, especially for "the unwise man." See Sandbach, pp. 48-52.

16. Many critics have seen this figure and his counterpart in X as Thomson and the dead woman as Matilda Weller, the fourteen-year-old Irish girl he was engaged to marry when he was eighteen. Apparently ending the poet's serious romantic life just when it had begun, Matilda's death suggested to him for the first time the pessimistic philosophy which would come to dominate his later work (see Ridler, p. xii and Schaefer, *James Thomson,* pp. 9-36).

17. According to Professor Schaefer, Thomson completed the last ten stanzas of IV on October 5, 1870, and wrote the first three of X on October 6, finishing the rest a week later ("The Two Cities of Dreadful Night," p. 616).

18. Thomson could be very hard on those who evidenced a sense of betrayal and loss, even to the extent of characterizing Christ's exclamation "My God, my God, why hast thou forsaken me?" (Matthew 27.46) as a "womanish cry of desperation" (quoted in Ridler, p. xviii). This condemnation of what one considers to be excess emotion is typically Stoic.

19. A much expanded earlier version of the procession can be found in "A Lady of Sorrow," *Essays and Phantasies,* pp. 18-21.

20. (New York, 1938), pp. 72ff.

21. In that poem Thomson had included a long catalogue of social injustices which could be consumed by a fiery "law of the Truth" if only men would cooperate with each other (see Part IV, Section IV, 183-208).

22. Two years before, in "Proposals for the Speedy Extinction of Evil and Misery" (1871), Thomson had asserted that *"the human race . . . can compel nature to do what it pleases, by resolving on instant universal suicide in case of her refusal"* (*Essays and Phantasies,* p. 90). The characteristic stress on collective action, as well as the vigor with which Thomson pursues this idea, suggests that he was not being entirely ironic here. For an extended examination of Thomson's relation to existentialism, see Kenneth Byron, *The Pessimism of James Thomson* (London, 1966), pp. 142ff.

23. Sections XVIII-XX have already been mentioned as misguided reactions to the City, and XVII exposes the pathetic fallacy: any emotion we read into nature is "a grand illusion," for "the empyrean is a void abyss" (ll. 27-28).

24. The simple family life is celebrated in much of Thomson's poetry, and he seems to have been happiest when living with the family of one friend or another. But he felt that his apparently hereditary alcoholism, coupled with Matilda's early death, had ended all such hopes in his own life forever (Ridler, p. xix).

25. Melville's remark is quoted by Henry S. Salt in *Company I Have Kept* (London, 1930), p. 108.

26. The Job epigraph is from the Morgan Library ms of *The City* (Ridler, pp. 270-271). Melville's intuitive grasp of the Job-like structure of *The City* was hardly accidental, for his own work may have provided a source for Thomson's poem. While there are similarities between *The City* and "Bartleby," *Pierre* (1852) most strikingly anticipates the structure, philosophy, and phrasing of the later work. Like *The City, Pierre* details an inverted quest for spiritual values and self-knowledge, brutally instructing its hero in the illusiveness of religion, morality, and familial security. Melville uses the same quotation from the *Inferno* to introduce a "city of Woe," dark, vast, and isolating, and like Thomson he writes of "strangely demented people;—composed of countenance, but wandering of mind; soul-composed and bodily-wandering. . . . Some were always talking about Hell, Eternity, and God; and some of all things as fixedly decreed" (*Pierre, or The Ambiguities,* ed. Harrison Hayford, Hershel Parker, and G. Thomas Tanselle [Northwestern Univ. Press, 1971], pp.

120-121). This remarkable prevision of the 1870 City (see sections I. 50-67; VI. 55-57; VII. 1-7; and XI. 1-20) is reinforced through many thematic parallels: the interrelation of all human action (p. 176), the controlling metaphor of life as a dream or nightmare (p. 274), the comparison of inscrutable nature to a sphinx (p. 343) or an abyss (pp. 284-285), a fatalism that mocks notions of free will (p. 182), and Pierre's joining in the perverse community of "Apostles" without a God (pp. 265-274). Moreover, both Melville and Thomson are convinced that the subversive truths of their work will reach only a small number of the initiated: "men are only made to comprehend things which they comprehended before" (p. 209). Such verbal echoes (cf. Proem, ll. 38-42) suggest that Thomson knew Melville's book as intimately as the despair behind it.

27. See Section III of "A Lady of Sorrow," *Essays and Phantasies,* pp. 16-21. For the quotations from Job, see pp. 31, 50.

28. From a letter by Thomson, printed in *Secular Review,* July 15, 1882, reprinted in Ridler, pp. 248-249. Thomson echoes Job 1.7.

Robert Greer Cohn (essay date spring 1985)

SOURCE: Cohn, Robert Greer. "Urban Mallarmé." *Stanford French Review* 9, no. 1 (spring 1985): 61-9.

[*In the following essay, Cohn examines Stéphane Mallarmé's treatment of urban settings and subjects in his poetry.*]

Poetry is situated, first and last, both above and below a hypothetical norm-line, that of chronology, history, narration. It is, as we now tend to say, primarily "metaphorical," which is to say not only vertical—"above and below"—but, in an ultimate *exchange* of our operational epistemological axes, also horizontal, Edenic, "first and last." So T. S. Eliot spoke of the poet as being both more civilized and more primitive than his more temperate brother. In other words, that steep up-down bipolar dialectic, we know, as Eliot surely did, is caught up, in advanced art, in a *dimensional* dialectic together with the horizontal axis of time, and also of sobriety, objectivity, realism, the prosaic in that sense, which includes of course the broad perspective of the modern city and some fits of urbanity.

Mallarmé absorbed this more complex atmosphere from his aesthetic era generally, going back as far as Sainte-Beuve's *Joseph Delorme* and snatches of Nerval, but Baudelaire was the obvious lesson here, the late Baudelaire who to his subjective axis of deep ambivalence in

fleurs and *mal* added the objectivity of the *Tableaux parisiens* and, as Eliot remarked, raised the imagery of the metropolis to poetry of the "*first intensity.*" On that initial vertical, of course, we find not only floral beauty and muddy evil but our sophisticated-primitive pair: high imaginative intellect and plunging sensuality characteristic of the child and the *naïf*; and we know that Baudelaire extolled the naïveté of Delacroix or Guys and the budding genius of the child. But this metaphorical profundity was *crossed* by the realism of the *Tableaux parisiens* and the prose poems where we find a subtle hint of the assimilated metonymic axis in the dirt-grooved paving stones on which he stumbled—the *heurté* effect of the preface to the *Petits Poèmes en prose* (on which Benjamin based a rambling essay)—and the parallel maturing rhythm of the wrinkles in his noble *petites vieilles* and the comparably fascinating *vieillards.*

All that dimensional play adds up to the often-fateful *croisement* in the swarming *grande ville* where his art crystallized solid as rocks in his poetic womb, as he elegiacally pronounced in *Le Cygne*: "Mes chers souvenirs sont plus lourds que des rocs": crystallized in Memory at the intersection of loss and recovery, gravity and grace.

Rimbaud too plunged toward the childishly pure and intimate even as his prose poetry rose to something well beyond the ordinary city—something in all-time and -space, metaphysic or cosmic or just sweepingly aesthetic, in the *Illuminations*. But again the art passes by way of the everyday of, particularly, London or Paris.

Mallarmé's art matured in the same way. The early Lamartine, Banville, and Hugo manner or bits of erotica went readily down to earthy nature and up to the stars, but the horizontal perspective tends to go past the limited locale of the city toward the oceanic in space and time, which will culminate in the *Coup de Dés*. Yet between these imitative-earliest and original-later manners there is much that is directly pertinent to the city, most typically, as we noted, in the prose poems proper and, inevitably, his fashion magazine but also in all sorts of other concrete imagery from beginning to end of his writing.

> Les sentiments de la vie parisienne pris au sérieux et vus à travers le prisme de la poésie, un idéal qui n'existe point par son propre rêve et soit le lyrisme de la réalité, telle est l'intention des *Poésies parisiennes.*[1]

In this youthful essay on the collection of his friend Emmanuel des Essarts, Mallarmé keeps his distance but at the same time is sincerely attracted to what he sees as authentic in Essarts:

> . . . il a senti que toute époque peut être lyrisée, et a compris qu'on pouvait chercher l'idéal hors de l'antiquité . . . dans la consciencieuse étude de son âme et dans la franche observation de son temps.
>
> (*OC,* p. 252)

This anticipates by a year Baudelaire's classic observation in "Le Peintre de la vie moderne," but Baudelaire had presented this view earlier, in the *Salons*.

Clearly, Mallarmé's view is complex already at this stage. One cannot at all agree with Georges Poulet, echoed by Guy Michaud, that the master symbolist's aesthetic would move in a diametrically opposite direction from Essart's. Not at all. Nothing in Mallarmé is that simple. Poulet's claim that Mallarmé's poetry exists by its own dream and is not the lyricism of reality goes with a whole train of weary clichés about his abstractness and idealism. Sartre, in his essay on "L'Engagement de Mallarmé" (*Obliques*, no. 18), effectively refutes this, seeing Mallarmé as an "existential" poet (saved!), adding bluntly that those who dub him a Platonist are "either dupes or knaves." But even this is problematic in Mallarmé: he is and is not a Platonist, and the word "existential" does not quite do it either. Some vibrant combination like "existential idealist" is closer. Mallarmé's idealism, above, must be complemented, on the metaphorical dimension, by an equal rootedness, gravity, and earthiness below, and this whole paradoxical axis is in dialectical relation with the horizontal: the metonymic, the historical, the real, including the city, as we noted earlier in speaking of Baudelaire.

One can call this position "ludic," thinking of his own "Jeu suprême," or holistic and organic, whatever. In any event, he is a poet of life in this rounded sense: "la vraie vie," as Proust put it. And it is indeed the atmosphere of Proust *avant la lettre* that we breathe in the moving tribute to Berthe Morisot who, though usually absent from Paris is described as "si sienne." He evokes: "une réminiscence parfaite, bonne, défunte, comme sîtot nous la résumions précieusement au sortir, dans les avenues du Bois ou des Champs-Elysées" (*OC*, p. 534). He calls up with deft impressionist touches her typical intimate interiors and adds:

> notre contemporaine aborde sa semblable comme il ne faut l'omettre, la créature de gala, agencée en vue d'usages étrangers, galbeuse ou fignolée relevant du calligraphe à moins que le genre n'induise, littérairement, le romancier; à miracle, elle la restitue, par quelle clairvoyance, le satin se vivifiant à un contact de peau, l'orient de perles, à l'atmosphère.
>
> (*OC*, p. 537)

Morisot could have ideally illustrated Mallarmé's fashion magazine, *La Dernière Mode*, in short, where he developed much of his elaborate later manner in connection with all that *mondanité*. I will not dwell on this, but clearly that aspect of the city, the *riches quartiers* and their feminine flowerings has a great deal to do with the liveliness of Mallarmé's final style. An elusive instance is the metaphor of the dressed-up stature as

writing, semiotic well before Barthes; it shows up in the *stature mignonne ténébreuse debout* of the twisting siren in the *Coup de Dés*, which is also a character of type. Here is another passage from the same essay, in the same urban setting, in a park:

> Féerie, oui, quotidienne—sans distance, par l'inspiration, plus que le plein air enflant un glissement, le matin ou après-midi, de cygnes à nous: ni au-delà que ne s'acclimate, des ailes détournée et de tous paradis, l'enthousiaste innéité de la jeunesse dans une profondeur de journée.
>
> (*OC*, p. 537)

The denial of traditional transcendence is patent but so is the complexity which subtly reintroduces Eden in modern understated form, through a sort of new testament of beauty and reality, which Proust will prolong.

Understated, urbanely, and no less powerful for that. One thinks of Mallarmé's quiet observation to René Ghil: "On ne peut se passer d'Eden." Perhaps we can speak of a sort of pantheism here as in the case of Debussy, implying a cosmopolitan belief beyond narrow parochialism, hence civilized and citified in that sense. We are on touchy ground here, and we must tread lightly. We are talking about something very subtle and in-between, dialectical, involving an advanced tension of opposites. Something like what Geo Norge had in mind when he spoke of there being nothing more *intimate* than formal French gardens. Or Richard Wilbur in *Ceremony*:

> But ceremony never did conceal,
> Save to the silly eye which all allows,
> How much we are the woods we wander in.
>
>
>
> What's lightly hid is deepest understood,
> And when with social smile and formal dress
> She teaches leaves to curtsey and quadrille,
> I think there are most tigers in the wood.[2]

Tigers or fauns. Whether framed in supple alexandrines or the elusive but rock-solid *tonal* score, we never quite forget that "L'Après-midi d'un faune" is French art. Mallarmé and Debussy, as well as Proust, were in fact born Parisians. One might pause here for a sigh like the one "Marcel" heaved on returning in later sadder years to the Bois, and momentarily conjure up a living representative of that *belle époque* of art, the daughter of Paul Valéry, Mme Agathe Rouart-Valéry, whose walls are lined with pictures by her Aunt Berthe as well as one of the finest Renoirs extant, a portrait of her mother.

Like Baudelaire, or Zola, Mallarmé finds poetry in the poorer neighborhoods too:

> Dans un de ces faubourgs où vont des caravanes
> De chiffonniers se battre et baiser galamment

Un vieux linge sentant la peau des courtisanes
Et lapider les chats dans l'amour s'abîmant

.

Mais ce qui me fit mal à voir, ce fut la porte
Lui semblant trop étroite ou l'escalier trop bas
Un croque-mort grimpant au logis de la morte
Par la lucarne, avec une échelle, à grands pas.

.

Du premier échelon jusqu'au dernier, cet être
Ainsi que Roméo fantasquement volait,
Quand, par galanterie, au bord de la fenêtre,
Il dépose sa pipe en tirant le volet.

("Galanterie macabre," *OC*, pp. 15-16)

Almost Hulot. This is mere juvenilia but it is in a vein Mallarmé goes on to develop in the prose poems as well as his "Tombeau de Charles Baudelaire." But many of his *poésies* are flecked with city-touches, not grimly *peuple* but rather everyday:

J'errais donc, l'oeil rivé sur le pavé vieilli
Quand avec du soleil aux cheveux, dans la rue
Et dans le soir, tu m'es en riant apparue.

Those old paving stones as I noted at the beginning are a part of the metonymic city-flavor, and those streets are the everyday setting of an epiphany; for Mallarmé, as for Kafka, miracles are in the streets. The pivoting of one dimension to the other, horizontal to vertical, occurs insensibly through the run-on line: "dans la rue / Et dans le soir." It takes off . . .

Then there is the Malte Laurids Brigge flavor of the hospital in "Les Fenêtres"; the lamp-post on which his miserable poet hangs himself in "Le Guignon"; the flag flapping outside his window for a parade in a sonnet to Méry; the "pot de fard gisant au pied d'un mur" in "L'Azur." "Remémoration des amis belges" is a reminiscence of the town of Bruges, its decaying walls and canals; "Aumône" describes an encounter with a beggar; "Brise marine" and "Don du poème" are city-bound: the poet dreams out of a window of escape from his urbanity and art. The whole of the "Tombeau de Charles Baudelaire" sets the mentor poet in his cityscape of gas lamps, sewers, prostitutes, and dusty trees.

Given the Mallarméan climate of mystery, these aspects of the metropolis come at one in an almost surreal scatter, and one can speak of modernist moods like cubism or *poésie éclatée*. But again caution is required. Mallarmé believed in coherence, strove for it, usually got it. He knew as well as we do that any art, like everything else human, is limited, fragmentary. But he also knew that if, along with an acute awareness of the former one did not simultaneously aim at coherence, integrity, harmony, and eventually total meaning, the art could not amount to much. This in-between position was exactly the one he expressed in the cognate matter of obscurity

(*Le Mystère dans les lettres*). The (old) New Critics and, later, Camus, called for tension in this sense. Obviously, a premature unity will not do it. But neither will certitude about the value of the fragment.

The "Tombeau de Charles Baudelaire" brings us, via the kindred imagery of "Le Phénomène futur," to the prose poems of which it is the first.

These, naturally, add a palpable dimension of realism in the sense of the median, the quotidian, and the broad perspective of the contemporary world. In a study of the prose poem generally, I observed that this particular *cross* of dimensions tended to produce imagery such as the *croisement,* in Baudelaire's preface and the *croisée,* or window-shape in the genre from Aloysius Bertrand through Mallarmé and beyond. In "Le Phénomène futur" it is the frame of the little *scène* on which the "Montreur de choses Passées" exhibits his vestigial and *originelle* stunningly vertical stature of beauty, "une femme d'autrefois," while the other dimension, of the decadent city, is spread in the background: "Les arbres s'ennuient . . . maint réverbère attend le crépuscule et ravive les visages d'une malheureuse foule . . ."

In the following piece, "Plainte d'automne," a true window looks out over a *faubourg*: the poet, through it, listens to an "orgue de barbarie," "joyeusement vulgaire," and the tone, with mixed sentimentality and irony, is almost campy, Brecht-Weill, very much of our time.

"Frisson d'hiver" is another domestic scene looking out of the window over a townscape: "les rues sont vides, je te parlerai de nos meubles." I skip over "Le Démon de l'analogie" to return to it later in fuller detail. "Pauvre enfant pâle" is about the little street singer who will grow up perhaps to crime, out of hunger, and die as a scapegoat for bourgeois society, the poet included, he thinks guiltily but snugly, again peering theough a window. "La Pipe" is a delicious surging up in Proustian memory, *avant la lettre,* of a London square, literally, and seen through a window's kindred shape: "J'ai revu par les fenêtres ces arbres malades du square désert . . ."

But this is sufficient, in our present little frame, to establish the stance of these enchanting pieces and, by extension, the whole development through prose in the dialectical way which led to the *Coup de Dés* and a great deal in modern writing after the celebrated "Crise de vers."

I do not, by the way, at all go along with the deconstructionist view of these matters. Poetry is not left behind or burned in the process, rather *aufgehoben,* in the universal pattern of the dimensional dialectic Hegel demonstrated, for example, in his on-going historical relations between the *Herr* and the *Knecht,* the master

and the so-called slave who is really a horizontal becoming, a worker leading to a bourgeois, all that in opposition to the proud, vertical and death-confronting, holistic "metaphoric" stance of the lord. Just as the *Herr* changes into later versions, such as Prince Hamlet and the artist-hero through deep dealings with ordinary folk and the sober Horatios of this world, so poetry becomes a less narrowly subjective affair through its truck with prose; the illustrations from Villon to our time are endless. The Kierkegaardian and post-Kierkegaardian critiques complicate this pattern, to be sure; but through Baudelaire, Rimbaud, Mallarmé, Valéry and beyond, the poetry continues to defy the repeated debunking assault.

Finally, I return to "Le Démon de l'analogie" to offer a smidgeon of what is fully available in no. 7 of *L'Infini*. The city is the backdrop: "je sortis de mon appartement . . . Je fis des pas dans la rue . . ." But the window here has become the "vitrine" through which he experiences the *déjà vu*. What he sees is another version of the *cristallisation* which is the window itself as a symbol of art, "ce cristal par le monstre insulté" as he called it in "Les Fenêtres," which makes us think of Baudelaire's most intense prose poem, by that name (it came a year later, curiously). And the crystallization, of haunting interlocking words and images, into *something* he does not yet fathom gives us the process of creation in the male womb, the same that occurred in "Le Cygne" where Baudelaire feels in his pregnant belly the elegiac strain of "Le vieux Paris n'est plus"; the embryonic stuff of art is in him as his "chers souvenirs" which are "plus lourds que des rocs."

In "Le Démon," too, the sense of a "glorieux Souvenir" goes with the stream of inspiration from a creative source, Eden way back there, lost as the old Paris—with overtones of paradise, no doubt—and childhood or farther back the womb. How this stuff stirs and brews involved with all sorts of other expressions running throughout Mallarmé's oeuvre is best left for that other place. Just this hint: it has enormously to do with the ambiguous sound *u* itself, repeated obsessively in phrases like "je fis de pas dans la rue et reconnus en le son *nul* la corde tendue de l'instrument de musique . . ." This *u* is tellingly ensconced in the central seminal symbol of the *plume* and its important echoes of *plus* as in the "Jamais plus" of Poe, "ne visite plus la plume" of the "Ouverture ancienne d'Hérodiade" and many another such cluster. The *plume* is anagrammatically in the key term "Pénultième," along with the obvious *penna* group: feather in his cap, feather pen in his hand, and the biologically creative equivalent in the *penna*-penis echo, whence the "Pénible jouissance" in part. All this swirls and expands into the kaleidoscopic complexities of the *Coup de Dés* through the "hilarité et

horreur" of the "Jeu suprême." "Le Démon de l'analogie" is squarely on this main route and solidly set in the true life of the poet.

And how solidly all that is embedded in our twentieth-century tradition is well put by Marshall McLuhan in his "Joyce, Mallarmé, and the Press": "it is the newspaper as seen by Mallarmé that provides most of the symbolist landscapes of Ulysses."[3] "Mallarmé is, before Joyce, the best spokesman of the new approach. In his "Shop Windows" ("Etalages") while analyzing the aesthetics of the commercial layout, he considers the relations between poetry and the press" (13). And McLuhan goes on to show how Mallarmé deprecates the finicky reactionaries of art: "Poetry (they suppose) will always be exclusive and the best of its pinions will never approach those pages of the newspaper where it is parodied" (16). Indeed, Mallarmé did bring the two together, and the *Coup de Dés* was the masterly expression of the new aesthetic in his own hands. McLuhan further enthuses: "The author of *Ulysses* was the only person to grasp the full artistic implications of this radically democratic aesthetic elaborated by the fabulous artificer, the modern Daedalus, Stéphane Mallarmé" (14). Finally: "It is the Mallarméan method of orchestration of the qualities of ordinary speech and experience that recurs, again and again, in the *Wake* (*Finnegans* . . .)" (18).

This is a far cry from the standard view of the aloof and hothouse, algebraic, Parnassian symbolist. That side exists, in truth, and there are many slighting references to the press as well as other vulgar expressions of modernity. But McLuhan is right in his insistence on the vein that runs in extenso through the late essays, "Crise de vers," "Etalages," and "Le Livre, Instrument spirituel" from 1892 to 1896. One can hardly say it too often: it is the two sides together that begin to tell us what Mallarmé is about and the cultured world growing with him.

The crystallization of mature poetry takes place at the intersection in Memory—"le glorieux Souvenir"—of loss and recovery, gravity and grace; moreover, at the crossroads of vision and sober reality; of space and time; of still, deep harmony and wandering-brook melody; of poetry and prose.

In the process of *organic* crystallization, which is the creative imagination, at every stage of the artist's special penetrating and structuring hardness there is a complementary feminine softness: at the peak, the icy diamonds of Mallarmé, but with the *clarté mélodieuse* ascribed to them in "Hérodiade"; these diamonds, like the ones in the sonnet to Méry, *weep*. At such privileged moments of supreme tendresse, the city appears through the eyes of Mallarmé or Proust:

> . . . et tout Londres, Londres tel que je le vécus en entier à moi seul, il y a un an, est apparu; d'abord les

chers brouillards qui emmitouflent nos cervelles et ont, là-bas, une odeur à eux, quand ils pénètrent sous la croisée. Mon tabac sentait une chambre sombre aux meubles de cuir saupoudrés par la poussière de charbon sur lesquels se roulait le maigre chat noir; les grands feux! et la bonne aux bras rouges versant les charbons, et le bruit de ces charbons tombant du seau de tôle dans la corbeille de fer, le matin—alors que le facteur frappait le double coup solennel qui me faisait vivre! J'ai revu par les fenêtres ces arbres malades du square désert . . .

(Mallarmé, "La Pipe")

Notes

1. *Oeuvres complètes* (*OC*), edited by Henri Mondor and G. Jean-Aubry (Pléiade, 1945), p. 249.

2. Richard Wilbur, *Ceremony and Other Poems* (New York: Harcourt Brace, 1978).

3. Marshall McLuhan, "Joyce, Mallarmé, and the Press," *The Interior Landscape* (New York, 1969), p. 17.

William Chapman Sharpe (essay date 1990)

SOURCE: Sharpe, William Chapman. "Walt Whitman's Urban Incarnation." In *Unreal Cities: Urban Figuration in Wordsworth, Baudelaire, Whitman, Eliot, and Williams,* pp. 69-101. Baltimore, Md.: The Johns Hopkins University Press, 1990.

[*In the following excerpt, Sharpe details what he regards as Walt Whitman's singular approach to urban poetry, asserting that Whitman exhibits a "preoccupation with the city's surface and depth, its textual reflection and physical reality."*]

Do you know what it is as you pass to be loved by
 strangers?
Do you know the talk of those turning eye-balls?

—"Song of the Open Road"[1]

What language speaks through the eyes of love? Of all the poets of the city, only Whitman so readily claims to have the answer. In *Leaves of Grass,*[2] to see eye to eye is to make the world exist, and to know oneself to be inseparable from it. By recording the casual contact between strangers, Whitman tries to capture the ephemerality of the street in the substance of the poem. He boldly asserts what Wordsworth dreaded to discover, that in the city no self can be held apart from the urban whirl, and he surpasses even Baudelaire in celebrating that belief. Arguing that the observer and the objects he sees engender each other, Whitman creates a poetry of the city that attempts to transcend the limits of the text by fashioning its own physical universe. Repeatedly he affirms the existence of a bodily relationship between himself and his urban surroundings, whether persons, objects, landscapes, or even his readers. His contact with the crowd becomes the means by which he builds his own identity, his own poetic city of the self. As he proclaims in "Salut au Monde!" (1856), "I see the cities of the earth and make myself at random a part of them" (*LG* 144). Because he seeks no less than utter "adhesiveness" between poet and world, Whitman's work is animated by the desire to possess the entire city, to turn sight into speech, and the poem into a palpable entity that can, like the electric glance between strangers, bring poet and reader into physical intimacy. The "act-poem" of making love becomes the model for his communion with the reader as well as with the passer-by.

This literary, almost literal, embrace becomes the means by which he authenticates his own being in a world whose reality, he suspects, can be established only by tactile apprehension. For Whitman, the perception of an object and his sexually imagined fusion with it are almost instantaneous, but everything rests upon the tangibility of what he sees. In translating sight into signs and the "talk" of eyeballs into images of desire, he repeatedly encounters limitations of both body and text that seem to threaten that reality. In poems such as "Of the Terrible Doubt of Appearances," Whitman voices the fear that the entire basis of his apprehension, and in particular the life-giving tide of the streets, may consist of no more than "specks and flashes" or "phantoms incessant." But by striving to make his poetry unite poet, word, and world, he discovers that the glance and the poem about it may be able to reach the reader with the force of a physical embrace. Only through "the mystery of eyesight" can the poet touch and animate the passer-by, the city, the reader; and from them he demands reciprocal creation: "O city! / Behold me—incarnate me as I have incarnated you!" (*LG,* 294).

This Never-Satisfied Appetite

From the start of his career, Whitman was confident that he would achieve fame as an urban poet.[3] In an early poem called "Pictures," he boldly set his own portrait between those of Dante and Shakespeare, depicting himself as a laureate of the city: "—And this—whose picture is this? / Who is this, with rapid feet, curious, gay—going up and down Mannahatta, through the streets, along the shores, working his way through the crowds, observant and singing?" (*LG,* 645).[4] Although much of Whitman's early life was passed on Long Island and in the still-rural town of Brooklyn, by the time he published *Leaves of Grass* in 1855 he had spent almost fifteen years working in and around New York as a printer, journalist, and editor.[5] In the Preface to the 1856 edition he declared his affection for the city: "Every day I go among the people of Manhattan Island . . . and among the young men, to discover the spirit of them, and to refresh myself" (*LG,* 733-34). In later

versions of "Song of Myself" he introduced himself as the quintessential New Yorker: "Walt Whitman, a kosmos, of Manhattan the son" (*LG*, 52). For, despite his occasional criticisms of the city, Whitman never really altered his belief that Manhattan was the center of the universe.[6]

Whitman's major city poetry belongs to the years between 1855 and 1860, during which he created the most compelling vision of the city yet seen in American poetry.[7] "Crossing Brooklyn Ferry" and the *Calamus* poems project an urban landscape thronging with crowds, permeated with longing, and insatiate for continual self-consummation. But the germ of this appetitive, sexualized city could already be found in his first great poem, "Song of Myself" (1855). With its sweeping certainties and nascent doubts, the poem anticipates the contest between appropriation and loss that underlies Whitman's entire *oeuvre*. In the sprawling catalogues of human activity that would become his trademark, Whitman seeks to encompass the city both imaginatively and sensuously. His inventory of urban life includes printers and machinists, factory girls and prostitutes, road builders, pedlars, and lunatics. The inhabitants of the city become a part of the poet who pays tribute to them, even as his identity is revealed to depend upon them: "Such as it is to be of these more or less I am" (*LG*, 44). The daily activity of the city thus produces not the strident cacophony of Babel, but the "song" of the poet who takes his identity from the multitude. As a line added later makes explicit, the poet regards himself as a harmonious textile woven of the crowd's urban multiplicity: "And of these one and all I weave the song of myself" (*LG*, 44).[8]

Yet beyond his presumption in claiming to contain multitudes within a single self, Whitman communicates what he called, in summing up *Leaves of Grass* in 1876, "this terrible, irrepressible yearning . . . this never-satisfied appetite" (*LG*, 753). The city that seems to offer him the substance he craves may, he implies, turn out to be only the echo of his own longing: "A call in the midst of the crowd, / My own voice, orotund sweeping and final" (*LG*, 76). For no city can ever be so full of life that Whitman cannot imagine wanting more of it, more from it, more than it. And this is precisely the void that must be filled by poetic assertion and literary self-completion. As he says of the relentless "procreant urge of the world," it paradoxically demands "always a knit of identity, always distinction" (*LG*, 31). The fusion between self and world is never entire, and the longing rekindles sexual, textual fires.

Thus despite Whitman's cosmic convictions and physical certitude, there remains room for literary mediation and interpretive risk:

I know I am solid and sound,
To me the converging objects of the universe perpetually flow,
All are written to me, and I must get what the writing means.

(*LG*, 47)

This three-line stanza, beginning with the self at the center of the universe and ending with it under pressure to decode hieroglyphic messages from an unknown author, represents concisely the obstacles which Whitman will face in subsequent poems. The more he seeks to establish his intuitive, unerring insight, his total interpenetration with the noumenal world, the more the very text that announces his omnipresence starts to confess its anxious insufficiency. "A word of reality . . . materialism first and last imbueing,"[9] he avows in 1855 (Murphy, 698). But he later revised the line to read, "I accept Reality and dare not question it" (*LG*, 51), thereby implying that he feared undoing the very authority he sought to assert. These doubts, and the reader-oriented strategy that Whitman developed to combat them, emerge clearly by the time of the 1860 edition of *Leaves of Grass*.[10]

THE LOVE OF STRANGERS

Between writing "Song of Myself" and the *Calamus* poems, Whitman moves from the long poem to shorter lyrics and in the process gives a more universal cast to the inhabitants of his town and their milieu. Forgoing detailed descriptions of his fellow citizens, as well as his mystic claims to have shared in their varied lives, Whitman curiously achieves a more personal effect by focusing instead on an archetypal moment: the poet's walk through the heart of the city. In these poems Whitman stakes everything on the emotional and physical contact he can establish with casual friends and instantaneous lovers. This pursuit of perceptual certainty through bodily knowledge not only underlies Whitman's vision of the ideal city but also, because it inescapably involves the mediation of the text, provokes a desperate effort to recreate the material world within the textual one.[11]

Whitman addresses his most powerful poems to unknown strangers seen in the streets as he passes. Occupations or physical traits do not matter; a look suffices to tell the poet all he needs to know about the new lovers he finds wherever he turns his head—for Whitman's supreme urban experience requires only a quick glance, and lasts as long. The momentary eye contact between strangers in the crowd both ignites their passion and fulfills it:

City of orgies, walks and joys,
City whom that I have lived and sung in your midst
 will one day make you illustrious,
Not the pageants of you, not your shifting tableaus,
 your spectacles, repay me,

Not the interminable rows of your houses, nor the
 ships at the wharves,
Nor the processions in the streets, nor the bright win-
 dows with goods in them,
Nor to converse with learn'd persons, or bear my share
 in the soiree or feast;
Not those, but as I pass O Manhattan, your frequent
 and swift flash of eyes offering me love,
Offering response to my own—these repay me,
Lovers, continual lovers, only repay me.

<div align="right">(LG, 125-26)[12]</div>

In "City of Orgies" (1860), Whitman fuses two of
Baudelaire's central motifs, bathing in the crowd and
the "swift flash of eyes" between strangers. In regard-
ing the city as a vast conglomeration of sexual desire
and promise, Whitman has much in common with the
French poet, who was his close contemporary.[13] Both
poets single out eye contact with strangers on a busy
street as a metaphor for the stimulating yet disjunctive
nature of modern city life. Mythicizing the vocation of
the *flâneur,* they delight in what Baudelaire called the
"bain de multitude." But if Baudelaire discovers in each
bizarre or beautiful stranger the depths of his own es-
trangement and the city's propensity to rupture human
connections, Whitman seizes his satisfaction from the
initial contact, ephemeral as it may be.[14]

For Whitman, the visual interplay between poet and
passers-by embodies the essence of the city's offerings,
and upon this momentary rapport all other friendships
and worthwhile communities build. Just as Baudelaire's
Tableaux parisiens revised the popular genre of the *tab-
leau de Paris,* the "tableaus" that Whitman rejects in
"City of Orgies" indicate the poet's preference for rapid,
repeated encounters with his fellow citizens rather than
static pictures. Processions, social occasions, and build-
ings seem paradoxically more transient than the linger-
ing intensity of glances exchanged with sudden lovers
in the streets.[15] As he writes in "Song of the Broad-
Axe" (1856), "How the floridness of the materials of
cities shrivels before a man's or woman's look!" (*LG,*
190). Casual but loving contact is the most permanent
feature of the city, a city where the word *orgies* has no
negative connotations, but is rather synonymous with
that quintessential urban activity, walking, and its re-
sult, joy. This intimacy between lasting friends and in-
stant lovers lies at the heart of Whitman's celebration
of the city; it forms the irreducible core of his poetic ef-
fort to convey that community to his readers.[16]

Whitman's roving eye delights not only in what Baude-
laire called "the bliss of multiplying numbers." Some-
times it fastens on a single member of the crowd, per-
haps someone already looking his way:

Among the men and women the multitude,
 I perceive one picking me out by secret and divine
 signs,

Acknowledging none else, not parent, wife, husband,
 brother, child, any nearer than I am,
Some are baffled, but that one is not—that one knows
 me.

Ah lover and perfect equal,
I meant that you should discover me so by faint indi-
 rections,
And I when I meet you mean to discover you by the
 like in you.

<div align="right">"Among the Multitude" (1860; LG, 135)</div>

The poem is rare among Whitman's descriptions of the
passing glance, for it shows the poet being caught in
the gaze of another.[17] The divinity of the eyesight that
bears a look of love, the instant rapport between sharers
of a gaze that transcends all other personal attach-
ments—these characteristic qualities of the encounter
are now being reported by the object of scrutiny. But
the poet is far from helpless in this visual field, far
from being discomfited by it; rather, he claims credit
for the situation ("I meant that you should discover me
so by faint indirections"). He salutes the onlooker as his
lover and equal, and announces that he will discover
him in return. Yet there is an element of narcissism in
these echoing, reciprocal actions, as though the poet
were looking in a mirror. Do such optic excursions en-
able the poet to reach out to others? Or is he just gaz-
ing at his own reflection? The poem hints at the voice-
less signs by which homosexual lovers recognize each
other;[18] if the gaze penetrates to no sexual difference,
the image of this "perfect equal" may produce just such
a sense of mirroring self-admiration. The actual contact
that could confer separate if similar identities upon poet
and Other is deferred beyond the poem's end: "And I
when I meet you mean to discover you by the like in
you."

Many of Whitman's poems pursue the endless stream
of potential lovers that the city streets provide.[19] Yet in
only one does Whitman match the finely poised ambi-
guities of Baudelaire's "A une passante." Though he
could not have known Baudelaire's poem, his own "To
a Stranger," written the same year (1860), provides an
uncannily direct reply:

Passing stranger! you do not know how longingly I
 look upon you,
You must be he I was seeking, or she I was seeking,
 (it comes to me as of a dream,)
I have somewhere surely lived a life of joy with you,
All is recall'd as we flit by each other, fluid, affection-
 ate, chaste, matured,
You grew up with me, were a boy with me or a girl
 with me,
I ate with you and slept with you, your body has be-
 come not yours only nor left my body mine only,
You give me pleasure of your eyes, face, flesh, as we
 pass, you take of my beard, breast, hands, in return,
I am not to speak to you, I am to think of you when I
 sit alone or wake at night alone,

I am to wait, I do not doubt I am to meet you again,
I am to see to it that I do not lose you.

(*LG,* 127)

Here the city, the presence of the crowd, and the eye contact between poet and stranger are so much a part of the moment that they are assumed and never mentioned. In contrast to "A une passante," where no words are possible in the deafening street, Whitman asserts that there is no need for words: "I am not to speak to you." Sight alone is enough, enabling the poet "to see to it" by his act of poetry and memory that the moment will not be lost. While Baudelaire cries hopelessly, "Fugitive beauté . . . ne te verrai-je que dans l'éternité?" Whitman tells his *passante,* "I do not doubt I am to meet you again." And yet, Whitman's stranger does *not* know the depth of his longing, while Baudelaire is convinced that the *passante does* know how the poet feels about her. Baudelaire's sense of loss is all the more poignant for what he and the *passante* have shared, once and finally; Whitman's satisfaction lies rather in the prospect ("I am to think of you when I sit alone or wake at night alone") and in the poem's memorializing of that possibility. Both poets make the poem a site of possession, but Baudelaire commemorates the past, while Whitman looks to the future.

Perhaps it is this anticipation that lends Whitman's encounter, for all its immediacy, an air of unreality, a quality of wish fulfillment:

You must be he I was seeking, or she I was seeking,
 (it comes to me as of a dream,)
I have somewhere surely lived a life of joy with you,
All is recall'd as we flit by each other, fluid, affection-
 ate, chaste, matured.

"As of a dream" the two halves of the fantasy, the yearner and the yearned for, come together in a hazy cloud of euphoria. In comparison to the particularized object of Baudelaire's poem—dressed in mourning, swinging her skirts as she walks, displaying a finely sculpted leg—Whitman's object of desire is discreetly sexless and undefined. The stranger may well be, in fact, like a brother or sister ("You grew up with me, were a boy with me or a girl with me"), further complicating the nature of the poet's longing.

Yet his "chaste" feelings can hardly be platonic. In three other *Calamus* poems, "Behold This Swarthy Face" (*LG,* 126), "A Glimpse" (*LG,* 131), and "What Think You I Take My Pen in Hand" (*LG,* 133), Whitman's urban lovers do make physical contact, sharing kisses, holding hands, and parting with loving hugs in the midst of a crowd. "To a Stranger" strives to achieve that established relationship for its participants as well: the intensity of the poet's conviction that the stranger is not really strange ("I ate with you and slept with you")

attempts to preclude the unfulfilled desire it expresses. Not only do the eyes and imagination find their consummation in the instant of crossing, but also does the body: "You give me pleasure of your eyes, face, flesh, as we pass, you take of my beard, breast, hands, in return." Here Whitman turns "the talk of the turning eyeballs" into a mutual offering, a transformation of self into Other: "your body has become not yours only nor left my body mine only;" it is, in William Carlos Williams' phrase, an "interpenetration, both ways." Possessing the body of the stranger in both the past and present moment, the poet announces his belief that the future will be his as well.

What initially appears as an instant, untroubled rapport with the anonymous Other becomes by the end of the lyric a psychic drama of desire as fraught with tension and contradiction as Baudelaire's sonnet. Even Whitman's enjoyment of the transience of the event seems contravened by his claim that he has already had "pleasure" of the stranger, and intends to do so again. The poet's quest for knowledge of the Other extends into both an intimately shared past and an anxious, wakeful future, leaving little room for the casual, present-tense encounter that the poem at first seems to represent. It is thus not so much a question of his stilling the stranger's motion as of their moving together in unison, and through all stages of life. Yet because all this passing, parallelism, and parting are mediated for us by the poet's aggressive omniscience, it is finally as difficult to believe that he has possessed the secrets of the stranger's life and body as it is to doubt it. The poem turns its gaze back on the reader, and only its first line seems certain: "you do not know how longingly I look upon you."

The possibility that you or I might be the passing stranger whom Whitman addresses attests to the evident power yet indeterminate depth of the poet's desire, his quest to possess even the crowd of his readers. If the reader is Whitman's *passant(e),* then the text is the fluid city in which they temporarily meet. The very indefiniteness of the "you" enables the poet to pull the reader into his textual crowd, swelling the ranks of the admirers he rejoices in having around him. But while Whitman's direct appeal to his unnamed auditor brings the reader closer to him as he strolls his poetic Mannahatta, another, complementary trajectory emerges: the poet is trying to break out of the text and into the city of his audience. As he says explicitly in another poem of 1860, "I spring from the pages into your arms" ("So Long!" *LG,* 505).[20]

Whitman usually takes care not to give this impulse too much rein, for it dangerously suggests that the poem may be more an inscription of emptiness than a cry of ecstatic repletion. Instead of containing multitudes, the poet may be exposed as a vast hollowness that craves

them. The significantly titled "Poem of Joys" (1860) demonstrates not only how closely Whitman associates the urban throng with sexual desire but also how painfully unrequited he sometimes feels his love to be:

> O for the girl, my mate! O for happiness with my
> mate!
> O the young man as I pass! O I am sick after the
> friendship of him who, I fear, is indifferent to me.
>
> O the streets of cities!
> The flitting faces—the expressions, eyes, feet, cos-
> tumes! O I cannot tell how welcome they are to me;
> O of men—of women toward me as I pass—The
> memory of only one look—the boy lingering and
> waiting.
>
> (Pearce, 261)[21]

The familiar "joys" of streets, faces, eyes, all in constant flux, are present; but they are compromised. Even more strongly than "To a Stranger," the passage confesses the ache amidst the excitement, the "sick" yearning for more satisfaction, more recognition, more love than "only one look" can provide. Enticing faces flit past at the boundary of the self, marking the lingering pain of their distance as well as the spontaneous pleasure of their brief proximity. In such moments Whitman, like Baudelaire, appears to depend upon the crowd for his own self-animation, the ardent vitality of his life ignited by the eyes and bodies of others around him and by the memory of unnamed possibility: "the boy lingering and waiting." In later versions of the poem, Whitman canceled these lines, perhaps because they gave away too much, not just about his sexual preferences, but about his yearning to be noticed by a city that did not always heed his advances. Here he has no "continual lovers" who "repay" him, as in "City of Orgies," nor can he maintain the emotional balance and mirrorlike coolness of "Among the Multitude."

But this is not his typical stance. Whitman prefers to stress his delight in belonging to the crowd, omnivorously devouring it. His awareness that others are as lonely as he is permits him to discover a paradoxical emotional unity in the very isolation that prevents their embrace.[22] A line from "Poem of Joys" celebrates that comforting revelation: "O the joy of that vast elemental sympathy which only the human soul is capable of generating and emitting in steady and limitless floods" (LG, 177). Such sentiments enable him to take a Baudelairean bath of multitude in the torrents of "elemental sympathy" that his own sense of human community produces. This belief is what justifies the earlier hyperbolic fantasies of "Song of Myself":

> My lovers suffocate me,
> Crowding my lips, thick in the pores of my skin,
> Jostling me through streets and public halls, coming
> naked to me at night.
>
> (LG, 81)

The suffocating, jostling proximity that for Wordsworth obliterates the self and its creativity provides Whitman with the very means of poetic life. This erotic bravado, publicly oversatisfying the private desires that prompt it, strikes the elaborate balance between sexual urges and textual gratification upon which Whitman's best poetry relies. It is almost inevitable, then, that his ideal city should be built around the free and open love of its citizens, easing the chronic tension between eye and Other.

.

"CROSSING BROOKLYN FERRY"

Whitman's greatest poem of the city, "Crossing Brooklyn Ferry" (1856), triumphantly meets the challenge of merging city and text, and it does so by joining site and sight, "I" and eye, to the moment of the poem's incarnation by the reader. Turning from present-day to future audiences of *Leaves of Grass,* Whitman transforms the reader into the longed-for passer-by of his landscape, validating himself, his poem, and his city through the reader's own physical situation, through the exchange of glances out of and beyond the page. Caught in the poet's vision, the reader changes from present stranger to future lover, and enters the ideal city of friends. While Whitman may not be able to guarantee the poem's "presence" as an extratextual entity, he can claim that immediacy by exploiting the poem's undeniable textual presence to the reader, and the reader's present-tense relation to it.

Whitman's preoccupation with the city's surface and depth, its textual reflection and physical reality, make it appropriate that he should begin his poem by confronting the mirroring surfaces of sea and sky. The first two lines enlarge the notion of visual rapport with a passing stranger to include the landscape itself:

> Flood-tide below me! I see you face to face!
> Clouds of the west—sun there half an hour high—I
> see you also face to face.
>
> (LG, 159)[23]

Just as the poet eliminates the difference between himself and others through a single glance, he now sees eye to eye with all the external world. The reiterated phrase "face to face" evokes St. Paul's relation to God, and implies that Whitman's experience of the city is providentially sanctioned, and more celestial than earthly. The poet inspects his subject, not through a glass darkly, but by looking directly into the natural manifestation of the Divine countenance—which, reflected in the water, will turn out to be the poet's own.[24]

Far from being a timeless, static moment, everything is in motion around the ferry—tide, shipping, sea-birds, snapping flags above shore and sail. And yet few poems

approach the sustained liminality of "Crossing Brooklyn Ferry"; even as landscape, poet, and reader all surge toward one another in countless ways, each seems balanced on a fulcrum. While the ferry traverses the river from Manhattan's business district toward Brooklyn's hills, poem and poet rest poised between city and country, day and night, amid earth, air, and water, with the fourth element, fire, visible in the setting sun and the brightening flares of foundry chimneys.

The reader, too, partakes of this motion and balance. The next few lines prepare for another and even more important crossing:

> Crowds of men and women attired in the usual costumes, how curious you are to me!
> On the ferry-boats the hundreds and hundreds that cross, returning home, are more curious to me than you suppose,
> And you that shall cross from shore to shore years hence are more to me, and more in my meditations, than you might suppose.
>
> (*LG,* 159-60)

Poet and reader begin to engage in a double motion, not just across the river in their respective eras, but across time and text, toward each other.[25] The shifting referent of "you" here indicates the line of the poet's attack: first he names fellow participants in the present scene, then an unsupposing contemporary reader, and finally ferry riders and readers of the years to come. In place of the delocalized encounter usual in lyric poetry, Whitman situates the reader as part of a specific urban landscape, the poet's own. As it develops, their bond will depend increasingly on their common experience of the scene they share, each inseparable from the harbor and its sights. The mirroring relationship that being "face to face" with water and sky implies thus prepares for the subsequent effort to bring poet and reader to a similar understanding.

Drawing his own breath from the objects around him— "The impalpable sustenance of me from all things at all hours of the day"—the poet dissolves his being into the city's: "The simple, compact, well-join'd scheme, myself disintegrated, every one disintegrated yet part of the scheme" (*LG,* 160). The myriad phenomena that seemed to Wordsworth to melt into an incomprehensible mass from the heat of the throng retain for Whitman their individuality even as they show their common substance. The enduring differences of the crowd are the means to and proof of the identity which assimilates them; the "certainty of others" cannot be denied, making urban perception a sort of divine rosary: "The glories strung like beads on my smallest sights and hearings, on the walk in the street and the passage over the river" (*LG,* 160). The "scheme" in which they share comprises the poem as well as the city and its citizens, and through it Whitman intends to bring them all to an awareness of their underlying union with the landscape.

Thus, in section 3 the poet insists on the converging parallels between his life, his city, and those of the reader:

> It avails not, time nor place—distance avails not,
> I am with you, you men and women of a generation, or ever so many generations hence,
> Just as you feel when you look on the river and sky, so I felt,
> Just as any of you is one of a living crowd, I was one of a crowd
>
>
>
> I too many and many a time cross'd the river of old
>
>
>
> Saw the reflection of the summer sky in the water,
> Had my eyes dazzled by the shimmering track of beams,
> Look'd at the fine centrifugal spokes of light round the shape of my head in the sunlit water.
>
> (*LG,* 160-61)

Like ripples spreading outward from his haloed head, the next twenty lines describe clouds, bay, ships, sailors, and shore as day deepens into night. Each line begins with or implies verbs of sight: "watched," "saw," "look'd." At this stage, visual interaction is primary, the intensity of the poem's sight becoming the reflection of the self-reflection that poet and reader see in the landscape. Like the paintings of John Kensett or Martin Heade, or the sporting pictures of Thomas Eakins, such as *Max Schmidt in Single Scull,* these passages depict a luminist world resting perfectly at the intersection of time and eternity.

But at the center of the poem, in section 5, vision gives way to the quest for a more immediate and physical rapport. Playing on the double sense of the question "What is it then between us?" Whitman provokes the reader to consider the nascent relationship they share while also discounting any obstacle to it: "Whatever it is, it avails not" (*LG,* 162). Through an increasingly passionate appeal to mutual experiences and desires, Whitman thrusts himself upon his audience, even those "ever so many generations hence." Yet as in other poems expressing this textual-material tension, he voices his fears about his unreality and solitude, in order to overcome them:

> I too walk'd the streets of Manhattan island, and bathed in the waters around it,
> I too felt the curious abrupt questionings stir within me,
> In the day among crowds of people sometimes they came upon me,
> In my walks home late at night or as I lay in my bed they came upon me,
> I too had been struck from the float forever held in solution,
> I too had receiv'd identity by my body,

That I was I knew was of my body, and what I should
be I knew I should be of my body.

(*LG*, 162)

It is only through the body, finally, that the poet can address the sexual and metaphysical questionings that have risen from the city to disturb him, and through which, in his isolation, he can feel his connection to countless others like him.

This is Whitman's strongest move, to draw boldly upon the reader's own body and personality to give substance to himself. As he ingenuously puts it in the 1876 Preface, "I meant *Leaves of Grass* . . . to be the Poem of Identity, (of *Yours*, whoever you are, now reading these lines)" (*LG*, 752). Anticipating that the reader may not always possess an identity and outlook conducive to reproducing the poet's own, he counters by skillfully insinuating just how "whoever you are" might feel deep down inside. Thus, in "A Song for Occupations" he remarks reassuringly, "If you meet some stranger in the streets and love him or her, why I often meet strangers in the street and love them" (*LG*, 212). This typical allusion to the fellowship of shared emotions cleverly assigns to the reader habits that actually belong to the poet. In practice, the intimate effect of Whitman's appeal transcends its shakiness as a rhetorical strategy. Built entirely on this principle, section 6 of "Crossing Brooklyn Ferry" not only contains Whitman's most convincing attempt to prove that he too "knew what it was to be evil," but also provides one of his most eloquent descriptions of casual urban love and longing: "I too," he says,

> Was call'd by my nighest name by clear loud voices
> of young men as they saw me approaching or pass-
> ing,
> Felt their arms on my neck as I stood, or the negligent
> leaning of their flesh against me as I sat,
> Saw many I loved in the street or ferry-boat or public
> assembly, yet never told them a word.

(*LG*, 162-63)

In the guise of recognizing in the reader traits indelibly his own, Whitman manages to convey what "identity by my body" might mean for the person who inhabits it beyond the scope of a poem.

With common ground now established, the two brief stanzas of section 7 take the decisive step:

> Closer yet I approach you,
> What thought you have of me now, I had as much of
> you—I laid in my stores in advance,
> I consider'd long and seriously of you before you
> were born.
>
> Who was to know what should come home to me?
> Who knows but I am enjoying this?

Who knows, for all the distance, but I am as good as
looking at you now, for all you cannot see me?

(*LG*, 163)

Here for the first time the reader is assumed to be thinking of the poet who has lain patiently in wait for so long. Calling attention to but dismissing the fact that he is present only by his words, Whitman assigns to the reader responsibility for any absence: the reader is blind, while the poet can see, reveling as usual in the pleasures of sight.

The crucial, consummatory visual contact has finally been made. But the poet remains hidden from the reader, and the circuit of sight must be completed indirectly by the landscape they both look upon, separately yet together. When the poet's glance shifts momentarily back to his surroundings at the start of section 8, the climax is reached: "Ah, what can ever be more stately and admirable to me than mast-hemm'd Manhattan?" (*LG*, 163). Nothing, comes the answer, except the people of the city, his readers, whom he now knows through the landscape and who are therefore inextricably bound to it, participating with him in its divinity as intimate friends:

> What gods can exceed these that clasp me by the hand,
> and with voices I love call me promptly and loudly
> by my nighest name as I approach?
> What is more subtle than this which ties me to the
> woman or man that looks in my face?
> Which fuses me into you now, and pours my meaning
> into you?

(*LG*, 164)

By returning to the archetypal "face to face" communion of poet and city with which he began, Whitman miraculously cures the blindness of the text and "fuses" sexually as well as spiritually with "the man or woman that looks in my face"—the reader. The amorous relationship with the city and its inhabitants that they now have in common makes them both contemporaries and lovers; the look they exchange through the page collapses their distance in time and space. Moreover, it annihilates textual as well as temporal gaps between them, and "pours my meaning" beyond any doubts into the reader. The rest of the section displays satisfaction after consummation: "We understand then do we not? / What I promis'd without mentioning it, have you not accepted?" (*LG*, 164). The lines emphasize the mystical nature of the union effected; we can note the steps leading to it, but cannot really specify how it has happened. Because Whitman courts the reader by indirection and glances, they meet only by a kind of peripheral vision, when each regards the city rather than the other.

Yet the final section leaves no doubt as to the outcome. Poet and reader return to the panorama of harbor, town, and sky, now in full rapport with it. Other writers may

engage our interest by investing their images with enough symbolic resonance to make us feel that we too share their urban sensibility. But Whitman makes himself and the reader co-eternal with the city, joined with it in a permanently orgasmic union:

> Flow on, river! flow with the flood-tide, and ebb with the ebb-tide!
> Frolic on, crested and scallop-edg'd waves!
> Gorgeous clouds of the sunset! drench with your splendor me, or the men and women generations after me!
> Cross from shore to shore, countless crowds of passengers!
> Stand up, tall masts of Mannahatta! stand up, beautiful hills of Brooklyn!
> Throb, baffled and curious brain! throw out questions and answers!
> Suspend here and everywhere, eternal float of solution!
> Gaze, loving and thirsty eyes, in the house or street or public assembly!
>
> (*LG*, 164)

The admonition to the "loving and thirsty eyes" points to the source of this giant procreation: flooding tides, drenching clouds, erect masts and hills, and ejaculating mind all leap almost visibly from the poet's animating glance. For Whitman, city life does not exist apart from his perception of it,[26] just as his own life would be empty without the city to stimulate poetry and even thought itself. Mingling with the material of his creation, the poet becomes a god, the mirroring environment of the opening lines now spontaneously providing halos for him and his city of saints: "Diverge, fine spokes of light, from the shape of my head, or any one's head, in the sunlit water!" (*LG*, 165).[27]

Corona'd all, poet, reader, and citizens of Mannahatta become members of a harmoniously pastoralized city of the Saved.[28] The four elements serve as the four-square walls of this New Jerusalem:

> Fly on, sea-birds! fly sideways, or wheel in large circles high in the air;
> Receive the summer sky, you water, and faithfully hold it till all downcast eyes have time to take it from you!
>
>
>
> Burn high your fires, foundry chimneys! cast black shadows at nightfall! cast red and yellow light over the tops of the houses!
>
>
>
> Thrive, cities—bring your freight, bring your shows. . . .
>
> (*LG*, 164-65)

As the godlike poet sets the city in motion with his exultant imperatives, Revelation's divine marriage of heaven and earth converges with the Wordsworthian marriage of man and nature, body and soul, to create an urban-pastoral synthesis, the prosperous, industrialized new garden of the West.[29] Arrayed for the holy union, the entire city participates in the wedding. Assuming the roles of bride and groom, the "beautiful hills of Brooklyn" meet the "tall masts of Mannahatta" that stand up to greet them at the poet's command. In the prefatorial letter to the 1856 edition of *Leaves of Grass*, Whitman speaks of "the divinity of sex" (*LG*, 738), and to the degree that "Crossing Brooklyn Ferry" merges city and nature, poet and reader, through that medium, the entire scene becomes a celestial landscape perfumed with the scent of the bodies that enclose and sustain the soul: "You necessary film, continue to envelop the soul, / About my body for me, and your body for you, be hung our divinest aromas" (*LG*, 165).

Earlier in section 6, in the context of "gnawing" uncertainties, the poet had confessed that he too played "the same old role" (*LG*, 163) in the self-conscious drama of life. But having now penetrated through the text to reader and landscape, he returns to the troubling image with renewed enthusiasm. Now he both accepts the divisions between self, object, and city that might encourage this inauthentic theatrical activity, and at the same time suggests that they have lost their power to mediate, to keep each apart from its essence:

> Live, old life! play the part that looks back on the actor or actress!
> Play the old role, the role that is great or small according as one makes it!
> Consider, you who peruse me, whether I may not in unknown ways be looking upon you.
>
> (*LG*, 164)

As he commands a moment later, "Appearances, now or henceforth, indicate what you are" (*LG*, 165). Reversing the opening passages where the poet scrutinizes the reader, the writer admits that to us he is only a text. Accepting that *his* role is to be perused, Whitman leaves to his readers the task of imagining the "unknown ways" that the poet's presence and empowering vision can reach us. The mutual exchange between eyes and mirroring sky and sea serves as a model for the loyal reciprocity that ought to obtain between them: "Receive the summer sky, you water, and faithfully hold it till all downcast eyes have time to take it from you!" Like the water he traverses and imprints with his own reflection, Whitman has been entrusted with impressions he must preserve until all the "downcast eyes" of his reading public remove them from him. As long as the bay mirrors the world above it, the poet can count on his poem being charged with elemental "questions and answers" (*LG*, 164) that the reader, through personal rapport with the scene, will then be able to draw from it.

The conclusion of this interchange carries with it the heightened awareness that all inanimate objects mani-

fest as much of the heavenly as the poet's silhouette in the water. The assimilation of matter and mind by one another is complete:

> You have waited, you always wait, you dumb, beautiful ministers,
> We receive you with free sense at last, and are insatiate henceforward,
> Not you any more shall be able to foil us, or withhold yourselves from us,
> We use you, and do not cast you aside—we plant you permanently within us,
> We fathom you not—we love you—there is perfection in you also,
> You furnish your parts toward eternity,
> Great or small, you furnish your parts toward the soul.
>
> (*LG*, 165)[30]

Creating a self commensurate with the city, and a city inseparable from the self, Whitman nevertheless does not claim to have mastered or subsumed the phenomena he addresses: "We fathom you not." The plural subject confirms that Whitman has decisively joined himself to the former "you" of the reader, both becoming fellow admirers of the harbor scene that lies open to them. The receptive "free sense" with which in turn they admit the "dumb, beautiful ministers" of the material world into their lives is the relaxed outcome of the poem's gradual but importunate processes of commingling observer, text, and world. Nonetheless, the fact of their being "insatiate henceforward" indicates that the old longing must continue, as part of the inevitable thrust of life, even in divine conditions. Though poet has crossed to reader, the rest of the scene guards its liminal quality, adding subject and object to the list of items suspended in transit. The city and its objects, although unable to withhold their substance from the desire of the poet who wishes to internalize them, still remain independent "parts toward eternity." With the realization of permanence and perfection, the poem claims for itself a lasting status in the field of entities penetrated by sight and born of the body. As the imagination and body are projected onto the urban landscape which has become cosmic, and material phenomena are planted within, the poem partakes of world and word in its own "unknown ways," the ever-retraceable record of the soul's embrace of the city.

Whitman himself was at times skeptical of the reality of this encounter. But through his amorous "face to face" apprehension of the city's stones, streets, and passing strangers, and his absorption of them in return, he builds in his poetry the almost palpable city of Mannahatta, a modern, secular, and sensuous New Jerusalem fabricated from the contemporary materials of thriving New York. Defying textuality by announcing it, he asserts the solidity of his city by claiming the reader's body for his own. Seen in this light, Whitman's program for self-incarnation appears both less assured and more daring than previously imagined. If his frank sexuality as a "lover of populous pavements" (*LG*, 15) makes him more thoroughly sympathetic to modern city life than Blake, Wordsworth, or even Baudelaire, his "terrible doubts" about the substance of his vision bind him to all the poets of the unreal city, and foreshadow the fractured cityscapes of *The Waste Land* and *Paterson*.

In a letter written in 1889, two years before his death, Whitman addresses for a final time the relation between his poems and the city, setting out in the process what would later become the underlying principle of William Carlos Williams' epic. He summarizes the bond with a characteristic appeal to the sexual conjunction that was always, for him, at the heart of both urban and literary existence:

> I can hardly tell why, but feel very positively that if any thing can justify my revolutionary attempts & utterances it is such *ensemble*—like a great city to modern civilization, & a whole combined clustering paradoxical identity a man, a woman.[31]

The worth of *Leaves of Grass* as innovative poetry, Whitman concludes, lies in the book's being itself like a city. In its variousness, its desires and frustrations, its sense of being separate from yet joined to the lovers on the other side of the page, it embodies the "whole combined clustering paradoxical identity" of male and female that marks the "ensemble" of Whitman's work. By the force of the analogy, Whitman completes a circuit that he had dedicated his poetic career to closing—from the physical body of the poet to the body of his work, and ultimately, mysteriously, to a city of sexual beings of whom he counts himself one. If the city is the concrete image of his life's work, then his life itself may seem to merge with that irresistible metropolis which, "insatiate," he takes such pains to make solid in his writing. That he can "hardly tell why" this incarnation should occur is the appropriate sendoff to such a city of texts, for they successfully resist logic each time they insist on "the mystery of the eyesight" and the tactile rewards it yields.

Notes

1. The epigraph is from *Leaves of Grass*, ed. Sculley Bradley and Harold W. Blodgett (1965; New York: Norton, 1973), 153.

2. Wherever possible, Whitman's poems are cited by page number from the above edition, hereafter abbreviated *LG*. This text is based on the final, "death-bed" edition of *Leaves of Grass* (Philadelphia: David McKay, 1891-1892). Dates indicate when poems first appeared in print, even if revised later; but unless noted, the text cited differs only minutely from that originally published. I have also relied on *Leaves of Grass: The First (1855) Edition*, ed. Malcolm Cowley (New York:

Viking, 1959) and *Walt Whitman: The Complete Poems,* ed. Francis Murphy (New York: Penguin, 1975) for some early texts, including the original "Song of Myself," and on *Leaves of Grass: Facsimile Edition of the 1860 Text,* ed. Roy Harvey Pearce (Ithaca: Cornell University Press, 1961).

3. Despite the centrality of the city in Whitman's life and work, relatively few critics have focused on its role in his poetry. Among the best essays are those of Kristiaan Versluys ("Walt Whitman's Mannahatta or the Joy of a Romantic," *The Poet in the City* [Tübingen: Narr, 1987], 43-71), James L. Machor ("Pastoralism and the American Urban Ideal: Hawthorne, Whitman, and the Literary Pattern," *American Literature* 54.3 [1982]: 329-53), and M. Wynn Thomas ("Walt Whitman and Mannahatta-New York," *American Quarterly* 34 [Fall 1982]: 362-78). Each explores the tension between Whitman's poetic city of Mannahatta and the actual city of New York. Burton Pike (*The Image of the City in Modern Literature* [Princeton: Princeton University Press, 1981]), John H. Johnston (*The Poet and the City* [Athens: University of Georgia Press, 1984]), and David Weimer (*The City as Metaphor* [New York: Random House, 1966]) discuss Whitman in the context of other urban literature, the last two contending that Whitman fails to unify his city poetry either aesthetically or morally. For other studies see Larzer Ziff, "Whitman and the Crowd," *Critical Inquiry* 10 (June 1984): 579-91; J. Thomas Chaffin, Jr., "Give Me Faces and Streets: Walt Whitman and the City," *Walt Whitman Review* 23 (1977): 109-20; and Stephen Tanner, "Walt Whitman as Urban Transcendentalist," *South Dakota Review* 14.2 (1976): 6-18. An earlier version of my analysis appeared as "City/Body/Text: Walt Whitman's Urban Incarnation," *Cycnos: Politique et Poétique de la Ville* (Nice: University of Nice, 1984), 39-48.

4. Like Wordsworth, Whitman imagines himself as the hero of a new epic extolling the life and thought of the poet, and thus later in "Pictures" he sets himself next to Rousseau and Emerson. The aspiration to achieve this within an urban context ("the young man of Mannahatta . . . him I sing for a thousand years" [*LG,* 647]) did not develop immediately. The early poem "Young Grimes" (1840) concludes by counseling its readers to remain on their farms: "Leave the wide city's noisy din— / The busy haunts of men— / And here enjoy a tranquil life, / Unvexed by guilt or pain" (Murphy, 635).

5. On the importance of the city in Whitman's journalism and prose, see Joseph Jay Rubin, *The Historic Whitman* (University Park: Pennsylvania State University Press, 1973); Joseph Jay Rubin and Charles Brown, eds., *Walt Whitman of the New York Aurora: Editor at Twenty-Two* (n.p.: Bald Eagle Press, 1950); Walt Whitman, *New York Dissected,* ed. Emory Holloway and Ralph Adimari (New York: R. R. Wilson, 1936); and Henry M. Christman, ed., *Walt Whitman's New York* (New York: Macmillan, 1963). The standard biographies also relate Whitman's activities as a journalist in New York to his growth as a poet: Gay Wilson Allen, *The Solitary Singer: A Critical Biography of Walt Whitman,* rev. ed. (1967; Chicago: University of Chicago Press, 1985); Justin Kaplan, *Walt Whitman: A Life* (New York: Simon & Schuster, 1980); and Paul Zweig, *Walt Whitman: The Making of the Poet* (New York: Basic Books, 1984). See Versluys, 43-49 and 65-69, for a consideration of the interplay between Whitman's poetry and his prose.

6. Thomas argues that Whitman's "chronic disappointment" over the materialism of New York emerges in the poems of 1865, and that in later years he "retreated to the consolations of the ideal" as his poetic Mannahatta "grew increasingly distant from the actual historical New York" (372-77). Similarly, Versluys claims that the intensity of Whitman's joy over New York's preparation for the Civil War can be explained only by his fear that the city had abandoned its democratic ideals (60). But both critics acknowledge that Whitman's declining gusto for urban life is balanced by his unflagging appreciation of its beauty and energy. As Versluys says, "Whitman's doubts about the city are real but intermittent, penetrating yet always adulterated" (70). The present chapter considers the view of the city that emerges in Whitman's early works, rather than how it might have been modified later. For an examination of Whitman's entire *oeuvre* in relation to the larger currents of nineteenth-century politics, see Betsy Erkkila, *Whitman the Political Poet* (New York: Oxford University Press, 1988).

7. On the city in American literature, see Leo Marx, *The Machine in the Garden* (New York: Oxford University Press, 1964) and "Pastoralism in America," *Ideology and Classic American Literature,* ed. Sacvan Bercovitch and Myra Jehlen (New York: Oxford University Press, 1986), 36-69; Blanche Gelfant, *The American City Novel,* 2nd ed. (Norman: University of Oklahoma Press, 1970); and Michael C. Jaye and Ann C. Watts, eds., *Literature and the Urban Experience* (New Brunswick, N.J.: Rutgers University Press, 1981). Conflicting images of the nineteenth-century city are explored in Janis P. Stout, *Sodoms in Eden: The City in American Fiction Before 1860* (Westport, Conn.: Greenwood, 1976), and Adri-

enne Siegel, *The Image of the American City in Popular Literature 1820-1870* (Port Washington, N.Y.: Kennikat, 1981). Joan Zlotnik in *Portrait of an American City: The Novelist's New York* (Port Washington, N.Y.: Kennikat, 1982) provides useful information on Whitman's city. John H. Johnston, *The Poet and the City,* offers the most extensive consideration to date of American city poetry, including Whitman, Eliot, Hart Crane, Auden, Ginsberg, and Williams.

8. While Whitman's encyclopedic technique argues for the equality of all endeavors and occupations, at the same time it accents the poet's special ability to participate in and record them. See Ziff, 582.

9. Whitman regularly uses ellipsis points, and in quoting passages containing them I have left the four periods unspaced. Where I have omitted material, the points forming the ellipsis have been spaced.

10. By 1860 almost all the major poems of the city were already in place in *Leaves of Grass,* in versions very close to those of the final 1892 edition. While Whitman subtly repressed the sexual content of some poems after 1866, none of the urban poems studied here was significantly altered. M. Jimmie Killingsworth analyzes the effect of the changes in "Whitman's Sexual Themes During a Decade of Revision: 1866-1876," *Walt Whitman Quarterly Review* 4.1 (1986): 7-15; he cites *Leaves of Grass: A Textual Variorum of the Printed Poems,* 3 vols., ed. Sculley Bradley, Harold W. Blodgett, Arthur Golden, and William White (New York: New York University Press, 1980).

11. Of the forty-five poems in the original *Calamus* section of the 1860 *Leaves of Grass,* nine deal explicitly with urban experience, and several others help define the relation between the poet and the physical world. According to Thomas, in *Calamus* Whitman approaches the city in two ways: first, by considering its "uncertain and perhaps unredeemable character," and second, by describing the ideal communities he would like to see in its place (370). But there is a crucial third approach that mediates between the other two: Whitman regards the intimate contact between citizens as the only way to settle qualms about the city's unreality, expressed in the first group of poems, and also as the only way to establish the ideal "city of friends," described in the second group.

12. In 1860 the untitled poem's first line read, "City of my walks and joys!" (Pearce, 363).

13. Whitman was born in 1819, Baudelaire in 1821; *Les Fleurs du mal* appeared just two years after *Leaves of Grass.* Apparently Whitman did not read Baudelaire until 1875, late in his career: "his sole mention of Baudelaire," writes F. O. Matthiessen, "was to quote one of the few beliefs they shared, 'The immoderate taste for beauty and art leads men into monstrous excesses'" (*American Renaissance* [New York: Oxford University Press, 1941], 518). On the source of Whitman's citation of Baudelaire, see W. T. Bandy, "Whitman and Baudelaire," *Walt Whitman Quarterly Review* 1.3 (1983): 53-55.

14. For further comparison of Whitman and Baudelaire, see Johnston, 148, 406; and Versluys, 52-53. The latter examines the two poets' treatment of urban lowlife, concluding that evil in the Baudelairean sense "never touches [Whitman] to the core and he can lay no claim, therefore, to being the poet of the dark side of the city" (53). But Whitman's urban torments, though of a different order from those of Baudelaire, do exist, and stem from his need for poetic self-incarnation through the melding of bodily and textual energies.

15. Whitman took care that in the final order he set for *Leaves of Grass,* his first city lyric should also sound this keynote: "Once I pass'd through a populous city imprinting my brain for future use with its shows, architecture, customs, traditions, / Yet now of all that city I remember only a woman I casually met there who detain'd me for love of me" ("Once I Passed Through a Populous City," 1860; *LG,* 109-10). The manuscript of the poem shows it was originally a man whom the poet met (Murphy, 798).

16. The city is clearly not the only sexual site for Whitman. What are perhaps Whitman's most graphic, "spermatic" evocations of sex and masturbation occur in sections 24, 28, and 29 of "Song of Myself," in pastoral settings. The city is more likely to be the arena of erotic activity with others, but the emphasis falls usually on what is permissible publicly (such as eye contact); what is unseen (all sorts of longings); and what is furtive (i.e., taking place at night or in bed). Often this secret behavior suggests the prolonging of a glance exchanged in the street, and deals in thoughts rather than actions. Thus the sexually charged quality of Whitman's city is due in large part to its sense of *potential* fulfillment—the constant interaction of attractive, attracted strangers who have little time or privacy to pursue physically the desires that their yearning looks signify. For an extended consideration of Whitman's sexual attitudes in their social context, see M. Jimmie Killingsworth, *Whitman's Poetry of the Body: Sexuality, Politics, and the Text* (Chapel Hill: University of North Carolina Press, 1989); see also

Harold Aspiz, "Walt Whitman: The Spermatic Imagination," *On Whitman: The Best from "American Literature,"* ed. Edwin H. Cady and Louis J. Budd (Durham: Duke University Press, 1987), 273-89.

17. Usually Whitman does the singling out, even in the most unlikely situations. See Ziff, 590.

18. Edwin H. Miller suggests that Whitman's language of the eyes animates a lonely cityscape through the momentary gratification of "achieving identity among fellow outlaws." Miller quotes J. A. Symonds' *Studies in Sexual Inversion*: "these [homosexual] men know each other at first sight. . . . 'We recognize each other at once,' says the writer of a report. . . . 'A mere glance of the eye suffices'" (*Walt Whitman's Poetry* [Boston: Houghton, Mifflin, 1968], 163).

19. For example, "I Dream'd in a Dream" (1860), "A Noiseless Patient Spider" (1862), "Poem of Joys" (1860), "Mannahatta" (1860), and "Faces" (1855).

20. Other poems that address the reader while making self-conscious reference to their being read in a book include "Now Lift Me Close" (1860), "How Solemn as One by One" (1865), and "Song of Myself."

21. The poem was not a part of the *Calamus* section in 1860 and was later much revised; see *LG,* 176-77.

22. Thomas makes a similar point about Sections 5 and 6 of "Crossing Brooklyn Ferry" (368).

23. The text cited here, from the 1892 *Leaves of Grass,* differs only slightly in phrasing and punctuation from the text of the 1860 edition, with the exception that a few lines, which Whitman rightly saw as redundant, are dropped. For the full 1860 text, see Pearce, 379-88. A major difference from the original 1856 text, the changed ending, is noted below.

24. See I Corinthians 13:12 and Susan Strom, "'Face to Face': Whitman's Biblical Reference in 'Crossing Brooklyn Ferry,'" *Walt Whitman Review* 24 (1978): 7-16. In *The Prelude,* Wordsworth too speaks of "The comers and the goers face to face— / Face after face" (1805; VII, 172-73). This is not a moment of lasting insight for Wordsworth, but rather its fleeting, ironic opposite.

25. As Ziff notes, "Whitman translates himself into his audience, joining it finally to view the 'I' of the poem as apart. . . . The 'we' at the close of the poem is the poet among the readers, and the 'you' . . . becomes the objects of their shared world, among which the poem now takes its place" (587-88).

26. Of Whitman's refusal to distinguish between city and self, Quentin Anderson writes, "bodies and images are simply correlative with 'soul.' They exist only in that they are apprehended; we exist only in the measure that we apprehend them. . . . It is an assertion that what is seen is correlative with a seer or seers. . . . In sum, there is no evidence that in the Whitman of 1856 there is a separate realm in which 'soul' enjoys an existence independent of a presented scene" (*The Imperial Self* [New York: Vintage, 1971], 127). I am indebted to Professor Anderson's reading of Whitman (119-65) throughout this section.

27. Cf. "To You" (1856): "I paint myriads of heads, but paint no head without its nimbus of gold-color'd light" (*LG,* 234). Ziff's comment on the passage is applicable to the disintegrated yet inviolable identities of "Crossing Brooklyn Ferry" as well: "What we must gaze upon is the wonder of the similarity of the halos for all the difference in the faces beneath them, the wonder of the difference in the faces for all the sameness of the halos that crown them. The one is not the salvation of the many; the many is the salvation of the one" (590).

28. "Song of Myself" anticipates this moment, the poet appearing to be a pilgrim whose progress has been guaranteed, one who already possesses a key to the Celestial City: "Our rendezvous is fitly appointed. . . . God will be there and wait till we come." Whitman even echoes St. John in Revelation as he beholds a city in the sky: "This day before dawn I ascended a hill and looked at the crowded heaven" (1855; Murphy, 731, 732).

29. See Machor, 339.

30. The original 1856 conclusion of the poem placed even more emphasis on the substantiality of the scene, and the capacity of its objects to shape the poet's own body and soul:

> We descend upon you and all things, we arrest you all,
> We realize the soul only by you faithful solids and fluids
> Through you color, form, location, sublimity, ideality,
> Through you every proof, comparison, and all the suggestions and determinations of ourselves.
>
> (Murphy, 806)

"Creator and receiver both"—in Wordsworth's phrase—of the world the mind intuits, Whitman cannot imagine himself without the objects of nature that lend him being. Similarly, Wordsworth recalls that "I was often unable to think of external things as having external existence, and I communed with all that I saw as something not apart

from, but inherent in, my own immaterial nature"
(*The Poetical Works of William Wordsworth,* ed.
E. de Selincourt and Helen Darbishire [Oxford:
Clarendon Press, 1947], IV: 463). But whereas for
Wordsworth soul seems to both underlie and un-
dermine substance, for Whitman "solids and flu-
ids" are what make the soul possible.

31. Edwin Haviland Miller, ed., *The Correspondence,*
5 vols. (New York: New York University Press,
1969), IV: 299 (5 March 1889).

URBAN LIFE AND INDIVIDUAL
IDENTITY

Linda Patterson Miller (essay date fall 1979)

SOURCE: Miller, Linda Patterson. "The Writer in the
Crowd: Poe's Urban Vision." *American Transcendental
Quarterly,* no. 44 (fall 1979): 325-39.

[*In the following essay, Miller appraises Edgar Allan
Poe's treatment of urban life as vivid, realistic, and
skillful representation of the complex personal and soci-
etal issues of identity stemming from nineteenth-century
urbanization.*]

Edgar Allan Poe has been well recognized as an artist
who created works which evoke a mood of otherworld-
liness—places located in the interiors of the mind or the
soul. Despite this, Poe's prose was spawned in, and in-
deed reflects, the city of his day; for like so many
Americans during the 1830's and 1840's, Poe moved to
the large urban centers of the East and it was these cit-
ies which provided him with the bulk of his literary
material during the last eleven years of his life. In Phila-
delphia and then in New York, Poe witnessed the evils
of urbanization—over-crowding, poverty, sickness,
crime, and an industrialization which threatened indi-
vidual integrity and human worth. Poe mulled over
these evils, yet he was not totally appalled by urbaniza-
tion. Although Morton and Lucia White emphasize the
tradition in American intellectual circles of anti-
urbanism, a pattern, they say, into which Poe fits well,
Poe's relationship with the city was seldom so one-
sided.[1] Poe did regret the grislier aspects of city life
which seemed to undermine both the American and the
human experience; yet he was also charmed by the
city's vitality and awed by its monetary and artistic
promise. As such, Poe joined his contemporaries, not in
denying the city, but in attempting through his tales and

essays to interpret and evaluate it. Essentially, Poe's ar-
tistic treatment of nineteenth-century urban phenomena
mirrors the ambivalences many Americans had toward
the burgeoning urban complex.[2]

Like his English counterpart Charles Dickens, Poe re-
garded the swelling urban masses, at their most unruly,
as a collectively mindless and uncontained beast which
defiled human dignity. In one of Poe's last stories, "Mel-
lonta Tauta" (*Godey's Lady's Book,* February 1849),
Poe characterized "the Mob" as "the most odious of all
men that ever encumbered the earth." "Giant in stat-
ure—insolent, rapacious, filthy," the Mob has "the gall
of a bullock with the heart of a hyena and the brains of
a peacock."[3] Although Poe primarily satirized democ-
racy, as well as his present day New Yorkers, in this
story which he set in the year 2848, he saw the inherent
dangers of democracy from the perspective of the urban
dilemma wherein crowds gather and seethe with a con-
vulsive turbulence.

Poe earlier demonstrated these same sentiments in "Four
Beasts in One; The Homo-Cameleopard" first printed as
"Epimanes" in 1836 (*Southern Literary Messenger*) and
later reprinted with only minor word changes in an
1845 issue of the *Broadway Journal.* Significantly,
Poe's intimacy with Philadelphia and New York by
1845 had not prompted him to alter in any way the cen-
tral message of this story in which the seemingly "noble
and free" citizens of Antioch, who gathered as a crowd
to celebrate their king, now garbed as a leopard, be-
come a "tumultuous mob of idiots and madmen." The
narrator has "difficulty in stemming the tide" as "the
sea of people" come his way, and the air, "horrible with
the clamor of a million throats," reinforces the precipi-
tous conditions of city life—its "jumble of all ranks and
ages," its "multiplicity of sects and nations," its "Babel
of languages," its "screaming of beasts." As individuals
become consumed by the crowd, their rationality is dis-
torted and they become wild and inhuman. And while
the city is alive with celebration, vital and active, it is,
in terms of humaneness, non-productive (II, 207-213).

Although Poe often used such crowds to represent the
chaotic state of mind or the internal oppression of an
individual character (such as William Wilson, who is
overcome by "the suffocating atmosphere of the
crowded rooms" in a large gathering during a Roman
carnival [III, 323]), he also portrayed crowds in order to
emphasize the very real dehumanizing character of man
en masse. As the narrator in "Mellonta Tauta" sarcasti-
cally "rejoices," "we live in an age [the year 2848] so
enlightened that no such thing as an individual is sup-
posed to exist. It is the mass for which the true Human-
ity cares" (VI, 199). Such dissolution of the individual,
which the compression of the city inevitably encour-
ages, too often breeds aberrant behavior. This Poe rec-

ognized. In "The Purloined Letter" (1845), Dupin's hired man fires what seems to be a pistol shot into the afternoon conflux of Paris, at which point people scream and shout. But finally, the crowd calms down, seemingly somewhat inured to the capricious violence of city life, as they suffer the fellow "to go his way as a lunatic or a drunkard" (VI, 51).

As reflected in such stories as "The Purloined Letter," city life during Poe's day did not engender calm. In fact, it was quite the opposite, and Poe merely recreated in several of his tales the dangerous realities of nineteenth-century city life wherein few urban citizens, rich or poor, were spared the violence of social unrest. As James F. Richardson notes, people at this time were frightened to walk the dangerous thoroughfares.[4] Rapidly doubling in population, inadequately policed, and seldom able to provide the "promised" comforts, both Philadelphia and New York suffered contagions of crime and major rioting.[5] Social historian Sam Bass Warner, Jr. contends that Philadelphia's period of unrest, largely extending from 1834 until 1849, "pressed every class and ethnic group into some kind of [aggressive] action."[6] Not surprisingly, the newspapers and the fiction of the 1840's increasingly described such acts as reflections of the often unspoken realization that beneath the glossy city veneer of "bustling activity, the growing commerce, the glittering stores, and the finery of dress," there festered "an incredible social decay."[7] Poe, like his fellow city dwellers, religiously poured over the daily newssheets to speculate upon the latest chronicle of crime. From this obsession with city violence resulted two of Poe's tales of ratiocination: "Murders in the Rue Morgue" (*Graham's Magazine,* April 1841) and "The Mystery of Marie Roget" (*Snowden's Lady's Companion,* November-December 1842, February 1843).[8]

In both of these stories, Poe vividly portrayed the textures of city life; and while he called his city Paris, it was actually an American phenomenon drawn from the Philadelphia and New York of the time. As ratiocinative genius Dupin and his cohort variously sally forth into the night streets in "Murders in the Rue Morgue," they garner fleeting glimpses of city backgrounds which are collectively enlightening: "the wild lights and shadows of the populous city"; a "long dirty street"; a "fruiterer, with a large basket upon his head, brushing quickly past"; a "pile of paving-stones collected at a spot where the causeway is undergoing repair"; many "loose fragments"; and "holes and ruts in the pavement." Through these descriptions one begins to absorb the city's "flavors," its feel, its dangerous excitements; one even recognizes the polygot, working-class population so typical of the large eastern city of America (IV, 152-55). As Dupin peruses the newspaper's account of witnesses at the scene of the murders in the Rue Morgue, he compiles a list of tradespeople of varied origins: a laun-

dress, tobacconist, silversmith, restaurateur, banker, clerk, tailor, undertaker, confectioner—even a physician and surgeon. One is from Amsterdam, another England, another Spain, another Italy (IV, 156-65). Alongside the local color, however, one begins to sense as well the seamier aspects of city life, and in particular, the predominance of crime. When Dupin reflects in "The Mystery of Marie Roget" upon the "numerous bands of blackguards which infest the vicinity" of Paris (V, 41), he merely repeats what the newspaper of both New York and Philadelphia during Poe's time regularly recorded. Muggers, rapists, and murderers, often in the form of organized gangs, stalked the darkened streets. Dupin doubts "if there were not a *dozen* gangs . . . in and about the vicinity . . . at *or about* the period of [Marie Roget's death]" (V, 58). And when Poe's Parisians understandably seek peace and security in the city's rural outskirts, they come to realize that the brutality of the peripatetic blackguards has even seeped into the farthest greenery. "With sickness of heart the wanderer [flees] back to the polluted Paris as to a less odious because less incongruous sink of pollution" (V, 49).[9]

By comparing the crime-infested city to the now spoiled countryside, Poe effectively emphasized the breadth of the urban ills which the blackguard gangs embodied. His sense of these ills, however, went beyond crime. In several of his tales as well as his journalistic essays, he suggested the ominous implications of widespread urban poverty. His 14 May letter to the *Columbia Spy* written in 1844, upon his arrival to New York, and his "Four Beasts in One" particularly synthesize Poe's conception of the debilitating penury associated with urban expansion. Although Poe fought his own battles with poverty, he nonetheless retained a characteristic sense of humor, albeit sardonic, regarding urban squalor. The "prevalent shanties of the Irish squatters," penned Poe from New York, look like "*tabernacles*"; and a typical immigrant abode is small, "nine feet by six, with a pigsty applied externally, by way of both portico and support. The whole fabric (which is of mud) has been erected in somewhat too obvious an imitation of the Tower of Pisa."[10] Despite Poe's sarcasm here, his description conveys the debasement which many an unskilled immigrant, too poor to buy land and locked into menial labor, experienced.[11] "Four Beasts in One" poignantly reinforces this truth. Although the city of Epidaphne contains "stately palaces" and "sumptuous and magnificent" temples, "an infinity of mud huts, and abominable hovels," and "a most intolerable stench" and "abundance of filth" overpower the splendor to evoke a pervasive sense of "gloom" and "desolation" (II, 205-206). In "The Man of the Crowd" as well, Poe's narrator describes "the most noisome quarter" of the city "where everything wore the worst impress of the most deplorable poverty, and of the most desperate crime." Here wooden tenements totter to their fall "in

directions so many and capricious, that scarce the semblance of a passage was discernible between them." Paving-stones "lay at random," and a "horrible filth festered in the dammed-up gutters." And as in "Four Beasts in One," "the whole atmosphere teemed with desolation" (IV, 144).

Such urban filth and overcrowding bred the more tangible reality of rampant disease along with gloom. As Poe well recognized, a city dweller during the cholera epidemics of the 1830's and 1840's had good reason to fear for his life. In the thickly populated eastern cities especially, cholera took a heavy human toll. Charles E. Rosenberg details how this highly contagious disease caused a "peculiar tension" in the city dweller which one young Bostonian described as "'a state about midway between hope and fear.'"[12] Those who could afford it, like the narrator of Poe's "The Sphinx" (*Arthur's Ladies Magazine,* January 1846), fled to the country in order to save their lives. This narrator accepts the "invitation of a relative to spend a fortnight with him in the retirement of his *cottage orné* on the banks of the Hudson," but while he and his relation have much to occupy them—"rambling in the woods, sketching, boating, fishing, bathing, music and books"—they cannot prevent their minds from wandering to "the gloom and desolation of the neighboring city." As the narrator relates, they "learned to expect daily the loss of some friend," and "the air from the South seemed . . . redolent with death." He can "neither speak, think, nor dream of anything else" (VI, 238-239).

Whereas the narrator and his friend have sought reprieve in the countryside from the epidemic, the denizens in "The Masque of the Red Death" (*Graham's Magazine,* May 1842; *Broadway Journal,* July 1845) attempt to defy the "fatal" and "hideous" pestilence which has "long devastated the country" by fleeing, with Prince Prospero, to a castellated abbey. Here they indulge in merry making for five or six months while they leave "the external world" to "take care of itself." Death's persistent toll makes its presence regularly felt, however, as Prospero's ebony clock chimes out the hour with "so peculiar a note and emphasis" that even the most giddy grow "pale" and then resolve to disregard these chimes the next time. When an unknown "masked figure" suddenly appears at one of Prospero's more lavish masquerade balls, the revellers become sobered if not horrified by this "tall and gaunt" figure who "had gone so far as to assume the type of the Red Death," his vesture "dabbled in *blood*—and his broad brow . . . besprinkled with the scarlet horror." As the figure stalks among the revellers, Prospero is at first immobilized but then takes action, rushing toward the figure intending to kill him. Instead, Prospero dies, as do the revellers, "one by one." The presence of the Red Death, even in this retreat supposedly fortified from the ravages of the disease outside, "had come like a thief in the night. . . . And Darkness and Decay and the Red Death held illimitable dominion over all" (IV, 250-258).

The effects of this dominion on the city and the city dweller are graphically depicted in Poe's "King Pest: A Tale Containing an Allegory" (*Southern Literary Messenger,* September 1835; *Broadway Journal,* October 1845). By describing the wanderings of two drunken sailors through the "dark, narrow, and filthy lanes and alleys of London," a city "in a great measure depopulated" by the "Demon of Disease," Poe conveys the "horrors" of the situation. Looters have ransacked the empty shops and homes, "fallen houses [choke] up the streets," and "fetid and poisonous smells everywhere" prevail. But most horribly, in this city of disease and death individuals in plague-stricken areas rot unnoticed in "windowless habitations" (II, 171-173). As Poe emphasizes here, cholera ravaged the city dweller both physically and psychologically. Personal despair, along with death, has established its own domain, and the city dweller seems defenseless against the ills which the city both harbors and fosters. Like the figure of the Red Death which shows itself finally to be "untenanted by any tangible form" (IV, 258), disease seems a far too pervasive yet illusive foe, and the sinister presence of the cholera as it hovers over the city becomes synonymous to the city dweller with all the worst effects of urban life.

Although Poe's characters may seek release from the city in outlying abbeys or country estates, or even in the city's outskirts (as in "The Mystery of Marie Roget"), they are seldom able permanently to escape from the far reaching influences of urban expansion. The cities prospered, but with a progress which too often seemed counterproductive. As Poe implied in his 14 May letter to the *Columbia Spy,* the spirit of modernization which molded the city was in essence a spirit of decay. The old "magnificent places [of New York] are doomed," he wrote, and it is "the spirit of Improvement [which] has withered them with its acrid breath." Envisioning once "picturesque sites" with streets already "'mapped' through them," Poe concluded his letter with a grim forecast: "In some thirty years every noble cliff will be a pier, and the whole island will be densely desecrated by buildings of brick" wherein a sense of human integrity disintegrates.[13]

Poe's story "Diddling Considered as One of the Exact Sciences" speaks to this disintegration by detailing a new breed of commercial crassness engendered by such "modernization." Published in the *Saturday Courier* of 14 October 1843, this tale depicts the city dweller as an animal who "diddles" (or cheats his fellow man). The diddler attempts to accumulate cash at his neighbor's expense. Man has always been a diddler, Poe wrote, but "the moderns . . . have brought it to a perfection never dreamed of by our thick-headed progenitors." For ex-

rounded by people but untouched and separate. He represents the city's enigma. The narrator finally decides that "it will be in vain to follow [him further]; for I shall learn no more of him, nor of his deeds" (IV, 140-45).

The narrator's resignation reflects Poe's own ambiguous response to the city and the quality of life which it produced. While he could not condone the city's ailments, he still remained fascinated by its mystery and intensity, and by its endless creative possibilities. Much like that other acute observer, Monsieur C. Auguste Dupin, Poe no doubt took delight in roaming the city's streets. They continually promised the unexpected, and as Dupin's companion noted in "The Murders in the Rue Morgue," Dupin relished their nightly sallies through Paris because of "that infinity of mental excitement" which observation "amid the wild lights and shadows of the populous city" afforded him. It was "at such times" that Dupin's friend "could not help remarking and admiring" the "peculiar analytic ability in Dupin" which these walks enhanced (IV, 152). Like Dupin then, Poe did not totally condemn the cities as the cesspools of humanity. Instead, he rather enjoyed the opportunity to observe mankind with all of its foibles which city life seemed to magnify. Poe's seven letters written to the *Columbia Spy* during his first months in New York City in 1844 capture his cynicism yet reveal his delight in American urbanity. Crime and poverty, decay and death aside, Poe "reported," often tongue-in-cheek, on a New York which was "not yet over the bustle of the first of May." "Thronged with strangers" and "brimful of all kinds of *legitimate* liveliness," Poe's New York abounds with foot races, literary doings, and political hoopla. It also breeds noise, fraud, and incongruity.[16]

The "amount of general annoyances wrought by street-noises is incalculable," Poe wrote. "Clam-and-cat-fish venders" chanting from their "leathern throats" could obscure conversation "for five or even ten minutes at a time"; and even the "round stones" of the street, because of their poor resiliency, caused too great a din. While Poe advocated a quieter more durable pavement, he also sought the reduction of such city fraud as the lamp-lighting functionaries' flat refusal to "light up; preferring to appropriate the oil to their own private and personal emolument." Poe also found the city's attempt to ban Sunday entertainments incongruous, for "to declare a thing immoral, and therefore expedient, at *all* times, is one thing—to declare it immoral on Sunday, and therefore to forbid it on that particular day, is quite another."[17] For Poe, however, New York's architecture, as typified by the elegant Trinity Church juxtaposed against "villas" of "silvered gingerbread," best represented urban incongruity. While the harbor of New York "in point of *natural* beauty," had "scarcely its equal in the northern hemisphere," Brooklyn had been "most

grievously disfigured . . . by displays of landscape and architectural *taste*. More atrocious *pagodas*, or what not . . . were certainly never imagined than the greater portion of those which affront the eye." As Poe concluded in his letter of 12 June 1844, "I know few towns which inspire me with so great disgust and contempt." These "palaces of painted white pine" are nothing short of "preposterous."[18]

Poe disliked New York's unnaturalness, and he found ludicrous man's attempt to reestablish a natural environment amidst the "silvered-gingerbread," the factories, and the shanties. Unable to anticipate the work of such city park advocates as Frederick Law Olmsted, Poe implied there could be no way to "reinstall" and sequester nature in the heart of the city, and the fountain at the Bowling-Green symbolized man's futile attempts. It is "an absurdity," wrote Poe. While "the original conception was rusticity—Nature, in short," the water which "was designed to fall and flow naturally, over natural rocks," instead pounds with "the air of a small country jail in a hard thunder shower."[19]

Partly to escape this ersatz city milieu, Poe lived on New York's borders, "about 13 miles . . . on the railroad leading north."[20] Previously, he had sought Philadelphia's more rural environment in Fairmont Park, an area of the city which conveniently offered both access to and shelter from the city; and in both cities, Poe seemingly attempted, like Hans Pfaall, "to leave the world" by living in "solitude" and scorning "all things present."[21] Nonetheless, Poe never lost sight of his artistic and economic dependence upon both Philadelphia and New York.

In looking to these cities, Poe's desires were moderate, though large in conception. He wished to found a magazine of literary merit.[22] He simultaneously longed to create for himself a literary reputation of national and international scope. Poe explained his goals in a letter to William Poe on 15 August 1840: "If I fully succeed in my purposes [by founding this magazine] I will not fail to produce some lasting effect upon the growing literature of the country, while I establish for myself individually a name which that country 'will not willingly let die.'"[23] As Ellis Paxson Oberholtzer has noted, only a large northern city such as Philadelphia could provide the "capitalists willing to assist [Poe] in realizing [these] greater ambitions"; and as Poe himself recognized, his magazine and thus his reputation could only triumph if he pushed it in "the chief northern cities" where he might also find "a connexion . . . with some gentleman of literary attainments, who could at the same time advance as much ready money as [would] be requisite for the first steps of the undertaking."[24]

By the summer of 1840, two years into his roughly six-year stay in Philadelphia, Poe had declined "a farther connexion with the Gentleman's Magazine" (where he

ample, a housekeeper goes to a furniture warehouse to buy a sofa, and the man whom she pays only pretends to work there. She never receives her sofa, yet the deceiver is several dollars richer. Another man ensconced at the end of a city bridge collects tolls from all passers by, respectfully informing them "of the new county law." "Some grumble but all submit, and the diddler goes home a wealthier man by some fifty or sixty dollars." And still another man places an ad in the newspapers asking for "three or four intelligent and competent clerks, to whom a liberal salary will be paid." Because of the job's great responsibilities, he states, "it is deemed advisable to demand a deposit of fifty dollars from each clerk employed." After interviewing "some fifteen or twenty young gentlemen piously inclined" who have all deposited their fifty dollars, the ingenious scoundrel absconds with the money and conveniently skips town. As this sarcastically humorous story confirms, the city entrepreneur too often eschewed principle for economic gain (V, 213, 217, 222-223). Called in those years "a contractor or capitalist," we today would describe this new kind of businessman as "a hustler."[14] As Poe's story stresses, in order to triumph or simply to survive amidst changing priorities, one sometimes sacrificed (and regrettably too easily) his most valuable asset—an individual sense of pride and honesty.

The disappearance of cottage industries intensified this loss of pride and integrity. Unable to compete with factory output, the master craftsman relinquished his hold upon the older cherished ways. In a time of transformation "from artisan towns into hives of small factories and wholesale outlets," the hand worker "lost ground"—"he lost status, he lost assurance of employment, and he lost personal control over his work."[15] "The Unparalleled Adventure of One Hans Pfaall" (*Southern Literary Messenger,* June 1835) recounts this attempt to reestablish personal priorities, to confront the essential question of how to live meaningfully in an age of "progress."

Hans Pfaall, "an humble artizan" like his father and his father before him, mended bellows, occupying "for the period of forty years . . . the little square brick building, at the head of the alley called Sauerkraut." It was a "respectable and indeed lucrative profession" until "the spirit of the age" made people forget Pfaall, who "grew as poor as a rat," his "burdens" becoming "intolerable." Finally, having decided he must either kill himself or flee the city, Pfaall proceeds "to force a passage . . . *to the moon.*" As Pfaall relates it, "I determined to depart, yet live—to leave the world, yet continue to exist." Though unable to live with the new ways, Pfaall uses them (a recently-discovered means of flight—the balloon) to escape (II, 47-49, 61). Progress destroys the individual self, while paradoxically proving the means of mankind's salvation. Thus while the nineteenth-century urban individual was sometimes overlooked in

the congested, mud-baked streets, humanity en masse and the progressive spirit of the times was booming.

This sense of isolation, the easy loss of individual recognition and personal accountability in the midst of progress, prompted him to write his most complete city tale, "The Man of the Crowd" (*Burton's Gentleman's Magazine,* December 1840). This story's graphic portrayal of city life—its physical terrain, its changing moods, its people—reveals Poe's own intimacy with the large urban center. Not so much the story of the man of the crowd, or of the narrator, the tale instead portrays the city as character. The narrator's nightlong perusal of "the tumultuous sea of human heads" and his circular journey from the main thoroughfare to the "verge of the city" and back again serves to catalog the city's "noisy and inordinate vivacity" along with its human despair. Through the "smoky panes" of a coffeehouse on one of the city's busiest avenues, the narrator enjoys observing the "continuous tide" of people: "clerks," "pick-pockets," "gamblers," "Jew pedlars," "street beggars," "feeble and ghastly invalids," "modest young girls" and "women of the town," "pie-men," "porters," "coal-heavers," "sweeps," "organ-grinders," "monkey-exhibitors and ballad mongers," "ragged artisans and exhausted laborers of every description" (IV, 134, 144, 136-39). One man in particular with an unusual face and demeanor captures the narrator's attention, and he decides to follow him.

Through the city's narrow back lanes and its "thick humid fog" and then "heavy rain," the narrator pursues the man from the coffeehouse to a "brilliantly lighted" square, a "large and busy bazaar," the "verge of the city" marked by poverty. This pursuit becomes marked by the narrator's increasing obsession with understanding the mystery of this man and the milieu which has produced him. The man's expression haunts the narrator, for it somehow embodies all of the city's potential coupled with its ills—"ideas of vast mental power, of caution, of penuriousness, of avarice, of coolness, of malice, of blood-thirstiness, of triumph, of merriment, of excessive terror, of intense—of extreme despair." Although the narrator pursues the man throughout the evening and the next day, he fails to comprehend "the waywardness of his actions," his attempt to avoid contact with people while simultaneously seeking out the areas of greatest population. "Wearied unto death" with his fruitless course throughout the city's best and worst areas, the narrator stops "fully in front of the wanderer" and gazes at him "steadfastly in the face." He hopes in this last penetrating glance to unravel the mystery of this man and of the environment which sustains him; but the narrator can only conclude that this man represents the most sinister aspects of urban existence, "the type and the genius of deep crime" which the city harbors and nurtures. The man "refuses to be alone," states the narrator, for "*He is the man of the crowd*"—sur-

had served in a quasi-editorial capacity for a little over a year) in order to establish this journal.[25] But despite letters to various writers and men of wealth throughout the country promoting Poe's proposed *Penn Magazine,* and despite indications that the magazine was variously ready for the press, if one can believe Poe's often exaggerated accounts, the Philadelphia journal never materialized. This failure drove Poe to New York in the spring of 1844 to try again with a new title, *The Stylus.* A few months after taking residence in the city, Poe asked his friend Dr. Thomas H. Chivers to join him. "I am only 'biding my time'—awaiting means and opportunity [to begin the journal]," Poe wrote. "Should you conclude to join me, we will not fail to make fame and fortune." As Poe reemphasized to Chivers, "you will find me here—at New York—where I live, at present, in strict seclusion, busied with books and ambitious thoughts, until the hour shall arrive when I may come forth with a certainty of success. A Magazine like Graham's will never do. We must do something far better."[26]

New York, however, like Philadelphia, failed to provide Poe with the "better" magazine or, for that matter, any magazine. Yet both cities gave Poe recognition and an artistic base, and they also, significantly, determined the tone and texture of many of Poe's tales and essays. When Poe's *Tales* came out in 1839, Poe wrote Joseph Evans Snodgrass that the Philadelphians had given him "the *very highest possible* praise."[27] New Yorkers also saw Poe in a position of relative artistic prominence. As Poe wrote in *Godey's Lady's Book* (May 1846), "New York literature may be taken as a fair representation of that of the country at large. The city itself is the focus of American letters."[28] The city was also, quite literally, the stimulus for a consciously "American" literature. When the Young Americans under the leadership of Cornelius Matthews admonished American writers to look to their own country, not to foreign soil, for recognition as well as rich backgrounds from which to write, they stressed the wealth of literary material inherent in the multi-faceted urban complexes of the 1830's and 1840's.[29] Poe somewhat allied himself with this group and perhaps followed its admonitions indirectly by drawing his stories from the city influences which dominated the last eleven years of his life. As Arthur Hobson Quinn emphasizes, Poe repeatedly began with what he knew and simply "changed scenery and other elements to suit his story."[30]

Poe seldom employed American names for his fictionalized urban centers—his Parises and Londons, or the more erotic Venice or classical Antioch—and in this he was in keeping with the American culture and artistic milieu of his day. Not unlike such contemporaries as Ralph Waldo Emerson who, as Michael Cowan nicely demonstrates, looked to the European city as "a functional background" against which to "study the rising cities of his own nation," Poe sometimes in his stories "transplanted" his American city locales into European settings.[31] He also, in keeping with his contemporaries, identified America with a classical tradition as a reinforcement of America's purpose. As Cowan emphasizes, America sometimes thought of itself as a new Rome—"not the Rome of . . . corruption, but a freshly emerging empire," full only of all that was vigorous and grand.[32] These "new Romes," however, were inherently duplicitous. Rome represented both a rise and a fall, decay as well as grandeur. Thus, when Poe alluded to the classical city of Antioch, which he did in "Four Beasts in One," these allusions bore contradictory overtones and became apt conveyors of his own ambivalence towards America's future as it lay in urban technological growth. Poe's profiles of distant, decaying cities do bear an air of prophecy—a thinly veiled warning regarding the American urban trends which he witnessed during his stay in Philadelphia and New York. But his portraits of vitally active as well as dangerous cities also convey a frank appraisal of, and a certain appreciation for, the complexities of man in a progressive era which did not lend itself to easy solutions. The "wild lights and shadows" and the "fitful and garish lustre" of Monsieur Dupin's Paris, and "the waver, the jostle, and the hum" of "The Man of the Crowd," could only be so vividly detailed by one who had himself been there to witness and to capture first hand on paper these new urban trends which enticed as well as frightened the American of Poe's day.

Notes

1. Morton and Lucia White in *The Intellectual vs. the City: From Thomas Jefferson to Frank Lloyd Wright* (Cambridge: Harvard University Press and the M. I. T. Press, 1962) emphasize Poe's largely negative, psychological reaction to the city. In this he joined with the American "literary tendency to denigrate the city," and those intellectuals who lived in the city criticized it most sharply (p. 2). "For them the city scene was a backdrop for frightening experiences, personal defeat, icy intellectualism, heartless commercialism, miserable poverty, crime and sin, smoke and noise, dusk and loneliness. Often they confronted the city in bad dreams and nightmares" (p. 37).

2. Poe, like many of his literary peers, had an admittedly pragmatic alliance with the large urban centers of the East. He believed that in Philadelphia and then New York he could best realize his twofold dream for a magazine and a name, and he became economically and artistically dependent upon both cities. Arthur Hobson Quinn, *Edgar Allan Poe: A Critical Biography* (New York: D. Appleton-Century Co., 1941) details Poe's years in the city but does not emphasize the effect which urban life had upon Poe's art. Edward Wagenknecht's more recent biography, *Edgar Allan Poe:*

The Man Behind the Legend (New York: Oxford University Press, 1963), notes but does not discuss to any extent the relationship of Poe's environment to this art. In general, as best represented by Daniel Hoffman's *Poe Poe Poe Poe Poe Poe Poe* (Garden City, New York: Doubleday, 1972), scholars have emphasized the "otherworldly" quality of Poe's art. No study has yet fully analyzed Poe's relationship to the city. Janis P. Stout's recent *Sodoms in Eden: The City in American Fiction Before 1860* (Westport, Connecticut: Greenwood Press, 1976) extends somewhat the Whites' earlier study by analyzing Poe's use of city imagery and underscoring his ambivalence to city life, "the attitude most characteristic of the period" (p. 7). Essentially, Stout sees Poe's cities as "devices for the creation of atmospheric effects and the exploration of abnormal psychological states. They are not objects for analysis in their own right." As such, it is the "sinister atmosphere" of his city views, and "not any convincingness as recognizable depictions, that is important" (pp. 54, 56). Yet Poe was concerned about the very real problems of the city dweller, and he did pay close attention to realistic city detail which he employed in his prose, not only to create the effects which Stout discusses, but also to evaluate indirectly the precipitous and exciting conditions of the large city of his day.

3. The Complete Works of Edgar Allan Poe, ed. James A. Harrison, 17 vols., 2nd ed. (1902; rpt. New York: AMS Press, Inc., 1965) VI, pp. 208-209. Future references will be cited by volume and page number within the text.

4. Richardson's work, *The New York Police: Colonial Times to 1901* (New York: Oxford University Press, 1970), focuses upon the growth of New York during Poe's day and the increase of crime which began "from the mid-1820's on." By the 1830's and 1840's, Richardson notes, the streets could well be described as "pathways of danger" (pp. 15, 26).

5. In New York, for example, the population "more than doubled" between 1825 and 1845 (Anselm L. Strauss, *Images of the American City* [New York: Free Press of Glencoe, 1961], p. 217.) The New York police system struggled to keep astride this growth and its attendant violence. As the *Commercial Advertiser* of 20 August 1840 stated, "It is notorious that the New York police is wretchedly inadequate to the arrest of offenders and the punishment of crime; as to *prevention* of crime, we might almost as well be without the name of a police, as we are all but without the substance" (Richardson, p. 26).

6. Warner, *The Private City: Philadelphia in Three Periods of Its Growth* (Philadelphia: University of Pennsylvania Press, 1968), pp. 125-126.

7. David Brion Davis, *Homicide in American Fiction, 1798-1860: A Study in Social Values* (Ithaca, New York: Cornell University Press, 1957), p. 259.

8. Poe acknowledged his debt to the well-publicized New York murder of Mary Cecilia Rogers as the basis of "The Mystery of Marie Roget"; and although scholars have fully discussed this background circumstance, they have not sufficiently recognized the accuracy of the story's environmental details. Ostensibly writing about New York and then naming the city Paris, Poe embellished his tale by drawing upon his five years in Philadelphia. The murder of Mary Cecilia Rogers with its "attention-arousing combination of illicit sex and violence . . . focused public opinion on the subject of a more efficient police," and Poe's story published after the murder served to keep alive the issue (Richardson, pp. 37-38).

9. Strauss emphasizes that there was a regular need in the midst of increasing city ills and lack of "any imaginable rural scenery" for the city dweller to be refreshed periodically with rural visits. Unfortunately, this ability to leave at will was open only to the affluent. See p. 218.

10. [Edgar Allan Poe,] *Doings of Gotham: Poe's Contributions to the Columbia Spy* . . . , ed. Jacob E. Spannuth with comments by Thomas Ollive Mabbott (Pottsville, Pennsylvania: Jacob E. Spannuth, 1929), p. 25.

11. Sam Bass Warner, Jr. in *The Urban Wilderness: A History of the American City* (New York: Harper & Row, 1972) emphasizes that "the nineteenth-century American city was a magnet for immigrants. From the 1820's onward, young men flocked to the city from American farms and towns as well as from European villages, towns and cities" p. 76. Robert S. Pickett in his *House of Refuge: Origins of Juvenile Reform in New York State, 1815-1857* (Syracuse: Syracuse University Press, 1969) succinctly summarizes the negative aspects of this movement wherein the cities became "a dumping ground for European paupers" and "a haven for a floating population of youths who had wandered from the supposed bedrock of American virtue, the countryside" p. 2. The people of the time, stresses Robert H. Bremner in *From the Depths: The Discovery of Poverty in the United States* (1956; rpt. New York: New York University Press, 1967), feared that the "Old World" was inundating the New to the point where "the simplest and most frequently advanced explanation for the

manifold problems created by the slums was immigration" (pp. 7-8).

12. As Rosenberg indicates in *The Cholera Years: The United States in 1832, 1849, and 1866* (Chicago: University of Chicago Press, 1962), people in the cities during the big cholera epidemics recognized that the disease spread most rapidly in the congested city areas, and they tried to escape the city if possible. "The country, especially clean and elevated places, seemed to offer the only security against the disease" (p. 38).

13. *Doings of Gotham,* pp. 25-26.

14. Warner, *The Urban Wilderness,* p. 73.

15. Warner, *The Urban Wilderness,* pp. 74 and 79.

16. *Doings of Gotham,* pp. 24, 31 and 39, respectively.

17. *Doings of Gotham,* pp. 61, 32 and 39, respectively.

18. *Doings of Gotham,* pp. 59 and 65.

19. *Doings of Gotham,* p. 26. Although the American romantic believed that the urban boom had defaced nature, he also felt that nature, when pressed, could retaliate. Thus, as Michael H. Cowan notes in his *City of the West: Emerson, America, and Urban Metaphor* (New Haven: Yale University Press, 1967), pp. 191-192), some of Poe's stories portray the ultimate futility of man's attempts to control his environment. In "The Masque of the Red Death" disease finally destroys the walled city, and in "The Fall of the House of Usher" gravity easily demolishes Usher's palatial domain. As always, nature remains the more powerful and vital force.

20. Poe to Thomas H. Chivers, 22 July 1846, Letter 239, *The Letters of Edgar Allan Poe,* ed. John Ward Ostrom, 2 vols. (Cambridge: Harvard University Press, 1948), II, p. 325.

21. Poe to James R. Lowell, 2 July 1844, Letter 179, *Letters,* I, pp. 256-258.

22. Talk of his proposed magazine dominates Poe's letters from 1840 until his death. As his letter to Washington Irving on 21 June 1841 spells out, Poe envisioned a definite type of magazine— higher class, at the price of $5. See Letter 113, *Letters,* I, pp. 161-163.

23. Poe to William Poe, Letter 97, *Letters,* I, pp. 140-142.

24. It was precisely for these reasons rather than "the hope of finding what he did, a sub-editor's desk in the office of an already established magazine" that

Poe "was drawn to Philadelphia," states Oberholtzer in his *The Literary History of Philadelphia* (1906; rpt. Detroit: Gale Research Co., 1969), p. 285. See also Poe to Charles W. Thomson, 28 June 1840, Letter 96, *Letters,* I, pp. 139-140.

25. Poe to Charles W. Thomson, 28 June 1840, Letter 96, *Letters,* I, pp. 139-140.

26. Poe to Thomas H. Chivers on 10 July, 1844, Letter 180, *Letters,* I, p. 259.

27. Poe to Joseph Evans Snodgrass on 19 December 1839, Letter 88, *Letters,* I, p. 125.

28. Introduction to *The Literati of New York City, Works,* XV, p. 5.

29. For a complete discussion of the composition, goals and effects upon American literature of this movement, see Perry Miller's *The Raven and the Whale: The War of Words and Wits in the Era of Poe and Melville,* "Book Two: Young America," (New York: Harcourt Brace and Company, 1956), pp. 69-117.

30. Quinn, p. 130.

31. Cowan, p. 12.

32. Cowan, pp. 126-128.

Nancy L. Paxton (essay date 1984)

SOURCE: Paxton, Nancy L. "George Eliot and the City: The Imprisonment of Culture." In *Women Writers and the City: Essays in Feminist Literary Criticism,* edited by Susan Merrill Squier, pp. 71-96. Knoxville: University of Tennessee Press, 1984.

[*In the following essay, Paxton argues that in her novel* Romola, *George Eliot "presents a paradigm for woman's experience in the city by disclosing how men in urban culture make women into subjects of art in order to reinforce their social preeminence by this apparent flattery."*]

There is a conspicuous silence in George Eliot's fiction regarding the Victorian woman's relation to the city. Eliot is most celebrated for her presentations of the quiet country life of the English Midlands before they were disturbed by Victorian industrial progress. Her fiction depicts the natural serenity of the rural worlds of Hayslope, St. Ogg's, Raveloe, Treby Magna, and, of course, Middlemarch. Though in *Daniel Deronda* she does describe London in some detail, it is less vividly realized than Gwendolen Harleth's country home at Offendene. Only in *Romola,* Eliot's single attempt to write an historical novel about the distant past, does she depict her heroine's life in a city by surrounding her by

quattrocento Florence, that "adorable city" that Eliot's contemporaries were rediscovering because of their interest in the Italian Risorgimento and in the epic poetry of Dante.[1]

Eliot's unwillingness to depict the urban life of a heroine as creative and unconventional as she was herself has seemed a puzzling, provoking, and—for some readers—an unforgivable omission in her fiction, but her silence seems to reflect her feelings that cities in general and London in particular were somehow threatening. In 1863, while she was writing *Romola,* she sent a letter to her beloved friend, Barbara Bodichon, in which she commented about living in London:

> I know you are enjoying the country. I have just been having the joy myself. The wide sky, the *not*-London makes a new creature of me in half an hour. I wonder then why I am ever depressed, why I am so shaken by agitation. I come back to London and again the air is full of demons.[2]

Though Eliot had long since rejected her initial puritanical reasons for disapproving of London as a "great Babel,"[3] and though she had come to enjoy with deep appreciation the music, art, literature, and intellectual ferment of the vast English city that she adopted as her home, she nonetheless continued to feel vaguely oppressed by it, and complaints like the one she sent to Bodichon reappear with regularity in her letters throughout her career.

Nonetheless, if Marian Evans had not come to London in 1850 after her father's death and begun to work as the silent editor of the *Westminster Review,* George Eliot would, perhaps, never have been born. At thirty-one, Marian Evans's dearest desire was to free herself from the parochial world of her childhood and to somehow escape from what John Cross has called the "slavery" of her domestic life, "shut up in a farmhouse in the remote country."[4] All the yearning of her "full passionate nature and hungry intellect" that he describes is expressed in a letter written a few months before her father's death:

> O the bliss of having a very high attic in a romantic continental town, such as Geneva—far away from morning callers, dinners and decencies; and then to pause for a year and think "de omnibus rebus et quibusdam aliis," and then return to life, and work for poor stricken humanity and never think of self again.[5]

Though she traveled to Geneva in the summer following her father's death, she characteristically did not spend that year of perfect intellectual self-indulgence that she longed for, and though she moved to London by November 1850, she did not easily find the fulfillment in life that she desired. Her career as novelist began, as we all know, only after she made her momentous choice to live unmarried with G. H. Lewes, and

only after she had signaled that choice publicly by leaving London with him to go to Weimar, Germany. The painful repercussions of both these choices defined Eliot's experience of London ever afterward, and perhaps some of the reasons for her silence about the city life of an emancipated, educated, and artistic woman like herself can be found in these circumstances of her biography.[6]

One of the most dazzling moments in *Middlemarch,* however, suggests a second dimension to Eliot's silence about the city beyond these details of her private life which illuminates her experiences as a woman writer and sheds a retrospective light on her conception and construction of *Romola,* that single novel about a woman's relation to the city. In describing Dorothea Brooke Casaubon standing in the sunlight before the statue of the reclining Cleopatra in the Vatican Museum, Eliot presents a paradigm for woman's experience in the city by disclosing how men in urban culture make women into subjects of art in order to reinforce their social pre-eminence by this apparent flattery. Dorothea, brooding about her sudden disillusionment with her "bridal life," does not actually see the statue in front of her, but she is viewed by her cousin Will Ladislaw and by the artist Naumann, who tries to transform her into a suitable subject for his art. Finding a "fine bit of antithesis" in the contrast between the image of the sensuous ideal of womanhood and the flesh and blood reality, he tells Will:

> There lies antique beauty, not corpse-like even in death, but arrested in the complete contentment of its sensuous perfection: and here stands beauty in its breathing life, with the consciousness of Christian centuries in its bosom. But she should be dressed like a nun; I think she looks almost what you call a Quaker; I would dress her as a nun in my picture.[7]

Though Dorothea is not herself aware that being transformed into an aesthetic object this way contributes to her sense of the oppressiveness of the Eternal City, Eliot goes on in *Middlemarch* to describe her heroine's struggle to compel Will to see her as a woman desiring love and not as a "poem" or a goddess.

Furthermore, Eliot describes the demoralizing effect that viewing the monumental art of Rome—that "Titanic life struggling on walls and ceilings"—has upon Dorothea:

> She had been led through the best galleries, had been taken to the best points of view, had been shown the greatest ruins and the most glorious churches, and she had ended oftenest choosing to drive out to the Campagna where she could feel alone with the earth and sky, away from the oppressive masquerade of ages, in which her own life seemed to become a masque with enigmatical costumes.

(ch. 20, pp. 224-25)

Dorothea feels distressed both by the "stupendous fragmentariness" and by the painfully "deep impressions" that this art makes on her, but her dismay is amplified because of her experience as a woman. Educated by that "toy-box history of the world adapted to young ladies" (ch. 10, p. 112), and encouraged to find moral order everywhere, Dorothea is especially shaken when she can find no intellectual or moral unity in this vast wreck of "spiritual and sensuous ideals," Measuring her ordinary woman's life against the conflicting images of heroic womanhood that she sees in the city's museums and churches makes Dorothea feel even more keenly the "moral imprisonment" of her chosen life with Casaubon.

Dorothea's feelings of humiliation, pain, and entrapment in her first confrontation with the art of the Eternal City apparently echo some of Eliot's own initial feelings of "humiliating passivity" in regarding the art of Rome and Florence, but Eliot's use of allusions to Charlotte Brontë's *Villette* suggests that she is describing a sense of oppression shared by other women writers and Victorian feminists.[8] By inviting readers familiar with literature of the female tradition to see parallels between Brontë's heroine, Lucy Snowe, who also stands before the image of the Cleopatra, and Dorothea, Eliot discloses a more subversive and feminist analysis of woman's relation to urban culture. Unlike Dorothea, Lucy actually examines and criticizes the reclining figure of the "indolent gypsy giantess," depicted on a vast canvas rather than carved in stone. While Lucy considers the Cleopatra as "on the whole an enormous piece of claptrap," she nonetheless prefers it to the images of women that her mentor, M. Paul, urges her to study instead: the "grim and grey" images, "cold and vapid as ghosts," which present the four stages of a woman's life: the "Jeune Fille," the "Mariée," the "Jeune Mère," and the "Veuve." Brontë directly describes in this scene how men convert art into propaganda to protect their power, and though Eliot is more subtle in her treatment of her heroine's confrontation with the conventionalized and prescriptive aesthetic ideals of femininity, she nonetheless reveals a similar wary cynicism about the female figures that are enshrined in the temples of culture. The depiction of the Cleopatra as only partially clad, in both cases, makes it graphically clear to both heroines that the power to design, utilize, and preserve particular versions of the feminine ideal and ignore others resides with men. Furthermore, Eliot reveals that the statue Dorothea stands before does not really represent Cleopatra but rather Antigone, and thus she indicates how readily the heroic representations of woman's spiritual perfection are misnamed and reinterpreted by succeeding generations who convert them into images of sensuous amorality. This process of renaming and reinterpreting the ideals of womanhood is particularly confusing to women; both Dorothea and Lucy regard such images of women as either utterly "alien" and "enigmatical" or "grim" and, as Eliot shows, it is no wonder.

While the scene from *Middlemarch* contains in miniature all the elements of Eliot's analysis of woman's entrapment by the city and its art, she presents her most comprehensive study not only of woman's moral but also of her physical confinement in *Romola*. This novel, published in installments in the *Cornhill Magazine,* describes the life of an aristocratic young woman living in Florence during Savonarola's ascendancy, fall, and martyrdom, from 1492 to 1498. Though famous historical figures like Niccolò Machiavelli, Luigi Pulci, Piero de' Medici, and Charles VIII of France move in the background, and the artist Piero di Cosimo and the passionate reformer Savonarola intervene more directly in Romola's life, Eliot focuses her novel deliberately on the historical, unrecorded, private life of a heroic woman. She presents two dimensions to Romola's entrapment by urban culture: the legal subordination imposed on her because she is a daughter, a wife, and a citizen of Florence, and the "moral imprisonment" that confines her because she is, by definition, the subject rather than the maker of the art and literature that surround her in this great center of Renaissance culture.

In choosing to set her novel in quattrocento Florence, Eliot made a choice that clarified and simplified her heroine's relation to the law because this city is the single agent of the state and serves the function later assumed by the nation-state. Even Eliot's less sympathetic Victorian readers recognized that Romola's struggle to free herself from the subjection imposed on her by civil and religious law paralleled the struggle of Victorian feminists.[9] A simple review of the plot makes clear Romola's efforts to escape her confinement by law. Eliot begins the novel by dramatizing the greater freedom of movement allowed Tessa, a young peasant woman from the countryside, in contrast to her heroine, who is completely innocent "about the world outside her father's books" (ch. 5, p. 104) and who does not leave her fortresslike home even to worship because her father has raised her to regard Christianity as mere superstition. Romola is therefore particularly susceptible to Tito Melema's charm when the beautiful young stranger comes to her father's library to offer his services to the blind old scholar. Tito courts and marries Romola and exploits his new family's social connections in his climb to power in the city government. After her marriage and after her father dies, Romola begins her slow and complicated disillusionment and tries twice to leave her husband. In describing this conflict, Eliot emphasizes Romola's legal subjection to Tito, for her heroine's first attempt to leave her husband occurs when she realizes that he has betrayed her father's dying request to donate the Bardo library to Florence and has sold it to the French invaders instead. Romola de-

cides to leave Tito, assuming she has the power to break "an outward tie that no longer represented the inward bond of love" (ch. 36, p. 391).

When Romola is safely outside the gates of Florence, she feels "for the first time in her life . . . alone in the presence of earth and sky, with no human presence interposing and making a law for her" (ch. 40, p. 428). Savonarola, however, interrupts her reverie and urges her to submit to God's law which makes unbreakable her bond to Tito and to Florence. Accepting his argument, Romola returns to the city, reassumes her role as wife, and begins her religious "discipleship" as Florence's "Visible Madonna," which prompts her to move outside her home to feed the hungry and care for the sick in the city's streets. When she discovers that Tito has sold his foster father into slavery and has established a "second marriage" with Tessa, the peasant woman who bears him two children, Romola determines again to leave her husband. Romola confronts Tito directly this time, saying, "I too am a human being. I have a soul of my own that abhors your actions. Our union is a pretence—as if a perpetual lie could be a sacred marriage" (ch. 58, p. 567). By thus refusing to accept the definitions of the good woman legislated by the civil and religious laws of the patriarchs of Florence, Romola claims her freedom from falsely restricting laws and successfully asserts her selfhood when she leaves the city a second time. Romola spends many weeks away from Florence in a primitive, mysterious, beautiful village in the countryside, and finally returns to Florence only to discover that Tito and Baldasarre have drowned together in the Arno and that Savonarola is under sentence of death. Eliot ends the novel with her heroine achieving a liberation from the misogynistic civil and religious laws enforced by father, husband, and priest.

Eliot makes it clear that Romola's subjection to civil and religious law is a function of urban society by sketching the parallels between her heroine's experience of marriage and that of the "contadina" who becomes Tito's "second wife." Like Romola, Tessa is also easily influenced by Tito, but Eliot shows how her ignorance and naiveté put her at special disadvantage in the sophisticated urban world of Florence. From the first, Tessa trusts Tito implicitly and responds with spontaneity to all his gestures of love. Coming from the countryside where domestic relations are less legalistically defined, Tessa innocently accepts the "sham" ceremony that Tito arranges for her as a genuine religious rite sanctifying and legitimizing their betrothal. Later, she takes the coral charm Tito offers her as a symbol of their marriage. In both these episodes, Eliot dramatizes Tito's superior power as symbol maker in the city that formally recognizes and protects male preeminence in both civil and religious law.

In the city, Tessa gladly surrenders her freedom when Tito provides her with a home and a duessa to care for her. Unlike Romola, she remains content with her enclosed domestic world; she is willing to honor Tito's request that she stay indoors, always out of sight, although she does not ever understand the real reason for this prohibition—that he does not want his legitimate wife to discover his "second wife" and children. Eventually, Tessa's love, enlarged by her maternity, becomes the only "uncontaminated" spring of kindness in Tito's otherwise corrupted life.[10] Eliot asserts the power of primitive blood bonds that tie Tito to his children and their mother:

> No guile was needed towards Tessa: she was too ignorant and too innocent to suspect him of anything. And the little voices calling him "Babbo" were very sweet in his ears for the short while that he heard them. When he thought of leaving Florence, he never thought of leaving Tessa and the little ones behind. He was very fond of these round-cheeked, wide-eyed human things that clung about him and knew no evil of him. And wherever affection can spring, it is like the green leaf and the blossom—pure, and breathing purity, whatever soil it may grow in.
>
> (ch. 50, pp. 501-502)

Nonetheless, Tito finally finds it expedient to abandon his second family along with his first when he plans his escape from the city, and without his protection, Tessa and her children are helpless. It is Romola who rescues them when she returns to Florence. Thus, Eliot contrasts Romola's marriage, sanctioned by the laws of the city and legitimized by the financial settlement that gives Tito the right to control the Bardo house and library, with Tessa's union, blessed only by the natural and erotic bonds that tie the lover to the beloved and the parent to the child, to show how marriage is transformed into a sterile economic contract by the city's laws.

Examining Romola's and Tessa's legal subordination this way, though, makes us ask why Romola fails to escape the city the first time, makes us question why Eliot shows her so responsive to Savonarola's appeal. Eliot demonstrates an answer to this question in her presentation of Romola's "moral imprisonment" by the literature and art of her city, and especially by the image of the Madonna in both its secular and religious manifestations. Eliot's treatment of Romola's "moral imprisonment" was especially complicated, because Eliot herself had tremendous difficulty escaping the patriarchal literature and art of Florence. Her own experiences researching and writing *Romola* and her response to and use of *The Divine Comedy* in her novel illustrate why it was so difficult for Eliot to liberate her heroine from the city.

Modern critics often remind us of the painstaking labor that Eliot expended on *Romola* by invoking her remark, "I began it as a young woman—I finished it an old

woman," but they do not adequately recognize the monumental challenge she faced in recreating with any degree of accuracy the "things which have not changed"[11] in the private lives of fifteenth-century women. Eliot clearly recognized the dilemma she faced in trying to unearth what is traditionally regarded as the ahistorical, the mundane, the irrelevant, and she articulated this awareness eloquently in a letter she wrote to her illustrator, Frederick Leighton, when she learned that he planned a trip to Florence:

> If you are going to see Ghirlandajo's frescoes, I wish you would especially notice if the women in his group have not that plain piece of opaque drapery over the head that haunts my memory. . . . We have in Varchi a sufficiently fit and clear description of the ordinary male costume of dignified Florentines in my period; but, for the corresponding feminine costume, the best authority I have seen is the very incomplete one of a certain Genevra's trousseau. . . . Approximate truth is the only truth available, but at least one must strive for that and not wander off into arbitrary falsehood.[12]

This letter makes us wonder where did Eliot turn to discover all the carefully researched and historically accurate details of Romola's life. What woman's history survives? Where did she discover what Romola would wear, what she could do to amuse herself, what she would think about? Though Eliot mentions Cassandre Fidele, a woman scholar of fifteenth-century Venice, she could find no counterpart for Romola in fifteenth-century Florence and was forced to rely primarily on the materials of culture that survive: on men's history, literature, and art.[13]

In depicting Romola, Eliot not only had to struggle to maintain historical accuracy consistent with her realistic aesthetic, she also had to work against one of the most powerful symbols of the Italian Renaissance, Dante's vision of the Virgin Mother, which was associated with Florence in the minds of Victorian readers. Dante defines woman's place in the city by presenting his Beloved Beatrice, who lived in the moral center of the earthly city of Florence, in relation to her spiritual counterpart, the Virgin Mother, who reigns enthroned in the Celestial Rose at the center of the Heavenly City of God. A. B. Giamatti describes how the metaphor of the city functions in *The Divine Comedy*:

> Finally, the city includes all; it is amphitheater and rose. Here where will and desire are one, where perfect stillness creates perfect motion, the twin images of Garden and City are married in the final, luminous vision.[14]

In the course of the poem, Beatrice is drawn into the center of the Heavenly City to her place beside the Holy Madonna, and thus Virgin and Mother are seen as one. In effect, Dante's Beatrice can only live in the poet's imagination in Florence, and even in Paradise she moves only to lead him on to the center of the City of God. Eliot, however, wished to reverse this paradigm in order to free her heroine from the city and the prescriptive images of selfless, humble womanhood embodied so powerfully in Dante's Virgin Mother. Thus, she found that while Dante's poetry helped her enormously in imagining the inner life of her characters, it also inhibited her imagination especially in the construction of her heroine.

When Eliot was writing the episode of the novel that describes Romola's first attempt to escape from Florence and her oppressive marriage, Eliot—as if in sympathy with her heroine—suffered from a period of paralyzing depression. In December 1862, she wrote:

> I am extremely spiritless—dead, and hopeless about my writing. The long state of headache has left me in depression and incapacity. . . . I am inwardly irritable, and unvisited by good thoughts. Reading the 'Purgatorio' again and the 'Compendium Revelationum' of Savonarola. After this record, I read over what I have written of Part IX to George [Lewes] and he, to my surprise, completely approved of it.[15]

Though G. H. Lewes's praise of this section of the novel apparently surprised the ever-doubting Eliot, it hardly does us, especially when we remember that he frequently called her "Madonna" during this period of their lives together. Some of Eliot's depression may have come from her despair of ever being able to invent a way to allow her heroine to escape from the role of the Divine Mother—when she, herself, nearly four centuries later, had not completely escaped from the confining image of the Madonna and from the oppression of another city that exalted it as an ideal.[16]

Thus, Eliot remained trapped, in part, by the paradox that faces all women writers: she must use what Adrienne Rich has called the "oppressor's language" if she is to communicate at all.[17] Because Eliot wished to lend heroic stature and spiritual authority to her heroine by using a historically accurate idiom like Dante's, *The Divine Comedy* remained a powerful presence in *Romola*. At the outset, Eliot reminds us that Romola's city is Dante's, and leads us to the "severely simple doorplace, bearing this description: 'Qu Nacque il Divino Poeta'" (ch. 1, p. 53), as a point of reference for the drama that follows.

Eliot evokes Dante frequently in her presentations of both Tessa and Romola. In her characterization of the former, Eliot uses the parallels between Beatrice and the Divine Madonna ironically to dramatize Tessa's unconscious sexuality and her instinctive apprehension of the fundamental appeal of the Christian symbol of the Virgin Mother. Tessa responds readily and intuitively to the beautiful icons of the Madonna that she sees in the churches of Florence. She feels a religious awe "over

something supernatural and heavenly" (ch. 14, p. 200) when she worships before the image of the Virgin Mother, and she acts out her naive understanding of the Madonna's significance in her subsequent relations with Tito, Baldasarre, and Romola.

Eliot planned originally to preface the chapter introducing Tessa with an epigraph from Dante's *Purgatorio* which refers to Beatrice's appearance in the Terrestrial Paradise.[18] The lines she selected, though, refer to Matilda, who acts as Beatrice's hand-maiden and leads the poet to the spring that restores memory. Certainly the similarities between Matilda's gentle submissiveness and Tessa's are clear; both act "as a gentle soul that makes no excuse but makes her will the will of another as soon as it is revealed by an outward sign" (*Purgatorio,* 33: 130-32). Yet this allusion to Dante becomes an ironic comment on Tessa's naiveté and intellectual incapacity, so evident in her first appearance, and similarly forecasts her later action when she unwittingly leads Tito away from his appointments in the city and invites him to fall asleep with his head in her lap as they sit outside the gates of Florence (ch. 10, pp. 153-65).

In her description of this second meeting between Tito and Tessa under the plane tree, Eliot lends the contadina a clam serenity that recalls Beatrice sitting under the great tree in the Terrestrial Paradise (*Purgatorio,* 32: 85-108), as she presents Tessa sitting at what seems to be the still point of the universe, watching over Tito as the world wheels slowly by. Again, though, the allusion functions ironically to display the pitiful inadequacy of Tessa's moral judgment, for, ignorant as she is about Tito's real place in the city and his anticipated marriage to Romola, she feels herself near "Paradise" in this moment they have stolen together outside the city's time and culture. While Tessa finds in the Christian Madonna an image that expresses her own spontaneously loving nature and her instinctive respect for the power of female sexuality and fertility associated with this image since before the advent of Christianity, she is incapable of understanding the symbol in Dante's sophisticated metaphysical terms, and perhaps this is one of the reasons why Eliot abandoned her plan to use epigraphs in *Romola.*

When Tessa becomes a mother, Eliot makes more explicit the contadina's solipsistic identification with the figure of the Holy Madonna. She shows that Tessa's naive responsiveness to the symbol, like her dependency upon Tito in their illegitimate marriage, makes her especially vulnerable in the urban world of Florence. Whenever Tessa leaves her home without Tito's permission, she finds herself helpless and powerless. The first time she steps outside her home, she meets Baldasarre, the man who raised Tito and who seeks revenge upon him. Knowing nothing of this man's relation to Tito,

Tessa simply observes his need for love, and, to cheer him, she brings her child to him as he sits sheltered in a barn outside her home. Naively calling attention to the parallels between herself and the Madonna, Tessa tells him, "This is my baby. . . . It is like the little Gesù, and I should think the Santa Madonna would be kinder to me now, is it not true?" (ch. 33, p. 367). Her remarks thus disclose the unconscious egoism which rules even in her religious life, for by her own analogy, she has become the Holy Madonna. Her altruism has precisely the opposite effect from the comfort she intended, however. As he holds the child, Baldasarre mutters, "Poor thing," with "something strangely threatening in his apparent pity." Of him, Eliot concludes, "It did not seem . . . as if this guileless, loving little woman could reconcile him to the world at all, but rather that she was with him against the world, that she was a creature who would need to be avenged" (ch. 33, p. 367). Baldasarre's transformation from a loving parent to a revengeful one, indicated in his response to Tessa, demonstrates how deeply hostile Florence is to the values of spontaneous love and familial affection that she embraces so instinctively, and in such a world, Tessa's naive identification with the Madonna prevents her from recognizing the real limits of her power as mother.

Eliot shows, though, that while Tessa's identification with the figure of the Christian Madonna is essentially ego-gratifying, she is able nonetheless to recognize that she is in the presence of a love greater and stronger than her own when she meets Romola in the streets of Florence the second time she ventures outside the protection of her home. Tessa is conscious of Romola's superior moral power and stature and associates her with the figure of the Madonna, when, thinking back on her encounter, she muses: "In the dream-like combination of small experience which made up Tessa's thoughts, Romola had remained confusedly associated with the pictures in the churches, and when she reappeared, the grateful remembrance of her protection was slightly tinctured with religious awe" (ch. 56, p. 546). When Tessa later asks Tito "who the heavenly lady that had come just when she wanted and vanished so soon was likely to be—whether she could be the Holy Madonna herself," he tries in his capacity as patriarchal authority to correct Tessa's perception of Romola (ch. 56, p. 546). In this exchange between Tessa and Tito, Eliot demonstrates how the symbol of the Holy Mother is aestheticized and disassociated from any earthly referent in Florence. Only an illiterate peasant woman like Tessa and uneducated followers of Savonarola acknowledge the primitive power that the Christian symbol of the Madonna embodies and find it to be an awe-inspiring force in their earthly world. For men at home in civilization, and for women like Romola who are educated by them, the image of the Madonna is emptied of the primitive meaning that Tessa apprehends and worships. All the men that Eliot describes in Florence—even

strangers like Tito and Baldasarre—claim the power to interpret, reshape, or redefine not only the symbol of the Madonna but all feminine images of spiritual and sensuous perfection in order to preserve their hegemony in the city.

Eliot's use of Dante in her characterization of Romola is even more complicated because without the defense of irony used in Tessa's portrait, Eliot had difficulty controlling the parallels between her heroine and Dante's Holy Virgin and Divine Madonna. She presents Romola's experiences with her father, husband, and priest, and her eventual escape from Florence by using some of the symbolical elements of Dante's epic vision of the Holy Virgin in the Terrestrial Paradise (*Purgatorio*, 27-33) and the Divine Mother in the Celestial City (*Paradiso*, 30-33). Nonetheless, Eliot adjusts these elements, as we shall see, so that they are consistent with her woman-centered vision and with her feminist sensibilities. While other critics have documented the ways that Eliot violates her realistic aesthetics by overidealizing Romola, especially by comparing her to the Madonna, they have failed to explain the function of Romola's two flights from the city or to acknowledge the imaginative difficulties Eliot faced in describing them. I would like to show how and why Eliot includes Romola's failed and successful attempts to achieve her extraordinary liberation from Florence and the sensuous and spiritual ideals of womanhood that it imposed.[19]

Because Eliot had to struggle so with Dante's influence in her characterization of Romola, she was forced to confront what it means for a woman to be defined by her culture as the Other. Both times Romola steps outside the walls of Florence, she experiences an existential crisis because she confronts a self that has been suppressed by patriarchal culture.[20] The first time she finds herself "free and alone" outside the city, Romola feels triumph: "A certain awe which inevitably accompanied this most momentous act of her life became a more conscious element in Romola's feeling as she found herself in the impalpable golden glory and the long shadow of herself which was not to be escaped" (ch. 37, p. 400). Yet accepting that which has been repressed by her civilization becomes frightening for Romola when she finds herself in the landscape her brother Dino foresaw in a visionary dream as he was dying. He correctly predicted Romola's two attempts to escape from Florence when he envisioned her marriage:

> And the priest who married you had the face of death; and the graves opened, and the dead in their shrouds rose and followed the bridal train. And you passed on through the streets and the gates into the valley, and it seemed that he who led you hurried you more than you could bear. . . . And at last you came to a stony place

where there was no water, and no trees or herbage; but instead of water, I saw men of bronze and marble springing up and crowding round you.

(ch. 15, p. 215)

Dino assumes the patriarch's privilege and interprets the dream for Romola as a warning against marriage, which he imagines in conventional Christian terms, as the temptation of an "angel of darkness." For a daughter of civilization like Romola, guilt overshadows the "golden glory" of the self when memory thus turns traitor; her first return, then, becomes the return of the repressed. Before Romola can successfully confront her own female nature outside the bounds of civilization, she must see through the symbols of her father's and husband's classicism and the images of her brother's and spiritual advisor's Christianity, those figures of bronze and marble and those scholastic parchments. Only then can Romola transcend them and find herself outside the gates of Florence in a world that has not been predetermined by male authority.

To illuminate Romola's struggle toward self-definition, Eliot demonstrates how her heroine's experiences with the secular and religious symbols of Florence parallel Tessa's but move in the opposite direction as she grows more and more skeptical about the sensuous and spiritual ideals by which the patriarchs define womanhood in her culture. Like Tessa, she begins willing to accept instruction as to the meaning of the female symbols inside the city, and thus she is taught to speak the "oppressor's language" in both words and symbols. Without that secure sense of her own sexual identity that makes the primitive meaning of the Christian symbol of the Madonna real to Tessa, Romola is ultimately compelled to resist the patriarchal authorities who indoctrinate her to the meaning of those symbols within the city. Though she fails to find relief and comfort when she escapes to the natural world the first time, Romola develops a critical consciousness about the sensuous and spiritual ideals defining womanhood in her city that made these images seem "alien" and "enigmatical" to both Lucy Snowe in *Villette* and Dorothea Brooke Casaubon in *Middlemarch*. Ironically, Romola develops this understanding of her place as Other in Florentine culture by playing the part of the "Visible Madonna"— that image that Dante used so effectively to unite the classical and Christian traditions in his *Divine Comedy*.

Romola's escape from her "moral imprisonment" is slow and difficult, though, precisely because she loves the men who act as her teachers, reflecting Eliot's parallel struggle to transcend Dante's vision of woman's place in the earthly and heavenly cities. Romola's indoctrination to the images of womanhood repeats Lucy Snowe's in *Villette*, but the schooling Eliot's heroine receives begins not with art but rather with literature and extends beyond both the library and the artist's studio

to the city's churches, those original temples of culture which Victorian museums imitated. In dramatizing how Romola is taught to see her life according to the images of the patriarchy, Eliot demonstrates how her mother-less heroine is protected from the influence of women because her father regards it as pernicious. In Romola's first appearance in the novel, Eliot reveals her heroine's pain as her father teaches her about the secular ideals of motherhood sanctioned by the classical texts in his library. Like one of Milton's daughters, Romola reads to her blind father a story about the redemptive power of the mother:

> There was a certain nymph of Thebes named Chariclo, especially dear to Pallas; and this nymph was the mother of Teiresias. But once . . . it happened that Teiresias coming as a hunter to quench his thirst at the fountain, inadvertently beheld Minerva unveiled, and immediately became blind. . . . When Teiresias had fallen into this calamity, Pallas, moved by the tears of Chariclo, endowed him with prophecy and length of days, and even caused his prudence and wisdom to continue after he had entered among the shades, so then an oracle spoke from his tomb.
>
> (ch. 5, p. 94)

Though this myth clearly expresses the sanctity and power of the mother, Bardo interprets it for Romola by reminding her of the "wandering, vagrant propensities of the feminine mind" and the "feeble powers of the feminine body" (ch. 5, p. 97). He recognizes none of the power of reconciliation expressed in Chariclo's story. Instead, he comments on the "debasing influence" of women "with their sparrow-like frivolity and their enslaving superstition," complimenting Romola with, "Thou has never fretted me . . . with thy petty desires as thy mother did" (ch. 5, p. 100). While Bardo does not perceive the irony in his juxtaposition of past and present mother's stories, Romola comprehends it viscerally as well as intellectually as her angry blush reveals, but her duty and love compel her to accept silently her father's definition of the mother and herself.[21] Romola must try twice before she can escape the self-doubt Bardo's misogyny has inspired. Furthermore, to heal the split between the images of the real and ideal mothers that he describes, she must finally leave the city that fosters it.

Romola's introduction to the sensuous ideals defining womanhood in art echoes Lucy Snowe's experience more directly and anticipates Dorothea's, for it is Tito, her beloved, who tries to flatter Romola into seeing herself in the image of Ariadne. On the day of their betrothal, Tito brings Romola a miniature that portrays Bacchus and Ariadne. Dutifully, like her father's daughter, Romola reads the language of the symbols of the painting as Tito instructs her: "Ah it is you—it is perfect. . . . And I am Ariadne and you are crowning me. Yes, it is true, Tito, you have crowned my poor life"

(ch. 20, p. 260). Playing the role of symbol maker that he assumes often with Tessa, Tito encourages Romola to forget her sorrow over her brother's death and enjoy the happiness imaged in the painting, saying, "My Ariadne must never look backward now" (ch. 20, p. 263).

Eliot indicates a further complication in Brontë's analysis of the sexual politics of art as male propaganda by describing the process by which Tito commissions this portrait. The image of womanhood that Tito prescribes actually looks like Romola because he has the wealth and authority to command the artist, Piero di Cosimo, to transform the original Ovidian tale of Theseus's abandonment of Ariadne into a more gratifying image of himself as Bacchus saving Ariadne:

> The young Bacchus must be seated in a ship, his head bound with clusters of grapes, and a spear intwined with vine-leaves in his hand. . . . But I want to have the fair-haired Ariadne with him, made immortal with her golden crown—that is not in Ovid's story, but no matter, you will conceive it all.
>
> (ch. 18, p. 244)

In this city where "truth is a riddle for the eyes and the wit to discover" (ch. 3, p. 82), Tito can manipulate art so that it falsifies his relation to Romola by granting the artist permission to depict Romola as Antigone with her aging father as Oedipus. Though Cosimo's version is clearly a more accurate representation of Romola, it is nonetheless distorted because it reshapes Romola to fit the classical myth valorizing a virgin's self-sacrifice for her brother and father.

Like Lucy and unlike Dorothea, Romola recognizes the falseness of Tito's idealizing portrait of her just before she tries to leave Florence the first time. Romola's decision to "renounce Ariadne's crown" and dissolve her marriage to Tito is accompanied by her heightened awareness of how the portrait has served Tito's purposes:

> Romola looked at the familiar images with new bitterness and repulsion; they seemed a more pitiable mockery than ever on this chill morning, when she had waked up to wander in loneliness. They had been no tomb of sorrow, but a lying screen. Foolish Ariadne! with her gaze of love, as if that bright face, with its hyacinthine curls like tendrils among the vines, held the deep secret of life!
>
> (ch. 37, pp. 397-98)

By describing Romola's bitterness over "foolish Ariadne," Eliot suggests how Tito has manipulated this female image of sensuous perfection. Romola experiences the rage of a woman who has seen how images of beatified wifehood and filial self-sacrifice have served to "screen" reality. The beauty of the former seduces women into imagining that their triumphant powerful-

ness in love is the perfect complement to their actual powerlessness in marriage. The latter image persuades heroic women that rebellion against the laws of the patriarchy can only be legitimized when it is undertaken not for the self but in the name of the father or brother. By leaving Florence this first time, Romola hopes to escape from these false images of the wife, having already been released from the filial relation because both her brother and father have since died.

Romola, like Dorothea, can only imagine her future life by a "pathetic mixture of childish romance with her woman's trials" (ch. 36, pp. 393-94). The failure of her imagination indicates the effects of living in a city and culture where she is always seen as the subject but never the maker of literature and art. Romola is completely unfamiliar with any exercise in self-definition. Before she sets off for Venice she muses: "She did not know that any Florentine woman had ever done exactly what she was going to do; . . . she had invented a lot for herself—to go to the most learned woman in the world—Cassandre Fidele, at Venice, and ask her how an instructed woman could support herself in a lonely life there" (ch. 36, p. 393). To expedite her flight from the city, Romola puts on a disguise; she wears the costume of a nun, for only so dressed can she move freely through the streets of Florence.[22]

Because Romola is only masquerading as a nun, though, Savonarola recognizes her and calls her back to Florence by playing on her guilt for "withdrawing in secrecy and disguise" and by reminding her of the duties she owes to Church and city (ch. 40, p. 430). Before she returns to Florence, Savonarola also instructs Romola about the meaning of Christian symbols just as Bardo and Tito have. The priest directs her to consider the meaning of the cross she wears by reminding her that it is the "image of a Supreme offering, made by Supreme love." He describes how the symbol should apply to her life: "Make your marriage-sorrows an offering, too, my daughter, to the great work by which sin and sorrow are being made to cease. . . . There is the vision which makes all life below it dross forever" (ch. 40, p. 436). But it is Savonarola's appeal to Romola's integrity that draws her back to Florence; it is not her faith in Church doctrine or her desire to martyr herself to earn a life hereafter. Moreover, it is the image of the Madonna that is the compelling ideal of her religious life; it is not the "image of the cross" that Savonarola prescribes.

When Romola returns to the city, she refuses to retire into the domestic seclusion of her earlier life with Tito, and in this way she offers an important contrast to Tessa. Under Savonarola's guidance, Romola takes up the role of the "Visible Madonna" of Florence and moves about the city ministering to the poor and sick,[23] but Eliot makes it clear that this role is not a natural one for her.

Unlike Tessa, she must struggle to transform herself into the semblance of the Madonna: "She had no innate taste for tending the sick and clothing the ragged, like some women to whom the details of such work are welcome in themselves. Her early training had kept her aloof from such womanly labors; and if she had not brought to them the inspiration of her deepest feelings, they would have been irksome to her" (ch. 44, p. 463). In assuming the part of the "Visible Madonna" of Florence, Romola actually takes part in the heroic pageant that seems a "masquerade" to Dorothea. Because of her "old contempt for their superstition," Romola is unwilling to join a religious order and take on the role of Holy Virgin; so she models herself after the only other female image that the Christians of Florence revere, the role of the Madonna. Thus she assumes a second costume, but one that allows her to maintain her personal integrity while it grants her free access to the ritual spaces inside and outside Florence's great churches.

Though Romola begins to recover a sense of the dignity and power of her own femaleness by acting as the Visible Madonna of the city, she recognizes finally that the Madonna too—in both its aesthetic and religious forms—is also a "screen" for the reality of a woman's life in patriarchal culture. The men in power in Florence regard the figure of the Madonna in a thoroughly egoistic light; one of the city's proverbs asserts that the Florentines had a "Madonna who would do what they pleased," a saying that Romola recalls when she watches a procession accompanying the ancient icon of the Madonna that is brought into the city during a famine (ch. 42, p. 445). Romola begins to see that the freedom and power she claimed in playing the part of the Visible Madonna are illusory; she, like Tessa, is really powerless as soon as she steps outside the female roles her culture sanctions. When she is threatened by a crowd of irreligious, rough, hungry men, she acknowledges the limits of a woman's power in Florence: "You have the power to take this bread if you will. It was saved for sick women and children. You are strong men; but if you do not choose to suffer because you are strong, you have the power to take everything from the weak" (ch. 42, p. 449). Thus, in her treatment of Romola's career as Florence's "Visible Madonna," Eliot displays how her heroine serves a Church and state which exalt the figure of maternal solicitude and supernatural goodness by the worship of the Virgin Mother, but yet deny and subvert the earthly expression of these values in the material world.

Romola's crisis of faith signals more, then, than a religious questioning; for in challenging the priest's vision of moral law, she sees finally the subjective nature of the entire fabric of classical and Christian myth by which the patriarchs of culture define her. She sees that she has been denied the power to interpret visions and symbols according to her own inward light by Savon-

arola just as she has been suppressed by the secular agents of the state—by her father and husband. As she kneels on the altar at the Badia before the image of Filippino Lippi's serene Virgin, Romola realizes how this revelation applies particularly to her experience as a woman living inside a city she does not and cannot control. Romola has just seen one of the sisters of a religious order imitate Savonarola by describing a religious vision that visited her. Recognizing the self-serving nature of the nun's vision and realizing at the same time why Savonarola will not denounce this woman or any of her "spirit-seeing sisters," Romola is forced to see the essential subjectivity of Savonarola's visions as well:

> The answer came with painful clearness: he was fettered inwardly by the consciousness that such revelations were not, in their basis, distinctly separable from his own visions; he was fettered outwardly by the foreseen consequences of raising a cry against himself even among members of his own party, as one who would suppress all Divine inspiration of which he himself was not the vehicle.
>
> (ch. 52, p. 526)

Just as she apprehended the limits of her father's and husband's authority in defining the secular images embodying perfect womanhood, so she sees now the prescriptive quality of Savonarola's visions. Indignantly, she confronts him:

> Do you, then, know so well what will further the coming of God's kingdom, father, that you dare despise the plea of mercy—of justice—of faithfulness to your own teaching? . . . Take care, father, lest your enemies have some reason when they say that in your visions of what will further God's kingdom, you see only what will strengthen your own party.
>
> (ch. 59, p. 578)

With this denunciation, Romola claims the right to define God's kingdom as something "wider" than Savonarola, as Church father, would declare. Thus, she rejects the principles he lives by which allow him to divide men into "sheep and goats by the easy mark of some political or religious symbol" (ch. 52, p. 527).

This is the rebellion that allows Romola to claim her own right to define a moral law and her proper relation to it. When she decides to leave Florence a second time, she determines to act in defiance of both civil and religious law, "in the face of a law which is not unarmed with Divine lightnings," just as Savonarola has done. "The law was sacred, but rebellion might be sacred, too. It flashed upon [Romola's] mind that the problem before her was essentially the same as that which had lain before Savonarola—the problem where the sacredness of obedience ended and where the sacredness of rebellion began. To her, as to him, there came a mo-

ment when her soul must dare to act on its own warrant" (ch. 56, pp. 552-53). In claiming this freedom, it is important to note, Romola does not rebel in the traditional way allowed women saints—the means the visionary nun and her sisterhood elected. Rather, she claims the right to describe God's kingdom as something "wider" than that envisioned by Christian visionaries and by Dante as well.

Casting aside all the ideals of her culture, however, is an even more terrifying crisis for Romola than accepting her sexuality, and Eliot presents this second existential crisis as a more devastating one for her heroine. Escaping civilization entails more, for Romola, than confronting her relation to nature; it means surviving the moment when all the classical and Christian myths that have shaped her life cease to hold their meaning. Again, Dino's dream foreshadows her crisis of faith and identity:

> And thou, Romola, didst wring thy hands and seek for water, and there was none. . . . And the bronze and marble figures seemed to turn into demons and snatch my father's body from thee, and the parchments shrivelled up, and blood ran everywhere instead of them, and fire upon the blood, till they all vanished, and the plain was bare and stony again, and thou wast alone in the midst of it.
>
> (ch. 15, p. 215)

Once she rejects the myths defining her role in the city, Romola's anger and despair are all-consuming, as Dino anticipated, but she turns them inward, good daughter of the city that she is, and contemplates suicide.

Romola sets herself adrift in a tiny boat and floats down the Arno, abandoning herself to her own "imagination," but miraculously she retreats beyond both the thoughts of death and the stories of "proud stoical heroism" that provided her first vision of escape. She recalls instead her girlhood daydreams of "floating naiad-like" down the river. She feels the agnostic's despair when she thinks of her past: "Memories hung upon her like the weight of broken wings that could never be lifted—memories of human sympathy that the Great Mother had no milk to still" (ch. 61, p. 590). By this image borrowed from Dante, Eliot reminds us that though Romola has imitated the role of the Great Mother in her work in Florence, she could find no reciprocity in the material world. Though she served the patriarchy by nurturing the poor and the sick, at the behest of the rich and powerful, she was not herself served or satisfied; her "thirst" for human sympathy persisted.

In recalling Dante's dream vision of the Holy Mother in the Celestial City at this moment of Romola's despair, Eliot discloses the difficulty of her heroine's—and her own—escape. Though Romola yearns for the "milk" of the Holy Mother, like the white radiances in Dante's

Celestial Rose that reach ever upward, imitating, in Dante's metaphor, "the infant that stretches out its arms to its mother after it has taken the milk" (*Paradiso,* 23: 121-22), Romola can find no Paradise like Dante's where her desire for perfect love and justice is satisfied. There is no complementing beatific vision for the woman who is defined by her culture as the Other. Thus, Romola is unable to trace the "message of love in the far-off symbolic writing of the heavens" that Dante learned to read when he was instructed by his Beatrice. Instead, Romola feels herself "orphaned in the wide spaces of sea and sky" (ch. 61, p. 590); her wings remain "crushed," and she thus renounces a place in both the earthly and heavenly cities.

Romola looks for meaning, then, in the Terrestrial rather than the other worldly Paradise. In her "cradle of new life" (ch. 68, p. 641), Romola discovers no reconciliation among the celestial spheres; instead, she finds an earthly world outside the city which retains the "awe for noble womanhood" and pays homage to its "primordial power." When Romola leaves her male mentors behind and passes her Lethe, she regains consciousness in a natural world of pregnant silence and primordial beauty. She turns to the past rather than the future and there discovers her fundamental identity among these images of serene beauty: the crescent-shaped valley, the sapphire blue sea, the green luxuriance, and the ripening corn, all symbolizing the attributes of a prehistoric mother goddess predating Florence's icon of the Madonna. The world that Romola retreats to also contains human suffering and is clearly of this world, for here she finds a crying child, a plague-stricken village, and a ruined hovel.

In this primitive, almost prehistoric world, Romola reconstructs a woman-centered culture and exercises her own power as a moral leader in it. In this rural world set apart from Renaissance culture, Romola recognizes the naturalness and power of her own maternal impulses, but she no longer feels obliged to assume the prescribed role of the "Visible Madonna." Though the priest and sick villagers that she meets initially mistake her for the "Mother with the glory about her tending the sick" (ch. 68, p. 646), Romola is no longer willing to cooperate with Christian mythology by acting the part of the divine and disembodied Holy Mother. She is not content with the "aves" of the priest and the villagers; she commands their active help in a way she could not in Florence. Though she cares for a child that she saves from the plague while she is in the village, she leaves him behind when she returns to Florence. Thus, she refuses to reenact the Virgin birth; for Romola, in this primitive world, as in Florence, there are no annunciations to lift her above humanity: "No radiant angel came across the gloom with a clear message for her" (ch. 36, p. 396).

When she departs, Romola leaves behind, as did the patriarchs of Florence, a myth that describes her. But there are no miracles in the many legends that were "afterwards told in that valley about the blessed Lady who came over the sea" (ch. 68, p. 649); there were no visions of supernaturally self-sacrificing Madonnas, no promises of perpetual help. She leaves, instead, "legends by which all who heard might know that in times gone by a woman had done beautiful loving deeds there, rescuing those who were ready to perish." For Romola, as for Eliot herself, such legends must suffice: "If everything else is doubtful, this suffering that I can help is certain: if the glory of the cross is an illusion, the sorrow is only the truer" (ch. 69, p. 650). Ultimately, Romola returns to Florence because Florentine women—and Victorian women writers like Eliot herself—could not imagine living out a utopian separatist vision of a woman-dominated world set apart from male civilization and culture.

Before she returns to Florence, however, Romola recognizes that the "simpler relations of the human being to his fellow men had been complicated for her with all the special ties of marriage, the State, and religious discipleship" (ch. 69, p. 650), and this revelation is like "a new baptism" to her. She does not, we must note, reassume any of her old functions. She returns, instead, to the family who remains, to her cousin Monna Brigida and to her husband's "second wife," Tessa, with her two children. Though her efforts to restore the simpler family-centered values may seem to reflect Eliot's notorious conservatism, we should observe that Eliot has made this saving remnant a community of women. It is a family that defies patriarchal laws of marriage and legitimacy; Romola accepts the responsibility of caring for Tessa's children as warmly as if they were her own. Furthermore, this is a family without living fathers, since both Tito and Baldasarre are dead.[24]

It is Romola who tells Lillo and Ninna about their natural and spiritual fathers' histories. And in repeating this domestic history, Romola reenacts the mother's role that Dante's Cacciguida so beautifully describes; she tends the cradle and soothes the child, using the "tongue that first delights fathers and mothers" (*Paradiso,* 15: 121-26). However, Eliot has moved beyond Dante's vision, beyond the paradisal world he imagines where Church fathers catechize and the lovely Beatrice instructs. She gives us instead a glimpse of a woman-centered world and reminds us that it is woman who first defines the language that delights the child and composes the history of the "things which have not changed" (Proem). Thus Romola asserts the matriarch's power by exercising her right to define such histories and by speaking of its beauty rather than silently representing it.

In the conclusion of *Romola,* Eliot evades all the apotheosis we might expect for a saint or a goddess and in-

sists that we look at Romola's "maimed life" in all its severe grandeur: she renounces Ariadne's crown; she avoids Antigone's self-destruction; she evades Beatrice's transcendence; she rejects the Madonna's motherhood. She comes to recognize the powerlessness of the Madonna's role in Florence, and her perception is clarified and confirmed when she lives, for a time, outside the gates of the city. Because of her splendid classical education and her moral insight into the Christian tradition, Romola is able to attain a more comprehensive understanding of her place in culture and in nature than either Lucy Snowe or Dorothea. She recognizes, at last, a self that transcends not only the legal and social definitions of womanhood constructed by her society but also the female ideals embodied by literature and art in Florence. Thus, she achieves a self-consciousness about urban life and culture that is, of all Eliot's heroines, perhaps closest to her own. We do Romola a great disservice to see her as a "goddess" and not as a woman; we do Eliot an even greater disservice.

Notes

1. See Andrew Sanders's introduction to *Romola* (Harmondsworth: Penguin, 1980), 10-11. All subsequent citations to *Romola* refer to this edition.

2. *The George Eliot Letters,* ed. Gordon Haight (New Haven: Yale Univ. Press, 1954-1980), IV, 102. For similar complaints especially relevant to *Romola,* see III, 293, 294, 360, 376.

3. *Letters,* I, 7.

4. John Cross's frankness in *The Life and Letters of George Eliot* (New York: Sproul, 1899) about the isolation Marian Evans faced as a young woman charged with the responsibilities of housekeeping is especially notable because he was otherwise zealous in suppressing evidence that she was less than a Victorian angel.

5. *Letters,* I, 261.

6. See, for example, Gordon Haight, *George Eliot: A Biography* (New York: Oxford Univ. Press, 1968, paper), 122-210; Ruby Redinger, *George Eliot: The Emergent Self* (New York: Knopf, 1975), 226-94.

7. All citations are to *Middlemarch,* ed. W. J. Harvey (Baltimore: Penguin, 1965), 219-35. This scene is, of course, often cited by critics but none has discussed it in relation to women and to *Villette,* to my knowledge.

8. See Charlotte Brontë, *Villette,* ed. Geoffrey Tillotson and Donald Hawes (Boston: Houghton Mifflin, 1971), 171-77. Eliot was deeply impressed by *Villette;* see *Letters,* II, 87.

9. See, for example, Henry James, *Partial Portraits* (London: Macmillan, 1888), 56. Eliot's feminism has been, of course, often debated, but Gordon Haight mentions her support for marriage and divorce reform in *George Eliot,* 204. For a more extended analysis of Eliot's involvement in this and other Victorian feminist causes, see my "Feminism and Positivism in George Eliot's *Romola,*" *Nineteenth-Century Women Writers* (Hofstra University Conference, 1980, proceedings forthcoming). John Goode has also confirmed my analysis in his lecture, "The Affections Clad with Knowledge: The Duty of Woman and the Public Life," George Eliot Conference, Nov. 22, 1980, Rutgers University.

10. Eliot's lack of prudishness in her treatment of Tessa reflects her feminist sympathies and her personal experience in sharing the responsibilities of parenting G. H. Lewes's three sons. Eliot seemed to grow more sympathetic to the situation of what Victorians called the "fallen woman," as is evident when we compare her treatment of Hetty Sorrel in *Adam Bede* to Tessa.

11. Gordon Haight seems to have established this tradition in *George Eliot,* 362. See George Levine, "Romola as 'Fable,'" in Barbara Hardy, ed. *Critical Essays on George Eliot* (New York: Barnes and Noble, 1970), 78-98.

12. *Letters,* IV, 42-43.

13. When I consider the frustrations I felt in simply researching the names, dates, and issues of nineteenth-century feminism, I find an entirely new meaning in Eliot's comment that writing *Romola* transformed her into an "old" woman.

14. In *The Earthly Paradise and the Renaissance Epic* (Princeton: Princeton Univ. Press, 1966), 118.

15. Cross, II, 431.

16. See Nina Auerbach's "Artists and Mothers: A False Alliance," in *Women and Literature* (Spring 1978), 6, no. 1, 3-15. Ironically, John Cross also adopted a nickname for Eliot during their nine-month marriage cut short by her death in December 1880; he called her "Beatrice." This association of Beatrice and Madonna evident in *Romola* is thus borne out by the private mythology shaping Eliot's personal life.

17. Adrienne Rich uses this evocative term in her "Burning of Paper Instead of Children," in *The Will to Change* (New York: Norton, 1971).

18. See Appendix B in Sanders's edition of *Romola,* 683. This is his translation. All subsequent citations from *The Divine Comedy* refer to John D. Sinclair (New York: Oxford Univ. Press, 1939, paper).

19. George Levine's "*Romola* as 'Fable'" presents perhaps the best analysis of Eliot's failures. See

also Joseph Wiesenfarth, *George Eliot's Mythmaking* (Heidelberg: Winter 1977), for an excellent summary of this critical tradition.

20. This is Carole Robinson's term from her "*Romola*: A Reading of the Novel," in *Victorian Studies* 6 (1966) 40. I find Dante to be a much less anachronistic parallel for *Romola* than Sartre.

21. Eliot stresses Romola's womanliness, in part, I think, to counter the reactionary Victorian arguments that too much education could "unsex" women. Providing an adequate education, of course, is a complicated problem as Eliot's subsequent treatment of Romola's experience with patriarchal culture reveals.

22. Needless to say, Romola's consciousness that she must wear a costume on the street for her own protection is another element that invites comparison to Victorian—and modern—women's experiences.

23. Eliot's description of Romola's career as a nurse, emphasizing her moral stature and chaste integrity, echoes Florence Nightingale's argument that nursing was a respectable profession for the Victorian woman.

24. The alliance between Romola and Tessa reflects the association that drew middle-class wives and mistresses together later in the agitation to repeal the Contagious Disease Acts in 1871. See Judy Walkowitz's excellent essay, "The Politics of Prostitution," in *Women: Sex and Sexuality,* ed. Catherine R. Stimpson (Chicago: Univ. of Chicago Press, 1980), 145-57.

David M. Craig (essay date 1987)

SOURCE: Craig, David M. "The Interplay of City and Self in *Oliver Twist, David Copperfield,* and *Great Expectations.*" *Dickens Studies Annual* 16 (1987): 17-38.

[*In the following essay, Craig illustrates Dickens's depiction of the reciprocal relationship between identity and external reality through the urban experiences of his novels' protagonists.*]

> the city
> the man, an identity, it can't be
> otherwise—an
> interpenetration both ways . . .
>
> W. C. Williams, *Paterson*

In imagining the London experiences of his autobiographical heroes, Oliver, David, and Pip, Charles Dickens records his changing conception of the relationship between city and self. For Dickens, the terms of urban experience evolve as he becomes increasingly aware of the way in which reality is created by consciousness and consciousness is itself shaped by external reality. In *Oliver Twist,* the city and the self have discrete identities, as Dickens systematically detaches Oliver from his urban surroundings, the subjective world from the objective. In *David Copperfield,* the city has a subjective identity, as backdrop to David's desire to become the "hero of [his] own life" (1). Cast by David's memory or transfigured by his imagination, the city stands in relation to the hopes and fears of the self. Only in *Great Expectations* does Dickens fuse the identities of the city and self. Through the act of perception, views of the city are always conditioned and framed by the concerns of the self. Conversely, the city encloses consciousness itself so that acts of consciousness are always shaped by their urban context. In *Great Expectations,* then, city and self represent inseparable phenomena—much as observer and event do in the new physics.

Dickens makes explicit the connection between the identity of the city and the perceptions of its inhabitants in a notebook entry late in his career. He conceives the possibility of "representing London—or Paris, or any great place—in the new light of being actually unknown to all the people in the story, and only taking the colour of their fears and fancies and opinions. So getting a new aspect, and being unlike itself. An *odd* unlikeness to itself" (*Letters,* III: 788). This city exists in the minds of those who know or experience it. Such an urban novel would mirror the way in which urban residents know the city: the city they see as outside themselves is the mental representation of the experience of the city that is inside themselves. This transformation of the city into an "*odd* unlikeness to itself" identifies the true nature of the Dickensian city. As J. Hillis Miller says of the Dickens city: "[it] is, first of all, the co-presence of an unimaginable number of people in an entirely humanized world" (*World,* 293). If Dickens never actually wrote the novel of London or Paris that he postulates, he does record the London of the "fears," "fancies," and "opinions" of his autobiographical heroes. These "Londons"—as the Smithfield scenes of *Oliver Twist* and *Great Expectations* indicate—are worlds as different as their heroes Oliver and Pip.

By examining the urban experiences of Dickens' heroes as a relationship rather than as an event, I am departing from the thematic approaches of Alexander Welsh and F. S. Schwarzbach.[1] While Welsh and Schwarzbach provide the groundwork for this study by documenting the way in which the city operated as a catalytic agent for Dickens' imagination and the way in which his imagination responded differently to the country and the city, their readings render Dickens' London as a fixed reality. Focusing on Dickens' efforts to cope with the destructive London of his experience, Welsh and Schwarzbach reduce urban scenes as varied as the Smithfield

scenes in *Oliver Twist* and *Great Expectations* to aspects of a single vision. Raymond Williams provides a more fruitful insight when he argues that the form of Dickens' novels unfolds "a way of seeing," because this formulation makes the city inseparable from Dickens' novelistic imagination (159). For Williams, this mode of seeing is ultimately social, a recognition of "relationships and connections . . . that are obscured, complicated, mystified, by the sheer rush and noise and miscellaneity of the new complex social order" (155). Unlike Williams, whose interest is in the vision, I want to focus on the process of seeing itself. As represented by *Oliver Twist, David Copperfield,* and *Great Expectations,* this process of seeing is more complicated than Williams's schema would indicate because it bonds the seer and the seen so that each shapes and is shaped by the other.

Oliver Twist, David Copperfield, and *Great Expectations* illuminate Dickens' increasingly self-conscious recognition of the interpenetration of city and self, for, as Berry Westburg argues, these novels "are systematically related" (xvi). They present striking similarities in their presentations of London and of urban experience.[2] On one level, there are suggestive geographical parallels, as for instance Dickens' use of Smithfield in *Oliver Twist* and *Great Expectations* as setting for the crucial scenes introducing the hero to the city. More importantly, Dickens reworks the same urban motifs in each successive novel. For example, Oliver's physical imprisonment in Fagin's lair becomes David's entrapment in his blacking house memories, which, in turn, becomes Pip's psychological entanglement in his own guilty consciousness. But the most important aspect for this study is the change in Dickens' style in representing moments of urban vision.[3] As a record of the dialogue between imagination and the city, Dickens' style embodies his recognition of a changing epistemological relationship between himself and the world. In this sense, style is an event, an experience; style is, to adapt Wallace Stevens, the "cry of its occasion / Part of the res itself and not about it" ("An Ordinary Evening in New Haven," xii: 473).

The shift in Dickens' style from the largely metonymic patterning of *Oliver Twist* to the metaphoric method of *Great Expectations* provides occasion and signal to the change in the way that his imagination conceives urban reality.[4] The metonymic style of *Oliver Twist* is dualistic, always distinguishing the subject from the object; the narrator's reportorial stance from that which he reports, Oliver's emotional responsiveness from the London world inside and out of Fagin's lair.[5] Dickens usually invests his rhetorical energy in the city as object of perception. Readers will recall the prominent role that extended passages of townscape description play in the scenes set at Jacob's island, at Smithfield, and in Fagin's den. By contrast, in *David Copperfield* a pattern

of stylistic overlay juxtaposes two modes of consciousness often in the same passages, that of the youthful David with that of the narrator David.[6] Rhetorically, the subject, David, is always in the foreground and the object in the background, much as in the relationship between the actor and the backdrop on a stage. London scenes, so prominent in *Oliver Twist,* almost disappear. Even the famous account of the blacking factory occupies a scant four paragraphs, themselves foreshortened from Dickens' autobiographical formulation. This turn in Dickens' metonymic method places the city—as it exists in David's memories or as it is rendered by his imagination—in relation to the concerns of the self. The metaphoric mode of *Great Expectations* unites the city and the self by placing in the foreground the process of consciousness itself, both of Pip the youth and Pip the narrator. Ernst Cassirer's account of the making of metaphor provides a useful description of the kind of consciousness which the text reproduces: perceptual "excitement caused by some object in the outer world furnishes both the occasion and the means of its denomination" (89). This metaphoric process conjoins city and self, the object and subject of sensation, and in doing so concentrates meaning in the relationship between them. In *Great Expectations,* urban identity necessarily partakes of the reciprocal principles of city and self.

II

Detaching the observer from that which is observed, the metonymic style of *Oliver Twist* depicts city and self as separate realities. The Smithfield scene, in which Oliver and Sikes pass through the market on the way to rob the Maylies, provides a paradigmatic instance of the city as distinct from its observers, the narrator and Oliver. The narrator observes the churning market with the detachment of a reporter and chronicles its myriad details with the fidelity of a camera. Its energy challenges his ability to perceive and order. Hence his rhetorical structures embody his efforts to know—to classify, to sequence, and to order the tumultuous market:

> It was market-morning. The ground was covered, nearly ankle-deep, with filth and mire; a thick steam, perpetually rising from the reeking bodies of the cattle, and mingling with the fog, which seemed to rest upon the chimney-tops, hung heavily above. All the pens in the centre of the large area, and as many temporary pens as could be crowded into the vacant space, were filled with sheep; tied up to posts by the gutter side were long lines of beasts and oxen, three or four deep. Countrymen, butchers, drovers, hawkers, boys, thieves, idlers, and vagabonds of very low grade, were mingled together in a mass; the whistling of drovers, the barking of dogs, the bellowing and plunging of oxen, the bleating of sheep, the grunting and squeaking of pigs, the cries of hawkers, the shouts, oaths, and quarreling on all sides; the ringing of bells and roar of voices, that issued from every public-house; the crowding, pushing, driving, beating, whooping and yelling; the hideous

and discordant din that resounded from every corner of the market; and the unwashed, unshaved, squalid, and dirty figures constantly running to and fro, and bursting in and out of the throng; rendered it a stunning and bewildering scene, which quite confounded the senses.

(153)

The passage presents an objective city, in contrast to the subjective city of the memorandum book, and works by enumerating and categorizing details: kinds of animals, varieties of people, and types of noise. The narrator's analysis gives the market the shape of the interpretive mind. Yet while each element in the classification schema is rendered individually, the totality becomes chaotic and confusing.[7] For example, the people, each classified so distinctly, become "mingled together in a mass" and the sounds combine to form the "hideous and discordant din." This anarchic world overcomes the order principles of the interpretive mind. Categorical distinctions disintegrate: "whistling drovers," "barking dogs," "bleating sheep," "cries of the hawkers" exist on the same level. The common element of this environment is noise, with human language just another variant. The collapse of the many details into a cacophonous whole negates the effort at classification, signifying a world which cannot be logically ordered and which dissolves upon analysis into shapelessness.

Like a solar flare, "crowding, pushing, driving," Smithfield reaches outward, its force threatening the narrative calm which attempts to contain, to form, and to analyze. Even in this early Dickens townscape, the object of perception is acting upon the subject. As the predominance of gerunds in the passage indicates, energy is the essential characteristic of the world. The gerunds provide a temporal representation of chaos—a continuous present that defies temporal order and sequence. The gerundial construction—a rhetorical synthesis of action and being—also illuminates the relationship between the narrative mind and the world. By literally rendering action as being, the gerunds provide moments of static perception, models of change. This rhetorical reordering of Smithfield's energy permits both the narrator and the reader to contemplate without becoming involved; it is the rhetoric of distance. Simultaneously, verbal nouns point to the limitations of language to represent and contain the anarchic market. They proclaim their own failure to represent motion as motion. The "stunning and bewildering scene . . . quite [confounding to the] senses" resists efforts at knowing, its energy and fluidity finally eluding the framing language of analysis and classification. Dickens' style undercuts the narrative control, pointing to an actuality that is beyond rational ordering.

Counterpoised to the narrator's rhetorical exploration is Oliver's movement through Smithfield, his urban journey. Dickens renders Oliver's journey with two com-

ments which frame the extended passage of description: "from which latter place arose a tumult of discordant sounds that filled Oliver Twist with amazement" (153) and "Mr. Sikes, dragging Oliver after him, elbowed his way through the thickest of the crowd, and bestowed very little attention on the numerous sights and sounds, which so astonished the boy" (153). The syntax of each sentence emphasizes Oliver's passivity—that he is acted upon rather than acting and that the scene imposes itself upon his mind. Rhetorically, Smithfield, not Oliver, is the subject of this scene. The words "amazement" and "astonishment" point out Oliver's primarily emotional response to the marketplace—a reaction only half formulated by consciousness. His generalized reaction contrasts with the particularity of the narrator's analysis. In the journey, this Dickensian innocent is untainted by the world and knowledge. Unlike the narrator, who can bring the interpretive mind to bear on what he sees, Oliver cannot comprehend Smithfield; unlike the narrator, he can see with no possibility for knowing.

One terminus of the narrator's and Oliver's urban journeys is Fagin's lair, Dickens' imaginative center of London and the novel. If the metonymic style detaches the narrator and Oliver from the city, it emphasizes the interdependence between Fagin, the urban man, and his environment. In introducing Fagin, the narrator depicts him as inseparable from his context:

> The walls and ceiling of the room were perfectly black with age and dirt. There was a deal table before the fire: upon which were a candle, stuck in a ginger-beer bottle, two or three pewter pots, a loaf and butter, and a plate. In a frying-pan, which was on the fire, and which was secured to the mantleshelf by a string, some sausages were cooking; and standing over them, with a toasting-fork in his hand, was a very old shrivelled Jew, whose villainous-looking and repulsive face was obscured by a quantity of matted red hair. He was dressed in a greasy flannel gown, with his throat bare; and seemed to be dividing his attention between the frying-pan and a clothes-horse, over which a great number of silk handkerchiefs were hanging. Several rough beds made of old sacks were huddled side by side on the floor. Seated round the table were four or five boys, none older than the Dodger, smoking long clay pipes, and drinking spirits with the air of middle-aged men. These all crowded about their associate as he whispered a few words to the Jew; and then turned round and grinned at Oliver. So did the Jew himself, toasting-fork in hand.

(56-57)

The narrative method is synecdochic (according to Jakobson, one of the characteristics of the metonymic style), with the table and its contents evoking the character of the room. The passage proceeds in a "this-is-the-house-that-Jack-built" fashion with a series of spatial connections all leading to the preparer of the domestic banquet, Fagin. The periodic sentence which

introduces Fagin momentarily arrests the movement of the passage, suspending the reader's attention until the "very old shrivelled Jew" materializes. Introduced as an appendage to the frying pan, which is in turn connected to the wall, Fagin comes into existence inseparable from his surroundings. And yet clearly, he is the center of the scene, its source of energy and power. When Fagin focuses on Oliver in the final sentence of the paragraph, this center radiates outward, an ever-expanding ripple. Even the passive voice construction does not diminish Fagin's energy. When Fagin's attention turns to Oliver, Oliver is enclosed.

At once prison and refuge, Fagin's lair affords Oliver another perspective on the city, this time from the inside out.

> There was a back-garret window with rusty bars outside, which had no shutter; and out of this, Oliver often gazed with a melancholy face for hours together; but nothing was to be descried from it but a confused and crowded mass of house-tops, blackened chimneys, and gable-ends. Sometimes, indeed, a grizzly head might be seen, peering over the parapet-wall of a distant house: but it was quickly withdrawn again; and as the window of Oliver's observatory was nailed down, and dimmed with the rain and smoke of years, it was as much as he could do to make out the forms of the different objects beyond, without making any attempt to be seen or heard,—which he had as much chance of being, as if he had lived inside the ball of St. Paul's Cathedral.
>
> (128-129)

This passage sets Oliver's confusion in relief.[8] Although he "gazes" upon the urban spectacle, he cannot apprehend what he sees. "The confused mass of house-tops, blackened chimneys, and gable-ends" are represented photographically—not filtered through Oliver's consciousness. The generalized details convey the confusion of the urban world: particulars proliferate, movement is always random, amid abundance there is only aloneness. Dickens' prose detaches Oliver from the very scene of which he is the observer. "Oliver's observatory" isolates him "as if he had lived inside the ball of St. Paul's Cathedral." This is one of the few metaphoric elements in the novel's townscape, and even it has a literal—not a metaphoric—referent. The simile calls attention to Dickens' willingness to expose the innocent to the city, but not to let it touch him; to let him gaze upon the city, but not to let him penetrate its mysteries.

There is an important exception to Dickens' systematic detachment of city and self, that in the story of Nancy and Sikes. In rendering deserted, fog-enshrouded Smithfield, Dickens shifts his attention to the minds of his human observers. In doing so, he demonstrates the identification with the criminal that Edmund Wilson so brilliantly examined in "The Two Scrooges." At this point in his career Dickens cannot yet directly expose his hero to the night city, the alienating city, but can explore it in his guise as outlaw. Carefully detaching Oliver from Smithfield with the narrative hyperbole, "it [Smithfield] might have been Grosvenor Square, for anything Oliver knew to the contrary" (109), Dickens probes the city of Sikes's and Nancy's fears.

> It was Smithfield that they were crossing. . . .
>
> They [Sikes, Nancy, and Oliver] had hurried on a few paces, when a deep church-bell struck the hour. With its first stroke, his two conductors stopped, and turned their heads in the direction whence the sound proceeded.
>
> "Eight o'clock, Bill," said Nancy, when the bell ceased.
>
> "What's the good of telling me that; I can hear it, can't I!" replied Sikes.
>
> "I wonder whether *they* can hear it," said Nancy.
>
> "Of course they can," replied Sikes. "It was Bartlemy time when I was shopped; and there warn't a penny trumpet in the fair, as I couldn't hear the squeaking on. Arter I was locked up for the night, the row and din outside made the thundering old jail so silent, that I could almost have beat my brains out against the iron plates of the door."
>
> "Poor fellows!" said Nancy. . . . "Oh, Bill, such fine young chaps as them!"
>
> (109-110)

Sikes and Nancy understand Smithfield in a way that Oliver does not. Their impressions take shape in their remembrances of their Newgate colleagues, for to the consciousness of the criminal even the empty marketplace underscores his status as fugitive.[9] Yet as the reaction to the tolling bells indicates, Sikes and Nancy do not have the same experience of Smithfield. For Nancy the bells are the catalyst for her empathetic reminiscences, while for Sikes the silence between the tolling bells partakes of the ominous quiet of Newgate that made him want to beat his "brains out against the iron plates of the door." Nancy's sense of place is shaped by her loyalties to others, hence her pledge to remain faithful to Sikes if he is imprisoned: "I'd walk round and round the place [Newgate] till I dropped, if the snow was on the ground and I hadn't a shawl to cover me" (110). By contrast, for Sikes, the chiming clock frames the silent market—much as the "row and din [of the St. Bartholomew Fair] made the thundering old jail so silent."

Sikes's and Nancy's different reactions dramatize the subjective city that will later capture Dickens' attention in the memorandum book; their reactions also show why Schwarzbach is wrong when he argues that before *Edwin Drood* the Dickens city "is invested with tonal qualities independent of the novels' characters" (217).

Nancy's plea to Sikes, "wait a minute," underscores the difference in their interpretations. By her plea, Nancy is telling Sikes of her loyalty to him and asking him to understand her "Smithfield." But of course Sikes cannot, for his "Smithfield" shares the silence of Newgate and prefigures the shape of death. His rejection of Nancy's sympathy on the grounds that only a "file and twenty yards of good stout rope" would help him reveals the workings of an alienated mind—a mind haunted by death and cut off from the sympathy it most needs (110). As their failure to communicate indicates, Sikes's and Nancy's interpretations of their Newgate memories place them in entirely different "Smithfields."

In the multiple Smithfields of Nancy, Sikes, the narrator, and Oliver, Dickens announces a central concern: exploring the relationship between the city's unaccommodating actuality and his protagonists' personal points of view. At root, his concern is epistemological, one of how best to know the city. In the novel's core story, Dickens contrasts the narrator's objective, taxonomic knowing and Oliver's subjective responsiveness—the latter which registers urban realities in the manner of a seismograph recording a far-off earthquake. By contrast, Dickens in the guise of outlaw can probe the alternative idea that city and self exist as relationship—that, as Sikes's and Nancy's Newgate memories demonstrate, the process of consciousness is necessarily shaped by its external context. Similarly, Sikes's and Nancy's Smithfield, while having an actual existence, cannot be entirely separated from their memories and perceptions. This city shaped by its viewers' needs and fears points to the London of David Copperfield's experience.

III

If the Oliver Twist story emphasizes the disjunction between the city's chaotic multiplicity and the hero's innocent consciousness, then *David Copperfield* brings the two into conjunction. The novel reproduces both the interpretative consciousness of the *Oliver Twist* narrator and the emotional innocence of Oliver's, but the two stories are joined with David's view of his youthful experience encased by the mature David's memories. When the two Davids view the city, there is an inward turn. The novel renders the central urban scenes—for instance, David's first passage through London, his time at Murdstone and Grinby's, and the search for Miss Emily—as interior events, experiences whose location is inside the self. In contrast to the simple metonymy of *Oliver Twist,* a pattern of overlay predominates in *David Copperfield.* This style juxtaposes past memories and present perspectives, thereby framing the external city with its subjective recording.

To the eyes of the youthful David, the city is the place of inclusion and confusion much as it was to Oliver. As he observes upon his first entrance into London, "we

went on through a great noise and roar that confused my weary head beyond description" (74). Surrounded by this external tumult, David alternately casts the story of his triumph and falls asleep, overwhelmed by the welter of urban sensations. Appropriately, his first view of London records not the sights and sounds, but the city of his imagination where the heroes of literature were "constantly enacting and re-enacting their adventures" (71). In this formulation, David's story documents the growth of imagination, his *Prelude,* and the dangers that the city poses to imagination. The coach-house story of his first London visit unfolds both parts of this tale. With no one to meet him, David casts a tale of abandonment and identifies himself as "more solitary than Robinson Crusoe, who had nobody to look at him and see that he was solitary" (72). This identification signifies the problem the city poses for David—his absolute sense of isolation and the pain of a consciousness which cannot communicate its feelings to others.

David's account of his coach-house experiences fills out the story of his desertion: "I couldn't hope to remain there when I began to starve" (73). Sitting amid the bundles, boxes, and debris, David becomes to his own imagination one more bit of baggage waiting to be picked up. In this nightmare formulation David, unlike Oliver, has become part of the urban environment. The arrival of Mr. Mell—who picks up David "as if I were weighed, bought, delivered and paid for"—completes his story (73). This resolution unfolds one possible ending for his tale, being reduced from subject to object of his own narrative.[10] If imagination provides a way of expressing the fears of the emotional orphan uncared for by the world, it also intensifies his aloneness, making him want to extinguish consciousness. Positing a connection between the coach-house baggage and himself, David has liberated his imagination to explore the relationship between his experience and the world around him, between city and self. But this imaginative liberation also brings confinement as the surroundings impose themselves on his imagination so that he begins to see himself as a part of this setting, as coach-house refuse.

In rendering David's urban journey away from the London coach house toward Mr. Creakles's school, Dickens' narrative overlay blends past and present perspectives and dramatizes David's urban confinement. In contrast to David's transforming consciousness upon entering London, his mind now is passive. The ride produces only fragments of memory: "we went . . . over a bridge which, no doubt, was London Bridge (indeed I think he [Mr. Mell] told me so, but I was half asleep)" (72). During the journey, the reader never sees London more directly than this. Rather the narrative reproduces the overwhelming fatigue that David felt during the coach ride. This fatigue—a kind of twilight of consciousness—is not rendered as time past, but as sen-

sation re-experienced. In the account of this sensation, the two Davids, youth and narrator, occupy the same narrative space, the stylistic overlay bringing the two into conjunction.

The account of the rest stop at Mrs. Fibbitson's almshouse in south London illustrates this conjunction of the two Davids and their two perspectives.

> My impression is, after many years of consideration, that there never can have been anybody in the world who played worse. He [Mr. Mell] made the most dismal sounds I have ever heard produced . . . but the influence of the strain upon me was, first, to make me think of all my sorrows until I could hardly keep my tears back; then to take away my appetite; and lastly, to make me so sleepy that I couldn't keep my eyes open. They begin to close again, and I begin to nod, as the recollection rises fresh upon me. Once more the little room, with its open corner cupboard, and its square-backed chairs, and its angular little staircase leading to the room above, and its three peacock's feathers displayed over the mantelpiece . . . fades from before me, and I nod, and sleep. The flute becomes inaudible, the wheels of the coach are heard instead, and I am on my journey. The coach jolts, I wake with a start, and the flute has come back again, and the Master of Salem House is sitting with his legs crossed, playing it dolefully, while the old woman of the house looks on delighted. She fades in her turn, and he fades, and all fades, and there is no flute, no Master, no Salem House, no David Copperfield, no anything but heavy sleep.

(75-76)

For David the narrator, the memory of Mr. Mell's flute is the catalyst for re-experiencing the entire episode—the melancholy strains bringing back memories of Mrs. Fibbitson's parlor still ornamented by the peacock feathers, recalling the pain of desertion that David fights to suppress, and once again invoking the sleep that will momentarily relieve the pain. In the recollection—as in the troubled sleep of the youthful David—past, present, and future are co-presences. And in the recollection, David the narrator and David the youth have a composite identity. They respond similarly to the pain of the experience—the youth to the pain of abandonment by his mother, the man to the pain of the youth. Both want a sleep that will extinguish sensation. Neither awake, listening to Mell's flute, nor asleep can the Davids find rest or solace; neither can the narrative. A resting place comes only with the extinction of consciousness: "all fades, and there is no flute, no Master, no Salem House, *no David Copperfield,* no anything but heavy sleep" (my emphasis). Here sleep does not bring rest or comfort, only momentary cessation of the treasured modes of David's mental life, memory and imagination. With David so "dead asleep," the narrative momentarily has the quiescence of death. Yet even this momentary narrative silence takes its shape from "the great noise and uproar" that surrounds it, from the London outside Mrs. Fibbitson's (74).

The temptation to extinguish his troubled consciousness and David's fear of becoming one more bit of London debris give shape to his experiences in London. Again and again, he wonders what people think of him and records such comments as that of the one-eyed man in gaiters: "they had better put a brass collar round my neck, and tie me up in the stable" (72). Such comments are included because David wants to be recognized, and he believes that if people will only see him they will realize his preeminence. Thus in the blacking factory chapter David describes his efforts to buy a tavern keeper's best ale and the wife's kiss as fully as he does his time at Murdstone and Grinby's. For David (as for Dickens) the episode, especially the kiss, is important because it validates his sense of distinction. Many of the Micawber episodes in which David becomes friend and confidant also serve this function. As David begins to be seen by others, he becomes the subject of his life and emerges from the urban backdrop.

If the youthful David seeks liberation, the mature narrator finds only enclosure. The blacking factory, Murdstone and Grinby's, typifies these urban enclosures, for this youthful trauma has its imaginative formulation in the mature David's experience.[11] Dickens' revisions from his original, autobiographical account of the experience call attention to his changing intentions. In the autobiographical version, the passage presents a memory long avoided; in *Copperfield,* the memory frames even the present moment.

> The blacking warehouse was the last house on the left-hand side of the way, at old Hugerford Stairs. It was a crazy, tumble-down old house, abutting of course on the river, and literally overrun with rats. Its wainscotted rooms and its rotten floors and staircase, and the grey rats' swarming and scuffling coming up the stairs at all times, and the dirt and decay of the place, rise up visibly before me, as if I were there again. The counting-house was on the first floor, looking over the coal-barges and the river. There was a recess in it, in which I was to sit and work.

(Forster I: 25)

> Murdstone and Grinby's warehouse was at the waterside. It was down in Blackfriars. Modern improvements have altered the place; but it was the last house at the bottom of a narrow street, curving down hill to the river, with some stairs at the end, where people took boat. It was a crazy old house with a wharf of its own, abutting on the water when the tide was in, and on the mud when the tide was out, and literally overrun with rats. Its panelled rooms, discoloured with the dirt and smoke of a hundred years, I dare say; its decaying floors and staircase; the squeaking and scuffling of the old grey rats down in the cellars; and the dirt and rottenness of the place; are things, not of many years ago, in my mind, but of the present instant. They are all before me, just as they were in the evil hour when I went among them for the first time, with my trembling hand in Mr. Quinion's.

(154)

The passage from the autobiography is of the past, a past which impinges on the present only in that its images "rise up visibly before [one]." Yet even when pressing against the present, this past is held at a rhetorical distance. The "as if" formulation of the simile "as if I were there again" signals that the details of Murdstone and Grinby's only can intrude on the present as the result of a deliberate act of mind. They remain at the distance of memory. By contrast, in the *Copperfield* passage the past encloses the present: "decaying floors and staircase . . . the squeaking and scuffling of the old grey rats [are] . . . of the present instant" still confining David. Unlike Oliver, whose enclosures were the physical and geographical reality of Fagin's den, David is enclosed by memories, memories which neither temporal nor geographical change affect. The *Copperfield* passage negates its initial assertion that "modern improvements have altered the place." In David's memory nothing has changed, and the physical details are as present as consciousness itself. It is not the blacking factory in which David "was to sit," rather the factory in which David's hand is still "trembling." As the image of David's trembling hand tells us, the scene does not locate the beginning of pain, but denominates David's continuing authorship of the self.

Unaltered by the accidents of historical change, the blacking factory is part of David's permanent psychic space. The narrative reproduces the mature David's, as well as the mature Dickens', active participations in the sensations of the child. Again Dickens' revisions from the autobiography are suggestive:

> The deep remembrance of the sense I had of being utterly *neglected and hopeless*; of the shame I felt in my position . . . cannot be written. My whole nature was so penetrated with the grief and humiliation of such considerations, that even now, famous and caressed and happy, I often forget in my dreams that I have a dear wife and children; even that I am a man; and wander desolately back to that time in my life.
>
> (my emphasis, Forster I: 26-27)

> The deep remembrance of the sense I had, of being utterly without hope *now*—of the shame I felt in my position . . . cannot be written.
>
> (my emphasis, 155)

The insertion of the word "now" and the deletions from the autobiographical account not only change the temporal character of the passage; they also call attention to David's narrative presence. The changes, particularly the omissions, dramatize what Dickens felt compelled to specify in the autobiography—the pain of insignificance and the fear of losing the self. The inserted "now" emphasizes the immediacy of the wounding, making the pain, fear, and guilt of the present moment. Dickens uses the *Copperfield* formulation of the passage to dramatize David's using a remembered "real" event to

identify the self—not to show David wandering "back to that time in my life." Dickens' David narrates the tale in order to accommodate himself to the pain of the experience. By casting the city as backdrop to his own story and by dramatizing the hazards of urban enclosures, this David emerges as subject of his own narrative—something that the passive Oliver never became.

David's hard-won subjectivity demonstrates the successful interaction between his urban experience and his writing. Through the course of his narrative, David literally finds his way in the city, in this "Modern Babylon" as Micawber calls it. The welter of sensations occasioned by the city are organized and systematized. The blacking factory episode continues with David learning under Micawber's guidance "the names of streets and the shapes of corner houses . . . that [he] might find [his] way back easily [to the blacking factory]" (157). As his memoir *David Copperfield* demonstrates, these lessons in urban navigation are not lost on David, who returns at will to Murdstone and Grinby's. But Dickens' David not only traverses the city by mapping its geography, he also makes his way by "fit[ting] my old books to my altered life, and ma[king] stories for myself, out of the streets, and out of men and women" (168). For David, these urban fictions give London a familiar shape by imposing on its landscape a textual map that he already knows. If this David can no longer believe in London as the place where "all [his] favourite heroes . . . [were] constantly enacting and re-enacting" (71) their adventures, he can transform its "sordid things" and his "strange experiences" there into his own "imaginative world" (169).

In this imaginative re-formation of the city, David encounters not only the city, but also the self. David continues his memories of his London experiences during this time by turning, as he so often does in his narrative, to himself: "I set down this remembrance here, because it is an instance . . . [of] how some main points in the character I shall unconsciously develop, I suppose, in writing my life, were gradually forming all this while" (168). This passage juxtaposes his transcription of his life story with the development of his character in the past. Its rhetorical formulation makes David the author of his character. But David's authorship, his "development of [his] character," is an act of the present, an act of writing. Not that this authorship is detached from the past or from what he was before he began to compose his autobiography, but rather the mature rememberer David is as responsible for developing his character as the youthful David was. In this passage, then, as in much of Wordsworth's *Prelude*, memory and imagination are co-extensive realms, and they mix and mingle until neither David nor Dickens can distinguish between them. As David says at chapter's end in turning from the events of blacking factory days, "When my thoughts go back now, to that slow agony of my

youth, I wonder how much of the histories I invented for such people hangs like a mist of fancy over well-remembered facts!" (169). The mature David like his youthful counterpart can only accommodate himself to his pain by encasing urban experience in memory and imagination—just as he himself remains encased in blacking factory days. As Pip will discover, however, to transform the city either by memory or imagination will have its own dangers.

IV

By presenting townscape in *Great Expectations* as inseparable from the act of conceiving it, Dickens depicts the reciprocity of city and self. Unlike *David Copperfield,* which keeps David in the narrative foreground, *Great Expectations* places the process of consciousness itself in the foreground. Even more than David, Pip uses urban experience as both present occasion and vehicle for asserting the identity of the self. Townscape becomes the backdrop against which the drama of the self is played. His brief comment upon entering London for the first time is typical of his method of rendering the city: "I think I might have had some faint doubts, whether it [London] was not rather ugly, crooked, narrow, and dirty" (153). But the city also shapes the responses that it occasions. As occasion for and object of sensation, the city plays a crucial role in the way Pip defines his experience. If the London of *Great Expectations* takes the form of Pip's "fears and fancies and opinions," it also provides the mold which forms them.

The scene in Jaggers's office, which serves a function similar to that of the scene in Fagin's lair in *Oliver Twist* and the coach-house scene in *David Copperfield,* introduces the interplay between Pip and his urban surroundings.

> Mr. Jaggers's room was lighted by a skylight only, and was a most dismal place; the skylight, eccentrically patched like a broken head, and the distorted adjoining houses looking as if they had twisted themselves to peep down at me through it. There were not so many papers about, as I should have expected to see; and there were some odd objects about, that I should not have expected to see—such as an old rusty pistol, a sword in a scabbard, several strange-looking boxes and packages, and two dreadful casts on a shelf, of faces peculiarly swollen and twitchy about the nose.
>
> (154)

Rendering the office in synecdochic details, Pip has the particularity of vision that Oliver and David lack. His description reproduces the play of consciousness with the world: the likening of the skylight to a patched head or the adjoining houses to peeping Toms. Pip's transforming imagination (like the romantic imagination of the young David) replaces the reportorial objectivity of the *Oliver Twist* narrator. The verbs of the scene in Jag-

gers's office place Pip's mental actions and reactions in the foreground: "I should not have expected to see," "I fancied" (twice), "I . . . became frustrated," "I called to mind," "I wondered" (154-155). In the scene Pip has a novelistic imagination busy constructing its own plot. "Mr. Jaggers's own high back chair was of deadly black horse hair, with rows of brass nails round it like a coffin, and I fancied I could see how he leaned back in it, and bit his forefinger at his clients." When Pip sits in the client's chair, he becomes an actor in the imagined story.

Having animated the room, Pip finds himself the victim of his imaginative exercise, when his surroundings begin to enclose him. Pip is haunted by the life he has given to the fixtures of Jaggers's office. For instance, Pip notes that the two grotesque plaster statues above Jaggers's chair have "faces peculiarly swollen and twitchy about the nose." As he gazes on them further, he supplies them with a history, deciding that they are Jaggers's relatives, and finds himself wondering "why he stuck them [these plaster 'relatives'] on that dusty perch for the blacks and flies to settle on, instead of giving them a place at home" (155). Finally Pip flees the room because he cannot "bear the two casts on the shelf above Mr. Jaggers's chair" (155). This understated formulation mutes the emotion underlying the scene—Pip's feelings of being smothered and constricted by the room. The city provides the molds—the "casts"—with which Pip's claustrophobic imagination encloses him.

Pip's flight from Jaggers's office through Smithfield and Newgate, which provides his first extended urban views, exemplifies this interpenetration of city and self. In contrast to the narrative richness of the *Oliver Twist* vision of Smithfield, Pip's initial apprehension of the marketplace is rendered in a single sentence, a generalization that reduces the multiplicity of Smithfield to a single image—filth. "So, I came into Smithfield; and the shameful place, being all asmear with filth and fat and blood and foam, seemed to stick to me" (155). Unlike Oliver, Pip is experiencing Smithfield and is, to his own consciousness, contaminated by its filthy debris. Pip's feelings of uncleanliness call attention to the workings of the imaginative consciousness which fuses city and self. In the Smithfield sentence we observe the making of metaphor: "that concentration and heightening of simple sensory experience which finds release in the representation of subjective impulses and excitations in definite objective forms and figures" (Cassirer, 88). This projection of inner experience upon the world is precisely what Pip enacts when he tries to cleanse himself of Smithfield's "fat" and "foam" by turning toward St. Paul's. To the metaphoric imagination, the city becomes the external representation of the sensations of the self—the clinging "fat and foam," an iconic representation of Pip's emotional life, of the one constant in

his experience, guilt. Smithfield has become a part of his self-consciousness. In the Smithfield passage, we can observe the interplay between city and self occurring on three simultaneous levels: his physical movement, his corresponding experiential movement, and the play of imagination which renders experience as metaphor.

On the first level, Pip's retreat from Smithfield transforms the townscape—Smithfield, Jaggers's office in Little Britain, Newgate, and St. Paul's—into a syntagmatic system in which the identity of each location is shaped by its proximity to its neighbors. Pip's movement towards St. Paul's through Newgate and back to Jaggers's office illustrates the workings of this system:

> So, I rubbed it [Smithfield's filth] off with all possible speed by turning into a street where I saw the great black dome of Saint Paul's bulging at me from behind a grim stone building which a bystander said was Newgate Prison. Following the wall of the jail, I found the roadway covered with straw to deaden the noise of passing vehicles; and from this, and from the quantity of people standing about smelling strongly of spirits and beer, I inferred that the trials were on.
>
> While I looked about me here, an exceedingly dirty and partially drunk minister of justice asked me if I would like to step in and hear a trial or so. . . . As I declined the proposal on the plea of an appointment, he was so good as to take me into a yard and show me . . . where people were publicly whipped, and then he showed me the Debtors' Door, out of which culprits came to be hanged. . . . Under these circumstances I thought myself well rid of him for a shilling.
>
> I dropped into the office to ask if Mr. Jaggers had come in yet. . . .
>
> (155-156)

As framed by Pip's perspective, the horror of Newgate is heightened by the blackness of St. Paul's looming behind it. And in this context, the church dome seems to take its blackness from the market refuse of Smithfield and the judicial corruption of Newgate. The succession of sites—the syntax of this geography—dramatizes Pip's flawed assumptions. By exposing him to increasingly appalling forms of corruption, this sequence unmasks Pip's illusory notions of progress. Ironically, while Pip's summary generalization of his walk, his "sickening idea of London," is entirely merited, he cannot see any connection between the city that he has just encountered and the London of his imagination—the setting which will seal and approve his aspirations toward gentility (156).

On the second level, Pip's experiential journey through Smithfield and Newgate parallels his physical movement, as he continually confronts the feelings of contamination and enclosure that he hopes to dispel. The claustrophobic "dirt and dust" of Jaggers's office are re-

placed by the clinging blood and foam of Smithfield, which are in turn replaced by the judicial contamination of Newgate. Succumbing to the "partially drunk minister of justice['s]" invitation to see the gallows, Pip not only finds the most repulsive form of corruption and most constricting feelings of enclosure, but also perceives a pattern that recurs regularly and seems to shape his life. As Pip will observe on a subsequent visit to Newgate with Wemmick:

> I consumed the whole time in thinking how strange it was that I should be encompassed by all this taint of prison and crime; that, in my childhood out on our lonely marshes on a winter evening, I should have first encountered it; that it should have reappeared on two occasions, starting out like a stain that was faded but not gone; that it should . . . pervade my fortune and advancement.
>
> (249)

The suggestive irony of the verb "encompassed" dramatizes the interchange between Newgate and Pip's expectations as well as signifies his constricted and constricting view of experience. Like Miss Havisham, who enshrouds herself in the darkness of Satis House, the Pip who pursues his expectations darkens his consciousness, giving it the shape of nightmare. As the Newgate image makes clear, Pip's constricted imagination denies its very aspirations; in his imaginative enclosures, Pip gives himself no exit.

On the third level, Pip's language in the Smithfield and Newgate passages is metaphoric, yoking his subjective experience and the world as if they were equivalent realms. The metaphors are self-reflexive, calling attention to Pip's language rhythms and to the movement of his mind. His choice of verbs describes not only his movement through the city but also the movement of his consciousness: "would take a turn," "came into Smithfield," "rubbed it off by turning into," "dropped into the office," "strolled out again," "turned into Bartholomew Close" (155-156). Pip's physical and linguistic turns are always circular, revealing the rhythms of his life. Continually seeking release, he finds only the enclosure of the city and of his own mind. His circling consciousness continually eddies back to the two poles of his experience, Newgate and Estella. Also Pip's metaphoric imagination presents the creation of its experience, in the process of representing the experience itself. For example, when Pip perceives the physical corruption of Smithfield or the social corruption of Newgate, he simultaneously casts the form of his experience, the necessity for cleansing that he continually seeks but never finds. Similarly, Pip's use of the verb "encompassed" during his second Newgate visit dramatizes both his guilty consciousness and his imaginative casting of his prison-house origins (the latter soon to be validated in Magwitch's revelations). As the Smithfield and Newgate narratives reveal, the self and the city are

equivalent realms, Pip's guilty consciousness and the urban corruption.

Because city and self are equivalent realms, exploration of one allows exploration of the other. As rendered by Pip's mature imagination, the Jaggers's office-Smithfield-Newgate excursion represents this dual exploration. The journey has been from the city to the self and back again, from a perception of urban filth and corruption to the realization this perception is spawned by Pip's own guilt-constricted consciousness. To Pip's metaphoric consciousness, as well as to the mature Dickens, city and self are reciprocal principles: townscape partakes of the identity of the perceiver and in turn shapes the perceiver's consciousness.[12]

As medium for the dialogue between city and self, Charles Dickens' style in *Oliver Twist, David Copperfield,* and *Great Expectations* embodies his changing conception of the "identity of things." His successive redescriptions of the city constitute a series of epistemological events and a record of urban consciousness. In reseeing London, Dickens becomes increasingly unwilling to separate townscape from the consciousness that observes it. Not that the objective city disappears, for as the example of Smithfield suggests, its tumultuous reality troubles Pip as much as it did Oliver, the *Oliver Twist* narrator, and, of course, Dickens himself. But more important than the objective city is the contingent relationship between city and self. In Smithfield and the other urban locales of *Great Expectations,* Dickens approximates the only city that Pip can ever know, that of his fear, guilt, and desire. Pip metamorphoses this city into a "skylight, eccentrically patched like a broken head" or into clinging "fat and foam." Such metaphors not only refigure the city's existence, but also denominate the experience of the self. Pip's metamorphic language proclaims his consciousness and the subjectivity that David's narrative strives to achieve. Dickens' style reproduces Pip's metaphoric imagination, thereby conjoining the city and the self as dual creators of Pip's—and human—experience. Anticipating the Modernist view of such writers as William Carlos Williams, Charles Dickens forges the urban identity of city and self, "an interpenetration both ways."

Notes

1. Grounding his argument on Dickens' journalistic and incidental pieces as well as on his fiction, Welsh persuasively argues that Dickens counterpoises the hearth and home to the modern city, which Dickens, inheriting the Christian tradition of his time, sees as a city of death. According to Welsh, Dickens' mythic rendering of domesticity "impose[s] its own religious construction of reality" (vi). Locating Dickens' understanding of urban experience at Warren's Blacking Factory,

Schwarzbach traces Dickens' treatment of the city chronologically from the early novels, in which characters must flee the city in order to live, to the later novels, in which they learn to accommodate themselves to the urban world. He argues that in response to the trauma of his blacking factory experience Dickens creates a personal urban myth which sees the country past as a paradisal whole and the city present as an "objective correlative of Hell" (16). Only in *Our Mutual Friend* and *The Mystery of Edwin Drood* does Schwarzbach see Dickens' presentation of the city itself changing.

2. Readers interested in Dickens' use of actual London settings should see Chancellor, Dexter, and Fletcher.

3. See Stoehr (1-65) and Garis (1-30), who explore the relationship between Dickens' style and novelistic stance.

4. See Jakobson and Halle. In using the terms metonymic and metaphoric, I am drawing upon Jakobson's distinction between two modes of language and two modes of mind. According to Jakobson, the principle underlying metonymy is contiguity—in language especially syntactic contiguity and in mind contextual association and combination. In the metonymic mode, an author explores contiguous relationships: for instance, between characters and their context, plot and the atmosphere it evokes, space and time. The metonymic mode provides a kind of portraiture which represents a subject in relation to its context or which renders it by isolating its characteristic details. By contrast the principle underlying metaphor is substitution—in language especially semantic substitution and in mind symbolic transformation. In the metaphoric mode an author focuses on the sign or symbol, rather than on the referent. For this reason, Jakobson associates the metaphoric style with poetry or romance. In the metaphoric mode, an author operates symbolically, working by association or identification. In practice, as Jakobson indicates, both modes are continually operative, but at the level of "style, preference is given to one of the processes" (76).

5. There are a number of other studies which use Jakobson's terminology to investigate Dickens, most notably by Arac, Garrett, Miller ("The Fiction of Realism"), and Romano. Among these studies, Arac's pursues a tack most similar to my own, for he explores the relationship between stylistic effects and Dickens' search for a comprehensive social vision: "if narrative prose seemed innovative and disruptive, an agency of mobility and transformation, it also worked toward a totalizing understanding. Through the interplay of 'metaphor and metonymy,' local stylistic effects combined to

build up the coherence of a book's world. . . . The search for continuity involved trying to see society as a whole extended to the search for figurative techniques to integrate a book" (8).

6. Professor Avrom Fleishman suggested the term "overlay" to describe Dickens' stylistic strategy of juxtaposing past and present moments within the same passage, even within the same sentence. This paper had its genesis in Professor Fleishman's "Literary Townscape" NEH seminar, and the ideas from his seminar are interwoven throughout my study.

7. The particularity of this description—its careful location in time and space—indicates that Stephen Marcus overstates his case when he argues: "*Oliver Twist,* however, issues from what we might call a generic imagination. . . . Even in describing so palpable a thing as the slums of London, Dickens repeatedly insists upon the labyrinthine, maze-like confusion of the streets, courts, and buildings" (63-64). This argument applies more to London as Oliver sees it, than to London as the omniscient narrator records it.

8. Readers of J. Hillis Miller's study of Dickens will recognize my debt to his analysis of this passage. Miller, however, sees Oliver as being much more active than I do in his perceptions of the world: "He [Oliver] spends long hours studying this disordered world, as if he had some faint chance of forcing it to yield up its secret which might be *his* secret too, the secret of his identity and the meaning of his life" (*World,* 54-55). Miller's analysis of Dickens' urban scenes has provided a stimulus for many of my own.

9. J. Hillis Miller's description of the metonymic logic of *Sketches by Boz* could also be applied to the underworld characters of *Oliver Twist:* "it is easy to see how, in the case of the *Sketches,* the predominance of metonymy reinforces that deterministic vision of man's life which is often said to be an essential aspect of realistic fiction. One narrative pattern recurring in the *Sketches* is an apparently inescapable progression of the city dwellers step by step toward starvation, sickness, degradation, crime, depravity, suicide, or execution. A character caught in this progression is 'impelled by sheer necessity, down the precipice that [has] led him to a lingering death'" ("The Fiction of Realism," 101).

10. As the novel's first sentence indicates, David's fear of losing his narrative preeminence and thus his self informs his story: "Whether I shall turn out to be the hero of my own life, or whether that station will be held by anybody else, these pages must show" (1). Written from the perspective of

the present, this sentence tells us that David's subjectivity must be continually established.

11. In modifying interpretations of the blacking factory episode—particularly those of Forster, Wilson, and Marcus—Albert D. Hutter argues that the episode gains its importance from Dickens' adult perspective: "I have suggested . . . that he continued to use his adult memory of Warren's to preserve a sense of his own boyishness, his own identity as a child. . . . We tend to forget that Warren's was not, as most biographers would have us believe, the beginning; it is the subject of autobiographical reconstruction" (13-14). Like Hutter, I see the adult perspective as the crucially important one.

12. *Great Expectations* does not conclude Dickens' examination of urban experience, for he can only allow Pip to realize his identity in the city, not to make his living or life there. These will be the issues of *Our Mutual Friend,* his most ambitious urban novel. In a work in progress, Avrom Fleishman is exploring *Our Mutual Friend* as Dickens' utopian effort, showing how humane life is possible in the city.

Works Cited

Arac, Jonathan. *Commissioned Spirits.* New Brunswick, N.J.: Rutgers University Press, 1979.

Cassirer, Ernst. *Language and Myth.* 1946. New York: Dover, 1953.

Chancellor, E. Beresford. *The London of Charles Dickens.* London: Grant Richards, 1924.

Dexter, Walter. *The London of Charles Dickens.* New York: Dutton, 1924.

Dickens, Charles. *Oliver Twist.* 1838. London: Oxford University Press, 1949.

———. *David Copperfield.* 1850. London: Oxford University Press, 1948.

———. *Great Expectations.* 1861. London: Oxford University Press, 1953.

———. *The Letters of Charles Dickens.* Ed. Walter Drexler. Vol. III. Bloomsbury: Nonesuch Press, 1938. 3 vols.

Fletcher, Geoffrey. *The London Dickens Knew.* London: Hutchinson, 1970.

Forster, John. *The Life of Charles Dickens.* Vol. I. New York: Scribner's, 1927. 2 vols.

Garis, Robert. *The Dickens Theatre.* Oxford: Clarendon, 1965.

Garrett, Peter K. *The Victorian Multiplot Novel.* New Haven, Conn.: Yale University Press, 1980.

Hutter, Albert D. "Reconstructive Autobiography: The Experience at Warren's Blacking." *Dickens Studies Annual,* 6. Carbondale and Edwardsville: Southern Illinois University Press, 1977.

Jakobson, Roman, and Morris Halle. *Fundamentals of Language.* The Hague: Mouton, 1956.

Marcus, Steven. *Dickens from Pickwick to Dombey.* 1965. New York: Simon and Schuster, 1968.

Miller, J. Hillis. *Charles Dickens: The World of His Novels.* Cambridge, Mass.: Harvard University Press, 1958.

———. "The Fiction of Realism: *Sketches by Boz, Oliver Twist,* and Cruikshank's Illustrations." *Dickens Centennial Essays.* Eds. Ada Nesbet and Blake Nevius. Los Angeles: University of California Press, 1971.

Romano, John. *Dickens and Reality.* New York: Columbia University Press, 1978.

Schwarzbach, F. S. *Dickens and the City.* London: Athlone, 1979.

Stevens, Wallace. *The Collected Poems of Wallace Stevens.* New York: Knopf, 1971.

Stoehr, Taylor. *Dickens: The Dreamer's Stance.* Ithaca, N.Y.: Cornell University Press, 1965.

Welsh, Alexander, *The City of Dickens.* Oxford: Clarendon, 1971.

Westburg, Barry. *The Confessional Fiction of Dickens.* DeKalb: Northern Illinois University Press, 1977.

Williams, Raymond. *The Country and the City.* 1970. New York: Oxford University Press, 1973.

Wilson, Edmund. "The Two Scrooges." *The Wound and the Bow.* Cambridge, Mass.: Harvard University Press, 1941.

FURTHER READING

Criticism

Autrey, Max L. "'My Kinsman, Major Molineux': Hawthorne's Allegory of the Urban Movement." *College Literature* 12, no. 3 (fall 1985): 211-21.

Asserts that Nathaniel Hawthorne's "My Kinsman, Major Molineux" offers a sociological examination of moving from the natural, rural world to an artificial, urban world.

Bramen, Carrie Tirado. "William Dean Howells and the Failure of the Urban Picturesque." *The New England Quarterly* 73, no. 1 (March 2000): 82-99.

Argues that "[William Dean] Howells's urban sketches reveal not an escape from the realities of the city but a commitment to radicalizing the aesthetic."

Burke, Alan R. "The Strategy and Theme of Urban Observation in *Bleak House.*" *Studies in English Literature, 1500-1900* 9, no. 4 (autumn 1969): 659-76.

Maintains that *Bleak House* represents Dickens's "first mature use of the city" in which the author explores the motif of observation by and of city dwellers.

Entin, Joseph. "'Unhuman Humanity': Bodies of the Urban Poor and the Collapse of Realist Legibility." *Novel: A Forum on Fiction* 34, no. 3 (summer 2001): 313-37.

Suggests that nineteenth-century "scenes of tramping and of urban looking . . . frequently destabilize the relation between seeing and social power that underwrites many dominant realist and naturalist narratives."

Sen, Sambudha. "*Bleak House, Vanity Fair,* and the Making of an Urban Aesthetic." *Nineteenth-Century Literature* 54, no. 4 (March 2000): 480-502.

Offers a comparison of Charles Dickens's and William Makepeace Thackeray's expression of urban aesthetic through an analysis of each author's approach to characterization.

Versluys, Kristiaan. "Western Wordsworthianism: Cities Reviled and Cities Idealized." *The Wordsworth Circle* 15, no. 1 (winter 1984): 20-2.

Surveys the ways in which the work of William Wordsworth has influenced other writers' approaches to representing urban life in their works.

How to Use This Index

The main references

Calvino, Italo
 1923-1985 CLC 5, 8, 11, 22, 33, 39,
 73; SSC 3, 48

list all author entries in the following Thomson Gale Literary Criticism series:

AAL = *Asian American Literature*
BG = *The Beat Generation: A Gale Critical Companion*
BLC = *Black Literature Criticism*
BLCS = *Black Literature Criticism Supplement*
CLC = *Contemporary Literary Criticism*
CLR = *Children's Literature Review*
CMLC = *Classical and Medieval Literature Criticism*
DC = *Drama Criticism*
FL = *Feminism in Literature: A Gale Critical Companion*
GL = *Gothic Literature: A Gale Critical Companion*
HLC = *Hispanic Literature Criticism*
HLCS = *Hispanic Literature Criticism Supplement*
HR = *Harlem Renaissance: A Gale Critical Companion*
LC = *Literature Criticism from 1400 to 1800*
NCLC = *Nineteenth-Century Literature Criticism*
NNAL = *Native North American Literature*
PC = *Poetry Criticism*
SSC = *Short Story Criticism*
TCLC = *Twentieth-Century Literary Criticism*
WLC = *World Literature Criticism, 1500 to the Present*
WLCS = *World Literature Criticism Supplement*

The cross-references

See also CA 85-88, 116; CANR 23, 61;
DAM NOV; DLB 196; EW 13; MTCW 1, 2;
RGSF 2; RGWL 2; SFW 4; SSFS 12

list all author entries in the following Thomson Gale biographical and literary sources:

AAYA = *Authors & Artists for Young Adults*
AFAW = *African American Writers*
AFW = *African Writers*
AITN = *Authors in the News*
AMW = *American Writers*
AMWR = *American Writers Retrospective Supplement*
AMWS = *American Writers Supplement*
ANW = *American Nature Writers*
AW = *Ancient Writers*
BEST = *Bestsellers*
BPFB = *Beacham's Encyclopedia of Popular Fiction: Biography and Resources*
BRW = *British Writers*
BRWS = *British Writers Supplement*
BW = *Black Writers*
BYA = *Beacham's Guide to Literature for Young Adults*
CA = *Contemporary Authors*
CAAS = *Contemporary Authors Autobiography Series*
CABS = *Contemporary Authors Bibliographical Series*
CAD = *Contemporary American Dramatists*
CANR = *Contemporary Authors New Revision Series*
CAP = *Contemporary Authors Permanent Series*
CBD = *Contemporary British Dramatists*
CCA = *Contemporary Canadian Authors*
CD = *Contemporary Dramatists*
CDALB = *Concise Dictionary of American Literary Biography*

CDALBS = *Concise Dictionary of American Literary Biography Supplement*
CDBLB = *Concise Dictionary of British Literary Biography*
CMW = *St. James Guide to Crime & Mystery Writers*
CN = *Contemporary Novelists*
CP = *Contemporary Poets*
CPW = *Contemporary Popular Writers*
CSW = *Contemporary Southern Writers*
CWD = *Contemporary Women Dramatists*
CWP = *Contemporary Women Poets*
CWRI = *St. James Guide to Children's Writers*
CWW = *Contemporary World Writers*
DA = *DISCovering Authors*
DA3 = *DISCovering Authors 3.0*
DAB = *DISCovering Authors: British Edition*
DAC = *DISCovering Authors: Canadian Edition*
DAM = *DISCovering Authors: Modules*
 DRAM: *Dramatists Module;* **MST:** *Most-studied Authors Module;*
 MULT: *Multicultural Authors Module;* **NOV:** *Novelists Module;*
 POET: *Poets Module;* **POP:** *Popular Fiction and Genre Authors Module*
DFS = *Drama for Students*
DLB = *Dictionary of Literary Biography*
DLBD = *Dictionary of Literary Biography Documentary Series*
DLBY = *Dictionary of Literary Biography Yearbook*
DNFS = *Literature of Developing Nations for Students*
EFS = *Epics for Students*
EXPN = *Exploring Novels*
EXPP = *Exploring Poetry*
EXPS = *Exploring Short Stories*
EW = *European Writers*
FANT = *St. James Guide to Fantasy Writers*
FW = *Feminist Writers*
GFL = *Guide to French Literature,* Beginnings to 1789, 1798 to the Present
GLL = *Gay and Lesbian Literature*
HGG = *St. James Guide to Horror, Ghost & Gothic Writers*
HW = *Hispanic Writers*
IDFW = *International Dictionary of Films and Filmmakers: Writers and Production Artists*
IDTP = *International Dictionary of Theatre: Playwrights*
LAIT = *Literature and Its Times*
LAW = *Latin American Writers*
JRDA = *Junior DISCovering Authors*
MAICYA = *Major Authors and Illustrators for Children and Young Adults*
MAICYAS = *Major Authors and Illustrators for Children and Young Adults Supplement*
MAWW = *Modern American Women Writers*
MJW = *Modern Japanese Writers*
MTCW = *Major 20th-Century Writers*
NCFS = *Nonfiction Classics for Students*
NFS = *Novels for Students*
PAB = *Poets: American and British*
PFS = *Poetry for Students*
RGAL = *Reference Guide to American Literature*
RGEL = *Reference Guide to English Literature*
RGSF = *Reference Guide to Short Fiction*
RGWL = *Reference Guide to World Literature*
RHW = *Twentieth-Century Romance and Historical Writers*
SAAS = *Something about the Author Autobiography Series*
SATA = *Something about the Author*
SFW = *St. James Guide to Science Fiction Writers*
SSFS = *Short Stories for Students*
TCWW = *Twentieth-Century Western Writers*
WLIT = *World Literature and Its Times*
WP = *World Poets*
YABC = *Yesterday's Authors of Books for Children*
YAW = *St. James Guide to Young Adult Writers*

Literary Criticism Series
Cumulative Author Index

20/1631
See Upward, Allen

A/C Cross
See Lawrence, T(homas) E(dward)

A. M.
See Megged, Aharon

Abasiyanik, Sait Faik 1906-1954
See Sait Faik
See also CA 123; 231

Abbey, Edward 1927-1989 **CLC 36, 59; TCLC 160**
See also AMWS 13; ANW; CA 45-48; 128; CANR 2, 41, 131; DA3; DLB 256, 275; LATS 1:2; MTCW 2; MTFW 2005; TCWW 1, 2

Abbott, Edwin A. 1838-1926 **TCLC 139**
See also DLB 178

Abbott, Lee K(ittredge) 1947- **CLC 48**
See also CA 124; CANR 51, 101; DLB 130

Abe, Kobo 1924-1993 **CLC 8, 22, 53, 81; SSC 61; TCLC 131**
See also CA 65-68; 140; CANR 24, 60; DAM NOV; DFS 14; DLB 182; EWL 3; MJW; MTCW 1, 2; MTFW 2005; NFS 22; RGWL 3; SFW 4

Abe Kobo
See Abe, Kobo

Abelard, Peter c. 1079-c. 1142 **CMLC 11, 77**
See also DLB 115, 208

Abell, Kjeld 1901-1961 **CLC 15**
See also CA 191; 111; DLB 214; EWL 3

Abercrombie, Lascelles
1881-1938 **TCLC 141**
See also CA 112; DLB 19; RGEL 2

Abish, Walter 1931- **CLC 22; SSC 44**
See also CA 101; CANR 37, 114, 153; CN 3, 4, 5, 6; DLB 130, 227; MAL 5; RGHL

Abrahams, Peter (Henry) 1919- **CLC 4**
See also AFW; BW 1; CA 57-60; CANR 26, 125; CDWLB 3; CN 1, 2, 3, 4, 5, 6; DLB 117, 225; EWL 3; MTCW 1, 2; RGEL 2; WLIT 2

Abrams, M(eyer) H(oward) 1912- ... **CLC 24**
See also CA 57-60; CANR 13, 33; DLB 67

Abse, Dannie 1923- **CLC 7, 29; PC 41**
See also CA 53-56; CAAS 1; CANR 4, 46, 74, 124; CBD; CN 1, 2, 3; CP 1, 2, 3, 4, 5, 6, 7; DAB; DAM POET; DLB 27, 245; MTCW 2

Abutsu 1222(?)-1283 **CMLC 46**
See Abutsu-ni

Abutsu-ni
See Abutsu
See also DLB 203

Achebe, (Albert) Chinua(lumogu)
1930- **BLC 1; CLC 1, 3, 5, 7, 11, 26, 51, 75, 127, 152; WLC 1**
See also AAYA 15; AFW; BPFB 1; BRWC 2; BW 2, 3; CA 1-4R; CANR 6, 26, 47, 124; CDWLB 3; CLR 20; CN 1, 2, 3, 4, 5, 6, 7; CP 2, 3, 4, 5, 6, 7; CWRI 5; DA; DA3; DAB; DAC; DAM MST, MULT, NOV; DLB 117; DNFS 1; EWL 3; EXPN; EXPS; LAIT 2; LATS 1:2; MAICYA 1, 2; MTCW 1, 2; MTFW 2005; NFS 2; RGEL 2; RGSF 2; SATA 38, 40; SATA-Brief 38; SSFS 3, 13; TWA; WLIT 2; WWE 1

Acker, Kathy 1948-1997 **CLC 45, 111**
See also AMWS 12; CA 117; 122; 162; CANR 55; CN 5, 6; MAL 5

Ackroyd, Peter 1949- **CLC 34, 52, 140**
See also BRWS 6; CA 123; 127; CANR 51, 74, 99, 132; CN 4, 5, 6, 7; DLB 155, 231; HGG; INT CA-127; MTCW 2; MTFW 2005; RHW; SATA 153; SUFW 2

Acorn, Milton 1923-1986 **CLC 15**
See also CA 103; CCA 1; CP 1, 2, 3, 4; DAC; DLB 53; INT CA-103

Adam de la Halle c. 1250-c.
1285 **CMLC 80**

Adamov, Arthur 1908-1970 **CLC 4, 25**
See also CA 17-18; 25-28R; CAP 2; DAM DRAM; DLB 321; EWL 3; GFL 1789 to the Present; MTCW 1; RGWL 2, 3

Adams, Alice (Boyd) 1926-1999 .. **CLC 6, 13, 46; SSC 24**
See also CA 81-84; 179; CANR 26, 53, 75, 88, 136; CN 4, 5, 6; CSW; DLB 234; DLBY 1986; INT CANR-26; MTCW 1, 2; MTFW 2005; SSFS 14, 21

Adams, Andy 1859-1935 **TCLC 56**
See also TCWW 1, 2; YABC 1

Adams, (Henry) Brooks
1848-1927 **TCLC 80**
See also CA 123; 193; DLB 47

Adams, Douglas (Noel) 1952-2001 .. **CLC 27, 60**
See also AAYA 4, 33; BEST 89:3; BYA 14; CA 106; 197; CANR 34, 64, 124; CPW; DA3; DAM POP; DLB 261; DLBY 1983; JRDA; MTCW 2; MTFW 2005; NFS 7; SATA 116; SATA-Obit 128; SFW 4

Adams, Francis 1862-1893 **NCLC 33**

Adams, Henry (Brooks)
1838-1918 **TCLC 4, 52**
See also AMW; CA 104; 133; CANR 77; DA; DAB; DAC; DAM MST; DLB 12, 47, 189, 284; EWL 3; MAL 5; MTCW 2; NCFS 1; RGAL 4; TUS

Adams, John 1735-1826 **NCLC 106**
See also DLB 31, 183

Adams, Mary
See Phelps, Elizabeth Stuart

Adams, Richard (George) 1920- ... **CLC 4, 5, 18**
See also AAYA 16; AITN 1, 2; BPFB 1; BYA 5; CA 49-52; CANR 3, 35, 128; CLR 20; CN 4, 5, 6, 7; DAM NOV; DLB 261; FANT; JRDA; LAIT 5; MAICYA 1, 2; MTCW 1, 2; NFS 11; SATA 7, 69; YAW

Adamson, Joy(-Friederike Victoria)
1910-1980 **CLC 17**
See also CA 69-72; 93-96; CANR 22; MTCW 1; SATA 11; SATA-Obit 22

Adcock, Fleur 1934- **CLC 41**
See also CA 25-28R, 182; CAAE 182; CAAS 23; CANR 11, 34, 69, 101; CP 1, 2, 3, 4, 5, 6, 7; CWP; DLB 40; FW; WWE 1

Addams, Charles 1912-1988 **CLC 30**
See also CA 61-64; 126; CANR 12, 79

Addams, Charles Samuel
See Addams, Charles

Addams, (Laura) Jane 1860-1935 . **TCLC 76**
See also AMWS 1; CA 194; DLB 303; FW

Addison, Joseph 1672-1719 **LC 18**
See also BRW 3; CDBLB 1660-1789; DLB 101; RGEL 2; WLIT 3

Adler, Alfred (F.) 1870-1937 **TCLC 61**
See also CA 119; 159

Adler, C(arole) S(chwerdtfeger)
1932- ... **CLC 35**
See also AAYA 4, 41; CA 89-92; CANR 19, 40, 101; CLR 78; JRDA; MAICYA 1, 2; SAAS 15; SATA 26, 63, 102, 126; YAW

Adler, Renata 1938- **CLC 8, 31**
See also CA 49-52; CANR 95; CN 4, 5, 6; MTCW 1

Adorno, Theodor W(iesengrund)
1903-1969 **TCLC 111**
See also CA 89-92; 25-28R; CANR 89; DLB 242; EWL 3

Ady, Endre 1877-1919 **TCLC 11**
See also CA 107; CDWLB 4; DLB 215; EW 9; EWL 3

A.E. **TCLC 3, 10**
See Russell, George William
See also DLB 19

Aelfric c. 955-c. 1010 **CMLC 46**
See also DLB 146

Aeschines c. 390B.C.-c. 320B.C. **CMLC 47**
See also DLB 176

Aeschylus 525(?)B.C.-456(?)B.C. .. **CMLC 11, 51; DC 8; WLCS**
See also AW 1; CDWLB 1; DA; DAB; DAC; DAM DRAM, MST; DFS 5, 10; DLB 176; LMFS 1; RGWL 2, 3; TWA; WLIT 8

Aesop 620(?)B.C.-560(?)B.C. **CMLC 24**
See also CLR 14; MAICYA 1, 2; SATA 64

Affable Hawk
 See MacCarthy, Sir (Charles Otto) Desmond
Africa, Ben
 See Bosman, Herman Charles
Afton, Effie
 See Harper, Frances Ellen Watkins
Agapida, Fray Antonio
 See Irving, Washington
Agee, James (Rufus) 1909-1955 **TCLC 1,
 19, 180**
 See also AAYA 44; AITN 1; AMW; CA 108;
 148; CANR 131; CDALB 1941-1968;
 DAM NOV; DLB 2, 26, 152; DLBY
 1989; EWL 3; LAIT 3; LATS 1:2; MAL
 5; MTCW 2; MTFW 2005; NFS 22;
 RGAL 4; TUS
Aghill, Gordon
 See Silverberg, Robert
Agnon, S(hmuel) Y(osef Halevi)
 1888-1970 **CLC 4, 8, 14; SSC 30;
 TCLC 151**
 See also CA 17-18; 25-28R; CANR 60, 102;
 CAP 2; EWL 3; MTCW 1, 2; RGHL;
 RGSF 2; RGWL 2, 3; WLIT 6
Agrippa von Nettesheim, Henry Cornelius
 1486-1535 **LC 27**
Aguilera Malta, Demetrio
 1909-1981 **HLCS 1**
 See also CA 111; 124; CANR 87; DAM
 MULT, NOV; DLB 145; EWL 3; HW 1;
 RGWL 3
Agustini, Delmira 1886-1914 **HLCS 1**
 See also CA 166; DLB 290; HW 1, 2; LAW
Aherne, Owen
 See Cassill, R(onald) V(erlin)
Ai 1947- **CLC 4, 14, 69; PC 72**
 See also CA 85-88; CAAS 13; CANR 70;
 CP 6, 7; DLB 120; PFS 16
Aickman, Robert (Fordyce)
 1914-1981 **CLC 57**
 See also CA 5-8R; CANR 3, 72, 100, DLB
 261; HGG; SUFW 1, 2
Aidoo, (Christina) Ama Ata
 1942- **BLCS; CLC 177**
 See also AFW; BW 1; CA 101; CANR 62,
 144; CD 5, 6; CDWLB 3; CN 6, 7; CWD;
 CWP; DLB 117; DNFS 1, 2; EWL 3; FW;
 WLIT 2
Aiken, Conrad (Potter) 1889-1973 **CLC 1,
 3, 5, 10, 52; PC 26; SSC 9**
 See also AMW; CA 5-8R; 45-48; CANR 4,
 60; CDALB 1929-1941; CN 1; CP 1;
 DAM NOV, POET; DLB 9, 45, 102; EWL
 3; EXPS; HGG; MAL 5; MTCW 1, 2;
 MTFW 2005; PFS 24; RGAL 4; RGSF 2;
 SATA 3, 30; SSFS 8; TUS
Aiken, Joan (Delano) 1924-2004 **CLC 35**
 See also AAYA 1, 25; CA 9-12R, 182; 223;
 CAAE 182; CANR 4, 23, 34, 64, 121;
 CLR 1, 19, 90; DLB 161; FANT; HGG;
 JRDA; MAICYA 1, 2; MTCW 1; RHW;
 SAAS 1; SATA 2, 30, 73; SATA-Essay
 109; SATA-Obit 152; SUFW 2; WYA;
 YAW
Ainsworth, William Harrison
 1805-1882 **NCLC 13**
 See also DLB 21; HGG; RGEL 2; SATA
 24; SUFW 1
Aitmatov, Chingiz (Torekulovich)
 1928- ... **CLC 71**
 See Aytmatov, Chingiz
 See also CA 103; CANR 38; CWW 2; DLB
 302; MTCW 1; RGSF 2; SATA 56
Akers, Floyd
 See Baum, L(yman) Frank
Akhmadulina, Bella Akhatovna
 1937- **CLC 53; PC 43**
 See also CA 65-68; CWP; CWW 2; DAM
 POET; EWL 3

Akhmatova, Anna 1888-1966 **CLC 11, 25,
 64, 126; PC 2, 55**
 See also CA 19-20; 25-28R; CANR 35;
 CAP 1; DA3; DAM POET; DLB 295; EW
 10; EWL 3; FL 1:5; MTCW 1, 2; PFS 18;
 RGWL 2, 3
Aksakov, Sergei Timofeyvich
 1791-1859 **NCLC 2**
 See also DLB 198
Aksenov, Vasilii (Pavlovich)
 See Aksyonov, Vassily (Pavlovich)
 See also CWW 2
Aksenov, Vassily
 See Aksyonov, Vassily (Pavlovich)
Akst, Daniel 1956- **CLC 109**
 See also CA 161; CANR 110
Aksyonov, Vassily (Pavlovich)
 1932- **CLC 22, 37, 101**
 See Aksenov, Vasilii (Pavlovich)
 See also CA 53-56; CANR 12, 48, 77; DLB
 302; EWL 3
Akutagawa Ryunosuke 1892-1927 ... **SSC 44;
 TCLC 16**
 See also CA 117; 154; DLB 180; EWL 3;
 MJW; RGSF 2; RGWL 2, 3
Alabaster, William 1568-1640 **LC 90**
 See also DLB 132; RGEL 2
Alain 1868-1951 **TCLC 41**
 See also CA 163; EWL 3; GFL 1789 to the
 Present
Alain de Lille c. 1116-c. 1203 **CMLC 53**
 See also DLB 208
Alain-Fournier **TCLC 6**
 See Fournier, Henri-Alban
 See also DLB 65; EWL 3; GFL 1789 to the
 Present; RGWL 2, 3
Al-Amin, Jamil Abdullah 1943- **BLC 1**
 See also BW 1, 3; CA 112; 125; CANR 82;
 DAM MULT
Alanus de Insluis
 See Alain de Lille
Alarcon, Pedro Antonio de
 1833-1891 **NCLC 1; SSC 64**
Alas (y Urena), Leopoldo (Enrique Garcia)
 1852-1901 **TCLC 29**
 See also CA 113; 131; HW 1; RGSF 2
Albee, Edward (Franklin) (III)
 1928- .. **CLC 1, 2, 3, 5, 9, 11, 13, 25, 53,
 86, 113; DC 11; WLC 1**
 See also AAYA 51; AITN 1; AMW; CA
 5-8R; CABS 3; CAD; CANR 8, 54, 74,
 124; CD 5, 6; CDALB 1941-1968; DA;
 DA3; DAB; DAC; DAM DRAM, MST;
 DFS 2, 3, 8, 10, 13, 14; DLB 7, 266; EWL
 3; INT CANR-8; LAIT 4; LMFS 2; MAL
 5; MTCW 1, 2; MTFW 2005; RGAL 4;
 TUS
Alberti (Merello), Rafael
 See Alberti, Rafael
 See also CWW 2
Alberti, Rafael 1902-1999 **CLC 7**
 See Alberti (Merello), Rafael
 See also CA 85-88; 185; CANR 81; DLB
 108; EWL 3; HW 2; RGWL 2, 3
Albert the Great 1193(?)-1280 **CMLC 16**
 See also DLB 115
Alcaeus c. 620B.C.- **CMLC 65**
 See also DLB 176
Alcala-Galiano, Juan Valera y
 See Valera y Alcala-Galiano, Juan
Alcayaga, Lucila Godoy
 See Godoy Alcayaga, Lucila
Alciato, Andrea 1492-1550 **LC 116**
Alcott, Amos Bronson 1799-1888 ... **NCLC 1,
 167**
 See also DLB 1, 223

Alcott, Louisa May 1832-1888 . **NCLC 6, 58,
 83; SSC 27; WLC 1**
 See also AAYA 20; AMWS 1; BPFB 1;
 BYA 2; CDALB 1865-1917; CLR 1, 38,
 109; DA; DA3; DAB; DAC; DAM MST,
 NOV; DLB 1, 42, 79, 223, 239, 242;
 DLBD 14; FL 1:2; FW; JRDA; LAIT 2;
 MAICYA 1, 2; NFS 12; RGAL 4; SATA
 100; TUS; WCH; WYA; YABC 1; YAW
Alcuin c. 730-804 **CMLC 69**
 See also DLB 148
Aldanov, M. A.
 See Aldanov, Mark (Alexandrovich)
Aldanov, Mark (Alexandrovich)
 1886-1957 **TCLC 23**
 See also CA 118; 181; DLB 317
Aldington, Richard 1892-1962 **CLC 49**
 See also CA 85-88; CANR 45; DLB 20, 36,
 100, 149; LMFS 2; RGEL 2
Aldiss, Brian W(ilson) 1925- . **CLC 5, 14, 40;
 SSC 36**
 See also AAYA 42; CA 5-8R, 190; CAAE
 190; CAAS 2; CANR 5, 28, 64, 121; CN
 1, 2, 3, 4, 5, 6, 7; DAM NOV; DLB 14,
 261, 271; MTCW 1, 2; MTFW 2005;
 SATA 34; SCFW 1, 2; SFW 4
Aldrich, Bess Streeter
 1881-1954 **TCLC 125**
 See also CLR 70; TCWW 2
Alegria, Claribel
 See Alegria, Claribel (Joy)
 See also CWW 2; DLB 145, 283
Alegria, Claribel (Joy) 1924- **CLC 75;
 HLCS 1; PC 26**
 See Alegria, Claribel
 See also CA 131; CAAS 15; CANR 66, 94,
 134; DAM MULT; EWL 3; HW 1;
 MTCW 2; MTFW 2005; PFS 21
Alegria, Fernando 1918-2005 **CLC 57**
 See also CA 9-12R; CANR 5, 32, 72; EWL
 3; HW 1, 2
Aleichem, Sholom **SSC 33; TCLC 1, 35**
 See Rabinovitch, Sholem
 See also TWA
Aleixandre, Vicente 1898-1984 **HLCS 1;
 TCLC 113**
 See also CANR 81; DLB 108; EWL 3; HW
 2; MTCW 1, 2; RGWL 2, 3
Aleman, Mateo 1547-1615(?) **LC 81**
Alencar, Jose de 1829-1877 **NCLC 157**
 See also DLB 307; LAW; WLIT 1
Alencon, Marguerite d'
 See de Navarre, Marguerite
Alepoudelis, Odysseus
 See Elytis, Odysseus
 See also CWW 2
Aleshkovsky, Joseph 1929-
 See Aleshkovsky, Yuz
 See also CA 121; 128
Aleshkovsky, Yuz **CLC 44**
 See Aleshkovsky, Joseph
 See also DLB 317
Alexander, Lloyd (Chudley) 1924- ... **CLC 35**
 See also AAYA 1, 27; BPFB 1; BYA 5, 6,
 7, 9, 10, 11; CA 1-4R; CANR 1, 24, 38,
 55, 113; CLR 1, 5, 48; CWRI 5; DLB 52;
 FANT; JRDA; MAICYA 1, 2; MAICYAS
 1; MTCW 1; SAAS 19; SATA 3, 49, 81,
 129, 135; SUFW; TUS; WYA; YAW
Alexander, Meena 1951- **CLC 121**
 See also CA 115; CANR 38, 70, 146; CP 5,
 6, 7; CWP; DLB 323; FW
Alexander, Samuel 1859-1938 **TCLC 77**
Alexeyev, Constantin (Sergeivich)
 See Stanislavsky, Konstantin (Sergeivich)

Anderson, C. Farley
See Mencken, H(enry) L(ouis); Nathan, George Jean
Anderson, Jessica (Margaret) Queale
1916- .. **CLC 37**
See also CA 9-12R; CANR 4, 62; CN 4, 5, 6, 7; DLB 325
Anderson, Jon (Victor) 1940- **CLC 9**
See also CA 25-28R; CANR 20; CP 1, 3, 4, 5; DAM POET
Anderson, Lindsay (Gordon)
1923-1994 **CLC 20**
See also CA 125; 128; 146; CANR 77
Anderson, Maxwell 1888-1959 **TCLC 2, 144**
See also CA 105; 152; DAM DRAM; DFS 16, 20; DLB 7, 228; MAL 5; MTCW 2; MTFW 2005; RGAL 4
Anderson, Poul (William)
1926-2001 **CLC 15**
See also AAYA 5, 34; BPFB 1; BYA 6, 8, 9; CA 1-4R, 181; 199; CAAE 181; CAAS 2; CANR 2, 15, 34, 64, 110; CLR 58; DLB 8; FANT; INT CANR-15; MTCW 1, 2; MTFW 2005; SATA 90; SATA-Brief 39; SATA-Essay 106; SCFW 1, 2; SFW 4; SUFW 1, 2
Anderson, Robert (Woodruff)
1917- ... **CLC 23**
See also AITN 1; CA 21-24R; CANR 32; CD 6; DAM DRAM; DLB 7; LAIT 5
Anderson, Roberta Joan
See Mitchell, Joni
Anderson, Sherwood 1876-1941 ... **SSC 1, 46, 91; TCLC 1, 10, 24, 123; WLC 1**
See also AAYA 30; AMW; AMWC 2; BPFB 1; CA 104; 121; CANR 61; CDALB 1917-1929; DA; DA3; DAB; DAC; DAM MST, NOV; DLB 4, 9, 86; DLBD 1; EWL 3; EXPS; GLL 2; MAL 5; MTCW 1, 2; MTFW 2005; NFS 4; RGAL 4; RGSF 2; SSFS 4, 10, 11; TUS
Andier, Pierre
See Desnos, Robert
Andouard
See Giraudoux, Jean(-Hippolyte)
Andrade, Carlos Drummond de **CLC 18**
See Drummond de Andrade, Carlos
See also EWL 3; RGWL 2, 3
Andrade, Mario de **TCLC 43**
See de Andrade, Mario
See also DLB 307; EWL 3; LAW; RGWL 2, 3; WLIT 1
Andreae, Johann V(alentin)
1586-1654 **LC 32**
See also DLB 164
Andreas Capellanus fl. c. 1185- **CMLC 45**
See also DLB 208
Andreas-Salome, Lou 1861-1937 ... **TCLC 56**
See also CA 178; DLB 66
Andreev, Leonid
See Andreyev, Leonid (Nikolaevich)
See also DLB 295; EWL 3
Andress, Lesley
See Sanders, Lawrence
Andrewes, Lancelot 1555-1626 **LC 5**
See also DLB 151, 172
Andrews, Cicily Fairfield
See West, Rebecca
Andrews, Elton V.
See Pohl, Frederik
Andrews, Peter
See Soderbergh, Steven
Andreyev, Leonid (Nikolaevich)
1871-1919 **TCLC 3**
See Andreev, Leonid
See also CA 104; 185

Andric, Ivo 1892-1975 **CLC 8; SSC 36; TCLC 135**
See also CA 81-84; 57-60; CANR 43, 60; CDWLB 4; DLB 147; EW 11; EWL 3; MTCW 1; RGSF 2; RGWL 2, 3
Androvar
See Prado (Calvo), Pedro
Angela of Foligno 1248(?)-1309 **CMLC 76**
Angelique, Pierre
See Bataille, Georges
Angell, Roger 1920- **CLC 26**
See also CA 57-60; CANR 13, 44, 70, 144; DLB 171, 185
Angelou, Maya 1928- ... **BLC 1; CLC 12, 35, 64, 77, 155; PC 32; WLCS**
See also AAYA 7, 20; AMWS 4; BPFB 1; BW 2, 3; BYA 2; CA 65-68; CANR 19, 42, 65, 111, 133; CDALBS; CLR 53; CP 4, 5, 6, 7; CPW; CSW; CWP; DA; DA3; DAB; DAC; DAM MST, MULT, POET, POP; DLB 38; EWL 3; EXPN; EXPP; FL 1:5; LAIT 4; MAICYA 2; MAICYAS 1; MAL 5; MAWW; MTCW 1, 2; MTFW 2005; NCFS 2; NFS 2; PFS 2, 3; RGAL 4; SATA 49, 136; TCLE 1:1; WYA; YAW
Angouleme, Marguerite d'
See de Navarre, Marguerite
Anna Comnena 1083-1153 **CMLC 25**
Annensky, Innokentii Fedorovich
See Annensky, Innokenty (Fyodorovich)
See also DLB 295
Annensky, Innokenty (Fyodorovich)
1856-1909 **TCLC 14**
See also CA 110; 155; EWL 3
Annunzio, Gabriele d'
See D'Annunzio, Gabriele
Anodos
See Coleridge, Mary E(lizabeth)
Anon, Charles Robert
See Pessoa, Fernando (Antonio Nogueira)
Anouilh, Jean (Marie Lucien Pierre)
1910-1987 . **CLC 1, 3, 8, 13, 40, 50; DC 8, 21**
See also AAYA 67; CA 17-20R; 123; CANR 32; DAM DRAM; DFS 9, 10, 19; DLB 321; EW 13; EWL 3; GFL 1789 to the Present; MTCW 1, 2; MTFW 2005; RGWL 2, 3; TWA
Anselm of Canterbury
1033(?)-1109 **CMLC 67**
See also DLB 115
Anthony, Florence
See Ai
Anthony, John
See Ciardi, John (Anthony)
Anthony, Peter
See Shaffer, Anthony (Joshua); Shaffer, Peter (Levin)
Anthony, Piers 1934- **CLC 35**
See also AAYA 11, 48; BYA 7; CA 200; CAAE 200; CANR 28, 56, 73, 102, 133; CPW; DAM POP; DLB 8; FANT; MAICYA 2; MAICYAS 1; MTCW 1, 2; MTFW 2005; SAAS 22; SATA 84, 129; SATA-Essay 129; SFW 4; SUFW 1, 2; YAW
Anthony, Susan B(rownell)
1820-1906 **TCLC 84**
See also CA 211; FW
Antiphon c. 480B.C.-c. 411B.C. **CMLC 55**
Antoine, Marc
See Proust, (Valentin-Louis-George-Eugene) Marcel
Antoninus, Brother
See Everson, William (Oliver)
See also CP 1
Antonioni, Michelangelo 1912- **CLC 20, 144**
See also CA 73-76; CANR 45, 77

Antschel, Paul 1920-1970
See Celan, Paul
See also CA 85-88; CANR 33, 61; MTCW 1; PFS 21
Anwar, Chairil 1922-1949 **TCLC 22**
See Chairil Anwar
See also CA 121; 219; RGWL 3
Anzaldua, Gloria (Evanjelina)
1942-2004 **CLC 200; HLCS 1**
See also CA 175; 227; CSW; CWP; DLB 122; FW; LLW; RGAL 4; SATA-Obit 154
Apess, William 1798-1839(?) **NCLC 73; NNAL**
See also DAM MULT; DLB 175, 243
Apollinaire, Guillaume 1880-1918 **PC 7; TCLC 3, 8, 51**
See Kostrowitzki, Wilhelm Apollinaris de
See also CA 152; DAM POET; DLB 258, 321; EW 9; EWL 3; GFL 1789 to the Present; MTCW 2; PFS 24; RGWL 2, 3; TWA; WP
Apollonius of Rhodes
See Apollonius Rhodius
See also AW 1; RGWL 2, 3
Apollonius Rhodius c. 300B.C.-c. 220B.C. **CMLC 28**
See Apollonius of Rhodes
See also DLB 176
Appelfeld, Aharon 1932- ... **CLC 23, 47; SSC 42**
See also CA 112; 133; CANR 86; CWW 2; DLB 299; EWL 3; RGHL; RGSF 2; WLIT 6
Apple, Max (Isaac) 1941- **CLC 9, 33; SSC 50**
See also CA 81-84; CANR 19, 54; DLB 130
Appleman, Philip (Dean) 1926- **CLC 51**
See also CA 13-16R; CAAS 18; CANR 6, 29, 56
Appleton, Lawrence
See Lovecraft, H. P.
Apteryx
See Eliot, T(homas) S(tearns)
Apuleius, (Lucius Madaurensis) c. 125-c. 164 **CMLC 1, 84**
See also AW 2; CDWLB 1; DLB 211; RGWL 2, 3; SUFW; WLIT 8
Aquin, Hubert 1929-1977 **CLC 15**
See also CA 105; DLB 53; EWL 3
Aquinas, Thomas 1224(?)-1274 **CMLC 33**
See also DLB 115; EW 1; TWA
Aragon, Louis 1897-1982 **CLC 3, 22; TCLC 123**
See also CA 69-72; 108; CANR 28, 71; DAM NOV, POET; DLB 72, 258; EW 11; EWL 3; GFL 1789 to the Present; GLL 2; LMFS 2; MTCW 1, 2; RGWL 2, 3
Arany, Janos 1817-1882 **NCLC 34**
Aranyos, Kakay 1847-1910
See Mikszath, Kalman
Aratus of Soli c. 315B.C.-c. 240B.C. **CMLC 64**
See also DLB 176
Arbuthnot, John 1667-1735 **LC 1**
See also DLB 101
Archer, Herbert Winslow
See Mencken, H(enry) L(ouis)
Archer, Jeffrey 1940- **CLC 28**
See also AAYA 16; BEST 89:3; BPFB 1; CA 77-80; CANR 22, 52, 95, 136; CPW; DA3; DAM POP; INT CANR-22; MTFW 2005
Archer, Jeffrey Howard
See Archer, Jeffrey
Archer, Jules 1915- **CLC 12**
See also CA 9-12R; CANR 6, 69; SAAS 5; SATA 4, 85

Alexie, Sherman (Joseph, Jr.)
1966- **CLC 96, 154; NNAL; PC 53**
See also AAYA 28; BYA 15; CA 138;
CANR 65, 95, 133; CN 7; DA3; DAM
MULT; DLB 175, 206, 278; LATS 1:2;
MTCW 2; MTFW 2005; NFS 17; SSFS
18
al-Farabi 870(?)-950 **CMLC 58**
See also DLB 115
Alfau, Felipe 1902-1999 **CLC 66**
See also CA 137
Alfieri, Vittorio 1749-1803 **NCLC 101**
See also EW 4; RGWL 2, 3; WLIT 7
Alfonso X 1221-1284 **CMLC 78**
Alfred, Jean Gaston
See Ponge, Francis
Alger, Horatio, Jr. 1832-1899 **NCLC 8, 83**
See also CLR 87; DLB 42; LAIT 2; RGAL
4; SATA 16; TUS
Al-Ghazali, Muhammad ibn Muhammad
1058-1111 **CMLC 50**
See also DLB 115
Algren, Nelson 1909-1981 **CLC 4, 10, 33;
SSC 33**
See also AMWS 9; BPFB 1; CA 13-16R;
103; CANR 20, 61; CDALB 1941-1968;
CN 1, 2; DLB 9; DLBY 1981, 1982,
2000; EWL 3; MAL 5; MTCW 1, 2;
MTFW 2005; RGAL 4; RGSF 2
**al-Hariri, al-Qasim ibn 'Ali Abu
Muhammad al-Basri**
1054-1122 **CMLC 63**
See also RGWL 3
Ali, Ahmed 1908-1998 **CLC 69**
See also CA 25-28R; CANR 15, 34; CN 1,
2, 3, 4, 5; DLB 323; EWL 3
Ali, Tariq 1943- **CLC 173**
See also CA 25-28R; CANR 10, 99
Alighieri, Dante
See Dante
See also WLIT 7
al-Kindi, Abu Yusuf Ya'qub ibn Ishaq c.
801-c. 873 **CMLC 80**
Allan, John B.
See Westlake, Donald E(dwin)
Allan, Sidney
See Hartmann, Sadakichi
Allan, Sydney
See Hartmann, Sadakichi
Allard, Janet **CLC 59**
Allen, Edward 1948- **CLC 59**
Allen, Fred 1894-1956 **TCLC 87**
Allen, Paula Gunn 1939- **CLC 84, 202;
NNAL**
See also AMWS 4; CA 112; 143; CANR
63, 130; CWP; DA3; DAM MULT; DLB
175; FW; MTCW 2; MTFW 2005; RGAL
4; TCWW 2
Allen, Roland
See Ayckbourn, Alan
Allen, Sarah A.
See Hopkins, Pauline Elizabeth
Allen, Sidney H.
See Hartmann, Sadakichi
Allen, Woody 1935- **CLC 16, 52, 195**
See also AAYA 10, 51; AMWS 15; CA 33-
36R; CANR 27, 38, 63, 128; DAM POP;
DLB 44; MTCW 1; SSFS 21
Allende, Isabel 1942- ... **CLC 39, 57, 97, 170;
HLC 1; SSC 65; WLCS**
See also AAYA 18, 70; CA 125; 130; CANR
51, 74, 129; CDWLB 3; CLR 99; CWW
2; DA3; DAM MULT, NOV; DLB 145;
DNFS 1; EWL 3; FL 1:5; FW; HW 1, 2;
INT CA-130; LAIT 5; LAWS 1; LMFS 2;
MTCW 1, 2; MTFW 2005; NCFS 1; NFS
6, 18; RGSF 2; RGWL 3; SATA 163;
SSFS 11, 16; WLIT 1

Alleyn, Ellen
See Rossetti, Christina
Alleyne, Carla D. **CLC 65**
Allingham, Margery (Louise)
1904-1966 **CLC 19**
See also CA 5-8R; 25-28R; CANR 4, 58;
CMW 4; DLB 77; MSW; MTCW 1, 2
Allingham, William 1824-1889 **NCLC 25**
See also DLB 35; RGEL 2
Allison, Dorothy E. 1949- **CLC 78, 153**
See also AAYA 53; CA 140; CANR 66, 107;
CN 7; CSW; DA3; FW; MTCW 2; MTFW
2005; NFS 11; RGAL 4
Alloula, Malek **CLC 65**
Allston, Washington 1779-1843 **NCLC 2**
See also DLB 1, 235
Almedingen, E. M. **CLC 12**
See Almedingen, Martha Edith von
See also SATA 3
Almedingen, Martha Edith von 1898-1971
See Almedingen, E. M.
See also CA 1-4R; CANR 1
Almodovar, Pedro 1949(?)- **CLC 114;
HLCS 1**
See also CA 133; CANR 72, 151; HW 2
Almqvist, Carl Jonas Love
1793-1866 **NCLC 42**
**al-Mutanabbi, Ahmad ibn al-Husayn Abu
al-Tayyib al-Jufi al-Kindi**
915-965 **CMLC 66**
See Mutanabbi, Al-
See also RGWL 3
Alonso, Damaso 1898-1990 **CLC 14**
See also CA 110; 131; 130; CANR 72; DLB
108; EWL 3; HW 1, 2
Alov
See Gogol, Nikolai (Vasilyevich)
al'Sadaawi, Nawal
See El Saadawi, Nawal
See also FW
al-Shaykh, Hanan 1945- **CLC 218**
See Shaykh, al- Hanan
See also CA 135; CANR 111; WLIT 6
Al Siddik
See Rolfe, Frederick (William Serafino Aus-
tin Lewis Mary)
See also GLL 1; RGEL 2
Alta 1942- .. **CLC 19**
See also CA 57-60
Alter, Robert B(ernard) 1935- **CLC 34**
See also CA 49-52; CANR 1, 47, 100
Alther, Lisa 1944- **CLC 7, 41**
See also BPFB 1; CA 65-68; CAAS 30;
CANR 12, 30, 51; CN 4, 5, 6, 7; CSW;
GLL 2; MTCW 1
Althusser, L.
See Althusser, Louis
Althusser, Louis 1918-1990 **CLC 106**
See also CA 131; 132; CANR 102; DLB
242
Altman, Robert 1925- **CLC 16, 116**
See also CA 73-76; CANR 43
Alurista **HLCS 1; PC 34**
See Urista (Heredia), Alberto (Baltazar)
See also DLB 82; LLW
Alvarez, A(lfred) 1929- **CLC 5, 13**
See also CA 1-4R; CANR 3, 33, 63, 101,
134; CN 3, 4, 5, 6; CP 1, 2, 3, 4, 5, 6, 7;
DLB 14, 40; MTFW 2005
Alvarez, Alejandro Rodriguez 1903-1965
See Casona, Alejandro
See also CA 131; 93-96; HW 1
Alvarez, Julia 1950- **CLC 93; HLCS 1**
See also AAYA 25; AMWS 7; CA 147;
CANR 69, 101, 133; DA3; DLB 282;
LATS 1:2; LLW; MTCW 2; MTFW 2005;
NFS 5, 9; SATA 129; WLIT 1
Alvaro, Corrado 1896-1956 **TCLC 60**
See also CA 163; DLB 264; EWL 3

Amado, Jorge 1912-2001 ... **CLC 13, 40, 106;
HLC 1**
See also CA 77-80; 201; CANR 35, 74, 135;
CWW 2; DAM MULT, NOV; DLB 113,
307; EWL 3; HW 2; LAW; LAWS 1;
MTCW 1, 2; MTFW 2005; RGWL 2, 3;
TWA; WLIT 1
Ambler, Eric 1909-1998 **CLC 4, 6, 9**
See also BRWS 4; CA 9-12R; 171; CANR
7, 38, 74; CMW 4; CN 1, 2, 3, 4, 5, 6;
DLB 77; MSW; MTCW 1, 2; TEA
Ambrose, Stephen E(dward)
1936-2002 **CLC 145**
See also AAYA 44; CA 1-4R; 209; CANR
3, 43, 57, 83, 105; MTFW 2005; NCFS 2;
SATA 40, 138
Amichai, Yehuda 1924-2000 .. **CLC 9, 22, 57,
116; PC 38**
See also CA 85-88; 189; CANR 46, 60, 99,
132; CWW 2; EWL 3; MTCW 1, 2;
MTFW 2005; PFS 24; RGHL; WLIT 6
Amichai, Yehudah
See Amichai, Yehuda
Amiel, Henri Frederic 1821-1881 **NCLC 4**
See also DLB 217
Amis, Kingsley (William)
1922-1995 **CLC 1, 2, 3, 5, 8, 13, 40,
44, 129**
See also AITN 2; BPFB 1; BRWS 2; CA
9-12R; 150; CANR 8, 28, 54; CDBLB
1945-1960; CN 1, 2, 3, 4, 5, 6; CP 1, 2,
3, 4; DA; DA3; DAB; DAC; DAM MST,
NOV; DLB 15, 27, 100, 139, 326; DLBY
1996; EWL 3; HGG; INT CANR-8;
MTCW 1, 2; MTFW 2005; RGEL 2;
RGSF 2; SFW 4
Amis, Martin (Louis) 1949- **CLC 4, 9, 38,
62, 101, 213**
See also BEST 90:3; BRWS 4; CA 65-68;
CANR 8, 27, 54, 73, 95, 132; CN 5, 6, 7;
DA3; DLB 14, 194; EWL 3; INT CANR-
27; MTCW 2; MTFW 2005
Ammianus Marcellinus c. 330-c.
395 ... **CMLC 60**
See also AW 2; DLB 211
Ammons, A(rchie) R(andolph)
1926-2001 ... **CLC 2, 3, 5, 8, 9, 25, 57,
108; PC 16**
See also AITN 1; AMWS 7; CA 9-12R;
193; CANR 6, 36, 51, 73, 107; CP 1, 2,
3, 4, 5, 6, 7; CSW; DAM POET; DLB 5,
165; EWL 3; MAL 5; MTCW 1, 2; PFS
19; RGAL 4; TCLE 1:1
Amo, Tauraatua i
See Adams, Henry (Brooks)
Amory, Thomas 1691(?)-1788 **LC 48**
See also DLB 39
Anand, Mulk Raj 1905-2004 **CLC 23, 93**
See also CA 65-68; 231; CANR 32, 64; CN
1, 2, 3, 4, 5, 6, 7; DAM NOV; DLB 323;
EWL 3; MTCW 1, 2; MTFW 2005; RGSF
2
Anatol
See Schnitzler, Arthur
Anaximander c. 611B.C.-c.
546B.C. **CMLC 22**
Anaya, Rudolfo A(lfonso) 1937- **CLC 23,
148; HLC 1**
See also AAYA 20; BYA 13; CA 45-48;
CAAS 4; CANR 1, 32, 51, 124; CN 4, 5,
6, 7; DAM MULT, NOV; DLB 82, 206,
278; HW 1; LAIT 4; LLW; MAL 5;
MTCW 1, 2; MTFW 2005; NFS 12;
RGAL 4; RGSF 2; TCWW 2; WLIT 1
Andersen, Hans Christian
1805-1875 **NCLC 7, 79; SSC 6, 56;
WLC 1**
See also AAYA 57; CLR 6; DA; DA3;
DAB; DAC; DAM MST, POP; EW 6;
MAICYA 1, 2; RGSF 2; RGWL 2, 3;
SATA 100; TWA; WCH; YABC 1

Archer, Lee
See Ellison, Harlan (Jay)

Archilochus c. 7th cent. B.C.- **CMLC 44**
See also DLB 176

Arden, John 1930- **CLC 6, 13, 15**
See also BRWS 2; CA 13-16R; CAAS 4;
CANR 31, 65, 67, 124; CBD; CD 5, 6;
DAM DRAM; DFS 9; DLB 13, 245;
EWL 3; MTCW 1

Arenas, Reinaldo 1943-1990 .. **CLC 41; HLC 1**
See also CA 124; 128; 133; CANR 73, 106;
DAM MULT; DLB 145; EWL 3; GLL 2;
HW 1; LAW; LAWS 1; MTCW 2; MTFW
2005; RGSF 2; RGWL 3; WLIT 1

Arendt, Hannah 1906-1975 **CLC 66, 98**
See also CA 17-20R; 61-64; CANR 26, 60;
DLB 242; MTCW 1, 2

Aretino, Pietro 1492-1556 **LC 12**
See also RGWL 2, 3

Arghezi, Tudor **CLC 80**
See Theodorescu, Ion N.
See also CA 167; CDWLB 4; DLB 220;
EWL 3

Arguedas, Jose Maria 1911-1969 **CLC 10, 18; HLCS 1; TCLC 147**
See also CA 89-92; CANR 73; DLB 113;
EWL 3; HW 1; LAW; RGWL 2, 3; WLIT 1

Argueta, Manlio 1936- **CLC 31**
See also CA 131; CANR 73; CWW 2; DLB
145; EWL 3; HW 1; RGWL 3

Arias, Ron(ald Francis) 1941- **HLC 1**
See also CA 131; CANR 81, 136; DAM
MULT; DLB 82; HW 1, 2; MTCW 2;
MTFW 2005

Ariosto, Lodovico
See Ariosto, Ludovico
See also WLIT 7

Ariosto, Ludovico 1474-1533 ... **LC 6, 87; PC 42**
See Ariosto, Lodovico
See also EW 2; RGWL 2, 3

Aristides
See Epstein, Joseph

Aristophanes 450B.C.-385B.C. **CMLC 4, 51; DC 2; WLCS**
See also AW 1; CDWLB 1; DA; DA3;
DAB; DAC; DAM DRAM, MST; DFS
10; DLB 176; LMFS 1; RGWL 2, 3;
TWA; WLIT 8

Aristotle 384B.C.-322B.C. **CMLC 31; WLCS**
See also AW 1; CDWLB 1; DA; DA3;
DAB; DAC; DAM MST; DLB 176;
RGWL 2, 3; TWA; WLIT 8

Arlt, Roberto (Godofredo Christophersen)
1900-1942 **HLC 1; TCLC 29**
See also CA 123; 131; CANR 67; DAM
MULT; DLB 305; EWL 3; HW 1, 2;
IDTP; LAW

Armah, Ayi Kwei 1939- . **BLC 1; CLC 5, 33, 136**
See also AFW; BRWS 10; BW 1; CA 61-
64; CANR 21, 64; CDWLB 3; CN 1, 2,
3, 4, 5, 6, 7; DAM MULT, POET; DLB
117; EWL 3; MTCW 1; WLIT 2

Armatrading, Joan 1950- **CLC 17**
See also CA 114; 186

Armin, Robert 1568(?)-1615(?) **LC 120**

Armitage, Frank
See Carpenter, John (Howard)

Armstrong, Jeannette (C.) 1948- **NNAL**
See also CA 149; CCA 1; CN 6, 7; DAC;
SATA 102

Arnette, Robert
See Silverberg, Robert

Arnim, Achim von (Ludwig Joachim von Arnim) 1781-1831 .. **NCLC 5, 159; SSC 29**
See also DLB 90

Arnim, Bettina von 1785-1859 **NCLC 38, 123**
See also DLB 90; RGWL 2, 3

Arnold, Matthew 1822-1888 **NCLC 6, 29, 89, 126; PC 5; WLC 1**
See also BRW 5; CDBLB 1832-1890; DA;
DAB; DAC; DAM MST, POET; DLB 32,
57; EXPP; PAB; PFS 2; TEA; WP

Arnold, Thomas 1795-1842 **NCLC 18**
See also DLB 55

Arnow, Harriette (Louisa) Simpson
1908-1986 **CLC 2, 7, 18**
See also BPFB 1; CA 9-12R; 118; CANR
14; CN 2, 3, 4; DLB 6; FW; MTCW 1, 2;
RHW; SATA 42; SATA-Obit 47

Arouet, Francois-Marie
See Voltaire

Arp, Hans
See Arp, Jean

Arp, Jean 1887-1966 **CLC 5; TCLC 115**
See also CA 81-84; 25-28R; CANR 42, 77;
EW 10

Arrabal
See Arrabal, Fernando

Arrabal (Teran), Fernando
See Arrabal, Fernando
See also CWW 2

Arrabal, Fernando 1932- ... **CLC 2, 9, 18, 58**
See Arrabal (Teran), Fernando
See also CA 9-12R; CANR 15; DLB 321;
EWL 3; LMFS 2

Arreola, Juan Jose 1918-2001 **CLC 147; HLC 1; SSC 38**
See also CA 113; 131; 200; CANR 81;
CWW 2; DAM MULT; DLB 113; DNFS
2; EWL 3; HW 1, 2; LAW; RGSF 2

Arrian c. 89(?)-c. 155(?) **CMLC 43**
See also DLB 176

Arrick, Fran **CLC 30**
See Gaberman, Judie Angell
See also BYA 6

Arrley, Richmond
See Delany, Samuel R(ay), Jr.

Artaud, Antonin (Marie Joseph)
1896-1948 **DC 14; TCLC 3, 36**
See also CA 104; 149; DA3; DAM DRAM;
DFS 22; DLB 258, 321; EW 11; EWL 3;
GFL 1789 to the Present; MTCW 2;
MTFW 2005; RGWL 2, 3

Arthur, Ruth M(abel) 1905-1979 **CLC 12**
See also CA 9-12R; 85-88; CANR 4; CWRI
5; SATA 7, 26

Artsybashev, Mikhail (Petrovich)
1878-1927 **TCLC 31**
See also CA 170; DLB 295

Arundel, Honor (Morfydd)
1919-1973 **CLC 17**
See also CA 21-22; 41-44R; CAP 2; CLR
35; CWRI 5; SATA 4; SATA-Obit 24

Arzner, Dorothy 1900-1979 **CLC 98**

Asch, Sholem 1880-1957 **TCLC 3**
See also CA 105; EWL 3; GLL 2; RGHL

Ascham, Roger 1516(?)-1568 **LC 101**
See also DLB 236

Ash, Shalom
See Asch, Sholem

Ashbery, John (Lawrence) 1927- .. **CLC 2, 3, 4, 6, 9, 13, 15, 25, 41, 77, 125, 221; PC 26**
See Berry, Jonas
See also AMWS 3; CA 5-8R; CANR 9, 37,
66, 102, 132; CP 1, 2, 3, 4, 5, 6, 7; DA3;
DAM POET; DLB 5, 165; DLBY 1981;
EWL 3; INT CANR-9; MAL 5; MTCW
1, 2; MTFW 2005; PAB; PFS 11; RGAL
4; TCLE 1:1; WP

Ashdown, Clifford
See Freeman, R(ichard) Austin

Ashe, Gordon
See Creasey, John

Ashton-Warner, Sylvia (Constance)
1908-1984 **CLC 19**
See also CA 69-72; 112; CANR 29; CN 1,
2, 3; MTCW 1, 2

Asimov, Isaac 1920-1992 **CLC 1, 3, 9, 19, 26, 76, 92**
See also AAYA 13; BEST 90:2; BPFB 1;
BYA 4, 6, 7, 9; CA 1-4R; 137; CANR 2,
19, 36, 60, 125; CLR 12, 79; CMW 4;
CN 1, 2, 3, 4, 5; CPW; DA3; DAM POP;
DLB 8; DLBY 1992; INT CANR-19;
JRDA; LAIT 5; LMFS 2; MAICYA 1, 2;
MAL 5; MTCW 1, 2; MTFW 2005;
RGAL 4; SATA 1, 26, 74; SCFW 1, 2;
SFW 4; SSFS 17; TUS; YAW

Askew, Anne 1521(?)-1546 **LC 81**
See also DLB 136

Assis, Joaquim Maria Machado de
See Machado de Assis, Joaquim Maria

Astell, Mary 1666-1731 **LC 68**
See also DLB 252; FW

Astley, Thea (Beatrice May)
1925-2004 **CLC 41**
See also CA 65-68; 229; CANR 11, 43, 78;
CN 1, 2, 3, 4, 5, 6, 7; DLB 289; EWL 3

Astley, William 1855-1911
See Warung, Price

Aston, James
See White, T(erence) H(anbury)

Asturias, Miguel Angel 1899-1974 **CLC 3, 8, 13; HLC 1**
See also CA 25-28; 49-52; CANR 32; CAP
2; CDWLB 3; DA3; DAM MULT, NOV;
DLB 113, 290; EWL 3; HW 1; LAW;
LMFS 2; MTCW 1, 2; RGWL 2, 3; WLIT
1

Atares, Carlos Saura
See Saura (Atares), Carlos

Athanasius c. 295-c. 373 **CMLC 48**

Atheling, William
See Pound, Ezra (Weston Loomis)

Atheling, William, Jr.
See Blish, James (Benjamin)

Atherton, Gertrude (Franklin Horn)
1857-1948 **TCLC 2**
See also CA 104; 155; DLB 9, 78, 186;
HGG; RGAL 4; SUFW 1; TCWW 1, 2

Atherton, Lucius
See Masters, Edgar Lee

Atkins, Jack
See Harris, Mark

Atkinson, Kate 1951- **CLC 99**
See also CA 166; CANR 101, 153; DLB
267

Attaway, William (Alexander)
1911-1986 **BLC 1; CLC 92**
See also BW 2, 3; CA 143; CANR 82;
DAM MULT; DLB 76; MAL 5

Atticus
See Fleming, Ian (Lancaster); Wilson,
(Thomas) Woodrow

Atwood, Margaret 1939- . **CLC 2, 3, 4, 8, 13, 15, 25, 44, 84, 135; PC 8; SSC 2, 46; WLC 1**
See also AAYA 12, 47; AMWS 13; BEST
89:2; BPFB 1; CA 49-52; CANR 3, 24,
33, 59, 95, 133; CN 2, 3, 4, 5, 6, 7; CP 1,
2, 3, 4, 5, 6, 7; CPW; CWP; DA; DA3;
DAB; DAC; DAM MST, NOV, POET;
DLB 53, 251, 326; EWL 3; EXPN; FL
1:5; FW; GL 2; INT CANR-24; LAIT 5;
MTCW 1, 2; MTFW 2005; NFS 4, 12,
13, 14, 19; PFS 7; RGSF 2; SATA 50,
170; SSFS 3, 13; TCLE 1:1; TWA; WWE
1; YAW

Atwood, Margaret Eleanor
See Atwood, Margaret

Aubigny, Pierre d'
See Mencken, H(enry) L(ouis)

Aubin, Penelope 1685-1731(?) **LC 9**
See also DLB 39

Auchincloss, Louis 1917- **CLC 4, 6, 9, 18, 45; SSC 22**
See also AMWS 4; CA 1-4R; CANR 6, 29, 55, 87, 130; CN 1, 2, 3, 4, 5, 6, 7; DAM NOV; DLB 2, 244; DLBY 1980; EWL 3; INT CANR-29; MAL 5; MTCW 1; RGAL 4

Auchincloss, Louis Stanton
See Auchincloss, Louis

Auden, W(ystan) H(ugh) 1907-1973 . **CLC 1, 2, 3, 4, 6, 9, 11, 14, 43, 123; PC 1; WLC 1**
See also AAYA 18; AMWS 2; BRW 7; BRWR 1; CA 9-12R; 45-48; CANR 5, 61, 105; CDBLB 1914-1945; CP 1, 2; DA; DA3; DAB; DAC; DAM DRAM, MST, POET; DLB 10, 20; EWL 3; EXPP; MAL 5; MTCW 1, 2; MTFW 2005; PAB; PFS 1, 3, 4, 10; TUS; WP

Audiberti, Jacques 1899-1965 **CLC 38**
See also CA 25-28R; DAM DRAM; DLB 321; EWL 3

Audubon, John James 1785-1851 . **NCLC 47**
See also ANW; DLB 248

Auel, Jean M(arie) 1936- **CLC 31, 107**
See also AAYA 7, 51; BEST 90:4; BPFB 1; CA 103; CANR 21, 64, 115; CPW; DA3; DAM POP; INT CANR-21; NFS 11; RHW; SATA 91

Auerbach, Berthold 1812-1882 **NCLC 171**
See also DLB 133

Auerbach, Erich 1892-1957 **TCLC 43**
See also CA 118; 155; EWL 3

Augier, Emile 1820-1889 **NCLC 31**
See also DLB 192; GFL 1789 to the Present

August, John
See De Voto, Bernard (Augustine)

Augustine, St. 354-430 **CMLC 6; WLCS**
See also DA; DA3; DAB; DAC; DAM MST; DLB 115; EW 1; RGWL 2, 3; WLIT 8

Aunt Belinda
See Braddon, Mary Elizabeth

Aunt Weedy
See Alcott, Louisa May

Aurelius
See Bourne, Randolph S(illiman)

Aurelius, Marcus 121-180 **CMLC 45**
See Marcus Aurelius
See also RGWL 2, 3

Aurobindo, Sri
See Ghose, Aurabinda

Aurobindo Ghose
See Ghose, Aurabinda

Austen, Jane 1775-1817 **NCLC 1, 13, 19, 33, 51, 81, 95, 119, 150; WLC 1**
See also AAYA 19; BRW 4; BRWC 1; BRWR 2; BYA 3; CDBLB 1789-1832; DA; DA3; DAB; DAC; DAM MST, NOV; DLB 116; EXPN; FL 1:2; GL 2; LAIT 2; LATS 1:1; LMFS 1; NFS 1, 14, 18, 20, 21; TEA; WLIT 3; WYAS 1

Auster, Paul 1947- **CLC 47, 131**
See also AMWS 12; CA 69-72; CANR 23, 52, 75, 129; CMW 4; CN 5, 6, 7; DA3; DLB 227; MAL 5; MTCW 2; MTFW 2005; SUFW 2; TCLE 1:1

Austin, Frank
See Faust, Frederick (Schiller)

Austin, Mary (Hunter) 1868-1934 . **TCLC 25**
See also ANW; CA 109; 178; DLB 9, 78, 206, 221, 275; FW; TCWW 1, 2

Averroes 1126-1198 **CMLC 7**
See also DLB 115

Avicenna 980-1037 **CMLC 16**
See also DLB 115

Avison, Margaret (Kirkland) 1918- .. **CLC 2, 4, 97**
See also CA 17-20R; CANR 134; CP 1, 2, 3, 4, 5, 6, 7; DAC; DAM POET; DLB 53; MTCW 1

Axton, David
See Koontz, Dean R.

Ayckbourn, Alan 1939- **CLC 5, 8, 18, 33, 74; DC 13**
See also BRWS 5; CA 21-24R; CANR 31, 59, 118; CBD; CD 5, 6; DAB; DAM DRAM; DFS 7; DLB 13, 245; EWL 3; MTCW 1, 2; MTFW 2005

Aydy, Catherine
See Tennant, Emma (Christina)

Ayme, Marcel (Andre) 1902-1967 ... **CLC 11; SSC 41**
See also CA 89-92; CANR 67, 137; CLR 25; DLB 72; EW 12; EWL 3; GFL 1789 to the Present; RGSF 2; RGWL 2, 3; SATA 91

Ayrton, Michael 1921-1975 **CLC 7**
See also CA 5-8R; 61-64; CANR 9, 21

Aytmatov, Chingiz
See Aitmatov, Chingiz (Torekulovich)
See also EWL 3

Azorin **CLC 11**
See Martinez Ruiz, Jose
See also DLB 322; EW 9; EWL 3

Azuela, Mariano 1873-1952 .. **HLC 1; TCLC 3, 145**
See also CA 104; 131; CANR 81; DAM MULT; EW 11; HW 1, 2; LAW; MTCW 1, 2; MTFW 2005

Ba, Mariama 1929-1981 **BLCS**
See also AFW; BW 2; CA 141; CANR 87; DNFS 2; WLIT 2

Baastad, Babbis Friis
See Friis-Baastad, Babbis Ellinor

Bab
See Gilbert, W(illiam) S(chwenck)

Babbis, Eleanor
See Friis-Baastad, Babbis Ellinor

Babel, Isaac
See Babel, Isaak (Emmanuilovich)
See also EW 11; SSFS 10

Babel, Isaak (Emmanuilovich) 1894-1941(?) . **SSC 16, 78; TCLC 2, 13, 171**
See Babel, Isaac
See also CA 104; 155; CANR 113; DLB 272; EWL 3; MTCW 2; MTFW 2005; RGSF 2; RGWL 2, 3; TWA

Babits, Mihaly 1883-1941 **TCLC 14**
See also CA 114; CDWLB 4; DLB 215; EWL 3

Babur 1483-1530 **LC 18**

Babylas 1898-1962
See Ghelderode, Michel de

Baca, Jimmy Santiago 1952- . **HLC 1; PC 41**
See also CA 131; CANR 81, 90, 146; CP 6, 7; DAM MULT; DLB 122; HW 1, 2; LLW; MAL 5

Baca, Jose Santiago
See Baca, Jimmy Santiago

Bacchelli, Riccardo 1891-1985 **CLC 19**
See also CA 29-32R; 117; DLB 264; EWL 3

Bach, Richard 1936- **CLC 14**
See also AITN 1; BEST 89:2; BPFB 1; BYA 5; CA 9-12R; CANR 18, 93, 151; CPW; DAM NOV, POP; FANT; MTCW 1; SATA 13

Bach, Richard David
See Bach, Richard

Bache, Benjamin Franklin 1769-1798 **LC 74**
See also DLB 43

Bachelard, Gaston 1884-1962 **TCLC 128**
See also CA 97-100; 89-92; DLB 296; GFL 1789 to the Present

Bachman, Richard
See King, Stephen

Bachmann, Ingeborg 1926-1973 **CLC 69**
See also CA 93-96; 45-48; CANR 69; DLB 85; EWL 3; RGHL; RGWL 2, 3

Bacon, Francis 1561-1626 **LC 18, 32**
See also BRW 1; CDBLB Before 1660; DLB 151, 236, 252; RGEL 2; TEA

Bacon, Roger 1214(?)-1294 **CMLC 14**
See also DLB 115

Bacovia, George 1881-1957 **TCLC 24**
See Vasiliu, Gheorghe
See also CDWLB 4; DLB 220; EWL 3

Badanes, Jerome 1937-1995 **CLC 59**
See also CA 234

Bagehot, Walter 1826-1877 **NCLC 10**
See also DLB 55

Bagnold, Enid 1889-1981 **CLC 25**
See also BYA 2; CA 5-8R; 103; CANR 5, 40; CBD; CN 2; CWD; CWRI 5; DAM DRAM; DLB 13, 160, 191, 245; FW; MAICYA 1, 2; RGEL 2; SATA 1, 25

Bagritsky, Eduard **TCLC 60**
See Dzyubin, Eduard Georgievich

Bagrjana, Elisaveta
See Belcheva, Elisaveta Lyubomirova

Bagryana, Elisaveta **CLC 10**
See Belcheva, Elisaveta Lyubomirova
See also CA 178; CDWLB 4; DLB 147; EWL 3

Bailey, Paul 1937- **CLC 45**
See also CA 21-24R; CANR 16, 62, 124; CN 1, 2, 3, 4, 5, 6, 7; DLB 14, 271; GLL 2

Baillie, Joanna 1762-1851 **NCLC 71, 151**
See also DLB 93; GL 2; RGEL 2

Bainbridge, Beryl (Margaret) 1934- . **CLC 4, 5, 8, 10, 14, 18, 22, 62, 130**
See also BRWS 6; CA 21-24R; CANR 24, 55, 75, 88, 128; CN 2, 3, 4, 5, 6, 7; DAM NOV; DLB 14, 231; EWL 3; MTCW 1, 2; MTFW 2005

Baker, Carlos (Heard) 1909-1987 **TCLC 119**
See also CA 5-8R; 122; CANR 3, 63; DLB 103

Baker, Elliott 1922- **CLC 8**
See also CA 45-48; CANR 2, 63; CN 1, 2, 3, 4, 5, 6, 7

Baker, Jean H. **TCLC 3, 10**
See Russell, George William

Baker, Nicholson 1957- **CLC 61, 165**
See also AMWS 13; CA 135; CANR 63, 120, 138; CN 6; CPW; DA3; DAM POP; DLB 227; MTFW 2005

Baker, Ray Stannard 1870-1946 **TCLC 47**
See also CA 118

Baker, Russell (Wayne) 1925- **CLC 31**
See also BEST 89:4; CA 57-60; CANR 11, 41, 59, 137; MTCW 1, 2; MTFW 2005

Bakhtin, M.
See Bakhtin, Mikhail Mikhailovich

Bakhtin, M. M.
See Bakhtin, Mikhail Mikhailovich

Bakhtin, Mikhail
See Bakhtin, Mikhail Mikhailovich

Bakhtin, Mikhail Mikhailovich 1895-1975 **CLC 83; TCLC 160**
See also CA 128; 113; DLB 242; EWL 3

Bakshi, Ralph 1938(?)- **CLC 26**
See also CA 112; 138; IDFW 3

Bakunin, Mikhail (Alexandrovich)
1814-1876 **NCLC 25, 58**
See also DLB 277

Baldwin, James (Arthur) 1924-1987 . **BLC 1;
CLC 1, 2, 3, 4, 5, 8, 13, 15, 17, 42, 50,
67, 90, 127; DC 1; SSC 10, 33; WLC 1**
See also AAYA 4, 34; AFAW 1, 2; AMWR
2; AMWS 1; BPFB 1; BW 1, CA 1-4R;
124; CABS 1; CAD; CANR 3, 24;
CDALB 1941-1968; CN 1, 2, 3, 4; CPW;
DA; DA3; DAB; DAC; DAM MST,
MULT, NOV, POP; DFS 11, 15; DLB 2,
7, 33, 249, 278; DLBY 1987; EWL 3;
EXPS; LAIT 5; MAL 5; MTCW 1, 2;
MTFW 2005; NCFS 4; NFS 4; RGAL 4;
RGSF 2; SATA 9; SATA-Obit 54; SSFS
2, 18; TUS

Baldwin, William c. 1515-1563 **LC 113**
See also DLB 132

Bale, John 1495-1563 **LC 62**
See also DLB 132; RGEL 2; TEA

Ball, Hugo 1886-1927 **TCLC 104**

Ballard, J(ames) G(raham) 1930- . **CLC 3, 6,
14, 36, 137; SSC 1, 53**
See also AAYA 3, 52; BRWS 5; CA 5-8R;
CANR 15, 39, 65, 107, 133; CN 1, 2, 3,
4, 5, 6, 7; DA3; DAM NOV, POP; DLB
14, 207, 261, 319; EWL 3; HGG; MTCW
1, 2; MTFW 2005; NFS 8; RGEL 2;
RGSF 2; SATA 93; SCFW 1, 2; SFW 4

Balmont, Konstantin (Dmitriyevich)
1867-1943 **TCLC 11**
See also CA 109; 155; DLB 295; EWL 3

Baltausis, Vincas 1847-1910
See Mikszath, Kalman

Balzac, Honore de 1799-1850 ... **NCLC 5, 35,
53, 153; SSC 5, 59; WLC 1**
See also DA; DA3; DAB; DAC; DAM
MST, NOV; DLB 119; EW 5; GFL 1789
to the Present; LMFS 1; RGSF 2; RGWL
2, 3; SSFS 10; SUFW; TWA

Bambara, Toni Cade 1939-1995 **BLC 1;
CLC 19, 88; SSC 35; TCLC 116;
WLCS**
See also AAYA 5, 49; AFAW 2; AMWS 11;
BW 2, 3; BYA 12, 14; CA 29-32R; 150;
CANR 24, 49, 81; CDALBS; DA; DA3;
DAC; DAM MST, MULT; DLB 38, 218;
EXPS; MAL 5; MTCW 1, 2; MTFW
2005; RGAL 4; RGSF 2; SATA 112; SSFS
4, 7, 12, 21

Bamdad, A.
See Shamlu, Ahmad

Bamdad, Alef
See Shamlu, Ahmad

Banat, D. R.
See Bradbury, Ray (Douglas)

Bancroft, Laura
See Baum, L(yman) Frank

Banim, John 1798-1842 **NCLC 13**
See also DLB 116, 158, 159; RGEL 2

Banim, Michael 1796-1874 **NCLC 13**
See also DLB 158, 159

Banjo, The
See Paterson, A(ndrew) B(arton)

Banks, Iain
See Banks, Iain M(enzies)
See also BRWS 11

Banks, Iain M(enzies) 1954- **CLC 34**
See Banks, Iain
See also CA 123; 128; CANR 61, 106; DLB
194, 261; EWL 3; HGG; INT CA-128;
MTFW 2005; SFW 4

Banks, Lynne Reid **CLC 23**
See Reid Banks, Lynne
See also AAYA 6; BYA 7; CLR 86; CN 4,
5, 6

Banks, Russell (Earl) 1940- **CLC 37, 72,
187; SSC 42**
See also AAYA 45; AMWS 5; CA 65-68;
CAAS 15; CANR 19, 52, 73, 118; CN 4,
5, 6, 7; DLB 130, 278; EWL 3; MAL 5;
MTCW 2; MTFW 2005; NFS 13

Banville, John 1945- **CLC 46, 118, 224**
See also CA 117; 128; CANR 104, 150; CN
4, 5, 6, 7; DLB 14, 271, 326; INT CA-
128

Banville, Theodore (Faullain) de
1832-1891 **NCLC 9**
See also DLB 217; GFL 1789 to the Present

Baraka, Amiri 1934- **BLC 1; CLC 1, 2, 3,
5, 10, 14, 33, 115, 213; DC 6; PC 4;
WLCS**
See Jones, LeRoi
See also AAYA 63; AFAW 1, 2; AMWS 2;
BW 2, 3; CA 21-24R; CABS 3; CAD;
CANR 27, 38, 61, 133; CD 3, 5, 6;
CDALB 1941-1968; CP 4, 5, 6, 7; CPW;
DA; DA3; DAC; DAM MST, MULT,
POET, POP; DFS 3, 11, 16; DLB 5, 7,
16, 38; DLBD 8; EWL 3; MAL 5; MTCW
1, 2; MTFW 2005; PFS 9; RGAL 4;
TCLE 1:1; TUS; WP

Baratynsky, Evgenii Abramovich
1800-1844 **NCLC 103**
See also DLB 205

Barbauld, Anna Laetitia
1743-1825 **NCLC 50**
See also DLB 107, 109, 142, 158; RGEL 2

Barbellion, W. N. P. **TCLC 24**
See Cummings, Bruce F(rederick)

Barber, Benjamin R. 1939- **CLC 141**
See also CA 29-32R; CANR 12, 32, 64, 119

Barbera, Jack (Vincent) 1945- **CLC 44**
See also CA 110; CANR 45

Barbey d'Aurevilly, Jules-Amedee
1808-1889 **NCLC 1; SSC 17**
See also DLB 119; GFL 1789 to the Present

Barbour, John c. 1316-1395 **CMLC 33**
See also DLB 146

Barbusse, Henri 1873-1935 **TCLC 5**
See also CA 105; 154; DLB 65; EWL 3;
RGWL 2, 3

Barclay, Alexander c. 1475-1552 **LC 109**
See also DLB 132

Barclay, Bill
See Moorcock, Michael

Barclay, William Ewert
See Moorcock, Michael

Barea, Arturo 1897-1957 **TCLC 14**
See also CA 111; 201

Barfoot, Joan 1946- **CLC 18**
See also CA 105; CANR 141

Barham, Richard Harris
1788-1845 **NCLC 77**
See also DLB 159

Baring, Maurice 1874-1945 **TCLC 8**
See also CA 105; 168; DLB 34; HGG

Baring-Gould, Sabine 1834-1924 ... **TCLC 88**
See also DLB 156, 190

Barker, Clive 1952- **CLC 52, 205; SSC 53**
See also AAYA 10, 54; BEST 90:3; BPFB
1; CA 121; 129; CANR 71, 111, 133;
CPW; DA3; DAM POP; DLB 261; HGG;
INT CA-129; MTCW 1, 2; MTFW 2005;
SUFW 2

Barker, George Granville
1913-1991 **CLC 8, 48**
See also CA 9-12R; 135; CANR 7, 38; CP
1, 2, 3, 4, 5; DAM POET; DLB 20; EWL
3; MTCW 1

Barker, Harley Granville
See Granville-Barker, Harley
See also DLB 10

Barker, Howard 1946- **CLC 37**
See also CA 102; CBD; CD 5, 6; DLB 13,
233

Barker, Jane 1652-1732 **LC 42, 82**
See also DLB 39, 131

Barker, Pat 1943- **CLC 32, 94, 146**
See also BRWS 4; CA 117; 122; CANR 50,
101, 148; CN 6, 7; DLB 271, 326; INT
CA-122

Barker, Patricia
See Barker, Pat

Barlach, Ernst (Heinrich)
1870-1938 **TCLC 84**
See also CA 178; DLB 56, 118; EWL 3

Barlow, Joel 1754-1812 **NCLC 23**
See also AMWS 2; DLB 37; RGAL 4

Barnard, Mary (Ethel) 1909- **CLC 48**
See also CA 21-22; CAP 2; CP 1

Barnes, Djuna 1892-1982 **CLC 3, 4, 8, 11,
29, 127; SSC 3**
See Steptoe, Lydia
See also AMWS 3; CA 9-12R; 107; CAD;
CANR 16, 55; CN 1, 2, 3; CWD; DLB 4,
9, 45; EWL 3; GLL 1; MAL 5; MTCW 1,
2; MTFW 2005; RGAL 4; TCLE 1:1;
TUS

Barnes, Jim 1933- **NNAL**
See also CA 108; 175; CAAE 175; CAAS
28; DLB 175

Barnes, Julian 1946- **CLC 42, 141**
See also BRWS 4; CA 102; CANR 19, 54,
115, 137; CN 4, 5, 6, 7; DAB; DLB 194;
DLBY 1993; EWL 3; MTCW 2; MTFW
2005

Barnes, Julian Patrick
See Barnes, Julian

Barnes, Peter 1931-2004 **CLC 5, 56**
See also CA 65-68; 230; CAAS 12; CANR
33, 34, 64, 113; CBD; CD 5, 6; DFS 6;
DLB 13, 233; MTCW 1

Barnes, William 1801-1886 **NCLC 75**
See also DLB 32

Baroja, Pio 1872-1956 **HLC 1; TCLC 8**
See also CA 104; 247; EW 9

Baroja y Nessi, Pio
See Baroja, Pio

Baron, David
See Pinter, Harold

Baron Corvo
See Rolfe, Frederick (William Serafino Aus-
tin Lewis Mary)

Barondess, Sue K(aufman)
1926-1977 **CLC 8**
See Kaufman, Sue
See also CA 1-4R; 69-72; CANR 1

Baron de Teive
See Pessoa, Fernando (Antonio Nogueira)

Baroness Von S.
See Zangwill, Israel

Barres, (Auguste-)Maurice
1862-1923 **TCLC 47**
See also CA 164; DLB 123; GFL 1789 to
the Present

Barreto, Afonso Henrique de Lima
See Lima Barreto, Afonso Henrique de

Barrett, Andrea 1954- **CLC 150**
See also CA 156; CANR 92; CN 7

Barrett, Michele **CLC 65**

Barrett, (Roger) Syd 1946-2006 **CLC 35**

Barrett, William (Christopher)
1913-1992 **CLC 27**
See also CA 13-16R; 139; CANR 11, 67;
INT CANR-11

Barrett Browning, Elizabeth
1806-1861 **NCLC 1, 16, 61, 66, 170;
PC 6, 62; WLC 1**
See also AAYA 63; BRW 4; CDBLB 1832-
1890; DA; DA3; DAB; DAC; DAM MST,
POET; DLB 32, 199; EXPP; FL 1:2; PAB;
PFS 2, 16, 23; TEA; WLIT 4; WP

Barrie, J(ames) M(atthew)
1860-1937 **TCLC 2, 164**
See also BRWS 3; BYA 4, 5; CA 104; 136;
CANR 77; CDBLB 1890-1914; CLR 16;
CWRI 5; DA3; DAB; DAM DRAM; DFS
7; DLB 10, 141, 156; EWL 3; FANT;
MAICYA 1, 2; MTCW 2; MTFW 2005;
SATA 100; SUFW; WCH; WLIT 4; YABC
1

Barrington, Michael
See Moorcock, Michael

Barrol, Grady
See Bograd, Larry

Barry, Mike
See Malzberg, Barry N(athaniel)

Barry, Philip 1896-1949 **TCLC 11**
See also CA 109; 199; DFS 9; DLB 7, 228;
MAL 5; RGAL 4

Bart, Andre Schwarz
See Schwarz-Bart, Andre

Barth, John (Simmons) 1930- ... **CLC 1, 2, 3,
5, 7, 9, 10, 14, 27, 51, 89, 214; SSC 10,
89**
See also AITN 1, 2; AMW; BPFB 1; CA
1-4R; CABS 1; CANR 5, 23, 49, 64, 113;
CN 1, 2, 3, 4, 5, 6, 7; DAM NOV; DLB
2, 227; EWL 3; FANT; MAL 5; MTCW
1; RGAL 4; RGSF 2; RHW; SSFS 6; TUS

Barthelme, Donald 1931-1989 ... **CLC 1, 2, 3,
5, 6, 8, 13, 23, 46, 59, 115; SSC 2, 55**
See also AMWS 4; BPFB 1; CA 21-24R;
129; CANR 20, 58; CN 1, 2, 3, 4; DA3;
DAM NOV; DLB 2, 234; DLBY 1980,
1989; EWL 3; FANT; LMFS 2; MAL 5;
MTCW 1, 2; MTFW 2005; RGAL 4;
RGSF 2; SATA 7; SATA-Obit 62; SSFS
17

Barthelme, Frederick 1943- **CLC 36, 117**
See also AMWS 11; CA 114; 122; CANR
77; CN 4, 5, 6, 7; CSW; DLB 244; DLBY
1985; EWL 3; INT CA-122

Barthes, Roland (Gerard)
1915-1980 **CLC 24, 83; TCLC 135**
See also CA 130; 97-100; CANR 66; DLB
296; EW 13; EWL 3; GFL 1789 to the
Present; MTCW 1, 2; TWA

Bartram, William 1739-1823 **NCLC 145**
See also ANW; DLB 37

Barzun, Jacques (Martin) 1907- **CLC 51,
145**
See also CA 61-64; CANR 22, 95

Bashevis, Isaac
See Singer, Isaac Bashevis

Bashkirtseff, Marie 1859-1884 **NCLC 27**

Basho, Matsuo
See Matsuo Basho
See also RGWL 2, 3; WP

Basil of Caesaria c. 330-379 **CMLC 35**

Basket, Raney
See Edgerton, Clyde (Carlyle)

Bass, Kingsley B., Jr.
See Bullins, Ed

Bass, Rick 1958- **CLC 79, 143; SSC 60**
See also ANW; CA 126; CANR 53, 93, 145;
CSW; DLB 212, 275

Bassani, Giorgio 1916-2000 **CLC 9**
See also CA 65-68; 190; CANR 33; CWW
2; DLB 128, 177, 299; EWL 3; MTCW 1;
RGHL; RGWL 2, 3

Bastian, Ann **CLC 70**

Bastos, Augusto Roa
See Roa Bastos, Augusto

Bataille, Georges 1897-1962 **CLC 29;
TCLC 155**
See also CA 101; 89-92; EWL 3

Bates, H(erbert) E(rnest)
1905-1974 **CLC 46; SSC 10**
See also CA 93-96; 45-48; CANR 34; CN
1; DA3; DAB; DAM POP; DLB 162, 191;
EWL 3; EXPS; MTCW 1, 2; RGSF 2;
SSFS 7

Bauchart
See Camus, Albert

Baudelaire, Charles 1821-1867 . **NCLC 6, 29,
55, 155; PC 1; SSC 18; WLC 1**
See also DA; DA3; DAB; DAC; DAM
MST, POET; DLB 217; EW 7; GFL 1789
to the Present; LMFS 2; PFS 21; RGWL
2, 3; TWA

Baudouin, Marcel
See Peguy, Charles (Pierre)

Baudouin, Pierre
See Peguy, Charles (Pierre)

Baudrillard, Jean 1929- **CLC 60**
See also DLB 296

Baum, L(yman) Frank 1856-1919 .. **TCLC 7,
132**
See also AAYA 46; BYA 16; CA 108; 133;
CLR 15, 107; CWRI 5; DLB 22; FANT;
JRDA; MAICYA 1, 2; MTCW 1, 2; NFS
13; RGAL 4; SATA 18, 100; WCH

Baum, Louis F.
See Baum, L(yman) Frank

Baumbach, Jonathan 1933- **CLC 6, 23**
See also CA 13-16R; CAAS 5; CANR 12,
66, 140; CN 3, 4, 5, 6, 7; DLBY 1980;
INT CANR-12; MTCW 1

Bausch, Richard (Carl) 1945- **CLC 51**
See also AMWS 7; CA 101; CAAS 14;
CANR 43, 61, 87; CN 7; CSW; DLB 130;
MAL 5

Baxter, Charles (Morley) 1947- . **CLC 45, 78**
See also CA 57-60; CANR 40, 64, 104, 133;
CPW; DAM POP; DLB 130; MAL 5;
MTCW 2; MTFW 2005; TCLE 1:1

Baxter, George Owen
See Faust, Frederick (Schiller)

Baxter, James K(eir) 1926-1972 **CLC 14**
See also CA 77-80; CP 1; EWL 3

Baxter, John
See Hunt, E(verette) Howard, (Jr.)

Bayer, Sylvia
See Glassco, John

Bayle, Pierre 1647-1706 **LC 126**
See also DLB 268, 313; GFL Beginnings to
1789

Baynton, Barbara 1857-1929 **TCLC 57**
See also DLB 230; RGSF 2

Beagle, Peter S(oyer) 1939- **CLC 7, 104**
See also AAYA 47; BPFB 1; BYA 9, 10,
16; CA 9-12R; CANR 4, 51, 73, 110;
DA3; DLBY 1980; FANT; INT CANR-4;
MTCW 2; MTFW 2005; SATA 60, 130;
SUFW 1, 2; YAW

Bean, Normal
See Burroughs, Edgar Rice

Beard, Charles A(ustin)
1874-1948 **TCLC 15**
See also CA 115; 189; DLB 17; SATA 18

Beardsley, Aubrey 1872-1898 **NCLC 6**

Beattie, Ann 1947- **CLC 8, 13, 18, 40, 63,
146; SSC 11**
See also AMWS 5; BEST 90:2; BPFB 1;
CA 81-84; CANR 53, 73, 128; CN 4, 5,
6, 7; CPW; DA3; DAM NOV, POP; DLB
218, 278; DLBY 1982; EWL 3; MAL 5;
MTCW 1, 2; MTFW 2005; RGAL 4;
RGSF 2; SSFS 9; TUS

Beattie, James 1735-1803 **NCLC 25**
See also DLB 109

Beauchamp, Kathleen Mansfield 1888-1923
See Mansfield, Katherine
See also CA 104; 134; DA; DA3; DAC;
DAM MST; MTCW 2; TEA

Beaumarchais, Pierre-Augustin Caron de
1732-1799 **DC 4; LC 61**
See also DAM DRAM; DFS 14, 16; DLB
313; EW 4; GFL Beginnings to 1789;
RGWL 2, 3

Beaumont, Francis 1584(?)-1616 .. **DC 6; LC
33**
See also BRW 2; CDBLB Before 1660;
DLB 58; TEA

Beauvoir, Simone de 1908-1986 **CLC 1, 2,
4, 8, 14, 31, 44, 50, 71, 124; SSC 35;
WLC 1**
See also BPFB 1; CA 9-12R; 118; CANR
28, 61; DA; DA3; DAB; DAC; DAM
MST, NOV; DLB 72; DLBY 1986; EW
12; EWL 3; FL 1:5; FW; GFL 1789 to the
Present; LMFS 2; MTCW 1, 2; MTFW
2005; RGSF 2; RGWL 2, 3; TWA

**Beauvoir, Simone Lucie Ernestine Marie
Bertrand de**
See Beauvoir, Simone de

Becker, Carl (Lotus) 1873-1945 **TCLC 63**
See also CA 157; DLB 17

Becker, Jurek 1937-1997 **CLC 7, 19**
See also CA 85-88; 157; CANR 60, 117;
CWW 2; DLB 75, 299; EWL 3; RGHL

Becker, Walter 1950- **CLC 26**

Becket, Thomas a 1118(?)-1170 **CMLC 83**

Beckett, Samuel (Barclay)
1906-1989 .. **CLC 1, 2, 3, 4, 6, 9, 10, 11,
14, 18, 29, 57, 59, 83; DC 22; SSC 16,
74; TCLC 145; WLC 1**
See also BRWC 2; BRWR 1; BRWS 1; CA
5-8R; 130; CANR 33, 61; CBD; CDBLB
1945-1960; CN 1, 2, 3, 4; CP 1, 2, 3, 4;
DA; DA3; DAB; DAC; DAM DRAM,
MST, NOV; DFS 2, 7, 18; DLB 13, 15,
233, 319, 321; DLBY 1990; EWL 3; GFL
1789 to the Present; LATS 1:2; LMFS 2;
MTCW 1, 2; MTFW 2005; RGSF 2;
RGWL 2, 3; SSFS 15; TEA; WLIT 4

Beckford, William 1760-1844 **NCLC 16**
See also BRW 3; DLB 39, 213; GL 2; HGG;
LMFS 1; SUFW

Beckham, Barry (Earl) 1944- **BLC 1**
See also BW 1; CA 29-32R; CANR 26, 62;
CN 1, 2, 3, 4, 5, 6; DAM MULT; DLB 33

Beckman, Gunnel 1910- **CLC 26**
See also CA 33-36R; CANR 15, 114; CLR
25; MAICYA 1, 2; SAAS 9; SATA 6

Becque, Henri 1837-1899 **DC 21; NCLC 3**
See also DLB 192; GFL 1789 to the Present

Becquer, Gustavo Adolfo
1836-1870 **HLCS 1; NCLC 106**
See also DAM MULT

Beddoes, Thomas Lovell 1803-1849 .. **DC 15;
NCLC 3, 154**
See also BRWS 11; DLB 96

Bede c. 673-735 **CMLC 20**
See also DLB 146; TEA

Bedford, Denton R. 1907-(?) **NNAL**

Bedford, Donald F.
See Fearing, Kenneth (Flexner)

Beecher, Catharine Esther
1800-1878 **NCLC 30**
See also DLB 1, 243

Beecher, John 1904-1980 **CLC 6**
See also AITN 1; CA 5-8R; 105; CANR 8;
CP 1, 2, 3

Beer, Johann 1655-1700 **LC 5**
See also DLB 168

Beer, Patricia 1924- **CLC 58**
See also CA 61-64; 183; CANR 13, 46; CP
1, 2, 3, 4, 5, 6; CWP; DLB 40; FW

Beerbohm, Max
See Beerbohm, (Henry) Max(imilian)

Beerbohm, (Henry) Max(imilian)
1872-1956 **TCLC 1, 24**
See also BRWS 2; CA 104; 154; CANR 79;
DLB 34, 100; FANT; MTCW 2

Beer-Hofmann, Richard
1866-1945 **TCLC 60**
See also CA 160; DLB 81

Beg, Shemus
See Stephens, James

Begiebing, Robert J(ohn) 1946- **CLC 70**
See also CA 122; CANR 40, 88

Begley, Louis 1933- **CLC 197**
See also CA 140; CANR 98; DLB 299;
RGHL; TCLE 1:1

Behan, Brendan (Francis)
1923-1964 **CLC 1, 8, 11, 15, 79**
See also BRWS 2; CA 73-76; CANR 33,
121; CBD; CDBLB 1945-1960; DAM
DRAM; DFS 7; DLB 13, 233; EWL 3;
MTCW 1, 2

Behn, Aphra 1640(?)-1689 .. **DC 4; LC 1, 30,
42; PC 13; WLC 1**
See also BRWS 3; DA; DA3; DAB; DAC;
DAM DRAM, MST, NOV, POET; DFS
16; DLB 39, 80, 131; FW; TEA; WLIT 3

Behrman, S(amuel) N(athaniel)
1893-1973 **CLC 40**
See also CA 13-16; 45-48; CAD; CAP 1;
DLB 7, 44; IDFW 3; MAL 5; RGAL 4

Bekederemo, J. P. Clark
See Clark Bekederemo, J(ohnson) P(epper)
See also CD 6

Belasco, David 1853-1931 **TCLC 3**
See also CA 104; 168; DLB 7; MAL 5;
RGAL 4

Belcheva, Elisaveta Lyubomirova
1893-1991 **CLC 10**
See Bagryana, Elisaveta

Beldone, Phil "Cheech"
See Ellison, Harlan (Jay)

Beleno
See Azuela, Mariano

Belinski, Vissarion Grigoryevich
1811-1848 **NCLC 5**
See also DLB 198

Belitt, Ben 1911- **CLC 22**
See also CA 13-16R; CAAS 4; CANR 7,
77; CP 1, 2, 3, 4, 5, 6; DLB 5

Belknap, Jeremy 1744-1798 **LC 115**
See also DLB 30, 37

Bell, Gertrude (Margaret Lowthian)
1868-1926 **TCLC 67**
See also CA 167; CANR 110; DLB 174

Bell, J. Freeman
See Zangwill, Israel

Bell, James Madison 1826-1902 **BLC 1;
TCLC 43**
See also BW 1; CA 122; 124; DAM MULT;
DLB 50

Bell, Madison Smartt 1957- **CLC 41, 102,
223**
See also AMWS 10; BPFB 1; CA 111, 183;
CAAE 183; CANR 28, 54, 73, 134; CN
5, 6, 7; CSW; DLB 218, 278; MTCW 2;
MTFW 2005

Bell, Marvin (Hartley) 1937- **CLC 8, 31**
See also CA 21-24R; CAAS 14; CANR 59,
102; CP 1, 2, 3, 4, 5, 6, 7; DAM POET;
DLB 5; MAL 5; MTCW 1

Bell, W. L. D.
See Mencken, H(enry) L(ouis)

Bellamy, Atwood C.
See Mencken, H(enry) L(ouis)

Bellamy, Edward 1850-1898 **NCLC 4, 86,
147**
See also DLB 12; NFS 15; RGAL 4; SFW 4

Belli, Gioconda 1948- **HLCS 1**
See also CA 152; CANR 143; CWW 2;
DLB 290; EWL 3; RGWL 3

Bellin, Edward J.
See Kuttner, Henry

Bello, Andres 1781-1865 **NCLC 131**
See also LAW

**Belloc, (Joseph) Hilaire (Pierre Sebastien
Rene Swanton)** 1870-1953 **PC 24;
TCLC 7, 18**
See also CA 106; 152; CLR 102; CWRI 5;
DAM POET; DLB 19, 100, 141, 174;
EWL 3; MTCW 2; MTFW 2005; SATA
112; WCH; YABC 1

Belloc, Joseph Peter Rene Hilaire
See Belloc, (Joseph) Hilaire (Pierre Sebas-
tien Rene Swanton)

Belloc, Joseph Pierre Hilaire
See Belloc, (Joseph) Hilaire (Pierre Sebas-
tien Rene Swanton)

Belloc, M. A.
See Lowndes, Marie Adelaide (Belloc)

Belloc-Lowndes, Mrs.
See Lowndes, Marie Adelaide (Belloc)

Bellow, Saul 1915-2005 **CLC 1, 2, 3, 6, 8,
10, 13, 15, 25, 33, 34, 63, 79, 190, 200;
SSC 14; WLC 1**
See also AITN 2; AMW; AMWC 2; AMWR
2; BEST 89:3; BPFB 1; CA 5-8R; 238;
CABS 1; CANR 29, 53, 95, 132; CDALB
1941-1968; CN 1, 2, 3, 4, 5, 6, 7; DA;
DA3; DAB; DAC; DAM MST, NOV,
POP; DLB 2, 28, 299; DLBD 3; DLBY
1982; EWL 3; MAL 5; MTCW 1, 2;
MTFW 2005; NFS 4, 14; RGAL 4;
RGHL; RGSF 2; SSFS 12; TUS

Belser, Reimond Karel Maria de 1929-
See Ruyslinck, Ward
See also CA 152

Bely, Andrey **PC 11; TCLC 7**
See Bugayev, Boris Nikolayevich
See also DLB 295; EW 9; EWL 3

Belyi, Andrei
See Bugayev, Boris Nikolayevich
See also RGWL 2, 3

Bembo, Pietro 1470-1547 **LC 79**
See also RGWL 2, 3

Benary, Margot
See Benary-Isbert, Margot

Benary-Isbert, Margot 1889-1979 **CLC 12**
See also CA 5-8R; 89-92; CANR 4, 72;
CLR 12; MAICYA 1, 2; SATA 2; SATA-
Obit 21

Benavente (y Martinez), Jacinto
1866-1954 **DC 26; HLCS 1; TCLC 3**
See also CA 106; 131; CANR 81; DAM
DRAM, MULT; EWL 3; GLL 2; HW 1,
2; MTCW 1, 2

Benchley, Peter 1940-2006 **CLC 4, 8**
See also AAYA 14; AITN 2; BPFB 1; CA
17-20R; 248; CANR 12, 35, 66, 115;
CPW; DAM NOV, POP; HGG; MTCW 1,
2; MTFW 2005; SATA 3, 89, 164

Benchley, Peter Bradford
See Benchley, Peter

Benchley, Robert (Charles)
1889-1945 **TCLC 1, 55**
See also CA 105; 153; DLB 11; MAL 5;
RGAL 4

Benda, Julien 1867-1956 **TCLC 60**
See also CA 120; 154; GFL 1789 to the
Present

Benedict, Ruth 1887-1948 **TCLC 60**
See also CA 158; CANR 146; DLB 246

Benedict, Ruth Fulton
See Benedict, Ruth

Benedikt, Michael 1935- **CLC 4, 14**
See also CA 13-16R; CANR 7; CP 1, 2, 3,
4, 5, 6, 7; DLB 5

Benet, Juan 1927-1993 **CLC 28**
See also CA 143; EWL 3

Benet, Stephen Vincent 1898-1943 **PC 64;
SSC 10, 86; TCLC 7**
See also AMWS 11; CA 104; 152; DA3;
DAM POET; DLB 4, 48, 102, 249, 284;
DLBY 1997; EWL 3; HGG; MAL 5;
MTCW 2; MTFW 2005; RGAL 4; RGSF
2; SUFW; WP; YABC 1

Benet, William Rose 1886-1950 **TCLC 28**
See also CA 118; 152; DAM POET; DLB
45; RGAL 4

Benford, Gregory (Albert) 1941- **CLC 52**
See also BPFB 1; CA 69-72, 175; CAAE
175; CAAS 27; CANR 12, 24, 49, 95,
134; CN 7; CSW; DLBY 1982; MTFW
2005; SCFW 2; SFW 4

Bengtsson, Frans (Gunnar)
1894-1954 **TCLC 48**
See also CA 170; EWL 3

Benjamin, David
See Slavitt, David R(ytman)

Benjamin, Lois
See Gould, Lois

Benjamin, Walter 1892-1940 **TCLC 39**
See also CA 164; DLB 242; EW 11; EWL
3

Ben Jelloun, Tahar 1944-
See Jelloun, Tahar ben
See also CA 135; CWW 2; EWL 3; RGWL
3; WLIT 2

Benn, Gottfried 1886-1956 .. **PC 35; TCLC 3**
See also CA 106; 153; DLB 56; EWL 3;
RGWL 2, 3

Bennett, Alan 1934- **CLC 45, 77**
See also BRWS 8; CA 103; CANR 35, 55,
106; CBD; CD 5, 6; DAB; DAM MST;
DLB 310; MTCW 1, 2; MTFW 2005

Bennett, (Enoch) Arnold
1867-1931 **TCLC 5, 20**
See also BRW 6; CA 106; 155; CDBLB
1890-1914; DLB 10, 34, 98, 135; EWL 3;
MTCW 2

Bennett, Elizabeth
See Mitchell, Margaret (Munnerlyn)

Bennett, George Harold 1930-
See Bennett, Hal
See also BW 1; CA 97-100; CANR 87

Bennett, Gwendolyn B. 1902-1981 **HR 1:2**
See also BW 1; CA 125; DLB 51; WP

Bennett, Hal **CLC 5**
See Bennett, George Harold
See also DLB 33

Bennett, Jay 1912- **CLC 35**
See also AAYA 10; CA 69-72; CANR 11,
42, 79; JRDA; SAAS 4; SATA 41, 87;
SATA-Brief 27; WYA; YAW

Bennett, Louise (Simone) 1919- **BLC 1;
CLC 28**
See also BW 2, 3; CA 151; CDWLB 3; CP
1, 2, 3, 4, 5, 6, 7; DAM MULT; DLB 117;
EWL 3

Benson, A. C. 1862-1925 **TCLC 123**
See also DLB 98

Benson, E(dward) F(rederic)
1867-1940 **TCLC 27**
See also CA 114; 157; DLB 135, 153;
HGG; SUFW 1

Benson, Jackson J. 1930- **CLC 34**
See also CA 25-28R; DLB 111

Benson, Sally 1900-1972 **CLC 17**
See also CA 19-20; 37-40R; CAP 1; SATA
1, 35; SATA-Obit 27

Benson, Stella 1892-1933 **TCLC 17**
See also CA 117; 154, 155; DLB 36, 162;
FANT; TEA

Bentham, Jeremy 1748-1832 **NCLC 38**
See also DLB 107, 158, 252

Bentley, E(dmund) C(lerihew)
1875-1956 **TCLC 12**
See also CA 108; 232; DLB 70; MSW

Bentley, Eric 1916- **CLC 24**
See also CA 5-8R; CAD; CANR 6, 67;
CBD; CD 5, 6; INT CANR-6

Bentley, Eric Russell
See Bentley, Eric

ben Uzair, Salem
See Horne, Richard Henry Hengist

Beranger, Pierre Jean de
1780-1857 **NCLC 34**

Berdyaev, Nicolas
See Berdyaev, Nikolai (Aleksandrovich)

Berdyaev, Nikolai (Aleksandrovich)
1874-1948 **TCLC 67**
See also CA 120; 157

Berdyayev, Nikolai (Aleksandrovich)
See Berdyaev, Nikolai (Aleksandrovich)

Berendt, John 1939- **CLC 86**
See also CA 146; CANR 75, 83, 151

Berendt, John Lawrence
See Berendt, John

Beresford, J(ohn) D(avys)
1873-1947 **TCLC 81**
See also CA 112; 155; DLB 162, 178, 197;
SFW 4; SUFW 1

Bergelson, David (Rafailovich)
1884-1952 **TCLC 81**
See Bergelson, Dovid
See also CA 220

Bergelson, Dovid
See Bergelson, David (Rafailovich)
See also EWL 3

Berger, Colonel
See Malraux, (Georges-)André

Berger, John (Peter) 1926- **CLC 2, 19**
See also BRWS 4; CA 81-84; CANR 51,
78, 117; CN 1, 2, 3, 4, 5, 6, 7; DLB 14,
207, 319, 326

Berger, Melvin H. 1927- **CLC 12**
See also CA 5-8R; CANR 4, 142; CLR 32;
SAAS 2; SATA 5, 88, 158; SATA-Essay
124

Berger, Thomas (Louis) 1924- .. **CLC 3, 5, 8,
11, 18, 38**
See also BPFB 1; CA 1-4R; CANR 5, 28,
51, 128; CN 1, 2, 3, 4, 5, 6, 7; DAM
NOV; DLB 2; DLBY 1980; EWL 3;
FANT; INT CANR-28; MAL 5; MTCW
1, 2; MTFW 2005; RHW; TCLE 1:1;
TCWW 1, 2

Bergman, (Ernst) Ingmar 1918- **CLC 16,
72, 210**
See also AAYA 61; CA 81-84; CANR 33,
70; CWW 2; DLB 257; MTCW 2; MTFW
2005

Bergson, Henri(-Louis) 1859-1941 . **TCLC 32**
See also CA 164; EW 8; EWL 3; GFL 1789
to the Present

Bergstein, Eleanor 1938- **CLC 4**
See also CA 53-56; CANR 5

Berkeley, George 1685-1753 **LC 65**
See also DLB 31, 101, 252

Berkoff, Steven 1937- **CLC 56**
See also CA 104; CANR 72; CBD; CD 5, 6

Berlin, Isaiah 1909-1997 **TCLC 105**
See also CA 85-88; 162

Bermant, Chaim (Icyk) 1929-1998 ... **CLC 40**
See also CA 57-60; CANR 6, 31, 57, 105;
CN 2, 3, 4, 5, 6

Bern, Victoria
See Fisher, M(ary) F(rances) K(ennedy)

Bernanos, (Paul Louis) Georges
1888-1948 **TCLC 3**
See also CA 104; 130; CANR 94; DLB 72;
EWL 3; GFL 1789 to the Present; RGWL
2, 3

Bernard, April 1956- **CLC 59**
See also CA 131; CANR 144

Bernard, Mary Ann
See Soderbergh, Steven

Bernard of Clairvaux 1090-1153 .. **CMLC 71**
See also DLB 208

Berne, Victoria
See Fisher, M(ary) F(rances) K(ennedy)

Bernhard, Thomas 1931-1989 **CLC 3, 32,
61; DC 14; TCLC 165**
See also CA 85-88; 127; CANR 32, 57; CD-
WLB 2; DLB 85, 124; EWL 3; MTCW 1;
RGHL; RGWL 2, 3

Bernhardt, Sarah (Henriette Rosine)
1844-1923 **TCLC 75**
See also CA 157

Bernstein, Charles 1950- **CLC 142**
See also CA 129; CAAS 24; CANR 90; CP
4, 5, 6, 7; DLB 169

Bernstein, Ingrid
See Kirsch, Sarah

Beroul fl. c. 12th cent. - **CMLC 75**

Berriault, Gina 1926-1999 **CLC 54, 109;
SSC 30**
See also CA 116; 129; 185; CANR 66; DLB
130; SSFS 7,11

Berrigan, Daniel 1921- **CLC 4**
See also CA 33-36R, 187; CAAE 187;
CAAS 1; CANR 11, 43, 78; CP 1, 2, 3, 4,
5, 6, 7; DLB 5

Berrigan, Edmund Joseph Michael, Jr.
1934-1983
See Berrigan, Ted
See also CA 61-64; 110; CANR 14, 102

Berrigan, Ted **CLC 37**
See Berrigan, Edmund Joseph Michael, Jr.
See also CP 1, 2, 3; DLB 5, 169; WP

Berry, Charles Edward Anderson 1931-
See Berry, Chuck
See also CA 115

Berry, Chuck **CLC 17**
See Berry, Charles Edward Anderson

Berry, Jonas
See Ashbery, John (Lawrence)
See also GLL 1

Berry, Wendell (Erdman) 1934- ... **CLC 4, 6,
8, 27, 46; PC 28**
See also AITN 1; AMWS 10; ANW; CA
73-76; CANR 50, 73, 101, 132; CP 1, 2,
3, 4, 5, 6, 7; CSW; DAM POET; DLB 5,
6, 234, 275; MTCW 2; MTFW 2005;
TCLE 1:1

Berryman, John 1914-1972 ... **CLC 1, 2, 3, 4,
6, 8, 10, 13, 25, 62; PC 64**
See also AMW; CA 13-16; 33-36R; CABS
2; CANR 35; CAP 1; CDALB 1941-1968;
CP 1; DAM POET; DLB 48; EWL 3;
MAL 5; MTCW 1, 2; MTFW 2005; PAB;
RGAL 4; WP

Bertolucci, Bernardo 1940- **CLC 16, 157**
See also CA 106; CANR 125

Berton, Pierre (Francis de Marigny)
1920-2004 **CLC 104**
See also CA 1-4R; 233; CANR 2, 56, 144;
CPW; DLB 68; SATA 99; SATA-Obit 158

Bertrand, Aloysius 1807-1841 **NCLC 31**
See Bertrand, Louis oAloysiusc

Bertrand, Louis oAloysiusc
See Bertrand, Aloysius
See also DLB 217

Bertran de Born c. 1140-1215 **CMLC 5**

Besant, Annie (Wood) 1847-1933 **TCLC 9**
See also CA 105; 185

Bessie, Alvah 1904-1985 **CLC 23**
See also CA 5-8R; 116; CANR 2, 80; DLB
26

Bestuzhev, Aleksandr Aleksandrovich
1797-1837 **NCLC 131**
See also DLB 198

Bethlen, T. D.
See Silverberg, Robert

Beti, Mongo **BLC 1; CLC 27**
See Biyidi, Alexandre
See also AFW; CANR 79; DAM MULT;
EWL 3; WLIT 2

Betjeman, John 1906-1984 **CLC 2, 6, 10,
34, 43**
See also BRW 7; CA 9-12R; 112; CANR
33, 56; CDBLB 1945-1960; CP 1, 2, 3;
DA3; DAB; DAM MST, POET; DLB 20;
DLBY 1984; EWL 3; MTCW 1, 2

Bettelheim, Bruno 1903-1990 **CLC 79;
TCLC 143**
See also CA 81-84; 131; CANR 23, 61;
DA3; MTCW 1, 2; RGHL

Betti, Ugo 1892-1953 **TCLC 5**
See also CA 104; 155; EWL 3; RGWL 2, 3

Betts, Doris (Waugh) 1932- **CLC 3, 6, 28;
SSC 45**
See also CA 13-16R; CANR 9, 66, 77; CN
6, 7; CSW; DLB 218; DLBY 1982; INT
CANR-9; RGAL 4

Bevan, Alistair
See Roberts, Keith (John Kingston)

Bey, Pilaff
See Douglas, (George) Norman

Bialik, Chaim Nachman
1873-1934 **TCLC 25**
See Bialik, Hayyim Nahman
See also CA 170; EWL 3

Bialik, Hayyim Nahman
See Bialik, Chaim Nachman
See also WLIT 6

Bickerstaff, Isaac
See Swift, Jonathan

Bidart, Frank 1939- **CLC 33**
See also AMWS 15; CA 140; CANR 106;
CP 5, 6, 7

Bienek, Horst 1930- **CLC 7, 11**
See also CA 73-76; DLB 75

Bierce, Ambrose (Gwinett)
1842-1914(?) **SSC 9, 72; TCLC 1, 7,
44; WLC 1**
See also AAYA 55; AMW; BYA 11; CA
104; 139; CANR 78; CDALB 1865-1917;
DA; DA3; DAC; DAM MST; DLB 11,
12, 23, 71, 74, 186; EWL 3; EXPS; HGG;
LAIT 2; MAL 5; RGAL 4; RGSF 2; SSFS
9; SUFW 1

Biggers, Earl Derr 1884-1933 **TCLC 65**
See also CA 108; 153; DLB 306

Billiken, Bud
See Motley, Willard (Francis)

Billings, Josh
See Shaw, Henry Wheeler

Billington, (Lady) Rachel (Mary)
1942- **CLC 43**
See also AITN 2; CA 33-36R; CANR 44;
CN 4, 5, 6, 7

Binchy, Maeve 1940- **CLC 153**
See also BEST 90:1; BPFB 1; CA 127; 134;
CANR 50, 96, 134; CN 5, 6, 7; CPW;
DA3; DAM POP; DLB 319; INT CA-134;
MTCW 2; MTFW 2005; RHW

Binyon, T(imothy) J(ohn)
1936-2004 **CLC 34**
See also CA 111; 232; CANR 28, 140

Bion 335B.C.-245B.C. **CMLC 39**

Bioy Casares, Adolfo 1914-1999 ... **CLC 4, 8,
13, 88; HLC 1; SSC 17**
See Casares, Adolfo Bioy; Miranda, Javier;
Sacastru, Martin
See also CA 29-32R; 177; CANR 19, 43,
66; CWW 2; DAM MULT; DLB 113;
EWL 3; HW 1, 2; LAW; MTCW 1, 2;
MTFW 2005

Birch, Allison **CLC 65**

Bird, Cordwainer
See Ellison, Harlan (Jay)
Bird, Robert Montgomery
1806-1854 **NCLC 1**
See also DLB 202; RGAL 4
Birkerts, Sven 1951- **CLC 116**
See also CA 128; 133, 176; CAAE 176;
CAAS 29; CANR 151; INT CA-133
Birney, (Alfred) Earle 1904-1995 .. **CLC 1, 4,**
6, 11; PC 52
See also CA 1-4R; CANR 5, 20; CN 1, 2,
3, 4; CP 1, 2, 3, 4, 5, 6; DAC; DAM MST,
POET; DLB 88; MTCW 1; PFS 8; RGEL
2
Biruni, al 973-1048(?) **CMLC 28**
Bishop, Elizabeth 1911-1979 **CLC 1, 4, 9,**
13, 15, 32; PC 3, 34; TCLC 121
See also AMWR 2; AMWS 1; CA 5-8R;
89-92; CABS 2; CANR 26, 61, 108;
CDALB 1968-1988; CP 1, 2, 3; DA;
DA3; DAC; DAM MST, POET; DLB 5,
169; EWL 3; GLL 2; MAL 5; MAWW;
MTCW 1, 2; PAB; PFS 6, 12; RGAL 4;
SATA-Obit 24; TUS; WP
Bishop, John 1935- **CLC 10**
See also CA 105
Bishop, John Peale 1892-1944 **TCLC 103**
See also CA 107; 155; DLB 4, 9, 45; MAL
5; RGAL 4
Bissett, Bill 1939- **CLC 18; PC 14**
See also CA 69-72; CAAS 19; CANR 15;
CCA 1; CP 1, 2, 3, 4, 5, 6, 7; DLB 53;
MTCW 1
Bissoondath, Neil (Devindra)
1955- .. **CLC 120**
See also CA 136; CANR 123; CN 6, 7;
DAC
Bitov, Andrei (Georgievich) 1937- ... **CLC 57**
See also CA 142; DLB 302
Biyidi, Alexandre 1932-
See Beti, Mongo
See also BW 1, 3; CA 114; 124; CANR 81;
DA3; MTCW 1, 2
Bjarme, Brynjolf
See Ibsen, Henrik (Johan)
Bjoernson, Bjoernstjerne (Martinius)
1832-1910 **TCLC 7, 37**
See also CA 104
Black, Benjamin
See Banville, John
Black, Robert
See Holdstock, Robert P.
Blackburn, Paul 1926-1971 **CLC 9, 43**
See also BG 1:2; CA 81-84; 33-36R; CANR
34; CP 1; DLB 16; DLBY 1981
Black Elk 1863-1950 **NNAL; TCLC 33**
See also CA 144; DAM MULT; MTCW 2;
MTFW 2005; WP
Black Hawk 1767-1838 **NNAL**
Black Hobart
See Sanders, (James) Ed(ward)
Blacklin, Malcolm
See Chambers, Aidan
Blackmore, R(ichard) D(oddridge)
1825-1900 **TCLC 27**
See also CA 120; DLB 18; RGEL 2
Blackmur, R(ichard) P(almer)
1904-1965 **CLC 2, 24**
See also AMWS 2; CA 11-12; 25-28R;
CANR 71; CAP 1; DLB 63; EWL 3;
MAL 5
Black Tarantula
See Acker, Kathy
Blackwood, Algernon (Henry)
1869-1951 **TCLC 5**
See also CA 105; 150; DLB 153, 156, 178;
HGG; SUFW 1

Blackwood, Caroline (Maureen)
1931-1996 **CLC 6, 9, 100**
See also BRWS 9; CA 85-88; 151; CANR
32, 61, 65; CN 3, 4, 5, 6; DLB 14, 207;
HGG; MTCW 1
Blade, Alexander
See Hamilton, Edmond; Silverberg, Robert
Blaga, Lucian 1895-1961 **CLC 75**
See also CA 157; DLB 220; EWL 3
Blair, Eric (Arthur) 1903-1950 **TCLC 123**
See Orwell, George
See also CA 104; 132; DA; DA3; DAB;
DAC; DAM MST, NOV; MTCW 1, 2;
MTFW 2005; SATA 29
Blair, Hugh 1718-1800 **NCLC 75**
Blais, Marie-Claire 1939- **CLC 2, 4, 6, 13,**
22
See also CA 21-24R; CAAS 4; CANR 38,
75, 93; CWW 2; DAC; DAM MST; DLB
53; EWL 3; FW; MTCW 1, 2; MTFW
2005; TWA
Blaise, Clark 1940- **CLC 29**
See also AITN 2; CA 53-56, 231; CAAE
231; CAAS 3; CANR 5, 66, 106; CN 4,
5, 6, 7; DLB 53; RGSF 2
Blake, Fairley
See De Voto, Bernard (Augustine)
Blake, Nicholas
See Day Lewis, C(ecil)
See also DLB 77; MSW
Blake, Sterling
See Benford, Gregory (Albert)
Blake, William 1757-1827 . **NCLC 13, 37, 57,**
127; PC 12, 63; WLC 1
See also AAYA 47; BRW 3; BRWR 1; CD-
BLB 1789-1832; CLR 52; DA; DA3;
DAB; DAC; DAM MST, POET; DLB 93,
163; EXPP; LATS 1:1; LMFS 1; MAI-
CYA 1, 2; PAB; PFS 2, 12, 24; SATA 30;
TEA; WCH; WLIT 3; WP
Blanchot, Maurice 1907-2003 **CLC 135**
See also CA 117; 144; 213; CANR 138;
DLB 72, 296; EWL 3
Blasco Ibanez, Vicente 1867-1928 . **TCLC 12**
See Ibanez, Vicente Blasco
See also BPFB 1; CA 110; 131; CANR 81;
DA3; DAM NOV; EW 8; EWL 3; HW 1,
2; MTCW 1
Blatty, William Peter 1928- **CLC 2**
See also CA 5-8R; CANR 9, 124; DAM
POP; HGG
Bleeck, Oliver
See Thomas, Ross (Elmore)
Blessing, Lee (Knowlton) 1949- **CLC 54**
See also CA 236; CAD; CD 5, 6; DFS 23
Blight, Rose
See Greer, Germaine
Blish, James (Benjamin) 1921-1975 . **CLC 14**
See also BPFB 1; CA 1-4R; 57-60; CANR
3; CN 2; DLB 8; MTCW 1; SATA 66;
SCFW 1, 2; SFW 4
Bliss, Frederick
See Card, Orson Scott
Bliss, Reginald
See Wells, H(erbert) G(eorge)
Blixen, Karen (Christentze Dinesen)
1885-1962
See Dinesen, Isak
See also CA 25-28; CANR 22, 50; CAP 2;
DA3; DLB 214; LMFS 1; MTCW 1, 2;
SATA 44; SSFS 20
Bloch, Robert (Albert) 1917-1994 **CLC 33**
See also AAYA 29; CA 5-8R, 179; 146;
CAAE 179; CAAS 20; CANR 5, 78;
DA3; DLB 44; HGG; INT CANR-5;
MTCW 2; SATA 12; SATA-Obit 82; SFW
4; SUFW 1, 2

Blok, Alexander (Alexandrovich)
1880-1921 **PC 21; TCLC 5**
See also CA 104; 183; DLB 295; EW 9;
EWL 3; LMFS 2; RGWL 2, 3
Blom, Jan
See Breytenbach, Breyten
Bloom, Harold 1930- **CLC 24, 103, 221**
See also CA 13-16R; CANR 39, 75, 92,
133; DLB 67; EWL 3; MTCW 2; MTFW
2005; RGAL 4
Bloomfield, Aurelius
See Bourne, Randolph S(illiman)
Bloomfield, Robert 1766-1823 **NCLC 145**
See also DLB 93
Blount, Roy (Alton), Jr. 1941- **CLC 38**
See also CA 53-56; CANR 10, 28, 61, 125;
CSW; INT CANR-28; MTCW 1, 2;
MTFW 2005
Blowsnake, Sam 1875-(?) **NNAL**
Bloy, Leon 1846-1917 **TCLC 22**
See also CA 121; 183; DLB 123; GFL 1789
to the Present
Blue Cloud, Peter (Aroniawenrate)
1933- ... **NNAL**
See also CA 117; CANR 40; DAM MULT
Bluggage, Oranthy
See Alcott, Louisa May
Blume, Judy (Sussman) 1938- **CLC 12, 30**
See also AAYA 3, 26; BYA 1, 8, 12; CA 29-
32R; CANR 13, 37, 66, 124; CLR 2, 15,
69; CPW; DA3; DAM NOV, POP; DLB
52; JRDA; MAICYA 1, 2; MAICYAS 1;
MTCW 1, 2; MTFW 2005; SATA 2, 31,
79, 142; WYA; YAW
Blunden, Edmund (Charles)
1896-1974 **CLC 2, 56; PC 66**
See also BRW 6; BRWS 11; CA 17-18; 45-
48; CANR 54; CAP 2; CP 1, 2; DLB 20,
100, 155; MTCW 1; PAB
Bly, Robert (Elwood) 1926- **CLC 1, 2, 5,**
10, 15, 38, 128; PC 39
See also AMWS 4; CA 5-8R; CANR 41,
73, 125; CP 1, 2, 3, 4, 5, 6, 7; DA3; DAM
POET; DLB 5; EWL 3; MAL 5; MTCW
1, 2; MTFW 2005; PFS 6, 17; RGAL 4
Boas, Franz 1858-1942 **TCLC 56**
See also CA 115; 181
Bobette
See Simenon, Georges (Jacques Christian)
Boccaccio, Giovanni 1313-1375 ... **CMLC 13,**
57; SSC 10, 87
See also EW 2; RGSF 2; RGWL 2, 3; TWA;
WLIT 7
Bochco, Steven 1943- **CLC 35**
See also AAYA 11, 71; CA 124; 138
Bode, Sigmund
See O'Doherty, Brian
Bodel, Jean 1167(?)-1210 **CMLC 28**
Bodenheim, Maxwell 1892-1954 **TCLC 44**
See also CA 110; 187; DLB 9, 45; MAL 5;
RGAL 4
Bodenheimer, Maxwell
See Bodenheim, Maxwell
Bodker, Cecil 1927-
See Bodker, Cecil
Bodker, Cecil 1927- **CLC 21**
See also CA 73-76; CANR 13, 44, 111;
CLR 23; MAICYA 1, 2; SATA 14, 133
Boell, Heinrich (Theodor)
1917-1985 **CLC 2, 3, 6, 9, 11, 15, 27,**
32, 72; SSC 23; WLC 1
See Boll, Heinrich (Theodor)
See also CA 21-24R; 116; CANR 24; DA;
DA3; DAB; DAC; DAM MST, NOV;
DLB 69; DLBY 1985; MTCW 1, 2;
MTFW 2005; SSFS 20; TWA
Boerne, Alfred
See Doeblin, Alfred

Boethius c. 480-c. 524 **CMLC 15**
See also DLB 115; RGWL 2, 3; WLIT 8
Boff, Leonardo (Genezio Darci)
1938- **CLC 70; HLC 1**
See also CA 150; DAM MULT; HW 2
Bogan, Louise 1897-1970 **CLC 4, 39, 46, 93; PC 12**
See also AMWS 3; CA 73-76; 25-28R; CANR 33, 82; CP 1; DAM POET; DLB 45, 169; EWL 3; MAL 5; MAWW; MTCW 1, 2; PFS 21; RGAL 4
Bogarde, Dirk
See Van Den Bogarde, Derek Jules Gaspard Ulric Niven
See also DLB 14
Bogosian, Eric 1953- **CLC 45, 141**
See also CA 138; CAD; CANR 102, 148; CD 5, 6
Bograd, Larry 1953- **CLC 35**
See also CA 93-96; CANR 57; SAAS 21; SATA 33, 89; WYA
Boiardo, Matteo Maria 1441-1494 **LC 6**
Boileau-Despreaux, Nicolas 1636-1711 . **LC 3**
See also DLB 268; EW 3; GFL Beginnings to 1789; RGWL 2, 3
Boissard, Maurice
See Leautaud, Paul
Bojer, Johan 1872-1959 **TCLC 64**
See also CA 189; EWL 3
Bok, Edward W(illiam)
1863-1930 **TCLC 101**
See also CA 217; DLB 91; DLBD 16
Boker, George Henry 1823-1890 . **NCLC 125**
See also RGAL 4
Boland, Eavan (Aisling) 1944- .. **CLC 40, 67, 113; PC 58**
See also BRWS 5; CA 143, 207; CAAE 207; CANR 61; CP 1, 6, 7; CWP; DAM POET; DLB 40; FW; MTCW 2; MTFW 2005; PFS 12, 22
Boll, Heinrich (Theodor)
See Boell, Heinrich (Theodor)
See also BPFB 1; CDWLB 2; EW 13; EWL 3; RGHL; RGSF 2; RGWL 2, 3
Bolt, Lee
See Faust, Frederick (Schiller)
Bolt, Robert (Oxton) 1924-1995 **CLC 14; TCLC 175**
See also CA 17-20R; 147; CANR 35, 67; CBD; DAM DRAM; DFS 2; DLB 13, 233; EWL 3; LAIT 1; MTCW 1
Bombal, Maria Luisa 1910-1980 **HLCS 1; SSC 37**
See also CA 127; CANR 72; EWL 3; HW 1; LAW; RGSF 2
Bombet, Louis-Alexandre-Cesar
See Stendhal
Bomkauf
See Kaufman, Bob (Garnell)
Bonaventura **NCLC 35**
See also DLB 90
Bonaventure 1217(?)-1274 **CMLC 79**
See also DLB 115; LMFS 1
Bond, Edward 1934- **CLC 4, 6, 13, 23**
See also AAYA 50; BRWS 1; CA 25-28R; CANR 38, 67, 106; CBD; CD 5, 6; DAM DRAM; DFS 3, 8; DLB 13, 310; EWL 3; MTCW 1
Bonham, Frank 1914-1989 **CLC 12**
See also AAYA 1, 70; BYA 1, 3; CA 9-12R; CANR 4, 36; JRDA; MAICYA 1, 2; SAAS 3; SATA 1, 49; SATA-Obit 62; TCWW 1, 2; YAW
Bonnefoy, Yves 1923- . **CLC 9, 15, 58; PC 58**
See also CA 85-88; CANR 33, 75, 97, 136; CWW 2; DAM MST, POET; DLB 258; EWL 3; GFL 1789 to the Present; MTCW 1, 2; MTFW 2005

Bonner, Marita . **HR 1:2; PC 72; TCLC 179**
See Occomy, Marita (Odette) Bonner
Bonnin, Gertrude 1876-1938 **NNAL**
See Zitkala-Sa
See also CA 150; DAM MULT
Bontemps, Arna(ud Wendell)
1902-1973 .. **BLC 1; CLC 1, 18; HR 1:2**
See also BW 1; CA 1-4R; 41-44R; CANR 4, 35; CLR 6; CP 1; CWRI 5; DA3; DAM MULT, NOV, POET; DLB 48, 51; JRDA; MAICYA 1, 2; MAL 5; MTCW 1, 2; SATA 2, 44; SATA-Obit 24; WCH; WP
Boot, William
See Stoppard, Tom
Booth, Martin 1944-2004 **CLC 13**
See also CA 93-96; 188; 223; CAAE 188; CAAS 2; CANR 92; CP 1, 2, 3, 4
Booth, Philip 1925- **CLC 23**
See also CA 5-8R; CANR 5, 88; CP 1, 2, 3, 4, 5, 6, 7; DLBY 1982
Booth, Wayne C. 1921-2005 **CLC 24**
See also CA 1-4R; 244; CAAS 5; CANR 3, 43, 117; DLB 67
Booth, Wayne Clayson
See Booth, Wayne C.
Borchert, Wolfgang 1921-1947 **TCLC 5**
See also CA 104; 188; DLB 69, 124; EWL 3
Borel, Petrus 1809-1859 **NCLC 41**
See also DLB 119; GFL 1789 to the Present
Borges, Jorge Luis 1899-1986 ... **CLC 1, 2, 3, 4, 6, 8, 9, 10, 13, 19, 44, 48, 83; HLC 1; PC 22, 32; SSC 4, 41; TCLC 109; WLC 1**
See also AAYA 26; BPFB 1; CA 21-24R; CANR 19, 33, 75, 105, 133; CDWLB 3; DA; DA3; DAB; DAC; DAM MST, MULT; DLB 113, 283; DLBY 1986; DNFS 1, 2; EWL 3; HW 1, 2; LAW; LMFS 2; MSW; MTCW 1, 2; MTFW 2005; RGHL; RGSF 2; RGWL 2, 3; SFW 4; SSFS 17; TWA; WLIT 1
Borowski, Tadeusz 1922-1951 **SSC 48; TCLC 9**
See also CA 106; 154; CDWLB 4; DLB 215; EWL 3; RGHL; RGSF 2; RGWL 3; SSFS 13
Borrow, George (Henry)
1803-1881 **NCLC 9**
See also DLB 21, 55, 166
Bosch (Gavino), Juan 1909-2001 **HLCS 1**
See also CA 151; 204; DAM MST, MULT; DLB 145; HW 1, 2
Bosman, Herman Charles
1905-1951 **TCLC 49**
See Malan, Herman
See also CA 160; DLB 225; RGSF 2
Bosschere, Jean de 1878(?)-1953 ... **TCLC 19**
See also CA 115; 186
Boswell, James 1740-1795 ... **LC 4, 50; WLC 1**
See also BRW 3; CDBLB 1660-1789; DA; DAB; DAC; DAM MST; DLB 104, 142; TEA; WLIT 3
Bottomley, Gordon 1874-1948 **TCLC 107**
See also CA 120; 192; DLB 10
Bottoms, David 1949- **CLC 53**
See also CA 105; CANR 22; CSW; DLB 120; DLBY 1983
Boucicault, Dion 1820-1890 **NCLC 41**
Boucolon, Maryse
See Conde, Maryse
Bourdieu, Pierre 1930-2002 **CLC 198**
See also CA 130; 204
Bourget, Paul (Charles Joseph)
1852-1935 **TCLC 12**
See also CA 107; 196; DLB 123; GFL 1789 to the Present

Bourjaily, Vance (Nye) 1922- **CLC 8, 62**
See also CA 1-4R; CAAS 1; CANR 2, 72; CN 1, 2, 3, 4, 5, 6, 7; DLB 2, 143; MAL 5
Bourne, Randolph S(illiman)
1886-1918 **TCLC 16**
See also AMW; CA 117; 155; DLB 63; MAL 5
Bova, Ben(jamin William) 1932- **CLC 45**
See also AAYA 16; CA 5-8R; CAAS 18; CANR 11, 56, 94, 111; CLR 3, 96; DLBY 1981; INT CANR-11; MAICYA 1, 2; MTCW 1; SATA 6, 68, 133; SFW 4
Bowen, Elizabeth (Dorothea Cole)
1899-1973 . **CLC 1, 3, 6, 11, 15, 22, 118; SSC 3, 28, 66; TCLC 148**
See also BRWS 2; CA 17-18; 41-44R; CANR 35, 105; CAP 2; CDBLB 1945-1960; CN 1; DA3; DAM NOV; DLB 15, 162; EWL 3; EXPS; FW; HGG; MTCW 1, 2; MTFW 2005; NFS 13; RGSF 2; SSFS 5; SUFW 1; TEA; WLIT 4
Bowering, George 1935- **CLC 15, 47**
See also CA 21-24R; CAAS 16; CANR 10; CN 7; CP 1, 2, 3, 4, 5, 6, 7; DLB 53
Bowering, Marilyn R(uthe) 1949- **CLC 32**
See also CA 101; CANR 49; CP 4, 5, 6, 7; CWP
Bowers, Edgar 1924-2000 **CLC 9**
See also CA 5-8R; 188; CANR 24; CP 1, 2, 3, 4, 5, 6, 7; CSW; DLB 5
Bowers, Mrs. J. Milton 1842-1914
See Bierce, Ambrose (Gwinett)
Bowie, David **CLC 17**
See Jones, David Robert
Bowles, Jane (Sydney) 1917-1973 **CLC 3, 68**
See Bowles, Jane Auer
See also CA 19-20; 41-44R; CAP 2; CN 1; MAL 5
Bowles, Jane Auer
See Bowles, Jane (Sydney)
See also EWL 3
Bowles, Paul (Frederick) 1910-1999 . **CLC 1, 2, 19, 53; SSC 3**
See also AMWS 4; CA 1-4R; 186; CAAS 1; CANR 1, 19, 50, 75; CN 1, 2, 3, 4, 5, 6; DA3; DLB 5, 6, 218; EWL 3; MAL 5; MTCW 1, 2; MTFW 2005; RGAL 4; SSFS 17
Bowles, William Lisle 1762-1850 . **NCLC 103**
See also DLB 93
Box, Edgar
See Vidal, Gore
See also GLL 1
Boyd, James 1888-1944 **TCLC 115**
See also CA 186; DLB 9; DLBD 16; RGAL 4; RHW
Boyd, Nancy
See Millay, Edna St. Vincent
See also GLL 1
Boyd, Thomas (Alexander)
1898-1935 **TCLC 111**
See also CA 111; 183; DLB 9; DLBD 16, 316
Boyd, William (Andrew Murray)
1952- **CLC 28, 53, 70**
See also CA 114; 120; CANR 51, 71, 131; CN 4, 5, 6, 7; DLB 231
Boyesen, Hjalmar Hjorth
1848-1895 **NCLC 135**
See also DLB 12, 71; DLBD 13; RGAL 4
Boyle, Kay 1902-1992 **CLC 1, 5, 19, 58, 121; SSC 5**
See also CA 13-16R; 140; CAAS 1; CANR 29, 61, 110; CN 1, 2, 3, 4, 5; CP 1, 2, 3, 4, 5; DLB 4, 9, 48, 86; DLBY 1993; EWL 3; MAL 5; MTCW 1, 2; MTFW 2005; RGAL 4; RGSF 2; SSFS 10, 13, 14

Boyle, Mark
 See Kienzle, William X(avier)
Boyle, Patrick 1905-1982 **CLC 19**
 See also CA 127
Boyle, T. C.
 See Boyle, T(homas) Coraghessan
 See also AMWS 8
Boyle, T(homas) Coraghessan
 1948- **CLC 36, 55, 90; SSC 16**
 See Boyle, T. C.
 See also AAYA 47; BEST 90:4; BPFB 1;
 CA 120; CANR 44, 76, 89, 132; CN 6, 7;
 CPW; DA3; DAM POP; DLB 218, 278;
 DLBY 1986; EWL 3; MAL 5; MTCW 2;
 MTFW 2005; SSFS 13, 19
Boz
 See Dickens, Charles (John Huffam)
Brackenridge, Hugh Henry
 1748-1816 **NCLC 7**
 See also DLB 11, 37; RGAL 4
Bradbury, Edward P.
 See Moorcock, Michael
 See also MTCW 2
Bradbury, Malcolm (Stanley)
 1932-2000 **CLC 32, 61**
 See also CA 1-4R; CANR 1, 33, 91, 98,
 137; CN 1, 2, 3, 4, 5, 6, 7; CP 1; DA3;
 DAM NOV; DLB 14, 207; EWL 3;
 MTCW 1, 2; MTFW 2005
Bradbury, Ray (Douglas) 1920- **CLC 1, 3,**
 10, 15, 42, 98; SSC 29, 53; WLC 1
 See also AAYA 15; AITN 1, 2; AMWS 4;
 BPFB 1; BYA 4, 5, 11; CA 1-4R; CANR
 2, 30, 75, 125; CDALB 1968-1988; CN
 1, 2, 3, 4, 5, 6, 7; CPW; DA; DA3; DAB;
 DAC; DAM MST, NOV, POP; DLB 2, 8;
 EXPN; EXPS; HGG; LAIT 3, 5; LATS
 1:2; LMFS 2; MAL 5; MTCW 1, 2;
 MTFW 2005; NFS 1, 22; RGAL 4; RGSF
 2; SATA 11, 64, 123; SCFW 1, 2; SFW 4;
 SSFS 1, 20; SUFW 1, 2; TUS; YAW
Braddon, Mary Elizabeth
 1837-1915 **TCLC 111**
 See also BRWS 8; CA 108; 179; CMW 4;
 DLB 18, 70, 156; HGG
Bradfield, Scott (Michael) 1955- **SSC 65**
 See also CA 147; CANR 90; HGG; SUFW
 2
Bradford, Gamaliel 1863-1932 **TCLC 36**
 See also CA 160; DLB 17
Bradford, William 1590-1657 **LC 64**
 See also DLB 24, 30; RGAL 4
Bradley, David (Henry), Jr. 1950- **BLC 1;**
 CLC 23, 118
 See also BW 1, 3; CA 104; CANR 26, 81;
 CN 4, 5, 6, 7; DAM MULT; DLB 33
Bradley, John Ed(mund, Jr.) 1958- . **CLC 55**
 See also CA 139; CANR 99; CN 6, 7; CSW
Bradley, Marion Zimmer
 1930-1999 **CLC 30**
 See Chapman, Lee; Dexter, John; Gardner,
 Miriam; Ives, Morgan; Rivers, Elfrida
 See also AAYA 40; BPFB 1; CA 57-60; 185;
 CAAS 10; CANR 7, 31, 51, 75, 107;
 CPW; DA3; DAM POP; DLB 8; FANT;
 FW; MTCW 1, 2; MTFW 2005; SATA 90,
 139; SATA-Obit 116; SFW 4; SUFW 2;
 YAW
Bradshaw, John 1933- **CLC 70**
 See also CA 138; CANR 61
Bradstreet, Anne 1612(?)-1672 **LC 4, 30;**
 PC 10
 See also AMWS 1; CDALB 1640-1865;
 DA; DA3; DAC; DAM MST, POET; DLB
 24; EXPP; FW; PFS 6; RGAL 4; TUS;
 WP
Brady, Joan 1939- **CLC 86**
 See also CA 141

Bragg, Melvyn 1939- **CLC 10**
 See also BEST 89:3; CA 57-60; CANR 10,
 48, 89; CN 1, 2, 3, 4, 5, 6, 7; DLB 14,
 271; RHW
Brahe, Tycho 1546-1601 **LC 45**
 See also DLB 300
Braine, John (Gerard) 1922-1986 . **CLC 1, 3,**
 41
 See also CA 1-4R; 120; CANR 1, 33; CD-
 BLB 1945-1960; CN 1, 2, 3, 4; DLB 15;
 DLBY 1986; EWL 3; MTCW 1
Braithwaite, William Stanley (Beaumont)
 1878-1962 **BLC 1; HR 1:2; PC 52**
 See also BW 1; CA 125; DAM MULT; DLB
 50, 54; MAL 5
Bramah, Ernest 1868-1942 **TCLC 72**
 See also CA 156; CMW 4; DLB 70; FANT
Brammer, Billy Lee
 See Brammer, William
Brammer, William 1929-1978 **CLC 31**
 See also CA 235; 77-80
Brancati, Vitaliano 1907-1954 **TCLC 12**
 See also CA 109; DLB 264; EWL 3
Brancato, Robin F(idler) 1936- **CLC 35**
 See also AAYA 9, 68; BYA 6; CA 69-72;
 CANR 11, 45; CLR 32; JRDA; MAICYA
 2; MAICYAS 1; SAAS 9; SATA 97;
 WYA; YAW
Brand, Dionne 1953- **CLC 192**
 See also BW 2; CA 143; CANR 143; CWP
Brand, Max
 See Faust, Frederick (Schiller)
 See also BPFB 1; TCWW 1, 2
Brand, Millen 1906-1980 **CLC 7**
 See also CA 21-24R; 97-100; CANR 72
Branden, Barbara **CLC 44**
 See also CA 148
Brandes, Georg (Morris Cohen)
 1842-1927 **TCLC 10**
 See also CA 105; 189; DLB 300
Brandys, Kazimierz 1916-2000 **CLC 62**
 See also CA 239; EWL 3
Branley, Franklyn M(ansfield)
 1915-2002 **CLC 21**
 See also CA 33-36R; 207; CANR 14, 39;
 CLR 13; MAICYA 1, 2; SAAS 16; SATA
 4, 68, 136
Brant, Beth (E.) 1941- **NNAL**
 See also CA 144; FW
Brant, Sebastian 1457-1521 **LC 112**
 See also DLB 179; RGWL 2, 3
Brathwaite, Edward Kamau
 1930- **BLCS; CLC 11; PC 56**
 See also BW 2, 3; CA 25-28R; CANR 11,
 26, 47, 107; CDWLB 3; CP 1, 2, 3, 4, 5,
 6, 7; DAM POET; DLB 125; EWL 3
Brathwaite, Kamau
 See Brathwaite, Edward Kamau
Brautigan, Richard (Gary)
 1935-1984 **CLC 1, 3, 5, 9, 12, 34, 42;**
 TCLC 133
 See also BPFB 1; CA 53-56; 113; CANR
 34; CN 1, 2, 3; DA3; DAM
 NOV; DLB 2, 5, 206; DLBY 1980, 1984;
 FANT; MAL 5; MTCW 1; RGAL 4;
 SATA 56
Brave Bird, Mary **NNAL**
 See Crow Dog, Mary (Ellen)
Braverman, Kate 1950- **CLC 67**
 See also CA 89-92; CANR 141
Brecht, (Eugen) Bertolt (Friedrich)
 1898-1956 **DC 3; TCLC 1, 6, 13, 35,**
 169; WLC 1
 See also CA 104; 133; CANR 62; CDWLB
 2; DA; DA3; DAB; DAC; DAM DRAM,
 MST; DFS 4, 5, 9; DLB 56, 124; EW 11;
 EWL 3; IDTP; MTCW 1, 2; MTFW 2005;
 RGHL; RGWL 2, 3; TWA

Brecht, Eugen Berthold Friedrich
 See Brecht, (Eugen) Bertolt (Friedrich)
Bremer, Fredrika 1801-1865 **NCLC 11**
 See also DLB 254
Brennan, Christopher John
 1870-1932 **TCLC 17**
 See also CA 117; 188; DLB 230; EWL 3
Brennan, Maeve 1917-1993 ... **CLC 5; TCLC**
 124
 See also CA 81-84; CANR 72, 100
Brenner, Jozef 1887-1919
 See Csath, Geza
 See also CA 240
Brent, Linda
 See Jacobs, Harriet A(nn)
Brentano, Clemens (Maria)
 1778-1842 **NCLC 1**
 See also DLB 90; RGWL 2, 3
Brent of Bin Bin
 See Franklin, (Stella Maria Sarah) Miles
 (Lampe)
Brenton, Howard 1942- **CLC 31**
 See also CA 69-72; CANR 33, 67; CBD;
 CD 5, 6; DLB 13; MTCW 1
Breslin, James 1930-
 See Breslin, Jimmy
 See also CA 73-76; CANR 31, 75, 139;
 DAM NOV; MTCW 1, 2; MTFW 2005
Breslin, Jimmy **CLC 4, 43**
 See Breslin, James
 See also AITN 1; DLB 185; MTCW 2
Bresson, Robert 1901(?)-1999 **CLC 16**
 See also CA 110; 187; CANR 49
Breton, Andre 1896-1966 .. **CLC 2, 9, 15, 54;**
 PC 15
 See also CA 19-20; 25-28R; CANR 40, 60;
 CAP 2; DLB 65, 258; EW 11; EWL 3;
 GFL 1789 to the Present; LMFS 2;
 MTCW 1, 2; MTFW 2005; RGWL 2, 3;
 TWA; WP
Breytenbach, Breyten 1939(?)- .. **CLC 23, 37,**
 126
 See also CA 113; 129; CANR 61, 122;
 CWW 2; DAM POET; DLB 225; EWL 3
Bridgers, Sue Ellen 1942- **CLC 26**
 See also AAYA 8, 49; BYA 7, 8; CA 65-68;
 CANR 11, 36; CLR 18; DLB 52; JRDA;
 MAICYA 1, 2; SAAS 1; SATA 22, 90;
 SATA-Essay 109; WYA; YAW
Bridges, Robert (Seymour)
 1844-1930 **PC 28; TCLC 1**
 See also BRW 6; CA 104; 152; CDBLB
 1890-1914; DAM POET; DLB 19, 98
Bridie, James **TCLC 3**
 See Mavor, Osborne Henry
 See also DLB 10; EWL 3
Brin, David 1950- **CLC 34**
 See also AAYA 21; CA 102; CANR 24, 70,
 125, 127; INT CANR-24; SATA 65;
 SCFW 2; SFW 4
Brink, Andre (Philippus) 1935- . **CLC 18, 36,**
 106
 See also AFW; BRWS 6; CA 104; CANR
 39, 62, 109, 133; CN 4, 5, 6, 7; DLB 225;
 EWL 3; INT CA-103; LATS 1:2; MTCW
 1, 2; MTFW 2005; WLIT 2
Brinsmead, H. F(ay)
 See Brinsmead, H(esba) F(ay)
Brinsmead, H. F.
 See Brinsmead, H(esba) F(ay)
Brinsmead, H(esba) F(ay) 1922- **CLC 21**
 See also CA 21-24R; CANR 10; CLR 47;
 CWRI 5; MAICYA 1, 2; SAAS 5; SATA
 18, 78
Brittain, Vera (Mary) 1893(?)-1970 . **CLC 23**
 See also BRWS 10; CA 13-16; 25-28R;
 CANR 58; CAP 1; DLB 191; FW; MTCW
 1, 2

Broch, Hermann 1886-1951 **TCLC 20**
See also CA 117; 211; CDWLB 2; DLB 85, 124; EW 10; EWL 3; RGWL 2, 3

Brock, Rose
See Hansen, Joseph
See also GLL 1

Brod, Max 1884-1968 **TCLC 115**
See also CA 5-8R; 25-28R; CANR 7; DLB 81; EWL 3

Brodkey, Harold (Roy) 1930-1996 .. **CLC 56; TCLC 123**
See also CA 111; 151; CANR 71; CN 4, 5, 6; DLB 130

Brodsky, Iosif Alexandrovich 1940-1996
See Brodsky, Joseph
See also AAYA 71; AITN 1; CA 41-44R; 151; CANR 37, 106; DA3; DAM POET; MTCW 1, 2; MTFW 2005; RGWL 2, 3

Brodsky, Joseph . **CLC 4, 6, 13, 36, 100; PC 9**
See Brodsky, Iosif Alexandrovich
See also AMWS 8; CWW 2; DLB 285; EWL 3; MTCW 1

Brodsky, Michael 1948- **CLC 19**
See also CA 102; CANR 18, 41, 58, 147; DLB 244

Brodsky, Michael Mark
See Brodsky, Michael

Brodzki, Bella ed. **CLC 65**

Brome, Richard 1590(?)-1652 **LC 61**
See also BRWS 10; DLB 58

Bromell, Henry 1947- **CLC 5**
See also CA 53-56; CANR 9, 115, 116

Bromfield, Louis (Brucker) 1896-1956 **TCLC 11**
See also CA 107; 155; DLB 4, 9, 86; RGAL 4; RHW

Broner, E(sther) M(asserman) 1930- ... **CLC 19**
See also CA 17-20R; CANR 8, 25, 72; CN 4, 5, 6; DLB 28

Bronk, William (M.) 1918-1999 **CLC 10**
See also CA 89-92; 177; CANR 23; CP 3, 4, 5, 6, 7; DLB 165

Bronstein, Lev Davidovich
See Trotsky, Leon

Bronte, Anne
See Bronte, Anne

Bronte, Anne 1820-1849 **NCLC 4, 71, 102**
See also BRW 5; BRWR 1; DA3; DLB 21, 199; TEA

Bronte, (Patrick) Branwell 1817-1848 **NCLC 109**

Bronte, Charlotte
See Bronte, Charlotte

Bronte, Charlotte 1816-1855 **NCLC 3, 8, 33, 58, 105, 155; WLC 1**
See also AAYA 17; BRW 5; BRWC 2; BRWR 1; BYA 2; CDBLB 1832-1890; DA; DA3; DAB; DAC; DAM MST, NOV; DLB 21, 159, 199; EXPN; FL 1:2; GL 2; LAIT 2; NFS 4; TEA; WLIT 4

Bronte, Emily
See Bronte, Emily (Jane)

Bronte, Emily (Jane) 1818-1848 ... **NCLC 16, 35, 165; PC 8; WLC 1**
See also AAYA 17; BPFB 1; BRW 5; BRWC 1; BRWR 1; BYA 3; CDBLB 1832-1890; DA; DA3; DAB; DAC; DAM MST, NOV, POET; DLB 21, 32, 199; EXPN; FL 1:2; GL 2; LAIT 1; TEA; WLIT 3

Brontes
See Bronte, Anne; Bronte, Charlotte; Bronte, Emily (Jane)

Brooke, Frances 1724-1789 **LC 6, 48**
See also DLB 39, 99

Brooke, Henry 1703(?)-1783 **LC 1**
See also DLB 39

Brooke, Rupert (Chawner) 1887-1915 .. **PC 24; TCLC 2, 7; WLC 1**
See also BRWS 3; CA 104; 132; CANR 61; CDBLB 1914-1945; DA; DAB; DAC; DAM MST, POET; DLB 19, 216; EXPP; GLL 2; MTCW 1, 2; MTFW 2005; PFS 7; TEA

Brooke-Haven, P.
See Wodehouse, P(elham) G(renville)

Brooke-Rose, Christine 1926(?)- **CLC 40, 184**
See also BRWS 4; CA 13-16R; CANR 58, 118; CN 1, 2, 3, 4, 5, 6, 7; DLB 14, 231; EWL 3; SFW 4

Brookner, Anita 1928- .. **CLC 32, 34, 51, 136**
See also BRWS 4; CA 114; 120; CANR 37, 56, 87, 130; CN 4, 5, 6, 7; CPW; DA3; DAB; DAM POP; DLB 194, 326; DLBY 1987; EWL 3; MTCW 1, 2; MTFW 2005; NFS 23; TEA

Brooks, Cleanth 1906-1994 . **CLC 24, 86, 110**
See also AMWS 14; CA 17-20R; 145; CANR 33, 35; CSW; DLB 63; DLBY 1994; EWL 3; INT CANR-35; MAL 5; MTCW 1, 2; MTFW 2005

Brooks, George
See Baum, L(yman) Frank

Brooks, Gwendolyn (Elizabeth) 1917-2000 ... **BLC 1; CLC 1, 2, 4, 5, 15, 49, 125; PC 7; WLC 1**
See also AAYA 20; AFAW 1, 2; AITN 1; AMWS 3; BW 2, 3; CA 1-4R; 190; CANR 1, 27, 52, 75, 132; CDALB 1941-1968; CLR 27; CP 1, 2, 3, 4, 5, 6, 7; CWP; DA; DA3; DAC; DAM MST, MULT, POET; DLB 5, 76, 165; EWL 3; EXPP; FL 1.5; MAL 5; MAWW; MTCW 1, 2; MTFW 2005; PFS 1, 2, 4, 6; RGAL 4; SATA 6; SATA-Obit 123; TUS; WP

Brooks, Mel 1926-
See Kaminsky, Melvin
See also CA 65-68; CANR 16; DFS 21

Brooks, Peter (Preston) 1938- **CLC 34**
See also CA 45-48; CANR 1, 107

Brooks, Van Wyck 1886-1963 **CLC 29**
See also AMW; CA 1-4R; CANR 6; DLB 45, 63, 103; MAL 5; TUS

Brophy, Brigid (Antonia) 1929-1995 **CLC 6, 11, 29, 105**
See also CA 5-8R; 149; CAAS 4; CANR 25, 53; CBD; CN 1, 2, 3, 4, 5, 6; CWD; DA3; DLB 14, 271; EWL 3; MTCW 1, 2

Brosman, Catharine Savage 1934- **CLC 9**
See also CA 61-64; CANR 21, 46, 149

Brossard, Nicole 1943- **CLC 115, 169**
See also CA 122; CAAS 16; CANR 140; CCA 1; CWP; CWW 2; DLB 53; EWL 3; FW; GLL 2; RGWL 3

Brother Antoninus
See Everson, William (Oliver)

Brothers Grimm
See Grimm, Jacob Ludwig Karl; Grimm, Wilhelm Karl

The Brothers Quay
See Quay, Stephen; Quay, Timothy

Broughton, T(homas) Alan 1936- **CLC 19**
See also CA 45-48; CANR 2, 23, 48, 111

Broumas, Olga 1949- **CLC 10, 73**
See also CA 85-88; CANR 20, 69, 110; CP 5, 6, 7; CWP; GLL 2

Broun, Heywood 1888-1939 **TCLC 104**
See also DLB 29, 171

Brown, Alan 1950- **CLC 99**
See also CA 156

Brown, Charles Brockden 1771-1810 **NCLC 22, 74, 122**
See also AMWS 1; CDALB 1640-1865; DLB 37, 59, 73; FW; GL 2; HGG; LMFS 1; RGAL 4; TUS

Brown, Christy 1932-1981 **CLC 63**
See also BYA 13; CA 105; 104; CANR 72; DLB 14

Brown, Claude 1937-2002 ... **BLC 1; CLC 30**
See also AAYA 7; BW 1, 3; CA 73-76; 205; CANR 81; DAM MULT

Brown, Dan 1964- **CLC 209**
See also AAYA 55; CA 217; MTFW 2005

Brown, Dee 1908-2002 **CLC 18, 47**
See also AAYA 30; CA 13-16R; 212; CAAS 6; CANR 11, 45, 60, 150; CPW; CSW; DA3; DAM POP; DLBY 1980; LAIT 2; MTCW 1, 2; MTFW 2005; NCFS 5; SATA 5, 110; SATA-Obit 141; TCWW 1, 2

Brown, Dee Alexander
See Brown, Dee

Brown, George
See Wertmueller, Lina

Brown, George Douglas 1869-1902 **TCLC 28**
See Douglas, George
See also CA 162

Brown, George Mackay 1921-1996 ... **CLC 5, 48, 100**
See also BRWS 6; CA 21-24R; 151; CAAS 6; CANR 12, 37, 67; CN 1, 2, 3, 4, 5, 6; CP 1, 2, 3, 4, 5, 6; DLB 14, 27, 139, 271; MTCW 1; RGSF 2; SATA 35

Brown, (William) Larry 1951-2004 . **CLC 73**
See also CA 130; 134; 233; CANR 117, 145; CSW; DLB 234; INT CA-134

Brown, Moses
See Barrett, William (Christopher)

Brown, Rita Mae 1944- **CLC 18, 43, 79**
See also BPFB 1; CA 45-48; CANR 2, 11, 35, 62, 95, 138; CN 5, 6, 7; CPW; CSW; DA3; DAM NOV, POP; FW; INT CANR-11; MAL 5; MTCW 1, 2; MTFW 2005; NFS 9; RGAL 4; TUS

Brown, Roderick (Langmere) Haig-
See Haig-Brown, Roderick (Langmere)

Brown, Rosellen 1939- **CLC 32, 170**
See also CA 77-80; CAAS 10; CANR 14, 44, 98; CN 6, 7

Brown, Sterling Allen 1901-1989 **BLC 1; CLC 1, 23, 59; HR 1:2; PC 55**
See also AFAW 1, 2; BW 1, 3; CA 85-88; 127; CANR 26; CP 3, 4; DA3; DAM MULT, POET; DLB 48, 51, 63; MAL 5; MTCW 1, 2; MTFW 2005; RGAL 4; WP

Brown, Will
See Ainsworth, William Harrison

Brown, William Hill 1765-1793 **LC 93**
See also DLB 37

Brown, William Wells 1815-1884 **BLC 1; DC 1; NCLC 2, 89**
See also DAM MULT; DLB 3, 50, 183, 248; RGAL 4

Browne, (Clyde) Jackson 1948(?)- ... **CLC 21**
See also CA 120

Browne, Sir Thomas 1605-1682 **LC 111**
See also BRW 2; DLB 151

Browning, Robert 1812-1889 . **NCLC 19, 79; PC 2, 61; WLCS**
See also BRW 4; BRWC 2; BRWR 2; CD-BLB 1832-1890; CLR 97; DA; DA3; DAB; DAC; DAM MST, POET; DLB 32, 163; EXPP; LATS 1:1; PAB; PFS 1, 15; RGEL 2; TEA; WLIT 4; WP; YABC 1

Browning, Tod 1882-1962 **CLC 16**
See also CA 141; 117

Brownmiller, Susan 1935- **CLC 159**
See also CA 103; CANR 35, 75, 137; DAM NOV; FW; MTCW 1, 2; MTFW 2005

Brownson, Orestes Augustus 1803-1876 **NCLC 50**
See also DLB 1, 59, 73, 243

Bruccoli, Matthew J(oseph) 1931- ... **CLC 34**
　　See also CA 9-12R; CANR 7, 87; DLB 103
Bruce, Lenny **CLC 21**
　　See Schneider, Leonard Alfred
Bruchac, Joseph III 1942- **NNAL**
　　See also AAYA 19; CA 33-36R; CANR 13,
　　47, 75, 94, 137; CLR 46; CWRI 5; DAM
　　MULT; JRDA; MAICYA 2; MAICYAS 1;
　　MTCW 2; MTFW 2005; SATA 42, 89,
　　131
Bruin, John
　　See Brutus, Dennis
Brulard, Henri
　　See Stendhal
Brulls, Christian
　　See Simenon, Georges (Jacques Christian)
Brunetto Latini c. 1220-1294 **CMLC 73**
Brunner, John (Kilian Houston)
　　1934-1995 **CLC 8, 10**
　　See also CA 1-4R; 149; CAAS 8; CANR 2,
　　37; CPW; DAM POP; DLB 261; MTCW
　　1, 2; SCFW 1, 2; SFW 4
Bruno, Giordano 1548-1600 **LC 27**
　　See also RGWL 2, 3
Brutus, Dennis 1924- ... **BLC 1; CLC 43; PC
24**
　　See also AFW; BW 2, 3; CA 49-52; CAAS
　　14; CANR 2, 27, 42, 81; CDWLB 3; CP
　　1, 2, 3, 4, 5, 6, 7; DAM MULT, POET;
　　DLB 117, 225; EWL 3
Bryan, C(ourtlandt) D(ixon) B(arnes)
　　1936- **CLC 29**
　　See also CA 73-76; CANR 13, 68; DLB
　　185; INT CANR-13
Bryan, Michael
　　See Moore, Brian
　　See also CCA 1
Bryan, William Jennings
　　1860-1925 **TCLC 99**
　　See also DLB 303
Bryant, William Cullen 1794-1878 . **NCLC 6,
46; PC 20**
　　See also AMWS 1; CDALB 1640-1865;
　　DA; DAB; DAC; DAM MST, POET;
　　DLB 3, 43, 59, 189, 250; EXPP; PAB;
　　RGAL 4; TUS
Bryusov, Valery Yakovlevich
　　1873-1924 **TCLC 10**
　　See also CA 107; 155; EWL 3; SFW 4
Buchan, John 1875-1940 **TCLC 41**
　　See also CA 108; 145; CMW 4; DAB;
　　DAM POP; DLB 34, 70, 156; HGG;
　　MSW; MTCW 2; RGEL 2; RHW; YABC
　　2
Buchanan, George 1506-1582 **LC 4**
　　See also DLB 132
Buchanan, Robert 1841-1901 **TCLC 107**
　　See also CA 179; DLB 18, 35
Buchheim, Lothar-Guenther 1918- **CLC 6**
　　See also CA 85-88
Buchner, (Karl) Georg
　　1813-1837 **NCLC 26, 146**
　　See also CDWLB 2; DLB 133; EW 6;
　　RGSF 2; RGWL 2, 3; TWA
Buchwald, Art(hur) 1925- **CLC 33**
　　See also AITN 1; CA 5-8R; CANR 21, 67,
　　107; MTCW 1, 2; SATA 10
Buck, Pearl S(ydenstricker)
　　1892-1973 **CLC 7, 11, 18, 127**
　　See also AAYA 42; AITN 1; AMWS 2;
　　BPFB 1; CA 1-4R; 41-44R; CANR 1, 34;
　　CDALBS; CN 1; DA; DA3; DAB; DAC;
　　DAM MST, NOV; DLB 9, 102; EWL 3;
　　LAIT 3; MAL 5; MTCW 1, 2; MTFW
　　2005; RGAL 4; RHW; SATA 1, 25; TUS
Buckler, Ernest 1908-1984 **CLC 13**
　　See also CA 11-12; 114; CAP 1; CCA 1;
　　CN 1, 2, 3; DAC; DAM MST; DLB 68;
　　SATA 47

Buckley, Christopher 1952- **CLC 165**
　　See also CA 139; CANR 119
Buckley, Christopher Taylor
　　See Buckley, Christopher
Buckley, Vincent (Thomas)
　　1925-1988 **CLC 57**
　　See also CA 101; CP 1, 2, 3, 4; DLB 289
Buckley, William F(rank), Jr. 1925- . **CLC 7,
18, 37**
　　See also AITN 1; BPFB 1; CA 1-4R; CANR
　　1, 24, 53, 93, 133; CMW 4; CPW; DA3;
　　DAM POP; DLB 137; DLBY 1980; INT
　　CANR-24; MTCW 1, 2; MTFW 2005;
　　TUS
Buechner, (Carl) Frederick 1926- . **CLC 2, 4,
6, 9**
　　See also AMWS 12; BPFB 1; CA 13-16R;
　　CANR 11, 39, 64, 114, 138; CN 1, 2, 3,
　　4, 5, 6, 7; DAM NOV; DLBY 1980; INT
　　CANR-11; MAL 5; MTCW 1, 2; MTFW
　　2005; TCLE 1:1
Buell, John (Edward) 1927- **CLC 10**
　　See also CA 1-4R; CANR 71; DLB 53
Buero Vallejo, Antonio 1916-2000 ... **CLC 15,
46, 139; DC 18**
　　See also CA 106; 189; CANR 24, 49, 75;
　　CWW 2; DFS 11; EWL 3; HW 1; MTCW
　　1, 2
Bufalino, Gesualdo 1920-1996 **CLC 74**
　　See also CA 209; CWW 2; DLB 196
Bugayev, Boris Nikolayevich
　　1880-1934 **PC 11; TCLC 7**
　　See Bely, Andrey; Belyi, Andrei
　　See also CA 104; 165; MTCW 2; MTFW
　　2005
Bukowski, Charles 1920-1994 ... **CLC 2, 5, 9,
41, 82, 108; PC 18; SSC 45**
　　See also CA 17-20R; 144; CANR 40, 62,
　　105; CN 4, 5; CP 1, 2, 3, 4, 5; CPW; DA3;
　　DAM NOV, POET; DLB 5, 130, 169;
　　EWL 3; MAL 5; MTCW 1, 2; MTFW
　　2005
Bulgakov, Mikhail 1891-1940 **SSC 18;
TCLC 2, 16, 159**
　　See also BPFB 1; CA 105; 152; DAM
　　DRAM, NOV; DLB 272; EWL 3; MTCW
　　2; MTFW 2005; NFS 8; RGSF 2; RGWL
　　2, 3; SFW 4; TWA
Bulgakov, Mikhail Afanasevich
　　See Bulgakov, Mikhail
Bulgya, Alexander Alexandrovich
　　1901-1956 **TCLC 53**
　　See Fadeev, Aleksandr Aleksandrovich;
　　Fadeev, Alexandr Alexandrovich; Fadeyev,
　　Alexander
　　See also CA 117; 181
Bullins, Ed 1935- ... **BLC 1; CLC 1, 5, 7; DC
6**
　　See also BW 2, 3; CA 49-52; CAAS 16;
　　CAD; CANR 24, 46, 73, 134; CD 5, 6;
　　DAM DRAM, MULT; DLB 7, 38, 249;
　　EWL 3; MAL 5; MTCW 1, 2; MTFW
　　2005; RGAL 4
Bulosan, Carlos 1911-1956 **AAL**
　　See also CA 216; DLB 312; RGAL 4
**Bulwer-Lytton, Edward (George Earle
Lytton)** 1803-1873 **NCLC 1, 45**
　　See also DLB 21; RGEL 2; SFW 4; SUFW
　　1; TEA
Bunin, Ivan Alexeyevich 1870-1953 ... **SSC 5;
TCLC 6**
　　See also CA 104; DLB 317; EWL 3; RGSF
　　2; RGWL 2, 3; TWA
Bunting, Basil 1900-1985 **CLC 10, 39, 47**
　　See also BRWS 7; CA 53-56; 115; CANR
　　7; CP 1, 2, 3, 4; DAM POET; DLB 20;
　　EWL 3; RGEL 2

Bunuel, Luis 1900-1983 ... **CLC 16, 80; HLC
1**
　　See also CA 101; 110; CANR 32, 77; DAM
　　MULT; HW 1
Bunyan, John 1628-1688 .. **LC 4, 69; WLC 1**
　　See also BRW 2; BYA 5; CDBLB 1660-
　　1789; DA; DAB; DAC; DAM MST; DLB
　　39; RGEL 2; TEA; WCH; WLIT 3
Buravsky, Alexandr **CLC 59**
Burckhardt, Jacob (Christoph)
　　1818-1897 **NCLC 49**
　　See also EW 6
Burford, Eleanor
　　See Hibbert, Eleanor Alice Burford
Burgess, Anthony . **CLC 1, 2, 4, 5, 8, 10, 13,
15, 22, 40, 62, 81, 94**
　　See Wilson, John (Anthony) Burgess
　　See also AAYA 25; AITN 1; BRWS 1; CD-
　　BLB 1960 to Present; CN 1, 2, 3, 4, 5;
　　DAB; DLB 14, 194, 261; DLBY 1998;
　　EWL 3; RGEL 2; RHW; SFW 4; YAW
Burke, Edmund 1729(?)-1797 **LC 7, 36;
WLC 1**
　　See also BRW 3; DA; DA3; DAB; DAC;
　　DAM MST; DLB 104, 252; RGEL 2;
　　TEA
Burke, Kenneth (Duva) 1897-1993 ... **CLC 2,
24**
　　See also AMW; CA 5-8R; 143; CANR 39,
　　74, 136; CN 1, 2; CP 1, 2, 3, 4, 5; DLB
　　45, 63; EWL 3; MAL 5; MTCW 1, 2;
　　MTFW 2005; RGAL 4
Burke, Leda
　　See Garnett, David
Burke, Ralph
　　See Silverberg, Robert
Burke, Thomas 1886-1945 **TCLC 63**
　　See also CA 113; 155; CMW 4; DLB 197
Burney, Fanny 1752-1840 **NCLC 12, 54,
107**
　　See also BRWS 3; DLB 39; FL 1:2; NFS
　　16; RGEL 2; TEA
Burney, Frances
　　See Burney, Fanny
Burns, Robert 1759-1796 ... **LC 3, 29, 40; PC
6; WLC 1**
　　See also AAYA 51; BRW 3; CDBLB 1789-
　　1832; DA; DA3; DAB; DAC; DAM MST,
　　POET; DLB 109; EXPP; PAB; RGEL 2;
　　TEA; WP
Burns, Tex
　　See L'Amour, Louis (Dearborn)
Burnshaw, Stanley 1906-2005 **CLC 3, 13,
44**
　　See also CA 9-12R; 243; CP 1, 2, 3, 4, 5, 6,
　　7; DLB 48; DLBY 1997
Burr, Anne 1937- **CLC 6**
　　See also CA 25-28R
Burroughs, Edgar Rice 1875-1950 . **TCLC 2,
32**
　　See also AAYA 11; BPFB 1; BYA 4, 9; CA
　　104; 132; CANR 131; DA3; DAM NOV;
　　DLB 8; FANT; MTCW 1, 2; MTFW
　　2005; RGAL 4; SATA 41; SCFW 1, 2;
　　SFW 4; TCWW 1, 2; TUS; YAW
Burroughs, William S. 1914-1997 . **CLC 1, 2,
5, 15, 22, 42, 75, 109; TCLC 121; WLC
1**
　　See Lee, William; Lee, Willy
　　See also AAYA 60; AITN 2; AMWS 3; BG
　　1:2; BPFB 1; CA 9-12R; 160; CANR 20,
　　52, 104; CN 1, 2, 3, 4, 5, 6; CPW; DA;
　　DA3; DAB; DAC; DAM MST, NOV,
　　POP; DLB 2, 8, 16, 152, 237; DLBY
　　1981, 1997; EWL 3; HGG; LMFS 2;
　　MAL 5; MTCW 1, 2; MTFW 2005;
　　RGAL 4; SFW 4
Burroughs, William Seward
　　See Burroughs, William S.

Burton, Sir Richard F(rancis)
1821-1890 **NCLC 42**
See also DLB 55, 166, 184; SSFS 21
Burton, Robert 1577-1640 **LC 74**
See also DLB 151; RGEL 2
Buruma, Ian 1951- **CLC 163**
See also CA 128; CANR 65, 141
Busch, Frederick 1941-2006 .. **CLC 7, 10, 18,**
47, 166
See also CA 33-36R; 248; CAAS 1; CANR
45, 73, 92; CN 1, 2, 3, 4, 5, 6, 7; DLB 6,
218
Busch, Frederick Matthew
See Busch, Frederick
Bush, Barney (Furman) 1946- **NNAL**
See also CA 145
Bush, Ronald 1946- **CLC 34**
See also CA 136
Bustos, F(rancisco)
See Borges, Jorge Luis
Bustos Domecq, H(onorio)
See Bioy Casares, Adolfo; Borges, Jorge
Luis
Butler, Octavia E. 1947-2006 **BLCS; CLC**
38, 121
See also AAYA 18, 48; AFAW 2; AMWS
13; BPFB 1; BW 2, 3; CA 73-76; 248;
CANR 12, 24, 38, 73, 145; CLR 65; CN
7; CPW; DA3; DAM MULT, POP; DLB
33; LATS 1:2; MTCW 1, 2; MTFW 2005;
NFS 8, 21; SATA 84; SCFW 2; SFW 4;
SSFS 6; TCLE 1:1; YAW
Butler, Octavia Estelle
See Butler, Octavia E.
Butler, Robert Olen, (Jr.) 1945- **CLC 81,**
162
See also AMWS 12; BPFB 1; CA 112;
CANR 66, 138; CN 7; CSW; DAM POP;
DLB 173; INT CA-112; MAL 5; MTCW
2; MTFW 2005; SSFS 11
Butler, Samuel 1612-1680 **LC 16, 43**
See also DLB 101, 126; RGEL 2
Butler, Samuel 1835-1902 **TCLC 1, 33;**
WLC 1
See also BRWS 2; CA 143; CDBLB 1890-
1914; DA; DA3; DAB; DAC; DAM MST,
NOV; DLB 18, 57, 174; RGEL 2; SFW 4;
TEA
Butler, Walter C.
See Faust, Frederick (Schiller)
Butor, Michel (Marie Francois)
1926- **CLC 1, 3, 8, 11, 15, 161**
See also CA 9-12R; CANR 33, 66; CWW
2; DLB 83; EW 13; EWL 3; GFL 1789 to
the Present; MTCW 1, 2; MTFW 2005
Butts, Mary 1890(?)-1937 **TCLC 77**
See also CA 148; DLB 240
Buxton, Ralph
See Silverstein, Alvin; Silverstein, Virginia
B(arbara Opshelor)
Buzo, Alex
See Buzo, Alexander (John)
See also DLB 289
Buzo, Alexander (John) 1944- **CLC 61**
See also CA 97-100; CANR 17, 39, 69; CD
5, 6
Buzzati, Dino 1906-1972 **CLC 36**
See also CA 160; 33-36R; DLB 177; RGWL
2, 3; SFW 4
Byars, Betsy 1928- **CLC 35**
See also AAYA 19; BYA 3; CA 33-36R,
183; CAAE 183; CANR 18, 36, 57, 102,
148; CLR 1, 16, 72; DLB 52; INT CANR-
18; JRDA; MAICYA 1, 2; MAICYAS 1;
MTCW 1; SAAS 1; SATA 4, 46, 80, 163;
SATA-Essay 108; WYA; YAW
Byars, Betsy Cromer
See Byars, Betsy

Byatt, Antonia Susan Drabble
See Byatt, A.S.
Byatt, A.S. 1936- **CLC 19, 65, 136, 223;**
SSC 91
See also BPFB 1; BRWC 2; BRWS 4; CA
13-16R; CANR 13, 33, 50, 75, 96, 133;
CN 1, 2, 3, 4, 5, 6; DA3; DAM NOV,
POP; DLB 14, 194, 319, 326; EWL 3;
MTCW 1, 2; MTFW 2005; RGSF 2;
RHW; TEA
Byrd, William II 1674-1744 **LC 112**
See also DLB 24, 140; RGAL 4
Byrne, David 1952- **CLC 26**
See also CA 127
Byrne, John Keyes 1926-
See Leonard, Hugh
See also CA 102; CANR 78, 140; INT CA-
102
Byron, George Gordon (Noel)
1788-1824 **DC 24; NCLC 2, 12, 109,**
149; PC 16; WLC 1
See also AAYA 64; BRW 4; BRWC 2; CD-
BLB 1789-1832; DA; DA3; DAB; DAC;
DAM MST, POET; DLB 96, 110; EXPP;
LMFS 1; PAB; PFS 1, 14; RGEL 2; TEA;
WLIT 3; WP
Byron, Robert 1905-1941 **TCLC 67**
See also CA 160; DLB 195
C. 3. 3.
See Wilde, Oscar (Fingal O'Flahertie Wills)
Caballero, Fernan 1796-1877 **NCLC 10**
Cabell, Branch
See Cabell, James Branch
Cabell, James Branch 1879-1958 **TCLC 6**
See also CA 105; 152; DLB 9, 78; FANT;
MAL 5; MTCW 2; RGAL 4; SUFW 1
Cabeza de Vaca, Alvar Nunez
1490-1557(?) **LC 61**
Cable, George Washington
1844-1925 **SSC 4; TCLC 4**
See also CA 104; 155; DLB 12, 74; DLBD
13; RGAL 4; TUS
Cabral de Melo Neto, Joao
1920-1999 **CLC 76**
See Melo Neto, Joao Cabral de
See also CA 151; DAM MULT; DLB 307;
LAW; LAWS 1
Cabrera Infante, G(uillermo)
1929-2005 **CLC 5, 25, 45, 120; HLC**
1; SSC 39
See also CA 85-88; 236; CANR 29, 65, 110;
CDWLB 3; CWW 2; DA3; DAM MULT;
DLB 113; EWL 3; HW 1, 2; LAW; LAWS
1; MTCW 1, 2; MTFW 2005; RGSF 2;
WLIT 1
Cade, Toni
See Bambara, Toni Cade
Cadmus and Harmonia
See Buchan, John
Caedmon fl. 658-680 **CMLC 7**
See also DLB 146
Caeiro, Alberto
See Pessoa, Fernando (Antonio Nogueira)
Caesar, Julius **CMLC 47**
See Julius Caesar
See also AW 1; RGWL 2, 3; WLIT 8
Cage, John (Milton), (Jr.)
1912-1992 **CLC 41; PC 58**
See also CA 13-16R; 169; CANR 9, 78;
DLB 193; INT CANR-9; TCLE 1:1
Cahan, Abraham 1860-1951 **TCLC 71**
See also CA 108; 154; DLB 9, 25, 28; MAL
5; RGAL 4
Cain, G.
See Cabrera Infante, G(uillermo)
Cain, Guillermo
See Cabrera Infante, G(uillermo)

Cain, James M(allahan) 1892-1977 .. **CLC 3,**
11, 28
See also AITN 1; BPFB 1; CA 17-20R; 73-
76; CANR 8, 34, 61; CMW 4; CN 1, 2;
DLB 226; EWL 3; MAL 5; MSW; MTCW
1; RGAL 4
Caine, Hall 1853-1931 **TCLC 97**
See also RHW
Caine, Mark
See Raphael, Frederic (Michael)
Calasso, Roberto 1941- **CLC 81**
See also CA 143; CANR 89
Calderon de la Barca, Pedro
1600-1681 **DC 3; HLCS 1; LC 23**
See also DFS 23; EW 2; RGWL 2, 3; TWA
Caldwell, Erskine (Preston)
1903-1987 **CLC 1, 8, 14, 50, 60; SSC**
19; TCLC 117
See also AITN 1; AMW; BPFB 1; CA 1-4R;
121; CAAS 1; CANR 2, 33; CN 1, 2, 3,
4; DA3; DAM NOV; DLB 9, 86; EWL 3;
MAL 5; MTCW 1, 2; MTFW 2005;
RGAL 4; RGSF 2; TUS
Caldwell, (Janet Miriam) Taylor (Holland)
1900-1985 **CLC 2, 28, 39**
See also BPFB 1; CA 5-8R; 116; CANR 5;
DA3; DAM NOV, POP; DLBD 17;
MTCW 2; RHW
Calhoun, John Caldwell
1782-1850 **NCLC 15**
See also DLB 3, 248
Calisher, Hortense 1911- **CLC 2, 4, 8, 38,**
134; SSC 15
See also CA 1-4R; CANR 1, 22, 117; CN
1, 2, 3, 4, 5, 6, 7; DA3; DAM NOV; DLB
2, 218; INT CANR-22; MAL 5; MTCW
1, 2; MTFW 2005; RGAL 4; RGSF 2
Callaghan, Morley Edward
1903-1990 **CLC 3, 14, 41, 65; TCLC**
145
See also CA 9-12R; 132; CANR 33, 73;
CN 1, 2, 3, 4; DAC; DAM MST; DLB
68; EWL 3; MTCW 1, 2; MTFW 2005;
RGEL 2; RGSF 2; SSFS 19
Callimachus c. 305B.C.-c.
240B.C. **CMLC 18**
See also AW 1; DLB 176; RGWL 2, 3
Calvin, Jean
See Calvin, John
See also GFL Beginnings to 1789
Calvin, John 1509-1564 **LC 37**
See Calvin, Jean
Calvino, Italo 1923-1985 **CLC 5, 8, 11, 22,**
33, 39, 73; SSC 3, 48
See also AAYA 58; CA 85-88; 116; CANR
23, 61, 132; DAM NOV; DLB 196; EW
13; EWL 3; MTCW 1, 2; MTFW 2005;
RGHL; RGSF 2; RGWL 2, 3; SFW 4;
SSFS 12; WLIT 7
Camara Laye
See Laye, Camara
See also EWL 3
Camden, William 1551-1623 **LC 77**
See also DLB 172
Cameron, Carey 1952- **CLC 59**
See also CA 135
Cameron, Peter 1959- **CLC 44**
See also AMWS 12; CA 125; CANR 50,
117; DLB 234; GLL 2
Camoens, Luis Vaz de 1524(?)-1580
See Camoes, Luis de
See also EW 2
Camoes, Luis de 1524(?)-1580 . **HLCS 1; LC**
62; PC 31
See Camoens, Luis Vaz de
See also DLB 287; RGWL 2, 3
Campana, Dino 1885-1932 **TCLC 20**
See also CA 117; 246; DLB 114; EWL 3

Campanella, Tommaso 1568-1639 **LC 32**
See also RGWL 2, 3
Campbell, John W(ood, Jr.)
1910-1971 **CLC 32**
See also CA 21-22; 29-32R; CANR 34;
CAP 2; DLB 8; MTCW 1; SCFW 1, 2;
SFW 4
Campbell, Joseph 1904-1987 **CLC 69;**
TCLC 140
See also AAYA 3, 66; BEST 89:2; CA 1-4R;
124; CANR 3, 28, 61, 107; DA3; MTCW
1, 2
Campbell, Maria 1940- **CLC 85; NNAL**
See also CA 102; CANR 54; CCA 1; DAC
Campbell, (John) Ramsey 1946- **CLC 42;**
SSC 19
See also AAYA 51; CA 57-60, 228; CAAE
228; CANR 7, 102; DLB 261; HGG; INT
CANR-7; SUFW 1, 2
Campbell, (Ignatius) Roy (Dunnachie)
1901-1957 **TCLC 5**
See also AFW; CA 104; 155; DLB 20, 225;
EWL 3; MTCW 2; RGEL 2
Campbell, Thomas 1777-1844 **NCLC 19**
See also DLB 93, 144; RGEL 2
Campbell, Wilfred **TCLC 9**
See Campbell, William
Campbell, William 1858(?)-1918
See Campbell, Wilfred
See also CA 106; DLB 92
Campbell, William Edward March
1893-1954
See March, William
See also CA 108
Campion, Jane 1954- **CLC 95**
See also AAYA 33; CA 138; CANR 87
Campion, Thomas 1567-1620 **LC 78**
See also CDBLB Before 1660; DAM POET;
DLB 58, 172; RGEL 2
Camus, Albert 1913-1960 **CLC 1, 2, 4, 9,**
11, 14, 32, 63, 69, 124; DC 2; SSC 9,
76; WLC 1
See also AAYA 36; AFW; BPFB 1; CA 89-
92; CANR 131; DA; DA3; DAB; DAC;
DAM DRAM, MST, NOV; DLB 72, 321;
EW 13; EWL 3; EXPN; EXPS; GFL 1789
to the Present; LATS 1:2; LMFS 2;
MTCW 1, 2; MTFW 2005; NFS 6, 16;
RGHL; RGSF 2; RGWL 2, 3; SSFS 4;
TWA
Canby, Vincent 1924-2000 **CLC 13**
See also CA 81-84; 191
Cancale
See Desnos, Robert
Canetti, Elias 1905-1994 .. **CLC 3, 14, 25, 75,**
86; TCLC 157
See also CA 21-24R; 146; CANR 23, 61,
79; CDWLB 2; CWW 2; DA3; DLB 85,
124; EW 12; EWL 3; MTCW 1, 2; MTFW
2005; RGWL 2, 3; TWA
Canfield, Dorothea F.
See Fisher, Dorothea (Frances) Canfield
Canfield, Dorothea Frances
See Fisher, Dorothy (Frances) Canfield
Canfield, Dorothy
See Fisher, Dorothy (Frances) Canfield
Canin, Ethan 1960- **CLC 55; SSC 70**
See also CA 131; 135; MAL 5
Cankar, Ivan 1876-1918 **TCLC 105**
See also CDWLB 4; DLB 147; EWL 3
Cannon, Curt
See Hunter, Evan
Cao, Lan 1961- **CLC 109**
See also CA 165
Cape, Judith
See Page, P(atricia) K(athleen)
See also CCA 1

Capek, Karel 1890-1938 **DC 1; SSC 36;**
TCLC 6, 37; WLC 1
See also CA 104; 140; CDWLB 4; DA;
DA3; DAB; DAC; DAM DRAM, MST,
NOV; DFS 7, 11; DLB 215; EW 10; EWL
3; MTCW 2; MTFW 2005; RGSF 2;
RGWL 2, 3; SCFW 1, 2; SFW 4
Capella, Martianus fl. 4th cent - **CMLC 84**
Capote, Truman 1924-1984 . **CLC 1, 3, 8, 13,**
19, 34, 38, 58; SSC 2, 47, 93; TCLC
164; WLC 1
See also AAYA 61; AMWS 3; BPFB 1; CA
5-8R; 113; CANR 18, 62; CDALB 1941-
1968; CN 1, 2, 3; CPW; DA; DA3; DAB;
DAC; DAM MST, NOV, POP; DLB 2,
185, 227; DLBY 1980, 1984; EWL 3;
EXPS; GLL 1; LAIT 3; MAL 5; MTCW
1, 2; MTFW 2005; NCFS 2; RGAL 4;
RGSF 2; SATA 91; SSFS; TUS
Capra, Frank 1897-1991 **CLC 16**
See also AAYA 52; CA 61-64; 135
Caputo, Philip 1941- **CLC 32**
See also AAYA 60; CA 73-76; CANR 40,
135; YAW
Caragiale, Ion Luca 1852-1912 **TCLC 76**
See also CA 157
Card, Orson Scott 1951- **CLC 44, 47, 50**
See also AAYA 11, 42; BPFB 1; BYA 5, 8;
CA 102; CANR 27, 47, 73, 102, 106, 133;
CPW; DA3; DAM POP; FANT; INT
CANR-27; MTCW 1, 2; MTFW 2005;
NFS 5; SATA 83, 127; SCFW 2; SFW 4;
SUFW 2; YAW
Cardenal, Ernesto 1925- **CLC 31, 161;**
HLC 1; PC 22
See also CA 49-52; CANR 2, 32, 66, 138;
CWW 2; DAM MULT, POET; DLB 290;
EWL 3; HW 1, 2; LAWS 1; MTCW 1, 2;
MTFW 2005; RGWL 2, 3
Cardinal, Marie 1929-2001 **CLC 189**
See also CA 177; CWW 2; DLB 83; FW
Cardozo, Benjamin N(athan)
1870-1938 **TCLC 65**
See also CA 117; 164
Carducci, Giosue (Alessandro Giuseppe)
1835-1907 **PC 46; TCLC 32**
See also CA 163; EW 7; RGWL 2, 3
Carew, Thomas 1595(?)-1640 . **LC 13; PC 29**
See also BRW 2; DLB 126; PAB; RGEL 2
Carey, Ernestine Gilbreth 1908- **CLC 17**
See also CA 5-8R; CANR 71; SATA 2
Carey, Peter 1943- **CLC 40, 55, 96, 183**
See also CA 123; 127; CANR 53, 76, 117;
CN 4, 5, 6, 7; DLB 289, 326; EWL 3;
INT CA-127; MTCW 1, 2; MTFW 2005;
RGSF 2; SATA 94
Carleton, William 1794-1869 **NCLC 3**
See also DLB 159; RGEL 2; RGSF 2
Carlisle, Henry (Coffin) 1926- **CLC 33**
See also CA 13-16R; CANR 15, 85
Carlsen, Chris
See Holdstock, Robert P.
Carlson, Ron(ald F.) 1947- **CLC 54**
See also CA 105, 189; CAAE 189; CANR
27; DLB 244
Carlyle, Thomas 1795-1881 **NCLC 22, 70**
See also BRW 4; CDBLB 1789-1832; DA;
DAB; DAC; DAM MST; DLB 55, 144,
254; RGEL 2; TEA
Carman, (William) Bliss 1861-1929 ... **PC 34;**
TCLC 7
See also CA 104; 152; DAC; DLB 92;
RGEL 2
Carnegie, Dale 1888-1955 **TCLC 53**
See also CA 218
Carossa, Hans 1878-1956 **TCLC 48**
See also CA 170; DLB 66; EWL 3

Carpenter, Don(ald Richard)
1931-1995 **CLC 41**
See also CA 45-48; 149; CANR 1, 71
Carpenter, Edward 1844-1929 **TCLC 88**
See also CA 163; GLL 1
Carpenter, John (Howard) 1948- ... **CLC 161**
See also AAYA 2; CA 134; SATA 58
Carpenter, Johnny
See Carpenter, John (Howard)
Carpentier (y Valmont), Alejo
1904-1980 . **CLC 8, 11, 38, 110; HLC 1;**
SSC 35
See also CA 65-68; 97-100; CANR 11, 70;
CDWLB 3; DAM MULT; DLB 113; EWL
3; HW 1, 2; LAW; LMFS 2; RGSF 2;
RGWL 2, 3; WLIT 1
Carr, Caleb 1955- **CLC 86**
See also CA 147; CANR 73, 134; DA3
Carr, Emily 1871-1945 **TCLC 32**
See also CA 159; DLB 68; FW; GLL 2
Carr, John Dickson 1906-1977 **CLC 3**
See Fairbairn, Roger
See also CA 49-52; 69-72; CANR 3, 33,
60; CMW 4; DLB 306; MSW; MTCW 1,
2
Carr, Philippa
See Hibbert, Eleanor Alice Burford
Carr, Virginia Spencer 1929- **CLC 34**
See also CA 61-64; DLB 111
Carrere, Emmanuel 1957- **CLC 89**
See also CA 200
Carrier, Roch 1937- **CLC 13, 78**
See also CA 130; CANR 61, 152; CCA 1;
DAC; DAM MST; DLB 53; SATA 105,
166
Carroll, James Dennis
See Carroll, Jim
Carroll, James P. 1943(?)- **CLC 38**
See also CA 81-84; CANR 73, 139; MTCW
2; MTFW 2005
Carroll, Jim 1951- **CLC 35, 143**
See also AAYA 17; CA 45-48; CANR 42,
115; NCFS 5
Carroll, Lewis **NCLC 2, 53, 139; PC 18;**
WLC 1
See Dodgson, Charles L(utwidge)
See also AAYA 39; BRW 5; BYA 5, 13; CD-
BLB 1832-1890; CLR 2, 18, 108; DLB
18, 163, 178; DLBY 1998; EXPN; EXPP;
FANT; JRDA; LAIT 1; NFS 7; PFS 11;
RGEL 2; SUFW 1; TEA; WCH
Carroll, Paul Vincent 1900-1968 **CLC 10**
See also CA 9-12R; 25-28R; DLB 10; EWL
3; RGEL 2
Carruth, Hayden 1921- **CLC 4, 7, 10, 18,**
84; PC 10
See also CA 9-12R; CANR 4, 38, 59, 110;
CP 1, 2, 3, 4, 5, 6, 7; DLB 5, 165; INT
CANR-4; MTCW 1, 2; MTFW 2005;
SATA 47
Carson, Anne 1950- **CLC 185; PC 64**
See also AMWS 12; CA 203; CP 7; DLB
193; PFS 18; TCLE 1:1
Carson, Ciaran 1948- **CLC 201**
See also CA 112; 153; CANR 113; CP 6, 7
Carson, Rachel
See Carson, Rachel Louise
See also AAYA 49; DLB 275
Carson, Rachel Louise 1907-1964 **CLC 71**
See Carson, Rachel
See also AMWS 9; ANW; CA 77-80; CANR
35; DAM POP; FW; LAIT 4; MAL
5; MTCW 1, 2; MTFW 2005; NCFS 1;
SATA 23
Carter, Angela (Olive) 1940-1992 **CLC 5,**
41, 76; SSC 13, 85; TCLC 139
See also BRWS 3; CA 53-56; 136; CANR
12, 36, 61, 106; CN 3, 4, 5; DA3; DLB
14, 207, 261, 319; EXPS; FANT; FW; GL

2; MTCW 1, 2; MTFW 2005; RGSF 2;
SATA 66; SATA-Obit 70; SFW 4; SSFS
4, 12; SUFW 2; WLIT 4

Carter, Nick
 See Smith, Martin Cruz

Carver, Raymond 1938-1988 **CLC 22, 36,**
 53, 55, 126; PC 54; SSC 8, 51
 See also AAYA 44; AMWS 3; BPFB 1; CA
 33-36R; 126; CANR 17, 34, 61, 103; CN
 4; CPW; DA3; DAM NOV; DLB 130;
 DLBY 1984, 1988; EWL 3; MAL 5;
 MTCW 1, 2; MTFW 2005; PFS 17;
 RGAL 4; RGSF 2; SSFS 3, 6, 12, 13, 23;
 TCLE 1:1; TCWW 2; TUS

Cary, Elizabeth, Lady Falkland
 1585-1639 **LC 30**

Cary, (Arthur) Joyce (Lunel)
 1888-1957 **TCLC 1, 29**
 See also BRW 7; CA 104; 164; CDBLB
 1914-1945; DLB 15, 100; EWL 3; MTCW
 2; RGEL 2; TEA

Casal, Julian del 1863-1893 **NCLC 131**
 See also DLB 283; LAW

Casanova, Giacomo
 See Casanova de Seingalt, Giovanni Jacopo
 See also WLIT 7

Casanova de Seingalt, Giovanni Jacopo
 1725-1798 **LC 13**
 See Casanova, Giacomo

Casares, Adolfo Bioy
 See Bioy Casares, Adolfo
 See also RGSF 2

Casas, Bartolome de las 1474-1566
 See Las Casas, Bartolome de
 See also WLIT 1

Casely-Hayford, J(oseph) E(phraim)
 1866-1903 **BLC 1; TCLC 24**
 See also BW 2; CA 123; 152; DAM MULT

Casey, John (Dudley) 1939- **CLC 59**
 See also BEST 90:2; CA 69-72; CANR 23,
 100

Casey, Michael 1947- **CLC 2**
 See also CA 65-68; CANR 109; CP 2, 3;
 DLB 5

Casey, Patrick
 See Thurman, Wallace (Henry)

Casey, Warren (Peter) 1935-1988 **CLC 12**
 See also CA 101; 127; INT CA-101

Casona, Alejandro **CLC 49**
 See Alvarez, Alejandro Rodriguez
 See also EWL 3

Cassavetes, John 1929-1989 **CLC 20**
 See also CA 85-88; 127; CANR 82

Cassian, Nina 1924- **PC 17**
 See also CWP; CWW 2

Cassill, R(onald) V(erlin)
 1919-2002 **CLC 4, 23**
 See also CA 9-12R; 208; CAAS 1; CANR
 7, 45; CN 1, 2, 3, 4, 5, 6, 7; DLB 6, 218;
 DLBY 2002

Cassiodorus, Flavius Magnus c. 490(?)-c.
 583(?) **CMLC 43**

Cassirer, Ernst 1874-1945 **TCLC 61**
 See also CA 157

Cassity, (Allen) Turner 1929- **CLC 6, 42**
 See also CA 17-20R; 223; CAAE 223;
 CAAS 8; CANR 11; CSW; DLB 105

Castaneda, Carlos (Cesar Aranha)
 1931(?)-1998 **CLC 12, 119**
 See also CA 25-28R; CANR 32, 66, 105;
 DNFS 1; HW 1; MTCW 1

Castedo, Elena 1937- **CLC 65**
 See also CA 132

Castedo-Ellerman, Elena
 See Castedo, Elena

Castellanos, Rosario 1925-1974 **CLC 66;**
 HLC 1; SSC 39, 68
 See also CA 131; 53-56; CANR 58; CD-
 WLB 3; DAM MULT; DLB 113, 290;
 EWL 3; FW; HW 1; LAW; MTCW 2;
 MTFW 2005; RGSF 2; RGWL 2, 3

Castelvetro, Lodovico 1505-1571 **LC 12**

Castiglione, Baldassare 1478-1529 **LC 12**
 See Castiglione, Baldesar
 See also LMFS 1; RGWL 2, 3

Castiglione, Baldesar
 See Castiglione, Baldassare
 See also EW 2; WLIT 7

Castillo, Ana 1953- **CLC 151**
 See also AAYA 42; CA 131; CANR 51, 86,
 128; CWP; DLB 122, 227; DNFS 2; FW;
 HW 1; LLW; PFS 21

Castle, Robert
 See Hamilton, Edmond

Castro (Ruz), Fidel 1926(?)- **HLC 1**
 See also CA 110; 129; CANR 81; DAM
 MULT; HW 2

Castro, Guillen de 1569-1631 **LC 19**

Castro, Rosalia de 1837-1885 ... **NCLC 3, 78;**
 PC 41
 See also DAM MULT

Cather, Willa (Sibert) 1873-1947 . **SSC 2, 50;**
 TCLC 1, 11, 31, 99, 132, 152; WLC 1
 See also AAYA 24; AMW; AMWC 1;
 AMWR 1; BPFB 1; CA 104; 128; CDALB
 1865-1917; CLR 98; DA; DA3; DAB;
 DAC; DAM MST, NOV; DLB 9, 54, 78,
 256; DLBD 1; EWL 3; EXPN; EXPS; FL
 1:5; LAIT 3; LATS 1:1; MAL 5; MAWW;
 MTCW 1, 2; MTFW 2005; NFS 2, 19;
 RGAL 4, RGSF 2; RHW; SATA 30; SSFS
 2, 7, 16; TCWW 1, 2; TUS

Catherine II
 See Catherine the Great
 See also DLB 150

Catherine the Great 1729-1796 **LC 69**
 See Catherine II

Cato, Marcus Porcius
 234B.C.-149B.C. **CMLC 21**
 See Cato the Elder

Cato, Marcus Porcius, the Elder
 See Cato, Marcus Porcius

Cato the Elder
 See Cato, Marcus Porcius
 See also DLB 211

Catton, (Charles) Bruce 1899-1978 . **CLC 35**
 See also AITN 1; CA 5-8R; 81-84; CANR
 7, 74; DLB 17; MTCW 2; MTFW 2005;
 SATA 2; SATA-Obit 24

Catullus c. 84B.C.-54B.C. **CMLC 18**
 See also AW 2; CDWLB 1; DLB 211;
 RGWL 2, 3; WLIT 8

Cauldwell, Frank
 See King, Francis (Henry)

Caunitz, William J. 1933-1996 **CLC 34**
 See also BEST 89:3; CA 125; 130; 152;
 CANR 73; INT CA-130

Causley, Charles (Stanley)
 1917-2003 **CLC 7**
 See also CA 9-12R; 223; CANR 5, 35, 94;
 CLR 30; CP 1, 2, 3, 4, 5; CWRI 5; DLB
 27; MTCW 1; SATA 3, 66; SATA-Obit
 149

Caute, (John) David 1936- **CLC 29**
 See also CA 1-4R; CAAS 4; CANR 1, 33,
 64, 120; CBD; CD 5, 6; CN 1, 2, 3, 4, 5,
 6, 7; DAM NOV; DLB 14, 231

Cavafy, C(onstantine) P(eter) **PC 36;**
 TCLC 2, 7
 See Kavafis, Konstantinos Petrou
 See also CA 148; DA3; DAM POET; EW
 8; EWL 3; MTCW 2; PFS 19; RGWL 2,
 3; WP

Cavalcanti, Guido c. 1250-c.
 1300 .. **CMLC 54**
 See also RGWL 2, 3; WLIT 7

Cavallo, Evelyn
 See Spark, Muriel (Sarah)

Cavanna, Betty **CLC 12**
 See Harrison, Elizabeth (Allen) Cavanna
 See also JRDA; MAICYA 1; SAAS 4;
 SATA 1, 30

Cavendish, Margaret Lucas
 1623-1673 **LC 30**
 See also DLB 131, 252, 281; RGEL 2

Caxton, William 1421(?)-1491(?) **LC 17**
 See also DLB 170

Cayer, D. M.
 See Duffy, Maureen (Patricia)

Cayrol, Jean 1911-2005 **CLC 11**
 See also CA 89-92; 236; DLB 83; EWL 3

Cela (y Trulock), Camilo Jose
 See Cela, Camilo Jose
 See also CWW 2

Cela, Camilo Jose 1916-2002 **CLC 4, 13,**
 59, 122; HLC 1; SSC 71
 See Cela (y Trulock), Camilo Jose
 See also BEST 90:2; CA 21-24R; 206;
 CAAS 10; CANR 21, 32, 76, 139; DAM
 MULT; DLB 322; DLBY 1989; EW 13;
 EWL 3; HW 1; MTCW 1, 2; MTFW
 2005; RGSF 2; RGWL 2, 3

Celan, Paul **CLC 10, 19, 53, 82; PC 10**
 See Antschel, Paul
 See also CDWLB 2; DLB 69; EWL 3;
 RGHL; RGWL 2, 3

Celine, Louis-Ferdinand .. **CLC 1, 3, 4, 7, 9,**
 15, 47, 124
 See Destouches, Louis-Ferdinand
 See also DLB 72; EW 11; EWL 3; GFL
 1789 to the Present; RGWL 2, 3

Cellini, Benvenuto 1500-1571 **LC 7**
 See also WLIT 7

Cendrars, Blaise **CLC 18, 106**
 See Sauser-Hall, Frederic
 See also DLB 258; EWL 3; GFL 1789 to
 the Present; RGWL 2, 3; WP

Centlivre, Susanna 1669(?)-1723 **DC 25;**
 LC 65
 See also DLB 84; RGEL 2

Cernuda (y Bidon), Luis
 1902-1963 **CLC 54; PC 62**
 See also CA 131; 89-92; DAM POET; DLB
 134; EWL 3; GLL 1; HW 1; RGWL 2, 3

Cervantes, Lorna Dee 1954- **HLCS 1; PC**
 35
 See also CA 131; CANR 80; CP 7; CWP;
 DLB 82; EXPP; HW 1; LLW

Cervantes (Saavedra), Miguel de
 1547-1616 **HLCS; LC 6, 23, 93; SSC**
 12; WLC 1
 See also AAYA 56; BYA 1, 14; DA; DAB;
 DAC; DAM MST, NOV; EW 2; LAIT 1;
 LATS 1:1; LMFS 1; NFS 8; RGSF 2;
 RGWL 2, 3; TWA

Cesaire, Aime (Fernand) 1913- **BLC 1;**
 CLC 19, 32, 112; DC 22; PC 25
 See also BW 2, 3; CA 65-68; CANR 24,
 43, 81; CWW 2; DA3; DAM MULT,
 POET; DLB 321; EWL 3; GFL 1789 to
 the Present; MTCW 1, 2; MTFW 2005;
 WP

Chabon, Michael 1963- ... **CLC 55, 149; SSC**
 59
 See also AAYA 45; AMWS 11; CA 139;
 CANR 57, 96, 127, 138; DLB 278; MAL
 5; MTFW 2005; SATA 145

Chabrol, Claude 1930- **CLC 16**
 See also CA 110

Chairil Anwar
 See Anwar, Chairil
 See also EWL 3

Challans, Mary 1905-1983
See Renault, Mary
See also CA 81-84; 111; CANR 74; DA3;
MTCW 2; MTFW 2005; SATA 23; SATA-
Obit 36; TEA

Challis, George
See Faust, Frederick (Schiller)

Chambers, Aidan 1934- **CLC 35**
See also AAYA 27; CA 25-28R; CANR 12,
31, 58, 116; JRDA; MAICYA 1, 2; SAAS
12; SATA 1, 69, 108, 171; WYA; YAW

Chambers, James 1948-
See Cliff, Jimmy
See also CA 124

Chambers, Jessie
See Lawrence, D(avid) H(erbert Richards)
See also GLL 1

Chambers, Robert W(illiam)
1865-1933 **SSC 92; TCLC 41**
See also CA 165; DLB 202; HGG; SATA
107; SUFW 1

Chambers, (David) Whittaker
1901-1961 **TCLC 129**
See also CA 89-92; DLB 303

Chamisso, Adelbert von
1781-1838 **NCLC 82**
See also DLB 90; RGWL 2, 3; SUFW 1

Chance, James T.
See Carpenter, John (Howard)

Chance, John T.
See Carpenter, John (Howard)

Chandler, Raymond (Thornton)
1888-1959 **SSC 23; TCLC 1, 7, 179**
See also AAYA 25; AMWC 2; AMWS 4;
BPFB 1; CA 104; 129; CANR 60, 107;
CDALB 1929-1941; CMW 4; DA3; DLB
226, 253; DLBD 6; EWL 3; MAL 5;
MSW; MTCW 1, 2; MTFW 2005; NFS
17; RGAL 4; TUS

Chang, Diana 1934- **AAL**
See also CA 228; CWP; DLB 312; EXPP

Chang, Eileen 1921-1995 **AAL; SSC 28**
See Chang Ai-Ling; Zhang Ailing
See also CA 166

Chang, Jung 1952- **CLC 71**
See also CA 142

Chang Ai-Ling
See Chang, Eileen
See also EWL 3

Channing, William Ellery
1780-1842 **NCLC 17**
See also DLB 1, 59, 235; RGAL 4

Chao, Patricia 1955- **CLC 119**
See also CA 163

Chaplin, Charles Spencer
1889-1977 **CLC 16**
See Chaplin, Charlie
See also CA 81-84; 73-76

Chaplin, Charlie
See Chaplin, Charles Spencer
See also AAYA 61; DLB 44

Chapman, George 1559(?)-1634 . **DC 19; LC
22, 116**
See also BRW 1; DAM DRAM; DLB 62,
121; LMFS 1; RGEL 2

Chapman, Graham 1941-1989 **CLC 21**
See Monty Python
See also CA 116; 129; CANR 35, 95

Chapman, John Jay 1862-1933 **TCLC 7**
See also AMWS 14; CA 104; 191

Chapman, Lee
See Bradley, Marion Zimmer
See also GLL 1

Chapman, Walker
See Silverberg, Robert

Chappell, Fred (Davis) 1936- **CLC 40, 78,
162**
See also CA 5-8R; 198; CAAE 198; CAAS
4; CANR 8, 33, 67, 110; CN 6; CP 6, 7;
CSW; DLB 6, 105; HGG

Char, Rene(-Emile) 1907-1988 **CLC 9, 11,
14, 55; PC 56**
See also CA 13-16R; 124; CANR 32; DAM
POET; DLB 258; EWL 3; GFL 1789 to
the Present; MTCW 1, 2; RGWL 2, 3

Charby, Jay
See Ellison, Harlan (Jay)

Chardin, Pierre Teilhard de
See Teilhard de Chardin, (Marie Joseph)
Pierre

Chariton fl. 1st cent. (?)- **CMLC 49**

Charlemagne 742-814 **CMLC 37**

Charles I 1600-1649 **LC 13**

Charriere, Isabelle de 1740-1805 .. **NCLC 66**
See also DLB 313

Chartier, Alain c. 1392-1430 **LC 94**
See also DLB 208

Chartier, Emile-Auguste
See Alain

Charyn, Jerome 1937- **CLC 5, 8, 18**
See also CA 5-8R; CAAS 1; CANR 7, 61,
101; CMW 4; CN 1, 2, 3, 4, 5, 6, 7;
DLBY 1983; MTCW 1

Chase, Adam
See Marlowe, Stephen

Chase, Mary (Coyle) 1907-1981 **DC 1**
See also CA 77-80; 105; CAD; CWD; DFS
11; DLB 228; SATA 17; SATA-Obit 29

Chase, Mary Ellen 1887-1973 **CLC 2;
TCLC 124**
See also CA 13-16; 41-44R; CAP 1; SATA
10

Chase, Nicholas
See Hyde, Anthony
See also CCA 1

Chateaubriand, Francois Rene de
1768-1848 **NCLC 3, 134**
See also DLB 119; EW 5; GFL 1789 to the
Present; RGWL 2, 3; TWA

Chatelet, Gabrielle-Emilie Du
See du Chatelet, Emilie
See also DLB 313

Chatterje, Sarat Chandra 1876-1936(?)
See Chatterji, Saratchandra
See also CA 109

Chatterji, Bankim Chandra
1838-1894 **NCLC 19**

Chatterji, Saratchandra **TCLC 13**
See Chatterje, Sarat Chandra
See also CA 186; EWL 3

Chatterton, Thomas 1752-1770 **LC 3, 54**
See also DAM POET; DLB 109; RGEL 2

Chatwin, (Charles) Bruce
1940-1989 **CLC 28, 57, 59**
See also AAYA 4; BEST 90:1; BRWS 4;
CA 85-88; 127; CPW; DAM POP; DLB
194, 204; EWL 3; MTFW 2005

Chaucer, Daniel
See Ford, Ford Madox
See also RHW

Chaucer, Geoffrey 1340(?)-1400 .. **LC 17, 56;
PC 19, 58; WLCS**
See also BRW 1; BRWC 1; BRWR 2; CD-
BLB Before 1660; DA; DA3; DAB;
DAC; DAM MST, POET; DLB 146;
LAIT 1; PAB; PFS 14; RGEL 2; TEA;
WLIT 3; WP

Chavez, Denise (Elia) 1948- **HLC 1**
See also CA 131; CANR 56, 81, 137; DAM
MULT; DLB 122; FW; HW 1, 2; LLW;
MAL 5; MTCW 2; MTFW 2005

Chaviaras, Strates 1935-
See Haviaras, Stratis
See also CA 105

Chayefsky, Paddy **CLC 23**
See Chayefsky, Sidney
See also CAD; DLB 7, 44; DLBY 1981;
RGAL 4

Chayefsky, Sidney 1923-1981
See Chayefsky, Paddy
See also CA 9-12R; 104; CANR 18; DAM
DRAM

Chedid, Andree 1920- **CLC 47**
See also CA 145; CANR 95; EWL 3

Cheever, John 1912-1982 **CLC 3, 7, 8, 11,
15, 25, 64; SSC 1, 38, 57; WLC 2**
See also AAYA 65; AMWS 1; BPFB 1; CA
5-8R; 106; CABS 1; CANR 5, 27, 76;
CDALB 1941-1968; CN 1, 2, 3; CPW;
DA; DA3; DAB; DAC; DAM MST, NOV,
POP; DLB 2, 102, 227; DLBY 1980,
1982; EWL 3; EXPS; INT CANR-5;
MAL 5; MTCW 1, 2; MTFW 2005;
RGAL 4; RGSF 2; SSFS 2, 14; TUS

Cheever, Susan 1943- **CLC 18, 48**
See also CA 103; CANR 27, 51, 92; DLBY
1982; INT CANR-27

Chekhonte, Antosha
See Chekhov, Anton (Pavlovich)

Chekhov, Anton (Pavlovich)
1860-1904 **DC 9; SSC 2, 28, 41, 51,
85; TCLC 3, 10, 31, 55, 96, 163; WLC
2**
See also AAYA 68; BYA 14; CA 104; 124;
DA; DA3; DAB; DAC; DAM DRAM,
MST; DFS 1, 5, 10, 12; DLB 277; EW 7;
EWL 3; EXPS; LAIT 3; LATS 1:1; RGSF
2; RGWL 2, 3; SATA 90; SSFS 5, 13, 14;
TWA

Cheney, Lynne V. 1941- **CLC 70**
See also CA 89-92; CANR 58, 117; SATA
152

Chernyshevsky, Nikolai Gavrilovich
See Chernyshevsky, Nikolay Gavrilovich
See also DLB 238

Chernyshevsky, Nikolay Gavrilovich
1828-1889 **NCLC 1**
See Chernyshevsky, Nikolai Gavrilovich

Cherry, Carolyn Janice **CLC 35**
See Cherryh, C. J.
See also AAYA 24; BPFB 1; DLBY 1980;
FANT; SATA 93; SCFW 2; SFW 4; YAW

Cherryh, C. J. 1942-
See Cherry, Carolyn Janice
See also CA 65-68; CANR 10, 147

Chesnutt, Charles W(addell)
1858-1932 **BLC 1; SSC 7, 54; TCLC
5, 39**
See also AFAW 1, 2; AMWS 14; BW 1, 3;
CA 106; 125; CANR 76; DAM MULT;
DLB 12, 50, 78; EWL 3; MAL 5; MTCW
1, 2; MTFW 2005; RGAL 4; RGSF 2;
SSFS 11

Chester, Alfred 1929(?)-1971 **CLC 49**
See also CA 196; 33-36R; DLB 130; MAL
5

Chesterton, G(ilbert) K(eith)
1874-1936 . **PC 28; SSC 1, 46; TCLC 1,
6, 64**
See also AAYA 57; BRW 6; CA 104; 132;
CANR 73, 131; CDBLB 1914-1945;
CMW 4; DAM NOV, POET; DLB 10, 19,
34, 70, 98, 149, 178; EWL 3; FANT;
MSW; MTCW 1, 2; MTFW 2005; RGEL
2; RGSF 2; SATA 27; SUFW 1

Chettle, Henry 1560-1607(?) **LC 112**
See also DLB 136; RGEL 2

Chiang, Pin-chin 1904-1986
See Ding Ling
See also CA 118

Chief Joseph 1840-1904 **NNAL**
See also CA 152; DA3; DAM MULT

Chief Seattle 1786(?)-1866 **NNAL**
See also DA3; DAM MULT

Ch'ien, Chung-shu 1910-1998 **CLC 22**
See Qian Zhongshu
See also CA 130; CANR 73; MTCW 1, 2
Chikamatsu Monzaemon 1653-1724 ... **LC 66**
See also RGWL 2, 3
Child, L. Maria
See Child, Lydia Maria
Child, Lydia Maria 1802-1880 .. **NCLC 6, 73**
See also DLB 1, 74, 243; RGAL 4; SATA 67
Child, Mrs.
See Child, Lydia Maria
Child, Philip 1898-1978 **CLC 19, 68**
See also CA 13-14; CAP 1; CP 1; DLB 68; RHW; SATA 47
Childers, (Robert) Erskine
1870-1922 **TCLC 65**
See also CA 113; 153; DLB 70
Childress, Alice 1920-1994 . **BLC 1; CLC 12, 15, 86, 96; DC 4; TCLC 116**
See also AAYA 8; BW 2, 3; BYA 2; CA 45-48; 146; CAD; CANR 3, 27, 50, 74; CLR 14; CWD; DA3; DAM DRAM, MULT, NOV; DFS 2, 8, 14; DLB 7, 38, 249; JRDA; LAIT 5; MAICYA 1, 2; MAICYAS 1; MAL 5; MTCW 1, 2; MTFW 2005; RGAL 4; SATA 7, 48, 81; TUS; WYA; YAW
Chin, Frank (Chew, Jr.) 1940- **AAL; CLC 135; DC 7**
See also CA 33-36R; CAD; CANR 71; CD 5, 6; DAM MULT; DLB 206, 312; LAIT 5; RGAL 4
Chin, Marilyn (Mei Ling) 1955- **PC 40**
See also CA 129; CANR 70, 113; CWP; DLB 312
Chislett, (Margaret) Anne 1943- **CLC 34**
See also CA 151
Chitty, Thomas Willes 1926- **CLC 11**
See Hinde, Thomas
See also CA 5-8R; CN 7
Chivers, Thomas Holley
1809-1858 **NCLC 49**
See also DLB 3, 248; RGAL 4
Choi, Susan 1969- **CLC 119**
See also CA 223
Chomette, Rene Lucien 1898-1981
See Clair, Rene
See also CA 103
Chomsky, Avram Noam
See Chomsky, Noam
Chomsky, Noam 1928- **CLC 132**
See also CA 17-20R; CANR 28, 62, 110, 132; DA3; DLB 246; MTCW 1, 2; MTFW 2005
Chona, Maria 1845(?)-1936 **NNAL**
See also CA 144
Chopin, Kate **SSC 8, 68; TCLC 127; WLCS**
See Chopin, Katherine
See also AAYA 33; AMWR 2; AMWS 1; BYA 11, 15; CDALB 1865-1917; DA; DAB; DLB 12, 78; EXPN; EXPS; FL 1:3; FW; LAIT 3; MAL 5; MAWW; NFS 3; RGAL 4; RGSF 2; SSFS 2, 13, 17; TUS
Chopin, Katherine 1851-1904
See Chopin, Kate
See also CA 104; 122; DA3; DAC; DAM MST, NOV
Chretien de Troyes c. 12th cent. - . **CMLC 10**
See also DLB 208; EW 1; RGWL 2, 3; TWA
Christie
See Ichikawa, Kon
Christie, Agatha (Mary Clarissa)
1890-1976 .. **CLC 1, 6, 8, 12, 39, 48, 110**
See also AAYA 9; AITN 1, 2; BPFB 1; BRWS 2; CA 17-20R; 61-64; CANR 10, 37, 108; CBD; CDBLB 1914-1945; CMW

4; CN 1, 2; CPW; CWD; DA3; DAB; DAC; DAM NOV; DFS 2; DLB 13, 77, 245; MSW; MTCW 1, 2; MTFW 2005; NFS 8; RGEL 2; RHW; SATA 36; TEA; YAW
Christie, Philippa **CLC 21**
See Pearce, Philippa
See also BYA 5; CANR 109; CLR 9; DLB 161; MAICYA 1; SATA 1, 67, 129
Christine de Pizan 1365(?)-1431(?) **LC 9; PC 68**
See also DLB 208; RGWL 2, 3
Chuang Tzu c. 369B.C.-c.
286B.C. **CMLC 57**
Chubb, Elmer
See Masters, Edgar Lee
Chulkov, Mikhail Dmitrievich
1743-1792 **LC 2**
See also DLB 150
Churchill, Caryl 1938- **CLC 31, 55, 157; DC 5**
See Churchill, Chick
See also BRWS 4; CA 102; CANR 22, 46, 108; CBD; CD 6; CWD; DFS 12, 16; DLB 13, 310; EWL 3; FW; MTCW 1; RGEL 2
Churchill, Charles 1731-1764 **LC 3**
See also DLB 109; RGEL 2
Churchill, Chick
See Churchill, Caryl
See also CD 5
Churchill, Sir Winston (Leonard Spencer)
1874-1965 **TCLC 113**
See also BRW 6; CA 97-100; CDBLB 1890-1914; DA3; DLB 100; DLBD 16; LAIT 4; MTCW 1, 2
Chute, Carolyn 1947- **CLC 39**
See also CA 123; CANR 135; CN 7
Ciardi, John (Anthony) 1916-1986 . **CLC 10, 40, 44, 129; PC 69**
Scc also CA 5-8R; 118; CAAS 2; CANR 5, 33; CLR 19; CP 1, 2, 3, 4; CWRI 5; DAM POET; DLB 5; DLBY 1986; INT CANR-5; MAICYA 1, 2; MAL 5; MTCW 1, 2; MTFW 2005; RGAL 4; SAAS 26; SATA 1, 65; SATA-Obit 46
Cibber, Colley 1671-1757 **LC 66**
See also DLB 84; RGEL 2
Cicero, Marcus Tullius
106B.C.-43B.C. **CMLC 3, 81**
See also AW 1; CDWLB 1; DLB 211; RGWL 2, 3; WLIT 8
Cimino, Michael 1943- **CLC 16**
See also CA 105
Cioran, E(mil) M. 1911-1995 **CLC 64**
See also CA 25-28R; 149; CANR 91; DLB 220; EWL 3
Cisneros, Sandra 1954- **CLC 69, 118, 193; HLC 1; PC 52; SSC 32, 72**
See also AAYA 9, 53; AMWS 7; CA 131; CANR 64, 118; CN 7; CWP; DA3; DAM MULT; DLB 122, 152; EWL 3; EXPN; FL 1:5; FW; HW 1, 2; LAIT 5; LATS 1:2; LLW; MAICYA 2; MAL 5; MTCW 2; MTFW 2005; NFS 2; PFS 19; RGAL 4; RGSF 2; SSFS 3, 13; WLIT 1; YAW
Cixous, Helene 1937- **CLC 92**
See also CA 126; CANR 55, 123; CWW 2; DLB 83, 242; EWL 3; FL 1:5; FW; GLL 2; MTCW 1, 2; MTFW 2005; TWA
Clair, Rene **CLC 20**
See Chomette, Rene Lucien
Clampitt, Amy 1920-1994 **CLC 32; PC 19**
See also AMWS 9; CA 110; 146; CANR 29, 79; CP 4, 5; DLB 105; MAL 5
Clancy, Thomas L., Jr. 1947-
See Clancy, Tom
See also CA 125; 131; CANR 62, 105; DA3; INT CA-131; MTCW 1, 2; MTFW 2005

Clancy, Tom **CLC 45, 112**
See Clancy, Thomas L., Jr.
See also AAYA 9, 51; BEST 89:1, 90:1; BPFB 1; BYA 10, 11; CANR 132; CMW 4; CPW; DAM NOV, POP; DLB 227
Clare, John 1793-1864 **NCLC 9, 86; PC 23**
See also BRWS 11; DAB; DAM POET; DLB 55, 96; RGEL 2
Clarin
See Alas (y Urena), Leopoldo (Enrique Garcia)
Clark, Al C.
See Goines, Donald
Clark, Brian (Robert)
See Clark, (Robert) Brian
See also CD 6
Clark, (Robert) Brian 1932- **CLC 29**
See Clark, Brian (Robert)
See also CA 41-44R; CANR 67; CBD; CD 5
Clark, Curt
See Westlake, Donald E(dwin)
Clark, Eleanor 1913-1996 **CLC 5, 19**
See also CA 9-12R; 151; CANR 41; CN 1, 2, 3, 4, 5, 6; DLB 6
Clark, J. P.
See Clark Bekederemo, J(ohnson) P(epper)
See also CDWLB 3; DLB 117
Clark, John Pepper
See Clark Bekederemo, J(ohnson) P(epper)
See also AFW; CD 5; CP 1, 2, 3, 4, 5, 6, 7; RGEL 2
Clark, Kenneth (Mackenzie)
1903-1983 **TCLC 147**
See also CA 93-96; 109; CANR 36; MTCW 1, 2; MTFW 2005
Clark, M. R.
See Clark, Mavis Thorpe
Clark, Mavis Thorpe 1909-1999 **CLC 12**
See also CA 57 60; CANR 8, 37, 107; CLR 30; CWRI 5; MAICYA 1, 2; SAAS 5; SATA 8, 74
Clark, Walter Van Tilburg
1909-1971 **CLC 28**
See also CA 9-12R; 33-36R; CANR 63, 113; CN 1; DLB 9, 206; LAIT 2; MAL 5; RGAL 4; SATA 8; TCWW 1, 2
Clark Bekederemo, J(ohnson) P(epper)
1935- **BLC 1; CLC 38; DC 5**
See Bekederemo, J. P. Clark; Clark, J. P.; Clark, John Pepper
See also BW 1; CA 65-68; CANR 16, 72; DAM DRAM, MULT; DFS 13; EWL 3; MTCW 2; MTFW 2005
Clarke, Arthur C(harles) 1917- **CLC 1, 4, 13, 18, 35, 136; SSC 3**
See also AAYA 4, 33; BPFB 1; BYA 13; CA 1-4R; CANR 2, 28, 55, 74, 130; CN 1, 2, 3, 4, 5, 6, 7; CPW; DA3; DAM POP; DLB 261; JRDA; LAIT 5; MAICYA 1, 2; MTCW 1, 2; MTFW 2005; SATA 13, 70, 115; SCFW 1, 2; SFW 4; SSFS 4, 18; TCLE 1:1; YAW
Clarke, Austin 1896-1974 **CLC 6, 9**
See also CA 29-32; 49-52; CAP 2; CP 1, 2; DAM POET; DLB 10, 20; EWL 3; RGEL 2
Clarke, Austin C(hesterfield) 1934- .. **BLC 1; CLC 8, 53; SSC 45**
See also BW 1; CA 25-28R; CAAS 16; CANR 14, 32, 68, 140; CN 1, 2, 3, 4, 5, 6, 7; DAC; DAM MULT; DLB 53, 125; DNFS 2; MTCW 2; MTFW 2005; RGSF 2
Clarke, Gillian 1937- **CLC 61**
See also CA 106; CP 3, 4, 5, 6, 7; CWP; DLB 40
Clarke, Marcus (Andrew Hislop)
1846-1881 **NCLC 19**
See also DLB 230; RGEL 2; RGSF 2

Clarke, Shirley 1925-1997 CLC 16
See also CA 189
Clash, The
See Headon, (Nicky) Topper; Jones, Mick; Simonon, Paul; Strummer, Joe
Claudel, Paul (Louis Charles Marie)
1868-1955 TCLC 2, 10
See also CA 104; 165; DLB 192, 258, 321; EW 8; EWL 3; GFL 1789 to the Present; RGWL 2, 3; TWA
Claudian 370(?)-404(?) CMLC 46
See also RGWL 2, 3
Claudius, Matthias 1740-1815 NCLC 75
See also DLB 97
Clavell, James (duMaresq)
1925-1994 CLC 6, 25, 87
See also BPFB 1; CA 25-28R; 146; CANR 26, 48; CN 5; CPW; DA3; DAM NOV, POP; MTCW 1, 2; MTFW 2005; NFS 10; RHW
Clayman, Gregory CLC 65
Cleaver, (Leroy) Eldridge
1935-1998 BLC 1; CLC 30, 119
See also BW 1, 3; CA 21-24R; 167; CANR 16, 75; DA3; DAM MULT; MTCW 2; YAW
Cleese, John (Marwood) 1939- CLC 21
See Monty Python
See also CA 112; 116; CANR 35; MTCW 1
Cleishbotham, Jebediah
See Scott, Sir Walter
Cleland, John 1710-1789 LC 2, 48
See also DLB 39; RGEL 2
Clemens, Samuel Langhorne 1835-1910
See Twain, Mark
See also CA 104; 135; CDALB 1865-1917; DA; DA3; DAB; DAC; DAM MST, NOV; DLB 12, 23, 64, 74, 186, 189; JRDA; LMFS 1; MAICYA 1, 2; NCFS 4; NFS 20; SATA 100; YABC 2
Clement of Alexandria
150(?)-215(?) CMLC 41
Cleophil
See Congreve, William
Clerihew, E.
See Bentley, E(dmund) C(lerihew)
Clerk, N. W.
See Lewis, C.S.
Cleveland, John 1613-1658 LC 106
See also DLB 126; RGEL 2
Cliff, Jimmy CLC 21
See Chambers, James
See also CA 193
Cliff, Michelle 1946- BLCS; CLC 120
See also BW 2; CA 116; CANR 39, 72; CD-WLB 3; DLB 157; FW; GLL 2
Clifford, Lady Anne 1590-1676 LC 76
See also DLB 151
Clifton, (Thelma) Lucille 1936- BLC 1;
CLC 19, 66, 162; PC 17
See also AFAW 2; BW 2, 3; CA 49-52; CANR 2, 24, 42, 76, 97, 138; CLR 5; CP 2, 3, 4, 5, 6, 7; CSW; CWP; CWRI 5; DA3; DAM MULT, POET; DLB 5, 41; EXPP; MAICYA 1, 2; MTCW 1, 2; MTFW 2005; PFS 1, 14; SATA 20, 69, 128; WP
Clinton, Dirk
See Silverberg, Robert
Clough, Arthur Hugh 1819-1861 .. NCLC 27, 163
See also BRW 5; DLB 32; RGEL 2
Clutha, Janet Paterson Frame 1924-2004
See Frame, Janet
See also CA 1-4R; 224; CANR 2, 36, 76, 135; MTCW 1, 2; SATA 119
Clyne, Terence
See Blatty, William Peter

Cobalt, Martin
See Mayne, William (James Carter)
Cobb, Irvin S(hrewsbury)
1876-1944 TCLC 77
See also CA 175; DLB 11, 25, 86
Cobbett, William 1763-1835 NCLC 49
See also DLB 43, 107, 158; RGEL 2
Coburn, D(onald) L(ee) 1938- CLC 10
See also CA 89-92; DFS 23
Cocteau, Jean (Maurice Eugene Clement)
1889-1963 CLC 1, 8, 15, 16, 43; DC 17; TCLC 119; WLC 2
See also CA 25-28; CANR 40; CAP 2; DA; DA3; DAB; DAC; DAM DRAM, MST, NOV; DLB 65, 258, 321; EW 10; EWL 3; GFL 1789 to the Present; MTCW 1, 2; RGWL 2, 3; TWA
Codrescu, Andrei 1946- CLC 46, 121
See also CA 33-36R; CAAS 19; CANR 13, 34, 53, 76, 125; CN 7; DA3; DAM POET; MAL 5; MTCW 2; MTFW 2005
Coe, Max
See Bourne, Randolph S(illiman)
Coe, Tucker
See Westlake, Donald E(dwin)
Coen, Ethan 1958- CLC 108
See also AAYA 54; CA 126; CANR 85
Coen, Joel 1955- CLC 108
See also AAYA 54; CA 126; CANR 119
The Coen Brothers
See Coen, Ethan; Coen, Joel
Coetzee, J. M. 1940- CLC 23, 33, 66, 117, 161, 162
See also AAYA 37; AFW; BRWS 6; CA 77-80; CANR 41, 54, 74, 114, 133; CN 4, 5, 6, 7; DA3; DAM NOV; DLB 225, 326; EWL 3; LMFS 2; MTCW 1, 2; MTFW 2005; NFS 21; WLIT 2; WWE 1
Coetzee, John Maxwell
See Coetzee, J. M.
Coffey, Brian
See Koontz, Dean R.
Coffin, Robert P(eter) Tristram
1892-1955 TCLC 95
See also CA 123; 169; DLB 45
Cohan, George M. 1878-1942 TCLC 60
See also CA 157; DLB 249; RGAL 4
Cohan, George Michael
See Cohan, George M.
Cohen, Arthur A(llen) 1928-1986 CLC 7, 31
See also CA 1-4R; 120; CANR 1, 17, 42; DLB 28; RGHL
Cohen, Leonard 1934- CLC 3, 38
See also CA 21-24R; CANR 14, 69; CN 1, 2, 3, 4, 5, 6; CP 1, 2, 3, 4, 5, 6, 7; DAC; DAM MST; DLB 53; EWL 3; MTCW 1
Cohen, Leonard Norman
See Cohen, Leonard
Cohen, Matt(hew) 1942-1999 CLC 19
See also CA 61-64; 187; CAAS 18; CANR 40; CN 1, 2, 3, 4, 5, 6; DAC; DLB 53
Cohen-Solal, Annie 1948- CLC 50
See also CA 239
Colegate, Isabel 1931- CLC 36
See also CA 17-20R; CANR 8, 22, 74; CN 4, 5, 6, 7; DLB 14, 231; INT CANR-22; MTCW 1
Coleman, Emmett
See Reed, Ishmael (Scott)
Coleridge, Hartley 1796-1849 NCLC 90
See also DLB 96
Coleridge, M. E.
See Coleridge, Mary E(lizabeth)
Coleridge, Mary E(lizabeth)
1861-1907 TCLC 73
See also CA 116; 166; DLB 19, 98

Coleridge, Samuel Taylor
1772-1834 NCLC 9, 54, 99, 111; PC 11, 39, 67; WLC 2
See also AAYA 66; BRW 4; BRWR 2; BYA 4; CDBLB 1789-1832; DA; DA3; DAB; DAC; DAM MST, POET; DLB 93, 107; EXPP; LATS 1:1; LMFS 1; PAB; PFS 4, 5; RGEL 2; TEA; WLIT 3; WP
Coleridge, Sara 1802-1852 NCLC 31
See also DLB 199
Coles, Don 1928- CLC 46
See also CA 115; CANR 38; CP 5, 6, 7
Coles, Robert (Martin) 1929- CLC 108
See also CA 45-48; CANR 3, 32, 66, 70, 135; INT CANR-32; SATA 23
Colette, (Sidonie-Gabrielle)
1873-1954 .. SSC 10, 93; TCLC 1, 5, 16
See Willy, Colette
See also CA 104; 131; DA3; DAM NOV; DLB 65; EW 9; EWL 3; GFL 1789 to the Present; MTCW 1, 2; MTFW 2005; RGWL 2, 3; TWA
Collett, (Jacobine) Camilla (Wergeland)
1813-1895 NCLC 22
Collier, Christopher 1930- CLC 30
See also AAYA 13; BYA 2; CA 33-36R; CANR 13, 33, 102; JRDA; MAICYA 1, 2; SATA 16, 70; WYA; YAW 1
Collier, James Lincoln 1928- CLC 30
See also AAYA 13; BYA 2; CA 9-12R; CANR 4, 33, 60, 102; CLR 3; DAM POP; JRDA; MAICYA 1, 2; SAAS 21; SATA 8, 70, 166; WYA; YAW 1
Collier, Jeremy 1650-1726 LC 6
Collier, John 1901-1980 . SSC 19; TCLC 127
See also CA 65-68; 97-100; CANR 10; CN 1, 2; DLB 77, 255; FANT; SUFW 1
Collier, Mary 1690-1762 LC 86
See also DLB 95
Collingwood, R(obin) G(eorge)
1889(?)-1943 TCLC 67
See also CA 117; 155; DLB 262
Collins, Billy 1941- PC 68
See also AAYA 64; CA 151; CANR 92; CP 7; MTFW 2005; PFS 18
Collins, Hunt
See Hunter, Evan
Collins, Linda 1931- CLC 44
See also CA 125
Collins, Tom
See Furphy, Joseph
See also RGEL 2
Collins, (William) Wilkie
1824-1889 NCLC 1, 18, 93; SSC 93
See also BRWS 6; CDBLB 1832-1890; CMW 4; DLB 18, 70, 159; GL 2; MSW; RGEL 2; RGSF 2; SUFW 1; WLIT 7
Collins, William 1721-1759 LC 4, 40; PC 72
See also BRW 3; DAM POET; DLB 109; RGEL 2
Collodi, Carlo NCLC 54
See Lorenzini, Carlo
See also CLR 5; WCH; WLIT 7
Colman, George
See Glassco, John
Colman, George, the Elder
1732-1794 LC 98
See also RGEL 2
Colonna, Vittoria 1492-1547 LC 71
See also RGWL 2, 3
Colt, Winchester Remington
See Hubbard, L. Ron
Colter, Cyrus J. 1910-2002 CLC 58
See also BW 1; CA 65-68; 205; CANR 10, 66; CN 2, 3, 4, 5, 6; DLB 33
Colton, James
See Hansen, Joseph
See also GLL 1

Colum, Padraic 1881-1972 **CLC 28**
See also BYA 4; CA 73-76; 33-36R; CANR 35; CLR 36; CP 1; CWRI 5; DLB 19; MAICYA 1, 2; MTCW 1; RGEL 2; SATA 15; WCH

Colvin, James
See Moorcock, Michael

Colwin, Laurie (E.) 1944-1992 **CLC 5, 13, 23, 84**
See also CA 89-92; 139; CANR 20, 46; DLB 218; DLBY 1980; MTCW 1

Comfort, Alex(ander) 1920-2000 **CLC 7**
See also CA 1-4R; 190; CANR 1, 45; CN 1, 2, 3, 4; CP 1, 2, 3, 4, 5, 6, 7; DAM POP; MTCW 2

Comfort, Montgomery
See Campbell, (John) Ramsey

Compton-Burnett, I(vy) 1892(?)-1969 **CLC 1, 3, 10, 15, 34; TCLC 180**
See also BRW 7; CA 1-4R; 25-28R; CANR 4; DAM NOV; DLB 36; EWL 3; MTCW 1, 2; RGEL 2

Comstock, Anthony 1844-1915 **TCLC 13**
See also CA 110; 169

Comte, Auguste 1798-1857 **NCLC 54**

Conan Doyle, Arthur
See Doyle, Sir Arthur Conan
See also BPFB 1; BYA 4, 5, 11

Conde (Abellan), Carmen 1901-1996 **HLCS 1**
See also CA 177; CWW 2; DLB 108; EWL 3; HW 2

Conde, Maryse 1937- **BLCS; CLC 52, 92**
See also BW 2, 3; CA 110; 190; CAAE 190; CANR 30, 53, 76; CWW 2; DAM MULT; EWL 3; MTCW 2; MTFW 2005

Condillac, Etienne Bonnot de 1714-1780 **LC 26**
See also DLB 313

Condon, Richard (Thomas) 1915-1996 **CLC 4, 6, 8, 10, 45, 100**
See also BEST 90:3; BPFB 1; CA 1-4R; 151; CAAS 1; CANR 2, 23; CMW 4; CN 1, 2, 3, 4, 5, 6; DAM NOV; INT CANR-23; MAL 5; MTCW 1, 2

Condorcet **LC 104**
See Condorcet, marquis de Marie-Jean-Antoine-Nicolas Caritat
See also GFL Beginnings to 1789

Condorcet, marquis de Marie-Jean-Antoine-Nicolas Caritat 1743-1794
See Condorcet
See also DLB 313

Confucius 551B.C.-479B.C. **CMLC 19, 65; WLCS**
See also DA; DA3; DAB; DAC; DAM MST

Congreve, William 1670-1729 ... **DC 2; LC 5, 21; WLC 2**
See also BRW 2; CDBLB 1660-1789; DA; DAB; DAC; DAM DRAM, MST, POET; DFS 15; DLB 39, 84; RGEL 2; WLIT 3

Conley, Robert J(ackson) 1940- **NNAL**
See also CA 41-44R; CANR 15, 34, 45, 96; DAM MULT; TCWW 2

Connell, Evan S(helby), Jr. 1924- . **CLC 4, 6, 45**
See also AAYA 7; AMWS 14; CA 1-4R; CAAS 2; CANR 2, 39, 76, 97, 140; CN 1, 2, 3, 4, 5, 6; DAM NOV; DLB 2; DLBY 1981; MAL 5; MTCW 1, 2; MTFW 2005

Connelly, Marc(us Cook) 1890-1980 . **CLC 7**
See also CA 85-88; 102; CAD; CANR 30; DFS 12; DLB 7; DLBY 1980; MAL 5; RGAL 4; SATA-Obit 25

Connor, Ralph **TCLC 31**
See Gordon, Charles William
See also DLB 92; TCWW 1, 2

Conrad, Joseph 1857-1924 **SSC 9, 67, 69, 71; TCLC 1, 6, 13, 25, 43, 57; WLC 2**
See also AAYA 26; BPFB 1; BRW 6; BRWC 1; BRWR 2; BYA 2; CA 104; 131; CANR 60; CDBLB 1890-1914; DA; DA3; DAB; DAC; DAM MST, NOV; DLB 10, 34, 98, 156; EWL 3; EXPN; EXPS; LAIT 2; LATS 1:1; LMFS 1; MTCW 1, 2; MTFW 2005; NFS 2, 16; RGEL 2; RGSF 2; SATA 27; SSFS 1, 12; TEA; WLIT 4

Conrad, Robert Arnold
See Hart, Moss

Conroy, (Donald) Pat(rick) 1945- ... **CLC 30, 74**
See also AAYA 8, 52; AITN 1; BPFB 1; CA 85-88; CANR 24, 53, 129; CN 7; CPW; CSW; DA3; DAM NOV, POP; DLB 6; LAIT 5; MAL 5; MTCW 1, 2; MTFW 2005

Constant (de Rebecque), (Henri) Benjamin 1767-1830 **NCLC 6**
See also DLB 119; EW 4; GFL 1789 to the Present

Conway, Jill K(er) 1934- **CLC 152**
See also CA 130; CANR 94

Conybeare, Charles Augustus
See Eliot, T(homas) S(tearns)

Cook, Michael 1933-1994 **CLC 58**
See also CA 93-96; CANR 68; DLB 53

Cook, Robin 1940- **CLC 14**
See also AAYA 32; BEST 90:2; BPFB 1; CA 108, 111, CANR 41, 90, 109; CPW; DA3; DAM POP; HGG; INT CA-111

Cook, Roy
See Silverberg, Robert

Cooke, Elizabeth 1948- **CLC 55**
See also CA 129

Cooke, John Esten 1830-1886 **NCLC 5**
See also DLB 3, 248; RGAL 4

Cooke, John Estes
See Baum, L(yman) Frank

Cooke, M. E.
See Creasey, John

Cooke, Margaret
See Creasey, John

Cooke, Rose Terry 1827-1892 **NCLC 110**
See also DLB 12, 74

Cook-Lynn, Elizabeth 1930- **CLC 93; NNAL**
See also CA 133; DAM MULT; DLB 175

Cooney, Ray **CLC 62**
See also CBD

Cooper, Anthony Ashley 1671-1713 .. **LC 107**
See also DLB 101

Cooper, Dennis 1953- **CLC 203**
See also CA 133; CANR 72, 86; GLL 1; HGG

Cooper, Douglas 1960- **CLC 86**

Cooper, Henry St. John
See Creasey, John

Cooper, J(oan) California (?)- **CLC 56**
See also AAYA 12; BW 1; CA 125; CANR 55; DAM MULT; DLB 212

Cooper, James Fenimore 1789-1851 **NCLC 1, 27, 54**
See also AAYA 22; AMW; BPFB 1; CDALB 1640-1865; CLR 105; DA3; DLB 3, 183, 250, 254; LAIT 1; NFS 9; RGAL 4; SATA 19; TUS; WCH

Cooper, Susan Fenimore 1813-1894 **NCLC 129**
See also ANW; DLB 239, 254

Coover, Robert (Lowell) 1932- **CLC 3, 7, 15, 32, 46, 87, 161; SSC 15**
See also AMWS 5; BPFB 1; CA 45-48; CANR 3, 37, 58, 115; CN 1, 2, 3, 4, 5, 6, 7; DAM NOV; DLB 2, 227; DLBY 1981; EWL 3; MAL 5; MTCW 1, 2; MTFW 2005; RGAL 4; RGSF 2

Copeland, Stewart (Armstrong) 1952- **CLC 26**

Copernicus, Nicolaus 1473-1543 **LC 45**

Coppard, A(lfred) E(dgar) 1878-1957 **SSC 21; TCLC 5**
See also BRWS 8; CA 114; 167; DLB 162; EWL 3; HGG; RGEL 2; RGSF 2; SUFW 1; YABC 1

Coppee, Francois 1842-1908 **TCLC 25**
See also CA 170; DLB 217

Coppola, Francis Ford 1939- ... **CLC 16, 126**
See also AAYA 39; CA 77-80; CANR 40, 78; DLB 44

Copway, George 1818-1869 **NNAL**
See also DAM MULT; DLB 175, 183

Corbiere, Tristan 1845-1875 **NCLC 43**
See also DLB 217; GFL 1789 to the Present

Corcoran, Barbara (Asenath) 1911- **CLC 17**
See also AAYA 14; CA 21-24R; 191; CAAE 191; CAAS 2; CANR 11, 28, 48; CLR 50; DLB 52; JRDA; MAICYA 2; MAIC-YAS 1; RHW; SAAS 20; SATA 3, 77; SATA-Essay 125

Cordelier, Maurice
See Giraudoux, Jean(-Hippolyte)

Corelli, Marie **TCLC 51**
See Mackay, Mary
See also DLB 34, 156; RGEL 2; SUFW 1

Corinna c. 225B.C.-c. 305B.C. **CMLC 72**

Corman, Cid **CLC 9**
See Corman, Sidney
See also CAAS 2; CP 1, 2, 3, 4, 5, 6, 7; DLB 5, 193

Corman, Sidney 1924-2004
See Corman, Cid
See also CA 85-88; 225; CANR 44; DAM POET

Cormier, Robert (Edmund) 1925-2000 **CLC 12, 30**
See also AAYA 3, 19; BYA 1, 2, 6, 8, 9; CA 1-4R; CANR 5, 23, 76, 93; CDALB 1968-1988; CLR 12, 55; DA; DAB; DAC; DAM MST, NOV; DLB 52; EXPN; INT CANR-23; JRDA; LAIT 5; MAICYA 1, 2; MTCW 1, 2; MTFW 2005; NFS 2, 18; SATA 10, 45, 83; SATA-Obit 122; WYA; YAW

Corn, Alfred (DeWitt III) 1943- **CLC 33**
See also CA 179; CAAE 179; CAAS 25; CANR 44; CP 3, 4, 5, 6, 7; CSW; DLB 120, 282; DLBY 1980

Corneille, Pierre 1606-1684 ... **DC 21; LC 28**
See also DAB; DAM MST; DFS 21; DLB 268; EW 3; GFL Beginnings to 1789; RGWL 2, 3; TWA

Cornwell, David (John Moore) 1931- **CLC 9, 15**
See le Carre, John
See also CA 5-8R; CANR 13, 33, 59, 107, 132; DA3; DAM POP; MTCW 1, 2; MTFW 2005

Cornwell, Patricia 1956- **CLC 155**
See also AAYA 16, 56; BPFB 1; CA 134; CANR 53, 131; CMW 4; CPW; CSW; DAM POP; DLB 306; MSW; MTCW 2; MTFW 2005

Cornwell, Patricia Daniels
See Cornwell, Patricia

Corso, (Nunzio) Gregory 1930-2001 . **CLC 1, 11; PC 33**
See also AMWS 12; BG 1:2; CA 5-8R; 193; CANR 41, 76, 132; CP 1, 2, 3, 4, 5, 6, 7; DA3; DLB 5, 16, 237; MAL 5; MTCW 1, 2; MTFW 2005; WP

Cortazar, Julio 1914-1984 ... **CLC 2, 3, 5, 10, 13, 15, 33, 34, 92; HLC 1; SSC 7, 76**
See also BPFB 2; CA 21-24R; CANR 12, 32, 81; CDWLB 3; DA3; DAM MULT, NOV; DLB 113; EWL 3; EXPS; HW 1, 2; LAW; MTCW 1, 2; MTFW 2005; RGSF 2; RGWL 2, 3; SSFS 3, 20; TWA; WLIT 1

Cortes, Hernan 1485-1547 **LC 31**

Corvinus, Jakob
See Raabe, Wilhelm (Karl)

Corwin, Cecil
See Kornbluth, C(yril) M.

Cosic, Dobrica 1921- **CLC 14**
See also CA 122; 138; CDWLB 4; CWW 2; DLB 181; EWL 3

Costain, Thomas B(ertram)
1885-1965 **CLC 30**
See also BYA 3; CA 5-8R; 25-28R; DLB 9; RHW

Costantini, Humberto 1924(?)-1987 . **CLC 49**
See also CA 131; 122; EWL 3; HW 1

Costello, Elvis 1954- **CLC 21**
See also CA 204

Costenoble, Philostene
See Ghelderode, Michel de

Cotes, Cecil V.
See Duncan, Sara Jeannette

Cotter, Joseph Seamon Sr.
1861-1949 **BLC 1; TCLC 28**
See also BW 1; CA 124; DAM MULT; DLB 50

Couch, Arthur Thomas Quiller
See Quiller-Couch, Sir Arthur (Thomas)

Coulton, James
See Hansen, Joseph

Couperus, Louis (Marie Anne)
1863-1923 **TCLC 15**
See also CA 115; EWL 3; RGWL 2, 3

Coupland, Douglas 1961- **CLC 85, 133**
See also AAYA 34; CA 142; CANR 57, 90, 130; CCA 1; CN 7; CPW; DAC; DAM POP

Court, Wesli
See Turco, Lewis (Putnam)

Courtenay, Bryce 1933- **CLC 59**
See also CA 138; CPW

Courtney, Robert
See Ellison, Harlan (Jay)

Cousteau, Jacques-Yves 1910-1997 .. **CLC 30**
See also CA 65-68; 159; CANR 15, 67; MTCW 1; SATA 38, 98

Coventry, Francis 1725-1754 **LC 46**

Coverdale, Miles c. 1487-1569 **LC 77**
See also DLB 167

Cowan, Peter (Walkinshaw)
1914-2002 **SSC 28**
See also CA 21-24R; CANR 9, 25, 50, 83; CN 1, 2, 3, 4, 5, 6, 7; DLB 260; RGSF 2

Coward, Noel (Peirce) 1899-1973 . **CLC 1, 9, 29, 51**
See also AITN 1; BRWS 2; CA 17-18; 41-44R; CANR 35, 132; CAP 2; CBD; CD-BLB 1914-1945; DA3; DAM DRAM; DFS 3, 6; DLB 10, 245; EWL 3; IDFW 3, 4; MTCW 1, 2; MTFW 2005; RGEL 2; TEA

Cowley, Abraham 1618-1667 **LC 43**
See also BRW 2; DLB 131, 151; PAB; RGEL 2

Cowley, Malcolm 1898-1989 **CLC 39**
See also AMWS 2; CA 5-8R; 128; CANR 3, 55; CP 1, 2, 3, 4; DLB 4, 48; DLBY 1981, 1989; EWL 3; MAL 5; MTCW 1, 2; MTFW 2005

Cowper, William 1731-1800 **NCLC 8, 94; PC 40**
See also BRW 3; DA3; DAM POET; DLB 104, 109; RGEL 2

Cox, William Trevor 1928-
See Trevor, William
See also CA 9-12R; CANR 4, 37, 55, 76, 102, 139; DAM NOV; INT CANR-37; MTCW 1, 2; MTFW 2005; TEA

Coyne, P. J.
See Masters, Hilary

Cozzens, James Gould 1903-1978 . **CLC 1, 4, 11, 92**
See also AMW; BPFB 1; CA 9-12R; 81-84; CANR 19; CDALB 1941-1968; CN 1, 2; DLB 9, 294; DLBD 2; DLBY 1984, 1997; EWL 3; MAL 5; MTCW 1, 2; MTFW 2005; RGAL 4

Crabbe, George 1754-1832 **NCLC 26, 121**
See also BRW 3; DLB 93; RGEL 2

Crace, Jim 1946- **CLC 157; SSC 61**
See also CA 128; 135; CANR 55, 70, 123; CN 5, 6, 7; DLB 231; INT CA-135

Craddock, Charles Egbert
See Murfree, Mary Noailles

Craig, A. A.
See Anderson, Poul (William)

Craik, Mrs.
See Craik, Dinah Maria (Mulock)
See also RGEL 2

Craik, Dinah Maria (Mulock)
1826-1887 **NCLC 38**
See Craik, Mrs.; Mulock, Dinah Maria
See also DLB 35, 163; MAICYA 1, 2; SATA 34

Cram, Ralph Adams 1863-1942 **TCLC 45**
See also CA 160

Cranch, Christopher Pearse
1813-1892 **NCLC 115**
See also DLB 1, 42, 243

Crane, (Harold) Hart 1899-1932 **PC 3; TCLC 2, 5, 80; WLC 2**
See also AMW; AMWR 2; CA 104; 127; CDALB 1917-1929; DA; DA3; DAB; DAC; DAM MST, POET; DLB 4, 48; EWL 3; MAL 5; MTCW 1, 2; MTFW 2005; RGAL 4; TUS

Crane, R(onald) S(almon)
1886-1967 **CLC 27**
See also CA 85-88; DLB 63

Crane, Stephen (Townley)
1871-1900 **SSC 7, 56, 70; TCLC 11, 17, 32; WLC 2**
See also AAYA 21; AMW; AMWC 1; BPFB 1; BYA 3; CA 109; 140; CANR 84; CDALB 1865-1917; DA; DA3; DAB; DAC; DAM MST, NOV, POET; DLB 12, 54, 78; EXPN; EXPS; LAIT 2; LMFS 2; MAL 5; NFS 4, 20; PFS 9; RGAL 4; RGSF 2; SSFS 4; TUS; WYA; YABC 2

Cranmer, Thomas 1489-1556 **LC 95**
See also DLB 132, 213

Cranshaw, Stanley
See Fisher, Dorothy (Frances) Canfield

Crase, Douglas 1944- **CLC 58**
See also CA 106

Crashaw, Richard 1612(?)-1649 **LC 24**
See also BRW 2; DLB 126; PAB; RGEL 2

Cratinus c. 519B.C.-c. 422B.C. **CMLC 54**
See also LMFS 1

Craven, Margaret 1901-1980 **CLC 17**
See also BYA 2; CA 103; CCA 1; DAC; LAIT 5

Crawford, F(rancis) Marion
1854-1909 **TCLC 10**
See also CA 107; 168; DLB 71; HGG; RGAL 4; SUFW 1

Crawford, Isabella Valancy
1850-1887 **NCLC 12, 127**
See also DLB 92; RGEL 2

Crayon, Geoffrey
See Irving, Washington

Creasey, John 1908-1973 **CLC 11**
See Marric, J. J.
See also CA 5-8R; 41-44R; CANR 8, 59; CMW 4; DLB 77; MTCW 1

Crebillon, Claude Prosper Jolyot de (fils)
1707-1777 **LC 1, 28**
See also DLB 313; GFL Beginnings to 1789

Credo
See Creasey, John

Credo, Alvaro J. de
See Prado (Calvo), Pedro

Creeley, Robert 1926-2005 **CLC 1, 2, 4, 8, 11, 15, 36, 78**
See also AMWS 4; CA 1-4R; 237; CAAS 10; CANR 23, 43, 89, 137; CP 1, 2, 3, 4, 5, 6, 7; DA3; DAM POET; DLB 5, 16, 169; DLBD 17; EWL 3; MAL 5; MTCW 1, 2; MTFW 2005; PFS 21; RGAL 4; WP

Creeley, Robert White
See Creeley, Robert

Crenne, Helisenne de 1510-1560 **LC 113**

Crevecoeur, Hector St. John de
See Crevecoeur, Michel Guillaume Jean de
See also ANW

Crevecoeur, Michel Guillaume Jean de
1735-1813 **NCLC 105**
See Crevecoeur, Hector St. John de
See also AMWS 1; DLB 37

Crevel, Rene 1900-1935 **TCLC 112**
See also GLL 2

Crews, Harry (Eugene) 1935- **CLC 6, 23, 49**
See also AITN 1; AMWS 11; BPFB 1; CA 25-28R; CANR 20, 57; CN 3, 4, 5, 6, 7; CSW; DA3; DLB 6, 143, 185; MTCW 1, 2; MTFW 2005; RGAL 4

Crichton, (John) Michael 1942- **CLC 2, 6, 54, 90**
See also AAYA 10, 49; AITN 2; BPFB 1; CA 25-28R; CANR 13, 40, 54, 76, 127; CMW 4; CN 2, 3, 6, 7; CPW; DA3; DAM NOV, POP; DLB 292; DLBY 1981; INT CANR-13; JRDA; MTCW 1, 2; MTFW 2005; SATA 9, 88; SFW 4; YAW

Crispin, Edmund **CLC 22**
See Montgomery, (Robert) Bruce
See also DLB 87; MSW

Cristina of Sweden 1626-1689 **LC 124**

Cristofer, Michael 1945(?)- **CLC 28**
See also CA 110; 152; CAD; CANR 150; CD 5, 6; DAM DRAM; DFS 15; DLB 7

Cristofer, Michael Ivan
See Cristofer, Michael

Criton
See Alain

Croce, Benedetto 1866-1952 **TCLC 37**
See also CA 120; 155; EW 8; EWL 3; WLIT 7

Crockett, David 1786-1836 **NCLC 8**
See also DLB 3, 11, 183, 248

Crockett, Davy
See Crockett, David

Crofts, Freeman Wills 1879-1957 .. **TCLC 55**
See also CA 115; 195; CMW 4; DLB 77; MSW

Croker, John Wilson 1780-1857 **NCLC 10**
See also DLB 110

Crommelynck, Fernand 1885-1970 .. **CLC 75**
See also CA 189; 89-92; EWL 3

Cromwell, Oliver 1599-1658 **LC 43**

Cronenberg, David 1943- **CLC 143**
　See also CA 138; CCA 1
Cronin, A(rchibald) J(oseph)
　1896-1981 **CLC 32**
　See also BPFB 1; CA 1-4R; 102; CANR 5;
　CN 2; DLB 191; SATA 47; SATA-Obit 25
Cross, Amanda
　See Heilbrun, Carolyn G(old)
　See also BPFB 1; CMW; CPW; DLB 306;
　MSW
Crothers, Rachel 1878-1958 **TCLC 19**
　See also CA 113; 194; CAD; CWD; DLB
　7, 266; RGAL 4
Croves, Hal
　See Traven, B.
Crow Dog, Mary (Ellen) (?)- **CLC 93**
　See Brave Bird, Mary
　See also CA 154
Crowfield, Christopher
　See Stowe, Harriet (Elizabeth) Beecher
Crowley, Aleister **TCLC 7**
　See Crowley, Edward Alexander
　See also GLL 1
Crowley, Edward Alexander 1875-1947
　See Crowley, Aleister
　See also CA 104; HGG
Crowley, John 1942- **CLC 57**
　See also AAYA 57; BPFB 1; CA 61-64;
　CANR 43, 98, 138; DLBY 1982; FANT;
　MTFW 2005; SATA 65, 140; SFW 4;
　SUFW 2
Crowne, John 1641-1712 **LC 104**
　See also DLB 80; RGEL 2
Crud
　See Crumb, R.
Crumarums
　See Crumb, R.
Crumb, R. 1943- **CLC 17**
　See also CA 106; CANR 107, 150
Crumb, Robert
　See Crumb, R.
Crumbum
　See Crumb, R.
Crumski
　See Crumb, R.
Crum the Bum
　See Crumb, R.
Crunk
　See Crumb, R.
Crustt
　See Crumb, R.
Crutchfield, Les
　See Trumbo, Dalton
Cruz, Victor Hernandez 1949- ... **HLC 1; PC
　37**
　See also BW 2; CA 65-68; CAAS 17;
　CANR 14, 32, 74, 132; CP 1, 2, 3, 4, 5,
　6, 7; DAM MULT, POET; DLB 41; DNFS
　1; EXPP; HW 1, 2; LLW; MTCW 2;
　MTFW 2005; PFS 16; WP
Cryer, Gretchen (Kiger) 1935- **CLC 21**
　See also CA 114; 123
Csath, Geza **TCLC 13**
　See Brenner, Jozef
　See also CA 111
Cudlip, David R(ockwell) 1933- **CLC 34**
　See also CA 177
Cullen, Countee 1903-1946 . **BLC 1; HR 1:2;
　PC 20; TCLC 4, 37; WLCS**
　See also AFAW 2; AMWS 4; BW 1; CA
　108; 124; CDALB 1917-1929; DA; DA3;
　DAC; DAM MST, MULT, POET; DLB 4,
　48, 51; EWL 3; EXPP; LMFS 2; MAL 5;
　MTCW 1, 2; MTFW 2005; PFS 3; RGAL
　4; SATA 18; WP
Culleton, Beatrice 1949- **NNAL**
　See also CA 120; CANR 83; DAC
Cum, R.
　See Crumb, R.

Cumberland, Richard
　1732-1811 **NCLC 167**
　See also DLB 89; RGEL 2
Cummings, Bruce F(rederick) 1889-1919
　See Barbellion, W. N. P.
　See also CA 123
Cummings, E(dward) E(stlin)
　1894-1962 .. **CLC 1, 3, 8, 12, 15, 68; PC
　5; TCLC 137; WLC 2**
　See also AAYA 41; AMW; CA 73-76;
　CANR 31; CDALB 1929-1941; DA;
　DA3; DAB; DAC; DAM MST, POET;
　DLB 4, 48; EWL 3; EXPP; MAL 5;
　MTCW 1, 2; MTFW 2005; PAB; PFS 1,
　3, 12, 13, 19; RGAL 4; TUS; WP
Cummins, Maria Susanna
　1827-1866 **NCLC 139**
　See also DLB 42; YABC 1
Cunha, Euclides (Rodrigues Pimenta) da
　1866-1909 **TCLC 24**
　See also CA 123; 219; DLB 307; LAW;
　WLIT 1
Cunningham, E. V.
　See Fast, Howard (Melvin)
Cunningham, J(ames) V(incent)
　1911-1985 **CLC 3, 31**
　See also CA 1-4R; 115; CANR 1, 72; CP 1,
　2, 3, 4; DLB 5
Cunningham, Julia (Woolfolk)
　1916- **CLC 12**
　See also CA 9-12R; CANR 4, 19, 36; CWRI
　5; JRDA; MAICYA 1, 2; SAAS 2; SATA
　1, 26, 132
Cunningham, Michael 1952- **CLC 34**
　See also AMWS 15; CA 136; CANR 96;
　CN 7; DLB 292; GLL 2; MTFW 2005;
　NFS 23
Cunninghame Graham, R. B.
　See Cunninghame Graham, Robert
　(Gallnigad) Bontine
**Cunninghame Graham, Robert (Gallnigad)
　Bontine** 1852-1936 **TCLC 19**
　See Graham, R(obert) B(ontine) Cunning-
　hame
　See also CA 119; 184
Curnow, (Thomas) Allen (Monro)
　1911-2001 **PC 48**
　See also CA 69-72; 202; CANR 48, 99; CP
　1, 2, 3, 4, 5, 6, 7; EWL 3; RGEL 2
Currie, Ellen 19(?)- **CLC 44**
Curtin, Philip
　See Lowndes, Marie Adelaide (Belloc)
Curtin, Phillip
　See Lowndes, Marie Adelaide (Belloc)
Curtis, Price
　See Ellison, Harlan (Jay)
Cusanus, Nicolaus 1401-1464 **LC 80**
　See Nicholas of Cusa
Cutrate, Joe
　See Spiegelman, Art
Cynewulf c. 770- **CMLC 23**
　See also DLB 146; RGEL 2
Cyrano de Bergerac, Savinien de
　1619-1655 **LC 65**
　See also DLB 268; GFL Beginnings to
　1789; RGWL 2, 3
Cyril of Alexandria c. 375-c. 430 . **CMLC 59**
Czaczkes, Shmuel Yosef Halevi
　See Agnon, S(hmuel) Y(osef Halevi)
Dabrowska, Maria (Szumska)
　1889-1965 **CLC 15**
　See also CA 106; CDWLB 4; DLB 215;
　EWL 3
Dabydeen, David 1955- **CLC 34**
　See also BW 1; CA 125; CANR 56, 92; CN
　6, 7; CP 5, 6, 7

Dacey, Philip 1939- **CLC 51**
　See also CA 37-40R, 231; CAAE 231;
　CAAS 17; CANR 14, 32, 64; CP 4, 5, 6,
　7; DLB 105
Dacre, Charlotte c. 1772-1825(?) . **NCLC 151**
Dafydd ap Gwilym c. 1320-c. 1380 **PC 56**
Dagerman, Stig (Halvard)
　1923-1954 **TCLC 17**
　See also CA 117; 155; DLB 259; EWL 3
D'Aguiar, Fred 1960- **CLC 145**
　See also CA 148; CANR 83, 101; CN 7;
　CP 5, 6, 7; DLB 157; EWL 3
Dahl, Roald 1916-1990 **CLC 1, 6, 18, 79;
　TCLC 173**
　See also AAYA 15; BPFB 1; BRWS 4; BYA
　5; CA 1-4R; 133; CANR 6, 32, 37, 62;
　CLR 1, 7, 41, 111; CN 1, 2, 3, 4; CPW;
　DA3; DAB; DAC; DAM MST, NOV,
　POP; DLB 139, 255; HGG; JRDA; MAI-
　CYA 1, 2; MTCW 1, 2; MTFW 2005;
　RGSF 2; SATA 1, 26, 73; SATA-Obit 65;
　SSFS 4; TEA; YAW
Dahlberg, Edward 1900-1977 .. **CLC 1, 7, 14**
　See also CA 9-12R; 69-72; CANR 31, 62;
　CN 1, 2; DLB 48; MAL 5; MTCW 1;
　RGAL 4
Daitch, Susan 1954- **CLC 103**
　See also CA 161
Dale, Colin **TCLC 18**
　See Lawrence, T(homas) E(dward)
Dale, George E.
　See Asimov, Isaac
d'Alembert, Jean Le Rond
　1717-1783 **LC 126**
Dalton, Roque 1935-1975(?) **HLCS 1; PC
　36**
　See also CA 176; DLB 283; HW 2
Daly, Elizabeth 1878-1967 **CLC 52**
　See also CA 23-24; 25-28R; CANR 60;
　CAP 2; CMW 4
Daly, Mary 1928- **CLC 173**
　See also CA 25-28R; CANR 30, 62; FW;
　GLL 1; MTCW 1
Daly, Maureen 1921- **CLC 17**
　See also AAYA 5, 58; BYA 6; CANR 37,
　83, 108; CLR 96; JRDA; MAICYA 1, 2;
　SAAS 1; SATA 2, 129; WYA; YAW
Damas, Leon-Gontran 1912-1978 **CLC 84**
　See also BW 1; CA 125; 73-76; EWL 3
Dana, Richard Henry Sr.
　1787-1879 **NCLC 53**
Daniel, Samuel 1562(?)-1619 **LC 24**
　See also DLB 62; RGEL 2
Daniels, Brett
　See Adler, Renata
Dannay, Frederic 1905-1982 **CLC 11**
　See Queen, Ellery
　See also CA 1-4R; 107; CANR 1, 39; CMW
　4; DAM POP; DLB 137; MTCW 1
D'Annunzio, Gabriele 1863-1938 ... **TCLC 6,
　40**
　See also CA 104; 155; EW 8; EWL 3;
　RGWL 2, 3; TWA; WLIT 7
Danois, N. le
　See Gourmont, Remy(-Marie-Charles) de
Dante 1265-1321 **CMLC 3, 18, 39, 70; PC
　21; WLCS**
　See Alighieri, Dante
　See also DA; DA3; DAB; DAC; DAM
　MST, POET; EFS 1; EW 1; LAIT 1;
　RGWL 2, 3; TWA; WP
d'Antibes, Germain
　See Simenon, Georges (Jacques Christian)
Danticat, Edwidge 1969- **CLC 94, 139**
　See also AAYA 29; CA 152, 192; CAAE
　192; CANR 73, 129; CN 7; DNFS 1;
　EXPS; LATS 1:2; MTCW 2; MTFW
　2005; SSFS 1; YAW
Danvers, Dennis 1947- **CLC 70**

Danziger, Paula 1944-2004 **CLC 21**
See also AAYA 4, 36; BYA 6, 7, 14; CA
112; 115; 229; CANR 37, 132; CLR 20;
JRDA; MAICYA 1, 2; MTFW 2005;
SATA 36, 63, 102, 149; SATA-Brief 30;
SATA-Obit 155; WYA; YAW

Da Ponte, Lorenzo 1749-1838 **NCLC 50**

d'Aragona, Tullia 1510(?)-1556 **LC 121**

Dario, Ruben 1867-1916 **HLC 1; PC 15; TCLC 4**
See also CA 131; CANR 81; DAM MULT;
DLB 290; EWL 3; HW 1, 2; LAW;
MTCW 1, 2; MTFW 2005; RGWL 2, 3

Darley, George 1795-1846 **NCLC 2**
See also DLB 96; RGEL 2

Darrow, Clarence (Seward)
1857-1938 **TCLC 81**
See also CA 164; DLB 303

Darwin, Charles 1809-1882 **NCLC 57**
See also BRWS 7; DLB 57, 166; LATS 1:1;
RGEL 2; TEA; WLIT 4

Darwin, Erasmus 1731-1802 **NCLC 106**
See also DLB 93; RGEL 2

Daryush, Elizabeth 1887-1977 **CLC 6, 19**
See also CA 49-52; CANR 3, 81; DLB 20

Das, Kamala 1934- **CLC 191; PC 43**
See also CA 101; CANR 27, 59; CP 1, 2, 3,
4, 5, 6, 7; CWP; DLB 323; FW

Dasgupta, Surendranath
1887-1952 **TCLC 81**
See also CA 157

**Dashwood, Edmee Elizabeth Monica de la
Pasture** 1890-1943
See Delafield, E. M.
See also CA 119; 154

da Silva, Antonio Jose
1705-1739 **NCLC 114**

Daudet, (Louis Marie) Alphonse
1840-1897 **NCLC 1**
See also DLB 123; GFL 1789 to the Present;
RGSF 2

d'Aulnoy, Marie-Catherine c.
1650-1705 **LC 100**

Daumal, Rene 1908-1944 **TCLC 14**
See also CA 114; 247; EWL 3

Davenant, William 1606-1668 **LC 13**
See also DLB 58, 126; RGEL 2

Davenport, Guy (Mattison, Jr.)
1927-2005 **CLC 6, 14, 38; SSC 16**
See also CA 33-36R; 235; CANR 23, 73;
CN 3, 4, 5, 6; CSW; DLB 130

David, Robert
See Nezval, Vitezslav

Davidson, Avram (James) 1923-1993
See Queen, Ellery
See also CA 101; 171; CANR 26; DLB 8;
FANT; SFW 4; SUFW 1, 2

Davidson, Donald (Grady)
1893-1968 **CLC 2, 13, 19**
See also CA 5-8R; 25-28R; CANR 4, 84;
DLB 45

Davidson, Hugh
See Hamilton, Edmond

Davidson, John 1857-1909 **TCLC 24**
See also CA 118; 217; DLB 19; RGEL 2

Davidson, Sara 1943- **CLC 9**
See also CA 81-84; CANR 44, 68; DLB
185

Davie, Donald (Alfred) 1922-1995 **CLC 5,
8, 10, 31; PC 29**
See also BRWS 6; CA 1-4R; 149; CAAS 3;
CANR 1, 44; CP 1, 2, 3, 4, 5, 6; DLB 27;
MTCW 1; RGEL 2

Davie, Elspeth 1918-1995 **SSC 52**
See also CA 120; 126; 150; CANR 141;
DLB 139

Davies, Ray(mond Douglas) 1944- ... **CLC 21**
See also CA 116; 146; CANR 92

Davies, Rhys 1901-1978 **CLC 23**
See also CA 9-12R; 81-84; CANR 4; CN 1,
2; DLB 139, 191

Davies, (William) Robertson
1913-1995 **CLC 2, 7, 13, 25, 42, 75,
91; WLC 2**
See Marchbanks, Samuel
See also BEST 89.2; BPFB 1; CA 33-36R;
150; CANR 17, 42, 103; CN 1, 2, 3, 4, 5,
6; CPW; DA; DA3; DAB; DAC; DAM
MST, NOV, POP; DLB 68; EWL 3; HGG;
INT CANR-17; MTCW 1, 2; MTFW
2005; RGEL 2; TWA

Davies, Sir John 1569-1626 **LC 85**
See also DLB 172

Davies, Walter C.
See Kornbluth, C(yril) M.

Davies, William Henry 1871-1940 ... **TCLC 5**
See also BRWS 11; CA 104; 179; DLB 19,
174; EWL 3; RGEL 2

Da Vinci, Leonardo 1452-1519 **LC 12, 57,
60**
See also AAYA 40

Davis, Angela (Yvonne) 1944- **CLC 77**
See also BW 2, 3; CA 57-60; CANR 10,
81; CSW; DA3; DAM MULT; FW

Davis, B. Lynch
See Bioy Casares, Adolfo; Borges, Jorge
Luis

Davis, Frank Marshall 1905-1987 **BLC 1**
See also BW 2, 3; CA 125; 123; CANR 42,
80; DAM MULT; DLB 51

Davis, Gordon
See Hunt, E(verette) Howard, (Jr.)

Davis, H(arold) L(enoir) 1896-1960 . **CLC 49**
See also ANW; CA 178; 89-92; DLB 9,
206; SATA 114; TCWW 1, 2

Davis, Natalie Zemon 1928- **CLC 204**
See also CA 53-56; CANR 58, 100

Davis, Rebecca (Blaine) Harding
1831-1910 **SSC 38; TCLC 6**
See also CA 104; 179; DLB 74, 239; FW;
NFS 14; RGAL 4; TUS

Davis, Richard Harding
1864-1916 **TCLC 24**
See also CA 114; 179; DLB 12, 23, 78, 79,
189; DLBD 13; RGAL 4

Davison, Frank Dalby 1893-1970 **CLC 15**
See also CA 217; 116; DLB 260

Davison, Lawrence H.
See Lawrence, D(avid) H(erbert Richards)

Davison, Peter (Hubert) 1928-2004 . **CLC 28**
See also CA 9-12R; 234; CAAS 4; CANR
3, 43, 84; CP 1, 2, 3, 4, 5, 6, 7; DLB 5

Davys, Mary 1674-1732 **LC 1, 46**
See also DLB 39

Dawson, (Guy) Fielding (Lewis)
1930-2002 **CLC 6**
See also CA 85-88; 202; CANR 108; DLB
130; DLBY 2002

Dawson, Peter
See Faust, Frederick (Schiller)
See also TCWW 1, 2

Day, Clarence (Shepard, Jr.)
1874-1935 **TCLC 25**
See also CA 108; 199; DLB 11

Day, John 1574(?)-1640(?) **LC 70**
See also DLB 62, 170; RGEL 2

Day, Thomas 1748-1789 **LC 1**
See also DLB 39; YABC 1

Day Lewis, C(ecil) 1904-1972 . **CLC 1, 6, 10;
PC 11**
See Blake, Nicholas; Lewis, C. Day
See also BRWS 3; CA 13-16; 33-36R;
CANR 34; CAP 1; CP 1; CWRI 5; DAM
POET; DLB 15, 20; EWL 3; MTCW 1, 2;
RGEL 2

Dazai Osamu **SSC 41; TCLC 11**
See Tsushima, Shuji
See also CA 164; DLB 182; EWL 3; MJW;
RGSF 2; RGWL 2, 3; TWA

de Andrade, Carlos Drummond
See Drummond de Andrade, Carlos

de Andrade, Mario 1892(?)-1945
See Andrade, Mario de
See also CA 178; HW 2

Deane, Norman
See Creasey, John

Deane, Seamus (Francis) 1940- **CLC 122**
See also CA 118; CANR 42

de Beauvoir, Simone
See Beauvoir, Simone de

de Beer, P.
See Bosman, Herman Charles

De Botton, Alain 1969- **CLC 203**
See also CA 159; CANR 96

de Brissac, Malcolm
See Dickinson, Peter (Malcolm de Brissac)

de Campos, Alvaro
See Pessoa, Fernando (Antonio Nogueira)

de Chardin, Pierre Teilhard
See Teilhard de Chardin, (Marie Joseph)
Pierre

de Crenne, Helisenne c. 1510-c.
1560 ... **LC 113**

Dee, John 1527-1608 **LC 20**
See also DLB 136, 213

Deer, Sandra 1940- **CLC 45**
See also CA 186

De Ferrari, Gabriella 1941- **CLC 65**
See also CA 146

de Filippo, Eduardo 1900-1984 ... **TCLC 127**
See also CA 132; 114; EWL 3; MTCW 1;
RGWL 2, 3

Defoe, Daniel 1660(?)-1731 **LC 1, 42, 108;
WLC 2**
See also AAYA 27; BRW 3; BRWR 1; BYA
4; CDBLB 1660-1789; CLR 61; DA;
DA3; DAB; DAC; DAM MST, NOV;
DLB 39, 95, 101; JRDA; LAIT 1; LMFS
1; MAICYA 1, 2; NFS 9, 13; RGEL 2;
SATA 22; TEA; WCH; WLIT 3

de Gouges, Olympe
See de Gouges, Olympe

de Gouges, Olympe 1748-1793 **LC 127**
See also DLB 313

de Gourmont, Remy(-Marie-Charles)
See Gourmont, Remy(-Marie-Charles) de

de Gournay, Marie le Jars
1566-1645 **LC 98**
See also FW

de Hartog, Jan 1914-2002 **CLC 19**
See also CA 1-4R; 210; CANR 1; DFS 12

de Hostos, E. M.
See Hostos (y Bonilla), Eugenio Maria de

de Hostos, Eugenio M.
See Hostos (y Bonilla), Eugenio Maria de

Deighton, Len **CLC 4, 7, 22, 46**
See Deighton, Leonard Cyril
See also AAYA 6; BEST 89:2; BPFB 1; CD-
BLB 1960 to Present; CMW 4; CN 1, 2,
3, 4, 5, 6, 7; CPW; DLB 87

Deighton, Leonard Cyril 1929-
See Deighton, Len
See also AAYA 57; CA 9-12R; CANR 19,
33, 68; DA3; DAM NOV, POP; MTCW
1, 2; MTFW 2005

Dekker, Thomas 1572(?)-1632 **DC 12; LC
22**
See also CDBLB Before 1660; DAM
DRAM; DLB 62, 172; LMFS 1; RGEL 2

de Laclos, Pierre Ambroise Franois
See Laclos, Pierre-Ambroise Francois

Delacroix, (Ferdinand-Victor-)Eugene
1798-1863 **NCLC 133**
See also EW 5

Delafield, E. M. **TCLC 61**
　See Dashwood, Edmee Elizabeth Monica
　　de la Pasture
　See also DLB 34; RHW

de la Mare, Walter (John)
　1873-1956 . **SSC 14; TCLC 4, 53; WLC 2**
　See also CA 163; CDBLB 1914-1945; CLR
　　23; CWRI 5; DA3; DAB; DAC; DAM
　　MST, POET; DLB 19, 153, 162, 255, 284;
　　EWL 3; EXPP; HGG; MAICYA 1, 2;
　　MTCW 2; MTFW 2005; RGEL 2; RGSF
　　2; SATA 16; SUFW 1; TEA; WCH

de Lamartine, Alphonse (Marie Louis Prat)
　See Lamartine, Alphonse (Marie Louis Prat)
　　de

Delaney, Franey
　See O'Hara, John (Henry)

Delaney, Shelagh 1939- **CLC 29**
　See also CA 17-20R; CANR 30, 67; CBD;
　　CD 5, 6; CDBLB 1960 to Present; CWD;
　　DAM DRAM; DFS 7; DLB 13; MTCW 1

Delany, Martin Robison
　1812-1885 **NCLC 93**
　See also DLB 50; RGAL 4

Delany, Mary (Granville Pendarves)
　1700-1788 **LC 12**

Delany, Samuel R(ay), Jr. 1942- **BLC 1; CLC 8, 14, 38, 141**
　See also AAYA 24; AFAW 2; BPFB 1; BW
　　2, 3; CA 81-84; CANR 27, 43, 116; CN
　　2, 3, 4, 5, 6, 7; DAM MULT; DLB 8, 33;
　　FANT; MAL 5; MTCW 1, 2; RGAL 4;
　　SATA 92; SCFW 1, 2; SFW 4; SUFW 2

De la Ramee, Marie Louise (Ouida)
　1839-1908
　See Ouida
　See also CA 204; SATA 20

de la Roche, Mazo 1879-1961 **CLC 14**
　See also CA 85-88; CANR 30; DLB 68;
　　RGEL 2; RHW; SATA 64

De La Salle, Innocent
　See Hartmann, Sadakichi

de Laureamont, Comte
　See Lautreamont

Delbanco, Nicholas 1942- **CLC 6, 13, 167**
　See also CA 17-20R, 189; CAAE 189;
　　CAAS 2; CANR 29, 55, 116, 150; CN 7;
　　DLB 6, 234

Delbanco, Nicholas Franklin
　See Delbanco, Nicholas

del Castillo, Michel 1933- **CLC 38**
　See also CA 109; CANR 77

Deledda, Grazia (Cosima)
　1875(?)-1936 **TCLC 23**
　See also CA 123; 205; DLB 264; EWL 3;
　　RGWL 2, 3; WLIT 7

Deleuze, Gilles 1925-1995 **TCLC 116**
　See also DLB 296

Delgado, Abelardo (Lalo) B(arrientos)
　1930-2004 **HLC 1**
　See also CA 131; 230; CAAS 15; CANR
　　90; DAM MST, MULT; DLB 82; HW 1,
　　2

Delibes, Miguel **CLC 8, 18**
　See Delibes Setien, Miguel
　See also DLB 322; EWL 3

Delibes Setien, Miguel 1920-
　See Delibes, Miguel
　See also CA 45-48; CANR 1, 32; CWW 2;
　　HW 1; MTCW 1

DeLillo, Don 1936- **CLC 8, 10, 13, 27, 39, 54, 76, 143, 210, 213**
　See also AMWC 2; AMWS 6; BEST 89:1;
　　BPFB 1; CA 81-84; CANR 21, 76, 92,
　　133; CN 3, 4, 5, 6, 7; CPW; DA3; DAM
　　NOV, POP; DLB 6, 173; EWL 3; MAL 5;
　　MTCW 1, 2; MTFW 2005; RGAL 4; TUS

de Lisser, H. G.
　See De Lisser, H(erbert) G(eorge)
　See also DLB 117

De Lisser, H(erbert) G(eorge)
　1878-1944 **TCLC 12**
　See de Lisser, H. G.
　See also BW 2; CA 109; 152

Deloire, Pierre
　See Peguy, Charles (Pierre)

Deloney, Thomas 1543(?)-1600 **LC 41**
　See also DLB 167; RGEL 2

Deloria, Ella (Cara) 1889-1971(?) **NNAL**
　See also CA 152; DAM MULT; DLB 175

Deloria, Vine, Jr. 1933-2005 **CLC 21, 122; NNAL**
　See also CA 53-56; 245; CANR 5, 20, 48,
　　98; DAM MULT; DLB 175; MTCW 1;
　　SATA 21; SATA-Obit 171

Deloria, Vine Victor
　See Deloria, Vine, Jr.

del Valle-Inclan, Ramon (Maria)
　See Valle-Inclan, Ramon (Maria) del
　See also DLB 322

Del Vecchio, John M(ichael) 1947- .. **CLC 29**
　See also CA 110; DLBD 9

de Man, Paul (Adolph Michel)
　1919-1983 **CLC 55**
　See also CA 128; 111; CANR 61; DLB 67;
　　MTCW 1, 2

DeMarinis, Rick 1934- **CLC 54**
　See also CA 57-60, 184; CAAE 184; CAAS
　　24; CANR 9, 25, 50; DLB 218; TCWW 2

de Maupassant, (Henri Rene Albert) Guy
　See Maupassant, (Henri Rene Albert) Guy
　　de

Dembry, R. Emmet
　See Murfree, Mary Noailles

Demby, William 1922- **BLC 1; CLC 53**
　See also BW 1, 3; CA 81-84; CANR 81;
　　DAM MULT; DLB 33

de Menton, Francisco
　See Chin, Frank (Chew, Jr.)

Demetrius of Phalerum c.
　307B.C.- **CMLC 34**

Demijohn, Thom
　See Disch, Thomas M(ichael)

De Mille, James 1833-1880 **NCLC 123**
　See also DLB 99, 251

Deming, Richard 1915-1983
　See Queen, Ellery
　See also CA 9-12R; CANR 3, 94; SATA 24

Democritus c. 460B.C.-c. 370B.C. . **CMLC 47**

de Montaigne, Michel (Eyquem)
　See Montaigne, Michel (Eyquem) de

de Montherlant, Henry (Milon)
　See Montherlant, Henry (Milon) de

Demosthenes 384B.C.-322B.C. **CMLC 13**
　See also AW 1; DLB 176; RGWL 2, 3;
　　WLIT 8

de Musset, (Louis Charles) Alfred
　See Musset, Alfred de

de Natale, Francine
　See Malzberg, Barry N(athaniel)

de Navarre, Marguerite 1492-1549 ... **LC 61; SSC 85**
　See Marguerite d'Angouleme; Marguerite
　　de Navarre

Denby, Edwin (Orr) 1903-1983 **CLC 48**
　See also CA 138; 110; CP 1

de Nerval, Gerard
　See Nerval, Gerard de

Denham, John 1615-1669 **LC 73**
　See also DLB 58, 126; RGEL 2

Denis, Julio
　See Cortazar, Julio

Denmark, Harrison
　See Zelazny, Roger (Joseph)

Dennis, John 1658-1734 **LC 11**
　See also DLB 101; RGEL 2

Dennis, Nigel (Forbes) 1912-1989 **CLC 8**
　See also CA 25-28R; 129; CN 1, 2, 3, 4;
　　DLB 13, 15, 233; EWL 3; MTCW 1

Dent, Lester 1904-1959 **TCLC 72**
　See also CA 112; 161; CMW 4; DLB 306;
　　SFW 4

De Palma, Brian 1940- **CLC 20**
　See also CA 109

De Palma, Brian Russell
　See De Palma, Brian

De Quincey, Thomas 1785-1859 **NCLC 4, 87**
　See also BRW 4; CDBLB 1789-1832; DLB
　　110, 144; RGEL 2

Deren, Eleanora 1908(?)-1961
　See Deren, Maya
　See also CA 192; 111

Deren, Maya **CLC 16, 102**
　See Deren, Eleanora

Derleth, August (William)
　1909-1971 **CLC 31**
　See also BPFB 1; BYA 9, 10; CA 1-4R; 29-
　　32R; CANR 4; CMW 4; CN 1; DLB 9;
　　DLBD 17; HGG; SATA 5; SUFW 1

Der Nister 1884-1950 **TCLC 56**
　See Nister, Der

de Routisie, Albert
　See Aragon, Louis

Derrida, Jacques 1930-2004 **CLC 24, 87, 225**
　See also CA 124; 127; 232; CANR 76, 98,
　　133; DLB 242; EWL 3; LMFS 2; MTCW
　　2; TWA

Derry Down Derry
　See Lear, Edward

Dersonnes, Jacques
　See Simenon, Georges (Jacques Christian)

Der Stricker c. 1190-c. 1250 **CMLC 75**
　See also DLB 138

Desai, Anita 1937- **CLC 19, 37, 97, 175**
　See also BRWS 5; CA 81-84; CANR 33,
　　53, 95, 133; CN 1, 2, 3, 4, 5, 6, 7; CWRI
　　5; DA3; DAB; DAM NOV; DLB 271,
　　323; DNFS 2; EWL 3; FW; MTCW 1, 2;
　　MTFW 2005; SATA 63, 126

Desai, Kiran 1971- **CLC 119**
　See also BYA 16; CA 171; CANR 127

de Saint-Luc, Jean
　See Glassco, John

de Saint Roman, Arnaud
　See Aragon, Louis

Desbordes-Valmore, Marceline
　1786-1859 **NCLC 97**
　See also DLB 217

Descartes, Rene 1596-1650 **LC 20, 35**
　See also DLB 268; EW 3; GFL Beginnings
　　to 1789

Deschamps, Eustache 1340(?)-1404 .. **LC 103**
　See also DLB 208

De Sica, Vittorio 1901(?)-1974 **CLC 20**
　See also CA 117

Desnos, Robert 1900-1945 **TCLC 22**
　See also CA 121; 151; CANR 107; DLB
　　258; EWL 3; LMFS 2

Destouches, Louis-Ferdinand
　1894-1961 **CLC 9, 15**
　See Celine, Louis-Ferdinand
　See also CA 85-88; CANR 28; MTCW 1

de Tolignac, Gaston
　See Griffith, D(avid Lewelyn) W(ark)

Deutsch, Babette 1895-1982 **CLC 18**
　See also BYA 3; CA 1-4R; 108; CANR 4,
　　79; CP 1, 2, 3; DLB 45; SATA 1; SATA-
　　Obit 33

Devenant, William 1606-1649 **LC 13**

Devkota, Laxmiprasad 1909-1959 . **TCLC 23**
　See also CA 123

De Voto, Bernard (Augustine)
1897-1955 **TCLC 29**
See also CA 113; 160; DLB 9, 256; MAL
5; TCWW 1, 2

De Vries, Peter 1910-1993 **CLC 1, 2, 3, 7, 10, 28, 46**
See also CA 17-20R; 142; CANR 41; CN
1, 2, 3, 4, 5; DAM NOV; DLB 6; DLBY
1982; MAL 5; MTCW 1, 2; MTFW 2005

Dewey, John 1859-1952 **TCLC 95**
See also CA 114; 170; CANR 144; DLB
246, 270; RGAL 4

Dexter, John
See Bradley, Marion Zimmer
See also GLL 1

Dexter, Martin
See Faust, Frederick (Schiller)

Dexter, Pete 1943- **CLC 34, 55**
See also BEST 89:2; CA 127; 131; CANR
129; CPW; DAM POP; INT CA-131;
MAL 5; MTCW 1; MTFW 2005

Diamano, Silmang
See Senghor, Leopold Sedar

Diamond, Neil 1941- **CLC 30**
See also CA 108

Diaz del Castillo, Bernal c.
1496-1584 **HLCS 1; LC 31**
See also DLB 318; LAW

di Bassetto, Corno
See Shaw, George Bernard

Dick, Philip K. 1928-1982 ... **CLC 10, 30, 72; SSC 57**
See also AAYA 24; BPFB 1; BYA 11; CA
49-52; 106; CANR 2, 16, 132; CN 2, 3;
CPW; DA3; DAM NOV, POP; DLB 8;
MTCW 1, 2; MTFW 2005; NFS 5; SCFW
1, 2; SFW 4

Dick, Philip Kindred
See Dick, Philip K.

Dickens, Charles (John Huffam)
1812-1870 **NCLC 3, 8, 18, 26, 37, 50, 86, 105, 113, 161; SSC 17, 49, 88; WLC 2**
See also AAYA 23; BRW 5; BRWC 1, 2;
BYA 1, 2, 3, 13, 14; CDBLB 1832-1890;
CLR 95; CMW 4; DA; DA3; DAB; DAC;
DAM MST, NOV; DLB 21, 55, 70, 159,
166; EXPN; GL 2; HGG; JRDA; LAIT 1,
2; LATS 1:1; LMFS 1; MAICYA 1, 2;
NFS 4, 5, 10, 14, 20; RGEL 2; RGSF 2;
SATA 15; SUFW 1; TEA; WCH; WLIT
4; WYA

Dickey, James (Lafayette)
1923-1997 **CLC 1, 2, 4, 7, 10, 15, 47, 109; PC 40; TCLC 151**
See also AAYA 50; AITN 1, 2; AMWS 4;
BPFB 1; CA 9-12R; 156; CABS 2; CANR
10, 48, 61, 105; CDALB 1968-1988; CP
1, 2, 3, 4, 5, 6; CPW; CSW; DA3; DAM
NOV, POET, POP; DLB 5, 193; DLBD 7;
DLBY 1982, 1993, 1996, 1997, 1998;
EWL 3; INT CANR-10; MAL 5; MTCW
1, 2; NFS 9; PFS 6, 11; RGAL 4; TUS

Dickey, William 1928-1994 **CLC 3, 28**
See also CA 9-12R; 145; CANR 24, 79; CP
1, 2, 3, 4; DLB 5

Dickinson, Charles 1951- **CLC 49**
See also CA 128; CANR 141

Dickinson, Emily (Elizabeth)
1830-1886 **NCLC 21, 77, 171; PC 1; WLC 2**
See also AAYA 22; AMW; AMWR 1;
CDALB 1865-1917; DA; DA3; DAB;
DAC; DAM MST, POET; DLB 1, 243;
EXPP; FL 1:3; MAWW; PAB; PFS 1, 2,
3, 4, 5, 6, 8, 10, 11, 13, 16; RGAL 4;
SATA 29; TUS; WP; WYA

Dickinson, Mrs. Herbert Ward
See Phelps, Elizabeth Stuart

Dickinson, Peter (Malcolm de Brissac)
1927- **CLC 12, 35**
See also AAYA 9, 49; BYA 5; CA 41-44R;
CANR 31, 58, 88, 134; CLR 29; CMW 4;
DLB 87, 161, 276; JRDA; MAICYA 1, 2;
SATA 5, 62, 95, 150; SFW 4; WYA; YAW

Dickson, Carr
See Carr, John Dickson

Dickson, Carter
See Carr, John Dickson

Diderot, Denis 1713-1784 **LC 26, 126**
See also DLB 313; EW 4; GFL Beginnings
to 1789; LMFS 1; RGWL 2, 3

Didion, Joan 1934- . **CLC 1, 3, 8, 14, 32, 129**
See also AITN 1; AMWS 4; CA 5-8R;
CANR 14, 52, 76, 125; CDALB 1968-
1988; CN 2, 3, 4, 5, 6, 7; DA3; DAM
NOV; DLB 2, 173, 185; DLBY 1981,
1986; EWL 3; MAL 5; MAWW; MTCW
1, 2; MTFW 2005; NFS 3; RGAL 4;
TCLE 1:1; TCWW 2; TUS

di Donato, Pietro 1911-1992 **TCLC 159**
See also CA 101; 136; DLB 9

Dietrich, Robert
See Hunt, E(verette) Howard, (Jr.)

Difusa, Pati
See Almodovar, Pedro

Dillard, Annie 1945- **CLC 9, 60, 115, 216**
See also AAYA 6, 43; AMWS 6; ANW; CA
49-52; CANR 3, 43, 62, 90, 125; DA3;
DAM NOV; DLB 275, 278; DLBY 1980;
LAIT 4, 5; MAL 5; MTCW 1, 2; MTFW
2005; NCFS 1; RGAL 4; SATA 10, 140;
TCLE 1:1; TUS

Dillard, R(ichard) H(enry) W(ilde)
1937- **CLC 5**
See also CA 21-24R; CAAS 7; CANR 10;
CP 2, 3, 4, 5, 6, 7; CSW; DLB 5, 244

Dillon, Eilis 1920-1994 **CLC 17**
See also CA 9-12R, 182; 147; CAAE 182;
CAAS 3; CANR 4, 38, 78; CLR 26; MAI-
CYA 1, 2; MAICYAS 1; SATA 2, 74;
SATA-Essay 105; SATA-Obit 83; YAW

Dimont, Penelope
See Mortimer, Penelope (Ruth)

Dinesen, Isak **CLC 10, 29, 95; SSC 7, 75**
See Blixen, Karen (Christentze Dinesen)
See also EW 10; EWL 3; EXPS; FW; GL
2; HGG; LAIT 3; MTCW 1; NCFS 2;
NFS 9; RGSF 2; RGWL 2, 3; SSFS 3, 6,
13; WLIT 2

Ding Ling ... **CLC 68**
See Chiang, Pin-chin
See also RGWL 3

Diphusa, Patty
See Almodovar, Pedro

Disch, Thomas M(ichael) 1940- ... **CLC 7, 36**
See Disch, Tom
See also AAYA 17; BPFB 1; CA 21-24R;
CAAS 4; CANR 17, 36, 54, 89; CLR 18;
CP 5, 6, 7; DA3; DLB 8; HGG; MAICYA
1, 2; MTCW 1, 2; MTFW 2005; SAAS
15; SATA 92; SCFW 1, 2; SFW 4; SUFW
2

Disch, Tom
See Disch, Thomas M(ichael)
See also DLB 282

d'Isly, Georges
See Simenon, Georges (Jacques Christian)

Disraeli, Benjamin 1804-1881 ... **NCLC 2, 39, 79**
See also BRW 4; DLB 21, 55; RGEL 2

Ditcum, Steve
See Crumb, R.

Dixon, Paige
See Corcoran, Barbara (Asenath)

Dixon, Stephen 1936- **CLC 52; SSC 16**
See also AMWS 12; CA 89-92; CANR 17,
40, 54, 91; CN 4, 5, 6, 7; DLB 130; MAL
5

Dixon, Thomas, Jr. 1864-1946 **TCLC 163**
See also RHW

Djebar, Assia 1936- **CLC 182**
See also CA 188; EWL 3; RGWL 3; WLIT
2

Doak, Annie
See Dillard, Annie

Dobell, Sydney Thompson
1824-1874 **NCLC 43**
See also DLB 32; RGEL 2

Doblin, Alfred **TCLC 13**
See Doeblin, Alfred
See also CDWLB 2; EWL 3; RGWL 2, 3

Dobroliubov, Nikolai Aleksandrovich
See Dobrolyubov, Nikolai Alexandrovich
See also DLB 277

Dobrolyubov, Nikolai Alexandrovich
1836-1861 **NCLC 5**
See Dobroliubov, Nikolai Aleksandrovich

Dobson, Austin 1840-1921 **TCLC 79**
See also DLB 35, 144

Dobyns, Stephen 1941- **CLC 37**
See also AMWS 13; CA 45-48; CANR 2,
18, 99; CMW 4; CP 4, 5, 6, 7; PFS 23

Doctorow, Edgar Laurence
See Doctorow, E.L.

Doctorow, E.L. 1931- . **CLC 6, 11, 15, 18, 37, 44, 65, 113, 214**
See also AAYA 22; AITN 2; AMWS 4;
BEST 89:3; BPFB 1; CA 45-48; CANR
2, 33, 51, 76, 97, 133; CDALB 1968-
1988; CN 3, 4, 5, 6, 7; CPW; DA3; DAM
NOV, POP; DLB 2, 28, 173; DLBY 1980;
EWL 3; LAIT 3; MAL 5; MTCW 1, 2;
MTFW 2005; NFS 6; RGAL 4; RGHL;
RHW; TCLE 1:1; TCWW 1, 2; TUS

Dodgson, Charles L(utwidge) 1832-1898
See Carroll, Lewis
See also CLR 2; DA; DA3; DAB; DAC;
DAM MST, NOV, POET; MAICYA 1, 2;
SATA 100; YABC 2

Dodsley, Robert 1703-1764 **LC 97**
See also DLB 95; RGEL 2

Dodson, Owen (Vincent) 1914-1983 .. **BLC 1; CLC 79**
See also BW 1; CA 65-68; 110; CANR 24;
DAM MULT; DLB 76

Doeblin, Alfred 1878-1957 **TCLC 13**
See Doblin, Alfred
See also CA 110; 141; DLB 66

Doerr, Harriet 1910-2002 **CLC 34**
See also CA 117; 122; 213; CANR 47; INT
CA-122; LATS 1:2

Domecq, H(onorio Bustos)
See Bioy Casares, Adolfo

Domecq, H(onorio) Bustos
See Bioy Casares, Adolfo; Borges, Jorge
Luis

Domini, Rey
See Lorde, Audre (Geraldine)
See also GLL 1

Dominique
See Proust, (Valentin-Louis-George-Eugene)
Marcel

Don, A
See Stephen, Sir Leslie

Donaldson, Stephen R(eeder)
1947- **CLC 46, 138**
See also AAYA 36; BPFB 1; CA 89-92;
CANR 13, 55, 99; CPW; DAM POP;
FANT; INT CANR-13; SATA 121; SFW
4; SUFW 1, 2

Donleavy, J(ames) P(atrick) 1926- **CLC 1, 4, 6, 10, 45**
See also AITN 2; BPFB 1; CA 9-12R; CANR 24, 49, 62, 80, 124; CBD; CD 5, 6; CN 1, 2, 3, 4, 5, 6, 7; DLB 6, 173; INT CANR-24; MAL 5; MTCW 1, 2; MTFW 2005; RGAL 4

Donnadieu, Marguerite
See Duras, Marguerite

Donne, John 1572-1631 ... **LC 10, 24, 91; PC 1, 43; WLC 2**
See also AAYA 67; BRW 1; BRWC 1; BRWR 2; CDBLB Before 1660; DA; DAB; DAC; DAM MST, POET; DLB 121, 151; EXPP; PAB; PFS 2, 11; RGEL 3; TEA; WLIT 3; WP

Donnell, David 1939(?)- **CLC 34**
See also CA 197

Donoghue, Denis 1928- **CLC 209**
See also CA 17-20R; CANR 16, 102

Donoghue, P. S.
See Hunt, E(verette) Howard, (Jr.)

Donoso (Yanez), Jose 1924-1996 ... **CLC 4, 8, 11, 32, 99; HLC 1; SSC 34; TCLC 133**
See also CA 81-84; 155; CANR 32, 73; CD-WLB 3; CWW 2; DAM MULT; DLB 113; EWL 3; HW 1, 2; LAW; LAWS 1; MTCW 1, 2; MTFW 2005; RGSF 2; WLIT 1

Donovan, John 1928-1992 **CLC 35**
See also AAYA 20; CA 97-100; 137; CLR 3; MAICYA 1, 2; SATA 72; SATA-Brief 29; YAW

Don Roberto
See Cunninghame Graham, Robert (Gallnigad) Bontine

Doolittle, Hilda 1886-1961 . **CLC 3, 8, 14, 31, 34, 73; PC 5; WLC 3**
See H. D.
See also AAYA 66; AMWS 1; CA 97-100; CANR 35, 131; DA; DAC; DAM MST, POET; DLB 4, 45; EWL 3; FW; GLL 1; LMFS 2; MAL 5; MAWW; MTCW 1, 2; MTFW 2005; PFS 6; RGAL 4

Doppo, Kunikida **TCLC 99**
See Kunikida Doppo

Dorfman, Ariel 1942- **CLC 48, 77, 189; HLC 1**
See also CA 124; 130; CANR 67, 70, 135; CWW 2; DAM MULT; DFS 4; EWL 3; HW 1, 2; INT CA-130; WLIT 1

Dorn, Edward (Merton)
1929-1999 **CLC 10, 18**
See also CA 93-96; 187; CANR 42, 79; CP 1, 2, 3, 4, 5, 6, 7; DLB 5; INT CA-93-96; WP

Dor-Ner, Zvi **CLC 70**

Dorris, Michael (Anthony)
1945-1997 **CLC 109; NNAL**
See also AAYA 20; BEST 90:1; BYA 12; CA 102; 157; CANR 19, 46, 75; CLR 58; DA3; DAM MULT, NOV; DLB 175; LAIT 5; MTCW 2; MTFW 2005; NFS 3; RGAL 4; SATA 75; SATA-Obit 94; TCWW 2; YAW

Dorris, Michael A.
See Dorris, Michael (Anthony)

Dorsan, Luc
See Simenon, Georges (Jacques Christian)

Dorsange, Jean
See Simenon, Georges (Jacques Christian)

Dorset
See Sackville, Thomas

Dos Passos, John (Roderigo)
1896-1970 ... **CLC 1, 4, 8, 11, 15, 25, 34, 82; WLC 2**
See also AMW; BPFB 1; CA 1-4R; 29-32R; CANR 3; CDALB 1929-1941; DA; DA3; DAB; DAC; DAM MST, NOV; DLB 4,

9, 274, 316; DLBD 1, 15; DLBY 1996; EWL 3; MAL 5; MTCW 1, 2; MTFW 2005; NFS 14; RGAL 4; TUS

Dossage, Jean
See Simenon, Georges (Jacques Christian)

Dostoevsky, Fedor Mikhailovich
1821-1881 .. **NCLC 2, 7, 21, 33, 43, 119, 167; SSC 2, 33, 44; WLC 2**
See Dostoevsky, Fyodor
See also AAYA 40; DA; DA3; DAB; DAC; DAM MST, NOV; EW 7; EXPN; NFS 3, 8; RGSF 2; RGWL 2, 3; SSFS 8; TWA

Dostoevsky, Fyodor
See Dostoevsky, Fedor Mikhailovich
See also DLB 238; LATS 1:1; LMFS 1, 2

Doty, M. R.
See Doty, Mark (Alan)

Doty, Mark
See Doty, Mark (Alan)

Doty, Mark (Alan) 1953(?)- **CLC 176; PC 53**
See also AMWS 11; CA 161, 183; CAAE 183; CANR 110; CP 7

Doty, Mark A.
See Doty, Mark (Alan)

Doughty, Charles M(ontagu)
1843-1926 **TCLC 27**
See also CA 115; 178; DLB 19, 57, 174

Douglas, Ellen **CLC 73**
See Haxton, Josephine Ayres; Williamson, Ellen Douglas
See also CN 5, 6, 7; CSW; DLB 292

Douglas, Gavin 1475(?)-1522 **LC 20**
See also DLB 132; RGEL 2

Douglas, George
See Brown, George Douglas
See also RGEL 2

Douglas, Keith (Castellain)
1920-1944 **TCLC 40**
See also BRW 7; CA 160; DLB 27; EWL 3; PAB; RGEL 2

Douglas, Leonard
See Bradbury, Ray (Douglas)

Douglas, Michael
See Crichton, (John) Michael

Douglas, (George) Norman
1868-1952 **TCLC 68**
See also BRW 6; CA 119; 157; DLB 34, 195; RGEL 2

Douglas, William
See Brown, George Douglas

Douglass, Frederick 1817(?)-1895 **BLC 1; NCLC 7, 55, 141; WLC 2**
See also AAYA 48; AFAW 1, 2; AMWC 1; AMWS 3; CDALB 1640-1865; DA; DA3; DAC; DAM MST, MULT; DLB 1, 43, 50, 79, 243; FW; LAIT 2; NCFS 2; RGAL 4; SATA 29

Dourado, (Waldomiro Freitas) Autran
1926- **CLC 23, 60**
See also CA 25-28R; 179; CANR 34, 81; DLB 145, 307; HW 2

Dourado, Waldomiro Freitas Autran
See Dourado, (Waldomiro Freitas) Autran

Dove, Rita (Frances) 1952- . **BLCS; CLC 50, 81; PC 6**
See also AAYA 46; AMWS 4; BW 2; CA 109; CAAS 19; CANR 27, 42, 68, 76, 97, 132; CDALBS; CP 5, 6, 7; CSW; CWP; DA3; DAM MULT, POET; DLB 120; EWL 3; EXPP; MAL 5; MTCW 2; MTFW 2005; PFS 1, 15; RGAL 4

Doveglion
See Villa, Jose Garcia

Dowell, Coleman 1925-1985 **CLC 60**
See also CA 25-28R; 117; CANR 10; DLB 130; GLL 2

Dowson, Ernest (Christopher)
1867-1900 **TCLC 4**
See also CA 105; 150; DLB 19, 135; RGEL 2

Doyle, A. Conan
See Doyle, Sir Arthur Conan

Doyle, Sir Arthur Conan
1859-1930 . **SSC 12, 83; TCLC 7; WLC 2**
See Conan Doyle, Arthur
See also AAYA 14; BRWS 2; CA 104; 122; CANR 131; CDBLB 1890-1914; CLR 106; CMW 4; DA; DA3; DAB; DAC; DAM MST, NOV; DLB 18, 70, 156, 178; EXPS; HGG; LAIT 2; MSW; MTCW 1, 2; MTFW 2005; RGEL 2; RGSF 2; RHW; SATA 24; SCFW 1, 2; SFW 4; SSFS 2; TEA; WCH; WLIT 4; WYA; YAW

Doyle, Conan
See Doyle, Sir Arthur Conan

Doyle, John
See Graves, Robert (von Ranke)

Doyle, Roddy 1958- **CLC 81, 178**
See also AAYA 14; BRWS 5; CA 143; CANR 73, 128; CN 6, 7; DA3; DLB 194, 326; MTCW 2; MTFW 2005

Doyle, Sir A. Conan
See Doyle, Sir Arthur Conan

Dr. A
See Asimov, Isaac; Silverstein, Alvin; Silverstein, Virginia B(arbara Opshelor)

Drabble, Margaret 1939- **CLC 2, 3, 5, 8, 10, 22, 53, 129**
See also BRWS 4; CA 13-16R; CANR 18, 35, 63, 112, 131; CDBLB 1960 to Present; CN 1, 2, 3, 4, 5, 6, 7; CPW; DA3; DAB; DAC; DAM MST, NOV, POP; DLB 14, 155, 231; EWL 3; FW; MTCW 1, 2; MTFW 2005; RGEL 2; SATA 48; TEA

Drakulic, Slavenka 1949- **CLC 173**
See also CA 144; CANR 92

Drakulic-Ilic, Slavenka
See Drakulic, Slavenka

Drapier, M. B.
See Swift, Jonathan

Drayham, James
See Mencken, H(enry) L(ouis)

Drayton, Michael 1563-1631 **LC 8**
See also DAM POET; DLB 121; RGEL 2

Dreadstone, Carl
See Campbell, (John) Ramsey

Dreiser, Theodore 1871-1945 **SSC 30; TCLC 10, 18, 35, 83; WLC 2**
See also AMW; AMWC 2; AMWR 2; BYA 15, 16; CA 106; 132; CDALB 1865-1917; DA; DA3; DAC; DAM MST, NOV; DLB 9, 12, 102, 137; DLBD 1; EWL 3; LAIT 2; LMFS 2; MAL 5; MTCW 1, 2; MTFW 2005; NFS 8, 17; RGAL 4; TUS

Dreiser, Theodore Herman Albert
See Dreiser, Theodore

Drexler, Rosalyn 1926- **CLC 2, 6**
See also CA 81-84; CAD; CANR 68, 124; CD 5, 6; CWD; MAL 5

Dreyer, Carl Theodor 1889-1968 **CLC 16**
See also CA 116

Drieu la Rochelle, Pierre(-Eugene)
1893-1945 **TCLC 21**
See also CA 117; DLB 72; EWL 3; GFL 1789 to the Present

Drinkwater, John 1882-1937 **TCLC 57**
See also CA 109; 149; DLB 10, 19, 149; RGEL 2

Drop Shot
See Cable, George Washington

Droste-Hulshoff, Annette Freiin von
1797-1848 **NCLC 3, 133**
See also CDWLB 2; DLB 133; RGSF 2; RGWL 2, 3

Drummond, Walter
See Silverberg, Robert
Drummond, William Henry
1854-1907 **TCLC 25**
See also CA 160; DLB 92
Drummond de Andrade, Carlos
1902-1987 **CLC 18; TCLC 139**
See Andrade, Carlos Drummond de
See also CA 132; 123; DLB 307; LAW
Drummond of Hawthornden, William
1585-1649 **LC 83**
See also DLB 121, 213; RGEL 2
Drury, Allen (Stuart) 1918-1998 **CLC 37**
See also CA 57-60; 170; CANR 18, 52; CN
1, 2, 3, 4, 5, 6; INT CANR-18
Druse, Eleanor
See King, Stephen
Dryden, John 1631-1700 **DC 3; LC 3, 21,**
115; PC 25; WLC 2
See also BRW 2; CDBLB 1660-1789; DA;
DAB; DAC; DAM DRAM, MST, POET;
DLB 80, 101, 131; EXPP; IDTP; LMFS
1; RGEL 2; TEA; WLIT 3
du Bellay, Joachim 1524-1560 **LC 92**
See also GFL Beginnings to 1789; RGWL
2, 3
Duberman, Martin (Bauml) 1930- **CLC 8**
See also CA 1-4R; CAD; CANR 2, 63, 137;
CD 5, 6
Dubie, Norman (Evans) 1945- **CLC 36**
See also CA 69-72; CANR 12, 115; CP 3,
4, 5, 6, 7; DLB 120; PFS 12
Du Bois, W(illiam) E(dward) B(urghardt)
1868-1963 **BLC 1; CLC 1, 2, 13, 64,**
96; HR 1:2; TCLC 169; WLC 2
See also AAYA 40; AFAW 1, 2; AMWC 1;
AMWS 2; BW 1, 3; CA 85-88; CANR
34, 82, 132; CDALB 1865-1917; DA;
DA3; DAC; DAM MST, MULT, NOV;
DLB 47, 50, 91, 246, 284; EWL 3; EXPP;
LAIT 2; LMFS 2; MAL 5; MTCW 1, 2;
MTFW 2005; NCFS 1; PFS 13; RGAL 4;
SATA 42
Dubus, Andre 1936-1999 **CLC 13, 36, 97;**
SSC 15
See also AMWS 7; CA 21-24R; 177; CANR
17; CN 5, 6; CSW; DLB 130; INT CANR-
17; RGAL 4; SSFS 10; TCLE 1:1
Duca Minimo
See D'Annunzio, Gabriele
Ducharme, Rejean 1941- **CLC 74**
See also CA 165; DLB 60
du Chatelet, Emilie 1706-1749 **LC 96**
See Chatelet, Gabrielle-Emilie Du
Duchen, Claire **CLC 65**
Duclos, Charles Pinot- 1704-1772 **LC 1**
See also GFL Beginnings to 1789
Dudek, Louis 1918-2001 **CLC 11, 19**
See also CA 45-48; 215; CAAS 14; CANR
1; CP 1, 2, 3, 4, 5, 6, 7; DLB 88
Duerrenmatt, Friedrich 1921-1990 ... **CLC 1,**
4, 8, 11, 15, 43, 102
See Durrenmatt, Friedrich
See also CA 17-20R; CANR 33; CMW 4;
DAM DRAM; DLB 69, 124; MTCW 1, 2
Duffy, Bruce 1953(?)- **CLC 50**
See also CA 172
Duffy, Maureen (Patricia) 1933- **CLC 37**
See also CA 25-28R; CANR 33, 68; CBD;
CN 1, 2, 3, 4, 5, 6, 7; CP 5, 6, 7; CWD;
CWP; DFS 15; DLB 14, 310; FW; MTCW
1
Du Fu
See Tu Fu
See also RGWL 2, 3
Dugan, Alan 1923-2003 **CLC 2, 6**
See also CA 81-84; 220; CANR 119; CP 1,
2, 3, 4, 5, 6, 7; DLB 5; MAL 5; PFS 10

du Gard, Roger Martin
See Martin du Gard, Roger
Duhamel, Georges 1884-1966 **CLC 8**
See also CA 81-84; 25-28R; CANR 35;
DLB 65; EWL 3; GFL 1789 to the
Present; MTCW 1
Dujardin, Edouard (Emile Louis)
1861-1949 **TCLC 13**
See also CA 109; DLB 123
Duke, Raoul
See Thompson, Hunter S(tockton)
Dulles, John Foster 1888-1959 **TCLC 72**
See also CA 115; 149
Dumas, Alexandre (pere)
1802-1870 **NCLC 11, 71; WLC 2**
See also AAYA 22; BYA 3; DA; DA3;
DAB; DAC; DAM MST, NOV; DLB 119,
192; EW 6; GFL 1789 to the Present;
LAIT 1, 2; NFS 14, 19; RGWL 2, 3;
SATA 18; TWA; WCH
Dumas, Alexandre (fils) 1824-1895 **DC 1;**
NCLC 9
See also DLB 192; GFL 1789 to the Present;
RGWL 2, 3
Dumas, Claudine
See Malzberg, Barry N(athaniel)
Dumas, Henry L. 1934-1968 **CLC 6, 62**
See also BW 1; CA 85-88; DLB 41; RGAL
4
du Maurier, Daphne 1907-1989 .. **CLC 6, 11,**
59; SSC 18
See also AAYA 37; BPFB 1; BRWS 3; CA
5-8R; 128; CANR 6, 55; CMW 4; CN 1,
2, 3, 4; CPW; DA3; DAB; DAC; DAM
MST, POP; DLB 191; GL 2; HGG; LAIT
3; MSW; MTCW 1, 2; NFS 12; RGEL 2;
RGSF 2; RHW; SATA 27; SATA-Obit 60;
SSFS 14, 16; TEA
Du Maurier, George 1834-1896 **NCLC 86**
See also DLB 153, 178; RGEL 2
Dunbar, Paul Laurence 1872-1906 ... **BLC 1;**
PC 5; SSC 8; TCLC 2, 12; WLC 2
See also AFAW 1, 2; AMWS 2; BW 1, 3;
CA 104; 124; CANR 79; CDALB 1865-
1917; DA; DA3; DAC; DAM MST,
MULT, POET; DLB 50, 54, 78; EXPP;
MAL 5; RGAL 4; SATA 34
Dunbar, William 1460(?)-1520(?) **LC 20;**
PC 67
See also BRWS 8; DLB 132, 146; RGEL 2
Dunbar-Nelson, Alice **HR 1:2**
See Nelson, Alice Ruth Moore Dunbar
Duncan, Dora Angela
See Duncan, Isadora
Duncan, Isadora 1877(?)-1927 **TCLC 68**
See also CA 118; 149
Duncan, Lois 1934- **CLC 26**
See also AAYA 4, 34; BYA 6, 8; CA 1-4R;
CANR 2, 23, 36, 111; CLR 29; JRDA;
MAICYA 1, 2; MAICYAS 1; MTFW
2005; SAAS 2; SATA 1, 36, 75, 133, 141;
SATA-Essay 141; WYA; YAW
Duncan, Robert (Edward)
1919-1988 **CLC 1, 2, 4, 7, 15, 41, 55;**
PC 2
See also BG 1:2; CA 9-12R; 124; CANR
28, 62; CP 1, 2, 3, 4; DAM POET; DLB
5, 16, 193; EWL 3; MAL 5; MTCW 1, 2;
MTFW 2005; PFS 13; RGAL 4; WP
Duncan, Sara Jeannette
1861-1922 **TCLC 60**
See also CA 157; DLB 92
Dunlap, William 1766-1839 **NCLC 2**
See also DLB 30, 37, 59; RGAL 4
Dunn, Douglas (Eaglesham) 1942- **CLC 6,**
40
See also BRWS 10; CA 45-48; CANR 2,
33, 126; CP 1, 2, 3, 4, 5, 6, 7; DLB 40;
MTCW 1

Dunn, Katherine (Karen) 1945- **CLC 71**
See also CA 33-36R; CANR 72; HGG;
MTCW 2; MTFW 2005
Dunn, Stephen (Elliott) 1939- .. **CLC 36, 206**
See also AMWS 11; CA 33-36R; CANR
12, 48, 53, 105; CP 3, 4, 5, 6, 7; DLB
105; PFS 21
Dunne, Finley Peter 1867-1936 **TCLC 28**
See also CA 108; 178; DLB 11, 23; RGAL
4
Dunne, John Gregory 1932-2003 **CLC 28**
See also CA 25-28R; 222; CANR 14, 50;
CN 5, 6, 7; DLBY 1980
Dunsany, Lord **TCLC 2, 59**
See Dunsany, Edward John Moreton Drax
Plunkett
See also DLB 77, 153, 156, 255; FANT;
IDTP; RGEL 2; SFW 4; SUFW 1
Dunsany, Edward John Moreton Drax
Plunkett 1878-1957
See Dunsany, Lord
See also CA 104; 148; DLB 10; MTCW 2
Duns Scotus, John 1266(?)-1308 ... **CMLC 59**
See also DLB 115
du Perry, Jean
See Simenon, Georges (Jacques Christian)
Durang, Christopher 1949- **CLC 27, 38**
See also CA 105; CAD; CANR 50, 76, 130;
CD 5, 6; MTCW 2; MTFW 2005
Durang, Christopher Ferdinand
See Durang, Christopher
Duras, Claire de 1777-1832 **NCLC 154**
Duras, Marguerite 1914-1996 . **CLC 3, 6, 11,**
20, 34, 40, 68, 100; SSC 40
See also BPFB 1; CA 25-28R; 151; CANR
50; CWW 2; DFS 21; DLB 83, 321; EWL
3; FL 1:5; GFL 1789 to the Present; IDFW
4; MTCW 1, 2; RGWL 2, 3; TWA
Durban, (Rosa) Pam 1947- **CLC 39**
See also CA 123; CANR 98; CSW
Durcan, Paul 1944- **CLC 43, 70**
See also CA 134; CANR 123; CP 1, 5, 6, 7;
DAM POET; EWL 3
Durfey, Thomas 1653-1723 **LC 94**
See also DLB 80; RGEL 2
Durkheim, Emile 1858-1917 **TCLC 55**
Durrell, Lawrence (George)
1912-1990 **CLC 1, 4, 6, 8, 13, 27, 41**
See also BPFB 1; BRWS 1; CA 9-12R; 132;
CANR 40, 77; CDBLB 1945-1960; CN 1,
2, 3, 4; CP 1, 2, 3, 4, 5; DAM NOV; DLB
15, 27, 204; DLBY 1990; EWL 3; MTCW
1, 2; RGEL 2; SFW 4; TEA
Durrenmatt, Friedrich
See Duerrenmatt, Friedrich
See also CDWLB 2; EW 13; EWL 3;
RGHL; RGWL 2, 3
Dutt, Michael Madhusudan
1824-1873 **NCLC 118**
Dutt, Toru 1856-1877 **NCLC 29**
See also DLB 240
Dwight, Timothy 1752-1817 **NCLC 13**
See also DLB 37; RGAL 4
Dworkin, Andrea 1946-2005 **CLC 43, 123**
See also CA 77-80; 238; CAAS 21; CANR
16, 39, 76, 96; FL 1:5; FW; GLL 1; INT
CANR-16; MTCW 1, 2; MTFW 2005
Dwyer, Deanna
See Koontz, Dean R.
Dwyer, K. R.
See Koontz, Dean R.
Dybek, Stuart 1942- **CLC 114; SSC 55**
See also CA 97-100; CANR 39; DLB 130;
SSFS 23
Dye, Richard
See De Voto, Bernard (Augustine)
Dyer, Geoff 1958- **CLC 149**
See also CA 125; CANR 88

Dyer, George 1755-1841 **NCLC 129**
See also DLB 93

Dylan, Bob 1941- **CLC 3, 4, 6, 12, 77; PC 37**
See also CA 41-44R; CANR 108; CP 1, 2, 3, 4, 5, 6, 7; DLB 16

Dyson, John 1943- **CLC 70**
See also CA 144

Dzyubin, Eduard Georgievich 1895-1934
See Bagritsky, Eduard
See also CA 170

E. V. L.
See Lucas, E(dward) V(errall)

Eagleton, Terence (Francis) 1943- .. **CLC 63, 132**
See also CA 57-60; CANR 7, 23, 68, 115; DLB 242; LMFS 2; MTCW 1, 2; MTFW 2005

Eagleton, Terry
See Eagleton, Terence (Francis)

Early, Jack
See Scoppettone, Sandra
See also GLL 1

East, Michael
See West, Morris L(anglo)

Eastaway, Edward
See Thomas, (Philip) Edward

Eastlake, William (Derry) 1917-1997 **CLC 8**
See also CA 5-8R; 158; CAAS 1; CANR 5, 63; CN 1, 2, 3, 4, 5, 6; DLB 6, 206; INT CANR-5; MAL 5; TCWW 1, 2

Eastman, Charles A(lexander) 1858-1939 **NNAL; TCLC 55**
See also CA 179; CANR 91; DAM MULT; DLB 175; YABC 1

Eaton, Edith Maude 1865-1914 **AAL**
See Far, Sui Sin
See also CA 154; DLB 221, 312; FW

Eaton, (Lillie) Winnifred 1875-1954 **AAL**
See also CA 217; DLB 221, 312; RGAL 4

Eberhart, Richard 1904-2005 **CLC 3, 11, 19, 56**
See also AMW; CA 1-4R; 240; CANR 2, 125; CDALB 1941-1968; CP 1, 2, 3, 4, 5, 6, 7; DAM POET; DLB 48; MAL 5; MTCW 1; RGAL 4

Eberhart, Richard Ghormley
See Eberhart, Richard

Eberstadt, Fernanda 1960- **CLC 39**
See also CA 136; CANR 69, 128

Echegaray (y Eizaguirre), Jose (Maria Waldo) 1832-1916 **HLCS 1; TCLC 4**
See also CA 104; CANR 32; EWL 3; HW 1; MTCW 1

Echeverria, (Jose) Esteban (Antonino) 1805-1851 **NCLC 18**
See also LAW

Echo
See Proust, (Valentin-Louis-George-Eugene) Marcel

Eckert, Allan W. 1931- **CLC 17**
See also AAYA 18; BYA 2; CA 13-16R; CANR 14, 45; INT CANR-14; MAICYA 2; MAICYAS 1; SAAS 21; SATA 29, 91; SATA-Brief 27

Eckhart, Meister 1260(?)-1327(?) .. **CMLC 9, 80**
See also DLB 115; LMFS 1

Eckmar, F. R.
See de Hartog, Jan

Eco, Umberto 1932- **CLC 28, 60, 142**
See also BEST 90:1; BPFB 1; CA 77-80; CANR 12, 33, 55, 110, 131; CPW; CWW 2; DA3; DAM NOV, POP; DLB 196, 242; EWL 3; MSW; MTCW 1, 2; MTFW 2005; NFS 22; RGWL 3; WLIT 7

Eddison, E(ric) R(ucker) 1882-1945 **TCLC 15**
See also CA 109; 156; DLB 255; FANT; SFW 4; SUFW 1

Eddy, Mary (Ann Morse) Baker 1821-1910 **TCLC 71**
See also CA 113; 174

Edel, (Joseph) Leon 1907-1997 .. **CLC 29, 34**
See also CA 1-4R; 161; CANR 1, 22, 112; DLB 103; INT CANR-22

Eden, Emily 1797-1869 **NCLC 10**

Edgar, David 1948- **CLC 42**
See also CA 57-60; CANR 12, 61, 112; CBD; CD 5, 6; DAM DRAM; DFS 15; DLB 13, 233; MTCW 1

Edgerton, Clyde (Carlyle) 1944- **CLC 39**
See also AAYA 17; CA 118; 134; CANR 64, 125; CN 7; CSW; DLB 278; INT CA-134; TCLE 1:1; YAW

Edgeworth, Maria 1768-1849 ... **NCLC 1, 51, 158; SSC 86**
See also BRWS 3; DLB 116, 159, 163; FL 1:3; FW; RGEL 2; SATA 21; TEA; WLIT 3

Edmonds, Paul
See Kuttner, Henry

Edmonds, Walter D(umaux) 1903-1998 **CLC 35**
See also BYA 2; CA 5-8R; CANR 2; CWRI 5; DLB 9; LAIT 1; MAICYA 1, 2; MAL 5; RHW; SAAS 4; SATA 1, 27; SATA-Obit 99

Edmondson, Wallace
See Ellison, Harlan (Jay)

Edson, Margaret 1961- **CLC 199; DC 24**
See also CA 190; DFS 13; DLB 266

Edson, Russell 1935- **CLC 13**
See also CA 33-36R; CANR 115; CP 2, 3, 4, 5, 6, 7; DLB 244; WP

Edwards, Bronwen Elizabeth
See Rose, Wendy

Edwards, G(erald) B(asil) 1899-1976 **CLC 25**
See also CA 201; 110

Edwards, Gus 1939- **CLC 43**
See also CA 108; INT CA-108

Edwards, Jonathan 1703-1758 **LC 7, 54**
See also AMW; DA; DAC; DAM MST; DLB 24, 270; RGAL 4; TUS

Edwards, Sarah Pierpont 1710-1758 .. **LC 87**
See also DLB 200

Efron, Marina Ivanovna Tsvetaeva
See Tsvetaeva (Efron), Marina (Ivanovna)

Egeria fl. 4th cent. - **CMLC 70**

Egoyan, Atom 1960- **CLC 151**
See also AAYA 63; CA 157; CANR 151

Ehle, John (Marsden, Jr.) 1925- **CLC 27**
See also CA 9-12R; CSW

Ehrenbourg, Ilya (Grigoryevich)
See Ehrenburg, Ilya (Grigoryevich)

Ehrenburg, Ilya (Grigoryevich) 1891-1967 **CLC 18, 34, 62**
See Erenburg, Il'ia Grigor'evich
See also CA 102; 25-28R; EWL 3

Ehrenburg, Ilyo (Grigoryevich)
See Ehrenburg, Ilya (Grigoryevich)

Ehrenreich, Barbara 1941- **CLC 110**
See also BEST 90:4; CA 73-76; CANR 16, 37, 62, 117; DLB 246; FW; MTCW 1, 2; MTFW 2005

Eich, Gunter
See Eich, Gunter
See also RGWL 2, 3

Eich, Gunter 1907-1972 **CLC 15**
See Eich, Gunter
See also CA 111; 93-96; DLB 69, 124; EWL 3

Eichendorff, Joseph 1788-1857 **NCLC 8**
See also DLB 90; RGWL 2, 3

Eigner, Larry **CLC 9**
See Eigner, Laurence (Joel)
See also CAAS 23; CP 1, 2, 3, 4, 5, 6; DLB 5; WP

Eigner, Laurence (Joel) 1927-1996
See Eigner, Larry
See also CA 9-12R; 151; CANR 6, 84; CP 7; DLB 193

Eilhart von Oberge c. 1140-c. 1195 .. **CMLC 67**
See also DLB 148

Einhard c. 770-840 **CMLC 50**
See also DLB 148

Einstein, Albert 1879-1955 **TCLC 65**
See also CA 121; 133; MTCW 1, 2

Eiseley, Loren
See Eiseley, Loren Corey
See also DLB 275

Eiseley, Loren Corey 1907-1977 **CLC 7**
See Eiseley, Loren
See also AAYA 5; ANW; CA 1-4R; 73-76; CANR 6; DLBD 17

Eisenstadt, Jill 1963- **CLC 50**
See also CA 140

Eisenstein, Sergei (Mikhailovich) 1898-1948 **TCLC 57**
See also CA 114; 149

Eisner, Simon
See Kornbluth, C(yril) M.

Ekeloef, (Bengt) Gunnar 1907-1968 **CLC 27; PC 23**
See Ekelof, (Bengt) Gunnar
See also CA 123; 25-28R; DAM POET

Ekelof, (Bengt) Gunnar 1907-1968
See Ekeloef, (Bengt) Gunnar
See also DLB 259; EW 12; EWL 3

Ekelund, Vilhelm 1880-1949 **TCLC 75**
See also CA 189; EWL 3

Ekwensi, C. O. D.
See Ekwensi, Cyprian (Odiatu Duaka)

Ekwensi, Cyprian (Odiatu Duaka) 1921- **BLC 1; CLC 4**
See also AFW; BW 2, 3; CA 29-32R; CANR 18, 42, 74, 125; CDWLB 3; CN 1, 2, 3, 4, 5, 6; CWRI 5; DAM MULT; DLB 117; EWL 3; MTCW 1, 2; RGEL 2; SATA 66; WLIT 2

Elaine ... **TCLC 18**
See Leverson, Ada Esther

El Crummo
See Crumb, R.

Elder, Lonne III 1931-1996 **BLC 1; DC 8**
See also BW 1, 3; CA 81-84; 152; CAD; CANR 25; DAM MULT; DLB 7, 38, 44; MAL 5

Eleanor of Aquitaine 1122-1204 ... **CMLC 39**

Elia
See Lamb, Charles

Eliade, Mircea 1907-1986 **CLC 19**
See also CA 65-68; 119; CANR 30, 62; CD-WLB 4; DLB 220; EWL 3; MTCW 1; RGWL 3; SFW 4

Eliot, A. D.
See Jewett, (Theodora) Sarah Orne

Eliot, Alice
See Jewett, (Theodora) Sarah Orne

Eliot, Dan
See Silverberg, Robert

Eliot, George 1819-1880 **NCLC 4, 13, 23, 41, 49, 89, 118; PC 20; SSC 72; WLC 2**
See Evans, Mary Ann
See also BRW 5; BRWC 1, 2; BRWR 2; CDBLB 1832-1890; CN 7; CPW; DA; DA3; DAB; DAC; DAM MST, NOV; DLB 21, 35, 55; FL 1:3; LATS 1:1; LMFS 1; NFS 17, 20; RGEL 2; RGSF 2; SSFS 8; TEA; WLIT 3

Eliot, John 1604-1690 **LC 5**
See also DLB 24

Eliot, T(homas) S(tearns)
1888-1965 **CLC 1, 2, 3, 6, 9, 10, 13, 15, 24, 34, 41, 55, 57, 113; PC 5, 31; WLC 2**
See also AAYA 28; AMW; AMWC 1; AMWR 1; BRW 7; BRWR 2; CA 5-8R; 25-28R; CANR 41; CBD; CDALB 1929-1941; DA; DA3; DAB; DAC; DAM DRAM, MST, POET; DFS 4, 13; DLB 7, 10, 45, 63, 245; DLBY 1988; EWL 3; EXPP; LAIT 3; LATS 1:1; LMFS 2; MAL 5; MTCW 1, 2; MTFW 2005; NCFS 5; PAB; PFS 1, 7, 20; RGAL 4; RGEL 2; TUS; WLIT 4; WP

Elisabeth of Schonau c.
1129-1165 **CMLC 82**

Elizabeth 1866-1941 **TCLC 41**

Elizabeth I 1533-1603 **LC 118**
See also DLB 136

Elkin, Stanley L(awrence)
1930-1995 .. **CLC 4, 6, 9, 14, 27, 51, 91; SSC 12**
See also AMWS 6; BPFB 1; CA 9-12R; 148; CANR 8, 46; CN 1, 2, 3, 4, 5, 6; CPW; DAM NOV, POP; DLB 2, 28, 218, 278; DLBY 1980; EWL 3; INT CANR-8; MAL 5; MTCW 1, 2; MTFW 2005; RGAL 4; TCLE 1:1

Elledge, Scott **CLC 34**

Eller, Scott
See Shepard, James R.

Elliott, Don
See Silverberg, Robert

Elliott, George P(aul) 1918-1980 **CLC 2**
See also CA 1-4R; 97-100; CANR 2; CN 1, 2; CP 3; DLB 244; MAL 5

Elliott, Janice 1931-1995 **CLC 47**
See also CA 13-16R; CANR 8, 29, 84; CN 5, 6, 7; DLB 14; SATA 119

Elliott, Sumner Locke 1917-1991 **CLC 38**
See also CA 5-8R; 134; CANR 2, 21; DLB 289

Elliott, William
See Bradbury, Ray (Douglas)

Ellis, A. E. ... **CLC 7**

Ellis, Alice Thomas **CLC 40**
See Haycraft, Anna
See also CN 4, 5, 6; DLB 194

Ellis, Bret Easton 1964- **CLC 39, 71, 117**
See also AAYA 2, 43; CA 118; 123; CANR 51, 74, 126; CN 6, 7; CPW; DA3; DAM POP; DLB 292; HGG; INT CA-123; MTCW 2; MTFW 2005; NFS 11

Ellis, (Henry) Havelock
1859-1939 **TCLC 14**
See also CA 109; 169; DLB 190

Ellis, Landon
See Ellison, Harlan (Jay)

Ellis, Trey 1962- **CLC 55**
See also CA 146; CANR 92; CN 7

Ellison, Harlan (Jay) 1934- ... **CLC 1, 13, 42, 139; SSC 14**
See also AAYA 29; BPFB 1; BYA 14; CA 5-8R; CANR 5, 46, 115; CPW; DAM POP; DLB 8; HGG; INT CANR-5; MTCW 1, 2; MTFW 2005; SCFW 2; SFW 4; SSFS 13, 14, 15, 21; SUFW 1, 2

Ellison, Ralph (Waldo) 1914-1994 **BLC 1; CLC 1, 3, 11, 54, 86, 114; SSC 26, 79; WLC 2**
See also AAYA 19; AFAW 1, 2; AMWC 2; AMWR 2; AMWS 2; BPFB 1; BW 1, 3; BYA 2; CA 9-12R; 145; CANR 24, 53; CDALB 1941-1968; CN 1, 2, 3, 4, 5; CSW; DA; DA3; DAB; DAC; DAM MST, MULT, NOV; DLB 2, 76, 227; DLBY 1994; EWL 3; EXPN; EXPS; LAIT 4; MAL 5; MTCW 1, 2; MTFW 2005; NCFS 3; NFS 2, 21; RGAL 4; RGSF 2; SSFS 1, 11; YAW

Ellmann, Lucy 1956- **CLC 61**
See also CA 128; CANR 154

Ellmann, Lucy Elizabeth
See Ellmann, Lucy

Ellmann, Richard (David)
1918-1987 **CLC 50**
See also BEST 89:2; CA 1-4R; 122; CANR 2, 28, 61; DLB 103; DLBY 1987; MTCW 1, 2; MTFW 2005

Elman, Richard (Martin)
1934-1997 **CLC 19**
See also CA 17-20R; 163; CAAS 3; CANR 47; TCLE 1:1

Elron
See Hubbard, L. Ron

El Saadawi, Nawal 1931- **CLC 196**
See al'Sadaawi, Nawal; Sa'adawi, al-Nawal; Saadawi, Nawal El; Sa'dawi, Nawal al-
See also CA 118; CAAS 11; CANR 44, 92

Eluard, Paul **PC 38; TCLC 7, 41**
See Grindel, Eugene
See also EWL 3; GFL 1789 to the Present; RGWL 2, 3

Elyot, Thomas 1490(?)-1546 **LC 11**
See also DLB 136; RGEL 2

Elytis, Odysseus 1911-1996 **CLC 15, 49, 100; PC 21**
See Alepoudelis, Odysseus
See also CA 102; 151; CANR 94; CWW 2; DAM POET; EW 13; EWL 3; MTCW 1, 2; RGWL 2, 3

Emecheta, (Florence Onye) Buchi
1944- **BLC 2; CLC 14, 48, 128, 214**
See also AAYA 67; AFW; BW 2, 3; CA 81-84; CANR 27, 81, 126; CDWLB 3; CN 4, 5, 6, 7; CWRI 5; DA3; DAM MULT; DLB 117; EWL 3; FL 1:5; FW; MTCW 1, 2; MTFW 2005; NFS 12, 14; SATA 66; WLIT 2

Emerson, Mary Moody
1774-1863 **NCLC 66**

Emerson, Ralph Waldo 1803-1882 . **NCLC 1, 38, 98; PC 18; WLC 2**
See also AAYA 60; AMW; ANW; CDALB 1640-1865; DA; DA3; DAB; DAC; DAM MST, POET; DLB 1, 59, 73, 183, 223, 270; EXPP; LAIT 2; LMFS 1; NCFS 3; PFS 4, 17; RGAL 4; TUS; WP

Eminescu, Mihail 1850-1889 .. **NCLC 33, 131**

Empedocles 5th cent. B.C.- **CMLC 50**
See also DLB 176

Empson, William 1906-1984 ... **CLC 3, 8, 19, 33, 34**
See also BRWS 2; CA 17-20R; 112; CANR 31, 61; CP 1, 2, 3; DLB 20; EWL 3; MTCW 1, 2; RGEL 2

Enchi, Fumiko (Ueda) 1905-1986 **CLC 31**
See Enchi Fumiko
See also CA 129; 121; FW; MJW

Enchi Fumiko
See Enchi, Fumiko (Ueda)
See also DLB 182; EWL 3

Ende, Michael (Andreas Helmuth)
1929-1995 **CLC 31**
See also BYA 5; CA 118; 124; 149; CANR 36, 110; CLR 14; DLB 75; MAICYA 1, 2; MAICYAS 1; SATA 61, 130; SATA-Brief 42; SATA-Obit 86

Endo, Shusaku 1923-1996 **CLC 7, 14, 19, 54, 99; SSC 48; TCLC 152**
See Endo Shusaku
See also CA 29-32R; 153; CANR 21, 54, 131; DA3; DAM NOV; MTCW 1, 2; MTFW 2005; RGSF 2; RGWL 2, 3

Endo Shusaku
See Endo, Shusaku
See also CWW 2; DLB 182; EWL 3

Engel, Marian 1933-1985 **CLC 36; TCLC 137**
See also CA 25-28R; CANR 12; CN 2, 3; DLB 53; FW; INT CANR-12

Engelhardt, Frederick
See Hubbard, L. Ron

Engels, Friedrich 1820-1895 .. **NCLC 85, 114**
See also DLB 129; LATS 1:1

Enright, D(ennis) J(oseph)
1920-2002 **CLC 4, 8, 31**
See also CA 1-4R; 211; CANR 1, 42, 83; CN 1, 2; CP 1, 2, 3, 4, 5, 6, 7; DLB 27; EWL 3; SATA 25; SATA-Obit 140

Ensler, Eve 1953- **CLC 212**
See also CA 172; CANR 126; DFS 23

Enzensberger, Hans Magnus
1929- **CLC 43; PC 28**
See also CA 116; 119; CANR 103; CWW 2; EWL 3

Ephron, Nora 1941- **CLC 17, 31**
See also AAYA 35; AITN 2; CA 65-68; CANR 12, 39, 83; DFS 22

Epicurus 341B.C.-270B.C. **CMLC 21**
See also DLB 176

Epsilon
See Betjeman, John

Epstein, Daniel Mark 1948- **CLC 7**
See also CA 49-52; CANR 2, 53, 90

Epstein, Jacob 1956- **CLC 19**
See also CA 114

Epstein, Jean 1897-1953 **TCLC 92**

Epstein, Joseph 1937- **CLC 39, 204**
See also AMWS 14; CA 112; 119; CANR 50, 65, 117

Epstein, Leslie 1938- **CLC 27**
See also AMWS 12; CA 73-76, 215; CAAE 215; CAAS 12; CANR 23, 69; DLB 299; RGHL

Equiano, Olaudah 1745(?)-1797 . **BLC 2; LC 16**
See also AFAW 1, 2; CDWLB 3; DAM MULT; DLB 37, 50; WLIT 2

Erasmus, Desiderius 1469(?)-1536 **LC 16, 93**
See also DLB 136; EW 2; LMFS 1; RGWL 2, 3; TWA

Erdman, Paul E(mil) 1932- **CLC 25**
See also AITN 1; CA 61-64; CANR 13, 43, 84

Erdrich, Karen Louise
See Erdrich, Louise

Erdrich, Louise 1954- **CLC 39, 54, 120, 176; NNAL; PC 52**
See also AAYA 10, 47; AMWS 4; BEST 89:1; BPFB 1; CA 114; CANR 41, 62, 118, 138; CDALBS 5, 6, 7; CP 6, 7; CPW; CWP; DA3; DAM MULT, NOV, POP; DLB 152, 175, 206; EWL 3; EXPP; FL 1:5; LAIT 5; LATS 1:2; MAL 5; MTCW 1, 2; MTFW 2005; NFS 5; PFS 14; RGAL 4; SATA 94, 141; SSFS 14; TCWW 2

Erenburg, Ilya (Grigoryevich)
See Ehrenburg, Ilya (Grigoryevich)

Erickson, Stephen Michael 1950-
See Erickson, Steve
See also CA 129; SFW 4

Erickson, Steve **CLC 64**
See Erickson, Stephen Michael
See also CANR 60, 68, 136; MTFW 2005; SUFW 2

Erickson, Walter
See Fast, Howard (Melvin)

Ericson, Walter
See Fast, Howard (Melvin)

Eriksson, Buntel
See Bergman, (Ernst) Ingmar

Eriugena, John Scottus c.
810-877 **CMLC 65**
See also DLB 115

Ernaux, Annie 1940- **CLC 88, 184**
See also CA 147; CANR 93; MTFW 2005;
NCFS 3, 5

Erskine, John 1879-1951 **TCLC 84**
See also CA 112; 159; DLB 9, 102; FANT

Eschenbach, Wolfram von
See Wolfram von Eschenbach
See also RGWL 3

Eseki, Bruno
See Mphahlele, Ezekiel

Esenin, Sergei (Alexandrovich)
1895-1925 **TCLC 4**
See Yesenin, Sergey
See also CA 104; RGWL 2, 3

Eshleman, Clayton 1935- **CLC 7**
See also CA 33-36R, 212; CAAE 212;
CAAS 6; CANR 93; CP 1, 2, 3, 4, 5, 6,
7; DLB 5

Espriella, Don Manuel Alvarez
See Southey, Robert

Espriu, Salvador 1913-1985 **CLC 9**
See also CA 154; 115; DLB 134; EWL 3

Espronceda, Jose de 1808-1842 **NCLC 39**

Esquivel, Laura 1951(?)- ... **CLC 141; HLCS
1**
See also AAYA 29; CA 143; CANR 68, 113;
DA3; DNFS 2; LAIT 3; LMFS 2; MTCW
2; MTFW 2005; NFS 5; WLIT 1

Esse, James
See Stephens, James

Esterbrook, Tom
See Hubbard, L. Ron

Estleman, Loren D. 1952- **CLC 48**
See also AAYA 27; CA 85-88; CANR 27,
74, 139; CMW 4; CPW; DA3; DAM
NOV, POP; DLB 226; INT CANR-27;
MTCW 1, 2; MTFW 2005; TCWW 1, 2

Etherege, Sir George 1636-1692 . **DC 23; LC
78**
See also BRW 2; DAM DRAM; DLB 80;
PAB; RGEL 2

Euclid 306B.C.-283B.C. **CMLC 25**

Eugenides, Jeffrey 1960(?)- **CLC 81, 212**
See also AAYA 51; CA 144; CANR 120;
MTFW 2005

Euripides c. 484B.C.-406B.C. **CMLC 23,
51; DC 4; WLCS**
See also AW 1; CDWLB 1; DA; DA3;
DAB; DAC; DAM DRAM, MST; DFS 1,
4, 6; DLB 176; LAIT 1; LMFS 1; RGWL
2, 3; WLIT 8

Evan, Evin
See Faust, Frederick (Schiller)

Evans, Caradoc 1878-1945 ... **SSC 43; TCLC
85**
See also DLB 162

Evans, Evan
See Faust, Frederick (Schiller)

Evans, Marian
See Eliot, George

Evans, Mary Ann
See Eliot, George
See also NFS 20

Evarts, Esther
See Benson, Sally

Everett, Percival
See Everett, Percival L.
See also CSW

Everett, Percival L. 1956- **CLC 57**
See Everett, Percival
See also BW 2; CA 129; CANR 94, 134;
CN 7; MTFW 2005

Everson, R(onald) G(ilmour)
1903-1992 **CLC 27**
See also CA 17-20R; CP 1, 2, 3, 4; DLB 88

Everson, William (Oliver)
1912-1994 **CLC 1, 5, 14**
See Antoninus, Brother
See also BG 1:2; CA 9-12R; 145; CANR
20; CP 2, 3, 4, 5; DLB 5, 16, 212; MTCW
1

Evtushenko, Evgenii Aleksandrovich
See Yevtushenko, Yevgeny (Alexandrovich)
See also CWW 2; RGWL 2, 3

Ewart, Gavin (Buchanan)
1916-1995 **CLC 13, 46**
See also BRWS 7; CA 89-92; 150; CANR
17, 46; CP 1, 2, 3, 4, 5, 6; DLB 40;
MTCW 1

Ewers, Hanns Heinz 1871-1943 **TCLC 12**
See also CA 109; 149

Ewing, Frederick R.
See Sturgeon, Theodore (Hamilton)

Exley, Frederick (Earl) 1929-1992 **CLC 6,
11**
See also AITN 2; BPFB 1; CA 81-84; 138;
CANR 117; DLB 143; DLBY 1981

Eynhardt, Guillermo
See Quiroga, Horacio (Sylvestre)

Ezekiel, Nissim (Moses) 1924-2004 .. **CLC 61**
See also CA 61-64; 223; CP 1, 2, 3, 4, 5, 6,
7; DLB 323; EWL 3

Ezekiel, Tish O'Dowd 1943- **CLC 34**
See also CA 129

Fadeev, Aleksandr Aleksandrovich
See Bulgya, Alexander Alexandrovich
See also DLB 272

Fadeev, Alexandr Alexandrovich
See Bulgya, Alexander Alexandrovich
See also EWL 3

Fadeyev, A.
See Bulgya, Alexander Alexandrovich

Fadeyev, Alexander **TCLC 53**
See Bulgya, Alexander Alexandrovich

Fagen, Donald 1948- **CLC 26**

Fainzilberg, Ilya Arnoldovich 1897-1937
See Ilf, Ilya
See also CA 120; 165

Fair, Ronald L. 1932- **CLC 18**
See also BW 1; CA 69-72; CANR 25; DLB
33

Fairbairn, Roger
See Carr, John Dickson

Fairbairns, Zoe (Ann) 1948- **CLC 32**
See also CA 103; CANR 21, 85; CN 4, 5,
6, 7

Fairfield, Flora
See Alcott, Louisa May

Fairman, Paul W. 1916-1977
See Queen, Ellery
See also CA 114; SFW 4

Falco, Gian
See Papini, Giovanni

Falconer, James
See Kirkup, James

Falconer, Kenneth
See Kornbluth, C(yril) M.

Falkland, Samuel
See Heijermans, Herman

Fallaci, Oriana 1930- **CLC 11, 110**
See also CA 77-80; CANR 15, 58, 134; FW;
MTCW 1

Faludi, Susan 1959- **CLC 140**
See also CA 138; CANR 126; FW; MTCW
2; MTFW 2005; NCFS 3

Faludy, George 1913- **CLC 42**
See also CA 21-24R

Faludy, Gyoergy
See Faludy, George

Fanon, Frantz 1925-1961 **BLC 2; CLC 74**
See also BW 1; CA 116; 89-92; DAM
MULT; DLB 296; LMFS 2; WLIT 2

Fanshawe, Ann 1625-1680 **LC 11**

Fante, John (Thomas) 1911-1983 **CLC 60;
SSC 65**
See also AMWS 11; CA 69-72; 109; CANR
23, 104; DLB 130; DLBY 1983

Far, Sui Sin .. **SSC 62**
See Eaton, Edith Maude
See also SSFS 4

Farah, Nuruddin 1945- **BLC 2; CLC 53,
137**
See also AFW; BW 2, 3; CA 106; CANR
81, 148; CDWLB 3; CN 4, 5, 6, 7; DAM
MULT; DLB 125; EWL 3; WLIT 2

Fargue, Leon-Paul 1876(?)-1947 **TCLC 11**
See also CA 109; CANR 107; DLB 258;
EWL 3

Farigoule, Louis
See Romains, Jules

Farina, Richard 1936(?)-1966 **CLC 9**
See also CA 81-84; 25-28R

Farley, Walter (Lorimer)
1915-1989 **CLC 17**
See also AAYA 58; BYA 14; CA 17-20R;
CANR 8, 29, 84; DLB 22; JRDA; MAI-
CYA 1, 2; SATA 2, 43, 132; YAW

Farmer, Philip Jose 1918- **CLC 1, 19**
See also AAYA 28; BPFB 1; CA 1-4R;
CANR 4, 35, 111; DLB 8; MTCW 1;
SATA 93; SCFW 1, 2; SFW 4

Farquhar, George 1677-1707 **LC 21**
See also BRW 2; DAM DRAM; DLB 84;
RGEL 2

Farrell, J(ames) G(ordon)
1935-1979 **CLC 6**
See also CA 73-76; 89-92; CANR 36; CN
1, 2; DLB 14, 271, 326; MTCW 1; RGEL
2; RHW, WLIT 4

Farrell, James T(homas) 1904-1979 . **CLC 1,
4, 8, 11, 66; SSC 28**
See also AMW; BPFB 1; CA 5-8R; 89-92;
CANR 9, 61; CN 1, 2; DLB 4, 9, 86;
DLBD 2; EWL 3; MAL 5; MTCW 1, 2;
MTFW 2005; RGAL 4

Farrell, Warren (Thomas) 1943- **CLC 70**
See also CA 146; CANR 120

Farren, Richard J.
See Betjeman, John

Farren, Richard M.
See Betjeman, John

Fassbinder, Rainer Werner
1946-1982 **CLC 20**
See also CA 93-96; 106; CANR 31

Fast, Howard (Melvin) 1914-2003 .. **CLC 23,
131**
See also AAYA 16; BPFB 1; CA 1-4R; 181;
214; CAAE 181; CAAS 18; CANR 1, 33,
54, 75, 98, 140; CMW 4; CN 1, 2, 3, 4, 5,
6, 7; CPW; DAM NOV; DLB 9; INT
CANR-33; LATS 1:1; MAL 5; MTCW 2;
MTFW 2005; RHW; SATA 7; SATA-
Essay 107; TCWW 1, 2; YAW

Faulcon, Robert
See Holdstock, Robert P.

Faulkner, William (Cuthbert)
1897-1962 **CLC 1, 3, 6, 8, 9, 11, 14,
18, 28, 52, 68; SSC 1, 35, 42, 92;
TCLC 141; WLC 2**
See also AAYA 7; AMW; AMWR 1; BPFB
1; BYA 5, 15; CA 81-84; CANR 33;
CDALB 1929-1941; DA; DA3; DAB;
DAC; DAM MST, NOV; DLB 9, 11, 44,
102, 316; DLBD 2; DLBY 1986, 1997;
EWL 3; EXPN; EXPS; GL 2; LAIT 2;
LATS 1:1; LMFS 2; MAL 5; MTCW 1,
2; MTFW 2005; NFS 4, 8, 13; RGAL 4;
RGSF 2; SSFS 2, 5, 6, 12; TUS

Fauset, Jessie Redmon
1882(?)-1961 .. **BLC 2; CLC 19, 54; HR
1:2**
See also AFAW 2; BW 1; CA 109; CANR
83; DAM MULT; DLB 51; FW; LMFS 2;
MAL 5; MAWW

Faust, Frederick (Schiller)
1892-1944 **TCLC 49**
See Brand, Max; Dawson, Peter; Frederick, John
See also CA 108; 152; CANR 143; DAM POP; DLB 256; TUS

Faust, Irvin 1924- **CLC 8**
See also CA 33-36R; CANR 28, 67; CN 1, 2, 3, 4, 5, 6, 7; DLB 2, 28, 218, 278; DLBY 1980

Fawkes, Guy
See Benchley, Robert (Charles)

Fearing, Kenneth (Flexner)
1902-1961 **CLC 51**
See also CA 93-96; CANR 59; CMW 4; DLB 9; MAL 5; RGAL 4

Fecamps, Elise
See Creasey, John

Federman, Raymond 1928- **CLC 6, 47**
See also CA 17-20R, 208; CAAE 208; CAAS 8; CANR 10, 43, 83, 108; CN 3, 4, 5, 6; DLBY 1980

Federspiel, J(uerg) F. 1931- **CLC 42**
See also CA 146

Feiffer, Jules (Ralph) 1929- **CLC 2, 8, 64**
See also AAYA 3, 62; CA 17-20R; CAD; CANR 30, 59, 129; CD 5, 6; DAM DRAM; DLB 7, 44; INT CANR-30; MTCW 1; SATA 8, 61, 111, 157

Feige, Hermann Albert Otto Maximilian
See Traven, B.

Feinberg, David B. 1956-1994 **CLC 59**
See also CA 135; 147

Feinstein, Elaine 1930- **CLC 36**
See also CA 69-72; CAAS 1; CANR 31, 68, 121; CN 3, 4, 5, 6, 7; CP 2, 3, 4, 5, 6, 7; CWP; DLB 14, 40; MTCW 1

Feke, Gilbert David **CLC 65**

Feldman, Irving (Mordecai) 1928- **CLC 7**
See also CA 1-4R; CANR 1; CP 1, 2, 3, 4, 5, 6, 7; DLB 169; TCLE 1:1

Felix-Tchicaya, Gerald
See Tchicaya, Gerald Felix

Fellini, Federico 1920-1993 **CLC 16, 85**
See also CA 65-68; 143; CANR 33

Felltham, Owen 1602(?)-1668 **LC 92**
See also DLB 126, 151

Felsen, Henry Gregor 1916-1995 **CLC 17**
See also CA 1-4R; 180; CANR 1; SAAS 2; SATA 1

Felski, Rita **CLC 65**

Fenno, Jack
See Calisher, Hortense

Fenollosa, Ernest (Francisco)
1853-1908 **TCLC 91**

Fenton, James Martin 1949- **CLC 32, 209**
See also CA 102; CANR 108; CP 2, 3, 4, 5, 6, 7; DLB 40; PFS 11

Ferber, Edna 1887-1968 **CLC 18, 93**
See also AITN 1; CA 5-8R; 25-28R; CANR 68, 105; DLB 9, 28, 86, 266; MAL 5; MTCW 1, 2; MTFW 2005; RGAL 4; RHW; SATA 7; TCWW 1, 2

Ferdowsi, Abu'l Qasem
940-1020(?) **CMLC 43**
See Firdawsi, Abu al-Qasim
See also RGWL 2, 3

Ferguson, Helen
See Kavan, Anna

Ferguson, Niall 1964- **CLC 134**
See also CA 190; CANR 154

Ferguson, Samuel 1810-1886 **NCLC 33**
See also DLB 32; RGEL 2

Fergusson, Robert 1750-1774 **LC 29**
See also DLB 109; RGEL 2

Ferling, Lawrence
See Ferlinghetti, Lawrence

Ferlinghetti, Lawrence 1919(?)- **CLC 2, 6, 10, 27, 111; PC 1**
See also BG 1:2; CA 5-8R; CAD; CANR 3, 41, 73, 125; CDALB 1941-1968; CP 1, 2, 3, 4, 5, 6, 7; DA3; DAM POET; DLB 5, 16; MAL 5; MTCW 1, 2; MTFW 2005; RGAL 4; WP

Ferlinghetti, Lawrence Monsanto
See Ferlinghetti, Lawrence

Fern, Fanny
See Parton, Sara Payson Willis

Fernandez, Vicente Garcia Huidobro
See Huidobro Fernandez, Vicente Garcia

Fernandez-Armesto, Felipe **CLC 70**
See Fernandez-Armesto, Felipe Fermin Ricardo
See also CANR 153

Fernandez-Armesto, Felipe Fermin Ricardo
1950-
See Fernandez-Armesto, Felipe
See also CA 142; CANR 93

Fernandez de Lizardi, Jose Joaquin
See Lizardi, Jose Joaquin Fernandez de

Ferre, Rosario 1938- **CLC 139; HLCS 1; SSC 36**
See also CA 131; CANR 55, 81, 134; CWW 2; DLB 145; EWL 3; HW 1, 2; LAWS 1; MTCW 2; MTFW 2005; WLIT 1

Ferrer, Gabriel (Francisco Victor) Miro
See Miro (Ferrer), Gabriel (Francisco Victor)

Ferrier, Susan (Edmonstone)
1782-1854 **NCLC 8**
See also DLB 116; RGEL 2

Ferrigno, Robert 1948(?)- **CLC 65**
See also CA 140; CANR 125

Ferron, Jacques 1921-1985 **CLC 94**
See also CA 117; 129; CCA 1; DAC; DLB 60; EWL 3

Feuchtwanger, Lion 1884-1958 **TCLC 3**
See also CA 104; 187; DLB 66; EWL 3; RGHL

Feuerbach, Ludwig 1804-1872 **NCLC 139**
See also DLB 133

Feuillet, Octave 1821-1890 **NCLC 45**
See also DLB 192

Feydeau, Georges (Leon Jules Marie)
1862-1921 **TCLC 22**
See also CA 113; 152; CANR 84; DAM DRAM; DLB 192; EWL 3; GFL 1789 to the Present; RGWL 2, 3

Fichte, Johann Gottlieb
1762-1814 **NCLC 62**
See also DLB 90

Ficino, Marsilio 1433-1499 **LC 12**
See also LMFS 1

Fiedeler, Hans
See Doeblin, Alfred

Fiedler, Leslie A(aron) 1917-2003 **CLC 4, 13, 24**
See also AMWS 13; CA 9-12R; 212; CANR 7, 63; CN 1, 2, 3, 4, 5, 6; DLB 28, 67; EWL 3; MAL 5; MTCW 1, 2; RGAL 4; TUS

Field, Andrew 1938- **CLC 44**
See also CA 97-100; CANR 25

Field, Eugene 1850-1895 **NCLC 3**
See also DLB 23, 42, 140; DLBD 13; MAICYA 1, 2; RGAL 4; SATA 16

Field, Gans T.
See Wellman, Manly Wade

Field, Michael 1915-1971 **TCLC 43**
See also CA 29-32R

Fielding, Helen 1958- **CLC 146, 217**
See also AAYA 65; CA 172; CANR 127; DLB 231; MTFW 2005

Fielding, Henry 1707-1754 **LC 1, 46, 85; WLC 2**
See also BRW 3; BRWR 1; CDBLB 1660-1789; DA; DA3; DAB; DAC; DAM DRAM, MST, NOV; DLB 39, 84, 101; NFS 18; RGEL 2; TEA; WLIT 3

Fielding, Sarah 1710-1768 **LC 1, 44**
See also DLB 39; RGEL 2; TEA

Fields, W. C. 1880-1946 **TCLC 80**
See also DLB 44

Fierstein, Harvey (Forbes) 1954- **CLC 33**
See also CA 123; 129; CAD; CD 5, 6; CPW; DA3; DAM DRAM, POP; DFS 6; DLB 266; GLL; MAL 5

Figes, Eva 1932- **CLC 31**
See also CA 53-56; CANR 4, 44, 83; CN 2, 3, 4, 5, 6, 7; DLB 14, 271; FW; RGHL

Filippo, Eduardo de
See de Filippo, Eduardo

Finch, Anne 1661-1720 **LC 3; PC 21**
See also BRWS 9; DLB 95

Finch, Robert (Duer Claydon)
1900-1995 **CLC 18**
See also CA 57-60; CANR 9, 24, 49; CP 1, 2, 3, 4, 5, 6; DLB 88

Findley, Timothy (Irving Frederick)
1930-2002 **CLC 27, 102**
See also CA 25-28R; 206; CANR 12, 42, 69, 109; CCA 1; CN 4, 5, 6, 7; DAC; DAM MST; DLB 53; FANT; RHW

Fink, William
See Mencken, H(enry) L(ouis)

Firbank, Louis 1942-
See Reed, Lou
See also CA 117

Firbank, (Arthur Annesley) Ronald
1886-1926 **TCLC 1**
See also BRWS 2; CA 104; 177; DLB 36; EWL 3; RGEL 2

Firdawsi, Abu al-Qasim
See Ferdowsi, Abu'l Qasem
See also WLIT 6

Fish, Stanley
See Fish, Stanley Eugene

Fish, Stanley E.
See Fish, Stanley Eugene

Fish, Stanley Eugene 1938- **CLC 142**
See also CA 112; 132; CANR 90; DLB 67

Fisher, Dorothy (Frances) Canfield
1879-1958 **TCLC 87**
See also CA 114; 136; CANR 80; CLR 71; CWRI 5; DLB 9, 102, 284; MAICYA 1, 2; MAL 5; YABC 1

Fisher, M(ary) F(rances) K(ennedy)
1908-1992 **CLC 76, 87**
See also CA 77-80; 138; CANR 44; MTCW 2

Fisher, Roy 1930- **CLC 25**
See also CA 81-84; CAAS 10; CANR 16; CP 1, 2, 3, 4, 5, 6, 7; DLB 40

Fisher, Rudolph 1897-1934 . **BLC 2; HR 1:2; SSC 25; TCLC 11**
See also BW 1, 3; CA 107; 124; CANR 80; DAM MULT; DLB 51, 102

Fisher, Vardis (Alvero) 1895-1968 **CLC 7; TCLC 140**
See also CA 5-8R; 25-28R; CANR 68; DLB 9, 206; MAL 5; RGAL 4; TCWW 1, 2

Fiske, Tarleton
See Bloch, Robert (Albert)

Fitch, Clarke
See Sinclair, Upton

Fitch, John IV
See Cormier, Robert (Edmund)

Fitzgerald, Captain Hugh
See Baum, L(yman) Frank

FitzGerald, Edward 1809-1883 **NCLC 9, 153**
See also BRW 4; DLB 32; RGEL 2

Fitzgerald, F(rancis) Scott (Key)
1896-1940 ... SSC 6, 31, 75; TCLC 1, 6,
14, 28, 55, 157; WLC 2
See also AAYA 24; AITN 1; AMW; AMWC
2; AMWR 1; BPFB 1; CA 110; 123;
CDALB 1917-1929; DA; DA3; DAB;
DAC; DAM MST, NOV; DLB 4, 9, 86,
219, 273; DLBD 1, 15, 16; DLBY 1981,
1996; EWL 3; EXPN; EXPS; LAIT 3;
MAL 5; MTCW 1, 2; MTFW 2005; NFS
2, 19, 20; RGAL 4; RGSF 2; SSFS 4, 15,
21; TUS

Fitzgerald, Penelope 1916-2000 . CLC 19, 51,
61, 143
See also BRWS 5; CA 85-88; 190; CAAS
10; CANR 56, 86, 131; CN 3, 4, 5, 6, 7;
DLB 14, 194, 326; EWL 3; MTCW 2;
MTFW 2005

Fitzgerald, Robert (Stuart)
1910-1985 CLC 39
See also CA 1-4R; 114; CANR 1; CP 1, 2,
3, 4; DLBY 1980; MAL 5

FitzGerald, Robert D(avid)
1902-1987 CLC 19
See also CA 17-20R; CP 1, 2, 3, 4; DLB
260; RGEL 2

Fitzgerald, Zelda (Sayre)
1900-1948 TCLC 52
See also AMWS 9; CA 117; 126; DLBY
1984

Flanagan, Thomas (James Bonner)
1923-2002 CLC 25, 52
See also CA 108; 206; CANR 55; CN 3, 4,
5, 6, 7; DLBY 1980; INT CA-108; MTCW
1; RHW; TCLE 1:1

Flaubert, Gustave 1821-1880 NCLC 2, 10,
19, 62, 66, 135; SSC 11, 60; WLC 2
See also DA; DA3; DAB; DAC; DAM
MST, NOV; DLB 119, 301; EW 7; EXPS;
GFL 1789 to the Present; LAIT 2; LMFS
1; NFS 14; RGSF 2; RGWL 2, 3; SSFS
6; TWA

Flavius Josephus
See Josephus, Flavius

Flecker, Herman Elroy
See Flecker, (Herman) James Elroy

Flecker, (Herman) James Elroy
1884-1915 TCLC 43
See also CA 109; 150; DLB 10, 19; RGEL
2

Fleming, Ian (Lancaster) 1908-1964 . CLC 3,
30
See also AAYA 26; BPFB 1; CA 5-8R;
CANR 59; CDBLB 1945-1960; CMW 4;
CPW; DA3; DAM POP; DLB 87, 201;
MSW; MTCW 1, 2; MTFW 2005; RGEL
2; SATA 9; TEA; YAW

Fleming, Thomas (James) 1927- CLC 37
See also CA 5-8R; CANR 10, 102; INT
CANR-10; SATA 8

Fletcher, John 1579-1625 DC 6; LC 33
See also BRW 2; CDBLB Before 1660;
DLB 58; RGEL 2; TEA

Fletcher, John Gould 1886-1950 TCLC 35
See also CA 107; 167; DLB 4, 45; LMFS
2; MAL 5; RGAL 4

Fleur, Paul
See Pohl, Frederik

Flieg, Helmut
See Heym, Stefan

Flooglebuckle, Al
See Spiegelman, Art

Flora, Fletcher 1914-1969
See Queen, Ellery
See also CA 1-4R; CANR 3, 85

Flying Officer X
See Bates, H(erbert) E(rnest)

Fo, Dario 1926- CLC 32, 109; DC 10
See also CA 116; 128; CANR 68, 114, 134;
CWW 2; DA3; DAM DRAM; DFS 23;
DLBY 1997; EWL 3; MTCW 1, 2; MTFW
2005; WLIT 7

Fogarty, Jonathan Titulescu Esq.
See Farrell, James T(homas)

Follett, Ken(neth Martin) 1949- CLC 18
See also AAYA 6, 50; BEST 89:4; BPFB 1;
CA 81-84; CANR 13, 33, 54, 102; CMW
4; CPW; DA3; DAM NOV, POP; DLB
87; DLBY 1981; INT CANR-33; MTCW
1

Fondane, Benjamin 1898-1944 TCLC 159

Fontane, Theodor 1819-1898 . NCLC 26, 163
See also CDWLB 2; DLB 129; EW 6;
RGWL 2, 3; TWA

Fonte, Moderata 1555-1592 LC 118

Fontenot, Chester CLC 65

Fonvizin, Denis Ivanovich
1744(?)-1792 LC 81
See also DLB 150; RGWL 2, 3

Foote, Horton 1916- CLC 51, 91
See also CA 73-76; CAD; CANR 34, 51,
110; CD 5, 6; CSW; DA3; DAM DRAM;
DFS 20; DLB 26, 266; EWL 3; INT
CANR-34; MTFW 2005

Foote, Mary Hallock 1847-1938 .. TCLC 108
See also DLB 186, 188, 202, 221; TCWW
2

Foote, Samuel 1721-1777 LC 106
See also DLB 89; RGEL 2

Foote, Shelby 1916-2005 CLC 75, 224
See also AAYA 40; CA 5-8R; 240; CANR
3, 45, 74, 131; CN 1, 2, 3, 4, 5, 6, 7;
CPW; CSW; DA3; DAM NOV, POP;
DLB 2, 17; MAL 5; MTCW 2; MTFW
2005; RHW

Forbes, Cosmo
See Lewton, Val

Forbes, Esther 1891-1967 CLC 12
See also AAYA 17; BYA 2; CA 13-14; 25-
28R; CAP 1; CLR 27; DLB 22; JRDA;
MAICYA 1, 2; RHW; SATA 2, 100; YAW

Forche, Carolyn (Louise) 1950- CLC 25,
83, 86; PC 10
See also CA 109; 117; CANR 50, 74, 138;
CP 4, 5, 6, 7; CWP; DA3; DAM POET;
DLB 5, 193; INT CA-117; MAL 5;
MTCW 2; MTFW 2005; PFS 18; RGAL
4

Ford, Elbur
See Hibbert, Eleanor Alice Burford

Ford, Ford Madox 1873-1939 ... TCLC 1, 15,
39, 57, 172
See Chaucer, Daniel
See also BRW 6; CA 104; 132; CANR 74;
CDBLB 1914-1945; DA3; DAM NOV;
DLB 34, 98, 162; EWL 3; MTCW 1, 2;
RGEL 2; TEA

Ford, Henry 1863-1947 TCLC 73
See also CA 115; 148

Ford, Jack
See Ford, John

Ford, John 1586-1639 DC 8; LC 68
See also BRW 2; CDBLB Before 1660;
DA3; DAM DRAM; DFS 7; DLB 58;
IDTP; RGEL 2

Ford, John 1895-1973 CLC 16
See also CA 187; 45-48

Ford, Richard 1944- CLC 46, 99, 205
See also AMWS 5; CA 69-72; CANR 11,
47, 86, 128; CN 5, 6, 7; CSW; DLB 227;
EWL 3; MAL 5; MTCW 2; MTFW 2005;
RGAL 4; RGSF 2

Ford, Webster
See Masters, Edgar Lee

Foreman, Richard 1937- CLC 50
See also CA 65-68; CAD; CANR 32, 63,
143; CD 5, 6

Forester, C(ecil) S(cott) 1899-1966 . CLC 35;
TCLC 152
See also CA 73-76; 25-28R; CANR 83;
DLB 191; RGEL 2; RHW; SATA 13

Forez
See Mauriac, Francois (Charles)

Forman, James
See Forman, James D(ouglas)

Forman, James D(ouglas) 1932- CLC 21
See also AAYA 17; CA 9-12R; CANR 4,
19, 42; JRDA; MAICYA 1, 2; SATA 8,
70; YAW

Forman, Milos 1932- CLC 164
See also AAYA 63; CA 109

Fornes, Maria Irene 1930- CLC 39, 61,
187; DC 10; HLCS 1
See also CA 25-28R; CAD; CANR 28, 81;
CD 5, 6; CWD; DLB 7; HW 1, 2; INT
CANR-28; LLW; MAL 5; MTCW 1;
RGAL 4

Forrest, Leon (Richard)
1937-1997 BLCS; CLC 4
See also AFAW 2; BW 2; CA 89-92; 162;
CAAS 7; CANR 25, 52, 87; CN 4, 5, 6;
DLB 33

Forster, E(dward) M(organ)
1879-1970 CLC 1, 2, 3, 4, 9, 10, 13,
15, 22, 45, 77; SSC 27; TCLC 125;
WLC 2
See also AAYA 2, 37; BRW 6; BRWR 2;
BYA 12; CA 13-14; 25-28R; CANR 45;
CAP 1; CDBLB 1914-1945; DA; DA3;
DAB; DAC; DAM MST, NOV; DLB 34,
98, 162, 178, 195; DLBD 10; EWL 3;
EXPN; LAIT 3; LMFS 1; MTCW 1, 2;
MTFW 2005; NCFS 1; NFS 3, 10, 11;
RGEL 2; RGSF 2; SATA 57; SUFW 1;
TEA; WLIT 4

Forster, John 1812-1876 NCLC 11
See also DLB 144, 184

Forster, Margaret 1938- CLC 149
See also CA 133; CANR 62, 115; CN 4, 5,
6, 7; DLB 155, 271

Forsyth, Frederick 1938- CLC 2, 5, 36
See also BEST 89:4; CA 85-88; CANR 38,
62, 115, 137; CMW 4; CN 3, 4, 5, 6, 7;
CPW; DAM NOV, POP; DLB 87; MTCW
1, 2; MTFW 2005

Forten, Charlotte L. 1837-1914 BLC 2;
TCLC 16
See Grimke, Charlotte L(ottie) Forten
See also DLB 50, 239

Fortinbras
See Grieg, (Johan) Nordahl (Brun)

Foscolo, Ugo 1778-1827 NCLC 8, 97
See also EW 5; WLIT 7

Fosse, Bob ... CLC 20
See Fosse, Robert Louis

Fosse, Robert Louis 1927-1987
See Fosse, Bob
See also CA 110; 123

Foster, Hannah Webster
1758-1840 NCLC 99
See also DLB 37, 200; RGAL 4

Foster, Stephen Collins
1826-1864 NCLC 26
See also RGAL 4

Foucault, Michel 1926-1984 . CLC 31, 34, 69
See also CA 105; 113; CANR 34; DLB 242;
EW 13; EWL 3; GFL 1789 to the Present;
GLL 1; LMFS 2; MTCW 1, 2; TWA

Fouque, Friedrich (Heinrich Karl) de la
Motte 1777-1843 NCLC 2
See also DLB 90; RGWL 2, 3; SUFW 1

Fourier, Charles 1772-1837 NCLC 51

Fournier, Henri-Alban 1886-1914
See Alain-Fournier
See also CA 104; 179

Fournier, Pierre 1916-1997 **CLC 11**
See Gascar, Pierre
See also CA 89-92; CANR 16, 40

Fowles, John 1926-2005 **CLC 1, 2, 3, 4, 6, 9, 10, 15, 33, 87; SSC 33**
See also BPFB 1; BRWS 1; CA 5-8R; 245;
CANR 25, 71, 103; CDBLB 1960 to
Present; CN 1, 2, 3, 4, 5, 6, 7; DA3; DAB;
DAC; DAM MST; DLB 14, 139, 207;
EWL 3; HGG; MTCW 1, 2; MTFW 2005;
NFS 21; RGEL 2; RHW; SATA 22; SATA-
Obit 171; TEA; WLIT 4

Fowles, John Robert
See Fowles, John

Fox, Paula 1923- **CLC 2, 8, 121**
See also AAYA 3, 37; BYA 3, 8; CA 73-76;
CANR 20, 36, 62, 105; CLR 1, 44, 96;
DLB 52; JRDA; MAICYA 1, 2; MTCW
1; NFS 12; SATA 17, 60, 120, 167; WYA;
YAW

Fox, William Price (Jr.) 1926- **CLC 22**
See also CA 17-20R; CAAS 19; CANR 11,
142; CSW; DLB 2; DLBY 1981

Foxe, John 1517(?)-1587 **LC 14**
See also DLB 132

Frame, Janet .. **CLC 2, 3, 6, 22, 66, 96; SSC 29**
See Clutha, Janet Paterson Frame
See also CN 1, 2, 3, 4, 5, 6, 7; CP 2, 3, 4;
CWP; EWL 3; RGEL 2; RGSF 2; TWA

France, Anatole **TCLC 9**
See Thibault, Jacques Anatole Francois
See also DLB 123; EWL 3; GFL 1789 to
the Present; RGWL 2, 3; SUFW 1

Francis, Claude **CLC 50**
See also CA 192

Francis, Dick
See Francis, Richard Stanley
See also CN 2, 3, 4, 5, 6

Francis, Richard Stanley 1920- ... **CLC 2, 22, 42, 102**
See Francis, Dick
See also AAYA 5, 21; BEST 89:3; BPFB 1;
CA 5-8R; CANR 9, 42, 68, 100, 141; CD-
BLB 1960 to Present; CMW 4; CN 7;
DA3; DAM POP; DLB 87; INT CANR-9;
MSW; MTCW 1, 2; MTFW 2005

Francis, Robert (Churchill)
1901-1987 **CLC 15; PC 34**
See also AMWS 9; CA 1-4R; 123; CANR
1; CP 1, 2, 3, 4; EXPP; PFS 12; TCLE
1:1

Francis, Lord Jeffrey
See Jeffrey, Francis
See also DLB 107

Frank, Anne(lies Marie)
1929-1945 **TCLC 17; WLC 2**
See also AAYA 12; BYA 1; CA 113; 133;
CANR 68; CLR 101; DA; DA3; DAB;
DAC; DAM MST; LAIT 4; MAICYA 1;
MAICYAS 1; MTCW 1, 2; MTFW 2005;
NCFS 2; RGHL; SATA 87; SATA-Brief
42; WYA; YAW

Frank, Bruno 1887-1945 **TCLC 81**
See also CA 189; DLB 118; EWL 3

Frank, Elizabeth 1945- **CLC 39**
See also CA 121; 126; CANR 78, 150; INT
CA-126

Frankl, Viktor E(mil) 1905-1997 **CLC 93**
See also CA 65-68; 161; RGHL

Franklin, Benjamin
See Hasek, Jaroslav (Matej Frantisek)

Franklin, Benjamin 1706-1790 **LC 25; WLCS**
See also AMW; CDALB 1640-1865; DA;
DA3; DAB; DAC; DAM MST; DLB 24,
43, 73, 183; LAIT 1; RGAL 4; TUS

**Franklin, (Stella Maria Sarah) Miles
(Lampe)** 1879-1954 **TCLC 7**
See also CA 104; 164; DLB 230; FW;
MTCW 2; RGEL 2; TWA

Franzen, Jonathan 1959- **CLC 202**
See also AAYA 65; CA 129; CANR 105

Fraser, Antonia (Pakenham) 1932- . **CLC 32, 107**
See also AAYA 57; CA 85-88; CANR 44,
65, 119; CMW; DLB 276; MTCW 1, 2;
MTFW 2005; SATA-Brief 32

Fraser, George MacDonald 1925- **CLC 7**
See also AAYA 48; CA 45-48; 180; CAAE
180; CANR 2, 48, 74; MTCW 2; RHW

Fraser, Sylvia 1935- **CLC 64**
See also CA 45-48; CANR 1, 16, 60; CCA
1

Frayn, Michael 1933- **CLC 3, 7, 31, 47, 176; DC 27**
See also AAYA 69; BRWC 2; BRWS 7; CA
5-8R; CANR 30, 69, 114, 133; CBD; CD
5, 6; CN 1, 2, 3, 4, 5, 6, 7; DAM DRAM,
NOV; DFS 22; DLB 13, 14, 194, 245;
FANT; MTCW 1, 2; MTFW 2005; SFW
4

Fraze, Candida (Merrill) 1945- **CLC 50**
See also CA 126

Frazer, Andrew
See Marlowe, Stephen

Frazer, J(ames) G(eorge)
1854-1941 **TCLC 32**
See also BRWS 3; CA 118; NCFS 5

Frazer, Robert Caine
See Creasey, John

Frazer, Sir James George
See Frazer, J(ames) G(eorge)

Frazier, Charles 1950- **CLC 109, 224**
See also AAYA 34; CA 161; CANR 126;
CSW; DLB 292; MTFW 2005

Frazier, Ian 1951- **CLC 46**
See also CA 130; CANR 54, 93

Frederic, Harold 1856-1898 **NCLC 10**
See also AMW; DLB 12, 23; DLBD 13;
MAL 5; NFS 22; RGAL 4

Frederick, John
See Faust, Frederick (Schiller)
See also TCWW 2

Frederick the Great 1712-1786 **LC 14**

Fredro, Aleksander 1793-1876 **NCLC 8**

Freeling, Nicolas 1927-2003 **CLC 38**
See also CA 49-52; 218; CAAS 12; CANR
1, 17, 50, 84; CMW 4; CN 1, 2, 3, 4, 5,
6; DLB 87

Freeman, Douglas Southall
1886-1953 **TCLC 11**
See also CA 109; 195; DLB 17; DLBD 17

Freeman, Judith 1946- **CLC 55**
See also CA 148; CANR 120; DLB 256

Freeman, Mary E(leanor) Wilkins
1852-1930 **SSC 1, 47; TCLC 9**
See also CA 106; 177; DLB 12, 78, 221;
EXPS; FW; HGG; MAWW; RGAL 4;
RGSF 2; SSFS 4, 8; SUFW 1; TUS

Freeman, R(ichard) Austin
1862-1943 **TCLC 21**
See also CA 113; CANR 84; CMW 4; DLB
70

French, Albert 1943- **CLC 86**
See also BW 3; CA 167

French, Antonia
See Kureishi, Hanif

French, Marilyn 1929- .. **CLC 10, 18, 60, 177**
See also BPFB 1; CA 69-72; CANR 3, 31,
134; CN 5, 6, 7; CPW; DAM DRAM,
NOV, POP; FL 1:5; FW; INT CANR-31;
MTCW 1, 2; MTFW 2005

French, Paul
See Asimov, Isaac

Freneau, Philip Morin 1752-1832 .. **NCLC 1, 111**
See also AMWS 2; DLB 37, 43; RGAL 4

Freud, Sigmund 1856-1939 **TCLC 52**
See also CA 115; 133; CANR 69; DLB 296;
EW 8; EWL 3; LATS 1:1; MTCW 1, 2;
MTFW 2005; NCFS 3; TWA

Freytag, Gustav 1816-1895 **NCLC 109**
See also DLB 129

Friedan, Betty 1921-2006 **CLC 74**
See also CA 65-68; 248; CANR 18, 45, 74;
DLB 246; FW; MTCW 1, 2; MTFW
2005; NCFS 5

Friedan, Betty Naomi
See Friedan, Betty

Friedlander, Saul 1932- **CLC 90**
See also CA 117; 130; CANR 72; RGHL

Friedman, B(ernard) H(arper)
1926- ... **CLC 7**
See also CA 1-4R; CANR 3, 48

Friedman, Bruce Jay 1930- **CLC 3, 5, 56**
See also CA 9-12R; CAD; CANR 25, 52,
101; CD 5, 6; CN 1, 2, 3, 4, 5, 6, 7; DLB
2, 28, 244; INT CANR-25; MAL 5; SSFS
18

Friel, Brian 1929- **CLC 5, 42, 59, 115; DC 8; SSC 76**
See also BRWS 5; CA 21-24R; CANR 33,
69, 131; CBD; CD 5, 6; DFS 11; DLB
13, 319; EWL 3; MTCW 1; RGEL 2; TEA

Friis-Baastad, Babbis Ellinor
1921-1970 **CLC 12**
See also CA 17-20R; 134; SATA 7

Frisch, Max (Rudolf) 1911-1991 ... **CLC 3, 9, 14, 18, 32, 44; TCLC 121**
See also CA 85-88; 134; CANR 32, 74; CD-
WLB 2; DAM DRAM, NOV; DLB 69,
124; EW 13; EWL 3; MTCW 1, 2; MTFW
2005; RGHL; RGWL 2, 3

Fromentin, Eugene (Samuel Auguste)
1820-1876 **NCLC 10, 125**
See also DLB 123; GFL 1789 to the Present

Frost, Frederick
See Faust, Frederick (Schiller)

Frost, Robert (Lee) 1874-1963 .. **CLC 1, 3, 4, 9, 10, 13, 15, 26, 34, 44; PC 1, 39, 71; WLC 2**
See also AAYA 21; AMW; AMWR 1; CA
89-92; CANR 33; CDALB 1917-1929;
CLR 67; DA; DA3; DAB; DAC; DAM
MST, POET; DLB 54, 284; DLBD 7;
EWL 3; EXPP; MAL 5; MTCW 1, 2;
MTFW 2005; PAB; PFS 1, 2, 3, 4, 5, 6,
7, 10, 13; RGAL 4; SATA 14; TUS; WP;
WYA

Froude, James Anthony
1818-1894 **NCLC 43**
See also DLB 18, 57, 144

Froy, Herald
See Waterhouse, Keith (Spencer)

Fry, Christopher 1907-2005 ... **CLC 2, 10, 14**
See also BRWS 3; CA 17-20R; 240; CAAS
23; CANR 9, 30, 74, 132; CBD; CD 5, 6;
CP 1, 2, 3, 4, 5, 6, 7; DAM DRAM; DLB
13; EWL 3; MTCW 1, 2; MTFW 2005;
RGEL 2; SATA 66; TEA

Frye, (Herman) Northrop
1912-1991 **CLC 24, 70; TCLC 165**
See also CA 5-8R; 133; CANR 8, 37; DLB
67, 68, 246; EWL 3; MTCW 1, 2; MTFW
2005; RGAL 4; TWA

Fuchs, Daniel 1909-1993 **CLC 8, 22**
See also CA 81-84; 142; CAAS 5; CANR
40; CN 1, 2, 3, 4, 5; DLB 9, 26, 28;
DLBY 1993; MAL 5

Fuchs, Daniel 1934- **CLC 34**
See also CA 37-40R; CANR 14, 48

Fuentes, Carlos 1928- .. **CLC 3, 8, 10, 13, 22, 41, 60, 113; HLC 1; SSC 24; WLC 2**
See also AAYA 4, 45; AITN 2; BPFB 1; CA 69-72; CANR 10, 32, 68, 104, 138; CDWLB 3; CWW 2; DA; DA3; DAB; DAC; DAM MST, MULT, NOV; DLB 113; DNFS 2; EWL 3; HW 1, 2; LAIT 3; LATS 1:2; LAW; LAWS 1; LMFS 2; MTCW 1, 2; MTFW 2005; NFS 8; RGSF 2; RGWL 2, 3; TWA; WLIT 1

Fuentes, Gregorio Lopez y
See Lopez y Fuentes, Gregorio

Fuertes, Gloria 1918-1998 **PC 27**
See also CA 178, 180; DLB 108; HW 2; SATA 115

Fugard, (Harold) Athol 1932- . **CLC 5, 9, 14, 25, 40, 80, 211; DC 3**
See also AAYA 17; AFW; CA 85-88; CANR 32, 54, 118; CD 5, 6; DAM DRAM; DFS 3, 6, 10; DLB 225; DNFS 1, 2; EWL 3; LATS 1:2; MTCW 1; MTFW 2005; RGEL 2; WLIT 2

Fugard, Sheila 1932- **CLC 48**
See also CA 125

Fujiwara no Teika 1162-1241 **CMLC 73**
See also DLB 203

Fukuyama, Francis 1952- **CLC 131**
See also CA 140; CANR 72, 125

Fuller, Charles (H.), (Jr.) 1939- **BLC 2; CLC 25; DC 1**
See also BW 2; CA 108; 112; CAD; CANR 87; CD 5, 6; DAM DRAM, MULT; DFS 8; DLB 38, 266; EWL 3; INT CA-112; MAL 5; MTCW 1

Fuller, Henry Blake 1857-1929 **TCLC 103**
See also CA 108; 177; DLB 12; RGAL 4

Fuller, John (Leopold) 1937- **CLC 62**
See also CA 21-24R; CANR 9, 44; CP 1, 2, 3, 4, 5, 6, 7; DLB 40

Fuller, Margaret
See Ossoli, Sarah Margaret (Fuller)
See also AMWS 2; DLB 183, 223, 239; FL 1:3

Fuller, Roy (Broadbent) 1912-1991 ... **CLC 4, 28**
See also BRWS 7; CA 5-8R; 135; CAAS 10; CANR 53, 83; CN 1, 2, 3, 4, 5; CP 1, 2, 3, 4, 5; CWRI 5; DLB 15, 20; EWL 3; RGEL 2; SATA 87

Fuller, Sarah Margaret
See Ossoli, Sarah Margaret (Fuller)

Fuller, Sarah Margaret
See Ossoli, Sarah Margaret (Fuller)
See also DLB 1, 59, 73

Fuller, Thomas 1608-1661 **LC 111**
See also DLB 151

Fulton, Alice 1952- **CLC 52**
See also CA 116; CANR 57, 88; CP 5, 6, 7; CWP; DLB 193

Furphy, Joseph 1843-1912 **TCLC 25**
See Collins, Tom
See also CA 163; DLB 230; EWL 3; RGEL 2

Fuson, Robert H(enderson) 1927- **CLC 70**
See also CA 89-92; CANR 103

Fussell, Paul 1924- **CLC 74**
See also BEST 90:1; CA 17-20R; CANR 8, 21, 35, 69, 135; INT CANR-21; MTCW 1, 2; MTFW 2005

Futabatei, Shimei 1864-1909 **TCLC 44**
See Futabatei Shimei
See also CA 162; MJW

Futabatei Shimei
See Futabatei, Shimei
See also DLB 180; EWL 3

Futrelle, Jacques 1875-1912 **TCLC 19**
See also CA 113; 155; CMW 4

Gaboriau, Emile 1835-1873 **NCLC 14**
See also CMW 4; MSW

Gadda, Carlo Emilio 1893-1973 **CLC 11; TCLC 144**
See also CA 89-92; DLB 177; EWL 3; WLIT 7

Gaddis, William 1922-1998 ... **CLC 1, 3, 6, 8, 10, 19, 43, 86**
See also AMWS 4; BPFB 1; CA 17-20R; 172; CANR 21, 48, 148; CN 1, 2, 3, 4, 5, 6; DLB 2, 278; EWL 3; MAL 5; MTCW 1, 2; MTFW 2005; RGAL 4

Gaelique, Moruen le
See Jacob, (Cyprien-)Max

Gage, Walter
See Inge, William (Motter)

Gaiman, Neil 1960- **CLC 195**
See also AAYA 19, 42; CA 133; CANR 81, 129; CLR 109; DLB 261; HGG; MTFW 2005; SATA 85, 146; SFW 4; SUFW 2

Gaiman, Neil Richard
See Gaiman, Neil

Gaines, Ernest J(ames) 1933- .. **BLC 2; CLC 3, 11, 18, 86, 181; SSC 68**
See also AAYA 18; AFAW 1, 2; AITN 1; BPFB 2; BW 2, 3; BYA 6; CA 9-12R; CANR 6, 24, 42, 75, 126; CDALB 1968-1988; CLR 62; CN 1, 2, 3, 4, 5, 6, 7; CSW; DA3; DAM MULT; DLB 2, 33, 152; DLBY 1980; EWL 3; EXPN; LAIT 5; LATS 1:2; MAL 5; MTCW 1, 2; MTFW 2005; NFS 5, 7, 16; RGAL 4; RGSF 2; RHW; SATA 86; SSFS 5; YAW

Gaitskill, Mary 1954- **CLC 69**
See also CA 128; CANR 61, 152; DLB 244; TCLE 1:1

Gaitskill, Mary Lawrence
See Gaitskill, Mary

Gaius Suetonius Tranquillus
See Suetonius

Galdos, Benito Perez
See Perez Galdos, Benito
See also EW 7

Gale, Zona 1874-1938 **TCLC 7**
See also CA 105; 153; CANR 84; DAM DRAM; DFS 17; DLB 9, 78, 228; RGAL 4

Galeano, Eduardo (Hughes) 1940- . **CLC 72; HLCS 1**
See also CA 29-32R; CANR 13, 32, 100; HW 1

Galiano, Juan Valera y Alcala
See Valera y Alcala-Galiano, Juan

Galilei, Galileo 1564-1642 **LC 45**

Gallagher, Tess 1943- **CLC 18, 63; PC 9**
See also CA 106; CP 3, 4, 5, 6, 7; CWP; DAM POET; DLB 120, 212, 244; PFS 16

Gallant, Mavis 1922- **CLC 7, 18, 38, 172; SSC 5, 78**
See also CA 69-72; CANR 29, 69, 117; CCA 1; CN 1, 2, 3, 4, 5, 6, 7; DAC; DAM MST; DLB 53; EWL 3; MTCW 1, 2; MTFW 2005; RGEL 2; RGSF 2

Gallant, Roy A(rthur) 1924- **CLC 17**
See also CA 5-8R; CANR 4, 29, 54, 117; CLR 30; MAICYA 1, 2; SATA 4, 68, 110

Gallico, Paul (William) 1897-1976 **CLC 2**
See also AITN 1; CA 5-8R; 69-72; CANR 23; CN 1, 2; DLB 9, 171; FANT; MAICYA 1; SATA 13

Gallo, Max Louis 1932- **CLC 95**
See also CA 85-88

Gallois, Lucien
See Desnos, Robert

Gallup, Ralph
See Whitemore, Hugh (John)

Galsworthy, John 1867-1933 **SSC 22; TCLC 1, 45; WLC 2**
See also BRW 6; CA 104; 141; CANR 75; CDBLB 1890-1914; DA; DA3; DAB; DAC; DAM DRAM, MST, NOV; DLB 10, 34, 98, 162; DLBD 16; EWL 3; MTCW 2; RGEL 2; SSFS 3; TEA

Galt, John 1779-1839 **NCLC 1, 110**
See also DLB 99, 116, 159; RGEL 2; RGSF 2

Galvin, James 1951- **CLC 38**
See also CA 108; CANR 26

Gamboa, Federico 1864-1939 **TCLC 36**
See also CA 167; HW 2; LAW

Gandhi, M. K.
See Gandhi, Mohandas Karamchand

Gandhi, Mahatma
See Gandhi, Mohandas Karamchand

Gandhi, Mohandas Karamchand
1869-1948 **TCLC 59**
See also CA 121; 132; DA3; DAM MULT; DLB 323; MTCW 1, 2

Gann, Ernest Kellogg 1910-1991 **CLC 23**
See also AITN 1; BPFB 2; CA 1-4R; 136; CANR 1, 83; RHW

Gao Xingjian 1940- **CLC 167**
See Xingjian, Gao
See also MTFW 2005

Garber, Eric 1943(?)-
See Holleran, Andrew
See also CANR 89

Garcia, Cristina 1958- **CLC 76**
See also AMWS 11; CA 141; CANR 73, 130; CN 7; DLB 292; DNFS 1; EWL 3; HW 2; LLW; MTFW 2005

Garcia Lorca, Federico 1898-1936 **DC 2; HLC 2; PC 3; TCLC 1, 7, 49; WLC 2**
See Lorca, Federico Garcia
See also AAYA 46; CA 104; 131; CANR 81; DA; DA3; DAB; DAC; DAM DRAM, MST, MULT, POET; DFS 4, 10; DLB 108; EWL 3; HW 1, 2; LATS 1:2; MTCW 1, 2; MTFW 2005; TWA

Garcia Marquez, Gabriel 1928- **CLC 2, 3, 8, 10, 15, 27, 47, 55, 68, 170; HLC 1; SSC 8, 83; WLC 3**
See also AAYA 3, 33; BEST 89:1, 90:4; BPFB 2; BYA 12, 16; CA 33-36R; CANR 10, 28, 50, 75, 82, 128; CDWLB 3; CPW; CWW 2; DA; DA3; DAB; DAC; DAM MST, MULT, NOV, POP; DLB 113; DNFS 1, 2; EWL 3; EXPN; EXPS; HW 1, 2; LAIT 2; LATS 1:2; LAW; LAWS 1; LMFS 2; MTCW 1, 2; MTFW 2005; NCFS 3; NFS 1, 5, 10; RGSF 2; RGWL 2, 3; SSFS 1, 6, 16, 21; TWA; WLIT 1

Garcia Marquez, Gabriel Jose
See Garcia Marquez, Gabriel

Garcilaso de la Vega, El Inca
1539-1616 **HLCS 1; LC 127**
See also DLB 318; LAW

Gard, Janice
See Latham, Jean Lee

Gard, Roger Martin du
See Martin du Gard, Roger

Gardam, Jane (Mary) 1928- **CLC 43**
See also CA 49-52; CANR 2, 18, 33, 54, 106; CLR 12; DLB 14, 161, 231; MAICYA 1, 2; MTCW 1; SAAS 9; SATA 39, 76, 130; SATA-Brief 28; YAW

Gardner, Herb(ert George)
1934-2003 **CLC 44**
See also CA 149; 220; CAD; CANR 119; CD 5, 6; DFS 18, 20

Gardner, John (Champlin), Jr.
1933-1982 **CLC 2, 3, 5, 7, 8, 10, 18, 28, 34; SSC 7**
See also AAYA 45; AITN 1; AMWS 6; BPFB 2; CA 65-68; 107; CANR 33, 73; CDALBS; CN 2, 3; CPW; DA3; DAM NOV, POP; DLB 2; DLBY 1982; EWL 3; FANT; LATS 1:2; MAL 5; MTCW 1, 2; MTFW 2005; NFS 3; RGAL 4; RGSF 2; SATA 40; SATA-Obit 31; SSFS 8

Gardner, John (Edmund) 1926- **CLC 30**
See also CA 103; CANR 15, 69, 127; CMW 4; CPW; DAM POP; MTCW 1

Gardner, Miriam
See Bradley, Marion Zimmer
See also GLL 1

Gardner, Noel
See Kuttner, Henry

Gardons, S. S.
See Snodgrass, W(illiam) D(e Witt)

Garfield, Leon 1921-1996 **CLC 12**
See also AAYA 8, 69; BYA 1, 3; CA 17-20R; 152; CANR 38, 41, 78; CLR 21; DLB 161; JRDA; MAICYA 1, 2; MAIC-YAS 1; SATA 1, 32, 76; SATA-Obit 90; TEA; WYA; YAW

Garland, (Hannibal) Hamlin
1860-1940 **SSC 18; TCLC 3**
See also CA 104; DLB 12, 71, 78, 186; MAL 5; RGAL 4; RGSF 2; TCWW 1, 2

Garneau, (Hector de) Saint-Denys
1912-1943 **TCLC 13**
See also CA 111; DLB 88

Garner, Alan 1934- **CLC 17**
See also AAYA 18; BYA 3, 5; CA 73-76, 178; CAAE 178; CANR 15, 64, 134; CLR 20; CPW; DAB; DAM POP; DLB 161, 261; FANT; MAICYA 1, 2; MTCW 1, 2; MTFW 2005; SATA 18, 69; SATA-Essay 108; SUFW 1, 2; YAW

Garner, Hugh 1913-1979 **CLC 13**
See Warwick, Jarvis
See also CA 69-72; CANR 31; CCA 1; CN 1, 2; DLB 68

Garnett, David 1892-1981 **CLC 3**
See also CA 5-8R; 103; CANR 17, 79; CN 1, 2; DLB 34; FANT; MTCW 2; RGEL 2; SFW 4; SUFW 1

Garnier, Robert c. 1545-1590 **LC 119**
See also GFL Beginnings to 1789

Garrett, George (Palmer, Jr.) 1929- . **CLC 3, 11, 51; SSC 30**
See also AMWS 7; BPFB 2; CA 1-4R, 202; CAAE 202; CAAS 5; CANR 1, 42, 67, 109; CN 1, 2, 3, 4, 5, 6, 7; CP 1, 2, 3, 4, 5, 6, 7; CSW; DLB 2, 5, 130, 152; DLBY 1983

Garrick, David 1717-1779 **LC 15**
See also DAM DRAM; DLB 84, 213; RGEL 2

Garrigue, Jean 1914-1972 **CLC 2, 8**
See also CA 5-8R; 37-40R; CANR 20; CP 1; MAL 5

Garrison, Frederick
See Sinclair, Upton

Garrison, William Lloyd
1805-1879 **NCLC 149**
See also CDALB 1640-1865; DLB 1, 43, 235

Garro, Elena 1920(?)-1998 .. **HLCS 1; TCLC 153**
See also CA 131; 169; CWW 2; DLB 145; EWL 3; HW 1; LAWS 1; WLIT 1

Garth, Will
See Hamilton, Edmond; Kuttner, Henry

Garvey, Marcus (Moziah, Jr.)
1887-1940 ... **BLC 2; HR 1:2; TCLC 41**
See also BW 1; CA 120; 124; CANR 79; DAM MULT

Gary, Romain **CLC 25**
See Kacew, Romain
See also DLB 83, 299; RGHL

Gascar, Pierre **CLC 11**
See Fournier, Pierre
See also EWL 3; RGHL

Gascoigne, George 1539-1577 **LC 108**
See also DLB 136; RGEL 2

Gascoyne, David (Emery)
1916-2001 **CLC 45**
See also CA 65-68; 200; CANR 10, 28, 54; CP 1, 2, 3, 4, 5, 6, 7; DLB 20; MTCW 1; RGEL 2

Gaskell, Elizabeth Cleghorn
1810-1865 **NCLC 5, 70, 97, 137; SSC 25**
See also BRW 5; CDBLB 1832-1890; DAB; DAM MST; DLB 21, 144, 159; RGEL 2; RGSF 2; TEA

Gass, William H(oward) 1924- . **CLC 1, 2, 8, 11, 15, 39, 132; SSC 12**
See also AMWS 6; CA 17-20R; CANR 30, 71, 100; CN 1, 2, 3, 4, 5, 6, 7; DLB 2, 227; EWL 3; MAL 5; MTCW 1, 2; MTFW 2005; RGAL 4

Gassendi, Pierre 1592-1655 **LC 54**
See also GFL Beginnings to 1789

Gasset, Jose Ortega y
See Ortega y Gasset, Jose

Gates, Henry Louis, Jr. 1950- ... **BLCS; CLC 65**
See also BW 2, 3; CA 109; CANR 25, 53, 75, 125; CSW; DA3; DAM MULT; DLB 67; EWL 3; MAL 5; MTCW 2; MTFW 2005; RGAL 4

Gatos, Stephanie
See Katz, Steve

Gautier, Theophile 1811-1872 .. **NCLC 1, 59; PC 18; SSC 20**
See also DAM POET; DLB 119; EW 6; GFL 1789 to the Present; RGWL 2, 3; SUFW; TWA

Gay, John 1685-1732 **LC 49**
See also BRW 3; DAM DRAM; DLB 84, 95; RGEL 2; WLIT 3

Gay, Oliver
See Gogarty, Oliver St. John

Gay, Peter 1923- **CLC 158**
See also CA 13-16R; CANR 18, 41, 77, 147; INT CANR-18; RGHL

Gay, Peter Jack
See Gay, Peter

Gaye, Marvin (Pentz, Jr.)
1939-1984 **CLC 26**
See also CA 195; 112

Gebler, Carlo (Ernest) 1954- **CLC 39**
See also CA 119; 133; CANR 96; DLB 271

Gee, Maggie (Mary) 1948- **CLC 57**
See also CA 130; CANR 125; CN 4, 5, 6, 7; DLB 207; MTFW 2005

Gee, Maurice 1931- **CLC 29**
See also AAYA 42; CA 97-100; CANR 67, 123; CLR 56; CN 2, 3, 4, 5, 6, 7; CWRI 5; EWL 3; MAICYA 2; RGSF 2; SATA 46, 101

Gee, Maurice Gough
See Gee, Maurice

Geiogamah, Hanay 1945- **NNAL**
See also CA 153; DAM MULT; DLB 175

Gelbart, Larry
See Gelbart, Larry (Simon)
See also CAD; CD 5, 6

Gelbart, Larry (Simon) 1928- **CLC 21, 61**
See Gelbart, Larry
See also CA 73-76; CANR 45, 94

Gelber, Jack 1932-2003 **CLC 1, 6, 14, 79**
See also CA 1-4R; 216; CAD; CANR 2; DLB 7, 228; MAL 5

Gellhorn, Martha (Ellis)
1908-1998 **CLC 14, 60**
See also CA 77-80; 164; CANR 44; CN 1, 2, 3, 4, 5, 6 7; DLBY 1982, 1998

Genet, Jean 1910-1986 .. **CLC 1, 2, 5, 10, 14, 44, 46; DC 25; TCLC 128**
See also CA 13-16R; CANR 18; DA3; DAM DRAM; DFS 10; DLB 72, 321; DLBY 1986; EW 13; EWL 3; GFL 1789 to the Present; GLL 1; LMFS 2; MTCW 1, 2; MTFW 2005; RGWL 2, 3; TWA

Genlis, Stephanie-Felicite Ducrest
1746-1830 **NCLC 166**
See also DLB 313

Gent, Peter 1942- **CLC 29**
See also AITN 1; CA 89-92; DLBY 1982

Gentile, Giovanni 1875-1944 **TCLC 96**
See also CA 119

Gentlewoman in New England, A
See Bradstreet, Anne

Gentlewoman in Those Parts, A
See Bradstreet, Anne

Geoffrey of Monmouth c.
1100-1155 **CMLC 44**
See also DLB 146; TEA

George, Jean
See George, Jean Craighead

George, Jean Craighead 1919- **CLC 35**
See also AAYA 8, 69; BYA 2, 4; CA 5-8R; CANR 25; CLR 1; 80; DLB 52; JRDA; MAICYA 1, 2; SATA 2, 68, 124, 170; WYA; YAW

George, Stefan (Anton) 1868-1933 . **TCLC 2, 14**
See also CA 104; 193; EW 8; EWL 3

Georges, Georges Martin
See Simenon, Georges (Jacques Christian)

Gerald of Wales c. 1146-c. 1223 ... **CMLC 60**

Gerhardi, William Alexander
See Gerhardie, William Alexander

Gerhardie, William Alexander
1895-1977 **CLC 5**
See also CA 25-28R; 73-76; CANR 18; CN 1, 2; DLB 36; RGEL 2

Gerson, Jean 1363-1429 **LC 77**
See also DLB 208

Gersonides 1288-1344 **CMLC 49**
See also DLB 115

Gerstler, Amy 1956- **CLC 70**
See also CA 146; CANR 99

Gertler, T. **CLC 34**
See also CA 116; 121

Gertsen, Aleksandr Ivanovich
See Herzen, Aleksandr Ivanovich

Ghalib **NCLC 39, 78**
See Ghalib, Asadullah Khan

Ghalib, Asadullah Khan 1797-1869
See Ghalib
See also DAM POET; RGWL 2, 3

Ghelderode, Michel de 1898-1962 **CLC 6, 11; DC 15**
See also CA 85-88; CANR 40, 77; DAM DRAM; DLB 321; EW 11; EWL 3; TWA

Ghiselin, Brewster 1903-2001 **CLC 23**
See also CA 13-16R; CAAS 10; CANR 13; CP 1, 2, 3, 4, 5, 6, 7

Ghose, Aurabinda 1872-1950 **TCLC 63**
See Ghose, Aurobindo
See also CA 163

Ghose, Aurobindo
See Ghose, Aurabinda
See also EWL 3

Ghose, Zulfikar 1935- **CLC 42, 200**
See also CA 65-68; CANR 67; CN 1, 2, 3, 4, 5, 6, 7; CP 1, 2, 3, 4, 5, 6, 7; DLB 323; EWL 3

Ghosh, Amitav 1956- **CLC 44, 153**
See also CA 147; CANR 80; CN 6, 7; DLB 323; WWE 1

Giacosa, Giuseppe 1847-1906 **TCLC 7**
See also CA 104

Gibb, Lee
See Waterhouse, Keith (Spencer)

Gibbon, Edward 1737-1794 **LC 97**
See also BRW 3; DLB 104; RGEL 2

Gibbon, Lewis Grassic **TCLC 4**
See Mitchell, James Leslie
See also RGEL 2

Gibbons, Kaye 1960- **CLC 50, 88, 145**
See also AAYA 34; AMWS 10; CA 151;
CANR 75, 127; CN 7; CSW; DA3; DAM
POP; DLB 292; MTCW 2; MTFW 2005;
NFS 3; RGAL 4; SATA 117
Gibran, Kahlil 1883-1931 . **PC 9; TCLC 1, 9**
See also CA 104; 150; DA3; DAM POET,
POP; EWL 3; MTCW 2; WLIT 6
Gibran, Khalil
See Gibran, Kahlil
Gibson, Mel 1956- **CLC 215**
Gibson, William 1914- **CLC 23**
See also CA 9-12R; CAD; CANR 9, 42, 75,
125; CD 5, 6; DA; DAB; DAC; DAM
DRAM, MST; DFS 2; DLB 7; LAIT 2;
MAL 5; MTCW 2; MTFW 2005; SATA
66; YAW
Gibson, William (Ford) 1948- ... **CLC 39, 63,
186, 192; SSC 52**
See also AAYA 12, 59; BPFB 2; CA 126;
133; CANR 52, 90, 106; CN 6, 7; CPW;
DA3; DAM POP; DLB 251; MTCW 2;
MTFW 2005; SCFW 2; SFW 4
Gide, Andre (Paul Guillaume)
1869-1951 **SSC 13; TCLC 5, 12, 36,
177; WLC 3**
See also CA 104; 124; DA; DA3; DAB;
DAC; DAM MST, NOV; DLB 65, 321;
EW 8; EWL 3; GFL 1789 to the Present;
MTCW 1, 2; MTFW 2005; NFS 21;
RGSF 2; RGWL 2, 3; TWA
Gifford, Barry (Colby) 1946- **CLC 34**
See also CA 65-68; CANR 9, 30, 40, 90
Gilbert, Frank
See De Voto, Bernard (Augustine)
Gilbert, W(illiam) S(chwenck)
1836-1911 **TCLC 3**
See also CA 104; 173; DAM DRAM, POET;
RGEL 2; SATA 36
Gilbert of Poitiers c. 1085-1154 **CMLC 85**
Gilbreth, Frank B(unker), Jr.
1911-2001 **CLC 17**
See also CA 9-12R; SATA 2
Gilchrist, Ellen (Louise) 1935- .. **CLC 34, 48,
143; SSC 14, 63**
See also BPFB 2; CA 113; 116; CANR 41,
61, 104; CN 4, 5, 6, 7; CPW; CSW; DAM
POP; DLB 130; EWL 3; EXPS; MTCW
1, 2; MTFW 2005; RGAL 4; RGSF 2;
SSFS 9
Giles, Molly 1942- **CLC 39**
See also CA 126; CANR 98
Gill, Eric .. **TCLC 85**
See Gill, (Arthur) Eric (Rowton Peter
Joseph)
Gill, (Arthur) Eric (Rowton Peter Joseph)
1882-1940
See Gill, Eric
See also CA 120; DLB 98
Gill, Patrick
See Creasey, John
Gillette, Douglas **CLC 70**
Gilliam, Terry (Vance) 1940- **CLC 21, 141**
See Monty Python
See also AAYA 19, 59; CA 108; 113; CANR
35; INT CA-113
Gillian, Jerry
See Gilliam, Terry (Vance)
Gilliatt, Penelope (Ann Douglass)
1932-1993 **CLC 2, 10, 13, 53**
See also AITN 2; CA 13-16R; 141; CANR
49; CN 1, 2, 3, 4, 5; DLB 14
Gilligan, Carol 1936- **CLC 208**
See also CA 142; CANR 121; FW
Gilman, Charlotte (Anna) Perkins (Stetson)
1860-1935 **SSC 13, 62; TCLC 9, 37,
117**
See also AMWS 11; BYA 11; CA 106; 150;
DLB 221; EXPS; FL 1:5; FW; HGG;

LAIT 2; MAWW; MTCW 2; MTFW
2005; RGAL 4; RGSF 2; SFW 4; SSFS 1,
18
Gilmour, David 1946- **CLC 35**
Gilpin, William 1724-1804 **NCLC 30**
Gilray, J. D.
See Mencken, H(enry) L(ouis)
Gilroy, Frank D(aniel) 1925- **CLC 2**
See also CA 81-84; CAD; CANR 32, 64,
86; CD 5, 6; DFS 17; DLB 7
Gilstrap, John 1957(?)- **CLC 99**
See also AAYA 67; CA 160; CANR 101
Ginsberg, Allen 1926-1997 **CLC 1, 2, 3, 4,
6, 13, 36, 69, 109; PC 4, 47; TCLC
120; WLC 3**
See also AAYA 33; AITN 1; AMWC 1;
AMWS 2; BG 1:2; CA 1-4R; 157; CANR
2, 41, 63, 95; CDALB 1941-1968; CP 1,
2, 3, 4, 5, 6; DA; DA3; DAB; DAC; DAM
MST, POET; DLB 5, 16, 169, 237; EWL
3; GLL 1; LMFS 2; MAL 5; MTCW 1, 2;
MTFW 2005; PAB; PFS 5; RGAL 4;
TUS; WP
Ginzburg, Eugenia **CLC 59**
See Ginzburg, Evgeniia
Ginzburg, Evgeniia 1904-1977
See Ginzburg, Eugenia
See also DLB 302
Ginzburg, Natalia 1916-1991 **CLC 5, 11,
54, 70; SSC 65; TCLC 156**
See also CA 85-88; 135; CANR 33; DFS
14; DLB 177; EW 13; EWL 3; MTCW 1,
2; MTFW 2005; RGHL; RGWL 2, 3
Giono, Jean 1895-1970 **CLC 4, 11; TCLC
124**
See also CA 45-48; 29-32R; CANR 2, 35;
DLB 72, 321; EWL 3; GFL 1789 to the
Present; MTCW 1; RGWL 2, 3
Giovanni, Nikki 1943- **BLC 2; CLC 2, 4,
19, 64, 117; PC 19; WLCS**
See also AAYA 22; AITN 1; BW 2, 3; CA
29-32R; CAAS 6; CANR 18, 41, 60, 91,
130; CDALBS; CLR 6, 73; CP 2, 3, 4, 5,
6, 7; CSW; CWP; CWRI 5; DA; DA3;
DAB; DAC; DAM MST, MULT, POET;
DLB 5, 41; EWL 3; EXPP; INT CANR-
18; MAICYA 1, 2; MAL 5; MTCW 1, 2;
MTFW 2005; PFS 17; RGAL 4; SATA
24, 107; TUS; YAW
Giovene, Andrea 1904-1998 **CLC 7**
See also CA 85-88
Gippius, Zinaida (Nikolaevna) 1869-1945
See Hippius, Zinaida (Nikolaevna)
See also CA 106; 212
Giraudoux, Jean(-Hippolyte)
1882-1944 **TCLC 2, 7**
See also CA 104; 196; DAM DRAM; DLB
65, 321; EW 9; EWL 3; GFL 1789 to the
Present; RGWL 2, 3; TWA
Gironella, Jose Maria (Pous)
1917-2003 **CLC 11**
See also CA 101; 212; EWL 3; RGWL 2, 3
Gissing, George (Robert)
1857-1903 **SSC 37; TCLC 3, 24, 47**
See also BRW 5; CA 105; 167; DLB 18,
135, 184; RGEL 2; TEA
Gitlin, Todd 1943- **CLC 201**
See also CA 29-32R; CANR 25, 50, 88
Giurlani, Aldo
See Palazzeschi, Aldo
Gladkov, Fedor Vasil'evich
See Gladkov, Fyodor (Vasilyevich)
See also DLB 272
Gladkov, Fyodor (Vasilyevich)
1883-1958 **TCLC 27**
See Gladkov, Fedor Vasil'evich
See also CA 170; EWL 3

Glancy, Diane 1941- **CLC 210; NNAL**
See also CA 136; 225; CAAE 225; CAAS
24; CANR 87; DLB 175
Glanville, Brian (Lester) 1931- **CLC 6**
See also CA 5-8R; CAAS 9; CANR 3, 70;
CN 1, 2, 3, 4, 5, 6, 7; DLB 15, 139; SATA
42
Glasgow, Ellen (Anderson Gholson)
1873-1945 **SSC 34; TCLC 2, 7**
See also AMW; CA 104; 164; DLB 9, 12;
MAL 5; MAWW; MTCW 2; MTFW 2005;
RGAL 4; RHW; SSFS 9; TUS
Glaspell, Susan 1882(?)-1948 **DC 10; SSC
41; TCLC 55, 175**
See also AMWS 3; CA 110; 154; DFS 8,
18; DLB 7, 9, 78, 228; MAWW; RGAL
4; SSFS 3; TCWW 2; TUS; YABC 2
Glassco, John 1909-1981 **CLC 9**
See also CA 13-16R; 102; CANR 15; CN
1, 2; CP 1, 2, 3; DLB 68
Glasscock, Amnesia
See Steinbeck, John (Ernst)
Glasser, Ronald J. 1940(?)- **CLC 37**
See also CA 209
Glassman, Joyce
See Johnson, Joyce
Gleick, James (W.) 1954- **CLC 147**
See also CA 131; 137; CANR 97; INT CA-
137
Glendinning, Victoria 1937- **CLC 50**
See also CA 120; 127; CANR 59, 89; DLB
155
Glissant, Edouard (Mathieu)
1928- **CLC 10, 68**
See also CA 153; CANR 111; CWW 2;
DAM MULT; EWL 3; RGWL 3
Gloag, Julian 1930- **CLC 40**
See also AITN 1; CA 65-68; CANR 10, 70;
CN 1, 2, 3, 4, 5, 6
Glowacki, Aleksander
See Prus, Boleslaw
Gluck, Louise (Elisabeth) 1943- .. **CLC 7, 22,
44, 81, 160; PC 16**
See also AMWS 5; CA 33-36R; CANR 40,
69, 108, 133; CP 1, 2, 3, 4, 5, 6, 7; CWP;
DA3; DAM POET; DLB 5; MAL 5;
MTCW 2; MTFW 2005; PFS 5, 15;
RGAL 4; TCLE 1:1
Glyn, Elinor 1864-1943 **TCLC 72**
See also DLB 153; RHW
Gobineau, Joseph-Arthur
1816-1882 **NCLC 17**
See also DLB 123; GFL 1789 to the Present
Godard, Jean-Luc 1930- **CLC 20**
See also CA 93-96
Godden, (Margaret) Rumer
1907-1998 **CLC 53**
See also AAYA 6; BPFB 2; BYA 2, 5; CA
5-8R; 172; CANR 4, 27, 36, 55, 80; CLR
20; CN 1, 2, 3, 4, 5, 6; CWRI 5; DLB
161; MAICYA 1, 2; RHW; SAAS 12;
SATA 3, 36; SATA-Obit 109; TEA
Godoy Alcayaga, Lucila 1899-1957 .. **HLC 2;
PC 32; TCLC 2**
See Mistral, Gabriela
See also BW 2; CA 104; 131; CANR 81;
DAM MULT; DNFS; HW 1, 2; MTCW 1,
2; MTFW 2005
Godwin, Gail 1937- **CLC 5, 8, 22, 31, 69,
125**
See also BPFB 2; CA 29-32R; CANR 15,
43, 69, 132; CN 3, 4, 5, 6, 7; CPW; CSW;
DA3; DAM POP; DLB 6, 234; INT
CANR-15; MAL 5; MTCW 1, 2; MTFW
2005
Godwin, Gail Kathleen
See Godwin, Gail

Godwin, William 1756-1836 .. **NCLC 14, 130**
See also CDBLB 1789-1832; CMW 4; DLB 39, 104, 142, 158, 163, 262; GL 2; HGG; RGEL 2

Goebbels, Josef
See Goebbels, (Paul) Joseph

Goebbels, (Paul) Joseph
1897-1945 **TCLC 68**
See also CA 115; 148

Goebbels, Joseph Paul
See Goebbels, (Paul) Joseph

Goethe, Johann Wolfgang von
1749-1832 . **DC 20; NCLC 4, 22, 34, 90, 154; PC 5; SSC 38; WLC 3**
See also CDWLB 2; DA; DA3; DAB; DAC; DAM DRAM, MST, POET; DLB 94; EW 5; GL 2; LATS 1; LMFS 1:1; RGWL 2, 3; TWA

Gogarty, Oliver St. John
1878-1957 **TCLC 15**
See also CA 109; 150; DLB 15, 19; RGEL 2

Gogol, Nikolai (Vasilyevich)
1809-1852 **DC 1; NCLC 5, 15, 31, 162; SSC 4, 29, 52; WLC 3**
See also DA; DAB; DAC; DAM DRAM, MST; DFS 12; DLB 198; EW 6; EXPS; RGSF 2; RGWL 2, 3; SSFS 7; TWA

Goines, Donald 1937(?)-1974 ... **BLC 2; CLC 80**
See also AITN 1; BW 1, 3; CA 124; 114; CANR 82; CMW 4; DA3; DAM MULT, POP; DLB 33

Gold, Herbert 1924- ... **CLC 4, 7, 14, 42, 152**
See also CA 9-12R; CANR 17, 45, 125; CN 1, 2, 3, 4, 5, 6, 7; DLB 2; DLBY 1981; MAL 5

Goldbarth, Albert 1948- **CLC 5, 38**
See also AMWS 12; CA 53-56; CANR 6, 40; CP 3, 4, 5, 6, 7; DLB 120

Goldberg, Anatol 1910-1982 **CLC 34**
See also CA 131; 117

Goldemberg, Isaac 1945- **CLC 52**
See also CA 69-72; CAAS 12; CANR 11, 32; EWL 3; HW 1; WLIT 1

Golding, Arthur 1536-1606 **LC 101**
See also DLB 136

Golding, William (Gerald)
1911-1993 **CLC 1, 2, 3, 8, 10, 17, 27, 58, 81; WLC 3**
See also AAYA 5, 44; BPFB 2; BRWR 1; BRWS 1; BYA 2; CA 5-8R; 141; CANR 13, 33, 54; CD 5; CDBLB 1945-1960; CLR 94; CN 1, 2, 3, 4; DA; DA3; DAB; DAC; DAM MST, NOV; DLB 15, 100, 255, 326; EWL 3; EXPN; HGG; LAIT 4; MTCW 1, 2; MTFW 2005; NFS 2; RGEL 2; RHW; SFW 4; TEA; WLIT 4; YAW

Goldman, Emma 1869-1940 **TCLC 13**
See also CA 110; 150; DLB 221; FW; RGAL 4; TUS

Goldman, Francisco 1954- **CLC 76**
See also CA 162

Goldman, William 1931- **CLC 1, 48**
See also BPFB 2; CA 9-12R; CANR 29, 69, 106; CN 1, 2, 3, 4, 5, 6, 7; DLB 44; FANT; IDFW 3, 4

Goldman, William W.
See Goldman, William

Goldmann, Lucien 1913-1970 **CLC 24**
See also CA 25-28; CAP 2

Goldoni, Carlo 1707-1793 **LC 4**
See also DAM DRAM; EW 4; RGWL 2, 3; WLIT 7

Goldsberry, Steven 1949- **CLC 34**
See also CA 131

Goldsmith, Oliver 1730-1774 **DC 8; LC 2, 48, 122; WLC 3**
See also BRW 3; CDBLB 1660-1789; DA; DAB; DAC; DAM DRAM, MST, NOV, POET; DFS 1; DLB 39, 89, 104, 109, 142; IDTP; RGEL 2; SATA 26; TEA; WLIT 3

Goldsmith, Peter
See Priestley, J(ohn) B(oynton)

Gombrowicz, Witold 1904-1969 **CLC 4, 7, 11, 49**
See also CA 19-20; 25-28R; CANR 105; CAP 2; CDWLB 4; DAM DRAM; DLB 215; EW 12; EWL 3; RGWL 2, 3; TWA

Gomez de Avellaneda, Gertrudis
1814-1873 **NCLC 111**
See also LAW

Gomez de la Serna, Ramon
1888-1963 **CLC 9**
See also CA 153; 116; CANR 79; EWL 3; HW 1, 2

Goncharov, Ivan Alexandrovich
1812-1891 **NCLC 1, 63**
See also DLB 238; EW 6; RGWL 2, 3

Goncourt, Edmond (Louis Antoine Huot) de
1822-1896 **NCLC 7**
See also DLB 123; EW 7; GFL 1789 to the Present; RGWL 2, 3

Goncourt, Jules (Alfred Huot) de
1830-1870 **NCLC 7**
See also DLB 123; EW 7; GFL 1789 to the Present; RGWL 2, 3

Gongora (y Argote), Luis de
1561-1627 **LC 72**
See also RGWL 2, 3

Gontier, Fernande 19(?)- **CLC 50**

Gonzalez Martinez, Enrique
See Gonzalez Martinez, Enrique
See also DLB 290

Gonzalez Martinez, Enrique
1871-1952 **TCLC 72**
See Gonzalez Martinez, Enrique
See also CA 166; CANR 81; EWL 3; HW 1, 2

Goodison, Lorna 1947- **PC 36**
See also CA 142; CANR 88; CP 5, 6, 7; CWP; DLB 157; EWL 3

Goodman, Paul 1911-1972 **CLC 1, 2, 4, 7**
See also CA 19-20; 37-40R; CAD; CANR 34; CAP 2; CN 1; DLB 130, 246; MAL 5; MTCW 1; RGAL 4

GoodWeather, Harley
See King, Thomas

Googe, Barnabe 1540-1594 **LC 94**
See also DLB 132; RGEL 2

Gordimer, Nadine 1923- **CLC 3, 5, 7, 10, 18, 33, 51, 70, 123, 160, 161; SSC 17, 80; WLCS**
See also AAYA 39; AFW; BRWS 2; CA 5-8R; CANR 3, 28, 56, 88, 131; CN 1, 2, 3, 4, 5, 6, 7; DA; DA3; DAB; DAC; DAM MST, NOV; DLB 225, 326; EWL 3; EXPS; INT CANR-28; LATS 1:2; MTCW 1, 2; MTFW 2005; NFS 4; RGEL 2; RGSF 2; SSFS 2, 14, 19; TWA; WLIT 2; YAW

Gordon, Adam Lindsay
1833-1870 **NCLC 21**
See also DLB 230

Gordon, Caroline 1895-1981 . **CLC 6, 13, 29, 83; SSC 15**
See also AMW; CA 11-12; 103; CANR 36; CAP 1; CN 1, 2; DLB 4, 9, 102; DLBD 17; DLBY 1981; EWL 3; MAL 5; MTCW 1, 2; MTFW 2005; RGAL 4; RGSF 2

Gordon, Charles William 1860-1937
See Connor, Ralph
See also CA 109

Gordon, Mary 1949- .. **CLC 13, 22, 128, 216; SSC 59**
See also AMWS 4; BPFB 2; CA 102; CANR 44, 92, 154; CN 4, 5, 6, 7; DLB 6; DLBY 1981; FW; INT CA-102; MAL 5; MTCW 1

Gordon, Mary Catherine
See Gordon, Mary

Gordon, N. J.
See Bosman, Herman Charles

Gordon, Sol 1923- **CLC 26**
See also CA 53-56; CANR 4; SATA 11

Gordone, Charles 1925-1995 .. **CLC 1, 4; DC 8**
See also BW 1, 3; CA 93-96, 180; 150; CAAE 180; CAD; CANR 55; DAM DRAM; DLB 7; INT CA-93-96; MTCW 1

Gore, Catherine 1800-1861 **NCLC 65**
See also DLB 116; RGEL 2

Gorenko, Anna Andreevna
See Akhmatova, Anna

Gorky, Maxim **SSC 28; TCLC 8; WLC 3**
See Peshkov, Alexei Maximovich
See also DAB; DFS 9; DLB 295; EW 8; EWL 3; TWA

Goryan, Sirak
See Saroyan, William

Gosse, Edmund (William)
1849-1928 **TCLC 28**
See also CA 117; DLB 57, 144, 184; RGEL 2

Gotlieb, Phyllis (Fay Bloom) 1926- .. **CLC 18**
See also CA 13-16R; CANR 7, 135; CN 7; CP 1, 2, 3, 4; DLB 88, 251; SFW 4

Gottesman, S. D.
See Kornbluth, C(yril) M.; Pohl, Frederik

Gottfried von Strassburg fl. c.
1170-1215 **CMLC 10**
See also CDWLB 2; DLB 138; EW 1; RGWL 2, 3

Gotthelf, Jeremias 1797-1854 **NCLC 117**
See also DLB 133; RGWL 2, 3

Gottschalk, Laura Riding
See Jackson, Laura (Riding)

Gould, Lois 1932(?)-2002 **CLC 4, 10**
See also CA 77-80; 208; CANR 29; MTCW 1

Gould, Stephen Jay 1941-2002 **CLC 163**
See also AAYA 26; BEST 90:2; CA 77-80; 205; CANR 10, 27, 56, 75, 125; CPW; INT CANR-27; MTCW 1, 2; MTFW 2005

Gourmont, Remy(-Marie-Charles) de
1858-1915 **TCLC 17**
See also CA 109; 150; GFL 1789 to the Present; MTCW 2

Gournay, Marie le Jars de
See de Gournay, Marie le Jars

Govier, Katherine 1948- **CLC 51**
See also CA 101; CANR 18, 40, 128; CCA 1

Gower, John c. 1330-1408 **LC 76; PC 59**
See also BRW 1; DLB 146; RGEL 2

Goyen, (Charles) William
1915-1983 **CLC 5, 8, 14, 40**
See also AITN 2; CA 5-8R; 110; CANR 6, 71; CN 1, 2, 3; DLB 2, 218; DLBY 1983; EWL 3; INT CANR-6; MAL 5

Goytisolo, Juan 1931- **CLC 5, 10, 23, 133; HLC 1**
See also CA 85-88; CANR 32, 61, 131; CWW 2; DAM MULT; DLB 322; EWL 3; GLL 2; HW 1, 2; MTCW 1, 2; MTFW 2005

Gozzano, Guido 1883-1916 **PC 10**
See also CA 154; DLB 114; EWL 3

Gozzi, (Conte) Carlo 1720-1806 **NCLC 23**

Grabbe, Christian Dietrich
1801-1836 NCLC 2
See also DLB 133; RGWL 2, 3

Grace, Patricia Frances 1937- CLC 56
See also CA 176; CANR 118; CN 4, 5, 6, 7; EWL 3; RGSF 2

Gracian y Morales, Baltasar
1601-1658 LC 15

Gracq, Julien CLC 11, 48
See Poirier, Louis
See also CWW 2; DLB 83; GFL 1789 to the Present

Grade, Chaim 1910-1982 CLC 10
See also CA 93-96; 107; EWL 3; RGHL

Graduate of Oxford, A
See Ruskin, John

Grafton, Garth
See Duncan, Sara Jeannette

Grafton, Sue 1940- CLC 163
See also AAYA 11, 49; BEST 90:3; CA 108; CANR 31, 55, 111, 134; CMW 4; CPW; CSW; DA3; DAM POP; DLB 226; FW; MSW; MTFW 2005

Graham, John
See Phillips, David Graham

Graham, Jorie 1950- CLC 48, 118; PC 59
See also AAYA 67; CA 111; CANR 63, 118; CP 4, 5, 6, 7; CWP; DLB 120; EWL 3; MTFW 2005; PFS 10, 17; TCLE 1:1

Graham, R(obert) B(ontine) Cunninghame
See Cunninghame Graham, Robert (Gallnigad) Bontine
See also DLB 98, 135, 174; RGEL 2; RGSF 2

Graham, Robert
See Haldeman, Joe

Graham, Tom
See Lewis, (Harry) Sinclair

Graham, W(illiam) S(idney)
1918-1986 CLC 29
See also BRWS 7; CA 73-76; 118; CP 1, 2, 3, 4; DLB 20; RGEL 2

Graham, Winston (Mawdsley)
1910-2003 CLC 23
See also CA 49-52; 218; CANR 2, 22, 45, 66; CMW 4; CN 1, 2, 3, 4, 5, 6, 7; DLB 77; RHW

Grahame, Kenneth 1859-1932 TCLC 64, 136
See also BYA 5; CA 108; 136; CANR 80; CLR 5; CWRI 5; DA3; DAB; DLB 34, 141, 178; FANT; MAICYA 1, 2; MTCW 2; NFS 20; RGEL 2; SATA 100; TEA; WCH; YABC 1

Granger, Darius John
See Marlowe, Stephen

Granin, Daniil 1918- CLC 59
See also DLB 302

Granovsky, Timofei Nikolaevich
1813-1855 NCLC 75
See also DLB 198

Grant, Skeeter
See Spiegelman, Art

Granville-Barker, Harley
1877-1946 TCLC 2
See Barker, Harley Granville
See also CA 104; 204; DAM DRAM; RGEL 2

Granzotto, Gianni
See Granzotto, Giovanni Battista

Granzotto, Giovanni Battista
1914-1985 CLC 70
See also CA 166

Grass, Guenter (Wilhelm) 1927- ... CLC 1, 2, 4, 6, 11, 15, 22, 32, 49, 88, 207; WLC 3
See Grass, Gunter (Wilhelm)
See also BPFB 2; CA 13-16R; CANR 20, 75, 93, 133; CDWLB 2; DA; DA3; DAB; DAC; DAM MST, NOV; DLB 75, 124; FW 13; EWL 3; MTCW 1, 2; MTFW 2005; RGWL 2, 3; TWA

Grass, Gunter (Wilhelm)
See Grass, Guenter (Wilhelm)
See also CWW 2; RGHL

Gratton, Thomas
See Hulme, T(homas) E(rnest)

Grau, Shirley Ann 1929- CLC 4, 9, 146; SSC 15
See also CA 89-92; CANR 22, 69; CN 1, 2, 3, 4, 5, 6, 7; CSW; DLB 2, 218; INT CA-89-92; CANR-22; MTCW 1

Gravel, Fern
See Hall, James Norman

Graver, Elizabeth 1964- CLC 70
See also CA 135; CANR 71, 129

Graves, Richard Perceval
1895-1985 CLC 44
See also CA 65-68; CANR 9, 26, 51

Graves, Robert (von Ranke)
1895-1985 .. CLC 1, 2, 6, 11, 39, 44, 45; PC 6
See also BPFB 2; BRW 7; BYA 4; CA 5-8R; 117; CANR 5, 36; CDBLB 1914-1945; CN 1, 2, 3; CP 1, 2, 3, 4; DA3; DAB; DAC; DAM MST, POET; DLB 20, 100, 191; DLBD 18; DLBY 1985; EWL 3; LATS 1:1; MTCW 1, 2; MTFW 2005; NCFS 2; NFS 21; RGEL 2; RHW; SATA 45; TEA

Graves, Valerie
See Bradley, Marion Zimmer

Gray, Alasdair (James) 1934- CLC 41
See also BRWS 9; CA 126; CANR 47, 69, 106, 140; CN 4, 5, 6, 7; DLB 194, 261, 319; HGG; INT CA-126; MTCW 1, 2; MTFW 2005; RGSF 2; SUFW 2

Gray, Amlin 1946- CLC 29
See also CA 138

Gray, Francine du Plessix 1930- CLC 22, 153
See also BEST 90:3; CA 61-64; CAAS 2; CANR 11, 33, 75, 81; DAM NOV; INT CANR-11; MTCW 1, 2; MTFW 2005

Gray, John (Henry) 1866-1934 TCLC 19
See also CA 119; 162; RGEL 2

Gray, John Lee
See Jakes, John (William)

Gray, Simon (James Holliday)
1936- CLC 9, 14, 36
See also AITN 1; CA 21-24R; CAAS 3; CANR 32, 69; CBD; CD 5, 6; CN 1, 2, 3; DLB 13; EWL 3; MTCW 1; RGEL 2

Gray, Spalding 1941-2004 CLC 49, 112; DC 7
See also AAYA 62; CA 128; 225; CAD; CANR 74, 138; CD 5, 6; CPW; DAM POP; MTCW 2; MTFW 2005

Gray, Thomas 1716-1771 LC 4, 40; PC 2; WLC 3
See also BRW 3; CDBLB 1660-1789; DA; DA3; DAB; DAC; DAM MST; DLB 109; EXPP; PAB; PFS 9; RGEL 2; TEA; WP

Grayson, David
See Baker, Ray Stannard

Grayson, Richard (A.) 1951- CLC 38
See also CA 85-88, 210; CAAE 210; CANR 14, 31, 57; DLB 234

Greeley, Andrew M(oran) 1928- CLC 28
See also BPFB 2; CA 5-8R; CAAS 7; CANR 7, 43, 69, 104, 136; CMW 4; CPW; DA3; DAM POP; MTCW 1, 2; MTFW 2005

Green, Anna Katharine
1846-1935 TCLC 63
See also CA 112; 159; CMW 4; DLB 202, 221; MSW

Green, Brian
See Card, Orson Scott

Green, Hannah
See Greenberg, Joanne (Goldenberg)

Green, Hannah 1927(?)-1996 CLC 3
See also CA 73-76; CANR 59, 93; NFS 10

Green, Henry CLC 2, 13, 97
See Yorke, Henry Vincent
See also BRWS 2; CA 175; DLB 15; EWL 3; RGEL 2

Green, Julian CLC 3, 11, 77
See Green, Julien (Hartridge)
See also EWL 3; GFL 1789 to the Present; MTCW 2

Green, Julien (Hartridge) 1900-1998
See Green, Julian
See also CA 21-24R; 169; CANR 33, 87; CWW 2; DLB 4, 72; MTCW 1, 2; MTFW 2005

Green, Paul (Eliot) 1894-1981 CLC 25
See also AITN 1; CA 5-8R; 103; CAD; CANR 3; DAM DRAM; DLB 7, 9, 249; DLBY 1981; MAL 5; RGAL 4

Greenaway, Peter 1942- CLC 159
See also CA 127

Greenberg, Ivan 1908-1973
See Rahv, Philip
See also CA 85-88

Greenberg, Joanne (Goldenberg)
1932- CLC 7, 30
See also AAYA 12, 67; CA 5-8R; CANR 14, 32, 69; CN 6, 7; NFS 23; SATA 25; YAW

Greenberg, Richard 1959(?)- CLC 57
See also CA 138; CAD; CD 5, 6

Greenblatt, Stephen J(ay) 1943- CLC 70
See also CA 49-52; CANR 115

Greene, Bette 1934- CLC 30
See also AAYA 7, 69; BYA 3; CA 53-56; CANR 4, 146; CLR 2; CWRI 5; JRDA; LAIT 4; MAICYA 1, 2; NFS 10; SAAS 16; SATA 8, 102, 161; WYA; YAW

Greene, Gael CLC 8
See also CA 13-16R; CANR 10

Greene, Graham (Henry)
1904-1991 CLC 1, 3, 6, 9, 14, 18, 27, 37, 70, 72, 125; SSC 29; WLC 3
See also AAYA 61; AITN 2; BPFB 2; BRWR 2; BRWS 1; BYA 3; CA 13-16R; 133; CANR 35, 61, 131; CBD; CDBLB 1945-1960; CMW 4; CN 1, 2, 3, 4; DA; DA3; DAB; DAC; DAM MST, NOV; DLB 13, 15, 77, 100, 162, 201, 204; DLBY 1991; EWL 3; MSW; MTCW 1, 2; MTFW 2005; NFS 16; RGEL 2; SATA 20; SSFS 14; TEA; WLIT 4

Greene, Robert 1558-1592 LC 41
See also BRWS 8; DLB 62, 167; IDTP; RGEL 2; TEA

Greer, Germaine 1939- CLC 131
See also AITN 1; CA 81-84; CANR 33, 70, 115, 133; FW; MTCW 1, 2; MTFW 2005

Greer, Richard
See Silverberg, Robert

Gregor, Arthur 1923- CLC 9
See also CA 25-28R; CAAS 10; CANR 11; CP 1, 2, 3, 4, 5, 6, 7; SATA 36

Gregor, Lee
See Pohl, Frederik

Gregory, Lady Isabella Augusta (Persse)
1852-1932 TCLC 1, 176
See also BRW 6; CA 104; 184; DLB 10; IDTP; RGEL 2

Gregory, J. Dennis
See Williams, John A(lfred)

Gregory of Nazianzus, St.
329-389 CMLC 82

Grekova, I. CLC 59
See Ventsel, Elena Sergeevna
See also CWW 2

Grendon, Stephen
See Derleth, August (William)

Grenville, Kate 1950- **CLC 61**
 See also CA 118; CANR 53, 93; CN 7; DLB
 325
Grenville, Pelham
 See Wodehouse, P(elham) G(renville)
Greve, Felix Paul (Berthold Friedrich)
 1879-1948
 See Grove, Frederick Philip
 See also CA 104; 141, 175; CANR 79;
 DAC; DAM MST
Greville, Fulke 1554-1628 **LC 79**
 See also BRWS 11; DLB 62, 172; RGEL 2
Grey, Lady Jane 1537-1554 **LC 93**
 See also DLB 132
Grey, Zane 1872-1939 **TCLC 6**
 See also BPFB 2; CA 104; 132; DA3; DAM
 POP; DLB 9, 212; MTCW 1, 2; MTFW
 2005; RGAL 4; TCWW 1, 2; TUS
Griboedov, Aleksandr Sergeevich
 1795(?)-1829 **NCLC 129**
 See also DLB 205; RGWL 2, 3
Grieg, (Johan) Nordahl (Brun)
 1902-1943 **TCLC 10**
 See also CA 107; 189; EWL 3
Grieve, C(hristopher) M(urray)
 1892-1978 **CLC 11, 19**
 See MacDiarmid, Hugh; Pteleon
 See also CA 5-8R; 85-88; CANR 33, 107;
 DAM POET; MTCW 1; RGEL 2
Griffin, Gerald 1803-1840 **NCLC 7**
 See also DLB 159; RGEL 2
Griffin, John Howard 1920-1980 **CLC 68**
 See also AITN 1; CA 1-4R; 101; CANR 2
Griffin, Peter 1942- **CLC 39**
 See also CA 136
Griffith, D(avid Lewelyn) W(ark)
 1875(?)-1948 **TCLC 68**
 See also CA 119; 150; CANR 80
Griffith, Lawrence
 See Griffith, D(avid Lewelyn) W(ark)
Griffiths, Trevor 1935- **CLC 13, 52**
 See also CA 97-100; CANR 45; CBD; CD
 5, 6; DLB 13, 245
Griggs, Sutton (Elbert)
 1872-1930 **TCLC 77**
 See also CA 123; 186; DLB 50
Grigson, Geoffrey (Edward Harvey)
 1905-1985 **CLC 7, 39**
 See also CA 25-28R; 118; CANR 20, 33;
 CP 1, 2, 3, 4; DLB 27; MTCW 1, 2
Grile, Dod
 See Bierce, Ambrose (Gwinett)
Grillparzer, Franz 1791-1872 **DC 14;**
 NCLC 1, 102; SSC 37
 See also CDWLB 2; DLB 133; EW 5;
 RGWL 2, 3; TWA
Grimble, Reverend Charles James
 See Eliot, T(homas) S(tearns)
Grimke, Angelina (Emily) Weld
 1880-1958 **HR 1:2**
 See Weld, Angelina (Emily) Grimke
 See also BW 1; CA 124; DAM POET; DLB
 50, 54
Grimke, Charlotte L(ottie) Forten
 1837(?)-1914
 See Forten, Charlotte L.
 See also BW 1; CA 117; 124; DAM MULT,
 POET
Grimm, Jacob Ludwig Karl
 1785-1863 **NCLC 3, 77; SSC 36**
 See Grimm Brothers
 See also CLR 112; DLB 90; MAICYA 1, 2;
 RGSF 2; RGWL 2, 3; SATA 22; WCH
Grimm, Wilhelm Karl 1786-1859 .. **NCLC 3,**
 77; SSC 36
 See Grimm Brothers
 See also CDWLB 2; CLR 112; DLB 90;
 MAICYA 1, 2; RGSF 2; RGWL 2, 3;
 SATA 22; WCH

Grimm and Grim
 See Grimm, Jacob Ludwig Karl; Grimm,
 Wilhelm Karl
Grimm Brothers **SSC 88**
 See Grimm, Jacob Ludwig Karl; Grimm,
 Wilhelm Karl
 See also CLR 112
Grimmelshausen, Hans Jakob Christoffel
 von
 See Grimmelshausen, Johann Jakob Christ-
 offel von
 See also RGWL 2, 3
Grimmelshausen, Johann Jakob Christoffel
 von 1621-1676 **LC 6**
 See Grimmelshausen, Hans Jakob Christof-
 fel von
 See also CDWLB 2; DLB 168
Grindel, Eugene 1895-1952
 See Eluard, Paul
 See also CA 104; 193; LMFS 2
Grisham, John 1955- **CLC 84**
 See also AAYA 14, 47; BPFB 2; CA 138;
 CANR 47, 69, 114, 133; CMW 4; CN 6,
 7; CPW; CSW; DA3; DAM POP; MSW;
 MTCW 2; MTFW 2005
Grosseteste, Robert 1175(?)-1253 . **CMLC 62**
 See also DLB 115
Grossman, David 1954- **CLC 67**
 See also CA 138; CANR 114; CWW 2;
 DLB 299; EWL 3; RGHL; WLIT 6
Grossman, Vasilii Semenovich
 See Grossman, Vasily (Semenovich)
 See also DLB 272
Grossman, Vasily (Semenovich)
 1905-1964 **CLC 41**
 See Grossman, Vasilii Semenovich
 See also CA 124; 130; MTCW 1; RGHL
Grove, Frederick Philip **TCLC 4**
 See Greve, Felix Paul (Berthold Friedrich)
 See also DLB 92; RGEL 2; TCWW 1, 2
Grubb
 See Crumb, R.
Grumbach, Doris (Isaac) 1918- . **CLC 13, 22,**
 64
 See also CA 5-8R; CAAS 2; CANR 9, 42,
 70, 127; CN 6, 7; INT CANR-9; MTCW
 2; MTFW 2005
Grundtvig, Nikolai Frederik Severin
 1783-1872 **NCLC 1, 158**
 See also DLB 300
Grunge
 See Crumb, R.
Grunwald, Lisa 1959- **CLC 44**
 See also CA 120; CANR 148
Gryphius, Andreas 1616-1664 **LC 89**
 See also CDWLB 2; DLB 164; RGWL 2, 3
Guare, John 1938- **CLC 8, 14, 29, 67; DC**
 20
 See also CA 73-76; CAD; CANR 21, 69,
 118; CD 5, 6; DAM DRAM; DFS 8, 13;
 DLB 7, 249; EWL 3; MAL 5; MTCW 1,
 2; RGAL 4
Guarini, Battista 1537-1612 **LC 102**
Gubar, Susan (David) 1944- **CLC 145**
 See also CA 108; CANR 45, 70, 139; FW;
 MTCW 1; RGAL 4
Gudjonsson, Halldor Kiljan 1902-1998
 See Halldor Laxness
 See also CA 103; 164
Guenter, Erich
 See Eich, Gunter
Guest, Barbara 1920-2006 ... **CLC 34; PC 55**
 See also BG 1:2; CA 25-28R; 248; CANR
 11, 44, 84; CP 1, 2, 3, 4, 5, 6, 7; CWP;
 DLB 5, 193
Guest, Edgar A(lbert) 1881-1959 ... **TCLC 95**
 See also CA 112; 168

Guest, Judith (Ann) 1936- **CLC 8, 30**
 See also AAYA 7, 66; CA 77-80; CANR
 15, 75, 138; DA3; DAM NOV, POP;
 EXPN; INT CANR-15; LAIT 5; MTCW
 1, 2; MTFW 2005; NFS 1
Guevara, Che **CLC 87; HLC 1**
 See Guevara (Serna), Ernesto
Guevara (Serna), Ernesto
 1928-1967 **CLC 87; HLC 1**
 See Guevara, Che
 See also CA 127; 111; CANR 56; DAM
 MULT; HW 1
Guicciardini, Francesco 1483-1540 **LC 49**
Guild, Nicholas M. 1944- **CLC 33**
 See also CA 93-96
Guillemin, Jacques
 See Sartre, Jean-Paul
Guillen, Jorge 1893-1984 . **CLC 11; HLCS 1;**
 PC 35
 See also CA 89-92; 112; DAM MULT,
 POET; DLB 108; EWL 3; HW 1; RGWL
 2, 3
Guillen, Nicolas (Cristobal)
 1902-1989 **BLC 2; CLC 48, 79; HLC**
 1; PC 23
 See also BW 2; CA 116; 125; 129; CANR
 84; DAM MST, MULT, POET; DLB 283;
 EWL 3; HW 1; LAW; RGWL 2, 3; WP
Guillen y Alvarez, Jorge
 See Guillen, Jorge
Guillevic, (Eugene) 1907-1997 **CLC 33**
 See also CA 93-96; CWW 2
Guillois
 See Desnos, Robert
Guillois, Valentin
 See Desnos, Robert
Guimaraes Rosa, Joao 1908-1967 **HLCS 2**
 See Rosa, Joao Guimaraes
 See also CA 175; LAW; RGSF 2; RGWL 2,
 3
Guiney, Louise Imogen
 1861-1920 **TCLC 41**
 See also CA 160; DLB 54; RGAL 4
Guinizelli, Guido c. 1230-1276 **CMLC 49**
 See Guinizzelli, Guido
Guinizzelli, Guido
 See Guinizelli, Guido
 See also WLIT 7
Guiraldes, Ricardo (Guillermo)
 1886-1927 **TCLC 39**
 See also CA 131; EWL 3; HW 1; LAW;
 MTCW 1
Gumilev, Nikolai (Stepanovich)
 1886-1921 **TCLC 60**
 See Gumilyov, Nikolay Stepanovich
 See also CA 165; DLB 295
Gumilyov, Nikolay Stepanovich
 See Gumilev, Nikolai (Stepanovich)
 See also EWL 3
Gump, P. Q.
 See Card, Orson Scott
Gunesekera, Romesh 1954- **CLC 91**
 See also BRWS 10; CA 159; CANR 140;
 CN 6, 7; DLB 267, 323
Gunn, Bill ... **CLC 5**
 See Gunn, William Harrison
 See also DLB 38
Gunn, Thom(son William)
 1929-2004 . **CLC 3, 6, 18, 32, 81; PC 26**
 See also BRWS 4; CA 17-20R; 227; CANR
 9, 33, 116; CDBLB 1960 to Present; CP
 1, 2, 3, 4, 5, 6, 7; DAM POET; DLB 27;
 INT CANR-33; MTCW 1; PFS 9; RGEL
 2
Gunn, William Harrison 1934(?)-1989
 See Gunn, Bill
 See also AITN 1; BW 1, 3; CA 13-16R;
 128; CANR 12, 25, 76

Gunn Allen, Paula
See Allen, Paula Gunn
Gunnars, Kristjana 1948- **CLC 69**
See also CA 113; CCA 1; CP 6, 7; CWP;
DLB 60
Gunter, Erich
See Eich, Gunter
Gurdjieff, G(eorgei) I(vanovich)
1877(?)-1949 **TCLC 71**
See also CA 157
Gurganus, Allan 1947- **CLC 70**
See also BEST 90:1; CA 135; CANR 114;
CN 6, 7; CPW; CSW; DAM POP; GLL 1
Gurney, A. R.
See Gurney, A(lbert) R(amsdell), Jr.
See also DLB 266
Gurney, A(lbert) R(amsdell), Jr.
1930- **CLC 32, 50, 54**
See Gurney, A. R.
See also AMWS 5; CA 77-80; CAD; CANR
32, 64, 121; CD 5, 6; DAM DRAM; EWL
3
Gurney, Ivor (Bertie) 1890-1937 ... **TCLC 33**
See also BRW 6; CA 167; DLBY 2002;
PAB; RGEL 2
Gurney, Peter
See Gurney, A(lbert) R(amsdell), Jr.
Guro, Elena (Genrikhovna)
1877-1913 **TCLC 56**
See also DLB 295
Gustafson, James M(oody) 1925- ... **CLC 100**
See also CA 25-28R; CANR 37
Gustafson, Ralph (Barker)
1909-1995 **CLC 36**
See also CA 21-24R; CANR 8, 45, 84; CP
1, 2, 3, 4, 5, 6; DLB 88; RGEL 2
Gut, Gom
See Simenon, Georges (Jacques Christian)
Guterson, David 1956- **CLC 91**
See also CA 132; CANR 73, 126; CN 7;
DLB 292; MTCW 2; MTFW 2005; NFS
13
Guthrie, A(lfred) B(ertram), Jr.
1901-1991 **CLC 23**
See also CA 57-60; 134; CANR 24; CN 1,
2, 3; DLB 6, 212; MAL 5; SATA 62;
SATA-Obit 67; TCWW 1, 2
Guthrie, Isobel
See Grieve, C(hristopher) M(urray)
Guthrie, Woodrow Wilson 1912-1967
See Guthrie, Woody
See also CA 113; 93-96
Guthrie, Woody **CLC 35**
See Guthrie, Woodrow Wilson
See also DLB 303; LAIT 3
Gutierrez Najera, Manuel
1859-1895 **HLCS 2; NCLC 133**
See also DLB 290; LAW
Guy, Rosa (Cuthbert) 1925- **CLC 26**
See also AAYA 4, 37; BW 2; CA 17-20R;
CANR 14, 34, 83; CLR 13; DLB 33;
DNFS 1; JRDA; MAICYA 1, 2; SATA 14,
62, 122; YAW
Gwendolyn
See Bennett, (Enoch) Arnold
H. D. **CLC 3, 8, 14, 31, 34, 73; PC 5**
See Doolittle, Hilda
See also FL 1:5
H. de V.
See Buchan, John
Haavikko, Paavo Juhani 1931- .. **CLC 18, 34**
See also CA 106; CWW 2; EWL 3
Habbema, Koos
See Heijermans, Herman
Habermas, Juergen 1929- **CLC 104**
See also CA 109; CANR 85; DLB 242
Habermas, Jurgen
See Habermas, Juergen

Hacker, Marilyn 1942- **CLC 5, 9, 23, 72,**
91; PC 47
See also CA 77-80; CANR 68, 129; CP 3,
4, 5, 6, 7; CWP; DAM POET; DLB 120,
282; FW; GLL 2; MAL 5; PFS 19
Hadewijch of Antwerp fl. 1250- ... **CMLC 61**
See also RGWL 3
Hadrian 76-138 **CMLC 52**
Haeckel, Ernst Heinrich (Philipp August)
1834-1919 **TCLC 83**
See also CA 157
Hafiz c. 1326-1389(?) **CMLC 34**
See also RGWL 2, 3; WLIT 6
Hagedorn, Jessica T(arahata)
1949- **CLC 185**
See also CA 139; CANR 69; CWP; DLB
312; RGAL 4
Haggard, H(enry) Rider
1856-1925 **TCLC 11**
See also BRWS 3; BYA 4, 5; CA 108; 148;
CANR 112; DLB 70, 156, 174, 178;
FANT; LMFS 1; MTCW 2; RGEL 2;
RHW; SATA 16; SCFW 1, 2; SFW 4;
SUFW 1; WLIT 4
Hagiosy, L.
See Larbaud, Valery (Nicolas)
Hagiwara, Sakutaro 1886-1942 **PC 18;**
TCLC 60
See Hagiwara Sakutaro
See also CA 154; RGWL 3
Hagiwara Sakutaro
See Hagiwara, Sakutaro
See also EWL 3
Haig, Fenil
See Ford, Ford Madox
Haig-Brown, Roderick (Langmere)
1908-1976 **CLC 21**
See also CA 5-8R; 69-72; CANR 4, 38, 83;
CLR 31; CWRI 5; DLB 88; MAICYA 1,
2; SATA 12; TCWW 2
Haight, Rip
See Carpenter, John (Howard)
Hailey, Arthur 1920-2004 **CLC 5**
See also AITN 2; BEST 90:3; BPFB 2; CA
1-4R; 233; CANR 2, 36, 75; CCA 1; CN
1, 2, 3, 4, 5, 6, 7; CPW; DAM NOV, POP;
DLB 88; DLBY 1982; MTCW 1, 2;
MTFW 2005
Hailey, Elizabeth Forsythe 1938- **CLC 40**
See also CA 93-96; 188; CAAE 188; CAAS
1; CANR 15, 48; INT CANR-15
Haines, John (Meade) 1924- **CLC 58**
See also AMWS 12; CA 17-20R; CANR
13, 34; CP 1, 2, 3, 4, 5; CSW; DLB 5,
212; TCLE 1:1
Hakluyt, Richard 1552-1616 **LC 31**
See also DLB 136; RGEL 2
Haldeman, Joe 1943- **CLC 61**
See Graham, Robert
See also AAYA 38; CA 53-56; 179; CAAE
179; CAAS 25; CANR 6, 70, 72, 130;
DLB 8; INT CANR-6; SCFW 2; SFW 4
Haldeman, Joe William
See Haldeman, Joe
Hale, Janet Campbell 1947- **NNAL**
See also CA 49-52; CANR 45, 75; DAM
MULT; DLB 175; MTCW 2; MTFW 2005
Hale, Sarah Josepha (Buell)
1788-1879 **NCLC 75**
See also DLB 1, 42, 73, 243
Halevy, Elie 1870-1937 **TCLC 104**
Haley, Alex(ander Murray Palmer)
1921-1992 **BLC 2; CLC 8, 12, 76;**
TCLC 147
See also AAYA 26; BPFB 2; BW 2, 3; CA
77-80; 136; CANR 61; CDALBS; CPW;
CSW; DA; DA3; DAB; DAC; DAM MST,
MULT, POP; DLB 38; LAIT 5; MTCW
1, 2; NFS 9

Haliburton, Thomas Chandler
1796-1865 **NCLC 15, 149**
See also DLB 11, 99; RGEL 2; RGSF 2
Hall, Donald 1928- .. **CLC 1, 13, 37, 59, 151;**
PC 70
See also AAYA 63; CA 5-8R; CAAS 7;
CANR 2, 44, 64, 106, 133; CP 1, 2, 3, 4,
5, 6, 7; DAM POET; DLB 5; MAL 5;
MTCW 2; MTFW 2005; RGAL 4; SATA
23, 97
Hall, Donald Andrew, Jr.
See Hall, Donald
Hall, Frederic Sauser
See Sauser-Hall, Frederic
Hall, James
See Kuttner, Henry
Hall, James Norman 1887-1951 **TCLC 23**
See also CA 123; 173; LAIT 1; RHW 1;
SATA 21
Hall, Joseph 1574-1656 **LC 91**
See also DLB 121, 151; RGEL 2
Hall, (Marguerite) Radclyffe
1880-1943 **TCLC 12**
See also BRWS 6; CA 110; 150; CANR 83;
DLB 191; MTCW 2; MTFW 2005; RGEL
2; RHW
Hall, Rodney 1935- **CLC 51**
See also CA 109; CANR 69; CN 6, 7; CP
1, 2, 3, 4, 5, 6, 7; DLB 289
Hallam, Arthur Henry
1811-1833 **NCLC 110**
See also DLB 32
Halldor Laxness **CLC 25**
See Gudjonsson, Halldor Kiljan
See also DLB 293; EW 12, EWL 3; RGWL
2, 3
Halleck, Fitz-Greene 1790-1867 **NCLC 47**
See also DLB 3, 250; RGAL 4
Halliday, Michael
See Creasey, John
Halpern, Daniel 1945- **CLC 14**
See also CA 33-36R; CANR 93; CP 3, 4, 5,
6, 7
Hamburger, Michael (Peter Leopold)
1924- **CLC 5, 14**
See also CA 5-8R, 196; CAAE 196; CAAS
4; CANR 2, 47; CP 1, 2, 3, 4, 5, 6, 7;
DLB 27
Hamill, Pete 1935- **CLC 10**
See also CA 25-28R; CANR 18, 71, 127
Hamilton, Alexander
1755(?)-1804 **NCLC 49**
See also DLB 37
Hamilton, Clive
See Lewis, C.S.
Hamilton, Edmond 1904-1977 **CLC 1**
See also CA 1-4R; CANR 3, 84; DLB 8;
SATA 118; SFW 4
Hamilton, Elizabeth 1758-1816 ... **NCLC 153**
See also DLB 116, 158
Hamilton, Eugene (Jacob) Lee
See Lee-Hamilton, Eugene (Jacob)
Hamilton, Franklin
See Silverberg, Robert
Hamilton, Gail
See Corcoran, Barbara (Asenath)
Hamilton, (Robert) Ian 1938-2001 . **CLC 191**
See also CA 106; 203; CANR 41, 67; CP 1,
2, 3, 4, 5, 6, 7; DLB 40, 155
Hamilton, Jane 1957- **CLC 179**
See also CA 147; CANR 85, 128; CN 7;
MTFW 2005
Hamilton, Mollie
See Kaye, M(ary) M(argaret)
Hamilton, (Anthony Walter) Patrick
1904-1962 **CLC 51**
See also CA 176; 113; DLB 10, 191

Hamilton, Virginia (Esther)
1936-2002 **CLC 26**
See also AAYA 2, 21; BW 2, 3; BYA 1, 2, 8; CA 25-28R; 206; CANR 20, 37, 73, 126; CLR 1, 11, 40; DAM MULT; DLB 33, 52; DLBY 2001; INT CANR-20; JRDA; LAIT 5; MAICYA 1, 2; MAICYAS 1; MTCW 1, 2; MTFW 2005; SATA 4, 56, 79, 123; SATA-Obit 132; WYA; YAW

Hammett, (Samuel) Dashiell
1894-1961 **CLC 3, 5, 10, 19, 47; SSC 17**
See also AAYA 59; AITN 1; AMWS 4; BPFB 2; CA 81-84; CANR 42; CDALB 1929-1941; CMW 4; DA3; DLB 226, 280; DLBD 6; DLBY 1996; EWL 3; LAIT 3; MAL 5; MSW; MTCW 1, 2; MTFW 2005; NFS 21; RGAL 4; RGSF 2; TUS

Hammon, Jupiter 1720(?)-1800(?) **BLC 2; NCLC 5; PC 16**
See also DAM MULT, POET; DLB 31, 50

Hammond, Keith
See Kuttner, Henry

Hamner, Earl (Henry), Jr. 1923- **CLC 12**
See also AITN 2; CA 73-76; DLB 6

Hampton, Christopher 1946- **CLC 4**
See also CA 25-28R; CD 5, 6; DLB 13; MTCW 1

Hampton, Christopher James
See Hampton, Christopher

Hamsun, Knut **TCLC 2, 14, 49, 151**
See Pedersen, Knut
See also DLB 297; EW 8; EWL 3; RGWL 2, 3

Handke, Peter 1942- **CLC 5, 8, 10, 15, 38, 134; DC 17**
See also CA 77-80; CANR 33, 75, 104, 133; CWW 2; DAM DRAM, NOV; DLB 85, 124; EWL 3; MTCW 1, 2; MTFW 2005; TWA

Handy, W(illiam) C(hristopher)
1873-1958 **TCLC 97**
See also BW 3; CA 121; 167

Hanley, James 1901-1985 **CLC 3, 5, 8, 13**
See also CA 73-76; 117; CANR 36; CBD; CN 1, 2, 3; DLB 191; EWL 3; MTCW 1; RGEL 2

Hannah, Barry 1942- **CLC 23, 38, 90**
See also BPFB 2; CA 108; 110; CANR 43, 68, 113; CN 4, 5, 6, 7; CSW; DLB 6, 234; INT CA-110; MTCW 1; RGSF 2

Hannon, Ezra
See Hunter, Evan

Hansberry, Lorraine (Vivian)
1930-1965 ... **BLC 2; CLC 17, 62; DC 2**
See also AAYA 25; AFAW 1, 2; AMWS 4; BW 1, 3; CA 109; 25-28R; CABS 3; CAD; CANR 58; CDALB 1941-1968; CWD; DA; DA3; DAB; DAC; DAM DRAM, MST, MULT; DFS 2; DLB 7, 38; EWL 3; FL 1:6; FW; LAIT 4; MAL 5; MTCW 1, 2; MTFW 2005; RGAL 4; TUS

Hansen, Joseph 1923-2004 **CLC 38**
See Brock, Rose; Colton, James
See also BPFB 2; CA 29-32R; 233; CAAS 17; CANR 16, 44, 66, 125; CMW 4; DLB 226; GLL 1; INT CANR-16

Hansen, Martin A(lfred)
1909-1955 **TCLC 32**
See also CA 167; DLB 214; EWL 3

Hansen and Philipson eds. **CLC 65**

Hanson, Kenneth O(stlin) 1922- **CLC 13**
See also CA 53-56; CANR 7; CP 1, 2, 3, 4, 5

Hardwick, Elizabeth (Bruce) 1916- . **CLC 13**
See also AMWS 3; CA 5-8R; CANR 3, 32, 70, 100, 139; CN 4, 5, 6; CSW; DA3; DAM NOV; DLB 6; MAWW; MTCW 1, 2; MTFW 2005; TCLE 1:1

Hardy, Thomas 1840-1928 **PC 8; SSC 2, 60; TCLC 4, 10, 18, 32, 48, 53, 72, 143, 153; WLC 3**
See also AAYA 69; BRW 6; BRWC 1, 2; BRWR 1; CA 104; 123; CDBLB 1890-1914; DA; DA3; DAB; DAC; DAM MST, NOV, POET; DLB 18, 19, 135, 284; EWL 3; EXPN; EXPP; LAIT 2; MTCW 1, 2; MTFW 2005; NFS 3, 11, 15, 19; PFS 3, 4, 18; RGEL 2; RGSF 2; TEA; WLIT 4

Hare, David 1947- . **CLC 29, 58, 136; DC 26**
See also BRWS 4; CA 97-100; CANR 39, 91; CBD; CD 5, 6; DFS 4, 7, 16; DLB 13, 310; MTCW 1; TEA

Harewood, John
See Van Druten, John (William)

Harford, Henry
See Hudson, W(illiam) H(enry)

Hargrave, Leonie
See Disch, Thomas M(ichael)

Hariri, Al- al-Qasim ibn 'Ali Abu Muhammad al-Basri
See al-Hariri, al-Qasim ibn 'Ali Abu Muhammad al-Basri

Harjo, Joy 1951- **CLC 83; NNAL; PC 27**
See also AMWS 12; CA 114; CANR 35, 67, 91, 129; CP 6, 7; CWP; DAM MULT; DLB 120, 175; EWL 3; MTCW 2; MTFW 2005; PFS 15; RGAL 4

Harlan, Louis R(udolph) 1922- **CLC 34**
See also CA 21-24R; CANR 25, 55, 80

Harling, Robert 1951(?)- **CLC 53**
See also CA 147

Harmon, William (Ruth) 1938- **CLC 38**
See also CA 33-36R; CANR 14, 32, 35; SATA 65

Harper, F. E. W.
See Harper, Frances Ellen Watkins

Harper, Frances E. W.
See Harper, Frances Ellen Watkins

Harper, Frances E. Watkins
See Harper, Frances Ellen Watkins

Harper, Frances Ellen
See Harper, Frances Ellen Watkins

Harper, Frances Ellen Watkins
1825-1911 **BLC 2; PC 21; TCLC 14**
See also AFAW 1, 2; BW 1, 3; CA 111; 125; CANR 79; DAM MULT, POET; DLB 50, 221; MAWW; RGAL 4

Harper, Michael S(teven) 1938- ... **CLC 7, 22**
See also AFAW 2; BW 1; CA 33-36R; 224; CAAE 224; CANR 24, 108; CP 2, 3, 4, 5, 6, 7; DLB 41; RGAL 4; TCLE 1:1

Harper, Mrs. F. E. W.
See Harper, Frances Ellen Watkins

Harpur, Charles 1813-1868 **NCLC 114**
See also DLB 230; RGEL 2

Harris, Christie
See Harris, Christie (Lucy) Irwin

Harris, Christie (Lucy) Irwin
1907-2002 **CLC 12**
See also CA 5-8R; CANR 6, 83; CLR 47; DLB 88; JRDA; MAICYA 1, 2; SAAS 10; SATA 6, 74; SATA-Essay 116

Harris, Frank 1856-1931 **TCLC 24**
See also CA 109; 150; CANR 80; DLB 156, 197; RGEL 2

Harris, George Washington
1814-1869 **NCLC 23, 165**
See also DLB 3, 11, 248; RGAL 4

Harris, Joel Chandler 1848-1908 **SSC 19; TCLC 2**
See also CA 104; 137; CANR 80; CLR 49; DLB 11, 23, 42, 78, 91; LAIT 2; MAICYA 1, 2; RGSF 2; SATA 100; WCH; YABC 1

Harris, John (Wyndham Parkes Lucas) Beynon 1903-1969
See Wyndham, John
See also CA 102; 89-92; CANR 84; SATA 118; SFW 4

Harris, MacDonald **CLC 9**
See Heiney, Donald (William)

Harris, Mark 1922- **CLC 19**
See also CA 5-8R; CAAS 3; CANR 2, 55, 83; CN 1, 2, 3, 4, 5, 6, 7; DLB 2; DLBY 1980

Harris, Norman **CLC 65**

Harris, (Theodore) Wilson 1921- **CLC 25, 159**
See also BRWS 5; BW 2, 3; CA 65-68; CAAS 16; CANR 11, 27, 69, 114; CD-WLB 3; CN 1, 2, 3, 4, 5, 6, 7; CP 1, 2, 3, 4, 5, 6, 7; DLB 117; EWL 3; MTCW 1; RGEL 2

Harrison, Barbara Grizzuti
1934-2002 **CLC 144**
See also CA 77-80; 205; CANR 15, 48; INT CANR-15

Harrison, Elizabeth (Allen) Cavanna
1909-2001
See Cavanna, Betty
See also CA 9-12R; 200; CANR 6, 27, 85, 104, 121; MAICYA 2; SATA 142; YAW

Harrison, Harry (Max) 1925- **CLC 42**
See also CA 1-4R; CANR 5, 21, 84; DLB 8; SATA 4; SCFW 2; SFW 4

Harrison, James (Thomas) 1937- **CLC 6, 14, 33, 66, 143; SSC 19**
See Harrison, Jim
See also CA 13-16R; CANR 8, 51, 79, 142; DLBY 1982; INT CANR-8

Harrison, Jim
See Harrison, James (Thomas)
See also AMWS 8; CN 5, 6; CP 1, 2, 3, 4, 5, 6, 7; RGAL 4; TCWW 2; TUS

Harrison, Kathryn 1961- **CLC 70, 151**
See also CA 144; CANR 68, 122

Harrison, Tony 1937- **CLC 43, 129**
See also BRWS 5; CA 65-68; CANR 44, 98; CBD; CD 5, 6; CP 2, 3, 4, 5, 6, 7; DLB 40, 245; MTCW 1; RGEL 2

Harriss, Will(ard Irvin) 1922- **CLC 34**
See also CA 111

Hart, Ellis
See Ellison, Harlan (Jay)

Hart, Josephine 1942(?)- **CLC 70**
See also CA 138; CANR 70, 149; CPW; DAM POP

Hart, Moss 1904-1961 **CLC 66**
See also CA 109; 89-92; CANR 84; DAM DRAM; DFS 1; DLB 7, 266; RGAL 4

Harte, (Francis) Bret(t)
1836(?)-1902 ... **SSC 8, 59; TCLC 1, 25; WLC 3**
See also AMWS 2; CA 104; 140; CANR 80; CDALB 1865-1917; DA; DA3; DAC; DAM MST; DLB 12, 64, 74, 79, 186; EXPS; LAIT 2; RGAL 4; RGSF 2; SATA 26; SSFS 3; TUS

Hartley, L(eslie) P(oles) 1895-1972 ... **CLC 2, 22**
See also BRWS 7; CA 45-48; 37-40R; CANR 33; CN 1; DLB 15, 139; EWL 3; HGG; MTCW 1, 2; MTFW 2005; RGEL 2; RGSF 2; SUFW 1

Hartmann, Geoffrey H. 1929- **CLC 27**
See also CA 117; 125; CANR 79; DLB 67

Hartmann, Sadakichi 1869-1944 ... **TCLC 73**
See also CA 157; DLB 54

Hartmann von Aue c. 1170-c. 1210 **CMLC 15**
See also CDWLB 2; DLB 138; RGWL 2, 3

Hartog, Jan de
See de Hartog, Jan

Haruf, Kent 1943- **CLC 34**
See also AAYA 44; CA 149; CANR 91, 131

Harvey, Caroline
See Trollope, Joanna

Harvey, Gabriel 1550(?)-1631 **LC 88**
See also DLB 167, 213, 281

Harwood, Ronald 1934- **CLC 32**
See also CA 1-4R; CANR 4, 55, 150; CBD;
CD 5, 6; DAM DRAM, MST; DLB 13

Hasegawa Tatsunosuke
See Futabatei, Shimei

Hasek, Jaroslav (Matej Frantisek)
1883-1923 **SSC 69; TCLC 4**
See also CA 104; 129; CDWLB 4; DLB
215; EW 9; EWL 3; MTCW 1, 2; RGSF
2; RGWL 2, 3

Hass, Robert 1941- ... **CLC 18, 39, 99; PC 16**
See also AMWS 6; CA 111; CANR 30, 50,
71; CP 3, 4, 5, 6, 7; DLB 105, 206; EWL
3; MAL 5; MTFW 2005; RGAL 4; SATA
94; TCLE 1:1

Hastings, Hudson
See Kuttner, Henry

Hastings, Selina **CLC 44**

Hathorne, John 1641-1717 **LC 38**

Hatteras, Amelia
See Mencken, H(enry) L(ouis)

Hatteras, Owen **TCLC 18**
See Mencken, H(enry) L(ouis); Nathan,
George Jean

Hauptmann, Gerhart (Johann Robert)
1862-1946 **SSC 37; TCLC 4**
See also CA 104; 153; CDWLB 2; DAM
DRAM; DLB 66, 118; EW 8; EWL 3;
RGSF 2; RGWL 2, 3; TWA

Havel, Vaclav 1936- **CLC 25, 58, 65, 123;
DC 6**
See also CA 104; CANR 36, 63, 124; CD-
WLB 4; CWW 2; DA3; DAM DRAM;
DFS 10; DLB 232; EWL 3; LMFS 2;
MTCW 1, 2; MTFW 2005; RGWL 3

Haviaras, Stratis **CLC 33**
See Chaviaras, Strates

Hawes, Stephen 1475(?)-1529(?) **LC 17**
See also DLB 132; RGEL 2

Hawkes, John (Clendennin Burne, Jr.)
1925-1998 .. **CLC 1, 2, 3, 4, 7, 9, 14, 15,
27, 49**
See also BPFB 2; CA 1-4R; 167; CANR 2,
47, 64; CN 1, 2, 3, 4, 5, 6; DLB 2, 7, 227;
DLBY 1980, 1998; EWL 3; MAL 5;
MTCW 1, 2; MTFW 2005; RGAL 4

Hawking, S. W.
See Hawking, Stephen W(illiam)

Hawking, Stephen W(illiam) 1942- . **CLC 63,
105**
See also AAYA 13; BEST 89:1; CA 126;
129; CANR 48, 115; CPW; DA3; MTCW
2; MTFW 2005

Hawkins, Anthony Hope
See Hope, Anthony

Hawthorne, Julian 1846-1934 **TCLC 25**
See also CA 165; HGG

Hawthorne, Nathaniel 1804-1864 ... **NCLC 2,
10, 17, 23, 39, 79, 95, 158, 171; SSC 3,
29, 39, 89; WLC 3**
See also AAYA 18; AMW; AMWC 1;
AMWR 1; BPFB 2; BYA 3; CDALB
1640-1865; CLR 103; DA; DA3; DAB;
DAC; DAM MST, NOV; DLB 1, 74, 183,
223, 269; EXPN; EXPS; GL 2; HGG;
LAIT 1; NFS 1, 20; RGAL 4; RGSF 2;
SSFS 5, 7, 11, 15; SUFW 1; TUS; WCH;
YABC 2

Hawthorne, Sophia Peabody
1809-1871 **NCLC 150**
See also DLB 183, 239

Haxton, Josephine Ayres 1921-
See Douglas, Ellen
See also CA 115; CANR 41, 83

Hayaseca y Eizaguirre, Jorge
See Echegaray (y Eizaguirre), Jose (Maria
Waldo)

Hayashi, Fumiko 1904-1951 **TCLC 27**
See Hayashi Fumiko
See also CA 161

Hayashi Fumiko
See Hayashi, Fumiko
See also DLB 180; EWL 3

Haycraft, Anna 1932-2005
See Ellis, Alice Thomas
See also CA 122; 237; CANR 90, 141;
MTCW 2; MTFW 2005

Hayden, Robert E(arl) 1913-1980 **BLC 2;
CLC 5, 9, 14, 37; PC 6**
See also AFAW 1, 2; AMWS 2; BW 1, 3;
CA 69-72; 97-100; CABS 2; CANR 24,
75, 82; CDALB 1941-1968; CP 1, 2, 3;
DA; DAC; DAM MST, MULT, POET;
DLB 5, 76; EWL 3; EXPP; MAL 5;
MTCW 1, 2; PFS 1; RGAL 4; SATA 19;
SATA-Obit 26; WP

Haydon, Benjamin Robert
1786-1846 **NCLC 146**
See also DLB 110

Hayek, F(riedrich) A(ugust von)
1899-1992 **TCLC 109**
See also CA 93-96; 137; CANR 20; MTCW
1, 2

Hayford, J(oseph) E(phraim) Casely
See Casely-Hayford, J(oseph) E(phraim)

Hayman, Ronald 1932- **CLC 44**
See also CA 25-28R; CANR 18, 50, 88; CD
5, 6; DLB 155

Hayne, Paul Hamilton 1830-1886 . **NCLC 94**
See also DLB 3, 64, 79, 248; RGAL 4

Hays, Mary 1760-1843 **NCLC 114**
See also DLB 142, 158; RGEL 2

Haywood, Eliza (Fowler)
1693(?)-1756 **LC 1, 44**
See also DLB 39; RGEL 2

Hazlitt, William 1778-1830 **NCLC 29, 82**
See also BRW 4; DLB 110, 158; RGEL 2;
TEA

Hazzard, Shirley 1931- **CLC 18, 218**
See also CA 9-12R; CANR 4, 70, 127; CN
1, 2, 3, 4, 5, 6, 7; DLB 289; DLBY 1982;
MTCW 1

Head, Bessie 1937-1986 **BLC 2; CLC 25,
67; SSC 52**
See also AFW; BW 2, 3; CA 29-32R; 119;
CANR 25, 82; CDWLB 3; CN 1, 2, 3, 4;
DA3; DAM MULT; DLB 117, 225; EWL
3; EXPS; FL 1:6; FW; MTCW 1, 2;
MTFW 2005; RGSF 2; SSFS 5, 13; WLIT
2; WWE 1

Headon, (Nicky) Topper 1956(?)- **CLC 30**

Heaney, Seamus (Justin) 1939- **CLC 5, 7,
14, 25, 37, 74, 91, 171, 225; PC 18;
WLCS**
See also AAYA 61; BRWR 1; BRWS 2; CA
85-88; CANR 25, 48, 75, 91, 128; CD-
BLB 1960 to Present; CP 1, 2, 3, 4, 5, 6,
7; DA3; DAB; DAM POET; DLB 40;
DLBY 1995; EWL 3; EXPP; MTCW 1,
2; MTFW 2005; PAB; PFS 2, 5, 8, 17;
RGEL 2; TEA; WLIT 4

Hearn, (Patricio) Lafcadio (Tessima Carlos)
1850-1904 **TCLC 9**
See also CA 105; 166; DLB 12, 78, 189;
HGG; MAL 5; RGAL 4

Hearne, Samuel 1745-1792 **LC 95**
See also DLB 99

Hearne, Vicki 1946-2001 **CLC 56**
See also CA 139; 201

Hearon, Shelby 1931- **CLC 63**
See also AITN 2; AMWS 8; CA 25-28R;
CANR 18, 48, 103, 146; CSW

Heat-Moon, William Least **CLC 29**
See Trogdon, William (Lewis)
See also AAYA 9

Hebbel, Friedrich 1813-1863 . **DC 21; NCLC
43**
See also CDWLB 2; DAM DRAM; DLB
129; EW 6; RGWL 2, 3

Hebert, Anne 1916-2000 **CLC 4, 13, 29**
See also CA 85-88; 187; CANR 69, 126;
CCA 1; CWP; CWW 2; DA3; DAC;
DAM MST, POET; DLB 68; EWL 3; GFL
1789 to the Present; MTCW 1, 2; MTFW
2005; PFS 20

Hecht, Anthony (Evan) 1923-2004 **CLC 8,
13, 19; PC 70**
See also AMWS 10; CA 9-12R; 232; CANR
6, 108; CP 1, 2, 3, 4, 5, 6, 7; DAM POET;
DLB 5, 169; EWL 3; PFS 6; WP

Hecht, Ben 1894-1964 **CLC 8; TCLC 101**
See also CA 85-88; DFS 9; DLB 7, 9, 25,
26, 28, 86; FANT; IDFW 3, 4; RGAL 4

Hedayat, Sadeq 1903-1951 **TCLC 21**
See also CA 120; EWL 3; RGSF 2

Hegel, Georg Wilhelm Friedrich
1770-1831 **NCLC 46, 151**
See also DLB 90; TWA

Heidegger, Martin 1889-1976 **CLC 24**
See also CA 81-84; 65-68; CANR 34; DLB
296; MTCW 1, 2; MTFW 2005

Heidenstam, (Carl Gustaf) Verner von
1859-1940 **TCLC 5**
See also CA 104

Heidi Louise
See Erdrich, Louise

Heifner, Jack 1946- **CLC 11**
See also CA 105; CANR 47

Heijermans, Herman 1864-1924 **TCLC 24**
See also CA 123; EWL 3

Heilbrun, Carolyn G(old)
1926-2003 **CLC 25, 173**
See Cross, Amanda
See also CA 45-48; 220; CANR 1, 28, 58,
94; FW

Hein, Christoph 1944- **CLC 154**
See also CA 158; CANR 108; CDWLB 2;
CWW 2; DLB 124

Heine, Heinrich 1797-1856 **NCLC 4, 54,
147; PC 25**
See also CDWLB 2; DLB 90; EW 5; RGWL
2, 3; TWA

Heinemann, Larry (Curtiss) 1944- .. **CLC 50**
See also CA 110; CAAS 21; CANR 31, 81;
DLBD 9; INT CANR-31

Heiney, Donald (William) 1921-1993
See Harris, MacDonald
See also CA 1-4R; 142; CANR 3, 58; FANT

Heinlein, Robert A(nson) 1907-1988 . **CLC 1,
3, 8, 14, 26, 55; SSC 55**
See also AAYA 17; BPFB 2; BYA 4, 13;
CA 1-4R; 125; CANR 1, 20, 53; CLR 75;
CN 1, 2, 3, 4; CPW; DA3; DAM POP;
DLB 8; EXPS; JRDA; LAIT 5; LMFS 2;
MAICYA 1, 2; MTCW 1, 2; MTFW 2005;
RGAL 4; SATA 9, 69; SATA-Obit 56;
SCFW 1, 2; SFW 4; SSFS 7; YAW

Helforth, John
See Doolittle, Hilda

Heliodorus fl. 3rd cent. - **CMLC 52**
See also WLIT 8

Hellenhofferu, Vojtech Kapristian z
See Hasek, Jaroslav (Matej Frantisek)

Heller, Joseph 1923-1999 . **CLC 1, 3, 5, 8, 11,
36, 63; TCLC 131, 151; WLC 3**
See also AAYA 24; AITN 1; AMWS 4;
BPFB 2; BYA 1; CA 5-8R; 187; CABS 1;
CANR 8, 42, 66, 126; CN 1, 2, 3, 4, 5, 6;

CPW; DA; DA3; DAB; DAC; DAM MST,
NOV, POP; DLB 2, 28, 227; DLBY 1980,
2002; EWL 3; EXPN; INT CANR-8;
LAIT 4; MAL 5; MTCW 1, 2; MTFW
2005; NFS 1; RGAL 4; TUS; YAW

Hellman, Lillian (Florence)
1906-1984 .. **CLC 2, 4, 8, 14, 18, 34, 44, 52; DC 1; TCLC 119**
See also AAYA 47; AITN 1, 2; AMWS 1;
CA 13-16R; 112; CAD; CANR 33; CWD;
DA3; DAM DRAM; DFS 1, 3, 14; DLB
7, 228; DLBY 1984; EWL 3; FL 1:6; FW;
LAIT 3; MAL 5; MAWW; MTCW 1, 2;
MTFW 2005; RGAL 4; TUS

Helprin, Mark 1947- **CLC 7, 10, 22, 32**
See also CA 81-84; CANR 47, 64, 124;
CDALBS; CN 7; CPW; DA3; DAM NOV,
POP; DLBY 1985; FANT; MAL 5;
MTCW 1, 2; MTFW 2005; SUFW 2

Helvetius, Claude-Adrien 1715-1771 .. **LC 26**
See also DLB 313

Helyar, Jane Penelope Josephine 1933-
See Poole, Josephine
See also CA 21-24R; CANR 10, 26; CWRI
5; SATA 82, 138; SATA-Essay 138

Hemans, Felicia 1793-1835 **NCLC 29, 71**
See also DLB 96; RGEL 2

Hemingway, Ernest (Miller)
1899-1961 **CLC 1, 3, 6, 8, 10, 13, 19, 30, 34, 39, 41, 44, 50, 61, 80; SSC 1, 25, 36, 40, 63; TCLC 115; WLC 3**
See also AAYA 19; AMW; AMWC 1;
AMWR 1; BPFB 2; BYA 2, 3, 13, 15; CA
77-80; CANR 34; CDALB 1917-1929;
DA; DA3; DAB; DAC; DAM MST, NOV;
DLB 4, 9, 102, 210, 308, 316; DLBD 1,
15, 16; DLBY 1981, 1987, 1996, 1998;
EWL 3; EXPN; EXPS; LAIT 3, 4; LATS
1:1; MAL 5; MTCW 1, 2; MTFW 2005;
NFS 1, 5, 6, 14; RGAL 4; RGSF 2; SSFS
17; TUS; WYA

Hempel, Amy 1951- **CLC 39**
See also CA 118; 137; CANR 70; DA3;
DLB 218; EXPS; MTCW 2; MTFW 2005;
SSFS 2

Henderson, F. C.
See Mencken, H(enry) L(ouis)

Henderson, Sylvia
See Ashton-Warner, Sylvia (Constance)

Henderson, Zenna (Chlarson)
1917-1983 **SSC 29**
See also CA 1-4R; 133; CANR 1, 84; DLB
8; SATA 5; SFW 4

Henkin, Joshua **CLC 119**
See also CA 161

Henley, Beth **CLC 23; DC 6, 14**
See Henley, Elizabeth Becker
See also AAYA 70; CABS 3; CAD; CD 5,
6; CSW; CWD; DFS 2, 21; DLBY 1986;
FW

Henley, Elizabeth Becker 1952-
See Henley, Beth
See also CA 107; CANR 32, 73, 140; DA3;
DAM DRAM, MST; MTCW 1, 2; MTFW
2005

Henley, William Ernest 1849-1903 .. **TCLC 8**
See also CA 105; 234; DLB 19; RGEL 2

Hennissart, Martha 1929-
See Lathen, Emma
See also CA 85-88; CANR 64

Henry VIII 1491-1547 **LC 10**
See also DLB 132

Henry, O. . **SSC 5, 49; TCLC 1, 19; WLC 3**
See Porter, William Sydney
See also AAYA 41; AMWS 2; EXPS; MAL
5; RGAL 4; RGSF 2; SSFS 2, 18; TCWW
1, 2

Henry, Patrick 1736-1799 **LC 25**
See also LAIT 1

Henryson, Robert 1430(?)-1506(?) **LC 20, 110; PC 65**
See also BRWS 7; DLB 146; RGEL 2

Henschke, Alfred
See Klabund

Henson, Lance 1944- **NNAL**
See also CA 146; DLB 175

Hentoff, Nat(han Irving) 1925- **CLC 26**
See also AAYA 4, 42; BYA 6; CA 1-4R;
CAAS 6; CANR 5, 25, 77, 114; CLR 1,
52; INT CANR-25; JRDA; MAICYA 1,
2; SATA 42, 69, 133; SATA-Brief 27;
WYA; YAW

Heppenstall, (John) Rayner
1911-1981 **CLC 10**
See also CA 1-4R; 103; CANR 29; CN 1,
2; CP 1, 2, 3; EWL 3

Heraclitus c. 540B.C.-c. 450B.C. ... **CMLC 22**
See also DLB 176

Herbert, Frank (Patrick)
1920-1986 **CLC 12, 23, 35, 44, 85**
See also AAYA 21; BPFB 2; BYA 4, 14;
CA 53-56; 118; CANR 5, 43; CDALBS;
CPW; DAM POP; DLB 8; INT CANR-5;
LAIT 5; MTCW 1, 2; MTFW 2005; NFS
17; SATA 9, 37; SATA-Obit 47; SCFW 1,
2; SFW 4; YAW

Herbert, George 1593-1633 . **LC 24, 121; PC 4**
See also BRW 2; BRWR 2; CDBLB Before
1660; DAB; DAM POET; DLB 126;
EXPP; RGEL 2; TEA; WP

Herbert, Zbigniew 1924-1998 **CLC 9, 43; PC 50; TCLC 168**
See also CA 89-92; 169; CANR 36, 74; CD-
WLB 4; CWW 2; DAM POET; DLB 232;
EWL 3; MTCW 1; PFS 22

Herbst, Josephine (Frey)
1897-1969 **CLC 34**
See also CA 5-8R; 25-28R; DLB 9

Herder, Johann Gottfried von
1744-1803 **NCLC 8**
See also DLB 97; EW 4; TWA

Heredia, Jose Maria 1803-1839 **HLCS 2**
See also LAW

Hergesheimer, Joseph 1880-1954 ... **TCLC 11**
See also CA 109; 194; DLB 102, 9; RGAL
4

Herlihy, James Leo 1927-1993 **CLC 6**
See also CA 1-4R; 143; CAD; CANR 2;
CN 1, 2, 3, 4, 5

Herman, William
See Bierce, Ambrose (Gwinett)

Hermogenes fl. c. 175- **CMLC 6**

Hernandez, Jose 1834-1886 **NCLC 17**
See also LAW; RGWL 2, 3; WLIT 1

Herodotus c. 484B.C.-c. 420B.C. .. **CMLC 17**
See also AW 1; CDWLB 1; DLB 176;
RGWL 2, 3; TWA; WLIT 8

Herrick, Robert 1591-1674 **LC 13; PC 9**
See also BRW 2; BRWC 2; DA; DAB;
DAC; DAM MST, POP; DLB 126; EXPP;
PFS 13; RGAL 4; RGEL 2; TEA; WP

Herring, Guilles
See Somerville, Edith Oenone

Herriot, James 1916-1995 **CLC 12**
See Wight, James Alfred
See also AAYA 1, 54; BPFB 2; CA 148;
CANR 40; CLR 80; CPW; DAM POP;
LAIT 3; MAICYA 2; MAICYAS 1;
MTCW 2; SATA 86, 135; TEA; YAW

Herris, Violet
See Hunt, Violet

Herrmann, Dorothy 1941- **CLC 44**
See also CA 107

Herrmann, Taffy
See Herrmann, Dorothy

Hersey, John (Richard) 1914-1993 **CLC 1, 2, 7, 9, 40, 81, 97**
See also AAYA 29; BPFB 2; CA 17-20R;
140; CANR 33; CDALBS; CN 1, 2, 3, 4,
5; CPW; DAM POP; DLB 6, 185, 278,
299; MAL 5; MTCW 1, 2; MTFW 2005;
RGHL; SATA 25; SATA-Obit 76; TUS

Herzen, Aleksandr Ivanovich
1812-1870 **NCLC 10, 61**
See Herzen, Alexander

Herzen, Alexander
See Herzen, Aleksandr Ivanovich
See also DLB 277

Herzl, Theodor 1860-1904 **TCLC 36**
See also CA 168

Herzog, Werner 1942- **CLC 16**
See also CA 89-92

Hesiod c. 8th cent. B.C.- **CMLC 5**
See also AW 1; DLB 176; RGWL 2, 3;
WLIT 8

Hesse, Hermann 1877-1962 ... **CLC 1, 2, 3, 6, 11, 17, 25, 69; SSC 9, 49; TCLC 148; WLC 3**
See also AAYA 43; BPFB 2; CA 17-18;
CAP 2; CDWLB 2; DA; DA3; DAB;
DAC; DAM MST, NOV; DLB 66; EW 9;
EWL 3; EXPN; LAIT 1; MTCW 1, 2;
MTFW 2005; NFS 6, 15; RGWL 2, 3;
SATA 50; TWA

Hewes, Cady
See De Voto, Bernard (Augustine)

Heyen, William 1940- **CLC 13, 18**
See also CA 33-36R, 220; CAAE 220;
CAAS 9; CANR 98; CP 3, 4, 5, 6, 7; DLB
5; RGHL

Heyerdahl, Thor 1914-2002 **CLC 26**
See also CA 5-8R; 207; CANR 5, 22, 66,
73; LAIT 4; MTCW 1, 2; MTFW 2005;
SATA 2, 52

Heym, Georg (Theodor Franz Arthur)
1887-1912 **TCLC 9**
See also CA 106; 181

Heym, Stefan 1913-2001 **CLC 41**
See also CA 9-12R; 203; CANR 4; CWW
2; DLB 69; EWL 3

Heyse, Paul (Johann Ludwig von)
1830-1914 **TCLC 8**
See also CA 104; 209; DLB 129

Heyward, (Edwin) DuBose
1885-1940 **HR 1:2; TCLC 59**
See also CA 108; 157; DLB 7, 9, 45, 249;
MAL 5; SATA 21

Heywood, John 1497(?)-1580(?) **LC 65**
See also DLB 136; RGEL 2

Heywood, Thomas 1573(?)-1641 **LC 111**
See also DAM DRAM; DLB 62; LMFS 1;
RGEL 2; TEA

Hibbert, Eleanor Alice Burford
1906-1993 **CLC 7**
See Holt, Victoria
See also BEST 90:4; CA 17-20R; 140;
CANR 9, 28, 59; CMW 4; CPW; DAM
POP; MTCW 2; MTFW 2005; RHW;
SATA 2; SATA-Obit 74

Hichens, Robert (Smythe)
1864-1950 **TCLC 64**
See also CA 162; DLB 153; HGG; RHW;
SUFW

Higgins, Aidan 1927- **SSC 68**
See also CA 9-12R; CANR 70, 115, 148;
CN 1, 2, 3, 4, 5, 6, 7; DLB 14

Higgins, George V(incent)
1939-1999 **CLC 4, 7, 10, 18**
See also BPFB 2; CA 77-80; 186; CAAS 9;
CANR 17, 51, 89, 96; CMW 4; CN 2, 3,
4, 5, 6; DLB 2; DLBY 1981, 1998; INT
CANR-17; MSW; MTCW 1

Higginson, Thomas Wentworth
1823-1911 **TCLC 36**
See also CA 162; DLB 1, 64, 243

Higgonet, Margaret ed. CLC 65

Highet, Helen
 See MacInnes, Helen (Clark)

Highsmith, (Mary) Patricia
 1921-1995 CLC 2, 4, 14, 42, 102
 See Morgan, Claire
 See also AAYA 48; BRWS 5; CA 1-4R; 147;
 CANR 1, 20, 48, 62, 108; CMW 4; CN 1,
 2, 3, 4, 5; CPW; DA3; DAM NOV, POP;
 DLB 306; MSW; MTCW 1, 2; MTFW
 2005

Highwater, Jamake (Mamake)
 1942(?)-2001 CLC 12
 See also AAYA 7, 69; BPFB 2; BYA 4; CA
 65-68; 199; CAAS 7; CANR 10, 34, 84;
 CLR 17; CWRI 5; DLB 52; DLBY 1985;
 JRDA; MAICYA 1, 2; SATA 32, 69;
 SATA-Brief 30

Highway, Tomson 1951- CLC 92; NNAL
 See also CA 151; CANR 75; CCA 1; CD 5,
 6; CN 7; DAC; DAM MULT; DFS 2;
 MTCW 2

Hijuelos, Oscar 1951- CLC 65; HLC 1
 See also AAYA 25; AMWS 8; BEST 90:1;
 CA 123; CANR 50, 75, 125; CPW; DA3;
 DAM MULT, POP; DLB 145; HW 1, 2;
 LLW; MAL 5; MTCW 2; MTFW 2005;
 NFS 17; RGAL 4; WLIT 1

Hikmet, Nazim 1902-1963 CLC 40
 See Nizami of Ganja
 See also CA 141; 93-96; EWL 3; WLIT 6

Hildegard von Bingen 1098-1179 . CMLC 20
 See also DLB 148

Hildesheimer, Wolfgang 1916-1991 .. CLC 49
 See also CA 101; 135; DLB 69, 124; EWL
 3; RGHL

Hill, Geoffrey (William) 1932- CLC 5, 8,
 18, 45
 See also BRWS 5; CA 81-84; CANR 21,
 89; CDBLB 1960 to Present; CP 1, 2, 3,
 4, 5, 6, 7; DAM POET; DLB 40; EWL 3;
 MTCW 1; RGEL 2; RGHL

Hill, George Roy 1921-2002 CLC 26
 See also CA 110; 122; 213

Hill, John
 See Koontz, Dean R.

Hill, Susan (Elizabeth) 1942- CLC 4, 113
 See also CA 33-36R; CANR 29, 69, 129;
 CN 2, 3, 4, 5, 6, 7; DAB; DAM MST,
 NOV; DLB 14, 139; HGG; MTCW 1;
 RHW

Hillard, Asa G. III CLC 70

Hillerman, Tony 1925- CLC 62, 170
 See also AAYA 40; BEST 89:1; BPFB 2;
 CA 29-32R; CANR 21, 42, 65, 97, 134;
 CMW 4; CPW; DA3; DAM POP; DLB
 206, 306; MAL 5; MSW; MTCW 2;
 MTFW 2005; RGAL 4; SATA 6; TCWW
 2; YAW

Hillesum, Etty 1914-1943 TCLC 49
 See also CA 137; RGHL

Hilliard, Noel (Harvey) 1929-1996 ... CLC 15
 See also CA 9-12R; CANR 7, 69; CN 1, 2,
 3, 4, 5, 6

Hillis, Rick 1956- CLC 66
 See also CA 134

Hilton, James 1900-1954 TCLC 21
 See also CA 108; 169; DLB 34, 77; FANT;
 SATA 34

Hilton, Walter (?)-1396 CMLC 58
 See also DLB 146; RGEL 2

Himes, Chester (Bomar) 1909-1984 .. BLC 2;
 CLC 2, 4, 7, 18, 58, 108; TCLC 139
 See also AFAW 2; BPFB 2; BW 2; CA 25-
 28R; 114; CANR 22, 89; CMW 4; CN 1,
 2, 3; DAM MULT; DLB 2, 76, 143, 226;
 EWL 3; MAL 5; MSW; MTCW 1, 2;
 MTFW 2005; RGAL 4

Himmelfarb, Gertrude 1922- CLC 202
 See also CA 49-52; CANR 28, 66, 102

Hinde, Thomas CLC 6, 11
 See Chitty, Thomas Willes
 See also CN 1, 2, 3, 4, 5, 6; EWL 3

Hine, (William) Daryl 1936- CLC 15
 See also CA 1-4R; CAAS 15; CANR 1, 20;
 CP 1, 2, 3, 4, 5, 6, 7; DLB 60

Hinkson, Katharine Tynan
 See Tynan, Katharine

Hinojosa(-Smith), Rolando (R.)
 1929- ... HLC 1
 See Hinojosa-Smith, Rolando
 See also CA 131; CAAS 16; CANR 62;
 DAM MULT; DLB 82; HW 1, 2; LLW;
 MTCW 2; MTFW 2005; RGAL 4

Hinton, S(usan) E(loise) 1950- .. CLC 30, 111
 See also AAYA 2, 33; BPFB 2; BYA 2, 3;
 CA 81-84; CANR 32, 62, 92, 133;
 CDALBS; CLR 3, 23; CPW; DA; DA3;
 DAB; DAC; DAM MST, NOV; JRDA;
 LAIT 5; MAICYA 1, 2; MTCW 1, 2;
 MTFW 2005 !**; NFS 5, 9, 15, 16; SATA
 19, 58, 115, 160; WYA; YAW

Hippius, Zinaida (Nikolaevna) TCLC 9
 See Gippius, Zinaida (Nikolaevna)
 See also DLB 295; EWL 3

Hiraoka, Kimitake 1925-1970
 See Mishima, Yukio
 See also CA 97-100; 29-32R; DA3; DAM
 DRAM; GLL 1; MTCW 1, 2

Hirsch, E.D., Jr. 1928- CLC 79
 See also CA 25-28R; CANR 27, 51, 146;
 DLB 67; INT CANR-27; MTCW 1

Hirsch, Edward 1950- CLC 31, 50
 See also CA 104; CANR 20, 42, 102; CP 6,
 7; DLB 120; PFS 22

Hirsch, Eric Donald, Jr.
 See Hirsch, E.D., Jr.

Hitchcock, Alfred (Joseph)
 1899-1980 CLC 16
 See also AAYA 22; CA 159; 97-100; SATA
 27; SATA-Obit 24

Hitchens, Christopher (Eric)
 1949- CLC 157
 See also CA 152; CANR 89

Hitler, Adolf 1889-1945 TCLC 53
 See also CA 117; 147

Hoagland, Edward (Morley) 1932- .. CLC 28
 See also ANW; CA 1-4R; CANR 2, 31, 57,
 107; CN 1, 2, 3, 4, 5, 6, 7; DLB 6; SATA
 51; TCWW 2

Hoban, Russell (Conwell) 1925- ... CLC 7, 25
 See also BPFB 2; CA 5-8R; CANR 23, 37,
 66, 114, 138; CLR 3, 69; CN 4, 5, 6, 7;
 CWRI 5; DAM NOV; DLB 52; FANT;
 MAICYA 1, 2; MTCW 1, 2; MTFW 2005;
 SATA 1, 40, 78, 136; SFW 4; SUFW 2;
 TCLE 1:1

Hobbes, Thomas 1588-1679 LC 36
 See also DLB 151, 252, 281; RGEL 2

Hobbs, Perry
 See Blackmur, R(ichard) P(almer)

Hobson, Laura Z(ametkin)
 1900-1986 CLC 7, 25
 See also BPFB 2; CA 17-20R; 118; CANR
 55; CN 1, 2, 3, 4; DLB 28; SATA 52

Hoccleve, Thomas c. 1368-c. 1437 LC 75
 See also DLB 146; RGEL 2

Hoch, Edward D(entinger) 1930-
 See Queen, Ellery
 See also CA 29-32R; CANR 11, 27, 51, 97;
 CMW 4; DLB 306; SFW 4

Hochhuth, Rolf 1931- CLC 4, 11, 18
 See also CA 5-8R; CANR 33, 75, 136;
 CWW 2; DAM DRAM; DLB 124; EWL
 3; MTCW 1, 2; MTFW 2005; RGHL

Hochman, Sandra 1936- CLC 3, 8
 See also CA 5-8R; CP 1, 2, 3, 4, 5; DLB 5

Hochwaelder, Fritz 1911-1986 CLC 36
 See Hochwalder, Fritz
 See also CA 29-32R; 120; CANR 42; DAM
 DRAM; MTCW 1; RGWL 3

Hochwalder, Fritz
 See Hochwaelder, Fritz
 See also EWL 3; RGWL 2

Hocking, Mary (Eunice) 1921- CLC 13
 See also CA 101; CANR 18, 40

Hodgins, Jack 1938- CLC 23
 See also CA 93-96; CN 4, 5, 6, 7; DLB 60

Hodgson, William Hope
 1877(?)-1918 TCLC 13
 See also CA 111; 164; CMW 4; DLB 70,
 153, 156, 178; HGG; MTCW 2; SFW 4;
 SUFW 1

Hoeg, Peter 1957- CLC 95, 156
 See also CA 151; CANR 75; CMW 4; DA3;
 DLB 214; EWL 3; MTCW 2; MTFW
 2005; NFS 17; RGWL 3; SSFS 18

Hoffman, Alice 1952- CLC 51
 See also AAYA 37; AMWS 10; CA 77-80;
 CANR 34, 66, 100, 138; CN 4, 5, 6, 7;
 CPW; DAM NOV; DLB 292; MAL 5;
 MTCW 1, 2; MTFW 2005; TCLE 1:1

Hoffman, Daniel (Gerard) 1923- . CLC 6, 13,
 23
 See also CA 1-4R; CANR 4, 142; CP 1, 2,
 3, 4, 5, 6, 7; DLB 5; TCLE 1:1

Hoffman, Eva 1945- CLC 182
 See also CA 132; CANR 146

Hoffman, Stanley 1944- CLC 5
 See also CA 77-80

Hoffman, William 1925- CLC 141
 See also CA 21-24R; CANR 9, 103; CSW;
 DLB 234; TCLE 1:1

Hoffman, William M.
 See Hoffman, William M(oses)
 See also CAD; CD 5, 6

Hoffman, William M(oses) 1939- CLC 40
 See Hoffman, William M.
 See also CA 57-60; CANR 11, 71

Hoffmann, E(rnst) T(heodor) A(madeus)
 1776-1822 NCLC 2; SSC 13, 92
 See also CDWLB 2; DLB 90; EW 5; GL 2;
 RGSF 2; RGWL 2, 3; SATA 27; SUFW
 1; WCH

Hofmann, Gert 1931-1993 CLC 54
 See also CA 128; CANR 145; EWL 3;
 RGHL

Hofmannsthal, Hugo von 1874-1929 ... DC 4;
 TCLC 11
 See also CA 106; 153; CDWLB 2; DAM
 DRAM; DFS 17; DLB 81, 118; EW 9;
 EWL 3; RGWL 2, 3

Hogan, Linda 1947- CLC 73; NNAL; PC
 35
 See also AMWS 4; ANW; BYA 12; CA 120,
 226; CANR 45, 73, 129; CAAE 226;
 CWP; DAM MULT; DLB 175; SATA
 132; TCWW 2

Hogarth, Charles
 See Creasey, John

Hogarth, Emmett
 See Polonsky, Abraham (Lincoln)

Hogarth, William 1697-1764 LC 112
 See also AAYA 56

Hogg, James 1770-1835 NCLC 4, 109
 See also BRWS 10; DLB 93, 116, 159; GL
 2; HGG; RGEL 2; SUFW 1

Holbach, Paul-Henri Thiry
 1723-1789 LC 14
 See also DLB 313

Holberg, Ludvig 1684-1754 LC 6
 See also DLB 300; RGWL 2, 3

Holcroft, Thomas 1745-1809 NCLC 85
 See also DLB 39, 89, 158; RGEL 2

Holden, Ursula 1921- CLC 18
 See also CA 101; CAAS 8; CANR 22

Holderlin, (Johann Christian) Friedrich
1770-1843 **NCLC 16; PC 4**
See also CDWLB 2; DLB 90; EW 5; RGWL
2, 3

Holdstock, Robert
See Holdstock, Robert P.

Holdstock, Robert P. 1948- **CLC 39**
See also CA 131; CANR 81; DLB 261;
FANT; HGG; SFW 4; SUFW 2

Holinshed, Raphael fl. 1580- **LC 69**
See also DLB 167; RGEL 2

Holland, Isabelle (Christian)
1920-2002 **CLC 21**
See also AAYA 11, 64; CA 21-24R; 205;
CAAE 181; CANR 10, 25, 47; CLR 57;
CWRI 5; JRDA; LAIT 4; MAICYA 1, 2;
SATA 8, 70; SATA-Essay 103; SATA-Obit
132; WYA

Holland, Marcus
See Caldwell, (Janet Miriam) Taylor
(Holland)

Hollander, John 1929- **CLC 2, 5, 8, 14**
See also CA 1-4R; CANR 1, 52, 136; CP 1,
2, 3, 4, 5, 6, 7; DLB 5; MAL 5; SATA 13

Hollander, Paul
See Silverberg, Robert

Holleran, Andrew **CLC 38**
See Garber, Eric
See also CA 144; GLL 1

Holley, Marietta 1836(?)-1926 **TCLC 99**
See also CA 118; DLB 11; FL 1:3

Hollinghurst, Alan 1954- **CLC 55, 91**
See also BRWS 10; CA 114; CN 5, 6, 7;
DLB 207, 326; GLL 1

Hollis, Jim
See Summers, Hollis (Spurgeon, Jr.)

Holly, Buddy 1936-1959 **TCLC 65**
See also CA 213

Holmes, Gordon
See Shiel, M(atthew) P(hipps)

Holmes, John
See Souster, (Holmes) Raymond

Holmes, John Clellon 1926-1988 **CLC 56**
See also BG 1:2; CA 9-12R; 125; CANR 4;
CN 1, 2, 3, 4; DLB 16, 237

Holmes, Oliver Wendell, Jr.
1841-1935 **TCLC 77**
See also CA 114; 186

Holmes, Oliver Wendell
1809-1894 **NCLC 14, 81; PC 71**
See also AMWS 1; CDALB 1640-1865;
DLB 1, 189, 235; EXPP; PFS 24; RGAL
4; SATA 34

Holmes, Raymond
See Souster, (Holmes) Raymond

Holt, Victoria
See Hibbert, Eleanor Alice Burford
See also BPFB 2

Holub, Miroslav 1923-1998 **CLC 4**
See also CA 21-24R; 169; CANR 10; CD-
WLB 4; CWW 2; DLB 232; EWL 3;
RGWL 3

Holz, Detlev
See Benjamin, Walter

Homer c. 8th cent. B.C.- **CMLC 1, 16, 61;
PC 23; WLCS**
See also AW 1; CDWLB 1; DA; DA3;
DAB; DAC; DAM MST, POET; DLB
176; EFS 1; LAIT 1; LMFS 1; RGWL 2,
3; TWA; WLIT 8; WP

Hongo, Garrett Kaoru 1951- **PC 23**
See also CA 133; CAAS 22; CP 5, 6, 7;
DLB 120, 312; EWL 3; EXPP; RGAL 4

Honig, Edwin 1919- **CLC 33**
See also CA 5-8R; CAAS 8; CANR 4, 45,
144; CP 1, 2, 3, 4, 5, 6, 7; DLB 5

Hood, Hugh (John Blagdon) 1928- . **CLC 15,
28; SSC 42**
See also CA 49-52; CAAS 17; CANR 1,
33, 87; CN 1, 2, 3, 4, 5, 6, 7; DLB 53;
RGSF 2

Hood, Thomas 1799-1845 **NCLC 16**
See also BRW 4; DLB 96; RGEL 2

Hooker, (Peter) Jeremy 1941- **CLC 43**
See also CA 77-80; CANR 22; CP 2, 3, 4,
5, 6, 7; DLB 40

Hooker, Richard 1554-1600 **LC 95**
See also BRW 1; DLB 132; RGEL 2

hooks, bell 1952(?)- **CLC 94**
See also BW 2; CA 143; CANR 87, 126;
DLB 246; MTCW 2; MTFW 2005; SATA
115, 170

Hope, A(lec) D(erwent) 1907-2000 **CLC 3,
51; PC 56**
See also BRWS 7; CA 21-24R; 188; CANR
33, 74; CP 1, 2, 3, 4, 5; DLB 289; EWL
3; MTCW 1, 2; MTFW 2005; PFS 8;
RGEL 2

Hope, Anthony 1863-1933 **TCLC 83**
See also CA 157; DLB 153, 156; RGEL 2;
RHW

Hope, Brian
See Creasey, John

Hope, Christopher (David Tully)
1944- **CLC 52**
See also AFW; CA 106; CANR 47, 101;
CN 4, 5, 6, 7; DLB 225; SATA 62

Hopkins, Gerard Manley
1844-1889 **NCLC 17; PC 15; WLC 3**
See also BRW 5; BRWR 2; CDBLB 1890-
1914; DA; DA3; DAB; DAC; DAM MST,
POET; DLB 35, 57; EXPP; PAB; RGEL
2; TEA; WP

Hopkins, John (Richard) 1931-1998 .. **CLC 4**
See also CA 85-88; 169; CBD; CD 5, 6

Hopkins, Pauline Elizabeth
1859-1930 **BLC 2; TCLC 28**
See also AFAW 2; BW 2, 3; CA 141; CANR
82; DAM MULT; DLB 50

Hopkinson, Francis 1737-1791 **LC 25**
See also DLB 31; RGAL 4

Hopley-Woolrich, Cornell George 1903-1968
See Woolrich, Cornell
See also CA 13-14; CANR 58; CAP 1;
CMW 4; DLB 226; MTCW 2

Horace 65B.C.-8B.C. **CMLC 39; PC 46**
See also AW 2; CDWLB 1; DLB 211;
RGWL 2, 3; WLIT 8

Horatio
See Proust, (Valentin-Louis-George-Eugene)
Marcel

Horgan, Paul (George Vincent
O'Shaughnessy) 1903-1995 .. **CLC 9, 53**
See also BPFB 2; CA 13-16R; 147; CANR
9, 35; CN 1, 2, 3, 4, 5; DAM NOV; DLB
102, 212; DLBY 1985; INT CANR-9;
MTCW 1, 2; MTFW 2005; SATA 13;
SATA-Obit 84; TCWW 1, 2

Horkheimer, Max 1895-1973 **TCLC 132**
See also CA 216; 41-44R; DLB 296

Horn, Peter
See Kuttner, Henry

Horne, Frank (Smith) 1899-1974 **HR 1:2**
See also BW 1; CA 125; 53-56; DLB 51;
WP

Horne, Richard Henry Hengist
1802(?)-1884 **NCLC 127**
See also DLB 32; SATA 29

Hornem, Horace Esq.
See Byron, George Gordon (Noel)

Horney, Karen (Clementine Theodore
Danielsen) 1885-1952 **TCLC 71**
See also CA 114; 165; DLB 246; FW

Hornung, E(rnest) W(illiam)
1866-1921 **TCLC 59**
See also CA 108; 160; CMW 4; DLB 70

Horovitz, Israel (Arthur) 1939- **CLC 56**
See also CA 33-36R; CAD; CANR 46, 59;
CD 5, 6; DAM DRAM; DLB 7; MAL 5

Horton, George Moses
1797(?)-1883(?) **NCLC 87**
See also DLB 50

Horvath, odon von 1901-1938
See von Horvath, Odon
See also EWL 3

Horvath, Oedoen von -1938
See von Horvath, Odon

Horwitz, Julius 1920-1986 **CLC 14**
See also CA 9-12R; 119; CANR 12

Horwitz, Ronald
See Harwood, Ronald

Hospital, Janette Turner 1942- **CLC 42,
145**
See also CA 108; CANR 48; CN 5, 6, 7;
DLB 325; DLBY 2002; RGSF 2

Hostos, E. M. de
See Hostos (y Bonilla), Eugenio Maria de

Hostos, Eugenio M. de
See Hostos (y Bonilla), Eugenio Maria de

Hostos, Eugenio Maria
See Hostos (y Bonilla), Eugenio Maria de

Hostos (y Bonilla), Eugenio Maria de
1839-1903 **TCLC 24**
See also CA 123; 131; HW 1

Houdini
See Lovecraft, H. P.

Houellebecq, Michel 1958- **CLC 179**
See also CA 185; CANR 140; MTFW 2005

Hougan, Carolyn 1943- **CLC 34**
See also CA 139

Household, Geoffrey (Edward West)
1900-1988 **CLC 11**
See also CA 77-80; 126; CANR 58; CMW
4; CN 1, 2, 3, 4; DLB 87; SATA 14;
SATA-Obit 59

Housman, A(lfred) E(dward)
1859-1936 **PC 2, 43; TCLC 1, 10;
WLCS**
See also AAYA 66; BRW 6; CA 104; 125;
DA; DA3; DAB; DAC; DAM MST,
POET; DLB 19, 284; EWL 3; EXPP;
MTCW 1, 2; MTFW 2005; PAB; PFS 4,
7; RGEL 2; TEA; WP

Housman, Laurence 1865-1959 **TCLC 7**
See also CA 106; 155; DLB 10; FANT;
RGEL 2; SATA 25

Houston, Jeanne Wakatsuki 1934- **AAL**
See also AAYA 49; CA 103; 232; CAAE
232; CAAS 16; CANR 29, 123; LAIT 4;
SATA 78, 168; SATA-Essay 168

Howard, Elizabeth Jane 1923- **CLC 7, 29**
See also BRWS 11; CA 5-8R; CANR 8, 62,
146; CN 1, 2, 3, 4, 5, 6, 7

Howard, Maureen 1930- **CLC 5, 14, 46,
151**
See also CA 53-56; CANR 31, 75, 140; CN
4, 5, 6, 7; DLBY 1983; INT CANR-31;
MTCW 1, 2; MTFW 2005

Howard, Richard 1929- **CLC 7, 10, 47**
See also AITN 1; CA 85-88; CANR 25, 80,
154; CP 1, 2, 3, 4, 5, 6, 7; DLB 5; INT
CANR-25; MAL 5

Howard, Robert E(rvin)
1906-1936 **TCLC 8**
See also BPFB 2; BYA 5; CA 105; 157;
FANT; SUFW 1; TCWW 1, 2

Howard, Warren F.
See Pohl, Frederik

Howe, Fanny (Quincy) 1940- **CLC 47**
See also CA 117; 187; CAAE 187; CAAS
27; CANR 70, 116; CP 6, 7; CWP; SATA-
Brief 52

Howe, Irving 1920-1993 **CLC 85**
See also AMWS 6; CA 9-12R; 141; CANR
21, 50; DLB 67; EWL 3; MAL 5; MTCW
1, 2; MTFW 2005

Howe, Julia Ward 1819-1910 **TCLC 21**
See also CA 117; 191; DLB 1, 189, 235;
FW

Howe, Susan 1937- **CLC 72, 152; PC 54**
See also AMWS 4; CA 160; CP 5, 6, 7;
CWP; DLB 120; FW; RGAL 4

Howe, Tina 1937- **CLC 48**
See also CA 109; CAD; CANR 125; CD 5,
6; CWD

Howell, James 1594(?)-1666 **LC 13**
See also DLB 151

Howells, W. D.
See Howells, William Dean

Howells, William D.
See Howells, William Dean

Howells, William Dean 1837-1920 ... **SSC 36;**
TCLC 7, 17, 41
See also AMW; CA 104; 134; CDALB
1865-1917; DLB 12, 64, 74, 79, 189;
LMFS 1; MAL 5; MTCW 2; RGAL 4;
TUS

Howes, Barbara 1914-1996 **CLC 15**
See also CA 9-12R; 151; CAAS 3; CANR
53; CP 1, 2, 3, 4, 5, 6; SATA 5; TCLE 1:1

Hrabal, Bohumil 1914-1997 **CLC 13, 67;**
TCLC 155
See also CA 106; 156; CAAS 12; CANR
57; CWW 2; DLB 232; EWL 3; RGSF 2

Hrabanus Maurus 776(?)-856 **CMLC 78**
See also DLB 148

Hrotsvit of Gandersheim c. 935-c.
1000 **CMLC 29**
See also DLB 148

Hsi, Chu 1130-1200 **CMLC 42**

Hsun, Lu
See Lu Hsun

Hubbard, L. Ron 1911-1986 **CLC 43**
See also AAYA 64; CA 77-80; 118; CANR
52; CPW; DA3; DAM POP; FANT;
MTCW 2; MTFW 2005; SFW 4

Hubbard, Lafayette Ronald
See Hubbard, L. Ron

Huch, Ricarda (Octavia)
1864-1947 **TCLC 13**
See also CA 111; 189; DLB 66; EWL 3

Huddle, David 1942- **CLC 49**
See also CA 57-60; CAAS 20; CANR 89;
DLB 130

Hudson, Jeffrey
See Crichton, (John) Michael

Hudson, W(illiam) H(enry)
1841-1922 **TCLC 29**
See also CA 115; 190; DLB 98, 153, 174;
RGEL 2; SATA 35

Hueffer, Ford Madox
See Ford, Ford Madox

Hughart, Barry 1934- **CLC 39**
See also CA 137; FANT; SFW 4; SUFW 2

Hughes, Colin
See Creasey, John

Hughes, David (John) 1930-2005 **CLC 48**
See also CA 116; 129; 238; CN 4, 5, 6, 7;
DLB 14

Hughes, Edward James
See Hughes, Ted
See also DA3; DAM MST, POET

Hughes, (James Mercer) Langston
1902-1967 **BLC 2; CLC 1, 5, 10, 15,**
35, 44, 108; DC 3; HR 1:2; PC 1, 53;
SSC 6, 90; WLC 3
See also AAYA 12; AFAW 1, 2; AMWR 1;
AMWS 1; BW 1, 3; CA 1-4R; 25-28R;
CANR 1, 34, 82; CDALB 1929-1941;
CLR 17; DA; DA3; DAB; DAC; DAM
DRAM, MST, MULT, POET; DFS 6, 18;

DLB 4, 7, 48, 51, 86, 228, 315; EWL 3;
EXPP; EXPS; JRDA; LAIT 3; LMFS 2;
MAICYA 1, 2; MAL 5; MTCW 1, 2;
MTFW 2005; NFS 21; PAB; PFS 1, 3, 6,
10, 15; RGAL 4; RGSF 2; SATA 4, 33;
SSFS 4, 7; TUS; WCH; WP; YAW

Hughes, Richard (Arthur Warren)
1900-1976 **CLC 1, 11**
See also CA 5-8R; 65-68; CANR 4; CN 1,
2; DAM NOV; DLB 15, 161; EWL 3;
MTCW 1; RGEL 2; SATA 8; SATA-Obit
25

Hughes, Ted 1930-1998 . **CLC 2, 4, 9, 14, 37,**
119; PC 7
See Hughes, Edward James
See also BRWC 2; BRWR 2; BRWS 1; CA
1-4R; 171; CANR 1, 33, 66, 108; CLR 3;
CP 1, 2, 3, 4, 5, 6; DAB; DAC; DLB 40,
161; EWL 3; EXPP; MAICYA 1, 2;
MTCW 1, 2; MTFW 2005; PAB; PFS 4,
19; RGEL 2; SATA 49; SATA-Brief 27;
SATA-Obit 107; TEA; YAW

Hugo, Richard
See Huch, Ricarda (Octavia)

Hugo, Richard F(ranklin)
1923-1982 **CLC 6, 18, 32; PC 68**
See also AMWS 6; CA 49-52; 108; CANR
3; CP 1, 2, 3; DAM POET; DLB 5, 206;
EWL 3; MAL 5; PFS 17; RGAL 4

Hugo, Victor (Marie) 1802-1885 **NCLC 3,**
10, 21, 161; PC 17; WLC 3
See also AAYA 28; DA; DA3; DAB; DAC;
DAM DRAM, MST, NOV, POET; DLB
119, 192, 217; EFS 2; EW 6; EXPN; GFL
1789 to the Present; LAIT 1, 2; NFS 5,
20; RGWL 2, 3; SATA 47; TWA

Huidobro, Vicente
See Huidobro Fernandez, Vicente Garcia
See also DLB 283; EWL 3; LAW

Huidobro Fernandez, Vicente Garcia
1893-1948 **TCLC 31**
See Huidobro, Vicente
See also CA 131; HW 1

Hulme, Keri 1947- **CLC 39, 130**
See also CA 125; CANR 69; CN 4, 5, 6, 7;
CP 6, 7; CWP; DLB 326; EWL 3; FW;
INT CA-125

Hulme, T(homas) E(rnest)
1883-1917 **TCLC 21**
See also BRWS 6; CA 117; 203; DLB 19

Humboldt, Alexander von
1769-1859 **NCLC 170**
See also DLB 90

Humboldt, Wilhelm von
1767-1835 **NCLC 134**
See also DLB 90

Hume, David 1711-1776 **LC 7, 56**
See also BRWS 3; DLB 104, 252; LMFS 1;
TEA

Humphrey, William 1924-1997 **CLC 45**
See also AMWS 9; CA 77-80; 160; CANR
68; CN 1, 2, 3, 4, 5, 6; CSW; DLB 6, 212,
234, 278; TCWW 1, 2

Humphreys, Emyr Owen 1919- **CLC 47**
See also CA 5-8R; CANR 3, 24; CN 1, 2,
3, 4, 5, 6, 7; DLB 15

Humphreys, Josephine 1945- **CLC 34, 57**
See also CA 121; 127; CANR 97; CSW;
DLB 292; INT CA-127

Huneker, James Gibbons
1860-1921 **TCLC 65**
See also CA 193; DLB 71; RGAL 4

Hungerford, Hesba Fay
See Brinsmead, H(esba) F(ay)

Hungerford, Pixie
See Brinsmead, H(esba) F(ay)

Hunt, E(verette) Howard, (Jr.)
1918- ,.. **CLC 3**
See also AITN 1; CA 45-48; CANR 2, 47,
103; CMW 4

Hunt, Francesca
See Holland, Isabelle (Christian)

Hunt, Howard
See Hunt, E(verette) Howard, (Jr.)

Hunt, Kyle
See Creasey, John

Hunt, (James Henry) Leigh
1784-1859 **NCLC 1, 70**
See also DAM POET; DLB 96, 110, 144;
RGEL 2; TEA

Hunt, Marsha 1946- **CLC 70**
See also BW 2, 3; CA 143; CANR 79

Hunt, Violet 1866(?)-1942 **TCLC 53**
See also CA 184; DLB 162, 197

Hunter, E. Waldo
See Sturgeon, Theodore (Hamilton)

Hunter, Evan 1926-2005 **CLC 11, 31**
See McBain, Ed
See also AAYA 39; BPFB 2; CA 5-8R; 241;
CANR 5, 38, 62, 97, 149; CMW 4; CN 1,
2, 3, 4, 5, 6, 7; CPW; DAM POP; DLB
306; DLBY 1982; INT CANR-5; MSW;
MTCW 1; SATA 25; SATA-Obit 167;
SFW 4

Hunter, Kristin
See Lattany, Kristin (Elaine Eggleston)
Hunter
See also CN 1, 2, 3, 4, 5, 6

Hunter, Mary
See Austin, Mary (Hunter)

Hunter, Mollie 1922- **CLC 21**
See McIlwraith, Maureen Mollie Hunter
See also AAYA 13, 71; BYA 6; CANR 37,
78; CLR 25; DLB 161; JRDA; MAICYA
1, 2; SAAS 7; SATA 54, 106, 139; SATA-
Essay 139; WYA; YAW

Hunter, Robert (?)-1734 **LC 7**

Hurston, Zora Neale 1891-1960 **BLC 2;**
CLC 7, 30, 61; DC 12; HR 1:2; SSC 4,
80; TCLC 121, 131; WLCS
See also AAYA 15, 71; AFAW 1, 2; AMWS
6; BW 1, 3; BYA 12; CA 85-88; CANR
61; CDALBS; DA; DA3; DAC; DAM
MST, MULT, NOV; DFS 6; DLB 51, 86;
EWL 3; EXPN; EXPS; FL 1:6; FW; LAIT
3; LATS 1:1; LMFS 2; MAL 5; MAWW;
MTCW 1, 2; MTFW 2005; NFS 3; RGAL
4; RGSF 2; SSFS 1, 6, 11, 19, 21; TUS;
YAW

Husserl, E. G.
See Husserl, Edmund (Gustav Albrecht)

Husserl, Edmund (Gustav Albrecht)
1859-1938 **TCLC 100**
See also CA 116; 133; DLB 296

Huston, John (Marcellus)
1906-1987 **CLC 20**
See also CA 73-76; 123; CANR 34; DLB
26

Hustvedt, Siri 1955- **CLC 76**
See also CA 137; CANR 149

Hutten, Ulrich von 1488-1523 **LC 16**
See also DLB 179

Huxley, Aldous (Leonard)
1894-1963 **CLC 1, 3, 4, 5, 8, 11, 18,**
35, 79; SSC 39; WLC 3
See also AAYA 11; BPFB 2; BRW 7; CA
85-88; CANR 44, 99; CDBLB 1914-1945;
DA; DA3; DAB; DAC; DAM MST, NOV;
DLB 36, 100, 162, 195, 255; EWL 3;
EXPN; LAIT 5; LMFS 2; MTCW 1, 2;
MTFW 2005; NFS 6; RGEL 2; SATA 63;
SCFW 1, 2; SFW 4; TEA; YAW

Huxley, T(homas) H(enry)
1825-1895 **NCLC 67**
See also DLB 57; TEA

Huygens, Constantijn 1596-1687 **LC 114**
See also RGWL 2, 3

Huysmans, Joris-Karl 1848-1907 ... **TCLC 7, 69**
See also CA 104; 165; DLB 123; EW 7; GFL 1789 to the Present; LMFS 2; RGWL 2, 3

Hwang, David Henry 1957- **CLC 55, 196; DC 4, 23**
See also CA 127; 132; CAD; CANR 76, 124; CD 5, 6; DA3; DAM DRAM; DFS 11, 18; DLB 212, 228, 312; INT CA-132; MAL 5; MTCW 2; MTFW 2005; RGAL 4

Hyde, Anthony 1946- **CLC 42**
See Chase, Nicholas
See also CA 136; CCA 1

Hyde, Margaret O(ldroyd) 1917- **CLC 21**
See also CA 1-4R; CANR 1, 36, 137; CLR 23; JRDA; MAICYA 1, 2; SAAS 8; SATA 1, 42, 76, 139

Hynes, James 1956(?)- **CLC 65**
See also CA 164; CANR 105

Hypatia c. 370-415 **CMLC 35**

Ian, Janis 1951- **CLC 21**
See also CA 105; 187

Ibanez, Vicente Blasco
See Blasco Ibanez, Vicente
See also DLB 322

Ibarbourou, Juana de 1895(?)-1979 **HLCS 2**
See also DLB 290; HW 1; LAW

Ibarguengoitia, Jorge 1928-1983 **CLC 37; TCLC 148**
See also CA 124; 113; EWL 3; HW 1

Ibn Battuta, Abu Abdalla 1304-1368(?) **CMLC 57**
See also WLIT 2

Ibn Hazm 994-1064 **CMLC 64**

Ibsen, Henrik (Johan) 1828-1906 **DC 2; TCLC 2, 8, 16, 37, 52; WLC 3**
See also AAYA 46; CA 104; 141; DA; DA3; DAB; DAC; DAM DRAM, MST; DFS 1, 6, 8, 10, 11, 15, 16; EW 7; LAIT 2; LATS 1:1; MTFW 2005; RGWL 2, 3

Ibuse, Masuji 1898-1993 **CLC 22**
See Ibuse Masuji
See also CA 127; 141; MJW; RGWL 3

Ibuse Masuji
See Ibuse, Masuji
See also CWW 2; DLB 180; EWL 3

Ichikawa, Kon 1915- **CLC 20**
See also CA 121

Ichiyo, Higuchi 1872-1896 **NCLC 49**
See also MJW

Idle, Eric 1943- **CLC 21**
See Monty Python
See also CA 116; CANR 35, 91, 148

Idris, Yusuf 1927-1991 **SSC 74**
See also AFW; EWL 3; RGSF 2, 3; RGWL 3; WLIT 2

Ignatow, David 1914-1997 **CLC 4, 7, 14, 40; PC 34**
See also CA 9-12R; 162; CAAS 3; CANR 31, 57, 96; CP 1, 2, 3, 4, 5, 6; DLB 5; EWL 3; MAL 5

Ignotus
See Strachey, (Giles) Lytton

Ihimaera, Witi (Tame) 1944- **CLC 46**
See also CA 77-80; CANR 130; CN 2, 3, 4, 5, 6, 7; RGSF 2; SATA 148

Ilf, Ilya .. **TCLC 21**
See Fainzilberg, Ilya Arnoldovich
See also EWL 3

Illyes, Gyula 1902-1983 **PC 16**
See also CA 114; 109; CDWLB 4; DLB 215; EWL 3; RGWL 2, 3

Imalayen, Fatima-Zohra
See Djebar, Assia

Immermann, Karl (Lebrecht) 1796-1840 **NCLC 4, 49**
See also DLB 133

Ince, Thomas H. 1882-1924 **TCLC 89**
See also IDFW 3, 4

Inchbald, Elizabeth 1753-1821 **NCLC 62**
See also DLB 39, 89; RGEL 2

Inclan, Ramon (Maria) del Valle
See Valle-Inclan, Ramon (Maria) del

Infante, G(uillermo) Cabrera
See Cabrera Infante, G(uillermo)

Ingalls, Rachel 1940- **CLC 42**
See also CA 123; 127; CANR 154

Ingalls, Rachel Holmes
See Ingalls, Rachel

Ingamells, Reginald Charles
See Ingamells, Rex

Ingamells, Rex 1913-1955 **TCLC 35**
See also CA 167; DLB 260

Inge, William (Motter) 1913-1973 **CLC 1, 8, 19**
See also CA 9-12R; CAD; CDALB 1941-1968; DA3; DAM DRAM; DFS 1, 3, 5, 8; DLB 7, 249; EWL 3; MAL 5; MTCW 1, 2; MTFW 2005; RGAL 4; TUS

Ingelow, Jean 1820-1897 **NCLC 39, 107**
See also DLB 35, 163; FANT; SATA 33

Ingram, Willis J.
See Harris, Mark

Innaurato, Albert (F.) 1948(?)- ... **CLC 21, 60**
See also CA 115; 122; CAD; CANR 78; CD 5, 6; INT CA-122

Innes, Michael
See Stewart, J(ohn) I(nnes) M(ackintosh)
See also DLB 276; MSW

Innis, Harold Adams 1894-1952 **TCLC 77**
See also CA 181; DLB 88

Insluis, Alanus de
See Alain de Lille

Iola
See Wells-Barnett, Ida B(ell)

Ionesco, Eugene 1912-1994 ... **CLC 1, 4, 6, 9, 11, 15, 41, 86; DC 12; WLC 3**
See also CA 9-12R; 144; CANR 55, 132; CWW 2; DA; DA3; DAB; DAC; DAM DRAM, MST; DFS 4, 9; DLB 321; EW 13; EWL 3; GFL 1789 to the Present; LMFS 2; MTCW 1, 2; MTFW 2005; RGWL 2, 3; SATA 7; SATA-Obit 79; TWA

Iqbal, Muhammad 1877-1938 **TCLC 28**
See also CA 215; EWL 3

Ireland, Patrick
See O'Doherty, Brian

Irenaeus St. 130- **CMLC 42**

Irigaray, Luce 1930- **CLC 164**
See also CA 154; CANR 121; FW

Iron, Ralph
See Schreiner, Olive (Emilie Albertina)

Irving, John (Winslow) 1942- ... **CLC 13, 23, 38, 112, 175**
See also AAYA 8, 62; AMWS 6; BEST 89:3; BPFB 2; CA 25-28R; CANR 28, 73, 112, 133; CN 3, 4, 5, 6, 7; CPW; DA3; DAM NOV, POP; DLB 6, 278; DLBY 1982; EWL 3; MAL 5; MTCW 1, 2; MTFW 2005; NFS 12, 14; RGAL 4; TUS

Irving, Washington 1783-1859 . **NCLC 2, 19, 95; SSC 2, 37; WLC 3**
See also AAYA 56; AMW; CDALB 1640-1865; CLR 97; DA; DA3; DAB; DAC; DAM MST; DLB 3, 11, 30, 59, 73, 74, 183, 186, 250, 254; EXPS; GL 2; LAIT 1; RGAL 4; RGSF 2; SSFS 1, 8, 16; SUFW 1; TUS; WCH; YABC 2

Irwin, P. K.
See Page, P(atricia) K(athleen)

Isaacs, Jorge Ricardo 1837-1895 ... **NCLC 70**
See also LAW

Isaacs, Susan 1943- **CLC 32**
See also BEST 89:1; BPFB 2; CA 89-92; CANR 20, 41, 65, 112, 134; CPW; DA3; DAM POP; INT CANR-20; MTCW 1, 2; MTFW 2005

Isherwood, Christopher (William Bradshaw) 1904-1986 **CLC 1, 9, 11, 14, 44; SSC 56**
See also AMWS 14; BRW 7; CA 13-16R; 117; CANR 35, 97, 133; CN 1, 2, 3; DA3; DAM DRAM, NOV; DLB 15, 195; DLBY 1986; EWL 3; IDTP; MTCW 1, 2; MTFW 2005; RGAL 4; RGEL 2; TUS; WLIT 4

Ishiguro, Kazuo 1954- . **CLC 27, 56, 59, 110, 119**
See also AAYA 58; BEST 90:2; BPFB 2; BRWS 4; CA 120; CANR 49, 95, 133; CN 5, 6, 7; DA3; DAM NOV; DLB 194, 326; EWL 3; MTCW 1, 2; MTFW 2005; NFS 13; WLIT 4; WWE 1

Ishikawa, Hakuhin
See Ishikawa, Takuboku

Ishikawa, Takuboku 1886(?)-1912 **PC 10; TCLC 15**
See Ishikawa Takuboku
See also CA 113; 153; DAM POET

Iskander, Fazil (Abdulovich) 1929- .. **CLC 47**
See Iskander, Fazil' Abdulevich
See also CA 102; EWL 3

Iskander, Fazil' Abdulevich
See Iskander, Fazil (Abdulovich)
See also DLB 302

Isler, Alan (David) 1934- **CLC 91**
See also CA 156; CANR 105

Ivan IV 1530-1584 **LC 17**

Ivanov, Vyacheslav Ivanovich 1866-1949 **TCLC 33**
See also CA 122; EWL 3

Ivask, Ivar Vidrik 1927-1992 **CLC 14**
See also CA 37-40R; 139; CANR 24

Ives, Morgan
See Bradley, Marion Zimmer
See also GLL 1

Izumi Shikibu c. 973-c. 1034 **CMLC 33**

J. R. S.
See Gogarty, Oliver St. John

Jabran, Kahlil
See Gibran, Kahlil

Jabran, Khalil
See Gibran, Kahlil

Jackson, Daniel
See Wingrove, David (John)

Jackson, Helen Hunt 1830-1885 **NCLC 90**
See also DLB 42, 47, 186, 189; RGAL 4

Jackson, Jesse 1908-1983 **CLC 12**
See also BW 1; CA 25-28R; 109; CANR 27; CLR 28; CWRI 5; MAICYA 1, 2; SATA 2, 29; SATA-Obit 48

Jackson, Laura (Riding) 1901-1991 **PC 44**
See Riding, Laura
See also CA 65-68; 135; CANR 28, 89; DLB 48

Jackson, Sam
See Trumbo, Dalton

Jackson, Sara
See Wingrove, David (John)

Jackson, Shirley 1919-1965 . **CLC 11, 60, 87; SSC 9, 39; WLC 3**
See also AAYA 9; AMWS 9; BPFB 2; CA 1-4R; 25-28R; CANR 4, 52; CDALB 1941-1968; DA; DA3; DAC; DAM MST; DLB 6, 234; EXPS; HGG; LAIT 4; MAL 5; MTCW 2; MTFW 2005; RGAL 4; RGSF 2; SATA 2; SSFS 1; SUFW 1, 2

Jacob, (Cyprien-)Max 1876-1944 **TCLC 6**
See also CA 104; 193; DLB 258; EWL 3; GFL 1789 to the Present; GLL 2; RGWL 2, 3

Jacobs, Harriet A(nn)
1813(?)-1897 NCLC 67, 162
See also AFAW 1, 2; DLB 239; FL 1:3; FW;
LAIT 2; RGAL 4
Jacobs, Jim 1942- CLC 12
See also CA 97-100; INT CA-97-100
Jacobs, W(illiam) W(ymark)
1863-1943 SSC 73; TCLC 22
See also CA 121; 167; DLB 135; EXPS;
HGG; RGEL 2; RGSF 2; SSFS 2; SUFW
1
Jacobsen, Jens Peter 1847-1885 NCLC 34
Jacobsen, Josephine (Winder)
1908-2003 CLC 48, 102; PC 62
See also CA 33-36R; 218; CAAS 18; CANR
23, 48; CCA 1; CP 2, 3, 4, 5, 6, 7; DLB
244; PFS 23; TCLE 1:1
Jacobson, Dan 1929- CLC 4, 14; SSC 91
See also AFW; CA 1-4R; CANR 2, 25, 66;
CN 1, 2, 3, 4, 5, 6, 7; DLB 14, 207, 225,
319; EWL 3; MTCW 1; RGSF 2
Jacqueline
See Carpentier (y Valmont), Alejo
Jacques de Vitry c. 1160-1240 CMLC 63
See also DLB 208
Jagger, Michael Philip
See Jagger, Mick
Jagger, Mick 1943- CLC 17
See also CA 239
Jahiz, al- c. 780-c. 869 CMLC 25
See also DLB 311
Jakes, John (William) 1932- CLC 29
See also AAYA 32; BEST 89:4; BPFB 2;
CA 57-60, 214; CAAE 214; CANR 10,
43, 66, 111, 142; CPW; CSW; DA3; DAM
NOV, POP; DLB 278; DLBY 1983;
FANT; INT CANR-10; MTCW 1, 2;
MTFW 2005; RHW; SATA 62; SFW 4;
TCWW 1, 2
James I 1394-1437 LC 20
See also RGEL 2
James, Andrew
See Kirkup, James
James, C(yril) L(ionel) R(obert)
1901-1989 BLCS; CLC 33
See also BW 2; CA 117; 125; 128; CANR
62; CN 1, 2, 3, 4; DLB 125; MTCW 1
James, Daniel (Lewis) 1911-1988
See Santiago, Danny
See also CA 174; 125
James, Dynely
See Mayne, William (James Carter)
James, Henry Sr. 1811-1882 NCLC 53
James, Henry 1843-1916 SSC 8, 32, 47;
TCLC 2, 11, 24, 40, 47, 64, 171; WLC
3
See also AMW; AMWC 1; AMWR 1; BPFB
2; BRW 6; CA 104; 132; CDALB 1865-
1917; DA; DA3; DAB; DAC; DAM MST,
NOV; DLB 12, 71, 74, 189; DLBD 13;
EWL 3; EXPS; GL 2; HGG; LAIT 2;
MAL 5; MTCW 1, 2; MTFW 2005; NFS
12, 16, 19; RGAL 4; RGEL 2; RGSF 2;
SSFS 9; SUFW 1; TUS
James, M. R. SSC 93
See James, Montague (Rhodes)
See also DLB 156, 201
James, Montague (Rhodes)
1862-1936 SSC 16; TCLC 6
See James, M. R.
See also CA 104; 203; HGG; RGEL 2;
RGSF 2; SUFW 1
James, P. D. CLC 18, 46, 122
See White, Phyllis Dorothy James
See also BEST 90:2; BPFB 2; BRWS 4;
CDBLB 1960 to Present; CN 4, 5, 6; DLB
87, 276; DLBD 17; MSW
James, Philip
See Moorcock, Michael

James, Samuel
See Stephens, James
James, Seumas
See Stephens, James
James, Stephen
See Stephens, James
James, William 1842-1910 TCLC 15, 32
See also AMW; CA 109; 193; DLB 270,
284; MAL 5; NCFS 5; RGAL 4
Jameson, Anna 1794-1860 NCLC 43
See also DLB 99, 166
Jameson, Fredric (R.) 1934- CLC 142
See also CA 196; DLB 67; LMFS 2
James VI of Scotland 1566-1625 LC 109
See also DLB 151, 172
Jami, Nur al-Din 'Abd al-Rahman
1414-1492 LC 9
Jammes, Francis 1868-1938 TCLC 75
See also CA 198; EWL 3; GFL 1789 to the
Present
Jandl, Ernst 1925-2000 CLC 34
See also CA 200; EWL 3
Janowitz, Tama 1957- CLC 43, 145
See also CA 106; CANR 52, 89, 129; CN
5, 6, 7; CPW; DAM POP; DLB 292;
MTFW 2005
Japrisot, Sebastien 1931- CLC 90
See Rossi, Jean-Baptiste
See also CMW 4; NFS 18
Jarrell, Randall 1914-1965 CLC 1, 2, 6, 9,
13, 49; PC 41; TCLC 177
See also AMW; BYA 5; CA 5-8R; 25-28R;
CABS 2; CANR 6, 34; CDALB 1941-
1968; CLR 6, 111; CWRI 5; DAM POET;
DLB 48, 52; FWL 3; EXPP; MAICYA 1,
2; MAL 5; MTCW 1, 2; PAB; PFS 2;
RGAL 4; SATA 7
Jarry, Alfred 1873-1907 SSC 20; TCLC 2,
14, 147
See also CA 104; 153; DA3; DAM DRAM;
DFS 8; DLB 192, 258; EW 9; EWL 3;
GFL 1789 to the Present; RGWL 2, 3;
TWA
Jarvis, E. K.
See Ellison, Harlan (Jay)
Jawien, Andrzej
See John Paul II, Pope
Jaynes, Roderick
See Coen, Ethan
Jeake, Samuel, Jr.
See Aiken, Conrad (Potter)
Jean Paul 1763-1825 NCLC 7
Jefferies, (John) Richard
1848-1887 NCLC 47
See also DLB 98, 141; RGEL 2; SATA 16;
SFW 4
Jeffers, (John) Robinson 1887-1962 .. CLC 2,
3, 11, 15, 54; PC 17; WLC 3
See also AMWS 2; CA 85-88; CANR 35;
CDALB 1917-1929; DA; DAC; DAM
MST, POET; DLB 45, 212; EWL 3; MAL
5; MTCW 1, 2; MTFW 2005; PAB; PFS
3, 4; RGAL 4
Jefferson, Janet
See Mencken, H(enry) L(ouis)
Jefferson, Thomas 1743-1826 . NCLC 11, 103
See also AAYA 54; ANW; CDALB 1640-
1865; DA3; DLB 31, 183; LAIT 1; RGAL
4
Jeffrey, Francis 1773-1850 NCLC 33
See Francis, Lord Jeffrey
Jelakowitch, Ivan
See Heijermans, Herman
Jelinek, Elfriede 1946- CLC 169
See also AAYA 68; CA 154; DLB 85; FW
Jellicoe, (Patricia) Ann 1927- CLC 27
See also CA 85-88; CBD; CD 5, 6; CWD;
CWRI 5; DLB 13, 233; FW

Jelloun, Tahar ben 1944- CLC 180
See Ben Jelloun, Tahar
See also CA 162; CANR 100
Jemyma
See Holley, Marietta
Jen, Gish AAL; CLC 70, 198
See Jen, Lillian
See also AMWC 2; CN 7; DLB 312
Jen, Lillian 1955-
See Jen, Gish
See also CA 135; CANR 89, 130
Jenkins, (John) Robin 1912- CLC 52
See also CA 1-4R; CANR 1, 135; CN 1, 2,
3, 4, 5, 6, 7; DLB 14, 271
Jennings, Elizabeth (Joan)
1926-2001 CLC 5, 14, 131
See also BRWS 5; CA 61-64; 200; CAAS
5; CANR 8, 39, 66, 127; CP 1, 2, 3, 4, 5,
6, 7; CWP; DLB 27; EWL 3; MTCW 1;
SATA 66
Jennings, Waylon 1937-2002 CLC 21
Jensen, Johannes V(ilhelm)
1873-1950 TCLC 41
See also CA 170; DLB 214; EWL 3; RGWL
3
Jensen, Laura (Linnea) 1948- CLC 37
See also CA 103
Jerome, Saint 345-420 CMLC 30
See also RGWL 3
Jerome, Jerome K(lapka)
1859-1927 TCLC 23
See also CA 119; 177; DLB 10, 34, 135;
RGEL 2
Jerrold, Douglas William
1803-1857 NCLC 2
See also DLB 158, 159; RGEL 2
Jewett, (Theodora) Sarah Orne
1849-1909 SSC 6, 44; TCLC 1, 22
See also AMW; AMWC 2; AMWR 2; CA
108; 127; CANR 71; DLB 12, 74, 221;
EXPS; FL 1:3; FW; MAL 5; MAWW;
NFS 15; RGAL 4; RGSF 2; SATA 15;
SSFS 4
Jewsbury, Geraldine (Endsor)
1812-1880 NCLC 22
See also DLB 21
Jhabvala, Ruth Prawer 1927- . CLC 4, 8, 29,
94, 138; SSC 91
See also BRWS 5; CA 1-4R; CANR 2, 29,
51, 74, 91, 128; CN 1, 2, 3, 4, 5, 6, 7;
DAB; DAM NOV; DLB 139, 194, 323,
326; EWL 3; IDFW 3, 4; INT CANR-29;
MTCW 1, 2; MTFW 2005; RGSF 2;
RGWL 2; RHW; TEA
Jibran, Kahlil
See Gibran, Kahlil
Jibran, Khalil
See Gibran, Kahlil
Jiles, Paulette 1943- CLC 13, 58
See also CA 101; CANR 70, 124; CP 5;
CWP
Jimenez (Mantecon), Juan Ramon
1881-1958 HLC 1; PC 7; TCLC 4
See also CA 104; 131; CANR 74; DAM
MULT, POET; DLB 134; EW 9; EWL 3;
HW 1; MTCW 1, 2; MTFW 2005; RGWL
2, 3
Jimenez, Ramon
See Jimenez (Mantecon), Juan Ramon
Jimenez Mantecon, Juan
See Jimenez (Mantecon), Juan Ramon
Jin, Ba 1904-2005
See Pa Chin
See also CA 244; CWW 2
Jin, Ha ... CLC 109
See Jin, Xuefei
See also CA 152; DLB 244, 292; SSFS 17

Jin, Xuefei 1956-
 See Jin, Ha
 See also CANR 91, 130; MTFW 2005;
 SSFS 17
Jodelle, Etienne 1532-1573 LC 119
 See also GFL Beginnings to 1789
Joel, Billy CLC 26
 See Joel, William Martin
Joel, William Martin 1949-
 See Joel, Billy
 See also CA 108
John, Saint 10(?)-100 CMLC 27, 63
John of Salisbury c. 1115-1180 CMLC 63
John of the Cross, St. 1542-1591 LC 18
 See also RGWL 2, 3
John Paul II, Pope 1920-2005 CLC 128
 See also CA 106; 133; 238
Johnson, B(ryan) S(tanley William)
 1933-1973 CLC 6, 9
 See also CA 9-12R; 53-56; CANR 9; CN 1;
 CP 1, 2; DLB 14, 40; EWL 3; RGEL 2
Johnson, Benjamin F., of Boone
 See Riley, James Whitcomb
Johnson, Charles (Richard) 1948- BLC 2;
 CLC 7, 51, 65, 163
 See also AFAW 2; AMWS 6; BW 2, 3; CA
 116; CAAS 18; CANR 42, 66, 82, 129;
 CN 5, 6, 7; DAM MULT; DLB 33, 278;
 MAL 5; MTCW 2; MTFW 2005; RGAL
 4; SSFS 16
Johnson, Charles S(purgeon)
 1893-1956 HR 1:3
 See also BW 1, 3; CA 125; CANR 82; DLB
 51, 91
Johnson, Denis 1949- . CLC 52, 160; SSC 56
 See also CA 117; 121; CANR 71, 99; CN
 4, 5, 6, 7; DLB 120
Johnson, Diane 1934- CLC 5, 13, 48
 See also BPFB 2; CA 41-44R; CANR 17,
 40, 62, 95; CN 4, 5, 6, 7; DLBY 1980;
 INT CANR-17; MTCW 1
Johnson, E(mily) Pauline 1861-1913 . NNAL
 See also CA 150; CCA 1; DAC; DAM
 MULT; DLB 92, 175; TCWW 2
Johnson, Eyvind (Olof Verner)
 1900-1976 CLC 14
 See also CA 73-76; 69-72; CANR 34, 101;
 DLB 259; EW 12; EWL 3
Johnson, Fenton 1888-1958 BLC 2
 See also BW 1; CA 118; 124; DAM MULT;
 DLB 45, 50
Johnson, Georgia Douglas (Camp)
 1880-1966 HR 1:3
 See also BW 1; CA 125; DLB 51, 249; WP
Johnson, Helene 1907-1995 HR 1:3
 See also CA 181; DLB 51; WP
Johnson, J. R.
 See James, C(yril) L(ionel) R(obert)
Johnson, James Weldon 1871-1938 .. BLC 2;
 HR 1:3; PC 24; TCLC 3, 19, 175
 See also AFAW 1, 2; BW 1, 3; CA 104;
 125; CANR 82; CDALB 1917-1929; CLR
 32; DA3; DAM MULT, POET; DLB 51;
 EWL 3; EXPP; LMFS 2; MAL 5; MTCW
 1, 2; MTFW 2005; NFS 22; PFS 1; RGAL
 4; SATA 31; TUS
Johnson, Joyce 1935- CLC 58
 See also BG 1:3; CA 125; 129; CANR 102
Johnson, Judith (Emlyn) 1936- CLC 7, 15
 See Sherwin, Judith Johnson
 See also CA 25-28R; 153; CANR 34; CP 6,
 7
Johnson, Lionel (Pigot)
 1867-1902 TCLC 19
 See also CA 117; 209; DLB 19; RGEL 2
Johnson, Marguerite Annie
 See Angelou, Maya
Johnson, Mel
 See Malzberg, Barry N(athaniel)

Johnson, Pamela Hansford
 1912-1981 CLC 1, 7, 27
 See also CA 1-4R; 104; CANR 2, 28; CN
 1, 2, 3; DLB 15; MTCW 1, 2; MTFW
 2005; RGEL 2
Johnson, Paul (Bede) 1928- CLC 147
 See also BEST 89:4; CA 17-20R; CANR
 34, 62, 100
Johnson, Robert CLC 70
Johnson, Robert 1911(?)-1938 TCLC 69
 See also BW 3; CA 174
Johnson, Samuel 1709-1784 . LC 15, 52, 128;
 WLC 3
 See also BRW 3; BRWR 1; CDBLB 1660-
 1789; DA; DAB; DAC; DAM MST; DLB
 39, 95, 104, 142, 213; LMFS 1; RGEL 2;
 TEA
Johnson, Uwe 1934-1984 .. CLC 5, 10, 15, 40
 See also CA 1-4R; 112; CANR 1, 39; CD-
 WLB 2; DLB 75; EWL 3; MTCW 1;
 RGWL 2, 3
Johnston, Basil H. 1929- NNAL
 See also CA 69-72; CANR 11, 28, 66;
 DAC; DAM MULT; DLB 60
Johnston, George (Benson) 1913- CLC 51
 See also CA 1-4R; CANR 5, 20; CP 1, 2, 3,
 4, 5, 6, 7; DLB 88
Johnston, Jennifer (Prudence)
 1930- CLC 7, 150
 See also CA 85-88; CANR 92; CN 4, 5, 6,
 7; DLB 14
Joinville, Jean de 1224(?)-1317 CMLC 38
Jolley, (Monica) Elizabeth 1923- CLC 46;
 SSC 19
 See also CA 127; CAAS 13; CANR 59; CN
 4, 5, 6, 7; DLB 325; EWL 3; RGSF 2
Jones, Arthur Llewellyn 1863-1947
 See Machen, Arthur
 See also CA 104; 179; HGG
Jones, D(ouglas) G(ordon) 1929- CLC 10
 See also CA 29-32R; CANR 13, 90; CP 1,
 2, 3, 4, 5, 6, 7; DLB 53
Jones, David (Michael) 1895-1974 CLC 2,
 4, 7, 13, 42
 See also BRW 6; BRWS 7; CA 9-12R; 53-
 56; CANR 28; CDBLB 1945-1960; CP 1,
 2; DLB 20, 100; EWL 3; MTCW 1; PAB;
 RGEL 2
Jones, David Robert 1947-
 See Bowie, David
 See also CA 103; CANR 104
Jones, Diana Wynne 1934- CLC 26
 See also AAYA 12; BYA 6, 7, 9, 11, 13, 16;
 CA 49-52; CANR 4, 26, 56, 120; CLR
 23; DLB 161; FANT; JRDA; MAICYA 1,
 2; MTFW 2005; SAAS 7; SATA 9, 70,
 108, 160; SFW 4; SUFW 2; YAW
Jones, Edward P. 1950- CLC 76, 223
 See also AAYA 71; BW 2, 3; CA 142;
 CANR 79, 134; CSW; MTFW 2005
Jones, Gayl 1949- BLC 2; CLC 6, 9, 131
 See also AFAW 1, 2; BW 2, 3; CA 77-80;
 CANR 27, 66, 122; CN 4, 5, 6, 7; CSW;
 DA3; DAM MULT; DLB 33, 278; MAL
 5; MTCW 1, 2; MTFW 2005; RGAL 4
Jones, James 1921-1977 CLC 1, 3, 10, 39
 See also AITN 1, 2; AMWS 11; BPFB 2;
 CA 1-4R; 69-72; CANR 6; CN 1, 2; DLB
 2, 143; DLBD 17; DLBY 1998; EWL 3;
 MAL 5; MTCW 1; RGAL 4
Jones, John J.
 See Lovecraft, H. P.
Jones, LeRoi CLC 1, 2, 3, 5, 10, 14
 See Baraka, Amiri
 See also CN 1, 2; CP 1, 2, 3; MTCW 2
Jones, Louis B. 1953- CLC 65
 See also CA 141; CANR 73

Jones, Madison (Percy, Jr.) 1925- CLC 4
 See also CA 13-16R; CAAS 11; CANR 7,
 54, 83; CN 1, 2, 3, 4, 5, 6, 7; CSW; DLB
 152
Jones, Mervyn 1922- CLC 10, 52
 See also CA 45-48; CAAS 5; CANR 1, 91;
 CN 1, 2, 3, 4, 5, 6, 7; MTCW 1
Jones, Mick 1956(?)- CLC 30
Jones, Nettie (Pearl) 1941- CLC 34
 See also BW 2; CA 137; CAAS 20; CANR
 88
Jones, Peter 1802-1856 NNAL
Jones, Preston 1936-1979 CLC 10
 See also CA 73-76; 89-92; DLB 7
Jones, Robert F(rancis) 1934-2003 CLC 7
 See also CA 49-52; CANR 2, 61, 118
Jones, Rod 1953- CLC 50
 See also CA 128
Jones, Terence Graham Parry
 1942- CLC 21
 See Jones, Terry; Monty Python
 See also CA 112; 116; CANR 35, 93; INT
 CA-116; SATA 127
Jones, Terry
 See Jones, Terence Graham Parry
 See also SATA 67; SATA-Brief 51
Jones, Thom (Douglas) 1945(?)- CLC 81;
 SSC 56
 See also CA 157; CANR 88; DLB 244;
 SSFS 23
Jong, Erica 1942- CLC 4, 6, 8, 18, 83
 See also AITN 1; AMWS 5; BEST 90:2;
 BPFB 2; CA 73-76; CANR 26, 52, 75,
 132; CN 3, 4, 5, 6, 7; CP 2, 3, 4, 5, 6, 7;
 CPW; DA3; DAM NOV, POP; DLB 2, 5,
 28, 152; FW; INT CANR-26; MAL 5;
 MTCW 1, 2; MTFW 2005
Jonson, Ben(jamin) 1572(?)-1637 . DC 4; LC
 6, 33, 110; PC 17; WLC 3
 See also BRW 1; BRWC 1; BRWR 1; CD-
 BLB Before 1660; DA; DAB; DAC;
 DAM DRAM, MST, POET; DFS 4, 10;
 DLB 62, 121; LMFS 1; PFS 23; RGEL 2;
 TEA; WLIT 3
Jordan, June 1936-2002 .. BLCS; CLC 5, 11,
 23, 114; PC 38
 See also AAYA 2, 66; AFAW 1, 2; BW 2,
 3; CA 33-36R; 206; CANR 25, 70, 114,
 154; CLR 10; CP 3, 4, 5, 6, 7; CWP;
 DAM MULT, POET; DLB 38; GLL 2;
 LAIT 5; MAICYA 1, 2; MTCW 1; SATA
 4, 136; YAW
Jordan, June Meyer
 See Jordan, June
Jordan, Neil 1950- CLC 110
 See also CA 124; 130; CANR 54, 154; CN
 4, 5, 6, 7; GLL 2; INT CA-130
Jordan, Neil Patrick
 See Jordan, Neil
Jordan, Pat(rick M.) 1941- CLC 37
 See also CA 33-36R; CANR 121
Jorgensen, Ivar
 See Ellison, Harlan (Jay)
Jorgenson, Ivar
 See Silverberg, Robert
Joseph, George Ghevarughese CLC 70
Josephson, Mary
 See O'Doherty, Brian
Josephus, Flavius c. 37-100 CMLC 13
 See also AW 2; DLB 176; WLIT 8
Josiah Allen's Wife
 See Holley, Marietta
Josipovici, Gabriel (David) 1940- CLC 6,
 43, 153
 See also CA 37-40R, 224; CAAE 224;
 CAAS 8; CANR 47, 84; CN 3, 4, 5, 6, 7;
 DLB 14, 319
Joubert, Joseph 1754-1824 NCLC 9

Jouve, Pierre Jean 1887-1976 **CLC 47**
 See also CA 65-68; DLB 258; EWL 3
Jovine, Francesco 1902-1950 **TCLC 79**
 See also DLB 264; EWL 3
Joyce, James (Augustine Aloysius)
 1882-1941 **DC 16; PC 22; SSC 3, 26,
 44, 64; TCLC 3, 8, 16, 35, 52, 159;
 WLC 3**
 See also AAYA 42; BRW 7; BRWC 1;
 BRWR 1; BYA 11, 13; CA 104; 126; CD-
 BLB 1914-1945; DA; DA3; DAB; DAC;
 DAM MST, NOV, POET; DLB 10, 19,
 36, 162, 247; EWL 3; EXPN; EXPS;
 LAIT 3; LMFS 1, 2; MTCW 1, 2; MTFW
 2005; NFS 7; RGSF 2; SSFS 1, 19; TEA;
 WLIT 4
Jozsef, Attila 1905-1937 **TCLC 22**
 See also CA 116; 230; CDWLB 4; DLB
 215; EWL 3
Juana Ines de la Cruz, Sor
 1651(?)-1695 **HLCS 1; LC 5; PC 24**
 See also DLB 305; FW; LAW; RGWL 2, 3;
 WLIT 1
Juana Inez de La Cruz, Sor
 See Juana Ines de la Cruz, Sor
Judd, Cyril
 See Kornbluth, C(yril) M.; Pohl, Frederik
Juenger, Ernst 1895-1998 **CLC 125**
 See Junger, Ernst
 See also CA 101; 167; CANR 21, 47, 106;
 DLB 56
Julian of Norwich 1342(?)-1416(?) . **LC 6, 52**
 See also DLB 146; LMFS 1
Julius Caesar 100B.C.-44B.C.
 See Caesar, Julius
 See also CDWLB 1; DLB 211
Junger, Ernst
 See Juenger, Ernst
 See also CDWLB 2; EWL 3; RGWL 2, 3
Junger, Sebastian 1962- **CLC 109**
 See also AAYA 28; CA 165; CANR 130;
 MTFW 2005
Juniper, Alex
 See Hospital, Janette Turner
Junius
 See Luxemburg, Rosa
Junzaburo, Nishiwaki
 See Nishiwaki, Junzaburo
 See also EWL 3
Just, Ward (Swift) 1935- **CLC 4, 27**
 See also CA 25-28R; CANR 32, 87; CN 6,
 7; INT CANR-32
Justice, Donald (Rodney)
 1925-2004 **CLC 6, 19, 102; PC 64**
 See also AMWS 7; CA 5-8R; 230; CANR
 26, 54, 74, 121, 122; CP 1, 2, 3, 4, 5, 6,
 7; CSW; DAM POET; DLBY 1983; EWL
 3; INT CANR-26; MAL 5; MTCW 2; PFS
 14; TCLE 1:1
Juvenal c. 60-c. 130 **CMLC 8**
 See also AW 2; CDWLB 1; DLB 211;
 RGWL 2, 3; WLIT 8
Juvenis
 See Bourne, Randolph S(illiman)
K., Alice
 See Knapp, Caroline
Kabakov, Sasha **CLC 59**
Kabir 1398(?)-1448(?) **LC 109; PC 56**
 See also RGWL 2, 3
Kacew, Romain 1914-1980
 See Gary, Romain
 See also CA 108; 102
Kadare, Ismail 1936- **CLC 52, 190**
 See also CA 161; EWL 3; RGWL 3
Kadohata, Cynthia (Lynn)
 1956(?)- **CLC 59, 122**
 See also AAYA 71; CA 140; CANR 124;
 SATA 155

Kafka, Franz 1883-1924 ... **SSC 5, 29, 35, 60;
 TCLC 2, 6, 13, 29, 47, 53, 112, 179;
 WLC 3**
 See also AAYA 31; BPFB 2; CA 105; 126;
 CDWLB 2; DA; DA3; DAB; DAC; DAM
 MST, NOV; DLB 81; EW 9; EWL 3;
 EXPS; LATS 1:1; LMFS 2; MTCW 1, 2;
 MTFW 2005; NFS 7; RGSF 2; RGWL 2,
 3; SFW 4; SSFS 3, 7, 12; TWA
Kahanovitsch, Pinkhes
 See Der Nister
Kahn, Roger 1927- **CLC 30**
 See also CA 25-28R; CANR 44, 69, 152;
 DLB 171; SATA 37
Kain, Saul
 See Sassoon, Siegfried (Lorraine)
Kaiser, Georg 1878-1945 **TCLC 9**
 See also CA 106; 190; CDWLB 2; DLB
 124; EWL 3; LMFS 2; RGWL 2, 3
Kaledin, Sergei **CLC 59**
Kaletski, Alexander 1946- **CLC 39**
 See also CA 118; 143
Kalidasa fl. c. 400-455 **CMLC 9; PC 22**
 See also RGWL 2, 3
Kallman, Chester (Simon)
 1921-1975 **CLC 2**
 See also CA 45-48; 53-56; CANR 3; CP 1,
 2
Kaminsky, Melvin **CLC 12, 217**
 See Brooks, Mel
 See also AAYA 13, 48; DLB 26
Kaminsky, Stuart M. 1934- **CLC 59**
 See also CA 73-76; CANR 29, 53, 89;
 CMW 4
Kaminsky, Stuart Melvin
 See Kaminsky, Stuart M.
Kamo no Chomei 1153(?)-1216 **CMLC 66**
 See also DLB 203
Kamo no Nagaakira
 See Kamo no Chomei
Kandinsky, Wassily 1866-1944 **TCLC 92**
 See also AAYA 64; CA 118; 155
Kane, Francis
 See Robbins, Harold
Kane, Henry 1918-
 See Queen, Ellery
 See also CA 156; CMW 4
Kane, Paul
 See Simon, Paul
Kanin, Garson 1912-1999 **CLC 22**
 See also AITN 1; CA 5-8R; 177; CAD;
 CANR 7, 78; DLB 7; IDFW 3, 4
Kaniuk, Yoram 1930- **CLC 19**
 See also CA 134; DLB 299; RGHL
Kant, Immanuel 1724-1804 **NCLC 27, 67**
 See also DLB 94
Kantor, MacKinlay 1904-1977 **CLC 7**
 See also CA 61-64; 73-76; CANR 60, 63;
 CN 1, 2; DLB 9, 102; MAL 5; MTCW 2;
 RHW; TCWW 1, 2
Kanze Motokiyo
 See Zeami
Kaplan, David Michael 1946- **CLC 50**
 See also CA 187
Kaplan, James 1951- **CLC 59**
 See also CA 135; CANR 121
Karadzic, Vuk Stefanovic
 1787-1864 **NCLC 115**
 See also CDWLB 4; DLB 147
Karageorge, Michael
 See Anderson, Poul (William)
Karamzin, Nikolai Mikhailovich
 1766-1826 **NCLC 3**
 See also DLB 150; RGSF 2
Karapanou, Margarita 1946- **CLC 13**
 See also CA 101
Karinthy, Frigyes 1887-1938 **TCLC 47**
 See also CA 170; DLB 215; EWL 3

Karl, Frederick R(obert)
 1927-2004 **CLC 34**
 See also CA 5-8R; 226; CANR 3, 44, 143
Karr, Mary 1955- **CLC 188**
 See also AMWS 11; CA 151; CANR 100;
 MTFW 2005; NCFS 5
Kastel, Warren
 See Silverberg, Robert
Kataev, Evgeny Petrovich 1903-1942
 See Petrov, Evgeny
 See also CA 120
Kataphusin
 See Ruskin, John
Katz, Steve 1935- **CLC 47**
 See also CA 25-28R; CAAS 14, 64; CANR
 12; CN 4, 5, 6, 7; DLBY 1983
Kauffman, Janet 1945- **CLC 42**
 See also CA 117; CANR 43, 84; DLB 218;
 DLBY 1986
Kaufman, Bob (Garnell) 1925-1986 . **CLC 49**
 See also BG 1:3; BW 1; CA 41-44R; 118;
 CANR 22; CP 1; DLB 16, 41
Kaufman, George S. 1889-1961 **CLC 38;
 DC 17**
 See also CA 108; 93-96; DAM DRAM;
 DFS 1, 10; DLB 7; INT CA-108; MTCW
 2; MTFW 2005; RGAL 4; TUS
Kaufman, Moises 1964- **DC 26**
 See also CA 211; DFS 22; MTFW 2005
Kaufman, Sue **CLC 3, 8**
 See Barondess, Sue K(aufman)
Kavafis, Konstantinos Petrou 1863-1933
 See Cavafy, C(onstantine) P(eter)
 See also CA 104
Kavan, Anna 1901-1968 **CLC 5, 13, 82**
 See also BRWS 7; CA 5-8R; CANR 6, 57;
 DLB 255; MTCW 1; RGEL 2; SFW 4
Kavanagh, Dan
 See Barnes, Julian
Kavanagh, Julie 1952- **CLC 119**
 See also CA 163
Kavanagh, Patrick (Joseph)
 1904-1967 **CLC 22; PC 33**
 See also BRWS 7; CA 123; 25-28R; DLB
 15, 20; EWL 3; MTCW 1; RGEL 2
Kawabata, Yasunari 1899-1972 **CLC 2, 5,
 9, 18, 107; SSC 17**
 See Kawabata Yasunari
 See also CA 93-96; 33-36R; CANR 88;
 DAM MULT; MJW; MTCW 2; MTFW
 2005; RGSF 2; RGWL 2, 3
Kawabata Yasunari
 See Kawabata, Yasunari
 See also DLB 180; EWL 3
Kaye, M(ary) M(argaret)
 1908-2004 **CLC 28**
 See also CA 89-92; 223; CANR 24, 60, 102,
 142; MTCW 1, 2; MTFW 2005; RHW;
 SATA 62; SATA-Obit 152
Kaye, Mollie
 See Kaye, M(ary) M(argaret)
Kaye-Smith, Sheila 1887-1956 **TCLC 20**
 See also CA 118; 203; DLB 36
Kaymor, Patrice Maguilene
 See Senghor, Leopold Sedar
Kazakov, Iurii Pavlovich
 See Kazakov, Yuri Pavlovich
 See also DLB 302
Kazakov, Yuri Pavlovich 1927-1982 . **SSC 43**
 See Kazakov, Iurii Pavlovich; Kazakov,
 Yury
 See also CA 5-8R; CANR 36; MTCW 1;
 RGSF 2
Kazakov, Yury
 See Kazakov, Yuri Pavlovich
 See also EWL 3
Kazan, Elia 1909-2003 **CLC 6, 16, 63**
 See also CA 21-24R; 220; CANR 32, 78

Kazantzakis, Nikos 1883(?)-1957 **TCLC 2, 5, 33**
See also BPFB 2; CA 105; 132; DA3; EW 9; EWL 3; MTCW 1, 2; MTFW 2005; RGWL 2, 3

Kazin, Alfred 1915-1998 **CLC 34, 38, 119**
See also AMWS 8; CA 1-4R; CAAS 7; CANR 1, 45, 79; DLB 67; EWL 3

Keane, Mary Nesta (Skrine) 1904-1996
See Keane, Molly
See also CA 108; 114; 151; RHW

Keane, Molly **CLC 31**
See Keane, Mary Nesta (Skrine)
See also CN 5, 6; INT CA-114; TCLE 1:1

Keates, Jonathan 1946(?)- **CLC 34**
See also CA 163; CANR 126

Keaton, Buster 1895-1966 **CLC 20**
See also CA 194

Keats, John 1795-1821 **NCLC 8, 73, 121; PC 1; WLC 3**
See also AAYA 58; BRW 4; BRWR 1; CD-BLB 1789-1832; DA; DA3; DAB; DAC; DAM MST, POET; DLB 96, 110; EXPP; LMFS 1; PAB; PFS 1, 2, 3, 9, 17; RGEL 2; TEA; WLIT 3; WP

Keble, John 1792-1866 **NCLC 87**
See also DLB 32, 55; RGEL 2

Keene, Donald 1922- **CLC 34**
See also CA 1-4R; CANR 5, 119

Keillor, Garrison 1942- **CLC 40, 115, 222**
See also AAYA 2, 62; BEST 89:3; BPFB 2; CA 111; 117; CANR 36, 59, 124; CPW; DA3; DAM POP; DLBY 1987; EWL 3; MTCW 1, 2; MTFW 2005; SATA 58; TUS

Keith, Carlos
See Lewton, Val

Keith, Michael
See Hubbard, L. Ron

Keller, Gottfried 1819-1890 **NCLC 2; SSC 26**
See also CDWLB 2; DLB 129; EW; RGSF 2; RGWL 2, 3

Keller, Nora Okja 1965- **CLC 109**
See also CA 187

Kellerman, Jonathan 1949- **CLC 44**
See also AAYA 35; BEST 90:1; CA 106; CANR 29, 51, 150; CMW 4; CPW; DA3; DAM POP; INT CANR-29

Kelley, William Melvin 1937- **CLC 22**
See also BW 1; CA 77-80; CANR 27, 83; CN 1, 2, 3, 4, 5, 6, 7; DLB 33; EWL 3

Kellogg, Marjorie 1922-2005 **CLC 2**
See also CA 81-84; 246

Kellow, Kathleen
See Hibbert, Eleanor Alice Burford

Kelly, Lauren
See Oates, Joyce Carol

Kelly, M(ilton) T(errence) 1947- **CLC 55**
See also CA 97-100; CAAS 22; CANR 19, 43, 84; CN 6

Kelly, Robert 1935- **SSC 50**
See also CA 17-20R; CAAS 19; CANR 47; CP 1, 2, 3, 4, 5, 6, 7; DLB 5, 130, 165

Kelman, James 1946- **CLC 58, 86**
See also BRWS 5; CA 148; CANR 85, 130; CN 5, 6, 7; DLB 194, 319, 326; RGSF 2; WLIT 4

Kemal, Yasar
See Kemal, Yashar
See also CWW 2; EWL 3; WLIT 6

Kemal, Yashar 1923(?)- **CLC 14, 29**
See also CA 89-92; CANR 44

Kemble, Fanny 1809-1893 **NCLC 18**
See also DLB 32

Kemelman, Harry 1908-1996 **CLC 2**
See also AITN 1; BPFB 2; CA 9-12R; 155; CANR 6, 71; CMW 4; DLB 28

Kempe, Margery 1373(?)-1440(?) ... **LC 6, 56**
See also DLB 146; FL 1:1; RGEL 2

Kempis, Thomas a 1380-1471 **LC 11**

Kendall, Henry 1839-1882 **NCLC 12**
See also DLB 230

Keneally, Thomas (Michael) 1935- ... **CLC 5, 8, 10, 14, 19, 27, 43, 117**
See also BRWS 4; CA 85-88; CANR 10, 50, 74, 130; CN 1, 2, 3, 4, 5, 6, 7; CPW; DA3; DAM NOV; DLB 289, 299, 326; EWL 3; MTCW 1, 2; MTFW 2005; NFS 17; RGEL 2; RGHL; RHW

Kennedy, A(lison) L(ouise) 1965- ... **CLC 188**
See also CA 168, 213; CAAE 213; CANR 108; CD 5, 6; CN 6, 7; DLB 271; RGSF 2

Kennedy, Adrienne (Lita) 1931- **BLC 2; CLC 66; DC 5**
See also AFAW 2; BW 2, 3; CA 103; CAAS 20; CABS 3; CAD; CANR 26, 53, 82; CD 5, 6; DAM MULT; DFS 9; DLB 38; FW; MAL 5

Kennedy, John Pendleton
1795-1870 **NCLC 2**
See also DLB 3, 248, 254; RGAL 4

Kennedy, Joseph Charles 1929-
See Kennedy, X. J.
See also CA 1-4R, 201; CAAE 201; CANR 4, 30, 40; CWRI 5; MAICYA 2; MAIC-YAS 1; SATA 14, 86, 130; SATA-Essay 130

Kennedy, William (Joseph) 1928- **CLC 6, 28, 34, 53**
See also AAYA 1; AMWS 7; BPFB 2; CA 85-88; CANR 14, 31, 76, 134; CN 4, 5, 6, 7; DA3; DAM NOV; DLB 143; DLBY 1985; EWL 3; INT CANR-31; MAL 5; MTCW 1, 2; MTFW 2005; SATA 57

Kennedy, X. J. **CLC 8, 42**
See Kennedy, Joseph Charles
See also AMWS 15; CAAS 9; CLR 27; CP 1, 2, 3, 4, 5, 6, 7; DLB 5; SAAS 22

Kenny, Maurice (Francis) 1929- **CLC 87; NNAL**
See also CA 144; CAAS 22; CANR 143; DAM MULT; DLB 175

Kent, Kelvin
See Kuttner, Henry

Kenton, Maxwell
See Southern, Terry

Kenyon, Jane 1947-1995 **PC 57**
See also AAYA 63; AMWS 7; CA 118; 148; CANR 44, 69; CP 6, 7; CWP; DLB 120; PFS 9, 17; RGAL 4

Kenyon, Robert O.
See Kuttner, Henry

Kepler, Johannes 1571-1630 **LC 45**

Ker, Jill
See Conway, Jill K(er)

Kerkow, H. C.
See Lewton, Val

Kerouac, Jack 1922-1969 **CLC 1, 2, 3, 5, 14, 29, 61; TCLC 117; WLC**
See Kerouac, Jean-Louis Lebris de
See also AAYA 25; AMWC 1; AMWS 3; BG 3; BPFB 2; CDALB 1941-1968; CP 1; CPW; DLB 2, 16, 237; DLBD 3; DLBY 1995; EWL 3; GLL 1; LATS 1:2; LMFS 2; MAL 5; NFS 8; RGAL 4; TUS; WP

Kerouac, Jean-Louis Lebris de 1922-1969
See Kerouac, Jack
See also AITN 1; CA 5-8R; 25-28R; CANR 26, 54, 95; DA; DA3; DAB; DAC; DAM MST, NOV, POET, POP; MTCW 1, 2; MTFW 2005

Kerr, (Bridget) Jean (Collins)
1923(?)-2003 **CLC 22**
See also CA 5-8R; 212; CANR 7; INT CANR-7

Kerr, M. E. **CLC 12, 35**
See Meaker, Marijane (Agnes)
See also AAYA 2, 23; BYA 1, 7, 8; CLR 29; SAAS 1; WYA

Kerr, Robert **CLC 55**

Kerrigan, (Thomas) Anthony 1918- .. **CLC 4, 6**
See also CA 49-52; CAAS 11; CANR 4

Kerry, Lois
See Duncan, Lois

Kesey, Ken (Elton) 1935-2001 ... **CLC 1, 3, 6, 11, 46, 64, 184; WLC 3**
See also AAYA 25; BG 1:3; BPFB 2; CA 1-4R; 204; CANR 22, 38, 66, 124; CDALB 1968-1988; CN 1, 2, 3, 4, 5, 6, 7; CPW; DA; DA3; DAB; DAC; DAM MST, NOV, POP; DLB 2, 16, 206; EWL 3; EXPN; LAIT 4; MAL 5; MTCW 1, 2; MTFW 2005; NFS 2; RGAL 4; SATA 66; SATA-Obit 131; TUS; YAW

Kesselring, Joseph (Otto)
1902-1967 **CLC 45**
See also CA 150; DAM DRAM, MST; DFS 20

Kessler, Jascha (Frederick) 1929- **CLC 4**
See also CA 17-20R; CANR 8, 48, 111; CP 1

Kettelkamp, Larry (Dale) 1933- **CLC 12**
See also CA 29-32R; CANR 16; SAAS 3; SATA 2

Key, Ellen (Karolina Sofia)
1849-1926 **TCLC 65**
See also DLB 259

Keyber, Conny
See Fielding, Henry

Keyes, Daniel 1927- **CLC 80**
See also AAYA 23; BYA 11; CA 17-20R, 181; CAAE 181; CANR 10, 26, 54, 74; DA; DA3; DAC; DAM MST, NOV; EXPN; LAIT 4; MTCW 2; MTFW 2005; NFS 2; SATA 37; SFW 4

Keynes, John Maynard
1883-1946 **TCLC 64**
See also CA 114; 162, 163; DLBD 10; MTCW 2; MTFW 2005

Khanshendel, Chiron
See Rose, Wendy

Khayyam, Omar 1048-1131 ... **CMLC 11; PC 8**
See Omar Khayyam
See also DA3; DAM POET; WLIT 6

Kherdian, David 1931- **CLC 6, 9**
See also AAYA 42; CA 21-24R, 192; CAAE 192; CAAS 2; CANR 39, 78; CLR 24; JRDA; LAIT 3; MAICYA 1, 2; SATA 16, 74; SATA-Essay 125

Khlebnikov, Velimir **TCLC 20**
See Khlebnikov, Viktor Vladimirovich
See also DLB 295; EW 10; EWL 3; RGWL 2, 3

Khlebnikov, Viktor Vladimirovich 1885-1922
See Khlebnikov, Velimir
See also CA 117; 217

Khodasevich, Vladislav (Felitsianovich)
1886-1939 **TCLC 15**
See also CA 115; DLB 317; EWL 3

Kielland, Alexander Lange
1849-1906 **TCLC 5**
See also CA 104

Kiely, Benedict 1919- ... **CLC 23, 43; SSC 58**
See also CA 1-4R; CANR 2, 84; CN 1, 2, 3, 4, 5, 6, 7; DLB 15, 319; TCLE 1:1

Kienzle, William X(avier)
1928-2001 **CLC 25**
See also CA 93-96; 203; CAAS 1; CANR 9, 31, 59, 111; CMW 4; DA3; DAM POP; INT CANR-31; MSW; MTCW 1, 2; MTFW 2005

Kierkegaard, Soren 1813-1855 **NCLC 34, 78, 125**
See also DLB 300; EW 6; LMFS 2; RGWL 3; TWA

Kieslowski, Krzysztof 1941-1996 **CLC 120**
See also CA 147; 151

Killens, John Oliver 1916-1987 **CLC 10**
See also BW 2; CA 77-80; 123; CAAS 2; CANR 26; CN 1, 2, 3, 4; DLB 33; EWL 3

Killigrew, Anne 1660-1685 **LC 4, 73**
See also DLB 131

Killigrew, Thomas 1612-1683 **LC 57**
See also DLB 58; RGEL 2

Kim
See Simenon, Georges (Jacques Christian)

Kincaid, Jamaica 1949- **BLC 2; CLC 43, 68, 137; SSC 72**
See also AAYA 13, 56; AFAW 2; AMWS 7; BRWS 7; BW 2, 3; CA 125; CANR 47, 59, 95, 133; CDALBS; CDWLB 3; CLR 63; CN 4, 5, 6, 7; DA3; DAM MULT, NOV; DLB 157, 227; DNFS 1; EWL 3; EXPS; FW; LATS 1:2; LMFS 2; MAL 5; MTCW 2; MTFW 2005; NCFS 1; NFS 3; SSFS 5, 7; TUS; WWE 1; YAW

King, Francis (Henry) 1923- **CLC 8, 53, 145**
See also CA 1-4R; CANR 1, 33, 86; CN 1, 2, 3, 4, 5, 6, 7; DAM NOV; DLB 15, 139; MTCW 1

King, Kennedy
See Brown, George Douglas

King, Martin Luther, Jr. 1929-1968 . **BLC 2; CLC 83; WLCS**
See also BW 2, 3; CA 25-28; CANR 27, 44; CAP 2; DA; DA3; DAB; DAC; DAM MST, MULT; LAIT 5; LATS 1:2; MTCW 1, 2; MTFW 2005; SATA 14

King, Stephen 1947- **CLC 12, 26, 37, 61, 113; SSC 17, 55**
See also AAYA 1, 17; AMWS 5; BEST 90:1; BPFB 2; CA 61-64; CANR 1, 30, 52, 76, 119, 134; CN 7; CPW; DA3; DAM NOV, POP; DLB 143; DLBY 1980; HGG; JRDA; LAIT 5; MTCW 1, 2; MTFW 2005; RGAL 4; SATA 9, 55, 161; SUFW 1, 2; WYAS 1; YAW

King, Stephen Edwin
See King, Stephen

King, Steve
See King, Stephen

King, Thomas 1943- **CLC 89, 171; NNAL**
See also CA 144; CANR 95; CCA 1; CN 6, 7; DAC; DAM MULT; DLB 175; SATA 96

Kingman, Lee **CLC 17**
See Natti, (Mary) Lee
See also CWRI 5; SAAS 3; SATA 1, 67

Kingsley, Charles 1819-1875 **NCLC 35**
See also CLR 77; DLB 21, 32, 163, 178, 190; FANT; MAICYA 2; MAICYAS 1; RGEL 2; WCH; YABC 2

Kingsley, Henry 1830-1876 **NCLC 107**
See also DLB 21, 230; RGEL 2

Kingsley, Sidney 1906-1995 **CLC 44**
See also CA 85-88; 147; CAD; DFS 14, 19; DLB 7; MAL 5; RGAL 4

Kingsolver, Barbara 1955- **CLC 55, 81, 130, 216**
See also AAYA 15; AMWS 7; CA 129; 134; CANR 60, 96, 133; CDALBS; CN 7; CPW; CSW; DA3; DAM POP; DLB 206; INT CA-134; LAIT 5; MTCW 2; MTFW 2005; NFS 5, 10, 12; RGAL 4; TCLE 1:1

Kingston, Maxine (Ting Ting) Hong 1940- **AAL; CLC 12, 19, 58, 121; WLCS**
See also AAYA 8, 55; AMWS 5; BPFB 2; CA 69-72; CANR 13, 38, 74, 87, 128; CDALBS; CN 6, 7; DA3; DAM MULT,
NOV; DLB 173, 212, 312; DLBY 1980; EWL 3; FL 1:6; FW; INT CANR-13; LAIT 5; MAL 5; MAWW; MTCW 1, 2; MTFW 2005; NFS 6; RGAL 4; SATA 53; SSFS 3; TCWW 2

Kinnell, Galway 1927- **CLC 1, 2, 3, 5, 13, 29, 129; PC 26**
See also AMWS 3; CA 9-12R; CANR 10, 34, 66, 116, 138; CP 1, 2, 3, 4, 5, 6, 7; DLB 5; DLBY 1987; EWL 3; INT CANR-34; MAL 5; MTCW 1, 2; MTFW 2005; PAB; PFS 9; RGAL 4; TCLE 1:1; WP

Kinsella, Thomas 1928- **CLC 4, 19, 138; PC 69**
See also BRWS 5; CA 17-20R; CANR 15, 122; CP 1, 2, 3, 4, 5, 6, 7; DLB 27; EWL 3; MTCW 1, 2; MTFW 2005; RGEL 2; TEA

Kinsella, W(illiam) P(atrick) 1935- . **CLC 27, 43, 166**
See also AAYA 7, 60; BPFB 2; CA 97-100, 222; CAAE 222; CAAS 7; CANR 21, 35, 66, 75, 129; CN 4, 5, 6, 7; CPW; DAC; DAM NOV, POP; FANT; INT CANR-21; LAIT 5; MTCW 1, 2; MTFW 2005; NFS 15; RGSF 2

Kinsey, Alfred C(harles) 1894-1956 **TCLC 91**
See also CA 115; 170; MTCW 2

Kipling, (Joseph) Rudyard 1865-1936 . **PC 3; SSC 5, 54; TCLC 8, 17, 167; WLC 3**
See also AAYA 32; BRW 6; BRWC 1, 2; BYA 4; CA 105; 120; CANR 33; CDBLB 1890-1914; CLR 39, 65; CWRI 5; DA; DA3; DAB; DAC; DAM MST, POET; DLB 19, 34, 141, 156; EWL 3; EXPS; FANT; LAIT 3; LMFS 1; MAICYA 1, 2; MTCW 1, 2; MTFW 2005; NFS 21; PFS 22; RGEL 2; RGSF 2; SATA 100; SFW 4; SSFS 8, 21; SUFW 1; TEA; WCH; WLIT 4; YABC 2

Kircher, Athanasius 1602-1680 **LC 121**
See also DLB 164

Kirk, Russell (Amos) 1918-1994 .. **TCLC 119**
See also AITN 1; CA 1-4R; 145; CAAS 9; CANR 1, 20, 60; HGG; INT CANR-20; MTCW 1, 2

Kirkham, Dinah
See Card, Orson Scott

Kirkland, Caroline M. 1801-1864 . **NCLC 85**
See also DLB 3, 73, 74, 250, 254; DLBD 13

Kirkup, James 1918- **CLC 1**
See also CA 1-4R; CAAS 4; CANR 2; CP 1, 2, 3, 4, 5, 6, 7; DLB 27; SATA 12

Kirkwood, James 1930(?)-1989 **CLC 9**
See also AITN 2; CA 1-4R; 128; CANR 6, 40; GLL 2

Kirsch, Sarah 1935- **CLC 176**
See also CA 178; CWW 2; DLB 75; EWL 3

Kirshner, Sidney
See Kingsley, Sidney

Kis, Danilo 1935-1989 **CLC 57**
See also CA 109; 118; 129; CANR 61; CDWLB 4; DLB 181; EWL 3; MTCW 1; RGSF 2; RGWL 2, 3

Kissinger, Henry A(lfred) 1923- **CLC 137**
See also CA 1-4R; CANR 2, 33, 66, 109; MTCW 1

Kittel, Frederick August
See Wilson, August

Kivi, Aleksis 1834-1872 **NCLC 30**

Kizer, Carolyn (Ashley) 1925- ... **CLC 15, 39, 80; PC 66**
See also CA 65-68; CAAS 5; CANR 24, 70, 134; CP 1, 2, 3, 4, 5, 6, 7; CWP; DAM POET; DLB 5, 169; EWL 3; MAL 5; MTCW 2; MTFW 2005; PFS 18; TCLE 1:1

Klabund 1890-1928 **TCLC 44**
See also CA 162; DLB 66

Klappert, Peter 1942- **CLC 57**
See also CA 33-36R; CSW; DLB 5

Klein, A(braham) M(oses) 1909-1972 **CLC 19**
See also CA 101; 37-40R; CP 1; DAB; DAC; DAM MST; DLB 68; EWL 3; RGEL 2; RGHL

Klein, Joe
See Klein, Joseph

Klein, Joseph 1946- **CLC 154**
See also CA 85-88; CANR 55

Klein, Norma 1938-1989 **CLC 30**
See also AAYA 2, 35; BPFB 2; BYA 6, 7, 8; CA 41-44R; 128; CANR 15, 37; CLR 2, 19; INT CANR-15; JRDA; MAICYA 1, 2; SAAS 1; SATA 7, 57; WYA; YAW

Klein, T(heodore) E(ibon) D(onald) 1947- **CLC 34**
See also CA 119; CANR 44, 75; HGG

Kleist, Heinrich von 1777-1811 **NCLC 2, 37; SSC 22**
See also CDWLB 2; DAM DRAM; DLB 90; EW 5; RGSF 2; RGWL 2, 3

Klima, Ivan 1931- **CLC 56, 172**
See also CA 25-28R; CANR 17, 50, 91; CDWLB 4; CWW 2; DAM NOV; DLB 232; EWL 3; RGWL 3

Klimentev, Andrei Platonovich
See Klimentov, Andrei Platonovich

Klimentov, Andrei Platonovich 1899-1951 **SSC 42; TCLC 14**
See Platonov, Andrei Platonovich; Platonov, Andrey Platonovich
See also CA 108; 232

Klinger, Friedrich Maximilian von 1752-1831 **NCLC 1**
See also DLB 94

Klingsor the Magician
See Hartmann, Sadakichi

Klopstock, Friedrich Gottlieb 1724-1803 **NCLC 11**
See also DLB 97; EW 4; RGWL 2, 3

Kluge, Alexander 1932- **SSC 61**
See also CA 81-84; DLB 75

Knapp, Caroline 1959-2002 **CLC 99**
See also CA 154; 207

Knebel, Fletcher 1911-1993 **CLC 14**
See also AITN 1; CA 1-4R; 140; CAAS 3; CANR 1, 36; CN 1, 2, 3, 4, 5; SATA 36; SATA-Obit 75

Knickerbocker, Diedrich
See Irving, Washington

Knight, Etheridge 1931-1991 ... **BLC 2; CLC 40; PC 14**
See also BW 1, 3; CA 21-24R; 133; CANR 23, 82; CP 1, 2, 3, 4, 5; DAM POET; DLB 41; MTCW 2; MTFW 2005; RGAL 4; TCLE 1:1

Knight, Sarah Kemble 1666-1727 **LC 7**
See also DLB 24, 200

Knister, Raymond 1899-1932 **TCLC 56**
See also CA 186; DLB 68; RGEL 2

Knowles, John 1926-2001 ... **CLC 1, 4, 10, 26**
See also AAYA 10; AMWS 12; BPFB 2; BYA 3; CA 17-20R; 203; CANR 40, 74, 76, 132; CDALB 1968-1988; CLR 98; CN 1, 2, 3, 4, 5, 6, 7; DA; DAC; DAM MST, NOV; DLB 6; EXPN; MTCW 1, 2; MTFW 2005; NFS 2; RGAL 4; SATA 8, 89; SATA-Obit 134; YAW

Knox, Calvin M.
See Silverberg, Robert

Knox, John c. 1505-1572 **LC 37**
See also DLB 132

Knye, Cassandra
See Disch, Thomas M(ichael)

Koch, C(hristopher) J(ohn) 1932- **CLC 42**
See also CA 127; CANR 84; CN 3, 4, 5, 6, 7; DLB 289

Koch, Christopher
See Koch, C(hristopher) J(ohn)

Koch, Kenneth (Jay) 1925-2002 **CLC 5, 8, 44**
See also AMWS 15; CA 1-4R; 207; CAD; CANR 6, 36, 57, 97, 131; CD 5, 6; CP 1, 2, 3, 4, 5, 6, 7; DAM POET; DLB 5; INT CANR-36; MAL 5; MTCW 2; MTFW 2005; PFS 20; SATA 65; WP

Kochanowski, Jan 1530-1584 **LC 10**
See also RGWL 2, 3

Kock, Charles Paul de 1794-1871 . **NCLC 16**

Koda Rohan
See Koda Shigeyuki

Koda Rohan
See Koda Shigeyuki
See also DLB 180

Koda Shigeyuki 1867-1947 **TCLC 22**
See Koda Rohan
See also CA 121; 183

Koestler, Arthur 1905-1983 ... **CLC 1, 3, 6, 8, 15, 33**
See also BRWS 1; CA 1-4R; 109; CANR 1, 33; CDBLB 1945-1960; CN 1, 2, 3; DLBY 1983; EWL 3; MTCW 1, 2; MTFW 2005; NFS 19; RGEL 2

Kogawa, Joy Nozomi 1935- **CLC 78, 129**
See also AAYA 47; CA 101; CANR 19, 62, 126; CN 6, 7; CP 1; CWP; DAC; DAM MST, MULT; FW; MTCW 2; MTFW 2005; NFS 3; SATA 99

Kohout, Pavel 1928- **CLC 13**
See also CA 45-48; CANR 3

Koizumi, Yakumo
See Hearn, (Patricio) Lafcadio (Tessima Carlos)

Kolmar, Gertrud 1894-1943 **TCLC 40**
See also CA 167; EWL 3; RGHL

Komunyakaa, Yusef 1947- .. **BLCS; CLC 86, 94, 207; PC 51**
See also AFAW 2; AMWS 13; CA 147; CANR 83; CP 6, 7; CSW; DLB 120; EWL 3; PFS 5, 20; RGAL 4

Konrad, George
See Konrad, Gyorgy

Konrad, Gyorgy 1933- **CLC 4, 10, 73**
See also CA 85-88; CANR 97; CDWLB 4; CWW 2; DLB 232; EWL 3

Konwicki, Tadeusz 1926- **CLC 8, 28, 54, 117**
See also CA 101; CAAS 9; CANR 39, 59; CWW 2; DLB 232; EWL 3; IDFW 3; MTCW 1

Koontz, Dean R. 1945- **CLC 78, 206**
See also AAYA 9, 31; BEST 89:3, 90:2; CA 108; CANR 19, 36, 52, 95, 138; CMW 4; CPW; DA3; DAM NOV, POP; DLB 292; HGG; MTCW 1; MTFW 2005; SATA 92, 165; SFW 4; SUFW 2; YAW

Koontz, Dean Ray
See Koontz, Dean R.

Koontz, Dean Ray
See Koontz, Dean R.

Kopernik, Mikolaj
See Copernicus, Nicolaus

Kopit, Arthur (Lee) 1937- **CLC 1, 18, 33**
See also AITN 1; CA 81-84; CABS 3; CAD; CD 5, 6; DAM DRAM; DFS 7, 14; DLB 7; MAL 5; MTCW 1; RGAL 4

Kopitar, Jernej (Bartholomaus)
1780-1844 **NCLC 117**

Kops, Bernard 1926- **CLC 4**
See also CA 5-8R; CANR 84; CBD; CN 1, 2, 3, 4, 5, 6, 7; CP 1, 2, 3, 4, 5, 6, 7; DLB 13; RGHL

Kornbluth, C(yril) M. 1923-1958 **TCLC 8**
See also CA 105; 160; DLB 8; SCFW 1, 2; SFW 4

Korolenko, V. G.
See Korolenko, Vladimir Galaktionovich

Korolenko, Vladimir
See Korolenko, Vladimir Galaktionovich

Korolenko, Vladimir G.
See Korolenko, Vladimir Galaktionovich

Korolenko, Vladimir Galaktionovich
1853-1921 **TCLC 22**
See also CA 121; DLB 277

Korzybski, Alfred (Habdank Skarbek)
1879-1950 **TCLC 61**
See also CA 123; 160

Kosinski, Jerzy (Nikodem)
1933-1991 **CLC 1, 2, 3, 6, 10, 15, 53, 70**
See also AMWS 7; BPFB 2; CA 17-20R; 134; CANR 9, 46; CN 1, 2, 3, 4; DA3; DAM NOV; DLB 2, 299; DLBY 1982; EWL 3; HGG; MAL 5; MTCW 1, 2; MTFW 2005; NFS 12; RGAL 4; RGHL; TUS

Kostelanetz, Richard (Cory) 1940- .. **CLC 28**
See also CA 13-16R; CAAS 8; CANR 38, 77; CN 4, 5, 6; CP 2, 3, 4, 5, 6, 7

Kostrowitzki, Wilhelm Apollinaris de
1880-1918
See Apollinaire, Guillaume
See also CA 104

Kotlowitz, Robert 1924- **CLC 4**
See also CA 33-36R; CANR 36

Kotzebue, August (Friedrich Ferdinand) von
1761-1819 **NCLC 25**
See also DLB 94

Kotzwinkle, William 1938- **CLC 5, 14, 35**
See also BPFB 2; CA 45-48; CANR 3, 44, 84, 129; CLR 6; CN 7; DLB 173; FANT; MAICYA 1, 2; SATA 24, 70, 146; SFW 4; SUFW 2; YAW

Kowna, Stancy
See Szymborska, Wislawa

Kozol, Jonathan 1936- **CLC 17**
See also AAYA 46; CA 61-64; CANR 16, 45, 96; MTFW 2005

Kozoll, Michael 1940(?)- **CLC 35**

Kramer, Kathryn 19(?)- **CLC 34**

Kramer, Larry 1935- **CLC 42; DC 8**
See also CA 124; 126; CANR 60, 132; DAM POP; DLB 249; GLL 1

Krasicki, Ignacy 1735-1801 **NCLC 8**

Krasinski, Zygmunt 1812-1859 **NCLC 4**
See also RGWL 2, 3

Kraus, Karl 1874-1936 **TCLC 5**
See also CA 104; 216; DLB 118; EWL 3

Kreve (Mickevicius), Vincas
1882-1954 **TCLC 27**
See also CA 170; DLB 220; EWL 3

Kristeva, Julia 1941- **CLC 77, 140**
See also CA 154; CANR 99; DLB 242; EWL 3; FW; LMFS 2

Kristofferson, Kris 1936- **CLC 26**
See also CA 104

Krizanc, John 1956- **CLC 57**
See also CA 187

Krleza, Miroslav 1893-1981 **CLC 8, 114**
See also CA 97-100; 105; CANR 50; CDWLB 4; DLB 147; EW 11; RGWL 2, 3

Kroetsch, Robert (Paul) 1927- **CLC 5, 23, 57, 132**
See also CA 17-20R; CANR 8, 38; CCA 1; CN 2, 3, 4, 5, 6, 7; CP 6, 7; DAC; DAM POET; DLB 53; MTCW 1

Kroetz, Franz
See Kroetz, Franz Xaver

Kroetz, Franz Xaver 1946- **CLC 41**
See also CA 130; CANR 142; CWW 2; EWL 3

Kroker, Arthur (W.) 1945- **CLC 77**
See also CA 161

Kroniuk, Lisa
See Berton, Pierre (Francis de Marigny)

Kropotkin, Peter (Aleksieevich)
1842-1921 **TCLC 36**
See Kropotkin, Petr Alekseevich
See also CA 119; 219

Kropotkin, Petr Alekseevich
See Kropotkin, Peter (Aleksieevich)
See also DLB 277

Krotkov, Yuri 1917-1981 **CLC 19**
See also CA 102

Krumb
See Crumb, R.

Krumgold, Joseph (Quincy)
1908-1980 **CLC 12**
See also BYA 1, 2; CA 9-12R; 101; CANR 7; MAICYA 1, 2; SATA 1, 48; SATA-Obit 23; YAW

Krumwitz
See Crumb, R.

Krutch, Joseph Wood 1893-1970 **CLC 24**
See also ANW; CA 1-4R; 25-28R; CANR 4; DLB 63, 206, 275

Krutzch, Gus
See Eliot, T(homas) S(tearns)

Krylov, Ivan Andreevich
1768(?)-1844 **NCLC 1**
See also DLB 150

Kubin, Alfred (Leopold Isidor)
1877-1959 **TCLC 23**
See also CA 112; 149; CANR 104; DLB 81

Kubrick, Stanley 1928-1999 **CLC 16; TCLC 112**
See also AAYA 30; CA 81-84; 177; CANR 33; DLB 26

Kumin, Maxine (Winokur) 1925- **CLC 5, 13, 28, 164; PC 15**
See also AITN 2; AMWS 4; ANW; CA 1-4R; CAAS 8; CANR 1, 21, 69, 115, 140; CP 2, 3, 4, 5, 6, 7; CWP; DA3; DAM POET; DLB 5; EWL 3; EXPP; MTCW 1, 2; MTFW 2005; PAB; PFS 18; SATA 12

Kundera, Milan 1929- . **CLC 4, 9, 19, 32, 68, 115, 135; SSC 24**
See also AAYA 2, 62; BPFB 2; CA 85-88; CANR 19, 52, 74, 144; CDWLB 4; CWW 2; DA3; DAM NOV; DLB 232; EW 13; EWL 3; MTCW 1, 2; MTFW 2005; NFS 18; RGSF 2; RGWL 3; SSFS 10

Kunene, Mazisi (Raymond) 1930- ... **CLC 85**
See also BW 1, 3; CA 125; CANR 81; CP 1, 6, 7; DLB 117

Kung, Hans **CLC 130**
See Kung, Hans

Kung, Hans 1928-
See Kung, Hans
See also CA 53-56; CANR 66, 134; MTCW 1, 2; MTFW 2005

Kunikida Doppo 1869(?)-1908
See Doppo, Kunikida
See also DLB 180; EWL 3

Kunitz, Stanley 1905-2006 **CLC 6, 11, 14, 148; PC 19**
See also AMWS 3; CA 41-44R; CANR 26, 57, 98; CP 1, 2, 3, 4, 5, 6, 7; DA3; DLB 48; INT CANR-26; MAL 5; MTCW 1, 2; MTFW 2005; PFS 11; RGAL 4

Kunitz, Stanley Jasspon
See Kunitz, Stanley

Kunze, Reiner 1933- **CLC 10**
See also CA 93-96; CWW 2; DLB 75; EWL 3

Kuprin, Aleksander Ivanovich
1870-1938 **TCLC 5**
See Kuprin, Aleksandr Ivanovich; Kuprin, Alexandr Ivanovich
See also CA 104; 182

Kuprin, Aleksandr Ivanovich
See Kuprin, Aleksander Ivanovich
See also DLB 295
Kuprin, Alexandr Ivanovich
See Kuprin, Aleksander Ivanovich
See also EWL 3
Kureishi, Hanif 1954- .. **CLC 64, 135; DC 26**
See also BRWS 11; CA 139; CANR 113;
CBD; CD 5, 6; CN 6, 7; DLB 194, 245;
GLL 2; IDFW 4; WLIT 4; WWE 1
Kurosawa, Akira 1910-1998 **CLC 16, 119**
See also AAYA 11, 64; CA 101; 170; CANR
46; DAM MULT
Kushner, Tony 1956- **CLC 81, 203; DC 10**
See also AAYA 61; AMWS 9; CA 144;
CAD; CANR 74, 130; CD 5, 6; DA3;
DAM DRAM; DFS 5; DLB 228; EWL 3;
GLL 1; LAIT 5; MAL 5; MTCW 2;
MTFW 2005; RGAL 4; RGHL; SATA 160
Kuttner, Henry 1915-1958 **TCLC 10**
See also CA 107; 157; DLB 8; FANT;
SCFW 1, 2; SFW 4
Kutty, Madhavi
See Das, Kamala
Kuzma, Greg 1944- **CLC 7**
See also CA 33-36R; CANR 70
Kuzmin, Mikhail (Alekseevich)
1872(?)-1936 **TCLC 40**
See also CA 170; DLB 295; EWL 3
Kyd, Thomas 1558-1594 .. **DC 3; LC 22, 125**
See also BRW 1; DAM DRAM; DFS 21;
DLB 62; IDTP; LMFS 1; RGEL 2; TEA;
WLIT 3
Kyprianos, Iossif
See Samarakis, Antonis
L. S.
See Stephen, Sir Leslie
Laȝamon
See Layamon
See also DLB 146
Labe, Louise 1521-1566 **LC 120**
Labrunie, Gerard
See Nerval, Gerard de
La Bruyere, Jean de 1645-1696 **LC 17**
See also DLB 268; EW 3; GFL Beginnings
to 1789
LaBute, Neil 1963- **CLC 225**
See also CA 240
Lacan, Jacques (Marie Emile)
1901-1981 **CLC 75**
See also CA 121; 104; DLB 296; EWL 3;
TWA
Laclos, Pierre-Ambroise Francois
1741-1803 **NCLC 4, 87**
See also DLB 313; EW 4; GFL Beginnings
to 1789; RGWL 2, 3
Lacolere, Francois
See Aragon, Louis
La Colere, Francois
See Aragon, Louis
La Deshabilleuse
See Simenon, Georges (Jacques Christian)
Lady Gregory
See Gregory, Lady Isabella Augusta (Persse)
Lady of Quality, A
See Bagnold, Enid
La Fayette, Marie-(Madelaine Pioche de la
Vergne) 1634-1693 **LC 2**
See Lafayette, Marie-Madeleine
See also GFL Beginnings to 1789; RGWL
2, 3
Lafayette, Marie-Madeleine
See La Fayette, Marie-(Madelaine Pioche
de la Vergne)
See also DLB 268
Lafayette, Rene
See Hubbard, L. Ron
La Flesche, Francis 1857(?)-1932 **NNAL**
See also CA 144; CANR 83; DLB 175

La Fontaine, Jean de 1621-1695 **LC 50**
See also DLB 268; EW 3; GFL Beginnings
to 1789; MAICYA 1, 2; RGWL 2, 3;
SATA 18
LaForet, Carmen 1921-2004 **CLC 219**
See also CA 246; CWW 2; DLB 322; EWL
3
LaForet Diaz, Carmen
See LaForet, Carmen
Laforgue, Jules 1860-1887 . **NCLC 5, 53; PC**
14; SSC 20
See also DLB 217; EW 7; GFL 1789 to the
Present; RGWL 2, 3
Lagerkvist, Paer (Fabian)
1891-1974 **CLC 7, 10, 13, 54; TCLC**
144
See Lagerkvist, Par
See also CA 85-88; 49-52; DA3; DAM
DRAM, NOV; MTCW 1, 2; MTFW 2005;
TWA
Lagerkvist, Par **SSC 12**
See Lagerkvist, Paer (Fabian)
See also DLB 259; EW 10; EWL 3; RGSF
2; RGWL 2, 3
Lagerloef, Selma (Ottiliana Lovisa)
... **TCLC 4, 36**
See Lagerlof, Selma (Ottiliana Lovisa)
See also CA 108; MTCW 2
Lagerlof, Selma (Ottiliana Lovisa)
1858-1940
See Lagerloef, Selma (Ottiliana Lovisa)
See also CA 188; CLR 7; DLB 259; RGWL
2, 3; SATA 15; SSFS 18
La Guma, (Justin) Alex(ander)
1925 1985 . **BLCS; CLC 19; TCLC 140**
See also AFW; BW 1, 3; CA 49-52; 118;
CANR 25, 81; CDWLB 3; CN 1, 2, 3;
CP 1; DAM NOV; DLB 117, 225; EWL
3; MTCW 1, 2; MTFW 2005; WLIT 2;
WWE 1
Laidlaw, A. K.
See Grieve, C(hristopher) M(urray)
Lainez, Manuel Mujica
See Mujica Lainez, Manuel
See also HW 1
Laing, R(onald) D(avid) 1927-1989 . **CLC 95**
See also CA 107; 129; CANR 34; MTCW 1
Laishley, Alex
See Booth, Martin
Lamartine, Alphonse (Marie Louis Prat) de
1790-1869 **NCLC 11; PC 16**
See also DAM POET; DLB 217; GFL 1789
to the Present; RGWL 2, 3
Lamb, Charles 1775-1834 **NCLC 10, 113;**
WLC 3
See also BRW 4; CDBLB 1789-1832; DA;
DAB; DAC; DAM MST; DLB 93, 107,
163; RGEL 2; SATA 17; TEA
Lamb, Lady Caroline 1785-1828 ... **NCLC 38**
See also DLB 116
Lamb, Mary Ann 1764-1847 **NCLC 125**
See also DLB 163; SATA 17
Lame Deer 1903(?)-1976 **NNAL**
See also CA 69-72
Lamming, George (William) 1927- ... **BLC 2;**
CLC 2, 4, 66, 144
See also BW 2, 3; CA 85-88; CANR 26,
76; CDWLB 3; CN 1, 2, 3, 4, 5, 6, 7; CP
1; DAM MULT; DLB 125; EWL 3;
MTCW 1, 2; MTFW 2005; NFS 15;
RGEL 2
L'Amour, Louis (Dearborn)
1908-1988 **CLC 25, 55**
See also AAYA 16; AITN 2; BEST 89:2;
BPFB 1; CA 1-4R; 125; CANR 3, 25, 40;
CPW; DA3; DAM NOV, POP; DLB 206;
DLBY 1980; MTCW 1, 2; MTFW 2005;
RGAL 4; TCWW 1, 2

Lampedusa, Giuseppe (Tomasi) di
... **TCLC 13**
See Tomasi di Lampedusa, Giuseppe
See also CA 164; EW 11; MTCW 2; MTFW
2005; RGWL 2, 3
Lampman, Archibald 1861-1899 ... **NCLC 25**
See also DLB 92; RGEL 2; TWA
Lancaster, Bruce 1896-1963 **CLC 36**
See also CA 9-10; CANR 70; CAP 1; SATA
9
Lanchester, John 1962- **CLC 99**
See also CA 194; DLB 267
Landau, Mark Alexandrovich
See Aldanov, Mark (Alexandrovich)
Landau-Aldanov, Mark Alexandrovich
See Aldanov, Mark (Alexandrovich)
Landis, Jerry
See Simon, Paul
Landis, John 1950- **CLC 26**
See also CA 112; 122; CANR 128
Landolfi, Tommaso 1908-1979 **CLC 11, 49**
See also CA 127; 117; DLB 177; EWL 3
Landon, Letitia Elizabeth
1802-1838 **NCLC 15**
See also DLB 96
Landor, Walter Savage
1775-1864 **NCLC 14**
See also BRW 4; DLB 93, 107; RGEL 2
Landwirth, Heinz 1927-
See Lind, Jakov
See also CA 9-12R; CANR 7
Lane, Patrick 1939- **CLC 25**
See also CA 97-100; CANR 54; CP 3, 4, 5,
6, 7; DAM POET; DLB 53; INT CA-97-
100
Lane, Rose Wilder 1887-1968 **TCLC 177**
See also CA 102; CANR 63; SATA 29;
SATA-Brief 28; TCWW 2
Lang, Andrew 1844-1912 **TCLC 16**
See also CA 114; 137; CANR 85; CLR 101;
DLB 98, 141, 184; FANT; MAICYA 1, 2;
RGEL 2; SATA 16; WCH
Lang, Fritz 1890-1976 **CLC 20, 103**
See also AAYA 65; CA 77-80; 69-72;
CANR 30
Lange, John
See Crichton, (John) Michael
Langer, Elinor 1939- **CLC 34**
See also CA 121
Langland, William 1332(?)-1400(?) **LC 19,**
120
See also BRW 1; DA; DAB; DAC; DAM
MST, POET; DLB 146; RGEL 2; TEA;
WLIT 3
Langstaff, Launcelot
See Irving, Washington
Lanier, Sidney 1842-1881 . **NCLC 6, 118; PC**
50
See also AMWS 1; DAM POET; DLB 64;
DLBD 13; EXPP; MAICYA 1; PFS 14;
RGAL 4; SATA 18
Lanyer, Aemilia 1569-1645 **LC 10, 30, 83;**
PC 60
See also DLB 121
Lao Tzu c. 6th cent. B.C.-3rd cent.
B.C. ... **CMLC 7**
Lao-Tzu
See Lao Tzu
Lapine, James (Elliot) 1949- **CLC 39**
See also CA 123; 130; CANR 54, 128; INT
CA-130
Larbaud, Valery (Nicolas)
1881-1957 **TCLC 9**
See also CA 106; 152; EWL 3; GFL 1789
to the Present

Lardner, Ring
See Lardner, Ring(gold) W(ilmer)
See also BPFB 2; CDALB 1917-1929; DLB
11, 25, 86, 171; DLBD 16; MAL 5;
RGAL 4; RGSF 2

Lardner, Ring W., Jr.
See Lardner, Ring(gold) W(ilmer)

Lardner, Ring(gold) W(ilmer)
1885-1933 **SSC 32; TCLC 2, 14**
See Lardner, Ring
See also AMW; CA 104; 131; MTCW 1, 2;
MTFW 2005; TUS

Laredo, Betty
See Codrescu, Andrei

Larkin, Maia
See Wojciechowska, Maia (Teresa)

Larkin, Philip (Arthur) 1922-1985 ... **CLC 3,
5, 8, 9, 13, 18, 33, 39, 64; PC 21**
See also BRWS 1; CA 5-8R; 117; CANR
24, 62; CDBLB 1960 to Present; CP 1, 2,
3, 4; DA3; DAB; DAM MST, POET;
DLB 27; EWL 3; MTCW 1, 2; MTFW
2005; PFS 3, 4, 12; RGEL 2

La Roche, Sophie von
1730-1807 **NCLC 121**
See also DLB 94

La Rochefoucauld, Francois
1613-1680 **LC 108**

**Larra (y Sanchez de Castro), Mariano Jose
de** 1809-1837 **NCLC 17, 130**

Larsen, Eric 1941- **CLC 55**
See also CA 132

Larsen, Nella 1893(?)-1963 **BLC 2; CLC
37; HR 1:3**
See also AFAW 1, 2; BW 1; CA 125; CANR
83; DAM MULT; DLB 51; FW; LATS
1:1; LMFS 2

Larson, Charles R(aymond) 1938- ... **CLC 31**
See also CA 53-56; CANR 4, 121

Larson, Jonathan 1960-1996 **CLC 99**
See also AAYA 28; CA 156; DFS 23;
MTFW 2005

La Sale, Antoine de c. 1386-1460(?) . **LC 104**
See also DLB 208

Las Casas, Bartolome de
1474-1566 **HLCS; LC 31**
See Casas, Bartolome de las
See also DLB 318; LAW

Lasch, Christopher 1932-1994 **CLC 102**
See also CA 73-76; 144; CANR 25, 118;
DLB 246; MTCW 1, 2; MTFW 2005

Lasker-Schueler, Else 1869-1945 ... **TCLC 57**
See Lasker-Schuler, Else
See also CA 183; DLB 66, 124

Lasker-Schuler, Else
See Lasker-Schueler, Else
See also EWL 3

Laski, Harold J(oseph) 1893-1950 . **TCLC 79**
See also CA 188

Latham, Jean Lee 1902-1995 **CLC 12**
See also AITN 1; BYA 1; CA 5-8R; CANR
7, 84; CLR 50; MAICYA 1, 2; SATA 2,
68; YAW

Latham, Mavis
See Clark, Mavis Thorpe

Lathen, Emma **CLC 2**
See Hennissart, Martha; Latsis, Mary J(ane)
See also BPFB 2; CMW 4; DLB 306

Lathrop, Francis
See Leiber, Fritz (Reuter, Jr.)

Latsis, Mary J(ane) 1927-1997
See Lathen, Emma
See also CA 85-88; 162; CMW 4

Lattany, Kristin
See Lattany, Kristin (Elaine Eggleston)
Hunter

Lattany, Kristin (Elaine Eggleston) Hunter
1931- .. **CLC 35**
See Hunter, Kristin
See also AITN 1; BW 1; BYA 3; CA 13-
16R; CANR 13, 108; CLR 3; CN 7; DLB
33; INT CANR-13; MAICYA 1, 2; SAAS
10; SATA 12, 132; YAW

Lattimore, Richmond (Alexander)
1906-1984 **CLC 3**
See also CA 1-4R; 112; CANR 1; CP 1, 2,
3; MAL 5

Laughlin, James 1914-1997 **CLC 49**
See also CA 21-24R; 162; CAAS 22; CANR
9, 47; CP 1, 2, 3, 4, 5, 6; DLB 48; DLBY
1996, 1997

Laurence, (Jean) Margaret (Wemyss)
1926-1987 . **CLC 3, 6, 13, 50, 62; SSC 7**
See also BYA 13; CA 5-8R; 121; CANR
33; CN 1, 2, 3, 4; DAC; DAM MST; DLB
53; EWL 3; FW; MTCW 1, 2; MTFW
2005; NFS 11; RGEL 2; RGSF 2; SATA-
Obit 50; TCWW 2

Laurent, Antoine 1952- **CLC 50**

Lauscher, Hermann
See Hesse, Hermann

Lautreamont 1846-1870 .. **NCLC 12; SSC 14**
See Lautreamont, Isidore Lucien Ducasse
See also GFL 1789 to the Present; RGWL
2, 3

Lautreamont, Isidore Lucien Ducasse
See Lautreamont
See also DLB 217

Lavater, Johann Kaspar
1741-1801 **NCLC 142**
See also DLB 97

Laverty, Donald
See Blish, James (Benjamin)

Lavin, Mary 1912-1996 . **CLC 4, 18, 99; SSC
4, 67**
See also CA 9-12R; 151; CANR 33; CN 1,
2, 3, 4, 5, 6; DLB 15, 319; FW; MTCW
1; RGEL 2; RGSF 2; SSFS 23

Lavond, Paul Dennis
See Kornbluth, C(yril) M.; Pohl, Frederik

Lawes, Henry 1596-1662 **LC 113**
See also DLB 126

Lawler, Ray
See Lawler, Raymond Evenor
See also DLB 289

Lawler, Raymond Evenor 1922- **CLC 58**
See Lawler, Ray
See also CA 103; CD 5, 6; RGEL 2

Lawrence, D(avid) H(erbert Richards)
1885-1930 **PC 54; SSC 4, 19, 73;
TCLC 2, 9, 16, 33, 48, 61, 93; WLC 3**
See Chambers, Jessie
See also BPFB 2; BRW 7; BRWR 2; CA
104; 121; CANR 131; CDBLB 1914-
1945; DA; DA3; DAB; DAC; DAM MST,
NOV, POET; DLB 10, 19, 36, 98, 162,
195; EWL 3; EXPP; EXPS; LAIT 2, 3;
MTCW 1, 2; MTFW 2005; NFS 18; PFS
6; RGEL 2; RGSF 2; SSFS 2, 6; TEA;
WLIT 4; WP

Lawrence, T(homas) E(dward)
1888-1935 **TCLC 18**
See Dale, Colin
See also BRWS 2; CA 115; 167; DLB 195

Lawrence of Arabia
See Lawrence, T(homas) E(dward)

Lawson, Henry (Archibald Hertzberg)
1867-1922 **SSC 18; TCLC 27**
See also CA 120; 181; DLB 230; RGEL 2;
RGSF 2

Lawton, Dennis
See Faust, Frederick (Schiller)

Layamon fl. c. 1200- **CMLC 10**
See Laȝamon
See also DLB 146; RGEL 2

Laye, Camara 1928-1980 **BLC 2; CLC 4,
38**
See Camara Laye
See also AFW; BW 1; CA 85-88; 97-100;
CANR 25; DAM MULT; MTCW 1, 2;
WLIT 2

Layton, Irving 1912-2006 **CLC 2, 15, 164**
See also CA 1-4R; 247; CANR 2, 33, 43,
66, 129; CP 1, 2, 3, 4, 5, 6, 7; DAC; DAM
MST, POET; DLB 88; EWL 3; MTCW 1,
2; PFS 12; RGEL 2

Layton, Irving Peter
See Layton, Irving

Lazarus, Emma 1849-1887 **NCLC 8, 109**

Lazarus, Felix
See Cable, George Washington

Lazarus, Henry
See Slavitt, David R(ytman)

Lea, Joan
See Neufeld, John (Arthur)

Leacock, Stephen (Butler)
1869-1944 **SSC 39; TCLC 2**
See also CA 104; 141; CANR 80; DAC;
DAM MST; DLB 92; EWL 3; MTCW 2;
MTFW 2005; RGEL 2; RGSF 2

Lead, Jane Ward 1623-1704 **LC 72**
See also DLB 131

Leapor, Mary 1722-1746 **LC 80**
See also DLB 109

Lear, Edward 1812-1888 **NCLC 3; PC 65**
See also AAYA 48; BRW 5; CLR 1, 75;
DLB 32, 163, 166; MAICYA 1, 2; RGEL
2; SATA 18, 100; WCH; WP

Lear, Norman (Milton) 1922- **CLC 12**
See also CA 73-76

Leautaud, Paul 1872-1956 **TCLC 83**
See also CA 203; DLB 65; GFL 1789 to the
Present

Leavis, F(rank) R(aymond)
1895-1978 **CLC 24**
See also BRW 7; CA 21-24R; 77-80; CANR
44; DLB 242; EWL 3; MTCW 1, 2;
RGEL 2

Leavitt, David 1961- **CLC 34**
See also CA 116; 122; CANR 50, 62, 101,
134; CPW; DA3; DAM POP; DLB 130;
GLL 1; INT CA-122; MAL 5; MTCW 2;
MTFW 2005

Leblanc, Maurice (Marie Emile)
1864-1941 **TCLC 49**
See also CA 110; CMW 4

Lebowitz, Fran(ces Ann) 1951(?)- ... **CLC 11,
36**
See also CA 81-84; CANR 14, 60, 70; INT
CANR-14; MTCW 1

Lebrecht, Peter
See Tieck, (Johann) Ludwig

le Carre, John **CLC 3, 5, 9, 15, 28, 220**
See Cornwell, David (John Moore)
See also AAYA 42; BEST 89:4; BPFB 2;
BRWS 2; CDBLB 1960 to Present; CMW
4; CN 1, 2, 3, 4, 5, 6, 7; CPW; DLB 87;
EWL 3; MSW; MTCW 2; RGEL 2; TEA

Le Clezio, J. M.G. 1940- **CLC 31, 155**
See also CA 116; 128; CANR 147; CWW
2; DLB 83; EWL 3; GFL 1789 to the
Present; RGSF 2

Le Clezio, Jean Marie Gustave
See Le Clezio, J. M.G.

Leconte de Lisle, Charles-Marie-Rene
1818-1894 **NCLC 29**
See also DLB 217; EW 6; GFL 1789 to the
Present

Le Coq, Monsieur
See Simenon, Georges (Jacques Christian)

Leduc, Violette 1907-1972 **CLC 22**
See also CA 13-14; 33-36R; CANR 69;
CAP 1; EWL 3; GFL 1789 to the Present;
GLL 1

Ledwidge, Francis 1887(?)-1917 **TCLC 23**
See also CA 123; 203; DLB 20
Lee, Andrea 1953- **BLC 2; CLC 36**
See also BW 1, 3; CA 125; CANR 82;
DAM MULT
Lee, Andrew
See Auchincloss, Louis
Lee, Chang-rae 1965- **CLC 91**
See also CA 148; CANR 89; CN 7; DLB
312; LATS 1:2
Lee, Don L. .. **CLC 2**
See Madhubuti, Haki R.
See also CP 2, 3, 4, 5
Lee, George W(ashington)
1894-1976 **BLC 2; CLC 52**
See also BW 1; CA 125; CANR 83; DAM
MULT; DLB 51
Lee, (Nelle) Harper 1926- . **CLC 12, 60, 194;**
WLC 4
See also AAYA 13; AMWS 8; BPFB 2;
BYA 3; CA 13-16R; CANR 51, 128;
CDALB 1941-1968; CSW; DA; DA3;
DAB; DAC; DAM MST, NOV; DLB 6;
EXPN; LAIT 3; MAL 5; MTCW 1, 2;
MTFW 2005; NFS 2; SATA 11; WYA;
YAW
Lee, Helen Elaine 1959(?)- **CLC 86**
See also CA 148
Lee, John **CLC 70**
Lee, Julian
See Latham, Jean Lee
Lee, Larry
See Lee, Lawrence
Lee, Laurie 1914-1997 **CLC 90**
See also CA 77-80; 158; CANR 33, 73; CP
1, 2, 3, 4, 5, 6; CPW; DAB; DAM POP;
DLB 27; MTCW 1; RGEL 2
Lee, Lawrence 1941-1990 **CLC 34**
See also CA 131; CANR 43
Lee, Li-Young 1957- **CLC 164; PC 24**
See also AMWS 15; CA 153; CANR 118;
CP 6, 7; DLB 165, 312; LMFS 2; PFS 11,
15, 17
Lee, Manfred B. 1905-1971 **CLC 11**
See Queen, Ellery
See also CA 1-4R; 29-32R; CANR 2, 150;
CMW 4; DLB 137
Lee, Manfred Bennington
See Lee, Manfred B.
Lee, Nathaniel 1645(?)-1692 **LC 103**
See also DLB 80; RGEL 2
Lee, Shelton Jackson 1957(?)- .. **BLCS; CLC**
105
See Lee, Spike
See also BW 2, 3; CA 125; CANR 42;
DAM MULT
Lee, Spike
See Lee, Shelton Jackson
See also AAYA 4, 29
Lee, Stan 1922- **CLC 17**
See also AAYA 5, 49; CA 108; 111; CANR
129; INT CA-111; MTFW 2005
Lee, Tanith 1947- **CLC 46**
See also AAYA 15; CA 37-40R; CANR 53,
102, 145; DLB 261; FANT; SATA 8, 88,
134; SFW 4; SUFW 1, 2; YAW
Lee, Vernon **SSC 33; TCLC 5**
See Paget, Violet
See also DLB 57, 153, 156, 174, 178; GLL
1; SUFW 1
Lee, William
See Burroughs, William S.
See also GLL 1
Lee, Willy
See Burroughs, William S.
See also GLL 1
Lee-Hamilton, Eugene (Jacob)
1845-1907 **TCLC 22**
See also CA 117; 234

Leet, Judith 1935- **CLC 11**
See also CA 187
Le Fanu, Joseph Sheridan
1814-1873 **NCLC 9, 58; SSC 14, 84**
See also CMW 4; DA3; DAM POP; DLB
21, 70, 159, 178; GL 3; HGG; RGEL 2;
RGSF 2; SUFW 1
Leffland, Ella 1931- **CLC 19**
See also CA 29-32R; CANR 35, 78, 82;
DLBY 1984; INT CANR-35; SATA 65
Leger, Alexis
See Leger, (Marie-Rene Auguste) Alexis
Saint-Leger
Leger, (Marie-Rene Auguste) Alexis
Saint-Leger 1887-1975 .. **CLC 4, 11, 46;**
PC 23
See Perse, Saint-John; Saint-John Perse
See also CA 13-16R; 61-64; CANR 43;
DAM POET; MTCW 1
Leger, Saintleger
See Leger, (Marie-Rene Auguste) Alexis
Saint-Leger
Le Guin, Ursula K(roeber) 1929- **CLC 8,**
13, 22, 45, 71, 136; SSC 12, 69
See also AAYA 9, 27; AITN 1; BPFB 2;
BYA 5, 8, 11, 14; CA 21-24R; CANR 9,
32, 52, 74, 132; CDALB 1968-1988; CLR
3, 28, 91; CN 2, 3, 4, 5, 6, 7; CPW; DA3;
DAB; DAC; DAM MST, POP; DLB 8,
52, 256, 275; EXPS; FANT; FW; INT
CANR-32; JRDA; LAIT 5; MAICYA 1,
2; MAL 5; MTCW 1, 2; MTFW 2005;
NFS 6, 9; SATA 4, 52, 99, 149; SCFW 1,
2; SFW 4; SSFS 2; SUFW 1, 2; WYA;
YAW
Lehmann, Rosamond (Nina)
1901-1990 **CLC 5**
See also CA 77-80; 131; CANR 8, 73; CN
1, 2, 3, 4; DLB 15; MTCW 2; RGEL 2;
RHW
Leiber, Fritz (Reuter, Jr.)
1910-1992 **CLC 25**
See also AAYA 65; BPFB 2; CA 45-48; 139;
CANR 2, 40, 86; CN 2, 3, 4, 5; DLB 8;
FANT; HGG; MTCW 1, 2; MTFW 2005;
SATA 45; SATA-Obit 73; SCFW 1, 2;
SFW 4; SUFW 1, 2
Leibniz, Gottfried Wilhelm von
1646-1716 **LC 35**
See also DLB 168
Leimbach, Martha 1963-
See Leimbach, Marti
See also CA 130
Leimbach, Marti **CLC 65**
See Leimbach, Martha
Leino, Eino **TCLC 24**
See Lonnbohm, Armas Eino Leopold
See also EWL 3
Leiris, Michel (Julien) 1901-1990 **CLC 61**
See also CA 119; 128; 132; EWL 3; GFL
1789 to the Present
Leithauser, Brad 1953- **CLC 27**
See also CA 107; CANR 27, 81; CP 5, 6, 7;
DLB 120, 282
le Jars de Gournay, Marie
See de Gournay, Marie le Jars
Lelchuk, Alan 1938- **CLC 5**
See also CA 45-48; CAAS 20; CANR 1,
70, 152; CN 3, 4, 5, 6, 7
Lem, Stanislaw 1921-2006 **CLC 8, 15, 40,**
149
See also CA 105; CAAS 1; CANR 32;
CWW 2; MTCW 1; SCFW 1, 2; SFW 4
Lemann, Nancy (Elise) 1956- **CLC 39**
See also CA 118; 136; CANR 121
Lemonnier, (Antoine Louis) Camille
1844-1913 **TCLC 22**
See also CA 121
Lenau, Nikolaus 1802-1850 **NCLC 16**

L'Engle, Madeleine (Camp Franklin)
1918- **CLC 12**
See also AAYA 28; AITN 2; BPFB 2; BYA
2, 4, 5, 7; CA 1-4R; CANR 3, 21, 39, 66,
107; CLR 1, 14, 57; CPW; CWRI 5; DA3;
DAM POP; DLB 52; JRDA; MAICYA 1,
2; MTCW 1, 2; MTFW 2005; SAAS 15;
SATA 1, 27, 75, 128; SFW 4; WYA; YAW
Lengyel, Jozsef 1896-1975 **CLC 7**
See also CA 85-88; 57-60; CANR 71;
RGSF 2
Lenin 1870-1924
See Lenin, V. I.
See also CA 121; 168
Lenin, V. I. **TCLC 67**
See Lenin
Lennon, John (Ono) 1940-1980 .. **CLC 12, 35**
See also CA 102; SATA 114
Lennox, Charlotte Ramsay
1729(?)-1804 **NCLC 23, 134**
See also DLB 39; RGEL 2
Lentricchia, Frank, Jr.
See Lentricchia, Frank
Lentricchia, Frank 1940- **CLC 34**
See also CA 25-28R; CANR 19, 106, 148;
DLB 246
Lenz, Gunter **CLC 65**
Lenz, Jakob Michael Reinhold
1751-1792 **LC 100**
See also DLB 94; RGWL 2, 3
Lenz, Siegfried 1926- **CLC 27; SSC 33**
See also CA 89-92; CANR 80, 149; CWW
2; DLB 75; EWL 3; RGSF 2; RGWL 2, 3
Leon, David
See Jacob, (Cyprien-)Max
Leonard, Elmore (John, Jr.) 1925- . **CLC 28,**
34, 71, 120, 222
See also AAYA 22, 59; AITN 1; BEST 89:1,
90:4; BPFB 2; CA 81-84; CANR 12, 28,
53, 76, 96, 133; CMW 4; CN 5, 6, 7;
CPW; DA3; DAM POP; DLB 173, 226;
INT CANR-28; MSW; MTCW 1, 2;
MTFW 2005; RGAL 4; SATA 163;
TCWW 1, 2
Leonard, Hugh **CLC 19**
See Byrne, John Keyes
See also CBD; CD 5, 6; DFS 13; DLB 13
Leonov, Leonid (Maximovich)
1899-1994 **CLC 92**
See Leonov, Leonid Maksimovich
See also CA 129; CANR 76; DAM NOV;
EWL 3; MTCW 1, 2; MTFW 2005
Leonov, Leonid Maksimovich
See Leonov, Leonid (Maximovich)
See also DLB 272
Leopardi, (Conte) Giacomo
1798-1837 **NCLC 22, 129; PC 37**
See also EW 5; RGWL 2, 3; WLIT 7; WP
Le Reveler
See Artaud, Antonin (Marie Joseph)
Lerman, Eleanor 1952- **CLC 9**
See also CA 85-88; CANR 69, 124
Lerman, Rhoda 1936- **CLC 56**
See also CA 49-52; CANR 70
Lermontov, Mikhail Iur'evich
See Lermontov, Mikhail Yuryevich
See also DLB 205
Lermontov, Mikhail Yuryevich
1814-1841 **NCLC 5, 47, 126; PC 18**
See Lermontov, Mikhail Iur'evich
See also EW 6; RGWL 2, 3; TWA
Leroux, Gaston 1868-1927 **TCLC 25**
See also CA 108; 136; CANR 69; CMW 4;
MTFW 2005; NFS 20; SATA 65
Lesage, Alain-Rene 1668-1747 **LC 2, 28**
See also DLB 313; EW 3; GFL Beginnings
to 1789; RGWL 2, 3
Leskov, N(ikolai) S(emenovich) 1831-1895
See Leskov, Nikolai (Semyonovich)

Leskov, Nikolai (Semyonovich) 1831-1895 **NCLC 25; SSC 34**
See Leskov, Nikolai Semenovich

Leskov, Nikolai Semenovich
See Leskov, Nikolai (Semyonovich)
See also DLB 238

Lesser, Milton
See Marlowe, Stephen

Lessing, Doris (May) 1919- ... **CLC 1, 2, 3, 6, 10, 15, 22, 40, 94, 170; SSC 6, 61; WLCS**
See also AAYA 57; AFW; BRWS 1; CA 9-12R; CAAS 14; CANR 33, 54, 76, 122; CBD; CD 5, 6; CDBLB 1960 to Present; CN 1, 2, 3, 4, 5, 6, 7; CWD; DA; DA3; DAB; DAC; DAM MST, NOV; DFS 20; DLB 15, 139; DLBY 1985; EWL 3; EXPS; FL 1:6; FW; LAIT 4; MTCW 1, 2; MTFW 2005; RGEL 2; RGSF 2; SFW 4; SSFS 1, 12, 20; TEA; WLIT 2, 4

Lessing, Gotthold Ephraim 1729-1781 **DC 26; LC 8, 124**
See also CDWLB 2; DLB 97; EW 4; RGWL 2, 3

Lester, Richard 1932- **CLC 20**

Levenson, Jay **CLC 70**

Lever, Charles (James) 1806-1872 **NCLC 23**
See also DLB 21; RGEL 2

Leverson, Ada Esther 1862(?)-1933(?) **TCLC 18**
See Elaine
See also CA 117; 202; DLB 153; RGEL 2

Levertov, Denise 1923-1997 .. **CLC 1, 2, 3, 5, 8, 15, 28, 66; PC 11**
See also AMWS 3; CA 1-4R, 178; 163; CAAE 178; CAAS 19; CANR 3, 29, 50, 108; CDALBS; CP 1, 2, 3, 4, 5, 6; CWP; DAM POET; DLB 5, 165; EWL 3; EXPP; FW; INT CANR-29; MAL 5; MTCW 1, 2; PAB; PFS 7, 17; RGAL 4; RGHL; TUS; WP

Levi, Carlo 1902-1975 **TCLC 125**
See also CA 65-68; 53-56; CANR 10; EWL 3; RGWL 2, 3

Levi, Jonathan **CLC 76**
See also CA 197

Levi, Peter (Chad Tigar) 1931-2000 **CLC 41**
See also CA 5-8R; 187; CANR 34, 80; CP 1, 2, 3, 4, 5, 6, 7; DLB 40

Levi, Primo 1919-1987 **CLC 37, 50; SSC 12; TCLC 109**
See also CA 13-16R; 122; CANR 12, 33, 61, 70, 132; DLB 177, 299; EWL 3; MTCW 1, 2; MTFW 2005; RGHL; RGWL 2, 3; WLIT 7

Levin, Ira 1929- **CLC 3, 6**
See also CA 21-24R; CANR 17, 44, 74, 139; CMW 4; CN 1, 2, 3, 4, 5, 6, 7; CPW; DA3; DAM POP; HGG; MTCW 1, 2; MTFW 2005; SATA 66; SFW 4

Levin, Meyer 1905-1981 **CLC 7**
See also AITN 1; CA 9-12R; 104; CANR 15; CN 1, 2, 3; DAM POP; DLB 9, 28; DLBY 1981; MAL 5; RGHL; SATA 21; SATA-Obit 27

Levine, Albert Norman 1923-2005
See Levine, Norman
See also CN 7

Levine, Norman 1923-2005 **CLC 54**
See also CA 73-76; 240; CAAS 23; CANR 14, 70; CN 1, 2, 3, 4, 5, 6; CP 1; DLB 88

Levine, Norman Albert
See Levine, Norman

Levine, Philip 1928- .. **CLC 2, 4, 5, 9, 14, 33, 118; PC 22**
See also AMWS 5; CA 9-12R; CANR 9, 37, 52, 116; CP 1, 2, 3, 4, 5, 6, 7; DAM POET; DLB 5; EWL 3; MAL 5; PFS 8

Levinson, Deirdre 1931- **CLC 49**
See also CA 73-76; CANR 70

Levi-Strauss, Claude 1908- **CLC 38**
See also CA 1-4R; CANR 6, 32, 57; DLB 242; EWL 3; GFL 1789 to the Present; MTCW 1, 2; TWA

Levitin, Sonia (Wolff) 1934- **CLC 17**
See also AAYA 13, 48; CA 29-32R; CANR 14, 32, 79; CLR 53; JRDA; MAICYA 1, 2; SAAS 2; SATA 4, 68, 119, 131; SATA-Essay 131; YAW

Levon, O. U.
See Kesey, Ken (Elton)

Levy, Amy 1861-1889 **NCLC 59**
See also DLB 156, 240

Lewes, George Henry 1817-1878 ... **NCLC 25**
See also DLB 55, 144

Lewis, Alun 1915-1944 **SSC 40; TCLC 3**
See also BRW 7; CA 104; 188; DLB 20, 162; PAB; RGEL 2

Lewis, C. Day
See Day Lewis, C(ecil)
See also CN 1

Lewis, Cecil Day
See Day Lewis, C(ecil)

Lewis, Clive Staples
See Lewis, C.S.

Lewis, C.S. 1898-1963 ... **CLC 1, 3, 6, 14, 27, 124; WLC 4**
See also AAYA 3, 39; BPFB 2; BRWS 3; BYA 15, 16; CA 81-84; CANR 33, 71, 132; CDBLB 1945-1960; CLR 3, 27, 109; CWRI 5; DA; DA3; DAB; DAC; DAM MST, NOV, POP; DLB 15, 100, 160, 255; EWL 3; FANT; JRDA; LMFS 2; MAICYA 1, 2; MTCW 1, 2; MTFW 2005; RGEL 2; SATA 13, 100; SCFW 1, 2; SFW 4; SUFW 1; TEA; WCH; WYA; YAW

Lewis, Janet 1899-1998 **CLC 41**
See Winters, Janet Lewis
See also CA 9-12R; 172; CANR 29, 63; CAP 1; CN 1, 2, 3, 4, 5, 6; DLBY 1987; RHW; TCWW 2

Lewis, Matthew Gregory 1775-1818 **NCLC 11, 62**
See also DLB 39, 158, 178; GL 3; HGG; LMFS 1; RGEL 2; SUFW

Lewis, (Harry) Sinclair 1885-1951 . **TCLC 4, 13, 23, 39; WLC 4**
See also AMW; AMWC 1; BPFB 2; CA 104; 133; CANR 132; CDALB 1917-1929; DA; DA3; DAB; DAC; DAM MST, NOV; DLB 9, 102, 284; DLBD 1; EWL 3; LAIT 3; MAL 5; MTCW 1, 2; MTFW 2005; NFS 15, 19, 22; RGAL 4; TUS

Lewis, (Percy) Wyndham 1884(?)-1957 .. **SSC 34; TCLC 2, 9, 104**
See also BRW 7; CA 104; 157; DLB 15; EWL 3; FANT; MTCW 2; MTFW 2005; RGEL 2

Lewisohn, Ludwig 1883-1955 **TCLC 19**
See also CA 107; 203; DLB 4, 9, 28, 102; MAL 5

Lewton, Val 1904-1951 **TCLC 76**
See also CA 199; IDFW 3, 4

Leyner, Mark 1956- **CLC 92**
See also CA 110; CANR 28, 53; DA3; DLB 292; MTCW 2; MTFW 2005

Lezama Lima, Jose 1910-1976 **CLC 4, 10, 101; HLCS 2**
See also CA 77-80; CANR 71; DAM MULT; DLB 113, 283; EWL 3; HW 1, 2; LAW; RGWL 2, 3

L'Heureux, John (Clarke) 1934- **CLC 52**
See also CA 13-16R; CANR 23, 45, 88; CP 1, 2, 3, 4; DLB 244

Li Ch'ing-chao 1081(?)-1141(?) **CMLC 71**

Liddell, C. H.
See Kuttner, Henry

Lie, Jonas (Lauritz Idemil) 1833-1908(?) **TCLC 5**
See also CA 115

Lieber, Joel 1937-1971 **CLC 6**
See also CA 73-76; 29-32R

Lieber, Stanley Martin
See Lee, Stan

Lieberman, Laurence (James) 1935- **CLC 4, 36**
See also CA 17-20R; CANR 8, 36, 89; CP 1, 2, 3, 4, 5, 6, 7

Lieh Tzu fl. 7th cent. B.C.-5th cent. B.C. **CMLC 27**

Lieksman, Anders
See Haavikko, Paavo Juhani

Lifton, Robert Jay 1926- **CLC 67**
See also CA 17-20R; CANR 27, 78; INT CANR-27; SATA 66

Lightfoot, Gordon 1938- **CLC 26**
See also CA 109; 242

Lightfoot, Gordon Meredith
See Lightfoot, Gordon

Lightman, Alan P(aige) 1948- **CLC 81**
See also CA 141; CANR 63, 105, 138; MTFW 2005

Ligotti, Thomas (Robert) 1953- **CLC 44; SSC 16**
See also CA 123; CANR 49, 135; HGG; SUFW 2

Li Ho 791-817 **PC 13**

Li Ju-chen c. 1763-c. 1830 **NCLC 137**

Lilar, Francoise
See Mallet-Joris, Francoise

Liliencron, (Friedrich Adolf Axel) Detlev von 1844-1909 **TCLC 18**
See also CA 117

Lille, Alain de
See Alain de Lille

Lilly, William 1602-1681 **LC 27**

Lima, Jose Lezama
See Lezama Lima, Jose

Lima Barreto, Afonso Henrique de 1881-1922 **TCLC 23**
See Lima Barreto, Afonso Henriques de
See also CA 117; 181; LAW

Lima Barreto, Afonso Henriques de
See Lima Barreto, Afonso Henrique de
See also DLB 307

Limonov, Eduard
See Limonov, Edward
See also DLB 317

Limonov, Edward 1944- **CLC 67**
See Limonov, Eduard
See also CA 137

Lin, Frank
See Atherton, Gertrude (Franklin Horn)

Lin, Yutang 1895-1976 **TCLC 149**
See also CA 45-48; 65-68; CANR 2; RGAL 4

Lincoln, Abraham 1809-1865 **NCLC 18**
See also LAIT 2

Lind, Jakov **CLC 1, 2, 4, 27, 82**
See Landwirth, Heinz
See also CAAS 4; DLB 299; EWL 3; RGHL

Lindbergh, Anne (Spencer) Morrow 1906-2001 **CLC 82**
See also BPFB 2; CA 17-20R; 193; CANR 16, 73; DAM NOV; MTCW 1, 2; MTFW 2005; SATA 33; SATA-Obit 125; TUS

Lindsay, David 1878(?)-1945 **TCLC 15**
See also CA 113; 187; DLB 255; FANT; SFW 4; SUFW 1

Lindsay, (Nicholas) Vachel 1879-1931 **PC 23; TCLC 17; WLC 4**
See also AMWS 1; CA 114; 135; CANR 79; CDALB 1865-1917; DA; DA3; DAC; DAM MST, POET; DLB 54; EWL 3; EXPP; MAL 5; RGAL 4; SATA 40; WP

Linke-Poot
　　See Doeblin, Alfred
Linney, Romulus 1930- **CLC 51**
　　See also CA 1-4R; CAD; CANR 40, 44,
　　79; CD 5, 6; CSW; RGAL 4
Linton, Eliza Lynn 1822-1898 **NCLC 41**
　　See also DLB 18
Li Po 701-763 **CMLC 2; PC 29**
　　See also PFS 20; WP
Lipsius, Justus 1547-1606 **LC 16**
Lipsyte, Robert 1938- **CLC 21**
　　See also AAYA 7, 45; CA 17-20R; CANR
　　8, 57, 146; CLR 23, 76; DA; DAC; DAM
　　MST, NOV; JRDA; LAIT 5; MAICYA 1,
　　2; SATA 5, 68, 113, 161; WYA; YAW
Lipsyte, Robert Michael
　　See Lipsyte, Robert
Lish, Gordon 1934- **CLC 45; SSC 18**
　　See also CA 113; 117; CANR 79, 151; DLB
　　130; INT CA-117
Lish, Gordon Jay
　　See Lish, Gordon
Lispector, Clarice 1925(?)-1977 **CLC 43;
　　HLCS 2; SSC 34**
　　See also CA 139; 116; CANR 71; CDWLB
　　3; DLB 113, 307; DNFS 1; EWL 3; FW;
　　HW 2; LAW; RGSF 2; RGWL 2, 3; WLIT
　　1
Littell, Robert 1935(?)- **CLC 42**
　　See also CA 109; 112; CANR 64, 115;
　　CMW 4
Little, Malcolm 1925-1965
　　See Malcolm X
　　See also BW 1, 3; CA 125; 111; CANR 82;
　　DA; DA3; DAB; DAC; DAM MST,
　　MULT; MTCW 1, 2; MTFW 2005
Littlewit, Humphrey Gent.
　　See Lovecraft, H. P.
Litwos
　　See Sienkiewicz, Henryk (Adam Alexander
　　Pius)
Liu, E. 1857-1909 **TCLC 15**
　　See also CA 115; 190
Lively, Penelope 1933- **CLC 32, 50**
　　See also BPFB 2; CA 41-44R; CANR 29,
　　67, 79, 131; CLR 7; CN 5, 6, 7; CWRI 5;
　　DAM NOV; DLB 14, 161, 207, 326;
　　FANT; JRDA; MAICYA 1, 2; MTCW 1,
　　2; MTFW 2005; SATA 7, 60, 101, 164;
　　TEA
Lively, Penelope Margaret
　　See Lively, Penelope
Livesay, Dorothy (Kathleen)
　　1909-1996 **CLC 4, 15, 79**
　　See also AITN 2; CA 25-28R; CAAS 8;
　　CANR 36, 67; CP 1, 2, 3, 4, 5; DAC;
　　DAM MST, POET; DLB 68; FW; MTCW
　　1; RGEL 2; TWA
Livy c. 59B.C.-c. 12 **CMLC 11**
　　See also AW 2; CDWLB 1; DLB 211;
　　RGWL 2, 3; WLIT 8
Lizardi, Jose Joaquin Fernandez de
　　1776-1827 **NCLC 30**
　　See also LAW
Llewellyn, Richard
　　See Llewellyn Lloyd, Richard Dafydd Viv-
　　ian
　　See also DLB 15
Llewellyn Lloyd, Richard Dafydd Vivian
　　1906-1983 **CLC 7, 80**
　　See Llewellyn, Richard
　　See also CA 53-56; 111; CANR 7, 71;
　　SATA 11; SATA-Obit 37
Llosa, Jorge Mario Pedro Vargas
　　See Vargas Llosa, Mario
　　See also RGWL 3
Llosa, Mario Vargas
　　See Vargas Llosa, Mario

Lloyd, Manda
　　See Mander, (Mary) Jane
Lloyd Webber, Andrew 1948-
　　See Webber, Andrew Lloyd
　　See also AAYA 1, 38; CA 116; 149; DAM
　　DRAM; SATA 56
Llull, Ramon c. 1235-c. 1316 **CMLC 12**
Lobb, Ebenezer
　　See Upward, Allen
Locke, Alain (Le Roy)
　　1886-1954 **BLCS; HR 1:3; TCLC 43**
　　See also AMWS 14; BW 1, 3; CA 106; 124;
　　CANR 79; DLB 51; LMFS 2; MAL 5;
　　RGAL 4
Locke, John 1632-1704 **LC 7, 35**
　　See also DLB 31, 101, 213, 252; RGEL 2;
　　WLIT 3
Locke-Elliott, Sumner
　　See Elliott, Sumner Locke
Lockhart, John Gibson 1794-1854 .. **NCLC 6**
　　See also DLB 110, 116, 144
Lockridge, Ross (Franklin), Jr.
　　1914-1948 **TCLC 111**
　　See also CA 108; 145; CANR 79; DLB 143;
　　DLBY 1980; MAL 5; RGAL 4; RHW
Lockwood, Robert
　　See Johnson, Robert
Lodge, David (John) 1935- **CLC 36, 141**
　　See also BEST 90:1; BRWS 4; CA 17-20R;
　　CANR 19, 53, 92, 139; CN 1, 2, 3, 4, 5,
　　6, 7; CPW; DAM POP; DLB 14, 194;
　　EWL 3; INT CANR-19; MTCW 1, 2;
　　MTFW 2005
Lodge, Thomas 1558-1625 **LC 41**
　　See also DLB 172; RGEL 2
Loewinsohn, Ron(ald William)
　　1937- **CLC 52**
　　See also CA 25-28R; CANR 71; CP 1, 2, 3,
　　4
Logan, Jake
　　See Smith, Martin Cruz
Logan, John (Burton) 1923-1987 **CLC 5**
　　See also CA 77-80; 124; CANR 45; CP 1,
　　2, 3, 4; DLB 5
Lo Kuan-chung 1330(?)-1400(?) **LC 12**
Lombard, Nap
　　See Johnson, Pamela Hansford
Lombard, Peter 1100(?)-1160(?) ... **CMLC 72**
Lombino, Salvatore
　　See Hunter, Evan
London, Jack 1876-1916 .. **SSC 4, 49; TCLC
　　9, 15, 39; WLC 4**
　　See London, John Griffith
　　See also AAYA 13; AITN 2; AMW; BPFB
　　2; BYA 4, 13; CDALB 1865-1917; CLR
　　108; DLB 8, 12, 78, 212; EWL 3; EXPS;
　　LAIT 3; MAL 5; NFS 8; RGAL 4; RGSF
　　2; SATA 18; SFW 4; SSFS 7; TCWW 1,
　　2; TUS; WYA; YAW
London, John Griffith 1876-1916
　　See London, Jack
　　See also CA 110; 119; CANR 73; DA; DA3;
　　DAB; DAC; DAM MST, NOV; JRDA;
　　MAICYA 1, 2; MTCW 1, 2; MTFW 2005;
　　NFS 19
Long, Emmett
　　See Leonard, Elmore (John, Jr.)
Longbaugh, Harry
　　See Goldman, William
Longfellow, Henry Wadsworth
　　1807-1882 **NCLC 2, 45, 101, 103; PC
　　30; WLCS**
　　See also AMW; AMWR 2; CDALB 1640-
　　1865; CLR 99; DA; DA3; DAB; DAC;
　　DAM MST, POET; DLB 1, 59, 235;
　　EXPP; PAB; PFS 2, 7, 17; RGAL 4;
　　SATA 19; TUS; WP
Longinus c. 1st cent. - **CMLC 27**
　　See also AW 2; DLB 176

Longley, Michael 1939- **CLC 29**
　　See also BRWS 8; CA 102; CP 1, 2, 3, 4, 5,
　　6, 7; DLB 40
Longstreet, Augustus Baldwin
　　1790-1870 **NCLC 159**
　　See also DLB 3, 11, 74, 248; RGAL 4
Longus fl. c. 2nd cent. - **CMLC 7**
Longway, A. Hugh
　　See Lang, Andrew
Lonnbohm, Armas Eino Leopold 1878-1926
　　See Leino, Eino
　　See also CA 123
Lonnrot, Elias 1802-1884 **NCLC 53**
　　See also EFS 1
Lonsdale, Roger ed. **CLC 65**
Lopate, Phillip 1943- **CLC 29**
　　See also CA 97-100; CANR 88; DLBY
　　1980; INT CA-97-100
Lopez, Barry (Holstun) 1945- **CLC 70**
　　See also AAYA 9, 63; ANW; CA 65-68;
　　CANR 7, 23, 47, 68, 92; DLB 256, 275;
　　INT CANR-7, -23; MTCW 1; RGAL 4;
　　SATA 67
Lopez de Mendoza, Inigo
　　See Santillana, Inigo Lopez de Mendoza,
　　Marques de
Lopez Portillo (y Pacheco), Jose
　　1920-2004 **CLC 46**
　　See also CA 129; 224; HW 1
Lopez y Fuentes, Gregorio
　　1897(?)-1966 **CLC 32**
　　See also CA 131; EWL 3; HW 1
Lorca, Federico Garcia
　　See Garcia Lorca, Federico
　　See also DFS 4; EW 11; PFS 20; RGWL 2,
　　3; WP
Lord, Audre
　　See Lorde, Audre (Geraldine)
　　See also EWL 3
Lord, Bette Bao 1938- **AAL; CLC 23**
　　See also BEST 90:3; BPFB 2; CA 107;
　　CANR 41, 79; INT CA-107; SATA 58
Lord Auch
　　See Bataille, Georges
Lord Brooke
　　See Greville, Fulke
Lord Byron
　　See Byron, George Gordon (Noel)
Lorde, Audre (Geraldine)
　　1934-1992 **BLC 2; CLC 18, 71; PC
　　12; TCLC 173**
　　See Domini, Rey; Lord, Audre
　　See also AFAW 1, 2; BW 1, 3; CA 25-28R;
　　142; CANR 16, 26, 46, 82; CP 2, 3, 4, 5;
　　DA3; DAM MULT, POET; DLB 41; FW;
　　MAL 5; MTCW 1, 2; MTFW 2005; PFS
　　16; RGAL 4
Lord Houghton
　　See Milnes, Richard Monckton
Lord Jeffrey
　　See Jeffrey, Francis
Loreaux, Nichol **CLC 65**
Lorenzini, Carlo 1826-1890
　　See Collodi, Carlo
　　See also MAICYA 1, 2; SATA 29, 100
Lorenzo, Heberto Padilla
　　See Padilla (Lorenzo), Heberto
Loris
　　See Hofmannsthal, Hugo von
Loti, Pierre **TCLC 11**
　　See Viaud, (Louis Marie) Julien
　　See also DLB 123; GFL 1789 to the Present
Lou, Henri
　　See Andreas-Salome, Lou
Louie, David Wong 1954- **CLC 70**
　　See also CA 139; CANR 120
Louis, Adrian C. **NNAL**
　　See also CA 223

Louis, Father M.
See Merton, Thomas (James)

Louise, Heidi
See Erdrich, Louise

Lovecraft, H. P. 1890-1937 **SSC 3, 52; TCLC 4, 22**
See also AAYA 14, BPFB 2; CA 104; 133; CANR 106; DA3; DAM POP; HGG; MTCW 1, 2; MTFW 2005; RGAL 4; SCFW 1, 2; SFW 4; SUFW

Lovecraft, Howard Phillips
See Lovecraft, H. P.

Lovelace, Earl 1935- **CLC 51**
See also BW 2; CA 77-80; CANR 41, 72, 114; CD 5, 6; CDWLB 3; CN 1, 2, 3, 4, 5, 6, 7; DLB 125; EWL 3; MTCW 1

Lovelace, Richard 1618-1657 . **LC 24; PC 69**
See also BRW 2; DLB 131; EXPP; PAB; RGEL 2

Lowe, Pardee 1904- **AAL**

Lowell, Amy 1874-1925 ... **PC 13; TCLC 1, 8**
See also AAYA 57; AMW; CA 104; 151; DAM POET; DLB 54, 140; EWL 3; EXPP; LMFS 2; MAL 5; MAWW; MTCW 2; MTFW 2005; RGAL 4; TUS

Lowell, James Russell 1819-1891 ... **NCLC 2, 90**
See also AMWS 1; CDALB 1640-1865; DLB 1, 11, 64, 79, 189, 235; RGAL 4

Lowell, Robert (Traill Spence, Jr.) 1917-1977 **CLC 1, 2, 3, 4, 5, 8, 9, 11, 15, 37, 124; PC 3; WLC 4**
See also AMW; AMWC 2; AMWR 2; CA 9-12R; 73-76; CABS 2; CAD; CANR 26, 60; CDALBS; CP 1, 2; DA; DA3; DAB; DAC; DAM MST, NOV; DLB 5, 169; EWL 3; MAL 5; MTCW 1, 2; MTFW 2005; PAB; PFS 6, 7; RGAL 4; WP

Lowenthal, Michael (Francis) 1969- **CLC 119**
See also CA 150; CANR 115

Lowndes, Marie Adelaide (Belloc) 1868-1947 **TCLC 12**
See also CA 107; CMW 4; DLB 70; RHW

Lowry, (Clarence) Malcolm 1909-1957 **SSC 31; TCLC 6, 40**
See also BPFB 2; BRWS 3; CA 105; 131; CANR 62, 105; CDBLB 1945-1960; DLB 15; EWL 3; MTCW 1, 2; MTFW 2005; RGEL 2

Lowry, Mina Gertrude 1882-1966
See Loy, Mina
See also CA 113

Lowry, Sam
See Soderbergh, Steven

Loxsmith, John
See Brunner, John (Kilian Houston)

Loy, Mina **CLC 28; PC 16**
See Lowry, Mina Gertrude
See also DAM POET; DLB 4, 54; PFS 20

Loyson-Bridet
See Schwob, Marcel (Mayer Andre)

Lucan 39-65 **CMLC 33**
See also AW 2; DLB 211; EFS 2; RGWL 2, 3

Lucas, Craig 1951- **CLC 64**
See also CA 137; CAD; CANR 71, 109, 142; CD 5, 6; GLL 2; MTFW 2005

Lucas, E(dward) V(errall) 1868-1938 **TCLC 73**
See also CA 176; DLB 98, 149, 153; SATA 20

Lucas, George 1944- **CLC 16**
See also AAYA 1, 23; CA 77-80; CANR 30; SATA 56

Lucas, Hans
See Godard, Jean-Luc

Lucas, Victoria
See Plath, Sylvia

Lucian c. 125-c. 180 **CMLC 32**
See also AW 2; DLB 176; RGWL 2, 3

Lucilius c. 180B.C.-102B.C. **CMLC 82**
See also DLB 211

Lucretius c. 94B.C.-c. 49B.C. **CMLC 48**
See also AW 2; CDWLB 1; DLB 211; EFS 2; RGWL 2, 3; WLIT 8

Ludlam, Charles 1943-1987 **CLC 46, 50**
See also CA 85-88; 122; CAD; CANR 72, 86; DLB 266

Ludlum, Robert 1927-2001 **CLC 22, 43**
See also AAYA 10, 59; BEST 89:1, 90:3; BPFB 2; CA 33-36R; 195; CANR 25, 41, 68, 105, 131; CMW 4; CPW; DA3; DAM NOV, POP; DLBY 1982; MSW; MTCW 1, 2; MTFW 2005

Ludwig, Ken 1950- **CLC 60**
See also CA 195; CAD; CD 6

Ludwig, Otto 1813-1865 **NCLC 4**
See also DLB 129

Lugones, Leopoldo 1874-1938 **HLCS 2; TCLC 15**
See also CA 116; 131; CANR 104; DLB 283; EWL 3; HW 1; LAW

Lu Hsun **SSC 20; TCLC 3**
See Shu-Jen, Chou
See also EWL 3

Lukacs, George **CLC 24**
See Lukacs, Gyorgy (Szegeny von)

Lukacs, Gyorgy (Szegeny von) 1885-1971
See Lukacs, George
See also CA 101; 29-32R; CANR 62; CD-WLB 4; DLB 215, 242; EW 10; EWL 3; MTCW 1, 2

Luke, Peter (Ambrose Cyprian) 1919-1995 **CLC 38**
See also CA 81-84; 147; CANR 72; CBD; CD 5, 6; DLB 13

Lunar, Dennis
See Mungo, Raymond

Lurie, Alison 1926- **CLC 4, 5, 18, 39, 175**
See also BPFB 2; CA 1-4R; CANR 2, 17, 50, 88; CN 1, 2, 3, 4, 5, 6, 7; DLB 2; MAL 5; MTCW 1; SATA 46, 112; TCLE 1:1

Lustig, Arnost 1926- **CLC 56**
See also AAYA 3; CA 69-72; CANR 47, 102; CWW 2; DLB 232, 299; EWL 3; RGHL; SATA 56

Luther, Martin 1483-1546 **LC 9, 37**
See also CDWLB 2; DLB 179; EW 2; RGWL 2, 3

Luxemburg, Rosa 1870(?)-1919 **TCLC 63**
See also CA 118

Luzi, Mario (Egidio Vincenzo) 1914-2005 **CLC 13**
See also CA 61-64; 236; CANR 9, 70; CWW 2; DLB 128; EWL 3

L'vov, Arkady **CLC 59**

Lydgate, John c. 1370-1450(?) **LC 81**
See also BRW 1; DLB 146; RGEL 2

Lyly, John 1554(?)-1606 **DC 7; LC 41**
See also BRW 1; DAM DRAM; DLB 62, 167; RGEL 2

L'Ymagier
See Gourmont, Remy(-Marie-Charles) de

Lynch, B. Suarez
See Borges, Jorge Luis

Lynch, David (Keith) 1946- **CLC 66, 162**
See also AAYA 55; CA 124; 129; CANR 111

Lynch, James
See Andreyev, Leonid (Nikolaevich)

Lyndsay, Sir David 1485-1555 **LC 20**
See also RGEL 2

Lynn, Kenneth S(chuyler) 1923-2001 **CLC 50**
See also CA 1-4R; 196; CANR 3, 27, 65

Lynx
See West, Rebecca

Lyons, Marcus
See Blish, James (Benjamin)

Lyotard, Jean-Francois 1924-1998 **TCLC 103**
See also DLB 242; EWL 3

Lyre, Pinchbeck
See Sassoon, Siegfried (Lorraine)

Lytle, Andrew (Nelson) 1902-1995 ... **CLC 22**
See also CA 9-12R; 150; CANR 70; CN 1, 2, 3, 4, 5, 6; CSW; DLB 6; DLBY 1995; RGAL 4; RHW

Lyttelton, George 1709-1773 **LC 10**
See also RGEL 2

Lytton of Knebworth, Baron
See Bulwer-Lytton, Edward (George Earle Lytton)

Maas, Peter 1929-2001 **CLC 29**
See also CA 93-96; 201; INT CA-93-96; MTCW 2; MTFW 2005

Mac A'Ghobhainn, Iain
See Smith, Iain Crichton

Macaulay, Catherine 1731-1791 **LC 64**
See also DLB 104

Macaulay, (Emilie) Rose 1881(?)-1958 **TCLC 7, 44**
See also CA 104; DLB 36; EWL 3; RGEL 2; RHW

Macaulay, Thomas Babington 1800-1859 **NCLC 42**
See also BRW 4; CDBLB 1832-1890; DLB 32, 55; RGEL 2

MacBeth, George (Mann) 1932-1992 **CLC 2, 5, 9**
See also CA 25-28R; 136; CANR 61, 66; CP 1, 2, 3, 4, 5; DLB 40; MTCW 1; PFS 8; SATA 4; SATA-Obit 70

MacCaig, Norman (Alexander) 1910-1996 **CLC 36**
See also BRWS 6; CA 9-12R; CANR 3, 34; CP 1, 2, 3, 4, 5, 6; DAB; DAM POET; DLB 27; EWL 3; RGEL 2

MacCarthy, Sir (Charles Otto) Desmond 1877-1952 **TCLC 36**
See also CA 167

MacDiarmid, Hugh **CLC 2, 4, 11, 19, 63; PC 9**
See Grieve, C(hristopher) M(urray)
See also CDBLB 1945-1960; CP 1, 2; DLB 20; EWL 3; RGEL 2

MacDonald, Anson
See Heinlein, Robert A(nson)

Macdonald, Cynthia 1928- **CLC 13, 19**
See also CA 49-52; CANR 4, 44, 146; DLB 105

MacDonald, George 1824-1905 **TCLC 9, 113**
See also AAYA 57; BYA 5; CA 106; 137; CANR 80; CLR 67; DLB 18, 163, 178; FANT; MAICYA 1, 2; RGEL 2; SATA 33, 100; SFW 4; SUFW; WCH

Macdonald, John
See Millar, Kenneth

MacDonald, John D(ann) 1916-1986 **CLC 3, 27, 44**
See also BPFB 2; CA 1-4R; 121; CANR 1, 19, 60; CMW 4; CPW; DAM NOV, POP; DLB 8, 306; DLBY 1986; MSW; MTCW 1, 2; MTFW 2005; SFW 4

Macdonald, John Ross
See Millar, Kenneth

Macdonald, Ross **CLC 1, 2, 3, 14, 34, 41**
See Millar, Kenneth
See also AMWS 4; BPFB 2; CN 1, 2, 3; DLBD 6; MAL 5; MSW; RGAL 4

MacDougal, John
See Blish, James (Benjamin)

MacDougal, John
See Blish, James (Benjamin)
MacDowell, John
See Parks, Tim(othy Harold)
MacEwen, Gwendolyn (Margaret)
1941-1987 CLC 13, 55
See also CA 9-12R; 124; CANR 7, 22; CP
1, 2, 3, 4; DLB 53, 251; SATA 50; SATA-
Obit 55
Macha, Karel Hynek 1810-1846 NCLC 46
Machado (y Ruiz), Antonio
1875-1939 TCLC 3
See also CA 104; 174; DLB 108; EW 9;
EWL 3; HW 2; PFS 23; RGWL 2, 3
Machado de Assis, Joaquim Maria
1839-1908 BLC 2; HLCS 2; SSC 24;
TCLC 10
See also CA 107; 153; CANR 91; DLB 307;
LAW; RGSF 2; RGWL 2, 3; TWA; WLIT
1
Machaut, Guillaume de c.
1300-1377 CMLC 64
See also DLB 208
Machen, Arthur SSC 20; TCLC 4
See Jones, Arthur Llewellyn
See also CA 179; DLB 156, 178; RGEL 2;
SUFW 1
Machiavelli, Niccolo 1469-1527 ... DC 16; LC
8, 36; WLCS
See also AAYA 58; DA; DAB; DAC; DAM
MST; EW 2; LAIT 1; LMFS 1; NFS 9;
RGWL 2, 3; TWA; WLIT 7
MacInnes, Colin 1914-1976 CLC 4, 23
See also CA 69-72; 65-68; CANR 21; CN
1, 2; DLB 14; MTCW 1, 2; RGEL 2;
RHW
MacInnes, Helen (Clark)
1907-1985 CLC 27, 39
See also BPFB 2; CA 1-4R; 117; CANR 1,
28, 58; CMW 4; CN 1, 2; CPW; DAM
POP; DLB 87; MSW; MTCW 1, 2;
MTFW 2005; SATA 22; SATA-Obit 44
Mackay, Mary 1855-1924
See Corelli, Marie
See also CA 118; 177; FANT; RHW
Mackay, Shena 1944- CLC 195
See also CA 104; CANR 88, 139; DLB 231,
319; MTFW 2005
Mackenzie, Compton (Edward Montague)
1883-1972 CLC 18; TCLC 116
See also CA 21-22; 37-40R; CAP 2; CN 1;
DLB 34, 100; RGEL 2
Mackenzie, Henry 1745-1831 NCLC 41
See also DLB 39; RGEL 2
Mackey, Nathaniel (Ernest) 1947- PC 49
See also CA 153; CANR 114; CP 6, 7; DLB
169
MacKinnon, Catharine A. 1946- CLC 181
See also CA 128; 132; CANR 73, 140; FW;
MTCW 2; MTFW 2005
Mackintosh, Elizabeth 1896(?)-1952
See Tey, Josephine
See also CA 110; CMW 4
MacLaren, James
See Grieve, C(hristopher) M(urray)
MacLaverty, Bernard 1942- CLC 31
See also CA 116; 118; CANR 43, 88; CN
5, 6, 7; DLB 267; INT CA-118; RGSF 2
MacLean, Alistair (Stuart)
1922(?)-1987 CLC 3, 13, 50, 63
See also CA 57-60; 121; CANR 28, 61;
CMW 4; CP 2, 3, 4, 5, 6, 7; CPW; DAM
POP; DLB 276; MTCW 1; SATA 23;
SATA-Obit 50; TCWW 2
Maclean, Norman (Fitzroy)
1902-1990 CLC 78; SSC 13
See also AMWS 14; CA 102; 132; CANR
49; CPW; DAM POP; DLB 206;
TCWW 2

MacLeish, Archibald 1892-1982 ... CLC 3, 8,
14, 68; PC 47
See also AMW; CA 9-12R; 106; CAD;
CANR 33, 63; CDALBS; CP 1, 2; DAM
POET; DFS 15; DLB 4, 7, 45; DLBY
1982; EWL 3; EXPP; MAL 5; MTCW 1,
2; MTFW 2005; PAB; PFS 5; RGAL 4;
TUS
MacLennan, (John) Hugh
1907-1990 CLC 2, 14, 92
See also CA 5-8R; 142; CANR 33; CN 1,
2, 3, 4; DAC; DAM MST; DLB 68; EWL
3; MTCW 1, 2; MTFW 2005; RGEL 2;
TWA
MacLeod, Alistair 1936- .. CLC 56, 165; SSC
90
See also CA 123; CCA 1; DAC; DAM
MST; DLB 60; MTCW 2; MTFW 2005;
RGSF 2; TCLE 1:2
Macleod, Fiona
See Sharp, William
See also RGEL 2; SUFW
MacNeice, (Frederick) Louis
1907-1963 CLC 1, 4, 10, 53; PC 61
See also BRW 7; CA 85-88; CANR 61;
DAB; DAM POET; DLB 10, 20; EWL 3;
MTCW 1, 2; MTFW 2005; RGEL 2
MacNeill, Dand
See Fraser, George MacDonald
Macpherson, James 1736-1796 LC 29
See Ossian
See also BRWS 8; DLB 109; RGEL 2
Macpherson, (Jean) Jay 1931- CLC 14
See also CA 5-8R; CANR 90; CP 1, 2, 3, 4,
6, 7; CWP; DLB 53
Macrobius fl. 430- CMLC 48
MacShane, Frank 1927-1999 CLC 39
See also CA 9-12R; 186; CANR 3, 33; DLB
111
Macumber, Mari
See Sandoz, Mari(e Susette)
Madach, Imre 1823-1864 NCLC 19
Madden, (Jerry) David 1933- CLC 5, 15
See also CA 1-4R; CAAS 3; CANR 4, 45;
CN 3, 4, 5, 6, 7; CSW; DLB 6; MTCW 1
Maddern, Al(an)
See Ellison, Harlan (Jay)
Madhubuti, Haki R. 1942- ... BLC 2; CLC 6,
73; PC 5
See Lee, Don L.
See also BW 2, 3; CA 73-76; CANR 24,
51, 73, 139; CP 6, 7; CSW; DAM MULT,
POET; DLB 5, 41; DLBD 8; EWL 3;
MAL 5; MTCW 2; MTFW 2005; RGAL
4
Madison, James 1751-1836 NCLC 126
See also DLB 37
Maepenn, Hugh
See Kuttner, Henry
Maepenn, K. H.
See Kuttner, Henry
Maeterlinck, Maurice 1862-1949 TCLC 3
See also CA 104; 136; CANR 80; DAM
DRAM; DLB 192; EW 8; EWL 3; GFL
1789 to the Present; LMFS 2; RGWL 2,
3; SATA 66; TWA
Maginn, William 1794-1842 NCLC 8
See also DLB 110, 159
Mahapatra, Jayanta 1928- CLC 33
See also CA 73-76; CAAS 9; CANR 15,
33, 66, 87; CP 4, 5, 6, 7; DAM MULT;
DLB 323
Mahfouz, Naguib (Abdel Aziz Al-Sabilgi)
1911(?)- CLC 153; SSC 66
See Mahfouz, Najib (Abdel Aziz al-Sabilgi)
See also AAYA 49; BEST 89:2; CA 128;
CANR 55, 101; DA3; DAM NOV;
MTCW 1, 2; MTFW 2005; RGWL 2, 3;
SSFS 9

Mahfuz, Najib (Abdel Aziz al-Sabilgi)
.. CLC 52, 55
See Mahfouz, Naguib (Abdel Aziz Al-
Sabilgi)
See also AFW; CWW 2; DLBY 1988; EWL
3; RGSF 2; WLIT 6
Mahon, Derek 1941- CLC 27; PC 60
See also BRWS 6; CA 113; 128; CANR 88;
CP 1, 2, 3, 4, 5, 6, 7; DLB 40; EWL 3
Maiakovskii, Vladimir
See Mayakovski, Vladimir (Vladimirovich)
See also IDTP; RGWL 2, 3
Mailer, Norman 1923- ... CLC 1, 2, 3, 4, 5, 8,
11, 14, 28, 39, 74, 111
See also AAYA 31; AITN 2; AMW; AMWC
2; AMWR 2; BPFB 2; CA 9-12R; CABS
1; CANR 28, 74, 77, 130; CDALB 1968-
1988; CN 1, 2, 3, 4, 5, 6, 7; CPW; DA;
DA3; DAB; DAC; DAM MST, NOV,
POP; DLB 2, 16, 28, 185, 278; DLBD 3;
DLBY 1980, 1983; EWL 3; MAL 5;
MTCW 1, 2; MTFW 2005; NFS 10;
RGAL 4; TUS
Mailer, Norman Kingsley
See Mailer, Norman
Maillet, Antonine 1929- CLC 54, 118
See also CA 115; 120; CANR 46, 74, 77,
134; CCA 1; CWW 2; DAC; DLB 60;
INT CA-120; MTCW 2; MTFW 2005
Maimonides, Moses 1135-1204 CMLC 76
See also DLB 115
Mais, Roger 1905-1955 TCLC 8
See also BW 1, 3; CA 105; 124; CANR 82;
CDWLB 3; DLB 125; EWL 3; MTCW 1;
RGEL 2
Maistre, Joseph 1753-1821 NCLC 37
See also GFL 1789 to the Present
Maitland, Frederic William
1850-1906 TCLC 65
Maitland, Sara (Louise) 1950- CLC 49
See also BRWS 11; CA 69-72; CANR 13,
59; DLB 271; FW
Major, Clarence 1936- ... BLC 2; CLC 3, 19,
48
See also AFAW 2; BW 2, 3; CA 21-24R;
CAAS 6; CANR 13, 25, 53, 82; CN 3, 4,
5, 6, 7; CP 2, 3, 4, 5, 6, 7; CSW; DAM
MULT; DLB 33; EWL 3; MAL 5; MSW
Major, Kevin (Gerald) 1949- CLC 26
See also AAYA 16; CA 97-100; CANR 21,
38, 112; CLR 11; DAC; DLB 60; INT
CANR-21; JRDA; MAICYA 1, 2; MAIC-
YAS 1; SATA 32, 82, 134; WYA; YAW
Maki, James
See Ozu, Yasujiro
Makine, Andrei 1957- CLC 198
See also CA 176; CANR 103; MTFW 2005
Malabaila, Damiano
See Levi, Primo
Malamud, Bernard 1914-1986 .. CLC 1, 2, 3,
5, 8, 9, 11, 18, 27, 44, 78, 85; SSC 15;
TCLC 129; WLC 4
See also AAYA 16; AMWS 1; BPFB 2;
BYA 15; CA 5-8R; 118; CABS 1; CANR
28, 62, 114; CDALB 1941-1968; CN 1, 2,
3, 4; CPW; DA; DA3; DAB; DAC; DAM
MST, NOV, POP; DLB 2, 28, 152; DLBY
1980, 1986; EWL 3; EXPS; LAIT 4;
LATS 1:1; MAL 5; MTCW 1, 2; MTFW
2005; NFS 4, 9; RGAL 4; RGHL; RGSF
2; SSFS 8, 13, 16; TUS
Malan, Herman
See Bosman, Herman Charles; Bosman,
Herman Charles
Malaparte, Curzio 1898-1957 TCLC 52
See also DLB 264
Malcolm, Dan
See Silverberg, Robert
Malcolm, Janet 1934- CLC 201
See also CA 123; CANR 89; NCFS 1

Malcolm X **BLC 2; CLC 82, 117; WLCS**
See Little, Malcolm
See also LAIT 5; NCFS 3

Malherbe, Francois de 1555-1628 **LC 5**
See also GFL Beginnings to 1789

Mallarme, Stephane 1842-1898 **NCLC 4, 41; PC 4**
See also DAM POET; DLB 217; EW 7; GFL 1789 to the Present; LMFS 2; RGWL 2, 3; TWA

Mallet-Joris, Francoise 1930- **CLC 11**
See also CA 65-68; CANR 17; CWW 2; DLB 83; EWL 3; GFL 1789 to the Present

Malley, Ern
See McAuley, James Phillip

Mallon, Thomas 1951- **CLC 172**
See also CA 110; CANR 29, 57, 92

Mallowan, Agatha Christie
See Christie, Agatha (Mary Clarissa)

Maloff, Saul 1922- **CLC 5**
See also CA 33-36R

Malone, Louis
See MacNeice, (Frederick) Louis

Malone, Michael (Christopher)
1942- .. **CLC 43**
See also CA 77-80; CANR 14, 32, 57, 114

Malory, Sir Thomas 1410(?)-1471(?) . **LC 11, 88; WLCS**
See also BRW 1; BRWR 2; CDBLB Before 1660; DA; DAB; DAC; DAM MST; DLB 146; EFS 2; RGEL 2; SATA 59; SATA-Brief 33; TEA; WLIT 3

Malouf, (George Joseph) David
1934- **CLC 28, 86**
See also CA 124; CANR 50, 76; CN 3, 4, 5, 6, 7; CP 1, 3, 4, 5, 6, 7; DLB 289; EWL 3; MTCW 1; MTFW 2005

Malraux, (Georges-)Andre
1901-1976 **CLC 1, 4, 9, 13, 15, 57**
See also BPFB 2; CA 21-22; 69-72; CANR 34, 58; CAP 2; DA3; DAM NOV; DLB 72; EW 12; EWL 3; GFL 1789 to the Present; MTCW 1, 2; MTFW 2005; RGWL 2, 3; TWA

Malthus, Thomas Robert
1766-1834 **NCLC 145**
See also DLB 107, 158; RGEL 2

Malzberg, Barry N(athaniel) 1939- ... **CLC 7**
See also CA 61-64; CAAS 4; CANR 16; CMW 4; DLB 8; SFW 4

Mamet, David 1947- .. **CLC 9, 15, 34, 46, 91, 166; DC 4, 24**
See also AAYA 3, 60; AMWS 14; CA 81-84; CABS 3; CAD; CANR 15, 41, 67, 72, 129; CD 5, 6; DA3; DAM DRAM; DFS 2, 3, 6, 12, 15; DLB 7; EWL 3; IDFW 4; MAL 5; MTCW 1, 2; MTFW 2005; RGAL 4

Mamet, David Alan
See Mamet, David

Mamoulian, Rouben (Zachary)
1897-1987 **CLC 16**
See also CA 25-28R; 124; CANR 85

Mandelshtam, Osip
See Mandelstam, Osip (Emilievich)
See also EW 10; EWL 3; RGWL 2, 3

Mandelstam, Osip (Emilievich)
1891(?)-1943(?) **PC 14; TCLC 2, 6**
See Mandelshtam, Osip
See also CA 104; 150; MTCW 2; TWA

Mander, (Mary) Jane 1877-1949 ... **TCLC 31**
See also CA 162; RGEL 2

Mandeville, Bernard 1670-1733 **LC 82**
See also DLB 101

Mandeville, Sir John fl. 1350- **CMLC 19**
See also DLB 146

Mandiargues, Andre Pieyre de **CLC 41**
See Pieyre de Mandiargues, Andre
See also DLB 83

Mandrake, Ethel Belle
See Thurman, Wallace (Henry)

Mangan, James Clarence
1803-1849 **NCLC 27**
See also RGEL 2

Maniere, J.-E.
See Giraudoux, Jean(-Hippolyte)

Mankiewicz, Herman (Jacob)
1897-1953 **TCLC 85**
See also CA 120; 169; DLB 26; IDFW 3, 4

Manley, (Mary) Delariviere
1672(?)-1724 **LC 1, 42**
See also DLB 39, 80; RGEL 2

Mann, Abel
See Creasey, John

Mann, Emily 1952- **DC 7**
See also CA 130; CAD; CANR 55; CD 5, 6; CWD; DLB 266

Mann, (Luiz) Heinrich 1871-1950 ... **TCLC 9**
See also CA 106; 164, 181; DLB 66, 118; EW 8; EWL 3; RGWL 2, 3

Mann, (Paul) Thomas 1875-1955 . **SSC 5, 80, 82; TCLC 2, 8, 14, 21, 35, 44, 60, 168; WLC 4**
See also BPFB 2; CA 104; 128; CANR 133; CDWLB 2; DA; DA3; DAB; DAC; DAM MST, NOV; DLB 66; EW 9; EWL 3; GLL 1; LATS 1:1; LMFS 1; MTCW 1, 2; MTFW 2005; NFS 17; RGSF 2; RGWL 2, 3; SSFS 4, 9; TWA

Mannheim, Karl 1893-1947 **TCLC 65**
See also CA 204

Manning, David
See Faust, Frederick (Schiller)

Manning, Frederic 1882-1935 **TCLC 25**
See also CA 124; 216; DLB 260

Manning, Olivia 1915-1980 **CLC 5, 19**
See also CA 5-8R; 101; CANR 29; CN 1, 2; EWL 3; FW; MTCW 1; RGEL 2

Mannyng, Robert c. 1264-c. 1340 **CMLC 83**
See also DLB 146

Mano, D. Keith 1942- **CLC 2, 10**
See also CA 25-28R; CAAS 6; CANR 26, 57; DLB 6

Mansfield, Katherine **SSC 9, 23, 38, 81; TCLC 2, 8, 39, 164; WLC 4**
See Beauchamp, Kathleen Mansfield
See also BPFB 2; BRW 7; DAB; DLB 162; EWL 3; EXPS; FW; GLL 1; RGEL 2; RGSF 2; SSFS 2, 8, 10, 11; WWE 1

Manso, Peter 1940- **CLC 39**
See also CA 29-32R; CANR 44

Mantecon, Juan Jimenez
See Jimenez (Mantecon), Juan Ramon

Mantel, Hilary (Mary) 1952- **CLC 144**
See also CA 125; CANR 54, 101; CN 5, 6, 7; DLB 271; RHW

Manton, Peter
See Creasey, John

Man Without a Spleen, A
See Chekhov, Anton (Pavlovich)

Manzano, Juan Franciso
1797(?)-1854 **NCLC 155**

Manzoni, Alessandro 1785-1873 ... **NCLC 29, 98**
See also EW 5; RGWL 2, 3; TWA; WLIT 7

Map, Walter 1140-1209 **CMLC 32**

Mapu, Abraham (ben Jekutiel)
1808-1867 **NCLC 18**

Mara, Sally
See Queneau, Raymond

Maracle, Lee 1950- **NNAL**
See also CA 149

Marat, Jean Paul 1743-1793 **LC 10**

Marcel, Gabriel Honore 1889-1973 . **CLC 15**
See also CA 102; 45-48; EWL 3; MTCW 1, 2

March, William **TCLC 96**
See Campbell, William Edward March
See also CA 216; DLB 9, 86, 316; MAL 5

Marchbanks, Samuel
See Davies, (William) Robertson
See also CCA 1

Marchi, Giacomo
See Bassani, Giorgio

Marcus Aurelius
See Aurelius, Marcus
See also AW 2

Marguerite
See de Navarre, Marguerite

Marguerite d'Angouleme
See de Navarre, Marguerite
See also GFL Beginnings to 1789

Marguerite de Navarre
See de Navarre, Marguerite
See also RGWL 2, 3

Margulies, Donald 1954- **CLC 76**
See also AAYA 57; CA 200; CD 6; DFS 13; DLB 228

Marie de France c. 12th cent. - **CMLC 8; PC 22**
See also DLB 208; FW; RGWL 2, 3

Marie de l'Incarnation 1599-1672 **LC 10**

Marier, Captain Victor
See Griffith, D(avid Lewelyn) W(ark)

Mariner, Scott
See Pohl, Frederik

Marinetti, Filippo Tommaso
1876-1944 **TCLC 10**
See also CA 107; DLB 114, 264; EW 9; EWL 3; WLIT 7

Marivaux, Pierre Carlet de Chamblain de
1688-1763 **DC 7; LC 4, 123**
See also DLB 314; GFL Beginnings to 1789; RGWL 2, 3; TWA

Markandaya, Kamala **CLC 8, 38**
See Taylor, Kamala (Purnaiya)
See also BYA 13; CN 1, 2, 3, 4, 5, 6, 7; DLB 323; EWL 3

Markfield, Wallace (Arthur)
1926-2002 **CLC 8**
See also CA 69-72; 208; CAAS 3; CN 1, 2, 3, 4, 5, 6, 7; DLB 2, 28; DLBY 2002

Markham, Edwin 1852-1940 **TCLC 47**
See also CA 160; DLB 54, 186; MAL 5; RGAL 4

Markham, Robert
See Amis, Kingsley (William)

Marks, J.
See Highwater, Jamake (Mamake)

Marks, J
See Highwater, Jamake (Mamake)

Marks-Highwater, J
See Highwater, Jamake (Mamake)

Marks-Highwater, J.
See Highwater, Jamake (Mamake)

Markson, David M(errill) 1927- **CLC 67**
See also CA 49-52; CANR 1, 91; CN 5, 6

Marlatt, Daphne (Buckle) 1942- **CLC 168**
See also CA 25-28R; CANR 17, 39; CN 6, 7; CP 4, 5, 6, 7; CWP; DLB 60; FW

Marley, Bob **CLC 17**
See Marley, Robert Nesta

Marley, Robert Nesta 1945-1981
See Marley, Bob
See also CA 107; 103

Marlowe, Christopher 1564-1593 . **DC 1; LC 22, 47, 117; PC 57; WLC 4**
See also BRW 1; BRWR 1; CDBLB Before 1660; DA; DA3; DAB; DAC; DAM DRAM, MST; DFS 1, 5, 13, 21; DLB 62; EXPP; LMFS 1; PFS 22; RGEL 2; TEA; WLIT 3

Marlowe, Stephen 1928- **CLC 70**
See Queen, Ellery
See also CA 13-16R; CANR 6, 55; CMW 4; SFW 4

Marmion, Shakerley 1603-1639 **LC 89**
See also DLB 58; RGEL 2

Marmontel, Jean-Francois 1723-1799 .. **LC 2**
See also DLB 314

Maron, Monika 1941- **CLC 165**
See also CA 201

Marquand, John P(hillips)
1893-1960 **CLC 2, 10**
See also AMW; BPFB 2; CA 85-88; CANR 73; CMW 4; DLB 9, 102; EWL 3; MAL 5; MTCW 2; RGAL 4

Marques, Rene 1919-1979 .. **CLC 96; HLC 2**
See also CA 97-100; 85-88; CANR 78; DAM MULT; DLB 305; EWL 3; HW 1, 2; LAW; RGSF 2

Marquez, Gabriel Garcia
See Garcia Marquez, Gabriel

Marquis, Don(ald Robert Perry)
1878-1937 **TCLC 7**
See also CA 104; 166; DLB 11, 25; MAL 5; RGAL 4

Marquis de Sade
See Sade, Donatien Alphonse Francois

Marric, J. J.
See Creasey, John
See also MSW

Marryat, Frederick 1792-1848 **NCLC 3**
See also DLB 21, 163; RGEL 2; WCH

Marsden, James
See Creasey, John

Marsh, Edward 1872-1953 **TCLC 99**

Marsh, (Edith) Ngaio 1895-1982 .. **CLC 7, 53**
See also CA 9-12R; CANR 6, 58; CMW 4; CN 1, 2, 3; CPW; DAM POP; DLB 77; MSW; MTCW 1, 2; RGEL 2; TEA

Marshall, Allen
See Westlake, Donald E(dwin)

Marshall, Garry 1934- **CLC 17**
See also AAYA 3; CA 111; SATA 60

Marshall, Paule 1929- .. **BLC 3; CLC 27, 72; SSC 3**
See also AFAW 1, 2; AMWS 11; BPFB 2; BW 2, 3; CA 77-80; CANR 25, 73, 129; CN 1, 2, 3, 4, 5, 6, 7; DAM MULT; DLB 33, 157, 227; EWL 3; LATS 1:2; MAL 5; MTCW 1, 2; MTFW 2005; RGAL 4; SSFS 15

Marshallik
See Zangwill, Israel

Marsten, Richard
See Hunter, Evan

Marston, John 1576-1634 **LC 33**
See also BRW 2; DAM DRAM; DLB 58, 172; RGEL 2

Martel, Yann 1963- **CLC 192**
See also AAYA 67; CA 146; CANR 114; DLB 326; MTFW 2005

Martens, Adolphe-Adhemar
See Ghelderode, Michel de

Martha, Henry
See Harris, Mark

Marti, Jose
See Marti (y Perez), Jose (Julian)
See also DLB 290

Marti (y Perez), Jose (Julian)
1853-1895 **HLC 2; NCLC 63**
See Marti, Jose
See also DAM MULT; HW 2; LAW; RGWL 2, 3; WLIT 1

Martial c. 40-c. 104 **CMLC 35; PC 10**
See also AW 2; CDWLB 1; DLB 211; RGWL 2, 3

Martin, Ken
See Hubbard, L. Ron

Martin, Richard
See Creasey, John

Martin, Steve 1945- **CLC 30, 217**
See also AAYA 53; CA 97-100; CANR 30, 100, 140; DFS 19; MTCW 1; MTFW 2005

Martin, Valerie 1948- **CLC 89**
See also BEST 90:2; CA 85-88; CANR 49, 89

Martin, Violet Florence 1862-1915 .. **SSC 56; TCLC 51**

Martin, Webber
See Silverberg, Robert

Martindale, Patrick Victor
See White, Patrick (Victor Martindale)

Martin du Gard, Roger
1881-1958 **TCLC 24**
See also CA 118; CANR 94; DLB 65; EWL 3; GFL 1789 to the Present; RGWL 2, 3

Martineau, Harriet 1802-1876 **NCLC 26, 137**
See also DLB 21, 55, 159, 163, 166, 190; FW; RGEL 2; YABC 2

Martines, Julia
See O'Faolain, Julia

Martinez, Enrique Gonzalez
See Gonzalez Martinez, Enrique

Martinez, Jacinto Benavente y
See Benavente (y Martinez), Jacinto

Martinez de la Rosa, Francisco de Paula
1787-1862 **NCLC 102**
See also TWA

Martinez Ruiz, Jose 1873-1967
See Azorin; Ruiz, Jose Martinez
See also CA 93-96; HW 1

Martinez Sierra, Gregorio
1881-1947 **TCLC 6**
See also CA 115; EWL 3

Martinez Sierra, Maria (de la O'LeJarraga)
1874-1974 **TCLC 6**
See also CA 115; EWL 3

Martinsen, Martin
See Follett, Ken(neth Martin)

Martinson, Harry (Edmund)
1904-1978 **CLC 14**
See also CA 77-80; CANR 34, 130; DLB 259; EWL 3

Martyn, Edward 1859-1923 **TCLC 131**
See also CA 179; DLB 10; RGEL 2

Marut, Ret
See Traven, B.

Marut, Robert
See Traven, B.

Marvell, Andrew 1621-1678 **LC 4, 43; PC 10; WLC 4**
See also BRW 2; BRWR 2; CDBLB 1660-1789; DA; DAB; DAC; DAM MST, POET; DLB 131; EXPP; PFS 5; RGEL 2; TEA; WP

Marx, Karl (Heinrich)
1818-1883 **NCLC 17, 114**
See also DLB 129; LATS 1:1; TWA

Masaoka, Shiki -1902 **TCLC 18**
See Masaoka, Tsunenori
See also RGWL 3

Masaoka, Tsunenori 1867-1902
See Masaoka, Shiki
See also CA 117; 191; TWA

Masefield, John (Edward)
1878-1967 **CLC 11, 47**
See also CA 19-20; 25-28R; CANR 33; CAP 2; CDBLB 1890-1914; DAM POET; DLB 10, 19, 153, 160; EWL 3; EXPP; FANT; MTCW 1, 2; PFS 5; RGEL 2; SATA 19

Maso, Carole 1955(?)- **CLC 44**
See also CA 170; CANR 148; CN 7; GLL 2; RGAL 4

Mason, Bobbie Ann 1940- ... **CLC 28, 43, 82, 154; SSC 4**
See also AAYA 5, 42; AMWS 8; BPFB 2; CA 53-56; CANR 11, 31, 58, 83, 125; CDALBS; CN 5, 6, 7; CSW; DA3; DLB 173; DLBY 1987; EWL 3; EXPS; INT CANR-31; MAL 5; MTCW 1, 2; MTFW 2005; NFS 4; RGAL 4; RGSF 2; SSFS 3, 8, 20; TCLE 1:2; YAW

Mason, Ernst
See Pohl, Frederik

Mason, Hunni B.
See Sternheim, (William Adolf) Carl

Mason, Lee W.
See Malzberg, Barry N(athaniel)

Mason, Nick 1945- **CLC 35**

Mason, Tally
See Derleth, August (William)

Mass, Anna **CLC 59**

Mass, William
See Gibson, William

Massinger, Philip 1583-1640 **LC 70**
See also BRWS 11; DLB 58; RGEL 2

Master Lao
See Lao Tzu

Masters, Edgar Lee 1868-1950 **PC 1, 36; TCLC 2, 25; WLCS**
See also AMWS 1; CA 104; 133; CDALB 1865-1917; DA; DAC; DAM MST, POET; DLB 54; EWL 3; EXPP; MAL 5; MTCW 1, 2; MTFW 2005; RGAL 4; TUS; WP

Masters, Hilary 1928- **CLC 48**
See also CA 25-28R; 217; CAAE 217; CANR 13, 47, 97; CN 6, 7; DLB 244

Mastrosimone, William 1947- **CLC 36**
See also CA 186; CAD; CD 5, 6

Mathe, Albert
See Camus, Albert

Mather, Cotton 1663-1728 **LC 38**
See also AMWS 2; CDALB 1640-1865; DLB 24, 30, 140; RGAL 4; TUS

Mather, Increase 1639-1723 **LC 38**
See also DLB 24

Matheson, Richard (Burton) 1926- .. **CLC 37**
See also AAYA 31; CA 97-100; CANR 88, 99; DLB 8, 44; HGG; INT CA-97-100; SCFW 1, 2; SFW 4; SUFW 2

Mathews, Harry (Burchell) 1930- **CLC 6, 52**
See also CA 21-24R; CAAS 6; CANR 18, 40, 98; CN 5, 6, 7

Mathews, John Joseph 1894-1979 .. **CLC 84; NNAL**
See also CA 19-20; 142; CANR 45; CAP 2; DAM MULT; DLB 175; TCWW 1, 2

Mathias, Roland (Glyn) 1915- **CLC 45**
See also CA 97-100; CANR 19, 41; CP 1, 2, 3, 4, 5, 6, 7; DLB 27

Matsuo Basho 1644(?)-1694 **LC 62; PC 3**
See Basho, Matsuo
See also DAM POET; PFS 2, 7, 18

Mattheson, Rodney
See Creasey, John

Matthews, (James) Brander
1852-1929 **TCLC 95**
See also CA 181; DLB 71, 78; DLBD 13

Matthews, Greg 1949- **CLC 45**
See also CA 135

Matthews, William (Procter III)
1942-1997 **CLC 40**
See also AMWS 9; CA 29-32R; 162; CAAS 18; CANR 12, 57; CP 2, 3, 4, 5, 6; DLB 5

Matthias, John (Edward) 1941- **CLC 9**
See also CA 33-36R; CANR 56; CP 4, 5, 6, 7

Matthiessen, F(rancis) O(tto)
1902-1950 **TCLC 100**
See also CA 185; DLB 63; MAL 5

Matthiessen, Peter 1927- ... **CLC 5, 7, 11, 32, 64**
See also AAYA 6, 40; AMWS 5; ANW; BEST 90:4; BPFB 2; CA 9-12R; CANR 21, 50, 73, 100, 138; CN 1, 2, 3, 4, 5, 6, 7; DA3; DAM NOV; DLB 6, 173, 275; MAL 5; MTCW 1, 2; MTFW 2005; SATA 27

Maturin, Charles Robert
1780(?)-1824 **NCLC 6, 169**
See also BRWS 8; DLB 178; GL 3; HGG; LMFS 1; RGEL 2; SUFW

Matute (Ausejo), Ana Maria 1925- .. **CLC 11**
See also CA 89-92; CANR 129; CWW 2; DLB 322; EWL 3; MTCW 1; RGSF 2

Maugham, W. S.
See Maugham, W(illiam) Somerset

Maugham, W(illiam) Somerset
1874-1965 .. **CLC 1, 11, 15, 67, 93; SSC 8; WLC 4**
See also AAYA 55; BPFB 2; BRW 6; CA 5-8R; 25-28R; CANR 40, 127; CDBLB 1914-1945; CMW 4; DA; DA3; DAB; DAC; DAM DRAM, MST, NOV; DFS 22; DLB 10, 36, 77, 100, 162, 195; EWL 3; LAIT 3; MTCW 1, 2; MTFW 2005; NFS 23; RGEL 2; RGSF 2; SATA 54; SSFS 17

Maugham, William Somerset
See Maugham, W(illiam) Somerset

Maupassant, (Henri Rene Albert) Guy de
1850-1893 . **NCLC 1, 42, 83; SSC 1, 64; WLC 4**
See also BYA 14; DA; DA3; DAB; DAC; DAM MST; DLB 123; EW 7; EXPS; GFL 1789 to the Present; LAIT 2; LMFS 1; RGSF 2; RGWL 2, 3; SSFS 4, 21; SUFW; TWA

Maupin, Armistead (Jones, Jr.)
1944- .. **CLC 95**
See also CA 125; 130; CANR 58, 101; CPW; DA3; DAM POP; DLB 278; GLL 1; INT CA-130; MTCW 2; MTFW 2005

Maurhut, Richard
See Traven, B.

Mauriac, Claude 1914-1996 **CLC 9**
See also CA 89-92; 152; CWW 2; DLB 83; EWL 3; GFL 1789 to the Present

Mauriac, Francois (Charles)
1885-1970 **CLC 4, 9, 56; SSC 24**
See also CA 25-28; CAP 2; DLB 65; EW 10; EWL 3; GFL 1789 to the Present; MTCW 1, 2; MTFW 2005; RGWL 2, 3; TWA

Mavor, Osborne Henry 1888-1951
See Bridie, James
See also CA 104

Maxwell, William (Keepers, Jr.)
1908-2000 **CLC 19**
See also AMWS 8; CA 93-96; 189; CANR 54, 95; CN 1, 2, 3, 4, 5, 6, 7; DLB 218, 278; DLBY 1980; INT CA-93-96; MAL 5; SATA-Obit 128

May, Elaine 1932- **CLC 16**
See also CA 124; 142; CAD; CWD; DLB 44

Mayakovski, Vladimir (Vladimirovich)
1893-1930 **TCLC 4, 18**
See Maiakovskii, Vladimir; Mayakovsky, Vladimir
See also CA 104; 158; EWL 3; MTCW 2; MTFW 2005; SFW 4; TWA

Mayakovsky, Vladimir
See Mayakovski, Vladimir (Vladimirovich)
See also EW 11; WP

Mayhew, Henry 1812-1887 **NCLC 31**
See also DLB 18, 55, 190

Mayle, Peter 1939(?)- **CLC 89**
See also CA 139; CANR 64, 109

Maynard, Joyce 1953- **CLC 23**
See also CA 111; 129; CANR 64

Mayne, William (James Carter)
1928- ... **CLC 12**
See also AAYA 20; CA 9-12R; CANR 37, 80, 100; CLR 25; FANT; JRDA; MAI-CYA 1, 2; MAICYAS 1; SAAS 11; SATA 6, 68, 122; SUFW 2; YAW

Mayo, Jim
See L'Amour, Louis (Dearborn)

Maysles, Albert 1926- **CLC 16**
See also CA 29-32R

Maysles, David 1932-1987 **CLC 16**
See also CA 191

Mazer, Norma Fox 1931- **CLC 26**
See also AAYA 5, 36; BYA 1, 8; CA 69-72; CANR 12, 32, 66, 129; CLR 23; JRDA; MAICYA 1, 2; SAAS 1; SATA 24, 67, 105, 168; WYA; YAW

Mazzini, Guiseppe 1805-1872 **NCLC 34**

McAlmon, Robert (Menzies)
1895-1956 **TCLC 97**
See also CA 107; 168; DLB 4, 45; DLBD 15; GLL 1

McAuley, James Phillip 1917-1976 .. **CLC 45**
See also CA 97-100; CP 1, 2; DLB 260; RGEL 2

McBain, Ed
See Hunter, Evan
See also MSW

McBrien, William (Augustine)
1930- ... **CLC 44**
See also CA 107; CANR 90

McCabe, Patrick 1955- **CLC 133**
See also BRWS 9; CA 130; CANR 50, 90; CN 6, 7; DLB 194

McCaffrey, Anne 1926- **CLC 17**
See also AAYA 6, 34; AITN 2; BEST 89:2; BPFB 2; BYA 5; CA 25-28R, 227; CAAE 227; CANR 15, 35, 55, 96; CLR 49; CPW; DA3; DAM NOV, POP; DLB 8; JRDA; MAICYA 1, 2; MTCW 1, 2; MTFW 2005; SAAS 11; SATA 8, 70, 116, 152; SATA-Essay 152; SFW 4; SUFW 2; WYA; YAW

McCaffrey, Anne Inez
See McCaffrey, Anne

McCall, Nathan 1955(?)- **CLC 86**
See also AAYA 59; BW 3; CA 146; CANR 88

McCann, Arthur
See Campbell, John W(ood, Jr.)

McCann, Edson
See Pohl, Frederik

McCarthy, Charles, Jr. 1933-
See McCarthy, Cormac
See also CANR 42, 69, 101; CPW; CSW; DA3; DAM POP; MTCW 2; MTFW 2005

McCarthy, Cormac **CLC 4, 57, 101, 204**
See McCarthy, Charles, Jr.
See also AAYA 41; AMWS 8; BPFB 2; CA 13-16R; CANR 10; CN 6, 7; DLB 6, 143, 256; EWL 3; LATS 1:2; MAL 5; TCLE 1:2; TCWW 2

McCarthy, Mary (Therese)
1912-1989 .. **CLC 1, 3, 5, 14, 24, 39, 59; SSC 24**
See also AMW; BPFB 2; CA 5-8R; 129; CANR 16, 50, 64; CN 1, 2, 3, 4; DA3; DLB 2; DLBY 1981; EWL 3; FW; INT CANR-16; MAL 5; MAWW; MTCW 1, 2; MTFW 2005; RGAL 4; TUS

McCartney, James Paul
See McCartney, Paul

McCartney, Paul 1942- **CLC 12, 35**
See also CA 146; CANR 111

McCauley, Stephen (D.) 1955- **CLC 50**
See also CA 141

McClaren, Peter **CLC 70**

McClure, Michael (Thomas) 1932- ... **CLC 6, 10**
See also BG 1:3; CA 21-24R; CAD; CANR 17, 46, 77, 131; CD 5, 6; CP 1, 2, 3, 4, 5, 6, 7; DLB 16; WP

McCorkle, Jill (Collins) 1958- **CLC 51**
See also CA 121; CANR 113; CSW; DLB 234; DLBY 1987

McCourt, Frank 1930- **CLC 109**
See also AAYA 61; AMWS 12; CA 157; CANR 97, 138; MTFW 2005; NCFS 1

McCourt, James 1941- **CLC 5**
See also CA 57-60; CANR 98, 152

McCourt, Malachy 1931- **CLC 119**
See also SATA 126

McCoy, Horace (Stanley)
1897-1955 **TCLC 28**
See also AMWS 13; CA 108; 155; CMW 4; DLB 9

McCrae, John 1872-1918 **TCLC 12**
See also CA 109; DLB 92; PFS 5

McCreigh, James
See Pohl, Frederik

McCullers, (Lula) Carson (Smith)
1917-1967 **CLC 1, 4, 10, 12, 48, 100; SSC 9, 24; TCLC 155; WLC 4**
See also AAYA 21; AMW; AMWC 2; BPFB 2; CA 5-8R; 25-28R; CABS 1, 3; CANR 18, 132; CDALB 1941-1968; DA; DA3; DAB; DAC; DAM MST, NOV; DFS 5, 18; DLB 2, 7, 173, 228; EWL 3; EXPS; FW; GLL 1; LAIT 3, 4; MAL 5; MAWW; MTCW 1, 2; MTFW 2005; NFS 6, 13; RGAL 4; RGSF 2; SATA 27; SSFS 5; TUS; YAW

McCulloch, John Tyler
See Burroughs, Edgar Rice

McCullough, Colleen 1937- **CLC 27, 107**
See also AAYA 36; BPFB 2; CA 81-84; CANR 17, 46, 67, 98, 139; CPW; DA3; DAM NOV, POP; MTCW 1, 2; MTFW 2005; RHW

McCunn, Ruthanne Lum 1946- **AAL**
See also CA 119; CANR 43, 96; DLB 312; LAIT 2; SATA 63

McDermott, Alice 1953- **CLC 90**
See also CA 109; CANR 40, 90, 126; CN 7; DLB 292; MTFW 2005; NFS 23

McElroy, Joseph 1930- **CLC 5, 47**
See also CA 17-20R; CANR 149; CN 3, 4, 5, 6, 7

McElroy, Joseph Prince
See McElroy, Joseph

McEwan, Ian (Russell) 1948- **CLC 13, 66, 169**
See also BEST 90:4; BRWS 4; CA 61-64; CANR 14, 41, 69, 87, 132; CN 3, 4, 5, 6, 7; DAM NOV; DLB 14, 194, 319, 326; HGG; MTCW 1, 2; MTFW 2005; RGSF 2; SUFW 2; TEA

McFadden, David 1940- **CLC 48**
See also CA 104; CP 1, 2, 3, 4, 5, 6, 7; DLB 60; INT CA-104

McFarland, Dennis 1950- **CLC 65**
See also CA 165; CANR 110

McGahern, John 1934-2006 **CLC 5, 9, 48, 156; SSC 17**
See also CA 17-20R; CANR 29, 68, 113; CN 1, 2, 3, 4, 5, 6, 7; DLB 14, 231, 319; MTCW 1

McGinley, Patrick (Anthony) 1937- . **CLC 41**
See also CA 120; 127; CANR 56; INT CA-127

McGinley, Phyllis 1905-1978 **CLC 14**
 See also CA 9-12R; 77-80; CANR 19; CP
 1, 2; CWRI 5; DLB 11, 48; MAL 5; PFS
 9, 13; SATA 2, 44; SATA-Obit 24
McGinniss, Joe 1942- **CLC 32**
 See also AITN 2; BEST 89:2; CA 25-28R;
 CANR 26, 70, 152; CPW; DLB 185; INT
 CANR-26
McGivern, Maureen Daly
 See Daly, Maureen
McGrath, Patrick 1950- **CLC 55**
 See also CA 136; CANR 65, 148; CN 5, 6,
 7; DLB 231; HGG; SUFW 2
McGrath, Thomas (Matthew)
 1916-1990 **CLC 28, 59**
 See also AMWS 10; CA 9-12R; 132; CANR
 6, 33, 95; CP 1, 2, 3, 4, 5; DAM POET;
 MAL 5; MTCW 1; SATA 41; SATA-Obit
 66
McGuane, Thomas (Francis III)
 1939- **CLC 3, 7, 18, 45, 127**
 See also AITN 2; BPFB 2; CA 49-52;
 CANR 5, 24, 49, 94; CN 2, 3, 4, 5, 6, 7;
 DLB 2, 212; DLBY 1980; EWL 3; INT
 CANR-24; MAL 5; MTCW 1; MTFW
 2005; TCWW 1, 2
McGuckian, Medbh 1950- **CLC 48, 174;**
 PC 27
 See also BRWS 5; CA 143; CP 4, 5, 6, 7;
 CWP; DAM POET; DLB 40
McHale, Tom 1942(?)-1982 **CLC 3, 5**
 See also AITN 1; CA 77-80; 106; CN 1, 2,
 3
McHugh, Heather 1948- **PC 61**
 See also CA 69-72; CANR 11, 28, 55, 92;
 CP 4, 5, 6, 7; CWP; PFS 24
McIlvanney, William 1936- **CLC 42**
 See also CA 25-28R; CANR 61; CMW 4;
 DLB 14, 207
McIlwraith, Maureen Mollie Hunter
 See Hunter, Mollie
 See also SATA 2
McInerney, Jay 1955- **CLC 34, 112**
 See also AAYA 18; BPFB 2; CA 116; 123;
 CANR 45, 68, 116; CN 5, 6, 7; CPW;
 DA3; DAM POP; DLB 292; INT CA-123;
 MAL 5; MTCW 2; MTFW 2005
McIntyre, Vonda N(eel) 1948- **CLC 18**
 See also CA 81-84; CANR 17, 34, 69;
 MTCW 1; SFW 4; YAW
McKay, Claude **BLC 3; HR 1:3; PC 2;**
 TCLC 7, 41; WLC 4
 See McKay, Festus Claudius
 See also AFAW 1, 2; AMWS 10; DAB;
 DLB 4, 45, 51, 117; EWL 3; EXPP; GLL
 2; LAIT 3; LMFS 2; MAL 5; PAB; PFS
 4; RGAL 4; WP
McKay, Festus Claudius 1889-1948
 See McKay, Claude
 See also BW 1, 3; CA 104; 124; CANR 73;
 DA; DAC; DAM MST, MULT, NOV,
 POET; MTCW 1, 2; MTFW 2005; TUS
McKuen, Rod 1933- **CLC 1, 3**
 See also AITN 1; CA 41-44R; CANR 40;
 CP 1
McLoughlin, R. B.
 See Mencken, H(enry) L(ouis)
McLuhan, (Herbert) Marshall
 1911-1980 **CLC 37, 83**
 See also CA 9-12R; 102; CANR 12, 34, 61;
 DLB 88; INT CANR-12; MTCW 1, 2;
 MTFW 2005
McManus, Declan Patrick Aloysius
 See Costello, Elvis
McMillan, Terry (L.) 1951- . **BLCS; CLC 50,**
 61, 112
 See also AAYA 21; AMWS 13; BPFB 2;
 BW 2, 3; CA 140; CANR 60, 104, 131;
 CN 7; CPW; DA3; DAM MULT, NOV,
 POP; MAL 5; MTCW 2; MTFW 2005;
 RGAL 4; YAW

McMurtry, Larry 1936- **CLC 2, 3, 7, 11,**
 27, 44, 127
 See also AAYA 15; AITN 2; AMWS 5;
 BEST 89:2; BPFB 2; CA 5-8R; CANR
 19, 43, 64, 103; CDALB 1968-1988; CN
 2, 3, 4, 5, 6, 7; CPW; CSW; DA3; DAM
 NOV, POP; DLB 2, 143, 256; DLBY
 1980, 1987; EWL 3; MAL 5; MTCW 1,
 2; MTFW 2005; RGAL 4; TCWW 1, 2
McMurtry, Larry Jeff
 See McMurtry, Larry
McNally, Terrence 1939- ... **CLC 4, 7, 41, 91;**
 DC 27
 See also AAYA 62; AMWS 13; CA 45-48;
 CAD; CANR 2, 56, 116; CD 5, 6; DA3;
 DAM DRAM; DFS 16, 19; DLB 7, 249;
 EWL 3; GLL 1; MTCW 2; MTFW 2005
McNally, Thomas Michael
 See McNally, T.M.
McNally, T.M. 1961- **CLC 82**
 See also CA 246
McNamer, Deirdre 1950- **CLC 70**
McNeal, Tom **CLC 119**
McNeile, Herman Cyril 1888-1937
 See Sapper
 See also CA 184; CMW 4; DLB 77
McNickle, (William) D'Arcy
 1904-1977 **CLC 89; NNAL**
 See also CA 9-12R; 85-88; CANR 5, 45;
 DAM MULT; DLB 175, 212; RGAL 4;
 SATA-Obit 22; TCWW 1, 2
McPhee, John (Angus) 1931- **CLC 36**
 See also AAYA 61; AMWS 3; ANW; BEST
 90:1; CA 65-68; CANR 20, 46, 64, 69,
 121; CPW; DLB 185, 275; MTCW 1, 2;
 MTFW 2005, TUS
McPherson, James Alan 1943- . **BLCS; CLC**
 19, 77
 See also BW 1, 3; CA 25-28R; CAAS 17;
 CANR 24, 74, 140; CN 3, 4, 5, 6; CSW;
 DLB 38, 244; EWL 3; MTCW 1, 2;
 MTFW 2005; RGAL 4; RGSF 2; SSFS
 23
McPherson, William (Alexander)
 1933- ... **CLC 34**
 See also CA 69-72; CANR 28; INT
 CANR-28
McTaggart, J. McT. Ellis
 See McTaggart, John McTaggart Ellis
McTaggart, John McTaggart Ellis
 1866-1925 **TCLC 105**
 See also CA 120; DLB 262
Mead, George Herbert 1863-1931 . **TCLC 89**
 See also CA 212; DLB 270
Mead, Margaret 1901-1978 **CLC 37**
 See also AITN 1; CA 1-4R; 81-84; CANR
 4; DA3; FW; MTCW 1, 2; SATA-Obit 20
Meaker, Marijane (Agnes) 1927-
 See Kerr, M. E.
 See also CA 107; CANR 37, 63, 145; INT
 CA-107; JRDA; MAICYA 1, 2; MAIC-
 YAS 1; MTCW 1; SATA 20, 61, 99, 160;
 SATA-Essay 111; YAW
Medoff, Mark (Howard) 1940- **CLC 6, 23**
 See also AITN 1; CA 53-56; CAD; CANR
 5; CD 5, 6; DAM DRAM; DFS 4; DLB
 7; INT CANR-5
Medvedev, P. N.
 See Bakhtin, Mikhail Mikhailovich
Meged, Aharon
 See Megged, Aharon
Meged, Aron
 See Megged, Aharon
Megged, Aharon 1920- **CLC 9**
 See also CA 49-52; CAAS 13; CANR 1,
 140; EWL 3; RGHL
Mehta, Deepa 1950- **CLC 208**
Mehta, Gita 1943- **CLC 179**
 See also CA 225; CN 7; DNFS 2

Mehta, Ved (Parkash) 1934- **CLC 37**
 See also CA 1-4R, 212; CAAE 212; CANR
 2, 23, 69; DLB 323; MTCW 1; MTFW
 2005
Melanchthon, Philipp 1497-1560 **LC 90**
 See also DLB 179
Melanter
 See Blackmore, R(ichard) D(oddridge)
Meleager c. 140B.C.-c. 70B.C. **CMLC 53**
Melies, Georges 1861-1938 **TCLC 81**
Melikow, Loris
 See Hofmannsthal, Hugo von
Melmoth, Sebastian
 See Wilde, Oscar (Fingal O'Flahertie Wills)
Melo Neto, Joao Cabral de
 See Cabral de Melo Neto, Joao
 See also CWW 2; EWL 3
Meltzer, Milton 1915- **CLC 26**
 See also AAYA 8, 45; BYA 2, 6; CA 13-
 16R; CANR 38, 92, 107; CLR 13; DLB
 61; JRDA; MAICYA 1, 2; SAAS 1; SATA
 1, 50, 80, 128; SATA-Essay 124; WYA;
 YAW
Melville, Herman 1819-1891 **NCLC 3, 12,**
 29, 45, 49, 91, 93, 123, 157; SSC 1, 17,
 46; WLC 4
 See also AAYA 25; AMW; AMWR 1;
 CDALB 1640-1865; DA; DA3; DAB;
 DAC; DAM MST, NOV; DLB 3, 74, 250,
 254; EXPN; EXPS; GL 3; LAIT 1, 2; NFS
 7, 9; RGAL 4; RGSF 2; SATA 59; SSFS
 3; TUS
Members, Mark
 See Powell, Anthony (Dymoke)
Membreno, Alejandro **CLC 59**
Menand, Louis 1952- **CLC 208**
 See also CA 200
Menander c. 342B.C.-c. 293B.C. **CMLC 9,**
 51; DC 3
 See also AW 1; CDWLB 1; DAM DRAM;
 DLB 176; LMFS 1; RGWL 2, 3
Menchu, Rigoberta 1959- .. **CLC 160; HLCS**
 2
 See also CA 175; CANR 135; DNFS 1;
 WLIT 1
Mencken, H(enry) L(ouis)
 1880-1956 **TCLC 13**
 See also AMW; CA 105; 125; CDALB
 1917-1929; DLB 11, 29, 63, 137, 222;
 EWL 3; MAL 5; MTCW 1, 2; MTFW
 2005; NCFS 4; RGAL 4; TUS
Mendelsohn, Jane 1965- **CLC 99**
 See also CA 154; CANR 94
Mendoza, Inigo Lopez de
 See Santillana, Inigo Lopez de Mendoza,
 Marques de
Menton, Francisco de
 See Chin, Frank (Chew, Jr.)
Mercer, David 1928-1980 **CLC 5**
 See also CA 9-12R; 102; CANR 23; CBD;
 DAM DRAM; DLB 13, 310; MTCW 1;
 RGEL 2
Merchant, Paul
 See Ellison, Harlan (Jay)
Meredith, George 1828-1909 .. **PC 60; TCLC**
 17, 43
 See also CA 117; 153; CANR 80; CDBLB
 1832-1890; DAM POET; DLB 18, 35, 57,
 159; RGEL 2; TEA
Meredith, William (Morris) 1919- **CLC 4,**
 13, 22, 55; PC 28
 See also CA 9-12R; CAAS 14; CANR 6,
 40, 129; CP 1, 2, 3, 4, 5, 6, 7; DAM
 POET; DLB 5; MAL 5
Merezhkovsky, Dmitrii Sergeevich
 See Merezhkovsky, Dmitry Sergeyevich
 See also DLB 295

Merezhkovsky, Dmitry Sergeevich
See Merezhkovsky, Dmitry Sergeyevich
See also EWL 3

Merezhkovsky, Dmitry Sergeyevich
1865-1941 **TCLC 29**
See Merezhkovsky, Dmitrii Sergeevich;
Merezhkovsky, Dmitry Sergeevich
See also CA 169

Merimee, Prosper 1803-1870 ... **NCLC 6, 65;
SSC 7, 77**
See also DLB 119, 192; EW 6; EXPS; GFL
1789 to the Present; RGSF 2; RGWL 2,
3; SSFS 8; SUFW

Merkin, Daphne 1954- **CLC 44**
See also CA 123

Merleau-Ponty, Maurice
1908-1961 **TCLC 156**
See also CA 114; 89-92; DLB 296; GFL
1789 to the Present

Merlin, Arthur
See Blish, James (Benjamin)

Mernissi, Fatima 1940- **CLC 171**
See also CA 152; FW

Merrill, James (Ingram) 1926-1995 .. **CLC 2,
3, 6, 8, 13, 18, 34, 91; PC 28; TCLC
173**
See also AMWS 3; CA 13-16R; 147; CANR
10, 49, 63, 108; CP 1, 2, 3, 4; DA3; DAM
POET; DLB 5, 165; DLBY 1985; EWL 3;
INT CANR-10; MAL 5; MTCW 1, 2;
MTFW 2005; PAB; PFS 23; RGAL 4

Merriman, Alex
See Silverberg, Robert

Merriman, Brian 1747-1805 **NCLC 70**

Merritt, E. B.
See Waddington, Miriam

Merton, Thomas (James)
1915-1968 . **CLC 1, 3, 11, 34, 83; PC 10**
See also AAYA 61; AMWS 8; CA 5-8R;
25-28R; CANR 22, 53, 111, 131; DA3;
DLB 48; DLBY 1981; MAL 5; MTCW 1,
2; MTFW 2005

Merwin, W(illiam) S(tanley) 1927- ... **CLC 1,
2, 3, 5, 8, 13, 18, 45, 88; PC 45**
See also AMWS 3; CA 13-16R; CANR 15,
51, 112, 140; CP 1, 2, 3, 4, 5, 6, 7; DA3;
DAM POET; DLB 5, 169; EWL 3; INT
CANR-15; MAL 5; MTCW 1, 2; MTFW
2005; PAB; PFS 5, 15; RGAL 4

Metastasio, Pietro 1698-1782 **LC 115**
See also RGWL 2, 3

Metcalf, John 1938- **CLC 37; SSC 43**
See also CA 113; CN 4, 5, 6, 7; DLB 60;
RGSF 2; TWA

Metcalf, Suzanne
See Baum, L(yman) Frank

Mew, Charlotte (Mary) 1870-1928 .. **TCLC 8**
See also CA 105; 189; DLB 19, 135; RGEL
2

Mewshaw, Michael 1943- **CLC 9**
See also CA 53-56; CANR 7, 47, 147;
DLBY 1980

Meyer, Conrad Ferdinand
1825-1898 **NCLC 81; SSC 30**
See also DLB 129; EW; RGWL 2, 3

Meyer, Gustav 1868-1932
See Meyrink, Gustav
See also CA 117; 190

Meyer, June
See Jordan, June

Meyer, Lynn
See Slavitt, David R(ytman)

Meyers, Jeffrey 1939- **CLC 39**
See also CA 73-76, 186; CAAE 186; CANR
54, 102; DLB 111

**Meynell, Alice (Christina Gertrude
Thompson)** 1847-1922 **TCLC 6**
See also CA 104; 177; DLB 19, 98; RGEL 2

Meyrink, Gustav **TCLC 21**
See Meyer, Gustav
See also DLB 81; EWL 3

Michaels, Leonard 1933-2003 **CLC 6, 25;
SSC 16**
See also CA 61-64; 216; CANR 21, 62, 119;
CN 3, 45, 6, 7; DLB 130; MTCW 1;
TCLE 1:2

Michaux, Henri 1899-1984 **CLC 8, 19**
See also CA 85-88; 114; DLB 258; EWL 3;
GFL 1789 to the Present; RGWL 2, 3

Micheaux, Oscar (Devereaux)
1884-1951 **TCLC 76**
See also BW 3; CA 174; DLB 50; TCWW
2

Michelangelo 1475-1564 **LC 12**
See also AAYA 43

Michelet, Jules 1798-1874 **NCLC 31**
See also EW 5; GFL 1789 to the Present

Michels, Robert 1876-1936 **TCLC 88**
See also CA 212

Michener, James A(lbert)
1907(?)-1997 .. **CLC 1, 5, 11, 29, 60, 109**
See also AAYA 27; AITN 1; BEST 90:1;
BPFB 2; CA 5-8R; 161; CANR 21, 45,
68; CN 1, 2, 3, 4, 5, 6; CPW; DA3; DAM
NOV, POP; DLB 6; MAL 5; MTCW 1, 2;
MTFW 2005; RHW; TCWW 1, 2

Mickiewicz, Adam 1798-1855 . **NCLC 3, 101;
PC 38**
See also EW 5; RGWL 2, 3

Middleton, (John) Christopher
1926- ... **CLC 13**
See also CA 13-16R; CANR 29, 54, 117;
CP 1, 2, 3, 4, 5, 6, 7; DLB 40

Middleton, Richard (Barham)
1882-1911 **TCLC 56**
See also CA 187; DLB 156; HGG

Middleton, Stanley 1919- **CLC 7, 38**
See also CA 25-28R; CAAS 23; CANR 21,
46, 81; CN 1, 2, 3, 4, 5, 6, 7; DLB 14,
326

Middleton, Thomas 1580-1627 **DC 5; LC
33, 123**
See also BRW 2; DAM DRAM, MST; DFS
18, 22; DLB 58; RGEL 2

Migueis, Jose Rodrigues 1901-1980 . **CLC 10**
See also DLB 287

Mikszath, Kalman 1847-1910 **TCLC 31**
See also CA 170

Miles, Jack **CLC 100**
See also CA 200

Miles, John Russiano
See Miles, Jack

Miles, Josephine (Louise)
1911-1985 **CLC 1, 2, 14, 34, 39**
See also CA 1-4R; 116; CANR 2, 55; CP 1,
2, 3, 4; DAM POET; DLB 48; MAL 5;
TCLE 1:2

Militant
See Sandburg, Carl (August)

Mill, Harriet (Hardy) Taylor
1807-1858 **NCLC 102**
See also FW

Mill, John Stuart 1806-1873 **NCLC 11, 58**
See also CDBLB 1832-1890; DLB 55, 190,
262; FW 1; RGEL 2; TEA

Millar, Kenneth 1915-1983 **CLC 14**
See Macdonald, Ross
See also CA 9-12R; 110; CANR 16, 63,
107; CMW 4; CPW; DA3; DAM POP;
DLB 2, 226; DLBD 6; DLBY 1983;
MTCW 1, 2; MTFW 2005

Millay, E. Vincent
See Millay, Edna St. Vincent

Millay, Edna St. Vincent 1892-1950 **PC 6,
61; TCLC 4, 49, 169; WLCS**
See Boyd, Nancy
See also AMW; CA 104; 130; CDALB
1917-1929; DA; DA3; DAB; DAC; DAM
MST, POET; DLB 45, 249; EWL 3;
EXPP; FL 1:6; MAL 5; MAWW; MTCW
1, 2; MTFW 2005; PAB; PFS 3, 17;
RGAL 4; TUS; WP

Miller, Arthur 1915-2005 **CLC 1, 2, 6, 10,
15, 26, 47, 78, 179; DC 1; WLC 4**
See also AAYA 15; AITN 1; AMW; AMWC
1; CA 1-4R; 236; CABS 3; CAD; CANR
2, 30, 54, 76, 132; CD 5, 6; CDALB
1941-1968; DA; DA3; DAB; DAC; DAM
DRAM, MST; DFS 1, 3, 8; DLB 7, 266;
EWL 3; LAIT 1, 4; LATS 1:2; MAL 5;
MTCW 1, 2; MTFW 2005; RGAL 4;
RGHL; TUS; WYAS 1

Miller, Henry (Valentine)
1891-1980 **CLC 1, 2, 4, 9, 14, 43, 84;
WLC 4**
See also AMW; BPFB 2; CA 9-12R; 97-
100; CANR 33, 64; CDALB 1929-1941;
CN 1, 2; DA; DA3; DAB; DAC; DAM
MST, NOV; DLB 4, 9; DLBY 1980; EWL
3; MAL 5; MTCW 1, 2; MTFW 2005;
RGAL 4; TUS

Miller, Hugh 1802-1856 **NCLC 143**
See also DLB 190

Miller, Jason 1939(?)-2001 **CLC 2**
See also AITN 1; CA 73-76; 197; CAD;
CANR 130; DFS 12; DLB 7

Miller, Sue 1943- **CLC 44**
See also AMWS 12; BEST 90:3; CA 139;
CANR 59, 91, 128; DA3; DAM POP;
DLB 143

Miller, Walter M(ichael, Jr.)
1923-1996 **CLC 4, 30**
See also BPFB 2; CA 85-88; CANR 108;
DLB 8; SCFW 1, 2; SFW 4

Millett, Kate 1934- **CLC 67**
See also AITN 1; CA 73-76; CANR 32, 53,
76, 110; DA3; DLB 246; FW; GLL 1;
MTCW 1, 2; MTFW 2005

Millhauser, Steven (Lewis) 1943- **CLC 21,
54, 109; SSC 57**
See also CA 110; 111; CANR 63, 114, 133;
CN 6, 7; DA3; DLB 2; FANT; INT CA-
111; MAL 5; MTCW 2; MTFW 2005

Millin, Sarah Gertrude 1889-1968 **CLC 49**
See also CA 102; 93-96; DLB 225; EWL 3

Milne, A. A. 1882-1956 **TCLC 6, 88**
See also BRWS 5; CA 104; 133; CLR 1,
26, 108; CMW 4; CWRI 5; DA3; DAB;
DAC; DAM MST; DLB 10, 77, 100, 160;
FANT; MAICYA 1, 2; MTCW 1, 2;
MTFW 2005; RGEL 2; SATA 100; WCH;
YABC 1

Milne, Alan Alexander
See Milne, A. A.

Milner, Ron(ald) 1938-2004 **BLC 3; CLC
56**
See also AITN 1; BW 1; CA 73-76; 230;
CAD; CANR 24, 81; CD 5, 6; DAM
MULT; DLB 38; MAL 5; MTCW 1

Milnes, Richard Monckton
1809-1885 **NCLC 61**
See also DLB 32, 184

Milosz, Czeslaw 1911-2004 **CLC 5, 11, 22,
31, 56, 82; PC 8; WLCS**
See also AAYA 62; CA 81-84; 230; CANR
23, 51, 91, 126; CDWLB 4; CWW 2;
DA3; DAM MST, POET; DLB 215; EW
13; EWL 3; MTCW 1, 2; MTFW 2005;
PFS 16; RGHL; RGWL 2, 3

Milton, John 1608-1674 **LC 9, 43, 92; PC
19, 29; WLC 4**
See also AAYA 65; BRW 2; BRWR 2; CD-
BLB 1660-1789; DA; DA3; DAB; DAC;

DAM MST, POET; DLB 131, 151, 281;
EFS 1; EXPP; LAIT 1; PAB; PFS 3, 17;
RGEL 2; TEA; WLIT 3; WP

Min, Anchee 1957- **CLC 86**
See also CA 146; CANR 94, 137; MTFW
2005

Minehaha, Cornelius
See Wedekind, Frank

Miner, Valerie 1947- **CLC 40**
See also CA 97-100; CANR 59; FW; GLL
2

Minimo, Duca
See D'Annunzio, Gabriele

Minot, Susan (Anderson) 1956- **CLC 44,
159**
See also AMWS 6; CA 134; CANR 118;
CN 6, 7

Minus, Ed 1938- **CLC 39**
See also CA 185

Mirabai 1498(?)-1550(?) **PC 48**
See also PFS 24

Miranda, Javier
See Bioy Casares, Adolfo
See also CWW 2

Mirbeau, Octave 1848-1917 **TCLC 55**
See also CA 216; DLB 123, 192; GFL 1789
to the Present

Mirikitani, Janice 1942- **AAL**
See also CA 211; DLB 312; RGAL 4

Mirk, John (?)-c. 1414 **LC 105**
See also DLB 146

Miro (Ferrer), Gabriel (Francisco Victor)
1879-1930 **TCLC 5**
See also CA 104; 185; DLB 322; EWL 3

Misharin, Alexandr **CLC 59**

**Mishima, Yukio ... CLC 2, 4, 6, 9, 27; DC 1;
SSC 4; TCLC 161; WLC 4**
See Hiraoka, Kimitake
See also AAYA 50; BPFB 2; GLL 1; MJW;
RGSF 2; RGWL 2, 3; SSFS 5, 12

Mistral, Frederic 1830-1914 **TCLC 51**
See also CA 122; 213; GFL 1789 to the
Present

Mistral, Gabriela
See Godoy Alcayaga, Lucila
See also DLB 283; DNFS 1; EWL 3; LAW;
RGWL 2, 3; WP

Mistry, Rohinton 1952- ... **CLC 71, 196; SSC
73**
See also BRWS 10; CA 141; CANR 86,
114; CCA 1; CN 6, 7; DAC; SSFS 6

Mitchell, Clyde
See Ellison, Harlan (Jay)

Mitchell, Emerson Blackhorse Barney
1945- .. **NNAL**
See also CA 45-48

Mitchell, James Leslie 1901-1935
See Gibbon, Lewis Grassic
See also CA 104; 188; DLB 15

Mitchell, Joni 1943- **CLC 12**
See also CA 112; CCA 1

Mitchell, Joseph (Quincy)
1908-1996 **CLC 98**
See also CA 77-80; 152; CANR 69; CN 1,
2, 3, 4, 5, 6; CSW; DLB 185; DLBY 1996

Mitchell, Margaret (Munnerlyn)
1900-1949 **TCLC 11, 170**
See also AAYA 23; BPFB 2; BYA 1; CA
109; 125; CANR 55, 94; CDALBS; DA3;
DAM NOV, POP; DLB 9; LAIT 2; MAL
5; MTCW 1, 2; MTFW 2005; NFS 9;
RGAL 4; RHW; TUS; WYAS 1; YAW

Mitchell, Peggy
See Mitchell, Margaret (Munnerlyn)

Mitchell, S(ilas) Weir 1829-1914 **TCLC 36**
See also CA 165; DLB 202; RGAL 4

Mitchell, W(illiam) O(rmond)
1914-1998 **CLC 25**
See also CA 77-80; 165; CANR 15, 43; CN
1, 2, 3, 4, 5, 6; DAC; DAM MST; DLB
88; TCLE 1:2

Mitchell, William (Lendrum)
1879-1936 **TCLC 81**
See also CA 213

Mitford, Mary Russell 1787-1855 ... **NCLC 4**
See also DLB 110, 116; RGEL 2

Mitford, Nancy 1904-1973 **CLC 44**
See also BRWS 10; CA 9-12R; CN 1; DLB
191; RGEL 2

Miyamoto, (Chujo) Yuriko
1899-1951 **TCLC 37**
See Miyamoto Yuriko
See also CA 170, 174

Miyamoto Yuriko
See Miyamoto, (Chujo) Yuriko
See also DLB 180

Miyazawa, Kenji 1896-1933 **TCLC 76**
See Miyazawa Kenji
See also CA 157; RGWL 3

Miyazawa Kenji
See Miyazawa, Kenji
See also EWL 3

Mizoguchi, Kenji 1898-1956 **TCLC 72**
See also CA 167

Mo, Timothy (Peter) 1950- **CLC 46, 134**
See also CA 117; CANR 128; CN 5, 6, 7;
DLB 194; MTCW 1; WLIT 4; WWE 1

Modarressi, Taghi (M.) 1931-1997 ... **CLC 44**
See also CA 121; 134; INT CA-134

Modiano, Patrick (Jean) 1945- **CLC 18,
218**
See also CA 85-88; CANR 17, 40, 115;
CWW 2; DLB 83, 299; EWL 3; RGHL

Mofolo, Thomas (Mokopu)
1875(?)-1948 **BLC 3; TCLC 22**
See also AFW; CA 121; 153; CANR 83;
DAM MULT; DLB 225; EWL 3; MTCW
2; MTFW 2005; WLIT 2

Mohr, Nicholasa 1938- **CLC 12; HLC 2**
See also AAYA 8, 46; CA 49-52; CANR 1,
32, 64; CLR 22; DAM MULT; DLB 145;
HW 1, 2; JRDA; LAIT 5; LLW; MAICYA
2; MAICYAS 1; RGAL 4; SAAS 8; SATA
8, 97; SATA-Essay 113; WYA; YAW

Moi, Toril 1953- **CLC 172**
See also CA 154; CANR 102; FW

Mojtabai, A(nn) G(race) 1938- **CLC 5, 9,
15, 29**
See also CA 85-88; CANR 88

Moliere 1622-1673 **DC 13; LC 10, 28, 64,
125, 127; WLC 4**
See also DA; DA3; DAB; DAC; DAM
DRAM, MST; DFS 13, 18, 20; DLB 268;
EW 3; GFL Beginnings to 1789; LATS
1:1; RGWL 2, 3; TWA

Molin, Charles
See Mayne, William (James Carter)

Molnar, Ferenc 1878-1952 **TCLC 20**
See also CA 109; 153; CANR 83; CDWLB
4; DAM DRAM; DLB 215; EWL 3;
RGWL 2, 3

Momaday, N(avarre) Scott 1934- **CLC 2,
19, 85, 95, 160; NNAL; PC 25; WLCS**
See also AAYA 11, 64; AMWS 4; ANW;
BPFB 2; BYA 12; CA 25-28R; CANR 14,
34, 68, 134; CDALBS; CN 2, 3, 4, 5, 6,
7; CPW; DA; DA3; DAB; DAC; DAM
MST, MULT, NOV, POP; DLB 143, 175,
256; EWL 3; EXPP; INT CANR-14;
LAIT 4; LATS 1:2; MAL 5; MTCW 1, 2;
MTFW 2005; NFS 10; PFS 2, 11; RGAL
4; SATA 48; SATA-Brief 30; TCWW 1,
2; WP; YAW

Monette, Paul 1945-1995 **CLC 82**
See also AMWS 10; CA 139; 147; CN 6;
GLL 1

Monroe, Harriet 1860-1936 **TCLC 12**
See also CA 109; 204; DLB 54, 91

Monroe, Lyle
See Heinlein, Robert A(nson)

Montagu, Elizabeth 1720-1800 **NCLC 7,
117**
See also FW

Montagu, Mary (Pierrepont) Wortley
1689-1762 **LC 9, 57; PC 16**
See also DLB 95, 101; FL 1:1; RGEL 2

Montagu, W. H.
See Coleridge, Samuel Taylor

Montague, John (Patrick) 1929- **CLC 13,
46**
See also CA 9-12R; CANR 9, 69, 121; CP
1, 2, 3, 4, 5, 6, 7; DLB 40; EWL 3;
MTCW 1; PFS 12; RGEL 2; TCLE 1:2

Montaigne, Michel (Eyquem) de
1533-1592 **LC 8, 105; WLC 4**
See also DA; DAB; DAC; DAM MST; EW
2; GFL Beginnings to 1789; LMFS 1;
RGWL 2, 3; TWA

Montale, Eugenio 1896-1981 ... **CLC 7, 9, 18;
PC 13**
See also CA 17-20R; 104; CANR 30; DLB
114; EW 11; EWL 3; MTCW 1; PFS 22;
RGWL 2, 3; TWA; WLIT 7

Montesquieu, Charles-Louis de Secondat
1689-1755 **LC 7, 69**
See also DLB 314; EW 3; GFL Beginnings
to 1789; TWA

Montessori, Maria 1870-1952 **TCLC 103**
See also CA 115; 147

Montgomery, (Robert) Bruce 1921(?)-1978
See Crispin, Edmund
See also CA 179; 104; CMW 4

Montgomery, L(ucy) M(aud)
1874-1942 **TCLC 51, 140**
See also AAYA 12; BYA 1; CA 108; 137;
CLR 8, 91; DA3; DAC; DAM MST; DLB
92; DLBD 14; JRDA; MAICYA 1, 2;
MTCW 2; MTFW 2005; RGEL 2; SATA
100; TWA; WCH; WYA; YABC 1

Montgomery, Marion H., Jr. 1925- **CLC 7**
See also AITN 1; CA 1-4R; CANR 3, 48;
CSW; DLB 6

Montgomery, Max
See Davenport, Guy (Mattison, Jr.)

Montherlant, Henry (Milon) de
1896-1972 **CLC 8, 19**
See also CA 85-88; 37-40R; DAM DRAM;
DLB 72, 321; EW 11; EWL 3; GFL 1789
to the Present; MTCW 1

Monty Python
See Chapman, Graham; Cleese, John
(Marwood); Gilliam, Terry (Vance); Idle,
Eric; Jones, Terence Graham Parry; Palin,
Michael (Edward)
See also AAYA 7

Moodie, Susanna (Strickland)
1803-1885 **NCLC 14, 113**
See also DLB 99

Moody, Hiram (F. III) 1961-
See Moody, Rick
See also CA 138; CANR 64, 112; MTFW
2005

Moody, Minerva
See Alcott, Louisa May

Moody, Rick **CLC 147**
See Moody, Hiram (F. III)

Moody, William Vaughan
1869-1910 **TCLC 105**
See also CA 110; 178; DLB 7, 54; MAL 5;
RGAL 4

Mooney, Edward 1951-
See Mooney, Ted
See also CA 130

Mooney, Ted **CLC 25**
See Mooney, Edward

Moorcock, Michael 1939- **CLC 5, 27, 58**
See Bradbury, Edward P.
See also AAYA 26; CA 45-48; CAAS 5;
CANR 2, 17, 38, 64, 122; CN 5, 6, 7;
DLB 14, 231, 261, 319; FANT; MTCW 1,
2; MTFW 2005; SATA 93, 166; SCFW 1,
2; SFW 4; SUFW 1, 2
Moorcock, Michael John
See Moorcock, Michael
Moore, Brian 1921-1999 ... **CLC 1, 3, 5, 7, 8,
19, 32, 90**
See Bryan, Michael
See also BRWS 9; CA 1-4R; 174; CANR 1,
25, 42, 63; CCA 1; CN 1, 2, 3, 4, 5, 6;
DAB; DAC; DAM MST; DLB 251; EWL
3; FANT; MTCW 1, 2; MTFW 2005;
RGEL 2
Moore, Edward
See Muir, Edwin
See also RGEL 2
Moore, G. E. 1873-1958 **TCLC 89**
See also DLB 262
Moore, George Augustus
1852-1933 **SSC 19; TCLC 7**
See also BRW 6; CA 104; 177; DLB 10,
18, 57, 135; EWL 3; RGEL 2; RGSF 2
Moore, Lorrie **CLC 39, 45, 68**
See Moore, Marie Lorena
See also AMWS 10; CN 5, 6, 7; DLB 234;
SSFS 19
Moore, Marianne (Craig)
1887-1972 **CLC 1, 2, 4, 8, 10, 13, 19,
47; PC 4, 49; WLCS**
See also AMW; CA 1-4R; 33-36R; CANR
3, 61; CDALB 1929-1941; CP 1; DA;
DA3; DAB; DAC; DAM MST; POET;
DLB 45; DLBD 7; EWL 3; EXPP; FL 1:6;
MAL 5; MAWW; MTCW 1, 2; MTFW
2005; PAB; PFS 14, 17; RGAL 4; SATA
20; TUS; WP
Moore, Marie Lorena 1957- **CLC 165**
See Moore, Lorrie
See also CA 116; CANR 39, 83, 139; DLB
234; MTFW 2005
Moore, Michael 1954- **CLC 218**
See also AAYA 53; CA 166; CANR 150
Moore, Thomas 1779-1852 **NCLC 6, 110**
See also DLB 96, 144; RGEL 2
Moorhouse, Frank 1938- **SSC 40**
See also CA 118; CANR 92; CN 3, 4, 5, 6,
7; DLB 289; RGSF 2
Mora, Pat(ricia) 1942- **HLC 2**
See also AMWS 13; CA 129; CANR 57,
81, 112; CLR 58; DAM MULT; DLB 209;
HW 1, 2; LLW; MAICYA 2; MTFW
2005; SATA 92, 134
Moraga, Cherríe 1952- **CLC 126; DC 22**
See also CA 131; CANR 66, 154; DAM
MULT; DLB 82, 249; FW; GLL 1; HW 1,
2; LLW
Morand, Paul 1888-1976 **CLC 41; SSC 22**
See also CA 184; 69-72; DLB 65; EWL 3
Morante, Elsa 1918-1985 **CLC 8, 47**
See also CA 85-88; 117; CANR 35; DLB
177; EWL 3; MTCW 1, 2; MTFW 2005;
RGHL; RGWL 2, 3; WLIT 7
Moravia, Alberto **CLC 2, 7, 11, 27, 46;
SSC 26**
See Pincherle, Alberto
See also DLB 177; EW 12; EWL 3; MTCW
2; RGSF 2; RGWL 2, 3; WLIT 7
More, Hannah 1745-1833 **NCLC 27, 141**
See also DLB 107, 109, 116, 158; RGEL 2
More, Henry 1614-1687 **LC 9**
See also DLB 126, 252
More, Sir Thomas 1478(?)-1535 **LC 10, 32**
See also BRWC 1; BRWS 7; DLB 136, 281;
LMFS 1; RGEL 2; TEA

Moreas, Jean **TCLC 18**
See Papadiamantopoulos, Johannes
See also GFL 1789 to the Present
Moreton, Andrew Esq.
See Defoe, Daniel
Morgan, Berry 1919-2002 **CLC 6**
See also CA 49-52; 208; DLB 6
Morgan, Claire
See Highsmith, (Mary) Patricia
See also GLL 1
Morgan, Edwin (George) 1920- **CLC 31**
See also BRWS 9; CA 5-8R; CANR 3, 43,
90; CP 1, 2, 3, 4, 5, 6, 7; DLB 27
Morgan, (George) Frederick
1922-2004 **CLC 23**
See also CA 17-20R; 224; CANR 21, 144;
CP 2, 3, 4, 5, 6, 7
Morgan, Harriet
See Mencken, H(enry) L(ouis)
Morgan, Jane
See Cooper, James Fenimore
Morgan, Janet 1945- **CLC 39**
See also CA 65-68
Morgan, Lady 1776(?)-1859 **NCLC 29**
See also DLB 116, 158; RGEL 2
Morgan, Robin (Evonne) 1941- **CLC 2**
See also CA 69-72; CANR 29, 68; FW;
GLL 2; MTCW 1; SATA 80
Morgan, Scott
See Kuttner, Henry
Morgan, Seth 1949(?)-1990 **CLC 65**
See also CA 185; 132
**Morgenstern, Christian (Otto Josef
Wolfgang)** 1871-1914 **TCLC 8**
See also CA 105; 191; EWL 3
Morgenstern, S.
See Goldman, William
Mori, Rintaro
See Mori Ogai
See also CA 110
Mori, Toshio 1910-1980 **SSC 83**
See also CA 116; 244; DLB 312; RGSF 2
Moricz, Zsigmond 1879-1942 **TCLC 33**
See also CA 165; DLB 215; EWL 3
Morike, Eduard (Friedrich)
1804-1875 **NCLC 10**
See also DLB 133; RGWL 2, 3
Mori Ogai 1862-1922 **TCLC 14**
See Ogai
See also CA 164; DLB 180; EWL 3; RGWL
3; TWA
Moritz, Karl Philipp 1756-1793 **LC 2**
See also DLB 94
Morland, Peter Henry
See Faust, Frederick (Schiller)
Morley, Christopher (Darlington)
1890-1957 **TCLC 87**
See also CA 112; 213; DLB 9; MAL 5;
RGAL 4
Morren, Theophil
See Hofmannsthal, Hugo von
Morris, Bill 1952- **CLC 76**
See also CA 225
Morris, Julian
See West, Morris L(anglo)
Morris, Steveland Judkins (?)-
See Wonder, Stevie
Morris, William 1834-1896 . **NCLC 4; PC 55**
See also BRW 5; CDBLB 1832-1890; DLB
18, 35, 57, 156, 178, 184; FANT; RGEL
2; SFW 4; SUFW
Morris, Wright (Marion) 1910-1998 . **CLC 1,
3, 7, 18, 37; TCLC 107**
See also AMW; CA 9-12R; 167; CANR 21,
81; CN 1, 2, 3, 4, 5, 6; DLB 2, 206, 218;
DLBY 1981; EWL 3; MAL 5; MTCW 1,
2; MTFW 2005; RGAL 4; TCWW 1, 2

Morrison, Arthur 1863-1945 **SSC 40;
TCLC 72**
See also CA 120; 157; CMW 4; DLB 70,
135, 197; RGEL 2
Morrison, Chloe Anthony Wofford
See Morrison, Toni
Morrison, James Douglas 1943-1971
See Morrison, Jim
See also CA 73-76; CANR 40
Morrison, Jim **CLC 17**
See Morrison, James Douglas
Morrison, John Gordon 1904-1998 ... **SSC 93**
See also CA 103; CANR 92; DLB 260
Morrison, Toni 1931- **BLC 3; CLC 4, 10,
22, 55, 81, 87, 173, 194; WLC 4**
See also AAYA 1, 22, 61; AFAW 1, 2;
AMWC 1; AMWS 3; BPFB 2; BW 2, 3;
CA 29-32R; CANR 27, 42, 67, 113, 124;
CDALB 1968-1988; CLR 99; CN 3, 4, 5,
6, 7; CPW; DA; DA3; DAB; DAC; DAM
MST, MULT, NOV, POP; DLB 6, 33, 143;
DLBY 1981; EWL 3; EXPN; FL 1:6; FW;
GL 3; LAIT 2, 4; LATS 1:2; LMFS 2;
MAL 5; MAWW; MTCW 1, 2; MTFW
2005; NFS 1, 6, 8, 14; RGAL 4; RHW;
SATA 57, 144; SSFS 5; TCLE 1:2; TUS;
YAW
Morrison, Van 1945- **CLC 21**
See also CA 116; 168
Morrissy, Mary 1957- **CLC 99**
See also CA 205; DLB 267
Mortimer, John (Clifford) 1923- **CLC 28,
43**
See also CA 13-16R; CANR 21, 69, 109;
CBD; CD 5, 6; CDBLB 1960 to Present;
CMW 4; CN 5, 6, 7; CPW; DA3; DAM
DRAM, POP; DLB 13, 245, 271; INT
CANR-21; MSW; MTCW 1, 2; MTFW
2005; RGEL 2
Mortimer, Penelope (Ruth)
1918-1999 **CLC 5**
See also CA 57-60; 187; CANR 45, 88; CN
1, 2, 3, 4, 5, 6
Mortimer, Sir John
See Mortimer, John (Clifford)
Morton, Anthony
See Creasey, John
Morton, Thomas 1579(?)-1647(?) **LC 72**
See also DLB 24; RGEL 2
Mosca, Gaetano 1858-1941 **TCLC 75**
Moses, Daniel David 1952- **NNAL**
See also CA 186
Mosher, Howard Frank 1943- **CLC 62**
See also CA 139; CANR 65, 115
Mosley, Nicholas 1923- **CLC 43, 70**
See also CA 69-72; CANR 41, 60, 108; CN
1, 2, 3, 4, 5, 6, 7; DLB 14, 207
Mosley, Walter 1952- **BLCS; CLC 97, 184**
See also AAYA 57; AMWS 13; BPFB 2;
BW 2; CA 142; CANR 57, 92, 136; CMW
4; CN 7; CPW; DA3; DAM MULT, POP;
DLB 306; MSW; MTCW 2; MTFW 2005
Moss, Howard 1922-1987 . **CLC 7, 14, 45, 50**
See also CA 1-4R; 123; CANR 1, 44; CP 1,
2, 3, 4; DAM POET; DLB 5
Mossgiel, Rab
See Burns, Robert
Motion, Andrew (Peter) 1952- **CLC 47**
See also BRWS 7; CA 146; CANR 90, 142;
CP 4, 5, 6, 7; DLB 40; MTFW 2005
Motley, Willard (Francis)
1909-1965 **CLC 18**
See also BW 1; CA 117; 106; CANR 88;
DLB 76, 143
Motoori, Norinaga 1730-1801 **NCLC 45**
Mott, Michael (Charles Alston)
1930- **CLC 15, 34**
See also CA 5-8R; CAAS 7; CANR 7, 29

Mountain Wolf Woman 1884-1960 . **CLC 92; NNAL**
See also CA 144; CANR 90

Moure, Erin 1955- **CLC 88**
See also CA 113; CP 5, 6, 7; CWP; DLB 60

Mourning Dove 1885(?)-1936 **NNAL**
See also CA 144; CANR 90; DAM MULT; DLB 175, 221

Mowat, Farley (McGill) 1921- **CLC 26**
See also AAYA 1, 50; BYA 2; CA 1-4R; CANR 4, 24, 42, 68, 108; CLR 20; CPW; DAC; DAM MST; DLB 68; INT CANR-24; JRDA; MAICYA 1, 2; MTCW 1, 2; MTFW 2005; SATA 3, 55; YAW

Mowatt, Anna Cora 1819-1870 **NCLC 74**
See also RGAL 4

Moyers, Bill 1934- **CLC 74**
See also AITN 2; CA 61-64; CANR 31, 52, 148

Mphahlele, Es'kia
See Mphahlele, Ezekiel
See also AFW; CDWLB 3; CN 4, 5, 6; DLB 125, 225; RGSF 2; SSFS 11

Mphahlele, Ezekiel 1919- ... **BLC 3; CLC 25, 133**
See Mphahlele, Es'kia
See also BW 2, 3; CA 81-84; CANR 26, 76; CN 1, 2, 3; DA3; DAM MULT; EWL 3; MTCW 2; MTFW 2005; SATA 119

Mqhayi, S(amuel) E(dward) K(rune Loliwe) 1875-1945 **BLC 3; TCLC 25**
See also CA 153; CANR 87; DAM MULT

Mrozek, Slawomir 1930- **CLC 3, 13**
See also CA 13-16R; CAAS 10; CANR 29; CDWLB 4; CWW 2; DLB 232; EWL 3; MTCW 1

Mrs. Belloc-Lowndes
See Lowndes, Marie Adelaide (Belloc)

Mrs. Fairstar
See Horne, Richard Henry Hengist

M'Taggart, John M'Taggart Ellis
See McTaggart, John McTaggart Ellis

Mtwa, Percy (?)- **CLC 47**
See also CD 6

Mueller, Lisel 1924- **CLC 13, 51; PC 33**
See also CA 93-96; CP 6, 7; DLB 105; PFS 9, 13

Muggeridge, Malcolm (Thomas) 1903-1990 **TCLC 120**
See also AITN 1; CA 101; CANR 33, 63; MTCW 1, 2

Muhammad 570-632 **WLCS**
See also DA; DAB; DAC; DAM MST; DLB 311

Muir, Edwin 1887-1959 . **PC 49; TCLC 2, 87**
See Moore, Edward
See also BRWS 6; CA 104; 193; DLB 20, 100, 191; EWL 3; RGEL 2

Muir, John 1838-1914 **TCLC 28**
See also AMWS 9; ANW; CA 165; DLB 186, 275

Mujica Lainez, Manuel 1910-1984 ... **CLC 31**
See Lainez, Manuel Mujica
See also CA 81-84; 112; CANR 32; EWL 3; HW 1

Mukherjee, Bharati 1940- **AAL; CLC 53, 115; SSC 38**
See also AAYA 46; BEST 89:2; CA 107, 232; CAAE 232; CANR 45, 72, 128; CN 5, 6, 7; DAM NOV; DLB 60, 218, 323; DNFS 1, 2; EWL 3; FW; MAL 5; MTCW 1, 2; MTFW 2005; RGAL 4; RGSF 2; SSFS 7; TUS; WWE 1

Muldoon, Paul 1951- **CLC 32, 72, 166**
See also BRWS 4; CA 113; 129; CANR 52, 91; CP 2, 3, 4, 5, 6, 7; DAM POET; DLB 40; INT CA-129; PFS 7, 22; TCLE 1:2

Mulisch, Harry (Kurt Victor) 1927- **CLC 42**
See also CA 9-12R; CANR 6, 26, 56, 110; CWW 2; DLB 299; EWL 3

Mull, Martin 1943- **CLC 17**
See also CA 105

Muller, Wilhelm **NCLC 73**

Mulock, Dinah Maria
See Craik, Dinah Maria (Mulock)
See also RGEL 2

Multatuli 1820-1881 **NCLC 165**
See also RGWL 2, 3

Munday, Anthony 1560-1633 **LC 87**
See also DLB 62, 172; RGEL 2

Munford, Robert 1737(?)-1783 **LC 5**
See also DLB 31

Mungo, Raymond 1946- **CLC 72**
See also CA 49-52; CANR 2

Munro, Alice (Anne) 1931- **CLC 6, 10, 19, 50, 95, 222; SSC 3; WLCS**
See also AITN 2; BPFB 2; CA 33-36R; CANR 33, 53, 75, 114; CCA 1; CN 1, 2, 3, 4, 5, 6, 7; DA3; DAC; DAM MST, NOV; DLB 53; EWL 3; MTCW 1, 2; MTFW 2005; RGEL 2; RGSF 2; SATA 29; SSFS 5, 13, 19; TCLE 1:2; WWE 1

Munro, H(ector) H(ugh) 1870-1916
See Saki
See also AAYA 56; CA 104; 130; CANR 104; CDBLB 1890-1914; DA; DA3; DAB; DAC; DAM MST, NOV; DLB 34, 162; EXPS; MTCW 1, 2; MTFW 2005; RGEL 2; RGSF 2; SSFS 15

Murakami, Haruki 1949- **CLC 150**
See Murakami Haruki
See also CA 165; CANR 102, 146; MJW; RGWL 3; SFW 4; SSFS 23

Murakami Haruki
See Murakami, Haruki
See also CWW 2; DLB 182; EWL 3

Murasaki, Lady
See Murasaki Shikibu

Murasaki Shikibu 978(?)-1026(?) .. **CMLC 1, 79**
See also EFS 2; LATS 1:1; RGWL 2, 3

Murdoch, (Jean) Iris 1919-1999 ... **CLC 1, 2, 3, 4, 6, 8, 11, 15, 22, 31, 51; TCLC 171**
See also BRWS 1; CA 13-16R; 179; CANR 8, 43, 68, 103, 142; CBD; CDBLB 1960 to Present; CN 1, 2, 3, 4, 5, 6; CWD; DA3; DAB; DAC; DAM MST, NOV; DLB 14, 194, 233, 326; EWL 3; INT CANR-8; MTCW 1, 2; MTFW 2005; NFS 18; RGEL 2; TCLE 1:2; TEA; WLIT 4

Murfree, Mary Noailles 1850-1922 .. **SSC 22; TCLC 135**
See also CA 122; 176; DLB 12, 74; RGAL 4

Murnau, Friedrich Wilhelm
See Plumpe, Friedrich Wilhelm

Murphy, Richard 1927- **CLC 41**
See also BRWS 5; CA 29-32R; CP 1, 2, 3, 4, 5, 6, 7; DLB 40; EWL 3

Murphy, Sylvia 1937- **CLC 34**
See also CA 121

Murphy, Thomas (Bernard) 1935- ... **CLC 51**
See Murphy, Tom
See also CA 101

Murphy, Tom
See Murphy, Thomas (Bernard)
See also DLB 310

Murray, Albert L. 1916- **CLC 73**
See also BW 2; CA 49-52; CANR 26, 52, 78; CN 7; CSW; DLB 38; MTFW 2005

Murray, James Augustus Henry 1837-1915 **TCLC 117**

Murray, Judith Sargent 1751-1820 **NCLC 63**
See also DLB 37, 200

Murray, Les(lie Allan) 1938- **CLC 40**
See also BRWS 7; CA 21-24R; CANR 11, 27, 56, 103; CP 1, 2, 3, 4, 5, 6, 7; DAM POET; DLB 289; DLBY 2001; EWL 3; RGEL 2

Murry, J. Middleton
See Murry, John Middleton

Murry, John Middleton 1889-1957 **TCLC 16**
See also CA 118; 217; DLB 149

Musgrave, Susan 1951- **CLC 13, 54**
See also CA 69-72; CANR 45, 84; CCA 1; CP 2, 3, 4, 5, 6, 7; CWP

Musil, Robert (Edler von) 1880-1942 **SSC 18; TCLC 12, 68**
See also CA 109; CANR 55, 84; CDWLB 2; DLB 81, 124; EW 9; EWL 3; MTCW 2; RGSF 2; RGWL 2, 3

Muske, Carol **CLC 90**
See Muske-Dukes, Carol (Anne)

Muske-Dukes, Carol (Anne) 1945-
See Muske, Carol
See also CA 65-68, 203; CAAE 203; CANR 32, 70; CWP; PFS 24

Musset, Alfred de 1810-1857 . **DC 27; NCLC 7, 150**
See also DLB 192, 217; EW 6; GFL 1789 to the Present; RGWL 2, 3; TWA

Musset, Louis Charles Alfred de
See Musset, Alfred de

Mussolini, Benito (Amilcare Andrea) 1883-1945 **TCLC 96**
See also CA 116

Mutanabbi, Al-
See al-Mutanabbi, Ahmad ibn al-Husayn Abu al-Tayyib al-Jufi al-Kindi
See also WLIT 6

My Brother's Brother
See Chekhov, Anton (Pavlovich)

Myers, L(eopold) H(amilton) 1881-1944 **TCLC 59**
See also CA 157; DLB 15; EWL 3; RGEL 2

Myers, Walter Dean 1937- .. **BLC 3; CLC 35**
See also AAYA 4, 23; BW 2; BYA 6, 8, 11; CA 33-36R; CANR 20, 42, 67, 108; CLR 4, 16, 35, 110; DAM MULT, NOV; DLB 33; INT CANR-20; JRDA; LAIT 5; MAICYA 1, 2; MAICYAS 1; MTCW 2; MTFW 2005; SAAS 2; SATA 41, 71, 109, 157; SATA-Brief 27; WYA; YAW

Myers, Walter M.
See Myers, Walter Dean

Myles, Symon
See Follett, Ken(neth Martin)

Nabokov, Vladimir (Vladimirovich) 1899-1977 **CLC 1, 2, 3, 6, 8, 11, 15, 23, 44, 46, 64; SSC 11, 86; TCLC 108; WLC 4**
See also AAYA 45; AMW; AMWC 1; AMWR 1; BPFB 2; CA 5-8R; 69-72; CANR 20, 102; CDALB 1941-1968; CN 1, 2; CP 2; DA; DA3; DAB; DAC; DAM MST, NOV; DLB 2, 244, 278, 317; DLBD 3; DLBY 1980, 1991; EWL 3; EXPS; LATS 1:2; MAL 5; MTCW 1, 2; MTFW 2005; NCFS 4; NFS 9; RGAL 4; RGSF 2; SSFS 6, 15; TUS

Naevius c. 265B.C.-201B.C. **CMLC 37**
See also DLB 211

Nagai, Kafu **TCLC 51**
See Nagai, Sokichi
See also DLB 180

Nagai, Sokichi 1879-1959
See Nagai, Kafu
See also CA 117

Nagy, Laszlo 1925-1978 **CLC 7**
See also CA 129; 112

Naidu, Sarojini 1879-1949 **TCLC 80**
 See also EWL 3; RGEL 2
Naipaul, Shiva(dhar Srinivasa)
 1945-1985 **CLC 32, 39; TCLC 153**
 See also CA 110; 112; 116; CANR 33; CN
 2, 3; DA3; DAM NOV; DLB 157; DLBY
 1985; EWL 3; MTCW 1, 2; MTFW 2005
Naipaul, V(idiadhar) S(urajprasad)
 1932- **CLC 4, 7, 9, 13, 18, 37, 105,**
 199; SSC 38
 See also BPFB 2; BRWS 1; CA 1-4R;
 CANR 1, 33, 51, 91, 126; CDBLB 1960
 to Present; CDWLB 3; CN 1, 2, 3, 4, 5,
 6, 7; DA3; DAB; DAC; DAM MST,
 NOV; DLB 125, 204, 207, 326; DLBY
 1985, 2001; EWL 3; LATS 1:2; MTCW
 1, 2; MTFW 2005; RGEL 2; RGSF 2;
 TWA; WLIT 4; WWE 1
Nakos, Lilika 1903(?)-1989 **CLC 29**
Napoleon
 See Yamamoto, Hisaye
Narayan, R(asipuram) K(rishnaswami)
 1906-2001 **CLC 7, 28, 47, 121, 211;**
 SSC 25
 See also BPFB 2; CA 81-84; 196; CANR
 33, 61, 112; CN 1, 2, 3, 4, 5, 6, 7; DA3;
 DAM NOV; DLB 323; DNFS 1; EWL 3;
 MTCW 1, 2; MTFW 2005; RGEL 2;
 RGSF 2; SATA 62; SSFS 5; WWE 1
Nash, (Frediric) Ogden 1902-1971 . **CLC 23;**
 PC 21; TCLC 109
 See also CA 13-14; 29-32R; CANR 34, 61;
 CAP 1; CP 1; DAM POET; DLB 11;
 MAICYA 1, 2; MAL 5; MTCW 1, 2;
 RGAL 4; SATA 2, 46; WP
Nashe, Thomas 1567-1601(?) **LC 41, 89**
 See also DLB 167; RGEL 2
Nathan, Daniel
 See Dannay, Frederic
Nathan, George Jean 1882-1958 **TCLC 18**
 See Hatteras, Owen
 See also CA 114; 169; DLB 137; MAL 5
Natsume, Kinnosuke
 See Natsume, Soseki
Natsume, Soseki 1867-1916 **TCLC 2, 10**
 See Natsume Soseki; Soseki
 See also CA 104; 195; RGWL 2, 3; TWA
Natsume Soseki
 See Natsume, Soseki
 See also DLB 180; EWL 3
Natti, (Mary) Lee 1919-
 See Kingman, Lee
 See also CA 5-8R; CANR 2
Navarre, Marguerite de
 See de Navarre, Marguerite
Naylor, Gloria 1950- **BLC 3; CLC 28, 52,**
 156; WLCS
 See also AAYA 6, 39; AFAW 1, 2; AMWS
 8; BW 2, 3; CA 107; CANR 27, 51, 74,
 130; CN 4, 5, 6, 7; CPW; DA; DA3;
 DAC; DAM MST, MULT, NOV, POP;
 DLB 173; EWL 3; FW; MAL 5; MTCW
 1, 2; MTFW 2005; NFS 4, 7; RGAL 4;
 TCLE 1:2; TUS
Neal, John 1793-1876 **NCLC 161**
 See also DLB 1, 59, 243; FW; RGAL 4
Neff, Debra ... **CLC 59**
Neihardt, John Gneisenau
 1881-1973 **CLC 32**
 See also CA 13-14; CANR 65; CAP 1; DLB
 9, 54, 256; LAIT 2; TCWW 1, 2
Nekrasov, Nikolai Alekseevich
 1821-1878 **NCLC 11**
 See also DLB 277
Nelligan, Emile 1879-1941 **TCLC 14**
 See also CA 114; 204; DLB 92; EWL 3
Nelson, Willie 1933- **CLC 17**
 See also CA 107; CANR 114

Nemerov, Howard (Stanley)
 1920-1991 **CLC 2, 6, 9, 36; PC 24;**
 TCLC 124
 See also AMW; CA 1-4R; 134; CABS 2;
 CANR 1, 27, 53; CN 1, 2, 3; CP 1, 2, 3,
 4, 5; DAM POET; DLB 5, 6; DLBY 1983;
 EWL 3; INT CANR-27; MAL 5; MTCW
 1, 2; MTFW 2005; PFS 10, 14; RGAL 4
Neruda, Pablo 1904-1973 .. **CLC 1, 2, 5, 7, 9,**
 28, 62; HLC 2; PC 4, 64; WLC 4
 See also CA 19-20; 45-48; CANR 131; CAP
 2; DA; DA3; DAB; DAC; DAM MST,
 MULT, POET; DLB 283; DNFS 2; EWL
 3; HW 1; LAW; MTCW 1, 2; MTFW
 2005; PFS 11; RGWL 2, 3; TWA; WLIT
 1; WP
Nerval, Gerard de 1808-1855 ... **NCLC 1, 67;**
 PC 13; SSC 18
 See also DLB 217; EW 6; GFL 1789 to the
 Present; RGSF 2; RGWL 2, 3
Nervo, (Jose) Amado (Ruiz de)
 1870-1919 **HLCS 2; TCLC 11**
 See also CA 109; 131; DLB 290; EWL 3;
 HW 1; LAW
Nesbit, Malcolm
 See Chester, Alfred
Nessi, Pio Baroja y
 See Baroja, Pio
Nestroy, Johann 1801-1862 **NCLC 42**
 See also DLB 133; RGWL 2, 3
Netterville, Luke
 See O'Grady, Standish (James)
Neufeld, John (Arthur) 1938- **CLC 17**
 See also AAYA 11; CA 25-28R; CANR 11,
 37, 56; CLR 52; MAICYA 1, 2; SAAS 3;
 SATA 6, 81, 131; SATA-Essay 131; YAW
Neumann, Alfred 1895-1952 **TCLC 100**
 See also CA 183; DLB 56
Neumann, Ferenc
 See Molnar, Ferenc
Neville, Emily Cheney 1919- **CLC 12**
 See also BYA 2; CA 5-8R; CANR 3, 37,
 85; JRDA; MAICYA 1, 2; SAAS 2; SATA
 1; YAW
Newbound, Bernard Slade 1930-
 See Slade, Bernard
 See also CA 81-84; CANR 49; CD 5; DAM
 DRAM
Newby, P(ercy) H(oward)
 1918-1997 **CLC 2, 13**
 See also CA 5-8R; 161; CANR 32, 67; CN
 1, 2, 3, 4, 5, 6; DAM NOV; DLB 15, 326;
 MTCW 1; RGEL 2
Newcastle
 See Cavendish, Margaret Lucas
Newlove, Donald 1928- **CLC 6**
 See also CA 29-32R; CANR 25
Newlove, John (Herbert) 1938- **CLC 14**
 See also CA 21-24R; CANR 9, 25; CP 1, 2,
 3, 4, 5, 6, 7
Newman, Charles 1938-2006 **CLC 2, 8**
 See also CA 21-24R; CANR 84; CN 3, 4,
 5, 6
Newman, Charles Hamilton
 See Newman, Charles
Newman, Edwin (Harold) 1919- **CLC 14**
 See also AITN 1; CA 69-72; CANR 5
Newman, John Henry 1801-1890 . **NCLC 38,**
 99
 See also BRWS 7; DLB 18, 32, 55; RGEL
 2
Newton, (Sir) Isaac 1642-1727 **LC 35, 53**
 See also DLB 252
Newton, Suzanne 1936- **CLC 35**
 See also BYA 7; CA 41-44R; CANR 14;
 JRDA; SATA 5, 77
New York Dept. of Ed. **CLC 70**

Nexo, Martin Andersen
 1869-1954 **TCLC 43**
 See also CA 202; DLB 214; EWL 3
Nezval, Vitezslav 1900-1958 **TCLC 44**
 See also CA 123; CDWLB 4; DLB 215;
 EWL 3
Ng, Fae Myenne 1957(?)- **CLC 81**
 See also BYA 11; CA 146
Ngema, Mbongeni 1955- **CLC 57**
 See also BW 2; CA 143; CANR 84; CD 5,
 6
Nguyen, James T(hiong'o) . **CLC 3, 7, 13, 182**
 See Ngugi wa Thiong'o
 See also CN 1, 2
Ngugi wa Thiong'o
 See Ngugi wa Thiong'o
 See also CD 3, 4, 5, 6, 7; DLB 125; EWL 3
Ngugi wa Thiong'o 1938- ... **BLC 3; CLC 36,**
 182
 See Ngugi, James T(hiong'o); Ngugi wa
 Thiong'o
 See also AFW; BRWS 8; BW 2; CA 81-84;
 CANR 27, 58; CDWLB 3; DAM MULT,
 NOV; DNFS 2; MTCW 1, 2; MTFW
 2005; RGEL 2; WWE 1
Niatum, Duane 1938- **NNAL**
 See also CA 41-44R; CANR 21, 45, 83;
 DLB 175
Nichol, B(arrie) P(hillip) 1944-1988 . **CLC 18**
 See also CA 53-56; CP 1, 2, 3, 4; DLB 53;
 SATA 66
Nicholas of Cusa 1401-1464 **LC 80**
 See also DLB 115
Nichols, John (Treadwell) 1940- **CLC 38**
 See also AMWS 13; CA 9-12R, 190; CAAE
 190; CAAS 2; CANR 6, 70, 121; DLBY
 1982; LATS 1:2; MTFW 2005; TCWW 1,
 2
Nichols, Leigh
 See Koontz, Dean R.
Nichols, Peter (Richard) 1927- **CLC 5, 36,**
 65
 See also CA 104; CANR 33, 86; CBD; CD
 5, 6; DLB 13, 245; MTCW 1
Nicholson, Linda ed. **CLC 65**
Ni Chuilleanain, Eilean 1942- **PC 34**
 See also CA 126; CANR 53, 83; CP 5, 6, 7;
 CWP; DLB 40
Nicolas, F. R. E.
 See Freeling, Nicolas
Niedecker, Lorine 1903-1970 **CLC 10, 42;**
 PC 42
 See also CA 25-28; CAP 2; DAM POET;
 DLB 48
Nietzsche, Friedrich (Wilhelm)
 1844-1900 **TCLC 10, 18, 55**
 See also CA 107; 121; CDWLB 2; DLB
 129; EW 7; RGWL 2, 3; TWA
Nievo, Ippolito 1831-1861 **NCLC 22**
Nightingale, Anne Redmon 1943-
 See Redmon, Anne
 See also CA 103
Nightingale, Florence 1820-1910 ... **TCLC 85**
 See also CA 188; DLB 166
Nijo Yoshimoto 1320-1388 **CMLC 49**
 See also DLB 203
Nik. T. O.
 See Annensky, Innokenty (Fyodorovich)
Nin, Anais 1903-1977 **CLC 1, 4, 8, 11, 14,**
 60, 127; SSC 10
 See also AITN 2; AMWS 10; BPFB 2; CA
 13-16R; 69-72; CANR 22, 53; CN 1, 2;
 DAM NOV, POP; DLB 2, 4, 152; EWL
 3; GLL 2; MAL 5; MAWW; MTCW 1, 2;
 MTFW 2005; RGAL 4; RGSF 2
Nisbet, Robert A(lexander)
 1913-1996 **TCLC 117**
 See also CA 25-28R; 153; CANR 17; INT
 CANR-17

Nishida, Kitaro 1870-1945 **TCLC 83**

Nishiwaki, Junzaburo 1894-1982 **PC 15**
See Junzaburo, Nishiwaki
See also CA 194; 107; MJW; RGWL 3

Nissenson, Hugh 1933- **CLC 4, 9**
See also CA 17-20R; CANR 27, 108, 151; CN 5, 6; DLB 28

Nister, Der
See Der Nister
See also EWL 3

Niven, Larry 1938-
See Niven, Lawrence VanCott
See also CA 21-24R, 207; CAAE 207; CAAS 12; CANR 14, 44, 66, 113; CPW; DAM POP; MTCW 1, 2; SATA 95, 171; SFW 4

Niven, Lawrence VanCott **CLC 8**
See Niven, Larry
See also AAYA 27; BPFB 2; BYA 10; DLB 8; SCFW 1, 2

Nixon, Agnes Eckhardt 1927- **CLC 21**
See also CA 110

Nizan, Paul 1905-1940 **TCLC 40**
See also CA 161; DLB 72; EWL 3; GFL 1789 to the Present

Nkosi, Lewis 1936- **BLC 3; CLC 45**
See also BW 1, 3; CA 65-68; CANR 27, 81; CBD; CD 5, 6; DAM MULT; DLB 157, 225; WWE 1

Nodier, (Jean) Charles (Emmanuel)
1780-1844 **NCLC 19**
See also DLB 119; GFL 1789 to the Present

Noguchi, Yone 1875-1947 **TCLC 80**

Nolan, Christopher 1965- **CLC 58**
See also CA 111; CANR 88

Noon, Jeff 1957- **CLC 91**
See also CA 148; CANR 83; DLB 267; SFW 4

Norden, Charles
See Durrell, Lawrence (George)

Nordhoff, Charles Bernard
1887-1947 **TCLC 23**
See also CA 108; 211; DLB 9; LAIT 1; RHW 1; SATA 23

Norfolk, Lawrence 1963- **CLC 76**
See also CA 144; CANR 85; CN 6, 7; DLB 267

Norman, Marsha (Williams) 1947- . **CLC 28, 186; DC 8**
See also CA 105; CABS 3; CAD; CANR 41, 131; CD 5, 6; CSW; CWD; DAM DRAM; DFS 2; DLB 266; DLBY 1984; FW; MAL 5

Normyx
See Douglas, (George) Norman

Norris, (Benjamin) Frank(lin, Jr.)
1870-1902 **SSC 28; TCLC 24, 155**
See also AAYA 57; AMW; AMWC 2; BPFB 2; CA 110; 160; CDALB 1865-1917; DLB 12, 71, 186; LMFS 2; MAL 5; NFS 12; RGAL 4; TCWW 1, 2; TUS

Norris, Leslie 1921-2006 **CLC 14**
See also CA 11-12; CANR 14, 117; CAP 1; CP 1, 2, 3, 4, 5, 6, 7; DLB 27, 256

North, Andrew
See Norton, Andre

North, Anthony
See Koontz, Dean R.

North, Captain George
See Stevenson, Robert Louis (Balfour)

North, Captain George
See Stevenson, Robert Louis (Balfour)

North, Milou
See Erdrich, Louise

Northrup, B. A.
See Hubbard, L. Ron

North Staffs
See Hulme, T(homas) E(rnest)

Northup, Solomon 1808-1863 **NCLC 105**

Norton, Alice Mary
See Norton, Andre
See also MAICYA 1; SATA 1, 43

Norton, Andre 1912-2005 **CLC 12**
See Norton, Alice Mary
See also AAYA 14; BPFB 2; BYA 4, 10, 12; CA 1-4R; 237; CANR 2, 31, 68, 108, 149; CLR 50; DLB 8, 52; JRDA; MAICYA 2; MTCW 1; SATA 91; SUFW 1, 2; YAW

Norton, Caroline 1808-1877 **NCLC 47**
See also DLB 21, 159, 199

Norway, Nevil Shute 1899-1960
See Shute, Nevil
See also CA 102; 93-96; CANR 85; MTCW 2

Norwid, Cyprian Kamil
1821-1883 **NCLC 17**
See also RGWL 3

Nosille, Nabrah
See Ellison, Harlan (Jay)

Nossack, Hans Erich 1901-1978 **CLC 6**
See also CA 93-96; 85-88; DLB 69; EWL 3

Nostradamus 1503-1566 **LC 27**

Nosu, Chuji
See Ozu, Yasujiro

Notenburg, Eleanora (Genrikhovna) von
See Guro, Elena (Genrikhovna)

Nova, Craig 1945- **CLC 7, 31**
See also CA 45-48; CANR 2, 53, 127

Novak, Joseph
See Kosinski, Jerzy (Nikodem)

Novalis 1772-1801 **NCLC 13**
See also CDWLB 2; DLB 90; EW 5; RGWL 2, 3

Novick, Peter 1934- **CLC 164**
See also CA 188

Novis, Emile
See Weil, Simone (Adolphine)

Nowlan, Alden (Albert) 1933-1983 ... **CLC 15**
See also CA 9-12R; CANR 5; CP 1, 2, 3; DAC; DAM MST; DLB 53; PFS 12

Noyes, Alfred 1880-1958 **PC 27; TCLC 7**
See also CA 104; 188; DLB 20; EXPP; FANT; PFS 4; RGEL 2

Nugent, Richard Bruce
1906(?)-1987 **HR 1:3**
See also BW 1; CA 125; DLB 51; GLL 2

Nunn, Kem **CLC 34**
See also CA 159

Nussbaum, Martha Craven 1947- .. **CLC 203**
See also CA 134; CANR 102

Nwapa, Flora (Nwanzuruaha)
1931-1993 **BLCS; CLC 133**
See also BW 2; CA 143; CANR 83; CDWLB 3; CWRI 5; DLB 125; EWL 3; WLIT 2

Nye, Robert 1939- **CLC 13, 42**
See also BRWS 10; CA 33-36R; CANR 29, 67, 107; CN 1, 2, 3, 4, 5, 6, 7; CP 1, 2, 3, 4, 5, 6, 7; CWRI 5; DAM NOV; DLB 14, 271; FANT; HGG; MTCW 1; RHW; SATA 6

Nyro, Laura 1947-1997 **CLC 17**
See also CA 194

Oates, Joyce Carol 1938- .. **CLC 1, 2, 3, 6, 9, 11, 15, 19, 33, 52, 108, 134; SSC 6, 70; WLC 4**
See also AAYA 15, 52; AITN 1; AMWS 2; BEST 89:2; BPFB 2; BYA 11; CA 5-8R; CANR 25, 45, 74, 113, 129; CDALB 1968-1988; CN 1, 2, 3, 4, 5, 6, 7; CP 5, 6, 7; CPW; CWP; DA; DA3; DAB; DAC; DAM MST, NOV, POP; DLB 2, 5, 130; DLBY 1981; EWL 3; EXPS; FL 1:6; FW; GL 3; HGG; INT CANR-25; LAIT 4; MAL 5; MAWW; MTCW 1, 2; MTFW 2005; NFS 8; RGAL 4; RGSF 2; SATA 159; SSFS 1, 8, 17; SUFW 2; TUS

O'Brian, E. G.
See Clarke, Arthur C(harles)

O'Brian, Patrick 1914-2000 **CLC 152**
See also AAYA 55; CA 144; 187; CANR 74; CPW; MTCW 2; MTFW 2005; RHW

O'Brien, Darcy 1939-1998 **CLC 11**
See also CA 21-24R; 167; CANR 8, 59

O'Brien, Edna 1932- **CLC 3, 5, 8, 13, 36, 65, 116; SSC 10, 77**
See also BRWS 5; CA 1-4R; CANR 6, 41, 65, 102; CDBLB 1960 to Present; CN 1, 2, 3, 4, 5, 6, 7; DA3; DAM NOV; DLB 14, 231, 319; EWL 3; FW; MTCW 1, 2; MTFW 2005; RGSF 2; WLIT 4

O'Brien, Fitz-James 1828-1862 **NCLC 21**
See also DLB 74; RGAL 4; SUFW

O'Brien, Flann **CLC 1, 4, 5, 7, 10, 47**
See O Nuallain, Brian
See also BRWS 2; DLB 231; EWL 3; RGEL 2

O'Brien, Richard 1942- **CLC 17**
See also CA 124

O'Brien, (William) Tim(othy) 1946- . **CLC 7, 19, 40, 103, 211; SSC 74**
See also AAYA 16; AMWS 5; CA 85-88; CANR 40, 58, 133; CDALBS; CN 5, 6, 7; CPW; DA3; DAM POP; DLB 152; DLBD 9; DLBY 1980; LATS 1:2; MAL 5; MTCW 2; MTFW 2005; RGAL 4; SSFS 5, 15; TCLE 1:2

Obstfelder, Sigbjoern 1866-1900 **TCLC 23**
See also CA 123

O'Casey, Sean 1880-1964 **CLC 1, 5, 9, 11, 15, 88; DC 12; WLCS**
See also BRW 7; CA 89-92; CANR 62; CBD; CDBLB 1914-1945; DA3; DAB; DAC; DAM DRAM, MST; DFS 19; DLB 10; EWL 3; MTCW 1, 2; MTFW 2005; RGEL 2; TEA; WLIT 4

O'Cathasaigh, Sean
See O'Casey, Sean

Occom, Samson 1723-1792 **LC 60; NNAL**
See also DLB 175

Occomy, Marita (Odette) Bonner
1899(?)-1971
See Bonner, Marita
See also BW 2; CA 142; DFS 13; DLB 51, 228

Ochs, Phil(ip David) 1940-1976 **CLC 17**
See also CA 185; 65-68

O'Connor, Edwin (Greene)
1918-1968 **CLC 14**
See also CA 93-96; 25-28R; MAL 5

O'Connor, (Mary) Flannery
1925-1964 **CLC 1, 2, 3, 6, 10, 13, 15, 21, 66, 104; SSC 1, 23, 61, 82; TCLC 132; WLC 4**
See also AAYA 7; AMW; AMWR 2; BPFB 3; BYA 16; CA 1-4R; CANR 3, 41; CDALB 1941-1968; DA; DA3; DAB; DAC; DAM MST, NOV; DLB 2, 152; DLBD 12; DLBY 1980; EWL 3; EXPS; LAIT 5; MAL 5; MAWW; MTCW 1, 2; MTFW 2005; NFS 3, 21; RGAL 4; RGSF 2; SSFS 2, 7, 10, 19; TUS

O'Connor, Frank **CLC 23; SSC 5**
See O'Donovan, Michael Francis
See also DLB 162; EWL 3; RGSF 2; SSFS 5

O'Dell, Scott 1898-1989 **CLC 30**
See also AAYA 3, 44; BPFB 3; BYA 1, 2, 3, 5; CA 61-64; 129; CANR 12, 30, 112; CLR 1, 16; DLB 52; JRDA; MAICYA 1, 2; SATA 12, 60, 134; WYA; YAW

Odets, Clifford 1906-1963 **CLC 2, 28, 98; DC 6**
See also AMWS 2; CA 85-88; CAD; CANR 62; DAM DRAM; DFS 3, 17, 20; DLB 7, 26; EWL 3; MAL 5; MTCW 1, 2; MTFW 2005; RGAL 4; TUS

O'Doherty, Brian 1928- **CLC 76**
See also CA 105; CANR 108
O'Donnell, K. M.
See Malzberg, Barry N(athaniel)
O'Donnell, Lawrence
See Kuttner, Henry
O'Donovan, Michael Francis
1903-1966 **CLC 14**
See O'Connor, Frank
See also CA 93-96; CANR 84
Oe, Kenzaburo 1935- .. **CLC 10, 36, 86, 187;**
SSC 20
See Oe Kenzaburo
See also CA 97-100; CANR 36, 50, 74, 126;
DA3; DAM NOV; DLB 182; DLBY 1994;
LATS 1:2; MJW; MTCW 1, 2; MTFW
2005; RGSF 2; RGWL 2, 3
Oe Kenzaburo
See Oe, Kenzaburo
See also CWW 2; EWL 3
O'Faolain, Julia 1932- **CLC 6, 19, 47, 108**
See also CA 81-84; CAAS 2; CANR 12,
61; CN 2, 3, 4, 5, 6, 7; DLB 14, 231, 319;
FW; MTCW 1; RHW
O'Faolain, Sean 1900-1991 **CLC 1, 7, 14,**
32, 70; SSC 13; TCLC 143
See also CA 61-64; 134; CANR 12, 66; CN
1, 2, 3, 4; DLB 15, 162; MTCW 1, 2;
MTFW 2005; RGEL 2; RGSF 2
O'Flaherty, Liam 1896-1984 **CLC 5, 34;**
SSC 6
See also CA 101; 113; CANR 35; CN 1, 2,
3; DLB 36, 162; DLBY 1984; MTCW 1,
2; MTFW 2005; RGEL 2; RGSF 2; SSFS
5, 20
Ogai
See Mori Ogai
See also MJW
Ogilvy, Gavin
See Barrie, J(ames) M(atthew)
O'Grady, Standish (James)
1846-1928 **TCLC 5**
See also CA 104; 157
O'Grady, Timothy 1951- **CLC 59**
See also CA 138
O'Hara, Frank 1926-1966 **CLC 2, 5, 13,**
78; PC 45
See also CA 9-12R; 25-28R; CANR 33;
DA3; DAM POET; DLB 5, 16, 193; EWL
3; MAL 5; MTCW 1, 2; MTFW 2005;
PFS 8, 12; RGAL 4; WP
O'Hara, John (Henry) 1905-1970 . **CLC 1, 2,**
3, 6, 11, 42; SSC 15
See also AMW; BPFB 3; CA 5-8R; 25-28R;
CANR 31, 60; CDALB 1929-1941; DAM
NOV; DLB 9, 86, 324; DLBD 2; EWL 3;
MAL 5; MTCW 1, 2; MTFW 2005; NFS
11; RGAL 4; RGSF 2
O'Hehir, Diana 1929- **CLC 41**
See also CA 245
Ohiyesa
See Eastman, Charles A(lexander)
Okada, John 1923-1971 **AAL**
See also BYA 14; CA 212; DLB 312
Okigbo, Christopher 1930-1967 **BLC 3;**
CLC 25, 84; PC 7; TCLC 171
See also AFW; BW 1, 3; CA 77-80; CANR
74; CDWLB 3; DAM MULT, POET; DLB
125; EWL 3; MTCW 1, 2; MTFW 2005;
RGEL 2
Okigbo, Christopher Ifenayichukwu
See Okigbo, Christopher
Okri, Ben 1959- **CLC 87, 223**
See also AFW; BRWS 5; BW 2, 3; CA 130;
138; CANR 65, 128; CN 5, 6, 7; DLB
157, 231, 319, 326; EWL 3; INT CA-138;
MTCW 2; MTFW 2005; RGSF 2; SSFS
20; WLIT 2; WWE 1

Olds, Sharon 1942- .. **CLC 32, 39, 85; PC 22**
See also AMWS 10; CA 101; CANR 18,
41, 66, 98, 135; CP 5, 6, 7; CPW; CWP;
DAM POET; DLB 120; MAL 5; MTCW
2; MTFW 2005; PFS 17
Oldstyle, Jonathan
See Irving, Washington
Olesha, Iurii
See Olesha, Yuri (Karlovich)
See also RGWL 2
Olesha, Iurii Karlovich
See Olesha, Yuri (Karlovich)
See also DLB 272
Olesha, Yuri (Karlovich) 1899-1960 . **CLC 8;**
SSC 69; TCLC 136
See Olesha, Iurii; Olesha, Iurii Karlovich;
Olesha, Yury Karlovich
See also CA 85-88; EW 11; RGWL 3
Olesha, Yury Karlovich
See Olesha, Yuri (Karlovich)
See also EWL 3
Oliphant, Mrs.
See Oliphant, Margaret (Oliphant Wilson)
See also SUFW
Oliphant, Laurence 1829(?)-1888 .. **NCLC 47**
See also DLB 18, 166
Oliphant, Margaret (Oliphant Wilson)
1828-1897 **NCLC 11, 61; SSC 25**
See Oliphant, Mrs.
See also BRWS 10; DLB 18, 159, 190;
HGG; RGEL 2; RGSF 2
Oliver, Mary 1935- **CLC 19, 34, 98**
See also AMWS 7; CA 21-24R; CANR 9,
43, 84, 92, 138; CP 4, 5, 6, 7; CWP; DLB
5, 193; EWL 3; MTFW 2005; PFS 15
Olivier, Laurence (Kerr) 1907-1989 . **CLC 20**
See also CA 111; 150; 129
Olsen, Tillie 1912- ... **CLC 4, 13, 114; SSC 11**
See also AAYA 51; AMWS 13; BYA 11;
CA 1-4R; CANR 1, 43, 74, 132;
CDALBS; CN 2, 3, 4, 5, 6, 7; DA; DA3;
DAB; DAC; DAM MST; DLB 28, 206;
DLBY 1980; EWL 3; EXPS; FW; MAL
5; MTCW 1, 2; MTFW 2005; RGAL 4;
RGSF 2; SSFS 1; TCLE 1:2; TCWW 2;
TUS
Olson, Charles (John) 1910-1970 .. **CLC 1, 2,**
5, 6, 9, 11, 29; PC 19
See also AMWS 2; CA 13-16; 25-28R;
CABS 2; CANR 35, 61; CAP 1; CP 1;
DAM POET; DLB 5, 16, 193; EWL 3;
MAL 5; MTCW 1, 2; RGAL 4; WP
Olson, Toby 1937- **CLC 28**
See also CA 65-68; CANR 9, 31, 84; CP 3,
4, 5, 6, 7
Olyesha, Yuri
See Olesha, Yuri (Karlovich)
Olympiodorus of Thebes c. 375-c.
430 **CMLC 59**
Omar Khayyam
See Khayyam, Omar
See also RGWL 2, 3
Ondaatje, Michael 1943- **CLC 14, 29, 51,**
76, 180; PC 28
See also AAYA 66; CA 77-80; CANR 42,
74, 109, 133; CN 5, 6, 7; CP 1, 2, 3, 4, 5,
6, 7; DA3; DAB; DAC; DAM MST; DLB
60, 323, 326; EWL 3; LATS 1:2; LMFS
2; MTCW 2; MTFW 2005; NFS 23; PFS
8, 19; TCLE 1:2; TWA; WWE 1
Ondaatje, Philip Michael
See Ondaatje, Michael
Oneal, Elizabeth 1934-
See Oneal, Zibby
See also CA 106; CANR 28, 84; MAICYA
1, 2; SATA 30, 82; YAW
Oneal, Zibby **CLC 30**
See Oneal, Elizabeth
See also AAYA 5, 41; BYA 13; CLR 13;
JRDA; WYA

O'Neill, Eugene (Gladstone)
1888-1953 ... **DC 20; TCLC 1, 6, 27, 49;**
WLC 4
See also AAYA 54; AITN 1; AMW; AMWC
1; CA 110; 132; CAD; CANR 131;
CDALB 1929-1941; DA; DA3; DAB;
DAC; DAM DRAM, MST; DFS 2, 4, 5,
6, 9, 11, 12, 16, 20; DLB 7; EWL 3; LAIT
3; LMFS 2; MAL 5, MTCW 1, 2; MTFW
2005; RGAL 4; TUS
Onetti, Juan Carlos 1909-1994 ... **CLC 7, 10;**
HLCS 2; SSC 23; TCLC 131
See also CA 85-88; 145; CANR 32, 63; CD-
WLB 3; CWW 2; DAM MULT, NOV;
DLB 113; EWL 3; HW 1, 2; LAW;
MTCW 1, 2; MTFW 2005; RGSF 2
O Nuallain, Brian 1911-1966
See O'Brien, Flann
See also CA 21-22; 25-28R; CAP 2; DLB
231; FANT; TEA
Ophuls, Max 1902-1957 **TCLC 79**
See also CA 113
Opie, Amelia 1769-1853 **NCLC 65**
See also DLB 116, 159; RGEL 2
Oppen, George 1908-1984 **CLC 7, 13, 34;**
PC 35; TCLC 107
See also CA 13-16R; 113; CANR 8, 82; CP
1, 2, 3; DLB 5, 165
Oppenheim, E(dward) Phillips
1866-1946 **TCLC 45**
See also CA 111; 202; CMW 4; DLB 70
Opuls, Max
See Ophuls, Max
Orage, A(lfred) R(ichard)
1873-1934 **TCLC 157**
See also CA 122
Origen c. 185-c. 254 **CMLC 19**
Orlovitz, Gil 1918-1973 **CLC 22**
See also CA 77-80; 45-48; CN 1; CP 1, 2;
DLB 2, 5
O'Rourke, P(atrick) J(ake) 1947- .. **CLC 209**
See also CA 77-80; CANR 13, 41, 67, 111;
CPW; DAM POP; DLB 185
Orris
See Ingelow, Jean
Ortega y Gasset, Jose 1883-1955 **HLC 2;**
TCLC 9
See also CA 106; 130; DAM MULT; EW 9;
EWL 3; HW 1, 2; MTCW 1, 2; MTFW
2005
Ortese, Anna Maria 1914-1998 **CLC 89**
See also DLB 177; EWL 3
Ortiz, Simon J(oseph) 1941- ... **CLC 45, 208;**
NNAL; PC 17
See also AMWS 4; CA 134; CANR 69, 118;
CP 3, 4, 5, 6, 7; DAM MULT, POET;
DLB 120, 175, 256; EXPP; MAL 5; PFS
4, 16; RGAL 4; TCWW 2
Orton, Joe **CLC 4, 13, 43; DC 3; TCLC**
157
See Orton, John Kingsley
See also BRWS 5; CBD; CDBLB 1960 to
Present; DFS 3, 6; DLB 13, 310; GLL 1;
RGEL 2; TEA; WLIT 4
Orton, John Kingsley 1933-1967
See Orton, Joe
See also CA 85-88; CANR 35, 66; DAM
DRAM; MTCW 1, 2; MTFW 2005
Orwell, George **SSC 68; TCLC 2, 6, 15,**
31, 51, 128, 129; WLC 4
See Blair, Eric (Arthur)
See also BPFB 3; BRW 7; BYA 5; CDBLB
1945-1960; CLR 68; DAB; DLB 15, 98,
195, 255; EWL 3; EXPN; LAIT 4, 5;
LATS 1:1; NFS 3, 7; RGEL 2; SCFW 1,
2; SFW 4; SSFS 4; TEA; WLIT 4; YAW
Osborne, David
See Silverberg, Robert
Osborne, George
See Silverberg, Robert

Author Index

Osborne, John (James) 1929-1994 **CLC 1, 2, 5, 11, 45; TCLC 153; WLC 4**
See also BRWS 1; CA 13-16R; 147; CANR 21, 56; CBD; CDBLB 1945-1960; DA; DAB; DAC; DAM DRAM, MST; DFS 4, 19; DLB 13; EWL 3; MTCW 1, 2; MTFW 2005; RGEL 2

Osborne, Lawrence 1958- **CLC 50**
See also CA 189; CANR 152

Osbourne, Lloyd 1868-1947 **TCLC 93**

Osgood, Frances Sargent
1811-1850 **NCLC 141**
See also DLB 250

Oshima, Nagisa 1932- **CLC 20**
See also CA 116; 121; CANR 78

Oskison, John Milton
1874-1947 **NNAL; TCLC 35**
See also CA 144; CANR 84; DAM MULT; DLB 175

Ossian c. 3rd cent. - **CMLC 28**
See Macpherson, James

Ossoli, Sarah Margaret (Fuller)
1810-1850 **NCLC 5, 50**
See Fuller, Margaret; Fuller, Sarah Margaret
See also CDALB 1640-1865; FW; LMFS 1; SATA 25

Ostriker, Alicia (Suskin) 1937- **CLC 132**
See also CA 25-28R; CAAS 24; CANR 10, 30, 62, 99; CWP; DLB 120; EXPP; PFS 19

Ostrovsky, Aleksandr Nikolaevich
See Ostrovsky, Alexander
See also DLB 277

Ostrovsky, Alexander 1823-1886 .. **NCLC 30, 57**
See Ostrovsky, Aleksandr Nikolaevich

Otero, Blas de 1916-1979 **CLC 11**
See also CA 89-92; DLB 134; EWL 3

O'Trigger, Sir Lucius
See Horne, Richard Henry Hengist

Otto, Rudolf 1869-1937 **TCLC 85**

Otto, Whitney 1955- **CLC 70**
See also CA 140; CANR 120

Otway, Thomas 1652-1685 ... **DC 24; LC 106**
See also DAM DRAM; DLB 80; RGEL 2

Ouida ... **TCLC 43**
See De la Ramee, Marie Louise (Ouida)
See also DLB 18, 156; RGEL 2

Ouologuem, Yambo 1940- **CLC 146**
See also CA 111; 176

Ousmane, Sembene 1923- ... **BLC 3; CLC 66**
See Sembene, Ousmane
See also BW 1, 3; CA 117; 125; CANR 81; CWW 2; MTCW 1

Ovid 43B.C.-17 **CMLC 7; PC 2**
See also AW 2; CDWLB 1; DA3; DAM POET; DLB 211; PFS 22; RGWL 2, 3; WLIT 8; WP

Owen, Hugh
See Faust, Frederick (Schiller)

Owen, Wilfred (Edward Salter)
1893-1918 ... **PC 19; TCLC 5, 27; WLC 4**
See also BRW 6; CA 104; 141; CDBLB 1914-1945; DA; DAB; DAC; DAM MST, POET; DLB 20; EWL 3; EXPP; MTCW 2; MTFW 2005; PFS 10; RGEL 2; WLIT 4

Owens, Louis (Dean) 1948-2002 **NNAL**
See also CA 137, 179; 207; CAAE 179; CAAS 24; CANR 71

Owens, Rochelle 1936- **CLC 8**
See also CA 17-20R; CAAS 2; CAD; CANR 39; CD 5, 6; CP 1, 2, 3, 4, 5, 6, 7; CWD; CWP

Oz, Amos 1939- **CLC 5, 8, 11, 27, 33, 54; SSC 66**
See also CA 53-56; CANR 27, 47, 65, 113, 138; CWW 2; DAM NOV; EWL 3; MTCW 1, 2; MTFW 2005; RGHL; RGSF 2; RGWL 3; WLIT 6

Ozick, Cynthia 1928- **CLC 3, 7, 28, 62, 155; SSC 15, 60**
See also AMWS 5; BEST 90:1; CA 17-20R; CANR 23, 58, 116; CN 3, 4, 5, 6, 7; CPW; DA3; DAM NOV, POP; DLB 28, 152, 299; DLBY 1982; EWL 3; EXPS; INT CANR-23; MAL 5; MTCW 1, 2; MTFW 2005; RGAL 4; RGHL; RGSF 2; SSFS 3, 12

Ozu, Yasujiro 1903-1963 **CLC 16**
See also CA 112

Pabst, G. W. 1885-1967 **TCLC 127**

Pacheco, C.
See Pessoa, Fernando (Antonio Nogueira)

Pacheco, Jose Emilio 1939- **HLC 2**
See also CA 111; 131; CANR 65; CWW 2; DAM MULT; DLB 290; EWL 3; HW 1, 2; RGSF 2

Pa Chin ... **CLC 18**
See Jin, Ba
See also EWL 3

Pack, Robert 1929- **CLC 13**
See also CA 1-4R; CANR 3, 44, 82; CP 1, 2, 3, 4, 5, 6, 7; DLB 5; SATA 118

Padgett, Lewis
See Kuttner, Henry

Padilla (Lorenzo), Heberto
1932-2000 **CLC 38**
See also AITN 1; CA 123; 131; 189; CWW 2; EWL 3, HW 1

Page, James Patrick 1944-
See Page, Jimmy
See also CA 204

Page, Jimmy 1944- **CLC 12**
See Page, James Patrick

Page, Louise 1955- **CLC 40**
See also CA 140; CANR 76; CBD; CD 5, 6; CWD; DLB 233

Page, P(atricia) K(athleen) 1916- **CLC 7, 18; PC 12**
See Cape, Judith
See also CA 53-56; CANR 4, 22, 65; CP 1, 2, 3, 4, 5, 6, 7; DAC; DAM MST; DLB 68; MTCW 1; RGEL 2

Page, Stanton
See Fuller, Henry Blake

Page, Stanton
See Fuller, Henry Blake

Page, Thomas Nelson 1853-1922 **SSC 23**
See also CA 118; 177; DLB 12, 78; DLBD 13; RGAL 4

Pagels, Elaine
See Pagels, Elaine Hiesey

Pagels, Elaine Hiesey 1943- **CLC 104**
See also CA 45-48; CANR 2, 24, 51, 151; FW; NCFS 4

Paget, Violet 1856-1935
See Lee, Vernon
See also CA 104; 166; GLL 1; HGG

Paget-Lowe, Henry
See Lovecraft, H. P.

Paglia, Camille (Anna) 1947- **CLC 68**
See also CA 140; CANR 72, 139; CPW; FW; GLL 2; MTCW 2; MTFW 2005

Paige, Richard
See Koontz, Dean R.

Paine, Thomas 1737-1809 **NCLC 62**
See also AMWS 1; CDALB 1640-1865; DLB 31, 43, 73, 158; LAIT 1; RGAL 4; RGEL 2; TUS

Pakenham, Antonia
See Fraser, Antonia (Pakenham)

Palamas, Costis
See Palamas, Kostes

Palamas, Kostes 1859-1943 **TCLC 5**
See Palamas, Kostis
See also CA 105; 190; RGWL 2, 3

Palamas, Kostis
See Palamas, Kostes
See also EWL 3

Palazzeschi, Aldo 1885-1974 **CLC 11**
See also CA 89-92; 53-56; DLB 114, 264; EWL 3

Pales Matos, Luis 1898-1959 **HLCS 2**
See Pales Matos, Luis
See also DLB 290; HW 1; LAW

Paley, Grace 1922- .. **CLC 4, 6, 37, 140; SSC 8**
See also AMWS 6; CA 25-28R; CANR 13, 46, 74, 118; CN 2, 3, 4, 5, 6, 7; CPW; DA3; DAM POP; DLB 28, 218; EWL 3; EXPS; FW; INT CANR-13; MAL 5; MAWW; MTCW 1, 2; MTFW 2005; RGAL 4; RGSF 2; SSFS 3, 20

Palin, Michael (Edward) 1943- **CLC 21**
See Monty Python
See also CA 107; CANR 35, 109; SATA 67

Palliser, Charles 1947- **CLC 65**
See also CA 136; CANR 76; CN 5, 6, 7

Palma, Ricardo 1833-1919 **TCLC 29**
See also CA 168; LAW

Pamuk, Orhan 1952- **CLC 185**
See also CA 142; CANR 75, 127; CWW 2; WLIT 6

Pancake, Breece Dexter 1952-1979
See Pancake, Breece D'J
See also CA 123; 109

Pancake, Breece D'J **CLC 29; SSC 61**
See Pancake, Breece Dexter
See also DLB 130

Panchenko, Nikolai **CLC 59**

Pankhurst, Emmeline (Goulden)
1858-1928 **TCLC 100**
See also CA 116; FW

Panko, Rudy
See Gogol, Nikolai (Vasilyevich)

Papadiamantis, Alexandros
1851-1911 **TCLC 29**
See also CA 168; EWL 3

Papadiamantopoulos, Johannes 1856-1910
See Moreas, Jean
See also CA 117; 242

Papini, Giovanni 1881-1956 **TCLC 22**
See also CA 121; 180; DLB 264

Paracelsus 1493-1541 **LC 14**
See also DLB 179

Parasol, Peter
See Stevens, Wallace

Pardo Bazan, Emilia 1851-1921 **SSC 30**
See also EWL 3; FW; RGSF 2; RGWL 2, 3

Pareto, Vilfredo 1848-1923 **TCLC 69**
See also CA 175

Paretsky, Sara 1947- **CLC 135**
See also AAYA 30; BEST 90:3; CA 125; 129; CANR 59, 95; CMW 4; CPW; DA3; DAM POP; DLB 306; INT CA-129; MSW; RGAL 4

Parfenie, Maria
See Codrescu, Andrei

Parini, Jay (Lee) 1948- **CLC 54, 133**
See also CA 97-100, 229; CAAE 229; CAAS 16; CANR 32, 87

Park, Jordan
See Kornbluth, C(yril) M.; Pohl, Frederik

Park, Robert E(zra) 1864-1944 **TCLC 73**
See also CA 122; 165

Parker, Bert
See Ellison, Harlan (Jay)

Parker, Dorothy (Rothschild)
1893-1967 . **CLC 15, 68; PC 28; SSC 2;
TCLC 143**
See also AMWS 9; CA 19-20; 25-28R; CAP
2; DA3; DAM POET; DLB 11, 45, 86;
EXPP; FW; MAL 5; MAWW; MTCW 1,
2; MTFW 2005; PFS 18; RGAL 4, RGSF
2; TUS

Parker, Robert B. 1932- **CLC 27**
See also AAYA 28; BEST 89:4; BPFB 3;
CA 49-52; CANR 1, 26, 52, 89, 128;
CMW 4; CPW; DAM NOV, POP; DLB
306; INT CANR-26; MSW; MTCW 1;
MTFW 2005

Parker, Robert Brown
See Parker, Robert B.

Parkin, Frank 1940- **CLC 43**
See also CA 147

Parkman, Francis, Jr. 1823-1893 .. **NCLC 12**
See also AMWS 2; DLB 1, 30, 183, 186,
235; RGAL 4

Parks, Gordon 1912-2006 **BLC 3; CLC 1,
16**
See also AAYA 36; AITN 2; BW 2, 3; CA
41-44R; CANR 26, 66, 145; DA3; DAM
MULT; DLB 33; MTCW 2; MTFW 2005;
SATA 8, 108

Parks, Gordon Alexander Buchanan
See Parks, Gordon

Parks, Suzan-Lori 1964(?)- **DC 23**
See also AAYA 55; CA 201; CAD; CD 5,
6; CWD; DFS 22; RGAL 4

Parks, Tim(othy Harold) 1954- **CLC 147**
See also CA 126; 131; CANR 77, 144; CN
7; DLB 231; INT CA-131

Parmenides c. 515B.C.-c.
450B.C. **CMLC 22**
See also DLB 176

Parnell, Thomas 1679-1718 **LC 3**
See also DLB 95; RGEL 2

Parr, Catherine c. 1513(?)-1548 **LC 86**
See also DLB 136

Parra, Nicanor 1914- ... **CLC 2, 102; HLC 2;
PC 39**
See also CA 85-88; CANR 32; CWW 2;
DAM MULT; DLB 283; EWL 3; HW 1;
LAW; MTCW 1

Parra Sanojo, Ana Teresa de la
1890-1936 **HLCS 2**
See de la Parra, (Ana) Teresa (Sonojo)
See also LAW

Parrish, Mary Frances
See Fisher, M(ary) F(rances) K(ennedy)

Parshchikov, Aleksei 1954- **CLC 59**
See Parshchikov, Aleksei Maksimovich

Parshchikov, Aleksei Maksimovich
See Parshchikov, Aleksei
See also DLB 285

Parson, Professor
See Coleridge, Samuel Taylor

Parson Lot
See Kingsley, Charles

Parton, Sara Payson Willis
1811-1872 **NCLC 86**
See also DLB 43, 74, 239

Partridge, Anthony
See Oppenheim, E(dward) Phillips

Pascal, Blaise 1623-1662 **LC 35**
See also DLB 268; EW 3; GFL Beginnings
to 1789; RGWL 2, 3; TWA

Pascoli, Giovanni 1855-1912 **TCLC 45**
See also CA 170; EW 7; EWL 3

Pasolini, Pier Paolo 1922-1975 .. **CLC 20, 37,
106; PC 17**
See also CA 93-96; 61-64; CANR 63; DLB
128, 177; EWL 3; MTCW 1; RGWL 2, 3

Pasquini
See Silone, Ignazio

Pastan, Linda (Olenik) 1932- **CLC 27**
See also CA 61-64; CANR 18, 40, 61, 113;
CP 3, 4, 5, 6, 7; CSW; CWP; DAM
POET; DLB 5; PFS 8

Pasternak, Boris (Leonidovich)
1890-1960 **CLC 7, 10, 18, 63; PC 6;
SSC 31; WLC 4**
See also BPFB 3; CA 127; 116; DA; DA3;
DAB; DAC; DAM MST, NOV, POET;
DLB 302; EW 10; MTCW 1, 2; MTFW
2005; RGSF 2; RGWL 2, 3; TWA; WP

Patchen, Kenneth 1911-1972 **CLC 1, 2, 18**
See also BG 1:3; CA 1-4R; 33-36R; CANR
3, 35; CN 1; CP 1; DAM POET; DLB 16,
48; EWL 3; MAL 5; MTCW 1; RGAL 4

Pater, Walter (Horatio) 1839-1894 . **NCLC 7,
90, 159**
See also BRW 5; CDBLB 1832-1890; DLB
57, 156; RGEL 2; TEA

Paterson, A(ndrew) B(arton)
1864-1941 **TCLC 32**
See also CA 155; DLB 230; RGEL 2; SATA
97

Paterson, Banjo
See Paterson, A(ndrew) B(arton)

Paterson, Katherine 1932- **CLC 12, 30**
See also AAYA 1, 31; BYA 1, 2, 7; CA 21-
24R; CANR 28, 59, 111; CLR 7, 50;
CWRI 5; DLB 52; JRDA; LAIT 4; MAI-
CYA 1, 2; MAICYAS 1; MTCW 1; SATA
13, 53, 92, 133; WYA; YAW

Paterson, Katherine Womeldorf
See Paterson, Katherine

Patmore, Coventry Kersey Dighton
1823-1896 **NCLC 9; PC 59**
See also DLB 35, 98; RGEL 2; TEA

Paton, Alan (Stewart) 1903-1988 **CLC 4,
10, 25, 55, 106; TCLC 165; WLC 4**
See also AAYA 26; AFW; BPFB 3; BRWS
2; BYA 1; CA 13-16; 125; CANR 22;
CAP 1; CN 1, 2, 3, 4; DA3; DAB;
DAC; DAM MST, NOV; DLB 225;
DLBD 17; EWL 3; EXPN; LAIT 4;
MTCW 1, 2; MTFW 2005; NFS 3, 12;
RGEL 2; SATA 11; SATA-Obit 56; TWA;
WLIT 2; WWE 1

Paton Walsh, Gillian 1937- **CLC 35**
See Paton Walsh, Jill; Walsh, Jill Paton
See also AAYA 11; CANR 38, 83; CLR 2,
65; DLB 161; JRDA; MAICYA 1, 2;
SAAS 3; SATA 4, 72, 109; YAW

Paton Walsh, Jill
See Paton Walsh, Gillian
See also AAYA 47; BYA 1, 8

Patsauq, Markoosie 1942- **NNAL**
See also CA 101; CLR 23; CWRI 5; DAM
MULT

Patterson, (Horace) Orlando (Lloyd)
1940- ... **BLCS**
See also BW 1; CA 65-68; CANR 27, 84;
CN 1, 2, 3, 4, 5, 6

Patton, George S(mith), Jr.
1885-1945 **TCLC 79**
See also CA 189

Paulding, James Kirke 1778-1860 ... **NCLC 2**
See also DLB 3, 59, 74, 250; RGAL 4

Paulin, Thomas Neilson 1949-
See Paulin, Tom
See also CA 123; 128; CANR 98

Paulin, Tom **CLC 37, 177**
See Paulin, Thomas Neilson
See also CP 3, 4, 5, 6, 7; DLB 40

Pausanias c. 1st cent. - **CMLC 36**

Paustovsky, Konstantin (Georgievich)
1892-1968 **CLC 40**
See also CA 93-96; 25-28R; DLB 272;
EWL 3

Pavese, Cesare 1908-1950 **PC 13; SSC 19;
TCLC 3**
See also CA 104; 169; DLB 128, 177; EW
12; EWL 3; PFS 20; RGSF 2; RGWL 2,
3; TWA; WLIT 7

Pavic, Milorad 1929- **CLC 60**
See also CA 136; CDWLB 4; CWW 2; DLB
181; EWL 3; RGWL 3

Pavlov, Ivan Petrovich 1849-1936 . **TCLC 91**
See also CA 118; 180

Pavlova, Karolina Karlovna
1807-1893 **NCLC 138**
See also DLB 205

Payne, Alan
See Jakes, John (William)

Payne, Rachel Ann
See Jakes, John (William)

Paz, Gil
See Lugones, Leopoldo

Paz, Octavio 1914-1998 . **CLC 3, 4, 6, 10, 19,
51, 65, 119; HLC 2; PC 1, 48; WLC 4**
See also AAYA 50; CA 73-76; 165; CANR
32, 65, 104; CWW 2; DA; DA3; DAB;
DAC; DAM MST, MULT, POET; DLB
290; DLBY 1990, 1998; DNFS 1; EWL
3; HW 1, 2; LAW; LAWS 1; MTCW 1, 2;
MTFW 2005; PFS 18; RGWL 2, 3; SSFS
13; TWA; WLIT 1

p'Bitek, Okot 1931-1982 **BLC 3; CLC 96;
TCLC 149**
See also AFW; BW 2, 3; CA 124; 107;
CANR 82; CP 1, 2, 3; DAM MULT; DLB
125; EWL 3; MTCW 1, 2; MTFW 2005;
RGEL 2; WLIT 2

Peabody, Elizabeth Palmer
1804-1894 **NCLC 169**
See also DLB 1, 223

Peacham, Henry 1578-1644(?) **LC 119**
See also DLB 151

Peacock, Molly 1947- **CLC 60**
See also CA 103; CAAS 21; CANR 52, 84;
CP 5, 6, 7; CWP; DLB 120, 282

Peacock, Thomas Love
1785-1866 **NCLC 22**
See also BRW 4; DLB 96, 116; RGEL 2;
RGSF 2

Peake, Mervyn 1911-1968 **CLC 7, 54**
See also CA 5-8R; 25-28R; CANR 3; DLB
15, 160, 255; FANT; MTCW 1; RGEL 2;
SATA 23; SFW 4

Pearce, Philippa
See Christie, Philippa
See also CA 5-8R; CANR 4, 109; CWRI 5;
FANT; MAICYA 2

Pearl, Eric
See Elman, Richard (Martin)

Pearson, T. R. 1956- **CLC 39**
See also CA 120; 130; CANR 97, 147;
CSW; INT CA-130

Pearson, Thomas Reid
See Pearson, T. R.

Peck, Dale 1967- **CLC 81**
See also CA 146; CANR 72, 127; GLL 2

Peck, John (Frederick) 1941- **CLC 3**
See also CA 49-52; CANR 3, 100; CP 4, 5,
6, 7

Peck, Richard (Wayne) 1934- **CLC 21**
See also AAYA 1, 24; BYA 1, 6, 8, 11; CA
85-88; CANR 19, 38, 129; CLR 15; INT
CANR-19; JRDA; MAICYA 1, 2; SAAS
2; SATA 18, 55, 97, 110, 158; SATA-
Essay 110; WYA; YAW

Peck, Robert Newton 1928- **CLC 17**
See also AAYA 3, 43; BYA 1, 6; CA 81-84,
182; CAAE 182; CANR 31, 63, 127; CLR
45; DA; DAC; DAM MST; JRDA; LAIT
3; MAICYA 1, 2; SAAS 1; SATA 21, 62,
111, 156; SATA-Essay 108; WYA; YAW

Peckinpah, David Samuel
See Peckinpah, Sam
Peckinpah, Sam 1925-1984 **CLC 20**
See also CA 109; 114; CANR 82
Pedersen, Knut 1859-1952
See Hamsun, Knut
See also CA 104; 119; CANR 63; MTCW 1, 2
Peele, George 1556-1596 **DC 27; LC 115**
See also BRW 1; DLB 62, 167; RGEL 2
Peeslake, Gaffer
See Durrell, Lawrence (George)
Peguy, Charles (Pierre)
1873-1914 **TCLC 10**
See also CA 107; 193; DLB 258; EWL 3; GFL 1789 to the Present
Peirce, Charles Sanders
1839-1914 **TCLC 81**
See also CA 194; DLB 270
Pellicer, Carlos 1897(?)-1977 **HLCS 2**
See also CA 153; 69-72; DLB 290; EWL 3; HW 1
Pena, Ramon del Valle y
See Valle-Inclan, Ramon (Maria) del
Pendennis, Arthur Esquir
See Thackeray, William Makepeace
Penn, Arthur
See Matthews, (James) Brander
Penn, William 1644-1718 **LC 25**
See also DLB 24
PEPECE
See Prado (Calvo), Pedro
Pepys, Samuel 1633-1703 ... **LC 11, 58; WLC 4**
See also BRW 2; CDBLB 1660-1789; DA; DA3; DAB; DAC; DAM MST; DLB 101, 213; NCFS 4; RGEL 2; TEA; WLIT 3
Percy, Thomas 1729-1811 **NCLC 95**
See also DLB 104
Percy, Walker 1916-1990 **CLC 2, 3, 6, 8, 14, 18, 47, 65**
See also AMWS 3; BPFB 3; CA 1-4R; 131; CANR 1, 23, 64; CN 1, 2, 3, 4; CPW; CSW; DA3; DAM NOV, POP; DLB 2; DLBY 1980, 1990; EWL 3; MAL 5; MTCW 1, 2; MTFW 2005; RGAL 4; TUS
Percy, William Alexander
1885-1942 **TCLC 84**
See also CA 163; MTCW 2
Perec, Georges 1936-1982 **CLC 56, 116**
See also CA 141; DLB 83, 299; EWL 3; GFL 1789 to the Present; RGHL; RGWL 3
Pereda (y Sanchez de Porrua), Jose Maria de 1833-1906 **TCLC 16**
See also CA 117
Pereda y Porrua, Jose Maria de
See Pereda (y Sanchez de Porrua), Jose Maria de
Peregoy, George Weems
See Mencken, H(enry) L(ouis)
Perelman, S(idney) J(oseph)
1904-1979 .. **CLC 3, 5, 9, 15, 23, 44, 49; SSC 32**
See also AITN 1, 2; BPFB 3; CA 73-76; 89-92; CANR 18; DAM DRAM; DLB 11, 44; MTCW 1, 2; MTFW 2005; RGAL 4
Peret, Benjamin 1899-1959 **PC 33; TCLC 20**
See also CA 117; 186; GFL 1789 to the Present
Peretz, Isaac Leib
See Peretz, Isaac Loeb
See also CA 201
Peretz, Isaac Loeb 1851(?)-1915 **SSC 26; TCLC 16**
See Peretz, Isaac Leib
See also CA 109

Peretz, Yitzhkok Leibush
See Peretz, Isaac Loeb
Perez Galdos, Benito 1843-1920 **HLCS 2; TCLC 27**
See Galdos, Benito Perez
See also CA 125; 153; EWL 3; HW 1; RGWL 2, 3
Peri Rossi, Cristina 1941- .. **CLC 156; HLCS 2**
See also CA 131; CANR 59, 81; CWW 2; DLB 145, 290; EWL 3; HW 1, 2
Perlata
See Peret, Benjamin
Perloff, Marjorie G(abrielle)
1931- .. **CLC 137**
See also CA 57-60; CANR 7, 22, 49, 104
Perrault, Charles 1628-1703 **LC 2, 56**
See also BYA 4; CLR 79; DLB 268; GFL Beginnings to 1789; MAICYA 1, 2; RGWL 2, 3; SATA 25; WCH
Perry, Anne 1938- **CLC 126**
See also CA 101; CANR 22, 50, 84, 150; CMW 4; CN 6, 7; CPW; DLB 276
Perry, Brighton
See Sherwood, Robert E(mmet)
Perse, St.-John
See Leger, (Marie-Rene Auguste) Alexis Saint-Leger
Perse, Saint-John
See Leger, (Marie-Rene Auguste) Alexis Saint-Leger
See also DLB 258; RGWL 3
Persius 34-62 **CMLC 74**
See also AW 2; DLB 211; RGWL 2, 3
Perutz, Leo(pold) 1882-1957 **TCLC 60**
See also CA 147; DLB 81
Peseenz, Tulio F.
See Lopez y Fuentes, Gregorio
Pesetsky, Bette 1932- **CLC 28**
See also CA 133; DLB 130
Peshkov, Alexei Maximovich 1868-1936
See Gorky, Maxim
See also CA 105; 141; CANR 83; DA; DAC; DAM DRAM, MST, NOV; MTCW 2; MTFW 2005
Pessoa, Fernando (Antonio Nogueira)
1888-1935 **HLC 2; PC 20; TCLC 27**
See also CA 125; 183; DAM MULT; DLB 287; EW 10; EWL 3; RGWL 2, 3; WP
Peterkin, Julia Mood 1880-1961 **CLC 31**
See also CA 102; DLB 9
Peters, Joan K(aren) 1945- **CLC 39**
See also CA 158; CANR 109
Peters, Robert L(ouis) 1924- **CLC 7**
See also CA 13-16R; CAAS 8; CP 1, 5, 6, 7; DLB 105
Petofi, Sandor 1823-1849 **NCLC 21**
See also RGWL 2, 3
Petrakis, Harry Mark 1923- **CLC 3**
See also CA 9-12R; CANR 4, 30, 85; CN 1, 2, 3, 4, 5, 6, 7
Petrarch 1304-1374 **CMLC 20; PC 8**
See also DA3; DAM POET; EW 2; LMFS 1; RGWL 2, 3; WLIT 7
Petronius c. 20-66 **CMLC 34**
See also AW 2; CDWLB 1; DLB 211; RGWL 2, 3; WLIT 8
Petrov, Evgeny **TCLC 21**
See Kataev, Evgeny Petrovich
Petry, Ann (Lane) 1908-1997 .. **CLC 1, 7, 18; TCLC 112**
See also AFAW 1, 2; BPFB 3; BW 1, 3; BYA 2; CA 5-8R; 157; CAAS 6; CANR 4, 46; CLR 12; CN 1, 2, 3, 4, 5, 6; DLB 76; EWL 3; JRDA; LAIT 1; MAICYA 1, 2; MAICYAS 1; MTCW 1; RGAL 4; SATA 5; SATA-Obit 94; TUS
Petursson, Halligrimur 1614-1674 **LC 8**

Peychinovich
See Vazov, Ivan (Minchov)
Phaedrus c. 15B.C.-c. 50 **CMLC 25**
See also DLB 211
Phelps (Ward), Elizabeth Stuart
See Phelps, Elizabeth Stuart
See also FW
Phelps, Elizabeth Stuart
1844-1911 **TCLC 113**
See Phelps (Ward), Elizabeth Stuart
See also CA 242; DLB 74
Philips, Katherine 1632-1664 . **LC 30; PC 40**
See also DLB 131; RGEL 2
Philipson, Morris H. 1926- **CLC 53**
See also CA 1-4R; CANR 4
Phillips, Caryl 1958- **BLCS; CLC 96, 224**
See also BRWS 5; BW 2; CA 141; CANR 63, 104, 140; CBD; CD 5, 6; CN 5, 6, 7; DA3; DAM MULT; DLB 157; EWL 3; MTCW 2; MTFW 2005; WLIT 4; WWE 1
Phillips, David Graham
1867-1911 **TCLC 44**
See also CA 108; 176; DLB 9, 12, 303; RGAL 4
Phillips, Jack
See Sandburg, Carl (August)
Phillips, Jayne Anne 1952- **CLC 15, 33, 139; SSC 16**
See also AAYA 57; BPFB 3; CA 101; CANR 24, 50, 96; CN 4, 5, 6, 7; CSW; DLBY 1980; INT CANR-24; MTCW 1, 2; MTFW 2005; RGAL 4; RGSF 2; SSFS 4
Phillips, Richard
See Dick, Philip K.
Phillips, Robert (Schaeffer) 1938- **CLC 28**
See also CA 17-20R; CAAS 13; CANR 8; DLB 105
Phillips, Ward
See Lovecraft, H. P.
Philostratus, Flavius c. 179-c.
244 .. **CMLC 62**
Piccolo, Lucio 1901-1969 **CLC 13**
See also CA 97-100; DLB 114; EWL 3
Pickthall, Marjorie L(owry) C(hristie)
1883-1922 **TCLC 21**
See also CA 107; DLB 92
Pico della Mirandola, Giovanni
1463-1494 **LC 15**
See also LMFS 1
Piercy, Marge 1936- **CLC 3, 6, 14, 18, 27, 62, 128; PC 29**
See also BPFB 3; CA 21-24R, 187; CAAE 187; CAAS 1; CANR 13, 43, 66, 111; CN 3, 4, 5, 6, 7; CP 1, 2, 3, 4, 5, 6, 7; CWP; DLB 120, 227; EXPP; FW; MAL 5; MTCW 1, 2; MTFW 2005; PFS 9, 22; SFW 4
Piers, Robert
See Anthony, Piers
Pieyre de Mandiargues, Andre 1909-1991
See Mandiargues, Andre Pieyre de
See also CA 103; 136; CANR 22, 82; EWL 3; GFL 1789 to the Present
Pilnyak, Boris 1894-1938 . **SSC 48; TCLC 23**
See Vogau, Boris Andreyevich
See also EWL 3
Pinchback, Eugene
See Toomer, Jean
Pincherle, Alberto 1907-1990 **CLC 11, 18**
See Moravia, Alberto
See also CA 25-28R; 132; CANR 33, 63, 142; DAM NOV; MTCW 1; MTFW 2005
Pinckney, Darryl 1953- **CLC 76**
See also BW 2, 3; CA 143; CANR 79

Pindar 518(?)B.C.-438(?)B.C. **CMLC 12; PC 19**
See also AW 1; CDWLB 1; DLB 176; RGWL 2

Pineda, Cecile 1942- **CLC 39**
See also CA 118; DLB 209

Pinero, Arthur Wing 1855-1934 **TCLC 32**
See also CA 110; 153; DAM DRAM; DLB 10; RGEL 2

Pinero, Miguel (Antonio Gomez) 1946-1988 **CLC 4, 55**
See also CA 61-64; 125; CAD; CANR 29, 90; DLB 266; HW 1; LLW

Pinget, Robert 1919-1997 **CLC 7, 13, 37**
See also CA 85-88; 160; CWW 2; DLB 83; EWL 3; GFL 1789 to the Present

Pink Floyd
See Barrett, (Roger) Syd; Gilmour, David; Mason, Nick; Waters, Roger; Wright, Rick

Pinkney, Edward 1802-1828 **NCLC 31**
See also DLB 248

Pinkwater, D. Manus
See Pinkwater, Daniel Manus

Pinkwater, Daniel
See Pinkwater, Daniel Manus

Pinkwater, Daniel M.
See Pinkwater, Daniel Manus

Pinkwater, Daniel Manus 1941- **CLC 35**
See also AAYA 1, 46; BYA 9; CA 29-32R; CANR 12, 38, 89, 143; CLR 4; CSW; FANT; JRDA; MAICYA 1, 2; SAAS 3; SATA 8, 46, 76, 114, 158; SFW 4; YAW

Pinkwater, Manus
See Pinkwater, Daniel Manus

Pinsky, Robert 1940- **CLC 9, 19, 38, 94, 121, 216; PC 27**
See also AMWS 6; CA 29-32R; CAAS 4; CANR 58, 97, 138; CP 3, 4, 5, 6, 7; DA3; DAM POET; DLBY 1982, 1998; MAL 5; MTCW 2; MTFW 2005; PFS 18; RGAL 4; TCLE 1:2

Pinta, Harold
See Pinter, Harold

Pinter, Harold 1930- .. **CLC 1, 3, 6, 9, 11, 15, 27, 58, 73, 199; DC 15; WLC 4**
See also BRWR 1; BRWS 1; CA 5-8R; CANR 33, 65, 112, 145; CBD; CD 5, 6; CDBLB 1960 to Present; CP 1; DA; DA3; DAB; DAC; DAM DRAM, MST; DFS 3, 5, 7, 14; DLB 13, 310; EWL 3; IDFW 3, 4; LMFS 2; MTCW 1, 2; MTFW 2005; RGEL 2; RGHL; TEA

Piozzi, Hester Lynch (Thrale) 1741-1821 **NCLC 57**
See also DLB 104, 142

Pirandello, Luigi 1867-1936 .. **DC 5; SSC 22; TCLC 4, 29, 172; WLC 4**
See also CA 104; 153; CANR 103; DA; DA3; DAB; DAC; DAM DRAM, MST; DFS 4, 9; DLB 264; EW 8; EWL 3; MTCW 2; MTFW 2005; RGSF 2; RGWL 2, 3; WLIT 7

Pirsig, Robert M(aynard) 1928- ... **CLC 4, 6, 73**
See also CA 53-56; CANR 42, 74; CPW 1; DA3; DAM POP; MTCW 1, 2; MTFW 2005; SATA 39

Pisarev, Dmitrii Ivanovich
See Pisarev, Dmitry Ivanovich
See also DLB 277

Pisarev, Dmitry Ivanovich 1840-1868 **NCLC 25**
See also Pisarev, Dmitrii Ivanovich

Pix, Mary (Griffith) 1666-1709 **LC 8**
See also DLB 80

Pixerecourt, (Rene Charles) Guilbert de 1773-1844 **NCLC 39**
See also DLB 192; GFL 1789 to the Present

Plaatje, Sol(omon) T(shekisho) 1878-1932 **BLCS; TCLC 73**
See also BW 2, 3; CA 141; CANR 79; DLB 125, 225

Plaidy, Jean
See Hibbert, Eleanor Alice Burford

Planche, James Robinson 1796-1880 **NCLC 42**
See also RGEL 2

Plant, Robert 1948- **CLC 12**

Plante, David 1940- **CLC 7, 23, 38**
See also CA 37-40R; CANR 12, 36, 58, 82, 152; CN 2, 3, 4, 5, 6, 7; DAM NOV; DLBY 1983; INT CANR-12; MTCW 1

Plante, David Robert
See Plante, David

Plath, Sylvia 1932-1963 **CLC 1, 2, 3, 5, 9, 11, 14, 17, 50, 51, 62, 111; PC 1, 37; WLC 4**
See also AAYA 13; AMWR 2; AMWS 1; BPFB 3; CA 19-20; CANR 34, 101; CAP 2; CDALB 1941-1968; DA; DA3; DAB; DAC; DAM MST, POET; DLB 5, 6, 152; EWL 3; EXPN; EXPP; FL 1:6; FW; LAIT 4; MAL 5; MAWW; MTCW 1, 2; MTFW 2005; NFS 1; PAB; PFS 1, 15; RGAL 4; SATA 96; TUS; WP; YAW

Plato c. 428B.C.-347B.C. **CMLC 8, 75; WLCS**
See also AW 1; CDWLB 1; DA; DA3; DAB; DAC; DAM MST; DLB 176; LAIT 1; LATS 1:1; RGWL 2, 3; WLIT 8

Platonov, Andrei
See Klimentov, Andrei Platonovich

Platonov, Andrei Platonovich
See Klimentov, Andrei Platonovich
See also DLB 272

Platonov, Andrey Platonovich
See Klimentov, Andrei Platonovich
See also EWL 3

Platt, Kin 1911- **CLC 26**
See also AAYA 11; CA 17-20R; CANR 11; JRDA; SAAS 17; SATA 21, 86; WYA

Plautus c. 254B.C.-c. 184B.C. **CMLC 24; DC 6**
See also AW 1; CDWLB 1; DLB 211; RGWL 2, 3; WLIT 8

Plick et Plock
See Simenon, Georges (Jacques Christian)

Plieksans, Janis
See Rainis, Janis

Plimpton, George (Ames) 1927-2003 **CLC 36**
See also AITN 1; CA 21-24R; 224; CANR 32, 70, 103, 133; DLB 185, 241; MTCW 1, 2; MTFW 2005; SATA 10; SATA-Obit 150

Pliny the Elder c. 23-79 **CMLC 23**
See also DLB 211

Pliny the Younger c. 61-c. 112 **CMLC 62**
See also AW 2; DLB 211

Plomer, William Charles Franklin 1903-1973 **CLC 4, 8**
See also AFW; BRWS 11; CA 21-22; CANR 34; CAP 2; CN 1; CP 1, 2; DLB 20, 162, 191, 225; EWL 3; MTCW 1; RGEL 2; RGSF 2; SATA 24

Plotinus 204-270 **CMLC 46**
See also CDWLB 1; DLB 176

Plowman, Piers
See Kavanagh, Patrick (Joseph)

Plum, J.
See Wodehouse, P(elham) G(renville)

Plumly, Stanley (Ross) 1939- **CLC 33**
See also CA 108; 110; CANR 97; CP 3, 4, 5, 6, 7; DLB 5, 193; INT CA-110

Plumpe, Friedrich Wilhelm 1888-1931 **TCLC 53**
See also CA 112

Plutarch c. 46-c. 120 **CMLC 60**
See also AW 2; CDWLB 1; DLB 176; RGWL 2, 3; TWA; WLIT 8

Po Chu-i 772-846 **CMLC 24**

Podhoretz, Norman 1930- **CLC 189**
See also AMWS 8; CA 9-12R; CANR 7, 78, 135

Poe, Edgar Allan 1809-1849 **NCLC 1, 16, 55, 78, 94, 97, 117; PC 1, 54; SSC 1, 22, 34, 35, 54, 88; WLC 4**
See also AAYA 14; AMW; AMWC 1; AMWR 2; BPFB 3; BYA 5, 11; CDALB 1640-1865; CMW 4; DA; DA3; DAB; DAC; DAM MST, POET; DLB 3, 59, 73, 74, 248, 254; EXPP; EXPS; GL 3; HGG; LAIT 2; LATS 1:1; LMFS 1; MSW; PAB; PFS 1, 3, 9; RGAL 4; RGSF 2; SATA 23; SCFW 1, 2; SFW 4; SSFS 2, 4, 7, 8, 16; SUFW; TUS; WP; WYA

Poet of Titchfield Street, The
See Pound, Ezra (Weston Loomis)

Poggio Bracciolini, Gian Francesco 1380-1459 **LC 125**

Pohl, Frederik 1919- **CLC 18; SSC 25**
See also AAYA 24; CA 61-64, 188; CAAE 188; CAAS 1; CANR 11, 37, 81, 140; CN 1, 2, 3, 4, 5, 6; DLB 8; INT CANR-11; MTCW 1, 2; MTFW 2005; SATA 24; SCFW 1, 2; SFW 4

Poirier, Louis 1910-
See Gracq, Julien
See also CA 122; 126; CANR 141

Poitier, Sidney 1927- **CLC 26**
See also AAYA 60; BW 1; CA 117; CANR 94

Pokagon, Simon 1830-1899 **NNAL**
See also DAM MULT

Polanski, Roman 1933- **CLC 16, 178**
See also CA 77-80

Poliakoff, Stephen 1952- **CLC 38**
See also CA 106; CANR 116; CBD; CD 5, 6; DLB 13

Police, The
See Copeland, Stewart (Armstrong); Summers, Andrew James

Polidori, John William 1795-1821 . **NCLC 51**
See also DLB 116; HGG

Poliziano, Angelo 1454-1494 **LC 120**
See also WLIT 7

Pollitt, Katha 1949- **CLC 28, 122**
See also CA 120; 122; CANR 66, 108; MTCW 1, 2; MTFW 2005

Pollock, (Mary) Sharon 1936- **CLC 50**
See also CA 141; CANR 132; CD 5; CWD; DAC; DAM DRAM, MST; DFS 3; DLB 60; FW

Pollock, Sharon 1936- **DC 20**
See also CD 6

Polo, Marco 1254-1324 **CMLC 15**
See also WLIT 7

Polonsky, Abraham (Lincoln) 1910-1999 **CLC 92**
See also CA 104; 187; DLB 26; INT CA-104

Polybius c. 200B.C.-c. 118B.C. **CMLC 17**
See also AW 1; DLB 176; RGWL 2, 3

Pomerance, Bernard 1940- **CLC 13**
See also CA 101; CAD; CANR 49, 134; CD 5, 6; DAM DRAM; DFS 9; LAIT 2

Ponge, Francis 1899-1988 **CLC 6, 18**
See also CA 85-88; 126; CANR 40, 86; DAM POET; DLBY 2002; EWL 3; GFL 1789 to the Present; RGWL 2, 3

Poniatowska, Elena 1933- . **CLC 140; HLC 2**
See also CA 101; CANR 32, 66, 107; CD-WLB 3; CWW 2; DAM MULT; DLB 113; EWL 3; HW 1, 2; LAWS 1; WLIT 1

Pontoppidan, Henrik 1857-1943 **TCLC 29**
See also CA 170; DLB 300

Ponty, Maurice Merleau
See Merleau-Ponty, Maurice

Poole, Josephine CLC 17
See Helyar, Jane Penelope Josephine
See also SAAS 2; SATA 5

Popa, Vasko 1922-1991 . CLC 19; TCLC 167
See also CA 112; 148; CDWLB 4; DLB
181; EWL 3; RGWL 2, 3

Pope, Alexander 1688-1744 LC 3, 58, 60,
64; PC 26; WLC 5
See also BRW 3; BRWC 1; BRWR 1; CD-
BLB 1660-1789; DA; DA3; DAB; DAC;
DAM MST, POET; DLB 95, 101, 213;
EXPP; PAB; PFS 12; RGEL 2; WLIT 3;
WP

Popov, Evgenii Anatol'evich
See Popov, Yevgeny
See also DLB 285

Popov, Yevgeny CLC 59
See Popov, Evgenii Anatol'evich

Poquelin, Jean-Baptiste
See Moliere

Porete, Marguerite (?)-1310 CMLC 73
See also DLB 208

Porphyry c. 233-c. 305 CMLC 71

Porter, Connie (Rose) 1959(?)- CLC 70
See also AAYA 65; BW 2, 3; CA 142;
CANR 90, 109; SATA 81, 129

Porter, Gene(va Grace) Stratton .. TCLC 21
See Stratton-Porter, Gene(va Grace)
See also BPFB 3; CA 112; CWRI 5; RHW

Porter, Katherine Anne 1890-1980 ... CLC 1,
3, 7, 10, 13, 15, 27, 101; SSC 4, 31, 43
See also AAYA 42; AITN 2; AMW; BPFB
3; CA 1-4R; 101; CANR 1, 65; CDALBS;
CN 1, 2; DA; DA3; DAB; DAC; DAM
MST, NOV; DLB 4, 9, 102; DLBD 12;
DLBY 1980; EWL 3; EXPS; LAIT 3;
MAL 5; MAWW; MTCW 1, 2; MTFW
2005; NFS 14; RGAL 4; RGSF 2; SATA
39; SATA-Obit 23; SSFS 1, 8, 11, 16, 23;
TCWW 2; TUS

Porter, Peter (Neville Frederick)
1929- CLC 5, 13, 33
See also CA 85-88; CP 1, 2, 3, 4, 5, 6, 7;
DLB 40, 289; WWE 1

Porter, William Sydney 1862-1910
See Henry, O.
See also CA 104; 131; CDALB 1865-1917;
DA; DA3; DAB; DAC; DAM MST; DLB
12, 78, 79; MTCW 1, 2; MTFW 2005;
TUS; YABC 2

Portillo (y Pacheco), Jose Lopez
See Lopez Portillo (y Pacheco), Jose

Portillo Trambley, Estela 1927-1998 .. HLC 2
See Trambley, Estela Portillo
See also CANR 32; DAM MULT; DLB
209; HW 1

Posey, Alexander (Lawrence)
1873-1908 NNAL
See also CA 144; CANR 80; DAM MULT;
DLB 175

Posse, Abel CLC 70

Post, Melville Davisson
1869-1930 TCLC 39
See also CA 110; 202; CMW 4

Potok, Chaim 1929-2002 ... CLC 2, 7, 14, 26,
112
See also AAYA 15, 50; AITN 1, 2; BPFB 3;
BYA 1; CA 17-20R; 208; CANR 19, 35,
64, 98; CLR 92; CN 4, 5, 6; DA3; DAM
NOV; DLB 28, 152; EXPN; INT CANR-
19; LAIT 4; MTCW 1, 2; MTFW 2005;
NFS 4; RGHL; SATA 33, 106; SATA-Obit
134; TUS; YAW

Potok, Herbert Harold -2002
See Potok, Chaim

Potok, Herman Harold
See Potok, Chaim

Potter, Dennis (Christopher George)
1935-1994 CLC 58, 86, 123
See also BRWS 10; CA 107; 145; CANR
33, 61; CBD; DLB 233; MTCW 1

Pound, Ezra (Weston Loomis)
1885-1972 .. CLC 1, 2, 3, 4, 5, 7, 10, 13,
18, 34, 48, 50, 112; PC 4; WLC 5
See also AAYA 47; AMW; AMWR 1; CA
5-8R; 37-40R; CANR 40; CDALB 1917-
1929; CP 1; DA; DA3; DAB; DAC; DAM
MST, POET; DLB 4, 45, 63; DLBD 15;
EFS 2; EWL 3; EXPP; LMFS 2; MAL 5;
MTCW 1, 2; MTFW 2005; PAB; PFS 2,
8, 16; RGAL 4; TUS; WP

Povod, Reinaldo 1959-1994 CLC 44
See also CA 136; 146; CANR 83

Powell, Adam Clayton, Jr.
1908-1972 BLC 3; CLC 89
See also BW 1, 3; CA 102; 33-36R; CANR
86; DAM MULT

Powell, Anthony (Dymoke)
1905-2000 CLC 1, 3, 7, 9, 10, 31
See also BRW 7; CA 1-4R; 189; CANR 1,
32, 62, 107; CDBLB 1945-1960; CN 1, 2,
3, 4, 5, 6; DLB 15; EWL 3; MTCW 1, 2;
MTFW 2005; RGEL 2; TEA

Powell, Dawn 1896(?)-1965 CLC 66
See also CA 5-8R; CANR 121; DLBY 1997

Powell, Padgett 1952- CLC 34
See also CA 126; CANR 63, 101; CSW;
DLB 234; DLBY 01

Powell, (Oval) Talmage 1920-2000
See Queen, Ellery
See also CA 5-8R; CANR 2, 80

Power, Susan 1961- CLC 91
See also BYA 14; CA 160; CANR 135; NFS
11

Powers, J(ames) F(arl) 1917-1999 CLC 1,
4, 8, 57; SSC 4
See also CA 1-4R; 181; CANR 2, 61; CN
1, 2, 3, 4, 5, 6; DLB 130; MTCW 1;
RGAL 4; RGSF 2

Powers, John J(ames) 1945-
See Powers, John R.
See also CA 69-72

Powers, John R. CLC 66
See Powers, John J(ames)

Powers, Richard (S.) 1957- CLC 93
See also AMWS 9; BPFB 3; CA 148;
CANR 80; CN 6, 7; MTFW 2005; TCLE
1:2

Pownall, David 1938- CLC 10
See also CA 89-92, 180; CAAS 18; CANR
49, 101; CBD; CD 5, 6; CN 4, 5, 6, 7;
DLB 14

Powys, John Cowper 1872-1963 ... CLC 7, 9,
15, 46, 125
See also CA 85-88; CANR 106; DLB 15,
255; EWL 3; FANT; MTCW 1, 2; MTFW
2005; RGEL 2; SUFW

Powys, T(heodore) F(rancis)
1875-1953 TCLC 9
See also BRWS 8; CA 106; 189; DLB 36,
162; EWL 3; FANT; RGEL 2; SUFW

Pozzo, Modesta
See Fonte, Moderata

Prado (Calvo), Pedro 1886-1952 ... TCLC 75
See also CA 131; DLB 283; HW 1; LAW

Prager, Emily 1952- CLC 56
See also CA 204

Pratchett, Terry 1948- CLC 197
See also AAYA 19, 54; BPFB 3; CA 143;
CANR 87, 126; CLR 64; CN 6, 7; CPW;
CWRI 5; FANT; MTFW 2005; SATA 82,
139; SFW 4; SUFW 2

Pratolini, Vasco 1913-1991 TCLC 124
See also CA 211; DLB 177; EWL 3; RGWL
2, 3

Pratt, E(dwin) J(ohn) 1883(?)-1964 . CLC 19
See also CA 141; 93-96; CANR 77; DAC;
DAM POET; DLB 92; EWL 3; RGEL 2;
TWA

Premchand TCLC 21
See Srivastava, Dhanpat Rai
See also EWL 3

Prescott, William Hickling
1796-1859 NCLC 163
See also DLB 1, 30, 59, 235

Preseren, France 1800-1849 NCLC 127
See also CDWLB 4; DLB 147

Preussler, Otfried 1923- CLC 17
See also CA 77-80; SATA 24

Prevert, Jacques (Henri Marie)
1900-1977 CLC 15
See also CA 77-80; 69-72; CANR 29, 61;
DLB 258; EWL 3; GFL 1789 to the
Present; IDFW 3, 4; MTCW 1; RGWL 2,
3; SATA-Obit 30

Prevost, (Antoine Francois)
1697-1763 LC 1
See also DLB 314; EW 4; GFL Beginnings
to 1789; RGWL 2, 3

Price, (Edward) Reynolds 1933- ... CLC 3, 6,
13, 43, 50, 63, 212; SSC 22
See also AMWS 6; CA 1-4R; CANR 1, 37,
57, 87, 128; CN 1, 2, 3, 4, 5, 6, 7; CSW;
DAM NOV; DLB 2, 218, 278; EWL 3;
INT CANR-37; MAL 5; MTFW 2005;
NFS 18

Price, Richard 1949- CLC 6, 12
See also CA 49-52; CANR 3, 147; CN 7;
DLBY 1981

Prichard, Katharine Susannah
1883-1969 CLC 46
See also CA 11-12; CANR 33; CAP 1; DLB
260; MTCW 1; RGEL 2; RGSF 2; SATA
66

Priestley, J(ohn) B(oynton)
1894-1984 CLC 2, 5, 9, 34
See also BRW 7; CA 9-12R; 113; CANR
33; CDBLB 1914-1945; CN 1, 2, 3; DA3;
DAM DRAM, NOV; DLB 10, 34, 77,
100, 139; DLBY 1984; EWL 3; MTCW
1, 2; MTFW 2005; RGEL 2; SFW 4

Prince 1958- CLC 35
See also CA 213

Prince, F(rank) T(empleton)
1912-2003 CLC 22
See also CA 101; 219; CANR 43, 79; CP 1,
2, 3, 4, 5, 6, 7; DLB 20

Prince Kropotkin
See Kropotkin, Peter (Aleksieevich)

Prior, Matthew 1664-1721 LC 4
See also DLB 95; RGEL 2

Prishvin, Mikhail 1873-1954 TCLC 75
See Prishvin, Mikhail Mikhailovich

Prishvin, Mikhail Mikhailovich
See Prishvin, Mikhail
See also DLB 272; EWL 3

Pritchard, William H(arrison)
1932- .. CLC 34
See also CA 65-68; CANR 23, 95; DLB
111

Pritchett, V(ictor) S(awdon)
1900-1997 ... CLC 5, 13, 15, 41; SSC 14
See also BPFB 3; BRWS 3; CA 61-64; 157;
CANR 31, 63; CN 1, 2, 3, 4, 5, 6; DA3;
DAM NOV; DLB 15, 139; EWL 3;
MTCW 1, 2; MTFW 2005; RGEL 2;
RGSF 2; TEA

Private 19022
See Manning, Frederic

Probst, Mark 1925- CLC 59
See also CA 130

Procaccino, Michael
See Cristofer, Michael

Proclus c. 412-c. 485 CMLC 81

Prokosch, Frederic 1908-1989 **CLC 4, 48**
See also CA 73-76; 128; CANR 82; CN 1, 2, 3, 4; CP 1, 2, 3, 4; DLB 48; MTCW 2

Propertius, Sextus c. 50B.C.-c. 16B.C. **CMLC 32**
See also AW 2; CDWLB 1; DLB 211; RGWL 2, 3; WLIT 8

Prophet, The
See Dreiser, Theodore

Prose, Francine 1947- **CLC 45**
See also CA 109; 112; CANR 46, 95, 132; DLB 234; MTFW 2005; SATA 101, 149

Protagoras c. 490B.C.-420B.C. **CMLC 85**
See also DLB 176

Proudhon
See Cunha, Euclides (Rodrigues Pimenta) da

Proulx, Annie
See Proulx, E. Annie

Proulx, E. Annie 1935- **CLC 81, 158**
See also AMWS 7; BPFB 3; CA 145; CANR 65, 110; CN 6, 7; CPW 1; DA3; DAM POP; MAL 5; MTCW 2; MTFW 2005; SSFS 18, 23

Proulx, Edna Annie
See Proulx, E. Annie

Proust, (Valentin-Louis-George-Eugene) Marcel 1871-1922 **SSC 75; TCLC 7, 13, 33; WLC 5**
See also AAYA 58; BPFB 3; CA 104; 120; CANR 110; DA; DA3; DAB; DAC; DAM MST, NOV; DLB 65; EW 8; EWL 3; GFL 1789 to the Present; MTCW 1, 2; MTFW 2005; RGWL 2, 3; TWA

Prowler, Harley
See Masters, Edgar Lee

Prudentius, Aurelius Clemens 348-c. 405 .. **CMLC 78**
See also EW 1; RGWL 2, 3

Prus, Boleslaw 1845-1912 **TCLC 48**
See also RGWL 2, 3

Pryor, Aaron Richard
See Pryor, Richard

Pryor, Richard 1940-2005 **CLC 26**
See also CA 122; 152; 246

Pryor, Richard Franklin Lenox Thomas
See Pryor, Richard

Przybyszewski, Stanislaw 1868-1927 **TCLC 36**
See also CA 160; DLB 66; EWL 3

Pteleon
See Grieve, C(hristopher) M(urray)
See also DAM POET

Puckett, Lute
See Masters, Edgar Lee

Puig, Manuel 1932-1990 **CLC 3, 5, 10, 28, 65, 133; HLC 2**
See also BPFB 3; CA 45-48; CANR 2, 32, 63; CDWLB 3; DA3; DAM MULT; DLB 113; DNFS 1; EWL 3; GLL 1; HW 1, 2; LAW; MTCW 1, 2; MTFW 2005; RGWL 2, 3; TWA; WLIT 1

Pulitzer, Joseph 1847-1911 **TCLC 76**
See also CA 114; DLB 23

Purchas, Samuel 1577(?)-1626 **LC 70**
See also DLB 151

Purdy, A(lfred) W(ellington) 1918-2000 **CLC 3, 6, 14, 50**
See also CA 81-84; 189; CAAS 17; CANR 42, 66; CP 1, 2, 3, 4, 5, 6, 7; DAC; DAM MST, POET; DLB 88; PFS 5; RGEL 2

Purdy, James (Amos) 1923- **CLC 2, 4, 10, 28, 52**
See also AMWS 7; CA 33-36R; CAAS 1; CANR 19, 51, 132; CN 1, 2, 3, 4, 5, 6, 7; DLB 2, 218; EWL 3; INT CANR-19; MAL 5; MTCW 1; RGAL 4

Pure, Simon
See Swinnerton, Frank Arthur

Pushkin, Aleksandr Sergeevich
See Pushkin, Alexander (Sergeyevich)
See also DLB 205

Pushkin, Alexander (Sergeyevich) 1799-1837 **NCLC 3, 27, 83; PC 10; SSC 27, 55; WLC 5**
See Pushkin, Aleksandr Sergeevich
See also DA; DA3; DAB; DAC; DAM DRAM, MST, POET; EW 5; EXPS; RGSF 2; RGWL 2, 3; SATA 61; SSFS 9; TWA

P'u Sung-ling 1640-1715 **LC 49; SSC 31**

Putnam, Arthur Lee
See Alger, Horatio, Jr.

Puttenham, George 1529(?)-1590 **LC 116**
See also DLB 281

Puzo, Mario 1920-1999 **CLC 1, 2, 6, 36, 107**
See also BPFB 3; CA 65-68; 185; CANR 4, 42, 65, 99, 131; CN 1, 2, 3, 4, 5, 6; CPW; DA3; DAM NOV, POP; DLB 6; MTCW 1, 2; MTFW 2005; NFS 16; RGAL 4

Pygge, Edward
See Barnes, Julian

Pyle, Ernest Taylor 1900-1945
See Pyle, Ernie
See also CA 115; 160

Pyle, Ernie .. **TCLC 75**
See Pyle, Ernest Taylor
See also DLB 29; MTCW 2

Pyle, Howard 1853-1911 **TCLC 81**
See also AAYA 57; BYA 2, 4; CA 109; 137; CLR 22; DLB 42, 188; DLBD 13; LAIT 1; MAICYA 1, 2; SATA 16, 100; WCH; YAW

Pym, Barbara (Mary Crampton) 1913-1980 **CLC 13, 19, 37, 111**
See also BPFB 3; BRWS 2; CA 13-14; 97-100; CANR 13, 34; CAP 1; DLB 14, 207; DLBY 1987; EWL 3; MTCW 1, 2; MTFW 2005; RGEL 2; TEA

Pynchon, Thomas (Ruggles, Jr.) 1937- **CLC 2, 3, 6, 9, 11, 18, 33, 62, 72, 123, 192, 213; SSC 14, 84; WLC 5**
See also AMWS 2; BEST 90:2; BPFB 3; CA 17-20R; CANR 22, 46, 73, 142; CN 1, 2, 3, 4, 5, 6, 7; CPW 1; DA; DA3; DAB; DAC; DAM MST, NOV, POP; DLB 2, 173; EWL 3; MAL 5; MTCW 1, 2; MTFW 2005; NFS 23; RGAL 4; SFW 4; TCLE 1:2; TUS

Pythagoras c. 582B.C.-c. 507B.C. . **CMLC 22**
See also DLB 176

Q
See Quiller-Couch, Sir Arthur (Thomas)

Qian, Chongzhu
See Ch'ien, Chung-shu

Qian, Sima 145B.C.-c. 89B.C. **CMLC 72**

Qian Zhongshu
See Ch'ien, Chung-shu
See also CWW 2

Qroll
See Dagerman, Stig (Halvard)

Quarles, Francis 1592-1644 **LC 117**
See also DLB 126; RGEL 2

Quarrington, Paul (Lewis) 1953- **CLC 65**
See also CA 129; CANR 62, 95

Quasimodo, Salvatore 1901-1968 **CLC 10; PC 47**
See also CA 13-16; 25-28R; CAP 1; DLB 114; EW 12; EWL 3; MTCW 1; RGWL 2, 3

Quatermass, Martin
See Carpenter, John (Howard)

Quay, Stephen 1947- **CLC 95**
See also CA 189

Quay, Timothy 1947- **CLC 95**
See also CA 189

Queen, Ellery **CLC 3, 11**
See Dannay, Frederic; Davidson, Avram (James); Deming, Richard; Fairman, Paul W.; Flora, Fletcher; Hoch, Edward D(entinger); Kane, Henry; Lee, Manfred B.; Marlowe, Stephen; Powell, (Oval) Talmage; Sheldon, Walter J(ames); Sturgeon, Theodore (Hamilton); Tracy, Don(ald Fiske); Vance, Jack
See also BPFB 3; CMW 4; MSW; RGAL 4

Queen, Ellery, Jr.
See Dannay, Frederic; Lee, Manfred B.

Queneau, Raymond 1903-1976 **CLC 2, 5, 10, 42**
See also CA 77-80; 69-72; CANR 32; DLB 72, 258; EW 12; EWL 3; GFL 1789 to the Present; MTCW 1, 2; RGWL 2, 3

Quevedo, Francisco de 1580-1645 **LC 23**

Quiller-Couch, Sir Arthur (Thomas) 1863-1944 **TCLC 53**
See also CA 118; 166; DLB 135, 153, 190; HGG; RGEL 2; SUFW 1

Quin, Ann 1936-1973 **CLC 6**
See also CA 9-12R; 45-48; CANR 148; CN 1; DLB 14, 231

Quin, Ann Marie
See Quin, Ann

Quincey, Thomas de
See De Quincey, Thomas

Quindlen, Anna 1953- **CLC 191**
See also AAYA 35; CA 138; CANR 73, 126; DA3; DLB 292; MTCW 2; MTFW 2005

Quinn, Martin
See Smith, Martin Cruz

Quinn, Peter 1947- **CLC 91**
See also CA 197; CANR 147

Quinn, Peter A.
See Quinn, Peter

Quinn, Simon
See Smith, Martin Cruz

Quintana, Leroy V. 1944- **HLC 2; PC 36**
See also CA 131; CANR 65, 139; DAM MULT; DLB 82; HW 1, 2

Quintilian c. 40-c. 100 **CMLC 77**
See also AW 2; DLB 211; RGWL 2, 3

Quintillian 0035-0100 **CMLC 77**

Quiroga, Horacio (Sylvestre) 1878-1937 ... **HLC 2; SSC 89; TCLC 20**
See also CA 117; 131; DAM MULT; EWL 3; HW 1; LAW; MTCW 1; RGSF 2; WLIT 1

Quoirez, Francoise 1935-2004 **CLC 9**
See Sagan, Francoise
See also CA 49-52; 231; CANR 6, 39, 73; MTCW 1, 2; MTFW 2005; TWA

Raabe, Wilhelm (Karl) 1831-1910 . **TCLC 45**
See also CA 167; DLB 129

Rabe, David (William) 1940- .. **CLC 4, 8, 33, 200; DC 16**
See also CA 85-88; CABS 3; CAD; CANR 59, 129; CD 5, 6; DAM DRAM; DFS 3, 8, 13; DLB 7, 228; EWL 3; MAL 5

Rabelais, Francois 1494-1553 **LC 5, 60; WLC 5**
See also DA; DAB; DAC; DAM MST; EW 2; GFL Beginnings to 1789; LMFS 1; RGWL 2, 3; TWA

Rabi'a al-'Adawiyya c. 717-c. 801 .. **CMLC 83**
See also DLB 311

Rabinovitch, Sholem 1859-1916
See Aleichem, Sholom
See also CA 104

Rabinyan, Dorit 1972- **CLC 119**
See also CA 170; CANR 147

Rachilde
See Vallette, Marguerite Eymery; Vallette, Marguerite Eymery
See also EWL 3

Racine, Jean 1639-1699 **LC 28, 113**
See also DA3; DAB; DAM MST; DLB 268;
EW 3; GFL Beginnings to 1789; LMFS
1; RGWL 2, 3; TWA

Radcliffe, Ann (Ward) 1764-1823 ... **NCLC 6,
55, 106**
See also DLB 39, 178; GL 3; HGG; LMFS
1; RGEL 2; SUFW; WLIT 3

Radclyffe-Hall, Marguerite
See Hall, (Marguerite) Radclyffe

Radiguet, Raymond 1903-1923 **TCLC 29**
See also CA 162; DLB 65; EWL 3; GFL
1789 to the Present; RGWL 2, 3

Radnoti, Miklos 1909-1944 **TCLC 16**
See also CA 118; 212; CDWLB 4; DLB
215; EWL 3; RGHL; RGWL 2, 3

Rado, James 1939- **CLC 17**
See also CA 105

Radvanyi, Netty 1900-1983
See Seghers, Anna
See also CA 85-88; 110; CANR 82

Rae, Ben
See Griffiths, Trevor

Raeburn, John (Hay) 1941- **CLC 34**
See also CA 57-60

Ragni, Gerome 1942-1991 **CLC 17**
See also CA 105; 134

Rahv, Philip **CLC 24**
See Greenberg, Ivan
See also DLB 137; MAL 5

Raimund, Ferdinand Jakob
1790-1836 **NCLC 69**
See also DLB 90

Raine, Craig (Anthony) 1944- .. **CLC 32, 103**
See also CA 108; CANR 29, 51, 103; CP 3,
4, 5, 6, 7; DLB 40; PFS 7

Raine, Kathleen (Jessie) 1908-2003 .. **CLC 7,
45**
See also CA 85-88; 218; CANR 46, 109;
CP 1, 2, 3, 4, 5, 6, 7; DLB 20; EWL 3;
MTCW 1; RGEL 2

Rainis, Janis 1865-1929 **TCLC 29**
See also CA 170; CDWLB 4; DLB 220;
EWL 3

Rakosi, Carl **CLC 47**
See Rawley, Callman
See also CA 228; CAAS 5; CP 1, 2, 3, 4, 5,
6, 7; DLB 193

Ralegh, Sir Walter
See Raleigh, Sir Walter
See also BRW 1; RGEL 2; WP

Raleigh, Richard
See Lovecraft, H. P.

Raleigh, Sir Walter 1554(?)-1618 **LC 31,
39; PC 31**
See Ralegh, Sir Walter
See also CDBLB Before 1660; DLB 172;
EXPP; PFS 14; TEA

Rallentando, H. P.
See Sayers, Dorothy L(eigh)

Ramal, Walter
See de la Mare, Walter (John)

Ramana Maharshi 1879-1950 **TCLC 84**

Ramoacn y Cajal, Santiago
1852-1934 **TCLC 93**

Ramon, Juan
See Jimenez (Mantecon), Juan Ramon

Ramos, Graciliano 1892-1953 **TCLC 32**
See also CA 167; DLB 307; EWL 3; HW 2;
LAW; WLIT 1

Rampersad, Arnold 1941- **CLC 44**
See also BW 2, 3; CA 127; 133; CANR 81;
DLB 111; INT CA-133

Rampling, Anne
See Rice, Anne
See also GLL 2

Ramsay, Allan 1686(?)-1758 **LC 29**
See also DLB 95; RGEL 2

Ramsay, Jay
See Campbell, (John) Ramsey

Ramuz, Charles-Ferdinand
1878-1947 **TCLC 33**
See also CA 165; EWL 3

Rand, Ayn 1905-1982 **CLC 3, 30, 44, 79;
WLC 5**
See also AAYA 10; AMWS 4; BPFB 3;
BYA 12; CA 13-16R; 105; CANR 27, 73;
CDALBS; CN 1, 2, 3; CPW; DA; DA3;
DAC; DAM MST, NOV, POP; DLB 227,
279; MTCW 1, 2; MTFW 2005; NFS 10,
16; RGAL 4; SFW 4; TUS; YAW

Randall, Dudley (Felker) 1914-2000 . **BLC 3;
CLC 1, 135**
See also BW 1, 3; CA 25-28R; 189; CANR
23, 82; CP 1, 2, 3, 4, 5; DAM MULT;
DLB 41; PFS 5

Randall, Robert
See Silverberg, Robert

Ranger, Ken
See Creasey, John

Rank, Otto 1884-1939 **TCLC 115**

Ransom, John Crowe 1888-1974 .. **CLC 2, 4,
5, 11, 24; PC 61**
See also AMW; CA 5-8R; 49-52; CANR 6,
34; CDALBS; CP 1, 2; DA3; DAM POET;
DLB 45, 63; EWL 3; EXPP; MAL 5;
MTCW 1, 2; MTFW 2005; RGAL 4; TUS

Rao, Raja 1908-2006 **CLC 25, 56**
See also CA 73-76; CANR 51; CN 1, 2, 3,
4, 5, 6; DAM NOV; DLB 323; EWL 3;
MTCW 1, 2; MTFW 2005; RGEL 2;
RGSF 2

Raphael, Frederic (Michael) 1931- ... **CLC 2,
14**
See also CA 1-4R; CANR 1, 86; CN 1, 2,
3, 4, 5, 6, 7; DLB 14, 319; TCLE 1:2

Ratcliffe, James P.
See Mencken, H(enry) L(ouis)

Rathbone, Julian 1935- **CLC 41**
See also CA 101; CANR 34, 73, 152

Rattigan, Terence (Mervyn)
1911-1977 **CLC 7; DC 18**
See also BRWS 7; CA 85-88; 73-76; CBD;
CDBLB 1945-1960; DAM DRAM; DFS
8; DLB 13; IDFW 3, 4; MTCW 1, 2;
MTFW 2005; RGEL 2

Ratushinskaya, Irina 1954- **CLC 54**
See also CA 129; CANR 68; CWW 2

Raven, Simon (Arthur Noel)
1927-2001 **CLC 14**
See also CA 81-84; 197; CANR 86; CN 1,
2, 3, 4, 5, 6; DLB 271

Ravenna, Michael
See Welty, Eudora

Rawley, Callman 1903-2004
See Rakosi, Carl
See also CA 21-24R; 228; CANR 12, 32,
91

Rawlings, Marjorie Kinnan
1896-1953 **TCLC 4**
See also AAYA 20; AMWS 10; ANW;
BPFB 3; BYA 3; CA 104; 137; CANR 74;
CLR 63; DLB 9, 22, 102; DLBD 17;
JRDA; MAICYA 1, 2; MAL 5; MTCW 2;
MTFW 2005; RGAL 4; SATA 100; WCH;
YABC 1; YAW

Ray, Satyajit 1921-1992 **CLC 16, 76**
See also CA 114; 137; DAM MULT

Read, Herbert Edward 1893-1968 **CLC 4**
See also BRW 6; CA 85-88; 25-28R; DLB
20, 149; EWL 3; PAB; RGEL 2

Read, Piers Paul 1941- **CLC 4, 10, 25**
See also CA 21-24R; CANR 38, 86, 150;
CN 2, 3, 4, 5, 6, 7; DLB 14; SATA 21

Reade, Charles 1814-1884 **NCLC 2, 74**
See also DLB 21; RGEL 2

Reade, Hamish
See Gray, Simon (James Holliday)

Reading, Peter 1946- **CLC 47**
See also BRWS 8; CA 103; CANR 46, 96;
CP 5, 6, 7; DLB 40

Reaney, James 1926- **CLC 13**
See also CA 41-44R; CAAS 15; CANR 42;
CD 5, 6; CP 1, 2, 3, 4, 5, 6, 7; DAC;
DAM MST; DLB 68; RGEL 2; SATA 43

Rebreanu, Liviu 1885-1944 **TCLC 28**
See also CA 165; DLB 220; EWL 3

Rechy, John 1934- **CLC 1, 7, 14, 18, 107;
HLC 2**
See also CA 5-8R, 195; CAAE 195; CAAS
4; CANR 6, 32, 64, 152; CN 1, 2, 3, 4, 5,
6, 7; DAM MULT; DLB 122, 278; DLBY
1982; HW 1, 2; INT CANR-6; LLW;
MAL 5; RGAL 4

Rechy, John Francisco
See Rechy, John

Redcam, Tom 1870-1933 **TCLC 25**

Reddin, Keith 1956- **CLC 67**
See also CAD; CD 6

Redgrove, Peter (William)
1932-2003 **CLC 6, 41**
See also BRWS 6; CA 1-4R; 217; CANR 3,
39, 77; CP 1, 2, 3, 4, 5, 6, 7; DLB 40;
TCLE 1:2

Redmon, Anne **CLC 22**
See Nightingale, Anne Redmon
See also DLBY 1986

Reed, Eliot
See Ambler, Eric

Reed, Ishmael (Scott) 1938 . **BLC 3; CLC 2,
3, 5, 6, 13, 32, 60, 174; PC 68**
See also AFAW 1, 2; AMWS 10; BPFB 3;
BW 2, 3; CA 21-24R; CANR 25, 48, 74,
128; CN 1, 2, 3, 4, 5, 6, 7; CP 1, 2, 3, 4,
5, 6, 7; CSW; DA3; DAM MULT; DLB
2, 5, 33, 169, 227; DLBD 8; EWL 3;
LMFS 2; MAL 5; MSW; MTCW 1, 2;
MTFW 2005; PFS 6; RGAL 4; TCWW 2

Reed, John (Silas) 1887-1920 **TCLC 9**
See also CA 106; 195; MAL 5; TUS

Reed, Lou ... **CLC 21**
See Firbank, Louis

Reese, Lizette Woodworth 1856-1935 . **PC 29**
See also CA 180; DLB 54

Reeve, Clara 1729-1807 **NCLC 19**
See also DLB 39; RGEL 2

Reich, Wilhelm 1897-1957 **TCLC 57**
See also CA 199

Reid, Christopher (John) 1949- **CLC 33**
See also CA 140; CANR 89; CP 4, 5, 6, 7;
DLB 40; EWL 3

Reid, Desmond
See Moorcock, Michael

Reid Banks, Lynne 1929-
See Banks, Lynne Reid
See also AAYA 49; CA 1-4R; CANR 6, 22,
38, 87; CLR 24; CN 1, 2, 3, 7; JRDA;
MAICYA 1, 2; SATA 22, 75, 111, 165;
YAW

Reilly, William K.
See Creasey, John

Reiner, Max
See Caldwell, (Janet Miriam) Taylor
(Holland)

Reis, Ricardo
See Pessoa, Fernando (Antonio Nogueira)

Reizenstein, Elmer Leopold
See Rice, Elmer (Leopold)
See also EWL 3

Remarque, Erich Maria 1898-1970 . **CLC 21**
See also AAYA 27; BPFB 3; CA 77-80; 29-
32R; CDWLB 2; DA; DA3; DAB; DAC;
DAM MST, NOV; DLB 56; EWL 3;
EXPN; LAIT 3; MTCW 1, 2; MTFW
2005; NFS 4; RGHL; RGWL 2, 3

Remington, Frederic S(ackrider)
1861-1909 **TCLC 89**
See also CA 108; 169; DLB 12, 186, 188;
SATA 41; TCWW 2

Remizov, A.
See Remizov, Aleksei (Mikhailovich)

Remizov, A. M.
See Remizov, Aleksei (Mikhailovich)

Remizov, Aleksei (Mikhailovich)
1877-1957 **TCLC 27**
See Remizov, Alexey Mikhaylovich
See also CA 125; 133; DLB 295

Remizov, Alexey Mikhaylovich
See Remizov, Aleksei (Mikhailovich)
See also EWL 3

Renan, Joseph Ernest 1823-1892 . **NCLC 26, 145**
See also GFL 1789 to the Present

Renard, Jules(-Pierre) 1864-1910 .. **TCLC 17**
See also CA 117; 202; GFL 1789 to the
Present

Renart, Jean fl. 13th cent. - **CMLC 83**

Renault, Mary **CLC 3, 11, 17**
See Challans, Mary
See also BPFB 3; BYA 2; CN 1, 2, 3;
DLBY 1983; EWL 3; GLL 1; LAIT 1;
RGEL 2; RHW

Rendell, Ruth (Barbara) 1930- .. **CLC 28, 48**
See Vine, Barbara
See also BPFB 3; BRWS 9; CA 109; CANR
32, 52, 74, 127; CN 5, 6, 7; CPW; DAM
POP; DLB 87, 276; INT CANR-32;
MSW; MTCW 1, 2; MTFW 2005

Renoir, Jean 1894-1979 **CLC 20**
See also CA 129; 85-88

Resnais, Alain 1922- **CLC 16**

Revard, Carter 1931- **NNAL**
See also CA 144; CANR 81, 153; PFS 5

Reverdy, Pierre 1889-1960 **CLC 53**
See also CA 97-100; 89-92; DLB 258; EWL
3; GFL 1789 to the Present

Rexroth, Kenneth 1905-1982 **CLC 1, 2, 6, 11, 22, 49, 112; PC 20**
See also BG 1:3; CA 5-8R; 107; CANR 14,
34, 63; CDALB 1941-1968; CP 1, 2, 3;
DAM POET; DLB 16, 48, 165, 212;
DLBY 1982; EWL 3; INT CANR-14;
MAL 5; MTCW 1, 2; MTFW 2005;
RGAL 4

Reyes, Alfonso 1889-1959 **HLCS 2; TCLC 33**
See also CA 131; EWL 3; HW 1; LAW

Reyes y Basoalto, Ricardo Eliecer Neftali
See Neruda, Pablo

Reymont, Wladyslaw (Stanislaw)
1868(?)-1925 **TCLC 5**
See also CA 104; EWL 3

Reynolds, John Hamilton
1794-1852 **NCLC 146**
See also DLB 96

Reynolds, Jonathan 1942- **CLC 6, 38**
See also CA 65-68; CANR 28

Reynolds, Joshua 1723-1792 **LC 15**
See also DLB 104

Reynolds, Michael S(hane)
1937-2000 **CLC 44**
See also CA 65-68; 189; CANR 9, 89, 97

Reznikoff, Charles 1894-1976 **CLC 9**
See also AMWS 14; CA 33-36; 61-64; CAP
2; CP 1, 2; DLB 28, 45; RGHL; WP

Rezzori, Gregor von
See Rezzori d'Arezzo, Gregor von

Rezzori d'Arezzo, Gregor von
1914-1998 **CLC 25**
See also CA 122; 136; 167

Rhine, Richard
See Silverstein, Alvin; Silverstein, Virginia
B(arbara Opshelor)

Rhodes, Eugene Manlove
1869-1934 **TCLC 53**
See also CA 198; DLB 256; TCWW 1, 2

R'hoone, Lord
See Balzac, Honore de

Rhys, Jean 1890-1979 **CLC 2, 4, 6, 14, 19, 51, 124; SSC 21, 76**
See also BRWS 2, CA 25-28R, 85-88,
CANR 35, 62; CDBLB 1945-1960; CD-
WLB 3; CN 1, 2; DLB 36, 117, 162; DNFS 2; EWL 3; LATS 1:1;
MTCW 1, 2; MTFW 2005; NFS 19;
RGEL 2; RGSF 2; RHW; TEA; WWE 1

Ribeiro, Darcy 1922-1997 **CLC 34**
See also CA 33-36R; 156; EWL 3

Ribeiro, Joao Ubaldo (Osorio Pimentel)
1941- **CLC 10, 67**
See also CA 81-84; CWW 2; EWL 3

Ribman, Ronald (Burt) 1932- **CLC 7**
See also CA 21-24R; CAD; CANR 46, 80;
CD 5, 6

Ricci, Nino (Pio) 1959- **CLC 70**
See also CA 137; CANR 130; CCA 1

Rice, Anne 1941- **CLC 41, 128**
See Rampling, Anne
See also AAYA 9, 53; AMWS 7; BEST
89:2; BPFB 3; CA 65-68; CANR 12, 36,
53, 74, 100, 133; CN 6, 7; CPW; CSW;
DA3; DAM POP; DLB 292; GL 3; GLL
2; HGG; MTCW 2; MTFW 2005; SUFW
2; YAW

Rice, Elmer (Leopold) 1892-1967 **CLC 7, 49**
See Reizenstein, Elmer Leopold
See also CA 21-22; 25-28R; CAP 2; DAM
DRAM; DFS 12; DLB 4, 7; IDTP; MAL
5; MTCW 1, 2; RGAL 4

Rice, Tim(othy Miles Bindon)
1944- **CLC 21**
See also CA 103; CANR 46; DFS 7

Rich, Adrienne (Cecile) 1929- ... **CLC 3, 6, 7, 11, 18, 36, 73, 76, 125; PC 5**
See also AAYA 69; AMWR 2; AMWS 1;
CA 9-12R; CANR 20, 53, 74, 128;
CDALBS; CP 1, 2, 3, 4, 5, 6, 7; CSW;
CWP; DA3; DAM POET; DLB 5, 67;
EWL 3; EXPP; FL 1:6; FW; MAL 5;
MAWW; MTCW 1, 2; MTFW 2005;
PAB; PFS 15; RGAL 4; RGHL; WP

Rich, Barbara
See Graves, Robert (von Ranke)

Rich, Robert
See Trumbo, Dalton

Richard, Keith **CLC 17**
See Richards, Keith

Richards, David Adams 1950- **CLC 59**
See also CA 93-96; CANR 60, 110; CN 7;
DAC; DLB 53; TCLE 1:2

Richards, I(vor) A(rmstrong)
1893-1979 **CLC 14, 24**
See also BRWS 2; CA 41-44R; 89-92;
CANR 34, 74; CP 1, 2; DLB 27; EWL 3;
MTCW 2; RGEL 2

Richards, Keith 1943-
See Richard, Keith
See also CA 107; CANR 77

Richardson, Anne
See Roiphe, Anne

Richardson, Dorothy Miller
1873-1957 **TCLC 3**
See also CA 104; 192; DLB 36; EWL 3;
FW; RGEL 2

**Richardson (Robertson), Ethel Florence
Lindesay** 1870-1946
See Richardson, Henry Handel
See also CA 105; 190; DLB 230; RHW

Richardson, Henry Handel **TCLC 4**
See Richardson (Robertson), Ethel Florence
Lindesay
See also DLB 197; EWL 3; RGEL 2; RGSF
2

Richardson, John 1796-1852 **NCLC 55**
See also CCA 1; DAC; DLB 99

Richardson, Samuel 1689-1761 **LC 1, 44; WLC 5**
See also BRW 3; CDBLB 1660-1789; DA;
DAB; DAC; DAM MST, NOV; DLB 39;
RGEL 2; TEA; WLIT 3

Richardson, Willis 1889-1977 **HR 1:3**
See also BW 1; CA 124; DLB 51; SATA 60

Richler, Mordecai 1931-2001 **CLC 3, 5, 9, 13, 18, 46, 70, 185**
See also AITN 1; CA 65-68; 201; CANR
31, 62, 111; CCA 1; CLR 17; CN 1, 2, 3,
4, 5, 7; CWRI 5; DAC; DAM MST, NOV;
DLB 53; EWL 3; MAICYA 1, 2; MTCW
1, 2; MTFW 2005; RGEL 2; RGHL;
SATA 44, 98; SATA-Brief 27; TWA

Richter, Conrad (Michael)
1890-1968 **CLC 30**
See also AAYA 21; BYA 2; CA 5-8R; 25-
28R; CANR 23; DLB 9, 212; LAIT 1;
MAL 5; MTCW 1, 2; MTFW 2005;
RGAL 4; SATA 3; TCWW 1, 2; TUS;
YAW

Ricostranza, Tom
See Ellis, Trey

Riddell, Charlotte 1832-1906 **TCLC 40**
See Riddell, Mrs. J. H.
See also CA 165; DLB 156

Riddell, Mrs. J. H.
See Riddell, Charlotte
See also HGG; SUFW

Ridge, John Rollin 1827-1867 **NCLC 82; NNAL**
See also CA 144; DAM MULT; DLB 175

Ridgeway, Jason
See Marlowe, Stephen

Ridgway, Keith 1965- **CLC 119**
See also CA 172; CANR 144

Riding, Laura **CLC 3, 7**
See Jackson, Laura (Riding)
See also CP 1, 2, 3, 4, 5; RGAL 4

Riefenstahl, Berta Helene Amalia 1902-2003
See Riefenstahl, Leni
See also CA 108; 220

Riefenstahl, Leni **CLC 16, 190**
See Riefenstahl, Berta Helene Amalia

Riffe, Ernest
See Bergman, (Ernst) Ingmar

Riggs, (Rolla) Lynn
1899-1954 **NNAL; TCLC 56**
See also CA 144; DAM MULT; DLB 175

Riis, Jacob A(ugust) 1849-1914 **TCLC 80**
See also CA 113; 168; DLB 23

Riley, James Whitcomb 1849-1916 **PC 48; TCLC 51**
See also CA 118; 137; DAM POET; MAI-
CYA 1, 2; RGAL 4; SATA 17

Riley, Tex
See Creasey, John

Rilke, Rainer Maria 1875-1926 **PC 2; TCLC 1, 6, 19**
See also CA 104; 132; CANR 62, 99; CD-
WLB 2; DA3; DAM POET; DLB 81; EW
9; EWL 3; MTCW 1, 2; MTFW 2005;
PFS 19; RGWL 2, 3; TWA; WP

Rimbaud, (Jean Nicolas) Arthur
1854-1891 ... **NCLC 4, 35, 82; PC 3, 57; WLC 5**
See also DA; DA3; DAB; DAC; DAM
MST, POET; DLB 217; EW 7; GFL 1789
to the Present; LMFS 2; RGWL 2, 3;
TWA; WP

Rinehart, Mary Roberts
1876-1958 **TCLC 52**
See also BPFB 3; CA 108; 166; RGAL 4;
RHW
Ringmaster, The
See Mencken, H(enry) L(ouis)
Ringwood, Gwen(dolyn Margaret) Pharis
1910-1984 **CLC 48**
See also CA 148; 112; DLB 88
Rio, Michel 1945(?)- **CLC 43**
See also CA 201
Rios, Alberto (Alvaro) 1952- **PC 57**
See also AAYA 66; AMWS 4; CA 113;
CANR 34, 79, 137; CP 6, 7; DLB 122;
HW 2; MTFW 2005; PFS 11
Ritsos, Giannes
See Ritsos, Yannis
Ritsos, Yannis 1909-1990 **CLC 6, 13, 31**
See also CA 77-80; 133; CANR 39, 61; EW
12; EWL 3; MTCW 1; RGWL 2, 3
Ritter, Erika 1948(?)- **CLC 52**
See also CD 5, 6; CWD
Rivera, Jose Eustasio 1889-1928 ... **TCLC 35**
See also CA 162; EWL 3; HW 1, 2; LAW
Rivera, Tomas 1935-1984 **HLCS 2**
See also CA 49-52; CANR 32; DLB 82;
HW 1; LLW; RGAL 4; SSFS 15; TCWW
2; WLIT 1
Rivers, Conrad Kent 1933-1968 **CLC 1**
See also BW 1; CA 85-88; DLB 41
Rivers, Elfrida
See Bradley, Marion Zimmer
See also GLL 1
Riverside, John
See Heinlein, Robert A(nson)
Rizal, Jose 1861-1896 **NCLC 27**
Roa Bastos, Augusto 1917-2005 **CLC 45;
HLC 2**
See also CA 131; 238; CWW 2; DAM
MULT; DLB 113; EWL 3; HW 1; LAW;
RGSF 2; WLIT 1
Roa Bastos, Augusto Jose Antonio
See Roa Bastos, Augusto
Robbe-Grillet, Alain 1922- **CLC 1, 2, 4, 6,
8, 10, 14, 43, 128**
See also BPFB 3; CA 9-12R; CANR 33,
65, 115; CWW 2; DLB 83; EW 13; EWL
3; GFL 1789 to the Present; IDFW 3, 4;
MTCW 1, 2; MTFW 2005; RGWL 2, 3;
SSFS 15
Robbins, Harold 1916-1997 **CLC 5**
See also BPFB 3; CA 73-76; 162; CANR
26, 54, 112; DA3; DAM NOV; MTCW 1,
2
Robbins, Thomas Eugene 1936-
See Robbins, Tom
See also CA 81-84; CANR 29, 59, 95, 139;
CN 7; CPW; CSW; DA3; DAM NOV,
POP; MTCW 1, 2; MTFW 2005
Robbins, Tom **CLC 9, 32, 64**
See Robbins, Thomas Eugene
See also BEST 90:3;
BPFB 3; CN 3, 4, 5, 6, 7; DLBY 1980
Robbins, Trina 1938- **CLC 21**
See also AAYA 61; CA 128; CANR 152
Roberts, Charles G(eorge) D(ouglas)
1860-1943 **SSC 91; TCLC 8**
See also CA 105; 188; CLR 33; CWRI 5;
DLB 92; RGEL 2; RGSF 2; SATA 88;
SATA-Brief 29
Roberts, Elizabeth Madox
1886-1941 **TCLC 68**
See also CA 111; 166; CLR 100; CWRI 5;
DLB 9, 54, 102; RGAL 4; RHW; SATA
33; SATA-Brief 27; TCWW 2; WCH
Roberts, Kate 1891-1985 **CLC 15**
See also CA 107; 116; DLB 319

Roberts, Keith (John Kingston)
1935-2000 **CLC 14**
See also BRWS 10; CA 25-28R; CANR 46;
DLB 261; SFW 4
Roberts, Kenneth (Lewis)
1885-1957 **TCLC 23**
See also CA 109; 199; DLB 9; MAL 5;
RGAL 4; RHW
Roberts, Michele (Brigitte) 1949- **CLC 48,
178**
See also CA 115; CANR 58, 120; CN 6, 7;
DLB 231; FW
Robertson, Ellis
See Ellison, Harlan (Jay); Silverberg, Robert
Robertson, Thomas William
1829-1871 **NCLC 35**
See Robertson, Tom
See also DAM DRAM
Robertson, Tom
See Robertson, Thomas William
See also RGEL 2
Robeson, Kenneth
See Dent, Lester
Robinson, Edwin Arlington
1869-1935 **PC 1, 35; TCLC 5, 101**
See also AMW; CA 104; 133; CDALB
1865-1917; DA; DAC; DAM MST,
POET; DLB 54; EWL 3; EXPP; MAL 5;
MTCW 1, 2; MTFW 2005; PAB; PFS 4;
RGAL 4; WP
Robinson, Henry Crabb
1775-1867 **NCLC 15**
See also DLB 107
Robinson, Jill 1936- **CLC 10**
See also CA 102; CANR 120; INT CA 102
Robinson, Kim Stanley 1952- **CLC 34**
See also AAYA 26; CA 126; CANR 113,
139; CN 6, 7; MTFW 2005; SATA 109;
SCFW 2; SFW 4
Robinson, Lloyd
See Silverberg, Robert
Robinson, Marilynne 1944- **CLC 25, 180**
See also AAYA 69; CA 116; CANR 80, 140;
CN 4, 5, 6, 7; DLB 206; MTFW 2005
Robinson, Mary 1758-1800 **NCLC 142**
See also DLB 158; FW
Robinson, Smokey **CLC 21**
See Robinson, William, Jr.
Robinson, William, Jr. 1940-
See Robinson, Smokey
See also CA 116
Robison, Mary 1949- **CLC 42, 98**
See also CA 113; 116; CANR 87; CN 4, 5,
6, 7; DLB 130; INT CA-116; RGSF 2
Roches, Catherine des 1542-1587 **LC 117**
Rochester
See Wilmot, John
See also RGEL 2
Rod, Edouard 1857-1910 **TCLC 52**
Roddenberry, Eugene Wesley 1921-1991
See Roddenberry, Gene
See also CA 110; 135; CANR 37; SATA 45;
SATA-Obit 69
Roddenberry, Gene **CLC 17**
See Roddenberry, Eugene Wesley
See also AAYA 5; SATA-Obit 69
Rodgers, Mary 1931- **CLC 12**
See also BYA 5; CA 49-52; CANR 8, 55,
90; CLR 20; CWRI 5; INT CANR-8;
JRDA; MAICYA 1, 2; SATA 8, 130
Rodgers, W(illiam) R(obert)
1909-1969 **CLC 7**
See also CA 85-88; DLB 20; RGEL 2
Rodman, Eric
See Silverberg, Robert
Rodman, Howard 1920(?)-1985 **CLC 65**
See also CA 118

Rodman, Maia
See Wojciechowska, Maia (Teresa)
Rodo, Jose Enrique 1871(?)-1917 **HLCS 2**
See also CA 178; EWL 3; HW 2; LAW
Rodolph, Utto
See Ouologuem, Yambo
Rodriguez, Claudio 1934-1999 **CLC 10**
See also CA 188; DLB 134
Rodriguez, Richard 1944- **CLC 155; HLC
2**
See also AMWS 14; CA 110; CANR 66,
116; DAM MULT; DLB 82, 256; HW 1,
2; LAIT 5; LLW; MTFW 2005; NCFS 3;
WLIT 1
Roelvaag, O(le) E(dvart) 1876-1931
See Rolvaag, O(le) E(dvart)
See also CA 117; 171
Roethke, Theodore (Huebner)
1908-1963 **CLC 1, 3, 8, 11, 19, 46,
101; PC 15**
See also AMW; CA 81-84; CABS 2;
CDALB 1941-1968; DA3; DAM POET;
DLB 5, 206; EWL 3; EXPP; MAL 5;
MTCW 1, 2; PAB; PFS 3; RGAL 4; WP
Rogers, Carl R(ansom)
1902-1987 **TCLC 125**
See also CA 1-4R; 121; CANR 1, 18;
MTCW 1
Rogers, Samuel 1763-1855 **NCLC 69**
See also DLB 93; RGEL 2
Rogers, Thomas Hunton 1927- **CLC 57**
See also CA 89-92; INT CA-89-92
Rogers, Will(iam Penn Adair)
1879-1935 **NNAL; TCLC 8, 71**
See also CA 105; 144; DA3; DAM MULT;
DLB 11; MTCW 2
Rogin, Gilbert 1929- **CLC 18**
See also CA 65-68; CANR 15
Rohan, Koda
See Koda Shigeyuki
Rohlfs, Anna Katharine Green
See Green, Anna Katharine
Rohmer, Eric **CLC 16**
See Scherer, Jean-Marie Maurice
Rohmer, Sax **TCLC 28**
See Ward, Arthur Henry Sarsfield
See also DLB 70; MSW; SUFW
Roiphe, Anne 1935- **CLC 3, 9**
See also CA 89-92; CANR 45, 73, 138;
DLBY 1980; INT CA-89-92
Roiphe, Anne Richardson
See Roiphe, Anne
Rojas, Fernando de 1475-1541 ... **HLCS 1, 2;
LC 23**
See also DLB 286; RGWL 2, 3
Rojas, Gonzalo 1917- **HLCS 2**
See also CA 178; HW 2; LAWS 1
Roland (de la Platiere), Marie-Jeanne
1754-1793 **LC 98**
See also DLB 314
**Rolfe, Frederick (William Serafino Austin
Lewis Mary)** 1860-1913 **TCLC 12**
See Al Siddik
See also CA 107; 210; DLB 34, 156; RGEL
2
Rolland, Romain 1866-1944 **TCLC 23**
See also CA 118; 197; DLB 65, 284; EWL
3; GFL 1789 to the Present; RGWL 2, 3
Rolle, Richard c. 1300-c. 1349 **CMLC 21**
See also DLB 146; LMFS 1; RGEL 2
Rolvaag, O(le) E(dvart) **TCLC 17**
See Roelvaag, O(le) E(dvart)
See also DLB 9, 212; MAL 5; NFS 5;
RGAL 4
Romain Arnaud, Saint
See Aragon, Louis

Romains, Jules 1885-1972 **CLC 7**
See also CA 85-88; CANR 34; DLB 65, 321; EWL 3; GFL 1789 to the Present; MTCW 1

Romero, Jose Ruben 1890-1952 **TCLC 14**
See also CA 114; 131; EWL 3; HW 1; LAW

Ronsard, Pierre de 1524-1585 . **LC 6, 54; PC 11**
See also EW 2; GFL Beginnings to 1789; RGWL 2, 3; TWA

Rooke, Leon 1934- **CLC 25, 34**
See also CA 25-28R; CANR 23, 53; CCA 1; CPW; DAM POP

Roosevelt, Franklin Delano
1882-1945 **TCLC 93**
See also CA 116; 173; LAIT 3

Roosevelt, Theodore 1858-1919 **TCLC 69**
See also CA 115; 170; DLB 47, 186, 275

Roper, William 1498-1578 **LC 10**

Roquelaure, A. N.
See Rice, Anne

Rosa, Joao Guimaraes 1908-1967 ... **CLC 23; HLCS 1**
See Guimaraes Rosa, Joao
See also CA 89-92; DLB 113, 307; EWL 3; WLIT 1

Rose, Wendy 1948- . **CLC 85; NNAL; PC 13**
See also CA 53-56; CANR 5, 51; CWP; DAM MULT; DLB 175; PFS 13; RGAL 4; SATA 12

Rosen, R. D.
See Rosen, Richard (Dean)

Rosen, Richard (Dean) 1949- **CLC 39**
See also CA 77-80; CANR 62, 120; CMW 4; INT CANR-30

Rosenberg, Isaac 1890-1918 **TCLC 12**
See also BRW 6; CA 107; 188; DLB 20, 216; EWL 3; PAB; RGEL 2

Rosenblatt, Joe **CLC 15**
See Rosenblatt, Joseph
See also CP 3, 4, 5, 6, 7

Rosenblatt, Joseph 1933-
See Rosenblatt, Joe
See also CA 89-92; CP 1, 2; INT CA-89-92

Rosenfeld, Samuel
See Tzara, Tristan

Rosenstock, Sami
See Tzara, Tristan

Rosenstock, Samuel
See Tzara, Tristan

Rosenthal, M(acha) L(ouis)
1917-1996 **CLC 28**
See also CA 1-4R; 152; CAAS 6; CANR 4, 51; CP 1, 2, 3, 4, 5, 6; DLB 5; SATA 59

Ross, Barnaby
See Dannay, Frederic; Lee, Manfred B.

Ross, Bernard L.
See Follett, Ken(neth Martin)

Ross, J. H.
See Lawrence, T(homas) E(dward)

Ross, John Hume
See Lawrence, T(homas) E(dward)

Ross, Martin 1862-1915
See Martin, Violet Florence
See also DLB 135; GLL 2; RGEL 2; RGSF 2

Ross, (James) Sinclair 1908-1996 ... **CLC 13; SSC 24**
See also CA 73-76; CANR 81; CN 1, 2, 3, 4, 5, 6; DAC; DAM MST; DLB 88; RGEL 2; RGSF 2; TCWW 1, 2

Rossetti, Christina 1830-1894 ... **NCLC 2, 50, 66; PC 7; WLC 5**
See also AAYA 51; BRW 5; BYA 4; DA; DA3; DAB; DAC; DAM MST, POET; DLB 35, 163, 240; EXPP; FL 1:3; LATS 1:1; MAICYA 1; PFS 10, 14; RGEL 2; SATA 20; TEA; WCH

Rossetti, Christina Georgina
See Rossetti, Christina

Rossetti, Dante Gabriel 1828-1882 . **NCLC 4, 77; PC 44; WLC 5**
See also AAYA 51; BRW 5; CDBLB 1832-1890; DA; DAB; DAC; DAM MST, POET; DLB 35; EXPP; RGEL 2; TEA

Rossi, Cristina Peri
See Peri Rossi, Cristina

Rossi, Jean-Baptiste 1931-2003
See Japrisot, Sebastien
See also CA 201; 215

Rossner, Judith 1935-2005 **CLC 6, 9, 29**
See also AITN 2; BEST 90:3; BPFB 3; CA 17-20R; 242; CANR 18, 51, 73; CN 4, 5, 6, 7; DLB 6; INT CANR-18; MAL 5; MTCW 1, 2; MTFW 2005

Rossner, Judith Perelman
See Rossner, Judith

Rostand, Edmond (Eugene Alexis)
1868-1918 **DC 10; TCLC 6, 37**
See also CA 104; 126; DA; DA3; DAB; DAC; DAM DRAM, MST; DFS 1; DLB 192; LAIT 1; MTCW 1; RGWL 2, 3; TWA

Roth, Henry 1906-1995 **CLC 2, 6, 11, 104**
See also AMWS 9; CA 11-12; 149; CANR 38, 63; CAP 1; CN 1, 2, 3, 4, 5, 6; DA3; DLB 28; EWL 3; MAL 5; MTCW 1, 2; MTFW 2005; RGAL 4

Roth, (Moses) Joseph 1894-1939 ... **TCLC 33**
See also CA 160; DLB 85; EWL 3; RGWL 2, 3

Roth, Philip 1933- ... **CLC 1, 2, 3, 4, 6, 9, 15, 22, 31, 47, 66, 86, 119, 201; SSC 26; WLC 5**
See also AAYA 67; AMWR 2; AMWS 3; BEST 90:3; BPFB 3; CA 1-4R; CANR 1, 22, 36, 55, 89, 132; CDALB 1968-1988; CN 3, 4, 5, 6, 7; CPW 1; DA; DA3; DAB; DAC; DAM MST, NOV, POP; DLB 2, 28, 173; DLBY 1982; EWL 3; MAL 5; MTCW 1, 2; MTFW 2005; RGAL 4; RGHL; RGSF 2; SSFS 12, 18; TUS

Roth, Philip Milton
See Roth, Philip

Rothenberg, Jerome 1931- **CLC 6, 57**
See also CA 45-48; CANR 1, 106; CP 1, 2, 3, 4, 5, 6, 7; DLB 5, 193

Rotter, Pat ed. **CLC 65**

Roumain, Jacques (Jean Baptiste)
1907-1944 **BLC 3; TCLC 19**
See also BW 1; CA 117; 125; DAM MULT; EWL 3

Rourke, Constance Mayfield
1885-1941 **TCLC 12**
See also CA 107; 200; MAL 5; YABC 1

Rousseau, Jean-Baptiste 1671-1741 **LC 9**

Rousseau, Jean-Jacques 1712-1778 **LC 14, 36, 122; WLC 5**
See also DA; DA3; DAB; DAC; DAM MST; DLB 314; EW 4; GFL Beginnings to 1789; LMFS 1; RGWL 2, 3; TWA

Roussel, Raymond 1877-1933 **TCLC 20**
See also CA 117; 201; EWL 3; GFL 1789 to the Present

Rovit, Earl (Herbert) 1927- **CLC 7**
See also CA 5-8R; CANR 12

Rowe, Elizabeth Singer 1674-1737 **LC 44**
See also DLB 39, 95

Rowe, Nicholas 1674-1718 **LC 8**
See also DLB 84; RGEL 2

Rowlandson, Mary 1637(?)-1678 **LC 66**
See also DLB 24, 200; RGAL 4

Rowley, Ames Dorrance
See Lovecraft, H. P.

Rowley, William 1585(?)-1626 ... **LC 100, 123**
See also DFS 22; DLB 58; RGEL 2

Rowling, J. K. 1966- **CLC 137, 217**
See also AAYA 34; BYA 11, 13, 14; CA 173; CANR 128; CLR 66, 80, 112; MAICYA 2; MTFW 2005; SATA 109; SUFW 2

Rowling, Joanne Kathleen
See Rowling, J. K.

Rowson, Susanna Haswell
1762(?)-1824 **NCLC 5, 69**
See also AMWS 15; DLB 37, 200; RGAL 4

Roy, Arundhati 1960(?)- **CLC 109, 210**
See also CA 163; CANR 90, 126; CN 7; DLB 323, 326; DLBY 1997; EWL 3; LATS 1:2; MTFW 2005; NFS 22; WWE 1

Roy, Gabrielle 1909-1983 **CLC 10, 14**
See also CA 53-56; 110; CANR 5, 61; CCA 1; DAB; DAC; DAM MST; DLB 68; EWL 3; MTCW 1; RGWL 2, 3; SATA 104; TCLE 1:2

Royko, Mike 1932-1997 **CLC 109**
See also CA 89-92; 157; CANR 26, 111; CPW

Rozanov, Vasilii Vasil'evich
See Rozanov, Vassili
See also DLB 295

Rozanov, Vasily Vasilyevich
See Rozanov, Vassili
See also EWL 3

Rozanov, Vassili 1856-1919 **TCLC 104**
See Rozanov, Vasilii Vasil'evich; Rozanov, Vasily Vasilyevich

Rozewicz, Tadeusz 1921- **CLC 9, 23, 139**
See also CA 108; CANR 36, 66; CWW 2; DA3; DAM POET; DLB 232; EWL 3; MTCW 1, 2; MTFW 2005; RGHL; RGWL 3

Ruark, Gibbons 1941- **CLC 3**
See also CA 33-36R; CAAS 23; CANR 14, 31, 57; DLB 120

Rubens, Bernice (Ruth) 1923-2004 . **CLC 19, 31**
See also CA 25-28R; 232; CANR 33, 65, 128; CN 1, 2, 3, 4, 5, 6, 7; DLB 14, 207, 326; MTCW 1

Rubin, Harold
See Robbins, Harold

Rudkin, (James) David 1936- **CLC 14**
See also CA 89-92; CBD; CD 5, 6; DLB 13

Rudnik, Raphael 1933- **CLC 7**
See also CA 29-32R

Ruffian, M.
See Hasek, Jaroslav (Matej Frantisek)

Ruiz, Jose Martinez **CLC 11**
See Martinez Ruiz, Jose

Ruiz, Juan c. 1283-c. 1350 **CMLC 66**

Rukeyser, Muriel 1913-1980 . **CLC 6, 10, 15, 27; PC 12**
See also AMWS 6; CA 5-8R; 93-96; CANR 26, 60; CP 1, 2, 3; DA3; DAM POET; DLB 48; EWL 3; FW; GLL 2; MAL 5; MTCW 1, 2; PFS 10; RGAL 4; SATA-Obit 22

Rule, Jane (Vance) 1931- **CLC 27**
See also CA 25-28R; CAAS 18; CANR 12, 87; CN 4, 5, 6, 7; DLB 60; FW

Rulfo, Juan 1918-1986 .. **CLC 8, 80; HLC 2; SSC 25**
See also CA 85-88; 118; CANR 26; CDWLB 3; DAM MULT; DLB 113; EWL 3; HW 1, 2; LAW; MTCW 1, 2; RGSF 2; RGWL 2, 3; WLIT 1

Rumi, Jalal al-Din 1207-1273 **CMLC 20; PC 45**
See also AAYA 64; RGWL 2, 3; WLIT 6; WP

Runeberg, Johan 1804-1877 **NCLC 41**

Runyon, (Alfred) Damon
1884(?)-1946 TCLC 10
See also CA 107; 165; DLB 11, 86, 171;
MAL 5; MTCW 2; RGAL 4
Rush, Norman 1933- CLC 44
See also CA 121; 126; CANR 130; INT CA-126
Rushdie, (Ahmed) Salman 1947- CLC 23,
31, 55, 100, 191; SSC 83; WLCS
See also AAYA 65; BEST 89:3; BPFB 3;
BRWS 4; CA 108; 111; CANR 33, 56,
108, 133; CN 4, 5, 6, 7; CPW 1; DA3;
DAB; DAC; DAM MST, NOV, POP;
DLB 194, 323, 326; EWL 3; FANT; INT
CA-111; LATS 1:2; LMFS 2; MTCW 1,
2; MTFW 2005; NFS 22, 23; RGEL 2;
RGSF 2; TEA; WLIT 4
Rushforth, Peter 1945-2005 CLC 19
See also CA 101; 243
Rushforth, Peter Scott
See Rushforth, Peter
Ruskin, John 1819-1900 TCLC 63
See also BRW 5; BYA 5; CA 114; 129; CD-
BLB 1832-1890; DLB 55, 163, 190;
RGEL 2; SATA 24; TEA; WCH
Russ, Joanna 1937- CLC 15
See also BPFB 3; CA 25-28; CANR 11, 31,
65; CN 4, 5, 6, 7; DLB 8; FW; GLL 1;
MTCW 1; SCFW 1, 2; SFW 4
Russ, Richard Patrick
See O'Brian, Patrick
Russell, George William 1867-1935
See A.E.; Baker, Jean H.
See also BRWS 8; CA 104; 153; CDBLB
1890-1914; DAM POET; EWL 3; RGEL
2
Russell, Jeffrey Burton 1934- CLC 70
See also CA 25-28R; CANR 11, 28, 52
Russell, (Henry) Ken(neth Alfred)
1927- CLC 16
See also CA 105
Russell, William Martin 1947-
See Russell, Willy
See also CA 164; CANR 107
Russell, Willy CLC 60
See Russell, William Martin
See also CBD; CD 5, 6; DLB 233
Russo, Richard 1949- CLC 181
See also AMWS 12; CA 127; 133; CANR
87, 114
Rutherford, Mark TCLC 25
See White, William Hale
See also DLB 18; RGEL 2
Ruysbroeck, Jan van 1293-1381 ... CMLC 85
Ruyslinck, Ward CLC 14
See Belser, Reimond Karel Maria de
Ryan, Cornelius (John) 1920-1974 CLC 7
See also CA 69-72; 53-56; CANR 38
Ryan, Michael 1946- CLC 65
See also CA 49-52; CANR 109; DLBY
1982
Ryan, Tim
See Dent, Lester
Rybakov, Anatoli (Naumovich)
1911-1998 CLC 23, 53
See Rybakov, Anatolii (Naumovich)
See also CA 126; 135; 172; SATA 79;
SATA-Obit 108
Rybakov, Anatolii (Naumovich)
See Rybakov, Anatoli (Naumovich)
See also DLB 302; RGHL
Ryder, Jonathan
See Ludlum, Robert
Ryga, George 1932-1987 CLC 14
See also CA 101; 124; CANR 43, 90; CCA
1; DAC; DAM MST; DLB 60
S. H.
See Hartmann, Sadakichi

S. S.
See Sassoon, Siegfried (Lorraine)
Sa'adawi, al- Nawal
See El Saadawi, Nawal
See also AFW; EWL 3
Saadawi, Nawal El
See El Saadawi, Nawal
See also WLIT 2
Saba, Umberto 1883-1957 TCLC 33
See also CA 144; CANR 79; DLB 114;
EWL 3; RGWL 2, 3
Sabatini, Rafael 1875-1950 TCLC 47
See also BPFB 3; CA 162; RHW
Sabato, Ernesto (R.) 1911- CLC 10, 23;
HLC 2
See also CA 97-100; CANR 32, 65; CD-
WLB 3; CWW 2; DAM MULT; DLB 145;
EWL 3; HW 1, 2; LAW; MTCW 1, 2;
MTFW 2005
Sa-Carneiro, Mario de 1890-1916 . TCLC 83
See also DLB 287; EWL 3
Sacastru, Martin
See Bioy Casares, Adolfo
See also CWW 2
Sacher-Masoch, Leopold von
1836(?)-1895 NCLC 31
Sachs, Hans 1494-1576 LC 95
See also CDWLB 2; DLB 179; RGWL 2, 3
Sachs, Marilyn 1927- CLC 35
See also AAYA 2; BYA 6; CA 17-20R;
CANR 13, 47, 150; CLR 2; JRDA; MAI-
CYA 1, 2; SAAS 2; SATA 3, 68, 164;
SATA-Essay 110; WYA; YAW
Sachs, Marilyn Stickle
See Sachs, Marilyn
Sachs, Nelly 1891-1970 CLC 14, 98
See also CA 17-18; 25-28R; CANR 87;
CAP 2; EWL 3; MTCW 2; MTFW 2005;
PFS 20; RGHL; RGWL 2, 3
Sackler, Howard (Oliver)
1929-1982 CLC 14
See also CA 61-64; 108; CAD; CANR 30;
DFS 15; DLB 7
Sacks, Oliver 1933- CLC 67, 202
See also CA 53-56; CANR 28, 50, 76, 146;
CPW; DA3; INT CANR-28; MTCW 1, 2;
MTFW 2005
Sacks, Oliver Wolf
See Sacks, Oliver
Sackville, Thomas 1536-1608 LC 98
See also DAM DRAM; DLB 62, 132;
RGEL 2
Sadakichi
See Hartmann, Sadakichi
Sa'dawi, Nawal al-
See El Saadawi, Nawal
See also CWW 2
Sade, Donatien Alphonse Francois
1740-1814 NCLC 3, 47
See also DLB 314; EW 4; GFL Beginnings
to 1789; RGWL 2, 3
Sade, Marquis de
See Sade, Donatien Alphonse Francois
Sadoff, Ira 1945- CLC 9
See also CA 53-56; CANR 5, 21, 109; DLB
120
Saetone
See Camus, Albert
Safire, William 1929- CLC 10
See also CA 17-20R; CANR 31, 54, 91, 148
Sagan, Carl (Edward) 1934-1996 CLC 30,
112
See also AAYA 2, 62; CA 25-28R; 155;
CANR 11, 36, 74; CPW; DA3; MTCW 1,
2; MTFW 2005; SATA 58; SATA-Obit 94
Sagan, Francoise CLC 3, 6, 9, 17, 36
See Quoirez, Francoise
See also CWW 2; DLB 83; EWL 3; GFL
1789 to the Present; MTCW 2

Sahgal, Nayantara (Pandit) 1927- CLC 41
See also CA 9-12R; CANR 11, 88; CN 1,
2, 3, 4, 5, 6, 7; DLB 323
Said, Edward W. 1935-2003 CLC 123
See also CA 21-24R; 220; CANR 45, 74,
107, 131; DLB 67; MTCW 2; MTFW
2005
Saint, H(arry) F. 1941- CLC 50
See also CA 127
St. Aubin de Teran, Lisa 1953-
See Teran, Lisa St. Aubin de
See also CA 118; 126; CN 6, 7; INT CA-
126
Saint Birgitta of Sweden c.
1303-1373 CMLC 24
Sainte-Beuve, Charles Augustin
1804-1869 NCLC 5
See also DLB 217; EW 6; GFL 1789 to the
Present
Saint-Exupery, Antoine de
1900-1944 TCLC 2, 56, 169; WLC
See also AAYA 63; BPFB 3; BYA 3; CA
108; 132; CLR 10; DA3; DAM NOV;
DLB 72; EW 12; EWL 3; GFL 1789 to
the Present; LAIT 3; MAICYA 1, 2;
MTCW 1, 2; MTFW 2005; RGWL 2, 3;
SATA 20; TWA
Saint-Exupery, Antoine Jean Baptiste Marie
Roger de
See Saint-Exupery, Antoine de
St. John, David
See Hunt, E(verette) Howard, (Jr.)
St. John, J. Hector
See Crevecoeur, Michel Guillaume Jean de
Saint-John Perse
See Leger, (Marie-Rene Auguste) Alexis
Saint-Leger
See also EW 10; EWL 3; GFL 1789 to the
Present; RGWL 2
Saintsbury, George (Edward Bateman)
1845-1933 TCLC 31
See also CA 160; DLB 57, 149
Sait Faik .. TCLC 23
See Abasiyanik, Sait Faik
Saki SSC 12; TCLC 3; WLC 5
See Munro, H(ector) H(ugh)
See also BRWS 6; BYA 11; LAIT 2; RGEL
2; SSFS 1; SUFW
Sala, George Augustus 1828-1895 . NCLC 46
Saladin 1138-1193 CMLC 38
Salama, Hannu 1936- CLC 18
See also CA 244; EWL 3
Salamanca, J(ack) R(ichard) 1922- .. CLC 4,
15
See also CA 25-28R, 193; CAAE 193
Salas, Floyd Francis 1931- HLC 2
See also CA 119; CAAS 27; CANR 44, 75,
93; DAM MULT; DLB 82; HW 1, 2;
MTCW 2; MTFW 2005
Sale, J. Kirkpatrick
See Sale, Kirkpatrick
Sale, John Kirkpatrick
See Sale, Kirkpatrick
Sale, Kirkpatrick 1937- CLC 68
See also CA 13-16R; CANR 10, 147
Salinas, Luis Omar 1937- ... CLC 90; HLC 2
See also AMWS 13; CA 131; CANR 81,
153; DAM MULT; DLB 82; HW 1, 2
Salinas (y Serrano), Pedro
1891(?)-1951 TCLC 17
See also CA 117; DLB 134; EWL 3
Salinger, J(erome) D(avid) 1919- .. CLC 1, 3,
8, 12, 55, 56, 138; SSC 2, 28, 65; WLC
5
See also AAYA 2, 36; AMW; AMWC 1;
BPFB 3; CA 5-8R; CANR 39, 129;
CDALB 1941-1968; CLR 18; CN 1, 2, 3,
4, 5, 6, 7; CPW 1; DA; DA3; DAB; DAC;
DAM MST, NOV, POP; DLB 2, 102, 173;

Romains, Jules 1885-1972 **CLC 7**
See also CA 85-88; CANR 34; DLB 65, 321; EWL 3; GFL 1789 to the Present; MTCW 1

Romero, Jose Ruben 1890-1952 **TCLC 14**
See also CA 114; 131; EWL 3; HW 1; LAW

Ronsard, Pierre de 1524-1585 . **LC 6, 54; PC 11**
See also EW 2; GFL Beginnings to 1789; RGWL 2, 3; TWA

Rooke, Leon 1934- **CLC 25, 34**
See also CA 25-28R; CANR 23, 53; CCA 1; CPW; DAM POP

Roosevelt, Franklin Delano 1882-1945 **TCLC 93**
See also CA 116; 173; LAIT 3

Roosevelt, Theodore 1858-1919 **TCLC 69**
See also CA 115; 170; DLB 47, 186, 275

Roper, William 1498-1578 **LC 10**

Roquelaure, A. N.
See Rice, Anne

Rosa, Joao Guimaraes 1908-1967 ... **CLC 23; HLCS 1**
See Guimaraes Rosa, Joao
See also CA 89-92; DLB 113, 307; EWL 3; WLIT 1

Rose, Wendy 1948- . **CLC 85; NNAL; PC 13**
See also CA 53-56; CANR 5, 51; CWP; DAM MULT; DLB 175; PFS 13; RGAL 4; SATA 12

Rosen, R. D.
See Rosen, Richard (Dean)

Rosen, Richard (Dean) 1949- **CLC 39**
See also CA 77-80; CANR 62, 120; CMW 4; INT CANR-30

Rosenberg, Isaac 1890-1918 **TCLC 12**
See also BRW 6; CA 107; 188; DLB 20, 216; EWL 3; PAB; RGEL 2

Rosenblatt, Joe **CLC 15**
See Rosenblatt, Joseph
See also CP 3, 4, 5, 6, 7

Rosenblatt, Joseph 1933-
See Rosenblatt, Joe
See also CA 89-92; CP 1, 2; INT CA-89-92

Rosenfeld, Samuel
See Tzara, Tristan

Rosenstock, Sami
See Tzara, Tristan

Rosenstock, Samuel
See Tzara, Tristan

Rosenthal, M(acha) L(ouis) 1917-1996 **CLC 28**
See also CA 1-4R; 152; CAAS 6; CANR 4, 51; CP 1, 2, 3, 4, 5, 6; DLB 5; SATA 59

Ross, Barnaby
See Dannay, Frederic; Lee, Manfred B.

Ross, Bernard L.
See Follett, Ken(neth Martin)

Ross, J. H.
See Lawrence, T(homas) E(dward)

Ross, John Hume
See Lawrence, T(homas) E(dward)

Ross, Martin 1862-1915
See Martin, Violet Florence
See also DLB 135; GLL 2; RGEL 2; RGSF 2

Ross, (James) Sinclair 1908-1996 ... **CLC 13; SSC 24**
See also CA 73-76; CANR 81; CN 1, 2, 3, 4, 5, 6; DAC; DAM MST; DLB 88; RGEL 2; RGSF 2; TCWW 1, 2

Rossetti, Christina 1830-1894 ... **NCLC 2, 50, 66; PC 7; WLC 5**
See also AAYA 51; BRW 5; BYA 4; DA; DA3; DAB; DAC; DAM MST, POET; DLB 35, 163, 240; EXPP; FL 1:3; LATS 1:1; MAICYA 1, 2; PFS 10, 14; RGEL 2; SATA 20; TEA; WCH

Rossetti, Christina Georgina
See Rossetti, Christina

Rossetti, Dante Gabriel 1828-1882 . **NCLC 4, 77; PC 44; WLC 5**
See also AAYA 51; BRW 5; CDBLB 1832-1890; DA; DAB; DAC; DAM MST, POET; DLB 35; EXPP; RGEL 2; TEA

Rossi, Cristina Peri
See Peri Rossi, Cristina

Rossi, Jean-Baptiste 1931-2003
See Japrisot, Sebastien
See also CA 201; 215

Rossner, Judith 1935-2005 **CLC 6, 9, 29**
See also AITN 2; BEST 90:3; BPFB 3; CA 17-20R; 242; CANR 18, 51, 73; CN 4, 5, 6, 7; DLB 6; INT CANR-18; MAL 5; MTCW 1, 2; MTFW 2005

Rossner, Judith Perelman
See Rossner, Judith

Rostand, Edmond (Eugene Alexis) 1868-1918 **DC 10; TCLC 6, 37**
See also CA 104; 126; DA; DA3; DAB; DAC; DAM DRAM, MST; DFS 1; DLB 192; LAIT 1; MTCW 1; RGWL 2, 3; TWA

Roth, Henry 1906-1995 **CLC 2, 6, 11, 104**
See also AMWS 9; CA 11-12; 149; CANR 38, 63; CAP 1; CN 1, 2, 3, 4, 5, 6; DA3; DLB 28; EWL 3; MAL 5; MTCW 1, 2; MTFW 2005; RGAL 4

Roth, (Moses) Joseph 1894-1939 ... **TCLC 33**
See also CA 160; DLB 85; EWL 3; RGWL 2, 3

Roth, Philip 1933- ... **CLC 1, 2, 3, 4, 6, 9, 15, 22, 31, 47, 66, 86, 119, 201; SSC 26; WLC 5**
See also AAYA 67; AMWR 2; AMWS 3; BEST 90:3; BPFB 3; CA 1-4R; CANR 1, 22, 36, 55, 89, 132; CDALB 1968-1988; CN 3, 4, 5, 6, 7; CPW 1; DA; DA3; DAB; DAC; DAM MST, NOV, POP; DLB 2, 28, 173; DLBY 1982; EWL 3; MAL 5; MTCW 1, 2; MTFW 2005; RGAL 4; RGHL; RGSF 2; SSFS 12, 18; TUS

Roth, Philip Milton
See Roth, Philip

Rothenberg, Jerome 1931- **CLC 6, 57**
See also CA 45-48; CANR 1, 106; CP 1, 2, 3, 4, 5, 6, 7; DLB 5, 193

Rotter, Pat ed. **CLC 65**

Roumain, Jacques (Jean Baptiste) 1907-1944 **BLC 3; TCLC 19**
See also BW 1; CA 117; 125; DAM MULT; EWL 3

Rourke, Constance Mayfield 1885-1941 **TCLC 12**
See also CA 107; 200; MAL 5; YABC 1

Rousseau, Jean-Baptiste 1671-1741 **LC 9**

Rousseau, Jean-Jacques 1712-1778 **LC 14, 36, 122; WLC 5**
See also DA; DA3; DAB; DAC; DAM MST; DLB 314; EW 4; GFL Beginnings to 1789; LMFS 1; RGWL 2, 3; TWA

Roussel, Raymond 1877-1933 **TCLC 20**
See also CA 117; 201; EWL 3; GFL 1789 to the Present

Rovit, Earl (Herbert) 1927- **CLC 7**
See also CA 5-8R; CANR 12

Rowe, Elizabeth Singer 1674-1737 **LC 44**
See also DLB 39, 95

Rowe, Nicholas 1674-1718 **LC 8**
See also DLB 84; RGEL 2

Rowlandson, Mary 1637(?)-1678 **LC 66**
See also DLB 24, 200; RGAL 4

Rowley, Ames Dorrance
See Lovecraft, H. P.

Rowley, William 1585(?)-1626 ... **LC 100, 123**
See also DFS 22; DLB 58; RGEL 2

Rowling, J. K. 1966- **CLC 137, 217**
See also AAYA 34; BYA 11, 13, 14; CA 173; CANR 128; CLR 66, 80, 112; MAICYA 2; MTFW 2005; SATA 109; SUFW 2

Rowling, Joanne Kathleen
See Rowling, J. K.

Rowson, Susanna Haswell 1762(?)-1824 **NCLC 5, 69**
See also AMWS 15; DLB 37, 200; RGAL 4

Roy, Arundhati 1960(?)- **CLC 109, 210**
See also CA 163; CANR 90, 126; CN 7; DLB 323, 326; DLBY 1997; EWL 3; LATS 1:2; MTFW 2005; NFS 22; WWE 1

Roy, Gabrielle 1909-1983 **CLC 10, 14**
See also CA 53-56; 110; CANR 5, 61; CCA 1; DAB; DAC; DAM MST; DLB 68; EWL 3; MTCW 1; RGWL 2, 3; SATA 104; TCLE 1:2

Royko, Mike 1932-1997 **CLC 109**
See also CA 89-92; 157; CANR 26, 111; CPW

Rozanov, Vasilii Vasil'evich
See Rozanov, Vassili
See also DLB 295

Rozanov, Vasily Vasilyevich
See Rozanov, Vassili
See also EWL 3

Rozanov, Vassili 1856-1919 **TCLC 104**
See Rozanov, Vasilii Vasil'evich; Rozanov, Vasily Vasilyevich

Rozewicz, Tadeusz 1921- **CLC 9, 23, 139**
See also CA 108; CANR 36, 66; CWW 2; DA3; DAM POET; DLB 232; EWL 3; MTCW 1, 2; MTFW 2005; RGHL; RGWL 3

Ruark, Gibbons 1941- **CLC 3**
See also CA 33-36R; CAAS 23; CANR 14, 31, 57; DLB 120

Rubens, Bernice (Ruth) 1923-2004 . **CLC 19, 31**
See also CA 25-28R; 232; CANR 33, 65, 128; CN 1, 2, 3, 4, 5, 6, 7; DLB 14, 207, 326; MTCW 1

Rubin, Harold
See Robbins, Harold

Rudkin, (James) David 1936- **CLC 14**
See also CA 89-92; CBD; CD 5, 6; DLB 13

Rudnik, Raphael 1933- **CLC 7**
See also CA 29-32R

Ruffian, M.
See Hasek, Jaroslav (Matej Frantisek)

Ruiz, Jose Martinez **CLC 11**
See Martinez Ruiz, Jose

Ruiz, Juan c. 1283-c. 1350 **CMLC 66**

Rukeyser, Muriel 1913-1980 . **CLC 6, 10, 15, 27; PC 12**
See also AMWS 6; CA 5-8R; 93-96; CANR 26, 60; CP 1, 2, 3; DA3; DAM POET; DLB 48; EWL 3; FW; GLL 2; MAL 5; MTCW 1, 2; PFS 10; RGAL 4; SATA-Obit 22

Rule, Jane (Vance) 1931- **CLC 27**
See also CA 25-28R; CAAS 18; CANR 12, 87; CN 4, 5, 6, 7; DLB 60; FW

Rulfo, Juan 1918-1986 .. **CLC 8, 80; HLC 2; SSC 25**
See also CA 85-88; 118; CANR 26; CD-WLB 3; DAM MULT; DLB 113; EWL 3; HW 1, 2; LAW; MTCW 1, 2; RGSF 2; RGWL 2, 3; WLIT 1

Rumi, Jalal al-Din 1207-1273 **CMLC 20; PC 45**
See also AAYA 64; RGWL 2, 3; WLIT 6; WP

Runeberg, Johan 1804-1877 **NCLC 41**

Runyon, (Alfred) Damon
 1884(?)-1946 **TCLC 10**
 See also CA 107; 165; DLB 11, 86, 171;
 MAL 5; MTCW 2; RGAL 4
Rush, Norman 1933- **CLC 44**
 See also CA 121; 126; CANR 130; INT CA-
 126
Rushdie, (Ahmed) Salman 1947- **CLC 23,**
 31, 55, 100, 191; SSC 83; WLCS
 See also AAYA 65; BEST 89:3; BPFB 3;
 BRWS 4; CA 108; 111; CANR 33, 56,
 108, 133; CN 4, 5, 6, 7; CPW 1; DA3;
 DAB; DAC; DAM MST, NOV, POP;
 DLB 194, 323, 326; EWL 3; FANT; INT
 CA-111; LATS 1:2; LMFS 2; MTCW 1,
 2; MTFW 2005; NFS 22, 23; RGEL 2;
 RGSF 2; TEA; WLIT 4
Rushforth, Peter 1945-2005 **CLC 19**
 See also CA 101; 243
Rushforth, Peter Scott
 See Rushforth, Peter
Ruskin, John 1819-1900 **TCLC 63**
 See also BRW 5; BYA 5; CA 114; 129; CD-
 BLB 1832-1890; DLB 55, 163, 190;
 RGEL 2; SATA 24; TEA; WCH
Russ, Joanna 1937- **CLC 15**
 See also BPFB 3; CA 25-28; CANR 11, 31,
 65; CN 4, 5, 6, 7; DLB 8; FW; GLL 1;
 MTCW 1; SCFW 1, 2; SFW 4
Russ, Richard Patrick
 See O'Brian, Patrick
Russell, George William 1867-1935
 See A.E.; Baker, Jean H.
 See also BRWS 8; CA 104; 153; CDBLB
 1890-1914; DAM POET; EWL 3; RGEL
 2
Russell, Jeffrey Burton 1934- **CLC 70**
 See also CA 25-28R; CANR 11, 28, 52
Russell, (Henry) Ken(neth Alfred)
 1927- .. **CLC 16**
 See also CA 105
Russell, William Martin 1947-
 See Russell, Willy
 See also CA 164; CANR 107
Russell, Willy **CLC 60**
 See Russell, William Martin
 See also CBD; CD 5, 6; DLB 233
Russo, Richard 1949- **CLC 181**
 See also AMWS 12; CA 127; 133; CANR
 87, 114
Rutherford, Mark **TCLC 25**
 See White, William Hale
 See also DLB 18; RGEL 2
Ruysbroeck, Jan van 1293-1381 ... **CMLC 85**
Ruyslinck, Ward **CLC 14**
 See Belser, Reimond Karel Maria de
Ryan, Cornelius (John) 1920-1974 **CLC 7**
 See also CA 69-72; 53-56; CANR 38
Ryan, Michael 1946- **CLC 65**
 See also CA 49-52; CANR 109; DLBY
 1982
Ryan, Tim
 See Dent, Lester
Rybakov, Anatoli (Naumovich)
 1911-1998 **CLC 23, 53**
 See Rybakov, Anatolii (Naumovich)
 See also CA 126; 135; 172; SATA 79;
 SATA-Obit 108
Rybakov, Anatolii (Naumovich)
 See Rybakov, Anatoli (Naumovich)
 See also DLB 302; RGHL
Ryder, Jonathan
 See Ludlum, Robert
Ryga, George 1932-1987 **CLC 14**
 See also CA 101; 124; CANR 43, 90; CCA
 1; DAC; DAM MST; DLB 60
S. H.
 See Hartmann, Sadakichi

S. S.
 See Sassoon, Siegfried (Lorraine)
Sa'adawi, al- Nawal
 See El Saadawi, Nawal
 See also AFW; EWL 3
Saadawi, Nawal El
 See El Saadawi, Nawal
 See also WLIT 2
Saba, Umberto 1883-1957 **TCLC 33**
 See also CA 144; CANR 79; DLB 114;
 EWL 3; RGWL 2, 3
Sabatini, Rafael 1875-1950 **TCLC 47**
 See also BPFB 3; CA 162; RHW
Sabato, Ernesto (R.) 1911- **CLC 10, 23;**
 HLC 2
 See also CA 97-100; CANR 32, 65; CD-
 WLB 3; CWW 2; DAM MULT; DLB 145;
 EWL 3; HW 1, 2; LAW; MTCW 1, 2;
 MTFW 2005
Sa-Carneiro, Mario de 1890-1916 . **TCLC 83**
 See also DLB 287; EWL 3
Sacastru, Martin
 See Bioy Casares, Adolfo
 See also CWW 2
Sacher-Masoch, Leopold von
 1836(?)-1895 **NCLC 31**
Sachs, Hans 1494-1576 **LC 95**
 See also CDWLB 2; DLB 179; RGWL 2, 3
Sachs, Marilyn 1927- **CLC 35**
 See also AAYA 2; BYA 6; CA 17-20R;
 CANR 13, 47, 150; CLR 2; JRDA; MAI-
 CYA 1, 2; SAAS 2; SATA 3, 68, 164;
 SATA-Essay 110; WYA; YAW
Sachs, Marilyn Stickle
 See Sachs, Marilyn
Sachs, Nelly 1891-1970 **CLC 14, 98**
 See also CA 17-18; 25-28R; CANR 87;
 CAP 2; EWL 3; MTCW 2; MTFW 2005;
 PFS 20; RGHL; RGWL 2, 3
Sackler, Howard (Oliver)
 1929-1982 **CLC 14**
 See also CA 61-64; 108; CAD; CANR 30;
 DFS 15; DLB 7
Sacks, Oliver 1933- **CLC 67, 202**
 See also CA 53-56; CANR 28, 50, 76, 146;
 CPW; DA3; INT CANR-28; MTCW 1, 2;
 MTFW 2005
Sacks, Oliver Wolf
 See Sacks, Oliver
Sackville, Thomas 1536-1608 **LC 98**
 See also DAM DRAM; DLB 62, 132;
 RGEL 2
Sadakichi
 See Hartmann, Sadakichi
Sa'dawi, Nawal al-
 See El Saadawi, Nawal
 See also CWW 2
Sade, Donatien Alphonse Francois
 1740-1814 **NCLC 3, 47**
 See also DLB 314; EW 4; GFL Beginnings
 to 1789; RGWL 2, 3
Sade, Marquis de
 See Sade, Donatien Alphonse Francois
Sadoff, Ira 1945- **CLC 9**
 See also CA 53-56; CANR 5, 21, 109; DLB
 120
Saetone
 See Camus, Albert
Safire, William 1929- **CLC 10**
 See also CA 17-20R; CANR 31, 54, 91, 148
Sagan, Carl (Edward) 1934-1996 **CLC 30,**
 112
 See also AAYA 2, 62; CA 25-28R; 155;
 CANR 11, 36, 74; CPW; DA3; MTCW 1,
 2; MTFW 2005; SATA 58; SATA-Obit 94
Sagan, Francoise **CLC 3, 6, 9, 17, 36**
 See Quoirez, Francoise
 See also CWW 2; DLB 83; EWL 3; GFL
 1789 to the Present; MTCW 2

Sahgal, Nayantara (Pandit) 1927- **CLC 41**
 See also CA 9-12R; CANR 11, 88; CN 1,
 2, 3, 4, 5, 6, 7; DLB 323
Said, Edward W. 1935-2003 **CLC 123**
 See also CA 21-24R; 220; CANR 45, 74,
 107, 131; DLB 67; MTCW 2; MTFW
 2005
Saint, H(arry) F. 1941- **CLC 50**
 See also CA 127
St. Aubin de Teran, Lisa 1953-
 See Teran, Lisa St. Aubin de
 See also CA 118; 126; CN 6, 7; INT CA-
 126
Saint Birgitta of Sweden c.
 1303-1373 **CMLC 24**
Sainte-Beuve, Charles Augustin
 1804-1869 **NCLC 5**
 See also DLB 217; EW 6; GFL 1789 to the
 Present
Saint-Exupery, Antoine de
 1900-1944 **TCLC 2, 56, 169; WLC**
 See also AAYA 63; BPFB 3; BYA 3; CA
 108; 132; CLR 10; DA3; DAM NOV;
 DLB 72; EW 12; EWL 3; GFL 1789 to
 the Present; LAIT 3; MAICYA 1, 2;
 MTCW 1, 2; MTFW 2005; RGWL 2, 3;
 SATA 20; TWA
Saint-Exupery, Antoine Jean Baptiste Marie
 Roger de
 See Saint-Exupery, Antoine de
St. John, David
 See Hunt, E(verette) Howard, (Jr.)
St. John, J. Hector
 See Crevecoeur, Michel Guillaume Jean de
Saint-John Perse
 See Leger, (Marie-Rene Auguste) Alexis
 Saint-Leger
 See also EW 10; EWL 3; GFL 1789 to the
 Present; RGWL 2
Saintsbury, George (Edward Bateman)
 1845-1933 **TCLC 31**
 See also CA 160; DLB 57, 149
Sait Faik **TCLC 23**
 See Abasiyanik, Sait Faik
Saki **SSC 12; TCLC 3; WLC 5**
 See Munro, H(ector) H(ugh)
 See also BRWS 6; BYA 11; LAIT 2; RGEL
 2; SSFS 1; SUFW
Sala, George Augustus 1828-1895 . **NCLC 46**
Saladin 1138-1193 **CMLC 38**
Salama, Hannu 1936- **CLC 18**
 See also CA 244; EWL 3
Salamanca, J(ack) R(ichard) 1922- .. **CLC 4,**
 15
 See also CA 25-28R; 193; CAAE 193
Salas, Floyd Francis 1931- **HLC 2**
 See also CA 119; CAAS 27; CANR 44, 75,
 93; DAM MULT; DLB 82; HW 1, 2;
 MTCW 2; MTFW 2005
Sale, J. Kirkpatrick
 See Sale, Kirkpatrick
Sale, John Kirkpatrick
 See Sale, Kirkpatrick
Sale, Kirkpatrick 1937- **CLC 68**
 See also CA 13-16R; CANR 10, 147
Salinas, Luis Omar 1937- ... **CLC 90; HLC 2**
 See also AMWS 13; CA 131; CANR 81,
 153; DAM MULT; DLB 82; HW 1, 2
Salinas (y Serrano), Pedro
 1891(?)-1951 **TCLC 17**
 See also CA 117; DLB 134; EWL 3
Salinger, J(erome) D(avid) 1919- .. **CLC 1, 3,**
 8, 12, 55, 56, 138; SSC 2, 28, 65; WLC
 5
 See also AAYA 2, 36; AMW; AMWC 1;
 BPFB 3; CA 5-8R; CANR 39, 129;
 CDALB 1941-1968; CLR 18; CN 1, 2, 3,
 4, 5, 6, 7; CPW 1; DA; DA3; DAB; DAC;
 DAM MST, NOV, POP; DLB 2, 102, 173;

EWL 3; EXPN; LAIT 4; MAICYA 1, 2;
MAL 5; MTCW 1, 2; MTFW 2005; NFS
1; RGAL 4; RGSF 2; SATA 67; SSFS 17;
TUS; WYA; YAW

Salisbury, John
See Caute, (John) David

Sallust c. 86B.C.-35B.C. **CMLC 68**
See also AW 2; CDWLB 1; DLB 211;
RGWL 2, 3

Salter, James 1925- .. **CLC 7, 52, 59; SSC 58**
See also AMWS 9; CA 73-76; CANR 107;
DLB 130

Saltus, Edgar (Everton) 1855-1921 . **TCLC 8**
See also CA 105; DLB 202; RGAL 4

Saltykov, Mikhail Evgrafovich
1826-1889 **NCLC 16**
See also DLB 238:

Saltykov-Shchedrin, N.
See Saltykov, Mikhail Evgrafovich

Samarakis, Andonis
See Samarakis, Antonis
See also EWL 3

Samarakis, Antonis 1919-2003 **CLC 5**
See Samarakis, Andonis
See also CA 25-28R; 224; CAAS 16; CANR
36

Sanchez, Florencio 1875-1910 **TCLC 37**
See also CA 153; DLB 305; EWL 3; HW 1;
LAW

Sanchez, Luis Rafael 1936- **CLC 23**
See also CA 128; DLB 305; EWL 3; HW 1;
WLIT 1

Sanchez, Sonia 1934- **BLC 3; CLC 5, 116, 215; PC 9**
See also BW 2, 3; CA 33-36R; CANR 24,
49, 74, 115; CLR 18; CP 2, 3, 4, 5, 6, 7;
CSW; CWP; DA3; DAM MULT; DLB 41;
DLBD 8; EWL 3; MAICYA 1, 2; MAL 5;
MTCW 1, 2; MTFW 2005; SATA 22, 136;
WP

Sancho, Ignatius 1729-1780 **LC 84**

Sand, George 1804-1876 **NCLC 2, 42, 57; WLC 5**
See also DA; DA3; DAB; DAC; DAM
MST, NOV; DLB 119, 192; EW 6; FL 1:3;
FW; GFL 1789 to the Present; RGWL 2,
3; TWA

Sandburg, Carl (August) 1878-1967 . **CLC 1, 4, 10, 15, 35; PC 2, 41; WLC 5**
See also AAYA 24; AMW; BYA 1, 3; CA
5-8R; 25-28R; CANR 35; CDALB 1865-
1917; CLR 67; DA; DA3; DAB; DAC;
DAM MST, POET; DLB 17, 54, 284;
EWL 3; EXPP; LAIT 2; MAICYA 1, 2;
MAL 5; MTCW 1, 2; MTFW 2005; PAB;
PFS 3, 6, 12; RGAL 4; SATA 8; TUS;
WCH; WP; WYA

Sandburg, Charles
See Sandburg, Carl (August)

Sandburg, Charles A.
See Sandburg, Carl (August)

Sanders, (James) Ed(ward) 1939- **CLC 53**
See Sanders, Edward
See also BG 1:3; CA 13-16R; CAAS 21;
CANR 13, 44, 78; CP 1, 2, 3, 4, 5, 6, 7;
DAM POET; DLB 16, 244

Sanders, Edward
See Sanders, (James) Ed(ward)
See also DLB 244

Sanders, Lawrence 1920-1998 **CLC 41**
See also BEST 89:4; BPFB 3; CA 81-84;
165; CANR 33, 62; CMW 4; CPW; DA3;
DAM POP; MTCW 1

Sanders, Noah
See Blount, Roy (Alton), Jr.

Sanders, Winston P.
See Anderson, Poul (William)

Sandoz, Mari(e Susette) 1900-1966 .. **CLC 28**
See also CA 1-4R; 25-28R; CANR 17, 64;
DLB 9, 212; LAIT 2; MTCW 1, 2; SATA
5; TCWW 1, 2

Sandys, George 1578-1644 **LC 80**
See also DLB 24, 121

Saner, Reg(inald Anthony) 1931- **CLC 9**
See also CA 65-68; CP 3, 4, 5, 6, 7

Sankara 788-820 **CMLC 32**

Sannazaro, Jacopo 1456(?)-1530 **LC 8**
See also RGWL 2, 3; WLIT 7

Sansom, William 1912-1976 . **CLC 2, 6; SSC 21**
See also CA 5-8R; 65-68; CANR 42; CN 1,
2; DAM NOV; DLB 139; EWL 3; MTCW
1; RGEL 2; RGSF 2

Santayana, George 1863-1952 **TCLC 40**
See also AMW; CA 115; 194; DLB 54, 71,
246, 270; DLBD 13; EWL 3; MAL 5;
RGAL 4; TUS

Santiago, Danny **CLC 33**
See James, Daniel (Lewis)
See also DLB 122

**Santillana, Inigo Lopez de Mendoza,
Marques de** 1398-1458 **LC 111**
See also DLB 286

Santmyer, Helen Hooven
1895-1986 **CLC 33; TCLC 133**
See also CA 1-4R; 118; CANR 15, 33;
DLBY 1984; MTCW 1; RHW

Santoka, Taneda 1882-1940 **TCLC 72**

Santos, Bienvenido N(uqui)
1911-1996 **AAL; CLC 22; TCLC 156**
See also CA 101; 151; CANR 19, 46; CP 1;
DAM MULT; DLB 312; EWL; RGAL 4;
SSFS 19

Sapir, Edward 1884-1939 **TCLC 108**
See also CA 211; DLB 92

Sapper **TCLC 44**
See McNeile, Herman Cyril

Sapphire
See Sapphire, Brenda

Sapphire, Brenda 1950- **CLC 99**

Sappho fl. 6th cent. B.C.- ... **CMLC 3, 67; PC 5**
See also CDWLB 1; DA3; DAM POET;
DLB 176; FL 1:1; PFS 20; RGWL 2, 3;
WLIT 8; WP

Saramago, Jose 1922- **CLC 119; HLCS 1**
See also CA 153; CANR 96; CWW 2; DLB
287; EWL 3; LATS 1:2; SSFS 23

Sarduy, Severo 1937-1993 **CLC 6, 97; HLCS 2; TCLC 167**
See also CA 89-92; 142; CANR 58, 81;
CWW 2; DLB 113; EWL 3; HW 1, 2;
LAW

Sargeson, Frank 1903-1982 **CLC 31**
See also CA 25-28R; 106; CANR 38, 79;
CN 1, 2, 3; EWL 3; GLL 2; RGEL 2;
RGSF 2; SSFS 20

Sarmiento, Domingo Faustino
1811-1888 **HLCS 2; NCLC 123**
See also LAW; WLIT 1

Sarmiento, Felix Ruben Garcia
See Dario, Ruben

Saro-Wiwa, Ken(ule Beeson)
1941-1995 **CLC 114**
See also BW 2; CA 142; 150; CANR 60;
DLB 157

Saroyan, William 1908-1981 ... **CLC 1, 8, 10, 29, 34, 56; SSC 21; TCLC 137; WLC 5**
See also AAYA 66; CA 5-8R; 103; CAD;
CANR 30; CDALBS; CN 1, 2; DA; DA3;
DAB; DAC; DAM DRAM, MST, NOV;
DFS 17; DLB 7, 9, 86; DLBY 1981; EWL
3; LAIT 4; MAL 5; MTCW 1, 2; MTFW
2005; RGAL 4; RGSF 2; SATA 23; SATA-
Obit 24; SSFS 14; TUS

Sarraute, Nathalie 1900-1999 **CLC 1, 2, 4, 8, 10, 31, 80; TCLC 145**
See also BPFB 3; CA 9-12R; 187; CANR
23, 66, 134; CWW 2; DLB 83, 321; EW
12; EWL 3; GFL 1789 to the Present;
MTCW 1, 2; MTFW 2005; RGWL 2, 3

Sarton, (Eleanor) May 1912-1995 **CLC 4, 14, 49, 91; PC 39; TCLC 120**
See also AMWS 8; CA 1-4R; 149; CANR
1, 34, 55, 116; CN 1, 2, 3, 4, 5, 6; CP 1,
2, 3, 4, 5, 6; DAM POET; DLB 48; DLBY
1981; EWL 3; FW; INT CANR-34; MAL
5; MTCW 1, 2; MTFW 2005; RGAL 4;
SATA 36; SATA-Obit 86; TUS

Sartre, Jean-Paul 1905-1980 . **CLC 1, 4, 7, 9, 13, 18, 24, 44, 50, 52; DC 3; SSC 32; WLC 5**
See also AAYA 62; CA 9-12R; 97-100;
CANR 21; DA; DA3; DAB; DAC; DAM
DRAM, MST, NOV; DFS 5; DLB 72,
296, 321; EW 12; EWL 3; GFL 1789 to
the Present; LMFS 2; MTCW 1, 2; MTFW
2005; NFS 21; RGHL; RGSF 2; RGWL
2, 3; SSFS 9; TWA

Sassoon, Siegfried (Lorraine)
1886-1967 **CLC 36, 130; PC 12**
See also BRW 6; CA 104; 25-28R; CANR
36; DAB; DAM MST, NOV, POET; DLB
20, 191; DLBD 18; EWL 3; MTCW 1, 2;
MTFW 2005; PAB; RGEL 2; TEA

Satterfield, Charles
See Pohl, Frederik

Satyremont
See Peret, Benjamin

Saul, John (W. III) 1942- **CLC 46**
See also AAYA 10, 62; BEST 90:4; CA 81-
84; CANR 16, 40, 81; CPW; DAM NOV,
POP; HGG; SATA 98

Saunders, Caleb
See Heinlein, Robert A(nson)

Saura (Atares), Carlos 1932-1998 **CLC 20**
See also CA 114; 131; CANR 79; HW 1

Sauser, Frederic Louis
See Sauser-Hall, Frederic

Sauser-Hall, Frederic 1887-1961 **CLC 18**
See Cendrars, Blaise
See also CA 102; 93-96; CANR 36, 62;
MTCW 1

Saussure, Ferdinand de
1857-1913 **TCLC 49**
See also DLB 242

Savage, Catharine
See Brosman, Catharine Savage

Savage, Richard 1697(?)-1743 **LC 96**
See also DLB 95; RGEL 2

Savage, Thomas 1915-2003 **CLC 40**
See also CA 126; 132; 218; CAAS 15; CN
6, 7; INT CA-132; SATA-Obit 147;
TCWW 2

Savan, Glenn 1953-2003 **CLC 50**
See also CA 225

Sax, Robert
See Johnson, Robert

Saxo Grammaticus c. 1150-c.
1222 **CMLC 58**

Saxton, Robert
See Johnson, Robert

Sayers, Dorothy L(eigh) 1893-1957 . **SSC 71; TCLC 2, 15**
See also BPFB 3; BRWS 3; CA 104; 119;
CANR 60; CDBLB 1914-1945; CMW 4;
DAM POP; DLB 10, 36, 77, 100; MSW;
MTCW 1, 2; MTFW 2005; RGEL 2;
SSFS 12; TEA

Sayers, Valerie 1952- **CLC 50, 122**
See also CA 134; CANR 61; CSW

Sayles, John (Thomas) 1950- **CLC 7, 10, 14, 198**
See also CA 57-60; CANR 41, 84; DLB 44

Scammell, Michael 1935- **CLC 34**
See also CA 156
Scammell, Vernon 1922- **CLC 49**
See also CA 5-8R; CANR 8, 24, 57, 143;
CN 1, 2; CP 1, 2, 3, 4, 5, 6, 7; CWRI 5;
DLB 27; SATA 59
Scarlett, Susan
See Streatfeild, (Mary) Noel
Scarron 1847-1910
See Mikszath, Kalman
Scarron, Paul 1610-1660 **LC 116**
See also GFL Beginnings to 1789; RGWL
2, 3
Schaeffer, Susan Fromberg 1941- **CLC 6,
11, 22**
See also CA 49-52; CANR 18, 65; CN 4, 5,
6, 7; DLB 28, 299; MTCW 1, 2; MTFW
2005; SATA 22
Schama, Simon (Michael) 1945- **CLC 150**
See also BEST 89:4; CA 105; CANR 39,
91
Schary, Jill
See Robinson, Jill
Schell, Jonathan 1943- **CLC 35**
See also CA 73-76; CANR 12, 117
Schelling, Friedrich Wilhelm Joseph von
1775-1854 **NCLC 30**
See also DLB 90
Scherer, Jean-Marie Maurice 1920-
See Rohmer, Eric
See also CA 110
Schevill, James (Erwin) 1920- **CLC 7**
See also CA 5-8R; CAAS 12; CAD; CD 5,
6; CP 1, 2, 3, 4, 5
Schiller, Friedrich von 1759-1805 **DC 12;
NCLC 39, 69, 166**
See also CDWLB 2; DAM DRAM; DLB
94; EW 5; RGWL 2, 3; TWA
Schisgal, Murray (Joseph) 1926- **CLC 6**
See also CA 21-24R; CAD; CANR 48, 86;
CD 5, 6; MAL 5
Schlee, Ann 1934- **CLC 35**
See also CA 101; CANR 29, 88; SATA 44;
SATA-Brief 36
Schlegel, August Wilhelm von
1767-1845 **NCLC 15, 142**
See also DLB 94; RGWL 2, 3
Schlegel, Friedrich 1772-1829 **NCLC 45**
See also DLB 90; EW 5; RGWL 2, 3; TWA
Schlegel, Johann Elias (von)
1719(?)-1749 **LC 5**
Schleiermacher, Friedrich
1768-1834 **NCLC 107**
See also DLB 90
Schlesinger, Arthur M(eier), Jr.
1917- **CLC 84**
See also AITN 1; CA 1-4R; CANR 1, 28,
58, 105; DLB 17; INT CANR-28; MTCW
1, 2; SATA 61
Schlink, Bernhard 1944- **CLC 174**
See also CA 163; CANR 116; RGHL
Schmidt, Arno (Otto) 1914-1979 **CLC 56**
See also CA 128; 109; DLB 69; EWL 3
Schmitz, Aron Hector 1861-1928
See Svevo, Italo
See also CA 104; 122; MTCW 1
Schnackenberg, Gjertrud (Cecelia)
1953- **CLC 40; PC 45**
See also AMWS 15; CA 116; CANR 100;
CP 5, 6, 7; CWP; DLB 120, 282; PFS 13
Schneider, Leonard Alfred 1925-1966
See Bruce, Lenny
See also CA 89-92
Schnitzler, Arthur 1862-1931 **DC 17; SSC
15, 61; TCLC 4**
See also CA 104; CDWLB 2; DLB 81, 118;
EW 8; EWL 3; RGSF 2; RGWL 2, 3

Schoenberg, Arnold Franz Walter
1874-1951 **TCLC 75**
See also CA 109; 188
Schonberg, Arnold
See Schoenberg, Arnold Franz Walter
Schopenhauer, Arthur 1788-1860 . **NCLC 51,
157**
See also DLB 90; EW 5
Schor, Sandra (M.) 1932(?)-1990 **CLC 65**
See also CA 132
Schorer, Mark 1908-1977 **CLC 9**
See also CA 5-8R; 73-76; CANR 7; CN 1,
2; DLB 103
Schrader, Paul (Joseph) 1946- . **CLC 26, 212**
See also CA 37-40R; CANR 41; DLB 44
Schreber, Daniel 1842-1911 **TCLC 123**
Schreiner, Olive (Emilie Albertina)
1855-1920 **TCLC 9**
See also AFW; BRWS 2; CA 105; 154;
DLB 18, 156, 190, 225; EWL 3; FW;
RGEL 2; TWA; WLIT 2; WWE 1
Schulberg, Budd (Wilson) 1914- .. **CLC 7, 48**
See also BPFB 3; CA 25-28R; CANR 19,
87; CN 1, 2, 3, 4, 5, 6, 7; DLB 6, 26, 28;
DLBY 1981, 2001; MAL 5
Schulman, Arnold
See Trumbo, Dalton
Schulz, Bruno 1892-1942 .. **SSC 13; TCLC 5,
51**
See also CA 115; 123; CANR 86; CDWLB
4; DLB 215; EWL 3; MTCW 2; MTFW
2005; RGSF 2; RGWL 2, 3
Schulz, Charles M. 1922-2000 **CLC 12**
See also AAYA 39; CA 9-12R; 187; CANR
6, 132; INT CANR-6; MTFW 2005;
SATA 10; SATA-Obit 118
Schulz, Charles Monroe
See Schulz, Charles M.
Schumacher, E(rnst) F(riedrich)
1911-1977 **CLC 80**
See also CA 81-84; 73-76; CANR 34, 85
Schumann, Robert 1810-1856 **NCLC 143**
Schuyler, George Samuel 1895-1977 . **HR 1:3**
See also BW 2; CA 81-84; 73-76; CANR
42; DLB 29, 51
Schuyler, James Marcus 1923-1991 .. **CLC 5,
23**
See also CA 101; 134; CP 1, 2, 3, 4, 5;
DAM POET; DLB 5, 169; EWL 3; INT
CA-101; MAL 5; WP
Schwartz, Delmore (David)
1913-1966 ... **CLC 2, 4, 10, 45, 87; PC 8**
See also AMWS 2; CA 17-18; 25-28R;
CANR 35; CAP 2; DLB 28, 48; EWL 3;
MAL 5; MTCW 1, 2; MTFW 2005; PAB;
RGAL 4; TUS
Schwartz, Ernst
See Ozu, Yasujiro
Schwartz, John Burnham 1965- **CLC 59**
See also CA 132; CANR 116
Schwartz, Lynne Sharon 1939- **CLC 31**
See also CA 103; CANR 44, 89; DLB 218;
MTCW 2; MTFW 2005
Schwartz, Muriel A.
See Eliot, T(homas) S(tearns)
Schwarz-Bart, Andre 1928- **CLC 2, 4**
See also CA 89-92; CANR 109; DLB 299;
RGHL
Schwarz-Bart, Simone 1938- . **BLCS; CLC 7**
See also BW 2; CA 97-100; CANR 117;
EWL 3
Schwerner, Armand 1927-1999 **PC 42**
See also CA 9-12R; 179; CANR 50, 85; CP
2, 3, 4, 5, 6; DLB 165
**Schwitters, Kurt (Hermann Edward Karl
Julius)** 1887-1948 **TCLC 95**
See also CA 158

Schwob, Marcel (Mayer Andre)
1867-1905 **TCLC 20**
See also CA 117; 168; DLB 123; GFL 1789
to the Present
Sciascia, Leonardo 1921-1989 .. **CLC 8, 9, 41**
See also CA 85-88; 130; CANR 35; DLB
177; EWL 3; MTCW 1; RGWL 2, 3
Scoppettone, Sandra 1936- **CLC 26**
See Early, Jack
See also AAYA 11, 65; BYA 8; CA 5-8R;
CANR 41, 73; GLL 1; MAICYA 2; MAI-
CYAS 1; SATA 9, 92; WYA; YAW
Scorsese, Martin 1942- **CLC 20, 89, 207**
See also AAYA 38; CA 110; 114; CANR
46, 85
Scotland, Jay
See Jakes, John (William)
Scott, Duncan Campbell
1862-1947 **TCLC 6**
See also CA 104; 153; DAC; DLB 92;
RGEL 2
Scott, Evelyn 1893-1963 **CLC 43**
See also CA 104; 112; CANR 64; DLB 9,
48; RHW
Scott, F(rancis) R(eginald)
1899-1985 **CLC 22**
See also CA 101; 114; CANR 87; CP 1, 2,
3, 4; DLB 88; INT CA-101; RGEL 2
Scott, Frank
See Scott, F(rancis) R(eginald)
Scott, Joan **CLC 65**
Scott, Joanna 1960- **CLC 50**
See also CA 126; CANR 53, 92
Scott, Paul (Mark) 1920-1978 **CLC 9, 60**
See also BRWS 1; CA 81-84; 77-80; CANR
33; CN 1, 2; DLB 14, 207, 326; EWL 3;
MTCW 1; RGEL 2; RHW; WWE 1
Scott, Ridley 1937- **CLC 183**
See also AAYA 13, 43
Scott, Sarah 1723-1795 **LC 44**
See also DLB 39
Scott, Sir Walter 1771-1832 **NCLC 15, 69,
110; PC 13; SSC 32; WLC 5**
See also AAYA 22; BRW 4; BYA 2; CD-
BLB 1789-1832; DA; DAB; DAC; DAM
MST, NOV, POET; DLB 93, 107, 116,
144, 159; GL 3; HGG; LAIT 1; RGEL 2;
RGSF 2; SSFS 10; SUFW 1; TEA; WLIT
3; YABC 2
Scribe, (Augustin) Eugene 1791-1861 . **DC 5;
NCLC 16**
See also DAM DRAM; DLB 192; GFL
1789 to the Present; RGWL 2, 3
Scrum, R.
See Crumb, R.
Scudery, Georges de 1601-1667 **LC 75**
See also GFL Beginnings to 1789
Scudery, Madeleine de 1607-1701 .. **LC 2, 58**
See also DLB 268; GFL Beginnings to 1789
Scum
See Crumb, R.
Scumbag, Little Bobby
See Crumb, R.
Seabrook, John
See Hubbard, L. Ron
Seacole, Mary Jane Grant
1805-1881 **NCLC 147**
See also DLB 166
Sealy, I(rwin) Allan 1951- **CLC 55**
See also CA 136; CN 6, 7
Search, Alexander
See Pessoa, Fernando (Antonio Nogueira)
Sebald, W(infried) G(eorg)
1944-2001 **CLC 194**
See also BRWS 8; CA 159; 202; CANR 98;
MTFW 2005; RGHL
Sebastian, Lee
See Silverberg, Robert

Sebastian Owl
See Thompson, Hunter S(tockton)
Sebestyen, Igen
See Sebestyen, Ouida
Sebestyen, Ouida 1924- **CLC 30**
See also AAYA 8; BYA 7; CA 107; CANR
40, 114; CLR 17; JRDA; MAICYA 1, 2;
SAAS 10; SATA 39, 140; WYA; YAW
Sebold, Alice 1963(?)- **CLC 193**
See also AAYA 56; CA 203; MTFW 2005
Second Duke of Buckingham
See Villiers, George
Secundus, H. Scriblerus
See Fielding, Henry
Sedges, John
See Buck, Pearl S(ydenstricker)
Sedgwick, Catharine Maria
1789-1867 **NCLC 19, 98**
See also DLB 1, 74, 183, 239, 243, 254; FL
1:3; RGAL 4
Seelye, John (Douglas) 1931- **CLC 7**
See also CA 97-100; CANR 70; INT CA-
97-100; TCWW 1, 2
Seferiades, Giorgos Stylianou 1900-1971
See Seferis, George
See also CA 5-8R; 33-36R; CANR 5, 36;
MTCW 1
Seferis, George **CLC 5, 11; PC 66**
See Seferiades, Giorgos Stylianou
See also EW 12; EWL 3; RGWL 2, 3
Segal, Erich (Wolf) 1937- **CLC 3, 10**
See also BEST 89:1; BPFB 3; CA 25-28R;
CANR 20, 36, 65, 113; CPW; DAM POP;
DLBY 1986; INT CANR-20; MTCW 1
Seger, Bob 1945- **CLC 35**
Seghers, Anna **CLC 7**
See Radvanyi, Netty
See also CDWLB 2; DLB 69; EWL 3
Seidel, Frederick (Lewis) 1936- **CLC 18**
See also CA 13-16R; CANR 8, 99; CP 1, 2,
3, 4, 5, 6, 7; DLBY 1984
Seifert, Jaroslav 1901-1986 . **CLC 34, 44, 93;
PC 47**
See also CA 127; CDWLB 4; DLB 215;
EWL 3; MTCW 1, 2
Sei Shonagon c. 966-1017(?) **CMLC 6**
Sejour, Victor 1817-1874 **DC 10**
See also DLB 50
Sejour Marcou et Ferrand, Juan Victor
See Sejour, Victor
Selby, Hubert, Jr. 1928-2004 **CLC 1, 2, 4,
8; SSC 20**
See also CA 13-16R; 226; CANR 33, 85;
CN 1, 2, 3, 4, 5, 6, 7; DLB 2, 227; MAL
5
Selzer, Richard 1928- **CLC 74**
See also CA 65-68; CANR 14, 106
Sembene, Ousmane
See Ousmane, Sembene
See also AFW; EWL 3; WLIT 2
Senancour, Etienne Pivert de
1770-1846 **NCLC 16**
See also DLB 119; GFL 1789 to the Present
Sender, Ramon (Jose) 1902-1982 **CLC 8;
HLC 2; TCLC 136**
See also CA 5-8R; 105; CANR 8; DAM
MULT; DLB 322; EWL 3; HW 1; MTCW
1; RGWL 2, 3
Seneca, Lucius Annaeus c. 4B.C.-c.
65 **CMLC 6; DC 5**
See also AW 2; CDWLB 1; DAM DRAM;
DLB 211; RGWL 2, 3; TWA; WLIT 8
Senghor, Leopold Sedar 1906-2001 ... **BLC 3;
CLC 54, 130; PC 25**
See also AFW; BW 2; CA 116; 125; 203;
CANR 47, 74, 134; CWW 2; DAM
MULT, POET; DNFS 2; EWL 3; GFL
1789 to the Present; MTCW 1, 2; MTFW
2005; TWA

Senior, Olive (Marjorie) 1941- **SSC 78**
See also BW 3; CA 154; CANR 86, 126;
CN 6; CP 6, 7; CWP; DLB 157; EWL 3;
RGSF 2
Senna, Danzy 1970- **CLC 119**
See also CA 169; CANR 130
Serling, (Edward) Rod(man)
1924-1975 **CLC 30**
See also AAYA 14; AITN 1; CA 162; 57-
60; DLB 26; SFW 4
Serna, Ramon Gomez de la
See Gomez de la Serna, Ramon
Serpieres
See Guillevic, (Eugene)
Service, Robert
See Service, Robert W(illiam)
See also BYA 4; DAB; DLB 92
Service, Robert W(illiam)
1874(?)-1958 ... **PC 70; TCLC 15; WLC
5**
See Service, Robert
See also CA 115; 140; CANR 84; DA;
DAC; DAM MST, POET; PFS 10; RGEL
2; SATA 20
Seth, Vikram 1952- **CLC 43, 90**
See also BRWS 10; CA 121; 127; CANR
50, 74, 131; CN 6, 7; CP 5, 6, 7; DA3;
DAM MULT; DLB 120, 271, 282, 323;
EWL 3; INT CA-127; MTCW 2; MTFW
2005; WWE 1
Seton, Cynthia Propper 1926-1982 .. **CLC 27**
See also CA 5-8R; 108; CANR 7
Seton, Ernest (Evan) Thompson
1860-1946 **TCLC 31**
See also ANW; BYA 3; CA 109; 204; CLR
59; DLB 92; DLBD 13; JRDA; SATA 18
Seton-Thompson, Ernest
See Seton, Ernest (Evan) Thompson
Settle, Mary Lee 1918-2005 **CLC 19, 61**
See also BPFB 3; CA 89-92; 243; CAAS 1;
CANR 44, 87, 126; CN 6, 7; CSW; DLB
6; INT CA-89-92
Seuphor, Michel
See Arp, Jean
Sevigne, Marie (de Rabutin-Chantal)
1626-1696 **LC 11**
See Sevigne, Marie de Rabutin Chantal
See also GFL Beginnings to 1789; TWA
Sevigne, Marie de Rabutin Chantal
See Sevigne, Marie (de Rabutin-Chantal)
See also DLB 268
Sewall, Samuel 1652-1730 **LC 38**
See also DLB 24; RGAL 4
Sexton, Anne (Harvey) 1928-1974 **CLC 2,
4, 6, 8, 10, 15, 53, 123; PC 2; WLC 5**
See also AMWS 2; CA 1-4R; 53-56; CABS
2; CANR 3, 36; CDALB 1941-1968; CP
1, 2; DA; DA3; DAB; DAC; DAM MST,
POET; DLB 5, 169; EWL 3; EXPP; FL
1:6; FW; MAL 5; MAWW; MTCW 1, 2;
MTFW 2005; PAB; PFS 4, 14; RGAL 4;
RGHL; SATA 10; TUS
Shaara, Jeff 1952- **CLC 119**
See also AAYA 70; CA 163; CANR 109;
CN 7; MTFW 2005
Shaara, Michael (Joseph, Jr.)
1929-1988 **CLC 15**
See also AAYA 71; AITN 1; BPFB 3; CA
102; 125; CANR 52, 85; DAM POP;
DLBY 1983; MTFW 2005
Shackleton, C. C.
See Aldiss, Brian W(ilson)
Shacochis, Bob **CLC 39**
See Shacochis, Robert G.
Shacochis, Robert G. 1951-
See Shacochis, Bob
See also CA 119; 124; CANR 100; INT CA-
124

Shadwell, Thomas 1641(?)-1692 **LC 114**
See also DLB 80; IDTP; RGEL 2
Shaffer, Anthony (Joshua)
1926-2001 **CLC 19**
See also CA 110; 116; 200; CBD; CD 5, 6;
DAM DRAM; DFS 13; DLB 13
Shaffer, Peter (Levin) 1926- .. **CLC 5, 14, 18,
37, 60; DC 7**
See also BRWS 1; CA 25-28R; CANR 25,
47, 74, 118; CBD; CD 5, 6; CDBLB 1960
to Present; DA3; DAB; DAM DRAM,
MST; DFS 5, 13; DLB 13, 233; EWL 3;
MTCW 1, 2; MTFW 2005; RGEL 2; TEA
Shakespeare, William 1564-1616 **WLC 5**
See also AAYA 35; BRW 1; CDBLB Be-
fore 1660; DA; DA3; DAB; DAC; DAM
DRAM, MST, POET; DFS 20, 21; DLB
62, 172, 263; EXPP; LAIT 1; LATS 1:1;
LMFS 1; PAB; PFS 1, 2, 3, 4, 5, 8, 9;
RGEL 2; TEA; WLIT 3; WP; WS; WYA
Shakey, Bernard
See Young, Neil
Shalamov, Varlam (Tikhonovich)
1907-1982 **CLC 18**
See also CA 129; 105; DLB 302; RGSF 2
Shamloo, Ahmad
See Shamlu, Ahmad
Shamlou, Ahmad
See Shamlu, Ahmad
Shamlu, Ahmad 1925-2000 **CLC 10**
See also CA 216; CWW 2
Shammas, Anton 1951- **CLC 55**
See also CA 199
Shandling, Arline
See Berriault, Gina
Shange, Ntozake 1948- ... **BLC 3; CLC 8, 25,
38, 74, 126; DC 3**
See also AAYA 9, 66; AFAW 1, 2; BW 2;
CA 85-88; CABS 3; CAD; CANR 27, 48,
74, 131; CD 5, 6; CP 5, 6, 7; CWD; CWP;
DA3; DAM DRAM, MULT; DFS 2, 11;
DLB 38, 249; FW; LAIT 4, 5; MAL 5;
MTCW 1, 2; MTFW 2005; NFS 11;
RGAL 4; SATA 157; YAW
Shanley, John Patrick 1950- **CLC 75**
See also AMWS 14; CA 128; 133; CAD;
CANR 83, 154; CD 5, 6; DFS 23
Shapcott, Thomas W(illiam) 1935- .. **CLC 38**
See also CA 69-72; CANR 49, 83, 103; CP
1, 2, 3, 4, 5, 6, 7; DLB 289
Shapiro, Jane 1942- **CLC 76**
See also CA 196
Shapiro, Karl (Jay) 1913-2000 **CLC 4, 8,
15, 53; PC 25**
See also AMWS 2; CA 1-4R; 188; CAAS
6; CANR 1, 36, 66; CP 1, 2, 3, 4, 5, 6;
DLB 48; EWL 3; EXPP; MAL 5; MTCW
1, 2; MTFW 2005; PFS 3; RGAL 4
Sharp, William 1855-1905 **TCLC 39**
See Macleod, Fiona
See also CA 160; DLB 156; RGEL 2
Sharpe, Thomas Ridley 1928-
See Sharpe, Tom
See also CA 114; 122; CANR 85; INT CA-
122
Sharpe, Tom **CLC 36**
See Sharpe, Thomas Ridley
See also CN 4, 5, 6, 7; DLB 14, 231
Shatrov, Mikhail **CLC 59**
Shaw, Bernard
See Shaw, George Bernard
See also DLB 10, 57, 190
Shaw, G. Bernard
See Shaw, George Bernard
Shaw, George Bernard 1856-1950 **DC 23;
TCLC 3, 9, 21, 45; WLC 5**
See Shaw, Bernard
See also AAYA 61; BRW 6; BRWC 1;
BRWR 2; CA 104; 128; CDBLB 1914-
1945; DA; DA3; DAB; DAC; DAM

DRAM, MST; DFS 1, 3, 6, 11, 19, 22;
EWL 3; LAIT 3; LATS 1:1; MTCW 1, 2;
MTFW 2005; RGEL 2; TEA; WLIT 4

Shaw, Henry Wheeler 1818-1885 .. **NCLC 15**
See also DLB 11; RGAL 4

Shaw, Irwin 1913-1984 **CLC 7, 23, 34**
See also AITN 1; BPFB 3; CA 13-16R; 112;
CANR 21; CDALB 1941-1968; CN 1, 2,
3; CPW; DAM DRAM, POP; DLB 6,
102; DLBY 1984; MAL 5; MTCW 1, 21;
MTFW 2005

Shaw, Robert (Archibald)
1927-1978 **CLC 5**
See also AITN 1; CA 1-4R; 81-84; CANR
4; CN 1, 2; DLB 13, 14

Shaw, T. E.
See Lawrence, T(homas) E(dward)

Shawn, Wallace 1943- **CLC 41**
See also CA 112; CAD; CD 5, 6; DLB 266

Shaykh, al- Hanan
See al-Shaykh, Hanan
See also CWW 2; EWL 3

Shchedrin, N.
See Saltykov, Mikhail Evgrafovich

Shea, Lisa 1953- **CLC 86**
See also CA 147

Sheed, Wilfrid (John Joseph) 1930- . **CLC 2, 4, 10, 53**
See also CA 65-68; CANR 30, 66; CN 1, 2,
3, 4, 5, 6, 7; DLB 6; MAL 5; MTCW 1,
2; MTFW 2005

Sheehy, Gail 1937- **CLC 171**
See also CA 49-52; CANR 1, 33, 55, 92;
CPW; MTCW 1

Sheldon, Alice Hastings Bradley
1915(?)-1987
See Tiptree, James, Jr.
See also CA 108; 122; CANR 34; INT CA-
108; MTCW 1

Sheldon, John
See Bloch, Robert (Albert)

Sheldon, Walter J(ames) 1917-1996
See Queen, Ellery
See also AITN 1; CA 25-28R; CANR 10

Shelley, Mary Wollstonecraft (Godwin)
1797-1851 **NCLC 14, 59, 103, 170;
SSC 92; WLC 5**
See also AAYA 20; BPFB 3; BRW 3;
BRWC 2; BRWS 3; BYA 5; CDBLB
1789-1832; DA; DA3; DAB; DAC; DAM
MST, NOV; DLB 110, 116, 159, 178;
EXPN; FL 1:3; GL 3; HGG; LAIT 1;
LMFS 1, 2; NFS 1; RGEL 2; SATA 29;
SCFW 1, 2; SFW 4; TEA; WLIT 3

Shelley, Percy Bysshe 1792-1822 .. **NCLC 18,
93, 143; PC 14, 67; WLC 5**
See also AAYA 61; BRW 4; BRWR 1; CD-
BLB 1789-1832; DA; DA3; DAB; DAC;
DAM MST, POET; DLB 96, 110, 158;
EXPP; LMFS 1; PAB; PFS 2; RGEL 2;
TEA; WLIT 3; WP

Shepard, James R. **CLC 36**
See also CA 137; CANR 59, 104; SATA 90,
164

Shepard, Jim
See Shepard, James R.

Shepard, Lucius 1947- **CLC 34**
See also CA 128; 141; CANR 81, 124;
HGG; SCFW 2; SFW 4; SUFW 2

Shepard, Sam 1943- **CLC 4, 6, 17, 34, 41,
44, 169; DC 5**
See also AAYA 1, 58; AMWS 3; CA 69-72;
CABS 3; CAD; CANR 22, 120, 140; CD
5, 6; DA3; DAM DRAM; DFS 3, 6, 7,
14; DLB 7, 212; EWL 3; IDFW 3, 4;
MAL 5; MTCW 1, 2; MTFW 2005;
RGAL 4

Shepherd, Jean (Parker)
1921-1999 **TCLC 177**
See also AAYA 69; AITN 2; CA 77-80; 187

Shepherd, Michael
See Ludlum, Robert

Sherburne, Zoa (Lillian Morin)
1912-1995 **CLC 30**
See also AAYA 13; CA 1-4R; 176; CANR
3, 37; MAICYA 1, 2; SAAS 18; SATA 3;
YAW

Sheridan, Frances 1724-1766 **LC 7**
See also DLB 39, 84

Sheridan, Richard Brinsley
1751-1816 . **DC 1; NCLC 5, 91; WLC 5**
See also BRW 3; CDBLB 1660-1789; DA;
DAB; DAC; DAM DRAM, MST; DFS
15; DLB 89; WLIT 3

Sherman, Jonathan Marc 1968- **CLC 55**
See also CA 230

Sherman, Martin 1941(?)- **CLC 19**
See also CA 116; 123; CAD; CANR 86;
CD 5, 6; DFS 20; DLB 228; GLL 1;
IDTP; RGHL

Sherwin, Judith Johnson
See Johnson, Judith (Emlyn)
See also CANR 85; CP 2, 3, 4, 5; CWP

Sherwood, Frances 1940- **CLC 81**
See also CA 146, 220; CAAE 220

Sherwood, Robert E(mmet)
1896-1955 **TCLC 3**
See also CA 104; 153; CANR 86; DAM
DRAM; DFS 11, 15, 17; DLB 7, 26, 249;
IDFW 3, 4; MAL 5; RGAL 4

Shestov, Lev 1866-1938 **TCLC 56**

Shevchenko, Taras 1814-1861 **NCLC 54**

Shiel, M(atthew) P(hipps)
1865-1947 **TCLC 8**
See Holmes, Gordon
See also CA 106; 160; DLB 153; HGG;
MTCW 2; MTFW 2005; SCFW 1, 2;
SFW 4; SUFW

Shields, Carol (Ann) 1935-2003 **CLC 91,
113, 193**
See also AMWS 7; CA 81-84; 218; CANR
51, 74, 98, 133; CCA 1; CN 6, 7; CPW;
DA3; DAC; MTCW 2; MTFW 2005; NFS
23

Shields, David (Jonathan) 1956- **CLC 97**
See also CA 124; CANR 48, 99, 112

Shiga, Naoya 1883-1971 **CLC 33; SSC 23;
TCLC 172**
See Shiga Naoya
See also CA 101; 33-36R; MJW; RGWL 3

Shiga Naoya
See Shiga, Naoya
See also DLB 180; EWL 3; RGWL 3

Shilts, Randy 1951-1994 **CLC 85**
See also AAYA 19; CA 115; 127; 144;
CANR 45; DA3; GLL 1; INT CA-127;
MTCW 2; MTFW 2005

Shimazaki, Haruki 1872-1943
See Shimazaki Toson
See also CA 105; 134; CANR 84; RGWL 3

Shimazaki Toson **TCLC 5**
See Shimazaki, Haruki
See also DLB 180; EWL 3

Shirley, James 1596-1666 **DC 25; LC 96**
See also DLB 58; RGEL 2

Sholokhov, Mikhail (Aleksandrovich)
1905-1984 **CLC 7, 15**
See also CA 101; 112; DLB 272; EWL 3;
MTCW 1, 2; MTFW 2005; RGWL 2, 3;
SATA-Obit 36

Shone, Patric
See Hanley, James

Showalter, Elaine 1941- **CLC 169**
See also CA 57-60; CANR 58, 106; DLB
67; FW; GLL 2

Shreve, Susan
See Shreve, Susan Richards

Shreve, Susan Richards 1939- **CLC 23**
See also CA 49-52; CAAS 5; CANR 5, 38,
69, 100; MAICYA 1, 2; SATA 46, 95, 152;
SATA-Brief 41

Shue, Larry 1946-1985 **CLC 52**
See also CA 145; 117; DAM DRAM; DFS
7

Shu-Jen, Chou 1881-1936
See Lu Hsun
See also CA 104

Shulman, Alix Kates 1932- **CLC 2, 10**
See also CA 29-32R; CANR 43; FW; SATA
7

Shuster, Joe 1914-1992 **CLC 21**
See also AAYA 50

Shute, Nevil **CLC 30**
See Norway, Nevil Shute
See also BPFB 3; DLB 255; NFS 9; RHW;
SFW 4

Shuttle, Penelope (Diane) 1947- **CLC 7**
See also CA 93-96; CANR 39, 84, 92, 108;
CP 3, 4, 5, 6, 7; CWP; DLB 14, 40

Shvarts, Elena 1948- **PC 50**
See also CA 147

Sidhwa, Bapsi 1939-
See Sidhwa, Bapsy (N.)
See also CN 6, 7; DLB 323

Sidhwa, Bapsy (N.) 1938- **CLC 168**
See Sidhwa, Bapsi
See also CA 108; CANR 25, 57; FW

Sidney, Mary 1561-1621 **LC 19, 39**
See Sidney Herbert, Mary

Sidney, Sir Philip 1554-1586 . **LC 19, 39; PC
32**
See also BRW 1; BRWR 2; CDBLB Before
1660; DA; DA3; DAB; DAC; DAM MST,
POET; DLB 167; EXPP; PAB; RGEL 2;
TEA; WP

Sidney Herbert, Mary
See Sidney, Mary
See also DLB 167

Siegel, Jerome 1914-1996 **CLC 21**
See Siegel, Jerry
See also CA 116; 169; 151

Siegel, Jerry
See Siegel, Jerome
See also AAYA 50

Sienkiewicz, Henryk (Adam Alexander Pius)
1846-1916 **TCLC 3**
See also CA 104; 134; CANR 84; EWL 3;
RGSF 2; RGWL 2, 3

Sierra, Gregorio Martinez
See Martinez Sierra, Gregorio

Sierra, Maria (de la O'LeJarraga) Martinez
See Martinez Sierra, Maria (de la
O'LeJarraga)

Sigal, Clancy 1926- **CLC 7**
See also CA 1-4R; CANR 85; CN 1, 2, 3,
4, 5, 6, 7

Siger of Brabant 1240(?)-1284(?) . **CMLC 69**
See also DLB 115

Sigourney, Lydia H.
See Sigourney, Lydia Howard (Huntley)
See also DLB 73, 183

Sigourney, Lydia Howard (Huntley)
1791-1865 **NCLC 21, 87**
See Sigourney, Lydia H.; Sigourney, Lydia
Huntley
See also DLB 1

Sigourney, Lydia Huntley
See Sigourney, Lydia Howard (Huntley)
See also DLB 42, 239, 243

Siguenza y Gongora, Carlos de
1645-1700 **HLCS 2; LC 8**
See also LAW

Sigurjonsson, Johann
See Sigurjonsson, Johann

Sigurjonsson, Johann 1880-1919 ... **TCLC 27**
See also CA 170; DLB 293; EWL 3

Sikelianos, Angelos 1884-1951 **PC 29; TCLC 39**
 See also EWL 3; RGWL 2, 3

Silkin, Jon 1930-1997 **CLC 2, 6, 43**
 See also CA 5-8R; CAAS 5; CANR 89; CP 1, 2, 3, 4, 5, 6; DLB 27

Silko, Leslie (Marmon) 1948- **CLC 23, 74, 114, 211; NNAL; SSC 37, 66; WLCS**
 See also AAYA 14; AMWS; ANW; BYA 12; CA 115; 122; CANR 45, 65, 118; CN 4, 5, 6, 7; CP 4, 5, 6, 7; CPW 1; CWP; DA; DA3; DAC; DAM MST, MULT, POP; DLB 143, 175, 256, 275; EWL 3; EXPP; EXPS; LAIT 4; MAL 5; MTCW 2; MTFW 2005; NFS 4; PFS 9, 16; RGAL 4; RGSF 2; SSFS 4, 8, 10, 11; TCWW 1, 2

Sillanpaa, Frans Eemil 1888-1964 ... **CLC 19**
 See also CA 129; 93-96; EWL 3; MTCW 1

Sillitoe, Alan 1928- .. **CLC 1, 3, 6, 10, 19, 57, 148**
 See also AITN 1; BRWS 5; CA 9-12R, 191; CAAE 191; CAAS 2; CANR 8, 26, 55, 139; CDBLB 1960 to Present; CN 1, 2, 3, 4, 5, 6; CP 1, 2, 3, 4, 5; DLB 14, 139; EWL 3; MTCW 1, 2; MTFW 2005; RGEL 2; RGSF 2; SATA 61

Silone, Ignazio 1900-1978 **CLC 4**
 See also CA 25-28; 81-84; CANR 34; CAP 2; DLB 264; EW 12; EWL 3; MTCW 1; RGSF 2; RGWL 2, 3

Silone, Ignazione
 See Silone, Ignazio

Silver, Joan Micklin 1935- **CLC 20**
 See also CA 114; 121; INT CA-121

Silver, Nicholas
 See Faust, Frederick (Schiller)

Silverberg, Robert 1935- **CLC 7, 140**
 See also AAYA 24; BPFB 3; BYA 7, 9; CA 1-4R, 186; CAAE 186; CAAS 3; CANR 1, 20, 36, 85, 140; CLR 59; CN 6, 7; CPW; DAM POP; DLB 8; INT CANR-20; MAICYA 1, 2; MTCW 1, 2; MTFW 2005; SATA 13, 91; SATA-Essay 104; SCFW 1, 2; SFW 4; SUFW 2

Silverstein, Alvin 1933- **CLC 17**
 See also CA 49-52; CANR 2; CLR 25; JRDA; MAICYA 1, 2; SATA 8, 69, 124

Silverstein, Shel(don Allan)
 1932-1999 **PC 49**
 See also AAYA 40; BW 3; CA 107; 179; CANR 47, 74, 81; CLR 5, 96; CWRI 5; JRDA; MAICYA 1, 2; MTCW 2; MTFW 2005; SATA 33, 92; SATA-Brief 27; SATA-Obit 116

Silverstein, Virginia B(arbara Opshelor)
 1937- .. **CLC 17**
 See also CA 49-52; CANR 2; CLR 25; JRDA; MAICYA 1, 2; SATA 8, 69, 124

Sim, Georges
 See Simenon, Georges (Jacques Christian)

Simak, Clifford D(onald) 1904-1988 . **CLC 1, 55**
 See also CA 1-4R; 125; CANR 1, 35; DLB 8; MTCW 1; SATA-Obit 56; SCFW 1, 2; SFW 4

Simenon, Georges (Jacques Christian)
 1903-1989 **CLC 1, 2, 3, 8, 18, 47**
 See also BPFB 3; CA 85-88; 129; CANR 35; CMW 4; DA3; DAM POP; DLB 72; DLBY 1989; EW 12; EWL 3; GFL 1789 to the Present; MSW; MTCW 1, 2; MTFW 2005; RGWL 2, 3

Simic, Charles 1938- **CLC 6, 9, 22, 49, 68, 130; PC 69**
 See also AMWS 8; CA 29-32R; CAAS 4; CANR 12, 33, 52, 61, 96, 140; CP 2, 3, 4, 5, 6, 7; DA3; DAM POET; DLB 105; MAL 5; MTCW 2; MTFW 2005; PFS 7; RGAL 4; WP

Simmel, Georg 1858-1918 **TCLC 64**
 See also CA 157; DLB 296

Simmons, Charles (Paul) 1924- **CLC 57**
 See also CA 89-92; INT CA-89-92

Simmons, Dan 1948- **CLC 44**
 See also AAYA 16, 54; CA 138; CANR 53, 81, 126; CPW; DAM POP; HGG; SUFW 2

Simmons, James (Stewart Alexander)
 1933- ... **CLC 43**
 See also CA 105; CAAS 21; CP 1, 2, 3, 4, 5, 6, 7; DLB 40

Simms, William Gilmore
 1806-1870 **NCLC 3**
 See also DLB 3, 30, 59, 73, 248, 254; RGAL 4

Simon, Carly 1945- **CLC 26**
 See also CA 105

Simon, Claude 1913-2005 ... **CLC 4, 9, 15, 39**
 See also CA 89-92; 241; CANR 33, 117; CWW 2; DAM NOV; DLB 83; EW 13; EWL 3; GFL 1789 to the Present; MTCW 1

Simon, Claude Eugene Henri
 See Simon, Claude

Simon, Claude Henri Eugene
 See Simon, Claude

Simon, Marvin Neil
 See Simon, Neil

Simon, Myles
 See Follett, Ken(neth Martin)

Simon, Neil 1927- **CLC 6, 11, 31, 39, 70; DC 14**
 See also AAYA 32; AITN 1; AMWS 4; CA 21-24R; CAD; CANR 26, 54, 87, 126; CD 5, 6; DA3; DAM DRAM; DFS 2, 6, 12, 18; DLB 7, 266; LAIT 4; MAL 5; MTCW 1, 2; MTFW 2005; RGAL 4; TUS

Simon, Paul 1941(?)- **CLC 17**
 See also CA 116; 153; CANR 152

Simon, Paul Frederick
 See Simon, Paul

Simonon, Paul 1956(?)- **CLC 30**

Simonson, Rick ed. **CLC 70**

Simpson, Harriette
 See Arnow, Harriette (Louisa) Simpson

Simpson, Louis (Aston Marantz)
 1923- **CLC 4, 7, 9, 32, 149**
 See also AMWS 9; CA 1-4R; CAAS 4; CANR 1, 61, 140; CP 1, 2, 3, 4, 5, 6, 7; DAM POET; DLB 5; MAL 5; MTCW 1, 2; MTFW 2005; PFS 7, 11, 14; RGAL 4

Simpson, Mona 1957- **CLC 44, 146**
 See also CA 122; 135; CANR 68, 103; CN 6, 7; EWL 3

Simpson, Mona Elizabeth
 See Simpson, Mona

Simpson, N(orman) F(rederick)
 1919- .. **CLC 29**
 See also CA 13-16R; CBD; DLB 13; RGEL 2

Sinclair, Andrew (Annandale) 1935- . **CLC 2, 14**
 See also CA 9-12R; CAAS 5; CANR 14, 38, 91; CN 1, 2, 3, 4, 5, 6, 7; DLB 14; FANT; MTCW 1

Sinclair, Emil
 See Hesse, Hermann

Sinclair, Iain 1943- **CLC 76**
 See also CA 132; CANR 81; CP 5, 6, 7; HGG

Sinclair, Iain MacGregor
 See Sinclair, Iain

Sinclair, Irene
 See Griffith, D(avid Lewelyn) W(ark)

Sinclair, Mary Amelia St. Clair 1865(?)-1946
 See Sinclair, May
 See also CA 104; HGG; RHW

Sinclair, May **TCLC 3, 11**
 See Sinclair, Mary Amelia St. Clair
 See also CA 166; DLB 36, 135; EWL 3; RGEL 2; SUFW

Sinclair, Roy
 See Griffith, D(avid Lewelyn) W(ark)

Sinclair, Upton 1878-1968 **CLC 1, 11, 15, 63; TCLC 160; WLC 5**
 See also AAYA 63; AMWS 5; BPFB 3; BYA 2; CA 5-8R; 25-28R; CANR 7; CDALB 1929-1941; DA; DA3; DAB; DAC; DAM MST, NOV; DLB 9; EWL 3; INT CANR-7; LAIT 3; MAL 5; MTCW 1, 2; MTFW 2005; NFS 6; RGAL 4; SATA 9; TUS; YAW

Sinclair, Upton Beall
 See Sinclair, Upton

Singe, (Edmund) J(ohn) M(illington)
 1871-1909 **WLC**

Singer, Isaac
 See Singer, Isaac Bashevis

Singer, Isaac Bashevis 1904-1991 .. **CLC 1, 3, 6, 9, 11, 15, 23, 38, 69, 111; SSC 3, 53, 80; WLC 5**
 See also AAYA 32; AITN 1, 2; AMW; AMWR 2; BPFB 3; BYA 1, 4; CA 1-4R; 134; CANR 1, 39, 106; CDALB 1941-1968; CLR 1; CN 1, 2, 3, 4; CWRI 5; DA; DA3; DAB; DAC; DAM MST, NOV; DLB 6, 28, 52, 278; DLBY 1991; EWL 3; EXPS; HGG; JRDA; LAIT 3; MAI-CYA 1, 2; MAL 5; MTCW 1, 2; MTFW 2005; RGAL 4; RGHL; RGSF 2; SATA 3, 27; SATA-Obit 68; SSFS 2, 12, 16; TUS; TWA

Singer, Israel Joshua 1893-1944 **TCLC 33**
 See also CA 169; EWL 3

Singh, Khushwant 1915- **CLC 11**
 See also CA 9-12R; CAAS 9; CANR 6, 84; CN 1, 2, 3, 4, 5, 6, 7; DLB 323; EWL 3; RGEL 2

Singleton, Ann
 See Benedict, Ruth

Singleton, John 1968(?)- **CLC 156**
 See also AAYA 50; BW 2, 3; CA 138; CANR 67, 82; DAM MULT

Siniavskii, Andrei
 See Sinyavsky, Andrei (Donatevich)
 See also CWW 2

Sinjohn, John
 See Galsworthy, John

Sinyavsky, Andrei (Donatevich)
 1925-1997 **CLC 8**
 See Siniavskii, Andrei; Sinyavsky, Andrey Donatovich; Tertz, Abram
 See also CA 85-88; 159

Sinyavsky, Andrey Donatovich
 See Sinyavsky, Andrei (Donatevich)
 See also EWL 3

Sirin, V.
 See Nabokov, Vladimir (Vladimirovich)

Sissman, L(ouis) E(dward)
 1928-1976 **CLC 9, 18**
 See also CA 21-24R; 65-68; CANR 13; CP 2; DLB 5

Sisson, C(harles) H(ubert)
 1914-2003 **CLC 8**
 See also BRWS 11; CA 1-4R; 220; CAAS 3; CANR 3, 48, 84; CP 1, 2, 3, 4, 5, 6, 7; DLB 27

Sitting Bull 1831(?)-1890 **NNAL**
 See also DA3; DAM MULT

Sitwell, Dame Edith 1887-1964 **CLC 2, 9, 67; PC 3**
 See also BRW 7; CA 9-12R; CANR 35; CDBLB 1945-1960; DAM POET; DLB 20; EWL 3; MTCW 1, 2; MTFW 2005; RGEL 2; TEA

Siwaarmill, H. P.
 See Sharp, William

Sjoewall, Maj 1935- CLC 7
See Sjowall, Maj
See also CA 65-68; CANR 73

Sjowall, Maj
See Sjoewall, Maj
See also BPFB 3; CMW 4; MSW

Skelton, John 1460(?)-1529 LC 71; PC 25
See also BRW 1; DLB 136; RGEL 2

Skelton, Robin 1925-1997 CLC 13
See Zuk, Georges
See also AITN 2; CA 5-8R; 160; CAAS 5;
CANR 28, 89; CCA 1; CP 1, 2, 3, 4, 5, 6;
DLB 27, 53

Skolimowski, Jerzy 1938- CLC 20
See also CA 128

Skram, Amalie (Bertha)
1847-1905 TCLC 25
See also CA 165

Skvorecky, Josef (Vaclav) 1924- CLC 15,
39, 69, 152
See also CA 61-64; CAAS 1; CANR 10,
34, 63, 108; CDWLB 4; CWW 2; DA3;
DAC; DAM NOV; DLB 232; EWL 3;
MTCW 1, 2; MTFW 2005

Slade, Bernard 1930- CLC 11, 46
See Newbound, Bernard Slade
See also CAAS 9; CCA 1; CD 6; DLB 53

Slaughter, Carolyn 1946- CLC 56
See also CA 85-88; CANR 85; CN 5, 6, 7

Slaughter, Frank G(ill) 1908-2001 ... CLC 29
See also AITN 2; CA 5-8R; 197; CANR 5,
85; INT CANR-5; RHW

Slavitt, David R(ytman) 1935- CLC 5, 14
See also CA 21-24R; CAAS 3; CANR 41,
83; CN 1, 2; CP 1, 2, 3, 4, 5, 6, 7; DLB
5, 6

Slesinger, Tess 1905-1945 TCLC 10
See also CA 107; 199; DLB 102

Slessor, Kenneth 1901-1971 CLC 14
See also CA 102; 89-92; DLB 260; RGEL
2

Slowacki, Juliusz 1809-1849 NCLC 15
See also RGWL 3

Smart, Christopher 1722-1771 . LC 3; PC 13
See also DAM POET; DLB 109; RGEL 2

Smart, Elizabeth 1913-1986 CLC 54
See also CA 81-84; 118; CN 4; DLB 88

Smiley, Jane (Graves) 1949- CLC 53, 76,
144
See also AAYA 66; AMWS 6; BPFB 3; CA
104; CANR 30, 50, 74, 96; CN 6, 7; CPW
1; DA3; DAM POP; DLB 227, 234; EWL
3; INT CANR-30; MAL 5; MTFW 2005;
SSFS 19

Smith, A(rthur) J(ames) M(arshall)
1902-1980 CLC 15
See also CA 1-4R; 102; CANR 4; CP 1, 2,
3; DAC; DLB 88; RGEL 2

Smith, Adam 1723(?)-1790 LC 36
See also DLB 104, 252; RGEL 2

Smith, Alexander 1829-1867 NCLC 59
See also DLB 32, 55

Smith, Anna Deavere 1950- CLC 86
See also CA 133; CANR 103; CD 5, 6; DFS
2, 22

Smith, Betty (Wehner) 1904-1972 CLC 19
See also BPFB 3; BYA 3; CA 5-8R; 33-
36R; DLBY 1982; LAIT 3; RGAL 4;
SATA 6

Smith, Charlotte (Turner)
1749-1806 NCLC 23, 115
See also DLB 39, 109; RGEL 2; TEA

Smith, Clark Ashton 1893-1961 CLC 43
See also CA 143; CANR 81; FANT; HGG;
MTCW 2; SCFW 1, 2; SFW 4; SUFW

Smith, Dave CLC 22, 42
See Smith, David (Jeddie)
See also CAAS 7; CP 3, 4, 5, 6, 7; DLB 5

Smith, David (Jeddie) 1942-
See Smith, Dave
See also CA 49-52; CANR 1, 59, 120;
CSW; DAM POET

Smith, Iain Crichton 1928-1998 CLC 64
See also BRWS 9; CA 21-24R; 171; CN 1,
2, 3, 4, 5, 6; CP 1, 2, 3, 4, 5, 6; DLB 40,
139, 319; RGSF 2

Smith, John 1580(?)-1631 LC 9
See also DLB 24, 30; TUS

Smith, Johnston
See Crane, Stephen (Townley)

Smith, Joseph, Jr. 1805-1844 NCLC 53

Smith, Kevin 1970- CLC 223
See also AAYA 37; CA 166; CANR 131

Smith, Lee 1944- CLC 25, 73
See also CA 114; 119; CANR 46, 118; CN
7; CSW; DLB 143; DLBY 1983; EWL 3;
INT CA-119; RGAL 4

Smith, Martin
See Smith, Martin Cruz

Smith, Martin Cruz 1942- .. CLC 25; NNAL
See also BEST 89:4; BPFB 3; CA 85-88;
CANR 6, 23, 43, 65, 119; CMW 4; CPW;
DAM MULT, POP; HGG; INT CANR-
23; MTCW 2; MTFW 2005; RGAL 4

Smith, Patti 1946- CLC 12
See also CA 93-96; CANR 63

Smith, Pauline (Urmson)
1882-1959 TCLC 25
See also DLB 225; EWL 3

Smith, Rosamond
See Oates, Joyce Carol

Smith, Sheila Kaye
See Kaye-Smith, Sheila

Smith, Stevie 1902-1971 CLC 3, 8, 25, 44;
PC 12
See also BRWS 2; CA 17-18; 29-32R;
CANR 35; CAP 2; CP 1; DAM POET;
DLB 20; EWL 3; MTCW 1, 2; PAB; PFS
3; RGEL 2; TEA

Smith, Wilbur (Addison) 1933- CLC 33
See also CA 13-16R; CANR 7, 46, 66, 134;
CPW; MTCW 1, 2; MTFW 2005

Smith, William Jay 1918- CLC 6
See also AMWS 13; CA 5-8R; CANR 44,
106; CP 1, 2, 3, 4, 5, 6, 7; CSW; CWRI
5; DLB 5; MAICYA 1, 2; SAAS 22;
SATA 2, 68, 154; SATA-Essay 154; TCLE
1:2

Smith, Woodrow Wilson
See Kuttner, Henry

Smith, Zadie 1975- CLC 158
See also AAYA 50; CA 193; MTFW 2005

Smolenskin, Peretz 1842-1885 NCLC 30

Smollett, Tobias (George) 1721-1771 ... LC 2,
46
See also BRW 3; CDBLB 1660-1789; DLB
39, 104; RGEL 2; TEA

Snodgrass, W(illiam) D(e Witt)
1926- CLC 2, 6, 10, 18, 68
See also AMWS 6; CA 1-4R; CANR 6, 36,
65, 85; CP 1, 2, 3, 4, 5, 6, 7; DAM POET;
DLB 5; MAL 5; MTCW 1, 2; MTFW
2005; RGAL 4; TCLE 1:2

Snorri Sturluson 1179-1241 CMLC 56
See also RGWL 2, 3

Snow, C(harles) P(ercy) 1905-1980 ... CLC 1,
4, 6, 9, 13, 19
See also BRW 7; CA 5-8R; 101; CANR 28;
CDBLB 1945-1960; CN 1, 2; DAM NOV;
DLB 15, 77; DLBD 17; EWL 3; MTCW
1, 2; MTFW 2005; RGEL 2; TEA

Snow, Frances Compton
See Adams, Henry (Brooks)

Snyder, Gary (Sherman) 1930- . CLC 1, 2, 5,
9, 32, 120; PC 21
See also AMWS 8; ANW; BG 1:3; CA 17-
20R; CANR 30, 60, 125; CP 1, 2, 3, 4, 5,
6, 7; DA3; DAM POET; DLB 5, 16, 165,
212, 237, 275; EWL 3; MAL 5; MTCW
2; MTFW 2005; PFS 9, 19; RGAL 4; WP

Snyder, Zilpha Keatley 1927- CLC 17
See also AAYA 15; BYA 1; CA 9-12R;
CANR 38; CLR 31; JRDA; MAICYA 1,
2; SAAS 2; SATA 1, 28, 75, 110, 163;
SATA-Essay 112, 163; YAW

Soares, Bernardo
See Pessoa, Fernando (Antonio Nogueira)

Sobh, A.
See Shamlu, Ahmad

Sobh, Alef
See Shamlu, Ahmad

Sobol, Joshua 1939- CLC 60
See Sobol, Yehoshua
See also CA 200; RGHL

Sobol, Yehoshua 1939-
See Sobol, Joshua
See also CWW 2

Socrates 470B.C.-399B.C. CMLC 27

Soderberg, Hjalmar 1869-1941 TCLC 39
See also DLB 259; EWL 3; RGSF 2

Soderbergh, Steven 1963- CLC 154
See also AAYA 43; CA 243

Soderbergh, Steven Andrew
See Soderbergh, Steven

Sodergran, Edith (Irene) 1892-1923
See Soedergran, Edith (Irene)
See also CA 202; DLB 259; EW 11; EWL
3; RGWL 2, 3

Soedergran, Edith (Irene)
1892-1923 TCLC 31
See Sodergran, Edith (Irene)

Softly, Edgar
See Lovecraft, H. P.

Softly, Edward
See Lovecraft, H. P.

Sokolov, Alexander V(sevolodovich) 1943-
See Sokolov, Sasha
See also CA 73-76

Sokolov, Raymond 1941- CLC 7
See also CA 85-88

Sokolov, Sasha CLC 59
See Sokolov, Alexander V(sevolodovich)
See also CWW 2; DLB 285; EWL 3; RGWL
2, 3

Solo, Jay
See Ellison, Harlan (Jay)

Sologub, Fyodor TCLC 9
See Teternikov, Fyodor Kuzmich
See also EWL 3

Solomons, Ikey Esquir
See Thackeray, William Makepeace

Solomos, Dionysios 1798-1857 NCLC 15

Solwoska, Mara
See French, Marilyn

Solzhenitsyn, Aleksandr I. 1918- .. CLC 1, 2,
4, 7, 9, 10, 18, 26, 34, 78, 134; SSC 32;
WLC 5
See Solzhenitsyn, Aleksandr Isayevich
See also AAYA 49; AITN 1; BPFB 3; CA
69-72; CANR 40, 65, 116; DA; DA3;
DAB; DAC; DAM MST, NOV; DLB 302;
EW 13; EXPS; LAIT 4; MTCW 1, 2;
MTFW 2005; NFS 6; RGSF 2; RGWL 2,
3; SSFS 9; TWA

Solzhenitsyn, Aleksandr Isayevich
See Solzhenitsyn, Aleksandr I.
See also CWW 2; EWL 3

Somers, Jane
See Lessing, Doris (May)

Somerville, Edith Oenone
1858-1949 SSC 56; TCLC 51
See also CA 196; DLB 135; RGEL 2; RGSF
2

Somerville & Ross
See Martin, Violet Florence; Somerville,
Edith Oenone

Sommer, Scott 1951- CLC 25
See also CA 106

Sommers, Christina Hoff 1950- CLC 197
See also CA 153; CANR 95

Sondheim, Stephen (Joshua) 1930- . CLC 30,
39, 147; DC 22
See also AAYA 11, 66; CA 103; CANR 47,
67, 125; DAM DRAM; LAIT 4

Sone, Monica 1919- AAL
See also DLB 312

Song, Cathy 1955- AAL; PC 21
See also CA 154; CANR 118; CWP; DLB
169, 312; EXPP; FW; PFS 5

Sontag, Susan 1933-2004 ... CLC 1, 2, 10, 13,
31, 105, 195
See also AMWS 3; CA 17-20R; 234; CANR
25, 51, 74, 97; CN 1, 2, 3, 4, 5, 6, 7;
CPW; DA3; DAM POP; DLB 2, 67; EWL
3; MAL 5; MAWW; MTCW 1, 2; MTFW
2005; RGAL 4; RHW; SSFS 10

Sophocles 496(?)B.C.-406(?)B.C. CMLC 2,
47, 51; DC 1; WLCS
See also AW 1; CDWLB 1; DA; DA3;
DAB; DAC; DAM DRAM, MST; DFS 1,
4, 8; DLB 176; LAIT 1; LATS 1:1; LMFS
1; RGWL 2, 3; TWA; WLIT 8

Sordello 1189-1269 CMLC 15

Sorel, Georges 1847-1922 TCLC 91
See also CA 118; 188

Sorel, Julia
See Drexler, Rosalyn

Sorokin, Vladimir CLC 59
See Sorokin, Vladimir Georgievich

Sorokin, Vladimir Georgievich
See Sorokin, Vladimir
See also DLB 285

Sorrentino, Gilbert 1929-2006 CLC 3, 7,
14, 22, 40
See also CA 77-80; CANR 14, 33, 115; CN
3, 4, 5, 6, 7; CP 1, 2, 3, 4, 5, 6, 7; DLB 5,
173; DLBY 1980; INT CANR-14

Soseki
See Natsume, Soseki
See also MJW

Soto, Gary 1952- ... CLC 32, 80; HLC 2; PC
28
See also AAYA 10, 37; BYA 11; CA 119;
125; CANR 50, 74, 107; CLR 38; CP 4,
5, 6, 7; DAM MULT; DLB 82; EWL 3;
EXPP; HW 1, 2; INT CA-125; JRDA;
LLW; MAICYA 2; MAICYAS 1; MAL 5;
MTFW 2005; PFS 7; RGAL 4;
SATA 80, 120; WYA; YAW

Soupault, Philippe 1897-1990 CLC 68
See also CA 116; 147; 131; EWL 3; GFL
1789 to the Present; LMFS 2

Souster, (Holmes) Raymond 1921- CLC 5,
14
See also CA 13-16R; CAAS 14; CANR 13,
29, 53; CP 1, 2, 3, 4, 5, 6, 7; DA3; DAC;
DAM POET; DLB 88; RGEL 2; SATA 63

Southern, Terry 1924(?)-1995 CLC 7
See also AMWS 11; BPFB 3; CA 1-4R;
150; CANR 1, 55, 107; CN 1, 2, 3, 4, 5,
6; DLB 2; IDFW 3, 4

Southerne, Thomas 1660-1746 LC 99
See also DLB 80; RGEL 2

Southey, Robert 1774-1843 NCLC 8, 97
See also BRW 4; DLB 93, 107, 142; RGEL
2; SATA 54

Southwell, Robert 1561(?)-1595 LC 108
See also DLB 167; RGEL 2; TEA

Southworth, Emma Dorothy Eliza Nevitte
1819-1899 NCLC 26
See also DLB 239

Souza, Ernest
See Scott, Evelyn

Soyinka, Wole 1934- .. BLC 3; CLC 3, 5, 14,
36, 44, 179; DC 2; WLC 5
See also AFW; BW 2, 3; CA 13-16R;
CANR 27, 39, 82, 136; CD 5, 6; CDWLB
3; CN 6, 7; CP 1, 2, 3, 4, 5, 6 ,7; DA;
DA3; DAB; DAC; DAM DRAM, MST,
MULT; DFS 10; DLB 125; EWL 3;
MTCW 1, 2; MTFW 2005; RGEL 2;
TWA; WLIT 2; WWE 1

Spackman, W(illiam) M(ode)
1905-1990 CLC 46
See also CA 81-84; 132

Spacks, Barry (Bernard) 1931- CLC 14
See also CA 154; CANR 33, 109; CP 3, 4,
5, 6, 7; DLB 105

Spanidou, Irini 1946- CLC 44
See also CA 185

Spark, Muriel (Sarah) 1918-2006 . CLC 2, 3,
5, 8, 13, 18, 40, 94; PC 72; SSC 10
See also BRWS 1; CA 5-8R; CANR 12, 36,
76, 89, 131; CDBLB 1945-1960; CN 1, 2,
3, 4, 5, 6, 7; CP 1, 2, 3, 4, 5, 6, 7; DA3;
DAB; DAC; DAM MST, NOV; DLB 15,
139; EWL 3; FW; INT CANR-12; LAIT
4; MTCW 1, 2; MTFW 2005; NFS 22;
RGEL 2; TEA; WLIT 4; YAW

Spaulding, Douglas
See Bradbury, Ray (Douglas)

Spaulding, Leonard
See Bradbury, Ray (Douglas)

Speght, Rachel 1597-c. 1630 LC 97
See also DLB 126

Spence, J. A. D.
See Eliot, T(homas) S(tearns)

Spencer, Anne 1882-1975 HR 1:3
See also BW 2; CA 161; DLB 51, 54

Spencer, Elizabeth 1921- CLC 22; SSC 57
See also CA 13-16R; CANR 32, 65, 87; CN
1, 2, 3, 4, 5, 6, 7; CSW; DLB 6, 218;
EWL 3; MTCW 1; RGAL 4; SATA 14

Spencer, Leonard G.
See Silverberg, Robert

Spencer, Scott 1945- CLC 30
See also CA 113; CANR 51, 148; DLBY
1986

Spender, Stephen (Harold)
1909-1995 .. CLC 1, 2, 5, 10, 41, 91; PC
71
See also BRWS 2; CA 9-12R; 149; CANR
31, 54; CDBLB 1945-1960; CP 1, 2, 3, 4,
5, 6; DA3; DAM POET; DLB 20; EWL
3; MTCW 1, 2; MTFW 2005; PAB; PFS
23; RGEL 2; TEA

Spengler, Oswald (Arnold Gottfried)
1880-1936 TCLC 25
See also CA 118; 189

Spenser, Edmund 1552(?)-1599 LC 5, 39,
117; PC 8, 42; WLC 5
See also AAYA 60; BRW 1; CDBLB Be-
fore 1660; DA; DA3; DAB; DAC; DAM
MST, POET; DLB 167; EFS 2; EXPP;
PAB; RGEL 2; TEA; WLIT 3; WP

Spicer, Jack 1925-1965 CLC 8, 18, 72
See also BG 1:3; CA 85-88; DAM POET;
DLB 5, 16, 193; GLL 1; WP

Spiegelman, Art 1948- CLC 76, 178
See also AAYA 10, 46; CA 125; CANR 41,
55, 74, 124; DLB 299; MTCW 2; MTFW
2005; RGHL; SATA 109, 158; YAW

Spielberg, Peter 1929- CLC 6
See also CA 5-8R; CANR 4, 48; DLBY
1981

Spielberg, Steven 1947- CLC 20, 188
See also AAYA 8, 24; CA 77-80; CANR
32; SATA 32

Spillane, Frank Morrison CLC 3, 13
See Spillane, Mickey
See also BPFB 3; CMW 4; DLB 226; MSW

Spillane, Mickey 1918-2006
See Spillane, Frank Morrison
See also CA 25-28R; CANR 28, 63, 125;
DA3; MTCW 1, 2; MTFW 2005; SATA
66

Spinoza, Benedictus de 1632-1677 .. LC 9, 58

Spinrad, Norman (Richard) 1940- ... CLC 46
See also BPFB 3; CA 37-40R, 233; CAAE
233; CAAS 19; CANR 20, 91; DLB 8;
INT CANR-20; SFW 4

Spitteler, Carl (Friedrich Georg)
1845-1924 TCLC 12
See also CA 109; DLB 129; EWL 3

Spivack, Kathleen (Romola Drucker)
1938- .. CLC 6
See also CA 49-52

Spofford, Harriet (Elizabeth) Prescott
1835-1921 SSC 87
See also CA 201; DLB 74, 221

Spoto, Donald 1941- CLC 39
See also CA 65-68; CANR 11, 57, 93

Springsteen, Bruce 1949- CLC 17
See also CA 111

Springsteen, Bruce F.
See Springsteen, Bruce

Spurling, Hilary 1940- CLC 34
See also CA 104; CANR 25, 52, 94

Spurling, Susan Hilary
See Spurling, Hilary

Spyker, John Howland
See Elman, Richard (Martin)

Squared, A.
See Abbott, Edwin A.

Squires, (James) Radcliffe
1917-1993 CLC 51
See also CA 1-4R; 140; CANR 6, 21; CP 1,
2, 3, 4, 5

Srivastava, Dhanpat Rai 1880(?)-1936
See Premchand
See also CA 118; 197

Stacy, Donald
See Pohl, Frederik

Stael
See Stael-Holstein, Anne Louise Germaine
Necker
See also EW 5; RGWL 2, 3

Stael, Germaine de
See Stael-Holstein, Anne Louise Germaine
Necker
See also DLB 119, 192; FL 1:3; FW; GFL
1789 to the Present; TWA

Stael-Holstein, Anne Louise Germaine
Necker 1766-1817ι.. NCLC 3, 91
See Stael; Stael, Germaine de

Stafford, Jean 1915-1979 .. CLC 4, 7, 19, 68;
SSC 26, 86
See also CA 1-4R; 85-88; CANR 3, 65; CN
1, 2; DLB 2, 173; MAL 5; MTCW 1, 2;
MTFW 2005; RGAL 4; RGSF 2; SATA-
Obit 22; SSFS 21; TCWW 1, 2; TUS

Stafford, William (Edgar)
1914-1993 CLC 4, 7, 29; PC 71
See also AMWS 11; CA 5-8R; 142; CAAS
3; CANR 5, 22; CP 1, 2, 3, 4, 5; DAM
POET; DLB 5, 206; EXPP; INT CANR-
22; MAL 5; PFS 2, 8, 16; RGAL 4; WP

Stagnelius, Eric Johan 1793-1823 . NCLC 61

Staines, Trevor
See Brunner, John (Kilian Houston)

Stairs, Gordon
See Austin, Mary (Hunter)

Stalin, Joseph 1879-1953 TCLC 92

Stampa, Gaspara c. 1524-1554 .. **LC 114; PC 43**
See also RGWL 2, 3; WLIT 7

Stampflinger, K. A.
See Benjamin, Walter

Stancykowna
See Szymborska, Wislawa

Standing Bear, Luther
1868(?)-1939(?) **NNAL**
See also CA 113; 144; DAM MULT

Stanislavsky, Konstantin (Sergeivich)
1863(?)-1938 **TCLC 167**
See also CA 118

Stannard, Martin 1947- **CLC 44**
See also CA 142; DLB 155

Stanton, Elizabeth Cady
1815-1902 **TCLC 73**
See also CA 171; DLB 79; FL 1:3; FW

Stanton, Maura 1946- **CLC 9**
See also CA 89-92; CANR 15, 123; DLB 120

Stanton, Schuyler
See Baum, L(yman) Frank

Stapledon, (William) Olaf
1886-1950 **TCLC 22**
See also CA 111; 162; DLB 15, 255; SCFW 1, 2; SFW 4

Starbuck, George (Edwin)
1931-1996 **CLC 53**
See also CA 21-24R; 153; CANR 23; CP 1, 2, 3, 4, 5, 6; DAM POET

Stark, Richard
See Westlake, Donald E(dwin)

Staunton, Schuyler
See Baum, L(yman) Frank

Stead, Christina (Ellen) 1902-1983 ... **CLC 2, 5, 8, 32, 80**
See also BRWS 4; CA 13-16R; 109; CANR 33, 40; CN 1, 2, 3; DLB 260; EWL 3; FW; MTCW 1, 2; MTFW 2005; RGEL 2; RGSF 2; WWE 1

Stead, William Thomas
1849-1912 **TCLC 48**
See also CA 167

Stebnitsky, M.
See Leskov, Nikolai (Semyonovich)

Steele, Richard 1672-1729 **LC 18**
See also BRW 3; CDBLB 1660-1789; DLB 84, 101; RGEL 2; WLIT 3

Steele, Timothy (Reid) 1948- **CLC 45**
See also CA 93-96; CANR 16, 50, 92; CP 5, 6, 7; DLB 120, 282

Steffens, (Joseph) Lincoln
1866-1936 **TCLC 20**
See also CA 117; 198; DLB 303; MAL 5

Stegner, Wallace (Earle) 1909-1993 .. **CLC 9, 49, 81; SSC 27**
See also AITN 1; AMWS 4; ANW; BEST 90:3; BPFB 3; CA 1-4R; 141; CAAS 9; CANR 1, 21, 46; CN 1, 2, 3, 4, 5; DAM NOV; DLB 9, 206, 275; DLBY 1993; EWL 3; MAL 5; MTCW 1, 2; MTFW 2005; RGAL 4; TCWW 1, 2; TUS

Stein, Gertrude 1874-1946 **DC 19; PC 18; SSC 42; TCLC 1, 6, 28, 48; WLC 5**
See also AAYA 64; AMW; AMWC 2; CA 104; 132; CANR 108; CDALB 1917-1929; DA; DA3; DAB; DAC; DAM MST, NOV, POET; DLB 4, 54, 86, 228; DLBD 15; EWL 3; EXPS; FL 1:6; GLL 1; MAL 5; MAWW; MTCW 1, 2; MTFW 2005; NCFS 4; RGAL 4; RGSF 2; SSFS 5; TUS; WP

Steinbeck, John (Ernst) 1902-1968 ... **CLC 1, 5, 9, 13, 21, 34, 45, 75, 124; SSC 11, 37, 77; TCLC 135; WLC 5**
See also AAYA 12; AMW; BPFB 3; BYA 2, 3, 13; CA 1-4R; 25-28R; CANR 1, 35; CDALB 1929-1941; DA; DA3; DAB; DAC; DAM DRAM, MST, NOV; DLB 7, 9, 212, 275, 309; DLBD 2; EWL 3; EXPS; LAIT 3; MAL 5; MTCW 1, 2; MTFW 2005; NFS 1, 5, 7, 17, 19; RGAL 4; RGSF 2; RHW; SATA 9; SSFS 3, 6; TCWW 1, 2; TUS; WYA; YAW

Steinem, Gloria 1934- **CLC 63**
See also CA 53-56; CANR 28, 51, 139; DLB 246; FW; MTCW 1, 2; MTFW 2005

Steiner, George 1929- **CLC 24, 221**
See also CA 73-76; CANR 31, 67, 108; DAM NOV; DLB 67, 299; EWL 3; MTCW 1, 2; MTFW 2005; RGHL; SATA 62

Steiner, K. Leslie
See Delany, Samuel R(ay), Jr.

Steiner, Rudolf 1861-1925 **TCLC 13**
Scc also CA 107

Stendhal 1783-1842 .. **NCLC 23, 46; SSC 27; WLC 5**
See also DA; DA3; DAB; DAC; DAM MST, NOV; DLB 119; EW 5; GFL 1789 to the Present; RGWL 2, 3; TWA

Stephen, Adeline Virginia
See Woolf, (Adeline) Virginia

Stephen, Sir Leslie 1832-1904 **TCLC 23**
See also BRW 5; CA 123; DLB 57, 144, 190

Stephen, Sir Leslie
See Stephen, Sir Leslie

Stephen, Virginia
See Woolf, (Adeline) Virginia

Stephens, James 1882(?)-1950 **SSC 50; TCLC 4**
See also CA 104; 192; DLB 19, 153, 162; EWL 3; FANT; RGEL 2; SUFW

Stephens, Reed
See Donaldson, Stephen R(eeder)

Steptoe, Lydia
See Barnes, Djuna
See also GLL 1

Sterchi, Beat 1949- **CLC 65**
See also CA 203

Sterling, Brett
See Bradbury, Ray (Douglas); Hamilton, Edmond

Sterling, Bruce 1954- **CLC 72**
See also CA 119; CANR 44, 135; CN 7; MTFW 2005; SCFW 2; SFW 4

Sterling, George 1869-1926 **TCLC 20**
See also CA 117; 165; DLB 54

Stern, Gerald 1925- **CLC 40, 100**
See also AMWS 9; CA 81-84; CANR 28, 94; CP 3, 4, 5, 6, 7; DLB 105; RGAL 4

Stern, Richard (Gustave) 1928- ... **CLC 4, 39**
See also CA 1-4R; CANR 1, 25, 52, 120; CN 1, 2, 3, 4, 5, 6, 7; DLB 218; DLBY 1987; INT CANR-25

Sternberg, Josef von 1894-1969 **CLC 20**
See also CA 81-84

Sterne, Laurence 1713-1768 **LC 2, 48; WLC 5**
See also BRW 3; BRWC 1; CDBLB 1660-1789; DA; DAB; DAC; DAM MST, NOV; DLB 39; RGEL 2; TEA

Sternheim, (William Adolf) Carl
1878-1942 **TCLC 8**
See also CA 105; 193; DLB 56, 118; EWL 3; IDTP; RGWL 2, 3

Stevens, Margaret Dean
See Aldrich, Bess Streeter

Stevens, Mark 1951- **CLC 34**
See also CA 122

Stevens, Wallace 1879-1955 . **PC 6; TCLC 3, 12, 45; WLC 5**
See also AMW; AMWR 1; CA 104; 124; CDALB 1929-1941; DA; DA3; DAB; DAC; DAM MST, POET; DLB 54; EWL 3; EXPP; MAL 5; MTCW 1, 2; PAB; PFS 13, 16; RGAL 4; TUS; WP

Stevenson, Anne (Katharine) 1933- .. **CLC 7, 33**
See also BRWS 6; CA 17-20R; CAAS 9; CANR 9, 33, 123; CP 3, 4, 5, 6, 7; CWP; DLB 40; MTCW 1; RHW

Stevenson, Robert Louis (Balfour)
1850-1894 **NCLC 5, 14, 63; SSC 11, 51; WLC 5**
See also AAYA 24; BPFB 3; BRW 5; BRWC 1; BRWR 1; BYA 1, 2, 4, 13; CD-BLB 1890-1914; CLR 10, 11, 107; DA; DA3; DAB; DAC; DAM MST, NOV; DLB 18, 57, 141, 156, 174; DLBD 13; GL 3; HGG; JRDA; LAIT 1, 3; MAICYA 1, 2; NFS 11, 20; RGEL 2; RGSF 2; SATA 100; SUFW; TEA; WCH; WLIT 4; WYA; YABC 2; YAW

Stewart, J(ohn) I(nnes) M(ackintosh)
1906-1994 **CLC 7, 14, 32**
See Innes, Michael
See also CA 85-88; 147; CAAS 3; CANR 47; CMW 4; CN 1, 2, 3, 4, 5; MTCW 1, 2

Stewart, Mary (Florence Elinor)
1916- **CLC 7, 35, 117**
See also AAYA 29; BPFB 3; CA 1-4R; CANR 1, 59, 130; CMW 4; CPW; DAB; FANT; RHW; SATA 12; YAW

Stewart, Mary Rainbow
See Stewart, Mary (Florence Elinor)

Stifle, June
See Campbell, Maria

Stifter, Adalbert 1805-1868 .. **NCLC 41; SSC 28**
See also CDWLB 2; DLB 133; RGSF 2; RGWL 2, 3

Still, James 1906-2001 **CLC 49**
See also CA 65-68; 195; CAAS 17; CANR 10, 26; CSW; DLB 9; DLBY 01; SATA 29; SATA-Obit 127

Sting 1951-
See Sumner, Gordon Matthew
See also CA 167

Stirling, Arthur
See Sinclair, Upton

Stitt, Milan 1941- **CLC 29**
See also CA 69-72

Stockton, Francis Richard 1834-1902
See Stockton, Frank R.
See also AAYA 68; CA 108; 137; MAICYA 1, 2; SATA 44; SFW 4

Stockton, Frank R. **TCLC 47**
See Stockton, Francis Richard
See also BYA 4, 13; DLB 42, 74; DLBD 13; EXPS; SATA-Brief 32; SSFS 3; SUFW; WCH

Stoddard, Charles
See Kuttner, Henry

Stoker, Abraham 1847-1912
See Stoker, Bram
See also CA 105; 150; DA; DA3; DAC; DAM MST, NOV; HGG; MTFW 2005; SATA 29

Stoker, Bram . **SSC 62; TCLC 8, 144; WLC 6**
See Stoker, Abraham
See also AAYA 23; BPFB 3; BRWS 3; BYA 5; CDBLB 1890-1914; DAB; DLB 304; GL 3; LATS 1:1; NFS 18; RGEL 2; SUFW; TEA; WLIT 4

Stolz, Mary (Slattery) 1920- **CLC 12**
See also AAYA 8; AITN 1; CA 5-8R; CANR 13, 41, 112; JRDA; MAICYA 1, 2; SAAS 3; SATA 10, 71, 133; YAW

Stone, Irving 1903-1989 **CLC 7**
See also AITN 1; BPFB 3; CA 1-4R; 129; CAAS 3; CANR 1, 23; CN 1, 2, 3, 4; CPW; DA3; DAM POP; INT CANR-23; MTCW 1, 2; MTFW 2005; RHW; SATA 3; SATA-Obit 64

Stone, Oliver (William) 1946- **CLC 73**
See also AAYA 15, 64; CA 110; CANR 55, 125

Stone, Robert (Anthony) 1937- ... **CLC 5, 23, 42, 175**
See also AMWS 5; BPFB 3; CA 85-88; CANR 23, 66, 95; CN 4, 5, 6, 7; DLB 152; EWL 3; INT CANR-23; MAL 5; MTCW 1; MTFW 2005

Stone, Ruth 1915- **PC 53**
See also CA 45-48; CANR 2, 91; CP 5, 6, 7; CSW; DLB 105; PFS 19

Stone, Zachary
See Follett, Ken(neth Martin)

Stoppard, Tom 1937- ... **CLC 1, 3, 4, 5, 8, 15, 29, 34, 63, 91; DC 6; WLC 6**
See also AAYA 63; BRWC 1; BRWR 2; BRWS 1; CA 81-84; CANR 39, 67, 125; CBD; CD 5, 6; CDBLB 1960 to Present; DA; DA3; DAB; DAC; DAM DRAM, MST; DFS 2, 5, 8, 11, 13, 16; DLB 13, 233; DLBY 1985; EWL 3; LATS 1:2; MTCW 1, 2; MTFW 2005; RGEL 2; TEA; WLIT 4

Storey, David (Malcolm) 1933- . **CLC 2, 4, 5, 8**
See also BRWS 1; CA 81-84; CANR 36; CBD; CD 5, 6; CN 1, 2, 3, 4, 5, 6; DAM DRAM; DLB 13, 14, 207, 245, 326; EWL 3; MTCW 1; RGEL 2

Storm, Hyemeyohsts 1935- ... **CLC 3; NNAL**
See also CA 81-84; CANR 45; DAM MULT

Storm, (Hans) Theodor (Woldsen) 1817-1888 **NCLC 1; SSC 27**
See also CDWLB 2; DLB 129; EW; RGSF 2; RGWL 2, 3

Storni, Alfonsina 1892-1938 . **HLC 2; PC 33; TCLC 5**
See also CA 104; 131; DAM MULT; DLB 283; HW 1; LAW

Stoughton, William 1631-1701 **LC 38**
See also DLB 24

Stout, Rex (Todhunter) 1886-1975 **CLC 3**
See also AITN 2; BPFB 3; CA 61-64; CANR 71; CMW 4; CN 2; DLB 306; MSW; RGAL 4

Stow, (Julian) Randolph 1935- ... **CLC 23, 48**
See also CA 13-16R; CANR 33; CN 1, 2, 3, 4, 5, 6, 7; CP 1, 2, 3, 4; DLB 260; MTCW 1; RGEL 2

Stowe, Harriet (Elizabeth) Beecher 1811-1896 **NCLC 3, 50, 133; WLC 6**
See also AAYA 53; AMWS 1; CDALB 1865-1917; DA; DA3; DAB; DAC; DAM MST, NOV; DLB 1, 12, 42, 74, 189, 239, 243; EXPN; FL 1:3; JRDA; LAIT 2; MAICYA 1, 2; NFS 6; RGAL 4; TUS; YABC 1

Strabo c. 64B.C.-c. 25 **CMLC 37**
See also DLB 176

Strachey, (Giles) Lytton 1880-1932 **TCLC 12**
See also BRWS 2; CA 110; 178; DLB 149; DLBD 10; EWL 3; MTCW 2; NCFS 4

Stramm, August 1874-1915 **PC 50**
See also CA 195; EWL 3

Strand, Mark 1934- .. **CLC 6, 18, 41, 71; PC 63**
See also AMWS 4; CA 21-24R; CANR 40, 65, 100; CP 1, 2, 3, 4, 5, 6, 7; DAM POET; DLB 5; EWL 3; MAL 5; PAB; PFS 9, 18; RGAL 4; SATA 41; TCLE 1:2

Stratton-Porter, Gene(va Grace) 1863-1924
See Porter, Gene(va Grace) Stratton
See also ANW; CA 137; CLR 87; DLB 221; DLBD 14; MAICYA 1, 2; SATA 15

Straub, Peter 1943- **CLC 28, 107**
See also BEST 89:1; BPFB 3; CA 85-88; CANR 28, 65, 109; CPW; DAM POP; DLBY 1984; HGG; MTCW 1, 2; MTFW 2005; SUFW 2

Straub, Peter Francis
See Straub, Peter

Strauss, Botho 1944- **CLC 22**
See also CA 157; CWW 2; DLB 124

Strauss, Leo 1899-1973 **TCLC 141**
See also CA 101; 45-48; CANR 122

Streatfeild, (Mary) Noel 1897(?)-1986 **CLC 21**
See also CA 81-84; 120; CANR 31; CLR 17, 83; CWRI 5; DLB 160; MAICYA 1, 2; SATA 20; SATA-Obit 48

Stribling, T(homas) S(igismund) 1881-1965 **CLC 23**
See also CA 189; 107; CMW 4; DLB 9; RGAL 4

Strindberg, (Johan) August 1849-1912 ... **DC 18; TCLC 1, 8, 21, 47; WLC 6**
See also CA 104; 135; DA; DA3; DAB; DAC; DAM DRAM, MST; DFS 4, 9; DLB 259; EW 7; EWL 3; IDTP; LMFS 2; MTCW 2; MTFW 2005; RGWL 2, 3; TWA

Stringer, Arthur 1874-1950 **TCLC 37**
See also CA 161; DLB 92

Stringer, David
See Roberts, Keith (John Kingston)

Stroheim, Erich von 1885-1957 **TCLC 71**

Strugatskii, Arkadii (Natanovich) 1925-1991 **CLC 27**
See Strugatsky, Arkadii Natanovich
See also CA 106; 135; SFW 4

Strugatskii, Boris (Natanovich) 1933- **CLC 27**
See Strugatsky, Boris (Natanovich)
See also CA 106; SFW 4

Strugatsky, Arkadii Natanovich
See Strugatskii, Arkadii (Natanovich)
See also DLB 302

Strugatsky, Boris (Natanovich)
See Strugatskii, Boris (Natanovich)
See also DLB 302

Strummer, Joe 1952-2002 **CLC 30**

Strunk, William, Jr. 1869-1946 **TCLC 92**
See also CA 118; 164; NCFS 5

Stryk, Lucien 1924- **PC 27**
See also CA 13-16R; CANR 10, 28, 55, 110; CP 1, 2, 3, 4, 5, 6, 7

Stuart, Don A.
See Campbell, John W(ood, Jr.)

Stuart, Ian
See MacLean, Alistair (Stuart)

Stuart, Jesse (Hilton) 1906-1984 ... **CLC 1, 8, 11, 14, 34; SSC 31**
See also CA 5-8R; 112; CANR 31; CN 1, 2, 3; DLB 9, 48, 102; DLBY 1984; SATA 2; SATA-Obit 36

Stubblefield, Sally
See Trumbo, Dalton

Sturgeon, Theodore (Hamilton) 1918-1985 **CLC 22, 39**
See Queen, Ellery
See also AAYA 51; BPFB 3; BYA 9, 10; CA 81-84; 116; CANR 32, 103; DLB 8; DLBY 1985; HGG; MTCW 1, 2; MTFW 2005; SCFW 2; SFW 4; SUFW

Sturges, Preston 1898-1959 **TCLC 48**
See also CA 114; 149; DLB 26

Styron, William 1925- **CLC 1, 3, 5, 11, 15, 60; SSC 25**
See also AMW; AMWC 2; BEST 90:4; BPFB 3; CA 5-8R; CANR 6, 33, 74, 126; CDALB 1968-1988; CN 1, 2, 3, 4, 5, 6, 7; CPW; CSW; DA3; DAM NOV, POP;

DLB 2, 143, 299; DLBY 1980; EWL 3; INT CANR-6; LAIT 2; MAL 5; MTCW 1, 2; MTFW 2005; NCFS 1; NFS 22; RGAL 4; RGHL; RHW; TUS

Su, Chien 1884-1918
See Su Man-shu
See also CA 123

Suarez Lynch, B.
See Bioy Casares, Adolfo; Borges, Jorge Luis

Suassuna, Ariano Vilar 1927- **HLCS 1**
See also CA 178; DLB 307; HW 2; LAW

Suckert, Kurt Erich
See Malaparte, Curzio

Suckling, Sir John 1609-1642 . **LC 75; PC 30**
See also BRW 2; DAM POET; DLB 58, 126; EXPP; PAB; RGEL 2

Suckow, Ruth 1892-1960 **SSC 18**
See also CA 193; 113; DLB 9, 102; RGAL 4; TCWW 2

Sudermann, Hermann 1857-1928 .. **TCLC 15**
See also CA 107; 201; DLB 118

Sue, Eugene 1804-1857 **NCLC 1**
See also DLB 119

Sueskind, Patrick 1949- **CLC 44, 182**
See Suskind, Patrick

Suetonius c. 70-c. 130 **CMLC 60**
See also AW 2; DLB 211; RGWL 2, 3; WLIT 8

Sukenick, Ronald 1932-2004 **CLC 3, 4, 6, 48**
See also CA 25-28R; 209; 229; CAAE 209; CAAS 8; CANR 32, 89; CN 3, 4, 5, 6, 7; DLB 173; DLBY 1981

Suknaski, Andrew 1942- **CLC 19**
See also CA 101; CP 3, 4, 5, 6, 7; DLB 53

Sullivan, Vernon
See Vian, Boris

Sully Prudhomme, Rene-Francois-Armand 1839-1907 **TCLC 31**
See also GFL 1789 to the Present

Su Man-shu **TCLC 24**
See Su, Chien
See also EWL 3

Sumarokov, Aleksandr Petrovich 1717-1777 **LC 104**
See also DLB 150

Summerforest, Ivy B.
See Kirkup, James

Summers, Andrew James 1942- **CLC 26**

Summers, Andy
See Summers, Andrew James

Summers, Hollis (Spurgeon, Jr.) 1916- .. **CLC 10**
See also CA 5-8R; CANR 3; CN 1, 2, 3; CP 1, 2, 3, 4; DLB 6; TCLE 1:2

Summers, (Alphonsus Joseph-Mary Augustus) Montague 1880-1948 **TCLC 16**
See also CA 118; 163

Sumner, Gordon Matthew **CLC 26**
See Police, The; Sting

Sun Tzu c. 400B.C.-c. 320B.C. **CMLC 56**

Surrey, Henry Howard 1517-1574 ... **LC 121; PC 59**
See also BRW 1; RGEL 2

Surtees, Robert Smith 1805-1864 .. **NCLC 14**
See also DLB 21; RGEL 2

Susann, Jacqueline 1921-1974 **CLC 3**
See also AITN 1; BPFB 3; CA 65-68; 53-56; MTCW 1, 2

Su Shi
See Su Shih
See also RGWL 2, 3

Su Shih 1036-1101 **CMLC 15**
See Su Shi

Suskind, Patrick **CLC 182**
See Sueskind, Patrick
See also BPFB 3; CA 145; CWW 2

Sutcliff, Rosemary 1920-1992 **CLC 26**
See also AAYA 10; BYA 1, 4; CA 5-8R;
139; CANR 37; CLR 1, 37; CPW; DAB;
DAC; DAM MST, POP; JRDA; LATS
1:1; MAICYA 1, 2; MAICYAS 1; RHW;
SATA 6, 44, 78; SATA-Obit 73; WYA;
YAW

Sutro, Alfred 1863-1933 **TCLC 6**
See also CA 105; 185; DLB 10; RGEL 2

Sutton, Henry
See Slavitt, David R(ytman)

Suzuki, D. T.
See Suzuki, Daisetz Teitaro

Suzuki, Daisetz T.
See Suzuki, Daisetz Teitaro

Suzuki, Daisetz Teitaro
1870-1966 **TCLC 109**
See also CA 121; 111; MTCW 1, 2; MTFW
2005

Suzuki, Teitaro
See Suzuki, Daisetz Teitaro

Svevo, Italo **SSC 25; TCLC 2, 35**
See Schmitz, Aron Hector
See also DLB 264; EW 8; EWL 3; RGWL
2, 3; WLIT 7

Swados, Elizabeth (A.) 1951- **CLC 12**
See also CA 97-100; CANR 49; INT CA-
97-100

Swados, Harvey 1920-1972 **CLC 5**
See also CA 5-8R; 37-40R; CANR 6; CN
1; DLB 2; MAL 5

Swan, Gladys 1934- **CLC 69**
See also CA 101; CANR 17, 39; TCLE 1:2

Swanson, Logan
See Matheson, Richard (Burton)

Swarthout, Glendon (Fred)
1918-1992 **CLC 35**
See also AAYA 55; CA 1-4R; 139; CANR
1, 47; CN 1, 2, 3, 4, 5; LAIT 5; SATA 26;
TCWW 1, 2; YAW

Swedenborg, Emanuel 1688-1772 **LC 105**

Sweet, Sarah C.
See Jewett, (Theodora) Sarah Orne

Swenson, May 1919-1989 **CLC 4, 14, 61,
106; PC 14**
See also AMWS 4; CA 5-8R; 130; CANR
36, 61, 131; CP 1, 2, 3, 4; DA; DAB;
DAC; DAM MST, POET; DLB 5; EXPP;
GLL 2; MAL 5; MTCW 1, 2; MTFW
2005; PFS 16; SATA 15; WP

Swift, Augustus
See Lovecraft, H. P.

Swift, Graham (Colin) 1949- **CLC 41, 88**
See also BRWC 2; BRWS 5; CA 117; 122;
CANR 46, 71, 128; CN 4, 5, 6, 7; DLB
194, 326; MTCW 2; MTFW 2005; NFS
18; RGSF 2

Swift, Jonathan 1667-1745 **LC 1, 42, 101;
PC 9; WLC 6**
See also AAYA 41; BRW 3; BRWC 1;
BRWR 1; BYA 5, 14; CDBLB 1660-1789;
CLR 53; DA; DA3; DAB; DAC; DAM
MST, NOV, POET; DLB 39, 95, 101;
EXPN; LAIT 1; NFS 6; RGEL 2; SATA
19; TEA; WCH; WLIT 3

Swinburne, Algernon Charles
1837-1909 ... **PC 24; TCLC 8, 36; WLC
6**
See also BRW 5; CA 105; 140; CDBLB
1832-1890; DA; DA3; DAB; DAC; DAM
MST, POET; DLB 35, 57; PAB; RGEL 2;
TEA

Swinfen, Ann **CLC 34**
See also CA 202

Swinnerton, Frank (Arthur)
1884-1982 **CLC 31**
See also CA 202; 108; CN 1, 2, 3; DLB 34

Swinnerton, Frank Arthur
1884-1982 **CLC 31**
See also CA 108; DLB 34

Swithen, John
See King, Stephen

Sylvia
See Ashton-Warner, Sylvia (Constance)

Symmes, Robert Edward
See Duncan, Robert (Edward)

Symonds, John Addington
1840-1893 **NCLC 34**
See also DLB 57, 144

Symons, Arthur 1865-1945 **TCLC 11**
See also CA 107; 189; DLB 19, 57, 149;
RGEL 2

Symons, Julian (Gustave)
1912-1994 **CLC 2, 14, 32**
See also CA 49-52; 147; CAAS 3; CANR
3, 33, 59; CMW 4; CN 1, 2, 3, 4, 5; CP 1,
3, 4; DLB 87, 155; DLBY 1992; MSW;
MTCW 1

Synge, (Edmund) J(ohn) M(illington)
1871-1909 **DC 2; TCLC 6, 37**
See also BRW 6; BRWR 1; CA 104; 141;
CDBLB 1890-1914; DAM DRAM; DFS
18; DLB 10, 19; EWL 3; RGEL 2; TEA;
WLIT 4

Syruc, J.
See Milosz, Czeslaw

Szirtes, George 1948- **CLC 46; PC 51**
See also CA 109; CANR 27, 61, 117; CP 4,
5, 6, 7

Szymborska, Wislawa 1923- ... **CLC 99, 190;
PC 44**
See also CA 154; CANR 91, 133; CDWLB
4; CWP; CWW 2; DA3; DLB 232; DLBY
1996; EWL 3; MTCW 2; MTFW 2005;
PFS 15; RGHL; RGWL 3

T. O., Nik
See Annensky, Innokenty (Fyodorovich)

Tabori, George 1914- **CLC 19**
See also CA 49-52; CANR 4, 69; CBD; CD
5, 6; DLB 245; RGHL

Tacitus c. 55-c. 117 **CMLC 56**
See also AW 2; CDWLB 1; DLB 211;
RGWL 2, 3; WLIT 8

Tagore, Rabindranath 1861-1941 **PC 8;
SSC 48; TCLC 3, 53**
See also CA 104; 120; DA3; DAM DRAM,
POET; DLB 323; EWL 3; MTCW 1, 2;
MTFW 2005; PFS 18; RGEL 2; RGSF 2;
RGWL 2, 3; TWA

Taine, Hippolyte Adolphe
1828-1893 **NCLC 15**
See also EW 7; GFL 1789 to the Present

Talayesva, Don C. 1890-(?) **NNAL**

Talese, Gay 1932- **CLC 37**
See also AITN 1; CA 1-4R; CANR 9, 58,
137; DLB 185; INT CANR-9; MTCW 1,
2; MTFW 2005

Tallent, Elizabeth (Ann) 1954- **CLC 45**
See also CA 117; CANR 72; DLB 130

Tallmountain, Mary 1918-1997 **NNAL**
See also CA 146; 161; DLB 193

Tally, Ted 1952- **CLC 42**
See also CA 120; 124; CAD; CANR 125;
CD 5, 6; INT CA-124

Talvik, Heiti 1904-1947 **TCLC 87**
See also EWL 3

Tamayo y Baus, Manuel
1829-1898 **NCLC 1**

Tammsaare, A(nton) H(ansen)
1878-1940 **TCLC 27**
See also CA 164; CDWLB 4; DLB 220;
EWL 3

Tam'si, Tchicaya U
See Tchicaya, Gerald Felix

Tan, Amy (Ruth) 1952- . **AAL; CLC 59, 120,
151**
See also AAYA 9, 48; AMWS 10; BEST
89:3; BPFB 3; CA 136; CANR 54, 105,
132; CDALBS; CN 6, 7; CPW 1; DA3;
DAM MULT, NOV, POP; DLB 173, 312;
EXPN; FL 1:6; FW; LAIT 3, 5; MAL 5;
MTCW 2; MTFW 2005; NFS 1, 13, 16;
RGAL 4; SATA 75; SSFS 9; YAW

Tandem, Felix
See Spitteler, Carl (Friedrich Georg)

Tanizaki, Jun'ichiro 1886-1965 ... **CLC 8, 14,
28; SSC 21**
See Tanizaki Jun'ichiro
See also CA 93-96; 25-28R; MJW; MTCW
2; MTFW 2005; RGSF 2; RGWL 2

Tanizaki Jun'ichiro
See Tanizaki, Jun'ichiro
See also DLB 180; EWL 3

Tannen, Deborah 1945- **CLC 206**
See also CA 118; CANR 95

Tannen, Deborah Frances
See Tannen, Deborah

Tanner, William
See Amis, Kingsley (William)

Tao Lao
See Storni, Alfonsina

Tapahonso, Luci 1953- **NNAL; PC 65**
See also CA 145; CANR 72, 127; DLB 175

Tarantino, Quentin (Jerome)
1963- **CLC 125**
See also AAYA 58; CA 171; CANR 125

Tarassoff, Lev
See Troyat, Henri

Tarbell, Ida M(inerva) 1857-1944 . **TCLC 40**
See also CA 122; 181; DLB 47

Tarkington, (Newton) Booth
1869-1946 **TCLC 9**
See also BPFB 3; BYA 3; CA 110; 143;
CWRI 5; DLB 9, 102; MAL 5; MTCW 2;
RGAL 4; SATA 17

Tarkovskii, Andrei Arsen'evich
See Tarkovsky, Andrei (Arsenyevich)

Tarkovsky, Andrei (Arsenyevich)
1932-1986 **CLC 75**
See also CA 127

Tartt, Donna 1964(?)- **CLC 76**
See also AAYA 56; CA 142; CANR 135;
MTFW 2005

Tasso, Torquato 1544-1595 **LC 5, 94**
See also EFS 2; EW 2; RGWL 2, 3; WLIT
7

Tate, (John Orley) Allen 1899-1979 .. **CLC 2,
4, 6, 9, 11, 14, 24; PC 50**
See also AMW; CA 5-8R; 85-88; CANR
32, 108; CN 1, 2; CP 1, 2; DLB 4, 45, 63;
DLBD 17; EWL 3; MAL 5; MTCW 1, 2;
MTFW 2005; RGAL 4; RHW

Tate, Ellalice
See Hibbert, Eleanor Alice Burford

Tate, James (Vincent) 1943- **CLC 2, 6, 25**
See also CA 21-24R; CANR 29, 57, 114;
CP 1, 2, 3, 4, 5, 6, 7; DLB 5, 169; EWL
3; PFS 10, 15; RGAL 4; WP

Tate, Nahum 1652(?)-1715 **LC 109**
See also DLB 80; RGEL 2

Tauler, Johannes c. 1300-1361 **CMLC 37**
See also DLB 179; LMFS 1

Tavel, Ronald 1940- **CLC 6**
See also CA 21-24R; CAD; CANR 33; CD
5, 6

Taviani, Paolo 1931- **CLC 70**
See also CA 153

Taylor, Bayard 1825-1878 **NCLC 89**
See also DLB 3, 189, 250, 254; RGAL 4

Taylor, C(ecil) P(hilip) 1929-1981 **CLC 27**
See also CA 25-28R; 105; CANR 47; CBD

Taylor, Edward 1642(?)-1729 . **LC 11; PC 63**
See also AMW; DA; DAB; DAC; DAM
MST, POET; DLB 24; EXPP; RGAL 4;
TUS

Taylor, Eleanor Ross 1920- **CLC 5**
See also CA 81-84; CANR 70

Taylor, Elizabeth 1912-1975 **CLC 2, 4, 29**
See also CA 13-16R; CANR 9, 70; CN 1,
2; DLB 139; MTCW 1; RGEL 2; SATA
13

Taylor, Frederick Winslow
1856-1915 **TCLC 76**
See also CA 188

Taylor, Henry (Splawn) 1942- **CLC 44**
See also CA 33-36R; CAAS 7; CANR 31;
CP 6, 7; DLB 5; PFS 10

Taylor, Kamala (Purnaiya) 1924-2004
See Markandaya, Kamala
See also CA 77-80; 227; MTFW 2005; NFS
13

Taylor, Mildred D(elois) 1943- **CLC 21**
See also AAYA 10, 47; BW 1; BYA 3, 8;
CA 85-88; CANR 25, 115, 136; CLR 9,
59, 90; CSW; DLB 52; JRDA; LAIT 3;
MAICYA 1, 2; MTFW 2005; SAAS 5;
SATA 135; WYA; YAW

Taylor, Peter (Hillsman) 1917-1994 .. **CLC 1,
4, 18, 37, 44, 50, 71; SSC 10, 84**
See also AMWS 5; BPFB 3; CA 13-16R;
147; CANR 9, 50; CN 1, 2, 3, 4, 5; CSW;
DLB 218, 278; DLBY 1981, 1994; EWL
3; EXPS; INT CANR-9; MAL 5; MTCW
1, 2; MTFW 2005; RGSF 2; SSFS 9; TUS

Taylor, Robert Lewis 1912-1998 **CLC 14**
See also CA 1-4R; 170; CANR 3, 64; CN
1, 2; SATA 10; TCWW 1, 2

Tchekhov, Anton
See Chekhov, Anton (Pavlovich)

Tchicaya, Gerald Felix 1931-1988 .. **CLC 101**
See Tchicaya U Tam'si
See also CA 129; 125; CANR 81

Tchicaya U Tam'si
See Tchicaya, Gerald Felix
See also EWL 3

Teasdale, Sara 1884-1933 **PC 31; TCLC 4**
See also CA 104; 163; DLB 45; GLL 1;
PFS 14; RGAL 4; SATA 32; TUS

Tecumseh 1768-1813 **NNAL**
See also DAM MULT

Tegner, Esaias 1782-1846 **NCLC 2**

Teilhard de Chardin, (Marie Joseph) Pierre
1881-1955 **TCLC 9**
See also CA 105; 210; GFL 1789 to the
Present

Temple, Ann
See Mortimer, Penelope (Ruth)

Tennant, Emma (Christina) 1937- .. **CLC 13,
52**
See also BRWS 9; CA 65-68; CAAS 9;
CANR 10, 38, 59, 88; CN 3, 4, 5, 6, 7;
DLB 14; EWL 3; SFW 4

Tenneshaw, S. M.
See Silverberg, Robert

Tenney, Tabitha Gilman
1762-1837 **NCLC 122**
See also DLB 37, 200

Tennyson, Alfred 1809-1892 ... **NCLC 30, 65,
115; PC 6; WLC 6**
See also AAYA 50; BRW 4; CDBLB 1832-
1890; DA; DA3; DAB; DAC; DAM MST,
POET; DLB 32; EXPP; PAB; PFS 1, 2, 4,
11, 15, 19; RGEL 2; TEA; WLIT 4; WP

Teran, Lisa St. Aubin de **CLC 36**
See St. Aubin de Teran, Lisa

Terence c. 184B.C.-c. 159B.C. **CMLC 14;
DC 7**
See also AW 1; CDWLB 1; DLB 211;
RGWL 2, 3; TWA; WLIT 8

Teresa de Jesus, St. 1515-1582 **LC 18**

Teresa of Avila, St.
See Teresa de Jesus, St.

Terkel, Louis **CLC 38**
See Terkel, Studs
See also AAYA 32; AITN 1; MTCW 2; TUS

Terkel, Studs 1912-
See Terkel, Louis
See also CA 57-60; CANR 18, 45, 67, 132;
DA3; MTCW 1, 2; MTFW 2005

Terry, C. V.
See Slaughter, Frank G(ill)

Terry, Megan 1932- **CLC 19; DC 13**
See also CA 77-80; CABS 3; CAD; CANR
43; CD 5, 6; CWD; DFS 18; DLB 7, 249;
GLL 2

Tertullian c. 155-c. 245 **CMLC 29**

Tertz, Abram
See Sinyavsky, Andrei (Donatevich)
See also RGSF 2

Tesich, Steve 1943(?)-1996 **CLC 40, 69**
See also CA 105; 152; CAD; DLBY 1983

Tesla, Nikola 1856-1943 **TCLC 88**

Teternikov, Fyodor Kuzmich 1863-1927
See Sologub, Fyodor
See also CA 104

Tevis, Walter 1928-1984 **CLC 42**
See also CA 113; SFW 4

Tey, Josephine **TCLC 14**
See Mackintosh, Elizabeth
See also DLB 77; MSW

Thackeray, William Makepeace
1811-1863 **NCLC 5, 14, 22, 43, 169;
WLC 6**
See also BRW 5; BRWC 2; CDBLB 1832-
1890; DA; DA3; DAB; DAC; DAM MST,
NOV; DLB 21, 55, 159, 163; NFS 13;
RGEL 2; SATA 23; TEA; WLIT 3

Thakura, Ravindranatha
See Tagore, Rabindranath

Thames, C. H.
See Marlowe, Stephen

Tharoor, Shashi 1956- **CLC 70**
See also CA 141; CANR 91; CN 6, 7

Thelwall, John 1764-1834 **NCLC 162**
See also DLB 93, 158

Thelwell, Michael Miles 1939- **CLC 22**
See also BW 2; CA 101

Theobald, Lewis, Jr.
See Lovecraft, H. P.

Theocritus c. 310B.C.- **CMLC 45**
See also AW 1; DLB 176; RGWL 2, 3

Theodorescu, Ion N. 1880-1967
See Arghezi, Tudor
See also CA 116

Theriault, Yves 1915-1983 **CLC 79**
See also CA 102; CANR 150; CCA 1;
DAC; DAM MST; DLB 88; EWL 3

Theroux, Alexander (Louis) 1939- **CLC 2,
25**
See also CA 85-88; CANR 20, 63; CN 4, 5,
6, 7

Theroux, Paul (Edward) 1941- **CLC 5, 8,
11, 15, 28, 46**
See also AAYA 28; AMWS 8; BEST 89:4;
BPFB 3; CA 33-36R; CANR 20, 45, 74,
133; CDALBS; CN 1, 2, 3, 4, 5, 6, 7; CP
1; CPW 1; DA3; DAM POP; DLB 2, 218;
EWL 3; HGG; MAL 5; MTCW 1, 2;
MTFW 2005; RGAL 4; SATA 44, 109;
TUS

Thesen, Sharon 1946- **CLC 56**
See also CA 163; CANR 125; CP 5, 6, 7;
CWP

Thespis fl. 6th cent. B.C.- **CMLC 51**
See also LMFS 1

Thevenin, Denis
See Duhamel, Georges

Thibault, Jacques Anatole Francois
1844-1924
See France, Anatole
See also CA 106; 127; DA3; DAM NOV;
MTCW 1, 2; TWA

Thiele, Colin (Milton) 1920- **CLC 17**
See also CA 29-32R; CANR 12, 28, 53,
105; CLR 27; CP 1, 2; DLB 289; MAI-
CYA 1, 2; SAAS 2; SATA 14, 72, 125;
YAW

Thistlethwaite, Bel
See Wetherald, Agnes Ethelwyn

Thomas, Audrey (Callahan) 1935- **CLC 7,
13, 37, 107; SSC 20**
See also AITN 2; CA 21-24R, 237; CAAE
237; CAAS 19; CANR 36, 58; CN 2, 3,
4, 5, 6, 7; DLB 60; MTCW 1; RGSF 2

Thomas, Augustus 1857-1934 **TCLC 97**
See also MAL 5

Thomas, D(onald) M(ichael) 1935- . **CLC 13,
22, 31, 132**
See also BPFB 3; BRWS 4; CA 61-64;
CAAS 11; CANR 17, 45, 75; CDBLB
1960 to Present; CN 4, 5, 6, 7; CP 1, 2, 3,
4, 5, 6, 7; DA3; DLB 40, 207, 299; HGG;
INT CANR-17; MTCW 1, 2; MTFW
2005; RGHL; SFW 4

Thomas, Dylan (Marlais) 1914-1953 **PC 2,
52; SSC 3, 44; TCLC 1, 8, 45, 105;
WLC 6**
See also AAYA 45; BRWS 1; CA 104; 120;
CANR 65; CDBLB 1945-1960; DA; DA3;
DAB; DAC; DAM DRAM, MST, POET;
DLB 13, 20, 139; EWL 3; EXPP; LAIT
3; MTCW 1, 2; MTFW 2005; PAB; PFS
1, 3, 8; RGEL 2; RGSF 2; SATA 60; TEA;
WLIT 4; WP

Thomas, (Philip) Edward 1878-1917 . **PC 53;
TCLC 10**
See also BRW 6; BRWS 3; CA 106; 153;
DAM POET; DLB 19, 98, 156, 216; EWL
3; PAB; RGEL 2

Thomas, Joyce Carol 1938- **CLC 35**
See also AAYA 12, 54; BW 2, 3; CA 113;
116; CANR 48, 114, 135; CLR 19; DLB
33; INT CA-116; JRDA; MAICYA 1, 2;
MTCW 1, 2; MTFW 2005; SAAS 7;
SATA 40, 78, 123, 137; SATA-Essay 137;
WYA; YAW

Thomas, Lewis 1913-1993 **CLC 35**
See also ANW; CA 85-88; 143; CANR 38,
60; DLB 275; MTCW 1, 2

Thomas, M. Carey 1857-1935 **TCLC 89**
See also FW

Thomas, Paul
See Mann, (Paul) Thomas

Thomas, Piri 1928- **CLC 17; HLCS 2**
See also CA 73-76; HW 1; LLW

Thomas, R(onald) S(tuart)
1913-2000 **CLC 6, 13, 48**
See also CA 89-92; 189; CAAS 4; CANR
30; CDBLB 1960 to Present; CP 1, 2, 3,
4, 5, 6, 7; DAB; DAM POET; DLB 27;
EWL 3; MTCW 1; RGEL 2

Thomas, Ross (Elmore) 1926-1995 .. **CLC 39**
See also CA 33-36R; 150; CANR 22, 63;
CMW 4

Thompson, Francis (Joseph)
1859-1907 **TCLC 4**
See also BRW 5; CA 104; 189; CDBLB
1890-1914; DLB 19; RGEL 2; TEA

Thompson, Francis Clegg
See Mencken, H(enry) L(ouis)

Thompson, Hunter S(tockton)
1937(?)-2005 **CLC 9, 17, 40, 104**
See also AAYA 45; BEST 89:1; BPFB 3;
CA 17-20R; 236; CANR 23, 46, 74, 77,
111, 133; CPW; CSW; DA3; DAM POP;
DLB 185; MTCW 1, 2; MTFW 2005;
TUS

Thompson, James Myers
 See Thompson, Jim (Myers)
Thompson, Jim (Myers)
 1906-1977(?) **CLC 69**
 See also BPFB 3; CA 140; CMW 4; CPW;
 DLB 226; MSW
Thompson, Judith (Clare Francesca)
 1954- .. **CLC 39**
 See also CA 143; CD 5, 6; CWD; DFS 22
Thomson, James 1700-1748 **LC 16, 29, 40**
 See also BRWS 3; DAM POET; DLB 95;
 RGEL 2
Thomson, James 1834-1882 **NCLC 18**
 See also DAM POET; DLB 35; RGEL 2
Thoreau, Henry David 1817-1862 .. **NCLC 7,
 21, 61, 138; PC 30; WLC 6**
 See also AAYA 42; AMW; ANW; BYA 3;
 CDALB 1640-1865; DA; DA3; DAB;
 DAC; DAM MST; DLB 1, 183, 223, 270,
 298; LAIT 2; LMFS 1; NCFS 3; RGAL
 4; TUS
Thorndike, E. L.
 See Thorndike, Edward L(ee)
Thorndike, Edward L(ee)
 1874-1949 **TCLC 107**
 See also CA 121
Thornton, Hall
 See Silverberg, Robert
Thorpe, Adam 1956- **CLC 176**
 See also CA 129; CANR 92; DLB 231
Thubron, Colin (Gerald Dryden)
 1939- .. **CLC 163**
 See also CA 25-28R; CANR 12, 29, 59, 95;
 CN 5, 6, 7; DLB 204, 231
Thucydides c. 455B.C.-c. 395B.C. . **CMLC 17**
 See also AW 1; DLB 176; RGWL 2, 3;
 WLIT 8
Thumboo, Edwin Nadason 1933- **PC 30**
 See also CA 194; CP 1
Thurber, James (Grover)
 1894-1961 .. **CLC 5, 11, 25, 125; SSC 1,
 47**
 See also AAYA 56; AMWS 1; BPFB 3;
 BYA 5; CA 73-76; CANR 17, 39; CDALB
 1929-1941; CWRI 5; DA; DA3; DAB;
 DAC; DAM DRAM, MST, NOV; DLB 4,
 11, 22, 102; EWL 3; EXPS; FANT; LAIT
 3; MAICYA 1, 2; MAL 5; MTCW 1, 2;
 MTFW 2005; RGAL 4; RGSF 2; SATA
 13; SSFS 1, 10, 19; SUFW; TUS
Thurman, Wallace (Henry)
 1902-1934 **BLC 3; HR 1:3; TCLC 6**
 See also BW 1, 3; CA 104; 124; CANR 81;
 DAM MULT; DLB 51
Tibullus c. 54B.C.-c. 18B.C. **CMLC 36**
 See also AW 2; DLB 211; RGWL 2, 3;
 WLIT 8
Ticheburn, Cheviot
 See Ainsworth, William Harrison
Tieck, (Johann) Ludwig
 1773-1853 **NCLC 5, 46; SSC 31**
 See also CDWLB 2; DLB 90; EW 5; IDTP;
 RGSF 2; RGWL 2, 3; SUFW
Tiger, Derry
 See Ellison, Harlan (Jay)
Tilghman, Christopher 1946- **CLC 65**
 See also CA 159; CANR 135, 151; CSW;
 DLB 244
Tillich, Paul (Johannes)
 1886-1965 **CLC 131**
 See also CA 5-8R; 25-28R; CANR 33;
 MTCW 1, 2
Tillinghast, Richard (Williford)
 1940- .. **CLC 29**
 See also CA 29-32R; CAAS 23; CANR 26,
 51, 96; CP 2, 3, 4, 5, 6, 7; CSW
Timrod, Henry 1828-1867 **NCLC 25**
 See also DLB 3, 248; RGAL 4

Tindall, Gillian (Elizabeth) 1938- **CLC 7**
 See also CA 21-24R; CANR 11, 65, 107;
 CN 1, 2, 3, 4, 5, 6, 7
Tiptree, James, Jr. **CLC 48, 50**
 See Sheldon, Alice Hastings Bradley
 See also DLB 8; SCFW 1, 2; SFW 4
Tirone Smith, Mary-Ann 1944- **CLC 39**
 See also CA 118; 136; CANR 113; SATA
 143
Tirso de Molina 1580(?)-1648 **DC 13;
 HLCS 2; LC 73**
 See also RGWL 2, 3
Titmarsh, Michael Angelo
 See Thackeray, William Makepeace
Tocqueville, Alexis (Charles Henri Maurice
 Clerel Comte) de 1805-1859 .. **NCLC 7,
 63**
 See also EW 6; GFL 1789 to the Present;
 TWA
Toer, Pramoedya Ananta
 1925-2006 **CLC 186**
 See also CA 197; RGWL 3
Toffler, Alvin 1928- **CLC 168**
 See also CA 13-16R; CANR 15, 46, 67;
 CPW; DAM POP; MTCW 1, 2
Toibin, Colm 1955- **CLC 162**
 See also CA 142; CANR 81, 149; CN 7;
 DLB 271
Tolkien, J(ohn) R(onald) R(euel)
 1892-1973 **CLC 1, 2, 3, 8, 12, 38;
 TCLC 137; WLC 6**
 See also AAYA 10; AITN 1; BPFB 3;
 BRWC 2; BRWS 2; CA 17-18; 45-48;
 CANR 36, 134; CAP 2; CDBLB 1914-
 1945; CLR 56; CN 1; CPW 1; CWRI 5;
 DA; DA3; DAB; DAC; DAM MST, NOV,
 POP; DLB 15, 160, 255; EFS 2; EWL 3;
 FANT; JRDA; LAIT 1; LATS 1:2; LMFS
 2; MAICYA 1, 2; MTCW 1, 2; MTFW
 2005; NFS 8; RGEL 2; SATA 2, 32, 100;
 SATA-Obit 24; SFW 4; SUFW; TEA;
 WCH; WYA; YAW
Toller, Ernst 1893-1939 **TCLC 10**
 See also CA 107; 186; DLB 124; EWL 3;
 RGWL 2, 3
Tolson, M. B.
 See Tolson, Melvin B(eaunorus)
Tolson, Melvin B(eaunorus)
 1898(?)-1966 **BLC 3; CLC 36, 105**
 See also AFAW 1, 2; BW 1, 3; CA 124; 89-
 92; CANR 80; DAM MULT, POET; DLB
 48, 76; MAL 5; RGAL 4
Tolstoi, Aleksei Nikolaevich
 See Tolstoy, Alexey Nikolaevich
Tolstoi, Lev
 See Tolstoy, Leo (Nikolaevich)
 See also RGSF 2; RGWL 2, 3
Tolstoy, Aleksei Nikolaevich
 See Tolstoy, Alexey Nikolaevich
 See also DLB 272
Tolstoy, Alexey Nikolaevich
 1882-1945 **TCLC 18**
 See Tolstoy, Aleksei Nikolaevich
 See also CA 107; 158; EWL 3; SFW 4
Tolstoy, Leo (Nikolaevich)
 1828-1910 . **SSC 9, 30, 45, 54; TCLC 4,
 11, 17, 28, 44, 79, 173; WLC 6**
 See Tolstoi, Lev
 See also AAYA 56; CA 104; 123; DA; DA3;
 DAB; DAC; DAM MST, NOV; DLB 238;
 EFS 2; EW 7; EXPS; IDTP; LAIT 2;
 LATS 1:1; LMFS 1; NFS 10; SATA 26;
 SSFS 5; TWA
Tolstoy, Count Leo
 See Tolstoy, Leo (Nikolaevich)
Tomalin, Claire 1933- **CLC 166**
 See also CA 89-92; CANR 52, 88; DLB
 155

Tomasi di Lampedusa, Giuseppe 1896-1957
 See Lampedusa, Giuseppe (Tomasi) di
 See also CA 111; DLB 177; EWL 3; WLIT
 7
Tomlin, Lily **CLC 17**
 See Tomlin, Mary Jean
Tomlin, Mary Jean 1939(?)-
 See Tomlin, Lily
 See also CA 117
Tomline, F. Latour
 See Gilbert, W(illiam) S(chwenck)
Tomlinson, (Alfred) Charles 1927- **CLC 2,
 4, 6, 13, 45; PC 17**
 See also CA 5-8R; CANR 33; CP 1, 2, 3, 4,
 5, 6, 7; DAM POET; DLB 40; TCLE 1:2
Tomlinson, H(enry) M(ajor)
 1873-1958 **TCLC 71**
 See also CA 118; 161; DLB 36, 100, 195
Tonna, Charlotte Elizabeth
 1790-1846 **NCLC 135**
 See also DLB 163
Tonson, Jacob fl. 1655(?)-1736 **LC 86**
 See also DLB 170
Toole, John Kennedy 1937-1969 **CLC 19,
 64**
 See also BPFB 3; CA 104; DLBY 1981;
 MTCW 2; MTFW 2005
Toomer, Eugene
 See Toomer, Jean
Toomer, Eugene Pinchback
 See Toomer, Jean
Toomer, Jean 1894-1967 .. **BLC 3; CLC 1, 4,
 13, 22; HR 1:3; PC 7; SSC 1, 45;
 TCLC 172; WLCS**
 See also AFAW 1, 2; AMWS 3, 9; BW 1;
 CA 85-88; CDALB 1917-1929; DA3;
 DAM MULT; DLB 45, 51; EWL 3; EXPP;
 EXPS; LMFS 2; MAL 5; MTCW 1, 2;
 MTFW 2005; NFS 11; RGAL 4; RGSF 2;
 SSFS 5
Toomer, Nathan Jean
 See Toomer, Jean
Toomer, Nathan Pinchback
 See Toomer, Jean
Torley, Luke
 See Blish, James (Benjamin)
Tornimparte, Alessandra
 See Ginzburg, Natalia
Torre, Raoul della
 See Mencken, H(enry) L(ouis)
Torrence, Ridgely 1874-1950 **TCLC 97**
 See also DLB 54, 249; MAL 5
Torrey, E(dwin) Fuller 1937- **CLC 34**
 See also CA 119; CANR 71
Torsvan, Ben Traven
 See Traven, B.
Torsvan, Benno Traven
 See Traven, B.
Torsvan, Berick Traven
 See Traven, B.
Torsvan, Berwick Traven
 See Traven, B.
Torsvan, Bruno Traven
 See Traven, B.
Torsvan, Traven
 See Traven, B.
Tourneur, Cyril 1575(?)-1626 **LC 66**
 See also BRW 2; DAM DRAM; DLB 58;
 RGEL 2
Tournier, Michel 1924- **CLC 6, 23, 36, 95;
 SSC 88**
 See also CA 49-52; CANR 3, 36, 74, 149;
 CWW 2; DLB 83; EWL 3; GFL 1789 to
 the Present; MTCW 1, 2; SATA 23
Tournier, Michel Edouard
 See Tournier, Michel
Tournimparte, Alessandra
 See Ginzburg, Natalia

Towers, Ivar
See Kornbluth, C(yril) M.

Towne, Robert (Burton) 1936(?)- **CLC 87**
See also CA 108; DLB 44; IDFW 3, 4

Townsend, Sue **CLC 61**
See Townsend, Susan Lilian
See also AAYA 28; CA 119; 127; CANR
65, 107; CBD; CD 5, 6; CPW; CWD;
DAB; DAC; DAM MST; DLB 271; INT
CA-127; SATA 55, 93; SATA-Brief 48;
YAW

Townsend, Susan Lilian 1946-
See Townsend, Sue

Townshend, Pete
See Townshend, Peter (Dennis Blandford)

Townshend, Peter (Dennis Blandford)
1945- **CLC 17, 42**
See also CA 107

Tozzi, Federigo 1883-1920 **TCLC 31**
See also CA 160; CANR 110; DLB 264;
EWL 3; WLIT 7

Tracy, Don(ald Fiske) 1905-1970(?)
See Queen, Ellery
See also CA 1-4R; 176; CANR 2

Trafford, F. G.
See Riddell, Charlotte

Traherne, Thomas 1637(?)-1674 .. **LC 99; PC 70**
See also BRW 2; BRWS 11; DLB 131;
PAB; RGEL 2

Traill, Catharine Parr 1802-1899 .. **NCLC 31**
See also DLB 99

Trakl, Georg 1887-1914 **PC 20; TCLC 5**
See also CA 104; 165; EW 10; EWL 3;
LMFS 2; MTCW 2; RGWL 2, 3

Trambley, Estela Portillo **TCLC 163**
See Portillo Trambley, Estela
See also CA 77-80; RGAL 4

Tranquilli, Secondino
See Silone, Ignazio

Transtroemer, Tomas Gosta
See Transtromer, Tomas (Goesta)

Transtromer, Tomas (Gosta)
See Transtromer, Tomas (Goesta)
See also CWW 2

Transtromer, Tomas (Goesta)
1931- **CLC 52, 65**
See Transtromer, Tomas (Gosta)
See also CA 117; 129; CAAS 17; CANR
115; DAM POET; DLB 257; EWL 3; PFS
21

Transtromer, Tomas Gosta
See Transtromer, Tomas (Goesta)

Traven, B. 1882(?)-1969 **CLC 8, 11**
See also CA 19-20; 25-28R; CAP 2; DLB
9, 56; EWL 3; MTCW 1; RGAL 4

Trediakovsky, Vasilii Kirillovich
1703-1769 **LC 68**
See also DLB 150

Treitel, Jonathan 1959- **CLC 70**
See also CA 210; DLB 267

Trelawny, Edward John
1792-1881 **NCLC 85**
See also DLB 110, 116, 144

Tremain, Rose 1943- **CLC 42**
See also CA 97-100; CANR 44, 95; CN 4,
5, 6, 7; DLB 14, 271; RGSF 2; RHW

Tremblay, Michel 1942- **CLC 29, 102, 225**
See also CA 116; 128; CCA 1; CWW 2;
DAC; DAM MST; DLB 60; EWL 3; GLL
1; MTCW 1, 2; MTFW 2005

Trevanian **CLC 29**
See Whitaker, Rod

Trevor, Glen
See Hilton, James

Trevor, William .. **CLC 7, 9, 14, 25, 71, 116; SSC 21, 58**
See Cox, William Trevor
See also BRWS 4; CBD; CD 5, 6; CN 1, 2,
3, 4, 5, 6, 7; DLB 14, 139; EWL 3; LATS
1:2; RGEL 2; RGSF 2; SSFS 10; TCLE
1:2

Trifonov, Iurii (Valentinovich)
See Trifonov, Yuri (Valentinovich)
See also DLB 302; RGWL 2, 3

Trifonov, Yuri (Valentinovich)
1925-1981 **CLC 45**
See Trifonov, Iurii (Valentinovich); Tri-
fonov, Yury Valentinovich
See also CA 126; 103; MTCW 1

Trifonov, Yury Valentinovich
See Trifonov, Yuri (Valentinovich)
See also EWL 3

Trilling, Diana (Rubin) 1905-1996 . **CLC 129**
See also CA 5-8R; 154; CANR 10, 46; INT
CANR-10; MTCW 1, 2

Trilling, Lionel 1905-1975 **CLC 9, 11, 24; SSC 75**
See also AMWS 3; CA 9-12R; 61-64;
CANR 10, 105; CN 1, 2; DLB 28, 63;
EWL 3; INT CANR-10; MAL 5; MTCW
1, 2; RGAL 4; TUS

Trimball, W. H.
See Mencken, H(enry) L(ouis)

Tristan
See Gomez de la Serna, Ramon

Tristram
See Housman, A(lfred) E(dward)

Trogdon, William (Lewis) 1939-
See Heat-Moon, William Least
See also AAYA 66; CA 115; 119; CANR
47, 89; CPW; INT CA-119

Trollope, Anthony 1815-1882 **NCLC 6, 33, 101; SSC 28; WLC 6**
See also BRW 5; CDBLB 1832-1890; DA;
DA3; DAB; DAC; DAM MST, NOV;
DLB 21, 57, 159; RGEL 2; RGSF 2;
SATA 22

Trollope, Frances 1779-1863 **NCLC 30**
See also DLB 21, 166

Trollope, Joanna 1943- **CLC 186**
See also CA 101; CANR 58, 95, 149; CN
7; CPW; DLB 207; RHW

Trotsky, Leon 1879-1940 **TCLC 22**
See also CA 118; 167

Trotter (Cockburn), Catharine
1679-1749 **LC 8**
See also DLB 84, 252

Trotter, Wilfred 1872-1939 **TCLC 97**

Trout, Kilgore
See Farmer, Philip Jose

Trow, George W. S. 1943- **CLC 52**
See also CA 126; CANR 91

Troyat, Henri 1911- **CLC 23**
See also CA 45-48; CANR 2, 33, 67, 117;
GFL 1789 to the Present; MTCW 1

Trudeau, Garry B. **CLC 12**
See Trudeau, G.B.
See also AAYA 10; AITN 2

Trudeau, G.B. 1948-
See Trudeau, Garry B.
See also AAYA 60; CA 81-84; CANR 31;
SATA 35, 168

Truffaut, Francois 1932-1984 ... **CLC 20, 101**
See also CA 81-84; 113; CANR 34

Trumbo, Dalton 1905-1976 **CLC 19**
See also CA 21-24R; 69-72; CANR 10; CN
1, 2; DLB 26; IDFW 3, 4; YAW

Trumbull, John 1750-1831 **NCLC 30**
See also DLB 31; RGAL 4

Trundlett, Helen B.
See Eliot, T(homas) S(tearns)

Truth, Sojourner 1797(?)-1883 **NCLC 94**
See also DLB 239; FW; LAIT 2

Tryon, Thomas 1926-1991 **CLC 3, 11**
See also AITN 1; BPFB 3; CA 29-32R; 135;
CANR 32, 77; CPW; DA3; DAM POP;
HGG; MTCW 1

Tryon, Tom
See Tryon, Thomas

Ts'ao Hsueh-ch'in 1715(?)-1763 **LC 1**

Tsushima, Shuji 1909-1948
See Dazai Osamu
See also CA 107

Tsvetaeva (Efron), Marina (Ivanovna)
1892-1941 **PC 14; TCLC 7, 35**
See also CA 104; 128; CANR 73; DLB 295;
EW 11; MTCW 1, 2; RGWL 2, 3

Tuck, Lily 1938- **CLC 70**
See also CA 139; CANR 90

Tu Fu 712-770 **PC 9**
See Du Fu
See also DAM MULT; TWA; WP

Tunis, John R(oberts) 1889-1975 **CLC 12**
See also BYA 1; CA 61-64; CANR 62; DLB
22, 171; JRDA; MAICYA 1, 2; SATA 37;
SATA-Brief 30; YAW

Tuohy, Frank **CLC 37**
See Tuohy, John Francis
See also CN 1, 2, 3, 4, 5, 6, 7; DLB 14,
139

Tuohy, John Francis 1925-
See Tuohy, Frank
See also CA 5-8R; 178; CANR 3, 47

Turco, Lewis (Putnam) 1934- **CLC 11, 63**
See also CA 13-16R; CAAS 22; CANR 24,
51; CP 1, 2, 3, 4, 5, 6, 7; DLBY 1984;
TCLE 1:2

Turgenev, Ivan (Sergeevich)
1818-1883 **DC 7; NCLC 21, 37, 122; SSC 7, 57; WLC 6**
See also AAYA 58; DA; DAB; DAC; DAM
MST, NOV; DFS 6; DLB 238, 284; EW
6; LATS 1:1; NFS 16; RGSF 2; RGWL 2,
3; TWA

Turgot, Anne-Robert-Jacques
1727-1781 **LC 26**
See also DLB 314

Turner, Frederick 1943- **CLC 48**
See also CA 73-76; 227; CAAE 227; CAAS
10; CANR 12, 30, 56; DLB 40, 282

Turton, James
See Crace, Jim

Tutu, Desmond M(pilo) 1931- .. **BLC 3; CLC 80**
See also BW 1, 3; CA 125; CANR 67, 81;
DAM MULT

Tutuola, Amos 1920-1997 **BLC 3; CLC 5, 14, 29**
See also AFW; BW 2, 3; CA 9-12R; 159;
CANR 27, 66; CDWLB 3; CN 1, 2, 3, 4,
5, 6; DA3; DAM MULT; DLB 125; DNFS
2; EWL 3; MTCW 1, 2; MTFW 2005;
RGEL 2; WLIT 2

Twain, Mark **SSC 6, 26, 34, 87; TCLC 6, 12, 19, 36, 48, 59, 161; WLC 6**
See Clemens, Samuel Langhorne
See also AAYA 20; AMW; AMWC 1; BPFB
3; BYA 2, 3, 11, 14; CLR 58, 60, 66; DLB
11; EXPN; EXPS; FANT; LAIT 2; MAL
5; NCFS 4; NFS 1, 6; RGAL 4; RGSF 2;
SFW 4; SSFS 1, 7, 16, 21; SUFW; TUS;
WCH; WYA; YAW

Tyler, Anne 1941- . **CLC 7, 11, 18, 28, 44, 59, 103, 205**
See also AAYA 18, 60; AMWS 4; BEST
89:1; BPFB 3; BYA 12; CA 9-12R; CANR
11, 33, 53, 109, 132; CDALBS; CN 1, 2,
3, 4, 5, 6, 7; CPW; CSW; DAM NOV,
POP; DLB 6, 143; DLBY 1982; EWL 3;
EXPN; LATS 1:2; MAL 5; MAWW;
MTCW 1, 2; MTFW 2005; NFS 2, 7, 10;
RGAL 4; SATA 7, 90; SSFS 17; TCLE
1:2; TUS; YAW

Tyler, Royall 1757-1826 **NCLC 3**
See also DLB 37; RGAL 4

Tynan, Katharine 1861-1931 **TCLC 3**
See also CA 104; 167; DLB 153, 240; FW

Tyndale, William c. 1484-1536 **LC 103**
See also DLB 132

Tyutchev, Fyodor 1803-1873 **NCLC 34**

Tzara, Tristan 1896-1963 **CLC 47; PC 27; TCLC 168**
See also CA 153; 89-92; DAM POET; EWL 3; MTCW 2

Uchida, Yoshiko 1921-1992 **AAL**
See also AAYA 16; BYA 2, 3; CA 13-16R; 139; CANR 6, 22, 47, 61; CDALBS; CLR 6, 56; CWRI 5; DLB 312; JRDA; MAI-CYA 1, 2; MTCW 1, 2; MTFW 2005; SAAS 1; SATA 1, 53; SATA-Obit 72

Udall, Nicholas 1504-1556 **LC 84**
See also DLB 62; RGEL 2

Ueda Akinari 1734-1809 **NCLC 131**

Uhry, Alfred 1936- **CLC 55**
See also CA 127; 133; CAD; CANR 112; CD 5, 6; CSW; DA3; DAM DRAM, POP; DFS 11, 15; INT CA-133; MTFW 2005

Ulf, Haerved
See Strindberg, (Johan) August

Ulf, Harved
See Strindberg, (Johan) August

Ulibarri, Sabine R(eyes)
1919-2003 **CLC 83; HLCS 2**
See also CA 131; 214; CANR 81; DAM MULT; DLB 82; HW 1, 2; RGSF 2

Unamuno (y Jugo), Miguel de
1864-1936 .. **HLC 2; SSC 11, 69; TCLC 2, 9, 148**
See also CA 104; 131; CANR 81; DAM MULT, NOV; DLB 108, 322; EW 8; EWL 3; HW 1, 2; MTCW 1, 2; MTFW 2005; RGSF 2; RGWL 2, 3; SSFS 20; TWA

Uncle Shelby
See Silverstein, Shel(don Allan)

Undercliffe, Errol
See Campbell, (John) Ramsey

Underwood, Miles
See Glassco, John

Undset, Sigrid 1882-1949 .. **TCLC 3; WLC 6**
See also CA 104; 129; DA; DA3; DAB; DAC; DAM MST, NOV; DLB 293; EW 9; EWL 3; FW; MTCW 1, 2; MTFW 2005; RGWL 2, 3

Ungaretti, Giuseppe 1888-1970 ... **CLC 7, 11, 15; PC 57**
See also CA 19-20; 25-28R; CAP 2; DLB 114; EW 10; EWL 3; PFS 20; RGWL 2, 3; WLIT 7

Unger, Douglas 1952- **CLC 34**
See also CA 130; CANR 94

Unsworth, Barry (Forster) 1930- **CLC 76, 127**
See also BRWS 7; CA 25-28R; CANR 30, 54, 125; CN 6, 7; DLB 194, 326

Updike, John 1932- . **CLC 1, 2, 3, 5, 7, 9, 13, 15, 23, 34, 43, 70, 139, 214; SSC 13, 27; WLC 6**
See also AAYA 36; AMW; AMWC 1; AMWR 1; BPFB 3; BYA 12; CA 1-4R; CABS 1; CANR 4, 33, 51, 94, 133; CDALB 1968-1988; CN 1, 2, 3, 4, 5, 6, 7; CP 1, 2, 3, 4, 5, 6, 7; CPW 1; DA; DA3; DAB; DAC; DAM MST, NOV, POET, POP; DLB 2, 5, 143, 218, 227; DLBD 3; DLBY 1980, 1982, 1997; EWL 3; EXPP; HGG; MAL 5; MTCW 1, 2; MTFW 2005; NFS 12; RGAL 4; RGSF 2; SSFS 3, 19; TUS

Updike, John Hoyer
See Updike, John

Upshaw, Margaret Mitchell
See Mitchell, Margaret (Munnerlyn)

Upton, Mark
See Sanders, Lawrence

Upward, Allen 1863-1926 **TCLC 85**
See also CA 117; 187; DLB 36

Urdang, Constance (Henriette)
1922-1996 **CLC 47**
See also CA 21-24R; CANR 9, 24; CP 1, 2, 3, 4, 5, 6; CWP

Uriel, Henry
See Faust, Frederick (Schiller)

Uris, Leon (Marcus) 1924-2003 ... **CLC 7, 32**
See also AITN 1, 2; BEST 89:2; BPFB 3; CA 1-4R; 217; CANR 1, 40, 65, 123; CN 1, 2, 3, 4, 5, 6; CPW 1; DA3; DAM NOV, POP; MTCW 1, 2; MTFW 2005; RGHL; SATA 49; SATA-Obit 146

Urista (Heredia), Alberto (Baltazar)
1947- .. **HLCS 1**
See Alurista
See also CA 182; CANR 2, 32; HW 1

Urmuz
See Codrescu, Andrei

Urquhart, Guy
See McAlmon, Robert (Menzies)

Urquhart, Jane 1949- **CLC 90**
See also CA 113; CANR 32, 68, 116; CCA 1; DAC

Usigli, Rodolfo 1905-1979 **HLCS 1**
See also CA 131; DLB 305; EWL 3; HW 1; LAW

Usk, Thomas (?)-1388 **CMLC 76**
See also DLB 146

Ustinov, Peter (Alexander)
1921-2004 **CLC 1**
See also AITN 1; CA 13-16R; 225; CANR 25, 51; CBD; CD 5, 6; DLB 13; MTCW 2

U Tam'si, Gerald Felix Tchicaya
See Tchicaya, Gerald Felix

U Tam'si, Tchicaya
See Tchicaya, Gerald Felix

Vachss, Andrew 1942- **CLC 106**
See also CA 118, 214; CAAE 214; CANR 44, 95, 153; CMW 4

Vachss, Andrew H.
See Vachss, Andrew

Vachss, Andrew Henry
See Vachss, Andrew

Vaculik, Ludvik 1926- **CLC 7**
See also CA 53-56; CANR 72; CWW 2; DLB 232; EWL 3

Vaihinger, Hans 1852-1933 **TCLC 71**
See also CA 116; 166

Valdez, Luis (Miguel) 1940- **CLC 84; DC 10; HLC 2**
See also CA 101; CAD; CANR 32, 81; CD 5, 6; DAM MULT; DFS 5; DLB 122; EWL 3; HW 1; LAIT 4; LLW

Valenzuela, Luisa 1938- **CLC 31, 104; HLCS 2; SSC 14, 82**
See also CA 101; CANR 32, 65, 123; CD-WLB 3; CWW 2; DAM MULT; DLB 113; EWL 3; FW; HW 1, 2; LAW; RGSF 2; RGWL 3

Valera y Alcala-Galiano, Juan
1824-1905 **TCLC 10**
See also CA 106

Valerius Maximus fl. 20- **CMLC 64**
See also DLB 211

Valery, (Ambroise) Paul (Toussaint Jules)
1871-1945 **PC 9; TCLC 4, 15**
See also CA 104; 122; DA3; DAM POET; DLB 258; EW 8; EWL 3; GFL 1789 to the Present; MTCW 1, 2; MTFW 2005; RGWL 2, 3; TWA

Valle-Inclan, Ramon (Maria) del
1866-1936 **HLC 2; TCLC 5**
See del Valle-Inclan, Ramon (Maria)
See also CA 106; 153; CANR 80; DAM MULT; DLB 134; EW 8; EWL 3; HW 2; RGSF 2; RGWL 2, 3

Vallejo, Antonio Buero
See Buero Vallejo, Antonio

Vallejo, Cesar (Abraham)
1892-1938 **HLC 2; TCLC 3, 56**
See also CA 105; 153; DAM MULT; DLB 290; EWL 3; HW 1; LAW; RGWL 2, 3

Valles, Jules 1832-1885 **NCLC 71**
See also DLB 123; GFL 1789 to the Present

Vallette, Marguerite Eymery
1860-1953 **TCLC 67**
See Rachilde
See also CA 182; DLB 123, 192

Valle Y Pena, Ramon del
See Valle-Inclan, Ramon (Maria) del

Van Ash, Cay 1918-1994 **CLC 34**
See also CA 220

Vanbrugh, Sir John 1664-1726 **LC 21**
See also BRW 2; DAM DRAM; DLB 80; IDTP; RGEL 2

Van Campen, Karl
See Campbell, John W(ood, Jr.)

Vance, Gerald
See Silverberg, Robert

Vance, Jack 1916-
See Queen, Ellery; Vance, John Holbrook
See also CA 29-32R; CANR 17, 65, 154; CMW 4; MTCW 1

Vance, John Holbrook **CLC 35**
See Vance, Jack
See also DLB 8; FANT; SCFW 1, 2; SFW 4; SUFW 1, 2

Van Den Bogarde, Derek Jules Gaspard Ulric Niven 1921-1999 **CLC 14**
See Bogarde, Dirk
See also CA 77-80; 179

Vandenburgh, Jane **CLC 59**
See also CA 168

Vanderhaeghe, Guy 1951- **CLC 41**
See also BPFB 3; CA 113; CANR 72, 145; CN 7

van der Post, Laurens (Jan)
1906-1996 **CLC 5**
See also AFW; CA 5-8R; 155; CANR 35; CN 1, 2, 3, 4, 5, 6; DLB 204; RGEL 2

van de Wetering, Janwillem 1931- ... **CLC 47**
See also CA 49-52; CANR 4, 62, 90; CMW 4

Van Dine, S. S. **TCLC 23**
See Wright, Willard Huntington
See also DLB 306; MSW

Van Doren, Carl (Clinton)
1885-1950 **TCLC 18**
See also CA 111; 168

Van Doren, Mark 1894-1972 **CLC 6, 10**
See also CA 1-4R; 37-40R; CANR 3; CN 1; CP 1; DLB 45, 284; MAL 5; MTCW 1, 2; RGAL 4

Van Druten, John (William)
1901-1957 **TCLC 2**
See also CA 104; 161; DLB 10; MAL 5; RGAL 4

Van Duyn, Mona (Jane) 1921-2004 .. **CLC 3, 7, 63, 116**
See also CA 9-12R; 234; CANR 7, 38, 60, 116; CP 1, 2, 3, 4, 5, 6, 7; CWP; DAM POET; DLB 5; MAL 5; MTFW 2005; PFS 20

Van Dyne, Edith
See Baum, L(yman) Frank

van Itallie, Jean-Claude 1936- **CLC 3**
See also CA 45-48; CAAS 2; CAD; CANR 1, 48; CD 5, 6; DLB 7

Towers, Ivar
See Kornbluth, C(yril) M.

Towne, Robert (Burton) 1936(?)- **CLC 87**
See also CA 108; DLB 44; IDFW 3, 4

Townsend, Sue **CLC 61**
See Townsend, Susan Lilian
See also AAYA 28; CA 119; 127; CANR
65, 107; CBD; CD 5, 6; CPW; CWD;
DAB; DAC; DAM MST; DLB 271; INT
CA-127; SATA 55, 93; SATA-Brief 48;
YAW

Townsend, Susan Lilian 1946-
See Townsend, Sue

Townshend, Pete
See Townshend, Peter (Dennis Blandford)

Townshend, Peter (Dennis Blandford)
1945- **CLC 17, 42**
See also CA 107

Tozzi, Federigo 1883-1920 **TCLC 31**
See also CA 160; CANR 110; DLB 264;
EWL 3; WLIT 7

Tracy, Don(ald Fiske) 1905-1970(?)
See Queen, Ellery
See also CA 1-4R; 176; CANR 2

Trafford, F. G.
See Riddell, Charlotte

Traherne, Thomas 1637(?)-1674 .. **LC 99; PC 70**
See also BRW 2; BRWS 11; DLB 131;
PAB; RGEL 2

Traill, Catharine Parr 1802-1899 .. **NCLC 31**
See also DLB 99

Trakl, Georg 1887-1914 **PC 20; TCLC 5**
See also CA 104; 165; EW 10; EWL 3;
LMFS 2; MTCW 2; RGWL 2, 3

Trambley, Estela Portillo **TCLC 163**
See Portillo Trambley, Estela
See also CA 77-80; RGAL 4

Tranquilli, Secondino
See Silone, Ignazio

Transtroemer, Tomas Gosta
See Transtromer, Tomas (Goesta)

Transtromer, Tomas (Gosta)
See Transtromer, Tomas (Goesta)
See also CWW 2

Transtromer, Tomas (Goesta)
1931- **CLC 52, 65**
See Transtromer, Tomas (Gosta)
See also CA 117; 129; CAAS 17; CANR
115; DAM POET; DLB 257; EWL 3; PFS
21

Transtromer, Tomas Gosta
See Transtromer, Tomas (Goesta)

Traven, B. 1882(?)-1969 **CLC 8, 11**
See also CA 19-20; 25-28R; CAP 2; DLB
9, 56; EWL 3; MTCW 1; RGAL 4

Trediakovsky, Vasilii Kirillovich
1703-1769 **LC 68**
See also DLB 150

Treitel, Jonathan 1959- **CLC 70**
See also CA 210; DLB 267

Trelawny, Edward John
1792-1881 **NCLC 85**
See also DLB 110, 116, 144

Tremain, Rose 1943- **CLC 42**
See also CA 97-100; CANR 44, 95; CN 4,
5, 6, 7; DLB 14, 271; RGSF 2; RHW

Tremblay, Michel 1942- **CLC 29, 102, 225**
See also CA 116; 128; CCA 1; CWW 2;
DAC; DAM MST; DLB 60; EWL 3; GLL
1; MTCW 1, 2; MTFW 2005

Trevanian **CLC 29**
See Whitaker, Rod

Trevor, Glen
See Hilton, James

Trevor, William .. **CLC 7, 9, 14, 25, 71, 116;
SSC 21, 58**
See Cox, William Trevor
See also BRWS 4; CBD; CD 5, 6; CN 1, 2,
3, 4, 5, 6, 7; DLB 14, 139; EWL 3; LATS
1:2; RGEL 2; RGSF 2; SSFS 10; TCLE
1:2

Trifonov, Iurii (Valentinovich)
See Trifonov, Yuri (Valentinovich)
See also DLB 302; RGWL 2, 3

Trifonov, Yuri (Valentinovich)
1925-1981 **CLC 45**
See Trifonov, Iurii (Valentinovich); Tri-
fonov, Yury Valentinovich
See also CA 126; 103; MTCW 1

Trifonov, Yury Valentinovich
See Trifonov, Yuri (Valentinovich)
See also EWL 3

Trilling, Diana (Rubin) 1905-1996 . **CLC 129**
See also CA 5-8R; 154; CANR 10, 46; INT
CANR-10; MTCW 1, 2

Trilling, Lionel 1905-1975 **CLC 9, 11, 24;
SSC 75**
See also AMWS 3; CA 9-12R; 61-64;
CANR 10, 105; CN 1, 2; DLB 28, 63;
EWL 3; INT CANR-10; MAL 5; MTCW
1, 2; RGAL 4; TUS

Trimball, W. H.
See Mencken, H(enry) L(ouis)

Tristan
See Gomez de la Serna, Ramon

Tristram
See Housman, A(lfred) E(dward)

Trogdon, William (Lewis) 1939-
See Heat-Moon, William Least
See also AAYA 66; CA 115; 119; CANR
47, 89; CPW; INT CA-119

Trollope, Anthony 1815-1882 **NCLC 6, 33,
101; SSC 28; WLC 6**
See also BRW 5; CDBLB 1832-1890; DA;
DA3; DAB; DAC; DAM MST, NOV;
DLB 21, 57, 159; RGEL 2; RGSF 2;
SATA 22

Trollope, Frances 1779-1863 **NCLC 30**
See also DLB 21, 166

Trollope, Joanna 1943- **CLC 186**
See also CA 101; CANR 58, 95, 149; CN
7; CPW; DLB 207; RHW

Trotsky, Leon 1879-1940 **TCLC 22**
See also CA 118; 167

Trotter (Cockburn), Catharine
1679-1749 **LC 8**
See also DLB 84, 252

Trotter, Wilfred 1872-1939 **TCLC 97**

Trout, Kilgore
See Farmer, Philip Jose

Trow, George W. S. 1943- **CLC 52**
See also CA 126; CANR 91

Troyat, Henri 1911- **CLC 23**
See also CA 45-48; CANR 2, 33, 67, 117;
GFL 1789 to the Present; MTCW 1

Trudeau, Garry B. **CLC 12**
See Trudeau, G.B.
See also AAYA 10; AITN 2

Trudeau, G.B. 1948-
See Trudeau, Garry B.
See also AAYA 60; CA 81-84; CANR 31;
SATA 35, 168

Truffaut, Francois 1932-1984 ... **CLC 20, 101**
See also CA 81-84; 113; CANR 34

Trumbo, Dalton 1905-1976 **CLC 19**
See also CA 21-24R; 69-72; CANR 10; CN
1, 2; DLB 26; IDFW 3, 4; YAW

Trumbull, John 1750-1831 **NCLC 30**
See also DLB 31; RGAL 4

Trundlett, Helen B.
See Eliot, T(homas) S(tearns)

Truth, Sojourner 1797(?)-1883 **NCLC 94**
See also DLB 239; FW; LAIT 2

Tryon, Thomas 1926-1991 **CLC 3, 11**
See also AITN 1; BPFB 3; CA 29-32R; 135;
CANR 32, 77; CPW; DA3; DAM POP;
HGG; MTCW 1

Tryon, Tom
See Tryon, Thomas

Ts'ao Hsueh-ch'in 1715(?)-1763 **LC 1**

Tsushima, Shuji 1909-1948
See Dazai Osamu
See also CA 107

Tsvetaeva (Efron), Marina (Ivanovna)
1892-1941 **PC 14; TCLC 7, 35**
See also CA 104; 128; CANR 73; DLB 295;
EW 11; MTCW 1, 2; RGWL 2, 3

Tuck, Lily 1938- **CLC 70**
See also CA 139; CANR 90

Tu Fu 712-770 **PC 9**
See Du Fu
See also DAM MULT; TWA; WP

Tunis, John R(oberts) 1889-1975 **CLC 12**
See also BYA 1; CA 61-64; CANR 62; DLB
22, 171; JRDA; MAICYA 1, 2; SATA 37;
SATA-Brief 30; YAW

Tuohy, Frank **CLC 37**
See Tuohy, John Francis
See also CN 1, 2, 3, 4, 5, 6, 7; DLB 14,
139

Tuohy, John Francis 1925-
See Tuohy, Frank
See also CA 5-8R; 178; CANR 3, 47

Turco, Lewis (Putnam) 1934- **CLC 11, 63**
See also CA 13-16R; CAAS 22; CANR 24,
51; CP 1, 2, 3, 4, 5, 6, 7; DLBY 1984;
TCLE 1:2

Turgenev, Ivan (Sergeevich)
1818-1883 **DC 7; NCLC 21, 37, 122;
SSC 7, 57; WLC 6**
See also AAYA 58; DA; DAB; DAC; DAM
MST, NOV; DFS 6; DLB 238, 284; EW
6; LATS 1:1; NFS 16; RGSF 2; RGWL 2,
3; TWA

Turgot, Anne-Robert-Jacques
1727-1781 **LC 26**
See also DLB 314

Turner, Frederick 1943- **CLC 48**
See also CA 73-76, 227; CAAE 227; CAAS
10; CANR 12, 30, 56; DLB 40, 282

Turton, James
See Crace, Jim

Tutu, Desmond M(pilo) 1931- .. **BLC 3; CLC
80**
See also BW 1, 3; CA 125; CANR 67, 81;
DAM MULT

Tutuola, Amos 1920-1997 **BLC 3; CLC 5,
14, 29**
See also AFW; BW 2, 3; CA 9-12R; 159;
CANR 27, 66; CDWLB 3; CN 1, 2, 3, 4,
5, 6; DAM MULT; DLB 125; DNFS
2; EWL 3; MTCW 1, 2; MTFW 2005;
RGEL 2; WLIT 2

Twain, Mark **SSC 6, 26, 34, 87; TCLC 6,
12, 19, 36, 48, 59, 161; WLC 6**
See Clemens, Samuel Langhorne
See also AAYA 20; AMW; AMWC 1; BPFB
3; BYA 2, 3, 11, 14; CLR 58, 60, 66; DLB
11; EXPN; EXPS; FANT; LAIT 2; MAL
5; NCFS 4; NFS 1, 6; RGAL 4; RGSF 2;
SFW 4; SSFS 1, 7, 16, 21; SUFW; TUS;
WCH; WYA; YAW

Tyler, Anne 1941- . **CLC 7, 11, 18, 28, 44, 59,
103, 205**
See also AAYA 18, 60; AMWS 4; BEST
89:1; BPFB 3; BYA 12; CA 9-12R; CANR
11, 33, 53, 109, 132; CDALBS; CN 1, 2,
3, 4, 5, 6, 7; CPW; CSW; DAM NOV,
POP; DLB 6, 143; DLBY 1982; EWL 3;
EXPN; LATS 1:2; MAL 5; MAWW;
MTCW 1, 2; MTFW 2005; NFS 2, 7, 10;
RGAL 4; SATA 7, 90; SSFS 17; TCLE
1:2; TUS; YAW

Tyler, Royall 1757-1826 **NCLC 3**
See also DLB 37; RGAL 4

Tynan, Katharine 1861-1931 **TCLC 3**
See also CA 104; 167; DLB 153, 240; FW

Tyndale, William c. 1484-1536 **LC 103**
See also DLB 132

Tyutchev, Fyodor 1803-1873 **NCLC 34**

Tzara, Tristan 1896-1963 **CLC 47; PC 27;
TCLC 168**
See also CA 153; 89-92; DAM POET; EWL
3; MTCW 2

Uchida, Yoshiko 1921-1992 **AAL**
See also AAYA 16; BYA 2, 3; CA 13-16R;
139; CANR 6, 22, 47, 61; CDALBS; CLR
6, 56; CWRI 5; DLB 312; JRDA; MAI-
CYA 1, 2; MTCW 1, 2; MTFW 2005;
SAAS 1; SATA 1, 53; SATA-Obit 72

Udall, Nicholas 1504-1556 **LC 84**
See also DLB 62; RGEL 2

Ueda Akinari 1734-1809 **NCLC 131**

Uhry, Alfred 1936- **CLC 55**
See also CA 127; 133; CAD; CANR 112;
CD 5, 6; CSW; DA3; DAM DRAM, POP;
DFS 11, 15; INT CA-133; MTFW 2005

Ulf, Haerved
See Strindberg, (Johan) August

Ulf, Harved
See Strindberg, (Johan) August

Ulibarri, Sabine R(eyes)
1919-2003 **CLC 83; HLCS 2**
See also CA 131; 214; CANR 81; DAM
MULT; DLB 82; HW 1, 2; RGSF 2

Unamuno (y Jugo), Miguel de
1864-1936 .. **HLC 2; SSC 11, 69; TCLC
2, 9, 148**
See also CA 104; 131; CANR 81; DAM
MULT, NOV; DLB 108, 322; EW 8; EWL
3; HW 1, 2; MTCW 1, 2; MTFW 2005;
RGSF 2; RGWL 2, 3; SSFS 20; TWA

Uncle Shelby
See Silverstein, Shel(don Allan)

Undercliffe, Errol
See Campbell, (John) Ramsey

Underwood, Miles
See Glassco, John

Undset, Sigrid 1882-1949 .. **TCLC 3; WLC 6**
See also CA 104; 129; DA; DA3; DAB;
DAC; DAM MST, NOV; DLB 293; EW
9; EWL 3; FW; MTCW 1, 2; MTFW
2005; RGWL 2, 3

Ungaretti, Giuseppe 1888-1970 ... **CLC 7, 11,
15; PC 57**
See also CA 19-20; 25-28R; CAP 2; DLB
114; EW 10; EWL 3; PFS 20; RGWL 2,
3; WLIT 7

Unger, Douglas 1952- **CLC 34**
See also CA 130; CANR 94

Unsworth, Barry (Forster) 1930- **CLC 76,
127**
See also BRWS 7; CA 25-28R; CANR 30,
54, 125; CN 6, 7; DLB 194, 326

Updike, John 1932- . **CLC 1, 2, 3, 5, 7, 9, 13,
15, 23, 34, 43, 70, 139, 214; SSC 13, 27;
WLC 6**
See also AAYA 36; AMW; AMWC 1;
AMWR 1; BPFB 3; BYA 12; CA 1-4R;
CABS 1; CANR 4, 33, 51, 94, 133;
CDALB 1968-1988; CN 1, 2, 3, 4, 5, 6,
7; CP 1, 3, 4, 5, 6, 7; CPW 1; DA;
DA3; DAB; DAC; DAM MST, NOV,
POET, POP; DLB 2, 5, 143, 218, 227;
DLBD 3; DLBY 1980, 1982, 1997; EWL
3; EXPP; HGG; MAL 5; MTCW 1, 2;
MTFW 2005; NFS 12; RGAL 4; RGSF 2;
SSFS 3, 19; TUS

Updike, John Hoyer
See Updike, John

Upshaw, Margaret Mitchell
See Mitchell, Margaret (Munnerlyn)

Upton, Mark
See Sanders, Lawrence

Upward, Allen 1863-1926 **TCLC 85**
See also CA 117; 187; DLB 36

Urdang, Constance (Henriette)
1922-1996 **CLC 47**
See also CA 21-24R; CANR 9, 24; CP 1, 2,
3, 4, 5, 6; CWP

Uriel, Henry
See Faust, Frederick (Schiller)

Uris, Leon (Marcus) 1924-2003 ... **CLC 7, 32**
See also AITN 1, 2; BEST 89:2; BPFB 3;
CA 1-4R; 217; CANR 1, 40, 65, 123; CN
1, 2, 3, 4, 5, 6; CPW 1; DA3; DAM NOV,
POP; MTCW 1, 2; MTFW 2005; RGHL;
SATA 49; SATA-Obit 146

Urista (Heredia), Alberto (Baltazar)
1947- .. **HLCS 1**
See Alurista
See also CA 182; CANR 2, 32; HW 1

Urmuz
See Codrescu, Andrei

Urquhart, Guy
See McAlmon, Robert (Menzies)

Urquhart, Jane 1949- **CLC 90**
See also CA 113; CANR 32, 68, 116; CCA
1; DAC

Usigli, Rodolfo 1905-1979 **HLCS 1**
See also CA 131; DLB 305; EWL 3; HW 1;
LAW

Usk, Thomas (?)-1388 **CMLC 76**
See also DLB 146

Ustinov, Peter (Alexander)
1921-2004 **CLC 1**
See also AITN 1; CA 13-16R; 225; CANR
25, 51; CBD; CD 5, 6; DLB 13; MTCW
2

U Tam'si, Gerald Felix Tchicaya
See Tchicaya, Gerald Felix

U Tam'si, Tchicaya
See Tchicaya, Gerald Felix

Vachss, Andrew 1942- **CLC 106**
See also CA 118; 214; CAAE 214; CANR
44, 95, 153; CMW 4

Vachss, Andrew H.
See Vachss, Andrew

Vachss, Andrew Henry
See Vachss, Andrew

Vaculik, Ludvik 1926- **CLC 7**
See also CA 53-56; CANR 72; CWW 2;
DLB 232; EWL 3

Vaihinger, Hans 1852-1933 **TCLC 71**
See also CA 116; 166

Valdez, Luis (Miguel) 1940- **CLC 84; DC
10; HLC 2**
See also CA 101; CAD; CANR 32, 81; CD
5, 6; DAM MULT; DFS 5; DLB 122;
EWL 3; HW 1; LAIT 4; LLW

Valenzuela, Luisa 1938- **CLC 31, 104;
HLCS 2; SSC 14, 82**
See also CA 101; CANR 32, 65, 123; CD-
WLB 3; CWW 2; DAM MULT; DLB 113;
EWL 3; FW; HW 1, 2; LAW; RGSF 2;
RGWL 3

Valera y Alcala-Galiano, Juan
1824-1905 **TCLC 10**
See also CA 106

Valerius Maximus fl. 20- **CMLC 64**
See also DLB 211

Valery, (Ambroise) Paul (Toussaint Jules)
1871-1945 **PC 9; TCLC 4, 15**
See also CA 104; 122; DA3; DAM POET;
DLB 258; EW 8; EWL 3; GFL 1789 to
the Present; MTCW 1, 2; MTFW 2005;
RGWL 2, 3; TWA

Valle-Inclan, Ramon (Maria) del
1866-1936 **HLC 2; TCLC 5**
See del Valle-Inclan, Ramon (Maria)
See also CA 106; 153; CANR 80; DAM
MULT; DLB 134; EW 8; EWL 3; HW 2;
RGSF 2; RGWL 2, 3

Vallejo, Antonio Buero
See Buero Vallejo, Antonio

Vallejo, Cesar (Abraham)
1892-1938 **HLC 2; TCLC 3, 56**
See also CA 105; 153; DAM MULT; DLB
290; EWL 3; HW 1; LAW; RGWL 2, 3

Valles, Jules 1832-1885 **NCLC 71**
See also DLB 123; GFL 1789 to the Present

Vallette, Marguerite Eymery
1860-1953 **TCLC 67**
See Rachilde
See also CA 182; DLB 123, 192

Valle Y Pena, Ramon del
See Valle-Inclan, Ramon (Maria) del

Van Ash, Cay 1918-1994 **CLC 34**
See also CA 220

Vanbrugh, Sir John 1664-1726 **LC 21**
See also BRW 2; DAM DRAM; DLB 80;
IDTP; RGEL 2

Van Campen, Karl
See Campbell, John W(ood, Jr.)

Vance, Gerald
See Silverberg, Robert

Vance, Jack 1916-
See Queen, Ellery; Vance, John Holbrook
See also CA 29-32R; CANR 17, 65, 154;
CMW 4; MTCW 1

Vance, John Holbrook **CLC 35**
See Vance, Jack
See also DLB 8, FANT, SCFW 1, 2; SFW
4; SUFW 1, 2

**Van Den Bogarde, Derek Jules Gaspard
Ulric Niven** 1921-1999 **CLC 14**
See Bogarde, Dirk
See also CA 77-80; 179

Vandenburgh, Jane **CLC 59**
See also CA 168

Vanderhaeghe, Guy 1951- **CLC 41**
See also BPFB 3; CA 113; CANR 72, 145;
CN 7

van der Post, Laurens (Jan)
1906-1996 **CLC 5**
See also AFW; CA 5-8R; 155; CANR 35;
CN 1, 2, 3, 4, 5, 6; DLB 204; RGEL 2

van de Wetering, Janwillem 1931- ... **CLC 47**
See also CA 49-52; CANR 4, 62, 90; CMW
4

Van Dine, S. S. **TCLC 23**
See Wright, Willard Huntington
See also DLB 306; MSW

Van Doren, Carl (Clinton)
1885-1950 **TCLC 18**
See also CA 111; 168

Van Doren, Mark 1894-1972 **CLC 6, 10**
See also CA 1-4R; 37-40R; CANR 3; CN
1; CP 1; DLB 45, 284; MAL 5; MTCW
1, 2; RGAL 4

Van Druten, John (William)
1901-1957 **TCLC 2**
See also CA 104; 161; DLB 10; MAL 5;
RGAL 4

Van Duyn, Mona (Jane) 1921-2004 .. **CLC 3,
7, 63, 116**
See also CA 9-12R; 234; CANR 7, 38, 60,
116; CP 1, 2, 3, 4, 5, 6, 7; CWP; DAM
POET; DLB 5; MAL 5; MTFW 2005;
PFS 20

Van Dyne, Edith
See Baum, L(yman) Frank

van Itallie, Jean-Claude 1936- **CLC 3**
See also CA 45-48; CAAS 2; CAD; CANR
1, 48; CD 5, 6; DLB 7

Van Loot, Cornelius Obenchain
 See Roberts, Kenneth (Lewis)
van Ostaijen, Paul 1896-1928 **TCLC 33**
 See also CA 163
Van Peebles, Melvin 1932- **CLC 2, 20**
 See also BW 2, 3, CA 85-88, CANR 27,
 67, 82; DAM MULT
van Schendel, Arthur(-Francois-Emile)
 1874-1946 **TCLC 56**
 See also EWL 3
Vansittart, Peter 1920- **CLC 42**
 See also CA 1-4R; CANR 3, 49, 90; CN 4,
 5, 6, 7; RHW
Van Vechten, Carl 1880-1964 ... **CLC 33; HR 1:3**
 See also AMWS 2; CA 183; 89-92; DLB 4,
 9, 51; RGAL 4
van Vogt, A(lfred) E(lton) 1912-2000 . **CLC 1**
 See also BPFB 3; BYA 13, 14; CA 21-24R;
 190; CANR 28; DLB 8, 251; SATA 14;
 SATA-Obit 124; SCFW 1, 2; SFW 4
Vara, Madeleine
 See Jackson, Laura (Riding)
Varda, Agnes 1928- **CLC 16**
 See also CA 116; 122
Vargas Llosa, Jorge Mario Pedro
 See Vargas Llosa, Mario
Vargas Llosa, Mario 1936- .. **CLC 3, 6, 9, 10, 15, 31, 42, 85, 181; HLC 2**
 See Llosa, Jorge Mario Pedro Vargas
 See also BPFB 3; CA 73-76; CANR 18, 32,
 42, 67, 116, 140; CDWLB 3; CWW 2;
 DA; DA3; DAB; DAC; DAM MST,
 MULT, NOV; DLB 145; DNFS 2; EWL
 3; HW 1, 2; LAIT 5; LATS 1:2; LAW;
 LAWS 1; MTCW 1, 2; MTFW 2005;
 RGWL 2; SSFS 14; TWA; WLIT 1
Varnhagen von Ense, Rahel
 1771-1833 **NCLC 130**
 See also DLB 90
Vasari, Giorgio 1511-1574 **LC 114**
Vasilikos, Vasiles
 See Vassilikos, Vassilis
Vasiliu, George
 See Bacovia, George
Vasiliu, Gheorghe
 See Bacovia, George
 See also CA 123; 189
Vassa, Gustavus
 See Equiano, Olaudah
Vassilikos, Vassilis 1933- **CLC 4, 8**
 See also CA 81-84; CANR 75, 149; EWL 3
Vaughan, Henry 1621-1695 **LC 27**
 See also BRW 2; DLB 131; PAB; RGEL 2
Vaughn, Stephanie **CLC 62**
Vazov, Ivan (Minchov) 1850-1921 . **TCLC 25**
 See also CA 121; 167; CDWLB 4; DLB
 147
Veblen, Thorstein B(unde)
 1857-1929 **TCLC 31**
 See also AMWS 1; CA 115; 165; DLB 246;
 MAL 5
Vega, Lope de 1562-1635 ... **HLCS 2; LC 23, 119**
 See also EW 2; RGWL 2, 3
Veldeke, Heinrich von c. 1145-c.
 1190 .. **CMLC 85**
Vendler, Helen (Hennessy) 1933- ... **CLC 138**
 See also CA 41-44R; CANR 25, 72, 136;
 MTCW 1, 2; MTFW 2005
Venison, Alfred
 See Pound, Ezra (Weston Loomis)
Ventsel, Elena Sergeevna 1907-2002
 See Grekova, I.
 See also CA 154
Verdi, Marie de
 See Mencken, H(enry) L(ouis)
Verdu, Matilde
 See Cela, Camilo Jose

Verga, Giovanni (Carmelo)
 1840-1922 **SSC 21, 87; TCLC 3**
 See also CA 104; 123; CANR 101; EW 7;
 EWL 3; RGSF 2; RGWL 2, 3; WLIT 7
Vergil 70B.C.-19B.C. ... **CMLC 9, 40; PC 12; WLCS**
 See Virgil
 See also AW 2; DA; DA3; DAB; DAC;
 DAM MST, POET; EFS 1; LMFS 1
Vergil, Polydore c. 1470-1555 **LC 108**
 See also DLB 132
Verhaeren, Emile (Adolphe Gustave)
 1855-1916 **TCLC 12**
 See also CA 109; EWL 3; GFL 1789 to the
 Present
Verlaine, Paul (Marie) 1844-1896 .. **NCLC 2, 51; PC 2, 32**
 See also DAM POET; DLB 217; EW 7;
 GFL 1789 to the Present; LMFS 2; RGWL
 2, 3; TWA
Verne, Jules (Gabriel) 1828-1905 ... **TCLC 6, 52**
 See also AAYA 16; BYA 4; CA 110; 131;
 CLR 88; DA3; DLB 123; GFL 1789 to
 the Present; JRDA; LAIT 2; LMFS 2;
 MAICYA 1, 2; MTFW 2005; RGWL 2, 3;
 SATA 21; SCFW 1, 2; SFW 4; TWA;
 WCH
Verus, Marcus Annius
 See Aurelius, Marcus
Very, Jones 1813-1880 **NCLC 9**
 See also DLB 1, 243; RGAL 4
Vesaas, Tarjei 1897-1970 **CLC 48**
 See also CA 190; 29-32R; DLB 297; EW
 11; EWL 3; RGWL 3
Vialis, Gaston
 See Simenon, Georges (Jacques Christian)
Vian, Boris 1920-1959(?) **TCLC 9**
 See also CA 106; 164; CANR 111; DLB
 72, 321; EWL 3; GFL 1789 to the Present;
 MTCW 2; RGWL 2, 3
Viaud, (Louis Marie) Julien 1850-1923
 See Loti, Pierre
 See also CA 107
Vicar, Henry
 See Felsen, Henry Gregor
Vicente, Gil 1465-c. 1536 **LC 99**
 See also DLB 318; IDTP; RGWL 2, 3
Vicker, Angus
 See Felsen, Henry Gregor
Vidal, Eugene Luther Gore
 See Vidal, Gore
Vidal, Gore 1925- **CLC 2, 4, 6, 8, 10, 22, 33, 72, 142**
 See Box, Edgar
 See also AAYA 64; AITN 1; AMWS 4;
 BEST 90:2; BPFB 3; CA 5-8R; CAD;
 CANR 13, 45, 65, 100, 132; CD 5, 6;
 CDALBS; CN 1, 2, 3, 4, 5, 6, 7; CPW;
 DA3; DAM NOV, POP; DFS 2; DLB 6,
 152; EWL 3; INT CANR-13; MAL 5;
 MTCW 1, 2; MTFW 2005; RGAL 4;
 RHW; TUS
Viereck, Peter 1916-2006 **CLC 4; PC 27**
 See also CA 1-4R; CANR 1, 47; CP 1, 2, 3,
 4, 5, 6, 7; DLB 5; MAL 5; PFS 9, 14
Viereck, Peter Robert Edwin
 See Viereck, Peter
Vigny, Alfred (Victor) de
 1797-1863 **NCLC 7, 102; PC 26**
 See also DAM POET; DLB 119, 192, 217;
 EW 5; GFL 1789 to the Present; RGWL
 2, 3
Vilakazi, Benedict Wallet
 1906-1947 **TCLC 37**
 See also CA 168

Villa, Jose Garcia 1914-1997 ... **AAL; PC 22; TCLC 176**
 See also CA 25-28R; CANR 12, 118; CP 1,
 2, 3, 4; DLB 312; EWL 3; EXPP
Villard, Oswald Garrison
 1872 1949 **TCLC 160**
 See also CA 113; 162; DLB 25, 91
Villarreal, Jose Antonio 1924- **HLC 2**
 See also CA 133; CANR 93; DAM MULT;
 DLB 82; HW 1; LAIT 4; RGAL 4
Villaurrutia, Xavier 1903-1950 **TCLC 80**
 See also CA 192; EWL 3; HW 1; LAW
Villaverde, Cirilo 1812-1894 **NCLC 121**
 See also LAW
Villehardouin, Geoffroi de
 1150(?)-1218(?) **CMLC 38**
Villiers, George 1628-1687 **LC 107**
 See also DLB 80; RGEL 2
Villiers de l'Isle Adam, Jean Marie Mathias Philippe Auguste 1838-1889 ... **NCLC 3; SSC 14**
 See also DLB 123, 192; GFL 1789 to the
 Present; RGSF 2
Villon, Francois 1431-1463(?) . **LC 62; PC 13**
 See also DLB 208; EW 2; RGWL 2, 3;
 TWA
Vine, Barbara **CLC 50**
 See Rendell, Ruth (Barbara)
 See also BEST 90:4
Vinge, Joan (Carol) D(ennison)
 1948- **CLC 30; SSC 24**
 See also AAYA 32; BPFB 3; CA 93-96;
 CANR 72; SATA 36, 113; SFW 4; YAW
Viola, Herman J(oseph) 1938- **CLC 70**
 See also CA 61-64; CANR 8, 23, 48, 91;
 SATA 126
Violis, G.
 See Simenon, Georges (Jacques Christian)
Viramontes, Helena Maria 1954- **HLCS 2**
 See also CA 159; DLB 122; HW 2; LLW
Virgil
 See Vergil
 See also CDWLB 1; DLB 211; LAIT 1;
 RGWL 2, 3; WLIT 8; WP
Visconti, Luchino 1906-1976 **CLC 16**
 See also CA 81-84; 65-68; CANR 39
Vitry, Jacques de
 See Jacques de Vitry
Vittorini, Elio 1908-1966 **CLC 6, 9, 14**
 See also CA 133; 25-28R; DLB 264; EW
 12; EWL 3; RGWL 2, 3
Vivekananda, Swami 1863-1902 **TCLC 88**
Vizenor, Gerald Robert 1934- **CLC 103; NNAL**
 See also CA 13-16R, 205; CAAE 205;
 CAAS 22; CANR 5, 21, 44, 67; DAM
 MULT; DLB 175, 227; MTCW 2; MTFW
 2005; TCWW 2
Vizinczey, Stephen 1933- **CLC 40**
 See also CA 128; CCA 1; INT CA-128
Vliet, R(ussell) G(ordon)
 1929-1984 **CLC 22**
 See also CA 37-40R; 112; CANR 18; CP 2,
 3
Vogau, Boris Andreyevich 1894-1938
 See Pilnyak, Boris
 See also CA 123; 218
Vogel, Paula A(nne) 1951- ... **CLC 76; DC 19**
 See also CA 108; CAD; CANR 119, 140;
 CD 5, 6; CWD; DFS 14; MTFW 2005;
 RGAL 4
Voigt, Cynthia 1942- **CLC 30**
 See also AAYA 3, 30; BYA 1, 3, 6, 7, 8;
 CA 106; CANR 18, 37, 40, 94, 145; CLR
 13, 48; INT CANR-18; JRDA; LAIT 5;
 MAICYA 1, 2; MAICYAS 1; MTFW
 2005; SATA 48, 79, 116, 160; SATA-Brief
 33; WYA; YAW

Voigt, Ellen Bryant 1943- CLC 54
See also CA 69-72; CANR 11, 29, 55, 115;
CP 5, 6, 7; CSW; CWP; DLB 120; PFS
23

Voinovich, Vladimir 1932- .. CLC 10, 49, 147
See also CA 81-84; CAAS 12; CANR 33,
67, 150; CWW 2; DLB 302; MTCW 1

Voinovich, Vladimir Nikolaevich
See Voinovich, Vladimir

Vollmann, William T. 1959- CLC 89
See also CA 134; CANR 67, 116; CN 7;
CPW; DA3; DAM NOV, POP; MTCW 2;
MTFW 2005

Voloshinov, V. N.
See Bakhtin, Mikhail Mikhailovich

Voltaire 1694-1778 . LC 14, 79, 110; SSC 12;
WLC 6
See also BYA 13; DA; DA3; DAB; DAC;
DAM DRAM, MST; DLB 314; EW 4;
GFL Beginnings to 1789; LATS 1:1;
LMFS 1; NFS 7; RGWL 2, 3; TWA

von Aschendrof, Baron Ignatz
See Ford, Ford Madox

von Chamisso, Adelbert
See Chamisso, Adelbert von

von Daeniken, Erich 1935- CLC 30
See also AITN 1; CA 37-40R; CANR 17,
44

von Daniken, Erich
See von Daeniken, Erich

von Hartmann, Eduard
1842-1906 TCLC 96

von Hayek, Friedrich August
See Hayek, F(riedrich) A(ugust von)

von Heidenstam, (Carl Gustaf) Verner
See Heidenstam, (Carl Gustaf) Verner von

von Heyse, Paul (Johann Ludwig)
See Heyse, Paul (Johann Ludwig von)

von Hofmannsthal, Hugo
See Hofmannsthal, Hugo von

von Horvath, Odon
See von Horvath, Odon

von Horvath, Odon
See von Horvath, Odon

von Horvath, Odon 1901-1938 TCLC 45
See von Horvath, Oedoen
See also CA 118; 194; DLB 85, 124; RGWL
2, 3

von Horvath, Oedoen
See von Horvath, Odon
See also CA 184

von Kleist, Heinrich
See Kleist, Heinrich von

von Liliencron, (Friedrich Adolf Axel)
Detlev
See Liliencron, (Friedrich Adolf Axel) De-
tlev von

Vonnegut, Kurt, Jr.
See Vonnegut, Kurt

Vonnegut, Kurt 1922- ... CLC 1, 2, 3, 4, 5, 8,
12, 22, 40, 60, 111, 212; SSC 8; WLC 6
See also AAYA 6, 44; AITN 1; AMWS 2;
BEST 90:4; BPFB 3; BYA 3, 14; CA
1-4R; CANR 1, 25, 49, 75, 92; CDALB
1968-1988; CN 1, 2, 3, 4, 5, 6, 7; CPW 1;
DA; DA3; DAB; DAC; DAM MST, NOV,
POP; DLB 2, 8, 152; DLBD 3; DLBY
1980; EWL 3; EXPN; EXPS; LAIT 4;
LMFS 2; MAL 5; MTCW 1, 2; MTFW
2005; NFS 3; RGAL 4; SCFW; SFW 4;
SSFS 5; TUS; YAW

Von Rachen, Kurt
See Hubbard, L. Ron

von Sternberg, Josef
See Sternberg, Josef von

Vorster, Gordon 1924- CLC 34
See also CA 133

Vosce, Trudie
See Ozick, Cynthia

Voznesensky, Andrei (Andreievich)
1933- CLC 1, 15, 57
See Voznesensky, Andrey
See also CA 89-92; CANR 37; CWW 2;
DAM POET; MTCW 1

Voznesensky, Andrey
See Voznesensky, Andrei (Andreievich)
See also EWL 3

Wace, Robert c. 1100-c. 1175 CMLC 55
See also DLB 146

Waddington, Miriam 1917-2004 CLC 28
See also CA 21-24R; 225; CANR 12, 30;
CCA 1; CP 1, 2, 3, 4, 5, 6, 7; DLB 68

Wagman, Fredrica 1937- CLC 7
See also CA 97-100; INT CA-97-100

Wagner, Linda W.
See Wagner-Martin, Linda (C.)

Wagner, Linda Welshimer
See Wagner-Martin, Linda (C.)

Wagner, Richard 1813-1883 NCLC 9, 119
See also DLB 129; EW 6

Wagner-Martin, Linda (C.) 1936- CLC 50
See also CA 159; CANR 135

Wagoner, David (Russell) 1926- CLC 3, 5,
15; PC 33
See also AMWS 9; CA 1-4R; CAAS 3;
CANR 2, 71; CN 1, 2, 3, 4, 5, 6, 7; CP 1,
2, 3, 4, 5, 6, 7; DLB 5, 256; SATA 14;
TCWW 1, 2

Wah, Fred(erick James) 1939- CLC 44
See also CA 107; 141; CP 1, 6, 7; DLB 60

Wahloo, Per 1926-1975 CLC 7
See also BPFB 3; CA 61-64; CANR 73;
CMW 4; MSW

Wahloo, Peter
See Wahloo, Per

Wain, John (Barrington) 1925-1994 . CLC 2,
11, 15, 46
See also CA 5-8R; 145; CAAS 4; CANR
23, 54; CDBLB 1960 to Present; CN 1, 2,
3, 4, 5; CP 1, 2, 3, 4, 5; DLB 15, 27, 139,
155; EWL 3; MTCW 1, 2; MTFW 2005

Wajda, Andrzej 1926- CLC 16, 219
See also CA 102

Wakefield, Dan 1932- CLC 7
See also CA 21-24R, 211; CAAE 211;
CAAS 7; CN 4, 5, 6, 7

Wakefield, Herbert Russell
1888-1965 TCLC 120
See also CA 5-8R; CANR 77; HGG; SUFW

Wakoski, Diane 1937- CLC 2, 4, 7, 9, 11,
40; PC 15
See also CA 13-16R, 216; CAAE 216;
CAAS 1; CANR 9, 60, 106; CP 1, 2, 3, 4,
5, 6, 7; CWP; DAM POET; DLB 5; INT
CANR-9; MAL 5; MTCW 2; MTFW
2005

Wakoski-Sherbell, Diane
See Wakoski, Diane

Walcott, Derek (Alton) 1930- ... BLC 3; CLC
2, 4, 9, 14, 25, 42, 67, 76, 160; DC 7;
PC 46
See also BW 2; CA 89-92; CANR 26, 47,
75, 80, 130; CBD; CD 5, 6; CDWLB 3;
CP 1, 2, 3, 4, 5, 6, 7; DA3; DAB; DAC;
DAM MST, MULT, POET; DLB 117;
DLBY 1981; DNFS 1; EFS 1; EWL 3;
LMFS 2; MTCW 1, 2; MTFW 2005; PFS
6; RGEL 2; TWA; WWE 1

Waldman, Anne (Lesley) 1945- CLC 7
See also BG 1:3; CA 37-40R; CAAS 17;
CANR 34, 69, 116; CP 1, 2, 3, 4, 5, 6, 7;
CWP; DLB 16

Waldo, E. Hunter
See Sturgeon, Theodore (Hamilton)

Waldo, Edward Hamilton
See Sturgeon, Theodore (Hamilton)

Walker, Alice 1944- BLC 3; CLC 5, 6, 9,
19, 27, 46, 58, 103, 167; PC 30; SSC 5;
WLCS
See also AAYA 3, 33; AFAW 1, 2; AMWS
3; BEST 89:4; BPFB 3; BW 2, 3; CA 37-
40R; CANR 9, 27, 49, 66, 82, 131;
CDALB 1968-1988; CN 4, 5, 6, 7; CPW;
CSW; DA; DA3; DAB; DAC; DAM MST,
MULT, NOV, POET, POP; DLB 6, 33,
143; EWL 3; EXPN; EXPS; FL 1:6; FW;
INT CANR-27; LAIT 3; MAL 5; MAWW;
MTCW 1, 2; MTFW 2005; NFS 5; RGAL
4; RGSF 2; SATA 31; SSFS 2, 11; TUS;
YAW

Walker, Alice Malsenior
See Walker, Alice

Walker, David Harry 1911-1992 CLC 14
See also CA 1-4R; 137; CANR 1; CN 1, 2;
CWRI 5; SATA 8; SATA-Obit 71

Walker, Edward Joseph 1934-2004
See Walker, Ted
See also CA 21-24R; 226; CANR 12, 28,
53

Walker, George F(rederick) 1947- .. CLC 44,
61
See also CA 103; CANR 21, 43, 59; CD 5,
6; DAB; DAC; DAM MST; DLB 60

Walker, Joseph A. 1935-2003 CLC 19
See also BW 1, 3; CA 89-92; CAD; CANR
26, 143; CD 5, 6; DAM DRAM, MST;
DFS 12; DLB 38

Walker, Margaret (Abigail)
1915-1998 BLC; CLC 1, 6; PC 20;
TCLC 129
See also AFAW 1, 2; BW 2, 3; CA 73-76;
172; CANR 26, 54, 76, 136; CN 1, 2, 3,
4, 5, 6; CP 1, 2, 3, 4, 5, 6; CSW; DAM
MULT; DLB 76, 152; EXPP; FW; MAL
5; MTCW 1, 2; MTFW 2005; RGAL 4;
RHW

Walker, Ted CLC 13
See Walker, Edward Joseph
See also CP 1, 2, 3, 4, 5, 6, 7; DLB 40

Wallace, David Foster 1962- ... CLC 50, 114;
SSC 68
See also AAYA 50; AMWS 10; CA 132;
CANR 59, 133; CN 7; DA3; MTCW 2;
MTFW 2005

Wallace, Dexter
See Masters, Edgar Lee

Wallace, (Richard Horatio) Edgar
1875-1932 TCLC 57
See also CA 115; 218; CMW 4; DLB 70;
MSW; RGEL 2

Wallace, Irving 1916-1990 CLC 7, 13
See also AITN 1; BPFB 3; CA 1-4R; 132;
CAAS 1; CANR 1, 27; CPW; DAM NOV,
POP; INT CANR-27; MTCW 1, 2

Wallant, Edward Lewis 1926-1962 ... CLC 5,
10
See also CA 1-4R; CANR 22; DLB 2, 28,
143, 299; EWL 3; MAL 5; MTCW 1, 2;
RGAL 4; RGHL

Wallas, Graham 1858-1932 TCLC 91

Waller, Edmund 1606-1687 LC 86; PC 72
See also BRW 2; DAM POET; DLB 126;
PAB; RGEL 2

Walley, Byron
See Card, Orson Scott

Walpole, Horace 1717-1797 LC 2, 49
See also BRW 3; DLB 39, 104, 213; GL 3;
HGG; LMFS 1; RGEL 2; SUFW 1; TEA

Walpole, Hugh (Seymour)
1884-1941 TCLC 5
See also CA 104; 165; DLB 34; HGG;
MTCW 2; RGEL 2; RHW

Walrond, Eric (Derwent) 1898-1966 . HR 1:3
See also BW 1; CA 125; DLB 51

Walser, Martin 1927- **CLC 27, 183**
See also CA 57-60; CANR 8, 46, 145;
CWW 2; DLB 75, 124; EWL 3

Walser, Robert 1878-1956 **SSC 20; TCLC 18**
See also CA 118; 165; CANR 100; DLB 66; EWL 3

Walsh, Gillian Paton
See Paton Walsh, Gillian

Walsh, Jill Paton **CLC 35**
See Paton Walsh, Gillian
See also CLR 2, 65; WYA

Walter, Villiam Christian
See Andersen, Hans Christian

Walters, Anna L(ee) 1946- **NNAL**
See also CA 73-76

Walther von der Vogelweide c.
1170-1228 **CMLC 56**

Walton, Izaak 1593-1683 **LC 72**
See also BRW 2; CDBLB Before 1660;
DLB 151, 213; RGEL 2

Wambaugh, Joseph (Aloysius), Jr.
1937- **CLC 3, 18**
See also AITN 1; BEST 89:3; BPFB 3; CA 33-36R; CANR 42, 65, 115; CMW 4;
CPW 1; DA3; DAM NOV, POP; DLB 6;
DLBY 1983; MSW; MTCW 1, 2

Wang Wei 699(?)-761(?) **PC 18**
See also TWA

Warburton, William 1698-1779 **LC 97**
See also DLB 104

Ward, Arthur Henry Sarsfield 1883-1959
See Rohmer, Sax
See also CA 108; 173; CMW 4; HGG

Ward, Douglas Turner 1930- **CLC 19**
See also BW 1; CA 81-84; CAD; CANR 27; CD 5, 6; DLB 7, 38

Ward, E. D.
See Lucas, E(dward) V(errall)

Ward, Mrs. Humphry 1851-1920
See Ward, Mary Augusta
See also RGEL 2

Ward, Mary Augusta 1851-1920 ... **TCLC 55**
See Ward, Mrs. Humphry
See also DLB 18

Ward, Nathaniel 1578(?)-1652 **LC 114**
See also DLB 24

Ward, Peter
See Faust, Frederick (Schiller)

Warhol, Andy 1928(?)-1987 **CLC 20**
See also AAYA 12; BEST 89:4; CA 89-92;
121; CANR 34

Warner, Francis (Robert le Plastrier)
1937- **CLC 14**
See also CA 53-56; CANR 11; CP 1, 2, 3, 4

Warner, Marina 1946- **CLC 59**
See also CA 65-68; CANR 21, 55, 118; CN 5, 6, 7; DLB 194; MTFW 2005

Warner, Rex (Ernest) 1905-1986 **CLC 45**
See also CA 89-92; 119; CN 1, 2, 3, 4; CP 1, 2, 3, 4; DLB 15; RGEL 2; RHW

Warner, Susan (Bogert)
1819-1885 **NCLC 31, 146**
See also DLB 3, 42, 239, 250, 254

Warner, Sylvia (Constance) Ashton
See Ashton-Warner, Sylvia (Constance)

Warner, Sylvia Townsend
1893-1978 .. **CLC 7, 19; SSC 23; TCLC 131**
See also BRWS 7; CA 61-64; 77-80; CANR 16, 60, 104; CN 1, 2; DLB 34, 139; EWL 3; FANT; FW; MTCW 1, 2; RGEL 2;
RGSF 2; RHW

Warren, Mercy Otis 1728-1814 **NCLC 13**
See also DLB 31, 200; RGAL 4; TUS

Warren, Robert Penn 1905-1989 .. **CLC 1, 4, 6, 8, 10, 13, 18, 39, 53, 59; PC 37; SSC 4, 58; WLC 6**
See also AITN 1; AMW; AMWC 2; BPFB 3; BYA 1; CA 13-16R; 129; CANR 10, 47; CDALB 1968-1988; CN 1, 2, 3, 4;
CP 1, 2, 3, 4; DA; DA3; DAB; DAC;
DAM MST, NOV, POET; DLB 2, 48, 152, 320; DLBY 1980, 1989; EWL 3; INT CANR-10; MAL 5; MTCW 1, 2; MTFW 2005; NFS 13; RGAL 4; RGSF 2; RHW;
SATA 46; SATA-Obit 63; SSFS 8; TUS

Warrigal, Jack
See Furphy, Joseph

Warshofsky, Isaac
See Singer, Isaac Bashevis

Warton, Joseph 1722-1800 ... **LC 128; NCLC 118**
See also DLB 104, 109; RGEL 2

Warton, Thomas 1728-1790 **LC 15, 82**
See also DAM POET; DLB 104, 109;
RGEL 2

Waruk, Kona
See Harris, (Theodore) Wilson

Warung, Price **TCLC 45**
See Astley, William
See also DLB 230; RGEL 2

Warwick, Jarvis
See Garner, Hugh
See also CCA 1

Washington, Alex
See Harris, Mark

Washington, Booker T(aliaferro)
1856-1915 **BLC 3; TCLC 10**
See also BW 1; CA 114; 125; DA3; DAM MULT; LAIT 2; RGAL 4; SATA 28

Washington, George 1732-1799 **LC 25**
See also DLB 31

Wassermann, (Karl) Jakob
1873-1934 **TCLC 6**
See also CA 104; 163; DLB 66; EWL 3

Wasserstein, Wendy 1950-2006 . **CLC 32, 59, 90, 183; DC 4**
See also AMWS 15; CA 121; 129; 247;
CABS 3; CAD; CANR 53, 75, 128; CD 5, 6; CWD; DA3; DAM DRAM; DFS 5, 17; DLB 228; EWL 3; FW; INT CA-129;
MAL 5; MTCW 2; MTFW 2005; SATA 94

Waterhouse, Keith (Spencer) 1929- . **CLC 47**
See also CA 5-8R; CANR 38, 67, 109;
CBD; CD 6; CN 1, 2, 3, 4, 5, 6, 7; DLB 13, 15; MTCW 1, 2; MTFW 2005

Waters, Frank (Joseph) 1902-1995 ... **CLC 88**
See also CA 5-8R; 149; CAAS 13; CANR 3, 18, 63, 121; DLB 212; DLBY 1986;
RGAL 4; TCWW 1, 2

Waters, Mary C. **CLC 70**

Waters, Roger 1944- **CLC 35**

Watkins, Frances Ellen
See Harper, Frances Ellen Watkins

Watkins, Gerrold
See Malzberg, Barry N(athaniel)

Watkins, Gloria Jean
See hooks, bell

Watkins, Paul 1964- **CLC 55**
See also CA 132; CANR 62, 98

Watkins, Vernon Phillips
1906-1967 **CLC 43**
See also CA 9-10; 25-28R; CAP 1; DLB 20; EWL 3; RGEL 2

Watson, Irving S.
See Mencken, H(enry) L(ouis)

Watson, John H.
See Farmer, Philip Jose

Watson, Richard F.
See Silverberg, Robert

Watts, Ephraim
See Horne, Richard Henry Hengist

Watts, Isaac 1674-1748 **LC 98**
See also DLB 95; RGEL 2; SATA 52

Waugh, Auberon (Alexander)
1939-2001 **CLC 7**
See also CA 45-48; 192; CANR 6, 22, 92;
CN 1, 2, 3; DLB 14, 194

Waugh, Evelyn (Arthur St. John)
1903-1966 .. **CLC 1, 3, 8, 13, 19, 27, 44, 107; SSC 41; WLC 6**
See also BPFB 3; BRW 7; CA 85-88; 25-28R; CANR 22; CDBLB 1914-1945; DA;
DA3; DAB; DAC; DAM MST, NOV, POP; DLB 15, 162, 195; EWL 3; MTCW 1, 2; MTFW 2005; NFS 13, 17; RGEL 2;
RGSF 2; TEA; WLIT 4

Waugh, Harriet 1944- **CLC 6**
See also CA 85-88; CANR 22

Ways, C. R.
See Blount, Roy (Alton), Jr.

Waystaff, Simon
See Swift, Jonathan

Webb, Beatrice (Martha Potter)
1858-1943 **TCLC 22**
See also CA 117; 162; DLB 190; FW

Webb, Charles (Richard) 1939- **CLC 7**
See also CA 25-28R; CANR 114

Webb, Frank J. **NCLC 143**
See also DLB 50

Webb, James H(enry), Jr. 1946- **CLC 22**
See also CA 81-84

Webb, Mary Gladys (Meredith)
1881-1927 **TCLC 24**
See also CA 182; 123; DLB 34; FW

Webb, Mrs. Sidney
See Webb, Beatrice (Martha Potter)

Webb, Phyllis 1927- **CLC 18**
See also CA 104; CANR 23; CCA 1; CP 1, 2, 3, 4, 5, 6, 7; CWP; DLB 53

Webb, Sidney (James) 1859-1947 .. **TCLC 22**
See also CA 117; 163; DLB 190

Webber, Andrew Lloyd **CLC 21**
See Lloyd Webber, Andrew
See also DFS 7

Weber, Lenora Mattingly
1895-1971 **CLC 12**
See also CA 19-20; 29-32R; CAP 1; SATA 2; SATA-Obit 26

Weber, Max 1864-1920 **TCLC 69**
See also CA 109; 189; DLB 296

Webster, John 1580(?)-1634(?) **DC 2; LC 33, 84, 124; WLC 6**
See also BRW 2; CDBLB Before 1660; DA;
DAB; DAC; DAM DRAM, MST; DFS 17, 19; DLB 58; IDTP; RGEL 2; WLIT 3

Webster, Noah 1758-1843 **NCLC 30**
See also DLB 1, 37, 42, 43, 73, 243

Wedekind, Benjamin Franklin
See Wedekind, Frank

Wedekind, Frank 1864-1918 **TCLC 7**
See also CA 104; 153; CANR 121, 122;
CDWLB 2; DAM DRAM; DLB 118; EW 8; EWL 3; LMFS 2; RGWL 2, 3

Wehr, Demaris **CLC 65**

Weidman, Jerome 1913-1998 **CLC 7**
See also AITN 2; CA 1-4R; 171; CAD;
CANR 1; CD 1, 2, 3, 4, 5; DLB 28

Weil, Simone (Adolphine)
1909-1943 **TCLC 23**
See also CA 117; 159; EW 12; EWL 3; FW;
GFL 1789 to the Present; MTCW 2

Weininger, Otto 1880-1903 **TCLC 84**

Weinstein, Nathan
See West, Nathanael

Weinstein, Nathan von Wallenstein
See West, Nathanael

Weir, Peter (Lindsay) 1944- **CLC 20**
See also CA 113; 123

Weiss, Peter (Ulrich) 1916-1982 .. **CLC 3, 15, 51; TCLC 152**
See also CA 45-48; 106; CANR 3; DAM DRAM; DFS 3; DLB 69, 124; EWL 3; RGHL; RGWL 2, 3

Weiss, Theodore (Russell)
1916-2003 **CLC 3, 8, 14**
See also CA 9-12R, 189; 216; CAAE 189; CAAS 2; CANR 46, 94; CP 1, 2, 3, 4, 5, 6, 7; DLB 5; TCLE 1:2

Welch, (Maurice) Denton
1915-1948 **TCLC 22**
See also BRWS 8, 9; CA 121; 148; RGEL 2

Welch, James (Phillip) 1940-2003 **CLC 6, 14, 52; NNAL; PC 62**
See also CA 85-88; 219; CANR 42, 66, 107; CN 5, 6, 7; CP 2, 3, 4, 5, 6, 7; CPW; DAM MULT, POP; DLB 175, 256; LATS 1:1; NFS 23; RGAL 4; TCWW 1, 2

Weldon, Fay 1931- . **CLC 6, 9, 11, 19, 36, 59, 122**
See also BRWS 4; CA 21-24R; CANR 16, 46, 63, 97, 137; CDBLB 1960 to Present; CN 3, 4, 5, 6, 7; CPW; DAM POP; DLB 14, 194, 319; EWL 3; FW; HGG; INT CANR-16; MTCW 1, 2; MTFW 2005; RGEL 2; RGSF 2

Wellek, Rene 1903-1995 **CLC 28**
See also CA 5-8R; 150; CAAS 7; CANR 8; DLB 63; EWL 3; INT CANR-8

Weller, Michael 1942- **CLC 10, 53**
See also CA 85-88; CAD; CD 5, 6

Weller, Paul 1958- **CLC 26**

Wellershoff, Dieter 1925- **CLC 46**
See also CA 89-92; CANR 16, 37

Welles, (George) Orson 1915-1985 .. **CLC 20, 80**
See also AAYA 40; CA 93-96; 117

Wellman, John McDowell 1945-
See Wellman, Mac
See also CA 166; CD 5

Wellman, Mac **CLC 65**
See Wellman, John McDowell; Wellman, John McDowell
See also CAD; CD 6; RGAL 4

Wellman, Manly Wade 1903-1986 ... **CLC 49**
See also CA 1-4R; 118; CANR 6, 16, 44; FANT; SATA 6; SATA-Obit 47; SFW; SUFW

Wells, Carolyn 1869(?)-1942 **TCLC 35**
See also CA 113; 185; CMW 4; DLB 11

Wells, H(erbert) G(eorge) 1866-1946 . **SSC 6, 70; TCLC 6, 12, 19, 133; WLC 6**
See also AAYA 18; BPFB 3; BRW 6; CA 110; 121; CDBLB 1914-1945; CLR 64; DA; DA3; DAB; DAC; DAM MST, NOV; DLB 34, 70, 156, 178; EWL 3; EXPS; HGG; LAIT 3; LMFS 2; MTCW 1, 2; MTFW 2005; NFS 17, 20; RGEL 2; RGSF 2; SATA 20; SCFW 1, 2; SFW 4; SSFS 3; SUFW; TEA; WCH; WLIT 4; YAW

Wells, Rosemary 1943- **CLC 12**
See also AAYA 13; BYA 7, 8; CA 85-88; CANR 48, 120; CLR 16, 69; CWRI 5; MAICYA 1, 2; SAAS 1; SATA 18, 69, 114, 156; YAW

Wells-Barnett, Ida B(ell)
1862-1931 **TCLC 125**
See also CA 182; DLB 23, 221

Welsh, Irvine 1958- **CLC 144**
See also CA 173; CANR 146; CN 7; DLB 271

Welty, Eudora 1909-2001 **CLC 1, 2, 5, 14, 22, 33, 105, 220; SSC 1, 27, 51; WLC 6**
See also AAYA 48; AMW; AMWR 1; BPFB 3; CA 9-12R; 199; CABS 1; CANR 32, 65, 128; CDALB 1941-1968; CN 1, 2, 3, 4, 5, 6, 7; CSW; DA; DA3; DAB; DAC;

DAM MST, NOV; DLB 2, 102, 143; DLBD 12; DLBY 1987, 2001; EWL 3; EXPS; HGG; LAIT 3; MAL 5; MAWW; MTCW 1, 2; MTFW 2005; NFS 13, 15; RGAL 4; RGSF 2; RHW; SSFS 2, 10; TUS

Welty, Eudora Alice
See Welty, Eudora

Wen I-to 1899-1946 **TCLC 28**
See also EWL 3

Wentworth, Robert
See Hamilton, Edmond

Werfel, Franz (Viktor) 1890-1945 ... **TCLC 8**
See also CA 104; 161; DLB 81, 124; EWL 3; RGWL 2, 3

Wergeland, Henrik Arnold
1808-1845 **NCLC 5**

Wersba, Barbara 1932- **CLC 30**
See also AAYA 2, 30; BYA 6, 12, 13; CA 29-32R, 182; CAAE 182; CANR 16, 38; CLR 3, 78; DLB 52; JRDA; MAICYA 1, 2; SAAS 2; SATA 1, 58; SATA-Essay 103; WYA; YAW

Wertmueller, Lina 1928- **CLC 16**
See also CA 97-100; CANR 39, 78

Wescott, Glenway 1901-1987 .. **CLC 13; SSC 35**
See also CA 13-16R; 121; CANR 23, 70; CN 1, 2, 3, 4; DLB 4, 9, 102; MAL 5; RGAL 4

Wesker, Arnold 1932- **CLC 3, 5, 42**
See also CA 1-4R; CAAS 7; CANR 1, 33; CBD; CD 5, 6; CDBLB 1960 to Present; DAB; DAM DRAM; DLB 13, 310, 319; EWL 3; MTCW 1; RGEL 2; TEA

Wesley, Charles 1707-1788 **LC 128**
See also DLB 95; RGEL 2

Wesley, John 1703-1791 **LC 88**
See also DLB 104

Wesley, Richard (Errol) 1945- **CLC 7**
See also BW 1; CA 57-60; CAD; CANR 27; CD 5, 6; DLB 38

Wessel, Johan Herman 1742-1785 **LC 7** ◆
See also DLB 300

West, Anthony (Panther)
1914-1987 **CLC 50**
See also CA 45-48; 124; CANR 3, 19; CN 1, 2, 3, 4; DLB 15

West, C. P.
See Wodehouse, P(elham) G(renville)

West, Cornel (Ronald) 1953- **BLCS; CLC 134**
See also CA 144; CANR 91; DLB 246

West, Delno C(loyde), Jr. 1936- **CLC 70**
See also CA 57-60

West, Dorothy 1907-1998 **HR 1:3; TCLC 108**
See also BW 2; CA 143; 169; DLB 76

West, (Mary) Jessamyn 1902-1984 ... **CLC 7, 17**
See also CA 9-12R; 112; CANR 27; CN 1, 2, 3; DLB 6; DLBY 1984; MTCW 1, 2; RGAL 4; RHW; SATA-Obit 37; TCWW 2; TUS; YAW

West, Morris L(anglo) 1916-1999 **CLC 6, 33**
See also BPFB 3; CA 5-8R; 187; CANR 24, 49, 64; CN 1, 2, 3, 4, 5, 6; CPW; DLB 289; MTCW 1, 2; MTFW 2005

West, Nathanael 1903-1940 .. **SSC 16; TCLC 1, 14, 44**
See also AMW; AMWR 2; BPFB 3; CA 104; 125; CDALB 1929-1941; DA3; DLB 4, 9, 28; EWL 3; MAL 5; MTCW 1, 2; MTFW 2005; NFS 16; RGAL 4; TUS

West, Owen
See Koontz, Dean R.

West, Paul 1930- **CLC 7, 14, 96**
See also CA 13-16R; CAAS 7; CANR 22, 53, 76, 89, 136; CN 1, 2, 3, 4, 5, 6, 7; DLB 14; INT CANR-22; MTCW 2; MTFW 2005

West, Rebecca 1892-1983 ... **CLC 7, 9, 31, 50**
See also BPFB 3; BRWS 3; CA 5-8R; 109; CANR 19; CN 1, 2, 3; DLB 36; DLBY 1983; EWL 3; FW; MTCW 1, 2; MTFW 2005; NCFS 4; RGEL 2; TEA

Westall, Robert (Atkinson)
1929-1993 **CLC 17**
See also AAYA 12; BYA 2, 6, 7, 8, 9, 15; CA 69-72; 141; CANR 18, 68; CLR 13; FANT; JRDA; MAICYA 1, 2; MAICYAS 1; SAAS 2; SATA 23, 69; SATA-Obit 75; WYA; YAW

Westermarck, Edward 1862-1939 . **TCLC 87**

Westlake, Donald E(dwin) 1933- . **CLC 7, 33**
See also BPFB 3; CA 17-20R; CAAS 13; CANR 16, 44, 65, 94, 137; CMW 4; CPW; DAM POP; INT CANR-16; MSW; MTCW 2; MTFW 2005

Westmacott, Mary
See Christie, Agatha (Mary Clarissa)

Weston, Allen
See Norton, Andre

Wetcheek, J. L.
See Feuchtwanger, Lion

Wetering, Janwillem van de
See van de Wetering, Janwillem

Wetherald, Agnes Ethelwyn
1857-1940 **TCLC 81**
See also CA 202; DLB 99

Wetherell, Elizabeth
See Warner, Susan (Bogert)

Whale, James 1889-1957 **TCLC 63**

Whalen, Philip (Glenn) 1923-2002 **CLC 6, 29**
See also BG 1:3; CA 9-12R; 209; CANR 5, 39; CP 1, 2, 3, 4, 5, 6, 7; DLB 16; WP

Wharton, Edith (Newbold Jones)
1862-1937 ... **SSC 6, 84; TCLC 3, 9, 27, 53, 129, 149; WLC 6**
See also AAYA 25; AMW; AMWC 2; AMWR 1; BPFB 3; CA 104; 132; CDALB 1865-1917; DA; DA3; DAB; DAC; DAM MST, NOV; DLB 4, 9, 12, 78, 189; DLBD 13; EWL 3; EXPS; FL 1:6; GL 3; HGG; LAIT 2, 3; LATS 1:1; MAL 5; MAWW; MTCW 1, 2; MTFW 2005; NFS 5, 11, 15, 20; RGAL 4; RGSF 2; RHW; SSFS 6, 7; SUFW; TUS

Wharton, James
See Mencken, H(enry) L(ouis)

Wharton, William (a pseudonym)
1925- **CLC 18, 37**
See also CA 93-96; CN 4, 5, 6, 7; DLBY 1980; INT CA-93-96

Wheatley (Peters), Phillis
1753(?)-1784 ... **BLC 3; LC 3, 50; PC 3; WLC 6**
See also AFAW 1, 2; CDALB 1640-1865; DA; DA3; DAC; DAM MST, MULT, POET; DLB 31, 50; EXPP; FL 1:1; PFS 13; RGAL 4

Wheelock, John Hall 1886-1978 **CLC 14**
See also CA 13-16R; 77-80; CANR 14; CP 1, 2; DLB 45; MAL 5

Whim-Wham
See Curnow, (Thomas) Allen (Monro)

Whitaker, Rod 1931-2005
See Trevanian
See also CA 29-32R; 246; CANR 45, 153; CMW 4

White, Babington
See Braddon, Mary Elizabeth

White, E. B. 1899-1985 **CLC 10, 34, 39**
See also AAYA 62; AITN 2; AMWS 1; CA 13-16R; 116; CANR 16, 37; CDALBS; CLR 1, 21, 107; CPW; DA3; DAM POP; DLB 11, 22; EWL 3; FANT; MAICYA 1, 2; MAL 5; MTCW 1, 2; MTFW 2005; NCFS 5; RGAL 4; SATA 2, 29, 100; SATA-Obit 44; TUS

White, Edmund (Valentine III)
1940- **CLC 27, 110**
See also AAYA 7; CA 45-48; CANR 3, 19, 36, 62, 107, 133; CN 5, 6, 7; DA3; DAM POP; DLB 227; MTCW 1, 2; MTFW 2005

White, Elwyn Brooks
See White, E. B.

White, Hayden V. 1928- **CLC 148**
See also CA 128; CANR 135; DLB 246

White, Patrick (Victor Martindale)
1912-1990 **CLC 3, 4, 5, 7, 9, 18, 65, 69; SSC 39; TCLC 176**
See also BRWS 1; CA 81-84; 132; CANR 43; CN 1, 2, 3, 4; DLB 260; EWL 3; MTCW 1; RGEL 2; RGSF 2; RHW; TWA; WWE 1

White, Phyllis Dorothy James 1920-
See James, P. D.
See also CA 21-24R; CANR 17, 43, 65, 112; CMW 4; CN 7; CPW; DA3; DAM POP; MTCW 1, 2; MTFW 2005; TEA

White, T(erence) H(anbury)
1906-1964 **CLC 30**
See also AAYA 22; BPFB 3; BYA 4, 5; CA 73-76; CANR 37; DLB 160; FANT; JRDA; LAIT 1; MAICYA 1, 2; RGEL 2; SATA 12; SUFW 1; YAW

White, Terence de Vere 1912-1994 ... **CLC 49**
See also CA 49-52; 145; CANR 3

White, Walter
See White, Walter F(rancis)

White, Walter F(rancis) 1893-1955 ... **BLC 3; HR 1:3; TCLC 15**
See also BW 1; CA 115; 124; DAM MULT; DLB 51

White, William Hale 1831-1913
See Rutherford, Mark
See also CA 121; 189

Whitehead, Alfred North
1861-1947 **TCLC 97**
See also CA 117; 165; DLB 100, 262

Whitehead, E(dward) A(nthony)
1933- **CLC 5**
See Whitehead, Ted
See also CA 65-68; CANR 58, 118; CBD; CD 5; DLB 310

Whitehead, Ted
See Whitehead, E(dward) A(nthony)
See also CD 6

Whiteman, Roberta J. Hill 1947- **NNAL**
See also CA 146

Whitemore, Hugh (John) 1936- **CLC 37**
See also CA 132; CANR 77; CBD; CD 5, 6; INT CA-132

Whitman, Sarah Helen (Power)
1803-1878 **NCLC 19**
See also DLB 1, 243

Whitman, Walt(er) 1819-1892 .. **NCLC 4, 31, 81; PC 3; WLC 6**
See also AAYA 42; AMW; AMWR 1; CDALB 1640-1865; DA; DA3; DAB; DAC; DAM MST, POET; DLB 3, 64, 224, 250; EXPP; LAIT 2; LMFS 1; PAB; PFS 2, 3, 13, 22; RGAL 4; SATA 20; TUS; WP; WYAS 1

Whitney, Phyllis A(yame) 1903- **CLC 42**
See also AAYA 36; AITN 2; BEST 90:3; CA 1-4R; CANR 3, 25, 38, 60; CLR 59; CMW 4; CPW; DA3; DAM POP; JRDA; MAICYA 1, 2; MTCW 2; RHW; SATA 1, 30; YAW

Whittemore, (Edward) Reed, Jr.
1919- .. **CLC 4**
See also CA 9-12R, 219; CAAE 219; CAAS 8; CANR 4, 119; CP 1, 2, 3, 4, 5, 6, 7; DLB 5; MAL 5

Whittier, John Greenleaf
1807-1892 **NCLC 8, 59**
See also AMWS 1; DLB 1, 243; RGAL 4

Whittlebot, Hernia
See Coward, Noel (Peirce)

Wicker, Thomas Grey 1926-
See Wicker, Tom
See also CA 65-68; CANR 21, 46, 141

Wicker, Tom **CLC 7**
See Wicker, Thomas Grey

Wideman, John Edgar 1941- ... **BLC 3; CLC 5, 34, 36, 67, 122; SSC 62**
See also AFAW 1, 2; AMWS 10; BPFB 4; BW 2, 3; CA 85-88; CANR 14, 42, 67, 109, 140; CN 4, 5, 6, 7; DAM MULT; DLB 33, 143; MAL 5; MTCW 2; MTFW 2005; RGAL 4; RGSF 2; SSFS 6, 12; TCLE 1:2

Wiebe, Rudy (Henry) 1934- .. **CLC 6, 11, 14, 138**
See also CA 37-40R; CANR 42, 67, 123; CN 1, 2, 3, 4, 5, 6, 7; DAC; DAM MST; DLB 60; RHW; SATA 156

Wieland, Christoph Martin
1733-1813 **NCLC 17**
See also DLB 97; EW 4; LMFS 1; RGWL 2, 3

Wiene, Robert 1881-1938 **TCLC 56**

Wieners, John 1934- **CLC 7**
See also BG 1:3; CA 13-16R; CP 1, 2, 3, 4, 5, 6, 7; DLB 16; WP

Wiesel, Elie 1928- **CLC 3, 5, 11, 37, 165; WLCS**
See also AAYA 7, 54; AITN 1; CA 5-8R; CAAS 4; CANR 8, 40, 65, 125; CDALBS; CWW 2; DA; DA3; DAB; DAC; DAM MST, NOV; DLB 83, 299; DLBY 1987; EWL 3; INT CANR-8; LAIT 4; MTCW 1, 2; MTFW 2005; NCFS 4; NFS 4; RGHL; RGWL 3; SATA 56; YAW

Wiesel, Eliezer
See Wiesel, Elie

Wiggins, Marianne 1947- **CLC 57**
See also AAYA 70; BEST 89:3; CA 130; CANR 60, 139; CN 7

Wigglesworth, Michael 1631-1705 **LC 106**
See also DLB 24; RGAL 4

Wiggs, Susan **CLC 70**
See also CA 201

Wight, James Alfred 1916-1995
See Herriot, James
See also CA 77-80; SATA 55; SATA-Brief 44

Wilbur, Richard (Purdy) 1921- **CLC 3, 6, 9, 14, 53, 110; PC 51**
See also AMWS 3; CA 1-4R; CABS 2; CANR 2, 29, 76, 93, 139; CDALBS; CP 1, 2, 3, 4, 5, 6, 7; DA; DAB; DAC; DAM MST, POET; DLB 5, 169; EWL 3; EXPP; INT CANR-29; MAL 5; MTCW 1, 2; MTFW 2005; PAB; PFS 11, 12, 16; RGAL 4; SATA 9, 108; WP

Wild, Peter 1940- **CLC 14**
See also CA 37-40R; CP 1, 2, 3, 4, 5, 6, 7; DLB 5

Wilde, Oscar (Fingal O'Flahertie Wills)
1854(?)-1900 **DC 17; SSC 11, 77; TCLC 1, 8, 23, 41, 175; WLC 6**
See also AAYA 49; BRW 5; BRWC 1, 2; BRWR 2; BYA 15; CA 104; 119; CANR 112; CDBLB 1890-1914; DA; DA3; DAB; DAC; DAM DRAM, MST, NOV; DFS 4, 8, 9, 21; DLB 10, 19, 34, 57, 141,

156, 190; EXPS; FANT; GL 3; LATS 1:1; NFS 20; RGEL 2; RGSF 2; SATA 24; SSFS 7; SUFW; TEA; WCH; WLIT 4

Wilder, Billy **CLC 20**
See Wilder, Samuel
See also AAYA 66; DLB 26

Wilder, Samuel 1906-2002
See Wilder, Billy
See also CA 89-92; 205

Wilder, Stephen
See Marlowe, Stephen

Wilder, Thornton (Niven)
1897-1975 .. **CLC 1, 5, 6, 10, 15, 35, 82; DC 1, 24; WLC 6**
See also AAYA 29; AITN 2; AMW; CA 13-16R; 61-64; CAD; CANR 40, 132; CDALBS; CN 1, 2; DA; DA3; DAB; DAC; DAM DRAM, MST, NOV; DFS 1, 4, 16; DLB 4, 7, 9, 228; DLBY 1997; EWL 3; LAIT 3; MAL 5; MTCW 1, 2; MTFW 2005; RGAL 4; RHW; WYAS 1

Wilding, Michael 1942- **CLC 73; SSC 50**
See also CA 104; CANR 24, 49, 106; CN 4, 5, 6, 7; DLB 325; RGSF 2

Wiley, Richard 1944- **CLC 44**
See also CA 121; 129; CANR 71

Wilhelm, Kate **CLC 7**
See Wilhelm, Katie (Gertrude)
See also AAYA 20; BYA 16; CAAS 5; DLB 8; INT CANR-17; SCFW 2

Wilhelm, Katie (Gertrude) 1928-
See Wilhelm, Kate
See also CA 37-40R; CANR 17, 36, 60, 94; MTCW 1; SFW 4

Wilkins, Mary
See Freeman, Mary E(leanor) Wilkins

Willard, Nancy 1936- **CLC 7, 37**
See also BYA 5; CA 89-92; CANR 10, 39, 68, 107, 152; CLR 5; CP 2, 3, 4, 5; CWP; CWRI 5; DLB 5, 52; FANT; MAICYA 1, 2; MTCW 1; SATA 37, 71, 127; SATA-Brief 30; SUFW 2; TCLE 1:2

William of Malmesbury c. 1090B.C.-c. 1140B.C. **CMLC 57**

William of Ockham 1290-1349 **CMLC 32**

Williams, Ben Ames 1889-1953 **TCLC 89**
See also CA 183; DLB 102

Williams, C(harles) K(enneth)
1936- **CLC 33, 56, 148**
See also CA 37-40R; CAAS 26; CANR 57, 106; CP 1, 2, 3, 4, 5, 6, 7; DAM POET; DLB 5; MAL 5

Williams, Charles
See Collier, James Lincoln

Williams, Charles (Walter Stansby)
1886-1945 **TCLC 1, 11**
See also BRWS 9; CA 104; 163; DLB 100, 153, 255; FANT; RGEL 2; SUFW 1

Williams, Ella Gwendolen Rees
See Rhys, Jean

Williams, (George) Emlyn
1905-1987 **CLC 15**
See also CA 104; 123; CANR 36; DAM DRAM; DLB 10, 77; IDTP; MTCW 1

Williams, Hank 1923-1953 **TCLC 81**
See Williams, Hiram King

Williams, Helen Maria
1761-1827 **NCLC 135**
See also DLB 158

Williams, Hiram Hank
See Williams, Hank

Williams, Hiram King
See Williams, Hank
See also CA 188

Williams, Hugo (Mordaunt) 1942- ... **CLC 42**
See also CA 17-20R; CANR 45, 119; CP 1, 2, 3, 4, 5, 6, 7; DLB 40

Williams, J. Walker
See Wodehouse, P(elham) G(renville)

Williams, John A(lfred) 1925- . **BLC 3; CLC 5, 13**
See also AFAW 2; BW 2, 3; CA 53-56, 195; CAAE 195; CAAS 3; CANR 6, 26, 51, 118; CN 1, 2, 3, 4, 5, 6, 7; CSW; DAM MULT; DLB 2, 33; EWL 3; INT CANR-6; MAL 5; RGAL 4; SFW 4

Williams, Jonathan (Chamberlain) 1929- **CLC 13**
See also CA 9-12R; CAAS 12; CANR 8, 108; CP 1, 2, 3, 4, 5, 6, 7; DLB 5

Williams, Joy 1944- **CLC 31**
See also CA 41-44R; CANR 22, 48, 97

Williams, Norman 1952- **CLC 39**
See also CA 118

Williams, Roger 1603(?)-1683 **LC 129**
See also DLB 24

Williams, Sherley Anne 1944-1999 ... **BLC 3; CLC 89**
See also AFAW 2; BW 2, 3; CA 73-76; 185; CANR 25, 82; DAM MULT, POET; DLB 41; INT CANR-25; SATA 78; SATA-Obit 116

Williams, Shirley
See Williams, Sherley Anne

Williams, Tennessee 1911-1983 . **CLC 1, 2, 5, 7, 8, 11, 15, 19, 30, 39, 45, 71, 111; DC 4; SSC 81; WLC 6**
See also AAYA 31; AITN 1, 2; AMW; AMWC 1; CA 5-8R; 108; CABS 3; CAD; CANR 31, 132; CDALB 1941-1968; CN 1, 2, 3; DA; DA3; DAB; DAC; DAM DRAM, MST; DFS 17; DLB 7; DLBD 4; DLBY 1983; EWL 3; GLL 1; LAIT 4; LATS 1:2; MAL 5; MTCW 1, 2; MTFW 2005; RGAL 4; TUS

Williams, Thomas (Alonzo) 1926-1990 **CLC 14**
See also CA 1-4R; 132; CANR 2

Williams, William C.
See Williams, William Carlos

Williams, William Carlos 1883-1963 **CLC 1, 2, 5, 9, 13, 22, 42, 67; PC 7; SSC 31; WLC 6**
See also AAYA 46; AMW; AMWR 1; CA 89-92; CANR 34; CDALB 1917-1929; DA; DA3; DAB; DAC; DAM MST, POET; DLB 4, 16, 54, 86; EWL 3; EXPP; MAL 5; MTCW 1, 2; MTFW 2005; NCFS 4; PAB; PFS 1, 6, 11; RGAL 4; RGSF 2; TUS; WP

Williamson, David (Keith) 1942- **CLC 56**
See also CA 103; CANR 41; CD 5, 6; DLB 289

Williamson, Ellen Douglas 1905-1984
See Douglas, Ellen
See also CA 17-20R; 114; CANR 39

Williamson, Jack **CLC 29**
See Williamson, John Stewart
See also CAAS 8; DLB 8; SCFW 1, 2

Williamson, John Stewart 1908-
See Williamson, Jack
See also CA 17-20R; CANR 23, 70, 153; SFW 4

Willie, Frederick
See Lovecraft, H. P.

Willingham, Calder (Baynard, Jr.) 1922-1995 **CLC 5, 51**
See also CA 5-8R; 147; CANR 3; CN 1, 2, 3, 4, 5; CSW; DLB 2, 44; IDFW 3, 4; MTCW 1

Willis, Charles
See Clarke, Arthur C(harles)

Willy
See Colette, (Sidonie-Gabrielle)

Willy, Colette
See Colette, (Sidonie-Gabrielle)
See also GLL 1

Wilmot, John 1647-1680 **LC 75; PC 66**
See Rochester
See also BRW 2; DLB 131; PAB

Wilson, A(ndrew) N(orman) 1950- .. **CLC 33**
See also BRWS 6; CA 112; 122; CN 4, 5, 6, 7; DLB 14, 155, 194; MTCW 2

Wilson, Angus (Frank Johnstone) 1913-1991 . **CLC 2, 3, 5, 25, 34; SSC 21**
See also BRWS 1; CA 5-8R; 134; CANR 21; CN 1, 2, 3, 4; DLB 15, 139, 155; EWL 3; MTCW 1, 2; MTFW 2005; RGEL 2; RGSF 2

Wilson, August 1945-2005 .. **BLC 3; CLC 39, 50, 63, 118, 222; DC 5; WLCS**
See also AAYA 16; AFAW 2; AMWS 8; BW 2, 3; CA 115; 122; 244; CAD; CANR 42, 54, 76, 128; CD 5, 6; DA; DA3; DAB; DAC; DAM DRAM, MST, MULT; DFS 3, 7, 15, 17; DLB 228; EWL 3; LAIT 4; LATS 1:2; MAL 5; MTCW 1, 2; MTFW 2005; RGAL 4

Wilson, Brian 1942- **CLC 12**

Wilson, Colin (Henry) 1931- **CLC 3, 14**
See also CA 1-4R; CAAS 5; CANR 1, 22, 33, 77; CMW 4; CN 1, 2, 3, 4, 5, 6; DLB 14, 194; HGG; MTCW 1; SFW 4

Wilson, Dirk
See Pohl, Frederik

Wilson, Edmund 1895-1972 .. **CLC 1, 2, 3, 8, 24**
See also AMW; CA 1-4R; 37-40R; CANR 1, 46, 110; CN 1; DLB 63; EWL 3; MAL 5; MTCW 1, 2; MTFW 2005; RGAL 4; TUS

Wilson, Ethel Davis (Bryant) 1888(?)-1980 **CLC 13**
See also CA 102; CN 1, 2, DAC; DAM POET; DLB 68; MTCW 1; RGEL 2

Wilson, Harriet
See Wilson, Harriet E. Adams
See also DLB 239

Wilson, Harriet E.
See Wilson, Harriet E. Adams
See also DLB 243

Wilson, Harriet E. Adams 1827(?)-1863(?) **BLC 3; NCLC 78**
See Wilson, Harriet; Wilson, Harriet E.
See also DAM MULT; DLB 50

Wilson, John 1785-1854 **NCLC 5**

Wilson, John (Anthony) Burgess 1917-1993
See Burgess, Anthony
See also CA 1-4R; 143; CANR 2, 46; DA3; DAC; DAM NOV; MTCW 1, 2; MTFW 2005; NFS 15; TEA

Wilson, Lanford 1937- .. **CLC 7, 14, 36, 197; DC 19**
See also CA 17-20R; CABS 3; CAD; CANR 45, 96; CD 5, 6; DAM DRAM; DFS 4, 9, 12, 16, 20; DLB 7; EWL 3; MAL 5; TUS

Wilson, Robert M. 1941- **CLC 7, 9**
See also CA 49-52; CAD; CANR 2, 41; CD 5, 6; MTCW 1

Wilson, Robert McLiam 1964- **CLC 59**
See also CA 132; DLB 267

Wilson, Sloan 1920-2003 **CLC 32**
See also CA 1-4R; 216; CANR 1, 44; CN 1, 2, 3, 4, 5, 6

Wilson, Snoo 1948- **CLC 33**
See also CA 69-72; CBD; CD 5, 6

Wilson, William S(mith) 1932- **CLC 49**
See also CA 81-84

Wilson, (Thomas) Woodrow 1856-1924 **TCLC 79**
See also CA 166; DLB 47

Wilson and Warnke eds. **CLC 65**

Winchilsea, Anne (Kingsmill) Finch 1661-1720
See Finch, Anne
See also RGEL 2

Winckelmann, Johann Joachim 1717-1768 **LC 129**
See also DLB 97

Windham, Basil
See Wodehouse, P(elham) G(renville)

Wingrove, David (John) 1954- **CLC 68**
See also CA 133; SFW 4

Winnemucca, Sarah 1844-1891 **NCLC 79; NNAL**
See also DAM MULT; DLB 175; RGAL 4

Winstanley, Gerrard 1609-1676 **LC 52**

Wintergreen, Jane
See Duncan, Sara Jeannette

Winters, Arthur Yvor
See Winters, Yvor

Winters, Janet Lewis **CLC 41**
See Lewis, Janet
See also DLBY 1987

Winters, Yvor 1900-1968 **CLC 4, 8, 32**
See also AMWS 2; CA 11-12; 25-28R; CAP 1; DLB 48; EWL 3; MAL 5; MTCW 1; RGAL 4

Winterson, Jeanette 1959- **CLC 64, 158**
See also BRWS 4; CA 136; CANR 58, 116; CN 5, 6, 7; CPW; DA3; DAM POP; DLB 207, 261; FANT; FW; GLL 1; MTCW 2; MTFW 2005; RHW

Winthrop, John 1588-1649 **LC 31, 107**
See also DLB 24, 30

Wirth, Louis 1897-1952 **TCLC 92**
See also CA 210

Wiseman, Frederick 1930- **CLC 20**
See also CA 159

Wister, Owen 1860-1938 **TCLC 21**
See also BPFB 3; CA 108; 162; DLB 9, 78, 186; RGAL 4; SATA 62; TCWW 1, 2

Wither, George 1588-1667 **LC 96**
See also DLB 121; RGEL 2

Witkacy
See Witkiewicz, Stanislaw Ignacy

Witkiewicz, Stanislaw Ignacy 1885-1939 **TCLC 8**
See also CA 105; 162; CDWLB 4; DLB 215; EW 10; EWL 3; RGWL 2, 3; SFW 4

Wittgenstein, Ludwig (Josef Johann) 1889-1951 **TCLC 59**
See also CA 113; 164; DLB 262; MTCW 2

Wittig, Monique 1935-2003 **CLC 22**
See also CA 116; 135; 212; CANR 143; CWW 2; DLB 83; EWL 3; FW; GLL 1

Wittlin, Jozef 1896-1976 **CLC 25**
See also CA 49-52; 65-68; CANR 3; EWL 3

Wodehouse, P(elham) G(renville) 1881-1975 . **CLC 1, 2, 5, 10, 22; SSC 2; TCLC 108**
See also AAYA 65; AITN 2; BRWS 3; CA 45-48; 57-60; CANR 3, 33; CDBLB 1914-1945; CN 1, 2; CPW 1; DA3; DAB; DAC; DAM NOV; DLB 34, 162; EWL 3; MTCW 1, 2; MTFW 2005; RGEL 2; RGSF 2; SATA 22; SSFS 10

Woiwode, L.
See Woiwode, Larry (Alfred)

Woiwode, Larry (Alfred) 1941- ... **CLC 6, 10**
See also CA 73-76; CANR 16, 94; CN 3, 4, 5, 6, 7; DLB 6; INT CANR-16

Wojciechowska, Maia (Teresa) 1927-2002 **CLC 26**
See also AAYA 8, 46; BYA 3; CA 9-12R; 183; 209; CAAE 183; CANR 4, 41; CLR 1; JRDA; MAICYA 1, 2; SAAS 1; SATA 1, 28, 83; SATA-Essay 104; SATA-Obit 134; YAW

Wojtyla, Karol (Josef)
See John Paul II, Pope

Wojtyla, Karol (Jozef)
See John Paul II, Pope

Wolf, Christa 1929- **CLC 14, 29, 58, 150**
See also CA 85-88; CANR 45, 123; CD-WLB 2; CWW 2; DLB 75; EWL 3; FW; MTCW 1; RGWL 2, 3; SSFS 14

Wolf, Naomi 1962- **CLC 157**
See also CA 141; CANR 110; FW; MTFW 2005

Wolfe, Gene 1931- **CLC 25**
See also AAYA 35; CA 57-60; CAAS 9; CANR 6, 32, 60, 152; CPW; DAM POP; DLB 8; FANT; MTCW 2; MTFW 2005; SATA 118, 165; SCFW 2; SFW 4; SUFW 2

Wolfe, Gene Rodman
See Wolfe, Gene.

Wolfe, George C. 1954- **BLCS; CLC 49**
See also CA 149; CAD; CD 5, 6

Wolfe, Thomas (Clayton)
1900-1938 **SSC 33; TCLC 4, 13, 29, 61; WLC 6**
See also AMW; BPFB 3; CA 104; 132; CANR 102; CDALB 1929-1941; DA; DA3; DAB; DAC; DAM MST, NOV; DLB 9, 102, 229; DLBD 2, 16; DLBY 1985, 1997; EWL 3; MAL 5; MTCW 1, 2; NFS 18; RGAL 4; SSFS 18; TUS

Wolfe, Thomas Kennerly, Jr.
1931- **CLC 147**
See Wolfe, Tom
See also CA 13-16R; CANR 9, 33, 70, 104; DA3; DAM POP; DLB 185; EWL 3; INT CANR-9; MTCW 1, 2; MTFW 2005; TUS

Wolfe, Tom **CLC 1, 2, 9, 15, 35, 51**
See Wolfe, Thomas Kennerly, Jr.
See also AAYA 8, 67; AITN 2; AMWS 3; BEST 89:1; BPFB 3; CN 5, 6, 7; CPW; CSW; DLB 152; LAIT 5; RGAL 4

Wolff, Geoffrey 1937- **CLC 41**
See also CA 29-32R; CANR 29, 43, 78, 154

Wolff, Geoffrey Ansell
See Wolff, Geoffrey

Wolff, Sonia
See Levitin, Sonia (Wolff)

Wolff, Tobias (Jonathan Ansell)
1945- **CLC 39, 64, 172; SSC 63**
See also AAYA 16; AMWS 7; BEST 90:2; BYA 12; CA 114; 117; CAAS 22; CANR 54, 76, 96; CN 5, 6, 7; CSW; DA3; DLB 130; EWL 3; INT CA-117; MTCW 2; MTFW 2005; RGAL 4; RGSF 2; SSFS 4, 11

Wolfram von Eschenbach c. 1170-c.
1220 .. **CMLC 5**
See Eschenbach, Wolfram von
See also CDWLB 2; DLB 138; EW 1; RGWL 2

Wolitzer, Hilma 1930- **CLC 17**
See also CA 65-68; CANR 18, 40; INT CANR-18; SATA 31; YAW

Wollstonecraft, Mary 1759-1797 **LC 5, 50, 90**
See also BRWS 3; CDBLB 1789-1832; DLB 39, 104, 158, 252; FL 1:1; FW; LAIT 1; RGEL 2; TEA; WLIT 3

Wonder, Stevie 1950- **CLC 12**
See also CA 111

Wong, Jade Snow 1922-2006 **CLC 17**
See also CA 109; CANR 91; SATA 112

Woodberry, George Edward
1855-1930 **TCLC 73**
See also CA 165; DLB 71, 103

Woodcott, Keith
See Brunner, John (Kilian Houston)

Woodruff, Robert W.
See Mencken, H(enry) L(ouis)

Woolf, (Adeline) Virginia 1882-1941 .. **SSC 7, 79; TCLC 1, 5, 20, 43, 56, 101, 123, 128; WLC 6**
See also AAYA 44; BPFB 3; BRW 7; BRWC 2; BRWR 1; CA 104; 130; CANR 64, 132; CDBLB 1914-1945; DA; DA3; DAB; DAC; DAM MST, NOV; DLB 36, 100, 162; DLBD 10; EWL 3; EXPS; FL 1:6; FW; LAIT 3; LATS 1:1; LMFS 2; MTCW 1, 2; MTFW 2005; NCFS 2; NFS 8, 12; RGEL 2; RGSF 2; SSFS 4, 12; TEA; WLIT 4

Woollcott, Alexander (Humphreys)
1887-1943 **TCLC 5**
See also CA 105; 161; DLB 29

Woolrich, Cornell **CLC 77**
See Hopley-Woolrich, Cornell George
See also MSW

Woolson, Constance Fenimore
1840-1894 **NCLC 82; SSC 90**
See also DLB 12, 74, 189, 221; RGAL 4

Wordsworth, Dorothy 1771-1855 . **NCLC 25, 138**
See also DLB 107

Wordsworth, William 1770-1850 .. **NCLC 12, 38, 111, 166; PC 4, 67; WLC 6**
See also AAYA 70; BRW 4; BRWC 1; CD-BLB 1789-1832; DA; DA3; DAB; DAC; DAM MST, POET; DLB 93, 107; EXPP; LATS 1:1; LMFS 1; PAB; PFS 2; RGEL 2; TEA; WLIT 3; WP

Wotton, Sir Henry 1568-1639 **LC 68**
See also DLB 121; RGEL 2

Wouk, Herman 1915- **CLC 1, 9, 38**
See also BPFB 2, 3; CA 5-8R; CANR 6, 33, 67, 146; CDALBS; CN 1, 2, 3, 4, 5, 6; CPW; DA3; DAM NOV, POP; DLBY 1982; INT CANR-6; LAIT 4; MAL 5; MTCW 1, 2; MTFW 2005; NFS 7; TUS

Wright, Charles (Penzel, Jr.) 1935- .. **CLC 6, 13, 28, 119, 146**
See also AMWS 5; CA 29-32R; CAAS 7; CANR 23, 36, 62, 88, 135; CP 3, 4, 5, 6, 7; DLB 165; DLBY 1982; EWL 3; MTCW 1, 2; MTFW 2005; PFS 10

Wright, Charles Stevenson 1932- **BLC 3; CLC 49**
See also BW 1; CA 9-12R; CANR 26; CN 1, 2, 3, 4, 5, 6, 7; DAM MULT, POET; DLB 33

Wright, Frances 1795-1852 **NCLC 74**
See also DLB 73

Wright, Frank Lloyd 1867-1959 **TCLC 95**
See also AAYA 33; CA 174

Wright, Jack R.
See Harris, Mark

Wright, James (Arlington)
1927-1980 **CLC 3, 5, 10, 28; PC 36**
See also AITN 2; AMWS 3; CA 49-52; 97-100; CANR 4, 34, 64; CDALBS; CP 1, 2; DAM POET; DLB 5, 169; EWL 3; EXPP; MAL 5; MTCW 1, 2; MTFW 2005; PFS 7, 8; RGAL 4; TUS; WP

Wright, Judith (Arundell)
1915-2000 **CLC 11, 53; PC 14**
See also CA 13-16R; 188; CANR 31, 76, 93; CP 1, 2, 3, 4, 5, 6, 7; CWP; DLB 260; EWL 3; MTCW 1, 2; MTFW 2005; PFS 8; RGEL 2; SATA 14; SATA-Obit 121

Wright, L(aurali) R. 1939- **CLC 44**
See also CA 138; CMW 4

Wright, Richard (Nathaniel)
1908-1960 ... **BLC 3; CLC 1, 3, 4, 9, 14, 21, 48, 74; SSC 2; TCLC 136, 180; WLC 6**
See also AAYA 5, 42; AFAW 1, 2; AMW; BPFB 3; BW 1; BYA 2; CA 108; CANR 64; CDALB 1929-1941; DA; DA3; DAB; DAC; DAM MST, MULT, NOV; DLB 76, 102; DLBD 2; EWL 3; EXPN; LAIT 3; 4; MAL 5; MTCW 1, 2; MTFW 2005; NCFS 1; NFS 1, 7; RGAL 4; RGSF 2; SSFS 3, 9, 15, 20; TUS; YAW

Wright, Richard B(ruce) 1937- **CLC 6**
See also CA 85-88; CANR 120; DLB 53

Wright, Rick 1945- **CLC 35**

Wright, Rowland
See Wells, Carolyn

Wright, Stephen 1946- **CLC 33**
See also CA 237

Wright, Willard Huntington 1888-1939
See Van Dine, S. S.
See also CA 115; 189; CMW 4; DLBD 16

Wright, William 1930- **CLC 44**
See also CA 53-56; CANR 7, 23, 154

Wroth, Lady Mary 1587-1653(?) **LC 30; PC 38**
See also DLB 121

Wu Ch'eng-en 1500(?)-1582(?) **LC 7**

Wu Ching-tzu 1701-1754 **LC 2**

Wulfstan c. 10th cent. -1023 **CMLC 59**

Wurlitzer, Rudolph 1938(?)- **CLC 2, 4, 15**
See also CA 85-88; CN 4, 5, 6, 7; DLB 173

Wyatt, Sir Thomas c. 1503-1542 . **LC 70; PC 27**
See also BRW 1; DLB 132; EXPP; RGEL 2; TEA

Wycherley, William 1640-1716 **LC 8, 21, 102**
See also BRW 2; CDBLB 1660-1789; DAM DRAM; DLB 80; RGEL 2

Wyclif, John c. 1330-1384 **CMLC 70**
See also DLB 146

Wylie, Elinor (Morton Hoyt)
1885-1928 **PC 23; TCLC 8**
See also AMWS 1; CA 105; 162; DLB 9, 45; EXPP; MAL 5; RGAL 4

Wylie, Philip (Gordon) 1902-1971 ... **CLC 43**
See also CA 21-22; 33-36R; CAP 2; CN 1; DLB 9; SFW 4

Wyndham, John **CLC 19**
See Harris, John (Wyndham Parkes Lucas) Beynon
See also DLB 255; SCFW 1, 2

Wyss, Johann David Von
1743-1818 **NCLC 10**
See also CLR 92; JRDA; MAICYA 1, 2; SATA 29; SATA-Brief 27

Xenophon c. 430B.C.-c. 354B.C. ... **CMLC 17**
See also AW 1; DLB 176; RGWL 2, 3; WLIT 8

Xingjian, Gao 1940-
See Gao Xingjian
See also CA 193; DFS 21; RGWL 3

Yakamochi 718-785 **CMLC 45; PC 48**

Yakumo Koizumi
See Hearn, (Patricio) Lafcadio (Tessima Carlos)

Yamada, Mitsuye (May) 1923- **PC 44**
See also CA 77-80

Yamamoto, Hisaye 1921- **AAL; SSC 34**
See also CA 214; DAM MULT; DLB 312; LAIT 4; SSFS 14

Yamauchi, Wakako 1924- **AAL**
See also CA 214; DLB 312

Yanez, Jose Donoso
See Donoso (Yanez), Jose

Yanovsky, Basile S.
See Yanovsky, V(assily) S(emenovich)

Yanovsky, V(assily) S(emenovich)
1906-1989 **CLC 2, 18**
See also CA 97-100; 129

Yates, Richard 1926-1992 **CLC 7, 8, 23**
See also AMWS 11; CA 5-8R; 139; CANR 10, 43; CN 1, 2, 3, 4, 5; DLB 2, 234; DLBY 1981, 1992; INT CANR-10

Yau, John 1950- **PC 61**
 See also CA 154; CANR 89; CP 4, 5, 6, 7;
 DLB 234, 312
Yeats, W. B.
 See Yeats, William Butler
Yeats, William Butler 1865-1939 . **PC 20, 51;**
 TCLC 1, 11, 18, 31, 93, 116; WLC 6
 See also AAYA 48; BRW 6; BRWR 1; CA
 104; 127; CANR 45; CDBLB 1890-1914;
 DA; DA3; DAB; DAC; DAM DRAM,
 MST, POET; DLB 10, 19, 98, 156; EWL
 3; EXPP; MTCW 1, 2; MTFW 2005;
 NCFS 3; PAB; PFS 1, 2, 5, 7, 13, 15;
 RGEL 2; TEA; WLIT 4; WP
Yehoshua, A(braham) B. 1936- .. **CLC 13, 31**
 See also CA 33-36R; CANR 43, 90, 145;
 CWW 2; EWL 3; RGHL; RGSF 2; RGWL
 3; WLIT 6
Yellow Bird
 See Ridge, John Rollin
Yep, Laurence Michael 1948- **CLC 35**
 See also AAYA 5, 31; BYA 7; CA 49-52;
 CANR 1, 46, 92; CLR 3, 17, 54; DLB 52,
 312; FANT; JRDA; MAICYA 1, 2; MAI-
 CYAS 1; SATA 7, 69, 123; WYA; YAW
Yerby, Frank G(arvin) 1916-1991 **BLC 3;**
 CLC 1, 7, 22
 See also BPFB 3; BW 1, 3; CA 9-12R; 136;
 CANR 16, 52; CN 1, 2, 3, 4, 5; DAM
 MULT; DLB 76; INT CANR-16; MTCW
 1; RGAL 4; RHW
Yesenin, Sergei Alexandrovich
 See Esenin, Sergei (Alexandrovich)
Yesenin, Sergey
 See Esenin, Sergei (Alexandrovich)
 See also EWL 3
Yevtushenko, Yevgeny (Alexandrovich)
 1933- **CLC 1, 3, 13, 26, 51, 126; PC**
 40
 See Evtushenko, Evgenii Aleksandrovich
 See also CA 81-84; CANR 33, 54; DAM
 POET; EWL 3; MTCW 1; RGHL
Yezierska, Anzia 1885(?)-1970 **CLC 46**
 See also CA 126; 89-92; DLB 28, 221; FW;
 MTCW 1; RGAL 4; SSFS 15
Yglesias, Helen 1915- **CLC 7, 22**
 See also CA 37-40R; CAAS 20; CANR 15,
 65, 95; CN 4, 5, 6, 7; INT CANR-15;
 MTCW 1
Yokomitsu, Riichi 1898-1947 **TCLC 47**
 See also CA 170; EWL 3
Yonge, Charlotte (Mary)
 1823-1901 **TCLC 48**
 See also CA 109; 163; DLB 18, 163; RGEL
 2; SATA 17; WCH
York, Jeremy
 See Creasey, John
York, Simon
 See Heinlein, Robert A(nson)
Yorke, Henry Vincent 1905-1974 **CLC 13**
 See Green, Henry
 See also CA 85-88; 49-52
Yosano, Akiko 1878-1942 ... **PC 11; TCLC 59**
 See also CA 161; EWL 3; RGWL 3
Yoshimoto, Banana **CLC 84**
 See Yoshimoto, Mahoko
 See also AAYA 50; NFS 7
Yoshimoto, Mahoko 1964-
 See Yoshimoto, Banana
 See also CA 144; CANR 98; SSFS 16
Young, Al(bert James) 1939- ... **BLC 3; CLC**
 19
 See also BW 2, 3; CA 29-32R; CANR 26,
 65, 109; CN 2, 3, 4, 5, 6, 7; CP 1, 2, 3, 4,
 5, 6, 7; DAM MULT; DLB 33
Young, Andrew (John) 1885-1971 **CLC 5**
 See also CA 5-8R; CANR 7, 29; CP 1;
 RGEL 2

Young, Collier
 See Bloch, Robert (Albert)
Young, Edward 1683-1765 **LC 3, 40**
 See also DLB 95; RGEL 2
Young, Marguerite (Vivian)
 1909-1995 **CLC 82**
 See also CA 13-16; 150; CAP 1; CN 1, 2,
 3, 4, 5, 6
Young, Neil 1945- **CLC 17**
 See also CA 110; CCA 1
Young Bear, Ray A. 1950- ... **CLC 94; NNAL**
 See also CA 146; DAM MULT; DLB 175;
 MAL 5
Yourcenar, Marguerite 1903-1987 ... **CLC 19,**
 38, 50, 87
 See also BPFB 3; CA 69-72; CANR 23, 60,
 93; DAM NOV; DLB 72; DLBY 1988;
 EW 12; EWL 3; GFL 1789 to the Present;
 GLL 1; MTCW 1, 2; MTFW 2005;
 RGWL 2, 3
Yuan, Chu 340(?)B.C.-278(?)B.C. . **CMLC 36**
Yurick, Sol 1925- **CLC 6**
 See also CA 13-16R; CANR 25; CN 1, 2,
 3, 4, 5, 6, 7; MAL 5
Zabolotsky, Nikolai Alekseevich
 1903-1958 **TCLC 52**
 See Zabolotsky, Nikolay Alekseevich
 See also CA 116; 164
Zabolotsky, Nikolay Alekseevich
 See Zabolotsky, Nikolai Alekseevich
 See also EWL 3
Zagajewski, Adam 1945- **PC 27**
 See also CA 186; DLB 232; EWL 3
Zalygin, Sergei -2000 **CLC 59**
Zalygin, Sergei (Pavlovich)
 1913-2000 **CLC 59**
 See also DLB 302
Zamiatin, Evgenii
 See Zamyatin, Evgeny Ivanovich
 See also RGSF 2; RGWL 2, 3
Zamiatin, Evgenii Ivanovich
 See Zamyatin, Evgeny Ivanovich
 See also DLB 272
Zamiatin, Yevgenii
 See Zamyatin, Evgeny Ivanovich
Zamora, Bernice (B. Ortiz) 1938- .. **CLC 89;**
 HLC 2
 See also CA 151; CANR 80; DAM MULT;
 DLB 82; HW 1, 2
Zamyatin, Evgeny Ivanovich
 1884-1937 **SSC 89; TCLC 8, 37**
 See Zamiatin, Evgenii; Zamiatin, Evgenii
 Ivanovich; Zamyatin, Yevgeny Ivanovich
 See also CA 105; 166; SFW 4
Zamyatin, Yevgeny Ivanovich
 See Zamyatin, Evgeny Ivanovich
 See also EW 10; EWL 3
Zangwill, Israel 1864-1926 ... **SSC 44; TCLC**
 16
 See also CA 109; 167; CMW 4; DLB 10,
 135, 197; RGEL 2
Zanzotto, Andrea 1921- **PC 65**
 See also CA 208; CWW 2; DLB 128; EWL
 3
Zappa, Francis Vincent, Jr. 1940-1993
 See Zappa, Frank
 See also CA 108; 143; CANR 57
Zappa, Frank **CLC 17**
 See Zappa, Francis Vincent, Jr.
Zaturenska, Marya 1902-1982 **CLC 6, 11**
 See also CA 13-16R; 105; CANR 22; CP 1,
 2, 3
Zayas y Sotomayor, Maria de 1590-c.
 1661 ... **LC 102**
 See also RGSF 2
Zeami 1363-1443 **DC 7; LC 86**
 See also DLB 203; RGWL 2, 3

Zelazny, Roger (Joseph) 1937-1995 . **CLC 21**
 See also AAYA 7, 68; BPFB 3; CA 21-24R;
 148; CANR 26, 60; CN 6; DLB 8; FANT;
 MTCW 1, 2; MTFW 2005; SATA 57;
 SATA-Brief 39; SCFW 1, 2; SFW 4;
 SUFW 1, 2
Zhang Ailing
 See Chang, Eileen
 See also CWW 2; RGSF 2
Zhdanov, Andrei Alexandrovich
 1896-1948 **TCLC 18**
 See also CA 117; 167
Zhukovsky, Vasilii Andreevich
 See Zhukovsky, Vasily (Andreevich)
 See also DLB 205
Zhukovsky, Vasily (Andreevich)
 1783-1852 **NCLC 35**
 See Zhukovsky, Vasilii Andreevich
Ziegenhagen, Eric **CLC 55**
Zimmer, Jill Schary
 See Robinson, Jill
Zimmerman, Robert
 See Dylan, Bob
Zindel, Paul 1936-2003 **CLC 6, 26; DC 5**
 See also AAYA 2, 37; BYA 2, 3, 8, 11, 14;
 CA 73-76; 213; CAD; CANR 31, 65, 108;
 CD 5, 6; CDALBS; CLR 3, 45, 85; DA;
 DA3; DAB; DAC; DAM DRAM, MST,
 NOV; DFS 12; DLB 7, 52; JRDA; LAIT
 5; MAICYA 1, 2; MTCW 1, 2; MTFW
 2005; NFS 14; SATA 16, 58, 102; SATA-
 Obit 142; WYA; YAW
Zinn, Howard 1922- **CLC 199**
 See also CA 1-4R; CANR 2, 33, 90
Zinov'Ev, A.A.
 See Zinoviev, Alexander
Zinov'ev, Aleksandr
 See Zinoviev, Alexander
 See also DLB 302
Zinoviev, Alexander 1922-2006 **CLC 19**
 See Zinov'ev, Aleksandr
 See also CA 116; 133; CAAS 10
Zinoviev, Alexander Aleksandrovich
 See Zinoviev, Alexander
Zizek, Slavoj 1949- **CLC 188**
 See also CA 201; MTFW 2005
Zoilus
 See Lovecraft, H. P.
Zola, Emile (Edouard Charles Antoine)
 1840-1902 .. **TCLC 1, 6, 21, 41; WLC 6**
 See also CA 104; 138; DA; DA3; DAB;
 DAC; DAM MST, NOV; DLB 123; EW
 7; GFL 1789 to the Present; IDTP; LMFS
 1, 2; RGWL 2; TWA
Zoline, Pamela 1941- **CLC 62**
 See also CA 161; SFW 4
Zoroaster 628(?)B.C.-551(?)B.C. ... **CMLC 40**
Zorrilla y Moral, Jose 1817-1893 **NCLC 6**
Zoshchenko, Mikhail (Mikhailovich)
 1895-1958 **SSC 15; TCLC 15**
 See also CA 115; 160; EWL 3; RGSF 2;
 RGWL 3
Zuckmayer, Carl 1896-1977 **CLC 18**
 See also CA 69-72; DLB 56, 124; EWL 3;
 RGWL 2, 3
Zuk, Georges
 See Skelton, Robin
 See also CCA 1
Zukofsky, Louis 1904-1978 ... **CLC 1, 2, 4, 7,**
 11, 18; PC 11
 See also AMWS 3; CA 9-12R; 77-80;
 CANR 39; CP 1, 2; DAM POET; DLB 5,
 165; EWL 3; MAL 5; MTCW 1; RGAL 4
Zweig, Paul 1935-1984 **CLC 34, 42**
 See also CA 85-88; 113
Zweig, Stefan 1881-1942 **TCLC 17**
 See also CA 112; 170; DLB 81, 118; EWL
 3; RGHL
Zwingli, Huldreich 1484-1531 **LC 37**
 See also DLB 179

Literary Criticism Series
Cumulative Topic Index

This index lists all topic entries in Thompson Gale's *Children's Literature Review* (CLR), *Classical and Medieval Literature Criticism* (CMLC), *Contemporary Literary Criticism* (CLC), *Drama Criticism* (DC), *Literature Criticism from 1400 to 1800* (LC), *Nineteenth-Century Literature Criticism* (NCLC), *Short Story Criticism* (SSC), and *Twentieth-Century Literary Criticism* (TCLC). The index also lists topic entries in the Gale Critical Companion Collection, which includes the following publications: *The Beat Generation* (BG), *Feminism in Literature* (FL), *Gothic Literature* (GL), and *Harlem Renaissance* (HR).

Abbey Theatre in the Irish Literary Renaissance TCLC 154: 1-114
 origins and development, 2-14
 major figures, 14-30
 plays and controversies, 30-59
 artistic vision and significance, 59-114

Abolitionist Literature of Cuba and Brazil, Nineteenth-Century NCLC 132: 1-94
 overviews, 2-11
 origins and development, 11-23
 sociopolitical concerns, 23-39
 poetry, 39-47
 prose, 47-93

The Aborigine in Nineteenth-Century Australian Literature NCLC 120: 1-88
 overviews, 2-27
 representations of the Aborigine in Australian literature, 27-58
 Aboriginal myth, literature, and oral tradition, 58-88

The Aesopic Fable LC 51: 1-100
 the British Aesopic Fable, 1-54
 the Aesopic tradition in non-English-speaking cultures, 55-66
 political uses of the Aesopic fable, 67-88
 the evolution of the Aesopic fable, 89-99

African-American Folklore and Literature TCLC 126: 1-67
 African-American folk tradition, 1-16
 representative writers, 16-34
 hallmark works, 35-48
 the study of African-American literature and folklore, 48-64

Age of al-Andalus CMLC 81: 1-174
 overviews, 1-48
 history, society, and culture, 48-127
 Andalusī poetry, 127-73

Age of Johnson LC 15: 1-87
 Johnson's London, 3-15
 aesthetics of neoclassicism, 15-36
 "age of prose and reason," 36-45
 clubmen and bluestockings, 45-56
 printing technology, 56-62
 periodicals: "a map of busy life," 62-74
 transition, 74-86

The Age of King Alfred the Great CMLC 79: 1-141
 overviews and historical background, 4-17

the Alfredian translations, 17-43
 King Alfred's prefaces, 43-84
 Alfred and Boethius, 84-140

Age of Spenser LC 39: 1-70
 overviews and general studies, 2-21
 literary style, 22-34
 poets and the crown, 34-70

AIDS in Literature CLC 81: 365-416

Alcohol and Literature TCLC 70: 1-58
 overview, 2-8
 fiction, 8-48
 poetry and drama, 48-58

American Abolitionism NCLC 44: 1-73
 overviews and general studies, 2-26
 abolitionist ideals, 26-46
 the literature of abolitionism, 46-72

American Autobiography TCLC 86: 1-115
 overviews and general studies, 3-36
 American authors and autobiography, 36-82
 African-American autobiography, 82-114

American Black Humor Fiction TCLC 54: 1-85
 characteristics of black humor, 2-13
 origins and development, 13-38
 black humor distinguished from related literary trends, 38-60
 black humor and society, 60-75
 black humor reconsidered, 75-83

American Civil War in Literature NCLC 32: 1-109
 overviews and general studies, 2-20
 regional perspectives, 20-54
 fiction popular during the war, 54-79
 the historical novel, 79-108

American Frontier in Literature NCLC 28: 1-103
 definitions, 2-12
 development, 12-17
 nonfiction writing about the frontier, 17-30
 frontier fiction, 30-45
 frontier protagonists, 45-66
 portrayals of Native Americans, 66-86
 feminist readings, 86-98
 twentieth-century reaction against frontier literature, 98-100

American Humor Writing NCLC 52: 1-59
 overviews and general studies, 2-12

the Old Southwest, 12-42
 broader impacts, 42-5
 women humorists, 45-58

American Naturalism in Short Fiction SSC 77: 1-103
 overviews and general studies, 2-30
 major authors of American literary Naturalism, 30-102
 Ambrose Bierce, 30
 Stephen Crane, 30-53
 Theodore Dreiser, 53-65
 Jack London, 65-80
 Frank Norris, 80-9
 Edith Wharton, 89-102

American Novel of Manners TCLC 130: 1-42
 history of the Novel of Manners in America, 4-10
 representative writers, 10-18
 relevancy of the Novel of Manners, 18-24
 hallmark works in the Novel of Manners, 24-36
 Novel of Manners and other media, 36-40

American Mercury, The TCLC 74: 1-80

American Popular Song, Golden Age of TCLC 42: 1-49
 background and major figures, 2-34
 the lyrics of popular songs, 34-47

American Proletarian Literature TCLC 54: 86-175
 overviews and general studies, 87-95
 American proletarian literature and the American Communist Party, 95-111
 ideology and literary merit, 111-17
 novels, 117-36
 Gastonia, 136-48
 drama, 148-54
 journalism, 154-9
 proletarian literature in the United States, 159-74

American Realism NCLC 120: 89-246
 overviews, 91-112
 background and sources, 112-72
 social issues, 172-223
 women and realism, 223-45

American Renaissance SSC 64: 46-193
 overviews and general studies, 47-103
 major authors of short fiction, 103-92

American Romanticism NCLC 44: 74-138
overviews and general studies, 74-84
sociopolitical influences, 84-104
Romanticism and the American frontier,
104-15
thematic concerns, 115-37

American Western Literature TCLC 46:
1-100
definition and development of American
Western literature, 2-7
characteristics of the Western novel, 8-23
Westerns as history and fiction, 23-34
critical reception of American Western lit-
erature, 34-41
the Western hero, 41-73
women in Western fiction, 73-91
later Western fiction, 91-9

American Writers in Paris TCLC 98: 1-156
overviews and general studies, 2-155

Anarchism NCLC 84: 1-97
overviews and general studies, 2-23
the French anarchist tradition, 23-56
Anglo-American anarchism, 56-68
anarchism: incidents and issues, 68-97

Angry Young Men TCLC 166: 1-80
overviews, 2-18
major figures, 18-58
themes and style, 58-79

Animals in Literature TCLC 106: 1-120
overviews and general studies, 2-8
animals in American literature, 8-45
animals in Canadian literature, 45-57
animals in European literature, 57-100
animals in Latin American literature,
100-06
animals in women's literature, 106-20

Antebellum South, Literature of the NCLC
112:1-188
overviews, 4-55
culture of the Old South, 55-68
antebellum fiction: pastoral and heroic ro-
mance, 68-120
role of women: a subdued rebellion, 120-59
slavery and the slave narrative, 159-85

Anti-Americanism TCLC 158: 1-98
overviews and general studies, 3-18
literary and intellectual perspectives, 18-36
social and political reactions, 36-98

Anti-Apartheid TCLC 162: 1-121
overviews, 3-45
major authors, 45-74
anti-apartheid literature and the liberal tra-
dition, 74-101
writing under apartheid: historical views,
101-20

The Apocalyptic Movement TCLC 106:
121-69

Aristotle CMLC 31:1-397
philosophy, 3-100
poetics, 101-219
rhetoric, 220-301
science, 302-397

Art and Literature TCLC 54: 176-248
overviews and general studies, 176-93
definitions, 193-219
influence of visual arts on literature, 219-31
spatial form in literature, 231-47

Arthurian Literature CMLC 10: 1-127
historical context and literary beginnings,
2-27
development of the legend through Malory,
27-64
development of the legend from Malory to
the Victorian Age, 65-81
themes and motifs, 81-95
principal characters, 95-125

Arthurian Revival NCLC 36: 1-77
overviews and general studies, 2-12
Tennyson and his influence, 12-43
other leading figures, 43-73
the Arthurian legend in the visual arts, 73-6

**The Audience and Nineteenth-Century Lit-
erature** NCLC 160: 1-158
overviews, 3-35
race, class, gender, 35-89
America, 89-102
Britain and Europe, 102-30
genre and audience, 130-57

**Australian Cultural Identity in Nineteenth-
Century Literature** NCLC 124: 1-164
overviews and general studies, 4-22
poetry, 22-67
fiction, 67-135
role of women writers, 135-64

Australian Literature TCLC 50: 1-94
origins and development, 2-21
characteristics of Australian literature,
21-33
historical and critical perspectives, 33-41
poetry, 41-58
fiction, 58-76
drama, 76-82
Aboriginal literature, 82-91

Aztec Myths and Literature LC 122: 1-182
Overviews and General Studies, 3-68
Cosmology, 68-136
Language and Literature, 136-81

The Beat Generation BG 1:1-562
the Beat Generation: an overview, 1-137
primary sources, 3-32
overviews and general studies, 32-47
Beat Generation as a social phenomenon,
47-65
drugs, inspiration, and the Beat Genera-
tion, 65-92
religion and the Beat Generation, 92-124
women of the Beat Generation, 124-36
Beat "scene": East and West, 139-259
primary sources, 141-77
Beat scene in the East, 177-218
Beat scene in the West, 218-59
Beat Generation publishing: periodicals,
small presses, and censorship, 261-349
primary sources, 263-74
overview, 274-88
Beat periodicals: "little magazines," 288-
311
Beat publishing: small presses, 311-24
Beat battles with censorship, 324-49
performing arts and the Beat Generation,
351-417
primary sources, 353-58
Beats and film, 358-81
Beats and music, 381-415
visual arts and the Beat Generation, 419-91
primary sources, 421-24
critical commentary, 424-90

Beat Generation, Literature of the TCLC 42:
50-102
overviews and general studies, 51-9
the Beat generation as a social phenom-
enon, 59-62
development, 62-5
Beat literature, 66-96
influence, 97-100

The Bell Curve Controversy CLC 91: 281-
330

***Bildungsroman* in Nineteenth-Century Lit-
erature** NCLC 20: 92-168
surveys, 93-113
in Germany, 113-40
in England, 140-56
female *Bildungsroman*, 156-67
NCLC 152: 1-129
overview, 3-16

definition and issues, 16-52
female *Bildungsromane* , 52-83
ideology and nationhood, 83-128

Black Humor, Contemporary CLC 196: 1-128
overviews and general studies, 2-18
black humor in American fiction, 18-28
development and history, 29-62
major authors, 62-115
technique and narrative, 115-127

The Bloomsbury Group TCLC 34: 1-73
history and major figures, 2-13
definitions, 13-7
influences, 17-27
thought, 27-40
prose, 40-52
and literary criticism, 52-4
political ideals, 54-61
response to, 61-71

The Bloomsbury Group TCLC 138: 1-59
representative members of the Bloomsbury
Group, 9-24
literary relevance of the Bloomsbury
Group, 24-36
Bloomsbury's hallmark works, 36-48
other modernists studied with the Blooms-
bury Group, 48-54

The Blues in Literature TCLC 82: 1-71

Bly, Robert, *Iron John: A Book about Men
and Men's Work* CLC 70: 414-62

The Book of J CLC 65: 289-311

The Book of Common Prayer LC 118: 1-76
overviews, 2-43
translation and diffusion, 44 63
influence of the Prayer Book, 63-76

Brazilian Literature TCLC 134: 1-126
overviews and general studies, 3-33
Brazilian poetry, 33-48
contemporary Brazilian writing, 48-76
culture, politics, and race in Brazilian writ-
ing, 76-100
modernism and postmodernism in Brazil,
100-25

British Ephemeral Literature LC 59: 1-70
overviews and general studies, 1-9
broadside ballads, 10-40
chapbooks, jestbooks, pamphlets, and
newspapers, 40-69

Buddhism and Literature TCLC 70: 59-164
eastern literature, 60-113
western literature, 113-63

**Buddhism in the Nineteenth-Century West-
ern World** NCLC 164: 1-88
overviews, 3-47
Buddhism and Western Philosophers, 47-74
Buddhism in Western Literature, 74-88

**The *Bulletin* and the Rise of Australian Lit-
erary Nationalism** NCLC 116: 1-121
overviews, 3-32
legend of the nineties, 32-55
Bulletin style, 55-71
Australian literary nationalism, 71-98
myth of the bush, 98-120

Businessman in American Literature TCLC
26: 1-48
portrayal of the businessman, 1-32
themes and techniques in business fiction,
32-47

The Calendar LC 55: 1-92
overviews and general studies, 2-19
measuring time, 19-28
calendars and culture, 28-60
calendar reform, 60-92

Captivity Narratives LC 82: 71-172
overviews, 72-107
captivity narratives and Puritanism, 108-34

captivity narratives and Native Americans, 134-49
influence on American literature, 149-72

Caribbean Literature TCLC 138: 60-135
overviews and general studies, 61-9
ethnic and national identity, 69-107
expatriate Caribbean literature, 107-23
literary histoiography, 123-35

Catholicism in Nineteenth-Century American Literature NCLC 64: 1-58
overviews, 3-14
polemical literature, 14-46
Catholicism in literature, 47-57

Cavalier Poetry and Drama LC 107: 1-71
overviews, 2-36
Cavalier drama, 36-48
major figures, 48-70

Celtic Mythology CMLC 26: 1-111
overviews and general studies, 2-22
Celtic myth as literature and history, 22-48
Celtic religion: Druids and divinities, 48-80
Fionn MacCuhaill and the Fenian cycle, 80-111

Celtic Twilight See Irish Literary Renaissance

Censorship and Contemporary World Literature CLC 194: 1-80
overviews and general studies, 2-19
notorious cases, 19-59
censorship in the global context, 59-79

Censorship of the Press in the Nineteenth Century NCLC 156: 1-133
overviews, 3-29
censorship in Austria, Germany, and Russia, 29-87
censorship in France and Spain, 87-120
censorship in England and America, 120-33

Censorship in Twentieth-Century Literature TCLC 154: 115-238
overviews and general studies, 117-25
censorship and obscenity trials, 125-61
censorship and sexual politics, 161-81
censorship and war, 181-207
political censorship and the state, 207-28
censorship and the writer, 228-38

The Chartist Movement and Literature NCLC 60: 1-84
overview: nineteenth-century working-class fiction, 2-19
Chartist fiction and poetry, 19-73
the Chartist press, 73-84

The Chicago Renaissance TCLC 154: 239-341
overviews and general studies, 240-60
definitions and growth, 260-82
the language debate, 282-318
major authors, 318-40

Chicano/a Literature, Contemporary CLC 205: 82-181
overviews, 84-124
Chicana studies, 124-40
some representative works, 140-80

Chick-Lit and Lad-Lit CLC 210: 115-64
overviews, 117-25
the debate over Chick Lit, 125-46
representative authors, 146-64

Child Labor in Nineteenth-Century Literature NCLC 108: 1-133
overviews, 3-10
climbing boys and chimney sweeps, 10-16
the international traffic in children, 16-45
critics and reformers, 45-82
fictional representations of child laborers, 83-132

Childhood in Nineteenth-Century Literature NCLC 172: 1-140
overviews, 2-20
Romanticism and childhood, 20-46
childhood in the works of William Wordsworth, 46-72
childhood in the works of Charles Dickens, 72-106
childhood in the works of Leo Tolstoy, 106-29
childhood in the works of Emily Dickinson, 129-39

Children's Literature, Nineteenth-Century NCLC 52: 60-135
overviews and general studies, 61-72
moral tales, 72-89
fairy tales and fantasy, 90-119
making men/making women, 119-34

Christianity in Twentieth-Century Literature TCLC 110: 1-79
overviews and general studies, 2-31
Christianity in twentieth-century fiction, 31-78

Chronicle Plays LC 89: 1-106
development of the genre, 2-33
historiography and literature, 33-56
genre and performance, 56-88
politics and ideology, 88-106

The City and Literature TCLC 90: 1-124
overviews and general studies, 2-9
the city in American literature, 9-86
the city in European literature, 86-124

City Comedy LC 118: 77-211
origins and development, 79-113
economic issues, 113-32
women and city comedy, 132-82
the plays of Thomas Middleton, 182-211

Civic Critics, Russian NCLC 20: 402-46
principal figures and background, 402-9
and Russian Nihilism, 410-6
aesthetic and critical views, 416-45

The Cockney School NCLC 68: 1-64
overview, 2-7
Blackwood's Magazine and the contemporary critical response, 7-24
the political and social import of the Cockneys and their critics, 24-63

Colonial America: The Intellectual Background LC 25: 1-98
overviews and general studies, 2-17
philosophy and politics, 17-31
early religious influences in Colonial America, 31-60
consequences of the Revolution, 60-78
religious influences in post-revolutionary America, 78-87
colonial literary genres, 87-97

Colonialism in Victorian English Literature NCLC 56: 1-77
overviews and general studies, 2-34
colonialism and gender, 34-51
monsters and the occult, 51-76

Columbus, Christopher, Books on the Quincentennial of His Arrival in the New World CLC 70: 329-60

Comic Books TCLC 66: 1-139
historical and critical perspectives, 2-48
superheroes, 48-67
underground comix, 67-88
comic books and society, 88-122
adult comics and graphic novels, 122-36

Comedy of Manners LC 92: 1-75
overviews, 2-21
comedy of manners and society, 21-47
comedy of manners and women, 47-74

Commedia dell'Arte LC 83: 1-147

overviews, 2-7
origins and development, 7-23
characters and actors, 23-45
performance, 45-62
texts and authors, 62-100
influence in Europe, 100-46

Conduct Books in Nineteenth-Century Literature NCLC 152: 130-229
women's education, 131-68
feminist revisions, 168-82
American behavioral literature: cultivating national identity, 182-209
English behavioral literature: defining a middle class, 209-27

Connecticut Wits NCLC 48: 1-95
overviews and general studies, 2-40
major works, 40-76
intellectual context, 76-95

Crime Fiction, Contemporary CLC 209: 34-192
overviews, 37-61
ethnicity and race in crime fiction, 61-105
literary traditions and crime fiction, 105-43
themes, 143-81
representative authors, 181-92

Crime in Literature TCLC 54: 249-307
evolution of the criminal figure in literature, 250-61
crime and society, 261-77
literary perspectives on crime and punishment, 277-88
writings by criminals, 288-306

Crime-Mystery-Detective Stories SSC 59: 89-226
overviews and general studies, 90-140
origins and early masters of the crime-mystery-detective story, 140-73
hard-boiled crime-mystery-detective fiction, 173-209
diversity in the crime-mystery-detective story, 210-25

The Crusades CMLC 38: 1-144
history of the Crusades, 3-60
literature of the Crusades, 60-116
the Crusades and the people: attitudes and influences, 116-44

Cuban Exile Literature, Contemporary CLC 207: 1-100
overviews, 2-20
Cubana writers and exile, 20-48
some representative works, 48-100

Cyberpunk TCLC 106: 170-366
overviews and general studies, 171-88
feminism and cyberpunk, 188-230
history and cyberpunk, 230-70
sexuality and cyberpunk, 270-98
social issues and cyberpunk, 299-366

Cyberpunk Short Fiction SSC 60: 44-108
overviews and general studies, 46-78
major writers of cyberpunk fiction, 78-81
sexuality and cyberpunk fiction, 81-97
additional pieces, 97-108

Czechoslovakian Literature of the Twentieth Century TCLC 42: 103-96
through World War II, 104-35
de-Stalinization, the Prague Spring, and contemporary literature, 135-72
Slovak literature, 172-85
Czech science fiction, 185-93

Dadaism TCLC 46: 101-71
background and major figures, 102-16
definitions, 116-26
manifestos and commentary by Dadaists, 126-40
theater and film, 140-58
nature and characteristics of Dadaist writing, 158-70

Danish Literature See Twentieth-Century Danish Literature

Darwinism and Literature NCLC 32: 110-206
 background, 110-31
 direct responses to Darwin, 131-71
 collateral effects of Darwinism, 171-205

Death in American Literature NCLC 92: 1-170
 overviews and general studies, 2-32
 death in the works of Emily Dickinson, 32-72
 death in the works of Herman Melville, 72-101
 death in the works of Edgar Allan Poe, 101-43
 death in the works of Walt Whitman, 143-70

Death in Nineteenth-Century British Literature NCLC 68: 65-142
 overviews and general studies, 66-92
 responses to death, 92-102
 feminist perspectives, 103-17
 striving for immortality, 117-41

Death in Literature TCLC 78: 1-183
 fiction, 2-115
 poetry, 115-46
 drama, 146-81

Decadence in Nineteenth-Century Literature NCLC 164: 90-191
 overviews, 90-132
 Decadent literary subjects, 132-44
 Decadence in British literature, 144-57
 Decadence in French literature, 158-79
 women writers and Decadence, 179-90

Deconstruction TCLC 138: 136-256
 overviews and general studies, 137-83
 deconstruction and literature, 183-221
 deconstruction in philosophy and history, 221-56

de Man, Paul, Wartime Journalism of CLC 55: 382-424

Depictions of Islam in Modern Literature TCLC 166: 81-198
 overviews, 82-115
 literature in the Muslim world, 115-56
 Western interpretations, 156-82
 women, Islam, and literature, 182-97

Detective Fiction, Nineteenth-Century NCLC 36: 78-148
 origins of the genre, 79-100
 history of nineteenth-century detective fiction, 101-33
 significance of nineteenth-century detective fiction, 133-46
 NCLC 148: 1-161
 overviews, 3-26
 origins and influences, 26-63
 major authors, 63-134
 Freud and detective fiction, 134-59

Detective Fiction, Twentieth-Century TCLC 38: 1-96
 genesis and history of the detective story, 3-22
 defining detective fiction, 22-32
 evolution and varieties, 32-77
 the appeal of detective fiction, 77-90

Detective Story See Crime-Mystery-Detective Stories

Dime Novels NCLC 84: 98-168
 overviews and general studies, 99-123
 popular characters, 123-39
 major figures and influences, 139-52
 socio-political concerns, 152-167

Disease and Literature TCLC 66: 140-283
 overviews and general studies, 141-65

disease in nineteenth-century literature, 165-81
tuberculosis and literature, 181-94
women and disease in literature, 194-221
plague literature, 221-53
AIDS in literature, 253-82

El Dorado, The Legend of See The Legend of El Dorado

The Double in Nineteenth-Century Literature NCLC 40: 1-95
 genesis and development of the theme, 2-15
 the double and Romanticism, 16-27
 sociological views, 27-52
 psychological interpretations, 52-87
 philosophical considerations, 87-95

Dramatic Realism NCLC 44: 139-202
 overviews and general studies, 140-50
 origins and definitions, 150-66
 impact and influence, 166-93
 realist drama and tragedy, 193-201

Drugs and Literature TCLC 78: 184-282
 overviews and general studies, 185-201
 pre-twentieth-century literature, 201-42
 twentieth-century literature, 242-82

Dystopias in Contemporary Literature CLC 168: 1-91
 overviews and general studies, 2-52
 dystopian views in Margaret Atwood's *The Handmaid's Tale* (1985), 52-71
 feminist readings of dystopias, 71-90

Eastern Mythology CMLC 26: 112-92
 heroes and kings, 113-51
 cross-cultural perspective, 151-69
 relations to history and society, 169-92

Ecocriticism and Nineteenth-Century Literature NCLC 140: 1-168
 overviews, 3-20
 American literature: Romantics and Realists, 20-76
 American explorers and naturalists, 76-123
 English literature: Romantics and Victorians, 123-67

Ecofeminism and Nineteenth-Century Literature NCLC 136: 1-110
 overviews, 2-24
 the local landscape, 24-72
 travel writing, 72-109

Eighteenth-Century British Periodicals LC 63: 1-123
 rise of periodicals, 2-31
 impact and influence of periodicals, 31-64
 periodicals and society, 64-122

Eighteenth-Century Travel Narratives LC 77: 252-355
 overviews and general studies, 254-79
 eighteenth-century European travel narratives, 279-334
 non-European eighteenth-century travel narratives, 334-55

Electronic "Books": Hypertext and Hyperfiction CLC 86: 367-404
 books vs. CD-ROMS, 367-76
 hypertext and hyperfiction, 376-95
 implications for publishing, libraries, and the public, 395-403

Eliot, T. S., Centenary of Birth CLC 55: 345-75

Elizabethan Drama LC 22: 140-240
 origins and influences, 142-67
 characteristics and conventions, 167-83
 theatrical production, 184-200
 histories, 200-12
 comedy, 213-20
 tragedy, 220-30

Elizabethan Prose Fiction LC 41: 1-70
 overviews and general studies, 1-15

origins and influences, 15-43
style and structure, 43-69

The Emergence of the Short Story in the Nineteenth Century NCLC 140: 169-279
 overviews, 171-74
 the American short story, 174-214
 the short story in Great Britain and Ireland, 214-235
 stories by women in English, 235-45
 the short story in France and Russia, 245-66
 the Latin American short story, 266-77

Enclosure of the English Common NCLC 88: 1-57
 overviews and general studies, 1-12
 early reaction to enclosure, 12-23
 nineteenth-century reaction to enclosure, 23-56

The Encyclopedists LC 26: 172-253
 overviews and general studies, 173-210
 intellectual background, 210-32
 views on esthetics, 232-41
 views on women, 241-52

English Abolitionist Literature of the Nineteenth Century NCLC 136: 111-235
 overview, 112-35
 origins and development, 135-42
 poetry, 142-58
 prose, 158-80
 sociopolitical concerns, 180-95
 English abolitionist literature and feminism, 195-233

English Caroline Literature LC 13: 221-307
 background, 222-41
 evolution and varieties, 241-62
 the Cavalier mode, 262-75
 court and society, 275-91
 politics and religion, 291-306

English Decadent Literature of the 1890s NCLC 28: 104-200
 fin de siècle: the Decadent period, 105-19
 definitions, 120-37
 major figures: "the tragic generation," 137-50
 French literature and English literary Decadence, 150-7
 themes, 157-61
 poetry, 161-82
 periodicals, 182-96

English Emblem Books LC 125: 1-99
 overviews, 2-27
 background and contexts, 27-63
 major emblem writers, 63-83
 religion and emblem books, 83-99

English Essay, Rise of the LC 18: 238-308
 definitions and origins, 236-54
 influence on the essay, 254-69
 historical background, 269-78
 the essay in the seventeenth century, 279-93
 the essay in the eighteenth century, 293-307

English Mystery Cycle Dramas LC 34: 1-88
 overviews and general studies, 1-27
 the nature of dramatic performances, 27-42
 the medieval worldview and the mystery cycles, 43-67
 the doctrine of repentance and the mystery cycles, 67-76
 the fall from grace in the mystery cycles, 76-88

The English Realist Novel, 1740-1771 LC 51: 102-98
 overviews and general studies, 103-22
 from Romanticism to Realism, 123-58
 women and the novel, 159-175
 the novel and other literary forms, 176-197

English Revolution, Literature of the LC 43: 1-58
overviews and general studies, 2-24
pamphlets of the English Revolution, 24-38
political sermons of the English Revolution, 38-48
poetry of the English Revolution, 48-57

English Romantic Hellenism NCLC 68: 143-250
overviews and general studies, 144-69
historical development of English Romantic Hellenism, 169-91
influence of Greek mythology on the Romantics, 191-229
influence of Greek literature, art, and culture on the Romantics, 229-50

English Romantic Poetry NCLC 28: 201-327
overviews and reputation, 202-37
major subjects and themes, 237-67
forms of Romantic poetry, 267-78
politics, society, and Romantic poetry, 278-99
philosophy, religion, and Romantic poetry, 299-324

The Epistolary Novel LC 59: 71-170
overviews and general studies, 72-96
women and the Epistolary novel, 96-138
principal figures: Britain, 138-53
principal figures: France, 153-69

Espionage Literature TCLC 50: 95-159
overviews and general studies, 96-113
espionage fiction/formula fiction, 113-26
spies in fact and fiction, 126-38
the female spy, 138-44
social and psychological perspectives, 144-58

European Debates on the Conquest of the Americas LC 67: 1-129
overviews and general studies, 3-56
major Spanish figures, 56-98
English perceptions of Native Americans, 98-129

European Romanticism NCLC 36: 149-284
definitions, 149-77
origins of the movement, 177-82
Romantic theory, 182-200
themes and techniques, 200-23
Romanticism in Germany, 223-39
Romanticism in France, 240-61
Romanticism in Italy, 261-4
Romanticism in Spain, 264-8
impact and legacy, 268-82

Exile in Literature TCLC 122: 1-129
overviews and general studies, 2-33
exile in fiction, 33-92
German literature in exile, 92-129

Exile in Nineteenth-Century European and American Literature NCLC 172: 141-248
overview, 143-51
exile in French literature, 151-81
exile in British literature, 181-202
exile in American literature, 202-27
women and exile, 227-47

Existentialism and Literature TCLC 42: 197-268
overviews and definitions, 198-209
history and influences, 209-19
Existentialism critiqued and defended, 220-35
philosophical and religious perspectives, 235-41
Existentialist fiction and drama, 241-67

Ezra Pound Controversy TCLC 150: 1-132
politics of Ezra Pound, 3-42
anti-semitism of Ezra Pound, 42-57
the Bollingen Award controversy, 57-76
Pound's later writing, 76-104
criticism of *The Pisan Cantos*, 104-32

Familiar Essay NCLC 48: 96-211
definitions and origins, 97-130
overview of the genre, 130-43
elements of form and style, 143-59
elements of content, 159-73
the Cockneys: Hazlitt, Lamb, and Hunt, 173-91
status of the genre, 191-210

Fantasy in Contemporary Literature CLC 193: 137-250
overviews and general studies, 139-57
language, form, and theory, 157-91
major writers, 191-230
women writers and fantasy, 230-50

Fashion in Nineteenth-Century Literature NCLC 128: 104-93
overviews and general studies, 105-38
fashion and American literature, 138-46
fashion and English literature, 146-74
fashion and French literature, 174-92

The Faust Legend LC 47: 1-117

Fear in Literature TCLC 74: 81-258
overviews and general studies, 81
pre-twentieth-century literature, 123
twentieth-century literature, 182

Feminism in the 1990s: Commentary on Works by Naomi Wolf, Susan Faludi, and Camille Paglia CLC 76: 377-415

Feminist Criticism, Contemporary CLC 180: 1-103
overviews and general studies, 2-59
modern French feminist theory, 59-102

Feminist Criticism in 1990 CLC 65: 312-60

Feminism in Literature FL 1: 1-279; 2: 1-295; 4: 1-626
women and women's writings from antiquity through the middle ages, 1:1-99
primary sources, 1:4-12
women in the ancient world, 1:12-34
women in the medieval world, 1:34-56
women in classical art and literature, 1:56-74
classical and medieval women writers, 1:74-96
women in the 16th, 17th, and 18th centuries: an overview, 1:101-91
primary sources, 1:104-11
overviews, 1:112-32
society, 1:132-64
politics, 1:164-77
women in literature, 1:177-90
women's literature in the 16th, 17th, and 18th centuries 1:193-279
primary sources, 1:195-201
overviews, 1:202-39
women's literature in the 16th, 17th, and 18th centuries, 1:239-79
women in the 19th century: an overview, 2:1-88
primary sources, 2:3-15
overviews, 2:15-50
early feminists, 2:50-67
representations of women in literature and art in the 19th century, 2:67-86
women's literature in the 19th century, 2:89-206
primary sources, 2:91-9
overviews, 2:99-140
American women writers, 2:141-77
British women writers, 2:177-204
United States suffrage movement in the 19th century, 2:207-95
primary sources, 2:209-29
overviews, 2:229-39
the civil war and its effect on suffrage, 2:239-53
suffrage: issues and individuals, 2:253-94
women in the early to mid-20th century (1900-1960): an overview, 4:1-126

primary sources, 4:1-14
overviews, 4:14-48
social and economic conditions, 4:48-67
women and the arts, 4:67-125
suffrage in the 20th century, 4:127-234
primary sources, 4:129-36
overviews, 4:136-77
major figures and organizations, 4:177-214
women and law, 4:214-32
women's literature from 1900 to 1960, 4:235-344
primary sources, 4:238-41
overviews, 4:241-61
impact of the world wars, 4:261-304
women and the dramatic tradition, 4:304-39
Asian American influences, 4:339-42
the feminist movement in the 20th century, 4:345-443
primary sources, 4:347-58
overviews, 4:358-403
feminist legal battles, 4:403-34
third-wave feminism, 4:434-42
women's literature from 1960 to the present, 4:445-536
primary sources, 4:448-60
overviews, 4:460-83
women authors of color, 4:483-97
feminist literary theory, 4:497-511
modern lesbian literature, 4:511-534

Fifteenth-Century English Literature LC 17: 248-334
background, 249-72
poetry, 272-315
drama, 315-23
prose, 323-33

Fifteenth-Century Spanish Poetry LC 100:82-173
overviews and general studies, 83-101
the Cancioneros, 101-57
major figures, 157-72

The Figure of La Malinche in Mexican Literature LC 127: 91-172
Overview 92-108
The Historical Malinche 108-33
Malinche Reinvented 133-72

Film and Literature TCLC 38: 97-226
overviews and general studies, 97-119
film and theater, 119-34
film and the novel, 134-45
the art of the screenplay, 145-66
genre literature/genre film, 167-79
the writer and the film industry, 179-90
authors on film adaptations of their works, 190-200
fiction into film: comparative essays, 200-23

Finance and Money as Represented in Nineteenth-Century Literature NCLC 76: 1-69
historical perspectives, 2-20
the image of money, 20-37
the dangers of money, 37-50
women and money, 50-69

Folklore and Literature TCLC 86: 116-293
overviews and general studies, 118-144
Native American literature, 144-67
African-American literature, 167-238
folklore and the American West, 238-57
modern and postmodern literature, 257-91

Food in Literature TCLC 114: 1-133
food and children's literature, 2-14
food as a literary device, 14-32
rituals invloving food, 33-45
food and social and ethnic identity, 45-90
women's relationship with food, 91-132

Food in Nineteenth-Century Literature
NCLC 108: 134-288
overviews, 136-74
food and social class, 174-85
food and gender, 185-219
food and love, 219-31
food and sex, 231-48
eating disorders, 248-70
vegetarians, carnivores, and cannibals,
270-87

French Drama in the Age of Louis XIV LC
28: 94-185
overview, 95-127
tragedy, 127-46
comedy, 146-66
tragicomedy, 166-84

French Enlightenment LC 14: 81-145
the question of definition, 82-9
le siècle des lumières, 89-94
women and the salons, 94-105
censorship, 105-15
the philosophy of reason, 115-31
influence and legacy, 131-44

French New Novel TCLC 98: 158-234
overviews and general studies, 158-92
influences, 192-213
themes, 213-33

French Realism NCLC 52: 136-216
origins and definitions, 137-70
issues and influence, 170-98
realism and representation, 198-215

French Revolution and English Literature
NCLC 40: 96-195
history and theory, 96-123
romantic poetry, 123-50
the novel, 150-81
drama, 181-92
children's literature, 192-5

French Symbolist Poetry NCLC 144: 1-107
overviews, 2-14
Symbolist aesthetics, 14-47
the Symbolist lyric, 47-60
history and influence, 60-105

Futurism TCLC 166: 199-338
overviews, 200-10
poetry, 210-23
theater, 223-32
music, 232-46
Futurism and Fascism, 246-312
women Futurist writers, 312-37

Futurism, Italian TCLC 42: 269-354
principles and formative influences, 271-9
manifestos, 279-88
literature, 288-303
theater, 303-19
art, 320-30
music, 330-6
architecture, 336-9
and politics, 339-46
reputation and significance, 346-51

Gaelic Revival See Irish Literary Renaissance

Gates, Henry Louis, Jr., and African-American Literary Criticism CLC 65: 361-405

Gaucho Literature TCLC 158: 99-195
overviews and general studies, 101-43
major works, 143-95

Gambling in Nineteenth-Century Literature
NCLC 168: 1-84
overview, 2-7
gambling in American literature, 7-39
gambling in British literature, 39-57
gambling in Russian literature, 57-84

Gay and Lesbian Literature CLC 76: 416-39

Gay and Lesbian Literature, Contemporary
CLC 171: 1-130
overviews and general studies, 2-43
contemporary gay literature, 44-95
lesbianism in contemporary literature, 95-129

Gender in Nineteenth-Century Literature
NCLC 168: 192-352
overviews, 195-256
gender and race, 256-83
gender and men, 283-309
gender and class, 309-20
gender and the text, 320-51

The Generation of 1927 TCLC 178: 1-109
overviews 2-17
literary and thematic assessments 17-59
major authors 59-108

Generation of 1898 Short Fiction SSC 75:
182-287
overviews and general studies, 182-210
major short story writers of the Generation
of 1898, 210-86
Azorín, 210-16
Emilia Pardo Bazán, 216-34
Vicente Blasco Ibáñez, 234-36
Gabriel Miró, 236-43
Miguel de Unamuno, 243-68
Ramon del Valle-Inclán, 268-86

German Exile Literature TCLC 30: 1-58
the writer and the Nazi state, 1-10
definition of, 10-4
life in exile, 14-32
surveys, 32-50
Austrian literature in exile, 50-2
German publishing in the United States,
52-7

German Expressionism TCLC 34: 74-160
history and major figures, 76-85
aesthetic theories, 85-109
drama, 109-26
poetry, 126-38
film, 138-42
painting, 142-7
music, 147-53
and politics, 153-8

The Ghost Story SSC 58: 1-142
overviews and general studies, 1-21
the ghost story in American literature,
21-49
the ghost story in Asian literature, 49-53
the ghost story in European and English
literature, 54-89
major figures, 89-141

The Gilded Age NCLC 84: 169-271
popular themes, 170-90
Realism, 190-208
Aestheticism, 208-26
socio-political concerns, 226-70

Glasnost and Contemporary Soviet Literature CLC 59: 355-97

Gone with the Wind as Cultural Phenomenon
TCLC 170: 1-103
overviews, 2-60
race, gender, and class in *Gone with the
Wind,* 60-102

Gothic Drama NCLC 132: 95-198
overviews, 97-125
sociopolitical contexts, 125-58
Gothic playwrights, 158-97

Gothic Literature GL 1: 1-577
Gothic Literature: an overview, 1-106
primary sources, 4-16
overviews, 16-40
origins of the Gothic, 40-57
American Gothic, 57-74
European Gothic, 74-104
society, culture, and the Gothic, 107-229

primary sources, 110-27
overviews, 127-80
race and the Gothic, 180-210
women and the Gothic, 210-28
gothic themes, settings, and figures, 231-387
primary sources, 236-49
overviews, 249-64
haunted dwellings and the supernatural,
264-301
psychology and the Gothic, 301-42
vampires, 342-85
performing arts and the Gothic, 389-474
primary sources, 394-401
drama, 401-15
film, 415-52
television, 452-60
music, 461-73
visual arts and the Gothic, 475-526
primary sources, 477-80
overviews, 480-86
architecture, 486-506
art, 506-525

Gothic Novel NCLC 28: 328-402
development and major works, 328-34
definitions, 334-50
themes and techniques, 350-78
in America, 378-85
in Scotland, 385-91
influence and legacy, 391-400

The Governess in Nineteenth-Century Literature NCLC 104: 1-131
overviews and general studies, 3-28
social roles and economic conditions, 28-86
fictional governesses, 86-131

The Grail Theme in Twentieth-Century Literature TCLC 142: 1-89
overviews and general studies, 2-20
major works, 20-89

Graphic Narratives CLC 86: 405-32
history and overviews, 406-21
the "Classics Illustrated" series, 421-2
reviews of recent works, 422-32

Graphic Novels CLC 177: 163-299
overviews and general studies, 165-198
critical readings of major works, 198-286
reviews of recent graphic novels, 286-299

Graveyard Poets LC 67: 131-212
origins and development, 131-52
major figures, 152-75
major works, 175-212

Greek Historiography CMLC 17: 1-49

Greek Lyric Poetry, The Rise of CMLC 77:
226-329
overviews, 229-46
literary history, 246-72
themes and style, 272-302
representative authors, 302-28

Greek Mythology CMLC 26: 193-320
overviews and general studies, 194-209
origins and development of Greek mythology, 209-29
cosmogonies and divinities in Greek mythology, 229-54
heroes and heroines in Greek mythology,
254-80
women in Greek mythology, 280-320

Greek Theater CMLC 51: 1-58
criticism, 2-58

Hard-Boiled Fiction TCLC 118: 1-109
overviews and general studies, 2-39
major authors, 39-76
women and hard-boiled fiction, 76-109

The Harlem Renaissance HR 1: 1-563
overviews and general studies of the Harlem Renaissance, 1-137
primary sources, 3-12

overviews, 12-38
background and sources of the Harlem
 Renaissance, 38-56
the New Negro aesthetic, 56-91
patrons, promoters, and the New York
 Public Library, 91-121
women of the Harlem Renaissance,
 121 37
social, economic, and political factors that
 influenced the Harlem Renaissance,
 139-240
 primary sources, 141-53
 overviews, 153-87
 social and economic factors, 187-213
 Black intellectual and political thought,
 213-40
publishing and periodicals during the Har-
 lem Renaissance, 243-339
 primary sources, 246-52
 overviews, 252-68
 African American writers and main-
 stream publishers, 268-91
 anthologies: *The New Negro* and others,
 291-309
 African American periodicals and the
 Harlem Renaissance, 309-39
performing arts during the Harlem Renais-
 sance, 341-465
 primary sources, 343-48
 overviews, 348-64
 drama of the Harlem Renaissance,
 364-92
 influence of music on Harlem Renais-
 sance writing, 437-65
visual arts during the Harlem Renaissance,
 467-563
 primary sources, 470-71
 overviews, 471-517
 painters, 517-36
 sculptors, 536-58
 photographers, 558-63

Harlem Renaissance TCLC 26: 49-125
 principal issues and figures, 50-67
 the literature and its audience, 67-74
 theme and technique in poetry, fiction, and
 drama, 74-115
 and American society, 115-21
 achievement and influence, 121-2

Havel, Václav, Playwright and President CLC
65: 406-63

Heroic Drama LC 91: 249-373
 definitions and overviews, 251-78
 politics and heroic drama, 278-303
 early plays: Dryden and Orrery, 303-51
 later plays: Lee and Otway, 351-73

Historical Fiction, Nineteenth-Century NCLC
48: 212-307
 definitions and characteristics, 213-36
 Victorian historical fiction, 236-65
 American historical fiction, 265-88
 realism in historical fiction, 288-306

Hollywood and Literature TCLC 118: 110-
251
 overviews and general studies, 111-20
 adaptations, 120-65
 socio-historical and cultural impact, 165-
 206
 theater and hollywood, 206-51

Holocaust and the Atomic Bomb: Fifty Years
Later CLC 91: 331-82
 the Holocaust remembered, 333-52
 Anne Frank revisited, 352-62
 the atomic bomb and American memory,
 362-81

Holocaust Denial Literature TCLC 58: 1-110
 overviews and general studies, 1-30
 Robert Faurisson and Noam Chomsky,
 30-52

Holocaust denial literature in America,
 52-71
library access to Holocaust denial litera-
 ture, 72-5
the authenticity of Anne Frank's diary,
 76-90
David Irving and the "normalization" of
 Hitler, 90-109

Holocaust, Literature of the TCLC 42: 355-
450
 historical overview, 357-61
 critical overview, 361-70
 diaries and memoirs, 370-95
 novels and short stories, 395-425
 poetry, 425-41
 drama, 441-8

Homosexuality in Nineteenth-Century Lit-
erature NCLC 56: 78-182
 defining homosexuality, 80-111
 Greek love, 111-44
 trial and danger, 144-81

Humors Comedy LC 85: 194-324
 overviews, 195-251
 major figures: Ben Jonson, 251-93
 major figures: William Shakespeare, 293-
 324

Hungarian Literature of the Twentieth Cen-
tury TCLC 26: 126-88
 surveys of, 126-47
 Nyugat and early twentieth-century litera-
 ture, 147-56
 mid-century literature, 156-68
 and politics, 168-78
 since the 1956 revolt, 178-87

Hysteria in Nineteenth-Century Literature
NCLC 64: 59-184
 the history of hysteria, 60-75
 the gender of hysteria, 75-103
 hysteria and women's narratives, 103-57
 hysteria in nineteenth-century poetry,
 157-83

Image of the Noble Savage in Literature LC
79: 136-252
 overviews and development, 136-76
 the Noble Savage in the New World, 176-
 221
 Rousseau and the French Enlightenment's
 view of the noble savage, 221-51

Imagism TCLC 74: 259-454
 history and development, 260
 major figures, 288
 sources and influences, 352
 Imagism and other movements, 397
 influence and legacy, 431

Immigrants in Nineteenth-Century Litera-
ture, Representation of NCLC 112: 188-298
 overview, 189-99
 immigrants in America, 199-223
 immigrants and labor, 223-60
 immigrants in England, 260-97

Incest in Nineteenth-Century American Lit-
erature NCLC 76: 70-141
 overview, 71-88
 the concern for social order, 88-117
 authority and authorship, 117-40

Incest in Victorian Literature NCLC 92: 172-
318
 overviews and general studies, 173-85
 novels, 185-276
 plays, 276-84
 poetry, 284-318

Indian Literature in English TCLC 54: 308-
406
 overview, 309-13
 origins and major figures, 313-25
 the Indo-English novel, 325-55
 Indo-English poetry, 355-67

Indo-English drama, 367-72
critical perspectives on Indo-English litera-
 ture, 372-80
modern Indo-English literature, 380-9
Indo-English authors on their work, 389-
 404

The Industrial Revolution in Literature
NCLC 56: 183 273
 historical and cultural perspectives, 184-
 201
 contemporary reactions to the machine,
 201-21
 themes and symbols in literature, 221-73

The Influence of Ernest Hemingway TCLC
162: 122-259
 overviews, 123-43
 writers on Hemingway, 143-58
 Hemingway's evocation of place, 158-84
 gender and identity, 184-229
 Hemingway and the quest for meaning,
 229-58

The Influence of William Faulkner TCLC
170: 104-255
 overviews, 105-16
 Faulkner and narrative, 116-60
 Faulkner and psychology, 160-80
 Faulkner and race, 180-219
 impact on contemporary culture, 219-43
 Faulkner and women, 243-54

The Irish Famine as Represented in
Nineteenth-Century Literature NCLC 64:
185-261
 overviews and general studies, 187-98
 historical background, 198-212
 famine novels, 212-34
 famine poetry, 234-44
 famine letters and eye-witness accounts,
 245-61

Irish Literary Renaissance TCLC 46: 172-
287
 overview, 173-83
 development and major figures, 184-202
 influence of Irish folklore and mythology,
 202-22
 Irish poetry, 222-34
 Irish drama and the Abbey Theatre, 234-56
 Irish fiction, 256-86

Irish Nationalism and Literature NCLC 44:
203-73
 the Celtic element in literature, 203-19
 anti-Irish sentiment and the Celtic response,
 219-34
 literary ideals in Ireland, 234-45
 literary expressions, 245-73

The Irish Novel NCLC 80: 1-130
 overviews and general studies, 3-9
 principal figures, 9-22
 peasant and middle class Irish novelists,
 22-76
 aristocratic Irish and Anglo-Irish novelists,
 76-129

Israeli Literature TCLC 94: 1-137
 overviews and general studies, 2-18
 Israeli fiction, 18-33
 Israeli poetry, 33-62
 Israeli drama, 62-91
 women and Israeli literature, 91-112
 Arab characters in Israeli literature, 112-36

Italian Futurism See Futurism, Italian

Italian Humanism LC 12: 205-77
 origins and early development, 206-18
 revival of classical letters, 218-23
 humanism and other philosophies, 224-39
 humanism and humanists, 239-46
 the plastic arts, 246-57
 achievement and significance, 258-76

Italian Romanticism NCLC 60: 85-145
origins and overviews, 86-101
Italian Romantic theory, 101-25
the language of Romanticism, 125-45

Jacobean Drama LC 33: 1-37
the Jacobean worldview: an era of transition, 2-14
the moral vision of Jacobean drama, 14-22
Jacobean tragedy, 22-3
the Jacobean masque, 23-36

Jazz and Literature TCLC 102: 3-124

Jewish-American Fiction TCLC 62: 1-181
overviews and general studies, 2-24
major figures, 24-48
Jewish writers and American life, 48-78
Jewish characters in American fiction, 78-108
themes in Jewish-American fiction, 108-43
Jewish-American women writers, 143-59
the Holocaust and Jewish-American fiction, 159-81

Jews in Literature TCLC 118: 252-417
overviews and general studies, 253-97
representing the Jew in literature, 297-351
the Holocaust in literature, 351-416

The Journals of Lewis and Clark NCLC 100: 1-88
overviews and general studies, 4-30
journal-keeping methods, 30-46
Fort Mandan, 46-51
the Clark journal, 51-65
the journals as literary texts, 65-87

Kabuki LC 73: 118-232
overviews and general studies, 120-40
the development of Kabuki, 140-65
major works, 165-95
Kabuki and society, 195-231

King Alfred the Great, The Age of See The Age of King Alfred the Great

The Kit-Kat Club LC 71: 66-112
overviews and general studies, 67-88
major figures, 88-107
attacks on the Kit-Kat Club, 107-12

The Knickerbocker Group NCLC 56: 274-341
overviews and general studies, 276-314
Knickerbocker periodicals, 314-26
writers and artists, 326-40

Künstlerroman TCLC 150: 133-260
overviews and general studies, 135-51
major works, 151-212
feminism in the *Künstlerroman,* 212-49
minority *Künstlerroman,* 249-59

The Lake Poets NCLC 52: 217-304
characteristics of the Lake Poets and their works, 218-27
literary influences and collaborations, 227-66
defining and developing Romantic ideals, 266-84
embracing Conservatism, 284-303

Language Poets TCLC 126: 66-172
overviews and general studies, 67-122
selected major figures in language poetry, 122-72

Larkin, Philip, Controversy CLC 81: 417-64

Latin American Literature, Twentieth-Century TCLC 58: 111-98
historical and critical perspectives, 112-36
the novel, 136-45
the short story, 145-9
drama, 149-60
poetry, 160-7

the writer and society, 167-86
Native Americans in Latin American literature, 186-97

Law and Literature TCLC 126: 173-347
overviews and general studies, 174-253
fiction critiquing the law, 253-88
literary responses to the law, 289-346

The Legend of El Dorado LC 74: 248-350
overviews, 249-308
major explorations for El Dorado, 308-50

The Legend of Pope Joan LC 123: 1-88
overviews and general studies, 3-87

The Levellers LC 51: 200-312
overviews and general studies, 201-29
principal figures, 230-86
religion, political philosophy, and pamphleteering, 287-311

The Lilith Legend in Modern Literature TCLC 170: 256-319
overviews, 257-67
historical and literary background, 267-89
the Lilith legend in twentieth-century literature, 289-319

Literary Criticism in the Nineteenth Century, American NCLC 128: 1-103
overviews and general studies, 2-44
the trancendentalists, 44-65
"young America," 65-71
James Russell Lowell, 71-9
Edgar Allan Poe, 79-97
Walt Whitman, 97-102

Literary Expressionism TCLC 142: 90-185
overviews and general studies, 91-138
themes in literary expressionism, 138-61
expressionism in Germany, 161-84

The Literary Marketplace Nineteenth-Century NCLC 128: 194-368
overviews and general studies, 197-228
British literary marketplace, 228-66
French literary marketplace, 266-82
American literary marketplace, 282-323
Women in the literary marketplace, 323-67

Literary Prizes TCLC 122: 130-203
overviews and general studies, 131-34
the Nobel Prize in Literature, 135-83
the Pulitzer Prize, 183-203

Literature and Millenial Lists CLC 119: 431-67
The Modern Library list, 433
The Waterstone list, 438-439

Literature in Response to the September 11 Attacks CLC 174: 1-46
Major works about September 11, 2001, 2-22
Critical, artistic, and journalistic responses, 22-45

Literature of the American Cowboy NCLC 96: 1-60
overview, 3-20
cowboy fiction, 20-36
cowboy poetry and songs, 36-59

Literature of the California Gold Rush NCLC 92: 320-85
overviews and general studies, 322-24
early California Gold Rush fiction, 324-44
Gold Rush folklore and legend, 344-51
the rise of Western local color, 351-60
social relations and social change, 360-385

Literature of the Counter-Reformation LC 109: 213-56
overviews and general studies, 214-33
influential figures, 233-56

The Living Theatre DC 16: 154-214

The Lost Generation See Writers of the Lost Generation

Luddism in Nineteenth-Century Literature NCLC 140: 280-365
overviews, 281-322
the literary response, 322-65

Lynching in Nineteenth-Century Literature NCLC 148: 162-247
lynching in literature and music, 163-92
Ida B. Wells-Barnett and the anti-lynching movement, 192-221
resistance to lynching in society and the press, 221-46

Madness in Nineteenth-Century Literature NCLC 76: 142-284
overview, 143-54
autobiography, 154-68
poetry, 168-215
fiction, 215-83

Madness in Twentieth-Century Literature TCLC 50: 160-225
overviews and general studies, 161-71
madness and the creative process, 171-86
suicide, 186-91
madness in American literature, 191-207
madness in German literature, 207-13
madness and feminist artists, 213-24

Magic Realism TCLC 110: 80-327
overviews and general studies, 81-94
magic realism in African literature, 95-110
magic realism in American literature, 110-32
magic realism in Canadian literature, 132-46
magic realism in European literature, 146-66
magic realism in Asian literature, 166-79
magic realism in Latin-American literature, 179-223
magic realism in Israeli literature and the novels of Salman Rushdie, 223-38
magic realism in literature written by women, 239-326

The Martin Marprelate Tracts LC 101: 165-240
criticism, 166-240

Marxist Criticism TCLC 134: 127-57
overviews and general studies, 128-67
Marxist interpretations, 167-209
cultural and literary Marxist theory, 209-49
Marxism and feminist critical theory, 250-56

The Masque LC 63: 124-265
development of the masque, 125-62
sources and structure, 162-220
race and gender in the masque, 221-64

Medical Writing LC 55: 93-195
colonial America, 94-110
enlightenment, 110-24
medieval writing, 124-40
sexuality, 140-83
vernacular, 185-95

Memoirs of Trauma CLC 109: 419-466
overview, 420
criticism, 429

Metafiction TCLC 130: 43-228
overviews and general studies, 44-85
Spanish metafiction, 85-117
studies of metafictional authors and works, 118-228

Metaphysical Poets LC 24: 356-439
early definitions, 358-67
surveys and overviews, 367-92
cultural and social influences, 392-406
stylistic and thematic variations, 407-38

Missionaries in the Nineteenth-Century, Literature of NCLC 112: 299-392
history and development, 300-16
uses of ethnography, 316-31
sociopolitical concerns, 331-82
David Livingstone, 382-91

The Modern Essay TCLC 58: 199-273
overview, 200-7
the essay in the early twentieth century, 207-19
characteristics of the modern essay, 219-32
modern essayists, 232-45
the essay as a literary genre, 245-73

Modern French Literature TCLC 122: 205-359
overviews and general studies, 207-43
French theater, 243-77
gender issues and French women writers, 277-315
ideology and politics, 315-24
modern French poetry, 324-41
resistance literature, 341-58

Modern Irish Literature TCLC 102: 125-321
overview, 129-44
dramas, 144-70
fiction, 170-247
poetry, 247-321

Modern Japanese Literature TCLC 66: 284-389
poetry, 285-305
drama, 305-29
fiction, 329-61
western influences, 361-87

Modernism TCLC 70: 165-275
definitions, 166-84
Modernism and earlier influences, 184-200
stylistic and thematic traits, 200-29
poetry and drama, 229-42
redefining Modernism, 242-75

Monasticism and Literature CMLC 74: 88-294
major figures, 89-132
secular influences, 132-54
monastic principles and literary practices, 154-232
women and monasticism, 232-93

Muckraking Movement in American Journalism TCLC 34: 161-242
development, principles, and major figures, 162-70
publications, 170-9
social and political ideas, 179-86
targets, 186-208
fiction, 208-19
decline, 219-29
impact and accomplishments, 229-40

Multiculturalism CLC 189: 167-254
overviews and general studies, 168-93
the effects of multiculturalism on global literature, 193-213
multicultural themes in specific contemporary works, 213-53

Multiculturalism in Literature and Education CLC 70: 361-413

Music and Modern Literature TCLC 62: 182-329
overviews and general studies, 182-211
musical form/literary form, 211-32
music in literature, 232-50
the influence of music on literature, 250-73
literature and popular music, 273-303
jazz and poetry, 303-28

Mystery Story See Crime-Mystery-Detective Stories

Native American Literature CLC 76: 440-76

Natural School, Russian NCLC 24: 205-40
history and characteristics, 205-25
contemporary criticism, 225-40

Naturalism NCLC 36: 285-382
definitions and theories, 286-305
critical debates on Naturalism, 305-16
Naturalism in theater, 316-32
European Naturalism, 332-61
American Naturalism, 361-72
the legacy of Naturalism, 372-81

Negritude TCLC 50: 226-361
origins and evolution, 227-56
definitions, 256-91
Negritude in literature, 291-343
Negritude reconsidered, 343-58

Negritude TCLC 158: 196-280
overviews and general studies, 197-208
major figures, 208-25
Negritude and humanism, 225-29
poetry of Negritude, 229-47
politics of Negritude, 247-68
the Negritude debate, 268-79

New Criticism TCLC 34: 243-318
development and ideas, 244-70
debate and defense, 270-99
influence and legacy, 299-315

New Criticism TCLC 146: 1-108
overviews and general studies, 3-19
defining New Criticism, 19-28
place in history, 28-51
poetry and New Criticism, 51-78
major authors, 78-108

The New Humanists TCLC 162: 260-341
overviews, 261-92
major figures, 292-310
New Humanism in education and literature, 310-41

New South, Literature of the NCLC 116: 122-240
overviews, 124-66
the novel in the New South, 166-209
myth of the Old South in the New, 209-39

The New Woman in Nineteenth-Century Literature NCLC 156: 134-281
overview, 136-39
historical and social context, 139-57
contemporary descriptions of the new woman, 157-65
the new woman and popular fiction, 165-86
the new woman and the decadents, 187-207
the new woman and the theater, 207-48
Henry James, Bram Stoker, and Others, 248-80

The New World in Renaissance Literature LC 31: 1-51
overview, 1-18
utopia vs. terror, 18-31
explorers and Native Americans, 31-51

New York Intellectuals and *Partisan Review* TCLC 30: 117-98
development and major figures, 118-28
influence of Judaism, 128-39
Partisan Review, 139-57
literary philosophy and practice, 157-75
political philosophy, 175-87
achievement and significance, 187-97

The New Yorker TCLC 58: 274-357
overviews and general studies, 274-95
major figures, 295-304
New Yorker style, 304-33
fiction, journalism, and humor at *The New Yorker,* 333-48
the new *New Yorker,* 348-56

Newgate Novel NCLC 24: 166-204
development of Newgate literature, 166-73
Newgate Calendar, 173-7
Newgate fiction, 177-95
Newgate drama, 195-204

New Zealand Literature TCLC 134: 258-368
overviews and general studies, 260-300
Maori literature, 300-22
New Zealand drama, 322-32
New Zealand fiction, 332-51
New Zealand poetry, 351-67

Nigerian Literature of the Twentieth Century TCLC 30: 199-265
surveys of, 199-227
English language and African life, 227-45
politics and the Nigerian writer, 245-54
Nigerian writers and society, 255-62

Nihilism and Literature TCLC 110: 328-93
overviews and general studies, 328-44
European and Russian nihilism, 344-73
nihilism in the works of Albert Camus, Franz Kafka, and John Barth, 373-92

Nineteenth-Century Captivity Narratives NCLC 80:131-218
overview, 132-37
the political significance of captivity narratives, 137-67
images of gender, 167-96
moral instruction, 197-217

Nineteenth-Century Euro-American Literary Representations of Native Americans NCLC 104: 132-264
overviews and general studies, 134-53
Native American history, 153-72
the Indians of the Northeast, 172-93
the Indians of the Southeast, 193-212
the Indians of the West, 212-27
Indian-hater fiction, 227-43
the Indian as exhibit, 243-63

Nineteenth-Century Native American Autobiography NCLC 64: 262-389
overview, 263-8
problems of authorship, 268-81
the evolution of Native American autobiography, 281-304
political issues, 304-15
gender and autobiography, 316-62
autobiographical works during the turn of the century, 362-88

Nineteenth-Century Pornography NCLC 144: 108-202
nineteenth-century pornographers, 110-64
pornography and literature, 164-91
pornography and censorship, 191-201

Nineteenth-Century Western Literature in Japan NCLC 156: 282-352
overviews, 283-305
European literature in Japan, 305-28
American literature in Japan, 328-52

Noh Drama LC 103: 189-270
overviews, 190-94
origins and development, 194-214
structure, 214-28
types of plays, 228-45
masks in Noh drama, 245-57
Noh drama and the audience, 257-69

Norse Mythology CMLC 26: 321-85
history and mythological tradition, 322-44
Eddic poetry, 344-74
Norse mythology and other traditions, 374-85

Northern Humanism LC 16: 281-356
 background, 282-305
 precursor of the Reformation, 305-14
 the Brethren of the Common Life, the Devotio Moderna, and education, 314-40
 the impact of printing, 340-56

The Novel of Manners NCLC 56: 342-96
 social and political order, 343-53
 domestic order, 353-73
 depictions of gender, 373-83
 the American novel of manners, 383-95

Novels of the Ming and Early Ch'ing Dynasties LC 76: 213-356
 overviews and historical development, 214-45
 major works—overview, 245-85
 genre studies, 285-325
 cultural and social themes, 325-55

Nuclear Literature: Writings and Criticism in the Nuclear Age TCLC 46: 288-390
 overviews and general studies, 290-301
 fiction, 301-35
 poetry, 335-8
 nuclear war in Russo-Japanese literature, 338-55
 nuclear war and women writers, 355-67
 the nuclear referent and literary criticism, 367-88

Occultism in Modern Literature TCLC 50: 362-406
 influence of occultism on literature, 363-72
 occultism, literature, and society, 372-87
 fiction, 387-96
 drama, 396-405

Opium and the Nineteenth-Century Literary Imagination NCLC 20:250-301
 original sources, 250-62
 historical background, 262-71
 and literary society, 271-9
 and literary creativity, 279-300

Orientalism NCLC 96: 149-364
 overviews and general studies, 150-98
 Orientalism and imperialism, 198-229
 Orientalism and gender, 229-59
 Orientalism and the nineteenth-century novel, 259-321
 Orientalism in nineteenth-century poetry, 321-63

The Oxford Movement NCLC 72: 1-197
 overviews and general studies, 2-24
 background, 24-59
 and education, 59-69
 religious responses, 69-128
 literary aspects, 128-178
 political implications, 178-196

The Parnassian Movement NCLC 72: 198-241
 overviews and general studies, 199-231
 and epic form, 231-38
 and positivism, 238-41

Pastoral Literature of the English Renaissance LC 59: 171-282
 overviews and general studies, 172-214
 principal figures of the Elizabethan period, 214-33
 principal figures of the later Renaissance, 233-50
 pastoral drama, 250-81

Periodicals, Nineteenth-Century American NCLC 132: 199-374
 overviews, chronology, and development, 200-41
 literary periodicals, 241-83
 regional periodicals, 283-317
 women's magazines and gender issues, 317-47
 minority periodicals, 347-72

Periodicals, Nineteenth-Century British NCLC 24: 100-65
 overviews and general studies, 100-30
 in the Romantic Age, 130-41
 in the Victorian era, 142-54
 and the reviewer, 154-64

Picaresque Literature of the Sixteenth and Seventeenth Centuries LC 78: 223-355
 context and development, 224-71
 genre, 271-98
 the picaro, 299-326
 the picara, 326-53

Plath, Sylvia, and the Nature of Biography CLC 86: 433-62
 the nature of biography, 433-52
 reviews of *The Silent Woman,* 452-61

Political Theory from the 15th to the 18th Century LC 36: 1-55
 overview, 1-26
 natural law, 26-42
 empiricism, 42-55

Polish Romanticism NCLC 52: 305-71
 overviews and general studies, 306-26
 major figures, 326-40
 Polish Romantic drama, 340-62
 influences, 362-71

Politics and Literature TCLC 94: 138-61
 overviews and general studies, 139-96
 Europe, 196-226
 Latin America, 226-48
 Africa and the Caribbean, 248-60

Popular Literature TCLC 70: 279-382
 overviews and general studies, 280-324
 "formula" fiction, 324-336
 readers of popular literature, 336-351
 evolution of popular literature, 351-382

The Portrayal of Jews in Nineteenth-Century English Literature NCLC 72: 242-368
 overviews and general studies, 244-77
 Anglo-Jewish novels, 277-303
 depictions by non-Jewish writers, 303-44
 Hebraism versus Hellenism, 344-67

The Portrayal of Mormonism NCLC 96: 61-148
 overview, 63-72
 early Mormon literature, 72-100
 Mormon periodicals and journals, 100-10
 women writers, 110-22
 Mormonism and nineteenth-century literature, 122-42
 Mormon poetry, 142-47

Post-apartheid Literature CLC 187: 284-382
 overviews and general studies, 286-318
 the post-apartheid novel, 318-65
 post-apartheid drama, 365-81

Postcolonial African Literature TCLC 146: 110-239
 overviews and general studies, 111-45
 ideology and theory, 145-62
 postcolonial testimonial literature, 162-99
 major authors, 199-239

Postcolonialism TCLC 114: 134-239
 overviews and general studies, 135-153
 African postcolonial writing, 153-72
 Asian/Pacific literature, 172-78
 postcolonial literary theory, 178-213
 postcolonial women's writing, 213-38

Postmodernism TCLC 90:125-307
 overview, 126-166
 criticism, 166-224
 fiction, 224-282
 poetry, 282-300
 drama, 300-307

Pragmatism in Nineteenth-Century Literature NCLC 168: 85-209
 overviews, 86-133

 pragmatism and literature, 133-52
 Charles Sanders Peirce, 152-65
 William James, 165-208

Pre-Raphaelite Movement NCLC 20: 302-401
 overview, 302-4
 genesis, 304-12
 Germ and *Oxford and Cambridge Magazine,* 312-20
 Robert Buchanan and the "Fleshly School of Poetry," 320-31
 satires and parodies, 331-4
 surveys, 334-51
 aesthetics, 351-75
 sister arts of poetry and painting, 375-94
 influence, 394-9

Pre-romanticism LC 40: 1-56
 overviews and general studies, 2-14
 defining the period, 14-23
 new directions in poetry and prose, 23-45
 the focus on the self, 45-56

The Presentation of Literature in the Nineteenth Century NCLC 160: 159-226
 book design, 160-71
 gift books, 172-91
 serial novels, 191-214
 dime novels, 214-226

Pre-Socratic Philosophy CMLC 22: 1-56
 overviews and general studies, 3-24
 the Ionians and the Pythagoreans, 25-35
 Heraclitus, the Eleatics, and the Atomists, 36-47
 the Sophists, 47-55

The Prison in Nineteenth-Century Literature NCLC 116: 241-357
 overview, 242-60
 romantic prison, 260-78
 domestic prison, 278-316
 America as prison, 316-24
 physical prisons and prison authors, 324-56

Protestant Hagiography and Martyrology LC 84: 106-217
 overview, 106-37
 John Foxe's *Book of Martyrs,* 137-97
 martyrology and the feminine perspective, 198-216

Protestant Reformation, Literature of the LC 37: 1-83
 overviews and general studies, 1-49
 humanism and scholasticism, 49-69
 the reformation and literature, 69-82

Psychoanalysis and Literature TCLC 38: 227-338
 overviews and general studies, 227-46
 Freud on literature, 246-51
 psychoanalytic views of the literary process, 251-61
 psychoanalytic theories of response to literature, 261-88
 psychoanalysis and literary criticism, 288-312
 psychoanalysis as literature/literature as psychoanalysis, 313-34

The Quarrel between the Ancients and the Moderns LC 63: 266-381
 overviews and general studies, 267-301
 Renaissance origins, 301-32
 Quarrel between the Ancients and the Moderns in France, 332-58
 Battle of the Books in England, 358-80

Racism in Literature TCLC 138: 257-373
 overviews and general studies, 257-326
 racism and literature by and about African Americans, 292-326
 theme of racism in literature, 326-773

Rap Music CLC 76: 477-50

Reader-Response Criticism TCLC 146: 240-357

overviews and general studies, 241-88
critical approaches to reader response, 288-342
reader-response interpretation, 342-57

Realism in Short Fiction SSC 63: 128-57

overviews and general studies, 129-37
realist short fiction in France, 137-62
realist short fiction in Russia, 162-215
realist short fiction in England, 215-31
realist short fiction in the United States, 231-56

Regionalism and Local Color in Short Fiction SSC 65: 160-289

overviews and general studies, 163-205
regionalism/local color fiction of the west, 205-42
regionalism/local color fiction of the midwest, 242-57
regionalism/local color fiction of the south, 257-88

Renaissance Natural Philosophy LC 27: 201-87

cosmology, 201-28
astrology, 228-54
magic, 254-86

Representations of Africa in Nineteenth-Century Literature NCLC 148: 248-351

overview, 251-66
Northeast and Central Africa, 266-76
South Africa, 276-301
West Africa, 301-49

Representations of the Devil in Nineteenth-Century Literature NCLC 100: 89-223

overviews and general studies, 90-115
the Devil in American fiction, 116-43
English Romanticism: the satanic school, 143-89
Luciferian discourse in European literature, 189-222

Restoration Drama LC 21: 184-275

general overviews and general studies, 185-230
Jeremy Collier stage controversy, 230-9
other critical interpretations, 240-75

Revenge Tragedy LC 71: 113-242

overviews and general studies, 113-51
Elizabethan attitudes toward revenge, 151-88
the morality of revenge, 188-216
reminders and remembrance, 217-41

Revising the Literary Canon CLC 81: 465-509

Revising the Literary Canon TCLC 114: 240-84

overviews and general studies, 241-85
canon change in American literature, 285-339
gender and the literary canon, 339-59
minority and third-world literature and the canon, 359-84

Revolutionary Astronomers LC 51: 314-65

overviews and general studies, 316-25
principal figures, 325-51
Revolutionary astronomical models, 352-64

Robin Hood, Legend of LC 19: 205-58

origins and development of the Robin Hood legend, 206-20
representations of Robin Hood, 220-44
Robin Hood as hero, 244-56

Romance Fiction, Contemporary CLC 206: 178-271

overviews, 180-93
literary conventions, 193-215
opposing viewpoints, 215-20

reader response to Romance literature, 220-37
Romance literature in the world, 237-70

Romantic Literary Criticism NCLC 144: 203-357

background and overviews, 205-30
literary reviews, 230-38
the German Romantics, 238-81
Wordsworth and Coleridge, 281-326
variations on Romantic critical theory, 326-56

Rushdie, Salman, *Satanic Verses* Controversy CLC 55: 214-63; 59:404-56

Russian Nihilism NCLC 28: 403-47

definitions and overviews, 404-17
women and Nihilism, 417-27
literature as reform: the Civic Critics, 427-33
Nihilism and the Russian novel: Turgenev and Dostoevsky, 433-47

Russian Thaw TCLC 26: 189-247

literary history of the period, 190-206
theoretical debate of socialist realism, 206-11
Novy Mir, 211-7
Literary Moscow, 217-24
Pasternak, *Zhivago*, and the Nobel prize, 224-7
poetry of liberation, 228-31
Brodsky trial and the end of the Thaw, 231-6
achievement and influence, 236-46

Salem Witch Trials LC 38: 1-145

overviews and general studies, 2-30
historical background, 30-65
judicial background, 65-78
the search for causes, 78-115
the role of women in the trials, 115-44

Salinger, J. D., Controversy Surrounding *In Search of J. D. Salinger* CLC 55: 325-44

Samizdat Literature TCLC 150: 261-342

overviews and general studies, 262-64
history and development, 264-309
politics and Samizdat, 309-22
voices of Samizdat, 322-42

Sanitation Reform, Nineteenth-Century NCLC 124: 165-257

overviews and general studies, 166
primary texts, 186-89
social context, 189-221
public health in literature, 221-56

Science and Modern Literature TCLC 90: 308-419

overviews and general studies, 295-333
fiction, 333-95
poetry, 395-405
drama, 405-19

Science in Nineteenth-Century Literature NCLC 100: 224-366

overviews and general studies, 225-65
major figures, 265-336
sociopolitical concerns, 336-65

Science Fiction, Nineteenth-Century NCLC 24: 241-306

background, 242-50
definitions of the genre, 251-56
representative works and writers, 256-75
themes and conventions, 276-305

Scottish Chaucerians LC 20: 363-412

Scottish Poetry, Eighteenth-Century LC 29: 95-167

overviews and general studies, 96-114
the Scottish Augustans, 114-28
the Scots Vernacular Revival, 132-63
Scottish poetry after Burns, 163-66

The Sea in Literature TCLC 82: 72-191

drama, 73-9
poetry, 79-119
fiction, 119-91

The Sea in Nineteenth-Century English and American Literature NCLC 104: 265-362

overviews and general studies, 267-306
major figures in American sea fiction—Cooper and Melville, 306-29
American sea poetry and short stories, 329-45
English sea literature, 345-61

The Sensation Novel NCLC 80: 219-330

overviews and general studies, 221-46
principal figures, 246-62
nineteenth-century reaction, 262-91
feminist criticism, 291-329

The Sentimental Novel NCLC 60: 146-245

overviews and general studies, 147-58
the politics of domestic fiction, 158-79
a literature of resistance and repression, 179-212
the reception of sentimental fiction, 213-44

September 11 Attacks See Literature in Response to the September 11 Attacks

Sex and Literature TCLC 82: 192-434

overviews and general studies, 193-216
drama, 216-63
poetry, 263-87
fiction, 287-431

Sherlock Holmes Centenary TCLC 26: 248-310

Doyle's life and the composition of the Holmes stories, 248-59
life and character of Holmes, 259-78
method, 278-79
Holmes and the Victorian world, 279-92
Sherlockian scholarship, 292-301
Doyle and the development of the detective story, 301-07
Holmes's continuing popularity, 307-09

Short Science Fiction, Golden Age of, 1938-1950 SSC 73: 1-145

overviews and general studies, 3-48
publishing history of Golden Age Short Science Fiction, 48-65
major Golden Age Short Science Fiction authors and editors
Isaac Asimov, 65-77
Ray Bradbury, 77-92
John W. Campbell, 92-106
Arthur C. Clarke, 106-15
Robert A. Heinlein, 115-29
Damon Knight, 129-40
Frederik Pohl, 141-43

Short-Short Fiction SSC 61: 311-36

overviews and general studies, 312-19
major short-short fiction writers, 319-35

The Silver Fork Novel NCLC 88: 58-140

criticism, 59-139

Slave Narratives, American NCLC 20: 1-91

background, 2-9
overviews and general studies, 9-24
contemporary responses, 24-7
language, theme, and technique, 27-70
historical authenticity, 70-5
antecedents, 75-83
role in development of Black American literature, 83-8

The Slave Trade in British and American Literature LC 59: 283-369

overviews and general studies, 284-91
depictions by white writers, 291-331
depictions by former slaves, 331-67

Social Conduct Literature LC 55: 196-298

overviews and general studies, 196-223
prescriptive ideology in other literary forms, 223-38

role of the press, 238-63
impact of conduct literature, 263-87
conduct literature and the perception of
women, 287-96
women writing for women, 296-98

**Social Protest Literature of Victorian En-
gland** NCLC 160: 227-359
overviews: protest in Victorian literature,
229-62
woman question, 262-304
condition-of-England novel, 304-58

**Social Protest Literature Outside England,
Nineteenth-Century** NCLC 124: 258-350
overviews and general studies, 259-72
oppression revealed, 272-306
literature to incite or prevent reform,
306-50

Socialism NCLC 88: 141-237
origins, 142-54
French socialism, 154-83
Anglo-American socialism, 183-205
Socialist-Feminism, 205-36

Southern Gothic Literature TCLC 142: 186-
270
overviews and general studies, 187-97
major authors in southern Gothic literature,
197-230
structure and technique in southern Gothic
literature, 230-50
themes in southern Gothic literature, 250-70

Southern Literature, Contemporary CLC
167: 1-132
criticism, 2-131

Southern Literature of the Reconstruction
NCLC 108: 289-369
overview, 290-91
reconstruction literature: the consequences
of war, 291-321
old south to new: continuities in southern
culture, 321-68

Southwestern Humor SSC 81: 105-248
overviews, 106-83
Mark Twain, 183-97
George Washington Harris, 197-208
other major figures, 208-46

Spanish Civil War Literature TCLC 26:
311-85
topics in, 312-33
British and American literature, 333-59
French literature, 359-62
Spanish literature, 362-73
German literature, 373-75
political idealism and war literature, 375-83

Spanish Golden Age Literature LC 23: 262-
332
overviews and general studies, 263-81
verse drama, 281-304
prose fiction, 304-19
lyric poetry, 319-31

Sparta in Literature CMLC 70: 145-271
overviews, 147-61
Spartan poetry, 161-72
the Spartan myth, 172-200
historical background, 200-27
Spartan society and culture, 227-69

Spasmodic School of Poetry NCLC 24: 307-52
history and major figures, 307-21
the Spasmodics on poetry, 321-7
Firmilian and critical disfavor, 327-39
theme and technique, 339-47
influence, 347-51

Sports in Literature TCLC 86: 294-445
overviews and general studies, 295-324
major writers and works, 324-402
sports, literature, and social issues, 402-45

Steinbeck, John, Fiftieth Anniversary of *The
Grapes of Wrath* CLC 59: 311-54

The Stream-of-Consciousness Novel TCLC
178: 110-95
style and development 111-43
representative authors 134-95

Sturm und Drang NCLC 40: 196-276
definitions, 197-238
poetry and poetics, 238-58
drama, 258-75

**Supernatural Fiction in the Nineteenth Cen-
tury** NCLC 32: 207-87
major figures and influences, 208-35
the Victorian ghost story, 236-54
the influence of science and occultism,
254-66
supernatural fiction and society, 266-86

Supernatural Fiction, Modern TCLC 30: 59-
116
evolution and varieties, 60-74
"decline" of the ghost story, 74-86
as a literary genre, 86-92
technique, 92-101
nature and appeal, 101-15

Surrealism TCLC 30: 334-406
history and formative influences, 335-43
manifestos, 343-54
philosophic, aesthetic, and political prin-
ciples, 354-75
poetry, 375-81
novel, 381-6
drama, 386-92
film, 392-8
painting and sculpture, 398-403
achievement, 403-5

Surrealism in Children's Literature CLR
103: 127-200
overviews and general studies, 130-52
critical analysis of surrealist children's au-
thors and works, 152-99

Sylvia Beach and Company TCLC 158: 281-
370
overviews and general studies, 282-97
Shakespeare and Company, 297-314
the business of publishing, 315-40
Sylvia Beach and James Joyce, 341-70

Symbolism, Russian TCLC 30: 266-333
doctrines and major figures, 267-92
theories, 293-8
and French Symbolism, 298-310
themes in poetry, 310-4
theater, 314-20
and the fine arts, 320-32

Symbolist Movement, French NCLC 20: 169-
249
background and characteristics, 170-86
principles, 186-91
attacked and defended, 191-7
influences and predecessors, 197-211
and Decadence, 211-6
theater, 216-26
prose, 226-33
decline and influence, 233-47

Television and Literature TCLC 78: 283-426
television and literacy, 283-98
reading vs. watching, 298-341
adaptations, 341-62
literary genres and television, 362-90
television genres and literature, 390-410
children's literature/children's television,
410-25

Theater of the Absurd TCLC 38: 339-415
"The Theater of the Absurd," 340-7
major plays and playwrights, 347-58
and the concept of the absurd, 358-86
theatrical techniques, 386-94

predecessors of, 394-402
influence of, 402-13

**Tin Pan Alley See American Popular Song,
Golden Age of**

Tobacco Culture LC 55: 299-366
social and economic attitudes toward to-
bacco, 299-344
tobacco trade between the old world and
the new world, 344-55
tobacco smuggling in Great Britain, 355-66

Transcendentalism, American NCLC 24: 1-99
overviews and general studies, 3-23
contemporary documents, 23-41
theological aspects of, 42-52
and social issues, 52-74
literature of, 74-96

**Travel Narratives in Contemporary Litera-
ture** CLC 204: 260-351
overviews, 261-76
major authors, 276-311
modern travel writing, 311-31
women writers and travel, 331-51

Travel Writing in the Nineteenth Century
NCLC 44: 274-392
the European grand tour, 275-303
the Orient, 303-47
North America, 347-91
NCLC 168: 210-347
overviews, 212-43
women's travel writing, 243-311
other notable travel writers and their works,
312-47

Travel Writing in the Twentieth Century
TCLC 30: 407-56
conventions and traditions, 407-27
and fiction writing, 427-43
comparative essays on travel writers,
443-54

Treatment of Death in Children's Literature
CLR 101: 152-201
overviews and general studies, 155-80
analytical and bibliographical reviews of
death in children's literature, 180-97
death of animals in children's literature,
197-200

Tristan and Isolde Legend CMLC 42: 311-
404

Troubadours CMLC 66: 244-383
overviews, 245-91
politics, economics, history, and the trouba-
dours, 291-344
troubadours and women, 344-82

True-Crime Literature CLC 99: 333-433
history and analysis, 334-407
reviews of true-crime publications, 407-23
writing instruction, 424-29
author profiles, 429-33

Twentieth-Century Danish Literature TCLC
142: 271-344
major works, 272-84
major authors, 284-344

Ulysses **and the Process of Textual Recon-
struction** TCLC 26:386-416
evaluations of the new *Ulysses,* 386-94
editorial principles and procedures, 394-
401
theoretical issues, 401-16

**Unconventional Family in Children's Litera-
ture** CLR 102: 146-213
overviews and general studies, 149-79
analytical and bibliographical reviews,
179-97
types of unconventional families: foster,
adopted, homosexual, 197-212

Urban Life in Nineteenth-Century Literature NCLC 172: 249-334
overviews, 250-77
urban poetry, 277-304
urban life and individual identity, 304-34

Utilitarianism NCLC 84: 272-340
J. S. Mill's Utilitarianism: liberty, equality, justice, 273-313
Jeremy Bentham's Utilitarianism: the science of happiness, 313-39

Utopianism NCLC 88: 238-346
overviews: Utopian literature, 239-59
Utopianism in American literature, 259-99
Utopianism in British literature, 299-311
Utopianism and Feminism, 311-45

Utopian Literature, Nineteenth-Century NCLC 24: 353-473
definitions, 354-74
overviews and general studies, 374-88
theory, 388-408
communities, 409-26
fiction, 426-53
women and fiction, 454-71

Utopian Literature, Renaissance LC 32: 1-63
overviews and general studies, 2-25
classical background, 25-33
utopia and the social contract, 33-9
origins in mythology, 39-48
utopia and the Renaissance country house, 48-52
influence of millenarianism, 52-62

Vampire in Literature TCLC 46: 391-454
origins and evolution, 392-412
social and psychological perspectives, 413-44
vampire fiction and science fiction, 445-53

Vernacular Bibles LC 67: 214-388
overviews and general studies, 215-59
the English Bible, 259-355
the German Bible, 355-88

Victorian Autobiography NCLC 40: 277-363
development and major characteristics, 278-88
themes and techniques, 289-313
the autobiographical tendency in Victorian prose and poetry, 313-47
Victorian women's autobiographies, 347-62
NCLC 152: 230-365
overviews and general studies, 232-61
autobiography and the self, 261-93
autobiography and gender, 293-307
autobiography and class, 307-36
autobiography and fiction, 336-64

Victorian Critical Theory NCLC 136: 236-379
overviews and general studies, 237-86
Matthew Arnold, 286-324
Walter Pater and aestheticism, 324-36
other Victorian critics, 336-78

Victorian Fantasy Literature NCLC 60: 246-384
overviews and general studies, 247-91
major figures, 292-366
women in Victorian fantasy literature, 366-83

Victorian Hellenism NCLC 68: 251-376
overviews and general studies, 252-78
the meanings of Hellenism, 278-335
the literary influence, 335-75

Victorian Illustrated Fiction NCLC 120: 247-356
overviews and development, 128-76
technical and material aspects of book illustration, 276-84
Charles Dickens and his illustrators, 284-320
William Makepeace Thackeray, 320-31
George Eliot and Frederic Leighton, 331-51
Lewis Carroll and John Tenniel, 351-56

Victorian Novel NCLC 32: 288-454
development and major characteristics, 290-310
themes and techniques, 310-58
social criticism in the Victorian novel, 359-97
urban and rural life in the Victorian novel, 397-406
women in the Victorian novel, 406-25
Mudie's Circulating Library, 425-34
the late-Victorian novel, 434-51

Vietnamese Literature TCLC 102: 322-386

Vietnam War in Literature and Film CLC 91: 383-437
overview, 384-8
prose, 388-412
film and drama, 412-24
poetry, 424-35

The Vietnam War in Short Fiction SSC 79: 83-177
overviews and general studies, 84-93
women authors of Vietnam War short fiction, 93-116
Robert Olen Butler: *A Good Scent from a Strange Mountain* (1992), 116-31
Barry Hannah: *Airships* (1978), 131-50
Tim O'Brien: *The Things They Carried* (1990), 150-65
Tobias Wolff: *Back in the World* (1985), 165-69
other authors and works, 169-76

Violence in Literature TCLC 98: 235-358
overviews and general studies, 236-74
violence in the works of modern authors, 274-358

Vorticism TCLC 62: 330-426
Wyndham Lewis and Vorticism, 330-8
characteristics and principles of Vorticism, 338-65
Lewis and Pound, 365-82
Vorticist writing, 382-416
Vorticist painting, 416-26

The Well-Made Play NCLC 80: 331-370
overviews and general studies, 332-45
Scribe's style, 345-56
the influence of the well-made play, 356-69

Women's Autobiography, Nineteenth Century NCLC 76: 285-368
overviews and general studies, 287-300
autobiographies concerned with religious and political issues, 300-15
autobiographies by women of color, 315-38

autobiographies by women pioneers, 338-51
autobiographies by women of letters, 351-68

Women's Diaries, Nineteenth-Century NCLC 48: 308-54
overview, 308-13
diary as history, 314-25
sociology of diaries, 325-34
diaries as psychological scholarship, 334-43
diary as autobiography, 343-8
diary as literature, 348-53

Women in Modern Literature TCLC 94: 262-425
overviews and general studies, 263-86
American literature, 286-304
other national literatures, 304-33
fiction, 333-94
poetry, 394-407
drama, 407-24

Women Writers, Seventeenth-Century LC 30: 2-58
overview, 2-15
women and education, 15-9
women and autobiography, 19-31
women's diaries, 31-9
early feminists, 39-58

World War I Literature TCLC 34: 392-486
overview, 393-403
English, 403-27
German, 427-50
American, 450-66
French, 466-74
and modern history, 474-82

World War I Short Fiction SSC 71: 187-347
overviews and general studies, 187-206
female short fiction writers of World War I, 206-36
Central Powers
Czechoslovakian writers of short fiction, 236-44
German writers of short fiction, 244-61
Entente/Allied Alliance
Australian writers of short fiction, 261-73
English writers of short fiction, 273-305
French writers of short fiction, 305-11
Associated Power: American writers of short fiction, 311-46

Writers of the Lost Generation TCLC 178: 196-369
overviews 197-225
major figures 225-98
women of the Lost Generation 298-341
expatriate writers and Paris 341-68

Yellow Journalism NCLC 36: 383-456
overviews and general studies, 384-96
major figures, 396-413

Yiddish Literature TCLC 130: 229-364
overviews and general studies, 230-54
major authors, 254-305
Yiddish literature in America, 305-34
Yiddish and Judaism, 334-64

Young Playwrights Festival
1988 CLC 55: 376-81
1989 CLC 59: 398-403
1990 CLC 65: 444-8

Topic Index

NCLC Cumulative Nationality Index

AMERICAN

Adams, John **106**
Alcott, Amos Bronson **1, 167**
Alcott, Louisa May **6, 58, 83**
Alger, Horatio Jr. **8, 83**
Allston, Washington **2**
Apess, William **73**
Audubon, John James **47**
Barlow, Joel **23**
Bartram, William **145**
Beecher, Catharine Esther **30**
Bellamy, Edward **4, 86, 147**
Bird, Robert Montgomery **1**
Boker, George Henry **125**
Boyesen, Hjalmar Hjorth **135**
Brackenridge, Hugh Henry **7**
Brentano, Clemens (Maria) **1**
Brown, Charles Brockden **22, 74, 122**
Brown, William Wells **2, 89**
Brownson, Orestes Augustus **50**
Bryant, William Cullen **6, 46**
Calhoun, John Caldwell **15**
Channing, William Ellery **17**
Child, Lydia Maria **6, 73**
Chivers, Thomas Holley **49**
Cooke, John Esten **5**
Cooke, Rose Terry **110**
Cooper, James Fenimore **1, 27, 54**
Cooper, Susan Fenimore **129**
Cranch, Christopher Pearse **115**
Crèvecoeur, Michel Guillaume Jean de **105**
Crockett, David **8**
Cummins, Maria Susanna **139**
Dana, Richard Henry Sr. **53**
Delany, Martin Robinson **93**
Dickinson, Emily (Elizabeth) **21, 77, 171**
Douglass, Frederick **7, 55, 141**
Dunlap, William **2**
Dwight, Timothy **13**
Emerson, Mary Moody **66**
Emerson, Ralph Waldo **1, 38, 98**
Field, Eugene **3**
Foster, Hannah Webster **99**
Foster, Stephen Collins **26**
Frederic, Harold **10**
Freneau, Philip Morin **1, 111**
Garrison, William Lloyd **149**
Hale, Sarah Josepha (Buell) **75**
Halleck, Fitz-Greene **47**
Hamilton, Alexander **49**
Hammon, Jupiter **5**
Harris, George Washington **23, 165**
Hawthorne, Nathaniel **2, 10, 17, 23, 39, 79, 95, 158, 171**
Hawthorne, Sophia Peabody **150**
Hayne, Paul Hamilton **94**
Holmes, Oliver Wendell **14, 81**
Horton, George Moses **87**
Irving, Washington **2, 19, 95**
Jackson, Helen Hunt **90**
Jacobs, Harriet A(nn) **67, 162**
James, Henry Sr. **53**

Jefferson, Thomas **11, 103**
Kennedy, John Pendleton **2**
Kirkland, Caroline M. **85**
Lanier, Sidney **6, 118**
Lazarus, Emma **8, 109**
Lincoln, Abraham **18**
Longfellow, Henry Wadsworth **2, 45, 101, 103**
Longstreet, Augustus Baldwin **159**
Lowell, James Russell **2, 90**
Madison, James **126**
Melville, Herman **3, 12, 29, 45, 49, 91, 93, 123, 157**
Mowatt, Anna Cora **74**
Murray, Judith Sargent **63**
Neal, John **161**
Osgood, Frances Sargent **141**
Parkman, Francis Jr. **12**
Parton, Sara Payson Willis **86**
Paulding, James Kirke **2**
Peabody, Elizabeth Palmer **169**
Pinkney, Edward **31**
Poe, Edgar Allan **1, 16, 55, 78, 94, 97, 117**
Prescott, William Hickling **163**
Rowson, Susanna Haswell **5, 69**
Sedgwick, Catharine Maria **19, 98**
Shaw, Henry Wheeler **15**
Sigourney, Lydia Howard (Huntley) **21, 87**
Simms, William Gilmore **3**
Smith, Joseph Jr. **53**
Solomon, Northup **105**
Southworth, Emma Dorothy Eliza Nevitte **26**
Stowe, Harriet (Elizabeth) Beecher **3, 50, 133**
Taylor, Bayard **89**
Tenney, Tabitha Gilman **122**
Thoreau, Henry David **7, 21, 61, 138**
Timrod, Henry **25**
Trumbull, John **30**
Truth, Sojourner **94**
Tyler, Royall **3**
Very, Jones **9**
Warner, Susan (Bogert) **31, 146**
Warren, Mercy Otis **13**
Webster, Noah **30**
Webb, Frank J. **143**
Whitman, Sarah Helen (Power) **19**
Whitman, Walt(er) **4, 31, 81**
Whittier, John Greenleaf **8, 59**
Wilson, Harriet E. Adams **78**
Winnemucca, Sarah **79**

ARGENTINIAN

Echeverria, (Jose) Esteban (Antonino) **18**
Hernández, José **17**
Sarmiento, Domingo Faustino **123**

AUSTRALIAN

Adams, Francis **33**
Clarke, Marcus (Andrew Hislop) **19**
Gordon, Adam Lindsay **21**
Harpur, Charles **114**

Kendall, Henry **12**

AUSTRIAN

Grillparzer, Franz **1, 102**
Lenau, Nikolaus **16**
Nestroy, Johann **42**
Raimund, Ferdinand Jakob **69**
Sacher-Masoch, Leopold von **31**
Stifter, Adalbert **41**

BRAZILIAN

Alencar, Jose de **157**

CANADIAN

Crawford, Isabella Valancy **12, 127**
De Mille, James **123**
Haliburton, Thomas Chandler **15, 149**
Lampman, Archibald **25**
Moodie, Susanna (Strickland) **14, 113**
Richardson, John **55**
Traill, Catharine Parr **31**

CHINESE

Li Ju-chen **137**

COLOMBIAN

Isaacs, Jorge Ricardo **70**
Silva, José Asunción **114**

CUBAN

Avellaneda, Gertrudis Gómez de **111**
Casal, Julián del **131**
Manzano, Juan Francisco **155**
Martí (y Pérez), José (Julian) **63**
Villaverde, Cirilo **121**

CZECH

Macha, Karel Hynek **46**

DANISH

Andersen, Hans Christian **7, 79**
Grundtvig, Nicolai Frederik Severin **1, 158**
Jacobsen, Jens Peter **34**
Kierkegaard, Søren **34, 78, 125**

DUTCH

Multatuli (Eduard Douwes Dekker) **165**

ENGLISH

Ainsworth, William Harrison **13**
Arnold, Matthew **6, 29, 89, 126**
Arnold, Thomas **18**
Austen, Jane **1, 13, 19, 33, 51, 81, 95, 119, 150**
Bagehot, Walter **10**
Barbauld, Anna Laetitia **50**
Barham, Richard Harris **77**
Barnes, William **75**
Beardsley, Aubrey **6**

Beckford, William 16
Beddoes, Thomas Lovell 3, 154
Bentham, Jeremy 38
Blake, William 13, 37, 57, 127
Bloomfield, Robert 145
Borrow, George (Henry) 9
Bowles, William Lisle 103
Brontë, Anne 4, 71, 102
Brontë, Charlotte 3, 8, 33, 58, 105, 155
Brontë, Emily (Jane) 16, 35, 165
Brontë, (Patrick) Branwell 109
Browning, Elizabeth Barrett 1, 16, 61, 66, 170
Browning, Robert 19, 79
Bulwer-Lytton, Edward (George Earle Lytton) 1, 45
Burney, Fanny 12, 54, 107
Burton, Richard F(rancis) 42
Byron, George Gordon (Noel) 2, 12, 109, 149
Carlyle, Thomas 22, 70
Carroll, Lewis 2, 53, 139
Clare, John 9, 86
Clough, Arthur Hugh 27, 163
Cobbett, William 49
Coleridge, Hartley 90
Coleridge, Samuel Taylor 9, 54, 99, 111
Coleridge, Sara 31
Collins, (William) Wilkie 1, 18, 93
Cowper, William 8, 94
Crabbe, George 26, 121
Craik, Dinah Maria (Mulock) 38
Cumberland, Richard 167
Dacre, Charlotte 151
Darwin, Charles 57
Darwin, Erasmus 106
De Quincey, Thomas 4, 87
Dickens, Charles (John Huffam) 3, 8, 18, 26, 37, 50, 86, 105, 113, 161
Disraeli, Benjamin 2, 39, 79
Dobell, Sydney Thompson 43
Du Maurier, George 86
Dyer, George 129
Eden, Emily 10
Eliot, George 4, 13, 23, 41, 49, 89, 118
FitzGerald, Edward 9, 153
Forster, John 11
Froude, James Anthony 43
Gaskell, Elizabeth Cleghorn 5, 70, 97, 137
Gilpin, William 30
Godwin, William 14, 130
Gore, Catherine 65
Hallam, Arthur Henry 110
Hamilton, Elizabeth 153
Haydon, Benjamin Robert 146
Hays, Mary 114
Hazlitt, William 29, 82
Hemans, Felicia 29, 71
Holcroft, Thomas 85
Hood, Thomas 16
Hopkins, Gerard Manley 17
Horne, Richard Hengist 127
Hunt, (James Henry) Leigh 1, 70
Huxley, T(homas) H(enry) 67
Inchbald, Elizabeth 62
Ingelow, Jean 39, 107
Jefferies, (John) Richard 47
Jerrold, Douglas William 2
Jewsbury, Geraldine (Endsor) 22
Keats, John 8, 73, 121
Keble, John 87
Kemble, Fanny 18
Kingsley, Charles 35
Kingsley, Henry 107
Lamb, Charles 10, 113
Lamb, Lady Caroline 38
Lamb, Mary 125
Landon, Letitia Elizabeth 15
Landor, Walter Savage 14
Lennox, Charlotte Ramsay 23, 134
Lewes, George Henry 25

Lewis, Matthew Gregory 11, 62
Linton, Eliza Lynn 41
Macaulay, Thomas Babington 42
Malthus, Thomas Robert 145
Marryat, Frederick 3
Martineau, Harriet 26, 137
Mayhew, Henry 31
Mill, Harriet (Hardy) Taylor 102
Mill, John Stuart 11, 58
Mitford, Mary Russell 4
Montagu, Elizabeth 117
More, Hannah 27, 141
Morris, William 4
Newman, John Henry 38, 99
Norton, Caroline 47
Oliphant, Laurence 47
Opie, Amelia 65
Paine, Thomas 62
Pater, Walter (Horatio) 7, 90, 159
Patmore, Coventry Kersey Dighton 9
Peacock, Thomas Love 22
Percy, Thomas 95
Piozzi, Hester Lynch (Thrale) 57
Planché, James Robinson 42
Polidori, John William 51
Radcliffe, Ann (Ward) 6, 55, 106
Reade, Charles 2, 74
Reeve, Clara 19
Reynolds, John Hamilton 146
Robertson, Thomas William 35
Robinson, Henry Crabb 15
Robinson, Mary 142
Rogers, Samuel 69
Rossetti, Christina (Georgina) 2, 50, 66
Rossetti, Dante Gabriel 4, 77
Sala, George Augustus 46
Shelley, Mary Wollstonecraft (Godwin) 14, 59, 103, 170
Shelley, Percy Bysshe 18, 93, 143
Smith, Charlotte (Turner) 23, 115
Southey, Robert 8, 97
Surtees, Robert Smith 14
Symonds, John Addington 34
Tennyson, Alfred 30, 65, 115
Thackeray, William Makepeace 5, 14, 22, 43, 169
Thelwall, John 162
Tonna, Charlotte Elizabeth 135
Trelawny, Edward John 85
Trollope, Anthony 6, 33, 101
Trollope, Frances 30
Warton, Joseph 118
Williams, Helen Maria 135
Wordsworth, Dorothy 25, 138
Wordsworth, William 12, 38, 111, 166

FILIPINO

Rizal, José 27

FINNISH

Kivi, Aleksis 30
Lonnrot, Elias 53
Runeberg, Johan 41

FRENCH

Augier, Emile 31
Balzac, Honoré de 5, 35, 53, 153
Banville, Théodore (Faullain) de 9
Barbey d'Aurevilly, Jules-Amédée 1
Baudelaire, Charles 6, 29, 55, 155
Becque, Henri 3
Beranger, Pierre Jean de 34
Bertrand, Aloysius 31
Borel, Pétrus 41
Chamisso, Adelbert von 82
Chateaubriand, François René de 3, 134
Comte, Auguste 54
Constant (de Rebecque), (Henri) Benjamin 6
Corbière, Tristan 43
Crèvecoeur, Michel Guillaume Jean de 105
Daudet, (Louis Marie) Alphonse 1

Delacroix, Eugene 133
Desbordes-Valmore, Marceline 97
Dumas, Alexandre (fils) 9
Dumas, Alexandre (pere) 11, 71
Duras, Claire de 154
Feuillet, Octave 45
Flaubert, Gustave 2, 10, 19, 62, 66, 135
Fourier, Charles 51
Fromentin, Eugène (Samuel Auguste) 10, 125
Gaboriau, émile 14
Gautier, Théophile 1, 59
Genlis, Stéphanie-Félicité de 166
Gobineau, Joseph-Arthur 17
Goncourt, Edmond (Louis Antoine Huot) de 7
Goncourt, Jules (Alfred Huot) de 7
Hugo, Victor (Marie) 3, 10, 21, 161
Joubert, Joseph 9
Kock, Charles Paul de 16
Laclos, Pierre Ambroise François 4, 87
Laforgue, Jules 5, 53
Lamartine, Alphonse (Marie Louis Prat) de 11
Lautréamont 12
Leconte de Lisle, Charles-Marie-René 29
Maistre, Joseph 37
Mallarmé, Stéphane 4, 41
Maupassant, (Henri René Albert) Guy de 1, 42, 83
Mérimée, Prosper 6, 65
Michelet, Jules 31
Musset, (Louis Charles) Alfred de 7, 150
Nerval, Gérard de 1, 67
Nodier, (Jean) Charles (Emmanuel) 19
Pixérécourt, (René Charles) Guilbert de 39
Renan, Joseph Ernest 26, 145
Rimbaud, (Jean Nicolas) Arthur 4, 35, 82
Sade, Donatien Alphonse François 3, 47
Sainte-Beuve, Charles Augustin 5
Sand, George 2, 42, 57
Scribe, (Augustin) Eugène 16
Senancour, Etienne Pivert de 16
Staël-Holstein, Anne Louise Germaine Necker 3
Stendhal 23, 46
Sue, Eugene 1
Taine, Hippolyte Adolphe 15
Tocqueville, Alexis (Charles Henri Maurice Clérel Comte) de 7, 63
Vallès, Jules 71
Verlaine, Paul (Marie) 2, 51
Vigny, Alfred (Victor) de 7, 102
Villiers de l'Isle Adam, Jean Marie Mathias Philippe Auguste 3

GERMAN

Arnim, Achim von (Ludwig Joachim von Arnim) 5, 159
Arnim, Bettina von 38, 123
Auerbach, Berthold 171
Bonaventura 35
Büchner, (Karl) Georg 26, 146
Chamisso, Adelbert von 82
Claudius, Matthias 75
Droste-Hülshoff, Annette Freiin von 3, 133
Eichendorff, Joseph 8
Engels, Friedrich 85, 114
Feuerbach, Ludwig 139
Fichte, Johann Gottlieb 62
Fontane, Theodor 26, 163
Fouqué, Friedrich (Heinrich Karl) de la Motte 2
Freytag, Gustav 109
Goethe, Johann Wolfgang von 4, 22, 34, 90, 154
Grabbe, Christian Dietrich 2
Grimm, Jacob Ludwig Karl 3, 77
Grimm, Wilhelm Karl 3, 77
Hebbel, Friedrich 43
Hegel, Georg Wilhelm Friedrich 46, 151
Heine, Heinrich 4, 54, 147

Herder, Johann Gottfried von **8**
Hoffmann, E(rnst) T(heodor) A(madeus) **2**
Hölderlin, (Johann Christian) Friedrich **16**
Humboldt, Alexander von **170**
Humboldt, Wilhelm von **134**
Immermann, Karl (Lebrecht) **4, 49**
Jean Paul **7**
Kant, Immanuel **27, 67**
Kleist, Heinrich von **2, 37**
Klinger, Friedrich Maximilian von **1**
Klopstock, Friedrich Gottlieb **11**
Kotzebue, August (Friedrich Ferdinand) von **25**
La Roche, Sophie von **121**
Ludwig, Otto **4**
Marx, Karl (Heinrich) **17, 114**
Mörike, Eduard (Friedrich) **10**
Novalis **13**
Schelling, Friedrich Wilhelm Joseph von **30**
Schiller, Friedrich von **39, 69, 166**
Schlegel, August Wilhelm von **15, 142**
Schlegel, Friedrich **45**
Schleiermacher, Friedrich **107**
Schopenhauer, Arthur **51, 157**
Schumann, Robert **143**
Storm, (Hans) Theodor (Woldsen) **1**
Tieck, (Johann) Ludwig **5, 46**
Varnhagen, Rahel **130**
Wagner, Richard **9, 119**
Wieland, Christoph Martin **17**

GREEK

Foscolo, Ugo **8, 97**
Solomos, Dionysios **15**

HUNGARIAN

Arany, Janos **34**
Madach, Imre **19**
Petofi, Sándor **21**

INDIAN

Chatterji, Bankim Chandra **19**
Dutt, Michael Madhusudan **118**
Dutt, Toru **29**

IRISH

Allingham, William **25**
Banim, John **13**
Banim, Michael **13**
Boucicault, Dion **41**
Carleton, William **3**
Croker, John Wilson **10**
Darley, George **2**
Edgeworth, Maria **1, 51, 158**
Ferguson, Samuel **33**
Griffin, Gerald **7**
Jameson, Anna **43**
Le Fanu, Joseph Sheridan **9, 58**
Lever, Charles (James) **23**
Maginn, William **8**
Mangan, James Clarence **27**
Maturin, Charles Robert **6, 169**
Merriman, Brian **70**
Moore, Thomas **6, 110**
Morgan, Lady **29**
O'Brien, Fitz-James **21**

Sheridan, Richard Brinsley **5, 91**

ITALIAN

Alfieri, Vittorio **101**
Collodi, Carlo **54**
Foscolo, Ugo **8, 97**
Gozzi, (Conte) Carlo **23**
Leopardi, Giacomo **22, 129**
Manzoni, Alessandro **29, 98**
Mazzini, Giuseppe **34**
Nievo, Ippolito **22**

JAMAICAN

Seacole, Mary Jane Grant **147**

JAPANESE

Akinari, Ueda **131**
Ichiyō, Higuchi **49**
Motoori, Norinaga **45**

LITHUANIAN

Mapu, Abraham (ben Jekutiel) **18**

MEXICAN

Lizardi, Jose Joaquin Fernandez de **30**
Najera, Manuel Gutierrez **133**

NORWEGIAN

Collett, (Jacobine) Camilla (Wergeland) **22**
Wergeland, Henrik Arnold **5**

POLISH

Fredro, Aleksander **8**
Krasicki, Ignacy **8**
Krasiński, Zygmunt **4**
Mickiewicz, Adam **3, 101**
Norwid, Cyprian Kamil **17**
Slowacki, Juliusz **15**

ROMANIAN

Eminescu, Mihail **33, 131**

RUSSIAN

Aksakov, Sergei Timofeyvich **2**
Bakunin, Mikhail (Alexandrovich) **25, 58**
Baratynsky, Evgenii Abramovich **103**
Bashkirtseff, Marie **27**
Belinski, Vissarion Grigoryevich **5**
Bestuzhev, Aleksandr Aleksandrovich **131**
Chernyshevsky, Nikolay Gavrilovich **1**
Dobrolyubov, Nikolai Alexandrovich **5**
Dostoevsky, Fedor Mikhailovich **2, 7, 21, 33, 43, 119, 167**
Gogol, Nikolai (Vasilyevich) **5, 15, 31, 162**
Goncharov, Ivan Alexandrovich **1, 63**
Granovsky, Timofei Nikolaevich **75**
Griboedov, Aleksandr Sergeevich **129**
Herzen, Aleksandr Ivanovich **10, 61**
Karamzin, Nikolai Mikhailovich **3**
Krylov, Ivan Andreevich **1**
Lermontov, Mikhail Yuryevich **5, 47, 126**
Leskov, Nikolai (Semyonovich) **25**
Nekrasov, Nikolai Alekseevich **11**
Ostrovsky, Alexander **30, 57**
Pavlova, Karolina Karlovna **138**

Pisarev, Dmitry Ivanovich **25**
Pushkin, Alexander (Sergeyevich) **3, 27, 83**
Saltykov, Mikhail Evgrafovich **16**
Smolenskin, Peretz **30**
Turgenev, Ivan **21, 37, 122**
Tyutchev, Fyodor **34**
Zhukovsky, Vasily (Andreevich) **35**

SCOTTISH

Baillie, Joanna **2, 151**
Beattie, James **25**
Blair, Hugh **75**
Campbell, Thomas **19**
Carlyle, Thomas **22, 70**
Ferrier, Susan (Edmonstone) **8**
Galt, John **1, 110**
Hogg, James **4, 109**
Jeffrey, Francis **33**
Lockhart, John Gibson **6**
Mackenzie, Henry **41**
Miller, Hugh **143**
Oliphant, Margaret (Oliphant Wilson) **11, 61**
Scott, Walter **15, 69, 110**
Stevenson, Robert Louis (Balfour) **5, 14, 63**
Thomson, James **18**
Wilson, John **5**
Wright, Frances **74**

SERBIAN

Karadžić, Vuk Stefanović **115**

SLOVENIAN

Kopitar, Jernej **117**
Prešeren, Francè **127**

SPANISH

Alarcon, Pedro Antonio de **1**
Bécquer, Gustavo Adolfo **106**
Caballero, Fernan **10**
Castro, Rosalia de **3, 78**
Espronceda, Jose de **39**
Larra (y Sanchez de Castro), Mariano Jose de **17, 130**
Martínez de la Rosa, Francisco de Paula **102**
Tamayo y Baus, Manuel **1**
Zorrilla y Moral, Jose **6**

SWEDISH

Almqvist, Carl Jonas Love **42**
Bremer, Fredrika **11**
Stagnelius, Eric Johan **61**
Tegner, Esaias **2**

SWISS

Amiel, Henri Frederic **4**
Burckhardt, Jacob (Christoph) **49**
Charriere, Isabelle de **66**
Gotthelf, Jeremias **117**
Keller, Gottfried **2**
Lavater, Johann Kaspar **142**
Meyer, Conrad Ferdinand **81**
Wyss, Johann David Von **10**

UKRAINIAN

Shevchenko, Taras **54**

VENEZUELAN

Bello, Andrés **131**

Nationality Index

ISBN-13: 978-0-7876-8656-7
ISBN-10: 0-7876-8656-5

Sedative, hypnotic, or anxiolytic
 dependence
 abuse
Polysubstance dependence
Psychoactive substance dependence NOS
Psychoactive substance abuse NOS

SCHIZOPHRENIA
Schizophrenia
 catatonic
 disorganized
 paranoid
 undifferentiated
 residual

DELUSIONAL (PARANOID) DISORDER
Delusional (paranoid) disorder
 erotomanic
 grandiose
 jealous
 persecutory
 somatic
 unspecified

PSYCHOTIC DISORDERS NOT ELSEWHERE CLASSIFIED
Brief reactive psychosis
Schizophreniform disorder
 without good prognostic features
 with good prognostic features
Schizoaffective disorder
 Specify bipolar type or depressive type
Induced psychotic disorder
Psychotic disorder NOS (atypical psychosis)

MOOD DISORDERS
Bipolar Disorders
Bipolar disorder
 mixed
 manic
 depressed
Cyclothymia
Bipolar disorder NOS

Depressive Disorders
Major depression
 single episode
 recurrent
Dysthymia (or depressive neurosis)
 Specify primary or secondary type
 Specify early or late onset
Depressive disorder NOS

ANXIETY DISORDERS (or Anxiety and Phobic Neuroses)
Panic disorder
 with agoraphobia
 without agoraphobia
Agoraphobia without history of panic disorder
Social phobia
 generalized type
Simple phobia
Obsessive compulsive disorder (or obsessive compulsive neurosis)
Post-traumatic stress disorder
 delayed onset
Generalized anxiety disorder
Anxiety disorder NOS

SOMATOFORM DISORDERS
Body dysmorphic disorder
Conversion disorder (or hysterical neurosis, conversion type)
 Specify single episode or recurrent
Hypochondriasis (or hypochondriacal neurosis)

Somatization disorder
Somatoform pain disorder
Undifferentiated somatoform disorder
Somatoform disorder NOS

DISSOCIATIVE DISORDERS
(or Hysterical Neuroses, Dissociative Type)
Multiple personality disorder
Psychogenic fugue
Psychogenic amnesia
Depersonalization disorder (or depersonalization neurosis)
Dissociative disorder NOS

SEXUAL DISORDERS
Paraphilias
Exhibitionism
Fetishism
Frotteurism
Pedophilia
Sexual masochism
Sexual sadism
Transvestic fetishism
Voyeurism
Paraphilia NOS

Sexual Dysfunctions
 Specify lifelong or acquired
 Specify generalized or situational
Sexual desire disorders
 hypoactive sexual desire disorder
 sexual aversion disorder
Sexual arousal disorders
 female sexual arousal disorder
 male erectile disorder
Orgasm disorders
 inhibited female orgasm
 inhibited male orgasm
 premature ejaculation
Sexual pain disorders
 dyspareunia
 vaginismus
Sexual dysfunction NOS

Other Sexual Disorders
Sexual disorder NOS

SLEEP DISORDERS
Dyssomnias
Insomnia disorder
 related to another mental disorder (nonorganic)
 related to known organic factor
Primary insomnia
Hypersomnia disorder
 related to another mental disorder (nonorganic)
 related to a known organic factor
Primary hypersomnia
Sleep-wake schedule disorder
 Specify advanced or delayed phase type, disorganized type, frequently changing type
Other dyssomnias
 dyssomnia NOS

Parasomnias
Dream anxiety disorder (nightmare disorder)
Sleep terror disorder
Sleepwalking disorder
Parasomnia NOS

FACTITIOUS DISORDER
Factitious disorder
 with physical symptoms
 with psychological symptoms
Factitious disorder NOS

IMPULSE CONTROL DISORDERS NOT ELSEWHERE CLASSIFIED
Intermittent explosive disorder
Kleptomania
Pathological gambling
Pyromania
Trichotillomania
Impulse control disorder NOS

ADJUSTMENT DISORDER
Adjustment disorder
 with anxious mood
 with depressed mood
 with disturbance of conduct
 with mixed disturbance of emotions and conduct
 with mixed emotional features
 with physical complaints
 with withdrawal
 with work (or academic) inhibition
Adjustment disorder NOS

PSYCHOLOGICAL FACTORS AFFECTING PHYSICAL CONDITION
Psychological factors affecting physical condition

PERSONALITY DISORDERS (AXIS II)
Cluster A
Paranoid
Schizoid
Schizotypal

Cluster B
Antisocial
Borderline
Histrionic
Narcissistic

Cluster C
Avoidant
Dependent
Obsessive compulsive
Passive aggressive
Personality disorder NOS

CONDITIONS NOT ATTRIBUTABLE TO A MENTAL DISORDER THAT ARE A FOCUS OF ATTENTION OR TREATMENT
Academic problem
Adult antisocial behavior
Borderline intellectual functioning (Axis II)
Childhood or adolescent antisocial behavior
Malingering
Marital problem
Noncompliance with medical treatment
Occupational problem
Parent-child problem
Other interpersonal problem
Other specified family circumstances
Phase of life problem or other life circumstance problem
Uncomplicated bereavement

ADDITIONAL CLASSIFICATIONS
Unspecified mental disorder (nonpsychotic)
No diagnosis or condition on Axis I
Diagnosis or condition deferred on Axis I
No diagnosis or condition on Axis II
Diagnosis or condition deferred on Axis II

Abnormal Psychology

Abnormal Psychology

The Problem of Maladaptive Behavior

SEVENTH EDITION

Irwin G. Sarason
University of Washington

Barbara R. Sarason
University of Washington

PRENTICE HALL, Englewood Cliffs, New Jersey 07632

Library of Congress Cataloging-in-Publication Data

Sarason, Irwin G.
 Abnormal psychology : the problem of maladaptive behavior / Irwin
G. Sarason, Barbara R. Sarason. -- 7th ed.
 p. cm.
 Includes bibliographical references and index.
 ISBN 0-13-007022-X
 1. Psychology, Pathological. I. Sarason, Barbara R. II. Title.
 [DNLM: 1. Psychopathology. 2. Social Behavior Disorders. WM 100
S2425a]
 RC454.28 1993
 616.89--dc20
DNLM/DLC
for Library of Congress 92-9191
 CIP

Editorial/production supervision: Marielle
 Reiter
Acquisitions editor: Susan Finnemore
 Brennan
Editor-in-chief: Charlyce Jones Owen
Development/copy editor: Lauren Shafer
Interior and cover design: Amy Rosen/
 Jerry Votta

Art director: Florence Dara Silverman/
 Anne T. Bonanno
Prepress buyer: Kelly Behr
Manufacturing buyer: Mary Ann Gloriande
Supplements editor: Sharon Chambliss
Editorial assistant: Jennie Katsaros
Photo research: Yvonne Gerin
Photo editor: Lori Morris-Nantz

Cover art: Pablo Picasso, *Femme assise devant la fenêtre,* 1937. Huile et pastel sur toile; 130 x 97, 3 cm. Musée Picasso, Paris. Art Resource.

1993, 1989, 1987, 1984, 1980, 1976, 1972 by Prentice-Hall, Inc.
A Simon & Schuster Company
Englewood Cliffs, New Jersey 07632

Printed in the United States of America
10 9 8 7 6 5 4 3 2 1

ISBN 0-13-007022-X

Prentice-Hall International (UK) Limited, *London*
Prentice-Hall of Australia Pty. Limited, *Sydney*
Prentice-Hall Canada Inc., *Toronto*
Prentice-Hall Hispanoamericana, S.A., *Mexico*
Prentice-Hall of India Private Limited, *New Delhi*
Prentice-Hall of Japan, Inc., *Tokyo*
Simon & Schuster Asia Pte. Ltd., *Singapore*
Editora Prentice-Hall do Brasil, Ltda., *Rio de Janeiro*

(Acknowledgments appear on pp. 636–637, which constitute a continuation of the copyright page.)

*To three individuals whose ability to adapt we admire
(in order of their appearance) Sue, Jane, and Don*

Brief Contents

1 Abnormal Psychology, 1

2 The Historical Background of Abnormal Psychology, 30

3 Theoretical Perspectives on Maladaptive Behavior, 54

4 Classification and Assessment, 90

5 Vulnerability, Stress, and Coping: Maladaptive Reactions, 124

6 Anxiety Disorders, 154

7 Psychological Factors and Physical Symptoms, 184

8 Sexual Variations and Disorders, 214

9 Personality Disorders, 248

10 Mood Disorders, 280

11 Schizophrenic Disorders, 320

12 Causes and Markers of Schizophrenia, 350

13 Brain Disorders and Changes Related to Aging, 380

14 Addictive Disorders, 410

15 Maladaptive Behaviors of Childhood and Adolescence, 448

16 Developmental Disorders, 484

17 Therapies and Their Evaluation, 514

18 Society's Response to Maladaptive Behavior, 548

Contents

Preface xvii
About the Authors xxi

1 Abnormal Psychology

WHAT IS ABNORMAL BEHAVIOR? 2
Box 1–1 Father Kills Two Young Sons 3
The Stigma of Abnormal Behavior 4
Adaptive and Maladaptive Behavior 5
STRESS, COPING, AND VULNERABILITY 6
REASONS FOR CLINICAL CONTACTS 7
Personal Unhappiness 8
The Concerns of Others 8
Legal and Community Problems 9
THE EPIDEMIOLOGY OF MALADAPTIVE
 BEHAVIOR 9
Prevalence, Incidence, and Risk Factors 10
SOURCES OF HELP 12

Types of Treatment Facilities 12
Types of Mental Health Specialists 13
RESEARCH IN ABNORMAL PSYCHOLOGY 14
Observing Behavior 14
The Role of Theory 17
The Research Journey 17
Types of Research 18
Box 1–2 Understanding Abnormal Behavior
 through Animal Research 22
Statistics and Research Design 26
ETHICAL ASPECTS OF RESEARCH 27
CHAPTER SUMMARY 27

2 The Historical Background of Abnormal Psychology

HISTORICAL VIEWS OF ABNORMAL
 BEHAVIOR 31
The Ancient Western World 34
The Middle Ages 35
The Renaissance 39
The Age of Reason and the
 Enlightenment 40
The Reform Movement 42

Box 2–1 A Protest That Had an Effect 47
PSYCHOLOGICAL VERSUS ORGANIC VIEWS
 OF ABNORMAL BEHAVIOR 48
The Psychological Approach 48
The Organic Approach 49
The Approaches Converge 49
THE STAGE IS SET 51
CHAPTER SUMMARY 52

3 Theoretical Perspectives on Maladaptive Behavior

THE ROLE OF THEORY IN ABNORMAL
 PSYCHOLOGY 56
THE BIOLOGICAL PERSPECTIVE 57
Biological Determinants of Abnormal
 Behavior 58
The Neurosciences Revolution 64

Box 3–1 What Goes On When We Sleep—
 and When We Can't 65
Integration of Biological and Psychological
 Systems 67
THE PSYCHODYNAMIC PERSPECTIVE 68
Freud and Psychoanalysis 69

Contemporary Approaches to
 Psychoanalysis 74
Evaluating Psychoanalytic Theory 75
THE BEHAVIORAL PERSPECTIVE 75
Classical Conditioning 77
Operant Conditiong 78
Social Learning Theory 79
THE COGNITIVE PERSPECTIVE 81
Maladaptive Bchavior and Cognition 81
Cognitive Therapies 83

**THE HUMANISTIC-EXISTENTIAL
 PERSPECTIVE 83**
Rogers' Conception of the Self 84
The Existential Point of View 85
THE COMMUNITY PERSPECTIVE 85
Social Roles and Labeling 86
Contributions of the Community
 Perspective 86
**THE VALUE OF AN INTERACTIONAL
 APPROACH 86**
CHAPTER SUMMARY 88

4 Classification and Assessment

CLASSIFICATION 92
Advantages and Disadvantages of
 Classification 92
Stress, Vulnerability, and Coping 94
The Multiaxial Approach 94
The Major Diagnostic Categories 95
Evaluation of the DSM Multiaxial
 Approach 96
Research on Classification 98
**ASSESSMENT: THE BASIS OF
 CLASSIFICATION 99**

The Interview 99
Intelligence Tests 104
**Box 4–1 Intelligence Tests and Report
 Writing 108**
Personality Assessment 110
Behavioral Assessment 115
Cognitive Assessment 117
Relational Assessment 118
Bodily Assessment 119
CHAPTER SUMMARY 121

5 Vulnerability, Stress, and Coping: Maladaptive Reactions

**VULNERABILITY, TEMPERAMENT, AND
 COPING 126**
Box 5–1 Two Weeks in the Hospital 130
Coping Techniques 131
Social Support 132
STRESS AROUSAL 134
Stress-Arousing Situations 135
Box 5–2 Date Rape 137
Life Transitions 138
CLINICAL REACTIONS TO STRESS 140
Adjustment Disorder 141

Posttraumatic Disorders 143
Dissociative Disorders 146
**TREATING STRESS-RELATED
 PROBLEMS 150**
Supportive Therapy 150
Drugs and Sedatives 151
Relaxation Training 151
Systematic Desensitization 151
Cognitive Modification 151
Social Intervention 151
CHAPTER SUMMARY 152

6 Anxiety Disorders

GENERALIZED ANXIETY DISORDER 158
PANIC DISORDER 158

**Box 6–1 An Anxious, Precise, Demanding
 Man Seeks Help 161**

PHOBIAS 162
Simple Phobias 164
Social phobias 165
Agoraphobia 166
OBSESSIVE-COMPULSIVE DISORDER 168
**INTERPRETING AND TREATING ANXIETY
 DISORDERS 173**

The Psychodynamic Perspective 173
The Behavioral Perspective 174
The Cognitive Perspective 176
The Biological Perspective 179
Box 6–2 Comorbidity 181
CHAPTER SUMMARY 182

7 Psychological Factors and Physical Symptoms

**PSYCHOLOGICAL, SOCIAL, AND BODILY
 INTERACTIONS 186**
Psychophysiological Approaches 186
The Biopsychosocial Model 187
Stress and Illness 187
**Box 7–1 Behavioral Medicine and Health
 Psychology 188**
PSYCHOPHYSIOLOGICAL DISORDERS 189
Headaches 190
Cardiovascular Disorders 193
**Box 7–2 Heredity, Life Style, and Coronary
 Heart Disease: A Study of Twins 196**
Cancer 202
The Immune System and Related
 Disorders 203

Allergies 203
Gastrointestinal Disorders 204
SOMATOFORM DISORDERS 205
Psychogenic Pain Disorder 205
Hypochondriasis 206
Somatization Disorders 207
Conversion Disorders 208
**FACTITIOUS DISORDERS AND
 MALINGERING 209**
**Box 7–3 Group Hysteria among
 Schoolchildren 210**
CHAPTER SUMMARY 212

8 Sexual Variations and Disorders

**CHANGING VIEWS OF SEXUAL
 BEHAVIOR 216**
SURVEYS OF SEXUAL BEHAVIOR 216
HOMOSEXUALITY 217
How Sexual Preference Develops 218
A Cross-cultural View 220
Psychological Adjustment 220
Relationship Patterns 221
Sexual Response 222
BISEXUALITY 223
SEXUAL DYSFUNCTION 224

Types of Sexual Dysfunction 224
Treatment of Sexual Dysfunction 226
The Effectiveness of Sex Therapy 230
GENDER IDENTITY DISORDER 230
Childhood Problems of Gender
 Identity 230
Gender Identity Disorder in Adults 231
**Box 8–1 The Stories of Two
 Transsexuals 232**
THE PARAPHILIAS 234
Fetishism 234

Transvestitism 235
Sexual Sadism and Masochism 237
Autoerotic Asphyxia 239
Voyeurism 240
Exhibitionism 241
Obscene Telephone Calls 241
Pedophilia 242

Perspectives on the Paraphilias 242
SEXUAL VICTIMIZATION 243
Rape 243
Child Sexual Abuse 244
Incest 245
CHAPTER SUMMARY 246

9 Personality Disorders

**CLASSIFYING PERSONALITY
 DISORDERS 251**
ODD OR ECCENTRIC BEHAVIORS 253
Paranoid Personality Disorder 253
Schizoid Personality Disorder 254
Schizotypal Personality Disorder 255
**DRAMATIC, EMOTIONAL, OR ERRATIC
 BEHAVIORS 257**
Histrionic Personality Disorder 257
Narcissistic Personality Disorder 259
Borderline Personality Disorder 260
Antisocial Personality Disorder 265
**Box 9–1 Antisocial Personality Disorder:
 A Frightening Example 266**

ANXIOUS OR FEARFUL BEHAVIORS 271
Avoidant Personality Disorder 271
Dependent Personality Disorder 272
Obsessive-Compulsive Personality
 Disorder 274
Passive-Aggressive Personality Disorder 275
**TREATMENT OR PERSONALITY
 DISORDERS 276**
**THE OUTLOOK FOR PERSONALITY
 DISORDER CLASSIFICATION 277**
CHAPTER SUMMARY 278

10 Mood Disorders

WHAT ARE MOOD DISORDERS? 282
How Common Are Mood Disorders? 282
DEPRESSION 283
Depressed Mood 283
Risk Factors 284
DEPRESSIVE DISORDER 285
Dysthymia 286
Major Depression 287
THEORIES OF DEPRESSION 289
Biological Theories 289
The Psychodynamic View 297
The Behavioral Perspective 298
The Cognitive Perspective 300
**Box 10–1 Abraham Lincoln: An Effective
 Leader Afflicted with Depression 305**

The Humanistic-Existential Perspective 306
Contrasting Psychological Theories of
 Depression 306
An Interactional View 307
THE BIPOLAR DISORDERS 307
Manic Episodes 308
Causes of Bipolar Disorder 313
**Box 10–2 Creativity, Leadership, and Bipolar
 Disorders 310**
Treatment of Bipolar Disorder 313
SUICIDE AND PARASUICIDE 313
Causes of Suicide 316
Box 10–3 Suicide and the Survivors 316
The Impact of Suicide on Others 317
CHAPTER SUMMARY 318

11 Schizophrenic Disorders

**THE IMPACT OF SCHIZOPHRENIC
DISORDERS 324**
DIAGNOSTIC CRITERIA 324
**CHARACTERISTICS OF SCHIZOPHRENIC
DISORDERS 326**
Delusions 326
Disordered Thinking 326
Hallucinations 328
Lack of Appropriate Emotion 330
Unclear Boundaries of the Self 330
Unpredictable Motor Behavior 331
Change in Motivational Level 331
Impaired Interpersonal Functioning 331
Attention Difficulties 331
**A HISTORICAL VIEW OF SCHIZOPHRENIC
DISORDERS 332**
Dementia Praecox 332
The Schizophrenias 332
First-Rank Symptoms 333

European and American Definitions 334
Positive and Negative Symptoms 334
TYPES OF SCHIZOPHRENIA 335
Traditional and Current DSM Subtypes 335
Schizophrenic Spectrum Disorders 337
**OUTCOME INDICATIONS AND LONG-TERM
STUDIES 337**
Box 11–1 Delusional Thinking 338
THERAPEUTIC APPROACHES 342
Biological Approaches 342
Psychodynamic Therapies 343
Behavioral Therapy 343
Ongoing Therapeutic Care 344
**Box 11–2 Lessening a Family's Guilt over
Schizophrenia 346**
A Comprehensive Approach 347
CHAPTER SUMMARY 348

12 Causes and Markers of Schizophrenia

GENETIC FACTORS 351
Family Studies 352
Twin Studies 353
**Box 12–1 Growing Up with a Mother Who
Has a Schizophrenic Disorder 354**
Adoption Studies 354
A Genetic Model 356
Genetic Counseling 357
VULNERABILITY AND STRESS FACTORS 359
**HIGH-RISK STUDIES AND THE SEARCH FOR
MARKERS 361**
**UNDERSTANDING THE SCHIZOPHRENIC
PROCESS 362**
Structural Abnormalities in the Brain 362

Biochemical Abnormalities in the
Brain 363
Psychophysiological Abnormalities 365
Attention Problems 366
Disordered Thinking 368
Language Use Abnormalities 369
FAMILY RELATIONSHIPS 370
Family Communication Deviance 371
Expressed Emotion 371
Parental Affective Style 373
THE ROLE OF THE COMMUNITY 374
**Box 12–2 Investigating a Single Case from a
Variety of Perspectives 375**
CHAPTER SUMMARY 378

13 Brain Disorders and Changes Related to Aging

THE BRAIN: AN INTERACTIONAL PERSPECTIVE 382
Vulnerability to Brain Disorders 382
Box 13–1 Sarah Fell and Her Life Was Changed Forever 383
The Normal Aging Process 384
ASSESSING BRAIN DAMAGE 385
Brain Imaging 386
CHARACTERISTICS OF ORGANIC MENTAL DISORDERS 387
Delirium 387
Dementia 389
MAJOR CAUSES OF DEMENTIA 391
Alzheimer's Disease 391
Box 13–2 Helping the Victim of Alzheimer's Disease 393
Pick's Disease 396
Multi-infarct Dementia 396
AIDS Dementia Complex 396

Other Organic Brain Syndromes 396
THE VARIETY OF CAUSES OF BRAIN DISORDERS 397
A Genetic Basis: Huntington's Disease 398
A Neurotransmitter Deficit: Parkinson's Disease 399
An Infectious Disorder: General Paresis 399
Nutritional Deficiencies: Pellagra and Korsakoff's Syndrome 400
Brain Trauma: Injuries and Tumors 400
Box 13–3 Mass Killer with Malignant Brain Tumor 401
Multiple Causal Factors: Epilepsy 402
Blockage of Blood Supply: Cerebrovascular Accidents 406
AN INTEGRATIVE APPROACH TO BRAIN DISORDERS 406
CHAPTER SUMMARY 408

14 Addictive Disorders

ADDICTIVE BEHAVIOR 412
ALCOHOL 414
Alcohol Abuse and Dependence 414
Box 14-1 Some Facts about the Alcohol Problem 415
Alcohol and Health 417
Perspectives on Alcohol Abuse 418
Treatment 424
Preventing Alcohol Abuse 429
Box 14–2 Drinking on Campus 430

OTHER DRUGS
Barbituates and Tranquilizers 432
The Opioids 433
Cocaine 436
Amphetamines 438
Psychedelics 438
Phencyclidine (PCP) 440
Marijuana 440
Nicotine 443
CHAPTER SUMMARY 446

15 Maladaptive Behaviors of Childhood and Adolescence

CHILDREN IN CLINICAL SETTINGS 450
THE SCOPE OF THE PROBLEM 451
Box 15–1 Effects of Child Abuse and Neglect 452
DISRUPTIVE BEHAVIOR 454

Attention-deficit Hyperactivity Disorder 454
Conduct Disorder 458
Box 15–2 The Beating and Rape of a Jogger in Central Park 462
INTERNALIZING DISORDERS 464

Anxiety Disorders of Childhood 464
Depression in Children and
 Adolescents 468
EATING DISORDERS 472
Anorexia Nervosa 474
Bulimia Nervosa 476
**THERAPY FOR CHILDREN AND
 ADOLESCENTS 478**

Play Therapy 478
Cognitive and Behavior Therapies 480
Family Therapy 480
Results of Therapy 481
CHAPTER SUMMARY 481

16 Developmental Disorders

AUTISTIC DISORDERS 486
Characteristics of Autistic Behavior 486
Research on Autistic Disorder 487
Box 16–1 Two Autistic Persons 488
Therapy 490
Prospects for Change 492
MENTAL RETARDATION 494
**Box 16–2 How Families Adapt to Retarded
 Children 495**

Degrees of Mental Retardation 496
Biological Causes 498
Psychosocial Disadvantage 507
Psychosocial Enrichment 507
Psychological and Social Problems 510
CHAPTER SUMMARY 511

17 Therapies and Their Evaluation

PSYCHOTHERAPY 516
Psychodynamic Therapy and
 Psychoanalysis 517
Humanistic and Existential Therapies 520
The Cognitive Psychotherapies 522
BEHAVIOR THERAPY 523
**COGNITIVE-BEHAVIORAL
 APPROACHES 524**
Cognitive-Behavioral Interventions 525
Relaxation Training 525
Exposure Therapy 526
Modeling 526
GROUP THERAPY 528
Cognitive-Behavioral Group Therapy 529
Family and Marital Therapy 529
Psychodrama 531

**INTEGRATION OF PSYCHOLOGICALLY
 BASED THERAPEUTIC APPROACHES 532**
Research on the Psychological
 Therapies 532
**Box 17–1 Examining the Process of
 Psychotherapy 534**
Outcome Studies 534
Comparing Therapies 536
Components of Effective Therapy 538
Improving Therapy Research 539
BIOLOGICAL THERAPIES 540
Electroconvulsive Therapy 540
Drug Therapies 542
HOSPITALIZATION 543
CHAPTER SUMMARY 546

18　Society's Response to Maladaptive Behavior

TYPES OF PREVENTION 550
Situation-focused and Competency-focused
　　Prevention 550
Levels of Prevention 552
SITES OF PREVENTION 556
The Family 556
The School 563
The Community 565
TREATMENT IN THE COMMUNITY 570
Problems with Community Programs 570
Improving Treatment Programs 571
Box 18–1 The Face of Homelessness 572

**LEGAL ASPECTS OF TREATMENT AND
　　PREVENTION 575**
Institutionalization 575
**Box 18–2 The Debate Over the Insanity
　　Defense 578**
The Rights of Patients 580
THE CHALLENGE OF PREVENTION 581
Paraprofessionals 582
Self-Help Groups 582
Community Psychology 584
A FINAL WORD 584
CHAPTER SUMMARY 585

Glossary 587
References 611
Photo References 636
Name Index 638
Subject Index 647

Preface

As authors, teachers, and active researchers we have a number of goals for this book. We want the seventh edition of *Abnormal Psychology* to interest students and make the field of abnormal psychology come alive for them. To accomplish this objective, throughout the book we have sought to link the material to students' life experiences, so that they can integrate their new knowledge into an existing framework to enhance its retention and use after the course is completed.

In writing this text, we have kept in mind four goals in particular, which we believe will enable students to obtain as clear an understanding of abnormal psychology as possible. Our first and most important goal in this edition, as in previous ones, is communicating to students the excitement and challenge of the field of abnormal psychology. Like all teachers of undergraduates, we want students to be knowledgeable, curious, and oriented to key issues that are being or should be explored. We work toward this goal in a number of ways. For example, we feature many issues of special interest to students, such as date rape, eating disorders, feelings of depression and suicidal thoughts, and the effects of substance abuse. These topics are discussed and then put into a larger interactional context. Rather than focusing on the sensational aspects of disordered behaviors, we help students understand how it may come about, how it is assessed and categorized, and what is known about its prevention and treatment. We have also provided a considerable amount of new and intriguing case material related to several types of disorders, including depersonalization, borderline and antisocial personality disorders, depression, bipolar disorder, brain disorders, and autism. Because maladaptive behavior's effects are not limited to the individual involved, we provide vivid illustrations of such behaviors' interpersonal effects. The text is laced not only with first-person accounts of experience with various types of mental illness but also includes descriptions of family members' efforts to cope with and help the affected person. These accounts greatly enhance both the interest value of the text and students' understanding of the personal and social consequences of maladaptive behaviors.

Our second goal is to provide students with an awareness of basic principles and a sufficiently broad theoretical perspective into which the findings can be placed. Our field constantly becomes more complex with increasing numbers of discrete findings. There is nothing so disorienting and discouraging for students as an overload of facts without a structure into which they fit; yet at the same time, there is nothing so simplistic as a theory that purports to account for everything. Thus, we have consistently worked to provide not a catalogue of findings and techniques but a theoretical structure in terms of which diverse perspectives, results, and methods can be integrated for students. Despite many positive changes from the preceding edition, we retain our general approach. The focus in this seventh edition continues to be on the interactions among determinants of abnormal behavior as seen from a variety of theoretical perspectives and vulnerability factors that may contribute to the development of disorders in the context of stressful situations. The book's structure allows students to analyze various types of vulnerability factors, including past experiences, current stressors, and a host of biological factors. We think the interactional and vulnerability models will help them view abnormal psychology as a coherent and integrated field.

A third goal of this edition is to enable students to understand the current exciting research developments in the field of abnormal psychology. We want students to know not only about the results of studies, but also about the research process that produces these findings. In this edition we have expanded our presentation of types of research and research designs, highlighting progress in especially promising areas. Chapter 1 has an entire section devoted to research design, and we have also illustrated the research enterprise throughout the book. For example, the study of the epidemiology of maladaptive behavior is addressed in many chapters.

While the number of intriguing new topics that this edition explores is too long to list here in full, we can mention some highlights. These include the comorbidity of maladaptive behavior; the neurosciences revolution and its implications for multidisciplinary research; the

increasing ability to predict genetic vulnerability to several disorders; the effect of AIDS on brain function as illustrated by AIDS dementia complex; the increasing use of group and family therapies in clinical work; the importance of relational assessment; and the broadening applications of cognitive techniques. We have added several examples of promising clinical techniques and processes, including novel assessment work-ups and approaches such as cognitive therapy and several of the biological therapies.

Presentation of the material in this edition takes into account the major features of DSM-IV whose publication is scheduled for 1994. While some details of the new DSM remain to be finalized, its major objectives, and how they are to be attained, are clear. DSM-IV will be a revision of DSM-III-R rather than an entirely new diagnostic system. Its emphasis is on improving user-friendliness and reliability, broadening comprehensiveness of coverage, and strengthening clinicians' ability to make differential diagnoses. In addition to fine tuning, DSM-IV is intended to be compatible with the World Health Organization's International Classification of Diseases (ICD-10) which will be published in 1995. Because some students have found confusing the many references to DSM-I, DSM-II, DSM-III, and DSM-III-R in abnormal psychology textbooks, and since references to DSM-IV will only add to this confusion, we have decided to refer to the American Psychiatric Association's classification system simply as DSM. Of course, whenever we make a point about a particular version of DSM we specify the edition. Unless otherwise specified, the concepts and diagnostic criteria are those of DSM-IV as they are expected to be presented or modified from DSM-III-R To help clarify the changes in diagnostic criteria over time we have designed the endpapers of this edition to reflect the major changes in classification since World War II. These diagnostic changes, in turn, reflect the many scientific and clinical advances of the past 50 years. A goal of the endpapers of this edition is to emphasize the fact that abnormal psychology, far from being static, is a dynamic and increasingly complex field in which the knowledge base continues to grow. Because of this growth and change, we believe emphasis rightly belongs on the concepts governing the diagnostic system rather than on details that may be changed many times during the student's lifetime.

With each new edition of *Abnormal Psychology* we have found ourselves impressed—and sometimes amazed—at the number of new developments that almost instantly become "hot topics." But these topics tell only part of the story needed to create a basic understanding of the field. While perhaps not so dramatic, the cumulative quality of research on maladaptive behavior is also impressive. We find the research discovery process exciting and challenging whether the topic is "hot" (like non-invasive brain imaging) or one that has been recognized for many years (such as gender differences in depression). A recent experience accidentally brought this cumulative aspect of the field of abnormal psychology home to us. We happened to leaf through the fourth edition of this book, which was published in 1984. An examination of the important topics of about ten years ago, as well as comparisons of the fifth and sixth edition texts with the seventh edition manuscipt, made clear how much has been learned in the field of abnormal psychology (as well as how much is still to be understood) and how the most prevalent research issues have shifted and been modified. For instance, some currently hot topics (such as psychoneuroimmunology) were nowhere to be found a decade ago. Other topics (such as the roles of expressed emotion in schizophrenic relapses and biological vulnerability in the development of schizophrenic disorders) were dealt with in 1984 and in successive editions, but research efforts have since come a long way in enhancing our understanding of these areas.

An especially good example of the cumulative impact of research is the nature–nurture issue. While the fourth edition accurately reflected the importance of this issue, expressed then as nature *versus* nurture, we now can see it as nature *interacting with* nurture. We try in the current edition to show students that pitting hereditary and environmental factors against each other is not nearly as valuable as using an interactional biopsychosocial approach to focus on how inheritance and experience jointly contribute to the shaping of behavior. Other topics that were merely touched upon in 1984 now occupy center stage because of recent research and clinical progress. These include the use of structured interviews in diagnosis, personality disorders in adults, and internalizing and externalizing disorders in children. In this edition we have increased our attention to research findings from both descriptive and interpretive standpoints.

We have devoted a great deal of attention to our fourth goal, making the text as pedagogically sound as possible. In addition to providing up-to-date information and what we hope is an engaging writing style, we have emphasized a variety of pedagogical features that contribute to coherence and integration. We have given special emphasis to *how* material is presented. For example, the tables and illustrations reflect the importance that we place on coherence and integration and on heightening the salience and interest level of the text material.

Many of the tables in this edition are integrative; that is, they make a meaningful Gestalt out of seemingly disparate facts. For instance, new integrative tables summarize the effects of frontal lobe lesions, risk factors for violent behavior, characteristics of a useful classification system, interpersonal features of testing situations,

clinical features in autistic disorders, and several other topics. In addition to case material that engages students' interest, we have carefully selected photographs and illustrations that depict the important conceptual and clinical points discussed in the text. We are especially pleased at the large number of color illustrations in this edition. In addition to adding new content, case examples, illustrations, and tables, we have carefully scrutinized every line of the previous edition, deleted material judiciously so that the new material added is not overwhelming, revised the writing on virtually every page of the book to maximize clarity, and intensified our efforts to provide a structure for theory, research, and practice. Wherever possible, we have sought to use nontechnical language and avoid jargon, to be comprehensive but not encyclopedic, broad as well as deep.

The current edition is cumulative, not only in content, but also in writing, teaching aids, illustrations, and features likely to spark students' interest. One of the dangers of such cumulation is an overly long and detailed text. Thus we have been careful not only to add, but to delete, to tighten the text and to keep in mind the amount of information students can assimilate in one academic term.

In the preface to the sixth edition we said we wanted to make the content of abnormal psychology accessible to students. This continues to be our guiding principle. We hope that the seventh edition's many attractive features, including comprehensive end-of-chapter summaries, an updated glossary, useful indexes, bold-faced key terms, engaging writing, and generous use of color, make it "user-friendly," thought-provoking, and motivating for students as well as an effective tool for instructors.

Many people had a hand in making this book. We want to thank first our editor, Susan Finnemore Brennan. She provided us with support, encouragement, and a first-class editorial and production team. Among those who worked with her at Prentice Hall, we especially want to take note of Lorinda Morris's work as art editor, and Marielle Reiter's efficiency and organization as production editor. Two people who made very significant

contributions to the book as an educational tool were Lauren Shafer who, as developmental editor, read the manuscript with a critical eye and contributed greatly to this edition's organization, clarity, and consistency, and Yvonne Gerin, whose photo research produced interesting and instructive illustrations and who excelled in detective work to track down the original source of hard-to-find but highly relevant illustrative material that we had come upon. We also want to express our gratitude to the reviewers for the seventh edition, each of whom read sections of the manuscript and provided many helpful suggestions:

- Ileana Arias, University of Georgia
- Patricia Barker, Schenectady County Community College
- Eric J. Cooley, Western Oregon State College
- Linda E. Flickinger, St. Clair County Community College
- Alan G. Glaros, University of Missouri—Kansas City
- James Huntermark, Missouri Western State College
- Linda Musun-Miller, University of Arkansas—Little Rock
- Joseph J. Palladino, University of Southern Indiana
- Mary E. Procidano, Fordham University
- Michael L. Raulin, State University of New York at Buffalo
- Louis W. Stamps, University of Wisconsin—La Crosse
- Thomas A. Widiger, University of Kentucky

In addition, we want to acknowledge the efforts of a number of our associates at the University of Washington. Betty Johnson typed much of the manuscript. Victoria Gradín played a leading role in helping us organize the many file boxes of reprints we had collected. Naomi Zavislak and Karen Robbins checked and verified references. Karen also made numerous trips to the library and became a first-class sleuth at turning up needed materials. She and Mark Maling were also very helpful in the last-minute rush that completing the name and subject indexes always entails.

Irwin G. Sarason
Barbara R. Sarason

The *New York Times* and Prentice Hall are sponsoring *A Contemporary View,* a program designed to enhance student access to current information of relevance in the classroom.

Through this program, the core subject matter presented in the Sarasons' text is supplemented by a collection of time-sensitive articles from one of the world's most distinguished newspapers, the *New York Times.* These articles are gathered into newspaper format to demonstrate the vital, ongoing connection between what is learned in the classroom and what is happening in the world around us. To enjoy the wealth of information in the *New York Times* daily, a reduced subscription rate is available in deliverable areas. For information, call toll-free: 1-800-631-1222.

Prentice Hall and the *New York Times* are proud to co-sponsor *A Contemporary View.* We hope it will make the reading of both textbooks and newspapers a more dynamic, involving process.

About the Authors

For many years, both Irwin Sarason and Barbara Sarason have been deeply interested in the multiple causes of maladaptive behavior and how it can be most effectively treated. They are especially intrigued by the human costs of psychological pain and behavioral problems for family members and the community, as well as for the person directly affected. Finding ways in which communities can be improved and become more supportive places to live has been a goal toward which they have worked throughout their careers. Some of the specific ways they have implemented this goal have been through their work with juvenile delinquents, high school students with poor academic motivation, and college students who experience uncomfortably high levels of test or social anxiety. The Sarasons are perhaps best known for their work on the role of social support as a modifier of stress and a promoter of mental health. They have worked extensively in a social-learning framework, most recently by using these principles to increase prosocial behavior among high school students. They are also actively involved in health psychology. At present they are conducting a large-scale project that uses psychological principles to produce social and environmental changes in a community setting to help motivate people to adopt healthier lifestyles.

The Sarasons are interested not only in maladaptation but also in how people overcome problems they confront in life. An important question for them is how success and happiness can be maximized given the seemingly overwhelming challenges each person must face throughout the life cycle. A current focus of their research is how people's individual relationships with family and friends not only aid them in coping with the stresses and strains of daily life but also help to promote their psychological adjustment. The topic of social support, in general and as a function of specific relationships, has implications for understanding individual development, abnormal behavior, health status, and the factors within the psychotherapeutic relationship that contribute to positive clinical outcomes. The Sarasons believe that an important ingredient of psychotherapy is the therapist's communication of acceptance and positive evaluation of the patient. Beyond the psychotherapeutic relationship, their work suggests that people who feel that they are accepted and valued by others are more likely to cope well with stress and are less likely to develop maladaptive symptoms.

Irwin Sarason received his B.A. degree from Rutgers University and Barbara Sarason received her B.A. degree from Depauw University. They first met while graduate students at the University of Iowa. Each has a Ph.D. degree with a specialization in Clinical Psychology from Indiana University. They moved to Seattle in 1956, after completing internships at the Veterans' Administration Hospital in West Haven, Connecticut. At present Irwin Sarason is professor and chairperson and Barbara Sarason is research professor in the Psychology Department at the University of Washington.

The Sarasons have published over 300 articles and many books on such topics as anxiety, stress and coping, personality research, social support, and techniques for facilitating behavioral change. They have both lectured extensively in the United States and in Europe.

Abnormal Psychology

CHAPTER 1

What Is Abnormal Behavior?
The Stigma of Abnormal Behavior
Adaptive and Maladaptive Behavior

Stress, Coping, and Vulnerability

Reasons for Clinical Contacts
Personal Unhappiness
The Concerns of Others
Legal and Community Problems

The Epidemiology of Maladaptive Behavior
Prevalence, Incidence, and Risk Factors

Sources of Help
Types of Treatment Facilities
Types of Mental Health Specialists

Research in Abnormal Psychology
Observing Behavior
The Role of Theory
The Research Journey
Types of Research
Statistics and Research Design

Ethical Aspects of Research

Chapter Summary

Pablo Picasso, *Brooding Woman*, 1904. Watercolor on paper, 10 5/8 × 14 1/2". Collection, Museum of Modern Art, New York. Gift of Mr. and Mrs. Werner E. Josten.

*I*t is worse to be sick in soul than in body, for those afflicted in body only suffer, but those afflicted in soul both suffer and do ill.

Plutarch, Moralia: Affections of soul and body, sec. 501 E. About 95 A.D.

Bob Cates had felt tense, anxious, and worried a lot of the time during his entire stay at the large university he attended. There seemed to be so much to do. However, in his senior year, despite the fact that he was usually an energetic person, even small things seemed to require a major effort. He felt particularly overwhelmed at pressure points like taking exams, writing papers, and having to say things in class.

For reasons that were not clear, Bob became increasingly depressed and began to feel that he couldn't go on much longer. His classes, and life in general, seemed less and less worth the effort they required. He couldn't concentrate on his school work and spent several hours each day sitting in his dormitory room—sometimes, just staring into space.

Bob Cates' friends noticed the changes in his behavior and mood and were concerned. As a result of their encouragement, Bob went to the University Counseling Service and had a series of sessions with a counselor. The questions that passed through the counselor's mind included the following:

What is Bob experiencing at the present time—what is he feeling and thinking about?

How serious is the problem that he is experiencing and to what degree is he aware of its seriousness?

What are the causes of Bob's problem—is the problem due to something that has

arisen in his current situation or is it a continuation of a long-term, perhaps lifelong, pattern?

What can be done to help Bob overcome his unhappy state?

What is going on in a particular person's life that results in unhappiness and disordered behavior? What can be done to alleviate the problem? These questions are the focus of abnormal psychology. In the case of Bob Cates, the problem was part of a long-term pattern, but was also related to things going on in his current life situation. His parents had always emphasized the importance of hard work and achievement. His excellent high school record showed to what degree he had learned to strive for success. What seemed to have happened at the university (many of the facts were far from clear) was that for the first time he began to question the values on which his need to achieve was based. As his counseling proceeded, he came to see that in many subtle ways his parents had shaped him to be a "producer." During his junior year, when he was beginning to think about what to do after completing his education, Bob began to feel that he could never achieve as much as his parents wanted him to. This thought had a nagging, depressing effect on him. The future seemed hopeless, and he felt helpless to do anything about it. After several counseling sessions Bob admitted that he had had suicidal thoughts, although he had never seriously considered taking his own life.

What Is Abnormal Behavior?

How abnormal is Bob Cates? While there is no basis for concluding that Bob is "crazy," he definitely has had serious difficulties in adjusting to college. Just how much pressure his parents actually placed on him is not answered by the available information. The fact that he spent hours just sitting in his room, together with his suicidal thoughts, suggests that he was experiencing adjustment difficulties that were much greater than those that are typical for college students.

In this book we will see cases of abnormal behavior both more and less serious than that of Bob Cates. Box 1–1 describes a man whose psychological problems dwarf those of Bob Cates and require that the community respond to them. Because our goal is not simply the description of abnormal behavior, we will review theoretical frameworks within which instances of human failure, inadequacy, and unhappiness have been conceptualized. At the same time we will also review basic research, pertinent to theories of abnormal behavior. This review of existing theory and research will give us a general framework within which to interpret the wide variety of human problems that find expression in abnormal behaviors. This framework emphasizes the roles played by stress, coping skills, and personal vulnerabilities.

Mental disorders, like anything unusual, may make us uncomfortable and even a little frightened. A mentally ill person should not be seen as evil, however, merely as different. **Abnormal psychology** is the area within psychology that is focused on maladaptive behavior—its causes, consequences and treatment. Abnormal psychology deals with how it feels to be different, the meanings that get attached to being different, and how society deals with people whom it considers to be different. The spectrum of differentness is wide, ranging from reality-defying delusions and severe debilitation to worries and behavioral quirks that we would be better off not having but that do not interfere significantly with our daily lives.

An example of this milder end of the spectrum is a man who was an eminently successful district attorney, was elected governor of New York on three occasions, and was almost elected president of the United States in 1948. This man, Thomas E. Dewey, reached the pinnacle of success, displaying such qualities as rectitude, efficiency, precision, and a nearly limitless capacity for hard work. Yet it was just this combination of traits that made Dewey seem too good to be true. For example, he was never late or absent in his first twelve years of schooling. He lacked a sense of humor and seemed to enjoy life only when he was achieving some goal. He also had personal rigidities that restricted the spontaneity so important in public figures. For example, he had a phobia about germs. When he toured prisons, he would not touch a doorknob without first wiping it off with a folded handkerchief concealed in his palm. He also drank three quarts of water a day because of its presumed healthful effects. Dewey achieved much, but had he been less rigid he might have achieved even more; perhaps more important, he might have been a happier person (R. N. Smith, 1982).

Governor Dewey's differentness was quite mild in comparison to problems like those experienced by Joan Houghton. Houghton's break with reality required intensive treatment during a 5-week period of hospitalization. After her recovery she wrote an account of her experiences.

My mother and I sat next to each other in the waiting room while my father investigated admission procedures. A young man was seated

BOX 1–1 Father Kills Two Young Sons

Sometimes people who have led a reasonably ordinary life begin to develop unusual behaviors. These changes may come about very quickly or they may be gradual. The case reported here shows a gradual buildup of pressures that finally brought about a tragedy. Most mental disorders do not involve violent behavior of any kind, let alone anything as horrifying as the act committed by the subject of this case, Bart Dobben. However, Bart Dobben (Figure 1–1), in his extreme and sudden violence, shares a trait common to many distressed individuals, even those with relatively mild disorders (such as Bob Cates). They are successful for long periods of time at masking their inner lives. Until they develop obvious behavioral symptoms, few people—even those who know them rather well—would guess the dimensions of the turmoil they are experiencing.

In some ways, the life of Bart Dobben was like that of everyone else on Amity Street. He mowed the lawn, tinkered with the car and doted on his two young sons.

Mr. Dobben was popular and active in school, said his mother, Mari Dobben. Like many young men in town, he went to work in the foundry, starting as a janitor after high school.

He soon moved into production, operating a huge vessel that purified and treated 10,000 pounds of molten iron at a time to produce various alloys, said Paul White, his partner in the vessel's control room for five years.

"He wasn't disliked," Mr. White said. "He was a friendly, outgoing person." He was energetic, his friend said, adding

that Mr. Dobben would ask the foreman for work when operations were slow.

"He took a lot of abuse from people he worked with," Mr. White said. "I felt a lot of people would take advantage of his nature and inability to come back with a lot of vulgar talk."

Mr. Dobben had a new house and a year-old baby when things began to unravel in late 1985. Mr. White, 31, said he noticed the change.

Mr. Dobben's wife, Susan, told officials that one day in September 1985, her husband took the family on a harrowing drive down twisting roads at speeds of up to 80 miles an hour "because he felt God told him that our baby was in danger."

The police were called and Mr. Dobben was taken to the psychiatric unit of a local hospital. But he refused psychiatric treatment.

Mrs. Dobben later filed a petition seeking to have her husband committed to the Kalamazoo Regional Psychiatric Hospital. In the petition, she said her husband once covered the house windows and the television set with towels, hung diapers over baby pictures and "anointed the baby and things in his room with olive oil."

Dr. Jadimpalli V. Raju, a psychiatrist, diagnosed Mr. Dobben as a schizophrenic who exhibited an "overreligious preoccupation" and who believed "God is going to come soon and take care of things."

On Thanksgiving Day, the police say, Mr. Dobben took his two

FIGURE 1–1 Bart Dobben.

sons, Bartley Joel, 2 years old, and Peter David, 15 months old, to the Cannon-Muskegon Corporation foundry where he worked and put them inside a giant ladle used to carry molten metal.

He then heated it to 1,300 degrees while his wife, unknowing, waited outside in the car. . . .

—Associated Press

So despite the outward similarity of his earlier life to that of his neighbors, Mr. Dobben was not like the rest of the people on Amity Street. His story culminated in a family tragedy.

near us. Perspiration dripped across his brow and down his cheeks. In silence I took a tissue from my purse, moved close to him and gently wiped the moisture from his face. I reassured him that everything would be fine.

Soon my father rejoined us. We went together to a small room where I met Kay, the psychiatric social worker assigned to my case, and a psychiatrist (whose name I don't recall). We talked a few minutes. I was presented with a

piece of paper and instructed to sign my name. Obediently, I wrote "Saint Joan" on the paper, not realizing that I was voluntarily admitting myself to a state mental hospital. . . . At the time of my hospitalization I had both a sense of death and a rebirth about me. My first psychotic episode appeared as a private mental exorcism, ending with the honor of sainthood and the gifts of hope and faith.

(Houghton, 1982, pp. 548–549)

The Stigma of Abnormal Behavior

Although Joan Houghton's recovery enabled her to obtain and hold a job at the National Institute of Mental Health and to write sensitively about her experience, she faced many barriers that made the recovery process more difficult than it had to be. Her ordeal continued after discharge from the hospital.

The crisis of mental illness appeared as a nuclear explosion in my life. All that I had known and enjoyed previously was suddenly transformed, like some strange reverse process of nature, from a butterfly's beauty into a pupa's cocoon. There was a binding, confining quality to my life, in part chosen, in part imposed. Repeated rejections, the awkwardness of others around me, and my own discomfort and self-consciousness propelled me into solitary confinement.

My recovery from mental illness and its aftermath involved a struggle—against my own body, which seemed to be without energy and stamina, and against a society that seemed reluctant to embrace me. It seemed that my greatest needs— to be wanted, needed, valued—were the very needs which others could not fulfill. At times, it felt as though I were trying to swim against a tidal wave.

(Houghton, 1980, p. 8)

The following incident illustrates what swimming against that tidal wave was like.

One Sunday I went to church alone after being absent for several weeks. The minister (who knew of my history, faith, and strong belief in God) began his sermon with reference to the devil. He said, "If you ever want to be convinced of the

existence of the devil, you should visit a mental institution." To illustrate his point, he described people who had lost control of their bodily functions, who screamed out obscenities. I left church after the sermon, drove home vowing never to return to that church as long as that minister preached from the pulpit. At home, however, I began to replace my anger with doubt. Maybe I misunderstood.

At my invitation the minister visited our home to discuss his philosophy about mental illness and the mentally ill. His visit was our last encounter. Not only did he see evil in mental illness but he conveyed an unforgiving attitude to those who have the misfortune of residing in mental hospitals.

(Houghton, 1980, p. 10)

As Houghton's account makes clear, people who are noticeably deviant may experience prejudice and discrimination. The stigma associated with mental illness may express itself directly, as when people outrightly reject individuals who behave in abnormal ways, or indirectly, as when former mental patients anticipate rejection even though they have not been rebuffed by anyone. In the course of socialization we all develop ideas about how mental patients are viewed and treated. If we are not mental patients ourselves, these beliefs may be relatively unimportant to us, applicable only to people on the margins of our lives. For those who do become patients, however, the beliefs become personally relevant. If they think that people devalue and discriminate against mental patients, they feel threatened. They may keep their personal worries and preoccupations a secret, or they may remove themselves from any social situation where they might be rejected. The resulting social withdrawal, uncertainty, and tentativeness affect their job performance, their relationship with others, and their opinion of themselves.

Although mental health professionals generally conclude that severe mental illness stems from organic or brain-based disorders, (Andreasen, 1984) the general public does not share this view. For example, a recent survey found that 71 percent of respondents thought severe mental illness was due to emotional weakness, 65 percent thought bad parenting was to blame, 35 percent cited sinful behavior, and 45 percent believed that the mentally ill bring on their illness and could will it away if they wished (Judd, 1990)[1]. Further, while psychologists believe much mental illness can be cured or most

[1]The percentage of responses across the categories adds to more than 100, because the respondents had the option of choosing more than one possible cause.

maladaptive behavior greatly reduced, a full 43 percent of survey respondents thought mental illnesses are incurable. Only 10 percent believed that severe mental disorders had a biological basis and involved the brain. A challenge to the field of abnormal psychology is to correct such misperceptions that distort the nature of abnormal behavior and may contribute to such stigmatization.

Adaptive and Maladaptive Behavior

The bulk of the behaviors studied by abnormal psychology are related to human failures and inadequacies. These failures in living are due mainly to failures in adaptation. **Adaptation** involves the balance between what people do and want to do, on the one hand, and what the environment (the community) requires, on the other.

Adaptation is a dynamic process. Each of us responds to our environment and to the changes that occur within it. How well we adapt depends on two factors: our personal characteristics (skills, attitudes, physical condition) and the nature of the situations that confront us (for example, family conflict or natural disaster). These two factors jointly determine whether we survive, are content, and prosper, or whether we fall by the wayside. Because nothing—neither ourselves nor the environment—stays the same for very long, adaptation must take place all the time. The extremely rapid rate of change in the modern world puts a particular strain on our ability to adapt. Moreover, successful adaptation to one set of conditions is not a guarantee of successful adaptation to others.

ADAPTATION AND ADJUSTMENT Scientists sometimes draw a distinction between adaptation and *adjustment*. Adaptation can refer to survival of the species, whereas **adjustment** refers to individual mastery of the environment and the sense of being at peace with oneself. In many instances this distinction is valid and useful. In certain cases, however, it oversimplifies the human situation. Unlike those of animals, the adaptive successes and failures of human beings cannot be measured simply in terms of the survival and reproduction of the species. For most people in the modern world, concerns about quality of life and level of contentment far overshadow the need to satisfy biological requirements. Human beings have developed subtle language forms, a refined level of thinking, superior problem-solving skills, intricate social relationships, and complex communication processes, all of which affect behavior and its interpretation. The notion that a failure to adapt may affect survival of the species has some credibility—individuals' feelings of failure may damage their social relationships, and the human gene pool might be significantly affected by the failure of such people to marry and have children. On the other hand, many individuals with certain types of inadequacies, who would probably be unable to hold their own in a subsistence economy, can survive and reproduce in the modern world because of social institutions such as welfare programs, Social Security, and health insurance.

Biological factors aside, how we live and how we feel about the way we live are important factors in human adaptation. For the authors of this book, adaptation refers to people's ability or inability to modify their behavior in response to changing environmental requirements. This book therefore, focuses primarily on people's personal and social adaptations.

MALADAPTIVE VERSUS DEVIANT BEHAVIOR All maladaptive behavior is deviant behavior. However, deviant or unusual behavior is not necessarily maladaptive. This can be seen in the case of Albert Einstein. At the age of 12 Einstein decided to devote his life to solving the "riddle of the huge world." Early in his career, while working as a patent office examiner, he wrote five papers that eventually changed our view of the universe. Although public recognition of the importance of Einstein's theory was many years away, his ability to think about the properties of matter in a completely new way began almost at once to influence the thought of physicists. While other kinds of deviant behaviors, such as wearing very bright ties, refusing to travel by airplane, drinking ten cups of coffee a day, and needing to read in bed for two hours before falling asleep, are not as productive as Einstein's behavior and may seem odd or annoying, people who act in these ways do not need major rehabilitative efforts to live happy, productive lives.

Describing behavior as **maladaptive** implies that a problem exists; it also suggests that either vulnerability in the individual, inability to cope, or exceptional stress in the environment has led to problems in living. Students of maladaptive behavior are especially interested in behavior that is not merely different or deviant but that also represents a source of concern to the individual, to his or her family and friends, or to society. This means, for example, that students of maladaptive behavior direct more of their attention toward those with very low IQs than toward those with high IQs, or toward those who are not happy rather than toward those who are extremely content.

There are many causes of maladaptations. In some instances—for example, in certain forms of brain damage—an organic cause is uncovered. In other cases, undesirable present or past social relationships—for example, an incestuous relationship—may be implicated. In still other cases, a combination of these factors along with a stressful event, such as the death of a loved one or the birth of a child, plays a decisive role.

Maladaptations range from chronic fears that are troubling but not disabling to severe distortion of reality, and inability to function independently. A person may simply be unhappy about his or her maladaptive behavior, or the community may be worried about what might happen if the person is not removed from society. Throughout this book many different kinds of maladaptive behavior will be described, along with the social reactions they evoke.

Stress, Coping, and Vulnerability

When we talk about how well people adapt, it is important to consider the conditions under which the adaptations are made. The same person may handle a frightening or difficult situation well at one time and maladaptively at others. Some people may behave adaptively in the same situation that others handle poorly. Why is this the case? Three concepts—stress, coping, and vulnerability—help us to understand these differences in behavior. Seven-year-old Denton may adapt well when he has a sympathetic teacher, when his parents are getting along well, and when he is healthy. However, if he has a teacher whom he hates, if his parents bicker half the night and are on the edge of divorce, and if he is constipated, he may become much more upset about not being a starting player in his soccer team than he might otherwise. Or if Mrs. Block has just lost an important client for her firm and comes home to find someone has smashed into her car as it sat parked in the driveway, and then her 12-year-old son tells her he has just left his violin on the school bus, she may not respond as constructively as she might have under other circumstances.

Stress refers to people's reactions to situations that pose demands, constraints, or opportunities. For example, a person could feel stressed by seeing a child fall into a rapidly flowing river, by being awakened by a fire alarm and smelling smoke, or by being promoted to a new job with more responsibility. People are likely to experience psychological stress when they have to deal with an unexpected or unusual change, such as a natural disaster. They are likely to experience even greater stress than usual when the change occurs at the same time as a severe life crisis (such as the death of a loved one) or at the beginning of a critical developmental period (such as adolescence). As Table 1–1 shows, the average number of stressful life events (such as family disturbances, serious illness of a parent, brother, or sister) is greater for clinical cases than for comparable control persons.

Coping refers to how people deal with difficulties and attempt to overcome them. **Coping skills** are the techniques available to an individual in making such attempts. A number of general skills are useful in handling stressful situations. These include thinking constructively, dealing with problems as they arise, behaving flexibly, and providing feedback to oneself about which tactics work in a given situation and which ones do not. How useful any particular skill will be depends upon the nature of the situation and the individual's vulnerabilities and assets. Having an effective repertoire of coping skills strengthens a person's sense of self-control and self-direction. By gaining greater control over our behavior, we may be able to alter environmental conditions that influence us.

Vulnerability refers to how likely we are to respond maladaptively to certain situations. An individual can be an effective coper in one situation but not in another. Vulnerability may be increased through heredity, such as having a schizophrenic parent, by certain personality characteristics such as a tendency to worry or

Table 1–1
Negative Life Events and Personal Maladjustment

Clinical Group		Average Number of Negative Life Events
Conduct disorders	Cases	1.18
	Controls	.36
Mild mood disorders	Cases	1.13
	Controls	.36
Severe mood disorders	Cases	.84
	Controls	.22
Somatic symptoms disorders	Cases	1.04
	Controls	.19

SOURCE: Based on Goodyer, Kolvin, and Gatzanis, (1985). Reprinted with permission from the *British Journal of Psychiatry*.

feel anxious, by the lack of certain skills such as the ability to make decisions calmly, or by a buildup of unexpected negative experiences. Some people are more vulnerable in all situations because they deal less effectively with what happens to them in daily life. Others are more vulnerable simply because of a combination of recent stressful events. Certainly people are more vulnerable in particular kinds of situations that remind them of former problems or difficulties. For example, upon seeing a child swept away in a river, a person who has seen one of her younger brothers killed in an accident when she was 5 might freeze, while someone who has not had such an experience might be able to act in time to save the child.

Certain life conditions in and of themselves increase people's vulnerability and increase their risk of maladaptive behavior. People who share these conditions become a part of a high-risk group that is more likely than the rest of the population to experience the negative effects of stress. Population groups that may be at high risk for certain conditions include children and adolescents, the aged and the disabled, and disadvantaged minority groups.

Stress, coping, and vulnerability are interrelated (see Figure 1–2). The greater the stress, the less vulnerability is required for a person to display maladaptive behavior. The less severe the stress, the greater the vulnerability needed to produce maladaptive behavior. The better people's coping repertoires, the less likely they are to be unable to function in situations in which they are vulnerable. Generally, it is easier and more effective to help people learn better ways of dealing with stress than to prevent the stresses to which they are vulnerable. Chapter 5 presents a more in-depth view of the effects of stress and the variety of ways people deal with them.

Clinical interventions are ways of helping people cope with stress more effectively. The intervention selected for someone who is experiencing a short-term crisis, such as the serious illness of a loved one, might be a tranquilizing drug. In this case, the tranquilizer reduces vulnerability to intense anxiety experienced over a specific period of time. In other cases, insight into the person's desires, motivations, and conflicts is needed in order to help the individual cope more effectively with stress and become less vulnerable to the crises that are the inevitable ingredients of every human life. Sometimes the person needs to learn new skills or behaviors that are effective in dealing with difficult situations. For some people, the way they think about a situation needs to be changed. If a low test grade makes you think, "I'm dumb; it's no use trying to finish this course," later academic performance might be very different than it would be if you thought, "I didn't study very effectively; I'd better organize my work better and check with the professor before the next test to ask about the points that aren't clear." Clinicians thus will vary their approaches depend-

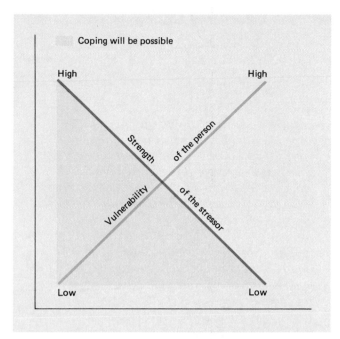

FIGURE 1–2 The interaction between stress and vulnerability determines whether coping will be possible. Whether a person has adequate coping skills determines whether coping will occur.

ing on their assessment of the factors in a given case and the psychological perspective or viewpoints they favor.

In this book we will present a number of different perspectives on why maladaptive behavior occurs and how adaptive behavior can be substituted for it. Running through our discussion of abnormal psychology will be a consideration of the effects of stress and individual vulnerability on the outcome of any particular situation. The more we understand what causes an individual to feel stressed, and the more we can identify the factors that produce vulnerability, the clearer the sources of the maladaptive behavior will be and the more likely we will be to come up with effective treatment procedures. This search for understanding is what the study of abnormal psychology is all about.

Reasons for Clinical Contacts

Some people seek professional help because they are dissatisfied with themselves and certain aspects of their lives; others do so because of concerns expressed by family members, friends, or co-workers; still others are forced to see clinicians because they have gotten into trouble in the community.

Personal Unhappiness

In the following case, personal unhappiness seems to have been the factor that led this person to seek help.

Jack Farmer was a 40-year-old executive in a large multinational corporation. From all outward appearances, any differences he might have had from other people were positive. Whatever weaknesses he had were minor. For example, his athletic ability was probably below average. The opinion of his company and community was that Jack Farmer was a very well-functioning individual. While he and his wife and two children got along reasonably well, Jack had some concerns that had shaped his family role, particularly as his children approached high school age. These concerns had to do with the burdens of family responsibility, especially the need he felt to ensure his family's happiness should anything happen to him. He occasionally commented to his wife that television commercials about the need to have plenty of life insurance seem to have been written specifically with him in mind. However, Jack was concerned about more than money. He felt that he should be a closer friend to his children and less distant from his wife than he often was. He was also very concerned about the issue of nuclear waste and the pollution of the natural environment. His concerns often led to his feeling blue and hopeless about the future.

One Sunday Jack read a newspaper article about a local mental health center that had opened recently. The article pointed out that the center's services were not restricted to severely disturbed individuals, that perfectly normal people who have hit a rough spot in their lives might find it valuable to talk with an expert about their personal problems. After several weeks of internal debate ("Could I be a little crazy?" "I'd be ashamed if my friends ever found out that I went to a shrink"), Jack decided to go to the mental health center.

By conventional standards, Jack Farmer's case is not serious. He sought help because of personal dissatisfactions and concerns. Wrestling further with his personal tensions seemed worse to him than his fear of being stigmatized if he sought professional help.

The Concerns of Others

Sometimes it is difficult even for professionals to decide what the dividing line should be between maladaptive and merely unusual behavior. In the following case, there was no agreement about whether the woman concerned was psychotic (out of touch with reality) and needed institutionalization, or whether her behavior was simply unusual and presented no hazard to her or her family.

Mary Waverly was in her late twenties. A university graduate, she had run a successful boutique in a large western city until shortly before the birth of her daughter, Alice, who is now 2 years old. During the year before Alice was born, Mary's mother had been treated for cancer. She died when Alice was fourteen months old. During Alice's first year and a half, the baby had surgery several times to correct a birth defect.

Recently, Mary's husband attempted to have her committed to a psychiatric hospital. He said he was concerned about their daughter's welfare. Mary had become preoccupied with rather unusual religious ideas. Although she came from a very religious family, until recently, when she joined a cult group, her behavior had not seemed out of the ordinary. Since joining the group she refused to have sexual relations with her husband because he was not a "believer." Although she seemed to take good care of her child, she made all decisions only after listening to the "voice of the Lord."

When Mary Waverly was examined, her judgment did not seem impaired, her intelligence was found to be above average, and her religious thoughts, although they took up a great deal of her time, did not seem to differ from those of other enthusiastic converts to cult groups. A pediatrician examined her daughter and reported that she was well cared for. A question was raised about what Mary Waverly might do if she thought God told her to harm her child or someone else. Neither of the clinicians who examined her was willing to give a definite answer to this question.

Mary Waverly didn't think she had a mental disorder and didn't think she needed treatment. One of the clinicians agreed. He believed that her behavior was unusual but that she was not mentally ill. Another clinician thought she was a paranoid schizophrenic who

should be hospitalized for drug therapy. What should be done when professionals disagree? In this case, after hearing the conflicting views Mr. Waverly decided not to press for hospitalization.

Legal and Community Problems

Mild personal maladaptations like Jack Farmer's affect the lives of the individual and possibly a small number of other people. Mary Waverly's behavior was a matter of concern to her husband because he was worried that she might harm their daughter. In the case of Charles Clay, a legal problem arose over something he had done.

Charles Clay, aged 45, owned what had been a successful 24-hour-a-day grocery store. Now, however, he was having increasing difficulty containing his anger toward his customers. Until five years ago he had been a cheerful, friendly merchant. Then his wife died, and his personality seemed to change. Increasingly he worried that people were trying to shoplift his merchandise. (There was a problem with a few high school students who frequented his store right after school.) As time went on, he began to confront customers with his suspicions and even to demand that some of them submit to being searched.

Not surprisingly, Charles' business began to decline. When this happened, he got very angry and even more suspicious. The culminating event occurred when a woman entered the store, walked around for a few minutes, and then bought a newspaper. When he tried to search her (at the same time yelling, "Don't tell me you were just looking around!"), she ran from the store and summoned the police. The ensuing police investigation led him to seek advice from his lawyer, who had been a friend since high school. Although Charles insisted that "there is nothing the matter with me," his anger and suspiciousness bothered his lawyer. Using tact and persuasion, the lawyer got him to agree to visit a psychiatrist. Unfortunately, the visit did not work out well. He was reluctant to talk about his concerns with the psychiatrist and was angered by what he viewed as the psychiatrist's inquisitiveness. He refused to return for a second visit. Nevertheless, the lawyer was able to get Charles out of trouble with the police. Unfortunately, several months later he was
arrested and convicted of physically attacking another customer.

Many people saw Charles Clay as having problems that he refused to recognize. In spite of the social consensus about the maladaptive quality of his behavior, he gave himself a clean bill of health. In part because of his failure to perceive his own behavior accurately, he eventually got into trouble with the law. His first contact with the police did not result in formal charges; the community's agents recognized his psychological difficulties, and the focus of their attention was on helping a citizen with his personal problems. The second contact, however, resulted in punishment for a crime. Society had decided that he was not going to help himself and moved to protect itself.

Gross failure to see oneself accurately, as illustrated by the case of Charles Clay, is characteristic of several of the most serious forms of maladaptive behavior. In such cases, it is a highly positive development if the person begins to suspect that his or her behavior is contributing to difficulties in getting along with others.

The Epidemiology of Maladaptive Behavior

Psychologists use findings from **epidemiological research** to help them understand patterns and possible relationships between maladaptive behaviors of certain populations or groups and a variety of environmental and behavioral factors. Information for epidemiological research may come from analyses of various types of data, such as hospital and clinic records, the geographical distribution of mental disorders, and the types of community facilities available for the treatment of the mentally disturbed. For example, a study of institutional records has shown that the northeastern and Pacific Coast regions of the United States have had consistently higher rates of schizophrenia over an 83-year period than have other regions of the country (Torrey & Bowler, 1990). Research is needed to identify the reasons for these geographical differences.

Another example of the role of epidemiological research emerges from the finding that a number of basic personal factors, such as age and sex, have been shown to be correlated with types of disorders and use of clinical facilities (National Institute of Mental Health, 1990). Table 1–2 shows the rates per 100,000 population for

Table 1-2
Admission to Outpatient Mental Health Services[a]

Age Group	Rate
Under 18	872.3
18–24	1098.9
24–44	1276.2
45–65	567.4
65 and over	229.6
All ages	888.6

[a]Rates per 100,000 civilian population

SOURCE: Based on National Institute of Mental Health (1990), p. 164.

different age groups admitted to outpatient facilities for the treatment of mental and behavioral problems. It is noteworthy that children and youth are admitted at a higher rate relative to their number in the population than are both the elderly and those aged 45 to 64. In contrast, the admission rates for the elderly are low relative to their number in the population.

Epidemiologists are interested in identifying the environmental causes of particular conditions, especially those causes associated with a community's way of life. The Broad Street pump incident is one of the most famous examples of epidemiological inquiry and its use in furthering public health. In 1848, during a severe cholera epidemic in London, a study of the disease's distribution within the city was carried out. The investigation showed that the outbreak had a geographical center, a water pump in Broad Street. It was further found that two groups of people within that area—inmates of an institution and employees of a brewery—did not develop the illness in anything like epidemic proportions. Each of these groups had its own well, and brewery workers drank beer rather than water at work. On the basis of this information, the Broad Street pump was dismantled and the epidemic was brought under control. This example is especially interesting because it shows how epidemiological detective work can contribute to human well-being even when the cause of a condition is unknown—in 1848 the microorganisms that cause cholera had not yet been identified.

Prevalence, Incidence, and Risk Factors

Epidemiologists conduct surveys to estimate the extent of a health problem. Epidemiological research has identified a number of factors that must be attended to in order to ensure the accuracy of survey results. These include representative sampling of the population, clearly worded questions asked, and careful training of interviewers. Table 1–3 gives the definitions of a number of concepts used in epidemiological research.

Two types of information are obtained in epidemiological surveys. **Prevalence** data describe the frequency of occurrence of a given condition among a certain population at a particular point in time. For example, if, on a given date, 100 cases of depression were counted in a community of 1,000 people, the prevalence rate would be 10 percent. A recent study has concluded that one in five Americans has an active behavioral disorder, and the best estimate is a 32 percent lifetime prevalence for a disorder of some type (Robins & Regier, 1991). **Incidence** data relate to the number of *new* cases of a specific condition that arise during a particular period of time. For example, if 10 people who had not been depressed at the time of the prevalence study became depressed during the next year, the incidence rate would be 1 percent.

In addition to prevalence and incidence, another important epidemiological concept is **risk factor.** This concept is based on the finding of a statistically significant association between a disorder and a factor (for example, lung cancer and smoking; cardiovascular disease and high cholesterol level). For example, the following are risk factors that have been identified for violent behavior (Reid & Balis, 1987):

- History of aggressive, destructive behavior
- History of repeated traffic violations (reckless driving, etc.)
- History of abuse and neglect in childhood
- Childhood history of severe hyperactivity and restlessness
- Habitual alcohol use and dependence
- Suicidal attempts and gestures
- Hypersexuality
- Low frustration tolerance
- Low self-esteem and failure to achieve
- Inability to examine one's own behavior
- Impulsivity
- Self-centeredness

When risk factors are identified, they may be useful in suggesting prevention efforts. For example, children who have been abused or neglected might be given the opportunity to have positive experiences with caring adults as a step toward preventing long-term frustration and anger. Risk factors can serve as early warning signs of the need for intervention regarding particular conditions.

The value of identifying risk factors is reflected in a study of the relationship between diagnosis of abnormal behavior and the likelihood of committing violent acts. Overall, mental abnormality by itself has not been found to contribute much to the prediction of violent behavior.

However, epidemiological research on a large representative sample of residents in several cities has yielded two important findings (Swanson and others, 1990). One is that some diagnoses are more predictive of violent behavior than others. In the Swanson investigation, substance abusers report committing very high rates of violent acts. Persons diagnosed with anxiety disorders have low rates of violence, and diagnoses of schizophrenia are associated with only slightly elevated rates. Young males of lower socioeconomic status are found to be at substantially higher risk levels. The other important finding of the Swanson study concerns the relationship between the number of diagnostic categories used in describing individuals and the risk of violent behavior. As Figure 1–3 shows, the rate of reported violent behavior increases sharply with the number of diagnostic categories assigned by clinical workers. A greater number of diagnostic categories might be taken as an indicator of the complexity of a case and the gross amount and variety of psychopathology present. Thus, the more symptoms and problems someone has, the more likely that violent behavior will be among them. We should bear in mind the limitations of this epidemiological survey, however. The reports of violent behavior came from the survey respondents themselves. The study's conclusions need to be confirmed by independent assessments of the occurrence of violent behavior.

In addition to establishing connections between various factors, epidemiological surveys have proven valuable in correcting some false assumptions. (Robins & Regier, 1991). It had been thought that minority groups must have high rates of antisocial personality and substance abuse disorders because they have high rates of arrest and incarceration. However, recent evidence suggests that the high arrest and incarceration rates among minority groups cannot be explained simply by diagnoses of antisocial personality and substance abuse disorders. Until recently it had been generally assumed that women are particularly liable to develop psychological problems. However, recent surveys have shown that psychological

FIGURE 1–3 Percentage of respondents reporting violent behavior by the number of diagnoses (Dx).
(Swanson, Holzer, Ganju, & Jono. (1990). *Hospital and Community Psychiatry,* p. 767)

disorders in men are as common or slightly more common than in women. Women are more likely to have depressive and anxiety disorders while men are more apt to have substance abuse and antisocial personality disorders (Robins & Regier, 1991).

Mental illness has an effect not only on diagnosed individuals, but also on their family members. An estimated 30 to 40 million people experience some direct consequences because of their close ties with mentally ill individuals (Research on Mental Illness and Addictive

Disorders, 1985). In this book, we will focus not only on the effect of maladaptive behavior on the person whose problems are described but also on the impact of the problem on family members—parents, husbands, wives, and children. Table 1–4 (on page 11) lists several factors that are significantly related to the presence of mental illness. It seems clear that interpersonal, economic, and educational factors play important roles in the frequency of abnormal behaviors. There is also evidence that people who have good coping skills and supportive friends and relatives are less likely to suffer psychological distress than those who do not (Horwitz, 1984).

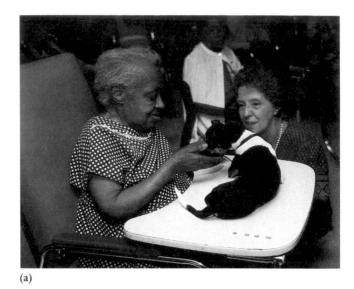

(a)

Sources of Help

Types of Treatment Facilities

Despite the decrease in recent years in number of beds in state mental hospitals, these institutions continue to play an important role in caring for the most disturbed and troublesome patients in the U.S. mental health system. State hospitals serve as 24-hour emergency backups, the institutions of last resort and ultimate responsibility (Rosenstein and others, 1986). Nevertheless, most experts agree about the desirability of treating people in the community as early as possible so as to avoid institutionalization.

Community-based treatment has become a more realistic possibility for some disturbed individuals because of an increase in the availability of community facilities, changes in state laws regarding involuntary hospitalization and the detaining of disturbed individuals in mental hospitals, and the discovery that a variety of drugs effectively control much of the violent and bizarre behavior associated with mental patients. The number of community treatment and care facilities has increased over threefold since 1955, and the trend toward treating people in the community is now firmly established. Figure 1–4 shows some of the mental health services that are available today.

(b)

FIGURE 1–4 A variety of community mental health services provide for the many different mental health needs that exist in any community. a) The therapist knows that contact with a pet can be an effective therapy for isolated people because it helps them to feel loved and cared for and provides a new interest in their lives. b) Not all mental health services are provided by professionals. This parent volunteer is discussing drug problems with a teen group. c) Sometimes the most effective way to understand how to deal with problems is discussion of them with a well-trained therapist.

(c)

Since the 1960's there has been a movement to **deinstitutionalize,** or return to the community, mental patients whose problems can be expected to continue for long periods. Under the banner of community-based care, many of them now live in nursing homes, boarding houses, residential hotels (often in undesirable neighborhoods), and subsidized apartments. This change, based partly on concern for the civil rights of the individual, is also a result of scientific advances like the use of antipsychotic drugs. These make it possible for many people to function adaptively enough so that they don't need to be institutionalized, although many of these individuals still behave in marginal, ineffective fashion. The development of community support programs in conjunction with established therapeutic programs for chronically mentally ill individuals offers promise of better lives for many people. At the present time, however, a comprehensive range of residential, therapeutic, and social services is not available in many communities. As a result, many people who might be able to function in a protected environment or with some types of psychological support or supervision of antipsychotic medication end up as part of the homeless population, often in large urban areas. Chapter 17 will look at this problem in more detail.

Types of Mental Health Specialists

Most of the behavior patterns with which this book deals are of special interest to four groups of mental health specialists: clinical psychologists, psychiatrists, psychiatric social workers, and psychiatric nurses. A **clinical psychologist** holds a graduate degree, usually a Ph.D., and specializes in abnormal behavior. Clinical psychologists are trained to diagnose and treat personality problems that are not medical or organic in nature. They also plan and conduct research investigations. A **psychiatrist** is a physician (an M.D.) with postgraduate training and experience in treating emotional disorders. Psychiatrists have legal responsibilities in commitment proceedings and in the supervision of mental hospitals. **Somatic therapies,** such as drugs and electroconvulsive therapy, are administered by psychiatrists. A **psychiatric social worker,** holder of a graduate degree in social work, is most often concerned with the link between a person who displays problematic behavior and his or her home environment. Psychiatric social workers are trained to work with families and help them utilize social agencies or other community resources to get practical help with such things as finances, as well as mental health care.

A **psychiatric nurse** has special training in the care of mentally-ill patients. Psychiatric nurses play a variety of roles. They are skilled in working closely with patients and understanding their needs so that all contacts the patient has with others during a hospitalization have as much of the therapeutic focus as possible. Within hospital settings they often supervise ward personnel and train them in the approach they should take with each patient.

The activities of these mental health workers, especially of psychiatrists, clinical psychologists, and social workers often overlap. For example, all three are trained to conduct psychotherapy and counseling. Table 1–5 shows the numbers of these mental health specialists among men and women.

The following account by a clinical psychologist accurately reflects the diversity of activities in which most clinicians engage.

I wish the time passed more slowly because there is just so much to do. From talking to my clinician friends I know I'm not alone in feeling that way. Part of the problem is that most of us don't just do one thing. Sure, some do mainly therapy and others are primarily diagnosticians. But most of us do many things.

Table 1–5

Number of Clinically Trained Mental Health Personnel

Professional Group	Total Number	Number of Men	Number of Women
Psychology	56,530	35,275	21,255
Psychiatry	30,642	25,348	5,294
Social work	81,737	23,050	58,687
Psychiatric nursing	10,567	444	10,123

SOURCE: Based on Mental Health, United States. (1990).

Take me, for example. I work in a big-city general hospital that has two wards for psychiatric cases and a large outpatient clinic. Many of these patients are not in very good contact with reality. In some cases police officers picked them up because they were wandering aimlessly around town in the middle of winter, in the dead of night. In other cases, they are people who have had some recent situational stress and are just not able to come to terms with it.

In still other cases, physicians who have patients on other wards in the hospital ask us for help. Yesterday, for example, a surgeon referred a case to me because the patient, who is supposed to undergo abdominal surgery tomorrow, has been in such a psychological panic that the doctor felt something had to be done—and he didn't know what to do. So far, I've talked with the patient twice. Really, all I did was listen and let her ventilate her feelings. You'd be amazed how much just listening in a sympathetic and supportive manner does to help a person who is going through a stressful situation. When I told the surgeon that this patient was very worried about getting too strong a dose of anesthetic and dying he was amazed. He said the patient had never mentioned that worry to him.

About 20 percent of my time is spent dealing with problems nonpsychiatric physicians need help with. Perhaps 30 percent is spent doing therapy either on the wards or in the outpatient clinic. Another 20 percent involves administering psychological tests to patients with particular problems. The rest of the time I do research. That's what usually gets squeezed out when a number of pressing clinical problems arise. That's when I most need a time-stretcher. But all the pressure is nothing compared to how much I like what I'm doing. I wouldn't trade with anybody.

The work of professionals in the mental health field is especially challenging because it requires the ability to think on one's feet correctly and quickly size up a problem ("Is this person depressed enough to be thinking about suicide?"), and devise appropriate and sometimes unusual treatment plans for clients. This means that while clinicians strive for complete objectivity in their work and try to use proven techniques, they often must devise on-the-spot tactics to deal with the particular problem confronting them.

Research in Abnormal Psychology

Scientific investigation, or the use of the scientific method, has greatly increased our understanding of abnormal behavior, how to treat it, and how to prevent it. As a consequence, observation and fact have replaced beliefs and hope in the effort to help people suffering from behavior disorders.

Some scientists have contributed to clinical progress either by accident or as an offshoot of some other interest. For example, some advances in developing tranquilizing drugs came from the observation that drugs that were being used for other purposes also decreased anxiety. However, most of the scientific information on which contemporary abnormal psychology is based comes from in-depth studies of deviant people. Although researchers may differ on their interpretation of data, they agree that careful observation is essential for scientific progress.

Observing Behavior

Certain sciences, such as astronomy and anatomy, are basically descriptive in nature. Scientists in those two disciplines concentrate on using careful observations to describe heavenly or earthly bodies. Psychologists also do research that is descriptive in nature. By describing various behaviors and the specific circumstances under which they seem to occur, researchers can obtain important information about potential cause-and-effect relationships. Observation and description are often the first steps in the scientific process; eventually they lead to the formulation of hypotheses that can be tested experimentally and applied in clinical situations. As can be seen in the following description, observation plays an important role in psychological treatment:

I noticed that Mr. R never looked directly at me. He answered my questions but always looked the other way. He seemed terribly shy and afraid. I was tempted to ask him what he was afraid of, but decided not to because he might take my comment as a criticism.

Some clinicians might have decided to ask Mr. R. about his apparent fearfulness. However, all would agree

on the importance of carefully observing and noting his anxious behavior.

The scientific process always begins with some kind of noteworthy observation. Researchers often stumble onto important discoveries quite by accident. When this happens, a good researcher heeds B. F. Skinner's advice: "When you run into something interesting, drop everything and study it" (Skinner, 1959).

One problem in psychological research is that people cannot be completely disinterested observers of themselves. Personal values, goals, and interests, together with cultural norms, influence our judgments about the success or failure of human adaptation. Maladaptation is neither a universal nor a timeless concept. Behavior that may be quite adaptive in one society may be a failure in another.

With this in mind, how do scientists study human behavior objectively? They record responses, describe events and the conditions surrounding them, and then draw inferences about causes. In order to overcome the effects of personal bias, several observers make reports on each of the individuals or events under study. Reliability increases when these observers have a common frame of reference, agree on which particular aspects of behavior to emphasize (and which not to emphasize), and when they do not have to draw too many inferences from their observations. Observational methods are used in specially created laboratory conditions as well as in naturally occurring situations.

Observation is more than simply using one's eyes in a seemingly straightforward way. Certain questions must be asked first: What types of responses should be selected for observation? How capable is the observer of making reliable and unbiased observations? Will the observer's presence influence the behavior that he or she wants to study? Is it preferable to observe behavior within naturally occurring settings or under controlled laboratory conditions? Should observations be limited to motor responses (walking, running), verbal responses (phone conversations, requests for help), or expressive behavior (smiling, crying)? How long a period of time is needed for reliable observation? Is time sampling needed—that is, should observations be gathered during several different time intervals? Even mental patients who hallucinate frequently do not engage in this kind of behavior all the time; time sampling can provide data on the conditions under which certain types of responses are most likely to occur.

Reliable observations can provide useful records of both the incidence of behavior in a given environment and the events that elicit and maintain it. An example of how observational research can correct commonsense but incorrect assumptions is found in a study of the frequency of interactions between patients and staff on a

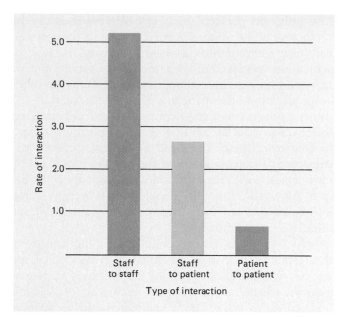

FIGURE 1–5 Rates of interaction for different patient and staff relationships.

(Adapted from Eldred, Bell, Longabaugh, & Sherman. (1964). p. 4)

mental hospital ward (Eldred and others, 1964). One might assume that the staff members' goal of helping their patients would lead them to spend most of their time interacting with the patients. However, as Figure 1–5 shows, the rate at which staff members interacted with other staff members was approximately double the rate at which they interacted with the patients. The low rate of interaction among the patients themselves also seems surprising, but it is typical of the social isolation found on the wards of many mental hospitals.

Although they are subjective and therefore are

FIGURE 1–6 The mood and activity changes in a patient treated for depression. The patient's mood ratings are based on her self-observations.

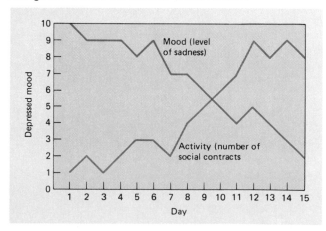

susceptible to personal bias, **self-observations** can be useful in clinical research. For example, a patient who had been admitted to a mental hospital because of depression was asked to keep track of her mood (level of sadness) and activity (number of social exchanges with hospital staff or other patients). Figure 1–6 (on page 15) shows a progressively less depressed mood and increased social activity during her first 15 days of hospitalization. In this case, there was good agreement between the patient's self-observations and the observations made by the hospital staff. This concordance will not always be the case. As we all know, the people with whom we come into contact in our daily lives may not see us as we see ourselves (see Figure 1–7).

Self-observations are useful in keeping records of the responses to clinical treatment. In the case of the patient whose self-observations are recorded in Figure 1–6 the treatment was complex, consisting of a benign hospital environment, daily individual and group psychotherapy, and medication. It would be interesting to compare the self-observation records of groups of comparable patients whose treatment consisted of only one of these elements—the hospital environment, psychotherapy, or medication alone—as well as all the possible combinations of these treatments.

TYPES OF OBSERVATIONAL DATA The value of observations is greatest when what is to be observed is defined explicitly. Four types of data are of special interest in observational research:

1. The stimuli that elicit particular types of responses—for example, the influence of family members' behavior (such as criticism or hostility) on a person who is prone to become depressed.

2. The subjective response to the stimuli—for example, the person's feelings when he or she is criticized.

3. The behavioral response to the stimuli—for example, the person's level of social activity after receiving criticism.

4. The consequences of the behavior—for example, how does the environment respond when the person behaves in a depressed manner?

The types of observations made and the observational methods employed depend on a number of factors, including the hypothesis being investigated and the situations in which the observations must be made. Observations might be made by means of hidden videotaping equipment, by visible observers who do not interact with the people they are studying, or by participant observers who become actively involved in the behavior they are observing. Each of these methods has advantages and disadvantages. For example, secret videotaping allows us to observe behavior without the knowledge of the individual who is being observed, but this technique is often questionable for ethical reasons. Participant and nonparticipant observations have been used by anthropologists and sociologists as well as by

FIGURE 1–7 (Drawing by Mankoff; © 1985 The New Yorker Magazine, Inc)

"You are fair, compassionate, and intelligent, but you are perceived as biased, callous, and dumb."

psychologists. However, any observer may affect people's behavior simply by being present. Participant observers may damage their objectivity by becoming overinvolved with the people they are studying. Nonparticipant observers may come to superficial conclusions because they are not involved enough. Each of these techniques can be valuable, and each has both supporters and critics.

The Role of Theory

While bird watchers, museumgoers, and children in the back seat of a car may observe—often very precisely—what is going on around them, scientists seek to make observations that not only describe what is going on but also explain it. Scientific study involves a continuous interplay between observations and attempts to explain and understand what was observed. Typically, the path of scientific understanding involves these steps:

1. Initial, often informal, observations

2. Tentative hypotheses to explain the meaning of the observations

3. Further observations (if possible, under controlled conditions), to test the hypotheses

4. Theory building

Scientists like to proceed from observation to theory because they want to figure out why or how a particular phenomenon occurs. Behaving just as lay people would, they use reason, logic, and sometimes simple guesswork to arrive at an initial and tentative explanation. However, whereas casual observers may be satisfied with such a tentative answer, scientists recognize it as only tentative and go on to test their understanding by "if . . . then . . ." hypotheses that can be evaluated (for example, "if patients are concerned about rejection by the therapist, then they will be uncomfortable in therapy," or "if children are frustrated, then they are likely to behave aggressively"). They then proceed to collect the observations needed either to support or refute the hypothesis. If the hypothesis is supported by their observations, they return to their original "Why?" question and attempt to formulate increasingly broad concepts and principles that go beyond initial observations. This is the way theories are developed.

Good theories have a number of functions. First, they are able to incorporate many existing facts, observations, and relationships within a single, broad explanatory framework. Second, additional hypotheses may be derived from the theory and tested, and may lead to new observations. In this way theories provide a foundation on which to build knowledge. If new observations do not support the theory, it may be modified or discarded.

However, it will still have served a valuable function by leading to the discovery of new knowledge and to the development of an even better and more inclusive theory.

In order for a theory to be useful, it must be capable of being tested and refuted. It should be able to specify the types of relationships that are not possible as well as those that are. If it seems able to account for everything and anything, even seemingly contradictory facts, it is not a good scientific theory. The essence of the scientific method is systematic observation and the use of objective procedures to identify cause-and-effect relationships.

The Research Journey

The path of research from observation to theory is a little like going on an automobile trip. There is a lot more to the journey than knowing where one is and where one wants to go. What route should be followed? Will there be detours? Would bad weather make a difference? How should one prepare for the trip? Following are some of the important steps in the scientist's research journey:

1. *Specifying the topic as clearly as possible.* Suppose you are intrigued by psychotherapy. Why are you drawn to that topic? Is it because you think verbal interchanges are crucial to achieving therapeutic change? Or are you more interested in the interpersonal relationship between client and therapist?

2. *Reviewing the relevant literature.* Some library work can save a researcher a lot of time and frustration. Studying the pertinent books and journals can answer many questions: How have other people dealt with this idea? What were the outcomes of their research?

3. *Defining the variables.* A variable is any aspect of a person, group, or setting that is measured for the purposes of the study in question. **Independent variables** are manipulated by the researcher in order to investigate their effects on particular outcomes that are called **dependent variables.**

4. *Developing a specific hypothesis.* A **hypothesis** is a statement to be proved, an idea that has been formulated so that it may be evaluated using scientific methods. A hypothesis is a kind of educated guess that states a predicted relationship between events or variables. It is typically stated in the form "If A exists, then B will occur."

5. *Selecting a research strategy.* What plan of action will permit the hypothesis to be tested? Does the researcher plan to see each subject on one occasion (for example, at the beginning or end of psychotherapy), or will several observations be necessary in

order to test the hypothesis? Should an experiment be conducted? Conducting an experiment means systematically varying one or more conditions for some groups but not for others. Is experimental research possible in a particular clinical setting?

6. *Conducting the study.* The research should be carried out objectively enough to permit others to replicate it. Therefore, all the steps in the research process must be specified. For example, how was the sample of subjects selected? Were the subjects chosen on the basis of age, sex, or intelligence? If so, the selection variables must be specified.

7. *Analyzing the results.* How did the group or groups perform? What is the likelihood that the results are simply due to chance? An analysis of research results usually includes making a distribution of the scores obtained by subjects; calculating relevant **descriptive statistics,** the numerical measures (scores) that enable a researcher to describe certain aspects of subjects' performance (for example, the mean or average); and calculating **inferential statistics,** the statistics that are used for judgments about the probability that the results are due to chance.

8. *Reporting research findings.* Writing up a piece of research not only permits communication of ideas and findings to others but also forces researchers to think through all that they have done and the meaning that might be attached to it. Going public serves an important communication function. The scientific journey would be much less valuable if research results were not written up and published.

Types of Research

Researchers use a variety of methods to better understand maladaptive behavior. We will focus on clinical observations here because of the valuable insights they provide about individual cases. Clinical studies also suggest profitable directions for projects involving various samples of subjects and methods. The following sections will discuss the most common types of clinical observations.

CASE STUDIES **Case studies** involve detailed observations of a single patient's behavior. The clinician tries to organize many observations conceptually. In most case studies, explanations of the events occur after the fact, and there is little, if any, opportunity to rule out other possible explanations by controlling for them. Even the most intensive study of an individual case cannot assure us that we have isolated the true causes of the

(b)

FIGURE 1–8 It is dangerous to infer causality from correlational data. (a) The witches are trying to infer causality on the basis of an association they have observed; (b) the man's data are recollections of past events, which can be notoriously unreliable. The recollections could be correlated with his current mood.

([a] By permission of Sidney Harris and *Saturday Review World*; © 1987 by Sidney Harris. [b] "Frank and Ernest" drawing by B. Thaves. Reprinted by permission of NEA, Inc.)

(a)

FIGURE 1–9 Research suggests that viewing of extremely aggressive behavior such as that seen in highly publicized boxing matches might contribute to temporary increases in the homicide rate.

behavior. Nevertheless, such studies can provide important leads for more controlled research. Clinicians recognize that each case is different because of the particular circumstances surrounding the case, and cases may become more complicated because of client's verbal reports. Troubled people more often than not leave out important information in telling their stories to clinicians. They frequently fail to remember significant experiences and the feelings and thoughts related to them. Each case study thus is unique, although with experience clinicians become sensitive to commonalities that aid them in understanding and helping people.

CORRELATIONAL STUDIES In **correlational studies,** researchers investigate relationships between uncontrolled events. These studies show us that two things are associated (see Figure 1–8), but they do not explain which factor causes what. For example, a correlational study may identify a significant relationship between socioeconomic or marital status and severity of psychopathology. Although we do not know which is the contributing factor, a potentially important association has been singled out.

A good example of a correlational study is one that analyzes the effects of mass media violence on aggressive behavior. Much of the evidence that televised violence increases the tendency of viewers to behave aggressively comes from controlled laboratory studies in which the aggressive behavior that occurred was not of a serious or brutal nature. Phillips (1983) hypothesized that news of a violent act is most likely to stimulate violence when the aggression in the news story is presented as (1) rewarded, (2) exciting, (3) real, and (4) justified. He reasoned that

one type of news story that meets all these standards is the heavyweight championship fight (see Figure 1–9). Accordingly, Phillips analyzed daily counts of all U.S. homicides from the National Center for Health Statistics and related them to the occurrence of 18 heavyweight championship boxing matches over a certain period.

Phillips found that on the days following highly publicized fights, homicides increased nearly 15 percent. Those fights that attracted the greatest media attention were associated with even larger increases in homicides. He attributed these increases in violent behavior to the modeling of successful aggression by the victorious fighter. Although a variety of factors might have contributed to Phillips' findings (for example, the critical factor might have been the day of the week or the amount of gambling involved), the association between highly publicized fights and homicides is potentially valuable information for policymakers concerned about the possible effects of media violence.

Both case studies and correlational studies provide bases for hypotheses. In evaluating a hypothesis it is important to decide on the observations that are relevant to it and the conditions under which those observations should be made. The conditions might be the same for all subjects or different for designated groups. In assessment studies, the conditions are the same, the aim being to gather information under standard conditions for purposes of description and prediction. In experimental studies, the conditions are varied so as to test hypotheses about the effects of the conditions.

ASSESSMENT STUDIES The purpose of **assessment studies** is to provide an objective account of

behavior at any given time. Assessment methods range from recording how often certain responses occur in natural situations to noting the types of behavior displayed in specially created settings such as interviews. Assessment is not simply a measuring device; it is a general approach to observing and interpreting behavior. As such, it extends beyond traditional procedures such as interviews and tests in much the same way that the concept of intelligence and the judgments based on it extend beyond the tests used to measure it.

Assessment data can be used in a number of ways. They might be employed to predict future behavior, to identify correlates of present behavior, or to measure the likelihood of a positive reaction to therapeutic procedures. For example, a study of junior high school students might indicate the type of person who is most likely to engage in antisocial behavior in the future; a comparison of the assessed characteristics of depressed individuals might point out those who are most likely to commit suicide; and a comparison of the personality traits of people who respond positively to psychotherapy and those who respond negatively might help in screening candidates for therapy. Assessment research ranges from in-depth studies of one or a few people to surveys of large populations.

When people are assessed, several kinds of data are usually gathered, including age, sex, personal history, and number of previous hospitalizations. This information can be intercorrelated and the degree of relationship among the various items determined. Assessment studies, which often involve large samples of subjects and sophisticated assessment techniques, are limited by their correlational nature; despite this limitation, they have much to contribute to the study of abnormal behavior. This is particularly true when, for practical or ethical reasons, it is not possible to manipulate conditions experimentally. Suppose, for example, that we wanted to study the possibility that having been abused as a child increases the likelihood that one will abuse one's own children. It would be highly unethical as well as impractical to subject an experimental group of children to severe abuse and then wait twenty years to see whether or not they beat their own children. However, information obtained through assessment about such a correlation could be of great value in understanding the causes of abuse, and could perhaps be used in selecting high-risk parents for programs designed to prevent abuse.

As an alternative, we might find ways to measure the amount of abuse parents received when they were children as well as the extent to which they now abuse their own children. For each of a large group of parents, we could obtain a score for each of the two abuse variables—each parent's reports of being abused as a child and some measure of his or her abusiveness as a

parent—and then determine what kind of relationship, if any, exists between the two sets of measures. If being abusive and having been abused are correlated that would provide a potentially useful clue to how child abuse could be prevented. For instance, perhaps parental counseling and training for people who were abused as children would be of preventive value.

If we find a positive correlation, we might be tempted to conclude from the data that child abuse is caused by parents having been abused as children. This is certainly a possibility, but it is important to remember that *correlation* is not the same as *cause*. There are other possible explanations for the positive correlation. It may be, for example, that guilt about abusing their own child causes parents to exaggerate the extent to which they were abused as children. Another possibility is that some other variable that was not measured in the study (such as some form of psychological disturbance) actually caused the parent to be the target of abuse as a child and causes him or her to become a child abuser as an adult. We simply cannot be certain which of these and other possible causal relationships may account for the positive correlation between recalled childhood experiences and present adult behavior.

Longitudinal Studies One way to deal with limitations inherent in assessment studies is the **longitudinal study,** whose goal is to observe and record the behavior of people over long periods—perhaps twenty or thirty years. This type of study is costly, time-consuming, and often frustrating to the investigator, who may not live to see the study completed. There are other problems as well. The nature of the group under study may change greatly as people move or die. The

FIGURE 1–10 Timing of life transitions by withdrawn behavior in childhood.

(Based on Caspi & Elder. (1988))

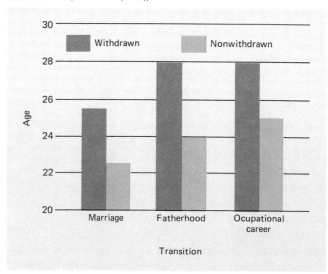

methods chosen at the beginning of the study may become outdated. The importance of new variables that were ignored in the study may become recognized by the scientific community. For these reasons, few longitudinal studies are done. Nevertheless because they deal so directly with the developmental process, the value of such studies is widely recognized.

Figure 1–10 illustrates the predictive value of longitudinal studies. Researchers were able to identify a group of men who at ages 8 to 10 had been socially withdrawn and inhibited (Caspi & Elder, 1988). Because they had been studied over a period of more than 20 years, it was possible to relate social withdrawal in childhood to these men's experiences at three adult life transitions: getting married, becoming a father, and beginning a work career. As Figure 1–10 shows, men with a childhood history of social withdrawal marry at a significantly older age than men with no such behavioral history—the difference between the groups is three years. Not surprisingly, delayed age at marriage corresponds with delayed parenthood. Finally, withdrawn behavior in childhood seems to hinder men's transition into an occupational career. Men with a childhood history of withdrawn behavior assumed a work career three years after the majority of their peers were already established in an occupation.

The delays in life transitions revealed by this study can generate conflicting obligations and options that may enhance stress and the risk of maladaptation. Evidence about the connection between withdrawn behavior in childhood and disorganization later in life could be of value in developing programs to improve the social adjustment of withdrawn children.

Follow-up Studies One type of research that avoids some of the logistical problems of longitudinal studies, but still has longitudinal features, is the **follow-up study.** In such studies, people are given an initial assessment and then are contacted again months or years later to see whether there have been any changes in their behavior during that time. Follow-up studies are used to assess the effects of different therapeutic approaches as well as to observe the development of particular conditions. For example, a follow-up study might be carried out to determine how well people who have been discharged from a mental hospital have adjusted to life in the community. Figure 1–11 summarizes the results of a study that explored the relationship between the amount of television viewing at 8 years of age and the seriousness of criminal acts at age 30. The figure shows that the seriousness of crimes was proportional to TV-viewing frequency at age 8 for both males and females. While this relationship may not be causal, the fact that child TV viewing was predictive of crime seriousness in adulthood suggests the need to investigate the TV-viewing experi-

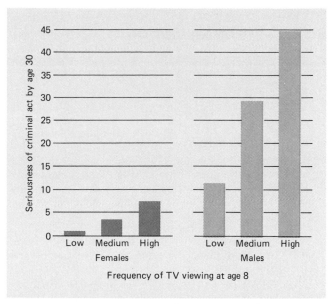

FIGURE 1–11 Seriousness of criminal acts by age 30 as a function of frequency of television viewing at age 8. (Eron. (1987). p. 440. Copyright © 1987 by the American Psychological Association. Reprinted by permission of the author)

ences of children. What are the characteristics of children who do a lot of TV viewing? What sorts of programs do they watch?

Cross-sectional Studies The **cross-sectional study** is a useful way to assess the views or status of one or more groups of people at any given point in time. Cross-sectional studies are the most common assessment method used by social scientists. Because no follow-up is required, these studies are less time-consuming and expensive than longitudinal studies. A public opinion poll is an example of a cross-sectional study that is carried out in the field. Developmental psychologists often use the cross-sectional approach in the laboratory or in natural settings to compare children's behavior, attributes, abilities, and concerns at different ages.

EXPERIMENTAL STUDIES Experimental research involves the observation and assessment of behavior, but with an important additional ingredient. In **experimental studies,** or **experiments,** variables can be manipulated. This degree of control is impossible in many real-life situations. Because experimenters can control the variables in the laboratory, they can more easily isolate and record the causes of the behavior they observe. For certain purposes research with animals is valuable because it permits the manipulation of experimental variables and the control of unwanted factors to an extent usually not possible with people (see Box 1–2).

The variables that are manipulated by researchers in experiments are **independent variables; dependent**

BOX 1–2 Understanding Abnormal Behavior through Animal Research

For obvious reasons, certain types of experimentation cannot be carried out using human subjects. For example, it would be impossible—and unethical, even if it were possible—to try to observe and control the course of a person's life. However, the telescoped life span of nonhuman primates like monkeys makes it possible to study the long-term consequences of early experiences. Under controlled conditions these experiences can be observed either as they unfold or after experimental manipulations. Animal studies permit levels of control and ways of carrying out experimental manipulations that are not possible with humans. As a consequence, animal experimentation plays an important role in the study of abnormal behavior.

Animal studies can be used to investigate both biological and social factors in behavior. One example of research with a biological focus is the investigation of the effects of drugs. Researchers have fed monkeys large doses of drugs that are believed to cause depression and have noted their effects on the animals' behavior. Such experiments have shown that depression-inducing drugs lead to decreases in the general activity and exploratory behavior of monkeys.

A group of drugs called amphetamines, which function as stimulants, produce psychotic symptoms in people. Once the effects of amphetamines on animals are shown to be similar, animals that had been injected with amphetamines can then be given antipsychotic drugs to determine whether they are able to counteract the amphetamine's psychosis-inducing action. Research has shown that rats and humans exhibit some similar symptoms when treated with amphetamines, and we now know that certain antipsychotic drugs are effective in reversing the effects of amphetamines on rats.

People who abuse amphetamines frequently engage in ritualized stereotyped behavior such as repetitively disassembling complex objects like radios. Not surprisingly, reassembly of such objects requires more concentration than they can muster. Rats that are given high doses of amphetamines develop a similar syndrome called **stereotypy.** They pace back and forth, sniffing the corners of their cages and chew repetitively on the bars. Studies are being conducted on the brains of rats treated with either or both amphetamines and antipsychotic drugs. These studies will help identify the areas of the brain and the mechanisms related to the drug effects.

Animal subjects have been used in another aspect of research on amphetamines and other stimulants. In a number of studies, stimulant drugs have been shown to increase an animal's sensitivity to reinforcement. That is, the drug increases the effects of reward and possibly even punishment so that the animal learns habits more quickly and with greater success. This finding is provocative because stimulant drugs often make hyperactive children more responsive to reward and punishment.

In the course of their research on dogs, Samuel Corson and his co-workers (1976) noticed that some of the dogs were quite restless and not very responsive to rewards and punishments. They administered a variety of drugs to the dogs with no beneficial effect until they tried amphetamines. The researchers found that the stimulant medication quieted the dogs and that, like hyperactive children, they were then better able to learn. An examination of the hyperactive dogs' brains showed that they were deficient in certain neurotransmitters, chemicals that make possible the movement of nerve impulses. The identification of this deficiency opens up the possibility of a better understanding of the nervous-system abnormalities that cause hyperactivity and the way therapeutic drugs like amphetamines act to alleviate this condition.

Another example of animal studies with a biological focus can be seen in the work of Harry Harlow and his co-workers. They were interested in the effects of early experience on the later development of monkeys. Infant monkeys show a number of innate behaviors, such as clinging and sucking. When the infants are separated from their mothers and reared with other young monkeys, their clinging behavior lasts much longer than it does for mother-reared monkeys (see Figure 1–12a). Young monkeys also begin to show innate fear behavior when they are about 2 months old. When they are reared with other monkeys, the fear behaviors do not disappear but last into adulthood (Suomi & Harlow, 1978).

variables are any observed changes in behavior due to the manipulation. Psychological experiments are designed to discover relationships between environmental conditions and behavior. Figure 1–13 illustrates a conventional experimental design. For example, an experiment might be done to discover the relationship between the temperature in a room and people's performance on a test. In this experiment the independent variable would be the temperature. The experimenter would use a different temperature for each experimental group. The dependent variable would be the test scores. If the average test scores for the groups were significantly different, the experimenter would conclude that this result was related to the different temperatures in the rooms in which the groups worked. Asking people how they felt under both conditions would be simpler, but the results would not be nearly as accurate or objective.

A study by Abrams and Wilson (1979) illustrates

FIGURE 1–12 (a) All monkeys go through a clinging stage, but monkeys who are reared without their mothers show a greatly prolonged period of clinging. (b) A young monkey, still in the clinging stage, can be an effective therapist for an older monkey who has been reared in isolation.

When infant monkeys are not only separated from their mothers but reared in isolation for 6 months, they show several disturbed behaviors. They suck themselves, constantly rock back and forth, and are very timid. When their isolation ends, they behave very aggressively toward other monkeys. The research showed, however, that monkeys that are reared in isolation for 6 months can later develop normally if they are "treated" by therapist monkeys. The most successful therapist monkeys were 3-month-olds who still showed a great deal of clinging behavior. They clung to the isolates affectionately (see Figure 1–12b). The isolates soon responded, and within 6 months their behavior was hard to distinguish from that of their therapists (Suomi & Harlow, 1972).

Young monkeys separated from their mothers often show symptoms similar to depression in humans. Depression in young monkeys may be preceded by a protest phase characterized by immediate frantic activity that appears to reflect attempts to communicate with and locate the missing mother. The depression is often followed by a detachment phase in which the young monkey shows an emotional detachment or aloofness from its mother upon reunion. This phase has been observed in human children when in the presence of mothers from whom they have been separated (Rosenblum & Paully, 1987).

the power of the experiment in identifying a factor that is relevant to a particular type of behavior. The researchers were interested in the relationship between alcohol and social anxiety in women. The subjects were paid female undergraduates selected from volunteers who reported only moderate drinking. Two independent variables, alcohol dose and expectancy, were manipulated by randomly assigning subjects to one of four groups: expect alcohol and receive alcohol, expect alcohol and receive placebo, expect placebo and receive alcohol, or expect placebo and receive placebo. (A **placebo** is an inactive substance whose effect on a person's behavior depends on his or her expectations.) The experimental manipulation was **double-blind;** that is, neither the subject nor the experimenter knew what the subject was drinking. Unlike the cartoon in Figure 1–14, records are kept of which subjects are assigned to each group, but those who evaluate the subjects' behavior or progress

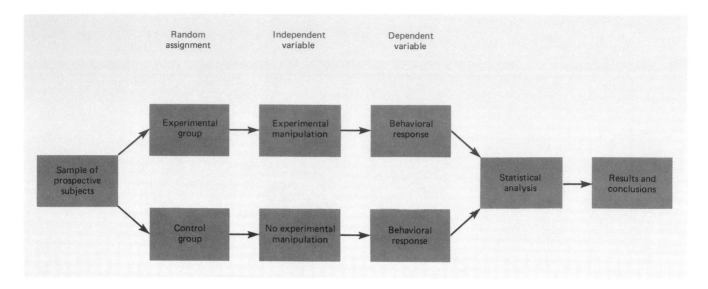

FIGURE 1–13 In a conventional experimental design, subjects are randomly assigned to an experimental or control group for manipulation of the independent variable. Their dependent variable behaviors are then measured; differences between the two groups of subjects are assessed through statistical analysis to determine the effects of the independent variable.

and the subjects themselves do not know the assignment. All of the subjects were told that both alcohol and

FIGURE 1–14

(© 1993 by Sidney Harris)

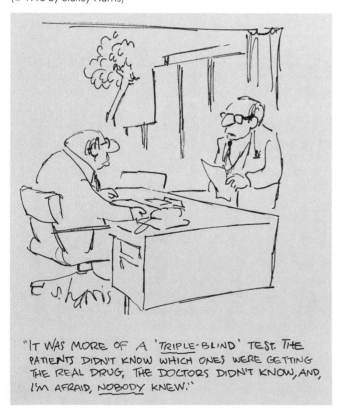

"IT WAS MORE OF A 'TRIPLE-BLIND' TEST. THE PATIENTS DIDN'T KNOW WHICH ONES WERE GETTING THE REAL DRUG, THE DOCTORS DIDN'T KNOW, AND, I'M AFRAID, NOBODY KNEW."

nonalcohol groups would be tested in the study and that they had been randomly assigned to either the alcohol-only group or the nonalcohol-only group. Under the guise of preparing for a breathalyzer test, the subjects gargled with a mouthwash that reduced their sensitivity to taste. The drinks were mixed from labeled bottles in full view of the subject, and the glasses in the "receive placebo" group were surreptitiously smeared with vodka. Finally, the breathalyzer was altered to give false feedback.

After the drink manipulation and breathalyzer test, the subjects were placed in a controlled social interaction with a male confederate. The dependent variables included physiological measures of anxiety (heart rate and skin conductance) taken before, during, and after the interaction; self-report measures of anxiety taken before and after the interaction; and observer ratings of the anxiety shown by each subject during the interaction.

The experiment showed that women who believed that they had consumed alcohol, whether or not their drinks actually contained it, showed significantly increased levels of physiological arousal compared with those who believed that they had drunk only tonic water. According to ratings made by observers, subjects who believed that they had consumed alcohol showed greater discomfort in the social interaction (see Figure 1–15). This experiment highlights the decisive role that subjects' expectations can play in their behavior and in their ability to cope.

There are two general types of experiments. The

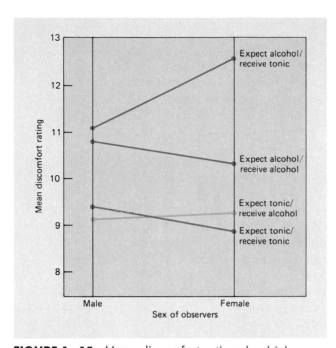

FIGURE 1–15 Mean discomfort ratings by drink content, expectancy, and sex made by observers who rated videotapes of subjects' social interactions.

(From Abrams, D.B., and Wilson, G.T. [1979]. Effects of alcohol on social anxiety in women. *Journal of Abnormal Psychology* 88: 161–173. Copyright © 1979 by the American Psychological Association. Reprinted by permission of the authors)

first type is the **hypothesis-testing experiment,** in which the researcher makes a prediction based on a theory and then conducts an experiment to see whether the prediction is correct. In the following excerpt, a psychologist outlines her plan for such a study.

> *I'm interested in determining whether, if children have an early close, secure relationship with an adult, what psychologists call attachment, they will have fewer problems getting along with other children when they enter school. My hypothesis is that if children are securely attached when they are very young, their social skills will be better and they will be less likely to be described as having behavior problems.*
>
> *I have some records of nursery school children's behavior in a situation designed to measure attachment. In that research setup, a young child and his or her mother sit together in an attractive room with some playthings. Then a "stranger" (a research worker) comes into the room and sits down. After awhile the mother leaves; she comes back a short time later. The way the child behaves, both while the mother is gone and when she returns, is a measure of*

attachment. If the child does not cling to the mother when the stranger enters, and if the child continues to play with the toys, is not distressed when she leaves, and greets her warmly but does not cling to her when she returns, the child is said to be securely attached.

Now those children are in the first grade, and I want to determine whether those who were securely attached in nursery school behave differently from the other children in either stressful or nonstressful situations. For one-half of each of the attachment groups, I am observing the children in a frustrating situation where they are given an impossible task to solve. For the other half of each group, I will give the children another task that is not difficult but takes a fairly long time to do. My hypothesis is that children who are securely attached will work longer at the impossible task than the other attachment group. For the other task, I expect no difference between the two groups. I base these predictions on the idea that children who are securely attached in their early years develop feelings of competence and tolerance of frustration superior to those of children who did not have a positive attachment experience.

The second type of experiment, the **behavior-change experiment** is concerned primarily with the development of therapeutic techniques. It is also designed to test hypotheses, but in this case the goal is to make an immediate contribution to the development of practical rehabilitative techniques. For example, a behavior-change experiment might test the hypothesis that supervised work experiences are significantly more effective than group psychotherapy in changing the attitudes and behavior of convicted criminals. The researcher who wrote the following account is studying schizophrenics. However, his goal is a very practical one: improving the social skills of schizophrenics.

> *I'm trying to devise procedures that will help hospitalized schizophrenics return to the community more quickly and be more effective when they make their return. My approach is to start with one obvious deficiency of schizophrenics: inadequate social skills. They just don't do a very good job of relating to other people. What I've been doing is finding out, by asking them questions and observing them, what social skills schizophrenics lack; for example, they have a lot of trouble introducing*

themselves to strangers and making small talk. I'm modeling—that is, demonstrating—for them various ways of being effective in social situations. I also have a control group that doesn't get the social skills training, as well as a group that participates in discussions about how to handle social situations but gets no modeling. If I'm on the right track, follow-ups should show that the modeling group is better able to adjust back into the community than the control group and maybe also better than the discussion group.

Statistics and Research Design

Scientific observation results in data that are usually numerical in nature. Statistical procedures allow the researcher to summarize and bring order to data, as well as to measure relationships among variables.

DESCRIPTIVE STATISTICS **Descriptive statistics** are used to summarize observations. The summaries might be of patients' responses to psychological tests, the ages at which various types of patients develop their conditions, and clinicians' ratings of patients' progress. **Measures of central tendency** provide descriptive numerical summaries of a groups' behavior. The three most commonly used measures of central tendency are the **mean** or arithmetic average; the **median,** the point that cuts the distribution of scores in half, so that half of the rank-ordered scores fall above it and half below it, and the **mode,** the score that the largest number of subjects obtained. Because of its desirable mathematical properties, the mean is typically favored in statistical analyses.

Measures of central tendency, such as the mean, provide information about the average score in a distribution. However, knowing the average score in a distribution does not provide all of the information required to describe a group of scores. In addition, **measures of variability** are required. The simplest idea of variability is the **range** which is merely the difference between the highest and lowest scores. The most commonly used measure of variability is the **standard deviation** which takes into account all of the scores in the distribution rather than only the highest and lowest. The standard deviation reflects the size of the deviation of the scores in the distribution from the group mean.

INFERENTIAL STATISTICS Whereas descriptive statistics help us characterize a group of subjects, it is often important to make comparisons among two or more groups (for example, the mean IQs of students at two high schools). **Inferential statistics** help us determine whether any observed differences between groups should be attributed to chance or to some systematic factor (the socioeconomic status of students at the schools, for example). Statistical tests, such as the *t-test,* evaluate the **null hypothesis,** the theory that the groups really do not differ. If the null hypothesis is rejected, it is unlikely that the observed differences could have arisen by chance. Statistical tests yield what is known as a *level of significance,* which is determined by comparing the results of the statistical tests with a set of probability tables.

CORRELATION COEFFICIENTS Quite commonly, clinicians or researchers are interested not so much in how groups might differ, but in how variables that represent characteristics of some particular sample or population are related to each other. The **correlation coefficient** provides this information. Correlation coefficients can range from −1.00 to +1.00. A coefficient of +1.00 means that there is a perfect positive association between two variables. A correlation of −1.00 signifies a perfect negative, or inverse, relationship, and a correlation of .00 means that there is no relationship between the variables.

INTERPRETING STATISTICS There are many types of statistical tests, some of which are complex. For example, some procedures involve evaluating the relationships among combinations of three or more variables. But regardless of the procedures employed, interpretation of the results obtained is required in light of the research design and methods employed. The experiment is a powerful scientific tool, but it is not infallible. Certain factors can seriously undermine the validity of research results. Four of the most serious issues that researchers must consider in conducting studies and interpreting results are confounding of variables, reactivity, demand characteristics, and expectancy effects. How we interpret the results of research depends not only on the outcomes of the statistical tests employed but also on how well the research was conducted; that is, how successful the researcher has been in eliminating these biasing factors.

Confounding occurs when uncontrolled variables affect the dependent variable in a way that is mistakenly attributed to the independent variable. For example, some depressed individuals might be given psychotherapy while others serve as control group. Comparing the two groups might show a statistically significant difference in depressed mood, with the group that received psychotherapy showing less depression after psychotherapy than the control group. This result would suggest that psychotherapy is a useful treatment for depression. But what if the experimental and control groups differed in age, sex, or initial level of depression? These possibly confounding variables would lead us to be very cautious about any statistically significant results we might obtain.

Reactivity refers to changes in behavior that occur

when subjects know they are being observed or studied. If subjects in a laboratory experiment react to being observed by behaving differently from the way they would outside the laboratory, we might easily draw false conclusions from the experimental results.

Demand characteristics are features of research situations that give subjects information about how they are expected to behave. Subjects may pick up these clues about the nature of a study and how they are "supposed" to behave. Some patients in psychoanalysis might report more dreams than patients in other forms of psychotherapy because their analysts may communicate that reporting and analyzing dreams is what they want their patients to do. Because demand characteristics can be a threat to valid results, researchers often feel a need to hide the true intent of their experiments.

Expectancy effects can be a source of bias in experiments if they lead to systematic errors in observations. In a study not involving tranquilizers, some experimenters might rate patients who have been taking tranquilizing drugs as being less anxious because in past research such drugs were found to reduce anxiety. In this case, scientists should be blind with regard to the drug being taken. Researchers' expectancies about what will happen in a given situation might actually influence the observations they make.

An additional factor that influences the results of research is **sampling.** A researcher virtually can never study every member of the larger group to which experimental results are expected to apply. We are almost always restricted to a segment, or sample, of that larger group, which is called the population. If valid conclusions are to be drawn, the sample must reflect the important characteristics of that larger population. Public opinion pollsters thus use samples that possess the important characteristics (age, gender, political party, geographical location, and so on) in the same proportion as contained in the general population. The responses of such a representative sample are therefore likely to mirror those of the larger population. Clearly, interpretation of research investigations depends on the nature of the samples studied—if the sample does not adequately reflect the general public, results will have a limited application.

Ethical Aspects of Research

Regardless of the scholarly merits of doing research, investigators should never place people in either physical or psychological jeopardy. Subjects should be informed regarding what the experiment is about and any hazards associated with participation in it. They also must be clearly told that they are free to withdraw from the experiment at any time. If deception must be used, the subjects must be completely debriefed after the experiment, and the entire procedure explained to them. Special measures must be taken to protect confidentiality.

As a result of the increasing emphasis on the protection and welfare of both human and animal subjects used in psychological research, psychologists now must restrict their experimentation with certain groups of people who are not in a position to give their consent, such as children, the mentally retarded, and seriously disturbed mental patients. When such people, or others who are not able to give consent, are involved, consent must be obtained from their parents or guardians. Strict guidelines are also being developed for research in prisons. No prisoner can be forced to participate in research or penalized for refusal to do so, and in the case of rehabilitative programs, prisoners must be permitted to share in decisions concerning program goals. Researchers must adhere to the ethics of research or risk serious legal and professional consequences.

Chapter Summary

WHAT IS ABNORMAL BEHAVIOR?

Abnormal psychology deals with how it feels to be different, how others interpret these differences, and how society deals with those it considers different. An understanding of the roles of **stress, coping skills,** and **personal vulnerabilities** is important in interpreting abnormal behavior.

The Stigma of Abnormal Behavior Beliefs and assumptions about mental illness affect the way people respond to someone who shows abnormal behavior. Those who behave in unusual ways or have been diagnosed as having a mental illness may be rejected by others either directly or indirectly. Many false beliefs exist about the causes and the outcome of mental illness.

Adaptive and Maladaptive Behavior **Adaptation,** as the term is used in this book, refers to people's ability or inability to modify their behavior in response to changes in their environment. Deviant or unusual behavior is often *not* maladaptive. **Maladaptive** behavior refers to behavior that causes problems

in living. Maladaptive behavior ranges from relatively minor but troubling fears to severe distortion of reality and inability to function independently.

STRESS, COPING, AND VULNERABILITY

Stress refers to people's reactions to situations that pose demands, constraints, or opportunities. **Coping skills** are the techniques such as constructive thinking and flexibility that people use to deal with stress. **Vulnerability** refers to the likelihood of maladaptive response. Vulnerability is affected by heredity, personality factors, lack of certain skills, a history of negative life events, and certain environmental conditions. Stress, coping, and vulnerability are interrelated. The greater the stress, the less vulnerability is required for a person to display maladaptive behavior.

REASONS FOR CLINICAL CONTACTS

Personal Unhappiness Although to an outsider a person may be functioning well, feelings of anxiety, depression, or a feeling of failure to reach one's potential may motivate an individual to seek therapeutic help.

The Concerns of Others Even if people do not view their own behavior as maladaptive or abnormal, others who know them well may see either present or potential problems and urge them to seek professional contact.

Legal and Community Problems If a person's maladaptive behavior is seen as a threat to others, legal or community agencies often become involved.

THE EPIDEMIOLOGY OF MALADAPTIVE BEHAVIOR

Epidemiologists look for clues about the causes of disorders by investigating environmental, personal, and behavioral characteristics that are associated with different rates of various disorders.

Prevalence, Incidence, and Risk Factors **Prevalence** data describe the frequency of occurrence of a condition at a given point in time. **Incidence** data are the number of *new* cases occurring during a given period. **Risk factors** are personal or situational characteristics that have been found to have a significant association with a disorder.

SOURCES OF HELP

Types of Treatment Facilities Facilities for the treatment of mental disorders range from inpatient treatment at state hospitals and in psychiatric wards of general hospitals to outpatient-based treatment in the community. These outpatient facilities include hospital emergency rooms, mental health clinics, and the services of mental health workers. The movement for **deinstitutionalization** returned many people to the community without providing sufficient community facilities to care for them adequately.

Types of Mental Health Specialists Mental health specialists include **clinical psychologists, psychiatrists, psychiatric social workers,** and **psychiatric nurses.** Each of these professional specialties requires different training. Although the responsibilities ordinarily given to each group differ, they often carry out similar therapeutic activities.

RESEARCH IN ABNORMAL PSYCHOLOGY

Observing Behavior Observation is the beginning stage in the scientific process. It is important to recognize that observations are susceptible to cultural and personal bias. To make observation useful it is necessary to determine such things as the types of responses to be observed, how the observer's presence will affect the behavior, and the period of time necessary for reliable observation. In addition to observation by others, **self-observation** by the client can provide useful research data. The data obtained from observation can include the stimuli that elicit particular responses, the subjective and behavioral responses to particular stimuli, and the environmental consequences of certain behaviors.

The Role of Theory Theories in abnormal psychology often begin with informal observations in clinical settings. Researchers then make hypotheses based on their observations and test these through further observations, preferably under controlled conditions. As these studies show whether or not each hypothesis is supported by research findings, a theory can be built. Theories are used to relate many facts into a single framework and also to provide new questions for researchers to test in a systematic manner. For this reason it is very important that theories are constructed to be testable and refutable.

The Research Journey The vital steps in scientific research are: specifying the topic, reviewing the literature, defining the variables to be measured, developing the hypothesis, selecting a research strategy, conducting the study, analyzing the data, and reporting the research findings. Both **independent variables,** or those that are manipulated by the researcher, and **dependent variables,** or outcomes, must be specified.

Types of Research **Case studies** provide descriptions of single individuals who are usually studied through many observations. **Correlational studies** provide information about how much variables are related or associated, but like case studies they do not show cause and effect. **Assessment studies** describe behavior at any given time. They can be used for prediction of future behavior or to identify correlates of present behavior, but, like case and correlational studies they cannot be used to show causality. **Experimental studies** can be used to infer causality. Two major types of experimental studies are the **hypothesis-testing experiment** and the **behavior-change experiment.**

Statistics and Research Design Statistical procedures enable a researcher to summarize data and measure relationships among variables. The results are calculated in terms of both **descriptive statistics,** or numerical measures, and **inferential statistics,** which are used to provide information about whether the results might be due to chance. Included among descriptive

statistics are **measures of central tendency,** which include the **mean, median,** and **mode.** The **range** of scores is a simple measure of variability. The most commonly used variability measure is the **standard deviation.** Inferential statistics are used to evaluate the **null hypothesis** (to determine whether the groups in an experimental study differ). These statistics can be used to determine the **level of significance** or the probability that the results occurred by chance. When the results of an experiment are interpreted, several factors that can negatively affect the validity of the results must be kept in mind. The factors include **confounding of variables, reactivity** of subject behavior, **demand characteristics** of the experiment, and **expectancy effects.**

ETHICAL ASPECTS OF RESEARCH

Researchers must not treat people without their informed consent, and must never treat them in a way that might possibly cause them either physical or psychological harm. Potential subjects must be informed about the nature of the experiment and any risks it might involve, and their written consent must be obtained. They must be given a chance to withdraw and if any deception is used, they must be debriefed afterwards by having the procedures explained. All data from research must be kept confidential so that no one except the researchers will know the subjects' responses.

The Historical Background
of Abnormal Psychology

C H A P T E R 2

Historical Views of Abnormal Behavior
The Ancient Western World
The Middle Ages
The Renaissance
The Age of Reason and the Enlightenment
The Reform Movement

Psychological versus Organic Views of Abnormal Behavior
The Psychological Approach
The Organic Approach
The Approaches Converge

The Stage Is Set

Chapter Summary

Johann Baptist Gumpp (1651–1728), *Self-Portrait*. Scala/Art Resource, New York.

Those who cannot remember the past are condemned to repeat it.

George Santayana, The Life of Reason, 1905–1908

To really understand people, we need to know what has happened in their lives. To really understand current ideas and practices concerning abnormal psychology, we need to learn about its origins and history.

Historical Views of Abnormal Behavior

Someone might observe that modern techniques are surely much more effective, enlightened, and sophisticated than those used in earlier times, and ask: Why not concentrate on them instead of getting bogged down in accounts of the past? The trouble with this approach is that it misses important links between the past and the present. Much of what seems modern is an outgrowth of the past, not a rejection of it. In abnormal psychology, as in other fields of study, there are fewer completely new ideas than one might think. A review of the history of abnormal psychology provides a context within which the best of the modern discipline can be understood.

People have always been concerned about their physical well-being, their social relationships, and their place in the universe. They have posed many questions about these issues and have evolved theories about them. Some of those theories seem almost universal. They can be observed in many parts of the world and in many periods of human history. Perhaps the greatest benefit of studying the history of abnormal psychology is the discovery that certain theories of maladaptive behavior have occurred over and over again.

One ancient theory that is still encountered today holds that abnormal behavior can be explained by the operation of supernatural and magical forces such as evil spirits or the devil. In societies that believe in this theory, therapy generally involves **exorcism,** that is, removing the evil that resides in the individual through counter-

magic and prayer. Although this view is most prevalent in nonliterate cultures, it is still found in industrialized societies and often exists side by side with more modern approaches. For example, many people who use folk healers also seek assistance from health care professionals. Professionals can improve the effectiveness of the help they provide by understanding what folk healers do and why their patients seek them out.

In many societies the **shaman** or medicine man, a magician who is believed to have contact with supernatural forces, is the medium through which spirits communicate with human beings (see Figure 2–1). Through the shaman, an afflicted person can learn which spirits are responsible for his or her problem and what needs to be done to appease them. To accomplish this, the shaman conducts a seance in which he displays intense excitement and often mimics the abnormal behavior he seeks to cure. Through mystical utterances, violent movements, and by acting out his dreams, the shaman reveals messages from spirits. Often the liberation of an evil spirit from the patient's body is expressed through what appears, through sleight of hand, to be the actual expulsion of an object, such as a stone, from the patient's ear or mouth. These rituals are based on specific theories about supernatural forces or evil powers as the cause of abnormal behavior and as the basis of therapeutic change.

It is tempting to view seemingly primitive beliefs about mental illness as part of the dead past. Yet the fact is that even in a relatively advanced and enlightened society like the United States there is a wide range of views about the causes of personal problems. The following case, reported in 1977, concerned a 33-year-old man from a rural area near Little Rock, Arkansas:

The patient had been having seizures recently and had become increasingly irritable and withdrawn from his family. When he could no longer be detained safely on the neurology service, he was transferred to the psychiatric ward, where he became increasingly more agitated, confused, and almost delirious. He became very fearful whenever people approached him, and he began to hallucinate. He finally slowed down after being given 1000 mg of chlorpromazine (a tranquilizer), but the necessity for bed restraint remained. All neurological findings, including a brain scan, proved normal. After two weeks of hospitalization the patient suffered a cardiac arrest. All efforts to revive him failed. An autopsy provided no reason for the death. After he died, the patient's wife told staff members that her husband had been seeing a "two-headed," an older woman considered by the community to be a witch who cast spells and healed people. The widow stated that her husband had angered the two-headed and that she had caused his death.

—Golden, 1977, p. 1425

Reports of "two-headeds" in Africa and other places describe them as people with voodoo powers who are able to cause sickness, insanity, and death. The power of such beings apparently is related to the victim's belief in them. The effect of the shaman's behavior both in curing disorders and causing them illustrates the interre-

FIGURE 2–1 A shaman anoints a man with holy water to protect him from evil spirits as the latter embarks on a pilgrimage.

FIGURE 2–2 The technique of trephining involved chipping a hole in the person's skull. The healing that took place on this skull shows that some individuals actually survived the operation.

FIGURE 2–2 The technique of trephining involved chipping a hole in the person's skull. The healing that took place on this skull shows that some individuals actually survived the operation.

lationship of people's beliefs and emotional reactions and their physical and psychological health.

Shamans are currently active in many countries. In Taiwan there are professional shamans, while in China the shamans are part-time practitioners of an illegal activity. Approximately 70 percent of rural Chinese with mental illnesses consult shamans (Shengxian & Phillips, 1990). Many of the families of these people are not even aware of the existence of mental hospitals. Since they often perceive disturbed behavior as the outcome of intervention by the spirit world, they seek out shamans for assistance.

A recurring theme in the history of abnormal behavior is the belief that individuals behave strangely because their bodies are not working right. Such people are thought to have something wrong with them, an organic defect that affects a specific organ rather than the whole body. The source of the presumed defect varies according to the nature of the abnormality, the society's cultural beliefs, and—particularly in the modern era—scientific knowledge.

The finding of ancient skulls with holes in them that were not caused by battle wounds has led some anthropologists to conjecture that abnormal behavior was sometimes treated by means of a procedure called **trephination.** In this technique a sharp tool such as a stone was used to make a hole in the skull about 2 centimeters in diameter (see Figure 2–2). Evidence that trephination was performed as early as 3000 to 2000 B.C.

FIGURE 2–3 A mural depicting the ancient Incas of Peru performing trephination.

has been uncovered in eastern Mediterranean and North African countries. Studies of trephined skulls suggest that the operation often was not fatal, a remarkable achievement given the difficulty of the procedure. Trephination may have been done to permit demonic spirits to escape. However, because of the absence of written records and the fact that our only data are the trephined skulls themselves, we need to be cautious in speculating about their significance (see Figure 2–3 on page 33).

Another general approach to the causes of abnormal behavior reflects what might be called the psychological perspective. According to this point of view, behavioral disturbances are caused by inadequacies in the way an individual thinks, feels, or perceives the world. According to the psychological perspective, people are at least potentially capable of examining their own thinking and modifying their behavior in light of that examination. Many modern psychotherapists see their task as helping people learn to think more rationally about themselves and their social relationships.

All three of these perspectives—mystical, organic, and psychological—have recurred throughout the history of Western civilization, beginning with the Greeks.

The Ancient Western World

The philosophers of ancient Greece were the earliest to write about the psychological and organic approaches to deviance. At the height of their civilization, the Greeks emphasized the rational analysis of the natural world. The concepts of motivation and intelligence were among those that they invented in their efforts to explain the behavior they observed in everyday life. Although we tend to see the modern era as the period in which human beings have sought to extend the boundaries of human understanding through the application of reason, the foundations for this period were laid by the writings of the ancient Greek philosophers. The main difference between us and the Greeks of antiquity is that we have access to all the knowledge that has accumulated in the past 2,000 years, as well as the tools of the scientific method.

Even in ancient Greece, knowledge evolved over a period of several centuries. At the time that Homer created the *Iliad* and the *Odyssey* (about 800 B.C.), disturbed or psychotic behavior was interpreted as a form of punishment for offenses against the gods. ("Those whom the gods would destroy, they first make mad.") In the battle scenes in the *Iliad,* Homer typically described his heroes as suddenly possessed by feelings of power that are engendered in them by the gods. States of insanity were believed to be created in the same way. Therapy took place in a group of temples dedicated to Asclepius, the god of healing. Each temple was a mazelike structure in which mental patients walked and slept and ultimately reached the center. In the process it was believed that Asclepius attended to their dreams and healed them.

In the centuries after Homer, the idea that a person's life is in the hands of the gods gradually declined, at least among educated citizens. The Greek philosophers became increasingly curious about aspects of the individual that might explain normal as well as abnormal behavior. Extreme mental deviations and disorders came to be viewed as natural phenomena for which rational treatments might be developed.

The ancient Egyptians, as well as the Mesopotamians and Hebrews, believed the seat of the mind to be in the heart. When the Pharaohs were embalmed, the heart was venerated, but the brain was removed and thrown away. For the Greeks, however, the brain was the seat of the mind. (Shakespeare referred to the lingering heart–mind controversy in Act III of *The Merchant of Venice* when he wrote: "Tell me where is fancie bred in the heart or in the head.") Despite his lack of anatomical knowledge, the Greek physician Hippocrates (460–377 B.C.) looked to the brain in his efforts to explain why people behave as they do. He described the brain as the interpreter of consciousness and the body's most important organ.

Hippocrates described epileptic seizures and concluded that they were caused by a diseased brain. He also wrote about depression, states of delirium, psychosis, irrational fears (what we now call phobias), and hysteria (organic symptoms in the absence of an organic disturbance). He and his followers became known for their ability to recognize and treat mental illness. Their therapeutic techniques consisted of rest, bathing, and dieting. There is even a record of Hippocrates appearing as an expert witness at the trial of an insane person. Today physicians continue to pay their debt to Hippocrates by taking the Hippocratic oath when they graduate from medical school (see Figure 2–4).

Three other Greek philosophers—Socrates (470–399 B.C.), Plato (427–347 B.C.), and Aristotle (384–322 B.C.)—also deserve mention for their contributions to abnormal psychology. Socrates was interested in self-exploration and considered reasoning to be the cornerstone of the good life and personal happiness. He believed in using inquiry to further knowledge; his goal was to teach by asking questions instead of giving answers. Today this procedure—called the Socratic method—is a valuable teaching tool as well as a component of the scientific method.

Socrates' most famous student, Plato, developed the **organismic point of view.** He saw behavior as a product of the totality of psychological processes. Like many modern writers, Plato believed that disturbed behavior grew out of conflicts between emotion and

FIGURE 2–4 Hippocrates, an older contemporary of Plato, was born in 460 B.C. He attended the medical school on the island of Cos and traveled to many cities both to practice and to teach. Over the centuries his influence grew. His writings include material that today would be called textbooks, articles, case histories, and speeches.

reason. In contrast to those who saw abnormal behavior as having a physical cause, he stressed the power of ideas, going so far as to say that the mind is the only true reality of human existence. According to Plato, the ideal individual is, above all, guided by reason. In his *Laws,* he expressed the belief that people who have lost their reason should be separated from society: "No lunatic shall be allowed to be at large in the community; the relatives of such persons shall keep them in safe custody at home by such methods as they contrive, on penalty of fine." Plato's belief is similar to that which has been held by many societies in the past. However, as time went on separation of the mentally ill from others in the commu-

nity became the responsibility of the government rather than of the family. The large institutions created to care for the mentally ill are described later in this chapter. Since the middle of the 1960s, an emphasis on the civil rights of those who are mentally ill has resulted in the closure of many of these institutions and the return of many patients to the community and, for those that have them, to the care of family members.

Aristotle, a pupil of Plato and the teacher of Alexander the Great, wrote extensively on the nature of reasoning and consciousness and also sought to analyze human emotions. He described and speculated about a number of emotional and motivational states, including anger, fear, envy, courage, hatred, and pity. He believed that anger occurred when a person was subjected to what he or she experienced as injustice and wrongdoing; he saw fear as the awareness of danger with an expectation of loss, defeat, or rejection. Like most of the Greek philosophers, Aristotle placed the highest value on reason and application. He also believed that the various forces in the body need to be in balance for reason to prevail.

Galen (130–200 A.D.), the greatest Roman physician, consolidated and augmented the Greek theories of mind and body. Galen extended ancient theories about the role of the four humors in personal character and temperament. The four **humors** (fluids of the body) were blood, black bile, yellow bile, and phlegm. Each of the humors was believed to be associated with a certain temperamental quality, and imbalances among the humors were believed to cause various disorders. For Galen, psychological characteristics were expressions of bodily processes and as such were influenced by the particular blend or balance of the four humors. Galen's theories were popular through the medieval period (see Figure 2–5 on page 36).

The rational approach of the ancient philosophers laid the groundwork for modern science. It led to attempts to classify abnormal behavior according to some consistent scheme. It temporarily replaced magic and religious explanations of abnormal behavior with a quest, through observation and reason, for natural causes. Except for a break during the Middle Ages, that quest has continued until the present time.

The Middle Ages

A host of changes accompanied the decline of ancient Greek culture and the rise and fall of the Roman Empire. Perhaps the two most obvious causes of these changes were the invasions of Western Europe by barbarian tribes and the growth of the Christian religion. The invaders, whose ideas were primitive compared to those of the Greeks and Romans, caused great social unrest, while the Christian religion served to comfort

FIGURE 2–5 These medieval woodcuts reflect the view that temperamental qualities result from excesses of the four humors. *From left to right:* The man with plenty of blood who has a changeable temperament; the hot-tempered man with an excess of yellow bile; the sluggish man with too much phlegm; and the man with too much black bile who is melancholic.

people in troubled times. The church also acted as a unifying force when the civil government of Rome finally fell.

The unrest of the Middle Ages was intensified by nearly constant warfare as well as by the Black Death and other epidemics that came without warning and wiped out hundreds of thousands of people. During this period

fear and terror spread like brush fires, causing many outbreaks of group hysteria. The nature of these outbreaks varied. Some groups of people behaved like packs of wolves, and others danced in the streets, making spiderlike movements.

During the early Middle Ages the importance of the Christian spirit of charity, particularly toward stigmatized groups such as the severely mentally disturbed, cannot be overestimated. For example, in Gheel, Belgium, the church established a special institution for the care of retarded and psychotic children. As they improved, these children were often placed with local sympathetic families (see Figure 2–6). Also during this period, music and dance were thought to cure insanity by restoring the chemical balance within the body (see Figure 2–7).

One figure in the early Christian era, the theologian and philosopher Saint Augustine (354–430 A.D.), stands out because he helped lay the groundwork for modern

FIGURE 2–6 One place where moral therapy has survived is Gheel, Belgium. Founded after the miracle cure of five "lunatics" at the shrine of St. Dymphna in the thirteenth century, the colony has continued its work to the present. Over 2,000 patients like this man live in private homes under few restrictions; there they work with their host families at everyday tasks until they have recovered.

FIGURE 2–7 In this medieval engraving, the insane are shown being led through a dance, in an effort to improve their mental condition.

psychodynamic theories of abnormal behavior. Writing extensively about feelings, mental anguish, and human conflict, he was perhaps the earliest forerunner of today's psychoanalysts. It was not so much the topics he dealt with as the way he approached them that most resembles the psychoanalytic method of today. Saint Augustine used introspection, or examination of his own thoughts, feelings, and motives, to discuss mental processes like the conflict between pleasure and discipline. He worked almost ruthlessly toward a complete, if painful, self-analysis, and in his *Confessions* he revealed his innermost thoughts, temptations, and fears.

By demonstrating that introspection and exploration of the individual's emotional life could be valuable sources of psychological knowledge, Saint Augustine made an important contribution to modern abnormal psychology. Unfortunately, these efforts were not followed up during the late Middle Ages. As the church's control and influence increased, so did its role in governmental affairs, and it was religious dogma, not civil law, that became the supreme voice of authority. The church came to control the practice of medicine, defining its goals and prescribing treatments for various conditions. To the degree that this control reflected a feeling of charity toward people suffering hardships of various kinds, the church played a positive role. To the extent that it was intolerant, authoritarian, and repressive, however, its role was decidedly negative.

The legacy of rationality that the Middle Ages had inherited from the Greek philosophers was quickly abandoned in the late medieval period. Demonology and superstition gained renewed importance in the explanation of abnormal behavior. Church authorities felt the need for a definitive document on the apprehension and

conviction of witches and sorcerers, whom they saw as the primary agents of evil. That need was met in 1484 with the publication of *Malleus Maleficarum (The Witches' Hammer)* by Fathers Henry Kramer and James Sprenger, a highly influential work that became a basic reference for investigators of diabolical phenomena.

In the late Middle Ages, although many people continued to take a benign, naturalistic view of mental illness, antiintellectualism and belief in magic and witchcraft increased. Many people believed strongly in exorcism, the casting out of evil spirits from the body of an afflicted person (see Figure 2–8). Nevertheless, it is difficult to draw firm conclusions about the mental status of the witches who were put on trial during the Middle Ages, since the available evidence is sparse and scattered. However, research has shown that many of the "witches" who were put on trial in New England during the sixteenth and seventeenth centuries were persecuted social outcasts rather than people suffering from mental disorders (Demos, 1982; Schoenman, 1984; Spanos, 1978).

History does not move in a simple, uncomplicated way. The *Malleus Maleficarum* described a case of a young man who could not restrain himself from protruding his tongue or shouting obscenities whenever he tried to pray. It attributed this problem to demonic possession. However, Paracelsus (1493–1541) vigorously attacked such notions. Like the Greeks before him, he pictured maladaptations as caused by natural phenomena, although, as a believer in astrology, he felt that such phenomena lay within the stars and planets, not within the individual. In the sixteenth century another rational thinker, Juan Huarte (1530–1589), wrote one of the first treatises on psychology, *Probe of the Mind*. In it he

FIGURE 2–8 This late fifteenth-century painting by Girolamo Di Benvenuto, *St. Catherine Exorcising a Possessed Woman*, shows St. Catherine of Siena casting the devil out of a possessed woman. The devil is seen fleeing from the woman's head.

distinguished between theology and psychology and argued forcefully for a rational explanation of the psychological development of children.

In addition to thoughtful individuals like Paracelsus and Huarte, there were some relatively enlightened governments and some serious efforts to care for mentally troubled individuals. In England, for example, the Crown had the right and duty to protect the mentally impaired, who were divided into two categories: natural fools and persons *non compos mentis*. A **natural fool** was a mentally retarded person whose intellectual capacities had never progressed beyond those of a child. **Persons** ***non compos mentis*** (Latin for "not of sound mind") did not show mental disability at birth. Their deviant behavior was not continuous, and they might show long periods of recovery. (For reasons that are not clear, by the fifteenth century the term "lunatic" had replaced the phrase *"non compos mentis"* and "idiot" had replaced "natural fool.")

There is also evidence that hearings to judge a person's mental status and legal competency were held as early as the thirteenth century (Neugebauer, 1979). Such examinations were designed to assess a person's orientation, memory, and intellect. The following description of Emma de Beston, which dates from 1383, is typical of the reports that were based on such examinations.

The said Emma, being caused to appear before them, was asked whence she came and said that she did not know. Being asked in what town she was, she said that she was at Ely. Being asked how many days there were in the week, she said seven but could not name them. Being asked how many husbands she had had in her time she said three, giving the name of one only and not knowing the names of the others. Being asked whether she had ever had issue by them, she said that she had had a husband with a son, but did not know his name. Being asked how many shillings were in forty pence, she said she did not know. Being asked whether she would rather have twenty silver groats than forty pence, she said they were of the same value. They examined her in all other ways which they thought best and found that she was not of sound mind, having neither sense nor memory nor sufficient intelligence to manage herself, her lands or her goods. As appeared by inspection she had the face and countenance of an idiot.

—O'Donoghue, 1914, pp. 127–128

FIGURE 2–9 This sixteenth-century woodcut shows a method for curing insanity. An insane man's head is held in an oven while demons and troublesome thoughts exit through the top of the oven.

The Renaissance

The Renaissance was a period of increased humanism, curiosity about nature, and interest in scholarship. Yet persecution of the people society did not like continued. Figure 2–9 is an example of the less than compassionate view of insanity that was commonplace. Many medical authorities devoted much time to investigating skin blemishes, which were believed to indicate points of contact with Satan. The idea of magical cures embodied in shamanism was evident in the popular therapy of removing stones from the head (see Figure 2–10).

Although the influence of *Malleus Maleficarum* (see page 37) continued to be felt for centuries, gradually the idea that irrational behavior could be explained rationally gained renewed attention. It followed that detailed descriptions of the behavior in question were needed. Johann Weyer (1515–1576), a sixteenth-century physician, was one of the major contributors to this development. In an age of unbridled superstition, Weyer emphasized psychological conflict and disturbed interpersonal relationships as causes of mental disorder. His enlightened humanism undoubtedly saved countless mentally ill people from death at the stake. Weyer had the courage to insist that witches were mentally disturbed individuals rather than creatures of Satan. He vigorously asserted the need to treat such people medically rather than theologically.

On the basis of careful psychological examination of mental patients, Weyer described a wide range of abnormal behavior, including the disorders known today as paranoia, epilepsy, psychosis, depression, and persistent nightmares. In *The Deception of Demons* he specifically attacked the preposterous claims of the *Malleus Maleficarum*. He argued that clinical treatment must be oriented toward meeting the needs of disturbed people

FIGURE 2–10 This early sixteenth-century painting by the Dutch painter Hieronymous Bosch shows an operation for removing stones from the head. An old phrase used even today to describe a mentally unbalanced person is "He has stones (or rocks) in his head." In the sixteenth and seventeenth centuries, quacks took advantage of this superstition and pretended to cure insanity by making a superficial incision in the patient's scalp and "extracting" small stones that were supplied by a confederate standing behind the patient.

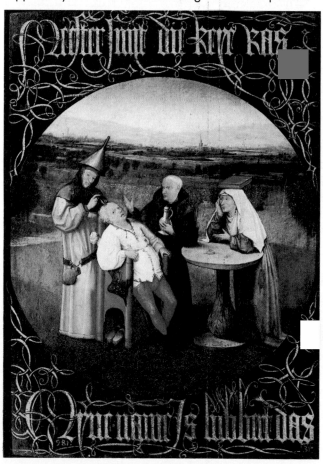

rather than merely following rules of clerical institutions. He spent much time talking with and observing his patients because he felt that he could not treat psychopathology without firsthand knowledge of it. The knowledge led him to the conclusion that inner experiences (such as psychological conflict) and disturbed relationships with others were significant causes of mental illness. Weyer's writings represent a major step toward the separation of abnormal psychology from theology.

The Age of Reason and the Enlightenment

The seventeenth century, known as the Age of Reason, and the eighteenth century, known as the Enlightenment, have been so labeled because during these two centuries reason and the scientific method came to replace faith and dogma as ways of understanding the natural world. During these two centuries major advances were made in such diverse fields as astronomy, biology, and chemistry. Scientists and philosophers alike emphasized the need to support assertions with observations of natural phenomena.

Although human emotions and motivations are less accessible to direct observation than the moon, the human circulatory system, or molecular structures, a number of philosophers and scientists focused on the subjective experiences of human beings. Baruch Spinoza (1632–1677) anticipated modern approaches to psychology and physiology with his argument that mind and body are inseparable. Much current writing in psychology is reminiscent of Spinoza's writings, in which he discussed psychological causation and the roles of emotions, ideas, and desires in human life. Spinoza even referred to unconscious mechanisms that influence behavior. His main contribution to abnormal psychology was his argument that psychological processes, though they are not directly observable, are equal in importance to the material processes of the natural world. The English physician William Harvey (1578–1657), best known for his work on the human circulatory system, also wrote about the relationships between the psychological and physiological sides of life.

Among the perceptive observers of the human experience in every age have been playwrights, novelists, and poets. During the Age of Reason, a number of authors probed especially deeply into the problems of human motivation and emotions. The clearest examples can be found in many plays of William Shakespeare (1564–1616), particularly *Hamlet*. Hamlet wants to take revenge on his uncle but consistently hesitates to act. Psychoanalysts have interpreted this hesitation as a reflection of Hamlet's neurotic conflicts concerning his mother, who had married the uncle after the death of Hamlet's father. Another literary work that dealt with

human emotions was *The Anatomy of Melancholy,* by Robert Burton (1577–1640) (see Figure 2–11). In this book Burton focused on the emotional core of depression and called attention to an observation that clinical workers have often made: depressed people tend to be very angry not only with themselves but with all others as well. Burton, a professor of divinity at Oxford, based his description and analysis of depression on his own experience.

These literary developments mirror the longstanding conflict between psychological and physical explanations of abnormal behavior. However, during the seventeenth and eighteenth centuries both groups—those who analyzed subjective experience and those who sought to identify physical defects—finally rejected the

FIGURE 2–11 The title page from Robert Burton's book, which was written under the name of Democritus Junior. At the top center is a picture of Democritus the Elder in his garden, while a portrait of the author is at the bottom. The three larger pictures on each side illustrate some of the causes of melancholy. Jealousy, love, and superstition are on the left; solitude, hypochondriasis, and mania are on the right. At the bottom are two herbs, borage and hellebore, that were thought to help cure melanchonia.

(a)

(b)

FIGURE 2–12 These statues, originally above the gates of the Bethlehem Hospital in London, are generally taken as representations of Raving Madness (a) and Melancholy Madness (b). They exemplify the then growing interest in physiognomy, or gauging emotions from the appearance of the body and face. (See page 43 for more on Bethlehem Hospital.)

idea that demons and supernatural forces were the causes of abnormal behavior. As a consequence, by the end of the eighteenth century superstition had been almost totally replaced by a commitment to rationality, scientific observation, and humane treatment of the mentally ill.

In England the movement toward humane treatment gained impetus as a result of the psychotic breakdown suffered by King George III in 1765. This event precipitated a constitutional crisis and made many people aware that even prominent individuals were not immune to mental derangement. Madhouses had existed in England for many years, but only in 1774 did Britain pass its first parliamentary act licensing such institutions and regulating the admission of patients to them.

From the late seventeenth to the nineteenth century interest rose in **physiognomy,** the art of judging character, personality, and feelings from the form of the body, particularly the face (see Figure 2–12). In the early nineteenth century another new approach to abnormal

psychology emerged. Franz Joseph Gall (1758–1828), a physician, studied the brains of different kinds of people (young, old, deranged) and gathered evidence suggesting that brain size and mental development are related. On the basis of this evidence he formulated the theory of **phrenology,** according to which discrete psychological "faculties" were located in specific areas of the brain. Gall believed that bumps and indentations on the surface of the skull were accurate reflections of the underlying brain parts. Figure 2–13 shows a device that was used to measure these irregularities. Interest in this now-discredited theory lasted a long time: the journal of the Ohio State Phrenological Society was published until 1938, and the British Phrenological Society was in existence until 1967.

Two additional examples that illustrate the growing interest in physical approaches to mental illness are the ideas of Cullen and Mesmer. The Scottish physician William Cullen (1712–1790) believed that neurotic behavior was caused by physical defects of the nervous

FIGURE 2–13 The Lavery electric phrenometer, invented in 1907, was designed to measure bumps on the head. Such bumps were thought to indicate the location of different psychological faculties.

system. Cullen's therapeutic efforts seem naive, but they were a logical outgrowth of his organic orientation. He treated his patients with cold dousings, bloodletting, inducing of vomiting, special diets, exercise programs, and physiotherapy. Like most of his contemporaries, Cullen used severe restraints and straitjackets to control violently disturbed individuals.

An even more famous example of the quest for organic explanations of abnormal behavior is the career of a Viennese physician, Franz Anton Mesmer (1734–1815). In 1774 Mesmer heard of the work of some English physicians who were treating certain diseases with magnets. He then treated a patient by making her swallow a preparation containing iron and attaching three magnets to her body, one on her stomach and two on her legs. Following her dramatic recovery, Mesmer speculated about the mechanisms that had brought about the cure. We would all agree with his first conclusion: the favorable result could not reasonably be explained by the action of the magnets alone. But Mesmer, a flamboyant and ambitious man, went on to assert that the magnets had simply reinforced or strengthened the primary cause of the cure: his personal or animal magnetism.

While Mesmer's idea of animal magnetism seems ridiculous today, it fit reasonably well with some of the scientific beliefs of his time. In the eighteenth century it was widely believed that the planets influenced both physiological and psychological aspects of behavior. Mesmer contended that all human beings were endowed with a special magnetic fluid, a kind of sixth sense that, when liberated, could cure and prevent all illnesses (see Figure 2–14). Furthermore, he was convinced that he possessed an unusual abundance of the fluid. Mesmer believed that a gesture with his hands was enough to make his patients feel the transmission of his magnetic force.

Mesmer's patients entered a thickly carpeted, dimly lit room amid soft music and perfumed air. They held hands, forming a circle around the *baquet,* a tub filled with magnetized water. Mesmer entered, dressed in an elegant cloak and carrying a sword. These dramatics were deliberately created to accomplish the emotional crisis needed for the cure.

Many testimonials claimed that Mesmer's treatment had been helpful. However, the mechanism of his therapy had more to do with the power of suggestion than with human magnetic fluids. His animal magnetism was a forerunner not of an organic cure, but rather of a complex psychological means of influencing attitudes and behavior. Mesmer thus was an important figure in the history of hypnosis, a clinical technique that, while far removed from Mesmer's *baquet,* still relies on suggestion as a means of influencing the patient's state of awareness.

The Reform Movement

The growth of a scientific attitude toward mental disorders that began in the eighteenth century contributed to an increase in compassion for people who suffered from them. This new compassion became the basis for the reform movement of the nineteenth century. Philippe Pinel (1745–1826), a leader in the reform of French mental hospitals, had expressed great sympathy for the plight of the deranged. He firmly believed that they required humane care and treatment. Although this orientation is widely accepted by both professional workers and the public today, Pinel's ideas were far from

FIGURE 2–14 Mesmer treated his patients using a *baquet,* a round tub in which he placed bottles of magnetized water. This eighteenth-century engraving shows patients using rods and ropes connected to the tub to touch the afflicted areas on their bodies.

commonplace in his time. Pinel had to fight against the view that institutions for the insane were needed more to protect society than to help the deranged.

An interesting aspect of the growth of Pinel's humanism was the influence of Jean-Baptiste Pussin, a former patient at a hospital where Pinel worked. After being discharged Pussin was given a job at the Hospice de Bicêtre, the major asylum for male patients, where he eventually became superintendent of the ward for incurable mental patients. Research has shown that it was Pussin, not Pinel, who removed the chains from patients at the Bicêtre. (Weiner, 1979). Pussin forbade cruelty toward patients and routinely dismissed attendants who mistreated them. Pinel learned much from Pussin, and when he was appointed head of the Salpêtrière, the women's asylum, he insisted that Pussin come with him.

Other reformers in Europe and America also had to fight many battles to achieve their goals. An example of the less-than-human methods that they opposed were the "ships of fools," or ships whose captains were paid to take the mentally ill away from the offended community. The community usually didn't seem to care that the lives of the passengers often ended at the bottom of the sea thousands of miles from home.

An important step toward humane treatment of the mentally ill occurred on May 25, 1815, when the British House of Commons ordered a "Parliamentary Inquiry into the Madhouses of England." One of these, the Hospital of St. Mary of Bethlehem in London, had become known for the noise and chaos prevailing within it. The activities in this "madhouse" were of such great interest to the public that visitors often came to observe the antics of the patients. Tickets were even sold to this popular tourist attraction (see Figure 2–15), from which the word *bedlam* is derived. A full-scale investigation was initiated after incidents of physical abuse at Bethlehem Hospital were revealed by a citizen's committee, which rallied public support for enlightened legislation on behalf of the mentally ill.

One of the leaders of the citizen's reform committee was William Hone, a political satirist. Hone described the formation of the committee as follows.

> *I was at a Coffee Shop in Fleet Street sitting next to Alderman Waithman, when the illustrator George Cruikshank came in. We talked, as we often did, on the subject of madhouses, of the abuses and cruelty to the patients—*
>
> *I then proposed forming a committee to investigate the Lunatic Asylums.*
>
> *Thus self-authorized, we knocked at the door of one Asylum after another. George Cruikshank drew the pictures and I took notes.*

FIGURE 2–15 This engraving shows one artist's conception of Bethlehem Hospital in London as it was in 1710. Note the visitors looking at the patients through the barred windows. It may be difficult to believe that a mental hospital would sell admission tickets, but until the late eighteenth century this is exactly what was done at this institution. Visitors were charged a penny a visit, for which they could view the antics of the inmates and tease them to their hearts' content.

Cruikshank's graphic portrayals of the inhuman conditions endured by the mentally ill were a major factor in bringing about reform (see Figure 2–16).

By the middle of the nineteenth century, the growing acceptance of humanitarian ideas had led to a broad recognition of the need to reform social institutions. Vigorous movements were begun to establish protective and benign asylums for the mentally ill. These movements were given impetus by Pinel's *Treatise on Insanity*, written at the beginning of the nineteenth century, in which he called for the application of scientific principles in place of guesswork in arriving at treatments for disturbed behavior. Classifying his patients according to observable characteristics, such as melancholy and delirium, Pinel sought to devise specific treatments for

FIGURE 2–16 The illustrator George Cruikshank's dramatic pictures of the mistreatment of mental patients helped bring about reform legislation. His portrait of William Norris, who was bound by foot-long chains to an iron rod at the head of his bed for 12 years, is an example of those illustrations.

them. For example, here is how he described the optimal treatment of melancholia and depression:

Patience, firmness, humane feeling in the manner of directing them, continuous watchfulness in the wards to prevent outbursts of anger and exasperations, pleasant occupations varied according to differences in taste, various types of physical exercise, spacious quarters among trees, all the enjoyments and tranquillity of country living, and from time to time soft and melodious music, all the easier to obtain since there is

almost always in these establishments some distinguished musician whose talents languish for want of exercise and cultivation.

—Pinel, 1809, pp. 258–260

The sometimes huge asylums for the insane that were built in the nineteenth century came into existence because it was felt that the only way to treat mentally disturbed people was to isolate them from the damaging influences of family, friends, and community. Accompanying this view was the belief in **moral treatment.** This approach mirrored Pinel's treatment plan for depression. It sought to control and rehabilitate the patient through a fixed schedule that encouraged regular habits; kind treatment with a minimum of restraint; a daily visit from the hospital superintendent, who assumed the role of persuader and inspirational leader; calm, pleasant surroundings; accommodations that separated patients with different degrees of disturbance; proper diet; some medication; and organized physical and mental activities (see Figure 2–17).

The programs of hospitals that employed moral-treatment approaches seemed to be most effective when the patients and staff shared common religious, ethnic, and cultural values; when caseloads were held to a relatively small size; when the hospital superintendent was charismatic and inspirational; and when adequate funds to run the hospitals were available (Morrissey & Goldman, 1986).

An important feature of the European reform movement was the creation of institutions for the treatment of psychologically troubled children. At the beginning of the nineteenth century, childhood was marked by a high infant mortality rate and an early entry into the adult work world, for example, in the coal mines,

FIGURE 2–17 This lithograph, called *Lunatic's Ball*, shows a dance that was held for patients at a county asylum in 1848. The contrast between this picture and that of Bethlehem Hospital illustrates the advances made in the 1800s. Note also the continued belief in the beneficial effects of music and the arts, also illustrated in Figure 2–7.

cotton mills, and other factories. Up to the 1850s children were placed into exactly the same institutions as adults. They were locked up in prisons—in 1816, 3,000 prisoners in various London jails were under 20, almost half under 17 years of age. Many were placed in workhouses. The inadequate or nonexistent facilities for children came about in part due to the then-standard definition of insanity as the loss of reason. Childhood, it was believed, was the time before reason was acquired. By the middle of the nineteenth century, however, textbooks dealing with psychological abnormalities included sections on children, using such terms as "the insanity of early life." Eventually, special institutions were developed not only for the care and treatment of disturbed children but also for those who were mentally retarded.

THE REFORM MOVEMENT IN AMERICA The eighteenth century was not a good time to be insane in the fledgling British Colonies; often the mentally ill simply languished in jail. In early colonial days the mentally ill generally were ignored until they required some action because they were thought to be a nuisance or a menace to the community. In this way, the insane became identified with criminals and paupers. In some communities, a group of these people would be loaded into a stagecoach in the middle of the night and dumped in the town square of some distant locale.

Gradually, however, a reform movement did evolve in the colonies. Virginia's royal governor, Francis Fauquier, persuaded the House of Burgesses to build a hospital for "ideots and lunaticks"; the hospital opened on October 12, 1773 (see Figure 2–18). Benjamin Rush (1745–1813), a signer of the Declaration of Independence, is often credited with the founding of American psychiatry. He believed that "madness" was caused by engorgement of the blood vessels of the brain. Although the treatment methods that he advocated (bleeding, purging, and water cures) today seem more like punishment than therapy, his work took place in a hospital rather than in a custodial institution, and his methods were intended to reduce pressure on the brain's blood vessels and thus reduce mental illness. The Pennsylvania Hospital, where Rush introduced his new treatment methods, was the first hospital in America to admit mentally ill patients. His *Medical Inquiries and Observations upon the Diseases of the Mind,* published in 1812, was the first American textbook on psychiatry and was used as a basic reference for over fifty years.

The lack of humane treatment and decent facilities for the insane in America appalled Dorothea Dix (1802–1887), a Boston schoolteacher who devoted much of her life to reforming institutions for the indigent. (See Figures 2–19 and 2–20.) By 1847 she had visited 18 penitentiaries, 300 county jails and houses of correction, and 500 almshouses where the mentally ill

(a)

(b)

(c)

FIGURE 2–18 (a) The Colonial Williamsburg restoration in Virginia features a reconstruction of the Public Hospital for Persons of Insane and Disordered Minds, America's first public institution exclusively for the mentally ill. (b) In the eighteenth century the inmates inhabited bare, depressing cells. (c) By the mid-nineteenth century, comfortable housing had become an important part of treatment.

were kept. Through her personal efforts 32 mental hospitals were constructed.

In 1908, an American businessman named Clifford Beers recorded his experiences as a mental patient in his book *A Mind that Found Itself* (see Box 2–1). After his recovery Beers became determined to make changes in the conditions of mental hospitals, and his book

helped him gather support for a citizens' reform group, the National Committee for Mental Hygiene (now called the National Association for Mental Health), which was founded in 1909. The group promoted social programs aimed at preventing mental illness as well as ensuring humane treatment of the mentally ill.

Despite the progress toward more humane treat-

FIGURE 2–20 The crib was one of the prescientific "therapies" for violent patients that Dorothea Dix sought to abolish.

BOX 2–1 A Protest That Had an Effect

Clifford Beers's book, *A Mind that Found Itself*, is the story of his treatment in mental hospitals during a period of psychosis and a protest against the often cruel treatment of patients in institutions for the mentally ill. Its description of what Beers endured gripped the imagination of readers and helped gain popular support for the American mental health movement (see Figure 2–21). After his recovery Beers carried on a lifelong crusade that helped revolutionize the care of the mentally ill. In the following excerpt Beers describes his agony when he was restrained in a camisole or straitjacket, a canvas device that was used to restrict movement of unruly patients. In this case Beers believed that the attending physician had laced the jacket unnecessarily tight because of his anger at Beers's behavior.

No incidents of my life have ever impressed themselves more indelibly on my memory than those of my first night in a straitjacket. Within one hour of the time I was placed in it I was suffering pain as intense as any I ever endured, and before the night had passed it had become almost unbearable. My right hand was so held that the tip of one of my fingers was all but cut by the nail of another, and soon knifelike pains began to shoot through my right arm as far as the shoulder. After four or five hours the excess of pain rendered me partially insensible to it. But for fifteen consecutive hours I remained in that instrument of torture; and not until the twelfth hour, about breakfast time the next morning did the attendant so much as loosen a cord.

During the first seven or eight hours, excruciating pains racked

not only my arms, but half of my body. Though I cried and moaned, in fact, screamed so loudly that the attendants must have heard me, little attention was paid to me. . . . I even begged the attendants to loosen the jacket enough to ease me a little. This they refused to do, and they even seemed to enjoy being in a position to add their considerable mite to my torture.

After fifteen interminable hours the straitjacket was removed. Whereas just prior to its putting on I had been in a vigorous enough condition to offer stout resistance when wantonly assaulted, now, on coming out of it, I was helpless. When my arms were released from their constricted position, the pain was intense. Every joint had been racked. I had no control over the fingers of either hand, and could not have dressed myself had I been promised my freedom for doing so.

For more than the following week I suffered as already described, though of course with gradually decreasing intensity as my racked body became accustomed to the unnatural positions it was forced to take. The first experience occurred on the night of October 18th, 1902. I was subjected to the same unfair, unnecessary, and unscientific ordeal for twenty-one consecutive nights and parts of the corresponding twenty-one days. On more than one occasion, indeed, the attendant placed me in the straitjacket during the day for refusing to obey some trivial command. This, too, without an explicit order from the doctor in charge, though perhaps he acted under a general order.

During most of the time I was held also in seclusion in a padded cell.

FIGURE 2–21 Clifford Beers became an effective advocate for humane treatment of mental disorders after his own experiences in a mental institution.

A padded cell is a vile hole. The side walls are padded as high as a man can reach, as is also the inside of the door. One of the worst features of such cells is the lack of ventilation, which deficiency of course aggravates their general unsanitary condition. The cell which I was forced to occupy was practically without heat, and as winter was coming on, I suffered intensely from the cold.

—Beers, 1981 [1907], pp. 107, 110–111

ment of mental patients in the nineteenth century, the mentally ill continued to be persecuted well into the twentieth century. An example is provided by Albert Deutsch, who published a shocking expose of the mistreatment of patients at the Philadelphia State Hospital for Mental Diseases during the 1940s:

The male "incontinent ward" was like a scene out of Dante's Inferno. Three hundred nude men, stood, squatted and sprawled in this bare room. . . . Winter or Summer, these creatures never were given any clothing at all. . . . Many patients . . . had to eat their meals with their hands. There weren't nearly enough spoons or other tableware to go around. . . . Four hundred patients were herded into one barn-like dayroom intended for only 80. There were only a few benches; most of the men had to stand all day or sit on the splintery floor. There was no supervised recreation, no occupational therapy. . . . Only two attendants were on this ward; at least 10 were needed. The hogs in a near-by pigpen were far better fed, in far greater comfort than these human beings.

—Deutsch, 1948, pp. 49–50

Today such conditions are unlikely to exist and many institutions provide a high standard of care. Figure 2–22 shows a scene from a contemporary mental hospital. While the quality of care in many mental hospitals has improved over time, the deinstitutionalization movement begun over twenty-five years ago has resulted in a lower standard of care for many people affected by mental illness and an increase in the suffering for some. For instance, the situation of homeless mentally ill persons in many ways parallels the less humane treatment of the mentally ill in earlier periods of history. Deinstitutionalization and some of its consequences are discussed further in both chapters 1 and 18.

Psychological versus Organic Views of Abnormal Behavior

The causes of abnormal behavior have yet to be determined fully, and debates on this issue recur continually. Is abnormal behavior caused by disturbances in bodily functioning or by subjective experiences, thoughts, and motivations? This question remains high on the agenda of contemporary clinicians and researchers, and the way it is approached today owes much to the way it has been phrased over the years, particularly during the nineteenth century.

The Psychological Approach

Eighteenth-century theories emphasized **rational thinking** as the way to achieve personal and social adjustment. During the first half of the nineteenth century, however, the important role of **irrational thought** in both normal and abnormal behavior attracted much more attention. This shift in emphasis took place as part of the so-called Romantic reaction against the view of philosophers and scientists who gave little weight to the role of emotions, motivations, and internal conflicts in human behavior. Many clinical workers and researchers began to view internal conflicts as a major cause of personal unhappiness and failure to adapt socially. This focus on emotion and irrational feelings laid the groundwork for Sigmund Freud's early twentieth century

FIGURE 2–22 Although present-day mental institutions may be barren facilities for "warehousing" patients, many hospitals are pleasant and stimulating institutions. These patients are in a well-run hospital whose staff recognizes the importance of positive social interactions in the recovery process.

writing about mental processes and their relationship to disturbed behavior (see chapter 3).

The reaction against pure rationalism directed more attention to the inner life of the person than to any other aspect of human existence. The German psychiatrist Johann Christian Heinroth (1773–1843) theorized that mental illness resulted from internal conflicts between unacceptable impulses and the guilt generated by those impulses, and that the individual is often unaware of these conflicts. What distinguished theories like Heinroth's from those of his predecessors was their attempts to provide an account of the whole person, the inner life, and the mental stresses and strains that underlie observable behavior. This was in contrast to the rationalist view that the scientific study of abnormal behavior primarily required meticulous observation and description of disordered behaviors, along with classification of those behaviors.

Heinroth's ideas are strikingly similar to Freud's notion that impulses clash with conscience and result in anxiety, unhappiness, and socially inappropriate behavior. Freud, like Heinroth, recognized that this clash might take place at an unconscious level and that awareness of these conflicts was a means of understanding and resolving them, and hence a way of correcting maladaptive behavior. Despite these similarities, Freud seems to have been only slightly acquainted with Heinroth and the other participants in the Romantic reaction. One reason for this was that by the mid-nineteenth century, long before Freud's work began, the pendulum had begun to swing in a quite different direction— toward the search for biological causes of abnormal behavior.

The Organic Approach

Just as Heinroth was the champion of the psychological approach to abnormal behavior, another German psychiatrist, Wilhelm Griesinger (1817–1868), led the search for bodily causes. He argued that most mental disorders were caused by the direct or indirect influence of disturbances in brain function. While he was a staunch advocate of humane treatment and was himself a sensitive observer of human conflict, Griesinger firmly believed that the organic, rather than the psychological, origins of human maladaptation and unhappiness were predominant. His slogan was "mental diseases are brain diseases."

Behind this perspective was the assumption that the material (brain cells) almost invariably causes the mental manifestation (personal unhappiness). The major implication of this viewpoint was that it was necessary to find out more about how the body (particularly the nervous system) works. One way of doing so was to dissect the brains of mentally disturbed individuals after their deaths. Researchers reasoned that the unusual behaviors exhibited by those individuals had been caused by structural abnormalities in the brain. Through direct examination of the brains of such people, they hoped to discover relationships between the brain and behavior. From this point of view, introspection as a path to understanding psychological disturbance held little appeal. Nor was there much interest in how thoughts direct observable behavior.

Emil Kraepelin (1856–1926), who was influenced by Griesinger, also believed that abnormal behavior was caused by organic disturbances. Kraepelin's major contribution was his attempt to construct a classification system that would encompass most of the disorders that required treatment and hospitalization. He distinguished between two especially serious and debilitating conditions, dementia praecox and manic-depressive psychosis, and believed that they were specific diseases with specific organic causes.

The Approaches Converge

Toward the end of the nineteenth century, important developments took place on both the physical and psychological fronts. The French neurologist Jean Martin Charcot (1825–1893) continued to believe that organic disturbances were of crucial importance, but he used a psychological approach in studying and treating his patients. The patients in whom Charcot was most interested were **hysterics,** people who suffered from physical complaints for which no organic causes could be found. Hysterics complained of loss of sensation in the skin, pains in various parts of the body, blindness and other visual impairments, tics, muscular contractions that resembled epileptic seizures, difficulty in walking, or paralysis. In addition to this wide variety of inexplicable symptoms, Charcot observed some psychological consistencies in hysterical patients, notably what he called *la belle indifference:* although a person who had become paralyzed could be expected to be depressed about it, Charcot's patients seemed unconcerned about their condition. Charcot also noticed that hysterical patients had their own incorrect theories of bodily functioning and that their physical symptoms were compatible with those theories. He diagnosed many of these cases as "traumatic paralysis."

Despite his orientation toward organic causes, Charcot became impressed with his psychological observations and came to the conclusion that mental states were indeed related to hysterical symptoms. He therefore developed a technique for hypnotizing hysterical patients. While they were in a hypnotic trance, he suggested

FIGURE 2–23 This portrait of Charcot shows him demonstrating the typical behavior of a hysteric, using a female patient as an example. Notice her fainting posture. Such dramatic behavior is typical of a hysterical episode.

to them that their symptoms (for example, paralysis of a part of the body) would disappear. In many cases the symptoms indeed vanished completely. Charcot also was able to induce hysterical symptoms in normal individuals by giving them appropriate suggestions while they were under hypnosis. Hypnosis is still used today in the treatment of some disorders, but the approach is much more complex than Charcot's reliance on mere suggestion as a way to remove symptoms.

Throughout France and Europe Charcot gained great prestige; he was referred to as the "Napoleon of neuroses." He became known as a charismatic clinician and teacher (see Figure 2–23). The following account describes some of his miraculous cures:

> *Many patients were brought to Charcot from all over the world, paralytics on stretchers or wearing complicated apparatuses. Charcot ordered the removal of those appliances and told the patients to walk. There was, for instance, a young lady who had been paralyzed for years. Charcot bade her stand up and walk, which she did under the astonished eyes of her parents and of the Mother Superior of the convent in which she had been staying. Another young lady was brought to Charcot with a paralysis of both legs. Charcot found no organic lesion; the consultation was not yet over when the patient stood up and walked*

> *back to the door where the cabman, who was waiting for her, took off his hat in amazement and crossed himself.*

> —Ellenberger, 1970, p. 95

One of Charcot's students, Pierre Janet (1859–1947), extended his work and concluded that hysteria was due to a splitting off from conscious experience of certain ideas that continued to influence behavior. He observed that under hypnosis many patients recalled upsetting events that seemed to be related to the onset of their symptoms. He found that in some cases, when patients expressed the strong feelings they had experienced at the time the original events took place, their symptoms weakened temporarily or disappeared.

Besides strengthening the view that psychological causes played a role in a significant number of behavioral disorders, Charcot and Janet helped broaden the scope of behavior that was studied by abnormal psychology. Their patients, though they were troubled people who needed help, were not thought of as insane or crazy.

One of the many clinical workers who came to France especially to study with Charcot was Sigmund Freud (1856–1939) (see Figure 2–24). Freud had received his medical training as a neurologist and initially believed that the ultimate causes of abnormal behavior were biological. Like Charcot, however, he chose to explore aspects of mental life that seemed to be related to psychological discomfort and maladaptive behavior. Also

PHOTOGRAPHIE des CHAMPS ÉLYSÉES

FIGURE 2–24 Charcot presented this inscribed photograph of himself to Sigmund Freud after Freud's visit to Paris. The visit had been possible because the University of Vienna had approved Freud's application for a travel grant, an excerpt of which follows.

> If the Honourable College of Professors will award me the traveling grant, it is my intention to spend 3–4 months with Professor Charcot in Paris studying the wealth of material provided by the Salpêtrière Clinic, such a favourable opportunity not being available to me in the Departments of the General Hospital.

(Macmillan, 1986)

like Charcot, Freud became increasingly interested in noncatastrophic conditions such as hysteria and phobias. Chapter 3 discusses Freud's theories in some depth.

The Stage Is Set

The history of abnormal psychology is the story of how communities have responded to people who were different and did not fit in. The ups and downs, the advances and retreats, leave us with a feeling of cautious optimism about the power of the intellect to comprehend and devise ways of helping individuals who are unable to adapt to community norms.

Ideas about abnormality are almost never brand new. As we have seen, they have a history that in some cases is very long. Moreover, they are often complex. Attitudes toward deviant individuals have always reflected the social dynamics that prevailed at the time. An example of the link between what is going on in a society (its values, prejudices, and the like) and how it conceives of mental illness has been provided by studies of the role of women in the nineteenth century. Theories that asserted that there were sex-based differences in the tendency to engage in abnormal behavior were an outgrowth of cultural stereotypes and the social status quo. Not only were women regarded as subordinate to men, they were also believed to be more prone to nervous and emotional disorders. Biological factors were assumed to play a role in these differences. Some of Sigmund Freud's writings reflect this sexist assessment; for example, early in his career he assumed that the strong sexual repression he observed in women was the cause of what he viewed as their intellectual inferiority (Ellenberger, 1970).

Because we are so close to our own times, we tend to lose sight of many of the basic assumptions and beliefs that direct the thinking of our contemporaries about a wide variety of topics. If we look back at earlier periods, these assumptions and beliefs are easier to see, and they often seem strange. For example, during the 1880s and 1890s, Freud's developing theories had to compete with ideas that seem naive today. One such idea was the notion that masturbation is a sign of serious personality disorder. People who masturbated were described as moral degenerates, as deceitful, selfish, and full of cunning. Excessive masturbation was believed to result in "masturbational insanity." Another popular idea was that there was a connection between blushing and psychological functioning: excessive blushing indicated inner moral failings, whereas inability to blush reflected psychological weakness (Skultans, 1979).

Policies regarding the treatment of abnormal behavior have been influenced by the public's concerns and priorities. For example, the American public puts a premium on speed and often seems to feel that a quick solution is best. Thus in the 1960s and 1970s public opinion favored a drastic reduction in the number of residents in mental hospitals. Because an effective system of halfway houses and other support services had not been established, masses of hurriedly discharged mental patients had to make their own way into unprepared and largely hostile communities. Few were able to make the transition successfully.

This book is devoted to modern theory, research,

and practice concerning abnormal behavior. Everyone has read dozens of newspaper and magazine articles describing breakthroughs that will soon eliminate certain types of mental disorders. Too often the solutions do not materialize, because the breakthrough has been interpreted too simplistically. As the scientific method has uncovered information on a variety of fronts, the need to recognize the complexity of most forms of maladaptation has become clearer.

Chapter Summary

HISTORICAL VIEWS OF ABNORMAL BEHAVIOR

It is important to know about the history of abnormal psychology because certain perspectives about deviance—mystical, organic, and psychological—have continued to recur throughout history. Some early mystical beliefs concerning the role of supernatural or magical forces in the origin of abnormal behavior are still found in many cultures. From this point of view, therapy often involves **exorcism,** or the removal of the evil through countermagic or prayer. This practice is often performed by a **shaman,** or folk healer. Another perspective links abnormal behavior with organic defect. Early evidence of this view is found in skulls from prehistoric times that show evidence of **trephination,** chipping holes in the skull. The psychological perspective suggests that abnormal behavior is related to disturbances in the way a person thinks or perceives the world and that these disturbances are potentially modifiable.

The Ancient Western World In ancient Greece disturbed behavior was originally interpreted as punishment for offenses against the gods. Later, several Greek philosophers, beginning with Socrates, held a more psychological view and considered reasoning to be basic to adaptive behavior. Plato developed the **organismic point of view,** which explained behavior as an overall expression of a person's psychological process. He thought of disturbed behavior as arising from internal conflicts between reason and emotion. Galen, a Roman physician, taught that psychological characteristics were expressions of bodily process influenced by a balance of the **four humors.**

The Middle Ages During the Middle Ages, contrasting views of mental illness existed. St. Augustine helped lay the groundwork for modern psychodynamic theory through his use of introspection to discuss mental processes. During the late Middle Ages, the church played both important positive and negative roles in the treatment of the mentally ill. The *Malleus Maleficarum* was an influential book that focused on the apprehension and conviction of witches and sorcerers. It played an important role in the persecution of the mentally ill who were often perceived as agents of diabolical forces. During this same period, rational thinkers Paracelsus and Juan Huarte attacked superstitious beliefs. Some governments, such as that in England, took responsibility for the protection of those who were mentally ill. There, two categories of persons, called **natural fools** and **persons non compos mentis,** were considered to need this protection.

The Renaissance During the late fifteenth and the sixteenth centuries, despite an increase in learning, witches were still persecuted and the influence of *Malleus Maleficarum* was still strong. However, Weyer, in an influential book, *The Deception of Demons,* argued for clinical treatment for the mentally ill rather than religious persecution. Weyer emphasized disturbed interpersonal relationships and psychological conflict as causes of mental disorder.

The Age of Reason and the Enlightenment In the seventeenth and eighteenth centuries, scientific knowledge increased greatly. Philosophers such as Spinoza wrote about the roles of emotions, ideas, and desires in life and made reference to unconscious mechanisms that influence behavior. Scientists such as Harvey wrote about the relationship between the physiological and psychological aspects of life. Literature also dealt with emotion and motivation. Many of Shakespeare's plays focus on the effects of emotion on behavior. Burton, in his book the *Anatomy of Melancholy,* described and analyzed depression from a psychological viewpoint. New ideas appeared such as **physiognomy,** the art of judging personality from physical appearance, and **phrenology,** the view that mental faculties could be "read" from feeling the bumps on a person's head. Mesmer developed the idea of animal magnetism, which led to the use of **hypnotism** as a treatment for mental disorder.

The Reform Movement The movement toward more humane treatment of the mentally ill began with the development of **moral treatment** by Pinel in France. In England, Hone and Cruikshank spearheaded a governmental review of conditions in London's St. Mary of Bethlehem hospital, the institution whose terrible conditions for patients was the origination of the word "bedlam." In the nineteenth century, special institutions were developed to care for and treat children who were mentally ill or retarded. The reform movement in the United States was led first by Rush, later by Dix, and then by Beers, who used his experiences as a patient to improve conditions in mental hospitals.

PSYCHOLOGICAL VERSUS ORGANIC VIEWS OF ABNORMAL BEHAVIOR

Because much is yet to be learned about the causes of abnormal behavior, the debate over the role of psychological factors and bodily functioning is ongoing.

The Psychological Approach The emphasis on **irrational thought** arose in the early nineteenth century as a reaction to the focus on **rational thinking** that characterized the Age of Reason. Heinroth described mental illness as the result of internal conflicts between unacceptable impulses and the guilt those impulses caused. About 100 years later, Freud had similar ideas despite the prevailing beliefs in his day about the biological basis for abnormal behavior.

The Organic Approach Griesinger argued that mental disorders are the result of disturbances in brain function. Later, Kraepelin used this view to construct a classification system for serious disorders. He distinguished between *dementia praecox* and *manic-depressive psychosis,* disorders that he believed had specific organic causes.

THE APPROACHES CONVERGE

Charcot was especially interested in **hysteria.** Although he believed in organic causes, he concluded that mental states were related to hysterical symptoms. He used hypnosis and suggestion to cure hysterical patients. Janet found that patients' symptoms were decreased by their expression of strong feelings that had been experienced earlier during an upsetting event. Freud's work with Charcot helped form his theoretical perspective.

THE STAGE IS SET

Attitudes about abnormal behavior and ideas about appropriate treatment are a reflection of the social values and prejudices of the time. It is important to keep this historical perspective in mind as emphasis shifts between biological and psychological explanations and treatments for abnormal behavior.

Theoretical Perspectives
on Maladaptive Behavior

C H A P T E R 3

The Role of Theory in Abnormal Psychology

The Biological Perspective
Biological Determinants of Abnormal Behavior
The Neurosciences Revolution
Integration of Biological and Psychological Systems

The Psychodynamic Perspective
Freud and Psychoanalysis
Contemporary Approaches to Psychoanalysis
Evaluating Psychoanalytic Theory

The Behavioral Perspective
Classical Conditioning
Operant Conditioning
Social Learning Theory

The Cognitive Perspective
Maladaptive Behavior and Cognition
Cognitive Therapies

The Humanistic–Existential Perspective
Rogers' Conception of the Self
The Existential Point of View

The Community Perspective
Social Roles and Labeling
Contributions of the Community Perspective

The Value of an Interactional Approach

Chapter Summary

Robert Anderson, *Tile Walls—Strange Angels*, 1991.
Wetherholt Galleries, Washington, D.C.

Fred Price, age 38, has been experiencing occasional pain in his chest for two months. He is a high school vice-principal in a large city, a high-pressure job requiring many daily contacts with teachers and students. The teachers often have complaints and the students almost always are having problems or causing them. Fred's task is to handle the problems effectively and quickly. He has put off seeing a doctor, attributing the chest pain to indigestion associated with stress at work. In fact, Alka Seltzer seemed to help somewhat. Recently he and his wife have been arguing a lot, often about money: braces for one child's teeth, tuition and living expenses for his oldest child who wants to go to college away from home, and nursing home expenses for his wife's mother. Last night, during an especially fierce argument with his wife, he had another bout of chest pains that took several hours to subside even after he took Alka Seltzer. Afterwards Fred began thinking about the fact that his father had his first heart attack at the age of 47. Like Fred, his father had had a demanding job that took a lot out of him, leaving him exhausted at night. In the morning Fred called his doctor for an appointment.

It would be difficult to summarize Fred Price's problems in a neat, straightforward manner. Is he a man who is about to have a heart attack? If so, is it because he has "bad" genes that make him prone to have one? Or, might his somatic problems simply be expressions of a high anxiety level engendered by a stressful job? Are his physical resources or stress-coping skills inadequate to handle the demands of being a vice-principal of an inner-city high school? What role do family pressures and marital discord play in his symptoms? Like most of us, Fred Price is a complex person. His thoughts, behavior,

and physical status probably have multiple determinants. From the information provided, it is not possible to determine the likely cause or causes of his symptoms and apparent unhappiness.

Clinicians and researchers have developed theories they hope will be helpful in identifying the causes of behavioral maladaptation and physical illness. These theories guide clinicians as they inquire into the determinants of maladaptation. While researchers occasionally joke about theories (and theorists) that promise more than they should (see Figure 3–1), theoretical concepts can and do play valuable roles in suggesting lines of inquiry, raising questions about commonly-held assumptions, and integrating available evidence. As we observed in Chapter 1, the concepts of stress, coping, and vulnerability weigh heavily in efforts to understand maladaptive behavior.

Stress arises when we must respond to challenges that may be unexpected and for which we do not feel prepared. The beginning of a new job, a death in the family, and living in an area with a high crime rate are examples of such challenges. People usually respond to stress by trying to alleviate it. How they respond reflects the effectiveness of their coping skills. For example, a person might install an alarm system after a neighbor's house has been robbed. Some people, however, choose less constructive responses. They may deal with the stress of living in a crime-ridden area by buying guns and vicious dogs or by never leaving their houses after dark. Abnormal psychology deals with behavior that results from failures to cope constructively with the demands, constraints, and opportunities that we all experience throughout our lives.

The failures to adapt that are the concern of

abnormal psychology usually cannot be explained by the presence of stress alone. It is necessary to investigate the coping styles and vulnerabilities of people who exhibit such failures if we are to understand their maladaptive behavior and help them correct it. There are large differences in how well particular individuals cope with stress. We are all vulnerable to experiences that are related to sensitive areas in our personalities. When these personally relevant buttons are pushed, our capacity for handling stress declines and we feel less competent and content than usual. The war hero who falls apart when his wife threatens to divorce him, the child who is the delight of her teachers but cannot get along with her playmates—both show that an individual may be more vulnerable to certain situational and developmental challenges than to others.

A variety of theories have been offered to explain the vulnerabilities and coping failures that increase the likelihood of personal breakdown. In this chapter we will review the major theoretical approaches as they apply to the relationships among stress, coping, and vulnerability and to other important aspects of maladaptive behavior.

The Role of Theory in Abnormal Psychology

Everyone wants to know why things happen. Scientific theories are created to organize what we know and explain what it means. Theories are never complete, because there are different ways of looking at what we do know and because there are always some pieces missing from our knowledge. Even an incomplete theory is useful, however, if it provides a perspective for examining the information we have. A good theory will also help us decide what new information we need.

Clinical workers and researchers operate on the basis of formal theories, but they also use informal theories or hunches based on past experience. A psychiatrist, clinical psychologist, or social worker who is assigned a case will use a particular theoretical perspective to analyze the available information. We all use theoretical perspectives in our lives, which serve as lenses that reflect and shape our conceptions of human nature. Thus according to one theoretical perspective a bad cold may be thought of as a viral infection; according to another it may be simply "God's will"; and according to your mother it may be "your own fault for getting your feet wet."

The diversity of theories in abnormal psychology is wide. We will review six theoretical perspectives that are particularly influential today: (1) the **biological perspec-**

FIGURE 3– 1 (© 1990 by Sidney Harris—Science Magazine)

tive, which emphasizes the role of bodily processes; (2) the **psychodynamic perspective,** which emphasizes the role of anxiety and inner conflict; (3) the **behavioral perspective,** which examines how the environment influences behavior; (4) the **cognitive perspective,** which looks to defective thinking and problem solving as causes of abnormal behavior; (5) the **humanistic–existential perspective,** which emphasizes our uniqueness as individuals and our freedom to make our own decisions; and (6) the **community perspective,** which is concerned with the roles of social relationships and the impact of socioeconomic conditions on maladaptive behavior.

Which of these theoretical perspectives is right? In Jewish lore there is a story about a couple who came to their rabbi for marriage counseling. The rabbi interviewed each partner separately about the problems in their relationship and then met with them together. They asked him who was right and who was wrong. The rabbi told the puzzled couple, "You are both right." The rabbi's observation also applies to these theoretical perspectives. Each one deals with pieces of reality, but the pieces are often quite different. Some theories are more pertinent to an understanding of the causes of stress, others to the ways in which we cope, and still others to the nature of human vulnerabilities. Consequently, there is no reason why we should commit ourselves to a particular theoretical position and feel called upon to explain all abnormal behavior in terms of its concepts. With a topic as complex as abnormal behavior, it is a good idea to remember that even a respected theory may be too simple an explanation.

It is also important to note that theories are not static. In the previous chapter we saw that through the centuries explanations of deviance have undergone wide swings. New facts exerted an influence on existing theories, but so did people's beliefs, which may or may not have scientific validity. Besides accommodating new facts or changes in public attitudes, a new theory may be developed as a reaction to weaknesses in a currently popular theory. Although all of the basic theoretical viewpoints discussed in this chapter are important and are actively used and researched today, it is worthwhile to keep in mind that each was a reaction to the situation prevailing at the time it was initially proposed.

The Biological Perspective

In our review of the history of abnormal psychology in Chapter 2, we saw that the idea that bodily disturbances cause disordered behavior has been around for a long time. It is not surprising that the biological perspective gained renewed popularity in the eighteenth and nineteenth centuries, when great leaps forward in anatomy, physiology, and genetics made it seem reasonable that a biological cause might eventually be found for every disorder, be it physical or behavioral. Major impetus for the biological point of view came from findings about the relationship between bodily infections and defects, on the one hand, and disordered behavior, on the other.

Recent information about the role of biological factors supports the argument that such factors are important to some, but certainly not all, mental conditions. Modern advances in several areas of biology and medicine have continued to motivate researchers. For example, equipment and techniques like the positron emission tomography (PET) scan and the computerized tomography (CT) scan, which make it possible to see how the brain works without the use of surgical or other invasive procedures, are beginning to permit previously unthought-of studies of the relationships between behavior and the brain. And research on heredity and genetics has shown that certain chromosomal defects are responsible for metabolic disorders, such as phenylketonuria, that in turn may lead to specific forms of mental retardation. The list of behavioral problems in which biological processes play at least some role is lengthening, as is the list of biologically based therapies.

Most people distinguish between the body and the mind, although the meanings attached to these words vary widely. **Body** refers to organs, muscles, bones, and brain; **mind** usually refers to attitudes, feelings, and thoughts. Although we generally speak as if the worlds of body and mind were totally separate, the separation between body and mind is actually an intellectual invention rather than a reality. Cognitive and bodily processes are closely intertwined, though how much weight one assigns to each process in accounting for maladaptive behavior depends on one's view. And new evidence may alter prevailing views from time to time.

At its most extreme, the biological viewpoint assumes that all maladaptive behavior is due to a disordered body structure or function. Such a disorder can be explained by an inherited defect that may cause permanent damage, by a defect acquired through injury or infection before or after birth or by a more or less temporary physiological malfunction caused by some condition that is present at a particular time such as a high fever caused by a temporary infection. A less extreme view, which still emphasizes the importance of biological functioning, recognizes that maladaptive behavior is a joint product of three types of disordered processes: in the body (for example, a hormonal deficiency), in psychological functioning (for example, a tendency toward shyness), and in the social environment

(for example, a high unemployment rate in the community). This interactional view is discussed later in the chapter.

Biological Determinants of Abnormal Behavior

A number of biological factors influence the behavior of organisms. How we behave and think depends not only on the action of each by itself but also on the interrelationships among them. Genetic factors, the brain and nervous system, and the endocrine glands all play important roles in psychological processes and in abnormal behavior.

GENETIC FACTORS The field of genetics has expanded dramatically in recent years. Evidence that genetic abnormalities account for a significant number of medical problems has led researchers to seek hereditary roots for maladaptive behavior as well. Available evidence suggests that genetic factors may contribute to such diverse disorders as schizophrenia, depression, criminality, and mental retardation. The idea that people can inherit certain behavioral tendencies arouses skepticism among some people who feel it conflicts with egalitarian ideals and conjures up a specter of "biological determinism." Yet research, particularly within the past two decades, has shown that few dimensions of behavior seem to be immune to the effects of genetic factors.

A major factor in some genetic abnormalities is irregularities in the structure or number of an individual's chromosomes. **Chromosomes** are threadlike bodies that are present in pairs in all body cells. Humans have 46 chromosomes in each cell. **Chromosomal anomalies** are likely to produce abnormalities in the brain. For instance, persons with Down syndrome, a type of mental retardation, have three # 21 chromosomes instead of two.

Arranged linearly along the chromosomes are the **genes,** each of which occupies its own characteristic position or **locus.** In contrast to the 46 chromosomes that are contained in a cell, an estimated 100,000 genes function as the elements of human heredity. More than 4,000 diseases are known that result from failure or abnormality of a gene, but in most cases the actual genes have not been identified or assigned to any particular chromosome. While maps of chromosomes, called **karyotypes,** have assisted geneticists in identifying chromosomal anomalies for some time, the prospect of mapping the human **genome,** the complete set of a person's genes, will revolutionize biology. To date, less than 1,000 human genes have been located—scientific expertise in gene mapping is indeed in its infancy. It is no exaggeration to say that current maps of human chromosomes compare in accuracy to the navigational charts that guided the explorers to the New World. But another decade of special efforts directed toward mapping the human genome could yield maps comparable to today's most detailed geological surveys. (See Figure 3–2.)

Scientists do know that faulty genes, or genes that are defective in some way, can exist in the absence of obvious chromosomal deviations and may cause metabolic or biochemical abnormalities. Particular genes influence behavior through a long series of steps. Their influence may be modified by events that happen before and after birth, as well as by the actions of other genes. The basis for gene action is a complex substance, **deoxyribonucleic acid (DNA),** that is found in the chromosomes. The discovery of DNA as the means by which genetic information is transferred led to the discovery of how genes work.

Sometimes a specific gene is present that has been identified as causing a certain characteristic or disease, yet the person may show no sign of the problem or perhaps only mild symptoms. The term **penetrance** has been used to refer to the percentage of cases in which, if a specific gene is present, a particular trait, characteristic, or disease will actually manifest itself in the fully developed organism. For example, the molecules of DNA you receive from your parents may carry the blueprint for a strong,

FIGURE 3–2 The development of radioactive markers now enables scientists to examine films of genetic material.

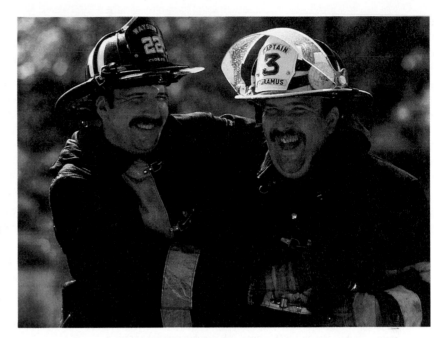

FIGURE 3–3 These identical twins were reunited at age 31 for the first time since they were adopted by two different families shortly after birth. They found that despite different upbringing they were very similar in many of their habits, interests and even in their choice of occupation, fire fighting.

sturdy body. But this will not automatically make you an athlete. Your nutrition, the amount of exercise and training you get, and your motivation, as well as any illnesses or injuries you experience before or after your birth, will all influence how your genetic predisposition toward physical strength is expressed.

Behavior Genetics A young but rapidly developing field is **population genetics,** the study of the distribution of genes throughout groups of people who mate with each other. Such information is used in predicting the incidence of certain genetically carried disorders. For example, Tay Sachs disease is a form of retardation that is caused by genes carried by some Jews whose ancestors came from a particular area of Europe.

Behavior geneticists study the effects of genetic inheritance on behavior. Behavioral genetic research with humans usually takes one of two forms: analysis of family histories or twin studies. Genealogical studies begin with an individual who manifests a particular trait. His or her relatives are then assessed to see whether they have the same trait. When such an analysis is carried out over at least two generations, some inferences about family genetics can be drawn. Twin studies are a more direct way of studying the effects of heredity on behavior. **Monozygotic** (identical) twins have been compared with **dizygotic** (fraternal) twins with respect to a variety of behaviors. Because monozygotic twins develop from the same fertilized egg, they have identical genes and hence identical heredities. Dizygotic twins, on the other hand, are the products of two entirely different eggs. If monozygotic twins exhibit a particular behavior disorder more often than dizygotic twins do, the identical heredity of the monozygotic pair may be the important factor.

The degree of **concordance** in twin studies refers to the relationship between twins or other family members with respect to a given characteristic or trait. If both twins show the trait, the pair is described as concordant (see Figure 3–3). If they do not, the pair is described as discordant. For example, studies have shown that the concordance rate of schizophrenics is high for monozygotic twins and drops precipitously for dizygotic twins of the same sex. The drop is even greater for dizygotic twins of opposite sexes. However, the fact that the concordance rate is not 100 percent for monozygotic twins suggests that environmental influences play a role. Although there is a very strong suggestion of a genetic component in schizophrenia, we must not forget that experience can lessen or emphasize the effects of any hereditary tendency.

The latter point is illustrated by a study of a set of identical triplets, all of whom suffered from serious chronic disorders (McGuffin and others, 1982). Two of the brothers had periods of auditory hallucinations and other clear schizophrenic symptoms. Between these periods they functioned at a low level and were unable to work. The third brother also had psychotic periods (although not as clearly schizophrenic), but he was able to function at a relatively high level and could hold a job between his psychotic episodes. His IQ was higher than that of his brothers, and his relationship with his father was much less stormy than theirs. This case demonstrates that even when people have identical heredities, their levels of functioning may vary in important ways.

The extent to which genes affect behavior has been a subject of debate for at least the last two centuries. In the nineteenth century fierce battles were fought in what

has come to be known as the nature–nurture controversy. Heredity (nature) and environment (nurture) were seen as separate and distinct forces that worked in an either/or fashion. Either nature determined a certain behavior, or nurture did; you couldn't have it both ways. Today, however, most psychologists hold the view that the interplay of many forces—in particular the interaction between the information carried by genes and the experience provided by the environment—determines behavioral patterns.

As the case above and others suggest, close and constant as it may seem, even the family environment affects children differently. Children growing up in the same household have different experiences. They may be at different ages when the family's income and social status rise and fall. They are treated differently by parents and their brothers and sisters. Birth order, age spacing, and sex differences are important. Furthermore, children have different experiences outside the family, with schoolmates, teachers, and friends. Random events of all kinds may also have effects that are compounded over time and make children in the same family different in unpredictable ways. Current work by behavioral geneticists suggests that differences in personality among family members are accounted for by a combination of genetic differences among the children and the effects of the **non-shared environment** (the unique relationships and life experiences of each child) (Plomin, 1990).

THE NERVOUS SYSTEM AND THE BRAIN

The Nervous System The nervous system has two major divisions: the **central nervous system,** which includes all the nerve cells (neurons) of the brain and spinal cord, and the **peripheral nervous system,** which includes all the neurons connecting the central nervous system with the glands, muscles, and sensory receptors (see Figure 3–4). The peripheral nervous system also has two divisions; the **somatic system,** which transmits information from sense organs to the muscles responsible for voluntary movement, and the **autonomic system,** which directs the activity of the glands and internal organs.

The fundamental unit of the entire nervous system is the **neuron,** or nerve cell, which has a long extension called the **axon** and several shorter extensions called **dendrites.** The function of nerve cells is to transmit electrical impulses to other nerve cells and to structures outside the nervous system (such as muscles and glands). A typical nerve cell receives a messenger chemical, or **neurotransmitter,** from other nerve cells through specific receptor sites on its dendrites. It changes the chemical signal to an electrical one and sends it through the axon. When the electrical signal reaches the tip of the axon, the nerve cell releases molecules of neurotransmitters that pass through a tiny region called the **synapse**

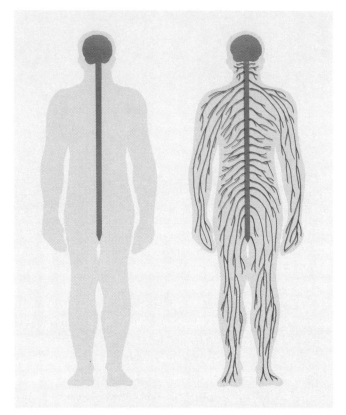

FIGURE 3–4 The central nervous system and the peripheral nervous system. The central nervous system (CNS) *(left)* consists of the brain, brain stem, and spinal cord; the peripheral nervous system (PNS) *(right)* includes all nerve fibers extending to and from the rest of the body. The CNS acts on the world through the PNS (a brain without a mouth cannot speak); it also learns about the world through the PNS (a brain without eyes cannot see).

and are taken up by specific receptors on the dendrites of adjacent nerve cells. This process can be repeated many times to transmit signals throughout the nervous system (see Figure 3–5).

The Brain The brain is easily the most complex part of the nervous system (see Figure 3–6). Its two cerebral hemispheres are highly developed centers for processing sensory information. The **cerebral cortex,** the convoluted layer of gray matter that covers each hemisphere, controls our distinctively human behavior. The cortex has areas that monitor hearing, vision, body sensations, and other processes. Disturbances in specific parts of the brain (caused, for example, by tumors) will result in specific behavioral deficits (for example, loss of speech). Electrical stimulation of certain areas of the cerebral cortex also produces specific motor responses or sensory effects.

The brain and its neurons are active continuously. This activity occurs spontaneously as well as in response to external stimulation. The activity of nerve cells

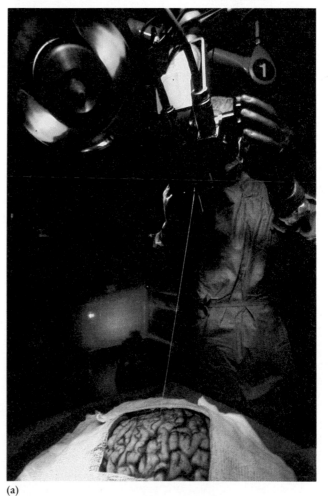

FIGURE 3–5 The relationship between a pair of typical neurons. A neuron consists of a cell body and two types of extensions—dendrites and an axon. Specific receptors or dendrites receive neurotransmitter molecules from the axons of adjacent neurons. This transfer sets up an electrical impulse in the receiving neuron that is in turn transmitted through the neuron by the nerve terminal at the tip of its axon. The arrival of the impulse at the nerve terminal causes the release of neurotransmitter molecules (shown by dots), which diffuse across a small gap (the synapse) to receptors on the dendrites of the next neuron. The process can be repeated many times to send signals throughout the brain and the rest of the nervous system.

FIGURE 3–6 The human brain. (a) View of exposed human brain during surgery. (b) The surface of the left hemisphere with major areas and their functions labeled. (c) A midline view of the right hemisphere with major areas and structures and their functions labeled.

(a)

generates electrical energy, and the voltage differences between cells or regions can be amplified and measured as brain potentials. A record of these brain potentials, called an **electroencephalogram (EEG),** shows a pattern of brain waves. Researchers have found that most behavioral states have distinct brain wave patterns. For example, the patterns designated as beta waves dominate during wakefulness, whereas theta and delta waves characterize deep sleep. Researchers have also been able to correlate brain wave patterns with psychological functions such as dreaming and attention, and with abnormalities caused by tumors or by the unusual electrical activity found in epilepsy (see Figure 3–7).

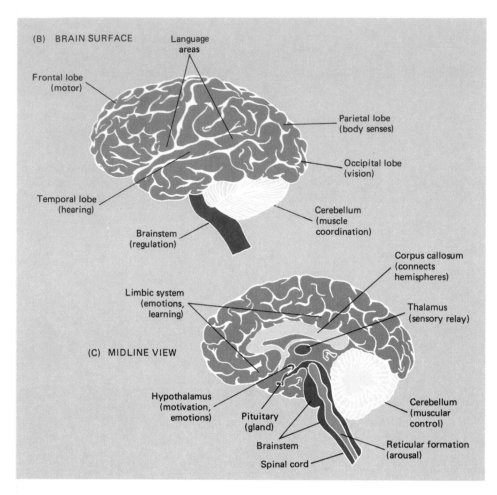

(B) BRAIN SURFACE

Language areas

Frontal lobe (motor)

Parietal lobe (body senses)

Occipital lobe (vision)

Temporal lobe (hearing)

Brainstem (regulation)

Cerebellum (muscle coordination)

Corpus callosum (connects hemispheres)

Limbic system (emotions, learning)

Thalamus (sensory relay)

(C) MIDLINE VIEW

Hypothalamus (motivation, emotions)

Pituitary (gland)

Brainstem

Spinal cord

Cerebellum (muscular control)

Reticular formation (arousal)

FIGURE 3–6 *(Continued)*

Behavioral state	EEG
Alert, awake	
Awake, resting, eyes closed (alpha waves)	
Light sleep	
Deep sleep	
Dreaming sleep "REM" (rapid-eye-movement)	1 sec

(A)

Normal (tracing 1)

Spontaneous petit mal epilepsy attack (tracing 2)

(B)

Cerebral tumor (tracing 3

FIGURE 3–7 An EEG and three EEG tracings. (a) An electroencephalogram (EEG) uses scalp electrodes to measure the activity of specific types of neurons. Particular EEG patterns are associated with certain behavioral states, as depicted here. (b) EEG tracings from patients who have different disorders are often visually distinguishable from one another and from those of normal subjects. Tracing 1 shows a normal EEG. Tracing 2 shows the onset of wave and spike discharges that are characteristic of petit mal epilepsy, a disorder in which sudden transitory disturbances of brain function may cause brief periods of loss of consciousness. Tracing 3 demonstrates the slow wave activity that is often associated with a cerebral tumor.

The Nervous System and Behavior Abundant evidence exists that various behavioral deficits result from defects in the central nervous system, but many questions remain unanswered. Frequently, neither the particular type of deficit nor the available information about possible organic damage is sufficiently clear-cut to permit a high degree of certainty about the causes of behavior. A person who experiences memory losses and thought disturbances may have fallen on his or her head,

but the actual effects of the fall on brain tissue may not be obvious.

An important part of current brain research concerns recently identified systems within the brain. For example, work on the basic psychology and biology of motivation has resulted in the discovery of the brain reward system in higher animals. The brain reward system involves the hypothalamus and structures of the limbic system. The **limbic system** is part of the primitive, lower part of the cortex and is associated with emotional and motivational functions; the **hypothalamus,** located above the roof of the mouth, plays a role in motivation and emotions but also has connections with many other areas of the brain. Activation of the brain reward system by electrical stimulation produces an intense feeling of pleasure that is much more powerful than ordinary reinforcers, such as food and sex. In experimental work with rats it has been found that if an electrode is implanted so that an animal can deliver a weak shock to its own brain reward system by pressing a lever, it will do so at a very fast rate. If the animal is starved and then given a choice between food and electrical self-stimulation, it will self-stimulate until it starves to death.

Early researchers who studied the brain reward system had no idea that their work might be related to addiction to substances like opium, but unexpected recent evidence is rapidly changing the situation. Researchers have discovered that there are chemical receptors on neurons in certain regions of the brain that respond to opiates. In fact, the greatest concentration of these opiate receptors is in the brain reward system. Moreover, the brain produces substances called **endorphins** that activate these receptors; they are even more powerful analgesics (pain relievers) than opium and, when administered directly, are addictive.

The endorphins work like keys in a lock. They fit only into sites, or receptors, that are specifically designed to accept them. Because the endorphins are similar to opium and related chemicals, knowledge of how they work may lead to a better understanding of drug addiction and its treatment. There are, of course, equally important environmental, psychosocial, and personality factors that influence the actual addictive behaviors. If scientists can create nonaddictive chemicals that function like the opiates, they may be able to ease pain of all kinds, including the pain connected with stopping a heroin habit. Before this can happen, however, much more information about the brain reward system and endorphins is needed.

THE ENDOCRINES Your body contains a marvelous system of glands and nerves which quickly organizes your heart, lungs, liver, kidneys, blood vessels, and bowels, causing them to work at top efficiency in an emergency. And when the threat ends, that same glandular system calms everything down.

Several glands, including the pituitary, thyroid, adrenal, and gonadal (sex) glands, as well as the part of the pancreas that produces insulin, make up the endocrine system (see Figure 3–8). These glands are ductless: the endocrines, unlike the salivary glands or tear glands, have no ducts for delivery of the substances they produce. Instead, they discharge those substances directly into the bloodstream, which carries them to all parts of the body. Hormones secreted by the endocrine glands act as chemical messengers (the word "hormone" is derived from a Greek word meaning "messenger"). They correlate our reactions to external events and coordinate bodily growth and development.

Hormones are very potent, so it takes very little of them to exert an influence over their specific target cells. Cells that respond to hormones are genetically endowed with special surface molecules, or "receptors," that detect even very low hormone concentrations. Once these cells receive a hormone, they initiate a series of adjustments within the cell that are dictated by the hormone. Hormones will usually increase the cell's activity temporarily.

FIGURE 3–8 The endocrine glands and their locations in the body.

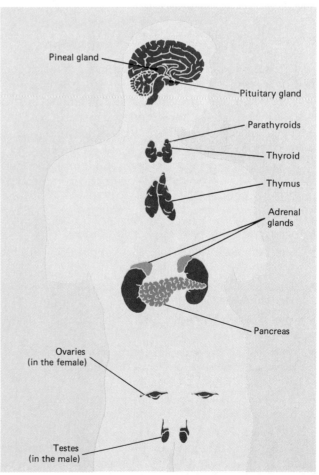

In the study of abnormal psychology there is particular interest in the role played by the endocrine glands in dealing with stress. The word **stressor** is often used to refer to a condition that makes it harder to achieve or maintain biological and psychological adaptation. Examples of stressors to which the endocrine glands respond are biological factors such as disease germs and psychological experiences such as receiving an insult or engaging in combat. The hormones secreted by the glands help us mobilize our physical resources to deal with stressors by fighting or escaping.

The stress response involves the pituitary gland and the part of the adrenal gland called the **adrenal cortex.** In times of stress the brain is activated and sends messages to one of its structures, the hypothalamus, which is close to the pituitary gland. The hypothalamus releases a substance called **corticotrophin-releasing factor** (CRF), which goes to the pituitary to form and release another chemical, **adrenocorticotrophic hormone** (ACTH). ACTH is released into the bloodstream and can go directly to the adrenal cortex, where it causes the adrenal cortex to form and release **adrenal corticosteroids,** which affect the brain's and the body's response to mental and physical stress. Some researchers have used the level of these steroids as an indicator of the degree of stress experienced by the individual.

The Neurosciences Revolution

Exciting as developments in the fields of genetics, neurology, and endocrinology have been, equally impressive are recent advances in our understanding of their interrelationships. A new interdisciplinary field has emerged, called **neuroscience.** Researchers in the neurosciences aim to understand the relationship between the structure and function of the brain and human thoughts, feelings, and behavior. The neuroscience disciplines include:

- neuroanatomy—the study of brain structure;
- neuropathology—the study of disease processes caused by disorders of brain structure;
- neurochemistry—the study of the chemical processes that control brain function;
- neuropharmacology—the study of the effects of drugs on the brain;
- neuropsychology—the study of the relationship between various psychological or mental functions and brain structure;
- neuroendocrinology—the study of the relationship between glandular function and brain function.

As more and more neuroscience research has been undertaken, it has become increasingly clear that a multitude of factors may cause mental illness. At present, we can only partially understand these causes. We do know, however, that several forms of mental illness are due to different types of brain abnormalities, including the loss of nerve cells and excesses or deficits in chemical transmissions between neurons. We can also attribute some maladaptive behaviors to defects in the wiring or circuitry pattern within the nervous system, to deficiencies in the command centers of the brain, or to the way messages move through the nervous system. The tendency to develop such abnormalities may run in families and therefore be partially hereditary. A broad range of environmental factors (for example, infections, nutrition, head injuries, or even the shocks and stresses of everyday life) may also play important roles in causing some mental illnesses.

The value of the neurosciences' multidisciplinary approach can be illustrated with the disorder Parkinson's disease. Parkinson's disease was described by James Parkinson in 1817. It has been called the "shaking palsy" because its victims suffer from a tendency to shake, most noticeably in their hands, as well as a tendency to become stiff and rigid, sometimes to such a degree that they are nearly paralyzed. A significant percentage of people with Parkinson's disease, particularly the elderly, develop lapses of memory, disorientation, and poor judgment. As techniques to study brain structures were developed, it was found that victims of this disease had a loss of nerve cells in a particular and quite small part of their brains called the *substantia nigra*. Neurochemists have shown that certain neurochemical abnormalities contributed to this loss. Spurred on by this clue, neuropharmacologists have found that giving Parkinson's patients the substance L-dopa could correct this neurochemical deficiency. The use of L-dopa has revolutionized the treatment of Parkinson's disease. Patients who receive it often have a marked decrease in their symptoms, particularly rigidity. Many patients who were nearly incapacitated are now able to live normal lives.

The case of Parkinson's disease illustrates how the neuroscience disciplines interrelate closely, with discoveries in one branch often put to use by researchers or clinicians in another branch. Neuroscientists have shown that behavior, perception, and cognition are results of integrated actions of networks of nerve cells. Understanding the complex activities of the nervous system requires identifying the relevant anatomical connections and chemical factors. Sensitive techniques now permit study of the discrete molecular events that take place at the synapses, the junctions between nerve cells where clinically useful treatments are known to exert their actions. Great strides have been made in identifying transmitter substances and the process of neural transmission pertinent to a number of types of maladaptive behavior. Box 3–1 presents an example of how the

BOX 3–1 What Goes on when We Sleep—and when We Can't?

The topic of sleep disturbance is not a new one. The Roman poet Lucretius wrote about the problems of sleep 2,000 years ago. Countless remedies for sleep disturbances have been suggested. In 1550, the French surgeon Ambroise Paré proposed the following treatment for insomnia: "One should make artificial rain by making water run from some high place into a cauldron that it may make such a noise that the patient can hear it. By these means sleep will be provoked in him."

Sleep disturbances affect about one third of the U.S. population. Patients with sleep problems are concerned not only about the immediate distress and discomfort caused by inability to sleep, but also about the effects of their sleep deficit on family life, employment status, and general social adjustment. Sleep disorders accompany a number of forms of maladaptive behavior (including depression, which is discussed in Chapter 10).

Today, valuable information about what goes on when we sleep is coming from neuroscience research conducted in sleep laboratories (see Figure 3–9), in which a number of biological processes are monitored while subjects sleep. Through such sleep studies, researchers in the neurosciences have significantly contributed to an understanding of the complex processes involved in sleep. Some of their findings include the following.

1. Stages of sleep can be marked by specific types of events, such as EEG patterns and eye blinking.

2. Sleep occurs in cycles. The distribution of wakefulness across an eight-hour nocturnal period has been described for each successive hour (the first hour has more wakefulness than any of the remaining seven hours).

3. Most bodily processes slow down at sleep onset and may be further reduced later in sleeping.

4. At least three groups of neurotransmitters play roles in sleep.

5. The secretion of certain hypothalamic–pituitary hormones are closely related to sleep–wake cycles.

The fact that these types of biological processes have been identified as significant contributors to whether and how deeply we sleep does not mean that an individual is powerless to change a faulty sleep pattern. Attention to the following behavioral and environmental factors can help us maximize the benefits of sleep (Hauri & Orr, 1982).

1. Sleep as much as needed to feel refreshed during the following day. Restricting the time in bed seems to solidify sleep, but excessively long times in bed seem related to fragmented and shallow sleep.

2. Get up at the same time each day, seven days a week. (A regular waking time in the morning leads to regular times of sleep onset.)

3. A steady daily amount of exercise probably deepens sleep.

4. Insulate your bedroom against sounds (carpeting, insulated curtains, closing the door).

5. Excessively warm rooms may disturb sleep; keep the room temperature moderate.

6. Hunger may disturb sleep. A light snack at bedtime may help sleep.

7. Try to avoid excessive liquids in the evening, in order to minimize the need for nighttime trips to the bathroom.

8. Avoid caffeinated beverages in the evening.

9. Avoid alcohol in the evening. Although alcohol helps tense people fall asleep more easily, the ensuing sleep is then broken up.

10. People who feel angry and frustrated because they cannot sleep

FIGURE 3–9 The electrodes connected to this woman's face and head allow scientists in the sleep laboratory to monitor and record the electrical activity from her heart and brain as well as the muscle activity from her face and neck throughout the night while she sleeps.

should not try harder and harder to fall asleep but should turn on the light, leave the bedroom, and do something different like reading a boring book. Don't engage in a stimulating activity. Return to bed only when sleepy. Get up at your regular time the next day, no matter how little you slept.

11. The chronic use of tobacco disturbs sleep.

12. If you find yourself waking up and looking at the clock, put the clock under the bed or cover it up.

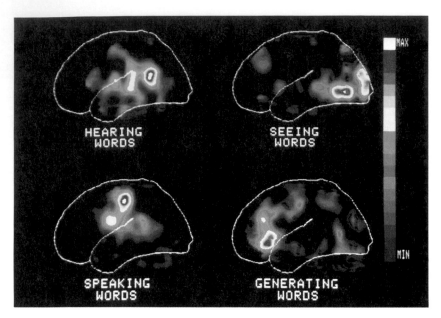

FIGURE 3–10 PET scans of normal subjects give researchers clues as to what areas of the brain are involved in everyday activities and how the metabolism in the brain is affected.

neurosciences have deepened our understanding of an aspect of behavior most of us take for granted, sleep.

In the 1970s, advances in applied physics and computer science laid the basis for the later development of instruments that permit the study of both brain anatomy and function in living individuals. New techniques for studying anatomy of the living brain include computerized tomography (CT) and magnetic resonance imaging (MRI). These techniques are based on the ability of electromagnetic waves (X-rays) and radio-frequency signals to penetrate bone tissue. With CT and MRI techniques a signal from the outside is transformed by the interior of the head into an outgoing signal that can then be used for information retrieval. Further refinements in CT and MRI techniques are expected to provide anatomical images of brain structure with a resolution of about 1 millimeter. This resolution will make feasible living brain comparisons among people with a wide variety of mental disorders. Another technique, positron emission tomography (PET), makes possible the study of brain physiology in living subjects and provides images of metabolic processes, cerebral blood flow, and features of neurotransmission (see Figure 3–10). Use of PET scans has provided greater understanding of the role of neurotransmitters in brain function and mental disorders. Prior to their development researchers had been hampered by the lack of techniques for directly assessing the way these substances function in the living human brain.

PSYCHONEUROIMMUNOLOGY Psychoneuroimmunology is a new field of study that links psychological, neural, and immunological processes. The case below illustrates how these processes may interact in an individual.

Larry Jackson, a 50-year-old high school teacher, was divorced five years ago, and had had a series of infections and fevers, swollen lymph nodes, and a nagging cough ever since his high-school-age daughter had died four years previously. Recently he had experienced severe respiratory difficulties, as a result of which he had been hospitalized. The three months prior to the hospitalization had been particularly stressful because of disagreements with the school principal, who seemed always to be annoyed with him. While he was in the hospital, treatment with antibiotics resulted in some symptomatic improvement, but he continued to feel weak and the lymph node swelling persisted. A lymph node biopsy showed the existence of some cancerous cells. His physician was not sure how Jackson's physical symptoms were related or caused, but the doctor concluded, after several conversations with his patient, that Jackson had not yet gotten over his daughter's death. Jackson seemed to work very hard at denying his grief over the daughter's death. He never expressed the feelings that the doctor felt would be normal under the circumstances.

Many physicians have noted associations between significant losses, like a daughter's death, and subsequent illness. The association often seems greatest when the person experiencing the loss is unable to express strong emotions, for example, the grief that normally accompa-

nies personal tragedies. Cases like Jackson's have led researchers to the hypothesis that the stress evoked by major losses and separations disrupts the body's immune system and thereby contributes to a host of physical illnesses.

The immune system has two major tasks: recognition of foreign materials (called **antigens**), and inactivation and/or removal of these materials. The immune system influences a person's susceptibility to the course of a disease. It consists of several distinct groups of cells called **lymphocytes.** Recent research has provided a preliminary understanding of how stress and emotional factors lead to hormonal changes that can sometimes decrease the efficiency of the immune system and thus increase susceptibility to disease.

The first demonstration of a relationship between bereavement and alterations in the functioning of the immune system was a study of 26 surviving spouses of patients who either had been fatally injured or had died after a prolonged illness (Bartrop and others, 1977). Although the effects were not large, the evidence suggested diminished immune system functioning among the survivors. Subsequent research has shown that bereavement caused by the death of a spouse is associated with a suppression of immunity and that the absence of a supportive social network also contributes to suppression of the immune system (Stein and others, 1987). Furthermore, certain psychological states, such as loneliness, depression, and feelings of helplessness, have a negative impact on the immune system. In this connection it is noteworthy that Jackson's divorce had occurred a year before his daughter's death. The divorce had greatly restricted his social network. He had fewer contacts with other people and lacked social relationships that made it easy for him to express his grief, loneliness, and anger at the terrible things that had happened to him.

Psychoneuroimmunologists study three bodily systems simultaneously—the nervous, endocrine, and immune systems—that can communicate with one another through complex chemical signals. It is possible that some people who exhibit severe emotional and behavioral abnormalities show psychoneuroimmunological abnormalities as well. This possibility is being investigated, particularly in people suffering from either of two severe psychological conditions, schizophrenia and depression.

Integration of Biological and Psychological Systems

For many years chemicals have been known to influence behavior—for example, to reduce pain and induce sleep. Chemicals are used extensively in treating maladaptive behavior. Several kinds of psychoactive drugs (antipsychotic, antianxiety, and antidepressant drugs) are often highly effective in reducing particular types of maladaptive behavior. Figure 3–11 illustrates how the use of antipsychotic drugs allows many individuals to be treated as outpatients instead of enduring long stays in mental hospitals.

The biological perspective has proven fruitful because of the therapies, such as drugs, that it has produced, and also because of the questions it has raised. If the abnormal behavior of schizophrenics can be muted or eliminated by certain chemical compounds, can schizophrenia be regarded merely as a sign of a specific chemical disorder in the nervous system? Unfortunately, this sort of question can almost never be answered in a true-or-false fashion. For example, there are also instances in which purely psychological treatment of schizophrenics has led to marked reductions in bizarre behavior.

To what degree can maladaptive behavior be viewed as a disease? The boundaries between health and disease are far from clear, partly because of the roles played by psychological, social, and cultural factors as well as biological ones. Given the multiple factors that affect people, an extreme organic perspective is likely to be overly simplified. More likely to stand the test of time is a model that views maladaptive behavior as a product of these interacting factors. Although it does not provide a final answer, the biological perspective has enhanced our understanding of one of these sets of factors.

From the standpoint of abnormal psychology, it is important to relate biological processes to maladaptive behavior. Theories about these relationships range from

FIGURE 3–11 The introduction of antipsychotic drugs resulted in a sharp decline in the number of patients in mental hospitals. This figure shows the number of resident patients in state and county mental hospitals before and after the introduction of chlorpromazine, a drug that is particularly effective in treating schizophrenia. Prior to the introduction of the antipsychotic drugs, there had been a steady increase in the number of hospitalized mental patients. The use of those drugs has greatly reduced and even eliminated hospital stays for many individuals.

(Based on data from National Institute of Mental Health)

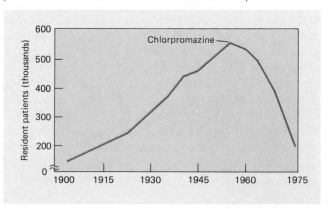

those that reject the importance of the relationship for most disorders, to those that see value in exploring them but do not draw many firm conclusions, to those that argue that mental illnesses are diseases in the same sense as cancer or high blood pressure. However, there is growing evidence that cancer and high blood pressure are not pure illustrations of physically caused conditions. Most diseases are probably caused by multiple determinants, including physical, environmental, psychological, and hereditary factors. Disentangling these various kinds of causes from one another can be a difficult scientific problem.

It is clear that the multiple causes of mental illness, like those of cancer and high blood pressure, are only partially understood. The biological perspective implies that many types of abnormal behavior are due largely to factors beyond people's control—primarily to the type of brain and body people are born with and the environment in which they are nourished. While this point of view may seem extremely deterministic, it is not totally so. Most theorists recognize that, to varying degrees, biological systems have plasticity. For example, the brain has built into it the ability to adapt and change in response to injury or changes in the environment. The limits that biological processes place on behavior and the degree to which those processes can be influenced represent topics of current research and theory.

The Psychodynamic Perspective

The **psychodynamic perspective** is based on the idea that thoughts and emotions are important causes of behavior. Psychodynamic approaches to behavior assume that, to varying degrees, observable behavior (overt responses) is a function of intrapsychic processes (covert events). Not all psychodynamic theorists emphasize the same inner events and the same sources of environmental stimulation, but they do agree that personality is shaped by a combination of inner and outer events, with emphasis on the inner ones. Sigmund Freud, the originator of the psychodynamic perspective, believed that eventually all behavior could be explained by bodily changes; however, because so little was known in his time about the relationships between the body and the personality, he actually gave biological factors little emphasis. Nevertheless, impressed by Charles Darwin's theory concerning the importance of emotions, Freud directed his attention to their influences over thought. Freud believed that to understand behavior it is necessary to analyze the thoughts preceding and associated with it,

and that to understand those thoughts, a person's deepest emotions and feelings must be explored.

Because thoughts and feelings are not directly observable, psychodynamic theorists must infer them. They relate their inferences about inner processes to important features of overt behavior. The following account by a psychotherapist illustrates how this process is done:

By the fourth session I realized that he had never mentioned his father. It seemed as if there wasn't and never had been a father. I asked myself: How could it be that this man who is so unhappy and has so many problems fails to even mention his father? I guessed that he was either so ashamed of his father that he couldn't talk about him or he harbored so much anger toward him that consciously or unconsciously he couldn't deal with it. I decided to wait and see what would happen rather than push the client in the direction of talking about something that was very sensitive for him.

During the ninth session he told me about a dream he had had the night before. A large dark man sat at a table and a small child watched from a corner as the man ate great quantities of food and ordered a small, frightened woman to bring him more and more. After he ate each helping he would raise a gun and shoot down a few people who were standing in a row against the wall.

The client reported how frightened he had felt during the dream. As we discussed his associations to the dream, it became clear to me that the man in the dream represented his father. After several more sessions he told me he felt very angry with me because I constantly told him what to do and verbally cut him down. After pointing out that in reality I had said almost nothing, I asked him if I seemed like the man in the dream. Finally the dike burst. For the rest of the session and the next one all of his seething hatred toward his father came out. He blurted out that when he was a child he had seen his father strike his mother several times. When he saw this happen, he had wanted to kill his father.

Apart from the contribution that psychodynamic theorics have made to our understanding of human behavior, they seem especially influential because they are

the systems out of which all types of psychotherapy developed. While clinical psychoanalysis as originated by Freud is infrequently used today, its basic elements and the theory of mental events underlying it have greatly influenced the development of the entire field of psychotherapy.

Freud and Psychoanalysis

Sigmund Freud, a Viennese neurologist, is clearly one of the most influential writers of this century, admired for his wit, intellect, and willingness to revise and improve his theories as his clinical experience grew. Freud began his practice at a time when there were few effective forms of treatment in most fields of medicine. Effective treatment generally depends on an understanding of the causes of a disorder, and at that time, although accurate diagnoses could sometimes be made, little was known about the causes of disease, whether physical or mental. A disorder that was particularly common during the late 1800s was hysteria, the presence of physical problems in the absence of any physical causes. Like other well-trained neurologists of his time, Freud originally used hypnosis to help his hysterical patients lose their symptoms. Then a friend, Joseph Breuer, told Freud that while under hypnosis one of his patients had recalled and understood the emotional experience that had led to the development of her symptoms, and that her symptoms had then disappeared. For a time Freud and Breuer used this method of recapturing memories with some success. However, because some patients were not easy to hypnotize and sometimes the positive effects did not last long, Freud began to develop his method of psychoanalysis, in which the patient recaptures forgotten memories without the use of hypnosis. Freud's psychoanalytical method made him enormously influential among European clinicians. When he visited the United States in 1909, his reputation had spread across the Atlantic (see Figure 3–12).

FREUD'S THEORIES OF PERSONALITY Freud's theories of personality may seem complicated because they incorporate many interlocking factors, but two basic assumptions underlie them all; psychic determinism and the conscious–unconscious dimension.

The principle of **psychic determinism** states that all behavior, whether overt (a muscle movement) or covert (a thought), is caused or determined by prior mental events. The outside world and the private psychic life of the individual combine to determine all aspects of behavior. As a clinical practitioner, Freud sought to modify unwanted behavior by identifying and eliminating its psychic determinants.

Freud assumed that mental events such as thoughts and fantasies vary in the ease with which they come to the individual's awareness. For example, aspects of mental life that are currently in awareness are **conscious.** Mental contents that are not currently at the level of awareness but can reach that level fairly easily are **preconscious.** Mental contents that can be brought to awareness only with great difficulty are **unconscious.** Freud was inter-

FIGURE 3–12 Freud's visit to the United States in 1908 was important in extending his influence in North America. He is shown here at Clark University in Worcester, Massachusetts with some of the pioneers of psychoanalysis and psychology. From left to right in the front row are Freud, G. Stanley Hall, and Carl Jung. Standing behind them are A.A. Brill, Ernest Jones, and Sandor Ferenczi.

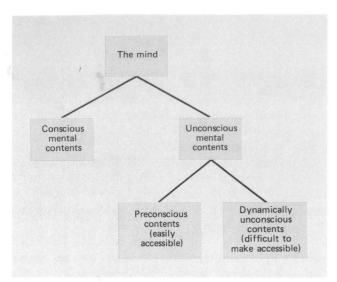

FIGURE 3–13 Freud's model of the mind. Freud viewed the mind as having conscious and unconscious portions. Material in the unconscious portion varies in the ease with which it can be brought to consciousness. The more intense the emotions linked with unconscious thoughts, the greater the difficulty in bringing them to the level of awareness.

ested mainly in how these unconscious mental contents could influence overt behavior (see Figure 3–13).

Freud was especially intrigued by thoughts and fantasies that seem to go underground but then reappear at the conscious level. He asserted that the level of intrapsychic conflict was a major factor in determining our awareness of particular mental events. According to Freud, the classic example of intrapsychic conflict results when a young boy desires to take his father's place in relation to his mother but at the same time feels love and affection for his father. Freud believed that the greater the degree of intrapsychic conflict, the greater the likelihood that the mental events connected with it would remain unconscious. The more massive the unconscious conflict, the greater the person's vulnerability to stress. Freud believed that behavior disorders that occur after childhood are caused by a combination of early traumatic experiences and later experiences that trigger the emotions and unresolved conflicts associated with the early events.

Freud contended that hidden emotions or drives are involved in human conflict. He referred to these drives as **libido** and believed that they were a form of psychic energy analogous to the individual's supply of physical energy. Just as some people are more athletic, some have stronger libidos. Freud also believed that the psychic energy or drive level of the individual sets up an inner state of tension that must somehow be reduced. In general, libido can be seen as desire for pleasure, particularly sexual gratification.

One novel feature of Freud's theory was his emphasis on sexuality. This emphasis was no doubt related to the often prudish, repressive atmosphere of Vienna at that time. The concept of sexuality within psychoanalytic theory is very broad and, rather than referring only to sexual intimacy, can be equated with the individual's total quest for pleasure and gratification. Freud also saw the process of development as being expressed in sexual terms.

Stages of Psychosexual Development
Freud's theory of personality development placed tremendous emphasis on the effects of experiences that occur during the first five years of life. During this period children pass through a number of stages during which their libido is focused on a series of pleasure-giving or erogenous zones in the body. Those zones are the mouth, the anus, and the genitals, resulting in the **oral, anal,** and **phallic psychosexual stages.** In the phallic period, which occurs at about age 3, the child's pleasure in touching his or her genitals is accompanied by fantasies related to the sexual and aggressive impulses the child feels toward his or her parents. The child then enters a more or less sexually inactive latency period, which lasts until adolescence, when the sexual impulses are once again activated. If all has gone well to this point, the individual reaches the **genital stage,** in which pleasure comes from a mature heterosexual relationship. In well-socialized adults the self-centered sexuality of earlier psychosexual stages blossoms into mature love and the individual becomes capable of genuine caring and adult sexual satisfaction.

What happens to children during these psychosexual stages helps mold their adult personalities. If they are unsuccessful in resolving the psychosexual conflicts that accompany a given stage or are severely deprived or overindulged, they may become fixated at one stage or another. **Fixation** is an arrest in personal development caused by the unresolved difficulties experienced at a given stage. Moreover, even if people resolve their conflicts successfully, severe difficulties later in life may cause them to **regress,** or adopt some of the feelings or behavior of earlier, more satisfying stages.

Freud's ideas about psychosexual development are undoubtedly the most controversial aspect of his theory. Although many theorists agree that childhood experiences are very important in personality development, many of them reject Freud's assertions about childhood sexuality.

The Psychic Apparatus For Freud, the mental world of the individual is divided into three structures: the **id,** the **ego,** and the **superego.** A basic distinction is made between the ego and the id. The id is a completely unorganized reservoir of psychic energy. The ego, on the other hand, is a problem-solving agent. Whereas the id is concerned simply with maximizing pleasure, the ego's efforts are directed toward maximizing pleasure within the constraints of reality. The id says, "I want it now."

The ego says, "Okay, but first we have to do our homework" or "No, that's illegal." The ego performs the valuable functions of avoiding danger or coping with it when avoidance is not possible. There are three major sources of danger for the individual: the environment, his or her id impulses, and guilt. Guilt comes from the third structure of the psychic apparatus, the superego, which represents the person's moral code and reflects social values as expressed by parents, schools, and so on. The superego uses guilt to keep the id in line. The superego might say, "You know that's wrong" or "Work is more important than pleasure" (see Figure 3–14).

In early infancy the id is in control of all phases of behavior. Freud described the thought processes of the infant as **primary process thinking,** or thinking that is characterized by inability to discriminate between the real and the unreal, between the "me" and the "nonme," as well as by inability to inhibit impulses. Primary process thinking reflects uninhibited adherence to the **pleasure principle**—the immediate satisfaction of needs and desires without regard for the requirements of reality.

The desire for immediate gratification that characterizes primary process thinking is dominant in childhood. Thus, most children, when given a piece of candy, eat it immediately, whereas an adult might wait until after lunch. A child who can't get immediate gratification often shifts its goal in order to achieve gratification in some other way. Thus, a baby that is crying for its bottle may gratify itself at least temporarily by sucking vigorously on its thumb.

Secondary process thinking is characteristic of older children and adults and is dependent on the development of the ego. The adult has learned to wait for gratification. Saving money for a goal—a new stereo system, a nest egg for old age—rather than going out for an expensive dinner on payday would be an example. The adult is also less likely than the child to substitute another object for gratification. An adult will generally keep working for the originally desired object even if setbacks occur.

Primary process thinking is still found in adults. It can be seen in humor, in dreams, in the parent who feels

FIGURE 3–14 The id, ego, and superego can give very different messages. See if you can identify which is the source of each message in this cartoon. The answers are at the bottom.

(Drawing by R. Chast; © 1983 The New Yorker Magazine, Inc.)

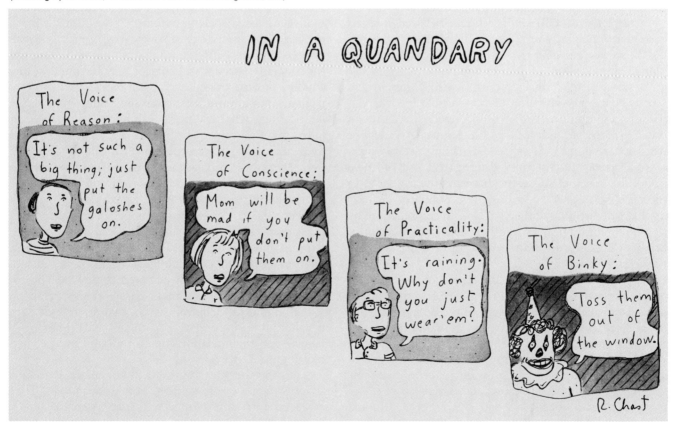

Answers: a, c ego b superego d id

better after coming home and yelling at the children because her boss criticized her on the job, and in the person who eats a pint of ice cream out of the container while standing right in front of the refrigerator. However, maladaptation is considered to exist only when the primary process plays an overriding role in the adult's behavior.

Anxiety Freud defined **anxiety** as a response to perceived danger or stress. He distinguished between two kinds of anxiety-provoking situations. In one, of which birth might be the best example, anxiety is caused by stimulation that exceeds the organism's capacity to handle it. In the other, Freud assumed that psychic energy (libido) accumulates if inhibitions and taboos keep it from being expressed. This accumulated energy may build up to the point where it may overwhelm the controls of the ego. When this happens, a panic or traumatic state results. Psychoanalysts believe that these traumatic states are likely to occur in infants and children who do not know how to cope with much of their environment.

Anxiety often arises in anticipation of danger rather than after a dangerous situation has actually occurred. Anxiety, like physical pain, thus serves a protective function by signaling the approach of danger and warning us to prepare our defenses. Anxiety can also indicate inability to cope with danger. The meaning of anxiety is a central problem of psychoanalysis.

Defense Mechanisms Freud believed that the ego was not helpless in the face of the demands of the id, the outside world, and the superego. Anxiety alerts the individual to danger, such as the presence of an intense unconscious conflict or unacceptable wish. If this anxiety cannot be managed by direct action, so that the wish can be gratified, the ego initiates unconscious defenses in order to ward off awareness of the conflict. A variety of defensive responses to perceived danger are possible. Since everyone experiences danger, the use of these responses, called **defense mechanisms,** clearly is not a special characteristic of maladaptive behavior. Defense mechanisms are used, either singly or in combination, by all people at one time or another. The level of adaptive behavior depends on the repertory of defenses available to the individual.

The most important and basic of the defense mechanisms is **repression.** Freud called it the cornerstone on which psychoanalysis rests. Repression, like other defenses, is directed at both external dangers, such as fear-arousing events, and internal dangers, such as wishes, impulses, and emotions that cry out for gratification but arouse guilt. Repression reduces anxiety by keeping anxiety-laden thoughts and impulses out of the person's consciousness.

Repression is often described as motivated forgetting. It is necessary to distinguish between two kinds of forgetting: forgetting neutral mental content such as an unimportant telephone number is not the same as forgetting a traumatic childhood experience. Psychoanalysts are not nearly as interested in neutral material as they are in personally significant events. For instance, a recent college graduate may forget to go for a job interview if she is afraid that she will fail and not be hired, or a man may forget to attend the wedding of his brother to a woman that he himself was attracted to. In each case, the forgetting is real. The person is not making an excuse but actually is unaware of the engagement at the time. The effort required to achieve such repression sometimes makes other behavior less effective. The person is, in a sense, preoccupied with the effort to maintain the repression. Sometimes repressed thoughts and wishes leak out and are expressed indirectly. Table 3–1 lists some other defense mechanisms.

CLINICAL PSYCHOANALYSIS Psychoanalysis is both a theoretical perspective and a clinical technique. As a clinical technique, it takes time. One of its conditions usually is that both patient and analyst make a commitment to the process for an indefinite period. Freud believes that much unhappiness and ineffectiveness are caused by forgotten conflicts that occurred long ago. Many a psychoanalyst has commented that a lifetime of difficulty cannot be straightened out in a few months.

Today most psychoanalysts are physicians who receive special training in the field of psychiatry and even more specialized analytic training. Some people without medical training, including psychologists, are also qualified to do psychoanalysis. All psychoanalysts believe that the roots of maladaptive behavior may be found in early childhood experiences and in infantile thoughts and feelings that persist into later life. They believe that insight into what went on in childhood enables the individual to adopt more mature and effective ways of living a happier, more productive adult life.

Many of Freud's ideas emerged from his studies of the dreams, fantasies, and memories of his patients. He developed the technique of **free association,** which calls for patients to express their thoughts and feelings as freely as possible during analysis. With censorship (defense) reduced in this way, Freud hoped to gain a clearer picture of the conflicts underlying maladaptive behavior. As his work proceeded, it occurred to him that dreams might provide evidence about the workings of unconscious impulses. Clinical psychoanalysis places great weight on the interpretation of dreams and other types of fantasy and their relationship to thought and behavior (see Figure 3–15 on page 74).

Psychotherapists agree that not all cases of maladaptive behavior are suitable for psychoanalysis. There are several reasons why psychoanalysis might not be recommended. For example, a person might not have adequate financial resources to pay for the many sessions

Table 3–1

Some Defense Mechanisms Used in Addition to Repression

Freud mentioned a number of defense mechanisms, but he devoted most of his attention to repression as an all-inclusive defense. His daughter, Anna Freud, defined most of the concepts we refer to today as defense mechanisms.

DISPLACEMENT

A shift of feelings and attitudes from one object to another, more acceptable substitute.

Examples:

A man is critized by his boss and then feels angry. He comes home and yells at his wife (yelling at the boss might be too dangerous).

A young woman feels sexually attracted to her older brother. She finds a person in her office who has the same dry sense of humor and curly hair as her brother and quickly becomes very attracted to him.

INTELLECTUALIZATION

Dealing with problems as interesting events that can be explained rationally and that have no anxiety or emotional content attached to them.

Examples:

A woman whose husband has just died discusses the inadequacy of America's mourning rituals, rather than her anger at her husband for leaving her.

A man who has just seen a bank robbery in which five people near him were gunned down talks about how interesting it was to observe the variety of ways that the people present reacted to the murders.

REACTION FORMATION

Expressing an unacceptable impulse by transforming it into its opposite.

Examples:

A person who is attracted by the excitement and brutality of war becomes an overly zealous pacifist.

A mother who feels angry and rejecting toward her child checks many times to see if the child is all right during the night and worries excessively about her safety on the way to and from school.

DENIAL

Refusal to acknowledge the anxiety-arousing aspects of the environment. The denial may be related only to the emotions connected to an idea or event or it may involve failure to acknowledge the event itself. Denial is often seen in adults who are under very severe stress often related to loss or failure.

Examples:

A husband, when told that his wife has incurable cancer, remains convinced that she will recover.

A student who has to take a final exam on material she doesn't understand, tells herself the exam is really not important and goes to a movie instead of studying the material with which she is having trouble.

IDENTIFICATION WITH THE AGGRESSOR

Adopting the traits or mannerisms of a feared person.

Examples:

A child who is afraid of his father takes on certain of his characteristics.

A member of the American Nazi Party who is the son of a concentration camp survivor.

PROJECTION

Characteristics or impulses that arouse anxiety are externalized by attributing them to others. Psychotics are particularly likely to use projection.

Examples:

Nazis in Germany who started World War II insisted that they did so because of aggressive threats from other countries.

A man who has a strong desire to have extramarital affairs but feels guilty about it constantly accuses his wife of being unfaithful to him even though he has no evidence.

REGRESSION

Going back to earlier ways of behaving that were characteristic of a previous development level. Typical of people who go to pieces under stress.

Examples:

A wife goes home to her mother every time she and her husband have a quarrel.

A student consoles himself, whenever things get rough, with several hot fudge sundaes, repeating behavior learned when mother gave him ice cream to make him feel better after a scraped elbow or a disappointment.

SUBLIMATION

A socially useful course of action developed when more direct forms of gratification are blocked.

Examples:

A teenager with strong aggressive feelings expresses them without danger by becoming a football player.

Someone with strong erotic feelings expresses them in a socially approved way by becoming a painter of nudes.

(A) Symptom Formation

Traumatic childhood experiences → Defense mechanisms forgetting → Symptoms

(B) Symptom Removal

Free associations dreams → Recovery of forgotten material → Awareness and interpretation of forgotten material → Symptom removal

FIGURE 3–15 Processes hypothesized by Freud to be involved in symptom formation and removal. Symptoms (abnormal behavior, worries, unhappiness) result from emotion-laden traumatic childhood experiences that, while defended against and forgotten, continue to exert unconscious influences that distort behavior, thought, and emotions. In the accepting, benign atmosphere of the psychoanalytic session, clues to the forgotten material come to the fore and are interpreted. Realization of the infantile quality of the forgotten material permits the individual to give up the symptoms.

needed, or might lack the necessary intellectual resources, particularly the verbal skill to engage in the required level of communication. Freud believed that the most severe mental disorders, psychoses, could not be treated successfully with psychoanalysis.

Contemporary Approaches to Psychoanalysis

Several psychoanalysts have disagreed with aspects of psychoanalytic theory as created by Freud. Among the early revisionists, Carl Jung (1875–1961) and Alfred Adler (1870–1937), both were originally members of Freud's inner circle of supporters. Both men had much more optimistic conceptions of human nature than Freud did. Jung did not think that all behavior is determined by earlier events. His emphasis on the need to emphasize spiritual qualities as well as rational ideas and his interest in Eastern religious thought have made him popular with many people today. Adler believed that people could be changed for the better through the creation of social conditions designed to develop realistic and adaptive lifestyles. For example, children have to be helped to overcome the inferiority that they naturally feel in comparison to adults. Consequently, Adler attached great importance to training parents in effective child-rearing techniques, and to the early education of children. He was a strong believer in the need to prevent psychological disorders rather than simply treat them after they occur.

Erik Erikson (b. 1902) is a central figure in contemporary psychoanalytic theory. His theory is a psychosocial one that emphasizes the "mutual fit between the individual and environment—that is, of the individ-

ual's capacity to relate to an ever-changing life space of people and institutions, on the one hand, and, on the other, the readiness of these people and institutions to make him part of an ongoing cultural concern" (Erikson, 1975, p. 102). Erikson stresses the role Freud assigned to the ego, but he gives it additional qualities such as the needs for trust and hope, industry, intimacy and love, and integrity. He thinks of the ego as a strong creative force that can deal effectively with problems.

Of special interest to psychologists is Erikson's idea of stages of development. Unlike Freud, who believed that development was essentially completed early in life, Erikson sees development as a lifelong process. Erikson's view reflects his interest in the interpersonal and cultural needs of the developing individual. He described a life cycle of stages, each of which presents the individual with tasks to be achieved. Whereas Freud centered development around psycho*sexual* stages of the infant and child, Erikson directed attention to psycho*social* stages throughout the life cycle. Failure to resolve the conflicts of a particular stage makes coping at succeeding stages more difficult. Erikson's stages range from the acquisition of a sense of trust in others—developed particularly in relation to the mother during the first year of life—to a satisfaction with oneself and one's accomplishments and a sense of order and meaning in life developed in later years. In between these stages, and at particular periods of life, individuals who successfully meet life cycle challenges develop a sense of autonomy and self-control, initiative and purpose, industriousness, a fulfilling self-concept and sense of identity, the ability to form satisfying intimate ties with others, and the ability to lose themselves in work and significant interpersonal relationships.

Object relations theorists offer another approach to psychoanalytic theory. While working within a psychoanalytic framework, these practitioners emphasize the view that the mind is made up of internal representations of significant others, who are referred to as objects. Object relations proponents focus attention on the emotional bonds between one person and another. Melanie Klein (1882–1960), a controversial British pioneer in the psychoanalysis of children, gave great emphasis to complex, presumably "pre-wired" object fantasies that she believed occurred in very young infants. Other object relations theorists, including those who differ with Klein, give central importance to the concept of **splitting,** the capacity of an infant to divide a single object (for example, mother) into separate good and bad mothers depending on the infant's experience of gratification or frustration. They believe that splitting is common in several types of maladaptive behavior in which an individual has developed a poor capacity for loving and reacting appropriately to others.

Self-psychology is a relatively recent theory put forth by Heinz Kohut (1913–1981), an Austrian psychoanalyst who spent much of his professional life in the United States. Kohut held that a person's self-concept is the central organizer of psychological development. His approach to personal development focuses on the maturation of the sense of self from its infantile state of fragility and fragmentation into the cohesive and stable structure of adulthood. The sexual and aggressive drives so emphasized by Freud are not the forces of psychological development for Kohut. That role is played instead by the self. Kohut believed that psychological disorder results when there are major deficits in the structure of the self. Undesirable early experiences—for example, inadequate mothering and attention—can interfere with development of the self. Therapists who adhere to self-psychology see their task as helping to repair the damage done by previous unloving relationships and environments. They seek to facilitate in the patient a healthy sense of self, a satisfactory and reasonably stable level of self-esteem, and the ability to take pride in accomplishments. These practitioners also aim to instill an awareness of and responsiveness to the needs of others while patients learn to respond to their own needs.

Contemporary theorists have helped broaden the perspectives of psychoanalysis, particularly through their emphasis on the role of distorted interpersonal relationships in maladaptive behavior. They have insisted that disordered behavior and thought must be viewed as outgrowths of the individual's efforts to cope with personal crises in a world peopled by others. In presenting their views, these theorists have deemphasized the role of biology in personality and instead have looked to the social environment for explanations of maladaptive behavior.

Evaluating Psychoanalytic Theory

Psychoanalytic theory contains many ideas about the nature of perception and thought, human development, psychopathology, and treatment. However, its formulations are difficult to study scientifically because the events they hypothesize are not directly observable. Because psychoanalytic theory contains many general and somewhat unclearly defined concepts, it is hard to evaluate objectively. It seems to be better at explaining what has already happened than at predicting future events.

Since psychoanalytic concepts are difficult to prove experimentally, some researchers have tended to reject them out of hand. Others recognize that certain psychoanalytic concepts are vaguely stated and in fact untestable, but nevertheless feel that scientific investigations should be conducted whenever possible.

Is psychoanalysis a theoretical framework within which human behavior can be studied scientifically, or is it a therapeutic method? These two possibilities are not inconsistent, as Freud pointed out on several occasions. A full evaluation of psychoanalysis will be possible only when its effectiveness as a therapy for maladaptive behavior has been objectively assessed and its links with the scientific method have been strengthened.

Two research areas pertinent to the psychoanalytic perspective have seemed particularly promising. One concerns efforts to relate hypothesized psychodynamic processes to specific areas of brain function (Winson, 1985); the other seeks to test experimentally such specific psychoanalytic concepts as primary process thinking, repression, and the superego's role as censor (Erdelyi, 1985; Bowers & Meichenbaum, 1985).

The Behavioral Perspective

Give me a dozen healthy infants, well-formed, and my own specified world to bring them up in and I'll guarantee to take any one at random and train him to become any type of specialist I might select, doctor, lawyer, artist, merchant-chief, and yes, even beggarman and thief, regardless of his talents, penchants, tendencies, abilities, vocations, and race of his ancestors.

—Watson, 1925, p. 82

For John B. Watson (1878–1958), an American psychologist who was the founder of behaviorism,

development was a thoroughly mechanical affair. The complete personality—by which Watson meant the whole system of overt behavior—was built up out of the conditioning process. Although many contemporary learning theorists are not as confident as Watson about the simplicity of the processes of behavior acquisition and behavior change, the behavioristic approach continues to exert a powerful influence.

Just as dissatisfaction with a narrow biological orientation was one factor in the development of the psychodynamic perspective, the **behavioral perspective** developed in part because psychologists found many of Freud's ideas about the mind vague, complicated, and untestable. These theorists thought that the same behaviors examined by Freud could be explained in a simpler fashion and in a way that would make it possible to study them experimentally.

Both the psychoanalytic and behavioral approaches are deterministic, but each finds the source of behavior in a different place. (**Determinism** means that every event or act is caused by what has happened before, not by the overt decisions of the individual.) Psychologists using the behavioral perspective focus on learning. They view behavior as a product of stimulus–response (S–R) relationships, not of intrapsychic events. They do not delve into the past or try to get people to figure out why they are the way they are. To change behavior, they concentrate on altering the relevant aspects of the environment, particularly sources of reinforcement.

A **reinforcer** is an event whose occurrence increases the probability that a certain stimulus will evoke a certain response. Reinforcers reward the individual for doing the right thing or not doing the wrong thing. If the reward is desirable enough, the individual is likely to keep on performing properly as long as the response is reinforced. The response can be either an approach response (asking for another glass of milk) or an escape or avoidance response (running from a pursuer or refusing to go out at night). A **positive reinforcer** increases the probability that the proper response will be made by giving the individual something pleasant. A **negative reinforcer,** on the other hand, increases the probability that the proper response will be made by taking away something unpleasant as soon as that desired response occurs.

Table 3–2

Some Mechanisms of Behavior Change

	Definition	Examples
Positive Reinforcement	Encouraging any behavior by using a desired reinforcer as a reward.	Giving a child candy when he brings in a homework assignment. Saying "good girl" when a baby swallows a spoonful of cereal.
Negative Reinforcement	Encouraging any behavior by removing an aversive stimulus when the behavior occurs.	Ceasing to scold a child when he hangs up his coat after throwing it on the floor. Allowing a child to go out if the child is having a tantrum because she must stay home.
Punishment	Aversive stimulus given as a result of an undesired behavior in an attempt to suppress that behavior in the future.	Slapping a child for swearing at you. Sending a child to her room because she broke her brother's toy.
Extinction	Supressing behavior by removing the reinforcers for it.	Ignoring a child when he has a temper tantrum. Removing all rock records from the record collection of your roommate, who likes only rock music and plays the stereo too often for your comfort.

Punishment, another way of changing behavior, is an unpleasant consequence for a wrong response. For example, a wife may positively reinforce her husband for not drinking by having sex with him only when he is sober; she may negatively reinforce his drinking by stopping her nagging when he stops drinking; and she may punish him for drunkenness by locking him out of the house. Table 3–2 illustrates the differences between reinforcement and punishment and contrasts them with **extinction,** still another way of changing behavior.

Positive and negative reinforcers and punishment have been applied to a variety of situations. Smiles, gold stars, and hugs are often highly effective in stimulating productive behavior in schoolchildren, and frowns or scolding may be used to discourage undesirable behavior. However, punishment, a negative consequence of behavior that is intended to discourage its repetition, is not very effective when used alone. It may cut down on undesired behavior, but it does not necessarily stimulate productive activity, since the person does not learn an acceptable substitute behavior.

The use of reinforcement in research on maladaptive behavior has followed two general paradigms: classical conditioning and operant conditioning.

Classical Conditioning

In **classical conditioning,** the response that an organism automatically makes to a certain stimulus is transferred to a new stimulus through an association between the two stimuli. The most famous classical conditioning experiment was the Russian physiologist Ivan Pavlov's (1849–1936) investigation of salivation in dogs. Pavlov placed a hungry dog in a harness and turned on a light at certain intervals. The dog did not salivate in response to the light, which was the **conditioned stimulus** (CS). After a few such trials, meat powder was delivered immediately after the CS had been turned on. Since the dog was hungry, it salivated—an **unconditioned response** (UR)—upon presentation of the **unconditioned stimulus** (US), the meat powder. After a number of trials in which turning on the light was followed by delivery of meat powder, Pavlov found that the dog salivated when the light was turned on even if food did not follow. A **conditioned response** (CR) to the light had been established. Pavlov also carried out experiments with sounds, such as bells, as the conditioned stimulus (see Figure 3–16).

In some classical conditioning situations, the US is painful. Unpleasant US's are used when the goal is to strengthen **avoidance** or **escape responses.** For instance, an electric fence gives pets or cattle a mild but uncomfortable shock when they touch it. The sight of the fence alone then becomes enough to cause them to stay within a certain limited area. Conditioned responses that are not

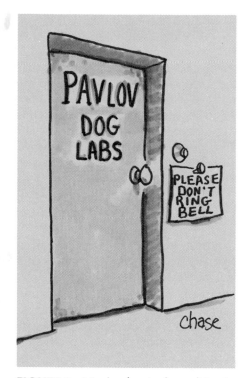

FIGURE 3–16 In classical conditioning, any neutral agent—like a bell—can become a conditioned stimulus. (*Science* 238 [October 1987]: 454)

reinforced periodically through the presence of the US become weaker and ultimately disappear from the organism's repertory of responses. This disappearance of a previously learned response is called **extinction.**

Students of maladaptive behavior have been intrigued by the process of classical conditioning because it seems to explain fear, anxiety, and other types of emotional reactions. Some of these reactions may come about because of accidental classical conditioning. A child who has been bitten by a dog may fear all dogs and, through generalization, other types of animals as well. Classical conditioning is also the basis for some therapies. An example is **systematic desensitization,** a therapeutic procedure whose goal is to extinguish a conditioned response. This procedure might be used to help a woman who has been afraid of cars ever since she was injured in a serious auto crash. At first she was merely uncomfortable in a car, but finally she became so fearful that she could not even look at a picture of a car. A diagram of the classical conditioning situation would look like this:

Unconditioned stimulus → Unconditioned response
Car crash and injury *Fear*

Conditioned stimulus → Conditioned response
Car *Fear*

Through a series of steps that break down the bond between the conditioned stimulus and the conditioned

response and substitute another conditioned response, the woman's fear could be removed. First she would be taught to relax, then to imagine she was looking at an automobile ad in a magazine. Her relaxed state would counteract the anxiety response. Once she could do this successfully, she might be asked to look at a real ad, then to look at a real car, to touch a car, to imagine herself in a car, and so on. At each step she would relax first and then experience the conditioned stimulus. In this way a new conditioning bond would be built up between a car and a relaxed state.

Operant Conditioning

In **operant conditioning,** the organism must make a particular response before the reinforcement occurs. The organism "operates" on its environment and produces an effect. The American psychologist B. F. Skinner (1904–1990) is famous for demonstrating the effectiveness of operant conditioning. Skinner devised an experimental "Skinner box," in which a rat will press a bar repeatedly if this activity is reinforced by pellets of food falling into a dish (see Figure 3–17). Whereas classical conditioning makes use of natural as well as contrived responses, operant conditioning deals with responses that occur relatively infrequently prior to being reinforced.

A diagram of operant conditioning looks like this:

<p style="text-align:center">

Response

↓

Reinforcement

↓

Increased probability

of repetition of response

</p>

For example, in teaching a child to talk, parents reward the child with smiles and hugs whenever she says a desired word. These parental behaviors are positive reinforcements; they increase the chance that the child will repeat the word.

We hear over and over again how complex human behavior is. We point to our lofty thoughts, fine feelings, and obscure motives. But those who use the behavioral perspective see human behavior as complex for other reasons. Even the simplest act can be seen as a chain of responses, each of which needs to be learned. Few of us get things right the first time. Children are particularly likely to become discouraged and give up if reinforcement is withheld until they do something perfectly. Thus, **shaping**—obtaining the desired response by reinforcing successfully better approximations of it—is one of the basic processes in operant conditioning.

Considerable thought and planning are needed to

FIGURE 3–17 B.F. Skinner, one of the most influential psychologists of the twentieth century, is shown here demonstrating the famous Skinner box used in many of his operant-conditioning experiments.

decide what sorts of reinforcers are best for achieving particular behavior-shaping goals. In some situations an effective reinforcer may be rejected for purely practical reasons. A teacher who wanted to control disruptive behavior in the classroom probably could not use candy as a reinforcer, because it might have an undesirable effect on the pupils' appetites. In addition to deciding which reinforcers would be most effective and practical, it is necessary to decide on a **schedule** for reinforcing particular types of responses. The following case, which involves shaping verbal behavior in a 13-year-old boy with a suspected hearing problem, illustrates these elements.

Benjie, who wore a hearing aid, had never been observed to make verbal responses (except for occasional grunts). He did not smile, cry, or interact meaningfully with others in any way. A reinforcement program was instituted in which

candy was used as both a positive and a negative reinforcer. In addition to negative reinforcement (removal of a previously earned piece of candy), mild punishment (a slap on the hand) was used. This was how the operant treatment of Benjie began:

a. *The experimenter sat across from Benjie and said, "Do you hear me, Benjie? If you do, nod your head." The experimenter nodded his head in the hope that Benjie would imitate him and gave Benjie some candy. Initially, Benjie made no head-nodding response.*

b. *Next, the basic procedure remained the same; however, candy was made contingent on the head-nodding response. Soon, Benjie was making 100 percent imitative head-nodding responses.*

c. *In the next procedure, the experimenter stood behind Benjie when giving the verbal cue. Benjie responded by nodding his head. This was the first indication to the experimenters that Benjie did, in fact, have the ability to hear verbalizations given at a normal conversational volume. From that point on Benjie did not wear his hearing aid in the laboratory or at home.*

This reinforcement procedure was not effective in inducing Benjie to make sounds. Because he seemed unresponsive to rewards, the experimenters decided to try a food deprivation schedule as a means of modifying Benjie's behavior. At breakfast, as soon as he made a sound he received a bite of food. This procedure proved to be effective. When he was hungry, he would make sounds at the command, "Benjie, tell me something." Eventually he came to respond to the command even when he was not hungry. After several months Benjie responded with a vocal sound every time a verbal command was directed toward him.

—Knowles and Prutsman, 1968, p. 2

Although the ethical guidelines for working with subjects would generally prohibit the use of food deprivation as a way of motivating behavior, this kind of approach may be used in very special situations such as this one. Here the acquisition of a new behavior is important for treatment, and less intrusive ways of promoting the needed change are not effective. Another example of this controversial approach to behavior change is the use of mild electric shock or other painful stimulus to treat disturbed and retarded children who are self-mutilating; that is, they constantly inflict injury on themselves by knocking their heads against the wall, pulling out their own hair, and so on. The use of this technique has been debated by both professionals and the courts, but because of the lack of any effective alternative is often considered to cause less damage to the patient than the self-inflicted behavior.

Social Learning Theory

Social learning theorists emphasize the idea that a number of factors combine to shape social behavior and mediate the influence of learning experiences. Although social learning theorists generally agree that covert events serve as mediators between external stimuli and overt behavior, the extent of the role of such events is not clear.

Modeling has received considerable attention from social learning theorists. They believe that reinforcement is not always necessary for learning to occur. **Modeling** can be used to change behavior because people are able to learn by watching how other people do things. Opportunities for observational learning arise when another person—a model—performs some response or group of responses. One of the first learning theorists to point this out was Albert Bandura (b. 1925). He emphasized that the observer does not need to have had practice in making the observed response and does not necessarily have to be reinforced in order to learn it. Exposure to models whose behavior and skills we admire plays an important role in our personal development and contributes to our self-esteem (see Figure 3–18). Models may have desirable or undesirable effects on those who observe their behavior.

Clinical studies support the conclusion that observational learning plays a part in the acquisition of maladaptive behavior. Anxiety in patients can often be traced to modeling experiences. A severe phobia, for example, may represent an exaggeration of a major or minor fear observed in a parent. Watching television is basically a symbolic modeling experience, especially for children. Noticeable and sometimes dramatic changes in behavior can result from modeling experiences. Terms like **vicarious learning, social facilitation, copying,** and **identification** are terms used to characterize this process.

Modeling exposes the observer to the specific responses displayed by the model. Even more important, it provides the observer with food for thought. A child who observes continual arguing between parents forms a concept of what marriage is like. Poor people who observe the parade of commercials on television come to believe that most other people are free from financial worries. Modeling, then, not only illustrates possible overt behavior but also contributes to the formation of concepts, attitudes, and needs. **Role playing,** or practic-

(a)

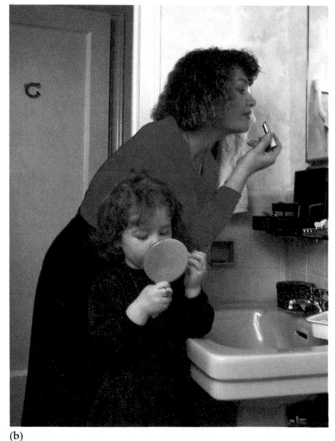

(b)

ing behavior shown by a model, is another important learning technique.

The way in which modeling and role playing can strengthen adaptive behavior is illustrated by the case of John R., an unemployed 18-year-old who had been placed in a juvenile correction facility for stealing a car. Therapists noted that his problem was not simply a failure to adhere to social norms but a weak behavioral repertory.

A particularly serious deficiency was his fear about and inadequacy in job interview situations. He had never had an opportunity to observe the effective behavior of others in situations that required putting one's best foot forward. In the institution he was given the opportunity to observe job interview behavior as modeled by persons (noninmates) who were effective in this area. On several occasions John observed simulated job interviews and then practiced being interviewed himself. After leaving the institution, he found that the modeling experience had helped him. He reported that while waiting for an actual job interview he had remembered and thought about the behavior he had observed. He then mentally rehearsed how he might handle himself when confronted by the personnel manager. He was hired, he felt, because of the new skill and security he brought to the previously traumatic job interview situation. His increased skill and security seemed to result from his having a better idea of what to expect in a job interview.

A strength of social learning theory is its recognition of two developmental aspects of behavior. One is the individual's history of experiences, including various types of events and associated conditioning and modeling. The other aspect, less well understood, but no less important, is how the individual analyzes and interprets past experiences. Much of what is learned, especially after the early years of childhood, occurs implicitly, that is, without being a direct consequence of external environmental effects. **Implicit learning** takes place when an individual arranges memories of experiences (such as his father's need to read the newspaper right after dinner) into new patterns of thought (such as the role of the reading as a barrier to family interaction). As the child

develops an extensive symbolic repertory of words and images, he is no longer dependent on actual environmental experience to learn. Instead, children can manipulate their growing storehouses of symbols and images, imagine new attainments, and thus develop new strategies for dealing with the environment. Similarly, by reorganizing their internal symbolic world, adults supplement the external world with novel thoughts that in turn provide new opportunities for learning and self-administered reinforcements. The emphasis that social learning theorists have placed on the role of the individual as an information processor has increased over time so that most researchers in this field now speak of their view as *cognitive* social learning theory.

The Cognitive Perspective

People are disturbed not by things, but by the views which they take of them.

—Epictetus, first century A.D.

If the Greek philosopher Epictetus were alive today, he would likely be a cognitive psychologist. The word "cognitive" comes from the Latin word *cognitare,* meaning "to have known." Cognitive psychology addresses human beings as information processors and problem solvers. The cognitive view seeks to account for behavior by studying the ways in which the person attends to, interprets, and uses available information.

Like the psychodynamic perspective, the **cognitive perspective** is concerned with internal processes. Rather than stressing urges, needs, and motivations, however, it emphasizes how people acquire and interpret information and use it in solving problems. Unlike psychoanalysis, it places great emphasis on mental processes that we are aware of or can rather easily be made aware of, as opposed to hidden motivations, feelings, and conflicts. Its approach has been contrasted with the learning perspective's emphasis on the external environment as a prime cause of behavior. Typically, the cognitive perspective pays more attention to our present thoughts and problem-solving strategies than to our personal histories. However, histories of cognitions also receive some attention (Sarason, 1979). The relationships among emotions, motivations, and cognitive processes and thus the overlap between the cognitive perspective and other approaches is becoming more evident.

In its view of the individual as information processor, the cognitive perspective holds that people are continually collecting, storing, modifying, interpreting, and understanding both internally generated information and environmental stimuli. Humans are seen as active, selective seekers, creators, and users of information, and behavior is viewed as both a product and an initiator of mental acts and environmental changes. The mental life of the individual is conceived of as consisting of **schemata** (plural of schema) that contain information in particular domains such as parents, work, and pets. Through their influence on cognitive processes, schemata enable people to identify stimuli quickly, cluster them into manageable units, fill in missing information, and select a strategy for obtaining further information, solving a problem, or reaching a goal.

From a clinical standpoint, self-schemata are especially important. They organize and guide not only our social experiences but any experiences that are personally relevant. Personally relevant experiences are often laden with emotions and are likely to reflect an individual's prior learning history. Self-schemata are capable of distorting a person's perceptions of reality. Schemata that concern our self-evaluations influence not only how we feel about ourselves but also how we relate to others. For example, **self-efficacy** refers to the strength of our convictions about our personal effectiveness. People may imagine potential difficulties as more formidable than they are in reality if they perceive themselves as ineffective in important types of situations. Inappropriate or maladaptive behavior in those situations may confirm the individual's self-perception as inadequate, helpless, or cowardly. This confirmation may cause the person to avoid problematic situations or reduce his or her task-relevant efforts. A vicious cycle is thereby created and perpetuated.

The cognitive perspective on personality has led to a variety of theories. Among the best known of these are those of Dollard and Miller, Kelly, and Bandura.

Maladaptive Behavior and Cognition

JOHN DOLLARD AND NEAL MILLER John Dollard (1900–1980) and Neal Miller (b. 1909) tried to relate human learning to psychodynamic processes as well as to external events. Although thinking, feeling, perceiving, and other covert processes cannot be observed, they can be inferred. They are usually called **hypothetical constructs** (because there is no way to prove that they really exist) or **intervening variables** (because they are presumed to intervene between environmental stimuli and behavior).

Dollard and Miller (1950) thought they saw parallels between learning theory and Freudian theory in the area of personality development. For example, the reinforcement principle and Freud's pleasure principle

have the same general function: people are more likely to do what makes them feel good. Dollard and Miller also made use of cognitive concepts by describing maladaptive behavior as a joint product of unfortunate life experiences and maladaptive thinking. They viewed gaining insight into the roots of one's behavior as acquiring self-awareness responses. Despite their preference for describing behavior in terms of habits and learning, they emphasized the individual's cognitive resolution of conflicts.

GEORGE KELLY The product of George Kelly's (1905–1966) extensive study of the nature of personal experience was his psychology of **personal constructs.** Kelly (1955) concluded that people's personal constructs reflect how they interpret or develop ideas about themselves, the world, and future events. Personal constructs are the way in which each person builds his or her own reality by sorting people and events into categories. Kelly believed that each person is constantly engaged in problem solving and that personal constructs are an important means of organizing information about interpersonal relationships.

There are wide differences between the personal constructs of different individuals. People may perceive the same event in entirely different ways. For example, suppose two lovers break up. One observer may describe the event as simple incompatibility, while another may believe that one person "jilted" the other. Another might say that the breakup was due to "parental meddling"; still another might see it as a "blessing in disguise."

Kelly was not a supporter of the concepts of hidden psychodynamics and the unconscious. He often referred to what he whimsically termed "Kelly's first principle": "If you don't know what is wrong with clients, ask them, they may tell you." Although he recognized that we might not be aware of all of our personal constructs at any given time, he tended to reject Freud's belief that the greater part of mental life is hidden from view. He also tended to reject the emphasis placed by psychoanalysis on what happened to a person in the past. For Kelly, the important thing was the distinctive set of personal constructs that guide a person's life at the present time.

Kelly stressed the role of personal constructs as causes of emotional reactions. We feel anxious when we don't know how to handle a situation, when we become aware that our system of constructs does not encompass a problem that has arisen. Thus, Kelly believed that cognitions precede emotions. He saw psychotherapy as a way of demonstrating to clients that their constructs are hypotheses rather than facts. Once clients realized this, he encouraged them to test their constructs so that the maladaptive ones could be replaced with more useful ones.

ALBERT BANDURA In addition to his emphasis on social learning theory, Albert Bandura has more recently emphasized the symbolic and cognitive aspects of learning as opposed to the stimulus–response aspects (see Figure 3–19). According to Bandura (1981), we can solve problems symbolically without having to resort to trial-and-error behavior because we can foresee the consequences of our behavior and act accordingly. For example, we buy fire insurance because we think about what might happen if our house burned down. Similarly, in preparing for our first winter camping trip, we assemble protective gear because we can anticipate the effects of a blizzard. The ability to anticipate consequences operates in more routine behaviors as well as in special instances like these.

Bandura (1978) is interested in studying self-regulation, or learning by internal reinforcement, as opposed to modifying behavior by external reinforcement alone. Many cognitive psychologists are developing techniques by which people who lack behavioral self-control can be helped to acquire it. The following examples illustrate techniques for strengthening self-control that make use of cognitive mechanisms.

1. A student studies every night even though no test has been announced.

2. A heavy smoker teaches herself nonsmoking behavior.

FIGURE 3–19 Albert Bandura's work on modeling, as well as his more recent work on self-regulation, has been important not only theoretically but also in the development of new therapeutic approaches.

In the first case, the student may motivate himself by means of cognitive representation of future consequences. That is, he may think about how bad he would feel if he scored poorly on the next test or how stressful it would be to try to learn all the information the night before the test. Another motivation may be his own goal-setting behavior. He wants to receive a high grade for the course. Whenever he feels like turning on the television set or stopping for a snack, he visualizes how he will feel if he attains his goal. When people evaluate their own behavior in this way, they tend to persist until they achieve their goals.

In the second example, each time the former smoker has the impulse to smoke, she may imagine an X-ray of lungs afflicted by cancer, or she may see herself coughing and unable to breathe. Such self-generated cognitive mechanisms would provide negative reinforcement for her thoughts about smoking.

Cognitive Therapies

The idea that maladaptive thoughts are the cause of maladaptive behavior and that people must be taught new ways of thinking has been used as a basic approach by many therapists. Several forms of therapy are based on the cognitive perspective.

Rational-emotive therapy, developed by Albert Ellis, is based on the belief that behavior depends more on individual belief systems and ways of interpreting situations than on objective conditions. Ellis contends that all effective psychotherapists, whether or not they realize it, function as teachers for their clients. They help their clients to review, reperceive, and rethink their lives; to question their irrational beliefs; and to modify their unrealistic and illogical thoughts, emotions, and behaviors. Ellis regards both intense emotions and maladaptive behavior as the modifiable consequences of thoughts. He admits that faulty beliefs are probably formed in childhood. However, he feels that finding out how people got to be the way they are is less important than helping them respond more constructively to their present situation.

In rational–emotive therapy the clinician explains and demonstrates productive thinking, persuades the client to think and behave in more effective ways, and discusses homework assignments. Through such assignments the client might practice ways of behaving more assertively with co-workers or family members without alienating them (Ellis, 1962, 1970; Smith, 1982).

George Kelly used a variety of tactics to help his clients explore and modify their personal constructs. Most often he used a traditional interview format in which he and his client talked about specific personal constructs and the roles they led the client to play in social relationships. In addition, he used **fixed-role therapy,** in which clients experimented with (by acting out) new roles that might result from particular revisions in their personal-construct systems. Kelly believed that people have difficulty simply trying out new ways of behaving; hence he was very supportive of these experimental efforts (Niemeyer, 1986).

Aaron Beck (1976) also thinks that the job of the therapist is to help clients restructure their thinking and replace maladaptive thoughts with thoughts that are more helpful in coping with stressful situations. Beck's work was originally focused on the cognitions of depressed individuals; but recently his approach has been extended to the problems of anxiety and personality disorders (Beck & Emery, 1985; Beck and others, 1990). Beck thinks that people's emotions and behavior are based largely on the way they view the world. In his view, many people exaggerate their difficulties and minimize the possibility that anything can be done about them. Applying this idea in therapy, it becomes important to identify those beliefs (for example, "People don't like me") that shape personal interpretations of events and facilitate or inhibit action. Beck believes that people generally have broad goals that are very important to them but that may not be completely in their awareness. The therapist's job is to help translate the client's stated aspirations and inhibitions into these underlying goals. Beck's cognitive therapeutic approach is illustrated in Chapter 10.

The Humanistic–Existential Perspective

The humanistic–existential perspective presents a sharp contrast to the theoretical approaches described so far. Its roots are found in a number of philosophical and religious systems that have stressed the dignity, inherent goodness, and freedom of human nature. The growth of this perspective within psychology was partly a product of this tradition and partly a reaction to the less flattering conceptions of human nature that are characteristic of psychoanalysis and radical behaviorism.

One of the central assumptions of the humanistic view is that in every person there is an active force toward **self-actualization,** a striving to be "all that you can be." When the human personality unfolds in a benign environment that gives these creative forces free rein, the positive inner nature of the human being emerges. Human misery and pathology, on the other hand, are fostered by environments that frustrate the individual's natural tendencies toward self-actualization.

Closely related to the humanistic movement is the existential perspective, which became popular in Europe after World War II, as psychologists and philosophers sought to understand how the horrors of the war could have occurred and how certain people were able to rise above them and find meaning in life. While the humanistic theories focus on the process of self-actualization, existential theorists emphasize self-determination, choice, and the responsibility of the individual to rise above environmental forces. "We are our choices," maintains the existentialist. "Our existence and its meaning are squarely in our own hands, for we alone can decide what our attitudes and behaviors will be."

Humanistic–existential theorists believe that scientific psychology is missing the mark when it dwells only on observable behavior and neglects the person's inner life. They believe that inner experiences and the search for the meaning of existence are the core of the individual and hence should be the focus of psychology. They therefore regard introspection as a valid and, indeed, indispensable source of psychological information.

Rogers' Conception of the Self

Carl Rogers (1902–1987), one of the leaders of humanistic psychology (see Figure 3–20) used the self-image as the centerpiece of his perspective on personality (1951, 1959, 1980). Rogers related the ability to achieve self-understanding and self-actualization to the individual's self-regard and perception of acceptance by others. An adult who felt wanted and highly valued as a child is likely to have a positive self-image, to be thought well of by others, and to have the capacity for self-actualization. Optimal adjustment results in what Rogers calls the fully functioning person and is characterized by a low level of anxiety. Anxiety is due to uneasiness or tension resulting from inconsistencies between people's self-perceptions and their ideas of what they would like to be.

Although the ways in which they conceptualized behavior contrast sharply, both Rogers and Freud developed their theoretical positions on the basis of similar observational data: the behavior of clients and therapists in psychotherapy. However, Rogers rejected the psychoanalytic notion that people are irrational and unsocial by nature. He asserted, on the contrary, that each person is basically rational, socialized, and constructive.

For Rogers, psychotherapy is a situation in which anxious, troubled people with low self-regard and distorted perceptions of themselves and the world seek help. Rogers thinks that healthy people are those who move away from roles created by the expectations of others,

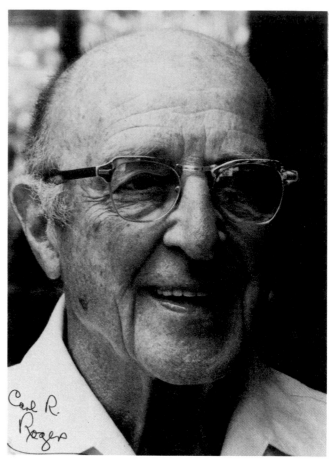

FIGURE 3–20 Carl Rogers

that is, they do not pretend to be something they are not. Instead, they learn to trust themselves and reject the false selves that others have created for them. Neurotic and psychotic people, on the other hand, have self-concepts that do not match their experiences. They are afraid to accept their own experiences as valid, so they distort them, either to protect themselves or to win approval from others. A therapist can help them give up these false selves.

The task for Rogerian therapists is neither to provide interpretations nor to give advice. Rather, the therapist must accept clients as having worth and dignity in their own right despite their problems. This acceptance means that the therapist must understand the client's feelings, no matter how positive or negative they are or how much they contradict the therapist's own attitudes.

Rogers believed that "there is no such thing as scientific knowledge; there are only individual perceptions of what appears to each person to be such knowledge" (1959). This statement expresses the humanistic–existentialist view that inner experience and a

search for individual meaning should be the focus of psychology.

The Existential Point of View

Existentialists believe that people are free to choose among alternative courses of action. If this is true, why are so many people unhappy and dissatisfied? Why does maladaptive behavior exist? For one thing, not everyone chooses wisely. A person can choose to act either authentically or inauthentically. To act **authentically** means to freely establish one's own goals. To act **inauthentically** means to let other people dictate those goals. For each person there are also certain givens that place definite limits on what he or she may become. These may be characteristics that are present at birth, such as learning ability, physical appearance, or the presence of a disabling disease, or they may be environmental, including the influence of parents and later of school and peers. These expand or contract the individual's chances for fulfillment based on the qualities present at birth. The primary task of the therapist, according to this view, is to help empty, lonely people expand their experiences and fulfill their own uniqueness, that is, to help them make constructive choices.

The Community Perspective

Most people see mental illness as a personal health problem or as a character defect. In contrast, from the **community perspective,** maladaptive behavior results from inability to cope effectively with stress. It is not viewed as a disease or problem that exists only within the individual; instead, it is seen as at least partly a failure of the individual's social support system. This system includes the person's spouse, parents, siblings, relatives, friends, teachers, employer, religious adviser, and others, as well as community organizations and government agencies.

Community psychologists, proponents of the community perspective, do not deny the role of life history or genetic makeup in causing maladaptive behavior, but these are not seen as necessarily sufficient to produce such behavior. For example, a person vulnerable to schizophrenia may develop hallucinations for many reasons: biochemical factors, traumatic early experiences, or unusual social relationships are all possibilities. However, the presence of an especially strong stressor or the breakdown of the person's social support system may be equally important in producing the schizophrenic behavior.

The community approach attempts to reduce maladaptive behavior through preventive measures, by intervening in people's lives before catastrophes occur. Such measures include a variety of special programs: discussion or mutual support programs for recently separated, divorced, or widowed people; preschool enrichment programs for children from low-income, single-parent homes; combined school programs and child care facilities for teenage single parents; day-care centers for elderly people who may not be able to live self-sufficiently. Implicit in community psychology is the belief that the effects of social disorganization (such as slums, bad schools, and high unemployment rates) are a major cause of many personal problems. For this reason, mental health professionals with a community orientation tend to become involved in efforts to change society by lobbying for legislation and becoming actively involved in community affairs.

Community psychologists study the social environment and factors related to it, such as socioeconomic status. When the living places of people who are identified as psychologically and socially impaired are plotted on a map, it can be shown that the frequency of such problems is much higher in certain areas than in others. **Social-causation theories** argue that the poor schools, crime, inadequate housing, and prejudice often found in low-income, deteriorating neighborhoods may increase the stress experienced by already vulnerable people. The **social-selection theory,** on the other hand, argues that lower socioeconomic groups show a greater incidence of maladaptive behavior because people who do not function well tend to experience downward social mobility. Recent research suggests that, while social causation is implicated in depression, antisocial behavior, and substance abuse, social selection is implicated in schizophrenia (Dohrenwend and others, 1992).

Those who believe in the community perspective are more likely to support the social-causation theory. They point out that, while social selection may be a factor, the theory does not rule out the stress-producing situations encountered by low income people that may aggravate existing disorders. Such people may have less power to control their environment as well as fewer resources for dealing with stress. For a variety of reasons, including the difficulty of carrying out controlled research in community settings, one cannot completely rule out either the social-selection or the social-causation theory. One or the other might apply to certain types of disorders. In either case, psychologists with a community perspective see a need to develop special programs aimed at counteracting undesirable aspects of urban life such as

poverty and overcrowding. Such programs would improve the lives of the general population as well as those of people with specific psychological problems.

Social Roles and Labeling

All individuals belong to social groups. These groups shape people's behavior by providing the distinctive reinforcements, punishments, and models that are part of life in a particular cultural setting. The members of a social group share a set of meanings or symbols, experience a feeling of unity, and participate in a network of mutual obligations. The group or groups to which a person belongs influence nearly every aspect of his or her life.

Social roles are particular functions that a person plays as a member of a social group. Some theorists have maintained that we always attempt to project an image and that, in fact, we have no true self. This position is presented by Erving Goffman (1959), who argues that in all of our encounters with other people we adopt particular roles. Each role is accompanied by a script that includes different actions and signals. In effect, we vary our behaviors continuously as the situation requires. This viewpoint implies that there is no such thing as a fixed personality.

Less extreme than this position, and more widely accepted, is the composite position: There is a basic personality that is overlaid with situational role playing. Research has shown that a number of factors influence the roles people play in social relationships. These factors are often important because they serve to label an individual in a particular way. **Labeling** occurs whenever people are categorized on some basis, whether that basis is relevant and fair or not. Labels can be destructive because they draw attention to one aspect of the person while ignoring other aspects that make him or her unique. (Would you like to be labeled as a slob simply because you don't like to put your shoes away at night?) Some labels, such as "good student" and "loyal friend," are desirable, but many others carry negative social connotations. For example, the role of mental patient is widely viewed as socially unacceptable, and the label of mentally ill often causes permanent damage. The damage takes many forms, including discrimination by others and feelings of self-doubt and inadequacy.

Contributions of the Community Perspective

What we know at present supports the emphasis that community psychology has given to the role of the social environment in emotions and maladaptive behavior. For example, children's levels of distress and depression increase sharply when they live in an environment in which adults express high levels of anger and behave aggressively. There is some evidence that this responsiveness to family discord is greater for boys than it is for girls (Cummings and others, 1985; Farber and others, 1985).

The community perspective has been influential in producing creative new approaches to maladaptive behavior and in reaching segments of the population whose psychological needs hitherto have been ignored. It has been effective both in changing the perspective of academic thinking and in altering social policy. As important, it has raised questions for future research whose answers will contribute to our understanding of both the social causes of maladaptive behavior and ways the social environment can enhance the lives of children and adults. Included among these questions are: How does stress in personal lives and in the community influence whether maladaptive behavior occurs? Can the community provide social support that either prevents maladaptive behavior or limits its undesirable effects? How can communities best meet the needs of special groups such as chronically mentally ill people and the homeless?

The Value of an Interactional Approach

We have reviewed six widely varying perspectives on the causes and treatment of maladaptive behavior. You may be wondering how these perspectives relate to the rest of the book. Which one is emphasized most? We think you should know our biases and how our views will affect what you learn in this book.

We have attempted to use the most valuable contributions of each viewpoint in our discussions of abnormal behavior. Abnormal behavior can result from any or all of a large number of factors. One perspective may contribute more than another under one set of conditions; under a different set, another viewpoint may be more useful. Our approach, which is shared by many other psychologists, is interactional. The way a situation influences behavior depends on the particular vulnerabilities, capabilities, and preoccupations of the person experiencing the particular set of conditions. These conditions and the person's characteristics can be thought of as interacting or combining to produce a special product, the individual's behavior. Why maladap-

tive behavior occurs in some people and not others can be understood in this way.

As Figure 3–21 shows, whether behavior is adaptive or maladaptive depends upon the individual's personal characteristics—biological and psychological factors that are vulnerabilities or assets—and the characteristics of the social environment—whether it poses difficult challenges or provides needed support from loved ones and social institutions. In addition to influencing final behavior, personal and environmental factors also can influence each other. For example, someone who is aggressive and always gets into fights is likely to alienate other people and thereby reduce social support. At the same time, someone who experiences a succession of stressful life events may become discouraged and feel pessimistic about a positive outcome.

This interactional approach not only provides a general framework for thinking about maladaptive behavior but also allows for specification of the factors that are especially pertinent to particular disorders. For example, while in the past schizophrenia may have been thought of as being caused by demonic possession, we now know that certain personal and environmental factors, as well as specific biological conditions, play roles in the incidence of this serious disorder. Researchers today are investigating the possible relevance to schizophrenia of a large variety of these factors, including the following personal variables (Gottesman, 1991).

1. A reduced capacity for information processing in situations requiring attention to complex stimuli

2. Hyperactivity of the autonomic nervous system to aversive stimuli in the environment

3. Poor social and coping skills

There is also evidence that these environmental factors contribute to the incidence of schizophrenia and its recurrence:

1. Stressful life events

2. A nonsupportive social network

Research has shown that it is particular combinations of these personal vulnerabilities and environmental handicaps, not their individual existence, that pose special risks for people with tendencies toward various types of maladaptive behavior.

Another example of the application of the interactional approach can be seen in the study of depression. For instance, there is evidence that many people do not become depressed for either purely mental or purely environmental reasons (Oatley & Bolton, 1985). A full

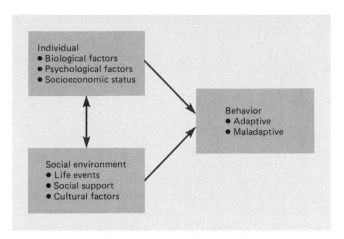

FIGURE 3–21 The interactional approach integrates factors in both individuals and their environments.

understanding of depression requires information about both the person's internal state and the state of his or her social and community ties. Depression can be viewed as despair over a severe loss or disappointment from which, for a longer or shorter time, there seems to be no escape. Recovery from this crisis depends on whether the situation changes and/or how the person's cognitions about the situation change.

Each of us has expectations and goals that color our thoughts. A stamp collector probably has different thoughts when going to the post office than a noncollector does. Our thoughts serve as **mediators:** they provide links between informational inputs and behavioral outputs, just as an intermediary in the business world links a manufacturer and a retailer. Several theories of abnormal behavior deal with the mediating process, though there are differences of opinion about which ones are most important. The various theoretical perspectives reflect these differences by focusing on such different mediators as chemical processes in the body, drives and emotions, thinking styles, values and needs, or the social milieu.

Each of us confronts diverse situations each day. They provide us with information (pleasant, unpleasant, frightening, reassuring) and often call forth certain reactions. The information available to us influences our way of looking at things. At the same time, our personal characteristics—our skills and vulnerabilities—help determine how we handle the situations to which we must respond. As psychologists and authors, we are interested in what makes an individual vulnerable to particular situations, what kind of stressors cause maladaptive behavior to appear, and how people can build coping skills that enable them to deal better with stressors and compensate for their vulnerabilities.

Chapter Summary

THE ROLE OF THEORY IN ABNORMAL PSYCHOLOGY

Theories play an important role in guiding research on the causes of behavioral maladaptations and physical illness. The six currently influential theoretical perspectives are: 1) the biological perspective, 2) the psychodynamic perspective, 3) the behavioral perspective, 4) the cognitive perspective, 5) the humanistic–existential perspective, and 6) the community perspective. Each of these theories has something to contribute to the understanding of maladaptive behavior.

THE BIOLOGICAL PERSPECTIVE

The **biological perspective** views bodily disturbances as the cause of disordered behavior. The bodily disturbance may be due to a genetic defect, an injury or infection before or after birth, or to a more or less temporary physiological malfunction caused by some condition present at a particular time.

Biological Determinants of Abnormal Behavior **Genes,** the elements of human heredity, are transmitted from parent to child in the form of **DNA.** DNA is found in the **chromosomes,** present in pairs in all body cells. **Behavior genetics** emphasizes the interaction of heredity and environment. Research in behavior genetics is carried out either through the study of family histories or through studies of twins. The two major divisions of the nervous system are the **central nervous system (CNS),** the nerve cells in the brain and spinal cord, and the **peripheral nervous system,** the neurons connecting the CNS with the glands, muscles, and sensory receptors.

The Neurosciences Revolution **Neuroscience** is a new interdisciplinary field aimed at understanding the relationship between thinking, feeling, and behavior and the structure and function of the brain. The use of new techniques to study molecular level events at the synapse as well as scanning techniques that make possible the study of the living brain are contributing to the understanding of relationships between brain and behavior. **Psychoneuroimmunology** is an area of research focused on the effects of psychological and neural events on immunological processes.

Integration of Biological and Psychological Systems One major contribution of the biological perspective is drug therapy. A variety of drugs are used in treating maladaptive behavior. However, it is important to recognize the multiple determinants of abnormal behavior that include interactions among the physical environment, psychological factors, and biological functioning.

THE PSYCHODYNAMIC PERSPECTIVE

The **psychodynamic perspective** is based on the idea that thoughts and emotions are important causes of behavior.

Freud and Psychoanalysis Freud developed **psychoanalysis,** a method in which the patient recaptures forgotten memories without the use of hypnosis. The two most basic assumptions of Freud's theories of personality are **psychic determinism** and the **conscious-unconscious dimension.** The latter includes three levels of consciousness: the **conscious, preconscious,** and **unconscious.** Freud's theory placed great emphasis on the first five years of life. During this period he thought that the **libido,** or basic human drives, was focused on a series of specific erogenous zones or sources of pleasure. His theory divided the mental world into three structures—the **id,** the **ego,** and the **superego.** Freud also placed great emphasis on the concept of **anxiety** and on the use of **defense mechanisms** to ward off anxiety. He believed the most important of the defense mechanisms was **repression.**

Contemporary Approaches to Psychoanalysis Psychoanalytic theory has been modified by many later theorists. Erikson developed a **psychosocial** theory. He described a series of stages of development over the entire life cycle. **Objects relations** theory was developed by psychoanalysts such as Klein. Kohut developed a theory of **self-psychology.**

Evaluating Psychoanalytic Theory Although much of psychoanalytic theory is difficult to test experimentally, in recent years two research areas have developed. One attempts to relate psychodynamic processes to brain function and the other focuses on testing specific psychoanalytic concepts such as repression.

THE BEHAVIORAL PERSPECTIVE

The behavioral perspective focuses on behavior as a response to stimuli in the environment. Behaviors that receive **reinforcement** or reward have an increased probability of occurring again. **Negative reinforcement** occurs when something unpleasant is taken away after the behavior occurs. **Punishment** provides a negative consequence for the behavior.

Classical Conditioning In **classical conditioning,** the response that occurs automatically to one stimulus is transferred to a new stimulus by pairing the two stimuli.

Operant Conditioning In **operant conditioning** the response precedes the reinforcement.

Social Learning Theory **Social learning** theorists do not believe that direct reinforcement is always necessary for learning. They stress the use of **modeling,** or observational learning, as the way a great deal of behavior, especially social behavior, is learned. **Role playing,** or practice of the modeled behavior, is also an important learning technique.

THE COGNITIVE PERSPECTIVE

The **cognitive perspective** focuses on how people acquire and interpret information and use it in problem-solving. Each

person develops **schemata** that contain information about different domains in a person's life and assist in information processing and strategy development. In the study of maladaptive behavior, **self-schemata** are particularly important.

Maladaptive Behavior and Cognition Dollard and Miller combined elements of the psychodynamic, learning, and cognitive perspectives. They saw maladaptive behavior as a result of both unfortunate life experiences and maladaptive thinking. According to Kelly, each person builds a view of the world by sorting people and events into categories. He called these categories **personal constructs,** and thought the role of psychotherapy was to help people replace maladaptive personal constructs with more adaptive ones. Bandura is especially interested in **self-regulation** through the use of internal rather than external reinforcement.

Cognitive Therapies **Rational-emotive therapy,** developed by Ellis, is based on the idea that behavior is more a function of belief systems than of actual conditions. The therapist's role is to explain, demonstrate, and assist the client in practicing more productive ways of thinking. **Fixed-role therapy,** developed by Kelly, focuses on assisting clients to act out new roles that may help them revise their personal-construct systems. Beck focuses on helping clients replace maladaptive thoughts with more effective coping techniques. His work initially focused on depression but now also includes problems with anxiety as the major symptom.

THE HUMANISTIC–EXISTENTIAL PERSPECTIVE

The **humanist perspective** assumes that in every person there is an active force toward **self-actualization.**

Rogers' Conception of the Self Rogers emphasized the importance of the **self-image.** He believed a primary role of the therapist was the total acceptance of the client as a person of worth.

The Existential Point of View Existentialists focus on the need to help people to establish their own goals and then to make constructive choices to reach these.

THE COMMUNITY PERSPECTIVE

Community psychologists focus on the failure of social support systems as the cause of maladaptations. They emphasize preventive intervention—such as special programs in schools—and programs for specific groups that are at high risk because they need help in solving problems of living.

Social Roles and Labeling **Social roles** are defined by the person's group and the functions of the person in that group. Each role has a script that determines how the person is expected to act in different situations. **Labeling** is the result of categorizing people on some basis, such as the social group to which they belong, without attention to their individual characteristics.

Contributions of the Community Perspective The community perspective has been influential in reaching people whose needs have been ignored by the other perspectives that focus more on treating the individual instead of changing the environment. How best to provide support in the community setting is still a question that needs extensive research.

THE VALUE OF AN INTERACTIONAL APPROACH

All of the perspectives make contributions to the **interactional approach.** This approach takes into account both personal vulnerabilities and the stressful aspects of the situation.

Classification and Assessment

CHAPTER 4

Classification
Advantages and Disadvantages of Classification
Stress, Vulnerability, and Coping
The Multiaxial Approach
The Major Diagnostic Categories
Evaluation of the DSM Multiaxial Approach
Research on Classification

Assessment: The Basis of Classification
The Interview
Intelligence Tests
Personality Assessment
Behavioral Assessment
Cognitive Assessment
Relational Assessment
Bodily Assessment

Chapter Summary

Dick Jemison, *Dreamwork I*, 1990. Elaine Horwitch Galleries, Scottsdale, AZ.

*R*obert Frank, a 37-year-old married man, has come to a community mental health center because some of his thoughts have been bothering him.

For as long as he can recall, he has been introverted and somewhat fearful of people. He has desired social contact but, because of his fearfulness, has usually been unsuccessful in forming relationships. At the time he has come to the center, he has been keeping certain disturbing thoughts to himself. In the past he had discussed these thoughts with his wife and with clinicians at a mental hospital. He thinks he is being spied upon by some unknown group, which he believes to be a government intelligence agency. He also feels that his television set is providing him with special messages and that an attempt is being made to control his will and thoughts. He has a job in a large corporation. In the judgment of his supervisor, he has performed well in the past but recently his work has deteriorated somewhat.

Frank has been hospitalized on two occasions, after which he seemed to make a good adjustment back into the community. Six months ago his mother's death upset him greatly. During the past few months he has increasingly restricted his social activities to members of his family and has been somewhat withdrawn even with them. He has come to the community mental health center because the thoughts were becoming more persistent. His discomfort level was increasing, and he realized that he was becoming more incoherent; he wanted to avoid another hospitalization if at all possible.

The clinical worker who talked with Frank wanted to get all this background information so that she could recommend the most practical and effective therapeutic program. She went through a series of steps in which information about Frank was gathered and interpreted. To increase the accuracy of their interpretations, clinicians often make use of the experiences of other professionals in evaluating behavior. Classification systems are particularly valuable because they represent attempts to organize what a great many clinical workers know about the various types of problems they deal with.

The classification of personal problems is based on assessments of what clients say and how they behave. Both present life conditions and past experiences are taken into account. Classification is not simply an intellectual exercise, however. It has far-reaching effects on the lives of people who exhibit maladaptive behavior and on the activities of clinical workers.

Classification

The need to classify various types of personalities and personal problems has been recognized for a long time. Since the time of Hippocrates, classification systems have continually been revised to incorporate new knowledge and changing viewpoints. Nevertheless, the classification of abnormal behavior is still in an early stage of evolution, partly because of the arbitrary nature of the process of attaching labels to people. For example, there is no precise point at which an excessive drinker becomes a full-blown alcoholic, or when the tension you feel when you are alone in a strange room becomes the intense dread known as claustrophobia.

A classification statement, or **diagnosis,** places a disorder within a system of conventional groupings based on significant similarities in symptoms. Most classification systems are organized in hierarchical fashion, just as they are in the natural sciences. Thus, in the system that is used to classify animal life, human beings are members of the species *Homo sapiens,* genus *Homo,* which is a subdivision of the family Hominidae, of the order Primates, of the class Mammalia, of the phylum Chordata, of the kingdom Animalia. Similarly, manic episode is a subdivision of bipolar disorder, which in turn is one of the major disorders in the family of mood disorders.

While classification is generally regarded as a scientific and clinical tool, we should remember that all people continually use some form of classification in their daily lives. The people we meet, the day's weather, and other everyday experiences are all put into groups on the

basis of similarities to past experiences or other ways of classifying events. Classification is a way of trying to understand and learn from experience. Without a classification system, everything that happens to us would be unique and we could not prepare for the future in any way (see Figure 4–1).

Advantages and Disadvantages of Classification

General use of a widely recognized classification system is very important. If every clinical worker made up his or her own system, communication problems would be enormous. It would be difficult to make use of research data on effective treatment, for example. Classification systems are also useful for statistical purposes. Government and other planning agencies need records of how often various types of maladaptation occur. Without such records, it would be impossible to say whether the incidence of certain forms of maladaptation was increasing or decreasing. Moreover, to the extent that the categories used in established classification systems are distinctive and can be rated reliably, they contribute to the planning of treatment programs and facilities.

Still, the usefulness of classification for understanding the causes of some disorders and treating them remains controversial, as shown by the following comments by an experienced clinician.

You would think that after working with troubled people for twenty years I'd know what their major problems are and what I should be diagnosing. Yet I'm not really sure what diagnosis is, what it should be, or how it can do more than just name and pigeonhole. I classify cases because it helps me keep records and communicate with other clinicians. At the same time, my major job is to treat people, to decide what I can do that will help them figure out what they should do to make their lives happier and more worthwhile. People are more different than they are similar. Two people may come in with a similar symptom, like delusions of grandeur, but the mechanisms that produce the symptom may be different. I wish diagnosis helped me better understand the basis for the conditions I diagnose.

The idea of classifying maladaptive behaviors has been criticized on several counts. Most important to many people is the fact that a diagnosis puts a label on a person. Labeling might make it difficult for a former patient to get a job, gain admission to a professional program, obtain custody of a child, and the like. Another argument is that many diagnoses are not useful because

FIGURE 4–1 In this cartoon, Linus is discovering how to classify an event ("I'll slug you right back") so he can better prepare for the future.

("Peanuts" drawing by Charles Schulz. Reprinted by permission of United Features Syndicate, Inc.)

the diagnostic categories are imperfect and the same label may be assigned to behaviors that appear similar but have different causes and different treatments.

On balance, the case for classification is a strong one. It is easy to defend the idea that each patient is unique, yet nothing can be done to help an individual without referring to general principles. What is known about an individual case, however detailed, can be utilized only if the case is viewed within the context of existing knowledge. At the same time, general principles will have validity only if they are based on observation of individuals.

There are two major sources of unreliability in diagnoses. One concerns clinical judgment: differences in therapists' clinical training and theoretical orientation may lead to different diagnoses. The other major source of unreliability is the fact that diagnostic labels are attached to people, and no two people (or their problems) are alike. The same person might also describe his or her problem differently on two separate occasions depending on how he or she was feeling at the time or

what events relating to the problem had occurred recently. Diagnosticians may change their original assessment of a case, or two people with similar problems might describe their conditions differently and therefore be classified differently.

Ambiguities and inconsistencies also arise because most clinics and hospitals are burdened with more cases than they can handle. Leisurely and protracted study aimed at accurate classification is often impossible. Another factor in classification difficulty is the range of problems treated by a particular clinical facility. The staff of a facility that treats a narrow range of disorders may tend to describe and interpret its cases differently than would the staff of a more broadly based institution. Diagnostic methods will achieve a firmer scientific basis as assessment becomes more standardized and less susceptible to distortion by such factors. Table 4–1 lists some of the important features of a good classification system. Currently, for most types of maladaptive behavior, the characteristics listed in Table 4–1 remain goals and are not yet achievements.

Table 4–1
Characteristics of a Good Clinical Classification System

1. Provides information about the cause or causes of a condition.
2. Provides a common language for communication among clinicians and researchers.
3. Enables clinicians to give patients and their families a short- and long-term outlook.
4. Provides clues to treatment.
5. Suggests paths to prevention.

Stress, Vulnerability, and Coping

The authors' approach to abnormal psychology has some definite implications for the process of classification. This approach argues that abnormal behavior must be understood in the context of several factors: the recent stressful events in a person's life, such as a bereavement or loss of a job; the person's general vulnerabilities, such as a tendency toward low self-esteem that may have been engendered by early childhood experiences or a highly reactive nervous system; and what the individual has going for him or her, such as coping skills, intellectual ability, and family and friends who are willing and able to help.

Classifying abnormal behavior should be a matter of drawing a picture of a person rather than simply marking a point on a graph. In classifying a person who is experiencing a problem, we want to know not only what the problem is—for example, Frank's belief that he is being spied on—but also the context of the problem. In Frank's case, the context includes (1) recent experiences that may have aroused stress and led to the worsening of his condition, (2) his vulnerabilities or weaknesses, and (3) his assets or strengths. The fact that Frank has experienced long periods of good adjustment (for example, being able to hold a job) is encouraging and should not be ignored. Optimally, the way we classify people should tell us something about their future prospects and likely responses to therapeutic efforts.

The Multiaxial Approach

Over the years, classification or diagnosis has meant many things, from the simple assignment of a name or label to a statement providing information about several aspects of a particular case. (The roots of "diagnostic" mean "thorough knowledge.") Official classifications of mental disorders first came into use in the United States in 1840, with the adoption of a one-item classification scheme. In the census that year, "idiocy" was the single label used to categorize mental illness. By the 1880 census, there were eight categories for mental disorders.

Today, practitioners make use of a **multiaxial classification system** designed to summarize the diverse information relevant to an individual case rather than to provide a single label. Instead of merely assigning a case to a category (such as schizophrenia), clinicians using a multiaxial system can describe an individual in terms of a set of clinically important factors, or *axes*. The American Psychiatric Association's multiaxial classification system is currently so widely accepted that it is easy to lose sight of the fact that the multiaxial feature is a relatively new development in the classification of mental disorders. The first multiaxial system was presented as recently as 1980, in the *Diagnostic and Statistical Manual of Mental Disorders* (referred to as DSM-III). A revision of DSM-III, referred to as DSM-III-R, was published in 1987. Like its predecessors, DSM-IV, scheduled to be published in the mid 1990's, is multiaxial in nature.

Multiaxial diagnostic systems are primarily concerned with the description of clinical problems. Its categories take note of the etiology, or cause, of the disorder when it can be identified (although some critics of DSM maintain that this system does not pay sufficient attention to etiology), as well as the subjective experiences of clients (for example, how worried or angry they seem to be) and their assets and liabilities. The current DSM system provides information about the context in which abnormal behavior occurs as well as a description of the behavior.

BUILDING A MULTIAXIAL CLASSIFICATION SYSTEM The basic DSM multiaxial concept is that several different domains of information about the biological, psychological, and social aspects of a person's condition need to be evaluated in an integrated way. The five axes of the DSM system illustrate this approach.

- Axis I contains the **primary classification** or diagnosis of the problem that requires attention (for example, fear of heights).
- Axis II classifies any **developmental and personality disorders** that begin in childhood or adolescence and usually persist in stable form into adult life. Examples are mental retardation and personality disorders such as an unwarranted tendency to interpret the actions of other people as threatening.
- Axis III refers to any **physical disorders** that seem relevant to a case (for example, the client's history of heart attacks).
- Axis IV rates the severity of **psychosocial stressors** in the client's recent past that may have contributed to the clinical problem and might influence the course of treatment (for example, divorce, death of a parent, loss of a job). Whether the stress is acute or chronic is also noted.

- Axis V contains a global assessment of **psychological functioning, social relationships, and occupational activities** attained by the client. Ratings are made for both current functioning and the highest level of functioning during the past year. The behavior of two severely disturbed people would probably be interpreted differently and even treated differently if one had a history of good relationships with others and an excellent work record while the other had a history of social inadequacy and inability to hold a job.

The case of Robert Frank presented at the beginning of the chapter might be classified as follows:

- Axis I: Paranoid schizophrenia
- Axis II: Avoidant personality disorder
- Axis III: No apparent medical problems
- Axis IV: Extreme
- Axis V: Serious impairment in several areas

An innovation of the DSM system is that it provides criteria for quantitatively coding the relatively subjective factors of Axes IV and V. Axis IV provides guidelines for rating the overall severity of recent events (for example, death of a child, retirement) and long-lasting circumstances (unemployment or serious chronic illness, for example). Guidelines for Axis V pertain to level of functioning (for example, violent to self or others, conflict with co-workers).

The more complete the available information about a given case, the more reliable the classification and ratings will be. Often, particularly in acute or emergency cases, a classification is made even though there are big informational gaps. In these cases, the classification is considered to be tentative and may be revised as more information is acquired.

The Major Diagnostic Categories

Beginning with DSM-III in 1980, a special effort has been made to be as specific as possible in describing major diagnostic categories and in listing the symptoms and factors relevant to particular disorders. These include the typical features of the disorder, the age at which it usually develops, its likely progression or outcome, the amount of social and occupational impairment involved, possible complications (for example, suicide attempts by depressed individuals), aspects of a person's life that increase the risk of a severe disorder, sex differences, and relevant family patterns. Table 4–2 lists indicators such as these, which the clinician attends to in making classifications.

AXIS I CATEGORIES Axis I includes all the major clinical disorders except personality and specific developmental disorders.

- **Disorders of Infancy, Childhood, or Adolescence.** Conditions first evident in these periods include disruptive behavior, gender identity disorders, and certain eating disorder.
- **Organic Mental Disorders.** Transient or permanent brain dysfunction attributable to such factors as the aging process or ingestion of a substance that affects the brain—for example, psychoses due to effects of excessive intake of alcohol, difficulty in directing attention, memory loss.
- **Psychoactive Substance Use Disorders.** Personal and social problems with use of certain substances—for example, dependence on and abuse of heroin, marijuana, and tobacco.
- **Sleep Disorders.** Insomnia or difficulty in going to sleep or staying asleep, excessive daytime sleepiness, complaints of sleep disturbance without objective evidence, impairment of respiration during sleep, disturbance of the sleep-wake schedule, sleepwalking, sleep terrors.
- **Schizophrenia.** Chronic disorganized behavior and thought of psychotic proportions (delusions, hallucinations), incoherence, and social isolation.
- **Delusional (Paranoid) Disorder.** Well-organized system of delusions (often of being persecuted) without the incoherence, bizarreness, and social isolation seen in schizophrenia.

Table 4–2
Clinical Observations and Symptoms Used in DSM Classification

While a given symptom may be part of several different clinical pictures (for example, headaches may be present in cases marked by high anxiety, hypochondriasis, or somatic complaints), this list suggests the kinds of data clinicians attend to and that go into a psychiatric diagnosis. The presence of *groups* of symptoms characteristic of a particular disorder increases the likelihood of accurate classification.

Anxiety
Behavior
Cognitive functioning (attention, memory)
Eating disturbance
Energy level
Mood
Motor activity
Occupational and social impairment
Perceptual disturbance
Personal appearance
Personality traits
Physical symptoms
Sleep disturbance
Speaking manner
Thought content

- **Psychotic Disorders Not Classified Elsewhere.** Includes schizophreniform disorders (similar to schizophrenia but of less than six months' duration), brief psychosis in reaction to a particular stress, and schizoaffective disorders (a combination of disorganization and delusional behavior with feelings of depression and elation).
- **Mood (Affective) Disorders.** Depression or manic excitement, or both.
- **Anxiety Disorders.** Anxiety, tension, and worry are major aspects of the clinical picture, with psychotic features (delusions, hallucinations) absent. Included also are posttraumatic (reactive, stress-caused) disorders. These may be brief or chronic.
- **Somatoform Disorders.** Physical symptoms for which no medical causes can be found. These symptoms are apparently not under voluntary control and are linked to psychological factors or conflicts.
- **Dissociative Disorders.** Sudden, temporary change in the normal functions of consciousness (for example, loss of memory).
- **Sexual Disorders.** Deviant sexual thoughts and behavior that are either personally anxiety-provoking or socially maladaptive.
- **Factitious Disorders.** Physical or behavior symptoms that are voluntarily produced by the individual, apparently in order to play the role of patient, and often involving chronic, blatant lying.
- **Impulse Control Disorders Not Classified Elsewhere.** Maladaptations characterized by failure to resist impulses (for example, pathological gambling, chronic stealing of desired objects, habitual fire-setting).
- **Adjustment Disorder.** Maladaptive reactions to identifiable life events or circumstances that are expected to lessen and cease when the stressor ceases. The reactions may be dominated by depressed mood, anxiety, withdrawal, conduct disorder such as truancy, or lessening in work or job performance.
- **Psychological Factors Affecting Physical Condition.** Used to describe what have been referred to as either psychophysiological or psychosomatic disorders. Common examples include migraine headaches, painful menstruation, asthma, and duodenal ulcer.

AXIS II CATEGORIES The disorders listed on Axis II begin in childhood or adolescence and continue into adult life without much change. Axis I and II are separated so that when adults are evaluated, these continuing characteristics, which may affect personality or cognitive, social, or motor skills, will be taken into consideration. Axis II contains two major categories, *Developmental Disorders* and *Personality Disorders.* In some instances, the classification statements of Axis II are used to provide additional information about the primary diagnosis of Axis I. In others, the disorder referred to on Axis II is the individual's major problem.

- **Developmental Disorders.** These include **Mental Retardation,** a significantly subaverage level of general intellectual functioning; **Pervasive Developmental Disorders,** in which there is an impairment in social interaction and communication that is accompanied by odd stereotyped behavior; and **Specific Developmental Disorders,** in which there are problems, for example, in particular aspects of speech, academic skills such as reading or arithmetic, or physical coordination.
- **Personality Disorders.** These are characterized by enduring, inflexible, and maladaptive patterns of relating to, perceiving, and thinking about the environment and oneself. These faulty patterns cause impairment in social and occupational functioning. Personality disorders may resemble personality characteristics that occur in people who are functioning adaptively. They may also resemble many different behaviors associated with anxiety disorders, psychoses, or mood disorders.

Axis II may not distinguish clearly enough between personality styles or traits that are commonly seen in the general population but appear to cause few problems for the individual and the rigid clearly maladaptive personality styles that lead to personal unhappiness or ineffectiveness. Imperfect as it may be, however, the attempt to include personality factors in psychiatric classification is a step forward.

Evaluation of the DSM Multiaxial Approach

DSM-III, DSM-III-R, and DSM-IV differ from earlier classification manuals in their emphasis on describing clinical problems rather than interpreting them and listing specific criteria for each diagnostic category. This change came about as a result of widespread concern that psychiatric diagnoses are often unreliable because they are based on guesses about the underlying causes of problems. A review of earlier diagnostic systems will illustrate the path clinicians have taken in classifying abnormal behavior.

DSM-I, published in 1952, and DSM-II, published in 1968, were significantly smaller volumes than DSM-III, DSM-III-R, and DSM-IV. Recent DSM's are so much larger due to their greater scope of maladaptations covered, greater use of examples of particular classifications, and the fact that the intent of the recent DSMs has been a reliable and unambiguous description of disorders. The language of both DSM-I and DSM-II was heavily influenced by psychoanalytic theory, and the manuals focused on internal nonobservable processes. As a result, clinicians' diagnoses often varied greatly. In contrast, the recent DSMs have used much more precise language. Another reason for the superiority of the most recent DSMs is that extensive field trials were carried out in their development. These trials, involving thousands of patients and hundreds of clinicians, made it possible to

check for ease of usage and reliability and to correct deficiencies before publication.

Although they represent advances in clinical classification, no one believes that the most recent DSMs are the final word on the subject of diagnosis. Among their limitations are continued reliance on impressionistic clinical judgments (for example, in estimating the severity of a disorder). The recent DSMs might best be viewed as sets of guidelines for characterizing clinical problems, and they are concerned primarily with the description of these problems.

The time intervals between the several versions of DSM have become progressively shorter. This acceleration is due to rapid advances in knowledge about the various types of maladaptive behavior that have to be taken into account in diagnosis and to efforts to improve the reliability of the diagnostic system. Whereas the first multiaxial DSM (DSM-III) represented a major innovation in the concept of classification, DSM-IV reflects the need for fine-tuning of the diagnostic system, and a new accessibility for its users more than new knowledge. Another important reason for producing DSM-IV such a short time after DSM-III-R is the desirability of an internationally standardized system. Extensive research throughout the world on mental disorders requires that world-wide diagnostic systems be as similar as possible if researchers in all countries are to be able to take advantage of new information. The tenth edition of the World Health Organization's International Classification of Diseases (ICD-10), which includes maladaptive behavior as one subsection and which is widely used through much of the world, will be published in the mid-1990's. Over the years those who developed the ICD and DSM systems have been cooperating and sharing information in an effort to make the systems more similar. Work on DSM-IV has been accelerated so that the two systems will have updated versions of increased similarity available at about the same time.

DSM-III and its successors have sought to be quite specific about the criteria for using each diagnostic category. It seems that these manuals have successfully achieved this objective. By emphasizing descriptions of behavior rather than theoretical ideas about its cause, the DSM approach has reduced the amount of inference needed to make a particular diagnosis, and has increased reliability. In addition to increasing the dimensions for describing particular disorders, recent manuals have greatly increased coverage of the range of disorders. This increase is especially evident in the extensive coverage of childhood disorders.

Although much more research is needed in order to make a definitive evaluation of the DSM multiaxial approach, practitioners agree that it has been successful in facilitating communication among clinicians and contributing to more reliable classification. For example, prior to DSM-III clinicians often complained about the difficulty, using available classification criteria, of distinguishing between certain affective disorders and schizophrenia. Furthermore, as a consequence of too-vague criteria, diagnoses of schizophrenia were made more often than this disorder actually occurs in the population. Evidence since introduction of DSM-III suggests that this overrepresentation of schizophrenia diagnoses has been much reduced (Adamson, 1989).

It is possible that comprehensiveness of the multiaxial approach is a mixed blessing. Clinicians show a high level of agreement in classifying patients on broad general diagnostic categories, such as depression and juvenile delinquency, and less consistency in classifying finer subdivisions within these general categories (Rutter & Shaffer, 1980). Much research will be required in order to determine the breadth and specificity needed to maximize the value of current multiaxial approaches.

Critics have argued that recent DSMs have paid too much attention to how a person appears at a particular point in time (for example, upon admission to a clinic or hospital) and not enough to his or her prior history and developmental crises. The DSM system has also been criticized for providing little information about the causes of abnormal behavior. Several writers argue that since the publication of DSM-III, etiology has not been given sufficient attention in classification, and that both description of and inferences about the processes involved in maladaptive behavior are needed (Vaillant, 1984).

Despite these criticisms, most practitioners recognize the unique value of the multiaxial approach. By introducing axes that pertain to severity of stress and previous level of adjustment, as well as to long-lasting personality patterns, DSM-III recognized the need for integrating what is known about people's vulnerabilities, assets, and stressful life events with what is observed in their behavior. Efforts are continuing to improve the existing axes in the light of both research findings and the needs of practicing clinicians.

Despite the shortcomings in the axis system, there nevertheless seems little doubt that DSM as it stands today is an improvement over previous diagnostic systems. Many of its limitations grow out of limitations in our understanding of what mental health and mental disorder are. Any classification system can be no better than available knowledge and attitudes about what is being classified. As we will see later in this chapter, experts who have devoted their entire careers to studying a specific topic such as schizophrenia have strong differences of opinion about what types of behavior should be examined. The greatest contributions of DSM-III, DSM-III-R, and DSM-IV may turn out to be

the new knowledge that results from the arguments they have stimulated.

Research on Classification

Research on the classification of abnormal behavior has focused on the role of clinical judgment in classification and on the effects of the labeling process. Information is also needed on how complex a classification system should be. How many categories should it have? Which variables must be assessed in making a diagnosis? Which ones should be optional? In what way should an individual's life story be taken into account in assessing his or her present behavior? The psychoanalytic perspective might lead to the conclusion that information about early childhood is essential to assessment, whereas a behavioristic viewpoint might emphasize a detailed description of present-day behavior. A diagnosis is not simply a label that is attached to a client by a clinician; it is a complex product of present knowledge and opinion about maladaptive behavior. As such, diagnosis is not an immutable process. Rather, it changes with advances in knowledge and alterations in what society defines as a problem.

Earlier we mentioned the importance of achieving agreement among clinicians in classifying cases. Until about twenty years ago, diagnosis was handicapped by the low reliability of diagnostic agreement. **Reliability** is concerned with whether a classification decision is reproducible, either by the same clinician at a different time or by different clinicians. In order to have high reliability the defining characteristics of a class or the criteria which must be met in order to establish class membership must be clearly defined. For example, it must be clearly specified which specific symptoms all patients in this class would have in common and which symptoms would cause their exclusion from the class. Reliability can be assessed with several specific statistical tools. Often, reliability is simply assessed by the degree of agreement when the same patient is diagnosed by several different clinicians. However, simply using the percentage of agreement overlooks the possibility that some clinical agreement might occur by chance. A clinician who sees schizophrenia in a high percentage of his or her cases will show a fair amount of chance agreement with other clinicians in using the label of schizophrenia. A reliability index, the **kappa statistic,** corrects the amount of observed agreement for the amount of chance agreement. This correction is based on information about the overall frequency with which clinicians use particular classifications. By correcting for chance agreement, use of the kappa statistic provides a truer estimate of diagnostic reliability and has become the standard method for indexing agreement in studies relating to classification.

Validity is concerned with whether or not the classification system groups together people whose symptoms arise from the same causes and respond to similar treatments. An ideal demonstration of the validity of a diagnosis calls for identifying similar causes and mechanisms underlying the symptoms of all those with the same diagnosis. A more usual way to view validity is the power of the class membership assigned to predict clinical course and outcome and the most effective treatment approach. The highly specific descriptions of most DSM categories have greatly increased the reliability of the diagnoses made using the system, but the validity of many of DSM classifications has yet to be fully established. One of the reasons for this is that not enough is known about the causes of many disorders. It is likely for instance, that some DSM categories may contain disorders with very different causes despite the similar symptoms that are the basis for the classification. Another problem is that the DSM system allows a diagnosis if the person has a certain number of symptoms from a much larger list. This means that two people who have the same diagnosis may have only a few symptoms in common. Determining more about the similarity of causation within the same diagnostic group is currently a major focus of research.

CLINICAL JUDGMENT A variety of data go into classification statements. In arriving at a diagnosis, the clinician goes through a series of problem-solving and decision-making steps. The more complete and standardized the data and the more explicit the intervening cognitive steps, the greater the reliability of the diagnosis. This holds true whether we are talking about a clinician making a diagnosis on two different occasions using the same data or about two clinicians making independent diagnoses on the basis of the same information.

Studies of clinical judgment have been carried out in order to determine just how the clinician's role affects the reliability of classification. When diagnostic criteria are described clearly and intensive training is given in their use, and when the clinicians using them employ comparable methods, the reliability of diagnoses increases significantly. Additional factors also affect clinical judgments. One of these is the fact that certain disorders are more easily classified than others (for example, the reliability of diagnoses for organic brain disorders is higher than those for schizophrenia). Irrelevant or tangential information, such as labels, may throw a clinician off course. In addition, the attitudes and characteristics of diagnosticians often influence the judgments they make.

Research on clinical judgment suggests that even though they may not carry out formal research projects, clinicians use a research process in making their diagnoses. Like more research-oriented scientists, clinicians

make observations, integrate them, and draw conclusions on the basis of the evidence they have gathered.

Evidence gathered in formal research on clinical judgment has helped identify factors that contribute to disagreement and error in day-to-day clinical research. Among them are the following.

1. *Client factors.* The client is not a constant. In fact, he or she may contribute to differences in clinical opinion by behaving in different ways at different times. If one clinician assesses an individual who is in the midst of an alcoholic delirium, while another clinician's assessment is carried out several days after the delirium has lifted, differences in classification would not be surprising.

2. *Method factors.* Clinicians who use different assessment techniques might describe people who are actually similar as being different.

3. *Criteria factors.* Clinicians who have different standards for classifying cases might differ in their diagnoses.

4. *Clinician factors.* Clinicians differ in how they assess data. Personality differences, as well as differences in training and theoretical orientation, influence the clinician's information processing.

Clinicians differ in how they process information and in how much they can keep track of. Computers may prove to be valuable aids to clinical assessment because they are capable of scanning and retaining larger amounts of information than a human diagnostician can. Whether or not clinicians are aided by computers, the process by which they form judgments and make decisions is an important part of research on classification.

Assessment: The Basis of Classification

While efforts are made to improve classification systems, clinical workers must employ currently available methods in their work. The major methods used to assess behavior in clinical settings include interviews, psychological tests, and behavioral assessment. Assessment of other aspects of individual's behavior have also been developed and are discussed later in the chapter.

Structured interviews are used primarily in two settings in which information obtained in a standard way is particularly important. One of these settings is in large institutions where a client will be assigned to treatment only after initial information is collected and a group of health professionals have discussed a diagnosis and agreed on an initial treatment plan. In this type of setting

it is especially important that information on all clients be obtained in a uniform manner so that the conference concerning the treatment plan is minimally affected by the particular person who gathered the data and so that all needed information is likely to be obtained. The other setting in which structured interviews are generally used is one in which research is being carried out. Again the ability to obtain data on a client that can be meaningfully compared with data on many other individuals is of crucial importance. In contrast to these situations, clinicians who will carry out the treatment program themselves often develop individual approaches to gathering data. They may find that a standardized interview makes it more difficult to begin forming a relationship with the client. In addition, they may fit their own interview approach to their own personalities and to information they have personally found important in treating other clients.

Although there is agreement about the need to develop valid ways of characterizing individuals, clinicians disagree on how this can best be accomplished. Because no single assessment tool is considered foolproof, assessment is commonly approached in more than one way in order to yield a more complete and accurate description of the individual.

Psychological tests differ from interviews in that they restrict the client's freedom of expression. Just as it is easier to quantify and compare scores on a multiple choice test than on an essay test, the responses obtained on psychological tests can be more readily quantified and compared than the more open-ended and unstructured responses obtained in interviews. To achieve a well-rounded picture of the individual, most clinicians interpret quantified psychometric results in light of behavioral observations made in less restricted situations.

The Interview

The interview continues to be the most widely used assessment tool. Clinical interviews are of two types: assessment and therapeutic. The purpose of the **assessment** or **diagnostic interview** is to gather information and assess behavior. On the basis of the client's verbal and nonverbal behavior during the interview, the interviewer tries to understand why the client is seeking help and what might be done from a therapeutic standpoint. The **therapeutic interview** (or therapy session) occurs after a preliminary assessment has been made. Its aim is the actual modification of maladaptive behavior and attitudes.

Interviews usually involve two individuals, the interviewer and the client, although other people, such as family members, are sometimes included. Family members may also be interviewed separately. Treatment decisions are often based largely on the data gathered in

Table 4–3
Four Components of the Clinical Interview

While these components are found in virtually all types of clinical interviews, they are especially pertinent to the diagnostic interview.

1. *Rapport.* Rapport relates to how the interviewer and client relate to each other. To achieve rapport, the interviewer seeks to put the client at ease and show interest in the problem being discussed.
2. *Technique.* Depending on the client and the problem, the interviewer selects techniques to build rapport and to obtain information. Techniques range from open-ended questions to a tactful challenge of something the client has said.
3. *Mental status.* To determine the mental level at which the client is functioning, the interviewer will evaluate his or her answers to questions. Are they clear or fuzzy, pleasant or angry, reality-oriented or full of strange and bizarre ideas?
4. *Diagnosis.* The interviewer is continually revising his or her formulation of the client's problems and personality. This process includes a diagnosis.

SOURCE: Othmer & Othmer, 1989

an assessment interview, which may begin as a telephone call and then be followed up in a face-to-face setting. Table 4–3 lists four important components of the clinical interview.

CONTENT OF THE INTERVIEW Assessment interviewers seek to identify problems and determine the nature and extent of maladaptive behavior. Typically, interviewers begin by trying to find out how the client describes, understands, and interprets his or her problem. In some cases, the complaint is nonspecific, such as "I feel tense and worried all the time." In other cases, it may seem deceptively clear, as in "My child is hyperactive—I can't control him." Then the interviewer may inquire into the history of the problem. In the course of obtaining this information, the interviewer may get a better understanding of the stressing agents that were present in the client's life as the problem was developing.

Initial interviews often are relatively unstructured. Depending on the problem and how it is described, the interviewer may have to move back and forth among a number of topics. However, an attempt is made to answer the following questions:

1. *Who is the client?* That is, what is his or her name, age, ethnic and cultural background, marital status, and occupation? What led to his or her decision to obtain professional help?
2. *How does the client think and feel about life at this time?* What are the client's preoccupations and feelings?

3. *What is the history of the problem and the client's developmental background?* Depending on the particular problem, an inquiry might be made into the physical and emotional climate of the home during the client's infancy and childhood, as well as the client's sleep patterns, physical and motor development, and sexual and social development.
4. *What is the client's present psychological state?* What is noteworthy about the client's speech, thought, judgment, cooperativeness, and social skills?

During an assessment interview, many aspects of behavior must be observed and noted. These include the client's general appearance and grooming, voice and speech patterns, the kinds of thoughts described, as well as facial expression, posture, and style of movement.

People with serious problems state facts, opinions, attitudes, and, in some cases, distortions and lies. They behave in a variety of ways: they may sigh, gesture, avert their eyes, tap their feet, smile, or grimace at the interviewer. As a consequence of this flood of responses, the interviewer usually can extract and use only a small percentage of the data presented during the interview. On the other hand, some clients hesitate to discuss their problems openly and provide very little information. Answers to questions such as, "How does your wife get on your nerves?" can differ widely in honesty, clarity, and feeling. Unanticipated reactions by the client must also be noted.

Interviewers need to observe the relationship between their clients' verbal and nonverbal behaviors. Often what interviewers hear contradicts what they see. The client's verbal manner may be calm and dispassionate even though tension is evident from nonverbal signs such as sweating and hand-wringing. In some cases, gestures, movements, and facial expressions yield clues to the sources of a client's anxiety. Experienced clinicians are adept at observing nuances of behavior that clients are unaware of or believe they are suppressing successfully, as can be seen in the following interview:

During the interview she held her small son on her lap. The child began to play with his genitals. The mother, without looking directly at the child, moved his hand away and held it securely for a while. Later in the interview the mother was asked what she ordinarily did when the child played with himself. She replied that he never did this—he was a very "good" boy. She was evidently entirely unconscious of what had transpired in the very presence of the interviewer.

—Maccoby and Maccoby, 1954, p. 484

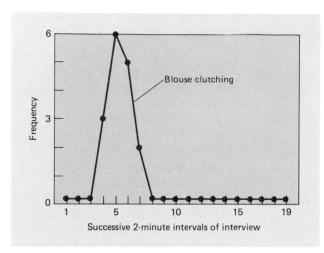

FIGURE 4–2 Frequency of one nonverbal response (blouse clutching) during an interview.

Another interviewer recorded the frequency of a client's "blouse-clutching" behavior during an assessment interview (see Figure 4–2), and noted a particularly high frequency of this behavior during one portion of the interview (Mahl, 1968). The client had at that time been describing how, at the age of 8, she and her twin sister had been told that they had "killed their mother" during their birth.

THE ROLE OF THE INTERVIEWER Every type of assessment involves taking a behavior sample for the purpose of predicting future behavior. Much of the behavior that is sampled in an interview is self-description. To facilitate the planning of treatment, the interviewer must establish valid relationships between the responses made during the interview and the client's behavior in current or future life situations. If the interview behavior is not representative of the client's characteristic response tendencies, inappropriate treatment decisions may be made. The interviewer attempts to construct a situation that, within a short period, provides reflections of complex lifelong patterns.

In most applied settings assessment interviewers make mental and written notes, subjectively interpreting the behavior sample as it unfolds. A truly objective evaluation of an interview, however, cannot focus on the client alone. Each interview involves a developing and distinctive relationship between the interviewer and the client, and their characteristics jointly influence what takes place during the interview. Research supports clinical impressions that interviewers are a major factor in the interview. Are they accurate observers of the client's behavior? Do they unduly influence the behavior of the person being interviewed? These questions arise frequently in discussions of interviewing. Interviewers don't always note or interpret correctly much of what goes on in an interview. The interviewer's behavior may influence the data obtained in an interview as well as how those data are analyzed. This is true for both assessment and therapeutic interviews. The following are some interviewer characteristics that might influence the course of an interview and its content (Beutler and others, 1986):

- age
- gender
- ethnicity
- professional background
- interviewing style
- personality pattern
- attitudes and values
- expectations

As the following case suggests, the unique characteristics and styles that both the client and interviewer bring to the clinical situation make it difficult to perfectly standardize clinical interviews.

The interviewer knew nothing about Robert Hatton except that he was 19 years old, had just begun his studies at a large university, and had a skin condition of apparently recent origin. The skin condition included redness, breaking out in large welts, and itchiness. Hatton had come to the Student Health Service for the skin condition, but the ointment prescribed gave only minor, temporary relief. Because the physician who treated him suspected that the problem might be a result, at least in part, of psychological factors she recommended that he talk with a clinical psychologist who was a consultant on the staff of the Student Health Service to investigate whether any psychological factors were playing a role in his symptoms.

The first thing Hatton mentioned to the psychologist was the skin condition, how annoying and disruptive it was because of the incessant itching, and his puzzlement at being referred to a psychologist. During the initial interview he sweated a lot, occasionally had to catch his breath, and tapped his foot continually. Noting the stigma Hatton seemed to feel about talking with what he called "a mental specialist," the psychologist made the following internal analysis of the situation: "If Robert's skin condition does have a psychological component, he has to learn that it is okay to talk to me. My main job right now is to listen and not to ask a lot of questions that make Robert think he's crazy."

The psychologist did ask some questions ("Have you had skin problems in the past? Under what circumstances?" "How do you like it at the university?"), but mainly she listened patiently, avoiding making quick judgments about what the client had to say, and carefully observed what the client said and did, as well as what topics seemed to be upsetting to him. While avoiding aloofness, the psychologist maintained a detached but friendly attitude. When Hatton expressed concern about his ability to succeed at the university, the clinician did not say, "You're obviously intelligent enough to be very successful at this university," even though Hatton's vocabulary and manner of expressing himself were obviously outstanding. (She mused to herself, "What good would it do if I told Robert what all his friends and relatives tell him? What he is saying is that he's scared and really is worried about flunking out. I've got to let him know I realize what he is going through. The flip reassurance of other people hasn't done him one bit of good.")

The interview was uncomfortable for both Hatton and the psychologist. Hatton was tense, and there were long pauses during which he seemed unable to think of anything to say. Each of these pauses posed a conflict for the interviewer. ("If the pause is too long and too uncomfortable, he might decide not to come to see me again. On the other hand, what clients say after pauses is often very significant. I've got to steer along just the right path with Robert.") The interviewer increased her level of activity whenever she detected that the client was experiencing too much anxiety or felt that he needed a show of interest and support.

The clinical psychologist had seen many cases in which physical problems (such as skin conditions) were related to the stress of university life. But she did not want to pigeonhole Hatton. Her main goal in the initial interview was to establish a relationship of mutual trust with him. She liked him, wanted to help him, and thought she could. But the first task was to accept him as a likable, unique person and hope that he would want to come back. Apparently her approach worked, because Hatton came back four times, as a result of which much information was brought out and the clinical picture became clearer. What emerged was a person of exceptional potential for whom the university created an intense stress because of the need he felt to be worthy of all the sacrifices his family was making for him. While he wanted to reward his parents for their help, he was also deeply angered at the way in which they blithely assumed he would make Phi Beta Kappa if he avoided being lazy.

On the basis of the series of interviews, the psychologist pieced together a picture of an intense stress reaction because of all the pressures to which Hatton felt he was being subjected. The psychologist did not know for sure what had caused the skin condition, but she felt that it might have been an accompaniment of the anxious thoughts connected with going to the university. Her recommendation to Hatton and to the referring physician was that psychotherapy might be helpful. Because the student health service did not provide psychotherapy sessions, the psychologist recommended to Hatton that he see a psychotherapist who might help him decide on his own goals in life, rather than uncritically accept his parents' goals for him. After a series of twenty therapy sessions, Hatton was much less anxious, his skin condition was gone, and he felt more accepting of both himself and his parents.

One important interviewing skill is the ability to size up a situation quickly and to devise an appropriate clinical strategy in light of the assessment. In the following case, the interviewer quickly picked up on the patient's denial of having a problem and turned the focus to how others might have perceived the problem. The 25-year-old patient was a man diagnosed as experiencing a manic episode, a condition marked by a euphoric, hyperactive state and impaired judgment.

Patient:	By the way, before we start, I just wanted to tell you that everything I say, there's no bullshit. It's the truth.
Interviewer:	Why don't we begin by your telling me exactly what it was that got you into the hospital?
Patient:	I was transferred from City Hospital.
Interviewer:	O.K., what got you into that hospital?
Patient:	I was pretending to be an undercover cop.
Interviewer:	You were pretending to be an undercover cop? How come?
Patient:	How come? I had just seen the movie Serpico. And I knew I could do a better job.

Interviewer:	Was it recently that you saw the film?
Patient:	About two months ago.
Interviewer:	This had been going on for some time then?
Patient:	Yeah.
Interviewer:	So, how long has it been since you were last feeling well?
Patient:	Last feeling well? Right now!
Interviewer:	You've been feeling well, then?
Patient:	Oh, yeah. I've been feeling well for the past . . . I've been feeling well for a long time.
Interviewer:	However, going into the hospital means that other people are not certain that you're well.
Patient:	Of course! That's what I've been dealing with.
Interviewer:	Well, then, let's rephrase the question. How long has it been since others have felt that there was something the matter with you?
Patient:	That began about three months ago. I was telling my sister that I could take any amount of cyanide or mescaline, or any other drug, and that it wouldn't have any effect on me at all. She didn't believe me.

THE STRUCTURED INTERVIEW We noted earlier that standardized procedures increase the reliability of classifications of abnormal behavior. This makes a lot of sense, since standardization guarantees that clinicians will at least ask the same questions of each person they interview. An argument against standardized interviews is that they do not give the clinician the flexibility needed to form a productive relationship with a client. However, there is no reason why a clinical worker could not use a standardized format in one interview and a more flexible one in another.

Structured, or **standardized, interviews** use a standard series of questions to determine whether specific symptoms are present. Standardization is achieved by providing the interviewer with a glossary of symptom definitions, a series of questions that are pertinent to symptoms, a set of topics about which information should be obtained, and cut-off points that indicate when to stop probing on a particular topic. The clinician also is given instructions for rating the presence and severity of symptoms in numerical terms. Most structured interviews permit the interviewer to depart from the standardized form under specified circumstances. The interviewer also has the option of pursuing lines of inquiry (including a return to a former line of questioning or a jump to a completely different section) that are suggested by the client's responses.

THE DIAGNOSTIC INTERVIEW SCHEDULE The **Diagnostic Interview Schedule (DIS)** illustrates the potential of the structured interview (Robins and others, 1981). The DIS is designed to permit diagnosis of selected disorders such as panic disorder. A person who has a panic disorder has recurrent anxiety attacks that often occur unpredictably, though certain situations, such as riding on a bus, may become associated with a panic attack. Panic attacks are noted for their frequency, severity, and symptoms, which include sweating, trembling, faintness, and heart palpitations. The section of the DIS that pertains to panic disorder provides the following questions and offers procedures for interpreting the answers and deriving the appropriate classification.

- Did a panic attack occur?
- How many attacks have occurred?
- What are the symptoms?
- Are the attacks repetitive rather than isolated?
- Are the attacks characteristic of the person's life rather than confined to a brief, atypical period?
- At what age did the attacks begin?
- Are the attacks explainable as symptoms of another disorder?
- Is the person tense, nervous, or high-strung between attacks?

The DIS has continued to evolve and now includes procedures, probes, and criteria appropriate for use with specific clusters of symptoms. New clusters are added periodically. Questions are asked not only about symptoms but also about recent and past experiences associated with their onset. For example, in the case of bulimia, whose main symptom is binge eating, questions are asked about the types of food eaten, the respondent's mood during and after the binge, the environment in which the eating is done, how the binges are terminated, associated weight gain, and efforts to prevent weight gain. The onset and most recent occurrence of the disorder are determined from the dates of the first and most recent binges.

The DIS can be employed by professional and nonprofessional interviewers who have been trained in its use. Table 4–4 lists examples of some of the types of interview questions used. Training (a week-long course), supervision, quality control in the use of the interview,

Table 4-4
Examples of Questions Used in Structured Interviews

How old were you the first time you were bothered by these particular fears?

Has there ever been a period of two weeks or more when you felt worthless, sinful, or guilty?

Have you ever gotten into physical fights while drinking?

For how many weeks, months, or years did you continue to have no interest in an activity that had meant a lot to you before?

Has there ever been a period of two weeks or more when you had a lot more trouble concentrating than is normal for you?

Has there ever been a period of two weeks or more when you wanted to die?

and periodic retraining sessions are recommended with the use of the DIS. Programs for computer scoring of interview data are available. Studies are being carried out to determine the feasibility of using computers either to directly administer the DIS or to aid the interviewer in administering it.

Research has shown that both professional and nonprofessional DIS users tend to agree with each other and with the impressions gained by clinicians in non-DIS psychiatric interviews (Helzer and others, 1985). While the goal of an instrument like the DIS is to assess the occurrence of specific symptoms determining whether that goal has been achieved is not a simple matter as there is no objective and absolute standard against which to measure results. Nevertheless, clear specification of diag-

nostic definitions is a major achievement because it makes possible uniform diagnostic methods for diverse populations and places.

Instruments like the DIS, based on specific clinical criteria, have the potential to make comparability across studies a reality. However, much more research will be needed to determine whether this potential can be fully realized. Table 4-5 presents some common sources of error in the use of the DIS. Research on the DIS and similar instruments is proceeding at an accelerating pace. One of the findings of that research is that lay interviewers (that is, nonprofessionals) are able to use the DIS in a reliable fashion and that their judgments tend to agree with those of professionals (Helzer and others, 1987).

Intelligence Tests

Intelligence tests were the first widely recognized psychological assessment tool. During the latter part of the nineteenth century, intelligence was equated with fast reflexes and sensitivity to the environment. Efforts to assess intelligence thus relied heavily on sensory and other discrimination tasks. The English scientist Francis Galton sought to evaluate intelligence by measuring such things as reaction time, ability to discriminate between weights, sensitivity to pain, and ability to differentiate tones.

As the study of intelligence has evolved, it has come to be thought of as having two components: general intelligence, demonstrated by a global capacity to solve problems, and specific abilities, such as spatial perception. In examining intelligence, psychologists have focused on two main areas of interest. One type of interest is theoretical and is broken down into three general

Table 4-5
Sources of Error (Misinformation) in Structured Interviews

Structure of the Interview	1. Lack of specificity in questions asked.
	2. Questions that are too complex (for example, more than one question embedded in a single question).
	3. Too many questions that result in fatigue effects.
The Client	1. Client's need to give socially desirable answers.
	2. Lack of understanding of the questions.
	3. Memory lapses.
	4. Anxiety and emotional arousal resulting in poor attention to some or all questions.
The Interviewer	1. Inability to establish rapport with client.
	2. Insufficient training in use of the structured interview.

categories: what intelligence is, where it comes from, and how it works. The second kind of interest is practical—the goal of constructing tests to measure intelligence that can be used for predicting future achievements. The tests that psychologists construct are related to their theories of intelligence. For example, theories about the relationship between brain damage and perceptual and motor skills have resulted in efforts to measure deficits in these skills (see Figure 4–3).

The Binet Tests In the late nineteenth and early twentieth centuries, the French psychologist Alfred Binet developed a series of tests that differed noticeably from those that had previously been used to measure intelligence. Binet viewed intelligence as something that grows with age; older children are, on the average, more intelligent than younger ones. He sought to measure reasoning, ability to understand and follow directions, and the exercise of judgment or good sense. The child's score on the original Binet test was expressed as a mental level corresponding to the age of normal children whose performance reached the same level.

Later the term "mental age" was substituted for "mental level" and an intelligence quotient (IQ) was computed by dividing the person's test score, or mental age (MA), by his or her chronological age (CA) and multiplying the result by 100. In equation form,

$$IQ = \frac{MA}{CA} \times 100$$

The current test, called the Stanford-Binet scales, has undergone periodic revisions. Stanford-Binet scores are now derived from norms based on how much the individual's score deviates from the mean score for a particular age.

In its first three editions the Binet test yielded one overall score. Use of the Binet-type tests declined beginning in the 1960s, partly because the tasks on the Binet scales did not lend themselves to separate, reliable, quantitative analyses. Perhaps the most important reason for the relative decline in the use of the Binet scales was that they were designed primarily for work with children. As a result of these criticisms, the fourth edition (Stanford-Binet, 1985) yields several different scores, and many of the items have been rewritten to apply to adults as well as children. The new edition resembles the widely used Wechsler tests, discussed below, more than did the earlier editions.

FIGURE 4–3a Perceptual performance in a case of organic brain damage. The Bender Visual-Motor Gestalt Test (1938) is a deceptively simple task in which the subject is asked to copy geometric forms like these.

(From Bender Visual-Motor Gestalt Test, published by American Orthopsychiatric Association, 1938)

FIGURE 4–3b The Bender-Gestalt protocol of a patient suffering from organic brain damage.

(From Lacks [1984], p. 34. Copyright 1984 by John Wiley & Sons. Reprinted by permission.)

(A)

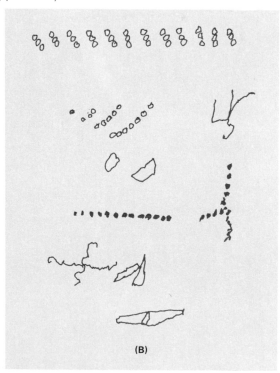

(B)

THE WECHSLER TESTS David Wechsler (1955, 1958) regarded the Binet tests as deficient because they produced only a single score. He believed that intelligence is an aggregate of abilities and should be measured as such. The current version of the Wechsler test for those 16 years and older, **Wechsler Adult Intelligence Scale** (WAIS-R), published in 1981, consists of eleven subtests, of which six are verbal and five nonverbal. An important advantage of a test like the WAIS is that in addition to yielding an aggregate score, each of its subtests can be scored separately.

Three IQs are obtained on the Wechsler scales. **Verbal IQ** reflects level of attainment on subtests dealing with general information, comprehension, ability to think in abstract terms, and arithmetic. **Performance IQ** reflects level of attainment on tasks requiring solution of puzzles, substitution of symbols for digits, and reproduction of designs. Finally, the **Full Scale IQ** represents the total score on the test. The WAIS-R is the most popular test for assessing adult intelligence. It is used in clinical, educational, and vocational evaluations of individuals aged 16 and up (Kaufman, 1990).

The success of Wechsler's Adult Intelligence Scales led to the development of the **Wechsler Intelligence Scale for Children (WISC).** The WISC was developed as a downward extension of the adult level WAIS (see Figure 4–4). It uses the same categories of subtests and

FIGURE 4–4 This child is completing one of the puzzle-like tasks that make up the object assembly subtest of the WISC.

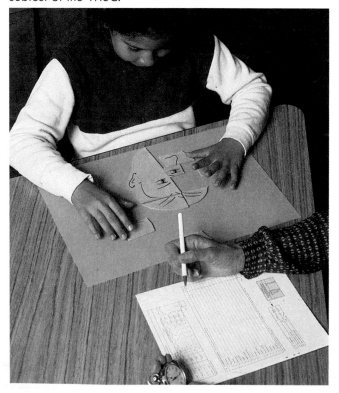

many of the same items as the WAIS with some easier items added. Like the WAIS, it also provides a Verbal IQ, a Performance IQ, and a Full Scale IQ. In addition to these IQ measures, a new set of factor scales was developed for WISC-III. These scales divide the subtests into four groups that provide scores on verbal comprehension, perceptual organization, freedom from distractibility, and information processing speed. These scales are intended to make the test more useful as a diagnostic instrument to pinpoint the source of a child's intellectual strengths and weaknesses. The latest edition of the WISC, WISC-III, published in 1991, updated and revised many items and standardized the instrument with a demographically representative norm sample of 2,200 children between the ages of 6 and 16, with equal numbers of males and females.

For use with even younger children, the **Wechsler Preschool and Primary Scale of Intelligence (WPPSI)** was developed. This test's revision in 1989 (WPPSI-R) improved the instrument's content, broadened its scope, and updated norms. Just as most subtests on the WISC are downward extensions and adaptations of the WAIS, the majority of the subtests on the WPPSI are downward extensions of the WISC subtests. The additional subtests cover the same general skills as subtests on the WAIS and WISC, but the material is presented differently because of the age of the children to be tested. For example, instead of being asked to use blocks to reproduce a series of designs, the child is asked to copy simple designs using a colored pencil. Like the WAIS and the WISC, the WPPSI provides verbal, performance, and full scale scores that then can be converted into IQ scores. The 1989 revision has norms based on a sample of 1,600 children, including 100 boys and 100 girls at each half year age level. The sample was selected to conform with the information in the 1980 census in terms of a variety of variables including geographical area, parent education, and proportion of children enrolled in preschool programs. The construction of test norms used in the WPPSI represents the most sophisticated approach to normative development used so far in any of the Wechsler tests. The age range of the WPPSI-R extends from age 3 to age 7 years. Thus, there is a one-year overlap between the WPPSI-R and the WISC-R. The WPSSI-R is intended for use as a measure of intellectual ability in a wide range of educational and clinical settings. Box 4–1 (on pages 108–9) describes a situation in which testing was recommended and gives an example of a report based on the testing session.

KAUFMAN ASSESSMENT BATTERY FOR CHILDREN The **Kaufman Assessment Battery for Children (K-ABC)** has come into frequent use because of concern about the effects of a child's cultural experiences on test results. The K-ABC is designed to incorporate ideas from cognitive psychology and neuropsychology into the

assessment of intelligence (Kaufman & Kaufman, 1983). The K-ABC consists of 16 subtests, some for older and some for younger children. The tests fall into several categories: sequential processing, such as remembering a series of digits or hand movements; simultaneous processing, such as arranging a series of related pictures in the correct order; and tests that measure school experi-

ence more directly, such as naming pictures of well-known places and objects (see Figure 4–5). Many of the tests do not require a verbal response, and those that do require a few words at most. In most cases, the child can respond by pointing or in other nonverbal ways. The test has been described as a way to learn more about the child's approach to problem-solving and learning tasks.

(a)

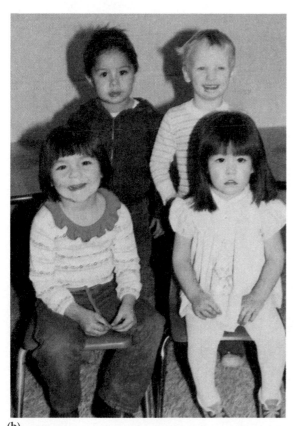

(b)

FIGURE 4–5 Some of the tasks from the Kaufman-ABC. In the Face Recognition subtest, the child is shown a picture of one or two faces such as (a) for five seconds. The child is then asked to select that face or faces from a group picture such as (b). The Gestalt Closure subtest, illustrated by (c), consists of a series of partially completed drawings. The child's task is to name the object pictured, in this case a bicycle. In the Word Order subtest (d) the child is shown a group of pictures and asked to touch them in the order they are named. Later the task is made more difficult by having the examiner name the items and then ask the child to do another task before pointing to the pictures in the correct sequence.

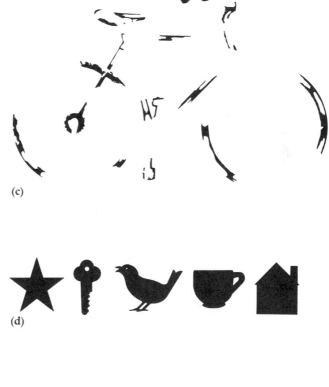

(c)

(d)

The test's emphasis on short-term memory has been questioned by some critics, but the test authors argue that what is being measured is not memory as such but the sequential and simultaneous processing abilities that are defined as intelligence by cognitive psychologists.

Although the K-ABC tests have been described as being particularly fair to minority children, scores on these tests show the same black–white differences that

BOX 4–1 Intelligence Tests and Report Writing

Table 4–6
Information That May Be Contributed by a Tester's Behavioral Observations

What do testers notice? In addition to the test responses themselves, testers are attentive to how clients approach tasks, their emotional reactions, and how they relate to the tester. These are some of the behavioral observations the tester may note and use in writing a case report.

1. How persistent is the client? Keeps trying? Gives up easily?
2. Is the client able to concentrate on the task at hand?
3. What is the client's attitude toward the test? Casual or serious? Competitive?
4. What is the client's problem-solving style? Methodical? Reasoned? Impulsive? Fragmented?
5. What emotions does the client exhibit? Is he or she anxious about being tested? Angry? Depressed?
6. How does the client react to failure or possible failure? Gets upset at failures? Expects to fail?
7. How does the client react to the tester? As an authority figure? As an adversary?
8. How verbally expressive is the client? Articulate? Monosyllabic?

Intelligence tests yield scores whose interpretation depends on the characteristics of the person tested (for example, is he or she depressed?) and behavioral observations of the individual made by the tester (such as whether the person is paying attention

or has trouble seeing or hearing test instructions). A useful report of test results helps the evaluator place the scores in the context of the individual's current situation. Table 4–6 lists some of the questions a tester may consider while administering an intelligence test.

In addition to presenting quantitative information, a report of an intelligence test makes use of the tester's behavioral observations, interprets the test scores, and offers pertinent recommendations. The following write up typifies a report based on a WPPSI-R given to a kindergartner.

Blue Grove Community School Corporation Report of WPPSI-R Testing

Date: May 7, 1990
Name: Aaron James
Date Tested: April 13 and 28, 1990
Date of Birth: June 6, 1984
Chronological Age: 5 years 10 months 7 days
Sex: Male
School: Blue Grove Elementary
Grade: Kindergarten
Teacher: Mrs. Davis
Parent: Mr. and Mrs. Michael James
Address: 123 Oak Drive, Blue Grove, IN
Telephone: 996-7291
Referred by: Teacher
Examiner: Dr. Theresa Stark

Reason for Referral
Aaron was referred for testing by his teacher because of learning difficulties. According to his teacher, he has a short attention span and gets frustrated easily. His teacher would like to know why he can't comprehend ver-

bal directions and why he needs one-to-one explanations.

Background Information
Aaron is a 5 year, 10 month old male who lives with his mother and father and two older brothers. He attended a preschool program and is presently in kindergarten. Pre-kindergarten screening results did not indicate any readiness problems. Aaron has received extra individual help with letter recognition and printing from the teacher's aide since October.

According to his mother, developmental milestones of sitting alone, crawling, standing alone, and walking alone were age appropriate. First words and short sentences were late. Aaron seemed less mature than his older brothers when he started kindergarten, according to his mother. No significant medical history is noted in his health record or reported by his parents.

Aaron was described by his mother as an excellent child to take anywhere because he will sit quietly and patiently. His father described him as unhappy and very quiet. His teacher described him as lacking in self-confidence because he often asks other students for confirmation that he is doing something correctly.

Concerning social behaviors, Aaron's teacher stated that he gets along well with others. It was also noted by his mother that he gets along well with others.

Behavioral Observations
Aaron was tested on April 13 and 28, 1990, at Blue Grove Elementary. Aaron came to the testing situation with a positive manner and was cooperative with the examiner. During testing his attention was focused. On difficult tasks he was persistent. During testing Aaron's attitude toward the

are seen on other intelligence tests. However, the K-ABC tests do demonstrate that if parental education is taken into account there is little racial or ethnic difference on many nonverbal reasoning tasks. When the education of the parents is taken into account, blacks of preschool age and Hispanics of preschool and school age perform as well as whites. These similarities are due primarily to the tests' emphasis on short term memory.

examiner showed an eagerness to please. Aaron's attitude toward his own performance was characterized as confident and he responded to directions appropriately. He appeared to view both the performance and verbal tasks as enjoyable. Rapport was easy to establish and easy to maintain.

Aaron's mother reported no motor, visual, or hearing impairments and that Aaron is not taking any medication which would affect test performance. Aaron's dominant language is English, and English is spoken in the home. During testing he demonstrated left hand dominance. Speech was observed to be fluent and articulate. No unusual behaviors were observed.

Considering these observations, the results of this evaluation are believed to represent an accurate estimation of Aaron's current level of functioning.

Test Results

Composite	IQ	Classification
Performance	104	Average
Verbal	86	Low Average
Full Scale	94	Average

Test Interpretation

Aaron obtained an IQ of 94 +/−6 on the Wechsler Preschool and Primary Scale of Intelligence–Revised. The chances that the range of scores from 88 to 100 includes his true IQ are about 95 out of 100. According to the classification ratings for the Wechsler Scales, Aaron is in the average range of intelligence.

There was a significant difference ($p<.05$) between the Performance Score of 104 and the Verbal Score of 86. Approximately 20 out of 100 chil-

dren the same age as Aaron would have such a difference in scores. This difference indicates that Aaron did better on tasks requiring perceptual organization and nonverbal responses than he did on tasks involving verbal comprehension and a spoken response.

Aaron's score on the Object Assembly subtest was significantly higher ($p<.05$) than his mean Performance Score and his mean Full Scale Score. This task required him to assemble a puzzle picturing a common object. His high score would suggest a strength with seeing the whole from its visual components. His score on the Similarities subtest was significantly lower ($p<.05$) than his mean Verbal Score and his mean Full Scale Score. This task required him to form analogies and demonstrate an understanding of the concept of similarity. His low score would suggest a weakness in verbalizing relationships.

By looking at patterns of scores on the various subtests of the WPPSI-R, it is hypothesized that Aaron's relative strengths are with tasks requiring the integration of numerous sources of information into a whole, visual perception of meaningful drawings (cars, people, animals, etc.), and a flexible problem solving style. It is hypothesized that Aaron's relative weaknesses are with tasks involving verbal concepts, reasoning ability with abstract categories, word definitions, the ability to compare/contrast and categorize words, verbal communication, and the ability to reason with words.

Summary

Aaron is a five year old boy of average intelligence who was referred for testing because of learning difficulties. Aaron appears to be more successful with tasks involving perceptual organization than verbal comprehension.

Recommendations

The following recommendations are based on background information and present test data.

1. Although no current hearing impairment was reported, an audiological screening and a review of Aaron's medical history for possible ear infections is suggested because of the discrepancy between verbal and performance test results.

2. Aaron should be evaluated by a speech and language clinician for receptive and expressive language abilities.

3. Further testing with an individual achievement measure and an assessment of basic conceptual knowledge.

4. Work with Aaron's parents to have them encourage his communication skills. For example, Aaron can retell the events of his school day at the supper table. The re-telling of short stories or simple riddles could be done while riding in the car.

5. Practice new skills at home and school in several different ways. For example, in order to learn the letter names, Aaron may finger paint them, write them with markers or crayons, construct them with "play-dough" ropes, practice them with flash cards, and point to them on cereal boxes and signs.

6. Plan a multidisciplinary conference to evaluate Aaron's current level of functioning and plan appropriate educational programming.

Dr. Theresa Stark
School Psychologist
NCSP #13-089

Personality Assessment

Research on personality has stimulated the development of a variety of tests, rating scales, and questionnaires aimed at measuring personality differences. These devices can be useful shortcuts to understanding behavior. Think how long it takes you to get to know a person; in many situations psychologists do not have that kind of time.

Personality tests and other assessment methods are used in clinical settings in making diagnoses, in deciding whether treatment is required, and in planning the treatment to be used. Personality tests may also be used in selecting employees. A third major use of personality measures is in psychological research, where the tests may be used as either independent or dependent variables. For example, as an independent variable, scores on a measure of test anxiety—that is, the feeling of tenseness and worry that people experience before an exam—might be used to divide people into groups according to how upset they get while taking exams. Researchers have investigated whether more test-anxious students behave differently than less anxious ones in an experimental situation. A less common use of personality tests is as a dependent variable to measure the effect of some experimental treatment. One group of subjects might see a war movie showing violent battle scenes while another views a nature film. A personality test might then be used to determine which group had the higher aggression score.

PERSONALITY INVENTORIES The success of intelligence tests in predicting future achievement led researchers to try to develop similar ways to measure personality. But personality isn't something that can be measured by a total score that is high, medium, or low. The testlike measures used in personality assessment are meant to indicate the types of characteristics that combine to make up an individual's personality.

Rather than testing general knowledge or specific skills, **personality inventories** ask people questions about themselves. These questions may take a variety of forms. When taking such a test, you might have to decide whether each of a series of statements is accurate as a self-description, or you might be asked to respond to a series of true–false questions about yourself and the world. Several inventories require the respondent to rate a set of statements on a scale based on how well they reflect his or her characteristics. Modern personality inventories yield several scores, each of which is intended to represent a distinct aspect of the personality.

Since its introduction in 1943, the **Minnesota Multiphasic Personality Inventory (MMPI)** has been one of the most widely used psychological tests. A revision, entitled MMPI-2, was published in 1989; it consists of 567 items. In developing MMPI-2, the wording of many of the original MMPI items was updated and a number of items were dropped, changed, or added. The standardization of MMPI-2 was superior to that of the original MMPI because of the new normative sample's larger size, geographic representativeness, and racial balance. Although there is still much work to be done in analyzing the MMPI-2, it appears to be a successful revision and should be used as widely as the original MMPI (Graham, 1990).

The MMPI-2 includes ten scales related to different groups of clinical disorders (the scales are usually referred to by the abbreviations in parentheses): hypochondriasis (Hs), depression (D), hysteria (Hy), psychopathic deviate (Pd), masculinity-femininity (Mf), paranoia (Pa), psychasthenia (Pt), schizophrenia (Sc), hypomania (Ma), and social introversion (Si). In addition to these standard clinical scales, there are numerous special scales—for example, the 16-item Anger scale reflects irritability, impatience, grouchiness, and hotheadedness. People who sometimes feel like swearing or smashing things may get high scores on this scale (Butcher, 1990). Scores on MMPI-2 scales can be compared with those of the normal standardization group and samples of reliably diagnosed clinical cases.

Besides the clinical scales, the MMPI-2 also includes several validity or control scales. These were designed to assess test-taking attitudes and response biases that might distort the picture presented by the clinical scale scores alone. High scores on these scales may indicate invalid clinical scale profiles. The validity scales consider the tendency of people to create a favorable impression, and consist of items dealing with minor flaws and weaknesses to which most people are willing to admit. People with high L (or Lie) scores appear impossibly good and virtuous. The F scale (or validity score) was designed to detect deviant or atypical ways of responding to test items. High scores on this scale indicate that people describe themselves as having a number of rare and improbable characteristics. While the F scale was included to reflect people's carelessness and confusion in taking the MMPI, it has also come to be seen as a good indicator of psychopathology.

The K scale (or defensiveness score) is more subtle than the L and F scales and covers several different content areas in which a person can deny problems (for example, suspiciousness, worry). Its construction was based on the observation that some open and frank people may obtain high scores on the clinical scales while others who are very defensive may obtain low scores. The K scale was devised to reduce these biasing factors. People who get high K scores are defensive; they tend to answer "False" to items like "I feel bad when others criticize me." K corrections are made on a number of clinical scales in order to compare the scores obtained by people who differ in these tendencies.

In addition to the L, F, and K scales that were part of the original MMPI, MMPI-2 has three new validity scales. The Fb scale is intended to reflect a subject's tendency to answer later items in the test booklet differently than those that occur earlier. The VRIN scale provides an indication of subjects' tendencies to respond inconsistently to MMPI-2 items. Inconsistencies can result when subjects do not read the content of the items and respond instead in a random or near random way. The TRIN scale was developed to identify subjects who respond indiscriminately by giving either mainly true responses (acquiescence) or mainly false responses (non-acquiescence) without taking into account the meaning of the item statement.

Table 4–7 describes the MMPI-2's clinical and validity scales. The principal application of the MMPI-2 is in deciding how to classify a given case. In general, the greater the number and magnitude of deviant scores on the MMPI-2, the more likely it is that the individual is severely disturbed. In making diagnostic decisions, the MMPI-2 user must be adept at interpreting not only the scores on the individual scales but also the pattern of those scores in a particular person's profile. For example,

the assessor cannot assume that a high score on the schizophrenia scale indicates the presence of schizophrenia. Other psychotic groups may show high elevation on this scale, and schizophrenics often score higher on other scales than on the Sc scale.

RATING SCALES There are many other personality assessment techniques. The **rating scale** is one of the most venerable and versatile of these. Rating scales present respondents with a question that focuses on a concept, person, or situation, and ask them to select from a number of choices. The rating scale is similar in some respects to a multiple choice test, but its options represent degrees of a particular characteristic.

An example of a rating scale item is "To what degree are you shy?" People might be asked to place this item on a scale ranging from "Not at all" to "Extremely." They can do this graphically by placing a check mark at an appropriate point on a continuum. Rating scales can be used to rate other people's behavior as well as one's own. For instance, a teacher might use rating scales to rate his or her students. In this case the item above might read "To what degree is this student shy?" An example of this use of rating scales in clinical work is the assessment

Table 4–7

The MMPI-2: Clinical and Validity Scales

The name, abbreviation, and number of each scale is given. (Clinical workers typically refer to the clinical scales by number rather than by name or abbreviation.) Interpretations are given for high scores on the scales.

Clinical Scales

NAME AND ABBREVIATION	SCALE NUMBER	INTERPRETATION OF HIGH SCORES
Hypochondriasis (Hs)	1	Bodily preoccupation; pessimistic
Depression (D)	2	Depressed; lacks self-confidence
Hysteria (Hy)	3	Psychologically motivated physical symptoms; lacks insight
Psychopathic deviate (Pd)	4	Antisocial tendencies: impulsive
Masculinity–femininity (Mf)	5	Sex-role conflict
Paranoia (Pa)	6	Suspiciousness; resentful
Psychasthenia (Pt)	7	Anxiety; insecure
Schizophrenia (Sc)	8	Bizarre thinking; withdrawn
Hypomania (Ma)	9	Excessive psychomotor activity; unrealistic goals
Social introversion (Si)	0	Social anxiety; shy

Validity Scales

L scale	—	Need to present unrealistically favorable impression
F scale	—	Severe psychological disturbance
K scale	—	Defensiveness; inhibited
Fb scale	—	Inattention to some items
VRIN scale	—	Inconsistent responses
TRIN scale	—	Acquiescence or nonacquiescence biases

of children's ability to pay attention to what is going on around them and to exercise self-control. The degree to which children possess these abilities is an indicator of their personal development. Many clinical problems in children are related to the inability to delay responding until the desired time, to plan activities, and to engage in socially appropriate behavior. Kendall and Wilcox (1978) devised a convenient series of rating scales to assess children's self-control. Their measure, the **Behavior Rating Scale for Children,** has proven reliable and can be used in a variety of settings and by untrained observers such as parents.

The Behavior Rating Scale for Children presents the rater with 33 questions, each of which is responded to on a 7-point rating scale (1 = always, 7 = never). The following are some representative items from the scale.

- Does the child sit still?
- Does the child disrupt games?
- Does the child think before he or she acts?

- Does the child grab for the belongings of others?
- Is the child easily distracted from his or her work or chores?

Another type of rating scale, the **visual analogue scale (VAS)** has been used in clinical and research settings to measure a variety of subjective phenomena, such as pain, anxiety, and craving for substances such as cigarettes. One or several VASs might be used in a given study. A VAS provides a convenient, easy, and rapidly-administered measurement strategy (Wewers & Lowe, 1990). However, the applicability of these scales is limited by subjects' ability to conceptually understand the method itself, that is, to provide a representation of a personal perception of an abstract concept as a linear unit. Figure 4–6 shows examples of different types visual analogue scales that measure pain and anxiety.

Rating scales, like self-report questionnaires, are not immune to inaccuracy. One possible biasing factor, the **halo effect,** results when an individual rates a person more favorably than is realistic on a specific characteristic

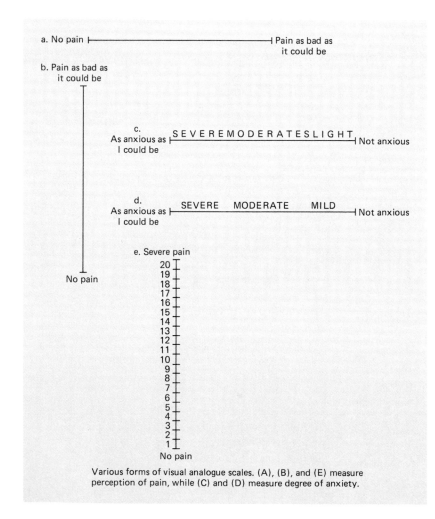

FIGURE 4–6 Various forms of visual analogue scales. (a), (b), and (e) measure perception of pain, while (c) and (d) assess the degree of anxiety.

Various forms of visual analogue scales. (A), (B), and (E) measure perception of pain, while (C) and (D) measure degree of anxiety.

(a)

(b)

FIGURE 4–7a As the client responds to the Rorschach card, the clinician records both verbal responses and behavior.

FIGURE 4–7b This inkblot, similar to those used in the Rorschach test, produced a variety of responses, including: 1. "Looks like a long tunnel or channel in the center." 2. "On its side, I see a crabby old man frowning, with a long nose. I don't like him." 3. "There is a head of a camel in the middle there—no body, just the head."

because the rater has a generally favorable reaction to the person. Other methodological problems include the tendency to want to say only nice things about oneself or someone else, and the tendency to use the midrange of the scales. Research has shown that many of these problems can be reduced through careful wording of items, instructions to the rater, use of minimally ambiguous concepts and scales, and in some cases, actual training in making ratings (Anastasi, 1988).

PROJECTIVE TECHNIQUES One group of assessment specialists believes that the more freedom people have in picking their responses, the more meaningful the description and classification that can be obtained. Because personality inventories do not permit much freedom of choice, some clinical psychologists prefer to use **projective techniques,** in which a person is shown ambiguous stimuli and asked what he or she thinks they are about. Some clinicians believe that projective techniques are very sensitive to unconscious dimensions of personality. Defense mechanisms, latent impulses, and anxieties have all been inferred from data gathered in projective situations.

The **Rorschach inkblots,** developed by the Swiss psychiatrist Hermann Rorschach (1884–1922), consist of ten cards, half colored and half black and white (see Figure 4–7). The test is administered by showing the cards, one at a time, and asking the person to describe what he or she sees in them. There are no right or wrong answers. After the person has reponded to the inkblots in

a free-association manner, the examiner asks questions about particular responses ("What gave you that impression?" "What made it seem like a _____?"). Besides recording what is said in response to the inkblots, the examiner also notes the person's mannerisms, gestures, and attitudes. Figure 4–8 offers a lighter view of the Rorschach test and its origins.

FIGURE 4–8

(Drawing by R. Chast; © 1989 The New Yorker Magazine, Inc.)

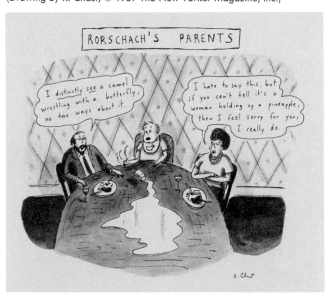

Rorschach developed the inkblot test as part of an experimental effort to relate perception to personality. He believed that people's responses to inkblots could serve as clues to their basic personality traits. However, negative research findings have caused many users of protective techniques to become dubious about the validity of the Rorschach inkblots as perceptual indicators of personality (Anastasi, 1988). Even if the inkblots are useless for this purpose, however, the test can be used in analyzing people's social behavior and the content of their verbal productions. Attempts to elicit assistance from the examiner and the use of stereotyped verbal responses are examples of the types of behavior that can be observed in the Rorschach situation (Aronow & Reznikoff, 1983). A number of attempts have also been made to develop a Rorschach scoring system that is more psychometrically sound. One ambitious effort to provide a uniform system for interpreting the Rorschach has been developed by Exner and his colleagues (Wiener-Levy & Exner, 1981). Research that has been completed so far suggests that the use of this system permits comparability among findings of different researchers.

Like the Rorschach test, the **Thematic Appreception tion Test (TAT)** employs ambiguous stimuli to which people can respond in a free manner. The TAT uses pictures that show people engaging in a variety of activities; hence, it is less ambiguous than the Rorschach inkblots. The total test consists of 30 picture cards and one blank card, although in most test situations not all of the cards are used. The cards are presented one at a time, and the client is asked to make up a story describing the scene in each picture, the events that led up to that scene, and the events that will grow from it. The client is also asked to describe the thoughts and feelings of the people in the story. As the client looks at the card and tells the story, the clinician not only records the story itself but notes behavior such as pauses, facial expressions, and changes in tone of voice.

Henry A. Murray (1893–1988), the author of the TAT (Murray, 1936), described the picture in Figure 4–9 (Card 12-F) as a portrait of a young woman, with a weird old woman grimacing in the background. Following is a story about that picture that was told by a 37-year-old woman who was diagnosed as a paranoid schizophrenic and was also depressed. How might her story be interpreted? Note the perceptual distortion that changed the usual mother–daughter relationship into a father–son relationship. (The examiner's questions are indicated in parentheses).

It's an old man standing behind a young man thinking, or knows what this young man should do, what he has ahead of him. He is

FIGURE 4–9 Cards from the Thematic Appreception Test are more structured than the Rorschach stimuli yet they also produce many different responses. This card produced the two very different stories in the text.

very tired [old man] and the young man has a lot more—I can't explain it. The young man hasn't had the experience and gone through as much as the old man. That's all I think of now. (Relationship?) There is no relationship. I said father and son though didn't I? (Related?) No. (Happening?) They're both concentrating on life. (Explain?) Well, the old man, as I said, is concentrating on what the young man has ahead of him. (?) Whatever he chooses. (What did old man go through?) He looked like he had gone through suffering. (Explain?) Suffering from living. (?) Working hard. (Else?) No. (?) Well, I thought of other things. The trouble he'd had. (?) Family troubles. (Story!) They lived way out in a lonely place, worked and existed. Nothing much to do, and they became very tired, and that's all.

—Schafer, 1948, pp. 188–189

Here is the response to the same card that was given by a 27-year-old married woman who would probably be diagnosed as having an anxiety disorder. How does it compare with the first response?

[Shakes head, swallows.] The old woman must be either the mother or the grandmother of the young woman. The young woman has a strong face. She has lots of character. The old woman has a sly expression on her face or around her mouth. If it wasn't for that expression on her face, I might try to interpret it. I can't imagine why she looks that way. The old woman looks like she worked hard all her life. (?) I don't know, just can't imagine. If this old lady had a different expression on her face, say, one of worry . . . (?) Then I'd say she must be cherishing a lot of ambitions for the girl. Maybe she would be hoping that the girl would do things she always wanted to do. Maybe her ambitions would be realized in this woman.

—Schafer, 1948, p. 258

Clinical interpretation of a TAT story usually begins with an effort to determine the character with whom the person seems to have identified. Attention is paid to such variables as the person's behavior in the testing situation, characteristics of his or her utterances, the way the stories are told, the stories' emotional tone, and the conscious and unconscious needs that are revealed by the story content.

Whereas Rorschach viewed his test as an experimental perceptual task, Murray conceived of the TAT as a probe of the unconscious. Most contemporary users of projective techniques such as these consider them to be methods of tapping unconscious processes, an emphasis that is derived largely from the influence of psychoanalytic theory. Some psychotherapists use TAT responses as clues to hidden problem areas that require in-depth exploration.

In addition to the Rorschach and the TAT, many types of tasks are used as projective stimuli. In a **word-association test,** for example, a list of words is presented one at a time, and the client is asked to respond with the first word or idea that comes to mind. Clinicians are most interested in how long it takes a person to respond and how unusual the associations are. The **sentence-completion technique** is a logical extension of word associations. Here the subject is presented with a series of incomplete sentences and asked to complete them. Sentence-completion methods are typically analyzed in terms of the attitudes, conflicts, and motives reflected in them. The following are typical sentence stems.

- I worry about _____.
- My mother _____.
- What makes me mad is _____.
- My greatest regret is _____.

Other widely used projective methods include asking people to draw pictures of themselves and others, to finger paint, or to tell stories. These approaches have been used as means of increasing knowledge about fantasy, its determinants, and its behavioral correlates. At times their clinical application has been based more on theoretical usefulness than on objectively demonstrated validity. Researchers who are concerned with the evaluation of clinical tools continue to study these techniques.

Behavioral Assessment

Behavioral assessment has grown out of the behavioral-therapy movement. It is often used to identify response deficits, which are then treated through the use of behavioral methods such as reinforcement schedules and modeling. Clinicians often use behavioral observations to get information that cannot be obtained by other means. Examples of such observations include the frequency of a particular type of response, such as physical attacks on others on the school playground, or observations by teachers of certain behaviors of a school child such as frequent interruptions in the classroom. In either case, observational data must meet the same standards of reliability as data obtained by more formal measures.

Consider the case of a 10-year-old boy who, according to his teacher, is doing poorly in his schoolwork and, according to his parents, is difficult to manage at home and doesn't get along with other children. In addition to using a measure of the boy's general intelligence, which might help to explain his poor schoolwork, personality tests, which might reveal trends that are related to his inadequate social relationships, an interview with him to provide insights into his view of the problem, and an interview with his parents since the boy's poor behavior in school may be symptomatic of problems at home, behavioral assessments could add valuable information. Appropriate types of behavioral observations might include observations of his activities and response patterns in school; observations of his behavior in a specially created situation, such as a playroom with many interesting toys and games; and observations of his behavior at home while he is interacting with one or both of his parents and while he is playing alone or with friends.

Making all of these assessments would be a major undertaking and not practical under most circumstances. Because of the variety of data that are potentially available, the assessor must decide which types of information are most feasible and desirable under a given

set of circumstances. In most cases, the clinician is interested in both subjective and objective information. Subjective information includes what clients think about, the emotions they experience, and their worries and preoccupations. Interviews, personality inventories, and projective techniques provide indications of subjective experience, although considerable clinical judgment is needed to infer what is going on within the client from the way he or she responds to a test. Objective information includes the person's observable behavior and usually does not require the assessor to draw complex inferences about such topics as attitudes toward parents, unconscious wishes, and deep-seated conflicts. Behavioral assessment is directed toward this type of observation (see Figure 4–10).

THE ASSESSMENT FOCUS The following are some of the questions likely to be covered in behavioral assessments. Notice the absence of references to unconscious motivations or intrapsychic tensions.

1. What is the problem as described by the clinician?
2. Who are the people involved in the problem (for example, parents, spouse)?
3. Under what circumstances is the problem most in evidence?
4. What reinforcers contribute to maintenance of the problematic behavior?
5. What is the developmental history of the problem?
6. What are the assets and liabilities of the client's behavioral repertoire?
7. How modifiable are aspects of the client's situation that bear on the problem, and how can modification be made?

Baseline, or **operant, observations** are a type of behavioral observation that is becoming increasingly popular. These are recordings of response frequencies in particular situations before any treatment intervention has been made. They can be used in several ways. Observations might be made simply to describe a person's response repertoire at a given time. For example, the number of aggressive responses made by children of different ages might be recorded. Such observations also provide a baseline for judging the effectiveness of behavior modification techniques. A similar set of observations, made after behavior modification procedures have been used, could be compared with the baseline measurement as a way of determining how well the therapy worked. For example, here are some questions that behavioral observations of schoolchildren can answer concerning the effectiveness of a special program to

(a)

FIGURE 4–10a This child's aggressive behavior in a playroom situation is being rated by observers through a one-way mirror. Behavioral observations made in a controlled environment are helpful to clinicians because they make comparisons among children more meaningful.

FIGURE 4–10b Children's behavior can also be observed in a natural setting. Aggressive behavior on a playground can be rated by observers. Because the situation is less standardized and other children are involved, these naturalistic ratings may be less easily compared. At the same time, the observed behavior may give important information about the child's everyday behaviors.

(b)

train teachers in the handling of children with particular types of behavioral problems:

1. Is the student engaged in an activity other than schoolwork?
2. Is the student looking around and not engaged in any other activity?
3. Is the student interacting with one or more other students?
4. Is the student interacting with the classroom teacher?

Cognitive Assessment

Just as it is important to know what a person does and how his or her behavior affects other people, it is also necessary to assess the thoughts that may lie behind the behavior. **Cognitive assessment** provides information about thoughts that precede, accompany, and follow maladaptive behavior. It also provides information about the effects of procedures whose goal is to modify both how someone thinks about a problem and how he or she behaves.

Cognitive assessment can be carried out in a variety of ways. For example, questionnaires have been developed to sample people's thoughts after an upsetting event. Electronic beepers have been used to signal subjects to record their thoughts at certain times of the day. There are also questionnaires to assess the directions people give themselves while working on a task and their theories about why things happen as they do.

Cognitions play an important role when a person is trying to concentrate on an intellectual task (see Figure 4–11). Anyone who has taken exams knows that worrying about one's ability, the possibility of failure, and what other students might be doing interferes with effective performance. But while thoughts that reflect worry have undesirable effects, thoughts that are directed toward the task at hand are helpful. The Cognitive Interference Questionnaire (Sarason & Stoops, 1978) was developed to assess the degree to which people working on important tasks have thoughts that interfere with their concentration. Subjects respond to the questionnaire by indicating how often thoughts like the following ones enter their minds while they are working on an assigned task.

- I thought about how others have done on this task.
- I thought about things completely unrelated to this task.
- I thought about how poorly I was doing.
- I thought about something that made me angry.
- I thought about something that happened earlier in the day.

The assessment of thoughts and ideas is a relatively new development. It has received impetus from the

FIGURE 4–11 People have different kinds of thoughts while taking an exam. Worries or thoughts that are unrelated to the exam interfere with good performance.

growing evidence that thought processes and the content of thoughts are related to emotions and behavior (Booth–Butterfield, 1991). Cognitive assessment provides information about adaptive and maladaptive aspects of people's thoughts and the role thoughts play in the processes of planning, making decisions, and interpreting reality.

Relational Assessment

Maladaptive behavior always occurs in some environmental context. One person might hallucinate only when other people are not present. Another person might become angry, and even violent, only when in the presence of certain other individuals. Because of the importance of an individual's social context, this book emphasizes an interactional approach to abnormal psychology that directs attention to the interrelationships among personal and situational variables. Our relationships with other people are important types of contextual variables; clinicians thus recognize the importance of making **relational assessments,** or evaluating key relationships, such as those within a family. Families are complex units of people who, while they may be alike in some ways, are unique individuals each with a particular set of needs, behavioral styles, emotions, and beliefs about themselves and the world in which they live (see Figure 4–12).

Clinicians try to develop ways of characterizing a

FIGURE 4–12

(Drawing by R. Chast; © 1987 The New Yorker Magazine, Inc.)

person's social relationships, both with the outside environment and with other individuals. In Chapter 5 we will discuss measures of social support that assess how supportive a person perceives the environment to be. In addition to this global sense of support, information is needed about specific features of a person's key close relationships. Each person can be viewed as one component of the numerous two-or-more-person interactions that fill daily activity. How does the person function in these interactions? What are his or her relational or interpersonal skills?

The family is one of the most powerful interactional systems affecting all people. To conceptualize patients without considering the dynamics of their family is to see half a picture at best. To plan treatment without considering the needs and opinions of the patient's family might represent an invitation to treatment failure. Moreover, whether clinicians admit it or not, the patient's family is often psychologically present, representing a powerful determining force in the patient's behavior. For this reason, interviewers need to make some type of assessment that gathers information about both individual family members and the family as a system. The following topics about the family might be brought up in a clinical interview.

- What were holidays like at your house?
- Who makes the decisions in your family?
- What kinds of things did your brothers and sisters like to do?
- Tell me a little about what kinds of things your parents used to argue about?

Because of the important role the family plays in shaping personality and the development of maladaptive behavior, researchers are beginning to develop ways of objectively measuring close relationships, such as those within a family. For example, Pierce (Pierce and others, 1991) has developed the *Quality of Relationships Inventory* to assess various aspects of close relationships with specific people (for example, with family members, romantic partners, or friends). This inventory obtains quantified responses from subjects to such questions as:

- To what extent could you turn to your mother for advice about problems?
- How much does your father like you?
- How much does your mother want you to change?
- How critical of you is your brother?
- How often does your sister make you angry?

Another relational assessment tool, the *Family Environment Scale* (Moos, 1974), asks subjects to de-

scribe the overall social climate within their families by responding to items like these:

- There are a lot of spontaneous discussions in our family.
- In our family each person has different ideas about what is right and wrong.
- In our family, we are strongly encouraged to be independent.

Clinicians can use the results of these assessments to understand more about the client's social network. If several family or network members complete these measures, the clinician has a better idea of how representative the client's views are of the quality of the relationships and the general atmosphere in the immediate social environment. If the client is being treated in a family setting, with other family members present at therapy sessions, the measures give the clinician valuable clues about family relationships.

Bodily Assessment

Another insight into clients' feelings and motivations is their expressive behavior. Clinicians pay particular attention to the nonverbal messages received through **bodily assessment.** Bodily functions may also reflect motivations and concerns, and some clinicians take note of these as well. Sophisticated devices have been developed to measure such physiological changes as pupil dilation, blood pressure, and electrical skin responses under specific conditions.

Technological advances are making it possible to monitor an individual's physiological state on a continuous basis. Sweat, heart rate, blood volume, the amounts of different substances in the bloodstream, and blood pressure can all be recorded and correlated with the presence or absence of certain psychological conditions such as stress. Although the automated assessment of bodily processes that are pertinent to behavior disorders is just getting under way, this approach seems promising.

An example of the use of automated assessment can be seen in the measurement of blood pressure. It is now possible to measure blood pressure while a person is engaged in everyday activities. This represents a considerable advance, since resting blood pressure readings may not give a full picture of changes in pressure or provide an accurate 24-hour average. Ambulatory monitors can show changes in a patient's blood pressure throughout the day and during sleep (see Figure 4–13a). Such data are useful in diagnosing cases of high blood pressure in which cognitive and behavioral factors play important roles. They may also be important in the selection and evaluation of treatment programs.

Figure 4–13b shows the pattern of blood pressure changes for a 45-year-old woman during a typical day. The patient had been diagnosed as having chronically elevated blood pressure, but as the figure shows, the readings actually covered a wide range. Other studies of patients who had been diagnosed as having high blood pressure have shown that blood pressure readings taken in the doctor's office may be significantly higher than readings taken during normal activity, even though the office readings are usually taken after a period of rest.

Another measure of emotional response is the **polygraph,** or lie detector. It records physiological reactions (heart rate, blood pressure, respiration rate, and galvanic skin response). Its use has been criticized because it violates the right of privacy and the right to avoid self-incrimination. Even more important, questions have been raised about its reliability and validity. Criminal cases suggest that the accuracy of the polygraph in judging guilt can be made with 75- to 97-percent accuracy, but the rate of false-positives (people who are innocent but whose polygraph records suggest guilt) is too high to use the polygraph as the sole basis of

FIGURE 4–13a The portable blood pressure monitor allows a person's blood pressure to be recorded automatically at predetermined times without interfering with his or her normal daily activities.

(a)

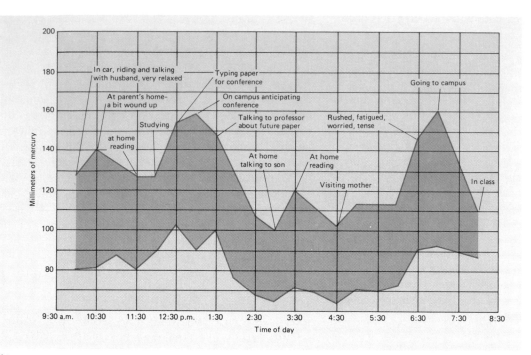

(b)

FIGURE 4–13b An ambulatory blood pressure monitor was used to record the changes in a 45-year-old woman's blood pressure during a one-day period. The chart is annotated with descriptions of the subject's daily activities. The top line charts systolic blood pressure and the bottom line diastolic blood pressure. Systolic pressure represents the higher point in the blood pressure cycle as the heart contracts and sends blood through the circulatory system. Diastolic pressure represents the low point in the pressure cycle, which occurs as the heart fills with blood.

(Werdegar et al., 1967, p. 103)

FIGURE 4–14 Polygraph tracing for one psychiatric patient. Stimulus words are numbered.

(Abrams, 1973, p. 95)

determining guilt or innocence (Council on Scientific Affairs, 1986).

Research might suggest novel applications of the polygraph in the field of mental health. For example, it may be possible to use the polygraph to determine what situations or topics caused a particular emotional reaction on the part of a client. This knowledge might provide some clues about areas that should be explored during therapy. In one study (Abrams, 1973), the polygraph was used in much the same way that a word-association test would be used. Stimulus words—some neutral, some thought to be especially relevant—were read to each of 20 psychiatric patients while they were attached to a polygraph. Figure 4–14 shows a typical set of polygraph tracings from this study. Respiration is at the top, galvanic skin response (GSR) in the center, and a combination of heart rate and blood pressure at the bottom. Stimulus word 23, *window,* was included as a neutral control word. However, instead of the expected lack of response, the patient showed a definite reaction to it. On the other hand, while there is a response to *sex,* it does not compare with the GSR to *window.* The patient later disclosed that he had considered committing suicide by jumping out a window. Word 26, the therapist's name, resulted in a large GSR, a slight rise in blood pressure, and suppression of breathing. In contrast, the patient reacted relatively little to neutral word 27, *pen.*

Biofeedback, which is described in Chapter 7, is being used increasingly in the treatment of certain bodily complaints. The patient receives continuous reports of a particular index of bodily functions, such as blood pressure, and is helped to find ways of bringing the index within normal limits. Thus, the opportunity to monitor one's own behavior and bodily functioning can have a therapeutic effect.

Techniques of bodily assessment are becoming more and more sophisticated and play increasingly important roles in diagnosis. At several points in this book we will describe a variety of **brain imaging techniques** such as those mentioned in Chapter 3 that enable clinicians to study brain anatomy in patients in great detail, to observe shifts in metabolic activity as the brain responds to cognitive and perceptual tasks, and to measure quantitatively the neurochemical activity of neurotransmitter circuits in the brain. These brain imaging techniques may make it possible to identify the anatomical, metabolic, and neurochemical bases of mental illnesses.

Assessment techniques help in defining the nature and scope of clinical problems, selecting appropriate treatments, and evaluating the results from treatment. The use of multiple techniques (for example, interview, projective techniques, and bodily assessment) may provide a particularly firm basis for valid clinical judgments.

As theories of maladaptive behavior become more comprehensive and more firmly based on scientific findings, approaches to classification can be expected to change. Assessment and classification methods help clinicians describe disordered behavior and plan therapeutic interventions to change it. What is assessed and how people are classified and treated depend on what we know about the factors involved in abnormal behavior.

Chapter Summary

CLASSIFICATION

Classification is necessary in all branches of knowledge. In the area of personality and abnormal behavior, classification is based on assessment of what clients say and how they behave; it also takes account of events they have experienced in the present as well as their past histories. In abnormal psychology the classification of a person is referred to as a **diagnosis.** The diagnosis places the person's disorder within an existing system or grouping of disorders.

Advantages and Disadvantages of Classification An ideal classification system for abnormal behavior would group together behaviors with similar causes. However, in the field of

abnormal psychology not enough is known about the causes of many disorders to do this. Therefore the classification is a descriptive one in which different types of disorders are described in detail. Even a descriptive classification system is important—for communication concerning treatment, in research, and for statistical purposes. On the negative side, classification may result in labeling that creates stigmatization. If the groupings in the system are incorrect because of incomplete knowledge, they make it harder for researchers to see true relationships between disorders.

Stress, Vulnerability, and Coping In classifying individuals, it is important to characterize their problems within the context of their stresses as well as their vulnerabilities and coping abilities.

The Multiaxial Approach A **multiaxial diagnostic system** is designed not to provide a simple label, but to summarize information about several aspects of the person's history and behavior. Since 1980, the diagnostic system used for most purposes in the United States, the **Diagnostic and Statistical Manual of Mental Disorders (DSM),** has used a multiaxial system. This began with DSM-III in 1980 and has continued with DSM-III-R and DSM-IV. DMS currently has five axes: Axis I, the primary diagnosis; Axis II, any pervasive developmental disorders and personality disorders; Axis III, relevant physical disorders; Axis IV, recent stresses; and Axis V, a global assessment of psychosocial functioning, both current and in the past year.

The Major Diagnostic Categories Axis I includes groupings for disorders of infancy, childhood or adolescence, organic mental disorders, substance use disorders, sleep disorders, schizophrenia and other psychotic disorders, mood disorders, anxiety disorders, somatoform disorders, dissociative disorders, sexual disorders, factitious disorders, impulse control disorders not classified elsewhere, adjustment disorder, and psychological factors that affect a physical condition. Axis II includes developmental disorders and personality disorders.

Evaluation of the DSM Multiaxial Approach The approach of DSM since the publication of DSM III has been to use very specific descriptive diagnostic criteria for each category. This approach has increased the reliability of diagnoses among clinicians. DSM has also grown much more comprehensive and includes many more disorders and subdivisions of different disorders. More research is needed to know whether this additional classification is justified. There are some problems with ratings required for each axis, but in general the axes should prove valuable over time. Overall, the changes in DSM-III, DSM-III-R, and DSM-IV have improved the usefulness of this diagnostic system.

Research on Classification Unreliability in diagnosis or classification made by the clinician is based on the characteristics of the diagnostic system and a variety of other factors. These include client factors—the way the client is behaving at a particular time; method factors such as the different assessment techniques used by clinicians; criteria factors that are a function of baselines the clinician develops as a result of the type of patients seen; and factors related to the clinician's own personality and theoretical orientation. Research on classification must take into account all of these factors and how they interact with the characteristics of the diagnostic system.

ASSESSMENT: THE BASIS OF CLASSIFICATION

Because no single assessment tool is perfect, a variety of different ways of characterizing individuals have been developed. The major methods include interviews, psychological tests and behavioral assessment as well as more specialized approaches.

The Interview The **interview** can be used for both diagnosis and therapy. Initial interviews are often relatively unstructured, but during this intake interview the clinician tries to determine why the client came for help, the current state of the client's mood and view of life, the history of the problem, and how the client is currently functioning. Interviewers typically note both verbal and nonverbal behavior of the client. Personal characteristics of the interviewer as well as the client determine how the interview will proceed. The clinician needs to have the ability to size up the situation quickly and adopt the appropriate clinical strategies to clearly assess the problem. In some circumstances, a structured interview format such as the **Diagnostic Interview Schedule** is useful to increase comparability across interviews and help to ensure that the same types of information are gathered about each client.

Intelligence Tests The first standardized **intelligence tests** were developed by Alfred Binet. These yield an **intelligence quotient (IQ)** score based on dividing the child's **mental age** by his or her actual or chronological age and multiplying by 100. Although this method is no longer used, the term "IQ" has remained in use. Currently, the scores on the Binet test as well as other intelligence tests are determined by deviation from a predetermined norm based on test results of a large and representative sample of people. At present, the **Wechsler tests** are the most frequently used intelligence tests. These tests report three different IQ scores: a **Verbal IQ,** a **Performance IQ,** and a **Full Scale IQ,** which represents the total score on the test. There is a series of Wechsler tests, each suitable for a different age group. These include the **Weschler Adult Intelligence Scale (WAIS-R),** the **Wechsler Intelligence Scale for Children (WISC),** and the **Wechsler Preschool and Primary Scale of Intelligence (WPPSI).** Currently, the **Kauffman Assessment Battery for Children (K-ABC),** a test based on ideas from cognitive psychology and neuropsychology and designed to reduce cultural bias in intelligence testing, is used extensively for testing children.

Personality Assessment Personality assessment includes many different approaches. These include personality inventories, rating scales, and projective tests. **Personality inventories** ask people questions about themselves. Because personality is not conceptualized as a single construct, most personality tests yield several scores. The **Minnesota Multiphasic Personality Inventory (MMPI)** is a widely used personality inventory. **Rating scales** present a series of items and allow the respondent to select from a number of choices, often concerning the degree to which the item is descriptive of him or her. A variation of the rating scale is the **visual analogue scale.** This approach is often used to measure the degree of some sensation experienced by the client.

Projective techniques use ambiguous stimuli to which the client is asked to respond. These are most often used by clinicians with a psychodynamic orientation. Two well-known projective techniques are the **Rorschach inkblots** and the **Thematic Apperception Test (TAT).**

Behavioral Assessment **Behavioral assessment** focuses on observations of the frequency of particular types or categories of response. It is often used to identify response deficits. **Baseline** or **operant** observations are used to describe a person's response repertory at a particular time. Behavioral

observations may be made either in a controlled setting or in the person's natural environment.

Cognitive Assessment **Cognitive Assessment** provides information about thoughts that precede, accompany, and follow maladaptive behavior. Questionnaires and beepers are often used in cognitive assessment. Cognitive assessment has been used most extensively in studying the factors that affect concentration on important tasks.

Relational Assessment Because people's behavior is affected by their interpersonal relationships, it is important to assess both general and specific social relationships. One important area of relationships for many people is family relationships. Relationships can be assessed either as general categories such as family or at the level of specific relationships such as mother, brother, or best friend.

Bodily Assessment A person's inner state can be assessed by measuring bodily functions such as blood pressure, heartbeat, respiration, and galvanic skin response. Biofeedback techniques have been developed that allow a person to monitor and to learn to control his or her own bodily responses.

Vulnerability, Stress, and Coping: Maladaptive Reactions

Vulnerability, Temperament, and Coping
Coping Techniques
Social Support

Stress Arousal
Stress-Arousing Situations
Life Transitions

Clinical Reactions to Stress
Adjustment Disorder
Posttraumatic Disorders
Dissociative Disorders

Treating Stress-Related Problems
Supportive Therapy
Drugs and Sedatives
Relaxation Training
Systematic Desensitization
Cognitive Modification
Social Intervention

Chapter Summary

Y. David Chung, *Subway*, 1989. Gallery K, Washington, D.C.

*O*ne morning, while brushing her teeth, Sheila Mason noticed a small lump on her gum. It didn't hurt, but she was sure that it had not been there before. She wondered whether it might be related to an upset stomach or a cold, but there had been no recent changes in her diet and she felt fine. She was worried about the lump, but at the same time she didn't want to bring a trivial symptom to the attention of her physician or dentist. After three days the lump was still there. It was no bigger than it had been when she had first noticed it, and it still didn't hurt. Sheila concluded that it was not her responsibility to decide whether or not the lump was a trivial symptom. That was the professional's job. Having decided to get an expert to look at the lump, Sheila was left with only one question: Should she call her physician or her dentist?

Grace Dolby, married and the mother of two children, felt a small but noticeable lump in her right breast. Her first reaction was one of alarm bordering on panic, but then she told herself it was really nothing. She must have been mistaken. Then she simply tried to stop thinking about the lump. She put it out of her mind whenever her thoughts strayed to the topic. She also said nothing to anyone else about it for over two months and made a tremendous effort to wish it away. Grace was usually outgoing and cheerful, but during those months her husband, Jack, noticed that she had become moody, tense, and depressed. At times she also seemed distant and preoccupied. Toward the end of the two-month period, Grace's moodiness and distance from others (including her children) increased. Her sleep became fitful, and she had frequent headaches (even though previously she had almost never had them). If her husband insisted that she tell him what the

125

matter was, her reply was always, "Nothing's the matter. I'm perfectly normal." Finally, one evening during lovemaking Jack felt the lump in her breast, and despite Grace's protests that it was "nothing" he insisted that she see the family physician.

Just about the only thing that Sheila Mason and Grace Dolby have in common is that they discovered lumps that worried them. The two women dealt with their worries in quite different ways. After some doubt about whether she should undergo a clinical examination, Sheila made a rational decision to seek help. She realized that there was a chance the lump could be serious but that she could not evaluate the possibility herself and that the longer she waited, the worse it would be.

In contrast, Grace Dolby seemed unable to act realistically and decisively. She first attempted to cope with the discovery of the lump in her breast by trying to deny that it was really there. But this was not completely successful. She then tried to tell herself that it "wasn't anything." The stress aroused by her discovery could be reduced only temporarily by denial and secrecy. She was still unable to deal with the reality of the lump.

Such a situation would be stressful for anyone. Most people who find themselves in such a situation go to a doctor immediately. Grace Dolby's response is considered maladaptive mainly because it did not work; the lump (or reality) did not go away. In fact, Grace's behavior simply increased the amount of stress she experienced. A clinician working with Grace would want to understand the personal needs, motivations, and dispositions that combined with the situation (discovery of the lump) to produce her decision to be secretive and not to act. What made Grace Dolby so much more vulnerable to stress than Sheila Mason?

In this chapter we describe ways in which people react to stress. We emphasize examples of maladaptive behavior in response to two types of situations: those, like Sheila Mason's and Grace Dolby's, that arise suddenly, and those that develop more gradually and represent turning points in life, such as making a career decision (see Figure 5–1). We examine the concept of stress, explore the different ways in which people handle it, and review three clinical conditions (adjustment disorders, posttraumatic disorders, and dissociative disorders) in which stress plays an identifiable role. Even though the behavioral reactions observed in the three conditions seem quite different, stress plays a crucial role in each, and its removal is often followed by improvement.

Because this is the first chapter in which we study particular disorders in some depth, it is worthwhile to anticipate an observation that has been made many times by both experienced clinicians and students: The various disorders are not conveniently arranged so that they have mutually exclusive features. Stress is the main topic of this chapter, but we will also refer to stress as we discuss other forms of maladaptation. What is distinctive about the disorders discussed here is that the exact sources of stress are more evident than they usually are in most forms of abnormal behavior. In the next chapter, where we review the anxiety disorders, we will find it more difficult to specify the exact sources of stress that result in intense anxiety.

Vulnerability, Temperament, and Coping

In Chapter 1 we said that the term "stress" refers to situations that pose demands, constraints, or opportunities. However, a situation that is stress-arousing for one person might be a neutral event for another. Whether a certain situation is stressful for us or not depends on how we appraise it and how we rate our ability to deal with it. There are two stages in the appraisal of any situation. During **primary appraisal,** individuals interpret a situation as either threatening or harmless. During **secondary appraisal,** they consider the kind of action that is called for, as well as the nature and potency of their resources for managing or coping with it. The extent to which people feel threatened depends on their estimate of the resources, which in turn is based largely on the information provided by the environment and by their own experiences and characteristics.

People differ not only in the life events they experience but also in their vulnerability to them. A person's **vulnerability** to stress is influenced by his or her temperament, coping skills, and the social support available. Vulnerability increases the likelihood of a maladaptive response to stress. For example, unloved children are more vulnerable and generally at greater risk of developing behavior disorders than those who are loved (Werner & Smith, 1982).

Temperament comprises those aspects of a person's behavior (particularly those having to do with feelings and emotions) that show some significant degree of consistency over time and from one life situation to another. Activity level, mood, and distractibility are examples of temperamental attributes. Throughout the life cycle, these attributes can be assets or liabilities depending on the life situations the individual confronts. For example, an abundance of energy in a highly active person can be an asset when it is used in the pursuit of specific, planned goals, and a liability in situations where

FIGURE 5–1 Sudden and sustained stress. Stress can be aroused by a sudden, shattering, and unexpected event (like a natural catastrophe) or it can be less intense, but last for a relatively long period of time. (a) The effects of the 1989 San Francisco earthquake illustrate stress caused by an instantaneous event. Situations like (b) searching for a job—especially during bad economic times—and (c) being both a parent and a student may be less dramatic than an earthquake, but they also pose major challenges to an individual's coping resources.

(a)

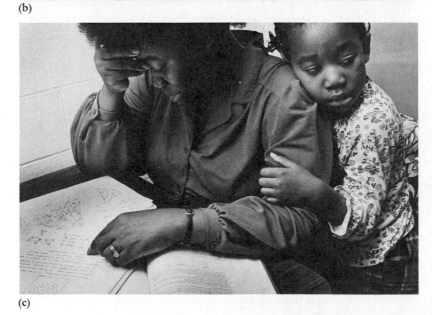

(b)

(c)

hasty judgments, commitments, and responses should be avoided. Table 5–1 describes several aspects of temperament that alone or combined can play roles in how people handle stress. Adjustment problems may occur when temperamental factors prevent people from meeting their own or others' expectations. For example, children with a tendency to withdraw from new stimuli may experience excessive stress if their parents or teachers demand rapid adjustment to new conditions (such as entering nursery school). Researchers are attempting to identify the origins of temperament (for example, heredity, biological make-up, parental attitudes, and sociocultural factors) (Chess, 1990).

Coping skills, characteristic ways of dealing with difficulties, influence how we identify and try to solve problems. People who cope successfully do not just know how to do things. They also know how to approach situations for which they do not have a readily available response.

The coping skills that people bring with them to life experiences (their expectations, fears, skills, hopes) influence how much stress they feel and how well they cope with it. Experience and success in coping with similar situations, well-founded self-confidence, and the ability to remain composed and "think on one's feet" instead of falling to pieces when faced with a problem, all contribute to realistic appraisals of and responses to situations. These characteristics are products of personality development, which, in turn, is influenced by social relationships.

A task-oriented, matter-of-fact response to a tough situation is usually more effective than becoming anxious, angry, or defensive. Failure to be task-oriented can happen for a variety of reasons. A person may simply lack the coping resources needed to take a matter-of-fact approach. In that case, the situation is beyond his or her capabilities. It could also be that certain elements of the situation may prevent an individual from taking a constructive approach to it. For example, a man might have the coping resources needed to be assertive with other men but not with women. His vulnerability with regard to women might keep him from complaining about being shortchanged by a waitress, whereas he would be quick to complain if he were shortchanged by a waiter. In trying to identify the basis for a particular behavioral coping response, it is necessary to analyze carefully what is going on in the situation, together with the person's assets and liabilities (coping resources and vulnerabilities). In addition, attention must be paid to how the person sizes up the situation (primary appraisal) and his or her coping resources (secondary appraisal).

Personal vulnerabilities and past experiences influence how much stress we experience in a given situation and how we deal with it. For example, Grace Dolby, the subject of the second case at the beginning of the chapter, had in the past experienced many physical symptoms that required action—such as high temperature and skin rash. The lump in her breast, however, was different because of its life-threatening implications. Her mother had died when Grace was 4 years old, and Grace was concerned about depriving her children of the maternal love and attention that she had missed as a result of her mother's early death. Perhaps her intense concern about abandoning her children made Grace particularly vulnerable to her symptom and resulted in her denial of its significance.

Like Grace, many people with bodily symptoms cope with them by denying them. They may intentionally ignore them and try to keep thoughts of them out of awareness or misinterpret them. A common response to

Table 5–1

Aspects of Temperament

Temperamental Attribute	Description
Activity level	The motor component of a person's life
Mood	The amount of pleasant and friendly feelings and behavior, as contrasted with those that are unpleasant and unfriendly
Distractibility	How much extraneous environmental stimuli interfere with or alter the direction of attention and behavior
Persistence	Continuation of an activity in the face of obstacles, in order to reach a desired goal
Reaction intensity	The energy level of response, irrespective of its quality
Approach-Withdrawal tendency	The nature of initial responses to new stimuli (such as a stranger, new food, a new place)
Adaptability	The ease with which initial responses (for example, approach or withdrawal) can be modified in direction

the chest pain of a heart attack is denial of its significance. It has been estimated that 80 to 90 percent of people who experience such pain attribute it to other causes, usually indigestion (Hackett & Cassem, 1975). Once the possibility that it might be a heart attack strikes them, they think, "It couldn't be happening to me." This thought alone seems to be enough to keep them from seeking medical help. Even some physicians, who should know better, have gone jogging when they experienced chest pains in order to "prove it's nothing." Thus, there is a common tendency to deny the true significance of pain despite its severity, intensity, or duration.

This is true for psychological pain as well. Many people deny the reality of an unhappy or unsatisfying marriage rather than seek counseling or even a divorce. People who have lost their jobs may blame their employers instead of recognizing their own inadequacies as employees. They may put off looking for work because they "deserve a rest," denying even to themselves that they are afraid of being fired again. As Table 5–2 shows, denial can play a reality-distorting role at various stages of a stressful experience.

Particular conditions might arouse stressful reactions in some people but not in others. At a memorial concert honoring the famous jazz musician Louis "Satchmo" Armstrong, his widow was stricken with a fatal heart attack as she played the final chord of a song that was identified with her husband, "The St. Louis Blues." According to a newspaper report, a 38-year-old father collapsed and died when his efforts to revive his 2-year-old daughter, who had fallen into a wading pool, failed. The report suggested that the girl had fallen into the pool while the father's attention wandered. An obituary noting the sudden death, at 51, of the newly appointed president of a television network stated that he

Table 5–2

Types of Denial of Stress

Type of Denial	Example
1. Denial of provided information	"No one ever told me about it."
2. Denial of information about a threat	"No one ever told me there was anything to worry about."
3. Denial of personal relevance	"It doesn't apply to me."
4. Denial of urgency	"No need to hurry."
5. Denial of vulnerability	"No matter what happens, it can't happen to me."
6. Denial of emotion	"I'm not scared."
7. Denial of the emotion's relevance	"I'm scared, but there is no reason to feel that way."

SOURCE: Adapted from Breznitz, 1988. Courtesy of Hemisphere Publishing Corporation.

was on his way to attend the funeral of his father, who had died the day before. Each of these examples suggests the importance of the appraisal process for each individual who experiences a particular type of event.

Another example of the importance of the appraisal process is found in hospitals, places to which we may turn in times of great stress. Hospitals are supposed to be places where people can recover from illness, but in fact

FIGURE 5–2 The combination of a serious illness or injury, the unfamiliar and impersonal high tech setting of the intensive care unit, and limited contact with friends and family can produce a highly stressful situation that may make recovery more difficult.

hospitalization is usually a highly stressful experience. For instance, the continuous monitoring of a patient's physical status in the intensive care unit can create a high degree of stress. The knowledge that one has a condition that is serious enough to require placement in an intensive care unit may be even more stressful (see Figure 5–2). Probably the most stressful aspect of hospitalization for both the patient and family members is the frequently occurring uncertainty about what the outcome of the treatment may be (see Box 5–1). Frustrations from dealing with bureaucratic hospital procedures can be stressful even to a patient who is familiar with hospital routines and who has excellent coping skills.

Heightened stress levels have detectable, although usually not immediately noticeable, psychological consequences. For example, a significantly higher percentage of depressed and suicidal people than of people with other disorders have had undesirable recent experiences. The undesirable events that contribute most to depression include the departure or loss of significant people in one's life during the previous year (see Chapter 10).

The psychological disorders discussed in this chapter begin with a specific event that has definable characteristics and has special meaning for the person involved. This event is then appraised or processed, and as a result of the appraisal, the person's emotions or

BOX 5–1 Two Weeks in the Hospital

John A. Talbott, the author of this account, was not just "any" patient. At the time of the accident he was President of the American Psychiatric Association. Although as a physician he was familiar with medical procedures, being a patient gave him a quite different view of his condition and treatment than he would have had as a hospital staff member. The effect of injuries and the hospitalization itself may be stressful, but this account shows how hospital procedures and medical personnel can add significantly to the problems of hospitalization.

> On November 30, 1981, while standing on the sidewalk near the Museum of Natural History in New York, I was hit by one of two cabs that had collided at the nearby intersection. . . . It was early in the morning. My physical injuries were substantial . . . but in retrospect, it was the way I was subsequently cared for, rather than treated, that sticks most in mind. . . ."

Some of Talbott's experiences show how interpersonal interactions can add to stress. For instance:

Each morning a new nurse would bounce cheerily into the room, introduce herself, and take a history. I assumed on the second day that my first day's nurse had the day off. But by the third or fourth day I realized that some bizarre rotational system ensured that no nurse would ever get to know me, my needs, and my care, since I'd never see the same one twice.

One evening I received no dinner. After calls to the kitchen from the nursing staff produced no result, they urged me to call—"they'll listen to you, you're a doctor." The nutrition person announced that it was too late for dinner, they were already immersed in setting up the breakfast trays. I asked if it wasn't possible to alter the routine so that I might be fed before 10 p.m. She then blew up at me for not understanding all the pressures she was under, and only after I reminded her that I was the patient and her job was to help patients, did she apologize and relent.

Finally, the day arrived, my few meager belongings marking a two-week stay were packed, and I was ready for the trip home. I

eagerly awaited my physician's arrival to deliver some parting words—I awaited his optimistic view of my recovery, his good cheer, his clinical enthusiasm. Instead, he said he hoped he'd be able to "save" my leg, since the damage done was extensive, the healing complicated, and the prognosis uncertain. But, if he wasn't, all sorts of things could be done, including bone grafts. And if worse came to worse there was always the possibility of an amputation. But I shouldn't worry, that wouldn't happen for a while. When my wife arrived I was in tears.

Going home was no picnic—with an enormous, heavy cast and limited energy, I could barely make it to the bathroom—but it was home, without the surly aides, constantly rotating nurses, inadequate medication, dashing house staff, uncoordinated treatment team, incredibly unappealing food, and dehumanized physicians.

—J. A. Talbott, Medical Humanism: A Personal Odyssey, in *Psychiatric News*, 2, 31, 1985. Copyright © 1985, The American Psychiatric Association. Reprinted by permission.

thoughts (fears, plans) are aroused and coping strategies are considered. The end product is some response that reflects the level of stress as well as the person's resources and vulnerabilities.

Coping Techniques

In coping, people use their personal resources to master a problem, overcome or sidestep an obstacle, answer a question, or resolve a dilemma. Different coping strategies are effective in different types of situations. People who generally cope successfully have a varied array of personal resources, which include the ability to:

1. Seek pertinent information.
2. Share concerns and find consolation when needed.
3. Redefine a situation so as to make it more solvable.
4. Consider alternatives and examine consequences.
5. Use humor to defuse a situation.

A growing body of research is devoted to the question of how people can be helped to cope with stress more effectively (Hodgkinson & Stewart, 1991; Lazarus, 1991). One finding of this research is that what you don't know *can* hurt you. People who know what to expect beforehand are better able to cope with stress than people who do not know what lies ahead. Many surgical patients, for example, suffer unnecessarily because they have not been warned that they will have considerable pain after the operation. It has been shown that patients are less anxious and recover faster when the surgery and recovery process are explained to them before the operation takes place.

In one study (Anderson, 1987), 60 men undergoing coronary bypass grafts were divided into three groups. One group received the hospital's standard preparation: a brochure on the procedures and a short visit from a nurse to answer questions. The other groups watched a videotape that followed a patient through the operation and recovery. In addition, one of these groups received advanced instructions in the physical therapy exercises—such as deep breathing to expand their lung capacity—that they would be doing to help recovery. While 75 percent of those with the standard preparation suffered after the surgery from acute hypertension—a condition that can endanger coronary bypass patients in the first 12 hours after surgery—less than 45 percent of those who saw the tape had the problem. The patients who viewed the tape also had less anxiety as they waited in the hospital before the surgery and reported less stress and seemed more relaxed to nurses in the week after the surgery. The group that received extra instruc-

tion in the physical therapy went into surgery feeling even less anxious than the other groups.

Learning the specific skills needed in stressful situations also helps individuals cope more effectively. Many people enter dangerous situations without proper training. For example, many hiking and mountain climbing accidents are a result of poor training and preparation. Besides learning specific skills, individuals can be trained for stressful situations by being put through a series of experiences that are graded from relatively low to relatively high in stress. In addition, observing a model who copes with stress in an effective way can help people who are about to enter a strange or dangerous situation.

People sometimes fail to cope with stress because a high level of arousal interferes with their ability to concentrate on adaptive thoughts. These people do not observe their own thoughts, feelings, and behaviors in challenging situations, and they fail to engage in constructive problem solving. Learning general skills for coping with stress involves learning how to think constructively, solve problems, behave flexibly, and provide feedback to oneself about which tactics work and which do not (see Table 5–3).

The following are examples of useful statements that people can make to themselves in preparing for and dealing with stressful situations. Such statements have been used in training programs directed toward strengthening cognitive skills. In this training, the statements are modeled for each participant, who is then given an opportunity to rehearse them while imagining being in stressful situations (Freeman and others, 1989).

PREPARING FOR A STRESSFUL SITUATION
- "I should work out a plan for dealing with this problem."
- "I'm not going to worry about what happens; I'll just prepare myself in the best way I can."

CONFRONTING A STRESSFUL SITUATION
- "I'm just going to take one step at a time. I can do it."
- "I want to be sure to stick to what's really important."

COPING WITH FEELINGS OF BEING OVERWHELMED
- "Sure I'm scared—but that's normal."
- "I know I'm afraid, but I've got to do things that will help me cope."

REINFORCING SELF-STATEMENTS
- "I controlled my tension—and I did it."
- "I must be pretty good to be able to handle a crisis like that one."

As the above statements show, people who cope effectively with stressful situations have learned to direct

Table 5–3

Aids to Behavioral Coping

1. *Be task-oriented.* Focus only on the task confronting you. It is not productive to spend time with thoughts or feelings that are unrelated to accomplishing the task. Being task-oriented means that you are concentrating completely on the job at hand. Negative or disruptive thoughts and emotions are the enemies of task orientation.

2. *Be yourself.* Don't role play. You will be more effective acting naturally than trying to fit a role. Place your confidence in *yourself,* not in the role.

3. *Self-monitor.* Pay attention to the way you are thinking and feeling in a given situation. It is important to learn about what causes stress for you and about your personal reactions to stress. Effective self-monitoring is your early warning system. It can alert you to the necessity of using the other coping skills to prevent a blowup.

4. *Be realistic about what you can achieve.* Know your own limits as well as your strengths. At times, laughter is the best medicine—don't lose your sense of humor.

5. *Have a constructive outlook.* Try to look for the positives in the people around you. Don't be too quick to conclude that people are behaving the way they are just to upset you. Put yourself in the other person's shoes—from that point of view his or her behavior may make perfect sense.

6. *Use supportive relationships.* Compare notes, blow off steam, and get support from your friends. Don't draw into yourself when you are feeling stressed. Remember that we all "get by with a little help from our friends."

7. *Be patient with yourself.* Don't punish yourself for not achieving perfection. Your mistakes should be learning experiences, not times for heavy self-criticism. Keep your expectations of yourself at a reasonable level.

their thoughts along productive lines and to avoid being distracted by fear and worry. Actors, quarterbacks, and other people who are often in the limelight soon learn that attention to the task at hand is more constructive than self-preoccupied thoughts ("There are 100,000 people out there waiting for me to fumble that ball"). They also learn to anticipate problems that might complicate a stressful situation and to think about the way to deal with them. Actors come to accept that they will occasionally get their lines mixed up and that deemphasizing their mistakes and moving on to the next line reduces the impact of their errors. On the other hand, the thoughts of some people who are prone to stress disorders are saturated with self-blame and catastrophizing ("The worst will surely happen").

Social Support

Our social network includes people on whom we can rely, people who let us know that they care about,

value, and love us. Someone who believes that he or she belongs to a social network experiences **social support.** Evidence is increasing that maladaptive ways of thinking and behaving occur disproportionately among people with few social supports. The amount and adequacy of social support available to a person plays a part in both vulnerability and coping (Sarason and others, 1990). Vulnerability to physical and psychological breakdown increases as social support decreases. That is, social support serves as a buffer against the upsets of living in a complex world. Not only is social support very helpful during a period of stress (it is nice to know that there are people pulling for us in a tough situation), but it is also helpful in times of relative calm. It gives us the security and self-confidence to try out new approaches and gain additional coping skills. With an expanded repertory of coping skills, we are in a better position to handle demands, frustrations, and challenges when they do arise.

Research aimed at measuring social support is under way. The Social Support Questionnaire (SSQ) provides information about how much social support people think they have and how satisfied they are with it (Sarason and others, 1983). This information is then scored on separate Availability and Satisfaction scores. Table 5–4 lists some of the items on the SSQ. One interesting finding of research using the SSQ is that there is only a moderate correlation between the Availability and Satisfaction scores. There appears to be no minimum number of social supports that ensures satisfaction for everyone. For some people, a small number of close friends and relatives is satisfying, whereas others seem to need ties to many different people.

Research with the SSQ has also revealed relationships between social support and physical health. In general, people who have had many recent undesirable experiences are more likely to get sick than those who have been more fortunate. However, people who have high levels of social support are less vulnerable to illness even when they have experienced a recent misfortune (Sarason and others, 1985).

Maladaptive ways of thinking and behaving are more common among people who have few social supports, particularly within their families. Strong family ties seem to encourage self-reliance. Self-reliance and reliance on others are not only compatible but complementary. Social support facilitates coping with crisis and adapting to change.

Why do some people have many rewarding ties that help them smooth out the rough spots in their lives, while others are lonely and socially isolated? Are the number and quality of social ties simply a matter of luck? There is evidence that people with high and low levels of social support as assessed by the SSQ differ in the social skills needed to attract the interest of others (Sarason and others, 1985). When engaging in a conversation with a

Table 5–4

The Social Support Questionnaire

The *Social Support Questionnaire (SSQ)* consists of 27 items, four of which are presented here. After answering each item, the test taker is asked to indicate his or her level of satisfaction with the support available by marking a 6-point rating scale that ranges from "very satisfied" to "very unsatisfied." The SSQ yields scores relating to *Availability* of and *Satisfaction* with social support.

Whom do you know whom you can trust with information that could get you in trouble? (This item is completed as an example).

_____ No one	A) R.N. (brother)	D) T.N. (father)	G)
	B) L.M. (friend)	E) L.M. (employer)	H)
	C) R.S. (friend)	F)	I)

Whose lives do you feel that you are an important part of?

_____ No one	A)	D)	G)
	B)	E)	H)
	C)	F)	I)

Whom can you really count on to distract you from your worries when you feel under stress?

_____ No one	A)	D)	G)
	B)	E)	H)
	C)	F)	I)

Who helps you feel that you truly have something positive to contribute to others?

_____ No one	A)	D)	G)
	B)	E)	H)
	C)	F)	I)

stranger, people who are high in social support feel more competent, comfortable, and assured than people who report having few social supports. In addition, people who are low in social support tend to be perceived by others as being less interesting, dependable, friendly, and considerate than people who are high in social support. They are also less wanted as friends and co-workers and report feeling more lonely. There appears to be a strong link between social skills and social support. People with low levels of support may not believe that other people could be interested in them. This belief would tend to

increase their vulnerability to stress, especially in situations that called for interactions with other people. Training in social skills might not only increase their interpersonal effectiveness but also help reduce their perception of social isolation.

As we have seen, the coping process involves a number of interacting factors. Figure 5–3 summarizes the role of three especially important factors in this process: individuals' coping resources, their vulnerabilities, and their perceptions of available social support.

FIGURE 5–3 The stress-coping process. How a person actually copes with a stress-arousing situation depends on the person's skills or coping resources, vulnerabilities, and having a supportive social network.

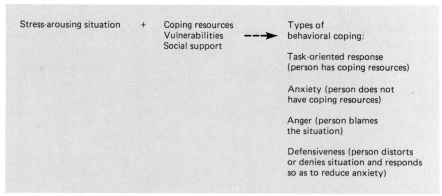

Stress Arousal

A variety of circumstances can evoke stress and require the individuals to adjust to it. Since stress has undesirable effects on behavior, thought, and bodily functioning, it is important to build up a person's resources for behavioral coping. Uncomfortable psychological feelings are present when people experience stress. Blood pressure, hormone levels, and brain waves are also affected by stress. Very high levels of stress can result in trembling, stuttering, and a decline in the effectiveness with which tasks are carried out.

There is often little consistency in people's reactions to stress. That is, one person might react to stress primarily in a bodily way, another might develop psychological symptoms, and yet another might show a profound deterioration in performance. Responses to stress involve bodily, psychological, and behavioral systems, but the correlation among these systems is often low. Table 5–5 lists ways in which the three systems may react to stress.

There seems to be some truth to the commonly held belief that everyone has a breaking point. The more stress people experience, the more likely they are to break down either physically or psychologically. Dealing with several stressful situations at the same time obviously places great demands on a person's resources, but stress can also have cumulative effects.

Research has shown that people who have experienced multiple stressors in the recent past are especially susceptible to depression, anxiety, and overreactivity of physiological systems (Noshpitz & Coddington, 1990). There is growing reason to believe that mental or physical breakdowns could be predicted if there were a way to quantify how stressful certain life experiences are. For this reason, researchers have sought ways of assessing those experiences. Because recent experiences often exert a more powerful influence and are more easily recalled than those that occurred many years before, efforts have been made to quantify stressful life changes for specific time periods, such as the past year. Questionnaires have been constructed to assess not only whether certain events have occurred in the recent past, but also how the individual perceived the event and felt its impact (Cohen, 1988; Sarason and others, 1978). These questionnaires deal with events such as being fired from a job, getting a new job, breaking up with a boyfriend or girlfriend, and experiencing financial difficulties. While the occurrence of any one particular event might not put a person at a greater risk for an adverse outcome (such as getting sick), the occurrence of several different kinds of events close together in a brief period of time would create significant added risk.

There is growing evidence that economic conditions such as poverty can affect the incidence of stressful life events, which in turn can cause health and behavioral problems. A number of studies have shown that low socioeconomic status is associated with a high frequency of stressful events and the lack of adequate methods for coping with them (Eron & Peterson, 1982). Thus, it is not necessarily socioeconomic status by itself that causes problems, but rather the life events and poor coping skills that are correlated with this status.

Regardless of socioeconomic status, unemployment can cause psychological as well as economic problems. Brenner (1973, 1984) has reported that when employment levels decline, admissions to state mental hospitals rise. He also found that economic reverses are correlated with increases in death rates from a variety of conditions, including suicide, homicide, and cirrhosis of the liver, a disorder that is often associated with heavy alcohol use. The physical and physiological effects of unemployment are not necessarily immediate. The entire impact of a rise in unemployment might not be felt for

Table 5–5
Some Psychological, Bodily, and Behavioral Reactions to Stress

Psychological Responses

Feeling upset
Inability to concentrate
Irritability
Loss of self-confidence
Worry
Difficulty making decisions
Racing thoughts
Absent-mindedness

Bodily Responses

Rapid pulse
Pounding heart
Increased perspiration
Tensing of arm and leg muscles
Shortness of breath
Gritting of teeth

Behavioral Responses

Deterioration in performance effectiveness
Smoking and use of alcohol or other "recreational" drugs
Accident proneness
Nervous mannerisms (foot tapping, nail biting)
Increased or decreased eating
Increased or decreased sleeping

several years after it occurred. People who have multiple stressors in their lives at the time that they lose their jobs run the greatest risk of some sort of breakdown.

Stress-Arousing Situations

Two broad types of stress-arousing conditions that require adjustment are situations that arise in life, often unexpectedly, and developmental transitions. The death of a close friend illustrates the need for a situational adjustment; going to college is an example of a transitional adjustment. Such stress-arousing conditions have varying characteristics. Following are some of the ways in which challenging situations and circumstances vary.

1. *Duration.* Stressful situations differ in duration. A job interview lasts for a short time, whereas a marital quarrel might last for hours or days.

2. *Severity.* Situations vary in the severity of the circumstances confronting the individual. In general, a minor injury is easier to cope with than a major injury.

3. *Predictability.* In some cases predictability is high (we know what is going to happen), whereas in others predictability is low. The amount of stress caused by a request to give an oral presentation in class would depend on whether the request was made on the spot or was a previously given assignment.

4. *Degree of loss of control.* One of the most upsetting aspects of a situation is the feeling that one is unable to exert any influence on the circumstances. For example, earthquake victims can do nothing to prevent or control the quake's initial impact and aftershocks.

5. *The individual's level of self-confidence.* Lack of self-confidence often results in reduced personal effectiveness, even though the person may really know how to handle the situation. For example, a recently divorced woman may feel ill at ease in social situations that she was able to handle very well during her marriage.

6. *Suddenness of onset.* Suddenness of onset influences how prepared we are to cope with a particular situation. An accident is usually completely unexpected, whereas the crises of adolescence build up gradually.

TRAUMATIC EVENTS Accidents, natural disasters, and military combat are examples of situations that typically evoke high levels of stress and may result in posttraumatic stress disorders. Their psychological impact comes from actual physical injury or threat of injury and from the possibility of loss of life.

An airplane crash has some special features that must be recognized if its victims are to be psychologically helped. The passengers on a flight are usually strangers to one another, often come from a variety of areas, and are usually far from home. Whereas natural disasters are frequently perceived as "acts of God," air crashes engender reactions of anger and, even more striking, of guilt on the part of some survivors.

There may be serious long-range problems related to airplane crashes as well as immediate effects. Survivors and crew members are likely to experience such chronic problems as psychological withdrawal from their work, family life, or society in general, as well as physical symptoms and habitual anxiety (Gist & Lubin, 1989). Survivors often torture themselves with such questions as "Why didn't I do more to save those who perished?" and "Why did I survive when others did not?" Victims may experience an "anniversary syndrome"—episodes of depression and anxiety on the anniversary of the disaster. This may happen without the victim's understanding the source of the strong feelings that well up at about the time of the anniversary.

Along with passengers and crew members, other groups feel the emotional effects of an airplane crash. These include ground crew members, air controllers, and those who witness the crash or have contact with the crash scene. For instance, after the collision of a commercial airliner and a small private plane, wreckage and bodies fell into a suburban area (see Figure 5–4). Efforts

FIGURE 5–4 Sometimes death strikes suddenly. This passenger jet has just collided with a small plane near the San Diego airport. The photographer snapped it as it plunged toward the ground in a crash that killed all 136 passengers aboard. The two passengers in the small plane were also killed.

were made to obtain information about witnesses' psychological reactions and to help them return to normal as quickly as possible. The following account of the experience of a young couple who witnessed the disaster illustrates some of the psychological, behavioral, and bodily reactions found in disaster victims.

At first they responded with great reservation, saying that they had been eyewitnesses to the crash from their home in North Park. They added that although their house was still intact, there had been approximately seventeen bodies scattered around their yard, trees, and roof. They had decided that they never wanted to live in the house again and had called the Salvation Army for help in finding a new home. After some initial reluctance to talk at all about their reactions, they began to freely disclose every detail. They were obviously quite anxious and angry, focusing their hostility at the media, police, and the councilman who was present. Recurrent images of bodies lying around their home were reported by the man, as were obsessions with the details of the tragedy. (Where did the body come from that hit their car and did $700 worth of damage? Did he die on impact or before? Was he on the ground and, if so, how could he have hit from that angle? Why did they put a sheet over him when there were so many other bodies and parts lying around and when "gawkers" just kept lifting the sheet off anyway?) He had attempted to remain busy and mentally occupied in order to keep his mind off these images. The woman had experienced multiple somatic disturbances including, most prominently, anorexia, nausea, and frequent sighing respirations. They both talked intensively and openly for an hour and a half; at the end, both agreed that they felt better having had the opportunity to get some of these thoughts out in the open.

—Shuchter and Zisook, 1984, p. 296

Extreme stressors set in motion a cycle of reactions aimed at restoring an equilibrium between the person's self-concept and the new realities of his or her life (Gist & Lubin, 1989). Preexisting personality characteristics may interfere with an adaptive response after a disaster. People who see themselves as incompetent, who tend to respond defensively to challenges (for example, by using denial or projection), who have conflicts involving

themes similar to some aspect of the disaster, or who believe that their past thoughts might somehow have influenced what happened—such people are likely to have long-lasting maladaptive reactions to traumatic situations. These prolonged reactions usually include feeling dazed and having intrusive thoughts and images about the traumatic event. Such thoughts and images may interfere with the ability to sleep.

As more becomes known about what traumatic events like airplane accidents do to people, steps can be taken to improve the effectiveness of personnel who have the job of dealing with them. Training in the ability to recognize emotional problems and provide emotional support would be of great value in the efforts of such personnel to reduce both the short-term and long-term effects of these events.

PERSONAL CRISES As we have seen, stressors can be widespread events that affect many people, such as an airplane crash, or they can be a highly personal crisis. The death of a loved one, the loss of a job, and the need to care for a parent who has an incurable illness are all examples of personal crises. Rape is another type of personal crisis whose frequency of occurrence and seriousness are now receiving increased attention. Rape affects men as well as women, married as well as single persons. Date rape is a particularly serious problem among adolescent- and college-age persons (see Box 5–2).

The fears that persist after the experience of rape tend to restrict and control the victim's life (Ruch and others, 1991). The most prevalent fears are of being alone, of strangers, of going out, and of darkness. Women who have been victims of sudden and violent assaults by strangers are especially likely to remain fearful and depressed for a long time, and they are also more likely to avoid dating for a long period. In one study, 36 percent of those raped had not recovered four to six years after the attack (Bateman, 1986). Generalized feelings of anxiety and fear were higher in the rape victims than in controls no matter how many years had passed since the rape. Estimates are that 80 percent of the rape victim's primary relationships break up within a year of the rape (Riesenberg, 1987). Male partners of female rape victims often show a predictable sequence of behavior (Bateman, 1986). First comes about a week of anger followed by a protective phase. Both of these are accompanied by avoidance of the victim and by anxiety. After about a month the partner becomes depressed and feels guilty, and sexual difficulties with the victim continue. At the end of three months of follow-up the partners still felt guilt and depression.

From the behavioral perspective, a rape is part of an in vivo classical-conditioning situation in which the threat of death or physical damage elicits a strong autonomic arousal, fear. Any stimulus that is present

BOX 5–2 Date Rape

College women are a high-risk group for sexual assault. Nationally, the age group with the highest rape victimization rate is the 16–19 year olds with the age 20–24 group having the second highest rate (Ward and others, 1991). About 16 percent of women college students in two different surveys reported that they had been raped by someone they knew or were dating (Sherman, 1985). In another survey of a representative sample of university students, 6 percent of the women replied "yes" to the question, "Have you ever been raped?" However, when the definition was broadened somewhat, percentages went up substantially; 21 percent of the women said that they had had sexual intercourse with a man when they didn't really want to because they had felt pressured by his continual arguments (Koss & Oros, 1982). Eleven percent of the college men in the surveys said they had forced a woman to have intercourse. A typical story was something like what happened to a 20-year-old college student in Pittsburgh.

> She met him two years ago at a fraternity party on a neighboring campus. His dashing good looks, she recalls now, coupled with his shy grin and friendly manner made him appear "sweet, but not macho." They talked and danced for hours, and later that evening, he took her in his arms and they kissed.
>
> When he asked if she would like to get something to eat, she agreed. But instead of heading toward a nearby restaurant, he swerved onto a side street, pulled over to the curb and stopped the car. Then he raped her.

—Sherman, 1985, p. 17

Sexual activity that goes farther than one of the participants would like is not new among college students, nor are the forces behind it. But the term "date rape" is recent, and this label itself may have given such activity a new identity, defining nonconsensual sex between dates or acquaintances as a form of male assault rather than a form of female fault.

Research with both high school and college students shows that a sizeable minority of students do not believe that date rape is definitely unacceptable behavior (Mahoney, 1983). Men who have been charged with rape by women they have known or dated are often befuddled by the current situation. Many of them have been conditioned to believe that initial refusals are an essential part of a "mating game" ritual, one that dictates that women must resist somewhat to make themselves more attractive to men. The material in Table 5–6 on page 138 provides information to counter this misperception of the social norm.

Several studies have examined the attitudes of college students toward date rape. In one such study, based on questionnaire responses of college students, those students who were more accepting of date rape were less sure that forcible date rape is really rape, were more traditional in their attitudes toward women, were more self-permissive about premarital sex with friends or acquaintances, and had less knowledge about sex than other students (Fischer, 1986). A measure of acceptance of force in sexual intercourse was found to be correlated with how often college men admitted using force to have intercourse, how much force was used, and with a lower degree of social responsibility and social conscience (Rapaport & Burkart, 1984). Research also has shown that alcohol and drugs play important roles in date or acquaintance rape. Approximately 75% of the men and 55% of the women involved in date rape had been drinking or taking drugs prior to the incident (Abbey, 1991; Ward, 1991). The role of alcohol was especially important in combination with participation in party-related activities.

Because research findings show that students' perceptions of what is sexually appropriate have an important influence on their behavior, many schools have begun to educate students about the role that attitudes play in sexual intimacy and about the relationship of behaviors that impair judgement, such as heavy drinking, to the occurrence of date rape. This type of educational program not only heightens student awareness of the problem, but also provides information about how to cope in situations that might be likely to result in unwanted sexual intercourse (See Figure 5–5).

FIGURE 5–5 These students are watching a video used in school—sponsored programs designed to combat date rape by increasing awareness about the rights of individuals and factors that increase vulnerability and to illustrate coping strategies.

Table 5–6
Typical Aspects of Sexual Assaults on Young Women and Guidelines for Prevention

The typical sexual assault is committed by a boyfriend or acquaintance and occurs during a date.

Most such assaults do not involve severe physical violence or the use of a weapon.

The kind of force typically used is verbal pressure.

Most victims are able to prevent an assault from being completed.

Often, drinking or drug use by the offender plays a part in causing the assault.

Although most victims do not have prolonged emotional reactions to sexual assaults, some express fears, depression, and anger years after the experience.

This type of sexual assault can often be prevented by remembering—and following—two simple guidelines:

Everyone has the right to say "no" to unwanted sexual contact.

No one has the right to force sexual contact on another person.

SOURCE: Ageton, 1985, p. iii.

during the rape—darkness, a man with a particular appearance, being alone—becomes associated with the fear response. These cues then become conditioned stimuli that independently evoke fear and anxiety. Because some of these stimuli are often encountered by the victim in her daily life, she may begin to use avoidance behavior to escape them. This decreases the likelihood that the conditioned fear response will dissipate over time. Behavior therapy offers a way of overcoming these problems. By using both cognitive and behavioral techniques, victims can learn to overcome their avoidance behavior and thus extinguish their anxiety (Veronen & Kilpatrick, 1983).

Since an estimated 10 to 20 percent of rape victims have continuing problems of sexual dysfunction several years after the rape, they may also be helped by sex therapy that takes into account anger and resentment toward men, guilt and self-blame, and attitudes toward their partners that may be a residue of the rape. Victims of uncontrollable events such as rape blame themselves for what has happened more than the objective situation suggests is realistic. Such self-blame is illustrated in this account of a rape victim's experience.

The young woman who was raped after the fraternity party berated herself initially for not

picking out some flaw in her assailant's character. She recalls wondering whether her blouse was too low-cut, or whether she had said or done anything to provoke the assault.

"It took me a long time," she says ruefully, "to realize that it wasn't my fault."

—Sherman, 1985, p. 19

Social-psychological research suggests that this self-blame by the victim might be a result of a desire to gain some control over the victimizing experience (Wortman, 1983). The self-perception that one is a victim and that others perceive one as a victim is unpleasant or aversive. Victims react to the aversiveness of their situation by evaluating in ways that are self-enhancing (Taylor, 1983). Some of these strategies include:

1. Minimizing the consequences by making comparisons with others who were less fortunate, or suggesting possible worse outcomes ("I might have been killed").

2. Thinking of one's own adjustment to the events as better than most people could attain ("I think I did extremely well under the circumstances. Some people would just fall apart").

3. Highlighting the gains from the victimization ("I was happy to find out that I am a very strong person. My life has been made better by this knowledge").

Rape victims need to know what to do and where to go after the rape in order to obtain medical, mental-health, social, and legal services. They also need immediate and follow-up medical care for physical trauma, collection of medicolegal evidence, prevention of venereal disease, and protection against unwanted pregnancy. Rape victims need to be listened to and helped to talk about their experience, as well as to be given basic information and assistance in making decisions about further steps to be taken. An important source of help for rape victims is rape-relief centers where information and psychological support may be obtained (see Figure 5–6).

Life Transitions

Whereas disasters and many personal crises are imposed on people from outside, other crises grow out of the individual's own path of personal development. Some of the transitions in the life cycle that can cause stress are the following.

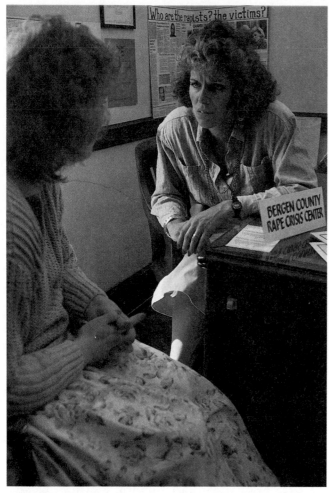

FIGURE 5–6 Rape relief centers provide information about medical and legal services for rape victims as well as immediate supportive interactions. Such centers attempt to reduce the feelings of social stigma experienced by many rape victims.

1. Birth and attainment of coordination between mother and infant

2. Initial steps toward independence and transition to an out-of-home facility (school, day-care center)

3. The biological and social changes that mark puberty and adolescence

4. Major educational transitions, such as going to college

5. Entry into the world of work

6. Marriage

7. Bearing and rearing children

8. Moving to a new place of residence

9. Children's milestones

10. Retirement

We will illustrate transitional stress with two examples: adolescence and old age.

ADOLESCENCE The role of cultural factors in adolescence cannot be overestimated. As a reasonably distinct period of life, adolescence might be described as a by-product of the Industrial Revolution. Prior to that event there had been no need to provide a special niche for people who were biologically no longer children but to whom society did not find it convenient to assign adult roles. Since the Industrial Revolution, the age at which individuals are admitted to adult occupational roles has repeatedly been raised, with the result that the period of adolescence has been lengthened. The stress experienced by adolescents has been increased by the lack of agreement about when adolescence ends as well as by the greater number of life choices young people have to make.

Adolescence can be divided into early, middle, and late periods. The dominant theme of early adolescence, approximately ages 12 to 14, is the individual's response to changes in sex hormone levels and a general growth spurt. For girls, the onset of puberty comes at an increasingly early age—the average age at first menstruation has declined from 16.5 years in 1860 to 12.5 years today. The comparable events of puberty for boys lag approximately two years behind those for girls.

By the end of this early period, the young teenager has acquired a body that is quite different from the one he or she had as a child. Changes in body image have a significant effect on an adolescent's self-concept. How well an adolescent likes his or her body often depends on how other people respond to it. For example, late-maturing boys generally show more personal and social maladjustment at all stages of adolescence than those who mature early. They tend to be characterized by negative self-concepts, prolonged dependency, and feelings of rejection by important peer groups. The picture is different for girls. Early-maturing girls often lack poise and are submissive in their social relationships. Late-maturing girls, on the other hand, seem more outgoing and self-assured (Conger, 1991).

The extent to which the unpredictable moodiness, depression, anger, and emotionality often seen in early adolescence are related to changes in sex hormone levels is unclear. It has been shown, however, that adolescence does not necessarily have to be a stormy and stressful time. Parental interest, reasonable guidelines, and support, particularly from the same-sex parent, play important roles in helping the younger teenager make the necessary developmental transitions.

During midadolescence (roughly 15 to 17 years of age), the teenager receives increasing responsibility and more privileges (for example, holding down a part-time job; driving a car). There are also increases in stress created by the fact that the adolescent is in many ways a marginal character: too old to be treated as a child, too young to have the rights of an adult. Perhaps the most

noteworthy developmental occurrence in midadolescence is the gradual shift from a here-and-now perspective to a point of view that is oriented toward the future. In addition, the individual becomes less self-absorbed and grows increasingly concerned with values and ideals.

In late adolescence, teenagers begin to relinquish their parents as primary attachment figures. Living with the family, which is seen as protection by some adolescents and as restraint by others, can now come to an end. Some individuals move directly into the adult roles of marriage and full-time work, whereas others enter a more or less extended adolescence through college or job-training experience. Major tasks of this period include development of a personal identity, renegotiation of the relationship to the family, and the development of stable and enduring ties to others. Late adolescence can be difficult for a variety of reasons, including high unemployment rates among teenagers and young adults as well as high crime rates and the problems posed by alcoholism and drug abuse.

During this period adolescents often feel isolated and in limbo. Various factors contribute to this adolescent loneliness. The adolescent experiences new desires and expectations that may not be readily satisfied but that disrupt existing personal relationships. A predisposition to loneliness may originate in such personality characteristics as shyness and low self-esteem and may be intensified by cultural factors such as the existing social network.

OLD AGE As people grow older, they often seem to slow down because of physiological changes. For example, chemical changes in bone structure make the bones more brittle. Age also seems to cause decreases in adrenal gland secretion, which results in hair loss. Changes in the central nervous system may result from the loss of cells that do not replace themselves, as well as from changes in hormone levels, oxygen deficiencies caused by impaired blood circulation, or changes in cell components. Finally, aging seems to be associated with increased susceptibility to disease.

Increased susceptibility to psychological disorders accompanies the physical debilities of old age. Depression is the most prevalent psychological disorder among older people, and paranoid thinking (for example, the belief that people are eavesdropping on one) seems to increase in the later years. Sleep patterns also change with age. Older people need less sleep and are more likely to awaken spontaneously during the night. A wide variety of physical complaints in the absence of a diagnosed physical problem is also frequent. Elderly people, who often have diminished physical and mental reserves, may face especially strong stressors, including illness and the adverse changes that typically accompany growing old, such as loss of loved ones, forced relocation, and increased dependence on others.

What makes for good adaptation to old age? People who adjust well to old age appear to have been able to enjoy themselves and to obtain gratification from social relationships throughout their lives. They are also able to express their feelings, have a positive self-image, and feel a sense of purpose in life. Maladjusted elderly people express distress and discontent and are problems for their family and often for their community. The following factors seem to encourage adaptation to old age.

1. Economic security
2. High educational level
3. Social independence (including the capacity for solitary enjoyment)
4. Good health

Clinical Reactions to Stress

Stress plays a role in most of the conditions that make up abnormal psychology. Stress disorders that require clinical attention are pathological because they go beyond expected and normal emotional and cognitive reactions to severe personal challenges. Table 5–7 lists some of the normal and abnormal responses to stress. As the table makes clear, many normal responses become abnormal reactions when symptoms persist and are excessive. Successful coping often involves the individual's somehow coming to terms with overwhelming feelings such as sadness or anger. For example, one researcher (Bohmfalk, 1991) documented the case of a physician who, while delivering terrible news to families of patients with dismal or hopeless prognoses, would develop an irrational urge to laugh. The doctor had to learn to face the overwhelming distress he felt in delivering the news. The physician described how he was finally able to face his own distress and free himself of his urge to laugh while conveying bad news to a particular patient's family.

The patient and her family were perfectly typical. The girl was neither beautiful nor brilliant, her family neither overbearing nor solicitous. Their deep concern for her fate was overblown by neither guilt nor persecution. Her severe injuries were ordinary, her operation went smoothly, and there was no problem over several days with any aspect of her care. She just wasn't going to

Table 5–7

Normal and Abnormal Responses to Stress

Normal Responses	Abnormal Responses
Feeling strong emotions subsequent to the event (for example, fear, sadness, rage)	Being overwhelmed by intense emotions; experiencing panic or exhaustion
Resistance to thinking about the event; denial	Extreme resistance to thinking about the event (for example, through use of drugs); massive denial
Having unwanted, intrusive thoughts about the event	Having disturbing, persistent images and thoughts that interfere with usual functioning
Temporary physical symptoms (headaches, stomach distress)	Strong, persistent bodily reactions (for example, continuing headaches, chronic stomach pains)
Resuming one's normal pattern of life	Long-term problems in ability to love and work

survive. This time, however, after bracing myself for the ultimate family conference and hoping I would be able to suppress an involuntary smile or chuckle, something wonderfully different happened. As the parents, grandparents, and siblings accepted my report and began to cry quietly, tears began flowing down my face. I had no guilt, I had nothing for which to apologize; I hadn't even come to know this family very well. But there I was, crying right along with them. I didn't want to cry, it just happened. I didn't feel stupid or self-conscious. I simply felt really sad.

. . . Since those initial belated tears, I never had to fight an inappropriate smile. Misery is no longer a laughing matter.

—Bohmfalk, 1991, p. 1245

This section will review three conditions, which, though dealt with by DSM in different ways, are all linked to stress arousal, strong emotional reactions—that may be denied—and clinical symptoms. In *adjustment disorders,* a recent increase in life stress precedes what is usually a temporary maladaptive reaction. *Posttraumatic disorders* are often more complicated because of the possibility of delayed and recurring reactions to stress. *Dissociative disorders* are among the most dramatic and puzzling forms of abnormal behavior and are almost always preceded by an upsurge of stress that the individual cannot handle.

Adjustment disorders are considered to be more straightforward than the other two conditions. This lack of ambiguity may be due to the fact that in an adjustment disorder specific stressful experiences can be identified as having occurred recently in the patient's life, and prospects of recovery are relatively good. While specific stressors can also be identified in a posttraumatic disorder, they are often more dramatic and overwhelming than those seen in adjustment disorders, their effects last over a longer period of time, and recovery prospects are less positive. One source of controversy about posttraumatic disorders is the question of the reliability of information about the patient's personality prior to the traumatic event. Clinicians must evaluate how much of the posttraumatic disorder is attributable to the event and how much to the patient's vulnerabilities before the event. Varying interpretations of dissociative disorders depend upon the weights given to a number of factors, including the stressors that immediately precede clinical flare-ups, stressors that may have occurred early in the person's life, and biological causes. A major challenge in the real world of maladaptive behavior is the multiplicity of factors involved in most cases.

Adjustment Disorder

A person with an **adjustment disorder** is someone who has not adapted as well as the average person to one or more stressors that have occurred in the previous three months. The stressors might involve a developmental transition (such as marriage, divorce, the death of a loved one, having a child, or menopause), or they might be situational (such as changing schools, getting a new supervisor at work, or having been socially rejected), or they might be multiple stressors that have accumulated recently. Most of the time a person's maladaptive

reactions to these stressors tend to disappear when the stressful circumstances dissipate or when the person learns how to live with new conditions. In the following case, the stressful transition to marriage resulted in an adjustment disorder.

Mark Catton, aged 23, had recently married. He and his wife had known each other for two years at college and were deeply in love. Their getting married seemed a perfectly logical consequence of their affection for each other. The first several weeks after the wedding were wonderful for the couple. They looked forward to their evenings together and often took short trips on the weekend.

One evening at dinner Dorothy talked about a new salesman at her office. She described him as intelligent, handsome, and charming. When Dorothy used the word "charming," something seemed to click inside Mark. He wondered why she had chosen that particular word to describe the new salesman, as well as why she talked so much about someone she had known for only a day. During the next few weeks Dorothy made several additional references to the salesman. Her liking for him was more obvious with each reference. Each time it came up, Mark became increasingly suspicious and depressed. When Dorothy worked until late in the evening twice in one week, his suspiciousness and depression increased. When he confronted her with his suspicion that she was dating the salesman, Dorothy displayed shock and outrage.

During the next few weeks Mark became increasingly depressed. His depression was interrupted only by occasional outbursts of venom directed toward Dorothy. Their sex life soon ceased to exist, and their evenings were filled with silence. The problem reached clinical proportions when Mark began to stay in bed all day. It took great effort for Dorothy to get him to see a psychotherapist, although by this time even Mark knew that something was very wrong.

During his sessions with the psychotherapist Mark came to see how unrealistic his expectations about marriage were. He also was able for the first time to bring all of his thoughts and feelings out into the open. One recollection about his parents seemed particularly important. He remembered that when he was about six or seven his parents had quarreled a great deal, apparently over his father's suspicion about his mother's activities at home while he was at work. His father had accused his mother of infidelity and had been very nasty. Mark couldn't remember exactly how the situation had been resolved. Although he had not thought about the incident for years, it became very meaningful to him, and discussing it in psychotherapy seemed to help him.

Mark Catton's case is interesting because it shows so clearly the interaction between past and present experiences. His own marital problems, created by his irrational suspicions about his wife's activities, seemed to be linked to things his wife had told him about the salesman and to his unrecognized fear that what his father had feared was actually being inflicted on him. One additional point about this case is that Mark had no history of suspiciousness and depression. Both reaction patterns had apparently been ignited simply by getting married. His psychological functioning deteriorated primarily because of the expectations and concerns he had brought to the marital situation, not because of a traumatic development within the marriage.

The severity of an adjustment disorder is not directly proportional to the severity of the stressor, because personality characteristics as well as cultural or group norms contribute to how well an individual copes with a given set of circumstances. However, one characteristic of adjustment disorders is that the behavior displayed is in excess of what would normally be expected under the circumstances. Depression over the death of a loved one would not be considered an adjustment disorder, because such a reaction is expected. Depression over a minor disagreement with a friend, on the other hand, would likely be considered an adjustment disorder.

An adjustment disorder usually does not involve extremely bizarre behavior and is not part of a lifelong pattern of maladaptation. The chances of complete recovery when the stress level comes down are good. Depression, anxiety, disturbances in conduct (truancy, fighting, reckless driving), disrupted sleep patterns, deterioration in performance at work or school, and social withdrawal are typical behaviors of individuals who have adjustment disorders.

BEREAVEMENT AND GRIEF **Bereavement** refers to the loss of someone significant through that person's death. The normal course of recovery from bereavement often extends to a year or more, and such a pattern of recovery is not considered to be an adjustment disorder. It is only when a person's response differs from this

normal pattern, and coping difficulties and emotional distress continue without gradual improvement, that the diagnosis of adjustment disorder would be given. Table 5–8 lists behavioral and physiological changes frequently observed in the period following the loss of a loved one.

Grief is the emotional or affective response to the loss. The symptoms of grief are part of a normal recovery process and not a sign of pathology. Nevertheless, grief takes more prolonged, pervasive, and complicated forms than many people realize. These forms vary greatly; there is no uniform and orderly succession of stages through which all bereaved people must pass. However, certain phases are observed often enough to be recognized as, if not typical, at least common after the death of a husband, wife, or child. The first reactions are often shock, numbness, bewilderment, and a sense of disbelief—even denial of the reality for a time. This reaction is common even when the death was anticipated. After a few days numbness turns to intense suffering. Grieving people feel empty. They are repeatedly reminded of the person who has died. Waves of crying sweep over them with each reminder; they may have dreams and even hallucinations in which the dead person is still alive (Clayton, 1990).

After this comes a period of despair, as the grieving person slowly accepts the loss. The dominant feelings are sadness and inability to feel pleasure. Tense, restless anxiety may alternate with lethargy and fatigue. Physical symptoms are common—weakness, sleep disturbances, loss of appetite, headaches, back pain, indigestion, shortness of breath, heart palpitations, and even occasional dizziness and nausea (Stroebe & Stroebe, 1987).

Grieving persons may alternate between avoiding reminders of the deceased and cultivating memories. Some desperately seek company, and others withdraw. Sadness is mixed with anger—at doctors who failed, at friends and relatives thought to be unappreciative, even

at the dead person for abandoning the living. The motives of people who try to help are sometimes suspected, and grieving persons may alienate their friends by irritability and quarrelsomeness. Most painful of all is self-reproach for having treated the deceased badly or having done too little to prevent the death. For example, there is evidence that a spouse's recovery from grief is quicker and more complete when the marriage was happy (Stroebe & Stroebe, 1987).

As we stated earlier, grief following bereavement is normal. However, sometimes the grieving process becomes abnormal. If that happens, the bereaved person may suffer persistent anxiety or depression produced by morbid or unresolved grief (Parkes, 1986). In such a case psychotherapy may be helpful.

Research on grief and the failure of some bereaved people to resume a normal life in a reasonable period of time is needed because bereavement is so common and because popular ideas about how people do or should respond to loss may not be correct. There is evidence that the grief process may be more complex than is generally thought to be the case (Wortman, 1987). In one study the effects of bereavement on several thousand men and women in semirural Washington County, Maryland, were investigated (Helsing, 1981). The bereaved subjects were compared with still-married individuals who were similar in such factors as age, sex, race, education, religious interests, and socioeconomic status. The major finding was that bereavement is much harder on men than on women. The overall mortality rate was 26 percent higher for widowers than for married men, compared with only a 3.8 percent difference between the rates for widows and married women. For widowers aged 55 to 64, the mortality rate was almost 61 percent higher than the rate for married men in the same age group. In men under 55 who remarried (at least half of them did), the death rate was at least 70 percent lower than for those who did not. In men aged 55 to 64, it was 50 percent lower. Death rates for widowers who remarried were even lower than the rates for men in the same age groups who were married throughout the period of the study. This study did not support the popular idea that the remaining spouse's risk of dying was significantly greater in the early months after bereavement. Only long-term death rates differed for the widowed and still-married subjects. Further research is being conducted to find out why wives are less affected by the loss of a spouse than husbands (Stroebe & Stroebe, 1987).

Table 5–8

Behavioral and Physiological Aspects of Bereavement in Adults

Behavioral Changes	Physiological Changes
Crying	Muscular weakness
Agitation, restlessness	Sighing
Preoccupation with image of the deceased	Sleep disturbance
Social withdrawal	Immunological changes
Decreased concentration and attention	Endocrine changes
Depressed mood	Cardiovascular changes
Anxiety	Decreased body weight

SOURCE: Based on Hofer, 1984.

Posttraumatic Disorders

Whereas the stressors in adjustment disorder are within the range of common experience, **posttraumatic**

disorders involve more extreme experiences (such as disasters) whose effects may extend over a long period. The onset of the clinical condition in posttraumatic disorders varies from soon after the trauma to a long time afterward. These disorders are considered to be acute if the condition begins within six months of the trauma and delayed if symptoms emerge more than six months after the event. The chances of complete recovery are better in the acute form than in the delayed form. Although preexisting psychological difficulties may intensify post-traumatic disorders, many people who develop these disorders do not have a history of psychiatric problems (Jones & Barlow, 1990).

A frequent characteristic of posttraumatic disorders is a tendency to reexperience the event. Painful and intrusive recollections and recurrent dreams or night-mares are common. The reexperiencing of a traumatic event may have an aura of unreality about it. When this happens, the person feels emotionally anesthetized amid an unstoppable flood of thoughts about the event.

In addition to reexperiencing the stressor, people who are suffering from posttraumatic disorders may show excessive autonomic arousal, hyperalertness, difficulty in concentrating on or completing tasks, and difficulty falling asleep. A symptom that often occurs in children who have experienced trauma is an exaggerated startle response. These symptoms may increase when the individual is exposed to cues related to the traumatic event (for example, when a victim of an automobile accident sees a car crash in a movie). Preoccupation with the traumatic event may also lead to decreased interest in social relationships, intimacy, and sexuality. Painful guilt feelings are common, as are depression, restlessness, and irritability. In some cases, there may be outbreaks of impulsive behavior, usually of a nonviolent nature (for example, unexplained absences from work), and abuse of alcohol or drugs.

In the following case, there was a short interval between the stressor and the onset of the posttraumatic condition. This case illustrates how denial can be used to blunt the strong feelings aroused by a stressful event.

Harry is a 40-year-old-truck dispatcher. He had worked his way up in a small trucking firm. One night he himself took a run because he was shorthanded. The load was steel pipes carried in an old truck. This improper vehicle had armor between the load bed and the driver's side of the forward compartment but did not fully protect the passenger's side.

Late at night Harry passed an attractive and solitary girl hitchhiking on a lonely stretch of highway. Making an impulsive decision to violate the company rule against passengers of any sort, he picked her up.

A short time later, a car veered across the divider line and entered his lane, threatening a head-on collision. He pulled over the shoulder of the road into an initially clear area, but crashed abruptly into a pile of gravel. The pipes shifted, penetrated the cab of the truck on the passenger's side and impaled the girl. Harry crashed into the steering wheel and windshield and was briefly unconscious. He regained consciousness and was met with the grisly sight of his dead companion.

The highway patrol found no identification on the girl, the other car had driven on, and Harry was taken by ambulance to a hospital emergency room. No fractures were found, his lacerations were sutured, and he remained overnight for observation. His wife, who sat with him, found him anxious and dazed that night, talking episodically of the events in a fragmentary and incoherent way so that the story was not clear.

The next day he was released. Against his wife's wishes, he returned to work. From then on, for several days, he continued his regular work as if nothing had happened. There was an immediate session with his superiors and with legal advisors. The result was that he was reprimanded for breaking the rule about passengers but also reassured that, otherwise, the accident was not his fault and he would not be held responsible. As it happened, the no passenger rule was frequently breached by other drivers, and this was well known throughout the group.

For several days after the accident Harry thought about it occasionally, but he was surprised at how little emotion he felt. However, despite his good performance at work, Harry's wife reported that he thrashed around in his sleep, ground his teeth, and seemed tenser and more irritable than usual. A month after the accident he had a nightmare in which mangled bodies appeared. He awoke in a state of anxiety. During the following days he had recurring, upsetting images of the girl's body. He developed a phobia about driving to and from work, increased his consumption of alcohol, had outbursts of temper at minor frustrations, and began feeling intense guilt about the accident.

In psychotherapy an effort was made to understand the significance of the accident for Harry. Initially Harry resisted describing to the

therapist the circumstances surrounding the accident. After this resistance subsided, his strong feelings—the guilt, fears, and anger—emerged and were discussed. Because of complex and defensive motives, Harry could not accept and integrate his traumatic perceptions of the accident. They were stored, but not forgotten. He came to understand that two themes had been most upsetting to him: guilt over his relief at the fact that the girl had been the victim instead of him, as well as guilt over his sexual fantasies about her; and anxiety over the realization that he had come so close to being the victim. Bringing these themes into focus enabled Harry to be more open about himself and to take a problem-solving rather than a defensive stance toward his situation. Psychotherapy enabled him to look at himself in a more realistic way, to feel comfortable doing so within the supportive-therapy situation, and to achieve an improved adaptation.

—Adapted from Horowitz, 1974, p. 769–771

Table 5–9

Symptoms of Intrusive Thinking and Denial in Posttraumatic Stress Disorders (Symptoms May Alternate)

Symptoms of Intrusive Thinking

Sleep and dream disturbances
Awareness of ideas and feelings related to the traumatic event
Preoccupation with the event
Compulsive repetitions of actions related to the event

Symptoms of Denial

Selective inattention
Amnesia (complete or partial)
Use of fantasy to counteract real conditions
Withdrawal

SOURCE: Adapted from Horowitz, 1986. Copyright © 1986 by the American Psychological Association. Reprinted by permission of the author.

What happens in posttraumatic stress? In coping with trauma, an individual uses a huge amount of psychological energy to fend off thoughts about it. Although the event has ended, it is relived daily, and there is an irrational fear that it will happen again. It is this fear that causes hypervigilance and agitation. Intrusive thoughts, images, and dreams may become so preoccupying that the person cannot engage in normal work or relationships.

In some cases of maladaptive reactions to trauma there may be an alternation of intrusive thinking and denial. In the intrusive state, the individual cannot stop having frightening thoughts related to the traumatic event. In the denial state, the individual ignores the implications of threats and losses, forgets important problems, and may show a withdrawal of interest in life. Table 5–9 lists symptoms of the intrusive and denial phases of posttraumatic disorders.

Posttraumatic stress disorder (PTSD), in which the reaction continues over a considerable period of time, is now an established psychiatric diagnosis, but it is still a controversial one. Epidemiological evidence suggests that the prevalence of PTSD is 1 percent in the general population and about 3.5 percent in civilians exposed to physical attack and in Vietnam veterans who were not wounded. About 20 percent of wounded veterans show symptoms of PTSD (Helzer and others, 1987). There is some evidence that preexisting emotional and behavioral difficulties increase the likelihood of PTSD. In one study,

72 percent of individuals with PTSD diagnoses had pre-stress histories of psychological disorders (Smith and others, 1990). Prominent among the pre-stress conditions diagnoses of adult PTSD patients were depression and alcohol abuse.

Certain symptoms may be related to the type of trauma experienced, such as whether or not the individual played a role in causing the traumatic event (for example, by driving a car recklessly or speeding). Victims of crimes involving violence and humiliation (for example, rape) often feel both intensely fearful and ashamed. Rape victims often show this type of reaction. Their anger at being victimized and the lack of control they feel concerning the event many times results in long term effects such as those discussed earlier in the chapter. Psychotherapy can often be helpful in reducing these effects because it helps victims to view the experience in a more objective way as well as to express the strong emotions they may have felt forced to suppress in conversations with friends and relatives.

The failure to confront a traumatic event is an important contributor to unhappiness and maladjustment, and the opportunity to tell a sympathetic listener about it can be therapeutic. After the worst fire in California history, a 1991 fire that burned thousands of acres in the Oakland-Berkeley hills, destroyed hundreds of homes, and killed 23 people, a coalition of artists and mental health experts launched a post-disaster art therapy program for students in the Oakland and Berkeley schools. Figure 5–7 shows the handiwork of a 10-year-old girl who had been very worried about her father's safety and had had to wait for hours to know whether he

FIGURE 5–7 Children who have experienced a disaster often feel anxiety for long afterwards. This sixth grader, from the area of Oakland that was devastated by the worst fire in California in recent times, displayed a Halloween mask of roaring flames. She made it as part of a post-disaster art therapy program and described her work as a "way to get my feelings out."

was safe. For younger students, art productions can be a way to express emotions beyond the capability of their vocabularies. For older children, they provide a way to express emotions without being embarrassed or feeling they have to respond correctly to adults' questions. The teachers had observed that after the severe earthquake that hit the area two years earlier, and again after the fire, the classroom behavior of children who were both directly and indirectly affected became much less constructive and harder to control. Many children showed symptoms of anxiety and some reported recurrent dreams of the fire experience.

Dissociative Disorders

Dissociative disorders are disturbances or alterations in the functions of identity, memory, and consciousness. The disturbance may come about suddenly or gradually and may last only a brief period or be long-lasting and chronic. The person's identity may be temporarily forgotten or a new identity assumed or there may be a feeling that one's sense of reality is lost. The maladaptive behaviors that arise from dissociative disorders provide a striking contrast to those that arise from posttraumatic stress disorders and adjustment disorders. Stress plays a major role in both, yet the reactions involved appear to be poles apart. Once again we see that

similar situations can elicit drastically different responses in people with different dispositions and vulnerabilities.

People with dissociative disorders use a variety of dramatic maneuvers to escape from the anxieties and conflicts aroused by stress. Their behavior involves sudden, temporary alterations of consciousness that serve to blot out painful experiences. In contrast, in posttraumatic stress disorders, individuals cannot get the distressing experiences that they have undergone out of their minds, and people with adjustment disorders show milder disturbances and decreased ability to cope, but their behavior clears up when they learn to adapt to a stressor, or when the stressor is removed.

Many dissociative disorders appear to begin and end abruptly and are precipitated by stressful experiences. Although these disorders usually occur after childhood, in most cases there is a history of serious family turmoil. Separation from parents in early childhood and abuse by parents have frequently been reported (Putnam, 1991).

The dissociation often involves feelings of unreality, estrangement, and depersonalization, and sometimes a loss or shift of self-identity. Less dramatic, but somewhat similar, examples of dissociation are commonly observed in normal adults and children. When the first impact of bad news or a catastrophe hits us, we may feel as if everything is suddenly strange, unnatural, and different (estrangement), or as if we are unreal and cannot actually be witnessing or feeling what is going on

(depersonalization). These are not classified as dissociative disorders but are useful to help in understanding what the much more severe dissociative disorder is like.

Four conditions classified as dissociative disorders are:

1. Psychogenic amnesia
2. Psychogenic fugue
3. Multiple personality
4. Depersonalization

All of these disorders involve large memory gaps and drastic changes in social roles (Braun, 1990).

PSYCHOGENIC AMNESIA Amnesia involves extensive, but selective, memory losses. Because some memory losses can also be traced to organic changes (for example, head injuries), the word **psychogenic** is used when no organic causes are discernible. The memory losses that are characteristic of amnesia are too extensive to be explained by ordinary forgetfulness. Some people cannot remember anything about their past. Others can no longer recall specific events, people, places, or objects while their memory for other, simultaneously experienced events remains intact.

Amnesia is usually precipitated by a physical accident or an emotionally traumatic event such as an intensely painful disappointment. Cases of psychogenic amnesia demonstrate, as Ernest Hilgard (1986) has noted, that the unity of consciousness is illusory. Our conscious representation of our actions is incomplete; our attention is usually divided among two or more streams of thought or courses of action. Unconscious systems of ideas may come to be split off from the major personality and exist as subordinate personalities, capable of becoming represented in consciousness under certain conditions. The following account illustrates the power of such unconscious forces.

A young man dressed in work clothes came to the emergency room of a hospital in the city in which he lived with the complaint that he did not know who he was. He seemed dazed, was not intoxicated, and carried no identification. After being kept in the hospital a few days, he woke up one morning in great distress, demanding to know why he was being kept in the hospital and announcing that he had to leave immediately to attend to urgent business.

With the recovery of his memory, the facts related to his amnesia emerged. The day his amnesia

began, he had been the driver in an automobile accident that resulted in the death of a pedestrian. Police officers on the scene were convinced that the driver had not been in the wrong: the accident had been the pedestrian's fault. The police told the driver to fill out a routine form and to plan to appear at the coroner's inquest. The man filled out the form at the home of a friend and accidentally left his wallet there. Later after mailing the form, he became dazed and amnesic. He was led to the hospital by a stranger. The amnesia was probably related to the stress of the fatal accident, fear of the inquest, and worry that he might actually have been responsible for the accident.

—Based on Cameron, 1963, pp. 355–56

While amnesia is probably the most common dissociative disorder, there are no accurate statistics on the incidence of any of the dissociative disorders. Psychogenic amnesias are seen more often in adolescents and young adults than in children and older people, and occur more often among females than males.

PSYCHOGENIC FUGUE Psychogenic fugue has as its essential feature unexpected travel away from home and customary workplace, the assumption of a new identity, and the inability to recall the previous identity. The travel and behavior seen in a person in a psychogenic fugue are more purposeful than any wandering that may take place in psychogenic amnesia. Such a person sets up a new life in some distant place as a seemingly different person. The fugue state, or amnesic flight, usually ends when he or she abruptly "wakes up," mystified and distressed at being in a strange place under strange circumstances (see Figure 5–8).

Fugues, like amnesia, are often precipitated by intolerable stresses such as marital quarrels, personal rejection, military conflict, and natural disasters. Fugues are usually of brief duration, with complete recovery and little likelihood of recurrence. After "waking up," the person frequently has no recollection of the events that took place during the fugue. The following case illustrates a fugue state with massive amnesia.

Samuel O., a graduate student, impoverished and far from home, was invited to dinner at the home of an instructor whom he had known when they were socioeconomic equals in another town. He accepted the invitation because he was lonely

the train and get away. When he acted on this
impulse, he apparently became amnesic.

—Based on Easton, 1959, pp. 505–513

FIGURE 5–8 Police distributed this photograph of a woman found wandering on a New Jersey highway in the hope that someone would recognize her. When she was found she was unable to remember her name, where she lived, or how she came to be walking along the highway.

and hungry, but he regretted it almost at once because his clothes were shabby. He thought, in retrospect, that the instructor had seemed condescending. That evening he left his rooming house in plenty of time for the dinner, but he failed to show up at the instructor's home. Two days later he was picked up by the police in a neighboring state. He could vaguely remember riding a freight train, talking with strangers, and sharing their food, but he had no idea who he was, where he had come from, or where he was going.

Later on, the young man was able to remember the events leading up to the fugue and something of what went on during it. When he started out for the instructor's house, he was still experiencing strong conflict about going there. He was ashamed of his appearance, resentful over the condescension, and afraid to express what he felt and call the dinner off. On his way, he was held up at a grade crossing by a slowly moving freight train. He had a sudden impulse to board

MULTIPLE PERSONALITY Multiple personality is the most dramatic of the dissociative disorders. In a multiple-personality reaction an individual assumes alternate personalities, like Dr. Jekyll and Mr. Hyde. Each personality has its own set of memories and typical behaviors. Frequently none of the personalities has any awareness of the others. In other cases, there is a one-way amnesia in which personality A is aware of the experiences of personality B while B remains unaware of A.

While multiple personality is a rare disorder, it is of increasing interest because of the marked increase in the number of cases currently being described in the clinical literature and the linkage that has been made in many of these cases between multiple personality and traumatic childhood experiences. The improved diagnostic criteria for the disorder that first appeared in DSM-III are thought to have contributed to the increased number of reported cases (Kluft, 1991). Many more female than male multiple personalities have been reported, the ratio being about 4 to 1 (Kluft, 1988).

Clinically, the personalities' behavioral differences and disparate self-concepts seem striking and puzzling. They may experience themselves as being of different genders, ages, and sexual orientations. They may have separate wardrobes, possessions, interests, and interpersonal styles. Their values, beliefs, and problems may diverge. They may even have different handwritings, handedness, speech patterns, and accents.

In the following case, a 38-year-old woman named Margaret B. was admitted to a hospital with paralysis of her legs following a minor car accident that had occurred six months earlier.

She reported that until three years before her admission to the hospital she had enjoyed smoking, drinking, visiting nightclubs, and otherwise indulging in parties and social activities. At that point, however, she and her husband, who was an alcoholic, were converted to a small, evangelical religious sect. Her husband achieved control of his drinking, she gave up her prior social indulgences, and the two of them became completely immersed in the activities of the church.

[The] history revealed that she often "heard a voice telling her to say things and do things." It was, she said, "a terrible voice" that sometimes threatened to "take over completely." When it was finally suggested to the patient that she let the voice "take over," she closed her eyes, clenched her fists, and grimaced for a few moments during which she was out of contact with those around her. Suddenly she opened her eyes and one was in the presence of another person. Her name, she said, was "Harriet." Whereas Margaret had been paralyzed, and complained of fatigue, headache and backache, Harriet felt well, and she at once proceeded to walk unaided around the interviewing room. She spoke scornfully of Margaret's religiousness, her invalidism and her puritanical life, professing that she herself liked to drink and "go partying" but that Margaret was always going to church and reading the Bible. "But," she said impishly and proudly, "I make her miserable—I make her say and do things she doesn't want to." At length, at the interviewer's suggestion, Harriet reluctantly agreed to "bring Margaret back," and after more grimacing and fist clenching, Margaret reappeared, paralyzed, complaining of her headache and backache, and completely amnesic for the brief period of Harriet's release from her prison.

—Nemiah, 1988, 247–248

The clash between Margaret's religiousness, on the one hand, and her inclinations to indulge in pleasure, on the other, is a frequent theme in cases of multiple personality. It is noteworthy that as a child Margaret had had a playmate, Harriet, to whom she had been very devoted. When they were both 6 years old Harriet had died of an acute infectious disease. Margaret had been deeply upset at her friend's death and wished that she had died in Harriet's place. Perhaps internalizing the image of her dead friend had in some way protected Margaret from prolonged despair and sorrow at her loss. As Margaret grew older, that internalization became the depository for all of her unacceptable impulses and feelings.

Many clinicians think of multiple personality as a psychological adaptation to traumatic experiences in early childhood. These experiences are severe and dramatic; examples are being dangled out of a window or being the victim of sexual sadism. In addition to having experienced harsh trauma in childhood, people with multiple personality seem prone to go into spontaneous hypnotic trances. This temporary defense may become

stabilized into multiple personality when the child faces repeated, overwhelming trauma.

Some researchers question whether multiple personality represents anything more than an extreme form of the normal ability to present a variety of distinctive "selves." An important reason for such disagreements about multiple personality is that cases of this disorder are rare, making it difficult to do good research and to compare cases seen at different times under different circumstances. Despite methodological difficulties, studies of multiple personality are proceeding on a number of fronts.

One provocative lead in multiple personality research relates to the possible role of brain abnormalities. Some studies have found that people with multiple personality have an elevated risk for epileptic seizures (Benson and others, 1986). It is possible that there is a connection between seizures and the switch between personalities. However, while some cases of epilepsy may involve a neurological condition that is associated with multiple personality, the strength and basis of the association are not yet established. Future work is needed to explore the possibility of a biological basis to the capacity to dissociate, the ways in which stress early in life and later on interact with biological factors, and the development of effective therapies. Clinicians believe that establishing a secure, trusting relationship with the therapist is essential for therapeutic progress (Kluft, 1988). When this is achieved, it becomes possible to deal with conflicts among the personalities and help the patient move toward cooperation among them and, optimally, integration of the personalities.

DEPERSONALIZATION While **depersonalization** is usually included among the dissociative disorders, some clinicians question its inclusion because it does not entail memory disturbances. In depersonalization there is a change in self-perception, and the person's sense of reality is temporarily lost or changed. Someone who is experiencing a state of depersonalization might say, "I feel as though I'm in a dream" or "I feel that I'm doing this mechanically." Frequently the individual has a feeling of not being in complete control of his or her actions, including speech. The onset of depersonalization is usually rapid and causes social or occupational impairment. The state of estrangement from oneself gradually disappears.

The following case illustrates several features of depersonalization:

A 24-year-old graduate student sought treatment because he felt he was losing his mind. He had begun to doubt his own reality. He felt he was

*living in a dream in which he saw himself from
without, and did not feel connected to his body
or his thoughts. When he saw himself through his
own eyes, he perceived his body parts as
distorted—his hands and feet seemed quite large.
As he walked across campus, he often felt the
people he saw might be robots; he began to
ruminate about his dizzy spells—did this mean
that he had a brain tumor?*

*. . . He often noted that he spent so much time
thinking about his situation that he lost contact
with all feelings except a pervasive discomfort
about his own predicament. . . .*

*. . . [H]e was preoccupied with his perception that
his feet had grown too large for his shoes, and
fretted over whether to break up with his
girlfriend because he doubted the reality of his
feelings for her, and had begun to perceive her in
a distorted manner.*

—Kluft, 1988, p. 580

People with depersonalization disorders may have
either a persistent sense of depersonalization or suffer
recurrent episodes. In either case, they perceive them-
selves as having lost their usual sense of reality, or as
having had it changed. They feel as if they are in a dream
and fear losing their sanity. A number of cases have been
reported in which depersonalization seemed to be a
response to extreme stress (Kluft, 1988).

INTERPRETING DISSOCIATIVE DISORDERS Dis-
sociation seems to represent a process whereby certain
mental functions that are ordinarily integrated with other
functions presumably operate in a more compartmental-
ized or automatic way, usually outside the sphere of
conscious awareness or memory recall. It might be
described as a condition in which information—incom-
ing, stored, or outgoing—is actively deflected from its
usual or expected associations. This phenomenon results
in alteration of the person's thoughts, feelings, or actions
so that information is not associated or integrated with
other information as it normally or logically would be.

The dissociative disorders are difficult to explain,
for several reasons. Often it is unclear whether a given
case involves dissociation or is some sort of psychotic
manifestation. Also, it is often difficult to obtain the
information needed to draw reasonable conclusions. In
the multiple personality case of Margaret, for example,
one wonders about the stressors that led to Harriet's
emergence. How important were the loss of the 6-year-
old playmate and the recent changes in Margaret's adult
life? While the source of stress is easy to identify in

adjustment and posttraumatic disorders, in the dissocia-
tive disorders, the source might not be obvious at all.
Dissociative disorders may be related to combinations of
vulnerability factors (for example, certain aspects of
biological makeup) and stresses that occurred many years
before maladaptation reached clinical proportions. Be-
cause human beings are able to distort their memories,
considerable probing is often needed to determine the
true nature of the stress.

Dissociative disorders are often discussed in psy-
chodynamic and cognitive terms. These disorders help
the individual escape from reality and seem to facilitate
the expression of a variety of pent-up emotions. They
have been interpreted as attempts to escape from exces-
sive tension, anxiety, and stimulation by separating some
parts of the personality from the rest. When there are no
indications of a recent experience that might have
functioned as a stressor, these perspectives raise questions
about earlier stressors that might still have symbolic
meaning for the individual. (Margaret's loss of Harriet
illustrates this possibility.) In treating dissociative disor-
ders, many clinicians seek to uncover the dissociated
memories and to help the individual face them and deal
with them more directly. Psychoanalysis, behavior ther-
apy, hypnosis, and videotaped interviews combined with
sedative drugs have all been useful for this purpose.

Treating Stress-Related Problems

People often overcome their maladaptive reactions
to stress in the course of time, but help from an expert
may speed up the process. The clinician has two broad
functions: (1) to provide social support for troubled
people, and (2) to strengthen their coping skills. Several
procedures are used in treating stress-related problems.

Supportive Therapy

It is hard to recover from a stress-related disorder if
one is or feels socially isolated. Because most stress
reactions involve feelings of inadequacy and isolation,
many people can be helped by sympathetic listening and
encouragement. Though they use different terms, both
psychodynamically and humanistically oriented clinicians
emphasize the client–therapist relationship as a means of
facilitating adaptive coping. Freudians describe their
efforts in this regard as strengthening the client's ego.
When the ego is able to manipulate reality more

effectively, it can handle the id's incessant demands with less stress. The Rogerian therapist's acceptance of clients as they are, coupled with recognition of their strengths and deemphasis of their failings, helps clients feel more positive about themselves and creates a supportive climate. Clients who receive supportive therapy often comment with relief that the therapist did not criticize them either directly or indirectly for their handling of difficult situations. Within a supportive environment clients can relax enough to engage in problem solving and the careful consideration of alternatives that had previously seemed impossible.

Drugs and Sedatives

A variety of anti-anxiety and antidepressive drugs are available to help people who have experienced trauma. While they are not a cure, such drugs can be of considerable value in overcoming panic states and other maladaptive reactions to intense short-term stress. Tranquilizers are often used along with psychological approaches such as supportive therapy.

Relaxation Training

It is possible for people to learn ways of helping themselves deal with stress. It is a well-known fact that people can learn to regulate voluntarily certain effects of the autonomic nervous system. Such regulation, in turn, can affect their emotional state. For example, anxiety can be caused by the sensation of tension that is experienced when muscle fibers are shortened or contracted, as they are during stress. Conversely, tension cannot be present when muscle fibers are lengthened or relaxed. Relaxation training involves the following steps.

1. Focusing attention on a series of specific muscle groups
2. Tensing each group
3. Maintaining tension for five to seven seconds
4. Telling oneself to relax and immediately releasing tension

5. Focusing attention on each muscle group as it relaxes

Relaxation training is used not only as a technique in its own right but also as a basis for other therapies. It is applicable to a wide variety of stress-related problems and can be readily taught both individually and in groups.

Systematic Desensitization

This procedure consists of combining relaxation training and a hierarchy of anxiety-producing stimuli to gradually eliminate the fear of a specific situation. The person learns to maintain the relaxed state while imagining anxiety-associated stimuli from the various stages of the hierarchy. In one study, soldiers with fears of airplanes, open places, and blood were treated with systematic desensitization (Kipper, 1977). The result was a significant reduction in their fears.

Cognitive Modification

Behavioral problems can arise in part because an individual persists in a particular maladaptive line of thought. If someone can be guided to think about a situation in a different, more productive way, adaptive coping may become possible. Cognitive modification involves learning new internal dialogues and new ways of thinking about situations and about oneself. In this sense, cognitive modification is a step toward productive problem solving.

Social Intervention

Some therapists prefer to treat troubled individuals alone, whereas others feel that they can be more helpful if they treat people within their social contexts. Family therapy, in which all members of the family go into treatment together, is based on the latter idea. In some instances the clinical worker might even decide to make one or more home visits to observe the family's interactions in more natural surroundings.

Chapter Summary

VULNERABILITY, TEMPERAMENT, AND COPING

People use two types of appraisal to determine how to deal with any situation. First, during **primary appraisal,** a situation is interpreted as either threatening or harmless. During **secondary appraisal,** assessment is made of the kind of action called for and also the effectiveness of personal resources to deal with the situation. **Vulnerability** to stress is influenced by a person's temperament, coping skills, and available social support. **Temperament** refers to consistent aspects of a person's behavior, especially those related to feelings and emotions. **Coping skills** refer to a person's characteristic ways of dealing with different types of situations.

Coping Techniques People who are effective copers usually have a variety of techniques available and are able to choose those most appropriate for the situation. These effective copers also learn to direct their thoughts toward problem solving and are able to avoid distraction caused by fear and worry.

Social Support **Social support,** the feeling of being cared about, valued, and loved by others, can help make people less vulnerable to stress. This belief that social support is available also encourages people to develop new ways to cope during periods that are not highly stressful. A relationship has been shown by many researchers between the availability of social support and both psychological and physical health.

STRESS AROUSAL

Stress can have undesirable effects on behavior, thought, and bodily functioning. Different people react to stressors in different ways so that the correlation between particular stressors and their effects on the different bodily symptoms is often low. It is particularly hard for people to deal with several stressors that occur nearly at the same time. However, the cumulative effects of stressors over a long period of time can also have a negative effect on a person's mental and physical health. Questionnaires are often used to assess what events a person has experienced in the recent past as well as how he or she perceived the events and reacted to them.

Stress-Arousing Situations Stress can arise either from specific situations or from developmental transitions. Stressful events vary in several ways: duration, severity, predictability, degree of loss of control, self-confidence of the person, and suddenness of onset. Accidents, natural disasters, and military combat all can bring about high levels of stress and may result in a posttraumatic stress disorder. Stress may also be the result of a personal crisis such as being victimized or raped.

Life Transitions Life transitions, such as going to college, getting a job, having a baby, and moving, may also be stressful. Adolescence is a time of particular stress because of physical changes, role changes, and changes in parent-child relationships. Another especially stressful period can be old age. Retirement, changes in family structure, increased susceptibility to disease, and lack of economic security can all contribute to increased stress.

CLINICAL REACTIONS TO STRESS

Among the disorders that seem most related to stress are adjustment disorders, posttraumatic disorders, and dissociative disorders.

Adjustment Disorder An **adjustment disorder** is a reaction to recent stress and usually disappears when the stress level decreases. Common symptoms of adjustment disorder are depression, anxiety, disruptive or reckless behavior, sleep problems, deterioration in performance, and social withdrawal. **Grief** following **bereavement** does not constitute an adjustment disorder unless it continues for an unusually long time.

Posttraumatic Disorders **Posttraumatic stress disorder** (PTSD) may occur after an extreme stress such as a natural disaster, a serious accident, or participation in battle or other war-related situations. PTSD symptoms vary widely, but may include recurrent dreams, flashbacks, impaired concentration, and emotional numbing. Those who experience PTSD after a stressful experience are likely to have had pre-stress histories of psychological disorder.

Dissociative Disorders Sudden temporary alterations of consciousness that blot out painful experiences are characteristic of **dissociative disorders.** Four conditions are included in this group: psychogenic amnesia, psychogenic fugue, multiple personality, and depersonalization. **Psychogenic amnesia** involves extensive, but selective, memory losses that have no known organic cause. This disorder is often associated with overwhelming stress. In a **psychogenic fugue,** the person loses identity, leaves home, and sets up a new life in a distant place. The fugue usually ends suddenly when the person suddenly "wakes up" with no memory of the events during the fugue. **Multiple personality** often seems to be associated with traumatic experiences in childhood. In this disorder the person assumes alternate personalities that may or may not be aware of each other. Although **depersonalization** is usually included in the dissociative disorder group, it does not involve memory disturbance. Instead it involves a dream-like state in which the person has a sense of being separated both from self and from reality. This state may be persistent or recurrent. In this disorder it is often difficult to identify the source of the stress.

TREATING STRESS-RELATED PROBLEMS

A variety of approaches are used either alone or in combination to treat stress-related disorders.

Supportive Therapy In **supportive therapy** the therapist provides acceptance and a non-critical attitude in order to give the client an opportunity to relax enough to engage in problem solving.

Drugs and Sedatives **Drugs and sedatives** act on the nervous system to allow the person to feel a temporary decrease in stress. This treatment is often combined with a psychological therapeutic approach.

Relaxation Training **Relaxation training** is a structured approach to tension reduction that also helps to decrease feelings of stress enough so that the person can focus on working out problems.

Systematic Desensitization **Systematic desensitization** is a process designed to eliminate fear in specific types of situations by pairing relaxation techniques with imagining the presence of the anxiety-associated stimuli.

Cognitive Modification **Cognitive modification** is the process of learning to think about or construe anxiety producing situations in a different way.

Social Intervention **Social intervention** involves treating not just the individual with the problem, but also involving family members in the treatment process.

Anxiety Disorders

CHAPTER 6

Generalized Anxiety Disorder

Panic Disorder

Phobias
Simple Phobias
Social Phobias
Agoraphobia

Obsessive–Compulsive Disorder

Interpreting and Treating Anxiety Disorders
The Psychodynamic Perspective
The Behavioral Perspective
The Cognitive Perspective
The Biological Perspective

Chapter Summary

Karel Appel, *Landscape Conversation*, 1973. Jane Kahan Gallery, New York.

CASE A: SUSAN

I wish I could tell you exactly what's the matter. Sometimes I feel like something terrible has just happened when actually nothing has happened at all. Other times I'm expecting the sky to fall down any minute. Most of the time I can't point my finger at something specific. Still, I feel tense and jumpy. The fact is that I am tense and jumpy almost all the time. Sometimes my heart beats so fast, I'm sure it's a heart attack.

Little things can set it off. The other day I thought a supermarket clerk had overcharged me a few cents on an item. She showed me that I was wrong, but that didn't end it. I worried the rest of the day. I kept going over the incident in my mind, feeling terribly embarrassed at having raised the possibility that the clerk had committed an error. The tension was so great, I wasn't sure I'd be able to go to work in the afternoon. That sort of thing is painful to live with.

CASE B: PAUL

It happened without any warning, a sudden wave of terror. My heart was pounding like mad, I couldn't catch my breath, and the ground underfoot seemed unstable. I was sure it was a heart attack. It was the worst experience of my life.

CASE C: SHARON

I can't tell you why I'm afraid of rats. They fill me with terror. Even if I just see the word "rat," my heart starts pounding. I worry about rats in restaurants I go to, in my kitchen cupboard, and anywhere I hear a noise that sounds like a small animal scratching or running.

CASE D: MIKE

Before I come home from work I spend half my time wondering whether a burglar has broken into the apartment. As soon as I get home I check every room, under the

bed, and in the closets. Before going to sleep I probably check the lock on the front door 50 times. I feel better after each check, but then my concern wells up and I have to go check again.

The problems described in these four cases are different, but they have one feature in common: the experience of strong anxiety. In Susan's case, which illustrates a *generalized anxiety disorder*, the anxiety is chronic and is felt in a variety of situations. Paul is suffering from a *panic disorder*, in which the anxiety is sudden and overwhelming. People who experience one or more panic attacks worry a great deal about whether and where another attack may take place. Sharon has a *phobic disorder*, in which anxiety is aroused by a specific type of situation, animal, or object. Mike's case is an example of an *obsessive–compulsive disorder*, in which thinking certain thoughts and not doing certain things (like checking the lock on the front door) arouse intense anxiety and concern.

Everyone has worries and fears, even the rich and famous (see Figure 6–1). Freud argued that anxiety can be adaptive if the discomfort that goes with it motivates people to learn new ways of approaching life's challenges. But whether it is adaptive or maladaptive, the discomfort can be intense. The anxious person who is waiting for the worst to happen is often unable to enjoy a personal life, or to gain gratification from work. Anxious people may

FIGURE 6–1 Even successful people known for their toughness and daring may have powerful fears that dictate their behavior. Tony Dorsett, one of football's greats, makes no secret of his fear of sleeping in the dark.

"I've always been a person afraid of the dark. I was taught that when you have complete darkness, that's when spirits walk. In our house when I was growing up, all the doors were always cracked a little bit at night so you could get light into the room. You come in my house now and you're gonna see light everywhere. Even now when I sleep, I leave the bathroom light on and leave the door cracked. And I'm not ashamed to tell you."

"Your order is not ready, nor will it ever be."

FIGURE 6–2

thus prevent themselves from experiencing positive outcomes in life (see Figure 6–2).

The term **anxiety** is usually defined as a diffuse, vague, very unpleasant feeling of fear and apprehension. The anxious person worries a lot, particularly about unknown dangers. In addition, the anxious individual shows combinations of the following symptoms: rapid heart rate, shortness of breath, diarrhea, loss of appetite, fainting, dizziness, sweating, sleeplessness, frequent urination, and tremors. All of these physical symptoms accompany fear as well as anxiety. Fear differs from anxiety because people who have fears can easily state what they are afraid of. People who feel anxious, on the other hand, are not aware of the reasons for their fear. Thus, even though fear and anxiety involve similar reactions, the cause of worry is readily apparent in the former case but is not at all clear in the latter.

This chapter focuses on the serious maladaptive aspects of anxiety, but it is useful to remember that anxiety has many causes and that all people experience it at some time in their lives. It is normal for people to experience anxiety when faced with stressful, threatening situations, but it is abnormal to feel strong, chronic anxiety in the absence of a visible cause.

The characteristics of anxiety include feelings of uncertainty, helplessness, and physiological arousal. A person who experiences anxiety complains of feeling nervous, tense, jumpy, and irritable. Often he or she has difficulty falling asleep at night. An anxious person becomes fatigued easily and has "butterflies in the stomach," as well as headaches, muscle tension, and difficulty in concentrating. There is growing evidence that people suffering from anxiety disorders are overly sensitive to threat cues. Such individuals may exhibit a heightened sensitivity, vigilance, or readiness to attend to potential threats (Litz & Keane, 1989). Table 6–1 lists common symptoms of anxiety and self-descriptions given by people with high levels of anxiety. The experience of intense anxiety may occur after an event has taken place, in anticipation of a future event, or when a person decides to resist a preoccupying idea, change an undesirable aspect of behavior, or approach a fear-arousing stimulus.

In the previous chapter we discussed one kind of anxiety disorder, the posttraumatic stress disorder, which occurs after an intensely traumatic event such as a serious accident or natural disaster. In this chapter we discuss four types of disorders in which the causes of anxiety usually are not so clear. A generalized anxiety disorder is marked by chronic anxiety over a long period (at least several months). A panic disorder consists of recurrent, sudden anxiety attacks in which the individual experiences intense terror and dread. In phobic disorders, the anxiety has an identifiable cause—for example, being near dogs or having to speak to a group. When the

Table 6–1
Common Anxiety Symptoms and Self-Descriptions Indicative of High Anxiety

Symptoms

1. Nervousness, jitteriness
2. Tension
3. Feeling tired
4. Dizziness
5. Frequency of urination
6. Heart palpitations
7. Feeling faint
8. Breathlessness
9. Sweating
10. Trembling
11. Worry and apprehension
12. Sleeplessness
13. Difficulty in concentrating
14. Vigilance

Self-Descriptions

1. I am often bothered by the thumping of my heart.
2. Little annoyances get on my nerves and irritate me.
3. I often suddenly become scared for no good reason.
4. I worry continuously and that gets me down.
5. I frequently get spells of complete exhaustion and fatigue.
6. It is always hard for me to make up my mind.
7. I always seem to be dreading something.
8. I feel nervous and high-strung all the time.
9. I often feel I can't overcome my difficulties.
10. I feel constantly under strain.

stimulus is not present, the phobic person's tension level is relatively low. In obsessive–compulsive disorder, anxiety results from efforts to prevent undesirable outcomes. The individual is plagued with a recurrent need to ward off disaster by thinking about certain ideas and/or performing certain acts.

Many clinicians used to describe people who were suffering from anxiety disorders as neurotic. In DSM-II, an early version of the classification system that was strongly influenced by the psychodynamic perspective, the word "neurosis" was used to describe disorders marked by anxiety, personal dissatisfaction, and inappropriate (but not psychotic) behavior. These disorders were grouped together because it was thought that they all arose from somewhat similar unconscious mental processes and motivations. Though this view may some day be substantiated, today such a view is not widely held. Most schemes for classifying maladaptive behavior in-

volve identifying its source and using the obvious presence of marked anxiety as the criterion for including maladaptive behavior in the group of **anxiety disorders**. This chapter is restricted to a discussion of disorders in which the individual is abnormally anxious, either generally or under certain circumstances, but still has adequate contact with reality and is rarely incapacitated enough to require institutionalization. The role of anxiety in several other disorders is described in later chapters. We will look first at specific characteristics of the various anxiety disorders as well as examine some similarities and differences among them. In the latter part of the chapter we will discuss particular therapeutic approaches to these disorders.

Generalized Anxiety Disorder

Generalized anxiety disorder might best be described as consisting of prolonged, vague, unexplained, but intense fears that do not seem to be attached to any particular object. They resemble normal fears, but there is no actual danger, and in most cases danger is not even imagined to be present. In one recent study, a group of patients with various types of anxiety disorders were asked, "Do you worry excessively about minor things?" Ninety-one percent of those diagnosed as having generalized anxiety disorder answered yes to this question, a much higher percentage than for any of the other anxiety disorder groups (Sanderson & Barlow, 1990).

In generalized anxiety disorder, anxiety persists for at least a month (usually much longer) and is not attributable to recent life experiences. The symptoms of generalized anxiety disorder are of four types: motor tension, hyperactivity of the autonomic nervous system, dread of the future, and hypervigilance. These symptoms may be experienced individually or in combination.

1. *Motor tension*. Individuals with this symptom are unable to relax, are keyed up, and are visibly shaky and tense. Strained facial expressions are common, as are furrowed brows and deep sighs. Such individuals are easily startled.
2. *Autonomic reactivity*. In individuals with this symptom, the sympathetic and parasympathetic nervous systems seem to be working overtime. There is some combination of sweating, dizziness, pounding or racing heart, hot or cold spells, cold and clammy hands, upset stomach, lightheadedness, frequent urination or defecation, lump in the throat, and high pulse and respiration rates.

3. *Apprehensive feelings about the future*. People with generalized anxiety disorders worry about what the future holds for them, for people close to them, or for their valued possessions.
4. *Hypervigilance*. People who suffer from generalized anxiety adopt a sentry like stance in their approach to life. They constantly scan the environment for dangers (not necessarily of a physical nature), although often they cannot specify what the dangers might be. This excessive vigilance is related to their hyperaroused state. Because they are always alert to potential threats, they are easily distracted from tasks on which they are working. Their hypervigilance also contributes to difficulty in falling asleep.

Generalized anxiety is a common disorder. One study conducted in three cities found that between 4.1 and 6.6 percent of the population had experienced a generalized anxiety disorder during their lives (Robins & Regier, 1991). The onset of generalized anxiety disorder can occur across the life cycle, but is most common in persons under the age of 30. The disorder was also found to be more prevalent in females and blacks.

While the cause of the anxiety is usually hard to identify, environmental events and recent experiences may play a role. One study found that in a large number of cases of generalized anxiety disorder, the sufferers had experienced important negative and unexpected events in the months before the anxiety reached clinical proportions (Blazer, 1987).

Panic Disorder

Pan, the Greek god of woods and fields, was blamed for the inexplicable dread sometimes felt by travelers in lonely places. His name has been given to a disorder identified by sudden, overwhelming, apparently senseless terror. **Panic disorders** may attack with no warning (see Figure 6–3). The indicators of panic disorder are similar to those of generalized anxiety disorder except that they are greatly magnified and usually have a sudden onset. However, there are differences between generalized anxiety disorder and panic disorder in their risk factors, rates of occurrence, and family relationships (Weissman, 1990).

People with panic disorder may not be anxious all the time. Instead, they have unanticipated anxiety attacks that recur after periods (perhaps several days) of normal functioning. Severe palpitations, extreme shortness of breath, chest pains or discomfort, trembling, sweating, dizziness, and a feeling of helplessness mark the panic

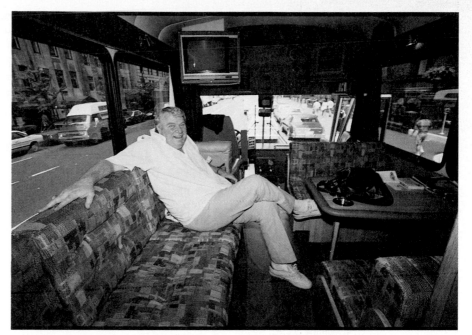

FIGURE 6–3 John Madden, a 6 foot four inch, 240-pound former football player and head coach of the Oakland Raiders professional football team, is now a well-known TV sports personality. While he was flying across the country, Madden experienced a severe panic attack, left the plane at a stop halfway across the United States, and has never flown again. He is shown here in the luxury bus donated for his use by Greyhound which now serves as his home as he travels across the country.

attacks. The victims fear that they will die, go crazy, or do something uncontrolled, and they report a variety of unusual psychosensory symptoms (Uhde and others, 1985). (see Table 6–2).

Panic attacks range in length from a few seconds to many hours and even days. They also differ in severity and in the degree of incapacitation involved. In the following case, frequent panic attacks had a definitely incapacitating effect.

A 30-year-old housewife comes to a psychiatric clinic complaining that she is afraid she will no longer be able to care for her three young children. In the past few months she has suffered repeated episodes of dizziness and shortness of breath, with chest pains, heart palpitations, headaches, and uncontrollable trembling. During these episodes the world seems strange and unreal, and she has a sense of impending doom. Once she went to a hospital, irresistibly convinced that she was having a heart attack. Her doctor told her that she was physically healthy and suggested that she relax, work less hard, and develop more interests outside her family, but the attacks became more intense and frequent, and finally he referred her to the clinic.

Although she used to be gregarious and outgoing, she is now afraid to leave home except in the company of her husband or her mother. She avoids supermarkets and department stores, and says that any crowded place makes her uneasy. When she has to be in an unfamiliar building, she tries to stay near the door and checks for windows and exits. She will no longer drive a car, ride a train, or board a boat. Bridges terrify her. She says that she trembled with fear even on the way to the clinic. Last summer the family did not take their usual vacation, because she did not think she could tolerate being so far from home. Now she wants her mother to stay with her when the children are at home, because she is afraid that if one of the children had an accident she would be unable to help.

—*The Harvard Mental Health Letter*, March 1990, p. 1

Table 6–2
Common Features of Panic Attacks

Shortness of breath or the feeling of being smothered

Dizziness, unsteadiness, or faintness

Trembling, shaking, or sweating

Heart palpitations or a racing heart rate

Choking, nausea, or stomach pain

Numbness or tingling; flushing or chills

Chest pain or discomfort

A sense of "strangeness," of being detached from oneself or one's surroundings

Fear of going crazy, losing control, or dying

The term **panic attack** denotes an abrupt surge of intense anxiety rising to a peak that is either cued by the presence or thoughts of particular stimuli or occurs without obvious cues and is spontaneous and unpredictable. In the former case (which is more common), persons experiencing panic often have persistent phobic fears and the stimuli evoke the fears. People who have panic attacks when evoking stimuli are not present typically do not have phobias as well.

Panic disorder is much less prevalent in the general population than other anxiety disorders (Robins & Regier, 1991). It affects women more than men, and younger age groups more than the elderly. Compared to other anxiety disorders, panic attacks appear to be particularly distressing experiences. Generalized anxiety and panic disorders both run in families, although the family incidence rate is much higher for panic disorder. There is no evidence that any specific type of childhood experience predisposes people to these states. Problems often arise in classifying these disorders, because many cases are complicated. Several types of maladaptive behavior may occur simultaneously. Obsessions, compulsions, and phobias might all be observed in a given individual. Severe panic states are sometimes followed by periods of psychotic disorganization in which there is a reduced capacity to test reality.

Box 6–1 presents a case of both anxiety and panic disorder along with an interpretation of its major features. A person who has had a panic attack develops anticipatory anxiety: He or she becomes worried and tense, and is afraid that the panic will recur. In some cases, this type of anticipatory anxiety seems to be a quite realistic fear. Recent research has revealed that persons who experience panic attacks perceive themselves as having impairments in their physical health and emotional well-being, and in occupational and financial functioning. They are heavy users of health-care facilities and emergency departments, and they are much more prone than the general population to think about committing suicide. Twenty percent of patients with panic disorder report that they have attempted suicide (Klerman and others, 1991). In addition to studying suicidal cognitions of people who experience panic attacks, research has revealed certain cognitive processes that occur during these attacks. Ottaviani and Beck (1987) asked persons who had had panic attacks about the types of thoughts they remembered having during the attacks. Subjects reported thoughts of humiliation, losing control, helplessness, and failure.

Drug research, another area of inquiry into panic disorders, has provided an interesting finding that suggests that panic and anticipatory anxiety have different sources. Imipramine, a drug used in the treatment of depression, has been shown to prevent the recurrence of panic attacks (Marks, 1987). However, it seems to have

Table 6–3
Percentages of Patients with Panic Disorder and Generalized Anxiety Disorder Reporting Particular Symptoms

Symptom	Panic Disorder	Generalized Anxiety Disorder
Sweating, flushing	58.3	22.2
Heart palpitations	89.5	61.1
Chest pain	68.8	11.1
Faintness, lightheadedness	52.1	11.1
Blurred vision	31.2	0
Feeling of muscular weakness	47.9	11.1

SOURCE: Based on Anderson, Noyes, and Crowe, 1984.

no effect on the anticipatory anxiety that panic attacks almost always arouse. That is, subjects treated with imipramine may feel anxious in anticipation of a panic attack but not experience one.

In the past, relatively few attempts had been made to identify and compare the anxiety disorder subgroups of generalized anxiety and panic disorders. Now that attention has been focused on the subgroups, these topics are being investigated more intensively. For example, one group of researchers has compared the patterns of symptoms, family characteristics, type of onset, and clinical course in generalized anxiety disorder and panic disorder (Anderson and others, 1984). Their findings support the assumption that these conditions are distinct from one another. Table 6–3 compares these disorders with regard to several bodily symptoms. Subjects with generalized anxiety disorder have fewer bodily symptoms than those with panic disorder. Their histories also show an earlier, more gradual onset. A generalized anxiety disorder has a more chronic course and is more likely to have a favorable outcome. Members of families in which a person suffers from a panic disorder tend to have a relatively high percentage of panic episodes. The compa-

Table 6–4
Characteristics of Panic Disorder in Comparison with Generalized Anxiety Disorder

1. Clinical onset is later.
2. The role of heredity seems to be greater.
3. The ratio of women to men is greater.
4. Alcoholism is more common.
5. While depression is common in both, it is unusually more so in panic disorder.

BOX 6–1 An Anxious, Precise, Demanding Man Seeks Help

Mr. E., 40 years old and recently married, sought clinical help because he was nervous and worried about his health. These lifelong concerns became worse during his courtship and honeymoon.

Mr. E. has trouble falling asleep if the room is too dark or too light, if he has eaten too much or too little, if the sheets are cold or wrinkled, if he forgets his nose spray, or if there is any noise. He fears nightmares, nocturnal asthma attacks, or dying in his sleep. He often awakes in a panicky sweat with nightmares, typically of being chased or suffocated. He worries that his lost sleep is shortening his life and ruining his work efficiency.

Mr. E. had always been anxious and worried. He expects the worst, dreads each time the phone rings lest it be bad news, and suspects that he has a serious illness. He experiences frequent palpitations, shortness of breath, dizziness, and numb fingers and has had numerous physical exams and electrocardiograms. The negative findings do not reassure him as Mr. E. is convinced that his doctors are withholding information, and he is determined to have additional checkups until his condition is diagnosed. He also has gastrointestinal flutters, frequent diarrhea or constipation, and occasional nausea and vomiting. His father died of heart disease and his mother of cancer, and he feels confident that he already has, or soon will have, one or both conditions.

Mr. E. is also extremely anxious about his work. He is a stockbroker responsible for large financial transactions and cannot ever relax his concentration, even on vacations. He has also felt considerable performance anxiety about his recently more active sex life and has suffered from consistent premature ejaculation. There are many specific situations that make him intolerably nervous—waiting in line, sitting in the middle of a row at a movie, riding public transportation, wearing a pair of pants a second time without having them cleaned, having dirty dollar bills, and so forth—but he is able to avoid most of them without great inconvenience. Mr. E. has panic attacks at least every few weeks. They tend to occur whenever something new is expected of him, when he is forced to do one of the things he fears, when he must give a talk, and, at times, for no apparent reason.

Mr. E. is a very precise and demanding man who is difficult to live or work with (or to treat). He is controlling, self-absorbed, maddeningly fastidious, and meticulous. He did not marry previously because he had very demanding expectations of a woman, and his worries and habits are intolerable to many women. His wife has begun to complain to him, and he is afraid she may leave unless he is able to change quickly.

—Frances, A.J. and Klein, D.F., Anxious, precise, demanding man seeks help soon after marriage. *Hospital and Community Psychiatry* 33, 89–90, 1982. Copyright © 1982, the American Psychiatric Association. Reprinted by permission.

An Evaluation of Mr. E.'s Condition

Because this is a real-life case, it is more complicated than a textbook outline of a disorder. Mr. E. might be described in terms of either generalized anxiety disorder or panic disorder. However, because of the definite recurring panic attacks, panic disorder seems the more likely primary diagnosis. Mr. E.'s concerns about being precise and meticulous also raise the possibility of an obsessive–compulsive personality disorder (see Chapter 9). Despite Mr. E.'s protestations to the contrary, he suffers from no apparent physical disorder. A reasonable rating of Mr. E.'s psychosocial stress (his recent marriage) would seem to be moderately severe. Mr. E. might be described as having a fair level of adaptive functioning in the past year. Despite his superior work performance, his social and leisure-time difficulties now suggest a decreased level of functioning.

Thus, Mr. E. might be described as having a panic disorder, features of an obsessive–compulsive personality disorder, no apparent physical disorders, moderately severe stress in the recent past, and moderate but increasing difficulty in functioning.

It is important to remember that experienced clinicians might disagree about this description either because of gaps in what is known about Mr. E. or because of emphasis on different known facts. With additional information, the classification might change. A clinician treating Mr. E. would want to better understand his sexual problems, his conviction that he has cancer or heart disease, and his somatic complaints, for which no bodily cause has been found.

rable percentage for family members of those with a generalized anxiety disorder is much lower.

Panic and generalized anxiety disorders differ most-clearly in the diffuseness of the anxiety seen in the latter and its focused intensity in the former. But research has shown that they differ in a number of other ways as well. Table 6–4 lists some of these differences. In addition to investigating the characteristics of panic disorders, researchers are also conducting experiments designed to better understand how the attacks come about. It has

been discovered that sodium lactate, when administered intravenously to patients with panic disorder, will often provoke a panic attack, while this does not happen to the general population. A number of research teams are seeking to identify the mechanisms by which sodium lactate causes panic attacks (see Figure 6–4). Imipramine significantly decreases the frequency of sodium lactate-provoked panic attacks. (Shear & Fyer, 1988).

Phobias

Phobos was the Greek god of fear. His likeness was painted on masks and shields to frighten enemies in battle. The word *phobia,* derived from his name, came to mean fear, panic, dread, or fright. Unlike people who have generalized anxiety disorders, people who have **phobic disorders** know exactly what they are afraid of. Except for their fears of specific objects, people, or situations, phobic individuals usually do not engage in gross distortions of reality. Nothing physical seems to be wrong with them. However, their fears are out of proportion with reality, seem inexplicable, and are beyond their voluntary control.

One question that inevitably arises in discussions of anxiety is why people spend so much time brooding about vague menaces when there are so many real dangers to worry about. Perhaps the degree of fear we feel about a potentially harmful event is linked not primarily to the degree of threat (in terms of the probability that it will actually happen to us) or even to the amount of injury that we imagine we might sustain if the worst did happen, but to the disturbing quality of the event or situation itself. For example, even though there are three times as many traffic fatalities as there are murders, our thoughts are rarely preoccupied by the danger of an automobile accident. Fear of violent crime, on the other hand, touches many of us. Crucial to the experience of fear is whether people feel that they will be able to respond meaningfully to a situation—that is, whether they will be able to cope.

Phobics do not need the actual presence of the feared object or situation to experience intense tension and discomfort. The following account by a psychiatrist with an airplane phobia shows that simply imagining a phobia-related event can elicit strong psychological and bodily reactions.

I was pampering my neurosis by taking the train to a meeting in Philadelphia. It was a nasty day out, the fog so thick you could see only a few feet ahead of your face, and the train, which had been late in leaving New York, was making up time by hurtling at a great rate across the flat land of New Jersey. As I sat there comfortably enjoying the ride, I happened to glance at the headlines of a late edition, which one of the passengers who had boarded in New York was reading. "TRAINS CRASH IN FOG," ran the banner headlines, "10 DEAD, MANY INJURED." I reflected on our speed, the dense fog outside, and had a mild,

FIGURE 6–4 The calm before the storm. A patient prepares for a sodium lactate infusion as part of a research study. Researchers are trying to determine why an infusion (constant flow) of sodium lactate often results in a panic attack for people prone to panic disorder but does not have this result in normal individuals.

transitory moment of concern that the fog might claim us victim, too, and then relaxed as I picked up the novel I had been reading. Some minutes later the thought suddenly entered my mind that had I not "chickened out" about flying, I might at that moment be overhead in a plane. At the mere image of sitting up there strapped in by a seat belt, my hands began to sweat, my heart to beat perceptibly faster, and I felt a kind of nervous uneasiness in my gut. The sensation lasted until I forced myself back to my book and forgot about the imagery.

I must say I found this experience a vivid lesson in the nature of phobias. Here I had reacted with hardly a flicker of concern to an admittedly small, but real danger of accident, as evidenced by the fog-caused train crash an hour or two earlier; at the same time I had responded to a purely imaginary situation with an unpleasant start of nervousness, experienced both as somatic symptoms and as an inner sense of indescribable dread so characteristic of anxiety. The unreasonableness of the latter was highlighted for me by its contrast with the absence of concern about the speeding train, which if I had worried about it, would have been an apprehension founded on real, external circumstances.

—Nemiah and Uhde, 1989, p. 973

The onset of many phobias is so gradual that it is difficult to tell whether there were any specific precipitating factors. In other cases, the apparent time of onset, although not necessarily the cause, can be pinpointed.

I was riding in my husband's car and I suddenly became terrified. I felt as if I would die. I made him turn around and take me home. I ran into the house and suddenly felt safe. I could not understand what had happened. I had never been afraid of cars. The next day it happened again, and it kept getting worse. Finally, just being on the street and seeing a car would bring on a terrible feeling. Now I just stay at home.

—De Nike and Tiber, 1968, p. 346

Phobias may begin with a generalized anxiety attack, but the anxiety then becomes crystallized around a particular object or situation (for example, elevators,

snakes, or darkness). As long as the feared object or situation can be avoided, the anxiety does not reach disturbing proportions. Some objects of phobias—such as cats, cars, and stairs—are considered aspects of everyday life by most of us. Other objects and situations—snakes, death, and heights—are disliked to some extent by most people. However, phobias involve levels of fear that, in addition to being overly intense, interfere with normal living patterns. One study of phobic patients showed that their fears fell into five categories related to (1) separations, (2) animals, (3) bodily mutilation, (4) social situations, and (5) nature (Torgersen, 1979). Table 6–5 gives examples of phobic content that fall into these categories.

Phobias tend to grow progressively broader. For example, one woman had a subway phobia that began with an inability to ride an express train between two fairly distant locations. Gradually the phobia developed until she would have to get off the train at each local stop, wait until her anxiety diminished, get on the next train, get off again at the next stop, and so on, until her destination was reached.

Phobic individuals usually develop ways of reducing their fears. The subway rider was able to get from one place to another. However, the often cumbersome procedures that phobics devise do not eliminate their fear; indeed, the fear seems always to be one step ahead of them. In one sense, phobic individuals who cannot cross the thresholds of certain rooms or cannot work may be as incapacitated as people with severe psychotic symptoms. In another sense, they are more fortunate than people who exhibit free-floating anxiety, since at least their fears are directed toward a specific object, and they can reduce their anxiety by simply avoiding that object.

Phobias, like other forms of maladaptive behavior, do not occur in isolation. They are usually intertwined

Table 6–5
Examples for Five Categories of Phobias

Separation fears	Social fears
Crowds	Eating with strangers
Traveling alone	Being watched writing
Being alone at home	Being watched working
Animal fears	Nature fears
Mice	Mountains
Rats	The ocean
Insects	Cliffs, heights
Mutilation fears	
Open wounds	
Surgical operations	
Blood	

SOURCE: From Torgersen, 1979.

with a host of other problems. In consequence, it is difficult to estimate their frequency accurately. While mild phobias are common, phobias that are serious enough to be clinically diagnosed occur relatively infrequently. They are the main complaint in perhaps 2 to 3 percent of all clinical cases (Kolb & Brodie, 1982). Phobias do not require hospitalization. Professional treatment, when it is given, is usually carried out on an outpatient basis.

One of the most interesting aspects of phobias is that the stimuli that evoke them are not random. The most common fear-arousing stimuli tend to be animals, objects, or events that presented real dangers in earlier stages of human evolution (McNally, 1987). Although extreme fear of dogs, snakes, and spiders seems maladaptive today, such fear may have been highly adaptive in earlier times. More "modern" phobias are rare. For example, pajama and electric-outlet phobias occur infrequently, even though these objects are often associated with trauma.

Traditionally, phobias have been named by means of Greek prefixes that stand for the object of the fear, as shown in the following examples:

- Acrophobia: fear of heights
- Agoraphobia: fear of open places and unfamiliar settings
- Aquaphobia: fear of water
- Claustrophobia: fear of closed places
- Xenophobia: fear of strangers

Recently, however, such names have been avoided. People's knowledge of Greek is not what it once was, and in any case, a staggering number of labels would be needed to take account of the great variety of phobias that have been observed. Today, therefore, phobias are grouped into three general categories: simple phobias, social phobias, and agoraphobia.

Phobias are very common disorders, being even more prevalent than generalized anxiety disorders (Robins & Regier, 1991). Rates of phobic disorder are about twice as high for females as males. In both sexes, blacks have higher rates than whites or Hispanics. Phobias typically have their onset in childhood or young adulthood and there is a sharp decline in new cases with age. The mean duration for phobias varies from 24 to 31 years—in other words, the duration tends to be chronic (Boyd and others, 1990).

Simple Phobias

Simple phobias are a miscellaneous category of irrational fears. Examples of simple phobias are intense fear of particular types of animals (for example, snakes, dogs, or rats), claustrophobia, and acrophobia (see Figure 6–5).

Simple phobia is the most common type of phobia, with about 11 percent of the population meeting the criteria for simple phobia during their lifetime. (The comparable figures for agoraphobia and social phobia are 5.6 percent and 2.7 percent, respectively.) Unreasonable fears of heights and bugs or other small animals are the most common fears, with over 18 percent of a large surveyed population responding positively to questions about these fears (Robins & Regier, 1991). Two other symptoms—unreasonable fears of water and public transport—were reported by over 10 percent of the sample surveyed.

If you have a simple phobia, it might have begun when you actually did face a risk that realistically provoked anxiety. Perhaps, for example, you found yourself in deep water before you learned to swim. Extreme fear was appropriate in such a situation. But if

FIGURE 6–5 This painting by George Tooker, titled *Cornice*, captures the fear of heights that acrophobics feel even when they are in situations much less threatening than the precarious perch shown in the painting, for instance when they are climbing ladders or standing near the railings of observation platforms.

(Columbus Museum of Art, Ohio: Museum Purchase: Howald Fund II)

you continue to avoid even the shallow end of a pool, your anxiety is excessive and may be of phobic proportions (see Figure 6–6). For the person with a simple phobia, the degree of distress varies with the prevalence of the avoided situation. For example, a hospital employee who fears blood may be in a constant state of fear because the probability of encountering blood in a hospital setting is high. When the probability of the feared stimulus is low, people with simple phobias are usually free of symptoms. The person who is phobic about drowning is usually not affected by that phobia except in the presence of water or when a beach party is being planned.

Children eventually overcome many of their fears. And while it is not unusual for adults with simple phobias to overcome their fear as a result of a positive experience involving contact with the fear-arousing stimulus, simple phobias tend to be chronic. A variety of therapeutic approaches have been used in treating simple phobias. Procedures that promote association between the fear-arousing stimulus and nonanxiety responses, and at the same time provide information countering mistaken beliefs about the stimulus (for example, that all dogs are ferocious), often have positive effects.

Mary, aged twenty-nine, had fainted at the sight of blood or injury ever since she was four years old. She and her therapist agreed on specific targets for treatment: watching blood samples being taken from someone else and from herself, coping with her children when they needed first aid for minor injuries, and getting her own

FIGURE 6–6 A simple phobia often can be traced to an intense, realistic childhood fear. For example, a child who was never taught to swim and remembers vividly desperate attempts to stay afloat might as an adult continue to be terrified by even shallow water.

varicose veins treated. In her first session, Mary was able to watch a blood sample being taken from her therapist's finger and then having her own finger pricked and a blood sample taken. In the next session, she was asked to imagine situations involving injury and to watch films depicting injuries to others. Between sessions, at home, Mary dealt successfully with some small emergencies with her children and she had her varicose veins injected. At follow-up eight months later, she reported that she was free of her problem. She was able to enroll in a first aid class and went freely to movies depicting blood and injury.

—Adapted from Marks, 1978, pp. 135–136

This case illustrates two important points. One is that exposure to fear-arousing stimuli contributes to overcoming simple phobias. The other is that a highly motivated client increases the likelihood of success.

Social Phobias

Social phobias are less common than simple phobias—they occur at only about 25 percent the rate of simple phobias—but they can attack with no less force (Robins & Regier, 1991). Social phobias are characterized by fear and embarrassment in dealings with others (see Figure 6–7). Often the individual's greatest fear is that signs of anxiety such as intense blushing, tremors of the hand, and a quavering voice will be detected by people with whom he or she comes into contact. Fear of public speaking and of eating in public are frequent complaints of socially phobic individuals. These problems often begin in late childhood or early adolescence, and may crystallize into a phobia in late adolescence.

I sometimes don't get to class because I think the teacher might call on me. My fear doesn't have anything to do with being unprepared if he asks me a question, because I'm almost always well prepared. My grades on exams are always near the top of the class. What I keep thinking about is that the teacher and all the students will see how red my face gets whenever I have to say something in a group.

Most phobias about interpersonal relationships involve one or more of the following fears: fear of

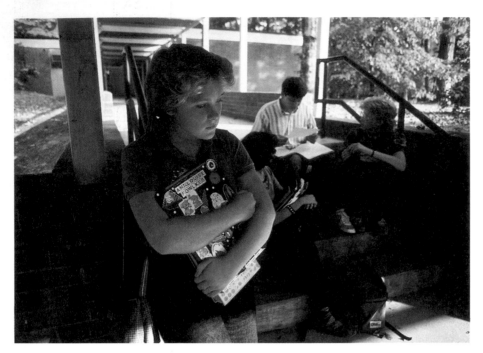

FIGURE 6–7 Social phobics avoid situations requiring contact. If they cannot stay away from contact with other people they often experience physical symptoms such as nausea, trembling, and profuse perspiration as well as disabling feelings of anxiety.

asserting oneself, fear of criticism, fear of making a mistake, and fear of public speaking. People who are afflicted in these ways have much in common. They go through life feeling generally inadequate and have many social and interpersonal difficulties. They attempt to compensate by immersing themselves in school and then in their work, never being really sure of their skills and talents. They dismiss their successes, if any, by saying, "My work isn't really good enough" or "I was just lucky—being in the right place at the right time." They may feel like impostors, fearing that they will be discovered and that the rug will be pulled out from under them.

Two types of social phobia are particularly stubborn, the fears of blushing and eating. Some people are terrified that they will blush in the company of others and are convinced that they will be highly visible and the center of painful attention. If questioned, these people cannot say what is so dreadful about blushing, but it is often evident that shame is an important component of their anxiety. In some cases, a change of color may not be at all evident to the observer, even though the individual insists that he or she feels bright red. The force of their fear, unfounded as it may be, often leads people to restrict their social lives severely. Fear of eating often involves a dread of eating in the company of others. Even this fear may be very specific. For instance, Emma, age 26, became very anxious when she had to eat or drink in the company of anyone she knew. However, she was able to eat or drink in public places without undue distress as long as the other people present were strangers. Table 6–6 gives some guidelines concerning interpersonal behavior that have been found to be helpful to social

phobics (Marks, 1987). Table 6–7 provides some hints that might be useful for a friend or spouse of a phobic person to help the fearful person.

Table 6–6
Interpersonal Self-Help Techniques for the Social Phobic Person

1. Respond to anxiety symptoms by approach rather than withdrawal.
2. Greet people properly, with eye contact.
3. Listen carefully to people and make a mental list of possible topics of conversation.
4. Show that you want to speak; initiate conversation (asking questions is easier, as it switches attention to the person expected to reply).
5. Speak up without mumbling.
6. Tolerate some silences.
7. Wait for cues from others in deciding where to sit, when to pick up a drink, and what to talk about.
8. Learn to tolerate criticism by introducing controversy deliberately at an appropriate point.

Agoraphobia

One ordinary day, while tending to some chore, taking a walk, driving to work—in other words, just going about his usual business—Leo Green was suddenly struck by a wave of awful terror. His heart started pounding, he trembled, he

perspired profusely, and he had difficulty catching his breath. He became convinced that something terrible was happening to him, maybe he was going crazy, maybe he was having a heart attack, maybe he was about to die. He desperately sought safety, reassurance from his family, treatment at a clinic or emergency room. His doctor could find nothing wrong with him, so he went about his business, until a panic attack struck him again. As the attacks became more frequent, he spent more and more time thinking about them. He worried, watched for danger, and waited with fear for the next one to hit.

He began to avoid situations where he had experienced an attack, then others where he might find it particularly difficult to cope with one by escaping and getting help. He started by making minor adjustments in his habits—going to a supermarket at midnight, for example, rather than on the way home from work when the store tended to be crowded. Gradually, Leo Green got to the point where he couldn't venture outside his immediate neighborhood, couldn't leave the house without his spouse, or sometimes couldn't leave at all. What started out as an inconvenience turned into a nightmare. Like a creature in a horror movie, fear expanded until it covered the entire screen of his life.

Table 6–7
Hints for Helping a Phobic Person

1. Never make the assumption that you know what is best; do not force your beliefs.
2. Always provide a way out if he or she is having difficulties (for example, leave the party).
3. Be aware of excuses to avoid the feared situation ("I'm not feeling well today"). Provide encouragement, but do not make a big issue if your suggestion is met with resistance.
4. Don't assume that because something was accomplished successfully one time that the next time will also be easy.
5. Never play tricks by doing something that is different from what you initially agreed upon.
6. If things are going well, suggest trying something a little more difficult.
7. Approach feared situations in gradual steps, never making the decision to go onto the next step yourself.
8. Encourage him or her to practice responses to the feared situation (a party, a dog).
9. While practicing or in the feared situation, don't constantly ask about the person's feelings.
10. If the phobic person practices alone and reports successes to you, share in his or her excitement.

This scenario describes a common path in the development of **agoraphobia,** the fear of entering unfamiliar situations. To the outside observer, a person with agoraphobia may look no different from one with a social phobia. Both may stay home from a party. But their reasons for doing so are different. While the social phobic is afraid of the scrutiny of other people, many investigators believe that the agoraphobic is afraid of his or her own internal cues. The agoraphobic dreads the awful anxiety of a panic attack, and is afraid of losing control in a crowd. Minor physical sensations may be interpreted as the prelude to some catastrophic threat to life. In severe cases, the individual may have an irrational fear of leaving the familiar setting of the home; in the most extreme cases, the victim is unable even to walk down the street or go shopping.

Like most other phobias, agoraphobia is more common among women than among men. It often begins in the late teens, although it is also observed in older people. And like other phobias, it waxes and wanes, and it is not uncommon for the object of the fear to change. Some cases of agoraphobia are preceded by panic attacks marked by intense anxiety. In many cases of agoraphobia, the phobic symptoms are a complication of panic disorder. People who experience the intense fears that are characteristic of agoraphobia strive to organize their lives in such a way as to minimize exposure to the fear-arousing stimuli.

Recent research suggests that agoraphobics can be divided into two groups, those with and those without panic attacks (Eaton & Keyl, 1990). A high percentage of people who experience panic attacks go on to develop agoraphobia unless they are treated early with certain drugs. One theory regarding the panic attack–agoraphobia linkage is that an individual is born with a biological vulnerability to panic attacks. Psychosocial factors, such as a pile-up of stressful life events and upsetting situations, can trigger a panic attack in a vulnerable individual. According to this theory, many patients, unaware of the biological roots of panic attacks, conclude that the situations in which the attacks take place must be the culprit. They become increasingly preoccupied with avoiding such situations and constrict their life styles—often at considerable economic and social expense—in the hope of eluding the attack. One patient confided that she had accumulated hundreds of dollars in fines by parking her car illegally in front of her office rather than face the anxiety associated with walking across the parking lot.

Panic attacks can be treated with certain drugs that are effective in treating depression (for example, the

tricyclic antidepressants and monoamine oxidase inhibitors) (Fyer & Sanberg, 1988). To a significant extent, agoraphobia is a complication of panic attacks that are untreated and therefore are allowed to recur. Antidepressants are effective in suppressing panic but not in reducing anticipatory anxiety and agoraphobia. Behavioral techniques, including graduated exposure to the situation the individual is afraid of, are effective in treating agoraphobia. Some highly motivated agoraphobics are able to carry out this exposure themselves, without the frequent aid of a therapist. The following case illustrates the successful use of this approach.

Ms. A., a 40-year-old woman, had been virtually housebound for 5 years because of classic agoraphobia. In a 1½-hour session, she, her husband, and I delineated her avoidance profile (those places she avoided regularly because they evoked panic) and worked out an exposure-homework program in which she would slowly habituate to one situation after another. I explained how she should keep a diary of her exposure-homework exercises and asked her to mail them to me. This she did regularly. She diligently carried out her exposure program and within weeks was mobile for the first time in years. She kept up her progress for 4 years without seeing me again, but then she had some family difficulties, which depressed her, and quickly relapsed. She saw me once more for an hour and was encouraged to revive her original exposure-homework program. On doing this she recovered her gains, which continued through follow-up for 9 years, when I last heard from her—a gratifying result for 2½ hours of time from a clinician.

—Marks, 1987, pp. 1163–1164

Agoraphobics are often clinging and dependent. Studies of the histories of severely impaired agoraphobics have shown that 50 percent of the patients exhibited separation anxiety in childhood, well before the onset of the agoraphobia (Gittelman & Klein, 1984). The association between childhood separation anxiety and agoraphobia is much stronger in women than in men. Perhaps, in some sense, agoraphobia is a delayed outbreak of childhood separation anxiety. Because separation anxiety is almost always measured by means of retrospective self-reports, there is a need for longitudinal studies that allow for the observation of subjects' behavior in addition to self-reports.

Obsessive–Compulsive Disorder

We forget to forgive ourselves. We certainly do not accept ourselves, nor trust ourselves. With the inevitable failures to live up to the outside standards we begin to fall into habits of pessimistic thinking about ourselves and the world. In psychological terms we are "other-directed." We are tormented by "shoulds" and "musts," rituals and perhaps prayers. We have no trust in ourselves, no strong ego, no self-esteem. . . . We, having no trust in ourselves go back, we check again, we tighten again, we wash again. We find new ways of feeling guilty and less full of self-esteem, we whip ourselves like a medieval flagellant with our hair shirts of responsibility for all. Sometimes we end up breaking the switch, over-tightening the screw, cutting too much off, talking too much about what we might have said to hurt someone, damaging a ligament or muscle in our arms, wrists, or fingers, and we end up crying (inside or outside) with confusion, more anxiety, more physical symptoms as described above. We are heading towards our greatest foe—despair or depression.

—Anonymous and Tiller, 1989, pages 279, 280.

This account by a member of a support group of persons with **obsessive–compulsive disorder** conveys the driven quality of the thoughts and rituals seen in people with this condition. It also illustrates the association often observed between obsessive–compulsive characteristics and depression. The specific forms these characteristics take vary from case to case. One man spends three hours in the bathroom every day, repeatedly washing himself, pursued by the thought that he might pass on a deadly disease to anyone he touches. Another man has stopped cooking for fear that he will poison his wife, and has stopped using electrical appliances for fear of causing a fire. The following case tells the story of a third man, who cannot prevent himself from driving back to reexamine every place on the road where he has hit a bump, because the thought that he has run someone over keeps forcing itself on him (see Figure 6–8).

I'm driving down the highway doing 55 MPH. I'm on my way to take a final exam. My seat belt is

FIGURE 6–8 For someone who has obsessive thoughts about the possibility of injuring another person while driving, a noneventful ride down an empty highway can become a highly upsetting experience.

buckled and I'm vigilantly following all the rules of the road. No one is on the highway—not a living soul.

Out of nowhere an Obsessive–Compulsive Disorder attack strikes. It's almost magical the way it distorts my perception of reality. While in reality no one is on the road, I'm intruded with the heinous thought that I might *have hit someone . . . a human being! God knows where such a fantasy comes from.*

I think about this for a second and then say to myself, "That's ridiculous. I didn't hit anybody." Nonetheless, a gnawing anxiety is born. An anxiety I will ultimately not be able to put away until an enormous emotional price has been paid.

I try to make reality chase away this fantasy. I reason, "Well, if I hit someone while driving, I would have felt *it." This brief trip into reality helps the pain dissipate . . . but only for a second. Why? Because the gnawing anxiety that I really did commit the illusionary accident is growing larger—so is the pain. . . .*

I start ruminating, "Maybe I did hit someone and didn't realize it . . . Oh my God! I might have killed somebody! I have to go back and check." Checking is the only way to calm the anxiety. It brings me closer to truth somehow. I can't live with the thought that I actually may have killed someone—I have to check it out.

Now I'm sweating . . . literally. I pray this outrageous act of negligence never happened. My fantasies run wild. I desperately hope the jury will be merciful.

—Rapoport, 1989, pp. 21–22

Another victim of this disorder vacuums and dusts her house thoroughly each day (see Figure 6–9). If a woman insists on cleaning the entire house each and every day, her family may jokingly accuse her of being compulsive. But for thousands of women, these cleaning urges may signal the beginning of obsessive–compulsive disorder.

Therapists say there are enormous differences between healthy people with compulsive streaks and those suffering from obsessive–compulsive disorder. Truly obsessive–compulsive people often have family histories of psychiatric disease, suggesting a genetic component to the disorder. They are wracked by self-doubt and often are unable to make even simple decisions.

By contrast, healthy people with a few compulsive tendencies tend to work efficiently and organize their daily activities to avoid confusion. They also take pride in

FIGURE 6–9 Cleaning the kitchen can be a constructive activity carried out by a well organized person. Cleaning the kitchen by someone with an obsessive-compulsive disorder is quite different, a task filled with concerns about whether the kitchen is really clean enough and countless repetitions of each cleaning activity.

their ability to control their emotions—an impossibility for those with obsessive–compulsive disorder. Although obsessive–compulsive people are wracked by guilt over their strange behavior's effects on their families, they continue because they believe their compulsive acts keep themselves and their families safe.

People who have an obsessive–compulsive disorder are tyrannized by repetitive acts or thoughts. **Obsessive** people are unable to get an idea out of their minds (for example, they are preoccupied by sexual, aggressive, or religious thoughts); **compulsive** people feel compelled to perform a particular act or series of acts over and over again (repetitive hand washing or stepping on cracks in the sidewalk, for example).

Obsessions usually involve doubt, hesitation, fear of contamination, or fear of one's own aggression. The most common forms of compulsive behavior are counting, ordering, checking, touching, and washing. A few victims of obsessive–compulsive disorder have purely mental rituals; for example, to ward off the obsessional thought or impulse they might recite a series of magic words or numbers. About 25 percent of people with an obsessive–compulsive disorder have intrusive thoughts but do not act on them. The rest are both obsessive and compulsive; compulsive behavior without obsessional thoughts is rare. (Skodol, 1989).

Compulsive rituals may become elaborate patterns of behavior that include many activities. For example, a man requires that his furniture never be left an inch out of place, and feels a need to dress and undress, brush his teeth, and use the toilet in a precise, unvarying order, all the time doubting whether he has performed this sequence of actions correctly, and often repeating it to make sure. Some theorists believe that compulsive behavior serves to divert attention from obsessive thoughts. In any case, compulsive rituals become a protection against anxiety, and so long as they are practiced correctly, the individual feels safe.

Because of their seemingly senseless character, obsessive–compulsive reactions, like phobias, are extremely intriguing and challenging to clinical workers, researchers, and lay observers. As Figure 6–10 shows, they have also intrigued cartoonists.

The exact incidence of obsessive–compulsive disorder is hard to determine. The victims tend to be secretive about their preoccupations and frequently are able to work effectively in spite of them; consequently, their "problems" are probably underestimated. Obsessive–compulsive disorder is more common among upper-income, somewhat more intelligent individuals. It tends to begin in late adolescence and early adulthood, and males and females are equally likely to suffer from it. A relatively high proportion of obsessive–compulsives—some surveys report up to 50 percent—remain unmarried.

FIGURE 6–10 Ralph seems to have a problem with at least one obsessional thought.

(Copyright © 1969. Reprinted by permission of the artist, Robert Censoni)

The most common features of obsessive–compulsive disorder are the following.

1. The obsession or compulsion intrudes insistently and persistently into the individual's awareness.

2. A feeling of anxious dread occurs if the thought or act is prevented for some reason.

3. The obsession or compulsion is experienced as foreign to oneself; it is unacceptable and uncontrollable.

4. The individual recognizes the absurdity and irrationality of the obsession or compulsion.

5. The individual feels a need to resist it.

The language used by those with an obsessive–compulsive disorder conveys their exaggerated attention to details, their air of detachment, and the difficulty they have in making a decision:

I seem to be stuck with them—the thoughts, I mean. They seem so unimportant and silly. Why can't I think about things I really want to think about? But I can't stop thinking about trivia like did I lock the garage door when I went to work this morning. I've never not locked it and my wife's home anyway. I get depressed when I realize how much time I waste on nothing.

I feel under such pressure, but I can't make a decision. I write out on 3-by-5 cards all the pros and cons, then I study them, consider all the

complications that perhaps might bear on the decision, and then I do it again—but I never seem to be able to make up my mind.

Obsessional thoughts often seem distasteful and shameful. Their content generally involves harming others, causing accidents to occur, swearing, or having abhorrent sexual or religious ideas. The person with these thoughts is often very fearful that he or she might act on them and as a result spends a great deal of time avoiding these situations or checking that everything is all right.

Susan, a quiet 30-year-old college graduate who has held the same responsible job for eight years, worries that she might put razor blades in other people's food. She refuses to drive a car because she fears she would deliberately smash it into another vehicle.

When she makes coffee at work, she worries that she might have slipped poison into it. She checks her clothing when she leaves work to make sure she hasn't tucked a razor blade into a pocket. She is afraid to hold babies or be around small children. She worries that she might suddenly commit some violent act, such as hurling them to the floor.

She won't shop by herself, afraid that she might slip something into the products on the store shelves. Even when accompanied by her boyfriend, she finds herself needing reassurance. "I was OK, wasn't I?" she asks.

Susan has never put sharp objects in food, hurt a baby, or poisoned coffee.

Depending on the situation and the nature of the obsession, the obsessive may feel some pride in his or her unwillingness to make a premature decision, or may feel self-contempt when indecisiveness prevents action and allows others to win acclaim. The founder of evolutionary theory, Charles Darwin, is an example of an obsessive. Only when Darwin faced the possibility of prior publication by a colleague was he able to overcome his obsessive indecisiveness and put *On the Origin of Species* into the hands of a publisher.

Compared with repetitive upsetting ideas, repetitive images are much less common among obsessives. A typical case is the following.

One of the patient's most distressing images consisted of four people lying dead in open coffins in an open grave. Once this image intruded she was unable to continue with her normal activities unless and until she put matters right by having one or more images in which she saw the same four people standing and walking about, seemingly healthy. Although the images appeared for the most part to be spontaneously (i.e., internally) generated, they could be provoked by exposure to violent or aggressive material of one sort or another—books or television programs. The images were extremely distressing and were capable of provoking her to tears in a matter of minutes.

—Rachman and Hodgson, 1980, p. 257

The variety of obsessive–compulsive rituals and thoughts is practically unlimited, but investigators have identified four broad types of preoccupations: (1) checking, (2) cleaning, (3) slowness, and (4) doubting and conscientiousness. The following statements illustrate each type.

CHECKING
- I frequently have to check things (gas or water taps, doors) several times.

CLEANING
- I avoid using public telephones because of possible contamination.

SLOWNESS
- I am often late because I can't seem to get through everything on time.

DOUBTING–CONSCIENTIOUSNESS
- Even when I do something very carefully, I often feel that it is not quite right.

Most of us have had similar feelings. One study compared the preoccupying thoughts of clinically diagnosed obsessives with those of normal individuals. Although the content of the two groups' thoughts showed many similarities, the clinical group's obsessions occurred more frequently, lasted longer, were more intense, and disrupted their lives more than those of the control group (Rachman & de Silva, 1978).

When the compulsive rituals or obsessive thoughts begin to interfere with important routines of daily life, they become significant problems that require professional attention. Their bases frequently are not well understood, but because all of us have had some

persistent preoccupations with particular acts and thoughts, their interfering effects can easily be appreciated. Obsessive–compulsive preoccupations—checking details, keeping things clean, and being deliberate—often increase during periods of stress. They can have undesirable effects when speedy decisions or actions are required.

Attempts to find out what obsessive–compulsives are afraid of usually fail. Many clinicians believe that fear of loss of control and the need for structure are at the core of the obsessions and compulsions. Whether the disorder reflects the impact of environmental factors or heredity, its incidence is greater among members of some families than among the general population.

A common feature of psychotic behavior is irrational thought, but an obsessive–compulsive person is not considered to be psychotic since he or she is usually aware of the irrationality. In some cases, however, the border between obsessive–compulsive disorder and true psychosis is imprecise.

People who suffer from obsessive–compulsive disorder are very cautious. Like victims of phobias and other anxiety disorders, they unreasonably anticipate catastrophe and loss of control. In general, victims of phobias fear what might happen to them, whereas victims of obsessive–compulsive disorders fear what they might do. There are mixed cases; for example, fear of knives might be associated with the obsessional thought that one will hurt someone if one picks up a knife, and fear of elevators might be brought on by a recurrent impulse to push someone down the shaft. An obsessional thought about shouting obscenities during a sermon might lead the victim to avoid attending church, just as a phobia about the sound of church bells would. Normally, the object of a phobia can be avoided while an obsession cannot be, but again there are mixed cases; a dirt phobia may be as intrusive as an obsession, because dirt is everywhere.

Obsessive thoughts and compulsive rituals shade into phobias to the extent that anxiety accompanies the thoughts or rituals and there is avoidance of situations that evoke them. For example, someone who has a washing ritual will try to avoid dirt, much as a person with a dog phobia avoids dogs. Clinical workers often observe that both obsessive–compulsives and phobics have an unusually high incidence of interpersonal problems. The two disorders differ in that the obsessive–compulsive's fear is directed not at the situation itself but, rather, at the consequences of becoming involved with it—for example, having to wash afterwards. Another difference is that obsessive–compulsives develop a more elaborate set of beliefs concerning their preoccupying thoughts and rituals than phobics do about their fears. Cognitions seem to play a larger role in obsession–compulsion than in phobia. This point is illustrated by the case of a 40-year-old man with a checking compulsion.

The other night my wife and I went to the movies. It was torture even though the movie was great. For about an hour before going I couldn't stop thinking about this need I have to check the doorknob in order to make sure it's locked. I had to get out of the car four times to check the doorknob. When I do that sort of thing, my wife tries to be understanding, but I know she is thinking, "How come once isn't enough?" On the way to the theater I kept worrying about whether the door was locked. I would bet I had similar thoughts a hundred times while at the theater. You can't enjoy yourself under those circumstances, can you?

Table 6–8
Similarities and Differences between Obsessive–Compulsive Disorders and Phobias

Similarities

1. An identifiable evoking stimulus results in increased anxiety.
2. Efforts are made to avoid or escape from the evoking stimulus.
3. Both disorders respond well to exposure therapy whose basic element is actual or imagined contact with the feared stimulus.

Differences

1. Phobics have persistent worries concerning a central theme, while obsessive–compulsives have more stereotyped repetitive thoughts and actions.
2. The two disorders have different evoking stimuli. Dirt, contagion, or harm to others are common obsessive–compulsive preoccupations, but cause few phobics much difficulty. Rituals are common in obsessive–compulsive disorders, but not in phobias.
3. Obsessive–compulsives usually look less tense and panic stricken when in contact with their evoking stimulus than do phobics.
4. Obsessive–compulsives take longer to feel better after they avoid or escape from their evoking stimulus (e.g., dirt) than is the case for phobics and their evoking stimuli (e.g., spiders).
5. Obsessive–compulsives spend more time thinking about improbable future contacts with the evoking stimulus than do phobics.

SOURCE: Adapted from I.M. Marks, Behavioral aspects of panic disorder. In *American Journal of Psychiatry*, 144, 1160–65, 1987. Copyright © 1987, the American Psychiatric Association. Reprinted by permission.

Table 6–8 compares significant characteristics of obsessive–compulsive disorders and phobias.

While obsessive–compulsive disorder has been traditionally regarded as rare, a recent and large epidemiological survey showed a sizeable lifetime prevalence of 2.6 percent in the population (Robins & Regier, 1991). While this figure is much lower than for phobias and generalized anxiety, it is higher than for panic disorder and several other diagnostic groupings. Obsessive–compulsive disorder tends to begin early in life and is most common among women ages 18 to 44. It is more common among the underemployed than the fully employed and the separated or divorced than the married. As public awareness of the high prevalence of obsessive–compulsive disorder increases, the social stigma associated with it may decrease and encourage those who suffer from it to seek professional help.

Interpreting and Treating Anxiety Disorders

Whether it is general or specific to certain situations, anxiety is a major component of the disorders dealt with in this chapter. Anxiety and the things that people do to keep it at manageable levels have been looked at from several theoretical perspectives.

The Psychodynamic Perspective

Psychodynamic theorists and many other clinicians believe that the major determinants of anxiety disorders are intrapsychic events and unconscious motivations. They believe that anxiety is an alarm reaction that appears whenever a person is threatened. How an individual adapts to the anxiety alarm depends on its intensity, the cue that evokes it, and the person's characteristic response to alarms. It is normal to experience some overt anxiety; the amount of anxiety and the nature of the threat determine whether an instance of anxiety is normal or pathological.

A distinguishing characteristic of clinical anxiety is that an alarm is frequently sounded in the absence of a consciously recognized source of danger. A danger exists, but its basis is vague or totally hidden from view. A tourist may understandably experience overwhelming anxiety while walking through a jungle. However, some individuals experience the same kind of anxiety in their own living rooms, for no apparent reason. According to the psychodynamic view, such people's defenses are inadequate to control or contain their anxiety. Figure 6–11 indicates, humorously, that it is possible to develop a defensive posture that effectively masks inner turmoil.

Psychodynamic theorists frequently mention the following as causes of anxiety that reaches clinical proportions: perception of oneself as helpless in coping with environmental pressures, separation or anticipation of abandonment, privation and loss of emotional supports as a result of sudden environmental changes, unacceptable or dangerous impulses that are close to breaking into consciousness, and threats or anticipation of disapproval and withdrawal of love.

The psychodynamic view of phobias stems from two fundamental concepts: (1) psychological conflict and (2) unconscious mental processes. From this standpoint the phobic situation or object has symbolic significance; it can be regarded as a stand-in for something else that one is frightened of, something that is completely beyond one's awareness. It represents an unresolved psychological conflict, a holdover from childhood. For example, a child who reaches school age at the same time that her brother is born might be very angry at her mother for sending her to school. She might feel that her mother is getting rid of her so that she can be alone with the new baby all day. On the way to school each day the little girl passes a house where a vicious German shepherd is chained up. The dog becomes associated with her fantasy about her mother's real reason for sending her to school. The girl manages to get through her childhood all right, but in her twenties she develops a phobia about dogs after her mother has expressed strong disapproval of her future husband.

Obsessive ideas and compulsive rituals may direct attention away from significant, distressing, unconscious

FIGURE 6–11 From a psychodynamic standpoint, inconsistencies between Snoopy's overt and covert behavior would be explained in terms of intrapsychic conflicts and attempts to resolve them.

(PEANUTS reprinted by permission of UFS, Inc.)

thoughts. Psychoanalysts believe that these thoughts often involve aggression and rage that may have first been aroused in the battle for autonomy between the growing child and the mother. When the mother is especially demanding and has unreasonably high expectations about when the child should meet certain developmental challenges (such as toilet training), the child may be forced to bottle up his or her anger. This unacceptable anger expresses itself deviously later in life.

Freud emphasized the roles of several defense mechanisms in the development of obsessive–compulsive disorders. These include isolation, undoing, and reaction formation. Through **isolation,** emotions are separated from a thought or act, which then becomes obsessive or compulsive. However, the emotion is not completely barred from consciousness and constantly threatens to break through the controls that have been imposed upon it. **Undoing** is illustrated by an individual who thinks obsessively, "My father will die" whenever he turns off a light. This thought compels him to turn around, touch the switch, and say, "I take back that thought." The compulsive act could be said to "undo" what he feared might result from the initial obsessive thought, which might be rooted in an underlying aggressive impulse toward the father. **Reaction formation** is illustrated by a mother who compulsively checks her children's rooms dozens of times while they are asleep; she is overly solicitous about her children because of her underlying resentment toward them.

Psychotherapy, the main clinical tool of the psychodynamically oriented clinician, is intended to help people expose and deal with the psychodynamic roots of their maladaptive behaviors. Most psychotherapists believe that such behaviors occur when a person becomes preoccupied with relieving or eliminating anxiety. They feel that by gaining insight into the unconscious roots of anxiety, the person can direct his or her activity toward altering or abandoning unwanted behavior. Chapter 17 reviews some of the major aspects of research on psychotherapy and other therapeutic approaches.

The Behavioral Perspective

Instead of speaking of symptoms caused by underlying events, behavioral psychologists focus on acquired responses and response tendencies. They believe that the general principles of learning can be applied to the understanding of all behavior, including anxiety disorders. According to behavioral theorists, anxiety that reaches clinical proportions is a learned or acquired response, a symptom that has been created by environmental conditions, often within the home.

B.F. Skinner, a leading behaviorist (see Chapter 3), objected to any references to mental events (thoughts or feelings) as explanations of behavior; he preferred to rely almost exclusively on observable stimulus and response (S and R) variables. Other theorists emphasize S and R variables but have gone one step beyond Skinner in dealing with internal events as well. Dollard and Miller (1950) were among the earliest theorists to broaden the psychology of learning to include mental events. They went so far as to agree with psychodynamic theorists that there is a personal history behind the development of neurotic disorders (now called anxiety disorders) and that psychotherapy (the "talking therapy") is the optimum means of modifying it.

> *If neurotic behavior is learned, it should be unlearned by some combination of the same principles by which it was taught. We believe this to be the case. Psychotherapy establishes a set of conditions by which neurotic habits may be unlearned and nonneurotic habits learned. Therefore, we view the therapist as a kind of teacher and the patient as a learner. In the same way and by the same principles that bad tennis habits can be corrected by a good coach, so bad mental and emotional habits can be corrected by a psychotherapist. There is this difference, however. Whereas only a few people want to play tennis, all the world wants a clear, free, efficient mind.*
>
> —Dollard and Miller, 1950, pp. 7–8

Learning concepts such as conditioning, reinforcement, and extinction have increasingly been applied to the study of anxiety disorders. Several new, clinically useful techniques, collectively referred to as **behavior therapy** are the most valuable outcomes of these applications. Research using behavior therapy has been directed at discovering the variables that help defuse highly emotional responses.

EXPOSURE THERAPIES A common element in most behavior therapies is exposing the client to stimuli that evoke discomfort until he or she becomes used to them. Much research has been carried out in which clients are exposed to feared stimuli and are prevented from making an avoidance or escape response. The client is strongly urged to continue to attend to the anxiety-eliciting stimuli despite the stressful effects that usually accompany this effort.

Exposure therapy has been used in treating both phobic and obsessive–compulsive disorders. A critical element of the treatment is motivating the client to maintain contact with the actual noxious stimuli or with their imagined presence until he or she becomes used to them. This might mean, for example, exposing a compulsive hand washer to dirt until the hand washing no longer occurs, or encouraging such a person to think about dirt, perhaps imagined first as household dust and

later as particularly noxious dirt such as vomit or feces. The therapist's task is to identify all components of the stimulus that evoke an avoidance or escape response and to continue the exposure until the evoked response no longer occurs.

Three types of therapy based on the exposure principle are systematic desensitization, implosive therapy, and in vivo exposure. In **systematic desensitization** a series of fear-arousing stimuli, carefully graded from mild to strongly fearful, are used. Only when a client is comfortable with one level of fear-producing stimuli is the next, slightly stronger stimulus introduced. **Implosive therapy** refers to therapist-controlled exposure to the imagined re-creation of a complex, high-intensity fear-arousing situation. **In vivo exposure** means that the individual experiences the actual feared situation rather than imagining it under the therapist's direction. In vivo exposure may be conducted gradually, beginning with low levels of stimulus intensity, or rapidly, by exposing the client immediately to high-intensity and prolonged stimulation. This rapid, intense exposure is called **flooding.**

Systematic desensitization, which is used primarily in the treatment of strong fears, is based on conditioning principles. The client is taught to relax and then is presented with a series of stimuli that are graded from low to high according to their capacity to evoke anxiety. The treatment of a death phobia illustrates how systematic desensitization is used. The patient's fears are arranged in a hierarchy, with the items in the hierarchy ranging, in descending order, from human corpses to funeral processions, black clothes, and floral wreaths. The therapy begins with items that are low in the hierarchy, such as seeing a wreath. The therapist tries to teach the client to remain relaxed while imagining or actually seeing a wreath. When the client can maintain a relaxed state consistently, the therapy proceeds with stimuli that are higher in the hierarchy.

A therapist does not try to produce cures overnight with conditioning procedures. Usually, the process of reducing the level of an emotional response to a stimulus that should be neutral is a gradual one. Clinical applications of systematic desensitization have shown that clients who are treated in this way become less upset by previously feared situations and better able to manage their anxiety. It is possible that the most effective part of systematic desensitization is the client's exposure to gradually increasing levels of fear-arousing stimuli under nonthreatening conditions. Individuals who can mentally rehearse being exposed to the upsetting, fear-arousing situations show particularly high levels of improvement.

Implosive therapy is based on the belief that many conditions, including anxiety disorders, are outgrowths of painful prior experiences. For the patient to unlearn them, the original situation must be re-created so that it can be experienced without pain. Therapists who use implosion ask their clients to imagine scenes related to particular personal conflicts and to recreate the anxiety felt in those scenes. The therapist strives to heighten the realism of the re-creation and to help the patient extinguish the anxiety that was created by the original aversive conditions. In addition, the client is helped to adopt more mature forms of behavior.

Implosive therapy uses the methods and ideas of both behavioral and psychodynamic theories. Although it is not uniformly effective in reducing anxiety, research to date suggests that it, like desensitization, can reduce many intense fears (Gelder and others, 1989).

The term in vivo exposure means that the exposure is carried out in a real-life setting, not simply in the imaginations of the client and the therapist as they sit in the therapist's office. The difference between in vivo exposure and flooding might be compared to the difference between wading into a swimming pool and jumping in at the deep end. An example of flooding might be an agoraphobic client who experienced intense anxiety anywhere outside her home who might be asked to go to a crowded shopping center with the therapist and remain there until her desire to escape disappeared. Researchers have reported that using this procedure, someone with a specific fear can lose it in only three sessions (Marks, 1987). Exposure, in combination with cognitive therapy, has also been found to be therapeutic for persons with panic disorder (Barlow and others, 1989; McNally, 1990).

In the treatment of most anxiety disorders, exposure has produced consistently good results, with improvements lasting for up to several years. The longer the exposure to the critical stimulus, the better the results. How well exposure treatment works depends on the client's motivation and on specific factors in his or her life. For example, when compulsive rituals are triggered by home cues (which is true in many cases), treatment needs to be conducted in the home setting. Failure to improve can usually be traced to failure to comply with treatment instructions, particularly by not seeking exposure to fear-arousing stimuli. In one study, compulsives received in vivo exposure therapy in their homes (Emmelkamp, 1980). The clients' task was to avoid responding compulsively when the evoking stimuli were present. Figure 6–12 shows changes in the clients' ratings of their levels of anxiety when exposed to the evoking stimuli. If the client refrained from compulsive behavior in the presence of the stimuli, the level of anxiety decreased immediately after exposure and the decrease was maintained one and six months later in the presence of the compulsion-evoking stimuli.

An important task for future research is to find out *why* exposure is effective. When a client "gets used to" an upsetting stimulus, what is going on? One possible

FIGURE 6–12 Changes in rated anxiety before exposure in vivo (pre), immediately afterwards (post), and at 1- and 6-month follow-up points.

(From Emmelkamp, van der Helm, van Zanten, and Plochg, 1980. Reprinted with permission from *Behavior Research and Therapy.* Copyright © 1980, Pergaman Journals, Ltd.)

explanation is that as clients find that they can handle a little exposure to upsetting stimuli and note that their anxiety levels subside, quickly they gain confidence in themselves and develop the courage to persist in their efforts to overcome their problems.

The most effective behavioral technique for treating compulsive rituals is a combination of exposure and response prevention. The therapist asks the patient to disclose all obsessions and compulsive patterns, and then prohibits them. A compulsive washer, for example, is allowed to become dirty, or is even made dirty, and then is ordered not to wash. A typical treatment might allow one ten-minute shower every fifth day. Exposure reduces hypersensitivity to dirt and the associated anxiety; response prevention eventually eliminates the compulsive ritual. Exposure usually has to be done outside the psychotherapist's office, and trained helpers may be needed—wives, husbands, friends, or nurse–therapists. Exposure in fantasy is less effective, but sometimes it is the only possible way—for example, a patient with a fear of causing a traffic fatality cannot actually run over someone.

Exposure therapy and other behavioral approaches are not highly effective with people who are "pure obsessives," that is, who do not engage in rituals or avoidant behavior. Because depression is a factor in many of these cases, antidepressant drugs are often used in the treatment of obsessions.

MODELING Another behavioral approach, **modeling,** is often combined with exposure to anxiety-provoking stimuli. While exposure therapies emphasize removing some of the overwhelming emotional response that may inhibit people who have an anxiety disorder, modeling emphasizes *acquiring* behavioral skills and a feeling of competence.

In addition to acting as a disinhibitor, modeling can function in the acquisition of new skills and response capabilities. This is especially true in **participant modeling,** which is often more effective than modeling alone. In participant modeling, a therapist models a response and then provides corrective feedback as the client performs the same behavior. In addition to the information provided by the modeled behavior, the client receives guidance on his or her own performance. Participant modeling works especially well with complex behaviors, such as those involved in certain social situations.

Modeling plays a role in **guided mastery,** in which the therapist guides the client toward mastery over frightening situations and maladaptive behavior. Guided mastery might involve modeling of adaptive behavior by the therapist, or it might take the form of directions to the client about how to cope with various aspects of a problematic situation. In either case, the guidance helps the client attain a sense of mastery or self-efficacy.

The Cognitive Perspective

The methods developed by behavioral therapists, although they are based on learning principles, have important implications for our understanding of cognitive processes, that is, private or internal processes such as imagery and how we think about ourselves and the world. Therapies like systematic desensitization, exposure, and modeling affect not only clients' behavior but also how they think about themselves. Furthermore, cognitive activity is often a specific step in behavioral therapy; for example, in systematic desensitization the client is asked to visualize, think about, or imagine certain fear-arousing situations. Cognitive rehearsal in combination with in vivo exposure has been used successfully with phobics and obsessive–compulsives. Available evidence suggests that this procedure is highly effective in ultimately reducing anxiety, regardless of whether the client feels relaxed or anxious during exposure.

Modeling can also have an important cognitive element. Someone who overcomes intense fears as a result of a behavioral-therapy program like participant modeling acquires more self-confidence and may begin to think about new ways of behaving in situations that were not covered in the modeling program. The way people think about things often changes when they acquire new response capabilities. These cognitive changes can then lead to important behavioral advances. The term **cogni-**

tive behavior therapy refers to clinical procedures based on principles of learning, such as extinction and reinforcement, that emphasize cognitive behavior.

COGNITIVE FACTORS IN MALADAPTIVE BEHAVIOR In addition to the increased interest in cognitive aspects of behavior therapy, there has been a rapid increase in the influence of the cognitive perspective on efforts to understand the anxiety disorders. This perspective emphasizes the ways in which certain thoughts and styles of thinking have undesirable effects on behavior. Thoughts that preoccupy people interfere with attention to the task at hand. Worries, daydreams, and ideas that have nothing to do with the immediate task are distracting and reduce behavioral effectiveness.

According to cognitive theorists, thinking disturbances that occur only in certain places or in relation to specific problems are the sources of anxiety. These types of thoughts include unrealistic appraisals of situations and consistent overestimation of their dangerous aspects; for example, the *degree* and *likelihood* of harm may both be exaggerated. Thus, a person's train of thought and mental set can be viewed as vulnerability factors that interact with the characteristics of situations. From this point of view, precipitating events (the situation) elicit or magnify an underlying attitude or fear (the vulnerability factor) and give rise to hypervigilance. As this attitude strengthens, danger-related thoughts become more easily activated by less specific, less avoidable situations ("If you look for it, you're sure to find it"). As a result, the anxious individual continually scans internal and external stimuli for danger signals.

An example of this sort of disturbance may be seen in an obsessive person who experiences intense anxiety when having to cross the street and may actually be unable to attempt a crossing. Most people would use the following train of thought.

1. Streets are safe for crossing at green lights or when free of traffic.
2. This street has a green light or is free of traffic.
3. Therefore, this street can be crossed.

The obsessive person's thinking, on the other hand, might go as follows.

1. Streets are safe for crossing at green lights or when free of traffic.
2. This street has a green light or is free of traffic, but if the light suddenly changes or a car appears unexpectedly. . .
3. Then this street is not safe for me to cross.

Studies of obsessive thinkers have revealed unreasonable beliefs and assumptions. Such people believe that they should be perfectly competent, must avoid criticism or disapproval, and will be severely punished for their mistakes and imperfections. In addition, at some level they seem to believe that thinking certain thoughts or performing certain rituals will help them avoid the disastrous outcomes they imagine are just around the corner. Obsessive–compulsives make arbitrary rules that they must follow (for example, stepping on every seventh crack in the sidewalk). Phobics also make up rules for themselves that are not based in reality (for example, "Elevators get stuck. If I use one it will get stuck and I might suffocate; therefore, I won't go in an elevator."). Unfortunately, "protective" rituals and rules become very intrusive and can interfere with normal activity.

COGNITIVE THERAPY Cognitive therapists employ a number of techniques. One of these is **cognitive restructuring.** Developed out of the rational–emotive therapy of Albert Ellis (see Chapter 3), cognitive restructuring calls the client's attention to the unrealistic thoughts that serve as cues for his or her maladaptive behavior. The therapist helps clients review their irrational beliefs and expectations and develop more rational ways of looking at their lives. For example, many people with anxiety disorders are perfectionists who expect too much of themselves and others and become overly emotional when their unattainable goals are not realized. During therapy sessions emphasis is placed on how the irrational things that people say to themselves can affect their emotions and behavior. The baseball pitcher in Figure 6–13 is being advised to do some cognitive restructuring in order to improve his chances of preventing this skilled batter from getting a hit.

FIGURE 6–13 The catcher is trying to help the pitcher overcome concern about pitching to a superhitter by encouraging the pitcher to think about the batter in a different way.

(From *The Wall Street Journal*—permission, Cartoon Features Syndicate)

By means of cognitive restructuring, people develop more realistic appraisals of themselves and others. For example, when taking an exam a person might think: "This test is hard. Everyone else seems to think it's going to be simple. They all must know a lot more than I do." Such thoughts are likely to lead to a high degree of anxiety. A cognitive therapist would help this client concentrate on a more adaptive type of thought such as: "I studied hard. I'll just try to answer one question at a time. If I don't know the answer, I'll go on to the next one. No reason for panic. Even people who do well don't know the answer to every question."

Thought stopping is another cognitive technique. It works on the assumption that a sudden distracting stimulus, such as an unpleasant noise, will serve to terminate obsessional thoughts. The client is asked to get the thought firmly in mind; then the therapist loudly says "Stop!" This sequence—obsessional thought followed by "Stop!"—is repeated several times with the client, rather than the therapist, yelling "Stop!" Finally, the client simply mentally says "Stop!" If it is successful, this procedure provides the client with a specific self-control technique for removing an obsessional thought when it occurs.

A third cognitive technique is **cognitive rehearsal,** through which the client can mentally rehearse adaptive approaches to problematic situations. Cognitive rehearsal is particularly useful for problems that cannot be conveniently simulated in a clinical setting. For example, behavioral rehearsal of social skills by socially phobic individuals requires the presence of a large group of people. However, someone who suffers from a social phobia can imagine being in a group and can mentally rehearse behaviors and internal statements designed to improve his or her interpersonal relationships.

Aaron Beck has developed one of the most influential types of cognitive therapy (Beck & Emery, 1985). He believes that the core psychological problem in anxiety disorders is a vulnerability that grows out of the individual's tendency to devalue his or her problem-solving ability as well as to exaggerate the degree of threat in a problematic situation. Such an individual perceives anxiety-provoking threats to social relationships, freedom, and self-identity.

Beck's cognitive therapy typically consists of five to twenty sessions. A minimal amount of time is spent acquiring background information, searching for the original causes of anxiety, or engaging in unfocused conversation with the patient. Most of the therapy is task-oriented, being devoted to solving problems brought up by the patient. The therapist encourages the patient to talk openly about his or her fears and concerns, and conveys empathy for the patient's anxiety. The Socratic method (see Chapter 2) is used to help the patient become aware of what his or her thoughts are,

examine them for cognitive distortions, and substitute more realistic thoughts. Three steps are involved in cognitive therapy: (1) conceptualizing the patient's problem, (2) choosing strategies and tactics to deal with the problem, and (3) assessing the effectiveness of those strategies and tactics.

In a sense, Beck is arguing that each of us has an inner voice. When that voice interferes with our ability to function adequately, the unproductive thoughts that result must be replaced by productive ones. This is done by correcting thinking errors and having the patient work on pertinent homework assignments. Using these techniques, the patient can develop not only improved ways of thinking but also more effective, less anxiety-producing ways of dealing with difficult situations.

The following exchange occurred in a therapy session in which Beck's approach was applied to a case of panic disorder. Because catastrophic misinterpretation of physiological sensations is a central component of panic disorder, the therapist sought a precise description of the patient's typical attack and helped the patient, an 18-year-old female, become more aware of her misinterpretations.

P (Patient): *I've felt a couple of times like I was going to have a heart attack.*

T (Therapist): *Tell me about that.*

P: *It's just like, it starts to beat so hard, and so fast, that, I mean, it* hurts, *and you just think, you're just like sitting there going* (breathes rapidly to demonstrate how she hyperventilates).

T: *What was the effect, do you think, of that particular image or idea on the symptoms themselves?*

P: *Oh, well, they get worse, as soon as you think . . .* (pause).

T: *So you have a bodily sensation here at this point in the spiral of anxiety* (pointing to diagram). *The next step, thoughts that the sensation is a sign of catastrophe, that you're going to have a heart attack. What do you think happens to your thoughts when your heart rate does in fact go up? Because you said it would increase when you had this fear . . .*

P: *Uh-huh.*

T: *What would you think then?*

P: *I just get really scared, and I have to get out of the situation that I'm in. I mean, I have to.*

T: *O.K. So you see what's happening there. You perceive a danger, which would lead to more anxiety; the anxiety would make the symptoms worse, would make the heart rate even faster; and you interpret that, then, as "I really am going to have a heart attack." Right?*

P: *Yeah, but only fleetingly, you know, and then I go "I'm not going to have a heart attack, but I've got to get out of here!"*

T: *O.K.*

P: *But, I mean,* fleetingly, *I've also thought all kinds of, you know, I'm sure . . .*

—Alford and others, 1990, pp. 231–232

Upon identification of her physiological sensations and negative automatic thoughts associated with the sensations, the patient was able to rapidly obtain some distance from her fearful thoughts. At a five-month follow-up, she reported having no panic attacks after the cognitive therapy ended.

COMBINING COGNITIVE AND BEHAVIORAL APPROACHES Some of the most promising efforts to apply psychological techniques to clinical problems involve combining approaches suggested by a variety of theoretical perspectives. Recent research on the treatment of anxiety disorders illustrates these attempts. Gillian Butler (1988) at Oxford University in England developed an anxiety management training program with the following components:

1. Information about the nature of anxiety and what might be expected from treatment;
2. A cognitive component to help with self-identification and response to specific anxiety-provoking thoughts;
3. Use of distractions and relaxation to cope with situations in which anxiety is anticipated;
4. Exposure training for overcoming avoidance behavior;
5. A component designed to instill self-confidence by identifying the person's strong points, by engaging in rewarding and pleasurable activities, and by paying attention to aspects of life in which the person is functioning relatively well.

The treatment program is described in an easy to understand self-help booklet that the client follows. Clients play an active role in setting goals, planning homework assignments, and monitoring their progress. The program has been used in a series of clinical studies with social phobia and generalized anxiety disorder patients. In one study of generalized anxiety disorder, clients were randomly assigned to either the treatment or control conditions. The program, which typically extended over fewer than nine sessions, resulted in significant reductions of anxiety. The therapeutic improvement was maintained at a six-month follow-up. The significance of these results is reflected in the finding that at post-treatment the anxiety ratings of half of the clients had fallen below the cutoff point that distinguishes a normal from a clinical population. There was some evidence that people with panic disorders also responded favorably to this type of treatment.

The Biological Perspective

Over the years several different types of reactions have been found to be caused by an individual's biological state. Some of these discoveries have led to the development of medical treatment methods. Although no direct organic cause has been found for most types of anxiety disorders, the findings of physical causation in other conditions suggest the possibility that there are some links between anxieties and biophysical functioning. People whose nervous systems are particularly sensitive to stimulation seem more likely to experience severe anxiety.

GENETIC AND ENVIRONMENTAL FACTORS Inbreeding experiments with animals have shown that heredity has a strong influence on such characteristics as timidity, fearfulness, and aggressiveness. Evidence also shows that anxiety disorders tend to run in families (Andreasen & Black, 1991).

One study found children of people treated for anxiety disorder were more anxious and fearful, had more school difficulties, worried more about family members and themselves, and had more somatic complaints than did the children of normal parents (Turner, 1987). These children also spent more time engaged in solitary activities and were seven times more likely to meet the criteria for an anxiety disorder than children whose families had no history of anxiety disorder. Another study of nearly 4,000 pairs of adult twins attempted to evaluate the separate effects of genetic and environmental factors in anxiety and depression (Kendler, 1986). There was strong evidence of a genetic factor and a statistically significant, but weaker, effect for a family environment factor.

DRUG THERAPIES During the 1950s new medications used in the treatment of severe psychotic disor-

ders were found to have dramatic positive effects. Subsequently, much biological research has also been directed toward developing medications that might be effective for less severe—and often more common—disorders. A number of drugs are now available for treating specific anxiety disorders. Research on their effects and how these are produced is ongoing.

Benzodiazepines Tranquilizing drugs are the most commonly used somatic therapy in the treatment of anxiety. Well over 55 million prescriptions for these substances are filled each year (Breier & Paul, 1990). Although placebo and enthusiasm reactions may account for some of their effectiveness, psychiatrists and other physicians who prescribe tranquilizers have found them valuable in reducing states of great tension. The literature on the behavioral effects of tranquilizers or anti-anxiety drugs suggests that these agents reduce the intensity of responses to stimuli that signal punishment and frustration.

In 1960 a group of drugs called **benzodiazepines** were introduced. They are marketed under trade names like Librium and Valium and are used for the treatment of anxiety, tension, behavioral excitement, and insomnia. Figure 6–14 shows the significantly lowering effect of one dose of a member of this group, diazepam (Valium), on the anxiety experienced when people who were phobic about cats and roaches were exposed to these animals. Similar results were obtained when the dependent measure was how close the person would come to the fear-arousing stimulus. It seems clear that a dose of diazepam made phobics better able to tolerate the animals they were afraid of. Although benzodiazepines have been proven effective in reducing anxiety, their side effects are quite problematic. Side effects include drowsiness, lethargy, motor impairment, and reduced ability to concentrate. The drugs also produce physiological and psychological dependence. Excessive use may lead to undesirable behavior, including disorientation, confusion, rage, and other symptoms that resemble drunkenness.

Several years ago researchers found that benzodiazepines bind to certain receptor sites in the receiving neuron and that the relative potencies of drugs in competing for these binding sites parallel their clinical effects. Receptor sites serve as receiving stations for the brain's nerve cells. They are analogous to locks into which the appropriate chemicals fit like keys.

The discovery of receptor sites for anti-anxiety drugs has set off a widespread search to map other specific receptor sites in the brain that mediate the effects of different types of drugs. Some experts believe that receptor sites are a key to a natural anxiety system and that anti-anxiety drugs act in the same way that natural body substances, perhaps still undiscovered, keep anxiety under control. One of the exciting questions now being investigated is that of what substances produced within the body attach to which types of receptors.

Recently, one benzodiazepine derivative, alprazolam, was approved by the United States Food and Drug Administration for the treatment of panic disorders. Alprazolam is fast-acting and has fewer unpleasant side effects than other drugs used in the treatment of panic disorders. Its side effects include drowsiness and withdrawal symptoms if a patient stops taking it after long-term use.

Antidepressants A major event in the development of drugs to treat anxiety disorders was the use of drugs developed as antidepressants in treating panic and obsessive–compulsive disorders. One group of antidepressants, the tricyclic drugs (imipramine, clomipramine), appears to have therapeutic effects on many people with these disorders. The tricyclics may be effective in up to two-thirds of those suffering with obsessive–compulsive disorder, reducing the obsessions and feelings of anxiety, and increasing the likelihood of a positive response to behavior therapy designed to eliminate ritualistic responding. Possible side effects of the tricyclic drugs include dry mouth, drowsiness, blurred vision, and seizures (Andreasen & Black, 1991).

The successful use of drugs to treat anxiety disorders not only has been of practical value and a stimulus for developing biological theories of anxiety, but also has raised some important questions. For example, why might drugs developed for the treatment of depression be helpful in cases of anxiety? Evidence that antidepressant drugs are useful in treating anxiety disorders suggests that the relationship between anxiety and depression needs careful examination. One study found that all patients in a sample of people diagnosed as

FIGURE 6–14 Subjective anxiety ratings when confronted with phobic stimuli. "After" measures were made two hours after the subject took either a pill containing diazepam (Valium) or a placebo.

(Adapted from Whitehead, Blackwell, and Robinson, 1978, p. 63)

depressed also showed anxiety symptoms (Barlow and others, 1986). Significant overlaps of symptoms in different disorders may partially explain some of the seemingly surprising effects that drugs have been found to have on certain groups of patients. These symptom overlaps are referred to as **comorbidity,** the co-occurrence of symptoms and conditions in different disorders. Box 6–2 deals with this topic, which is now being widely discussed among clinicians and researchers.

BOX 6–2 Comorbidity

Patients with anxiety disorders often have features of multiple mental disorders, especially the disturbances of mood found in depression. Although such co-occurrences of thoughts, behaviors, and symptoms appear in a number of other disorders as well, surprisingly little attention has been paid to this phenomenon. Table 6–9 shows the wide range of comorbidity, the co-occurrence of clinical symptoms, among various types of maladaptive behavior. The table indicates, for example, that 77.2 percent of cases of schizophrenia and paranoid disorders in the population studied had only that diagnosis, while 22.8 percent of these cases had multiple diagnoses (that is, diagnoses in addition to the primary one). Comorbidity estimates vary from study to study for several reasons, including the methods employed in making diagnoses and characteristics of the sample surveyed. For example, while 29.8 percent of the cases of anxiety disorder in

Table 6–9 involved multiple diagnoses, other studies using different populations and diagnostic methods have found greater comorbidity for anxiety and depressive disorders (Hecht and others, 1989). One study found that, while the risk of suicide in people with panic disorder is high, the risk is even higher in panic disorder cases that involved comorbidity with other disorders (Johnson and others, 1990).

Studies of comorbidity have led clinicians to attend to the fact that more than one disorder can be diagnosed in the same individual. In addition, an individual who meets the full diagnostic criteria for only one disorder may still have an increased frequency of symptoms from other categories—but to an extent that is insufficient to diagnose another disorder. Patients diagnosed as having a particular disorder may have relatively greater or lesser risk of also having other disorders being diag-

nosed or other symptoms observed.

Comorbidity can occur within a given diagnostic category as well as between different ones. For example, there is evidence that the presence of one type of anxiety disorder increases the likelihood of the presence of another. We know persons diagnosed as having social phobias often receive a secondary diagnosis of panic disorder (de Ruiter and others, 1989). Knowing that comorbidity may be high in certain types of cases is valuable to clinicians because it alerts them to the need to probe carefully regarding the possibility of co-occurrences.

Epidemiological studies of anxiety and mood disorders have revealed several intriguing findings. One is that the risk of depression in individuals with chronic anxiety disorders is greater than the risk of anxiety in individuals with depressive disorders (Maser & Cloninger, 1990). Another is that depressive disorders are more likely to remain free of comorbid anxiety while anxiety disorders are more often complicated by depression after long-term follow-up. There are many issues raised by the comorbidity of mental disorders. One pertains to the role of heredity. Is there a common genetic cause or predisposition for both depression and anxiety or are different environmental exposures responsible for comorbidity? At present we do not have an answer to this question. The association between anxiety and depression could be due to one of the disorders causing or leading to the other. Another possible explanation is that the two disorders have some common genetic cause. Because of increasing attention being given to the topic of comorbidity, research on which of these possibilities is most likely is accelerating (Merikangas, 1990).

Table 6–9
Percentages of Single and Multiple Diagnoses for Various Diagnostic Categories

Diagnostic Categories	(%) Single Diagnoses	(%) Multiple Diagnoses
Anxiety disorders	70.2	29.8
Affective disorders (depression)	57.4	42.6
Dissociative disorders	50.0	50.0
Adjustment disorders	69.0	31.0
Alcohol use disorders	13.5	86.5
Psychosexual disorders	13.8	86.2
Schizophrenic and paranoid disorders	77.2	22.8
Mental retardation	14.7	85.3
Organic brain disorders	67.0	33.0

SOURCE: Based on Mezzich, Ahn, Fabrega, & Pilkonis, 1990

Chapter Summary

GENERALIZED ANXIETY DISORDER

Anxiety is a vague, diffuse feeling that includes both worried thoughts and a combination of physical symptoms. Anxiety differs from ordinary fear in that fear is related to an identifiable cause, while the reasons for the anxiety are often not clear to the anxious person. A person with **generalized anxiety disorder** experiences vague, but intense, concerns and fearfulness that persist over a long period, at least a month, and includes four types of symptoms: motor tension, autonomic reactivity, apprehension about the future, and hypervigilance.

PANIC DISORDER

Panic attacks are severe anxiety attacks that occur unexpectedly and involve severe physical symptoms as well as very strong fears that often involve concern over dying, going crazy, or behaving in an uncontrolled way. Persons with panic disorder experience panic attacks unexpectedly and therefore become very anxious as they worry that another attack may occur. Panic disorder is the least prevalent of all the anxiety disorders. Some panic attacks can be prevented by **imipramine,** a drug used to treat depression. Both generalized anxiety disorder and panic disorder seem to run in families.

PHOBIAS

People who have **phobias** have fears related to specific objects, people, or situations. Phobias often develop gradually or begin with a generalized anxiety attack. Phobias are common disorders that affect women about twice as frequently as men. The rate of this disorder is higher among African-Americans than among either whites or Hispanics. Phobias often begin before adulthood and are likely to become chronic. Phobias can be grouped into three main types: simple phobias, social phobias, and agoraphobia.

Simple Phobias **Simple phobias** are the most commonly occurring type of phobia. This group includes miscellaneous irrational fears such as intense fear of a certain type of animal or of being in an enclosed place. Simple phobias may arise from an earlier frightening or anxiety producing situation that originally involved the type of person or situation that later became associated with the phobia. Procedures that use the classical conditioning approach of pairing the phobic stimulus with a nonanxiety response are often used successfully to treat simple phobias.

Social Phobias Intense and incapacitating fear and embarrassment when dealing with others characterize **social phobias.** Social phobias are the least common type of specific phobia. Fears of blushing when in a social situation or of eating with others present are two social phobias that are especially difficult to treat successfully.

Agoraphobia **Agoraphobia** is the term used when people develop a fear of entering unfamiliar situations. Many agoraphobics are afraid to leave their homes so their ability to carry on normal life activities is severely limited. There are two major types of agoraphobia, that with and that without panic attacks. In the latter group panic attacks often begin first and lead to agoraphobia. Panic attacks can often be treated with antidepressant drugs. Agoraphobia can be successfully treated with behavioral techniques in which the agoraphobic is exposed to the feared stimulus under controlled conditions with the support of a therapist.

OBSESSIVE-COMPULSIVE DISORDER

People affected by an **obsessive-compulsive disorder** are unable to control their preoccupation with specific ideas or are unable to prevent themselves from repeatedly carrying out a particular act or series of acts that affect their ability to carry out normal activities. The inability to stop thinking about a particular idea or topic is called an **obsession.** The topic of these thoughts is often felt by the person involved to be unpleasant and shameful. The need to perform certain behaviors over and over is called a **compulsion.** Many compulsions deal with counting, ordering, checking, touching, and washing. Compulsive rituals may become very elaborate and contain many activities. Like phobias, obsessive–compulsive disorder tends to begin before adulthood and is more common in women than in men.

INTERPRETING AND TREATING ANXIETY DISORDERS

The Psychodynamic Perspective Psychodynamic theorists suggest several possible causes of anxiety disorders. These include perceptions of helplessness and inability to cope with life situations, fear of abandonment or loss of love, sudden loss of emotional support, and unacceptable impulses that while still unconscious, are threatening to break into awareness. Freud defined several defense mechanisms that may play a role in obsessive-compulsive disorders. The mechanisms include **isolation, undoing, and reaction formation.** Psychodynamically oriented therapists typically deal with anxiety disorders by psychotherapy directed at helping clients gain insight into the unconscious roots of their anxiety.

The Behavioral Perspective The behavioral-learning concepts of conditioning, reinforcement, and extinction are all applied in **behavior therapy.** Behavioral therapists commonly use **exposure therapy** in treating phobic and obsessive–compulsive clients. Three types of therapy based on the exposure principle are **systematic desensitization** in which fear-arousing stimuli are presented in a graded series paired with relaxation exercises,

implosive therapy in which the client imagines a complex and highly arousing fear situation, and **in vivo exposure** in which the person actually is present in the feared situation. **Flooding** refers to the rapid, intense exposure of stimulation in an in vivo exposure situation. **Modeling** and **guided mastery** are often used by the therapist together with exposure therapy.

The Cognitive Perspective Many of the behavioral therapies such as systematic desensitization include cognitive rehearsal. **Cognitive behavior therapy** is based on the learning principles of extinction and reinforcement that include emphasis on cognitive behavior. Cognitive therapy focuses on a number of techniques that are usually combined with various behavioral exercises. These include **cognitive restructuring, thought stopping,** and **cognitive rehearsal.**

The Biological Perspective Strong evidence for a genetic factor in anxiety disorders is shown in studies of both animals and humans. There is also some weaker evidence of an environmental factor. A number of drugs are now used for treating specific anxiety disorders. The **benzodiazepines** or tranquilizing drugs such as Valium are the most frequently prescribed drugs used in the general treatment of anxiety. One benzodiazepine derivative, alprazolam, has recently become popular for treating panic disorders. One group of antidepressant drugs, the **tricyclics** are used successfully in treating obsessive–compulsive disorder especially in combination with behavior therapy. It is thought that one reason antidepressant drugs are useful in treating anxiety is because of the overlap in symptoms and conditions in the different disorders. This overlap is referred to as **comorbidity.**

Psychological Factors
and Physical Symptoms

C H A P T E R 7

Psychological, Social, and Bodily Interactions
Psychophysiological Approaches
The Biopsychosocial Model
Stress and Illness

Psychophysiological Disorders
Headaches
Cardiovascular Disorders
Cancer
The Immune System and Related Disorders
Allergies
Gastrointestinal Disorder

Somatoform Disorders
Psychogenic Pain Disorder
Hypochondriasis
Somatization Disorders
Conversion Disorders

Factitious Disorders and Malingering

Chapter Summary

Egon Schiele, *Standing Boy in Striped Shirt*, 1910. Private Collection. Courtesy of Serge Sabarsky, Inc., New York.

People get upset when they hear that someone they know has been diagnosed with cancer. A number of people I told began to cry. People said they would pray for me. All this might sound like an outpouring of love and support, but it was also scary. For awhile I reacted to any expression from others with anger, feeling that everyone thought I was dying. At times I worried that my understanding of my illness was incorrect, reasoning that others must know something that I don't about my prognosis or that I was denying the seriousness of my condition. I spent a lot of time reassuring others, trying to feel that they weren't viewing me as a person with "one foot in the grave."

These reactions make social support a more complex issue than it might at first appear. While having people around me to help and support me was invaluable, it also was a burden, taking energy I needed for other things. There is, however, one exception to this ambivalence. I quickly discovered the comfort of being with other people who were diagnosed with cancer.

. . . [O]ne day some colleagues asked about my chemotherapy. After telling them about the regimen one listener invited me to agree with her that it was wonderful that such potentially lifesaving drugs were available. I couldn't respond. You see, I hate my chemotherapy drugs. I loathe ordering them from the pharmacy, smelling them, feeling them in my hand, and taking them. But to express this to her would involve a lot of explaining, assuring her that I don't intend to stop my treatments, stating that, of course, I am glad we have these drugs, etc. I don't have to do that with another cancer patient. When a woman also being treated for breast cancer fairly spit out the name of one of her drugs I understood what she was feeling. When I complained that I was

tired of being bald, a colleague with cancer didn't tell me I looked great, urge me to hang in there, or get teary. He simply said "I know." Similarly, when he and I joke about our experiences we are being funny, not poignant, touching, or brave. It's good to be able to gripe and joke unselfconsciously.

—Shore, 1989, p. 25

Elsie Shore's account of her experience with cancer conveys some of the psychological stress that accompanies serious illness. It also shows the value of social support. Research findings suggest that informal, warm, accepting relationships, such as those she described, can have significant influences over bodily function. For example, there is evidence that the quality of close relationships (that is, the degree to which warmth and conflict characterize them) can influence the functioning of the immune system (Kennedy and others, 1990).

Evidence suggesting that psychological and social factors may play important roles in health and fitness—an idea that has intrigued both clinical workers and patients alike for a long time—is increasing. In this chapter we will review existing information about the relationships among personality, environment, and illness, and examine how psychological and social variables operate in health and illness. We will then emphasize several groups of conditions that are marked by actual tissue damage or impairment and that appear to be linked to certain personality and environmental factors. These conditions are often referred to as **psychophysiological** or **psychosomatic disorders.**

After reviewing these disorders, we will discuss another group of conditions, those that involve physical complaints with no detectable tissue damage or impairment. These conditions have been referred to as **somatoform disorders** because they suggest somatic impairment when there is no evidence that any exists. A third group of conditions that will be dealt with are **factitious disorders.** People with factitious conditions, as the name implies, have physical or psychological complaints that appear to be simulated and under their voluntary control. In other words, they seem to be faking.

Many of the disorders covered in this chapter are thought to result from frequent, intense, and prolonged physiological arousal. Whereas some people respond to stress primarily with bizarre thoughts and behavior, others respond primarily with physical symptoms ranging from cancer to migraine headaches. But while it is known that there are wide differences in individual patterns of physiological, cognitive, and behavioral reactions to stress, the mechanisms behind those patterns remain unclear. Whatever the mechanisms turn out to be,

it is now certain that they involve interactions among personal variables (for example, attitudes and physiological patterns) and situational variables (such as past and recent life experiences and social supports): Illness clearly results from multiple factors.

Psychological, Social, and Bodily Interactions

Awareness that one's state of mind can influence one's body has a long history (see Chapter 2). In the eighteenth century Mesmer claimed that he could modify the course of physical symptoms by using his personal "magnetism." In the nineteenth century Charcot pioneered the use of hypnosis in the treatment of bodily complaints, and early in this century Freud applied psychoanalytic concepts to physical symptoms. Freud believed that somatic symptoms had symbolic significance; they represented compromises among forbidden impulses, intrapsychic conflicts, and the need to defend oneself from anxiety. In the 1930s and 1940s a number of clinicians attempted to integrate Freudian ideas into a growing body of knowledge concerning the bodily aspects of emotional experiences. During this period the **psychosomatic hypothesis** became popular. According to this theory, bodily symptoms can be caused by a blocking of emotional expression.

Psychophysiological Approaches

More recent research work has focused on how bodily reactions change when people are exposed to various emotion-arousing stimuli. For example, emotional tension has been shown to influence the autonomic nervous system and the endocrine glands. One of the endocrine glands, the adrenal medulla, releases its hormones when the situation calls for "fight or flight." As a result, the rates of breathing and heartbeat and muscle tension increase. These and other bodily changes caused by emotional responses to stress prepare the organism to struggle for survival.

Much of the basic research on the endocrines' responses to stress had used animals as experimental subjects. Experimental studies have dealt with two central questions: (1) How does stress affect endocrine function? and (2) How do different levels of biochemical substances influence bodily functioning and behavior?

In his studies of the physiology of stress, Hans Selye subjected a variety of laboratory animals to many kinds of stressful situations. He invariably found that the endocrines spring into action when there are bodily or environmental threats of damage to the organism (Selye,

1976). Selye coined the phrase **general adaptation syndrome** to refer to an organism's pattern of reactions to prolonged stress. This pattern begins with an initial shock or alarm response, which is followed by a recovery or resistance phase. During the alarm phase the adrenal glands show particularly striking changes. They become enlarged and discharge their supply of steroids, a process that causes them to change color from yellow to brown. When Selye's animals were removed from stress, the adrenal glands returned to their normal size and seemed to resume normal functioning, but this recovery was only temporary. After several weeks of renewed stress, the glands again enlarged and lost their store of steroids. Selye found that if the stress is very great and continues for a long time, the animal finally dies from exhaustion.

Not surprisingly, demonstration of the general adaptation syndrome in animals has led to research on its existence in human beings. Studies of professional hockey players and of psychiatric patients appearing at staff conferences found increases in subjects' hormonal secretions during emotional stress that were similar to those found in Selye's animals (Elmadjian, 1963). Because of such changes in body functioning, severe and prolonged psychological pressures can cause physical diseases such as high blood pressure and stomach ulcers. Recent research has focused on the effects of varying degrees of stress on specific bodily systems and the mechanisms that produce the effects (Taylor, 1991).

The Biopsychosocial Model

Today most researchers look at physical symptoms from an interactional viewpoint: Bodily defects may cause psychological problems, and psychological problems may in turn cause bodily defects. When psychological factors are involved in illness, their roles are usually indirect. For example, personality characteristics by themselves may not cause an illness like asthma, but in combination with hypersensitive lungs and certain situational stresses, they may play an important role.

In the last two decades, emphasis has been placed on the interaction between psychological states and social and biological variables. According to the **biopsychosocial model,** a person can be regarded as a system with interacting biological, psychological, and social subsystems (Engel, 1977). This model can be illustrated by some of the complex activities involved in brain function. The brain processes both physical and nonphysical inputs (environmental events, ideas); it generates thoughts and behavior; and it regulates bodily functions. At any given moment the brain's circuitry permits simultaneous "programming" of data pertaining to the biological, psychological, and social spheres. The challenge facing researchers is to identify the factors and conditions that play roles in this complex type of information processing.

Biopsychosocial problems often arise when people's lives are disrupted by environmental changes, challenges, and constraints. The word **homeostasis** refers to the mechanism by which an organism mobilizes itself to restore a dynamic equilibrium in the face of these disruptions. At present most researchers and clinicians believe that, for any given individual, a host of variables—physical, psychological, and social—contribute to the phenomenon that we call "getting sick." The idea that illness is due simply to the influence of external agents seems outmoded. While it is true that there are individual differences in the vulnerability of bodily organs to disease, these differences must be considered in light of personality characteristics, environmental factors, and the general condition of the body. The biopsychosocial point of view is not limited to the causes of illness. It is also relevant to prevention and treatment, major fields of concern to the specialty areas of behavioral medicine and health psychology (see Box 7–1).

Stress and Illness

There is growing evidence that stress plays an important role in illness and health. We have observed that stress leads to diverse bodily reactions. The heart, lungs, and digestive, endocrine, and nervous systems, among others, work overtime when people experience stress. When these symptoms are consistently overloaded throughout long periods of a person's life, the likelihood increases that some sort of physical weakness or disturbance will occur. It makes good medical sense, therefore, to study the personal characteristics and aspects of life that go along with strong and persistent stress reactions or might predispose a person to psychological or physical breakdown. Stress is created when individuals face difficult situations and have to ask themselves, "How am I going to handle this one?" or "Can I do it?" These are some of the skills whose absence increases stress and the risk of illness:

1. Inability to adapt to changes in environmental demands

2. Inability to handle strong feelings and emotions, and to express them realistically

3. Inability to interpret demands, constraints, and opportunities correctly

4. Inability to form rewarding, lasting interpersonal ties, particularly love relationships

Only some of the people who are biologically predisposed to a particular condition actually fall ill. Others who are equally biologically vulnerable are able to cope effectively and thus reduce the negative effects of stress on health. The chance of onset of illness may vary

BOX 7–1 **Behavioral Medicine and Health Psychology**

The biopsychosocial model's emphasis on interrelating factors has contributed to the development of two new fields, behavioral medicine and health psychology. These fields are based on the idea that combinations of biological, psychological, and social factors influence an individual's health, vulnerability to disease, and reactions to disease. Studies in these fields strongly indicate that virtually every ill that can befall the body—from the common cold to cancer and heart disease—can be influenced, positively or negatively, by a person's mental state, lifestyle, and social relationships. By unveiling the mechanisms behind these effects, research may point to new ways of preventing and treating disease.

Behavioral medicine is concerned with ways of improving diagnosis, treatment, and rehabilitation by using psychological techniques that help people adopt healthier ways of living. An important goal of behavioral medicine is the improvement of service delivery by providers of health care. Researchers in behavioral medicine are particularly concerned with direct patient evaluation and treatment.

The related field of **health psychology** is directed toward the prevention of disease. Health psychologists seek to reduce health risks by changing people's thinking and living habits. Researchers in health psychology tend to be concerned with broader topics, including the acquisition and modification of behavior that influences health or is guided by concerns about health. Since as much as 50 percent of mortality from the leading causes of death can be traced to such behaviors as inactivity, poor nutrition, and smoking, health psychologists seek to strengthen those behaviors that contribute to good health (Taylor, 1991).

Both behavioral medicine and health psychology are concerned with reducing the stressfulness of illness and, wherever possible, preventing it.

Prevention often involves helping people to make healthful life style changes. Examples of targets of prevention efforts are smoking, a form of voluntary behavior clearly harmful to health and a major cause of cancer; alcohol abuse, which contributes to cirrhosis of the liver; injuries from accidents and violence; and overeating and underexercising which contribute to obesity, high blood pressure, and diabetes.

The great need for effective health-promotion techniques is suggested by the facts presented in Table 7–1 showing the results of a national survey of health-related behaviors. If only a small proportion of the people who either are failing to promote their own health or are engaging in activities harmful to their health could be helped to change their behavior, both personal suffering and economic costs would be significantly reduced.

Behavioral medicine and health psychology are interdisciplinary fields that integrate the behavioral and biomedical sciences. Common to both of these fields is a philosophy that emphasizes individual responsibility as a means of maximizing health. According to this view, health is a personal achievement, and people's behavior influences whether they attain it or not. Physical, mental, social, and economic factors all influence health and recovery from illness.

Of course, the degree to which health is a personal achievement depends on how many of the determinants of health are controllable. For example, air pollution, a cause of lung disease and asthma, is controlled to a significant degree by the decisions society makes; while the fat content of diet which is related to heart disease and cancer can be reduced when individuals decide to reduce the fat content in their own diets. However, the incidence of diseases strongly influenced by genetic factors is much less modifiable.

One significant factor in longevity is gender. While women live longer

Table 7–1
Facts about Health in the United States

About one-fourth of the adult population is 20 percent or more above desirable body weight.

About one-half of adults experience at least a moderate amount of stress in a 2 week period.

Forty percent of the population say they exercise or play sports, but only 28 percent are very physically active.

About 30 percent of persons 18 years of age and over smoke cigarettes.

Fifty percent of young mothers, 18 to 24 years of age, with less than 12 years of education have smoked in the year preceding the birth of their last child.

SOURCE: Adapted from *Health Promotion and Disease Prevention,* 1988.

than men, the cause of this difference is unclear. Probably both genetic and life style factors play roles. Sex differences in longevity are smaller in nonindustrial than in industrial societies. To a large extent this distinction reflects smaller sex differences in mortality for coronary heart disease in nonindustrial societies. In industrial societies like the United States, higher male mortality rates seem to be related to society's expectations that men be more aggressive, adventurous, ambitious, and hard-driving than women. If these expectations were changed, would male mortality rates become lower as a result? As more and more women hold jobs and support families, will their mortality rates go up? We do not have definite answers to these questions. Research that compares mortality among men who differ in their need to adopt traditional male roles and among women who differ in their conceptions of female roles may clarify this issue.

with a number of factors, including age, the particular form of the illness, and what is going on in the person's life. These interacting factors provide a clue to why it is practically impossible to make statements like, "John Jones got pneumonia because he had been working overtime for two months" or "Mary Smith developed ulcers because she is such a nervous person." Many people develop pneumonia without working overtime, and most people can work overtime without becoming sick. Similarly, many people who develop ulcers do not appear to be especially nervous, and most nervous people do not develop ulcers.

As noted earlier, stress causes a variety of physical changes. Among other things, it stimulates hormonal secretions (particularly those of the pituitary and adrenal glands), activates the autonomic system, brings about biochemical changes, and alters the brain's electrical level. Although all people have these reactions to stress, the strength and pattern of the reactions depend not only on the nature of the stressful stimulus but also on the individual's biological characteristics, personality, and life experiences. Recent and past life experiences play important roles in influencing our appraisal of situations and the coping mechanisms we use to deal with stress.

Psychophysiological Disorders

The body is made up of many millions of cells that, grouped together, form organs whose functions overlap to produce the body's systems. In this section, we review a number of bodily systems that have been approached from a biopsychosocial point of view and that are believed to be related to psychological processes.

Several groups of such physical disorders in which personality and social factors may play a part have been studied over the years. There is no evidence that these conditions are directly attributable to the mental state of the individual or that a person suffering from one of these disorders has a completely different personality from a person suffering from another disorder or none at all. What is becoming increasingly clear, however, is that people—not just cells or organs—have diseases, and that diseases must be studied in the context of people's physical, psychological, social, and cultural environments.

The term **psychophysiological disorder** has traditionally been applied to physical conditions in which psychologically meaningful events are closely related to bodily symptoms. Psychophysiological disorders might be thought of as end products of biopsychosocial processes. A large number of physical problems have been studied from a psychophysiological standpoint. These include disorders of the cardiovascular, respiratory, gastrointestinal, musculoskeletal, and genitourinary systems, as well as the skin. Both clinical data and informal observations suggest the importance of psychological factors in many of these disorders. Consider the following case.

A 38-year-old mother of four children had a five-year history of attacks of hives, a skin condition characterized by itching, burning, and stinging. During these attacks, areas of her face, trunk, waist, thighs, and arms would swell. There would be swelling even on her tongue and inside her respiratory passages. The attacks initially occurred about once a month, but at the time that she sought help, their frequency was closer to once every four or five days. Each attack was accompanied by depression and nausea.

An examination in an allergy clinic yielded negative results. After a psychiatrist placed the patient on tranquilizing drugs, the incidence of hives declined markedly. Further study indicated that her attacks usually occurred when she was experiencing intense stress. For example, when she was having marital difficulties and was forced to face the possibility that her husband might leave her, she had an especially severe series of attacks. At one point she felt so overwhelmed by situational stresses that she was hospitalized. During this period she was protected from family tensions, and her hives disappeared completely.

After leaving the hospital the patient entered psychotherapy on a twice-a-week basis. In these sessions she was able to express her frustrations at leading a very restricted life because of her small children's demands and her husband's inability to see why she might need time away from home. Another point that emerged in therapy was the patient's inability to express to her husband how much she needed to have him acknowledge her value as a person, not just as the mother of his children. After several months of therapy, she felt able to tell her husband about her unfulfilled psychological needs as well as her resentment and frustration. At the time that therapy ended, she had been completely free from hives for four months.

In this case, it seems clear that this particular woman's skin condition was linked to events and conditions in her personal life. A major hurdle for the researcher is figuring out how to proceed from relationships that may be at work in a given case to generalizations that could apply to whole groups of people.

Headaches

Headaches may be the most commonly reported painful bodily signal. Although the majority of headaches are not associated with significant organic disease, they nonetheless can be debilitating. Every year an estimated 80 percent of Americans suffer from at least one headache, and 10 to 20 percent go to a physician with headaches as their primary complaint. Headaches also are a major reason given for absenteeism from work or avoidance of other undesired social or personal activities (Thompson, 1982).

The pain of a headache has three components.

1. Physiological changes (usually either muscular contractions or blood vessel dilation)
2. The subjective experience of pain (aching, distress, fatigue, and so on)
3. Behavior motivated by the pain (for example, pill taking, withdrawal from family and social activities, absence from work).

Not all headaches are alike and there are wide differences in people's sensitivity to the physiological changes that signal the beginning of a headache (see Table 7–2).

Muscle-contraction or **tension headaches,** distinguished by changes in skeletal muscles, are probably the most common form of head pain. The person reports an aching, dull, pressing feeling; the scalp may feel tender if pressed with the hand; and there are persistent sensations of band-like pain or tightness in the head. The exact cause of muscle-contraction headaches has not yet been pinpointed. Research suggests that tension headache sufferers are emotionally hyperreactive to pain and to stress (Lehrer & Murphy, 1991).

Migraine headaches are localized on one side or on the front of the head. They are severe, tend to recur, and are often accompanied by a variety of somatic symptoms. The throbbing, pulsating pain characteristic of migraines may last for several hours. Nausea and vomiting are common. In some cases, the dilated cranial artery is visible and tender.

Unlike muscle-contraction headaches, migraines are usually preceded by a sensory, motor, or mood disturbance, called an *aura*. There may be ringing in the ears; tingling, numbness, or weakness of a limb; extreme sensitivity to light; visual blurring; distorted depth perception; nausea; or unaccountable emotional changes.

Many migraine sufferers have a family history of such headaches, but whether this is due to heredity or to common living experiences is unclear. Migraine attacks

Table 7–2

Differentiating Features of Common Types of Headaches

	Muscle–contraction headache	Migraine	Cluster headache
Sex	No difference	More frequent in women	More frequent in men
Quality of pain	Pressure, tightness, band-like	Throbbing	Piercing, burning, excruciating
Time of onset	Often afternoon or evening	Often early mornings and weekends	Soon after onset of sleep, and daytime
Mode of onset	Gradual	Abrupt or gradual	Abrupt
Duration	Hours, days, or weeks	Hours, 1 to 2 days	20 minutes to 2 hours
Precipitating or aggravating factors	Emotional stress or not apparent	Emotional stress, menstruation, alcohol, certain foods, change in weather	Alcohol, lying down, REM sleep
Associated symptoms or signs	No specific symptoms except tenderness of scalp or neck muscles	Nausea, vomiting, irritability, tender scalp	Tearing of eyes, nasal stuffiness and discharge
Personality traits	Competitive, conscientious	Perfectionistic, neat, efficient	Specific traits not identified
Age of onset	Adolescence; early adulthood	Puberty to menopause	20 to 50 years of age

may begin with stressful life changes such as puberty, going to college, or starting a job. Migraines occur more often in women.

To someone unfamiliar with migraines the agony of them may be hard to appreciate. An account by the prominent novelist Joan Didion (Figure 7–1) describes what the experience is like.

Three, four, sometimes five times a month, I spend the day in bed with a migraine headache, insensible to the world around me. Almost every day of every month, between these attacks, I feel the sudden irrational irritation and the flush of blood into the cerebral arteries which tell me that migraine is on its way, and I take certain drugs to avert its arrival. If I did not take the drugs, I would be able to function perhaps one day in four. . . .

Once an attack is under way, no drug touches it. When I am in a migraine aura (for some people the aura lasts fifteen minutes, for others several hours), I will drive through red lights, lose the house keys, spill whatever I am holding, lose the ability to focus my eyes or frame coherent sentences, and generally give the appearance of being on drugs, or drunk. The actual headache, when it comes, brings with it chills, sweating, nausea, a debility that seems to stretch the very limits of endurance. That no one dies of migraine seems, to someone deep into an attack, an ambiguous blessing.

—Didion, 1979, pp. 168–172

In the past, it was believed that migraine is caused by narrowing followed by dilation of blood vessels. This idea is now being replaced by the idea that a wave of cerebral electrical activity may cause the aura, or warning sensation, and headaches develop when the wave reaches pain-sensitive blood vessels. What triggers this wave? Stress, hunger, hormone fluctuations, foods, alcohol, too much sleep, caffeine withdrawal or noise are chief suspects. It has recently been found that serotonin, a nerve cell messenger, becomes depleted in the brain during a migraine attack. Some disturbance in serotonin function seems to be a central component, if not the primary culprit, in producing the pain and other symptoms of migraines. Drug companies are now working on the development of compounds that can correct a dysfunction in the brain chemistry of migraine sufferers.

Migraine headaches often respond positively to drugs that constrict the arteries in the scalp. Psychotherapists have observed significant improvement in some people who suffer from chronic headaches, but little or no improvement in people who have migraines only occasionally. There have been reports of the successful use of behavior therapy and biofeedback in some cases of migraine.

Cluster headaches are often confined to one side of the head with pain that is excruciating, the pain hitting a peak in three to five minutes and disappearing within an hour. Patients often are pain-free for long periods of time but then experience a series of headaches over several weeks, sometimes several in one day. The headaches often occur at night and wake people from sound sleep. Patients often pace and sometimes bang their heads against the wall in an attempt to quell the pain. Cluster headaches are more common in men.

BIOFEEDBACK Pain has to do with bodily signals that are so amplified they hurt us. Some other types of

FIGURE 7–1 Joan Didion, a prominent novelist, suffers from frequent migraine headaches. Her description of them conveys a clear picture of what the experience is like.

FIGURE 7–2 Biofeedback training can help clients control a variety of physiological responses. The top photo shows a client with the biofeedback apparatus. The photo at bottom is of the video monitor that visually presents the responses as they occur.

bodily signals are not so readily perceived and require amplification. As mentioned in Chapter 4, **biofeedback** is an amplification technique used in behavioral medicine to treat such problems as hypertension, highly volatile blood pressure, and epilepsy (see Figure 7–2). This technique provides a way of extending self-control procedures to deal with a variety of physiological behaviors that were formerly thought to be involuntary responses, such as heart rate, blood pressure, and brain waves. Such behaviors were thought to be beyond conscious control until researchers became aware of individuals who apparently are able to control them. One such person, a Yoga practitioner named Swami Rama, was studied intensively at the Menninger Foundation (Green, 1972). Laboratory tests showed that, among other things, Rama was able to speed up and slow down his heart rate at will, to stop his heart from pumping blood for 17 seconds, to cause two areas of his palm a few inches apart to change temperature in opposite directions until their temperature differed by 10 degrees F (the "hot" side of his palm became rosy whereas the "cold" side became ashen), and to produce widely differing brain wave patterns at will.

Rama was not unique, although the extent of his control is startling. Humans and animals can learn to control their heart rate, blood pressure, brain waves, and other behaviors. For humans, no external reinforcement of the behavior seems to be necessary. All that is required is that the individual be given information in the form of feedback from the response system in question. Just as we could never learn to shoot a basketball accurately if we did not receive visual feedback and feedback from our muscles, we cannot learn to control our heart rate or brain waves unless we receive some kind of feedback on physiological changes as they occur. The feedback then serves as a reinforcer for the desired change.

Ordinarily we do not get feedback on responses like blood pressure and brain waves, but through biofeedback which precisely measures physiological events and converts the electronic signals into visual or auditory feedback, we can be made aware of our own physiological responses. This process has been used to train people to control the physiological responses of the brain, muscles, and cardiovascular and glandular systems, and has been applied to a variety of clinical problems, including cardiac disorders, high blood pressure, headaches, anxiety, and neuromuscular disorders like cerebral palsy. Clients come in for regular biofeedback sessions until they learn to recognize and control their bodily

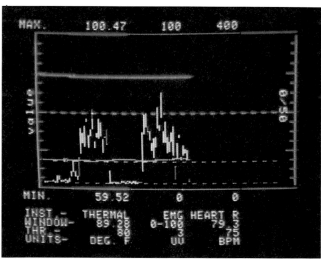

(b)

signals reliably without the help of the biofeedback apparatus.

Although there is no longer any question that people can learn to control a wide range of bodily functions, there are questions about the overall effective-

ness of biofeedback compared to relaxation training for migraine headaches or assertiveness training for tension headaches (Kellner, 1989). There is evidence that skills learned through biofeedback training are lost rather quickly when training stops. As researchers continue to identify the limitations of biofeedback, it becomes more apparent that these techniques are not the cure-all that overenthusiastic proponents initially believed they would be. But it is equally clear that biofeedback can be successfully applied to certain problems. An important goal of current research is to determine how and when biofeedback techniques can be used most effectively to enhance control over physiological and psychological responses.

Cardiovascular Disorders

Every affection of the mind that is attended with either pain or pleasure, hope or fear, is the cause of an agitation whose influence extends to the heart.

—William Harvey, 1628

Written more than 350 years ago, Harvey's allusion to an intimate association between neural factors and the heart received some attention in anecdote and fable, yet was not subjected to systematic scientific inquiry until the second half of the twentieth century. The heart is a highly specialized muscle that pumps blood to the body. The blood flows through the body in an unending loop of blood vessels called the circulatory system. Each day the human heart beats approximately 100,000 times, delivering the equivalent of 4,300 gallons of blood to all parts of the body. The arteries provide food and oxygen to the cells, while the veins remove carbon dioxide and waste products. The term **cardiovascular disorders** refers to pathological conditions that are related to the functioning of the heart and blood vessels. There is growing evidence that psychological and social factors play a role in two major cardiovascular disorders: coronary heart disease and hypertension. These conditions have caused over half of all deaths in the United States for more than 40 years.

CORONARY HEART DISEASE The leading cause of death and disability in the United States is **coronary heart disease (CHD),** accounting for 40% of all deaths. A million new cases are identified annually (Taylor, 1991). CHD is produced by lesions of the coronary arteries, the arteries that circulate blood within the heart itself. In CHD one or more of the three coronary arteries are partially or totally obstructed by deposits, called **plaques,** that thicken the arterial wall. When the coronary arteries become rigid and narrow as a result of these plaque deposits, the supply of blood to various portions of the heart muscle is temporarily or permanently cut off.

CHD takes a variety of forms. In **angina pectoris,** people suffer from periodic chest pains caused by an insufficient supply of oxygen-rich blood to the heart. The insufficient blood supply is related to plaque buildup (referred to as **atherosclerosis**) in the arteries. A **myocardial infarction,** also caused by an insufficient blood supply to the heart, is more serious than angina pectoris because it involves a more complete curtailment of the heart's blood supply. When people speak of a heart attack, they are usually referring to a myocardial infarction.

A significant factor in heart attacks is stress. From the Stone Age to the present day, human beings have responded to environmental challenges and threats by releasing larger amounts of adrenal and other stress hormones, followed by increases in heart rate and respiration and dilation of the vessels that transport blood to the muscles. Although these responses are adaptive or even life-saving when the threat is a wolf pack, you would do better without them if you are stuck in a traffic jam. In fact, not only are these primitive physiological responses of little help in dealing with most modern-day problems, but they may actually be related to the development of disease.

Stress seems to contribute to coronary disease through the body's general reactions to aversive stimulation. Under arousing conditions, hormonal substances called **catecholamines** are secreted. Two of the catecholamines, **epinephrine** and **norepinephrine,** accelerate the rate of arterial damage and ultimately can lead to heart attacks. Which people are most likely to have heart attacks under high levels of stress, and what steps lead from psychological stress to cardiac damage, are both topics of current research.

Personal Factors and CHD Factors known to increase the risk of CHD include age (older people are at greater risk), cigarette smoking, high blood pressure, high cholesterol level, and diabetes. Some studies have also implicated such factors as obesity, heredity, and lack of physical exercise. These factors may not be causes of CHD; they may simply be correlated with it. Even the most predictive of the risk factors still fails to identify more than half of the new cases of CHD. How these factors are related to the incidence of heart attack in a given individual is not yet known precisely.

There are important differences between men and women (Taylor, 1991). While most middle-aged heart attack victims are men, heart attacks that occur in later life are a principal cause of death for both men and women. Heart disease is the leading cause of death in women after the age of 66; in men it is the leading killer beginning at age 39. Women often have chest pains for a long time before a heart attack; in men, such pains more often mean a heart attack has already begun. Researchers

are currently examining the reasons for these differences. There may be important biological distinctions between the sexes in the functioning and development of the heart and cardiovascular system.

Death due to CHD has decreased more than 35 percent in the last 40 years, and recently this decrease has accelerated. Factors that may be contributing to the decline in mortality are improved medical services, the development of coronary care units in hospitals, advances in surgical and medical treatment of CHD, and improved control of blood pressure. Life-style changes such as less smoking, better eating habits, and increased physical fitness, also seem to play an important preventive role.

Stressful Events and CHD Researchers have found that particular stressful episodes—meeting a deadline, for example, or getting fired—affect the cardiovascular system temporarily (such as by raising blood pressure). Also, some sudden, personally meaningful events seem to set off major cardiovascular reactions. For example, separations from and losses of loved ones often bring about the need for sudden life-style changes and may culminate in a heart attack, as shown in the following case.

Harry Allen's wife had suffered from lung cancer for many months. Her death came slowly and painfully. For Allen, aged 54, the loss and grief were overwhelming. Everyone knew that the cancer was incurable and that death was approaching. Yet it came as a terrible shock to Allen. Four months before his wife's death, Harry had had a thorough physical examination that

included an electrocardiogram. The electrocardiogram as well as the other studies relevant to heart function were completely negative. Yet two days after his wife's death Allen collapsed and died of a massive heart attack.

The role of social losses and social isolation in recovery from heart attacks has been explored in a large number of studies. In one investigation, 2,320 male survivors of myocardial infarctions were assessed to identify factors that were predictive of how long they would live after having had a heart attack (Ruberman, 1984). One important factor was education, with the better-educated subjects living longer. Life stress and social isolation, both alone and in combination, also emerged as significant predictors of mortality. Life stress was defined by subjects' reports concerning such problems as job difficulties, divorces and separations, accidents, and criminal victimization. Social isolation was defined in terms of contacts with friends and relatives and membership in social, church, and fraternal organizations.

In Figure 7–3, graphs *a* and *b* show that when the effects of life stress and social isolation were evaluated separately, each of these factors was significantly associated with increased probability of mortality. The risk of death for men who were high in life stress was double the risk for men who were low in life stress. A similar relationship was found when men who were high and low in social isolation were compared. The combined effect of these two factors is shown in graph *c* of Figure 7–3. For men who were high in both life stress and

FIGURE 7–3 Cumulative probability of death under conditions of stress, social isolation or both as a function of number of months that subjects were followed up after myocardial infarction.

(Adapted from Ruberman, Weinblatt, Goldberg, and Chaudhary, 1984, p. 555. Reprinted by permission of *The New England Journal of Medicine, 9* (1984), p. 555)

social isolation, the risk of dying was four times greater than for men who were low in both life stress and social isolation. The middle line in graph *c* presents the risk of dying for men who were high in either life stress or social isolation.

As Figure 7–3 makes clear, it is valuable to have evidence concerning the relationship between sudden personal cataclysms, such as the death of a loved one or loss of a job, and coronary heart disease; equally significant is information about the effects of less intense, but persistent aspects of a person's life style.

Community Life Style and CHD Life style refers to a way of life that reflects the values and attitudes of an individual or group. Our jobs, interests, and social relationships show the effects of our life styles, but the type of community in which we live may also play a role. A recent study has provided evidence that there may be an important relationship between the general pace of life in a community and the incidence of cardiovascular disorders (Levine and others 1989). Thirty-six small, medium, and large metropolitan areas across the United States were compared using four indicators of pace of life:

1. How fast people walked
2. How fast people talked
3. The speed with which bank tellers worked
4. The proportion of individuals wearing watches (presumed to be an indicator of concern with time.)

The researchers found that pace of life was strongly related to death rates from coronary heart disease both across cities and across regions of the country. A faster pace played a role in higher rates of CHD, while communities with slower paces of life had lower rates of CHD.

Cultural Factors and CHD Studies that compare different cultures and the process of social change also provide evidence concerning the role of life-style factors in disease. In general, low rates of CHD tend to be found in parts of the world where tradition and family ties are strong. Cross-cultural data have provided a broader perspective on the relationship between psychosocial experience and physical breakdown. Japan, for example, has one of the lowest rates of heart disease in the world, while the United States has one of the highest. The rate of death from CHD for Japanese men between the ages of 35 and 64 is 64 per 100,000 population; the comparable figure for American men is 400 per 100,000. Could the nature of life in the United States be responsible for this high mortality rate? A study in which Japanese living in Japan were compared with Japanese-Americans living in Hawaii and California highlights the importance of cultural factors in the development of CHD (Marmot & Syme, 1976). The native Japanese had the lowest incidence of CHD; the Japanese-Americans living in Hawaii had a somewhat higher rate; and the Japanese-Americans living in California had the highest frequency of heart disease. Although diet probably accounts for some of these differences, societal and cultural differences also play a substantial role. For example, Japanese-Americans who believed in preserving traditional Japanese culture developed fewer cases of CHD than Japanese-Americans who had strongly accepted American culture.

There are wide regional and cultural differences in a large country like the United States. For example, according to a survey done some years ago, the town of Roseto, Pennsylvania, had a remarkably low death rate, especially from heart attacks. The coronary death rate for men was 100 per 100,000, and the rate for women was almost half that figure (Wolf, 1969). Moreover, residents of Roseto had low rates of several other stress-related disorders, such as stomach ulcers.

These low rates might seem surprising, since both the men and women of Roseto tended to be overweight and their diets, smoking, and exercise patterns were similar to those in other communities. What seemed to contribute most to the relatively low death rate was the way in which the people lived. Almost all Roseto's residents were of Italian descent and the town's neighborhoods were very cohesive. Family relationships were extremely close, supportive, and traditional. Men were likely to be the uncontested heads of their families. Personal and family problems tended to be worked out with the help of relatives, friends, and the local priest.

Although Roseto had these stable features, like all American communities, it had begun undergoing constant change. Young men and women were marrying non-Italians from other towns. The birth rate was declining, church attendance was down, and people were moving outside the old areas into more distant suburban neighborhoods. By the mid-1970s after many of these changes had occurred, a striking increase in the rate of heart attacks and sudden death was noticed, particularly among men under 55 (Greenberg, 1978). Apparently this social change was weakening Roseto's sources of social and emotional security, with important consequences for the health and longevity of its inhabitants.

Personal Life Styles and CHD Might the personal life-style patterns that are linked with CHD be related to basic aspects of personality? Is there a heart-attack-prone personal way of life? Box 7–2 summarizes a study of twins that addressed these questions.

On the basis of their observations of many heart attack patients, Friedman and Rosenman (1974) concluded that such a heart-attack-prone personality exists.

Twin studies allow the researcher to control for genetic factors and thus highlight the effects of life style and environmental factors. A study conducted in Sweden (Liljefors & Rahe, 1970) provided a unique set of data about the relationship between CHD, personality, and life style. The sample consisted of 32 pairs of identical male twins, 42 to 67 years of age, who were discordant for CHD—that is, only one member of each pair had a heart condition. Virtually all the twins had been raised together at least until their early teens.

The twins' characteristic behavior patterns in four areas—devotion to work, lack of leisure, home problems, and life dissatisfactions—were assessed through interviews. Table 7–3 shows the differences in one twin pair. Although the twins were at the same hereditary risk, the twin with CHD had a high pressure job during parts of the year and because he was self-employed may have experienced more stress throughout the year because of concerns about the success of his business. He reported continuing to feel a lack of sufficient time for his

tasks and perhaps for this reason had fewer periods of relaxation than his twin. In addition, he seemed dissatisfied with his achievements and his ability to carry out his business dealings effectively while his twin was relatively satisfied with his progress. Since the twins examined were discordant for CHD, the researchers concluded that life style as well as heredity is an important factor in the disease. A more recent study (Kringlen, 1981) has provided further support for this hypothesis.

Table 7-3

Twin-Pair Members Who Were Discordant for Coronary Heart Disease (CHD)

Twin without CHD	Twin with CHD
Devotion to Work	
The subject has been an auto repairman for the past 33 years. His workday is 8 hours long, and he works less than 5 hours per week overtime. At one time during his life for a 5–10 year period he worked about 8 hours per week overtime.	The subject is an owner of a small fur shop. During his high season he works up to 18 hours per day. The rest of the year he averages 9 hours per day.
Lack of Leisure	
The subject visits friends and family less than once per month. He reads the newspapers and watches TV about once per week. In the summer he rents a "sommarstuga," where he goes once a week. In the winter he goes skiing now and then. He takes a 45-minute lunch break along with a 20-minute coffee break during the day, and he usually relaxes then.	The subject visits friends less than once per month and has a hobby in the summer which he follows at a once-per-week frequency. He reads the newspapers and watches TV frequently. He manages to take regular vacations. The subject's lunch periods are 30 minutes long; he sometimes relaxes then and sometimes does not.
Home Problems	
He was married at 27 years of age. His wife is three years younger than he is. They have three children with one still living at home. He recalls having some arguments with his wife and having had some financial difficulties.	He was married at 33 years of age. His wife is eight years younger than he is. There are two children—both still reside in the home. He generally has had a good home life. He has had considerable economic difficulties.
Life Dissatisfactions	
The subject thinks that neither twin dominated. He had a comfortable childhood and was quite happy with his education. The problems in his marriage he sees as primarily due to his alcohol consumption prior to the last eight years. Since then he has not had much alcohol to drink, primarily because it interfered with his sexual relations. He is quite satisfied with his work.	The subject makes no comment about which twin might have dominated. He recalls a good childhood experience and was satisfied with his level of education. Throughout his working life he has felt constantly rushed and never had enough time for himself. He has had considerable trouble with his creditors in his business and feels he has particular difficulty in being tough enough to collect the money owed him. He feels he has strived a good deal to achieve the luxuries of life and has not succeeded very well.

SOURCE: From Liljefors and Rahe, 1970, pp. 540–541.

These people, called **Type A personalities** (see Figure 7–4), tend to operate under high pressure and to be very demanding both of themselves and of others. Type A people typically are more cynical and distrustful of others, and may harbor a good deal of hostility toward the world. Because of these characteristics, Type A people are believed to run an inordinate risk of suffering heart attacks. People with **Type B personalities,** on the other hand, are less pressured and driving than Type A's, and do not appear to run as high a risk for heart disease. The characteristics that seem to typify the Type A person include the following.

1. Talking rapidly and at times explosively.

2. Moving, walking, and eating rapidly

3. Becoming unduly irritated at delay (for example, waiting in line)

4. Attempting to schedule more and more in less and less time

5. Feeling vaguely guilty while relaxing

6. Trying to do two things at once

Type A attributes are assessed by means of specially designed questionnaires and interviews. The Type A pattern exists on a continuum, with some people show-ing more of the characteristic traits than others. Table 7–4 lists some items from a questionnaire designed to assess the Type A personality.

While all the findings concerning the Type A life style are not completely consistent, several research efforts have yielded positive relationships. One study showed that during eight and a half years of follow-up Type A men had more than twice as much heart disease as Type B men (Rosenman and others, 1975). This difference could not be explained simply in terms of traditional risk factors, such as cigarette smoking, because those factors had been equalized for the two groups.

One type of investigation that may help chart the relationship between personality and CHD and also clarify how known risk factors combine to bring about physical illness is the longitudinal or prospective study. Most clinical problems have been studied retrospectively, that is, after the fact. After someone gets sick, the doctor inquires about past illnesses and experiences that might explain the current problem. More powerful—but also more time-consuming and costly—is the prospective, or before-the-fact, investigation. Such a study gathers information over a relatively long period. Because prospective studies are longitudinal, they can provide a picture of how a person's thinking, behavior, and bodily reactions unfold over time. Depending on the data gathered, this approach permits the researcher to identify interactions between particular personality variables and important life events and the effects of those interactions on the person's health.

An example of a prospective investigation that reveals the strengths and weaknesses of this approach is

FIGURE 7–4 Type A individuals work rapidly, feel pressured, and frequently try to do two or more things at once.

(© 1984 by Sidney Harris–Chicago Magazine)

Table 7–4
Questionnaire Items Designed to Reflect Type A Characteristics

The subject's task is to rate each item on a scale ranging from *not at all like me* to *a great deal like me.*

1. I don't get upset when I have to wait in line at a store or theater.
2. I usually don't find it necessary to hurry.
3. When I play games, winning is very important to me.
4. I like competing with other people.
5. Second best is not good enough for me.
6. I'm often so busy that I have trouble finding the time for things like a haircut, shopping, and household chores.
7. I often feel like letting someone have it.
8. I get tense at work when I am competing for recognition.

Note: Scoring is reversed for items 1 and 2.

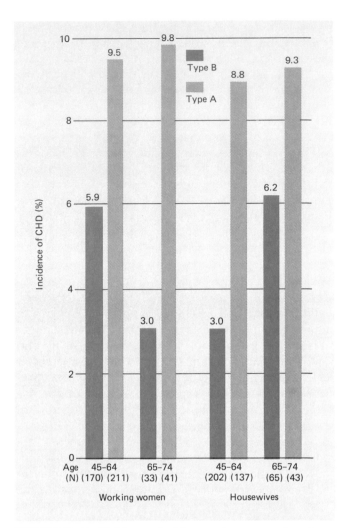

FIGURE 7–5 Eight-year incidence of coronary heart disease among Framingham working women and housewives with Type A and Type B behavior patterns.

(Findings from the Framingham study; Adapted from Haynes, Feinleib, & Kannel, 1980)

the Framingham study (Haynes and others, 1980). A group of 5,127 adult residents of Framingham, Massachusetts, have volunteered to participate in a study on coronary heart disease for the rest of their lives. They have been monitored for the incidence of illness, hospitalization, and death since 1948. Every two years each participant is given a physical examination that includes blood tests, electrocardiograms, X rays, and blood pressure readings. Several physical risk factors have been identified by the Framingham study, including elevated blood pressure, cholesterol level, and cigarette smoking. The study has confirmed that weight gains result in elevated blood pressure and thus indirectly increased the risk of coronary heart disease.

A subgroup of 1,674 Framingham participants between the ages of 45 and 77 was assessed for Type A tendencies and then followed up over an eight-year period (Haynes, and others, 1980). Women between the ages of 45 and 64 who developed CHD scored significantly higher on the Type A measure and exhibited more suppressed hostility (not showing or discussing anger), tension, and anxiety than women who remained free of CHD. Type A women developed twice as much CHD as Type B women. Although working women tended to have higher Type A scores than housewives, being a housewife did not protect Type A women from higher rates of CHD. Figure 7–5 shows that working women under 65 years of age were almost twice as likely to develop CHD if they exhibited Type A rather than Type B behavior. Among housewives in the under-65 age group, CHD incidence among Type As was almost three times greater than among Type Bs. Figure 7–6 shows the association of Type A behavior with CHD incidence among white- and blue-collar men in the 45 to 64 and 65 to 74 age groups. The association was significant only

FIGURE 7–6 Eight-year incidence of coronary heart disease among white-collar and blue-collar Type A and Type B men in the Framingham study.

(Adapted from Haynes, Feinleib, & Kannel, 1980)

among men holding white-collar jobs. The results of the Framingham study suggest that the Type A behavior pattern operates independently of the usual coronary risk factors (such as blood pressure, age, and weight).

Despite many positive results concerning this relationship there have also been some contradictory findings. For example, one study found that Type A men who had had heart attacks were *less* likely than Type Bs to have recurrences (Ragland & Brand, 1988). This unexpected result, as well as other findings not consistent with the Type A formulation, might have been due to methodological aspects of the particular investigations or to some factor that has not yet been identified (Dimsdale, 1988). In any case, there is good reason to believe that the original Type A–CHD relationship proposed by Friedman and Rosenman needs some revision.

Because the Type A pattern has many elements, researchers are exploring facets of the pattern that might be of special importance. Work on two topics currently being investigated, hostility and physiological reactivity, may help clarify relationships among personality, behavior, and CHD.

According to one hypothesis, hostility may be the most active Type A ingredient, and there is evidence that people who are hostile, angry, cynical, and suspicious of others have an especially high risk of fatal coronary disease (Barefoot and others, 1987). The results found for women in the Framingham study who were classified as Type A were consistent with this hypothesis. They showed showed that suppressed hostility was an important predictor of CHD for this group. It may be that the impatience, ambition, and work drive seen in so many Type A people is not nearly as important from a cardiovascular standpoint as their hostility (expressed or suppressed) and cynical view of other people's motivations. Table 7–5 presents sample questionnaire items designed to measure such cynical hostility. Because hostility has a number of aspects, it will be necessary to isolate its components and relate these to clinically significant events, such as whether people have heart attacks. Three components that merit study are (1) distrust of others (expecting someone to cheat or take advantage of you), (2) feeling very angry when you find someone cheating (the person in the ten-item supermarket express line who has twelve items) and (3) showing anger (telling the person with twelve items that he is a cheater). If cynical attitudes and hostile emotions cause biological responses that lead to coronary disease, clinicians may be able to devise ways of changing disease-producing thoughts and feelings. Further research on hostility and CHD is needed to assess this relationship and possible responses to it (Helmer and others, 1991; Houston & Vavek, 1991; Barefoot and others, 1991).

Another possible reformulation of the Type A pattern is suggested by evidence that Type As are more

Table 7–5

Questionnaire Items Used to Assess Cynical Hostility

Subjects are asked to circle the word "Never," "Sometimes," "Often," or "Always" as it best describes their behavior in these situations. It is believed that people who circle "Often" or "Always" in answer to these items are in a high-risk heart disease group. (MacDougall, 1981).

1. When anybody slows down or stops what I want to do, I think they are selfish, mean and inconsiderate.
2. When anybody does something that seems incompetent, messy, selfish or inconsiderate to me, I quickly feel angry or enraged. At the same time, my heart races, my breath comes quickly and my palms sweat.
3. When I have such thoughts or feelings (No. 2), I let fly with words, gestures, a raised voice and frowns.

physiologically reactive than other people. This excitability might be the most active ingredient in the Type A personality (Manuck and others, 1989). It has been hypothesized that perhaps there are two groups of people, hot and cold reactors, with the cold reactors showing normal cardiovascular responses (blood pressure, heart rate) to stress, and hot reactors displaying abnormally intense cardiovascular responses (Eliot & Buell, 1983). Hot and cold reactors might not differ in terms of their overt behavior, but the hot reactors might experience steep blood pressure surges under stress. If this proves to be the case, measurements of the Type A pattern by means of questionnaires and interviews may not be as direct a predictor of cardiac disorders as measurements of actual cardiovascular responses under stressful conditions.

Can CHD-prone Life Styles Be Changed?

Researchers are exploring the possibility of reducing the susceptibility to CHD using psychological training (Haaga, 1987). A variety of cognitive and behavioral techniques have been tried with Type As, including self-control training, learning to think about situations in less intense ways, and being attentive to the problems created by personal beliefs that emphasize urgency and the need to gain immediate control over events. There is some basis for believing that learning to think and act differently exerts a positive influence on the health of Type As. For example, one study found that Type A men who had already had a heart attack were less likely to have another attack if they had participated in a cognitive-behavior counseling program after the first heart attack (Thoresen and others, 1982). In regard to the connection between hostility and CHD, perhaps angry people can become more aware of their hostile tendencies and modify them, or perhaps they can learn to be more

trusting of and have more empathy with other people.

Another group of researchers has tried to help healthy successful Army colonels engage in fewer Type A behaviors (Gill and others, 1985). The colonels participated in a series of counseling sessions that dealt with ways of modifying beliefs and attributions that underlie Type A behavior. They were also given advice on how to avoid potentially stressful situations, and engaged in role plays in which they practiced less highly pressured ways of coping with situations. The findings support the conclusion that the Type A attributes of anger, irritation, and impatience are not necessary aspects of the drive, ambition, creativity, and hard work needed by military leaders. The study showed that the colonels became less prone to Type A behaviors and that their ability to function as leaders was in no way impaired, but actually may have been improved.

HYPERTENSION **Hypertension** is what most people describe as high blood pressure. A blood pressure level that is over 140 when the heart contracts (systolic pressure) and does not fall below 90 when the heart relaxes (diastolic pressure) is usually considered high. High blood pressure indicates that there is resistance to the flow of blood through the cardiovascular system. This condition places pressure on the arteries and forces the heart to work harder to overcome the resistance. Among younger adults (aged 25 to 44), men have higher blood pressures than women. Among older adults (aged 65 to 74), this pattern is reversed. Blood pressure readings of black adults typically exceed those of white adults.

High blood pressure is a major contributor to cardiovascular disorders and is one of the conditions that creates increased risk of heart attacks. Usually it is a silent or symptomless risk because the hypertensive individual might show no observable signs of a medical problem for many years. Hypertension may be the most common major chronic disease in the United States today.

Clinical observations indicating that many hypertensives show wide variability in blood pressure readings and seem emotionally on edge much of the time have led to speculation about the causes and treatment of this disorder. Chronic anger and anger suppression have been identified as particularly important factors (Chesney & Rosenman, 1985) (see Table 7–6). While everybody is exposed to anger-provoking situations, according to one theory, hypertensives experience chronic anger because of their inability to express it or assert themselves in a socially desirable manner. Psychotherapists believe that within the warm acceptance of the psychotherapeutic setting, angry, anxious people can gain insight into and mastery over their tendency to experience strong emotional reactions. However, firm empirical support for this approach is not yet available.

Some support is emerging for a behavioral approach to hypertension that directs attention to the specific types of situations associated with elevated blood pressure. Lack of competence in dealing with situations that call for assertiveness may be a specific behavioral deficit of many hypertensives. Assertiveness, defined as the ability to stand up for one's rights, express feelings, and avoid mistreatment by others, is a vital interpersonal skill and an indicator of social competence. People who are low in assertiveness tend to be mistreated, fail to express their feelings, and are frequently unable to have their needs met. Researchers have been able to show that hypertensives respond positively to behavioral training that involves the modeling and role-playing of appropriate assertiveness. As the social competence of these individuals increases, in many cases their blood pressure declines (Manuck and others, 1985); thus, strengthening the social skills of hypertensives may prove to be of clinical value.

Table 7–6

The Assessment of Anger

It is important to measure accurately the tendency to become angry and the ways in which people cope with it. If hypertensive people bottle up anger, a way is needed to assess this tendency. Since it can be experienced and expressed in different ways, reliable measures of anger are needed. These are some of the aspects that require assessment together with sample items.

General Anger

It is easy to make me angry.
At times, I feel angry for no specific reason.

Situations That Arouse Anger

I get angry when I am delayed.
I get angry when I do something stupid.
I get angry when people are unfair.

Anger Directed Outward

When I am angry with someone, I let that person know.

Anger Directed Inward

I harbor grudges that I don't tell anyone about.

Guilt Over Anger

I feel guilty about expressing my anger.

SOURCE: Based on Siegel, 1985. Courtesy of Hemisphere Publishing Corporation.

Another line of research concerns the relationship between relaxation and blood pressure. Some reduction in blood pressure can be achieved by teaching relaxation skills to hypertensives. Herbert Benson (1977) has developed relaxation exercises that involve four elements: a repetitive mental device, a passive attitude, decreased muscle tension, and a quiet environment. His approach uses instructions like the following.

Sit quietly in a comfortable position. Close your eyes. Deeply relax all your muscles, beginning at your feet and progressing up to your face. Keep them deeply relaxed.

Breathe through your nose. Become aware of your breathing. As you breathe out, say the word "one" silently to yourself. Continue for 20 minutes. You may open your eyes to check the time, but do not use an alarm. When you have finished, sit quietly for several minutes, at first with closed eyes and later with opened eyes.

Do not worry about whether you are successful in achieving a deep level of relaxation. Maintain a passive attitude and permit relaxation to occur at its own pace. Expect distracting thoughts. When these distracting thoughts occur, ignore them and continue repeating "one."

Practice the technique once or twice daily, but not within two hours after a meal, since the digestive processes seem to interfere with elicitation of anticipated changes.

—Benson, 1977, p. 153

The simple method outlined by Benson leads to lower blood pressure as well as to other bodily changes that accompany relaxation. Figure 7–7 shows the types of results that have encouraged clinicians to use relaxation techniques with hypertensives. As the figure makes clear, relaxation led to lower systolic blood pressure during the day and also while the subjects were asleep. There were similar results obtained for diastolic pressure.

There is also evidence that the combined use of relaxation and biofeedback has particularly good long-term effects on blood pressure (Jacob and others, 1987). These benefits must be considered along with certain drawbacks, including cost, side effects, and difficulty in getting some patients to take antihypertensive medications. These medications have been shown to be effective in reducing blood pressure.

A recent study relating job strain to blood pressure elevations has focused attention on the environment's role in hypertension (Schnall and others, 1990). In a study of 215 male workers (ranging from garbage

FIGURE 7–7 Systolic blood pressures for hypertensives who were given relaxation training and for an untreated control group. Blood pressure readings were taken during six time periods beginning with 7:31 to 9:30 a.m. (Adapted from Agras, Taylor, Kraemer, Allen, & Schneider, *Archives of General Psychiatry, 37*, p. 861. © 1980 American Medical Association)

collectors to stockbrokers) who were between the ages of 30 and 60, difficult work environments were found to have sustained round-the-clock effects on hypertension. The most problematic work environments were relatively low-level jobs in which high psychological demands were combined with little control over the work process and little use of skills. Inability to exert an influence on the work situation increased the likelihood of high blood pressure. If a high-stress job included latitude to control the situation there was no increase in blood pressure. Twenty-one percent of all subjects suffered job strain. These men faced as much as three times greater risk of having high blood pressure than did those without job strain. The men between the ages 30 to 40 who had high-stress jobs showed a thickening of the heart's left ventricle, or chamber, a condition that often precedes coronary disease and heart attacks. These men had all worked on the job for at least three years, none was more than 20 percent overweight and none had suffered heart disease before the study began. The finding of a significant relationship between high job stress and increased heart mass held regardless of the subject's alcohol intake, and whether or not the subject was a smoker.

Further research is needed to deal with several specific questions. What is it that hypertensives are doing when their blood pressure goes up or down? Might some of the positive effects of relaxation and biofeedback be placebo effects—that is, might lowered blood pressure following relaxation or biofeedback training be due partly to the expectation that the treatment will be

effective? Follow-up studies are needed to determine how lasting the results of behavioral procedures are, and comparative studies are needed that evaluate the effectiveness of several treatment methods (biofeedback, psychotherapy, and so on). Behavioral techniques might prove particularly useful in conjunction with antihypertensive drugs in treating high blood pressure (Bennett & Carroll, 1990).

Cancer

A growing number of research efforts are investigating whether psychological variables are related in some way to the occurrence and growth of cancer and to recovery from the disease.

Animal studies suggest that certain early life experiences (for example, daily handling or maternal separation) result in different patterns of cancer susceptibility in rats. Another critical factor is the animal's ability to develop an adaptive coping response. Exposure to acute *escapable* stress does not influence tumor growth appreciably; however, the identical amount of *uncontrollable* stress markedly exacerbates tumor growth (O'Leary, 1990). Both animal studies and clinical observations of humans have revealed that uncontrollable stress is related to cancer growth (Sklar & Anisman, 1981). Stimulated by such findings, research is now being carried out on the roles of stress and personality in human cancers. One of these studies has shown that medical students whose psychological profiles indicated a relatively restricted capacity for close interpersonal relationships were especially prone to develop cancers 20 to 25 years later (Shaffer and others, 1987).

One emerging hypothesis is that people who have difficulty handling strong feelings are more prone to develop cancers than people who can appropriately ventilate their emotions. In one psychological study of cancer patients, only about 30 percent of the group admitted feeling any discouragement whatever about the future, although many of them had large tumors for which no treatment was available (Plumb & Holland, 1977). In another study, patients with malignant melanoma, a type of cancer, were asked to rate on a scale of 1 to 100 the amount of personal adjustment needed to handle or cope with a serious illness (Rogentine and others, 1979). All of the patients reported that they had made the rating with their melanomas in mind. One year later each patient's clinical status was evaluated. Patients who had low scores (low ratings of the need for adjustment) were clinically worse off at the one-year follow-up than patients with high scores. This result seems consistent with the view that subjects who score low on the scale are using denial or repression of the

impact of the disease (lack of concern), whereas those who report a need for more adjustment are more realistic in their appraisal of the illness.

Another hypothesis that is being investigated concerns the relationship between depression and cancer. In one study, the MMPI (see Chapter 4) was administered to over 2,000 middle-aged employed men. Two decades later only the MMPI Depression score was associated with increased risk of death (Persky and others, 1987; Shekelle and others 1981). Whether psychological depression can be described as a direct or indirect cause of increased risk of death from cancer was not answered by this study. To answer that question we will need more information about the biology of psychological depression and its relationship to the growth of cancer cells.

The results of a recent clinical study suggest that group psychotherapy may be useful in helping cancer patients cope with their disease (Spiegel, 1989). The lives of women with breast cancer were lengthened by a year and a half when they participated in group psychotherapy; these women also reported significant reductions in their anxiety and pain. This study is particularly impressive because the 86 subjects had been randomly assigned to therapy and control groups, and all patients in both groups received standard medical treatment, including surgery and radiation or chemotherapy.

The evidence implicating psychological factors in cancer is still tentative; similar emotional states have been associated with a variety of physical disorders. Although we are a long way from identifying a "cancer-prone personality" or using psychological methods in treating cancers, the increasing attention being given to the relationships between personality and cancer is encouraging (Eysenck, 1987). Research does suggest the following personality characteristics as being typical of people who develop cancer.

- Denial and repression of emotion.
- Rigidity and conventionality.
- Diminished expression of anger.
- A tendency to feel hopeless and depressed.

One of the greatest needs in cancer research is for longitudinal studies that begin before people develop cancer symptoms. Obviously, such studies are difficult to conduct because no one can tell in advance that a person will develop a malignancy. The ideal study would be one in which a large representative sample of apparently healthy people is assessed psychologically and then followed up to determine which individuals develop cancer and whether its incidence can be predicted by psychological data collected before the cancer was identified.

Researchers who study possible behavioral factors in cancer must take into account some important facts and issues. Cancer is not a single disease but a group of different diseases sharing a common pattern of destructive, uncontrolled cellular growth. Psychosocial factors could theoretically affect at least two different stages of cancer: the initiation of a new cancer and the progression of an established cancer. Research to this point suggests that the main behavioral contributions to cancer initiation include smoking and poor nutrition. And although current research—such as some of the studies discussed in this section—point to a link between psychosocial factors and cancer outcome, the role of morale, mood, and attitude remains less well-established and is controversial.

The Immune System and Related Disorders

In Chapter 3 we described the new field of psychoneuroimmunology and noted that the immune system plays a role in the onset of cancer. The immune system is the body's surveillance system; it protects the body from disease-causing microorganisms. It is integrated with other physiological processes and is sensitive to changes in the functioning of the central nervous system and the endocrine glands. The immune system regulates susceptibility to cancers, infectious diseases, allergies, and auto-immune disorders (diseases in which cells of the immune system attack the normal tissue).

Recent research has provided evidence that psychological, behavioral, and environmental factors influence the functioning of the immune system in humans. Immunological consequences of stressors have been observed in such diverse situations as space flight, sleep deprivation, school examinations, bereavement, and depressive states. Not only exposure to multiple or chronic life stressors, but also loneliness, low levels of social support, and poor coping skills seem to lower the effectiveness of a person's immune system (Justice, 1987).

There is increasing evidence that stress and emotional arousal can lower the immune system's resistance to disease (Vollhardt, 1991). For example, many college students show decreased immune system functioning during exam periods (Jemmott & Locke, 1984; McClelland and others, 1985). This may help explain why they have so many illnesses during these periods. Another example of this relationship is a Canadian study of accountants which was conducted during the eight weeks preceding the deadline for filing income taxes and six months thereafter (Dorian & Garfinkel, 1987). The accountants not only experienced high levels of psychological distress, but they also showed a decline in immune

system function at the peak tax-filing periods. Studies like these suggest that high performance demands may be significantly associated with alterations in the immune system, which, in turn, may increase susceptibility to disease.

While earlier studies have found benefits for the immune system from such practices as exercise and relaxation, positive effects have recently been found for confronting traumatic memories, from learning to look at life more optimistically, and, perhaps surprisingly, from the excitement of living at a mildly hectic pace. (Kennedy and others, 1990; Pennebaker and others, 1990). Researchers do not know yet whether any of the documented immune system changes are medically significant; ways of better understanding the linkages between psychological variables and the functioning of the immune system are being explored. How the immune system may be related to other bodily systems is also being explored. Recent discoveries have shown that cells in the immune system have receptors for brain chemicals and that there are direct physiological links between the nervous system and the lymph nodes and spleen, where some immune cells are stored or made (Daruna & Morgan, 1990).

Allergies

Allergies are a common problem, affecting at least 15 percent of the population. Normally, when an **allergen,** a substance capable of causing an allergic reaction, enters the body, the antibodies produced by the immune system attack it. An allergy is an "abnormal" reaction to an ordinarily harmless substance; it is frequently described as immunity "gone wrong." While most research on allergies is directed toward understanding components of the immune system that are involved in the allergic response, recently there has been interest in the psychological as well as the physical aspects of allergies. One finding of this new line of research is that a person's total stress load, as well as exposure and adaptation to allergens, contributes to allergic reactions. Because asthma is one of the oldest forms of chronic allergy and has been studied most from a psychological standpoint, we will use it to illustrate the contribution of psychological factors to allergic reactions.

ASTHMA Although the cause is unknown, **asthma** appears to be an allergic condition that results in reversible obstruction of the bronchial passages. People who have asthma chronically wheeze, cough, and have difficulty breathing. To the patient, asthma means labored breathing, a feeling of constriction in the chest, gasping, and apprehension. About 30 out of 1,000 people in the United States have asthma.

Asthma patients often report that intense emo-

tional states accompany acute attacks of labored breathing. This is not surprising: One can quickly measure one's emotional state by how easy it is to breathe. It has long been recognized that psychological variables contribute to asthma attacks. According to one theory, asthmatics share a common personality type and similar unconscious conflicts. However, there is little evidence to indicate that asthmatics are psychologically any more deviant than the general population. Another theory holds that characteristic personality features are the result, rather than the cause, of the restricted activities of severe asthmatics (Vachon, 1989).

Although the search for the cause and cure of asthma continues, a number of psychological and situational factors that seem to maintain or worsen asthma attacks have been studied successfully. The value of objective study of clinical cases is suggested by an experiment conducted with asthmatic children in Denver (Purcell and others, 1969). Parents of asthmatic children have been described as overcontrolling people who create an emotionally tense home environment. Clinical evidence has indicated that removing the children from the home and placing them in an institutional setting often reduces their asthmatic symptoms. Purcell and his colleagues wished to discover the effects of separating asthmatic children from their families while keeping their home environment relatively constant.

The experimental design involved an initial qualification period during which asthmatic symptoms were assessed, a preseparation period, a separation period, and reunion. During the two-week separation period the child's family lived in a nearby motel or hotel and had no contact with the asthmatic child, who remained within the family home, playing and attending school as usual. A substitute parent cared for the child at home during the separation period. Wheezing declined precipitously during the separation and increased again during reunion (see Figure 7–8). Family relationships rather than physical aspects of the home environment thus appear to be conducive to asthmatic symptoms, although the psychological mechanism involved is unclear. One possibility is that the breathing obstruction that is characteristic of asthma may be produced by stress-induced activity of the autonomic nervous system, which stimulates mucus secretion, increased blood flow, and constriction of the bronchial tubes. Situational variables and personal vulnerability appear to combine in producing symptoms of asthma.

The importance of psychological factors in the clinical course of asthma is suggested by a study comparing children who died of asthmatic attacks with children who did not (Strunk and others, 1985). Depressive symptoms in the children and conflicts between the children's parents and medical personnel treating the children were especially likely to be associ-

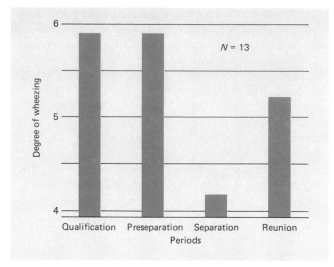

FIGURE 7–8 Mean daily scores for clinical evidence of wheezing during each period in the Denver asthma study.

(Reprinted by permission of Elsevier Science Publishing Co., Inc.; From K. Purcell, K. Brady, H. Schall, J. Muser, L. Molk, N. Gordon, and J. Means, The effect of asthma in children of experimental separation from the family. *Psychosomatic Medicine, 31*, pp. 144–164. Copyright © 1969 by the American Psychosomatic Society, Inc.)

ated with the deaths. The evidence thus suggested that the fatal cases were not due only to the severity of the disease, but also to psychological factors.

Gastrointestinal Disorders

Gastrointestinal disorders are abnormalities of the digestive system. The number of television commercials for stomach remedies clearly indicates that many people have trouble with their digestive processes. Scientists still do not know exactly how emotional processes are linked to pathological changes in the gastrointestinal tract. There is evidence that anger and hostility increase stomach acidity and that gastric symptoms commonly follow worry, business reverses, family quarrels, and other emotionally disturbing experiences. For example, one gastrointestinal disorder, diarrhea, has plagued troops going into battle for as long as wars have been fought.

Many studies of stress and gastrointestinal disease relate to **ulcers,** which are open sores in the skin or on some mucous membrane such as the lining of the stomach or intestine. Ulcerated tissue disintegrates, and the sores often discharge pus. Peptic ulcers—those related to the digestive system—include ulcers in the stomach (gastric ulcers) and in the first part of the small intestine (duodenal ulcers). The incidence of peptic ulcers ebbs and rises. It rose in the 1950s but has declined recently—a seeming paradox if our society is, as many people believe, more stressful now than it was in the past.

Cases of peptic ulcer often highlight the interacting roles of a number of relevant variables. The following case of duodenal ulcers in one member of a pair of twins is of particular interest.

John M., an identical twin, developed a series of severe ulcer symptoms, including bleeding, when he was 46 years old. His condition deteriorated to the point where he required hospitalization. He was described as passive, shy, dependent, and anxious. His wife had had several near-psychotic episodes, and John's ulcer symptoms developed about the time she was experiencing a particularly frightening breakdown. She was having an affair with another man and had threatened to kill her children.

John's twin brother Fred was studied because some clinical workers have speculated that psychophysiological disorders may be attributed partly to hereditary features. As in many cases of identical twins, Fred's personality was remarkably similar to John's; he was also shy and dependent. However, he was completely free of ulcer symptoms. The twins had been inseparable until they were 25, when Fred met his future wife; John married three years later. The major difference in the lives of the twins after age 25 was their marriages. Because John, the ulcer victim, had married a disturbed woman, he was forced to live under great tension, which increased his anxiety level. Fred, on the other hand, had married a motherly woman who managed the family affairs dependably. The ulcer-free identical twin had apparently found a psychosocial situation in which his passivity and dependency needs could be gratified, while his brother found only frustration in his marriage.

—Gottschalk, 1978, p. 91

Although John's case does not seem to support a genetic interpretation of duodenal ulcers, that conclusion is not completely justified. Ulcers occur mainly in people with high levels of blood pepsinogen (a gastric secretion). Both John and Fred had high blood pepsinogen levels, so they were both susceptible to developing ulcers. If they had swapped wives, John might have been cured while Fred got the ulcers. Thus, heredity may be a predisposing factor in ulcer cases, but the level of stress experienced by the individual may determine whether structural damage actually occurs.

Somatoform Disorders

Many of the bodily complaints that physicians are asked to treat suggest physical pathology, but no actual impairment can be found. Although failure to diagnose a case medically might be due to a doctor's lack of knowledge or to a faulty laboratory test, in a large group of cases psychological rather than physiological factors are responsible for the symptoms. These cases, which do not seem to be produced consciously, are characterized as **somatoform disorders.** This category includes psychogenic pain disorders and hypochondriasis, as well as somatization and conversion disorders.

Psychogenic Pain Disorder

Severe prolonged pain either without organic symptoms or greatly in excess of what might be expected to accompany organic symptoms is classified as a **psychogenic pain disorder.** There is often a temporal relationship between the occurrence of an actual, threatened, or fantasized interpersonal loss and complaints of pain. The complaints may be used to evoke social responses, such as attention, from others.

PAIN Saying "It hurts" is the result of an appraisal process that often leads to going to the doctor. Pain is influenced by biological, psychological, and social factors. The condition of our bodily systems obviously plays an important role in how we interpret signals coming from within our body. But our psychological state is also involved and, for this reason, pain is one of the more mysterious and elusive aspects of illness and its treatment. Social factors influence the perception of pain as well. When one member of a family reports pain the other members may respond with attention and expressions of concern. This response may serve as a stimulus for more reports of pain.

The word pain is derived from the Greek *poine*, meaning "punishment." By the middle of this century, it became clear that pain was a complex, multiply-determined experience. One barrier to the treatment of pain is the difficulty people have describing it objectively. If you have a lump you can point to it, or if a bone is broken, it can be seen in an x-ray. Pain does not have these objective references. A number of recent approaches to pain have focused on pain behaviors (for example, complaining about pain) and the conditions that strengthen or weaken them. In some cases pain is related to a physical disorder that can be identified, for example pain related to a deterioration of the disks that separate and cushion the bones in the spinal column. Even in situations where

the source of the pain can be identified in bodily changes, some people experience incapacitating pain while others with what seems to be very similar changes do not. Psychological approaches have focused on these behaviors and the conditions that strengthen or weaken them. Another class of pain behaviors have no such clear antecedents. Despite careful medical investigations, no organic changes can be found. The following case shows how operant conditioning procedures are clinically effective in bringing about behavioral changes related to pain when no physical cause can be identified.

The patient was a 19-year-old man who had been admitted to a hospital with complaints of pain in the lower back, hips, and both legs, and great difficulty in walking, sitting, and standing. An exhaustive medical study determined that his symptoms were unrelated to physical causes, and the case was diagnosed as a psychological disorder.

The operant therapy consisted of visits by a young assistant to the patient's room three times daily. During these visits the assistant spent approximately ten minutes talking to the patient about topics unrelated to his disorder. During an initial three-day period she encouraged him to walk but provided him with no reinforcement for doing so. During the next three-day sequence she instructed the patient to walk and reinforced him when this happened. Reinforcement consisted of comments such as "Good," "That's great," and "You're doing fine," accompanied by attention, friendliness, and smiling. Reinforcements were not given during the following three-day period, but they were reinstituted during the final three days of the experimental therapeutic program

—Hersen and others, 1972, pp. 720–721

This pattern of intervention is called an **A-B-A-B research design.** Such a design is useful in assessing the reasons for clinical change in a particular case because it can be carried out with only one subject who also serves as his or her own control in the period when no reinforcement is given. The A-B-A-B approach is used most often to determine whether operant-conditioning procedures are effective in bringing about behavioral changes. It consists of obtaining a baseline measure of the target behavior (A), instituting reinforcement-contingency procedures (B), removing the contingency so that the conditions that were present during the baseline

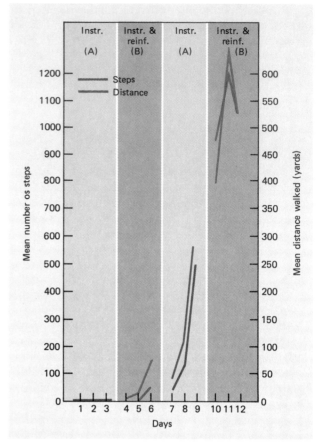

FIGURE 7–9 The chart shows changes in walking behavior during the four conditions of the repeated-measures design. Mean number of steps and distance are shown as a function of instructions and reinforcements.

period are reinstated (A), and reintroducing the phase-B contingency (B). This *repeated-measures design* is a very powerful method for isolating the conditions that control behavior.

Figure 7–9 summarizes the results of the program described in the above case. During the instruction period there was no increase in walking, but the addition of reinforcement resulted in increased walking. When reinforcing contingencies are discontinued, there is usually a decrement in the target behavior. In this case, contrary to what might be expected however, improvement continued during the second period in which no reinforcement was given. Uncontrolled and unscheduled reinforcement by other patients may have contributed to this continued improvement. The greatest improvement occurred during the final phase of the program when reinforcement by the assistant had resumed.

Hypochondriasis

Hypochondriasis is diagnosed if a person shows an unrealistic fear of disease in spite of reassurance that

his or her social or occupational functioning is not impaired. Hypochondriacs have an obsessive preoccupation and concern with the condition of their bodily organs and continually worry about their health. Because they fear developing a disease they keep careful track of all potential symptoms by keeping themselves attuned to even the most minute changes in bodily functioning (see Figure 7–10). They tend to misunderstand the nature of the significance of physiological activity and to exaggerate symptoms when they occur (Kellner, 1987). Here is a physician's account of one of his hypochondriacal patients:

Harold Yocum kept the most extensive diary of any patient I have ever seen. Harold was a dapper little guy, standing perhaps five feet four. A local retail clerk, he was always impeccably dressed: sharp creases on his suit trousers (always a suit), carefully knotted ties, handkerchief in the breast pocket just so, highly polished wing tips, carefully clipped nails, and sharply parted hair with the long sweep over the bald spot.

Harold was single and I could never get much social history from him—perhaps he didn't have much social history. He had some college education and had worked as a clerk for many years, but he never chatted about personal activities, friends, or hobbies. Efforts to engage him in such conversation made him uncomfortable, so after a few visits, I stopped

FIGURE 7–10 This woman seems to be an unusually well-organized hypochondriac.
(*Prevention*, September 1982, p. 75)

" THE DOCTOR WILL EXPECT TO HEAR MY SYMPTOMS."

trying. Indeed, after a few visits there was no opportunity to try. We had to review the diary. . . . He began to include more and more in his diary—time and dose of medication, general feelings, minor aches and pains, food-stuffs consumed, coffee and cola intake. He even developed his own stress scale and described evacuations in great detail—time, quantity, color.

Soon the volume of material was too much for his spiral-bound notebook and he began to bring in laboriously typed reports.

—Burnside, 1987, p. 1802

Somatization Disorders

Somatization disorders are marked by multiple somatic complaints that are recurrent or chronic. This condition is often referred to as *Briquet's syndrome* because a physician by that name described it in detail in 1859. The most common complaints are headaches, fatigue, heart palpitations, fainting spells, nausea, vomiting, abdominal pains, bowel troubles, allergies, and menstrual and sexual problems. With this wide assortment of complaints, it is not surprising that somatizing patients are constantly going to the doctor, changing doctors, and undergoing probably unneeded surgery. Figure 7–11 compares the frequency of major surgical procedures for patients who were classified as somatizers and for normal controls.

Patients with somatization disorders believe that they are sick, provide long and detailed histories in support of their belief, and take large quantities of medicines. Almost always, the chronic multiple complaints of somatizers are accompanied by a characteristic personality pattern and by difficulties in social relationships. They share many of the features of histrionic personality disorders, including a self-centered attitude and exaggerated expressions of emotion. Anxiety and depression are common features, as is manipulativeness, which may take the form of suicide threats and attempts. Somatizers impress people as being immature and overly excitable (Kellner, 1990). Somatization disorder differs from hypochondriasis in that hypochondriacs focus on the *fear* of having a specific disease or diseases while the person with a somatization disorder tends to be preoccupied with the symptoms.

The complaints in somatization disorders are usually presented in a dramatic, vague, or exaggerated way. Somatizers tend to use vivid images in describing events and their reactions to them. For example:

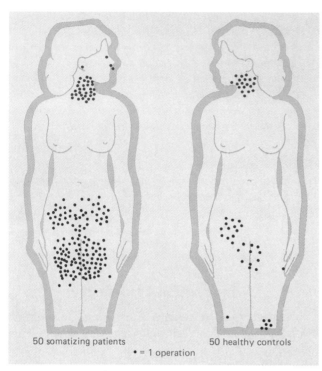

50 somatizing patients 50 healthy controls

• = 1 operation

FIGURE 7–11 The complaints of somatizing patients often lead to unnecessary surgery. These two figures compare the number and location of major surgical procedures in 50 somatizing patients and 50 control subjects. Three times as much body tissue was removed from the somatizing patients as from the controls.

(Based on Cohen and others, 1953)

- I wake up in the morning stiff as a board.
- My heart feels as if iron bands were being tightened around it.
- I throw up every half hour.
- I can't even take liquids.
- I feel as weak as a cat.
- I really can't take it much longer.

Somatizing patients usually have long medical histories that go back at least to early adulthood. These disorders seem to occur mainly in women; approximately 1 percent of women have the condition. It is not uncommon for a family to have more than one somatizer. Since people who are classified as having a somatizing disorder tend to be suggestible, the high prevalence of the disorder in certain families may reflect the influence of a somatizing parent (usually the mother) rather than heredity. The vagueness of somatization complaints makes it difficult to do good research on the disorder (for example, the researcher is frequently left to wonder about possible organic causes of the symptoms) (Barsky, 1989).

Conversion Disorders

People with **conversion disorders** report that they have lost part or all of some basic bodily function. The disturbance does not seem to be under voluntary control and cannot be explained in terms of the principles of medical science. Paralysis, blindness, deafness, and difficulty in walking are among the symptoms reported by these patients. The onset of symptoms in conversion disorders often follows a stressful experience and may be quite sudden. Psychodynamic theorists believe that the symptoms represent an underlying psychological conflict.

Conversion symptoms seem to be naive inventions developed without regard for the actual facts of anatomy. In the case of **glove anesthesia,** for example, the individual may be unable to feel anything in one hand, although the arm has normal sensation. This is anatomically impossible because the sensory nerve supply to this part of the body is organized so that glove anesthesia could not be a result of a neurological disorder.

Although conversion symptoms often seem to appear for no obvious reason, they can frequently be traced to specific precipitating events. Complicating the task of diagnosing conversion disorders is the fact that at times they cannot easily be distinguished from somatically rooted symptoms. One clue that helps make the distinction is a characteristic feature of conversion disorders that has been termed *la belle indifférence* (the beautiful indifference): Whereas the individual may experience intense anxiety in other areas of life, his or her lack of concern about what seems to be an incapacitating physical disturbance is remarkable and not typically associated with similar symptoms associated with true somatic disorders (Ford & Folks, 1985).

Clinical conversion cases usually involve a single disturbance during any one period. Different bodily sites might be affected in subsequent episodes. The symptoms often allow the person to escape from frustrating or challenging situations through physical incapacity. When the pressures of these experiences wane, the physical symptoms weaken. Secondary gain may also occur when the person derives something from a physical symptom (such as attention, affection, or a pension) that he or she might not get otherwise.

Because histrionic tendencies and excitability are characteristic of people who have these bodily reactions, their symptoms often tend to be highly dramatic as well as incapacitating. The drama is perhaps most intense in cases of **group hysteria,** outbreaks of conversion symptoms among people who live, work, or go to school together (see Box 7–3 on pages 210–11). The mass outbreak of hysteria is a vivid illustration of what social psychologists call *group contagion.*

Factitious Disorders and Malingering

Although somatoform disorders and problems that have traditionally been described as psychophysiological (for example, asthma and peptic ulcers) are different in a number of respects, they have in common the fact that the person with the disorder assumes the role of a patient—someone who receives attention and care. Another group of conditions that are characterized by the same feature is **factitious disorders.** However, in these conditions physical and psychological symptoms are voluntarily self-induced by the patient. They may involve a total fabrication or an exaggeration of a preexisting condition.

In a factitious disorder the only apparent goal is the *desire* to assume the role of patient. The person often has a history of uncontrollable lying, demands for attention from professional people, and dramatic accounts of vague pains. Classifying a set of symptoms as factitious may be quite difficult. The dramatic way in which the patient presents his or her problems usually arouses suspicion; however, many individuals with this disorder have managed to gather quite a bit of medical information and, as a consequence, may be good enough actors to make their symptoms seem credible (Sutherland & Rodin, 1990).

Factitious disorders typically begin during early adulthood and are often stimulated by hospitalization for a genuine physical problem. Because of their dramatically presented but vague symptoms, individuals with factitious disorders undergo frequent hospitalizations during which unnecessary surgery may be performed. While somatization disorders are more common in women, factitious disorders are more prevalent among men. Although the symptoms of somaticizers and those with factitious disorders are the same, the somaticizers believe they are really ill but those with factitious disorder are merely seeking attention by manufacturing symptoms.

The term **Munchausen syndrome** refers to an extreme type of factitious disorder that is marked by repeated, knowing simulation of disease for the sole purpose of obtaining medical attention. A patient with this syndrome may travel great distances to appear at hospitals with dramatic and plausible, yet false, histories that convince physicians and staff members that he or she is suffering from an acute illness. The syndrome is named after Baron von Munchausen, an eighteenth-century German cavalry officer who became legendary for concocting elaborate lies. Patients with this syndrome tell incredible tales about their medical histories. They also fake symptoms; for example, they may pretend to be in pain, put blood in a urine sample, or manipulate a thermometer to create an impression of fever. Sometimes they go even further, inflicting real injury on themselves by burning or cutting themselves, taking dangerous drugs, or injecting foreign material into their veins. Often they persuade doctors to perform unnecessary surgery. They may spend most of their lives moving from one hospital to another, trying to be admitted. Once in a hospital, they refuse to comply with its rules and make constant demands for attention. The following case illustrates a typical example of Munchausen syndrome.

A woman staggered into the emergency room of a New York City hospital bleeding from the mouth, clutching her stomach and wailing with pain. It was some entrance. Even in that setting, forever serving bleeders and clutchers and wailers, there was something about her, some terrible star quality that held stage center. Her pain was larger than life.

She told a harrowing story: A man had seduced her, then tied her up, beaten her, forced her to surrender money and jewelry on threat of death. She had severe pain in her lower left side, and an unbearable headache.

She was admitted, and exhaustively tested. Nothing could be found; no reason for the bleeding or the pain; the specialists were left scratching their heads.

Then, one day, a hospital aide came upon these items in her bedside table: a needle, syringe, and a blood thinner called heparin. Eureka. Inject yourself with enough blood thinner and you, too, can take stage center in an emergency room.

Confronted, she denied all charges. The stuff was not hers; someone was trying to frame her; if nobody believed her, she would check out of this place and find doctors who really cared. And off she went. Later, it was learned that she had recently been in two other hospitals: the same story, same symptoms and same sequence of events.

—Lear, 1988, p. 21

A particularly disturbing variant of Munchausen syndrome is one in which a mother produces symptoms of disease in her child and then presents the child for treatment. The mother's concern may be convincing

BOX 7-3 Group Hysteria among Schoolchildren

Two hundred twenty-four elementary-school students assembled in their school auditorium in Norwood, Mass., on the morning of May 21, 1979. The program, a play by the sixth graders honoring their graduation, marked the last formal gathering of the student body for the year. The performance came to an abrupt halt. A sixth-grade boy, a class leader, experienced dizziness, fell from the stage, lacerated his chin, and bled profusely. As a few teachers assisted the boy, several students became ill, and their symptoms began to spread rapidly. First, weakness, dizziness, chills, and faintness developed in four girls and one boy, all sixth graders. Then four more sixth-grade girls complained of the same symptoms. As more and more children became ill, teachers hurriedly dismissed the assembly. They directed the afflicted students to the auditorium floor and covered them with blankets. Alarmed and bewildered by these events, school officials summoned the fire department. The firemen, suspecting an environmental contaminant, ordered immediate evacuation of the building.

Authorities then moved the stricken children to one area of the school grounds. Sirens of approaching vehicles intensified the chaos. Once police arrived, they directed ambulances to transport the children to a local hospital (see Figure 7-12). Evacuation of the building and isolation of the afflicted students, however, failed to contain the spread of illness; the symptoms struck a new child every few minutes. The illness spread so rapidly that the number of afflicted children exhausted the capacity of the available vehicles.

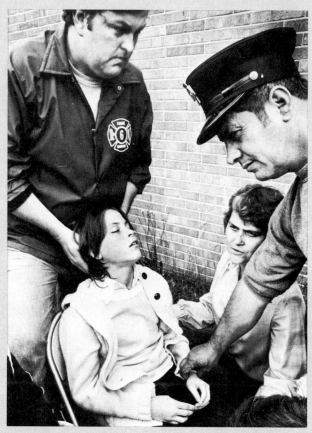

FIGURE 7-12 Rescue workers attend one of the many students who mysteriously fell ill in a Massachusetts elementary school.

because she herself feels a need to be cared for; it is as though she regards the child's body as an extension of her own. The child goes along with the mother because the relationship is so close and intense and the activity so exciting.

Having a factitious disorder is not the same thing as **malingering.** People with factitious disorders simply crave attention and want to be taken care of. Malingerers, on the other hand, seek medical care and hospitalization in order to achieve some specific goal such as compensation, a disability pension, or evasion of the police. Whereas multiple complaints and hospitalizations seem almost a continuous pattern in factitious disorders, malingering often ends abruptly when the patient gets what he or she wants. In contrast, people with factitious disorders seem incapable of stopping their lying and

With 34 of the more severely ill already hospitalized, the hospital dispatched a team of physicians and nurses to treat another 40 or 50 mildly symptomatic children lying on the lawn. As the physicians examined and reassured these patients, their symptoms began to subside. Within four hours of its precipitous beginning, the epidemic was over. . . .

During the outbreak, rumors spread rapidly throughout the school and the surrounding community. For example, two priests arrived to attend the families and friends of the "deceased" as a result of a rumor that 12 children had died of food poisoning. Another rumor circulated among the students that the boy who lacerated his chin underwent open-heart surgery when hospitalized. Mosquito spray, toxic fumes, gas leaks, water contamination, infectious agents, and psychological influences included some of the causes of the epidemic proffered by both professional and laymen. As the epidemic subsided, the more exaggerated rumors subsided. The cause of the outbreak, however, remained controversial in the community: one segment of the population thought "it was only in their minds," others insisted "it was something harmful in the air."

—Small and Nicholi, 1982, p. 721

Although most instances of group hysteria are treated somewhat like curiosities, the Norwood incident was investigated from a research standpoint. The research had to do with two questions: Were the hysterical symptoms related to events in the current lives of the children? Were the symptoms related to events experienced earlier in their lives?

One of the striking features of the Norwood incident was that the sixth grade had by far the highest number of hysterical cases (most of them girls). The researchers (Small & Nicholi, 1982) found that

1. A few days prior to the epidemic, local newspapers had reported that the school principal, who was respected and admired by both children and parents, would be transferred to another school. Many of the families had become disturbed about his transfer and signed a petition protesting his departure.

2. The epidemic began during the sixth graders' play, which marked their impending graduation and departure from school.

3. The sixth graders had planned a camping trip to follow graduation; those attending would sleep away from home for an entire week, many for the first time.

Thus, the sixth graders experienced or were about to experience the loss of their principal, separation from familiar school surroundings, and an exciting trip that included a new experience for many. Most children take such experiences in their stride. Did other features exist in the backgrounds of the affected children that, within the current climate of loss and change, made them more vulnerable to symptoms of mass hysteria?

By administering questionnaires to parents and children, the researchers were able to make some valuable comparisons between the children who required hospitalization and those who did not. They found that 47 percent of the hospitalized children had lost a parent, whereas only 10 percent of those who were not hospitalized had, and that 74 percent of the hospitalized children had experienced a death in the family, whereas only 39 percent of the nonhospitalized children had had such an experience.

The Norwood epidemic had several characteristics that are typical of group hysteria, particularly psychological stress, which in this case took the form of anticipated loss. In addition, there was a significant link between previous loss and hysterical symptoms. Although this does not prove that early loss causes hysterical symptoms, it does suggest that such loss may be an important vulnerability factor in hysteria.

manufacturing of symptoms. However, both of these conditions are self-induced, and both increase in response to high levels of stress.

Distinguishing factitious disorder or malingering from other conditions can be difficult. The judgment that a particular symptom is under voluntary control occasionally is made by excluding all other possible causes. Distinguishing between a factitious disorder and malingering also poses problems. When the clinician is not fully aware of the particular purpose for which the malingerer manufactures his or her symptoms, the chances of misdiagnosis increase. An act of malingering might, under certain circumstances, be considered adaptive (for example, when a prisoner of war fakes an illness), but factitious disorders are almost always seen in people with severe, lifelong personality disturbances.

Chapter Summary

PSYCHOLOGICAL, SOCIAL, AND BODILY INTERACTIONS

The **psychosomatic hypothesis,** popular 50–60 years ago, linked a person's development of certain bodily symptoms with the lack of emotional expression.

Psychophysiological Approaches Contemporary research has focused on bodily reactions to various emotion-arousing stimuli or stressors. The **general adaptation syndrome** was the term used by Selye to describe an organism's patterns of bodily reactions to prolonged stress.

The Biopsychosocial Model The **biopsychosocial model** considers the interaction of the person's biological, psychological, and social subsystems. In this view, psychological factors usually play indirect roles in illness in which they combine with biological vulnerabilities of the person and the product of their interaction determines the effect of different levels of stress on the individual. This view emphasizes the concept of **homeostasis** in which a living organism attempts to restore its dynamic equilibrium when it is exposed to stressors. Stress occurs when a person feels unable to control important aspects of life. Skills whose presence decrease stress and risk of illness include ability to adapt to environmental change, to handle strong emotions, to interpret the situation correctly, and to form positive close relationships. Pain is an example of a stressor influenced by this interaction of the three subsystems of psychological characteristics, biological vulnerabilities, and stress level.

Stress and Illness There is growing evidence that stress can play a role in illness. Stress occurs when a person feels unable to control important aspects of life. Skills whose presence decrease stress and risk of illness include the ability to adapt to environmental change, to handle strong emotions, to interpret a situation correctly, and to form close positive relationships.

PSYCHOPHYSIOLOGICAL DISORDERS

Headaches Headache pain, which may have a variety of causes, is often treated with **biofeedback,** a technique which helps the clients use self-control procedures to gain more control over body functions such as muscle tension and other reactions to stress.

Cardiovascular Disorders **Cardiovascular disorders** are pathological conditions related to the functioning of the heart and blood vessels. In coronary heart disease deposits, called **plaques,** thicken the walls of the coronary arteries and decrease the supply of blood available to produce a condition called **atherosclerosis.** This buildup can result in **angina pectoris** (chest pain) or in a **myocardial infarction** (what is usually called a heart attack). **Stress** is thought to contribute to the risk of coronary heart disease because in stressful situations the body secretes more of hormonal substances called **catecholamines.** Two of these, **epinephrine** and **norepinephrine** accelerate the rate of arterial damage. Many personal lifestyle factors can increase stress as can separation from or loss of a loved one. Living in a fast-paced society also increases risk of heart disease, presumably because it increases stress. When stress and social isolation are both present in a person's life, the risk of dying from heart disease is much higher than for people who are low in stress experiences and high in social support. People who have **Type A** personalities, that is they are very demanding of themselves and others and tend to operate under high pressure, are at higher risk for coronary heart disease than others. The hostile emotions that characterize many Type A people are also thought to be a risk factor. **Hypertension,** or high blood pressure, is also a risk factor for heart disease. Behavioral methods, including assertiveness training and relaxation training and biofeedback are helpful in lowering blood pressure in some cases.

Cancer Uncontrollable stress seems to be related to cancer growth. Some research indicates that inability to express strong feelings and depression may both be associated with greater risk of cancer. Although evidence linking psychological forces and cancer is still tentative, group psychotherapy has been shown to be associated with longer life expectancy for women with breast cancer.

The Immune System and Related Disorders The immune system regulates susceptibility to disease in the body. There seems to be a complex relationship between stress and disease susceptibility. Psychological approaches to stress regulation have been shown to affect the immune system.

Allergies An **allergy** is an abnormal reaction to a normally harmless substance. **Asthma** is an allergy that seems to have an important psychological component.

Gastrointestinal Disorder **Gastrointestinal disorders** such as **diarrhea** and **ulcers** seem to have both psychological causes related to stress and bodily causes.

SOMATOFORM DISORDERS

Somatoform disorders are bodily complaints for which no actual physical impairment can be found. Included in this category are psychogenic pain disorders, hypochondriasis, and somatization and conversion disorders.

Psychogenic Pain Disorder **Psychogenic pain disorder** involves reports of extreme and incapacitating pain without any identifiable organic symptoms or greatly in excess of what would be expected based on the organic symptoms found.

Hypochondriasis People affected with **hypochondriasis** show unrealistic fears of illness and are excessively preoccupied about their health.

Somatization Disorders Patients with **somatization disorders** (also called *Briquet's syndrome*) have multiple and recurrent or chronic bodily complaints. These complaints are likely to be presented in a dramatic and exaggerated way.

Conversion Disorders The symptoms of **conversion disorders** are the reported loss of part or all of some basic body function, for instance the paralysis of some portion of the body or a sensory function such as ability to see. This loss does not seem under voluntary control although the symptoms do not fit with the facts of anatomical structures. One symptom of conversion disorder is *belle indifference,* the lack of concern about what seem to be incapacitating physical symptoms.

FACTITIOUS DISORDERS AND MALINGERING

Factitious disorders have symptoms that are voluntarily induced by the patient, presumably in an effort to receive attention and care. **Munchausen syndrome** is an extreme form of this disorder in which the person deliberately simulates the symptoms of disease by faking symptoms and even manipulating the results of medical tests. **Malingering** differs from factitious disorder because the person reports the symptoms to achieve some specific goal such as an insurance settlement.

Sexual Variations
and Disorders

C H A P T E R 8

Changing Views of Sexual Behavior

Surveys of Sexual Behavior

Homosexuality
How Sexual Preference Develops
A Cross-cultural View
Psychological Adjustment
Relationship Patterns
Sexual Response

Bisexuality

Sexual Dysfunction
Types of Sexual Dysfunction
Treatment of Sexual Dysfunction
The Effectiveness of Sex Therapy

Gender Identity Disorder
Childhood Problems of Gender
Identity
Gender Identity Disorder in Adults

The Paraphilias
Fetishism
Transvestism
Sexual Sadism and Masochism
Autoerotic Asphyxia
Voyeurism
Exhibitionism
Obscene Telephone Calls
Pedophilia
Perspectives on the Paraphilias

Sexual Victimization
Rape
Child Sexual Abuse
Incest

Chapter Summary

George Tooker, *Embrace IV*, 1984. Marisa del Re Gallery, New York.

CASE A: LAURA
I told my parents because I wanted to share with them. Now I would tell people NEVER to tell their parents. DO NOT. I suppose it depends on the family. If you have a working relationship or communication with them. No, I'd say keep the relationship you now have. They don't need to know. I remember all the agony I went through in telling them. . . .

CASE B: JAMES
Well, when I first told my mother she said, "Well, it's no news to me. You're the same person." When I told my sister and brothers, they were scared. But I told them that I didn't choose to be gay, but I do choose to be happy. But I made it very clear to them. I told them that if they couldn't accept me for the person I am and always will be, then that was too bad. . . . When my sister first met Steve, she loved him. She said, "You better hang on to him. You've really got yourself a catch!"

—Meyer, 1990, p. 71

These two experiences of announcing to family members that one is homosexual show how varied responses to the "news" can be. The prevalence of homosexuality, how it is expressed, and how family and community respond to it, varies from culture to culture and from time to time. For example, in ancient Greece homosexuality was commonly accepted, and even encouraged. Today, many Americans disapprove of homosexuality and believe that it is a kind of mental illness. Others see it simply as one of several acceptable types of sexual orientation. Both of these views might be considered an improvement over earlier beliefs that regarded this type of sexual orientation as a sin or heresy.

This chapter deals with many variations in sexual behavior, ranging from behavior that is universally regarded as disturbed to behavior that some people simply don't like. Although the focus of this book is primarily on abnormal behavior, it is important to have a broad frame of reference in reviewing highly charged and often controversial topics like sexual variation.

Changing Views of Sexual Behavior

Sexual behavior of all types has never ceased to be a topic of great interest. Over the centuries ideas about sexuality and sexual deviance have undergone drastic changes. During the fourth century B.C. the Greeks regarded sex as a pleasurable part of nature, to be enjoyed with partners of either sex. This open view of sexuality contrasts sharply with the prevailing view during the period between the fall of Rome and the fifteenth century, when church authorities were obsessed with the notion of sex as a sin. During that period many thousands of Europeans were tortured into confessing erotic encounters with the devil, after which they were publicly burned alive. Entire villages in southern Germany and Switzerland were exterminated in this way.

The price that women had to pay to be rescued from this fate was to renounce all sexual or erotic thoughts. By the mid-nineteenth century, the idea of women as morally pure, erotically apathetic, and sexually inert had reached a peak. Women were expected to engage in sexual behavior only as a way of satisfying their husbands and carrying out their obligation to become mothers. Despite these expectations, however, pornography, prostitution, and venereal disease flourished.

From time to time, some brave souls have been willing to question popularly held ideas about the role of sexuality in human behavior. One of these individuals, Sigmund Freud, used material gathered from many patients to illustrate the negative effects of a repressive view of sexuality. Freud traced the sexual deviations of adults to significant events in childhood. Although some aspects of his theories continue to be controversial, Freud stimulated a rethinking of the role of sexual feelings in development. He argued that all people are innately bisexual. Although psychosexual development usually progresses along a heterosexual course, some circumstances, such as inability to resolve the Oedipus complex, might result in adult homosexual behavior. In general, Freud's view of homosexuality was that it is simply a variation of sexual development. In a letter to a mother who had written to him asking for therapy for her son, he wrote:

Homosexuality is assuredly no advantage, but it is nothing to be ashamed of, no vice, no degradation, it cannot be classified as an illness; we consider it to be a variation of sexual function produced by a certain arrest of sexual development. Many highly respectable individuals of ancient and modern times have been homosexuals, several of the greatest men among them (Plato, Michelangelo, Leonardo de Vinci, etc.). It is a great injustice to persecute homosexuality as a crime, and cruelty too.

—Freud, 1935/1951, p. 786

Havelock Ellis was another important influence on views about sexuality. Ellis wrote books and articles that focused on the range of sexual behavior that occurred in the lives of ordinary people. He recognized that it was common for both men and women to masturbate, and emphasized the psychological rather than physical causes of many sexual problems. It was Ellis who suggested that objective surveys be taken to find out what happens in ordinary sexual relationships. This useful suggestion was not acted upon until fairly recently.

Surveys of Sexual Behavior

Most of the information about the frequency of different sexual practices come from survey research. Alfred Kinsey, a biologist, was one of the pioneers in this approach to the study of sexual behavior. In 1938 he was asked to take charge of a new course on marriage at Indiana University and to give lectures on the biological aspects of sex and marriage. As he prepared for the course, Kinsey was amazed to find that there were only a few statistical studies on sexual behavior and no scientific data that he could pass on to students when they asked such questions as "Is masturbation harmful?" or "Is homosexuality abnormal?" In his class one night he stated that no one knew the answers to these questions because of a lack of information. He asked whether his students would be willing to submit their case histories so that scientists could discover enough about human sexual behavior to be able to answer some of these questions. The students agreed and this was the beginning of several important research studies and ultimately of the Institute for Sex Research at Indiana University.

Kinsey believed that human sexual behavior could be studied objectively. To find out about people's sex lives, he interviewed them about a wide variety of sexual practices. In each interview he asked hundreds of exceedingly personal questions in an accepting and matter-of-fact manner. One of Kinsey's colleagues, the psychologist Wardell Pomeroy, provided this account of Kinsey's approach to interviewing.

We asked our questions directly without hesitancy or apology. Kinsey correctly pointed out that if we were uncertain or embarrassed

in our questioning we could not expect to get anything but a corresponding response. Unlike previous researchers, we did not say "touching yourself" when we meant masturbation, or "relations with other persons" when "sexual intercourse" was intended. "Evasive terms invite dishonest answers," was Kinsey's dictum. We also never asked whether a subject had ever engaged in a particular activity; we assumed that everyone had engaged in everything, and so we began by asking when he had first done it. Thus the subject who might want to deny an experience had a heavier burden placed on him, and since he knew from the way the question was asked that it would not surprise us if he had done it, there seemed little reason to deny it.

—Pomeroy, 1972, p. 112

Although change in public attitudes and legal codes rarely comes about because of a single person or event, it would be difficult to overestimate Kinsey's contribution to knowledge about sexual behavior. In addition to promoting scientific research on human sexuality, Kinsey influenced public attitudes through his objective reporting of results showing that sexual behaviors that had been considered unusual or abnormal were in fact widely practiced.

The first Kinsey Report (Kinsey and others, 1948) presented a detailed statistical picture of the sexual behavior of 5,300 American males ranging in age from 10 to 90. Five years later a second report (Kinsey and others, 1953) provided similar information based on interviews with almost 6,000 women. Teams of researchers issued reports on homosexuality in 1978 and 1981 (Bell & Weinberg, 1978; Bell and others, 1981).

Obviously, surveys of sexual practices 40 or 50 years ago may not be applicable today. For example, the proportion of college-age males and females reporting that they are sexually active has changed. Not only has there been a great increase in the proportion of members of each sex who report having had intercourse, but the proportion of females has increased much more rapidly than that of males.

Another change has been in the increase in and acceptance of oral–genital sexual behavior among college students. In one survey about oral sex among college women, about two-thirds of the respondents reported that they had experienced it and most reported feeling no guilt about it. The women were just as likely to have performed oral sex as to have received it (Herold & Way, 1983). Kinsey had found that oral sex was considered more intimate than intercourse and seldom occurred until intercourse had been experienced. Herold and Way

found just the reverse. In their study, two-thirds of the women who were still virgins had experienced oral sex. This suggests a change in attitudes regarding the level of intimacy represented by oral sex as compared to intercourse.

The passage of time since these earlier surveys has brought with it changes in social customs, especially those related to increased acceptance of sexual relationships of non-traditional types, increased frequency of cohabitation before marriage, and increased rates of divorce and remarriage. In addition, concerns about AIDS and contracting the HIV virus seem to have had an impact on the sexual behaviors of many individuals. For all these reasons there is a need for current surveys of sexual practices.

Homosexuality

Homosexual behavior is sexual behavior with a member of one's own sex. **Homosexuals** are individuals who prefer to engage in sexual activity with members of their own sex over an extended period. Female homosexuality is often called **lesbianism.** Many homosexuals engage in sexual activity only with members of the same sex and are not attracted to members of the opposite sex. However, many homosexuals have heterosexual fantasies and can be sexually aroused by members of the opposite sex. A person's belief that he or she is a homosexual does not depend on actual behavior. Someone with no sexual experience at all may think of himself or herself as a homosexual. In recent years the term "gay" has been used by homosexuals to describe their life style because they feel that the term has fewer negative implications than "homosexual." Individuals, both males and females, who wish to publicly acknowledge their homosexual orientation usually use the term "gay."

Homosexuality illustrates the changing character of views about sexual behavior, and the degree to which sexual behavior can become a sociopolitical issue. Society's stigmatizing of homosexuals can be very harmful and lead to anxiety, self-doubt ("What's wrong with me?"; "I'm not normal"), and a perceived need to be "cured."

In the bad old days, when homosexuality was considered a mental illness, a friend of mine was trying to go straight. He was seeing a distinguished psychoanalyst who believed (and still believes) that what some call a life style and still others call a crime is a psychiatrically

treatable disorder. Through six years of anguished analysis, my friend changed his sexual orientation and married. His wife was wonderful—they had been friends for years—but he died unexpectedly of a heart attack at the age of 42, six months after the wedding. I am not superstitious, and I don't blame anyone, least of all his wife; he was happy with her. But a nagging question remains: Is it possible that my friend's doctor was trying to change something that should have been left alone?

He had been homosexual for years, and had had at least one stable long-term relationship. But he lived in a society that condemned him on religious and medical grounds. He "freely" chose to change through psychoanalysis. But this was a limited sort of freedom, and though he in fact did change—as some have—he did not live to find out how the change would work.

—Konner, 1989, p. 60

Public attitudes have tended to stigmatize homosexual activity to such an extent that many of those engaging in it have suffered social and legal mistreatment far beyond the domain of sexual behavior. During recent years, gay activism has increased markedly, as homosexuals have battled discrimination and social stigmatization.

All indications point to the conclusion that homosexual behavior is common. The Kinsey study in 1948 found that it probably occurs in more than one male in three during late adolescence, and this prevalence rate is believed to be true today, too. However, it cannot be assumed that these adolescents are predominantly homosexual or that they will continue either homosexual behaviors or even homosexual orientation into adulthood. The same thing can be said about heterosexual behavior. Its occurrence in adolescence may or may not predict the same kinds of sexual expression in adulthood.

However, there is some evidence that the foundations for homosexual or heterosexual preference can be seen in childhood and adolescence. Homosexual adult men are more likely than heterosexuals to report feelings of being different from their peers in childhood, to have had gender-atypical interests, greater sexual interest in other boys, and more intense homosexual fantasies (Green, 1987; Saghir & Robins, 1973). In the groups studied, homosexual adult men reported that the average age of awareness of same-sex attraction was about 13 years and that self-designation as homosexual occurred from ages 19 to 21.

Studies of adolescents and younger men confirm

these findings (Remafedi, 1987). Some of the young men studied self-labeled themselves as the result of sexual experiences with either men or women, but most of them adopted the self-label as a result of persistent homosexual feelings or attractions. This self-identification often came about over a long period in which they felt extreme emotional turmoil and may have thought about or attempted suicide mainly as a result of concern over their sexual orientation.

Another type of evidence that supports the findings of development of homosexual identification before adulthood comes from longitudinal studies of boys who were referred to mental-health professionals because of gender-atypical behavior during their preschool years. This behavior included dressing in girl's clothing and preferring female roles in play activities. The majority of the boys for whom these problems were severe can be expected to ultimately develop an adolescent or adult homosexual identity (Green, 1987; Money & Russe, 1979). This suggests that at least for a subgroup of the male homosexual population, adult sexual orientation may be determined early in life.

The evidence on homosexuality suggests the following.

1. Homosexual activity is not unusual in adolescence but does not necessarily predict adult sexual preference.

2. There is a subset of adolescents who clearly identify themselves as homosexual.

3. The roots of this sexual orientation may extend back to early childhood.

How Sexual Preference Develops

Recently researchers have focused attention on the roles of biological factors and learning in the development of sexual preferences. For example, one recent study suggested that there may be anatomical differences between the brains of homosexual and heterosexual men (LeVay, 1991). The study found that among men who had died from AIDS-related diseases, in homosexual men part of the hypothalamus (a brain region that influences sexual behavior) had the anatomical form usually found in women rather than the form typical of heterosexual men. This finding is not direct evidence that brain structure causes homosexuality, but it suggests the need to explore areas of the brain that might relate to sexual preference. One problem in this study is that because all the subjects had AIDS, this could have affected the result. However, there is growing speculation that the brain plays an important role in sexual behavior. It has previously been found that adult men's brains are on average 15 percent larger than adult women's brains.

This difference is equal to about twice the relative difference in average body size between men and women. Men's brains don't start out to be bigger though. The brains of male and female infants are about the same size until age 2 or 3. After that, male brains grow faster until about age 6. Some researchers think this pattern reflects the fact that the basic structure of the brain is female and it is modified when the activity of male sex hormones intensifies (Gibbons, 1991).

Animal studies have shown that prenatal hormone treatments may play a role in later homosexual behavior patterns. There are a few reports that a prenatal excess or deficiency of sex hormones can also affect human sexual behavior. Females who had experienced an excess of prenatal androgen (hormones that develop secondary sex characteristics in males) were more likely to have a lesbian sexual orientation (Money & Schwartz, 1977). However, treating adults with male or female hormones does not alter their sexual orientation in any way. It is possible, although far from proven, that prenatal hormones could predispose individuals to certain patterns of sexual behavior in adulthood. However, a person's sexual orientation is also thought to be strongly dependent on socialization after birth (Money, 1987).

The view that homosexuality is primarily a learned phenomenon suggests that pleasant early sexual experiences with members of the same sex or unpleasant experiences with members of the opposite sex can condition sexual thoughts and fantasies. This perspective can also be used to explain why some individuals change their sexual preference as adults. Some investigators have found that individuals who have changed their preference may have had unpleasant heterosexual experiences followed by rewarding homosexual ones (Masters & Johnson, 1979). Other investigators have stressed parent–child relationships in explaining homosexuality (Gadpaille, 1989). Bieber and others (1962) found that the predominant pattern among homosexual psychiatric patients was that of a close-binding, seductive mother who devalued and dominated a passive, distant, hostile father. However, more recent research with non-patients suggested that the family relationships of homosexual and heterosexual individuals do not differ (Bell and others, 1981). How accurate are the explanations of the various theoretical viewpoints? How well do they explain what has been found through research? In general, the answer is not very well. In a large and sophisticated study, Bell and his co-workers (Bell and others, 1981) concluded that neither a psychodynamic nor a behavioral view of homosexuality was supported by the evidence. Their findings include the following.

1. No evidence that parent–child relationships are important in determining sexual preference.

2. No evidence that homosexuality results from atypical experiences with members of the opposite sex during childhood—these atypical experiences include rape, parental punishment for sex play with members of the opposite sex, seductive behavior by opposite-sex parents, or actual seduction by an older male or female.

The study also provided evidence that sexual preference begins early.

1. Sexual preference is likely to be established by adolescence, even before there is much sexual activity.

2. Sexual feelings of attraction seemed much more important than early sexual activity in the determination of homosexual preference.

3. Adult homosexuals did not lack heterosexual experiences in childhood; however, they did not tend to find these gratifying.

4. Children who did not conform to gender roles in childhood had a somewhat increased probability of homosexual feelings and behavior in adolescence.

Gender nonconformity in childhood means that a person was typically interested in activities that are culturally associated with the opposite sex—for example, girls playing baseball and boys playing house. Although gender nonconformity is associated with a higher probability of homosexual orientation, it is not a very accurate clue. At least half the homosexual men in the study were typically masculine in both personal identity and interests while they were growing up, and at least one-fourth of the heterosexual men were nonconforming to male sex roles while growing up. The situation was similar for women. This means that while gender nonconformity in childhood increases the likelihood that the child will be homosexual in adulthood, it does not automatically signal later homosexuality.

Bell and his co-workers concluded that the development of a homosexual preference is probably biologically based. Although their study does not deal with biological data, their findings make that conclusion reasonable. However, as was explained above, any biological explanation requires much further research.

Despite a growing body of information about homosexuality, we still must conclude that its causes are not yet known. Perhaps one source of confusion concerning this topic has been the tendency to think of homosexuals as a homogeneous group. This belief may not be correct; more likely, there are different categories of homosexuals, which vary with regard to the reasons for sexual orientation. Biological factors may play especially important roles in certain types of sexual orienta-

tion, while factors in the social environment may be especially important in others. Researchers need to develop more studies of sexual orientation and sexual practices over time that take both biological and environmental factors into account. Unfortunately, most developmental research on sexuality has been retrospective, based on adults' reconstructions of their childhoods (Boxer & Cohler, 1989; Savin-Williams, 1990).

A Cross-cultural View

Since 1973 annual surveys reveal very little change in the proportion of Americans who think homosexual relations are wrong (Blendon and others, 1992) (see Table 8–1). Although heterosexual behavior generally has been the preferred pattern in the United States and most other cultures, in many societies certain forms of homosexual behavior are accepted or expected. For instance, in a large area of the southern Pacific Ocean stretching from Sumatra through Papua–New Guinea to the island of Melanesia homosexuality has an accepted role in the social institutions of the various tribal peoples (Herdt, 1984). In these groups, cultural tradition says that when males become nine years old they must leave their families and live in a single long house in the village center. From that time until they are 19 and at the age for marriage they all participate in homosexual activities. After marriage homosexual activity either ceases or occurs only occasionally. Thus, the prescribed male norm in this society is sequential bisexuality. In this culture, omission of the homosexual period rather than its inclusion is what is classified as deviant (Money, 1987).

Historically, homosexuality has been condemned by the dominant religions of the Western world; in the eighteenth and nineteenth centuries it was considered an illness. In recent years tolerance of homosexuality has increased. Many cities have enacted ordinances that make discrimination on account of sexual orientation illegal. As one author pointed out, "Homosexuals are being slowly redefined in less value-laden terms as practitioners of an alternative lifestyle, members of a new community" (Altman, 1982) (see Figure 8–1). This view may be changing, however, because of concern about AIDS. AIDS, the result of the HIV virus which can be sexually transmitted, has a high fatality rate, and the number of cases has grown quite rapidly. Although heterosexual transmission of the HIV virus has become increasingly common as has its transmission to unborn children from HIV positive mothers, many people still identify AIDS risk mainly with either homosexual behavior or illegal drug use. As a result, in at least some segments of the public, negative attitudes toward homosexuality may again increase.

Psychological Adjustment

Relatively few differences in psychological adjustment have been found between heterosexual and homosexual groups. The majority of homosexual individuals are well adjusted and productive people (Saghir & Robins, 1973). In a review of dozens of studies, there was no difference between homosexual and heterosexual groups in the rates of emotional instability or illness. No psychological tests could discriminate between the two groups (Reiss, 1980). Homosexuals, like heterosexuals, may be anxious or depressed and are not always emotionally stable, but homosexuality is clearly not a form of mental illness (Marmor, 1980). The psycholog-

Table 8–1

Attitudes of Adult Americans toward Homosexuality, 1973 and 1987

	Percentage of Sample	
Questions and Responses	1973	1987
1. Are sexual relations between two adults of the same sex:		
Always wrong	74	75
Almost always wrong	7	4
Wrong only sometimes	8	7
Not wrong at all	11	12
2. Should an admitted homosexual man be allowed to teach in a college or university?		
Yes	49	57
No	51	40

SOURCE: Based on Davis and Smith, 1987

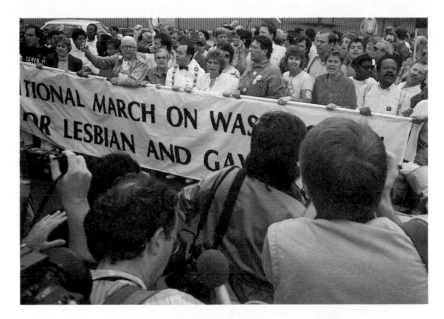

FIGURE 8–1 Gay Pride activities provide social support for homosexuals by visibly demonstrating their numbers. They also provide a way for homosexuals to publicly state their sexual preferences rather than hide them.

ical impact of the current high AIDS-associated death rate in the gay community as well as the personal loss of friends as a result of AIDS is likely to result in an increased amount of stress experienced by gay individuals. As we have stated throughout this book (see especially chapters 1 and 5), high stress is associated with a higher role of disorders of various types. Research has shown that mean levels of psychological distress among gay men at risk for AIDS are significantly higher than in the general population (Chuang and others, 1989; Joseph and others, 1990).

In 1973 the American Psychiatric Association removed homosexuality from its list of mental illnesses, and in 1975 the American Psychological Association also took this position. DSM-IV does not include homosexuality in its list of disorders. Many clinicians believe that maladaptive behavior in homosexuals, when it does occur, is often due to the social stigma attached to homosexuality rather than to anything pathological in the nature of homosexuality itself.

Relationship Patterns

Just as there is no single personality type or life-style pattern that is characteristic of heterosexuals, there is no single homosexual personality or life style. The Institute for Sex Research carried on an intensive ten-year study of homosexuals based on a large-scale survey of 1,500 individuals in the San Francisco Bay Area (Bell & Weinberg, 1978; Bell and others, 1981). This survey was the first to investigate how homosexuals differed from each other, not just from heterosexuals. The findings suggested not one but several consistent homosexual life styles:

1. *Close-Coupleds.* Respondents in this category were closely bonded partners whose relationships were similar to those in heterosexual marriages. Close-coupleds did not seek other partners and reported that they had no regrets about their homosexuality (see Figure 8–2).

2. *Open-Coupleds.* These respondents lived with a special partner but reported themselves to be less happy than close-coupled respondents. They had more outside sexual partners, whom they often picked up by cruising.

3. *Functionals.* This group consisted of "swinging singles" whose lives were organized around sexual experiences. They engaged in frequent cruising, had many friends, and felt that they were well adjusted.

4. *Dysfunctionals.* Respondents in this group were more poorly adjusted than the functionals. They had a large number of partners and a high level of sexual activity, but they saw themselves as sexually unappealing and their lives were marked by distress and conflict.

5. *Asexuals.* These people lacked involvements with others. They had few partners and engaged in little sexual activity. People in this group were less likely than those in other groups to say that they were exclusively homosexual. They were lonely and unhappy.

Few homosexual men and women in this study conformed to society's stereotypes. For example, respondents were not easily identifiable as homosexuals, and few were completely uninvolved with the opposite sex. One-third of the female and one-fifth of the male homosexuals who were interviewed had been married.

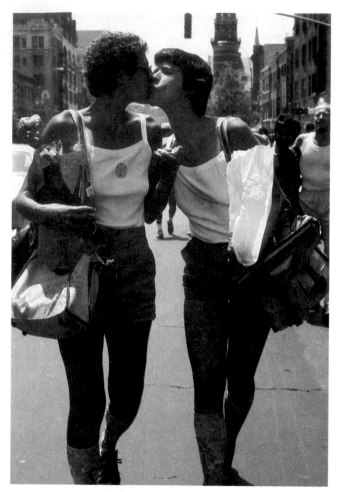

FIGURE 8–2 According to Bell and Weinberg's study of homosexual life styles, close-coupled lesbian partners seem to have more satisfying and stable relationships than close-coupled males.

One-fourth of the respondents' employers knew that they were homosexuals, as did one-fifth of their neighbors and one-half of their brothers and sisters. Their mothers were the most likely to know.

The sexual problems most frequently mentioned by homosexuals were lack of sexual outlets and the difficulty in finding suitable partners. Homosexual males reported many more sexual partners than female homosexuals did. Many of the men had had hundreds of partners; in contrast, the women tended to have had fewer than ten. Lesbians were more likely to have a relationship resembling a marriage than were male homosexuals. Men seem to be more interested in sexual activity, while women emphasized companionship, affection, and emotional support.

This research into the diversity of homosexual behaviors represents a valuable starting point for further inquiries. However, its limitations even at the time it was carried out should be recognized. The subjects may be representative neither of the population as a whole nor of homosexuals in general. The homosexuals in the study were volunteers recruited through public advertising, gay bars, and homosexual organizations. In addition, the homosexual climate in San Francisco is more permissive than that in most other communities in the United States. (Homosexuals living in less permissive places report a much higher incidence of social difficulties.) Unskilled and semiskilled people accounted for only 18 percent of the people in the study, and 73 percent of the black male respondents reported having had at least some college education—a much higher percentage than that found in the general population of black males. For these reasons further research is needed before we can decide whether the conclusions from this study correctly describe the entire homosexual population.

What are the similarities and differences between homosexual and heterosexual life styles? There are big gaps in our knowledge pertinent to this question. However, we do know that it is in the number and nature of sexual partnerships that homosexuals in our culture differ perhaps the most from heterosexuals. While close-coupled homosexuals are an identifiable group, overall, homosexuals report having had more sexual partners than do heterosexuals. Furthermore, many of these partners are strangers. While homosexuals of both sexes change partners more frequently than heterosexuals, the difference is much greater between homosexual and heterosexual males (Gadpaille, 1989). Because of concern about contracting the HIV virus and ultimately AIDS, it is not clear how the frequency of the different life style patterns among the gay population have changed. A variety of reports have suggested that in addition to an increased use of safe sex practices, some individuals have opted for fewer partners or for a reduced number of sexual contacts. Documentation of these lifestyle changes in a larger sample is needed to determine the actual as opposed to the perceived degree of change and whether the proportion of individuals in each of the life style groups described in the study by Bell and his associates is still applicable.

Sexual Response

Is the sexual experience of homosexuals different from that of heterosexuals? The answer is both yes and no. Masters and Johnson (1979) compared the physiological responses of male and female homosexual and heterosexual couples under laboratory conditions. They found no differences in physiological response during sexual activity and orgasm. But they did find that homosexual couples were more leisurely in their sexual activity, communicated more, and were more sensitive to their partners' needs than were heterosexual couples.

Bisexuality

Bisexual behavior, in which partners of either sex may be preferred at different times, is reported by a small but significant number of survey respondents. **Bisexuals** are sexually attracted to members of either sex and often engage in sexual activity with both men and women.

The incidence of bisexuality in Western societies is difficult to estimate. Probably about five percent of adults are bisexual if bisexuality is defined as sexual activity with both males and females in the past year (Masters and others, 1988). Patterns of bisexuality differ. Sometimes the bisexual individual has a long heterosexual relationship and then a long homosexual relationship. Or the order might be reversed. Sometimes both relationships go on during the same period. One 23-year-old woman described her bisexual experience as follows.

I had been dating a guy I was very friendly with for about a year with a good sexual relationship. Then I suddenly found myself making it with my roommate, who slowly but expertly introduced me to how two women make love. I really enjoyed both kinds of sex and both personal

relationships, so I continued them for some while until my graduate school career was over and I moved to a new town.

—Masters, Johnson, and Kolodny, 1988, p. 439

Both bisexuals and gays may have conventional heterosexual marriages. This may be due to a desire to have children or to have a conventional life style. Another reason may be that the person does not begin to experience other sexual feelings until later in life. Sometimes bisexuals are aware of their attraction to members of the same sex before marriage, but relatively few of them reveal this fact to their prospective spouses (Coleman, 1981/1982). If the spouse later discovers a homosexual relationship, an explosive situation may be created. Husbands seem to feel especially threatened because they tend to see their wives' lesbian preferences as a negative statement about the husband's performance as a lover (Masters and others, 1988).

If bisexuality culminates in a move to a homosexual life style, other problems can arise. A substantial number of active homosexuals are also parents (see Figure 8–3). Being both homosexual and a parent may produce two somewhat conflicting identities.

This double identity may also create problems in the homosexual relationship, especially for partners in

FIGURE 8–3 These men, photographed at a Gay Freedom Day parade in San Francisco, live openly as both parents and homosexuals. In a less liberal environment they might be denied not only custody but even access to their children.

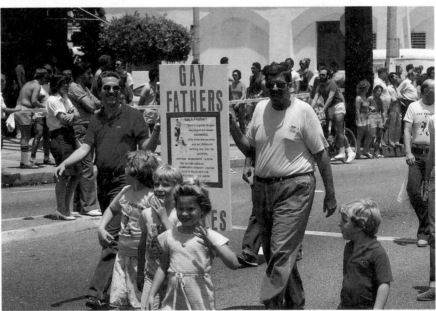

close- or open-coupled relationships. Another problem that sometimes arises is that of child custody. We don't really know how growing up in a household with a homosexual parent (and, in some cases, the parent's lover) can affect a child's development. Although the question has arisen in several court cases, little research on this subject is available.

Sexual Dysfunction

Homosexuals may experience psychological distress because of their social stigmatization. The distress caused by sexual dysfunction, on the other hand, is usually a very private matter about which other people have no knowledge. Both heterosexuals and homosexuals can experience sexual dysfunction.

A **sexual dysfunction** or **disorder** can be defined as persistent impairment of sexual interest or response that causes interpersonal difficulty or personal distress. Sometimes the dysfunction is independent of, and sometimes it results from, other psychological disorders or physical conditions (Catalan and others, 1990). If the problem is due *entirely* to organic factors it is not given this diagnosis. A predisposition may be created by upbringing, personality, lack of information, or early sexual trauma. More immediate, precipitating causes include conflict with the partner, infidelity, age, depression, or an accidental failure produced by fatigue, stress, anxiety, or alcohol. The disorder may be sustained by anticipation of failure, the partner's reaction, poor communication, and limited sexual skills. Because of the large number of factors that might be involved in sexual disorders, clinicians must sensitively inquire about many aspects of sexual activity (see Table 8–2).

Sexuality is a biological function like digestion or respiration, and adequate sexual functioning, like good digestion or normal breathing, requires freedom from agitated feelings or excessive tension and control. A psychophysiological disorder may develop through the mutual reinforcement of fears, excessive expectations, physical responses, and the partner's reaction. For example, a man may become anxious when his female partner is slow to achieve orgasm; his anxiety may make it still more difficult for her, which may increase his anxiety level further and lead to erectile dysfunction.

Types of Sexual Dysfunction

Problems people encounter in sexual activity may occur in any of four stages of the sexual-response cycle. The stages include the following periods.

Table 8–2

Information Needed in Diagnosing and Treating Sexual Dysfunction

1. The nature of the dysfunction (e.g., lack of interest in sexual activity, inability to achieve orgasm)
2. When the sexual difficulty first became apparent (how long ago? in what situation?)
3. With what frequency has the difficulty been encountered (with each sexual partner? frequently or occasionally?)
4. The course of the dysfunction (acute or gradual in onset?)
5. What the patient thinks is the cause of the difficulty (e.g., "Maybe I'm just getting older")
6. What have the patient and partner done to correct the dysfunction, and with what results?

SOURCE: Based on Moore, 1989

1. *Appetitive:* the presence of fantasy about sexual activity and a feeling of desire
2. *Excitement:* a period of subjective pleasure and physiological changes, including penile erection in the male and swelling and lubrication of the female genitals
3. *Orgasm:* the peaking of sexual pleasure and the release of sexual tension, as shown by ejaculation in the male and rhythmic muscle contraction in the pelvic area for both males and females
4. *Resolution:* a sense of relaxation and well-being. Men cannot produce an erection or experience orgasm during the resolution period, while women may be able to respond almost immediately to additional stimulation.

Sexual problems can occur during any of these stages. In the appetitive stage, physical conditions such as high blood pressure or diabetes can inhibit sexual desire. Some people simply seem to be at the low end of the normal distribution of sexual desire. These problems usually come to the attention of a clinician only when they become a source of concern to the individual or his or her partner.

Sexual problems can also occur at the excitement stage of the cycle. The male may fail to attain or hold an erection until the completion of intercourse. This problem is called **erectile dysfunction.** In females, a problem at this stage is inability to attain or maintain the swelling-lubrication response until the sex act is completed. This inability is often brought about by **inhibited sexual excitement.** Problems at each stage of sexual response may be a function of the individual and occur no matter who the partner is or they may be a function of some aspects of a particular relationship and occur only with a specific partner.

Inhibited sexual desire in either men or women was not regarded as a distinct problem or even named as a separate diagnosis until about ten years ago. This diagnosis now encompasses both lack of interest in and active aversion to sex. Low sexual desire is not always easy to define and cannot be judged merely by the frequency of sexual activity, which varies a great deal. (Mohr & Beutler, 1990).

In women, inhibited sexual excitement means insufficient lubrication of the vagina to allow entry of the penis. Inhibited excitement or arousal in men means failure to attain or hold an erection sufficiently to complete coitus (sexual intercourse). It may be either primary (that is, the man has never been able to sustain an erection long enough for coitus) or secondary (the man has been able to complete intercourse successfully in the past). The former is rare, the latter common. About one-eighth of men fail to retain an erection long enough to permit entry into the vagina and ejaculation at least a quarter of the time, and the proportion rises with age. Erectile dysfunction is the main problem of more than half of men who request treatment for sexual disorders (Sadock, 1989).

One technique that is used in evaluating a man's capacity to have an erection is measurement of changes in penis size during sleep, or **nocturnal penile tumescence (NPT).** Erection normally occurs during rapid eye movement (REM) sleep—the period of sleep associated with dreaming and indicated by the rapid darting of the eyeballs beneath the closed lids. Researchers have developed physiological recording instruments to measure NPT (Meisler & Carey, 1990). A fairly reliable test for nocturnal erections is the use of a snap gauge—a device that springs open when the penis enlarges. There are also several techniques for measuring blood flow and blood pressure in the penis. If the man experiences NPT, the cause of the erectile problem is likely to be psychological rather than physiological.

Anxiety stemming from personal conflict or from concern over a physical problem is often an important psychological factor in erectile dysfunction. Physical causes include early undiagnosed diabetes, hormonal imbalances, and the use of narcotics and alcohol. In the past, hidden psychopathology or psychodynamic conflicts was believed to be the main psychological cause of this type of sexual dysfunction. More recently, however, recognition has been given to **performance anxiety,** in which a man's preoccupation with sexual adequacy interferes with his performance. One 34-year-old man's comment is typical.

After awhile, the problem becomes so predictable that you start to make excuses in advance. It's as though you lose any chance of having sexual pleasure because you become preoccupied with the notion of failure. And that failure hits you right in the gut—you don't feel like much of a man.

—Masters and others, 1985, p. 502

Figure 8–4 illustrates the many sources of stress that may interact with biological vulnerabilities to result in problems of sexual performance for men.

Both males and females may experience problems in the orgasm phase of the sexual-response cycle. In the male, these take the form of premature ejaculation or

FIGURE 8–4 A variety of types of stress both remote and immediate can contribute to sexual dysfunction in men.
(Cole, 1985, p. 341. Reprinted with permission of the *British Journal of Psychiatry*)

delayed or absent ejaculation. In the female, they take the form of a delay or absence of orgasm after a normal excitement phase. **Premature ejaculation,** in which the man is unable to inhibit ejaculation long enough for his female partner to experience orgasm through intercourse, is probably the most common type of male sexual dysfunction. The man's failure to control his orgasm often results in his feeling sexually inadequate. According to one viewpoint, the male experiences anxiety as he reaches high levels of erotic arousal, and the anxiety triggers the involuntary orgasm.

In **retarded ejaculation,** on the other hand, the ejaculatory response is inhibited. Men with this problem respond to sexual stimuli with erotic feelings and a firm erection, but they are unable to ejaculate. In severe cases, the male may prolong intercourse for a long time, engage in fantasy, and drink alcohol, all to no avail. Although physical injuries may be responsible for the problem in some cases, a variety of psychological factors that contribute to the occurrence of retarded ejaculation include ambivalence toward the sexual partner, strongly suppressed anger, and a religious upbringing that engenders sexual guilt.

The chief disorder of the orgasm phase in females is **anorgasmia**—inability to achieve orgasm after normal excitement either through masturbation or coitus. About five to ten percent of women suffer from primary anorgasmia; they have never been able to achieve orgasm. Secondary anorgasmia is the main problem for the vast majority of women who come to clinics for the treatment of sexual disorders. Some women with anorgasmia have few other symptoms; others suffer from inhibited excitement, tension, irritability, and physical symptoms during sexual activity.

Psychological and situational factors can be an important cause of inhibited female orgasm. Psychological factors include unresolved conflicts over sexual activity and disturbances in the relationship between the partners. In many cases, however, the explanation is simpler: Inadequate stimulation during lovemaking can damage a woman's ability to become sexually responsive. In such cases, the therapist attempts to sensitize both partners to each other's sexual needs, explaining, for example, that a woman is more difficult to arouse than a man. Some women are unable to experience an orgasm without manual stimulation of the clitoris, which has a larger number of sensitive nerve endings than the vagina. This may represent a normal variation in sexual response. Most women do not have an orgasm each time they have intercourse, and about 15 percent of women never have orgasms (Cole, 1985). Anorgasmia can decrease a woman's overall sexual responsiveness as well as lead to depression and a decreased sense of self-esteem. As one 19-year-old college student said,

There's so much talk about orgasms that I've been wondering what's wrong with me, that I don't have them. I used to enjoy sex a lot, but lately it's a bad scene because I just get reminded of problems.

—Masters and others, 1988, p. 506

Other problems can also occur that often make sexual intercourse difficult. Both men and women may experience **dyspareunia,** a recurrent or persistent genital pain that occurs before, during, or after intercourse. Women also may be affected by **vaginismus.** This disorder makes intercourse difficult or impossible because of involuntary spasms of the outer portion of the vagina.

Because many cases never come to a clinician's attention, no one knows how prevalent sexual dysfunction is. In a study of 100 couples who had not sought sex therapy, 60 percent of the women reported difficulties in reaching orgasm, and 40 percent of the men reported problems with erection or ejaculation (Frank and others, 1978). Most of these couples described their marriages as at least moderately satisfying.

Treatment of Sexual Dysfunction

The decision to request help for a sexual disorder is difficult for most people, and the attitude of the person who hears the complaint is important. Whether a sexual problem is ultimately mentioned at all and the vagueness of the problem presented often depend on whether the therapist seems to have some knowledge of the sexual problems and can discuss them without embarrassment. Once the client has indicated that the problem involves sexual activity it is important for the interviewer to get detailed information about the patient's medical history and physical symptoms as well as family background, early sexual development, work history, and use of drugs and alcohol. For some disorders both a physical examination and a psychological evaluation are necessary. The therapist should have a clear and detailed idea of the patient's physical acts, emotional responses, fantasies during sex, and expectations. Figure 8–5 suggests that the man's expectations do not mesh with the experience of his sexual partner.

Usually sex therapy is requested by a couple. It is important to know how the partners feel about each other apart from the sexual relationship, how the relationship has changed (sexually or otherwise), how well they communicate, whether one partner is more interested in sex than the other, and which one is more

FIGURE 8–5

(Playboy, February 1979. Reproduced by special permission of Playboy Magazine; Copyright © 1979 by Playboy)

"Multiple? Are you kidding? It wasn't even fractional!"

eager for treatment. The therapist must see each partner separately in case there are subjects they do not want to discuss in each other's presence, such as fantasies, masturbation, infidelity, or feelings about their partner's sexual attractiveness.

In addition to dealing with factors specific to a given case, sex therapists have three general goals for the couple:

1. to engender an atmosphere of mutual communication;

2. to decrease the fear of failure;

3. to shift attention away from the fear of failure to the experience of sensory pleasure.

THE MASTERS AND JOHNSON APPROACH Over a ten-year period the research team of William Masters, a gynecologist, and Virginia Johnson, a behavioral scientist, studied the sexual responses of 694 men and women under controlled laboratory conditions. Masters and Johnson's studies (1966, 1970) have been largely responsible for giving the laboratory study of human sexual behavior and the treatment of sexual dysfunctions scientific credibility and respectability.

Since the publication of Masters and Johnson's first two books in 1966 and 1970, sex therapy has emerged as a discipline in its own right. While they recognize that many sexually dysfunctional people are dysfunctional in other areas of their personal and social lives, Masters and Johnson believe that short-term treatment directed primarily at sexual problems can help most people who experience such dysfunctions. They have observed that becoming sexually functional has a positive influence on a person's anxiety level as well as on his or her self-esteem. A man who is anxious but has a good sex life is probably happier than a man who has to deal with a sex problem in addition to anxiety.

Masters and Johnson emphasize the treatment of couples, not just the person who seems to have a problem. This does not mean that the partner is seen as the cause of the difficulty, but rather that both members of the relationship are affected by the problem. The Masters and Johnson approach uses a man and a woman working together as therapists. The therapy program is intensive and takes place daily over a two-week period. It emphasizes instruction in the sexual needs of both partners, together with exercises in erotic stimulation. Specific homework assignments are given that are designed to help couples become more aware of their own sexual sensations. The therapy procedure includes basic information about the sexual organs and the physiology of the sexual response for clients who lack this information (most of the people who come for treatment, in fact). The presentation of this basic information often has important therapeutic benefits in itself.

Emphasis is also placed on communication, nonverbal as well as verbal, between partners. Because couples who seek treatment typically place lovemaking exclusively under the man's control, sexual intercourse may be attempted only when he indicates that he is interested. The belief of many women that they will be rejected if they are sexually assertive continues to be widespread. In many cases of sexual dysfunction, the most effective treatment may not be complex physical or psychotherapeutic tactics, but simply providing information about sexual relationships and encouraging meaningful communication between sex partners.

Sensate focus is probably the best known of Masters and Johnson's sexual-retraining techniques. The rationale behind sensate focus is that sexually dysfunctional couples have lost the ability to think and feel in a sensual way because of the various stresses and pressures they associate with intercourse. They therefore have to be reacquainted with the pleasures of tactile contact. Each partner learns not only that being touched is pleasurable, but that exploring and caressing the partner's body can be exciting and stimulating in itself. The couple is encouraged to engage in sensate focus under conditions that are dissimilar to those associated with the anxieties, frustrations, and resentments of their former lovemaking. Intercourse is prohibited throughout the early stages of treatment because that simple requirement can reduce tension in both sexual and nonsexual areas of the relationship. Masters and Johnson thought this ban on intercourse made sensate focus particularly effective in treating performance anxiety. However, other therapists have suggested that a deemphasis rather than a ban is more helpful to couples (Lipsius, 1987).

The couples technique of therapy is especially appropriate in treating premature ejaculation, since this is often more upsetting to the woman than to the man. If premature ejaculation is the problem, the therapists often introduce a method known as the "squeeze technique" that helps recondition the ejaculatory reflex. The woman is taught to apply a firm, grasping pressure on the penis several times during the beginning stages of intercourse. This technique reduces the urgency of the need to ejaculate.

When the couple's problem is related to an orgasmic dysfunction in the woman, the treatment includes an exploratory discussion to identify attitudes that may be related to the woman's inability to attain orgasm. Then the couple is given a series of graduated homework assignments. If the woman is willing, she begins by exploring her own bodily sensations, stimulating herself by masturbating. As she becomes more comfortable with this technique, her partner begins to participate in the sessions through kissing and tactile stimulation. The importance of the woman's clear and assertive communication of her reactions and desires to her partner is strongly emphasized.

Masters and Johnson have reported very low failure rates of their treatment programs for both heterosexual and homosexual couples. However, their findings have been criticized, primarily because their reports are not completely clear on such topics as who is selected and who is rejected for the program and how success and failure are defined (Cole, 1985). Nevertheless, their techniques are far superior to earlier methods of treating sexual disorders.

THE BEHAVIORAL APPROACH Looked at from a behavioral perspective, the Masters and Johnson technique of sensate focus is reminiscent of systematic desensitization in that it leads to the substitution of a pleasurable response for anxiety. Sex therapists often create a sort of hierarchy in which certain parts of the body initially are designated as "out of bounds" and then are gradually included as progress is made. Although orthodox systematic desensitization can be used to eliminate specific anxieties (such as feeling uncomfortable while looking at a man's genitals), the more global sensate focus appears to be appropriate in dealing with the various diffuse anxieties experienced by sexually dysfunctional individuals.

The methods used by Masters and Johnson have been further refined by many behaviorally oriented therapists. For instance, relaxation and modeling may be combined in treating dysfunctional women whose major problem is sexual anxiety. Another behavioral approach to the treatment of interpersonal problems related to sexual performance is described in the following case. Notice the importance of cognitive elements in this treatment plan.

The client was a 24-year-old lawyer who after six months of marriage was upset by his frequent inability to obtain or retain an erection. His history suggested that his mother had been a dominating woman of whom he was fearful and that he was also unwilling to challenge or criticize his wife in any way even though he often felt considerable resentment toward her. He seemed to feel that expressing his feelings was not manly. After several therapeutic sessions directed at his irrational attitudes, he and the therapist composed a carefully worded speech for the client to deliver to his wife.

"Grace, I have something very important and very serious to discuss with you. It concerns you, me, our marriage, and life in general. I want you to please hear me out without interrupting me. . . . I was raised by my mother to bottle up my feelings, especially in relation to women. In thinking over this attitude, I now realize that this is crazy and even dishonest. I feel, for instance, that if I resent the fact that you turn to your father for advice in matters about which I have more knowledge than he, I ought to express my resentment instead of hiding it from you. I feel that when you order me about and treat me like a child, I ought to tell you how I really feel about it instead of acting like an obedient puppy dog. And most important of all, when you go ahead and make plans for me without consulting me, and especially when you yell at me in front of your parents, maybe I should quit acting as if I didn't mind and let you know how strongly I really react inside. What I am getting at is simply that in spite of my love and affection for you, I would really rather be unmarried than be a henpecked husband like my father."

This little monologue was rehearsed several times during a one-hour session until playbacks on a tape recorder convinced the therapist that the client was ready to confront his wife and that he would do so in a forthright and sincere manner. Rehearsal techniques were used in preparing the patient to cope with tears, interruptions, denials, counterallegations, etc. His assignment was then put into effect. The patient reported that his wife "heard me out without interruption. . . . [She] seemed a little upset, but agreed that I should not withhold or conceal my feelings. I felt incredibly close to her and that night we had very good sex."

—Lazarus, 1971, pp. 156–157

Researchers are paying increasing attention to both the cognitive and fantasy underpinnings of sexual behavior. Sexual fantasies can occur while daydreaming or during masturbation or sexual intercourse (see Figure 8–6). It is now recognized that being aroused by a given fantasy (for example, linking sex to physical violence or an exotic locale or someone other than one's partner) is not necessarily a sign of maladaptation (Meuwissen & Over, 1991). Fantasies can be a means of self-stimulation that heighten the experience of sex with another person. Among the most common sex fantasies are thinking of an imaginary lover, imagining being overpowered or forced to surrender, pretending to engage in a sex act that is usually regarded as repugnant, and reliving a previous sexual experience. Analyzing the emotional meanings of sexual fantasies and how the fantasies become linked to behavior is a challenge being taken up by researchers. Fantasy can be a useful technique for some individuals with sexual dysfunctions. They may be able to utilize it to heighten their level of arousal during sexual activity.

THE KAPLAN APPROACH Some therapists believe that behavioral methods are useful for many sexual problems, but that other problems require a combination of behavioral approaches with psychodynamically oriented therapy for one or both partners. One of the foremost proponents of this view is Helen Singer Kaplan (1974, 1979). Kaplan, a psychoanalyst, believes that standard sex therapy methods are effective when sexual problems are based on mild and easily diminished anxieties and conflicts. However, there are many individuals whose symptoms are rooted in more profound conflicts. Kaplan thinks that this is especially true in the

cases of men and women who lack sexual desire and men who have difficulty maintaining an erection. For these problems, Kaplan and her coworkers have developed a lengthy and individualized treatment program that involves traditional sex therapy and psychodynamically oriented sessions, sometimes with one of the clients and sometimes with both partners. The case of Sam and Susie illustrates Kaplan's approach.

Susie, 28, and Sam, 30, had been married four years and have 3-year-old twin sons. The chief complaint was Susie's lack of desire. The couple had a good relationship, each felt in love with the other and they were judged to be good parents. During their marriage they had had intercourse only three times. During the last two years they had had no physical contact because any attempt by Sam to hold or kiss Susie resulted in "hysterics," that is, she had an anxiety attack. The couple were referred to Kaplan after nine months of weekly sessions at a sex therapy clinic had not produced improvement.

The ordinary sensate focusing or pleasuring activities threw Susie into an anxiety state. In addition, when there was any improvement Susie would effectively resist or sabotage the treatment by trying to do too much. For example, if the assignment were to lie next to Sam in bed and hold his hand, she might try to have him caress her breast as well. This would then precipitate her

FIGURE 8–6 This eighteenth-century block print by Harunobu shows a young girl fantasizing about her lover while she masturbates.

(Harunobu, *A Fantasy* (late 1760s): Trustees of the British Museum)

anxious feelings. The therapist discussed this behavior with Susie and gave her the job of controlling the progress of desensitizing her anxiety. She was to select only tasks that were within her comfort-zone, that is, those that produced only tolerable anxiety.

Susie also had a more general problem with fun and pleasure. Whenever she allowed herself to experience them, she developed sharp headaches. As the desensitizing of her phobic avoidance of sexual contact progressed, Susie had a series of dreams about "dead relatives buried in the basement that needed to be removed." A central threatening figure was her deceased father. After discussions with the therapist about Oedipal feelings toward her father and the transfer of some of these feelings to her husband, Susie's father disappeared from her dreams.

After further sessions along with her husband that focused on guilt over pleasure, Susie's pleasure anxiety had decreased, her relationship with her husband was more open, and the couple was having satisfying intercourse at least once per week.

—Adapted from Kaplan, 1979, pp. 73–75

The Effectiveness of Sex Therapy

Great variations in the success rate for sex therapy have been reported by researchers (Cole, 1985). Successes reported range from 39 to 98 percent. Part of the problem in assessing effectiveness is that the measurement of success is often poorly defined in the research and few follow-up studies are reported so long-term changes are unknown. The particular treatment approach used does not seem to affect the success rate. One study compared Masters and Johnson's technique, with both a modified technique using only one therapist, and a technique that combined efforts to improve communication with behavioral methods such as relaxation training and contracts (Crowe and others, 1981). All three approaches led to improvement lasting at least one year for couples with problems of erectile dysfunction, anorgasmia, and loss of sexual interest. There was no difference in effectiveness among the various therapies.

Findings like these suggest that research is needed to determine which therapeutic elements are actually helpful and which elements are unnecessary. For instance, decreasing anxiety about sexual performance has been a focus of many approaches to sex therapy. However, anxiety is a complex construct that has behavioral, cognitive, and physiological aspects. The heightened physiological response that is part of anxiety has been shown to increase, not decrease, sexual response (Beck & Barlow, 1984). However, the cognitive aspects—for instance, interfering thoughts and problems of focusing attention—have a negative effect on arousal. Such thoughts may increase because of the demand for performance when the partner is clearly aroused. These findings suggest that attempts to decrease the physiological aspects of anxiety may be ineffective or even counterproductive whereas practice in screening out distracting thoughts might be most helpful.

If sex therapy is unsuccessful, its effects and the feelings it arouses may provide new insight for both the patient and the therapist. Some patients find the exercises mechanical or boring; this reaction may indicate hostility toward the partner, fear of rejection, or even performance anxiety about touching and caressing. Some people feel guilty about their own fantasies or are jealous of their partner's fantasies. The partner may sabotage the therapy by a critical attitude, detachment, or loss of interest. A common source of sexual problems is the relationship between the partners. Sometimes they have greatly differing expectations of the marriage or love affair. They may be chronically angry at each other or engaged in a power struggle. Sometimes both partners are unsure about how close they want to be, but this ambivalence takes a peculiar form in which one demands sexual intimacy and the other retreats. The recommended treatment for such problems is psychotherapy. What kind depends more on the therapist and patient than on the specific sexual disorder.

Gender Identity Disorder

Gender identity, a basic feature of personality, refers to an individual's feeling of being male or female. Children become aware that they are male or female at an early age, and once formed, their gender identity is highly resistant to change. Gender identity is different from sexual preference. Sexual preference refers to whether a person desires a sexual partner of the same or the opposite sex; it does not refer to the person's sexual self-concept.

Childhood Problems of Gender Identity

In **gender identity disorder of childhood,** children who have not yet reached puberty may show considerable distress at being male or female and will express intense desires to be of the opposite sex. For

instance a girl may vehemently state her desire to be a boy or even insist that she is a boy. She may refuse to wear ordinary feminine clothing and insist on wearing the clothing typical of males including boys' underwear and other accessories. She may also deny her gender by such behaviors as refusing to urinate while in a sitting position or by the insistence that she either already has or will grow a penis. Boys show the same types of behavior in reverse. In addition to playing with girls' toys and wanting to dress as a girl, a boy may say that he wants to be a woman when he grows up and that his penis and testes are disgusting or that they will disappear as he grows older (Bradley & Zucker, 1990).

Problems that may relate to gender identity come to clinical attention when parents become concerned because their child's behavior and social relationships are not like those of other children of the same sex and age. For instance, this mother is worried that her son is and will continue to be sexually abnormal.

My boy is showing feminine tendencies and has ever since he was two years old. It started out real cute. His sister had dress-up clothes at her grandparents', and when he got to be about two years old, he'd dress up in these clothes and hats and high heels, and he was just real cute. We thought it was something he'd pass. Now he will be eleven years old this month, and he does this in secret. I just felt like now was the time to investigate it.

—Green, 1974, p. xxi

If a young child's behavior is typical of that of children of the opposite sex, it does not always mean that the child has a gender identity problem. Often parents are not aware of how much their own behavior contributes to the behavior of their children. The mother quoted earlier may have encouraged her son to dress in women's clothes by telling him how cute he was then, and at no other time. When this is the case, counseling may be helpful. Parents can be trained to reinforce sex-appropriate behavior in the home—for example, by giving the child special attention or a material reinforcer when he or she is behaving appropriately. This approach has been found to be effective in helping children acquire new sex roles (Rekers, 1977).

Despite advances in the study of sexual practices, questions frequently arise as to how maladaptive a certain type of behavior is. Children who act out inappropriate sex roles early in their development may drop this behavior as they get older. The five-year-old tomboy or

sissy may simply be going through a phase. However, children who dress in the clothes of the opposite sex and whose play follows the patterns of the other sex, have an increased likelihood of developing a homosexual orientation in adulthood (Money, 1987). A longitudinal study compared boys with extremely feminine interests and behavior in childhood with boys in a control group (Green, 1987). Eleven years later 75 percent of the previously feminine boys were either bisexual or homosexual in fantasy and/or behavior. All but one of the boys in the control group were heterosexual.

Gender Identity Disorder in Adults

Gender identity disorders in adults can take two forms: **transsexualism** and **nontranssexual gender identity disorder.** Transsexuals experience an intense desire and need to change their sexual status, including their anatomical structure. In contrast, although adults with nontranssexual gender-identity disorder feel a discomfort and inappropriateness about their assigned sex and often cross-dress, they are not preoccupied with getting rid of their primary and secondary sexual characteristics and acquiring those of the other sex.

Although the number of cases of transsexualism is very small (according to one estimate, only 1 per 100,000 people for females and 1 per 30,000 for males), the behavior has aroused a great deal of curiosity. Scientific interest in transsexualism derives mainly from the light that such cases may shed on the general nature and development of gender identity. When a child's strong desire to be a member of the opposite sex continues into adulthood, transsexualism may result. The problem begins to surface at puberty, when maturational changes in the body emphasize biological gender. In the follow-up study of feminine boys described in the last section (Green, 1987), one boy seemed to have transsexual feelings. Though clinicians agree on the value of studying the lives of transsexuals, the use of medical techniques to bring about bodily changes that conform to the transsexual's gender identity remains controversial.

Changing a male transsexual into a female involves administering female hormones to reduce hair growth and stimulate development of the breasts, removing the male genitals, and creating an artificial vagina. Changing a female into a sexually functioning male is more difficult because the artificially constructed penis cannot become erect by natural means or feel tactile stimulation. An inflation device is sometimes implanted in the penis to make artificial erection possible. The long-term success of this method, however, is still in doubt.

Many of the candidates who apply to clinics for what is called sexual-reassignment surgery show considerable psychological disturbance. In one group of pa-

tients who applied to a university gender identity clinic, 92 percent of the males and 60 percent of the females showed other psychological disturbances in addition to problems with sexual identity (Levine, 1980). For this reason, clinicians stress the need to assess each candidate carefully before deciding whether to carry out the medical steps needed for a sex change. After people who are emotionally stable and likely to adjust well to surgery are selected, most reputable centers still require a number of preliminary steps before the surgery is carried out. This degree of caution is needed because the surgical procedures are irreversible.

After patients have been selected, they usually are required to spend one or two years prior to the surgery

BOX 8-1 The Stories of Two Transsexuals

Jan Morris

Several transsexuals have written about their experiences. One is Jan Morris, whose autobiography is entitled *Conundrum* (1974). James Humphrey Morris was a highly regarded English foreign correspondent. At age 17 he had been an officer in one of Britain's crack cavalry regiments. As a correspondent for *The Times* of London, he covered the successful attempt by Hilary and Tenzing to climb Mount Everest. He covered wars and rebellions the world over and also wrote fifteen books on history and travel. Then James became Jan. Jan Morris refers to her former self as a woman trapped in a man's body.

At age 3 or 4 James Morris realized that he was a girl who had been born into the wrong body. As an adult he enjoyed the company of women but did not desire to sleep with them. He married at 22, and he and his wife had five children. As middle age neared, he became depressed, had suicidal thoughts, and finally sought a transsexual change. Hormones were used to enlarge his breasts and soften his body to more feminine lines. After surgery to complete the process begun by the hormone pills, Morris divorced his wife. Jan Morris reports that she feels like the person she always wanted to be. (See Figure 8–7a–c.) She says the children of her former marriage treat her as an aunt.

FIGURE 8–7 (a) James Morris in 1964. (b) Jan Morris in 1977. (c) A note written by Morris to the authors.

(a)

(b)

Fancy putting me in a book of Hormonal Psychology — nobody could be much more Normal, psychologically speaking — or better Adapted, either! Let's meet some time, & you can judge for yourself!

Jan Morris

(c)

Susan Cannon

Not all sex-reassignment surgery is as successful as that of Jan Morris. Some time ago the Princeton alumni weekly carried a memorial notice that included the following description.

He was a courtly southern gentleman. He was soft-spoken and intelligent, one of the few authentic geniuses in our class. He was to many of us a drinking companion, a sympathetic listener, a friend.

Professionally, he did well. He had a severe stuttering problem, so he became a world-class debater at Princeton. He earned a physics degree.

living in the community as a member of the opposite sex. During this period hormone injections are used to alter secondary sex characteristics such as breast size or muscle definition. This period serves as psychological preparation for life as a member of the other sex and also provides a realistic experience of what that life may be like. Psychotherapy is also often required during the presurgical period. Sometimes clients have what might be called "magical" hopes regarding the surgery. The psychotherapeutic sessions can give them a chance to look at their underlying feelings and perhaps become more comfortable as hetero- or homosexuals.

What happens to those who undergo the surgery? Box 8–1 describes two different outcomes. In general,

Don Hegstrom, a former graduate and lifelong friend, convinced him that physics, in his context, was dull and he should maybe go for his Ph.D. in the history of science at Harvard. He did.

Walter was a scholar, and a certified intellectual (a label he wore with modesty and grace), a voracious reader, a creative thinker, a historian of national note, a teacher, a poet, an author, an editor ("The Smithsonian Journal of History"), and a curator of the Smithsonian Institution.

Walter Faw Cannon was also Susan Faye Cannon, a fact that she did not recognize until several years ago. Several years ago, Walter publicly proclaimed that he was a female in a male body. And just last year, he had a surgical sex change against the advice of his doctors. Three months before she died, she called and told a classmate that it had been demonstrated conclusively that genetically she had always been a woman. She was very glad, because she had always suspected it and, in more recent years, known it to be a fact.

—*Princeton Alumni Weekly*, April 5, 1982

Cannon began discovering his female identity during his undergraduate days at Princeton and during his stint in the U.S. Navy. At the age of 51 Cannon applied to Superior Court in the District of Columbia to change his first name to Faye, his mother's family name, and during the same period he began dressing as a woman. In an interview with the *Washington Post*,

(d) (e)

FIGURE 8–7 *(continued) (d)* Walter Cannon before he began receiving hormone treatments. *(e)* Walter Cannon after receiving hormone treatments and shortly before his sex-reassignment surgery.

Cannon described his situation. "I don't classify myself as gay, because I don't know what the word means. I define myself as a male woman. Then I know what the words mean" (Levey, 1977, C1).

Cannon's behavior created problems for him in his job at the Smithsonian. In spite of his reputation as a scholar he received a disability retirement in 1979. At the age of 55 he decided to undergo sex-reassignment surgery (see Figure 8–7d and e). Cannon had been a heavy user of painkillers before the surgery because of an arthritic problem. After

surgery, her use of these drugs escalated because of the extreme postsurgical pain. In 1981, Susan Cannon was found dead of acute codeine intoxication. It was not clear whether her death was a result of an accidental overdose.

These two cases involving well-educated, successful men who decided in midlife to reconcile their physical appearance with their sexual identification show how hard it is to generalize about the desirability of surgical sex reassignment even for those who clearly seem to be among the small group of true transsexuals.

however, the results have been disappointing. During the 1980s several prominent medical centers stopped doing transsexual surgery because the benefits were doubtful. In a long-term follow-up in male-to-female transsexuals, only one-third were judged to have a fair or good sexual adjustment (Lindemalm and others, 1986). More than half of the patients were unchanged in social adjustment. Almost one-third considered their sex-reassignment surgery to have been a mistake.

Transsexualism is a prime example of the interactional point of view. Sex is a matter of anatomy and physiology, but gender identity is strongly influenced by psychological, social, and cultural factors. It is likely that there may be a small group of transsexuals for whom sexual-reassignment therapy is an effective treatment. For many more, who are likely to have significant personality problems and other psychopathology, the surgery does not provide an answer to their mental health problems; instead, the problems may worsen. Some individuals become deeply depressed after surgery, while others have transient psychotic episodes.

Nontranssexual gender-identity disorder also produces discomfort about one's assigned sex. However, people with this disorder lack the preoccupation for acquiring the sexual organs and other physical characteristics of the opposite sex that is characteristic of transsexuals. Instead they focus on fantasizing that they are of the opposite sex or actually acting out that role through cross-dressing. This cross-dressing differs from that of transvestites, discussed later. Although transvestites obtain sexual gratification from cross-dressing they are not dissatisfied with their biological sex. They wish to remain male but become sexually excited by wearing women's clothes.

The Paraphilias

Not everyone is sexually excited by the same stimuli. Some individuals can gain sexual gratification only from particular objects or situations. Most of these sexual behaviors are tolerated by society if they are practiced in private or with consenting adult partners. The behaviors are likely to cause problems only if others are harmed or if social customs are openly flouted. DSM classifies these disorders as subcategories of **paraphilia,** which means attraction to the deviant. There are three general classes of paraphilias:

1. preference for the use of a nonhuman object for sexual arousal;
2. repetitive sexual activity with humans that involves real or simulated suffering or humiliation;
3. repetitive sexual activity with nonconsenting partners.

Fetishism

Fetishism, a psychological state in which a nonliving object (fetish) serves as a primary source of sexual arousal and consummation, is an example of a sexual deviation that is not usually addressed by the law. Most fetishists are solitary in their activities, although in some cases they commit crimes to acquire their favorite fetishes (often undergarments, boots, or shoes). Fetishists are almost always male, and the fetish varies widely from the clearly erotic (such as an article of women's underwear, especially underwear that has been worn, stained, and not yet laundered) to objects with little apparent connection with sexuality. Fetishism often begins in adolescence.

Rubber fetishes are particularly popular. In England the Mackintosh Society, named for rubberized raincoats, provides reassurance for individuals who feel embarrassed or isolated by their sexual interests. Some rubber fetishists derive sexual excitement merely from wearing rubber garments. Others dress in them or want their partner to wear them during sexual activity because the garments are necessary for them to become sexually aroused. One rubber fetishist describes the role played by rubber boots in his sexual behavior.

I always seem to have been fascinated by rubber boots. I cannot say exactly when the fascination first started, but I must have been very young. Their spell is almost hypnotic and should I see someone walking along with rubber boots, I become very excited and may follow the person for a great distance. I quickly get an erection under such circumstances and I might easily ejaculate. I often will take the boots to bed with me, caress them, kiss them, and ejaculate into them.

—Epstein, 1965, pp. 515–516

Fetishism is one of the most puzzling of all forms of sexual behavior. It is chronic, and in some cases the collection of fetishistic objects is the main activity in the individual's life. No one has been able to explain adequately fetishists' sexual attachment to diverse objects. Although theories range from those that stress unconscious motivation to those that hypothesize impaired neural mechanisms such as are found among epileptics,

the causes of this unusual type of sexual behavior remain shrouded in mystery (Wise, 1985).

Fetishists do not often seek therapy. In one large London hospital only 60 cases were diagnosed in a 20-year period (Chalkley & Powell, 1983). Of these, about 30 percent were referred by the courts, mainly because of their theft of fetishistic objects (see Figure 8–8). About a third of the patients came for treatment because of anxiety about their fetishistic behavior. About 20 percent came for other reasons and the fetish was identified only after they had begun treatment. Treatment based on learning principles has been applied to fetishism with some success. In aversion therapy, for example, the fetish object is paired, either actually or in fantasy, with an unpleasant stimulus such as electric shock or a sense of overwhelming embarrassment.

Transvestism

A transvestite uses clothing as a sexual stimulant or fetish. **Transvestism** literally means "cross-dressing" (see Figure 8–9). Women are not usually considered to be transvestites, probably because our society allows them to dress in most masculine styles. References to cross-dressing can be found throughout history. King Henry III of France cross-dressed publicly and wished to be addressed and treated as a woman. Joan of Arc wore her hair short and preferred to dress as a man. Most transvestites are heterosexual men who dress in women's clothes, often starting in adolescence. When not cross-dressed, the transvestite usually exhibits masculine behavior and interests.

FIGURE 8–8 The Seattle "shoe bandit" attacked women on the street and stole a single shoe from each. Here some of the shoes found in his apartment are surveyed by police.

FIGURE 8–9 Male transvestites gain sexual gratification from playing a female role but continue to identify themselves as males. (a) "Pete" in his everyday attire. (b) "Pete" in his role as a woman.

(a)

(b)

Although some clinicians have contended that transvestism and transsexualism are basically similar, there are a number of differences between these two conditions (Docter, 1988). Transsexuals desire to change their genitals and live as members of the opposite sex. They do not experience sexual arousal when cross-dressing. Transvestites, on the other hand, become sexually aroused when cross-dressing but continue to identify themselves as members of their biological sex.

A male transvestite gave this explanation for his behavior in a letter to his wife.

The personal masculine attributes that first attracted you to me are, as you know, an integral part of my personality, just as my transvestism is. It has always been a part of me. . . . We are only make-believe girls, and we know always that we are really men, so don't worry that we are ever dissatisfied with manhood, or want to change forever into a woman. When we are dressed in feminine clothes and attain as close a resemblance as possible to a real girl, we do certainly pretend that we are girls for that short time, but it is a pretense and definitely not a reality.

—Prince, 1967, pp. 80–81

An unusual study some years ago of a nationwide sample of transvestites provided comprehensive descriptions of their behavior and attitudes (Bentler & Prince, 1969, 1970). Compared with a nontransvestite group, the transvestites were more inhibited in their interpersonal relationships, less involved with other individuals, and more independent. In general, they gave evidence of being less able to seek sympathy, love, and help from others and seemed to be happier when they felt no obligations to others. However, in many areas of personality they did not differ significantly from nontransvestites.

Psychologists have emphasized several perspectives—psychodynamic processes, conditioning, and biological predisposition—in discussing transvestism. Many clinicians believe that transvestism develops in the context of disturbed parent–child relationships. Others see it as a product of aberrant psychosexual development. Behaviorists see it as a conditioned response that is susceptible to aversion therapy in which dressing in women's clothing is paired with an aversive stimulus. Behavioral training aimed at fostering confidence and adequacy in playing a conventional sex role has also been suggested.

Covert sensitization seems to be particularly useful in treating transvestism and other paraphilias. In this procedure clients are first asked to imagine as vividly as possible the sexually arousing behavior that they are trying to eradicate, and to follow these thoughts with equally vivid aversion imagery (for example, being discovered and embarrassed). This approach was used for a 31-year-old transvestite, a married police officer who sought help for uncontrollable urges to dress in women's clothing and appear in public. The client had a 16-year history of transvestism that had earlier resulted in his discharge from the Marine Corps. His wife had threatened to divorce him because of his cross-dressing. In treatment, he was asked to form images of deviant sexual scenes as well as aversive images of their undesirable consequences. The following is an example of the material used in the covert sensitization for this case.

You are in your house alone, and you are feeling lonely. You get the urge to put on the clothing, so you enter the bedroom and open the closet. You begin to get aroused as you decide what to wear. As you put on the clothing, you can see the colors and feel the clothing on your hands. You really are turned on as you put on the bra, panties, nylons, wig. You feel like playing with yourself as you apply your makeup, but you can't wait to go out. As you leave the house, you get very excited. You are touching your penis through the panties as you're driving.

And then you hear sirens! The police pull you over, and it's your fellow policemen. They start to laugh and call for other police cars. A crowd is gathering, and they know you're a man. The officers throw you around and take you to the station. The women are disgusted, and the chief will take your gun and badge. You are humiliated, and they call you "sick." Your kids are crying as they return from school because others tease them about having a perverted father. Look what you've done to yourself!

—Brownell and others, 1977, pp. 1146–1147

Covert sensitization has been quite successful in treating transvestism. Figure 8–10 shows the average percentages of full erection (measured by penis circumference) during a baseline period, during covert sensitization, and upon follow-up. The figure also shows self-reported changes in sexual arousal to transvestite stimuli. Both the physiological and self-report measures revealed a sizable decrease in sexual arousal. In addition, physiological and self-reported arousal in response to heterosexual stimuli increased. The client, who had received prior treatment for his sexual difficulties, was surprised at the effectiveness of the covert sensitization.

For some transvestites, it is not the clothes themselves that are exciting, but rather the ability to fool the

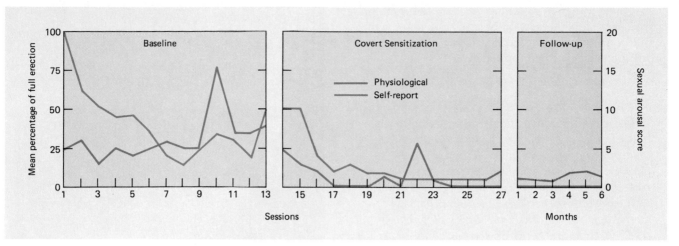

FIGURE 8–10 Mean percentages of full erection and sexual arousal scores (based on actual measurements and self-reports) for a transvestite man during baseline, treatment (covert sensitization), and follow-up periods.

(Adapted from Brownell, Hayes, and Barlow, 1977. Copyright © 1977 by the American Psychological Association. Adapted by permission of the authors.)

public and be taken for a woman. One transvestite was asked if he would feel happier if social custom allowed people to dress as they wished in public.

"Heavens, no," he smiled. "Merely to be allowed to wear women's clothes in public is nothing. It is the challenge of being so much like a woman that no one knows I'm a man that turns me on. The combination of doing something that I want to, that everyone says is impossible and is forbidden anyway, produces in me an arousal which, because it is in a sexual context, becomes sexual arousal."

—Gosselin and Wilson, 1980, p. 67

Sexual Sadism and Masochism

For some people, inflicting or experiencing pain and indignity is linked to sexual gratification. Many people incorporate mildly painful acts—such as biting, nipping, and spanking—into their sexual practices. When both partners enjoy them, these activities can enhance sexual pleasure. However, sadists and masochists often go beyond mild pain and, moreover, cannot enjoy sex any other way. To the **sadist,** achieving orgasm depends on humiliating others or inflicting pain on them. This is often referred to as "discipline." To the **masochist,** sexual satisfaction depends on "bondage"—suffering, humiliation, pain, and ill treatment at the hands of others. Sadism and masochism occur in both heterosex-

ual and homosexual relationships, but, like other sexual deviations, they are poorly understood. Some clinical workers have conjectured that the roots of sadism and masochism are to be found in childhood; others have mentioned possible biological factors. One area that would seem to merit study is the fantasy life of these individuals; for example, the thoughts associated with their sexual activities.

The sexual masochist experiences arousal through his or her own suffering, preferably by being humiliated and beaten. Masochists have fantasies, often beginning in childhood, in which they are bound, tortured, raped, or otherwise abused in ways that they cannot prevent. These fantasies and acts are far more common in males than in females. Five features are found in most cases of sadomasochism: (1) agreement as to which partner is to be dominant and which one submissive; (2) awareness by both partners that they are role playing; (3) the consent of both participants; (4) a sexual context; and (5) a shared understanding by both participants that their behavior is sadomasochistic (Weinberg and others, 1984).

In sadomasochistic relationships the participants agree on the limits beforehand.

My wife and I do play dominance and submission games, and maybe we have the marks to prove it on occasion. But the one playing top dog watches like a hawk to make sure we stop when the other one doesn't like it any more.

—Gosselin & Wilson, 1980, p. 69

Often a signal is set up so that the submissive partner can stop the session at any time if the agreed-upon boundaries are exceeded. One sadomasochistic prostitute explained her approach.

When you have a new client, what I used to do was I used to sit down and I would talk to them first and find out exactly what they wanted. Because sometimes you can get into a session with somebody and get very brutal and that's not what they want. There's heavy dominance and there's light dominance and there's play acting, roles, all different kinds. So the best thing to do is to sit down and talk to somebody first, initially.

—Weinberg, 1978, p. 290

When sadomasochism is a person's predominant sexual style, the most common way of reaching other sadomasochistic devotees is the use of ads in sadomasochistic magazines. For example:

Beautiful Dominatrix, 24. A true sophisticate of the bizarre and unusual. I have a well equipped dungeon in my luxurious home. You will submit to prolonged periods of degradation for my pleasure. Toilet servitude a must. I know what you crave and can fulfill your every need.

A very pretty 30-year-old female has fantasies about receiving hand spankings on bare behind. I've never allowed myself to act out any of the fantasies. Is there anyone out there who'd like to correspond with me about their fantasies or experience with spanking?

—Weinberg & Falk, 1980, pp. 385–386

As these examples show, the ads contain code messages. "Toilet servitude," for instance, refers to handling feces or being defecated on. Sadomasochistic experiences can also be enhanced by hoods, paddles, enema equipment, adult diapers, and other paraphernalia sold in sex shops (see Figure 8–11). Many of these "sex boutiques" can be found in middle-class neighborhoods.

Masochistic needs can also be satisfied without actually inflicting pain. For many couples, the fantasied aspect of violence is most important.

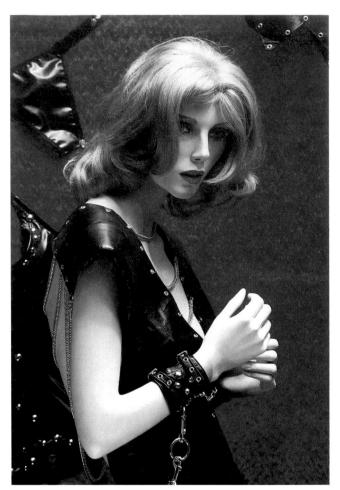

FIGURE 8–11 This sex shop mannequin is dressed in the leather, restraints, and chains that are attractive to many sadists and masochists.

Of course, he doesn't really hurt me. I mean quite recently he tied me down ready to receive "punishment," then by mistake he kicked my heel with his toe as he walked by. I gave a yelp, and he said "Sorry love—did I hurt you?"

—Gosselin and Wilson, 1980, pp. 54–55

My wife believes in discipline. If she gets angry and yells at me, I get an erection. If she ever raises her hand as if to hit me, I get so excited I can't stand it. Actually she has never hit me. When I have fantasies of her hitting or slapping me, my penis becomes erect immediately.

—Gosselin and Wilson, 1980, p. 54

Sadomasochists may be heterosexual, bisexual, or homosexual in their choice of partners. A questionnaire study showed few differences among these groups (Breslow and others, 1986). In general, subjects in all three groups felt that their sadomasochistic interests were natural ones that were present in childhood. People in all three groups used ads to make contact with others with similar interests. Few subjects in any of the groups reported being sexually abused as children although a sizeable minority felt emotionally abused. In general, the homosexual respondents tended to sometimes take the dominant and sometimes the submissive role in their sadomasochistic activities. Heterosexual and bisexual subjects were about equally divided into "predominantly dominant," "predominantly submissive," or "adopting either" roles. Although more men than women seem to be interested in sadomasochism, in one survey using questionnaires placed in a sadomasochistic contact magazine, 40 percent of those who responded were female (Breslow and others, 1985).

Few studies of fetishists, transvestites, and sado-masochists have been carried out because of the many difficulties involved in obtaining subjects. The results of the studies that have been done so far are hard to interpret because of the unrepresentative samples that investigators are forced to use. Researchers have become very creative in searching for these hard-to-find subjects. For example, one study utilized the membership lists of organizations for fetishists, sadomasochists, and transvestites (Gosselin & Wilson, 1980). The subjects, all males, were given the Eysenck Personality Questionnaire (Eysenck & Eysenck, 1975), a paper-and-pencil test that measures extraversion, neuroticism, and psychoticism and includes a "lie scale" intended to screen out test takers who do not answer candidly. A questionnaire on life style, sexual characteristics, sexual fantasies, and child-hood and adolescent experiences was also included. On the basis of these measures, all three sexually deviant groups were found to be more introverted and more inclined to fantasy than a control group. In the control group, 18 percent of the men could be considered fetishistic on the basis of their sexual fantasies, but only 2 to 5 percent could be called sadomasochistic or had transvestite fantasies.

Many of the subjects in one group—for example, the fetishists—had sexual interests that overlapped those in the other groups (see Figure 8–12). Thirty-five percent of any group had all three sets of interests. The biggest overlaps were between fetishists and sadomasochists and between fetishists and transvestites. This research suggests that very often sadomasochism and transvestism are elaborations of an early-learned fetish. Gosselin and Wilson conclude that these sexually variant behaviors are not the deliberate choice of an individual

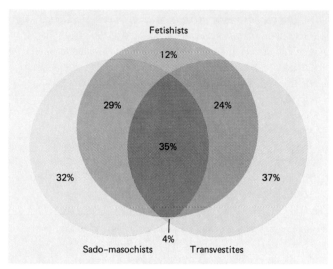

FIGURE 8–12 The overlap of sexual interests among groups of male fetishists, transvestites, and sadomasochists.

(From *Sexual Variations*. Copyright © 1980 by Glenn Wilson and Chris Gosselin. Reprinted by permission of Simon & Schuster)

looking for "kicks," but rather a logical, if unfortunate, reaction of a shy, introverted, emotionally sensitive child to a restrictive sexual upbringing.

Autoerotic Asphyxia

Sometimes sadomasochistic needs are satisfied by dangerous **autoerotic practices** or solo sex-related activities. One of the most common types of autoerotic practices that may lead to death is **autoerotic asphyxia,** the practice of artificially restricting the oxygen supply during sexual self-stimulation in order to enhance sexual enjoyment. Unintended deaths may result from all these practices, but such deaths are rather rare. In the United States an estimated 500 to 1,000 deaths per year result from autoerotic activities (Hazelwood and others, 1983). Little research has been done on this group, but a study of 70 consecutive cases received by the FBI showed that two-thirds of the victims had died while using materials or devices such as ropes, handcuffs, chains, hoods, gags, blindfolds, and belts to physically restrain or mentally humiliate themselves (Hazelwood and others, 1983). The following is a typical case.

The victim, a 32-year-old married father of three, was discovered dead on his bed by his 11-year-old daughter. The victim was dressed in pantyhose, a lady's sweater, and a brassiere. His hands were restrained to his sides by a soft belt. A sanitary pad was in his mouth and a pink brassiere was

wrapped over the mouth and around the head. His scrotum was swollen and exhibited two round areas resembling old cigarette burns. A similar type burn was located on the inner aspect of the left thigh near the scrotum. The cause of death was determined to be accidental asphyxiation. Because of the slack in the belt restraining his wrists, it would have been possible for the victim to slip his feet between his arms, thereby allowing him to remove the gag. Apparently his judgment was impaired due to his asphyxial state.

—Hazelwood and others, 1981, p. 131

This victim's sadomasochistic needs apparently led him to inflict burns on his own body as well as to use physical restraints. It seems likely that many individuals who inflict pain on themselves also have sadistic fantasies. Drawings of sadistic fantasies done by a man who ultimately died as a result of his autoerotic practices are shown in Figure 8–13.

The majority of autoerotic deaths occur in teenagers and young adult males, although the reported age range is 9 to 77 and a small number of female deaths have been reported (Brody, 1984).

Table 8–3 lists some warning signs that may suggest autoerotic asphyxial practices.

Voyeurism

Some sexual variations are not physically harmful but may victimize innocent people. One example is

Table 8–3
Signs of Possible Autoerotic Asphyxial Practices

1. Frequently bloodshot eyes
2. Marks on the neck
3. Disoriented or foggy behavior, especially after having gone off alone for awhile
4. Great interest in or possession of ropes, chains, plastic bags, or gas inhalation devices

voyeurism, the impulse to spy on others, usually strangers. The French word "voyeur" means "watcher." The voyeur is subject to an irresistible, repetitive urge to spy on others through windows or doors, in public toilets, in parks, or on beaches, and particularly enjoys watching other people have sex. Like the exhibitionist (to be described shortly), the voyeur or "peeping Tom" is male and achieves sexual gratification from doing something forbidden. Also like the exhibitionist, the voyeur is usually harmless and will run if he is discovered. In some cases, however, usually after feeling intensely stimulated or provoked, the voyeur will let his presence be known—for example, he may exhibit his genitals and ask his victim to touch him or even to masturbate him. Cases have been known in which the voyeur tried to force the victim to have sexual intercourse with him, but such cases are exceptional.

Voyeurism begins in early childhood and usually continues over a long period. Fifty percent of those arrested for voyeurism are later rearrested for similar acts. About one-fourth of the men who are arrested for peeping are married. When voyeuristic acts are related to

FIGURE 8–13 Sketches of sadistic sexual fantasies drawn by a victim of autoerotic asphyxia.

(Reprinted by permission of the publisher, from *Autoerotic Fatalities* by Robert R. Hazelwood, Park Elliott Dietz, and Ann Wolbert Burgess. Lexington, MA: Lexington Books, D.C. Heath and Company, Copyright © 1983, D.C. Heath and Company.)

life stress, the impulse to commit them usually decreases when the stress dissipates. While voyeurs show few signs of serious mental disorders, they usually have unsatisfying heterosexual relationships.

Exhibitionism

Exhibitionists, who are always males, repeatedly expose their genitals to unsuspecting strangers in public places as a way of experiencing sexual arousal. The exhibitionist does not want to harm anyone; his act of exposure is done for his own sexual gratification. His arousal is apparently heightened by seeing people react with amazement or shock when he unexpectedly shows his penis (see Figure 8–14). Exhibitionists expose their genitals mainly to women and children. One-third of all people arrested for sex offenses are exhibitionists, and about 20 percent of these are arrested more than once (Hyde, 1990).

Exhibitionism can begin between preadolescence and middle age, but it occurs most frequently during the twenties. An exhibitionist has an irresistible, compulsive need to expose his genitals, and he does so despite the

FIGURE 8–14 Exhibitionists receive sexual gratification from the shock and alarm expressed by their victims. A response of this kind would provide no sexual gratification.

(© Punch/Rothko)

"You don't often see a real silk lining, these days . . ."

anxiety, depression, and shame he feels as a result. Acts of genital exposure often seem to be triggered by feelings of excitement, fear, restlessness, and sexual arousal. When overcome by these feelings, the exhibitionist is driven to find relief. Both psychodynamic and behavioral therapies (particularly aversion therapy) have been tried with exhibitionists. Although both methods seem to achieve some success, the results are unpredictable (Hyde, 1990).

Obscene Telephone Calls

Another way of obtaining sexual gratification with a nonconsenting individual is by making obscene telephone calls. The caller almost always tries to get his victim to give him intimate information, often of a sexual nature, by pretending to be conducting a survey about menstruation, contraception, or sexual practices. In another type of obscene call, the caller masturbates while graphically describing the process to the victim.

Obscene callers often have trouble maintaining normal sexual relationships and their calls are often linked to fantasies concerning aggressive acts. Some clinicians believe that by making the calls, the callers are trying to recreate a childhood situation in which they were sexually abused. The recreation may in some way be an attempt to repair the situation. In 1990, Richard Berendzen resigned as president of American University because of accusations that he had made obscene phone calls to women running day-care centers in northern Virginia. He admitted making the calls and underwent treatment. Berendzen recalled having been sexually abused as a child (see Figure 8–15).

FIGURE 8–15 Richard Berendzen, a former university president, pleaded guilty to making a large number of obscene telephone calls.

Pedophilia

Pedophilia is the term used to describe a disorder that includes intense and recurrent sexual urges and sexually arousing fantasies involving some form of sexual activity with a child who has not reached the age of puberty. To be classified as a pedophile the person must either have acted on these urges or be very distressed by them. The sexual attractions of pedophiles are very specific. For instance, the only children who may be seen as arousing may be girls from the ages of 8 to 10. The behavior is usually a chronic one that continues over a long time. However, periods of high stress tend to increase the frequency of pedophilic behavior. In about 90 percent of all cases, the pedophile is someone whom the child knows (Hyde, 1990).

Pedophilic behavior may take a variety of forms, including exposure of the pedophile's sexual body parts to the child; kissing, hugging, and fondling the child in a sexual way; touching sexual parts of the child's body or inducing the child to touch or fondle the pedophile's sexual organs; or attempted or actual intercourse with the child. A Canadian survey found that a high proportion of people reported having been the victims of pedophilic behavior (Badgley, 1984). Most of the victims did not seek the assistance of public services. Clearly, better preventive and therapeutic measures are needed. Youngsters need to be taught to protect themselves and the public needs to be educated about the nature of the problem.

Pedophiles are likely to repeat the behavior after being apprehended. Some, but not all, child sex abusers can be classified as pedophiles. Some child sexual abuse occurs within families simply because the abuser does not have a satisfactory sexual partner. In most cases, a pedophile will have had sexual contacts with children both in and outside of the family and prefers children for sexual targets. Many pedophiles do report being sexually abused as children although researchers do not have much data on this disorder.

Perspectives on the Paraphilias

Human sexual behavior is varied. It has its underpinnings in a biological substrate for physiological expression and is strongly influenced by the socialization process. When sexual behavior greatly diverges from the norm, and especially when it is harmful to others, researchers attempt to understand it better by defining its characteristics. Defining and classifying these deviant sexual behaviors has been difficult, however, because they are: (1) committed by a small percentage of the population; (2) usually concealed by their participants; and (3) constantly modified by adaptations to social changes.

One hallmark of the paraphilias that researchers have been able to identify is that these unusual or bizarre acts are insistently and involuntarily repetitive (Hyde, 1990).

No single theory has so far been able to explain the development of paraphilic behavior. Each of the theoretical perspectives have implications for research in terms of definition of the variant behavior, preferred type of treatment, appropriate treatment goals, and ways of assessing treatment outcome.

The psychodynamic perspective views paraphilic behavior as a reflection of unresolved conflicts during psychosexual development (Freud, 1969). This view leads to long-term treatment that aims to change personality structure and dynamics and also alter overt behavior and sexual fantasies.

The behavioral perspective views sexual variance as something learned by the same rules as more usual sexual behavior—through conditioning, modeling, reinforcement, generalization, and punishment. From this perspective the definition of variant sexual behavior would be based on any personal discomfort of the individual with the behavior and any conflict between this behavior and the rules of society. The treatment, which can be as short as one day or much longer, is based on understanding the immediate antecedents and consequences of the behavior and on developing alternate forms of sexual arousal. Treatment effectiveness is based on overt behavior as measured by self-monitoring and psychophysiological measures. Various types of aversion therapy have been tried with paraphiliacs, but this approach has generated a great deal of controversy because of the pain and discomfort created. Covert sensitization which involves imagined unpleasant events seems to avoid some of the ethical questions surrounding the use of physical punishment. A broader behavioral view from the social-learning perspective explains the variant behavior as a substitute for deficits in social and sexual functioning, or inability to form a satisfactory marital relationship. The treatment goal is to assist the client to form satisfactory relationships through teaching interpersonal skills. Outcome measures here are client's self-reports of satisfying relationships with significant others as well as of satisfactory sexual relationships.

The biological perspective deals with heredity, prenatal hormonal environment, and a focus on the biological causes of gender identity. The treatment goals include suppression of the variant behaviors and of sexual responsiveness in general and may involve the use of hormonal treatments or surgery. But until the side-effects of hormonal treatments and long-term behavior changes can be assessed accurately, it is difficult to draw any conclusions about the therapeutic effects of this type of treatment for paraphiliacs. The outcome is usually measured in terms of psychophysiological responses as well as sexual activity.

No one type of treatment seems to be clearly superior for the paraphilias. Much of the research has severe shortcomings and consists of single-subject studies without control subjects. These shortcomings are not surprising when the difficulty of doing research in this area is considered. There is tentative evidence across many studies that behavioral treatment may be effective in reducing or eliminating some paraphilic sexual behavior and increasing appropriate sexual behavior instead (Kilmann and others, 1982). Many of the therapeutic efforts reported used a variety of behavioral treatments that included aversion therapy. The programs were most effective when they were tailored for the specific problems of the individual paraphiliac. Conventional counseling or psychotherapy has not been very effective in modifying paraphiliacs' behavior. The reasons for resistance to treatment are unclear.

Sexual Victimization

Some sexual deviations involve a participant who is either unwilling, uninformed, vulnerable, or too young to give legal consent. Among the clearest examples of such deviations are rape and child sexual abuse. When individuals who practice these deviations come into contact with the law, they are usually known as **sex offenders** and are subjected to a variety of treatments as well as to imprisonment. Some cases of rape and child sexual abuse are examples of paraphilias; others are examples of gratification through aggression or, in the case of child sexual abuse, desire for an easily obtainable and easily coerced sexual partner.

Research on sexual victimization has proceeded in two directions, one dealing with the effects on the victim and the other with the characteristics of perpetrators and the settings in which victimizations occur. Together, these two areas of investigation help us view a complete picture of these abhorrent crimes.

Rape

Rape, or having sexual intercourse forcibly and without the partner's consent, is a seriously underreported crime. Only about 15 to 20 percent of all rapes are reported to authorities—probably because of the emotional trauma experienced by the victim. In the United States, a rape occurs about every six minutes (Riesenberg, 1987) (see Figure 8–16). The great majority of convicted rapists are sent to civil prisons for fixed sentences, but some states maintain special treatment facilities for sexual offenders, particularly those who are violent. While both male and female rapes occur, females are overwhelmingly the victims of sexual assaults. However, many cases of male rape—by other males—have been reported in prison populations.

Rapes fall into three general categories: power rape, anger rape, and sadistic rape. In **power rape,** the rapist, who usually feels inadequate and awkward in interpersonal relationships, intimidates the victim with threats of physical harm. In **anger rape,** the rapist seems to be seeking revenge on women in general and expresses

FIGURE 8–16 The powerlessness and sense of physical violation felt by a rape victim may make psychological recovery a slow process.

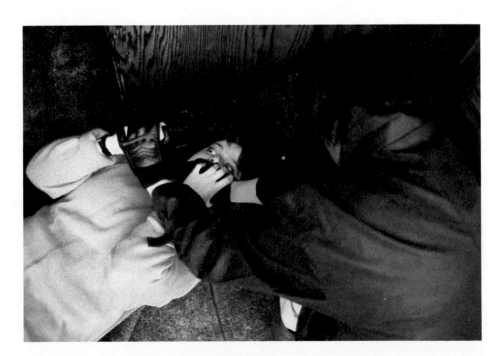

his rage through physical and verbal abuse. He seems to get little or no sexual satisfaction from the rape. The third and rarest type, **sadistic rape,** combines sexuality and aggression and focuses on the suffering of the victim (Prentky & Knight, 1991).

In Chapter 5, we looked at the effects of rape on its victims. Here the focus is on the rapist. What kinds of men commit these crimes? Can sexual aggression be predicted? Past sexual aggression against adults does tend to be predictive of future sexual aggression against adults (Hall, 1990). But while it is useful to have this information, it is also important to know how persons who have not previously been sexually aggressive develop this trait. Many variables may play roles in sexual aggression, including past sexual experiences such as victimization and deviant sexual arousal, general level of willingness to commit aggression, impulsivity, lack of respect for society's rules, deficient social skill, and a tendency to lose control under the influence of alcohol. More research is needed on the effects of these variables individually and in combination (Blader & Marshall, 1989).

Men between the ages of 20 and 24 form the largest group arrested for rape. The next most-frequent group are 15- to 19-year-old males. Adolescent males aged 12 through 19 account for almost a quarter of the forcible rapes and attempted rapes against all ages of victims (Davis & Leitenberg, 1987). As might be expected, rapes committed by adolescents tend to occur on weekends, at night, and in the summer. Burglary is often committed along with these rapes. Peer pressure seems to be a large factor in rape by adolescents, since sexual assaults are frequently committed as part of a group. In one study, 27 percent of rapes committed by offenders under the age of 21 involved multiple offenders. The proportion of adolescent rapists who are complete strangers to the victim varies widely, ranging from 42 to 91 percent (Virogradov and others, 1988).

Child Sexual Abuse

As was explained in the section on pedophilia, although pedophilics engage in child sexual abuse, not all child sexual abusers are pedophilics. The child abuser may seek sexual gratification from children because they are available, rather than because of particular attraction to them as is seen in pedophilia. Those child abusers who are not pedophilics often will choose any of a variety of sexual targets that are available to them. Unlike pedophilics, these other child abusers are not drawn exclusively to children as sexual objects.

Several major surveys have been carried out to determine how frequently child sexual victimization occurs (Painter, 1986). In all these surveys information was gathered from adults about their experience of sexual abuse during their own childhoods. Very different rates were reported in these surveys because they used varying definitions of sexual abuse. Some defined sexual abuse in terms of physical contact, ranging from touching or fondling to sexual intercourse or oral–genital or anal–genital contact. Other surveys also included noncontact abuse, such as exposure of the offender's genitals or requests for sexual involvement. Partly as a result of these different definitions, and partly as a result of different survey techniques, the rates of abuse reported range from about 12 percent to over 50 percent. When these rates are compared with the number of cases reported to social agencies or the police, there is a large difference. Probably only about one-quarter of the cases are actually reported (Finkelhor & Hotaling, 1984). One reason for the low percentage of cases reported is that abuse by family members is usually not made known to the authorities. In one study of victims, 73 percent of the cases researchers were told about by victims had been reported to authorities when the offender was a stranger; when the offender was a family member, no cases had been reported to authorities. When adults were reporting on their own past experiences, family members were said to be the offenders one-third of the time. But when parents reported on their children's experiences, only 10 percent of offenses were said to involve family members (Finkelhor, 1984). This difference also points to an underreporting of child sexual abuse. Of even greater concern, the very acts that may be the most harmful, those carried out by someone with continued access to the child, are the least likely to be reported. Special materials have been developed to help clinicians interview young children to determine whether sexual abuse has occurred (see Figure 8–17). Research is needed to determine their usefulness.

Because child abuse often becomes a legal issue, questions have been raised about whether the truthfulness of children's reports of child abuse could be relied upon. A survey of professionals who frequently deal with child abuse found that in general they believed the reports were accurate (Conte and others, 1991). The factors they considered in authenticating the reports included physical indicators of abuse such as sexually transmitted diseases, tears or enlargements of tissue, age-inappropriate sexual knowledge, children's descriptions that were consistent over time or that detailed a progression of sexual activity, and sexualized play or precocious or seductive behavior during the interview. The only factor that these experts felt might contribute to distortions in the children's reports was their status as subjects in custody battles.

What are the characteristics of families and individuals that may mean a high risk of sexual abuse? Children

FIGURE 8–17 Anatomically correct dolls such as these can be used to aid in interviewing child victims of sexual abuse, for court testimony and play therapy. The dolls, available in several racial types, have anal, oral, and genital openings, breasts or penises, and pubic hair. They also have movable tongues and fingers to aid in the description of oral molestation or masturbation.

(From Real People Dolls, Hylands Anatomical Dolls, Inc., 4455 Torrance Blvd., Suite 310, Torrance, CA 90503)

in step-, foster, and adoptive families seem to be most likely to be victimized (Russell, 1984). Other high-risk groups are children in families where there is marital discord and families in which physical violence and spouse abuse are frequent (Walker, 1984). These groups usually show disruption in family relationships, lack of supervision of children, and focus of attention by the parents on their own concerns rather than on those of the children.

What are the effects of sexual abuse in childhood? In the short term the child may show sexual preoccupation including excessive or public masturbation and an unusual interest in sexual organs and sex play. Another likely result is frequent physical complaints and problems such as rashes, vomiting, and headaches, none of which can be explained by medical examination. Some researchers think that at puberty the problems may intensify. What results carry over into adulthood is unclear. Sexual abuse in childhood may result in problems of depression and low self-esteem as well as in sexual difficulties, either avoidance of sexual contact or promiscuity or prostitution. In a study of college women, a relationship was found between a history of childhood sexual abuse and several measures of adjustment (Fromuth, 1986).

Although many people seem to emerge from childhood sexual abuse with no long-term effects, we do not yet have a very good idea of how others may be affected. Research studies suggest that the kinds of abuse that appear to be the most damaging are those that involve father figures, genital contact, and force (Browne & Finkelhor, 1986).

As reports of sexual abuse of children have increased, ways to protect children are now being carried out. Some information campaigns have concentrated on children's contacts with strangers—for example, "Never get into a car with anyone you don't know," "Never go with someone who says he or she has some candy for you." However, in the majority of reported assaults children are victimized by people they know. To prevent this kind of assault, children need to be taught to recognize signs of trouble and to be assertive enough to report them to a responsible adult. How to accomplish this task represents an important challenge to prevention-oriented researchers (Repucci & Haugaard, 1989).

INCEST While definitions of **incest** vary, it is generally recognized as sexual contact between persons who are closely biologically related (for example, father–daughter, mother–son, brother–sister). Most attention has been given to sexual abuse involving a father and daughter. Incest differs from pedophilia in that pedophiles are usually not biologically related to the child they victimize. An important question concerning incest is whether those who commit it also are a danger to children outside the family. One study found that 49 percent of one group of incestuous fathers abused children outside of the family at the same time they were

abusing their own children. Of these men, 18 percent were also raping adult women (Abel and others, 1988). Studies on the effects of incest on victims' adjustment confirm the results for sexual abuse of children generally.

Regardless of the relationship between the perpetrator and the victim, childhood sexual abuse is often associated with poor psychological adjustment and behavior disorders (Cahill and others, 1991; Swett and others, 1990).

Chapter Summary

CHANGING VIEWS OF SEXUAL BEHAVIOR

A look at history shows that views concerning sexuality have at some times been permissive and at other times restrictive. One area of sexuality in which views have varied both over time and across cultures is sexual preference. Currently the biological perspective is receiving the most attention in understanding sexual preference.

SURVEYS OF SEXUAL BEHAVIOR

Most information concerning sexual practices comes from survey research. The first two Kinsey Reports, published about forty years ago, still serve as a basis for much of what is known. Because patterns of sexual practices are known to have changed over time, there is need for new surveys that focus on representative samples of the population.

HOMOSEXUALITY

Homosexual behavior refers to sexual behavior with members of one's own sex. Surveys indicate that it is not unusual for people to have at least some experience with homosexual behavior in their lifetimes. **Homosexuality** refers to sexual preference for one's own sex that endures over an extended period. The term **gay** is increasingly used to refer to this behavior because of the feeling that the term has fewer negative associations. Many people who identify themselves as gay adopt this self-label during adolescence.

How Sexual Preference Develops Sexual preference may be related to biological factors such as the level of sex hormones to which the fetus is exposed during the prenatal period. Research on family relationships during early life does not seem to explain differences in sexual preference.

A Cross-cultural View Study of sexuality across cultures shows that homosexuality may be culturally expected for adolescents in some cultural settings. In recent years many people in western cultures have begun to view homosexuality in less value laden terms and more as an alternate life style that is followed by a segment of the population.

Psychological Adjustment Studies of the psychological adjustment of homosexual and heterosexual individuals have found that while a range of levels of adjustment can be found in each group, there are no overall group differences in adjustment.

Relationship Patterns Just as the types of relationships heterosexual individuals have differ, so do those of homosexuals.

Sexual Response In general there seems to be no difference in physiological responses to sexual experience for heterosexual and homosexual couples under laboratory conditions.

BISEXUALITY

Bisexual behavior means that at different times the person prefers sexual activity with the same or opposite sex partners. Patterns of bisexuality differ. Some people move from a relatively long lasting heterosexual relationship to a similar same-sex relationship or the reverse. Others tend to continue to move back and forth between these types of relationships.

SEXUAL DYSFUNCTION

A persistent impairment of sexual interest or response is called a **sexual dysfunction.** A sexual dysfunction is often associated with anxiety about performance or cultural inhibitions.

Types of Sexual Dysfunction Sexual problems can occur in any of four stages of the sexual response: appetitive, excitement, orgasm, or resolution. **Erectile dysfunction** refers to the inability of a man to maintain an erection until the completion of intercourse. Problems of erectile dysfunction are often associated with **performance anxiety.** Women may have similar problems of **inhibited sexual excitement** that result in an inability to maintain a swelling-lubrication response. For women, a problem that often brings them to clinics is **secondary anorgasmia** or the frequent inability to achieve orgasm. If the causes of the problem include both some aspects of physical condition and psychological factors the problem is called a **sexual disorder.**

Treatment of Sexual Dysfunction When a person seeks therapy for a sexual dysfunction or disorder, the clinician should get detailed information about medical history, physical symptoms, developmental history, drug and alcohol use, present relationships, and stressors. Sex therapy is often carried out by working with the couple rather than one person. The therapist attempts to decrease fear of failure and to focus on sensory pleasure rather than on the sex act itself. A frequent way of carrying this out is to use **sensate focus,** a sexual retraining technique developed by Masters and Johnson in their pioneering work on sex therapy. Behavioral and cognitive elements are

246 CHAPTER 8 Sexual Variations and Disorders

widely used in current treatment of sexual dysfunction. Some therapists use an approach that combines these elements with a more traditional psychodynamic approach. One advocate of this approach is Kaplan.

The Effectiveness of Sex Therapy More research is needed to interpret the widely differing results reported for sex therapy. Many therapists believe that aspects of the relationship between the members of the couple may be a major force in a negative therapeutic outcome.

GENDER IDENTITY DISORDER

Childhood Problems of Gender Identity Gender identity refers to a person's sexual self concept, the feeling of being male or female. In **gender identity disorder of childhood,** children who have not yet reached puberty express extreme distress at their gender and intense desires to be of the opposite sex.

Gender Identity Disorder in Adults Transsexualism refers to the intense desire by adults to change not only their sexual identity, but also their anatomical status. Adults who have **nontranssexual gender identity disorder** are uncomfortable with their assigned sex and may frequently **cross-dress,** that is wear clothes of the opposite sex. However, they are not preoccupied with changing their physical sexual characteristics as transsexuals are.

THE PARAPHILIAS

The term **paraphilia** means attraction to the deviant. Three general classes of paraphilias include: preference for use of nonhuman objects for sexual arousal, sexual activity with humans with sexual arousal based on real or simulated suffering or humiliation, and repetitive sexual activity with nonconsenting partners.

Fetishism Fetishism refers to the use of a nonliving object as a primary source of sexual arousal and consummation.

Transvestism A **transvestite** is someone who seeks sexual stimulation through crossdressing, wearing the clothing of the opposite sex. Transvestites continue to identify with their biological sex, and when not crossdressed, show behaviors and interests consistent with their sex.

Sexual Sadism and Masochism A **sadist** achieves orgasm through humiliating or inflicting pain on others. A **masochist** achieves sexual gratification and orgasm under circumstances of humiliation and ill treatment by others. Sadism and masochism occur in both heterosexual and homosexual relationships.

Autoerotic Asphyxia **Autoerotic practices** are activities a person engages in alone to bring about sexual gratification. **Autoerotic asphyxia** refers to heightening of sexual excitement in orgasm by partially restricting breathing. Because the resulting lack of oxygen may impair judgement, this practice can result in death from asphyxiation.

Voyeurism Voyeurism refers to the achievement of sexual gratification through watching or spying upon others particu-

larly when they are dressing, undressing, or engaging in sexual activity. The socially forbidden nature of the activity seems to be a major factor in producing the voyeur's sexual excitement.

Exhibitionism Exhibitionists are males who gain sexual arousal from exposing their genitals to strangers in public settings.

Obscene Telephone Calls A telephone call to an unconsenting victim that seeks sexual information or focuses on sexually explicit comments and threats is a way of gaining sexual arousal for some individuals.

Pedophilia A **pedophile** targets children as the main source of sexual gratification. Pedophilic behavior includes a variety of types: forcing the child to fondle the adult's sexual organs, the sexual fondling and caressing of the child by an adult, and attempted or actual intercourse.

Perspectives on the Paraphilias Each of the perspectives have something to offer in understanding the paraphilias. Because many of the pedophilic behaviors are carried out in private and only occasionally come to public attention, and because they vary so greatly, little research has been carried out on them and their causes are poorly understood. Conventional psychotherapy seems ineffective in treating paraphilias. Biological treatments involving hormones have been used but long term effects of these have not yet been evaluated. Behavioral therapy using aversion techniques has been tried but is found objectionable by many people on ethical grounds. Cognitive-behavioral approaches involving covert desensitization may be helpful in some cases.

SEXUAL VICTIMIZATION

Sex offenders are those who come into contact with the law because their sexual deviations involve a participant who is unwilling, uninformed, vulnerable, or too young to give legal consent. Some of these sexual offenses are examples of paraphilias, while others are related to gratification of aggressive impulses or the desire for an easily obtainable sexual partner.

Rape Rape is defined as forcible sexual intercourse with an unconsenting partner. A number of personal characteristics may play a role in the likelihood of carrying out a rape. These include past experiences of sexual victimization, deviant sexual arousal, aggressive or impulsive behaviors, social skills deficits, and a tendency to lose control under the influence of alcohol.

Child Sexual Abuse Because of differences in the definition of child sexual abuse, results of surveys concerning its frequency vary widely. The number of cases reported is also much smaller than those presumed to have occurred, partly because abuse by a family member is often not reported at the time.

Incest Incest refers to sexual contact between persons who are biologically related. An incestuous relationship as a child is often associated with poor psychological adjustment and behavior disorders in adulthood.

Personality Disorders

C H A P T E R 9

Classifying Personality Disorders

Odd or Eccentric Behaviors
Paranoid Personality Disorder
Schizoid Personality Disorder
Schizotypal Personality Disorder

Dramatic, Emotional, or Erratic Behaviors
Histrionic Personality Disorder
Narcissistic Personality Disorder
Borderline Personality Disorder
Antisocial Personality Disorder

Anxious or Fearful Behaviors
Avoidant Personality Disorder
Dependent Personality Disorder
Obsessive–Compulsive Personality Disorder
Passive–Aggressive Personality Disorder

Treatment of Personality Disorders

The Outlook For Personality Disorder Classification

Chapter Summary

Richard Hull, *Undertow*, 1986. Phyllis Kind Gallery, New York/Chicago.

*J*ohn, a 50-year-old retired policeman, sought treatment a few weeks after his dog had been run over and died. Since that time he had felt sad, tired, and had had trouble sleeping and concentrating.

John lived alone, and for many years had virtually no conversational contacts with other human beings beyond a "Hello" or "How are you?" He preferred to be by himself, found talk a waste of time, and felt awkward when other people tried to initiate a relationship. He occasionally spent some time in a bar, but always off by himself and not really following the general conversation. He read newspapers avidly, and was well informed in many areas, but took no particular interest in the people around him. He was employed as a security guard, but was known by fellow workers as a "cold fish" and a "loner." They no longer even noticed or teased him, especially since he never seemed to notice or care about their teasing anyway.

John floated through life without relationships except for that with his dog, which he dearly loved. At Christmas he would buy the dog elaborate gifts and, in return, would receive a wrapped bottle of scotch that he bought for himself as a gift from the dog. The loss of his pets had been the only events in his life that had caused him sadness. He experienced the death of his parents without emotion, and felt no regret whatever at being completely out of contact with the rest of his family. He considered himself different from other people, and regarded emotionality in others with bewilderment.

—Adapted from Spitzer and others, 1989, pp. 249–250

Dr. B., a 41-year-old family practitioner, was getting ready to leave his office at 6 P.M. to rush home and have supper before attending his son's final high school basketball game. The hospital called to inform him that one of his obstetric patients had arrived in Labor and Delivery and was currently showing 5 cm of cervical dilation. He knew that one of his partners was covering obstetrics that night, but he felt compelled to run by the hospital to check her before going home. After checking her, he decided to stay through the delivery, necessitating his missing his son's last game. After the delivery, the physician sat in the locker room and wept. He felt terribly guilt-ridden over missing the game, and as he reflected on the evening, he could not understand why he had not simply handed the case over to his partner. He poignantly stated later that he was not even emotionally attached to this particular patient. His own narcissism had gotten the best of him; i.e., he felt that he and he alone had to be the one to deliver the baby, as though his partner could not have performed exactly the same function.

—Gabbard, 1985, p. 2928

What do these two men have in common? How are they different? Do they have problems of clinical proportions?

John sought treatment because he feels terribly distraught. However, most clinicians would be confident that John also has some sort of mental disorder because of the extreme intensity of his reaction to the death of his dog and the time the reaction has lasted. His Axis I diagnosis (see Chapter 4) would probably be adjustment disorder with depressed mood because his distress is clearly linked to an identifiable stressor, the dog's death. But this Axis I classification does not completely capture all the major features of John's life. His longstanding pattern of not wanting or enjoying close relationships with other people, including his family, always choosing solitary activities, and only rarely experiencing strong emotions, coupled with an absence of oddities and eccentricities of behavior, speech, or thought, is indicative of schizoid personality disorder, an Axis II classification. Clinicians would maintain that it was the presence of the schizoid personality disorder that made John particularly vulnerable to the stress of his pet's death.

Dr. B. is probably not suffering from a mental disorder of any kind, but he may be somewhat compulsive when it comes to feeling responsible for his patients' welfare. When that compulsivity gets out of hand it can

cause him temporary distress as it did in this case. Yet he seems to be functioning well in his medical practice and his personality style is shared by many physicians who often feel an exaggerated sense of responsibility (Gabbard, 1985). This style may show itself in both adaptive and maladaptive ways. In one poll of 100 randomly selected physicians, all of them described themselves as "compulsive personalities" (Krakowski, 1982).

John's and Dr. B.'s cases illustrate what both clinicians and the public would all agree on—that everyone has a distinctive set of personal characteristics and that these traits affect behavior. John's life style seems to have contributed to his protracted bereavement, while Dr. B.'s compulsivity probably makes him the dedicated doctor he is (although, along with that dedication, there are occasional temporary personal upsets, such as missing his son's game).

A person's characteristic ways of responding are often referred to as his or her **personality.** Most people's personality styles do not affect their behavior similarly in all situations. Personality styles can be maladaptive if an individual is unable to modify his or her behavior when the environment undergoes significant changes that call for different approaches. If personality characteristics are not flexible enough to allow an individual to respond adaptively to at least an ordinary variety of situations, a disorder may be present.

When personality styles become pathological, they can impair an individual's functioning in important situations and can lead to anxiety, feelings of distress, and unhappiness. The point at which a personality style becomes a personality disorder is unclear. **Personality disorders** are longstanding, maladaptive, and inflexible ways of relating to the environment. Such disorders can usually be noticed in childhood or at least by early adolescence, and may continue through adult life. They severely limit an individual's approach to stress-producing situations because his or her characteristic styles of thinking and behavior allow for only a rigid and narrow range of responses. Studies of personality disorders within the general population estimate a prevalence rate between 6 and 11 percent (Merikangas & Weissman, 1986; Reich and others, 1989).

Personality disorders pose problems for people who construct classification systems, as well as for textbook writers and teachers of abnormal psychology. They seem important, and their existence can easily be recognized even by nonprofessional observers, yet little is known about their origins and development. With the exception of the antisocial personality disorder, and until recently the borderline personality disorder, very little research has been done on these problems, probably because they often are not dramatic or severely incapacitating and many people who might have such a disorder never seek help in dealing with their problems.

Although the maladaptive behavior that is typical of personality disorders sometimes causes great distress to the people involved, they find it difficult to change the way they think about and respond to situations. The clinical problems are intensified when, as is usually the case, the person does not regard his or her behavior patterns as maladaptive or undesirable, even if the unpleasant and counterproductive consequences of those behaviors are obvious to others. As we will see in this chapter, this situation is perhaps most evident in cases of antisocial personality.

Classifying Personality Disorders

Personality disorders are diagnosed on DSM's Axis II. Developmental disorders and mental retardation are also diagnosed on this axis. These three problems have in common a lifetime or near-lifetime duration and stability so that there are not likely to be periods of improvement or change. A diagnosis of personality disorder is made only when a person's inflexible long-lasting behavior pattern or personality style causes important problems in social situations or on the job, or when it results in a high level of personal distress. Table 9–1 lists three groups of major personality disorders; Figure 9–1 shows their frequency as well as how that frequency is divided between men and women.

Unlike the near permanent disorders diagnosed on Axis II, Axis I disorders, called **symptom disorders,** may come or go. Symptom disorders may be triggered by events or environmental factors and may disappear when conditions change, or when a person is taught new behaviors. People with Axis I disorders often see themselves as having personal problems (symptoms) that are troublesome and for which treatment is needed. People with Axis II disorders are far more likely to say that their difficulties are attributable to the environment (for example, their family or co-workers) and that they do not need clinical treatment.

A person often has both a personality disorder and a symptom disorder. The relationship between personality disorders and symptom disorders is unclear, but the relationship is obviously a close one. One theory holds that personality disorders may be thought of as vulnera-

Table 9–1

Major Personality Disorders and Their Characteristics

Odd or Eccentric Behavior

1. *Paranoid:* Tense; guarded; suspicious; holds grudges
2. *Schizoid:* Socially isolated with restricted emotional expression
3. *Schizotypal:* Peculiarities of thought, appearance, and behavior that are disconcerting to others; emotionally detached and isolated

Dramatic, Emotional, or Erratic Behavior

1. *Antisocial:* Manipulative; exploitive; dishonest; disloyal; lacking in guilt; habitually breaks social rules; childhood history of such behavior; often in trouble with the law
2. *Borderline:* Cannot stand to be alone; intense, unstable moods and personal relationships; chronic anger; drug and alcohol abuse
3. *Histrionic:* Seductive behavior; needs immediate gratification and constant reassurance; rapidly changing moods; shallow emotions
4. *Narcissistic:* Self-absorbed; expects special treatment and adulation; envious of attention to others

Anxious or Fearful Behavior

1. *Avoidant:* Easily hurt and embarrassed; few close friends; sticks to routines to avoid new and possibly stressful experiences
2. *Dependent:* Wants others to make decisions; needs constant advice and reassurance; fears being abandoned
3. *Obsessive–compulsive:* Perfectionistic; overconscientious; indecisive; preoccupied with details; stiff; unable to express affection
4. *Passive–aggressive:* Resents demands and suggestions; procrastinates; sulks; "forgets" obligations, or is deliberately inefficient

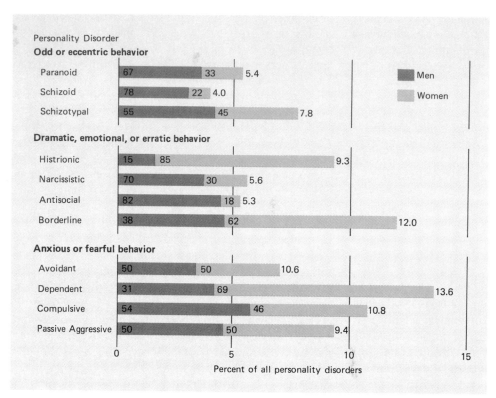

Personality Disorder

Odd or eccentric behavior

	Men	Women	
Paranoid	67	33	5.4
Schizoid	78	22	4.0
Schizotypal	55	45	7.8

Dramatic, emotional, or erratic behavior

	Men	Women	
Histrionic	15	85	9.3
Narcissistic	70	30	5.6
Antisocial	82	18	5.3
Borderline	38	62	12.0

Anxious or fearful behavior

	Men	Women	
Avoidant	50	50	10.6
Dependent	31	69	13.6
Compulsive	54	46	10.8
Passive Aggressive	50	50	9.4

Percent of all personality disorders

FIGURE 9–1 Not all personality disorders occur with equal frequency and not all affect men and women equally. Each bar shows what percent of all personality disorders are represented by each disorder. The different colored portions of each bar represent the proportion of men and women given this diagnosis. The total does not add up to 100 percent because a few personality disorders do not fit any of these categories.

(Data from Millon, 1986)

bilities, with each personality disorder associated with vulnerability to only some of the symptom disorders. For example, schizotypal personalities are thought to be susceptible to schizophrenia, dependent personalities to depression, avoidant personalities to social phobias, and borderline and antisocial personalities to drug and alcohol abuse. While this idea of increased vulnerability has some support, it is not a certainty. Another classification scheme includes personality disorders as milder forms of symptom disorders. Schizotypal disorder might be a mild form of schizophrenia and borderline disorder might be a form of mood disorder, for example.

In some instances, the classification statements of Axis II are used to provide information that bears on the primary diagnosis of Axis I. In other cases, a personality disorder referred to on Axis II is the individual's major problem. Many combinations are possible. A person may have a diagnosis on both Axes I and II. For example, Henry A. had psychotic symptoms that called for a diagnosis of schizophrenia. Before his present schizophrenic episode, however, Henry A. had shown several characteristics—odd speech, social isolation, suspiciousness, and hypersensitivity to real or imagined criticism—

that had significantly impaired his effectiveness in a variety of situations. Because of the different types of behaviors Henry A. showed, he was diagnosed using both Axis I and Axis II. The term "premorbid" means that before the schizophrenic symptoms developed, the personality disorder already existed.

- Axis I: Schizophrenia, paranoid, chronic
- Axis II: Schizotypal personality disorder (premorbid)

In another case, Gerry B. showed similar personality characteristics, but there was no basis for an Axis I diagnosis. Her diagnosis would be as follows.

- AXIS I: _____
- AXIS II: Schizotypal personality disorder

A third individual, Deborah C., had characteristics of the same personality disorder seen in Henry A. and Gerry B. However, she had additional characteristics that fit another personality disorder. In this case both personality disorders would be diagnosed.

- AXIS I: _____
- AXIS II: Schizotypal personality disorder; borderline personality disorder

Personality disorders produce the least reliable diagnoses of any DSM classification. One difficulty in deciding on the appropriateness of an Axis II diagnosis is the unclear boundary between those personality characteristics within normal limits and those that represent disordered behavior. Another problem is that some of the Axis II categories overlap a great deal. Rather than being separate disorders, they represent different degrees of the same general behaviors. In fact, about two-thirds of the patients who meet the criteria for one personality disorder will also meet the criteria for at least one more (Widiger, 1991). A third problem is that some personality disorders also overlap Axis I categories. For instance, in one study more than half of the individuals who were diagnosed as borderline also had a major affective disorder (Frances & Widiger, 1986).

If disorders are to be classified into separate types, their criteria should be distinct and mutually exclusive, and the number of ambiguous cases should be relatively few. Some DSM categories—for example, schizophrenia, the affective disorders, and the organic disorders—are relatively distinct from each other, although there are some fuzzy areas between them. But as we have seen, this is not true of personality disorders, many of whose diagnostic criteria overlap.

Some of these classification problems come about because so little is known about most personality disorders. Another difficulty stems from the so-called **prototypal approach** used in DSM. Each disorder has a list of possible characteristics, and if more than a specific number are met, the diagnosis of that disorder is given. This means that no one of the listed characteristics must be shared by everyone diagnosed with a particular personality disorder. For instance, for a diagnosis of paranoid personality disorder, a person must have any four from a list of seven characteristics. This means that any two people given this classification might have quite different characteristics.

Despite the drawbacks and uncertainties associated with the disorders listed in DSM's Axis II, the attempt to incorporate personality disorders into the classification process still represents a major advance. Prior to DSM-III, the diagnosis of mental disorders gave primary attention to the more obvious conditions now classified on Axis I. DSM-III's placement of the personality disorders on a separate axis highlights their importance to, co-existence with, and contribution to other disorders. In this way, Axis II represents a pioneering step toward a classification system applicable to the whole person. As research proceeds on this novel approach to diagnosis, it is likely that ways will be found to solve some of the classification problems mentioned above.

In this chapter, we will discuss the personality disorders in terms of the three groupings outlined in Table 9–1: odd or eccentric behaviors; dramatic, emotional or erratic behaviors; and fearful or anxious behaviors. While there are a number of other reasonable categorizations, this grouping provides an approachable structure for understanding these disorders.

Odd or Eccentric Behaviors

Paranoid Personality Disorder

People with **paranoid personality disorder** have several outstanding characteristics: unwarranted feelings of suspiciousness and mistrust of other people; hypersensitivity; the expectation—without sufficient justification—that they will be exploited or harmed by others; and a tendency to read hidden demeaning or threatening messages into benign remarks or events (for example, suspecting that a neighbor put out trash early to annoy them). It is very difficult for such people to have close relationships with others because they are constantly expecting treachery. The following case provides an account of a typical paranoid personality.

A 36-year-old single white male engineer was referred for psychiatric evaluation, with his grudging cooperation, by his project manager. He described his current work situation as very tense because his co-workers had been "ganging up" on him, giving him the most difficult assignments and sometimes removing the crucial information he needed from the relevant files. He said they did this "because they like to see me sweat." He had changed jobs four times in the past six years because of similar problems at previous jobs. Aside from his frequent contact with a sibling, the patient was socially isolated. He stated, "I've never trusted people. All they want to do is take advantage of you." He was tense, aloof, and obviously very angry at his co-workers. He was hypervigilant and made several comments indicating that he felt that the interviewer might not "see things my way." There was no evidence of psychosis or depression.

—Siever and Kendler, 1986, p. 199

Table 9–2

Clinical Features of Paranoid Personality Disorder

A person having several of these characteristics might be considered to have a paranoid personality disorder.

1. Expects, without sufficient basis, to be exploited or harmed by others.
2. Questions, without justification, the loyalty or trustworthiness of peers and associates.
3. Reads hidden demeaning or threatening meanings into benign remarks or events.
4. Bears grudges or is unforgiving of insults or slights.
5. Is reluctant to confide in others because of unwarranted fear that the information will be used against him or her.
6. Perceives attacks on his or her character or reputation that are not apparent to others and is quick to react with anger or to counterattack.
7. Has recurrent suspicions, without justification, regarding fidelity of spouse or sexual partner.

Paranoid individuals rarely seek clinical help. If a situation becomes so difficult that they are forced to seek help (for example, if they are required to work closely with other people), the therapist's hardest task is to penetrate the barrier of suspiciousness. They are also hypersensitive to criticism, making it especially difficult for them to function in subordinate positions. They have a strong fear of losing independence and the power to shape events. Just the feeling of being in a position of lower rank or lesser power might be intolerable (Akhtar, 1990).

People with paranoid personality disorder often seem cold, humorless, devious, and scheming. These characteristics do not promote close, rewarding relationships. Perhaps because people with this kind of personality keep to themselves and rarely become intimate with others, many of their unusual ideas remain unnoticed. Their performance is often impaired because their preoccupation with searching for hidden motives and special meanings limits their ability to consider and understand whole situations. When problems occur, they are often work-related, since work is an area in which interpersonal contacts are difficult to avoid.

Table 9–2 lists the major clinical features in DSM Axis II of paranoid personalities. As we stated earlier, all of the features do not have to be present for this classification to be used—four or more of the characteristics might justify use of the diagnosis.

Schizoid Personality Disorder

Individuals with **schizoid personality disorder** are reserved, socially withdrawn, and seclusive (see Figure 9–2). They prefer solitary work activities and hobbies and lack the capacity for warm, close relationships. Such people rarely express their feelings directly. Not only do they have few relationships with others, but they also seem to have little desire for them. In any case, they often have poor social skills, although their speech and behavior patterns are not unusual or eccentric. They also lack a sense of humor and seem detached from their environ-

FIGURE 9–2 Spending time alone, withdrawn from others, is typical of people with schizoid personality disorders. They often appear quite detached from life around them.

ment. When, in her book *The White Album,* Joan Didion uses the phrase "only marginally engaged in the dailiness of life," she could be describing the detachment of people with schizoid personality disorders. Perhaps because of this detachment, males with schizoid personality disorder seldom marry. Females are more likely to marry, possibly by accepting a marriage offer rather than seeking it.

Although the man in the following example did not complain of social isolation (and schizoid individuals rarely do) his stable solitary existence was a central part of his personality. He also showed a rigidity in his personal life and was not concerned about others' opinions of him as long as they let him alone.

A 46-year-old single white male accountant sought professional consultation on the advice of a colleague because of persistent feelings of dissatisfaction and depression following a change in his work situation. Although he retained his position at his firm, where he had worked for 20 years, many of his more important responsibilities had been shifted to a younger colleague. He had always worked well in a rather autonomous position in the firm but now felt that his daily work routine had been disrupted and he no longer had meaningful tasks to accomplish. It turned out that he had always been socially isolated, with social contacts limited to acquaintances at work, and followed a rather prescribed pattern of reading the newspaper and watching television as his evening recreation. He at times saw a married sister and her family on weekends. This limited life style had been tolerable for him for some time and he appeared relatively indifferent to the opinions of co-workers as long as he could count on being assigned his quota of accounts. His redefined position left him

with less work to do and an unclear role in the firm. He felt as if "the rug had been pulled out from under me." In the consultation, he was a quiet man who although cooperative was difficult to engage affectively. He spoke with little emotion and mumbled at times, exhibiting no sense of attachment to other people in his life, but only to his "way of doing things," which he had great difficulty in changing.

—Siever and Kendler, 1986, p. 192

The emotional responses of schizoid individuals seem rather flat as well as cold. The kinds of frustrations that arouse expressions of anger in most people elicit little observable hostility from these individuals. They often seem vague, self-absorbed, absent-minded, and not very aware of or interested in what is going on around them. Some of these people can support themselves if they find socially isolated jobs. Many of them, however, have problems at work because of the contact with other people that most jobs require. Since schizoid people are not bothered by their lack of personal relationships, they are poor prospects for therapy (Akhtar, 1987).

Table 9–3 lists the clinical features of schizoid personalities. As with all the personality disorders, the presence of every feature is not required for use of the classification.

Schizotypal Personality Disorder

People with **schizotypal personality disorder** are characterized by oddities of thinking, perceiving, communicating, and behaving. These deviations are never as extreme as those found in cases of full-blown schizophrenia. Still, clinicians often feel the need to probe for the possibility of major distortions, such as hearing voices.

Table 9–3

Clinical Features of Schizoid Personality Disorder

A person having several of these characteristics might be considered to have a schizoid personality disorder.

1. Neither desires nor enjoys close relationships, including being part of a family.
2. Almost always chooses solitary activities.
3. Few, if any, activities provide pleasure.
4. Indicates little, if any, desire to have sexual experiences with another person.
5. Appears indifferent to the praise or criticism of others.
6. No close friends or confidants (or only one).
7. Shows emotional coldness, detachment, and little variation in emotions.

I (Interviewer):	*Have you heard any voices ever?*
P (Patient):	*My own thoughts, I think them in words. I imagine how they would sound if I were to speak them out loud. There is the quality of sound in thoughts. Thoughts go beyond people. They interconnect and survive.*
I:	*Do you have access to those interconnecting thoughts? Are you familiar with ESP?*
P:	*I can sense them, I can sense the hostile thoughts of the character disorders.*
I:	*Tell me about these character disorders! Who are they?*
P:	*Those people who impose on your thoughts—you meet them everywhere. These thoughtless, callous mental morons.*
I:	*Do you think they are like a fraternity? Sticking together and conspiring against you?*
P:	*No, they are not like a conspiracy— more here and there, you know, just like people you meet and don't like. I don't think they are organized. It's more like a mind game.*

—Othmer and Othmer, 1989, p. 388

People with schizotypal personality disorder, like schizoid individuals, are seclusive, emotionally shallow, and socially unskilled. The speech patterns of the two groups are quite different. People with a schizoid personality disorder have no oddities of speech although they may lack social skills. Those with a schizotypal personality disorder, on the other hand, often are not understood because they either use unusual words and phrases or use common words in unusual ways. They also are likely to express ideas unclearly. At times—usually when they are under stress—their thinking deteriorates and they may express ideas that seem delusional. These cognitive and perceptual characteristics are probably the most important in distinguishing schizotypal personality disorder from borderline and schizoid personality disorders (Widiger and others, 1987).

The behavior of people with a schizotypal personality disorder may, at times, border on the bizarre. Much of the time they seem suspicious, superstitious, and aloof.

The following case illustrates a number of the characteristics of schizotypal personality disorder.

A 41-year-old man was referred to a community mental health center's activities program for help in improving his social skills. He had a lifelong pattern of social isolation, with no real friends, and spent long hours worrying that his angry thoughts about his older brother would cause his brother harm. He had previously worked as a clerk in civil service, but had lost his job because of poor attendance and low productivity.

On interview the patient was distant and somewhat distrustful. He described in elaborate and often irrelevant detail his rather uneventful and routine daily life. He told the interviewer that he had spent an hour and a half in a pet store deciding which of two brands of fish food to buy, and explained their relative merits. For two days he had studied the washing instructions on a new pair of jeans—Did "Wash before wearing" mean that the jeans were to be washed before wearing the first time, or did they need, for some reason, to be washed each time before they were worn? He did not regard concerns such as these as senseless, though he acknowledged that the amount of time spent thinking about them might be excessive. When asked about his finances, he could recite from memory his most recent monthly bank statement, including the amount of every check and the running balance as each check was written. He knew his balance on any particular day, but sometimes got anxious if he considered whether a certain check or deposit had actually cleared.

He asked the interviewer whether, if he joined the program, he would be required to participate in groups. He said that groups made him very nervous, and he was unsure if he could "stand" participating in them.

—Spitzer and others, 1989, p. 154

Noteworthy features of this case include the absence of close friends or confidants, thinking that one has magical powers (worrying that his angry thoughts would cause his brother harm), constricted affect (reflected in his being "distant" in the interview), odd speech (providing elaborate and often irrelevant details), and social anxiety. Because of this man's eccentricities of thought

Table 9–4

Clinical Features of Schizotypal Personality Disorder

A person having several of these characteristics might be considered to have a schizotypal personality disorder.

1. Ideas of reference (the belief that the conversation, smiling, or other actions of people have reference to oneself).
2. Excessive social anxiety that does not diminish with familiarity and tends to be associated with paranoid fears rather than negative judgments.
3. Odd beliefs or thinking that one has magical powers (e.g., "others can feel my feelings").
4. Unusual perceptual experiences including bodily illusions.
5. Odd speech and thinking (e.g., very vague, circumstantial, overelaborate).
6. Paranoid ideas or suspiciousness.
7. Odd or eccentric behavior or appearance (e.g., unusual mannerisms, talking to self, odd speech).
8. No close friends or confidants (or perhaps only one) other than relatives, primarily because of lack of desire for contact, pervasive discomfort with others, or eccentricities.
9. Inappropriate or constricted affect (e.g., is cold, aloof).

and speech he would be classified as schizotypal rather than schizoid.

Schizotypal individuals probably have more than the average risk of an episode of schizophrenia later in life. A 15-year follow-up of patients with schizotypal personality disorder suggests that this category represents a borderline group between health and schizophrenia (McGlashan, 1986). Since many cases of schizophrenia are presumed to have a hereditary, biological component, schizotypal individuals probably share this genetic characteristic. Table 9–4 lists clinical features of schizotypal personality disorder.

Persons with paranoid, schizoid, and schizotypal personality disorders have in common a degree of social detachment and the presence of "odd" or idiosyncratic behavior that can be observed in much more extreme form in schizophrenia. Paranoid personality disorder focuses attention on suspiciousness and mistrust of others; schizoid personality disorder on the preference for solitary activities, without there necessarily being distortions in perceptions of reality; and schizotypal personality disorder focuses on eccentricity and cognitive–perceptual distortions. Because of overlaps among these odd and eccentric behaviors and between them and some other Axis II and Axis I classifications, there is not complete agreement about their clinical uniqueness. Agreement is probably least for schizotypal personality disorder because research has shown that it is often closely related to schizophrenia and might simply be a weak form of that disorder (Siever and others, 1991). However, the schizotypal classification does meet the Axis II requirements of enduring patterns of perceiving,

relating to, and thinking about the environment and oneself. The criteria for schizotypal personality disorder refer to persistent disturbances in perception and cognition of relations between self and others. These disturbances are not limited to periods of stress; they are present virtually all the time. Research is needed to establish the contribution this Axis II classification can make to the diagnostic process.

Dramatic, Emotional, or Erratic Behaviors

The first group of personality disorders, which we have just reviewed, is composed of individuals with withdrawn behavior. The second category contains people who seek attention and whose behavior is often highly noticeable and very unpredictable.

Histrionic Personality Disorder

For people with **histrionic personality disorder**, getting the attention of others is a high priority (see Figure 9–3). Their motto might be "All the world's a stage"; in interpersonal relationships, they often act out a role, such as "the star" or "the victim." These people strike others as vain and immature and tend to speak in a dramatic, exaggerated, and gushing manner.

This classification is used in cases that are marked

FIGURE 9–3 Histrionic personalities may be overly concerned with making a striking or dramatic impression.

Histrionic individuals often operate on hunches and tend to stop at the obvious. Not only are they suggestible and easily influenced by the opinions of others, but they are also easy to distract. Their attention is easily captured and just as easily turned toward something else. Thus, their behavior has a scattered quality. These problems of attention also lead histrionic people to appear incredibly naive about many commonplace things.

Psychoanalyst Anthony Storr (1980) has interpreted histrionic behavior as a pattern that is often adopted by individuals who do not feel able to compete with others on equal terms and believe that no one is paying attention to them. Storr thinks that such people may have been disregarded by their parents as children. Although the child repeatedly tried to get the parents to think of him or her as an individual, those attempts failed. The child then became demanding and resorted to all kinds of dramatic behaviors in order to be noticed. This interpretation may help to explain another characteristic of these histrionic individuals—their frequent complaints of poor health, for example, weakness or headaches. The less attention the parents paid to the child, the more the child had to shout or dramatize to get their attention. Histrionic individuals carry these extreme behaviors into adulthood.

Perhaps because of such childhood experience, histrionic people may also feel unlovable and may react to this feeling by trying to make themselves sexually irresistible. Women in particular may dress and behave seductively yet not really desire intimate sexual activity. Women are more likely than men to be diagnosed as histrionic (Pfohl, 1991). Table 9–5 lists several clinical features frequently observed in cases of histrionic personality disorder. In the following case, the interviewer inquires about a sleep problem for which the patient was seeking clinical consultation.

I: Tell me about your sleep problems.

P: Oh, it's terrible. There are whole nights when I can't sleep at all. I toss and turn, and I get up in the morning without having closed my eyes for even a second.

I: This happens only some nights?

P: It happens when I have these terrible, terrible fights with my husband. He just tears me to pieces. (Patient rolls her eyes dramatically upward.)

I: Does he or anybody else notice what you are going through?

P: They don't have the foggiest idea. I can scream and yell and they still don't understand.

by exaggerated expression of emotion, stormy interpersonal relationships, a self-centered attitude, and manipulativeness. The manipulativeness might manifest itself in suicidal gestures, threats, or attempts, as well as in other attention-getting behaviors such as dramatic physical complaints. Histrionic patients often come to the attention of therapists because of a drug overdose or other form of suicide attempt.

Histrionic individuals often react too quickly to situations that require some analysis and thought. They don't always focus their attention long enough to perceive the details of a situation, and as a result they tend to respond with emotionally tinged generalities. When people with histrionic personalities are asked to describe something, they generally respond with impressions rather than facts. For example, a therapist who was taking a case history from a client and had made repeated efforts to get a description of the client's father reported that the patient "seemed . . . hardly to understand the sort of data I was interested in, and the best she could provide was, 'My father? He was wham-bang! That's all—just wham-bang!' " (Shapiro, 1965, p. 111).

Table 9–5

Clinical Features of Histrionic Personality Disorder

A person having several of these characteristics might be considered to have a histrionic personality disorder.

1. Rapidly shifting, but basically shallow expressions of emotions.
2. Overly concerned with physical attractiveness.
3. Inappropriately sexually seductive in appearance or behavior.
4. Uncomfortable when not the center of attention.
5. Excessively impressionistic speech, which lacks detail.
6. Intolerant of, or excessively frustrated by, situations that do not work out exactly as desired.
7. Apparent view of relationships as possessing greater intimacy than is actually the case (e.g., refers to an acquaintance as a "dear, dear friend").
8. Exaggerated expressions of emotion with much self-dramatization.

I: *When you have these fights, is your mood affected?*

P: *I get these devastating depressions and I have to cry the whole time.*

 —Othmer and Othmer, 1989, p. 402

Even though this patient talks freely, she isn't able to provide needed information. For example, she is unable to describe precisely the circumstances of the fights with her husband. She expresses her suffering in an exaggerated way typical of histrionic personality disorder and she is reluctant to furnish the facts.

Narcissistic Personality Disorder

The word "narcissism" comes from the classical myth about a young man, Narcissus, who fell in love with his reflection in a pond. Because he could never grasp his own image, he despaired and died of his own anguish.

Several critical factors play roles in **narcissistic personality disorder:** an extreme sense of self-importance and the expectation of special favors, a need for constant attention, fragile self-esteem, and lack of empathy or caring for others (see Figure 9–4). People with a narcissistic personality disorder are often preoccupied with fantasies of unlimited success and brilliance, power, beauty, and ideal love relationships. They may think of their problems as unique and feel that only other equally special people are able to understand them. The case of Robert Graham illustrates many of the characteristics of narcissistic personality disorder.

FIGURE 9–4 Even if they do not have the characteristics that would result in a diagnosis of narcissistic personality disorder, many theatrical performers are very high in narcissism. The characteristics of performers' jobs may increase whatever narcissistic tendencies they already possess. Their success often demands that they focus great attention on their youthful appearance, personal attractiveness, and other aspects of their self-image. Adoration by fans may also increase performers' feelings of self-absorption and of being special people.

Graham, a successful 30-year-old actor, contacted a therapist because he was having trouble with a new stage role. In it he had to play a character who was deeply depressed by the death of his wife. As Graham said, he had trouble portraying "a character who was so involved with a woman that his life essentially ended simply because she died."

In his first interview he told the therapist what a good actor he was. "I don't wish to be immodest, but I am uniquely talented." Throughout his life he had been told he was "uniquely cute" and "gifted." He could be charming and entertaining and used these abilities to make other people feel "special" as a way of furthering his career. He seemed to respond to others with a feeling of contempt and remarked that other people were gullible and "easily taken in by experiences."

Graham's relations with women puzzled him. He began dating and had sexual activity early and had romances with a series of women as he grew older. However, in each romance he would gradually lose interest after a short period and usually start an affair with another woman before breaking off with the first. He gave little thought to his former partner after breaking off each relationship. "It is almost as if people are playthings and I need lots and lots of new toys." His account of his life sounded as if he had never grieved or been depressed.

—Adapted from Spitzer and others, 1983, pp. 71–74

Table 9–6 lists characteristics frequently seen in narcissistic personality disorder. As with other personality disorders, all clinical features do not have to be present for the classification to be used. Rather, the characteristics in the table can be viewed as a prototype or composite of narcissistic disorders. The presence of more than half the features in a given case would justify use of the diagnosis.

The category of narcissistic personality disorder was introduced into DSM because mental-health professionals were seeing an increase in cases in which the problem seemed to be excessive self-concern and an inflated sense of one's own importance and uniqueness (see Figure 9–5). In addition, in recent years several psychoanalysts have focused on personal development in the early years of life, the development of the self as a separate entity, and narcissism as an aspect of self-development.

Relatively little research has been done on the classification of narcissistic personality disorder. One study used a structured interview, the Diagnostic Interview for Narcissism (DIN), designed to cover content areas that might be especially relevant to the diagnostic picture in narcissistic personality disorder (Gunderson and others, 1990). After the interviews were completed, the answers were coded into content areas and the results were statistically analyzed to determine the categories of response that best identified people with this disorder.

Borderline Personality Disorder

Borderline personality disorder was officially recognized as a diagnosis in 1980. Since that time the

Table 9–6
Clinical Features of Narcissistic Personality Disorder

A person having at least five of these characteristics might be considered to have a narcissistic personality disorder.

1. Grandiose sense of self-importance, exaggeration of personal achievements and talents, and need for recognition by others of one's superiority.
2. Preoccupations with fantasies of unlimited success, power, and beauty.
3. Sense of one's specialness and uniqueness that can be appreciated only by other special or high-status people or institutions (e.g., employers).
4. Requires excessive admiration and attention.
5. Sense of entitlement, expects especially favorable treatment or automatic compliance with personal expectations.
6. Exploits other people, takes advantage of them.
7. Lacks empathy for other people's needs and feelings.
8. Often envious of others or believes others are envious of him/her (resents privileges or achievements of those regarded less special or deserving).
9. Arrogant, haughty behavior or attitudes.

FIGURE 9–5 This sign suggests that Dr. Holgdbrn may have become a specialist in narcissistic personalities from observing his own behavior.

(Harley Schwadron)

self-destructive behavior, chronic range of cognitive distortions, fears of abandonment, and impulsivity.

Intense clinging dependency and manipulation characterize the interpersonal relationships of those with borderline personality disorder and make interaction with these people very difficult. They seem to wish for a dependent and exclusive relationship with another person. This desire for dependency is clear to outside observers but vehemently denied by the borderline individual. As a part of this vehement denial, such individuals devalue or discredit the strengths and personal significance of others. This often takes the form of extreme anger when the other person sets limits for the relationship, or when a separation is about to occur. In addition to anger, the borderline individual uses manipulative behavior to control relationships, such as complaining about physical symptoms and making and carrying out self-destructive threats. Table 9–7 lists major clinical features of borderline personality disorder.

Self-destructive behaviors have been called "the behavioral specialty" of those with borderline personality disorder. Table 9–8 shows the frequency of self-destructive acts in one group of borderline individuals. Overdosing with drugs and wrist-slashing are most common. In recent years severe bulimia (an eating disorder discussed in Chapter 15) has become a common self-destructive tactic (Gunderson & Zanarini, 1987). Such behaviors are designed to call forth a "saving" response from another significant person.

Self-destructiveness is the characteristic of borderline individuals that generates the most discomfort in those who attempt to help them. The therapist's hope of saving an endangered life is alternately encouraged and then dashed by the client's spiteful efforts at self-

borderline category has been used so widely that 20 percent of psychiatric patients are given this diagnosis and it is estimated to occur in three to five percent of the general population (Frances & Widiger, 1986). About two-thirds of those with borderline personality disorder are female. A heterogeneous group of individuals receive this diagnosis, but they share a number of characteristics, including unstable personal relationships, threats of

Table 9–7
Clinical Features of Borderline Personality Disorder

A person having several of these characteristics might be considered to have a borderline personality disorder.

1. Frantic efforts to avoid real or imagined abandonment.
2. Unstable and intense interpersonal relationships.
3. Persistent and markedly disturbed, distorted, or unstable sense of self (e.g., a feeling that one doesn't exist or embodies evil).
4. Impulsiveness in such areas as sex, substance use, crime, and reckless driving.
5. Recurrent suicidal thoughts, gestures, or behavior.
6. Emotional instability with periods of extreme depression, irritability, or anxiety.
7. Chronic feelings of emptiness.
8. Inappropriate intense anger or lack of control of anger (e.g., loss of temper, recurrent physical fights).
9. Under stress, transient psychotic-like experiences (e.g., paranoid thinking, depersonalization).

Table 9–8

Total Number of Self-destructive Acts Described by 57 People with Borderline Personality Disorder

Category	Number of Acts	Behavior Pattern
Suicide threats	42	To get attention To cause trouble In rage
Overdose	40	No usual pattern Barbiturates most frequent
Self-mutilation	36	Wrist-slashing most frequent, then body banging, then burning, puncturing, or hair removal
Drug abuse	38	Polydrug abuse most frequent, next amphetamines or alcohol binges, then marijuana
Promiscuity	36	Usually under the influence of drugs or alcohol
Accidents	14	Reckless driving

SOURCE: Adapted from Gunderson, 1984, p. 86.

destruction. Therapists often experience intense feelings of responsibility for borderline clients. The therapist's initial efforts to be supportive when the client threatens suicide can lead to increased responsibility for the client's life and increased involvement outside of the therapy sessions. Unless the controlling nature of the client's responses are interpreted in the therapy sessions, the situation may become unworkable for the therapist. It is necessary to make the client understand that the therapist cannot be manipulated by threats of suicide and that the client must work to understand these self-destructive urges without acting them out. If this effort is not successful, the threats of self-destruction will recur, and the risk to the client will be even greater if the therapist fails to respond on cue. This danger is illustrated by the following example.

A borderline patient periodically rented a motel room and, with a stockpile of pills nearby, would call her therapist's home with an urgent message. He would respond by engaging in long conversations in which he "talked her down." Even as he told her that she could not count on his always being available, he became more wary

of going out evenings without detailed instructions about how he could be reached. One night the patient couldn't reach him due to a bad phone connection. She fatally overdosed from what was probably a miscalculated manipulation.

—Gunderson, 1984, p. 93

Their strong need for a relationship leads borderline persons to have chronic and long-lasting fears that the people on whom they are dependent will abandon them. These fears are related to the extreme panic they feel when alone. As a defense against this fear, borderline people are compulsively social. But despite this need for social interaction, many of their behaviors repel people. These include their intense anger and demands, suspiciousness, and their impulsivity. They deal with stress by being sexually promiscuous, getting into fights, and binge eating and purging.

Marked emotional instability with sudden shifts to anxiety, and continued depression or irritability—which may last only a few hours and never more than a few days—are typical of borderline personality disorder, as is illustrated in the following description by a patient.

"I was alone at home a few months ago; I was frightened! I was trying to get in touch with my boyfriend and I couldn't. . . . He was nowhere to be found. All my friends seemed to be busy that night and I had no one to talk to. . . . I just got more and more nervous and more and more agitated. Finally—bang!—I took out a cigarette and lit it and stuck it into my forearm. I don't know why I did it because I didn't really care for him all that much. I guess I felt I had to do something dramatic."

—Stone, 1980, p. 400

Borderline individuals also show disturbance in their concepts of identity: uncertainties about self-image, gender identity, values, loyalties, and goals. They may have chronic feelings of emptiness or boredom and be unable to tolerate being alone. The following anecdote illustrates the behavior of a borderline individual.

A 27-year-old woman was married and had two small children. She had had a stormy adolescence, having been forced into sexual

relations with a brother six years her senior whom she at first idolized and later feared. Their relationship continued until just before she left home for college, when she told her parents of it. In the ensuing emotional turmoil, she made a gesture of suicide (overdose of aspirin) but was not hospitalized. . . . Outwardly flirtatious, although inwardly shy and ill at ease, she felt intensely lonely and went through a period of mild alcohol abuse and brief sexual affairs in an effort to cope with her anxiety and sense of inner emptiness. At age 19, she married a classmate and dropped out of school.

Fairly at ease in the first years of her marriage, she became anxious, bored, and given to fits of sadness and tearfulness after the birth of her second child. Her mood fluctuated widely from hour to hour, day to day, but negative feelings were greatly intensified on the three or four days before her period. Her husband had grown less attentive as the family expanded, in response to which she became increasingly irritable, provocative, and at times abusive (smashing plates, hurling insults). Her husband began to carry on an extramarital relationship, which she eventually discovered. At that point, she became seriously depressed, lost sleep and appetite, began to abuse alcohol and sedatives, and made several gestures of suicide, including one instance of cutting her wrist. On two occasions she hid for several nights in motels without informing anyone where she was. Each time she took her eight-year-old daughter with her, as though to protect her from the "designs" she imagined her husband had on their elder girl. After the wrist-cutting incident, when she had also left a note apologizing for being a "failure" as a wife and mother, she was hospitalized. She understood the unrealistic nature of her suspicions, as she explained to the hospital staff, but could not shake off the morbid doubts she experienced.

—Stone, 1986, p. 210

DISTINGUISHING BORDERLINES FROM OTHER GROUPS The word "borderline" suggests a marginal level of functioning, something that borders on becoming something else. Originally the term was used to describe a marginal or milder form of schizophrenia. Today, some researchers argue that borderline patients actually represent the boundary between personality disorders and mood disorders. Indeed, about half of those with borderline personality disorder can also be diagnosed as having a mood disorder. Such individuals are also likely to have a family history of mood disorder. However, people with several other types of personality disorders are equally as likely to be depressed. Relatives of those with borderline personality disorder are more likely to share this diagnosis than are family members of those with other personality disorders—that is, the disorder seems to "breed true" (Zanarini and others, 1988). This likelihood supports the view that borderline personality is a disorder in its own right.

Despite the evidence obtained from family studies, some researchers have been unable to distinguish borderline disorder from histrionic personality disorder and antisocial personality disorder (Pope and others, 1983). Figure 9–6 shows the overlapping characteristics between borderline personality disorder and the other personality disorders in the same diagnostic cluster. Overlap may also occur with a personality disorder in another cluster. Sometimes patients who are diagnosed as borderline and those who are diagnosed as schizotypal seem similar. However, the schizotypal and borderline categories have different emphases. The schizotypal category stresses cognitive symptoms: thinking that one has magical powers, ideas of reference, suspicious thought. The borderline category stresses affective or emotional symptoms: feelings of emotional instability, emptiness, boredom, and inappropriate and intense anger (Gunderson, 1984). Schizotypal individuals are socially isolated; in contrast, borderline individuals cannot stand being alone. Despite these problems of overlap with depression and with other personality disorders, research findings provide support for the borderline personality disorder as a true category of pathologies rather than as a combination of several groups (Zalewski & Archer, 1991).

RESEARCH INTO CAUSES OF BORDERLINE PERSONALITY DISORDER Probably because of the relatively large number of cases diagnosed as borderline personality disorders and also because borderline individuals are likely to make frequent suicidal gestures, more research on causes and treatment has been carried out with this disorder than with many of the other personality disorders. Most of the theories about its cause also focus on a disturbed early relationship between a preborderline child and his or her parents. There are a variety of descriptions of what this relationship might be like (Gunderson & Zanarini, 1987). Some focus on the attachment experience in early childhood, while others point to parents who fail to provide adequate attention to the child's own feelings so that he or she never develops an adequate sense of self (Alder & Buie, 1979). Some theorists focus on parental abuse (both sexual and physical) in adolescence as well as divorce, alcoholism, and other stressors (Linehan, 1987). It is clear from all these examples, however, that such stressors in the family often occur and the children do not develop borderline

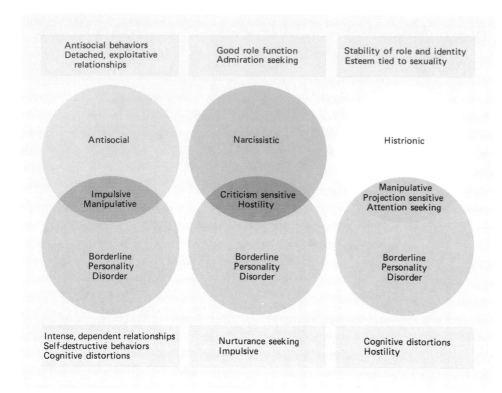

Antisocial behaviors
Detached, exploitative
relationships

Good role function
Admiration seeking

Stability of role and identity
Esteem tied to sexuality

Antisocial

Narcissistic

Histrionic

Impulsive
Manipulative

Criticism sensitive
Hostility

Manipulative
Projection sensitive
Attention seeking

Borderline
Personality
Disorder

Borderline
Personality
Disorder

Borderline
Personality
Disorder

Intense, dependent relationships
Self-destructive behaviors
Cognitive distortions

Nurturance seeking
Impulsive

Cognitive distortions
Hostility

FIGURE 9–6 The borderline personality disorder has some characteristics that overlap with other personality disorders in the dramatic, emotional, or erratic behavior category. The similar characteristics are shown in the overlapping circle segments. Characteristics that distinguish between the two disorders are shown in the boxes above and below each pair.

(Adapted from Gunderson and Zanarini, 1987, p. 7)

personality disorder. This finding suggests that borderline disorder may be associated with some genetic vulnerability. The disorder probably develops through a combination of neurobiological, early developmental, and later socializing factors. Splitting is Kernberg's (1975) theoretical explanation of the extreme changeability that can be seen in the borderline person's relationships to others. He defined **splitting** as the failure to integrate the positive and negative experiences that occur between the individual and other people. Rather than perceiving another individual as a loving person who sometimes accepts and sometimes rejects—for example, a mother who sometimes hugs and sometimes disciplines a young child—the borderline individual shifts back and forth between these contradictory images.

CLINICAL TREATMENT OF BORDERLINE PERSONALITY DISORDER A first step in planning treatment for any disorder is to identify its most distinctive features. Recent research has suggested three especially important problems in cases of borderline personality disorder (Hurt & Clarkin, 1990):

1. *Identity disturbances* reflected in borderlines' chronic feelings of emptiness or boredom and intolerance of being alone. These people have a strong need for involvement with others and a reliance on external support for self-definition.

2. *Affective disturbances* reflected in their intense, inappropriate anger, instability of emotions, and unsta-

ble interpersonal relationships. Borderlines often lead stormy, dramatic lives.

3. *Impulse disturbances* reflected in their self-damaging acts and impulsive behaviors.

Various therapeutic approaches deal with these core issues in different ways. Psychodynamically oriented clinicians believe that most borderline individuals can best be treated in intensive face-to-face psychotherapy sessions at least three times a week over a period of several years. In these sessions the therapist plays a more active structuring role than is usual in classical psychoanalysis. At the beginning the emphasis is on present behavior rather than childhood experiences, and rather than allowing the transference relationship to develop fully, the therapist explicitly describes and discusses the client's apparent distortions of reality—for example, the client's perceptions of the therapist.

Although psychoanalysts were among the first clinicians to describe and treat borderlines, clinicians of several theoretical perspectives are now developing therapies for these people. Cognitively oriented therapists focus on the borderline's limitations in three areas: automatic thoughts, cognitive distortions, and unrealistic underlying assumptions (for example, that people are either all good or all bad) (Linehan, 1989). Cognitive therapy thus concentrates on identifying and changing cognitions so as to permit better reality testing. Behavior therapists direct attention elsewhere, to the borderline's

defective behavioral repertory. They try to teach patients better social skills and to help them manage their anxiety so as to not become overwhelmed with affective reactions. Biologically oriented clinicians make use of various types of medication in treating borderlines. In general, medication alone is mildly effective, with patients perhaps improving from severely to moderately impaired. Combinations of several therapeutic approaches may prove to be particularly effective. For example, medications together with psychotherapy and family support could be useful in dealing with the borderline person's multiple problems. Further research is needed in developing therapeutic approaches that will help these unstable people who lead such chaotic lives (Linehan and others, 1991).

LONG-TERM PROSPECTS It was originally thought that because of their depressive and sometimes psychoticlike symptoms, borderline individuals would eventually develop a traditional illness such as schizophrenia or a major mood disorder. However, several follow-up studies show that this rarely happens; instead, borderline personality disorder tends to remain roughly the same over time (Plakun and others, 1985; Stone & Stone, 1988).

Follow-ups over ten years or less show that the unstable relationships, poor work performance, and symptom levels usually continue. Longer-term follow-up studies show that borderline individuals who have received intensive treatment and are from high socioeconomic levels have a fairly good chance of developing full-time employment. Interpersonal relations also improve after a long unstable period during the young adult years (Stone and others, 1987). About a third of these borderline patients eventually marry and establish their own families. However, the range of outcomes is wide

and many of those with borderline personality disorder continue to have severe interpersonal and occupational problems. One negative outcome is suicide. Probably eight to ten percent of borderline individuals actually kill themselves, although this figure is small compared to the number of suicide attempts by these people. Another frequent negative outcome is alcohol abuse. Figure 9–7 compares some of the positive and negative outcomes in studies of borderline personality disorder to those found in schizophrenia and major mood disorders.

Antisocial Personality Disorder

Antisocial personality disorder is associated with crime, violence, and delinquency. The essential characteristics of this disorder include a history of continuous and chronic conduct disorder. This behavior begins before the age of 15 and continues into adult life.

Evidence of a conduct disorder before the age of 15 can be found in some of the following behaviors: truancy; school suspension; arrest; running away from home; lying; engaging in sexual intercourse; using liquor, tobacco, or other nonprescribed drugs, unusually early compared to those in the peer group; stealing; vandalism; fighting; and violating rules at home or school. The pattern of irresponsible and antisocial behavior after the age of 15 includes several of these characteristics: inability to sustain a consistent work record; repeated antisocial acts such as stealing, destroying property, and harassing others; repeated fights or assaults; failure to honor financial obligations; failure to plan ahead; recklessness, especially in driving; mistreatment or neglect of one's children; sexual promiscuity; and lack of remorse upon harming others. Convicted murderer Gary Gilmore, whose life is described in Box 9–1, fits this description well.

FIGURE 9–7 The long-term outcome for borderline personality disorder is generally better than that for patients with either schizophrenia or a major mood disorder.

(Adapted from Gunderson and Zanarini, 1987, p. 10)

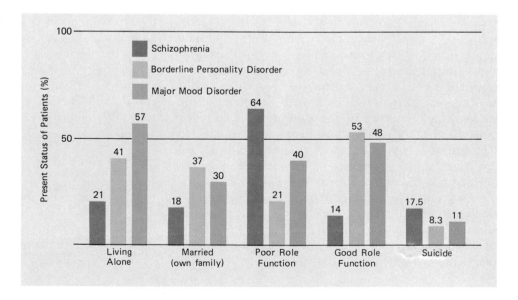

BOX 9–1 Antisocial Personality Disorder: A Frightening Example

The case of Gary Gilmore (Figure 9–8) illustrates many characteristics of antisocial personality disorder.

FIGURE 9–8 Gary Gilmore in 1976.

Gilmore was convicted of two murders and sentenced to death. When he was executed in 1977, he was the first person to be put to death in the United States in 11 years. Although he refused to appeal his conviction, several appeals were made on his behalf and his execution was delayed three times. During this period, while newspapers featured stories on his "fight for the right to be executed," he attempted suicide twice.

Gilmore displayed an antisocial personality pattern very early. In spite of his high intelligence, his school grades were poor, he was often truant, and he was repeatedly accused of stealing from his schoolmates. At age 14 he was sent to a juvenile center for stealing a car; after his release he was sent to jail several times for burglaries; and at age 20 he was sent to the state penitentiary for burglary and robbery. After his release from the penitentiary he spent 2 years in jail for reckless and drunk driving. After this imprisonment he spent 11 years in the state penitentiary for several armed robberies.

Gilmore reported that he had begun drinking at the age of 10 and later had used a variety of illegal drugs—amphetamines, cocaine, and LSD. During his prison stays, he drank when he could and smoked marijuana. He was a talented tattoo artist. Several times he tattooed obscene words and pictures on inmates whom he disliked. "I thought it was a good way to get back at the snitches. I would tatoo them on their bodies where they could not watch what I was doing. It wasn't until they looked at their tattoo in the mirror that they saw what I had done to them." When he was released from prison, Gilmore went to Utah to work in his uncle's shop. When that job didn't work out, he went on to several others. He met a woman and moved in with her the next day. He said that this was the first time he had ever had a close relationship with anyone. It didn't go smoothly. Her two children irritated him, and he often hit them. His drinking and his tendency to get into fights at parties also caused problems.

Before long Gilmore felt increas-

Although Gary Gilmore's antisocial traits may have led him to commit crimes, it is important to distinguish between criminal or aggressive behavior and antisocial personality disorder. While criminal or aggressive behavior could be related to any of a variety of circumstances and conditions (for example, certain forms of brain impairment), when it grows out of an antisocial personality disorder these behaviors are usually part of a recurrent pattern of antisocial behavior marked by lack of remorse or concern over the harm done to others. A large epidemiological survey of the community found that more than half the people whose histories caused them to be classified as having antisocial personality disorder did not have a significant history of arrests despite continuous and chronic antisocial behavior (Robins & Regier, 1991). Yet such people were also unlikely to be seen in a traditional clinical setting except under circumstances when it seemed to them that seeking clinical help would enable them to avoid legal consequences arising from their antisocial actions.

From the standpoint of abnormal psychology, the defining properties of antisocial personalities are not so much the particular acts they perform (for example, robbing a bank or shoplifting), as their distinctive deeply ingrained approach to life. They always seem to be participating in a game in which other individuals exist as pieces to be manipulated and utilized, and it is this game playing that leads these people to get into trouble with the law. At their worst, these people can be cruel, sadistic, or violent. They seldom show anxiety and don't feel guilt. Freudians would maintain that the mind of the antisocial personality is totally lacking the "moral police officer" role of the superego. Antisocial personalities do not see themselves as the cause of their problems, but rather see the tough spots they find themselves in as due to flaws in other people.

Table 9–9 lists characteristic features of those with antisocial personality disorder. These features create obvious difficulties in interpersonal relationships because of the antisocial personality's callousness, incapacity to

ingly frustrated. He seemed unable to succeed outside prison. He broke parole by getting drunk, but his parole officer decided not to report him. After an argument with the woman he lived with, he walked into a store and forcibly carried out a stereo, but he dropped it and fled when two security guards attempted to grab him. After a chase by the police, he got away. Again through the intervention of his parole officer, no charges were brought. When he went back to his house, his woman friend ordered him out with a gun.

In July he pulled into a gas station, ordered the attendant to give him all his cash, and then took the attendant into the station restroom and shot him twice in the head as the man knelt before him. The next morning he walked into a motel.

After being arrested for the crime, Gilmore provided this account of the shooting, as well as some background about himself.

I went in and told the guy to give me the money. I told him to lay on the floor and then I shot him. I then walked out and was carrying the cash drawer with me. I took the money and threw the cash drawer in a bush and I tried to push the gun in the bush, too. But as I was pushing it in the bush, it went off and that's how come I was shot in the arm. It seems like things have always gone bad for me. It seems like I've always done dumb things that just caused trouble for me. I remember when I was a boy I would feel like I had to do things like sit on a railroad track until just before the train came and then I would dash off. Or I would put my finger over the end of a BB gun and pull the trigger to see if a BB was really in it. Sometimes I would stick my finger in water and then put my finger in a light socket to see if it would really shock me.

—Spitzer, and others, 1983, p. 68

Gilmore was evaluated to determine whether he was competent to stand trial. His IQ was found to be 129, in the superior range. His general knowledge was surprisingly good for someone with so little education. He was proud of his vocabulary and read both fiction and news magazines avidly. There was no indication of any organic problems. He reported no bizarre or unusual thoughts except when on drugs. Personality tests revealed no thought or mood disturbances. He slept soundly, had a good appetite, and was not depressed or worried. "I almost never get blue. Though I've made a mess of my life, I never stew about the things I have done."

Gilmore showed the characteristic behaviors of an antisocial personality. He disobeyed rules at home and at school, drank, and used illegal drugs at an early age. By 14 he had been arrested for car theft. While he was in prison he was known for his cruel and violent behavior. He seemed to lack sympathy and felt no guilt. He never had a steady job or a long-lasting relationship.

Table 9–9
Clinical Features of Antisocial Personality Disorder

A person having several of these characteristics might be considered to have an antisocial personality disorder.

1. Glibness, superficiality.
2. Egocentricity, grandiosity.
3. Deceitfulness, manipulativeness.
4. Lacking in remorse.
5. Lacking in empathy.
6. Impulsivity.
7. Irresponsibility.
8. Angry and frustrated.
9. History of persistent, varied, and serious behavioral problems as a child and an adolescent.
10. Antisocial behavior as an adult.

have meaningful enduring ties to others, and disregard for social norms. In the following case, Bert illustrates a number of the characteristics seen in antisocial personality disorder. Bert's case is not as dramatic as that of Gary Gilmore, but Bert is representative of many people who are diagnosed as having an antisocial personality disorder yet who never come in contact with the law or if they do, are not convicted of a crime. These people treat others callously without any apparent concern. They seem to feel no guilt even at harming those closest to them. The excitement of taking chances and of manipulating others seems to be their prime motivators. They either lack an ability to foresee consequences or they consider the consequences unimportant.

After graduating from high school and having a few dead-end jobs, Bert wanted to go into business for himself. He asked his parents, who

had a modest income and some savings for their retirement, to lend him the money he needed to get started. Within five months Bert was out of business, his parents' money "lost," as he put it. Several months later, having found a new business opportunity, Bert again pleaded with his parents to borrow the money he needed. They agreed, and again Bert's opportunity fizzled. His parents desperately wanted to help Bert and to believe in him. So great was their need and so successful was Bert in "conning" his parents that they repeatedly helped him engage in activities that were doomed to failure. Bert craved the excitement of going into business for himself, but was unable either to attend to all the details involved in running a business or to plan ahead. He was magnificent in playing the role of the charming young man on the way up. When he failed, he felt no regrets concerning his failure's implications for his parents and others who had helped him.

RESEARCH INTO CAUSES OF ANTISOCIAL PERSONALITY DISORDER Researchers of antisocial personality have been hampered by the fact that it is so much easier to identify antisocial personalities among individuals who have been convicted of crimes than among the general population. Consequently, the group on which research is based may not be typical of all people with an antisocial personality disorder. One researcher approached this methodological problem in a unique way: She inserted the following ad in a Boston counterculture newspaper.

> ***Wanted: charming, aggressive, carefree people who are impulsively irresponsible but are good at handling people and at looking after number one. Send name, address, phone, and short biography proving how interesting you are to . . .***
>
> —Widom, 1978, p. 72

Widom's ad drew 73 responses, of which about two-thirds were from males. About one-third of the responses seemed to meet the criteria for a diagnosis of antisocial personality disorder. The respondents were interviewed and given a battery of psychological tests. Some of the characteristics of the group are shown in Table 9–10. The researcher concluded that the main difference between her sample and prison samples was that the people who answered her ad had somehow been able to avoid conviction after arrest or detention by the police. In other respects they seemed very similar to prison inmates.

Researchers have looked at many aspects of antiso-

Table 9–10

Characteristics of Subjects Interviewed by Widom[a]

Characteristic	Percentage of Subjects
Arrest Records:	
Detained	17.9
Arrested as an adult	64.3
Convicted as an adult	17.9
Incarceration:	
As a juvenile	10.7
As an adult	32.1
Psychiatric Hospitalization:	
Hospitalized at some time	21.4
Treated as an outpatient only	46.4
Suicide attempts	28.6
Number with both psychiatric and arrest records	46.4
Parental separation:	
Broken homes	21.4
Divorce	7.1
Parental psychopathology	7.1
Parental alcoholism	17.8

[a]The subjects averaged 25 years of age (from 19 to 47 years old). All except one were white.

SOURCE: Widom, 1978

cial individuals—their life histories, psychological and physiological functioning, and personality characteristics—in order to understand why these people behave as they do. The biological perspective has yielded a number of interesting findings. There is increasing evidence that heredity may play a role in both criminality and antisocial behavior. A Swedish study revealed that adopted children who were separated at birth from their parents with antisocial personality disorder show more antisocial behavior later in life than control subjects (Bohman and others, 1982).

How antisocial behavior might be inherited is not yet clear. Researchers have connected habitually violent and antisocial tendencies with the neurochemistry of the body. Impulsive physical violence and aggression in humans is related to very low levels of one of the neurotransmitters, serotonin, and one of its metabolites in the spinal fluid (Virkkunen, 1983). Another idea is that left-handedness and right-brain dominance may somehow be associated with antisocial personality disorder, but so far the evidence is not convincing (Hare & Forth, 1985). Other research has focused on patterns of brain wave activity. For example, some researchers have demonstrated a relationship between one type of electrical brain activity, slow alpha waves, and later antisocial behavior (Volavka, 1990). In normal individuals alpha-wave frequency is known to decrease with relaxation and

drowsiness and to increase with tension, so the slow alpha waves suggest that some antisocial individuals have a lower than normal arousal level. This may mean that sensory inputs that would be disturbing to most people would not be strong enough to excite antisocial individuals. Such people may crave increased stimulation and may therefore seek out unusual forms of excitement.

The brain wave patterns found in people who fit the criteria of antisocial personality disorder have some resemblance to those that occur normally in children and adolescents rather than those of adults. This similarity suggests that at least one subgroup of people with this disorder may have delayed cerebral maturation (Reid, 1986). This fits in with the observation that many psychopaths seem to "burn out" as they grow older. An example of this delayed maturation is shown in the life of Jackroller, a young mugger whose development was studied intensively in the 1920s (Shaw, 1930). Fifty years later, Jackroller told the story of his later life (Jackroller & Snodgrass, 1982). He saw what had happened to him as a series of injustices through which he had struggled. He had a history of trouble keeping jobs and blamed others for most of his difficulties, but he was no longer involved in criminal activity.

Another physiological factor—anxiety—has been studied in antisocial individuals. It had seemed reasonable to assume that people who met the criteria for antisocial personality would also show little anxiety compared to other individuals. But this assumption may be true only in a limited sense. Schalling (1978) found that while antisocial personalities seem to worry less than other people, they nevertheless experience all of the common somatic and muscular indicators of anxiety (high heart rate, shortness of breath, tense muscles). If we divide anxiety into its cognitive part—worry—and its physiological components—the body's responses to fear—antisocial individuals seem to lack the cognitive component of anxiety.

From a cognitive perspective, the study of antisocial behavior focuses on moral development (Kegan, 1986). Just as in the case of psychophysiological factors, the idea of a delay in moral development has been suggested. Between the ages of 7 and 11, normal children can tell when someone else treats them unfairly. If they have been treated unfairly in the past, when an opportunity arises they will "make up" for the past unfairness by striking back when someone else is vulnerable. For example, after being teased for being the shortest player on the peewee basketball team and then growing several inches, instead of feeling empathy for smaller kids the child will think, "Now it's my turn," not, "I'll treat younger kids differently."

A new morality normally begins to develop at about the age of 13. Then children think about the fairness of their own actions rather than concentrating on getting even. Cognitive theorists describe this as the development of the ability to reason in abstract terms and to understand the concept of partnership. From this point of view, those with antisocial personality disorder are developmentally arrested at the 7- to 11-year-old level because they are not concerned about the effects of their behavior on others.

In general, antisocial personality disorder cannot be explained simply by social class, bad associates, membership in a deviant subgroup, residence in a high-crime neighborhood, or brain damage. The disorder does seem to occur frequently in chaotic home environments. In all likelihood, its explanation will require approaches that simultaneously examine environmental, physiological, genetic, and temperamental variables.

CLINICAL TREATMENT OF ANTISOCIAL PERSONALITY DISORDER The following excerpt from a therapy session is interesting in two ways. The subject, 29-year-old Brett, illustrates some of the important features of antisocial personality disorder. For most of his late adolescence and early adult life, Brett had frequently schemed to cheat "the system" and to take what he wanted without paying for it. He used this approach not so much from lack of money to pay as for the excitement and pleasure that resulted when he was successful. Notice how the cognitively-oriented therapist deftly tries to get Brett to think about costs associated with "beating the system."

Therapist: How well has the "beat-the-system" approach actually worked out for you over time?

Brett: It works great . . . until someone catches on or starts to catch on. Then you have to scrap that plan and come up with a new one.

Therapist: How difficult was it, you know, to cover up one scheme and come up with a new one?

Brett: Sometimes it was really easy. There are some real pigeons out there.

Therapist: Was it always easy?

Brett: Well, no. Sometimes it was a real bitch. Like beating the phone system. That really ended up in a big hassle. There was really no way to cover it up, and everyone gave me such a hard time.

Therapist: Was it very easy to come up with an alternative plan?

Brett: Not for the phones. I never did come up with another plan.

Therapist:	How about at other times? Did beat-the-system plans come to you very easily—I mean, ones that actually worked?
Brett:	Well, I came up with lots of good ones, but it was tough coming up with something that would really pay off.
Therapist:	Did a good plan last a long time, or were new ones frequently required?
Brett:	Seems like I'm always needing a good plan to beat the system.
Therapist:	Do you think it's ever easier to go with the system instead of trying to beat it in some way?
Brett:	Well, after all that I have been through, I would have to say yes, there have been times that going with the system would have been easier in the long run. By the time I'm done paying legal fees, I will have shelled out more than my tuition would ever have cost me. But . . . it's such a challenge to beat the system. It feels exciting when I come up with a new plan and think I can make it work. Going with the system might not even occur to me.

—Beck, Freeman, and Associates, 1990, p. 171

The following excerpt from an interview with a person diagnosed as antisocial personality disorder illustrates the sensitivity with which clinicians must approach aspects of a patient's life that the individual might prefer not to admit to or discuss. In this case, the clinician needs to inquire into the patient's fighting. Does he get into fights because of living in a violent neighborhood or is he frequently the instigator?

Clinician:	Do some of them try to hassle you?
Patient:	Yeah sure, but that's all part of the game.
Clinician:	Have any of them tried to push you around?
Patient:	Yeah, a couple of them but I set them straight.
Clinician:	How do you mean?
Patient:	I kicked their asses.
Clinician:	Well, you look like you're in pretty good shape. I imagine you can take care of yourself pretty well. What about in the past, what types of fights have you been in?
Patient:	Oh, I been in a few now and then. People know not to mess with me. I grew up in a tough neighborhood and you had to know how to fight to survive.
Clinician:	When you were fairly young, let's say between the ages of say 15 and 25, how many fights do you think you were in, 20, 30?
Patient:	I'm bad but not that bad . . . oh, let's see, maybe about 15, who knows, it could have been as high as 20.
Clinician:	Did you ever get hurt?
Patient:	Nah, not really, but I did a number on a few of those guys.
Clinician:	Did you ever put anyone in the hospital?
Patient:	Yeah, there was one dude that I cut up pretty good, but he really deserved it, trust me.
Clinician:	Earlier you told me that you drank a fair amount in the past but have completely stopped now, which you deserve a lot of credit for. Back when you were drinking, did you sometimes feel on edge, almost like you needed a good fight, so you went looking for one, perhaps the alcohol making it a little more difficult to control your anger?
Patient:	Sometimes, yeah, sometimes. . . . especially if I was pretty strung out, I would be just plain nasty, and I started my fair share of fights. But usually I was just protecting myself or the guy really had it coming to him.
Clinician:	It certainly sounds like you know how to handle yourself in a fight. Did you used to run in a gang or how did you learn how to defend yourself so well?
Patient:	Like I said, where I grew up you had to learn how to fight, and I did hang out with a gang for a couple of years.

—Shea, 1988, pp. 375–376

In this interview, the clinician discovers that while the patient comes from a tough neighborhood, he is a frequent instigator of fights. The clinician enters the

potentially loaded topic of fighting by asking, "Do some of them try to hassle you?", referring to the patient's fellow residents at a drug rehabilitation center. Asking the question in this way enables the topic of fighting to be brought up without attributing blame to the patient. Once the patient is talking freely about fights, the clinician focuses on his history of fights and his role in them. Had the clinician prematurely asked, "Do you pick a lot of fights?" he probably would have gotten a defensive answer. The clinician skillfully compliments the patient ("Well, you look like you're in pretty good shape . . .") and makes it easy for the patient to admit to fighting by associating it with the use of alcohol. This approach not only provides needed diagnostic information, but it also helps build a working relationship with the patient.

People with antisocial personality disorder are not usually helped by traditional methods of psychotherapy. Their lack of empathy and social responsibility are major deterrents to establishing therapeutic rapport and commitment to change. The antisocial patient may at times experience a greater investment in outwitting the therapist than in effecting positive changes. Whenever possible, the therapist tries to raise questions in the patient's mind about beliefs that might result in antisocial behavior and negative outcomes—for example, the idea that wanting something or wanting to avoid something justifies a particular course of action.

A correctional facility or other type of highly structured, well-controlled setting may be the only means of managing some antisocial patients. An effective residential treatment center forces antisocial personalities to stay for months or years in a program with rigid rules so firm that they cannot talk their way out (Reid & Balis, 1987). In such a situation, the participants initially become depressed because they are forced to face their lack of inner feelings and their inability to establish meaningful relationships with others. The major goals of the entire program are to increase the person's ability to feel emotions, to think constructively about the future, to trust other people, and to develop empathy. Such a program emphasizes *milieu therapy,* an approach in which all the staff work together to provide consistent support and long-term stable relationships.

Another type of program has similar goals but can be carried out in the community. A judge may sentence young male first-offenders, or other men who are good prospects for improvement, to the program or to prison as an alternate. The offender is required to begin schooling or a job immediately and to return to an unlocked treatment center for the remaining time. Gradually he is given more physical freedom. Throughout the program he is also expected to be responsible for his behavior and that of others in the program. He is also expected to repay his victims for their losses and to pay

his living expenses. If he fails in the program, his alternate sentence, prison, immediately takes effect. Many people with antisocial personalities find this type of program very stressful. Often as many as 50 percent drop out and return to prison. For those who do successfully complete the program, however, the re-arrest rate has been significantly lower than the rate for similar people from traditional prison or halfway house settings.

Anxious or Fearful Behaviors

Disorders in this group share many characteristics with the personality disorders already described. What sets them apart is that each of these disorders has a prominent component of anxiety or fear.

Avoidant Personality Disorder

Avoidant personality disorder is characterized by low self-esteem, fear of negative evaluation, and a pervasive behavioral, emotional, and cognitive avoidance of social interaction. In therapy, avoidant personalities express a desire for affection, acceptance, and friendship; yet frequently, they have few friends and share little intimacy with anyone. Fear of rejection plays a key role in influencing these people to keep away from personal attachments. They won't enter into a relationship unless the other person provides unusually strong guarantees of uncritical acceptance. Table 9–11 lists clinical features of this disorder.

The seclusiveness of avoidant personalities differs from that of people with schizoid personality disorder because, unlike schizoids, avoidant people do want to enter into relationships. The conflict they feel is over wanting affection and, at the same time, doubting their acceptance by others. They cannot seem to rid themselves of the belief that any overtures of friendship will end in pain and disillusion. They are caught between wanting human contact and dreading it. People with avoidant personality disorder seem timid and withdrawn and perhaps also cold and strange to those who have superficial contact with them. However, to those who know them well, they appear anxious and extremely sensitive. Some of these feelings come from doubts about their own competence.

One coping mechanism that those with avoidant personality disorder are likely to use is hypervigilance. They continuously assess all their human contacts for signs of deception, humiliation, and negative reactions. As a result, they are able to detect the most minute traces

Table 9-11

Clinical Features of Avoidant Personality Disorder

A person having several of these characteristics might be considered to have an avoidant personality disorder.

1. Anticipates and worries about being rejected or criticized in social situations.
2. Has few friends despite the desire for them.
3. Is unwilling to get involved with people unless certain of being liked.
4. Avoids social or occupational activities that involve significant interpersonal contact.
5. Inhibits development of intimate relationships (despite wishing for them) because of fear of seeming foolish, being ridiculed, and feeling shamed.
6. Possesses low self-worth because of self-perceived social ineptness and lack of personally appealing qualities.
7. Unusually reluctant to engage in new situations or activities for fear of embarrassment.

of indifference or annoyance. They make mountains out of molehills. This technique of constantly scanning the environment is a self-defeating one, however, because it increases the likelihood that they will pick up just the kind of negative response they expect. In addition, their nervousness can result in making their companions uncomfortable, which can further damage the quality of their relationships with others.

Another maneuver that avoidant personalities use is to narrow their range of activities in order to cut off upsetting stimuli. Someone with an avoidant personality disorder may patronize only a small number of shops and restaurants so as to avoid encountering unfamiliar people or situations, or may even avoid shopping and other everyday activities because they seem too tiring or uncomfortable. Such people may also exaggerate the potential dangers of certain situations; for example, they may refuse to use buses or trains even though others do not doubt their safety. The lives of people with avoidant personality disorders are controlled by fears of looking foolish or being embarrassed. One unfortunate consequence of this retreat from contact with others and from new experiences is that it gives these individuals more time to be preoccupied with their own thoughts and to relive earlier painful experiences. The retreat also inhibits the development of social skills that might provide increased feelings of self-efficacy in dealing with interpersonal situations. Both these factors lead to a vicious cycle which makes new social contacts harder.

Avoidant personality disorder was added to the official DSM classification system in 1980. As yet little research has been done that gives insight into its causes or the most effective treatment approaches. One question concerning this disorder has to do with its discriminability from social phobia. One study compared individuals with social phobia and those diagnosed as avoidant personality disorder as they performed in a social

role-play test and gave a speech (Turner and others, 1986). Although the two groups reported equal levels of anxiety and similar anxious thoughts, those patients diagnosed as avoidant personality showed poorer social skills than those with social phobia. Further research is needed to evaluate overlaps between avoidant personality disorder and other classifications.

Dependent Personality Disorder

People with **dependent personality disorder** have two basic characteristics. First, they passively allow other people to make all the important decisions in their lives because they lack confidence and feel that they are unable to function independently. Second, to ensure that they will not lose this dependent position, such people subordinate their own needs to the needs and demands of others. Dependent personalities fear separation and have an excessive need to be taken care of. As a consequence, they are submissive and clinging.

Dependent individuals try to make themselves so pleasing that no one could possibly wish to abandon them. They are self-effacing, ever agreeable, and continually ingratiating. If left on their own, they feel empty, extremely anxious, and unable to function. They may feel anxiety even when the dependent relationship is intact because of the pervasive worry that the dominant figure might be lost in some way—for example, through death or divorce. Table 9-12 lists the clinical features of dependent personality disorder.

Dependent individuals feel that they must act meek and obedient in order to hold onto other people. They also behave affectionately and admiringly toward their protectors. In many cases this behavior may actually be an effective coping technique. The dominant partner will then feel useful, strong, and competent and will want to

Table 9-12
Clinical Features of Dependent Personality Disorder

A person having several of these characteristics might be considered to have a dependent personality disorder.

1. Is unable to make everyday decisions without excessive advice and reassurance from others.
2. Allows or encourages others to make important life decisions (e.g., getting married, where to live, having children).
3. Has difficulty expressing disagreement with others because of fear of their anger or loss of support.
4. Has difficulty independently initiating activities because of lack of confidence in personal judgment or abilities.
5. Goes to excessive lengths to obtain nurturance and support from others.
6. Feels uncomfortable or helpless when alone because of exaggerated fears of inability to care for himself or herself.
7. Indiscriminately seeks another relationship to provide nurturing and support when a close relationship ends.
8. Is frequently preoccupied with fears of being left to care for himself or herself.

encourage the relationship. Sometimes, however, things go wrong. The dominant individual may tire of the constant need to demonstrate affection and support and may behave abusively or seek to be rid of the leechlike attachment of the dependent partner. (Hirschfeld and others, 1991.)

The following case is an example of a dependent personality. The subject has allowed his mother to make the important decision as to whether he should marry his girl friend.

Matthew is a 34-year-old single man who lives with his mother and works as an accountant. He sought treatment because he was very unhappy after having just broken up with his girl friend. His mother had disapproved of his marriage plans, ostensibly because the woman was of a different religion. Matthew felt trapped and forced to choose between his mother and his girl friend, and since "blood is thicker than water," he had decided not to go against his mother's wishes. Nonetheless, he was angry at himself and at his mother, and believed that she would never let him marry and was possessively hanging on to him. His mother "wore the pants" in the family, and was a very domineering woman who was used to getting her way. Matthew was afraid of her and criticized himself for being weak, but also admired his mother and respected her judgment—"Maybe Carol wasn't right for me after all." He alternated between resentment and

a "Mother knows best" attitude. He felt that his own judgment was poor.

—Adapted from Spitzer & others, 1989, pp. 123–124

The causes of dependent personality disorders are unclear. One suggestion is that dependent individuals had overprotective parents who made life so easy for them as children that they never learned coping skills. Some theorists have suggested that dependent children were insecurely attached to their mothers or other caregivers or did not have close and trusting relationships with others during childhood. So far both of these ideas are interesting but untested hypotheses (Hirschfeld and others, 1991).

As with avoidant personalities, assertiveness training may be useful in treating dependent people. It may be difficult to convince these individuals that their coping styles need to be changed; sometimes a consciousness-raising therapy group is used before direct treatment is attempted.

As with other personality disorders we have discussed, more research is needed on this disorder's overlap with other conditions, its causes, and effective treatment strategies. Working with clients who have dependent personality disorders can be rewarding to the therapist when they develop the ability to function independently, but reaching that point can be difficult and frustrating. Many dependent people revel in the early stages of therapy. Then at some point they come to the realization that therapy isn't a passive experience. They begin to understand that therapy isn't just a matter of someone

(the therapist) showing an interest in them. What happens then can be a turning point in therapy—or the therapy can turn into a dead end.

Obsessive–Compulsive Personality Disorder

Obsessive–compulsive personality disorder is similar to obsessive–compulsive anxiety disorder (discussed in Chapter 6), but the two disorders are different. People with obsessive–compulsive personality disorder are rigid and restricted in their behavior, but they do not show obsessional thinking that seems to force itself into consciousness, nor do they engage in the kinds of irrational rituals that are performed by people with obsessive–compulsive anxiety disorder. People with the anxiety disorder see their behavior as nonadaptive and distressing, but they cannot stop behaving that way. People with a personality disorder, on the other hand, usually exhibit behavior that is rigid and unadaptive but that they feel is under their control.

Compulsive people have been described as "living machines" (Reich, 1933, 1949). As one patient put it, his life was like "a train that was running efficiently, fast, pulling a substantial load, but on a track laid out for it" (Shapiro, 1965). An obsessive–compulsive personality disorder has several characteristics. One is lack of ability to express many warm and tender emotions. Instead, a person with this disorder seems stiff, formal, and unusually serious. Such an individual is likely to be overly conscientious and inflexible about matters of morality. Extreme perfectionism is also a problem because it focuses on small details, lists, and rulemaking rather than on getting the job done. This rigidity leads to an inability to grasp the "big picture." For instance, in the following example two friends are discussing a house that K is interested in buying. L shows his rigidity in not really listening to what K says but going by his own "rule of house ownership."

K: *So you think I shouldn't buy it?*

L: *Never buy a house with a bad roof. It will cost you its price again in repairs before you're finished.*

K: *But the builder I hired to look it over did say it was in good condition otherwise.*

L: *The roof is only the beginning. First it's the roof and then comes the plumbing and then the heating and then the plaster.*

K: *Still, those things seem to be all right.*

L: *And, after the plaster, it will be the wiring.*

K: *But the wiring is . . .*

L [interrupts with calm assurance]: *It will cost double the price before you're finished.*

—Shapiro, 1965, p. 25

This example also illustrates another aspect of compulsive personalities: insistence that their way of doing things be followed, without any awareness of the feelings this creates in other people. K probably really wants to buy the house, and if L's criticisms are, as we suspect, simply evidence of his compulsive personality without any facts attached, K's self-esteem and his positive feelings toward L are not likely to increase as a result of this encounter. People with this disorder focus on rules and neatness and may be disturbed by anything out of place (see Figure 9–9). Excessive concentration on work and productivity is also typical. Even pleasure becomes work.

One such person carefully scheduled his Sundays with certain activities in order to produce "maximum enjoyment." He determinedly set about enjoying himself and became quite upset if anything interfered with his schedule, not merely because he missed the activity, but because his holiday had been spent inefficiently. Another compulsive patient always tried hard, in his social life, to be "spontaneous."

—Shapiro, 1965, p. 32

Finally, obsessive–compulsive personality disorder is characterized by indecisiveness. Individuals with this disorder have great difficulty making decisions because they might be wrong. Their inability to make decisions can be so extreme that they can accomplish relatively little. Their pleasure comes from planning a job, not from doing it. The early psychoanalyst Karl Abraham expressed this problem in the following passage.

Pleasure in indexing and classifying . . . in drawing up programmes and regulating work by timesheets . . . is so marked . . . that the forepleasure they get in working out a plan is stronger than their gratification in its execution, so that they often leave it undone.

—Abraham, 1921, 1927, pp. 378, 388

Despite job problems such as those referred to previously, obsessive–compulsiveness is relatively less likely than other personality disorders to inhibit job

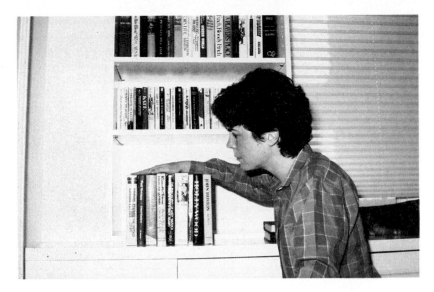

FIGURE 9-9 Housekeeping routines or other cleaning or straightening rituals occupy a great deal of time for some obsessive–compulsive people. This person's home library is a source of worry and frustration because of her concern about how to arrange the books. If they are arranged alphabetically by author, then she finds that the different sizes mixed together are visually unpleasing. If she arranges them by size, although they look better, she cannot find a particular book quickly. The result is that she spends a great deal of time both arranging the books and feeling dissatisfied with what she has done.

performance and is least often confused with misbehavior. Table 9–13 lists the clinical features of this personality disorder.

Someone with an obsessive–compulsive personality disorder usually seeks treatment only when his or her carefully built-up life style is threatened. This may happen when a spouse is exasperated and leaves, when a boss decides to fire the difficult employee, or when there is an accumulation of stressful events that make it impossible to carry on as usual. Psychotherapy is often recommended in these circumstances. Although in the past the therapeutic approach was usually psychodynamic and focused on unconscious processes that might underlie the disorder, in recent years other approaches have also come to the fore. A cognitive approach directs attention to the content, style, and structure of the individual's thought processes in the belief that it is irrational and dysfunctional thoughts that lead to maladaptive behavior (Beck and others, 1990). For example, automatic thoughts such as "I need to get this assignment done perfectly" may inhibit spontaneity and the expression of feelings. Behavioral approaches that use techniques like exposure therapy (see Chapter 6) are also being used, as is group therapy.

Passive–Aggressive Personality Disorder

People with **passive–aggressive personality disorder** habitually resist demands for adequate perfor-

Table 9–13
Clinical Features of Obsessive–Compulsive Personality Disorder

A person having several of these characteristics might be considered to have an obsessive–compulsive personality.

1. Perfectionism that interferes with completing tasks.
2. Preoccupation with details, rules, lists, and schedules.
3. Reluctance to delegate tasks or to work with others unless they follow exactly his or her way of doing things.
4. Excessive devotion to work and productivity to the exclusion of leisure activities and friendships.
5. Overconscientiousness and inflexibility about matters of morality or ethics.
6. Restricted expression of warm emotions.
7. Money is viewed as something to be saved for future catastrophes and spending for self and others is miserly.
8. Inability to discard worn out or worthless objects even when they have no sentimental value.
9. Behavior that is typically rigid and stubborn.

Table 9–14

Clinical Features of Passive–Aggressive Personality Disorder

A person having several of these characteristics might be considered to have a passive–aggressive personality disorder.

1. Procrastinates completion of routine tasks that need to be done, especially those that others ask to have completed.
2. Becomes sulky, irritable, or argumentative when asked to do something he or she does not want to do.
3. Seems to work deliberately slowly or to do a bad job on tasks that he or she really does not want to do.
4. Protests, without justification, that others make unreasonable demands.
5. Avoids obligations by claiming to have forgotten.
6. Fails to do his or her share of the work and thus obstructs the efforts of others.
7. Criticizes or scorns people in positions of power to an unreasonable degree.

mance both on the job and in their social lives. Although they have the skills to behave more effectively, they sabotage their accomplishments through procrastination, intentional inefficiency, stubbornness, and forgetfulness. As the name suggests, people with passive–aggressive personalities resent the demands that are made on them, but rather than expressing these feelings directly, they express their anger through passive resistance and obstruction of goal attainment. For example, if a supervisor comes in at quitting time and requests a complex report by early the next morning, a passive–aggressive person would be more likely to mislay some of the needed data than to directly tell the supervisor that the request is unreasonable.

The behavior of a passive–aggressive individual might be compared to a situation that is often found in child-rearing. The child pushes the parents to the limits of their control and then backs off just in time to prevent retaliation. Like the child, the passive–aggressive individual is extremely sensitive to the limits of others and goes that far and no farther. Interacting with a passive–aggressive person can be immobilizing because it requires one either to give in or to violate one's own ideas of what is appropriate and reasonable behavior.

Passive–aggressive coping mechanisms are not usually an effective way of living, but passive–aggressive individuals seem to have no awareness of how their own behavior contributes to difficult situations. A 30-year follow-up study of a group of college men found that the degree to which passive–aggressive behavior was used in early adulthood correlated negatively with good adjustment in middle age (Vaillant, 1976). Perhaps because most passive–aggressive individuals do not seek clinical help, this classification is one of the least used of those in the Axis II personality disorder group. Because it is a relatively recent classification, little research has been conducted on the topic and the clinical value of passive–

agressive personality disorder has not yet been demonstrated. As a consequence, some clinicians question its inclusion in DSM in its present form. They believe the criteria should either be broadened to include general types of negativistic behavior or the category should be deleted from the DSM list of personality disorders. Table 9–14 includes the major features of this disorder recognized by DSM.

Treatment of Personality Disorders

Our knowledge of personality disorders is limited because professionals see a restricted sample of people with these disorders. Unless their difficulties become overwhelming, such individuals tend to be satisfied with their behavior, not intensely unhappy the way an anxious or depressed person might be. As we have seen, people with personality disorders perceive their environment—not their rigid behavior patterns—as the cause of any difficulties they may encounter.

It is important to remember that even individuals who are classified as having a personality disorder may behave appropriately or normally some of the time. However, when coping behaviors are called for, each personality disorder is distinguished by the frequency and intensity with which certain characteristic behaviors appear. For example, someone with a paranoid personality disorder does not always appear to be suspicious, but he or she is much more likely than most people to be inappropriately suspicious. Many people with personality disorders go through life without ever coming into contact with a mental health professional. However, their rigid response styles often lead them to cope ineffectively

with their environment. If the environmental stresses become too great, their response styles may become clearly ineffective.

A variety of therapies have been used in treating personality disorders. Although most of these disorders have not been found to be very responsive to drugs in the past, clinicians have recently been using certain psychoactive drugs to treat some people with personality disorders. The drugs currently being assessed include certain antipsychotic drugs; one group of antidepressant drugs, the MAO inhibitors; and lithium. So far the results of drug therapy are not entirely clear. Behavioral techniques such as assertiveness training and systematic desensitization may be helpful for avoidant and dependent patients, and assertiveness training is also sometimes useful for passive–aggressive clients. Although cognitive therapies seem to be appropriate for deviant cognitive styles, little information on their effectiveness is available. However, dealing with the cognitions that underlie the personality disorders would seem to be a promising approach. Psychodynamic therapy is used especially for borderline, narcissistic, histrionic, and obsessive–compulsive personality disorders. An intensive milieu therapy that provides clear rules and a stable environment as well as clear penalties for failure to take personal responsibility for behavior is being tried as a way to help those with antisocial personality disorder.

Because personality disorders affect interpersonal relationships, they also tend to elicit certain patterns of behaviors from family members or friends. For this reason, any behavior changes that come about through therapy will have an impact on the patterns of these relationships. Group or family therapy thus may be a useful part of the treatment of many individuals with personality disorders. Therapists need to focus the client's attention on the effect of his or her behavior on the behavior of others.

The Outlook for the Personality Disorder Classification

The idea of personality disorders as independent conditions (listed in DSM's Axis II), that might or might not be related to the more traditional disorders (listed in Axis I), is relatively new. Even though clinicians have responded positively to this new system of classifying various personality patterns, many questions and issues remain.

Two questions that inevitably arise are: Are the personality disorders included in DSM the right ones— that is, are they defined in ways that contribute to diagnostic reliability and validity? Are there personality disorders not included in DSM that should be part of the classification system? It has been difficult for professionals to answer these questions because, except for a few of the personality disorders (most notably the borderline classification), research on these conditions has been quite limited. With increased use of Axis II by clinicians and as research evidence accrues, it seems likely that conceptualizations of the personality disorders will change, as well as the diagnostic criteria for their use.

Clinical experience and research may also suggest including in Axis II classifications of personality patterns not currently represented. For example, some people show a pervasive sadistic pattern of cruel, demanding, and aggressive behavior to other people; others show a self-defeating or masochistic pattern that leads to disappointment, failure, or mistreatment by others; and still others show mild, but persistent, depressive mood that is dominated by dejection and cheerlessness. Whether these or other personality patterns should also be included within Axis II is currently a topic of considerable discussion among clinicians and researchers.

Another important topic concerns how information about the personality disorders can most effectively be presented. Currently, Axis II uses a **categorical model** of classification, in which a disorder is considered to be diagnosed if a certain threshold of criteria is reached or exceeded. As we have seen in the clinical features tables presented throughout this chapter, it is not required that all listed criteria be present in order to use a particular classification. Contrasted with this classification model a **dimensional model** focuses attention on *patterns* of personality characteristics. In a dimensional approach, an individual would be classified not as having a dependent or antisocial personality disorder, but rather as having a personality pattern that reflects the individual's standing on a variety of dimensions. The value of a dimensional approach is that it results in a profile for each person classified. One possibility would be a profile of ratings of the severity of various types of maladaptive personality patterns. While the time for dimensional classification might not yet have come (it involves somewhat novel and complex procedures), with further research to support its value, it might be incorporated into future DSMs.

Chapter Summary

CLASSIFYING PERSONALITY DISORDERS

Personality disorders are longstanding, maladaptive, inflexible ways of relating to the environment. These disorders are diagnosed on Axis II of the DSM system. Many people with personality disorders also have a diagnosis on DSM Axis I. Personality disorders can be grouped into three categories: odd or eccentric behaviors; dramatic, emotional or erratic behaviors; and anxious or fearful behaviors.

ODD OR ECCENTRIC BEHAVIORS

Paranoid Personality Disorder People with **paranoid personality disorder** are suspicious and mistrusting of others and hypersensitive; they expect to be taken advantage of, and read hidden meanings into benign remarks or events. It is unusual for people with this personality disorder to seek clinical help, and if they do, their personality characteristics make them very difficult to treat.

Schizoid Personality Disorder Those diagnosed with **schizoid personality disorder** are withdrawn and seclusive, prefer to work alone, and do not seem interested in warm close relationships with others.

Schizotypal Personality Disorder **Schizotypal personality disorder** is associated with odd ways of thinking, perceiving, communicating, and behaving—although these deviations are not as extreme as those seen in people diagnosed with a schizophrenic disorder. Some research suggests that this disorder may be related to schizophrenia as a weak form of that disorder.

DRAMATIC, EMOTIONAL, OR ERRATIC BEHAVIORS

Histrionic Personality Disorder People with **histrionic personality disorder** place a high priority on getting others' attention. They are self-centered, manipulative, and have stormy interpersonal relationships.

Narcissistic Personality Disorder Factors that are important in the diagnosis of **narcissistic personality disorder** are an extreme sense of self-importance, need for constant attention, fragility of self-esteem, and a lack of empathy for others. Such people are likely to be preoccupied with fantasies concerning their power, brilliance, and success.

Borderline Personality Disorder Those diagnosed as having a **borderline personality disorder** have unstable personal relationships, often threaten and frequently engage in self-destructive behavior, are very impulsive, and tend to have relationships characterized by intense clinging dependency and manipulation of others. Because of the frequency of the borderline diagnosis, more work is done on treatment of this disorder than on the

other personality disorders. Although psychodynamic, behavioral, cognitive, and biological therapies have all been used extensively, a combination of these may be particularly effective.

Antisocial Personality Disorder **Antisocial personality disorder** is typified by a chronic and continuous history of behavior that violates the rights of others. This history begins before age 15 and continues into adulthood. In adulthood they continue to have a history of antisocial acts against property and other people, and are likely to be reckless and sexually promiscuous, and to lack remorse for hurting others. Many people in this category are able to avoid arrest for their actions. Many acts of criminal and antisocial behavior are committed by people who do not fit the classification of antisocial personality disorder. Traditional psychotherapy does not seem effective with individuals with antisocial personality. Confinement in a residential treatment center where the staff focuses on issues concerning emotions, building trust, and developing empathy, as well as constructive thinking about the future seems promising as a treatment.

ANXIOUS OR FEARFUL BEHAVIORS

Avoidant Personality Disorder People diagnosed as having **avoidant personality disorder** have low self-esteem, worry about negative evaluation by others, and avoid social interactions. Although they desire affection and close relationships, fear of rejection seems to keep these people from seeking such relationships.

Dependent Personality Disorder People with **dependent personality disorder** lack confidence in their ability to function independently and therefore allow others to make decisions for them. In order to maintain their dependent relationships, they are willing to subordinate their own needs and wishes to those of others.

Obsessive–Compulsive Personality Disorder **Obsessive–Compulsive personality disorder** is characterized by lack of ability to express warm emotions, extreme perfectionism, and a rigid approach to the way things "should" be done.

Passive–Aggressive Personality Disorder People who have **passive–aggressive personality disorder** use passive resistance and obstruction as an indirect way to express anger at the demands of others. They sabotage their own accomplishments through procrastination, forgetfulness, and intentional inefficiency.

TREATMENT OF PERSONALITY DISORDERS

Because many people with personality disorders never come to clinicians' attention, researchers have only studied a limited sample of this group. People with personality disorders may not seek clinical help because they see the environment as the source

of any problems. They are also likely to behave appropriately much of the time so that their problems do not cause others to refer them for treatment. Therapeutic approaches from each of the perspectives, sometimes in combination, are used for treating these individuals. These include a variety of psychoactive drugs, behavioral techniques such as assertiveness training and systematic desensitization, cognitive therapies, and psychodynamic therapies. Family or group therapies focus on the effects of the behaviors on others.

THE OUTLOOK FOR PERSONALITY DISORDER CLASSIFICATION

Because the current classifications of personality disorders overlap with each other, it is likely that as more research is done the conceptualizations of the disorders may change and new categories may be added. Another possibility is that a dimensional model that focuses on personality patterns might be preferable to the categorical model in current use.

Mood Disorders

CHAPTER 10

What Are Mood Disorders?
How Common Are Mood
Disorders?

Depression
Depressed Mood
Risk Factors

Depressive Disorder
Dysthymia
Major Depression

Theories of Depression
Biological Theories
The Psychodynamic View
The Behavioral Perspective
The Cognitive Perspective
The Humanistic–Existential
Perspective
Contrasting Psychological Theories
of Depression
An Interactional View

The Bipolar Disorders
Manic Episodes
Causes of Bipolar Disorder
Treatment of Bipolar Disorder

Suicide and Parasuicide
Causes of Suicide
The Impact of Suicide on Others

Chapter Summary

Fritz Scholder, *Mystery Woman with Shadows*, 1989.
Charlotte Jackson Fine Art, Santa Fe, NM.

It is difficult to put into words how I felt at that time. I guess my major reaction was one of despair—a despair of ever being human again. I honestly felt subhuman, lower than the lowest vermin. Furthermore, I was self-deprecatory and could not understand why anyone would want to associate with me, let alone love me. I became mistrustful and suspicious of others and was certain that they were checking up on me to prove that I was incompetent myself. . . . I had become increasingly concerned about finances. On one hand, I thought that I was receiving extra money that I didn't deserve and, on the other, I was certain that we were going bankrupt. In any case, I was positive that I was going to wind up in jail. When I received my July salary statement it appeared to me that the total was larger than it should be. This frightened me and I told my wife that we should phone the university immediately and arrange to return the extra money before I got into trouble. Gently, my wife told me that she thought the amount of money was correct and there was nothing to worry about. Of course, she was right. . . . I not only pondered my current situation but my whole career as well. I was positive that I was a fraud and a phony and that I didn't deserve my Ph.D. I didn't deserve to have tenure; I didn't deserve to be a Full Professor . . . I didn't deserve the research grants I had been awarded; I couldn't understand how I had written books and journal articles that I had and how they had been accepted for publication. I must have conned a lot of people.

—Endler, 1982, pp. 45–49

These were the thoughts of a well-known psychologist during a period of severe depression. They illustrate how drastically depression may alter mood, perception,

and behavior. A period of mania, on the other hand, leads to quite different thoughts and feelings, as described here:

> *When I am high I couldn't worry about money if I tried. So I don't. The money will come from somewhere, I am entitled, God will provide. Credit cards are disastrous, personal checks worse. . . . So, I bought twelve snake bite kits, with a sense of urgency and importance. I bought precious stones, elegant and unnecessary furniture, three watches within an hour of one another (in the Rolex rather than Timex class: champagne tastes bubble to the surface, are the surface, in mania), and totally inappropriate siren-like clothes. During one spree I spent several hundreds on books having titles or covers that somehow caught my fancy. . . . Once I shoplifted a blouse because I could not wait a minute longer for the woman-with-molasses-feet in front of me in line. I imagine I must have spent far more than $30,000 during my two manic episodes, and God only knows how much more during my frequent hypomanias. I haven't any idea where most of the money went.*

—Goodwin and Jamison, 1990, p. 29

What Are Mood Disorders?

The two examples above illustrate the range of behavior included in DSM's **mood disorder** category. The essential feature of disorders in this category is that they all reflect a disturbance in mood or emotional reaction that is not due to any other physical or mental disorder. Mood disorders are often referred to as **affective disorders.** Table 10–1 describes the major types of mood disorder. Mood disorders can be broken down into two groups, **bipolar disorders** and the much more common **depressive disorders.** All of the conditions outlined in the table will be discussed in this chapter.

How Common Are Mood Disorders?

For any disorder, it is important to know how many people are affected. One of the best ways to get this information is through an epidemiological study in

Table 10–1

Types of Mood Disorder

Depressive Disorders

Major Depression	One or more major depressive episodes
Dysthymia	History of depressed mood a majority of the time

Bipolar Disorders

Bipolar Disorder	One or more manic episodes and usually one or more major depressive episodes
Cyclothymia	Numerous hypomanic episodes and numerous periods of depressive symptoms
Bipolar II	At least one hypomanic episode and one major depressive episode but no manic episode or cyclothymia

which a large number of people are surveyed. A team of researchers (Weissman and others, 1990) used a sample of 20,000 scientifically selected people from five areas in the United States to carry out the Epidemiological Catchment Area study (ECA). All these people were interviewed and 7.8 percent of them were found to have met the criteria for a mood disorder one or more times in the past. The ECA study found that the reported rate of mood disorder was *generally similar* for whites, Hispanics, and African-Americans, although African-Americans did report slightly lower rates of mood disorder than the other two groups. Although few racial or ethnic differences were found, there was a dramatic difference in the rate of mood disorder for men and women. Twice as many women as men reported a mood disorder of some type in either the present or the past. This same difference was found for all time periods considered, including a lifetime, one year, or one month. The difference was completely accounted for by the higher rate of depressive disorders women reported; the rate of bipolar disorder for men and women did not differ significantly.

The overall rates of depressive disorder found in the ECA study were similar to the findings of other large epidemiological studies from other countries. In a 15-year study of a semirural area in Sweden, the Lundby Study (Rorsman and others, 1990), and a study of a rural Canadian area, the Stirling County Study (Murphy and others, 1988), the results were generally comparable with those from the ECA study of the United States, although the rates were somewhat lower. This difference might be expected since the ECA study focused mainly on urban areas where the rates of mood disorder tend to be higher

than they are outside of large cities. This international comparability lends confidence that the results of these studies are an accurate estimate of the overall incidence of mood disorder. The agreement is even more impressive because of some important differences in how the studies were carried out. The ECA study was a cross-sectional one in which people were asked to remember how they had felt at different times in the past as well as to recount the symptoms they had when interviewed. The foreign studies were longitudinal—the subjects were followed across time. It is important to study mood disorders in the general population (as these epidemiological studies do) as well as in the clinical population. It is estimated that in the United States only about 20 percent of all people with depressive symptoms will ever be treated for their depression (Holden, 1986). Studies that focus only on information from the treated group will thus come up with a very different picture of depressive symptoms and the patterns of recovery than if those who never came to professional attention were examined.

Depression

Depressed mood is found in a variety of disorders, so that its mere presence does not mean the person has a mood disorder. The term **depression** can refer to a symptom or to a disorder.

Depressed Mood

People use the word "depression" in their everyday language to refer to symptoms. These may be the result of an emotional state, a reaction to a situation, or a person's characteristic style of behavior. The feeling of depression is usually known as "the blues." It may occur in rainy weather, during an annoying cold, or after an argument with a friend. Often an event that is usually expected to be happy ends with such sad feelings. People may experience the blues after holidays such as Christmas or New Year's Day or after moving to a new home. Feelings of depression that are based on these temporary situations usually fade away quickly. Adults who have a major depressive disorder make a sharp distinction between the "black cloud" of depression and the unhappiness they feel when they are not ill (Hamilton, 1982).

The term depression is also used to describe a sadness that comes from a death in the family. After the death of someone they care deeply about, most survivors experience a depressed mood that is usually called grief. These feelings of depression are entirely normal. In fact, the absence of such emotions might create problems for the person in the long run. As we discussed in Chapter 5, common features of grief include physical distress such as sighing, tightness of the throat, an empty feeling in the abdomen, and a feeling of muscular weakness. In addition, there may be preoccupation with the visual image of the dead person, along with guilt and hostile reactions. During the normal process of grieving, the guilt, hostility, feelings of loss, and physical symptoms gradually disappear.

These same symptoms may be the result of any other kind of important loss. For example, the breakup of a dating relationship, or divorce or separation, may also bring about these feelings; they are likely to occur regardless of who wanted to end the relationship. Other kinds of stressful life events—losing a job, being turned down for a graduate school program, or losing everything in a fire—may also bring on feelings of depression. These feelings are not severe enough to be called mood disorders but may be classified as an adjustment disorder with depressed mood (adjustment disorders are discussed in Chapter 5). Severe feelings of depression are also frequent for people who have just had a heart attack or found they have a serious illness. In addition, depressed mood is an important symptom in a variety of other disorders including borderline personality disorder, schizophrenia, and physical changes in the brain such as those seen in Alzheimer's disease. Withdrawal from a variety of drugs—including amphetamines, cocaine, and alcohol—is also likely to produce symptoms of depression. In such instances, depression is seen as a response or symptom of a life stress or physical change and is not usually considered to reflect a mood disorder.

The following case presents a short-term response to stress, and is an example of depressed feelings that does not fall into the category of mood disorder.

A 24-year-old, single, female nursery-school teacher terminated brief psychotherapy after ten sessions. She had entered treatment two weeks after she discovered that the man she had been involved with for four months was married and wanted to stop seeing her. She reacted with bouts of sadness and crying, felt she was falling apart, took a week's sick leave from her job, and had vague thoughts that the future was so bleak that life might not be worth the effort. She felt that she must be in some essential way "flawed"; otherwise she would not have gotten so involved with someone who had no intentions of maintaining a long-term relationship. She felt that others "would have seen it," that only she was "so stupid" as to have been deceived. There were no other signs of a depressive syndrome, such as loss of interest or appetite or trouble concentrating.

She responded to mixed supportive–insight psychotherapy and, toward the end of treatment, began dating a law student whom she met at a local cafe.

—Spitzer and others, 1981, p. 261

Risk Factors

One of the greatest risk factors for depression is simply being female. Women are at least twice as likely to experience all types of depressed states than are men. Past researchers have tried to understand this difference in cultural terms. In American culture it has been thought to be more acceptable in general for women than for men to seek help for emotional problems. Women are more likely to consult physicians or mental health experts and to take a psychological view of their problems rather than to see them only in terms of physical symptoms. However, these explanations of more women *seeking treatment* for depression do not explain the higher overall *rate* for depression because the same difference in rate of depressive disorder for women and men has been consistently found in community surveys, such as the ECA study described earlier, where people are contacted on a randomized basis and not because they have sought help. Prospective studies that have followed the same group over time—such as the Stirling County and Lundby studies mentioned earlier—have also reported the same findings. One explanation that has been suggested by researchers interested in social support and its effect on health is that while women in general receive more social support than do men, they are also expected to offer more support (Shumaker & Hill, 1991). Because support-giving often involves them in the problems and stressors experienced by others, women may thus experience more stress than men. Results of a recent study support the idea that women may experience more stress because of their role as suppliers of support to others. The study found that for the age range of 25 to 45 years much of the difference in rates of depression between men and women was explained by the particularly high rate for married women, compared to the rates either for other women or for men (Paykel, 1991). During this age period married women are likely to have an especially high level of stress because of their role in caring for young children in addition to their roles in providing support to their extended families and to their responsibilities in the employment arena.

Another risk factor for depression is age. The risk for a first episode of any degree of depression is highest in women between the ages of 20 and 29. For men, the similar risk period is between the ages of 40 and 49 (Rorsman and others, 1990). Marital history and current marital status are also related to relative risk of depression. Table 10–2 shows the rates for major depression according to past and present marital status. Caution is needed in making assumptions about causality in the relationship between depression and marital status. A marriage might break up because of the difficulties for both spouses created by the depressed state of one, or the breakup itself can be a risk factor for depression because of the loss of a close social tie. Very likely the personal characteristics (depression) and the environmental stress and loss (divorce) have reciprocal effects (Henderson, 1977; Bruce and others, 1990). Living alone in itself does not appear to be a risk factor, especially for women.

Several other factors may also increase a person's risk of depression. A pileup of stressful events in a short time period, which might include such things as a move to another town, a new job, loss of a close relationship, or a major disappointment such as failing to get a desired job or admission to an academic program, makes a person more vulnerable to depression. Other long-term factors may play a role, such as a family history of depression or living with a depressed parent (Weissman, 1987).

In addition to personal factors, other more general factors are also thought to relate to increased risk of depression, most notably urban living and unemployment. Other socioeconomic factors that might seem to be related to increased stress—low income, low status employment, and little education—were not found to be related to depressive disorders in the ECA study (Weissman and others, 1990). Overall, this study suggests that increased risk for depression is associated with severing

Table 10–2
One-year Rates of Major Depression According to Past and Present Marital Status

Past Marital Status	Rate per Hundred
Married (no divorce)	1.5
Never married	2.4
Divorced once	4.1
Divorced twice	5.8
Cohabiting	5.1
Present Marital Status	
Married	2.1
Widowed	2.1
Separated/divorced	6.3
Never married	2.8

SOURCE: Adapted from Weissman, Bruce, Leaf, Florio, and Holzer, 1990, p. 72.

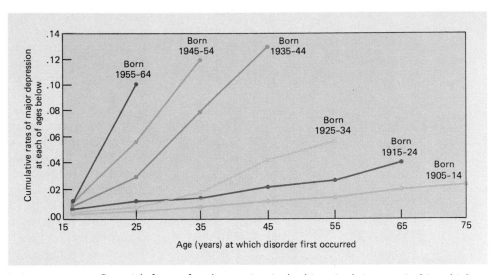

FIGURE 10–1 One risk factor for depression is the historical time period in which a person is born. Cohorts, or groups, born in each of the ten-year periods since 1935 have an increasing risk of depression just as a result of the period of their birth. The figure does not show data for those born in the 1965–1974 decade because many of them have as yet not reached the highest risk period.

(Adapted from *Archives of General Psychiatry*, 1984, 41, 13–21. Copyright © 1984, American Medical Association)

of intimate ties, unemployment, and urban living. These results may help to explain another quite puzzling finding that has been observed for some time: Birth cohort—or the year of one's birth—is an important risk factor in depression.

In recent years the prevalence of depression (the number of people depressed at any one time) and the incidence (the number of new cases in any given period) seem to be rising among younger people and decreasing among older people (Klerman, 1988). These changes have been observed in several large studies both in the United States and in Europe. Figure 10–1 illustrates these varying rates.

Depressive Disorder

Even if a person's depressed feelings are not a part of some other disorder, we still have to answer the question of how to distinguish between the blues or "normal depression" we all feel once in a while and a **depressive disorder** (depression that fits DSM criteria). Sadness often is experienced by people who are depressed, but sadness itself is not the same as depression.

Some of the symptoms of depressive disorder include dissatisfaction and anxiety, changes in appetite, sleep, and psychomotor functions, loss of interest and energy, feelings of guilt, thoughts of death, and dimin-

ished concentration. Many of these symptoms are experienced by the general population some time or other. The thoughts of clinically depressed people contain three key elements. People with a depressive disorder think of themselves as unworthy or to blame for what has happened, they think they are helpless to change their situation, and they do not think things will improve in the future (Rutter, 1986). The term **unipolar disorder** is often used when discussing different types of depressive disorder to distinguish between people who have experienced one or more episodes of depression but no manic episode and those who have a past history that includes at least one episode of mania. Individuals who have one or more episodes of mania as well as periods of depression are diagnosed as having bipolar disorder which is discussed later in the chapter. Figure 10–2 shows that many of the symptoms of depression are frequently reported by people who are not classified as having a depressive disorder. For instance, almost 23 percent of men and 36 percent of women in the ECA study reported a period lasting two weeks or more when they felt sad and blue ("dysphoric mood" in the figure). However, despite the frequency of this and other symptoms as shown in this figure, only a much smaller proportion of the population (about 3.6 percent of men and 8.7 percent of women) have enough of these symptoms at any one time so that they would be classified as experiencing a depressive episode. If you compare Figure 10–2 with Figure 10–4 you can see that although these symptoms occur relatively frequently

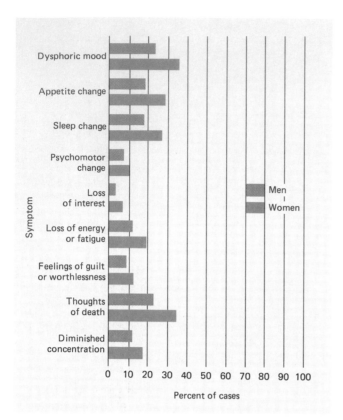

FIGURE 10–2 Percent of all individuals in the general population surveyed by the Epidemiological Area Catchment Study who reported having experienced each of these symptoms of depression for two weeks or longer.

(Reprinted with the permission of The Free Press, a Division of Macmillan, Inc. from *Psychiatric Disorders in America* by Lee N. Robins, Ph.D. and Darrel A. Regier, M.D. Copyright © 1991 by Lee N. Robins, Ph.D. and Darrel A. Regier, M.D.)

in the general population, they are much more frequent in people who are clinically depressed.

Dysthymia

The milder, less incapacitating form of depressive disorder is **dysthymia.** (The term "dysthymia" comes from the Greek words meaning "defective or diseased mood.") Dysthymia tends to be chronic, often lasting for years, and sometimes is hard to distinguish from a personality disorder. In order to be classified as a dysthymic disorder, the depressed mood or loss of interest or pleasure and other symptoms must be of longstanding duration. Even though this longstanding depressed mood may be interrupted by periods of a few days or a few weeks of normal mood, the depressed feelings are those that dominate over time.

People with dysthymia tend to be depressed most of the day, more days than not, based on their own description or the description of others. They also have at least several of the following problems: difficulties with eating (either poor appetite or overeating), difficulties

with sleeping (either insomnia or sleeping too much), constant feelings of tiredness, difficulty concentrating or making decisions, a low opinion of themselves, and feelings of hopelessness. Dysthymia, unlike major depression, shows little variability with age. The rate is stable from age 18 through age 64 and only declines after age 65. The length of a period of dysthymia has been found to extend from between 2 to at least 20 years. The median duration is about 5 years (Keller, 1990).

Dysthymia can coexist with any of the other mood disorders, but it is most likely to occur along with a major depressive episode. Periods of intense depression are usually described as time-limited, which means that either as a result of treatment or by some naturally occurring process the symptoms tend to lessen over time. This is in contrast to dysthymic disorder which tends to be chronic and persist for long periods, often over years of a person's life. If a person with dysthymic disorder develops symptoms of major depression as well, they are said to have "double depression" because at that time they meet the criteria for both diagnoses. This dual state occurs quite frequently. Almost half of the people studied in the ECA study who had dysthymia also had at least one episode of major depression in their lifetime. Figure 10–3 shows the overlap of the two disorders. If recovery is defined as recovery from both dysthymic disorder and the depressive episode, more than 60 percent of patients had not yet recovered after two years (Keller, 1990).

The following case describes a dysthymic woman whose problems with depression have persisted in spite of extensive psychotherapy. Throughout her adult life she has continued to show dysthymic symptoms. She continually feels inferior and without attraction for others. Even when events should suggest to her that she is attractive or competent, she seems to go out of her way to prove to herself that such is not the case.

FIGURE 10–3 Overlapping diagnoses—or comorbidity—of major depression and dysthymia over the lifetime.

(Weissman and others, 1990, p. 67)

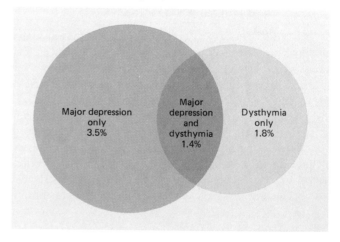

The 28-year-old junior executive had obtained a master's degree in business administration and moved to California a year and a half earlier to begin work in a large firm. She told the therapist in her initial interview that she was "depressed" about everything: her job, her husband, and her prospects for the future.

She had had extensive psychotherapy previously. Her complaints were of persistent feelings of depressed mood, inferiority, and pessimism, which she claims to have had since she was 16 or 17 years old. Although she did reasonably well in college, she consistently ruminated about those students who were "genuinely intelligent." She dated during college and graduate school, but claimed that she would never go after a guy she thought was "special," always feeling inferior and intimidated. Whenever she saw or met such a man, she acted stiff and aloof, or actually walked away as quickly as possible, only to berate herself afterward and then fantasize about him for many months. She claimed that her therapy had helped, although she still could not remember a time when she didn't feel somewhat depressed.

Just after graduation, she married the man she was going out with at the time primarily because she felt she "needed a husband" for companionship. Shortly after their marriage, the couple started to bicker. She was very critical of his clothes, his job, and his parents; and he, in turn, found her rejecting, controlling, and moody. She began to feel that she had made a mistake in marrying him. Her social life with her husband involves several other couples. The man in these couples is usually a friend of her husband's. She is sure that the women find her uninteresting and unimpressive, and that the people who seem to like her are probably no better off than she.

Recently she has also been having difficulties at work. She is assigned the most menial tasks at the firm and is never given an assignment of importance or responsibility. She admits that she frequently does a "slipshod" job of what is given her, never does more than is required, and never demonstrates any assertiveness or initiative to her supervisors. She views her boss as self-centered, unconcerned, and unfair, but nevertheless admires his success.

—Spitzer and others, 1981, pp. 10–11

Major Depression

A major depressive episode is marked by either or both a depressed mood and a loss of interest or pleasure in almost all activities. Some of the following problems are also noted in a major depressive episode: marked weight loss or gain when not dieting, constant sleeping problems, agitated or greatly slowed-down behavior, fatigue, inability to think clearly, feelings of worthlessness, and frequent thoughts about death or suicide. Figure 10–4 shows the incidence of these symptoms among those diagnosed as depressed.

The description of Mrs. B. provides a typical example of a major depressive episode. She was brought to a psychiatrist's office by her concerned husband. When he had called to make an appointment and was told that the first one available was in ten days, he had responded that he didn't think his wife could wait that long. Mrs. B., the mother of two children, was a 45-year-old legal secretary.

FIGURE 10–4 Percent of all individuals diagnosed as clinically depressed who report having each of these symptoms of depression. In general, some symptoms are more common among people who are depressed than are others. Men and women who are depressed vary in the frequency with which they report different types of symptoms.

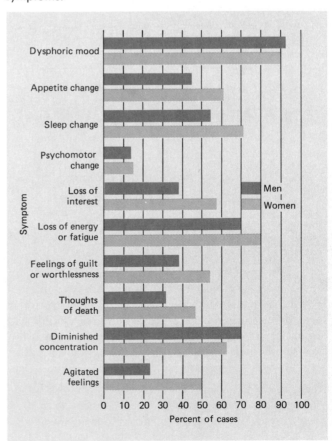

Mrs. B was dressed in wrinkled and slightly soiled clothing. Her hair was carelessly combed and there was a faint body odor about her. Her face was drawn and expressionless. She was helped by her husband into the office where she sat motionless, staring at the floor and occasionally sighing audibly. She said nothing unless asked a simple direct question. Even then her answers were delayed, spoken slowly, and of a droning, monotonous quality. A portion of the interview went as follows:

Dr. R: What's the trouble that brings you in?

Mrs. B: I don't care about anything.

Dr. R: What do you mean?

Mrs. B: (no response)

Dr. R: You look sad.

Mrs. B: Yes . . . not sad . . . just nothing.

Dr. R: How long have you been like this?

Mrs. B: About three weeks . . . getting worse.

Dr. R: Has anything like this ever happened to you before?

Mrs. B: No.

Dr. R: How's your appetite?

Mrs. B: No appetite.

Dr. R: Have you lost weight these three weeks?

Mrs. B: I don't know . . . maybe 10 or 12 lbs.

Dr. R: How's your sleeping?

Mrs. B: Bad. I wake up every morning about 3 and just lay there.

Dr. R: Do you feel bad about anything?

Mrs. B: Everything . . . I wish I were dead.

—Tomb and Christensen, 1987, p. 198

After her interview, Mrs. B.'s husband spoke with the psychiatrist. He said he and his wife had been married 26 years and this behavior was very different from any she had ever shown before. He thought the trouble had begun about a month earlier. At that time she was too tired to take part in her favorite activity, boating.

Gradually she has withdrawn. She doesn't want to see anybody, just wants to rest but I never see her sleeping. I force her to eat. I guess I panicked yesterday when she said she wanted to die.

—Tomb and Christensen, 1987, p. 198

If a person has one or more major depressive episodes but has never had a manic episode, he or she is said to have a **major depression.** The period a depressive episode lasts is variable. If it is not treated it may last about six months and then the person returns to his or her usual behavior pattern. It is estimated that half of the people who have a major depressive episode will have at least one more in their lifetime. If depression does recur, it is most likely to do so within two years. People who have recurrent major depressive episodes have an average of seven of them over their lifetimes (Cancro, 1985). About 15 percent of people with a major depression have some psychotic symptoms, usually delusions (false beliefs about reality). The delusions typically have the quality of despair—"I have an incurable illness and I'm dying," or self-blame—"I am not well because of my sinful behavior."

A 58-year-old man was brought to an emergency room by his wife and son. His behavior illustrates a psychotic depression:

. . . He was working as an architect and doing well until three weeks ago. At that time, he became noticeably more quiet and began to withdraw to his room immediately after dinner. One week ago he refused to go to work, stopped eating, and began to pace the floor at night. He would wring his hands, clench his fists, and cry. He talked of many minor life events as being "major sins" and today began to warn his family that he was really "the devil." "All these years you've mistaken me for your father. I am the devil, Satan himself. No one is more evil and wretched than me. I bring death and disease to the world and I will burn in Hell forever." This is the third time in five years he has presented himself in such a state. Each time he has professed the belief that his identity has been mistaken and he is really the devil.

—Tomb and Christensen, 1987, p. 49

Figure 10–5 shows an artist's version of a characteristic pose of severely depressed people who seem immersed in their own misery. People with major depressive disorder are often treated with antidepressant drugs or with electroconvulsive therapy. These types of treatment are described later in the chapter.

FIGURE 10–5 In his painting *Depression,* artist Jacob Lawrence has shown the downcast eyes, the drooping head and shoulders, and the shrunken posture of people who are deeply depressed.

Theories of Depression

Most researchers think that depression results from an interaction between a person's biological characteristics and psychological vulnerabilities and the occurrence of stressful events or difficult ongoing situations in his or her life (Akiskal, 1985). Despite this widely-held view that both characteristics of the person and of the situation are important, each of the perspectives discussed in this book has been used to try to understand the causes of depression and to find effective treatment approaches. As is usually the case, the different theoretical approaches to depression have produced different types of studies and different data, all of which may add to our understanding of the causes and treatment of this complex disorder.

Biological Theories

Biological theories assume that the cause of depression lies either in the genes or in some physiological malfunction that may or may not have an inherited base.

ROLE OF HEREDITY Twin studies and studies of families clearly suggest a genetic component in both major depression and bipolar disorders. One study (Gershon and others, 1988) has revealed that there is a much greater risk of developing a major depression if one's identical twin has had this disorder (54 percent) than if one's parent, brother, or sister has experienced it (16.6 percent). The chances of developing this disorder are even less if a person has no close relatives that have ever been given this diagnosis (5.8 percent). The

Gershon study also indicates that those with relatives with a bipolar diagnosis have almost three times as great a chance of developing a major depression as those who have no family member with this diagnosis (14.9 percent compared to 5.8 percent). These figures indicate that both major depression and bipolar disorders may be associated with the same genetic makeup.

Family studies have also shown that the younger people are when their first major depression occurs, the more likely it is that their relatives will also experience periods of depression (Weissman and others, 1984*a*). (See Figure 10–6.) Relatives of people who had a major depressive episode before the age of 20 had an eight-times greater chance of becoming depressed than relatives of normal subjects. Relatives of people who were over 40 when they first had a major depression had little more than the normal risk of depression. This increased risk was found both for relatives of patients who were hospitalized and for relatives of individuals who did not need to be hospitalized (Weissman and others, 1984*b*).

Although genetic factors seem important in many cases of depression, the exact mechanism of inheritance of depression is not clear and may even vary from one family to another. It is also obvious that nongenetic factors, either physical or related to a person's environment or relationships, may be required to produce depression even in people with a genetic vulnerability.

BIOCHEMICAL ASPECTS OF DEPRESSION: NEURO-TRANSMITTERS Whatever the mechanism by which the genetic factor is inherited, its influences are biochemical. Depression is probably the result of a lack of certain chemical neurotransmitters at particular sites in the brain. Neurotransmitter systems, especially the **monoamine neurotransmitters,** have been the most widely studied

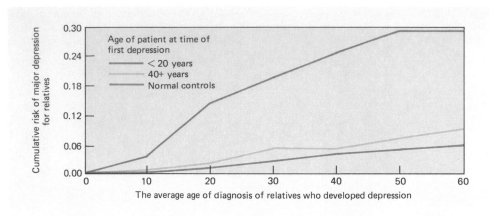

FIGURE 10-6 Cumulative risk of major depression for relatives of depressed people varies according to the age at which the person first becomes depressed.

(Modified from *Archives of General Psychiatry*, 1984, 41, 1136–1143. Copyright © 1984, American Medical Association)

biological phenomena in depression. The most important monoamines are the **catecholamines** norepinephrine and dopamine and the **indolamine** serotonin. All these monoamine systems originate from a small number of cell bodies in the limbic system. Other neurotransmitters that have been thought to play a role in depression include **gamma aminobutyric acid (GABA),** which seems to inhibit neurotransmitter action and is widely found in the central nervous system, and **acetylcholine,** which is found in both the central and the peripheral nervous systems and can be either an inhibitor or a stimulator of transmission between neurons.

Each of the billions of neurons in the brain interacts with others by electrochemical means. When the neuron is stimulated, it releases neurotransmitters, chemical substances, from **vesicles,** or storage areas in the nerve ending. The neurotransmitter diffuses across the *synapse* or space between two neurons (see Chapter 3) and interacts with a receptor, which is really a highly specialized protein substance, on the outside surface of the postsynaptic neuron. (Figure 10–7 is a greatly simplified diagram of the components of a synapse.) Biological changes occur within the postsynaptic nerve as a result of contact with the neurotransmitter. In nerve cells, this receptor stimulation often results in an electrical impulse or action potential.

Neurons regulate their own activity by feedback mechanisms that involve receptors on the nerve ending, called *autoreceptors.* When an autoreceptor is stimulated it inhibits further release of the neurotransmitter. Neurotransmitters such as *norepinephrine, dopamine,* and *serotonin* are normally inactivated at the synapse. Part of this inactivation takes place by their being taken back into the nerve endings from which they have been released.

An early hypothesis about the role of neurotransmitters in mood disorders was the **catecholamine theory.** In its simplest form, this theory proposed that depression might be the result of a deficiency of catecholamines, especially norepinephrine, at important

synapses in the brain and that mania might be due to an excess of catecholamines at those synapses. Antidepressant medication, as well as many environmental stimuli, work by altering this neurotransmitter activity. Some antidepressant drugs work to prevent the reuptake of the neurotransmitters, which results in a higher neurotransmitter level in the synapse. Another way that the amount of neurotransmitter at some synapses can be increased is by inhibiting the release or effectiveness of the chemical **monoamine oxidase (MAO)** which is contained in sac-like receptacles—called *mitochondria*—in the presynaptic nerve ending. MAO is an enzyme that causes a degradation or loss of effectiveness in catecholamine and serotonin neurotransmitters.

Even though the catecholamine hypothesis was known to be an oversimplification from the very beginning, it led to much useful research. Several types of

FIGURE 10-7 Diagram of a synapse.

(Reproduced with permission from Richelson, E.: Antidepressants and brain neurochemistry. *Mayo Clinic Proceedings,* 65, 1227–1236)

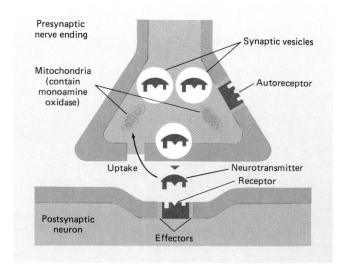

research findings soon showed that the role of the neurotransmitter in depression was more complex than was previously believed. Most important, the hypothesis could not account for the finding that some antidepressant drugs produced very rapid changes (in a few hours) in a person's amine uptake, but changes in the person's depressed state were usually not seen for 7 to 14 days after the treatment had begun. Further, some effective antidepressant drugs did not affect amine uptake to any great extent. This puzzling finding was explained to some extent by research on antidepressant effects in rats, which showed that long-term but not short-term treatment with antidepressant drugs caused a loss of sensitivity in postsynaptic receptors (Ventulani and others, 1976).

After this discovery, many researchers changed their focus from *pre*synaptic action to *post*synaptic, in order to investigate a newer hypothesis. The **desensitization hypothesis** assumes that certain catecholamine receptors are supersensitive in people who are depressed and that the role of antidepressant drugs is to reduce this sensitivity to normal levels. However, clinical studies to show the presence of these supersensitive receptors have not yet produced results to support this hypothesis (Heninger and others, 1988). It is important to remember that these postsynaptic effects may be the result of activity on the presynaptic side. Most antidepressant drugs can increase the level of catecholamines at postsynaptic receptor sites either by inhibiting their reuptake into the presynaptic neuron or affecting MAO activity. This increase in turn leads to a desensitization of the presynaptic receptors and thus increases their release of neurotransmitters.

Research on how the neurotransmitters function was handicapped for a long time by inadequate means of testing hypotheses. Changes in monoamine levels had to be assessed from urine, plasma, and cerebrospinal fluid and could not be directly measured. New methods in basic neuroscience led to the discovery of specific types and locations of receptor sites. For instance, the distribution of different types of receptors can be seen by studying brain tissue through a microscope after the receptors have been tagged using radioactive compounds. The same approach can be applied to the living human brain using positron emission tomography (PET). These techniques have led to identification of several subtypes of receptors that are each capable of responding to a specific neurotransmitter, which in turn has helped to increase our understanding of drug actions. So far two general classes of receptors are recognized. One group works to allow fast, precise signalling between neurons. The other type sets up a slow sequence of events that allows the incoming signal to be greatly amplified and distributed widely within the neuron. The location of receptors on the presynaptic terminal has also been verified by this method.

THE SEARCH FOR MARKERS OF DEPRESSION

Since most scientists agree that not all depressions have similar causes, a great deal of effort has been spent on finding subgroups of depressed patients that have similar characteristics. The study of such subgroups should not only make it easier to understand the causes of depression but, even more important, provide clues to the most effective treatment for a particular individual. A major focus of research in this area is the effort to develop a test that could be used to identify various subgroups.

Hormonal Studies Although much of the biological research on mood disorders is aimed at learning more about biochemical activity, it is also becoming clear that the disorders involve many different organ systems in the body. The close connections of mood disorders with the endocrine system are just beginning to be understood. Because of advances in understanding brain chemistry, especially the way in which the brain releases hormones from the pituitary gland, research on the hypothalamic-pituitary adrenal system's role in depression has recently increased greatly. A high level of cortisol, a hormone produced in the cortex of the brain, has been consistently found in depressed patients. Actions of a variety of neurotransmitters have been thought to be basic steps in this cortisol excess. Research efforts have used neuroendocrine strategies to develop diagnostic tests or markers to define subgroups of patients who respond in specific ways. If these neuroendocrine-based tests could successfully divide patients into meaningful groups, the results might be potentially useful both in understanding more about the role of hormones in depression and in defining subgroups of depressed patients for whom specific types of treatment or specific antidepressant drugs might be particularly helpful. So far, these efforts have added to general knowledge but have not been useful in a clinical setting.

One example of such a strategy is the **dexamethasone suppression test (DST)** (Carroll, 1985). In this test, patients are given dexamethasone, a steroid that suppresses the production of cortisol. Normally, dexamethasone suppresses the level of cortisol in the blood for about 24 hours. In some depressed patients, however, the suppression does not last that long (see Figure 10–8).

To date, research findings have not provided enough evidence to justify using the DST on a routine basis (APA Task Force, 1987). One problem is that the test does not differentiate between depressive disorder and the depressed phase of bipolar disorders. Many patients whose depressions appear to be biologically related show no response to the test. Another problem is that the dexamethasone suppressor response has been reported in many other conditions besides depression—for example, alcoholism, schizophrenia, and eating disorders—as well as in normal individuals who were

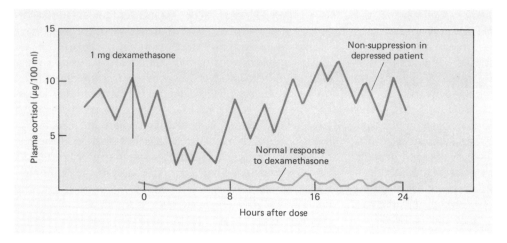

FIGURE 10–8 The dexamethasone suppression test identifies individuals whose hormonal systems do not react in a normal way. In most normal people, a dose of dexamethasone will suppress the secretion of blood cortisol. In some depressed people, however, the blood cortisol level does not decrease over a 24-hour period.

(Lingjaerde, 1983, p. 44)

dieting. It seems unlikely that all these disorders share a common cause. More likely, DST reflects a nonspecific aspect of the severity of the person's disorder (Hirschfeld & Goodwin, 1988). Thus, the DST cannot be viewed as a clear diagnostic sign of depression. Another shortcoming of the DST is that it does not discriminate between people who may be helped by antidepressant drugs and those who would not. Since gaining such information to make appropriate clinical treatment more quickly available is one of the purposes of the search for markers, results of research with the DST have so far been disappointing.

Scanning Techniques The use of scanning techniques to locate specific receptor sites has already been described. Brain imaging techniques such as positron emission tomography (PET) allow a nonintru-

sive assessment of neurotransmitter biochemistry in patients. PET scans can be used in a variety of ways. They can provide biochemical maps of the living brain, enable the neural circuits involved in specific behaviors to be visualized, and demonstrate how drugs affect the brain. An important advantage of these techniques for the study of behavior is their ability to define behavior changes in an objective manner. Figure 10–9 illustrates how scanning techniques can link observed behavioral changes in patients with depressive disorders to changes in brain activity. A variety of scanning techniques are described in Chapter 13.

Biological Rhythms Differences in biological rhythms may be a way to identify subgroups of depressed individuals; this approach may also be a way to clarify how biological functioning differs for people who are

FIGURE 10–9 Three series of PET scans of unipolar depression illustrate how this technique can be used as an objective measure of the changes in biological activity that accompany certain behavior changes. The center row illustrates the decreased glucose metabolism found in a unipolar depressed patient. (The darker green the area, the less the metabolic activity.) The top row shows how the glucose metabolism increases as a patient naturally recovers from a period of depression. The lower row shows a similar increase in glucose metabolism when a test drug improves a patient's behavior.

(O. Lingjaerde, 1983. The biochemistry of depression, *Acta Psychiatrica Scandinavica Supplementum, 302,* pp. 36–51. Copyright © 1983 Munksgaard International Publishers Ltd., Copenhagen, Denmark [University of California, Los Angeles])

depressed as compared to those who are not. Regular rhythms in the functioning of human beings and other animals have been recognized for a long time. Of these, the 24-hour or circadian rhythms have been studied most. These circadian rhythms are controlled or influenced by internal factors, including neurotransmitters, as well as by external factors, such as light (Steiner, 1989). Circadian rhythms can be shown for a large number of biological functions. Some of them, such as body temperature and sleep activity, are usually synchronized so that their peaks occur at the same time. When these rhythms get out of synchrony, other changes occur. For instance, sleep lasts a long time if a person goes to sleep at the top of the body temperature curve. If, instead, the person goes to sleep near the bottom of the temperature curve, sleep lasts a much shorter time. Sleep disturbance is frequent in depressed individuals. They tend to have trouble going to sleep and staying asleep. They also are likely to waken early in the morning and to feel most depressed in the morning. Table 10–3 lists some of the characteristics of sleep of depressed people.

Normal sleep has a number of phases that can be measured by monitoring the electrical impulses of the brain. The one that is of most interest from the standpoint of depression is REM sleep, during which the eyes rapidly move from side to side and brain wave patterns indicate a peak in brain activity. One characteristic in some depressed individuals is a shortened period between falling asleep and the beginning of the first REM period as well as increased length and intensity of the first REM period of the night (Kupfer and others, 1985). This characteristic, together with early wakening, may be due to an advance in temperature rhythm that causes the person to go to sleep nearer to the bottom than to the top of his or her temperature curve (see Figure 10–10).

Researchers studying the causes of depression had noted that treatment with antidepressant drugs and also with electroconvulsive therapy (ECT) cause these sleep disturbances to disappear. From this observation, they theorized that sleep deprivation might provide some clues to the physiological mechanisms of depression. In one study (Wu & Bunney, 1990), it was found that about two-thirds of depressed patients who have symptoms including disordered sleep are actually *less* depressed after total sleep deprivation for 24 hours. However, a high percentage of these same people show a return of depressive symptoms after one night of recovery sleep or even after a nap. Sleep studies such as these give researchers an opportunity to anticipate closely the timing of mood change and make it easier for them to measure psychobiological variables both before and after the change points. Sleep studies with EEG monitoring can also be used to help clarify what type of sleep—slow wave or REM—is more important for the relapse.

Table 10–3
Major Sleep Disturbances Common to Depression

Generalization	Findings
Shallow sleep	Decreased Stage 3 and 4 (Delta) sleep Increased Stage 1 sleep Greater sensitivity to noises
Fragmented sleep	Increased awakenings Increased stage shifts Decreased sleep efficiency
Short sleep	Decreased total sleep time Increased time to fall asleep Increased early morning awakening
"Intense" REM sleep	Increased REM density (increased eye movement during REM sleep)
REM sleep is advanced toward sleep onset	REM begins sooner after falling asleep Increased length and REM density of first REM period Increased proportion of REM in first half of night

SOURCE: From S.S. Campbell and J.C. Gillin (1987). Sleep measures in depression: How sensitive? How specific? *Psychiatric Annals,* 17, 647–653.

FIGURE 10–10 The relationship between duration of sleep and the circadian temperature rhythm.

(Adapted from Czeisler and others, *Science, 210,* p. 267. Copyright © 1980 by the AAAS)

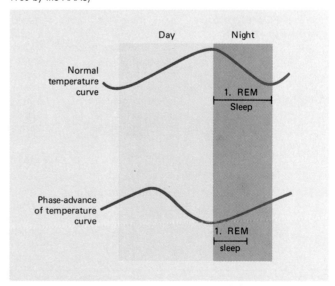

Another important question is whether the easing up of depression occurs in response to the total time over which the sleeplessness extends or because the deprivation includes some particular time in the course of sleep. It is possible, for instance, that some substance released in the body during sleep produces the depression. Studies of sleep patterns and depression might help isolate such a substance. Finally, if researchers can find out the variables that differentiate people who are not helped by sleep deprivation from those who are, they can learn more about different processes that are associated with depression.

TREATMENT BASED ON BIOLOGICAL THEORIES

Antidepressant Drugs and Lithium

The first effective antidepressants were from two chemical groups, **tricyclics** (named from their three-ring chemical structure) and **monoamine oxidase (MAO) inhibitors.** More recently a new group of antidepressants with a variety of ring structures have been developed. This group is often referred to as **second generation antidepressants.** Because of the varied ring structures, non-MAO inhibitor antidepressants are now more properly described as **heterocyclics.** Although it had been hoped that these heterocyclic antidepressants would produce a more complete and rapid lifting of mood than did the older group, so far those hopes have not been realized. Some of the second generation drugs do produce fewer side effects and are less toxic if there is an overdose, however. In addition to these drugs, the element **lithium** is used to treat depression, usually when it is a result of bipolar disorder. Table 10–4 lists some of the more widely known drugs in each category. Although these antidepressants may be effective in removing depressive symptoms or at least lessening them, they must be taken under careful medical supervision because they also have a variety of side effects. Because tricyclics work by blocking acetylcholine, a neurotransmitter in the parasympathetic nervous system, their effects include such things as dry mouth, constipation, dizziness, irregular heartbeat, blurred vision, ringing in the ears, retention of urine, and excessive sweating. In addition, tricyclics may cause tremors and, in older patients, confusion and

Table 10–4

Drugs Used in the Treatment of Mood Disorders

Generic Name	Trade Name (Example)	General Description
ANTIDEPRESSANT DRUGS		
Heterocyclics		
Tricyclic Type		
amitriptyline	Elavil	Used to treat relatively severe depressive symptoms of the unipolar type. Variable effectiveness in moderating symptoms. Slow acting. May take up to three weeks before response is seen. Many side effects, some dangerous. MAO inhibitors require restrictions in diet because of serious interactive effects with certain food chemicals.
doxepin	Sinequan	
imipramine	Tofranil	
trimipramine	Surmontil	
Second Generation Antidepressants		
amoxapine	Asendin	
fluoxetine	Prozac	
magnesium pemoline	Cylert	
maprotiline	Ludiomil	
trazodone	Desyrel	
MAO Inhibitors		
isocarboxazid	Marplan	
phenelzine	Nardil	
tranylcypromine	Parnate	
ANTIMANIC DRUGS		
lithium carbonate	Carbolith	Used to treat manic episodes and some severe depressions, especially those that alternate with mania. Effective in reducing or preventing manic episodes but variable with depressions. Many possible side effects if use not closely monitored. High toxic potential.
	Eskalith	
	Lithonate	
	Lithotabs	

delirium. They also may affect male sexual functioning by causing difficulties in ejaculation. Many of these side effects decrease after taking the drugs for several weeks. Patients who experience certain side effects may find that shifting to a drug with a different chemical composition will decrease them.

Some of the second generation antidepressants were developed in order to lessen side effects. One of these, fluoxetine (Prozac), has been available in the United States since 1988. It became popular very rapidly because of these lessened side effects and because it was effective with some patients who had not responded to the older tricyclics. In less than two years, more than half a million prescriptions were being written for it each month. However, several cases were reported that linked the drug to a preoccupation with suicide that lasted for two to four months after the drug was withdrawn. Questions over fluoxetine's safety resulted in lawsuits and in some physicians' discontinuing prescriptions of the drug. Although the controversy persists, experts so far do not believe convincing evidence links fluoxetine to suicidal thoughts (Fava, 1991).

Which group of drugs and which particular drug within a group will be effective is still usually a matter of trial and error on the part of the physician. Usually, one of the tricyclic drugs is preferred because the MAO inhibitors have more potentially dangerous side effects. Use of the MAO inhibitors also requires stricter supervision because when these drugs are taken with foods that contain a substance called tyramine they may produce a toxic reaction and cause blood pressure to rise to a life-threatening level. Because many common foods, including cheese, chocolate, sour cream, and wine, contain tyramine, the use of MAO inhibitors requires careful dietary monitoring.

Lithium is used to treat depression that occurs as a part of the mood swings of bipolar disorder. Lithium may change the chemical balance of the body fluids by replacing calcium, magnesium, potassium, and/or sodium, or it may slow down the release or increase the absorption of norepinephrine. Whatever the process, it seems effective in calming manic behavior and also serves to prevent the depressed phase of the bipolar cycle.

Electroconvulsive Therapy One of the problems in treating a severe episode of depression with either tricyclics or MAO inhibitors is the time lag between their initial use and the first signs of improvement of the patient's mood. Several weeks may go by before any improvement is seen. If there is concern about suicide, a wait of three weeks or so may seem too great a risk. In such situations, or if drugs are not effective, electroconvulsive therapy may be the treatment used because it produces a more rapid effect. **Electroconvulsive therapy (ECT)** involves passing a current of between 70 and 130 volts through the patient's head. First an anesthetic and a

muscle relaxant are administered. (The muscle relaxant is given to prevent injury from the convulsion caused by the electric charge.) The current is then administered through electrodes placed on one or both sides of the head.

ECT is very effective in treating severe depression in which there is a great deal of delusional thinking. ECT is also effective for some severe depressions that have not responded to tricyclics or MAO inhibitors. It is not effective for mild depressions (dysthymic disorder and adjustment disorder with depressed mood). Despite its effectiveness the use of ECT has brought forth a good deal of controversy.

ECT causes many changes. It produces massive discharges of neurons in much of the brain, activates the autonomic nervous system, releases secretions from the endocrine glands, and causes convulsions of many of the muscles. So many chemical changes occur in the body that it is difficult to determine which ones have an effect on the depression. It is likely that the seizure activity produces changes in the level of neurotransmitters or changes in the electrical responsiveness of the neuron. One change that results from ECT is an increased density of at least one type of serotonin receptor on postsynaptic neurons (Richelson, 1990).

ECT can result in memory loss, most of which disappears within a few weeks. The patient's ability to learn and retain information may also be affected for several weeks. Some people who have been treated with ECT report memory lapses several years later. Side effects related to memory may be reduced by placing the electrodes on only one side of the head and also by using brief pulses of electricity (Weiner and others, 1988). Unfortunately, these same modifications in the procedure often make ECT less effective in decreasing the depressive symptoms (Persad, 1990).

In general, ECT is used only after other treatments, usually antidepressant drugs, have been tried. The use of ECT has decreased at least until recently (Persad, 1990). An increase in use has been predicted by some authorities because ECT reduces time in the hospital and therefore also medical costs (Markowitz and others, 1987). In the early years of its use, ECT was estimated to produce improvement in between 80 and 90 percent of patients for whom it was used. Currently, ECT is rarely used unless treatment with antidepressant drugs has been tried and has been unsuccessful. Under those conditions, about 50 percent of patients show marked improvement after ECT (Sackeim and others, 1990).

Sometimes ECT can produce dramatic changes in mood. Norman Endler, the psychologist whose description of his own depression (later diagnosed as a bipolar type) appears at the beginning of this chapter, also described his experience with ECT after both tricyclic and MAO-inhibiting drugs had proved ineffective and

the depression was still incapacitating him after five months. Endler was faced with a choice between ECT and hospitalization; he reluctantly chose ECT.

Dr. Persad met us on the sixth floor at seven forty-five. He tried to calm me down, and I recall his saying that he had never seen anyone so agitated as I. The prospect of ECT really frightened me.

Beatty [Endler's wife] remained in the waiting area and Dr. Persad and I went into the ECT room. I changed into my pajamas and a nurse took my vital signs [blood pressure, pulse, and temperature]. The nurse and other attendants were friendly and reassuring. I began to feel at ease. The anesthetist arrived and informed me that she was going to give me an injection. I was asked to lie down on a cot and was wheeled into the ECT room proper. It was about eight o'clock. A needle was injected into my arm and I was told to count back from 100. I got about as far as 91. The next thing I knew I was in the recovery room and it was about eight-fifteen. I was slightly groggy and tired but not confused. My memory was not impaired. I certainly knew where I was. Shortly after eight-thirty, I got dressed, went down the hall to fetch Beatty, and she drove me home. At home I enjoyed breakfast and then lay down for a few hours. Late in the morning I got dressed. I felt no pain, no confusion, and no agitation. I felt neither less depressed nor more depressed than I had before the ECT. . . . After about the third or fourth treatment I went up to Dr. Persad's office and spoke to him briefly. He asked me if I had noticed any improvement and to what degree. I believed that I had improved 35 to 40 percent. Dr. Persad believed that the improvement was more likely to be 70 to 75 percent.

—Endler 1982, pp. 81–83

After the fifth and sixth treatments had been completed Endler returned to his office. A colleague who had been helping to manage the psychology department in his absence was there.

I asked her to remain. She stated that she would be glad to stay as long as I needed her assistance. By early afternoon Kathy looked at me and said "Norm, you are perfectly fine, you do not need

me here." She left and I stayed the rest of the day. As of then I resumed the chairmanship full time. A miracle had happened in two weeks. I had gone from feeling like an emotional cripple to feeling well.

—Endler, 1982, p. 83

Like many people who have a bipolar disorder, Endler experienced another depression about a year after the first. This time, although ECT produced improvement and made it possible for him to work effectively, the depressed mood hung on for several months. The long-term outcome was more favorable for Endler. Treatment with a combination of antidepressants and lithium led to a quick recovery. In 1989 he wrote that he had been "symptom free for eight years and am functioning as effectively as I did prior to my depression" without using any medication (Endler, 1989).

ASSESSMENT OF BIOLOGICAL TREATMENT OPTIONS Although both ECT and the various drug therapies can be helpful to those with depressive disorders, each option has both positive and negative features. ECT, although helpful to about half of those that neither the tricyclics nor the MAO inhibitors have helped, is not acceptable to many people. As in the case described above, the treatment may help relieve a depression but may not be able to prevent a recurrence. Repeated series of ECT administered if the depression does recur may not be as effective as they were for the first depressive episode. In addition, the long-term effects of repeated series of ECT treatments are not known.

Treatment with antidepressant drugs also presents difficulties. Because as yet it is difficult to predict which chemical compound will be most effective for a particular person, choosing the best drug is often a trial and error affair even for an experienced clinician. This means that the period before effective treatment begins may be long delayed and the severely depressed person may be at risk for suicide as well as being further demoralized by the concern that effective treatment may not be available. Also, as we have seen, many of the antidepressant drugs have side effects that may range from the merely annoying or uncomfortable, such as dry mouth or constipation, to the life-threatening, such as sudden changes in blood pressure. People who use antidepressant drugs should have frequent monitoring by a physician. Just as in the case of ECT, the effects these drugs may have after many years of use is also not known. Moreover, some researchers argue that dependence on drugs makes unipolar or bipolar individuals less likely to improve their coping mechanisms and thus increases the chances of their having further affective problems. The attitude of many therapists toward using biological treatment alone is expressed by Silvano Arieti, a well-

known psychoanalyst and researcher: "I have never met a patient about whom I could say that his depression came from nowhere and its origin had to be sought exclusively in metabolic disorder" (Arieti & Bemporad, 1978, p. 5).

The Psychodynamic View

The psychological study of depression was begun by Sigmund Freud and Karl Abraham, a German physician. Both described depression as a complex reaction to loss (Abraham, 1911/1968; Freud, 1917/1957). Depression, or melancholy, as Freud called it, was grief gone haywire—excessive, drawn out, often unrelated to the environment, and seemingly unjustified. Freud described both normal mourning and depression as responses to the loss of someone or something that was loved. However, in contrast to the mourner, the depressed person suffers "an extraordinary diminution of his self-regard, an impoverishment of his ego on a grand scale" (Freud, 1917/1957, p. 246). Freud believed that a depressed person has a strong and punishing conscience or superego. He thought that one reason the conscience becomes so strong is to control the anger and aggressive feelings that otherwise might come forth to hurt others (Freud, 1930).

A different way of conceptualizing depression from a psychodynamic view was suggested by Edward Bibring, an Austrian psychoanalyst (1953). He viewed depression as the emotional expression of the ego's helplessness in maintaining a desired sense of self. He changed the focus from an internal conflict to situations that made a person feel helpless. Later, Bibring's ideas were elaborated by others who suggested that depression be considered a negative emotion much like anxiety (Sandler & Joffee, 1965). According to this view, depression after the loss of a loved one was not so much due to the loss of the person but rather of the state of well-being that the presence of that person supplied. Sandler and Joffee saw depression as a two-part sequence. In the first state, immediately after the loss, they thought a "psychobiological reaction" occurred. After this strong emotional response to loss, they believed that most people are able to overcome their feelings by effectively coping with the situation and finding ways to regain their state of well-being. However, some people are unable to do this and, instead of beginning to recover, go on to experience what is called a clinical episode, which means that their grief and depressed feelings are then viewed as abnormal.

Psychoanalytic theorists have suggested that these clinical episodes happen because the events that set off the depression revive dimly conscious, threatening views of the self and others that are based on childhood experience. These assumptions appear to be related to a childhood belief that one will never be loved by others, never become worthwhile, and will always lack the ability to control what happens. John Bowlby, a British psychoanalyst, was one of the more prominent theorists who emphasized the importance of loss or separation in childhood to later development. Bowlby thought that separation of a child from its mother or another important figure during early childhood, whether because of illness, travel, or other reasons, created feelings of sadness, anger, and continuing anxiety that might affect the person's emotional relationships in adult life (Bowlby, 1980). Bowlby believed that the childhood experiences that contribute to these feelings are not single events, but develop from long-term patterns of familial interaction. Among these are children's inability to obtain a stable, secure relationship with a parent despite many efforts to be pleasing on the child's part, or children growing up in an atmosphere in which they hear repeatedly about how unlovable or incompetent they are.

The first phase in psychodynamic therapy is to reveal the unconscious processes that determine the client's behavior. These discoveries are usually made by discussion and interpretation of the client's thoughts and feelings in interaction with the therapist. When evidence emerges of distortions of reality, perhaps based on earlier relationships, the therapist helps the client understand the distortions. The second phase of treatment is to help the client understand how the present is different from the distant past in which the client lacked autonomy and control. The following case illustrates how past experiences contribute to depression and anxiety in the present.

One depressed woman stated that she became symptomatic when she could no longer keep up with her work and felt herself to be a failure. This explanation was partially true but did not go far enough in describing her actual situation. Later it was revealed that she began to feel anxious and dysphoric when her boss, upon whom she depended for a sense of worth . . . hired another female assistant. This threatened the patient's imagined special status with the boss, and she anticipated that he would favor the new employee, who was erroneously perceived as more able, attractive, and likeable than the patient. Much of this reaction was a recapitulation of the events surrounding the birth of a younger sibling when the patient was five years old. Just as in childhood, she attempted to win back the father's preferential regard by working harder and harder, in order to obtain praise and reassurance.

However, in contrast to her father, the boss did not sufficiently recognize her increased effort,

causing her to apply herself even harder so that her work did become too much for her. Therefore, she did become depressed as a result of being overwhelmed by her work; however, the initiative to do more and more was of her own choosing, and the basic reason for it was to become reinstated as the boss/father's favorite.

—Bemporad and Vasile, 1990, pp. 57–58

With the help of the therapist, the client gradually began to understand that her beliefs originated in childhood. As she became aware of these distorted views, other "transference distortions" in her reactions to the therapist appeared. Although she was unaware of doing so, she began to defer toward the therapist as a parental figure. But the therapist, instead of acting out the parental role she expected, helped her to identify and examine the reactions she anticipated. As a result, the client then began to understand how the nature of her past relationships affected her present behavior, that inside this adult was a helpless, needy child who had never felt able to act as she wanted to because of the fear of losing her father's favor. As these old assumptions began to alter, the client was able to be comfortable with the idea that perfection either in one's own eyes or in the eyes of others is not necessary for happiness or love. **Interpersonal psychotherapy** is often used with depressed clients. Interpersonal therapy has some of the same basic concepts as more traditional psychodynamic treatment. Therapists who use this approach believe that depression is best understood in an interpersonal context that emphasizes both people's social effectiveness and the degree to which they experience social support. This therapeutic approach focuses on helping people learn to be more socially effective.

Therapy that focuses on both feelings about the past and interpersonal skills seems particularly appropriate in treating depression because people who are depressed tend to come from troubled backgrounds and to have particular difficulty with close or intimate relationships with others (Becker & Schmaling, 1991). For many people who are depressed, effective long-term treatment seems to be associated with improvement in their relationships with their most significant others. Biologically based treatments for depression do not seem to modify these relational problems for many people who are depressed.

The Behavioral Perspective

Behaviorists view depression from a different perspective. When depressed people find themselves in stressful situations, they tend to cope by delaying (seeking more information before taking any action) and attempting to get emotional support from others. Excessive support seeking may be what makes other people feel uncomfortable and guilty and causes them to try to avoid contact with the depressed person. Depressed people may also make many complaints to elicit sympathy and affection. Although those who are on the receiving end of this treatment may respond appropriately at first, after a while they may begin to be annoyed or frustrated. Eventually a vicious cycle develops in which the display of symptoms and frustration of the depressed person's companions increase until the companions begin to say things like, "You could get better if you try," "No one has to act like that," and so forth (see Figure 10–11). These statements merely serve to worsen an already bad situation. Such feelings, whether expressed or not, are probably one reason why people tend to avoid the company of depressed individuals.

FIGURE 10–11 This poster, part of a campaign to inform the public about the need to seek treatment for depression, portrays a common reaction to the irritating qualities of depressed behavior.

"Why doesn't he just snap out of it."

Some research has suggested that many depressed people are capable of acting differently in different social roles (McNiel and others, 1987). When they meet people casually they may be able to conceal their negative behavior and behave in a socially desirable way. According to this view, it is mainly in long-term relationships, especially marital relationships, that we see the negative actions and negative responses predicted by the behavioral perspective.

A major focus of work on the interaction of depressed people with others is on married couples. The negative attitudes of depressed people and their spouses are usually obvious to others. These attitudes influence the spouses' interpretations of their interactions. There is usually both hostility and an attempt to hide negative feelings when disagreements are discussed (Coyne and others, 1987). Depression in one marital partner often seems to cause significant distress or depression in the other partner.

Although people who are depressed often seem to take a negative view of their interactions with others, there is considerable evidence that they also make a negative impression on others because of deficits in their social skills (Dykman and others, 1991). A negative spiral results, in which real deficits in performance compound the effects of the negative self-views. Depressed people not only are likely to think others respond to them negatively, but others are more likely to respond negatively because of the depressed people's lack of social skills.

SOCIAL SKILLS TRAINING One way to break this type of vicious cycle is through **social skills training,** one of the primary behavioral techniques used in treating depressed clients. This training has some overlap with interpersonal therapy discussed earlier; however, the two differ greatly because social skills training does not deal with any psychodynamic issues and concentrates solely on appropriate behavior and perhaps also on the cognitions that accompany it. Social skills training normally consists of four parts. First the client is taught basic verbal and nonverbal skills that focus on small segments of the desired behavior and then when these are learned, he or she practices gradually putting the segments together. After rehearsing these larger and larger parts with the therapist, the client then is given "homework" assignments in which the goal is to adapt the new skill so it is useful in the everyday environment. Next, the client is trained to be more perceptive about cues other people in the environment give and learns how to change his or her own behavior according to these environmental changes. Finally the client learns to adopt realistic criteria for performance and is taught how to be self-reinforcing. The following case illustrates the effectiveness of social skills training.

Ms. SJ is a 43-year-old single woman with a master's degree in chemistry. She has worked as a laboratory assistant for a number of years. She came to the clinic complaining of (a) sad mood, (b) low energy, (c) trouble making decisions, (d) feeling worthless, (e) pessimism about her future, and (f) guilt about her unsuccessful past. She was involved in a three-year intimate relationship, which has just ended. This event has rekindled symptoms of depression and a fear that this new episode would be as bad as a previous one ten years earlier.

. . . She reports a few very close girlfriends who, she says, tell her that she tends to be aloof and difficult to know. . . . She described her childhood family as discouraging any display of affection or anger. . . . As a result, she was very compliant, but she then felt very resentful.

Standardized role plays revealed difficulties with display of positive and negative assertion, as well as with conversation. She could not give a compliment to another person, particularly a male, and she could not touch a person. . . .

The first focus of clinical treatment was greeting people. Role plays focused on making eye contact with the other person, saying "Hello, I'm Sarah," and smiling. This behavior contrasted sharply with her current style of avoiding eye contact, not smiling, and only speaking if directly spoken to. Many role plays were carried out to train these skills. She continued to feel that this behavior was much too forward.

As she began to improve in this skill, touching the other person was added. Reverse role plays were first used, and her initial response to a touch on the hand was to become quite scared, to be silent, and to withdraw as fast as possible. Several practices were carried out in conjunction with a homework assignment . . . to observe other people in her clubs and to log each time one person touched another. After one week of observational data, she was astounded at how often people touched. . . .

Conversation role plays were repeated to include touching. After many repetitions, she became comfortable and began to enjoy the contact. Two further existing conversation behaviors were addressed before the first homework: First, she never wore a name tag because she believed that if someone really wanted to know her, they

would find out her name. Second, she would always position herself to be out of the way in order not to impede other people. . . . She attended her meetings with instructions (a) to introduce herself and say "Hello, I'm Sarah" to everyone, (b) to wear her name tag, (c) to locate herself in high-traffic areas, and (d) to smile with her greeting and with her departure. . . .

This homework assignment resulted in an astonishing response. People were friendly to her, included her in their conversations, and invited her into some of their activities. Not one person complained about the touching or about her being in the way. None of the men made any sexual overtures to her. This was such a success for her that she wondered why she had not done it before. These behaviors were practiced once more and then monitored. She continued these new behaviors, and they produced invitations to go sailing, to attend a special program in Florida, and to attend a meeting in Massachusetts as well. Her mood brightened considerably. She felt less alone, less like an outsider, and more worthwhile.

—Becker, 1990, pp. 99–100

Therapists who use a social skills training approach usually find it works well with depressed clients (Becker, 1990). If problems do occur, they tend to fall into certain categories. Clients may refuse to role play or to do the homework assignments. Role play is necessary so that the client gets the practice needed to use new behaviors in the real-life situations called for in the homework assignments. The practice gained from these assignments is in turn critical for success in learning new habits. Problems may also arise if the client experiences a series of crises that need attention, which take the focus away from the treatment. Of course, if the therapist does not attend to the crisis, a serious situation may result. Some clients continually bring new crises to therapy, with the result that they never learn the skills to solve their own problems. In dealing with a client's life crises, therefore, the therapist must steer a middle ground between focusing exclusively on social skills training and attending to the crisis at hand. Finally, problems in this type of therapeutic approach may occur if an inexperienced therapist tries to move through the training too quickly to get to the primary problem facing the client. This acceleration often results in the client's falling back on old and ineffective methods of dealing with other people.

The Cognitive Perspective

Probably the most influential psychological theories of depression today are derived from the cognitive perspective. The basis of these theories is the idea that the same experience may affect two people very differently. Part of this difference may be due to the way each person thinks about the event, to what cognitions each has about it. One person who does not receive an expected

Table 10–5
Cognitive Errors and the Assumptions from Which They Are Derived

Cognitive Error	Assumption
1. Overgeneralizing	1. If it is true in one case, it applies to any case that is even slightly similar.
2. Selective abstraction	2. The only events that matter are failures, deprivation, etc. Should measure self by errors, weaknesses, etc.
3. Excessive responsibility (assuming personal causality)	3. I am responsible for all bad things, failures, etc.
4. Assuming temporal causality (predicting without sufficient evidence)	4. If it has been true in the past, then it is always going to be true.
5. Self-references	5. I am the center of everyone's attention, especially of bad performances or personal attributes.
6. "Catastrophizing"	6. Always think of the worst. It is most likely to happen to you.
7. Dichotomous thinking	7. Everything is either one extreme or another (black or white; good or bad).

SOURCE: A. T. Beck (1976), *Cognitive Therapy and the Emotional Disorders.* New York: International Universities Press. Copyright © 1976 by Aaron T. Beck, M. D. Reprinted by permission of the publisher.

FIGURE 10–12 The cartoonist Roz Chast illustrates the negative focus about the past that is typical of a depressed person.

promotion might think: "I am a worthless person. Everyone thinks poorly of me. If they did not, I would have been selected for the job." A second person in the same situation might think: "R. was chosen for that job I wanted because he had more experience in negotiation. I know I could have done the job, but my qualifications didn't look as impressive on paper."

BECK'S COGNITIVE-DISTORTION MODEL Aaron Beck's cognitive-distortion model of depression (Beck, 1967, 1976; Beck and others, 1979) is the most original and influential of the cognitive approaches to depression. Beck argues that depression is primarily a disorder of thinking rather than of mood. He believes that depression can best be described as a **cognitive triad** of negative thoughts about oneself, the situation, and the future. A person who is depressed misinterprets facts in a negative way, focuses on the negative aspects of any situation, and also has pessimistic and hopeless expectations about the future. Table 10–5 illustrates some of these cognitive errors on the part of depressed individuals; Figure 10–12 takes a comical look at these negative thoughts.

Beck maintains that the cognitions of depressed people differ from the thoughts of people with anxiety disorders (Beck and others, 1987). Those with anxiety as their primary symptom have thoughts that focus on uncertainty and worry about the future. The thoughts of depressed people either focus on negative aspects of the past or reflect a negative outlook on what the future will bring. The anxious person worries about what might happen and *whether* he or she will be able to deal with it. The depressed person thinks about how terrible the future will be and how he or she will be *unable* to deal with it or improve it.

Beck believes that a person who is depressed blames any misfortune on his or her personal defects. Awareness of these presumed defects becomes so intense that it completely overwhelms any positive self-concepts. Any ambiguous situation is interpreted as evidence of the defect, even if there are more plausible explanations.

A good example is provided by Norman Endler's description of his thoughts during his bout of depression (Endler, 1982). Endler went through a period of fear

(not at all based on reality) that his family would desert him and he would be unable to cope with everyday living.

I recall a time during the end of August when I took the subway with my wife. She had gone through the turnstile before I did and I was positive that she was going to desert me. She probably had had enough of me and my shenanigans and was fed up with my behavior.

—Endler, 1982, p. 49

After his recovery from this period of depression, Endler recognized the irrationality of such a thought.

Of course nothing could have been further from the truth. Her kindness and devotion, her concern, compassion, and her love, more than anything else, sustained me during my ordeal. If I had to single out the one person who was most instrumental in my getting better, it would be my wife.

—Endler, 1982, p. 49

Beck also thinks that depressed people tend to compare themselves with others, which further lowers their self-esteem. Every encounter with another person becomes the opportunity for a negative self-evaluation. For instance, when talking with others the depressed person thinks: "I'm not a good conversationalist. I'm not as interesting as other people." Beck thinks that the tendency to have these negative cognitions may be related to particular ways of evaluating situations that grow out of childhood experiences. These thought patterns, called **schemata,** affect all the elements of the cognitive triad in later life. A list of the characteristics of these schemata is shown in Table 10–6.

Research on the outcome or effects of psychotherapy has raised some questions about whether these negative cognitions cause depression. It is possible that negative thoughts are merely the result of depression, not its causal agent. At present the answer to this question of causality is not clear. When clients involved in cognitive therapy were compared with those receiving antidepressant drugs, the decrease in depressed cognitions midway through the therapy sessions predicted good final outcome only for those in cognitive therapy (DeRubeis and others, 1990). Positive outcome for those receiving antidepressant drugs was not predicted by the degree to

Table 10–6
Schemata Used in Beck's Cognitive Theory of Depression

Schemata (silent assumptions)
Consist of unspoken, inflexible assumptions or beliefs
Result from past (early) experience
Form basis for screening, discriminating, weighing, and encoding stimuli
Form basis for categorizing, evaluating experiences, and making judgments and distorting actual experience
Determine the content of cognitions formed in situations and the affective response to them
Increase vulnerability to relapse

SOURCE: Beck, 1976.

which they experienced depressed cognitions at the same point in therapy. These results suggest that although changes in cognitions may play some role in recovery, they do not necessarily bring about the recovery by themselves.

COGNITIVE THERAPY FOR DEPRESSION Cognitive therapy is often referred to as **cognitive behavioral therapy** because it makes use of both types of theories. The proportion of cognitive and behavioral techniques that are used depends on the client's skills and degree of depression as well as the chosen goals of the therapy. In general, the more severely depressed the client, the more likely the therapist is to use behavioral techniques. In such cases, the first goals would be to mobilize the client to perform some simple self-help tasks. Later, as the client improves, the therapist may begin to work to help change some dysfunctional thinking by challenging parts of the client's belief system. Figure 10–13 illustrates the proportion of behavioral and cognitive techniques that are appropriate as a function of the client's level of functioning.

Among the behavioral techniques used by cognitive therapists is *activity scheduling,* in which the client plans his or her use of time and then keeps a record of how the time was spent. Activity listing is especially useful for clients who feel overwhelmed with their lives. Taking time to list what really must be accomplished each day helps them plan a realistic schedule. The activity schedule is also useful for evaluation by the client of the effectiveness with which each activity was carried out and the kind of emotional response it generated. The client is asked to make two numerical ratings for each activity concerning personal effectiveness (mastery) and personal pleasure. The therapist also gives the client assignments that are focused on particular problems. These tasks progress from minimal to greater difficulty and are matched to the client's level of functioning.

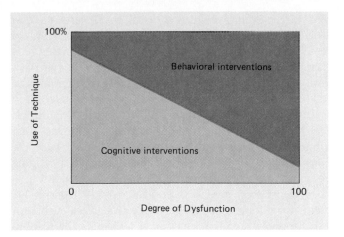

FIGURE 10–13 The proportion of behavioral to cognitive intervention is determined by the degree of the client's dysfunction.

(Freeman, 1990, p. 71)

Just as in social skills training, the therapist asks the client to rehearse and role play how to handle situations thought to be difficult. The therapist can serve as a model to show the client how to behave and can also provide helpful feedback. These approaches are identical to the behavioral approach discussed earlier. What cognitive therapy adds is a testing of the personal meanings assigned by the client to the behavior and a questioning of the evidence used by the client to assess a situation.

The following dialogue is an example of the cognitive technique used by Beck. The client, a 38-year-old executive, had just given the therapist his activity schedule and they were discussing his mastery ratings. One item, "wallpaper kitchen," stood out. This should have been an achievement for a severely depressed person, yet the client gave it a 0 for both mastery and pleasure.

Therapist: Why didn't you rate wallpapering the kitchen as a mastery experience?

Patient: Because the flowers didn't line up.

Therapist: You did in fact complete the job?

Patient: Yes.

Therapist: Your kitchen?

Patient: No. I helped a neighbor do his kitchen.

Therapist: Did he do most of the work? (Note that the therapist inquires about reasons for feelings of failure that might not be offered spontaneously.)

Patient: No. I really did almost all of it. He hadn't wallpapered before.

Therapist: Did anything else go wrong? Did you spill the paste all over? Ruin a lot of wallpaper? Leave a big mess?

Patient: No, no, the only problem was that the flowers did not line up.

Therapist: So, since it was not perfect, you get no credit at all.

Patient: Well . . . yes. (Note that the irrational belief that "if I don't do everything perfectly, I am useless, inadequate, and a failure" is implied by this reasoning. However, the correction of this assumption will be left to a later phase of therapy, when the patient is less depressed. For now, the correction of the cognitive distortion is the objective.)

Therapist: Just how far off was the alignment of the flowers?

Patient: (holds out fingers about 1/8 in. apart): About that much.

Therapist: On each strip of paper?

Patient: No . . . on two or three pieces.

Therapist: Out of how many?

Patient: About 20 to 25.

Therapist: Did anyone else notice it?

Patient: No. In fact, my neighbor thought it was great.

Therapist: Did your wife see it?

Patient: Yeh, she admired the job.

Therapist: Could you see the defect when you stood back and looked at the whole wall?

Patient: Well . . . not really.

Therapist: So you've selectively attended to a real but very small flaw in your effort to wallpaper. Is it logical that such a small defect should entirely cancel the credit you deserve?

Patient: Well, it wasn't as good as it should have been.

Therapist: If your neighbor had done the same quality job in your kitchen, what would you say?

Patient: . . . pretty good job!

—Beck and others, 1979, pp. 85–86

ATTRIBUTIONAL MODELS OF DEPRESSION The term **attribution** is used by social psychologists to refer to the causes a person assigns to things that happen. Beck's cognitive approach predicts that depressed individuals' attributions will be personal—that is, depressed people will blame themselves when anything bad happens. When something good does happen, it is usually attributed to luck. For instance, one woman was not especially pleased when a short story she had written was accepted for publication; she attributed the acceptance to sheer luck. On the other hand, when one of her articles was rejected, she was distressed because she thought the rejection reflected badly on her. Most nondepressed people do the opposite: They accept responsibility for the good in their lives but tend to blame the situation on others when things do not work out. Figure 10–14 illustrates this difference in attributional thinking. Attributional models of depression do not claim that attributional style alone is enough to cause depression. These models suggest that attributional style is important only when a person experiences intense or frequent negative events in his or her life (Abramson and others, 1989).

People who are depressed seem to feel helpless to control their environment. They think that, no matter what they do, they will be unable to affect the way things turn out. It is possible that such people learn to be helpless as a result of certain situations they have encountered in the past. Martin Seligman (1974, 1975) first popularized this concept, which is termed **learned helplessness.** Research on the concept of learned helplessness soon showed that some people feel generally helpless and others feel helpless only in certain situations. The explanation of this appeared to lie in the kinds of attributions people make about stressful situations (Abramson and others, 1989). The attribution model fits best in situations that have to do with achievement, such as college performance or vocational success. Other kinds

of negative events, such as a death or a friend moving away, may call up different sets of attributions from the same person. Another problem for this theory is that only about one-third of depressed people show this attributional style and those that do change their attributional style in periods when they are not depressed (Hamilton & Abramson, 1983). These findings imply two things. First, they suggest that attributions play a role only for a subgroup of depressed people. Second, they raise the question of whether this attributional style is a product or symptom rather than a causal factor in depression.

Depression has been associated with negative life events for a long time. It is clear that negative events for which people see themselves as at least partially responsible may be more important than negative events for which there is usually no responsibility, such as death or illness; sometimes, however, people who experience many negative events and who are clearly depressed can still function well much of the time (see Box 10–1). In addition it is clear that many people experience a great many stressful life events and do not become depressed. In order to understand the role of stressful life events in depression it is necessary to take into account their interaction with biological vulnerabilities, the availability of social support, and the person's cognitive attributions (Monroe & Depue, 1991). In order to determine the role that each of these plays in depression, it is important to study people over time.

As we have stated earlier in this text, theories change over time as their effectiveness in predicting future outcomes is tested. The learned helplessness hypothesis was revised to take into account the different kinds of attributions people make. In a further revision of the theory, it has been suggested that there is a subtype of depression, **hopelessness depression,** that links attributional style in a causal chain that leads to the occurrence of depression (Abramson and others, 1989). This chain starts with the perceived occurrence of negative life events or the nonoccurrence of positive life events. It also includes the person's characteristic way of viewing the causes and consequences of events as well as him- or herself. These personal characteristics work together to determine how the person will respond to the life event. The theory maintains that if the response is one of hopelessness, either about dealing with the event or changing oneself, depression will result.

The hopelessness theory is more similar to the other cognitive theories of depression than is the helplessness theory. It closely resembles Beck's ideas, although with some differences. The hopelessness theory describes a particular subclass of depression, whereas Beck focuses on the role cognitions play in depressions in general. The hopelessness theory also suggests that some people may be invulnerable, or at least much less vulnerable, to depression because of their tendency to

FIGURE 10–14 A comparison of the attribution process in depressed and nondepressed people.

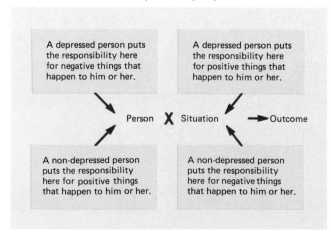

Although the ordinary picture of a depressed person is that of someone ineffective, withdrawn, and without energy, Abraham Lincoln was able to overcome a lifetime of periods of deep melancholy to be elected President of the United States and to effectively lead the country through one of its most trying periods, the Civil War (see Figure 10-15a).

In 1841, Lincoln was described by a physician as having "social and personal inadequacies and other guilt," with a diagnosis of hypochondria (quoted in Grinker, 1979). At this time Lincoln could not speak above a whisper. That same year he wrote to his law partner in Washington, D.C., "If what I feel were equally distributed to the whole human family, there would not be one cheerful face on the earth. Whether I shall ever be better, I cannot tell. I awefully [sic] forebode I shall not."

Despite his apprehension about the future, Lincoln of course did carry on. He enjoyed and was successful in national politics. However, even during his presidency he experienced periods of depression. The terrible loss of life in the Civil War and the lack of success of the northern forces in the early part of the war affected him greatly. During this period many members of Congress and in the public turned against him and doubted his leadership. His visits to the wounded in military hospitals were also deeply upsetting. He often sat silent, his "soul filled with sadness" (quoted in

FIGURE 10-15(b) One of the tragedies in Lincoln's life was the death, in childhood, of his son Tod who is shown here reading a book with his father.

FIGURE 10-15(a) Despite periods of depression that plagued him through much of his life, Abraham Lincoln was an effective leader throughout the continuing crises caused by the American civil war. Here he is shown delivering an inspiring and deeply moving speech to a large crowd at Gettysburg, Pennsylvania, the site of one of the important battles of the war.

Grinker, 1979). He felt guilty and full of self-reproach, wanted to die, and had dreams about assassination.

Lincoln not only experienced war-related problems, but his personal life was also filled by negative life events. His marriage to Mary Todd was an unhappy one with frequent explosive scenes, his wife was bitterly criticized and villified by Washington society, and two of his children died in childhood (see Figure 10-15b). His early life was also difficult: He grew up in extreme poverty, his mother died when he was young, and his father treated him harshly. Despite these adverse conditions, Lincoln managed to educate himself, become a successful lawyer and politician, be elected to Congress and finally to the presidency. Often virtually immobilized by periods of depression, Lincoln nevertheless became one of the United States' most revered presidents.

attribute negative events not to themselves or ongoing conditions in their environment, but to specific causes or situations that can be expected to come to an end soon.

COGNITIVE ACCURACY IN DEPRESSION Both Beck's theory and the revised learned helplessness hypothesis stress the inaccuracy of self-perception in depression. But the attributions of depressed people may be more accurate than these theories predict. Experimenters, studying how well people assessed their own social competence, found that depressed patients were quite

realistic about their own social skills (Lewinsohn and others, 1980). In contrast, other psychiatric patients and control subjects tended to see themselves as more competent than other people saw them. Even more interesting, the realism of the depressed patients' self-perceptions tended to decrease as therapy progressed. In short, as they became less depressed, the patients became less realistic about their effect on others; they deluded themselves more in the same way the nonpatients do. According to this view the result of cognitive therapy may actually be to encourage a normal lack of realism (Sackeim & Wegner, 1986).

Researchers who study cognitive distortion have focused primarily on negative events. However, attributions concerning positive events may also be important and may play a role in recovery from depression (Needles & Abramson, 1990). As yet the question of the degree of cognitive distortion in depression is far from settled. Many aspects of the cognitive theory of depression have been supported by research including increased negativity of cognitions about the self, increased hopelessness, and the focus on themes of loss. However, evidence that depressive thinking is especially inaccurate or illogical is still weak (Haaga and others, 1991).

The Humanistic–Existential Perspective

Whereas psychodynamic theorists emphasize the loss of a loved object as a central cause of depression, existential theorists focus on the loss of self-esteem. The lost object can be real or symbolic—power, social rank, or money—but the loss itself is not as important as the change in an individual's self-assessment as a result of the loss. Many people base their self-concepts on who they are or what they have: I'm the leader of the factory assembly team; I'm the boss; I'm a member of the exclusive city athletic club; I'm the husband of a famous movie star. Identifications of this kind offer external verification of people's worth in their own minds. The philosopher Kierkegaard expressed this view of the effects of loss very well in the following quotation:

> *Despair is never ultimately over the external object but always over ourselves. A girl loses her sweetheart and she despairs. It is not over the sweetheart, but over herself-without-the-sweetheart. And so it is with all cases of loss, whether it be money, power, or social rank. The unbearable loss is not really in itself unbearable. What we cannot bear is being stripped of the external object. We stand denuded and see the intolerable abyss of ourselves.*

Humanistic theorists such as Carl Rogers (1951, 1980) emphasize the difference between a person's ideal self and his or her perceptions of the actual state of things as the source of depression and anxiety. They, like Kierkegaard, believe that depression is likely to result when the difference between the ideal and the real selves becomes too great for the individual to tolerate. This discrepancy occurs frequently, especially among people who have high aspirations for achievement and are trying to fill several roles simultaneously. A current example of this problem is the dilemma of many women today. These women may be trying to fill multiple roles—a successful career, a wife who manages the household effectively, and a mother who provides adequate attention for her children. In such a situation it is inevitable that each role is not carried out to its highest potential and therefore the resulting discrepancy between the ideal self and the actual self in each of the multiple roles is often difficult for these women to deal with and is likely to create stress and depressed feelings as well as possible clinical depression in those women who are especially vulnerable.

Contrasting Psychological Theories of Depression

It is sometimes difficult to distinguish clearly how the various psychological theories of depression and the therapies derived from them differ. The behavioral approach and Beck's cognitive-distortion theory started out quite differently, but as their related therapies developed, many of the techniques used became more similar. The behavioral approach increasingly emphasized cognitive attributions, and Beck included learning-theory techniques like behavioral checklists of events and moods and homework assignments.

The same emphasis on feelings of hopelessness and helplessness is found in the humanistic–existential approach, in which loss of self-esteem and a perceived inability to alter the oppressive demands of society are central ideas. The therapeutic approach of the humanistic-existential group is much less structured than the cognitive or learning therapies but somewhat more direct than psychoanalysis. Like the learning and cognitive therapies, it is centered on the present rather than on the client's past history, as psychoanalysis is. Existential therapy is essentially a talking therapy and does not use the checklists and specific behavioral observations used in learning and cognitive approaches. Psychodynamic therapists stress cognitive distortions, but they tend to focus not only on how these affect present behavior but also on their origins in the client's earlier life. Cognitive theories are also concerned with a person's past experiences as a source of current schema that may produce distorted

perceptions or interpretations of others' behavior, but these theories focus less on the past and more on the distortion. For instance, in the information-processing approach, the linking of stressful events and past memories is clarified for the client. It is important to remember that while the psychological theories and their related therapies differ in emphasis, some of their basic ideas have become surprisingly similar.

A review of the results of different methods of psychological therapy for depression suggests that there is not much difference between them in effectiveness and that the gains clients make with these therapies are similar to those achieved from therapies using antidepressive drugs as the main intervention (Robinson and others, 1990). Among the studies that have compared cognitive therapy alone, antidepressant drug therapy alone, and a combination of the two therapies, the results suggest that the combination of cognitive and drug therapy may produce the best effects. However, the size of the outcome differences for these treatment groups is likely to be small (Hollon and others, 1991). The studies also suggest that those who receive cognitive therapy either alone or in combination with antidepressants are less likely to have another episode of depression in the next year than are people treated with antidepressants only. The high cost of studies of therapy has made it difficult for researchers to use adequate numbers of therapy cases in a single study to make likely the detection of small differences in outcome.

Rather than trying to determine which type of therapy is most effective, the most important and potentially rewarding task researchers presently have before them is to find out more about the factors responsible for improvement. The interactional view recognizes the important contributions of each therapeutic approach.

An Interactional View

Each of the approaches to depression has something to contribute to understanding and treatment of this disorder. Biological factors, events in early and present life, and thinking patterns may all interact to produce depression. We also know that some people may be genetically vulnerable or vulnerable due to certain prenatal or postnatal conditions.

No one type of therapy is best for unipolar depression. A large research project, the Treatment of Depression Collaborative Research Program, was set up to compare the effectiveness of therapy groups employing different treatment approaches: cognitive therapy; interpersonal therapy, which assumes that some depression is caused by role conflicts, grief, and deficient

interpersonal relationships; and drug therapy using a tricyclic antidepressant. The performances of the groups were compared with one another and with an untreated control group. In general the people in the therapy groups improved faster than the controls, but there were no differences in improvement among the groups treated with the different therapies after 16 weeks of treatment (Holden, 1986). These findings suggest that because of the interactive biological and psychological factors in depression, for many people changing any part of the interactive system may result in a lessening of depression.

The Bipolar Disorders

Bipolar disorders, or manic-depressive disorders, are characterized by phases of both depression and mania. This type of mood disorder is much less common than depression. The ECA study discussed at the beginning of this chapter found that only about 0.8 percent of the general population ever experience a manic episode. Table 10–7 contrasts manic and depressive behavior. The periods of depression that occur in bipolar disorder are not any different from the depression that has already been described in this chapter. The peak incidence of bipolar disorders is during young adulthood, although many people show evidence of the disorder as adolescents.

The occurrence of mania is a prerequisite for the diagnosis of bipolar disorder. **Mania** is characterized by a flight of ideas, elevated mood, and increased psychomotor activity. Although mania itself represents an extreme type of behavior, it is probably more useful to describe mania as one extreme on a spectrum of elated behavior. This spectrum includes mood states ranging from normal joy and happiness to extreme and hostile overactivity. A very small number of people may experience one or more periods of mania without ever experiencing depression (Goodwin & Jamison, 1987). Because this happens so infrequently these people are classified as having a bipolar disorder with the expectation that a period of depression will ultimately occur. Mania may also be caused by certain biochemical factors not related to bipolar disorder. Certain drugs can cause people with no history of affective disorders to experience episodes of mania. Drugs that produce this response include steroids, MAO inhibitors and tricyclic drugs used to treat depression, and L-dopa (used to treat Parkinson's disease). Mania can also result from infections, metabolic disturbances, and the growth of tumors. Mania in these cases is considered a symptom of the change in a person's biochemical state and is not classified as a mood disorder.

Table 10–7
Differing Patterns in Manic and Depressive Behavior Found in Bipolar Disorder

	Manic Behavior	Depressive Behavior
Emotional Characteristics	Elated, euphoric	Gloomy, hopeless
	Very sociable	Socially withdrawn
	Impatient at any hindrance	Irritable
Cognitive Characteristics	Racing thoughts, flight of ideas	Slowness of thought processes
	Desire for action	Obsessive worrying
	Impulsive behavior	Inability to make decisions
	Positive self-image	Negative self-image, self-blame
	Delusions of grandeur	Delusions of guilt and disease
	Talkative	
Motor Characteristics	Hyperactive	Decreased motor activity
	Does not become tired	Tired
	Needs less sleep than usual	Difficulty in sleeping
	Increased sex drive	Decreased sex drive
	Fluctuating appetite	Decreased appetite

A variant of bipolar disorder called **bipolar II** includes no manic episodes but instead at least one episode of hypomania as well as at least one major depressive episode. A **hypomanic episode** occurs when there is a distinct period of elevated, expansive, or irritable mood and other manic behaviors, but social or on-the-job functioning is not greatly impaired and the person does not have to be hospitalized. Bipolar II seems to be a separate type of disorder and not a preliminary problem that will later develop into a typical bipolar disorder (Dunner, 1987). Another disorder in this group is **cyclothymia.** In this disorder there is a chronic mood disturbance lasting at least two years that includes both hypomanic episodes and frequent mild periods of depressed mood.

People with bipolar disorder usually have episodes of disturbed behavior rather than consistent difficulties. How do people with bipolar disorders behave when they are not in either the depressed or the manic phase? It has often been assumed that even during a period of remission they behave less adaptively than the average person and are more conforming and dependent. This assumption may not be true, at least for individuals receiving lithium treatment. The intellectual functioning of bipolar patients may be less effective during periods of depression or mania, but it improves when the symptoms decrease. Intelligence test scores may actually increase during periods of hypomania (Clark and others, 1985). The personality test scores of many bipolar individuals return to the normal range between episodes of mania and depression (Lumry and others, 1982). Not all the effects of bipolar disorder are negative. The feelings of elation and creativity and the driving energy characteristic of the hypomanic state can be positive forces (see Box 10–2 on pages 310–11).

In a typical bipolar disorder a person will have episodes of both mania and depression and these may tend to recur in a pattern of the person's lifetime. There are several risk factors that increase the probability of additional episodes (Ambelas & George, 1986):

1. The younger the age at first manic episode;
2. The lower the stress of the event associated with the first episode;
3. Close family members who have some disorder defined by DSM.

Manic Episodes

Most episodes of mania occur as part of a bipolar disorder. The very word "manic" conjures up an image of the stereotypical crazy person—the maniac, a stock character in many older works of fiction—with frantic

behavior, staring eyes, and dramatic gestures. But what is mania really like? One of the two cases at the beginning of the chapter illustrates the impairment of judgment and the grandiose ideas that typically accompany mania. A reaction to a personal experience of mania is described in the following autobiographical account.

First and foremost comes a general sense of intense well-being. I know of course that this sense is illusory and transient, and that my behavior while it persists is so abnormal that I have to be confined, so that a good deal of the gilt is taken off the gingerbread. It is only when I have been free in the manic state that the ecstatic sensations accompanying it have their full effect, but they are apt to produce dire results in the real world, as will be seen. Although, however, the restrictions of confinement are apt at times to produce extreme irritation and even paroxysms of anger, the general sense of well-being, the pleasurable and sometimes ecstatic feeling-tone, remains as a sort of permanent background of all experience during the manic period.

—Custance, 1952

Environmental factors can sometimes be important in setting off a manic episode. Two-thirds of the first manic episodes experienced by patients in one study were preceded by a life-related stress of some kind (Ambelas, 1987). Stressful events can also cause a manic episode in people with a past history of manic episodes or bipolar disorder. For example, when a major hurricane struck Long Island, New York, in 1985, there was a dramatic increase in manic episodes among patients with bipolar disorder who were being treated with lithium (Aronson & Shukla, 1987). All the people who relapsed already had a high level of stress in their lives and most lacked social support from a close, confiding relationship. For each of these people the hurricane resulted in additional stress. For example, two people had to move into their parents' homes where there was a high tension level, another person went into a temporary shelter where she knew no one, and yet another wrecked her boyfriend's new car during the storm and their relationship deteriorated.

Causes of Bipolar Disorder

THE ROLE OF HEREDITY There seems to be a strong hereditary factor in bipolar disorders. Overall, the hereditary risk for bipolar disorders is about five times greater than that for unipolar depression (Rice and others, 1987). The overall risk for relatives of people who had their first episode of bipolar disorder at an early age is greater than for others and these relatives in turn are likely to develop bipolar disorder at an early age.

In particular, the children of people with bipolar disorder are much more likely than others to develop bipolar disorder themselves. They also show a high rate of unipolar disorder. In a study of the 37 children of 21 families in which at least one parent was bipolar, 24 percent of the children had received a DSM diagnosis, usually of some type of mood disorder (LaRoche and others, 1987). Although heredity is an important factor, stressful family life may also contribute to the appearance of bipolar disorder in vulnerable people. Lithium treatment may help the affected parent stabilize mood swings but, even with this improvement, treatment for the whole family may be useful. Children of a bipolar parent who also develop a disorder themselves are most likely to live in families in which the bipolar parent has frequent episodes of mania or depression (LaRoche and others, 1985).

Several studies have reported genetic markers for manic depression. One study focused on members of the Old Order Amish, a group living in relative isolation in Lancaster County, Pennsylvania, who are all descended from a small number of ancestors. The researcher found that a dominant gene on the tip of the short arm of chromosome 11 was associated with inherited bipolar disorder (Egeland, 1987). Two other investigations, one in Israel and one in Belgium, also found genetic markers, but those they found were located on an X chromosome of the 23rd chromosome pair (Baron and others, 1987). These differing results could mean several things. It may be that similar patterns of behavior can be the result of different genes. It may also be that because many different comparisons were made in each study, the one significant difference found was due to chance rather than to a meaningful relationship. Thus far a clear answer to the question of whether a genetic marker for bipolar disorder exists is not available.

Another question that has not been settled is whether bipolar and unipolar disorders are genetically related. Some researchers have suggested that the forms of mood disorder differ quantitatively rather than qualitatively; this would mean that different amounts of the same genetically transmitted factor would produce different mood disorders. It has been observed that while people who have bipolar disorder have a high rate of relatives with either bipolar or unipolar disorder, in contrast people with unipolar disorder generally have relatives with unipolar but not bipolar disorder (Faraone and others, 1990).

BOX 10-2 Creativity, Leadership, and Bipolar Disorder

A few years ago, a study of British artists and writers revealed that these highly creative people had received treatment for a mood disorder in much higher proportions than would be expected in the general population (Jamison, 1989). Moreover, the incidence for bipolar disorder, relatively rare in the general public, was significantly higher in this creative group. Figure 10–16 summarizes key findings from this study. This scientific study confirms what letters, diaries, and biographical accounts of well-known poets, artists, and composers have related for years: Highly creative people tend to experience extremes of mood, which in turn may fuel the creative process (see Figure 10–17). Such accounts provide fascinating information for those interested in understanding mood disorders.

Leonard Woolf, the husband of Virginia Woolf, a highly creative writer who was affected by bipolar disorder and ultimately killed herself while depressed, described the relationship of her disorder to her creativity this way:

> I am quite sure that Virginia's genius was closely connected with what manifested itself as mental instability and insanity. The creative imagination in her novels, her ability to "leave the ground" in conversation, and the voluble delusions of the breakdowns all came from the same place in her mind—she "stumbled after her own voice" and followed "the voices that fly ahead." And that in itself was the crux of her life, the tragedy of her genius.
> —Woolf, 1964, p. 80

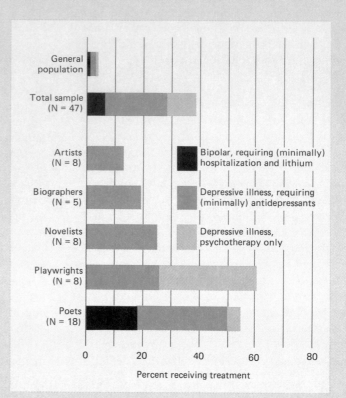

FIGURE 10–16 A sample of British writers and artists were found to have much higher rates for treatment of affective illness than the general British population. (Jamison, 1989)

FIGURE 10–17 Although poets seem to be affected by bipolar disorder more frequently than other writers, many well-known novelists, playwrights, and other writers also experienced some form of severe cyclothymia or bipolar illness. Of those pictured here, Virginia Woolf and Ernest Hemingway took their own lives during periods of depression.

(a) Virginia Woolf, English novelist and essayist.

(b) Eugene O'Neill, American playwright.

(c) Ernest Hemingway, American novelist.

Virginia Woolf seemed to agree. She wrote:

As an experience, madness is terrific. I can assure you, and not to be sniffed at; and in its lava I still find most of the things I write about. It shoots out of one everything shaped, final, not in mere driblets, as sanity does.

—Woolf, 1978, p. 180

Certain creative professions seem more prone to bipolar disorder than others. Novelists, playwrights, and composers all appear more likely than average to have a bipolar illness, while poets appear the most likely to be affected. For instance, 36 American poets born since 1900 are represented in *The New Oxford Book of American Verse*, a collection of outstanding poetry. Eight of these, listed in Table 10–8, have well-documented histories of bipolar disorder. This figure may be a low estimate of the total, since the biographical materials for all 36 poets have not yet been researched (Goodwin & Jamison, 1990). Since the rate for bipolar disorder in the general population is less than 1 percent, this group of very talented poets clearly has a significantly higher rate.

Creativity can be shown not only in the arts, but also in political leadership. Some outstanding political leaders of the past, for instance Napoleon Bonaparte, Oliver Cromwell, and Winston Churchill, all experienced periods of both quite severe depression and of high energy, elevated mood, impetuousness, and at times questionable judgment. People who worked with Churchill were impressed by the fertility of his mind and his inexhaustible stream of inventive thought. However, "all those who worked with him also agreed that he needed the most severe restraint put on him, and that many of his ideas, if they had been put into practice, would have been utterly disastrous" (Storr, 1988, pp. 14–15). The other side of his mood swings was documented by his personal physician, who described many conversations with Churchill. In one of them, Churchill ruminated that:

For two or three years the light faded out of the picture. I did my work. I sat in the House of Commons, but the black depression settled on me. . . . I don't like standing near the edge of a platform when an express train is passing through. I like to stand right back and if possible to get a pillar between me and the train. I don't like to stand by the side of a ship and look down into the water. A second's action would end everything.

—Moran, 1966, p. 167

Theodore Roosevelt is an example of a leader who was chronically hypomanic and although he was at times mildly depressed, he did not seem to have the periods of deep depressed mood that characterized the above-mentioned leaders. His life went on at a fast pace. He was overtalkative, often grandiose, restless, and extremely enthusiastic. He was able to get along with very little sleep and worked, wrote, or explored at a frenzied pace. During his lifetime he wrote more than 150,000 letters and a large number of books ranging in topic from naval history to a record of his experiences living in the wilderness.

For all these leaders, even those who were at times incapacitated by depression, their hypomanic periods produced inspired leadership and a large number of accomplishments. For both these leaders and the creative artists discussed earlier, their bipolar tendencies had a positive effect and enabled them to achieve a great deal. Their enormous accomplishments suggest that sometimes the negative aspects of these serious disorders are so preoccupying to researchers and clinicians that other important aspects of behavior may be overlooked. In spite of findings such as these, it is important to remember that many creative artists and successful leaders have no mood disorder or other type of psychopathology and that many people with mood disorders are not unusually creative or talented in leadership.

Table 10–8

Partial Listing of Major 20th Century American Poets, Born Between 1895 and 1935, with Documented Histories of Bipolar Illness

Poet	Pulitzer Prize in Poetry	Treated for Major Depressive Illness	Treated for Mania	Committed Suicide
Hart Crane (1899–1932)		X	X	X
Theodore Roethke (1908–1963)	X	X	X	
Delmore Schwartz (1913–1966)		X	X	
John Berryman (1914–1972)	X	X	X	X
Randall Jarrell (1914–1965)		X	X	X
Robert Lowell (1917–1977)	X	X	X	
Anne Sexton (1928–1974)	X	X	X	X
Sylvia Plath[a] (1932–1963)	X	X		X

[a]Plath, although not treated for mania, was probably bipolar II.

SOURCE: From *Manic-Depressive Illness* by Frederick K. Goodwin and Kay Redfield Jamison. Copyright © 1990 by Oxford University Press, Inc. Reprinted by permission.

BRAIN METABOLISM The use of noninvasive methods like PET scans has provided some information about brain metabolism in bipolar disorders. In general, the metabolic rate for glucose increases when a person moves from depression to a more normal state or to mania (see Figure 10–18). The use of PET scans may ultimately make it possible to distinguish between those with bipolar and unipolar disorders when their initial state is depression. About six percent of those who were originally diagnosed as having unipolar depression will later report an episode of mania and be reclassified as having a bipolar disorder (Schlesser & Altschuler, 1983). Identifying the disorder correctly when it begins is important because the most effective treatments for unipolar and bipolar disorders differ. Bipolar individuals are more likely to be helped by lithium and less likely to be helped by tricyclic antidepressants.

SLEEP STUDIES Sleep disturbance is often observed as a symptom of depression and of mania. Some researchers have wondered if perhaps the situation might be reversed and the sleep disturbance could be the cause of these disorders. As discussed earlier (see page 293), researchers have discovered that sleep deprivation may alleviate symptoms of depression. A dramatic but temporary improvement is experienced by almost two-thirds of patients with major depression if they are kept awake for one night (Wehr & Sack, 1987). The next period of sleep then causes the symptoms of depression to return.

FIGURE 10–18 PET scans of the brain of a bipolar individual who experienced rapid cycles of mania and depression. The top and bottom rows were taken on depressed days and the middle row on a hypomanic day. The colors of the scans correspond to glucose metabolic rates, which are indicated in the color bar on the right. The overall brain metabolic rates for glucose were 36 percent higher on the hypomanic day than the average rates for depressed days, which were within 10 percent of each other.

Improvements in depression can also come about through waking the patient after only about half the usual sleeping time, or shifting the time of sleep several hours earlier. This approach to treatment may have some practical applications. For example, a physician with a hypomanic temperament and a family history of bipolar illness became depressed. After one night of partial sleep deprivation (sleep from 10 P.M. to 2 A.M. only) he no longer felt depressed. By carrying out this partial deprivation pattern three or four nights a week for several weeks he continued to avoid depression. (Wehr & Sack, 1987.)

Sleep deprivation can also cause a manic episode in bipolar patients. This has been observed in ordinary life and also produced experimentally. A bipolar patient who was neither depressed nor manic went to an emergency room one evening because of a sore throat. She was kept waiting until five o'clock in the morning, and by then she was so manic that she had to be involuntarily hospitalized. In a study of one night's sleep deprivation of 12 depressed bipolar patients, nine switched into mania or hypomania during the night or the following day. Six of these remained manic for days or weeks (Wehr and others, 1982). The mechanisms by which sleep deprivation produces these antidepressant effects is unknown. It may not be the sleep deprivation itself that accounts for the change, but the greater exposure to light.

PHOTOTHERAPY Before an effective treatment for bipolar disorder was known, it was possible to observe the manic and depressed patterns over long periods. Researchers noted that in some cases the pattern was seasonal. For some people, periods of depression are more likely to occur in the winter months when there are fewer hours of daylight, and mania—or more often hypomanic behavior—occurs in the spring and summer, at the time of greatest daylight. The most prominent form of this **seasonal affective disorder (SAD)** is winter depression. One treatment that has been found to be at least temporarily effective for this depression is **phototherapy.**

Phototherapy involves exposing the depressed person for two to four hours per day to very bright light, several times brighter than what is normally used indoors. In most of the studies using phototherapy the light is generated from eight four-foot fluorescent bulbs behind a diffusion panel that is placed about three feet away from the person receiving treatment. The effectiveness of the phototherapy appears to be directly related to the degree of exposure, so that four hours of light exposure is more effective than two (Terman and others, 1987).

Phototherapy treatment produces a rapid improvement in less than a week. However, when the light treatment ends, the deterioration of the person's moods is just as rapid. Although studies of sleep deprivation and phototherapy might seem to be focused on the same

process because sleep deprivation usually increases exposure to light, the two types of treatment seem to operate independently (Rosenthal and others, 1988). Both these experimental therapies show the important role of biological rhythms in bipolar disorder.

Treatment of Bipolar Disorder

Although both sleep therapy and phototherapy hold promise for the future, the most common treatment for bipolar disorder today is lithium. Lithium may also be used for someone who is depressed and has had no manic periods if the person has relatives who have had bipolar disorder. Giving antidepressant drugs such as tricyclics or MAO inhibitors may induce manic episodes in such people. Lithium may have dangerous side effects if the amount is not regulated carefully, although the side effects of the antidepressants may be even more serious. Although it has been assumed that lithium is an effective treatment for mania, a two-year follow-up of patients for whom lithium carbonate was prescribed has raised some doubts about patients' use of this medication except under careful monitoring (Harrow and others, 1990). Only about one-fourth of the patients in that study had a very favorable outcome and about one-third had a very poor outcome. One cause of the poor outcomes was the tendency of many patients either wholly or temporarily to discontinue their medication against medical advice. This is a common response of bipolar patients to the effects of lithium. There are several possible reasons why this discontinuation occurs. One may be that lithium is abandoned when the person is in a low, although not depressed, period in the hope that stopping its use will elevate his or her mood. An even more intriguing reason is unwillingness to give up some of the pleasant cognitive and behavioral changes that come with an elevated mood (Goodwin & Jamison, 1990). These include increased sensitivity to the environment, sexual intensity, creativity, and social ease (see Box 10–2).

In any book on abnormal psychology, the negative or maladaptive aspects of abnormal behavior and the various disorders are likely to be emphasized. It is worth remembering, though, that at least in the case of bipolar disorder, the abnormal mood state may include some positive aspects. Although certainly all those with bipolar disorder are not creative people, and all creative people do not have bipolar disorder, a sizeable proportion of highly creative artists and writers seem to have been affected. For these people, mood changes that preceded or accompanied intense creative episodes have often been indistinguishable from hypomania.

The reaction of creative individuals with bipolar disorder to taking lithium suggests that, for them at least, hypomania and creativity may be closely connected (Polatin & Fieve, 1971). Such people complain that the continued use of lithium carbonate acts as a "brake" and inhibits creativity so that they are unable to express themselves. They feel that if lithium prevents the high, even if it also might prevent the "low," they would prefer not to take something that would deprive them of a pleasurable and productive state. This effect of lithium on productivity may occur only at the top rung of the creative spectrum (Goodwin & Jamison, 1990; Polatin & Fieve, 1971).

Suicide and Parasuicide

Those affected by mood disorder of either the unipolar or bipolar type are far more likely to commit suicide than are people in the general population or those in any other DSM diagnostic group. In one study carried out in Sweden, those with a mood disorder (either unipolar or bipolar) had a 78 percent greater risk of suicide than those with no diagnosed psychiatric disorder (Hagnell and others, 1981). The suicide rate for the bipolar category alone is also much higher than that for the general population. Results of a large number of studies to determine the frequency of suicide attempts by people with a bipolar disorder have shown that between 25 and 50 percent of these patients have attempted suicide at least once (Goodwin & Jamison, 1990). About 90 percent of the suicide attempts studied were serious enough to require hospitalization. Some studies comparing suicide attempts and completed suicides have found no bipolar-unipolar differences (Black and others, 1988) while others suggest that bipolar depression carries with it a bigger risk of suicide (Brent and others, 1988).

The pain and fear of experiencing another bipolar episode is shown clearly in this excerpt from the suicide letter written by the writer Virginia Woolf to her husband before she drowned herself:

> *Dearest, I feel certain I am going mad again. I feel we can't go through another of those terrible times. And I shan't recover this time. . . . So I am doing what seems the best thing to do. . . . I don't think two people could have been happier until this terrible disease came. I can't fight any longer.*
>
> —Bell, 1972, p. 266

Because of this high risk of suicide by those with a mood disorder, it is very important to be able to identify those within the group who are at highest risk so that they can be treated and protected. Table 10–9 lists a number of predictors that have been found. The majority

Table 10–9
Factors Related to Increased Risk of Suicide in Those with Mood Disorders

For treated or untreated individuals:

1. History of suicide among family members;
2. High level of anxiety;
3. Feelings of hopelessness;
4. Talk about or threats of suicide;
5. Previous suicide attempts.

In addition, for those who have had treatment for mood disorder:

1. Inadequate treatment;
2. Overprescription of tranquilizers;
3. Inadequate doses of antidepressant medication (tricyclics);
4. Inconsistent and poor outpatient care and follow-up after hospital discharge.

of people who commit suicide have seen a general physician in the three months before their deaths (Goodwin & Jamison, 1990), suggesting that they were experiencing problems but perhaps did not express them adequately. Past studies have shown that physicians tend to underdiagnose depression and often miss histories of suicidal behaviors. In addition, about half of those who die from an overdose of medication have obtained that lethal dose from a physician in a single prescription. Many of the medications used to treat depression and many tranquilizers prescribed for patients experiencing stress and anxiety are highly lethal if taken in large quantities.

Those seeking help do not always share their true feelings with a general physician or even with a therapist. In one study, 71 percent of patients had either threatened or attempted to kill themselves, but only 39 percent of the physicians who later saw them were aware of this (Murphy, 1975a, 1975b). Perhaps one reason that physicians and others are not aware of a suicide risk is that for many people much of the motivation to commit suicide seems to come from internal factors, not external ones.

It goes without saying that external misery has relatively little to do with suicide. . . . Suicide often seems to the outsider a supremely motiveless perversity performed . . . "in the very bosom of happiness," and for reasons which seem trivial or even imperceptible. . . . The real motives . . . belong to the internal world, devious, contradictory, labyrinthine, and mostly out of sight.

—Alvarez, 1973, pp. 95, 97

Suicide is a statistically rare event in the United States; only 13 out of every 100,000 deaths are due to suicide. Although those with mood disorders are at higher risk for suicide, it is important to remember that a sizeable number of people who commit or attempt suicide are not diagnosed with a mood disorder. Rates of suicide differ by age. Table 10–10 shows how the rates generally increase through age 84 and decrease after that. Because people are at greater risk for death from many causes as they grow older, this increase in rate does not mean that suicide is a relatively more significant cause of death in older age groups. Its peak impact is between ages 15 and 24 when it is the third-leading cause of death; it then drops to the fourth-leading cause between ages 25 and 44. Even though suicide rates are the highest for those 65 and over, it is not even in the ten top causes in this age group.

Many studies have focused on suicide among college students. The young-adult age group has a higher risk of suicide than many other groups. Further, because college students are generally healthy their overall death rate is low. For these reasons suicide is the second-most frequent cause of death among college students. (Accidents are the most frequent cause.)

Although the rate of suicides reported in college health service records is low, ranging from about 1 to 5 per 100,000 students, about 80 percent of the students in a study carried out at three universities reported some feelings of depression, 32 percent had thoughts about suicide, 4.5 percent had attempted suicide at some time, and 1 percent had attempted suicide while in college (Westefeld & Furr, 1987). Figure 10–19 shows the relative importance of different factors that students reported either made them think about suicide or attempt it. In general, social problems (love relation-

Table 10–10
Suicide Rates Per 100,000 by Age for 1986

Age	Rate
Under 1 year	—
1–4	—
5–14	0.8
15–24	13.1
25–34	15.7
35–44	15.2
45–54	16.4
55–64	17.0
65–74	19.7
75–84	25.2
85+	20.8
All ages	12.8

SOURCE: National Center for Health Statistics, *Advance Report of Final Mortality Statistics, 1986,* p. 38, September 30, 1988.

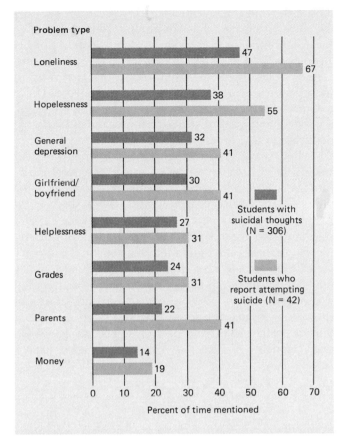

FIGURE 10–19 The percent of the time each of several problem areas was mentioned by students with thoughts about suicide or who reported attempting suicide.

(Adapted from Westefeld and Furr, 1987. Copyright © 1987 by the American Psychological Association. Adapted by permission of the authors.)

ships, dating, friends) were most important and family problems were relatively low on the list.

Twice as many men as women actually kill themselves, but twice as many women as men attempt suicide. Although very few children commit suicide, suicide threats and attempts are common reasons for therapeutic referrals of children. Since 1949 people born in each successive five-year period have started with a higher chance of suicide than the preceding group, so it seems likely that the overall rate will continue to increase. For instance, between 1950 and 1985 the rate of suicide for white men age 20 to 24 had increased from 9 to 27 suicides per 100,000 men. The rate for African-American men is lower, about two-thirds the white male rate, but is also increasing.

Suicide and **parasuicide** (suicide attempts that do not end in death) seem to be fundamentally different. People who kill themselves successfully seem to have planned the event carefully. They arrange not to be interrupted and to use effective means. Suicide attempters, on the other hand, may act impulsively, make sure of rescue, and use a method that is slow to take effect or is completely ineffective. The main purpose of parasuicides seems to be to manipulate others. People with borderline personality disorder often use suicide threats this way.

Different cultures interpret suicide differently. Most Western societies seek to prevent suicide and to interfere with its completion whenever possible. In some other cultures, for example in Japan, long-held traditions considered it an honorable action, perhaps the only acceptable one for a disgraced person.

If the urge to commit suicide is an outgrowth of a profound psychological disturbance, most people would agree that every effort should be made to keep the individual alive so that the problem can be treated. Nevertheless, one may certainly wonder whether there are any circumstances under which no effort should be made to prevent an individual from taking his or her life. What of the aged, the chronically infirm, and the incurably ill who want to terminate what they feel is a hopeless existence? Although the attention of clinical workers is directed primarily toward suicide as an outgrowth of personal problems and feelings of inadequacy and depression, we should bear in mind that there is a broader, more subjective context within which suicide can be considered.

In a study that investigated the influence of the potential suicide victim's situation on others' attitudes toward acceptability of suicide, college students read one of several fictitious scenarios about a man who decided to kill himself. The different scenarios portrayed the man as suffering from different conditions, including depression of different types, severe physical pain, or terminal bone cancer. This was one scenario:

> *John, a 45-year-old factory worker, has been suffering for the past 20 years from severe depression. His doctors believe the depression is likely due to a biochemical disorder of the central nervous system. Despite having received a wide variety of therapies (including drug treatments, psychotherapy, and behavior modification), the depression has gotten worse over time. John feels that the doctors have already done all they can, and he has no hope that his symptoms will be reduced. John is currently experiencing a great deal of psychological pain, and is very upset over the fact that his condition is draining the emotional and financial resources of his family and friends. John feels that the quality of his life now is very poor and will only get worse, and he fears that he will be an increasingly large burden to his loved ones. Despite protests from his family and friends, John has decided to kill himself.*
>
> —Deluty, 1988/89, p. 83

Students answered a series of evaluative questions about the man and his decision. The evaluations were most favorable when the suicide occurred in response to terminal bone cancer, and least favorable when they described chronic depression.

Similar results were obtained in a survey of health professionals' views about suicide. Suicide as a response to physical illness was judged as more acceptable than suicide in the face of chronic psychological illness (Hammond & Deluty, 1991). The majority of those who responded to the survey believed that it was possible to make a rational decision to commit suicide. However, although these professionals did not see suicide as morally wrong, they thought it was wrong because of the consequences for the survivors, who often feel extreme guilt and responsibility for not understanding and helping the dead person's distress (see Box 10–3).

Causes of Suicide

Ideas about the causes of suicide are divided into two main groups: those that see society as a reason and those that focus on the individual. In a few cases a society literally demands that a person commit suicide. In Japan, for instance, hara-kiri, a ritual suicide, was traditionally an honorable death that atoned for a serious personal failure. Sociologists also point out that in Western society most suicidal people are socially isolated and have few ties with the community. Psychological theories, on the other hand, tend to stress the role of the individual in the decision to commit suicide.

Behavioral theory emphasizes the importance of suicidal behavior in a person's learned behavioral repertory. Certain reinforcing cognitions may also be present—such as revenge, reunion with a deceased partner, or simply peace. Past suicidal behavior and suicide threats make suicide more likely. Social learning theory emphasizes the imitation of behavior. Temporary increases in suicide rates that often occur after a widely publicized suicide show the importance of imitation (Lesyna and others, 1990). Even fictional suicide stories shown on popular television have produced this effect. Suicidal behavior on the part of significant people in one's own environment also makes suicide more likely.

BOX 10–3 Suicide and the Survivors

Suicide has a strong impact on the families of those who killed themselves and on others who knew them. It is more painful for the family than other kinds of death and often harder to accept or acknowledge. Parents may think of the suicide of their adolescent child as an accidental death. They may also experience strong feelings of guilt and shame that may make normal mourning impossible. Young children of a parent who commits suicide are also likely to be seriously disturbed. The surviving parent may claim the suicide was an accident. The child then begins to distrust the parent or doubt the reality of what he or she had observed, or both. Children often feel responsible for a parental suicide or think they should have prevented it. The result of these misperceptions may be a child who is depressed, passive, and self-destructive. Because of the social stigma that surrounds suicide the survivors often avoid talking to others.

In the following paragraphs a wife describes her reactions and those of her 12-year-old son, Richard, to her husband's death.

For me the days that followed [her husband's suicide] were full of pain. The questions pounded at me. Why? Why? But shock numbs; somehow I could cope with memorial-service plans. Like a robot, I did what I had to do. People came and went, and I sat for hours without moving much. I remember not taking my clothes off for two days. I didn't want to move or change anything. Talking was an effort. Eating was an effort.

At the end of a week, after the service was over, the relatives had left, the real loneliness set in, and the guilt. Each night I dreamed that I was soothing Dick, telling him how much I loved him and still love him, feeling in my dreams that if only he knew, then he would be back and safe. . . . Two months later on the plane as we came home from a Christmas trip to visit Dick's family, Richard said, "I feel like I really miss somebody and I don't even know who." I said, "Don't you think it's Dad?" and the only tears I saw him cry came then. We talk often and he tells me that now he mostly feels mad. "When I start to feel angry or sad," he says, "I try to concentrate really hard on whatever I happen to be doing at the time, like playing ball or riding my bike."

I've found it difficult to be that sensible, to avoid guilt and constant questioning. The notes Dick left said it was his job, that I had nothing to do with what he did. Still, why couldn't I have seen what was happening? Why couldn't I have saved him? He had been the best friend I ever had. I must not have been a good enough friend to him. I wanted to piece it together; I relived every conversation. But there were no answers, and it didn't fit together.
—Kenyon, 1979, p. 17

The psychodynamic perspective is the source of most of the prominent psychological theories in the clinical literature on suicide. Psychodynamic theories describe suicide as an extreme case of a person's turning hostile or aggressive impulses toward him- or herself. However, this view is not supported by research findings, which indicate that hostile motives are infrequent in suicide (Linehan, 1981). However, the absence of a feeling of social support, of being cared about by others, is important in suicidal feelings and behavior. Feeling needed may also be significant. For example, being the parent of a child younger than 18 years of age has been shown to be a protective factor (Fawcett and others, 1987).

A series of negative events beyond the person's control frequently occurs during the year before someone makes a suicide attempt. A series of psychological losses, or **exit events,** in which a strong source of social support is removed, seems most likely to precede a suicide attempt. Such events might include a death, a divorce, or a breakup with a partner. Personality factors probably play a role also. People who behave impulsively or who abuse alcohol or drugs are more likely to make suicide attempts or successfully kill themselves (Roy & Linnoila, 1986). According to the cognitive view, suicide may result from a person's cognitive assessment of a situation as hopeless and of death as a way of getting rid of problems. People who attempt suicide are often quite rigid in their approach to situations and simply try to force negative thoughts out of awareness. This cognitive state helps prevent meaningful self-awareness and emotion and makes irrational and drastic measures such as suicide seem acceptable (Baumeister, 1990). For such people, the world appears to be divided into only two parts—good and bad. This outlook recalls the depressed thinking described by cognitive theorists like Beck (1976). This rigidity may include narrow perceptions of situations and of behavioral options. Figure 10–20 illustrates some of the cognitions that may preoccupy someone who feels there is no way for things to improve.

The Impact of Suicide on Others

Suicide is a traumatic event for the surviving family members, co-workers, or classmates. When a member of a group has committed suicide, group discussion and intervention can sometimes be helpful. This type of

FIGURE 10–20 As this lithograph by Traviés de DeVillers shows, the thoughts of someone who is depressed may focus on suicide.

intervention, called **postvention,** can help survivors deal with their grief and possible feelings of responsibility and guilt as well as serve as a way to prevent others from focusing on the usefulness of suicide as a way of coping with personal difficulties. Such a program is described in the discussion of prevention strategies in Chapter 18. Another type of program focuses more specifically on survivors' emotions and on helping them express their grief. Box 10–3 illustrates how important expressions of grief can be as well as the devastating impact and guilt felt by survivors. Even in the days immediately after the suicide survivors can be helped by a chance to express their feelings, obtain reassurance, and interpret what happened.

Chapter Summary

WHAT ARE MOOD DISORDERS?

Mood disorders reflect a disturbance in mood or emotional response that is not due to any other physical or mental disorder. They are often referred to as **affective disorders.** The two major types of mood disorder are **depressive disorders** and **bipolar disorders.**

How Common Are Mood Disorders? Mood disorder is relatively common. Twice as many women as men report mood disorder. Bipolar disorders are much less common than depressive disorders.

DEPRESSION

Depression can refer to a symptom or a disorder. The symptom of depressed mood does not necessarily mean a person has a mood disorder.

Depressed Mood In everyday language, the word "depression" is usually used to refer to depressed mood in connection with some aspects of the environment or with some mild physical symptoms. The term "depression" is also used to refer to normal feelings experienced after a significant loss, either a death, a relationship break-up, or failure to attain a significant goal.

Risk Factors Women are at greater risk for depression than are men. One possible reason is that women may experience more stress than men because they are expected, to a greater degree than men, to give support to others who are stressed. Age is also a risk factor. Women are particularly at risk during young adulthood, while for men the risk is highest in early middle age. Marital break-up, a pile-up of stressful life events, and a family history of depression also contribute to increased risk.

DEPRESSIVE DISORDER

A **depressive disorder** is defined as depressive symptoms that fit the DSM criteria. Depressive disorders are sometimes referred to as **unipolar disorders** to differentiate these types of depression from that found in bipolar disorder. There are several categories of depressive disorder.

Dysthymia Dysthymia is a stable condition in which a depressed mood is dominant over long periods of time even if it is interrupted by short periods of normal mood.

Major Depression A **major depressive episode** is defined as a period of either or both depressed mood and loss of interest or pleasure in most activities, together with some other symptoms, which may include marked change in body weight, constant sleep problems, tiredness, inability to think clearly, agitation or greatly slowed behavior, and thoughts of death. Depressive episodes tend to recur over a person's lifetime. One or more depressive episodes without any manic episode are classified as a **major depression.**

THEORIES OF DEPRESSION

It is generally thought that depression is the result of an interaction between biological characteristics, psychological vulnerabilities, and stressful events or ongoing stressful life situations. Each of the theoretical perspectives has contributed to the understanding of and the treatments available for depression.

Biological Theories Twin and family studies suggest a genetic component for both major depression and bipolar disorder. The mechanism for the depressed or manic behavior may be the neurotransmitter systems. The **monoamine neurotransmitters,** including the **catecholamines** *norepinephrine* and *dopamine* and the **indolamine** *serotonin*, have been most widely studied. The **catecholamine theory,** and later, the **desensitization hypothesis,** have been important in stimulating research on the biological aspects of depression. The search for markers of depression has been an important research strategy. Treatments based on biological theories include antidepressant drugs, especially those from the **heterocyclic** chemical group (including tricyclics and second generation antidepressants), **MAO inhibitors,** and **lithium** compounds. Another biological approach to treatment is **electroconvulsive therapy (ECT).**

The Psychodynamic View Freud's view of depression focused on a decrease in self-regard and a punishing conscience that was an attempt to control feelings of anger and aggression. Later psychodynamic theorists believed feelings of helplessness in coping with loss were central to depression. Psychodynamic therapy focuses on helping clients to discover and clarify distortions of reality and to see how past experiences and beliefs can distort interpretations of the present.

The Behavioral Perspective Depressed people may engage in excessive support-seeking, which eventually causes distress in those who have contact with them. An effective behavioral approach to treating depression is **social skills training,** focused both on appropriate behavior and on improved skills in understanding the cues other people give in social interactions.

The Cognitive Perspective Beck's **cognitive distortion model** of depression was the original cognitive view of depression and remains highly influential. The model explains depression as a **cognitive triad** of negative thoughts about oneself, the situation, and the future. Therapy from the cognitive perspective utilizes both cognitive and behavioral elements and is often called **cognitive behavioral therapy.** A subtype of depression may be **hopelessness depression,** in which the assignment of cause to an event, or the **attribution** process, is important in initiating the depression. The occurrence of stressful life events and attribution patterns may interact in producing both positive and negative changes in mood.

The Humanistic–Existential Perspective In the humanistic–existential view the loss focused on in psychodynamic theory is the loss of self-esteem. These theorists emphasize the difference

between the person's ideal self and his or her perception of the actual self. If the difference is too great, depression is likely to result.

Contrasting Psychological Theories of Depression Although the psychological theories differ in their approach and emphasis, they have increasingly come to include similar elements. In general, results from these different psychological therapies for depression suggest that there may not be much difference among them in their effectiveness and that such results are not very different than those from therapeutic intervention using only antidepressant drugs. Some research suggests that at least for certain patients, a combination of antidepressive drugs and cognitive therapy may produce the best effects. Comparisons of all therapies in effectiveness is difficult because of the high cost of that type of research.

An Interactional View Because of the interactive biological and psychological factors in depression, each of the perspectives may make an important contribution to recovery. This is because a change in any part of the interactive system may help alleviate the depression.

THE BIPOLAR DISORDERS

Bipolar disorders, sometimes referred to as manic-depressive disorders, include phases of both depression and mania. These disorders are most likely to be diagnosed during young adulthood. **Mania,** or a state of elevated mood, flight of ideas, and increased psychomotor activity, must have been present at some time before bipolar disorder can be diagnosed. A **hypomanic episode** refers to a period of manic behavior that is not extreme enough to greatly impair functioning. **Bipolar II** is a variant of bipolar disorder in which there has been no manic episode but at least one hypomanic period as well as a major depressive episode. **Cyclothymia** is a disorder with chronic mood disturbance; it includes both hypomanic episodes and frequent periods of mild depressed mood. Bipolar disorder seems to occur more frequently among highly creative people than among the rest of the population.

Manic Episodes Most manic episodes occur in the context of bipolar disorder. Stressors such as environmental disasters or lack of sleep can set off manic episodes in vulnerable people.

Causes of Bipolar Disorder The hereditary risk for bipolar disorder is greater than for depressive disorder. The use of PET scans may provide a better understanding of the development of manic episodes through a study of changes in brain metabolism. Sleep disturbance may also be causally related to depression and mania rather than a result of these mood changes. Another possible relationship being investigated in relation to both depression and mania is the seasonal patterns of daylight. The investigation of **seasonal affective disorder** and its treatment by **phototherapy** also can provide information about possible causes of bipolar disorder and depression.

Treatment of Bipolar Disorder Bipolar disorder is most commonly treated with lithium. However, lithium may be effective only under careful monitoring. Many people, especially those who are in occupations demanding high creativity, are likely to discontinue the medication because they find that the mood changes it causes are aversive.

SUICIDE AND PARASUICIDE

The possibility of suicide for people with either bipolar disorder or major depression is much higher than that for the general population. In the overall population, suicide is one of the leading causes of death for people between the ages of 15 and 44. Women are twice as likely as men to attempt suicide, while men are twice as likely as women to actually kill themselves. **Parasuicide** is the term used for suicide attempts that do not end in death.

Causes of Suicide Suicide may be culturally approved in some circumstances, for example in Japan for a person who has had a serious failure or been dishonored. In Western society social isolation is a risk factor. Some theorists think people are likely to attempt suicide as a kind of imitative behavior or copying style learned from media reports of dramatic suicides. Suicide is also considered to be an expression of self-anger or anger at others. A series of psychological losses or **exit events** also may increase suicide risk.

The Impact of Suicide on Others Suicide may have a devastating impact on survivors who may feel both grief and guilt for having failed to prevent the death. Opportunity for survivors to express their feelings in a group or individual setting can help them recover.

Schizophrenic Disorders

C H A P T E R 1 1

The Impact of Schizophrenic Disorders

Diagnostic Criteria

Characteristics of Schizophrenic Disorders
Delusions
Disordered Thinking
Hallucinations
Lack of Appropriate Emotion
Unclear Boundaries of the Self
Unpredictable Motor Behavior
Change in Motivational Level
Impaired Interpersonal Functioning
Attention Difficulties

A Historical View of Schizophrenic Disorders
Dementia Praecox
The Schizophrenias
First-Rank Symptoms
European and American Definitions
Positive and Negative Symptoms

Types of Schizophrenia
Traditional and Current DSM Subtypes
Schizophrenic Spectrum Disorders

Outcome Indicators and Long-Term Studies

Therapeutic Approaches
Biological Therapies
Psychodynamic Therapies
Behavioral Therapy
Ongoing Therapeutic Care
A Comprehensive Approach

Chapter Summary

Alfredo Casteneda, *Clairvoyance*, 1988. Mary-Anne Martin/ Fine Art, New York.

"*All of a sudden things weren't going so well. I began to lose control of my life and, most of all, myself. I couldn't concentrate on my school work, I couldn't sleep, and when I did sleep, I had dreams about dying. I was afraid to go to class, imagined that people were talking about me, and on top of that I heard voices. I called my mother in Pittsburgh and asked for advice. She told me to move off campus into an apartment with my sister.*

"*After I moved in with my sister, things got worse. I was afraid to go outside and when I looked out of the window, it seemed that everyone outside was yelling 'Kill her, kill her.' My sister forced me to go to school. I would go out of the house until I knew she had gone to work; then I would return home. Things continued to get worse. I imagined that I had a foul body odor and I sometimes took up to six showers a day. . . . Things worsened—I couldn't remember a thing. I had a notebook full of reminders telling me what to do on that particular day. I couldn't remember my school work, and I would study from 6 P.M. until 4 A.M.; but never had the courage to go to class on the following day. I tried to tell my sister about it, but she didn't understand. She suggested that I see a psychiatrist, but I was afraid to go out of the house to see him.*

"*One day I decided that I couldn't take the trauma anymore so I took an overdose of 35 Darvon pills. At the same moment, a voice inside me said, 'What did you do that for? Now you won't go to heaven.' At that instant I realized that I really didn't want to die, I wanted to live, and I was afraid. So I got on the phone and called the psychiatrist whom my sister had recommended.*"

After more than a year on medication, first in the hospital and then out, J.

decided she was well and stopped both medication and therapy. She got a job but quickly lost it. "My friends and family said I was behaving strangely, but I took no notice. I went out dancing practically every night to make up for the time lost while being afraid. . . ."

In the fall she went back to school in Atlanta to finish her senior year. Then she was hospitalized again. "This time things were twice as bad as the first. I no longer heard voices, but the things I saw and dreamed about were far more traumatic. I recall at one point thinking I was Jesus Christ and that I was placed on this earth to bear everyone's sins."

After a month in the hospital J. returned home and received both antipsychotic drugs and psychotherapy as an outpatient. Two years later, still on medication, she was back in college, president of her sorority, "more confident and happy than I have ever been in my life."

—Adapted from O'Neal, 1984, pp. 109–110

This young woman seems to have made a good recovery from several schizophrenic episodes. Before they began, she had been functioning at a high level. She was a good student, an officer in her sorority chapter, and president of a campus club, and she had a part-time job and a satisfying relationship with her boyfriend. As we will see later in this chapter, one predictor of improvement from a schizophrenic disorder is the person's level of adjustment before the symptoms appeared.

Not all people who develop schizophrenia experience such a dramatic recovery, even when they continue to use antipsychotic drugs. The following passage, written by the mother of a schizophrenic son, describes a more common pattern.

When Dan first began to suffer from schizophrenia, our family thought it was just a case of teenage blues. We sent him off to college. By the time he began attacking the refrigerator for reading his mind and threatening family members for using the word "right," we had learned to recognize the disease. We have six children. It was a happy family, and I wish I could say it hasn't changed. Our family isn't destroyed, but it is badly damaged.

We did everything we could to be helpful to Dan. We took him weekly to a psychiatrist, and then tried to see that he took his medicine. Whenever he was released from a hospital, we helped him find a job. We took him around until he found a suitable room in the area, and then once more

helped him move his drafting table and other belongings to his new home.

He never took his medicine once he was away from us. Each time he finally began breaking things, and we once more brought the drafting table, suitcases, and sometimes cockroaches back home. Eventually, he would be reaccepted by the hospital, and we sat with heavy hearts while heaving sighs of relief. . . . There has never been a time when we would be surprised to look out the window and see Dan coming up the driveway. This was true especially in the year we were testing adult homes, though we continued calling on Dan, taking him places, and inviting him home for visits. Here is an example of Dan's life during this period:

On August 6, 1981, we drove Dan to Richmond, stopping on the way to buy him a new pair of shoes. Ten days later, we called to find out Dan was in jail. He had eaten a restaurant meal he couldn't pay for and assaulted a policeman.

The manager of the adult home explained Dan's problem to the police, and they released him, but Dan was not happy to be back at the home. . . . He sold his new shoes, pawned his watch, ran up a bill in a friendly Vietnamese cafe, and found new places where he could order a meal only to discover later that he didn't have his billfold. He was constantly asking John to raise his allowance from $20 to $35 a week. Whenever we went to visit him, he would spoil our time together by badgering his father.

[Later, during a period at home,] Dan was getting more and more upset over people "messing with his mind." He finally threatened to kill his younger brother, who moved out to live temporarily with a friend. It wasn't long before Dan was back in the hospital. Though the doctor said there was nothing wrong with him, his lawyer had talked him into volunteering.

While Dan was in the hospital, we once more investigated adult homes, hoping to find one which would please him. By the time he was to be dismissed, we hadn't found anything suitable, and in the end, we presented him with a plan for living at home. He was now 34 years old, and his younger brother, Fred, was away at college, so it would be just the three of us. Here was our proposition:

We welcome you to live at home with us if you take your medicine regularly, eat at meal time,

and smoke only in a restricted area. We will give you $30 a week for your expenses, and you will have occasional use of the car after you get your driver's license.

For over a year now, he has been going to the clinic to get his shots. He knows a good thing when he sees it. That $30 never makes it to the end of the week, but if he talks hard enough, he can always get a couple more dollars out of his Dad, who would rather toss him the bills than risk building up his blood pressure.

—Adapted from Piercey, 1985, pp. 155–157

Schizophrenic disorders are a prominent part of the category of mental disorders known as *psychoses*.

A **psychosis** is a disorder that involves alterations of perception, thought, or consciousness. Someone who is psychotic makes incorrect inferences about reality based on these alterations, and believes that the inferences are real and actual. When the person can understand that the inferences are not real but are the products of fantasy or misperception, the psychosis is no longer present.

Many of the psychoses produce the kind of behaviors that were formerly called "madness," "lunacy," or "insanity." Causal factors have been found for some disorders with these symptoms. The causes may be temporary, such as the effect of drugs, reduced availability of oxygen to the brain during high fevers, or extreme vitamin deficiencies, or they may be permanent, for example the consequence of infections such as syphilis. However, a specific cause has not been found for many disorders that produce psychosis. Such disorders include, in addition to schizophrenic disorders, some manias, certain severe depressions, paranoid states, and brief psychotic reactions. Despite the similarity in psychotic behaviors that result from different causes, there are differences that help to identify the various psychoses (see Table 11–1).

Because schizophrenia is such a serious disorder and has been the focus of a great deal of research for many years, two chapters in this book, rather than one, seem appropriate. Schizophrenic disorder has long term impacts not only on those who develop it, but also on their families, and on society. This chapter describes the

Table 11–1

Differences among the Acute Psychoses

Type	Behavioral Characteristics
Schizophrenia	Loose associations Flat affect Bizarre delusions Alert, not dazed or confused Aware of time and place
Mania	Hyperactivity Pressured speech Elevated or irritable mood Usually aware of time and place
Organic brain syndrome	Loss of intellectual abilities Poor memory Impaired orientation Possible hallucinations or delusions
Brief reactive psychosis (response to particular conditions or physiological states)	Sudden onset Dramatic array of hallucinations and delusions Visual hallucinations more common than auditory hallucinations Mood tends to be expansive and effervescent Symptoms decline or disappear in a day or two
Psychotic depression	Somatic delusions (e.g., spine being eaten by worms) Hallucinations with negative, critical tone Delusions of guilt and self-reproach Paranoid thinking Biological signs—sleep disturbance, change in appetite, altered sex drive

typical behaviors and thinking patterns associated with schizophrenia because unlike the symptoms of many other disorders, many of them are very different from anything most people have ever experienced. Then, because ideas about schizophrenia have a long history, a history that still has impacts on current thinking and research, the chapter continues with a brief review of changes in the conceptualization of schizophrenia across time. Finally, this chapter describes what is known about long-term outcome of schizophrenic disorder and the different approaches to its treatment. After this groundwork has been laid, Chapter 12 then describes the different research approaches that are currently in use in an effort to understand both the biological and environmental bases for schizophrenic disorder. It reviews studies from a variety of perspectives that show how genetic vulnerability may be expressed in behavior both before and after the appearance of schizophrenic disorder.

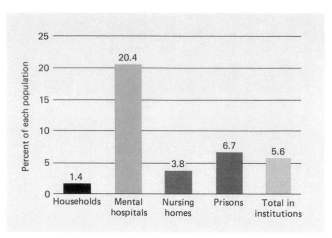

FIGURE 11–1 Although people who meet the diagnostic criteria for schizophrenic disorder make up only a small proportion of the general population, they represent a much higher proportion of the population of many types of institutions.

(Data from Keith and others, 1991, p. 37)

The Impact of Schizophrenic Disorders

Of all the psychoses, schizophrenic disorders have the most severe impact on people's lives and on the health care system. The ECA Catchment Study described in Chapter 10 found that about 14 in every 1,000 adults (1.4 percent) who live outside of institutions have met the criterion for a diagnosis of a schizophrenic disorder sometime in their lives (Keith and others, 1991). This means that more than 2,300,000 of the approximately 165 million adults in the United States could be diagnosed at some time in their lives as having a schizophrenic disorder. In any given year, about 1 percent of the population is affected by schizophrenia. This means that the schizophrenic disorders are five times more prevalent than multiple sclerosis and six times more than insulin-dependent diabetes. Figure 11–1 shows that the rates for people in institutions are much higher. In the United States, the direct cost of treatment of schizophrenic disorders is more than $7 billion dollars per year. Indirect costs, which include social services and loss of productivity, total at least another $14 billion. These costs make the economic burden of schizophrenia approximately equal to that for all types of cancer combined (Keith and others, 1991).

As an example of the high costs of treating schizophrenia, consider the case of one 32-year-old American woman who became ill when she was 14. In 18 years the direct costs for her care in inpatient settings or in community outpatient settings totaled more than $636,000 in 1983 dollars (Moran and others, 1984).

This figure did not include costs for outpatient therapy, health care, emergency room care, and social services, or the costs to her parents, who supported her financially when she was not in a hospital or halfway house.

In addition to the cost in money, the social and psychological costs of the schizophrenic disorders are tremendous both to patients and their families and to society. The psychological cost to patients is shown in the very high rates of attempted and completed suicide by those with a schizophrenic diagnosis. About one in every four patients with schizophrenia will try to kill him-or herself, and one in every ten will succeed (Roy, 1986). Those who elect suicide have certain characteristics in common with those in the general population who turn to suicide. They tend to be living alone, unmarried, unemployed, feeling hopeless, and to have made previous suicide attempts. However, people with a schizophrenic disorder who kill themselves also have certain distinctive characteristics. These include youth, a college education, a chronic course of illness with many worsenings and improvements, an awareness of the effects of schizophrenia, fear of further disintegration, and a nondelusional negative view concerning the future (Caldwell & Gottesman, 1990).

Diagnostic Criteria

The characteristics of schizophrenic disorder cover a wide range of behaviors, not all of which may occur in any one person. For a diagnosis of schizophrenic disorder to be given, there must be a significant period of

time in which a person shows changes to a markedly less satisfactory level of functioning in one or more major areas of life; for instance, work, social relations, or self-care. There must also be a period of at least one month when the person is actively psychotic, as shown by bizarre delusions, prominent hallucinations, or other clear signs of disorganized and strange behavior. These behaviors are described in the next section of this chapter. Table 11–2 lists the major clinical features of schizophrenia. These include two general types of symptoms, which may be described as positive and negative. The presence of some positive symptoms is essential for the diagnosis to be made; however, the negative symptoms are not required to be present. Positive and negative symptoms are discussed in more detail later in this chapter.

A number of other disorders are thought to be related to schizophrenia, but vary from it in important ways. Whether there is a connection between these disorders and schizophrenia is not clear. Some of these other disorders are described below.

Schizophreniform disorder is defined in the same way as is schizophrenic disorder, except that the schizophreniform disorder has not lasted long enough to be included in the schizophrenic category. **Schizoaffective disorder** is, as its name indicates, an overlapping of symptoms of schizophrenia and mood disorders. To be classified as schizoaffective disorder, these two types of symptoms must occur together for a substantial period of time, rather than one or the other occurring only briefly. **Schizotypal personality disorder** represents the category that was in the past referred to as simple schizophrenia. To use this diagnosis, the symptoms must last

FIGURE 11–2 Positive and negative symptoms typically occur with different frequencies in schizophrenia and disorders thought to be related to it. This figure depicts the relationship graphically.

(Pogue–Geile, M.F., M. Keshavan: Negative symptomatology in schizophrenia: Syndrome and subtype status, in Negative Schizophrenic Symptoms: Pathophysiology and Clinical Implications. Edited by Greden, J.F. and R. Tandon, Washington, DC, American Psychiatric Press. Copyright © 1991 American Psychiatric Press, Inc.)

for a considerable period of time (see Chapter 9). It includes a variety of symptoms that are similar to those found in some schizophrenic patients, including excessive social anxiety, odd beliefs and perceptual experiences, odd behavior and speech, suspiciousness, and a lack of close friends or confidants. Figure 11–2 shows how these disorders may be related in terms of the severity of both positive and negative symptoms. Those who are high on both dimensions are likely to be diagnosed as schizophrenic. Those low on both dimensions would not be likely to be considered ill. Those high on the negative symptom dimension and low on the positive symptom dimension would be diagnosed as having a schizoid personality disorder (described in Chapter 9). The reverse situation, high on the positive symptom dimension and low on the negative symptom dimension would define those with a schizophrenic diagnosis who would be thought to be likely to have a good outcome—or those diagnosed as having a schizophreniform disorder. Those who are more moderate in negative symptoms and have some positive symptoms would be classified as schizotypal personality disorder.

Symptoms that might occur before or after the active psychotic phase of a schizophrenic episode include marked social isolation and withdrawal; impairment in functioning in a previous role as a worker, student, or homemaker; impairment in personal hygiene and grooming; inappropriate affect; vague, digressive speech or contentless speech; odd beliefs or thinking one has magical powers; and/or marked lack of initiative, interests, or energy.

Table 11–2
The Clinical Picture of Schizophrenia

Positive symptoms, some of which are present at least during the active or acute phase of the disorder

Delusions
Hallucinations
Disorganized speech
Unusual motor behaviors
Disorganized and bizarre behavior

Negative symptoms, which may be present during the acute phase and also before and after the acute phase has subsided

Flat affect
Loss of motivation
Loss of energy
Loss of feelings of pleasure

Characteristics of Schizophrenic Disorders

The major characteristics of a schizophrenic disorder include specific patterns in content of thoughts; the form or structure in which thoughts are expressed; perception of the environment; changes in emotional response; an imperfect differentiation between oneself and the environment; and changes in degree of motivation, in relationships, in level of functioning, and in patterns of body movement. The next sections describe each of these aspects of schizophrenic behavior in more detail. When reading them it is important to remember that no single characteristic is always present or is unique to schizophrenia.

Delusions

A **delusion** is essentially a faulty interpretation of reality that cannot be shaken despite clear evidence to the contrary. Delusions occur in other disorders besides schizophrenia, but in each disorder they have a somewhat different content (See Table 11–3).

Delusions may be expressed in many ways. Some types of delusions occur more often in schizophrenia than in any other type of psychoses. Among these are the belief that everyone can hear the person's thoughts, the belief that others are either inserting thoughts into the person's mind or removing them, or the belief that the person's thoughts, feelings, and impulses are controlled by some external force. Other kinds of delusions that are typical of schizophrenia but that occur less often include the belief of being persecuted, grandiose thoughts about being an extremely important person, or ideas with a religious theme. The artist who created the picture in Figure 11–3 expressed some of his delusional thinking through his painting. Another example comes from an author who wrote about a variety of delusions that she had experienced while psychotic. Some of these delusions were somatic—for example, she believed she was able to stop her heart on command. Others were both religious and grandiose. She believed that people were worshipping her as the Madonna and that her child (not yet born) would be the savior of the world (Thelmar, 1932). In the case at the beginning of the chapter, the college student described her belief that she was Jesus Christ.

Delusions can result in violent behavior that harms others. In one tragic case, for instance, a mother severed a hand from each of her two daughters with a butcher knife and then chopped off her own hand. She then ran to neighbors and told them that she was John the Baptist and was going to be beheaded (*Seattle Times,* April 1, 1979, p. A13). At other times the behavior, although based on delusional thinking, is highly organized and requires immense concentration. The following case gives an example of such intense behavior. For eight hours a 22-year-old male student performed surgery deep in his abdomen, and carried out the operation in his college dormitory room with a precision that astonished surgeons. He had spent months preparing for the surgery, which, he said, was intended to "denervate his adrenal glands." He had read surgical texts and acquired instruments. Before the operation he sterilized his room, anesthetized himself with barbiturates, donned a sterile mask and gloves, and draped his body in sheets.

Lying supine and looking into strategically placed mirrors to obtain an optimum view, he began by cleansing his abdomen with alcohol. The incision was made with a scalpel, exposure obtained by retractors, and the dissection carried out with surgical instruments. . . .

After eight hours he had had a minimal blood loss but was unable to obtain adequate exposure to enter the retroperitoneal space because of the unexpected pain in retracting his liver. Exhausted, he bandaged his wound, cleaned up his room, and called the police for transport to the hospital because of a "rupture."

—Kalin, 1979, p. 2188

Disordered Thinking

Schizophrenia has been frequently referred to as a **formal-thought disorder.** This description refers to the structure or organization of thoughts and is different

Table 11–3
The Typical Content of Delusions Differs in Different Types of Psychoses

Disorder	Typical Delusional Content
Schizophrenia	Very bizarre Control by others Persecution
Paranoid Disorder	Jealousy Persecution
Depression (In either unipolar or bipolar disorder)	Guilt Bodily changes
Mania	Self-grandiosity

FIGURE 11–3 The artist who created this picture was, at the time, a hospitalized psychiatric patient who was troubled by a variety of tormenting thoughts. Here he represents his negative view of life and some of the topics that were special areas of conflict for him. Talented as an artist, he made painting his vocation after his recovery.

from the thought content problems just described. A frequent type of disordered thought is **loosening of associations,** in which the speaker's ideas shift from one topic to another in a way that seems unrelated to everyone else. When the loosening of association is severe the person's speech becomes incomprehensible. An example of loose associations is the answer given by someone with a schizophrenic disorder to the question, "What does this proverb mean, 'Strike while the iron is hot!'"

> *It could mean (pause) Hercules! (Could you say more?) I saw the movie Hercules. (Yes . . .) And it means don't iron over your hands and don't strike anybody before you cast the first stone.*
>
> —Marengo and others, 1986, p. 498

The word "autistic" has been used to describe schizophrenic thought patterns. Derived from the Greek word *autos,* meaning "self," **autistic thinking** is defined as thinking that is so self-centered that it is fully intelligible only to the person doing the thinking. Researchers have found that schizophrenic individuals ask inappropriate questions and give inappropriate answers (Rutter, 1985). What seems to be missing is the predictability and the repetitions of meaning that are present in normal speech. This may be the reason that interviewers who talk to someone with a schizophrenic disorder may come away confused about the conversation's meaning.

It is important to remember that not all people with a schizophrenic disorder display peculiar speech. The majority speak coherently most of the time, and peculiar speech is found in other patients about as frequently as it is in schizophrenics (Andreasen & Grove, 1979). To appreciate this point, rate the following examples on a five-point scale from 1, schizophrenic, to 5, normal.

> a. *Then, I always liked geography. My last teacher in the subject was Professor August A. He was a man with black eyes. I also*

like black eyes. There are also blue and gray eyes and other sorts, too. I have heard it said that snakes have green eyes. All people have eyes. There are some, too, who are blind. These blind people are led by a boy. It must be terrible not to be able to see. There are people who can't see, and in addition, can't hear. I know some who hear too much. One can hear too much. There are many sick people in Bürgholzli; they are called patients.

—Bleuler, 1950, p. 17

b. *Yes, of course, the whole thing wasn't my idea. So, I suppose I'd be perfectly happy if he came back and decided to do it all on his own. If I could make two trips myself, I don't see why he can't.*

—Laffal, 1965, p. 309

c. *Well, I wonder if that part of it can't be—I wonder if that doesn't—let me put it frankly; I wonder if that doesn't have to be continued? Let me put it this way: Let us suppose you get the million bucks, and you get the proper way to handle it. You could hold that side?*

—Gold, 1974, p. 117

When these excerpts were informally rated by several psychologists, item *a* was usually rated as schizophrenic. It represents the way people think schizophrenics speak. Item *b* was rated as normal because it is neither bizarre nor obscure. Item *c* was rated moderately schizophrenic because, while it is not bizarre, it is repetitious, loose, and difficult to follow (Schwartz, 1982). How do these ratings agree with yours? The results may cause you to readjust your ideas about schizophrenics, because *a* and *b* were produced by patients who were diagnosed as schizophrenic and *c* is from a conversation by former U.S. President Richard Nixon. According to one study, many of Nixon's colleagues produced similar speech (Gold, 1974).

Hard-to-follow communications may also come from people who have been given diagnoses other than schizophrenia. The following excerpt was produced by a hypomaniac patient.

Women of America, it behooves you one and all to help at this, the most interesting epoch of the World's History, in every way possible, the march of civilization, the march of victory! I will play you Beethoven's Great Symphony with

its four fateful opening notes—sol, sol, sol, mi V.V.V.V. the Day of the Century has dawned.

—Cohen, 1975, p. 1020

Schizophrenic individuals may be highly intelligent, not at all confused, and very painstaking in working out logical solutions to problems. However, their thought processes do not lead to conclusions based on reality or universal logic.

Another characteristic of schizophrenic speech is **poverty of content:** Even though the speaker talks for quite a while, little information is transmitted because what is said is vague, repetitive, stereotyped, and either too abstract or too concrete.

Hallucinations

Hallucinations account for most of the difficulties a person with schizophrenia experiences in perceiving reality. **Hallucinations** are projections of internal impulses and experiences onto perceptual images in the external world. Although they may occur in other disorders—for example, during the delirium associated with a high fever or as a result of the effects of drugs or other chemicals on the nervous system—only in schizophrenia do hallucinations occur when the person is in a clear, conscious state. Hallucinations can be associated with any of the senses. In the case at the beginning of the chapter, J. had the hallucination of hearing voices threatening to kill her. This kind of *auditory* hallucination is the most common type found in schizophrenia. Many schizophrenics report voices making a running commentary on their behavior or speaking directly to them and issuing orders or accusing them of terrible crimes or actions (see Figure 11–4). Hallucinations may also be related to touch. For instance, the person may feel burning or tingling sensations. Hallucinations associated with smell, while less common, are also typical. Foul odors are perceived as coming from one's body as a sign of decay and death or of some sexual change. Sometimes hallucinations are somatic, or reflect internal sensations.

I was drawing the head of a cat which meanwhile gnawed at my vitals. It was ghastly, intolerable.

—Sechehaye, 1951, p. 37

Hallucinations are often visual. While Figure 11–5 shows a reaction to frightening hallucinations, not all

FIGURE 11–4 Some hallucinations are extremely unpleasant. This person hears voices accusing her of horrible crimes that she has not committed.

I began to hallucinate at the age of nine. My classmates quickly noticed that I was "different" and reacted to me "differently." . . . Simple skills such as balancing in hopscotch, catching a ball, or running into a twirling jump rope were extremely difficult for me My classmates ridiculed my efforts and I reacted to their rejection by isolating myself from them, knowing that I did not belong. I would giggle at odd times as I would "see" a troop of elves jump merrily from desk to desk and tweak the teacher's nose. At other times, I would cry out at the sight of my desk biting my dress like a hungry animal. My behavior was annoying, and my explanations were seen as fanciful lies to cover up my disruptive behavior. . . . By late adolescence, I had learned that I could trust no one with the truth, and after two unsuccessful suicide attempts had decided stoically to see my life through to the bitter end.

—Lovejoy, 1982, p. 605

hallucinations are accusatory or unpleasant. Sometimes those who experience hallucinations find them so comfortable they are unwilling to give them up because they serve as protections from negative aspects of reality. At times, however, even nonthreatening hallucinations can have a negative effect, as the recollection of childhood hallucinations by a female patient illustrates.

One way to study the perceptions of schizophrenic individuals as they occur is to use a **thought sampling** method. In one study using this method, the patient wore a beeper; when it went off, her task was to record in a notebook what she was experiencing at that time. The patient, Jennifer, was a young woman living in a halfway house after several years of on-and-off hospitalization. At the time of the study she had improved and was considering moving to a cooperative apartment. But even at that time, she experienced thought patterns typical of schizophrenia.

FIGURE 11–5 This crayon drawing expresses the artist's perception of his mental illness. Unless he keeps busy, he has visual hallucinations of animals that frighten him greatly.

The technique of thought sampling can help us see that perceptual distortions may occur often in everyday schizophrenic thinking. In contrast to the dramatic memories from their period of psychoses by patients who have recovered, the thought-sampling technique conveys an idea of just how disabling the disordered perception in schizophrenia may be even when an observer would notice no unusual behavior.

Hallucinations have been investigated from several perspectives (Asaad & Shapiro, 1986). From a biological perspective they have been linked to abnormal brain excitability. PET scans have shown greater biochemical activity in the temporal lobe and auditory areas during auditory hallucinations. The neurotransmitter dopamine may also play a role. From the psychodynamic perspective, hallucinations are thought to represent a breakthrough into consciousness of material from the unconscious. Their content is believed to have psychodynamic meaning such as wish fulfillment, aggressive impulses, or a projection of a critical superego or conscience. From a cognitive viewpoint, intelligence level may play an important role in auditory hallucinations because these occur more frequently in people with lower intellectual and development levels. Perhaps auditory hallucinations represent the best way that less intellectually able people can describe stressful experience (Zigler & Levine, 1983).

Lack of Appropriate Emotion

One of the most common results of schizophrenia is change in emotional expression. People with a schizophrenic disorder are often described as showing emotional flatness, and this is especially true after the period of acute psychosis has passed. Such people are often apathetic, and display little emotion no matter what the situation. Talking with someone who behaves this way is very unsatisfactory because it seems that no emotional contact can be made. The person who expresses this lack

of affect may also complain that he or she no longer "feels" and cannot experience emotion. Although this flattened affect is a frequent symptom of schizophrenia, it also can occur as a result of antipsychotic drugs used to treat many schizophrenic patients.

Sometimes rather than showing flat affect, a schizophrenic person may show what seems to others to be an inappropriate emotional response. As an example, recall the young woman's account of her childhood giggles when she "saw" elves dancing across her desk. Because her schoolmates could not see the hallucinatory elves, her behavior seemed quite strange and inappropriate. Another inappropriate emotional response that may occur in schizophrenia is sudden, unpredictable, and seemingly inexplicable outbursts of anger. Whether all these inappropriate expressions of emotion are connected to hallucinations and delusions is not known.

Unclear Boundaries of the Self

A person with schizophrenia often has what is called a **loss of ego boundaries.** This description means that the normal feelings of personal uniqueness, of being a separate individual, and of being in control of one's own behavior are missing. Sometimes these feelings are related to delusions that focus on one's thoughts being known to others or of being controlled by others. Such feelings are illustrated in this description from an autobiographical account of a schizophrenic experience.

In other instances this sense of unclear boundaries takes the form of losing the sense of being a coherent person, as described here.

body. It is as if something is thrown in me, bursts me asunder. Why do I divide myself in different pieces? I feel that I am without poise, that my personality is melting and that my ego disappears and that I do not exist anymore. Everything pulls me apart. . . . The skin is the only possible means of keeping the different pieces together. There is no connection between the different parts of my body.

—Jaynes, 1976, p. 425

Unpredictable Motor Behavior

Just as the emotions expressed during schizophrenia are unpredictable, so is the motor activity. At times schizophrenic patients may become wildly aggressive and difficult to control, or they may move about constantly, much like a person experiencing a manic episode, stopping only when exhaustion sets in. One schizophrenic patient described the feeling of lack of control in this way:

I get shaky in the knees and my chest is like a mountain in front of me, and my body actions are different. The arms and legs are apart and away from me and they go on their own. That's when I feel I am the other person and copy their movements, or else stop and stand like a statue. I have to stop to find out whether my hand is in my pocket or not.

—Sass, 1987, p. 16

In contrast to the hyperactivity described here, however, some patients may remain motionless in strange postures for many hours, to the point at which circulation is impaired and swelling of body parts such as the feet and ankles occurs.

Change in Motivational Level

Another change that almost always accompanies a schizophrenic disorder is a change in motivation or interest level. Such changes are most likely to occur in the early phases of the disorder and again in the period after acute psychosis has passed. Parents often notice the first symptoms of what may become a schizophrenic disorder when their child's school grades begin to fall and the child does nothing but sit around listening to music or watching TV, constantly retreats to his or her bedroom, and avoids contact with others.

Some people who have experienced a schizophrenic disorder report a slowing down of thought processes. Their thoughts seemed to creep at a snail's pace. One person described her great sense of exhaustion, all concentrated in her head, as if a cogwheel had stuck (Thelmar, 1932). Another former patient described it this way:

The process of thought is like a chain that has become clogged with muddy oil . . . my mind was moving at the slowest possible rate; the real process of thought entered my consciousness like a slow rhythm or circular movement.

—Ogden, 1947, pp. 37, 92

Impaired Interpersonal Functioning

A behavior that is almost always present in schizophrenia in all its phases is social withdrawal and emotional detachment. The schizophrenic patient may be caught up in personal fantasies and inner experiences to the degree that the outer world is excluded. At some times, too, other problems with social interactions arise because the person seems unable to comprehend the most basic social conventions. For example, during at least some phases of the disorder, the schizophrenic person may intrude so much on others' personal space that they become uncomfortable and avoid contact. Such intrusions might involve inserting him- or herself into an ongoing interaction with strangers—for example, joining strangers at a lunch table and interacting in an overly familiar way. Another behavior of this kind involves clinging to others or simply standing only inches away when asking a question.

Attention Difficulties

One way to understand behavior typical of a schizophrenic disorder is to think about much of it in terms of problems with attention. A review of over 50 autobiographical books and articles by people who had been diagnosed as schizophrenic showed that difficulty in focusing attention and lack of concentration were mentioned most often (Freedman, 1974). For example:

I couldn't read (newspapers) because everything that I read had a large number of associations with it. I mean, I'd just read a headline, and the

headline of this item of news would have . . . very much wider associations in my mind. It seemed to start off everything that I read, and everything that sort of caught my attention seemed to start off, bang-bang-bang, like that, with an enormous number of associations, moving off into things so that it became so difficult for me to deal with, that I couldn't read.

—Laing, 1967, pp. 51–52

There are many possible reasons for these attentional problems. One may be that hallucinations compete with reality for attentional focus. Another possibility is that the problems in content of thought may produce distortions in the meaning of what is observed. Another reason for attention difficulty might be that disturbance in the sense of self and the anxiety it produces may result in an inability to screen out all the distracting stimuli that normally-functioning people ordinarily ignore. These are only a few of many ideas that may explain the kinds of behavior that are common in schizophrenia.

The period when psychotic symptoms first appear is often a time of great anxiety. The case of J. at the beginning of this chapter illustrates the impact of these anxious feelings. Many people make desperate attempts to control their thinking as they become aware of the onset of psychosis. They often concoct elaborate schemes for character development or body building in an attempt to occupy their thoughts and ward off the psychosis.

It is clear that people who are labeled as schizophrenic do not perceive situations in the same way that most other people do. What is not clear is whether such people focus on too many factors in a situation and become confused by too much information, or whether they notice only certain details and thus become incapable of accurately assessing what is happening.

I went to the teacher and said to her, "I am afraid. . . ." She smiled gently at me. But her smile, instead of reassuring me, only increased the anxiety and confusion, for I saw her teeth, white and even in the gleam of the light. Remaining all the while like themselves, soon they monopolized my entire vision as if the whole room were nothing but teeth under a remorseless light. Ghastly fear gripped me.

—U.S. Dept. of Health and Human Services, 1981, p. 2

A Historical View of Schizophrenic Disorders

Brief descriptions of what today would probably be called schizophrenic disorders are found in the Hindu *Ayur Veda*, which dates from 1400 B.C. and in the writings of the Roman physician Aretaeus in the first century A.D. (Kendell, 1983). However, for many centuries descriptions of schizophrenia were much less common and detailed than descriptions of psychotic behavior characterized by mania, probably because manic symptoms are more attention getting and less complex than the varied symptoms shown in schizophrenia. Schizophrenic disorders were not clearly defined until the nineteenth century.

Dementia Praecox

One of the first writers to classify schizophrenia as a distinct disorder was Emil Kraepelin (1856–1926), a German physician, who called it **dementia praecox.** Kraepelin was the author of the most influential psychiatric textbook of his period. He emphasized that classification depended on the cause of the illness, not just the symptoms observed at a particular time. Kraepelin used the term "dementia praecox" (premature madness) because the onset of the disorder occurred early in life, typically in adolescence. He believed the cause of dementia praecox was irreversible organic deterioration, which would eventually be found to have a specific organic cause and pathology. He thus considered recovery from the disorder to be impossible. Despite this belief he noted the great variability in the speed and extent of different individuals' declines and pointed out that there might even be remissions, or periods when the disorder was no longer obvious. In fact, out of 127 cases that Kraepelin studied, 16 seemed to have ended in complete recovery (Kraepelin, 1909, vol. 2, p. 865).

Kraepelin paid no attention to the psychological aspects of schizophrenia; his entire focus was on the symptoms of the underlying deterioration. Consequently, he ignored the person's life history, personality, and experiences with the illness. When he did mention psychological features, Kraepelin considered them temporary expedients, expecting that findings from microscopes and test tubes would make it possible to investigate the disease objectively.

The Schizophrenias

One of the first people to emphasize the psychological aspects of the disorder was Eugen Bleuler (1857–

1939), a Swiss physician, who was influenced by Freud's work on the neuroses. According to Bleuler, whatever the underlying process might be, many of the symptoms had a psychological cause. Bleuler spoke of "the schizophrenias" instead of using the term "dementia praecox" and broadened the concept of the disorder as well as changing its name. He believed that the symptoms might represent a group of disorders with different causes and outcomes, not a single cause and outcome as Kraepelin had thought. Bleuler noted that although some people with schizophrenic disorders deteriorate, others remain unchanged and some improve. He divided people with schizophrenic symptoms into two groups, chronic and acute, and thought that the acute cases had a good chance of recovery. Bleuler also emphasized the role of the environment in schizophrenic disorder. In his view, some individuals might have the potential for developing these disorders, but because particular types of environmental situations did not occur, the disorder remained latent and these people never showed visible signs of schizophrenia. This idea is still current in the concept of vulnerability, discussed in Chapter 12.

Bleuler spoke of this group of disorders as characterized by loss of integration of thinking, emotion, and motivation rather than by gradual deterioration. He summed up the primary characteristics of schizophrenic behavior as the "four A's": alterations in affect, alterations in association, ambivalence, and autism. Associated with these changes, in Bleuler's view, were the secondary symptoms of hallucinations and delusions.

Bleuler's ideas became popular in the United States, but in Europe, Kraepelin's ideas continued to be more influential. Because Bleuler had defined the criteria of schizophrenia vaguely, the diagnosis of schizophrenia came to be used for behaviors that differed greatly both in kind and in severity. In addition, American-trained clinicians began to interpret these definitions very broadly so that the diagnosis was frequently applied even when the person had only some of the specified characteristics.

From the 1930s until the 1960s, several important figures in American psychiatry, such as Adolf Meyer and Harry Stack Sullivan, emphasized a broad concept of schizophrenia and psychosis in general, and a concern with the psychodynamics of the behavior and emphasis on interpersonal relationships as causal factors. As a result, emphasis on differential diagnosis—discriminating, for example, between affective disorders and schizophrenia—was thought to be of little importance and the proportion of people who were called schizophrenic increased sharply. For example, in the 1930s about 20 percent of patients at the New York Psychiatric Institute were diagnosed as schizophrenic. By the 1950s, the figure had reached 80 percent (Kuriansky and others,

1974). During this same period, in Maudsley Hospital in London, where the more narrowly defined Kraepelin definition continued to be used, the proportion of patients diagnosed as schizophrenic remained at about 20 percent. This difference suggests that what on first glance seemed to be an epidemic of schizophrenia in the United States was actually the result of a change in the definition by which the diagnosis was made. When such a large number of people with different symptoms and different outcomes of illness were given the same diagnosis, the chances of effective treatment greatly decreased. As a result of this problem, work began to be focused on narrowing the definition of schizophrenic disorders.

First-Rank Symptoms

Kurt Schneider (1887–1967) was one of the leaders in the effort to make the definition of schizophrenia more concise and easier to reach agreement over. Schneider did not deny that Kraepelin's idea of bodily changes was correct, but he believed that since these changes had not been identified, it was important to divide people into types on the basis of their psychological symptoms. Moreover, Schneider felt that Bleuler's characterization system of the four A's seemed too vague to be interpreted reliably.

Schneider dealt with these problems by describing a series of first- and second-rank symptoms. If first-rank symptoms were present and no organic cause was evident, a diagnosis of schizophrenia was justified. **First-rank symptoms** were all related to hallucinations and delusional thinking; they are now described as the positive signs (see the following section). The hallucinations are likely to be auditory, such as voices keeping up a running commentary on the person's current behavior. The delusions include the belief that thoughts are no longer confined only to the person's mind but are simultaneously broadcast for all to hear. For example, a 21-year-old student said:

As I think, my thoughts leave my head on a type of mental ticker-tape. Everyone around has only to pass the tape through their mind and they know my thoughts.

—Mellor, 1970, p. 17

First-rank symptoms also include experiences of external control, such as having thoughts inserted into one's head or arbitrarily taken away. Patients might report feeling hypnotized or having become robot-like,

under the control of others. A female patient reported this type of feeling:

> *I cry, tears roll down my cheeks and I look unhappy, but inside I have a cold anger because they are using me in this way, and it is not me who is unhappy, but they are projecting unhappiness into my brain. They project upon me laughter, for no reason, and you have no idea how terrible it is to laugh and look happy and know it is not you, but their emotions.*
>
> —Mellor, 1970, p. 17

Second-rank symptoms included other symptoms usually associated with schizophrenia that were not included as first-rank symptoms. Such symptoms, in Schneider's view, could also be found in other psychotic disorders, although a diagnosis of schizophrenia could be made without first-rank symptoms. Schneider considered the abnormal inner experiences of the individual to be the most telling characteristics of the illness. His classification system attempted to identify behavioral symptoms that would be readily noticed by an examiner, could be easily agreed upon by several observers, and could occur only in schizophrenia.

Schneider was only partially successful in meeting his goals. The first-rank symptoms are easily noticed and are easy for examiners to agree on. However, they have a serious disadvantage. Although these first-rank symptoms occur frequently in schizophrenia, they are not unique to it. At least one-fourth of patients with bipolar affective disorders also show some of these symptoms (Hoenig, 1984). In addition, the presence or absence of these symptoms does not seem to be related to later functioning and improvement (Silverstein & Harrow, 1981).

European and American Definitions

As a result of emphasis in the United States on narrowing the diagnosis for schizophrenic disorders, the concept of schizophrenia is now narrower than it is in Europe. This narrowing began with DSM III. Currently, the European diagnostic system is focused primarily on the first-rank symptoms of Schneider (Angst, 1988); and as a result, the diagnosis of schizophrenia is made only in the presence of clear psychotic symptoms. However, this differentiation also means that many patients who have depressive or affective symptoms along with the psychotic symptoms are classified as having schizophrenic disorder in Europe but would be excluded from that diagnosis in the United States. Thus, the European and American concepts of schizophrenia are still too different to make many comparisons meaningful. Researchers must consider the importance of recording a complete description of symptoms and behavior in addition to the diagnosis to make research findings useful across national boundaries.

Positive and Negative Symptoms

Due to initial enthusiasm over the ease of distinction of Schneider's first- and second-rank symptoms, interest in the delusional, or what are usually called the more active, symptoms of schizophrenia rose. Such interest was tempered, however, with the understanding that other symptoms also needed emphasis. Beginning with the work of Kraepelin, active symptoms were considered to be coupled with a characteristic deterioration in emotional functioning and motivation. Since it was clear from past research that many people who were diagnosed as schizophrenic passed through a period of active psychosis and also an extended period characterized by deficits in responding, it seemed to many researchers and clinicians that emphasis on both active and deficiency symptoms was needed.

Another reason for interest in both types of symptoms was the belief that they might be associated with different causal factors and different expectations for recovery. Interest in making the distinction had been part of the original conceptions of Kraepelin, Bleuler, and others, and was rekindled by the work of Crow in the early 1980s (1980a, 1980b, 1985).

Positive symptoms, or behavioral excesses, include hallucinations, delusions, bizarre behavior, and disordered thinking. Positive symptoms are thought to be a result of problems with the chemical neurotransmitter dopamine. **Negative symptoms,** or behavior deficits, are such behaviors as poverty of speech and of speech content, flattened affect, apathy, seclusiveness, and impaired attention (see Table 11–4). Although they are not found only in people with a diagnosis of schizophrenia, negative symptoms do appear to be more common among schizophrenic patients than among other diagnostic groups (Pogue-Geile & Zubin, 1988).

Several competing theories have arisen about the relationship of positive and negative symptoms. Crow's idea was that these symptoms represent two independent dimensions of pathology (Crowe, 1980a, 1980b). He suggested that there may be two different types of schizophrenia, one characterized by the florid positive symptoms and also by disturbances in dopamine transmission, and the other characterized by enduring negative symptoms and structural brain abnormalities. According to this view, positive and negative symptoms

Table 11–4

Examples of Negative Symptom Behavior[a]

Poverty of Speech	Flat Affect	Psychomotor Retardation
1. Long lapses before replying to questions	1. Avoids looking at interviewer	1. Slowed in movements
2. Restriction of quantity of speech	2. Blank, expressionless face	2. Reducation of voluntary movements
3. Failure to answer	3. Reduced emotion shown when emotional material discussed	
4. Speech slowed	4. Apathetic and uninterested	
5. Blocking	5. Monotonous voice	
	6. Low voice, difficult to hear	

[a]Items are from the Behavior Rating Inventory of the Psychiatric Assessment Interview.

SOURCE: Adapted from Carpenter and others, 1976. Reprinted with permission from the *British Journal of Psychiatry*.

should not be correlated, or if they are, the correlations should be positive but very small. An opposing view, presented by Andreasen, is that the positive and negative symptoms represent two opposite dimensions of the same general process; they should thus be negatively correlated to each other (Andreasen, 1982, 1985). Although the research findings so far have sometimes favored one view and sometimes the other, in general, Crow's view that the two groups of symptoms are uncorrelated has received the most support (Lenzenweger and others, 1989; Mortimer and others, 1990). If this theory is correct, it would be misleading to categorize those with schizophrenic symptoms into positive and negative symptom groups. The decision to categorize symptoms remains controversial, but many studies have continued to categorize patients into these two groups.

Most of the research with positive and negative symptoms has been done with chronic patients, those who have had a schizophrenic disorder over a long period. In general, studies of chronic patients have found that patients with positive symptoms have a better chance of resuming effective functioning than do patients with negative symptoms. Patients with predominantly negative symptoms not only tend to have consistently poor functioning over the long term, but they are likely to have had a history of poor functioning before their initial period of psychosis.

In studies of chronic patients, the type of symptoms initially assessed at the time of first hospitalization did not predict the type of symptoms the person had two years later. Negative symptoms after two years were associated with poor functioning and poor outcome, but negative symptoms during the first phase of the disorder were not necessarily related to a later poor outcome (Lindenmayer and others, 1986). One reason for this difference might be that for some people, depression associated with the experience of the initial psychotic symptoms of schizophrenic disorder may have produced a picture of negative symptoms that had a very different meaning than the negative symptoms found in patients who had been ill for a long time. Like other ways of trying to subdivide schizophrenia, the concept of positive and negative symptoms is helpful but needs further refinement.

One clue to the potential usefulness of positive and negative symptoms as indicators of outcome was supplied by a longitudinal study of long-term schizophrenia patients who were hospitalized at the National Institute of Mental Health (Breier and others, 1991). The positive and negative symptoms observed when patients were not being treated with antipsychotic drugs were not a good predictor of outcome. However, the type of symptoms that occurred during the period of antipsychotic drug treatment at the time of first hospitalization turned out to be a good predictor of symptoms, level of functioning, and time out of the hospital.

Types of Schizophrenia

Traditional and Current DSM Subtypes

Kraepelin described three subtypes of schizophrenia or dementia praecox—*paranoid, hebephrenic,* and *catatonic*. When Bleuler broadened the description of the disorder, he added a fourth category, simple schizophrenia. These four categories were used for many years. Current DSM categories reflect a modification of these traditional types. They include: *paranoid, disorganized, catatonic,* and a catchall or *undifferentiated* group. In

addition, there is a *residual* category for cases in which the psychotic features are no longer prominent.

The diagnosis most often given to patients with a schizophrenic disorder on their first admission to a mental hospital is **paranoid schizophrenia.** This disorder seems to display itself primarily in cognitive behavior, characterized by delusions and sustained, extreme suspiciousness. Figure 11–6 illustrates how an artist who experienced psychosis felt he was watched by others, a common belief of those with paranoid symptoms. Since some aspects of intellectual functioning may be unaffected by the delusional thoughts, under certain circumstances paranoid schizophrenics may seem to function relatively well. They also are more likely than those with other types of schizophrenic disorders to have a good outcome.

The following account was given by a medical student with a Ph.D. in psychology who developed an acute psychotic reaction in which delusions played a prominent role. His case illustrates the extreme fright that is felt by someone experiencing the beginning of such a delusional state. During his acute episode, the student had the haunting notion that there was something wrong with him, that he could not breathe, and that he might die. One morning, after an especially fearful, sleepless night, he reported the following experience.

FIGURE 11–6 Paranoid symptoms often take the form of feeling constantly watched by others—as portrayed in this painting by an artist who experienced psychosis.

I got up at 7 A.M., depressed, and drove to the hospital. I felt my breathing trouble might be due to an old heart lesion. . . . I decided that I was in heart failure and that people felt I wasn't strong enough to accept this, so they weren't telling me. I looked up heart failure in a textbook and found that the section had been removed, so I concluded that someone had removed it to protect me. I remembered other comments. A friend had talked about a "walkie-talkie," and the thought occurred to me that I might be getting medicine without my knowledge, perhaps by radio. I remembered someone talking about a one-way plane ticket; to me that meant a trip to Houston and a heart operation. I remembered an unusual smell in the lab and thought that might be due to the medicine they were giving me in secret. I began to think I might have a machine inside of me which secreted medicine into my blood stream. . . .

—Bowers, 1968, p. 353.

Paranoid schizophrenics misinterpret the world around them. Although they are capable of evaluating the situation correctly, they resist the feedback cues that most people use. Well-defined systems of delusional paranoid thinking can also occur in people who in other respects show well-integrated behavior. Such people are diagnosed as having a delusional disorder rather than schizophrenia of the paranoid type (see Box 11–1 on pages 338–39).

A person with **disorganized schizophrenia** shows incoherence in expression, grossly disorganized behavior, and either flat or extremely inappropriate emotional reactions. Such people behave actively but aimlessly. They may show a childish disregard for social conventions and may resist wearing clothes, or urinate or defecate at inappropriate times. Giggling, silly mannerisms, and inexplicable gestures are common. Usually the long-term outlook for recovery is poor. People with disorganized schizophrenia are likely to have shown symptoms early and to have been poorly adapted even before that time.

Disturbance in motor activity is the major symptom of **catatonic schizophrenia.** People with this disorder may refuse to speak and remain stiffly immobile or may be extremely agitated. **Waxy flexibility** is an extreme form of immobility in which the catatonic's arm or leg remains passively in the position in which it is placed. At the opposite extreme, the agitated catatonic shows

extreme psychomotor excitement, talking and shouting almost continuously. Patients who experience prolonged catatonic excitement may be very destructive and violent toward others. As with manic excitement, there is a danger of personal injury or collapse due to exhaustion. This form of schizophrenia is now rarely seen, although it was common until 30 or 40 years ago. This change is thought to be a result of the almost universal treatment with antipsychotic drugs received by patients with symptoms of a schizophrenic disorder.

People who formerly would have been diagnosed as simple or borderline schizophrenics, that is, those who exhibit a lifelong pattern of seclusiveness and withdrawal from others and also have hallucinations or delusions—are now placed in the category of *schizotypal personality disorder*. (Schizotypal personality disorder is described in Chapter 9.) A person with schizotypal personality disorder usually comes to the attention of clinicians only if some dramatic life change occurs. Loss of a job or the death or disability of a parent or other caretaker may bring such people into contact with the medical or welfare system because they lack the ability to function on their own. People with schizotypal personality disorder may be eccentric, but they do not fit the DSM definition of schizophrenic disorder.

The diagnostic subgroups of schizophrenia vary in how frequently each occurs and also in expected outcome after the active phase has ended. A problem in evaluating the probable outcome is that over time a person's behavioral picture may change so that his or her classification into one or another of these types may be different at different periods.

Schizophrenic Spectrum Disorders

When the families of schizophrenic individuals are studied, they seem to include more than the expected number of relatives who are somewhat unusual in their behavior. These relatives dress eccentrically, behave in unusual ways, and seem somewhat limited emotionally or somewhat asocial. A greater than anticipated number of relatives of schizophrenics may also show peculiarities in thinking—believing one has magical powers, for instance. Many researchers believe that there may be some genetic relationship between these behaviors and the schizophrenic disorders. They maintain that the whole spectrum of disordered behaviors should be investigated together and usually discuss all of these under the label of **schizophrenic spectrum disorders.**

Schizophrenic spectrum disorders include not only these unusual emotional responses and cognitive behaviors but also certain personality disorders. For instance, *schizotypal* and *paranoid personality disorders* occur more frequently in the families of people who have schizo-

phrenic disorders (Baron & Risch, 1987). Other disorders that have sometimes been linked to the schizophrenic spectrum are *schizoaffective disorder* (a category that includes individuals who show significant depression or manic symptoms along with the development of thought disorder), *atypical psychoses,* and *paranoid disorder* (Kendler and others, 1985). The study of the relationships among these disordered behaviors may provide clues to the causes of schizophrenic behavior.

Outcome Indicators and Long-Term Studies

There are two schools of thought regarding the outcome or prognosis for schizophrenia. One is derived from Kraepelin's original concept of dementia praecox. This view of schizophrenia as a nonreversible deteriorative disorder assumes that the prognosis is negative. The second viewpoint stems from Bleuler's concept of the schizophrenias, which emphasizes the symptoms rather than the course of the disease. From this viewpoint, a certain number and kind of symptoms are necessary for the diagnosis, but the outcome may range from complete recovery to permanent and severe disability. Currently, a generally accepted view is that some individuals who have been affected by a schizophrenic disorder do fully recover, but that percentage is low (Rund, 1990). However, mental health professionals make a distinction between *recovered* and *cured*. They do not consider it possible for those who recover from a schizophrenic disorder to be "cured" because they believe that any person who has had a schizophrenic disorder must live with the vulnerability to new psychotic episodes for the rest of his or her life.

Information about whether or not there ever is or can be a complete recovery from schizophrenia is very important for individuals who have been diagnosed as having a schizophrenic disorder and for their families. The implications are considerable even for those whose behavior seems to have returned to a preschizophrenic level. These points are dramatically illustrated by a letter written by someone who had earlier been diagnosed as schizophrenic.

A few years ago, during my training in medical school, I was hospitalized at a reputable institution and, at some time during my stay, diagnosed as schizophrenic. Fortunately, I am doing very well now, and am pursuing a career in research on schizophrenia. . . . During the

BOX 11–1 Delusional Thinking

Everyone engages in paranoid thinking at one time or another. You could probably think of at least one occasion when you have felt that you were being discriminated against or talked about or were suspicious of someone else's motives without adequate proof that such things had actually occurred. We can consider paranoid thinking to be a kind of cognitive style. People vary in how frequently they use it and in how much they let reality influence what they perceive. Paranoid thinking thus can be expressed as a kind of continuum extending from the everyday type to severe delusional thinking that affects all of a person's life (see Table 11–5).

Illness, drugs, damage to the brain, some effects of aging, and the experience of severe stress can also produce paranoid thinking, but these do not qualify as paranoid disorder or fit on the continuum in Table 11–5.

Sometimes people who have not thought in this way before suddenly begin to do so. Such varied factors as liver failure, vitamin B_{12} deficiency, hearing loss, brain tumors, syphilis, and a variety of drugs may produce paranoid thinking along with other symptoms. At least 65 different physical and mental conditions have features of paranoia (Manschreck & Petri, 1978).

Paranoid thinking is more common in older people. Often it is caused by social isolation and perhaps by a progressive hearing loss or a loss of vision that makes it harder for the person to verify his or her perceptions of what is actually happening. Sometimes the small strokes or bloodclots in the brain that occur in older people can lead to such symptoms. Another possible cause is atrophy or degeneration of brain tissue. Any of these conditions may produce severe enough maladaptive behavior to require that the person be institutionalized.

A 73-year-old man had lived in the community for years. He was not very sociable but was always thought of as a harmless crank.

Table 11–5

The Range of Disordered Perceptions of Reality with Paranoid Elements

Mild	Moderate			Severe
AVERAGE PERSON	**PARANOID PERSONALITY**	**PARANOID PERSONALITY DISORDER**	**DELUSIONAL (PARANOID) DISORDER**	**PARANOID SCHIZOPHRENIA**
Occasional suspicious thoughts	A suspicious cognitive style	A suspicious cognitive style so strong that it impairs effective behavior; there are no delusions; reality testing is intact	A stable and chronic delusional system; reality testing good in all other areas	Multiple delusions that are likely to be fragmented, accompanied by marked loosening of associations, obvious hallucinations, and other evidence of disorganization; reality markedly distorted

years since my hospitalization, however, I have often been fraught with profound guilt over my diagnosis of schizophrenia. . . . I felt that for some people I would be forevermore something of a subhuman creature. I grieved and mourned over my loss for several months. . . . Returning to work as a fellow in a department of psychiatry, I was repeatedly in contact with psychiatrists, psychologists, and other mental health

professionals. Quite frequently amidst such contacts there were derogatory and slanderous remarks of persons labeled as schizophrenic. Dismayed, I soon had repeated dreams in which I had a brain tumor, dreams that were not in the least bit frightening to me. Having an organic disorder seemed far easier to live with then—preferable to experiencing the full psychological impact of this label of

Then his hearing began to fail and he became afraid that his house was going to be broken into and all his things stolen. He thought his family was after his money and wanted to get rid of him. As a result, he barricaded himself in his house and refused to see anyone. He was finally hospitalized and given antipsychotic drugs. As a result, his hostile, angry behavior decreased but his delusional beliefs were unchanged.

Stress caused by environmental changes can also bring on a temporary episode of paranoid thinking. For example, immigrants experience paranoid disturbances at a much higher rate than native-born citizens. The move to any new place, especially one in which people feel different and perhaps inferior to others, usually produces high levels of stress. The following case shows how not only immigrant status, but any characteristic that makes a person different, can become a vulnerability under stressful conditions.

After being told by his recruiting officer not to report his bedwetting problem during his induction physical, an 18-year-old enuretic male from the rural South enlisted in the military. The other recruits began to tease him unmercifully with the discovery of his secret soon after the beginning of basic training. He began to believe that his recruiting officer and drill instructor were plotting to murder him so that his bedwetting would remain undiscovered by higher authorities. When he was examined, he exhibited hypersensitivity to criticism, paranoid thinking, and ideas of reference. After two months' hospitalization his delusions cleared. On one-year follow-up, although his social contact was minimal and he remained periodically enuretic, he continued to be free of psychotic thinking while he was living and working on his father's farm.

—Adapted from Walker and Brodie, 1985, p. 751

Paranoid delusions usually fall into one of several categories: the feeling of being persecuted by others; unwarranted jealousy and suspicion of sexual unfaithfulness by one's lover or mate; the feeling that another person has fallen in love with one when there is no evidence for this; and delusions of illness when none exists. The following descriptions illustrate some of these types.

T.Y. became suspicious that his wife was having an affair with her obstetrician during her pregnancy. The baby did not resemble the father, but he thought it did look like the obstetrician. T.Y. then threatened to kill the physician. After antipsychotic drugs and psychotherapy, his anger and threats of murder disappeared but he continued to believe the child was not his.

B.Z., an accountant, met a famous writer when the writer came to the accounting firm for advice about his financial planning. Although he was courteous and pleasant, he showed no special attention to her. She became convinced that he was irresistibly attracted to her, and she was soon entirely preoccupied with thoughts about his love and their future life together. Her feelings became so clear that he soon found another accounting firm. Antipsychotic medication was of no help, but after some psychotherapy sessions B.Z. agreed to stop calling the writer and waiting for him in the lobby of his apartment building.

Delusional disorder is rare. It is estimated that it affects only about .03 percent of the population or 3 in every 10,000 people. Although it can occur in young people, it is most likely to appear around ages 40 to 45. Once developed the delusional thinking may remain stable over long periods or it may come and go. Little is known about the causes or the most effective means of treatment of delusional disorder. Antipsychotic medications may be helpful in some crisis situations. Psychotherapy may also be helpful. The most effective way to deal with the delusions seems to be to suggest to the client the ways in which they interfere with his or her goals, rather than attempting to meet them head on. The client can sometimes be taught to recognize and avoid situations that produce or increase the delusions.

schizophrenia. . . . But I continually have a need to ask myself certain questions. Am I now committed to schizophrenia for life? Or is schizophrenia committed to me?

—Anonymous, 1977, p. 4

One frequently asked question is, What happens to people who are diagnosed as schizophrenic? Studies that follow individuals over long periods provide important information about the long-term implications of this diagnosis. However, the definition of schizophrenia has changed over time. Unless we know the particular definition used in the study, the results are hard to interpret. Another drawback of follow-up studies is that, because of their cost, they are often done on the basis of hospital records and the individual is never actually interviewed or personally evaluated. This methodological

problem introduces a good deal of uncertainty—for example, did all the record keepers use the same definition of level of adaptation? Despite all these problems, long-term follow-up studies provide information of interest to researchers, to clinicians, to those who have received a diagnosis of schizophrenia, and to their families. In general schizophrenia is a chronic disease with an outcome that is usually worse than that of other major mental illnesses, yet there are exceptions.

A review of long-term follow-up studies done since the early 1970s showed a consistency across their findings (McGlashan, 1988). These studies covered an average period of ten years since initial diagnosis. The review provided confirmation of the poor long-term outcome for those with a diagnosis of schizophrenia compared to those with other mental illnesses. It also confirmed that the course of schizophrenic illness should not be described as a continuous process of deterioration as some researchers had thought, but rather that the schizophrenic process seemed to bottom out or reach a plateau between five and ten years after the psychosis became apparent. For most of the studies reviewed, the level of recovery achieved five to ten years after the diagnosis was likely to continue unchanged in the future. The studies also showed that the diagnosis of schizophrenia was associated with an increased risk for physical illness, for suicide, and for mortality not associated with either accidents or suicide.

These follow-up studies showed that no treatment was clearly beneficial in promoting improvement. However, the outcomes in the different studies varied greatly. The percent of positive outcomes reported across the studies ranged from 6 to 61 percent. It is important to recognize that many patients recover from an acute schizophrenic episode and function adequately or even at a high level afterwards. Outcome from an episode of schizophrenic disorder can vary from continuous incapacity to recovery of previous level of function. Depending on the viewpoint of the researcher, patients who have regained or nearly returned to their former level of function can be considered to have made a complete recovery or they may be thought of as functioning well but continuing to be at high risk for another episode of the disorder. The important point to recognize is that a substantial number of patients, not just a few unusual cases, do show enough improvement that they no longer currently meet the criteria for a schizophrenic disorder. Some of this variation in outcome seems to be a result of the original characteristics of the sample in each study. Certain factors may make an individual more likely to experience a positive outcome. Table 11–6 shows some of the differences in the follow-up study populations that were associated with positive or negative outcomes.

These long-term follow-up studies have provided important information about predictors of individual outcome. Table 11–7 shows some of these predictors that were found in two or more of the studies. Because the criteria used to diagnose schizophrenia have differed over time, these follow-up studies also provide important information about how the criteria used in the diagnosis are related to outcome. In general, Schneider's first-rank symptoms did not strongly predict poor outcome (Bland & Orn, 1979; Tsuang and others, 1979). The first-rank symptoms used to make a diagnosis of schizophrenic disorder did not remain stable over the follow-up period. In contrast, several types of criteria used in research, some of which were ultimately incorporated into revisions of DSM, showed moderate to strong correlation with poor outcome and were relatively stable over time. These **narrow criteria** exclude many people who would otherwise be given the diagnosis. The presence of such criteria makes it highly likely that a person diagnosed

Table 11–6

Characteristics of Follow-Up Populations Associated with Different Percentages of Positive and Negative Outcome

Predictor	Positive Outcome	Negative Outcome
Length of illness	Shorter (less than 6–12 months)	Longer (more than 6–12 months)
Age at onset of illness	Young	Older
Type of residential community	Rural	Urban
Gender	Female	Male
Premorbid function	Good	Poor
Response to antipsychotic medication	Good	Poor
Diagnosis subtype	Paranoid subtypes	Other subtypes

SOURCE: Compiled from McGlashan, 1988, p. 535

Table 11–7
Patient Characteristics that Determined Outcome of Schizophrenia in Two or More Follow-Up Studies

Patient Predictor Characteristics	Value or Direction Associated with Better Outcome
GENETICS	
Family history of affective disorder	Present
Family history of schizophrenia	Absent
PREMORBID	
Schizoid personality	Absent
Loner	Absent
Married	Ever
Skills & interests	Present
Work functioning	Better
IQ	Higher
ILLNESS ONSET	
Acute (<6 months)	Present
Precipitating factors	Present
PSYCHOPATHOLOGY	
Depressive features	Present
Disorganized thought	Absent
Assaultiveness	Absent
Emotional blunting	Absent
Confusion or perplexity	Present
COURSE (BEFORE ADMISSION)	
Duration of prior hospitalizations	Shorter

SOURCE: Adapted from McGlashan, 1988, p. 535

with schizophrenia will experience a long-term negative outcome, while the absence of these criteria also eliminates many people who quite clearly are experiencing a schizophrenic episode. The narrow criteria include only those who have shown symptoms over an extended period of time and who are presumed to have a negative outcome.

The long-term follow-up studies have demonstrated that schizophrenia is not just a single disorder but is probably several disorders that have been grouped together because we do not yet understand the causal factors involved. This variability is evident when we look at patients at first diagnosis and then at follow-up. Some people who appear to have positive prospects for recovery turn out in the long run to develop a chronic and unremitting course of the disease. In contrast, some

patients do well at follow-up who appeared very severely affected at the time of their initial diagnosis.

Until more is known about the causes of schizophrenia, complete records of all symptoms shown by each patient should be obtained in addition to the diagnosis. Such records should include not only those symptoms related to the schizophrenic diagnosis, but also others that appear unrelated. Record-keeping like this allows many of those studied who were diagnosed using older systems to be rediagnosed on the basis of their original hospital records; thus, meaningful long-term follow-ups are possible.

One good example of the usefulness of this approach is the long-term study done of patients in a hospital in Vermont (Harding and others, 1987*a*, 1987*b*). In this study, long-term hospitalized patients

who had participated in a comprehensive rehabilitation program and been deinstitutionalized 20 to 30 years earlier were rediagnosed from their records. Those who met the DSM-III criteria for schizophrenia were traced and they or their families were interviewed. Between half and two-thirds of these individuals had recovered or were significantly improved. Figure 11–7 shows how many were functioning at least fairly well.

Although many of these people had made a poor adjustment for at least five years after the rehabilitation program, later on many had returned to their previous level of functioning or had even improved. Some of those who were classified as functioning well apparently did so only because they had learned to live with certain symptoms. Some were employed and had good social relationships but still experienced some hallucinations or delusions. Others, who did not work, nevertheless had developed extensive social networks. Because the patients in this study had been hospitalized for up to 25 years and were middle-aged when the rehabilitation program began, these results suggest that with younger, more recently hospitalized patients, the outcome might be even better.

The Vermont study also suggests that schizophrenia, rather than being unremitting, may be affected by prolonged environmental or psychosocial changes. Such changes may have a positive potential if applied in a supportive manner in the course of a stable and continuous care situation in which the patient is not shunted in and out of the hospital setting many times over a long period.

FIGURE 11–7 Many of the long-term patients followed up 30 years after they had left the hospital had at least a marginally adequate level of functioning. The figure shows the percent of the 168 patients who met or exceeded each criterion.

(Data from Harding and others, 1987a)

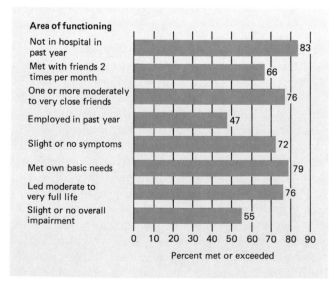

Therapeutic Approaches

Because the cause or causes of schizophrenic disorders are not well understood, clinicians have explored a variety of therapies. Therapies based on the different psychological perspectives are often combined together.

Biological Therapies

Probably the most standard treatment for schizophrenia today is antipsychotic drugs. The introduction of these drugs in the 1950s revolutionized the hospital treatment of psychosis because the drugs decreased the unusual and hard-to-control behaviors of many patients. The number of patients who had to be hospitalized for long periods was correspondingly reduced, although the number of hospitalizations per patient increased because an in-and-out pattern of hospital stays developed.

Although therapy with antipsychotic drugs is the most usual treatment for schizophrenia, there are no good predictors of which type of drug will be most effective during a psychotic episode. Clinicians, therefore, usually must implement what is essentially a trial-and-error approach to find the most beneficial drug for a particular patient. It is necessary to try a new drug for several weeks to determine if it will be helpful, so this method is problematic. Another serious drawback for the use of most antipsychotic drugs is the potentially irreversible damage to the nervous system that occasionally occurs as a result of their overuse. This damage usually appears in the form of **tardive dyskinesia,** or involuntary movements of the mouth, lips, tongue, legs, or body. The development of tardive dyskinesia is generally related to length of treatment and the amount of drugs given, and the risk seems to increase with age. At present there is no way to identify people who are at special risk for other factors. About 10 to 20 percent of patients in mental hospitals and 40 percent of chronically ill hospitalized and nonhospitalized schizophrenic patients show signs of tardive dyskinesia linked with drug treatment (Keck and others, 1989). Because antipsychotic drugs are sometimes given inappropriately or used for too long a time, the risk of these side effects is unnecessarily high for some patients. In 1985, the American Psychiatric Association issued a warning about the need for "cautious use" of antipsychotic drugs. Emphasis has been given to determining the lowest effective dose and the drugs with the least side effects.

For those with schizophrenic disorder antipsychotic medications available today do not offer a cure, but they are often effective in reducing acute psychotic symptoms. For some patients, the drugs do appear to

suppress ongoing psychotic behaviors but they may not prevent a new episode or relapse. Not all schizophrenic patients are helped by these drugs and some who receive them may deteriorate in their psychosocial functioning as a result (Awad, 1989). Even for those who benefit in some ways from antipsychotic drugs, medication does not affect negative symptoms of apathy and withdrawal (Carpenter and others, 1985).

In general, those who do improve as a result of drug therapy are likely to remain on a drug program after being discharged from the hospital in the hope that continuing medication for a few years after the first episode of schizophrenia may reduce relapses. One important problem with the use of antipsychotic drugs for nonhospitalized patients is noncompliance, the irregular or unreliable use of the antipsychotic drugs as directed by the physician. As many as half of all those for whom antipsychotic drug treatment is prescribed are noncompliant (Weiner and others, 1989). They may discontinue the drug because of its unpleasant side effects, because they refuse to accept the fact that it is necessary to take medicine when they no longer have symptoms, or simply because they forget. Socially isolated patients with a poor educational background are at an especially high risk for noncompliance. However, even of those who respond to antipsychotic drugs, and continue to use them, at least half will relapse or experience another psychotic episode within two years. Those who do not relapse and who make a good recovery are not likely to continue to use antipsychotic medication over a long period. In one study, most of those who appeared to have made a complete recovery (17 percent of the total group) were not using medication when contacted five years later. Those who were continuing to use it were less well functioning and were also likely to have experienced periodic relapses (Carone and others, 1991).

A significant percent of those with psychotic symptoms do not respond to the typical antipsychotic drugs, so that for them, other treatment approaches must be made. One approach has been to combine these drugs with antidepressants. Some patients have responded well to a combination of an antipsychotic drug with fluoxetine (Prozac), a new-generation antidepressant that was discussed in Chapter 10. Another approach to these patients who do not respond to traditional antipsychotic drugs has been to use the drug clozapine (Clozaril). This drug has been found to provide some improvement in about two-thirds of patients who had not responded to treatment with other antipsychotic drugs. It also has the benefit of not being linked to tardive dyskinesia.

Clozapine was developed in 1972, but its use was delayed because it was found to cause bone marrow failure and death in some patients (Terkelsen & Grosser, 1990). Now that this risk has been recognized, it can be reduced if physicians who prescribe clozapine carefully monitor their patients. Although the apparent effectiveness of clozapine, and the reduced risk if weekly blood samples are checked, suggests its widespread use, the high cost of treatment has created another type of controversy concerning the use of this drug. Most of the patients who might be helped by the drug have already exhausted any medical insurance they might have had and because of the severity of their schizophrenic disorder have no jobs or money to pay for treatment. Because of the patient management costs that go with the use of the drug, a year's treatment may cost as much as $9,000. It has been estimated that to care for those who might improve with this treatment might cost from 1.2 to 1.7 billion dollars annually in public funds. The ethical and financial issues involved in the use of clozapine have yet to be completely resolved.

Psychodynamic Therapies

In general, the results of psychotherapy with schizophrenics have not been impressive. Studies comparing the results of psychotherapy with those of drug therapies have indicated that when each is used alone, drug therapy is more effective than psychotherapy in shortening the hospital stay and in preventing readmissions. However, when combined with drug therapy, psychologically based therapies that are not psychodynamic in nature, such as supportive therapy, social skills training, and some types of family therapy, may help prevent a return to the hospital. These are discussed in more detail later in the chapter.

Only a few articles are currently published each year on psychodynamic treatment of schizophrenia and some researchers have suggested that because of scarce resources for research, no new studies comparing this form of treatment to others are appropriate (Mueser & Berenbaum, 1990). One reason for psychotherapy's lack of success may be that psychodynamically oriented therapy provides too much stimulation for some patients, especially chronic patients. These people need help in focusing their attention on practical skills such as learning more appropriate techniques of social interaction and skills related to everyday living and self-management. Psychotherapy may make it harder for patients with a schizophrenic disorder to maintain the cognitive control necessary for these tasks by further diminishing their fragile concept of self versus the environment.

Behavioral Therapy

It is generally recognized that many chronic schizophrenic patients are deficient in social skills. Many have

had this problem throughout life, while others are not prepared to be self-sufficient after a period of acute illness and hospitalization. *Social skills training*, based on social learning theory, is often an effective way to improve quality of life outside the hospital and to decrease the chances of rehospitalization (Morrison & Wixted, 1989).

Just as it is applied to mood disorders (see Chapter 10), social skills training for schizophrenics includes modeling, role playing, and real-life practice that is focused on teaching new, more adaptive interpersonal behavior. The training may initially focus on very basic components of social skills, such as voice volume and pitch, eye contact, and turn-taking. Later, or with people whose basic skills remain adequate, the therapy may be directed toward more complex behaviors. Even these are broken down into simpler components. As an example, Table 11–8 shows how the behavioral skills for carrying on an ordinary conversation might be divided for training purposes. Other skills, such as assertiveness or on the job skills can be treated in the same way.

Social skills training leads to significant improvements in the social behavior of those with impairments from schizophrenic disorder and also has a positive effect on their self-perceptions. In the few studies that provide follow-up data, it appeared that the differences in behavior between patients in the trained and untrained groups increased as time went on (Benton & Schroeder, 1990). These studies also suggest that social skills training may be related to earlier release from the hospital and a smaller likelihood of relapse.

Table 11–8
Behavior Skills Necessary for a Conversation

The teaching of these skills can be useful in therapy with patients with mood or personality disorders as well as those with schizophrenic disorders. However, for many patients with schizophrenia the training must initially focus on more basic, lower level skills than for the other diagnostic groups.

Initiating conversations
 Initiating a brief conversation with an acquaintance
 Initiating a brief conversation with a stranger
 Social telephone calls
Maintaining conversations
 Asking questions
 Providing information
 Social reinforcement
 Social perception
Ending conversations
 Timing
 How to break off
 Good-byes
 Judging when the partner wants to leave

SOURCE: Morrison and Wixted, 1989, p. 243

In addition to poor social skills, chronic patients are likely to have inadequate self-care skills. They are often poorly groomed, fail to wash regularly, have poor table manners, and are unable to use public transportation, manage their money, or prepare meals. Behavioral-training methods can also focus on the improvement of these skills. Successful transition for patients from the hospital to the community is predicted better by these skills than by the characteristics of behavior at or during hospitalization (Presly and others, 1982).

Ongoing Therapeutic Care

For many patients, the use of antipsychotic drugs has shortened their first hospital stay by reducing the period during which their psychotic symptoms are most evident. Reducing hospital stays has some very positive effects, since just being hospitalized for a long period, even in the best of institutions, can have negative effects on a person's coping abilities. For that reason, as well as cost factors and concerns about patient rights, increased emphasis has been placed on short hospital stays, mainly to begin and assess drug treatment, followed by discharge to aftercare in the community.

Many patients are repeatedly treated by crisis teams that have the ability to intervene in acute psychosis in the emergency room. While this practice may provide an alternative to hospitalization, many of the follow-up studies have shown that people with a schizophrenic disorder do best when they experience continuity of care over a long period. The case of Dennis, who very likely had been treated in the emergency room on a number of past occasions, illustrates the tragedies that can occur as a function of lack of continuity of care.

Dennis was apprehended by police inside a fast-food restaurant. He had been screaming and throwing tomatoes from the salad bar after he was unable to pay for his order and was asked to leave. The police officers could not calm him, and they felt he was talking in a confusing way about being followed and tortured. After being seen in an emergency room, Dennis was admitted to a public mental hospital. His delusions and auditory hallucinations seemed to respond to medication, and he became cooperative in talking about himself and his treatment history. The hospital staff learned that he had no home or job, but they saw no need to contact his family in California. He was discharged with a prescription, an address for a city shelter, and an appointment slip indicating a time the following week that someone at a

nearby clinic could see him. A nurse loaned him money for bus fare, but he never made any of those contacts. There was no further information about him until one day about five weeks later; police in an eastern city called his parents to say Dennis had been killed the night before when he walked in front of a truck on an interstate highway.

—National Institute of Mental Health, 1991, p. 1

FAMILY EDUCATION The kind of setting to which schizophrenics return after hospitalization and the forms of support available there are crucial to their recovery. One effective source of support and continuity can be the patient's family. If the family's attitude toward the patient is positive, the chances of a relapse are much lower than if the family is judgmental, hostile, and overinvolved (Leff, 1987).

Programs for family information and training have been found to prevent relapse and rehospitalization (Clarkin, 1989). These training programs provide family members with information about the nature of schizophrenia (diagnosis, symptoms, future expectations), its treatment (both medication and family management), and how the family can work together to take into account both the needs of the patient and the needs of the rest of the family. In some education programs, the patient participates in some or all of the sessions, while in others only the other family members take part. Some programs focus on one family at a time, others combine several family groups. Most programs begin by discussing what the diagnosis means, and stress that it is a means of communication rather than a condemnation of the affected person. The therapist might next try to dispel common myths about schizophrenia, such as the idea of split personality. Family members also find it helpful to know about the prevalence of schizophrenia so that they realize they are not alone in their frustration and difficulties.

One aspect of many of these programs that seems especially helpful is a detailed discussion of the common symptoms of schizophrenia such as thought disorder, delusions, hallucinations, and withdrawal, so that family members can understand what the patient is experiencing. The therapist tries to personalize this material, either by having the patient and the family talk about these symptoms and asking the patient to describe those that he or she has experienced, or by using autobiographical accounts similar to the quotations presented throughout this chapter.

Families also receive an explanation of what is known about the psychobiology of schizophrenia to help them understand the underlying mechanisms of the symptoms. Since one of the major goals of these programs is to decrease the feelings of guilt of the family that their behavior in some way caused the illness, most programs stress schizophrenia's genetic aspects (see Box 11–2 on page 346).

Programs are also likely to stress environmental factors, in the sense that schizophrenic disorder is a condition responsive to stress. The role of the family in managing the stress the patient experiences is emphasized as a way of possibly improving the course of the illness and making relapse less likely. Finally, and perhaps most importantly, family members are given guidelines about how to cope with living with someone with a schizophrenic disorder. Such guidelines might include constructive ways to handle guilt, embarrassment, frustration, and anger. Family members also learn why behavioral tactics that they might be likely to employ may not work, and receive instruction about how to keep the home atmosphere low-keyed, not overstimulating, and adequately structured.

MILIEU THERAPY Because many patients may not have a family to return to, other kinds of support programs also need to be provided. These include halfway houses or group homes, day-care facilities, and mental health clinics that provide both treatment and practical help. Some of these supports may be transitional; they help the discharged patient readjust to life in the community. Others are used to help a person who is functioning at a low level stay out of the hospital. Most support programs help people maintain the same level of adaptive behavior they had at the time of their hospital discharge, but they do not increase their level of performance. Despite their effectiveness at preventing relapse, good aftercare programs and sheltered living accommodations are in very short supply.

A number of types of therapeutic homelike environments in the community have been shown to be successful in preventing relapse in patients. These residential environments are usually developed around the idea of milieu therapy. **Milieu therapy** refers to providing a therapeutic environment on the part of all those involved with the patient. In a properly functioning mental health system, such residential treatment facilities—in combination with crisis teams—should be able to prevent much of the need for the traditional psychiatric hospital (Mosher, 1989). Table 11–9 describes the important characteristics of the milieu approach both for those experiencing an initial episode or an acute flare-up and for those who are chronic patients likely to remain in a protected setting for a long period. Milieu therapy has several central functions. The sheltered setting provides support and protection for the person as well as structure and containment. At the same time it provides opportunities for socialization and for validation of the symptoms experienced as part of a schizophrenic disorder. Those

BOX 11–2 **Lessening a Family's Guilt over Schizophrenia**

Donna Lee and her twin sons, Malcolm and Michael, are participants in a twin study at the National Institute of Mental Health. Malcolm is affected with schizophrenia while Michael is normal. The 25-year-old twins and their mother traveled from their home in Canada to Washington, D.C., for five days of testing that included MRI scans and neuropsychological exams. The study will eventually include 60 pairs of identical twins, 30 pairs in which one twin is healthy and one has schizophrenia, 20 pairs in which both twins have schizophrenia, and 10 pairs of healthy twins who will serve as controls.

Donna and Michael described some of their feelings when they first learned that Malcolm had been diagnosed with a schizophrenic disorder.

When Malcolm was first hospitalized, Donna said, "I was taken into a room, told he has schizophrenia, and asked if I had any questions. Well, you go into a total state of shock. And nobody sat there and explained exactly what schizophrenia is."

Relatives should receive a thorough explanation of the illness after they've recovered from the initial shock, because at that point, she said, "you're really not hearing anything—all you're hearing is that one word and you can't think of anything else." . . .

*"Don't blame the families,"
Michael said adamantly, emphasizing the "psychological*

and emotional damage" such an approach causes. "You're making a bad situation terrible." His mother agreed, adding that many relatives automatically blame themselves anyway. "I didn't know anything about schizophrenia and I blamed myself totally and thoroughly. . . . I sort of let Malcolm walk all over me once I found out what was wrong with him because . . . I thought, I've done this to him."

In Washington the Lees spoke openly about their experiences with mental illness. But at home, Michael said, "I don't really talk about it at all. If I have to say anything, I just say that [Malcolm] has a brain disease."

"I've got relatives that I haven't even gotten in touch with," Donna said, "because I know . . . they have the general view that it's caused by your being a bad parent . . . and also they wouldn't want Malcolm near them."

She added that she's "never even written" to one of her sisters. "She probably knows, but I can't . . . talk to her." Donna's voice trailed off. "We were very close before it happened."

"It's really helped all of us in our family, coming here," Donna commented. Learning that schizophrenia has a biological basis "made me feel better, made my ex-husband feel better. Even my youngest son is starting to accept it now. And it's made me

feel easier with Malcolm to realize that this is just an illness."

Both Donna and Michael Lee had experienced many frustrations in trying to deal with Malcolm after his disorder became apparent, but they were also aware of how much more difficult it had been for him than for them.

"No matter what any of us has gone through, Malcolm has gone through ten times worse," said his mother. He's "tried to commit suicide I don't know how many times since he found out about [his diagnosis]. Because when you think you're different and people avoid you and some are even afraid of you . . . what kind of life have you got to look forward to?"

Still, Michael observed that his twin recently obtained his high school equivalency. ". . . [H]e's doing better than some people who aren't plagued with mental disease."

—Adapted from *Psychiatric News*, March 17, 1989, pp. 2, 34

The experience of the Lees shows the importance of helping family members understand that there are biological causes of schizophrenia in order to avoid needless and crippling guilt. It illustrates how this knowledge can aid families to deal more effectively with the problems that a schizophrenic disorder creates and thus help both the person with the disorder and themselves.

working in the milieu setting validate affected persons' feelings by letting them know their delusions or hallucinations are quite real experiences. What they are, how they make the person feel, and what they mean can all be discussed.

Two examples of milieu intervention are the **surrogate parent model** and **day** or **partial hospitalization.** In a project that used the surrogate parent model, older couples who had extra space in their homes were

recruited through local advertising (Polack and others, 1979). These couples were carefully screened; those who had been successful parents to their own children and who had some previous record of community service were preferred. They were paid to keep rooms available in their homes to accept patients quickly when a placement was needed. Most of the patients stayed with them for two or three weeks and then severed their ties gradually, often returning for meals or visits over a long

Table 11-9

Characteristics of Effective Environments for Acute and Chronic Schizophrenic Disorder

For Those with Acute Psychosis

1. Small (6–10 patients) unit
2. High staff-to-patient ratio
3. High interaction of staff and patients
4. Involvement of both staff and patients in decisions
5. Emphasis on autonomy of patients
6. Focus on practical problems (e.g., living arrangements, money)
7. Positive expectations for and by patients
8. Minimal bureaucratic structure

For Those with Chronic Psychosis

1. Emphasis on clearly defined, specific behaviors requiring change
2. Action-, not explanation-oriented, structured program
3. Reasonable, positive, progressive, practical expectations with increasing patient responsibility
4. Continuation of residential treatment program into real community settings
5. Continuity of persons working with patients
6. Extensive use of groups to facilitate socialization and network building

SOURCE: Adapted from Mosher & Gunderson (1979); Paul (1969); Paul and Lentz (1977).

period. All patients were treated with antipsychotic drugs during their stay and crisis help was available if needed. The program was most successful with young psychotic patients for whom family intervention in their own homes had not been helpful.

Day or partial hospitalization is not a new idea. It was originally tested as an alternative to full long-term hospitalization. Currently, however, since long-term hospitalization for patients with schizophrenic disorder is relatively rare, day hospitals have been studied as alternatives to other kinds of outpatient care and generally have been found to be superior (Linn, 1989).

Several types of day hospitals have been tried. The **intensive care partial hospital** provides many of the same services that inpatient hospital units provide and is intended for short patient stays. The **chronic care model** has much lower expectations for symptom and behavioral change and no expected length of stay. This type of facility focuses on a practical approach and on provision of level of stimulation that can be equated with the patient's needs. This is important because too much stimulation can result in a high level of arousal which in turn leads to patient withdrawal. If the situation is one in

which the patient cannot withdraw, delusions or odd behaviors are likely to increase. The **rehabilitation model** serves to meet patient needs somewhere between the other two models. The rehabilitation milieu is intended to help patients who have severe social impairments and problems in vocational functioning. Although this approach takes into account the importance of not overstimulating the patients, it does not allow a great deal of tolerance of disruptive symptoms. Although the treatment is intended to be of limited length, the time allowed is considerably longer than in acute, emergency hospitalization.

Although there have been some encouraging results from day or partial hospital programs, they have not yet been tested sufficiently. One problem that has not been adequately dealt with is the matching of the type of patient to the type of program (Linn, 1989). This fit is important in order to avoid overstimulating patients with severe levels of schizophrenic disorder and thus worsening their symptoms.

Probably the biggest problem in establishing milieu therapy settings is that of funding. Although many research programs have demonstrated that this approach can be successful, successful milieu projects usually go out of existence when their special research funding is no longer available. Only when reimbursement for this type of treatment is included in insurance coverage will those with schizophrenic disorder have available the variety of treatment approaches that seem to produce long-term improvement and protection from the environmental stresses that may make relapse more likely (Mosher, 1989).

A Comprehensive Approach

Although several approaches to treatment of schizophrenia—antipsychotic drugs, behavioral skills training, and changes in the person's living environment and personal relationships—all can have positive effects on decreasing symptoms and helping the person function at a higher level, what is needed for most of those affected by a schizophrenic disorder is a comprehensive program that provides a continuity of care over time. The important elements of such a comprehensive program are listed in Table 11–10.

Although the focus on deinstitutionalization and care in the person's home community instead of long-term hospitalization in large state psychiatric hospitals was motivated by good intentions, the result has been that most people do not have any continuity of care. One of the results of this situation is that these patients become part of a "revolving door syndrome." They often have as many as three hospital admissions per year in addition to a large number of emergency room visits

Table 11–10

A Comprehensive Care Program Appropriate for Most People with Schizophrenic Disorder

Treatment
 Medication
 Family therapy
 Social skills training
 Medical care
 Crisis intervention
Rehabilitation
 Housekeeping
 Nutrition and hygiene
 Job training
 Transportation

Social services
 Income support
 Housing
 Social support
 Recreation
Continuity of care
 Active coordination of
 above services

SOURCE: Bellack, 1989, p. 7

(Bellack, 1989). Only a small number are effectively reintegrated as part of the community. More than half are unable to take care of the ordinary tasks of daily living, manage their own money, or take their medication as prescribed. They occupy inadequate housing, in general have poor health care, and are easy targets for criminal victimization. The case of Dennis illustrates what may result when poorly functioning people are not provided with continuity of care.

One approach that would serve these individuals better would be to regard and treat schizophrenia as a chronic condition in the same way that other chronic diseases such as diabetes or kidney failure are treated. Patients would benefit from a comprehensive program of long-term care so that they experience some continuity in caregivers and a variety of available coordinated services.

Chapter Summary

THE IMPACT OF SCHIZOPHRENIC DISORDERS

A **psychosis** is a disorder that involves alterations in perception, thought, or consciousness. **Schizophrenic disorders** are a subgroup of the psychoses and the group that has the most severe impact both on people's lives and on the mental health system.

DIAGNOSTIC CRITERIA

The diagnosis of schizophrenic disorder requires that the person show changes to a clearly less satisfactory level of functioning in one or more major areas of life and also that he or she experience at least a one-month period when active psychosis is present as shown by bizarre delusions, prominent hallucinations, and other clear signs of disorganized, strange behavior. **Schizophreniform disorder** has the same types of behavioral characteristics, but they have not lasted long enough to meet the schizophrenic disorder criteria. **Schizoaffective disorder** requires that symptoms of both schizophrenia and mood disorder be present together for a considerable period of time. **Schizotypal personality disorder** (see Chapter 9) has long-lasting symptoms including excessive social anxiety, odd beliefs and perceptual experiences, odd behavior and speech, suspiciousness, and lack of close friends.

CHARACTERISTICS OF SCHIZOPHRENIC DISORDERS

Delusions A **delusion** is a faulty interpretation of reality that cannot be shaken by contrary evidence. Although delusions can occur in other disorders, certain types of delusions occur more often in schizophrenia.

Disordered Thinking Because schizophrenia is typified by unusual structure or organization of thoughts, it is often referred to as a **formal-thought disorder**. Types of disordered thought include **loosening of associations, autistic thinking,** and **poverty of content.**

Hallucinations **Hallucinations,** projections of internal impulses and experiences onto perceptions in the external world, account for most of the difficulties in perception experienced by a person with schizophrenia. Hallucinations can be associated with any of the senses, but are most commonly visual or auditory.

Lack of Appropriate Emotion After the acute psychotic phase has passed, people with a schizophrenic disorder often show emotional flatness or lack of emotional responsiveness and general apathy. Sometimes the person's emotional responses seem inappropriate, perhaps because they are associated with hallucinations and delusions of which the observer is unaware.

Unclear Boundaries of the Self In schizophrenia, the normal feelings of being a separate person and of being in control of one's own behavior are missing. This is sometimes referred to as **loss of ego boundaries.**

Unpredictable Motor Behavior Motor activity may be unpredictable, ranging from episodes of wild aggression to long periods of motionlessness in a single posture.

Change in Motivational Level Either before or after the initial psychotic phase, a person with a schizophrenic disorder is likely to show a profound lack of motivation.

Impaired Interpersonal Functioning Because those with schizophrenic disorder are likely to be caught up in fantasies, they often are withdrawn and socially detached. They are also likely to ignore social conventions and as a result make others uncomfortable in social situations.

Attention Difficulties Many of the behaviors typical of those with a schizophrenic disorder can be summarized under problems of attention. These difficulties may be related to hallucinations as well as to extreme anxiety and a fragmented sense of self.

A HISTORICAL VIEW OF SCHIZOPHRENIC DISORDERS

Dementia Praecox Kraepelin defined **dementia praecox** as an irreversible organic deterioration that typically began in adolescence. He disregarded the psychological aspects of the disorder.

The Schizophrenias Bleuler used the term **"the schizophrenias"** because he believed that the symptoms might represent a group of disorders with different causes and outcomes.

First-Rank Symptoms Schneider developed a series of **first-rank** and **second-rank symptoms** in an effort to make diagnosis more reliable. First-rank symptoms were related to hallucinations and delusions and are now referred to as positive symptoms.

European and American Definitions At present, a diagnosis of schizophrenia made in Europe only requires the presence of clear psychotic symptoms. Practitioners in the United States use a much narrower diagnosis.

Positive and Negative Symptoms **Positive symptoms** include hallucinations, delusions, bizarre behavior, and disordered thinking. **Negative symptoms** reflect behavioral deficits in amount and content of speech, flattened affect, apathy, seclusiveness, and problems of attention. Researchers currently disagree about the relationship of positive and negative symptoms and their prognostic value.

TYPES OF SCHIZOPHRENIA

Traditional and Current DSM Subtypes Kraepelin described three subtypes—paranoid, hebephrenic, and catatonic. Bleuler added a fourth subtype, simple schizophrenia. Current DSM categories include **paranoid, disorganized, catatonic,** and residual (no longer showing prominent psychotic features). People formerly given the diagnosis of simple schizophrenia or borderline schizophrenia are now categorized as *schizotypal personality disorder.*

Schizophrenic Spectrum Disorders Because families of schizophrenic patients often include other members who show a variety of unusual behaviors or styles of thinking, the idea of **schizophrenic spectrum disorders** developed. These include some personality disorders as well as other psychotic disorders that involve disordered affect.

OUTCOME INDICATORS AND LONG-TERM STUDIES

Findings from long-term studies suggest that some people affected by schizophrenia do fully recover, but that the percentage is low. Many others improve greatly but may not reach their former level of adjustment. Even those who do recover are considered to be vulnerable to another episode.

Long-term studies consistently show that a poor long-term outcome is more likely in schizophrenia than in other types of mental illness. The studies also show that five to ten years after the diagnosis of schizophrenic disorder, most people's degree of recovery tends to stabilize and continue unchanged in the future. The studies also show that no one treatment is clearly beneficial for everyone.

THERAPEUTIC APPROACHES

Biological Therapies The most common treatment for schizophrenia at present is antipsychotic drugs. These do not produce a cure, but instead reduce acute psychotic symptoms. The drugs do not help all patients and may not prevent a relapse for those they do help. To be effective, the drugs must be taken consistently. However, many patients stop taking their medication when they are not under close supervision. For those not helped by antipsychotic drugs, these drugs are sometimes combined with antidepressants. A problem related to antipsychotic drug treatment is the risk of **tardive dyskinesia,** a condition in which a person experiences involuntary facial and body movements.

Psychodynamic Therapies Most researchers believe psychodynamic therapies are not suitable for treating schizophrenic disorder, perhaps because they provide too much stimulation for the patients.

Behavioral Therapy Social skills training, sometimes at a very basic level, may be helpful in keeping the person in the community once the acute psychotic phase of the disorder is over or is controlled by antipsychotic drugs.

Ongoing Therapeutic Care Programs for family intervention and training have been found to prevent relapse and rehospitalization. The programs provide information about schizophrenia and the treatment used, help the family in understanding the symptoms and the effect of these on the patient, and offer the family support in helping the patient on his or her return home while not feeling overburdened with that person's needs. **Milieu therapy** means the contribution to the provision of a therapeutic environment by all those in contact with the patient. Two examples of milieu interventions that have been used with some success are the **surrogate parent model** and **day** or **partial hospitalization.**

A Comprehensive Approach Most of those affected by schizophrenia could benefit from a combined approach that includes antipsychotic drugs, behavioral skills training, and efforts to improve the living environment and the patient's personal relationships. Deinstitutionalization has resulted in a fragmented approach to treatment in which many patients move in and out of the hospital with great frequency.

Causes and Markers
of Schizophrenia

C H A P T E R 1 2

Genetic Factors
Family Studies
Twin Studies
Adoption Studies
A Genetic Model
Genetic Counseling

Vulnerability and Stress Factors

High-Risk Studies and the Search for Markers

Understanding the Schizophrenic Process
Structural Abnormalities in the Brain
Biochemical Abnormalities in the Brain
Psychophysiological Abnormalities
Attention Problems
Disordered Thinking
Language Use Abnormalities

Family Relationships
Family Communication Deviance
Expressed Emotion
Parental Affective Style

The Role of the Community

Chapter Summary

Joan Miró, *Pitre Rose*, 1974, Jane Kahan Gallery, New York.

The cause of schizophrenic disorders is not known, although it seems likely that schizophrenia is produced by the interaction of vulnerability factors with some kind of environmental stress. This stress may come from disturbed family relationships, but it might also come from many other sources.

Schizophrenic disorders have been investigated from many points of view. Experimental manipulation and observational research have both been used in attempts to determine how people who exhibit schizophrenic behavior differ from those who do not. Such factors as heredity, family structure, and biochemistry have been examined. Recently, attempts have been made to find out why some people who have a hereditary risk of schizophrenia develop it while others do not. Such research is referred to as high-risk studies. *Much current work in these high-risk studies is focused on* markers *or characteristics that may predict a person's vulnerability to schizophrenic disorders. If these markers can be identified, they may provide clues to how the disorders come about and how they can be prevented.*

Genetic Factors

Research suggests that there is a genetic factor in schizophrenia. The importance of genetic factors in the development of schizophrenic disorders has emerged from the results of many family, twin, and adoption studies conducted over at least 75 years. These studies have shown that the risk of development of a schizophrenic disorder is correlated with the closeness of genetic relationship, or the percentage of genes that each relative has in common with the **index case**, as the person under study is often called. Genetic overlap with the index case ranges from 100 percent for identical twins

to 12.5 percent for great-grandchildren, first cousins, and great nieces and nephews.

Figure 12–1, based on a large number of family and twin studies, shows the average risk for developing schizophrenia when family members with different degrees of relationship have been diagnosed with the disorder. The lifetime risk of developing schizophrenia correlates quite well with the proportion of genes shared with an affected family member (Gottesman, 1991). In other words, the more genes two people have in common, the higher the risk. However, the fact that even for identical twins, who have identical genes, the risk is only about 50 percent, suggests other factors at work besides genetics. Later in this chapter we will discuss the implications of this finding from identical twin studies. But first we will present a description of how family, twin, and adoption studies are carried out. This description should illuminate the research tactics used to try to disentangle genetic and environmental aspects of family relationships, and to get the kind of information shown in Figure 12–1.

Family Studies

A common first step in studying the genetics of any disorder is to compare prevalence in relatives of affected individuals with prevalence in the general population. Systematic family studies were started early in this century and have continued ever since. A common way to conduct a family study is to construct a comprehensive diagram of a family tree going back several generations. Then all those people in this family tree who showed symptoms of any disorder are identified. In this way it is possible to see whether a disorder seems to occur in any particular pattern throughout the generations. This pattern can then be matched with predictions based on theoretical models. A family tree to study the occurrence of Fragile X disorder, a condition discussed later in this text, is shown in Chapter 16.

ASSORTATIVE MATING One factor that may affect the risk for schizophrenia or other disorders is **assortative mating.** This term refers to the tendency for people to mate with others who are more similar to them than would be the case if their choices were random. Assortative mating occurs for physical traits, psychological traits, and behavior disorders. The spouses of schizophrenic individuals are more likely than members of the general public to be diagnosed as schizophrenic. Their children may get "double doses" of genes associated with disordered behaviors.

Although families with both a schizophrenic mother and father are rare, at least five studies of the adult offspring of two schizophrenic parents have been carried out (Gottesman, 1991). The results of all these studies are similar. In each, about one-third of the children of these parents had developed a schizophrenic disorder. Because some of the children studied were not yet old enough to have passed through the entire period of risk for developing schizophrenia, the estimated lifetime maximum risk for the group as a whole was 46 percent. This risk is much higher than the 17 percent lifetime risk of developing schizophrenic disorder for children with only one parent affected by schizophrenia. The researchers in these studies also found that even the children of these marriages who did not develop schizophrenia had a considerably higher risk of having another psychiatric diagnosis than does the average child. However, the studies also were in agreement about another,

FIGURE 12–1 The degree of risk of developing a schizophrenic disorder correlates highly with the degree of genetic relationship with someone who has that disorder. These higher risks contrast with the general population risk of 1 percent. The column on the left shows the degree of relationship and the length of the bar indicates the lifetime percentage of risk of developing schizophrenia.

(From *Schizophrenia Genesis: The Origins of Madness* by Irving I. Gottesman. Copyright © 1991 by I.I. Gottesman. Reprinted with permission of W.H. Freeman and Company)

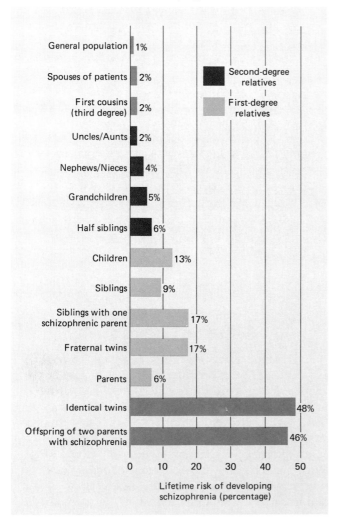

and perhaps quite surprising, finding. About one-quarter of the children in these families showed no disordered behavior. This finding is startling considering not only their genetic inheritance, but also the likelihood these children had experienced a good deal of stress from living in a family with two schizophrenic parents. Box 12–1 presents accounts of the stress experienced by two daughters who grew up with schizophrenic mothers. Although the daughters describe some positive aspects of these relationships, their accounts make clear the difficulties faced by a child growing up in such a household.

GENETIC SPECIFICITY AND THE SPECTRUM CONCEPT Family studies focus not only on the overall risks for different family relationships but also on exactly how the hereditary mechanisms work. Early in the history of genetic studies of disordered behavior, it was assumed that what people inherited was simply an increased chance of developing some "mental disease." Current knowledge of heredity suggests that various disorders, or at least different groups of disorders, have different genetic causes. This quality is called their **genetic specificity.** In addition to determining specific patterns of heredity for different disorders, family studies provide information about the relationships between schizophrenia and other disorders that may appear in families. If several particular disorders typically occur together in families, this suggests that those disorders may be genetically similar. Such similarity is called the **spectrum concept.**

In spite of the fact that schizophrenia includes many different symptom patterns, the genetic factors seem to have specificity because they do not also increase the risk for major mood disorder or delusional disorder (Gottesman and others, 1987). In addition to this specificity, genetic studies provide some support for the idea of a group of related disorders that may have a common genetic base with schizophrenia. These *schizophrenic spectrum disorders* all include eccentric behavior and disordered and unusual styles of thinking, but they differ in how severely they disrupt a person's functioning. Disorders usually included in the schizophrenic spectrum, in addition to schizophrenia, include schizotypal personality, paranoid personality, and schizoaffective disorders. (Schizoaffective disorders have characteristics of schizophrenia combined at some times with major depression or manic behavior.) Chapter 11 discusses the relationship among these disorders.

In one large study designed to investigate the spectrum concept, the rate of occurrence of mental disorders in relatives of patients who had been hospitalized for schizophrenia was compared with the rate for relatives of surgical patients from the same hospital (Kendler and others, 1985). When family groups were compared, nine percent of the families of schizophrenic patients and less than one percent of the families of surgical patients contained at least one other schizophrenic member. Overall, the relatives of the patients with schizophrenic disorders had higher rates of nonaffective psychosis, especially schizophrenia and schizoaffective disorders. These findings supported the idea of a schizophrenic spectrum of genetically related disorders.

Twin Studies

While family studies can give an overall picture of hereditary risks in schizophrenia and the possible genetic relationships among disorders, twin studies provide a way to focus on the environmental factors that contribute to schizophrenic disorders while keeping the hereditary factors constant. This is possible because identical, or monozygotic (MZ), twins are produced from the same fertilized egg and therefore have identical genetic makeup. Fraternal, or dizygotic (DZ), twins are produced from two fertilized eggs; they have the same genetic relationship as any other siblings.

About a dozen major twin studies have been carried out. All show that MZ twins have a much greater chance of being concordant for schizophrenia than DZ twins do.

As we saw earlier in Figure 12–1, the concordance rate for schizophrenia in MZ twins is only about 50 percent. This finding makes it clear that heredity alone is not enough to produce a schizophrenic disorder, at least in most people. For this reason, researchers are focusing on environmental variables that may interact with inherited predispositions.

One environmental variable that can differ even for identical twins is the environment experienced before birth. One study compared 100 pairs of MZ twins in which one member had schizophrenia and the other did not. The schizophrenic twin was twice as likely to have weighed less at birth than the normal twin (Stabenau & Pollin, 1967). The differences in birth weight might have been due to an *in utero* condition that influenced one twin but not the other. For example, one twin may have suffered mild brain damage that predisposed it to develop schizophrenia. The study also found that the schizophrenic twin was more likely to have had an illness in which the central nervous system was affected.

Twins do not occur frequently in the population, and twins who are adopted at or near birth—so that they grow up in clearly different environments—are extremely rare. This means that twin adoption studies base their conclusions on scanty evidence. Even rarer are pairs of twins reared apart in which at least one twin develops a schizophrenic disorder. One researcher found only nine such pairs in her review of all the twin studies that had been done (Farber, 1983).

In order to put these hereditary factors in perspective, it may help to compare the hereditary risk for schizophrenia with the hereditary risk for other disor-

BOX 12-1 Growing Up with a Mother Who Has a Schizophrenic Disorder

These two accounts written by daughters who spent their early lives with mothers who had a schizophrenic disorder show some of the stresses they experienced. They also show how, despite the mothers' illness, there were positive aspects to the mother–daughter relationship.

In the first excerpt, the mother and daughter shared some warmth and positive moments over their mutual love of music and dance.

My mother is a paranoid schizophrenic. In the past I was afraid to admit it, but now that I've put it down on paper, I'll be able to say it again and again: Mother, schizophrenic, Mother, paranoid, shame, guilt, Mother, crazy, different, Mother, schizophrenia.

I have been teaching inpatient children on the children's ward of Bellevue Psychiatric Hospital in New York City for 13 years, and yet I'm still wary of revealing the nature of my mother's illness. When I tell my friends about my mother, even psychiatrist friends, I regret my openness and worry that they will find me peculiar. . . .

On the outside our house resembled those of our neighbors, but on the inside it was so different that there was no basis of comparison. Our house was a disaster. Everything was a mess. Nothing matched, furniture was

broken, dishes were cracked, and there were coffee rings and cigarette burns clear across our grand piano. I was ashamed of our house. It was impossible to bring friends home. I never knew what my mother might be doing or how she would look.

She was totally unpredictable. At best she was working on a sculpture or practicing the piano, chain smoking and sipping stale coffee, with a dress too ragged to give to charity hanging from her emaciated body. At worst she was screaming at my father, still wearing her nightgown at six o'clock in the evening, a wild look on her face. I was never popular as a youngster, and I blamed my lack of popularity on my mother. . . .

Mother was quite interested in music and ballet, and she took me to every ballet and concert in Kansas City. She always looked terrible when she went out, and more than once she arrived at the theater in her bedroom slippers. I was embarrassed to be seen with her, and before we left home, I would try to convince her to dress properly. She never listened and sometimes became angry, but chic or not, I accompanied her.

I loved music and dance as much as she did. I even gave up Saturday afternoons to stay home with her and listen to the Metropolitan Opera broadcasts,

and I loved her most and felt closest to her sitting in front of a gas fire, feeling her bony arm around my shoulders as we listened to the music together. . . .

When I was in high school, Mother and I shared a room with twin beds. When Mother was lying down, she would start to moan as if she were talking in her sleep. "I can't stand that girl. She's evil; she's a bitch. She's just like her father." I was terrorized, but I dared not move. I felt I had to pretend to be asleep, because I didn't want her to know I was listening. . . .

I used to lie in bed, wishing I were dead, believing that I was the worthless girl she was describing. . . . My oldest brother was the target of the same kinds of insults, and we comforted each other. . . .

—Adapted from Lanquetot, 1984, pp. 467–471

In this second account, after a long period of estrangement, the daughter was finally able to understand that her mother cared about her despite the problems that the symptoms of schizophrenia placed in the way.

The period of time during which my mother began to withdraw and isolate herself from others—from my father, from myself, and from my younger sister— I remember only feeling a sort of desperate

ders. In general, twin studies show that genetic factors are at least as important in the development of schizophrenic disorders as they are in diabetes, hypertension, coronary artery disease, and ulcers, all of which have a strong genetic component.

Adoption Studies

Another way of studying the effects of heredity on the development of schizophrenia is through adoption studies. Adoption studies can give researchers a clearer understanding of the role environment and heredity may play in schizophrenia. There are three basic kinds of adoption studies in research on schizophrenia: those that compare adopted children whose biological parents were diagnosed as schizophrenic with adopted children whose parents did not have this disorder; those that examine the incidence of schizophrenia in the biological and adoptive families of adopted people who became schizophrenic; and those that study the relatively rare individuals who

denial of anything being wrong or out of the ordinary. Unfortunately, my father . . . was in the Navy and he went overseas a lot. It was during these absences that I would come home from the second or third grade to find my mother sitting alone in our living room, the blinds pulled down, the TV and radio off. On the table next to her chair would be a stack of three to five pieces of burnt, butterless toast and she would stare off into space as she crunched her way through the afternoon. She might greet me then as I came in or she might not. I hurried by, trying not to look at her too closely. . . .

I was aware of her paranoia, and I was aware it was not based on facts. She barricaded the back door with an ironing board after locking it at night. She accused the next door neighbor of stealing our clothes off the clothesline and taking our mail out of the mailbox.

Soon no one visited anymore, not the landlord and his wife, who were our personal friends, not the relatives who lived nearby—no one. It was just we two little girls with our mother who was slipping further and further away from us and, more importantly, from reality. . . .

Later on, this woman's mother was periodically hospitalized.

When my mother would return [from the hospital], her memory fogged from the electric shock treatments or coming out of a daze from drugs, . . . things would be mellow for awhile, and then she would wonder where all her jewelry was?! I would patiently remind her of how she threw it over the fence in the backyard, right before she checked into the hospital the last time. She would look confused first, then suspicious, and finally the paranoia would begin to unravel her life again. Some months later, after hurling all the contents of the refrigerator into the dining room or some other sort of frenzied behavior that our fragile family unit just could not handle, she would be taken back to the hospital. Sometimes my father would have to call the police to escort her away!

Finally, when this woman was 13, her parents were divorced and her mother lived elsewhere.

Life went on for all of us. My mother finally stopped spending time in mental hospitals shortly after I graduated from high school. She seemed to stabilize and find her niche somehow. She also remarried. Later she separated from her new husband, tried living with relatives, tried living alone, reunited with her husband, tried employment, even

tried suicide—in short, she began living her life and growing, in her own way, as we all do. She gets an injection once a month now that keeps her from hearing "the voices." She considers this a miracle, and so do I!

For over ten years, the woman's mother called her about once a month.

[She] endured many shallow and resentful conversations on my part. She never complained; she endured patiently. She never judged me, although I was judging her so harshly at that time, for not really being there for me as I was growing up. She always blessed me, was proud of me, and loved me.

Only after her own experience in psychotherapy was this daughter able to understand and accept her mother.

[Now] I have been gifted with the rediscovery of my love for my mother. Words cannot effectively describe the feeling of setting aside the broken heart I have been carrying around within me and nursing for some 30 years now. I love my mother just as she is, and that is exactly the way she has always loved me.

—Adapted from Crosby, 1989, pp. 507–509

have nonschizophrenic biological parents but whose adoptive parents became schizophrenic.

One of the first large adoption studies ever conducted was reported by a group of Danish and American researchers working in Denmark (Rosenthal and others, 1968, 1975). First the researchers searched the government adoption register of the Copenhagen area to find the names of parents who had given up their children to nonfamily members for adoption. Then they searched the official psychiatric register to see if they could find the names of any of those parents. The records of those who were found were rated, and those that clearly fit a strict definition of schizophrenia were selected. The children who had been given up for adoption by these parents became the index cases. The control group consisted of the adopted children whose parents had no psychiatric history. Three of the 39 index cases and none of the 47 controls were diagnosed as definitely schizophrenic. This high rate (8 percent compared to 0 percent) in the index group points to a hereditary factor. The children of

schizophrenic parents also had a higher risk of other schizophrenic spectrum disorders (26 percent compared to 15 percent).

In another kind of adoption study, Kety and his colleagues (1978) took advantage of the comprehensive records kept by the Danish government to locate people who had been adopted and had later become schizophrenic. They compared the frequencies of schizophrenia or other disturbances in the adoptees' biological and adoptive relatives. They also compared these findings with those for relatives of a control group of adoptees who had not been diagnosed as schizophrenic. They found that about twice as many blood relatives as adoptive relatives of schizophrenics had been diagnosed as definitely or possibly schizophrenic. Both rates were higher than those for the control group.

This study also contained an important subsample: half-brothers and half-sisters of the adopted individual who had the same father. Half-siblings share 25 percent of their genes, rather than 50 percent as full siblings do. However, half-siblings with a common father do not share the environment in the uterus before birth, nor do they share the same early mothering experience. These paternal half-brothers and half-sisters were also found to have a greater risk of schizophrenia and schizophrenic spectrum disorders than the control group. This finding gave increased weight to the importance of genetic factors in schizophrenia. Because the DSM definition of schizophrenia has been narrowed or made more restrictive over time, some of the index cases in these studies would not now be classified as schizophrenic; instead they would be considered to fall within one of the schizophrenic spectrum disorders. Nonetheless, once redefined in this way, the schizophrenic index cases and those now defined as spectrum index cases both had many more relatives with schizophrenic spectrum disorders than did the control subjects (Kendler & Gruenberg, 1984).

A third kind of adoption study is called a **cross-fostering study.** Such a study asks whether children whose biological parents are nonschizophrenic but who are reared by a schizophrenic adoptive parent are more likely to become schizophrenic than either of two other groups: children with a schizophrenic biological parent or children with nonschizophrenic heredity who are reared by normal individuals. Wender and others (1974) found that it made no difference in the incidence of schizophrenia of the children whether they were reared by schizophrenic or normal adoptive parents. Almost twice as many children with schizophrenic heredity as children without such heredity became schizophrenic in both types of homes. This study suggests that rearing by a schizophrenic adoptive parent does not increase a nonvulnerable person's chances of developing schizophrenia. As we will see later in the chapter, however, the stress of growing up in a home with a schizophrenic parent may increase the risk of developing schizophrenia in adopted children who are already genetically vulnerable to this disorder.

A Genetic Model

In studies of heredity, predictions based on theoretical models are compared with the observed frequency of occurrence of various characteristics. If the model is a good one, the agreement between prediction and observation should be close. The two major types of models show the transmission of inherited traits by one gene and by more than one gene.

Monogenic models are based on the idea that the genetic transmission that occurs at one locus (the place occupied by a gene pair on a particular chromosome) is all that is necessary to produce a particular characteristic. At any one locus, one gene of the pair may be dominant over the other. That means that the characteristic carried by that dominant gene—say, brown eyes—will be **expressed;** that is, the person will have brown eyes. A recessive trait—for example, blue eyes—will not be expressed unless both members of the gene pair carry the characteristic for blue eyes.

In investigating the genetics of schizophrenia, researchers originally looked for distributions based on a monogenic model, but they did not find them. The number of cases of schizophrenia in relatives of schizophrenics is always less than would be expected by monogenic models. One way of explaining this is to use the concept of **penetrance.** According to this idea, a predicted number of individuals will carry the potential for schizophrenia—they will have the right genetic makeup—but not all of them will become schizophrenic because they are not exposed to significant environmental stress. Another way to explain this difference in predicted and observed frequency is to use the schizophrenic spectrum view to broaden the diagnostic criteria so that relatives of schizophrenics who show related disorders are included.

Polygenic models assume that a number of genes found at specific locations must interact to produce a trait. Many characteristics, including height, weight, and skin color, are thought to be influenced by more than one gene. Some models suggest that a limited number of genes and locations are involved. Other polygenic models, called **multifactorial polygenic models,** do not specify the number of gene loci involved in schizophrenia. Instead, they assume that there are many of them and that they are interchangeable. Genes at all of these loci may have small additive effects on a person's vulnerability to schizophrenia. According to this view, many people have some predisposition to develop schizophrenia. If their predisposition is over a certain threshold, they will develop a schizophrenic disorder; if their liability is

below that threshold, they will not (McGue & Gottesman, 1989). This kind of polygenic model can be expanded to include two different levels of liability. Figure 12–2 illustrates such a model. People to the *right* of the *right-hand* threshold (for severe symptom) would develop a severe form of schizophrenia while those to the *left* of the *left-hand* threshold (for mild symptoms) would not be schizophrenic. Those *between* the two thresholds would develop a mild form of the disorder. Using a complex statistical technique called *path analysis,* this model seems to predict outcome fairly well for several large sets of data that have been collected to date (McGue and others, 1985; Faraone & Tsuang, 1985).

Genetic theorists tend to favor multifactorial polygenic models of heredity over single major locus models, but some combination of the two cannot yet be

FIGURE 12–2 These distributions show the liability of mild and severe disorders within the schizophrenic spectrum for the general population and for relatives of those with mild and severe disorders. If the liability is greater than the threshold, the disorder can be noted. Relatives of those who are severely affected have themselves a greater risk for both mild and severe diagnoses than the relatives of those who are mildly affected.

(Adapted from *Journal of Psychiatric Research,* 21, M. Baron and N. Risch, The spectrum concept of schizophrenia: Evidence for a continuum, Copyright © 1987. Reprinted with permission)

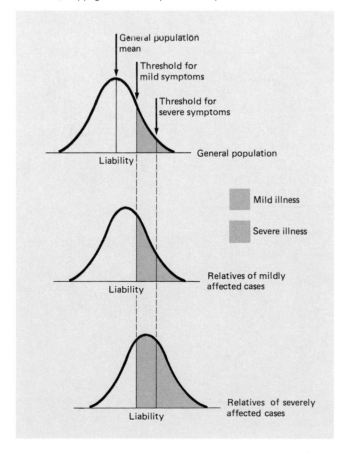

ruled out. The varying results from one study to another make it seem likely that schizophrenic disorders are not all based on the same genetic transmission.

Recent advances in molecular biology and molecular genetic linkage techniques have made it possible to study variations in DNA sequence. This new technology has been used to understand the genetic contributions to various illnesses such as Huntington's disease and muscular dystrophy. Although this technique is a promising one for understanding more about the genetics of schizophrenia, there are many problems. One has to do with how to define exactly what is being studied. For example, should only schizophrenic disorder be studied or should some or all of the associated disorders in the schizophrenic spectrum be included? Another problem is that schizophrenia is thought to be genetically heterogeneous, caused by genes at any of several different locations on the chromosomes.

Several studies have identified gene locations associated with schizophrenia using several generations of family groups in which there was more than one member with a diagnosis of schizophrenia. So far the findings differ. At least two of these studies have identified some abnormality in chromosome 5 (Bassett, 1989; Gurling and others, 1989). These results have not been supported in at least two other studies of family groups (Kaufmann and others, 1989; Kennedy and others, 1989). There are many possible reasons for this disagreement in findings. One is that schizophrenia is genetically heterogeneous. Another is that the techniques for reading the results from this technology are not as yet highly reliable, so that two readings from a blood sample of the same person may not always yield exactly the same result. However, despite its complexity, the techniques of molecular genetic research hold promise for new insights into the genetic aspects of schizophrenia.

Genetic Counseling

Genetic counseling is the provision of genetic information to help people make decisions about marriage, divorce, childbearing, and abortion. People who believe they may carry a genetic risk factor for schizophrenia seek genetic counseling to learn more about the risk of schizophrenia for themselves, their relatives, or their potential children. Genetic counselors are specialists in the study of the distribution of genes in normal and abnormal populations and have also received special training in how to relate this knowledge to specific genetic information gained from a history of disorders in a client's family. In addition, these counselors are trained to present this complex information to the client in an understandable way and to deal with the client's feelings concerning the information. A genetic counselor does not ordinarily give advice but instead presents whatever

is known about the risk factors. Because the inheritance of schizophrenia is complex and is not clearly understood at present, a genetic counselor must judge the risks for a particular family on the basis of both theoretical and practical information.

Computer programs are available to calculate the theoretical risk based on varying combinations of affected and nonaffected relatives. An example of part of a computer analysis of risk is shown in Table 12–1. This program is based on the hypothesis that the genetic pattern for schizophrenia is a multifactorial one—the more healthy relatives a person has and the closer they are to the person genetically, the lower the risk. For example, if neither parent is schizophrenic, but their two children both have the disorder, the risk for the next child is 14 percent. If there are two schizophrenic children and one healthy one, the risk for the next sibling is about 13 percent, and so forth (Gottesman, 1991). The table also shows that risk is greater if the relatives affected with schizophrenic disorder come from both the paternal and maternal sides of the family than if they come from only one side of the family. This increase in risk comes about because it is likely that an unaffected parent with a schizophrenic relative may be carrying some of the genes involved in schizophrenia. When these are combined with genes from another parent with one or more schizophrenic relatives they produce additional risks for a child of these parents.

Computer programs are helpful because of all these obvious complexities in prediction. However, it is necessary to remember that these programs are built on theories about the genetics of schizophrenia and are only general guidelines that *predict* risk or probability. The programs are only as good as the theories that support them and it is not yet certain which theory is correct or whether any of the current theories is appropriate.

Table 12–1
Computer Estimates of Risk for Schizophrenia with Different Combinations of Affected Family Members

Pedigree	Number of Schizophrenic Parents		
	None	One	Both
No sibs	0.9	8.5	41.1
1 sib *un*affected (U)	0.9	7.6	36.5
1 sib *a*ffected (A)	6.7	18.7	45.9
1 sib A + 1 sib U	6.2	16.6	41.9
1 sib A + 2 sibs U	5.5	14.8	38.9
2 sibs A	14.5	27.8	50.6
2 sibs A + 1 sib U	13.3	25.0	46.4
2 sibs A + 2 sibs U	12.0	22.4	43.4

	None	One		Both
		WITH RELATIVES ON SAME SIDE	WITH RELATIVES ON OPPOSITE SIDES	
1 2nd-degree relative A	2.7	10.6	19.0	45.3
1 sib A + 1 2nd-degree A	10.3	21.5	28.3	50.5
1 sib A + 1 2nd-degree A + 1 sib U	9.4	19.0	25.4	46.0
2 sibs A + 1 2nd-degree A	18.6	30.8	35.7	54.9
2 sibs A + 2 2nd-degree A + 1 sib U	19.9	30.0	38.0	54.1
1 3rd-degree relative A	1.7	9.6	13.3	42.8
1 sib A + 1 3rd-degree A	8.6	20.2	23.8	48.3
1 sib A + 3rd-degree A + 1 sib U	7.9	17.8	21.2	44.0
1 sib A + 1 2nd-degree A + 1 3rd-degree A	11.9	23.1	32.3	52.9
2 sibs A + 1 2nd-degree A + 1 3rd-degree A + 1 sib U	18.5	28.9	35.5	52.3

SOURCE: From *Schizophrenia Genesis: The Origins of Madness* by Irving I. Gottesman. Copyright © 1991 by I.I. Gottesman. Reprinted with permission of W.H. Freeman and Company

Further, just knowing the *number* of relatives involved does not take into account all the relevant variables. Several other factors are known to be related to risk. These include: the severity of the disorder, how chronic the disorder is, and the age at which the disorder began in each affected relative. If some of those in the family have not yet passed through the age range where the risk of schizophrenia is greatest, they may still have a chance of developing it and thus changing the predictive risk greatly. If work on genetic markers leads to more certain identification of those at greater risk, genetic counseling for schizophrenia can become more precise.

In addition to providing information on probable risk, genetic counselors can also be helpful by pointing out that both stress and genetic vulnerability are important in producing schizophrenic disorder.

Vulnerability and Stress Factors

Genetic factors are thought to be essential for the development of a schizophrenic disorder, but not sufficient in themselves. This way of thinking about the causes of schizophrenia is referred to as the **diathesis-stress theory.** The word "diathesis" means predisposition; the theory means that only people who have some genetic vulnerability will develop schizophrenia, and only if they are exposed to so much stress that they are unable to cope will they experience a range of schizophrenic symptoms. Although the diathesis-stress model can be applied to all behavior, in the area of schizophrenia it has been particularly clearly defined by Joseph Zubin (Zubin and others, 1982; Zubin & Spring, 1977). Zubin's hypothesis assumes that schizophrenia is not a permanent disorder but rather a permanent *vulnerability* to a disorder. According to this theory, each person has a level of vulnerability to schizophrenia determined by both genetic inheritance and prenatal and postnatal physical factors. This level, which may range from no risk to high risk, interacts with stressful events or conditions in a person's life. If the combination exceeds a certain critical level, schizophrenic behavior will occur. This concept of vulnerability offers one way of understanding why, if one identical twin has a schizophrenic disorder, the other twin's chances of also having the disorder are not 100 percent.

Zubin's model assumes that when the stressors decrease, the schizophrenic disorder will abate and the person will return to his or her earlier level of functioning (see Figure 12–3). Indeed, some of the findings reported in Chapter 11 support the idea that schizophrenia may be

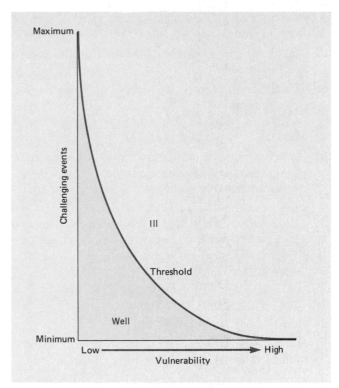

FIGURE 12–3 The relationship between vulnerability and challenging events.
(Adapted from Zubin and Spring, 1977)

an episodic disorder, at least for some people. Most present-day researchers, regardless of whether or not they accept Zubin's theories, would agree that a schizophrenic disorder is almost always a product of several factors, including biological make-up, coping skills, environmental condition, and life events.

An adoption study carried out in Finland supports this point of view (Tienari and others, 1990). The study paired adopted children whose biological mothers were schizophrenic with adopted children whose biological parents were not schizophrenic. First, the researchers collected information about the nearly 20,000 women who had been treated in psychiatric hospitals in Finland at some time during a ten-year period. From this group they found 171 women who had been diagnosed as schizophrenic and who had a child who was adopted by a nonrelative Finnish family before the child was four years old. We can appreciate how complex are the tasks required to complete an adoption study by considering the following. First, in this study a large number of cases had to be investigated to determine which of the women in the original sample were diagnosed as schizophrenic, had had a baby and had given up the baby for adoption. Fewer than 1 in 100 of the original cases qualified. All that effort had to be expended before the study could even get under way. Some of the other tasks the researchers faced were:

1. Selecting two adopted children as matched controls for each index case;

2. Checking the psychiatric histories of the control children's parents;

3. Administering structured interviews to all the biological mothers, thus providing a diagnosis with which to compare the diagnosis in the hospital records;

4. Interviewing the biological father of each index group member to evaluate whether he had a psychiatric disorder that would add to risk for the child.

In addition, the research team performed an evaluation of the child-rearing environment of each adoptive family for each index and control child, which included the following steps:

1. Interview with the entire family;

2. Joint interview with both adoptive parents;

3. Psychological testing of adoptive parents together and then also with their adoptive child;

4. Comprehensive test battery for each child and each adoptive parent, separately;

5. Follow-up assessments five to seven years after the initial assessment.

Because some of the adopted children have yet to reach or complete the age span of greatest risk for schizophrenia, data from this Finnish study will not be complete for a long time. Thus far in the study the people in the control group are much healthier than those in the index group. Fourteen percent of the control group have a severe psychological disorder, compared to 29 percent of the index group. One and one-half percent of the control group have developed a psychotic disorder compared to more than seven percent of the index group. Most interesting of all is the relationship between frequency of psychological problems and the adoptive family environment of the index cases.

The study's findings about the index children, shown in Figure 12–4, support the idea that healthy family environment has a protective effect for children who may be at risk for schizophrenia. In the group of index children reared in psychologically healthy families, none had become psychotic and only 4 percent had a severe psychological disorder. For the index children brought up in severely disturbed families, 11 percent were psychotic and 41 percent had a severe psychological disorder. Compared to the control children in each corresponding family type, the index children were less likely to be psychologically healthy as well as more likely to have a psychosis. These findings, although preliminary until the children have all passed the age of maximum

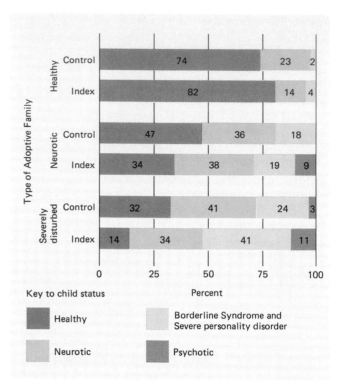

FIGURE 12–4 Even though adopted children whose biological mothers had a schizophrenic disorder (the index group) are more at risk than adopted children with normal biological mothers (the control group), the atmosphere in the adoptive families is important in the children's psychological outcome.

(Adapted from Tienari and others, 1990, p. 327)

risk, support the view that genetically transmitted vulnerability may be necessary for, or at least increase the likelihood of, occurrence of a schizophrenic disorder, but that disturbed family environment may play an important role in development of that vulnerability into a schizophrenic disorder.

The vulnerability theory suggests that research efforts in the areas of genetics and psychophysiology can be of great use in pointing out markers that can be used to identify vulnerable people. Efforts can then be directed toward helping these individuals avoid the degree of stress that might produce a schizophrenic disorder. Such efforts might include providing a supportive environment and helping vulnerable individuals develop better coping skills so that the unavoidable stressors of life will not affect them so severely.

Although these positive steps may help people cope with stressful life situations, there are a number of types of stressors that people are likely to inflict upon themselves through their behaviors. Although some of these do not have long term bad effects on those without a vulnerability to schizophrenia, for those at high risk these behaviors may have a devastating effect, perhaps as a result of their impact on an already malfunctioning

neurotransmitter system. People who are vulnerable to schizophrenia would be wise to avoid certain types of situations that could be linked to the onset of a schizophrenic episode. These include extreme sleep deprivation, encounter groups and sensitivity training that involve extreme emotional experiences, and the use of certain drugs that are known to have dopamine stimulating properties (marijuana, cocaine/crack, PCP, amphetamines, and LSD) (Gottesman, 1991). Use of one of these drugs by a vulnerable person may result in an irreparable case of genuine schizophrenia (Andreasen and others, 1987). These risk factors make clear the desirability of developing markers to identify those who may be vulnerable. Most of the remainder of this chapter will be devoted to a discussion of the search for markers of vulnerability to schizophrenia.

High-risk Studies and the Search for Markers

One way of examining the causal factors in schizophrenia is to study children beginning in infancy or early childhood and compare the records of those who later become schizophrenic with those who do not. This type of research has several advantages.

1. The subjects can be studied before those who develop disorders have experienced hospitalization and drugs.

2. None of the researchers, relatives, teachers, or subjects know who will become schizophrenic. Potential sources of bias in their observations and reports are thus removed.

3. The information obtained is relatively current when it is gathered. Questions about teenage dating patterns and frequency, for example, are answered more accurately by adolescents than they would be by a 30-year-old schizophrenic patient and his or her 55-year-old mother.

4. The data can be obtained uniformly, not by relying on records from various agencies and individuals working in different ways.

This type of study avoids many problems that arise in dealing with an individual who is already schizophrenic. For example, it is not necessary to rely on the patients' and their families' sometimes faulty and selective memories of past events. This is especially important because once a diagnosis of schizophrenic disorder has been made, everyone in the family may see past events in a different light. Studying the person and his or her family after schizophrenia has developed tells more about the consequences of having a schizophrenic disorder than about its causes. The diagnosis of schizophrenia means that the person likely has already suffered educational, economic, and social failures and may also have experienced hospitalization and extensive drug therapy. These factors alone may explain many of the differences that researchers find between schizophrenic and control groups.

In spite of these advantages, there is one important problem with studies that test people before they become ill and later compare the records for those who develop schizophrenia with those who do not. Since no more than 1.4 percent of all people ever develop a schizophrenic disorder, many thousands of people would have to be tested in order to be sure that the schizophrenic group would be large enough. One way to cope with this problem is to do a **high-risk** study. This means that the researcher selects for study a group that is thought to have a higher potential or risk of schizophrenia than the population in general. One such group consists of children who have at least one schizophrenic parent.

Most high-risk studies of children of schizophrenic parents focus on understanding the differences among children who do and do not develop problems despite the fact that all may have a potential genetic vulnerability. The Finnish study described earlier represents a sophisticated high-risk study in which the interaction between environment and heredity can be studied because the subjects were all adopted.

A pioneering high-risk study was carried out in Denmark beginning in 1962 (Kety and others, 1968). Since this study began, many other high-risk studies have been started. Most of the studies are longitudinal and compare children of a schizophrenic parent or parents with children of parents who have no identified disorder. However, a study underway at the University of Minnesota is cross-sectional with a short-term follow-up, and compares not only children who are vulnerable because they have schizophrenic parents but also children who are vulnerable because they have engaged in aggressive, bullying behavior or hyperactivity (Garmezy & Devine, 1984). A high-risk study completed at the University of Rochester combined cross-sectional and longitudinal approaches by comparing boys in several age groups at initial testing and over time (Wynne and others, 1987). Some of the results from these studies are presented in Table 12–2.

Much research on high-risk subjects has focused on identifying markers for schizophrenia by determining the distinctive early characteristics of children who ultimately become schizophrenic. Table 12–3 lists the characteristics a marker should have to make it useful in detecting genetic biological risk. So far the search for markers suggests several conclusions (Lewine, 1984).

Table 12–2
Markers from High-Risk Studies of Increased Risk of Schizophrenia

Birth problems—low birthweight and difficult birth

Poor emotional bonding—lack of a close relationship with the mother in the first three years of life

Poor motor coordination in infancy

Separation from parents—being raised in an institution or foster home

Intellectual deficits—poor performance on intelligence tests, especially in verbal abilities

Cognitive deficits—distractability and problems in focusing attention

Social deficits—aggressive behavior, anger, abrasiveness

Confusion and hostility in parent–child communication

SOURCE: N. F. Watt (Ed.), *Children at Risk for Schizophrenia: A Longitudinal Perspective.* New York: Cambridge University Press, 1984

Table 12–3
Characteristics Necessary for Useful Markers of Biological Risk for Schizophrenic Spectrum Disorder

1. The marker is distributed differently in psychotic than in control populations.
2. The marker is a stable trait rather than one associated with a particular set of temporary circumstances.
3. The marker occurs with higher frequency in family members of those with schizophrenic spectrum disorder than in the general population.
4. The marker occurs with higher frequency in offspring at high risk before they develop any schizophrenic spectrum disorder.
5. The presence of the marker in the offspring is a predictor of later development of a schizophrenic spectrum disease.
6. Determination of the marker is relatively noninvasive and can be used by a variety of investigators with high reliability.

SOURCE: Adapted from Garver, 1987, p. 526.

1. A marker, if it exists, may reflect vulnerability to psychosis in general rather than specifically to schizophrenia or schizophrenic spectrum disorder. Children whose parents have nonschizophrenic psychoses also differ from normal controls.
2. Changes over time, rather than particular traits, may be the most important markers.
3. Among the children in the high-risk group, only some (11 to 14 percent) are clearly deviant.

High-risk studies are making an important contribution to knowledge about schizophrenia. However, they have an important drawback. Since only about 11 percent of all people who become schizophrenic have one or more schizophrenic parents, it may be that the data from these studies apply only to a specific subtype of schizophrenia (Gottesman, 1991). As is true of other research carried out on a specific population—such as college students, members of the armed forces, or relatives of hospital patients—it is not clear what general statements can be made from findings based on a particular group. However, because they focus attention on vulnerabilities, the results of high-risk studies may play an important role in the design of prevention programs.

Understanding the Schizophrenic Process

Structural Abnormalities in the Brain

The search for structural abnormalities in the brain that are related to schizophrenia or other disordered behavior has a long history, but for many years it did not produce important insights into possible causes or processes of schizophrenia. Recent technological advances have increased interest in research in this area, however. Development of a variety of scanning techniques has made it possible to look at the structure and the function of the living brain without physically intrusive procedures that might harm the patient. More about these scanning techniques is presented in Chapter 13.

One finding that has emerged from the use of scanning techniques is that some schizophrenics have significantly larger **cerebral ventricles** (cavities that contain cerebrospinal fluid) than those found in the brains of nonschizophrenics. Researchers think that it is not the size of the ventricles themselves that is important, but rather the changes in the adjacent tissues. When the ventricles are enlarged, these tissues are smaller in volume, but it is not clear whether this size reduction is due to tissue shrinkage and the death of neurons or to failure of the tissues to develop. Some enlargement of ventricles seems to occur naturally; in general, people's ventricles become larger with age. Enlarged ventricles are also found in other conditions such as alcoholism, traumatic head injuries, and severe mood disorders involving psychosis (Raz & Raz, 1990). Another difficulty in understanding the meaning of enlarged ventricles is that these and other significant brain effects occur in only about one-third of people with schizophrenic disorder who are examined by radiologists.

The results of a study of 15 sets of MZ twins discordant for schizophrenia was of particular interest in understanding the role of enlarged ventricles, because the anatomy of the brains of each pair would be expected to be highly similar (Suddath and others, 1990). The twins with the schizophrenic disorder not only had enlarged lateral and third ventricles compared to their nonschizophrenic twins, but they also were found to have a reduction in the size of their temporal lobes, anterior hippocampus, and left temporal lobe gray matter. Since these areas of the brain are involved in thinking, concentration, memory and perception, these differences may be associated with some of the characteristic symptoms of schizophrenia discussed in Chapter 11. In 14 of the pairs, the twin with the schizophrenic disorder had reduced brain volume when compared to his or her healthy twin.

Figure 12–5 shows a diagram of the brain indicating the area scanned, along with scans of one pair of twins that illustrate the difference found in ventricle size. One possibility to explain this difference in MZ twins is that the twin with the enlarged ventricles might have experienced some injury before birth. Another interesting finding in this study was that the enlargement in many cases would not have been considered by a specialist to be of abnormal size. It was only in comparison with the healthy twin that the difference in size was apparent. This observation suggests that even subtle changes in ventricle size may be important in the development of schizophrenia.

Ventricular enlargement is often associated with the negative symptoms and poor outcome described in

Chapter 11 (Andreasen and others, 1990). It may have potential as a biological marker for schizophrenia. However, it is also associated with other disorders so perhaps it may be a marker of risk for psychotic disorder in general rather than schizophrenia in particular. In order to determine what these differences in brain anatomy mean, it will be necessary to track high-risk people over time to see when and how these anatomical changes occur in relation to the development of the disorder. One question is whether they continue to worsen over the course of the illness or whether they may have existed since birth. Some patients are found to have enlarged ventricles at the time they first are diagnosed with the disorder, suggesting that the enlargement may be present before the psychotic symptoms become apparent. Only by following patients, or preferably high-risk subjects, over time will such questions be answered.

Biochemical Abnormalities in the Brain

There are strong arguments for the assumption that biochemical factors play a role in at least some of the schizophrenias. An impetus to the search for biochemical clues has been provided by the effectiveness of some antipsychotic drugs, which are known to produce certain biochemical changes. Recent developments in technology and the discovery of new neurochemical systems in the body have enabled researchers to take a more sophisticated approach to biological differences than was possible in the past. Investigators are now able to look for abnormalities in biochemical *functioning*.

PET SCANS A technology that may provide breakthroughs in the study of chemical activity in the living human brain is the positron emission tomography (PET) scan. As we saw in Chapter 10, PET scans depict chemical activity inside the brain by recording radiation from a glucoselike substance injected into the individual's bloodstream. The injected material enters the brain and is used by the working brain cells, and the PET scanner records this activity in a series of thin cross sections of the brain. Use of this technique with psychiatric patients suggests that the PET scan can be used to distinguish between the brain activity of control subjects and patients with a diagnosis of schizophrenia. In addition, the PET scan has been used to observe changes in biochemical action in the brain caused by antipsychotic drugs.

Research using PET scans shows that people who are chronically schizophrenic tend to have a lower level of metabolism in the frontal and temporal lobes of their brains and a somewhat higher flow at the base of the skull than control subjects (see Figure 12–6).

THE DOPAMINE HYPOTHESIS Just as neurotransmitters are currently thought to be important in at least

FIGURE 12–5 When one identical (MZ) twin develops schizophrenia and the other twin does not, one difference found between them is likely to be enlarged ventricles in the affected twin, especially an enlarged third ventricle. The region of the brain scanned by MRI is shown in (a). The MRI scans in (b) show the difference in ventricle size in an unaffected twin and her twin sister who has a diagnosis of schizophrenic disorder.

(a)

(b)

(a)

(b)

(c)

FIGURE 12–6 PET scan photos show brain metabolism, the chemical activity currently going on in a living brain. Photo (a) shows how a patient is prepared for a PET scan. Photo (b) shows a PET scan of the brain of a normal individual and photo (c) shows a PET scan for a person with schizophrenic disorder who has never received any antipsychotic medication. Notice the relatively higher frontal metabolism in the normal person and the higher posterior metabolism in the patient. (Colors toward the red-yellow end of the spectrum indicate a higher rate of metabolic activity and those at the blue-green end a lower rate.)

some types of affective disorders (see Chapter 10), biologically oriented research on schizophrenia also stresses the importance of neurotransmitter functioning. In schizophrenia, current research focuses on dopamine. The **dopamine hypothesis,** simply stated, says that there is an excess of dopamine at certain synapses in the brain.

Theoretically this excess could result from any of three processes.

1. The transmitter neurons could produce too much dopamine.

2. Too much dopamine could remain in the synapses either because it might not break down fast enough or because reuptake into the vesicles of the transmitter neuron might not occur fast enough.

3. The receptor neurons might be overactive in their function either because the receptors are too sensitive or there are too many of them.

Currently the third explanation, overactive-receptor function, is best supported by research findings (Reynolds, 1989).

The idea that dopamine is involved in schizophrenia comes from two sources. One is the finding that large doses of amphetamines are capable of producing behavior in individuals with no history of psychological difficulties that is very similar to behavior typical of paranoid schizophrenics. Even more important, low doses of amphetamines make the symptoms of some schizophrenic individuals worse. Biochemically, amphetamines increase the amounts of both the catecholamines—dopamine and norepinephrine—that are present at the synapse.

The second reason to suspect that dopamine is involved comes from knowledge of the effects of the antipsychotic drugs used to treat schizophrenia. Dopamine receptors can now be identified by PET scans; this

FIGURE 12–7 The PET scan makes it possible for researchers to see the effect of various antipsychotic drugs on the receptors that would ordinarily receive the dopamine after it crossed the synapse. Scan (a) shows a patient treated with two different drugs that produce a complete blockade of these receptors. Scan (b) shows the same patient two weeks after the drug was discontinued. The receptors are no longer blocked and uptake and binding occur.

(a) (b)

may provide the best way of investigating the dopamine hypothesis (Sedvall and others, 1986) (see Figure 12–7). The effectiveness of antipsychotic drugs in reducing psychotic symptoms is directly related to their success at binding to (that is, blocking) postsynaptic dopamine receptors. Antipsychotic drugs that work by blocking brain receptors for dopamine are able to control positive symptoms in about 80 percent of patients. Clozapine, a drug discussed in Chapter 11, affects both serotonin and dopamine receptors, and sometimes can reduce both positive and negative symptoms.

Although the dopamine hypothesis is supported by these and other data, it is too simple to explain all the findings. For instance, even when antipsychotic drugs are effective, they typically require about six weeks to produce a maximum level of improvement. What appears to happen is that initially the blockage of the dopamine receptor results in feedback that increases the activity of the dopamine transmitters in the midbrain. However, after some time the neurons are firing so quickly that their effectiveness is actually decreased.

Psychophysiological Abnormalities

The study of the psychophysiology of behavior concentrates on the relationship between behavior and variations in the functioning of the central and peripheral nervous systems, as well as on the ways in which these systems mediate the responses of other systems (for example, the cardiovascular system). Psychophysiological measurement includes methods of recording and processing bioelectric signals from the surface of the skin.

Psychophysiological responses can be studied using a variety of techniques, including measures of the electrical conductance of the skin, analysis of brain wave patterns by means of an electroencephalograph (EEG), and analysis of heart rate by means of an electrocardiograph (EKG). Researchers in this area still face many technical problems. For example, some measures of nervous system activity are especially sensitive to the drugs used to treat schizophrenic patients. Since many patients are started on these drugs when they first come to clinical attention, untreated patients are rare.

Psychophysiological experimentation was formerly very tedious and time-consuming because the responses were recorded as tracings on polygraph paper, which had to be analyzed by hand. Today computers not only can present a complex series of visual or auditory stimuli but can convert the subject's responses directly into numbers that can be analyzed using sophisticated programs. Under these conditions, research on psychophysiological responses has grown rapidly.

BRAIN ELECTRICAL ACTIVITY MAPPING One technique, **brain electrical activity mapping (BEAM)**, summarizes EEG and evoked electrical potential in the form of color maps (see Figure 12–8). In one study, schizophrenic subjects had more slow wave activity (delta waves), especially in their frontal brain regions, than did controls (Morihisa and others, 1983). The greatest difference was found when the subjects' eyes were open. These findings are related to PET scan findings of reduced frontal lobe activity in schizophrenic patients and to the lower cerebral blood flow found by some researchers. In addition to the difference in delta waves, research with BEAM has shown increased beta wave activity in the left rear portion of the brain. Beta waves occur in a relatively rapid rhythm and are associated with alertness, so this response may be an indication of overarousal. The BEAM technique may provide another way to identify markers of vulnerability to schizophrenia.

AUTONOMIC NERVOUS SYSTEM RESPONSE Some researchers have grouped persons with schizophrenic disorders into those with an overreactive autonomic nervous system (ANS) and those with an underreactive ANS (Cannon and others, 1990). An overreactive ANS is thought to be related to positive symptoms, at least in the initial phases of the schizophrenic disorder, and an underreactive ANS is thought to be related to negative symptoms. It has been theorized that genetic vulnerability may be associated with positive symptoms and genetic vulnerability together with brain damage before or at birth with negative symptoms (Carpenter and others,

FIGURE 12–8 Brain electrical activity mapping (BEAM) provides a new way of studying electrical activity in the brain. The left-hand column shows the average activity at four time intervals for ten control subjects. The right-hand column represents the averaged data of ten schizophrenic subjects. In all these records, the lowest level of activity is represented by blue, with higher values represented by yellow, red, and white, in that order. The single record at the bottom center illustrates the differences between the control and schizophrenic groups. Blue represents the smallest difference and white the greatest.

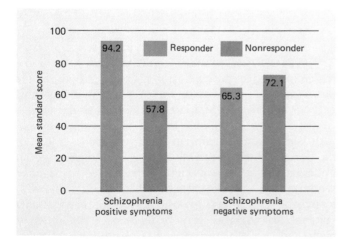

1991). The area of damage has been thought to be the anterior hypothalamus, which is the most important excitatory center of autonomic activity in the brain. Damage to this part of the brain might be expected to reduce ANS responsiveness and to contribute to negative symptoms of schizophrenia in high-risk individuals. Figure 12–9 shows how the high or low ANS response status of children in a high-risk sample was associated with the likelihood of positive or negative symptoms when they were adults. However, the study illustrated in the figure also showed that only some of the children with poor ANS regulation later became schizophrenic (Cannon and others, 1990). This finding suggests that lack of ANS regulation may be a marker of vulnerability but not a cause of schizophrenia. Development of schizophrenic disorder may also require environmental stressors combined with this vulnerability.

Attention Problems

Anyone who has contact with schizophrenics is struck by their attentional deficits. Emil Kraepelin noted long ago that schizophrenic disorder was associated with the lack of both the inclination and the initiative to keep attention focused for any length of time. Attentional problems are of interest, not only in understanding the deficits experienced in schizophrenia, but also in the search for markers of high-risk individuals.

Researchers have tried to understand what factors contribute to the problems of attention. One possibility is that people who have a schizophrenic disorder are only able to devote part of their information processing resources to the task at hand. The remainder of their attention is abnormally focused on task-irrelevant stimuli. This idea has been supported in some research studies. For instance, in one study patients and controls were asked to push a button as soon as a target tone was heard, and their reaction time was measured (Grillon and others, 1990). Although in general the patients' time was somewhat slower than that of controls, the difference in speed between the groups was greatly increased when a distractor tone was added to the task. Under the distractor condition the patient group's response time was much slower than that of the control group. A

FIGURE 12–9 Children in a high-risk study who were classified in childhood as high autonomic nervous system responders were more likely to show positive symptoms (hallucinations, delusions, and thought disorder) if they later became schizophrenic than were children who had been classified as ANS nonresponders. The difference in the two groups was not so large for negative symptoms because after the schizophrenic disorder had continued for some time, many of the high responders also developed negative symptoms.

(Adapted from Cannon and others, 1990, p. 341)

measure of electrical activity in various parts of the brain was used in this study as a way to link differences in cognitive processing and attention to the difference in reaction time. The brain electrical activity patterns showed that the patients attended much more to the distracting tones than did the control group. This finding supported the hypothesis that the difference in performance under the distracting condition was at least partly a result of an inability of the patients to focus their attention on one set of stimuli and to ignore others, thus possibly diverting too much of their information processing resources from the assigned task.

Although this experiment did provide some important information about the reason for poor performance on attentional tasks by patients with schizophrenic disorder, a study of this kind cannot answer the question of whether this distractibility might be a marker for schizophrenia or whether it is merely a symptom of the disorder when it becomes acute. Another study investigated this question by comparing performance on a distraction task by several different groups. The groups included those who had been diagnosed with schizophrenic disorder, those who had a relative with schizophrenia, and a number of normal controls (Spring and others, 1989). Subjects listened over a headphone to strings of words that included both distractor and target words. The study showed that when distractors were words unassociated with the target words, only the performance of hospitalized patients with schizophrenic disorder was disrupted and the performance of the other groups was not. This result suggested that disruptions of selective attention might be a sign of an acute schizophrenic episode rather than a marker of risk. However, the study also found that certain kinds of errors were more frequent in all the at-risk groups than in the normal controls. The findings in this study indicate that certain deficits in attention may be a marker of vulnerability to schizophrenia, but that these deficits become more general and more apparent during an acute psychotic episode. Figure 12–10 illustrates the results.

Two measures of attention look especially promising as biological markers of risk for schizophrenia in children of schizophrenic mothers (Erlenmeyer-Kimling, 1987). These are deficiencies in sustained attention, measured by a procedure called the Continuous Performance Test, and eye tracking dysfunction.

THE CONTINUOUS PERFORMANCE TEST The **Continuous Performance Test** (Rosvold and others, 1956) measures sustained visual attention for periods of up to 20 minutes. The subject is exposed to a series of different stimuli after he or she has been instructed to respond to one particular type of stimulus by pressing a key. Schizophrenic individuals make more errors both by pressing the button for the wrong stimulus and by not pressing the button when it would have been correct to

FIGURE 12–10 Performance of patients hospitalized with schizophrenic disorder on an attentional task compared with performance of outpatients with the same diagnosis, patients' relatives, and a control group showed that some types of attentional problems seem to be related to acute psychosis, but other types seem to be relatively enduring and are perhaps markers of vulnerability. (a) Only the group of currently hospitalized patients differed significantly in accuracy from the normal controls when the distracting words were not associated in meaning to the target words. (b) All groups of patients as well as their relatives differed significantly from normal controls, when only intrusion errors, those that contained some portion of the distractor word combined with the target word, were counted.

(B. Spring, M. Lemon, L. Weinstein, and A. Haskell (1989), "Distractibility in schizophrenia: State and trait aspects," in *British Journal of Psychiatry,* 155, 63–68. By permission of The Royal College of Psychiatrists)

do so. This poor performance may be related to a dysfunction in the reticular system in the brain stem (Mirsky & Bakay Pragay, 1984).

Children of schizophrenic mothers scored worse on the Continuous Performance Test than either children of mothers with other disorders or other children in their classrooms (Nuechterlein, 1983). In another study those children with a schizophrenic parent who also scored

FIGURE 12–11 Samples of visual-tracking performance by a control subject (C) and five patients with schizophrenia (S1–S5). (The target moved back and forth across a 20 degree arc every 2.5 seconds.)

(Iacono and Koenig, 1983, p. 39)

poorly on measures of attention were most likely to show behavioral difficulties in adulthood that might be early signs of schizophrenia (Cornblatt & Erlenmeyer-Kimling, 1985). These findings, along with the results of the distractibility study discussed above, indicate that a group of tasks measuring attention may be a useful marker in high-risk groups.

EYE TRACKING Smooth-pursuit eye movements, which, strictly speaking, are not voluntary and cannot be faked, occur only when a person tracks a slowly moving target such as a pendulum. About 85 percent of schizophrenics show abnormal patterns of these smooth-pursuit movements (Siever & Coursey, 1985). Figure 12–11 illustrates the difference between the typical tracking pattern of someone with a schizophrenic disorder and that of a normal control. About 50 percent of close relatives of schizophrenics also show this deviant pattern, but only 13 percent of relatives of other types of patients do.

It is important to note that these deviant tracking patterns are also found in other disorders, including bipolar disorders, brain lesions, brain damage, and some forms of drug intoxication. Poor trackers, even among people who have not received any psychiatric diagnosis, are likely to show interpersonal difficulties and neurological impairment. Why these relationships exist is not known at present, but even if causal processes are unclear, eye tracking patterns may be useful as markers for early identification of those at risk.

Disordered Thinking

Although schizophrenia is often described as thought disorder, some degree of disordered thinking is not unique to schizophrenia. Disordered thinking is part of a continuum that also includes normal thinking. In one study tape recordings of verbalizations of responses on the Rorschach personality test were compared for a number of groups, including normal controls (Solavoy and others, 1987). The responses were all rated on a thought disorder index. Although the group diagnosed with schizophrenic disorder had the highest overall number of thought-disordered responses, all groups showed some examples of disordered thought (see Figure 12–12).

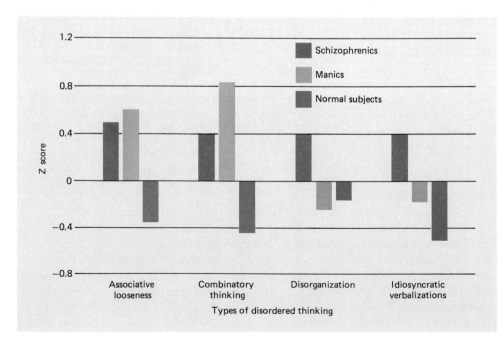

FIGURE 12–12 The frequency of thought-disordered responses of schizophrenic and manic patients was compared with that of normal subjects. The figure shows how each group differed from the overall mean (0) in each of several aspects of their performance. (The data were transformed for statistical purposes and the results are reported in terms of Z scores).

(*Archives of General Psychiatry*, 1987, 44, 13–20. Copyright © 1987, American Medical Association)

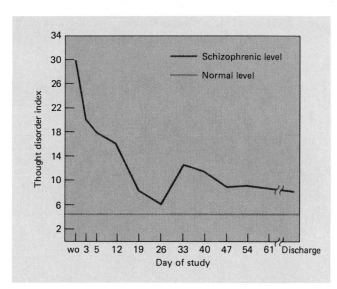

FIGURE 12–13 Mean Thought Disorder Index of 18 schizophrenic patients during their hospital stays. Effects of antipsychotic medications appear quickly and the index reaches a stable level that is higher than the level for normal individuals (wo = end of drug-free "wash-out" period to remove effects of previous medication).

(Holzman, 1978, p. 367)

Researchers have attempted to determine whether an above average degree of thought disorder is simply a symptom of acute psychosis or whether it is also a marker of vulnerability to schizophrenia. They have found that some degree of disordered thought may show up long before other signs of a schizophrenic disorder appear and that it may be a permanent characteristic of at least some people who are vulnerable to schizophrenia. For instance, in the Danish high-risk study of children of severely schizophrenic mothers, a significantly larger percent of children who later developed one of the schizophrenic spectrum disorders showed cognitive disturbance when they were tested at age 15 compared to the control subjects (Parnas and others, 1982).

A measure of thought disorder can also be useful in assessing the effects of antipsychotic medication. For example, in one study the responses of schizophrenic patients were evaluated on a thought disorder index before the patients began drug treatment. The results showed that thought disorder as measured by the index dropped dramatically after the drug treatment began (see Figure 12–13). The maximum effect was reached in about three weeks, and then a relatively stable level was maintained. These results suggest that the drug therapy was effective in maintaining better cognitive performance, although it is important to note that the level of disordered thinking shown by the schizophrenic patients remained consistently higher than that of nonschizophrenic individuals. Some of those who experience an episode of acute psychosis continue to show bizarre and idiosyncratic speech even after their overall condition improves and the psychosis fades.

Language Use Abnormalities

The language used by some schizophrenic individuals makes their speech difficult to follow, but this does not seem to be due to their lack of knowledge of grammatical rules. What is perceived as abnormal seems to lie in the thought communicated, not in the language used in the communication. The language pattern of schizophrenics has been found to differ from those of other patient groups and of normal controls in the way the thoughts are organized. Normal speech has a treelike structure that schizophrenic speech may lack. To see this difference in structure, read the next two examples and then look at the diagrams in Figure 12–14. The first segment was produced by someone hospitalized for depression.

Interviewer: *Can you describe where you live?*

Patient: *Yes, I live in Connecticut. We live in a 50-year-old Tudor house. It's a house that's very much a home . . . ah . . . I live there with my husband and son. It's a home where people are drawn to feel comfortable, walk in, let's see . . . a home that is furnished comfortably—not expensive—a home that shows very much my personality.*

The overall message of the above segment is fairly obvious—the woman is extolling the virtues of her house in terms of how it reflects on herself as a person. This message is represented by the tree-shaped plan in Figure 12–14.

The second speech segment was produced by a patient with a schizophrenic disorder.

Interviewer: *Did you ever try to hurt yourself? (Interviewer asks about patient's feelings about suicide after being admitted to a psychiatric hospital.)*

Patient: *I cut myself once when I was in the kitchen trying to please David. I was scared for [sic] life because David didn't want me and if David didn't want me then no man would.*

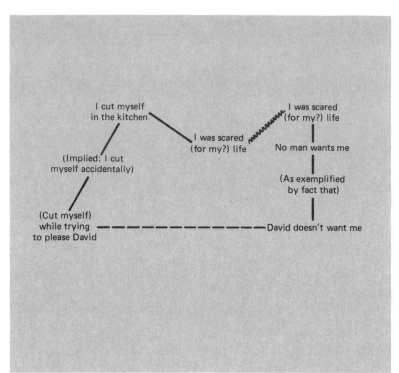

FIGURE 12–14 Hierarchical analyses of speech may provide understanding of schizophrenic thought processes. In the "house is like my personality" segment, certain statements can be located at different sites in the tree depending on how one interprets the communicative intention of the speaker. If "50-year-old Tudor" is metaphorically interpreted as referring to certain human qualities, then this statement is subordinate to the "house shows my personality" statement; otherwise, the statement would be subordinate to the superordinate "house" statement. A hierarchical analysis of the "I cut myself" segment interpretations of the text could potentially restore a strict hierarchical structure, but this requires assuming that the speaker disregarded the suicide theme without acknowledging that she changed the topic.

(Archives of General Psychiatry, 1986, 831–838. Copyright © 1986, American Medical Association)

This segment suggests a condensation of two disjointed messages. The right-hand chain of statements describes stress-related thoughts of the type that might lead to suicidal behavior. The left-hand hierarchy seemingly refers to an incident in which the speaker accidentally cuts herself. In this context, "I was scared for life" seems to refer to her reaction to seeing that she had accidentally cut herself. The result is a departure from a strict hierarchical ordering of statements, since "no man wants me" and "David doesn't want me" presuppose the "I was scared for life" statement and are referable to the suicide theme, but the statement "I [accidentally] cut myself" is not. This break is represented in Figure 12–14 by a jagged line.

By experimentally studying various aspects of schizophrenics' language, cognitive theorists look for clues to the specific ways in which schizophrenics differ from controls and how conditions can be varied to improve schizophrenics' performance. Through these procedures, they hope to obtain a better understanding of the thought processes that characterize schizophrenia.

Family Relationships

The experience of stressful life events is thought to be a risk factor for those who are already vulnerable to schizophrenia. One source of stress may be extremely frustrating interpersonal relationships during the early years of life. For some people, such experiences may result in a failure to develop emotional ties to other people and to expect support and warmth from the social environment. Stress in the family environment may have

a particularly strong effect on children who are genetically vulnerable. As we saw earlier in this chapter, studies of adopted children who had a genetic risk for schizophrenia have shown that the characteristics of an adoptive family affect the likelihood that a schizophrenic disorder will develop in their adopted child.

When we look at biological families rather than adoptive ones, it is extremely difficult to untangle causes and effects of stress and vulnerability. Some early research about families who had a child who developed a schizophrenic disorder had the unfortunate effect of appearing to blame the family for the child's illness. Box 11−2 illustrated the burden of guilt many families bear in wondering if their behavior was in some way the cause of the schizophrenic disorder. In reviewing studies that concern the family environment as a factor in schizophrenic disorder, it is important to remember that the characteristics researchers see in such families are probably the result of the interaction of family members' personalities and typical behaviors with those of a vulnerable child who may provide quite different kinds of stimuli for parents than other children do. Researchers should keep this interactional perspective in mind when observing parents and children together (Gottesman, 1991).

Research on family environment and schizophrenic disorder has focused both on the family prior to the time the disorder developed and on how the family interacts with a family member who has experienced an acute episode and has improved to the point of being discharged from the hospital. One aspect of behavior that both types of studies focus on is family communication. Communication deviance is often studied in families of children at high risk. In particular, researchers have looked at the way family members express emotion toward the affected person—both through interviews and direct observation.

Family Communication Deviance

Communication deviance refers to the inability of the parent or parents to maintain a shared focus of attention during interactions with another person. Cross-sectional studies have shown that high communication deviance is associated with schizophrenia in the children of such parents. However, some of the research on communication deviance has raised questions about causality. The parents' communication problems may be a response to unclear communications from the children.

One way to understand the causes and effects of communication problems is through long-term prospective studies. In a high-risk study carried out at the University of California at Los Angeles, the participating families each contained a mild- to moderately-disturbed

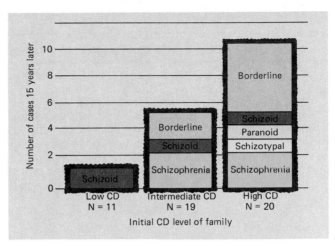

FIGURE 12−15 When families were divided into three levels of communication deviance (CD), the number of children who were later diagnosed as having a schizophrenic spectrum disorder was clearly different for each type of family.

(Adapted from Goldstein, 1985, p. 12. Copyright © 1985 Munksgaard International Publishers, Ltd., Copenhagen, Denmark)

teenage member (Goldstein, 1985). All of the families had contacted the university-based psychology clinic for help. At the time they were originally seen, the parents were given the Thematic Apperception Test (see Chapter 4), which was scored for communication deviance. Fifteen years later the children were rediagnosed and grouped according to the original assessment of parental communication deviance. The number of cases of schizophrenia and schizophrenic spectrum disorders was clearly related to the earlier assessments of communication deviance (see Figure 12−15). Fifty percent of the children in the families with high communication deviance had a diagnosis in the schizophrenic spectrum, compared to 26 percent in the intermediate- and 9 percent in the low-deviance families.

Expressed Emotion

In addition to how clearly families communicate, the emotional impact of what they communicate is important. **Expressed emotion** (EE) is a measure of the attitudes expressed by family members when talking about the person whose behavior is disturbed (Leff & Vaughn, 1985). Table 12−4 lists the categories of expressed emotion that are measured.

Researchers found that patients hospitalized for schizophrenic disorder who were subsequently discharged and who returned to families high in negative EE were not likely to stay out of the hospital as long as patients whose families were less critical. This was true whether or not the patient was also taking antipsychotic drugs (Leff & Vaughn, 1981; Vaughn & Leff, 1976)

Table 12–4

Scales of Expressed Emotion

1. *Critical comments about family members.* Criticisms are rated on the basis of content and/or tone. Remarks are considered to be critical if there is a clear and unambiguous statement that the relative dislikes, disapproves of, or resents a behavior or characteristic. The dissatisfaction is expressed intensely and emphatically; the relative must use phrases such as "It annoys me" or "I don't like it." Vocal aspects of speech such as pitch, speed, inflection, and loudness are used to identify critical tone.

2. *Hostility.* Hostility is rated as present when the patient is attacked for what he or she *is* rather than for what he or she *does*. Negative feeling is generalized in such a way that it is expressed about the person him- or herself rather than about particular behaviors or attributes.

3. *Emotional overinvolvement.* Emotional overinvolvement is rated when there is either an exaggerated emotional response to the patient's illness, marked concern reflected in unusually self-sacrificing and devoted behaviors, or extremely overprotective behaviors.

4. *Warmth.* Ratings of warmth are based on the sympathy, concern, and empathy relatives show when talking about the patient, the enthusiasm for and interest in the patient's activities, the number of spontaneous expressions of affection, and the tone of voice used when talking about the patient.

5. *Positive remarks.* Positive remarks are statements that express praise, approval, or appreciation of the behavior or personality of the patient.

SOURCE: From Leff and Vaughn, 1985. Reprinted with permission from the *British Journal of Psychiatry.*

(see Figure 12–16). Studies carried out in England and Los Angeles produced similar results (Vaughn and others, 1984). Negative EE includes criticism, hostility, and emotional overinvolvement (exaggerated emotional response to the illness or extreme protectiveness). Relatives who were rated high in negative EE made remarks like the following.

> *I always say, "why don't you pick up a book, do a crossword or something like that to keep your mind off it." That's even too much trouble.*
>
> *I've tried to jolly him out of it and pestered him into doing things. Maybe I've overdone it, I don't know.*
>
> *He went round the garden 90 times, in the door, back out the door. I said "Have a chair, sit out in the sun." Well, he nearly bit my head off.*

—Hooley, 1985, p. 134

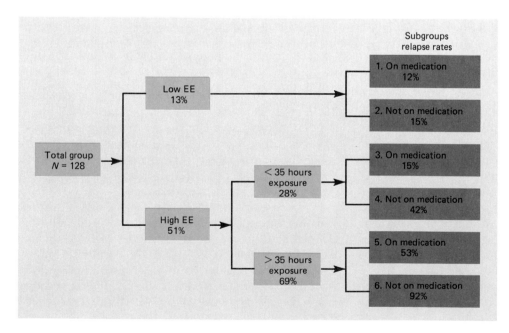

FIGURE 12–16 The relapse rates (after nine months) of 128 schizophrenic patients grouped by whether their families were high or low in negative expressed emotion (EE), the amount of time per week they were exposed to EE, and whether or not the patient was taking antipsychotic drugs.

(From C.E. Vaughn and J.P. Leff [1976], *British Journal of Psychiatry*, 129, p. 132. Copyright © 1976 by the *British Journal of Psychiatry.* Reprinted by permission)

Relatives who were low in negative EE were likely to make very different comments.

I know it's better for her to be on her own, to get away from me and try to do things on her own.

Whatever she does suits me.

I just tend to let it go because I know that when she wants to speak she will speak.

—Ibid.

As research on EE has continued, several findings have emerged:

1. Expressed emotion in a family may change over time. It may be a product both of the degree of agitation in the patient and of the family interaction style. Half the families high in negative expressed emotion at the patient's first admission are low one year later. A change from high to low negative expressed emotion in a family is associated with lower relapse rates (Hogarty and others, 1986).

2. The culture in which people live or from which they come plays a role in the amount of EE they express. In India relatives show relatively lower levels of negative expressed emotion toward patients than that shown to Anglo-American patients in the United States by their relatives. Mexican-Americans who live in the United States but who follow traditional cultural practices also show typically lower levels of expressed emotion toward their relatives than do Anglo-Americans (Leff & Vaughn, 1985; Jenkins and others, 1986).

3. Expressed emotion research has implications for patients who do not live with their families. High negative expressed emotion is associated with over-stimulating treatment and high expectations in foster homes and day-treatment centers, which in turn may lead to high rates of relapse.

EE research has become a focus of controversy because some practitioners reason that it blames families for the development of a member's schizophrenia. The research should not be thought of in this way, however. It is focused not on the cause of schizophrenic disorder but on conditions that increase the chance of rehospitalization. The term "expressed emotion" became an indication of a negative interactive style because early work showed how negative aspects of EE predict a high *relapse* rate. Later research has shown that warmth and positive comments may also help protect *against* relapse (Leff & Vaughn, 1985). The most important results of the work on EE have been positive. It stimulated the development of training programs to help families learn how to interact more effectively with patients when they return from the hospital after an acute episode. This type of family approach is discussed in detail in Chapter 11.

The term "expressed emotion" can also be misleading because research on negative EE may suggest that families should not express their emotional reactions to each other. What has been found is quite the reverse, however; in general, a high level of emotional expression in the sense of communicating feelings among family members has been found to help prevent relapse (Spiegel & Wissler, 1986). This finding indicates that some expression of feelings creates a healthier emotional atmosphere for everyone and prevents the festering of anger and irritation until full-blown emotional flare-ups occur.

The work on EE suggests several ways that the patient's outcome could be improved. As we saw in Chapter 11, family education can be extremely beneficial. When families know more about the symptoms and typical behaviors associated with schizophrenic disorders, they become more understanding of what the patient is experiencing and often less critical and hostile. Another way to help families is to focus on the social functioning of the patient through behavioral intervention. In one study, behavioral intervention consisted of education, stress management, stress innoculation, and goal planning for the family including the patient (Barrowclough & Tarrier, 1990). Before the intervention began, patients living in families rated high on negative EE were poorer in their social functioning that those with families low in negative EE. At the end of the 9-month intervention, patients from the high negative EE families who were in the experimental group had improved in their social functioning and patients from high negative EE families who were in the control group had declined. The high EE patients in the experimental intervention group also showed a lower rate of relapse than those in the high EE control group. In addition, more family members of high EE patients in the experimental group no longer were so critical and negative, but had changed their status to low EE. These results suggest that the work on EE has resulted in effective interventions for both patients and families.

Parental Affective Style

Expressed emotion is measured from interviews in which relatives talk about patients. **Parental affective style,** on the other hand, is assessed by means of directly observed interactions, in which family members including the patient or client discuss problems that tend to upset the family. Although negative expressed emotion and negative parental affective style may coexist in many individuals, they are not perfectly correlated. Analysis of

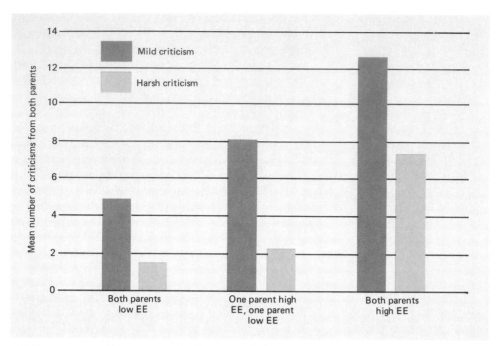

FIGURE 12–17 Expression of affective style by parents grouped by their expressed emotion (EE).

(Valone, K., Norton, J.P., Goldstein, M.J., & Doane, J.A. (1983). Parental expressed emotion and affective style in an adolescent sample at risk for schizophrenia spectrum disorders. *Journal of Abnormal Psychology, 92*, 399–407)

the interactions of parents and children and parents with each other reveals a complex pattern (Valone and others, 1983).

When both parents and their child all interact together, the behavior of a high EE parent is modified by the presence of the other parent. Figure 12–17 shows that when one parent is high and one low in negative EE, the number of harsh criticisms directed at the child is similar to the number directed at the child in an interaction with parents who are both low in negative EE. In spite of this modification in parental affective style by the presence of the other parent, a parent's EE seems to be a stable personal characteristic. In this study neither parent's EE level was related to the type of problem for which the family had come to the clinic or the way the child behaved during the interaction.

When both parents were high in expressed emotion, the family interaction has been shown to be more emotionally arousing (as measured by electrical skin conductance) than when the parents were low or mixed in negative expressed emotion (Valone and others, 1984). This arousal was shown not only by both parents but also by the adolescent child, who seemed most aroused when anticipating what the parents' next comments would be. This high level of arousal shows that families with high levels of negative expressed emotion experience a great deal of stress in their interactions.

The Role of the Community

More than 50 studies conducted in Canada, Denmark, Finland, Great Britain, Norway, Sweden, and Taiwan, as well as in the United States, have found that people of lower socioeconomic status (SES) are diagnosed as schizophrenic more frequently than people of middle or upper SES. However, researchers have not been able to discover why social class is related to schizophrenia. Two theories—social selection and the social-causation or increased-stress theory—have been posed to explain this relationship. The **social-selection theory** assumes that people who cannot make it in society gradually become lower in SES because of their poor coping skills. This idea has been supported by a number of studies, and stands in contrast to the idea that people who experience the stress of lower-class living develop poor coping skills. A review of research on the community and interpersonal functioning of people who have had a schizophrenic disorder shows that in at least one subgroup, poor functioning in these areas can be found before the disorder is noticed (Wallace, 1984). Poor functioning also is related to poor outcome after

the disorder has been diagnosed. This means that, for at least some people, poor social functioning may be a marker of vulnerability to schizophrenia.

Whereas the social-selection theory points to flaws in the individual as the cause of schizophrenia, an alternative explanation for the greater incidence of schizophrenia in the lower SES group points to flaws in the society itself. The **increased-stress theory** refers to the amount of stress experienced by people in different socioeconomic classes. Living in areas with high crime rates, run-down housing, and inadequate schools may be more difficult and stressful than living in more affluent communities. At the same time, lower-SES people have little money or power to cope with the stresses they encounter.

High density, or the presence of a large number of people in a living unit or neighborhood, has often been thought to be related to psychopathology. However, an analysis of the living conditions of people who were admitted for the first time to mental hospitals in Chicago showed that, after differences in socioeconomic status and race were taken into account, most of the cases came from areas where there were both a higher proportion of people living alone and a low population density (Magaziner, 1980). It might be that people who are vulnerable to schizophrenia often choose to live alone because they find personal interactions stressful. However, living alone may be a disadvantage in a crisis.

This chapter has discussed what is known about schizophrenia, drawing upon research based on a variety of perspectives. Box 12–2 illustrates how focusing on a unique group of people from several perspectives can produce a fuller picture of schizophrenic disorders.

BOX 12–2 Investigating a Single Case from a Variety of Perspectives

Investigation of schizophrenic behavior from several perspectives can help in understanding both the disorder and its symptoms. The case of the Genain sisters illustrates how investigations of heredity, brain anatomy and activity, psychophysiological measures, and family interactions can complement one another.

The sisters, who were identical quadruplets, shared the same heredity (see Figures 12–18 and 12–19). Because the odds for identical quadruplets are one in 16 million births, they became celebrities in their home town soon after their birth in 1930. During their childhood, they performed song and dance routines and were so popular that they had a police escort on one early local tour. As they grew older, however, it became clear that they were not developing in a normal way. One sister dropped out of high school. The other three graduated but had trouble holding jobs. During their twenties, all four sisters developed schizophrenic disorders.

Because of the uniqueness of this case (four individuals with identical heredity who all showed schizo-

FIGURE 12–18 The Genain sisters as young children.

phrenic behavior could be expected to occur only once in tens of billions of births), a local physician alerted scientists at the National Institute of Mental Health. The sisters came to Washington, D.C., and were hospitalized there for intensive study in the mid 1950's. During the three years that they spent at NIMH, they were examined from a number of perspectives. To protect their privacy, the sisters were given pseudonyms, corre-

FIGURE 12–19 The Genain sisters as adults.

BOX 12–2 (continued)

sponding to NIMH's initials—Nora, Iris, Myra, and Hester—and the family was given the name Genain, from the Greek words meaning "dire birth."

Several of the quadruplets' family members had histories of psychological problems. Not only was their father's behavior often bizarre, but his brother, his mother, and his paternal uncle had each had a nervous breakdown.

Even though they had the same genetic risk, the sisters' schizophrenia could have been at least partly the result of environmental factors. For example, as is usual in multiple births, they were all small at birth. All of them spent time in incubators and did not go home from the hospital until they were six weeks old. They grew up in the glare of publicity and constantly heard comments about their similarity. Their father restricted their interactions with other people by refusing to allow them to play with other children or, later, to take part in school activities or to date.

The girls' father also objected to their stay at NIMH and often threatened to take them out of the hospital. Although he was cooperative and cordial at times, he also had considerable hostility toward people. His wife reported that he had tried to choke her several times and said that she had considered leaving him. At times, he accused his wife of having sexual relationships with his daughters' psychiatrists. During the quadruplets' third year at the hospital, he died.

This report, which reflects the psychodynamic perspective, describes the family relationships in detail:

Mrs. Genain's unfulfilled needs for maternal nurturing found expression in her closeness to Nora. It was the symbiotic tie of mother and infant, one in which the mother does not see the infant as a separate individual but as part of herself. . . . The closeness between them supported a report that Nora was not only her father's "favorite," but her mother's also. . . . Nora was

always the first of the babies to be burped after feeding. . . . Nora was also the daughter Mrs. Genain took home for trial visits from the hospital, although Iris' adjustment was also appropriate for home visits.

The central role for Myra was the "independent positive." Mrs. Genain identified Myra with her own independent strivings and actions. . . . Myra was the daughter upon whom Mrs. Genain was prone to lean in times of stress, who often strove for the favored position (which in this family was the protected one) with her mother. . . . She tried to live out the role her mother assigned to her of becoming independent, and the dependent-independent conflict became acute for her when she tried to move out on her own.

The central theme of the role Mrs. Genain assigned to Iris was the "repressed" one. She identified in Iris her own feeling that she must put up with anything. . . . In areas that concerned Iris as an individual, e.g., her abilities and appearance, Mrs. Genain was neither concerned nor interested.

The central theme assigned to Hester was the "negative" one. . . . Hester personified that which Mrs. Genain regarded as undesirable—hostility and sexuality, for example. The perception of these feelings in Hester appeared to have blocked her mother's perception of other human qualities in her. She was the last to be regarded as sick (she had been "bad") and she was not hospitalized before coming to the Clinical Center. Later Mrs. Genain did not even consider a time when Hester might come home for home visits from the hospital.

—Adapted from Rosenthal, 1963, pp. 463–465

The Genains were invited back to NIMH for a follow-up in 1981. During

that period Myra had lived the most normal life. She went to business college and later worked as a secretary. She was the only one of the four sisters to marry and have children. Nora was next best in adjustment. She had worked at least seven years, partly in government training programs. Hester and Iris had each spent more than 15 years in hospitals and had received more antipsychotic drug treatment than either Myra or Nora.

Researchers wondered if scanning techniques, developed after the early study of the sisters, could shed light on the differences in their behavior. The sisters' CT scans appeared normal, but other types of scans showed abnormal patterns. Their PET scans, made when the women were resting, showed activity in the visual areas (see Figure 12–20). Scientists wondered if this was an indication of hallucinations. The PET scans of Myra and Nora, the two sisters who had made the best adjustment, were closer to the normal PET scans than those of the two sisters whose behavior was less adaptive. The Genains also showed much less alpha brain wave activity than is normal. Since alpha waves appear when people relax or let their minds go blank, the low frequency of alpha waves may also suggest hallucinations.

The sisters were also given Computer Electroencephalographic Tomography scans (CET). CET scans show the electrical activity in the brain, in contrast to PET scans, which show chemical activity (see Figure 12–21). Since CET scans are much cheaper and safer for the subject than PET scans, they can be repeated at frequent intervals. All four Genain sisters showed low levels of alpha waves on the CET scans compared to a control subject. The correspondence between PET and CET scan patterns both in this case and in general research findings seems fairly close (Buchsbaum & Haier, 1987). These findings, when matched with the sisters' behavioral histories and with the earlier test data, may prove a help in relating specific behaviors with environmental factors and biological functioning.

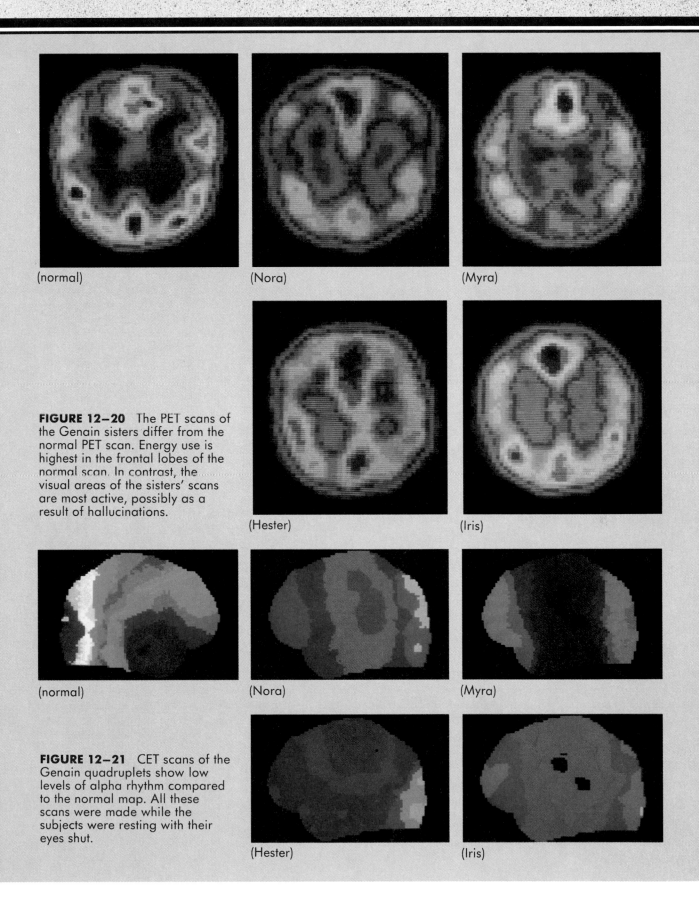

(normal) (Nora) (Myra)

(Hester) (Iris)

FIGURE 12–20 The PET scans of the Genain sisters differ from the normal PET scan. Energy use is highest in the frontal lobes of the normal scan. In contrast, the visual areas of the sisters' scans are most active, possibly as a result of hallucinations.

(normal) (Nora) (Myra)

(Hester) (Iris)

FIGURE 12–21 CET scans of the Genain quadruplets show low levels of alpha rhythm compared to the normal map. All these scans were made while the subjects were resting with their eyes shut.

Chapter Summary

GENETIC FACTORS

The person under study is often called the **index case.** Genetic relationships are carried out through family, twin, and adoption studies.

Family Studies The lifetime risk of developing schizophrenia correlates well with the proportion of genes shared with an affected family member. In family studies a family tree is constructed to give information about hereditary factors for a disorder. The risk for schizophrenia and other disorders is affected by **assortative mating,** the tendency for people to mate with others similar to themselves. **Genetic specificity** refers to findings that show that different disorders are caused by different genes. The **spectrum concept** refers to the situation in which several genetically related disorders typically occur in the same family.

Twin Studies Twin studies can help to disentangle heredity and environmental factors. Because monozygotic (MZ) twins have identical heredity, and dizygotic twins (DZ) share as many genes as a sibling pair, difference in rates of disorders in MZ and DZ twins suggest the relative contribution of heredity and environment.

Adoption Studies Adoption studies can also help provide information about heredity and environmental factors. The most common pattern for an adoption study is to use medical records to determine whether adopted children who had a biological parent with a schizophrenic disorder were more likely to develop a schizophrenic spectrum disorder than children without this genetic history. Some of these studies have relied only on medical records for both child and biological parent. Others that are more complex have assessed children and their adoptive families at several times over a period of years.

A Genetic Model **Monogenic models** are based on the idea that genetic transmission occurs at a specific gene pair locus. If the two genes in the pair differ, only one, the dominant gene, is **expressed. Penetrance** refers to the idea that a number of people in a family might have the right genetic makeup, but that only some of them may develop the disorder. **Polygenic models** assume that a number of genes found at specific locations must interact to produce the disorder. **Multifactorial polygenic models** assume that many gene loci are involved but they are interchangeable. Variations in DNA sequence can now be studied with modern methods and this knowledge may lead to a better understanding of schizophrenia and other disorders.

Genetic Counseling People concerned about their own genetic makeup may seek **genetic counseling** to get some estimate of their risk for a disorder seen in their family or the risk for any children they might have. Computer programs are helpful in these predictions, but they can only provide general statements of risk.

VULNERABILITY AND STRESS FACTORS

The **diathesis-stress theory** of schizophrenia emphasizes the interaction of biological vulnerability and environmental stress in the development of schizophrenic disorder. Data from adoption studies support this theory.

High-risk Studies and the Search for Markers Longitudinal studies are useful in examining causal factors in schizophrenia for many reasons. In disorders that occur in a relatively small percent of the population, longitudinal studies usually focus on subjects who are at high risk for the disorder because of the economic cost of including a large number who are extremely unlikely to develop the disorder. Research with high risk subjects has emphasized the identification of **markers** because an early indicator of especially high vulnerability would be helpful in providing early treatment. To be useful a marker should have several characteristics. Especially important among them are measurement of a stable personal trait, the occurrence or observability of the trait before a disorder develops, and the availability of a reliable and relatively noninvasive manner of assessment.

UNDERSTANDING THE SCHIZOPHRENIC PROCESS

Structural Abnormalities in the Brain The brains of some people with schizophrenic disorder have been found to have enlarged **cerebral ventricles.** Enlarged ventricles have been associated with negative symptoms and with a poor outcome.

Biochemical Abnormalities in the Brain Biochemical factors may play an important role in schizophrenia. Techniques such as PET scans can record the activity of working brain cells. Neurotransmitter functioning is thought to be important in schizophrenia. The **dopamine hypothesis** suggests that schizophrenic disorder is associated with an excess of dopamine at certain brain synapses. The effectiveness of drugs in reducing psychotic symptoms of schizophrenia is directly related to their effectiveness at blocking postsynaptic dopamine receptors.

Psychophysiological Abnormalities Subjects with schizophrenic disorder show more slow wave brain activity than do controls. This may be related to reduced frontal lobe activity. Positive and negative symptoms are thought to be related to overactivity and underactivity, respectively, in the autonomic nervous system. The study of brain wave activity has been made much easier by the development of the scanning technique called **brain electrical activity mapping (BEAM).**

Attention Problems Attention seems to be a central problem for those with schizophrenic disorder. Research findings suggest that attention may be a marker of vulnerability and that attentional deficits may be more general and acute during a

psychotic episode than at other times. Two measures of attention that seem particularly promising as risk markers are the Continuous Performance Test and eye tracking to measure **smooth-pursuit eye movements.**

Disordered Thinking Everyone probably shows some examples of disordered thinking, but those with schizophrenic disorder generally show the largest amount. Thus, a greater than usual degree of disordered thinking may be a marker of vulnerability to schizophrenia.

Language Use Abnormalities The structural organization of language used by those with schizophrenia is different from both the speech of other patient groups and of normal control groups.

FAMILY RELATIONSHIPS

Adoption studies of children at genetic risk for schizophrenia have shown that characteristics of the adoptive family environment are important in determining which children will develop a schizophrenic disorder. Stress in the family environment is likely to have a particularly negative effect on children who are genetically vulnerable.

Family Communication Deviance **Communication deviance** refers to an inability to maintain a shared focus of attention with another person. Parental communication devi-

ance may be associated with increased risk of later development of schizophrenic spectrum disorder in their child.

Expressed Emotion **Expressed emotion** (EE) is measured by the attitudes expressed toward a patient by a family member in a structured interview. High negative EE is associated with relapse for patients with schizophrenic disorder who have been discharged from the hospital after a psychotic episode. Results of EE research have been used to help families learn to interact more effectively with patients.

Parental Affective Style **Parental affective style** is measured during actual interactions of parents and children rather than through an interview. Expressed emotion and parental affective style are not perfectly correlated. When both parents are high in negative expressed emotion they and the child are all more physiologically aroused during family interactions.

THE ROLE OF THE COMMUNITY

The lower a person's socioeconomic status the greater the risk of a diagnosis of schizophrenic disorder. This finding has been explained in two ways. The **social-selection theory** assumes that people who have poor coping skills drift toward lower socioeconomic status. The **increased-stress theory** suggests that lower socioeconomic status is associated with greater stress in terms of poorer living conditions and increased crime.

Brain Disorders and Changes Related to Aging

C H A P T E R 1 3

The Brain: An Interactional Perspective
Vulnerability to Brain Disorders
The Normal Aging Process

Assessing Brain Damage
Brain Imaging

Characteristics of Organic Mental Disorders
Delirium
Dementia

Major Causes of Dementia
Alzheimer's Disease
Pick's Disease
Multi-Infarct Dementia
AIDS Dementia Complex
Other Organic Brain Syndromes

The Variety of Causes of Brain Disorders
A Genetic Basis: Huntington's Disease
A Neurotransmitter Deficit: Parkinson's Disease
An Infectious Disorder: General Paresis
Nutritional Deficiencies: Pellagra and Korsakoff's Syndrome
Brain Trauma: Injuries and Tumors
Multiple Causal Factors: Epilepsy
Blockage of Blood Supply: Cerebrovascular Accidents

An Integrative Approach to Brain Disorders

Chapter Summary

Edvard Munch (1863–1944), *Spanish Flu.* Scala/Art Resource, New York.

*B*ob Oxley, age 39, had been a long distance runner and, until recently, seemed to be in excellent condition. One morning he awoke with the worst headache he had ever had, became too nauseated to eat, and lay in bed caught between dreams and delirium. After a great effort, he dragged himself to his office, but the pain intensified and he could barely call his wife to take him home. When she got him to the hospital, a CT scan detected a white haze of blood in the fluid-filled spaces around his brain. Swollen tissue cast a shadow across both of his frontal lobes. A dye injected into his blood vessels filled a grapelike enlargement that ballooned out from a weakened artery in the front of his brain. Blood had leaked from a tiny tear in this bulge, causing the severe headache, and then clotted—preventing Bob's death. However, Bob was left with a condition called aphasia, in which the individual has a problem finding words and expressing what he might want to say. The aphasia resulted from the fact that the language center in his left frontal lobe had been injured. When Bob wanted to refer to his doctor, he said "blotcher." When asked to name ten animals he could not utter the names of more than two ("dog" and "cat"). When asked about his work, he said that he worked with "climates" (he was a stockbroker and worked with his clients). In most cases, Bob did not look distressed after his errors.

Ann Martin used to have an enviable memory. Now, at age 58, she forgets recent events and shows poor judgment. (She recently threw out a pair of valuable sterling silver salt and pepper shakers.) Because she can no longer balance her household budget, plan her meals, and take care of herself in other ways, she now

lives in a retirement home, even though she is still relatively young. Her condition has been diagnosed as Alzheimer's disease, which is caused by physical degeneration in the brain. This disease results in loss of intellectual ability and changes in personality and behavior.

These two cases show both similarities and differences. They are different because Ann Martin's behavior was the result of a deterioration of brain tissue as the result of a disease process that affected many aspects of her intellectual functioning. Bob Oxley's problem was due to an injury that affected a specific brain function—his ability to translate thoughts into speech. Despite these differences, these two people are similar in that they are each experiencing the effects of changes in the brain that are classified as an organic brain disorder. Our knowledge of the conditions that cause these disorders and their specific effects on brain function is increasing, not only because of new tools for study of the living brain, but also because of information about the interaction between organic functioning and personal characteristics and environmental variables. Despite these new techniques and new knowledge, for many people like Bob Oxley and Ann Martin who develop an organic brain disorder, their lives will never be the same again.

The Brain: An Interactional Perspective

The brain is an organ, like the kidney, the heart, or the liver, and organs are known to fail because of hereditary factors as well as environmental ones. Yet, to believe that the brain is merely a series of chemical reactions is to remove humans from any effects of their environment and their own actions. In fact, part of brain functions are "hard-wired" in advance of birth and part are designed to be shaped by experience.

At one time the prevailing view held that the brain grows through childhood, takes its final shape during adolescence, and then slowly ages. New work shows, however, that each area of the brain develops in unique ways throughout life. While some parts of the brain deteriorate, most brain cells continue to form new connections.

Three areas of brain research seem especially pertinent to an understanding of both normal and abnormal behavior:

1. Specifying how the brain grows and maintains itself;
2. Identifying the mechanisms by which the brain

acquires, stores, and uses information at the cellular and molecular levels, as well as the level of behavior and social interaction;

3. Making clear the role played by the brain in monitoring and regulating internal bodily processes.

In the past, people looked for physical causes for all forms of maladaptive behavior. If people behaved in odd ways, it was because there was something physically wrong with them. People could be "born criminals" or have "bad blood." Then scientists became aware of the psychological and social causes of behavioral problems. Physical explanations came to be seen as inadequate and even as somewhat simple-minded. Today, however, psychologists are developing a more complete picture of how intertwined the psychological, social, and physical domains of human behavior are.

We learn social skills, interact with others, and acquire personal attitudes within a framework of physical development. Human functioning is influenced by organic events that occur during intrauterine life, the birth process, and the long period of development after birth. The brain may become damaged suddenly, for example, when a person has a stroke or receives a head injury in an accident (see Box 13–1). In other cases certain diseases cause slow deterioration in the brain. These changes in the brain's physical nature, whether they happen quickly or slowly, and whether they involve large or small areas, are often the cause of unusual behavior. Damage to the brain can lead to a wide variety of behavioral problems, depending on what part of the brain is affected and the extent of the damage.

What is known today about brain disorders is consistent with what we have said throughout this text about the interaction among personal and environmental factors, vulnerability, and stress. It would simplify the lives of clinicians and researchers if they could assume that certain types of maladaptation are due to personal variables and others to situational pressures. Unfortunately, such an assumption would be incorrect. Behavior is a joint product of individual differences and environmental variables. The particular mix of these variables determines how people act and what they think about. There is no standard type of psychological effect for each type and degree of brain defect.

Vulnerability to Brain Disorders

Not only are there many differences in the actual damage to the brain through injury or disease that occur in different individuals, but the same amount of brain damage or deterioration can have varying effects. To some degree, these effects depend on the individual's personality and abilities and the social supports available

BOX 13–1 Sarah Fell and Her Life Was Changed Forever

One April day ten-year-old Sarah Monahan lost control of her bike and fell. She landed on a spiked piece of farm equipment and a two-inch spike punctured her left temple. Today, there is only a small scar, nothing to show the quarter-size hole where the spike shattered Sarah's skull and drove bone splinters into her brain. The accident left Sarah permanently brain-damaged, emotionally like a five year old, and academically at the third-grade level (see Figures 13–1 and 13–2). Her moods change in an instant, and she is increasingly aggressive toward her family and classmates. Her parents have been advised to lock up scissors and knives. Sarah once pushed her two-year-old brother into a rock bed, cutting his head and requiring a trip to the emergency room. She had no concept she had done anything wrong. Sometimes Sarah hears voices. One evening while the family was watching television, she stood up and yelled, "If you say that again, I'll kill you." No one had said a word.

—Based on *Seattle Times*, March 15, 1991, pp. A1, A3

FIGURE 13–1 Sarah's external wounds have healed and she appears unaffected by her injury.

FIGURE 13–2 Sarah and her teacher rejoice in Sarah's success in completing a computer problem.

to cushion the organic blow. Thus, there are many cases in which the psychological and behavioral effects of brain injuries and tumors do not conform to what would be expected on the basis of the amount of brain damage suffered.

The following are among the factors that influence vulnerability to brain damage and brain disorders:

1. *Age*. The age at which a brain condition develops can have both long- and short-term effects. Although in some instances an infant brain is better able to compensate for an injury than an adult brain, the infant brain may also be more susceptible to a variety of pathological conditions. Many behavioral deficits that are caused by damage to the brain in infancy are not noticed until considerably later.

2. *Social support*. The presence of caring, accepting people on whom the individual can rely usually eases

adjustment to a brain condition. Social isolation, on the other hand, increases cognitive deficits and, thus, abnormal behavior.

3. *Stress*. The greater the stress, the greater both the cognitive and behavioral deficits will be. Elderly people with chronic brain conditions often show marked deterioration following a piling up of stressful life events such as retirement or the death of a spouse.

4. *Personality factors*. It is a common clinical observation that some people react with intense anxiety, feelings of depersonalization, paranoid thinking, defensiveness, and hallucinations to any condition that causes even mild clouding of consciousness and impairment of cognitive and perceptual functioning.

5. *Physical condition*. The site of brain disorder, the rate of onset of the disorder, and the duration of the disorder all influence the clinical picture. In addition,

the individual's general level of health plays a role in his or her adjustment.

An individual's psychological state and social relationships at the onset of an organic condition can influence the impact of the condition on his or her behavior. A person with a stable personal life, for example, usually responds differently, and more adaptively, to treatment than someone in the throes of marital turmoil or financial reversal. When personal problems complicate an organic condition, both medical and psychological treatment may be necessary. In addition to its personal effects, impairment of brain function has a profound influence on interpersonal relationships. For example, people with epilepsy suffer from undesirable social consequences as well as from the seizures themselves.

Because determining the presence and extent of brain damage is complicated by the need to isolate its effects from those caused by personal and social factors, clinicians must avoid overly simple diagnoses. Clearly, a person who is noticeably disoriented, has trouble solving problems, and displays shallow or very changeable moods and emotions is suffering from some sort of behavioral problem. But the primary aspects of the diagnosis—an estimate of the roles played by organic damage, personality, and life stress in causing the disturbance—are not so easily determined.

The Normal Aging Process

For many years most of the problems of older people were lumped together under the heading of "senile disorders." We now know that several different types of psychological and behavioral problems occur among old people. The elderly are vulnerable both to serious consequences of brain changes such as senile dementia and to certain other psychological conditions such as those in which the role of organic factors is much less clear-cut. For example, depressive episodes increase in both frequency and depth in the later years of life (Hamilton, 1989). Depression is likely to be provoked by the beginning of an illness or disability, or the death of a spouse, but given time, most people adjust to these changes. The majority of severe depressions in old age are relapses, although new cases may occur even after the age of 75. Paranoid and hypochondriacal disorders are also common in older people.

Overall, the major clinical challenge facing the elderly is the greater likelihood of disorders in which there is brain degeneration. However, the problems of the elderly also reflect a number of other psychological problems that often accompany increased age. These problems seem to be outgrowths of personal insecurities evoked by such life changes as having to live alone or

being supported by others. At the same time, physiological changes may create additional stress as the person seeks to maintain self-esteem and competent, satisfying interactions. It would not be an exaggeration to say that the daily stresses the elderly have to cope with are often so numerous and so severe that they would probably tax the coping resources of young adults.

One of the few longitudinal studies of the relationship between age and intellectual functioning is the Seattle Longitudinal Study (Schaie, 1983). The original subjects, who ranged in age from 18 to 67, have now been tested 4 times over a 21-year period. The results have given a reasonably good picture of longitudinal change in cognitive abilities. The data show that there are only small changes in the kinds of abilities measured by intelligence tests before the age of 60, and no reliable decrease can be shown in these abilities before the age of 74. Although there is some decrease in measured ability beginning in the late 60s, it is not until age 81 that the average person falls below the middle range of performance for young adults. The data from the Seattle Longitudinal Study also suggest that there are very great individual differences in intellectual change throughout adulthood. Figure 13–3 illustrates some of the results of the study.

Three points need to be kept in mind about the elderly. One is that there are many examples of successful old people—people who are active, feel that they have

FIGURE 13–3 Performance on a variety of tasks used to measure intelligence shown as a percent of performance at age 25.

(From *Longitudinal Studies of Adult Psychological Development*, p. 114 by K.W. Schaie (ed.), published by Guilford Publications, Inc. Copyright © 1983 Guilford Publications, Inc. Reprinted by permission)

FIGURE 13–4 Grandma Moses was untrained and did not start painting in earnest until she was 75. *The Daughter's Homecoming* was painted in Grandma Moses' midcareer when she was 87. She did more than just live a long time and paint. She took the commonplaces of daily life, things we rarely look at because they are so homely, and gave them back their sense of wonder. As she looked at her extraordinary life, Grandma Moses said: "I look back on my life like a good day's work, it was done and I feel satisfied with it. I was happy and contented, I knew nothing better, and made the best out of what life offered. And life is what we make it, always has been, always will be."

something to offer, and make contributions to their families and communities. There is no better example of successful aging than the artist Anna Mary Robertson, better known as Grandma Moses (1860–1961), who first exhibited her paintings at age 78 (see Figure 13–4).

People who age successfully may suffer the physical declines that are frequent among the elderly, but they have found ways to work around them. A second point is that there is every reason to believe that most people can adapt successfully to the developmental transitions they encounter throughout life (Schaie, 1989). The third point is that there has been an unfortunate clinical neglect of older people. This is particularly true with regard to their psychological needs. Counseling and psychotherapy for the aged have often been dismissed as a waste of time. Yet many older people need opportunities to express their reactions to the variety of problems they face and to receive the support and advice of trusted clinicians.

Assessing Brain Damage

While the list of rare brain disorders is long, many brain disorders that have major impacts on thought and behavior are fairly common. For example, brain injuries, epilepsy, and acute cerebrovascular diseases are more common than schizophrenia and panic disorders (Silver and others, 1990). Consequently, the task of correctly identifying conditions that might be due to brain malfunction is an important one. This task is complicated by the fact that damage to a particular area of the brain can have diverse effects. This point is illustrated in Table 13–1, which lists symptoms often seen in patients who have disorders related to malfunction of the brain's frontal lobes.

A variety of procedures are used in assessing the extent of damage or deterioration of the brain. In

Table 13–1

Personality and Cognitive Changes in Patients with Disorders Related to Frontal Lobe Malfunctions

Apathy; loss of interest in social interactions
Inattention to personal appearance
Boisterousness; profanity; increased volume of speech
Irritability; violence
Increased risk-taking
Overeating; overdrinking
Reduced capacity to use language, symbols, and logic
Diminished ability to concentrate
Loss of orientation of time or place

SOURCE: Adapted from Silver and others, 1990

addition to a general physical evaluation, clinical tests may include a mental-status examination, neuropsychological testing, and both traditional x-rays and newer radiological techniques such as CT and PET scans that provide information on the brain's soft tissues and chemical activity.

The **mental-status examination** consists of an interview, which is useful for clinical observation as well as for any statements the individual might make. The mental-status examination is often supplemented by psychological testing and a neurological examination. Clinicians use the mental-status examination to elicit the following information.

1. Level of consciousness—how aware is the individual of what is going on?

2. General appearance (behavior, dress, cooperation)

3. Attention span

4. Orientation with regard to time and place

5. Short-term memory (events of past life or common knowledge)

6. Language (spontaneous speech, comprehension, repetition, reading, writing)

7. Stream of thought—do the individual's ideas fit together logically?

8. Mood

9. Judgment and insight

Use of the mental status examination is not limited to cases of suspected brain damage. It is employed generally to describe patients' behavior at the time they are seen clinically. It provides an objective record that is important for diagnosis and for assessing the course of a disorder and its subsequent response to treatment.

Careful and precise descriptions of behavior, without speculations and inferences, are necessary in recording the mental status examination. Its results are interpreted in conjunction with information about a patient's history, data from a physical examination, and the results of laboratory tests.

Neurologists, or physicians who specialize in diseases of the nervous system, use various techniques to assess brain damage and its cause. As discussed in Chapter 3, neuropsychology is a relatively new branch of psychology that deals with relationships between behavior and the condition of the brain. Clinical neuropsychologists are particularly interested in the effects of brain lesions on behavior. Neuropsychological tests are used to assess impairment in such areas as awareness of and responsiveness to sensory stimulation, ability to understand verbal communication and to express oneself, and emotional expression. Neuropsychological testing is sensitive to impaired functioning of various regions of the brain.

Brain Imaging

Progress in constructing tests to measure disturbances in various regions of the brain has been limited by the lack of direct information about what actually goes on in the brain. As we have seen in previous chapters, new technology using a variety of brain-imaging techniques is rapidly changing this situation. This technology contributes to clarifying the relationship between damage to specific regions of the brain and its effects on psychological functioning. This chapter which focuses on brain disorders is a good place to summarize some of the information about scanning techniques. Figure 13–5 shows the basic principles involved in three of the most widely used scanning techniques—computerized tomography (CT scan), positron emission tomography (PET scan), and magnetic resonance imaging (MRI).

The CT scan provides films that show where injuries, deterioration, or enlargement occurred. The PET scan allows researchers to visualize the activity of different parts of the human brain. A PET scan shows patterns of glucose utilization—an index of brain activity—in different parts of the brain. Much as weather maps show various levels of rainfall, a PET scan shows the levels of glucose metabolism in different parts of the brain as they vary with the person's mental state and behavior. The PET scan enables scientists to study biochemical changes in the brain that could never be charted before. Whereas the CT scan shows the brain's anatomy, the PET scan reveals the varying strength of biochemical processes that occur in different areas of the brain.

Magnetic resonance imaging (MRI) uses arrays of

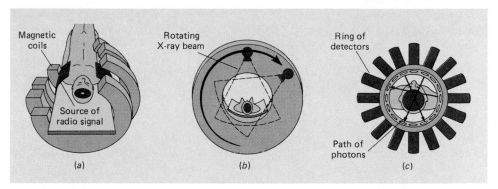

FIGURE 13–5 Each of the three major scanning techniques used to study the brain produces images in a different way and as the text explains, each type of scan may have somewhat different uses.

Magnetic resonance imaging (MRI) uses energy in the form of radio waves. After the patient is placed inside the imaging device, a strong magnetic field is created. Under these conditions atoms in each type of tissue resonate differently. A computer uses these resonation patterns to recreate a composite picture or scan.

Computer tomography (CT) operates through a narrowly focused X-ray that is rotated rapidly around the patient's body as the patient lies in the scanner. A computer then builds an image of a thin slice of the body from measures of the radiation passing through the patient as the X-ray source moves from one location to another.

In order to use positron emission tomography (PET) scanning procedures, radioactive chemicals must first be injected into the patient's body. As these chemicals are metabolized and move through the patient's body they emit positively charged electrons or positrons. Electrons and positrons then collide and emit pairs of photons that create signals by hitting detectors in the apparatus. These signals are then converted by a computer into a map of chemical activity.

sensitive detectors placed over the head to locate and measure precise sites of neural activity deep within the brain's furrows and creases. Both the MRI and the CT scan provide visualizations of brain anatomy and possible structural abnormalities. Unlike the CT, which is limited to imaging brain regions in a transverse plane, the MRI can image in all planes. The PET scan is the most elegant of the available imaging techniques because of its sensitivity and flexibility. PET scans permit the assessment of metabolic activity and the measurement of neurotransmitter function.

Characteristics of Organic Mental Disorders

Many of the organic mental disorders are basically physical disorders that have clusters of psychological symptoms associated with them. Clusters of symptoms that tend to appear together form a **syndrome.** Clusters of psychological and behavioral symptoms that are connected with temporary or permanent brain dysfunction are called **organic brain syndromes.** Cognitive loss is generally thought to be the hallmark of these organic

brain syndromes. This loss can affect perception, memory, imagination, thought processing, problem-solving skills, and judgment. The most common syndromes are delirium, dementia, intoxication, and withdrawal. This chapter will emphasize delirium and dementia; Chapter 14 will discuss intoxication and withdrawal.

Delirium affects the person's state of consciousness or attention while dementia refers to loss of intellectual ability. Delirium is often a short-term condition that is reversible, whereas dementia generally implies a nonreversible and often progressive condition.

Delirium

The symptoms of **delirium** include relatively global cognitive impairment, disorientation, and confusion. In delirium, an individual has difficulty mobilizing, focusing, shifting, and sustaining attention. A wide and changeable range of strong emotions that do not seem related to environmental events may be evident. The presence of several of the following symptoms permits diagnosis of this condition.

1. Perceptual disturbances (for example, misinterpreting actual occurrences)

2. Incoherent speech

3. Insomnia or daytime sleepiness

4. Increased or decreased psychomotor activity (for example, hyperactivity)

5. Disorientation and memory impairment.

Delirium can occur as a result of either an acute or a chronic brain condition. There are four general organic causes of delirium:

1. Brain disease (for example, an infection or tumor)

2. A disease or infection in another part of the body that affects the brain (for example, a metabolic condition)

3. Intoxication (for example, with alcohol)

4. Withdrawal from a substance to which an individual is addicted (for example, drugs).

Delirium generally accompanies some other serious physical problem; about 10 percent of hospitalized medical and surgical patients become delirious (Lipowski, 1987). A person who is hospitalized after a heart attack may become delirious because the amount of oxygen the brain receives could depend on whether the patient is sitting up or lying down. Inadequate excretion of body wastes can also cause delirium. For example, if the kidneys fail to function, the toxins that are usually filtered out by the kidneys and excreted in the urine will accumulate in the bloodstream and the blood will have less room for oxygen. As a result of such physical disturbances, the brain begins to starve for oxygen, and symptoms of delirium may occur. The symptoms generally disappear shortly after the precipitating condition has been corrected.

Psychological stress, sleep and sensory deprivation, prolonged immobilization, and severe fatigue are likely to contribute to the onset of delirium and to increase its severity. It is believed that a general derangement of brain metabolism coupled with an imbalance in the neurotransmitters underlies all cases of delirium.

Although everyone has the potential to develop delirium, there appear to be wide variations in susceptibility. Some people become delirious in response to metabolic changes or medications that do not produce delirium in others, whereas others fail to become delirious under metabolic conditions that are likely to produce delirium in most people. The incidence of delirium is highest among old people. It is not known to what extent this increase is a function of age itself rather than the frequency of organic brain disease and systemic disease in old age.

Patients with organic brain lesions are especially liable to develop delirium, as are people with long histories of alcohol or drug addiction. Delirium is frequent following surgery—either immediately or after a lucid period of several days—and seems to be due to the physical stress of the surgery itself and to the psychological stress of the surgery and the postoperative period. In a sense, delirium is a threshold phenomenon; that is, each individual probably has a specific threshold for this condition. Preexisting brain damage, addiction, and certain chronic medical disorders probably bring people close to this threshold even if they do not exceed it; relatively small metabolic changes may then push the patient over the threshold.

DELIRIUM TREMENS One of the most dramatic examples of delirium can be seen in an acute brain condition called **delirium tremens** (or "the DTs") that may sometimes result from excessive alcohol consumption. People with the DTs may be unable to follow directions like "stick out your tongue" or to attend to events going on around them. In addition to delirium, the DTs are characterized by tremors and visual hallucinations that result in a state of terror. The following excerpt from Mark Twain's *Huckleberry Finn* is a vivid description of the DTs experienced by Pap, a heavy user of alcohol for many years.

I don't know how long I was asleep, but all of a sudden there was an awful scream and I was up. There was Pap looking wild, and skipping around every which way and yelling about snakes. He said they was crawling up his legs; and then he would give a jump and scream, and say one had bit him on the cheek—but I couldn't see no snakes. He started running round and round the cabin, hollering, "Take him off, take him off; he's biting me on the neck." I never see a man look so wild in the eyes. Pretty soon he was all fagged out, and fell down panting; then he rolled over and over wonderful fast, kicking things every which way, and striking and grabbing at the air with his hands, and screaming and saying there was devils a-hold of him. He wore out by and by, and laid still awhile, moaning. Then he laid stiller, and didn't make a sound. I could hear the owls and wolves away off in the woods, and it seemed terrible still. He was lying over by the corner. By and by he raised up part way and listened, with his head to one side. He says, very low: "Tramp-tramp-tramp; they're coming after me but I won't go. Oh, they're here, don't touch me—don't! Hands off—they're cold; let go. Oh, let a poor devil alone." Then he went down on all fours and crawled off, begging them to let him alone, and he rolled himself up in his

blanket and wallowed in under the old pine table, still a-begging; and then he went to crying. I could hear him through the blanket.

The symptoms of delirium tremens usually are not evident until after the person has stopped drinking. Several aspects of the mechanism that causes its symptoms are not well understood, but the DTs seem to be due to the prolonged interference of alcohol with the metabolism of neurons. The condition occurs in about five percent of alcoholics. Regardless of the cause (alcohol, infection, and so on), diffuse slowing of brainwave patterns is a regular finding.

Delirium tremens can last for a week or longer and the affected person must usually be hospitalized. During an episode of the DTs, the patient's physical condition deteriorates and he or she becomes highly susceptible to infections. Tranquilizing drugs and a quiet and orderly environment are essential, since even routine conversations among hospital personnel may frighten the patient and heighten his or her hallucinatory experiences. Renewed ability to sleep and rest usually indicates that an episode of DTs is coming to an end. However, recovery depends on restoration of metabolic equilibrium. In some cases equilibrium cannot be restored and death occurs.

Dementia

I fear I am not in my perfect mind.
Methinks I should know you, and know this
 man;
Yet I am doubtful; for I am mainly ignorant
What place this is; and all the skill I have
Remembers not these garments; nor I know not
Where I did lodge last night. Do not laugh at
 me . . .

—Shakespeare, *King Lear*, Act IV, Scene 7

The onset of King Lear's madness shows the symptoms of dementia that people have witnessed for centuries. The essential feature of **brain deterioration,** or **dementia,** is a gradual loss of intellectual abilities that is sufficient to interfere with social or occupational functioning. Memory impairment, decline in ability to exercise good judgment and engage in abstract thinking, loss of self-control, and personality changes also occur. Dementia may be progressive, static, or even reversible if an effective treatment is available. Because individuals with dementia are not able to think clearly and often have difficulty making rational judgments, they are particularly vulnerable to physical, psychological, and social stress. Demented individuals are more likely than other people to experience delirium.

The onset of dementia is insidious, and the course of the disorder is usually gradual. The term **senile dementia** is often used to refer to the condition when it occurs in people over 65 (see Figure 13–6). Autopsies show that most senile dementias have the characteristics of *Alzheimer's disease,* which will be discussed later in the chapter. If dementia occurs in younger individuals, it is termed **presenile dementia.** In people with this condition there is a progressive atrophy (degeneration) of brain tissue, and their brainwave patterns are almost invariably abnormal. The individual becomes increasingly subject to lapses of memory, poor judgment, and disorientation. Deterioration in personal habits is common, and behavior may become unpredictable and impulsive. Because the person often remembers past events better than recent ones, he or she seems to live in the past much of the time (Heston and White, 1991).

The rate at which behavior is affected and the

FIGURE 13–6 Dementia was not a major public health concern prior to the twentieth century because few people lived beyond the age of 75, and dementia is largely a problem associated with advanced age. Today, more than 50 percent of the entire U.S. population reaches age 75 years and 25 percent live to be 85. The U.S. Census Bureau estimates that by the year 2000 there will be 35 million persons older than 65 years and that by the year 2050 this number will rise to 67 million. A large number of older people in nursing homes have some degree of dementia. The economic impact of dementia is great, running into billions of health care dollars each year.

manner in which it changes are influenced by many factors, not the least of which is the individual's reaction to the physical and psychological deterioration. A sizable percentage of senile people seem to undergo profound personality changes. However, these changes may be in degree rather than basic alterations of personality. For these people reconstruction of their earlier personalities may uncover the presence of maladaptive behavior patterns before the onset of senility, including actual and severe psychotic or neurotic reaction patterns, or more likely, tendencies in those directions. These tendencies are made worse by the onset of senility, but they are not caused by it. Over half of the cases that are diagnosed as senile dementia show various combinations of agitation, paranoid and schizophreniclike reactions, and depression. One common symptom is **confabulation:** when faced with loss of particular memories, the individual fills in memory gaps with detailed, but inaccurate, accounts of his or her activities (Horvath & others, 1989).

The following case describes symptoms that are often seen in primary degenerative dementia. **Primary degenerative dementia** refers to a condition in which the changed behavior appears to be the result of permanent, rather than temporary, changes in brain tissue and the central nervous system. These include a progressive memory deficit, at first for recent events but later for remote ones, along with narrowing of interests, loss of initiative, sluggishness of thought, apathy, irritability, and restlessness at night. Some of these symptoms are similar to those of depression; Table 13–2 lists some of the ways to differentiate the two.

A talented artist was referred by his wife; he had become anxious and mildly depressed when his first symptoms emerged. In many respects he was very fortunate. At the age of 65 he had achieved a national, even international, reputation as an illustrator . . . [he] had devised a special process used to produce color covers and prints. . . .

Recognition of his work gained him election to one of the distinguished clubs of artists in the city.

There had been some beginning failure in his memory. He complained of some difficulty in the use of his hands and arms, a clumsiness and lack of precision that did not exist before. When first seen, he advised that his father had become senile . . . and had had a slowly progressive course of increasing mental impairment, which the patient feared for himself. . . . He was accompanied on his first visit by his wife. . . . They had been married 30 years and had two daughters, both married.

She declared that at home he had become critical and querulous. He seemed to avoid going out to meet his artist friends. Furthermore, in contrast to his usual self-assurance at his work he seemed anxious and upset when requested to take on a new contract. His concern over his abilities, his doubts, and even refusal of work were reflected in his relations with his wife. [Over the succeeding months it was learned that she had commenced to drink and did not seem as interested in the care of the house.] Also, he said his daughters were hounding him. Although he was able to talk most interestingly of his past work and life, it was clear that he had difficulty in recalling his earlier visits with his physician, when they occurred, or what had been discussed. The course was slowly progressive. As time went on, the tension and near panic he felt over inability to perform, on the recognition of his slowly progressive impairment of perception and skill, accompanied by much anxiety in meeting his business and social acquaintances, continued to increase. . . .

The failure in this mental functioning proceeded slowly. Periods of disorientation were first noticed at night when he arose to go to the bathroom. Some six years after onset he became seriously

Table 13–2

Signs and Symptoms that Help Distinguish Depression from Dementia

Dementia	Depression
Even progression over months or years	Uneven progression over weeks
Attempts to hide memory loss	Complaints of memory loss
Worse later in day or when fatigued	Often worse in morning, better as day goes on
Unawareness of or minimizing of disability	Awareness of and exaggeration of disability
Abuse of drugs rare	Possible abuse of alcohol or other drugs

SOURCE: Based on Hestin and White, 1991

disturbed, had the delusion that men were attempting to kill him, and hallucinated voices. . . . He would talk to[his wife] of planning a Christmas card, but would forget that his daughters were married. His death, in a local general hospital, occurred quickly from cardiac arrest seven years after he was first seen.

—Kolb and Brodie, 1982, pp. 238–239

Major Causes of Dementia

Alzheimer's Disease

I visited Margo at her home each day. On my way, I'd pick up whatever she needed from the store, or sometimes a treat. Her favorite is peanut butter and jelly sandwiches on white bread. She can devour two in one sitting, especially if milk is at hand. Given her size, this always amazes me.

At the apartment, Margo's Jamaican home attendant, Louise, welcomed me with giggles and smiles, probably because my visit signaled a relief from her duties. It took Louise a few minutes to open the door since it was rigged with an array of locks and chains designed to keep Margo from slipping out in the night. Before the locks were installed, Margo had, on occasion, satisfied her understandable desire to explore the city on her own. We usually found her a couple of days later when we learned of a police report describing a woman in a nightgown seen roaming Central Park. Bad things have happened during these excursions. Does Margo understand that she is locked inside for her own safety? . . .

Margo never called me by name. I never figured out if she just forgot it from one day to the next

FIGURE 13–7 Alzheimer's disease destroys minds, but there have been few opportunities to study the disorder's impact on artistic creativity, one of the highest expressions of the human mind. These paintings and the sketch were created by an artist who began to show signs of Alzheimer's disease in his late 60s. When examined at the age of 74, he could not remember words three minutes after they were addressed to him. He was able to copy complex abstract figures, but his artistic ability had deteriorated.

A painting (a) completed at the time behavioral changes were first apparent shows good perspective, color sense, and attention to detail. A second (b), done seven years later, shows deterioration of all of these qualities, but retains some artistry. In a third picture (c), a sketch of the same subject done two years after that, the artist could only copy gross details from previous paintings. Testing over several years indicated that he first lost motivation, memory, and organizational ability, while visual perception and the physical ability to draw lasted longer.

(a)

(b)

(c)

or whether she ever actually remembered me at all. If I asked her, she would say she knew who I was. But that could have just been adaptive politeness; I probably looked like I wanted to be remembered.

—Firlik, 1991, p. 201

This account, written by a medical student, conveys some of the reality of **Alzheimer's disease,** an insidious, heartbreaking malady that is associated with advancing age. The memory lapses, confusion, and dementia associated with this disease inevitably worsen. People with Alzheimer's disease forget how to cook, go on wild spending sprees, lose the ability to balance their checkbooks and count change, forget how to drive a car, and lose creative abilities (see Figure 13–7 on page 391). Nearly total bodily and behavioral deterioration is typical in its final stages.

By far the leading cause of mental deterioration among the elderly, Alzheimer's disease affects over 10 percent of all people over 65 (Evans and others, 1989). In one family out of three, one parent will die of the disease. The disease tends to run in families and to be more frequent among females than among males. Because most Alzheimer's patients must eventually be placed in institutions, the disease (which has an average duration of about seven years) places tremendous demands on health-care resources. Alzheimer's victims constitute 50 to 60 percent of the 1.3 million people in nursing homes, accounting for more than half of the many billions of dollars spent annually on nursing home care. The disease will become more common and take an even greater toll as the average age of the U.S. population continues to increase. The part of the population over age 85 is particularly at risk for Alzheimer's disease (Advisory Panel on Alzheimer's Disease, 1991). By the year 2040 the number of people in this age group, the fastest growing segment of the United States population, is expected to be five times greater than it is currently. Based on the proportion of cases currently in that age group, it has been estimated that at that time the number of cases of Alzheimer's disease may exceed 6 million.

Alzheimer's disease is also the most common form of presenile dementia. In these cases also, it usually causes gradual intellectual deterioration with growing lapses of memory (see Table 13–3). The progressive destruction of nervous tissue leads to slurring of speech, involuntary movements of arms and legs, and in some cases, seizures. When the disease manifests itself primarily in the intellectual sphere, the individual may experience great anxiety about the deterioration of his or her abilities.

Research and experience with the increasing number of Alzheimer's patients have increased knowledge of the symptoms of the disease and ways of helping victims adjust. Box 13–2 summarizes current knowledge in these two areas.

RESEARCH DIRECTIONS Alzheimer's disease was first identified in 1906 by a German physician, Alois Alzheimer. His patient, a 51-year-old woman, suffered loss of memory, disorientation, and later, severe dementia. After her death, Alzheimer performed an autopsy on her brain and found the two distinctive characteristics of the disease: tangled clumps of nerve cells and patches of disintegrated nerve-cell branches called plaques. Because the patients Alzheimer studied were relatively young, he thought the disease to be one of middle age; similar symptoms in elderly people were generally regarded as a natural consequence of aging by Alzheimer and his contemporaries. Today this view has been discarded. Dementias of the Alzheimer's type seem to involve a

Table 13–3
Phases in the Cognitive Decline Accompanying Alzheimer's Disease

Phase	Examples
1. Complaints of memory deficit	Forgetting names that one formerly knew well
2. Increased cognitive decline and signs of confusion	Losing or misplacing an object of value
3. Moderately severe cognitive decline and intensified confusion (early dementia)	Inability to recall major aspects of one's life, such as the names of close family members
4. Severe cognitive decline and confusion (middle dementia)	Largely unaware of all recent events and experiences
5. Very severe cognitive decline and confusion (late dementia)	Loss of all verbal abilities, need for assistance in eating and toileting

SOURCE: Based on Reisberg, 1985.

BOX 13-2 Helping the Victim of Alzheimer's Disease

Caretakers of Alzheimer's patients need to be familiar with both the symptoms of the disease and ways to deal with them. Table 13–4 shows the frequencies with which various symptoms occur as the disease progresses. A basic ground rule for caring for Alzheimer's patients is: Take nothing for granted. Although no one patient will be like another, certain types of behaviors appear with a greater frequency than others. The following overview presents some of the most common behavioral concerns and coping strategies useful to caretaking family members.

SYMPTOM

1. *Depression.* Unhappiness and withdrawal are common in Alzheimer's disease patients.

2. *Hostility, Belligerence, and Aggression.* Alzheimer's patients can be selfish and hostile.

3. *Disorientation.* The Alzheimer's patient will become increasingly confused about people, places, and time.

4. *Wandering.* Wandering and restlessness are common problems.

5. *Anxiety and Suspiciousness.* Worries and paranoid thinking occur.

COPING STRATEGY

1. Caregivers can try to increase activities that patients formerly enjoyed and can still manage. Try to involve them in such activities, perhaps with another family member or a friend. Talk with them; reminisce about family, friends, and activities.

2. Confronting the situation head-on and trying to reason with Alzheimer's patients will not work. Being reassuring and calm may help to reduce the hostility. Trying to distract the patient with questions about the problem and gradually moving his or her attention to something else may also help.

3. Labeling items, or color coding rooms such as the bathroom or bedroom, can alleviate some problems in the early stages of the disease (see Figure 13–8). Talking in a calm voice,

Table 13–4
Percentages of Alzheimer's Disease Patients at Three Levels of Severity Showing Specific Problems

Type of Problem	Severity Level of Illness			Total Sample
	MILD	MODERATE	SEVERE	
Restlessness	60	40	50	45
Suspiciousness	20	24	29	24
Falling	20	33	29	28
Hallucinations	10	24	30	21
Wandering	18	22	50	26
Agitation	10	27	38	24
Hygiene	8	24	71	28
Incontinence	5	16	30	16

and reassuring patients of where they are and whom they are with, may help ease feelings of being lost and alone.

4. Keeping the household free of clutter is a major consideration so that there is not added confusion or harm to the patient as he or she wanders through what was once a familiar environment. Identification bracelets and safety locks are other useful devices for those individuals who are given to wandering. Walking and other physical exercises may help alleviate such problems.

5. Patient fears and anxieties cannot really be dealt with in a rational and normal manner. Identifying what is frightening patients may be helpful, but directly confronting and telling them there is nothing to their concerns will not work. It is often useful to develop calming answers to the situation that is frightening and then to distract the patient to another subject.

FIGURE 13–8 Alzheimer's disease has a profound effect, not only on the person who develops it, but also on the lives of all the members of the family. In this home, reminder signs are used to lessen the memory problems Alzheimer's disease creates.

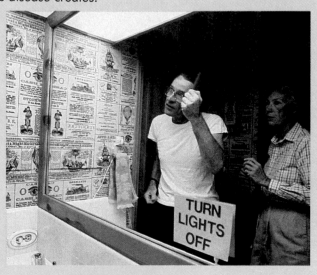

specific pathological process rather than being a normal consequence of aging. Researchers have looked to many sources for information about possible causes of the disease. There is growing reason to believe that different cases of Alzheimer's disease can spring from different causes. Rather than a single illness, the disease may be a group of closely associated disorders that involve both genetic and nongenetic factors.

Neurochemicals One of the keys to Alzheimer's disease may be a certain type of brain cell, the cholinergic cell, that is involved in memory and learning. These cells release an important chemical messenger called **acetylcholine.** Acetylcholine is a key player in brain activity. When it is released by the cholinergic cell, it stimulates neighboring cells and causes them to release other chemicals and these chemicals in turn influence still other cells. Alzheimer's disease evidently throws a wrench into this process. For reasons that are not yet understood, people with advanced Alzheimer's disease lose up to 80 percent of their cholinergic cells in key brain areas. As a result, there also is a dramatic reduction in the amount of acetylcholine produced in the brain. There is a strong correlation between the amount of loss of acetylcholine or cholinergic cells in an individual's brain and the severity of that person's dementia. One focus of current research is the development of drugs that will increase the formation of acetylcholine, prevent its destruction, or directly stimulate acetylcholine receptors. Current research also suggests that biochemical abnormalities in Alzheimer's disease are not limited to the cholinergic system. There are deficiencies in other systems as well, for example cell loss in the noradrenergic system which is another chemical messenger system (Advisory Panel on Alzheimer's Disease, 1991; Coyle and others, 1983).

Genes The fact that Alzheimer's disease often occurs in several members of the same family suggests that a genetic factor is at work. Half the immediate family members of patients with Alzheimer's disease may develop the devastating mental disorder if they live into their nineties. Growing evidence indicates that Alzheimer's disease is a hereditary disease, governed by a gene or genes that cause damage to the patient's brain late in life. (Horvath & others, 1989). The disease has been linked to abnormalities on chromosome 21, which has been identified as the location of the gene for a protein called beta amyloid found in the characteristic clumps and plaques of Alzheimer's disease. Laboratory studies have shown that beta amyloid fragments can kill nerve cells. Evidence also exists of an association between Alzheimer's disease in some families and chromosome 19 abnormalities.

Screening for hereditary influences in Alzheimer's disease might reveal genetic markers, and it might be possible to identify environmental factors that influence the age of onset and the progress of the disease. However, experts are divided on whether all cases of Alzheimer's disease will turn out to be caused by genes. Research on this topic is complicated by the fact that because the disease occurs so late in life, many people who might be destined to get it die from other causes first.

Alzheimer's Effect on the Family In addition to searching for the causes of Alzheimer's disease, researchers are attempting to find ways of treating not only the patient but caregivers as well. Those who care for people with Alzheimer's disease often experience severe stress. Marian Roach has provided the following description of her reactions and those of her sister, Margaret, to their mother's deterioration as a result of Alzheimer's disease.

I noticed that she had stopped taking phone messages. One friend said she sounded "jealous and hostile." She would abruptly hang up on people. She became obsessed with the plumbing: She would look under the sinks and start to take apart the pipes, convinced there was a drip. She would walk away in the middle of conversation. She became repetitive, depressed.

—Roach, 1983, p. 23

As the deterioration continued, the pressures and emotional strain worsened.

Margaret and I have no relatives but my mother. The decisions we make are made together. Margaret works until 11 at night and on weekends. We have a young woman who lives in the house from Monday through Friday. Another woman comes on Friday and Saturday nights. Yet another takes my mother out—for rides or to the movies—three afternoons a week. But the burden of care is on my patient sister, who manages the schedules and sees my mother daily. I work during the day. I am with my mother on Sundays.

As I have gotten to know this disease, I have felt ashamed at my own embarrassment. I find myself explaining her condition to people, to excuse her behavior. Sometimes I do this in front of her and, for an instant, my mother will look terribly embarrassed. I see it in her face and I feel very unlike a daughter. I feel like a traitor. And then

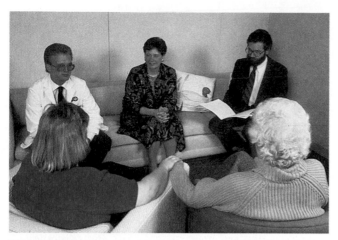

FIGURE 13–9 Not only those affected by Alzheimer's disease, but also other members of their families, feel the impact of the behavioral and cognitive changes brought about by the disorder. Counseling sessions for the entire family, including the patient, are often helpful not only for developing strategies for care, but also for reducing the stress felt by all family members.

she will forget my explanation of her "memory problem," and her questions and repetitions, along with my embarrassment, will continue. Alzheimer's victims are likely to say or do anything during the stages just before they can do literally nothing for themselves. It is difficult to know what to expect. The anticipation is sometimes the worst part.

I sometimes dread the weekends. I try not to cry in front of Margaret, who tries not to cry in front of me. Margaret and I have discussed the possibility of our contracting the disease. If I get it, I have said that I'd want Margaret to kill me; she has said the same.

—Roach, 1983, p. 31

Research on the particularly stressful aspects of caring for Alzheimer's victims has shown that the sense of lack of control over what will happen next is of great importance. In addition, caregivers feel isolated, unable to deal effectively with the continuing stress, and confused about their own reactions. Support groups and group therapy can be valuable in allowing family members to express their feelings, particularly those that they consider unacceptable (for example, anger and disappointment). The opportunity to compare their experiences with those of other people who are going through the same trial often makes them aware that such feelings are normal and understandable (see Figure 13–9) (Light & Lebowitz, 1989).

TREATMENT Little progress has been made in the treatment of Alzheimer's disease since Alois Alzheimer's day, and even diagnosis remains difficult. While the patient is alive, the diagnosis must be arrived at by a careful process of elimination. Through brain imaging and other tests, it is possible to determine that the patient has not suffered a series of small strokes and does not have Parkinson's disease, a brain tumor, depression, an adverse drug reaction, or other disorders that can cause dementia. The chances of making an accurate diagnosis of Alzheimer's disease in the living patient have been improved by the finding that 70 to 80 percent of patients with the disease show a characteristic pattern of decrease in metabolic function or cerebral blood flow in certain areas of the brain (see Figure 13–10). Because no other illness with symptoms of confusion and intellectual deterioration has so far been found that shows this pattern, scanning techniques provide a valuable clue to diagnosis although they do not as yet provide enough information to be certain that the patient has Alzheimer's disease. The only way to be absolutely certain that a patient has the disorder is to examine the brain after death. An autopsy is needed because so far it is the only way to determine whether the plaques and tangles characteristic of the disease are present.

Although much remains to be discovered about this disease, two critical crossroads reached in the approach to treatment for Alzheimer's disease have been (1) the recognition of Alzheimer's disease as a disorder distinct from the normal aging process, and (2) the realization that in developing therapeutic and social interventions for a major illness or disability the concept of *care* can be as important as that of *cure*.

FIGURE 13–10 These PET scans show the characteristic pattern of decrease in metabolic function seen in the brain of an Alzheimer's patient *(bottom)* compared to that of an age- and sex-matched control *(top)*.

Increasing knowledge about the role of genetic abnormalities in Alzheimer's disease may lead to effective treatment methods. There are several ways in which formation of beta amyloid might be stopped from killing nerve cells in the brain. For example, certain drugs might accomplish this task.

Four scientific and clinical care challenges now face researchers and clinicians who deal with Alzheimer's disease:

1. Determining the fundamental neurobiological causes;
2. Developing more effective treatments that would prevent its occurrence and impede or reverse its progression;
3. Providing sensitive clinical care for those already diagnosed with Alzheimer's disease;
4. Supporting family members throughout the course of the disease with expert advice, treatment, and caring.

Pick's Disease

Pick's disease is much less common than Alzheimer's disease. Whereas the risk of Alzheimer's disease increases steadily through adult life, Pick's disease is most likely to develop between the ages of 60 and 70. After that period the risk decreases (Heston & Mastri, 1982). Its symptoms are so similar to those of Alzheimer's disease that it takes an autopsy to tell the two disorders apart. People who have died from Pick's disease show a characteristic form of brain atrophy. Among people over age 40, 24 out of 100,000 can be expected to die of the disease. There appears to be a strong genetic factor, and men are at greater risk of developing the disease than women (Heston and others, 1987).

As is the case with Alzheimer's disease, there are no known cures for Pick's disease or any of the other senile and presenile dementias. Their treatment consists mainly of emotional support and sedative drugs. Efforts are made to structure the individual's life so that his or her days are uncomplicated and structured so as to avoid pressure and tension.

Multi-infarct Dementia

Another less common dementia, which is more likely to occur after age 65 than before, is **multi-infarct dementia.** This disorder is caused by a series of minor strokes that occur at different times. The onset is abrupt and the course of the disorder is fluctuating rather than uniformly progressive. The pattern of deficits is "patchy," depending on which areas of the brain have been destroyed. As the condition worsens, the relatively intact areas of intellectual functioning decrease and there is increased disturbance in several functions, including memory, abstract thinking, judgment, and impulse control. Hypertension may be a major factor in multi-infarct dementia. Controlling high blood pressure helps prevent this type of dementia and reduces the likelihood of additional minor strokes when multi-infarct dementia is already present.

AIDS Dementia Complex

AIDS dementia complex (ADC) is receiving increased attention from neurologists and psychologists because many AIDS patients display cognitive impairment (Dickson & Ranseen, 1990). In addition, some people who are positive for the human immunodeficiency virus (HIV) but have not developed any overt symptoms of AIDS show impairment in neuropsychological testing. The symptoms associated with ADC include: forgetfulness, concentration difficulties, mental slowness, mild motor difficulties, and apathetic, withdrawn behavior. The early symptoms of ADC are similar to the dementias of the elderly and may closely resemble a major depression. (See Table 13–2 for noticeable differences between the dementias and depression.) As ADC progresses, the majority of patients develop a severe dementia with global loss of cognitive functions, severe psychomotor retardation, mutism, and motor weakness. Psychotic symptoms develop in some patients. CT scans of ADC patients reveal cortical atrophy.

ADC is a newly recognized type of dementia. Its early recognition is complicated by its similarities to largely psychological disorders such as depression. Because the disorder usually appears in younger people who are not normally expected to develop dementing illnesses, the problem may be misdiagnosed. The typical psychological reactions to a diagnosis of AIDS may further hinder a correct diagnosis of ADC. Because many young individuals have a variety of self-defeating behaviors, such as drug abuse and promiscuous sexual activity, at the time they develop ADC the illness is particularly difficult to treat and to research carefully.

Other Organic Brain Syndromes

Many other organic brain syndromes exist, which, while less common than delirium and dementia, also involve major changes in overall functioning. In **amnestic syndrome,** for instance, there is a memory disturbance marked by inability to learn new material or recall information acquired in the past. Table 13–5 describes the three main diagnostic features of amnestic syn-

Table 13–5

Diagnostic Features of Amnestic Syndrome

1. *Anterograde amnesia*—impaired ability to learn, retain, and reproduce new information.
2. *Retrograde amnesia*—impaired ability to recall memories that were established prior to the onset of the disorder.
3. *Confabulation*—expression of inaccurate and at times inappropriate answers to straightforward and simple questions.

dromes. Neither the confusion and clouding of consciousness seen in delirium nor the general loss of intellectual abilities seen in dementia are characteristic of amnestic syndromes. The most common forms of amnestic syndrome result from thiamine deficiency and chronic alcohol use. The syndrome may also follow head injuries, surgery, or anything else that interferes with the flow of blood through the brain. Treatment depends entirely on the cause; no specific treatment is available for most of the disorders that cause this condition.

The diagnosis of **organic delusional syndrome** applies when there are delusions that seem to be attributable to an organic process. Intellectual impairment is absent or slight, and the confusion of delirium is absent. A number of substances discussed in Chapter 14 (for example, amphetamines, cannabis, and psychedelics) may cause this syndrome.

Organic hallucinosis refers to a syndrome characterized by recurrent or persistent hallucinations experienced in a state of clear awareness. This diagnosis is used when an organic factor is believed to be involved. Use of psychedelics is a common cause of this syndrome. The types of hallucinations manifested are often related to the substance involved. For example, alcohol tends to induce auditory hallucinations.

Organic affective syndrome features an abnormal mood, either depressive or manic, that is judged to be a consequence of a brain disorder rather than a personal response to an event or situation. This syndrome is often caused by toxic or metabolic factors. Disorders of the endocrine system can also play a role.

Organic anxiety syndrome is marked by recurrent panic attacks or generalized anxiety. This diagnosis is made when there is evidence from the patient's medical history, physical examination, or laboratory tests that a specific organic factor is causally related to the disturbance.

In an **organic personality syndrome** there are changes in the person's motivation, emotions, and impulse control. He or she may seem uncharacteristically apathetic, irritable, or euphoric. As with other organic brain syndromes, the diagnosis of organic personality syndrome is used when an organic factor is believed to be involved in the personality change. Structural damage to the brain—caused, for example, by a tumor or head injury—is common in this syndrome. Table 13–6 describes the diagnostic criteria for organic personality syndrome. The clinical picture depends to a great extent on the size and location of the brain lesion. The syndrome is more likely to be diagnosed in people who are over 50 years of age, who have no history of mental disorder, and in whom a personality change takes place abruptly over a relatively short period.

Table 13–6

Diagnostic Features of Organic Personality Syndrome

Feature	Examples
Emotional instability	Temper outbursts, sudden crying
Impaired impulse control	Poor social judgment, shoplifting
Marked apathy and indifference	No interest in usual hobbies
Paranoid thinking	Extreme suspiciousness

The Variety of Causes of Brain Disorders

To illustrate the range of problems that produce symptoms of organic brain disorder, we will discuss a number of additional disorders that alter behavior, emotions, and cognitive functioning. These disorders include those that are related to heredity, to the lack of a particular neurotransmitter, to infection, to a nutritional deficiency, or to brain damage caused by outside forces, the growth of a tumor within the brain, or cerebrovascular problems.

A Genetic Basis: Huntington's Disease

Huntington's disease, or **Huntington's chorea,** is a rare hereditary disorder that is transmitted by a single dominant gene and is characterized by progressive degeneration of brain tissue. It can begin at any time from childhood to late in life, but most commonly the onset occurs between the ages of 30 and 50. Four types of symptoms are observed in Huntington's disease: dementia, irritability and apathy, depression, and hallucinations and delusions. In addition, there are *choreiform* movements—involuntary, spasmodic jerking and twisting movements of the neck, trunk, and extremities, and much facial grimacing. (The word "chorea" refers to these movements.)

The psychological and behavioral symptoms of Huntington's disease are even more devastating than the physical ones. As the disease develops, the person experiences increasing difficulty in memory storage and retrieval. There is also evidence that intelligence test scores get progressively lower in the period just before the appearance of the characteristic choreiform movements. This suggests that the gene for Huntington's disease does not suddenly "turn on" at the time that the involuntary movements appear.

Impulsiveness in behavior and paranoid and depressive thinking are likely to occur as the disorder progresses and family life becomes disrupted. It is not clear whether these behavioral components of Huntington's disease are organically caused or whether they are psychological reactions to physical deterioration. Recently it has become known that people with Huntington's disease have a deficiency of one neurotransmitter, gamma-amino-butyric-acid (GABA).

The disorder usually begins in middle life, although the onset can occur much earlier. The folksinger and composer Woody Guthrie died in 1967 at the age of 55 after suffering from Huntington's disease for 13 years. As a result of a misdiagnosis, Guthrie had been considered an alcoholic and had been placed in a series of mental hospitals for years before the correct diagnosis was made. Guthrie had eight children, one of whom has already died of Huntington's disease.

Since the disease is inherited through a single dominant gene, each child of an affected parent has a 50-percent chance of inheriting the disorder. There is no skipping of generations, and until recently there has been no way of distinguishing carriers of the gene from noncarriers until the symptoms appear. The fact that Huntington's disease does not manifest itself until middle life has meant that family members that might be affected by it must spend their childhood, adolescence, and early adult years not knowing whether they will develop the disorder or not.

In the San Luis region of Venezuela, the prevalence of Huntington's disease is 700 times higher than in the United States. Within a population of about 3,000, about 150 people have been stricken by the disease and 1,500 more have a substantial risk of developing it. This is because San Luis is the home of a handful of families with many affected members. By far the largest of these families is the Soto family, which has the highest known concentration of Huntington's disease of any family in the world. This high incidence of the disease in one family has given scientists an unusual opportunity to study this rare disorder (see Figure 13–11).

By carefully studying the blood of Iris del Valle Soto and other members of her extended family of almost 4,000 people covering eight generations, researchers

FIGURE 13–11 Some of the members of a large Venezuelan family whose members are at exceptionally high risk for Huntington's disease enjoy a watermelon party. By donating their DNA for study, family members have helped in the search for the location of the gene that causes this disease.

achieved a startling breakthrough. They pinpointed the location in the specific chromosome pair (chromosome pair 4) at which the gene for Huntington's disease is located (Wexler and others, 1985). This was an important first step toward developing a diagnostic test for the disease and perhaps, eventually, a treatment. The diagnostic genetic test is now being used at several clinical centers in Canada and the United States on an experimental basis.

At present many people to whom the test is available, have not chosen to take it. In a study carried out in Canada, those at risk who volunteered to be tested also were assessed for psychological well-being both before the genetic testing and at several intervals afterwards (Hayden, 1991). As might be expected, those who learned that they were likely to develop the disease were very distressed when they first heard this result. However, six months later their psychological state was better than it had been prior to testing although they became distressed whenever they noticed something about their behavior, stumbling over a curb, for instance, that could possibly be an early symptom. People for whom the test indicated freedom from the Huntington's gene were elated at first but then seemed to go into a slump for a variety of reasons. Those who had made irreversible decisions based on concern for their genetic status, for example by being sterilized in order to avoid passing on the Huntington's gene, were particularly negatively affected. Another group negatively affected by the news that they did not carry the gene were those who had had unrealistic expectations about how the predictive testing would change their lives. There were similar numbers of negative psychological reactions in the groups that got good and bad news. In general, people who had experienced psychological problems prior to the test had the worst outcome regardless of the test outcome. The results of the study show clearly the importance of including counseling and support services into genetic testing programs.

A Neurotransmitter Deficit: Parkinson's Disease

Like Huntington's disease, **Parkinson's disease** is progressive and may begin by the age of 50. Its symptoms include tremor, rigidity, an expressionless, masklike facial appearance, and loss of vocal power. A person with Parkinson's disease typically exhibits social withdrawal, reduced intellectual ability, and rigidity in coping with his or her problems. Most Parkinson's patients seem emotionally overcontrolled. As with Huntington's disease, it is difficult to determine how much of the behavioral maladaptation associated with Parkinson's disease is due to organic processes and how much to the

patient's psychological reaction to them. The prevalence of the disease is about 250 per 100,000.

There is evidence that the brains of Parkinson's patients are deficient in the neurotransmitter dopamine. Unlike the dementias discussed so far, this disorder can be treated. A drug called L-dopa is used to relieve some of the symptoms. One study found that Parkinson's patients treated with L-dopa showed clinical improvement that persisted over a ten-year period (Bauer and others, 1982).

Recently, surgeons have carried out tissue implantations into the human brain as a possible way of relieving Parkinson's symptoms. In one case, the right adrenal gland was removed from a 35-year-old man suffering from Parkinson's disease and part of the gland—the medulla—was transplanted to the patient's brain. The hope was that the adrenal tissue would manufacture needed dopamine (Lewin, 1988). While success with tissue implantations has been reported in some cases, there have also been a number of failures. The prospects for use of this procedure for repairing some diseases of the brain are not yet clear.

An Infectious Disorder: General Paresis

Infectious disorders often have an acute onset, although the possibility of slow-acting viral infections should not be ruled out. The central nervous system often is more susceptible to bodily infections than other tissues of the body. Some of these infections do not last long, and successful treatments have been worked out for many of them. If left untreated, however, some infections can lead to irreversible brain disorders.

Untreated **syphilitic infections** are an example of this type of condition. If syphilis is diagnosed before its terminal stages, it can be treated with drugs, usually penicillin. The aim of the drugs is to return the cerebrospinal fluid to normal, which may require many months. These drugs may cure the patient, but the degree of improvement depends on how many neurons were destroyed before the treatment began. When the destruction is great, losses in intellectual functioning cannot be restored.

One of the results of untreated syphilis in its late stage is **general paresis,** or **dementia paralytica,** a progressive deterioration in psychological and motor functioning that results in paralysis, psychosis, and ultimately, death. Among the symptoms of general paresis are loss of cognitive functions, slurring of speech, tremors of the tongue and lips, and poor motor coordination. These symptoms are progressive and eventually lead to a helpless condition. Before the cause and treatment of syphilis were discovered, patients with

general paresis represented between one-tenth and one-third of all admissions to mental hospitals.

Because of the negative relationship between the degree of possible improvement and the extent of irreversible brain damage, prompt diagnosis and medical treatment of syphilitic infections is clearly the best approach to reducing the incidence of general paresis.

Nutritional Deficiencies: Pellagra and Korsakoff's Syndrome

Vitamin and other nutritional deficiencies can affect the nervous system. For example, **pellagra** is a reversible disease caused by a deficiency of the vitamin niacin (nicotinic acid) or its derivatives. The deficiency affects cells in the area of the cerebral cortex that controls body movement and in other parts of the brain. Symptoms of pellagra are varied, including a skin disorder (the skin looks as if it has been severely sunburned), diarrhea, and psychological deterioration. The signs of psychological impairment are similar to those of anxiety disorders and depression: anxiety, irritability, loss of recent memory, and difficulty in concentration. Untreated cases may result in delirium, hallucinations, and a variety of psychotic behaviors.

The incidence of pellagra has declined sharply in the United States as a result of improved diet, but it is still common in many underdeveloped countries. Chronic alcoholics who have poorly balanced diets may show symptoms of pellagra. On the basis of behavior alone, it is difficult to distinguish between pellagra and conditions like anxiety or schizophrenia, but when a niacin deficiency is suspected (usually on the basis of skin and digestive symptoms), diagnosis is relatively simple. Except in very severe cases, nutritional therapy is highly effective. The individual is placed on a protein-rich diet that is also high in B vitamins (niacin, thiamine, and vitamin B complex). Mild cases improve noticeably within 48 hours.

While the results of pellagra are reversible with nutrional therapy, sometimes nutritional deficiencies combine with toxic substances to produce substantial and irreversible damage to brain tissue. **Korsakoff's syndrome,** which occurs in some chronic alcoholics, results from a combination of alcoholism and vitamin B_1 (thiamine) deficiency. Recent and past memories are lost, and the person seems unable to form new memories. In addition, there are perceptual deficits, loss of initiative, and confabulation. Delirium tremens frequently is part of the patient's medical history. The longer the vitamin deficiency has persisted, the less responsive the individual will be to vitamin therapy.

Brain Trauma: Injuries and Tumors

Traumatic brain injury is the most common cause of organic mental disorders (Silver and others, 1990). Each year in the United States, over 500,000 people suffer severe injuries to the brain. As the case of Sarah Monahan presented in Box 13–1 makes clear, major brain injuries can have profound cognitive and behavioral consequences. Patients with less severe injuries also may suffer from prolonged psychological disability. They may have difficulties in a number of areas of functioning, including work, school, and leisure activities, and may show extreme personality changes.

In addition to head injuries, intracranial growths (brain tumors) can lead to both acute and chronic disorders. In many cases it is difficult to determine how much of the abnormal behavior is a result of damage and how much represents a lifelong behavior pattern or simply a reaction to knowledge of the injury. These factors can interact in many ways. A startling or traumatic event, whether or not it involves physical injury, usually has some specific and symbolic significance for the individual. The term **traumatic neurosis** has been used to describe reactions that follow such an event. A blow to the head that caused little physical damage might be exploited by the injured person, as in some hysterical disorders. The reaction may be reinforced by secondary gains, such as family sympathy or permission to quit one's job. Table 13–7 lists some of the factors that influence the effects of a brain injury.

Brain injuries are usually classified into three groups: **concussions,** or transient states that momentarily change the physical condition of the brain but do not cause structural damage; **contusions,** in which diffuse, fine structural damage—for example, the rupturing of tiny blood vessels—takes place; and **lacerations,** which involve major tears or ruptures in the brain tissue.

Although a concussion might include a temporary loss of consciousness, the person can be expected to recover completely within 24 to 48 hours. Sometimes it is difficult to diagnose precisely the extent of brain injury

Table 13–7
Factors that Influence the Effects of a Brain Injury

1. Age
2. Site of injury
3. Extent of damage
4. Emotional reactions to resulting physical and mental deficits
5. Personality and social competence
6. Social support available after injury

and its potential effect on brain functioning. A variety of tests and observations are used to analyze each case, including x-ray evidence of skull fracture, a CT scan to determine tissue damage, a test for blood in the spinal fluid, and observation of symptoms such as bleeding from the skull orifices (for example, the ears), throbbing headaches, prolonged loss of consciousness, and sluggish cognitive behavior. Head injuries can lead to highly specific losses in motor or cognitive functioning, with the extent of the loss depending on the kind of injury and where it is located.

Sometimes the brain is injured not by an accident or a blow but by pressure inside the skull, perhaps from a tumor. In such cases the speed with which the intruding body develops also influences the amount of loss. A tumor might grow slowly for a long time before there is evidence of intracranial pressure or behavioral change (see Box 13–3). A good prognosis in cases of brain injury or tumor depends on how early and how accurately the condition is diagnosed and how effective a treatment for the condition exists.

In some cases in which there is known physical damage, only minor behavioral deficits develop. Apparently some people adapt to minor brain damage better

BOX 13–3 Mass Killer with Malignant Brain Tumor

Most brain tumor victims don't become violent, but the behavioral effects of brain injuries and tumors can sometimes be puzzling and dramatic. For example, the evening of July 31, 1966, Charles Whitman, a student at the University of Texas, wrote the following note.

I don't really understand myself these days. I am supposed to be an average, reasonable, and intelligent young man. However, lately (I can't recall when it started) I have been the victim of many unusual and irrational thoughts. These thoughts constantly recur, and it requires a tremendous mental effort to concentrate on useful and progressive tasks. In March when my parents made a physical break I noticed a great deal of stress. I consulted Dr. Cochran at the University Health Center and asked him to recommend someone that I could consult with about some psychiatric disorders I felt I had. I talked with a doctor once for about two hours and tried to convey to him my fears that I felt overcome by overwhelming violent impulses. After one session I never saw the doctor again, and since then I have been fighting my mental turmoil alone, and seemingly to no avail. After my death I wish that an autopsy would be performed on me to see if there is any visible physical disorder. I have had some tremendous headaches in the past and have consumed two large bottles of Excedrin in the past three months.

Later that night Whitman killed his wife and his mother. The next morning he went to the tower on the university campus with a high-powered hunting rifle and opened fire. Ninety minutes later he was shot to death, but by that time he had shot 38 people, killing 14, (see Figure 13–12).

Because of the shocking nature of this incident, it attracted widespread attention. There were many attempts to explain Whitman's murderous acts. The letter that Whitman had written provided a number of clues. It referred to intense headaches, and a postmortem examination revealed a highly malignant tumor in a region of the brain that is known to be involved in aggressive behavior. Some experts suggested that Whitman's actions had been caused by brain damage. Others viewed them as products of the "unusual and irrational thoughts" to which he referred in his letter. A study of Whitman's life revealed that he had had many positive experiences with guns, and some authorities on violent behavior pointed to these experiences as a possible causal factor. Still others cited Whitman's reference to "overwhelming violent impulses" and suggested that those impulses had been bottled up for many years and had finally exploded into action because of the recent life stresses described in his letter.

We cannot be certain which of these potential causes was most important. Perhaps all of them contributed to his actions to varying degrees. The Whitman case dramatically illustrates the many perspectives from which a single act can be viewed and explained.

FIGURE 13–12 Charles Whitman, shown here in a college photo, killed his wife, mother, and 14 strangers who were hit by bullets he sprayed from a perch high in the tower of the administration building at the University of Texas.

than others do. While brain damage can cause maladaptive behavior, the opposite can occur: An individual can respond maladaptively to the knowledge of having a damaged brain. Furthermore, any type of major injury or traumatic condition might set off a maladaptive psychological reaction such as a psychosis. **Posttraumatic psychoses** are similar to other psychoses. They involve confusion, delirium, and temporary catatonic, manic, or depressive reactions. A posttraumatic psychosis might develop abruptly when a person begins to regain consciousness after receiving a head injury.

Unfortunately, it is usually unclear whether a latent psychosis existed before the traumatic event occurred. The patient cannot, of course, remember the period of unconsciousness following brain trauma, and recollections of the confused state that occurs just after regaining consciousness usually are hazy. In addition, there may be amnesia (loss of memory) of the time period prior to the injury (see Figure 13–13). Even after relatively minor injuries, many patients complain of headaches, dizziness, fatigue, lack of concentration, and anxiety. In most cases these complaints are of short duration.

Tumors produce a variety of physiological and psychological changes because their presence causes a rise in intracranial pressure or interferes with the blood supply to the brain. As with head injuries, the symptoms of tumors depend on their location in the brain. For example, tumors growing in or near the frontal lobe frequently lead to a gradual onset of mental changes, but again, the symptoms depend on the site of the tumor. One group of people with frontal-lobe tumors may become exuberant and euphoric, with their conversation punctuated by laughter and jokes. Another group may show general apathy and slowness in responding. Memory disorders are very common in people with cerebral tumors and are often the first noticeable indication that a problem exists. Researchers are investigating the degree to which training in attentional and cognitive skills can aid in the rehabilitation of brain-damaged individuals.

Early in their development some brain tumors result in changes that neurologists can assess. However, in the absence of other evidence to suggest the presence of a tumor, emphasis on personality and behavioral changes often results in misdiagnosis and the symptoms are attributed to nonorganic factors. The role of organic factors may become evident later. For example, the composer George Gershwin underwent psychoanalysis because he suffered severe headaches. It was not until shortly before his death that the diagnosis of a brain tumor was made.

Multiple Causal Factors: Epilepsy

Epilepsy is a transitory disturbance of brain function that develops suddenly, ceases spontaneously, and is likely to reoccur. The form that this disturbance takes depends on the site in the brain at which it originates, the extent of the brain area involved, and other factors. Epilepsy is not a disease but instead is a symptom consisting of recurrent episodes of changes in state of consciousness with or without an accompanying motor or sensory involvement.

Throughout history epilepsy has inspired awe, fear, a sense of mystery, and puzzlement. The Greek physician Hippocrates argued that epilepsy was a naturally caused disease, but for much of modern history it was seen as a sign of demonic possession. Many famous people, including Julius Caesar, the elder William Pitt, and Fyodor Dostoyevsky, were epileptics. Dostoyevsky, one of the world's great novelists, suffered his first epileptic seizure while he was in prison in Siberia. He believed that the agony of living in chains, the stench, and hard labor had precipitated his attacks which persisted for years even after he was permitted to leave the prison.

It was the English neurologist Hughlings Jackson (1834–1911) who first accounted for epileptic seizures in terms of brain lesions. He believed that the seizures resulted from excessive discharging by nerve cells in the gray matter of the brain and that irritation of specific areas of the brain caused the particular symptoms manifested by epileptics. Today, we know that many

FIGURE 13–13 On Christmas Day, 1985, James McDonnell came home to his wife in Larchmont, New York, after 14 years of amnesia. He had lost his memory after suffering head injuries in two automobile accidents, had gone to Philadelphia, and had found a job in a restaurant. McDonnell said that his memory had returned on Christmas Eve when he bumped his head.

mechanisms, not a single one, may make cells behave abnormally, as they do in epilepsy. The cells involved in epileptic seizures share several abnormal characteristics. During seizures they fire electrical discharges at high rates and in short bursts, with quiet periods in between. In contrast, most normal cells fire fewer discharges spaced more evenly over time. Groups of epileptic cells also tend to fire at the same time, whereas normal cells fire relatively independently of each other. This synchrony of cell discharge is an important factor in a seizure, although how seizures start is poorly understood. It is clear, however, that once a seizure begins, neurons in large portions of the brain fire excessively and simultaneously. Surprisingly, most of the brain's activity recorded between seizures is normal.

Most forms of epilepsy are not believed to be hereditary, but there seems to be a predisposition toward epilepsy in some families. Although it is difficult to give a precise estimate, perhaps half of all cases of epilepsy result from such nongenetic factors as head injuries at birth, infectious diseases of childhood, or brain infections and injuries later in life. The clinical problem of epilepsy is particularly challenging because its solution usually requires establishing the particular combination of causes at work in a given case.

Epilepsy is relatively common and has many forms (Horvath & others, 1989). Approximately one percent of the U.S. population has the condition, and two to three percent of the population has had a seizure at some time in life. Young children are prone to have seizures, often associated with high fevers. Many children "outgrow" their seizures, but the long-term consequences are not known. Victims of head trauma or brain tumors also are prone to develop epilepsy. The disease is more common in less affluent countries where health care is poor, because minor or moderate central nervous system infection and trauma are more likely to be neglected.

Researchers put the many forms of epilepsy, which may involve different brain structures, into two categories. Some epileptics have generalized seizures, with electrical activity of unknown origin occurring simultaneously throughout the brain. The second category includes epilepsies in which seizures can be traced to a particular area of the brain—for example, the hippocampus.

GRAND MAL AND PETIT MAL SEIZURES An epileptic seizure is a result of transient electrical instability of some cells in the brain, which sometimes triggers an "electrical storm" that spreads through part or all of the brain. This electrical activity culminates in a seizure, which can take one of many forms. Many epileptics have only one type of seizure, but a sizable minority experience two or more types. The major types include *grand mal* and *petit mal* seizures and *psychomotor epilepsy*. The brainwave patterns that are characteristic of each type are shown in Figure 13–14.

The most severe form of epileptic disorder is the **grand mal** (French for "great illness") **seizure** which typically lasts from two to five minutes. This type of attack leaves a painful impression on anyone who witnesses it. The victim of a grand mal seizure displays a set of very striking symptoms. The seizure often begins with a cry, followed by loss of consciousness, falling to the floor, and extreme spasms. These uncontrollable

FIGURE 13–14 EEG patterns of various types of epileptic seizures.

(*Archives of Neurology and Psychiatry*, 1939, 41, 1111–1116. Copyright © 1939, American Medical Association)

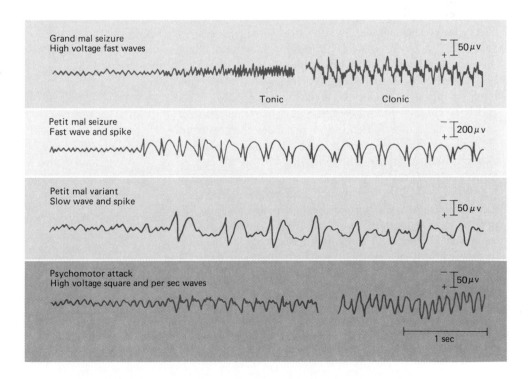

spasms can cause serious harm to the victim. Among the greatest dangers are head injuries and severe biting of the tongue or mouth. The muscular movements of a grand mal seizure are usually preceded by an *aura*, in which the individual experiences a clouded state of consciousness, including feelings of unreality and depersonalization (feelings of strangeness about oneself). The aura may last only a few seconds, but it is often remembered very vividly.

Following the aura, the *tonic phase* of the seizure begins. The body is in an extended position, the eyes remain open, the pupils are dilated, and the corneal and light reflexes are absent. The tonic phase lasts for 15 to 30 seconds and is followed by the *clonic phase*, during which the body alternates between marked muscular rigidity and relaxation. Bladder and bowel control may be lost. Following the convulsive part of a grand mal seizure, there may be a deep sleep that lasts for an hour or two. As the victim regains consciousness, he or she may be bewildered and amnesic. While some grand mal epileptics have daily attacks, cases have been reported in which there were only a few seizures in an entire lifetime.

In the **petit mal** ("small illness" in French) **seizure,** which is particularly common in children, there is no convulsion. Rather, there is a lapse of consciousness characterized by blank staring and lack of responsiveness lasting up to about half a minute. The individual usually does not lose consciousness. These seizures may occur many times a day.

Petit mal attacks may be difficult to identify unless the person is known to be epileptic or an attack is actually observed. They commonly start in early childhood. Some children have so many attacks daily that they have difficulty attending to what is going on around them. Most petit mal attacks result from disturbances in subcortical brain structures, although the cause of these disturbances is usually unknown.

PSYCHOMOTOR EPILEPSY In **psychomotor epilepsy,** a type that includes 15 percent of epilepsy cases and is rarely seen in children, the patient retains control of his or her motor functioning but loses the ability to exercise good judgment in carrying out activities. During a psychomotor attack, the individual is in a kind of trance; his or her movements may be repetitive and highly organized but are in fact semiautomatic. Psychomotor seizures may resemble those of petit mal epilepsy, but they last longer (up to two minutes), involve muscle movements related to chewing and speech, and show more clouding of consciousness. The occasional visual hallucinations and the confused state that characterize psychomotor epilepsy are similar to some symptoms of psychosis.

In some cases fear, terror, rage, and depression are among the emotional side effects of psychomotor seizures. These outbursts of emotion come on suddenly.

They are apparently automatic and unpremeditated, and they cannot be recalled later. Another feature of this syndrome is inability to shift attention to new objects and situations. There is some evidence suggesting that this syndrome may be associated with temporal lobe lesions; hence, this symptom pattern is referred to as **temporal lobe epilepsy.**

Psychological Factors Over the years there has been much conjecture about the role of psychological factors in epilepsy. Are epileptics helpless victims of their condition, or is it possible that the disease is part of their psychological adjustment to some other aspect of their lives? Clinicians have observed that epileptics' seizures tend to become more frequent when they are confronted with challenges and problems they do not feel competent to handle. In support of this clinical conclusion, research findings have shown that an increased number of stressful life events is associated with an increase in seizures (Hermann and others, 1990).

From a psychological point of view, the disease often creates overwhelming stress for both epileptics and their families. Much of this stress is related to lack of knowledge about epilepsy, its causes, and its treatment. Other important factors are the role of general life stresses in bringing on seizures and the effect of the stress caused by the ever-present possibility of a seizure, the need to lead a somewhat restricted life, and the stigma that attaches itself to people who are known to be epileptic.

There is increasing recognition of the developmental problems posed by epilepsy. For example, approximately 60 percent of all epileptics experience their first seizure before they are ten years old. This condition represents a major handicap during a formative period of physical and psychological growth. Writer Kurt Eichenwald, who has epilepsy, has described some of his college experiences.

My staring spells—periods of a few seconds of mental absence—had been going on for as long as I could remember. Although I mentioned them to my doctor and my parents occasionally, the events did not seem significant.

Then, in my first semester at college, I was horsing around in the dorm with my roommates, and I fell, hitting my head against a chair. I had a concussion. No one to this day knows if the concussion affected my seizures, but the staring spells soon increased in frequency and severity. I learned they were different from other people's passing moments of distraction.

I remember once, in the dining hall, suddenly realizing everyone was looking at me. My lap

was wet. I thought someone had thrown something at me. In fact, I had begun to stare while holding a glass of Coca-Cola in my hand. It had fallen in between my legs and shattered.

—Eichenwald, 1987, p. 30

Later, he began having more major seizures.

I experience what is called an "aura" as random brain cells start to fire. I feel a sense of separation. My head throbs, and I see a flash of lights. Even today, I am not sure of the order of these feelings or the amount of time separating them.

As the electrical firestorm sweeps across my brain, I lose consciousness and fall to the ground. The muscles in my body tighten up and my jaw clenches, the teeth possibly biting and bloodying my lips, tongue or cheek. My body jerks for a period, usually for less than a minute. During that time, I often get excessive amounts of saliva in my mouth, creating a froth. My breathing becomes irregular, sometimes even stopping. I also can become incontinent.

The convulsion ends, and I fall into a deep, though brief, sleep. As I wake up, another seizure can be triggered, starting the process again.

While unconscious, I do not respond to pain, such as the injection of needles. I have awakened half-frozen in a snowdrift but unaware, until my waking, of the cold.

When fully awake, I am very confused and panicked. Often, it takes time for me to realize a seizure has occurred. I am unsure where I am, who is with me or even what day it is. My speech is broken, and I stutter horribly, so that I am unable to ask questions except of the most patient observers.

—Eichenwald, 1987, p. 31

TREATMENT There are three major ways to treat epilepsy: drugs, surgery, and psychological management. Certain drugs, such as Dilantin and phenobarbitol, can reduce the frequency and severity of seizures. Unfortunately, there is considerable variation in the way people react to these drugs. The only way to establish the optimal dosage is through trial and error. In some cases

the epileptic may use substances (alcohol, for example) that interfere with the effectiveness of anticonvulsive drugs.

If the seizures are a result of some identifiable structural defect and drugs either are not effective or have strong side effects, surgical intervention may be considered. The seizures of temporal lobe epilepsy are especially difficult to control by means of medication, but some studies have reported successful results following removal of parts of the temporal lobe. Because brain surgery entails obvious risks, it is used only when it is clear that some abnormality of brain tissue is causing the seizures. The brain is such a complex structure that it is not always possible to be absolutely certain where the abnormality is although scanning techniques have helped to localize areas involved. In some cases diagnosed as temporal lobe epilepsy, the temporal lobe has been removed and has been found to have no lesions. For this reason, surgery is seen as a treatment of last resort, to be attempted only after drugs and psychological approaches have failed.

A variety of psychological methods have been used in treating epileptics. Operant conditioning procedures have been tried successfully with some epileptics who cannot be helped by medication. For example, epileptic children have been rewarded with attention and care following seizure-free periods. After a seizure occurs, these reinforcers are withdrawn or reduced in strength. Avoiding or changing certain cognitive cues can also be helpful because it is known that the aura preceding a grand mal seizure can be induced by thinking certain thoughts. Epileptics who have this form of the disorder can be trained to direct their attention to pleasant thoughts when they feel an aura coming on. Desensitization and relaxation training have been found to be helpful in reducing the frequency of epileptic attacks. Biofeedback, in which patients receive visual or auditory information about their brainwave patterns, can also be an effective treatment.

Many epileptics need help to cope with their condition. Because the disorder frequently begins before adulthood, the emotional responses of the epileptic's family must also be dealt with. Often the patient and the family see epilepsy as a kind of disgrace and react to it with shame and guilt. Because an atmosphere of emotional tension and frustration can increase the severity of an epileptic's seizures, psychotherapy and counseling are frequently recommended both for victims and for their families. Many people still view epilepsy as frightening and mysterious. As a result of such attitudes, an epileptic often feels socially stigmatized. Organizations like the Epilepsy Foundation work to provide information about epilepsy and to decrease occupational, social, and legal discrimination against epileptics. They publicize facts like the following.

1. Epileptics have the same intellectual capabilities as the general population.

2. Between seizures an epileptic suffers no disturbance in psychological function.

3. Most cases of epilepsy (about 80 percent) can be controlled with anticonvulsive drugs.

4. The genetic factor in epilepsy is probably no greater than in many other common diseases. A person with epilepsy who marries a nonepileptic may expect a two percent risk of having a child who also has the disorder. In many cases the risk is even less, especially if the epilepsy is associated with a birth injury or later accident or infection.

Blockage of Blood Supply: Cerebrovascular Accidents

Cerebrovascular accidents (CVAs), or **strokes,** are blockages or ruptures of the blood vessels in the cerebrum. When these blood vessels break or are blocked by a clot, a portion of the brain is deprived of its supply of oxygen and blood. Extensive damage to the brain and obvious changes in behavior may result. When the affected blood vessels are small and the interference with blood flow is temporary, the symptoms are milder— perhaps only confusion, unsteadiness, and excessive emotionality. Some of the behavioral effects of a stroke may be similar to the dementia that occurs in cases of brain deterioration. However, the symptoms of stroke characteristically have an abrupt onset.

Eric Hodgins, an editor and author, suffered a severe stroke that resulted in **aphasia,** a disturbance in the ability to use words, and paralysis of the left side of his body. He later recovered from the aphasia, and wrote about the experience. His account of his stroke vividly portrays the psychological as well as the physical aspects of a severe stroke.

The first thing to be said about it, is that it is like nothing else on earth. . . . The victim—patient is confused, or stunned, or shocked, or unconscious. Whatever his state he is not in good condition to give any fellow layman a clear and coherent account of what happened. Perhaps he can talk—perhaps not. Even with speech, he can't say "It hurts"—because it probably doesn't. So, stroke exists in no focal plane the uninitiated layman can understand or recognize, or on which he can practice his own brand of differential diagnosis. Thus, as with the traffic

accident, a variable period of total confusion elapses after the stroke has struck before the cry goes up, "Somebody get a doctor!". . .

Unlike other patient types I can think of, the stroke patient goes to the hospital with profound relief, and gladly. Although he is probably not in pain, he is in considerable fear—more than he can express. Something has gone very, very wrong, but "Somebody will fix it": this child-like phrase describes the depth of the patient's need for support and reassurance . . .

In my own case I found it both depressing and infuriating that I encountered no physician with the willingness or capacity to say, as my acute symptoms subsided, "I freely concede you are in a jam—in fact, in several jams. I have no ready-made solutions—but I will help you think your way out of your jams, because I conceive it part of my job, my medical job." Perhaps it is a contentious suggestion that medicine should reach this far out from its examination rooms and its prescription pads to help the stroke patient. But in that case, whose job is it?

—Quoted in Eisenson, 1973, pp. 204–207

Although Hodgins made a stunning recovery, strokes are in fact the third-ranking cause of death after heart attacks and cancer. There are approximately 500,000 new strokes and 200,000 deaths due to strokes in the United States each year. Over 80 percent of these involve people over the age of 65. In addition to age, high blood pressure plays a major role in strokes. The single most important way in which strokes can be prevented is through the treatment and control of high blood pressure. Many clinicians have observed that strokes occur especially often in people who live pressured lives. These people tend to have their strokes while they are relaxing or vacationing, the reasons for which are not clear.

An Integrative Approach to Brain Disorders

Because the conditions discussed in this chapter involve actual organic defects, it is tempting to see them as purely medical problems. Why do we consider brain

disorders to be different from other organic problems, such as broken arms or gallstones? A physical defect lies at the root of all of these conditions, but the brain has a complex effect on our behavior as well as on our body. This effect is not as clear and predictable as the effects of damage to other parts of the body. Once a broken arm has been set and healed, for example, the person can return to the condition he or she was in before the accident. This is not the case with brain injuries, and it is for this reason that they are of interest to psychologists.

To comprehend the effects of a brain injury on behavior, we require information about the person's life history, personality, and environmental and biophysical factors. Purely physical conditions such as broken arms, however, can be treated successfully without such data. Although brain disorders can be treated medically, psychodynamic, learning, cognitive, and community concepts are also important. Thus, from both the scientific and clinical standpoints, the most fruitful approach to brain disorders is one that integrates knowledge from these diverse fields.

From a psychodynamic perspective, although certain forms of maladaptive behavior may be organically caused, the way people respond to their condition involves psychological factors such as personality, earlier experience, and ways of coping. For example, the more outgoing a person is, the greater the likelihood of improvement in his or her condition. Many cases of brain disorder indicate that an individual's personality at the time of the organic damage has an effect on the degree and form of his or her behavioral deterioration. For example, the content of hallucinations and the ease with which they are expressed depend on personality characteristics.

Behavioral psychologists are less interested in the effects of personality and experience than psychologists who emphasize other perspectives. Behaviorists focus instead on people's ability to adapt to even the most drastic situations. Teaching new responses to compensate for those that have been lost is seen as more important for adjustment than simply helping people accept their new lot in life. Moreover, the way people respond to such training can provide more relevant information about their present psychological state than an examination of their personality before the illness occurred. Because of their emphasis on revising people's maladaptive responses as quickly as possible, behavioral psychol-

ogists have a major contribution to make in the treatment of organic brain disorders.

Cognitively oriented psychologists have contributed a variety of techniques to help people in the early stages of dementia deal with the deterioration in their abilities. Memory-aiding techniques such as list making can help Alzheimer's disease victims, for example. Cognitive techniques are also useful in counteracting the depression that often accompanies the development of physical problems and declining intellectual competence.

Damage to the brain and central nervous system would not seem to be a condition that is influenced by community variables. Yet, from all indications, central nervous system dysfunction is not randomly distributed. Cases of brain damage are highly concentrated in the segments of the population lowest in socioeconomic status. Within this group such problems seem to be most prevalent among African-American children. This is true for sociological, not biological, reasons. Poor black infants may become biologically vulnerable shortly after the moment of conception. Inadequate nutrition and prenatal care result in complications of pregnancy, which take their toll in high rates of premature births and congenital defects. These abnormalities include neurological damage that results in impaired intellectual functioning and in behavioral difficulties such as hyperactivity and short attention span. No single complication of pregnancy is more clearly associated with a wide range of neurological dysfunctions than premature birth. For these reasons, those who focus on the community perspective emphasize the prevention of brain disorders through preventive medical care, especially good prenatal care.

The stigma attached to many of the behavioral maladaptations stemming from brain damage often makes the situation worse. People tend to avoid and isolate individuals who are markedly deviant. The behavior of old people provides one of the clearest illustrations of the effects of this social rejection. Mild brain deterioration in a socially rejected older person may lead to greater behavioral maladaptation than moderate deterioration in a person who lives in a friendlier, more accepting environment. From the community perspective, changing people's attitudes toward those who behave differently because of brain disorders can sometimes lessen the behavioral effects of these biological changes.

Chapter Summary

THE BRAIN: AN INTERACTIONAL PERSPECTIVE

Areas of brain research that are especially important in understanding normal and abnormal behavior are those dealing with how the brain grows and maintains itself, the mechanisms by which it acquires, stores, and uses information, and the role it plays in monitoring and regulating internal bodily processes.

Vulnerability to Brain Disorders Factors that influence vulnerability to brain damage are age, social support, stress, personality factors, and physical conditions of the disorder, and overall health. Three of the most widely used scanning techniques are computerized tomography (CT), positron emission tomography (PET) and magnetic resonance imaging (MRI). Each of these techniques is based on different technology and their uses often complement each other.

The Normal Aging Process Elderly persons are at greater risk than the general population for developing disorders involving brain degeneration. They are also at greater risk for depression as a result of increased life stress that may be age-related. It is important to remember, however, that there are many examples of successful aging.

ASSESSING BRAIN DAMAGE

Brain disorders that have important effects on thought and behavior are fairly common, and occur more frequently than such disorders as schizophrenia or panic disorder. The presence of brain damage is assessed by clinical tests, neuropsychological testing, and a variety of scanning techniques. The **mental-status examination** is an interview that assesses a person's general awareness, appearance, mood, and a number of aspects of cognitive functioning. **Neurologists,** physicians who specialize in diseases of the nervous system, usually oversee cases of brain damage. **Neuropsychology** is a branch of psychology that deals with relationships between behavior and the condition of the brain.

Brain Imaging Noninvasive brain imaging techniques can supply researchers with detailed information about brain anatomy and the biochemical processes that occur in different areas of the brain.

CHARACTERISTICS OF ORGANIC MENTAL DISORDERS

A **syndrome** is a cluster of symptoms that tend to appear together. **Organic brain syndromes** are clusters of psychological and behavioral symptoms connected with temporary or permanent brain dysfunction.

Delirium Delirium is a state of relatively global cognitive impairment, disorientation, and confusion, in which a person has difficulty with all aspects of attention. It can occur as a result of many factors, including an acute brain disease or infection, a disease or infection in other parts of the body that affects the brain, intoxication, or withdrawal from an addicting substance. People differ widely in their vulnerability to delirium. **Delirium tremens,** which includes not only the symptoms common to delirium but also tremors and visual hallucinations, may sometimes result from excessive alcohol consumption.

Dementia Dementia, or **brain deterioration,** involves a gradual loss of intellectual abilities that interferes with normal functioning. Depending on its cause, dementia may be stable, progressive, or reversible. **Senile dementia** refers to this condition if it first occurs after age 65. In younger people, it is called **presenile dementia.** A common symptom of dementia is **confabulation,** in which a person compensates for loss of particular memories by filling in the gaps with inaccurate details. **Primary degenerative dementia** has a number of symptoms including progressive memory loss, apathy and loss of initiative, irritability, and restlessness during the night.

MAJOR CAUSES OF DEMENTIA

Alzheimer's Disease **Alzheimer's disease** is the most common form of both senile and presenile dementia. This disease's characteristic loss of neurons from the frontal and temporal lobes of the cerebral cortex leads to memory lapses, confusion, and eventual physical and mental deterioration. Research on Alzheimer's disease has focused on neurochemical changes in the brain and on genetic factors. Researchers also have explored ways to help families adapt to the stress of caring for a person with this disease.

Pick's Disease **Pick's disease** is much less common than Alzheimer's disease. This disorder can be diagnosed only at autopsy by a characteristic form of brain atrophy.

Multi-Infarct Dementia **Multi-infarct dementia** is caused by a series of minor strokes that occur over a period of time.

AIDS Dementia Complex **AIDS dementia complex (ADC)** is associated with cortical atrophy and includes symptoms of forgetfulness, problems in concentration, mental slowness, motor difficulties, and behavioral withdrawal. Both those who are HIV positive only and those who have overt symptoms of AIDS may show these impairments. Early symptoms of ADC are often mistaken for a psychological disorder.

Other Organic Brain Syndromes Several other brain syndromes, although less common, also cause major changes in overall functioning. These include **amnestic syndrome, organic delusional syndrome, organic hallucinosis, organic affective syndrome, organic anxiety syndrome,** and **organic personality syndrome.**

THE VARIETY OF CAUSES OF BRAIN DISORDERS

A Genetic Basis: Huntington's Disease **Huntington's disease,** or **Huntington's chorea,** is a rare hereditary disorder transmitted by a single dominant gene. It results in a progressive degeneration of brain tissue. Its symptoms have been found to be related to a deficiency of one neurotransmitter, GABA, and are thought to be related to a gene pair on chromosome 4.

A Neurotransmitter Deficit: Parkinson's Disease Symptoms of **Parkinson's disease** are progressive deterioration in intellectual ability, increased rigidity in coping, tremor, and mask-like facial appearance. This disease is believed to be related to a dopamine deficiency and can be treated with the drug L-dopa.

An Infectious Disorder: General Paresis Untreated **syphilitic infections** can lead to **general paresis,** or **dementia paralytica,** which results in a loss of neurons in the brain.

Nutritional Deficiencies: Pellagra and Korsakoff's Syndrome **Pellagra** is a reversible disease caused by a deficiency of the vitamin niacin. **Korsakoff's syndrome** is the result of a combination of alcoholism and vitamin B_1 deficiency.

Brain Trauma: Injuries and Tumors Brain injuries and tumors can result in profound cognitive and behavioral consequences. Some of the changed behavior may be the result of psychological factors related to the injury. Such changes are referred to as **traumatic neurosis.** Brain injuries are classified into three groups: **concussions,** which result in transient problems; **contusions,** where there is diffuse damage; and **lacerations,** which involve major tears or ruptures in the brain tissue. Brain tumors can result in a variety of behavioral changes depending on the location of the tumor. **Postraumatic psychoses** develop as a result of head injuries. Although the cause is different, and the disturbance is sometimes short lasting, the symptoms include the same type found in other psychoses.

Multiple Causal Factors: Epilepsy **Epilepsy** is due to an abnormality in brain cell behavior that may have many causes. Some epilepsies are related to generalized seizures and others can be traced to a source in a specific area of the brain. **Grand mal seizures** last several minutes and include loss of consciousness and convulsions. **Petit mal seizures** are lapses of consciousness that last less than a minute and do not include convulsions. **Psychomotor epilepsy** involves a trance-like state lasting up to two minutes and may include outbursts of emotion. Epilepsy may be treated with drugs, surgery, or psychological management depending on the symptoms.

Blockage of Blood Supply: Cerebrovascular Accidents **Cerebrovascular accidents (CVAs),** or **strokes,** are blockages or ruptures of the blood vessels in the cerebrum. Some of the effects may be similar to those of dementia, but the onset is sudden rather than gradual.

AN INTEGRATIVE APPROACH TO BRAIN DISORDERS

Although brain disorders involve organic problems, knowledge of psychological factors is very important in predicting exactly how a person's behavior will be affected. Each of the psychological perspectives is useful in understanding the impact of these disorders.

Addictive Disorders

C H A P T E R 1 4

Addictive Behavior

Alcohol
Alcohol Abuse and Dependence
Alcohol and Health
Perspectives on Alcohol Abuse
Treatment
Preventing Alcohol Abuse

Other Drugs
Barbiturates and Tranquilizers
The Opioids
Cocaine
Amphetamines
Psychedelics
Phencyclidine (PCP)
Marijuana
Nicotine

Chapter Summary

Raul Guerrero, *Coco Club*, 1989. Daniel Saxon Gallery, Los Angeles.

*T*he gentleman in the corner had been regarded as a true American success, lanky and deep-voiced, brilliant and beloved, the master of all he surveyed. Now, he gazed out defiantly, as if still on the summit, too high to see the cat feces at his feet or the unopened mail or the mirror that would have told him he was master of nothing but his own delusions.

Those who were to thrust the mirror in front of the 62-year-old man, whom I will call James B., were his daughter Isabel, myself, and three of the friends who loved him best.

If James B. had denied his problem, so had we. He had been depressed over the death of his wife and the loss of his architectural business. He had been presenting different excuses to each of us for his growing isolation. He had kept us at bay by clever use of the telephone, until it was cut off for nonpayment of a bill he had never opened.

Yet at last we had gathered into a crisis intervention team and surprised him, hung over, before he could perfect his alibis. . . .

"Daddy, we are here because we love you." Isabel's voice wavered, but the 9-month-old baby on her knee stared at her grandfather unblinkingly. James B., very gingerly, poured out coffee. "I can understand your concern," he said. He had thrown on a shirt—even a tie—but below his bathrobe, his thin, red legs had the look of arms flung down in defeat. "I've had this local flu. I've been going to my doctor for shots every day."

"I checked with your doctor, Daddy, and he hasn't seen you for two years. We think your disease is alcoholism."

All of James B.'s roles now seemed to collide and fall away, revealing the

obsession which shone in his eyes like unrequited love. "That's preposterous! My problems have nothing to do with alcohol."

Mel, his former business partner, said he had watched the most brilliant man he had ever known become addled into dull predictability. George, his former chess opponent, blushed and said that James B. had begun to cheat at the game. Lisa, his former lover, tremulously said she was going to marry a man she didn't love because the one she did had not preferred her to the bottle. I reminded him of the stars, and all of the people, including my baby and Isabel's, who could still learn from him.

Coached about the new science of alcohol and the liver, we tried to convince James B. that there was no shame in being an alcoholic.

"Look, can't you understand?" James B. said. "I'm sick, yes; depressed, yes; getting old, yes. But that's all."

"Jim," Mel said, in a voice that resonated with the tension we all felt, "it sounds like you would rather be anything at all than an alcoholic."

After 14 hours of this scenario, some of us began to question whether he really was an alcoholic. Maybe it was some other illness. Then he let spill a few words. "Geez, if I couldn't go down to the pub for a few, I think I'd go nuts!"

"Aaah," Isabel said. "You just admitted it." She put the baby on her father's knee. "Look at your granddaughter. This is your immortality, Daddy, and she needs you. Please don't die. Please choose life, for us."

James B. put his face, the color of gravel, in his hands. No one spoke. When he looked up, he said he would go to a local hospital.

—Franks, 1985, p. 48. Copyright © 1985 by the New York Times Company. Reprinted by permission

Alcohol is one of a group of substances that have ruined the lives of countless numbers of people. Although there are many differences among them, all of these substances are **psychoactive drugs;** that is, they affect thought, emotions, and behavior. A generalized reduction in goal-directed behavior (for example, going to school or work), together with cognitive deficits (such as inability to concentrate), is a common consequence of prolonged heavy use of a psychoactive substance. As the case of James B. shows, they are capable of causing not only changes in motivation and ability to concentrate and think clearly but also serious physical symptoms. This case also illustrates the tendency of abusers to deny that the substance they are using excessively is a major factor

in their problems. There are two broad categories of disorders related to the use of psychoactive substances. **Psychoactive substance dependence disorders** have both behavioral and physical features. Someone with one of these disorders gives drug use a much higher priority than other behaviors that once had higher value. Physically, there are alterations in bodily systems (particularly the nervous system) when drug use is discontinued, there is a need for increased frequency and amount of the substance to get the same effects as previously, and withdrawal symptoms occur if use of the drug is discontinued. The individual spends a great deal of time in activities necessary to get the substance, use it, and recover from its effects (Frances & Miller, 1991). In **substance abuse disorders** the syndrome is not so full-blown and the main problem is impaired social and/or occupational functioning. The individual feels a strong need to use the substance; at the same time, he or she makes repeated efforts to control or reduce use, but is unable to do so. Overlap exists between dependence and abuse disorders and they might best be thought of as lying along a continuum with dependence indicating drug use that is more hazardous than that found in abuse.

People with substance dependence disorders may have periods of intoxication or withdrawal symptoms. **Intoxication** is a process following ingestion of a psychoactive substance (such as alcohol) that results in deteriorating states ranging from exhilaration to stupefaction. Various types of maladaptive behavior, such as belligerence and poor judgment, are associated with intoxication. In **withdrawal,** a substance-specific syndrome follows cessation of or reduction in intake of a psychoactive substance that was previously used regularly to induce a state of intoxication. There may also be **flashbacks** in which the person reexperiences one or more of the perceptual symptoms, such as hallucinations, that were originally experienced while intoxicated.

Addictive Behavior

Throughout history people have used a variety of substances to modify their moods and behavior. The use of some substances has become so common that such use is considered normal and even appropriate; examples include champagne toasts for the New Year and a cigar to celebrate the new baby. A majority of adults use alcohol as a recreational drink; many individuals, from children to the elderly, use caffeine in the form of coffee, tea, or cola drinks as a stimulant; and a great many teenagers and adults use nicotine in the form of cigarettes. Some mood and behavior-modifying substances have medical

uses. Physicians prescribe these substances to reduce pain, relieve tension, or aid in limiting food intake by suppressing appetite. There is a wide spectrum of notions of acceptability of psychoactive substances.

While the use of many substances may be considered appropriate, excessive intake can lead to substance abuse and dependence. These conditions involve **addictive behavior** because of the presence of a repetitive habit pattern that increases the risk of disease and is associated with personal and social problems. Addictive behaviors are often perceived by the individual, as well as by others, as being out of control. However, the behavior continues to occur despite attempts to abstain or moderate use. Addictive habits are typically characterized by the need for immediate gratification and are often coupled with delayed, deleterious effects. Individuals thus seek short-term rewards at the expense of long-term costs. Attempts to change an addictive behavior are typically marked by high relapse rates (Marlatt and others, 1988).

Of course, we are all creatures of habit and we are all dependent on people, situations, and experiences. The formation of habits can be an instrument of survival that regulates social interactions, maintains the health of the body, and allows us to react quickly when reflection is impossible or unnecessary. However, a habitual activity or reaction can be maladaptive when it is inflexible and becomes a person's chief source of gratification. In addictions, behavior is simplified and experience is impoverished as the dominant habit becomes the central focus of life.

Addictive behavior that involves dependence is particularly serious because of the increased likelihood of severe and long-lasting impairment in functioning. Getting drunk at the company New Year's Eve party would not qualify as a substance abuse disorder; neither would a single drunken binge after a family quarrel. Instead, there must be significant, ongoing maladaptive behavior that interferes with social functioning and/or effectiveness on the job and continues even though the person knows that use of the substance is having significant negative consequences.

Another characteristic of substance dependence is that when not actually using the substance, the person spends a lot of time looking forward to using it and devotes a great deal of effort to making it available. For example, an office worker might have a three-martini lunch and keep the glow going by nipping at a bottle he keeps hidden in his desk. He would be unable to restrict his use of alcohol to certain times of the day, such as after working hours, even though his accuracy in preparing reports had slipped and he had received several warnings from his boss. A factory worker might know that her safety depended on being alert around a drill press, yet she might still drink on the job. A retiree might continue to drink even though he knew that the resultant damage to his liver was creating a life-threatening situation. All of these examples involve alcohol, but we could have substituted marijuana, heroin, or tranquilizers. The critical factor is not the particular substance used but its effects on the person's life.

Physiological dependence on a substance is reflected in tolerance and withdrawal. **Withdrawal** refers to a particular set of physical symptoms that occur when a person stops or cuts down on the use of a psychoactive substance. The severe physical reaction that occurs when heroin use is curtailed is probably the best-known form of withdrawal. **Tolerance** means that the person has to use more and more of a substance to get the same effect, or that the same sized dose has progressively less effect as time goes by. Reactions to morphine and alcohol are examples of tolerance build-up. The pain-reducing power of morphine decreases if the drug is given over a long period. As alcoholics consume increasing amounts of alcohol, their cell membranes are altered so that less and less of the alcohol permeates the membranes. If less alcohol is actually penetrating cell membranes, an alcoholic may have less alcohol in his or her brain than a normal person with the same blood level of alcohol would. This is interesting in view of the fact that some alcoholics can perform well after consuming an amount of alcohol that would put a nonalcoholic into a coma.

Table 14–1 lists the criteria for dependence on psychoactive substances. The substances that can produce physiological dependence include alcohol, amphetamines, barbiturates, opioids, and tobacco. Four types of substances are related to psychological dependence only —they have not been shown to produce physiological dependence. They are cannabis, cocaine, psychedelics, and PCP. Table 14–9, later in this chapter, will give more information about these substances.

Psychologists are interested in substance abuse and dependence because a person's response to drugs seems to be due to a combination of physiological and psychological factors. Some people can control their use of many psychoactive substances; others seem unable to do so. Some individuals who are addicted have severe withdrawal symptoms; others do not. The effects that drugs produce also differ from one user to another.

Probably both the personality and physiological characteristics of the user and the environment or setting in which the substance is used influence the reaction observed. This is another case in which the interaction between the person and the situation, which has been referred to so often throughout this book, is important in understanding individual behavior. However, although these individual characteristics have a major influence on a person's response to a mood- or behavior-modifying substance, such substances do have certain general effects that are experienced by most people who use them.

Table 14–1

Criteria for Dependence on Psychoactive Substances

1. Repeated (unsuccessful) effort to cut down or control substance abuse;
2. Frequent intoxication or impairment by substance abuse when one is expected to fulfill social or occupational obligations (for example, absence from work because of being hung over or high, going to work high, driving when drunk);
3. Need for increased amounts of the substance in order to achieve intoxication or the desired effect, or experiencing diminished effect with continued use of the same amount of the substance (tolerance);
4. Experiencing of a substance-specific syndrome following cessation or reduction of intake of the substance (withdrawal);
5. Frequent preoccupation with seeking or taking the substance;
6. Relinquishing of some important social, occupational, or recreational activity in order to seek or take the substance;
7. Frequent use of a psychoactive substance to relieve or avoid withdrawal symptoms (for example, taking a drink to relieve morning shakes);
8. Frequent use of the substance in larger doses or over a longer period;
9. Continuation of substance use despite a physical or mental disorder, or despite a significant social problem that the individual knows is made worse by the use of the substance;
10. Presence of a mental or physical disorder or condition that is usually a complication of prolonged substance use.

SOURCE: Based on Millman, 1986

Alcohol

Alcohol has been used for recreational, medicinal, and ceremonial purposes for at least ten thousand years. The oldest of all archaeological records contain reference to its use. The **alcohol** that is contained in beer, wine and hard liquor is a chemical compound known as ethyl alcohol or ethanol. Only ethanol is safe for human consumption—other kinds of alcohol are isopropyl alcohol (rubbing alcohol) and methyl alcohol (wood alcohol). Ethanol is manufactured by two methods, distillation (hard liquors) or fermentation (beer and wine).

Despite the different production methods used, the ethanol contained in all these beverages is the same drug. The only difference is in the amount of alcohol as a percentage of total volume. In beer and wine, the percentage usually varies from 3 to 14 percent. In hard liquor, sometimes called distilled spirits, the percentage varies from 40 percent (80 proof) to 75 percent (150 proof). The amount of pure ethanol is generally about the same in a one ounce shot of whiskey (or other hard liquor), a four ounce glass of wine, or a twelve-ounce bottle of beer.

In the short term, alcohol acts on the central nervous system as a "blocker" of messages transmitted from one nerve cell to the next. It first affects the frontal lobes of the brain, the seat of inhibitions, reasoning powers, memory, and judgment. After continued consumption, it next affects the cerebellum, the seat of motor muscle control, balance, and the five senses. Finally, it affects the spinal cord and medulla, the seat of involuntary functions such as breathing, heart rate, and body temperature control. If enough alcohol is consumed, to the point of a blood-alcohol level of .50 percent or more, the involuntary function system can shut down and the person may die from acute alcohol poisoning.

Alcohol Abuse and Dependence

Negative effects of overuse of alcohol have been considered a serious problem for many years. About 70 percent of adults in America drink alcohol on occasion; 12 percent of these Americans are heavy drinkers, people who drink almost every day and become intoxicated several times a month. More men than women are heavy drinkers. For both men and women, the prevalence of drinking is highest and abstention is lowest in the 21- to 34-year age range. (*Alcohol and Health,* 1990). Table 14–2 provides estimates of the percent of alcohol in the blood as a function of amount of alcohol consumed and body weight. Box 14–1 summarizes information about the pervasiveness of alcohol-related problems in today's society.

Alcohol abuse shows several typical patterns: regular daily intake of a large amount, regular heavy drinking confined to weekends, and unpredictable binge

Table 14–2

Are You Drunk?

This table shows the estimated percent of alcohol in the blood according to body weight and the number of drinks consumed. One drink is calculated as equal to one ounce of 100-proof alcohol, a 4-ounce glass of wine, or a 12-ounce bottle of beer. Alcohol in the blood decreases over time. To calculate how much time decreases blood-alcohol level, subtract .015 for each hour that has passed since the first drink.

Body Weight	Drinks						Interpreting the Results	
	1	2	3	4	5	6	BLOOD ALCOHOL PERCENT	INTOXICATED?
100 lbs.	.038	.075	.113	.150	.188	.225	.000 to .050%	No
120	.031	.063	.094	.125	.156	.188	.050 to .100	Maybe[a]
140	.027	.054	.080	.107	.134	.161	.100 to .150	Probably
160	.023	.047	.070	.094	.117	.141	.150 and above	Yes
180	.021	.042	.063	.083	.104	.125		
200	.019	.038	.056	.075	.094	.113		
220	.017	.034	.051	.068	.085	.102		
240	.016	.031	.047	.063	.078	.094		

[a]In most states, .100 is proof of illegal intoxication.

SOURCE: Government of the District of Columbia.

BOX 14–1 Some Facts about the Alcohol Problem

- Nearly half of all violent deaths are alcohol-related.
- More than 20,000 vehicle fatalities in the United States annually are attributed to alcohol abuse; these deaths are relatively more frequent among young people.
- After two decades of steady increases, the 1980s saw a gradual but consistent downturn in per capita alcohol consumption in the United States.
- Men are more likely than women to be drinkers and to be heavy drinkers.
- Women at highest risk for drinking-related problems are unmarried but living with a partner, are in their twenties or early thirties, and/or have a heavy-drinking husband or partner.
- Alcohol is twice as popular among college students as the next leading drug, marijuana, and more than five times as popular as cocaine (see Figure 14–1).
- Two-thirds of the adult U.S. population drink; however, the 10 percent of these (6.7 percent of the total adult population) who drink most heavily drink half of the total amount of alcohol consumed.

FIGURE 14–1 College students often find that many student organized social activities are focused around drinking.

drinking (long periods without alcohol interrupted by episodes of heavy drinking lasting for weeks or months). Alcohol abuse is often referred to as **problem drinking.** Problem drinking should not be viewed as an inevitable step on the way to alcoholism. However, one study found that over a four-year period 30 percent of people initially categorized as alcohol abusers had become alcohol dependent (Hasin and others, 1990). Alcohol dependence is referred to as **alcoholism.** Figure 14–2 shows the change from drinking as part of a social activity to the solitary drinking behavior typical of alcoholism. The following excerpt presents a first-person account of the downward spiral of an alcoholic.

My alcoholism took years to develop into a chronic affliction, and during much of that time I went to bars after work, one of the guys. The

(a)

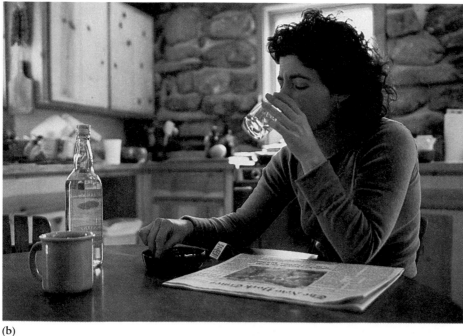

(b)

FIGURE 14–2 Drinking takes place in many different settings. (a) These couples have incorporated a drink with friends as one aspect of a pleasant social interaction. (b) This solitary drinker is likely to be using alcohol as a way of dealing with worries or depressed feelings.

delusion was gradually reinforced by gravitation. I mingled more and more with other persistent drinkers who took longer and longer to call for their bar tabs. Most of us were actually alcoholics in varying stages of development. The nonalcoholics had long ago selected themselves out. Those of us who remained agreed that we were "normal." Unhappy, but normal.

Alcoholic perceptions are like that, in a hundred insidious and distorting ways. All of them are aimed at protecting a drunkard's notion that he is possessed of free will. My drinking buddies and I agreed that we did not have a drinking problem. Everything in our increasingly narrow world, though, was a problem that required drinking: the wife, the kids, the boss, the government. In dingy watering holes from which everyone with a healthy life to lead had gone home, we conspired to overlook the obvious, that our bodily cells were addicted, and our minds were along for the ride.

Inexorably, the need for alcohol grew, while the lies wore thin. As my alcoholism accelerated, I abandoned most drinking partners and joined the ranks of solitary topers bellied up to countless bars. I lost any sense at all of what would happen after I started drinking; I became completely unpredictable. Sometimes I would go home after a couple of drinks (there was usually more booze there). More often, I would join the lineup of other alcoholics at the bar telephone stalls, fumbling with worn-out excuses about unexpected visitors and urgent business meetings.

Sometimes I would simply hole up in my office with a bottle after everyone else had gone home. There simply wasn't anything else in my life. Most frightening of all, I began to suffer alcoholic blackouts during drinking episodes. I would swim back into consciousness with no recollection of where I had been or what I had done. Once, I came to late at night on a downtown city street with my suit trousers slashed down one side by a razor.

Alcohol and Health

PHYSICAL HEALTH Alcohol abuse and dependence are linked to physical, as well as behavioral, impairment. Table 14−3 describes the negative effects of alcohol on various bodily organs and systems. People who drink heavily even on occasion face an increased risk of death associated with accidents, especially those caused by drunken driving. Alcohol acts like a general anesthetic, thereby impairing driving skills. Drivers aged 16 to 24 have the highest rate of alcohol-related crashes. Figure 14−3 shows the relationship between blood alcohol concentration and the probability that the person will cause a fatal automobile accident.

Research data show that alcohol is also involved in a high percentage of nontraffic accidents: Almost 50 percent of people who die from falls had been drinking; 52 percent of the fires that lead to adult deaths involved alcohol; and 38 percent of drowning victims had been drinking (*Alcohol and Health*, 1990).

Highway accidents in which alcohol is involved are the primary cause of death for young people. After

Table 14−3

The Effects of Alcohol on the Body

Bodily Organ or System	Effect
Brain	Brain cells are altered, and many die. Memory formation is blocked. Senses are dulled. Physical coordination is impaired.
Stomach and Intestines	Alcohol can trigger bleeding and can cause cancer.
Heart	Deterioration of the heart muscle can occur.
Immune System	Infection-fighting cells are prevented from functioning properly. Risk of bacterial disease is increased.
Reproduction	In men: hormone levels change, causing lower sex drive and enlarged breasts In women: menstrual cycles become irregular and ovaries malfunction.

FIGURE 14–3 The relative probability of being responsible for a fatal crash rises with rising blood-alcohol concentrations.

(*Journal of the American Medical Association*, 1986, 225, 522–527. Copyright © 1986, American Medical Association)

18-year-olds received the right to vote in 1971, the legal drinking age was lowered in many states. Studies of auto accident statistics from these states produced convincing evidence that the age reduction had resulted in an increased proportion of auto crashes and fatalities involving youthful drivers. Since 1976, therefore, many states have raised the drinking age. In the 12 months after Michigan raised the drinking age, accidents resulting in death or injury among 18- to 20-year-olds dropped by 28 percent.

Surprisingly, alcohol may also have some beneficial effects. Moderate use of alcohol (two ounces per day) may lessen the chances of a heart attack (*Alcohol and Health,* 1990). It is not clear why this should be the case, but researchers have suggested a number of possibilities. Alcohol may reduce psychological stress, or it may promote the formation of substances that help prevent or remove the plaque that can clog coronary arteries. Some researchers and public health officials are concerned that announcing positive effects of alcohol use will be interpreted as a suggestion that drinking is desirable for everyone. They point out that it is premature to recommend alcohol as a heart-attack preventative. A moderate amount for one person may be too much for another because of individual differences in tolerance for alcohol.

When alcohol is abused extensively, brain damage can result. For example, CT scans of young chronic alcoholics show reductions in the density of their left brain hemispheres compared to those of nonalcoholic individuals (Golden and others, 1981). Brain dysfunction is present in from 50 to 70 percent of detoxified alcoholics at the beginning of treatment. Certain cognitive abilities of people who use alcohol only moderately in social situations have been found to be impaired even 24 hours after they last used alcohol (Eckhardt and others, 1981).

The damaging effects of alcohol use by pregnant women on their unborn children has also been clearly documented. Because alcohol freely crosses the placenta, the developing fetus's blood alcohol level will be equal to that of the mother. As a result the child may develop **fetal alcohol syndrome** which produces physical malformations and mental retardation. It was at first thought that fetal alcohol syndrome was related to the mother's heavy alcohol use and to binge drinking in particular. More recent research has shown that even light to moderate alcohol use may have negative effects on the unborn child. (Fetal alcohol syndrome is discussed in detail in Chapter 16.)

MENTAL HEALTH In addition to what alcohol does to the body, its role in behavioral maladaptation is also powerful (Cox, 1990). This fact is reflected in recent comorbidity data showing that among people with alcohol disorders, another mental disorder appears in 37 percent of cases (Robins & Regier, 1991). Alcohol disorders in men are associated with an eightfold risk for psychotic episodes; in women, there is a threefold risk (Tien & Anthony, 1990). The highest comorbidity rates are for affective, anxiety, and antisocial personality disorders. Comorbidity rates are generally higher in women than men. The causes of high comorbidity rates related to alcohol abuse and dependence have not yet been discovered. When two disorders are associated, the one that occurs first might be a risk for the other. Overall, alcoholism precedes depression in the majority of cases. However, among women, depression comes first (Meyer, 1989).

Perspectives on Alcohol Abuse

THE BIOLOGICAL VIEW Ingestion of alcohol is associated with numerous behavioral, biophysical, and psychological changes. After the first drink, the average person experiences a lessening of anxiety. As more alcohol is consumed, the depressant action of alcohol affects brain functions. The individual staggers, and his or her mood becomes markedly unstable. Sensory perception is seriously impaired (see Table 14–4).

Table 14–4

Is It Safe to Drive?

The amount of alcohol that seriously interferes with driving skills varies from person to person, and even an individual's tolerance can vary over time. In general, however, impairment increases with each drink and the subsequent rise in blood-alcohol level. As little as one drink, especially if you do not drink regularly or if you drink on an empty stomach, can make you an unsafe driver.

| .05 | Blood-alcohol concentrations of 0.05 percent and above can mean lax thought, judgment, and restraint. There may be a significant increase in mistakes in tasks requiring divided attention. Steering errors increase and vision is affected.

| .10 | Around 0.10 percent, virtually all drivers are significantly impaired. Reaction to novel situations requiring choices is slowed, as are reactions to sounds or visual stimulation. Voluntary motor action is affected, with arm movements, walking, and speech usually becoming noticeably clumsy. At this blood-alcohol level, the likelihood of being involved in a crash is six times that of a sober driver.

| .20 | At 0.20 percent, the entire motor area of the brain is significantly depressed, and the person is very drunk. Staggering is likely. Reaction time is even slower, especially in divided-attention tasks. The person may become loud, incoherent, and emotionally unstable. At this level, the risk of a crash is 100 times that of a sober person.

Influenced by evidence that heavy drinking leads to a variety of bodily changes, writers have often characterized alcoholism itself as a disease. E. M. Jellinek (1960), often referred to as the father of the modern study of alcoholism, believed that alcoholism is a permanent and irreversible condition and that alcoholics are essentially different from nonalcoholics. Alcoholics, he contended, experience an irresistible physical craving for alcohol. Satisfaction of this craving leads to loss of control as a result of increasing physical dependence on alcohol. Alcoholic individuals feel compelled to continue drinking even after ingesting only a small amount of alcohol. Jellinek believed that the only way alcoholics can return to a normal life is through complete abstinence.

Some of Jellinek's ideas have been questioned on the basis of research findings that seem inconsistent with them. However, Jellinek's concept of alcoholism as a disease did succeed in changing people's attitude toward alcoholics from one of condemnation and blame to one of concern. In addition, it focused researchers' attention on the biological aspects of alcohol abuse.

Genetic Factors in Susceptibility to Alcohol

Studies using animals have shown that it is possible to breed strains of mice or rats that differ in the way they metabolize alcohol. (Goodwin, 1986). It has been demonstrated many times that alcoholism runs in human families as well. Sons of alcoholics are about four times more likely to be alcoholic than are sons of nonalcoholics. Adoption studies show this is true even when children have no exposure to their biological parents after the first few weeks of life (Schuckit, 1987). Evidence for genetic

predisposition to alcoholism is growing, and it is now widely accepted by researchers that alcoholism can result from the interaction of heredity and environment.

Studies of individuals who had a biological parent with alcoholism but were removed from the alcoholic environment through adoption at an early age have allowed assessment of the relative contributions of genetic and environmental factors in the genesis of alcoholism. Some studies have identified two types of genetic predisposition to alcoholism—*male-limited* and *milieu-limited* (Cloninger and others, 1981). In the male-limited type, susceptibility occurs only in males and early in their lives. In the milieu-limited form, a combination of genetic susceptibility and environmental provocation is needed to produce alcoholism that is usually less severe than the male-limited type.

Researchers are attempting to identify the specific gene or genes that might be linked to alcoholism. Although some researchers believe there are genes specific to alcoholism, others think alcoholism results from a set of biological factors that are heavily influenced by environmental events.

Knowledge that alcoholism has both genetic and environmental components can have important practical applications. If reliable biological indicators of a predisposition toward alcoholism can be found, individuals who have those indicators can know the risks they face and can make informed choices about drinking (see Figure 14–4). Another practical application is improved treatment. It is already clear that alcoholism is not a single disease. By clarifying the nature of various subcat-

(a)

(b)

FIGURE 14–4 Use of computerized scanning techniques has made it possible to work toward determining patterns of electrical activity in the brain that may identify those at high risk for alcoholism. These maps of differential electrical brain activity in controls (a) and individuals at high risk for alcoholism (b) were constructed by recording event-related brain potentials from 32 scalp electrodes and then using a mathematical computer program to construct the visual images. In the two photos, the electrical activity, represented as color shading, forms a somewhat different pattern for the controls and the at risk groups.

egories of alcoholism, genetic studies can point the way to more specific and effective therapies based on the genetic uniqueness of individuals.

Genetic molecular variations in alcohol-metabolizing enzymes are a major area of research on the heredity of alcoholism because a mutation that produces a slight alteration in the molecular structure of these enzymes could be expected to have a pronounced effect on their ability to remove alcohol from the body. Many investigators believe that such studies have the potential of explaining fundamental mechanisms of alcoholism and of identifying genetic markers of susceptibility (Newlin and Thomson, 1990).

Alcohol and the Nervous System Alcohol affects every system of the body, but its greatest, most immediate, and most visible effects are on the central nervous system. All the complex features of an individual—thoughts, emotions, actions—are based on chemical and electrical processes which occur in billions of nerve cells at any instant. Several features of this system could be involved in inherited predisposition to alcoholism. Alcohol could interfere with numerous processes involved in nerve cell function, and if there is inherited variation in these processes it could result in either neurochemical vulnerability or resistance to alcoholism. Among the leading neurochemical hypotheses are the following.

- Individuals who are predisposed toward alcoholism might have nerve cell membranes that are less sensitive to the permeability-altering effects of alcohol, which would affect the movement of sodium and potassium ions and the propagation of nerve impulses.

- Predisposition toward alcoholism might be based on inherited variations in the sensitivity of certain enzymes to inhibition by alcohol. This also would affect the transmission of nerve impulses, which depend on the enzyme's regulation of the flow of ions through the nerve cell membrane.

- Predisposition toward alcoholism may be based on inherited variations in the neurotransmitter release and uptake systems involved in the chemical propagation of nerve impulses between nerve cells.

- People who are predisposed to alcoholism may produce abnormal amounts of certain morphinelike compounds that may be involved in alcohol addiction.

- Predisposition toward alcoholism may be based on inherited variations in the brain's neurochemical mechanisms for reinforcing certain behaviors.

Sensitivity to Alcohol Individual sensitivity to the effects of alcohol varies greatly. As noted earlier, some people can remain conscious after drinking a quantity of alcohol that would cause others to pass out, become comatose, or even die. Others are so sensitive to alcohol that just one or two drinks can produce acute discomfort accompanied by obvious physiological changes. These individual variations are probably due to differences in the ability to metabolize alcohol or to innate differences in the central nervous system's sensitivity to alcohol.

When compared with men, women have much less of a specific stomach enzyme (alcohol hydrogenase) that neutralizes and breaks down alcohol. As a result, when a woman and a man drink the same amount, proportionately, for their size and weight, about 30 percent more alcohol enters the woman's bloodstream. When women drink too much alcohol, the small amount of the enzyme that they do have loses its ability to break down alcohol in the stomach. For alcoholic women, drinking alcohol is essentially the equivalent of injecting it intravenously, bypassing stomach digestion entirely. In male alcoholics, however, the enzyme still can neutralize alcohol, but not so well as in men who do not drink to excess. This enzyme may be one reason that women's livers get diseased more quickly than men's.

A comparison of people of different racial stock may shed light on the genetic component of these differences in alcohol metabolism. There is evidence of a high prevalence of sensitivity to alcohol among people of Oriental derivation (Chinese, Japanese, Koreans, Native Americans, and Eskimos). Signs of sensitivity—rapid facial flushing, elevated skin temperature, and increased pulse rate—after consuming moderate amounts of alcohol appear to be common among these groups but are seen in only 5 percent of Caucasians. Recent studies suggest that these differences are based on genetic variations in the enzymes involved in alcohol metabolism (*Alcoholism: An inherited disease*, 1985).

THE PSYCHODYNAMIC VIEW Psychodynamic theorists often describe the typical person who develops an alcohol problem as an **oral-dependent personality.** They believe that such a person's basic need for oral gratification was not satisfied early in life. This lack of satisfaction resulted in the development of an individual who is driven to secure oral satisfaction through such devices as drinking, smoking, and eating, and whose personality is characterized by self-doubt, passivity, and dependence.

Although there is no conclusive evidence that personality factors are involved in the development of alcoholism, a study reported by Jones (1981) demonstrated a consistent set of personality attributes among some alcoholics. The study drew upon data from a longitudinal research project that had begun when the subjects were ten-and-a-half years old. In middle age the subjects were interviewed about their drinking patterns. Jones found that as adults, male problem drinkers were likely to be described as relatively hostile, submissive, socially unsuccessful, and anxious. In general, these men had been rated as rather extroverted in adolescence. However, at that time they also described themselves as having less satisfactory social relationships and greater feelings of inferiority than did other males in the study. Jones believed that these men were rather impulsive and unsure of themselves in adolescence and that they had difficulty forming deeper, more lasting friendships. Additional longitudinal studies are needed to clarify the roles of personality and psychodynamic factors in alcohol use.

LEARNING FACTORS Some people drink as a way of coping with problems of living. They learn this behavior through reinforcement (being accepted by friends who value drinking), modeling (seeing others "solve" their problems with alcohol), and other learning mechanisms (see Figure 14–5). Short-term use of alcohol may be reinforcing for many people because of the pleasurable feeling of relaxation it produces. But since drinking is not an effective coping mechanism, their life situation does not improve. Feeling even less able to cope constructively, they increase their maladaptive coping behavior.

It is also possible that alcohol is sought for its short-term excitatory actions and is reinforcing because it makes people "feel good." Like all psychological phenomena, reinforcement has underlying neurochemical mechanisms. Most researchers agree that alcohol is a

FIGURE 14—5 This poster illustrates a modeling approach to discouraging alcohol use with its "Say No" message. Its focus is to help young people resist peer pressure to use alcohol.

reinforcer, that its reinforcement arises from specific mechanisms within the brain, and that these mechanisms, which constitute the brain's reward system, are probably located in a specific cluster of nerve cells.

Several studies have implicated certain neurochemicals in the reinforcing properties of alcohol. Alcohol may make many people "feel good" because it alters the levels of dopamine and norepinephrine, as well as opioid peptides, in a specific brain region. Subjectively, these neurochemical changes are experienced as excitation, and because that experience can be pleasurable, people will seek alcohol again (*Alcoholism: An inherited disease,* 1985).

COGNITIVE FACTORS Behavior is influenced by expectations about the consequences of behaving in a particular way as well as by what actually does happen.

Behavior thus can be shaped and maintained by cognitive appraisals of what has happened and what is likely to happen. A problem drinker learns to expect positive effects from drinking and interprets the experience in that way, despite the fact that the predominant quality of the actual experience is negative.

The importance of expectancy is illustrated by an experiment reported by Marlatt and others (1973). These investigators used a taste-rating task to determine whether drinking rates are affected by the actual presence of alcohol or merely by the expectancy of alcohol. The taste-rating task was an unobtrusive measure of drinking because the person's attention was focused on the taste of the drinks. The drinks used were vodka and tonic, and tonic alone. The subjects were permitted to drink as much of the beverages as they wished in the time allotted.

FIGURE 14–6 Student volunteers pose as research participants in an Alcohol Skills Training Program session held at the Behavioral Alcohol Research Laboratory (BARLAB) at the University of Washington.

The researchers found that the only significant determinant of the amount of alcohol consumed was the subjects' expectations regarding what they were drinking; those who expected alcohol drank more. This finding supports a cognitive interpretation of drinking. (Later in the chapter we discuss the applications of this cognitive perspective to therapy for problem drinkers.) Figure 14–6 shows a naturalistic setting for experiments on drinking behavior.

There is evidence that a person's belief about the alcohol content of a drink, regardless of its actual content, can be a significant determiner not only of alcohol consumption but also of various behaviors that may accompany or result from drinking, such as depression, delay of gratification, social anxiety, and sexual responsiveness in men. This evidence comes from studies, like the one described above, using the *balanced placebo design,* in which half of the subjects are given a drink containing alcohol and half are given a nonalcoholic beverage. By varying both drink content and expectancy set, this design permits joint and separate evaluation of the behavioral consequences of a subject's belief that he or she has consumed alcohol and the consequences of actual alcohol consumption.

SOCIAL AND COMMUNITY FACTORS The problem of excessive use of alcohol has sociocultural as well as psychological dimensions. The values and customs of the community influence attitudes toward drinking. In the past, problems of alcohol use were extremely frequent among certain ethnic groups, such as the Irish and Swedish, relatively infrequent for Italians, and particularly infrequent for Jews. Today, however, alcoholism is decreasing among Irish- and Swedish-Americans but rising among second- and third-generation Italian-Amer-

icans and Jews. Changing social customs within the cultural group seem to be a significant factor in these patterns of alcohol consumption.

Rates of alcoholism are low in groups in which the drinking customs, values, and sanctions are well known, agreed to by all, and consistent with the rest of the culture (see Figure 14–7). Among the sociocultural conditions that minimize alcohol problems are the following:

1. Exposure of children to alcohol at an early age in a strong family or religious setting. The alcoholic beverage is served in diluted form (wine as opposed to distilled spirits, for example) and in small quantities.

2. The beverage is considered a food and is served mainly at meals.

3. Drinking is not considered either a virtue—for example, a proof of manhood or virility—or a sin.

4. Abstinence is socially acceptable but excessive drinking or drunkenness is not.

A variety of social and interpersonal factors also influence alcohol consumption. These include the level of stress in the community and in the individual's personal life. Among the personal factors are friendships, family situation, and employment and financial status (Linsky and others, 1985).

AN INTERACTIONAL VIEW During recent years, a more complex biopsychosocial view of alcoholism has developed. At the core of this newer concept of alcoholism is an addictive cycle that results in a perpetuation of

FIGURE 14–7 The context in which alcoholic beverages are consumed is an important factor in alcoholism. Drinking wine at family gatherings, like this Jewish Passover ceremony, is much less likely to lead to problem drinking than imbibing in situations in which there is pressure for the individual to "excel at drinking."

harmful drinking. This cycle involves the following elements:

1. Certain susceptible individuals are more likely to develop alcohol dependence because of biological, psychological, or social predisposing factors (for example, genetics, depression, or peer influence).

2. Heavy drinking is intensified by precipitating factors such as stressful life events or psychological instigators (for example, anxiety or insomnia).

3. The susceptible individual finds alcohol rewarding, either because of the euphoria produced or the dysphoria assuaged.

4. Primary psychological dependence is developed as a consequence, resulting in tolerance and increased drinking.

5. Physical dependence follows, along with the need to drink to prevent withdrawal symptoms (secondary psychological dependence).

6. The addictive cycle is further intensified by persistent physiological craving.

7. Physical dependence mechanisms tend to become reactivated by alcohol ingestion after a period of abstinence, with accompanying reinstatement of the addictive cycle.

Treatment

The first step in treating an addicted alcohol user is usually **detoxification,** or "drying out." Detoxification, which usually is carried out in a protected, well-supervised setting such as a hospital, is aimed at removing the effects of a toxic substance (e.g., alcohol)

from the body. Physiological withdrawal symptoms often begin 6 to 24 hours after heavy drinking has stopped, although they can occur as soon as alcoholics simply reduce their intake of alcohol. Withdrawal signs can include tremors, delirium, sweating, confusion, increased blood pressure, and agitation. There is no established sobering agent—nothing that counteracts the effects of alcohol or speeds its breakdown and passage out of the body. Many alcoholics can withdraw on their own, but some are so severely dependent that they have to be detoxified—supervised as they go through a gradual withdrawal. Once detoxification is complete, insomnia, depression, and anxiety may persist for weeks or months. However, these conditions usually receive no treatment after the detoxification period has ended.

Most recovery from alcoholism is not the result of treatment. Probably no more than 10 percent of alcohol abusers are ever treated at all, but as many as 40 percent recover on their own. Alcoholics with a stable job and family life have the best chance; age, sex and the duration of alcohol abuse matter less. An important step in overcoming alcoholism is the alcoholic's acknowledgment of the disorder. As the case of James B. at the beginning of this chapter pointed out, alcohol abusers, feeling ashamed and guilty, often refuse to admit the problem to themselves and try to conceal it from their families and friends, who in turn may avoid acknowledging it for fear of being intrusive or having to take responsibility. It is valuable in clinical interviews to determine the patient's willingness to admit the seriousness of his or her drinking problem (see Table 14–5).

Denial and obliviousness are not the only sources of misunderstanding. In a society that has so many heavy drinkers, it is not always easy to decide when a drinking

Table 14-5
Determining Extent of Drinking Problem and Alcoholic's Willingness to Admit the Problem—The Initial Steps in Treatment Planning

It is not necessarily useful simply to ask how much a person drinks, because the response is likely to be vague and may be influenced by denial. One of the best ways of determining the extent of denial of the symptoms is a series of questions that can be addressed to alcoholics. Some helpful questions about drinking patterns or habits are the following:

Do you sometimes drink heavily after a disappointment or quarrel?
Do you always drink more heavily when you feel under pressure?
Are you drinking more often without eating?
Do you try to sneak in extra drinks on social occasions?
Have you attempted various ways to control your drinking?
Have you failed to keep promises to yourself to cut down?
Do you avoid your family and close friends while drinking?

Useful questions about feelings include:

Do you feel guilty about your drinking?
Do you want to go on drinking when your friends have had enough?
Do you often regret what you have said or done while drinking?
Do you feel uncomfortable if alcohol is not available in certain situations?
Are you annoyed by the way others talk about your drinking?

If friends or family members can be interviewed these questions might be addressed to them:

Does this person's drinking ever worry or embarrass you?
Does it spoil family holidays?
Does it create a tense atmosphere?
Do you lie to conceal it?
Does he or she try to justify the drinking or avoid discussion of it?
Do you or your children fear physical or verbal assault from this person when he or she is drinking?
Does this person become remorseful and apologize after a drinking episode?
Do others talk about this person's drinking?

problem has become so serious that special help is needed. Alcoholism can be hard to observe day by day, even if it's easily recognizable over a period of years. Patterns of abuse through a lifetime are variable, the symptoms come and go. Alcoholics are not always drinking uncontrollably; some drink only on weekends, and many succeed in remaining abstinent or nearly abstinent for months at a time (*Broadening the base of treatment for alcohol problems,* 1990). In the following sections we describe several treatment programs for problem drinkers and detoxified alcoholics.

THE BIOLOGICAL APPROACH Earlier in the chapter we mentioned that biological theories regarding susceptibility to alcohol might someday lead to effective physical therapies for alcoholism. While such therapies have not yet been developed, in the past decade, research into the pharmacological treatment of alcoholism has become increasingly active. Several drugs have been developed for the treatment for alcohol dependence and are used in the management of withdrawal symptoms, the treatment of certain psychological problems (for example, anxiety) in heavy drinkers, and in other aspects of rehabilitation. Research is also being conducted with the aim of developing a pharmacological agent that

might reduce alcohol cravings. Achieving this goal will require more knowledge concerning the behavioral and biological factors that regulate alcohol intake. Several neurotransmitters and neurohormones may play roles in the acquisition, maintenance, and cessation of alcohol consumption. Continued research on the mechanisms underlying these behaviors may yield more clinically useful drug treatments.

Another biological approach to alcohol problems is to alter the body's response to alcohol. The drug disulfiram provides one way to do this because it causes extreme and sometimes violent discomfort (nausea, vomiting, cold sweats) when a person drinks alcohol within 12 hours of taking it. Since disulfiram is self-administered, the success of this technique depends on the individual's motivation to reduce or eliminate drinking. If the person wants to drink, disulfiram therapy will fail. It may be useful, however, as part of a therapeutic approach that also deals with motivations or situational cues that lead to alcohol use (*Alcohol and Health,* 1990).

THE COMMUNITY APPROACH One outgrowth of the view that alcoholism is a disease, caused perhaps by physiological sensitivity to alcohol, is the belief that the alcoholic needs to avoid alcoholic beverages completely.

According to the disease model, losing control of drinking is an involuntary manifestation of an internal addictive disorder. If one drink is enough to set off a drinking binge in alcoholics who want to rehabilitate themselves, that drink must not be taken. Because Alcoholics Anonymous (AA) attempts to help the alcoholic resist taking that one drink, the AA program is widely recommended by adherents of the disease model. It is the most widely used group treatment for alcoholism.

Alcoholics Anonymous is a community-based approach to alcoholism. There are more than 73,000 groups throughout the world. Most members are referred to AA by other AA members and by rehabilitation and counseling programs. AA expects recovering alcoholics to admit their personal powerlessness over alcohol and seek help from a higher power, which can be understood in any way an individual member chooses. Members are urged to pray or meditate to get in touch with that power. They are asked to make a "moral inventory," confess the wrongs they have done, beg forgiveness, make amends, and carry the message to other alcoholics. AA takes the position that anyone who has once been an alcoholic is always an alcoholic; the disease can be arrested but vulnerability is permanent.

The most famous AA slogans are "It's the first drink that gets you drunk," which states the goal of abstinence, and "One day at a time," which places present action before long-term planning. AA members are told that although alcohol is the source of their problems they must assume responsibility for their own recovery. They must also resolve to devote themselves to helping others in need as part of their own rehabilitation.

The effectiveness of AA has not been scientifically documented and methodological problems make such an evaluation difficult. Many alcoholics drop out of the program, presumably as failures so they are not counted when the percentage of members who successfully abstain is calculated. In addition, not all people with alcohol problems are willing to join AA. Because the organization is committed to the idea of total abstinence from alcohol, individuals who believe they have a problem with alcohol but want to reduce rather than cease their drinking probably would not join the group. Because its members represent a selected population of those with alcohol-related problems their percentage of success in remaining abstinent does not necessarily represent the success rate for all alcohol-dependent people if they belonged to AA.

One of AA's most important rehabilitative ingredients is the social support it provides for members. Members know they can call upon fellow members at any time for aid in resisting the temptations of alcohol. Although AA may not be the right approach for every alcoholic, for those who find it congenial it can be a valuable source of support, belongingness, and security. While not formally affiliated with any professional organization or institution, AA now represents a major referral resource for alcoholic patients.

THE PSYCHODYNAMIC APPROACH Clinicians who take a psychodynamic perspective advocate psychotherapy for alcoholics. Although there have been some encouraging clinical reports on the usefulness of psychotherapy, research on the topic has not yet produced definitive conclusions. Most studies of psychotherapy with alcoholics are not comparable with respect to such important variables as the setting in which the treatment was applied, the duration of the therapy, and the criteria by which the therapy was evaluated.

The use of psychotherapy to help people with alcohol problems may be limited by the fact that they often need help at odd hours in their efforts to stay sober. The low self-esteem of some overusers of alcohol may be even further lowered by having to depend on people who do not have an alcohol problem.

In the past, psychotherapists believed that alcoholism was merely a symptom of underlying psychological difficulties. The logical conclusion was that such patients would improve in regard to their drinking, if such difficulties were successfully addressed. Today, it is widely recognized that psychotherapeutic exploration for someone who is still drinking not only provides very little benefit but may be barely remembered from one session to the next.

An increasing number of psychodynamically-oriented clinicians recognize the value of looking at alcohol problems from the standpoint of the family system rather than the individual. These therapists acknowledge that alcohol abuse not only affects families but is also influenced by how the family interacts and functions as a system. For this reason, it is necessary to find out whether family behavior patterns have been organized and altered to accommodate the unique demands of the alcoholic member. Family therapists view the whole family, not the alcoholic member alone, as the primary patient. While treatment goals vary from case to case, family therapists often focus their attention on restabilizing family behavior after cessation (or reduction) of drinking has taken place. In some cases, a major effort is needed to restructure relationships within the family.

THE LEARNING APPROACH Learning theorists may make use of **aversive conditioning** in their treatment of alcoholics. Aversive conditioning is based on the principles of classical conditioning (see Chapter 3). If a glass of alcohol (conditioned stimulus) regularly precedes an aversive stimulus such as a nausea-producing drug (unconditioned stimulus), the alcohol will eventually elicit some part of the unconditioned response—in this case, vomiting. Once the unpleasant response has been conditioned to alcohol, the habit of avoiding alcohol will

be established through operant conditioning. The response of abstinence is strengthened because it reduces the unpleasant feeling (nausea) that the conditioning situation has associated with alcohol. Electric shock is sometimes used in place of nausea-producing drugs in this procedure, but it seems to be less effective. Aversive conditioning approaches often require "booster sessions" because the threat of an unpleasant reaction tends to weaken over time. Long-term follow-up studies are needed to establish the success rate of this therapeutic method.

Another learning approach, *covert sensitization,* uses aversive images and fantasies rather than actual shocks and chemicals. Alcoholic patients are told that they can eliminate their "faulty habit" by associating it with unpleasant stimuli. They are instructed to close their eyes and imagine that they are about to drink an alcoholic beverage. They are then taught to imagine the sensations of nausea and vomiting. If it is repeated often enough, the association between nausea and the sight, smell, and taste of alcohol is presumed to establish a conditioned aversion to alcohol.

THE COGNITIVE APPROACH Many cognitively based alcohol programs are focused on controlled drinking rather than on abstinence. The **controlled drinking** approach means that the emphasis is on building participants' coping skills so that they can keep their alcohol consumption to the level they have previously determined is acceptable. In this approach, clients are oriented toward monitoring their own behavior by noting the situational and environmental antecedents and consequences of heavy drinking. Their past learning in relation to drinking is reviewed, and their expectations about the effects of alcohol are discussed. Participants in controlled-drinking programs are encouraged to ask themselves questions like the following.

- At what places am I most likely to overdrink?
- With which people am I most likely to overdrink?
- When am I most likely to overdrink?
- How do I feel emotionally just before I begin to overdrink?

Special emphasis is placed on drinking as a response to stress. This approach makes sense, since a high percentage of people with alcohol problems report that their heavy drinking often begins when they are faced with unpleasant, frustrating, or challenging situations. Improved problem-solving skills, particularly in the area of interpersonal relationships, learning how to anticipate and plan for stressful experiences, and acquiring the ability to say "No, thanks" when offered a drink have been shown to have therapeutic value for alcoholics (Marlatt & Gordon, 1985).

One reason that learning approaches may not be effective is that the short-term effects of alcohol often are positively reinforcing. Only the effects of overconsumption, ending in intoxication, dangerous or socially frowned-upon behavior, or a period of binge drinking have negative-reinforcement properties. The cognitive perspective deals with this problem by focusing the client's thoughts on the consequences of the drinking behavior as well as on the specific situations in which drinking is most likely to appear tempting. The client and the therapist work together to develop cognitive coping techniques to deal with these situations.

Relapse Prevention While the goal of therapeutic efforts is to help alcoholics stop drinking, or drinking to excess, maintaining sobriety over the long term is also of great importance. Alcoholics who undergo treatment have a high relapse rate. Many go through treatment a number of times or through a number of treatments and still relapse into uncontrolled drinking.

For those who view alcoholism as a disease, a relapse is a failure that the victim is powerless to control. From the cognitive viewpoint, a relapse is a slip or error. The cognitive approach views a relapse as a fork in the road. One fork leads back to the abusing behavior, the other toward the goal of positive change.

Relapse-prevention programs combine a cognitive approach with a variety of treatment procedures designed to change the individual's drinking pattern (Marlatt & Gordon, 1985). Such programs can be used whether the goal is abstinence or controlled drinking. The only requirement is that the client make a voluntary decision to change. The relapse-prevention approach assumes that the person experiences a sense of control over his or her behavior as long as the treatment program continues. If the person encounters a high-risk situation, this sense of control is threatened and a relapse is likely. High-risk situations include negative moods such as frustration, anger, or depression; interpersonal conflicts such as an argument with an employer or family member; and social pressure to indulge in drinking. If the person is able to make an effective coping response—for example, denying the offer assertively when friends suggest "just one drink"—the probability of a relapse decreases. Figure 14–8 describes the cognitive–behavioral approach to the relapse process.

An important factor in relapses is the **abstinence-violation effect.** When a relapse occurs, the individual has two kinds of cognitive and emotional responses. One is conflict and guilt; the other is an attribution to temporary situational factors rather than a permanent personal weakness or lack of self-efficacy. An alcoholic who breaks abstinence for the first time may continue to drink after the lapse in order to relieve the conflict and guilt related to the first drink. The individual may also reduce the conflict between the drinking behavior and the goal of avoiding relapses by thinking: "This just

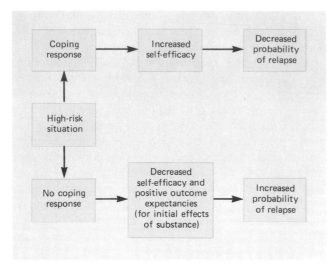

FIGURE 14–8 A cognitive–behavioral analysis of the relapse process begins with exposure to a high-risk situation. A high-risk situation is any situation that arouses stress, negative emotions, strong urges and temptations, and interpersonal conflict. Having a coping response increases the sense of self-efficacy (feeling that one is in control) and decreases the probability of relapse. Not having a coping response decreases self-efficacy (and heightens the feeling of not being in control) and, together with positive expectations about the favorable effects of the substance, increases the probability of relapse.

proves I'm an alcoholic. I can't control my drinking once I start it." Rather than attributing the lapse to the difficult situation, people who use these cognitions are likely to blame themselves for lack of willpower or inability to resist temptation. Such thoughts increase the probability that a single drink may snowball into a full-strength alcoholic binge and a total relapse.

In addition to viewing any slip into drinking as a temporary lapse and not necessarily a permanent relapse and a sign of personal failure, one of the primary goals of the relapse-prevention program is to train the individual

to recognize the early-warning signals that may precede a relapse and to plan and carry out a series of intervention or coping strategies before it is too late. The relapse-prevention technique holds promise not only for alcohol abuse but also for drug use, smoking, and other problems of self-control such as dieting. Its main components—identifying high-risk situations and learning pertinent coping and behavioral skills—are applicable to many types of situations. Table 14–6 lists some ways in which lapses can be handled in a positive manner. Many relapse-prevention programs recommend that individuals carry a card with them listing some coping techniques. Further research is needed that explores short- and long-term effects of relapse-prevention techniques.

Abstinence versus Controlled Drinking A sometimes intense and angry dispute about the necessity for abstinence began in the 1960s when studies reported that some former alcoholics could continue to drink moderately. Most advocates of controlled drinking are behavioral or cognitive–behavioral therapists who see alcohol abuse as a bad habit or a personal or social problem. Defenders of abstinence, including Alcoholics Anonymous and many medical and mental health professionals, believe that loss of control is inevitable for an alcoholic once drinking starts. They tend to regard alcoholism as a disease whose progress can be arrested only by removing the poison that causes it.

Critics of the disease perspective argue that while abstinence can work well for some individuals, it is very hard to live up to; moreover, recovery from alcoholism may not require such a drastic step. One study suggested that alcohol abusers can recover without abstinence (Polich and others, 1980). In this investigation, known as the Rand study, over 900 individuals with severe alcohol problems were studied for four years after they had been admitted to one of eight federal alcoholism treatment centers. The researchers found that at the end of this period almost half of the subjects were either

Table 14–6

Learning from a Lapse

A temporary lapse can be used as an opportunity for learning and need not signal defeat. The first priority is to prevent slips by anticipating high-risk situations and preparing ways to handle them. When a lapse does occur, it helps to carry a card listing coping tactics tailored to personal needs. Such advice might include:

1. Treat the slip as an emergency requiring immediate action.
2. Remember that a slip is not a relapse.
3. Renew your commitment.
4. Review the actions that led to the lapse so you won't repeat them.
5. Make an immediate plan for recovery.
6. Ask someone for help.

abstaining from alcohol or drinking in a controlled manner.

Another longitudinal study also found that some alcohol abusers can return to drinking on a controlled basis without abusing alcohol (Vaillant & Milofsky, 1982). However, subjects who were alcohol dependent and/or had many alcohol-related problems generally achieved successful results only if they became abstinent (see Figure 14–9).

These findings suggest that there may be two groups of alcohol abusers. Some can successfully resume drinking on a controlled basis. Others must abstain entirely if they are to cope with their alcohol problem. Both studies show that level of abuse before treatment plays an important role in the success of various treatment strategies. However, most researchers in this area would agree that the success rates of treatment procedures are not high enough.

Further research on such issues as the value of abstinence versus controlled drinking needs to be sufficiently complex to take account not only of subjects' drinking histories but also of their motivations and expectations about what would constitute success in coping with their drinking problems. For example, how much does abstinence change the life of an alcoholic? Alcoholics in the first few years of abstinence have been compared with returning prisoners of war. Their world is unfamiliar, because they have been living in an environ-ment created by alcohol. Feelings that have been blunted or suppressed come back to trouble them. They have lost a great deal of time and must start where they left off. Being sober, like being free after imprisonment, entails new responsibilities. Alcoholics in the early stages of abstinence thus often suffer from anxiety and depression and may find it difficult to hold a job or preserve a marriage. The resolution of these problems comes when they establish new personal relationships, rebuild old ones, and begin to develop confidence in their power to control their lives.

Preventing Alcohol Abuse

Although there has been much research related to the treatment of alcoholism, expert opinions differ concerning which treatments are particularly effective. One difficulty in interpreting the available evidence is that many people (perhaps over 50 percent) who enter alcohol treatment programs drop out of them, and no one knows what happens to these dropouts. Studies comparing inpatient and outpatient programs have produced conflicting results. It is becoming clear that much treatment research has failed to identify differential effectiveness because different types of patients have been lumped together in study populations. Despite conflicting findings concerning treatment programs, a picture of which alcohol abusers are likely to do well, regardless of the treatment, is emerging: people with jobs, stable relationships, minimal psychopathology, no history of past treatment failures, and minimal involvement with other drugs.

Research on treatment for alcoholism is improving and should yield practical results. Preventing alcohol abuse, however, would obviously be better than having to treat it. Unfortunately, less is known about prevention than about treatment. According to some studies, taxes that raise the price of alcohol and therefore reduce a society's total consumption have a more than proportionate effect on serious alcohol abuse. There are usually fewer alcohol problems in countries where the price of alcohol is high relative to the average income. It is less clear whether merely limiting alcohol advertising is effective.

Other community-level strategies that can be useful from the standpoint of prevention are raising the minimum drinking age, regulating the types of outlets and the hours during which alcohol may be sold, establishing tough drinking-and-driving laws, and carrying out various types of educational programs directed at important target groups. Box 14–2 presents information about the scope of the alcohol-abuse problem in one setting, the college campus, and suggests some practical approaches to prevention.

FIGURE 14–9 A return to controlled social drinking has a greater chance of success if the person has only a few symptoms of alcohol abuse. Only four men who had seven or more problems were able to return to social drinking. Most of these multiproblem people who did not resume alcohol abuse eventually became abstinent.

(*Archives of General Psychiatry*, 1982, 39, 127–133. Copyright ©1982, American Medical Association)

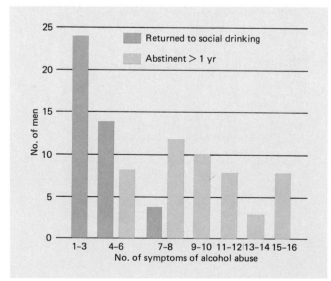

BOX 14-2 Drinking on Campus

In stark contrast to the purposeful bustle along the hospital corridor that crisp February dawn, a cluster of bewildered students glanced silently at each other as they waited to find out whether Jim Callahan was dead or alive.

Full of fear, for him and for themselves, the fraternity brothers replayed the previous night in their minds, again and again. The initiation ritual was supposed to have been funny—a test of the fraternity's power over its new pledges. Wasn't it a good job, to order them to drink "kamikazes" in the frat house basement until they were sick? The freshmen could sleep it off, after all. But when 18-year-old Jim Callahan passed out early on the morning of February 12, 1988, he never woke up.

Later, doctors would explain that Callahan died from acute alcohol poisoning caused by drinking a huge quantity of alcohol in a very short time. He drank about 24 ounces—nearly three-fourths of a liter—in 30 to 45 minutes following a Lambda Chi Alpha pledge-pinning ceremony.

This tragedy took place at Rutgers University, but there have been similar events at other educational institutions (see Figure 14–10). Although drinking among college students as a whole has declined from 89 percent in 1981 to 80 percent in 1991, surveys show that the rate of abusive drinking among college students has held relatively steady. This is in contrast to a decline in the rate of binge drinking among people in the same age group who are not college students (see Figure 14–11). The universities surveyed reported that the number of cases involving alcohol poisoning of students that are treated at medical centers has generally doubled (Celis, 1992).

One prevention approach taken by two University of Washington researchers, G. Alan Marlatt and John Baer, has been the development of a

six- to eight-week college course on sensible approaches to alcohol. Can merely taking a class alter harmful drinking habits? Marlatt and Baer found that course participants signifi-

FIGURE 14–10 Sometimes a tragedy in the family prompts social action. Larry Wooten, a university junior, died as the result of the challenge from an old friend with whom he competed in sports, for grades, and in social activities. The pair challenged each other while watching a football game in a bar as to who could drink more in an hour. Larry drank one more drink than his friend, a total of 23 shots of liquor, but later died as a result. His parents, shown here, have mounted a campaign against alcohol abuse. Their efforts are part of many by parents, fraternities, and universities to try to control the trend toward abusive drinking by college students.

cantly reduced their alcohol consumption and maintained that reduction even two years later. Furthermore, two other groups—one that only read the class manual and another that received only brief verbal information—also cut their drinking significantly. These results are even more impressive because all those selected for the class were at high risk for alcohol problems through heavy drinking or factors such as a family history of alcoholism. This prevention program does not tell students they

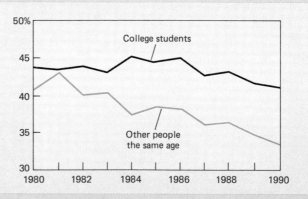

FIGURE 14–11 People between 19 and 22 years of age who reported that they had drunk at least five alcoholic drinks in a row at some time in the last two weeks.

(National Institute of Drug Abuse as published in the New York Times, Dec. 21, 1991, p. A8)

must abstain from liquor (except for those who are alcoholics), which may be a contributing factor to the program's success. The course provides information from which students can assess whether they have a problem and decide what, if anything, they want to do about it. Emphasis is placed on sensible drinking as a skill. Drinking is compared with driving, both of which can be dangerous if practiced by an unskilled person. The course tells students that, as with driving, one must learn to drink by experience—what, when, where, and how much—one can't learn simply by being told how (Kivlahan and others, 1990). The course also asks students to monitor their own drinking behavior by providing answers to questions such as those in Table 14–7.

One of the myths dispelled by the course is that the effects of alcohol are always a consequence of its chemical properties. Although this is undoubtedly true for motor performance, coordination, and reaction time, alcohol's effects on other functions—such as social behavior and moods—depend less on the actual content of a drink than on a person's prior perceptions and expectations.

The Social Side of College Drinking

Drinking is a preferred way to socialize; few students drink alone. Those whose drinking is getting out of hand are often threatened by those who don't drink. As long as others are consuming alcohol in large amounts, heavy drinkers rationalize that the amount they consume must be all right. Motives for drinking can vary quite a bit, however. For most students, college years are a time of experimentation with a range of adult behaviors; drinking, especially when it is not one's family pattern, is one of these. For some students, college years are also a time for rebellion; under-age drinking is a way to flout the rules that say they are "too

young." For some too, on campus as in society in general, drinking is a popular way to relieve stress. Other factors, such as ethnic patterns and heredity, may also play a role in drinking habits.

What Can You Do?

Here are some ways students can help themselves before they drink:

- Before a party, agree as a group on a designated driver—someone who will stay sober.
- Agree on ways to let someone know that he or she is drinking too much.

- Before drinking alcoholic beverages, provide and eat foods high in protein and carbohydrates.
- Pace drinks to one per hour.
- Have nonalcoholic beverages available, and switch to them after you reach your alcohol limit.
- Focus an event on dancing, dinner, or other activities, not on drinking.
- If someone becomes intoxicated, strongly suggest that he or she not drive, and drive the person home yourself or call a taxi. If necessary, let the person sleep overnight on the couch.
- If someone passes out, keep the person on his or her side, not on the back, and call for medical help.

Table 14–7
Understanding Personal Drinking Patterns Is the First Step to Sensible Alcohol Use

In order to help students understand the personal reasons for their alcohol use and the kinds of situations that are likely to lead to more drinking, one assignment to a class on sensible approaches to drinking involves thinking about and answering the following questions. The answers may give each student some important insights into his or her drinking patterns.

Are there any *places* where you are more likely to overdrink?
 (Yes/No) Where?

Are there any *people* with whom you are more likely to overdrink?
 (Yes/No) Who?

Are there any *times* or *days* when you are more likely to overdrink?
 (Yes/No) When?

Are there any *activities* that make it more likely that you will overdrink?
 (Yes/No) Describe them.

Do you think that you overdrink when you are *feeling* certain ways?
 (Yes/No) Describe those feelings.

Could you take a "vacation" from (avoid) any of the places or people involved in your overdrinking?
 (Yes/No) Which ones?

Are there places where you are *less likely* to overdrink?
 (Yes/No) Where?

Are there people with whom you are *less likely* to overdrink?
 (Yes/No) Who?

Other Drugs

Strictly speaking, alcohol is a drug—it is a chemical substance that leads to physiological and psychological changes when ingested. But for most people the word "drugs" means pills, powders, and pot. In addition to alcohol, psychoactive drugs may be classified into several groups: barbiturates and tranquilizers, the opioids, cocaine, amphetamines, psychedelics, phencyclidine (PCP), marijuana, and nicotine.

Barbiturates and Tranquilizers

Barbiturates (such as phenobarbitol) and tranquilizers (such as Valium) are grouped together because they both have a depressing effect on the central nervous system. They probably do this by interfering with synaptic transmission. Either they inhibit the secretion of excitatory neurotransmitters or they cause the release of inhibitory transmitter substances. Both types of drugs reduce anxiety and insomnia and affect a wide range of bodily functions. They are both very popular. Each year Americans consume over 300 tons of barbiturates; tranquilizers are an even bigger business.

Barbiturates, or derivatives of barbituric acid, are prescribed by physicians for relief of anxiety or to prevent convulsions. Mild doses of barbiturates are effective as sleeping pills, although they may actually cause sleep disorders if used over a long period. Higher doses, such as those used by addicted individuals, trigger an initial period of excitement that is followed by slurred speech, loss of coordination, severe depression, and impairment of thinking and memory. Illicit use of barbiturates often occurs in conjunction with the use of other drugs, notably alcohol and heroin. The effects of alcohol and barbiturates are addictive, and this combination is especially dangerous.

The body quickly develops a tolerance to barbiturates and tranquilizers. As tolerance develops, the amount of the substance needed to maintain the same level of intoxication is increased. The margin between an intoxicating dose and a fatal one also becomes smaller (see Figure 14–12). These drugs can cause both physical and psychological dependence. After addiction has developed, sudden abstinence can cause withdrawal symptoms including delirium, convulsions, and death. The following case describes the results of an accidental overdose of one type of barbiturates, secobarbital (Seconal). Because seconal is packaged in red capsules they are often referred to as *reds, red birds,* or *red devils.*

Judi A. was a young, attractive girl from a middle-class family who apparently was seeking something that eluded her. She died of an overdose of barbiturates.

Judi A. had lived only 17 years, 5 months and 27 days before her nude body was found on a grimy bed which had been made up on the floor of a rundown apartment in Newport Beach [California]. A small pill was found on the bed near the body, another was discovered on the floor.

Judi's death was classified as an accident because there was no evidence that she intended to take her own life. Actually it was about as accidental as if she'd killed herself while playing Russian roulette. Judi didn't intentionally take too many reds. She was familiar with them, had taken them before, knew what to expect. She'd even had an earlier scare from a nonfatal overdose. But her mind, clouded by the first few pills, lost count and she ingested a lethal number. She was dying before she swallowed the last pill.

—Adapted from Hazlett, 1971, p. 1

There are three types of barbiturate abuse.

1. *Chronic intoxication,* in which people obtain prescriptions, often from more than one physician. Initially they seek barbiturates to reduce insomnia and anxiety, and may then become addicted to the drugs.

FIGURE 14–12 The relative relationship between lethal and intoxicating doses of short-acting barbiturates in the blood changes as tolerance develops. (Dosages are only approximate because of individual differences in tolerance to the drug and patterns of use.)

(Adapted from Wesson & Smith, 1977, p. 35)

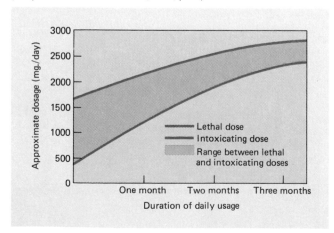

Chronic use leads to slurred speech and decreased effectiveness on the job.

2. *Episodic intoxication,* in which individuals take barbiturates orally to produce a "high" or state of well-being.

3. *Intravenous injections,* in which the drug is injected, often in combination with other drugs (such as heroin). Intravenous use produces a "rush" of pleasant, warm, drowsy feelings. Many complications are associated with prolonged use of the drug in this manner.

Relapses are common among barbiturate users because use of the drug is an easy way of escaping tension, anxiety, and feelings of inadequacy.

Some tranquilizers act like barbiturates, while others act quite differently. **Tranquilizers** are derived from several chemical groups. Overuse of tranquilizers is common. They are frequently prescribed to reduce anxiety, and perhaps half a million Americans use them for nonmedical purposes. As with barbiturates, the body develops a tolerance to many tranquilizers. Physical and psychological dependence and serious withdrawal symptoms may occur. Apparently unaware that they are addictive or that they can cause death, many people use tranquilizers freely. The undesirable effects of these substances increase when they are used in combination with alcohol and other drugs, just as they do with barbiturates.

Valium is a member of the *benzodiazepine* group of tranquilizers. Drugs in this group produce less euphoria than other tranquilizing drugs, so the risk of dependence and abuse is relatively low. Nevertheless, tolerance and withdrawal can develop.

The Opioids

The term **opioid** refers to any natural or synthetic substance that acts on the body in a way that is similar to the action of derivatives of the opium poppy. These substances bind to and act upon opioid receptor sites in the brain. The opioids include a variety of substances, some of which occur naturally while others are synthetic. Heroin is the most well-known synthetic opioid.

NATURAL OPIOIDS Several forms of opioids that resemble opium and heroin in their effects are manufactured by the brain and the pituitary gland. Three such distinct opioids are the **endorphins, enkephalins,** and **dynorphins.** Some of these substances can also be made artificially for experimental use. Research using natural opioids may provide insights into the mechanisms of pain, pleasure, emotion, and perception. The endorphins have been the most widely studied.

There is already some evidence that when individuals suffering from chronic spinal pain are treated effectively with acupuncture, endorphins are released into the spinal fluid (Jaffe, 1989). The endorphin levels seem to peak at the moments when the pain-relieving effects of the acupuncture are most pronounced.

Study of the endorphins has led to the mapping of the entire opioid-receptor system. The nerves of the brain and spinal cord have been found to contain specific sites to which opioids must bind in order to produce their effects. Morphine and similar drugs block pain signals to the brain because they fit into these sites like a key into a lock.

Work on the possibility that drug addiction may respond to endorphin therapy has begun in several laboratories. Some scientists suspect that addiction is a deficiency disease: The addict's craving for and dependence on opioids may be caused by chronic underproduction of natural endorphins. If this is the case, it may be possible to use synthesized endorphins to correct the underlying cause of addiction. Two possibilities might account for endorphin deficiencies. One is that the opioids themselves suppress endorphin production; the other is that some people have a genetically caused deficiency in endorphin production.

While the endorphins have been isolated and examined directly by biochemists, behavioral researchers have been able to study their action either by injecting endorphins into subjects and observing their analgesic (pain-killing) effects or by injecting a drug called *naloxone,* which blocks the effects of the endorphin. If a procedure produces analgesia when naloxone is not used but does not affect pain when naloxone is present, there is indirect evidence that endorphins mediate the pain-reducing effects of the procedure. For example, research done in China has shown that injections of naloxone greatly reduce the analgesic effects of acupuncture.

THE OPIATES The word **opiate** refers only to drugs of this type that are derived from the juice of the opium poppy, *Papaver somniferum.* Archaeologists think that the opium poppy's seemingly miraculous powers were first discovered by Neolithic farmers on the eastern shores of the Mediterranean Sea. This knowledge spread from Asia Minor across the ancient world, as the drug manufactured from the poppy, *opium,* became a valued commodity. In the seventeenth century opium was praised by a prominent physician as God's greatest gift to humanity for the relief of its sufferings.

In 1804 the most important active ingredient of opium, **morphine,** was identified. Physicians applauded it as a painkiller of known reliability. Opium and its derivatives were also used to treat coughs, diarrhea, fever, epilepsy, melancholy, diabetes, skin ulcers, constipation, and a variety of other ills well into the 1800s. Many people became addicted to opium and its derivatives after it was given to them for medicinal purposes; nineteenth-

century English writers Thomas De Quincy and Samuel Coleridge are examples. Opium derivatives were popular as home remedies, and until the 1860s there were few restrictions on who might sell or purchase them. One of the largest abuses of the drug was to sedate infants. Working mothers and women who tended babies for pay used these home remedies to keep infants sleepy and calm. By the late 1800s many physicians were becoming concerned about the problems of morphine addiction.

Just as morphine was at first considered a safe substitute for opium, **heroin,** which was produced for the first time in 1874 by boiling morphine in acetic acid, was at first hailed as a safe and effective substitute for morphine. This assertion soon proved to be horribly untrue, and today heroin is involved in over 90 percent of narcotic-addiction cases.

Heroin can be injected, smoked, or inhaled. Heroin addicts go through a characteristic sequence of experiences. After the drug is injected, the user feels a "rush" or "flash" as the nervous system reacts to its presence. Addicts describe the rush as an extraordinarily pleasurable sensation, one that is similar in many ways to sexual orgasm, only more intense and involving the whole body. Following the rush, the user experiences the "nods," a lingering state of euphoric bliss. Fatigue, tension, and anxiety fade away. Feelings of inadequacy are replaced by relaxed contentment. One young addict reported that after experiencing his first heroin high he had exclaimed to himself: "Why didn't they tell me such wonderful feelings existed?" A significant number of heroin addicts have stated that unless the world could provide them with a feeling to compensate for the loss of the high, they would never be able to give up heroin. The negative aspects associated with heroin, however, far outweigh the temporary feelings of well-being.

THE EFFECTS OF OPIOIDS Opioids have both sedative and analgesic effects. The opioids are sometimes called **narcotics,** but because this term is used differently by those who study drugs and by the legal system, it does not always have the same meaning to law enforcement personnel, laypeople, physicians, and scientists.

The opioids cause mood changes, sleepiness, mental clouding, constipation, and slowing of the activity of the brain's respiratory center. An overdose may cause death due to cessation of breathing. The withdrawal reaction can be severe and is manifested by sweating, muscle pains, nausea, vomiting, diarrhea, and other symptoms that may last for two or three days; less severe symptoms may persist for four to six months. Heroin use is likely to be associated with serious deterioration of both the individual's social life and family relations.

CAUSES OF OPIOID ADDICTION The finding that many veterans who used opiates in Vietnam were able to abstain upon returning home stimulated interest in the idea that controlled use of at least some addictive substances is possible for some people. Additional support for this view was provided by reports of people who have used opioids in a controlled manner for long periods. Although some users require drugs in increasingly large dosages every day, other daily users seem able to limit their intake. Perhaps the reason that controlled use of opioids has received relatively little attention is that people who are able to achieve such use do not come to the attention of clinicians. In any case, a better understanding of the process of opioid addiction is necessary so that effective social policies—for example, drug use laws and treatment procedures—can be formulated.

At present there are two competing views of opioid addiction: the exposure orientation and the interactional orientation. According to the **exposure orientation,** the cause of addiction is simply exposure to opioids. When a person experiences stress, endorphins are secreted and produce a stress-induced analgesia (increased tolerance for pain). The use of heroin and other opioids may cause a long-term breakdown in the biochemical system that synthesizes the endorphins. An addict may continue to use opioids because drug use has broken down the body's normal pain-relief system. It is also thought that opioid drugs are reinforcing because they postpone painful withdrawal symptoms. This view does not explain why some addicts have severe withdrawal symptoms while others do not. Moreover, some people become seriously addicted to other drugs that do not produce severe withdrawal symptoms, such as nicotine and coffee.

From the **interactional orientation,** both the person and the situation are important factors in the development of addiction: People's characteristics (their expectations, worries, etc.) and the situations they face in life, particularly those that create stress, jointly influence their need for and reactions to drugs. The available evidence is consistent with this interpretation. This view can explain why some military personnel who had served in Vietnam could so easily leave heavy drug use behind when they returned to the United States. In Vietnam, they were faced with strange people and places, boredom, danger, feelings of helplessness, and other emotions and situations that made their coping mechanisms appear inadequate. Once they had returned home, the situational cues that were related to a craving for opioids were absent.

One recurring finding of research on opioid addicts is that they frequently have severe personality problems (Kosten & Rounsaville, 1986). They suffer particularly from depression and their suicide rate is thought to be five times the average. Depression often continues after withdrawal and even becomes worse. Some authorities believe that the drugs cause depression, and others think that more often depression—or at least a vulnerability to depressive symptoms under stress—leads to opioid

abuse when the drugs are available. Depression in addicts may have been overestimated, since there is some evidence that the ones who seek treatment are more depressed than those who do not.

TREATMENT FOR OPIOID DEPENDENCE Clinicians do not agree on how opioid addiction should be treated. Since the nineteenth century, treatment has consisted primarily of hospitalization for withdrawal from the drug. Aside from being expensive, hospitalization generally seems to be ineffective, although positive findings have been reported in a 20-year follow-up study of hospitalized addicts (Vaillant, 1973). Although 23 percent had died (mostly from unnatural causes) and 25 percent were still known to be using drugs, somewhat more than one-third had achieved stable abstinence, mainly as a result of strict supervision after discharge from the hospital.

There is currently no single accepted standard of treatment for opioid dependence. One difficulty is that opioid dependence is now rarely the sole clinical problem; most patients with opioid dependence also abuse drugs other than opioids and commonly have severe psychological problems as well. Depression, antisocial behavior, and anxiety disorders are among the comorbidity features found in opioid dependence.

Methadone maintenance is the most widely used treatment for opioid addicts. Methadone is a synthetic substance that blocks the effects of heroin. It can be taken orally, prevents withdrawal symptoms for 24 hours, and prevents or decreases the euphoric effects or rushes that occur if heroin is taken while the methadone is active. Its withdrawal effects are also less intense (though somewhat more prolonged) than those of heroin, and their appearance is delayed. While the biochemical and physiological properties of methadone are not fully understood, it apparently blocks all the ordinary effects of morphinelike drugs by competing with them at receptor sites in the central nervous system. Through the use of methadone, the craving for heroin is relieved. Methadone allows a heroin-dependent person to function in society.

Methadone-maintenance programs seem suitable to a wide range of opioid-dependent individuals, and since they can be carried out on an outpatient basis, they cost less than institutional treatment. However, despite its relative effectiveness methadone maintenance is not universally supported. Critics claim that it does not really cure addicts but merely transfers their dependence from one drug to another.

For all patients not assigned to methadone maintenance, the first step is detoxification. It is usually attempted, for example, with any patient who is in treatment for the first time or has been dependent on opioids for no more than a year or two. Hospitalization may be convenient but is not necessary. It is now standard practice to substitute oral methadone for whatever drug the patient is taking and then gradually to lower the dose to zero over a period of a week or two as the detoxification proceeds. When the methadone dose becomes very low withdrawal symptoms may intensify and the user may wish to stop the detoxification process. Clonidine, a nonopiate drug originally marketed to lower blood pressure, has proved to be effective at this point in detoxification in easing withdrawal because it acts at some of the same nerve endings as opioids.

Another drug that may be helpful in achieving abstinence is **naltrexone,** which specifically blocks opioid receptors. While the drug is present, it prevents readdiction to heroin and other opioid drugs. It is relatively safe and nontoxic and one dose can last for up to three days. Unfortunately, although it is an excellent treatment for highly motivated patients who prefer to be opioid-free, most street heroin addicts are not interested in naltrexone because it keeps them from getting high. Naltrexone will effectively block the effects of opioids; thus, the individual cannot experience euphoria or calming from the use of heroin but it does not eliminate the psychological craving for opioids. The optimum duration of naltrexone therapy has not yet been established, but motivated patients should probably take it for at least three months after detoxification.

Dealing with drug addicts and with the traffic in illegal drugs is a major problem in many countries. One British program tries to control heroin abuse through a system of outpatient drug-dependence clinics. These clinics give addicts daily maintenance doses not only of methadone but even of heroin and cocaine. By providing a legal daily maintenance dose, the clinics hope to draw the addicts into contact with the helping system and make it unnecessary for them to support their habit through crime. The ultimate goal is to gradually wean addicts from the drugs if possible, or at least to stabilize them on a fixed dose of heroin or methadone in a lifetime program. In a ten-year follow-up study of the effectiveness of the system, investigators found that 40 percent of a group of addicts who had attended the clinics in 1969 were still attending a clinic and receiving heroin or methadone (Wille, 1981). The majority of these continuing users had been socially stable for at least ten years. Most of them were employed and were not currently in trouble with the law. Of the group who were no longer attending the clinics, at least half had become abstinent.

There are few follow-up studies from other countries with which these data may be compared. However, the data that exist suggest that the British program is at least as effective as approaches used in other countries (Jaffee, 1985). Moral objections to the government's providing heroin and cocaine for addicts have been a constant threat to the existence of the British program as more than a methadone-maintenance plan.

Is abstinence the solution to the addict's problems? One study suggests that merely abstaining from opioids has disappointingly little effect on the other medical, emotional, and social problems of addicts (Kosten and others, 1987). The subjects of the study were 150 patients who applied for treatment at an addiction clinic. Three-fourths were men, and they had used opioids for an average of ten years. Two-and-a-half years later the researchers interviewed most of them again. Some were now abstinent, and some were using even more opioids than before; most were in-between.

At the time of the follow-up, the general level of patients' problems had improved and their drug problems had improved the most. However, neither the original severity of the patients' drug problem nor the amount of time they were drug-free during the study predicted the severity of their drug problem at the time of follow-up. The severity of medical, family, and psychological problems of the patients at follow-up also did not predict their levels of drug use at follow-up but instead were related to the original severity of these problems at the beginning of the program.

Based on these results, the authors concluded that addicts need family therapy, psychotherapy for depression, vocational counseling, and other types of treatment at least as much as they need help in achieving abstinence. Psychodynamically and cognitively oriented therapies have been found to be helpful with some opioid addicts, particularly those with longstanding addictions and severe psychiatric disorders (Woody and others, 1986).

Cocaine

Cocaine is the main active drug in the leaves of the coca bush that grows on the eastern slopes of the Andes Mountains in South America. The Indians of Peru and Bolivia have used its leaves for centuries to increase endurance and decrease hunger so that they can cope better with the rigors of their economically marginal, high-altitude existence. In 1860 cocaine was isolated and purified.

Like heroin, cocaine initially had a positive, even benign image. Freud, who periodically used cocaine himself, recommended it for use in treating depression and other conditions, including morphine withdrawal. Its use as a local anesthetic led to the discovery of synthetic substitutes with low toxicity, while its use in treating morphine withdrawal indirectly led to self-administration of the drug. From about 1880 to 1900 cocaine was actually an ingredient in some popular brands of soda. Cocaine can be "snorted" or sniffed, smoked (often in a water pipe), or injected intravenously.

Cocaine is a naturally-occurring central nervous system stimulant. Whereas the opioids are "downers" that slow the body's responses, cocaine is an "upper" that increases heart rate, raises blood pressure and body temperature, and decreases appetite. It puts the body in an emergency state in much the same way that a rush of adrenaline would in a stressful situation. Although it is not clear how cocaine produces this effect, it is likely that it causes the release of large amounts of dopamine in the brain. Cocaine also affects at least three parts of the brain itself: the cerebral cortex, which governs reasoning and memory; the hypothalamus, which controls appetite, body temperature, sleep, and emotions such as fear and anger; and the cerebellum, which regulates motor activities such as walking and balance.

This case illustrates cocaine psychosis which can result from high dosages of the drug.

After a while, I was convinced that there were people trying to break into my house. I didn't know who they were, but I was sure that people were after me. There was probably some reality to it too, since I really was scared that the police would come in and bust me. The only way that I felt that I could protect myself was by getting a knife. So I started sleeping with a butcher knife next to me. That didn't work for long, though, because I still felt insecure. So I felt that I had to get a gun. Every night, I went to bed with a gun on one side of me and a butcher knife on the other side. I was just waiting for someone to come in the house so that I could blow his brains out. God knows what I was going to do with the knife. I swear, I was a maniac. It wouldn't have mattered who had come to the door. If someone had come to my door at the wrong time to borrow a cup of sugar, I can tell you with 100 percent certainty, he would have been dead.

—Weiss and Mirin, 1987, p. 39

Despite an overall decline in cocaine use, the potency of cocaine products now available is much greater than in the past with the wide availability of **crack** cocaine, a concentrated form of the drug. Crack has greatly increased the use of the drug among adolescents because of relatively low price. People who use crack experience high-dose, high-intensity effects that greatly increase the probability of extremely negative long term effects such as panic states, toxic psychoses, and paranoid schizophrenia. High-dose effects also include markedly altered perceptions of reality including aggressive or homicidal behavior against imagined persecution by others. Crack represents a serious problem because it seems to become addicting extremely rapidly.

The use of crack has produced one of the great tragedies of the last decade, the birth of thousands of "crack babies." Women who use cocaine in any form during pregnancy are likely to place the fetus at risk because of the greater chance of spontaneous abortion or fetal death late in pregnancy, or the reduction of infant birth weight if the pregnancy is carried to term. These effects are thought to be related to a lack of oxygen and reduced blood flow to the fetus as a result of the intense vasoconstriction or temporary narrowing of the mother's blood vessels induced by the cocaine. Some crack babies are born with visible birth defects, but many more have neurological defects. Nearly all these infants are irritable and difficult to soothe and as a result are less likely to receive adequate mothering. As these crack babies enter the school system, it appears that they have cognitive difficulties in structuring information and also have low tolerance for frustration. Crack babies have been referred to as a "bio-underclass," children for whom a combination of physiological damage and socioeconomic disadvantage may result in a life of inferiority (Rist, 1990). Estimates of the number of babies affected by crack use ranges from between 50,000 to 200,000 births per year (Julien, 1992).

Cocaine produces feelings of wittiness and hyperalertness and is often praised by users as being almost risk free: no hangovers like those produced by alcohol, no injection scars like those caused by heroin use, and no lung cancer, which is associated with use of marijuana and tobacco. Unfortunately, its action is more complex and less benign than most users believe. Since its effects are highly reinforcing and psychologically addicting to the user, desire for it is hard to control. A damaging habit usually develops over a period of several months to several years. Compulsive users cannot turn the drug down; they think about it constantly, dream about it, spend all their savings on it, and borrow, steal, or deal to pay for it.

Physical tolerance also develops quickly so an increased dose is needed to produce the same effects, thus increasing the danger of overdose. Users often say that they never quite recapture the euphoria of the first snort. Whether cocaine can be said to produce a withdrawal reaction depends partly on definitions but recent research suggests withdrawal does occur after extensive cocaine use (Grilly, 1989). Researchers are zeroing in on how cocaine produces euphoria and the depression and craving that result from chronic use. The drug interferes with the normal functioning of neurotransmitters, chemicals that activate nerves in an area of the brain associated with pleasurable feelings (Gawin, 1991).

High doses or repeated use of cocaine can produce a state resembling mania, with impaired judgment, incessant rambling talk, hyperactivity, and paranoia that may lead to violence or accidents. There is also an acute anxiety reaction that is sometimes severe enough to be called panic. Serious acute physical reactions are also possible. By constricting blood vessels and increasing the heart rate, cocaine can produce cardiac symptoms, including irregular heartbeat, angina, and myocardial infarction. High doses may also cause nausea, headache, cold sweats, tremors, and fast, irregular, shallow breathing. People who have high blood pressure or damaged arteries may suffer strokes as a result of cocaine use. Table 14-8 summarizes the effects of cocaine use. Death usually results from convulsions followed by paralysis of

Table 14-8

Effects of Cocaine[a]

1. Euphoria
2. Increased energy
3. Enhanced mental acuity and alertness
4. Increased sensory awareness (sexual, auditory, visual)
5. Decreased appetite
6. Decreased need for sleep
7. Increased self-confidence
8. Impaired judgment
9. Loss of motivation
10. Delusions and paranoid thinking
11. Convulsions
12. A variety of problems in the cardiovascular system including constricted blood vessels, increased heart rate, myocardial infarction, stroke, brain hemorrhages

[a]The effects depend on dosage and degree of habitual use.

the brain centers controlling respiration, which in turn leads to cardiac arrest; in serious cases an acute overdose must be treated with oxygen and anticonvulsant drugs. A common cause of death is intravenous injection of a "speedball"—a combination of heroin and cocaine.

TREATING COCAINE DEPENDENCE The cocaine dependent person must first become convinced that treatment is necessary. As in all types of drug and alcohol dependence, more or less subtle forms of denial are common; for example, abusers may want relief for some of the side effects without giving up the habit itself. Sometimes they are induced to come in for treatment only by pressure from family members, employers, or the law. People seek treatment at different stages of dependency, and the severity of the symptoms varies greatly.

Many cocaine users have joined mutual-help groups such as Cocaine Anonymous or Narcotics Anonymous. These programs use more or less the same approach, which was developed from Alcoholics Anonymous: They encourage their members to confide in others who have the same problem, to share their feelings, to make a resolution to overcome dependency, and to support the resolutions of other members. Members admit their powerlessness to control their drug use and seek help from a higher power while taking a "moral inventory" of themselves and pledging abstinence one day at a time.

Many cocaine users have histories of dysfunctional family lives. Cocaine use has been associated with family patterns of alcoholism, domestic violence, separation or divorce, as well as with physical, sexual, or emotional abuse within the family (Wallace, 1991). In such cases psychotherapy can be an important part of treatment—although psychotherapy alone rarely solves drug problems. Supportive psychotherapy is a relationship with a sympathetic professional who provides comfort and encourages the abuser to stay away from sources of cocaine. Interpretive or exploratory psychotherapy can help some abusers understand what functions cocaine has been fulfilling in their lives and find other ways of coping.

Amphetamines

Amphetamines, like cocaine, are potent psychomotor stimulants. Various drugs in this group are called speed, crystal, pep pills, bennies, meth, and many other names, depending on the specific active agent. Despite their dissimilar chemical structures, amphetamines and cocaine have many similar properties. They both probably act by influencing the norepinephrine and dopamine receptor systems. Antipsychotic drugs block not only the dopamine receptors but some of the norepinephrine receptors as well. If antipsychotic drugs are given prior to amphetamine or cocaine use, they inhibit most of their behavioral effects.

Moderate amphetamine use results in increased wakefulness, alertness, and elevation of mood. Psychomotor performance is improved temporarily, but the improvement may be followed by a compensatory rebound or letdown in which the user feels fatigued, less alert, and somewhat depressed.

The medical uses of amphetamines include suppression of appetite and improvement of mood in mild depressions. Amphetamines are also helpful in treating certain neurological and behavioral disorders. College students who use amphetamines when "cramming" for exams not only notice increased energy and tolerance for sleeplessness but also increased productivity on the next day's exam. Although this may be useful at times, the "improved" performance may not be truly better. Many students have the disillusioning experience of looking at their wondrous performance later and finding it to be of poor quality. The drug impaired their critical thinking at the same time that it increased their output.

High doses of amphetamines have significant effects on the central nervous system and the cardiovascular system; they lead to nervousness, headache, dizziness, agitation, apprehension, confusion, palpitations, and elevated blood pressure. Regular use of large amounts leads to greater tolerance for the drug and increased intolerance for being without it. Users become malnourished, exhausted, careless, and indifferent to normal responsibilities. Their thinking is often characterized by a paranoia that may develop into a full-blown psychosis accompanied by hallucinations. Withdrawal symptoms, if they occur, are mild compared with those that often accompany cessation of opioid use; they also differ qualitatively. Since tolerance for amphetamines develops rapidly, many users inject it into a vein to obtain more intense effects. This high-dose, long-term use of amphetamines is dangerous and self-destructive. Since the initial effects are stimulating and pleasant, unwary individuals often proceed to higher doses and eventually to a state of dependence.

Psychedelics

Psychedelics or **hallucinogens** act on the central nervous system to produce alteration of consciousness. They change the user's perceptions of both the internal and the external world. There is usually sensory displacement, which can drastically alter color perception and hearing. Auditory, visual, and tactile hallucinations accompany the experience, along with a changed perception of self. Among the natural psychedelic substances are mescaline, psilocybin, and dimethyl tryptamine (DMT). Synthetic psychedelics include diethyltryptamine (STP),

and **lysergic acid diethylamide (LSD).** The following case describes some of the effects of LSD.

A 21-year-old woman was admitted to the hospital after ingesting a large amount of LSD. About half an hour after ingestion she perceived that light affected her strangely and that the bricks in the wall had begun to move in and out. She became frightened when she realized that she was unable to distinguish her body from the chair she was sitting on or from her lover's body. Her fear became more marked as she began to think that she would not get back into herself. At the time of her admission she was hyperactive and laughed inappropriately. Her stream of talk was illogical and her emotions extremely variable. After two days this reaction had ceased, but she was still afraid of the drug and convinced that she would not take it again because of her frightening experience.

—Adapted from Kolb and Brodie, 1982, p. 666

In many cultures psychedelics have been used for hundreds of years. Mescaline, which is derived from the peyote cactus, and psilocybin, which is obtained from certain mushrooms, are used for religious ceremonies by Indians in Mexico and Central America. West Africans and Congolese have traditionally chewed the ibogaine root, which contains tryptamine, to "release the gods."

LSD (popularly called "acid") is a colorless, odorless, and tasteless material. Effects are produced by as little as 50 micrograms (a microgram is a millionth of a gram), an amount that in pure form would not be visible to the naked eye. No legally manufactured LSD is available to the general public, and the output of illegal, often amateur, laboratories is rarely pure LSD. In the course of research on certain groups of therapeutic compounds, LSD was first synthesized in 1938 by Albert Hoffman, a Swiss chemist. His description of the drugs' effects on him in the laboratory gave a more benign view than the case described above.

I was forced to stop my work in the laboratory . . . and to go home, as I was seized by a particular restlessness associated with the sensation of mild dizziness. On arriving home, I lay down and sank into a kind of drunkenness which was not unpleasant and which was characterized by extreme activity of imagination. As I lay in a dazed condition with my eyes closed (I experienced daylight as disagreeably bright) there surged upon me an uninterrupted stream of fantastic images of extraordinary plasticity and vividness and accompanied by an intense, kaleidoscope-like play of colours. This condition gradually passed off after about two hours.

—Hoffman, 1971, p. 23

The immediate effects of LSD usually last about 8 to 12 hours. The mechanism of its action is not well understood, but it is known to stimulate the sympathetic nervous system and to produce physiological changes like those seen in a person who is aroused, excited, or under stress. The most common subjective effects are euphoria, quick shifts from one mood to another, and altered awareness of the color, size, and shape of stimuli. Time perception is so altered that minutes may seem like hours. Bizarre sensations may be experienced, frequently including feelings of separation or disintegration of some part of the body. The user typically realizes that these effects are due to the drug and are not "out there." Some users experience bewilderment, disorganization, personal and sexual identity confusion, and fears of losing control. They may experience intense emotions that they cannot label. In fact, one of the most unfortunate effects of LSD is the feeling of being overwhelmed by confusing emotions that cannot be sorted out because they are going by so fast.

LSD sometimes produces extreme anxiety or panic reactions. Such "bad trips" are generally short-lived and can often be modified by supportive reassurance. Bad trips may be terminated by appropriate medication and occasionally by hospitalization. The most serious effects of LSD are paranoid symptoms (feelings of being followed, spied on, or persecuted), psychosis resembling that found in schizophrenia, and severe depression that occasionally leads to suicide attempts. Negative effects of a single large dose of LSD may persist for months, require long hospitalization, and resist the usual forms of treatment. The frequency of such reactions is difficult to determine but is probably less than one percent. When such problems arise, it is often difficult to separate the effects of LSD from those of prior drug use, personality characteristics, and a variety of other factors.

A more common effect of LSD use is "flashbacks": spontaneous recurrences of parts of the LSD experience long after the action of the drug has ceased. Such recurrences can take place in the first few weeks and have been reported as long as two years following the last dose

of the drug. It is not clear why these flashbacks occur. One possibility is that LSD causes biochemical changes in the body that last long after drug use. The aftereffects may have serious consequences if they occur in situations that require attentive thinking and decision making.

Treatment for abuse of psychedelics depends on the severity of the reaction. Severely affected people must have medical attention to prevent cardiovascular or respiratory collapse. If psychotic behavior is present, antipsychotic drugs of the type used to treat schizophrenia may be helpful, although about ten percent of drug users who become acutely psychotic never recover. Psychologically based therapy, particularly group psychotherapy and supportive drug-free groups, can be helpful because users of psychedelic drugs often have feelings of low self-worth and use the drugs to improve their relationships with other people. Many of these abusers need psychological help with their social responses so that they can substitute rewarding social experiences for the reinforcement they get from drugs.

Phencyclidine (PCP)

PCP (phencyclidine) has several street names, including "angel dust" and "crystal." It was first developed as an anesthetic in the 1950s. However, it was taken off the market for human use because it sometimes caused disorientation and hallucinations. It is available in a number of forms. It can be a pure, white crystallike powder, or a tablet or capsule. It also can be swallowed, smoked, sniffed, or injected. PCP is sometimes sprinkled on marijuana or parsley and smoked.

Although PCP is illegal, it is easily manufactured. Users can never be sure what they are buying since it is manufactured illegally. Sometimes it may not even be PCP, but a lethal by-product of the drug.

The effects of PCP depend on how much is taken, the way it is used, and the individual. Effects include increased heart rate and blood pressure, flushing, sweating, dizziness, and numbness. When large doses are taken, effects include drowsiness, convulsions, and coma. Taking large amounts of PCP can also cause death from repeated convulsions, heart and lung failure, or ruptured blood vessels in the brain.

PCP is classified as a dissociative anesthetic because it makes the individual feel dissociated or detached from the environment. In small doses, it produces insensitivity to pain; in large doses, it produces a comalike state and blank stare. People who take larger doses feel as if they are being bombarded by stimuli. They may lose the ability to distinguish between fantasy and reality and suffer severe intellectual and emotional disorganization. PCP users sometimes develop severe depression or a severe psychotic state that is not easily reversible.

Whether these outcomes are a result of the drug alone or of underlying personality characteristics is not clear.

Researchers studying areas of the brain affected by PCP have discovered that PCP can protect the brain from permanent damage after a stroke or heart attack. Scientists do not yet fully understand this process, but they have proven that it works in a series of animal studies. PCP has diverse effects because it works at two different sites on nerve cells, named PCP and sigma receptors, that have quite different characteristics. Pharmaceutical companies are working to develop new synthetic drugs with the same action as PCP but without its undesirable qualities. MK-801, the first compound of this type that is readily available to researchers, has reduced neuronal damage when given before or after trauma to animals (Myers, 1988).

Marijuana

The cannabis plant has been harvested throughout history for its fibers, oils, and psychoactive resin (see Figure 14–13). **Marijuana,** which consists of the dried leaves and flower tops of the plant, is the form in which it is most often used in the United States. The solidified resin, called **hashish** (or, colloquially, "hash"), can also be used to produce psychoactive effects.

Many Americans have used marijuana at least once, in spite of the fact that it is classified as an illegal substance and its cultivation, possession, distribution, and use are prohibited. Despite the prohibitions and the controversy over its safety, the use of marijuana increased sharply during the 1960s and 1970s. However, its use has been declining ever since (See Figure 14–14).

Figure 14–14 summarizes three surveys of college

FIGURE 14–13 Leaves from a marijuana plant.

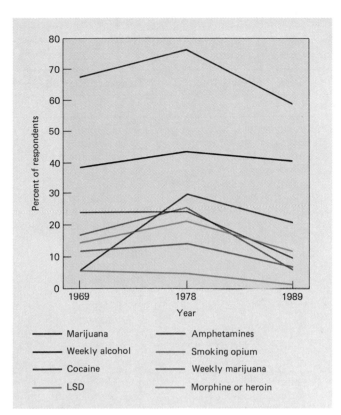

FIGURE 14–14 College student drug use: twenty-year trends. This figure gives the percent of students who had ever used a given drug in their lifetime (except for the categories of weekly marijuana and weekly alcohol, which represent the percent of students reporting current weekly use of these substances).

(*American Journal of Psychiatry*, 147, 998–1001, 1990. Copyright ©1990, the American Psychiatric Association. Reprinted by permission)

Legend:
— Marijuana
— Weekly alcohol
— Cocaine
— LSD
— Amphetamines
— Smoking opium
— Weekly marijuana
— Morphine or heroin

students that illustrate trends in drug use (Pope and others, 1990). The answers to a questionnaire given to 369 seniors at an eastern college in 1989 were compared with answers given on questionnaires in 1969 and 1978. Alcohol use had not declined much but illicit drug use showed a greater decline. The proportion of seniors using marijuana at least once a week was 18 percent in 1969, 29 percent in 1978, and only 6 percent in 1989. Between 1978 and 1989 the proportion of students who had ever used cocaine dropped from 30 percent to 20 percent, and the proportion who had ever used LSD declined from 20 percent to 12 percent.

More important, in 1989, as in 1978 and 1969, there were few differences between students who had used illicit drugs and those who had not, or even between occasional and long-term users. Drug users had about the same grades as other students, and participated to the same extent in college activities. One difference was that in all three surveys, drug users reported more sexual activity.

Marijuana is not pharmacologically a narcotic, although in the United States it has been legally classified

as one since 1937. The mechanisms of its action is not well understood, but its more common effects have been identified. (Table 14–9 compares the properties of marijuana with those of other drugs.) An important advance in research was the isolation of the major active ingredient in marijuana, THC (delta-9-tetrahydrocannabinol). Only barely detectable concentrations of THC are present in the brain of a rat after one dose. But with repeated administration THC and the products of its metabolism gradually build up and are detectable as long as eight days after the administration of a single dose.

Marijuana can be taken by either eating or smoking parts of the cannabis plant. Smoking is the fastest way to feel the drug's effects. When the smoke is inhaled, it is spread across the surface of the lungs, quickly absorbed into the bloodstream, and carried to the brain in a few seconds. When marijuana is ingested, THC enters the bloodstream from the digestive system and is carried to the liver. There enzymes break it down into other substances, which are carried to the brain by the circulatory system.

The psychological effects of marijuana use are illustrated in the following descriptions.

Usually the first puff doesn't affect me, but the second brings a slight feeling of dizziness and I get a real "buzz" on the third. By this I mean a sudden wave of something akin to dizziness hits me. It's difficult to describe. The best idea I can give is to say that for a moment the whole room, people, and sounds around me recede into the distance and I feel as if my mind contracted for an instant. When it has passed I feel "normal" but a bit "airy-fairy."

—Berke and Hernton, 1974, p. 96

The first time I smoked I had the feeling of being entirely outside of my body, hovering above it and as I was lying on the bed, I was exceptionally conscious of my body for part of the time, realizing how, and feeling how, each individual part was working.

—Berke and Hernton, 1974, p. 97

Marijuana became popular as a recreational drug partly because it is cheap and readily available but also because many people believe that when used in moderation it is not a risk to physical or mental health. Despite this widespread attitude, the federal government has

Table 14-9

Drugs: Characteristics and Effects

	Typical Effects	Effects of Overdose	Tolerance/Dependence
DEPRESSANTS			
Alcohol	Biphasic: tension reduction "high," followed by depressed physical and psychological functioning	Disorientation, loss of consciousness, death at extremely high blood-alcohol levels	Tolerance; physical and psychological dependence; withdrawal symptoms
Barbiturates Tranquilizers	Depressed reflexes and impaired motor functioning, tension reduction	Shallow respiration, clammy skin, dilated pupils, weak and rapid pulse, coma, possible death	Tolerance; high psychological and physical dependence on barbiturates, low to moderate physical dependence on such tranquilizers as Valium, although high psychological dependence; withdrawal symptoms
STIMULANTS			
Amphetamines Cocaine Caffeine Nicotine	Increased alertness, excitation, euphoria, increased pulse rate and blood pressure, sleeplessness	For amphetamines and cocaine: agitation, and with chronic high doses, hallucinations, paranoid delusions, convulsions, death	For amphetamines and cocaine: tolerance; psychological; possible physical dependence and withdrawal symptoms for cocaine
		For caffeine and nicotine: restlessness, insomnia, rambling thoughts, heart arrythmia, possible circulatory failure. For nicotine: increased blood pressure	For caffeine and nicotine: tolerance; physical and psychological dependence; withdrawal symptoms
OPIOIDS			
Opium Morphine Heroin	Euphoria, drowsiness, "rush" of pleasure, little impairment of psychological functions	Slow, shallow breathing, clammy skin, nausea, vomiting, pinpoint pupils, convulsions, coma, possible death	High tolerance; physical and psychological dependence; severe withdrawal symptoms
PSYCHEDELICS AND PCP			
LSD PCP (dissociative anesthetic)	Illusions, hallucinations, distortions in time perception, loss of contact with reality	Psychotic reactions, particularly with PCP; possible death with PCP	No physical dependence for LSD, degree unknown for PCP; psychological dependence for PCP, degree unknown for LSD
MARIJUANA			
	Euphoria, relaxed inhibitions, increased appetite, possible disorientation	Fatigue, disoriented behavior, possible psychosis	Psychological dependence

conducted a vigorous and costly campaign to prevent the entry of marijuana into this country. As a result, a great deal of marijuana is grown illegally in the United States and Canada. Several authoritative reports have been issued on the effects of marijuana on health, but scientific controversy and public confusion still exist as to whether marijuana should be legalized or whether the laws against it should be strengthened.

In the early 1980s a committee of the National Academy of Science was asked to make a critical review of current knowledge about the effects of marijuana on health (National Academy of Sciences, 1982). The committee's report concluded that marijuana has a variety of effects, some of which are harmful to human health. Marijuana use causes changes in the heart and circulation that are similar to those caused by stress. These changes might be a threat for individuals with high blood pressure or heart disease. Marijuana smoke causes changes in the lungs that may lead to respiratory problems, but cancer-producing agents in marijuana smoke are even more of a problem. Marijuana smoke contains about 50 percent more carcinogens than does tobacco smoke.

In males, marijuana suppresses the production of male hormones, decreases the size and weight of the prostate gland and testes, and inhibits sperm production, although these effects appear to be reversible. Such specific reproductive effects have not been found for non-pregnant women. In pregnant women, however, THC crosses the placental barrier and may harm the unborn child. It can also be secreted in breast milk, thereby affecting nursing infants. Various studies have shown that marijuana blocks ovulation and can cause birth defects in animals (Jaffe, 1989). The belief that marijuana use is associated with chromosome breaks, which are thought to be indicators of genetic damage, does not appear to be correct. Contradictory evidence exists as to whether the drug causes atrophy or other gross changes in the brain.

Marijuana impairs motor coordination and perception and makes driving and machine operation more hazardous. It also impairs short-term memory and slows learning. One particularly important point is that the impairment lasts for four to eight hours after the feeling of intoxication is over. This means that behavior may be affected even when the user is no longer aware of the presence of the drug.

One positive aspect of marijuana and its chemical derivatives is its therapeutic potential. Evidence suggests that marijuana is useful in the treatment of glaucoma, an eye disorder that may cause blindness, and that it helps control the severe nausea and vomiting that accompany chemotherapy for cancer. It may also be useful in treating asthma and certain types of epileptic seizures. However, the stress it puts on the cardiovascular system may make marijuana an inappropriate drug for treating older people.

Government agencies are reluctant to legalize the sale and use of marijuana because of vocal public opposition. Some legalization opponents argue that the most potent deterrent of marijuana use is the possibility of arrest and imprisonment. However, while enforcement of marijuana laws is a major drain on the resources of the criminal justice system, it does not seem to be effective. Some people have proposed licensing the sale of marijuana, as is done with alcohol, and writing laws regulating its potency. Endangering the lives or well-being of others—for example, by operating a motor vehicle while intoxicated—would be penalized, but safe recreational use would not be illegal. Others have suggested eliminating criminal penalties for users but not for sellers of marijuana. These proposals reflect the trend toward increasing acceptance of marijuana use.

Peer pressure is the strongest factor influencing adolescents toward marijuana use. Marijuana use by high school students appears to have peaked in 1978 and has declined significantly since then, perhaps because the fashion shifted toward alcohol. Because of the prevalence of its use and the public controversy about whether it should be decriminalized, over 20 percent of the states have dropped criminal penalties for minor marijuana offenses in the last few years. Several other states permit the use of marijuana for certain medical purposes.

There is a great need to base laws and social policies concerning marijuana and other drugs on facts rather than on opinions and fears. Laboratory research and studies of the longer-term effects of drugs and therapies are a first step toward providing the facts.

Nicotine

I can quit smoking if I wish;
I've done it a thousand times.

—Mark Twain

Nicotine and cancer-causing tars are the only pharmacologically active ingredients in tobacco. Nicotine acts at least in part by directly stimulating certain receptors that are sensitive to the neurotransmitter acetylcholine and as a result exerts powerful effects on the brain and spinal cord, the peripheral nervous system, and the heart. Its initial use causes nausea and vomiting by stimulating the vomiting center in the brain stem as well as receptors in the stomach, but tolerance of this effect develops quickly. Normal doses of nicotine can increase heart rate and blood pressure, and the heart's need for oxygen. If this increased need for oxygen cannot be met, for instance in people who have atherosclerosis or hardening of the arteries, the result may be angina or

chest pains or a heart attack. Smoking by pregnant women tends to reduce the birth weight of their babies. In addition to the effects of nicotine, the tars contained in tobacco are a major cause of lung cancer.

Despite these consequences, smoking is a difficult habit to give up even for those who try (see Figure 14–15). Some smokers experience psychological distress in the form of anxiety and guilt because they cannot stop smoking. The difficulty of giving up tobacco use on a long-term basis may be due to the unpleasant nature of the withdrawal experience, the importance of social or environmental cues, and the highly overlearned nature of the habit (the pack-a-day smoker is reinforced by the rapid effects of nicotine in each of about 75,000 puffs per year). Withdrawal symptoms—irritability, anxiety, headache, excessive appetite, and difficulty in concentrating—do not occur in all smokers, but in some heavy smokers withdrawal symptoms can be detected within two hours after the last cigarette. Since many smokers use cigarettes as a way of coping with stress, it is not clear whether these symptoms are related to the withdrawal of nicotine or whether some of them may be due to

psychological characteristics that helped start the addictive behavior.

Primarily due to more public awareness of the negative effects of tobacco, smoking rates have recently declined in the United States and Canada. Many long-term smokers have given up the habit. Most cigarette smokers who try to quit do so on their own and they are more likely to be successful than those who seek help in quitting through formal programs. Furthermore, persons who seek help tend to be heavier smokers and to have made more cessation attempts than those who quit unaided. While stopping smoking unaided is a simple, direct, and effective path to getting rid of nicotine dependence, special smoking cessation programs have an important role to play. According to one estimate, over two million people per year are helped by such programs (Keleman and others, 1990).

Therapeutic efforts to help people stop smoking take several forms. Some of these methods use the biological perspective. From this viewpoint, the problem is not so much that smoking calms the nerves as that nonsmoking sets up the negative reinforcement of

FIGURE 14–15

(Drawing by Handelsman, © 1985 The New Yorker Magazine, Inc.)

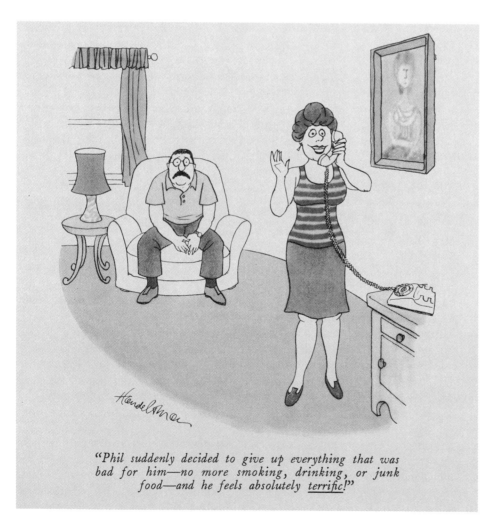

"Phil suddenly decided to give up everything that was bad for him—no more smoking, drinking, or junk food—and he feels absolutely terrific!"

withdrawal symptoms, which can be ended by having another cigarette. By resuming the use of cigarettes, the individual is attempting to regulate the nicotine level in his or her body. This may have important physiological effects because nicotine stimulates the release of *central peptides,* hormones that have a powerful effect on key mental and physical functions. This suggests that smokers who are heavily dependent but want to quit smoking may require, on a temporary basis, some pharmacological substitute for the nicotine they are deriving from cigarettes.

Chewing gum containing nicotine was developed to ease withdrawal from tobacco by providing both an alternate source of nicotine and a substitute oral activity. Nicotine gum probably does not give the same positive pleasure as smoking a cigarette because nicotine is absorbed more slowly through the lining of the mouth than through the lungs. However, the gum may enable a smoker to break the habit in two stages. First the smoker can focus on overcoming the behavioral and psychological components of tobacco dependence without having to cope with nicotine withdrawal at the same time. Linked with each smoker's puffing habits are the many other actions involved in handling cigarettes and responding to cues that call for lighting up. Because smoking is a complex behavior, all components of that behavior need to be addressed in helping a person stop smoking. Once these behavior patterns are controlled, withdrawal from the nicotine gum might be accomplished more easily.

Research is needed to evaluate the effects of nicotine gum by itself and in combination with other factors. For example, one recent experiment evaluated the gum using a balanced placebo design (Gottlieb, 1985). An advantage of this design is that it permits an answer to the question, what is the effect of receiving a drug alone and in combination with the subject's expectancies about the drug's effects? Gottlieb found that nicotine gum helped people stop smoking, but he also found that its effects were weaker than those of smokers' positive expectancies. Many smokers who were given a placebo but were told that it was nicotine gum showed a strong positive effect. Thus, cognitive factors are an important influence on the success of efforts to stop smoking.

Cognitive research has identified three "stages of change" relevant to smoking cessation (Marlatt & Gordon, 1985). The first stage involves the individual's commitment to making a change and setting goals—for example, stopping smoking. Unfortunately, smokers are often ambivalent about quitting and reluctant to take personal responsibility for quitting. They need help in developing their commitment and motivation to change. Once the individual has made the commitment to stop smoking, a specific plan can be developed and implemented. This is an action phase for actual change. The third stages involves maintenance of change, with relapse prevention playing an important role in maintenance. Change is facilitated when people can identify the situations in which they are most likely to be tempted to smoke, learn cognitive coping techniques as alternatives to smoking, and can use self-reinforcement when they are successful in resisting the temptation to smoke. Table 14–10 summarizes the stages of change concept.

One study assessed the way callers to a relapse-counseling hotline described how they dealt with the temptation to smoke (Shiffman, 1982). The relapse crises were usually brought on by situational factors: either positive feeling states related to other smokers, eating, or alcohol consumption, or (more frequently) negative feelings, especially anxiety, anger, and depression. Ex-smokers who performed any coping response in these situations were more likely to avoid a relapse. Behavioral responses such as getting up and leaving the situation were useful, but a combination of behavioral and cognitive coping responses worked best, especially in situations involving alcohol. Cognitive coping consisted of such things as reviewing the reasons for not smoking.

Substance dependence continues to be a major problem throughout the world. Recent developments in the study of pain regulators and pain receptors in the body are providing some valuable clues, particularly in the area of opioid abuse. Information about the health consequences of using some substances—for example,

Table 14–10

Stages of Change

1. *Contemplation and commitment.* Usually preceded by a precontemplation stage in which people do not see themselves as having a problem ("What's bad about smoking?").
2. *Action.* A specific plan for change is established and implemented (for example, use of nicotine substitutes, activating social support of friends, family, and coworkers).
3. *Maintenance.* Changing smoking patterns takes time, and self-monitoring and relapse prevention strategies are necessary during the action and maintenance phases.

marijuana and tobacco—have decreased their overall use. Some therapeutic procedures, especially those that emphasize cognitive techniques for relapse prevention, show promise as treatments for alcohol and tobacco abuse. Still unanswered, however, is the question of whether social policy should be changed—for example, to decriminalize marijuana or provide maintenance doses for heroin addicts in government clinics. In part because of lack of knowledge about the consequences of these actions—such as whether they would increase or decrease use of the substance—and in part because of philosophical differences among citizens, lawmakers, and scientists, these policy issues seem likely to remain unresolved.

Chapter Summary

A major area of addictive behavior involves **psychoactive substances,** those that affect thought, emotions, and behavior. Two categories of disorders are related to psychoactive substances: **Substance abuse disorders** involve impaired social or occupational functioning and a strong or uncontrollable desire to use the substance, while **psychoactive substance dependence disorders** involve alterations in bodily systems, the need to increase frequency and amount of use, and withdrawal symptoms. In the **withdrawal** period, a substance-specific syndrome follows the decrease or cessation of use of the substance. This syndrome may include **flashbacks** of the symptoms experienced while intoxicated.

ADDICTIVE BEHAVIOR

Both substance abuse and substance dependence involve **addictive behavior**—the presence of a repetitive habit pattern increasing the risk of disease and associated with personal and social problems. Psychologists are interested in substance dependence because a person's response to drugs is determined by a combination of physiological and psychological factors. Physiological dependence is reflected in the withdrawal symptoms described above. **Tolerance** means the person has to use more of a substance to get the same effect.

ALCOHOL

Ethanol is the only type of **alcohol** intended for human consumption. The ethanol contained in various types of alcoholic drinks—beer, wine, and hard or distilled liquor—is the same drug. However, these types of drinks differ in percentage of their total volume that is made up of alcohol. Alcohol acts on the central nervous system as a blocker of messages from one nerve cell to the next. Initially it acts on frontal lobe functions such as memory and judgment. In greater amounts it affects the cerebellum and motor muscle control. In very large amounts it affects the medulla and spinal cord and the involuntary functions of the body such as breathing and heart rate.

Alcohol Abuse and Dependence Alcohol abuse or **problem drinking** involves different drinking patterns ranging from large amounts daily to weekend binges. Alcohol dependence is referred to as **alcoholism.** About 30 percent of alcohol abusers may become alcoholics in a four-year period.

Alcohol and Health Alcohol abuse and dependence shorten life expectancy through negative effects on body organs and systems and also through a higher death rate from both traffic and nontraffic accidents. Extensive alcohol abuse is also a cause of brain damage. Pregnant women who drink may risk affecting their unborn children with **fetal alcohol syndrome,** a disorder that produces mental retardation as well as physical malformations. People who abuse alcohol are more likely also to have another diagnosable mental disorder. The most frequent problems that co-exist with alcohol abuse are affective disorders, anxiety disorders, and antisocial personality disorder.

Perspectives on Alcohol Abuse Ingestion of alcohol first reduces anxiety and then has a depressant effect on the body. The biological perspective views alcoholism as a permanent and irreversible condition. According to this view a person with alcohol problems must stop drinking entirely in order to control alcohol use. Researchers believe that there may be a genetic predisposition for alcoholism. People vary greatly in their sensitivity to the effects of alcohol. Women may be more sensitive to alcohol than men because they have less of a specific enzyme that neutralizes alcohol and because of their lower body weight. The psychodynamic perspective suggests that people who abuse alcohol may have an **oral-dependent personality;** that is, they have a larger than normal need for oral gratification because of early life experiences. The learning perspective suggests that, through both social and physiological reinforcement and through modeling, people learn to use alcohol as a way of coping. The cognitive perspective focuses on people's expectations about the effects of alcohol. The community perspective emphasizes the importance of the values and customs of the community in forming attitudes toward alcohol use. The more complex biopsychosocial view considers some individuals to have a predisposition for alcohol dependence and focuses on stress as a precipitating factor in drinking. In this view an addictive cycle develops.

Treatment Treatment for alcohol dependence begins with **detoxification,** "drying out," which is accompanied by physical symptoms of withdrawal. Specific types of drugs have been developed to ease the withdrawal symptoms. A community

approach is used by Alcoholics Anonymous, an organization dedicated to helping alcoholics become abstinent and rehabilitate themselves through mutual social support. Individual psychotherapy does not tend to be helpful for alcoholics, but family therapy may be useful to restructure relationships after drinking has stopped. Learning approaches including **aversive conditioning** and covert sensitization have been used to help people stop drinking. In the cognitive approach, drinkers are taught to monitor their behavior and determine the types of situations that are likely to tempt them to drink. **Relapse-prevention programs** help people gain effective coping responses to prevent drinking. These programs also help people cope with the **abstinence-violation effect,** the guilt and self-blame people feel when their coping lapses and they take one or more drinks. Some researchers and therapists believe that some people who have a history of alcohol abuse can learn to practice controlled drinking and use alcohol in moderation. Others believe that abstinence from all alcohol is the only way to deal with problem drinkers.

Preventing Alcohol Abuse Community level programs regulating access to alcohol and penalizing driving after alcohol use may be helpful. Prevention programs that teach young people about alcohol's effects and that help them to learn effective coping responses in situations where alcohol is served may be even more useful.

OTHER DRUGS

Barbiturates and Tranquilizers Both barbiturates and tranquilizers have a depressing effect on the central nervous system. Both groups of drugs are especially dangerous in combination with alcohol. **Barbiturates** are often prescribed by physicians to decrease anxiety or prevent convulsions. **Tranquilizers** are derived from several chemical groups. They are overused in the United States. Both barbiturates and tranquilizers are dangerous because tolerance develops and the user often increases the dose to dangerous levels to get the desired effect.

The Opioids Opioids is the term used to describe all drugs with morphine-like effects that bind to the opioid receptors in the brain. Some opioids occur naturally and some are chemically synthesized. Natural opioids include **endorphins, enkephalins,** and **dynorphins,** all of which are manufactured by the brain and the pituitary gland. **Opiates** are members of the opioid group that are derived from the juice of the opium poppy—for example, **morphine** and **heroin.** Opioids cause changes in mood, sleepiness, mental clouding, constipation, and slowing of the activity of the respiratory center in the brain. Opioids are sometimes called **narcotics,** but this term does not have the same meaning to law officers, physicians, scientists, and the public. The withdrawal reaction from opioid use can be severe. According to the **exposure orientation** theory of opioid addiction, the use of opiates shuts down the body's synthesis of natural opioids. The **interactional orientation** holds that the situation in which drugs are used is significant. The most widely used treatment for opioid addicts is **methadone maintenance. Naltrexone,** a drug that blocks opioid receptors, can be used effectively as treatment to prevent readdiction after detoxification.

Cocaine Cocaine, a drug from the leaves of the coca bush, stimulates the central nervous system and increases heart rate, raises blood pressure and temperature, and decreases appetite. It can produce feelings of hyperalertness, but in larger doses can produce a manic-like state, paranoia, and impaired judgment. **Crack** is a more potent form of cocaine that is highly addictive. Cocaine users may benefit from aversive conditioning and contingency contracts. Many cocaine users have dysfunctional families. Mutual help groups similar to Alcoholics Anonymous can be an effective way to provide the social support that is lacking.

Amphetamines Amphetamines are powerful psychomotor stimulants that affect both the central nervous system and the cardiovascular system. In moderate doses they result in wakefulness, alertness, and elevated mood. Tolerance develops rapidly, so many users begin injecting amphetamines to get more intense effects. High doses lead to nervousness, dizziness, confusion, heart palpitations and elevated blood pressure.

Psychedelics **Psychedelics** or **hallucinogens** produce alterations in consciousness by their action on the central nervous system. Natural psychedelics include mescaline, psilocybin, and DMT. Synthetic psychedelics include STP and LSD. Natural psychedelics have been used in religious ceremonies by many primitive cultures for hundreds of years. Abuse of psychedelic drugs can result in respiratory or cardiovascular collapse or in psychotic behavior. Prevention of recurrence of psychedelic drug use seems more effective with support groups and through teaching of social skills.

Phencyclidine (PCP) PCP is a synthetic chemical that may cause disorientation and hallucinations and make the user feel dissociated from the environment. Users sometimes develop a severe depression or a severe psychotic state that may be difficult to reverse.

Marijuana **Marijuana** is produced from the cannabis plant. **Hashish** is a solidified resin from this plant. The major active ingredient in marijuana is THC. Marijuana use impairs motor coordination and perception and affects short-term memory and learning even after the feeling of intoxication from the drug has passed.

Nicotine **Nicotine,** a chemical found in tobacco, acts at least in part by directly stimulating certain receptors that are sensitive to the neurotransmitter acetylcholine. Normal doses of nicotine can increase heart rate and blood pressure, and increases the heart's need for oxygen and may cause chest pains or a heart attack in people with atherosclerosis. Despite their knowledge that smoking is hazardous to health, many people find the habit of smoking difficult to give up. Such difficulty may be due to withdrawal symptoms, social and environmental cues, the overlearned nature of the habit, and the frequent reinforcement that is delivered with every puff. Although many smokers are able to quit on their own, smoking cessation programs can be effective for those who would like to quit. Cognitive research has identified three stages of change relevant to smoking cessation. These include commitment to change, implementation of the change, and maintenance of the change with emphasis on relapse prevention.

Maladaptive Behaviors
of Childhood and Adolescence

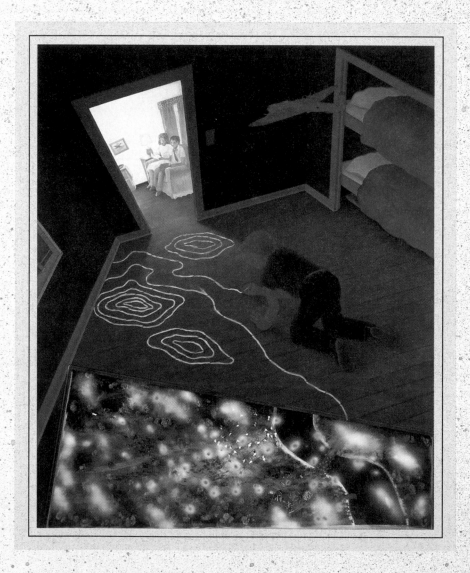

At three years of age, Anna was a quiet child. She spent a great deal of time sucking her thumb and hugging a teddy bear that was almost without fur as a result of constant loving. When her mother went into the bedroom to make the beds, Anna followed. The same things happened when her mother went to the telephone or took the wash out of the washing machine. She cried every day when her mother left her at the day-care center. The teachers there reported much the same behavior that she showed at home. At Anna's age her older sister had been a whirlwind of activity and spent her time playing with blocks or riding her trike. Anna's mother wondered whether Anna's behavior was cause for concern.

Children in Clinical Settings

The Scope of the Problem

Disruptive Behavior
Attention-deficit Hyperactivity Disorder
Conduct Disorder

Internalizing Disorders
Anxiety Disorders of Childhood
Depression in Children and Adolescents

Eating Disorders
Anorexia Nervosa
Bulimia Nervosa

Therapy for Children and Adolescents
Play Therapy
Cognitive and Behavior Therapies
Family Therapy
Results of Therapy

Chapter Summary

Lee N. Smith, *The Last Stand*, 1984. Courtesy of the artist.

Deciding to do something about unwanted behavior in a child can be much more agonizing than making a similar decision about an adult. Parents often feel responsible for everything their children do, and may feel especially guilty about admitting that their child has a problem that is serious enough to require professional help. And when parents or others do intervene, they may make things worse by emphasizing a problem that might disappear if it were ignored. On the other hand, many behavioral problems are easier to treat in children, since their behavior patterns and interaction styles have not yet become firmly established.

Behavioral problems sometimes interfere with a child's development by delaying the learning of all kinds of academic and social skills. Despite these potential handicaps, however, many children with psychological problems are brought to the attention of mental-health workers only when some crisis occurs. By then the problem may be difficult to treat because it has become so severe that the child had been labeled as a "problem." Withdrawn children like Anna are less likely to be referred for problem behavior than children who are extremely active, damage property or belongings, or who in other ways make life difficult for those around them. Yet Anna's behavior may be cause for concern if it

continues at its present level. Like every three year-old, she wants to make sure that important figures in her life are available, but in Anna's case those concerns seem to dominate most of her thinking. If Anna still follows this pattern by the age of four, her mother might consider consulting a clinical psychologist who specializes in the problems of young children. In the meantime, she might try to spend some time each day alone with Anna, playing or reading to her to give Anna a time when she can feel important and cared for as the center of her mother's attention.

Normal or healthy development comes about through a series of interlocking social, emotional, and cognitive competencies. Competencies at one developmental period not only help the child adapt to the environment, but also help prepare the way for new competencies to come. These developing competencies also integrate the old ones into new patterns of functioning. Pathological development, on the other hand, may be thought of as a lack of growth and integration of these competencies. Because of the important role early competencies play in later ones, an early disturbance may ultimately result in the emergence of a much larger disturbance some years later.

Because of the interlocking aspects of development as time goes on, attention should be paid to unusual patterns of childhood behavior whether these are hard to live with or not. Antisocial and acting-out behavior and severe reading problems in children are often correlated with adult disorders. Such childhood problems as shyness, fears, tics, nervousness, hypersensitivity, speech defects, and anxiety reactions may leave fewer discernible effects on later development. However, because adults who had these problems in childhood may be described as at least mildly maladjusted compared to the average person (Rutter & Hersov, 1985) intervention in childhood, perhaps in the manner suggested above for Anna, might enhance happiness in adulthood.

Psychological disorders that affect children run the gamut from extremely serious to quite minor. Some of these are unique to childhood, whereas others may be experienced by both children and adults. Some disorders, such as depression and schizophrenia, include behaviors that would be abnormal at any developmental stage. Others, such as phobias of early childhood, represent exaggerations of normal developmental trends. These disorders can affect the child's mood (as in anxiety disorders or depression) or behavior (as in hyperactivity or conduct disorders). They can also produce physical symptoms, as in eating disorders like anorexia nervosa or bulimia nervosa. In addition, there are more severe disorders, such as mental retardation and autism, in which the child does not develop normally over a long period and the outlook for significant change is poor.

These severe developmental disorders are discussed in Chapter 16.

Children in Clinical Settings

Many children who require clinical care because of maladaptive behavior are unable to understand their situations or to voice their complaints directly. Clinicians who evaluate and treat childhood disorders must be skilled at eliciting information from and about the child. Clinicians must know how to stay out of children's way as they reveal, at their own pace and in their own style, the character and contents of their personal worlds. Clinicians must also be highly skilled observers, able to see, hear, and in other ways sense all the data the child provides. A basic requirement of being an effective clinical worker with children is to resist the tendency to jump to conclusions on the basis of either insufficient evidence or erroneous assumptions. The following example illustrates the pitfalls of false assumptions. Jonah, a bright, normal little boy, surprised everyone by seeming to remember experiences others assumed he had forgotten.

Jonah's parents spent the first years of their married life in a small college town in the Midwest. It was there that Jonah was born and spent the first nine months of his life.

It was a peaceful existence. Since both parents were employed on the campus, a third adult took care of Jonah. Peter, a graduate student in psychology, was the regular baby-sitter. He sat with the little boy for a number of hours every day, and he and Jonah became very fond of one another. Then, when Jonah was nine months old, the family moved to a different campus because of a better job opportunity, and Jonah's friendship with Peter was rudely interrupted. Jonah did not seem to mind. His mother had more time for him in the new location, and Jonah developed into a cheerful and active toddler.

One day, Jonah's parents received a letter from Peter in which he announced his impending visit to their new home. Peter missed Jonah, and he had decided he would like to visit his former

charge. It would be their first encounter after 21 months.

When Peter arrived at the house, both Peter and Jonah smiled politely by way of greeting, and then Jonah did something quite extraordinary: He got down on all fours and repeated all the little games, which he had since outgrown, that he had played with Peter in the good old days—activities such as finger games and peek-a-boo. Peter complied, and the silent dialogue of reminiscing went on for a while.

But then Jonah put his hand on Peter's knee and said clearly and urgently, "backpack," referring to his once favorite mode of transportation—for which, at nine months, he had not yet had a term.

—Garbarino and others, 1990, pp. xii–xiii

Jonah's reunion with Peter demonstrates in a positive way the fact that events and people may leave strong impressions on and create strong feelings in small children that under certain conditions (often not well understood) they are capable of recalling. In the time that had passed since his early association with Peter, Jonah had acquired and learned to use properly the term for a pleasurable experience of long ago. Very young children may not be able to speak about some of their feelings. The difference in developmental stage between children and adults can constitute a barrier to communication and prevent sharing experiences. While Jonah remembered distant happy experiences, there is evidence that traumatic childhood experiences may also persist for long periods of time and come into active memory when current circumstances present cues that recall the past.

The case of a 40-year-old mental health professional, who had begun a new job at a facility for male juvenile delinquents, found his association with these boys began to bring back long-buried memories. On his long rides home he began seeing himself as a toddler—attacked in a shack by a group of older children. The man drove to the town where he had lived until he was four years old, and he found the shack that he had "pictured." The shack stood catercornered to his old house.

—Terr, 1991, p. 12

Four characteristics related to childhood trauma that appear to last for long periods are:

1. Visualized or otherwise repeatedly perceived memories of the traumatic event;

2. Repetitive behaviors (often in the form of play and behavioral reenactments);

3. Trauma-specific fears (fears of specific things related to the traumatic events);

4. Changed attitudes about people, life, and the future (e.g., "You can't count on anything or anyone to protect you").

In some cases, it is evident to the clinician that some fairly specific traumatic event is a key determinant of the abnormal behavior. However, in other cases multiple or vague determinants may seem to cause the behavior. Diagnostic interviews with children enable clinicians to learn as much as possible about the children's past and present and to establish rapport so that they will not be afraid to return for further sessions. Establishing rapport does not mean making the session a "fun" experience for the child, however. In fact, to be a good, noninterfering observer, the clinician must be able to tolerate discomfort in the child. For example, if a child shows anxiety by disrupting play or crying and the clinician moves in too quickly to provide support, information will be lost about how the child copes with anxiety. The clinician needs to find out from children's communications their understanding of why they have been brought to the clinical setting, how they view the clinician, and how they understand the situation. The clinician must answer similar questions pertaining to the child's parents. Because of the child's dependent status, parental involvement is often of great importance. The interaction of several systems (family, school, social services, social networks, and the legal system) may impact on assessing children's problems and planning therapeutic programs.

The Scope of the Problem

According to a recent conservative estimate, at least 12 percent of all children in the United States who are under age 18 meet the diagnostic criteria for one or more mental disorders (Institute of Medicine, 1990). Nearly half of these children are severely disordered or handicapped by their mental illness. One survey of clinical services available to mentally disturbed children found that fewer than one in five receives treatment of any kind

BOX 15–1 **Effects of Child Abuse and Neglect**

Parents who are guilty of **child neglect** may fail to provide food, clothing, warmth, a clean environment, and the supervision necessary to keep their children safe. Or they may provide these things but express no interest in their children and fail to interact with them more than is absolutely necessary. Parents who commit **child abuse,** on the other hand, may use severe physical punishment and even permanently harm their children, or they may use psychological forms of abuse that leave their children feeling like innately bad people who are unworthy of love.

Neglected children show the effects of lack of parental stimulation. They talk less and make fewer social responses. In addition, they engage in little exploratory or inquisitive behavior. They also are likely to be depressed (Conaway & Hansen, 1989).

Child abuse can leave both psychological and physical scars. Physically abused children are often seriously damaged. Many suffer neurological damage, and one-third have

problems severe enough to handicap them in everyday life. Children who have been physically abused tend to be deficient in motor skills such as those involved in running, skipping, or riding a tricycle. These deficiencies may be caused by their fear of exploring and taking risks, but poor motor development has been noted as early as four months of age, so lack of exploratory behavior is not a complete answer. Abused children also show delayed development of speech and language. Preschool children may be abused for talking, so they simply don't practice speaking. Instead, much of their communication is nonverbal.

The IQs of abused children are lower than might be expected (Salter and others, 1985). The delay in their cognitive development might be due to the unpredictable and dangerous environment in which such children live. Instead of concentrating on learning, they are anxious, preoccupied by fantasy, and concerned with ways of surviving. Fear of failure and

difficulty in paying attention to instructions seem to handicap abused children in testing situations.

For abused children, the world is an unpredictable and hateful place. The adults they live with may be hostile and impatient and can become violent without warning. These children must be prepared to anticipate and meet the needs of their parents and are constantly afraid of harsh punishment and verbal abuse. As a result, the children look unhappy and take little pleasure in their surroundings. They may have sleep disturbances, wet their beds, be apathetic, fearful, or phobic, and underachieve in school. They are also likely to be depressed, to have low self-esteem, and to think of themselves as innately bad (Gelardo & Sanford, 1987).

Much research on child abuse and neglect has lumped both kinds of parents together. However, although they overlap somewhat, these two groups differ in important respects. In one study, abusive, neglectful, and normal control-group mothers were

FIGURE 15–1 Frequency of different types of behaviors of abusive, neglectful, and control-group mothers when interacting with their children.
(Adapted from Bousha & Twentyman, 1984, p. 110)

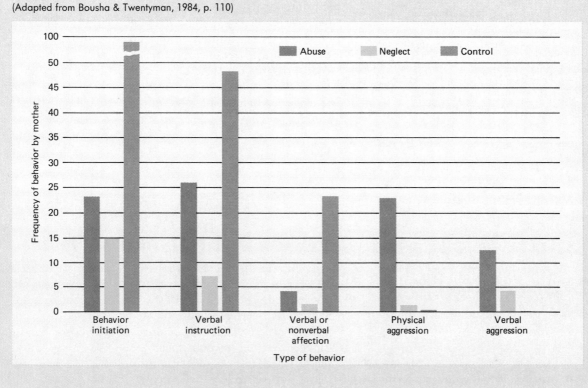

observed in their homes for 90 minutes on each of three consecutive days (Bousha & Twentyman, 1984). The abusive mothers had the highest rates of physical and verbal aggression and neglectful mothers the lowest rate of interaction. Figure 15–1 shows some of the differences among the three groups of mothers. The children of these mothers also behaved differently (see Figure 15–2). The control children showed less aggressive verbal and physical behavior and more initiations of social behavior than either of the other two groups. The neglected children initiated very little social behavior.

The following pattern is common in cases of child abuse and neglect (Twentyman and others, 1984):

1. The parent has unrealistic expectations for the child.

2. The child acts in a way that does not confirm these expectations.

3. The parent misattributes the child's actions to intentional and negative motivations.

4. The parent overreacts and excessively punishes the child.

Child abuse and neglect may have implications for the child's development, behavior, and mental health both in childhood and as an adult. Researchers are beginning to try to understand the behaviors and thoughts that lead to abuse and to devise ways of helping abused and neglected children and their parents.

While working with abused children and their families is difficult and stressful, it can also be gratifying to the clinician. A clinician with twenty years of experience in this work described his experience this way:

At times, it has been very discouraging. The parents are usually defensive and angry, at least initially, and the children are sometimes so damaged that the work feels overwhelming. These kids need love, acceptance, and understanding so much and yet when it is offered, it seems to frighten and confuse them. They test over and over again your patience and caring. . . . Whether or not they appreciated my efforts and my worry about them was unimportant. Just seeing some of them get out of the destructive cycle they were in and experience more feelings of success and self-worth was all the reward I needed. Sometimes even that was hard to come by. All in all, these families have taught me a lot, not only in a professional sense, but about myself. It has been humbling, but in the final analysis it has been worth the effort and pain.

—Jorgensen, 1990, pp. 31–32

FIGURE 15–2 Frequency of different types of behaviors by children when they interacted with their mothers who were abusive, neglectful, or from a control group. (Adapted from Bousha & Twentyman, 1984, p. 110)

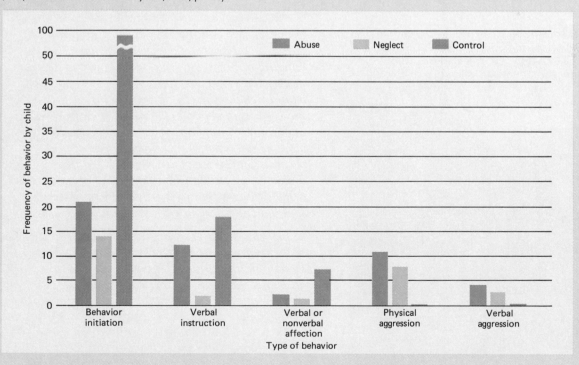

(*Childhood Disorders*, 1988). By comparison, 74 percent of children suffering from physical handicaps are treated professionally. In other words, maladaptive behavior in children is a major problem and society is not doing an adequate job in solving it. A number of risk factors for childhood disorders have been identified. They include parental psychopathology, family discord and divorce, low socioeconomic status, the child's temperamental characteristics, and stressful experiences (Jensen and others, 1990). Child abuse is an especially damaging stressor. Children who are abused have a very high rate of psychological problems (Erickson & Egeland, 1987) (see Box 15–1). For many of these children, their problems will extend into adulthood.

Helping troubled youngsters is often problematic, for several reasons. Lack of understanding of the nature of childhood disorders and their causes is one important factor. For example, it is not known whether some disorders of childhood, such as psychoses, depression, and anxiety disorders, are extensions of the adult categories or whether they are separate disorders with different causes. One piece of evidence that suggests that many childhood disorders are distinct from their adult versions is the difference in the sex ratios in these disorders for children and adults. In childhood, boys are affected more often than girls in almost all categories. Beginning in adolescence, however, affective disorders and anxiety disorders are more frequent in women, and there is no sex difference in schizophrenic disorders (Rutter & Garmezy, 1983).

Some maladaptive behavior in childhood results from normal variations in rates of development. Children who develop later than their age-mates often carry feelings of inadequacy and inferiority into adulthood. Personalities of children who are early or late in maturing physically may be permanently affected. Problems can also result from lateness in acquiring cognitive skills. Children who are unable to master academic work when their classmates are ready for it are at a serious disadvantage both in school and in later life, even if they catch up afterward (see Figure 15–3).

Disruptive Behavior

Disruptive behavior is an obvious indication of a potential problem. Two kinds of children who behave disruptively are of special concern to parents, teachers, and clinicians; children who do not pay attention and seem exceptionally active, and children who behave aggressively, break rules, and cause significant harm to other people and their property. The first type is diagnosed as having *attention-deficit hyperactivity disorder (ADHD)* while the latter group have *conduct disorder*.

Attention-deficit Hyperactivity Disorder

FIGURE 15–3 Learning to write requires a certain degree of coordination and cognitive skill. Children develop these skills at different rates. Those who develop them later than average often are at a disadvantage in kindergarten and in early school years.

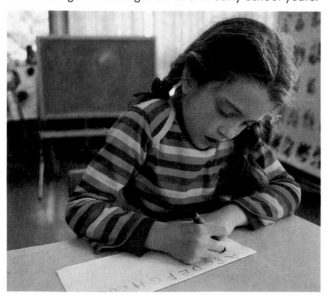

By his second year, he seemed to be ignorant of danger, walking on the edge of counters and hanging from the top shelf of the bookcase. If his mother did not watch him closely in the park, he would wander off. On one occasion, she became involved in discussion with another mother and later found Jimmy on another block, staring in a window and seemingly unaware that he had become lost. Temperamentally, he could be described as a child with a high level of motor activity, fluctuating mood, intensity of reaction, and difficulty adapting to new situations. . . .

In his third-grade class Jimmy sat near the front of the room, where the teacher could quietly direct him and answer his endless stream of questions. As usual, Jimmy made noise (squirming in his seat, humming, and drumming with two pencils) while the teacher was working at the board. His desk was disorganized, with papers falling out and crayons under the seat that occasionally were ground into the floor. He often did not sit in his seat but positioned himself

on his knees and leaned out into the aisle. Mrs. Johnson gave up ordering him to be quiet because threats each day had been greeted with verbal agreement but no change in Jimmy's behavior.

—Garfinkel and others, 1990, pp. 157–158

Jimmy illustrates a number of features seen in **attention-deficit hyperactivity disorder (ADHD).** Table 15–1 lists the symptoms of inattention, hyperactivity and impulsiveness commonly found in this disorder. According to DSM, the presence of a number of these symptoms for at least the past six months supports the use of an ADHD classification. The features listed in Table 15–1 make it clear that ADHD involves more than the high levels of exuberance and motor activity displayed by many normal children. Estimates of the prevalence of ADHD range from 3 to 15 percent of children in the general population (Whalen, 1989).

Children who have ADHD show degrees of impulsiveness, hyperactivity, and inattention that are inappropriate for their developmental level. They usually have some disturbance in each of these three areas of behavior although the degree of each may not be the same. **Impulsiveness** is shown by acting out of turn, starting a task without getting directions, and interrupting when others are talking. Impulsiveness also manifests itself in accident-prone behavior or doing dangerous things without thinking about the consequences. **Hyperactivity** includes jumping around, fidgeting, constantly manipulating or fiddling with objects, excessive twisting and wiggling when sitting down, and an inability to remain seated. **Inattention** is shown by a failure to follow through on tasks, frequent shifts from one activity to another, and failure to follow rules and to listen to what others say. About half the time ADHD develops before age four. At least three times as many boys as girls in the general population fit this description. Of children brought to clinics because of these behaviors, boys outnumber girls by as many as nine to one.

Table 15–1
Clinical Features of Attention-deficit Hyperactivity Disorder

Inattention

1. Easily distracted by extraneous stimuli.
2. Difficulty following through on instructions in the absence of close supervision (e.g., fails to finish schoolwork).
3. Difficulty sustaining attention in tasks or play activities.
4. Often does not seem to listen to what is being said to him or her.
5. Often loses things necessary for tasks or activities (e.g., toys, pencils).
6. Often fails to give close attention to details in schoolwork or other activities.
7. Has difficulty organizing goal-directed activities.
8. Often shifts from one uncompleted activity to another.

Hyperactivity

1. Often leaves seat in classroom or in other situations in which remaining seated is expected.
2. Has difficulty playing quietly.
3. Runs about or climbs excessively in inappropriate situations.
4. Often fidgets with hands or feet or squirms in seat.
5. Often interrupts or intrudes on others.
6. Often talks excessively.

Impulsiveness

1. Often acts before thinking.
2. Has difficulty awaiting turn in games or group situations.
3. Often blurts out answers to questions before they have been completed.
4. Often engages in physically dangerous activities without considering consequences (e.g., runs into street without looking).

Children who are classified in the ADHD category have more serious problems than children who are merely very active. They may have deficiencies in visual and auditory discrimination as well as in reading, writing, and language development. ADHD children are likely to fail not only in school but also in social situations, both outcomes that cause them to have a low opinion of themselves. As a result, they make few friends and are likely to develop various physical complaints as well as emotional problems, especially depression (Ross & Ross, 1982).

In a study comparing the behavior of hyperactive boys and their nonhyperactive brothers, mothers were asked to rate the severity of various behavior problems in both sons (Tarver-Behring and others, 1985). For all the behaviors rated, the hyperactive sons created more severe problems (see Figure 15–4). This was especially true in interpersonal situations involving play with other children or when the mother's attention was focused on other things such as talking on the phone, entertaining visitors, taking the child to public places, or driving.

In order to see whether the mothers played a role in creating the hyperactive behavior by interacting differently with their two sons, the mothers were observed alone with each son in two kinds of situations: free play and a series of structured tasks. During free play the boys diagnosed with ADHD were less likely than their brothers to answer their mothers' questions and were more likely to be distracted. Their behaviors differed in the same way during the structured task; in addition, the ADHD sons were less likely to follow instructions from their mothers. In this study, the mothers' behavior toward their two sons did not differ, but it is likely that

over time the hyperactive sons' lack of responsiveness might lead their mothers to interact with them less.

Children with ADHD experience difficulty in social interaction in school as well as at home. In both situations, others feel under pressure as a result of their behavior. Teachers are more intense and controlling with hyperactive boys than with their peers. The presence of such a child seems to alter the teacher's behavior for the whole class (Whalen & Henker, 1985). In classrooms with a hyperactive child, the rate of the teacher's negative interactions with the other children in the class also increases.

Boys with ADHD have social difficulties with their peers as well as with parents and teachers. Parents often report that their hyperactive children have no friends or get along only with children several years younger than they are. One reason for these social difficulties is that hyperactive children have deficits both in their social knowledge and in their performance of socially skilled behaviors (Grenell and others, 1987). These deficits do not carry over into all behaviors. The biggest problem for these children comes when they need to maintain an already established relationship. When conflict arises they are less friendly, more impulsive, and more assertive toward the other child. They have difficulty in following the rules in games or in cooperating on joint projects.

In order to help hyperactive children improve their social performance we need to know more about specific deficits associated with this disorder (Du Paul and others, 1991). One research project that dealt with this question took place at a summer camp (Whalen and Henker, 1985). Pairs of boys, one with ADHD and one a control, played a game where they alternated playing the roles of an astronaut and of mission control. The astronaut was to be the follower, to listen carefully to mission control messages, comply with instructions, and give appropriate feedback. Mission control was to be the leader who conveyed the needed information and guided the astronaut. Each boy played the game twice in each role, each time with a different partner. The most interesting finding was that unlike the normal boys, the ADHD boys seemed not to benefit from the opportunity to observe another boy in the more difficult role of mission control before playing the role themselves (see Figure 15–5). This difference in ability to learn vicariously in a situation may be related to the poorer social skills demonstrated by hyperactive children.

FOLLOW-UP STUDIES OF ADHD CHILDREN While many ADHD children may improve as they grow older, they have an elevated risk for mental and behavioral disorders later on. A substantial minority of these children enter the criminal justice system in adolescence or young adulthood, and drug use disorders are also frequently noted (Mannuzza and others, 1991). An important question requiring further research concerns

FIGURE 15–4 Mean severity of child behavior problems in 14 situations as rated by mothers for both their hyperactive and nonhyperactive sons.

(Tarver-Behring and others, 1985, p. 207)

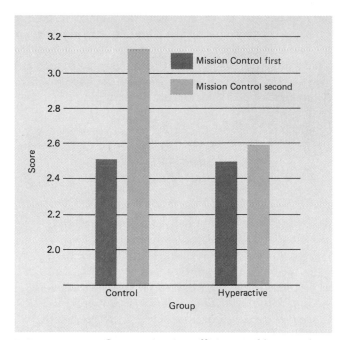

FIGURE 15–5 Communicative efficiency of boys with ADHD and control boys when serving as mission control during the first versus the second game. Although both groups of boys performed at about the same level when they played the role of mission control first, a notable difference emerged when the boys were first able to see another in that role. When they repeated the space-travel game, hyperactive boys showed much less change in their behavior than did the control boys.

(Whalen & Henker, 1985, p. 469)

the link between ADHD, conduct disorders, and antisocial personality disorder. There is strong evidence that ADHD is associated with later behaviors that harm others or create problems with the law (Biederman and others, 1991). It is also possible that tendencies toward conduct disorder accompany ADHD from an early age. When ADHD is not accompanied at an early age by conduct problems or aggression, the likelihood of adult antisocial behavior is relatively low (Lilienfeld & Waldman, 1990).

POSSIBLE CAUSES The causes of attention-deficit hyperactivity disorder are unknown. Children who have this disorder appear to have all the "basic equipment" needed to develop and function adequately. Neither their family climates or other environment nor their early childhood experiences appear different from those of their peers. Theories have been offered that diet (specifically, ingestion of too much sugar) is a cause of ADHD. However, strong support for nutritional explanations remains to be established.

Most children who have the disorder show no obvious evidence of actual brain damage, but individuals with ADHD may suffer from a metabolic dysfunction in the brain. Delayed maturation of the central nervous system may also contribute to the behavioral pattern seen in ADHD (Hynd and others, 1991). In a study of adults who have been hyperactive since childhood (and who are parents of hyperactive children), a team of researchers found reduced activity in those areas of the brain that control attention and movement (Zametkin and others, 1990). The researchers discovered that hyperactive adults were metabolizing glucose, the body's main source of energy, at a rate eight percent lower than control subjects.

Complications during pregnancy or birth and illnesses of early infancy have been found to be associated with hyperactive behavior, but the relationship is not strong enough to be used in predicting future school or behavior problems (Hartsough & Lambert, 1985). Another possible cause may be a genetic component. Often the father of an ADHD child also had a troubled childhood, was a school dropout, and remains restless and short-tempered (Whalen, 1989). In addition, some researchers have found high rates of antisocial personality disorder in male relatives of ADHD children and histrionic personality disorder in female relatives (Rie & Rie, 1980). Another possibility is that the disorder may be a result of a deficiency of neurotransmitters such as dopamine or norepinephrine.

TREATMENT By far the most common treatment for hyperactive children is the use of drugs, like methylphenidate (Ritalin) or dextroamphetamine (Dexedrine), that stimulate the central nervous system. A large number of studies reveal that these drugs have positive short-term effects: Many children show improved behavior and a decreased disruptiveness in the classroom, although their school performance may not change much (Rapport & Kelly, 1991). However, stimulants can have side effects, including insomnia, headaches, nausea, and impaired cognitive performance. Some children also develop incessant talking or explosive outbursts of rage when they are treated with these medications. In some cases the drugs depress the appetite so that weight gain is below normal.

A significant minority of children who use stimulant medication do not improve or have unpleasant side effects (Whalen and others, 1985). Some parents refuse stimulant therapy for their children, while others discontinue it prematurely, often because the children dislike taking the drugs. These problems, together with the growing awareness that attention-deficit hyperactivity disorder may have lifelong effects, have encouraged researchers to look at other therapeutic possibilities.

One problem that occurs with the use of these stimulant drugs is that the medication, rather than any personal action, may be seen as the sole reason for any changes in the child's behavior. As a result, the child may feel no responsibility for his or her behavior. Social psychologists might see this as a demonstration of

attribution theory, which emphasizes the importance of self-statements about cause on the behavior that follows. The importance of attribution can be seen in the following example, in which stimulant therapy for a nine-year-old boy was terminated:

The result was marked behavioral deterioration accompanied by such spontaneous attributional statements as "My pills help me get done with the work" and "I get angry without my pill." After four days, Tom was given pills again, but this time they were placebos. Even so, task attention and productivity returned to high levels, and the teacher attempted "reattribution therapy" by emphasizing that Tom, not the pills, was controlling his behavior. When he was allowed to earn his way off medication by finishing his work four days in a row, Tom met this criterion and continued to perform well in the classroom with neither medication nor placebo.

—Whalen and others, 1985, p. 404

Another approach to drug therapy in the treatment of ADHD is the use of imipramine and other tricyclic antidepressants. In general, stimulant drugs are preferred because they seem more effective and because they have fewer negative side effects. However, there may be a subgroup of hyperactive children who are also anxious or depressed in addition to their hyperactivity who respond better to imipramine (Pliszka, 1987).

There is a growing consensus that a combination of pharmacological and behavioral interventions provides the optimal treatment of ADHD (Goldstein & Goldstein, 1990). For instance, in one study short-term measures showed that such a combined treatment produces performance in ADHD children that is very similar to that of a normal control group. The two treatments seemed to have an additive effect, that is, the combined treatment group was superior in result to either of the two treatments alone (Gittelman-Klein and others, 1980). Further research is needed to clarify the condition under which psychological interventions add to the benefit of stimulant therapy.

Counseling the parents of ADHD children can be helpful. Parents need to be informed about the disorder—including its natural course, possible causes, and likely prognosis with and without treatment. They also should be given practical suggestions for the daily management of an ADHD child. For example, parents must learn the importance of avoiding stressful situations known to cause difficulty, overstimulation, and excessive fatigue. Almost all parents can be taught the general principle of structuring the child's environment to include regular routines and proper limits set on the child's behavior. Parental involvement is particularly valuable because complete reliance on drugs may reduce the interest of parents and teachers in finding other ways to help.

Conduct Disorder

The police received a call from Harry. He told them that he had come home and found his parents and brother murdered. Suspicion first focused on another brother, who was missing. When his body was later found stuffed in a trunk, suspicion finally turned to Harry. At first he seemed an unlikely candidate. He was a first-year student at a prestigious military academy and had been a quiet and somewhat lonely boy in high school. The family had been described as a close one with strong religious beliefs. As the story unfolded, Harry began to appear in a somewhat different light. He wanted to quit school. He hated the hazing the first-year students received. He seemed to have been marked as a loser and was frequently the target of jokes and punishment. His father had refused to allow him to quit school, just as he had earlier refused to allow him to quit Little League baseball even when Harry pleaded. Other students reported that during high school Harry was often teased and mistreated by his classmates.

On the night of the murders, Harry, home for Thanksgiving vacation, apparently felt he could stand the frustration no longer. One way to avoid returning to school was to remove the main obstacle to his quitting—his father.

—Adapted from *The New York Times*, November 29, 1976, pp. 1, 31

Ever since his parents could remember, Robbie has been in trouble. For example, when he was a young child he pushed his sister down the stairs and turned the switch on the electric garage door when his brother was riding his tricycle under it. As he grew older this behavior continued. At 15 Robbie raped his 6-year-old cousin and beat the elderly lady next door when he demanded her purse and then found only $1 in it. His parents and his teachers were all afraid of him. He never

seemed to feel sorry for his victims, and no one around him felt safe whenever he was out of the various institutions to which he had been sent during his adolescence.

Jeremy, age nine, was brought by his mother to a mental health clinic because he had become increasingly disobedient and difficult to manage at school. Several events that occurred during the previous month had convinced his mother that she must do something about his behavior. Several weeks ago he had sworn at his teacher and was suspended from school for three days. Last week he was reprimanded by the police for riding his three-wheeler in the street, something his mother had repeatedly cautioned him about. The next day he failed to use his pedal brakes and rode his bike into a store window, shattering it. He has not been caught in any more serious offenses, though once before he broke a window when he was riding his bike with a friend.

Jeremy had been difficult to manage since nursery school. Since that time the problems slowly escalated. Whenever he is without close supervision, he gets into trouble. He has been reprimanded at school for teasing and kicking other children, tripping them, and calling them names. He is described as bad-tempered and irritable, even though at times he seems to enjoy school. Often he appears to be deliberately trying to annoy other children, though he always claims that others have started the arguments. He does not become involved in serious fights, but does occasionally exchange a few blows with another child.

—Spitzer and others, 1989, pp. 307–308

Harry, Robbie, and Jeremy are similar in that each of them *acts out:* Each has acted maliciously toward other people. But the three boys' situations have important differences.

Adolescents like Harry are often found to be psychotic or greatly disturbed. Such individuals usually demonstrate a long-term pattern of turmoil and emotional hurts that they have held beneath the surface. At last some incident, sometimes very minor, triggers violent behavior. Robbie's behavior is impulsive and aggressive. He seems to have no mercy for his victims and attacks people who have been kind to him as readily as strangers or enemies. Despite the punishment he has

received and the institutions he has been sent to, he shows little concern about the harm his behavior has caused. Although Jeremy has annoyed other children and adults, he has not violated their basic rights or displayed any of the more serious forms of acting out behavior.

Children and adolescents who are classified in the category of **conduct disorder** go far beyond the pranks and mischief that are characteristic of their age group. Their behavior seriously violates the basic rights of others or the major rules of society and they may seek to physically dominate others (see Figure 15–6). Children who have conduct disorders are often truant and may lie, steal, run away from home, and molest animals and other people. They may begin voluntary sexual activity very

FIGURE 15–6 An aggressive boy with a need to dominate others drew this picture of himself as a flame-breathing dragon.

(Courtesy of John Lochman, Ph.D., Duke University Medical Center)

early and regularly use illegal drugs. Conduct disorders may occur mainly during group activity with peers or when a single child makes an unprovoked attack on animals or people. For example, Robbie would be diagnosed by most clinicians as having a longstanding conduct disorder, while Harry's horrifying crime appeared to be an isolated event related to some type of psychotic process. Researchers have found that this disorder affects more boys than girls.

This description of conduct disorder may sound similar to the characteristics of antisocial personality disorder (see Chapter 9). Remember, however, that by definition, antisocial personality disorder occurs only in individuals over 18 years of age. The DSM category of conduct disorder was devised for those below that age. This category is used to describe many individuals who are later diagnosed as having an antisocial personality disorder. The term can also be used for adults who do not meet all the criteria for antisocial personality disorders. Conduct disorder is not only a common childhood disorder, but a costly one because of society's need to deal with the consequences.

Jeremy's behavior places him within another group of children, who show a variety of annoying behaviors that include argumentativeness, irritability, defiance, negativism, and resentfulness. They might be diagnosed as having an **Oppositional Defiant Disorder.** This term is applied to a child whose problems are less serious than a conduct disorder but more severe than simply those of a difficult child. An oppositional defiant disorder usually begins by the age of eight and may eventually develop into a conduct or mood disorder. Before puberty it is more common in boys; after puberty it is equally common in both sexes. In adolescents oppositional defiant disorder is often associated with alcohol and drug abuse. Children with conduct disorder usually have all the symptoms of oppositional defiant disorder as well. Oppositional defiant disorder is a relatively new classification that was incorporated into DSM to distinguish milder cases, particularly those involving young children, from cases that fit the diagnosis of conduct disorder. How much the classification adds to reliable diagnosis is not yet clear and research on it is needed. Available evidence suggests that, while nearly all youths with conduct disorder have a history of oppositional defiant behavior, not all cases of oppositional defiant disorder develop into conduct disorder (Loeber, Lakey, & Thomas, 1991).

DEFINING CONDUCT DISORDER While the category of conduct disorder includes a wide variety of individuals and behaviors, experts do not agree on how this category can be meaningfully subdivided. Table 15–2 lists some of the behaviors characteristic of conduct disorders. The conduct disorders are diagnosed on DSM's Axis I, not on Axis II as personality disorders are. The conduct disorder diagnosis is given when a repetitive pattern exists over a period of six months or more of actions that either violate the basic rights of others or violate social norms or rules appropriate for the patient's age group. Some children with conduct disorder may be conforming to a group norm as part of a gang, for instance; others may carry out their aggressive activity on a solitary basis. Figure 15–7 illustrates behavior seen in conduct disorder.

Estimates of the frequency of conduct disorder in the general population vary across age groups and from study to study; for example 3.2 to 6.7 percent in ten year olds; 5.5 percent in children between four and sixteen years of age; and 6.9 percent in seven year olds (Robins, 1991). While the estimates may differ because of the

Table 15–2

Clinical Features of Conduct Disorder

1. School truancy.
2. Running away from home.
3. Onset of alcohol or other psychoactive substance use before age 13 and recurrent use thereafter.
4. Stealing items of significant value (e.g., shoplifting, burglary).
5. Breaking into someone else's home or car.
6. Engaging in mugging, armed robbery, purse-snatching, or extortion.
7. Deliberately destroying other people's property.
8. Initiating physical fights (e.g., at school, in the playground).
9. Being physically cruel to people and/or animals.
10. Using a weapon on more than one occasion that could cause serious physical harm to others.
11. Engaging in sexual activities in order to obtain money, goods, or drugs.
12. Forcing someone into sexual activity.

"The little dears! They still believe in Santa Claus."

FIGURE 15—7 Charles Addams illustrates the deliberate cruelty to others often practiced by children and adolescents with conduct disorder. Santa's basic rights are about to be violated by his reception into this household.

(Drawing by Chas. Addams; © 1952, 1980 The New Yorker Magazine, Inc.)

populations and locations studied, there is no question over the serious problems that conduct disorder represents in most communities. It is typically the most common reason for the referral of children to clinical settings (Robins, 1991).

It is clear, however, that there are important differences between occasional minor delinquency, which is common in some settings, and persistent antisocial behavior that causes severe harm to the victim (see Box 15—2 on page 462). A true conduct disorder shows a distinctive unfolding and consistency over time.

Table 15—3 presents the typical stages of disruptive and antisocial behaviors found in conduct disorder. Researchers have found that the long-term outcome for conduct disorder is clearly worse than for other disorders, for example childhood depression and anxiety (Robins & Price, 1991).

There are a number of factors that seem to increase the chances that a child will develop a conduct disorder. These include problems of focusing attention and hyperactive behavior as well as parental rejection, harsh discipline, absence of a father, and association with a

Table 15—3

The Unfolding of Disruptive and Antisocial Behaviors Typical of Conduct Disorder, from the Preschool Period to Adolescence

1. Difficult temperament
2. Hyperactivity
3. Overt conduct problems and aggressiveness
4. Poor social relationships
5. Academic problems
6. Truancy, stealing, substance use
7. Association with deviant peers
8. Delinquency (arrest)
9. Recidivism (repeated crime)

SOURCE: R.R. Loeber, Development and risk factors of juvenile antisocial behavior and delinquency (1990), in *Clinical Psychology Review,* 10, 1–41. Reprinted with permission of Pergamon Press plc.

group of delinquent children. Parents of children with conduct disorder are more likely to have antisocial personality disorder and problems with alcohol than parents in general.

Identifying a conduct disorder can be difficult. Children are constantly changing as they mature, and it is not always easy to tell when a problem is persistent enough to deserve a diagnosis. Most of what we know about conduct disorders comes from studies of delinquent adolescents, but "juvenile delinquent" is a legal and not a clinical term. Children's misbehavior is more likely to come to clinical attention if parents cannot cope with the problem behavior. Further, clinicians must bear in mind that misbehavior means different things in different circumstances. A boy who has failed in a woodworking class and is stealing from his father, a carpenter, does not display the same kind of problem as a boy who has injured two classmates by hitting them on the head with a heavy metal object. In both instances, however, the boys can be described as misbehaving.

In some cases, what appears to be a conduct disorder is simply a problem in adjusting to acute or chronic stress. In the situation described below, the boy's misconduct can be interpreted as a jealous battle with his mother and her lover over her affections.

Jeffrey, a 14-year-old boy, appeared in family court on a third felony charge. For several months he had stolen and lied, and been physically and verbally abusive and short-tempered. He has also been spending a lot of time lifting weights in an effort to develop strong muscles. Some four months ago his divorced mother began to live with a new man

BOX 15–2 **The Beating and Rape of a Jogger in Central Park**

In the spring of 1989, a young woman on her accustomed evening jog through New York's Central Park was severely beaten, raped, and left unconscious and bleeding by a group of about a dozen youths who were roaming the park in a vicious spree. The jogger was found nearly naked, bound, and gagged, close to death with a body temperature of only 80 degrees. Among her injuries were two severe skull fractures from a beating on her head with a brick and piece of pipe. The case of the "Central Park Jogger," as the victim came to be known, attracted national attention as professionals and lay people alike sought to understand the social and psychological forces behind this savage, random attack.

Police were able to reconstruct the activity of the jogger's attackers earlier that evening (see Figure 15–8). These included robbing an elderly man outside the park (which netted them only a sandwich), throwing rocks at a taxicab, and chasing two bicyclists. After the rape took place, the youths went on to attack a male jogger, beating him and hitting him on the head with a pipe. The teenagers, on a school holiday, had little to do and had taken part in what has come to be called a "wilding," described by some sociologists as a rite of passage or way to prove manhood. According to their testimony after the assault they described their mood as "joyous." One boy portrayed the group as laughing, leaping around, and just acting "stupid."

Police investigation showed that although most of those accused lived in a transitional neighborhood between poor and luxurious areas, most had parents with adequate incomes, who cared about and supervised their children and had high aims for their futures. Many of those accused took part in school and church activities, and their teachers and friends described them positively, not as trouble makers. They were apparently not using drugs at the time of the attack, and most had no criminal records.

—*New York Times*, 23 April 1989, p. B1; 26 April 1989, pp. A1, B24; 2 May 1989, p. C1.

Sociologists and anthropologists who have studied the youth's neighborhood say the attack may have emerged from several factors in the community (Kolata, 1989). One is the area's strong underground drug economy, which has resulted, especially since the introduction of crack cocaine, in a transfer of power to teenagers, even those who are not part of the drug trade. Not only are adults afraid to resist these drug dealers, but children and teenagers feel they must be seen as tough in order not to be picked on. Another factor seems to be the existence of loose groups of youths rather than formal gangs. Because the membership of these groups may change from night to night, they lack structure and it is easier for a few people who are out of control to influence the group so that unpredictable behavior results.

Comparing the behavior of the accused group of attackers to the characteristics of conduct disorder listed in Table 15–3 suggests that although many of the youths' behaviors during that evening fit the DSM criteria, the teens would not be classified as having a conduct disorder. Their behavior did not seem to be part of a characteristic pattern, but rather occurred as a social phenomenon. They were swept into these antisocial and violent acts through wanting to be seen as manly, daring, and unafraid by their peers. Their acts represent a social phenomenon, which while of great professional concern, is not the same as the behavior that is the focus of abnormal psychology or DSM.

FIGURE 15–8 Police officers search for clues in the area where a group of teenagers raped and beat a jogger in Central Park.

who has been trying to discipline Jeffrey. His mother seems to get some pleasure from his behavior and alternately indulges and punishes him.

TREATMENT Probably the most effective treatment for conduct disorder is prevention. Preventive measures involve helping children to develop skills that will give them successful experiences both now as youngsters and as they grow older. A project designed to enhance preschool children's cognitive development provides an example of the importance of learning skills in preventing later delinquent behavior. In the follow-up to this study the children, then adolescents, were compared to a group of similar background who had not attended the special preschool (Schweinhart & Weikart, 1980). Although the intelligence test scores of children who had been in the preschool group did not differ from those of children in the control group, their motivation and achievement in school and their classroom behavior were superior to those of the controls. Even more important in terms of the treatment of conduct disorders, their self-reports of delinquent behavior were much lower than those reported by the controls. These findings suggest that skill-building may be an important tool for modifying the aggressive behavior that is typical of conduct disorder. If family members are involved in the skill-building program so that they are more likely to reinforce the child's skills at home, school-based programs that teach cognitive or social skills are especially likely to be effective (Miller & Prinz, 1990).

For skill-building to be helpful, the way the child customarily evaluates situations must be taken into account. One interesting difference between aggressive and nonaggressive children is that the former show more bias in interpreting the causes of social interactions (Milich & Dodge, 1984). In situations in which the cause was not obvious—for example, being hit on the back with a ball—aggressive children are more likely to interpret the act as hostile. Sometimes this response may be caused by past experiences. For example, a psychologist reported the following incident:

I was treating an aggressive adolescent boy named Rocky twice per week on a long-term basis. We had built a good, warm relationship. One day I saw Rocky in the hallway and approached him from behind as he talked to a peer. I touched him on the shoulder and began to say hello when he turned around and impulsively punched me in the jaw. As soon as he realized whom he had hit, he apologized profusely saying

that he thought I must have been another patient on the ward. It was painfully clear to me that Rocky had been perceptually ready to perceive an attack from another.

—Dodge, 1985, p. 93

One way of dealing with these aggressive responses might be to devise interventions that aim at debiasing perceptions (Kendall and others, 1990). In this type of intervention, children learn to cognitively review the answers to a series of questions before acting. These include not only what led up to the situation and what happened, but also the long as well as the short term outcomes of the response that might be made. In this intervention the children practice the skill of cognitive review by first listening as the instructor reviews appropriate thoughts for a particular situation aloud, then verbally rehearsing appropriate thoughts themselves. As the children learn to apply this technique in other situations they are taught to begin by saying their thoughts aloud. A child might be taught to use the following "think-aloud" procedure when he or she finds a pencil is missing.

Uh oh, my pencil is missing. There, I see that Ronald has it. Now before I go and get it back, let me think about what happened. I'll do it out loud, like my skills leader has told me. Let's see, first I'll say to myself "What happened?" Well, I lost my pencil and Ronald has it. Ronald could have stolen it. Or maybe he just found it and was using it. Or maybe he doesn't know that it is mine. I wonder what Ronald is thinking. I guess I could ask him. I'm not sure which of these is right, but I don't want to get into a fight. I'd rather stay friends with Ronald, because we play basketball together. So I'll give him the benefit of the doubt. Maybe he just found it. I'll go ask him to return it.

—Dodge, 1985, p. 101

For this kind of approach to be effective, the child must have a warm working relationship with a clinician or some other person with whom he or she can have a series of positive social encounters. The positive encounter must happen over and over again to demonstrate to the child that his or her initial negative expectations were not accurate. Even then it may be difficult for the child to generalize the experience to other people, especially peers (Kazdin and others, 1989).

Early aggression and the attributions that evoke it

is an especially important problem because of evidence of a strong connection between aggressiveness from ages 10 to 13 and adult delinquency, including violent crime and damage to public property (Stattin & Magnusson, 1989).

Internalizing Disorders

While it is hard not to notice the disruptive behavior of children with hyperactivity and conduct disorder, it may be easy to overlook the problems of children who are quiet and struggle with inner concerns. We might think of hyperactivity and conduct disorders as *externalizing* disorders, and conditions in which anxiety and depression predominate as **internalizing disorders.** While *overt* activity (undesirable behavior) is the outstanding feature of externalizing disorders, *covert* activity (worries, disturbing thoughts) is the clinical problem in internalizing disorders. Internalizing disorders are often difficult to detect and their seriousness may tend to be underestimated by parents and teachers.

Internalizing disorders occur about equally in boys and girls, although they tend to be somewhat more frequent in girls. In contrast, as we have seen, externalizing disorders are much more frequent in boys. Another distinction is that children with internalizing disorders do not usually have the academic problems found with ADHD children or youngsters with conduct disorder.

In general, internalizing disorders respond better to treatment and are less likely to continue into adolescence and adulthood than childhood behavior disorders. Only about one-third of children with internalizing disorders still have those disorders four or five years later (Richman and others, 1982).

The internalizing disorders that are most common in children include several kinds of anxiety disorders—separation anxiety, generalized anxiety, phobias, obsessive–compulsive disorders—and depression. As children grow older, anxiety symptoms may decrease. However, children who are very high in anxiety, although they may no longer have an anxiety disorder, seldom move to the low end of the anxiety scale. Depression becomes more frequent in adolescence.

Children report fewer specific fears as they grow older. There are also changes in many fear patterns that seem to be related to the child's developmental progress. Some fears occur so frequently in infancy that they are not considered abnormal. These include fear of noises, falling, and strange objects or people. Such fears reach a peak about the age of two and usually decline rapidly after that.

As children grow older, they acquire the ability to both remember the accustomed pattern of past events and to anticipate the future. When this happens, their fears are likely to change. Instead of being afraid of what is happening in a given situation, children begin to anticipate and to worry about what may happen. The sections that follow will examine the most common forms of internalizing disorders, for children of different ages.

Anxiety Disorders of Childhood

Anxiety in children takes many forms. Some children are preoccupied with thoughts about terrible (and unlikely) things that might happen to them or their families; others show a general social anxiety in which they shrink from contact with people or even refuse to speak for long periods. Still others have phobias, or unrealistic fears of specific objects or places, that may greatly interfere with their everyday living. Some children develop obsessive–compulsive behaviors. Some of these problems are unique to children, and others occur in adults as well. Clinicians' interest in childhood anxiety disorders is increasing as it becomes clear that these anxiety disorders are far more common during childhood than previously had been believed.

FEARS AND PHOBIAS Most children's fears disappear as they grow older, even without treatment (see Figure 15–9). On the other hand, some children's fears

FIGURE 15–9 Frequency of fears across age.
(Based on King and others, 1989)

FIGURE 15–10 When a child witnesses a trusted person calmly modeling a non-fearful response, he or she may ultimately be able to take the next step and try the behavior, find it does not produce a negative result, and extinguish the former phobic response.

are intense and disturbing and are appropriate objects of professional concern even if they may disappear spontaneously later. To appreciate the impact of a childhood phobia on the child and her family, imagine Cindy, age 8, who has an unreasonable fear of dogs. She will not go out to play even in her own fenced yard because a dog might come near. She is unable to walk to school or go on errands, so she must be chauffeured everywhere.

Animal phobias, social phobias, and other fears that continue beyond the age at which they normally would disappear can often be treated effectively using some kind of behavioral approach such as systematic desensitization or modeling (see Figure 15–10). At the beginning of therapy the fearful child observes another child or adult interacting in the feared situation. Then, after a number of sessions, the fearful child is encouraged to approach the feared object gradually until finally he or she interacts with it as the model does. This adaptation of social-learning theory, stimulated by the work of Albert Bandura and others (Bandura & Menlove, 1968), is often used successfully in treating frequently occurring fears.

Modeling of a somewhat different sort, called **symbolic modeling,** can be used to prepare children for frightening and unfamiliar situations such as hospitalization and dental work. This procedure typically uses a realistic film that shows the child what to expect. Studies have shown that symbolic modeling may be an effective aid in reducing anxiety (Melamed & Bush, 1986).

The perspective from which a phobia is viewed is important in determining both the cause of its develop-

ment and the kind of therapy used. A psychodynamically oriented clinician would help a phobic child identify the feelings that may have aroused the phobic reaction. A behaviorally oriented clinician would concentrate on helping the child tolerate the feared object by exposing him or her to the fear-producing situation. A cognitive therapist would be interested in the history of the fear, at least in order to determine what thoughts the feared stimulus evokes. Cognitive therapy would teach the child to be aware of the irrationality of these thoughts and help him or her substitute more adaptive ways of thinking in the phobic situation.

OVERANXIOUS DISORDER While some children are anxious primarily in a situation with a specific fear-provoking stimulus, other children seem to be more generally anxious and to worry excessively and have unrealistic fears most of the time. Figure 15–11 offers a humorous look at some of the thoughts a child like this may have. Children who have such excessive worries for six months or longer have been described as having an **overanxious disorder.** Children with this disorder tend to worry a great deal about upcoming events such as regular visits to the doctor or school examinations. Even routine events such as keeping appointments and deadlines are sources of considerable worry and preoccupation for them. Such children usually have a poor self-concept and worry a great deal about social acceptance and other types of social evaluation.

Children with overanxious disorder often have a variety of physical complaints such as headaches or stomachaches for which no physical cause can be found.

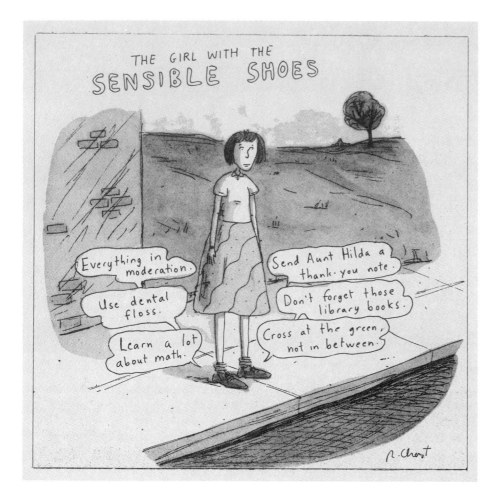

FIGURE 15–11 Sometimes worries of anxious children seem like a replay of all the worries and concerns they may have heard from anxious parents.

(Drawing b/ R. Chast; © 1981 The New Yorker Magazine, Inc.)

Children who are the oldest in small families and those who have families that put a focus on achievement are especially likely to develop this disorder. The child's mother is also more likely than average to have an anxiety disorder herself. Children who are excessively anxious in early life are more likely than others to develop some kind of anxiety disorder—either generalized anxiety or a phobic disorder—in their adult lives (Klein & Last, 1989).

OBSESSIVE–COMPULSIVE DISORDERS Obsessions involve the persistent intrusion of intense, unwanted senseless thoughts, while compulsions are marked by repetitive, ritualistic behaviors. Many children engage in mild rituals and obsessions as part of their normal development. Bedtime and dressing rituals are common in toddlers, preschool children, and younger grade school children. Compulsions, such as trivial motor acts, are also common. A young child may stroke his or her blanket continuously before falling asleep or may suck his or her thumb only at bedtime. Even children's games reflect these rituals. Children often chant rhymes or songs in a repetitive fashion or feel compelled to avoid certain objects, such as sidewalk cracks. Such behaviors rarely are maladaptive in childhood. Sometimes, however, certain acts develop into more disruptive **obsessive–compulsive** and **ritualistic** behaviors that require treatment.

In general the outlook for children who engage in severe obsessive–compulsive behavior often is not promising; about 50 percent do not make a substantial recovery (Elkins and others, 1980). They spend most of their day in rituals and obsessive thoughts, and this severely restricts their functioning. Fortunately, such a severe degree of obsessive–compulsive behavior in childhood is rare. Two cases, adolescent patients who were hospitalized because of the severity of their problems, are described in the following excerpt:

Patient A was a 14-year-old boy who began washing eight to ten times a day after his family moved to a new neighborhood when he was four. After that, he had only occasional episodes until about two years ago, when he began washing excessively because of fear of sperm on his body.

Table 15–4

Major Symptoms in Children and Adolescents with Severe Obsessive–compulsive Disorder

Symptom	Percentage Reporting Symptom
Excessive or ritualized handwashing, showering, bathing, tooth brushing	85
Repeating rituals (e.g., going in and out of doors)	51
Checking (e.g., doors, locks, stoves, appliances)	46

SOURCE: Based on Swedo and others, 1989

He also had obsessive thoughts of death and compulsively checked light switches. He had been treated both by psychotherapy and with antipsychotic drugs. At school, he was quiet and unaggressive, participated in many activities, and was a good student. His parents had a mutually supportive relationship and were of middle class socioeconomic status. All his siblings were well; however, his father was mildly depressed.

Patient B was also 14 years old. For the last two years, she had washed herself excessively, and was preoccupied by number rituals, such as the compulsion to perform all her daily acts in multiples of six. Until her symptoms developed, she had no obsessive traits, was a good student, and had many friends. She had been treated by psychotherapy for one year. Her symptoms began suddenly at a time when her father's business failed. Both parents, of middle class socioeconomic status, were alcoholic.

—Adapted from Rapoport and others, 1981, p. 1548

These adolescents were among nine hospitalized children who were studied by Judith Rapoport and her co-workers. Although none of the children could function effectively because of the severity of their obsessive–compulsive problems, none showed any signs of disordered thinking and all were able to discuss their problems sensibly. All of the children showed some depressive symptoms. Only three met the criteria for major depressive disorder at the time of hospitalization, but all would have met those criteria at some time in the past. Before their symptoms began, their development had not been particularly unusual. In general, they were good, but not outstanding students, and they seemed somewhat timid, although they were not excessively withdrawn.

Clinical research is uncovering information that may prove useful in understanding and treating obsessive–compulsive disorders in children. In general, these disorders resemble adult obsessive–compulsive disorders (see Chapters 6 and 9). The disorder is more common in boys than in girls, and perhaps 25 percent of immediate family members of children with obsessive–compulsive disorder have had somewhat similar disorders. Children with the disorder may have psychological problems over a long period of time (Flament, 1990). Table 15–4 lists the most common symptoms seen in severe childhood obsessive–compulsive disorders.

SEPARATION ANXIETY DISORDER One disorder that occurs mainly in childhood is **separation anxiety disorder.** Children with this disorder show excessive anxiety or even panic when they are not with major attachment figures, usually parents, or in familiar surroundings. Such children may be unable to stay in rooms by themselves and may refuse to go to school or visit friends' homes. When such children are asked why they are afraid, they may express fear of getting lost and never finding their parents again. Or they may have greatly exaggerated fears of animals, monsters, kidnappers, muggers, and of accidents or illness that may strike them or their parents. Very often such children complain of nausea, headaches, abdominal pains, or rapid heart rate. Sometimes, especially in older children, anxiety or panic is anticipated and seen when the time for the separation approaches.

In early childhood all children experience some separation anxiety (see Figure 15–12). This normal developmental stage is different from the excessive reaction to separation that may occur if older children develop a separation anxiety disorder. Another important point is that even older children may react strongly at the time of a separation from a parent or other person with whom they have a close relationship without being diagnosed with separation anxiety disorder. This diagnosis is given only if the disturbed behavior lasts an unusually long time—at least two weeks. It is this lasting quality, rather than the occurrence of distress and

FIGURE 15–12 For the period beginning before an infant's first birthday and extending for about 18 months, most children experience distress when they are about to be separated from a parent. This desire to stay in contact with the attachment figure may have biological roots. Through natural selection, infants of all species who stayed close to their mothers were more likely to survive.

concern about separation when it occurs, that distinguishes this disorder.

Children with separation anxiety disorder often have trouble going to sleep and insist that someone stay with them until they do fall asleep. Another way children express this anxiety is by waking during the night and getting into bed with a parent or sibling. Although these children may have no interpersonal difficulties when separation is not an issue, if they are away from home they may be extremely homesick and miserable or even panic. Under such circumstances they withdraw from social activity and are unable to concentrate on work or play.

Many times separation anxiety disorder develops after the child experiences some life stress. This could be a loss through death of a relative or pet or a threatened loss such as a serious illness in the family. Parental

separation or divorce or moving to a new neighborhood also may help precipitate this disorder. Why some children have this reaction to stress and others don't isn't clear. Neglected children are not likely to develop separation anxiety disorder; instead, children with this disorder are likely to come from families that are caring and close-knit. Some tendency to experience separation anxiety may run in families: It seems to be more common in close biological relatives of children with the disorder than in the general population.

It may be that children who develop a separation disorder have experienced some difficulties during the attachment process that many theorists believe takes place in the first two years of the child's life. The establishment of a secure attachment is considered important in preventing later psychological disorders, especially depression (Bowlby, 1980). Research on children who are securely attached shows that as they grow older they become more independent and better able to form good social relationships than other children.

The treatment of separation anxiety can be approached in a variety of ways depending on the features of particular cases. In some instances, the key to treatment is a behavioral approach in which an attempt is made to extinguish anxiety by increasing separation time. This approach requires the cooperation of both parents and the child and the help of the therapist in preparing the child for the separation attempts. Sometimes puppet play and role play with the therapist assuming the role of the child and displaying adaptive reactions to fantasied separations are helpful. The same puppet play technique might be used from a psychodynamic perspective in attempts to deal with the causes of the separation anxiety. A common cause of treatment failure with separation anxiety disorder lies in the inability of the parents to cooperate with the therapeutic program. This is particularly true when the child lives with a single parent who is socially isolated and highly dependent on the child. It is also a problem if parents have unresolved separation anxiety of their own that makes them powerless to stand aside. In such cases, a family therapy approach might be helpful for the child's problem.

Depression in Children and Adolescents

Helen knew something was wrong with her 12-year-old daughter, but she couldn't quite put her finger on it. Some days Nancy moped in her room, other days she was just quiet. There were times when she had angry outbursts for no reason at all, and she was terribly irritable. In

Table 15–5

Common Signs of Depression in Children and Adolescents

While either boys or girls may show these symptoms, they tend to be more common in one sex than the other.

More Common in Girls

1. Body image distortion. Feeling "ugly" or otherwise unattractive.
2. Loss of appetite and weight; eating less and eating erratically.
3. Lack of satisfaction. Being upset about herself, about life at school and at home, and about social life.

More Common in Boys

1. Irritability. Being easily angered and hostile; snapping at family, friends and teachers.
2. Social withdrawal. Ceasing to spend time with friends; spending most of the time alone.
3. Drop in school performance. Loss of interest in and enthusiasm about school and other activities.

addition, she seemed to have lost interest in eating. At first, Helen wrote it off as typical "preteen stuff." When her husband disagreed, they took Nancy to her pediatrician who referred her to a child psychiatrist. The diagnosis was depression.

Childhood is often pictured as a happy time of little responsibility, endless play, and infinite enjoyment. In fact, though, many children often think such thoughts as: "I'm dumb, ugly, and stupid," "I wish I were dead," and "You don't love me." Studies confirm that many youngsters often feel sad. In one study, about 10 to 12 percent of the 10-year-olds in a school district population were described by parents and teachers as often appearing miserable, unhappy, tearful, or distressed. When the children were interviewed, their responses created the same impression (Rutter and others, 1981). Table 15–5 lists common signs of depression in children and adolescents.

Depressed mood occurs less frequently in young children and becomes more common in adolescence. Among pre-adolescents, studies have found prevalence rates ranging from .5 to 2.7 percent. Among adolescents, the percentages show a threefold increase over the pre-adolescent figures (Fleming and others, 1989). DSM does not contain a special diagnostic category or description for depression in childhood; instead, it uses the adult criteria with minor modifications. Many questions remain to be answered about childhood depression because its characteristics are variable depending upon the age of the child and his or her cognitive and social abilities. The consequences of childhood-onset depression for future development are not yet clear (Kovacs & Goldstein, 1991).

LONG-TERM PATTERNS Depression is frequent among children who come to clinical attention and may also be relatively long-lasting. In one study of children 8 to 13 years old (Kovacs, 1985), it took one-and-a-half years before 92 percent of children who met the criteria for major depressive disorder (see Chapter 10) had recovered (see Figure 15–13). The chances of another occurrence of depression were also high. Seventy-two percent of these children had a second episode within five

FIGURE 15–13 Duration of depressive disorders in children.

(Data from Kovacs, 1985)

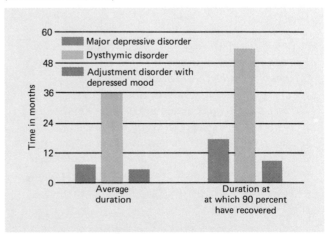

years. While depression in childhood sometimes is relatively brief, some children experience depression through a large part of their lives. In general, the earlier the onset of the syndrome the more severe mood disturbances are likely to be in adulthood (Harrington and others, 1990). In one longitudinal study, several children showed differing but long-continuing patterns of depression (Chess and others, 1983).

At 8 years of age, Harold had been having behavioral problems for a year. He disliked school, was shy, and had few friends. He was moody, quiet, and afraid of new situations. Because there had been several problems in his life—his parents had separated when he was 6 and his mother had been briefly hospitalized for severe depression—it was unclear whether his depression was due to these events or to other causes. Things improved, but at 12 Harold became depressed again and disliked school intensely. At 17 he reported that he could "step into an unhappy mood for no apparent reason" and then would feel tired and irritable and would avoid people. Shortly after this he became severely depressed for about two weeks and was treated with antidepressant drugs. At 22 he had moved to his own apartment. He made some money mopping floors but was basically supported by his mother. He spent most of his time practicing music—he had taught himself to play the piano, banjo, and guitar. He summarized his existence as going from "slow deadness to acute crisis" and described recurrent depressions at ages 9, 15, 18, and 19, each of which lasted months even when treated with antidepressant drugs.

—Adapted from Chess and others, 1983, pp. 413–414

Sylvia's depression was not noted until she was 21, after months of an intense obsessive preoccupation that her skin and hair were terribly ugly, which was not true. She threatened to drop out of college, and although she had top grades and was attending a top-level school she had changed colleges twice. She was hospitalized briefly and for the next year made many suicidal threats and a few suicidal attempts and then gradually improved.

During her therapy sessions she reported that she had been depressed even as far back as age 8

and had always covered it over with a veneer of cheerfulness and friendliness. This was substantiated by some poems she had written from ages 12 to 15 which were filled with melancholy and hopelessness. She did not report any life events that could explain the cause of her depression, although she did have several family members who had been depressed.

—Adapted from Chess and others, 1983, p. 415

Below, we will look at a few possible causes of longstanding patterns of depression in young people such as Harold and Sylvia.

CAUSES OF DEPRESSIVE DISORDERS Clinically depressed children and adolescents often seem similar to depressed adults when differences in developmental stages are taken into account. This correspondence might suggest that depressive disorders in youngsters and adults have similar causes. However, current evidence does not yet support such a conclusion.

Heredity is believed to be an important factor in the development of depression. Two types of studies concerning this possibility have been conducted. In *top-down studies*, the subjects are children, one or both of whose parents is depressed. In *bottom-up* studies, the adult relatives of depressed children are studied (Gelfand & Teti, 1990). Both types of studies find a clustering of depression within families. Environmental factors are also important, as suggested by the fact that undesirable family environments and poor relationships with parents, siblings, and peers are common in children with mood disorders. Behavioral approaches to these disorders direct attention to learning processes, environmental influences, and skill acquisition and deficits. Symptoms of depression are considered to result from problems of interacting with the environment. There is evidence that having a mother who is depressed is especially detrimental to a child. Maternal depression is associated with undesirable parenting practices such as unresponsiveness, inattentiveness, intrusiveness, inept discipline, and negative perceptions of children (Gelfand & Teti, 1990). Chapter 10 reviews several theories of depression in general, many of which apply to affective disorders in children and adolescents. In order to work effectively with young people suffering from these disorders, clinicians could benefit from an interactive view of depression's causes.

SUICIDAL BEHAVIOR IN CHILDHOOD AND ADOLESCENCE Thoughts of suicide and even suicide attempts do occur in young children. In one group of children between the ages of 6 and 12 who were seen at a mental health outpatient clinic, more than one-third had thought about suicide or had threatened or at-

tempted suicide (Pfeffer and others, 1980). The suicide methods tried or considered included jumping from high places, hanging themselves, running in front of cars, stabbing themselves, and swallowing pills. Negative perception of family environment is one of the strongest predictors of suicide, of suicidal attempts, and of suicidal thoughts among depressed children (Kranz & Moos, 1987). Suicidal children see their family environment as unsupportive, stressful, and high in conflict.

Not all children who kill themselves are depressed. Children who are angry or have personality disorders and problems of impulse control also are likely to kill themselves (Stillion and others, 1989). Feelings of hopelessness may also increase the probability of suicide attempts.

Rates of suicide and attempted suicide increase sharply during adolescence. Younger children do kill themselves, but suicide before age 10 is rare. From ages 10 to 14 the rate of suicide increases a hundredfold, and between age 15 and 19 there is an additional tenfold increase. In the United States a teenager tries to commit suicide every 1.1 seconds. Every 80 seconds, a teenager succeeds (Federal Centers for Disease Control, 1987). Suicide among teenagers is now the second-most likely cause of death among this group.

A number of possible factors for increased suicide in young people have been suggested, including changes in family structure, an increase in alcohol and substance abuse, and pessimism about the future over such things as a lack of personal opportunities in adulthood and the threat of nuclear war. Each of these has some data to support it (Simmons, 1987). For example, teenagers who attempt suicide are likely to come from families that are violent and often in the process of breaking apart. These families frequently show disturbed, dysfunctional communication patterns, histories of abnormal behavior in the parents, and evidence of sexual abuse (Spirit and others, 1989).

Drug use also may play a role. More than half of the adolescent suicides in one study had received a primary diagnosis of substance abuse (Murphy and others, 1986). Another explanation for the increased suicide rate lies in the idea that if there are more people in a particular cohort group, as has been the case with adolescents during most of this period, there is more competition for jobs and health services and also for teacher attention and academic honors.

WORKING CLINICALLY WITH DEPRESSED CHILDREN Depression is hardest to assess in very young children, since they have difficulty describing their emotional state. While fear can be inferred from behavior, facial expressions, and physiological responses, depression is harder to assess because of the importance of its cognitive components. It is important when interviewing a child about possible depression to ask questions in simple, concrete language. For example, few preschoolers spontaneously volunteer they feel sad but will express sad feelings when carefully questioned.

When a child is thought to be depressed, the first step is to establish whether that diagnosis fits. One way to do this is by conducting a structured interview with parents about developmental history, duration of symptoms, present behavior, and functioning in the family. The teacher can add information about school behavior and performance. However, many parents and teachers fail to note depression until the symptoms become quite severe, even in adolescents whose cognitive development should allow them to communicate these feelings. Agreement among the reports of parents, teachers, and the child about a variety of emotional problems is greater for 6- to 11-year-olds than for adolescents (Achenbach and others, 1987).

A structured interview with the child can convey important information. One approach is to use an adaptation of an interview used to diagnose depressed adults. A child's version of the Schedule for Affective Disorders and Schizophrenia (known as "Kiddie SADS") has been shown to measure depression in children reliably although not as well as in adults (Chambers and others, 1985). Because an individual interview with the child by a mental health professional is costly, other less expensive methods of getting information such as questionnaires are often used. One questionnaire frequently used for screening children is the Children's Depression Inventory (Kovacs & Beck, 1977).

The traditional approach to treating depressed children has been psychodynamically oriented therapy. More recently, behavioral therapy and family therapy have also been frequent choices. Behavioral therapy is often oriented toward helping the child learn social skills or assertive behavior. In many cases researchers have found that depressed children have depressed parents. Although this correlation may suggest a genetic link, it may also indicate that such children have learned to cope with stress in the same maladaptive way that their depressed parents do. Behavioral therapists can provide models of nondepressed coping styles by demonstrating effective behavior for the child. Family therapy can be an effective way to work with depressed children and their parents. Interacting with the parents and child together may help the therapist evaluate family interaction styles and also serve as a vehicle for increasing family member's understanding of their psychological impacts on each other.

Cognitive therapy is also appropriate because of the evidence that depressed children feel incompetent. One study of children 8 to 17 years old found that depressed adolescents and preadolescents had strong beliefs in their own incompetence (Weisz and others, 1987). The depression did not seem to be related to their perception

of a lack of connection between their behavior and the outcome. In other words, unlike what is sometimes seen in adults, these children did not view what happened to them as a lack of available reinforcement. Instead, as do some other depressed adults, they believed the lack of reinforcement occurred because they deserved none.

Antidepressant drugs are used to treat depression in children and adolescents as well as in adults. Tricyclic medication is as readily prescribed for adolescents as it is for adults. Among younger children, only those who are severely depressed seem to respond to tricyclics in the same way that adults do (Toolan, 1981). Because of the lack of information about the effects of such drugs during these crucial years of physical and cognitive development, most clinicians use them with great care.

The following case, involving an adolescent girl, shows the effectiveness of an intervention that combines psychotherapy and antidepressant medication.

Bridget is a depressed 16-year-old who went to a hospital emergency room after cutting her wrists with a razor blade. She was withdrawn, downcast, at times crying quietly, and nervously avoiding eye contact with the interviewer. She reported that she first began feeling miserable and hopeless about two months ago. She found she could not concentrate at school, her grades dropped from A's and B's to C's and D's, she stopped calling her friends, and she showed no interest in her piano lessons despite her aspiration to be a musician. Two weeks ago she stopped attending school, stating that she had neither the energy nor the interest to continue. She eats very little, thinks she may have lost some weight, and for the past month has been waking up at about five o'clock in the morning and is unable to get back to sleep. She thinks frequently of suicide, believing that her family would be better off without her. She used to have hopes for the future but now sees nothing good for herself, explaining that she will never complete school or obtain a good job.

Bridget recalls that life was always hard but never this hard. Her parents separated when she was three, and for the past 12 years she has lived with her mother and stepfather, who is also an alcoholic. Bridget reported that her stepfather beat her mother when he was drunk but never hit her. At the time of referral, Bridget and her mother were living in a downtown shelter for battered women, and the staff there had encouraged her to seek help.

Bridget has had a good initial response to treatment. She was put on antidepressant medication and began twice-weekly psychotherapy sessions. Five weeks after the initial referral, her depressive symptoms had abated markedly. She was back in school and was preparing an application for entry into a music conservatory. She was living in a one-room apartment with her mother, who had found a part-time job. Although Bridget's course of treatment is far from completed, her doctor is cautiously optimistic about the eventual outcome.

Institute of Medicine, 1990, pp. 29–30

Eating Disorders

Among the eating disorders that occur in childhood and adolescence are **pica,** in which the child persistently eats nonfood substances such as paint, string, leaves, or pebbles; **rumination disorder of infancy,** in which the infant regurgitates partially digested food; **anorexia nervosa,** in which adolescents become preoccupied with "feeling fat" and may diet virtually to the point of starvation; and **bulimia nervosa,** or binge eating that is often followed by purging through self-induced vomiting or the use of large doses of laxatives or diuretics. The two disorders that we discuss in this section, anorexia nervosa and bulimia nervosa, are especially prevalent throughout adolescence as well as young adulthood, and are more likely to be found in females than in males.

Anorexia Nervosa

Deborah developed anorexia nervosa when she was 16. A rather shy, studious teenager, she tried hard to please everyone. Nevertheless, she was not particularly popular with boys. When her father jokingly remarked that she would never get a date if she didn't lose ten pounds, she began to diet relentlessly—never stopping or believing she was thin enough. She developed a skeletal appearance. Shortly after the pounds started dropping off, Deborah's menstrual periods ceased. As her anorexia worsened, she became obsessed with food and developed strange eating rituals. She weighed all the food she would eat on a kitchen scale daily, cutting solids into miniscule

pieces and precisely measuring liquids in ounces. She would then put her daily ration in small containers, lining them up in neat rows. She also exercised compulsively, even after she weakened and began fainting. She never took an elevator if she could walk steps. No one was able to convince Deborah that she was in danger. Finally, her doctor insisted she be hospitalized for treatment of her illness. Even in the hospital she secretly continued her exercise regimen in the bathroom, doing numerous sit-ups and knee-bends. It took several hospitalizations and a good deal of individual and family outpatient therapy for Deborah to confront and solve her problems.

Deborah's story is a typical example of anorexia, or self-induced starvation. Sometimes this disorder is not recognized until victims become seriously underweight. No matter how much weight anorexics lose, even if they become emaciated, they are never satisfied, always seeing themselves as too fat.

Although anorexia nervosa has been recognized since the late 1700s and was given its present name in 1874, only recently have its psychological features become a subject of clinical interest. For many years medical opinion held that anorexia nervosa was a result of an endocrine disturbance; the possibility remains today that the condition is due to a disorder of the hypothalamus. (Certain hypothalamic tumors are known to give rise to a distaste for food.) However, most clinicians look to sociocultural pressures and other factors as causes of the disorder.

CHARACTERISTICS OF ANOREXICS Although the term **anorexia nervosa** means "nervous loss of appetite," researchers have found that anorexics are indeed hungry. They have both physiological and cognitive feelings of hunger, together with a strong preoccupation with food. Anorexics are likely to discuss recipes and cook elaborate meals for their families or friends, but do not eat what they prepare. If they do go through the motions of eating with others, most of the time is spent cutting food into tiny pieces and moving it around on the plate. When they actually do consume food, it is usually when they are alone.

To be considered anorexic, a person must refuse to eat to such an extent that his or her body weight is at least 15 percent below the normal level, or fail to gain weight during a period of growth so that his or her body weight is 15 percent below what would be expected. For women, the weight loss must be great enough to result in the absence of at least three consecutive menstrual cycles. Table 15–6 lists the typical characteristics of anorexia nervosa.

Anorexia is most common in middle- and upper-class adolescent females. The first case of anorexia in a black female was not reported until relatively recently (Jones and others, 1980). The disorder is also found in men, but it is much rarer. In a study conducted at a large hospital over a 20-year period, only 9 percent of the patients diagnosed as anorexic were men (Crisp & Burns, 1983).

The primary feature of anorexia nervosa is the obsessive preoccupation with losing weight. Unlike the true reduction of appetite in depressive disorders, there is in anorexia a conscious and deliberate refusal of food. The anorexic is not only preoccupied with weight regulation but also takes pride in the ability to control the

Table 15–6

Behavioral Features of Anorexia Nervosa

Substantial weight loss in a relatively short period

Diet continues although individual becomes bone-thin

Continual setting of new weight goals after one is reached

Dissatisfaction with appearance, claims of feeling fat, even after weight loss goal is reached

Isolated dieting rather than in a diet group

Development of unusual interest in food

Development of strange eating rituals, e.g., cuts food into tiny pieces or measures everything before eating extremely small amounts

Secret eating

Obsessiveness about exercising

Appearance of depression much of the time

Binging and purging

urge to eat (Mizes, 1990). As the following excerpt points out, anorexics often either do not see their weight loss, cessation of menstruation, and other symptoms as important or they are defensive about the subject.

Therapist: *What types of problems are you currently having with eating or weight related matters?*

Patient: *None.*

Therapist: *Why did your doctor refer you here for an evaluation?*

Patient: *Well, she thinks I might have an eating disorder.*

Therapist: *Why would Dr. Smith think that?*

Patient: *Because she thinks I am too skinny, and I haven't had a menstrual period in a year. The doctor talked to my parents, and they told her I never eat, but I eat. I just don't like a lot of stuff that they eat, so I don't eat with them.*

Therapist: *What do you typically eat?*

Patient: *Salads, mostly, and diet frozen dinners.*

—Williamson, 1990, p. 32

CAUSES OF ANOREXIA While the causes of anorexia are unknown, most clinicians and researchers believe that several risk factors play important roles. Prejudice against being fat is strong and emphasis on thinness is high in many cultural groups. Some career choices link thinness and achievement. Special populations (notably dancers and fashion models) are especially at risk for the development of anorexia (Goldbloom & Garfinkel, 1990).

Only one in every 100 to 150 teenage girls age 15 and over becomes anorexic, and the rate is even lower for younger girls. Since most adolescents are exposed to similar sociocultural pressures, the relatively low prevalence of anorexia suggests that other factors may play a role in the development of the disorder.

In their attempts to understand this disorder, researchers have divided anorexics into subgroups: those who are thin primarily because of restricted food intake (the *restrictor* group) and those who, in addition to restricting food intake, use vomiting and purging with laxatives to control their weight (the *bulimic anorexia* group). (Not all bulimics are anorexic. Some are of average weight and use purging only to compensate for the extremely high calorie intake during binges.) There

are a number of differences between the two subgroups: Those in the bulimic anorexic group are more likely than those in the restrictor group to abuse alcohol or drugs and to have other problems of impulse control, such as stealing (Leon & Phelan, 1984). Families of the bulimic anorexics are less stable, have more parental discord and physical health problems, and have experienced more negative events in the recent past. Such families have much higher rates of mood disorders and substance abuse disorders than the families of restrictors (Kog & Vandereycken, 1985). These correlations suggest that genetic factors may play a role in the development of bulimic anorexic disorders.

Some researchers look to dynamics within the family as a possible cause of anorexia. One family therapist who has taken a special interest in anorexic adolescents is Salvador Minuchin (Minuchin and others, 1978). Minuchin has found predominant characteristics in families with an anorexic child: enmeshment, overprotectiveness, rigidity, and lack of conflict resolution. The enmeshed family is one in which no one can be an individual or have a separate identity and the insistence on togetherness results in the lack of privacy. Family members are overprotective; they frequently express concern for each other's welfare and respond protectively to the least sign of distress. Families of anorexics also tend to be very rigid and to resist change. They have what amounts to a storybook image of themselves, and the growth of individuality in an adolescent child is a threat to this picture of perfection. Tolerance for conflict is also extremely low in these families. Some deny that any differences exist among their members, others deal with differences by shifting conversation to other topics. When such tactics are used, conflicts within the family are not resolved. Instead, natural differences accumulate and stress builds up.

CONSEQUENCES OF ANOREXIA Anorexia disturbs the body's functioning in many ways, resulting in such conditions as retarded bone growth, anemia, dry skin, low body temperature and basal metabolism rate, slow heart rate, and lack of tolerance for cold (Rock & Yager, 1987). As we have noted anorexia results in a least a temporary absence of menstrual periods. A number of additional physiological changes are likely to accompany anorexia, especially if there is vomiting. One of these, a low level of serum potassium, may cause cardiac arrhythmia, a tendency toward changes in heart rate that can result in death.

Some researchers believe that these physiological changes may be due to malfunctioning of the hypothalamus (Halmi and others, 1983). The hypothalamus controls the body's water balance, maintenance of body temperature, secretion of the endocrine glands, and fat metabolism. As noted earlier, some physicians believe that hypothalamic malfunctioning may be a cause rather

than a symptom of anorexia. Indeed, it is not clear whether the hypothalamic changes occur before the anorexic behavior begins or as a result of changes in eating behavior. Hypothalamic malfunction may also be related to impairment in dopamine regulation and, thus, to the development of depression. Both types of anorexics show obsessive preoccupations and feel a great deal of stress. Test results from the MMPI personality test (see Chapter 4) also indicate that anorexics are likely to be depressed (Leon and others, 1985) and this depression is likely to continue even after successful treatment for their weight problem (Toner and others, 1986).

One study compared the long-term outcome for both restricting and bulimic anorexic groups and found it to be much the same when either anorexic symptoms or social functioning was considered (Toner and others, 1986) (see Figure 15–14). Both groups were much more likely than a control group to have had an affective or anxiety disorder sometime in their lives. The only differences were that the bulimic group was more likely to have a substance abuse disorder than the restricting group. Depression seems to be a continuing problem for anorexic patients. A long-term follow-up study of 151 former anorexia patients found that nine had died an average of seven years after their first medical contact with anorexia, seven of them by suicide (Tolstrup and others, 1985).

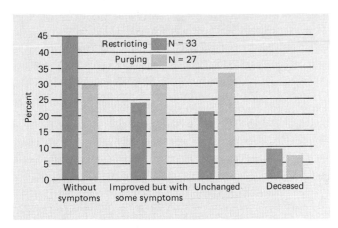

FIGURE 15–14 Groups of anorexic individuals who restrict their food intake and those that use purging for weight control show little difference in outcome after treatment.

(Adapted from Toner and others, 1986, p. 526)

THERAPY FOR ANOREXIA Psychologists have only recently begun to develop treatment plans for eating disorders. Treatments range from individual approaches (including psychotherapy and drugs) to family therapy, group therapy, and intensive inpatient or outpatient programs involving all of these approaches (see Figure 15–15). Anorexics may also receive coping skills train-

FIGURE 15–15 For some people who are severely affected by anorexia, a residential treatment center, such as the one shown here, may offer the most effective treatment setting.

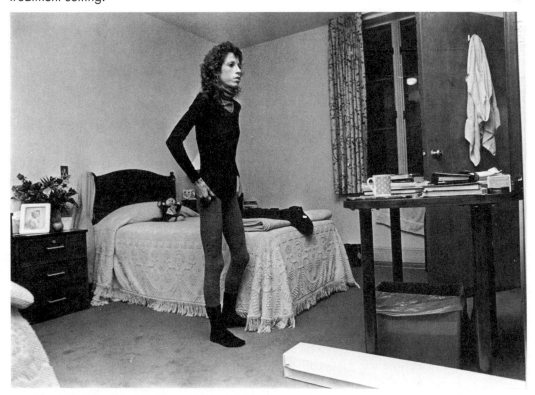

ing, assertiveness training, and nutritional education. The scientific merits of the various approaches remain to be established.

Two major therapeutic approaches used in treating anorexics are behavioral methods and family therapy; these techniques are often used together and combined with nutrition management. In behavioral programs hospital privileges are made dependent on weight gain. While this technique often leads to increases in body weight, it has some negative features. If the weight gain required is too great (some programs have required a half-pound gain per day), patients may develop bulimia and use laxatives and vomiting as a method of weight control (Leon & Phelan, 1984). They are also likely to show poor social adjustment. Cognitive–behavioral approaches have also been used to treat anorexia. These therapeutic methods focus on the faulty thinking that seems to contribute to the unrealistic body image of some anorexics. Cognitive interventions are usually combined with other approaches. Nutritional counseling is usually included as well. Emphasis is placed on establishing normal eating patterns.

Some researchers have focused on family therapy, especially for younger anorexics. Family therapist Salvadore Minuchin employed a specific course of family therapy that proved very effective. Minuchin and his co-workers followed most of their first 50 anorexic cases for at least two-and-a-half years after treatment began. They reported a recovery rate of 86 percent, with recovery defined as no symptom of eating disturbance or psychosocial difficulty at home, at school, or with peers (Minuchin and others, 1978). This study focused on young girls (average age 14) who had very recently begun to show anorexic symptoms. It is possible that this high recovery rate might not occur with older anorexics with more established eating (or noneating) habits.

Bulimia Nervosa

In **bulimia nervosa**, or binge eating, the person is aware of his or her abnormal eating patterns, afraid of being unable to stop eating, and likely to be depressed and self-critical about this behavior. In bulimia, binge eating occurs at least twice a week for at least three months and is often accompanied by laxative use, self-induced vomiting, or rigorous dieting in order to compensate for the binge behavior. Many anorexic patients have symptoms of bulimia; they are called bulimic anorexics or purging anorexics. But other people are bulimic without being very thin. Bulimics may be of average or above-average weight. Some researchers have suggested that bulimia is a type of depression and should be classified as an affective disorder. But as of now the evidence does not uphold this view (Hinz and William-

son, 1987). We can only say with surety that bulimia, like many other chronic disorders, is often accompanied by depression. The following case gives an example of a typical bulemic.

Lisa became bulimic at 18. Her strange eating behavior began when she started to diet. Although she dieted and exercised to lose weight, periodically she ate huge amounts of food and attempted to counter the effects of the extra calories and to maintain her normal weight by forcing herself to vomit.

Lisa often felt like an emotional powder keg, by turns, angry, frightened, and depressed. Sometimes she stole things on impulse; sometimes she drank too much. Sometimes she couldn't stop eating for hours. Unable to understand her own behavior, she thought no one else would either. She felt isolated and lonely. Typically, when things were not going well, she would be overcome with an uncontrollable desire for sweets. She literally ate pounds of candy and cake at a time, and often didn't stop until she was exhausted or in severe pain. Then, overwhelmed with guilt and disgust, she would force herself to vomit.

Her eating habits so embarrassed her that she kept them secret until, depressed by her mounting problems, she attempted suicide. Luckily, she didn't succeed. While recuperating in the hospital, she was referred to an eating disorders clinic where she became involved in group therapy. There she received the understanding and help she so desperately needed from others who had bulimia.

THE BINGE–PURGE CYCLE Binge eaters are generally on some sort of weight-reduction diet, and the binge represents their falling "off the wagon." They may binge only at certain times rather than continuously, and may hide food and eat in secret. Bulimics may consume prodigious amounts of food during one of these binges. Between 2000 and 5000 calories are usually consumed per binge, up to twice as many calories as most people consume in a day. Most binge eaters consume easily prepared, high-calorie foods such as potato chips, fast food, bread, and sweets, and many focus their binges on particular foods. Binges often occur while the person is at home alone watching TV or browsing through a magazine, or in a car or fast-food restaurant. If food runs

Table 15–7

Features of Bulimia Nervosa

Regular binges (large amounts of food eaten over a short period of time)

Binges often accompanied by regular forced vomiting and/or drugs used to stimulate vomiting, bowel movements, and urination

Despite frequent diet and exercise, individual maintains or regains weight

Secret eating

Enormous amounts of food eaten at one sitting, but no weight gain

Drug or alcohol abuse; may steal regularly

Appearance of depression much of the time

Swollen neck glands

Scars on the back of hands from forced vomiting

out during a binge, the bulimic may rush out to buy more. Bulimics tend to eat in an unsystematic manner; they binge, do not eat for a day, and then binge again. Table 15–7 lists some common characteristics of bulimia.

Binge eating is quite common among college women, but clinically significant bulimic behavior is not. And even when the criteria for bulimic behavior are met, the condition may not be long lasting. Even though bulimia is sometimes described as an epidemic on college campuses, that is not true unless one is referring to self-reported overeating with or without occasional purging. Although two-thirds of college women report eating binges, these are not as severe or frequent as those of bulimics and are not usually accompanied by self-induced vomiting or the use of laxatives. Only 1.3 percent of college women can be classified as bulimic (Schotte & Stunkard, 1987).

Attempts to explain bulimia have focused on the role of negative cognitive–emotional states in bringing on binge episodes. Pressure at work or school and problems with personal relationships often precede binges, and most bulimics feel anxious, depressed, and somewhat guilty before a binge. They also report that their binges are prompted by contact with certain people, most frequently their mothers but sometimes their boyfriends, fathers, and sisters (Carrol & Leon, 1981).

During their binges most bulimics feel immediate relief from anxiety and depression. This suggests that they may be using binge eating as a means of coping with stress. If this is the case, teaching them alternative coping skills should be an important part of therapy.

In the postbinge period most bulimics feel disgust and anger at their lack of self-control, guilt over having eaten "forbidden" foods that violate their strict and unrealistic diet standards, and depression at their inability to stop binging. These negative postbinge feelings are

thought to serve as a cue for purging which undoes the eating act and leads to a decrease in negative feelings. Postbinge purging in the form of vomiting has been reported by most bulimics. Purging alone often is not enough to produce a better mood, however. In one study, most bulimic individuals reported thoughts about suicide at the conclusion of the binge–purge cycle (Goldbloom & Garfinkel, 1990). This negative state can serve as a precipitating factor for another cycle.

Bulimia is not just an eating problem. It is associated with poor overall adjustment. Not only do bulimics experience depression and anxiety unusually strongly, but they also have poor skills for coping with these feelings. In addition to the psychological consequences of anxiety, depression, and guilt, the binge–purge cycle can also have distressing physical results. The most serious of these are due to the potassium imbalance from frequent vomiting, which can lead to muscle weakness and also to heart problems. Vomiting can also damage the esophagus and tooth enamel and increase tooth decay.

Bulimia may be related to a genetic component of mood disorders, as is suggested by the higher incidence of both mood disorders and alcoholism in relatives of bulimic individuals. However, other psychological factors may also contribute to bulimic behavior. It seems likely that certain personality factors make some people more vulnerable to family and social experiences that have a negative effect on self-esteem and feelings of self-efficacy.

TREATMENT OF BULIMIA A variety of cognitive and behavioral techniques have been used with bulimics. Treatment, focused on breaking the binge–purge cycle either by preventing binges or by preventing purges, often involves self-monitoring (keeping records of antecedents and consequences related to binge eating and purging); relaxation training; identifying and modifying

cognitive distortions; and altering the environment as necessary.

Antidepressant drugs are also used to treat bulimia. In some cases these are initially helpful in reducing the rate of binging, but relapses may occur when the medication is stopped. Some clinicians have combined antidepressants with other therapeutic approaches. One study found that, while a combination of group therapy and antidepressants yielded positive results, most of the therapeutic effect was attributable to the group therapy (Mitchell & others, 1990). Behavioral, cognitive, and psychodynamic treatment may be more effective than the use of antidepressant drugs in enhancing coping skills and thereby preventing relapse.

Therapy for Children and Adolescents

Although many of the therapeutic approaches developed for adults can be used directly, or in slightly modified form, with older children and adolescents, many times the most effective approach to therapy for young children is to work with the parent instead of the child. This type of therapy may have several purposes:

1. To help the parent understand the way children develop and the kinds of behavior typical of different ages.
2. To show the parent adaptive ways to deal with the child, for instance, how to play with a young child or how to use constructive methods of motivation rather than harsh discipline.
3. To suggest ways to improve family interactions that may be causing stress for the parents or the child or both.

When therapy focused on the child seems more appropriate, several differences between therapy for children and for adults must be considered:

1. Children rarely initiate treatment for themselves and typically do not understand the purpose of mental health services. Therefore, some children actively resist being taken for treatment.
2. The child's parents must have ongoing participation in the therapy process. Not only must the parents initiate, continue, and finance treatment, but they usually must modify their own behavior in certain respects.
3. Often children are referred for therapy because they are deviating from the normal pattern of develop-

ment. This means therapy must be at least partly directed toward attaining those norms if that is possible.

While many therapies that are used with adults have been adapted for use with children, researchers have also developed some methods that are uniquely suited to young children. Play therapy, storytelling techniques, and parent-administered behavior-modification programs are examples of therapies specially tailored for children.

Play Therapy

Because young children's limited verbal skills make traditional "talking" therapy inappropriate, many therapists employ **play therapy.** They meet with the child in a playroom and use the child's play activities or play interactions between the child and the therapist as a therapeutic vehicle (see Figure 15–16). Therapists use play to help children act out their feelings, face them, and learn to control them:

Joann, age six, comes into the playroom and begins to play with the clay. This is her fourth play therapy session. She is usually very quiet and does very little talking. Every time she comes in she plays with the clay and makes the same thing—a figure of a man carrying a cane. Each time, after she is finished, awful things happen to him. He is punched full of holes, beaten with a stick, run over by the toy truck, buried under a pile of blocks. The fourth time the clay figure emerges, the therapist says, "Here comes that man again."

Joann: Yes. (Her voice is tense, determined.)

Therapist: The man with the cane?

Joann: Yes. (She begins to punch him full of holes.)

Therapist: You're putting holes in the clay man.

Joann: Stab! Stab! Stab!

Therapist: You're stabbing him.

Joann (in small voice): Ouch. You hurt me. (Voice changing) I don't care. I want to hurt you.

Therapist: The clay man is crying because he is hurt.

Joann (interrupting): I want to hurt him.

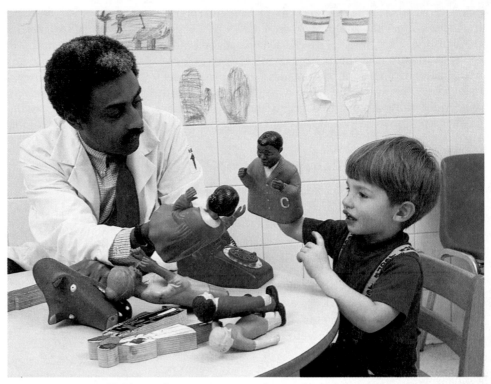

FIGURE 15–16 Children often communicate better through play than through speech. Play therapy is designed to take advantage of this fact and to give children a symbolic way to express their fears, aggressions, and insecurities.

Therapist: You want to hurt him.

Joann (emphatically): I don't like him.

Therapist: You don't like him.

Joann: I don't like him. I hate him. Look. This hole went clear through him. It went in his front and out his back.

Therapist: He gets holes punched clear through him. You fixed him.

Joann: Yes. I'll tear his head off.

Therapist: You'll even tear his head off?

Joann: I know, I know. I'll put him clear down in the bottom of the jar and then I'll put the clay in on top of him and he'll smother. (She tears him into little pieces and gouges her thumb through the clay and carefully puts the pieces down in the bottom of the jar and then covers it with all the rest of the clay.)

Therapist: You tore him into little pieces and buried him in the bottom of the jar. (Joann nods—and smiles at the therapist. Then she goes over to the baby doll, pretends to feed it, holds it tenderly in her arms, puts it

in bed, sets the table, and plays house very quietly.)

This was the pattern of Joann's behavior while in the playroom. She always made the clay man, tore him up, got rid of him, and then played with the baby doll. This continued through the seventh interview, and then she stopped making the clay man. She sometimes played with the clay, but made cats or toy dishes or candles. She was very fond of the doll and continued with this play.

—Axline, 1947, pp. 179–180

In the course of the therapy, Joann's nervous, tense, withdrawn behavior greatly improved. The therapist later learned that Joann's mother, who had been a widow for three years, was considering remarriage to a man who limped and carried a cane. Expressing her feelings without discussing them had apparently enabled Joann to accept her mother's marriage plans.

Note that the therapist offered no interpretations. Simply being able to express these negative thoughts in the presence of an accepting adult seemed beneficial to Joann. A psychodynamically oriented therapist might have handled this situation differently. Using the play

behavior as a base, the therapist might have interpreted the behavior to the child. For example, when Joann stabbed the clay man, a psychodynamically oriented therapist might have begun by saying, "You're angry with the man. You want to hurt him." Eventually, after many play therapy sessions, Joann would have come to understand why she felt as angry as she did about her mother's proposed marriage.

Cognitive and Behavior Therapies

Cognitive approaches are becoming increasingly popular in work with children and adolescents, particularly when combined with behavioral techniques. Cognitive aspects of therapy address children's distortions of reality, their expectations, and their "theories" of family life and school. Behavioral aspects focus on the stimuli that elicit maladaptive behavior in the child, the child's behavioral repertoire, and changes in reinforcement patterns by others who may unwittingly encourage such behavior to new patterns of reinforcement to discourage the maladaptive behavior.

Therapy for children often deals with cognitive issues such as their erroneous beliefs, distorted body image, and misinterpretations of environmental "messages." Teaching children to label these cognitive distortions can help them combat such thoughts. As in cognitive therapy with adults, therapists working with children might seek to combat anxiety resulting from negative anticipation of an event by asking what realistically might happen if the particular event were to occur.

Probably the most often used treatments for children involve behavioral methods of various kinds. One example can be seen in the following case:

Valerie, an eight-year-old girl from a low-income area, started to miss school in the second grade and in third grade the problem became worse. Whenever her mother attempted to take her to school, Valerie threw a temper tantrum or said she felt sick, so her mother left her with the neighbor. The therapist concluded that Val was getting reinforcement for staying away from school. By staying home, she gained extra contact with her mother and fun at the neighbor's house while her mother was at work. Some of the things Val liked most—chewing gum, ice cream, soda pop, and having her cousin stay all night—were combined as reinforcers to reward Val for going to school. Her mother no longer took Val to the neighbor's. Instead she reinforced Val by leaving home early before the children left for school and meeting her at the school door each morning, and by giving her candy when she returned from school and special treats when she had completed a week of school attendance. She also ignored Val's complaints of illness. Val's school attendance improved markedly as a result of this treatment. In addition, Val's grade-point average changed from C's before the treatment to A's and B's.

—Adapted from Ayllon and others, 1970

Figure 15–17 presents the results of behavioral therapy on Val's school attendance. A unique aspect of behavioral therapy for children is that one or both parents can be trained as "therapists" so that behavior modification can be carried out at home. The case of Valerie is an example of therapy in which a parent implemented the actual treatment. Although in many cases a clinician must plan the behavioral interventions and train the parents to carry them out, in some instances, particularly for less severe but still disruptive behaviors, group training sessions can be used to teach parents how to develop successful home treatment programs.

Family Therapy

As we have seen throughout this text, the family systems approach to therapy holds that it is the system of family interaction, not one individual, that is disturbed. Even though one person is usually identified as the

FIGURE 15–17 Valerie's voluntary school attendance. The behavioral intervention (including positive reinforcement) was initiated during the second quarter of the third year of school.

(Reprinted with permission from *Journal of Behavior Therapy and Experimental Psychiatry,* 1, T. Ayllon et al., Behavioral management of school phobia. Copyright © 1970, Pergamon Press, plc.)

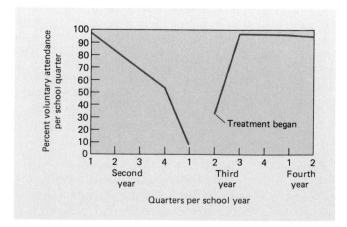

member with the problem, that person's symptoms are a reflection of a disturbance in a larger family unit. For example, a hyperactive boy was referred for treatment. Although he was labeled as the problem, a look at the family showed a more pervasive problem.

In this family the husband and wife did not get along. The husband spent all his time caring for his own dependent parents. He felt burdened by his wife and three children and felt no one looked after his needs. The wife felt neglected and uncared for and got satisfaction from the antics of her youngest child, the hyperactive boy. The other two older children who were well behaved seemed excessively mature in their actions. The problems in this interconnected system could be seen by looking at any of the members, not just at the young boy labeled as hyperactive.

—Andolphi and others, 1983

Family therapy has much in common with the psychodynamic approach because it often focuses on the meanings behind the behavior of each of the family members. The family therapist seeks to get a picture of the actual experience of the problem by the family. What is going on in the family now? What was going on in the family when the problem developed? How have family members responded? The first task of the therapist often is to reframe the child's problem in terms of family dysfunction and help develop alternative, healthier ways of dealing with these issues.

Results of Therapy

As is true with adults, therapy helps, at least to some degree, most children who receive it. This conclusion comes from an analysis of 75 studies of the effectiveness of therapy for children (Casey & Berman, 1985). As in therapy with adults, therapy with children is most effective in decreasing fear and anxiety. Unlike adults, however, children tend to show relatively little change in self-esteem, overall adjustment, and social adjustment.

Reports of the effects of therapy from parents and therapists have been encouraging. In contrast, reports from teachers and classmates seem more restrained. Another indicator of therapeutic outcome emerges when children's behavior changes are compared with their self-reports. Although their actual performance is often better, positive self-reports from the children are rare. One reason for this may be that children are not usually introspective and so have difficulty thinking about how they see themselves.

As in therapy with adults, evaluation of therapeutic efforts with children is an important scientific issue with several methodological problems (Kazdin, 1988). One of these concerns the subject population. A particular therapy might be effective with certain types of children, but not others. The treatment must also be specified, as must relevant characteristics of the therapists studied. It is important to determine how much of the results are attributable to the techniques employed and how much to the skills and personalities of the particular therapists included in the study. The researcher must also consider the question of which aspects of the child's adjustment are the ones most pertinent in evaluating the therapy and then use these as outcome measures.

Chapter Summary

CHILDREN IN CLINICAL SETTINGS

Memories of childhood trauma may last through long periods of life. They may result in repeatedly visualized memories of the event, its repetitive reenactment, trauma-specific fears, and changed attitudes toward others and events. Diagnostic interviews with children focus on trying to learn as much as possible about them and at the same time establishing rapport so they will want to return. The clinician needs to understand how the child perceives his or her situation. Parents, school personnel, social networks, and the legal system may also play roles in assessing the problem and planning treatment.

THE SCOPE OF THE PROBLEM

Maladaptive behavior in children is a major problem that society does not adequately address. Risk factors for childhood disorders include parental psychopathology, family discord and divorce, low socioeconomic status, the child's temperament, and stressful experiences. Child abuse is a particularly damaging stressor.

DISRUPTIVE BEHAVIOR

Attention-deficit Hyperactivity Disorder Symptoms of **attention-deficit hyperactivity disorder (ADHD)** include both

difficulty in focusing attention and a high level of disruptive activity that has continued for a period of at least six months. Although many children with ADHD improve as they grow older, children who have this disorder are at greater risk for other mental and behavioral disorders. In adolescence or young adulthood, those with ADHD who had conduct or aggression problems in childhood are more likely than their peers to become involved with the criminal justice system and to be drug abusers. ADHD may be associated with a metabolic dysfunction of the brain. Psychostimulant drugs such as Ritalin or Dexedrine are the most common treatment for hyperactive children. However, behavioral intervention together with pharmacological treatment may be the most effective treatment approach. Cognitive–behavioral therapy often helps improve academic achievement.

Conduct Disorder Children who are classified as having a **conduct disorder** carry out actions over at least a six-month period that either violate the basic rights of others or the social norms or rules for their age group. Many children who have a conduct disorder are classified as having an antisocial personality disorder when they become adults. Conduct disorder should not be confused with socialized delinquency, in which the child may carry out harmful or destructive behavior as part of a social group. Problems less serious than those found in conduct disorder, but more serious than those of a child who might be called difficult, are classified as an **oppositional defiant disorder.** This type of disorder may eventually develop into either a mood or conduct disorder. The best way of dealing with conduct disorder is prevention. Effective prevention efforts often use skill-building as a way of modifying aggressive behavior. An effective cognitive approach focuses on identifying and helping the child modify hostile attributions that may lead to aggressive behavior.

INTERNALIZING DISORDERS

Instead of being characterized by acting out, **internalizing disorders** are indicated by covert activities such as worries and disturbing thoughts. Internalizing disorders include several kinds of anxiety disorders and depression. In general these disorders respond to treatment better and are less likely to continue into adulthood than are disruptive behavior disorders.

Anxiety Disorders of Childhood Most children's fears disappear as they grow older. However, some fears and phobias have such an immediate impact on the child and the family that treatment is appropriate. Animal and social phobias can be treated effectively using the behavioral methods of desensitization or modeling. **Symbolic modeling** is a procedure used to help prepare children for frightening situations that they must experience such as surgery. Children who tend to be generally anxious and worry excessively over periods of six months or longer may be classified as having an **overanxious disorder.** Such children may have a poor self-concept and often have physical complaints such as headaches and stomachaches for which no physical cause can be found. These children are more likely to develop some kind of anxiety disorder in their adult lives. Although most children develop mild rituals and obsessions, those who develop more disruptive **obsessive–compulsive** and **ritualistic** behaviors may require treatment. For some

of these children behavioral methods are helpful. However, children whose obsessive–compulsive behavior is severe may not respond to treatment. A disorder that occurs mainly in childhood is **separation anxiety disorder,** in which children show panic or excessive anxiety when they are separated from their major attachment figure.

Depression in Children and Adolescents Depression is frequent among children who come to clinical attention. The period of depression may be brief or it may be either recurring or long-lasting. The frequency of depression among adolescents is much higher than that among pre-adolescents. Children who are depressed are more likely than others to experience depression in adulthood. Heredity appears to be important in childhood depression and depression tends to cluster within families. Maternal depression seems to have especially detrimental effects on children. Suicidal thoughts and attempts at suicide can occur even in very young children, although the frequency of these increases greatly in adolescence. Negative perceptions of the family environment are among the strongest predictors of suicidal thoughts and attempts in childhood. Depression is hardest to assess in young children, so clinicians often obtain additional information from parents and teachers. Involvement of the entire family appears to be very important in the treatment of depression and other childhood disorders.

EATING DISORDERS

Anorexia Nervosa **Anorexia nervosa** is self-induced starvation that occurs even though the person has both physiological and cognitive feelings of hunger. Such people "feel fat" and seem to have distorted body images that lead them to have an obsessive preoccupation with weight loss. Anorexia is most common in middle- and upper-class adolescent females. Some anorexics lose weight by limiting food intake; others, **bulimic anorexics,** use vomiting and laxatives to control calorie intake. Depression is often a long-term problem for people with anorexia. Treatment approaches most commonly used include behavioral methods and family therapy.

Bulimia Nervosa People who have **bulimia nervosa** practice binge eating although they are likely to be depressed and self-critical about such behavior. The binge eating occurs at least twice a week and is usually accompanied by laxative use or self-induced vomiting for weight control as part of a binge-purge cycle. Binge eaters are also likely to be on weight reducing diets from which their binges represent relapses. Bulimics may be thin, average, or above average in weight. Bulimia is thought by some researchers to be a form of depression in which the binges are used to get relief from anxiety and depression. Like anorexia nervosa, binge eating is not simply an eating problem but is associated with poor overall adjustment. Bulimia is treated with a variety of cognitive and behavioral techniques, group therapy, and antidepressant drugs.

THERAPY FOR CHILDREN AND ADOLESCENTS

With young children the most effective therapeutic approach is often to work with the parents to show them adaptive ways to

deal with their child and improve stressful family interactions. Because children often do not initiate therapy themselves, they may be unwilling participants. Parents, who typically initiate and finance the treatment of the child's problems, must usually also be willing to modify their own behavior.

Play Therapy Interaction with the therapist in a play setting is often the most appropriate direct treatment for young children because of their limited verbal skills.

Cognitive and Behavior Therapies As with adults, cognitive aspects of therapy for children are focused on their distortions of reality, their expectations, and their theories concerning their family and school. Behavioral methods are the most frequently used therapeutic techniques with children. In some cases the parent is trained in behavior modification techniques and becomes a quasi therapist.

Family Therapy The family systems approach focuses on patterns of family interaction rather than the individual as the source of the difficulty. The therapist tries to assess family dynamics and then to develop more adaptive ways for the family to interact.

Results of Therapy The outcome of therapy with children is similar to the outcome for adults: most patients are helped by it at least to some degree.

Developmental Disorders

CHAPTER 16

Autistic Disorder
Characteristics of Autistic Behavior
Research on Autistic Disorder
Therapy
Prospects for Change

Mental Retardation
Degrees of Mental Retardation
Biological Causes
Psychosocial Disadvantage
Psychosocial Enrichment
Psychological and Social Problems

Chapter Summary

Joan Miro, *L'Epouvante de l'oiseau portemalheur*, 1965.
Art Resource, New York.

Peter nursed eagerly, sat and walked at the expected ages. Yet some of his behavior made us vaguely uneasy. He never put anything in his mouth. Not his fingers nor his toys—nothing. More troubling was the fact that Peter didn't look at us, or smile, and wouldn't play the games that seemed as much a part of babyhood as diapers. While he didn't cry, he rarely laughed, and when he did, it was at things that didn't seem funny to us. He didn't cuddle, but sat upright in my lap, even when I rocked him. But children differ and we were content to let Peter be himself. We thought it hilarious when my brother, visiting us when Peter was eight months old, observed that "that kid has no social instincts, whatsoever." Although Peter was a first child, he was not isolated. I frequently put him in his playpen in front of the house, where the school children stopped to play with him as they passed. He ignored them too. . . .

Peter's babbling had not turned into speech by the time he was three. His play was solitary and repetitious. He tore paper into long thin strips, bushel baskets of it every day. He spun the lids from canning jars and became upset if we tried to divert him. Only rarely could I catch his eye, and then saw his focus change from me to the reflection in my glasses. It was like trying to pick up mercury with chopsticks.

—Quoted in Eberhardy, 1967, pp. 257–258

Peter's case is an example of one of the serious developmental disorders known as **autistic disorder.** Autistic disorder (autism) and mental retardation are two developmental disorders that greatly affect children's overall development. Other developmental disorders are more specific: They affect speech (stuttering or difficulties in pronunciation), academic skills (reading disorder,

expressive-writing disorder, or arithmetic disorder), or motor skills (coordination disorder). None of these specific disorders has as great an impact on children and their families as do autism and mental retardation. This chapter is devoted to these two major developmental disorders.

Autistic Disorder

John is five years old. He was referred to a child psychiatrist because of delayed speech development and poor peer relationships. His mother describes him as "living in a shell" and feels he never developed a close, loving relationship with her. He did not begin to speak until the age of three, and even now has a limited vocabulary of only about 200 words. Most of his speech consists of repetitive phrases heard on television, or simple requests or demands. He is unable to initiate or sustain a conversation with peers or adults.

John demonstrates a number of unusual behaviors and interests. For example, he is fascinated with water and often will spend long periods of time intently watching water dripping into a basin. He shows no interest in playing with toys in a usual way but would rather arrange objects in a straight line or else talk jargon to himself while rocking back and forth. He shows little interest in usual children's shows on television; he would rather watch adult game shows. He becomes very upset if furniture is moved around in the house and was inconsolable when his parents bought a new car.

His nursery school teacher says he has an amazing facility for numbers and letters, but she is concerned because he would rather stay by himself than play with other children. John communicates little with his teacher and seems odd and aloof, "in his own world."

When John was three, his mother was told by the family doctor that John probably would grow out of these problems. John's mother senses now that John is suffering from a severe and chronic condition.

Institute of Medicine, 1990, pp. 26–27

Autistic disorders, like John's, occur in about three children out of every 10,000 under the age of 15. Two-thirds of autistic children are mentally retarded and most require lifelong care. Boys are three to four times as likely to be autistic as girls. While autism is not common, its effects are devastating.

Characteristics of Autistic Behavior

Children with autistic disorder show several kinds of impairment—in social relationships, communication, and activities. Their social interactions are highly unusual. In general, such children have a noticeable lack of awareness of the existence or feelings of others. They may treat people as though they are objects. Autistic children do not seek out an adult for comfort if they are hurt or upset. They don't like to be held and they avoid eye contact. Children with autism prefer solitary play and have a poor understanding of social conventions. Even as young children, autistic children do not enjoy the usual parent–child kiss-and-cuddle routines. For example, they do not wave good-by or play peek-a-boo, and as toddlers, they do not follow their parents around the house or run to meet them when they come home.

Communication impairment is even more dramatic than impaired social behavior in autism. About half of all autistic children do not develop speech at all. Rather than a response to someone's action or an attempt to get an interaction going, the babble seems to an observer to occur randomly. If they do learn to talk, autistic children's speech is likely to be unusual. For instance, they may simply repeat what is said to them or repeat commercials they have heard on television. They also tend to reverse "you" and "I"; thus, when asking for a drink they might say "You want a drink" instead of "I want a drink." In addition, their tone of voice may be unusual—singsong or monotonous.

Autistic children have a very narrow range of interests and activities; they may spend a great deal of time spinning objects, flicking their fingers, or twisting or rocking their bodies. Sameness and routine are very important. Moving a piece of furniture or changing the daily routine in any way can be terribly distressing to an autistic child. Table 16–1 lists the major characteristics seen in autistic disorder.

As they grow older, autistic children may spend their time repetitively feeling or smelling objects or lining up items in a row. Bus timetables and the like may be fascinating to them and they sometimes spend hours studying such items. Because autistic children have a tremendous drive to carry out these fixations, the channeling of this behavior into somewhat similar

Table 16–1

Clinical Features of Autistic Disorder

Social Interaction

1. Marked lack of awareness of others.
2. Lack of social or emotional reciprocity.
3. Rarely seeks comfort or affection in times of distress.
4. Failure to develop peer relationships.
5. Absent or impaired imitation (lack of responsiveness to modeling).

Communication

1. Delay in or total absence of spoken language with markedly abnormal nonverbal communication (e.g., in eye-to-eye gaze).
2. Failure to use social or emotional cues to regulate communication.
3. Speech abnormalities (pitch, intonation, rate, rhythm, stress).
4. Stereotyped and repetitive use of language or idiosyncratic language (e.g., repeats words or phrases whether or not they have communicative value).

Behavior

1. Insistence on sameness (e.g., distress over small changes).
2. Persistent preoccupation with parts of objects.
3. Stereotyped body movements.
4. Markedly restricted range of interests.
5. Absent or markedly impaired imaginative play.

productive activities has been suggested as a therapeutic approach by one woman who has successfully overcome most of her autistic symptoms (Grandin, 1987). Box 16–1 describes the lives of two autistic persons.

AUTISM VERSUS CHILDHOOD SCHIZOPHRENIA Although autism was originally thought of as a psychosis, it is now considered to be a developmental disorder. However, psychosis can occur in children, and some childhood psychoses may be the same disorder as schizophrenia in adults. Childhood schizophrenia is rare—much rarer than schizophrenia in adulthood and rarely occurs before age seven or eight. It is not clear whether schizophrenia that occurs before age 15 has the same consequences and outcome as schizophrenia in adulthood; however, the symptoms are similar and include hallucinations, bizarre fantasies, ideas of being controlled by others, and paranoid ideas. Most researchers and clinicians agree that complete recovery from childhood schizophrenia is unlikely (Dawson & Castelloe, in press).

Research on Autistic Disorder

Autism was first described by Leo Kanner, a child psychiatrist, in 1943. Kanner presented cases of children who exhibited a unique pattern of behavior in which they were unable to relate in an ordinary way to people and situations from the beginning of life. In addition to this "extreme autistic aloneness," he stressed the children's "obsessive desire for the maintenance of sameness." Kanner thought of autism as a child psychosis and believed that most autistic children were basically very intelligent.

We now know that in the majority of cases autism is connected with global mental retardation. Although research on autism usually groups all autistic children together, such children seem to fall into at least two groups: those who are normal or near normal in intelligence and those who function at a retarded level (Prior, 1984). One important area for future research is the separate study of these two groups who may be very different despite the similarities in their social functioning.

THE PSYCHOLOGICAL PERSPECTIVE Autistic persons are profoundly impaired in several ways, with cognitive deficits and social and affective deficits being paramount.

Cognitive Deficits While most autistic children can see and hear normally, they respond to sensory input in a distorted way. From a very early age they are either under- or overresponsive to all kinds of stimuli. Often both ways of responding can be seen in the same person. Some of the perceptual disturbances of autistic children

BOX 16–1 Two Autistic Persons

Johnny

At ten years of age, Johnny's days and nights are marked by strict habits and inflexible preferences. There seems to be an order to his world, but it often escapes his family and teachers. When he was a baby, his mother reports, Johnny was a kind of loner. He never asked for attention; he just played by himself. Johnny's older brother is also autistic.

Shortly after he turned five, Johnny began to make curious hissing sounds. Later on, he began screaming (sometimes all day long) and had prolonged temper tantrums. His mother grew to dread the return of the school bus because she was so embarrassed by the impatience and angry looks of the bus driver. Johnny often hit himself (often his leg and face) and he cried a lot.

Two years ago, Johnny was placed in a residential–

educational center for young people with autism and other developmental disabilities. The children have their own rooms and are constantly supervised. A complex program of education, rules, and reinforcement has been designed for Johnny. While the staff have made no promises to Johnny's parents, he no longer screams and is learning to communicate by voice, sign language, and by pointing to pictures. He is better able to follow rules and seems happier (see Figure 16–1).

Adapted from *Tacoma News Tribune*, August 22, 1989, p. C1.

Ted

Nineteen-year-old Ted appeared to be developing normally until he was almost three. Then his parents became concerned because he still showed no interest in playing with other children and had begun

to use unusual speech patterns and show other unusual behaviors. At nine he could read and remember the spelling of five-syllable Greek names for dinosaurs but he couldn't tie his shoes or differentiate the fantasy on television or in books from reality. He knows the number of toes on exotic animals and names the day of the week a person's birthday will fall on far into the future. Ted has strange and irrational phobias of shower curtains, kites, and chicken soup. Ted's paternal uncle is also autistic.

Ted has been placed in a special center, comes home for holidays, and has made progress. An important goal for the center is to help Ted achieve a measure of independence during his adult life (see Figure 16–21).

Adapted from *Seattle Times*, January 9, 1990, p. H1.

FIGURE 16–1 Although he has become more attentive to environmental events, Johnny rarely interacts with other people. Like most autistic children, his play is solitary even when there is close contact with playmates. Johnny is on the right in the foreground.

FIGURE 16–2 Ted with his father, Charles. Because his older brother was autistic, Charles has been sensitive to the needs of autistic persons for a long time and is a leader in the state of Washington and throughout the country in creating facilities and conditions within communities that will improve the lives of autistic persons. He has written a book that describes his experiences with his brother and son (Hart, 1989).

seem to decrease with age, especially if the child responds well to treatment for the overall disorder, but there seems to be no doubt that early cognitive development in autistic children is abnormal (Leslie & Frith, 1990).

The most universal symptom of autistic disorder is language disturbance. More than half of all autistic children remain mute, and for those who do speak, specific aspects of language disorder remain. The "I" and "you" reversal is characteristic of autistic speech. Another characteristic is **echolalia** in which the child simply echoes or repeats all or part of what has been said to him or her. Both the language and manner of speaking of autistic children seem mechanical and monotonous.

Autistic children have problems with the social aspects of language, too. Even those who function well have difficulty initiating conversations or maintaining them. The usual kinds of expressions people use for these things, such as, "Speaking of," or "By the way," don't seem to be easy for autistic people to use. They also have trouble in social situations because they seem generally oblivious of their impact on others.

Another indication of the cognitive difficulties of autistic children is their lack of development of symbolic play. Using a stick for a horse or a big box for a playhouse are examples of symbolic play, which usually develops in normal children by about 21 months of age and becomes elaborated as they grow older. At least half of autistic children show a complete absence of symbolic play.

The cognitive problems of autistic children don't seem to be a function of poor memory. Autistic children's short-term recall is not deficient. For instance, when asked to repeat strings of words, verbal autistic children can repeat random meaningless strings as well as they can meaningful sentences (Dawson, 1989). In general, research on cognition suggests that, while their basic input and simple memory may not be impaired, autistic individuals have a problem with higher-level cognitive processing in which stimuli are organized by meaning. Autistic children have more problems with symbolic thought than with real-life examples. For example, one group did better at puzzles that required thinking about alternatives if the material they used was three-dimensional (colored wooden shapes) instead of two-dimensional (line drawings) (Prior & McGillivray, 1980). These cognitive deficiencies are probably related to the absence of symbolic or representational play in autistic children (Wulff, 1985).

Social and Affective Deficits

Autistic individuals have abnormal interpersonal relationships that seem to be related to their affective and emotional abnormalities. Research studies have shown that the emotional facial expressions, gestures, and vocalizations of autistic children are often idiosyncratic. (Dawson, 1989). Autistic children seem to lack the normal child's ability to coordinate affective expression and behavior. They seem neither to recognize the signals sent out by other people nor to display normally coherent patterns of feelings. Researchers suggest that they thus fail to participate in the coordinated patterns of feelings and action that usually occur between people. Related to this may be the fact that autistic children have difficulty in imitating a diversity of actions (Hobson, 1989). The abnormal interpersonal relationships that stem from autistic children's social comprehension deficit may lead to impaired verbal ability.

THE BIOLOGICAL PERSPECTIVE Many research efforts have focused on identifying a biological cause for autism. Researchers have made significant discoveries, but to date, no biological factor can be said with absolute certainty to be the determining factor. Because of autism's pattern of cognitive disabilities, researchers have focused on the left hemisphere of the brain, where language and symbolic material are assumed to be processed (Dawson, 1989). They have found that the cognitive problems of autistic children especially those of language, seem different from those that occur from either left-hemisphere or bilateral damage to the brain. These difficulties might be caused by early damage to the limbic system, which then affects other parts of the nervous system. Another possibility is that autism's symptoms can be explained in terms of a dysfunction of behavioral systems in the brain stem that is further distorted by dysfunctioning of the midbrain and the cortex.

Some kind of brain pathology seems likely in autistic individuals, since at least one-fifth of autistic children develop epileptic seizures in adolescence (Deykin & MacMahon, 1979). The risk of seizures is much greater for those autistic children who are severely retarded than for those who are not. Researchers have also noted a correlation between autism and brain injury at or after birth. In a study of 17 sets of identical twins in which only one of each set was autistic, 12 of the affected twins probably had experienced brain damage (for example, from convulsions shortly after birth) (Folstein & Rutter, 1977).

Through modern scanning technology, researchers are seeking to identify specific features of brain anatomy or brain biochemistry that differentiate autistic individuals from other groups. In one study, 18 autistic children and adults underwent nuclear magnetic resonance imaging (MRI), a procedure in which a magnetic field is used to create three-dimensional images of the brain (see Chapter 10). When they were compared with people who had either no neurological problems or neurological damage unrelated to autism, 14 of the 18 showed stunted development in a part of the cerebellum known as the superior posterior cerebellar vermis (Piven & others, 1990). The main function of the cerebellum is to coordinate complex movements. It is essential for bal-

ance, fine motor control, and muscle coordination. The cerebellar vermis is connected to brain regions that govern attention, arousal level, and the assimilation of sensory information (Courchesne and others, 1988).

Researchers speculate that the stunted development may occur in the first few months after conception or during the first or second years of life. Its causes are also unclear. Possibly the same process that damages the cerebellar vermis also harms other regions of the brain associated with symptoms of autism. Another possibility is that damage to the cerebellum alters the development of related brain regions. The unusual behavior of autistic children might be either a cause or an effect of underdevelopment in the cerebellum and other regions of the brain. According to one theory, autistic behavior is an attempt to relieve persistent overstimulation by uncontrolled brain activity (Dawson, 1989). There is some evidence that autistic persons have a shortage of a type of nerve cell that transmits inhibiting messages from the cerebellum to the cerebral cortex, the seat of thinking and judgment.

Research suggests there may also be a hereditary factor in autism. A survey conducted in Utah found that, while the rate of the disorder is low in the general population, there is a high prevalence among members of an autistic child's family (Ritvo and others, 1989). Among children born after the first autistic child, the rate is close to nine percent, or 215 times higher than that of the general population. In the rare case of two autistic children born in the same family, the chance of a third child with autism is 35 percent.

There is also evidence that a family history of delayed speech is much more common in families of a child who is autistic (25 percent of all of the families) than in the average family (Bartak and others, 1975). Another clue comes from a study of twins in which one member was autistic. The probability that the other twin would also be autistic or would have other cognitive abnormalities was greatly increased when the twins were monozygotic rather than dizygotic (see Figure 16–3). Knowledge about the genetics of autism suggests that what is inherited is probably not autism but some general tendency to have language or cognitive abnormalities (Rutter & Garmezy, 1983).

It has also been suggested that the parents of autistic children share human leukocyte antigens (HLA). Antigens are substances that stimulate the production of antibodies in the blood. The antibodies are blood proteins generated by the immune system and protect a person against specific microorganisms or toxins in the blood. When antigens of the parents are the same, this may increase the likelihood that the unborn child will be attacked by its mother's immune system (Stubbs and others, 1985). A finding supporting this idea is that mothers of autistic children report a greater frequency of

FIGURE 16–3 Differences between monozygotic and dizygotic twin pairs in which at least one twin is autistic. (Adapted from Folstein & Rutter, 1978, p. 226)

both spontaneous abortions and bleeding during pregnancy; these may be due in part to immune system attacks. Although this theory is still somewhat speculative, comparison of HLA antigen samples from parents of autistic children with samples from parents who did not have an autistic child showed the predicted differences. Seventy-five percent of the parents of autistic children shared antigens, but only 25 percent of the control parents did so.

Another area of research focuses on whether prenatal illness of the mother or other prenatal, birth-injury, or postnatal factors are related to autism. So far a variety of findings have been made about these relationships, but no single variable accounts for a large proportion of cases of autism or distinguishes between autistic children and controls (Tsai, 1987).

Therapy

Behavior-modification programs have often been used with children who are severely autistic. These programs have shown promise in improving such children's language and self-help skills, which, in turn, improve their chances for social adjustment.

At the beginning of a behavior-modification program, it may take 15 to 30 minutes to get a correct response from the child, even for simple tasks such as looking at the instructor on command. Once the child can consistently follow simple commands, he or she may be asked to perform imitative behavior, first by following visual instructions (such as raising an arm when the instructor does) and then by following verbal instructions (such as raising an arm when the instructor asks for

(a)

(b)

(c)

(d)

FIGURE 16—4 Autistic children receive special learning programs. *(a)* The therapist is hand-prompting a mute child to make the "wh" sound. *(b)* The therapist is using food as a reinforcer for the child to attend to him and make eye contact. *(c)* The therapist is teaching a child to identify parts of the face from a picture after he has learned to name the parts from his face and hers. She uses verbal reinforcement. *(d)* Autistic children have difficulty playing with other children. The therapist is using food to reinforce joint play activity.

that movement). An entire program such as this one takes several hours a day for months at a time. For this reason, at least one parent is trained to work with the child between visits to a professional. As the child progresses, the parent takes over a great deal of the training.

Although they help autistic children with specific skills, behavioral approaches to autism have often met with limited success (Franks, 1985). One of the biggest problems is the child's inability to generalize the responses that have been learned to other situations.

One follow-up study of children who had participated in intensive behavioral training suggests that this type of treatment may be effective for some autistic children (Lovaas, 1987). As preschoolers, the children were treated by trained therapists for 40 hours a week for at least two years. Their parents were also trained in the treatment procedures so that they could continue the treatment during all the child's waking hours. During the treatment each child's behavioral deficiencies were specifically targeted and special programs to encourage desired behaviors were developed. Some of these are shown in Figure 16—4.

The treatment procedure dealt with high rates of aggressive and self-stimulation behaviors in a graded series of methods. First these behaviors were ignored. If

that did not reduce them a "time-out" procedure was used in which the activity was interrupted until the child's objectionable behaviors ceased. More acceptable forms of behavior were shaped as replacements. Finally, if these methods were ineffective, the therapist said "no" very loudly or gave the child a slap on the thigh while the undesirable behavior was going on. Despite the therapists' general reluctance to use physically aversive behavior, work on the project showed that this was an essential element in producing behavior change. Children who improved in the program were placed in regular preschool and primary school programs. The rate of improvement in the intensive therapy group was compared to that for a similar group of children who were given the same type of therapy only ten hours a week and to that of a group treated in other programs. A comparison of the groups is shown in Figure 16–5.

Children who received the intensive training were more likely to be placed in regular classrooms than children in either of the other two groups. Results for those other two groups—the group that received a limited 10 hour per week intervention and the group that received other types of treatment—were quite similar to each other. Neither of these treatment approaches was found to be nearly as effective as the intensive training in helping autistic children to develop needed skills. The three programs did not differ in improving language skills. Nearly half of the children in each group were placed in classes for those with delayed language. The results of this project suggest that intensive behavioral training may allow some autistic children to reach an average level of functioning, and that this approach is superior to less intensive training and to the usual therapies that autistic children may receive.

Prospects for Change

As with other children, the intelligence test scores of autistic children predict their school achievement, later occupations, and social status. One key indicator of later outcome is whether the child has developed fairly good language skills by the age of five.

A follow-up study at a Canadian regional research center of children who had earlier been diagnosed as autistic showed that more than half the children were being cared for in institutions, that most had experienced a persistence of symptoms, and that few were living independently or were capable of holding a job (Wolf & Goldberg, 1986). About 90 percent of the group was mentally retarded.

A few autistic children who have made a good adjustment later in life have written about their experiences and provided some insight into what it must feel like to be autistic.

FIGURE 16–5 School placement at second grade for autistic children who were treated with an intensive behavioral therapy intervention during their preschool years compared to school placement of control groups. Note that none of the children in the ten-hour-per-week control group was able to be placed in a regular classroom.

(Data from Lovaas, 1987. Copyright © 1987 by the American Psychological Association. Reprinted by permission of the author.)

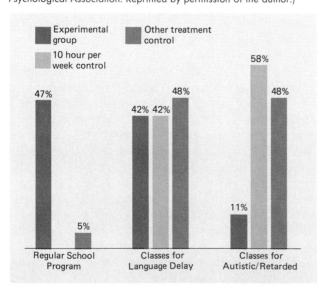

Tony was referred to a children's clinic when he was 26 months old. He did not speak at all and he did not seem to respond to his parents or the clinic staff in the way a young child might be expected to do; instead he ignored their approaches. His parents said he had always seemed stiff and hard to hold, he never smiled back at them, and he spent most of his time spinning objects or watching his hands as he moved his fingers.

Tony spent several years in a therapeutic nursery school and by age three had learned to communicate although he was severely echolalic. By the time he was six his intelligence test score was just slightly below average. During high school he was very aware of his feelings of being different. He quit high school in tenth grade and joined the army but was quickly discharged for fighting. Then he worked as an assembler in a manufacturing plant. He tried to get a girlfriend, but had been unsuccessful. He said he has difficulties with anxiety, periodic overuse of

alcohol, and unusual sensory experiences. This is a portion of what Tony wrote about himself [Tony's original spellings are retained here]:

"In school I learned some things very quickly but others were beyond learning comprehension. I used to disrupt the whole class and love to drive the teachers nuts. When I first started talking—five years old—I started talking about an incident that happened a year before. I was obsessed with certain things and played in my own way. I make things with Garbage or Junk and Play with them. I like mechanical Battery Power toys or electronic toys. . . . IN tenth grade I quit school and worked washing cars and work(ed) many other Jobs too. I was verry derpressed and Hyper at wok. I got along with my boss at all my Jobs. I tend to get lazy and had trouble getting along with other people. So in effort to keep my Jobs I avoided many people. I found It a lot easeyer to get along with older people and FEARED People my age because of school. I went into the army and got in lots of Fights with people. So I got dicarged. I allso have great Trouble getting thing organized and missunderstand allmost everything.

"And had and still have some mental blocks and great difficulty paying attention and listining to people and was verry easly distracted. I damanded to be amused by people and got board verry eas(i)ly and cant deal with stress. And had great difficulty fullfilling oblagations. I woudl hear electronic Noises and have quick siezious in bed and many other phsical problems. Often I have to be Force to get things done and verry uncoordinated. And was verry Nervious about everything. And Feared People and Social Activity Greatly . . . I never got Fired from a job. My problems havn't changed at ALL from early childhood. I was Just able to Function. And it still the same today."

—Volkmar and Cohen, 1985, pp. 49, 51

Another person, Temple Grandin, who was autistic in childhood but was above average in intelligence had fewer difficulties than Tony but still has some characteristics of autism:

I am now 36 years old and work as a consultant, designing livestock facilities for feedlots, ranches, and meat plants throughout the U.S. and abroad. I have also authored articles in both national and international livestock publications. At the present time I am doing research on animal behavior and neurophysiology and working on my doctorate in animal science at the University of Illinois. . . .

At the age of 1-1/2 to 3 I had many of the standard autistic behaviors such as fixation on spinning objects, refusing to be touched or held, preferring to be alone, destructive behavior, temper tantrums, inability to speak, sensitivity to sudden noises, appearance of deafness, and an intense interest in odors. . . .

At the age of 3 to 3-1/2 my behavior greatly improved, but I did not learn to speak until 3-1/2. At the age of 3 to 4 my behavior was more normal until I became tired. When I became tired, bouts of impulsive behavior would return. . . .

In college I was on the Dean's honor list, but getting through the foreign language requirement was difficult. I scraped by with Ds and Cs. Learning sequential things such as math was also very hard. My mind is completely visual and spatial work such as drawing is easy. I taught myself drafting in six months. I have designed big steel and concrete cattle facilities, but remembering a phone number or adding up numbers in my head is still difficult. I have to write them down. Every piece of information I have memorized is visual. If I have to remember an abstract concept I "see" the page of the book or my notes in my mind and "read" information from it. Melodies are the only things I can memorize without a visual image. I remember very little that I hear unless it is emotionally arousing or I can form a visual image. In class I take careful notes, because I would forget the auditory material. When I think about abstract concepts such as human relationships I use visual similes. For example, relationships between people are like a glass sliding door. The door must be opened gently, if it is kicked it may shatter. If I had to learn a foreign language, I would have to do it by reading, and make it visual.

—Grandin, 1984, pp. 144–145

In 1991, Temple Grandin, who now teaches animal science at Colorado State University and works as an

agricultural consultant designing livestock equipment, observed that:

> . . . *For me and for other autistic people, a challenging career or hobby makes life satisfying. Almost all my friends are people interested in either autism or livestock management. I cannot emphasize enough the importance to a high-functioning autistic person of developing an area of interest and building social contacts through it.*

—Grandin, 1991, p. 6

Successful adjustment is achieved by only a small proportion of autistic children. More typical is the case of Bruce:

> *During his preschool years he was involved in extensive therapy but he remained mute, bizarre, and socially isolated. During Bruce's school years no special program was available, so his mother took special courses to prepare herself to teach him. Through her efforts he learned about 100 words. He never used them voluntarily and relied on simple signs for communication.*
>
> *At 20 Bruce is physically healthy. He remains mute, but does use signs to express his wishes. As a child, he had unusual skill at assembling puzzle pieces. He still has this ability which helps him in his prevocational training. If left alone he still rocks his body for hours and twirls objects in front of his face, much as he did when he was a preschooler.*

—Adapted from Cohen and others, 1978, pp. 68–69

Mental Retardation

Mental retardation can be defined as a significantly below-average level of intellectual functioning as measured by an individually administered intelligence test. To be classified as mentally retarded, a person's social as well as intellectual functioning must be impaired (see Figure 16–6).

Mental retardation is regarded as a chronic, irreversible condition that begins before the age of 18. If

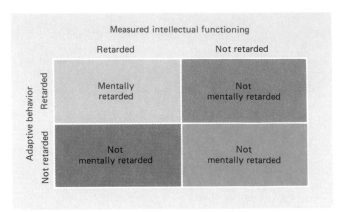

FIGURE 16–6 Only people who are significantly below average in both intellectual functioning and adaptive behavior are classified as mentally retarded.

intellectual functioning drops to retarded levels after age 18, the problem is classified as a dementia rather than mental retardation.

Although many children with autistic disorder are also retarded, there are several differences between autism and retardation.

1. Retarded children may have a cognitive development that is equal to their social development. In autism the child's social development is always lower than the cognitive development.

2. Retarded children show delays in language but autistic children show severe language deficits and more language deviance.

3. Self-stimulation, preoccupation by visual and auditory stimuli, and bizarre behaviors like spinning objects and flapping and twirling the body are common in autism but not in retardation.

4. Retarded children are motivated to please adults, but autistic children are not concerned about their impact on others.

Mental retardation can arise as a result of several factors. Genetic and prenatal factors may affect fetal development and result in retardation. Factors related to birth and early postnatal development (for example, traumatic deliveries that cause brain injury and head injuries occurring during infancy or early childhood) may also play roles. Psychosocial factors may be involved either by themselves or in addition to biological factors. Poverty, teenage parenthood, and substance abuse often produce a self-perpetuating familial pattern of retardation. In this chapter, we will review a number of the factors involved in mental retardation. Regardless of the cause or causes, mental retardation usually has a profound effect on the family of the affected child (see Box 16–2).

BOX 16–2 How Families Adapt to Retarded Children

From the parents' point of view, the birth of a mentally retarded child is a stressful and often devastating event. For nine months they have looked forward to the arrival of a healthy, normal child. When those expectations are shattered, they often go through a grieving process similar to that following the death of a family member. In the past, many professionals emphasized the parents' need for help until they could accept the situation. They viewed the process as time limited. One parent of a retarded child comments on this view.

Parents of retarded people, the theorists tell us, learn to live with their children's handicaps. They go through stages of reaction, moving through shock, guilt, and rejection to the promised land of acceptance and adjustment.

My own experience as the father of a retarded child did not fit this pattern. Instead, it convinced me that most people seriously misunderstand a parent's response to this situation. The standard view does not reflect the reality of parents' experience or lead to helpful conclusions.

Professionals could help parents more—and they would be more realistic—if they discarded their ideas about stages and progress. They could then begin to understand something about the deep, lasting changes that life with a retarded son or daughter brings to parents. And they could begin to see that the negative feelings—the shock, the guilt, and the bitterness—never disappear but stay on as a part of the parent's emotional life.

Most parents, I believe, never fully resolve the complexity of feelings about their child's retardation. They don't "adjust to" or "accept" that fact, at least not in the way psychology books describe it.

—Searl, 1978, p. 27

Many parents of retarded children retain some optimism about their child's future progress while the child is still young. For example, they may overestimate the child's academic potential and underestimate problems in

learning. This is illustrated by the observation that parents of young children are more supportive of the concept of mainstreaming (combining children of all abilities into one school program) than parents of older children, who see a greater need for special education programs (Suelzle & Keenan, 1981). In general, just as the grieving process goes on over a lifetime, the parents' acceptance of the severity of their child's disability is not steady and gradual. Instead, problems of acceptance flare up acutely at particular stages in the child's development.

Families of retarded children go through a series of crises as the child reaches various developmental stages. In one survey, three-quarters of the parents described life with their retarded child as a series of ups and progressively greater downs. Only one-quarter described their grief as being healed by time (Wikler and others, 1981). The parents were asked to evaluate the extent to which they were upset at a number of points, including early events such as the time of diagnosis, the time for walking and talking, and decisions on school placement, and later events such as the onset of puberty, the 21st birthday, and discussion and decisions about the care of the child after the parents' death.

When the parents' responses were compared with the predictions of social workers, the results showed that the social workers tended to overestimate the extent to which the parents'

were upset over the earlier experiences and to underestimate the extent to which they were upset over the later experiences. For example, the social workers overestimated the degree of the parents' upset at the times when the child would normally have been expected to walk, when the child entered a special-education class rather than the regular school program, and when younger siblings surpassed the retarded child in functioning. They markedly underestimated how upsetting the child's 21st birthday was to the parents.

The unmet needs of parents seem to form a U-shaped curve. These needs are high among parents of preschoolers, drop off when the children enter some kind of school program, and rise again, even beyond the original levels, when the children become young adults.

Periods of transition in the children's lives are also associated with increased family stress. Both entry into adolescence and to young adulthood seem particularly stressful to the family. Figure 16–7 shows the stress levels of families with retarded children of different ages. Two samplings two years apart showed similar findings.

In the past, parents of severely retarded children were urged to institutionalize such children shortly after birth, before they had had a chance to become attached to them. More recently, they have been urged to care for their children at home. However, the presence of a retarded child puts great stress on a family. Parents re-

FIGURE 16–7 The amount of stress reported by families of retarded children varies with the age of the children. Developmental transitions seem to produce especially high levels of stress.
(Wikler, 1986, p. 705)

Box 16–2 (Continued)

port a sense of loss and hopelessness, a decrease in self-esteem, and increases in shame, guilt, and marital disharmony (Lobato, 1983). The father of one autistic and retarded child wrote movingly in his diary about the stresses that his son's problems imposed on him and his wife, Foumi.

I notice that I have become more distrustful of Foumi, have lost some of my faith in her, so necessary for our marriage, or any marriage, because she has borne me Noah. Even though genetically, I suspect, it is I who am the wreck. But worse than cheating or mutual suspicion when it comes to unfixing the mystique that glues a marriage, I guess, is to have a disturbed kid. At first I thought it would draw us closer together, necessarily cement our relationship. Now Foumi and I have to be wary that it doesn't draw us apart. We have to be intelligent enough to realize there is a strain on any marriage whenever a baby is sick. And we always have a sick baby.

—Greenfeld, 1970, pp. 66–67

Very little research has been done on how parents cope with these stresses. A study of parents whose children were in a preschool program found that some parents, especially those who were younger and less well educated, used religion as a coping device (Friedrich and others, 1986). These parents believed that "God specifically chose me to be the parent of this special child." This belief appeared to give them comfort and increase their feeling that things were under control. Another group of parents in the same study believed that they were in control of their lives and could deal with the situation. These parents tended to be older and better educated. The results of this study suggest that the belief that someone or some force is in control can be helpful in withstanding the stress of having a retarded child. These feelings could be enhanced through support groups formed by the families themselves. Such groups could not only provide emotional support but increase feelings of control by sharing advice about parenting techniques and information about the availability of community facilities.

The brothers and sisters of retarded children may also be affected by the child's presence. Again, there has not been much research on these effects. What we do know suggests that the parents of a retarded child often place increased demands on their other children. They are expected to care for the retarded child and to subordinate their needs to those of their sibling. Their parents expect more of them and at the same time often have less time and attention to give them. These children sometimes feel pressure to excel in order to "make up" for their retarded sibling.

Much of the research on the effects of a retarded child on other family members was done some years ago, when many children were institutionalized, and in many cases there were no control groups. This is an area where more facts are needed. What is known at present is that, not surprisingly, the parents' attitudes toward the retarded child and their ways of dealing with the situation have an important effect on their other children's adjustment.

Degrees of Mental Retardation

Clinicians use four categories of mental retardation, which are based on intelligence-test scores: *mild, moderate, severe,* and *profound* (see Table 16–2). The following cases illustrate these categories and Table 16–3 presents highest levels of adaptive behavior for each group.

Mild Retardation: *Alice is 16 and has been in special classes since preschool. She can feed and dress herself well, but she needs help in deciding on appropriate clothes to wear. She can write simple letters and use the telephone. She can carry on an ordinary conversation, but she does not seem aware of important current events and is unable to talk or write about abstractions. She rides a bicycle and seems well coordinated. She can find her way*

around her neighborhood but can't go farther without aid. She can cook simple meals and go shopping for specific items by herself.

Table 16–2
Levels of Mental Retardation

	IQ	Percent of All Retardation
Mild mental retardation	50–70	85
Moderate mental retardation	35–49	10
Severe mental retardation	20–34	4
Profound mental retardation	Below 20	Less than 1

Table 16–3

Behavior of Retarded Individuals at Various Stages of Development

Level of Retardation	Highest Level of Adaptive Behavior		
	AGE 3	**AGE 9**	**AGE 15 AND OVER**
Profound	Drinks from a cup with help; sits unsupported or pulls self up; imitates sounds, repeats Ma-Ma. Indicates knowledge of familiar people and interacts with them nonverbally.	Tries to feed self but spills; can pull off pants and socks; walks alone; uses 4–10 words; may play with others briefly.	Feeds self; can dress except for small buttons and zippers; toilet trained but may have accidents; can climb steps and throw a ball; vocabulary of up to 300–400 words and uses grammatically correct sentences; if nonverbal, may use gestures for communication; understands simple questions and directions; participates in simple group games.
Severe	Feeds self with finger foods; can remove clothes, but often does so inappropriately; stands alone or walks unsteadily; says 1 or 2 words; plays "patty cake" or with toys.	Feeds self with spoon, may be messy; drinks unassisted; may indicate need for toilet; runs and jumps; speaks 2–3 word sentences; interacts with others in simple play.	Feeds self adequately with spoon and fork; can dress with zippers and buttons; is toilet trained. Can run, go up and down stairs alternating feet; may communicate in complex sentences; participates in group activities; does simple tasks and errands.
Moderate	Tries to feed self but spills; can pull off pants and socks; walks alone; uses 4–10 words; may play with others briefly.	Feeds self; can dress except for small buttons and zippers; toilet trained but may have accidents; can climb steps and throw a ball; vocabulary of up to 300–400 words and uses grammatically correct sentences; if nonverbal, may use gestures for communication; understands simple questions and directions; participates in simple group games.	Feeds, bathes, and dresses self; selects daily clothing; can wash and iron own clothes; has good body control; can carry on simple conversation and can interact cooperatively with others; can go on errand without a list; can assume responsibility for simple household tasks.
Mild	Feeds self with spoon, may be messy; drinks unassisted; may indicate need for toilet; runs and jumps; speaks 2–3 word sentences; interacts with others in simple play.	Feeds self adequately with spoon and fork; can dress with zippers and buttons; is toilet trained; can run, go up and down stairs alternating feet; may communicate in complex sentences; participates in group activities; does simple tasks and errands.	Cares for own personal grooming, sometimes with reminders; can go around own neighborhood easily; carries on everyday conversation; writes simple letters and uses telephone; can go shopping, prepare simple meals, and initiate most of own activities.

Moderate Retardation: *Bob, age 17, has been in a special educational program since he was six. He can dress himself but needs to be checked over to be sure he is completely dressed before going out. He can go to a nearby store by himself but cannot tell if he has been given the correct change. He cannot take buses alone. In his group home he makes his bed, helps set the table, and sweeps the floor. He works in a sheltered workshop stuffing envelopes. His speech is barely understandable, but he responds to directions and requests.*

Severe Retardation: Jason, age 21, has been in educational programs since he was six. He can feed himself with a spoon and can dress himself if the clothing is not too difficult to get on. He gets lost if he goes more than a block from home. He can talk, but his speech is repetitive and his vocabulary small. He enjoys going to the store with others but has no concept of making purchases. He cannot select three objects from a group. Jason has been enrolled in two different shelter workshop programs but has been unable to learn the job routine.

Profound Retardation: Peggy is 30. She has been slow in development since birth and has been in a special educational program since preschool. She cannot dress herself completely. She can use a spoon but not a knife and fork. She does not interact much with other people except by smiling or laughing; she does not talk. She can respond to simple commands like "Come here" and to her name. She spends a great deal of time rocking her body back and forth. Although she likes TV, she pays attention for only brief periods and seems to be watching only the movement.

Mental retardation has many causes, but these may be grouped into two general categories: nonenvironmental factors (including both genetic factors and biological causes such as prenatal exposure to alcohol or birth injuries) and psychosocial reasons. Retarded children who are also **psychosocially disadvantaged** may show no specific disabilities but may resemble their parents in low intellectual achievement. They are likely to experience little intellectual stimulation in their environment, receive poor medical care, and have unhealthful diets and living conditions. Thus, their heredity and/or environmental experiences may combine to cause their intelligence test scores to fall in the lower end of the distribution.

For a long time it has been thought that most mild mental retardation was usually explained by this combination of heredity and environmental conditions. In contrast, lower intelligence scores—those in moderate, severe, and profound retardation levels—were thought to be the result of some kind of pathology, such as disease, injury, chromosomal abnormality, or specific genetic disorder. Modern epidemiological research has cast doubt on this theory. A Swedish study has shown that at least half and often a much greater proportion of mildly retarded people in the population have some chromosomal defect, specific genetic disease, or some other specific pre- or postnatal disease or injury (Akesson, 1986). This suggests that such factors play a role at all levels of retardation. However, it is also true that compared to people in other retarded groups those in the mildly retarded group are more likely to have family members who also fall in the mildly retarded category. For instance, the IQ scores of the brothers and sisters of one group of retarded children were measured (Nichols, 1984). None of the siblings of the severely retarded children were retarded, but 20 percent of the siblings of mildly retarded children were also retarded (see Figure 16–8). These findings indicate that although there is some overlap, mild and severe cases of mental retardation probably have different causes.

Biological Causes

Whenever nonenvironmental causes of retardation are discussed, a number of overlapping terms are used. The predictable gene-based qualities that are transmitted from parents to children are **hereditary.** However, some of the genes available at the moment of conception are not quite like those of either parent and are called **mutants.** In addition, in certain polygenic disorders, each nonaffected parent may contribute enough pathologically related genes so that together these genes move the child over the threshold from nondisordered to disordered.

Disorders caused by mutations, superthreshold doses of affected genes, and disorders caused by predictable parental contribution are all referred to as **innate.** In addition, certain disorders can be acquired prenatally, for example, as a result of chemical substances passed to the child through the mother's placenta. These factors, together with the innate factors mentioned above, make up what are called **congenital** factors. **Constitutional**

FIGURE 16–8 IQ distribution for siblings of severely retarded (IQ less than 50) and mildly retarded (IQ 50–69) white children.
(Nichols, 1984, p. 163)

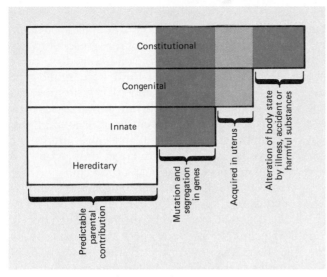

FIGURE 16–9 Definitions of nonenvironmental contributors to mental retardation.

factors include all these congenital factors and also factors that are due to illness or injury after birth.

Figure 16–9 explains the differences among these terms used to discuss biological causes of retardation.

HEREDITARY DISORDERS Some disorders are caused by specific genes that have been identified. If the disorder is caused by a dominant gene, only one gene of that particular gene pair needs to be affected to produce the disorder. In contrast, in recessive disorders, both members of the gene pair must be affected.

Disorders Caused by Specific Dominant Genes The number of known dominant genes that cause severe retardation is small because people who are afflicted by these disorders do not usually have children. Often a mutation, or spontaneous variation in a gene, seems to be responsible for the first case of a dominant gene disorder recognized in a family. In many of these disorders the symptoms do not become apparent immediately after birth. An example of such a disorder is **tuberous sclerosis.** In addition to severe retardation and seizures, this condition produces small fibrous tumors, often beside the nose, as well as internal tumors and skin abnormalities. The seizures may not begin until the child is three, and the tumors may not appear until several years later. In some mild cases the tumors appear but retardation may be minimal or absent.

Disorders Caused by Specific Recessive Genes A parent may carry only one recessive gene in a particular gene pair without showing symptoms of the problem transmitted by the gene. If both parents carry the same recessive gene, each of their children has a one in four chance of being affected by the problem and a two in four chance of becoming a carrier like the parents. Many of these inherited problems involve disorders of metabolism.

Phenylketonuria (PKU) is a disorder in which the body is unable to oxidize the chemical phenylalanine, which therefore accumulates in the body. If this accumulation is allowed to continue, severe mental retardation may result. Very few untreated PKU victims have IQs above 50. If treatment, which involves a restrictive diet, is started early, most of these changes can be prevented, although earlier damage cannot be reversed. Children who received treatment at an early age are usually in the normal range on intelligence tests and neurological examinations, although they score lower on intelligence tests than their siblings did at comparable ages.

Newborn infants can be tested for PKU although, because only one in 17,000 children has PKU, the costs of such testing are high per case actually identified. But the costs of caring for the retarded are also high. In one program the saving from detecting and treating each infant with PKU and thus preventing retardation was over $200,000 (Barden and others, 1984). Testing of newborns for PKU is now required in many states.

A lifelong adherence to a restrictive low protein diet is advisable for those with PKU. It had been thought that these children could go off their special diet when they became adults, but it is now known that change to a normal diet has negative long-term effects (Matthews and others, 1986). Adults who go off the diet may develop problems with short-term memory, coordination, and ability to concentrate. Based on this research, teaching dietary management beginning in early childhood can prevent retardation in the next generation.

Before treatment for PKU was developed most people who had PKU did not have children. Now that treatment has saved them from retardation, PKU women are more likely to have children. If pregnant women with PKU do not continue to follow a restrictive diet, their children are likely to be retarded. The retardation does not arise from a particular pair of recessive genes but instead comes from the environmental characteristics within the mother's uterus. A high phenylalanine level in the uterus is almost certain to result in severe fetal brain damage. This problem may be avoided or the risk decreased if the PKU mother follows the special low protein diet designed to control blood phenylalanine level.

Tay-Sachs disease, another inherited metabolic disorder, is inevitably fatal. This condition, which is caused by a recessive gene, occurs most often in Ashkenazi Jews whose ancestors came from a small area in Eastern Europe. It causes progressive degeneration of the nervous system, degeneration of the brain, and death, usually before the age of four.

Disorders Carried by the Sex Cells Every person has one chromosome pair that determines his or her sex. A woman has a pair of X chromosomes, one inherited from each parent. A man has one X chromo-

some inherited from his mother and one Y chromosome inherited from his father. If an abnormality occurs in this chromosome pair, called the sex cells, it does not always produce defects as severe as those produced by abnormalities in the nonsex chromosomes. (When an abnormality affects the nonsex chromosomes, mental retardation is almost always present.) However, certain sex cell abnormalities have been found to produce defects involving mental retardation.

One abnormality of the sex cells is called **Fragile X syndrome.** The Fragile X is so named because a small portion at the tip of the X chromosome seems susceptible to breakage under certain conditions. The Fragile X syndrome is the second-most common identifiable cause of mental retardation in males. The most common is Down syndrome, which we will discuss in the next section. Males with the Fragile X syndrome have long faces, big ears, and, as adults, large testes. Men who have this syndrome are more likely than women to be severely retarded. The syndrome usually results in severe to profound retardation, although some of those affected are only mildly retarded. Autistic behaviors and speech problems are often seen in people who have Fragile X syndrome (Brown and others, 1986; Hanson and others, 1986).

Because the Fragile X syndrome is transmitted through the X chromosome, men must inherit the disease from their mothers. If only one of a woman's X chromosomes is affected by the Fragile X syndrome the woman may or may not be retarded herself, but she may be a carrier who can transmit the problem to her children. One study examined four generations of one family in which the great grandmother was a carrier of the disorder (Saul, 1982). In the 40 people who were in the next three generations of her family, there were seven men with Fragile X syndrome, six women who were carriers and passed the disorder on to their children, and nine other women who were potential carriers but who had not yet given birth to a child with the syndrome. Several of these female carriers were at least mildly retarded.

Scientists have recently made the important discovery of the gene that causes the Fragile X syndrome. With this advance, it should now be possible to diagnose the disease unequivocally and to do prenatal genetic screening for the disease. It will also be possible to identify syndrome patients whose retardation or behavioral difficulties had been attributed to factors such as autism or a lack of oxygen during birth. Although no treatments currently exist for the syndrome, identification of the gene will enable researchers to study how the gene operates to influence intelligence and why flaws in it cause retardation.

DISORDERS DUE TO CHROMOSOME MUTATION

More than half of the children who are severely or profoundly retarded have genetic disorders that are not transmitted directly through specific dominant or recessive genes. In these cases, defects of the nonsex chromosomes, or **autosomes,** lead to conditions that cause mental retardation. About one-third have single-gene mutations and most of the remainder have chromosomal mutations or abnormalities. **Chromosomal abnormality** actually occurs in about 10 percent of all conceptions. However, since most of these abnormal fetuses are naturally aborted through miscarriage, only about 1.5 percent of all newborns have such a problem.

The most frequent chromosomal abnormality is **Down syndrome** (named for the physician who first described its symptoms), which occurs about once in every 800 births. Down syndrome is also called **trisomy 21.** The term trisomy refers to the presence of 3 chromosomes of a particular type rather than the usual two. In the case of Down syndrome there are 3 number 21 chromosomes (shown in Figure 16–14a). In addition to Down syndrome, there are other chromosomal abnormalities that are related to retardation: **trisomy 13** and **trisomy 18.** These conditions, which are much rarer than Down syndrome, cause more severe retardation and a shorter life expectancy. The parents of an infant with any of these trisomies face an increased risk of trisomy in future pregnancies.

Down Syndrome Children who are affected by Down syndrome have many characteristic physical features that make this disorder easy to recognize. These include a flat face and a small nose, eyes that appear to slant upward because of small folds of skin at the inside corners, slightly protruding lips and tongue, small ears, and small square hands with short fingers and a curved fifth finger. Children with Down syndrome tend to be shorter than average, with especially short arms and legs in proportion to their bodies. They also are likely to be somewhat obese in childhood and adolescence. Further, such a child is apt to have a congenital heart abnormality.

Children with Down syndrome have about a 99 percent chance of being retarded. There is considerable variability in the level of retardation, however, which may range from mild to severe. In general, Down children seem especially weak in tactile perception, higher-level abstraction and reasoning, and auditory perception.

Programs to provide increased stimulation to very young Down syndrome children have attempted to modify the typical downward trend of development (Cicchetti & Beeghly, 1990). Intervention often begins a few days after birth with physical therapy programs. Programs for young children provide a variety of activities to help develop both physical and cognitive skills (see Figure 16–10). Parents are also trained to take part in activities to stimulate their children.

As infants, Down syndrome children explore their

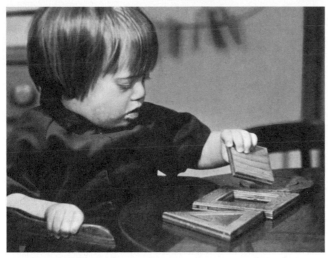

FIGURE 16–10 Enrichment activities for young Down syndrome children may help them achieve far more as they grow older than would have been previously expected.

environment in the same ways that other children do (MacTurk and others, 1985). During the preschool period, their development, although slower than that of nonhandicapped children, seems to follow a similar pattern. One difference is that these children show less exploration behavior and so are not as active in investigating their surroundings. Through their childhood and adolescence, Down syndrome children have poorer muscle tone and coordination than other children. As a result, they are less active, carry out tasks more slowly, and have poorer balance than other children. As Down syndrome children reach school age their delays in physical and cognitive development begin to cause more problems. Deficits in short-term memory often mean that information overload occurs, which can result in poor performance. Auditory memory is especially poor, making the child less able to learn from verbal information (Varnhagen and others, 1987). Other problems of Down children that can be major hindrances in pursuing a normal life are inability to comprehend instructions, to pay attention to several things at once, and to express clearly what they are thinking or what they need. Often even older Down syndrome children use a kind of telegraphic speech in which connecting words like "and" or "but" and other words such as prepositions and adverbs are missing. Such a teenager might say "Cat. Jump. Roof. Tree," instead of "The cat jumped off the roof and into the tree."

Because Down syndrome children often learn better by seeing material rather than hearing it, some researchers have tried using computers to improve this telegraphic speech (see Figure 16–11). Teenagers were able to improve their language structure by using special computers that read back what they wrote. One boy,

FIGURE 16–11 The use of computers may be a way to help Down syndrome adolescents overcome some of their problems in expressing their thoughts. Here, Christine, a 13-year-old, is using a computer to write more eloquently about her thoughts than she can say them. She wrote the poetic statement, "I like God's finest whispers."

who before the project could only describe his father who had recently died by saying "Dad. Talk. Down. Boom," was able to write: "My father and I went to his office. We would eat lunch and drink Diet 7-Up. I love you, Dad" (Kolata, 1987). Such efforts cannot cure retardation, but can help people function more effectively.

The average adolescent or adult with Down syndrome has the intellectual abilities of a young child. Mental development for people with Down syndrome can continue into their thirties and forties if they are in a stimulating environment (Berry and others, 1984). An increasing number of mentally retarded persons, including some with Down syndrome, are being placed in carefully selected and supervised jobs (see Figure 16–12). However, for many older people with Down syndrome, aging appears to occur early and brings with it a decrease in cognitive abilities. This may occur because their brains contain fewer neurons than the average, with the result that the normal loss of neurons with aging

FIGURE 16–12 A growing number of retarded people are working in paying jobs. Matthew R. Starr, who has Down syndrome, cleans cooking pots in the kitchen of a hotel in Maryland. Although he does not discriminate particularly well among clean and dirty pots, he wants to do a good job so he scrubs every one, even those that do not need it.

affects them with unusual severity. Researchers have discovered that the brains of young adults with Down syndrome tend to show plaques and tangles that appear similar although not identical to those found in Alzheimer's disease (see Figure 16–13). As in Alzheimer's disease, these changes seem to be concentrated in the hippocampus, the area of the brain that plays a selective role in learning and memory. About 25 to 40 percent of Down syndrome adults actually become demented, that is, lose their memories and the ability to care for themselves.

Causes of Down Syndrome As was mentioned earlier, in most cases Down syndrome results from the presence of an extra number 21 chromosome (Figure 16–14*a*). The trisomy usually results from a mistake in the cell division of either the egg or the sperm and occurs by accident.

FIGURE 16–13 Almost all adults with Down syndrome who live to be 30 or older develop brain lesions like those seen in patients with Alzheimer's disease. However, only a minority of the Down syndrome group become demented as Alzheimer's patients do. Photo (*a*) shows brain tissue from a normal adult. The neurons are marked with arrows. Photo (*b*) shows brain tissue from an adult with Down syndrome. Arrows show neurons with neurofibrillary tangles. Plaques are marked with a P and normal neurons with an N.

(a)

(b)

FIGURE 16–14 Chromosomal abnormalities are detected with relatively high frequency, and are the cause of many spontaneous abortions. The most common abnormality in children who are born alive is trisomy 21, which causes Down syndrome. In more than 95 percent of Down syndrome cases there are 47 chromosomes, with 3, rather than 2, twenty-first chromosomes. In a few other cases there are only 46 chromosomes but one member of the number 21 chromosome pair is defective. Part (a) shows the chromosomal analysis of a girl with Down syndrome. Note the extra chromosome 21 indicated by the arrow. The drawing in part (b) illustrates the process by which a chromosome translocation takes place. This "translocation chromosome" has been formed by the breaking and rejoining of chromosomes 14 and 21 (with loss of the little pieces).

(Adapted from *Facts about Down Syndrome*, U.S. Dept. of Health & Human Services, 1984)

In a few cases Down syndrome is produced by the process of translocation. **Translocation** occurs when a piece of one chromosome breaks off and attaches itself to a different chromosome (see Figure 16–14b). A parent can carry a translocation without showing symptoms of Down syndrome because the correct amount of genetic material is there even though it is out of place. But if the parent passes on both the normal chromosome 21 and the translocated parts of chromosome 21 to a child, the child will end up with too much genetic material for chromosome 21 just as in the case of the trisomy 21 process.

Mosaicism is another, very rare, cause of Down syndrome. **Mosaicism** means that not all the cells in a person's body have the same chromosome count. For example, some cells might have 46 chromosomes and some cells 47. Mosaicism is not transmitted from a parent, but instead results from an error in cell division in the fertilized egg. Infants who have mosaic Down syndrome may have only some of the characteristics features of the disorder because only some of their cells have an abnormal number of chromosomes.

The risk of having a child with Down syndrome increases dramatically with the age at which a woman becomes pregnant (see Figure 16–15). It is not clear why age of the mother has this effect. It might be that since women are born with all the eggs they will ever have, the eggs of an older mother may have passed their prime because of aging. Another possibility is that the eggs have been damaged over the years by such influences as medication, radiation, or other harmful sub-

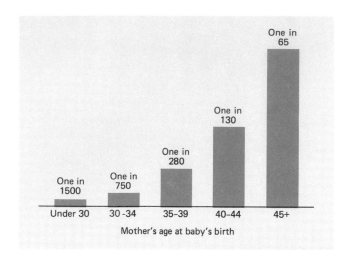

FIGURE 16-15 The chances of giving birth to a child with Down syndrome increase with the mother's age. (Smith & Wilson, 1973, p. 17)

stances in the environment. Since older fathers also seem to increase the child's risk for other genetic disorders, researchers are now looking at what factors related to the father's age might produce Down syndrome. Because men's supply of sperm is renewed continually, unlike women's egg supply, the answer does not seem to be in the aging of the genetic material itself.

PRENATAL DIAGNOSIS Help is available for parents who believe their unborn child is at risk for trisomy or a disorder caused by dominant or recessive genes. For a number of years **sonograms** or **ultrasound scans,** which show the fetus on a TV screen, and **amniocentesis,** an analysis of the amniotic fluid inside the amniotic sac surrounding the infant, have helped to detect the presence of Down syndrome and other genetic defects including some inherited disorders (see Figure 16–16). Amniocentesis cannot be used until about the fourth month of pregnancy and the cells must be cultured for two weeks after the test, so the pregnancy is well advanced before the result is known. This means that if the tests show a defect in the fetus the parents may face a very difficult decision over continuing the pregnancy.

FIGURE 16-16 The process of amniocentesis.

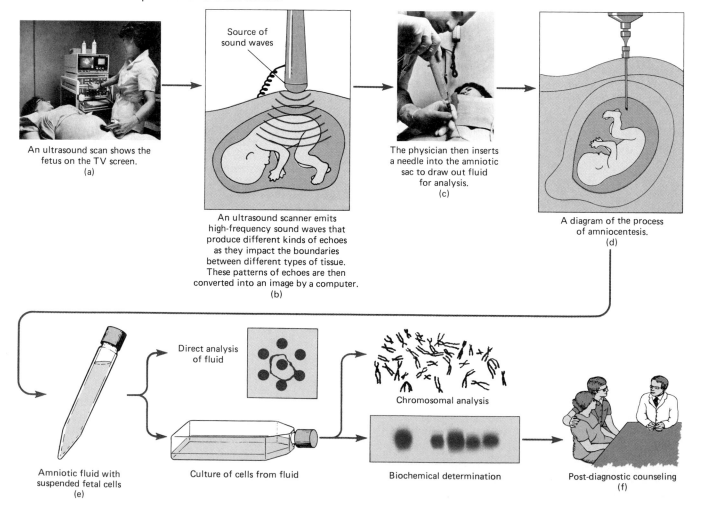

Amniocentesis may be suggested if the risk of a retarded or otherwise genetically damaged child is high—for example, if the mother is over 35 or if there is another child with genetic problems in the family. The results, together with information about the parents' genetic history, are used to counsel parents regarding the probable outcome of the pregnancy. Given this knowledge, the prospective parents can decide to terminate the pregnancy, or they can prepare themselves for the birth of a child with a specific problem. In the majority of cases the procedure reveals that the fetus does not have the defect, and the parents are spared months of needless anxiety.

A more recently developed procedure, **chorionic villus sampling,** is an alternative to amniocentesis and can be performed after only nine weeks of pregnancy. Test results are available in only a few days. Both amniocentesis and chorionic villi sampling can be carried out by using a needle inserted in the pregnant woman's abdomen, or the chorionic test can be done with a tube inserted into the cervix. One danger of amniocentesis has been that between one-half and one percent of the tests are followed by a miscarriage, so their use involves some risk to the fetus. The chorionic test may have a larger miscarriage rate, close to two percent. However, miscarriages also occur naturally as pregnancy progresses so some part of this increased risk might be explained by a miscarriage which would have occurred even if the chorionic procedure had not been used.

Another new test, the **alpha-fetoprotein test,** requires only a blood sample at the end of the fourth month of pregnancy. It can indicate not only possible genetic disorders such as Down syndrome but also neural tube defects such as *anencephaly,* in which the baby is born with a rudimentary brain or no brain at all, and *spina bifida,* in which a portion of the spine does not close and the nerve column is exposed. The alpha-fetoprotein blood test is not conclusive, so if the test is positive the pregnant woman needs a sonogram and perhaps amniocentesis as well.

Although these tests can save heartbreak for parents if a defect is detected, they may cause an unneeded risk for the fetus if the test shows no disorder to be present. They may also pose a difficult decision for couples who do not believe in abortion. The use of these tests is growing rapidly, however, in part because of fears by physicians of legal liability if the tests are not offered and the child has a birth defect.

DISORDERS CAUSED BY PRENATAL ENVIRON-MENT The environment in which the fetus lives before birth is a frequent cause of below-average intellectual functioning. In fact, mental retardation of prenatal origin is the most common of all birth defects. Prenatal factors that have been linked to mental retardation include maternal infections, blood incompatibilities and chronic maternal conditions, chemicals in the fetal environment, radiation, malnutrition, the age of the parents, and maternal stress.

Maternal Infections The placental sac surrounding the unborn infant acts as a barrier that prevents many infections from being transferred from the mother to the fetus, but a number of viruses may cross this barrier. Three viruses that are known to cause congenital malformations are **rubella virus** (German measles), **cytomegalovirus,** and **herpes virus hominus (herpes simplex).**

About half of all fetuses whose mothers contract rubella in the first three months of pregnancy are also infected. The virus destroys cells and may interfere with the fetal blood supply. In one group of children of mothers who had rubella while pregnant, about one-third were retarded (Chess, 1978). Retardation can also result if the mother has a bacterial infection such as syphilis or a chronic viral illness like herpes. Syphilis in the mother causes miscarriages and stillbirths as well as mental retardation, blindness, deafness, and other birth defects. Herpes infections in adults and older children are usually quite mild, but in a fetus or newborn child the same virus can cause widespread infection that can result in death. Although the herpes virus can pass through the placenta and infect the fetus, the most common way in which herpes is passed from mother to child is through direct contact during the birth process.

Rubella can be controlled by a general vaccination program. Syphilis can be treated with penicillin, preferably given to the mother, although damage may still occur if treatment is not begun as soon as the infection is discovered. Herpes simplex has no known cure, but since the child is usually infected by contact with the virus during the birth process, Caesarean section may avoid this contact and lower the risk of infection to the child.

Blood Incompatibilities and Chronic Maternal Conditions Sometimes biochemical substances in the fetus cause the mother to develop an antibody response to the baby. These antibodies may damage fetal tissues in much the same way that people sometimes reject organ transplants. Some chronic medical conditions in the mother may also cause retardation in the fetus. Hypertension (high blood pressure) and diabetes are examples of chronic disorders that may interfere with fetal nutrition and lead to brain damage. Both of these conditions can be treated in the pregnant woman if they are diagnosed early.

Drugs Drugs taken by the mother can pass through the placenta to the fetus. Even mild tranquilizers such as Librium are associated with an increase in the rate of serious fetal malformations. In addition, chemicals in the air, food, and water may affect the child before birth.

In recent years alcohol use during pregnancy has become recognized as an important cause of retardation.

FIGURE 16–17 This child shows a number of facial characteristics typical of fetal alcohol syndrome.

Even women who drink moderately during pregnancy may have children who are affected to some degree. So far no safe limits of alcohol use during pregnancy have been established.

Children born to mothers who drink heavily often exhibit **fetal alcohol syndrome (FAS),** a specific set of characteristics that includes retarded growth, physical defects and deformities, mental retardation, and other abnormalities of brain functioning and behavior. In severe cases, facial deformities are apparent at birth or in early childhood: small eyes, drooping eyelids, a short, upturned nose with a low bridge, flat cheeks, a thin upper lip, low-set ears, a receding chin, a bulging forehead, and an unusually large space between the nose and the mouth. Children with FAS are short and thin, with small heads. They grow slowly and their appetite is poor (see Figure 16–17).

Consistent with other evidence, a recent study found an average IQ of 68 in a group of adolescent and adult FAS individuals (Streissguth and others, 1991). Their academic functioning was typically at the second- to fourth-grade level, with arithmetic deficits most

common. Poor judgment, distractibility, and difficulty perceiving social cues were frequently noted. The individuals studied seemed to have little conception of the future or capacity to learn from experience. They ignored warnings and needed to have the simplest instructions repeated many, many times.

Not all children affected by alcohol in the womb develop the full FAS. If the mother's drinking is only moderately heavy, both physical and mental abnormalities may be subtler. For chronically alcoholic women who have one child with FAS, the chance that another child will also have it is 100 to 400 times higher than in the general population. (Streissguth and others, 1991).

It is hard to say how common fetal alcohol effects are because symptoms range from minor to incapacitating on a continuum without obvious breaks. One estimate of the prevalence rate of the full syndrome is one in 700 live births (Streissguth and others, 1991).

Children affected with FAS face many difficulties because of their cognitive disabilities. Michael Dorris, a professor at Dartmouth College who adopted a boy with FAS, described his son's life in this way:

> *My son will forever travel through a moonless night with only the roar of wind for company. Don't talk to him of mountains, of tropical beaches. Don't ask him to swoon at sunrises or marvel at the filter of light through leaves. He's never had time for such things, and he does not believe in them. He may pass by them close enough to touch on either side, but his hands are stretched forward, grasping for balance instead of pleasure. He doesn't wonder where he came from, where he's going. He doesn't ask who he is, or why. Questions are a luxury, the province of those at a distance from the periodic shock of rain. Gravity presses Adam so hard against reality that he doesn't feel the points at which he touches it. A drowning man is not separated from the lust for air by a bridge of thought—he is one with it— and my son, conceived and grown in an ethanol bath, lives each day in the act of drowning. For him there is no shore.*

—Dorris, 1989, p. 264

PROBLEMS AT AND AFTER BIRTH Certain conditions occurring at birth are known to increase the probability of mental retardation, although these are not nearly as frequent causes of retardation as some of the prenatal causes. Two of the most common birth complications are **asphyxia,** lack of oxygen, and **prematurity,**

birth three weeks or more before term. Some infants do not get enough oxygen during or before the birth process. If death does not result from this asphyxia, seizures, retardation, and other problems are likely to occur. Premature infants usually are low in birth weight. When a child weighs three pounds or less at birth, the risk of retardation as well as health problems becomes much greater. Because adolescents often give birth to small infants and—especially in the case of unmarried mothers—often do not have adequate medical care, their infants are at high risk for retardation and other problems (Andreasen & Black, 1991). For this reason alone, the increase in pregnancies among adolescent girls should be viewed with concern.

Damage to the central nervous system after birth can also cause retardation. Among the causes of such damage are infections, blows to the head, tumors, asphyxiation, and poisons. Some poisonous substances damage the brain cells by depriving them of oxygen. Carbon monoxide, barbiturates, and cyanide work in this way. Other poisons damage specific sites in the brain. Of these, lead, arsenic, and mercury are the most common.

Severe meningitis or encephalitis, which sometimes develops as a complication of mumps, measles, or chicken pox, can cause inflammation of the brain and the surrounding tissue. Often this results in retardation, seizures, or both. Some ear and blood infections can also damage brain tissues. Probably the most frequent causes of head injury are automobile accidents and child abuse. In an English institution for the retarded, researchers found that 11 percent of the children were handicapped because of brain damage associated with abuse (Buchanan & Oliver, 1977).

Psychosocial Disadvantage

About three-quarters of all retarded people are in the mildly retarded category. In many of these cases there are no obvious causal factors like the ones just discussed. However, careful epidemiological study often points to some contributing biological factors (Akesson, 1986). In many instances, these mildly retarded individuals cannot be singled out on the basis of their appearance, and often they are not identified as retarded until the early years of school. A very large number of children in this group come from families of low socioeconomic status. Because in many cases their parents' IQs also fall in the mildly retarded range, the question is often asked whether heredity is the predominant factor in their retardation.

Environment has been referred to by some as a threshold variable (Jensen, 1969), meaning that once a certain minimal quality of environment has been reached, further environmental stimulation is unimportant when compared to inherited capability. To put it another way, heredity provides a range of possibilities for the develop-

ing child, but the child's level of achievement within that rather wide range might be attributable to the environment in which he or she grows up. The results of many studies show that between 50 and 80 percent of the variation in intelligence factors is due to inheritance and the remainder to environmental influences (Zigler and others, 1984).

Psychosocial Enrichment

Some investigators have tried to manipulate the environment to determine the effect of an enriched environment on children who are thought to have low intellectual potential. In a program carried out in North Carolina, pregnant women with IQs averaging 80 were recruited for study (Ramey & Haskins, 1981). After their babies' births, half of the infants were cared for during the day at an educational day-care center and half were reared at home by their mothers. Both groups of children received medical care and dietary supplements, and their families were given social services if they requested them. At the age of three, the experimental children had significantly higher IQs than the control group. This difference seemed to be due to a decline in IQs of the control infants during the 12- to 18-month age period. By the time the children were five years old, 39 percent of the control group had IQs below 85, whereas only 11 percent of the experimental group had IQs in this range. This study suggests that educational day care beginning before three months of age results in normal intellectual development, at least until the age of five, for children of high-risk families.

Whether interventions that enrich the environment of economically deprived children who are at risk for retardation have a long-term effect on their intellectual performance is still an open question. Some investigators believe that interventions that begin in the very early years of life, such as the program described above, are most likely to succeed. Others believe that the early period of life is not uniquely critical and that later interventions also have a good chance of success (Clarke & Clarke, 1979). Most investigators would agree that work with the parents of young children, as well as with the children themselves, enhances the success potential for any program (Garber, 1988).

Typically, intervention programs produce improved scores during and immediately after the program. The same effect can be seen in the increased intelligence-test scores of culturally deprived children after their first year in school. However, in both cases these at-risk children seem to lose their early gains, and in later grades their performance worsens compared to that of other children. This change might be a function of the changing demands of school programs as children grow older. In the higher grades greater emphasis is placed on

abstract thinking. This is also true of the content of intelligence test questions aimed at older children. Perhaps many of these at-risk children are deficient in the ability to think abstractly. On the other hand, perhaps the special help in cognitive skills that the children obtained in the program was not complete enough to enable them to use those skills independently or to apply them to more complex levels of problem solving. This area of research is filled with many unanswered questions.

While in the past, retarded people were usually institutionalized for life, the current emphasis is on helping retarded people live more independent lives. The largest group of retarded individuals are classified as mildly retarded and this group has the greatest chance for living in the community on their own or with minimal support. Children who are mildly retarded, because they appear physically similar to other children and may have social or manual skills that partially mask their inability to handle intellectual tasks, may not be identified as retarded until they have been in school for several years. They may even remain unidentified throughout their entire school careers. However, people who are profoundly, severely, or moderately retarded are often identified soon after birth and may ultimately be placed in an institutional setting.

PUBLIC EDUCATIONAL PROGRAMS School programs for the retarded have changed greatly over the last 35 years. Special classes have been established for severely and moderately retarded students who previously were totally excluded from school programs, and many slow-learner classes for mildly retarded children have been abolished. The children from such classes have been **mainstreamed,** or integrated into regular classes. Both these changes have come about as a result of court decisions in cases dealing with the civil rights of the retarded.

The Education for All Handicapped Children Act of 1975 required public schools to provide free appropriate education to all handicapped children. Because of this law and recent court decisions, school districts are obligated to provide training for severely and profoundly retarded children. Such programs concentrate on basic communication and social skills. Although it is too early to assess whether they improve the child's performance, these programs do seem to prevent many severely and profoundly retarded children from being institutionalized in early childhood. Instead, a large number are now cared for at home, sometimes through adolescence or longer.

School classes for slow learners have been affected by a series of legal decisions, beginning with the *Brown v. Board of Education* case of 1954. In that decision, which marked the end of legally segregated schools and "separate but equal" education, special-education classes were criticized as offering poor education. Students were usually placed in classes for slow learners on the basis of intelligence tests, and critics argued that intelligence tests were unfair to lower-class or minority children because they were heavily loaded with socially and culturally biased items. These items would be familiar to middle-class children but might not be part of the experience of a child from a lower-class or minority family. Pressure to place mildly retarded children in regular classrooms has also come from laws requiring the "least restrictive" placement possible for any given child. There is a growing movement to avoid identifying and labeling the children as retarded because of concern that such labels may stigmatize them. For minority children in particular, it is feared that such labels may be a result of test bias rather than valid estimates of their abilities. Despite the potential benefits of "least restrictive" placement, however, some researchers believe that in certain states children who need special services may be denied them (Zigler & Hodapp, 1991).

Education in a mainstreamed or regular class is believed to be desirable for retarded children because exposure to normal role models and the absence of labeling might help them improve their achievement level and social adjustment. So far, however, this belief has not been supported by research findings. There seems to be little difference in performance between children who have been mainstreamed and those who have been placed in special classes. In one large study, both groups scored in the lowest one percent on standardized tests of reading and arithmetic (Kaufman and others, 1982). Nor does mainstreaming by itself improve the social status of a retarded child. In a study of more than 300 mainstreamed classrooms, the students were asked to rate each other's behavior. The mean rating for the retarded children was one standard deviation below that for their nonretarded classmates (Gottlieb and others, 1978) despite the fact that the basis of the ratings was not the label "retarded" but the *behavior* of the retarded children. Many retarded children lack social skills and an idea of what behaviors are socially appropriate. In addition, because retardation puts children at risk for lower academic performance than others of their age, those who feel they are achieving poorly may express frustration by aggressive behavior or by attention-getting actions that are annoying to their classmates.

COMMUNITY-LIVING PROGRAMS Emphasis on normalizing the lives of the retarded has increased in recent years. The same changes in the law requiring that even severely retarded individuals receive the least restrictive educational placement possible have been applied to the concept of overall care, too. As a result, many people who have been in institutions for many years have been discharged and have returned to the community. Young children who formerly would have been sent to institu-

FIGURE 16–18 In addition to providing shelter, group homes are a place where retarded adolescents and adults learn valuable homemaking and self-management skills.

tions often live at home and attend special school programs that include job training. At present, more retarded persons in residential care live in small, private facilities than in public institutions. New admissions to large state institutions, especially for children, are becoming increasingly rare.

Deinstitutionalization can have a major impact, not only on retarded individuals, but on their families as well. In one study, residents of a large institution were moved into small community-based living groups because of a court order (Latib and others, 1984). Initially most of their families opposed deinstitutionalization. Many of them had made the decision to institutionalize their relatives many years earlier, often under great stress. In general, they believed that their relatives had reached their highest level of development and had little chance of learning new skills. They thought they were adequately cared for and worried that they would not be protected in small residential settings. They also wondered how long funding would be available for community-based homes. Six months after the move, however, the families felt positively about it. Not only did they feel that deinstitutionalization was good for the member of their family who was now living in the community, but they felt happier themselves.

For retarded individuals who are discharged from large institutions, several kinds of living arrangements are possible. The most frequent choice is a group home for up to 15 residents. Other possibilities are a return to the retarded person's own family or to a foster home, or, less frequently, a move to a medium-sized institution or a nursing home (Craig & McCarver, 1984).

Group homes for the retarded function both as a permanent home for those who are unable to live independently and as a transition point for those who are

learning living skills that will help them live on their own (see Figure 16–18). Staff members work to broaden the resident's experiences—for example, by taking them on excursions. One problem in opening new group homes is the opposition of potential neighbors. Once the home is established, the opposition generally decreases and the neighbors' unrealistic fears about crime, property values, and quality of life dissipate (Okolo & Guskin, 1984).

An important part of community-living programs is the job training offered to residents through subsidized

FIGURE 16–19 A sheltered workshop offers both a place to learn job skills and a working environment for people who cannot compete for jobs on an equal basis.

sheltered workshops or special training programs where employees are not expected to work at the pace necessary to be economically feasible (see Figure 16–19). The woman described in the following excerpt illustrates how such programs enhance the lives of retarded individuals.

Linda had been in an institution for nearly 17 years before coming to the Community Residential Facility just two years ago. At 25, she has an estimated IQ of 21 and is physically handicapped. The home she lives in is near a large city and is a contemporary family house which has very homey and personalized living areas. Linda's home responsibilities include making her own bed and cleaning her own room; occasionally she helps clean the rest of the house and helps with the gardening. Linda works in a sheltered workshop doing piecework and other small jobs such as collating, assembling, and stapling, and she has been working for over one year. For working a half-day, two days per week, she earns over $20, which she puts into an account for clothing and recreation. Thirty hours a week, Linda attends an adult education class where she learns basic living skills. Linda gets along very well with other residents, but the facility operator doubts she will ever be able to live without supervised care.

—O'Connor, 1976, pp. 46–47

VOCATIONAL AND SOCIAL SKILLS TRAINING

Knowledge and use of appropriate vocational and social skills are key factors in success both in competitive job environments and in sheltered workshops. Skills training through modeling has been found to be a very effective technique. One study compared the effects of modeling with coaching the same skills (LaGreca and others, 1983). Several problem situations were modeled so that prospective workers could learn to identify both problem behaviors and appropriate ways of dealing with such situations.

You come to work in the morning and can't find one of the materials you need to do your job (for example, the napkins). Inappropriate solution: walk around, talking to co-workers; sit at table and do nothing. Appropriate solution: request help from supervisor politely.

You are working in the morning and the person working next to you is being very loud, talking and laughing. You are finding it hard

to concentrate on your work because of the noise. Inappropriate solution: yell at co-worker to "shut up"; throw something at co-worker; insult co-worker; threaten co-worker. Appropriate solution: politely request quiet behavior; ignore co-worker.

—LaGreca and others, 1983, p. 272

The effectiveness of modeling is shown by a comparison with both a coaching group and a control group. After seven weeks on the job only one of the 11 people in the modeling group had been fired. Half of the coaching group had been fired; in the control group, ten had been fired and only two were still on the job.

Another important aspect of retarded people's lives is a supportive network of people. One way to increase the amount of support available is to help the individual learn social skills. Another is to make sure that decisions about living and working conditions take friendships into account. If friendship networks are kept in mind when residents of facilities for the retarded have to be relocated, the outcome is likely to be much better. In one study, residents who had moved to a new home with chosen friends were more sociable several years later than residents who had been separated from friends (Romer & Heller, 1983). They were also better able to care for themselves.

While mentally retarded individuals are being integrated into the community, they are vulnerable to personal, sexual, and financial exploitation. One source of this problem is the tendency of the retarded to answer "yes" to all questions, regardless of content. Such readiness to agree clearly can have negative consequences. For one thing, it means that retarded people are likely to agree to inappropriate or unfair requests.

One way to prevent exploitation of retarded individuals is to pay special attention to teaching them what is expected of a person and how to say "no" (Schilling & Schinke, 1984). For example, participants in a training program for food service workers were taught how to handle their earnings and how to say "no" to people who asked to borrow money. Another problem area is sexual behavior. Training programs have taught retarded people how to recognize and escape from sexually exploitive situations. Mentally retarded individuals also need to be trained to understand what society views as appropriate sexual behavior and to avoid such acts as public masturbation and inappropriate sexual approaches to others.

Psychological and Social Problems

Retarded individuals are likely to experience psychological problems as well as intellectual retardation. In

one study, up to 40 percent of retarded children were rated by their parents or teachers as psychologically disturbed (Rutter and others, 1970). Severely retarded children exhibit an even higher rate of disturbance: Nearly half may be diagnosed as having a behavior disorder. The same types of disorders are seen in retarded children as in nonretarded children, although the frequencies of different types of disorders differ in the two groups. Those who are severely retarded are more likely to have a psychosis or to be hyperactive and less likely to have a conduct disorder (Rutter and others, 1975). This difference is probably explained by the likelihood that severely retarded children also have central nervous system damage.

Retarded children living with their parents may have more problems during adolescence than nonretarded children do. Mildly retarded adolescents in particular may experience a "friendship void." They tend to be socially isolated. Most of their contacts with others are at school, not in social activities. If they do have social interactions, these tend to be with younger children, not those of the same age (Brier, 1986). In one study, 84 percent of retarded children developed emotional or behavioral problems during adolescence (Zetlin & Turner, 1985). These included temper tantrums, violent or destructive behavior, use of drugs and alcohol, and an increase in withdrawal behavior. Many of these problems seemed to be related to the young people's growing awareness of the gap between themselves and other teenagers in terms of expectations for the future and ability to be independent. The retarded adolescents' desire for dating relationships was another source of problems. When these young people became adults, only one-third were still in conflict with their parents. The rest either had adjusted to dependence on their parents or had been able to establish fairly independent life styles that gave them satisfaction.

Retarded individuals often have a low opinion of themselves. When they live in the community this problem becomes more severe because there are more

FIGURE 16–20 This photo shows Victor, 30, and Kathy, 29, after they had announced their marriage plans. A few years ago such an announcement would have been almost unthinkable because both Kathy and Victor are retarded.

opportunities for comparisons with nonretarded people. In one study, retarded individuals living in an institution were more likely to rate themselves as smart and attractive than retarded people living in a community setting (Gibbons, 1985). Since the intellectual level of those in the institution was lower and the rated attractiveness no different, the community group's exposure to and self-comparisons with nonretarded individuals probably accounted for the difference.

The kinds of problems these adolescents and adults face can be helped by psychotherapy. Family therapy is often used, especially for adolescents. Individual psychotherapy can be useful in the same way that it may be helpful for nonretarded adolescents. Social skills training and job preparation also contribute to adjustment. Such techniques have helped many retarded people to adjust well, marry, and live semiindependent lives (see Figure 16–20).

Chapter Summary

AUTISTIC DISORDER

Autism is a relatively rare disorder, but one with profound effects. Two-thirds of those with autistic disorder are retarded.

Characteristics of Autistic Behavior Children with **autistic disorder** are impaired in social relationships, communication,

and activities. Many autistic children never develop speech. Those who do may have unusual speech patterns such as **echolalia,** the tendency to reply by repeating back what was said to them. They are likely to spend a great deal of time in repetitive motions or activities. Autism, although originally considered to be a psychosis, is now considered to be a

developmental disorder. Psychosis, although rare, does occur in childhood. Childhood schizophrenia, much less common than adult schizophrenia, does not usually occur before age seven or eight. Although the symptoms are similar, it is not known whether childhood schizophrenia is the same disorder as adult schizophrenia.

Research on Autistic Disorder Language disturbance is the most universal symptom of autism. The autistic person's cognitive problems don't seem to be the result of poor memory, but instead stem from difficulties with higher-level cognitive processing and symbolic thought. Autistic individuals also have social deficits because they seem unable to coordinate affective expression and behavior. This results in an inability to understand the signals sent out by others. Some type of brain pathology seems likely in autism. One-fifth of autistic children develop epileptic seizures in adolescence, the likelihood of developing these seizures is much higher in those who are severely retarded. Brain imaging techniques have shown that autistic children may be more likely to have stunted brain development in the cerebellum. If one child in a family is autistic, the chances of autism in subsequent children is much higher than that in the general population. Research on the genetics of autism suggests that what is inherited is some general tendency toward cognitive or language abnormalities rather than autism itself.

Therapy Severely autistic children are often treated by using a behavior modification program. Such programs' success is limited, although it may be successful with a subgroup of autistic children.

Prospects for Change A key predictor of outcome for an autistic child is development of language by age five. Intelligence test scores predict school and occupational outcome for these children just as they do for non-autistic children.

MENTAL RETARDATION

Mental retardation is defined as a significantly below-average level of intellectual functioning that is accompanied by impaired social functioning. Mental retardation is a chronic, irreversible condition that begins before age 18. Autistic children may also be retarded, but they form a special group that differs from other retarded children in several ways. Retarded children may have comparable levels of social and intellectual development, but autistic children have lower social than cognitive development. Autistic children also show severe language deficits and unusual behaviors that are not common in retardation.

Degrees of Mental Retardation Mental retardation is divided into four levels based on intelligence test scores. They include mild, moderate, severe, and profound retardation. There are two general categories of retardation: One is based on **psychosocial disadvantage** and one on biological factors not related to the child's social environment.

Biological Causes Retardation can be a result of a variety of **congenital** factors: inheritance of certain genes; **mutation** or changes in certain genes or chromosomes caused by a variety of

factors; gene contributions from each parent that together move the child over the threshold for retardation; or by chemical substances passed on to the fetus through the mother's placenta. Illness or injury after birth can also cause retardation. Both congenital factors and problems after birth are grouped together and termed **constitutional factors.** Those disorders caused by **dominant** genes require only one gene in the gene pair to produce the effect. Sometimes mutation of a parent's gene causes the first case of a dominant gene disorder found in a family. One example is **tuberous sclerosis.** Disorders caused by specific recessive genes require that the individual inherit that gene from both parents before symptoms appear. Examples of this type of disorder are **phenylketonuria (PKU)** and **Tay-Sachs disease.** Genetic defects carried on the **autosomes,** or nonsex cells, may produce more severe defects than those carried on the chromosome pair that determines sex. One abnormality carried by a sex-cell located gene pair is **Fragile X syndrome,** which is often associated with autistic behaviors and speech problems as well as retardation. **Chromosomal abnormality** occurs in ten percent of all conceptions, but most of these abnormal fetuses are spontaneously aborted. Of those that are not, the most frequent chromosomal abnormality is **Down syndrome.** Most children with Down syndrome are retarded, but the level of retardation varies. Children with Down syndrome have characteristic physical features and also seem to have specific cognitive deficits. Most cases of Down syndrome are the result of the presence of an extra number-21 chromosome, hence the name **trisomy-21.** A few cases of Down syndrome are caused by **translocation,** a process in which a piece of one chromosome breaks off and attaches itself to a different chromosome. Another even rarer cause of Down syndrome is **mosaicism,** a condition in which all cells in a person's body do not have the same chromosome count. The risk of having a child with Down syndrome increases dramatically with a mother's age. One way to determine if a fetus is affected by a trisomy or a disorder caused by dominant or recessive genes is through **amniocentesis,** an analysis of the amniotic fluid surrounding the fetus. Other prenatal procedures that are used to screen for a variety of defects include **ultrasound scans, chorionic villus sampling,** and an **alpha-fetoprotein** test. The most common cause of all birth defects is related to the **prenatal environment.** Retardation can be caused by maternal infections such as **rubella virus** (German measles), **cytomegalovirus,** and **herpes simplex.** If the mother has chronic high blood pressure or diabetes this may also interfere with fetal nutrition and produce retardation. An important cause of retardation is drugs that pass through the mother's placenta. **Fetal alcohol syndrome (FAS)** is an example of an important cause of both physical and mental abnormalities in children. Birth complications, prematurity, accidents, tumors, asphyxiation and severe illness such as encephalitis may also result in brain damage and retardation. A particularly important and preventable cause of retardation and brain damage is child abuse.

Psychosocial Disadvantage A large number of children, especially those with mild retardation, come from families of low socioeconomic status. Because many of their parents are also mildly retarded, it is not clear whether the children's retardation is related to heredity, environment, or a combination of both.

Psychosocial Enrichment If children from psychosocially dis-advantaged homes are given educational day care from an early age, they are less likely to be classified as retarded on intelligence tests. Little is known about the long-term effects of such programs, however. Another aspect of psychosocial enrichment is the current emphasis on helping retarded people live as independent lives as possible. One way this is done is through public education programs for the retarded. These have changed greatly, largely through the impetus of the Education for All Handicapped Children Act of 1975 that required public schools to provide appropriate education for all handicapped children. Programs include those for severely and profoundly retarded children where the emphasis is on basic communication and social skills. Such programs seem to delay institutionalization for these children because more of them are cared for at home through adolescence or longer. Another legal decision, the *Brown v. Board of Education* case of 1954 not only ended legal racial segregation of schools, but it also placed pressure on schools to integrate or **mainstream** retarded children into their regular classes. Although it was anticipated that doing away with special classes for the retarded would improve the quality of their educational experience, research findings have not demonstrated that this has happened. Deinstitutionalization efforts have meant that several kinds of living arrangements are possible for many retarded individuals. These include a return to their families, foster homes, group homes, or nursing homes. For those who can profit from them, sheltered workshops that teach job skills and also may provide subsidized employment have been valuable. Both vocational and social skills training are important for the success of retarded people in all these living and working situations.

Psychological and Social Problems Retarded persons are likely to experience psychological problems. Although these prob-lems are the same types found in the general population, the frequencies differ. Adolescence is a particularly difficult time for retarded children living at home and for their parents, at least in part because the teenagers experience a growing gap between their social expectations and ability to function independently and the expectations and abilities of non-retarded adolescents. Psychotherapy can be useful in dealing with these problems.

Therapies and Their Evaluation

C H A P T E R 1 7

Psychotherapy
Psychodynamic Therapy and Psychoanalysis
Humanistic and Existential Therapies
The Cognitive Psychotherapies

Behavior Therapy

Cognitive-Behavioral Approaches
Cognitive-Behavioral Interventions
Relaxation Training
Exposure Therapy
Modeling

Group Therapy
Cognitive-Behavioral Group Therapy
Family and Marital Therapy
Psychodrama

Integration of Psychologically Based Therapeutic Approaches

Research on the Psychological Therapies
Outcome Studies
Comparing Therapies
Components of Effective Therapy
Improving Therapy Research

Biological Therapies
Electroconvulsive Therapy
Drug Therapies

Hospitalization

Chapter Summary

Jan Sawka, *Memory*, 1991. Courtesy Carolyn Hill Gallery, New York.

*B*etty Rouse, housewife and mother of three adolescent children, had been in psychotherapy for two years. She had sought therapy because she felt herself to be an unhappy, inadequate person, who, as she put it, "was not good for much besides cooking dinner and chauffeuring the kids around to Scout meetings.

During the first several months of therapy, she talked mainly about herself. As time passed, however, her husband Fred was mentioned with increasing frequency and strong emotion. By the end of therapy, Betty concluded that, while many of her problems were of her own making, Fred had consistently made them worse by showing that he saw her as "just a housewife and mother," not as someone who was admirable for her own sake. After trying fruitlessly to talk with Fred about how he always belittled her, Betty concluded that her self-esteem was more important to her than she had ever realized and that Fred would only hinder its growth. With great pain and guilt, mainly because of the effect it might have on the children, Betty decided to get a job, live apart from Fred, and eventually get a divorce. She hoped one day to meet a man who would both love her and value her as a person.

Did Betty Rouse's psychotherapy have good or bad effects? The answer depends on a number of things, including her past life and one's own values. Therapy situations involve a special relationship between a professional clinician and a person with a problem. A therapist's job is difficult and hard to evaluate because each person's problem is unique and because the various therapeutic approaches differ greatly. Would the outcome of Betty Rouse's therapy have been different if she had been seeing a behavior therapist, a biologically oriented psychiatrist, or a family therapist? So many factors are involved that we cannot answer this question,

but it is possible to make comparisons among the therapeutic approaches used for different types of cases.

It is important to keep in mind the similarities as well as the differences among the various therapeutic approaches. All therapeutic relationships aim to provide clients with certain ingredients that are missing from their lives. Regardless of their therapeutic orientation, all clinicians must deal with the patient's psychological state and with his or her expectation of receiving help. All therapists attempt to form some sort of supportive therapeutic relationship. All clinicians must create a problem-solving setting, communicate their views of the problems presented, and help the client devise possible solutions to those problems.

In preceding chapters we have described major therapeutic approaches to specific types of maladaptive behavior. We have discussed the "talking therapies," such as psychoanalysis and client-centered counseling, in which conversations between the client and the therapist are the vehicle for achieving change; cognitive–behavioral therapies, such as systematic desensitization and building of social skills and confidence in using them, which involve applications of learning and cognitive principles in specially structured clinical situations; and biological therapies, such as antipsychotic, antidepressive, or tranquilizing drugs and electroconvulsive treatments, which are aimed at achieving behavior change through physical means.

Although we have talked about these approaches in relation to specific disorders, it is useful to summarize what we know about the various therapeutic methods in general. Reviewing these methods toward the end of the book will highlight how much we have learned along the way and also lay the groundwork for a discussion of how different therapies can be evaluated and compared. Do most or all of the different therapeutic approaches have common elements? Is a particular therapy effective for certain types of problems but not for others? What gaps exist in current knowledge about therapies and their rates of success? In the following pages, we will attempt to answer these and other questions. First we will discuss the psychologically based therapies. These include psychodynamic therapy and psychoanalysis, cognitive therapies, and behavioral and cognitive behavioral therapies either used with individuals or with groups. Next we will survey the uses of biologically based therapies, and finally cover the effects of hospitalization both in its therapeutic and protective aspects.

Psychotherapy

All forms of psychotherapy involve interchanges between a client and a therapist. These interchanges, which are nonverbal as well as verbal, are aimed at understanding what is on the client's mind. This understanding is then used as a basis for efforts to change the client's maladaptive ways of thinking, reacting to situations, and relating to others.

Most psychotherapists adhere to some type of psychodynamic or cognitive theory. Psychodynamic orientations emphasize the role of unconscious conflict in causing personal problems, whereas cognitive orientations emphasize the role of unrealistic or irrational thinking. Many psychotherapists utilize both psychodynamic and cognitive concepts in working with clients.

In the course of their work, and regardless of their theoretical orientations, psychotherapists must perform three tasks: (1) listen, (2) understand, and (3) respond. The therapist listens to the patient in order to learn about his or her preoccupations, worries, and concerns. Listening serves two functions: It lets the therapist hear about topics that the client brings up spontaneously, and it provides information pertinent to the therapist's hypotheses about the client's problems. Listening provides a basis for the therapist's understanding of the client's self-concept and view of the world.

Through listening and understanding, the therapist becomes able to respond. The response might be a question aimed at eliciting more information, or it might be a comment. The comment might be an interpretation of what has been going on in the session or in the client's interpersonal relationships. Those relationships can be divided into three categories.

1. Current in-treatment relationship
2. Current out-of-treatment relationships
3. Past relationships

The current in-treatment relationship has to do with interaction between the therapist and the client. (Do they like each other? Is there tension between them?) Current out-of-treatment relationships involve significant others such as the client's spouse, friends, families, or employer. (Is the patient experiencing more tension at work? Are there opportunities for good social relationships?) Psychodynamically oriented therapists in particular attempt to explore past relationships in order to uncover clues to the causes of current difficulties. (Are current difficulties with friends consistent with or a continuation of undesirable relationships in early childhood?)

Therapists are interested in determining the degree to which these three types of relationships may be related; for example, are conflicts between the client and the therapist similar to the client's earlier conflicts with parents or current conflicts between the client and a spouse or friend? In addition to searching for continu-

ities in interpersonal relationships, the therapist is attentive to themes that recur over several sessions. How similar is the way the client and the therapist relate to each other in the twentieth session to the way they related during their first therapeutic meeting? Are similar or different emotions and motives expressed as the therapy progresses?

Psychodynamic Therapy and Psychoanalysis

Although psychoanalysis greatly influenced the development of psychodynamic therapy, there are now a great variety of psychodynamic therapeutic approaches. Because psychoanalysis takes a long time and is expensive, only a small fraction of the people who desire it can experience that form of therapy. However, psychoanalytic concepts and techniques are widely used in ways that make them more suitable for the treatment of larger numbers of clients by many psychodynamically-oriented therapists.

Psychodynamic therapy is typically conducted with the client and the therapist sitting facing or almost facing each other. The client is encouraged to review early relationships with parents and significant others, but the therapist also directs attention to the situations facing the client at present. The client is expected to do most of the talking, while the psychodynamic therapist occasionally interjects clarifications to assist the client in understanding the dynamics of the problem that led him or her to seek professional help.

Psychoanalysis is a specific subtype of psychotherapy. Before a psychoanalysis formally begins, the psychoanalyst has a series of sessions with the client to determine the suitability of this therapeutic approach (See Table 17–1). A psychoanalysis requires on the average between two and five years, usually with four to five sessions per week. Over the years, the total number of sessions has increased. In contrast to psychodynamic therapy, the client lies on a couch and the therapist sits out of the client's line of sight in order to avoid distracting the client from the process of free association. In **free association,** the client expresses thoughts and feelings in as free and uninhibited a manner as possible. This expression results in a natural flow of ideas unencumbered by interruptions or explanations. The examination of dreams and fantasies is also important in psychoanalysis to a greater degree than in other psychodynamic therapies. Although the following example is not drawn from a psychoanalytic session, it illustrates the therapeutic use of fantasy material.

A 26-year-old patient reported that he was feeling rejected by his fiancée although she had done nothing to justify his reaction. He then reported that the feeling had started the previous day when he had been at a picnic with his fiancée and his best friend. Although his fiancée and his friend had been attentive to him, he felt uncomfortable. He then recalled that during the picnic he had experienced the following daydream. "Jane (his fiancée) and Bob (his friend) began to look at each other in a loving way. They passed signals back and forth of getting rid of me. They arranged to get together later that night. I got the old feeling of being rejected—wanting to be in but kept out and not wanted. They sneaked off at night and necked and had sex. Then they told me about it and I gave her up although I felt a deep loss at the same time." After having experienced this fantasy, he had felt rejected by his fiancée

Table 17–1

Who Is a Good Candidate for Psychoanalysis?

The cost of psychoanalysis, its length, and the relatively small number of certified psychoanalysts place an obvious limit on the number of people who can enter this type of therapy. Beyond these practical limitations, psychoanalysts are in general agreement that four personal characteristics are important factors in whether or not a course of analysis is likely to be successful.

1. *Motivation*. The client needs strong motivation to persevere in light of the intense, lengthy treatment.
2. *Ability to form a relationship*. The patient must have the capacity to form, maintain, and ultimately detach from, a close, trusting relationship.
3. *Introspection and capacity for insight*. Psychoanalysis requires curiosity about one's self and the capacity for self-scrutiny.
4. *Ego strength*. The client must be able to accept the "rules" of psychoanalysis and be open to sometimes painful facts and interpretations.

even though in reality she continued to be very affectionate to him.

After recounting the fantasy in the therapeutic hour, the patient had a stream of associations. "I feel sad and low, almost as though she actually was unfaithful. Bob reminds me of competing with my brother. I was always second fiddle to him. . . . I never made it up to his level. I was always losing out. . . . He was always better than me. Everybody liked him more than me."

The patient was then able to view his unpleasant reaction at the picnic as analogous to his early pattern of expecting to be pushed to one side by his brother. He visualized Bob's displacing him as his brother had previously triumphed over him. It became clear to him that his current reactions of jealousy and vulnerability were not justified on the basis of the reality situation. With this realization, his feelings of estrangement from his fiancée disappeared.

—Beck, 1970, pp. 6–7

Bob's discovery of the relationship between his early experiences and his current tendency to distort reality is an example of the **insight,** or understanding of one's inner life that is an important goal of psychoanalysis as well as other psychodynamic therapies. The following case presents another example.

After months of talking about her husband as a demanding, overbearing man who was always gloomy, Rose Francis, aged 50, remarked to her therapist: "You know, I guess I really don't like him." There was a tone of wonder and surprise in her voice when she said this. After recognizing her strong negative feelings toward her husband, Mrs. Francis found it possible to identify and sympathize with some of her husband's worries and concerns. She became better able to see the world through his eyes. The opportunity to tell her therapist, "You know, I guess I really don't like him," enabled Rose to be more accepting of her husband than she had been for years. Gaining insight into negative feelings often enables an individual to be more objective about the situation that gave rise to the feelings in the first place. In this case, Rose was able to ask herself the question, "Why does he behave as he does toward me?" and this thought then allowed her to think about the specific behaviors in the situation rather than about her angry feelings.

An important feature of many forms of psychotherapy is **transference,** the displacement by the client of affect and feelings from one important person (mother, father, spouse) to another, specifically, the therapist. In **positive transference,** the patient feels predominantly friendly and affectionate toward the therapist. In **negative transference** hostility predominates. **Countertransference** refers to the therapist's emotional reactions to a patient. It is important for the success of treatment that the therapist be aware of the countertransference reactions. They may also provide important clues to the client's relationships with others. Psychoanalysts must be analyzed themselves because of the belief that their self-insight will increase their awareness of their countertransference reactions (see Figure 17–1).

The case of Bill Jenkins, a 40-year-old construction supervisor who sought psychotherapy because of the increasing number of arguments he was having with his wife, provides an example of transference.

During the first twenty sessions he described in detail to the therapist frustrations connected with his marital and work situations. In these sessions, he never referred to any thoughts he might have had about the therapist. In the twenty-first session, Jenkins noticed a small crack in one of the walls of the therapist's office. He said to the therapist: "It looks like the construction company that put up that wall didn't do a very good job." After several uncomfortable pauses, he went on, "You know, Doc, I feel embarrassed saying this but somehow I keep feeling sorry for you, feeling like, in a way, you've been a loser. Like that lousy construction job over there (pointing to the crack in the wall).

FIGURE 17–1 Therapists may have negative reactions to patients because of countertransference.

(Drawing by D. Reilly; © 1991 The New Yorker Magazine, Inc.)

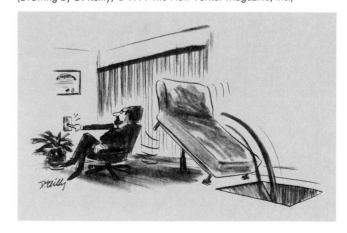

Some of those construction guys are pretty smart fellows who don't mind taking advantage of innocent people."

The characteristic Jenkins was attributing to the therapist (being a loser) could not have been based on facts available to him because Jenkins knew little about the therapist's background. What he said was the first outward expression of his developing relationship with and fantasies concerning the therapist. In subsequent sessions, Jenkins himself observed the similarity between his pictures of the therapist and his father, who was an alcoholic and a "loser." At one point he said, "It doesn't make sense, does it, for me to see you as being like my father?"

In asking that question, Jenkins showed insight and came close to making an interpretation of his behavior toward the therapist (seeing him as a loser like his father). Interpretations of behavior that arise during psychotherapy sessions may be made by either the therapist or the client. Many people go into psychotherapy expecting to be told what is wrong with them and what to do about it, but psychotherapists usually limit their intervention to making interpretations when they seem especially appropriate and the client seems unable to make or express them. Through these interpretations, therapists seek to expose areas of conflict, portions of which have been unconscious, and to help the client understand past psychological events. During therapy, individuals may be confronted with an interpretation that they have an interest in not acknowledging. They may become irritated with the therapist for confronting them, and in an effort to protect themselves they may try to think of more acceptable, but incorrect, explanations for their behavior. Most therapists prefer that clients evolve their own interpretations and then use them to achieve self-understanding with the help of the therapist. Psychodynamic treatment is aimed at helping the clients place their motivations in perspective and redirect the influence of the motivations on everyday life.

In psychoanalysis, transference and countertransference reactions are ultimately addressed. In other forms of psychotherapy, interpretations of these processes might be less important than dealing with the pressing problems in the client's day-to-day life. This does not mean that transference and countertransference do not occur or that the therapist doesn't think they are important. It means that the therapist has decided to give the highest priority to the problems that the client feels are most crucial. In some cases psychotherapists wish that they could explore certain aspects of the client's thinking but conclude that the client isn't ready to engage in such exploration.

In the initial stages of psychotherapy, tentative answers must be sought to a number of questions:

- Why did the client come to me?
- What are the pressing problems from the client's point of view?
- What underlying problems is the client not aware of?
- Will it be possible to help the client explore these underlying problems?

The answers to these questions help the therapist set objectives and decide on tactics for later stages of therapy. Clients often feel that as a result of their therapy experience they are able to see themselves, their past lives, and the people in their lives in a more objective light.

Identifying the subjective reactions of both clients and therapists to what goes on in therapy sessions is an important research task. Illustrative of how this task can be approached is the study of "good" and "bad" psychotherapy sessions. For example, Hoyt and others (1983) had psychotherapists and independent observers rate the quality of therapy sessions. The ratings were then related to what had gone on in the sessions. One finding was that therapists and independent observers often disagreed about the relationship between specific occurrences in the sessions and their degree of "goodness" or "badness." Therapists seemed to believe that a session was not particularly "good" if the client seemed resistant or difficult to relate to. On the other hand, outside observers often felt that a session was productive if the client was difficult and the therapist had to take a more active role as a result. Table 17–2 lists factors that

Table 17–2

Factors Contributing to "Good" and "Bad" Psychotherapy Sessions as Rated by Independent Observers

Factors Contributing to "Good" Sessions

1. The patient was encouraged to express thoughts and feelings.
2. The meaning of the patient's behavior was discussed.
3. The patient's avoidance of painful material was discussed.
4. The patient's responsibility for what went on in the session was discussed.

Factors Contributing to "Bad" Sessions

1. There were long silences.
2. The therapist used humor in discussing topics.

SOURCE: Adapted from Hoyt and others, 1983. The *Journal of Nervous and Mental Disease.* Copyright © 1983 by Williams and Wilkins.

independent observers rated as contributing to either "good" or "bad" sessions.

HYPNOSIS Hypnosis is the process of inducing a trance-like state in which the person being hypnotized is receptive to suggestions made by the hypnotist. In addition to receptivity to suggestion, the hypnotic state is characterized by an altered state of consciousness in which focused attention and concentration appear to be maximized. The hypnotized person seems exceptionally attentive to inner experience during the hypnotic session. Some psychotherapists use hypnosis for a variety of purposes: to suggest specific changes in thinking or behavior, as an aid in psychotherapy (for example, to help a client overcome anxiety or deal with upsetting ideas), and to enhance relaxation. Although the technique has been used clinically for years, research on hypnosis is in its infancy. There is considerable controversy over what hypnosis actually is and whether it really involves a special trance-like state. Because of its success in inducing states that appear to involve relaxation, it has aroused the interest of behavior therapists as well as psychotherapists (Weitzenhoffer, 1989).

It is now known that hypnosis is an altered state of consciousness—an intense alertness in which the mind can screen out extraneous matters and focus on particular details. The hypnotic trance is characterized by extreme relaxation and heightened susceptibility to suggestion. It allows people to suspend logical reasoning and draw upon psychological strengths that they do not normally command voluntarily. The focused concentration and heightened suggestibility of the trance state help the individual accept the therapist's directions and come to grips with problems more rapidly.

Hypnotists typically begin their sessions by asking subjects to stare at an object, suggesting in a soothing voice that they are relaxing and becoming hypnotized, and that they will find it easy to comply with the hypnotist's suggestions (see Figure 17–2). In experimental settings this "hypnotic induction" typically lasts for about 15 minutes. If the subjects are willing to be hypnotized, they appear relaxed and drowsy and become responsive to test suggestions from the hypnotist. Afterward they report changes in bodily sensations and claim that they have been hypnotized. People who are susceptible to hypnosis have beliefs and expectations that motivate them to adopt the hypnotic state. They usually have better than average ability to focus attention as well as a vivid imagination.

While the potential for emotional exploitation or deception is inherent in all forms of psychotherapy and all forms of human influence, this potential is a particular danger of hypnosis. For this reason, therapists disapprove of stage magicians who use hypnosis casually as entertainment. Inappropriate suggestions may create turmoil and conflict even though the patient does not act on them. That kind of harm is most likely when hypnosis is performed for its own sake or for the therapist's gratification. Hypnosis is not a treatment for severe mental disorders such as schizophrenia and major depression, but it has been used for almost everything else—from phobias to sexual problems and psychosomatic illnesses, to bedwetting and nail-biting in children.

Humanistic and Existential Therapies

Several forms of psychotherapy either disagree with the assumptions of psychodynamic theory or modify

FIGURE 17–2 A competent hypnotist can induce a trance in a variety of ways in about 10 minutes. A traditional method is to relax the subject and to direct attention—in a confident, rhythmic, monotonous, repetitive voice—to sensations that are usually ignored: "Your hand is getting heavier and heavier, it feels so heavy it is hard to keep it raised, it is becoming even heavier."

them in certain ways. The neo-Freudians accept most psychodynamic principles but reject the emphasis placed by psychoanalytic theory on instinctual unconscious impulses. **Humanistic therapies** emphasize people's desire to achieve self-respect. Existential therapists, whose viewpoints often overlap those of humanistic therapists, emphasize the need to confront basic questions of existence, such as: What is the meaning of my life? Am I hiding from myself?

CLIENT-CENTERED THERAPY Carl Rogers, the founder of **client-centered therapy,** saw the individual as seeking personal growth but needing the support of an appreciative, accepting therapist. The therapist is a nondirective facilitator who encourages the client's self-exploration and efforts to achieve greater maturity and self-confidence. Whereas in traditional psychodynamic therapy the therapeutic relationship—including transference and countertransference—and the therapist's interpretations help clients solve personal problems, in client-centered therapy a nonjudgmental therapist facilitates the process of self-understanding by serving as a mirror for the client.

As a group, client-centered therapists have been among the leaders in research about what actually goes on in psychotherapy. Rogers saw psychotherapy as a growth process and encouraged objective study of the events that occur as therapy progresses. He recognized that people's ideas and ways of looking at the world influence their emotional lives.

The client-centered therapist believes that perceptions and cognitions determine whether an individual has warm, positive interpersonal relationships or strained relationships that stir up unpleasant emotions. As the client restructures his or her view of the world, troubling emotions such as anxiety and anger become less potent. For example:

When I started coming here, I saw my problem as anger—toward other people as well as myself. There were times I felt like a seething inferno. You sat there as I ranted and raved and I really appreciated the fact that you listened so attentively to everything I said. Sometimes you would reflect back to me what I had just said, sometimes you would just ask a question about a comment I had made. I don't really know how it happened but I began thinking about why I get so angry at home. Then a lot of things fell into place. I was angry because I was doing things I didn't want to do. I was doing those things out of guilt and obligation. Why should I think I had to be nice to people I can't stand? When I finally

realized that I didn't have to do certain things, I became more spontaneous and less angry.

Client-centered therapists believe that people are not innately destructive, but they do have negative feelings. From the client-centered perspective, these feelings are considered to be an outgrowth of externally imposed distortions that force people to alter their behaviors and feelings much as a seed, trapped under a brick is forced to contort its growth to reach air and sun. Rogers thought of therapy as present-oriented and existential. Labels and diagnoses were not useful. What was needed was **unconditional positive regard,** reflected in the therapist's nonjudgmental, empathetic listening. Whereas a behavior therapist would concentrate on getting clients to change their behavior, a Rogerian therapist would focus on supplying an environment in which the client feels free to express thoughts and feelings. The client-centered therapists assume that unconditional positive regard will increase the client's self-acceptance and self-knowledge, which, in turn, will lead the client to change his or her behavior.

EXISTENTIAL THERAPY Existential therapies also emphasize the present and the need to recognize the uniqueness of each client. Existential therapists work as partners with their clients. Many combine humanistic and psychodynamic approaches in dealing with anxiety, its causes, and the defenses that the client erects to cope with it. In this sense, the existential approach is a therapeutic hybrid.

The emphasis of existential therapy is on helping clients come to terms with basic issues concerning the meaning and direction of their lives and the choices by which they shape their own destinies. Like the majority of clinicians who see nonhospitalized clients, most existential therapists work with people who are troubled by anxiety and depression. Existential therapists see their primary role as helping lonely people make constructive choices and become confident enough to fulfill their unique selves rather than repressing or distorting their experiences.

GESTALT THERAPY **Gestalt therapy** focuses on clients' perceptions of themselves and the world. It is based on the recognition that people unconsciously organize their perceptions as a *Gestalt:* a meaningful, integrated whole. A Gestalt therapist uses a variety of techniques, including role playing, in an effort to stimulate the client to express strong emotions.

Fritz Perls, the founder of Gestalt therapy, stressed the relationships among distorted perceptions, motivations, and emotions. Perls's therapy was a function of his personality. He could be inspiring and manipulative, perceptive and hostile. He said in his autobiography, "I

believe I am the best therapist for any type of neurosis in the States, maybe in the world. . . . At the same time I have to admit that I cannot work successfully with everybody" (Perls, 1969). Unlike most humanistic therapists, who stress the importance of unconditional positive regard for the client, Perls believed that the therapist's main task was to frustrate the client, to make him or her angry enough to fight out conflicts with authority and thereby develop enhanced feelings of self-worth. Perls believed that instead of trying to reconstruct the history of the client's relationships with others as is done in traditional psychodynamic therapy and psychoanalysis, the therapist should stress the client's moment-to-moment experiences as each session progresses.

Gestalt therapists believe that anxiety and personality disorders arise when people dissociate parts of themselves, particularly their need for personal gratification, from awareness. Because dreams often contain clues to dissociated parts of the self, Gestalt therapists encourage discussion and acting out of dreams.

The Cognitive Psychotherapies

The **cognitive psychotherapies** seek to correct misconceptions that contribute to maladjustment, defeat, and unhappiness. Imagine someone who, as a result of the vicissitudes of life, develops a faulty belief to the effect that "no one could possibly like me if I reveal my true self." Such a person is likely to avoid others, refrain from spontaneous behavior, and pine away in loneliness. Another set of circumstances may convince someone that a series of incidents of "bad luck" means that whatever happens next is likely to be disastrous. Thereupon the individual becomes fearful of the immediate future. Or, after many frustrations and conflicts, a person becomes so anxious that he or she is convinced that a "nervous breakdown" is imminent. The person then tries to avoid all stress even though the best approach would probably be coping with normal stresses—since success in handling them would provide the only convincing evidence of mental well-being. As Figure 17–3 indicates, even misconceptions that might seem positive may cause people problems and can also be a focus in cognitive therapy.

Since opinions, beliefs, or conceptions are ordinarily formed on the basis of evidence, adequate or inadequate, we can also assume that beliefs may be modified by evidence. Psychotherapy may, in fact, provide one of the few situations in which individuals are encouraged to think somewhat systematically about their beliefs, particularly their beliefs about themselves. A number of psychotherapeutic approaches share the assumption that maladaptive behavior is a product of unrealistic perceptions and conditions. The various cog-

FIGURE 17–3 Is this the real world? If this man believes that he deserves this sort of hero's welcome all the time, he may need help in coping with the letdowns that will occur when he is not welcomed as a conquering hero.

(Drawing by Frascino; © 1987 The New Yorker Magazine, Inc.)

nitive therapies use different tactics in redirecting the way people see and interpret their experiences, but they all generally reject the Freudian emphasis on the powerful role of unconscious drives.

An early cognitive approach to therapy was developed by George Kelly. Kelly's (1955) **psychology of personal constructs** led him to ask clients to examine the roles they played in interacting with others and the assumptions underlying those roles. In his **fixed-role therapy** Kelly encouraged his clients to practice new roles and relationships. Kelly saw people as problem-solvers whose faulty beliefs and assumptions often lead to undesirable solutions to the problems of living. According to Kelly, by encouraging the client to discuss personal constructs and social roles, the therapist helps the client question and reevaluate aspects of his or her life that arouse anxiety.

Another clinical approach based on cognitive theory is Albert Ellis's **rational–emotive therapy.** Ellis (1970) believes that self-defeating thinking is at the root of maladaptive behavior. Such thinking is based on arbitrary, inaccurate assumptions about oneself and others. It is often marked by a preoccupation with "musts": "I *must* always be friendly to people," I *must* not disappoint my parents," "I *must* be a big success." In rational–emotive therapy these musts are seen as causes of emotional arousal, which, if maintained at too high a level for too long a time, result in psychological and physical wearing down. Therapists who adhere to this approach believe that most of these and other self-

defeating musts are pounded into our heads as children, and we tend to accept them without question. Thus, rational–emotive therapy has two goals: to get people to question these fundamental, but mistaken, beliefs, and then to exchange them for more constructive ones (Rorer, 1989*a,* 1989*b*).

During the course of therapy the cognitive therapist actually demonstrates the ways in which unrealistic self-verbalizations can create or worsen emotional problems. The therapist also actively questions and contradicts faulty, unreasonable assumptions by the client and suggests alternative ways of thinking. Role playing is often used, with the therapist demonstrating the behavioral consequences of different types of beliefs.

Aaron Beck's (1976) cognitive therapy is also directed toward the thoughts that underlie intense, persistent emotional reactions. Beck's technique involves frequent, gentle questioning of the client about the basis for what he or she is saying. Beck speaks of "automatic thoughts" that seem to arise by themselves, without reasoning. These thoughts are accepted as valid even though they are not the products of rational consideration of alternatives. Children who simply accept their parents' values without questioning them are engaging in automatic thought. According to Beck, therapy should be aimed at terminating automatic thinking and replacing it with thoughts that result from rational consideration of alternatives.

Beck's cognitive therapy has been used with various forms of maladaptive behavior, but he has specialized in work with depressed people. In this work, emphasis is placed on the irrational ideas that contribute to feelings of depression and thoughts of suicide. The approach basically consists of a collaborative inquiry into the validity of clients' false beliefs about themselves, the world at large, or the future. For example, a client who believes he or she is a worthless individual may be encouraged to offer evidence in support of that view and then be asked to consider possible alternative interpretations of such evidence. In addition, the client might be assigned the task of empirically testing the validity of a depressive belief. Eventually, the weight of evidence should serve to undermine the depressive attitude (Beck & Weishaar, 1989).

Cognitive therapy may be an effective treatment for panic reactions as well as for depression. In one experiment, 17 patients averaged four panic attacks a week at the start; they had only one a week after six weeks of cognitive therapy and none at all when they completed treatment (Sokol and others, 1989). All were still free of symptoms after a year, and their depression and general anxiety were also greatly reduced. Figure 17–4 illustrates some results of this study. In contrast to the long-term success of cognitive therapy, people given drug treatment for panic attacks tend to relapse within a few months

FIGURE 17–4 Mean number of panic attacks as a function of weeks in treatment.

(Sokol, L., A.T. Beck, R.L. Greenberg, F.D. Wright, and R.J. Berchick, Cognitive therapy of panic disorder: A nonpharmacological alternative, *The Journal of Nervous and Mental Disease,* 177, 711–716, Coyright © 1989 by Williams & Wilkins)

when they are taken off the drug (Sokol and others, 1989).

The working hypothesis of cognitive therapy is that the best way to solve emotional problems is to alter the patient's thinking through cognitive restructuring. This form of psychotherapy concentrates mainly on the way people perceive the world and how they reason about it in everyday situations. Various techniques are used to expose and correct biased attention and recall, misinterpretation of events and statements, false assumptions, rigid beliefs, unjustified generalizations, inferences based on insufficient evidence, and other errors.

Behavior Therapy

Behavior therapy uses operant and classical conditioning based techniques in efforts to change maladaptive behavior. Table 17–3 lists the basic assumptions of behavior therapy. The operant techniques used in behavior therapy led to an approach referred to as behavior modification. The classical conditioning approach resulted in a variety of desensitization techniques that are used to reduce people's fear of specific situations or particular objects. **Behavior modification** refers to the application of operant learning principles to bring about a specific change in behavior. Although behavior modification originated as a technique based on operant conditioning, combinations of behavioral and cognitive approaches are now the most used approach to programs for behavior change. Operant conditioning methods use schedules of reinforcement and shaping to gradually achieve a desired response. Special prompts might be

Table 17–3

Basic Assumptions of Behavior Therapy

1. Most abnormal behavior is acquired and maintained according to the same principles as normal behavior.
2. Most abnormal behavior can be modified through the application of social-learning principles.
3. The current determinants of behavior must be assessed.
4. People are best described by what they think, feel, and do in specific life situations.
5. Treatment methods are precisely specified and objectively evaluated.
6. Treatment outcome is evaluated in terms of generalization to the real-life setting and its maintenance over time.
7. Treatment strategies are individually tailored to different problems in different individuals.
8. Extensive use is made of psychological assistance; from parents and teachers and others, to modify problem behavior in the settings in which it occurs.

SOURCE: Based on O'Leary and Wilson, 1987.

employed to highlight a situation that calls for a particular response. **Fading** refers to gradual elimination of these special cues when they are no longer needed. Positive reinforcers (such as praise or money) are used to strengthen desired responses. The **token economy** is one of the most common applications of operant principles to modify maladaptive behavior. In a token economy, patients are given reward tokens, such as poker chips, for socially constructive behaviors. The tokens can later be exchanged for desirable items or activities. Extinction procedures and punishment might be used to eliminate undesirable responses. When punishment is employed to eliminate a response, it is a good idea to positively reinforce an alternative, more desirable, response at the same time.

Another major development of recent years is the use of **biofeedback** procedures in which the individual is reinforced whenever a designated change in bodily functioning takes place. Through biofeedback the individual becomes better able to control internal processes, such as body temperature and heart rate, that are related to maladaptation.

Cognitive-Behavioral Approaches

Cognitive therapies, such as those devised by Kelly and Beck, were developed within traditional psychotherapeutic settings. **Cognitive-behavior therapy** reflects the increasing interest of behavior therapists in cognitive

modification as a means of influencing emotions and behaviors. This approach to therapy makes use of a variety of behavioral techniques, such as a graded program of activities, homework, and role playing, along with an effort to identify and modify unrealistic cognitions. In recent years, cognitive therapists and behavior therapists have freely borrowed techniques from one another. For example, Beck now employs homework assignments in his therapeutic work. Cognitive-behavior therapy builds on behavior therapy.

Psychodynamically oriented therapists often assume that symptoms will disappear after in-depth, lengthy analysis and insight gained about hidden complexes, fantasies, and anxieties. As this joke that pokes fun at these traditional psychodynamic approaches suggests, behavior therapists take a more direct approach to their clients' problems:

> *A man named John had a maddening compulsion to tear paper. After years of psychoanalysis, John was still tearing paper, and his family was losing all hope. They finally brought John to a new therapist, who walked John around the room, talking quietly to him. When he left the office, John was cured. A year later, John's compulsion was still gone, and the grateful family asked the therapist what he had said to John on that fateful day. The therapist said: "I told him, 'Don't tear paper.' "*

Even though they might laugh at this joke, both behaviorally and psychodynamically oriented therapists would perceive it as a great oversimplification of the therapeutic process.

Cognitive–Behavioral Interventions

In recent years increased recognition has been given to the simultaneous influences of environmental manipulations, such as those used in behavior modification programs, and cognitive processes. The resulting **cognitive–behavioral interventions** aim to correct people's misconceptions, strengthen their coping skills and feelings of control over their own lives, and facilitate constructive self-talk, or the things people typically say to themselves as they confront different types of situations. For instance, rather than saying "I'll never be able to do all that" they might tell themselves, "I'll just take it one step at a time."

There is growing evidence that cognitive–behavioral training can be quite effective in helping people overcome fears and inhibitions and increase their coping skills. While the mechanism by which this training leads to improvements in behavior has not been completely described, an important factor seems to be the client's sense of self-efficacy, that is, the client's belief that he or she is effective at carrying out tasks. Feelings of self-efficacy increase when individuals acquire new skills, which in turn encourages them to strengthen their skills even further.

Self-efficacy expectations refer to the belief that one is able to execute successfully the behavior required to produce a particular outcome. If people possess the necessary skills and there are adequate incentives, efficacy expectations can be major determinants of whether coping behavior will be initiated, how much effort will be expended, and how long that behavior will be sustained in the face of stress-arousing circumstances. Self-efficacy expectations may be altered through performance accomplishments, vicarious experiences, verbal persuasion, or emotional arousal. Of these, performance accomplishments have the most positive effect on feeling of self-efficacy (Bandura, 1982, 1986). It seems possible that self-efficacy expectations are among the most important contributors to behavioral change.

Relaxation Training

Relaxation training often helps people who are tense and generally anxious. In one approach, emphasis is placed on learning to contrast muscular tension with muscular relaxation. In another, meditation procedures are employed. Relaxation therapies appear to be helpful for a variety of psychosomatic disorders, particularly tension headaches and migraine headaches (see Chapter 7). However, they usually are not sufficient by themselves. Life styles, social environments, and views of the world can create or compound people's problems in living. Such factors as the quality and nature of available social support and the individual's goals, attitudes, and values often must be addressed. Table 17–4 lists a number of factors that bear on the advisability of using relaxation techniques in a given case.

Research on relaxation skills requires answers to two questions: Has the individual learned the relaxation skill? Does use of the skill lead to beneficial clinical results? Obviously, if the skills were never learned, there would be little reason to expect positive results from relaxation training. Appropriate control groups are needed to provide an adequate basis for judging the effectiveness of the training. There is also a need for studies that explore the effectiveness of relaxation training both alone and in combination with other types of therapy.

Muscular Relaxation Muscular relaxation involves tensing and then relaxing various muscle groups. The individual is encouraged to note the differences between feeling tense and feeling relaxed. Relaxation training is used in many methods of natural childbirth and in yoga. People who have difficulty falling asleep often find that relaxation exercises help them get to sleep more quickly. At first, individuals use relaxation exercises mainly in the therapy situation. But as their ability to relax themselves improves, they are encouraged to perform relaxation exercises in stressful situations that they encounter in everyday life.

Meditation In relaxation training involving meditation, the individual learns to concentrate on a thought, a sensation, a word, an object, or some mental state. Some techniques are very active and require that the person make a strenuous effort to focus on a specific thing. Certain yoga techniques, for example, require that the practitioner maintain specific postures and deliberately control his or her breathing or other bodily

Table 17–4
Factors in Successful Use of Relaxation Training

1. The individual's problems do not have an organic basis.
2. The individual is not psychotic, depressed, or subject to panic attacks.
3. The individual is able to assume responsibility for active participation in treatment, with special emphasis on home practice.
4. Family members are cooperative with and supportive of the individual's treatment.
5. The individual has reasonable expectations of the training's effectiveness.

functions. Other meditation techniques, such as transcendental meditation (TM), are passive approaches. Practitioners simply remain in a quiet atmosphere and make a relaxed attempt to achieve a state of inner peace. The individual concentrates on a *mantra* (a specially selected word) and tries, but does not strain, to exclude all other thoughts. Most passive techniques are practiced for 20-minute periods each day, typically once in the morning and again before dinner.

Exposure Therapy

Exposure therapies are based on the principle that continued exposure to anxiety-provoking stimuli will decrease anxiety to manageable levels and reduce phobic responses. **Exposure** consists of a gradual approach to an anxiety-provoking situation. Under such conditions the distress experienced in the situation is kept at a relatively low level.

Exposure to fear-arousing situations is one of the most effective ways of overcoming fear. However, there are positive results only if clients are willing to expose themselves to the situations they are afraid of. Although **in vivo exposure** (actually being in the situation) usually works best, **fantasized exposure** (thinking about being in the situation) is also effective. Exposure treatment is appropriate for many unpleasant or disadvantageous emotional responses. If the treatment is effective, improvement can usually be observed within five or six sessions.

Flooding is a form of exposure therapy in which the client is exposed to a flood of fear-arousing stimuli that is not terminated simply because the client experiences a high level of tension. In flooding, the clinical session is saturated with frightening thoughts and images in the hope that emotional responses to them will be extinguished through "burnout." If this happens, **extinction** is said to have occurred.

In **implosive therapy** the client experiences higher and higher levels of anxiety through imaginal presentation of scenes depicting behavior and situations that he or she has strenuously avoided in the past. The imagery used in treatment is intended to represent conflict areas that are thought to be the source of the avoidance behavior. The imaginal material used in implosion therapy tends to be much more intense than that used in flooding.

Systematic desensitization combines behavioral training (muscular relaxation) with cognitive activity. It begins with the induction of a relaxed state. While the client is relaxed, he or she imagines scenes that are related to his or her specific fear. Desensitization begins with scenes or images that are only mildly fear-arousing. The client is encouraged to concentrate on perpetuating the relaxed state while imagining those situations. Once the

client is able to remain relaxed, progressively more upsetting scenes are imagined.

The theory behind systematic desensitization is that the relaxation response competes with previously learned anxiety responses, such as fears and phobias. Research has shown that practicing relaxation when the fear-arousing stimulus is actually present (*in vivo* desensitization) yields superior results to simply imagining the stimulus. Desensitization works best with people who habitually show noticeable increases in physiological arousal (e.g., accelerated heart rate, moist palms) when exposed to the fear-arousing stimulus.

Paradoxical intention is a technique in which the therapist instructs the client to perform behaviors that appear to be in opposition to the client's therapeutic goal. For example, an individual who complains of inability to fall asleep within a satisfactory interval might be asked to remain awake as long as possible. An agoraphobic who cannot go into crowded places for fear of suffering severe heart palpitations might be instructed to go into crowded places and try to become anxious. Paradoxical intention is a relatively new technique that requires more research. It is not yet clear when it is appropriate or why it seems to be effective in particular cases. Perhaps it is effective because it requires the client to maintain the very behavior that he or she seeks to change under conditions that cannot support continuation of that behavior. Exposure to anxiety-provoking situations is an element of paradoxical intention and may contribute to its effectiveness (Shoham-Salomon and others, 1989).

Modeling

Often people are unaware that habit controls much of their behavior. Through **modeling,** they can be shown that there are other ways of doing things. Although modeling can take place when an individual observes someone demonstrating specific social skills, it also occurs informally, for example, when children imitate the heroes of television shows. In clinical applications of modeling, demonstrations by models are often combined with **guided rehearsals,** in which the individual is encouraged to imitate the behavior of the model with the model helping whenever necessary. When people imitate the adaptive behavior of models, their new responses are strengthened by positive reinforcement. The success of a modeling program depends on several factors.

1. How carefully the observer attends to the modeled behavior.
2. How well what was observed is retained.
3. The observer's ability to reproduce the modeled behavior.

4. How motivated the observer is to use the modeled behavior.

Live modeling involves direct observation of a model. **Participant modeling,** or **behavioral rehearsal,** goes one step further by requiring the client to practice the behavior, often in interaction with the model. **Symbolic modeling** refers to observation of a model who is presented indirectly through film, video or audio tape, or printed word. **Covert modeling** is a logical extension of symbolic modeling in which the individual is asked to imagine observing a model and a particular consequence. For example, a male cross-dresser was asked to engage in covert modeling by imagining the following scene.

> *You are standing behind a one-way mirror. You see a bare room except for two single beds with clothes on them. One bed has male clothes on it and the other has female clothes on it. Straight ahead at the other end of the room, you see a door open and a naked man about your age walks into the room. He walks toward the beds which are next to each other about four feet apart. He starts to go toward the bed with the female clothes on it. He looks at the clothes; suddenly you can see a painful expression on his face. He sits down on the bed. Now he starts to sweat and looks sick. He reaches for a bra and he starts to gag. As he puts the bra on he starts to vomit all over the clothes and on himself. He groans in agony as he doubles over and falls down to the ground. He is lying with the bra on and wallowing in vomit.*
>
> —Cautela, 1985, p. 93

A covert modeling scene was then presented in which the model puts on the male clothes and looks happy. In general, covert modeling involves constructing scenes or situations in which the client can picture the behavior that is to be changed.

Like other cognitive–behavioral therapies, modeling is often combined with other approaches. For example, while reinforcing adaptive overt behavior, the therapist might help the client acquire more realistic ideas about problem areas. In treating a complex problem such as intense anger in a child, the therapist might: (1) teach the parents to be more effective in reacting to temper tantrums (modeling might be used to accomplish this); (2) help the child identify the situations and thoughts that evoke the tantrums; (3) model cognitive and behavioral responses to stress and frustration that are more effective than anger; and (4) use guided rehearsal and praise to strengthen the child's adaptive behavior.

ASSERTIVENESS TRAINING Lack of assertive behavior is often related to deficits in social skills or to interfering emotional reactions and thoughts. If appropriate behaviors are available but are not performed because of anxiety, a useful focus may be on enhancing the client's anxiety management skills. **Assertiveness training** is specifically designed to enhance the interpersonal skills one needs to stand up for one's rights, such as refusing unwanted requests, expressing opinions, and making requests. Assertiveness training is preceded by a careful assessment of the client's responses in certain types of situations. The assessment is designed to answer these questions: What situations are of concern to the client? What does the client typically do in these situations? What are the personal and environmental blocks to more assertiveness in these situations?

Modeling and behavioral rehearsal play important roles in assertiveness training programs (see Figure 17–5). Positive feedback is offered after each rehearsal, and prompting is provided when needed. Homework assignments are used if, as is desirable, the client agrees to

FIGURE 17–5 Modeling and behavioral rehearsal can be effective techniques in assertiveness training. In these photos, the therapist demonstrates an introduction for a shy client.

(a)

(b)

carry out tasks that require assertiveness outside the training sessions. If the assertiveness deficits extend over a broad range of social behaviors, a number of training sessions may be needed. However, if the problem is fairly specific, a few sessions may be sufficient.

Group Therapy

Group approaches to psychotherapy are used not only because they are less costly but because many clinicians believe that therapy can be at least as effective with groups as it is with individuals. One appealing feature of group psychotherapy is that clients can learn both by observing other group members' adaptive and maladaptive attempts to solve personal problems and by comparing their own relationship with the therapist with those of the other members (see Figure 17–6).

Group therapy is usually seen as a means of broadening the application of psychotherapeutic concepts. Some advocates of group psychotherapy believe it may actually produce better results than individual therapy. Groups are particularly effective when they give participants opportunities to acquire new social skills through modeling. Opportunities to rehearse or practice these skills in the group increase the chances that the participants will actually use their newly acquired skills in everyday life. The following are among the most frequently observed features of group therapy:

1. *Self-disclosure*—the opportunity to tell the group about one's personal problems and concerns.

2. *Acceptance and support*—feeling a sense of belongingness and being valued by the group members.

3. *Norm clarification*—learning that one's problems are neither unique nor more serious than is true for other group members.

4. *Social learning*—being able to relate constructively and adaptively within the group.

5. *Vicarious learning*—learning about oneself through the observation of other group members, including the therapist.

6. *Self-understanding*—finding out about one's behavior in the group setting and the motivations contributing to the behavior.

Although group therapy initially was carried out from a psychodynamic perspective, humanistic, cognitive, and behavioral therapists have developed their own group techniques.

The experience of group therapy differs not only because of the theoretical perspective and methods of the group leader, but also because of a number of other factors. These include the types of problems or disorders confronting the group members, the therapeutic goals that have been established, the role the leader takes, the setting in which the group meets, and the individual characteristics of the group members. Clients are usually screened before being admitted to a therapy group to ensure that they will be able to participate at an effective level and that they will not be disruptive to the group as a whole. An important factor in many long-terms groups in which members enter and leave the group at different times is the presence of a few "senior" members who are doing well and serve as models for identification, stimulate hope, and offer practical advice and suggestions that have helped them improve their situation. These persons often have a special relationship with the group

FIGURE 17–6 Members of a therapy group have opportunities to learn and gather support from other members and from the therapist.

leader, who in turn must take care that the relationship is not seen as excluding others in the group.

Group therapy provides an opportunity for members to observe how their behavior affects other people and to receive personally relevant feedback. To maximize the likelihood that this will happen, group therapists often emphasize not only what members reveal about themselves, but also how the others react to what is said in the group setting. The following account gives an example of this process.

John, usually a silent member, opened a group meeting with a carefully planned statement about an episode of sexual abuse he had experienced as a child. He told the story in a deliberate manner with a flat expression. When he finished, there were a couple of minutes of silence, whereupon John said, half-jokingly, that he didn't give a damn if the group responded to him or not. Soon the disclosure evoked many reactions in the rest of the group. Another member, Steven, began to weep, recalling a past experience of sexual molestation and its subsequent influence on his sexual identity. Two other members offered him some words of support, which fell on deaf ears; this permitted the leader to point out how hard it is for Steven to accept comfort from others. One member commented that she felt confused by the discrepancy between how much John revealed and his flat, rehearsed manner of revelation. Another member, Mary, had an entirely different set of responses to John: She felt that his overwhelming self-disclosure put pressure on other group members to respond in kind. She resented this pressure and felt manipulated by John. A lively and engaging session ensued, with many complex variations on the theme of self-disclosure.

—Vinogradov and Yalom, 1990, p. 191

How did John's revelation affect the other members? How did John feel about his self-disclosure? The group leader encouraged John to examine his feelings and to comment on the support offered to him by other group members (both the explicit support of other members and the implicit support of Steven, who revealed similar painful material). The leader also encouraged a discussion of Mary's observations about John's style of delivery and her feelings of having been coerced and manipulated. A productive discussion took place, not so much about the content of John's early sexual

abuse, but about how the group functioned in dealing with it. Later sessions suggested that John benefited both from having made his self-disclosures and from learning about how the other members of the group reacted to them.

Cognitive–Behavioral Group Therapy

The focus of cognitive–behavioral group therapy is on increasing the skills and comfort of people in social situations. Group members role-play specific social situations that they find difficult. The themes of particular sessions are often selected by the therapist from prior knowledge of the members' problems. The therapist may model alternative ways of handling these situations. The role playing is accompanied by social reinforcement and feedback, and homework tasks are assigned. Other techniques are used as well, including graded task assignments, examination of specific types of distortions that may arise in social interactions (such as overgeneralization and imagining catastrophes), and discussion of types of cognitions that have negative and positive influences in group situations.

Cognitive–behavioral group therapy is more highly structured than group therapy conducted along psychodynamic lines. From a psychodynamic point of view, group psychotherapy represents an opportunity to deal with transference in a social situation and to compare one's attitude toward participation in a group with those of other group members. The group is often seen as an extension of the family. For example, a frequent topic that arises in group therapy is the competition of group members for the therapist's attention. A psychoanalyst might see echoes of the members' relationships to parents and siblings in their performances in the group. A cognitively oriented clinician, on the other hand, would be interested primarily in the often irrational ideas of group members concerning what goes on, or should go on, in social situations. Client-centered therapists see the therapist's role in groups as basically the same as in individual counseling; in both situations the therapist is a facilitator of personal growth. Cognitive–behavioral therapists are increasingly using techniques such as modeling and behavior rehearsal in groups.

Family and Marital Therapy

Sometimes therapy focuses on individuals who already constitute a group. Two examples are family therapy and marital therapy.

Family therapy is based on the idea that many problems both arise from family behavior patterns and are affected by them. It often is recommended when one

FIGURE 17-7 During family therapy sessions the therapist observes how the members of the family interact. For example, the therapist is using what has just been said by a family member to help the others see how one person's behavior affects other family members.

member of a family, especially a child, is referred to a mental-health professional. If maladaptive interactions with other members of the family are suspected as part of the problem, one of the most effective ways that a therapist can help the child is to work with all the family members together (see Figure 17–7). The following are some of the core problems that family therapy addresses:

1. Inability to resolve conflicts, make decisions, or solve problems

2. Chaotic organization and lack of agreed-upon responsibilities

3. Too rigid an organization resulting in an inability to respond to changing circumstances and stress

4. Overcloseness to the point that individual family members may lose any sense of individuality

5. Lack of emotional ties and communication among family members

6. Failure of the parents to agree on child-rearing practices.

Instead of treating family members individually, the therapist encourages the family to work as a group, dealing together with their attitudes and feelings toward one another and their resistance to cooperation and sharing. Family therapy often provides a valuable forum for airing hostilities, reviewing emotional ties, and dealing with crises. It is important for the therapist to be fair and impartial in discussing disagreements between family members and to bear in mind that families usually are characterized by a hierarchy in which parents are expected to assume some authority and responsibility for the behavior of their children. The degree of hierarchy will vary, depending on the parents' philosophy of child-rearing and the ages of the children. For adolescents and young adults, one important problem may be that their growing independence requires modification of the hierarchical structure.

Most family therapists begin by focusing on here-and-now problems. For example, a 12 year old boy may be intermittently truant from school, tell lies, and seek out parties on weekends where he had been known to drink beer. The child may complain of parental pressure and repeated criticism, whereas the parents express their fears about the child's unreliability and poor school performance. The therapist seeks to help the family develop plans which the parents and child then can implement together for dealing with these problems. The therapist's approach is designed to minimize guilt, scapegoating, and blame among family members and to maximize open-mindedness and cooperation among them.

Roles in the drama of family life, assumed perhaps out of loyalty or a need for belonging, may become destructive over time yet hard to abandon because they help to maintain the family. For example, a child who takes on the role of a parent because of a mother's or father's incapacity is likely to play this adult role poorly, using authority too harshly or making it a vehicle of rivalry with younger brothers and sisters. Another child may be assigned the role of bad boy so that one of the parents can play disciplinarian. Such roles must be openly recognized and the assignments altered if the family is to become more healthy. The family members often develop an unspoken family mythology that has important effects on all family members. The mythology may be some-

thing like, "John is the stupid one," "Father can't work." These myths are especially likely to create conflict when they are incompatible with family ideals or are not accepted by all members of the family. Therapists often find that bringing the myths out in the open in family discussion is helpful in focusing on the problems these distorted role assignments create.

THE FAMILY AS A SYSTEM If any single idea could be said to guide family therapy, it is probably the notion of a family system. Human life can be organized hierarchically into systems of varying size and complexity: the individual, the family, the society, the culture. The family is seen as a self-maintaining system which, like the human body, has feedback mechanisms that preserve its identity and integrity by restoring homeostasis—the internal status quo—after a disturbance. A change in one part of the family system thus is often compensated elsewhere. Families have mechanisms for adapting to changed circumstances, and, like individuals, they have biologically and socially determined states of development.

A family that functions poorly cannot adjust to change because its mechanisms are either inflexible or ineffectual. The family's daily habits and internal communication—its *transactional patterns,* as they are called—harm its individual members. The pathology is in the system as a whole. Individual disorders not only serve as a source of protection and power for the disturbed person but may also preserve the family system and act as a distorted means of communication within that system. They fulfill the same function that neurotic symptoms are said to fulfill for individuals in psychodynamic theory.

Some families are highly interdependent; everyone in them is overresponsive to everyone else. They develop habits of intimate quarreling and complaining that become difficult to change. In other families, the family members have little mutual contact or concern; their boundaries are rigid. Family systems that are too closely knit, or enmeshed, respond too intensely to change; every disturbance may turn into a crisis. Systems in which the family members are distant, or disengaged, do not respond strongly enough; serious problems are ignored and issues are avoided.

Systems theory defines influences as mutual and causality as circular, so family therapists tend to avoid blaming and attributing causes—although there are exceptions to this as to every other generalization about the field. The symptoms of a defective family system are said to take different forms in different members of the system. A husband and wife, for example, may seem to have very different personalities, but this may be due not to their intrinsic characteristics as individuals but rather to their functions within that system. For this reason, family therapists often make limited use of ordinary psychiatric diagnoses, which describe individual pathology, and diagnose family situations instead.

MARITAL THERAPY Marital therapy can be viewed as a subtype of family therapy. The overlap is seen in the couple who battle about how to handle their six-year-old son who sets fires: The wife blames the husband's permissiveness, he blames her strictness, and both see the child as the one needing treatment. To the therapist, the problem is the parental pulling and hauling for control over the child, and the child's fire-setting is a search for clarification. The therapist points this out and coaches the parents in making changes in the rules by which they operate. Those changes may not be directed at individual feelings, yet such therapy, usually short-term, often yields personality changes as the problem and its accompanying stress disappear.

Couples frequently seek marital therapy because one or both of the partners believe that the relationship is troubled or are contemplating ending it through divorce or separation. By seeing the therapist together, the partners can more easily identify problems and alter the ways in which they relate to each other. The main advantage of couple's therapy is that the therapist, as an impartial observer, can actually witness the couple's interactions rather than hearing about them in a second-hand and perhaps one-sided report. Both family therapy and marital therapy can be carried out from one of several perspectives. Family therapy is likely to include behavioral or psychodynamic approaches. Couples therapy often utilizes a cognitive focus as well. Regardless of the type of marital therapy practiced, a current trend is to focus attention on specific relevant issues such as helping the couple increase communication, express feelings, help each other, and enjoy shared experiences.

Marital therapists report distinct patterns of symptoms among couples. In some cases, each partner in a marriage demands too much of the same thing from the other: service, protection, care, and so forth. In other cases, spouses compound each other's problems by complementing each other. One partner takes charge and the other becomes incompetent: an overbearing and emotionally distant husband has a "hysterical" wife whose erratic behavior makes him still more overbearing; a strong, angry wife has a passive, alcoholic husband who is a suitable object of her anger, and that anger makes him even more passive; the husband of a depressed and hypochondriacal woman needs to be a healer and savior. Often marital therapy aims to reveal what is hidden: the passive partner's suppressed anger, the savior's feelings of helplessness.

Psychodrama

Although most group therapy is essentially an expanded, more complicated, and more realistic version

of individual therapy, a number of approaches have been designed especially for groups. One of these is **psychodrama,** which was created by Jacob Moreno in the 1920s. Moreno led impromptu activity groups of children in the public gardens of Vienna. He noticed that when the children were encouraged to act out stories instead of merely reading or listening to them, they often displayed unexpected depths of feeling and understanding. He later experimented with a form of theater, the "theater of spontaneity," in which players were encouraged to draw upon their inner resources in creating the dramatic action rather than following a script.

In psychodrama a group of individuals assembles under the leadership of a therapist (often called the director). The group enacts events of emotional significance in order to resolve conflicts and release members from inhibitions that limit their capacity for spontaneous and creative activity, particularly social activity. Behavior therapists use role playing to give clients practice in new social skills, but in psychodrama role playing tends to be more spontaneous and oriented toward expressing strongly felt emotions (see Figure 17–8).

Moreno saw psychodrama as a vehicle for express-ing strong emotions, acquiring insight into one's own behavior, and realistically evaluating the behavior of others. Psychodrama is a directive treatment in that the therapist controls the mechanics of the therapy situation. However, it is nondirective in that the emotional content of sessions arises spontaneously from the activities of the participants.

Integration of Psychologically Based Therapeutic Approaches

When therapists who base their techniques on different perspectives discuss their work, there are inevitable differences of opinion. The issues that separate the various schools of thought seem substantial. Should therapists actively direct clients toward behavioral change, or should they focus on the clients' development of insight? Should therapy delve into the past or examine the present? Should its duration be long or short? Despite the different ways in which these questions are answered, there is evidence of a movement toward the integration of therapeutic approaches. "Talking therapies," such as psychodynamic therapy, are placing more emphasis on clients' need to take responsibility for themselves and develop self-mastery. Behavioral therapies are giving increased attention to the cognitive underpinnings of behavioral change. Often this means helping clients acquire insight into their misconceptions about themselves and their social relationships. Many cognitive–behavioral therapists rely heavily on imagery as a means of achieving therapeutic goals. The use of imagery for treatment purposes clearly acknowledges the potentially crucial role of private events.

There is growing evidence that performance-based therapies, in which individuals concretely deal with problematic situations, can be very effective. However, cognitive processes, such as insight, may play an important role in helping people develop more adaptive approaches to their problems of living. As more therapists attend to the relative roles of cognition, emotion, and behavior, steps toward greater integration of therapeutic approaches are becoming noticeable.

Research on the Psychological Therapies

Many groups have a stake in the evaluation of therapeutic effectiveness. Patients, their families, thera-

FIGURE 17–8 Both role play and psychodrama are effective psychotherapeutic tools. These boys, confined to an institution for juveniles, are shown acting out a situation as the therapist watches.

pists, researchers, insurance companies, legislators, and planners of mental-health services all want to know which therapy is most effective. Furthermore, evaluation is not just a matter of identifying the best therapy. A generally effective therapy in the hands of an ineffective therapist could be harmful to patients. Beyond that, there are misdiagnoses that can lead to poor matches between therapies and therapists, on the one hand, and patients, on the other. In some cases, therapy helps a person, but only after one or more frustrating experiences with a therapist who is not helpful. Clearly, evaluating therapies and therapists is an important task for clinicians and the public (see Box 17–1 on pages 534–35).

Given the number of psychological therapies, it is obvious that researchers who study these areas have their work cut out for them. Obtaining information about therapeutic effectiveness is not easy for a number of reasons. For example, individual therapists differ in their ability to carry out particular therapies. Furthermore, some therapies may be more effective with certain types of patients than others. As we have seen, psychotherapy is not a single process applied to a single problem. Research on therapy is improving as studies become more complex and incorporate more relevant factors into their research designs. For many reasons, researchers cannot conduct studies on the effectiveness of different therapies in the same way that laboratory studies are usually carried out. Table 17–5 summarizes some of the practical differences between these types of studies.

Comparison of a particular therapy with a control condition is useful, but studies that compare the effectiveness of several treatment approaches for similar groups of clients are even more significant. A well-designed experiment, therefore, would set up the independent variable as a specific therapeutic procedure (such as group therapy or systematic desensitization) and the dependent variable as some aspect of behavior (such as frequency of suicidal thoughts). Even with this careful design, however, researchers must be cautious in making conclusions. Most clinicians agree that the same therapy will have varying effects on different types of patients.

Before a research project is carried out, there must be agreement on how to measure the results. For example, suppose a researcher intends to assess the effectiveness of different therapies designed to reduce the tendency to hallucinate. One way to measure the dependent variable would be to count the number of times people report having hallucinatory experiences. But people might have hallucinations that they did not report, or might make up such experiences just to have something to report. Thus, whereas some clinicians might contend that frequency of reported hallucinations is a reasonable index of the general tendency to hallucinate, others might not be satisfied with this conclusion.

In any research, all groups of subjects must be as similar or equal as possible before the experiment begins. The therapists in the various groups should also be comparable. Many other factors must also be controlled. For instance, suppose the staff on the ward of a mental hospital believe that their program is a significant therapeutic innovation. Their enthusiasm for the program might, *by itself,* influence the patients in their care. Actually, there is evidence that such an **enthusiasm effect** operates in a variety of situations, including hospitals, schools, and private consulting rooms.

Most studies of therapy techniques compare a group of people who receive treatment with one or two groups of people who do not. But such comparisons do not show how individuals within the groups are affected by specific aspects of the treatment. Clinicians also need to know how changes in the client's behavior are related to what the clinician does or says.

Table 17–5
Differences Between Experimental Laboratory Studies and Evaluation of Therapy

Factor	Laboratory Study	Psychotherapy
Independent variables	Usually quite clearly defined	Complex, often difficult to define clearly
Dependent variables	Usually quite clearly defined	Often involve complex set of responses that change over time
Experimental situation	Well-controlled	Not possible to eliminate unexpected events
Other situations	Researchers usually not concerned about what happens to subject outside experimental situation	Therapist is interested in outcome for client outside therapy situation

BOX 17-1 **Examining the Process of Psychotherapy**

Studies of therapeutic effectiveness contain valuable information but by no means tell the whole story of psychotherapy. Also needed are analyses of the ingredients of effective therapy. After all, if something works, we want to know *why* it works. **Process research** is concerned with the elements of psychotherapy; that is, what actually happens in therapy. This research explores such topics as the following:

1. The therapist–patient relationship;

2. The patient's goals, and whether they change over time (See Figure 17–9);

3. The therapist's goals, and whether they change over time;

4. The content of therapeutic sessions and changes in content over time;

5. Types of emotional expression at different phases of the therapeutic process;

6. How the patient and therapist perceive the sessions;

7. Whether the sessions focus on achieving insight or direct behavior modification.

"But what if you get me back to reality and I don't *like* it?"

FIGURE 17–9

(© 1989; reprinted courtesy of Bunny Hoest and Parade Magazine)

Researchers who study the therapeutic process seek to identify the events, beliefs, and attitudes in psychotherapy that contribute to patient improvement. Such improvement is displayed in patients' behavior and feelings. For example, researchers need to determine if therapists' and patients' goals in therapy are the same. There is evidence that psychodynamically-oriented therapists place greater value on the achievement of insight than do their patients.

On the other hand, patients rate reassurance and support from the therapist more highly than do their therapists (Llewelyn, 1988). Further inquiry is needed into how patients' and therapists' perceptions of their relationship and of events in psychotherapy relate to clinical outcomes (Garfield, 1990; Strupp, 1989).

Video and audio recordings of therapy sessions provide objective evidence of the events that take place in them and the tactics employed by

Outcome Studies

As we have emphasized throughout this chapter, there are disagreements about the relative effectiveness of the different psychological therapies. Researchers with different criteria and expectations have obtained different results from such comparisons. For example, after reviewing the literature, Eysenck (1952, 1961) concluded that psychotherapy was an ineffective clinical method. He argued that many apparent successes could be explained by **spontaneous remissions,** in which the client's symptoms would have disappeared in time with or without treatment. Bergin and Lambert (1978) found that psychotherapy had an effect but that the effect was not necessarily positive. Some patients actually seemed to deteriorate because of psychotherapy.

One of the most important questions in outcome studies is what the criteria for improvement should be.

Table 17–6 (on page 536) organizes a number of ways of thinking about *outcome measures,* which can be thought of as changes in the dependent variable described in the preceding section. Which are more important, changes in how the client feels and behaves, or changes in what he or she thinks about? Would the opinions of the client's family or co-workers be helpful in evaluating improvement? How important is the therapist's evaluation of the outcome? Sometimes the therapist and the client don't agree. Anthony Storr, a British psychoanalyst, gives this example of what he had considered an "unsuccessful" case:

Some time ago I had a letter from a man whom I had treated some 25 years previously asking whether I would see, or at any rate advise

therapists. In the following case, the taped session provided the following verbatim account as the therapist skillfully enabled the patient to express her fears of being rejected by the therapist.

Therapist: *We've gotten to know each other a lot better since our first session. Is there anything you've been afraid to tell me?*

Patient: *I'm not sure.*

Therapist: *Sometimes patients are afraid to tell their therapist something, especially if they think it'll put them in a bad light. Could that be true for you?*

Patient: *Yes. There is something. But I don't want to tell you.*

Therapist: *How are you predicting I'll react?*

Patient: *You'll think I'm terrible.*

—Beck and Freeman, 1990, p. 268

After a discussion of the patient's fear of rejection and with support from the therapist, the patient revealed a traumatic pattern of childhood sexual abuse of which she felt very ashamed. The discussion that ensued permitted valuable progress to be made in establishing a nondefensive working relationship between the patient and therapist. Had the therapist not taken the initiative in bringing out the patient's fears, the patient might never have been able to experience the therapist's acceptance of her as a person.

In addition to providing support and acceptance, good therapists give their patients the opportunities to learn that the world may not be as punishing a place as they think it is. The therapist may serve as a model who disconfirms the patient's irrational or unnecessarily pessimistic beliefs about the nature of interpersonal relationships—as shown in the following case.

A patient complained that she could not feel close to men. She was burdened by the unconscious belief that unless she was totally compliant with a man's wishes, he would feel insulted and reject her. She soon began to respond to the male therapist in the same way, withdrawing from him out of fear that she might feel forced to accept damaging interpretations or follow bad advice. So she unconsciously decided that before confronting any other problems she would have to change her belief in the need for compliance. Encouraged by her therapist, she decided to test the belief through trial actions.

Once she questioned some of the therapist's comments and felt relieved when the therapist was not upset; he had passed her test. He pointed out her exaggerated fear of hurting him. As a result, she felt less constrained by her unrealistic belief, less anxious and defensive. She relaxed some of the repression she had maintained in obedience to the belief and recalled that her father used to sulk whenever she challenged him. She then began to challenge the therapist more directly, and at the same time felt more able to cooperate with him. Once she knew that she did not have to agree with his ideas, she could like him and take his ideas seriously. She also began to feel more comfortable with her boyfriend and was able to work on problems she would have been afraid to confront before.

treatment for, his daughter. He assumed, wrongly, that I would not remember him, and, in the course of his letter, wrote as follows: "I can quite truthfully say that six months of your patient listening to my woes made a most important contribution to my life style. Although my transvestism was not cured, my approach to life and to other people was re-oriented and for that I am most grateful. It is part of my life that I have never forgotten."

Looked at from one point of view, my treatment of this man was a failure. His major symptom, the complaint which drove him to seek my help, was not abolished. And yet I think it is clear that he did get something from his short period of psychotherapy which was of considerable value to him. A man does not write to a psychotherapist

asking him to see his daughter, 25 years after his own treatment was over, using the terms employed in this letter, unless he believes that what happened during his period of treatment was important.

—Storr, 1980, p. 146

If all the measures of improvement do not agree, which is most important? How can we compare studies that use different outcome measures to evaluate the effectiveness of various therapies? Clearly, although outcome research is progressing in sophistication, many of the important questions will be difficult to answer. Personal accounts of experiences in psychotherapy provide researchers with hypotheses for future research.

Table 17-6
Important Dimensions of Therapy Outcome Measures

Dimensions	
Focus	Emotions
	Thoughts
	Behaviors
Possible processes	Evaluation
	Description
	Observation
Possible sources of data	Self-report
	Therapist rating
	Ratings of significant others
	Trained observation by others
	Trained self-monitoring
	Instrumental behavior

The three dimensions may be combined in many ways, but all contributions may not yield similar results.

Identifying the elements of personal growth and the factors that foster it will contribute to the development of better formal and informal therapies.

It is not unusual for clients to see themselves as cured while their therapists see them as unimproved or even as being worse. Studies of improvement therefore should include three independent measures: the client's evaluation of the progress made; the therapist's evaluation; and the judgments of people who know the client well, such as family members and friends.

Another approach to evaluating the effectiveness of therapy is to assess the resultant behavior change. Although one of the goals of psychotherapy is enhancement of the client's self-awareness and insight, most people would consider therapy a failure if the person's behavior remained the same. It is not enough to be a source of insight.

Changes in overt behavior are easier to describe and assess objectively than changes in attitudes, feelings, and beliefs. But questions remain. To what degree should behavioral change be used as a criterion? Who should determine the kinds and amounts of change desired? How lasting should the change be? How long-standing and disabling has the patient's condition been? It seems reasonable that criteria for success should be related to the difficulty of the hurdle to be overcome. Implicit in this conclusion is the recognition that criteria that are appropriate in one case may be inappropriate in others.

Comparing Therapies

There is growing support for the conclusion that psychological therapies are worthwhile for many people.

But are the different therapeutic approaches equally effective?

COMPARATIVE STUDIES In one widely cited comparative study (Sloane and others, 1975), the subjects were college students who had applied for treatment—mostly for anxiety and personality disorders—at a psychiatric outpatient clinic. The goal of the study was to compare the relative effectiveness of behavioral therapy (desensitization, assertiveness training, and so on) and more traditional, short-term, psychodynamically oriented therapy. In addition to these two groups, there was a control group whose members were told that they would have to wait about four months to receive treatment.

The clients were followed up 4 and 12 months after completing therapy. The measures used in the treatment comparisons were derived from interviews with the clients at these times, from the clients' ratings of their own improvement, and from improvement ratings made by an independent assessor. At four months, the psychotherapy and behavioral-therapy groups had improved equally, and significantly more than the waiting-list group. At the one-year follow-up, the behavioral-therapy clients, but not the psychotherapy group, showed some significant improvement with regard to the problems that had led them to seek therapy. However, there were no significant differences between the two groups with regard to social adjustment. The one-year follow-up results were complicated by the fact that some of the clients continued to receive treatment even though the therapy sessions were supposed to end after four months. The researchers concluded that their study provided no clear evidence that behavioral therapy was superior to psychotherapy.

The same researchers reported an interesting additional set of comparisons for some of the subjects in their treatment study (Sloane and others, 1977). One year after beginning treatment, the subjects were mailed questionnaires in which they were asked to rate the importance of 32 factors in the success of their treatment. What was most striking about their responses was the similarity between the psychotherapy and behavioral-therapy groups. Both groups emphasized the importance of gaining insight into one's problems, the client–therapist relationship, the opportunity to give vent to emotions, a sense of trust in the therapist, and the development of confidence. Thus, even though the two treatment approaches are based on different assumptions and use different methods, they were described similarly by the clients. This similarity held both for the sample as a whole and for subgroups of clients who were judged to have responded most positively to the treatments offered them.

In a more recent project, researchers analyzed four studies on the outcome of psychotherapy and concluded

that who performs the therapy matters much more than what kind of therapy it is (Luborsky and others, 1986). The studies were conducted at Johns Hopkins University, the University of Pennsylvania, the University of Pittsburgh, and McGill University. Altogether, 25 therapists and 240 patients were involved. In three studies, the patients were average psychiatric outpatients; in the Pennsylvania study, they were heroin addicts taking methadone. The techniques included individual psychodynamic therapy, cognitive–behavioral therapy, and group therapy, all in various combinations and for varying lengths of time. Among the many measures of outcome were judgments of improvement by both patients and therapists and ratings of interpersonal behavior, social adjustment, depression, severity of addiction, and other symptoms.

In all four studies some therapists had a significantly higher success rate than others. Differences among therapists were much greater than differences among therapies in producing a favorable outcome. There was little evidence to show that any individual therapist did better with a particular kind of patient. The researchers suggested that more might be learned about how psychotherapy works by studying the most effective therapists than by comparing different forms of treatment.

While evidence suggests that the various psychological approaches to treating cases that do not involve extreme psychopathology are all often effective, one should not conclude that it makes no difference which techniques are employed in clinical work. Psychological therapies have been less successful with serious conditions such as schizophrenia, some types of affective disorders, alcoholism, and drug abuse. However, psychological therapies can play an important role in treating some of these conditions when used in combination with biologically based treatments like drug therapy and ECT. The value of the psychological component of these combinations frequently lies in helping the patient deal realistically with problems of day-to-day living. For example, social-skills training has been used effectively to help psychotic individuals taking antipsychotic drugs to adjust better to hospital or community settings. Perhaps as more is learned about the distinctive features of particular therapies, it will be possible to combine them in ways that are optimal for clients (see Figure 17–10).

Evaluating the effectiveness of therapeutic efforts requires carefully planned large-scale projects. Conclusions about the relative effectiveness of these different techniques cannot be drawn from research that is too limited in scope or methodologically weak. We noted earlier that there is no best index of clinical outcome. That being the case, research studies should include several measures of outcome, such as clients' self-reports and behavioral measures gathered before and after

"I UTILIZE THE BEST FROM FREUD, THE BEST FROM JUNG AND THE BEST FROM MY UNCLE MARTY, A VERY SMART FELLOW."

FIGURE 17–10
(© 1983 by Sidney Harris—The Wall Street Journal)

therapy, as well as expert judgments of clinical progress. There might be significant differences between therapeutic approaches to specific problems with respect to some outcome measures but not others. Furthermore, a therapeutic procedure may be valuable even if it doesn't bring about a complete cure. A person who is less anxious after therapy will be grateful for that benefit despite the failure to achieve a total release from anxiety.

An example of the kind of large-scale project needed to compare different therapeutic approaches is a study of 250 patients who were either moderately or severely depressed (Klerman, 1987). The patients were divided at random into three experimental groups: The first and second groups were treated with one of two types of brief psychotherapy, designed to last 16 weeks, while the third group was given the drug imipramine. A control group of patients received placebos plus weekly supportive consultations with a psychiatrist. While 50 to 60 percent of the patients who received either the psychotherapeutic treatments or the drug reached "full recovery" with no serious symptoms, fewer than 30 percent of those in the control group reached full recovery.

These findings strengthen earlier research suggesting that some forms of psychotherapy are as effective as drugs in treating depression. They are also in accord with other research showing that the effects of behavior therapy and antidepressant drugs are similar (Christensen and others, 1987).

Arguments over the effectiveness of therapeutic programs can be expected to continue for several reasons: people's problems, expectations, and the extent to which their lives can be changed vary; therapists use different methods and have different expectations; and there are no uniform criteria for judging therapeutic effectiveness. Many people are helped by therapy, but some get worse.

Even though psychological therapies are not for everyone, they seem to help a sizable number of people sort out their problems and develop new ways of handling stress and the challenges of life.

META-ANALYSIS Recently a new statistical technique has been used in research on therapeutic outcome. Smith, Glass, and Miller (1980) pioneered this method in their comprehensive review of the research literature. Their results led them to conclude that the average client receiving therapy was generally better off in a measurable way than 75 percent of people who receive no treatment, and was also better off with respect to the alleviation of fear and anxiety than 83 percent of untreated controls. This method is known as **meta-analysis,** a way of quantifying outcome measures so that they can be combined over many studies. Whether meta-analysis is the best way to answer questions about therapeutic effectiveness is still being debated.

Meta-analysis involves (1) grouping studies in which treatment conditions have been compared with an untreated control condition on one or more measures of outcome; (2) statistically determining the therapeutic effects on different groups using the available measures; and (3) averaging the sizes of the effects across the studies that the researcher wants to compare. In this way groups receiving psychotherapy can be compared with untreated control groups and groups receiving other therapeutic approaches, such as systematic desensitization and behavior modification. Figure 17–11 provides an example of a meta-analysis of 475 studies of the effects of psychotherapy.

The number of meta-analytic studies is increasing, and so is their complexity (Rosenthal, 1991). Greater complexity is needed, in part, because researchers do not want to be criticized for mixing apples and oranges. The results of meta-analysis are harder to interpret if the effect sizes from fundamentally different types of studies are lumped together. Perhaps the sharpest criticism of meta-analysis is that comparisons of studies that are methodologically weak can add little to an ultimate evaluation of therapeutic effects. On the other hand, meta-analysis of tighter, more homogeneous studies could prove very enlightening.

Components of Effective Therapy

Research on the nature of psychological therapies has explored the characteristics, attitudes, and behavior of the client and therapist in addition to the therapeutic technique used. What goes on in therapy sessions can be characterized in terms of the operation of two sets of factors. **Technique factors** are the procedures employed by the therapist, which may or may not match the descriptions of those procedures found in books and manuals. **Interpersonal factors** refer to the social chem-

istry or dynamics of the relationship between the therapist and the client. To minimize the effects of individual differences among therapists, Freud struggled hard to establish technique factors as the single most important therapeutic influence in psychoanalysis. More recently, behavioral theorists have also emphasized the need to specify the procedures they employ. While it would be convenient if technique factors were the only ingredients in therapy, interpersonal factors not only are important but can be decisive in influencing the outcome.

An example of the importance of interpersonal factors is provided by a study that included groups of trained and untrained therapists (Strupp & Hadley, 1979). One group consisted of experienced professional psychotherapists; the other group of Vanderbilt University professors who were selected on the basis of their widely recognized interest in their students, their accessibility, and their willingness to listen to and help students solve personal problems. None of the professors had worked in the field of psychology or in any other "helping" profession. The subjects were college students, most of whom complained of anxiety. Each student was assigned to either a professional or a nonprofessional therapist. A third group of subjects constituted a control group. Each control subject went through an assessment procedure, but the start of therapy was delayed.

FIGURE 17–11 Meta-analysis involves the statistical combination of many separate and often very different studies. This figure illustrates the general findings of an analysis that combined 475 controlled studies of therapeutic effectiveness. The average person in the treated group was 0.85 standard deviations above the mean for the control group on the measures used to evaluate therapeutic outcome. This difference is a large one when compared to the effects of many experimental interventions used in psychology or education. For example, cutting the size of a school class in half causes an increase in achievement of 0.15 standard deviation units. The effect of nine months of instruction in reading is an improvement in reading skills of 0.67 standard deviation units.

(Smith, Mary Lee, Gene V. Glass, and Thomas I. Miller, The Benefits of Psychotherapy. The Johns Hopkins University Press, Baltimore/London, 1980, p. 88)

(a)

(b)

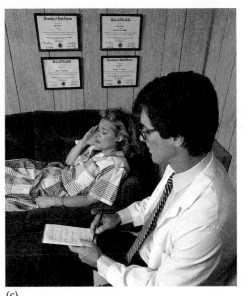

(c)

FIGURE 17–12 There is evidence that what goes on early in the patient–therapist relationship may be an important predictor of outcome. Although a patient who has an early negative reaction to his or her therapist may eventually be able to work productively with the therapist, a successful therapeutic outcome is more likely if the reaction is warm and positive. One factor in positive or negative reactions to the therapy situation is the patient's first impression of the therapist. Which of these therapists would you prefer to go to? Rank order your preferences and think about the basis for the rank ordering.

The study found no significant differences that could be attributed to the type of therapist to which a given client had been assigned. Clients who were treated by either psychotherapists or professors showed more improvement than the control subjects. The measures of change included the students' own ratings, judgments by independent experts, MMPI scores, and clinicians' evaluations of their clients' progress. Favorable outcomes were most prevalent among clients whose therapists actively provided them with information, encouragement, and opinions. The therapists whose clients improved were those who made special efforts to facilitate the discussion of problems, focused on the here and now rather than on early-childhood experiences, and encouraged the client to seek new social activities. Thus, the personal qualities of the therapist clearly are a very important factor in therapeutic process.

If psychological therapies are effective in treating specific clinical problems, an important question is, which events in therapy sessions are the active ingredients, the ones that actually bring about change? Evidence from studies like the one just described suggests that the active ingredients might be interpersonal factors and not the therapeutic process as usually described in textbooks. The following characteristics of therapists may influence the process of change and, thus, the outcome of therapy: warmth, friendliness, genuineness, interpersonal style, beliefs, values, and prejudices. In addition to the therapist's personality, his or her age, sex, and socioeconomic background may also play a role in the therapeutic process (see Figure 17–12). The means by which therapists' characteristics are communicated to the client include the therapist's appearance and his or her verbal and nonverbal behavior.

Improving Therapy Research

We have seen that in addition to technique factors such as the type of therapy practiced by the clinician, researchers must consider client and therapist factors and the tone or quality of the therapeutic relationship. Table 17–7 summarizes the research and clinical questions

Table 17–7

Issues Concerning Client, Therapist, and Relationship Factors

Client factors	What role do the personal characteristics of clients play in the outcome of therapy? Among the factors that often play important roles are the attitudes of clients toward therapy, their educational and socioeconomic levels, their levels of psychological distress, the social supports available to them in their environment, and the nature of the problem for which they are seeking help.
Therapist factors	What contributions do the characteristics of the therapist make to the process of therapy and its outcome? Among the important therapist variables are training, experience, clinical orientation, and personal qualities. The therapist's sex, age, ethnicity, and cultural background may also play important roles.
The therapeutic relationship	Does the therapist–client relationship make a difference? Available evidence suggests that the psychological chemistry that takes place when a therapist with a particular personality meets a client with a particular personality is an important factor in several types of therapy. Although therapist–client relationships have been explored more deeply in psychotherapy, there is evidence that they are also very important in other forms of therapy.

raised by these factors. The design of therapy research will improve as these questions stimulate methodological advances.

A number of clues are already available to permit the strengthening of research designs. These pertain to sample size, patient specificity, treatment specificity, and outcome measures.

1. *Sample size*. Because of the need to incorporate a large number of factors in the design of therapy research, large enough sample sizes are needed to allow for appropriate statistical analyses and justifiable inferences from results.

2. *Patient specificity*. Firm conclusions are more likely if subjects are relatively homogeneous in terms of factors that are not the target of the treatment intervention. So many factors may influence outcome that it is important to control as many extraneous variables as possible.

3. *Treatment specificity*. The more clearly defined the treatment or treatments, the more likely it is that reasonable inferences can be drawn from the research. This requires careful specification of the therapeutic techniques used in the research.

4. *Outcome measures*. The more relevant the outcome measures are to the type of case being treated, the more useful the study will be. For example, since obsessive–compulsives rarely hallucinate, there would be little value in using the frequency of hallucinations as an outcome variable. A more useful variable would be the frequency of obsessive thoughts and compulsive behaviors.

Control and comparison groups are needed in therapy studies because many influences beyond those that are of special interest to the researcher may be at work during the period covered by therapeutic intervention. Without adequate control or comparison groups, researchers cannot rule out the possibility of alternative explanations such as spontaneous remission.

No single control group is appropriate for testing all hypotheses. The control group or groups for a particular study must be chosen on the basis of the particular question under investigation. Table 17–8 describes some types of control groups that have been used in therapy outcome research. The type of control group or groups used in a given study depends on the number of subjects available and on the nature of the setting in which the research is carried out.

Biological Therapies

In Chapter 3 we discussed the biological orientation to maladaptive behavior and the therapies that have been generated by this point of view. The most widely used biological therapies today are **electroconvulsive therapy (ECT)** and a growing variety of drugs that influence psychological functioning.

Electroconvulsive Therapy

Until recently, use of ECT had been declining for about 20 years. The basis for the decline was the public's

Table 17–8
The Variety of Control Groups in Therapy Outcome Research

Wait-listed Controls

People who have asked for treatment but who have been placed on a waiting list usually for a specific period of time.

Dropout Controls

Clients who were included in the original study who discontinued their participation prematurely and did not complete the required series of treatments.

Placebo Controls

Clients who are seen by a therapist but receive only personal attention and not an active treatment.

Crossover Control Groups

For a predetermined period one group receives active treatment and the other a placebo or no-treatment. At a specified time the two groups switch so that the former no-treatment individuals begins the series of treatment sessions and those who initially received treatment experience placebo or no-treatment.

Clients as Their Own Controls

Behaviors are assessed before treatment begins and measures of change are calculated between the baseline measures and the same behaviors after the treatment.

Current Standard Treatment Controls

This type of control has largely replaced placebo or wait-listed controls for ethical reasons. These clients are treated with the usual treatment given prior to the development of the experimental treatment.

Untreated Controls

For ethical reasons this type of control group is rarely used in research on therapy. Untreated controls might be used in the case where they were determined, for instance through an epidemiological survey, to meet the diagnostic criteria of the problem under study but they had never sought treatment for their symptoms.

perception (shared by many clinicians) that ECT is dangerous, inhumane, and overused. Some municipalities have urged that its use be restricted. Nevertheless, ECT is now in the midst of a quiet revival. In improved forms, it has emerged as the treatment of choice for the most severe depression when drugs and other therapy fail to help (see Chapter 10). Patients for whom ECT is recommended are so severely depressed that they do not eat, sleep very little, and are suicidal. Many suffer from delusions. In about 80 percent of cases, ECT can lift depression within a few weeks (Andreasen & Black, 1991). The response to ECT of Norman Endler described in Chapter 10 is an example of the method's effectiveness.

Available evidence suggests that ECT is a relatively safe procedure, particularly when used with anesthetics and muscle relaxants that substantially lessen the trau-matic effects of the treatment. Risks are further reduced by applying the electric current to only one side of the head. Several such improvements in reducing ECT's side effects have contributed to its comeback (see Table 17–9). However, there is concern about the cognitive consequences of passing an electric current through a person's head. The major risk is memory loss, although this can be reduced by using ECT on the nondominant side of the brain and in the lowest possible dose.

Even though it has been used for many years, the mechanism by which ECT works is not yet clear. However, recent evidence suggests that the active ingredients in ECT are the electrical-biochemical events that follow the seizures triggered by the electrical impulses (Hay & Hay, 1990). Progress is now being made in understanding these events.

A clinician who is considering the use of ECT must

Table 17–9

Improvements in ECT that Have Increased Its Safety

1. *Length of electrical charge.* Reduced from one second to one twenty-fifth of a second.
2. *Intensity of electrical charge.* Reduced by up to one-half.
3. *Timing of sessions.* Reduced from as often as every day or even two or three a day to no more than three times a week.
4. *Length of treatment.* Formerly, up to 20 sessions or more; now, typically ten or fewer.
5. *Use of anesthetics and muscle relaxants.* Formerly, no anesthetics or muscle relaxants were used; now both are employed.
6. *Monitoring.* Both brain waves and the electrical functioning of the heart are now monitored, through EEG and EKG.
7. *Placement of ectrodes.* Formerly, on both sides of the head; now, on the nondominant side only.

perform a risk-benefit analysis. On the benefit side is the probability of rapid improvement and, for depressives, the reduced likelihood of death due to suicide. On the risk side, however, are the possibility of death in the course of receiving ECT (this risk is low, with an incidence of about one in 10,000 treatments), the chance of memory impairment (which is short-term and becomes less noticeable with time), and the risk of spontaneous seizures (which are infrequent). In weighing the advantages against the risks, clinicians might reasonably consider ECT when there is severe depression or a possibility of suicide, or when drugs and other therapies are ineffective or seem inappropriate (Coffey & Weiner, 1990).

Drug Therapies

Many drugs have been used clinically and in research. Drug treatment has been notably effective with four types of disorders, those in which schizophrenia, mania, depression, and anxiety play important roles:

1. **Antipsychotic drugs** (e.g., phenothiazines) are used primarily to treat people who have a schizophrenic disorder. These drugs are described in Chapter 11.

2. **Antimanic drugs** (e.g., lithium) are used to treat those who have a bipolar disorder. Chapter 10 includes a description of these drugs.

3. **Antidepressant drugs** (e.g., tricyclics, MAO inhibitors) are used to treat patients who have been diagnosed as having a mood disorder of the unipolar type, that is, characterized by relatively long-lasting

depression but without any history of manic or hypomanic episodes. More information about these drugs is found in Chapter 10.

4. **Antianxiety drugs** (e.g., benzodiazepines) are used with people who have a high level or prolonged state of anxiety that is strong enough to incapacitate them or at least cause them difficulty in carrying out many activities of daily life (See Chapter 6 for more information about these drugs.)

These types of medication differ in their effectiveness, mechanisms of action, and side effects. The antipsychotic drugs usually produce improvement in 4 to 6 weeks. Antimanic drugs are often effective by themselves, but at times they need to be combined with an antipsychotic drug in highly agitated patients. The effects of antimanic drugs are usually noticeable within a week. Among the antidepressants, tricyclic drugs are often tried initially, with other types of antidepressants reserved for those patients who do not respond to the tricyclics. The therapeutic effects of the antidepressants usually require between 2 and 4 weeks to be apparent. Antianxiety drugs, whose therapeutic effects may be noticed within a week, are usually employed for limited time periods (up to a few months) to avoid the problem of drug dependence.

Although psychoactive drugs have helped many people live normal or almost normal lives and the safety of their use has improved, there are many unanswered questions about them. A number of risks must still be considered including a variety of side effects. Depending on the drug employed, side effects may include drowsiness, confusion, nightmares, poor appetite, insomnia, blurred vision, lethargy, and changes in blood pressure. Some of the drugs may be fatal if the patient's condition is not monitored regularly and some of the drugs expose the patient to the risk of having a fatal overdose available.

Like those of psychological therapies, the effects of drug therapy are not always predictable. Factors such as age, sex, and genetic background can influence a person's response to a drug. The effectiveness of a particular drug may also depend on how it is metabolized, whether the patient takes it as prescribed, and whether other drugs are being taken at the same time.

DRUG RESEARCH Physicians who prescribe drugs want to maximize their therapeutic effects and minimize their undesirable consequences. These goals require the use of carefully designed research procedures. First, extensive preliminary research is done to study the effects of varying doses of a drug on laboratory animals. If these tests suggest that the drug is effective and does not have harmful side effects, if properly used, the drug is administered to human beings under carefully controlled conditions. If these results are also positive, the drug may be approved for large-scale clinical trials in which its

effectiveness is scientifically compared with other treatment methods.

Clinical Trials **Clinical trials** involving drugs and other therapeutic procedures can be complex and costly, and may extend over many years. They often include samples of subjects located throughout the country and even the world. The following are some of the steps in a clinical trial.

1. Planning the research design and statistical analyses.
2. Deciding on the dependent measures to be used in evaluating the trial.
3. Organizing procedures for gathering data.
4. Recruiting subjects and assigning them to treatments.
5. Assuring that clinical personnel are "blind" to the assigned treatment whenever possible.

In the course of conducting clinical trials, scientists must be careful to rule out alternative explanations for the results they get. In addition to the enthusiasm effect discussed earlier, researchers have to be aware of **placebo effects.** A placebo (often referred to as a "sugar pill") is an inactive substance that has no pharmacological effects but under certain conditions may produce noticeable improvements in patients (see Figure 17–13).

FIGURE 17–13

(© 1993 by Sidney Harris)

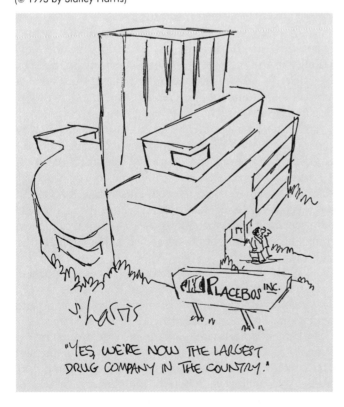

"YES, WE'RE NOW THE LARGEST DRUG COMPANY IN THE COUNTRY."

When a placebo is effective, it is because it has some of the same suggestive properties as a real treatment. Physicians know that the confidence with which they prescribe given medicines can influence their patients' reactions. Suggestible patients often show great improvement if a drug, even a chemically inactive one, is presented to them as a highly effective "wonder drug."

It might seem sufficient to evaluate drugs by comparing placebo groups with groups that are given chemically potent drugs. Actually, this is not the case, because the knowledge of which patients have received active substances and which ones have not can have a considerable influence on a physician's behavior or evaluations. Thus, the **double-blind method** is used to ensure that none of the participants knows whether the drug given to a particular patient is active or inert.

Hospitalization

Serious psychological illness may require hospitalization not only because the hospital provides round-the-clock care but also because it can offer all the complex therapies that a patient might need. But while some comprehensive mental hospitals provide an enriched program of therapies, offering such benefits as psychotherapy, drug therapy, and active social, educational, and recreational programs, the budgets of most state hospitals do not permit such varied fare. As a result, many patients in state hospitals receive drugs but few psychological therapies, and live in a relatively impoverished, unstimulating social environment. This is unfortunate because a hospital can be a place that helps a person cope with a crisis and experience personal growth.

No matter what kind of hospital is available, the major reasons for psychiatric hospitalization are as follows.

1. Thought or behavior that poses a threat to self or others.
2. Thought or behavior that is intolerable to members of the patient's community.
3. Failure of outpatient treatment and the hope that inpatient treatment will reverse the process.
4. A treatment procedure that requires a degree of control that is possible only in a hospital.
5. Withdrawal from alcohol or drugs.
6. Physical illness that is complicated by a mental disorder that requires continuous care.

Researchers have studied the kinds of hospital activities that are helpful to patients when they are not in

an acute phase of their disorder. One experiment compared a fairly traditional mental hospital routine with a routine based on social-learning principles (Paul & Lentz, 1977). Under the traditional routine, patients spent six percent of their time taking drugs, five percent in classes and meetings, and 63 percent in unstructured activities. This last percentage represents a great deal of boredom and a waste of therapeutic opportunities. Under the social-learning routine, however, 59 percent of the patients' time was devoted to classes, meetings, and structured activities. Only 12 percent of their time was unstructured. The ward employed a token economy to motivate the patients to engage in productive behavior. A comparison of the effects of the two approaches showed that the social-learning group had a significantly higher percentage of discharges to the community than the traditional group. However, regardless of the treatment used, only a small percentage of the patients were able to function in a self-supporting way.

Research on the process of resocialization may contribute answers to such questions as, what steps could help chronic patients adjust successfully to the community? Gordon Paul has suggested ten steps that mental hospitals might take to provide greater happiness and effectiveness among patients, higher morale among staff members, and a more positive social-rehabilitation role for the institution.

1. *Emphasize a "resident" rather than "patient" status through informal dress of staff, open channels of communication in all directions, and broad (but clear) authority structure.*

2. *Make clear, through a set of rules and attitudes, that the residents are responsible human beings; are expected to follow certain minimal rules of group living; and are expected to do their share in participating in self-care, work, recreational, and social activities.*

3. *Utilize step systems which gradually increase the expectations placed on the residents in terms of their degree of independence and level of responsibility, with community return emphasized from the outset.*

4. *Encourage social interactions and skills and provide a range of activities as well as regular large and small group meetings.*

5. *Emphasize clarity of communication, with concrete instruction in appropriate behavior and focus on utilitarian "action" rather than "explanation."*

6. *Provide opportunity to practice vocational and housekeeping skills, with feedback, and*

specific training in marketable skills when needed.

7. *Reacquaint residents with the "outside world" by exposing them to the community and bringing in community volunteers for discussions.*

8. *Identify the specific unique areas for change and support in concrete terms for each individual.*

9. *Prepare residents and significant others to live in mutually supportive ways in the community through prerelease training and scheduled aftercare.*

10. *When no significant other exists, train and release residents in groups of two to three as a "family" to provide significant others for one another.*

—Paul, 1969, p. 91

The effectiveness of a hospital depends on the needs of its residents, the quality and scope of its programs, and the community and family resources available to the patient. Because of variations in all of these areas, it is not surprising that there are strong differences of opinion about the effectiveness of hospitalization. When all factors are considered, it seems reasonable to conclude that some severely disturbed people can benefit from life in a socially active, therapeutic hospital. The precise percentage of currently institutionalized individuals who might benefit from this experience is very difficult to estimate.

If a ward is run mainly to satisfy the staff, or if a latent goal of the hospital is to maintain order and stability in the institution, the patients get the message. No therapy takes place because patients' behavior is aimed at minimizing conflict with the system and disruption of routine.

An unfortunate hospitalization is a special kind of experience whose mark may be visible long after its completion. It can increase patients' sense that they bear a stigma and make it easy for them to acquire "sick roles"—that is, to come to see themselves as sick people who will always have to be taken care of. It can also lead to a weakening of social and work skills. When these things happen, patients become less able to function in the community.

When complete hospitalization is not required, **partial hospitalization** may be employed (Rosie, 1987). This may include either day or night hospitalization and perhaps evening and weekend care in the hospital.

Day hospitals are used to provide treatment for patients who can live at home but need the structure and social interaction available in the treatment center. Day hospitals also allow members of the patients' families to

function more normally because they can carry on their usual activities during the day. Day hospitals often concentrate on teaching social and interpersonal behaviors as well as helping patients learn practical skills such as how to use the bus system or a pay telephone. They may also include training in basic work skills so that patients can get jobs in sheltered workshops that will provide the satisfaction of doing useful work and some payment as well.

Evening, night, and weekend programs are designed primarily to help hospitalized patients make the transition from the hospital to the community. Such programs are especially useful for people who are able to return to their jobs, schools, or training programs but do not have adequate family or social supports to go from inpatient to outpatient status without a partially protected transition period. The concept of night hospitals has gained some acceptance, but relatively few such hospitals have been established on a formal basis.

Over the past few decades hospitalizations for mental illness have become less frequent. While this fact in itself is not necessarily undesirable, public hospital beds available to people with low incomes have declined in number, while there has been an increase in private hospitals (Dorwart and others, 1991). As a consequence, access to hospital care is unevenly distributed in the population. Patients in public hospitals are being discharged after shorter periods of hospitalization, largely because of the effectiveness of psychoactive drugs and an increase in efforts to return patients to the community as quickly as possible. This **deinstitutionalization** process can be a boon to personal development if the individual has a good place to live, sufficient social support, and supervision when needed. Unfortunately, many people who have been discharged from mental hospitals live in furnished rooms in undesirable neighborhoods, are socially isolated, and receive little professional help beyond brief contacts with physicians who prescribe antipsychotic drugs.

The lack of adequate care in the community for chronic mental patients has contributed to the large numbers of homeless people in American cities (see Figure 17–14). Thousands of deinstitutionalized people have nowhere to live. They wander about city centers, sleep where they can, and carry their belongings with

FIGURE 17–14 The "dumping" of chronic mental patients on communities with inadequate clinical and rehabilitation programs contributes to the problem of homelessness.

them. While the problem of homelessness is complex, the "dumping" of deinstitutionalized people on a community only contributes to human misery. We will look further at this problem in the next chapter.

Chapter Summary

PSYCHOTHERAPY

No matter what their theoretical orientations psychotherapists perform three tasks: listening, understanding, and responding to the client.

Psychodynamic Therapy and Psychoanalysis **Psychoanalysis** is a special type of psychodynamic therapy carried on by specially trained therapists who use the technique of **free association** and place special emphasis on the examination of both dreams and fantasies. All psychodynamically oriented therapists emphasize **insight,** the understanding of one's inner life, as the goal of psychotherapy. They use the interpretation of **transference,** the client's displacement of affect and feeling about others onto the therapist, as an important part of therapy. They also take into account **countertransference,** the therapist's emotional response to the client.

Humanistic and Existential Therapies **Humanistic therapies** place emphasis on people's desire to achieve self-respect. An example of a humanistic therapy is Rogers's **client-centered therapy,** which stresses a nondirective, nonjudgmental approach in which the therapist provides an atmosphere of **unconditional positive regard.** The therapy is focused on increasing clients' self-acceptance and self-knowledge as a way to facilitate changes in their behavior. **Existential therapies** emphasize clients' needs to confront basic questions regarding the meaning and direction of their lives. Existential therapies are likely to combine humanistic and psychodynamic techniques. Perls's **Gestalt therapy** stresses that problems arise when people dissociate parts of themselves, especially their needs for personal gratification, from awareness.

The Cognitive Psychotherapies The theory of **cognitive psychotherapy** is that the best way to alter emotional problems is to alter the client's thinking through cognitive restructuring. An early cognitive approach was Kelly's **psychology of personal constructs,** which focused on the roles people played in interacting with others and the assumptions underlying those roles. Kelly developed **fixed-role therapy,** in which clients were encouraged to practice new roles and relationships. Ellis originated **rational–emotive therapy,** which emphasizes the need for clients to question and change their self-defeating thinking and mistaken beliefs. Beck's cognitive therapy focuses on automatic thoughts that may govern behavior although they are not produced by rational considerations. The client and therapist jointly explore the validity of the clients' false beliefs about themselves, the world at large, and the future.

BEHAVIOR THERAPY

Behavior therapy, the forerunner of cognitive behavioral therapies, began as a way of using operant and classical conditioning techniques to change behavior. **Behavior modification** developed from the operant techniques. Many operant conditioning methods use reinforcement and shaping to gradually achieve a desired response. **Fading** is the process of eliminating special cues used in the shaping process. A **token economy** uses operant methods to reinforce desired behaviors. **Biofeedback** is a method used to develop control of internal processes. **Desensitization** used in the treatment of phobias and other fears was developed from the classical conditioning techniques.

COGNITIVE BEHAVIORAL APPROACHES

Cognitive-Behavioral Interventions **Cognitive-behavioral therapy** is the result of combining behavior therapy and cognitive restructuring techniques. Cognitive-behavioral therapies are used to correct misconceptions, strengthen coping skills through behavioral techniques and enhance **self-efficacy expectations.**

Relaxation Training In **relaxation training** the relaxation effect is achieved either by focusing on muscle groups or through meditation techniques.

Exposure Therapy **Exposure therapy** is based on the idea that continuous exposure to anxiety-provoking stimuli will decrease anxiety. **Flooding** is a form of exposure therapy in which the client is exposed to a high level of fear arousing stimuli that is not terminated just as a function of client anxiety. Flooding is based on the idea that **extinction** of the fears will occur if the client remains in the anxiety-provoking situation long enough. In **implosive therapy** the client imagines scenes of behaviors or situations that he or she has avoided in the past and then experiences the intense anxiety these create until that anxiety is extinguished. **Systematic desensitization** combines muscular relaxation with cognitive activity in which the client imagines a series of increasingly anxiety arousing scenes related to specific fears. **In vivo desensitization** involves the same techniques when the fear-arousing stimulus is actually present. **Paradoxical intention** is a treatment in which the clinician asks the client to perform exactly the behavior the client is trying to stop.

Modeling **Modeling** is a "how to" approach that involves the demonstration of the behaviors involved in specific social skills for the client. The procedure may be carried out through **live modeling** or the direct observation of the model, **symbolic modeling** or observation of a recorded performance of the model, or **covert modeling** in which the client is asked to imagine observing a model and the consequences of the model's behavior. **Guided rehearsals** allow the client to practice the modeled behavior. **Assertiveness training** is the use of modeling and rehearsal to teach a person the interpersonal skills needed to keep them from being imposed on by others.

GROUP THERAPY

Group therapy sessions include a group of several clients usually with similar problems who meet together with a

therapist in regular sessions. In addition to being lower in cost than individual therapy, group therapy may be more effective for some problems. Group membership provides acceptance and support, normative information about behaviors and feelings, and an opportunity to learn through modeling and behavioral rehearsal. Group therapy is likely to be carried out from either a psychodynamic or a cognitive-behavioral perspective.

Cognitive–Behavioral Group Therapy The focus of **cognitive-behavioral group therapy** is on development of social skills and comfort in social situations.

Family and Marital Therapy Both family therapy and marital therapy focus on individuals who already constitute a group. Family therapists view the family as a system. In family therapy the family members work together with the therapist to deal with their attitudes and feelings toward each other and to understand how the behavior of each affects the others. Marital therapy can be viewed as a subtype of family therapy. Family therapy is likely to include psychodynamic or cognitive–behavioral approaches.

Psychodrama **Psychodrama** is a special kind of group therapy in which the group acts out events of emotional significance in order to express strongly-felt emotions.

INTEGRATION OF PSYCHOLOGICALLY BASED THERAPEUTIC APPROACHES

Aspects of many of the different therapeutic approaches have been found to be useful. Most therapists believe that therapeutic techniques addressing emotion, cognition, and behavior are all important in helping clients. As a result there is a trend toward a greater integration of therapeutic techniques based on the different perspectives.

RESEARCH ON THE PSYCHOLOGICAL THERAPIES

Simply comparing a single therapeutic technique with a control group is not very helpful. **Process research** in psychotherapy is concerned with understanding how each of the elements of the therapeutic effort affect the outcome for the client. The **enthusiasm effect** means that interest in the research project may modify many other aspects of the institutional setting or the therapist's behavior.

Outcome Studies One of the most important questions in studies of therapy is what the outcome measures should be. Possible choices are the therapist's opinion, the client's behavior or feelings, or the view of others such as family members or co-workers. There is often disagreement about outcome among these different sources.

Comparing Therapies Studies that compare different therapies have also found that there is considerable difference in the success of individual therapists, even those that use the same therapeutic approach. In general, psychological approaches have been found to be useful in cases without extreme psychopathology. Psychological therapies are often not successful alone in the treatment of schizophrenia, bipolar disorder, alcoholism, and drug abuse, but frequently produce a better result when used in combination with drug therapies than the drug therapies produce when used alone. Studies that compare several therapies are extremely expensive to carry out. As a result, a technique called **meta-analysis** has been used to evaluate jointly a group of separate studies so as to produce a statistical result.

Components of Effective Therapy Research on psychological therapies suggests that both **technique factors,** or procedures used by the therapist, and **interpersonal factors,** or the relationship between therapist and client, are important in therapeutic outcome.

Improving Therapy Research Several important considerations in therapy outcome research are adequate sample size, patients' similarity in factors not targeted in treatment, clearly specified treatment techniques, and careful choice of outcome measures. Adequate control and comparison groups are also important.

BIOLOGICAL THERAPIES

Electroconvulsive Therapy Electroconvulsive therapy (ECT) is most likely to be used for severe depression, especially as treatment for those who are at high risk for suicide, when drugs and other types of therapy have failed to help.

Drug Therapies Four general types of drugs have been found to be effective in treating mental disorders: **antipsychotic drugs, antimanic drugs, antidepressant drugs,** and **antianxiety drugs.** Before drugs can be used to treat patients the medications must be thoroughly tested for effectiveness and for negative side effects. Drugs and other therapeutic procedures are evaluated through **clinical trials** that compare outcomes for patients who receive different treatments. In these trials, alternative explanations of the results such as **placebo effects** must be considered.

HOSPITALIZATION

Some of the reasons that psychiatric hospitalization is recommended include behavior that poses a threat to self or others, failure of outpatient treatment, or a treatment procedure that requires a high degree of control. As a result of the **deinstitutionalization** movement of the past several decades, hospital treatment in the United States has become less frequent and those who are hospitalized tend to remain there for shorter periods of time.

Society's Response
to Maladaptive Behavior

C H A P T E R 1 8

Types of Prevention
Situation-focused and Competency-focused Prevention
Levels of Prevention

Sites of Prevention
The Family
The School
The Community

Treatment in the Community
Problems with Community Programs
Improving Treatment Programs

Legal Aspects of Treatment and Prevention
Institutionalization
The Rights of Patients

The Challenge of Prevention
Paraprofessionals
Self-help Groups
Community Psychology

A Final Word

Chapter Summary

Inger Jirby, *Moon at Sena Plaza*, 1991. Sena Galleries, Santa Fe, NM.

Ann Jackson had taught at Buchanan High School for eight years. She was 33 years old, still had some ideals, and had a reputation among both students and faculty of being a nice person. She was also a discouraged person who too often felt she wasn't able to reach several of her students. One who fell into this group was 16-year-old Bill Hadley. Bill paid little attention in class, did not complete assignments, and frequently did not show up at all. But what worried Ann Jackson the most was what she knew about Bill's activities outside class. Other students were afraid of him because of his imposing size, his bullying attitude, and his history of antisocial behavior. He had had numerous contacts with the police for a variety of reasons. He had been accused of puncturing the tires of a dozen cars parked along a street, extorting money from other students, and shoplifting at neighborhood stores. The most serious offense was a severe beating Bill had given to another student. According to those present at the fight, Bill was in such an uncontrollable rage that he couldn't stop hitting and kicking the other student even though it was evident that the student was helpless and in pain, and he started fighting with the spectators when they intervened. Ann Jackson couldn't get Bill out of her mind. She continually worried about what was going to happen to him.

Relatively small problems have a way of becoming big problems if nothing is done about them. Ann Jackson wished that something could be done to redirect Bill Hadley's life while he was still young, but she didn't know what she, the school, or the community could do now or what could have been done earlier to prevent Bill's current unhappiness, anger, and counterproductive behavior.

Many well-meaning and intelligent people feel

helpless when confronted with obvious mental distress in another individual. At the same time, everyday life is full of examples of people who are able to either help people in distress or help prevent distress from occurring. In the following example an exceptionally accomplished young college graduate was found to have had a chaotic, stress-inducing family life. Yet an informal relationship with a neighboring family had given him valuable opportunities for personal growth.

He came from an extremely disturbed home setting in which every member of his family except himself had been hospitalized for severe mental illness; and yet he had graduated from a renowned university with honors, had starred on the football team, and was unusually popular. During his government training he was held in the highest esteem by staff members and was rated as best liked and most likely to succeed by his peers.

In examining this young man's history we discovered that during his elementary school years he had essentially adopted a neighborhood family as his own and spent endless hours with them. Certain characteristics of this family appear most significant. They were a helping family in the sense that love emanated from them and was freely available to all. Of special significance for the fellow under consideration was his relationship with a boy in the family, a year older than he, who formed for him a positive role model with whom he closely identified. . . .

An even more crucial factor was his relationship with the mother in this family, who became his guide, counselor, and chief source of emotional nurturance. His reports indicate that while this relationship was intense, it was not symbiotic, and seemed to foster his independence and self-development. Although there are probably few like her, she represents a dimension of socially indigenous therapy that may be more significant than is usually recognized. Her home became a neighborhood gathering place. It might be characterized as an informal therapy agency, a kitchen clinic.

—Bergin and Lambert, 1978, pp. 149–150

In this chapter we discuss the role played by society in dealing with deviance and preventing problems of living.

Types of Prevention

Throughout this book we have considered methods of assessing, treating, and caring for individuals with behavior problems, but we have only briefly mentioned the possibility that the actual occurrence of maladaptive behavior in the population can be reduced. This is the focus of *prevention*.

Situation-focused and Competency-focused Prevention

Prevention can be approached from two perspectives. **Situation-focused prevention** is aimed at reducing or eliminating the environmental causes of disordered behavior, while **competency-focused prevention** is concerned with enhancing people's ability to cope with conditions that might lead to maladaptive behaviors. Situation-focused approaches seek to change the environment, for example, by making it less stressful. Competency-focused approaches seek to strengthen people's coping skills so as to make them more resistant should various types of stress-arousing situations arise.

Divorce is a common example of a stress-arousing situation. Its occurrence has increased dramatically over the last several decades and has resulted in changes in life styles and in the environments in which children are brought up. Nearly half of all children can expect to spend some time—an average of about six years—living in a single-parent family. Divorce and parental discord are related to impaired functioning and social behavior in children. Divorced people are likely to be overrepresented among people who make suicide attempts, become alcoholics, go through periods of depression, and seek help from mental-health professionals.

Programs are needed that can reduce the likelihood of maladjustment in divorced couples and their children. An example of such a program is one developed for newly separated individuals. The program provided the participants with psychological support and special training over a six-month period after the separation (Bloom & Hodges, 1988). Staff members made themselves available to participants when advice and counseling were needed. Training was provided in such practical areas as employment and child-rearing. Compared with newly separated people who did not participate in the program, the participants experienced less anxiety, fatigue, and physical illness, along with improved coping ability. There was some evidence that the intervention program was more effective for women than for men. Participants' comments after the program ended sug-

gested that their knowledge that interested people and special services were available if needed may have been the most powerful ingredient in the program. Future research will be needed to determine the long-term effects on both parents and children of programs that are designed to reduce the traumatic effects of an inevitably distressing situation.

Although the program just described can be seen as a competency-focused approach, it was activated only after the participants had already taken steps toward divorce. Another type of competency-focused prevention effort might aim to strengthen skills that are important in interpersonal relationships, particularly with one's spouse, long before thoughts of divorce might arise. The idea behind such an effort would be to increase coping skills and thereby enable couples to handle the stresses of marriage in more effective ways. Research on this type of preventive intervention is under way. For example, Markman and his colleagues (1988) have sought to strengthen skills that seem to help couples weather the stresses that challenge a marriage. Their program emphasizes communication skills. The couples are taught to focus on one topic at a time and to make their concerns and irritations clear, as in "I may seem angry because I had a bad day at work." They are also trained to "stop the action" until the partners cool down when repetitive cycles of conflict begin. One of the major signs of distress in a couple is escalating hostility, often in the form of nagging that provokes an angry response.

Early-education programs also illustrate competency-focused prevention. Their aim is to prevent or reduce problems in subsequent years. One project began with the frequent observation that maladapted children (and adults) tend to have weak interpersonal cognitive problem-solving skills (Shure & Spivack, 1982, 1987). These skills include the ability to identify problems and feelings (in oneself and others), to think of alternative solutions to a problem, to see relationships between alternative approaches and the achievement of goals, and to appreciate the consequences of one's actions. Interpersonal problem-solving skills can be thought of as mediating effective behavioral adjustment as well as fostering academic competence (see Figure 18–1).

The following is an excerpt from one of the lessons used by Spivack and his co-workers in teaching young children to be more sensitive to their feelings and those of others.

Now this is just a game. *Have each child hold a toy previously used from trinket box.* Peter, you snatch Kevin's toy from him.

Kevin, how do you feel about that? *Kevin responds.*

Peter, now let him have it back.

Now, how do you feel, Kevin? *After child answers, repeat with other pairs.*

Use a picture of a firetruck. Larry, how would going for a ride on this firetruck make you feel? *Let child respond.*

Let's pretend that a man came and drove the truck away and you could NOT have a ride. How would you feel now? *Same child responds.*

FIGURE 18–1 Children often act directly. When they want something they take it or they express displeasure by hitting another child. Cognitive games created by a team of researchers attempt to create greater empathy with others and in this way change the self-centered aggressive behavior often seen in childhood.

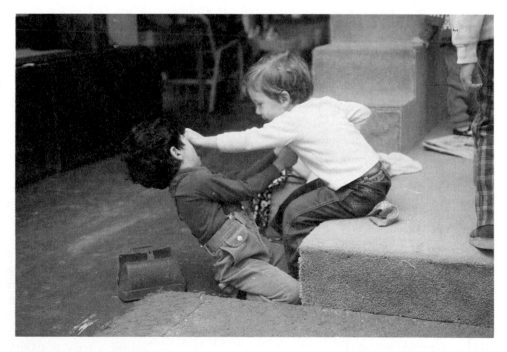

Now let's pretend he came back and said, "Okay, now you can go for a ride." How would that make you feel? *Same child responds.*

Use a picture of a ball. How do you think Steven might feel if we let him play with this ball? *Group answers.*

Maybe he would feel happy and maybe he would not feel happy. Let's find out. How can we find out? *Encourage children to ask.*

Let's pretend someone came along and threw the ball out the window so Steven could not play with it anymore. Now how do you think Steven might feel?

He might feel sad or he might feel mad. How can we find out?

Encourage children to ask.

—Spivack and others, 1976, pp. 183–184

These researchers found that behavioral adjustment was positively influenced by training in cognitive and social skills. This positive effect was greatest for children who originally seemed most maladjusted, and positive results were still evident a year later. In a related project inner-city mothers who were given training in interpersonal cognitive problem-solving skills were able to pass their training on to their children. Research with older children and adults supports the idea that the skills involved in academic and social effectiveness are learnable. Furthermore, it has been shown that improved teacher training—for example, teaching them to reinforce students' adaptive behavior—contributes to a more productive learning environment in the classroom. Sometimes situation-focused and competency-focused prevention efforts can occur as part of the same project. An approach that involves parenting classes and a chance to earn a high school diploma for teenage mothers combined with in-school day care for their children provides a competency focus for the mothers and situation-focused prevention for their preschool children. Because the mothers have few financial resources, few job-related skills, and usually lack maturity and knowledge about how to care for their children, the children are at high risk. In addition to earning a high school diploma and acquiring job-related skills, the young mothers in the Teenage Pregnancy and Parenting Program (TAPP) at Marshall Alternative High School in Seattle take courses in nutrition, anger management, household finances, and child rearing. Participants say the TAPP program also provides a support group and a gathering place for young mothers. Figure 18–2 shows one young mother and her son on the way to the school child care center.

FIGURE 18–2 In–high school day care facilities provide young mothers with a chance to earn a diploma and learn both work-related and parenting skills.

Levels of Prevention

"An ounce of prevention is worth a pound of cure" is a well-known truism. Why, then, aren't preventive measures more common? In some cases it is not clear what steps are needed to achieve the goal of prevention, and in others society does not seem willing or able to take the needed steps. Prevention of mental or physical disorder can take place on three levels. **Primary prevention** is concerned with the general reduction of new cases of these disorders and is administered to everyone in a particular population, for instance all students at a school or all pregnant women whether or not they may be at particular risk. Scientific information about cause and effect is very important in primary prevention. For example, knowledge of the possibility of harm to the unborn child has persuaded many women not to smoke or drink during pregnancy. Physicians are much more careful about prescribing medication for pregnant women because of information linking even seemingly harmless drugs with birth defects. And knowledge of the harmful effects of nicotine addiction has led psycholo-

gists to conduct research on ways to discourage children from beginning to smoke cigarettes (Flay and others, 1985). Another example of primary prevention is premarital counseling. Marital problems and divorce are highly correlated with maladaptive behavior. Premarital counseling is aimed at encouraging couples to anticipate any problems and to develop ways of coping with them before marriage.

The aim of **secondary prevention** is to reduce the potential disability of an existing abnormal condition. For example, if a child with phenylketonuria (PKU) is identified early, a special diet can prevent serious retardation. Children who are behind in intellectual and social development as a result of living in homes where little stimulation and individual attention are available can be helped to gain more normal development through special enrichment programs. These programs can help the child catch up in the developmental process and gain skills that will make later school achievement more likely.

Whereas secondary prevention refers to the diagnosis and treatment of disorders or problems as soon as possible, **tertiary prevention** is aimed at reducing the impairment that has resulted from a given disorder or event. This is achieved through rehabilitation and resocialization. For example, behavioral therapy for a hyperactive child may help him or her become more attentive in school and more accepted by other children despite the continuing problems associated with the condition. Counseling or group therapy after a traumatic event such as injury and permanent paralysis from an automobile accident may provide the social supports that reduce a person's vulnerability to the added stress of coping with the new disability. Rehabilitation of those who have committed crimes is another important area of tertiary prevention. Often offenders serve a prison sentence and are discharged back into the community without either adequate skills of impulse-control or the practical skills to get a job. The same difficult transitional situation is often faced by people who have been hospitalized for a schizophrenic disorder and later discharged directly into the community without any further attention or support.

Preventive measures have been developed in many cases in which biophysical factors are known to cause maladaptive behavior. However, the effects of detrimental social factors have frequently been ignored or neglected. It is much easier to detect and control the effects of an enzyme deficiency in newborn infants than it is to detect and control the pervasive influence of poverty and racism. But ignoring these causes and correlates of maladaptive behavior will not decrease their influence.

When prevention methods are successful, risk factors that lead to abnormal behavior are reduced or eliminated. In general, priority in efforts to achieve prevention is given to serious conditions that have high rates of incidence, and for which effective methods are available. For example, prevention efforts have been directed at one of the most serious and prevalent maladaptive behaviors of childhood, juvenile delinquency.

Juvenile delinquency is a legal term used to designate lawbreaking by minors. Each year between four and five percent of American teenagers, or approximately 1,300,000, are referred to the courts for suspected offenses other than traffic violations (Dryfoos, 1990) (see Figure 18–3). The following case gives an example of the troubled youngsters to whom the police, the legal system, and the community must respond.

Carl is a 16-year-old high school dropout who was placed in a locked correctional institution for seven months. He had been charged with breaking and entering, robbery, and parole violation offenses in which he admitted involvement. He first started getting into trouble at age 12 when he assaulted two women during a purse-snatching incident. By the time he entered high school, he had been in juvenile court for offenses involving theft, destruction of property, and unauthorized use of an automobile. When he was fifteen, he and his friends broke into an appliance store, and stole several color TVs, tape recorders, and portable radios. Carl's father is an accountant and his mother is a high school teacher. Carl describes himself as a "bad ass." He thinks his parents believe that hanging around with the wrong people is the source of his many difficulties with established authority and the law.

Delinquent behavior seems to have many causes, ranging from poor living conditions to a psychopathic or antisocial personality disorder to psychosis. Some of the following conditions have also been identified with delinquency.

1. Poor physical and economic conditions in the home and neighborhood.
2. Rejection or lack of security at home.
3. Exposure to antisocial role models within or outside the home, and antisocial pressures from peer-group relationships.
4. Lack of support for achievement in school.
5. The expectation of hostility on the part of others.

Juvenile delinquency can be approached at different levels of prevention. Primary prevention often takes the

(a)

(b)

(c)

FIGURE 18–3 Helping juvenile offenders to become productive members of society is a challenge to the court system, those who work to rehabilitate these young people and to society as a whole. (a) The judge often tries to assess the adolescent's attitudes about the offense. (b) Some juveniles can be treated most effectively in a residential institution where they are removed from their everyday environments and can receive intensive treatment. (c) Another effective way of helping some young offenders is to require that they spend time in community service rather than institutionalizing them.

form of programs aimed at improving living conditions and school achievement. For example, provision of low-cost subsidized housing that would enable families to move into low crime areas might provide less exposure to other delinquents. Special school programs that make individualized instruction available to help children with deficiencies in academic skills might not only help them become successful in school but might also have a long-term positive effect on their lives by giving them hope for the future as well as later opportunities for success. Although such programs are important and can be helpful to potential delinquents, perhaps the most effective primary prevention comes about through personal relationships. There is some evidence that if children growing up in high-crime areas have a positive role model, their behavior may be more influenced by that person than by their antisocial peers. The value of a positive model is shown in the following example.

Caesar and Richard are two brothers who live in a high-crime community. Neither has become delinquent. Talking with them gives us some clues to why this is so. Caesar has had one year of community college. He quit because he had to support the family, but at present he is unemployed. He spends his time with gang members but does not participate in their antisocial activities. He thinks he is able to do this because the others admire him for his skill at restoring old cars. This admiration makes it possible for him to socialize with them without participating in their activities, to dress differently, and to see himself as a potentially achieving person who will contribute to the community. Caesar attributes his goals and behavior to his efforts to be like an older, retired gang member, Hood. He describes his admiration for Hood this way:

"Hood's been through it all. He's lived here all his life—he's done time—he's been a user but now he's clean. He is harassed by the cops so much that he had to get a letter from a judge saying that he was clean and that he should be left alone. He helps all of us in the barrio. He tells it like it really is, takes us to the ball game, helps raise money for bail, whatever. He does it all for nothing. Not even teachers and counselors work for nothing."

Caesar's younger brother Richard is classified as a slow learner in school and has problems in math and reading. But he has learned how to repair bicycles and sees this as a way to gain status in the community. He believes Caesar was instrumental in the development of his own prosocial behavior. He explains their relationship as follows.

"My mother told my brother when my father left that he was responsible for me, she wasn't. My brother counseled me, looked out for me, and told me what to do. He told me never to steal— that if I wanted something to come to him and he'd try to get it for me or see if I could earn it. If my brother thought that I was getting into trouble, he would probably kick my butt."

—Based on Aiken and others, 1977, pp. 214–220

Some adolescents develop their own cognitive mechanisms to help them resist peer pressure.

Linda Carmichael, who lived in a Chicago tenement inhabited by winos, junkies, and petty hustlers, wanted to get out of the ghetto, and went to college. This is how she described the cognitions that helped her keep on her track when her peers sneered and when she "wanted to be out partying and goofing off like everyone else": "I'd start thinking about all those people on the street with nothing to look forward to and where would I be without school. That kept me going." Linda's teachers, impressed by her efforts, provided her with support, advice, and information that helped her achieve her goal.

—Goldman & Williams, 1978, p. 34

Secondary prevention programs concentrate on young people who have shown early signs of delinquency. For example, there might be a special intervention focused on helping youngsters who have committed minor nonviolent offenses (such as theft or truancy) behave less impulsively.

Sometimes changing delinquent behavior might be classified as tertiary prevention. The youth might be involved in seriously maladaptive behavior. The following case presents an example of the type of preventive measures that may be taken in such a situation.

A 14-year-old boy was referred to a therapist by the court because he had set several large grass fires that had endangered houses. He could not explain his behavior, and neither could his parents since he had always behaved responsibly at home.

The boy's family was seen for six family-therapy sessions. These sessions revealed that the family could not discuss problems openly but tended to communicate nonverbally. Several recent family crises had caused tension. The father seemed to handle his unhappiness by withdrawing from the family into club activities. The son seemed to express his anger at family problems by setting fires. Once they began to meet in therapy sessions and these problems became evident, all of the family members were able to change their behavior. One year later there had been no more fire-setting.

—Based on Eisler, 1972, pp. 77–78

At all levels of prevention, the problems of delinquency and the therapeutic treatment of delinquents are far from solved. The number of delinquents who go on to commit more antisocial acts is high. Different approaches work best with different types of cases, but as yet all methods produce more failures than successes. Understanding delinquency requires a better grasp of the variables involved in the interaction between the person and the situation.

Sites of Prevention

This chapter especially emphasizes research that is relevant to the prevention of maladaptive behavior. Where data are lacking, we speculate about the use of social experimentation. We do not attempt a comprehensive analysis of all the components of a complex social structure; instead, we direct our attention toward three areas that definitely affect the growth and development of children and adults: the family, the school, and the community.

The Family

Parents play a significant role in their children's development because of the genes they contribute and the environment they provide. This environment begins in the uterus during the nine months before birth. Whatever can improve prenatal care and thus reduce the incidence of premature birth and other foreseeable difficulties might help reduce several types of problems, such as low intelligence. Improved prenatal and neonatal care can be expected to reduce brain damage, which, among other conditions, is related to certain types of epilepsy.

From the standpoint of prevention, the family is important because much of the child's earliest learning and development takes place within the family setting. Self-help groups can be useful for parents of young children. These groups provide parents with a way of understanding the typical ways that children behave as well as a way of learning about how others have coped successfully with child-rearing problems. Meeting with others with similar interests also provides an important opportunity for social relationships with other adults, something that is often lacking for parents with young children. Parents' ideas about child-rearing and the development process make important contributions to the day-to-day environment of children (see Figure 18–4). The relationship between certain parental practices and aggression in children demonstrates the effect of parental attitudes on their children. Many aggressive children come from homes in which the parents make the child feel insecure and rejected, bombard the child with commands, taunts, and threats, and teach the child that force is the only way to get what is wanted. The following parenting practices have been linked reliably to children's aggression (Perry and others, 1990):

1. *Monitoring failures.* Parents of aggressive and delinquent children are less aware of their children's whereabouts, activities, and social contacts.

FIGURE 18–4 A self-help or mutual support group for parents of young children can provide both learning opportunities and social support.

2. *Parental aggression.* Many aggressive children come from homes in which at least one parent is exceptionally violent.

3. *Permissiveness.* Parents of aggressive children frequently decline to set limits on their children's behavior and are ineffective at stopping their children's deviant behavior.

4. *Inconsistency.* Inconsistency both between parents and within one parent in disciplinary practices have been implicated in aggressive development.

5. *Rejection.* Highly aggressive individuals often have a history of parental rejection.

Because parents' behavior may play a role in their children's problems, many clinicians who specialize in treating childhood disorders stress the importance of parenting training, family therapy, or in some cases, therapeutic work with the parents as the most effective way of helping children. However, some parents experience tremendous, and often unwarranted, personal guilt if their children develop problems (See Figure 18–5).

The following are some additional examples of the influence parents with certain disorders may have on their children (Rutter, 1988). Children of psychotic parents are slow in developing speech and bladder control, have more eating and sleeping problems, and are more likely to be delinquent than other children. Alcoholic parents have a disproportionately large number of hyperactive children, and alcoholic mothers are overrepresented among mothers of babies with low birthweight and low IQs. There is also a relationship between criminality in parents and delinquency in their children.

CHILD ABUSE Children who have been physically abused, malnourished, and neglected by their parents are more prone to various forms of maladaption than other children. Under certain circumstances even "normal" parents—that is, parents who are not obviously disturbed—can have negative effects on their children's development. One of the most tragic examples of this is child abuse.

A Spokane man who was once convicted of assaulting his 13-month-old daughter is sought by police on a recent charge of fracturing the skull of his 12-day-old daughter.

Parental failure is most blatant when parents physically harm their children. There are varying estimates of the number of children who are physically

WHAT WENT WRONG?

FIGURE 18–5 Some well-intentioned, overly conscientious parents worry too much about what children need early in life to lay the groundwork for a good life later. On the other hand, some parents do not devote enough attention to their children's needs.

(Drawing by R. Chast; © 1987 The New Yorker Magazine, Inc.)

mistreated in the United States each year. It is difficult to make such an estimate, because **child abuse** varies in degree and is often hidden from view by embarrassed and ashamed parents. But thousands of children, many under three years of age, are seriously—often fatally—mistreated each year. When emotional abuse is included as well as physical abuse, the figure becomes much larger. A sizable percentage of abuse cases involve sexual assault.

Abusive parents tend to be less intelligent and more aggressive, impulsive, immature, self-centered, tense, and self-critical than nonabusive parents. They are more likely to have been abused themselves as children; thus, child abuse is a vicious cycle (Cicchetti & Carlson, 1989). Table 18–1 lists family characteristics often associated with child abuse. The physical and psychological damage done to children by abusive parents can sometimes be observed immediately.

Table 18-1
Characteristics of Abusing Families

Parents' Histories

Experience of abuse or neglect
Lack of affection from parents
Large families
Married as teenagers

Current Family Situation

Socially isolated, parents lack social support
Marital discord
Parental impulsivity
Parental retardation or illiteracy
Stressful living conditions (e.g., inadequate housing)

Parents' Approach to Child-rearing

Infrequent praise of children
Strict demands on child
Low level of child supervision
Early toilet training
Maternal dislike of caretaking
Parental disagreements over child-rearing practices

SOURCE: Based on Nietzel and Himelein, 1986.

The blond-haired boy was curled unresponsive in the fetal position in a crib that was wheeled into the courtroom. Doctors recited the abuse the child had endured: a beating which caused gangrene and permanent brain damage; and having the words "I cry" burned into his back with a cigarette.

Often less observable are the long-term effects. The following report describes Rick, a 26-year-old college junior who sought psychotherapy. The case is interesting because it suggests how problems of adult life may be related to the experience of childhood abuse. Rick seemed to be able to function effectively. Unfortunately, many victims of child abuse do not turn out so well.

When he was two months old, he was hospitalized in traction with multiple broken bones in his legs, hips, and rib area. His mother had claimed that he had fallen from her lap to the floor, an

impossible story in view of the extent of the injury. He remained immobilized in the hospital for six months. Then he was sent home in a partial body cast, and two weeks later he returned to the hospital with a similar set of fractures and put back in traction. This time the doctor suggested to his father that Rick should be placed in a foster home or his mother should be admitted to a mental hospital. The father refused and Rick returned home. Three times during the next four years Rick's father took him to the doctor when he appeared sick and the doctor diagnosed starvation, saying the child clearly wasn't being fed. These events are known to Rick through his father, his father's relatives, and his family physician. Rick himself has only one memory before age ten—that is of at age seven playing with his grandfather whom he saw only a few times in his life. From the time Rick can remember, his mother totally ignored him, never talked to him or fed him, nor did she strike him again. His only sibling is a brother 16 months older than Rick, who suffered similar malnutrition but no violent injuries. Rick recalls believing his brother was the mother's favorite because he can recall her fixing the brother a meal once, which he claims she never did for him.

Rick's presenting complaints were anxiety during tests (although he does quite well on them) and a recurring nightmare which he had no insight into although it was found to be strikingly transparent: He is driving along in a car and passes a terribly injured man in a ditch—the injury varies, most commonly his leg is cut off. He drives into a nearby town and approaches people asking them to help the man in the ditch, and each one gives him an excuse why they cannot. A feeling of horror surfaces, not upon first seeing the man but when he realizes no one will help. At this point Rick awakens.

—Barrett and Fine, 1980, p. 290

Rick's nightmares suggest that he is still reliving his childhood situation, in which he was helpless and no one would help him.

An abusive parent is usually a very troubled person who seems to be a victim of uncontrollable impulses and frustrations. The following is an excerpt from a group therapy session in which the participants were mothers who had abused their children.

Mother 1:	*I was just at my breaking point and I knew if I didn't get help somewhere, it would just go on and on and end up a vicious circle. I think that everyone who has had this problem at one time has thought "my goodness, I must be the only person in the world that feels this way." And when I found out that I wasn't, that was a load off my mind.*
Therapist:	*Feels what way?*
Mother 1:	*Desperation with their children. Not knowing how to cope. Afraid that you would just lose control completely and knock their head off, you know. I think we were all brought up to believe that women are supposed to have children and they're supposed to have the mother-instinct and if you don't have it, there is something definitely wrong. And I think it took this group to make me realize that women just aren't born with the mothering instinct . . . that has helped me.*
Another mother:	*If you're going to pound your child, the best thing to do is separate yourself from your child.*
Mother 1:	*That's fine to say, but what if you're like me and you can go on beautifully for a month, two months, three months and all of a sudden like last week I was feeling just fine and I cleaned house like I do every Monday . . . I got all them damn floors waxed and _____ wakes up from her nap and she couldn't get her body shirt undone so she got all upset and she wet all over my new waxed floor. And I just went berserk and I threw her around like she had killed somebody, because right at that moment I just snapped, I didn't feel it coming. I was fine, everything*

was hunky-dory, nothing was wrong, I wasn't in a bad mood, there was no warning . . .

This type of behavior is typical of abusive parents. Behavioral training in impulse control and coping skills can be helpful for parents who want to stop harming their children. Numerous kinds of preventive programs have been attempted. These include parental education and the use of parents as therapists. A promising mutual-aid approach is Parents Anonymous (PA), an organization modeled after the social support approach of Alcoholics Anonymous (see Chapter 14).

An example of preventive research on abuse is a study in which abusing parents received training in parenting skills (Wolfe and others, 1981). The parents' training consisted of reading about effective parenting techniques, observing modeled demonstrations of how to handle common child-rearing problems, and learning relaxation and other coping skills. In addition, project staff members made weekly home visits to help the parents implement what they had learned. When parents who participated in this program were compared with a control group of abusers, the parents in the special program showed significant improvement in parenting skills. A follow-up showed that none of the specially treated abusers harmed their children during the year after their participation in the program. This study suggests that effective child management skills can be taught to abusive parents with a relatively small investment of time and labor.

Similarly, encouraging results were obtained in a study in which the subjects were 400 pregnant women who had at least one of a cluster of risk factors for child abuse (teenaged, poor, unmarried, first pregnancy) (Olds & Henderson, 1989). The pregnant women were randomly assigned to four treatment groups. The first group was a "no intervention" control, which included a screening of the child at one and two years of age. The second group included these screenings and provided free transportation to prenatal and well-baby medical appointments. The third group built upon that plan by adding to it nine visits to the home by a nurse during the pregnancy. The fourth group extended regular nurse's visits to the child's second birthday. The nurse's visits were designed to promote linkage with formal service agencies when appropriate and to enhance the social support of the mother (and father when present). Furthermore, the nurse provided parenting and health education and consultation. Finally, clarification of values around social and family issues was included. Clearly,

the fourth group received relatively broad and intensive family services.

The clearest benefits were reaped by the subjects who received the most extensive treatment. Nineteen percent of those in the control group abused or neglected their children within the first two years of life. In contrast, only four percent of those in the group who received long-term nurses' visits maltreated their children. The other two groups had better results than did the control group, but these were not nearly as impressive as the results for the group that received the extended intervention. Other evidence of the extended intervention's effectiveness were also found for scolding rates, provision of appropriate play materials, and avoidance of restriction. Moreover, their children showed a trend toward better developmental progress and fewer emergency room visits than their peers in the control group. These findings suggest that a comprehensive intervention program can prevent child maltreatment and promote good parenting in groups at high risk for parenting dysfunction.

SPOUSE ABUSE "To have and to hold . . . to love and to cherish. . . ." This sentiment reflects the feelings of most people toward marriage—but these feelings are not shared by everyone. Beginning in the 1970s, largely as a result of the women's movement, attention has been drawn to the problem of **spouse abuse,** or the plight of abused women—those who are browbeaten psychologically as well as those who are physically assaulted—who cower in bedrooms and kitchens, are patched up in emergency rooms, and, not infrequently, are beaten, shot, or stabbed to death in their own living rooms. Spouse abuse occurs in several million homes in the United States each year and more than 8 percent of homicides involve the killing of one spouse by another. An estimated 25 to 30 percent of all women with a spouse or cohabiting partner have been beaten at least once while in such a relationship (Sadock, 1989).

A woman who has been abused over a long period is afraid. Fear might be a woman's first and most immediate feeling during or after a beating, but other negative feelings may surface when she is not in physical danger. The abused woman is likely to develop doubts about herself. She might wonder whether she is justified in fearing for her life and calling herself "abused." Most likely, however, a woman who thinks or feels that she is being abused is probably correct.

An abused woman may also feel guilty, even though she has done nothing wrong. An abused wife may feel responsible for her husband's violence because she believes she may have provoked him in some way. She then places the blame on herself instead of on her abuser. Along with the feelings of being a failure, both as a woman and in her marriage, may come a real fear of being trapped and powerless.

A wife abuser tends to be filled with anger, resentment, suspicion, and tension. He also, underneath all his aggressive behavior, can be insecure and feel like a loser. He may use violence to give vent to the bad feelings he has about himself or his lot in life. Home is one place where he can express those feelings without punishment to himself. If he were angry with his boss and struck him, he would pay the price; but all too often he gets away without any penalty when he beats his wife. One study found that compared with nonabusive husbands, abusive husbands were less assertive in social relationships than their wives, more likely to have been abused as children and more likely to have witnessed spouse abuse between their own parents (Rosenbaum & O'Leary, 1981).

Efforts to help abused spouses include not only emergency care, safety, and shelter but also long-range planning. Because abused spouses need to develop better feelings about themselves—that is, change their self-image—they need to strengthen their self-related positive cognitions. Counseling often emphasizes the following types of self-statements.

- I am not to blame for being beaten and abused.
- I am not the cause of another person's violent behavior.
- I do not have to take it.
- I deserve to be treated with respect.
- I do have power over my own life.
- I can use my power to take good care of myself.
- I can make changes in my life if I want to.
- I am not alone. I can ask others to help me.
- I deserve to make my own life safe and happy.

The three levels of prevention can all be applied to spouse abuse. Premarital counseling is an example of primary prevention; marital counseling to reduce discord illustrates secondary prevention; and providing abused spouses with safety, shelter, and counseling exemplifies tertiary prevention.

PARENTAL CONFLICT AND DIVORCE The earlier discussion of divorce in this chapter emphasized minimizing maladjustment in the couple. There is also a sizable literature on the negative effects of divorce on children, and growing evidence that these effects can be reduced by taking certain preventive steps (Wallerstein, 1991).

Research on this topic is complicated, because it is not possible to separate the effects of divorce from the effects of family conflict and parental inadequacy. Divorce might be regarded as a special case of family conflict in which legal dissolution of the family results. While divorce is public and measurable, parental conflict occurs mainly in private and cannot be reduced to a

statistic. Researchers have tried to pinpoint the kinds of negative outcomes that family conflict tends to promote. Boys in most cases have been found to be more obviously vulnerable than girls are and they often respond in more easily noticed ways. Common reactions in boys are increased aggression, troubled peer relations, and lack of impulse control (Cherlin and others, 1991).

The degree to which divorce is upsetting to children has been recognized for a long time. Children of divorced parents show up much more frequently in psychiatric outpatient clinic populations than their proportion in the population would predict. Even children in nonclinical samples are likely to exhibit dramatic divorce-related changes in play behavior and relationships with others (Hetherington, 1991). Not only do children have to deal with their own stress, but they must cope with parents who are also experiencing high levels of stress and whose own emotional health and financial well-being may have significantly deteriorated. Children and their parents must adjust to new living and custody arrangements (see Figure 18–6). The clinical experience of many therapists and counselors has provided some ideas that may help parents soften the blow of divorce for their children.

1. *Tell the children ahead of time.* This lets them prepare for one parent's moving out.

2. *Tell the children the reasons that the decision was made.* This helps prevent children's frequent belief that they were the cause of the breakup. Make the explanation brief but honest and suitable for the age of the child.

3. *Emphasize that the divorce is a permanent decision.* Many children harbor the belief that their parents will eventually get back together.

4. *Explain what changes there will be in the child's life.* These may include moving, a new school, and much less money to spend. Emphasize the positive challenge of adapting to the new situation.

5. *Let the children be free to express their anger.* This is an effective way to prevent long-term problems. At the same time, the parents should avoid using their children as a dumping ground for their own sense of anger or despair. Instead, they should share their negative feelings with an adult friend or with a therapist or counselor.

6. *Avoid forcing the child to choose between the parents or to take sides.* Custody and visitation rights that are fair to both parents should be agreed upon. Both parents should make continued contact with the children a high priority.

PARENTS AS THERAPISTS While parents sometimes fail to help their children develop optimally, there are numerous instances in which they can play very positive roles. For example, there is growing evidence that parents can be trained to respond therapeutically to their children's behavioral problems. Training parents to be effective behavior-change agents has positive consequences for children's development (Kramer, 1990). Not only can the parent help the child learn needed cognitive or social skills, but because the parent learns to help in a positive way, the relationship between the parent and

FIGURE 18–6 Divorce has many effects on the lives of both parents and children. The majority of children live with their mothers, often in reduced economic circumstances. Children may have infrequent contact with their noncustodial parent and that relationship may be based on what are often rather superficial interactions but little ongoing attention. *(a)* A single mother prepares a meal for her children. *(b)* A child and noncustodial father spend an afternoon together on an outing.

(a)

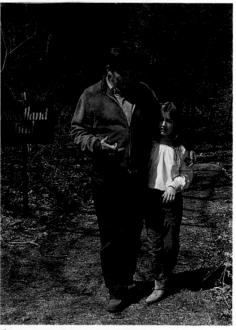

(b)

child can be improved. Training parents in helping skills can change the child's view of the parent from that of someone who is not satisfied with the child's behavior to someone supportive who cares about the child and is helping the child to change the situation to achieve a positive outcome. The main techniques for bringing this about are modeling, behavioral rehearsal, and reinforcement (see Figure 18–7).

Many demonstrations of the use of parents as therapists have focused on extreme forms of behavior such as autism and some forms of mental retardation. Parents of autistic children have been taught to observe behavior, to identify responses that need to be strengthened or weakened, and to use reinforcers skillfully. The following is an interchange between a mother and a psychologist who was training her to deal more effectively with her six-year-old autistic son Dorian. The mother had already learned several principles of behavioral therapy in preparation for her conference with the psychologist. She had made a list of behaviors that she felt Dorian had to learn, as well as a number of points that she and her husband would have to learn simultaneously.

Mrs. Cooper: *We would like Dorian to respond to instructions in various arts and crafts activities which would eventually lead to his learning of reading, writing, numbers, colors, and appropriate behavior in the classroom. In order to achieve this broad objective, he has to learn the following. The following are most of his problems. . . .*

a) The proper use of objects, such as crayons, paste, paper, pencils, and books.

FIGURE 18–7 This mother is teaching her child, who is a slow learner, how to write her name. Notice how she uses modeling, how the child practices what the mother has shown, and the mother's reinforcement of the child's progress.

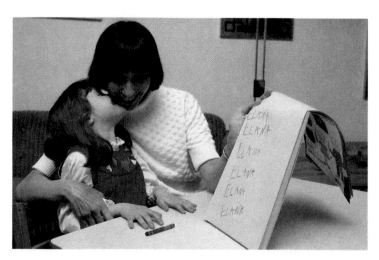

b) Sit still and pay attention. (They are not necessarily in that order. That is how they came to my mind.)

c) Focus his vision on what we point out.

d) He has to perceive the whole picture rather than focusing or fixating on a small part of it. (Perception, I feel, is somewhat of a problem.)

e) I would like him to learn to take pride and enjoy his success. Pride in his own achievement will, I hope, be his strongest reinforcer as he grows. These are his problems as well as what I feel our goals are and what we have to work for.

Dr. W.: The implication when you list all of these behaviors is that the behaviors are there, either too weakly. . . .

Mrs. Cooper: Yes, I feel they are there and could be brought out, but he's not willing to do it, as of now, so this is what I feel are his problems.

—Walder and others, 1967, pp. 57–58

Mrs. Cooper became skillful at recognizing environmental events that might reinforce appropriate responses emitted by Dorian. She planned and wrote up records of her "reinforcement experiments" with him.

We know the following about Dorian already:

a) He imitates what we say and, with some positive reinforcement, successfully learned a great deal of behavior.

b) He loves chocolate in any way, shape, or form. He imitates what we say and because of this, and in addition, with positive reinforcers such as the chocolate he has successfully learned a great deal of verbal behavior. This we know.

c) He loves chocolate and trains, lights, vacuum cleaners, cleaning objects, dearly.

d) He fixates on certain pages of books, and verbalizes quite accurately what he sees there.

e) He is beginning to explore the environment and loves to walk, looks into people's homes, and occasionally stops to talk to them.

—Walder and others, 1967, p. 59

Mrs. Cooper's experiments became more and more successful, and her son's autistic behavior, although it was not eliminated, became less of a problem.

Other studies have demonstrated that through special tutorial programs parents can become more effective in fostering desirable behavior in children who exhibit the more common types of problem behavior. For example, one child continually tried to command and control the behavior of his parents ("You go over there and I'll stay here"). When his parents learned to identify and differentially respond to this autocratic behavior, its frequency declined. The child became more socially cooperative when his parents ignored his commands; they also gave him special attention when he cooperated. Parents and teachers of highly aggressive boys have been taught to note the occurrence of particular types of undesirable behavior and to reduce its frequency through the use of reinforcement and other appropriate behavioral techniques (Patterson, 1982).

The School

School districts, schools, and classrooms are larger and more complex social systems than families. Often they seem unwieldy and unmanageable. However, in some respects it is more feasible to attack problems of behavior in the school situation than in the home. Dorian's mother invited a behavior modification specialist to visit her home and observe what went on there, but many parents, even while admitting that their families have problems, would be neither eager nor willing to have their privacy invaded by observers.

EARLY DETECTION PROGRAMS Teachers, school psychologists, and social workers can cite many instances in which longstanding family problems are not identified until the child reaches school age. But even when a problem is recognized at school, it may not be possible to deal with it effectively. The parent may refuse to cooperate with the school, or the realities of the child's life may make any significant change in his or her condition impossible—for example, if the child's home is unstable because of continual fighting between the parents or because the parents are immature and irresponsible.

Despite such barriers, early-detection projects in schools have attempted to identify children on the basis of their current behavior and school performance who

are likely to have more severe adjustment problems later in life. The results of these projects show that early observation of the child, together with data available to school mental-health workers (for example, nurses' notes, teachers' reports, and test scores), can predict later psychological difficulties. In addition, classmates' ratings of each other seem to have predictive value. On the basis of such information, secondary prevention studies have been carried out to help vulnerable children before their problems become serious enough to require clinical help. For example, in one project nonprofessional aides worked under close professional supervision for an entire school year with children who were judged to be at risk for school maladjustment. The children who received this one-to-one contact showed significant changes in a number of areas, including social and academic skills and overall adjustment (Chandler and others, 1984). Special training for teachers, workshops to help parents develop their child-rearing skills, and carefully planned in-school and after-school activity programs can help prevent a significant number of behavior disorders in children (Bond & Compas, 1989; Cowen & Hightower, 1990).

DROPPING OUT Some children are never comfortable in school, and by the time they reach high school they are ready to leave. The dropout problem is a social as well as an educational one. In prosperous times, when jobs are not difficult to obtain, the economic cost to the dropout may not seem great. However, when competition in the job market intensifies, poorly educated, unskilled people tend to fall by the wayside.

An example of primary prevention is a study aimed at teaching cognitive and social skills to high school students (Sarason & Sarason, 1981). The school in which the research was conducted had a history of high dropout and delinquency rates and a low percentage of graduates who went on to college. The research was carried out in class sessions as part of a regular course. The basic procedure involved using modeling to demonstrate social and cognitive skills, followed by rehearsal of the modeled behavior. The subjects saw demonstrations of the cognitive antecedents of effective behavior (for example, deciding between alternative courses of action) and effective overt responses (such as how to ask a teacher a question). Repeated emphasis was placed on the links between thought and action. The following is an excerpt from a modeling videotape that was shown in the experimental program ("Jim's cognitions" refers to voiceovers in which Jim's thoughts were spoken aloud).

Tom:	Hey Jim, you want to go down to Green Lake fourth period?
Jim:	What are you gonna do down at Green Lake?
Tom:	A bunch of us are gonna take the afternoon off and party it up.
Jim:	I don't think I can go. Sixth period Mr. Smith is reviewing for the algebra exam.
Tom:	What about coming over and staying until sixth?
Jim:	Well, I kind of like Mr. Jones's class. Besides, it's too hard to get to Green Lake and back in an hour and forty minutes. I could come after school.
Tom:	You know Lydia is going to be there.
Jim	(with noticeable interest): She is?
Tom:	Yeah. And by the time school is over, who knows if the party will still be there. We might go over to someone's house.
Jim's cognitions:	Gee, I really want to go to that party. Maybe I can get up the nerve to ask Lydia out. But I should stay for that algebra review, at least. The test will be hard enough without missing the review.
Tom:	You know, it is Friday afternoon and a beautiful day.
Jim's cognitions:	I wish Tom would let me make my own decision. This isn't easy. Maybe I could study hard this weekend. Then I won't need to go to the review. But will I really study Saturday?
Tom:	Well are you going to come?
Jim:	I don't know, Tom. I'll have to think about it some more. Maybe I'll see you there fourth. If not, I'll probably come later.
Tom:	Okay, I hope you come.

One year after the completion of the study, the experimental subjects had better school-attendance records, less tardiness, and fewer referrals to school counselors and psychologists because of behavioral problems than similar students who did not participate in the program.

Table 18–2 lists certain measures schools can take to prevent dropping out.

Table 18–2
Recommendations for Preventing School Failure and Dropping Out

1. Early identification of high-risk students, with particular attention to transition difficulties, such as from junior high to senior high school.
2. Small-size classes appear to be especially beneficial to high-risk students.
3. Individualized attention and instruction are necessities for children with problems in school.
4. Teachers should have reasonable but high expectations for behavior and achievement and be sensitive to gender, race, and cultural issues.
5. Counseling services are needed by potential dropouts who often have personal and family problems.

SOURCE: Based on Dreyfoos, 1990.

The Community

After people leave school they are pretty much on their own. Most of their activities are not supervised by authority figures, and a certain degree of independence is expected of them. At the same time, they are expected to fit into the community by working and by adhering to societal laws, values, norms, and priorities.

Work is the major postschool activity for most people. Finding employment that is satisfying and sufficient to earn a livelihood is obviously a major ingredient in an individual's satisfaction with life. How can maladaptive work behavior be prevented?

A study by Ross and Glaser (1973) compared several variables related to childhood experiences and the home environments of two groups of male residents of a ghetto in a large city. Both groups grew up under decidedly disadvantaged circumstances, but while half continued to live in poverty, the other half managed to change their lives for the better in significant ways. There were two successful "A" groups consisting of African-American and Mexican-American men and two unsuccessful "B" groups of the same ethnic makeup. The A groups had worked more or less steadily during the two years preceding the study; the B groups had been unemployed or underemployed. The investigators hypothesized that parental attitudes and aspirations made the difference between people who did and did not overcome the developmental barriers posed by poverty and discrimination.

Interviews with respondents in the two groups uncovered a number of differences that supported the hypothesis and were consistent for both ethnic groups. Members of the A groups received greater support, encouragement, and discipline at home. They also had developed a sense of self-esteem through involvement in productive activities. The results indicate the need to help relatively unsuccessful people overcome low self-esteem and self-confidence. Another personality characteristic of members of the B groups that might be modified through imaginative programs is their dependence on approval from peers. We might expect that many unproductive people would benefit from a close relationship with a nonpeer—teachers, athletic coaches, or employment counselors, for example—who would make demands, motivate achievement, provide information about productive skills, and act as both models and reinforcers of good performance.

COMMUNITY AGENCIES Every person is influenced by the way in which society and its institutions are organized. Although some institutions are concerned with specific segments of the population (for example, day-care centers, schools, social centers for senior citizens), several are capable of reaching a majority of the society's members. Because of our tendency to take these institutions for granted, we may lose sight of their potential for contributing to personal growth and reducing the likelihood of maladaptation. For example, a public library can be a powerful force in a person's life by providing access to books that can offer young people positive models and a broader view of the world. If the library can also provide positive personal experiences, these may make important contributions to the prevention of maladaptive behavior. Kenneth Clark, an influential educator who grew up in Harlem, met a librarian at the New York Public Library who became an important model and source of support for him.

I met Schomburg when I was about twelve years old, a crucial period in my life. It was at this time I clearly recognized that I was not ever going to be able to compete with my classmates in athletic skills.

I went to the library not only to escape the athletic competition, but also to escape the streets.

On one of my trips to the library, I decided that I was going to go upstairs to the third floor to the forbidden and mysterious area reserved for adults. I fully expected to be turned away unceremoniously. As I climbed the last flight of stairs, I felt the excitement of an interloper. I was prepared for the risk of either a polite or a more direct rejection. When I entered the room, a large man, whom I later came to know as Arthur Schomburg, got up from his desk and came over to me and smiled. He didn't ask me what I wanted. He merely put one arm around my shoulder and assumed that I was interested in the books. We went over to a table and sat down and began to talk. . . . We talked about books. We talked about wonderful things: about the history of human beings, about the contributions of Negroes which were to be found in books. He showed me portraits of Negroes who had contributed something important.

On that first day of meeting Schomburg, I knew I had met a friend. He accepted me as a human being and through his acceptance helped me to share his love of, and his excitement in, the world of books.

—Clark, 1965

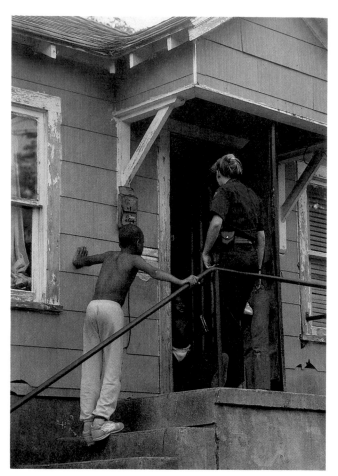

FIGURE 18—8 Police officers frequently must intervene in family disputes. This officer is trying to calm a domestic disturbance.

Sometimes community support comes about informally. Most people deal with everyday crises in the best way they can using available resources. Just as we don't go to a doctor every time we have a sniffle, we don't run to a clinical psychologist every time we are upset. The availability of nonprofessional "therapists" may be one reason for this. For example, people like hairdressers and bartenders do a lot of therapeutic listening to the troubles of their customers (Cowen, 1982). However, some social institutions have been specifically assigned the task of handling crises.

Although they are not usually included in lists of mental-health workers, police officers frequently modify behavior—whether for good or ill and whether they are aware of it or not. Police officers are not in a position to remove the causes of crime, but as their skills in human relations develop, their contributions to the prevention of crime could increase. A crime prevention experiment in New York City provided some information about the effects of increasing police officers' psychological sophistication and expertise (Bard, 1970). The focus of training and preventive work was on handling family disputes, since a high percentage of violent crimes are committed by close relatives. Another reason for developing more skill in handling family disturbances is that 22 percent of fatalities and 40 percent of injuries to police officers

occur while they are intervening in these situations (see Figure 18–8). Psychological training does help police officers handle violence more effectively. In addition, it can help them deal with many other problems, such as the usually harmless but often bizarre behavior of former mental hospital patients, with more tact and discretion.

SUICIDE PREVENTION Aside from the police, many communities offer specialized programs directed toward people who are going through a personal crisis or who share particular types of problems. For example, suicide and crisis prevention centers have been established in many communities (see Figure 18–9). The purpose of these centers is to encourage troubled people to seek help, either through telephone contact or in person. Such efforts may provide a means of reducing social isolation and bringing destructive and self-destructive thoughts out into the open. However, because it usually is not possible to conduct well-controlled studies of sudden crisis events such as potential suicides, there is continuing debate about the nature and effectiveness of crisis prevention centers. One study presented evidence

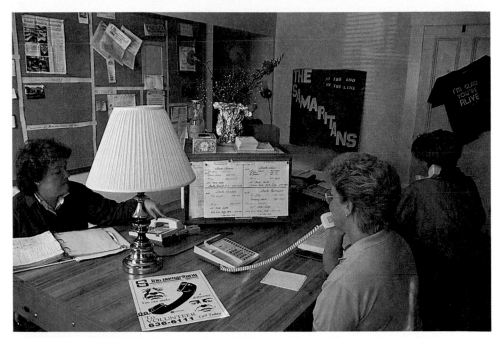

FIGURE 18–9 Crisis hotlines and suicide-prevention centers provide help for people who feel unable to cope with events in their lives. Sometimes just talking to an understanding listener is all that is needed. If more help is required, hotline staffers can provide callers with additional resources for assistance.

suggesting that suicide-prevention centers do lower suicide rates, particularly among young white females (Miller and others, 1984).

Many suicides can be prevented if friends and relatives recognize the danger signs and take appropriate actions. Some of these signs are listed in Table 18–3. There is no specific treatment for those who make suicide attempts, because the reasons for those attempts are extremely varied. Therapists who treat clients at risk for suicide must show that they are not surprised or discouraged by the client's suicidal urges. Several strategies are often employed by therapists to deal with the possibility of suicide. One approach is to be very active

and tell the client to get rid of pills, guns, ropes, or other potential means of suicide. Therapists must also be available at all times and may ask the client to call if he or she is uncertain about controlling suicidal impulses. Sometimes it is helpful to insist that the client make an explicit promise not to commit suicide. Because people contemplating suicide often are not thinking clearly and see no other options open to them, the therapist can be helpful in suggesting other possibilities to solve the problem. When a therapist or other person is in contact with someone threatening suicide, bargaining may be useful. For instance, someone threatening to jump from a high place can be urged to delay and keep all options

Table 18–3

Warning Signs of Suicide

Verbal comments. Statements such as "I wish I'd never been born," and "You'll be sorry when I'm gone," should be taken just as seriously as the direct threat, "I'm going to kill myself."

Behavior changes. These cover a wide range and include giving away treasured possessions, taking life-threatening risks, and having frequent accidents. Other signs may be complaints of intense loneliness or boredom, a marked increase in agitation or irritability, or getting into trouble with the police. There may also be the more customary signs of depression; changes in appetite and sleep habits, complaints of inability to concentrate, and withdrawal from friends and from favorite activities.

Situational factors. Inability to communicate with family and friends, recent problems at work or school, end of a love relationship, and recent involvement with drugs or alcohol all increase the situational risk for suicide.

FIGURE 18–10 Sometimes emergency physical intervention is necessary to prevent suicide. This woman had threatened to jump from a ledge outside her third floor apartment. Police and paramedics had to pull her to safety after their attempts to persuade her to reenter the building failed.

open by discussing the problem (see Figure 18–10). Sometimes despite these efforts it is necessary, if physically possible, to intervene to save the life of a potential suicide.

The prevention of suicide requires knowledge of the profile of people at risk for suicide. Studies have shown that people who commit suicide are nearly all psychologically disturbed (Murphy, 1988). There is a sharp rise in the incidence of suicide in the first few weeks following discharge from mental hospitals. Forty to 50 percent of those who commit suicide are clinically depressed and another 25 percent are alcoholics. These figures suggest that the major group at risk is a particular, highly recognizable, specific segment of the population. Bearing this profile in mind, Table 18–4 lists some

important contributions to suicide prevention that can be made by clinicians, family, and friends.

To prevent suicide, if family members or friends see any warning signs they should not hesitate to take action by asking questions such as "Are you very unhappy?" "Do you have a plan about taking your life?" "Do you think you really don't want to live anymore?" Asking direct questions about suicide doesn't put ideas into someone's head. Instead it may be a lifesaving measure if the answers are taken seriously. Both family and friends often don't believe that such statements might be carried out or they may be too frightened to take action. If the suicidal threat seems immediate, the nearest suicide prevention center (usually listed under "suicide" or "crisis" in the phone book) should be contacted.

Table 18–4

Steps to Preventing Suicide

1. Heightened awareness (for example, by family physicians) of the roles that depression, alcoholism, and other factors play in suicidal risk.
2. Early treatment of the psychological problems that underlie suicide attempts.
3. Careful questioning about suicidal intention ("Do you ever wish you were dead?", "Do you ever think about harming yourself or taking your life?", "Have you ever made a suicide attempt?")
4. Hospitalization of individuals who are known to have formulated a plan to kill themselves.
5. Removal of all access to firearms whenever the slightest hint of suicide is detected.
6. Restricted access of high-risk individuals to drugs that can be lethal in high doses.
7. Follow-up of high-risk individuals after treatment.

SOURCE: G.E. Murphy, Prevention of suicide in *American Psychiatric Press Review of Psychiatry, 7,* edited by A.J. Frances and R.E. Hales, Washington, D.C., American Psychiatric Press. Copyright © 1988 American Press, Inc. pp. 403–421.

SUICIDE POSTVENTION Suicide **postvention** refers to efforts to help those who knew the person who died. Suicides among young people are often particularly shocking and difficult for those who knew them to understand. If the person who killed him or herself was part of a larger group, for instance a student in school, the whole group may feel the impact of the death. Those who knew the person may have many conflicting feelings of anger, guilt, and shock. The suicide act may also take on a certain glamour among some other students who see it as exciting and glamorous way to deal with problems. In order to help the survivors and to prevent future suicides, programs involving professionals, school faculty, and students can be very effective. One such program used in schools after a student suicide is the Suicide Prevention Project of the New Jersey Community Mental Health Center at Piscataway. The **postvention** program has three basic principles.

1. Nothing should be done to glamorize or dramatize a suicide.

2. Doing nothing can be as dangerous as doing too much.

3. The students cannot be helped until the faculty is helped.

The postvention team usually meets first with school administrators, then with the faculty, and finally with all the members of the student group. During these meetings all participants have a chance to challenge their own feelings of guilt or self-blame by learning something about the dynamics of adolescent suicide. They also have opportunity to express the varying emotions that are typical after a suicide—shock, guilt, anger, and anxiety. Table 18–5 summarizes the postvention process and goals.

Table 18–5

The Postvention Process

Student Reaction	Postvention Staff Response
1. Shock. Students may initially appear remarkably unreactive. In fact, they are in a state of shock and not yet able to accept the reality of the suicide.	1. Staff needs to assume a stance of anticipatory waiting, acknowledging the shock and showing a willingness to talk about the suicide when students are ready. Hill (1984) suggests waiting 24 to 48 hours before initiating more direct action.
2. Anger and projection. Students will look for someone to blame. Initially, this may be directed at important adults in the victim's life, including school staff. "Why did they let it happen?"	2. Some expressions of anger must be allowed. Staff members may share the similar feeling they have had. However, at the same time, reality must be introduced. There are limits on how much one person can be responsible for actions of another.
3. Guilt. Typically, students who knew the victim may move from blaming others to blaming themselves. "If only I had talked to him more."	3. Here, particularly, staff can be helpful by sharing their own similar reactions. And again, the reality principle is also introduced. One person cannot assume total responsibility for the act of another.
4. Anger at victim. This is a common reaction by students, even those not closely connected to the victim. "How could he do this to us?"	4. Staff needs to give permission for such expressions by normalizing them, perhaps tempered by questioning if the victim fully realized the impact of his act.
5. Anxiety. Students will begin worrying about themselves. "If he could kill himself because he was upset, maybe I (or my friends) could too."	5. Discussion should be guided towards helping students differentiate between themselves and the victim and towards other options for problem-solving.
6. Relief. Once the normal distortions of feelings are resolved, students can allow themselves to feel the sadness of the loss and begin the healing process.	6. Staff must guard against encouraging a pseudo-mourning process before students have worked at resolving their conflicts over the suicide.

SOURCE: Lamb & Dunne–Maxim, 1987, p. 257

Treatment in the Community

Whether people receive mental-health services in the community or in institutions, society has a definite interest in how those services are provided, their effectiveness, and their cost. The mix of available services can influence not only the recipients' sense of well-being but also their economic productivity. In one study, matched groups of schizophrenic patients in Portland, Oregon, and Vancouver, British Columbia, were compared approximately one year following discharge from a mental hospital (Beiser and others, 1985). Whereas Vancouver had a rich network of accessible community services for the chronically mentally ill, Portland's services at the time of the study were limited. One year after discharge, the Vancouver group had experienced fewer readmissions, were more likely to be employed, and reported a higher level of well-being than was the case for the former patients in Portland. These results suggest that the effects of deinstitutionalization depend on the resources available to help former patients.

Many people who would otherwise have to be hospitalized could remain in the community if facilities that provide additional social support and supervision were available. An example of such a facility is the halfway house or community lodge. In one study, a group of institutionalized patients who had volunteered to do so moved from the mental hospital to a lodge in the community (Fairweather and others, 1969). The members decided who their leaders would be and the work that each would perform. Initially, extensive supervision was needed, and the group frequently found it necessary to seek help. However, as time passed, the lodge patients significantly increased their employment level and the length of time they were able to be out of the hospital. The median percentage of time in full employment for the lodge group was as high as 70 percent, while virtually all of the control subjects were totally unemployed. Unfortunately, funding for this type of facility is rarely available from either public sources, private organizations, or health or insurance coverage of patients.

Problems with Community Programs

A look at one mentally ill woman's journey through the mental health system illustrates many problems endemic to community programs. Writer Susan Sheehan (1982) followed the story of Sylvia Frumkin over nearly 20 years of treatment. Frumkin (the name is fictitious, but the story is true) had a long and disheartening journey through what is commonly called "the system." In fact, she encountered the disjointed, fragmented, and ineffective system at every turn. Following her first psychotic break in 1964 at the age of 15, she was repeatedly hospitalized or placed in various types of institutions. At different times she was diagnosed as manic-depressive or as schizophrenic, either undifferentiated or paranoid type. At one time or another she was given individual psychotherapy, antipsychotic medications, lithium, insulin coma therapy, electroconvulsive therapy, "Christian psychotherapy," and megavitamin therapy. Over the years she saw a constantly changing array of therapists, often for very short periods. These therapists treated her with nearly every available medication, sometimes without reference to her history, and they sometimes changed, suddenly decreased, or altogether stopped her medication in a seemingly arbitrary manner.

Sylvia Frumkin was not the kind of patient most therapists enjoy; she was described as slovenly, unappreciative, and uncooperative. She drained the energies of clinical personnel by being loud, abusive, and even violent during the acute phases of her illness. Even when she was not acutely ill, Frumkin was characterized by a staff member as "arrogant, nasty, and demanding." As Figure 18–11 shows, Sylvia Frumkin experienced 45 changes in treatment settings in 17 years. She was repeatedly bounced back and forth between her family home, various hospital settings, and community residential facilities. She was admitted 27 separate times to eight different hospitals (state, municipal, general, voluntary, and private), where she spent a total of nine years. She spent almost seven years in a state hospital. For slightly less than six years she lived with her family, cycling in and out of their home nine different times. She spent a total of three years in several different types of community settings, such as halfway houses, a foster home, a YWCA residence and a religious community. The cost of her care was estimated to be $636,000 in 1982 and would be considerably greater today if the costs of inflation were taken into account.

Unfortunately, Sylvia Frumkin's story is not unique. There are an estimated 1.7 to 2.4 million chronically mentally ill people in the United States. Policy makers and the public can learn a great deal from the experiences of people like Sylvia Frumkin. Her story clearly illustrates the profound impact of chronic mental illness on patients, families, and communities, as well as on the staggering costs of providing care. It may well be that Frumkin would have continued to deteriorate even if the conditions of her treatment had been more favorable, but the behavior of the system certainly seems to have been a contributing factor. In her various hospitalizations, Frumkin never experienced a prolonged relationship with a caring person. She perceived no one as having

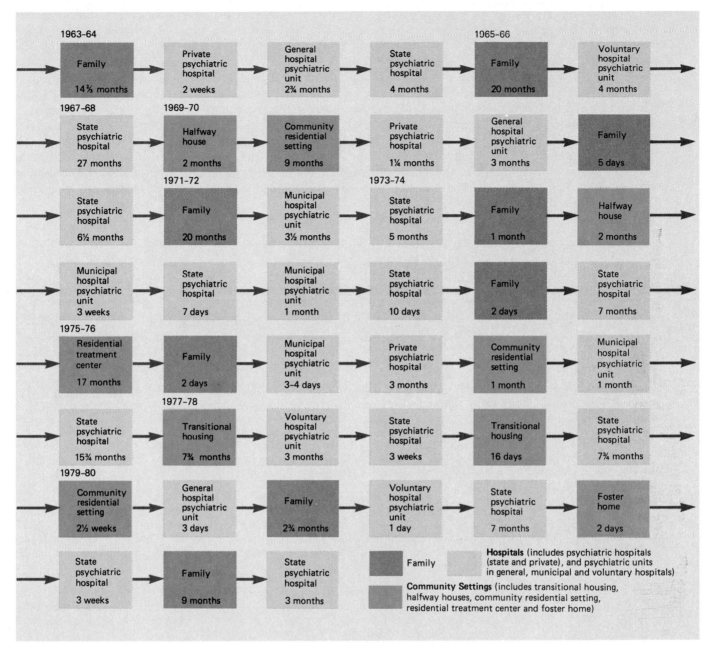

FIGURE 18–11 Sylvia Frumkin's odyssey as a chronic mental patient, 1963–1980.

(Moran, A.E., Freedman, R.I., and Sharfstein, S.S., The journey of Sylvia Frumkin: A case study for policymakers. *Hospital and Community Psychiatry, 35,* 887–893, 1984. Copyright © 1984, the American Psychiatric Association. Reprinted by permission)

her interests continuously at heart during a period of 17 years. Cases like Frumkin's have led mental-health workers, judges, and other government officials to think about ways to reform both the system and the laws that place disturbed individuals in public institutions.

Improving Treatment Programs

Experiments designed to improve the mix of available mental-health services are under way in a number of states. For example, the Massachusetts Mental Health Center provides an alternative for patients who traditionally would have been admitted and retained on inpatient services. In the system all patients who are thought to need inpatient hospitalization are first admitted to a day hospital. Those who do not require residential facilities return to their homes or community living situations at night and on weekends. Those who are admitted for day hospitalization but are found to require 24-hour inpatient care because they are dangerous or unable to care for themselves are transferred to an

acute intensive-care unit within the hospital. As soon as is warranted by the clinical situation, these patients are returned to the day hospital or to a day hospital and dormitory-inn. The dormitory-inn is a special facility that provides care for patients for whom the intensive-care unit is no longer appropriate, who need treatment in the day hospital, and who have no other place to sleep. It is a time-limited residence with an anticipated three-week length of stay (Gudeman and others, 1985). The development of this type of facility clearly reflects growing awareness of the need for an expanded array of treatment facilities in the community.

Long-term mental-hospital patients do not usually fare well when they return to the community unless effective aftercare programs are available to them. The Vancouver–Portland and community-lodge studies mentioned earlier, as well as other evidence, suggest that carefully planned aftercare programs both in hospitals and in the community can enable long-term patients to help themselves attain an impressive degree of autonomy. The opportunity for resocialization is an important element of these programs. Also of importance is the ability of the program to adapt to the special needs of its residents and workers. Halfway houses can, at a lower

BOX 18–1 The Face of Homelessness

Johnny, who would give no last name, said he was afraid of shelters and "opposed" to medication. Social workers guessed that he might have a breakdown, possibly a violent one, within two weeks—the time it would take for his last shot of medication to wear off. Meantime, they said, there was no good place to put him—no temporary quarters more inviting than a shelter or armory. There was no halfway house, no ready permanent housing.

FIGURE 18–12 Homeless woman in downtown Seattle uses an umbrella to protect herself during a recent snow flurry.

He clearly did not need hospitalization. So, they handed him a sandwich and another piece of paper, with a number to call when the crisis came. Johnny is a homeless person. Is he a "typical" homeless person? We know that there *is* no typical homeless person. Prior to the 1980s, the stereotype of a homeless person was a middle-aged, unattached man, frequently living on Skid Row and drinking excessively. Recently, many more young men, homeless women, and families with young children have joined the ranks of the homeless (see Figure 18–12), but at least three quarters of the homeless group are single men and less than 15 percent are families. Although they may differ in many ways, homeless people have several things in common. A majority lack supportive family and friends who can help during times of personal crises (Rossi, 1989). According to one comprehensive study (Burt, 1992), many homeless people are unlikely to become or remain self-sufficient because of severe impairments including mental illness, intellectual limitations, and addictions of various kinds. This means that because they are so vulnerable, a small setback that might not impair others' ability to be self-sufficient is enough to send them into homelessness. Similarities among the homeless include receiving few benefits from the public safety-net programs, not having a steady job, a high probability of having been institutionalized in the past in a mental

hospital, chemical dependency program or jail, and a three to five times higher chance of being depressed than the average person.

In studies of both shelter and street samples of adult homeless, from 10 to 36 percent had a history of previous psychiatric hospitalizations (Caton, 1990). However, estimating diagnosable mental illness and hospitalization histories among the homeless is difficult because investigators have employed different research approaches and the self-reports of some homeless individuals may not be reliable. Research carried out in Baltimore has shown that many homeless people suffer from a wide range of physical and mental health disorders (Breakey and others, 1989). The researchers found that disorders associated with alcohol and drug abuse were particularly prevalent. In addition to schizophrenia and bipolar disorders, homeless people often have less severe disorders such as anxiety and phobias. The large number of chronically mentally ill individuals among the homeless suggests the need for improving the accessibility and availability of community mental health services and supervised, supportive housing settings for the homeless. These improvements might significantly reduce the need for costly long-term, restrictive hospital care.

In many cities, the shelters available to the homeless are too few in number and lack adequate facilities. However, some communities are de-

cost to society, increase the personal freedom and self-confidence of many former mental-hospital patients and decrease the stigma attached to mental illness.

Although the concept of community care for the chronically mentally ill is a good one, as Chapter 17 pointed out, most deinstitutionalized people have simply been dumped into communities that fear them because of their eccentric behaviors and do not look after them in any systematic way.

Once the mentally ill are out on their own, they will more than likely stop taking their medications. The lack of professional care on the streets and the effects of alcohol and other drug abuse are further serious complications. They may now be too disorganized to extricate themselves from living on the streets—except by exhibiting blatantly bizarre or disruptive behavior that leads to their being taken to a hospital or jail (see Box 18–1).

Few deinstitutionalized people are given the vocational training, guidance in self-care, recreation, or opportunities for socializing that are required for any sort of meaningful existence. The need for follow-up care, the hard realities of insufficient funding, the impact of patients on communities, and the uncertainties as to what constitutes effective community programs have all

veloping innovative ways of dealing with homeless people who are psychologically disturbed. New York City's Project Help uses an active outreach program to identify those who are in need of help, provides immediate treatment, and places them in community residences, group homes, or their own apartments (see Figure 18–13). Daniel B. is an example of the success of Project Help:

Daniel B. had been surviving, just barely, on the streets of the Upper East Side of Manhattan. Emaciated and lice-infested, he foraged for food in garbage cans and slept in doorways. With his schizophrenia untreated, he was plagued by hallucinations. Now, Daniel has a clean, secure room of his own, and a sense of order about his days. He enjoys simple pleasures: a movie once a week, a nap in the afternoon, a cup of coffee with his caseworker. Regular medication controls his hallucinations. Daniel, who is in his 40s, now lives at a single-room-occupancy residence in Manhattan.

—*New York Times* July 18, 1989, p. A16

Unfortunately, because of their serious and chronic mental illnesses, about 30 percent of homeless people aided by Project Help have ended up back on the streets. Perhaps even more significant, programs like Project Help are thought to reach only a small percentage of New York's homeless, who number approximately 200,000 people (*Harvard Mental Health Letter*, 1990).

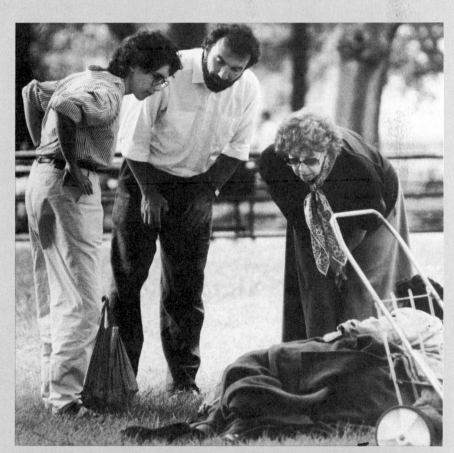

FIGURE 18–13 Workers from Project Help, a New York City program for the homeless, talk with a homeless person to determine whether he is severely mentally ill and needs hospitalization.

FIGURE 18–14 Deinstitutionalization may not live up to its promise if the trade-off for not being hospitalized is inadequate housing, isolation, and lack of therapeutic contact.

Label sighed. He wrapped a robe around her, coaxed her gently to a chair and talked constantly to her, "This is Rubie. You're all right now. No one is going to hurt you. Rubie is here now."

She looked at him, wide-eyed, questioning. She began to sob and the tears dampened long dark hair cascading around her face. Label put his arms around her, comforting her.

Afterward, after he had drawn her out of her trance and promised to return, Label stepped outside and leaned a sagging shoulder against the corridor wall. His eyes, too, were wet.

He knew that for this young woman there were no solutions, only problems. She was one of dozens, perhaps hundreds of people with mental problems who are in downtown Seattle now.

Few can be taken in for hospital care. More refuse to commit themselves to a hospital. Most are not considered dangerous to themselves or others, the criteria for an involuntary commitment.

—*Seattle Times*, December 16, 1977, p. A17

been largely ignored. As a result, a growing number of people who would otherwise be enthusiastic about deinstitutionalization have become at least somewhat disillusioned.

For some individuals, hospitalization denies them their freedom and further decreases their ability to cope with their problems. For others, the psychiatric hospital provides a haven where, in a protected atmosphere, they can regroup their defenses for reentry into the community (see Figure 18–14). The following excerpt from a Seattle newspaper illustrates how the deinstitutionalized movement may result in inadequate protection and help.

Rubie Label rapped gently at the door of the small housekeeping unit in the Frye Apartments, which he manages.

There was no answer.

Label pushed open the door and stepped inside. No one was in the kitchenette. He looked in the sitting room. Empty.

He glanced toward the open bathroom door. A young woman, without clothing, was standing rigid and transfixed in front of the mirror, her back to the doorway, apparently in deep shock.

This article stimulated the following letter from a reader.

After reading the article in the paper about the little psychotic lady who is living in abject misery in the hotel on First Avenue (The Times, December 16); I feel compelled to write this letter.

It is not an easy letter to write, as my past history of hospitalization in a mental institution is not one I am proud of or like to recall.

However, I must speak out on the issue of the commitment law in the State of Washington.

The crux of the whole problem of voluntary versus involuntary commitment to a mental hospital seems to lie in the simple fact that a person in the midst of a mental crisis is not capable of making the decision to commit himself to a hospital for treatment.

In a state of mental confusion or breakdown, one's mental processes are in such a muddle that one is unable to make any rational decision about life. Also, most times a mentally

confused person has the feeling that if "so-and-so would only keep me, I could make it." Well, so-and-so doesn't have the time, the interest, or the expertise to do or say the things you may need.

Most of the time, one's family and friends are just as confused as you are about what is best to do.

One of the things one is painfully aware of in any mental hospital is that the staff is being paid to care. But at least they care, and if they are up to snuff, they know how to help you.

A large mental hospital is not a happy place to be, but tell me this—what's so great about being in a flea-bitten hotel room where no one knows you exist or cares? Freedom and rights are great rhetoric, but what is freedom to one who is unable to use it for one's own best interests?

Is the right to starve to death in a wretched hotel room, and be so zonked out of your mind that you don't know who you are, really all that precious?

—*Seattle Times*, December 25, 1977, p. A13

The incident described in the newspaper article reflects the lack of community help and supervision for the mentally disturbed; the letter explains why the mental hospital remains a needed haven for some people.

One consequence of the large number of failures of deinstitutionalization has been an increase in readmissions to state hospitals. Patients now stay in the hospital for shorter periods but, because of their inability to function in the community, return more often. About half of the patients who are released from state hospitals are readmitted within a year of discharge.

What lessons can be learned from the way deinstitutionalization has been practiced up to now? Perhaps the most important lesson of the bad experiences of the past two decades is that deinstitutionalization as it is now being carried out is not helpful to many individuals. As happens so often, society neglects many of the nuts and bolts needed to reach a worthy objective. More money and more trained personnel are needed.

More education is also essential. Public-information programs about mental illness and retardation and more citizen involvement in planning for the reentry of former patients into the community can help make deinstitutionalization a positive experience for both the patients and the community. The entry of formerly hospitalized patients into the neighborhood has frequently been perceived as a threat, even though the

overwhelming majority of ex-mental patients and retarded individuals are harmless (Rabkin, 1979). Nothing can arouse negative feelings in a neighborhood more effectively than the proposed establishment of a halfway house or aftercare center in the vicinity. Yet there is no evidence that simply being a discharged mental patient makes a person more likely to commit crimes or endanger the community. However, there is an increasing tendency to place people with criminal records in mental hospitals, and people with previous arrest records are likely to be arrested again after they are discharged from mental hospitals.

The problems of the chronically mentally ill living in the community require a comprehensive system of care that includes:

1. An adequate number of supervised community-housing settings

2. Community clinical services ranging from professional mental-health workers who can provide crisis intervention to hospitalization for acute conditions

3. Recognition of the importance of families in treatment, along with adequate support for family members as well as for the patient.

Legal Aspects of Treatment and Prevention

In this and the previous chapter we have discussed ways to help people avoid having problems and, if that isn't possible, to overcome them to the extent possible. Because people live in groups, the community has an interest in preventing behavior that is maladaptive. Although historically it has not always been the case, governmental bodies now have laws that deal with both helping people who behave deviantly and protecting the public from the dangers posed by certain types of deviant individuals (for example, criminals). In reality, such laws may be problematic if our judgment of what constitutes help happens to be wrong or if the person doesn't want to be helped.

Institutionalization

The process of placing a person in an institution is called **commitment**. Prisoners are committed to prisons for punishment, and mental patients are committed to mental hospitals for treatment. **Criminal commitment** of an individual to a mental hospital may occur when a criminal act is legally declared to be a result of insanity

and it is determined that the interests of society and the individual would be best served by commitment to a mental hospital rather than to a prison. Some mental patients voluntarily commit themselves, but others are involuntarily hospitalized through a legal procedure called **civil commitment.** Civil commitment can only be carried out if a person is judged to be a risk to him- or herself or to others. The forced institutionalization of a person poses serious problems. On the one hand, civil commitment aims at providing help, but to do that, it may deprive the person of basic human rights.

One example of the logistical difficulties posed by commitment laws is the case of Anna May Peoples, a Seattle woman who was diagnosed as a paranoid schizo-phrenic. Because of her paranoia, she said, she took refuge in the city's Public Safety Building. Peoples made the building her home for two years, but authorities had to dismiss trespassing charges against her. She was judged not competent to stand trial, but not dangerous enough to institutionalize (see Figure 18–15). A newspaper article described her situation as follows.

. . . But the 64-year-old transient was arrested again last night, charged again with criminal trespass for being in the Public Safety Building after hours. Officers escorted her out of the building at 10:45 P.M., then arrested her five minutes later when she came back in.

To the consternation of the Police Department, Peoples insists on making her home in the building at Third Avenue and James Street. She bathes in the restroom sinks, dresses in the elevators, and sleeps on the rock-hard floors.

One night, police found her naked in an elevator. Another time, she fell asleep and plunged through a plate-glass door.

Social workers tried to find the woman a home, but Peoples refused help. She preferred the Public Safety Building, despite being dragged out by police on various occasions.

—Adapted from Guillen, 1982, p. B1

CRIMINAL COMMITMENT To convict a person of a crime, the state must establish beyond a reasonable doubt not only that the person committed the prohibited act but also that the act was committed with criminal intent. If criminal intent cannot be proven, the insanity defense becomes possible. The concept of insanity is often confused with that of competence to stand trial. **Insanity** refers to a person's state of mind at the time that an act was carried out, while **competency** refers to a person's state of mind at the time of a judicial proceeding. In a legal sense, an **incompetent person** is one who lacks the capacity to consult with a lawyer and to understand the nature of legal proceedings. Both insanity and competency are legal terms whose applicability in a given case is determined by a judge after considering all evidence, including the opinions of expert witnesses.

Insanity is a legal term, not a psychiatric diagnosis. Early English law did not recognize insanity as an excuse for criminal behavior. However, by the thirteenth century proof of criminal intentions was necessary to convict a person of a felony. If accused individuals could prove that they were completely "mad," they could successfully defend themselves against a criminal charge. In 1843 Daniel M'Naghten, a Scottish woodturner, assassinated

FIGURE 18–15 Anna May Peoples, caught between the technicalities of legal incompetence and lack of dangerousness, waits to hear her fate during a court appearance.

Edward Drummond, secretary to the prime minister of England. He was found not guilty because the judges stated that he was "labouring under such a defect of reason, from disease of the mind, as not to know the nature and quality of the act he was doing; or, if he did know, that he did not know he was doing what was wrong."

This ruling, known as the **M'Naghten rule,** became the "right and wrong" test of insanity and was widely adopted. As belief in this interpretation grew, statutes were introduced that permitted the court to defer sentencing decisions until the offender could be studied and recommendations made to the judge. Psychiatrists, psychologists, social workers, and probation officers became advisers to the court. Sentencing became more flexible, and parole was used increasingly.

An example of an attempt to invoke the M'Naghten rule occurred in the case of Jack Ruby, who was convicted of the murder of President Kennedy's assassin, Lee Harvey Oswald, in 1964. In appealing his death sentence, Ruby claimed that he suffered from psychomotor epilepsy and that this prevented him from determining right and wrong. However, this claim was rejected by the judge and Ruby was found legally sane. He eventually died in prison.

The M'Naghten rule and subsequent court decisions have been controversial largely because of the difficulty defining precisely what knowing right from wrong really means. In 1962 the American Law Institute (ALI) proposed a set of guidelines that have since been incorporated into the laws of several states. The ALI's guidelines focus on impairment that grows out of a defendant's mental illness and include the following ideas.

> 1. *A person is not responsible for criminal conduct if at the time of such conduct as a result of mental disease or defect he lacks substantial capacity either to appreciate the criminality (wrongfulness) of his conduct or to conform his conduct to the requirements of law.*
> 2. *. . . The terms "mental disease or defect" do not include an abnormality manifested only by repeated criminal or otherwise antisocial conduct.*
>
> —American Law Institute, 1962, p. 66

With each passing year, the ALI guidelines have gained increased acceptance throughout the country. In 1983, in the case of *Jones* v. *United States,* the Supreme Court ruled that people who are found not guilty by reason of insanity can be held indefinitely in a mental hospital under a less rigorous standard of proof of dangerousness than is required for civilly committed individuals. The Court ruled that acquitted insanity defendants "constitute a special class that should be treated differently."

The number of insanity defenses that are successful is very small. In the entire state of New York, for example, there are on the average fewer than 50 successful insanity defenses each year. Thus, the insanity defense contributes only a tiny fraction to the problem of crime in the United States. In part, this is because juries have difficulty applying the fine legal points involved in the insanity defense. The following excerpt from a news article illustrates this point.

Roderick Stoudamire, whose previous trial ended in a hung jury three months ago, was found guilty in Superior Court today of first-degree murder in the stabbing death last summer of a woman jogger at Seward Park.

The jury of six women and six men announced its verdict for the second trial at 10:40 A.M. in a courtroom packed with spectators. They deliberated about five hours.

The jury also found Stoudamire guilty of assaulting two other women joggers.

Stoudamire, 16, had pleaded not guilty by reason of insanity. It was his insanity defense that caused the deadlock in the first trial. After deliberating more than two days, jurors in that case said they were confused by the definition of criminal insanity, and could not decide whether it applied to Stoudamire.

The tall, slender youth sat quietly, usually with a vacant look on his face, as witnesses testified during both of the long and often dramatic trials. He wore the same look this morning when the decision against him was read.

A mistrial was declared in the youth's first trial after jurors announced they were deadlocked. In that trial, ten said they did not believe Stoudamire was legally insane, while the two others said they were convinced the youth was schizophrenic and voted to acquit him.

—Horne, 1979, p. C11

In 1981, John Hinckley's acquittal by reason of insanity from charges of attempting to assassinate President Ronald Reagan caused many people to question the fairness of the insanity defense. The American Psychiatric Association argued that people should be acquitted for

insanity only if they have a serious mental disorder such as psychosis. Those who have personality disorders—for example, antisocial personality disorder—or abuse drugs or alcohol should be held responsible for their actions. The Association further stated that expert witnesses should not be allowed to testify about whether the

BOX 18–2 The Debate Over the Insanity Defense

Will the insanity defense be retained in, or banished from, the federal and state criminal codes throughout the country? Legal and clinical experts—abolitionists and retentionists—continue to disagree. Throughout the controversy, however, one major point seems clear: Whatever happens to the insanity defense, the judicial system cannot ignore the mental aberrations that a defendant may have experienced at the time of an unlawful act. The public outcry against "criminals getting away with murder" also cannot be ignored, even though the insanity defense is only rarely successful. Understandably, the public remembers highly publicized cases in which the insanity defense is invoked and someone who has clearly committed a crime is found not guilty by reason of insanity (see Figure 18–16). Sometimes such people are released after a short hospitalization, and later commit another crime.

During the trial of John W. Hinckley, Jr., the man who shot Ronald Reagan and an aide, the barrage of contradictory expert testimony damaged the image of psychiatry in the public mind. Those who would abolish the insanity defense believe that one way to end this type of spectacle would be to restrict psychiatric testimony to evidence of mental abnormality that bears on the defendant's conscious awareness and perception—his or her "intent" to commit the crime. Other testimony concerning more subtle impairments of understanding, judgment, or behavior control would no longer be relevant at the guilt stage of the trial, but could be introduced at the time of sentencing. Another proposal calls for a pool of expert witnesses to be selected by the court. These experts would no longer testify for the prosecution or the defense. Instead, the impartial panel would attempt to arrive at a conclusion regarding the defendant's mental state when the crime was committed.

(a) (b) (c) (d)

FIGURE 18–16 Edmund E. Kemper, III (a) was acquitted by reason of insanity from the charge of murdering his grandparents in 1964, and was released from a mental hospital in 1969 as "cured"; he later murdered six college students, his mother, and one of her friends—for which he was found sane and guilty. Dennis Sweeney (b) was sent to the Mid-Hudson Psychiatric Center when a judge accepted his plea of "not guilty by reason of mental disease" for killing Congressman Allard Lowenstein in 1980. After the slaying of his parents, Gregory Shaddy (c) was acquitted by reason of insanity; he spent two years in a hospital and was then pronounced cured and released. The case of John W. Hinckley, Jr. (d) revived debate over the insanity defense after he was acquitted from the charge of attempting to assassinate President Ronald Reagan in 1981, and was committed to a mental hospital.

defendant was able to control his or her behavior (*Psychiatric News*, February 4, 1983). The use of expert opinion poses profound interpretive problems (see Box 18–2). So far none of the guidelines that have been proposed for dealing with the problem of insanity have provided a completely satisfactory solution.

CIVIL COMMITMENT All fifty states have civil commitment laws. These laws are based on the doctrine of **parens patriae**, (Latin for "parenthood to the state"), according to which the state can act in what it takes to be the best interest of a minor or of an adult who is incapacitated. The principal features of the process are a petition, a hearing, and a decision about the place to which the individual is to be committed. In some states, the judgments of psychiatrists are decisive in reaching commitment decisions. In others, physicians who are not psychiatrists play dominant roles. Until fairly recently, standards for commitment were loosely worded and protections for the patient either did not exist or were ignored. Then, in a 1979 decision (*Addington* v. *Texas*), the U.S. Supreme Court ruled that people may not be committed to mental institutions unless the state has presented "clear and convincing" evidence that they require hospitalization.

Growing awareness of abuses like the one described in the following newspaper article led to reforms of commitment codes in many states. The patient in this article had been sent to a medical hospital during a severe attack of asthma in 1956. Twenty days later she was committed to a county mental hospital. She was not discharged until 1960, even though the staff of the mental hospital had considered her sane since 1957. *The New York Times* gave the following report of the proceedings at her release trial.

At today's hearing in Judge Pindar's court, Dr. John J. Scott, assistant medical director of the county medical hospital, testified that as far back as 1957, at a hospital staff conference, Miss Dean had been adjudged sane.

Asked why she had not been released in view of her many requests for her freedom since that time, Dr. Scott said that the woman was without relatives and it had been feared that she would become a public charge.

When a patient at the hospital, Miss Dean performed the duties of a registered nurse, without pay.

Miss Dean's release was effected through the effort of a friend, who remembered that Raymond H. Chasan, a lawyer, had won the release of another

mental patient in 1947, under somewhat similar circumstances.

—Copyright © 1960 by The New York Times Company. Reprinted by permission

All civil commitment laws involve two judgments: whether the individual is suffering from a disabling mental illness and whether he or she is dangerous. The first criterion is relatively easy to establish. The second is more of a problem. "Dangerousness" refers to the potential to inflict harm on other people as well as on oneself. Judging how dangerous a person might be is often a difficult matter.

In the beginning, Jane's older neighbor seemed friendly enough.

Stuart, who lived alone, would often stop to chat. Sometimes he'd borrow a gardening tool, or Jane would borrow one from him. But two years ago, the relationship changed dramatically.

Stuart, who is in his 60s, became infatuated with Jane, 36. He recited Bible verses to her, then broke into her home while she was gone. He wrote Jane long love letters, tried to accost her and kiss her in church, and attempted to lure her three children into his house with candy and baseball cards.

He bought an expensive van identical to Jane's, and said he was planning to kidnap Jane and her children and drive them across the country.

—Based on *Seattle Times*, August 27, 1990, pp. A1, A5

Is Stuart harmless, or a serious danger to his neighbors? Although a judge declared Stuart harmless, he subsequently was jailed for several misdemeanors and also harassed Jane over a long period of time.

Because dangerousness involves a prediction of future behavior, its application to individual cases creates enormous problems. Can a clinical expert tell the court whether a person is dangerous and when he or she has stopped being dangerous?

In 1985 a 22-year-old accountant was pushed in front of a speeding subway train at rush hour. A large team of doctors, nurses, and technicians operated on her for 22 hours, trying to save her life and repair her severe head injuries and numerous broken bones. Her assailant, who had been held by another subway rider until police

arrived, turned out to be a 19-year-old unemployed woman with a history of mental problems. She had been released from a psychiatric ward less than a month before her crime, despite violent behavior while incarcerated and a psychiatrist's warning that she was dangerous. On two occasions she had attacked fellow patients and had to be subdued by means of a straitjacket.

Although the psychiatrist in this case was correct in thinking that the 19-year-old woman was dangerous, available evidence suggests that clinicians' predictions of whether a given individual will do something dangerous in the future are often inaccurate. Mental health specialists can do the best job of predicting dangerous behavior that might occur in the near future, but even then studies show they are only from 40 to 60 percent accurate (Appelbaum, 1991). For longer term predictions the record is much worse. In several studies that followed patients over several years, only 14 to 35 percent of those considered to be potentially dangerous to others were actually arrested for violent crimes. At present, the best indication of future dangerousness is dangerousness in the past unless the particular circumstances that led to the past behavior no longer exist.

Studies of dangerousness have consistently found that few patients are dangerous only to others. In a study of one thousand patients seen in psychiatric emergency rooms only 4 percent were dangerous to others, three times that many were suicidal or dangerous to themselves, and only 0.6 percent were dangerous only to others and not to themselves (Appelbaum, 1991).

The goal of protecting the rights of people who might be committed to an institution against their will is accepted by all. However, it is by no means clear how to protect those rights while simultaneously assuring the welfare of the individual and of society. At present, civil commitments seem to be increasing in frequency. This trend is being reinforced by recent court decisions that have emphasized the *parens patriae* role of the state in treating a patient for his or her own good. Also contributing to the trend is the failure of many states to develop community treatment networks to supplement hospital systems, as well as health insurance programs that provide only marginal subsidies for outpatient care.

The Rights of Patients

In the not-so-distant past, people were treated as if admission to a mental hospital justified taking away all their rights. However, according to court decisions over the past 20 years, patients' rights must be upheld and adequate treatment must be provided. In a 1971 case that attracted national attention (*Wyatt* v. *Stickney*), a court ruled that a state must provide adequate treatment for mental hospital patients who are confined involuntarily. Beyond recognizing the patient's right to treatment, the court specified basic hospital staffing ratios and qualifications and also required individualized treatment plans.

In a 1975 Supreme Court decision (*O'Connor* v. *Donaldson*), Kenneth Donaldson was awarded compensatory and punitive damages of $38,500 against two staff psychiatrists at the Florida State Hospital because they had not provided adequate treatment for him during the 14 years of his involuntary commitment. The significance of the *O'Connor* v. *Donaldson* ruling was its recognition that hospitalized people who are not dangerous have a constitutional right to treatment. Whether or not a dangerous patient has a similar right has not yet been decided. The *O'Connor* v. *Donaldson* decision strengthened the rights of involuntarily hospitalized patients, but it did not make the task of determining whether or not a patient is dangerous any easier.

The courts have opened the door to long-overdue improvement in the treatment of the mentally ill. A federal judge in New Jersey has ruled that an involuntarily committed mental patient who objected to the drug therapy administered to him may not be forced to take the medicine (*Rennie* v. *Klein*, 1978). Since drugs now constitute the primary mode of behavior control in institutions, and virtually all involuntarily committed patients are routinely given antipsychotic medications, this and similar rulings may have widespread effects on the way in which treatment is defined in state institutions. In addition to strengthening patients' right to get treatment (and their right to refuse it), the courts have also supported patients' right to receive the least restrictive treatment available. The "least restrictive treatment" is only as restrictive and confining as is necessary to achieve the purposes of the commitments.

Increasingly, both patients and judges are questioning the safety and effectiveness of present-day treatment methods. Physical treatments such as drugs and electroconvulsive therapy do have the potential to cause permanent injury. Certain patients appear to deteriorate as a result of receiving psychotherapy. Some experts also believe that behavior-modification procedures such as token economies are too coercive. Some critics believe that merely being institutionalized is therapeutically counterproductive, regardless of the quality of the institution. Until recently a hospital's power to deny patients the right to examine their own files was taken for granted. Now patients can see their charts, but some hospitals do not voluntarily tell patients that they are entitled to do so.

As the rights of patients have been extended, the requirement of informed consent has been strengthened.

Informed consent requires that patients receive adequate information about the nature of a planned treatment before they agree to submit to it. The clinician must communicate this information in language that is meaningful to the patient, rather than in medical jargon, and must clearly explain the potential risks and benefits, including any discomfort that might arise from the treatment. Frequently, if the patient is incompetent to evaluate the information provided (for example, because of a psychotic condition), a lawyer assigned to look out for the patient's interests plays a role in the decision-making process. The requirement of informed consent applies to people who serve as subjects in experiments as well as to patients who are undergoing treatment. Patients and experimental subjects both have the right to terminate their participation in treatment or research even if they had previously consented to participate.

Should patients have the right to discontinue treatment that most people would agree was helping them? The difficulty of answering this question can be seen in this daughter's account of her mother's changed behavior after discontinuing the use of antipsychotic medication. Her mother came to New York to join her children after being discharged from a mental institution in Kansas. She was taking Haldol, an antipsychotic drug.

On Haldol Mother's behavior improved tremendously, and we even harbored false hopes of her return to normal living. We never suspected that she might cease taking medication and regress. . . .

Not only did Mother rediscover art and music in New York, but she soon became familiar with the liberal New York laws regarding "patients' rights." She refused to continue to take Haldol and slowly began the reverse trip to "No Man's Land," where she now dwells. The first sign of her decompensation was a refusal to come to my apartment, and then she rejected me completely. Next the manager of her middle class apartment hotel asked us to remove her. She was annoying the guests with her outbursts. She had become known to all the shopkeepers on the block as "The Crazy Lady of West 72nd Street." Looking like a zombie, she paraded down West 72nd Street, accusing aunts, uncles, and brother of stealing her father's fortune, screaming at people who frightened her. . . .

Whether or not it's preferable for her to be forcefed Haldol and incarcerated in Kansas or allowed to do as she pleases in liberal New York, as destructive as her life is now, is paradoxical. She was not able to enjoy life and pursue her

artistic interests in the former situation, but she is even less able to do so in the latter. Without medication, she can only exist. I believe that basically she is less free in her present life, a prisoner of her delusions and paranoia. My brother, however, disagrees. He thinks that Mother is better off having the choice to live as she wishes, wandering aimlessly in the streets, constructing the world to fit her delusions.

—Adapted from Lanquetot, 1984, p. 471

The institutionalization of children brings with it special problems that the courts are only beginning to address. Among the questions that must be considered are: How much freedom may parents exercise in seeking to institutionalize a son or daughter? When, and under what conditions, can the state institutionalize children against the parents' will? What procedures are needed to protect the child's rights? What are those rights? The United States Supreme Court has ruled that parents may commit their children to state institutions as long as "neutral fact-finders" approve. The quality of the treatment provided is an important factor in approving institutionalization for children as well as for adults. For example, questions have been raised concerning the constitutionality of institutions for the mentally retarded that provide little or no special training.

The issue of informed consent in therapy has been recognized most clearly in the case of biological treatments such as electroconvulsive therapy, but it is also relevant to the psychological therapies. Whenever possible, the goals of therapy should be determined jointly by the therapist and the client, without undue influence exerted by the therapist. Should a therapist encourage a young man to go to college because the client's parents, who are paying the therapy bills, want him to? The client should be the main concern of the therapist, but external influences like the parents' desires might become coercive factors in treatment. Clinicians also must not unduly impose their personal values on the therapy they offer to clients. A respectful attitude toward the client, an undogmatic approach, and healthy questioning of therapeutic tactics are important ingredients in all types of treatment.

The Challenge of Prevention

At the beginning of this chapter we said that prevention can take more than one form. It can involve taking the steps needed to keep a disorder from arising in

the first place as well as efforts to limit its impact on the life of the individual. In this sense prevention and treatment are closely related. Common to both is the concept of vulnerability. Vulnerability arises when an individual's personal characteristics are insufficient to deal with the situation. The challenges of deinstitutionalization and prevention are the identification of opportunities for growth and stability and the provision of such opportunities to people who need them. These opportunities differ depending on the nature of the people to be served. For example, as they grow older, children need situations that give them increasing opportunities for independence. On the other hand, the aged usually need increasing care and attention.

Society inevitably must be involved in meeting the challenge of prevention because it controls or influences so many of the situations of modern life. We have seen many examples of the impact of community and social forces on our lives. Certain types of maladaptive behavior (for example, phobias and delusions) can be attacked on an individual basis with the clinical methods we have described (psychotherapy, behavioral therapy, drugs). But lasting solutions to many problems of living require social change. Children living in crowded slum apartments or with abusive or neglectful parents have only limited opportunities to generalize from what they learn in a stimulating school or preschool program. Medication may help deinstitutionalized patients hallucinate less frequently, but they still need a supportive environment and a chance to acquire new social and occupational skills.

Preventing maladaptive behavior and responding therapeutically to it when it does occur require an examination of society, its components, and how they are interrelated. This examination should include elements that a community lacks as well as positive steps that it may take. Examples of such steps are houses for runaway children, drop-in centers for teenagers, and crisis centers. Virtually all such programs have been started by citizens without government support, and, at least initially, on a nonprofessional basis. As a result of such efforts, professionals in many areas have broadened the scope of their clinical services and have increased their involvement in community programs.

Paraprofessionals

Programs have also been created to train and use nonprofessionals and paraprofessionals for significant roles in a variety of community settings. A wide culture-related gap often exists between middle-class professional workers (clinical psychologists, psychiatrists, and social workers) and people from lower socioeconomic groups who need help. Much of the success of **paraprofessionals** seems to be due to similarities be-

tween their backgrounds and those of their clients. For this reason, some community psychologists devote a major portion of their activities to training paraprofessionals.

Paraprofessionals vary widely in age, education, and cultural background. They often make up a large part of the staff in neighborhood service centers, residential youth centers, and mental-health programs in both urban and rural areas. There they may serve as bridges between an established agency and a target group in the community that the agency has failed to serve effectively. Although relatively little research has been done on how to select, train, and evaluate the effectiveness of these workers, it has been shown that in some situations paraprofessionals may be as effective as the experts (Hattie and others, 1984). The responsibilities of paraprofessionals and their role in professional and community power structures need to be defined.

Self-help Groups

Self-help groups can also contribute to prevention. For many human problems there are no easy answers or easy cures, but there is an alternative to coping with them alone. Millions of people whose problems and needs are not met through formal health care, social services, and counseling programs can find the hope and personal support they need in self-help groups. Within these groups, whose members share common concerns, they are offered the understanding and help of others who have gone through similar experiences. People like those in the following examples might find the help they need by contacting the appropriate group.

Margaret and Bill are parents of a young child diagnosed with terminal cancer. For two years they have shared suffering, dashed hopes, and heartbreak. In spite of caring friends and professional support, they feel alone in their grief.

Jean is a divorced mother who has custody of her three children. She now finds herself overwhelmed by the problems of single parenthood. Her teenage son has become difficult to handle and she is increasingly discouraged in trying to provide for her children's needs and the demands of her job.

Roger has a serious drinking problem. He has been fired from two jobs in the last year and is deeply in debt. He has lost the respect of his family and friends. He entered treatment at an alcoholism clinic but began to drink again two

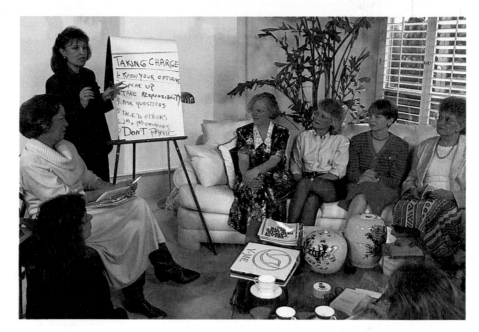

FIGURE 18–17 Self-help groups are based on the belief that some problems can be helped most through mutual support from those who have experienced the same difficulties. In this photo, a support group for women who have had breast cancer meets to hear a presentation and to talk about ways of dealing with the experience of being a cancer patient.

months after the treatment ended. He realizes that his addiction is ruining his life but feels helpless to control it.

As social beings, all of us need to be accepted, cared for, and emotionally supported; we also find it satisfying to care for and support those around us. Within the most natural "self-help networks"—families and friends—we establish the one-to-one contact so important to our happiness and well-being. This informal support is such a basic part of our social character that we tend to take it for granted, but it clearly influences our ability to handle distressing events in our lives. Many of our daily conversations are actually mutual counseling sessions in which we exchange the reassurance and advice that help us deal with routine stresses. In fact, research scientists have found that there is a strong link between the strength of our social support systems, our health, and our response to illness (see Figure 18–17). Further research is needed to determine when, under what conditions, and for which types of problems self-help groups are most effective (Videka-Sherman and Lieberman, 1985). Table 18–6 lists some of the characteristics of self-help groups and ways in which they benefit their members. Some self-help groups are well known and have been in existence for many years. An example of such a group is Alcoholics Anonymous. Based on the success of this group, similar groups such as Gamblers

Table 18–6

Self-help Groups

The Major Characteristics of Self-help Groups

1. Avoidance of professional leadership and direction
2. A homogeneous membership that has a common problem, affliction, or deviant status
3. Meeting places outside such traditional therapy settings as hospitals and clinics
4. Open-ended membership in which the group's composition is rarely constant

Ways in Which Self-help Groups Benefit Their Members

1. Emotional support and understanding
2. An accepting reference group that reduces social isolation
3. Information and advice
4. Models on how to cope effectively with stress
5. Enhancement of members' awareness of alternatives available in dealing with problems

Anonymous have been formed to help people with other types of problems. A group that is focused on the rehabilitation of mentally troubled persons is Compeer. This organization, with headquarters in Rochester, New York, began with ten mental patients and ten volunteers. It is now active in most states and in Canada as well. Compeer has helped more than 10,000 mentally and emotionally handicapped people. Mentally ill persons are put in contact with a "compeer"—a volunteer—who spends at least one hour per week with the client for a year. The volunteers, who invariably become the clients' friends, undergo brief training, meet with the clients' therapists if needed, and submit written monthly reports. Compeer seems to significantly cut the rate of clients' reentry to a mental institution. Its success may be attributed to the social support provided in frequent informal and meaningful contacts with a caring friend.

Community Psychology

Community psychology is concerned with the role of social systems in preventing human distress and maladaptive behavior. Community psychologists attempt to work in settings that have an impact on prevention. For example, they might serve as human-relations consultants to a police department, work to increase the skills of individuals who staff welfare offices, or develop prevention programs in homes or schools. Outreach programs are aimed at either preventing breakdowns or dealing with problems in the community before more drastic treatment programs, such as hospitalization, become necessary. Making communities livable requires good ideas about social planning as well as awareness that various segments of the population, including the aged, minorities, and the unemployed, have special needs. Community psychologists are interested in the environmental facts of life in particular communities as well as the impact of those facts on individual lives.

However, if pitfalls and problems cannot be anticipated, tampering with the mechanisms of society could do more harm than good. As a result, there is an urgent need for indexes of current social and psychological conditions in a community, roughly similar to the economic indicators that public and private officials use in setting economic goals. Some of these indicators are more visible than others. For example, national income statistics provide a measure of the level of material well-being; crime, accident, and drug use statistics provide clues to the moral condition of society; infant-mortality figures tell us something about the level of

health care. Indicators that are less easily indexed are the effectiveness of an educational system, the influence of mass media on behavior, and the cohesiveness of a neighborhood.

A reliable group of social and psychological indicators would not only tell us where society is at a given time but also provide useful dependent measures of the effects of social, political, and economic programs. The community exerts potent psychological influences on its members, and the task of community planners and behavioral scientists is to make those influences as adaptive as possible for the community's residents.

A Final Word

In Chapter 2 we traced the history of abnormal psychology and noted the enormous conceptual changes that have taken place over the centuries. This concluding chapter, perhaps more than any other in the book, illustrates the optimistic outlook of many researchers and therapists today. It is easy to point out the gaps in our knowledge: Why does schizophrenia primarily occur in the late teens and early twenties? What causes panic attacks? What can be done about senility? But perhaps more significant than the lack of knowledge implied by these questions is the current consensus that (1) the scientific method can fruitfully be applied to them, and (2) the resulting knowledge can be used to reduce the occurrence of maladaptive behavior.

There are many leads to effective prevention, but systematic research is needed to develop effective interventions. While the preventive approaches reviewed in this chapter seem promising, only scientific studies can validate them.

The formula for achieving prevention might be written $P = K \times W$. Prevention (P) is achieved when the needed knowledge (K) is available and society has the will (W) to use that knowledge to prevent unwanted outcomes. One of the great achievements of the present era is the widespread awareness that little good and much harm is done by blaming or stigmatizing people for their abnormalities, whether physical or behavioral. One of the great challenges is finding a way to motivate both individuals and society to do things to increase happiness, personal effectiveness, and the common good of the human family. The social need for prevention is, and will continue to be, one of the most powerful motivators for objective research in abnormal psychology.

Chapter Summary

TYPES OF PREVENTION

Situation-focused and Competency-focused Prevention **Situation-focused prevention** is aimed at reducing or eliminating the environmental causes of maladaptive behavior. The emphasis of **competency-focused prevention** is enhancing people's abilities to cope with the conditions that can lead to maladaptive behavior. Either of these approaches might be applied to divorce, an example of a stressful situation that often leads to maladaptive behavior. Early education programs illustrate a competency-focused prevention. The training they provide in cognitive and social skills facilitates the child's early school adjustment and may also have positive long-term effects.

Levels of Prevention **Primary prevention** focuses on reducing new cases that would otherwise occur in a population. The role of **secondary prevention** is to reduce the potential impact of an existing abnormal condition by decreasing its duration, intensity, or the disability it creates. **Tertiary prevention** is aimed at reducing the disability that has already resulted from a disorder or event. **Juvenile delinquency** is one area where all three types of prevention are relevant.

SITES OF PREVENTION

The Family The family is an important focus for prevention efforts. Parents affect their children's development from the moment of conception, through the genes they contribute, the prenatal environment, and the physical and psychological environment in which the children grow up. Parenting practices that have been linked to aggressive behavior in children include failure of supervision or monitoring, aggressive or abusive behavior, overpermissiveness, inconsistency, and rejection. Parental conflict and divorce are also areas where interventions at any of the three prevention levels can be helpful to the entire family. **Child abuse** and **spouse abuse** are other examples of harmful behaviors that can be treated by intervention at all levels of prevention. For some other types of problems parents can be trained to act as therapists toward their children.

The School Many family problems, behavior problems, and problems associated with learning are not identified until a child begins school. Special interventions by the classroom teacher and by school mental-health workers can prevent many behavior disorders in children. Interventions that strengthen children's social and cognitive skills can also help prevent their later dropping out of school.

The Community Community agencies or organizations can provide satisfying experiences for children that may help them develop positive interests and skills. They can bring children into contact with caring adults as well as provide access to new ideas. Police officers may play an important role in prevention. They may serve as positive role models and if trained in prevention techniques may help deter family violence by defusing confrontations. Crisis and suicide prevention centers can lower suicide rates and reduce social isolation. Suicide **postvention** programs are designed to help those who knew the person who died. They are usually presented in organizational settings to help those who knew and worked with the suicide victim deal with feelings of guilt and anger and to decrease the chances of additional suicides.

TREATMENT IN THE COMMUNITY

An integrated network of community services can help prevent hospital readmission for the chronically mentally ill. Communities also may prevent institutionalization by making adequate treatment facilities and housing such as group homes available.

Problems with Community Programs Community programs need to provide integrated treatment and support services as well as more continuity in service delivery for those who have chronic problems with maladaptive behavior.

Improving Treatment Programs A variety of treatment programs can offer alternatives to full time residential hospitalization. These include partial hospitalization through day hospitals or dormitory inns. Once patients are discharged from the hospital half-way houses an adequate case management system can be important in keeping them out of the hospital. Although deinstitutionalization has helped to empty hospitals of long term patients, the lack of funding of alternative programs has resulted in an increased frequency of readmissions of patients to hospitals for short term stays. Treatment programs of all types should offer support for family members as well as the patient and recognize the importance of families in treatment.

LEGAL ASPECTS OF TREATMENT AND PREVENTION

Institutionalization **Commitment,** or placement in an institution, may be either voluntary when patients agree to enter the hospital or involuntary when they are hospitalized through a legal procedure called **civil commitment. Criminal commitment** of a person to a mental hospital may occur when that person's criminal act is legally declared to be the result of insanity and it is in the interests of society to protect itself. **Insanity** is a legal term that refers to a person's state of mind when a criminal act was carried out; **competency** refers to a person's state of mind at the time of a judicial proceeding. A legally **incompetent person** lacks the capacity to consult a lawyer and to understand what the legal proceeding is about. The insanity defense arose from the recognition that a crime was not necessarily a deliberate violation of social norms but might be a result of a psychological disturbance. Although the

number of successful insanity defenses is very small, the defense has been the source of controversy of many years. The **M'Naghten rule,** or the knowledge of right and wrong test of insanity, was widely used for many years. More recently, the American Law Institute proposed a set of guidelines that have been incorporated into the laws of many states. The American Psychiatric Association has argued that people should be acquitted for insanity only if they have a severe disorder such as a psychosis. Civil commitment laws are based on the doctrine of **parens patriae,** the idea that the state can act in the best interest of a minor or incapacitated adult. The process includes a petition, a hearing, and a decision about the place of commitment. Current law requires that the state present "clear and convincing" reasons why hospitalization is required. Patient rights while hospitalized have also been the focus of court decisions. The state must provide adequate treatment for those who are confined involuntarily. In addition court decisions have upheld patients' rights to refuse specific types of treatment.

The Rights of Patients Patients' rights include the right of **informed consent** which means that they must have explained to them the nature of the treatment and its possible benefits and negative consequences before they agree to the treatment. They also have the right to terminate the treatment even if they had previously consented to it.

THE CHALLENGE OF PREVENTION

Prevention of maladaptive behavior and providing appropriate therapeutic responses when it does occur have implications for our basic social institutions as well as for specific programs for groups or treatment with individuals.

Paraprofessionals **Paraprofessionals,** who do not themselves have specialized mental health training but who are similar in cultural background to those to be served, often make important contributions to prevention and treatment.

Self-help Groups **Self-help groups** made up of people with a common problem can be helpful to many people who experience extreme stress or loss.

Community Psychology **Community psychology** is concerned with the role of social systems and community environment in prevention.

A FINAL WORD

The social need for prevention is one of the most powerful motivators for research in the field of abnormal psychology. The formula for prevention can be expressed: Prevention equals necessary knowledge multiplied by the will of society to use that knowledge.

Glossary

Abnormal psychology Study of deviant and maladaptive behaviors.

Abstinence-violation effect The reaction of conflict and guilt when an individual fails to resist the temptation to indulge in a behavior that he or she is trying to stop—for example, using alcohol. This response often triggers a binge or total relapse.

Acetylcholine Chemical involved in the transmission of nerve impulses.

Acid Slang term for LSD.

ACTH See *adrenocorticotrophic hormone.*

Adaptation Dynamic process by which an individual responds to his or her environment and the changes that occur within it; ability to modify one's behavior to meet changing environmental requirements. Adaptation to a given situation is influenced by one's personal characteristics and the type of situation. Term often used in a biological, Darwinian sense.

Addictive behavior The presence of a repetitive habit pattern that is associated with problems in the personal and social spheres as well as the risk of disease. This behavior must be perceived by the person and by others to be out of control.

Adjustment An individual's ability to harmonize with the environment.

Adjustment disorder Maladaptive reaction to a particular stressful condition that results in impaired functioning and symptoms in excess of what might be a normal response to the stressor. The reaction must occur soon after the beginning of the stress and the reaction can be expected to decrease when the stressor ceases.

Adjustment disorder with depressed mood Depression that occurs as a result of an identifiable life event and that is expected to disappear when the event's impact ceases. (Not classified as mood disorder.)

Adoption studies An attempt to understand the genetics of a disorder and separate them from the effects of environment by comparing children adopted in infancy whose biological parents are affected by a disorder with adopted children without such heredity.

Adrenal cortex The outer layer of the adrenal gland; a source of hormone secretion in the body.

Adrenal corticosteroids Hormones released by the adrenal cortex which affect the body's response to stress.

Adrenaline A secretion of the adrenal glands; also called *epinephrine.*

Adrenal medulla One of the two principle parts of the adrenal glands, the part of the endocrine system located just above the kidneys. A principle function is the secretion of hormones in emergency-type situations.

Adrenocortico-trophic Hormone (ACTH) Hormone secreted by the pituitary gland that goes to the adrenal cortex to release adrenal corticosteroids, chemicals that stimulate the body's response to stress.

Affect Emotion, feeling, or mood: pleasant or unpleasant, intense or mild; also, a tone of feeling accompanying a thought.

Affective disorder See *mood disorder.*

Agoraphobia Pathological fear of open spaces.

AIDS dementia complex (ADC) A type of dementia that is secondary to the development of the autoimmune disease syndrome (AIDS) or positive status of the human immunodeficiency virus (HIV).

Alcohol amnestic disorder Another term for Korsakoff's disease or syndrome.

Alcoholism Alcohol dependence or addiction.

Allergen The substance that causes an allergic reaction by causing antibodies to attack the immune system.

Allergy An abnormal immune system reaction to an ordinarily harmless substance.

Alpha-fetoprotein test A blood test used to assess the presence of genetic disorder or neural defects in the fetus.

Alpha wave A particular kind of electrical brain activity often seen when a person is tense and the frequency of which decreases with drowsiness or relaxation.

Alzheimer's disease Chronic brain disorder, occurring as early as the fourth decade of life and involving progressive destruction of nervous tissue, which results in slurring of speech, involuntary muscular movements, and gradual intellectual deterioration with growing lapses of memory.

Amnesia Total or partial memory loss—often acute—following emotional or physical trauma.

Amnestic syndrome A memory disturbance without confusion or delirium in which there is both inability to learn new material and to remember information learned in the past.

Amniocentesis Technique of removing a sample of amniotic fluid from a pregnant woman and analyzing it to determine whether there are chromosomal defects in the fetus.

Amphetamines Nervous system (particularly cerebral cortex) stimulants, such as dexedrine, which bring a sense of well-being and exhilaration. The stimulation effect is succeeded by fatigue and depression. Psychologically but probably not physiologically addicting.

Anal stage Stage of psychosexual development in which the child derives intense pleasure from activities associated with elimination.

Anencephaly A condition in which a child is born without a developed brain.

Angina pectoris Periodic chest pains resulting from an insufficient supply of oxygen to the heart. A type of coronary heart disease.

Anomaly A deviation from the norm; an abnormality.

Anorexia nervosa An intense and irrational feeling of being fat that leads to excessive restriction of food intake and weight loss that may be life threatening. Usually occurs in adolescence or early adulthood and is much more common in females than males.

Anorgasmia In women, the inability to achieve an orgasm after a normal level of sexual excitement.

Antianxiety drugs Commonly called *tranquilizers.* Used to calm anxious people.

Antidepressant drugs General term for a number of drugs used to relieve depression and to elevate mood.

Antigens Foreign substances that, when introduced into the body, induce the formation of antibodies and then react with these antibodies in a specifiable manner.

Antimanic drugs A family of drugs based on a compound of lithium carbonate that are used to treat mania, bipolar disorder, and some depressions.

Antipsychotic drugs Group of chemical compounds used to treat individuals who show severely disturbed behavior and thought processes, especially in cases of schizophrenia.

Antisocial personality disorder Characterized by continuous, chronic antisocial behavior, beginning before the age of 15 and continuing into adult life; before the age of 18 such behavior is called a *conduct disorder*. Behavior tends to impair the rights of others and to be characterized by an impaired capacity for close relationships.

Anxiety An affect with both psychological and physiological aspects. Generally, an unpleasant emotional state accompanied by physiological arousal and the cognitive elements of apprehension, guilt, and a sense of impending disaster. Distinguished from fear, which is an emotional reaction to a specific or identifiable object.

Anxiety disorder Formerly called *neurosis* or *neurotic disorder*. Characterized by some form of anxiety as the most prominent symptom. Includes panic disorders, phobic disorders, obsessive-compulsive disorder, generalized anxiety disorders, and reactions to stressors.

Aphasia Partial or total loss of the ability to convey thoughts through speech.

Appetitive Referring to a physical craving or desire.

Asexual Characterized by lack of response to sexual stimulation and lack of interest in sexual activity.

Asphyxia Unconsciousness or death caused by a lack of oxygen. May result in retardation or seizures as a result of brain damage.

Assertiveness training Combined cognitive and behavioral approach designed to increase the frequency of aggressive behavior that is socially desirable.

Assessment Information gathering aimed at describing and predicting behavior. Assessment specialists devise tests that measure various aspects of behavior.

Assessment interview Same as diagnostic interview.

Assessment study A study aimed at gathering information to describe a particular group in which variables are not manipulated. Such data can be used for prediction and are usually expressed in the form of correlations between variables.

Assortative mating The tendency for people to marry those who have characteristics similar to their own. For instance, chronic schizophrenics tend to marry individuals who have a schizophrenic spectrum disorder or other psychotic disorder. This genetic loading must be taken into account when estimating genetic risk for a variety of disorders.

Asthma Disorder of a chronic nature, often psycho-physiological in nature, characterized by coughing, wheezing, breathing difficulty, and a feeling of suffocating.

Atherosclerosis A disorder caused by a build up of plaque (deposits on the blood vessel walls) that narrow the vessels and result in insufficient blood supply to the heart.

Attention-deficit hyperactivity disorder Inability to focus attention together with an impulsive behavior pattern, which could not be expected from the child's developmental level. Often referred to as *hyperactivity* or by other similar labels.

Attribution A term used by social psychologists to describe the way a person assigns responsibility for cause and effect.

Aura Clouded state of consciousness, accompanied by feelings of unreality, which precedes an epileptic attack. Also, the sensory, motor, or mood disturbance preceding migraine headache.

Authentic behavior Term used by some existential theorists to describe behavior dictated by a person's own goals rather than by the goals of society.

Autistic Term used to describe a certain type of schizophrenic thought pattern characterized by self-centered thinking understandable only to the individual.

Autistic disorder A developmental disorder usually occurring early in childhood characterized by severe impairment in social relationships, communication, and activity. Frequently includes mental retardation.

Autistic savant One of a small number of persons who have the symptoms of autism, but who have special aptitudes that are remarkable not only compared to people with the same diagnosis, but compared to the aptitudes of the ordinary person.

Autoerotic asphyxia The self-limiting of oxygen into the body in order to increase sexual sensations. May result in death because of impaired judgement about when to release the oxygen restriction as a result of lessened cognitive function due to the oxygen deprivation.

Autoerotic practices Sexual stimulation practiced by an individual on him or herself.

Autonomic reactivity Excessive action of the sympathetic and parasympathetic portions of the autonomic nervous system.

Autonomic system Functional division of the nervous system concerned with visceral activities, smooth muscles, and endocrine glands. Name comes from the fact that it was formerly thought to function independently of the central nervous system.

Autosome Chromosome that does not determine the sex of the individual.

Aversion therapies Group of behavior therapies which attempt to condition avoidance responses in patients by pairing the behavior to be extinguished with punishing stimuli—for example, electric shock, social criticism, drugs that cause vomiting. Also known as *aversive conditioning*.

Aversive conditioning See *aversion therapies*.

Avoidance response Attempt to leave a situation in which an aversive stimulus is expected to occur.

Avoidant personality disorder Characterized by social withdrawal based on fear of social rejection.

Axon Part of the cell that transmits impulses away from the cell body and across the synapse to the dendrites of another cell.

Balanced placebo design An experimental design in which some subjects receive an inactive substance and others a psychoactive substance. Part of each group is led to expect that they have received the other category of substance and part of each group is accurately informed about what substance they are given.

Baquet A water-filled tub used by Mesmer as a focus for treatment of hysterical complaints.

Barbiturates Family of drugs that depress central nervous system action and may be addictive.

Baseline observation Operant conditioning procedure in which an initial rate of some response is established. Can be used for descriptive purposes or as a control condition before introducing behavior modifi-

cation procedures and subsequent response-rate comparisons.

BEAM See *brain electrical activity mapping.*

Bedlam Noisy uproar or confusion. A word derived from conditions at Bethlehem Hospital, an institution for the insane.

Behavioral assessment The objective recording of particular categories of observable behavior prior to beginning behavior therapy. The assessment may take place in specially contrived situations or under real life conditions.

Behavioral coping What a person actually does when confronted by a stressor.

Behavioral medicine An area focused on ways to improve health, treatment, and rehabilitation by using behavioral techniques to help people adopt generally healthier ways of living and to follow treatment plans for specific problems. Also focuses on helping health care providers improve their service delivery.

Behavioral Rating Scale for Children A type of rating scale designed to be used by untrained observers to quantify different aspects of children's behavior.

Behavior change experiment The test of a therapeutic manipulation to determine whether the individual's maladaptive behavior is lessened.

Behavior genetics Study of the transmission of certain kinds of behavior through selective mating.

Behaviorism School of psychology whose adherents contend that the study of overt and observable behaviors provides the only legitimate data of science. Covert events, such as consciousness, are disregarded or considered only as mediation processes between stimulus and response contingencies.

Behavior modification Type of therapy based on the principles of operant conditioning.

Behavior therapy Includes several techniques of behavior modification based on laboratory-derived principles of learning and conditioning. Behavior therapies focus on modifying overt behaviors with minimal reference to internal or covert events.

Benzodiazepines Group of drugs, such as Librium and Valium, used primarily to treat anxiety.

Bereavement The state of having lost someone through death.

Binet tests The intelligence test concept originated by Binet in which the person tested is asked to complete a variety of tasks that assess reasoning, ability to follow directions, and judgment. The results originally were based on the concept of the intelligence quotient or IQ as the ratio of test score or mental level to chronological age but are now computed in terms of how much the person's score deviates from the mean of scores for that particular chronological age.

Biofeedback Method for inducing behavioral change in which the client learns to alter autonomic nervous system responses by monitoring them on recording instruments.

Biological perspective Theoretical perspective that suggests that all disorders, physical or behavioral, have biological causes. Causes may lie in heredity, genetic accident, or bodily infection or trauma.

Biopsychosocial model Interactional view that emphasizes the interaction among biological, psychological, and social factors in determining behavior and body functioning.

Bipolar II A type of bipolar disorder in which the person has experienced at least one major depressive episode and one hypomanic episode but has never had a manic episode or cyclothymia.

Bipolar disorder Mood disorder in which the individual experiences both periods of mania and periods of depression. Formerly called *manic-depressive order.*

Bisexual Someone who is sexually attracted to members of both sexes.

Bisexual behavior The preference, at different times, for male and for female sex partners.

Bodily assessment Measures of some aspects of an individual's physiological state, for example heart rate, blood pressure, or amount of sweating. Many of these can be assessed automatically on a continuous basis over time.

Booster session An additional treatment carried out after a period of time has elapsed since the original treatment series. Intended to counteract any weakening of the treatment effect.

Borderline personality disorder Characterized by impulsive and unpredictable behavior and marked shifts in mood. Instability may affect personal relationships, behavior, mood, and image of self.

Bottom-up studies In the study of hereditary factors in disorder, this approach focuses first on identifying children with a disorder and then investigates the clinical status of their parents and other relatives. Contrast with *top-down studies.*

Brain deterioration See *dementia.*

Brain electrical activity mapping (BEAM) A technique for study of electrical brain activity in which the electrical impulses are summarized in color maps.

Brain imaging techniques A variety of non-intrusive computer based techniques that provide views of the structural or metabolic activity in the living brain.

Brainstem Portion of the central nervous system that includes the hindbrain, midbrain, and forebrain up to the thalamus.

Briquet's syndrome Another name for somatization disorder.

Bulimia nervosa Episodes of binge eating with the awareness that this behavior is abnormal. Vomiting is often self-induced by the individual at the end of the eating session.

Burnout Condition found most often among people in the helping professions whose work involves intense interpersonal contact. Symptoms includes loss of effectiveness and self-confidence and the general feeling of inability to deal with particular situations.

Caffeine Crystalline compound that is found in coffee, tea, and kola nuts and which acts as a stimulant of the central nervous system and also as a diuretic.

Cannabis Plant whose resin produces a psychoactive substance. In solid form the resin is called *hashish.*

Cardiovascular disorder Disorder affecting the blood vessel system and the heart.

Case study Detailed observations of a client's behavior, symptoms, and reported thoughts over a period of time with inferences about cause and effect supplied by the clinician. Often called clinical method.

Catatonic schizophrenia Type of schizophrenic disorder characterized by psychomotor disturbance. Often takes the form of body rigidity or posturing. Other behavior may include waxy flexibility or mutism.

Catecholamines Group of hormones, including epinephrine, norepinephrine, and dopamine, that are important in the response to stress. Some catecholamines are produced in the brain, where they are important in nerve transmission.

Categorical model An approach to classification used in the *Diagnostic and Statistical Manual.* In this

method the diagnosis may be made if a certain number of criteria are satisfied, rather than requiring all criteria to be met.

Cell body The part of the cell that contains the nucleus.

Central nervous system (CNS) Brain and spinal cord; does not include the nerve trunks and their peripheral connections.

Cerebellum Portion of the brain consisting of two hemispheres located behind and above the medulla; coordinates motor activities and maintains bodily equilibrium.

Cerebral cortex Convoluted layer of gray matter of the brain; outer layer of the cerebrum.

Cerebral hemispheres One of the two lateral halves of the cerebrum or upper part of the brain.

Cerebral ventricles Cavities in the brain that are connected to the central canal of the spinal cord and contain cerebrospinal fluid.

Cerebrovascular accident (CVA) Rupture or blockage of blood vessels in the cerebrum that disrupt or prevent blood flow. Commonly referred to as a *stroke*.

CHD See *coronary heart disease*.

Child abuse Harm, usually physical, deliberately inflicted on children by their parent(s), often by repeated beatings.

Child neglect Failure by the caretaker to provide a child with healthful environment, adequate food, clothing, or supervision.

Choline acetylcholine transferase Enzyme that forms acetylcholine.

Chorionic villus sampling A method of determining genetic damage in the fetus.

Chromosomal anomaly Abnormality in chromosome structure or number of chromosomes.

Chromosomes Gene-bearing structures within cells.

Chronic care model A type of full time or day hospitalization in which an attempt is made to improve the patient's level of social skills and to reduce symptoms. Expectations for patient change are limited to improvement rather than recovery.

Civil commitment Commitment of a person to an institution based on a judgment that the person is a potential danger to him or herself and/or to others.

Classical conditioning Pavlov's experimental method by which a conditioned stimulus is paired with an unconditioned stimulus. Procedure involves presenting the two stimuli in close temporal proximity. The first, or unconditioned, stimulus elicits a reflex. After a number of trials the second, or conditioned, stimulus acquires the potentiality of evoking a similar reflex.

Classification The establishment of a hierarchical system of categories based on the relationship or presumed relationship among the things to be classified, for instance, disorders of behavior and cognition.

Client-centered therapy Carl Rogers' therapeutic approach, which views the subject matter of psychotherapy as the client's world of immediate experience that should be approached from the client's frame of reference. In the Rogerian system, the therapist's main task is to create the opportunity for the individual to achieve a reorganization of his or her subjective world and to reach self-actualization.

Clinical method Case study of the individual through observation. May rely heavily upon intuitive judgments of the clinician rather than upon experimentation and systematic measurement.

Clinical psychologist Psychologist, usually with a Ph.D., who has special training and skills in assessing and treating maladaptive behavior.

Clinical trial The use of a research design including one or more experimental groups and a control group in testing the usefulness of a particular approach in treatment of patients.

Clinician Professional who deals directly with the examination or treatment of patients or clients.

Clitoris In females, a small organ at the front of the vulva that is highly sensitive to sexual stimulation. The analogue of the penis in the male.

Clonic phase An aspect of seizure activity in which there is rapid alternation of muscle contractions and muscle relaxation.

Cluster headache Very painful headaches that peak quickly and often last no more than an hour. Long pain free periods tend to alternate with series of headaches over a day or week.

Cocaine Stimulant with a number of characteristics in common with the amphetamines.

Codeine Derivative of opium that is less potent than morphine.

Cognitive assessment Specification and enumeration of the typical thoughts that precede, accompany, and follow maladaptive behavior. Used in research and by cognitive behavior therapists especially in working with depressed individuals.

Cognitive-behavioral interventions A therapeutic approach that includes structured training sessions and prescribed exercises to help clients change maladaptive behavior by changing specific types of thoughts about themselves and others that typically occur in certain situations.

Cognitive coping skills Particular ways of thinking that aid in behaving effectively in stressful situations.

Cognitive distortion model (*of depression*) Proposed by Aaron Beck and suggests that depression is a disorder of thought.

Cognitive modification Technique whereby individuals learn to modify maladaptive thought patterns or to substitute new internal dialogues for old maladaptive ones.

Cognitive perspective Point of view that considers behavior to be the result of information processing and problem solving. Emphasis is on mental processes of which the individual is aware or can easily become aware.

Cognitive psychology Study of human beings as information processors and problem solvers. Focus has recently been extended from the traditional studies of memory, attention, and problem solving to include the effects of personality factors and emotions on learning and performance.

Cognitive psychotherapy A talking therapy that is focused on clarifying the client's belief system and how it relates to maladjustment and unhappiness. The focus is on challenging inaccurate and maladaptive beliefs.

Cognitive rehearsal Procedure in which a client learns to rehearse ways to handle problem situations mentally. Such rehearsal makes it easier for the client to behave effectively in the actual situations.

Cognitive restructuring A technique used by Albert Ellis and other cognitive therapists in which the client is made aware of a connection between unrealistic thoughts and the maladaptive behavior these evoke. Clients are helped to develop more rational ways of looking at their behavior.

Cognitive set A person's habitual way of viewing the world and distorting it in terms of his or her personality characteristics and expectations.

Cognitive triad Description of depression in terms of negative thinking

about oneself, the current situation, and the future. Part of Beck's cognitive distortion model.

Coming out Term used by homosexuals to indicate the occasion of openly declaring their sexual orientation.

Commitment Placement in an institution, usually without the consent of the person committed, through a legal procedure. See also *civil commitment, criminal commitment*.

Communication deviance Term referring to the inability of a person to maintain a shared focus of attention with another. Studied in parent–child communications in families with a schizophrenic child.

Community perspective Viewpoint that much maladaptive behavior results from poor living conditions, discrimination, and so on. Emphasis is on preventive activities.

Community psychology Branch of applied psychology concerned with modifying both the individual and the structure of the social system to produce optimal benefits for both society and the individual. Community psychologists are often primarily interested in preventing maladaptive behavior.

Co-morbidity The significant overlap or co-occurance of symptoms and conditions in different disorders. The common finding of co-morbidity in depression and anxiety, for instance, makes it important to understand the relationship between these two disorders.

Competency May refer to adequacy of coping skills. In a legal sense refers to whether a person who is the object of a legal proceeding has the capacity to profit from consultation with a lawyer and to understand the purpose of the legal proceedings.

Competency-focused prevention Actions to prevent maladaptive behavior through helping those at risk develop coping skills.

Compulsive behavior Characterized by an individual's need to repeat a series of acts again and again even though he or she perceives them as senseless and interfering with desirable activities.

Computerized axial tomography (CT scan) Technique that uses a narrow beam of x-rays to photograph an area of the body from many angles. A computer then analyzes this information to provide a clear picture of soft tissues as well as the tissue seen in conventional x-rays.

Concordance Term describing the degree of relationship among twins and other family members with respect to a given characteristic or trait. They are referred to as *concordant* if they both show a particular trait; if they do not, the pair is described as *discordant* for that trait.

Concussion Head injury that does not cause lasting structural damage. Rate of recovery is proportional to the severity of the injury.

Conditioned response (CR) In classical conditioning, the response that occurs after training has taken place and after the conditioned stimulus has been presented.

Conditioned stimulus (CS) In classical conditioning, the neutral stimulus that does not elicit a response prior to training.

Conditioning See *classical conditioning; operant conditioning*.

Conduct disorder Diagnostic classification for those under 18 who commit antisocial acts. Adults may also be classified this way if they do not meet the criteria for the antisocial personality disorder.

Confabulation The process of filling in missing memories with fabricated information; to replace forgotten facts with fantasy.

Congenital Characteristics that are either innate or acquired, usually through chemical action, while the child is in the uterus.

Conscious Aspects of one's mental life of which a person is aware at any particular time.

Constitutional Any characteristics acquired by heredity, uterine environment, or illness or injury at or after birth.

Continuous Performance Test Test of sustained visual attention in which the subject is required to indicate whenever a certain stimulus is presented and to ignore all other stimuli.

Contusion Brain condition in which diffuse structural damage has occurred (e.g., rupture of blood vessels). Typically, cerebrospinal fluid pressure is raised, causing such symptoms as coma and stupor.

Conversion disorder Type of somatoform disorder in which there is a loss or change in physical functioning that suggests a physical disorder but seems to be a direct expression of a psychological conflict.

Coping Contending with difficulties and overcoming them.

Coping skills The characteristic way a person deals with difficulties or

stress. Commonly used skills include task-directed activity, working on a problem step by step, appropriate control of emotion.

Coping style Characteristic way a person deals with the stimuli in his or her environment.

Coronary heart disease (CHD) Disorder in which one or more of the coronary arteries is partially or totally obstructed by deposits. This results in a temporary or permanent cut off of blood to portions of the heart muscle.

Correlation Degree of correspondence between two variables; a statistical index of covariation that varies from$+ 1.00$ to$- 1.00$.

Correlational study Type of research in which the relationship of two or more characteristics is measured. No statement about cause and effect can be made from correlational research.

Cortex Outer layer of an organ such as the cerebrum, cerebellum, or adrenal gland.

Corticotrophin-releasing factor (CRF) Substance secreted by the hypothalamus that releases the chemical ACTH when it reaches the pituitary gland.

Countertransference Psychoanalytic term that refers to the therapist's emotional reactions to the patient. See also *transference*.

Covert Behavior that is internal and not directly observable. Includes unexpressed thoughts and feelings and other conscious and unconscious mental phenomena.

Covert modeling Learning through imagining how someone else would perform a task or by anticipating what response might be given to certain types of behavior.

Covert sensitization Behavioral therapy in which anxiety is created toward a particular stimulus situation that is likely to produce undesirable behavior. Usually the stimulus is paired with cognitions relating to the possible negative consequences if the person continues a given behavior. A treatment often used in changing the focus of sexual excitement.

CPT See *Continuous Performance Test*.

Crack A street name for a smokable form of very potent, concentrated cocaine.

Criminal commitment Commitment of a person to an institution based on a judgment that the person is guilty of a criminal act and is also legally insane.

Crisis A decisive turning point in a series of events.

Criteria The standards against which behaviors are measured.

Cross-cultural approach Method of studying the causes of various psychological and physical problems by studying their occurrence in a variety of cultures and then attempting to identify factors that are correlated with high and low frequency of the problems.

Cross-fostering study Method of evaluating hereditary factors in behavioral disorders by comparing frequency of a disorder in groups with genetic vulnerability reared by healthy adoptive parent(s) and groups without known genetic vulnerability reared by adoptive parent(s) who have a particular behavior disorder.

Cross-sectional study Research design in which different groups are sampled at the same time and the results compared. Technique often used to study human development.

CT scan See *computerized axial tomography.*

Culture General values, attitudes, achievements, and behavior patterns shared by members of the same society.

Cyclothymia A long lasting disorder that includes both mania and depressive episodes, neither of which meet the criteria for major episodes. Lasts for at least 2 years.

Cytomegalovirus One of a number of viral diseases which, if present in a pregnant woman, may result in retardation and other congenital problems in the child.

Date rape Rape committed by a person who is a social acquaintance of the person who is raped.

Day hospitalization Treatment approach used for either chronic or acutely ill patients or for patients in need of rehabilitation. Patients attend a hospital program during the day and return home in the evening. Activities during the day are focused on social skills and practical problem solving.

Defense mechanism (ego defense) Psychoanalytic term for various psychic operations used by the ego to avoid awareness of unpleasant and anxiety-provoking stimuli. The ego selectively uses defense mechanisms to ward off anxiety originating in the id, the superego, or dangers in external reality.

Deficiency needs According to Maslow, the most basic needs of life, which must be met before higher needs, such as social and intellectual needs, can be considered.

Deinstitutionalization Movement whose purpose is to remove patients from large mental hospitals and to obtain treatment and sheltered living conditions for them in the community.

Deinstitutionalize Efforts to remove from care-giving institutions all those individuals who do not present a clear danger to others or to themselves.

Delirium Condition characterized by a confused mental state, usually resulting from shock or fever, accompanied by alterations in attention and by hallucinations, delusions, and incoherence.

Delirium tremens Acute delirium caused by overdoses of alcohol and consisting of severe alterations in consciousness and attention. Also referred to as the DTs.

Delusion Incorrect belief maintained despite clear evidence to the contrary.

Delusional disorder The presence of a persistent but not bizarre delusion that is not due to any other mental disorder such as schizophrenia. Apart from the delusion the person's behavior is not obviously unusual.

Dementia Progressive atrophy of brain tissue that results in lapses of memory, poor judgment, and disorientation. Called *presenile dementia* if it occurs before age 65, and *senile dementia* if it begins after age 65.

Dementia paralytica Another term for general paresis.

Dementia praecox Older term for schizophrenia; used by Kraepelin to emphasize the early onset and irreversibility of the disorder as he defined it.

Demographic The description of human populations in terms of growth, density, distribution, and vital statistics.

Dendrite Branched part of a cell that serves as a receptor for nerve impulses from the axons of other cells and transmits them toward the cell body.

Denial Defense mechanism that allows rejection of elements of reality that would be consciously intolerable; negation of experiences or reality through unacceptance.

Deoxyribonucleic acid See *DNA.*

Dependent personality disorder Characterized by an inability to make major decisions and a belittling of a person's own abilities and assets. Intense discomfort is experienced if the person remains alone for more than a brief period.

Dependent variable Aspect of behavior which changes according to manipulation of the independent variable in an experiment.

Depersonalization Feelings of unreality or a loss of personal identity; often experienced as one's being someone else or as watching oneself in a movie.

Depression Pervasive feeling of sadness that may begin after some loss or stressful event, but that continues long afterwards. Inappropriate thought patterns that generalize every event as a calamity are characteristic.

Depressive disorder Depressive symptoms that meet diagnostic criteria for either a single episode of major depression, or recurrent episodes. If manic or hypomanic behavior has been observed in the past, depressed symptoms should not be classified as a major depression even if they meet the other criteria.

Descriptive statistics Procedures used to summarize groups of individual observations. The most common descriptive statistics are measures of central tendency (e.g., mean) and measures of variability (e.g., standard deviation).

Desensitization hypothesis The idea that antidepressant drugs are effective because they reduce abnormal sensitivity in the catecholamine receptors of people who are depressed.

Determinism The philosophical idea that all acts are the inevitable result of what has happened before and that human choice or free will plays no role in what happens.

Detoxification Ridding the body of the particular toxic substance that is causing the problem. In drug or alcohol detoxification, withdrawal signs are usually experienced as the amount of toxic substance declines.

Developmental disorder One of a group of disorders that involve distortions in the development of basic psychological functions that are involved in social skills, language, perception, and motor behavior. The disorder can be pervasive and involve many functions (e.g., autism) or specific and involve only a single aspect of development (e.g., developmental arithmetic disorder).

Dexamethasone Suppression Test Chemical test used in an attempt to differentiate depressed individuals

who may be helped by different treatments.

Dexedrine See *dextroamphetamine*.

Dextroamphetamine (e.g., Dexedrine) Stimulant drug sometimes used in the treatment of hyperactivity.

Diagnosis Classification of behavior disorders in terms of relatively homogeneous groups based on similar behaviors or correlates. Shorthand description of the behavioral and personality correlates associated with a particular classification. In medicine, the act or process of deciding the nature of a diseased condition.

Diagnostic and Statistical Manual (DSM) Classification system for abnormal behavior published by the American Psychiatric Association. The system is generally used in the United States for official diagnostic and record-keeping purposes.

Diagnostic interview Interview designed to gather information and assess behavior, usually for the purpose of determining seriousness and outcome or deciding what treatment approach would be appropriate.

Diagnostic Interview Schedule (DIS) Standardized interview format designed to yield information necessary to make a DMS diagnosis. At present the schedule covers only a few disorders.

Diastolic Term used to describe the blood pressure reading at the time the heart dilates to allow more blood to enter.

Diathesis stress theory The idea that only people with an underlying vulnerability to a disorder will develop that disorder when they are exposed to overwhelming stress. This approach is used particularly in understanding why some people develop symptoms of one of the schizophrenic spectrum disorders when exposed to stress.

Diazepam One of the benzodiazepines, a group of antianxiety tranquilizers. Known by trade name, Valium.

Dimensional model An approach to classification that focuses on patterns of characteristics to determine profiles of characteristics differentiate the different categories. The Minnesota Multiphasic Personality Inventory is used in this way.

Discordant Term often used in twin studies to describe particular characteristics on which the twins differ. Characteristics that are the same for both are referred to as *concordant*.

Disorders of infancy, childhood, or adolescence Conditions that begin at one of these developmental periods in a person's life.

Disorganized schizophrenia (hebephrenic) Type of schizophrenia distinguished by incoherent speech and flat, incongruous, or silly affect. Often associated with extreme oddities of behavior such as gesturing or grimacing.

Displacement Defense mechanism in which an emotional attitude is transferred from one object to a substitute object.

Dissociative disorder Sudden, temporary alteration in the functions of consciousness, identity, or motor behavior in which some part of one or more of these functions is lost. If consciousness is affected, the person cannot remember important personal events. If identity is affected, a new identity that dominates behavior is temporarily assumed. If motor behavior is affected, then consciousness and/or identity are also affected. Wandering behavior is the most common resulting motor behavior.

Dizygotic twins Fraternal twins developed from two fertilized eggs. The two individuals have the same genetic relationship as any pair of siblings.

DNA Abbreviation for deoxyribonucleic acid, a complex chemical found in chromosomes within living cell nuclei. The sequence of its units determines genetic inheritance.

Dominant gene Member of the gene pair that determines whether the individual will show the trait controlled by that gene. Other member of the pair may be the same (also dominant) or different (recessive).

Dopamine One of the neurotransmitter systems included under the category of catecholamines and also under the larger category of monoamine neurotransmitter.

Dopamine hypothesis Idea that schizophrenia involves an excess of the neurotransmitter dopamine at certain sites in the brain.

Double-blind method Experimental design used in drug research. Neither the subjects nor the experimenters know whether the medication given to different comparison groups are active or inert (placebos).

Down syndrome Condition related to some inequality in the chromosome pair designated as number 21. Usually associated with a trisomy, or presence of an extra chromosome in addition to the usual pair. Also called trisomy 21.

Drug therapy Use of a variety of psychoactive drugs to treat different types of maladaptive behavior. Drugs are most often used to treat schizophrenia, bipolar disorder, some depressions, and anxiety. Drug treatment is often combined with other types of therapy.

DSM See *Diagnostic and Statistical Manual*.

DST See *dexamethasone suppression test*.

DTs See *delirium tremens*.

Dymorphin One of the naturally occurring opioids in the body that are part of a signaling system related to pain, mood regulation, and learning.

Dyspareunia (functional) Type of sexual dysfunction in which persistent and recurrent genital pain is associated with coitus without any apparent physical cause.

Dysphoria Feelings of anxiety, depression, and restlessness.

Dysphoric mood Characterized by symptoms of depression, sadness, feeling blue and hopeless.

Dysthymia A long standing depressed mood accompanied by loss of interest and lack of pleasure in situations which most people would find enjoyable.

Dysthymic disorder Long lasting chronic depressed mood or loss of pleasure in most usual activities. Does not meet the criteria for a major depressive episode.

Echolalia Meaningless repetition of words.

ECT See *electroconvulsive therapy*.

EEG See *electroencephalogram*.

Efficacy expectation The belief that one can successfully carry out a particular behavior.

Ego In psychoanalytic theory, the part of the psyche which makes up the self or the "I." Part of the psyche that is conscious and most closely in touch with reality and that functions as the "executive officer" of the personality.

Ego boundaries, loss of A state of being unable to distinguish between oneself and another person as separate individuals each of whom has his/her own unique thoughts and feelings. Often associated with feelings of being controlled by others. May be found in schizophrenic disorder or borderline personality disorder.

Electroconvulsive therapy (ECT) Treatment for depression in which electrical current is passed through a patient's head. Used if a quick treatment is needed because of a high suicide risk or if antidepressant drugs have not been effective.

Electroencephalogram (EEG) Graphic record of minute electrical impulses arising from brain cells. Measured by an electronic device called an *electroencephalograph.*

Encephalitis Inflammation of the white matter of the brain. Symptoms include visual failure, mental deterioration, and spastic paralysis.

Encopresis Repeated voluntary or involuntary bowel movements of normal consistency that occur in inappropriate surroundings and are not a result of any organic disorder.

Endocrine Referring to any of the ductless glands of the body. These pass their secretions directly from the gland cells to the bloodstream.

Endorphin Pain-killing substance that occurs naturally in the brain.

Enkephalin A protein that naturally occurs in the body and that produces a morphine-like activity.

Epidemiological research Studies designed to link the occurrence of a disorder with a specified population. One focus of this research is the study of the association between mental disorders and various population variables. Results are often expressed in terms of *incidence,* or the number of new cases that appear during a specific time period, and *prevalence,* the number of cases that currently exist within the population.

Epidemiology The scientific study of the associations between diseases or behavioral deviations and social class variables, geographical variables, or environmental variables. These associations, derived from the study of large population groups, help to suggest possible causes for the health problems observed.

Epilepsy Transitory disturbance of brain function which is characterized by a sudden onset and loss of consciousness and which may involve tonic and clonic muscle spasms. Epileptic seizures may be minor (petit mal) or major (grand mal) and tend to recur.

Epinephrine One of the hormones secreted by the adrenal medulla, active in emotional excitement and in response to stress.

Erectile disorder Type of sexual dysfunction in which the male is occasionally or chronically unable to achieve or maintain a penile erection. The condition may have physical or psychological causes. Also known as *impotence.*

Erectile dysfunction See *erectile disorder.*

Erogenous zone Parts of the body sensitive to sexual stimulation.

Escape response The attempt to get out of an unpleasant or aversive situation.

Etiology Assignment of a cause; scientific study of causes and origins of maladaptive behavior.

Excitement (sexual) The initial response to sexual stimulation marked by vaginal lubrication or penile erection.

Exhibitionism Exposure of the genitals in public for purposes of obtaining sexual pleasure and gratification.

Exhibitionist One who practices exhibitionism.

Existential therapy Type of psychotherapy which uses both humanistic and psychodynamic approaches. Emphasis is placed on each person's ability to affect his or her life course by the particular choices made.

Exit event A psychological loss of social support through death, divorce, or the breakup of a relationship.

Exorcism Expelling of evil spirits.

Experiment A study using the experimental method.

Experimental method Study of the factors influencing a result by the manipulation of one or more experimental variables rather than simply observing what occurs naturally.

Exposure Requiring the client to participate in anxiety provoking situations under supportive supervision until the anxiety response is extinguished. Based on the classical conditioning approach.

Exposure orientation In drug addiction, the idea that addiction is brought about by an environment that provides availability of drugs.

Exposure therapy Behavioral therapy that has as its basic element maintaining contact with or imagining contact with the feared stimulus.

Expressed emotion (EE) A measure of emotional involvement and attitudes of family members when talking about a behaviorally disturbed family member.

Expressed trait A trait that dominates in the individual and is determined either by at least one dominant gene or by a pair of recessive genes. If only one recessive gene is present the individual has the potential to pass on a genetic characteristic, but that characteristic is not observable in the person him or herself.

Extinction Weakening of a response following removal of reinforcement.

Eye-tracking movements Study of smooth pursuit and saccadic eye movements as an individual attempts to visually follow a rhythmically moving stimulus. One goal of such study is to uncover genetic markers of vulnerability.

Factitious disorder Symptoms, either fabricated or self-induced, that are designed to produce attention and care from medical personnel.

Fading Technique for gradually eliminating cues used in behavior modification after an individual begins to achieve a desired response.

Family study Study of characteristics of a group of related individuals to uncover genetic patterns.

Family systems approach A therapeutic approach in which the disturbance experienced by the client is viewed as the result of the way the family interacts rather than a problem caused by the client alone.

Family therapy Specialized type of group therapy in which the members of the family of the client all participate in group-treatment sessions. The basic idea is that the family, not just the individual client, has to alter behavior to solve the problem.

Fantasized exposure Exposure therapy in which the upsetting stimuli are imagined rather than presented in actuality.

Fetal alcohol syndrome Condition that may occur in the children of alcoholic mothers or mothers who used excessive alcohol during pregnancy. Characterized by retardation and unusual physical characteristics.

Fetishism Sexual deviation in which sexual interest is centered upon some body part or inanimate object which becomes capable of stimulating sexual excitement.

First rank symptoms Group of symptoms described by Kurt Schneider in an attempt to establish clear behavioral criteria for schizophrenia. One of the bases of the DSM-III-R definition of schizophrenic disorders.

Fixation Inappropriately strong attachment for someone or something. Also refers to an abnormal arrest of development during infancy or childhood which persists in adult life as an inappropriate constellation of attitudes, habits, or interests.

Fixed-role therapy Cognitive approach developed by George Kelly in which the client is asked to practice or try out new roles in relationships.

Flashback The reexperiencing of hallucinations or other perceptual symp-

toms which had originally occurred while the person was intoxicated by a psychoactive substance.

Flooding Behavioral therapeutic technique used particularly in the treatment of phobias. Treatment consists of exposing the client to the feared stimulus until the fear response has extinguished.

Follow-up study A method in which individuals listed at one point in time are contacted again at a later time to reassess behavior so that any changes can be noted.

Four humours The four body fluids (blood, black bile, yellow bile, and phlegm) that were thought by the ancients to play a role in character and temperament.

Fragile X syndrome An abnormality of the X chromosome that is the most frequent cause of mental retardation except for Down syndrome.

Free association Basic technique of the psychoanalytic method by which a patient expresses his or her thoughts as freely and in as uninhibited a manner as possible. Free associations provide a natural flow of thought processes unencumbered by interruptions or explanations.

Frontal lobe Portion of each cerebral hemisphere involved in abstract thinking processes.

Fugue state Flight from reality in which the individual may leave his or her present environment and life situation and establish a new lifestyle in another geographical location. Such a person is usually totally amnesic concerning his or her past life, although other abilities remain unimpaired; he or she may appear essentially normal to others.

Full Scale IQ One of three intelligence test scores obtained from any of the Wechsler tests. This IQ score takes into account both verbal ability and performance and spatial skills.

Fully functioning person Term used by Carl Rogers to describe the optimal level of adjustment at which an individual can function with minimal anxiety.

GABA Term for gamma-amino-butyric-acid, a neurotransmitter. A deficiency of GABA, associated with hereditary causes, is thought to be involved in Huntington's disease.

Galvanic skin response (GSR) Change in the electrical resistance of the skin. This response serves as a dependent variable in conditioning and is used in lie detector tests.

Gastrointestinal disorders Disorders of the digestive system, the stomach, and intestines.

Gay Term used to describe a homosexual lifestyle by those who feel the term homosexual has too many negative connotations.

Gender identity Basic feature of personality encompassing an individual's conviction of being male or female.

Gender-identity disorder (transsexualism) Disorder in which the individual has a strong desire to become a member of the opposite sex by changing his or her anatomical structure.

Gender-identity disorder of childhood A disorder occurring before puberty in which the child shows intense distress over its assigned sex. Such children may deny their assigned sex or assert that they will develop the genital characteristics of the opposite sex.

Gender nonconformity in childhood Situation in which the child is primarily interested in the activities culturally associated with the opposite sex. Not necessarily associated with later sexual deviance.

Gene Microscopic structure in the chromosome; physical unit of hereditary transmission.

General adaptation syndrome Concept proposed by Selye. Three-stage reaction of an organism to excessive and prolonged stress, including (1) an alarm or mobilization reaction; (2) a resistance stage; and (3) a final stage of exhaustion.

Generalized anxiety disorder Persistent anxiety that lasts at least 1 month and includes several of the following: motor tension, autonomic hyperactivity, apprehensive expectation, vigilance, and scanning. The symptoms do not include phobias, panic attacks, obsessions, or compulsions.

General paresis See *paresis*.

Genetic counseling The giving of information about risk for inheritance of certain disorders based on general information about heredity, knowledge of family history, and genetic characteristics of the person or couple seeking information.

Genetic heterogeneity In genetics, the idea that more than one gene is necessary for the inheritance of a characteristic. However, the genes each have a separate effect, not an additive one.

Genetic specificity A gene pattern that is unique to a particular disorder or group of disorders.

Genital stage According to Freud, if maturation proceeds without problems, after adolescence the individual reaches this stage in which the focus of pleasure is on a mature heterosexual relationship.

Genome The specification or mapping of all the gene locations on the human chromosomes and the specification of the functions of the gene at each locus.

Gestalt A unified configuration that has many properties or meanings that could not be derived from the total of its individual parts.

Gestalt therapy Humanistic approach that emphasizes removing distortions in self-perception and in the perception of others. Originated by Perls.

Glove anesthesia Condition in which a person cannot move or feel the part of the arm and hand that a glove would normally cover.

Grand mal Severe form of epilepsy involving major convulsive attacks and loss of consciousness.

Grief Sorrow, usually over a loss.

Group home A sheltered living environment that may be either transitional or permanent. Often used for retarded persons and those with chronic schizophrenia. Emphasis is on self-care and self-regulation to the extent the individual's ability and condition permit.

Group hysteria Hysterical symptoms, often of a conversion disorder-like nature, that seem to spread contagiously through a group of individuals.

Group therapy Psychotherapy of several persons at the same time in small groups.

Guided mastery A therapeutic approach in which the therapist enhances the client's feelings of self-efficacy through modeling, information, or suggestions.

Guided rehearsal Aspect of modeling in which the client practices the previously modeled behavior and is coached by the therapist in order to improve the performance.

Gyri Raised portions of the brain's surface between the sulci (plural of gyrus).

Habituation Decrease of the orienting response after the repeated presentation of a stimuli.

Halfway house Transitional living facility that accommodates, for a short period of time, newly discharged psychiatric patients or those who have functioned maladaptively.

Hallucination Sensory perception in the absence of an external stimulus. Hallucinations are usually visual ("seeing things") but may occur in other sensory modalities as well.

Hallucinogen General name for a group of drugs or chemicals capable of producing hallucinations.

Halo effect Tendency to rate an individual improperly high or low on a particular factor because of prior information or a general impression of the individual.

Hashish Hallucinogenic substance that is the solidified resin of *cannabis sativa* (marijuana).

Headache, cluster Headaches that occur in groups over a relatively short time period. Each headache is very painful for several minutes and fades away completely within an hour.

Headache, migraine Severe headache caused by a constriction followed by a dilation of the cranial artery. Usually preceded by some sensory or emotional cues called an *aura*. The disorder is thought to have some stress-related components.

Health psychology Area of psychology concerned both with calling attention to ways that disease can be prevented by changing living habits and with helping people modify behavior that increases health risk.

Hebephrenic schizophrenia See *disorganized schizophrenia*.

Helplessness See *learned helplessness*.

Hereditary Qualities transmitted from parent to child through genetic transmission.

Heredity The process by which characteristics of an organism are basically determined by genes received from the parents.

Heroin Extremely addictive opiate derived from morphine.

Herpes virus hominus (herpes simplex) Chronic viral illness which, if present in a pregnant woman, may cause retardation and other congenital malformations in her child.

Heterocyclics Recent terminology used to describe the overall group comprising the tricyclics and second generation antidepressants and to distinguish them from the monoamine oxydase inhibitor group of antidepressant medications.

Heterosexual Characterized by attraction to the opposite sex.

Hierarchy of needs View, especially as described by Abraham Maslow, that certain basic needs of the individual must be met before the person becomes interested in such topics as personal growth and self-actualization.

High-risk study Research strategy entailing the longitudinal study of persons who might be vulnerable to breakdown.

Histrionic personality disorder Characterized by overly reactive behavior of a histrionic, exhibitionistic type. Individuals with this disorder are egocentric and self-absorbed and usually have poor sexual adjustment.

Homeostasis Maintenance of equilibrium and constancy among the bodily processes.

Homosexual A person who prefers to engage in sexual activity with persons of his or her own sex and who continues this behavior over a long period of time.

Homosexual behavior Sexual activity between persons of the same sex.

Hopelessness depression A suggested subtype of depression in which attributional style is important in producing the depressed state.

Hormones Glandular secretions that function as coordinators of bodily reactions to external events and body growth and development.

Humanistic-existentialist perspective Idea that all individuals are unique and should be free to make their own choices about life directions. Emphasizes the creative freedom and potential of the individual.

Humanistic therapies Psychotherapies with special emphasis on human beings' fundamental desires to obtain self-respect and their needs for it. Carl Rogers' approach is an example.

Huntington's disease Uncommon degenerative disease occurring in families. Symptoms include jerking and twisting movement, facial grimaces, and psychotic symptoms. Also called Huntington's chorea.

Hyperactivity See *attention-deficit hyperactivity disorder*.

Hypertension High blood pressure, usually considered a psychophysiologic disorder.

Hypervigilance Tendency to constantly survey the environment for negative stimuli. A coping mechanism often used by avoidant personalities and by anxious individuals.

Hypnosis Altered state of consciousness induced by suggestion. Ranges from mild hypersuggestibility to deep, trancelike states.

Hypochondriasis (Hypochondria) Disorder in which a person is preoccupied by fear of disease and worries a great deal about his or her health without any realistic cause.

Hypomania A disorder characterized by unusual elevation in mood that is not as extreme as that found in mania.

Hypomanic episode A distinct period of elevated expansive or irritable mood and other manic behaviors that is not severe enough to greatly impair social or occupational functioning and does not require hospitalization.

Hypothalamus Part of the brain that lies below the thalamus. Controls various activities of the autonomic nervous system, including regulation of body temperature.

Hypothesis A statement of relationship or cause and effect stated in terms that allow a scientific test.

Hypothesis-testing experiment Evaluation of the correctness of an idea by experimental test.

Hypothetical construct Inferred intermediate mechanism; a concept conceived of as having properties of its own (e.g., a memory trace).

Hysteria Presence of a physical problem without any physical causes. A person with hysteria is called an *hysteric*.

Hysteric Term used by Charcot to describe an individual who complains of organic symptoms such as pain, blindness, or paralysis for which no organic cause can be found.

Id In psychoanalysis, that division of the psyche which is a repository of all instinctual impulses and repressed mental contents. Represents the true unconscious or the "deepest" part of the psyche.

Identification Feeling of association with another person or group such that an individual takes on the viewpoint and behavior of the other(s).

Idiot Term formerly used for a retarded individual whose intelligence fell in the lowest measurable range.

Imipramine One of the tricyclic drugs used in the treatment of some depressed individuals.

Immune system Body system that fights disease through inactivation of foreign substances by means of lymphocyte cells.

Implicit learning Learning that derives from observations of behavior that are analyzed and interpreted some time after they actually occurred.

Implosive therapy Behavior therapy technique based on the principle of extinction. Client is repeatedly presented with strong anxiety-pro-

voking stimuli until he or she no longer reacts in an anxious manner.

Impotence Failure of a male to attain or maintain a penile erection even when sexually excited.

Impulse control disorder A disorder in which the person seems unable to resist impulses (gambling, stealing, fire setting) that do not occur as part of any other disorder.

Impulse control disorder not classified elsewhere A disorder that clearly has the characteristics of impulse control but does not meet the criteria for any of the types specified.

Impulsive Characterized by a lack of forethought or planning.

Inauthentic behavior According to existential theorists, the determination of behavioral goals by others, not one's self.

Incest Sexual relations between close family members, such as brother and sister or parent and child.

Incidence A count of the number of new cases that begin during a certain period of time; used in epidemiology. Contrast with *prevalence data*.

Incompetent person Legal term used to describe individuals who are not able to understand the meaning of legal proceedings in which they are involved and who are unable to consult with an attorney in a way that might assist their defense.

Increased-stress theory Idea that the negative impact of the condition of poverty and crime make mental illness, especially schizophrenia, more likely because of the increased pressures of living. Contrast with *social selection theory*.

Independent variable Experimental factor (e.g., time of food deprivation) that is manipulated or altered in some manner while others are held constant.

Index case Term used in the study of genetics to indicate the individual with a disorder whose heredity is under study.

Indoleamine Type of neurotransmitter of the monoamine group—e.g., serotonin—appears especially closely related to mood.

Infantile sexuality View held by Sigmund Freud that children as well as adults have sexual feelings and experience erotic stimulation.

Inferential statistics Methods based on the laws of probability that are used to draw conclusions about relationships among variables studied.

Inflexibility Inability to change; in personality, those coping styles habit-

ually used even if they are unsuitable to a given situation.

Information processing A view of cognitive behavior that compares the human senses and brain function and behavior to a computer.

Informed consent Requirement that patients must be given adequate information about the benefits and risks of planned treatments before they agree to the procedures.

Inhibited sexual excitement A sexual disorder characterized by either low sexual desire or aversion to sexual activity. In men, this disorder means failure to achieve or maintain an erection sufficient to complete sexual intercourse.

Innate Characteristics acquired through general inheritance or the mutation of a gene or genes passed on from the parent.

Insanity Legal term connoting mental incompetence, inability to distinguish "right from wrong," and inability to care for oneself.

Insight Self-knowledge; understanding the significance and purpose of one's motives or behavior, including the ability to recognize inappropriateness and irrationality.

Intellectualization A defense mechanism in which a person separates the description or meaning of an event from its emotional impact.

Intelligence test Standardized test used to establish an intelligence-level rating by measuring an individual's ability in a variety of tasks including information, word meaning, concept formation, and various performance skills.

Intensive care partial hospitalization Part time hospitalization that is focused on short patient stays for acutely ill patients.

Interactional orientation (*in addiction*) The idea that both aspects of the person and of the situation are important in determining whether addiction will occur. People who may use drugs while they are in a long term stressful situation may not show signs of addiction such as withdrawal when they transfer to a less stressful environment in which the cues that accompanied drug use are absent.

Interactional view of behavior Viewpoint that directs attention to the joint effects or interactions of many of the variables emphasized by different theoretical viewpoints in producing abnormal behavior.

Internalizing disorders A group of childhood disorders that are characterized less by overt activity than by

cognitive activity consisting of worries or disturbing thoughts.

Interpersonal factors In therapy refers to the relationship between the therapist and the client as a consequence of the personalities of the two rather than as a result of the techniques the therapist uses.

Interpersonal psychotherapy A form of psychotherapy that focuses on increasing clients' social effectiveness and the extent that they feel cared about by others.

Intervening variable An inferred variable functionally connected with antecedents and consequences; such variables are abstractions and have no properties other than those defined by the empirical data.

Interview See *diagnostic interview; therapeutic interview.*

Intravenous injection The injection of a drug or chemical directly into the bloodstream by inserting a hollow needle into a vein.

Intoxication Mental disorder and the presence of maladaptive behavior due to the use and present effect on the body of some substance. The most common behavior changes are inattention and impaired thinking, judgment, emotional control, and motor activity.

Intrapsychic conflict Lack of acceptance of certain areas of thought or emotion that make it necessary for an individual to attempt to keep some material out of awareness.

In vivo exposure A technique used in cognitive therapy or desensitization in which the individual practices adaptive cognitions or relaxation behavior in the actual presence of the anxiety-producing object or situation.

Irrational thought Ideas and beliefs that are derived from emotional response rather than reasoning.

Isolation Defense mechanism by which inconsistent or contradictory attitudes and feelings are walled off from each other in consciousness. Similar to repression, except that in isolation the impulse or wish is consciously recognized, but is separated from present behavior; in repression, neither the wish nor its relation to action is recognized. Intellectualization is a special form of isolation.

Juvenile delinquency Violations of the law committed by adolescents (usually defined as persons 18 years of age or younger).

Kappa statistic A type of reliability index that corrects for chance agree-

ment to provide a true estimate of reliability.

Karyotype A microphotograph of an individual's chromosomes in a standard array.

Kaufman Assessment Battery for Children (K-ABC) An intelligence test for children that is based on ideas from cognitive psychology and neuropsychology to measure simultaneous and sequential processing abilities. Designed to be less culturally biased than conventional intelligence tests.

Kinsey Report First detailed statistical report that attempted to present the variations in human sexual behavior from a descriptive, scientific view.

Korsakoff's syndrome Chronic brain disorder precipitated by a vitamin deficiency stemming from alcoholism. Characterized by marked disorientation, amnesia, and falsification of memory.

Labeling Cognitive device by which a person classifies his or her own emotional responses as a way of controlling behavior, especially in stress-producing situations. Also, a way people are categorized by others, a way of stereotyping.

La Belle indifference Marked lack of concern about one's disability, occasionally seen in patients with conversion disorder.

Laceration Gross tear or rupture in tissue. Cerebral lacerations may occur through head injuries.

Latency period According to Freud, the period from age 5 until adolescence during which the child's sexual impulses are not a primary focus of his or her pleasure-seeking activities.

Learned helplessness Acquired belief in one's helplessness to deal with a situation or control one's environment. Concept has been applied to explain depression in humans.

Learning perspective Idea that what one experiences is the most important aspect of behavior, which is considered as a product of stimulus—response relationships. One group of learning theorists were called behaviorists.

Lesbianism The practice of homosexual behavior by women.

Librium (chlordiazepoxide) Tranquilizer often prescribed for anxiety problems.

Limbic system Part of the brain that controls visceral and bodily changes associated with emotion; also regulates drive-motivated behavior. Lower parts of the cerebrum.

Lithium (lithium carbonate) Chemical salt used in the treatment of bipolar disorder.

Live modeling Learning through direct observation of another person who performs the act or acts which are to be learned.

Locus, gene The characteristic position within a chromosome in which a particular gene pair are located.

Locus of control Personality characteristic described by Julian Rotter in which an individual believes either that he or she has the power to affect the outcome of situations (internal locus of control) or that he or she has little control over what happens (external locus of control).

Longitudinal study Research strategy based on observing and recording the behavior of people over periods of time. Involves obtaining measures on the same people either continuously or at specific or regular intervals.

LSD (Lysergic acid dimethylamide) Chemically produced synthetic hallucinogen with psychotomimetic properties.

Lunatic Term used in the past to describe the insane. The word *luna* (moon) refers to the old belief that those who were insane were moonstruck.

Lycanthropy Term for the magical change believed to overcome individuals and cause them to behave like wolves.

Lymphocyte A general term that includes several types of cells in the immune system that fight disease.

Magnetic resonance imaging (MRI) A type of scanning technique that uses the changing form of magnetic fields around the head to map the electrical activity in the brain.

Mainstreamed An educational policy in which children with physical and mental disabilities participate at least to some degree in regular school classes. Some special classes during the school day may be provided that are focused on their special learning difficulties.

Major depressive disorder or episode A severe depression characterized by dysphoric mood as well as poor appetite, sleep problems, feelings of restlessness or being slowed down, loss of pleasure, loss of energy, feelings of inability to concentrate or indecisiveness, recurrent thoughts of death or suicide attempts. These occur without mood-incongruent delusions or hallucinations and are not due to schizophrenia, paranoid disor-

der, organic mental disorder, or recent death of a loved one.

Maladaptive behavior Behavior that deals inadequately with a situation, especially one that is stressful.

Male limited Hereditary pattern that seems to be transmitted only from fathers and only to male offspring.

Malingering Behavior designed to get financial or other rewards by pretending to have some disorder. *Contrast with* factitious disorder.

Mania Euphoric, hyperactive state in which an individual's judgment is impaired.

Manic depressive psychosis See *bipolar disorder*.

Mantra See *meditation*.

MAO inhibitor See *Monoamine oxidase inhibitor*.

Marijuana Substance derived from the leaves or flowering tops of the cannabis plant. Smoking it leads to a dreamy state of altered consciousness in which ideas are disconnected, uncontrollable, and plentiful. Under the influence of marijuana, behavior is impulsive and mood is elevated.

Marital therapy A subtype of group therapy in which a couple meet together with a therapist in an attempt to improve the couple's interaction.

Markers Biological or behavioral characteristics that may make it possible to identify people who are vulnerable to certain disorders.

Masochism Deviation in which sexual pleasure is attained from pain inflicted on oneself, from being dominated, or from being mistreated.

Masochist One who practices masochism.

Masturbation Self-stimulation of the genitals for the purposes of deriving sexual pleasure.

Mediator A link (for example, between a stimulus and the resulting behavior).

Meditation The technique of relaxing through concentrating on a thought, sensation, or special word or mantra.

Medroxyprogesterone acetate (MPA) A chemical used to reduce the level of male sex hormone in the blood which is used experimentally for treating some of the paraphilias. Trade name Depo-provera.

Meninges Any of the membranes enclosing the brain or spinal cord in vertebrates.

Meningitis Inflammation of any or all of the meninges of the brain and spinal cord. Usually caused by a bacterial infection.

Mental age The age equivalent at which a person's intelligence behav-

ior places him or her. Contrasted to chronological age, the person's actual age as determined by birth date. The ratio between the two [(MA ÷ CA) × 100] was the original formulation of the intelligence quotient.

Mental retardation Intellectual functioning significantly below average. Generally defined as an intelligence test score of 70 or below together with a poor level of social functioning. The degree of retardation is further defined. Scores of 50 to 70 together with a poor level of social functioning are called mild retardation, 35 to 49 moderate, 20 to 34 severe, and below 20 profound retardation.

Mental-status examination An interview, sometimes supplemented with psychological and neurological tests, used to assess an individual's intellectual function and ability to interact appropriately with the environment.

Meta-analysis Technique used to combine the data from many studies in a meaningful way. Has been used to investigate the effects of psychotherapy on clients.

Metacognition A person's knowledge of his or her own cognitive processes and the products of these processes.

Methadone Synthetic chemical whose action is similar to that of morphine. Because its use allegedly does not lead to escalation of dosage, it is prescribed by some authorities as a treatment for heroin addiction.

Methadone maintenance Use of methadone as a substitute for heroin. Methadone prevents withdrawal and suppresses the desire for heroin, although methadone also has undesirable side effects.

Method factors Variations in results that are caused by the way a study was conducted, the type of questionnaire used, or other factors not associated with a real difference in what has been measured.

Methylphenidate Stimulant drug (e.g., Ritalin) sometimes used in the treatment of hyperactivity.

Migraine headache A severe headache, often on one side only, accompanied by nausea and dilation of the cranial artery. These headaches are usually preceded by a sensory, motor, or mood disturbance called an aura.

Mileau-limited Term for a hereditary pattern in which a disorder seems to appear only under certain environmental conditions.

Mileau therapy Effort to provide a totally therapeutic environment within an institution by enlisting the efforts of all staff members as providers of some form of therapeutic contact.

Mind Human consciousness as shown in thought, perception, and memory. Reflects the artificial dichotomy often made between mind and body.

Minnesota Multiphasic Personality Inventory (MMPI) Self-report personality questionnaire designed to facilitate psychiatric diagnosis.

M'Naghten rule Legal precedent in English law, originating in 1843, which provides for acquittal if an accused person is found to be not responsible for the crime—that is, if he or she could not distinguish between "right and wrong." The rule did not take into account that a person might be held to be insane even though he or she knew the difference between right and wrong.

Modeling Behavior learned or modified as a result of observing the behavior of others. Learner does not have to make the observed response him- or herself, or be reinforced for making it, to learn the new behavior. Term used interchangeably with observational learning. See also, *covert, live,* and *symbolic modeling.*

Monoamine neurotransmitter Type of neurotransmitter with a distinctive single amino acid (NH_2) in its molecular structure. There are two types of monoamines: catecholamines and indoleamines.

Monoamine oxidase (MAO) Enzyme in the neuron receptors that inactivates the various amines, including the catecholamines.

Monoamine oxidase (MAO) inhibitor One of a group of drugs used to treat depression. Works by preventing the degrading of monoamines and thus allowing more norepinephrine and serotonin to collect at the receptor sites.

Monogenic (single-gene) theory Refers to theory of inheritance in which a gene at one particular locus (e.g., one site on a chromosome) is sufficient to produce an inherited characteristic.

Monozygotic twins Identical twins developed from one fertilized egg.

Mood disorder One of a group of disorders primarily affecting emotional tone. Can be depression, manic excitement, or both. May be episodic or chronic.

Moral treatment Technique of treating mental-hospital patients which prevailed in the nineteenth century. Emphasized removal of restraints, allowing religious conviction, and ensuring humanitarian treatment.

Morphine Principle derivative of opium, which has been used extensively to relieve pain.

Mosaicism The condition in which all a person's cells do not have the same chromosome count as a result of an error in cell division in the fertilized egg.

Multiaxial classification system System that rates an individual separately on a number of different criteria or axes. The DSM system is an example.

Multiaxial diagnostic system A multiaxial classification system developed to diagnose disordered behavior.

Multifactorial polygenic model Theory that a number of genes from a variety of loci may combine to produce a particular characteristic or disorder.

Multi-infarct dementia Intellectual deficit resulting from a series of minor strokes that occur over a period of time.

Multiple personality Rare form of dissociative disorder characterized by development and existence of two or more relatively independent and co-existing personality systems within the same individual.

Munchausen syndrome A factitious disorder in which the person pretends to have a particular disorder in order to get medical treatment. Involves faking of symptoms, and often self-injury.

Muscle contraction headache See *tension headache.*

Mutant A cell in which the hereditary material has been altered. This mutation may be spontaneous (occurring naturally) or induced by internal factors such as radiation and certain chemicals.

Mutation Sudden change in the composition of a gene, which usually causes abnormal characteristics in the progeny.

Myocardial infarction Tissue damage to the heart muscle from a drastic decrease in the amount of blood that reaches the heart; commonly called a heart attack.

Naloxone A drug that blocks the pain relieving effects of endorphins.

Naltrexone A drug that prevents readdiction to heroin and other opioids by blocking opioid receptors.

Narcissism Term for self-love or self-absorption derived from the Greek

myth about Narcissus who fell in love with what he thought was a water nymph but was in reality his own reflection in a pond.

Narcissistic personality disorder Characterized by a sense of self-importance and a preoccupation with fantasies of unlimited success. Individuals are preoccupied with how well they are doing and how well others think of them. Disorder is often accompanied by depressed mood.

Narcotics Legal term for addicting drugs, the most common of which are the opiates, derived from the Oriental poppy.

Narrow criteria In schizophrenia, research criteria that exclude those who are clearly have experienced a schizophrenic process but who have not had the symptoms for an extended period of time and who are presumed to have a possible positive outcome. These criteria may make outcome prediction better but may not add to a complete understanding of the schizophrenic process.

Natural disaster Overwhelming event caused by the forces of nature rather than human intervention—for example, a tornado, earthquake, or flood.

Natural fool Old term for a retarded person. It means one who is born deficient in judgment.

Negative symptoms, in schizophrenia Symptoms characterized by behavior deficits such as flattened affect, poverty of speech and apathy. Sometimes called Type II schizophrenia.

Negative transference Feelings of hostility a client carries over from earlier relationships into his or her relationship with a therapist.

Neoanalyst Theorist who agrees with a revised version of Freud's concepts.

Neo-Freudian Pertaining to former followers of Freud who departed in several major doctrinal ways from orthodox psychoanalysis. Whereas ego psychologists view themselves as psychoanalysts, neo-Freudians do not. Prominent among the neo-Freudians are Adler, Jung, and Sullivan. Their writings emphasize the social and cultural determinants of behavior.

Neuroleptic drugs Name for a group of psychoactive drugs that are used to treat schizophrenic disorders. These reduce psychotic symptoms but may have side effects resembling neurological disorders.

Neurologist Specialist in the diagnosis and treatment of disorders of the nervous system.

Neuron Individual nerve cell.

Neuropsychology Branch of psychology dealing with brain-behavior relationships.

Neuroscience An interdisciplinary field of science that is focused on understanding the relationship between brain structure and function and behavior, affect, and cognitions.

Neurosis Older term for what are now called *anxiety disorders*.

Neurotic depression Older term for *dysthymic disorder*.

Neurotransmitter Chemical product of the nervous system that makes possible the movement of the nerve impulse across the synapse.

Nicotine Volatile psychoactive substance that is the chief active chemical in tobacco.

Nocturnal penile tumescence (NPT) Enlargement and erection of the penis that occurs during rapid-eye-movement sleep.

Non compos mentis Latin term meaning not of sound mind and therefore not legally responsible.

Non-shared environment Term used in the study of twins or siblings to contrast the environmental effects that both experience in the family with those that differ because of unique events, personal characteristics, or experiences or relationships outside the family.

Nontranssexual gender identity disorder Persistent discomfort about one's assigned sex; frequently involves cross dressing or fantasies about cross dressing. Differs from transsexualism in that there is no persistent preoccupation to acquire the primary and secondary sexual characteristics of the other sex.

Norepinephrine Hormone also called *noradrenalin,* produced by the adrenal medulla. One of the catecholamine group.

NPT See *nocturnal penile tumescence.*

Object relations The psychoanalytic approach that focuses attention on the emotional bonds between persons rather than on a person's view of him or herself.

Observational research A method in which no variables are manipulated and relationships are studied as they naturally occur. Contrast with *experimental method.*

Obsessive behavior Characterized by preoccupation with a particular type of thought that keeps occurring repetitively.

Obsessive-compulsive behavior Behavior that combines ritualistic behavior and compulsive thinking.

Obsessive-compulsive disorder Characterized by recurrent obsessions and/or compulsions, often accompanied by depression or anxiety.

Obsessive-compulsive disorder of childhood Disorders that occur in children that are similar in symptoms to adult obsessive-compulsive disorders. This disorder is often associated with long-term problems.

Obsessive-compulsive personality disorder Distinguished by lack of ability to express warmth, a stiff and formal way of relating to others, and extreme perfectionism that leads an individual to focus on details rather than on the whole picture.

Occipital lobe Major division of either cerebral hemisphere located in the dorsal area.

Occupational activities Diagnosed on axis V of DSM. This information provides an assessment of how well a person is currently functioning.

Operant conditioning Form of conditioning in which a desired response occurs and is subsequently reinforced to increase its probability of more frequent occurrence; also called *instrumental conditioning.*

Operant response Response originally occurring rarely that has been increased in frequency through reinforcement.

Opiate Natural or synthetic substance that is similar in action to morphine or other derivatives of the opium poppy.

Opioid Drug with a morphine-like action. Can be either a natural or synthetic substance.

Oppositional defiant disorder Although less serious than conduct disorder, this disorder begins by age eight and is characterized by negative behaviors and unwillingness to accept the authority of others. Often develops into conduct or mood disorder.

Oral dependent Psychodynamic term to describe individuals who secure a major part of their psychological gratification from such activities as eating, drinking, and smoking, and who may show dependent personality characteristics.

Oral stage First developmental stage of infancy, during which pleasure is derived from lip and mouth contact with need-fulfilling objects (e.g., breast).

Organic affective syndrome Abnormal changes in mood thought to

be the result of changes in brain metabolism or toxic conditions.

Organic anxiety syndrome Panic attacks or generalized anxiety thought to be causally related to some specific organic factor.

Organic brain syndrome Group of symptoms characteristic of acute and chronic brain disorders.

Organic defect theory Idea that a particular bodily organ that is working improperly is the cause of maladaptive behavior.

Organic delusional syndrome Delusional thinking that occurs as the result of some organic condition, often associated with abuse of a variety of substances including amphetamines, cannabis, and hallucinogens.

Organic hallucinosis Hallucinations caused by some organic factor. Often the result of use of hallucinogenic drugs or large quantities of alcohol.

Organic mental disorder Brain dysfunction based on either aging or the ingestion of substances that affect brain activity. May be temporary or permanent.

Organic personality syndrome Diagnosis used when major personality changes occur that are believed to be the result of some change in or injury to brain tissue.

Organismic point of view Pertaining to the organism as a whole rather than to particular parts. Behavior is considered an interrelated and interactive function of the integrated organism.

Organ-susceptibility hypothesis Idea that emotional stress might cause a psychophysiological problem in a bodily organ in a particular individual because that organ had some inherent weakness.

Orgasm Third stage of sexual response, which involves rhythmic muscular contractions and high physical arousal. In the male ejaculation of semen takes place during this stage.

Orienting response Measurable psychophysiological changes that come about when a person notices an environmental stimulus and prepares to receive some information from it.

Overanxious disorder A childhood disorder in which excessive or unrealistic worry is observed over at least a 6-month period.

Overgeneralization According to Aaron Beck, characteristic way of thinking found in some depressed individuals. Tendency to exaggerate

the meaning of an event into a general principle.

Panic disorder Type of anxiety disorder characterized by recurring panic or anxiety attacks and extreme nervousness not necessarily related to exposure to threatening situations.

Paradigm A model or example.

Paradoxical intention Therapeutic technique in which the client is instructed to perform behaviors that seem to be counter to the therapeutic goal. For instance, someone who is afraid of crowds may be instructed to go into a crowd and concentrate on feeling as fearful as possible.

Paranoid disorder Disorder characterized by the persistence of delusions that are usually well organized; does not include prominent hallucinations, incoherent speech, thought derailment, or many of the delusions associated with schizophrenia.

Paranoid personality disorder Personality disorder similar in some ways to schizoid personality disorder, but notable for extreme sensitivity in interpersonal relationships; suspicious, jealous, and stubborn behavior; and a tendency to use the defense mechanism of projection.

Paranoid schizophrenia Type of schizophrenia characterized by persistent delusions, often either grandiose or accusatory.

Paraphilia Sexual deviation that involves choice of inappropriate sex partners or inappropriate goals for the sex act. Pedophilia, sadism, and voyeurism are examples.

Paraprofessional Term used to describe workers who have received certain basic training that enables them to perform tasks formerly performed by professional workers. Paraprofessionals often come from the same communities and educational backgrounds as the people whom they treat or aid.

Parasuicide Term used to describe any act that does not end in death in which a person deliberately causes self-injury or takes a drug overdose with the apparent intention of suicide.

Parens patriae Legal doctrine that gives the state power to act in what it believes to be the best interest of an incapacitated adult or a minor.

Parental affective style A measure of negative feelings expressed by family members as the family discusses upsetting problems together. Compare with *expressed emotion*.

Paresis Chronic and progressively deteriorating brain condition caused

by syphilitic infection and characterized by loss of cognitive and motor functions, speech disorder, and eventual death.

Parietal lobe Middle division of each cerebral hemisphere of the brain, behind the central sulcus, above the fissure of Sylvius, and in front of the parieto-occipital fissure.

Parkinson's disease Chronic and progressive neurological disorder characterized by motor tremor, rigidity, loss of vocal power, and psychotic symptoms. Believed to be caused by an acquired defect in brain metabolism.

Partial hospitalization Use of either day, night, or weekend hospital care for patients who do not need 24-hour care. Designed particularly to aid transition back to the community. Also used to prevent complete hospitalization if the family can provide partial care, for instance, outside of their own working hours.

Participant modeling Therapeutic procedure in which the response is first demonstrated for the client, who then produces the same response with suggestions from the therapist.

Passive–aggressive personality disorder Usually characterized by aggressive behavior exhibited in passive ways (e.g., pouting). Three types are often distinguished: (1) passive-aggressive type: hostility and aggression expressed by passive means such as obstructionism, stubbornness, inefficiency, and procrastination; (2) aggressive type: hostility and aggressiveness expressed directly through temper tantrums, destructive behavior, argumentativeness, and negativism; and (3) passive-dependent type: characterized by overdependency, helplessness, indecisiveness, and the childlike tendency to cling to others. Reactions are grouped together on the basis that they seem to represent different reactions to common-core conflicts over dependency and aggression.

Pathology Disease or abnormal physical condition.

PCP (phencyclidine) Hallucinogenic drug popularly known as "angel dust."

Pedophilia Sexual deviation in which an adult desires or engages in sexual relations with a child. May be either homosexual or heterosexual in nature.

Pedophile, fixated A person who begins to display pedophilia during adolescence and usually has no other important sexual relationships.

Pedophile, regressed A person who begins pedophilic behavior only after some negative life events.

Pellagra Chronic disease caused by niacin deficiency. Symptoms include skin eruptions, digestive disturbances, and disturbances of the nervous system which may cause psychoticlike behavior.

Penetrance Percentage of cases in which a particular trait or characteristic, derived from a specific gene, will manifest itself in subsequent organisms of the species.

Pepsinogen Substance found in the gastric system that is converted to a digestive enzyme by hydrochloric acid in the digestive system. Individuals with high natural pepsinogen levels are prone to develop ulcers under stressful conditions.

Peptide A compound containing two or more amino acids linked together in a specific chemical fashion.

Performance anxiety (sexual) High degree of concern in males about the ability to maintain an erection until orgasm. The anxiety has a negative effect on sexual performance.

Performance IQ One of the two subscores of the Wechsler intelligence test series. Reflects ability to solve puzzles, copy designs, and perform other similar tasks.

Peripheral nervous system System that includes all outlying nerve structures not included in the central nervous system.

Personal constructs A term originated by George Kelly for categories used by someone about his or her personal effectiveness in acting in specific or general types of situations.

Personality Particular constellation of attributes that defines one's individuality.

Personality disorder Deeply ingrained, inflexible, maladaptive patterns of thought and behavior which persist throughout a person's life.

Personality inventories Paper-and-pencil tests in which the person describes him- or herself by answering a series of true-false questions or by rating a series of self-descriptive phases. Most personality inventories yield several scores, each of which is intended to describe an aspect of personality.

Personal maladaptation Perception by an individual of personal dissatisfactions and concerns that interfere with happiness but not significantly with social adjustment or work achievement.

Pervasive developmental disorder A life-long disorder in which the quality of the person's social interactions, communication skills, and ability to engage in imaginative activities and other cognitive tasks is impaired. Autistic disorder is one subtype of this disorder that has been defined so far.

Petit mal Mild form of epilepsy which involves partial alterations of consciousness.

PET scan See *positron emission tomography*.

Phallic stage Stage of psychosexual development during which a child begins to perceive his or her body as a source of gratification. Feelings of narcissism are heightened during this period.

Phenobarbitol Barbiturate sometimes used as a sedative and in the control of epileptic seizure activity.

Phenothiazine One of a family of antipsychotic drugs.

Phenylketonuria (PKU) Form of mental retardation caused by a metabolic deficiency.

Phobia Excessive or inappropriate fear of some particular object or situation which is not in fact dangerous.

Phobic disorder Type of anxiety disorder mainly characterized by irrational and highly specific fears (for example, of dirt, water, high places).

Phototherapy The use of exposure to very bright light for several hours a day as a treatment for seasonal depression.

Phrenology Obsolete theory that different psychological behaviors were related to different parts of the brain and that these could be assessed by touching the surface of the skull.

Physical disorder Term used to refer to a medical as opposed to a psychological problem. Included in the DSM system on axis IV.

Physiognomy The art of judging human character or personality from facial features.

Pica Repeated eating of nonnutritive substances such as paint, clay, animal droppings, or laundry starch at a time when there is no evidence of hunger, malnutrition, or aversion.

Pick's disease Type of progressive dementia caused by atrophy of the cerebral cortex.

Placebo Inactive or inert substance that is presented as effective remedy for some problem in order to determine what role suggestibility plays in symptom change.

Placebo effect Changes in behavior as a result of the expectancy that a placebo, or inactive substance, is an active or "real" drug; type of suggestion effect.

Plaque Abnormal structure found in nerve cells of individuals who have Alzheimer's disease.

Plateau stage Second stage of sexual response, which includes increases in heart rate and muscle tension as well as swelling of genital tissue.

Play therapy Treatment approach used with children; based on the assumption that young children can express thoughts and fantasies more directly in play than through verbal means.

Pleasure principle Psychoanalytic term for the regulatory mechanism for mental life that functions to reduce tension and gain gratification. Principle that governs the functioning of the id to obtain gratification without regard to reality considerations.

Polygenic model Theory in genetics that several genes at different loci must interact to produce a particular inherited characteristic.

Polygraph Instrument that measures emotional responses through physiological reactions, such as blood pressure and galvanic skin response. Commonly called a *lie detector*.

Population genetics Study of the ways genes are distributed in a population through the mating of individuals.

Positive reinforcer See *reinforcer*.

Positive symptoms, in schizophrenia Generally, symptoms that show behavioral excesses: hallucinations, delusions, bizarre behavior, and so forth. Sometimes called Type I schizophrenia.

Positive transference Carrying over of positive feelings about other relationships onto the therapist-client relationship.

Positron emission tomography (PET) Technique for studying the dynamic chemical activity of the brain by using a scanning device that produces a series of cross-section images of the brain.

Posttraumatic psychosis Psychotic symptoms that appear suddenly after an injury to the brain or a stressful life event.

Posttraumatic stress disorder (PTSD) Development of symptoms in response to events of such severity that most people would be stressed by them. Symptoms often include a feeling of numbness in response or

psychological reexperiencing of the event in thoughts, dreams, or nightmares.

Postvention A therapeutic intervention in which survivors are given supportive treatment.

Poverty of content A characteristic of some schizophrenic speech in which little information is transmitted through speaking because of factors such as vagueness of meaning, repetition of phrases, or inappropriate degree of abstraction of the thoughts expressed.

Preconscious Thoughts that are not held in a person's mind at a particular time but which can easily be brought into awareness.

Premature ejaculation Inability of the male to inhibit ejaculation long enough for his female partner to experience orgasm.

Prematurity Before the expected time. In referring to infants, birth before the completion of the usual gestation period. Prematurity is a risk factor for psychological as well as physical difficulties later in development.

Premorbid adjustment Achievement level and adjustment to interpersonal activities shown by an individual earlier in life before a disorder becomes apparent.

Presenile dementia See *dementia*.

Prevalence Information concerning the number of cases of a particular disorder that are ongoing at any particular time. Contrast with *incidence data*.

Primary appraisal First stage of assessing the meaning of a situation. In this stage the situation is interpreted as threatening or harmless. In the following stage, secondary appraisal, the individual decides how to deal with the situation.

Primary classification In the DSM system, the problem diagnosed on axis I.

Primary degenerative dementia Dementia which is the specific result of a disease process rather than an additional symptom resulting from some other disorder.

Primary prevention Efforts at preventing the development of maladaptation by removing factors that might cause it to develop.

Primary process thinking Primary cognitive mode, characteristic of infants and children, that is not based on rules of organization or logic. The presence of primary process thinking, free association in its purest form, is characteristic of the id. Primary pro-

cess thought is illogical, is entirely pleasure oriented, has no sense of time or order, and does not discriminate between reality and fantasy. Compare with *secondary process thinking*.

Primitive emotion node A hypothetical memory unit that organizes memories related to a particular mood.

Problem drinking Term for the pattern of alcohol abuse that does not include alcohol dependence or physiological addiction.

Process research In psychotherapy research, the attempt to understand what happens during the course of psychotherapy in contrast to interest only in the desirability of the outcome.

Prognosis Forecast; probable course and outcome of a disorder.

Projection Defense mechanism that involves attributing to others the undesirable characteristics or impulses which belong to but are not acceptable to oneself.

Projective technique Ambiguous stimulus materials that elicit subjective responses of an associative or fantasy nature. So named because an individual is believed to "project" aspects of his or her personality into the task. Tasks may include inkblot interpretation (Rorschach Test), and various associative completion techniques (word association, incomplete sentences).

Prototypal approach The use of a checklist in making a diagnostic decision. If more than a predetermined number of characteristics are found, the diagnosis is made. As a result people with the same diagnosis may have different sets of characteristics.

Psilocybin One of the two psychoactive substances isolated from the psilocybin mushroom.

Psychedelic drug A drug that is able to alter sensory perceptions.

Psychiatric nurse A registered nurse who has taken specialized training on the care of those with mental illness.

Psychiatric social work Field of social work in which the professional specializes in helping those with maladaptive behaviors in a clinical, usually medical, setting.

Psychiatric social worker A person with a graduate degree in social work and specialized training in treating and practically assisting both patients with behavioral problems and their families.

Psychiatrist Physician with postgraduate training in the diagnosis

and treatment of emotional disorders.

Psychic determinism Principle of causality, one of the basic assumptions of psychoanalysis, which states that all events, overt and covert, are determined by prior and often multiple mental events.

Psychoactive drug Term including several types of drugs that may reduce maladaptive behavior. Includes antipsychotic, antianxiety, and antidepressant drugs.

Psychoactive substance A chemical that affects a person's thoughts, emotions, and behavior.

Psychoactive substance-induced organic mental disorder Organic changes that occur as a result of the use of psychoactive substances.

Psychoactive substance use disorders Behavioral or cognitive problems that are related to the use of some substance that affects the emotions, cognitions, and behavior such as alcohol, marijuana, and cocaine.

Psychoanalysis Term has three meanings: (1) theory of psychology and psychopathology developed by Freud from his clinical experiences with patients; (2) procedure for investigating the mental life, conflicts, and coping processes, which employs the techniques of free association, dream analysis, and interpretation of transference and resistance phenomena; and (3) form of therapy that uses the psychoanalytic procedure and the theories of personality and psychopathology just described.

Psychodrama Method of group therapy in which individuals both act out their emotional responses in situations they find difficult and also practice new, constructive roles.

Psychodynamic perspective Point of view that emphasizes thoughts and emotions as the most important determiners of behavior. Basic ideas come from the work of Sigmund Freud.

Psychodynamic therapy A therapeutic approach based on the psychodynamic perspective originating in the theories of Freud, but not limited to psychoanalysis.

Psychogenic Adjective referring to symptoms for which an organic cause cannot be specified.

Psychogenic amnesia Disturbance in the ability to recall important personal information in the absence of an organic disorder and without the assumption of a new identity such as that found in a psychogenic fugue.

Psychogenic fugue See *fugue state*.

Psychogenic pain disorder Characterized by severe pain that does not have an identifiable physical cause.

Psychoimmunology Study of the relationship between changes in immune system functioning and psychological events.

Psychological dependence Habit or need that requires continued or repeated administration of a drug to produce pleasure or to avoid conflict.

Psychological factors affecting physical condition Another term used for psychophysiological disorders or psychosomatic disorders.

Psychological functioning Ratings of both current functioning and highest level of functioning achieved in the past are recorded on axis V of the DSM. This information helps to determine how handicapped the person currently is by the disorder as well as the potential for change.

Psychological numbing Reduced capacity for emotion, and symptoms of apathy, withdrawal, and depression. These are likely to occur after a disaster.

Psychological perspective View that maladaptive behavior is caused by problems of perception, cognition, or emotion rather than by biological causes.

Psychological tests Procedures to measure in a standardized way some aspect of behavior such as intelligence or personality characteristics.

Psychology of personal constructs The approach of George Kelly, who was interested in helping his clients understand the unique way in which they viewed themselves and other people and also to see that their behavior was designed to fill certain roles. Kelly urged his clients to try out new roles rather than be stuck in nonadaptive ways of interacting.

Psychometric Refers to measures of psychological functioning.

Psychomotor Term used to describe muscular action resulting from prior mental activity, especially conscious mental activity.

Psychomotor epilepsy Trancelike state with recurring episodes of confusion during which repetitive and semiautomatic muscle movements occur. Often accompanied by confusion and visual hallucinations.

Psychoneuroimmunology A field of scientific specialization devoted to an understanding of the relationships among behavior, neural activity, and the immune system.

Psychopath Term used by Hervey Cleckley to describe antisocial individuals who met a certain set of characteristics including charm, lack of anxiety or guilt, poor judgment, and failure to learn from experience.

Psychopharmacology Study of the effects of drugs on psychological functioning and behavior.

Psychophysiological assessment Measurement of various body functions such as blood pressure, heart rate, breathing, and galvanic skin response in an attempt to understand feelings and emotions. One commercial use is the polygraph or lie detector.

Psychophysiological (psychosomatic) disorder Physical pathology and actual tissue damage that results from continued emotional mobilization of the body during periods of sustained stress.

Psychophysiology of behavior Study of the relationship between observed behavior and the functions of the central and peripheral nervous systems.

Psychosexual disorder Deviant sexual thoughts and/or behavior that are either personally anxiety-provoking, or are injurious to others.

Psychosexual stage One of several developmental stages of life as defined by Sigmund Freud. These differ in terms of the source of primary gratification and include oral, anal, phallic, and genital stages.

Psychosis (plural: psychoses) Disorder that includes any of the following: delusions, hallucinations, incoherence, repeated derailment of thought, marked poverty of thought content, marked illogicality, and grossly disorganized or catatonic behavior.

Psychosis, atypical A disorder in which there are psychotic symptoms (hallucinations, delusions, etc.) but the symptom pattern does not meet the criteria for any of the nonorganic psychotic disorders.

Psychosocial disadvantage Growing up in an intellectually, culturally, and financially impoverished environment.

Psychosocial stressor Feeling of stress arising from relationships with other people in the environment.

Psychosomatic disorder See *psychophysiological disorder*.

Psychosomatic hypothesis Idea popular in the 1930s and 1940s that physical symptoms can be caused by an inability to express strong emotions.

Psychotherapy General term referring to psychological, verbal, and expressive techniques used in treating maladaptive behavior. The client works on resolving inner conflicts and modifying his or her behavior by means of verbal interchanges with the therapist. Insight into feelings and behavior is the goal of most psychotherapy.

Psychotic An adjective indicating the presence of psychosis.

Psychotic disorder A disorder in which there is gross impairment in reality testing and the creation of a new reality. Psychotic disorders include schizophrenia, delusional disorders, some organic mental disorder, and some mood disorders.

Psychotic disorder not classified elsewhere Disorders in which psychosis is clearly present but which do not fit the criteria for any of the specific types of psychosis.

Punishment Aversive stimulus given as a result of an undesired behavior in an attempt to suppress that behavior in the future.

Rape Sexual intercourse accomplished by force and without the partner's consent.

Rape-relief center Organization, often composed in part of volunteers, designed to provide information about medical and legal services for those who have been raped and also to offer psychological support for the victims.

Rating scale Type of test in which a person can indicate on a scale the degree of his or her agreement with each item.

Rational approach Idea that only the use of reason and not experimental evidence or observation is the prime source of truth.

Rational-emotive therapy Therapy developed by Albert Ellis to modify unrealistic and illogical thought.

Rational thinking Based on reasoning and logic, not on observation or experimental evidence.

Reaction formation Defense mechanism that enables the individual to express an unacceptable impulse by transforming it into its opposite.

Recessive gene Member of a gene pair which determines the characteristic trait or appearance of the individual only if the other member of the pair matches it. Compare to *dominant gene*.

Recognition A measure of information retention in which the subject is asked to select which of several stim-

ulus items have been presented previously.

Refractory period (sexual) In males, the period after orgasm when no additional arousal can occur. Females may or may not have a refractory period.

Regress To go backward or return to an earlier level of functioning. Interpreted in psychoanalytic theory as a defense mechanism. See *regression*.

Regression Defense mechanism characterized by a return to earlier and more primitive modes of responding. Through regression, the ego returns to an earlier developmental phase of functioning which had met with some success.

Rehabilitation model A type of full time or day hospital in which attention is given to improving social and vocational functioning. The treatment is usually of limited length but may last longer than acute care.

Reinforcement Any event (stimulus) which, if contingent upon response by an organism, changes the probability that the response will be made again. Reinforcements may be positive (reward) or negative (aversive) and may be presented according to a prescribed schedule (continuous, intermittent). May also be primary (drive reducing—e.g., food) or secondary (derived from prior association with a primary reinforcer—e.g., money, praise).

Reinforcer A consequence of behavior that makes it more likely the behavior will occur again. A *positive reinforcer* achieves this result by provoking a reward or pleasure. A *negative reinforcer* is a stimulus that ceases when the desired behavior is performed. See also *punishment*.

Relapse prevention In treatment of alcohol problems from a cognitive viewpoint, the emphasis on identifying problem situations and helping the client to identify coping devices that may give him or her a feeling of control over such situations.

Relational assessment Testing instruments to assess a person's key social relationships.

Relaxation training Series of specified exercises that the client learns to perform in order to remove a tension response that may be characteristic in certain situations.

Reliability The tendency of a measure or procedure to produce the same results when administered on two different occasions. Also refers to the internal homogeneity of a multiple-item test.

Remission Cessation of the symptoms of a disorder. Implies that the basic problem may still exist.

REM sleep Stage of sleep characterized by rapid eye movements and a characteristic brain-wave pattern. Reducing the amount of REM sleep can help decrease some types of depressive symptoms.

Repression Psychoanalytic defense mechanism that involves a "stopping-thinking" or not-being-able-to-remember response. Repression actively forces traumatic events, intolerable and dangerous impulses, and other undesirable mental affects out of consciousness into the less-accessible realm of the unconscious.

Resolution phase The period after sexual orgasm in which the arousal decreases and the body's physiological status returns to normal.

Retardation Level of intellectual functioning that is significantly below average and is accompanied by an inability to behave adaptively in society because of this lack of cognitive ability.

Retarded ejaculation Inhibition of the sexual response of males that results in an inability to eject semen even when sexually excited.

Rheumatoid arthritis Chronic joint disease with inflammation caused by immune-system activity.

Risk factor A personal characteristic that is correlated with some disorder. Indicates an increased probability that the person will develop a particular type of problem or illness. People with high risk factors are said to be especially vulnerable to a particular disorder.

Ritalin See *methylphenidate*.

Ritualistic behavior Behavior that follows a series of prescribed actions that are repeated even though they may be maladaptive. Thought to be a way of reducing anxiety.

Role playing In psychotherapy, a technique that requires an individual to enact a social role other than his or her own, or to try out new roles. In sociology, an individual's assumption of the role expected of him or her in a particular type of situation.

Rorschach inkblots Projective test developed by Hermann Rorschach in which the individual is shown a series of ambiguous inkblots and asked to describe what is seen in them.

Rubella virus Virus which, if present in a pregnant woman, particularly during the first 3 months of pregnancy, can cause retardation and other congenital disorders in her child; commonly called *German measles*.

Rumination disorder of infancy Disorder in which partially digested food is brought up into the infant's mouth without nausea or vomiting. The infant loses weight or fails to gain weight after a period of normal functioning.

Saccadic eye movement Quick jerks of the eye interspersed with steady fixations that are under voluntary control.

SAD See *seasonal affective disorder*.

Sadism Sexual deviation in which sexual gratification is obtained through inflicting physical pain on other people.

Sadist One who practices sadism.

Sadistic personality disorder A longstanding behavioral pattern in which the person seems to enjoy inflicting psychological or physiological suffering on other people or on animals. The disorder differs from sexual sadism because the sadistic behavior is not carried out for sexual arousal.

Schedule A plan of what will happen and the time it is to occur.

Schemata The plural of schema. Schemata are the expectations people have as to the way others behave and the appropriate behaviors for various types of situations. A person's schemata are important in addition to what actually occurred in determining the way that he or she will respond to particular types of situations.

Schizoaffective disorder Separate category from either schizophrenia or affective disorders for individuals who show depressive or manic symptoms as well as those of thought disorder.

Schizoid personality disorder Classification used for withdrawn individuals who are not disturbed by their lack of social relationships. These people have flat emotional responses and often seem cold and detached.

Schizophrenia See *schizophrenic disorder*.

Schizophrenia, residual type A stage of schizophrenic disorder in which psychotic features, especially hallucinations or delusions, are no longer prominent although eccentric behavior, illogical thinking, social withdrawal, and so forth continue to be observed.

Schizophrenia in remission A lessening or disappearance of symptoms that had been apparent when the

person was diagnosed as having a schizophrenic disorder. The term reflects the view that schizophrenia is a life-long disease for which there is no cure, only the possibility of at least temporarily reduced symptoms.

Schizophrenic disorders Group of disorders that always involves at least one of the following at some time: delusions, hallucinations, or certain characteristics of thought disorder.

Schizophrenic spectrum disorder One of a group of disorders including schizotypal and paranoid personality disorders, and sometimes schizoaffective disorder, atypical psychosis, and paranoid disorder, which are thought by some researchers to be produced by the same genetic factors as schizophrenia. Used as an explanation for the fact that the incidence of narrowly defined schizophrenia alone is less than would be expected by monogenetic theory.

Schizotypal personality disorder Shows some of the symptoms of schizophrenia, but not in as extreme a form. People with this disorder include those formerly diagnosed as having simple schizophrenia. Differs from schizoid personality disorder in that it includes eccentricities of communication and behavior not seen in that group.

Seasonal affective disorder (SAD) A form of affective disorder in which depression is more likely to occur in winter when the hours of natural light are limited and mania is more likely to occur in spring and summer when the number of hours of daylight are at a maximum. Depression of this type is often treated with phototherapy (the use of bright lighting).

Secondary appraisal Second stage of appraisal of a situation in which an individual considers the kind of action necessary and whether he or she has the skills to deal with the situation.

Secondary prevention Efforts directed toward detecting early signs or symptoms to prevent a more serious condition.

Secondary process thinking Psychoanalytic concept referring to organized, logical, and reality-oriented adult thinking. Whereas primary process thinking is characteristic of the id and is based on the pleasure principle, secondary process thought is an ego function based on the reality principle.

Second generation antidepressants A group of more recently developed antidepressants that do not have the three-ring chemical structure of the tricyclic antidepressants.

Second rank symptoms Those symptoms classified by Schneider as typical of schizophrenia but which are also found in other psychotic disorders.

Self-actualization Synonymous with self-fulfillment. Process by which the development of one's potentials and abilities is achieved.

Self-defeating personality disorder A longstanding behavioral pattern in which a person seeks out situations or relationships that seem bound to end negatively. Such a person avoids situations that are potentially pleasureful or where the outcome may be successful.

Self-determination Viewpoint of existential theorists that individuals have control of their own lives through the choices they make.

Self-help group A group of people with the same problem who meet together to share experiences and ways to handle situations in an attempt to help themselves improve their own ability to cope with these problems.

Self-monitoring Keeping detailed records of one's behavior.

Self-observations Records kept by the client or patient that detail the frequency of certain specified types of behavior and usually include any specific environmental factors or personal thoughts that occurred just before, during, or after the behavior.

Self-psychology A theory developed by Kohut that considers the individual's self-concept as the central organizing factor in psychological development.

Self-regulation Technique of controlling one's own behavior through internal reinforcement often in the form of cognitions.

Senile dementia See *dementia*.

Sensate focus Approach to sex therapy advocated by Masters and Johnson in which an individual learns to focus on erotic sensation to the exclusion of other stimuli.

Sensorimotor Pertaining to the functions of the sensing and motor activities of the individual—for example, the sensorimotor nerves.

Sentence completion test Projection test in which the client is presented with a series of incomplete sentences and is asked to complete each one.

Separation anxiety disorder Some children's irrational fear of being apart from the parent(s) because of worries of what will happen to themselves or to their parent(s) in their absence.

Serotonin (5HT) One of a group of chemical neurotransmitters that implement neural transmission across the synapse. Thought to be involved in some types of depression.

Sex offender Term used for individuals who come into contact with the legal system because of their practice of sexual deviations that are prohibited by law.

Sex-reassignment surgery Surgery in which male or female genital organs are removed and facsimiles of genital organs of the opposite sex are created. Surgery is usually combined with hormone treatment to modify secondary sexual characteristics.

Sexual disorders Includes two types—paraphilias and sexual dysfunction. The first relates to obtaining sexual satisfaction through inappropriate partners or activities. The second is the inability to carry out normal sexual activities because of physiological difficulties thought to have psychological causes.

Sexual dysfunction Problems in one or more phases of sexual intercourse that decrease the pleasure derived by the participants or make successful culmination impossible.

Shaman Inspired priest or medium who can summon up and communicate with good and evil spirits.

Shaping Basic process of operant conditioning involving the reinforcement of successively closer approximations to a desired behavior.

Sheltered workshops Organizations, often run by charitable groups, that provide job training and experience and sometimes long term jobs for those unable to compete in the marketplace because of physical or mental disability.

Simple phobia Relatively rare type of phobia that involves irrational fear not related to either unfamiliar situations or social interactions; for example, fear of shut-in places (claustrophobia) or fear of specific animals.

Simple schizophrenia See *schizotypal personality disorder*.

Situation-focused prevention Actions to prevent maladaptive behavior through changing aspects of the environment. For example, providing after-school activities to keep children off the street or changing to non-leaded paint as a way to prevent

children from ingesting lead and possibly developing retardation.

Sleep disorders Disorders characterized either by problems with the amount, quality, and timing of sleep, or by abnormal events occurring during sleep such as night terrors or sleepwalking.

Smooth pursuit eye movements Type of essentially involuntary movement that occurs when an individual visually follows the movements of a rhythmically moving object such as a pendulum.

Social causation theory Theory that maladaptive behavior is a result of poor economic circumstances, poor housing, and inadequate social services.

Social facilitation Acquisition of social competence skills through observing the behavior of others.

Social intervention Treatment approach that involves not only interacting with the client but also attempting to modify the client's environment at home or at work.

Social-learning theories Refers to several similar theoretical viewpoints which hold that social behavior and inner thoughts and feelings are learned through social interactions.

Social phobia Type of irrational fear of situations in which a person will be exposed to the scrutiny of others. Most common types are fear of blushing, public speaking, eating in public, writing in public, and using public toilet facilities.

Social relationships Those interpersonal relationships that play a role in a person's life. Diagnosed on axis V of DSM.

Social role The function a particular person plays in society, which is determined by the particular role he or she fills. Most people have a variety of overlapping social roles, such as an occupational role, several family roles, and perhaps some recreational roles as well.

Social-selection theory Idea that the lower socioeconomic class contains many people who drifted there from higher classes because of their poor functioning. Higher incidence of maladaptive behavior in the lower class is explained in this way.

Social skills training Behavioral or cognitive-behavioral therapeutic approach that emphasizes learning more effective ways of interacting with other people in a variety of situations.

Social support The positive aspects of interpersonal ties that assist in coping and promote both physical and mental health.

Somatic system Part of the peripheral nervous system that sends nerve impulses from the sense organs to the muscles that determine voluntary movement.

Somatic therapy Treatment, such as drugs, surgery, or electroconvulsive therapy, that directly affects a person's physical state.

Somatization disorder (Briquet's syndrome) Disorder characterized by a variety of dramatic but vague complaints that are often chronic but which have no discernible physical cause.

Somatoform disorders Characterized by physical symptoms that suggest a physical disorder but for which there are (1) no organic findings to explain the symptom and (2) strong evidence or suggestion that the symptoms are linked to psychological factors or conflicts; formerly called *hysterical neurosis* or *conversion reaction*.

Sonogram See *ultrasound scanning technique*.

Specific developmental disorder Problems in specific area of development not due to another more general disorder such as retardation or autism. Examples are reading disorder, arithmetic disorder, inability to articulate certain sounds clearly.

Specificity The now discredited idea that specific types of emotional conflicts and types of stress were associated with the development of certain physical conditions in vulnerable persons.

Spectrum concept The idea that several differently classified disorders maybe caused by the same general genetic pattern. These disorders are then considered genetically related.

Spina bifida A condition in which the spinal cord does not close over the nerve column during the prenatal period. The amount of the spinal column that remains open determines how many nerves will be affected. This condition is often associated with an abnormal buildup of pressure of spinal fluid in the brain which can produce retardation unless it is surgically treated.

Splitting Term used to describe the inability of the borderline individual to integrate the positive and negative experiences he or she has with another individual into a coherent relationship. A term used by object relations theorists.

Spontaneous remission Disappearance of symptoms or maladaptive behavior in the absence of therapeutic intervention.

Spouse abuse Physical harm done to wives or husbands by their marital partners. Physical assaults by husbands on wives are most common. Abuse may also be psychological.

Squeeze technique Technique used in sex therapy to assist the male in retarding ejaculation by gently squeezing the end of the penis when ejaculation is imminent.

Standardized interview See *structured interview*.

Stanford-Binet Modification of the Binet test developed at Stanford University by Louis Terman, which has been the Binet format most often used in North America.

Statutory rape Crime defined as having sexual intercourse with someone below the age of legal consent. Force is not necessarily involved.

Stereotypy Development of a ritualized or highly repetitive behavior. Sometimes seen as a result of stress or of the use of certain drugs such as amphetamines.

STP (2, 5 dimethoxy-4-methyl amphetamine) Hallucinogenic agent similar to LSD.

Straight jacket Confining garment used to bind the arms tightly against the body. Often used for violent patients.

Stress Feeling or reaction individuals have when faced with a situation that demands action from them, especially action that may be beyond their capabilities.

Stressor Source of stress, pressure, or strain. Something that upsets the equilibrium of an organism.

Stroke See *cerebrovascular accident*.

Structured interview Also called a standardized interview. An interview procedure in which the interviewer is given a set of instructions that includes definitions of symptoms, numerical ratings for different symptom severities, a series of questions related to each type of symptoms, a set of topics to be covered, and information about how extensively the interviewer is to probe for information about each type of question. The interviewer is allowed flexibility in ordering of the questions.

Sublimation Defense mechanism and developmental concept which involves the refinement or redirection of undesirable impulses into new and more socially acceptable channels. Whereas displacement involves an alteration in choice of object, sublimation alters both the aim (unaccept-

able drive) and the object to a personally acceptable one.

Substance abuse Use of a psychoactive substance to the degree that a severe and long-lasting impairment in function results.

Substance abuse disorder A severe and long lasting impairment resulting from use of a psychoactive substance.

Substance-induced organic mental disorder Result of direct effects on the central nervous system of mood- or behavior-modifying substances. Examples are intoxication or drug-withdrawal symptoms.

Sulci (singular: sulcus) Shallow valleys on the surface of the brain separating the convolutions.

Superego Structure of the psyche in psychoanalytic theory which is developed by internalization of parental standards and by identification with parents. Contains two parts: the ego-ideal and the conscience. The ego-ideal represents the total of positive identifications with accepting and loving parents and desired standards of excellence and good conduct. The conscience includes those attitudes and values which are moralistic (good-bad) in nature.

Support group Group of individuals with the same or similar problems who meet to discuss their problems and how to deal with them.

Supportive therapy Brief form of psychotherapy in which the therapist provides acceptance for the patient and affords him or her some opportunity to be dependent.

Surrogate parent model An example of milieu intervention in which a patient lives for a few weeks during a critical phase of a disorder such as schizophrenia with a carefully screened couple who have been successful parents and who are trained to work with patients in crisis.

Survival guilt Feeling that is unfair to be alive when others in the same situation have died. Overwhelming feelings of guilt, unworthiness, and helplessness.

Symbolic modeling Learning through watching film or videotaped sequences of someone performing the act or acts to be learned or alternately learning appropriate responses through listening to audiotapes or reading text.

Symptom disorder Disorders diagnosed on axis I of the Diagnostic and Statistical Manual. These disorders have symptoms that may come and go unlike the disorders diagnosed on axis II which generally continue throughout life.

Synapse Point at which a nerve impulse passes from an axon of one neuron to the dendrite of another neuron.

Synaptic vesicle Container on the axon terminal button that serves as a storage point for a chemical neurotransmitter.

Syndrome A group of symptoms that often appear together.

Syphilitic infection Chronic infectious veneral disease, transmitted through direct contact, caused by a spirochete, *Trepenema pallidum*.

Systematic desensitization Learning-theory-based therapeutic technique in which a client is first trained in muscle relaxation and then imagines a series of increasingly anxiety-provoking situations until he or she no longer experiences anxiety while thinking about the stimuli. Learning principle involved is reciprocal inhibition, according to which two incompatible responses (e.g., anxiety and relaxation) cannot be made simultaneously by one person.

Systolic Term used to describe the blood pressure reading at the time the heart contracts to drive the blood through. Compare to *diastolic*.

Tactile Referring to the sense of touch.

Tangles Abnormal structure found in nerve cells of individuals who have Alzheimer's disease.

Tarantism Uncontrollable urge to dance, believed to be the result of the bite of a tarantula. This was frequent in Southern Italy from the fifteenth to seventeenth centuries.

Tardive dyskinesia Disorder involving uncontrolled body movements, often of the lips and tongue, that may result from treatment with antipsychotic drugs.

TAT See *Thematic Apperception Test*.

Tay-Sachs disease Inherited metabolic disorder, inevitably fatal, that causes progressive deterioration of the nervous system.

Technique factors The particular procedures used by a therapist in treating a client. Distinguished from the effects of the therapist's personality on the treatment.

Temperament The general nature of a person consistent across time and situations that is thought to arise from constitutional factors present at birth.

Temporal lobe Part of the cerebral hemisphere lying behind the temples and below the lateral fissure in front of the occipital lobe.

Tension headache Probably the most common form of headache; characterized by bandlike pains and tender scalp. Gradual in onset and often longlasting. Thought to be a result of stress.

Tertiary prevention Efforts aimed at reducing the impairment that may result from a given disorder.

Test anxiety Unusually apprehensive response to evaluative situations. Often a factor in poor performance because of worry and interfering thoughts.

THC (tetrahydrocannabinol) Major active ingredient in marijuana.

Thematic Apperception Test (TAT) Projective test consisting of somewhat ambiguous pictures. Subject is asked to tell a story about each picture. From these stories personality dynamics are inferred.

Theoretical perspective The particular set of beliefs or ideas that determine what people notice in behavior, how they interpret what they observe, and how they believe problems should be approached.

Therapeutic interview Interaction between a client and therapist although perhaps including other family members as well. Designed to help promote change in behavior and attitudes.

Thorazine Trade name for chlorpromazine, one of a group of tranquilizing drugs used in the treatment of schizophrenia.

Thought stopping A cognitive technique that uses a specific command as a distraction to end a period of obsessive thinking.

Tic Involuntary, repetitive, rapid muscle contractions often occurring in the face. Thought to be related to tension and anxiety.

Tolerance (drug) Condition in which an individual must use increasing doses of a substance to produce the same physiological effect.

Tonic phase Phase of seizure in which the body is extended and stiff and during which reflexes to light and to pressure on the cornea are absent. See also *clonic phase*.

Top-down studies In the study of heredity factors in disorder, this approach focuses first on identifying parents with a particular diagnosis and then ascertaining the clinical status of their children.

Tranquilizing drugs Drugs (for example, of the chlorpromazine and phenothiazine families) which are

used to reduce agitation and anxiety. Drug action inhibits the activities of the hypothalamus.

Transference Psychoanalytic term that refers to the displacement of affect from one person to another. Patterns of feelings and behavior originally experienced with significant figures in childhood are displaced or attached to individuals in one's current relationships (e.g., a psychotherapist). Current person is reacted to as if he or she were some significant other from the respondent's past. Transference reactions may be positive or negative.

Translocation The breaking off of a piece of one chromosome and the attachment of that piece to another chromosome. May result in the transmission of too much genetic material to the child of a person with a translocation.

Transsexualism Intense desire or need to change one's sexual status, including anatomical structure.

Transvestism Sexual deviation in which an individual derives gratification from wearing the clothing of the opposite sex.

Traumatic neurosis Psychological symptoms that occur after a traumatic event but which are not a direct result of physical injury.

Trephination Process of making a circular hole in the skull. In early times this was done to allow evil spirits to escape.

Tricyclics Group of drugs used to treat depression. An example is Imipramine. Common trade names of tricyclic drugs are Tofranil and Elavil.

Trisomy Occurrence in an individual of three chromosomes of one kind rather than the usual pair. Usually associated with an abnormality of some type.

Trisomy 13 Presence of three number 13 chromosomes rather than the usual pair. Occurs in one of every 5000 births and causes severe mental retardation and a number of specific physical defects. Only about 18 percent of affected infants survive the first year.

Trisomy 18 Presence of three number 18 chromosomes rather than the usual pair. The next most common trisomy after trisomy 21. Occurs in one of every 3000 births. Most such infants die before birth; only 10 percent of those born alive survive to age 1. Results in severe retardation and many physical abnormalities.

Trisomy 21 See *Down syndrome.*

Tuberous sclerosis Disorder caused by a dominant gene and characterized by severe retardation, seizures, and the appearance of small, fibrous tumors.

Type-A personality Term used to describe a personality type hypothesized to be heart-attack prone.

Type-B personality Term used to describe people who do not show the characteristics of Type-A personality. Type Bs are less pressured and hard driving than Type As.

Type I schizophrenia See *positive symptoms.*

Type II schizophrenia See *negative symptoms.*

Ulcer Sore on the skin or internal mucous tissue that results in the death of the tissue involved.

Ultrasound scan technique The use of sound waves to produce a visual image of a fetus or of the form and action of body organs. Also called *sonogram.*

Unauthentic behavior According to existentialist theory, that behavior governed not by an individual's desire but by the desires of other people.

Unconditional positive regard Term used by Carl Rogers to emphasize the importance of a therapist's unqualified acceptance of a client as a person of worth.

Unconditioned response (UR) In classical conditioning, the response that occurs automatically, before training, when the unconditioned stimulus is presented.

Unconditioned stimulus (US) In classical conditioning, the stimulus that automatically elicits the desired response before training has taken place.

Unconscious Out of awareness; mental contents that can be brought to awareness only with great difficulty (or not at all).

Undifferentiated type schizophrenia Clearly psychotic symptoms that either do not fit any of the other categories of schizophrenia or that meet the requirements for more than one category.

Undoing Defense mechanism aimed at negating or atoning for some disapproved impulse or act.

Unipolar disorder Term for an affective disorder in which only depression occurs and there is no history of episodes of mania.

Vaginal Pertaining to the vagina, the passage leading from the external genital opening to the uterus in female mammals.

Vaginismus (functional) Type of sexual dysfunction in women in which an involuntary spasm of the muscles of the outer third of the vagina interferes with sexual activity.

Validity In statistics, the extent to which a test measures what it is intended to or purports to measure.

Valium One of the minor tranquilizing drugs often prescribed to reduce anxiety.

Venereal disease Contagious disease for example, syphilis and gonorrhea, contracted through sexual intercourse.

Ventricles System of communicating cavities in the brain that are linked with the central canal of the spinal cord.

Verbal IQ One of the two subscores of the Wechsler intelligence test series. Tests reflect general information or knowledge and the ability to make abstractions.

Vesicle Storage area in the nerve endings that holds neurotransmitter chemicals.

Vicarious learning Learning that occurs merely by watching the behavior of others.

Visual analogue scales (VAS) A type of rating scale used to assess a variety of subjective phenomena by using portions of a line to represent a personal perception of the phenomena.

Voyeurism (scopophilia) Attaining sexual gratification from observing the sexual behavior of others. Synonymous with *peeping tomism.*

Vulnerability Tendency to react maladaptively, to be insufficiently defended especially in particular situations.

WAIS See *Wechsler Adult Intelligence Scale.*

Wechsler Adult Intelligence Scale (WAIS-R) A widely used individually administered intelligence test for those over 16 years of age. A series of subtests of different types yield a Verbal IQ, Performance IQ, and Full Scale IQ.

Wechsler Intelligence Scale for Children (WISC-III) Intended for children between ages 6 and 16. Uses the same general format as the Wechsler Adult Intelligence Scale and provides Verbal, Performance, and Full Scale IQs.

Wechsler Preschool and Primary Scale of Intelligence (WPPSI) Intended for children between ages 3 and 7. Uses the same general format as the Wechsler Adult Intelligence

Scale and provides Verbal, Performance, and Full Scale IQs.

WISC See *Wechsler Intelligence Scale for Children*.

Withdrawal Physiological changes, varying from mild to extremely unpleasant, that take place after an individual's discontinuation of a habit-forming substance. The symptoms of heroin withdrawal are perhaps best known.

Word association test Projective technique in which a list of words is presented one by one. Client is asked to respond to each item with the first word that comes to mind.

WPPSI See *Wechsler Preschool and Primary Scale of Intelligence*.

X-linked dominance Genes carried on the X sex chromosome that determine a characteristic by their presence. Females have two X chromosomes. Males have one X and one Y chromosome. This means that characteristics that are a result of X-linked dominance can occur in males only through inheritance from the mother. In females it can be inherited from either parent.

References

ABBEY, A. (1991). Acquaintance rape and alcohol consumption on college campuses: How are they linked? *Journal of American College Health, 39,* 165–169.

ABEL, G., BECHER, J., & CUNNINGHAM-RATHNER, J. (1988). Multiple paraphiliac diagnoses among sex offenders. *Bulletin of the American Academy of Psychiatry and the Law, 16,* 153–168.

ABRAHAM, K. (1953). Contributions to the theory of the anal character (1921). In K. Abraham, *Selected papers on psychoanalysis.* New York: Basic Books.

ABRAHAM, K. (1968). Notes on the psychoanalytic investigation and treatment of manic-depressive insanity and allied conditions (1911). In K. Abraham, *Selected papers of Karl Abraham.* New York: Basic Books.

ABRAMS, D. B., & WILSON, G. T. (1979). Effects of alcohol on social anxiety in women: Cognitive versus physiological processes. *Journal of Abnormal Psychology, 88,* 161–173.

ABRAMS, S. (1973). The polygraph in a psychiatric setting. *American Journal of Psychiatry, 130,* 94–98.

ABRAMSON, L. Y., METALSKY, G. I., & ALLOY, L. B. (1989). Hopelessness depression: A theory-based subtype of depression. *Psychological Review, 96,* 358–372.

ABRAMSON, L. Y., SELIGMAN, M.E.P., & TEASDALE, J. D. (1978). Learned helplessness in humans: Critique and reformulation. *Journal of Abnormal Psychology, 87,* 49–74.

ACHENBACH, T. M., MCCONAUGHY, S. H., & HOWELL, C. T. (1987). Child/adolescent behavioral and emotional problems: Implications of cross-informant correlations for situational specificity. *Psychological Bulletin, 101,* 213–232.

ACKERMAN, S. H., MANAKER, S., & COHEN, M. I. (1981). Recent separation and the onset of peptic ulcer disease in older children and adolescents. *Psychosomatic Medicine, 43,* 305–310.

ADAMSON, J. (1989). An appraisal of the DSM-III system. *Canadian Journal of Psychiatry, 34,* 303–310.

ADLER, G., & BYIE, D. (1979). Aloneness and borderline psychopathology: The possible relevance of child development issues. *International Journal of Psychoanalysis, 60,* 83–96.

ADVISORY PANEL ON ALZHEIMER'S DISEASE. DHHS Pub. No. (ADM)91-1791. Washington, DC: Superintendent of Documents, U.S. Government Printing Office.

AGETON, S. (1985). *Facts about sexual assault: A research report for teenagers.* Rockville, MD: U.S. Department of Health and Human Services.

AGRAS, W. S., TAYLOR, O. B., KRAEMER, H. C., ALLEN, R. A., & SCHNEIDER, M. S. (1980). Relaxation training: Twenty-four hour blood pressure reductions. *Archives of General Psychiatry, 37,* 859–863.

AIKEN, T. W., STUMPHAUZER, J. S., & VELOZ, E. V. (1977). Behavioral analysis of non-delinquent brothers in a high juvenile crime community. *Behavioral Disorders, 2,* 212–222.

AKESSON, H. O. (1986). The biological origin of mild mental retardation. *Acta Psychiatrica Scandinavica, 74,* 3–7.

AKHTAR, S. (1987). Schizoid personality disorder: A synthesis of developmental, dynamic, and descriptive features. *American Journal of Psychotherapy, 41,* 499–518.

AKHTAR, S. (1990). Paranoid personality disorder: A synthesis of developmental, dynamic, and descriptive features. *American Journal of Psychotherapy, 44,* 5–25.

AKISKAL, H. S. (1985). Interaction of biologic and psychologic factors in the origin of depressive disorders. *Acta Psychiatrica Scandinavica,* Supplementum, No. 319, 131–139.

ALCOHOL AND HEALTH (1990). Rockville, MD: National Institute of Alcohol Abuse and Alcoholism.

ALCOHOLISM: AN INHERITED DISEASE. (1985). Rockville, MD: National Institute of Alcohol Abuse and Alcoholism.

ALDRICH, C. K. (1966). *An introduction to dynamic psychiatry.* New York: McGraw-Hill.

ALFORD, B. A., BECK, A. T., FREEMAN, A., & WRIGHT, F. D. (1990). Brief focused cognitive therapy of panic disorder. *Psychotherapy, 27,* 230–234.

ALLOY, L. B., & ABRAMSON, L. Y. (1979). Judgment of contingency of depressed and nondepressed students: Sadder but wiser. *Journal of Experimental Psychology, 108,* 441–485.

ALLSOP, D., KIDD, M., LANDON, M., & TOMLINSON, A. (1986). Isolated senile plaque cores in Alzheimer's disease and Down's syndrome show differences in morphology. *Journal of Neurology, Neurosurgery, and Psychiatry, 49,* 886–892.

ALTMAN, D. (1982). *The homosexualization of America.* Boston: Beacon Press.

ALVAREZ, A. (1973). *The savage god: A study of suicide.* New York: Random House.

AMBELAS, A. (1987). Life events and mania: A special relationship. *British Journal of Psychiatry, 150,* 235–240.

AMBELAS, A., & GEORGE, M. (1986). Predictability of course of illness in manic patients with positive life events. *Journal of Nervous and Mental Disease, 1974,* 693–695.

AMERICAN LAW INSTITUTE. (1962). *Model penal code: Proposed official draft.* Philadelphia: American Law Institute.

AMERICAN PSYCHIATRIC ASSOCIATION. (1968). *Diagnostic and statistical manual of mental disorders,* 2nd ed. Washington, DC: American Psychiatric Association.

AMERICAN PSYCHIATRIC ASSOCIATION. (1980). *Diagnostic and statistical manual of mental disorders,* 3rd ed. Washington, DC: American Psychiatric Association.

AMERICAN PSYCHIATRIC ASSOCIATION. (1987). *Diagnostic and statistical manual of mental disorders,* 3rd ed. rev. Washington, DC: American Psychiatric Association.

ANASTASI, A. (1988). *Psychological testing,* 6th ed. New York: Macmillan.

ANDERSON, D. J., NOYES, R., JR., & CROWE, R. R. (1984). A comparison of panic disorder and generalized anxiety disorder. *American Journal of Psychiatry, 141,* 572–575.

ANDERSON, E. A. (1987). Preoperative preparation for cardiac surgery facilitates recovery, reduces psychological distress, and reduces the incidence of acute postoperative hypertension. *Journal of Consulting and Clinical Psychology, 55,* 513–520.

ANDOLPHI, M., ANGELO, C., MENGHI, P., & NICOLO-CORIGLIANO, A. (1983). *Behind the family mask: Therapeutic changes in rigid family systems.* New York: Brunner/Mazel.

ANDREASEN, N. C. (1982). Negative symptoms in schizophrenia: Definitions and reliability. *Archives of General Psychiatry, 39,* 784–788.

ANDREASEN, N. C. (1984). *The broken brain: The biological revolution in psychiatry.* New York: Harper & Row.

ANDREASEN, N. C. (1985). Positive vs. negative symptoms: A critical evaluation. *Schizophrenia Bulletin, 11,* 380–389.

ANDREASEN, N. C., ALLEBECK, P., ENGSTROM, A. & RYDBERG, U. (1987). Cannabis and schizophrenia: A longitudinal study of Swedish conscripts. *Lancet, 2,* 1483–1485.

ANDREASEN, N. C., & BLACK, D. W. (1991). *Introductory textbook of psychiatry.* Washington, DC: American Psychiatric Press.

ANDREASEN, N. C., EHRHARDT, J. C., SWAYZE, V. W., II, ALLIGER, R. J., YUH, W. T. C., COHEN, G., & ZIEBELL, S. (1990). Magnetic resonance imaging of the brain in schizophrenia. *Archives of General Psychiatry, 47,* 35–44.

ANDREASEN, N. C., & GROVE, W. (1979). The relationship between schizophrenic language, manic language, and aphasia. In J. Gruzelier & P. Flor-Henry, eds., *Hemisphere symmetries of function in psychopathology.* Amsterdam: Elsevier/North Holland.

ANDREASEN, N. C., & GROVE, W. M. (1986). Thought, language, and communication in schizophrenia: Diagnosis and prognosis. *Schizophrenia Bulletin, 12,* 348–359.

ANDREASEN, N. C., & POWERS, P. S. (1975). Creativity and psychosis. *Archives of General Psychiatry, 32*, 70–73.

ANDREWS, S., VAUGHN, K., HARVEY, R., & ANDREWS, G. (1986). A survey of practising psychiatrist's view on the treatment of schizophrenia. *British Journal of Psychiatry, 149*, 357–364.

ANGST, J. (1988). European long-term follow-up studies of schizophrenia. *Schizophrenia Bulletin, 14*, 501–513.

ANONYMOUS. (1965). A practicing psychiatrist: The experience of electroconvulsive therapy. *British Journal of Psychiatry, 111*, 365–367.

ANONYMOUS. (1977). Psychosocial implications of schizophrenic diagnoses (personal account). *Schizophrenia Bulletin, 3*, 4(b).

ANONYMOUS, & J. TILLER (1989). Obsessive–compulsive disorder: A sufferer's viewpoint. *Australian and New Zealand Journal of Psychiatry, 23*, 279–281.

ANTHONY, E. J. (1975). The influences of a manic-depressive environment on the developing child. In E. J. Anthony & T. Benedek, eds., *Depression and human existence*. Boston: Little, Brown.

APA TASK FORCE ON LABORATORY TESTS IN PSYCHIATRY. (1987). The Dexamethasone Suppression Test: An overview of the current status in psychiatry. *American Journal of Psychiatry, 144*, 1253–1262.

APPELBAUM, P. S. (1991). What are the current standards for involuntary commitment to a mental hospital? *Harvard Mental Health Letter, 7* (11), 8.

ARIETI, S., & BEMPORAD, J. (1978). *Severe and mild depression*. New York: Basic Books.

ARONOW, E., & RESNIKOFF, M. (1976). *Rorschach content interpretation*. Orlando, FL: Grune & Stratton.

ARONSON, T. A., & SHUKLA, S. (1987). Life events and relapse in bipolar disorder. The impact of a catastrophic event. *Acta Psychiatrica Scandinavica, 57*, 571–576.

ASAAD, G., & SHAPIRO, B. (1986). Hallucinations: Theoretical and clinical overview. *American Journal of Psychiatry, 143*, 1088–1097.

ASARNOW, J. R., & GOLDSTEIN, M. J. (1986). Schizophrenia during adolescence and early adulthood: A developmental perspective on risk research. *Clinical Psychology Review, 6*, 211–325.

AWAD, A. G. (1989). Drug therapy in schizophrenia—Variability of outcome and prediction of response. *Canadian Journal of Psychiatry, 34*, 711–720.

AXLINE, V. M. (1947). *Play therapy: The inner dynamics of childhood*. Boston: Houghton Mifflin.

AYLLON, T., GARBER, S. W., & ALLISON, M. G. (1977). Behavioral treatment of childhood neurosis. *Psychiatry, 40*, 315–322.

AYLLON, T., SMITH, D., & RODGERS, M. (1970). Behavioral management of school phobia. *Journal of Behavior Therapy and Experimental Psychiatry, 1*, 124–138.

BACHMAN, J. G., JOHNSTON, L. D., & O'MALLEY, P. M. (1990). Explaining the recent decline in cocaine use among young adults: Further evidence that perceived risks and disapproval lead to reduced drug use. *Journal of Health and Social Behavior, 31*, 173–184.

BADGLEY, R. F. (1984). *Sexual offences against children: Report of the Committee of Sexual Offences Against Children and Youth*. Ottawa: Minister of Supply Services.

BANDURA, A. (1969). *Principles of behavior modification*. New York: Holt, Rinehart & Winston.

BANDURA, A. (1977). Self-efficacy: Toward a unifying theory of behavior change. *Psychological Review, 84*, 191–215.

BANDURA, A. (1978). The self-system in reciprocal determinism. *American Psychologist, 33*, 344–358.

BANDURA, A. (1982). Self-efficacy mechanism in human agency. *American Psychologist, 37*, 122–147.

BANDURA, A. (1986). *Social foundations of thought and action: A social cognitive theory*. Englewood Cliffs, NJ: Prentice Hall.

BANDURA, A., & MENLOVE, F. L. (1968). Factors determining vicarious extinction of avoidance behavior through symbolic modeling. *Journal of Personality and Social Psychology, 8*, 99–108.

BANNON, N. J., & ROTH, R. H. (1983). Pharmacology of mesocortical dopamine neurons. *Pharmacological Reviews, 35(1)*, 53–68.

BARD, M. (1970). Alternatives to traditional law enforcement. In F. Korten, S. W. Cook, & J. I. Lacey, eds., *Psychology and the problems of society*. Washington, D.C.: American Psychological Association, 128–132.

BARDEN, H. S., KESSEL, R. & SCHUETT, V. E. (1984). The costs and benefits of screening for PKU in Wisconsin. *Social Biology, 31*, 1–17.

BAREFOOT, J. C., PETERSON, B. L., DAHLSTROM, W. G., SIEGLER, I. C., ANDERSON, N. B., & WILLIAMS, R. B., JR. (1991). Hostility patterns and health implications: Correlates of Cook-Medley Hostility Scale scores in a national survey. *Health Psychology, 10*, 18–24.

BAREFOOT, J. C., SIEGLER, I. C., NOWLING, J. B., PETERSON, B. L., HANEY, T. L., & WILLIAMS, R. B., JR. (1987). Suspiciousness, health, and mortality: A follow-up study of 500 older adults. *Psychosomatic Medicine, 49*, 450–457.

BARLOW, D. H., CRASKE, M. G., CERNY, J. A., & KLOSKO, J. S. (1989). Behavioral treatment of panic disorder. *Behavior Therapy, 20*, 261–282.

BARLOW, D. H., DiNARDO, P. A., VERMILYEA, B. B., VERMILYEA, J., & BLANCHARD, E. B. (1986). Co-morbidity and depression among the anxiety disorders: Issues in diagnosis and classification. *Journal of Nervous and Mental Disease, 174*, 63–72.

BARON, M., & RISCH, N. (1987). The spectrum concept of schizophrenia: Evidence for a genetic-environmental continuum. *Journal of Psychiatric Research, 21*, 257–267.

BARON, M., RISCH, N., HAMBORGER, R., MANDEL, B., KOSHNER, S., NEWMAN, M., DRUMER, D., & BELMAKER, R. H. (1987). Genetic linkage between X-chromosome markers and bipolar affective illness. *Nature, 326*, 289–292.

BARRETT, D., & FINE, H. (1980). A child was being beaten: The therapy of battered children as adults. *Psychotherapy: Theory, Research and Practice, 17*, 285–293.

BARROWCLOUGH, C., & TARRIER, N. (1990). Social functioning in schizophrenic patients. I. The effects of expressed emotion and family intervention. *Social Psychiatry and Psychiatric Epidemiology, 25*, 125–129.

BARSKY, A. J. (1989). Somatoform disorders. In H. I. Kaplan & B. J. Sadock, eds. *Comprehensive textbook of psychiatry*, 5th ed. Baltimore: Williams & Wilkins.

BARTAK, L., RUTTER, M., & COX, M. (1975). A comparative study of infantile autism and specific developmental receptive language disorder. I. The children. *British Journal of Psychiatry, 126*, 127–145.

BARTROP, R. W., LUCKHURST, E., LAZARUS, L., KILOH, L. G., & PENNY, R. (1977). Depressed lymphocyte function after bereavement. *Lancet, 1*, 834–836.

BASSETT, A. S. (1989). Chromosome 5 and schizophrenia: Implications for genetic linkage studies. *Schizophrenia Bulletin, 15*, 393–402.

BATEMAN, A. W. (1986). Rape: The forgotten victim. *British Medical Journal, 292*, 1306.

BAUER, R. B., STEVENS, C., REVENO, W. S., & ROSENBAUM, H. (1982). L-Dopa treatment of Parkinson's disease: A ten year follow-up study. *Journal of the American Geriatric Society, 30*, 322–325.

BAUMEISTER, R. F. (1990). Suicide as escape from self. *Psychological Bulletin, 97*, 90–113.

BECK, A. T. (1967). *Depression: Clinical, experimental and theoretical aspects*. New York: Hoeber.

BECK, A. T. (1970). Role of fantasies in psychotherapy and psychopathology. *Journal of Nervous and Mental Disease, 150*, 3–17.

BECK, A. T. (1976). *Cognitive therapy and the emotional disorders*. New York: International Universities Press.

BECK, A. T., BROWN, G., STEER, R. A., EIDELSON, J. L., & RISKIND, J. H. (1987). Differentiating anxiety and depression: A test of the cognitive content-specificity hypothesis. *Journal of Abnormal Psychology, 96*, 179–183.

BECK, A. T., & EMERY, G. (1985). *Anxiety disorders and phobias: A cognitive perspective*. New York: Basic Books.

BECK, A. T., FREEMAN, A., & ASSOCIATES (1990). *Cognitive therapy of personality disorders*. New York: Guilford.

BECK, A. T., KOVACS, M., & WEISSMAN, A. (1979). Assessment of suicidal ideation: The scale for suicide ideation. *Journal of Consulting and Clinical Psychology, 47*, 343–352.

BECK, A. T., RUSH, A. J., SHAW, B., & EMERY, G. (1979). *Cognitive therapy of depression*. New York: Guilford.

BECK, A. T., STEER, R. A., KOVACS, M., & GARRISON, B. (1985). Hopelessness and eventual suicide: A ten year prospective study of patients hospitalized with suicidal ideation. *American Journal of Psychiatry, 175*, 559–563.

BECK, A. T., & WEISHAAR, M. (1989). In A. Freeman, K. M. Simon, L. E. Beutler, & H. Arkowitz, eds., *Comprehensive handbook of cognitive therapy*. New York: Plenum.

BECK, J. G., & BARLOW, D. H. (1984). Current conceptualizations of sexual dysfunction: A review and an alternative perspective. *Clinical Psychology Review, 4,* 363–378.

BECKER, J., & SCHMALING, K. (1991). Interpersonal aspects of depression from psychodynamic and attachment perspectives. In J. Becker & A. Kleinman, eds., *Psychosocial aspects of depression.* Hillsdale, NJ: Erlbaum.

BECKER, R. E. (1990). Social skills training. In A. S. Bellack & M. Hersen, eds., *Comparative treatments for adult disorders.* New York: Wiley.

BEERS, C. (1908). *A mind that found itself.* Garden City, NY: Doubleday.

BEISER, M., SHORE, J. H., PETERS, R., & TATUM, E. (1985). Does community care for the mentally ill make a difference? A tale of two cities. *American Journal of Psychiatry, 142,* 1047–1105.

BELL, A. P., & WEINBERG, M. S. (1978). *Homosexualities: A study of diversity among men and women.* New York: Simon & Schuster.

BELL, A. P., WEINBERG, M. S., & HAMMERSMITH, S. F. (1981). *Sexual preference.* Bloomington: Indiana University Press.

BELL, Q. (1972). *Virginia Woolf: A biography.* New York: Harcourt Brace.

BELLACK, A. S. (1989). A comprehensive model for treatment of schizophrenia. In A. S. Bellack, ed., *A clinical guide for the treatment of schizophrenia.* New York: Plenum.

BELLACK, A. S., & MUESER, K. T. (1986). A comprehensive treatment program for schizophrenia and chronic mental illness. Special Issue: Systems aspects of chronic mental illness. *Community Mental Health, 22,* 175–189.

BEMPORAD, J. R. (1983). Cognitive, affective and psychologic changes in the depressed process. *Journal of the American Academy of Psychoanalysis, 11,* 159–172.

BEMPORAD, J. R., & VASILE, R. G. (1990). Psychotherapy. In A. S. Bellack and M. Hersen, eds., *Comparative treatments for adult disorders.* New York: Wiley.

BENDER, L. (1938). A visual motor Gestalt test and its clinical use. *American Orthopsychiatric Association,* Research Monographs, No. 3.

BENNETT, P., & CARROLL, D. (1990). Stress management approaches to the prevention of coronary heart disease. *British Journal of Clinical Psychology, 29,* 1–12.

BENSON, D. F., MILLER, B. L., & SIGNER, S. F. (1986). Dual personality associated with epilepsy. *Archives of Neurology, 43,* 471–474.

BENSON, H. (1977). Systemic hypertension and the relaxation response. *New England Journal of Medicine, 296,* 1152–1156.

BENTLER, P. M., & PRINCE, C. (1969). Personality characteristics of male transvestites. *Journal of Abnormal Psychology, 74,* 140–143.

BENTON, M. K., & SCHROEDER, H. E. (1990). Social skills training with schizophrenics: A meta-analytic evaluation. *Journal of Consulting and Clinical Psychology, 6,* 741–747.

BERGIN, A. E., & LAMBERT, M. J. (1978). The evaluation of therapeutic outcomes. In S. L. Garfield, & A. E. Bergin, eds., *Handbook of psychotherapy and behavior change: An empirical analysis,* 2nd ed. New York: John Wiley.

BERKE, J., & HERNTON, C. (1974). *The cannabis experience.* London: Peter Owen.

BERRY, P., GROENEWEG, G., GIBSON, D., & BROWN, R. I. (1984). Mental development of adults with Down syndrome. *American Journal of Mental Deficiency, 89,* 252–256.

BERTELSEN, A. (1979). A Danish twin study of manic-depressive disorders. In M. Schou & E. Stromgren, eds., *Origin, prevention and treatment of affective disorders.* London: Academic Press.

BEUTLER, L. E., CRAGO, M., & ARIZMENDI, T. G. (1986). Therapist variables in psychotherapy process and outcome. In S. L. Garfield & A. E. Bergin, eds., *Handbook of psychotherapy and behavior change,* 3rd ed. NY: John Wiley.

BIBRING, E. (1953). The mechanism of depression. In P. Greenacre, ed., *Affective disorders.* New York: International.

BIEBER, I. (1980). *Cognitive psychoanalysis.* New York: Jason Aronson.

BIEBER, I., DAIN, H. J., DINCE, P. R., DRELLICH, M. G., GRAND, H. J., GRUNDLACK, R. H., KREMER, M. W., RIFKIN, A. H., WILBUR, C. B., & BIEBER, T. B. (1962). *Homosexuality.* New York: Basic Books.

BIEDERMAN, J. (1991). Attention deficit hyperactivity disorder (ADHD). *Annals of Clinical Psychiatry, 3*(1), 9–22.

BIEGON, A., & ISRAELI, M. (1988). Regionally selective increases in beta-adrenergic receptor density in the brains of suicide victims. *Brain Research, 442,* 199–203.

BLACK, D. W., WARRACK, G., & WINOKUR, G. (1985). The Iowa Record-Linkage Study: II. Excess mortality among patients with organic mental disorders. *Archives of General Psychiatry, 42,* 78–81.

BLACK, D. W., WINOKUR, G., HULBERT, J., & NASRALLAH, A. (1988). Effect of psychosis on suicide risk in 1,593 patients with unipolar and bipolar affective disorders. *American Journal of Psychiatry, 145,* 849–852.

BLACK, D. W., YATES, W. R., & ANDREASEN, N. C. (1988). Schizophrenia, schizophreniform disorder, and delusional paranoid disorders. In J. A. Talbott, R. E. Hales, & S. C. Yudofsky, eds., *Textbook of psychiatry.* Washington, DC: American Psychiatric Press.

BLADER, J. C., & MARSHALL, W. C. (1989). Is assessment of sexual arousal in rapists worthwhile? A critique of current methods and the development of a response compatibility approach. *Clinical Psychology Review, 9,* 569–587.

BLAND, R. C., & ORNE, H. (1980). Schizophrenia: Schneider's first-rank symptoms and outcome. *British Journal of Psychiatry, 137,* 63–68.

BLAZER, D., HUGHES, D., & GEORGE, L. D. (1987). Stressful life events and the onset of a generalized anxiety syndrome. *American Journal of Psychiatry, 144,* 1178–1183.

BLEULER, E. (1950). *Dementia praecox or the group of schizophrenias (1911)* (J. Zinkin, trans.). New York: International Universities Press.

BLEULER, M. (1972). *The schizophrenic psychoses in the light of long-term case and family histories.* Stuttgart: Georg Theime Verlag.

BLEULER, M. (1978). *The schizophrenic disorders: Long term patient and family studies.* New Haven: Yale University Press.

BLOOM, B. L., & HODGES, W. F. (1988). The Colorado Separation and Divorce Program: A preventive intervention program for newly separated persons. In R. H. Price, E. L. Cowen, R. P. Lorian, & J. Ramos-McKay, eds., *Fourteen ounces of prevention: A casebook for practitioners.* Washington, DC: American Psychological Association.

BLUMSTEIN, P. W., & SCHWARTZ, P. (1976). Bisexuality in women. *Archives of Sexual Behavior, 5,* 171–181.

BOHMAN, M., CLONINGER, C. R., SIGVARDSSON, S., & VON KNORRING, A. L. (1982). Predisposition to petty criminality of Swedish adoptees I. Genetic and Rh environmental heterogeneity. *Archives of General Psychiatry, 39,* 1233–1241.

BOHMFALK, G. C. (1991). No laughing matter. *Journal of the American Medical Association, 265,* 1245.

BOND, L. A., & COMPAS, B. E. (1991). *Primary prevention and promotion in the schools.* Newbury Park, CA: Sage Publications.

BOOR, M. (1982). The multiple personality epidemic. *Journal of Nervous and Mental Disease, 170,* 302–304.

BOOTH-BUTTERFIELD, M., ED. (1991). *Communication, cognition, and anxiety.* Newbury Park, CA: Sage Publications.

BOUSHA, D. M., & TWENTYMAN, C. T. (1984). Mother-child interactional style in abuse, neglect, and control groups: Naturalistic observations in the home. *Journal of Abnormal Psychology, 93,* 106–114.

BOWERS, K. S., & MEICHENBAUM, D., EDS. (1985). *The unconscious reconsidered.* New York: Wiley Interscience.

BOWERS, M. B., JR. (1968). Pathogenesis of acute schizophrenic psychosis. *Archives of General Psychiatry, 19,* 348–355.

BOWLBY, J. (1973). *Separation: Anxiety and anger.* New York: Basic Books.

BOWLBY, J. (1980). *Loss, sadness, and depression.* New York: Basic Books.

BOXER, A. M., & COHLER, B. J. (1989). The life course of gay and lesbian youth: An immodest proposal for the study of lives. *Journal of Homosexuality, 17,* 315–355.

BOYD, J. H., RAE, D. S., THOMPSON, J. W., BURNS, B. J., BOURDON, K., LOCKE, B. Z., & REGIER, D. A. (1990). Phobia: Prevalence and risk factors. *Social Psychiatry and Psychiatric Epidemiology, 25,* 314–323.

BOZETT, F. W. (1981). Gay fathers: Evolution of the gay-father identity. *American Journal of Orthopsychiatry, 51,* 552–559.

BRADLEY, S. J., & ZUCKER, K. A. (1990). Gender identity disorder and psychosexual problems in children and adolescents. *Canadian Journal of Psychiatry, 35*(6), 477–486.

BRANDT, J., QUAID, K. A., FOLSTEIN, S. E., GARBER, P., MAESTRI, N. E., ABBOTT, M. H., SLAVNEY, P. R., FRANZ, M. L., KASCH, L., & KAZAZIAN, H. H. (1989). Presymptomatic diagnosis of delayed-onset disease with linked DNA markers: The experience in Huntington's disease. *Journal of the American Medical Association, 261,* 3108–3114.

BRAUN, B. G. (1983). Neurophysic changes in multiple personality due to integration: A preliminary report. *American Journal of Clinical Hypnosis, 26,* 84–92.

BRAUN, B. G. (1984). Toward a theory of multiple personality and other dissociative phenomena. *Psychiatric Clinics of North America, 7,* 171–193.

BRAUN, B. G. (1990). Multiple personality disorder: An overview. *The American Journal of Occupational Therapy, 44,* 971–976.

BREAKEY, W. R., FISCHER, P. J., KRAMER, M., NESTADT, G., ROMANOSKI, A. J., ROSS, A., ROYALL, R. M., & STINE, O. C. (1989). Health and mental health problems of homeless men and women in Baltimore. *Journal of the American Medical Association, 262,* 1352–1357.

BREIER, A., & PAUL, S. M. (1990). The GABA$_A$/benzodiazepine receptor: Implications for the molecular basis of anxiety. *Journal of Psychiatric Research, 24,* 91–104.

BRENNER, M. H. (1973). *Mental illness and the economy.* Cambridge, MA: Harvard University Press.

BRENNER, M. H. (1984). *Estimating the effects of economic change on national health and social well-being.* (Joint Economic Committee of the U.S. Congress). Washington, DC: U.S. Government Printing Office.

BRENT, D. A., PERPER, J. A., GOLDSTEIN, C. E., KOLKO, D. J., ALLAN, M. J., ALLMAN, C. J., & ZELENAK, J. P. (1988). Risk factors for adolescent suicide: A comparison of adolescent suicide victims with suicidal inpatients. *Archives of General Psychiatry, 45,* 581–588.

BRESLOW, N., EVANS, L., & LANGLEY, J. (1985). On the prevalence and roles of females in the sadomasochistic subculture: Report of an empirical study. *Archives of Sexual Behavior, 14,* 303–317.

BRESLOW, N., EVANS, L., & LANGLEY, J. (1986). Comparisons among heterosexual, bisexual, and homosexual male sadomasochists. *Journal of Homosexuality, 13,* 83–107.

BREZNITZ, S. (1988). The seven kinds of denial. In C. D. Spielberger, I. G. Sarason, & P. B. Defares, eds., *Stress and Anxiety,* vol. 11. Washington, D.C.: Hemisphere, 73–90.

BRIER, A., SCHREIBER, J. L., DYER, J., & PICKAR, D. (1991). National Institute of Mental Health longitudinal study of chronic schizophrenia: Prognosis and predictors of outcome. *Archives of General Psychiatry, 48,* 239–246.

BRIER, N. (1986). The mildly retarded adolescent: A psychosocial perspective. *Developmental and Behavioral Pediatrics, 7,* 320–323.

Broadening the base of treatment for alcohol problems. INSTITUTE OF MEDICINE (U.S.). (1990). Washington, D.C.: National Academy Press.

BRODY, G. H., & STONEMAN, Z. (1984). Children with atypical siblings. In B. B. Lahey & A. E. Kazdin, eds. *Advances in child clinical psychology,* vol. 6. New York: Plenum.

BRODY, J. E. (1984). Autoerotic death of youths causes widening concern. *New York Times,* March 27, 17, 20.

BROGA, M. I., & NEUFELD, R. W. (1981). Multivariate cognitive performance variables and response styles among paranoid and nonparanoid schizophrenics. *Journal of Abnormal Psychology, 90,* 495–509.

BROWN, G., & HARRIS, T. (1978). *Social origins of depression: A study of psychiatric disorder in women.* New York: Free Press.

BROWN, G. W., HARRIS, T., & COPELAND, J. R. (1977). Depression and loss. *British Journal of Psychiatry, 130,* 1–18.

BROWN, W. T., JENKINS, E. C., COHEN, I. L., FISCH, G. S., WOLF-SCHEIN, E. G., GROSS, A., WATERHOUSE, L., FEIN, D., MASON-BROTHERS, A., RITVO, E., RUTTENBERG, B. A., BENTLEY, W., & CASTELLS, S. (1986). Fragile X and autism: A multicenter survey. *American Journal of Medical Genetics, 23,* 341–352.

BROWNE, A., & FINKELHOR, D. (1986). Impact of child sexual abuse: A review of research. *Psychological Bulletin, 99,* 66–77.

BROWNELL, K. D., HAYES, S. C., & BARLOW, D. H. (1977). Patterns of appropriate and deviant sexual arousal: The behavioral treatment of multiple sexual deviations. *Journal of Consulting and Clinical Psychology, 45,* 1144–1155.

BRUCE, M. L., KIM, K., LEAF, P., & JACOBS, S. (1990). Depressive episodes and dysphoria resulting from conjugal bereavement in a prospective community sample. *American Journal of Psychiatry, 147,* 608–611.

BUCHANAN, A., & OLIVER, J. F. (1977). Abuse and neglect as a cause of mental retardation. *British Journal of Psychology, 131,* 458–467.

BUCHSBAUM, M. S. (1986). Brain imaging in the search for biological markers in affective disorder. *Journal of Clinical Psychiatry, 47,* 7–10.

BUCHSBAUM, M. S. (1990). The frontal lobes, basal ganglia, and temporal lobes as sites for schizophrenia. *Schizophrenia Bulletin, 16*(3), 379–389.

BUCHSBAUM, M. S., & HAIER, R. J. (1987). Functional and anatomical brain imaging: Impact on schizophrenia research. *Schizophrenia Bulletin, 13,* 115–132.

BURNSIDE, J. W. 1987. The diary. *Journal of the American Medical Association, 257,* 1802.

BURT, M. (1992) *Over the edge: The growth of homelessness in the 1980's.* New York: Russell Sage Foundation.

BUTCHER, J. N. (1990). *The MMPI-2 in psychological treatment.* New York: Oxford University Press.

BUTLER, G. (1989). Issues in the application of cognitive and behavioral strategies to the treatment of social phobia. *Clinical Psychology Review, 9,* 91–106.

CADORET, R. J. (1986). Adoption studies: Historical and methodological critique. *Psychiatric Developments, 1,* 45–64.

CAHILL, C., LLEWELYN, S. P., & PEARSON, C. (1991). Treatment of sexual abuse which occurred in childhood: A review. *British Journal of Clinical Psychology, 30,* 1–12.

CALDWELL, C. B., & GOTTESMAN, I. I. (1990). Schizophrenics kill themselves too: A review of risk factors for suicide. *Schizophrenia Bulletin, 16,* 571–589.

CALEV, A. (1984). Recall and recognition in chronic nondemented schizophrenics: Use of matched tasks. *Journal of Abnormal Psychology, 93,* 172–177.

CAMERON, N. (1963). *Personality development and psychopathology.* Boston: Houghton Mifflin.

CAMPBELL, S. S., & GILLIN, J. C. (1987). Sleep measures in depression: How sensitive? How specific? *Psychiatric Annals, 17,* 647–653.

CANCRO, R. (1985). Schizophrenic disorders. In H. I. Kaplan & B. J. Sadock, eds. *Comprehensive textbook of psychiatry,* 4th ed., vol. 1. Baltimore: Williams & Wilkins.

CANNON, T. D., MEDNICK, S. A., & PARNAS, J. (1990). Two pathways to schizophrenia in children at risk. In L. Robins & M. Rutter, eds., *Straight and devious pathways from childhood to adulthood.* New York: Cambridge University Press.

CANTON, C. L. M. (1990). *Homeless in America.* New York: Oxford University Press.

CAPUTO, P. A. (1977). *A rumor of war.* New York: Holt, Rinehart & Winston.

CAREY, G., & GOTTESMAN, I. I. (1981). Twin and family studies of anxiety, phobic, and obsessive disorders. In D. F. Klein & J. Rabkin, eds., *Anxiety: New research and changing concepts.* New York: Raven Press, 117–136.

CARONE, B. J., HARROW, M., & WESTERMEYER, J. F. (1991). Posthospital course and outcome in schizophrenia. *Archives of General Psychiatry, 48,* 247–253.

CARPENTER, W. T., JR., BUCHANAN, R. W., & KIRKPATRICK, B. (1991). The concept of negative symptoms in schizophrenia. In J. F. Greden & R. Tandon, eds., *Negative schizophrenic symptoms: Pathophysiology and clinical implications.* Washington, DC: American Psychiatric Press.

CARPENTER, W. T., JR., HEINRICHS, D. W., & ALPHS, L. D. (1985). Treatment of negative symptoms. *Schizophrenia Bulletin, 11,* 440–452.

CARPENTER, W. T., JR., SACKS, M. H., STRAUSS, J. S., BARTKO, J. J., & RAYNER, J. (1976). Evaluating signs and symptoms: Comparisons of structured interview and clinical approaches. *British Journal of Psychiatry, 128,* 397–403.

CARROL, K., & LEON, G. R. (1981). The bulimia-vomiting disorder within a generalized substance abuse pattern. Paper presented at the

15th Annual Convention of the Association for the Advancement of Behavior Therapy, Toronto.

CARROLL, B. J. (1985). Dexamethasone Suppression Test: A review of contemporary confusion. *Journal of Clinical Psychiatry, 46*, 13–24.

CASEY, R. J., & BERMAN, J. S. (1985). The outcome of psychotherapy with children. *Psychological Bulletin, 98*(2), 388–400.

CASPI, A. & ELDER, A. H., JR., (1988). Early personality and life disorganization. In E. M. Hetherington, R. M. Lerner, & M. Perlmutter, eds., *Child development in life-span perspective*. Hillsdale, NJ: Lawrence Erlbaum Associates.

CATALAN, J., HAWTON, K., & DAY, A. (1990). Couples referred to a sexual dysfunction clinic: Psychological and physical morbidity. *British Journal of Psychiatry, 156*, 61–67.

CAUTELA, J. R. (1985). Covert modeling. In A. S. Bellack & M. Hersen, eds., *Dictionary of behavior therapy techniques*. New York: Pergamon.

CELIS, W. (1991). As fewer students drink, abuse of alcohol persists. *The New York Times*, December 31, 1991, 1, A8.

CHALKLEY, A. J., & POWELL, G. E. (1983). The clinical description of forty-eight cases of sexual fetishisms. *British Journal of Psychiatry, 142*, 292–295.

CHAMBERS, W. J., PUIG-ANTICH, J., HIRSCH, M., PAEZ, P., AMBROSINI, P. J., TABRIZI, M. A., & DAVIES, M. (1985). The assessment of affective disorders in children and adolescents by semistructured interview. *Archives of General Psychiatry, 42*, 696–702.

CHANDLER, C. L., WEISSBERG, R. P., COWEN, E. L., & GUARE, J. 1984. Long term effects of a school-based secondary prevention program for young maladapting children. *Journal of Consulting and Clinical Psychology, 52*, 165–170.

CHARNEY, D. S., MENKES, D. B., & HENINGER, G. R. (1981). Receptor sensitivity and the mechanism of action of antidepressant treatment. *Archives of General Psychiatry, 38*, 1160–1180.

CHEETHAM, S. C., CROMPTON, M. R., KATONA, C. L. E., & HORTON, R. W. (1988). Brain 5-HT$_2$ receptor binding sites in depressed suicide victims. *Brain Research, 443*, 272–280.

CHESNEY, M. A., & ROSENMAN, R. H., EDS. (1985). *Anger and hostility in cardiovascular and behavioral disorders*. Washington, D.C.: Hemisphere.

CHESS, S. (1978). The plasticity of human development. *American Academy of Child Psychiatry, 17*, 80–91.

CHESS, S. (1990). Pathogenesis of the adjustment disorders: Vulnerabilities due to temperamental factors. In J. D. Noshpitz & R. D. Coddington, eds., *Stressors and the adjustment disorders*. New York: John Wiley.

CHESS, S., THOMAS, A., & HASSIBI, M. (1983). Depression in childhood and adolescence: A prospective study of six cases. *Journal of Nervous and Mental Disease, 171*, 411–420.

CHILDHOOD DISORDERS. (1988). Washington, DC: American Psychiatric Association.

CHRISTENSEN, H., HADZI-PAVLOVIC, D., ANDREWS, G., & MATTICK, R. (1987). Behavior therapy and tricyclic medication in the treatment of obsessive-compulsive disorder: A quantitative review. *Journal of Consulting and Clinical Psychology, 55*, 701–711.

CHUANG, H. T., DEVINS, G. M., HUNSLEY, J., & GILL, M. J. (1989). Psychosocial distress and well-being among gay and bisexual men with human immunodeficiency virus infection. *American Journal of Psychiatry, 146*, 876–880.

CICCHETTI, D., & BEEGHLY, M. (1990). *Children with Down Syndrome: A developmental perspective*. Cambridge, England: Cambridge University Press.

CICCHETTI, D., & CARLSON, V. (1989). *Child maltreatment: Theory and research on the causes and consequences of child abuse and neglect*. New York: Cambridge University Press.

CLARK, D. C., CLAYTON, P. J., ANDREASON, N. C., LEWIS, D., FAWCETT, J., & SCHEFTNER, W. A. (1985). Intellectual functioning and abstraction ability in major affective disorders. *Comprehensive Psychiatry, 26*, 313–325.

CLARK, K. A. (1965). A role for librarians in the relevant war against poverty. Wilson Library Bulletin, Sept. 1965 (Quoted in A. MacLeod, *Growing up in America*.) Rockville, MD: National Institute of Mental Health.

CLARKE, A. M., & CLARKE, A. D. D. (1979). *Early experience: Myths and evidence*. New York: Free Press.

CLARKIN, J. F. (1989). Family education. In A. S. Bellack, ed., *A clinical guide for the treatment of schizophrenia*. New York: Plenum.

CLAYTON, P. J. (1990). Bereavement and depression. *Journal of Clinical Psychiatry, 51*, 34–38.

CLONINGER, C. R., BOHMAN, M., & SIGVARDSSON, S. (1981). Inheritance of alcohol abuse. *Archives of General Psychiatry, 38*, 861–868.

COFFEY, C. E., & WEINER, R. D. (1990). Electroconvulsive therapy: An update. *Hospital and Community Psychology, 41*, 515–521.

COHEN, D. J., CAPARULO, B. K., & SHAYWITZ, B. A. (1978). Neurochemical and developmental models of childhood autism. In G. Serban, ed., *Cognitive defects in the development of mental illness*. New York: Brunner/Mazel.

COHEN, L. H. (1988). *Life events and psychological functioning: Theoretical and methodological issues*. Newbury Park, CA: Sage Publications.

COHEN, M. E., ROBINS, E., PURTELL, J. J., ALTMANN, M. W., & REED, D. E. (1953). Excessive surgery in hysteria. *Journal of the American Medical Association, 151*, 977–986.

COHEN, R. A. (1975). Manic-depressive illness. In A. M. Freedman, J. I. Kaplan, & B. J. Sadock, *Comprehensive textbook of psychiatry*, 2nd ed. Baltimore, MD: Williams & Wilkins.

COLE, N. (1985). Sex therapy—A critical appraisal. *British Journal of Psychiatry, 147*, 337–351.

COLEMAN, E. (1981–1982). Developmental stages of the coming out process. *Journal of Homosexuality, 7*(2/3), 31–43.

CONAWAY, L., & HANSEN, D. J. (1989). Social behavior of physically abused and neglected children: A critical review. *Clinical Psychology Review, 9*, 627–652.

CONGER, J. J. (1991). *Adolescence and youth*, 4th ed. New York: HarperCollins.

CONTE, J. R. (1991). Evaluating children's reports of sexual abuse: Results from a survey of professionals. *American Journal of Orthopsychiatry, 61*, 428–437.

COOPER, J., & SARTORIUS, M. (1977). Cultural and temporal variations in schizophrenia: A speculation on the importance of industrialization. *British Journal of Psychiatry, 130*, 50–55.

CORNBLATT, B. A., & ERLENMEYER-KIMLING, L. (1985). Global attentional deviance as a marker of risk for schizophrenia: Specificity and predictive validity. *Journal of Abnormal Psychology, 94*, 470–486.

CORSON, S. A., CORSON, E. O., ARNOLD, L. E., & KNOPP, W. (1976). Animal models of violence and hyperkinesis. In G. Serban & A. Kling, eds. *Animal models in human psychology*. New York: Plenum.

COUNCIL ON SCIENTIFIC AFFAIRS, AMERICAN MEDICAL ASSOCIATION. (1986). Alcohol and the driver. *Journal of the American Medical Association, 255*, 522–527.

COUNCIL ON SCIENTIFIC AFFAIRS, AMERICAN MEDICAL ASSOCIATION. (1986). Polygraph. *Journal of the American Medical Association, 256*, 1172–1175.

COURCHESNE, E., YOUNG-COURCHESNE, N., PRESS, G. A., HESSELINK, J. R., and JERNIGAN, T. L. (1988). Hypoplasia of cerebellar vermal lobules VI and VII in autism. *New England Journal of Medicine, 318*, 1349–1354.

COWEN, E. L. (1982). Help is where you find it: Four informal helping groups. *American Psychologist, 37*, 385–395.

COWEN, E. L., & HIGHTOWER, A. D. (1990). The Primary Mental Health Project: Alternative approaches in school-based preventive intervention. In T. B. Gutkin & C. R. Reynolds, eds., *Handbook of school psychology*. New York: John Wiley.

COX, B. J. (1990). Substance abuse and panic-related anxiety: A critical review. *Behavior Research and Therapy, 28*(5), 385–393.

COYLE, J. T., PRICE, D. L. C., & DELONG, M. R. (1983). Alzheimer's disease: A disorder of cortical cholinergic innervation. *Science, 219*, 1184–1190.

COYNE, J. C., KAHN, J., & GOTLIB, I. H. (1987). Depression. In T. Jacob, ed., *Family interaction and psychopathology*. New York: Pergamon.

CRAIG, E. M., & MCCARVER, R. B. (1984). Community placement and adjustment of deinstitutionalized clients: Issues and findings. *International Review of Research in Mental Retardation, 12*, 95–122.

CREESE, I., BURT, D. R., & SNYDER, S. H. (1976). Dopamine receptor binding predicts clinical and pharmacological potencies of antischizophrenic drugs. *Science, 192*, 481–483.

CRISP, A. H., & BURNS, T. (1983). The clinical presentation of anorexia nervosa in the male. *International Journal of Eating Disorders, 2,* 5–10.

CROOK, T., & ELIOT, J. (1980). Parental death during childhood and adult depression: A critical review of the literature. *Psychological Bulletin, 87,* 252–259.

CROSBY, D. (1989). First person account: Growing up with a schizophrenic mother. *Schizophrenia Bulletin, 15,* 507–509.

CROW, T. J. (1980a). Molecular pathology of schizophrenia: More than one disease process? *British Medical Journal, 280,* 66–68.

CROW, T. J. (1980b). Positive and negative schizophrenia symptoms and the role of dopamine. *British Journal of Psychiatry, 137,* 383–386.

CROW, T. J. (1985). The two syndrome concept: Origins and current status. *Schizophrenia Bulletin, 11,* 471–486.

CROWE, M. J., GILLAN, P., & GOLOMBOK, S. (1981). Form and content in the conjoint treatment of sexual dysfunction: A controlled study. *Behaviour Research and Therapy, 19,* 47–54.

CROWLEY, T. J. (1987). Clinical issues in cocaine abuse. In S. Fisher, A. Raskin, & E. H. Uhlenhuth, eds., *Clinical issues in cocaine abuse.* (pp. 193–211). New York: Oxford University Press.

CUMMINGS, E. M., IANNOTTI, R. J., & ZAHN-WAXLER, C. (1985). Influence of conflict between adults on the emotions and aggression of young children. *Developmental Psychology, 21,* 495–507.

CUMMINGS, J. L., & ZARIT, J. M. (1987). Probable Alzheimer's disease in an artist. *Journal of the American Medical Association, 258,* 2731–2734.

CUSTANCE, J. (1952). *Wisdom, madness and folly.* New York: Pelligrini & Cuddahy.

CZEISLER, C. A., WEITZMAN, G. D., MOORE-EDE, M. C., ZIMMERMAN, J. C., & KNAUER, R. S. (1980). Human sleep: Its duration and organization depend on its circadian phase. *Science, 210,* 1264–1267.

DARUNA, J. H., & MORGAN, J. E. (1990). Psychosocial effects on immune function: Neuroendocrine pathways. *Psychosomatics, 31,* 1–12.

DAVENPORT, Y. B., ADLAND, M. L., GOLD, P. W., & GOODWIN, F. K. (1979). Manic-depressive illness: Psychodynamic features of multi-generational families. *American Journal of Orthopsychiatry, 49,* 24–35.

DAVIS, G. E., & LEITENBERG, H. (1987). Adolescent sex offenders. *Psychological Bulletin, 101,* 417–427.

DAVIS, J. A., & SMITH, T. (1987). *General social surveys, 1972–1987: Cumulative data.* Storrs, CT: University of Connecticut, Roper Center for Public Opinion Research.

DAVIS, J. M. (1985). Antipsychotic drugs. In H. I. Kaplan & B. J. Sadock, eds. *Comprehensive textbook of psychiatry,* 4th ed., vol. 2. Baltimore, MD: Williams & Wilkins.

DAWSON, G., ED. (1989). *Autism: Nature, diagnosis, and treatment.* New York: Guilford.

DAWSON, G. & CASTELLOE, P. (in press). Autism. In C. E. Walker & M. C. Roberts, eds., *Handbook of clinical child psychology* (rev. ed.). New York: Wiley.

DAWSON, M. E., & NUECHTERLEIN, K. H. (1987). The role of autonomic dysfunctions within a vulnerability: Stress model of schizophrenic disorders. In D. Magnusson & A. Ohman, eds., *Psychopathology: An interactional perspective.* New York: Academic Press.

DAYEE, F. S. (1982). *Private zones.* Edmonds, WA: Charles Franklin Press.

DELUTY, R. H. (1988–89). Physical illness, psychiatric illness and the acceptability of suicide. *Omega: The Journal of Death and Dying, 1,* 79–91.

DEMOS, J. P. (1982). *Entertaining Satan: Witchcraft and the culture of early New England.* New York: Oxford University Press.

DE NIKE, L. D., & TIBER, N. (1968). Neurotic behavior. In P. London & D. Rosenham, eds., *Foundations of abnormal psychology.* New York: Holt, Rinehart & Winston.

DERRY, P. A., & KUIPER, N. A. (1981). Schematic processing and self reference in clinical depression. *Journal of Abnormal Psychology, 90,* 286–297.

DeRUBEIS, R. J., EVANS, M. D., HOLLON, S. D., GARVEY, M. J., GROVE, W. M., & TUASON, V. B. (1990). How does cognitive therapy work? Cognitive change and symptom change in cognitive therapy and pharmacotherapy for depression. *Journal of Consulting and Clinical Psychology, 38,* 862–869.

DE RUITER, C., RIJKEN, H., GARSSEN, B., VAN SCHAIK, A., & KRAAIMAAT, F. (1989). Comorbidity among the anxiety disorders. *Journal of Anxiety Disorders, 3,* 57–68.

DEUTSCH, A. (1948). *The shame of the states.* New York: Arno.

DEUTSCH, S. I., & DAVIS, K. L. (1983). Schizophrenia: A review of diagnostic and biological issues. II. Biological issues. *Hospital and Community Psychiatry, 34,* 423–437.

DEYKIN, E. Y., & MACMAHON, B. (1979). The incidence of seizures among children with autistic symptoms. *American Journal of Psychiatry, 136,* 1310–1312.

DICKSON, L. R., & RANSEEN, J. D. (1990). An update on selected organic mental syndromes. *Hospital and Community Psychiatry, 41,* 290–300.

DIDION, J. (1979). *The White Album.* New York: Simon & Schuster.

DIGDON, N., & GOTLIB, I. H. (1985). Developmental considerations in the study of childhood depression. *Developmental Review, 5,* 162–199.

DIMSDALE, J. E. (1988). A perspective on Type A behavior and coronary disease. *New England Journal of Medicine, 318,* 110–112.

DOCTER, R. F. (1988). *Transvestites and transsexuals.* New York: Plenum.

DODGE, K. A. (1985). Attributional bias in aggressive children. *Advances in Cognitive Behavioral Research and Therapy, 4,* 73–110.

DOHRENWEND, B. P., LEVAV, I., SHROUT, P. E., SCHWARTZ, S., NAVEH, G., LINK, B. G., SKODOL, A. E., & STUEVE, A. (1992). Socioeconomic status and psychiatric disorders: The causation-selection issue. *Science, 255,* 946–952.

DOLLARD, J., & MILLER, N. (1950). *Personality and psychotherapy.* New York: McGraw-Hill.

DORIAN, B., & GARFINKEL, P. E. (1987). Stress, immunity and illness—a review. *Psychological Medicine, 17,* 393–407.

DORRIS, M. (1989). *The broken cord.* New York: Harper & Row.

DORWART, R. A., SCHLESINGER, M., DAVISON, H., EPSTEIN, S., & HOOVER, C. (1991). A national study of psychiatric hospital care. *American Journal of Psychiatry, 148,* 204–210.

DOUGLAS, W. O. (1974). *Go east, young man.* New York: Random House.

DRYFOOS, J. G. (1990). *Adolescents at risk.* New York: Oxford University Press.

DULCAN, M. K. (1986). Comprehensive treatment of children and adolescents with attention deficit disorders: The state of the art. *Clinical Psychology Review, 6,* 539–569.

DUNNER, D. L. (1987). Stability of Bipolar II affective disorder as a diagnostic entity. *Psychiatric Annals, 17,* 18–20.

DU PAUL, G. J., GUEVREMONT, D. C., & BARKLEY, R. J. (1991). Attention deficit-hyperactivity disorder in adolescence: Critical assessment parameters. *Clinical Psychology Review, 11,* 231–245.

DYKMAN, B. M., HOROWITZ, L. M., ABRAMSON, L. Y., & USHER, M. (1991). Schematic and situational determinants of depressed and nonde-pressed students' interpretation of feedback. *Journal of Abnormal Psychology, 100,* 45–55.

EASTON, K. (1959). An unusual case of fugue and orality. *Psychoanalytic Quarterly, 28,* 505–513.

EATON, W. W., & KEYL, P. M. (1990). Risk factors for the onset of Diagnostic Interview Schedule/DSM-III: Agoraphobia in a prospective, population-based study. *Archives of General Psychiatry, 47,* 819–824.

EBERHARDY, F. (1967). The view from "the couch." *Journal of Child Psychology and Psychiatry, 8,* 257–263.

ECKARDT, M. J., HARFORD, T. C., KAELBER, C. T., PARKER, E. S., ROSENTHAL, L. S., RYBACK, R. S., SALMOIRAGHI, G. C., VANDERVEEN, E., & WARREN, K. R. (1981). Health hazards associated with alcohol consumption. *Journal of the American Medical Association, 246,* 648–666.

EGELAND, J. A., GERHARD, D. S., PAULS, D. L., SUSSEX, J. N., KIDD, K. K., ALLEN, C. R., HOSTETTER, A. M., & HOUSMAN, D. E. (1987). Bipolar affective disorders linked to DNA markers on chromosome II. *Nature, 325,* 783–787.

EICHENWALD, K. (1987). Braving epilepsy's storm. *New York Times Magazine,* January 11, 30–36.

EISENSON, J. (1973). *Adult aphasia: Assessment and treatment.* Englewood Cliffs, NJ: Prentice-Hall.

EISLER, R. M. (1972). Crisis intervention in the family of a firesetter. *Psychotherapy: Theory, research and practice, 9,* 76–79.

ELDRED, S. H., BELL, N. W., LONGABAUGH, R., & SHERMAN, L. J. (1964). Interactional correlates of chronicity in schizophrenia. *Psychiatric Research Report 19*, December 1–12. Washington, D.C.: American Psychiatric Association.

ELIOT, R. S., & BUELL, J. C. (1983). The role of the CNS in cardiovascular disorders. *Hospital Practice*, May, 189–199.

ELKINS, R., RAPOPORT, J., & LIPSKY, A. (1980). Childhood obsessive-compulsive disorder: A neurobiological perspective. *Journal of the American Academy of Child Psychiatry, 19*, 551–554.

ELLENBERGER, H. F. (1970). *The discovery of the unconscious.* New York: Basic Books.

ELLIS, A. (1962). *Reason and emotion in psychotherapy.* New York: Lyle Stuart.

ELLIS, A. (1970). Rational-emotive therapy. In L. Hersher, ed., *Four psychotherapies.* New York: Appleton-Century-Crofts.

ELMADJIAN, E. (1963). Excretion and metabolism effect in the epinephrine and norepinephrine in various emotional states. *Proceedings of the Fifth Pan-American Conference of Endocrinology*, Lima, Peru.

ENDLER, N. S. (1982). *Holiday of darkness.* New York: Wiley-Interscience.

ENDLER, N. S. (1989). *Holiday of darkness: A psychologist's personal journey out of his depression.* Revised Edition. Toronto: Wall & Thompson.

ENGEL, G. L. (1977). The need for a new medical model: A challenge for biomedicine. *Science, 196*, 129–136.

EMMELKAMP, P. M. G., VAN DER HELM, M., VAN ZANTEN, B. L., & PLOCHG, I. (1980). Treatment of obsessive-compulsive patients: The contribution of self-instructional training to the effectiveness of exposure. *Behavior Research and Therapy, 18*, 61–66.

EPSTEIN, A. W. (1965). Fetishism. In R. Slovenko, ed., *Sexual behavior and the law.* Springfield, IL: Thomas.

ERDELYI, M. (1985). *Psychoanalysis: Freud's cognitive psychology.* New York: W. H. Freeman.

ERICKSON, M. F., & EGELAND, B. (1987). A developmental view of the psychological consequences of maltreatment. *School Psychology Review, 16*, 156–168.

ERIKSON, E. H. (1975). *Life history and the historical moment.* New York: W. W. Norton.

ERLENMEYER-KIMLING, L. (1987). Biological markers for the liability to schizophrenia. In H. Helmchen & F. A. Henn, eds., *Biological perspectives of schizophrenia.* New York: John Wiley.

ERLENMEYER-KIMLING, L., & CORNBLATT, B. (1987). High risk research in schizophrenia: A summary of what has been learned. *British Journal of Psychiatry, 21*, 401–411.

ERON, L. D. (1987). The development of aggressive behavior from the perspective of a developing behaviorism. *American Psychologist, 42*, 435–442.

ERON, L. D., & PETERSON, R. A. (1982). Abnormal behavior: Social approaches. In M. R. Rosenzweig & L. W. Porter, eds., *Annual Review of Psychology.* Palo Alto, CA: Annual Reviews.

EVANS, D. E., FUNKENSTEIN, H. H., ALBERT, M. S., SCHERR, P. A., COOK, N. R., CHOWN, M. J., HEBERT, L. E., HENNEKENS, C. H., & TAYLOR, J. O. (1989). Prevalence of Alzheimer's disease in a community population of older persons: Higher than previously reported. *Journal of the American Medical Association, 262*, 2551–2556.

EYSENCK, H. J. (1952). The effects of psychotherapy: An evaluation. *Journal of Consulting Psychology, 16*, 319–324.

EYSENCK, H. J. (1961). The effects of psychotherapy. In H. J. Eysenck, ed., *Handbook of abnormal psychology.* New York: Basic Books.

EYSENCK, H. J. (1987). Anxiety, learned helplessness, and cancer: A causal theory. *Journal of Anxiety Disorders, 1*, 87–104.

EYSENCK, H. J., & EYSENCK, S. B. G. (1975). *Manual of the Eysenck Personality Questionnaire.* London: University of London Press.

FABREGA, H., MEZZICH, J. E., MEZZICH, A. C., & COFFMAN, G. A. (1986). Descriptive validity of DSM-III Depressions. *Journal of Nervous and Mental Disease, 174*, 573–584.

FAIRWEATHER, G. W., SANDERS, D. H., MAYNARD, H., CRESSLER, D. L., & BLECK, D. S. (1969). *Community life for the mentally ill: An alternative to institutional care.* Chicago: Aldine.

FARAONE, S., KREMEN, W., & TSUANG, M. (1990). Genetic transmission of major affective disorders: Quantitative models and linkage analyses. *Psychological Bulletin, 108*, 109–127.

FARAONE, S. V., & TSUANG, M. T. (1985). Quantitative models of the genetic transmission of schizophrenia. *Psychological Bulletin, 98*, 41–66.

FARBER, S. L. (1983). *Identical twins reared apart: A reanalysis.* New York: Basic Books.

FARBER, S. S., FELNER, R. D., & PRIMAVERA, J. (1985). Parental separation/divorce and adolescents: An examination of factors mediating adaptation. *American Journal of Community Psychiatry, 13*, 171–185.

FARINA, A., GHILA, D., BOUDREAU, L. A., ALLEN, J. G., & SHERMAN, M. (1971). Mental illness and the impact of believing others know about it. *Journal of Abnormal Psychology, 77*, 1–5.

FARMER, A., JACKSON, R., McGUFFIN, P., & STOREY, P. (1987). Cerebral ventricular enlargement in chronic schizophrenia: Consistencies and contradictions. *British Journal of Psychiatry, 150*, 324–330.

FAVA, M. (1991). Does fluoxetine increase the risk of suicide? *The Harvard Mental Health Letter, 7*(7), 8.

FAWCETT, J., SCHEFTNER, W., CLARK, D., HEDEKER, D., GIBBONS, R., & CORYELL, W. (1987). Clinical predictors of suicide in patients with major affective disorders: A controlled prospective study. *American Journal of Psychiatry, 144*, 35–46.

FELDMAN, D. (1987). A social work student's reaction to client suicide. *Social Casework, 63*(3), 184–187.

FERREL, R. B. (1980). Schizophrenia: The diagnoses and misdiagnoses. *Carrier Foundation Letter, 65* (Nov.), 1–5.

FINKELHOR, D. (1984). *Child sexual abuse: New theory and research.* New York: Free Press.

FINKELHOR, D., & HOTALING, G. (1984). Sexual abuse in the national incidence study of child abuse and neglect: An appraisal. *Child Abuse and Neglect, 8*, 23–33.

FIORE, M. C., NOVOTNY, T. E., PIERCE, J. P., GIOVINO, G. A., HATZIANDREU, E. J., NEWCOMB, P. A., SURAWICZ, T. S., & DAVIS, R. M. (1990). Methods used to quit smoking in the United States: Do cessation programs help? *Journal of the American Medical Association, 263*, 2760–2765.

FIRLIK, A. D. (1991). Margo's logo. *Journal of the American Medical Association, 265*, 201.

FISCHER, G. J. (1986). College student attitudes toward forcible date rape: I. Cognitive predictors. *Archives of Sexual Behavior, 15*, 457–466.

FLAMENT, M. F., KOBY, E., RAPOPORT, J. L., BERG, C. J., ZAHN, T., COX, C., DENCKLA, M., & LENANE, M. (1990). Childhood obsessive–compulsive disorder: A prospective follow-up study. *Journal of Child Psychology and Psychiatry, 31*, 363–380.

FLAY, B. R., RYAN, K. B., BEST, J. A., BROWN, K. S., KERSELL, M. W., d'AVERNAS, J. R., & ZANNA, M. P. (1985). Are social psychological smoking prevention programs effective? The Waterloo study. *Journal of Behavioral Medicine, 8*, 37–59.

FLEMING, J. E., OFFORD, D. R., & BOYLE, M. H. (1989). Prevalence of childhood and adolescent depression in the community. *British Journal of Psychiatry, 155*, 647–654.

FOLSTEIN, S., & RUTTER, M. (1977). Infantile autism: A genetic study of 21 twin pairs. *Journal of Child Psychology and Psychiatry, 18*, 297–321.

FOLSTEIN, S., & RUTTER, M. (1978). A twin study of individuals with infantile autism. In M. Rutter & E. Schopler, eds., *Autism: A reappraisal of concepts and treatment.* New York: Plenum.

FORD, C. V., & FOLKS, D. G. (1985). Conversion disorders: An overview. *Psychosomatics, 26*, 371–374, 380–383.

FOWLER, R., RICH, C., & YOUNG, D. (1986). San Diego suicide study. *Archives of General Psychiatry, 43*, 962–965.

FRAEBERG, S., ADELSON, E., & SHAPIRO, V. (1975). Ghosts in the nursery: A psychoanalytic approach to the problem of impaired infant-mother relationships. *Journal of the American Academy of Child Psychology, 14*, 387–421.

FRANCES, A. J., & KLEIN, D. F. (1982). Anxious, precise, demanding man seeks help soon after marriage. *Hospital and Community Psychiatry, 33*, 89–90.

FRANCES, R. J., & MILLER, S. I. (1991). *Clinical textbook of addictive disorders.* New York: Gardner.

FRANCES, R. J., & WIDIGER, T. (1986). The classification of personality disorders: An overview of problems and solutions. *Annual Review of Psychiatry, 5*, 240–257.

FRANK, E., ANDERSON, C., & RUBENSTEIN, D. (1978). Frequency of sexual dysfunction in "normal" couples. *New England Journal of Medicine, 299,* 111–115.

FRANKS, C. (1985). Behavior therapy with children and adolescents. *Annual Review of Behavior Therapy, 10,* 236–290.

FRANKS, L. (1985). The story of "James B." *New York Times Magazine,* Oct. 20, p. 48.

FREEDMAN, B. J. (1974). The subjective experience of perceptual and cognitive disturbances in schizophrenia: A review of autobiographical accounts. *Archives of General Psychiatry, 30,* 333–340.

FREEMAN, A. (1990). Cognitive therapy. In A. S. Bellack & M. Hersen, eds., *Handbook of comparative treatments for adult disorders.* New York: Wiley.

FREEMAN, A., SIMON, K. M., BEUTLER, L. E., & ARKOWITZ, H., EDS. (1989). *Comprehensive handbook of cognitive therapy.* New York: Plenum.

FREEMAN, B. J., RITVO, E. R., NEEDLEMAN, R., & YOKOTA, A. (1985). The stability of cognitive and linguistic parameters in autism: A five-year study. *Journal of the American Academy of Child Psychiatry, 24,* 459–464.

FREUD, S. (1930). Civilization and its discontents. In J. Strachey, ed., *The standard edition of the complete psychological works of Sigmund Freud,* vol. 21. London: Hogarth.

FREUD, S. (1950). (originally published 1909) Selected papers. In J. Strachey, ed., *The standard edition of the complete psychological works of Sigmund Freud,* vol. 3. London: Hogarth.

FREUD, S. (1951). A letter from Freud (April 9, 1935). *American Journal of Psychiatry, 107,* 786–787.

FREUD, S. (1957). (originally published 1917) Mourning and melancholia. In J. Strachey, ed., *The standard edition of the complete psychological works of Sigmund Freud,* vol. 14. London: Hogarth.

FREUD, S. (1963). *The cocaine papers.* New York: Dunquin.

FREUD, S. (1964). (originally published 1936) A disturbance of memory on the Acropolis. In J. Strachey, ed., *The standard edition of the complete psychological works of Sigmund Freud,* vol. 22. London: Hogarth.

FREUD, S. (1969). *Collected works,* vol. 5. New York: Basic Books.

FRIEDMAN, H. S., & BOOTH-KEWLEY, S. (1987). The "disease-prone personality." *American Psychologist, 42,* 539–555.

FRIEDMAN, M., & ROSENMAN, R. (1974). *Type A behavior and your heart.* New York: Knopf.

FRIEDRICH, W. N., WILTURNER, L. T., & COHEN, D. S. (1985). Coping resources and parenting mentally retarded children. *American Journal of Mental Deficiency, 90*(2), 130–139.

FROMUTH, M. E. (1986). The relationship of childhood sexual abuse with later psychological and sexual adjustment in a sample of college women. *Child Abuse and Neglect, 10,* 5–15.

FULLER, A. K. (1989). Child molestation and pedophilia: An overview for the physician. *Journal of the American Medical Association, 261,* 602–606.

FYER, A. J., & SANDBERG, D. P. (1988). Pharmacologic treatment of panic disorder. In A. J. Frances & R. E. Hales, eds., *Review of psychiatry,* vol. 7. Washington, DC: American Psychiatric Press.

GABBARD, G. O. (1985). The role of compulsiveness in the normal physician. *Journal of the American Medical Association, 254,* 2926–2929.

GADPAILLE, W. J. (1989). Homosexuality. In H. I. Kaplan & B. J. Sadock, eds., *Comprehensive textbook of psychiatry,* 5th ed., vol. 1. Baltimore: Williams & Wilkins.

GARBARINO, J., STOTT, F. M., AND OTHERS (1990). *What children can tell us: Eliciting, interpreting, and evaluating information from children.* San Francisco: Jossey-Bass.

GARBER, H. L. (1988). *The Milwaukee Project: Preventing mental retardation in children at risk.* Washington, DC: American Association on Mental Retardation.

GARFIELD, S. L. (1990). Issues and methods in psychotherapy process research. *Journal of Consulting and Clinical Psychology, 58,* 273–280.

GARFINKEL, B. D., CARLSON, G. A., & WELLER, E. B. (1990). *Psychiatric disorders in children and adolescents.* Philadelphia: Saunders.

GARMEZY, N., & DEVINE, E. (1984). Project competence: The Minnesota studies of children vulnerable to psychopathology. In N. F. Watt, E. J. Anthony, N. F. Wynne, & J. E. Rolf, eds. *Children at risk for schizophrenia: A longitudinal perspective.* New York: Cambridge University Press, 289–303.

GARNER, D. M., & GARFINKEL, P. E. (1980). Socio-cultural factors in the development of anorexia nervosa. *Psychological Medicine, 10,* 647–656.

GARNER, D. M., GARFINKEL, P. E., SCHWARTZ, D., & THOMPSON, M. (1980). Cultural expectations of thinness in women. *Psychological Reports, 47,* 438–491.

GARVER, D. L. (1987). Methodological issues facing the interpretation of high risk studies: Biological heterogeneity. *Schizophrenia Bulletin, 13,* 525–529.

GAWIN, F. H. (1991). Cocaine addiction: Psychology and neurophysiology. *Science, 251*(5001), 1580–1586.

GEBHARD, P. H. (1972). Incidence of overt homosexuality in the United States and Western Europe. In J. M. Livingood, ed., *National Institute of Mental Health Task Force on Homosexuality: Final Report and Background Papers,* Publication 72-9116. Dept. of Health, Education, & Welfare, 22–29.

GELARDO, M. S., & SANFORD, E. E. (1987). Child abuse and neglect: A review of the literature. *School Psychology Review, 2,* 137–155.

GELDER, M., GATH, D., & MAYOU, R, (1989). *Oxford textbook of psychiatry,* 2nd ed. Oxford, England: Oxford University Press.

GELFAND, D., & TETI, D. M. (1990). The effects of maternal depression on children. *Clinical Psychology Review, 10,* 329–353.

GEORGE, L., & NEUFELD, R. W. J. (1985). Cognition and symptomatology in schizophrenia. *Schizophrenia Bulletin, 11,* 264–285.

GERSHON, E. S., BERRETTINI, W. H., & GOLDIN, L. R. (1989). Mood disorders: Genetic aspects. In H. I. Kaplan & B. J. Sadock, eds., *Textbook of psychiatry,* 5th ed. Baltimore: Williams & Wilkins.

GERSHON, E. S., HAMOVIT, J., GUROFF, J. J., DIBBLE, E., LECKMAN, J. F., SCEERY, W., TARGUM, S. D., NURNBERGER, J. I., GOLDIN, L. R., & BUNNEY, W. E., JR. (1982). A family study of schizoaffective, bipolar I, bipolar II, unipolar and normal control probands. *Archives of General Psychiatry, 39,* 1157–1167.

GERSHON, L., & SHAW, F. H. (1961). Psychiatric sequelae of chronic exposure to organophosphorous insecticides. *Lancet, 1,* 1371–1374.

GERSTEIN, D. R. (1987). *Toward the prevention of alcohol problems: Government, business, and community action.* Washington, DC: National Academy Press.

GIBBONS, A. (1991). The brain as "sexual organ." *Science, 253,* 957–959.

GIBBONS, F. X. (1985). Stigma perception: Social comparison among mentally retarded persons. *American Journal of Mental Deficiency, 90,* 98–106.

GIBBS, F. A., GIBBS, E. L., & LENNOX, W. G. (1939). Influence of the blood sugar level on the wave and spike formation in petit mal epilepsy. *Archives of Neurology and Psychiatry, 41,* 1111–1116.

GILL, J. J., PRICE, V. A., FRIEDMAN, M., THORESEN, C. E., POWELL, L. H., ULMER, D., BROWN, B., & DREWS, F. R. (1985). Reduction in Type-A behavior in healthy middle-aged American military officers. *American Heart Journal, 110,* 503–514.

GIST, R., & LUBIN, B., EDS. (1989). *Psychosocial aspects of disaster.* New York: Wiley.

GITTELMAN, R., & KLEIN, D. F. (1984). Relationships between separation anxiety and panic and agoraphobic disorders. *Psychopathology, 17* (supplement), 56–65.

GITTELMAN-KLEIN, R., ABIKOFF, H., POLLACK, E., KLEIN, D., KATZ, S., & MATTES, J. (1980). A controlled trial of behavior modification and methylphenidate in hyperactive children. In C. Whalen & B. Henker, eds., *Hyperactive children: The social ecology of identification and treatment.* New York: Academic Press.

GOFF, D. C., BROTMAN, A. W., WAITES, M., & McCORMICK, S. (1990). Trial of fluoxetine added to neuroleptics for treatment-resistant schizophrenic patients. *American Journal of Psychiatry, 147,* 492–494.

GOFFMAN, E. (1959). *The presentation of self in everyday life.* New York: Doubleday.

GOLD, G. (1974). *The White House transcripts.* New York: Bantam Books.

GOLDBLOOM, D. S., & GARFINKEL, P. E. (1990). Eating disorders: Anorexia nervosa and bulimia nervosa. In B. D. Garfinkel, G. A. Carson, & E. B. Weller eds., *Psychiatric disorders in children and adolescents.* Philadelphia: Saunders.

GOLDEN, J. C., GRAVER, B., BLOSE, I., BERG, R., COFFMAN, J., & BLOCH, S. (1981). Differences in brain densities between chronic alcoholic and normal control patients. *Science, 211,* 508–510.

GOLDEN, K. M. (1977). Voodoo in Africa and the United States. *American Journal of Psychiatry, 134,* 1425–1427.

GOLDMAN, P., & WILLIAMS, D. A. (1978). Black youth, a lost generation? *Newsweek,* August 7, 22–34.

GOLDSTEIN, M. J. (1985). Family factors that antedate the onset of schizophrenia and related disorders: The results of a fifteen-year prospective longitudinal study. *Acta Psychiatrica Scandinavica Supplementum,* No. 319, *71,* 7–18.

GOLDSTEIN, S., & GOLDSTEIN, M. (1990). *Managing attention disorders in children.* New York: John Wiley.

GOODWIN, D. W. (1981). Alcoholism and alcoholic psychoses. In H. I. Kaplan & B. J. Sadock, eds. *Comprehensive textbook of psychiatry III,* 4th ed., vol. 1. Baltimore: Williams and Wilkins.

GOODWIN, D. W. (1986). Genetic factors in the development of alcoholism. *Psychiatric Clinics of North America, 9,* 427–433.

GOODWIN, F. K., & JAMISON, K. R. (1987). Bipolar disorders. In R. E. Hales & A. J. Frances, eds., *American Psychiatric Association Annual Review,* vol. 6. Washington, D.C.: American Psychiatric Press.

GOODWIN, F. K., & JAMISON, K. R. (1990). *Manic-depressive illness.* New York: Oxford University Press.

GOODYER, I., KOLVIN, I., & GATZANIS, S. (1985). Recent undesirable life events and psychiatric disorder in childhood and adolescence. *British Journal of Psychiatry, 147,* 517–523.

GOSSELIN, C., & WILSON, G. (1980). *Sexual variations.* New York: Simon & Schuster.

GOTLIB, I. H. & COLBY, C. A. (1987). *Treatment of depression.* New York: Pergamon Press.

GOTTESMAN, I. I. (1991). *Schizophrenia genesis: The origins of madness.* New York: Freeman.

GOTTESMAN, I. I., McGUFFIN, P., & FARMER, A. E. (1987). Clinical genetics as clues to the "real" genetics of schizophrenia. *Schizophrenia Bulletin, 13,* 23–47.

GOTTESMAN, I. I., & SHIELDS, J. (WITH THE ASSISTANCE OF D. R. HANSON). (1982). *Schizophrenia: The epigenetic puzzle.* New York: Cambridge University Press.

GOTTLIEB, A. (1985). *Nicotine chewing gum, smoking withdrawal symptoms, and relapse: A controlled study.* Unpublished dissertation, University of Washington, Seattle.

GOTTLIEB, J., SEMMEL, M. I., & VELDMAN, D. J. (1978). Correlates of social status among mainstreamed mentally retarded children. *Journal of Educational Psychology, 70,* 396–405.

GOTTSCHALK, L. A. (1978). Psychosomatic medicine today: An overview. *Psychosomatics, 19,* 89–93.

GOULD, M. S., & SHAFFER, D. (1986). The impact of suicide in television movies (Evidence of imitation). *New England Journal of Medicine, 316,* 690–694.

GOVE, W. R., & HUGHES, M. (1980). Reexamining the ecological fallacy: A study in which aggregate data are critical in investigating the pathological effects of living alone. *Social Forces, 58,* 1157–1177.

GRAHAM, J. R. (1990). *MMPI-2: Assessing personality and psychopathology.* New York: Oxford University Press.

GRAHAM, S. (1974). *A Lecture to young men.* Salem, NH: Ayer Publishers.

GRANDIN, T. (1984). My experiences as an autistic child and review of selected literature. *Journal of Orthomolecular Psychiatry, 13,* 144–174.

GRANDIN, T. (1987). Motivating autistic children. *Academic Therapy, 22(3),* 297–302.

GRANDIN, T. (1991). Overcoming autism: A first person account. *Harvard Mental Health Letter,* March 4–7.

GRAWBOWSKI, J., ED. (1985). *Pharmacological adjuncts in smoking cessation.* Rockville, MD: National Institute on Drug Abuse.

GREEN, E. (1972). Biofeedback for mind/body self-regulation: Feeling and creativity. *Biofeedback and self-control.* Chicago: Aldine.

GREEN, R. (1974). *Sexual identity conflicts in children and adults.* New York: Basic Books.

GREEN, R. (1985). Gender identity in childhood and later sexual orientation: Follow-up on 78 males. *American Journal of Psychiatry, 142,* 339–341.

GREEN, R. (1987). *The "sissy boy syndrome" and the development of homosexuality.* New Haven: Yale University Press.

GREEN, W. H., CAMPBELL, M., HARDESTY, A. S., GREGG, D. M., PADRON-GAYOL, M., SHELL, J., & ERLENMEYER-KIMLING, L. A comparison of schizophrenic and autistic children. *Journal of the American Academy of Child Psychiatry, 23,* 399–409.

GREENBERG, J. (1978). The Americanization of Roseto. *Science News, 113,* 378–382.

GREENFELD, J. A. (1970). A child called Noah. *Life,* October 23, 60–72.

GRENELL, M. M., GLASS, C. R., & KATZ, K. S. (1987). Hyperactive children and peer interaction: Knowledge and performance of social skills. *Journal of Abnormal Child Psychology, 15,* 1–13.

GRILLON, C., COURCHESNE, E., AMELI, R., GEYER, M. A., & BRAFF, D. L. (1990). Increased distractibility in schizophrenic patients. *Archives of General Psychiatry, 47,* 171–179.

GRILLY, D. (1989). *Drugs and human behavior.* Boston: Allyn and Bacon.

GRINKER, R. (1979). *Historical perspectives on depression.* Roche Laboratories Professional Services Department.

GROTH, A. N. (1979). *Men who rape.* New York: Plenum Press.

GROTH, A. N., LONGO, R. E., & McFADIN, J. B. (1982). Undetected recidivism among rapists and child molesters. *Crime and Delinquency, 28,* 450–458.

GROVE, W. M., & ANDREASEN, N. C. (1985). Language and thinking in psychosis. *Archives of General Psychiatry, 42,* 26–32.

GUDEMAN, J. E., DICKEY, B., HELLMAN, S., & BUFFETT, W. (1985). From inpatient to inn status: A new residential model. *Psychiatric Clinics of North America, 8,* 461–469.

GUILLEN, T. (1982). Competency ruling frees Safety Building squatter. *Seattle Times,* Jan. 27, B1.

GUNDERSON, J. G. (1984). *Borderline Personality Disorder.* Washington, D.C.: American Psychiatric Press.

GUNDERSON, J. G., RONNINGSTAM, E., & BODKIN, A. (1990). The diagnostic interview for narcissistic patients. *Archives of General Psychiatry, 47,* 676–680.

GUNDERSON, J. G., & ZANARINI, M. C. (1987). Current overview of the borderline diagnosis. *Journal of Clinical Psychiatry, 48(8)* (Supplement), 5–11.

GURLING, H. M. D., SHERRINGTON, R. P., BRYNJOLFSSON, J., READ, T., CURTIS, D., MANKOO, B. J., & PETURSSON, H. (1989). Recent and future molecular genetic research into schizophrenia. *Schizophrenia Bulletin, 15,* 373–382.

HAAGA, D. A. (1987). Treatment of the Type A behavior pattern. *Clinical Psychology Review, 7,* 557–574.

HAAGA, D. F., DYCK, M. J., & ERNST, D. (1991). Empirical status of cognitive theory of depression. *Psychological Bulletin, 110,* 215–236.

HACKETT, T. P., & CASSEM, N. H. (1975). The psychologic reactions of patients in the pre- and post-hospital phases of myocardial infarction. *Postgraduate Medicine, 57,* 43–46.

HAGNELL, O., LANKE, J., RORSMAN, B., & OJESJO, L. (1981). Mental illness as a risk factor for suicide. *Neuropsychobiology, 7,* 248–253.

HALL, G. C. (1990). Prediction of sexual aggression. *Clinical Psychology Review, 10(2),* 229–245.

HALL, W., GOLDSTEIN, G., ANDREWS, G., LAPSLEY, H., BARTELS, R., & SILOVE, D. (1985). Estimating the economic costs of schizophrenia. *Schizophrenia Bulletin, 11,* 598–610.

HALMI, K. A., OWEN, W., LASKY, E., & STOKES, P. (1983). Dopaminergic regulation in anorexia nervosa. *International Journal of Eating Disorders, 22,* 129–134.

HAMILTON, E., & ABRAMSON, L. 1983. Cognitive patterns and major depressive disorders: A longitudinal study in a hospital setting. *Journal of Abnormal Psychology, 92,* 173–184.

HAMILTON, M. (1982). Symptoms and assessment of depression. In E. S. Paykel, ed., *Handbook of affective disorders.* Edinburgh: Churchill-Livingston.

HAMILTON, M. (1989). Mood disorders: Clinical features. In H. I. Kaplan & B. J. Sadock, eds., *Comprehensive textbook of psychiatry,* 5th ed. Baltimore: Williams and Wilkins.

HAMMEN, C., & DeMAYO, R. (1982). Cognitive correlates of teacher stress and depressive symptoms: Implications for attributional models of depression. *Journal of Abnormal Psychology, 91,* 96–101.

HAMMEN, C. L. (1985). Predicting depression: A cognitive-behavioral perspective. In P. C. Kendall, ed., *Advances in cognitive-behavioral research and therapy*, vol. 4. Orlando, FL: Academic Press.

HAMMOND, L. K., & DELUTY, R. H. (June, 1991). *Attitudes of clinical psychologists, psychiatrists, and oncologists toward suicide*. Paper presented at the annual meeting of the American Association of Applied and Preventive Psychology, Washington, DC.

HANSON, D. M., JACKSON, A. W., & HAGERMAN, R. J. (1986). Speech disturbances (cluttering) in mildly impaired males with the Martin-Bell/Fragile X syndrome. *American Journal of Medical Genetics, 23*, 195–206.

HANSON, J. W., STREISSGUTH, A. P., & SMITH, D. W. (1978). The effects of moderate alcohol consumption during pregnancy on fetal growth and morphogenesis. *Journal of Pediatrics, 92*, 457–460.

HARDING, C. M., BROOKS, G. W., ASHIKAGA, T., STRAUSS, J. S., & BREIER, A. (1987a). The Vermont longitudinal study of persons with severe mental illness, I: Methodology, study sample and overall status 32 years later. *American Journal of Psychiatry, 144*, 718–726.

HARDING, C. M., ZUBIN, J., & STRAUSS, J. S. (1987b). Chronicity in schizophrenia: Fact, partial fact or artifact. *Hospital and Community Psychiatry, 38*, 477–486.

HARE, E. H. (1985). Old familiar faces: Some aspects of the asylum era in Britain, Part II. *Psychiatric Developments, 4*, 383–392.

HARE, R. D., & FORTH, A. E. (1985). Psychopathy and lateral preferences. *Journal of Abnormal Psychology, 94*, 541–546.

HARLOW, H. F., & SUOMI, S. J. (1974). Induced depression in monkeys. *Behavioral Biology, 12*, 273–296.

HARRINGTON, R., FUDGE, H., RUTTER, M., PICKLES, A., & HILL, J. (1990). Adult outcomes of childhood and adolescent depression. *Archives of General Psychiatry, 47*, 465–473.

HARROW, M., GOLDBERG, J. F., GROSSMAN, L. S., & MELTZER, H. Y. (1990). Outcome in manic disorders: A naturalistic follow-up study. *Archives of General Psychiatry, 47*, 666–671.

HART, C. (1989). *Without reason*. New York: Harper and Row.

HARTSOUGH, C. S., & LAMBERT, N. M. (1985). Medical factors in hyperactive and normal children: Prenatal, developmental and health history findings. *American Journal of Orthopsychiatry, 55*, 190–201.

HARVARD MENTAL HEALTH LETTER. (1990). Mental illness and homelessness: Part I. *7(1)*, 1–4.

HARVARD MENTAL HEALTH LETTER. (1990). Panic disorder: Part I. Boston. *7(3)*, 1.

HASIN, D. S., GRANT, B., & ENDICOTT, J. (1990). The natural history of alcohol abuse: Implications for definitions of alcohol use disorders. *American Journal of Psychiatry, 147*, 1537–1541.

HATHAWAY, S. R., & MCKINLEY, J. C. (1967). *Minnesota Multiphasic Personality Inventory: Manual for administration and scoring*. New York: Psychological Corporation.

HATTIE, J. A., SHARPLEY, C. F., & ROGERS, H. J. (1984). Comparative effectiveness of professional and paraprofessional helpers. *Psychological Bulletin, 95*, 534–541.

HAURI, P., & ORR, W. C. (1982). *The sleep disorders: A current concepts monograph*. Kalamazoo, MI: Upjohn.

HAY, D. P., & HAY, L. K. (1990). The role of ECT in the treatment of depression. In C. D. McCann & N. S. Endler, eds., *Depression: New directions in theory, research, and practice*. 255–272. Toronto: Wall & Emerson.

HAYDEN, M. R. (1991). *Predictive testing for Huntington's disease*. Paper presented at the International Congress of Human Genetics in Washington, DC.

HAYNES, S. G., FEINLEIB, M., & KANNEL, W. B. (1980). The relationship of psychological factors to coronary heart disease in the Framingham study: III. Eight-year incidence of coronary heart disease. *American Journal of Epidemiology, 111*, 37–58.

HAZELWOOD, R. R., BURGESS, A. W., & GROTH, A. N. (1981). Death during dangerous autoerotic practice. *Social Science Medicine, 15E*, 129–133.

HAZELWOOD, R. R., DIETZ, P. E., & BURGESS, A. W. (1983). *Autoerotic fatalities*. Lexington, MA: Lexington Books.

HAZLETT, B. (1971). Two who played with death—and lost the game. *Los Angeles Times*, November 1, 5.

HEALTH PROMOTION AND DISEASE PREVENTION: UNITED STATES, 1985. (1988). *Vital and Health Statistics*, Series 10, Number 183. Hyattsville, MD: U.S. Dept. of Health and Human Services.

HECHT, H., VON ZERSSEN, D., KRIEG, C., PÖSSL, J., & WITTCHEN, H. (1989). Anxiety and depression: Comorbidity, psychopathology, and social functioning. *Comprehensive Psychiatry, 30*, 420–433.

HELGASON, T. (1979). Prevalence and incidence of mental disorders estimated by a health questionnaire and psychiatric case register. *Acta Psychiatrica Scandinavica, 58*, 256–266.

HELMER, D. C., RAGLAND, D. R., & SYME, S. L. (1991). Hostility and coronary artery disease. *The American Journal of Epidemiology, 133*, 112–122.

HELSING, K. J., SZELO, M., & COMSTOCK, G. W. (1981). Factors associated with mortality after widowhood. *American Journal of Public Health, 71*, 802–809.

HELZER, J. E., ROBINS, L. N., & MCEVOY, L. (1987). Posttraumatic stress disorder in the general population. *New England Journal of Medicine, 317*, 1630–1634.

HELZER, J. E., ROBINS, L. N., MCEVOY, L. T., SPITZNAGEL, E. L., STOLZMAN, R. K., & FARMER, A. (1985). A comparison clinical and diagnostic interview schedule diagnoses. *Archives of General Psychiatry, 42*, 657–666.

HELZER, J. E., SPITZNAGEL, E. L., & MCEVOY, L. (1987). The predictive validity of lay diagnostic interview schedule diagnoses in the general population. *Archives of General Psychiatry, 44*, 1069–1077.

HENDEN, H. (1981). Psychotherapy and suicide. *American Journal of Psychotherapy, 35*, 469–480.

HENDERSON, S. (1977). The social network, support and neurosis: The function of attachment in adult life. *British Journal of Psychiatry, 131*, 185–191.

HENINGER, G. R., CHARNEY, D. S., & PRICE, L. H. (1988). Alpha$_2$-adrenergic receptor sensitivity in depression: The plasma MHPG, behavioral, and cardiovascular responses to yohimbine. *Archives of General Psychiatry, 45*, 718–726.

HENNELL, T. (1967). *The witnesses*. New Hyde Park, New York: University Books.

HENNIGAN, K. M., HEATH, L., WHARTON, J. D., DELROSARIO, M. L., COOK, T. D., & CALDER, B. J. (1982). Impact of the introduction of television on crime in the United States: Empirical findings and theoretical implications. *Journal of Personality and Social Psychology, 42*, 461–477.

HERDT, G. H., ED. (1984). *Ritualized homosexuality in Melanesia* Berkelev: University of California Press.

HERMANN, B. P., WHITMAN, S., WYLER, A. R., ANTON, M. T., & VANDERZWAGG, R. (1990). Psychosocial predictors of psychopathology in epilepsy. *British Journal of Psychiatry, 156*, 98–105.

HEROLD, E. S., & WAY, L. (1983). Oral-genital sexual behavior in a sample of university females. *Journal of Sex Research, 19*, 327–338.

HERSEN, M., GULLICK, E. L., MATHERNE, P. M., & HARBERT, T. L. (1972). Instructions and reinforcement in the modification of a conversion reaction. *Psychological Reports, 31*, 719–722.

HESSE, H. (1969). *Peter Camenzind*. New York: Farrar, Straus, and Giroux.

HESTON, L. L., & MASTRI, A. R. (1982). Age of onset of Pick's and Alzheimer's dementia: Implications for diagnosis and research. *Journal of Gerontology, 37*, 422–424.

HESTON, L. L., & WHITE, J. (1991). *The vanishing mind: A practical guide to Alzheimer's disease and other dementias*. New York: W. H. Freeman.

HESTON, L. L., WHITE, J. A., & MASTRI, A. R. (1987). Pick's disease. *Archives of General Psychiatry, 44*, 409–411.

HETHERINGTON, E. M. (1991). The role of individual differences and family relationships in children's coping with divorce and remarriage. In P. A. Cowan & E. M. Hetherington, eds., *Family transitions*. Hillsdale, NJ: Lawrence Erlbaum Associates.

HILGARD, E. R. (1986). *Divided consciousness*. New York: John Wiley.

HINZ, L. D., & WILLIAMSON, D. A. (1987). Bulimia and depression: A review of the affective variant hypothesis. *Psychological Bulletin, 102*, 150–158.

HIRSCHFELD, R. M. A., SHEA, M. T., & WEISE, R. (1991). Dependent personality disorder: Perspectives for DSM-IV. *Journal of Personality Disorders, 5*, 135–149.

HOBSON, R. P. (1989). Beyond cognition: A theory of autism. In G. Dawson, ed., *Autism: Nature, diagnosis, and treatment*. New York: Guilford.

HODGKINSON, P. E., & STEWART, M. (1991). *Coping with catastrophe*. London, England: Routledge.

HOENIG, J. (1984). Schneider's first rank symptoms and the tabulators. *Comprehensive Psychiatry, 25,* 77–87.

HOFER, M. A. (1984). Relationships as regulators: A psychobiologic perspective on bereavement. *Psychosomatic Medicine, 46,* 183–197.

HOFFMAN, A. (1971). LSD discoverer disputes "chance factor" in finding. *Psychiatric News, 16,* 23–26.

HOFFMAN, R., STOPEK, S., & ANDREASEN, N. C. (1986). A discourse analysis comparing manic versus schizophrenic speech disorganization. *Archives of General Psychiatry, 43,* 831–838.

HOFFMAN, R. E. (1986). Verbal hallucinations and language production processes in schizophrenia. *Behavioral and Brain Sciences, 9,* 503–548.

HOFLING, C. K. (1968). *Textbook of psychiatry for medical practice,* 2nd ed. Philadelphia: Lippincott.

HOGARTY, G. E., ANDERSON, C. M., REISS, D. J., KORNBLITH, S. J., GREENWALD, D. P., JAVNA, C. D., MADONIA, M. J., & THE EPICS SCHIZOPHRENIA RESEARCH GROUP. (1986). Family psychoeducation, social skills training, and maintenance chemotherapy in the aftercare treatment of schizophrenia I. *Archives of General Psychiatry, 43,* 633–642.

HOGARTY, G. E., SCHOOLER, N. R., ULRICH, R., MUSSARE, F., FERRO, P. & HERRON, E. (1979). Fluphenazine and social therapy in the aftercare of schizophrenic patients. *Archives of General Psychiatry, 36,* 1283–1294.

HOLDEN, C. (1985). A guarded endorsement for shock therapy. *Science, 228,* 1510–1511.

HOLDEN, C. (1986). Depression research advances: Treatment lags. *Science, 233,* 723–726.

HOLLON, S. D., DeRUBEIS, R. J., & EVANS, M. D. (1987). Causal mediation of change in treatment for depression: Discriminating between nonspecificity and noncausality. *Psychological Bulletin, 102,* 139–149.

HOLLON, S. D., SHELTON, R. C., & LOOSEN, P. T. (1991). Cognitive therapy and pharmacotherapy for depression. *Journal of Consulting and Clinical Psychology, 59,* 88–99.

HOLZMAN, P. S. (1978). Cognitive impairment and cognitive stability: Toward a theory of thought disorder. In G. Serban, ed., *Cognitive defects in the development of mental illness.* New York: Brunner/Mazel.

HOLZMAN, P. S., SOLOMON, C. M., LEVIN, S., & WATERNAUX, C. S. (1984). Pursuit eye movement dysfunctions in schizophrenia: Family evidence for specificity. *Archives of General Psychiatry, 41,* 136–139.

HOOLEY, J. M. (1985). Expressed emotion: A review of the critical literature. *Clinical Psychology Review, 5,* 119–139.

HORNE, J. (1979). Defendant found guilty of murdering jogger. *Seattle Times,* May 31, C11.

HOROWITZ, M. J. (1974). Stress response syndromes. *Archives of General Psychiatry, 31,* 768–781.

HOROWITZ, M. J. (1986). Stress-response syndromes: A review of posttraumatic and adjustment disorders. *Hospital and Community Psychiatry, 37,* 241–249.

HORVATH, T. B., SIEVER, L. J., MOHS, R. C., & DAVIS, K. (1989). Organic mental syndromes and disorders. In H. I. Kaplan & B. J. Sadock eds., *Comprehensive textbook of psychiatry,* 5th ed. Baltimore: Williams and Wilkins.

HORWITZ, A. V. (1984). The economy and social pathology. *Annual Review of Sociology, 10,* 95–119.

HOUGHTON, J. F. (1980). One personal experience: Before and after mental illness. In J. G. Rabkin, L. Gelb, & J. B. Lazar, eds., *Attitudes toward the mentally ill: Research perspectives.* Rockville, MD: National Institute of Mental Health.

HOUGHTON, J. F. (1982). First person account: Maintaining mental health in a turbulent world. *Schizophrenia Bulletin, 8,* 548–552.

HOUSTON, B. K., & VAVAK, C. R. (1991). Cynical hostility: Developmental factors, psychosocial correlates, and health behaviors. *Health Psychology, 10,* 9–17.

HOYT, M. F., XENAKIS, S. N., MARMAR, C. R., & HOROWITZ, M. J. (1983). Therapists' actions that influence their perceptions of "good" psychotherapy sessions. *The Journal of Nervous and Mental Diseases, 171,* 400–404.

HUDGENS, R. W. (1973). Mental health of political candidates: Notes on Abraham Lincoln. *American Journal of Psychiatry, 130,* 110.

HUNT, W. A., & BESPALIC, D. A. (1974). An evaluation of current methods of modifying smoking behavior. *Journal of Clinical Psychology, 30,* 430–438.

HURLBURT, R. T., & MELANCON, S. M. (1987). Single case study. Goofed up images: Thought sampling with a schizophrenic woman. *Journal of Nervous and Mental Disease, 175,* 575–578.

HURT, S. W., & CLARKIN, J. F. (1990). Borderline personality disorder: Prototypic typology and the development of treatment manuals. *Psychiatric Annals, 20,* 13–18.

HYDE, J. S. (1990). *Understanding human sexuality.* New York: McGraw-Hill.

HYND, G. W., HERN, K. L., VOELLER, K. K., & MARSHALL, R. M. (1991). Neurobiological basis of attention-deficit hyperactivity disorder (ADHD). *School Psychology Review, 20,* 174–186.

IANOCO, W. G., & KOENIG, W. G. R. (1983). Features that distinguish the smooth-pursuit eye-tracking performance of schizophrenic, affective disorder, and normal individuals. *Journal of Abnormal Psychology, 92,* 29–41.

INGRAM, R. E. (1984). Toward an information-processing analysis of depression. *Cognitive Therapy and Research, 8,* 443–478.

INSTITUTE OF MEDICINE (1990). *Research on children and adolescents with mental, behavioral, and developmental disorders.* Rockville, MD: National Institute of Mental Health.

ITIL, T. M. (1977). Qualitative and quantitative EEG findings in schizophrenics. *Schizophrenia Bulletin, 3,* 61–79.

ITIL, T. M., SALETU, B., & DAVIS, R. (1974). Stability studies of schizophrenics and normals using computer-analyzed EEG. *Biological Psychiatry, 8,* 321–325.

JACK-ROLLER, & SNODGRASS, J. (1982). The Jack-Roller at seventy. Lexington, MA.: Lexington Books.

JACOB, R. G., WING, R., & SHAPIRO, A. P. (1987). The behavioral treatment of hypertension: Long-term effects. *Behavior Therapy, 18,* 325–352.

JAFFEE, J. H. (1985). Opioid dependence. In H. I. Kaplan & B. J. Sadock, eds., *Comprehensive textbook of psychiatry,* 4th ed., vol. 1. Baltimore: Williams & Wilkins.

JAFFEE, J. H. (1989). Drug dependence: Opiods, nonnarcotics, nicotine (tobacco), and caffeine. In H. I. Kaplan & B. J. Sadock, eds., *Comprehensive textbook of psychiatry (Fifth Edition).* Baltimore: Williams and Wilkins.

JAMISON, K. R. (1989). Mood disorders and seasonal patterns in British writers and artists. *Psychiatry, 52,* 125–134.

JAMISON, K. R., GERNER, R. H., HAMMEN, C., & PADESKY, C. (1980). Clouds and silver linings: Positive experiences associated with primary affective disorders. *American Journal of Psychiatry, 137,* 198–202.

JANICAK, P. G., & BUSHES, R. A. (1987). Advances in the treatment of mania and other acute psychotic disorders. *Psychiatric Annals, 17,* 145–149.

JAYNES, J. (1976). *The origins of consciousness in the breakdown of the bicameral mind.* Boston: Houghton Mifflin.

JELLINEK, E. M. (1960). *The disease concept of alcoholism.* New Haven: Hillhouse Press.

JEMMOTT, J. B., III, & LOCKE, S. E. (1984). Psychosocial factors, immunologic mediation, and human susceptibility to infectious diseases: How much do we know? *Psychological Bulletin, 95,* 78–108.

JENKINS, J. H., KARNO, M. N., DE LA SELVA, A., SANTANA, F., TELLIS, C., LOPEZ, S., & MINTZ, J. (1986). Expressed emotion, maintenance psychotherapy and schizophrenic relapse among Mexican-Americans. *Psychopharmacology Bulletin, 22,* 621–627.

JENSEN, A. R. (1969). How much can we boost IQ and scholastic achievement? *Harvard Educational Review, 39,* 1–123.

JENSEN, P. S., BLOEDAU, L., DEGROOT, J., USSERY, T., & DAVIS, H. (1990). Children at risk: I. Risk factors and child symptomatology. *Journal of American Academy of Child Adolescent Psychiatry, 29,* 51–59.

JOEL-NIELSON, N. (1979). Suicide risk in manic-depressive disorder. In M. Schov & E. Stromgren, eds., *Origin, prevention and treatment of affective disorders.* London: Academic Press.

JOHNSON, J., WEISSMAN, M. M., & KLERMAN, G. L. (1990). Panic disorder, comorbidity, and suicide attempts. *Archives of General Psychiatry, 47,* 805–808.

JONES, D. J., FOX, M. M., BABIGAN, H. M., & HUTTON, H. E. (1980). Epidemiology of anorexia nervosa in Monroe County, New York: 1960–1976. *Psychosomatic Medicine, 42,* 551–558.

JONES, J. C., & BARLOW, D. H. (1990). The etiology of posttraumatic stress disorder. *Clinical Psychology Review, 10,* 299–328.

JONES, K. W., SMITH, D. W., STREISSGUTH, A. P., & MYRIANTHOPOULOS, N. C. (1974). Outcomes in offspring of chronic alcoholic women. *Lancet, 1*, 1076–1078.

JONES, M. C. (1981). Midlife drinking patterns. Correlates and antecedents. In D. H. Eichorn, ed., *Present and past in middle life.* New York: Academic Press, 223–242.

JORGENSEN, E. C. (1990). *Child abuse: A practical guide for those who help others.* New York: Continuum.

JOSEPH, J. G., CAUMARTIN, S. M., MARGALITTAL, M. P. H., KIRSCHT, J. P., KESSLER, R. C., OSTROW, D. G., & WORTMAN, C. B. (1990). Psychological functioning in a cohort of gay men at risk for AIDS: A three-year descriptive study. *The Journal of Nervous and Mental Disease, 178*, 607–615.

JUDD, L. L. (1990). Putting mental health on the nation's agenda. *Hospital and Community Psychiatry, 41*, 131–134.

JULIEN, R. M. (1992). *A primer of drug action,* 6th ed. New York: Freeman.

JUSTICE, B. (1987). *Who gets sick: Thinking and health.* Houston, TX: Peak Press.

KALIN, N. H. (1979). Genital and abdominal surgery: A case report. *Journal of the American Medical Association, 241*, 2188–2189.

KANE, J. M. (1987). Treatment of schizophrenia. *Schizophrenia Bulletin, 13*, 133–156.

KANFER, R., & ZEISS, A. M. (1983). Depression, interpersonal standard setting, and judgments of self-efficacy. *Journal of Abnormal Psychology, 92*, 319–329.

KAPLAN, H. S. (1974). *The new sex therapy: Active treatment of sexual dysfunctions.* New York: Quadrangle Books.

KAPLAN, H. S. (1979). *Disorders of sexual desire.* New York: Simon & Schuster.

KARLINSKY, H. (1986). Alzheimer's disease in Down's syndrome: A review. *Journal of the American Geriatrics Society, 34*, 728–734.

KAUFMAN, A. S. (1990). *Assessing adolescent and adult intelligence.* Boston: Allyn & Bacon.

KAUFMAN, A. S., & KAUFMAN, N. L. (1983). *Kaufman Assessment Battery for Children: Interpretive manual.* Circle Pines, NM: American Guidance Service.

KAUFMAN, M. J., AGARD, J. A., & SEMMEL, M. I. (1982). *Mainstreaming: Learners and their environments.* Baltimore: University Park Press.

KAUFMANN, C. A., DELISI, L. E., LEHNER, T., & GILLIAM, T. C. (1989). Physical mapping, linkage analysis of a putative schizophrenia locus on chromosome 5q. *Schizophrenia Bulletin, 15*, 441–452.

KAZDIN, A. E. (1988). *Child psychotherapy: Developing and identifying effective treatments.* New York: Pergamon.

KAZDIN, A. E., BASS, D., SIEGEL, T., & THOMAS, C. (1989). Cognitive-behavioral therapy and relationship therapy in the treatment of children referred for antisocial behavior. *Journal of Consulting and Clinical Psychology, 57*, 522–535.

KECK, P. E., JR., POPE, H. G., JR., & COHEN, B. M. (1989). Risk factors for neuroleptic malignant syndrome. *Archives of General Psychiatry, 46*, 914–918.

KEGAN, R. G. (1986). The child behind the mask: Sociopathy as developmental delay. In W. H. Reid, D. Dorr, J. I. Walker, & J. W. Bonner, eds., *Unmasking the Psychopath.* New York: W. W. Norton.

KEITH, S. J., REGIER, D. A., & RAE, D. S. (1991). Schizophrenic disorders. In L. N. Robins & D. A. Regier, eds., *Psychiatric disorders in America: The epidemiological catchment area study.* New York: The Free Press.

KELLER, M. B. (1987). Differential diagnosis, natural course, and epidemiology of bipolar disorder. In R. E. Hales & A. J. Francis, eds., *American Psychiatric Association Annual Review,* vol. 6. Washington, D.C.: American Psychiatric Press.

KELLER, M. B. (1990). Diagnostic and course of illness variables pertinent to refractory depression. In A. Tasman, S. M. Goldfinger, & C. A. Kaufmann, *Review of Psychiatry,* vol. 9. Washington, DC: American Psychiatric Press.

KELLNER, R. (1987). Hypochondriasis and somatization. *Journal of the American Medical Association, 258*, 2718–2722.

KELLNER, R. (1989). Undifferentiated somatoform disorder and somatoform disorder not otherwise specified. In Task Force Report of the American Psychiatric Association, *Treatments of psychiatric disorders.* Washington, DC: American Psychiatric Association.

KELLNER, R. (1990). Somatization: Theories and research. *The Journal of Nervous and Mental Disease, 178*, 150–160.

KELLY, G. A. (1955). *The psychology of personal constructs,* vols. 1 & 2. New York: W. W. Norton.

KENDALL, P. C., REBER, M., McLEER, S., EPPS, J., & RONAN, K. R. (1990). Cognitive-behavioral treatment of conduct-disordered children. *Cognitive Therapy and Research, 14*, 279–289.

KENDALL, P. C., & WILCOX, L. E. (1978). Self-control in children: Development of a rating scale. *Journal of Consulting and Clinical Psychology, 47*, 1020–1029.

KENDELL, R. E. (1983). Schizophrenia. In R. E. Kendall & A. K. Zealley, eds., *Companion to psychiatric studies.* Edinburgh: Churchill Livingstone.

KENDELL, R. E. (1989). Clinical validity. *Psychological Medicine, 19*, 45–55.

KENDLER, K. S. (1983). Overview: A current perspective on twin studies of schizophrenia. *American Journal of Psychiatry, 140*, 1413–1425.

KENDLER, K. S., & GRUENBERG, A. M. (1984). An independent analysis of the Copenhagen sample of the Danish adoption study of schizophrenia: IV. The pattern of psychiatric illness, as defined by DSM-III in adoptees and relatives. *Archives of General Psychiatry IV, 41*, 555–564.

KENDLER, K. S., GRUENBERG, M., & TSUANG, M. T. (1985). Psychiatric illness in first-degree relatives of schizophrenic and surgical control patients. *Archives of General Psychiatry, 42*, 770–779.

KENDLER, K. S., HEATH, A., MARTIN, N. G., & EAVES, L. J. (1986). Symptoms of anxiety and depression in a volunteer twin population: The etiologic role of genetic and environmental factors. *Archives of General Psychiatry, 43*, 213–221.

KENNEDY, J. L., GIUFFRA, L. A., MOISES, H. W., WETTERBERG, L., SJOGREN, B., CAVALLI-SFORZA, L. L., PAKSTIS, A. J., KIDD, J. R., & KIDD, K. K. (1989). Molecular genetic studies in schizophrenia. *Schizophrenia Bulletin, 15*, 383–391.

KENNEDY, S., KIECOLT-GLASER, J. K., & GLASER, R. (1990). Social support, stress, and the immune system. In B. R. Sarason, I. G. Sarason, & G. R. Pierce, eds., *Social support: An interactional view.* New York: John Wiley.

KENYON, K. (1979). A survivor's notes. *Newsweek,* April 30, 17.

KERNBERG, O. F. (1975). *Borderline conditions and pathological narcissism.* New York: Jason Aronson.

KETY, S. S., ROSENTHAL, D., WENDER, P., & SCHULSINGER, F. (1968). The type and prevalence of mental illness in the biological and adoptive families of adopted schizophrenics. In D. Rosenthal & S. S. Kety, eds., *The transmission of schizophrenia.* New York: Pergamon Press.

KETY, S. S., ROSENTHAL, D., WENDER, P. H., SCHULSINGER, F., & JACOBSON, B. (1978). The biological and adoptive families of adopted individuals who become schizophrenic: Prevalence of mental illness and other characteristics. In L. C. Wynne, R. L. Cromwell, & S. Matthysse, eds., *The nature of schizophrenia: New approaches to research and treatment.* New York: Wiley.

KILMANN, P. R., SABALIS, R. F., GEARING, M. I., BUKSTEL, L. H., & SCOVERN, A. W. (1982). The treatment of sexual paraphilias: A review of outcome research. *Journal of Sex Research, 18*, 193–252.

KING, N. J., OLLIER, K., IACUONE, R., SCHUSTER, S., BAYS, K., GULLONE, E., & OLLENDICK, T. H. (1989). Fears of children and adolescents: A cross-sectional Australian study using the Revised-Fear Survey Schedule for children. *Journal of Child Psychology and Psychiatry, 30*, 775–784.

KINSEY, A. C., POMEROY, W. B., & MARTIN, C. E. (1948). *Sexual behavior in the human male.* Philadelphia: W. B. Saunders.

KINSEY, A. C., POMEROY, W. B., MARTIN, C. E., & GEBHARD, P. H. (1953). Sexual behavior in the human female. Philadelphia: W. B. Saunders.

KIPPER, D. A. (1977). Behavior therapy for fears brought on by war experiences. *Journal of Consulting and Clinical Psychology, 45*, 216–221.

KIRBY, E. A., & KHAZINDAR, N. (1985). *Durable and generalized effects of cognitive-behavior modifications with attention deficit disorder children.* (Unpublished manuscript).

KIVLAHAN, D. R., MARLATT, G. A., FROMME, K., COPPEL, D. B., & WILLIAMS, E. (1990). Secondary prevention with college drinkers: Evalua-

tions of an alcohol skills training program. *Journal of Consulting and Clinical Psychology*, 58(6), 805–810.

KLEIN, R. G., & LAST, C. G. (1989). *Anxiety disorders in children.* Newbury Park, CA: Sage Publications.

KLERMAN, G. L. (1987). *The treatment of depressive conditions: Perspectives on depressive disorders.* Rockville, MD: National Institute of Mental Health.

KLERMAN, G. L. (1988). The current age of youthful melancholia: Evidence for increase in depression among adolescents and young adults. *British Journal of Psychiatry*, 152, 4–14.

KLERMAN, G. L., LAVORI, P. W., RICE, J., REICH, T., ENDICOTT, J., ANDREASEN, N. C., KELLER, M. D., & HIRSCHFIELD, R. M. A. (1985). Birth-cohort trends in rates of major depressive disorder among relatives of patients with affective disorder. *Archives of General Psychiatry*, 42, 689–693.

KLERMAN, G. L., WEISSMAN, M. M., OUELLETTE, R., JOHNSON, J., & GREENWALD, S. (1991). Panic attacks in the community: Social morbidity and health care utilization. *Journal of the American Medical Association*, 265, 742–746.

KLINE, N. S. (1977). Depression. *Swarthmore College Bulletin*, July, 8–11.

KLUFT, R. P. (1988). The dissociative disorders. In J. A. Talbott, R. E. Hales, & S. C. Yudofsky, eds., *The American Psychiatric Association textbook of psychiatry.* Washington, DC: American Psychiatric Press.

KLUFT, R. P. (1991). Multiple personality disorder. In A. Tasman & S. M. Goldfinger, eds., *Review of psychiatry*, vol. 10. Washington, DC: American Psychiatric Press.

KNOWLES, P. A. L., & PRUTSMAN, T. D. (1968). *The case of Benjie.* Unpublished manuscript, Florida Atlantic University.

KOG, E., & VANDEREYCKEN, W. (1985). Family characteristics of anorexia nervosa and bulimia: A review of the research literature. *Clinical Psychology Review*, 5, 159–180.

KOLATA, G. (1987). The poignant thoughts of Down's children are given voice. *New York Times*, December 22, 15.

KOLB, L. D., & BRODIE, H. K. H. (1982). *Modern clinical psychiatry*, 10th ed. Philadelphia: W. B. Saunders.

KONNER, M. (1989). Homosexuality: Who and why? *New York Times Magazine*, April 2, 60–61.

KOSS, M. P., & OROS, C. J. (1982). Sexual experiences survey: A research instrument investigating sexual aggression and victimization. *Journal of Consulting and Clinical Psychology*, 50, 455–457.

KOSTEN, T. R., & ROUNSAVILLE, B. J. (1986). Psychopathology in opioid addicts. *Psychiatric Clinics of North America*, 9, 515–532.

KOSTEN, T. R., ROUNSAVILLE, B. J., & KLEBER, H. D. (1987). Multidimensionality and prediction of treatment outcome in opioid addicts: 2.5-year follow-up. *Comprehensive Psychiatry*, 28, 3–13.

KOVACS, M. (1985). The natural history and course of depressive disorders in childhood. *Psychiatric Annals*, 15, 387–389.

KOVACS, M., & BECK, A. T. (1977). An empirical-clinical approach toward a definition of childhood depression. In J. G. Schulterbrandt & A. Raskin, eds., *Depression in childhood: Diagnosing treatment and conceptual models.* New York: Raven Press.

KOVACS, M., BECK, A. T., & WEISSMAN, A. (1975). The use of suicidal motives in the psychotherapy of attempted suicides. *American Journal of Psychotherapy*, 29, 363–368.

KOVACS, M., & GOLDSTON, D. (1991). Cognitive and social cognitive development in depressed children and adolescents. *Journal of the American Academy of Childhood and Adolescent Psychiatry*, 30, 388–392.

KRAEPELIN, E. 1909–1913. *Psychiatrie*, 8th ed. Leipzig: J. A. Barth.

KRAKOWSKI, A. J. (1982). Stress and the practice of medicine: II. Stressors, stresses, and strains. *Psychotherapy and Psychosomatics*, 38, 11–23.

KRAMER, J. J. (1990). Training parents as behavior change agents: Successes, failures, and suggestions for school psychologists. In T. B. Gutkin & C. R. Reynolds, eds., *Handbook of school psychology.* New York: John Wiley.

KRANTZ, S., & HAMMEN, C. L. (1979). Assessment of cognitive bias in depression. *Journal of Abnormal Psychology*, 88, 611–619.

KRINGLEN, E. (1981). Stress and coronary heart disease. *Twin Research 3: Epidemiological and clinical studies.* New York: Alan R. Liss.

KUPFER, D. J., ULRICH, R. F., COBLE, P. A., JARRETT, D. B., GROCHOCINSKI, V. J., DOMAN, J., MATTHEWS, G., & BORBELY, A. A. (1985). Electroencephalographic sleep of younger depressives. *Archives of General Psychiatry*, 42, 806–810.

KURIANSKY, J. B., DEMING, U. E., & GURLAND, B. J. (1974). On trends in the diagnosis of schizophrenia. *American Journal of Psychiatry*, 131, 402–408.

LACKS, P. (1984). *Bender-Gestalt screening for brain dysfunction.* New York: John Wiley.

LAFFAL, J. (1965). *Pathological and normal language.* New York: Atherton.

LAGRECA, A. M., STONE, W. L., & BELL, C. R., III. (1983). Facilitating the vocational-interpersonal skills of mentally retarded individuals. *American Journal of Mental Deficiency*, 88, 270–278.

LAING, R. D. (1967). *The politics of experience.* New York: Harper Torch Books.

LAMB, F., & DUNNE-MAXIM. K. (1987). Postvention in schools: Policy and progress. In Dunne, E. J., McIntosh, J. L., & Dunne-Maxim, K., eds., *Suicide and its aftermath: Understanding and counseling the survivors.* 245–262. New York: Norton.

LAMBERT, N. M., SANDOVAL, J., & SASSONE, D. (1978). Prevalence of hyperactivity in elementary school children as a function of social system defenses. *American Journal of Orthopsychiatry*, 48, 446–463.

LANQUETOT, R. (1984). First person account: Confessions of the daughter of a schizophrenic. *Schizophrenia Bulletin*, 10, 467–471.

LAROCHE, C., CHEIFETZ, P., LESTER, E. P., SHIBUR, L. D., TOMMASO, E., & ENGELSMANN, F. (1985). Psychopathology in the offspring of parents with bipolar affective disorders. *Canadian Journal of Psychiatry*, 30, 337–343.

LAROCHE, C., SHEINER, R., LESTER, E., BENIERAKIS, C., MARRACHE, M., ENGELMANN, F., & CHEIFETZ, P. (1987). Children of parents with manic-depressive illness: A follow-up study. *Canadian Journal of Psychiatry*, 32, 563–569.

LATIB, A., CONROY, J., & HESS, C. M. (1984). Family attitudes toward deinstitutionalization. *International Review of Research on Mental Retardation*, 12, 67–93.

LAUDENSLAGER, M. L., & REITE, M. L. (1984). Losses and separations: Immunological consequences and health implications. In P. Shaver, ed., *Review of personality and social psychology.* Beverly Hills, CA: Sage Publications.

LAZARUS, A. A. (1971). *Behavior therapy and beyond.* New York: McGraw-Hill.

LAZARUS, R. S. (1991). *Emotion and adaptation.* New York: Oxford University Press.

LEAF, P. J., WEISSMAN, M. M., MYERS, J. K., HOLZER, C., & TISCHLER, G. (1986). *Psychosocial risks and correlates of major depression in one United States urban community: Progress and challenge.* New York: Guilford Press.

LEAF, P. J., WEISSMAN, M. M., MYERS, J. K., TISCHLER, G. L., & HOLZER, C. E., III. (1984). Social factors related to psychiatric disorder: The Yale Epidemiological Catchment Area Study. *Social Psychiatry*, 19, 53–61.

LEAR, M. W. (1988). Mad malady. *The New York Times Magazine*, July 3, 21.

LEE, T., SEEMAN, P., TOURTELLOTTE, W. W., FARLEY, I. J., & HORNYKEIWICZ, O. (1978). Binding of ^3H-neuroleptics and ^3H-apomorphine in schizophrenic brains. *Nature*, 274, 897–900.

LEFF, J. (1987). The influence of life events and relatives' expressed emotion on the course of schizophrenia. In D. Magnusson & A. Ohman, eds., *Psychopathology: An interactional perspective.* New York: Academic Press.

LEFF, J., KUIPERS, L., BERKOWITZ, R., & STURGEON, D. (1985). A controlled trial of social intervention in the families of schizophrenic patients: Two-year follow-up. *British Journal of Psychiatry*, 146, 594–600.

LEFF, J., & VAUGHN, C. (1981). The role of maintenance therapy and relatives' expressed emotion in relapse schizophrenia: A two-year follow-up. *British Journal of Psychiatry*, 139, 102–104.

LEFF, J., & VAUGHN, C. (1985). *Expressed emotion in families.* New York: Guilford Press.

LEHMAN, H. E., & CANCRO, R. (1985). Schizophrenia: Clinical features. In H. I. Kaplan & B. J. Sadock, *Comprehensive textbook of psychiatry*, 4th ed., vol. 1. Baltimore: Williams & Wilkins.

LEHRER, P. M., & MURPHY, A. I. (1991). Stress reactivity and perception of pain among tension headache sufferers. *Behavioral Research Therapy*, 29, 61–69.

LEITENBERG, H., GROSS, J., PETERSON, J., & ROSEN, J. (1984). Analyses of an anxiety model and the process of change during exposure plus response prevention treatment of bulimia nervosa. *Behavior Therapy, 15*, 3–20.

LENZENWEGER, M. F., DWORKIN, R. H., & WETHINGTON, E. (1989). Models of positive and negative symptoms in schizophrenia: An empirical evaluation of latent structures. *Journal of Abnormal Psychology, 98*, 62–70.

LEON, G. R., LUCAS, A. R., COLLIGAN, R. C., FERINANDE, R. J., & KAMP, J. (1985). Sexual, body image, and personality attitudes in anorexia nervosa. *Journal of Abnormal Child Psychology, 13*, 245–257.

LEON, G. R., & PHELAN, P. W. (1984). Anorexia nervosa. In B. Lahey & A. Kazdin, eds., *Advances in Clinical Child Psychology, 8*, 81–111.

LESLIE, A. M., & FRITH, U. (1990). Prospects for a cognitive neuropsychology of autism: Hobson's choice. *Psychological Review, 97*, 122–131.

LESYNA, K., & PHILLIPS, D. P. (1990). Suicide and the media: Research and policy implications. In R. F. W. Diekstra, ed., *Preventive strategies on suicide*. Zurich: World Health Organization.

LEVAY, S. (1991). A difference in hypothalamic structure between heterosexual and homosexual men. *Science, 253*, 1034–1037.

LEVINE, R. V., LYNCH, K., MIYAKE, K., & LUCIA, M. (1989). The Type A city: Coronary heart disease and the pace of life. *Journal of Behavioral Medicine, 12*, 509–524.

LEVINE, S. B. (1980). Psychiatric diagnosis of patients requesting sex reassignment surgery. *Journal of Sex and Marital Therapy, 6*, 164–173.

LEVY, L. (1976). Self-help groups: Types and psychological processes. *Journal of Applied Behavioral Science, 12*, 310–323.

LEVY, R. F. (1977). "Male woman" finds self. *Washington Post*, May 11, C1, C3.

LEVY, R. I., & MOSKOWITZ, J. (1982). Cardiovascular research: Decades of progress, a decade of promise. *Science, 217*, 121–129.

LEWIN, R. (1988). Cloud over Parkinson's therapy. *Science, 240*, 390–392.

LEWINE, R. R. J. (1984). Stalking the schizophrenia marker: Evidence for a general vulnerability model of psychopathology. In N. F. Watt, E. J. Anthony, L. C. Wynne, & J. E. Rolf, eds., *Children at risk for schizophrenia: A longitudinal perspective*. Cambridge: Cambridge University Press.

LEWINSOHN, P. M., & ARCONAD, M. (1981). Behavioral treatment in depression: A social learning approach. In J. Clarkin & H. Glazer, eds., *Behavioral and directive treatment strategies*. New York: Garland Press.

LEWINSOHN, P. M., & HOBERMAN, H. M. (1982). Depression. In A. S. Bellak, M. Hersen, & A. E. Kazdin, eds. *International handbook of behavior modification and therapy*. New York: Plenum.

LEWINSOHN, P. M., MISCHEL, W., CHAPLAIN, W., & BARTON, R. (1980). Social competence and depression. The role of illusory self-perceptions. *Journal of Abnormal Psychology, 89*, 203–212.

LEWIS, D. O. (1989). Adult antisocial behavior and criminality. In H. I. Kaplan & B. J. Sadock, eds., *Comprehensive textbook of psychiatry*, (5th ed.). Baltimore: Williams & Wilkins.

LIGHT, E., & LEBOWITZ, B. D., EDS. (1989). *Alzheimer's disease treatment and family stress: Directions for research*. Rockville, MD: National Institute of Mental Health.

LILIENFELD, S. O., & WALDMAN, I. D. (1990). The relation between childhood attention-deficit hyperactivity disorder and adult antisocial behavior reexamined: The problem of heterogeneity. *Clinical Psychology Review, 10*, 699–725.

LILJEFORS, I., & RAHE, R. H. (1970). An identical twin study of psychosocial factors in coronary heart disease in Sweden. *Psychosomatic Medicine, 32*, 523–542.

LINDEMALM, G., KORLIN, D., & UDDENBERG, N. (1986). Long-term follow-up of "sex change" in 13 male to female transsexuals. *Archives of Sexual Behavior, 15*, 187–210.

LINDENMAYER, J. P., KAY, S. R., & FRIEDMAN, C. (1986). Negative and positive schizophrenic syndromes after the acute phase: A prospective follow-up. *Comprehensive Psychiatry, 27*, 276–286.

LINEHAN, M. M. (1981). A social-behavioral analysis of suicide and parasuicide. In J. F. Clarkin & H. I. Glazer, eds., *Depression: Behavioral and directive intervention strategies*. New York: Garland STPM Press.

LINEHAN, M. M. (1987). Dialectical behavior therapy for borderline personality disorder. *Bulletin of the Menninger Clinic, 51*, 261–276.

LINEHAN, M. M. (1989). Cognitive and behavior therapy for borderline personality disorder. In A. Tasman, R. E. Hales, & A. J. Frances, eds., *Annual Review of Psychiatry*, vol. 8. Washington, DC: American Psychiatric Press.

LINEHAN, M. M., ARMSTRONG, H. E., SUAREZ, A., ALLMON, D., & HEARD, H. L. (1991). Cognitive behavioral treatment of chronically parasuicidal borderline patients. *Archives of General Psychiatry, 48*, 1060–1064.

LINGJAERDE, O. (1983). The biochemistry of depression. *Acta Psychiatrica Scandinavica Supplementum, 69* (302), 36–51.

LINN, M. V., CAFFEY, E. M., KLETT, C. J., HOGARTY, G. E., & LAMB, H. R. (1979). Day treatment and psychotropic drugs in aftercare of schizophrenic patients. *Archives of General Psychiatry, 36*, 1055–1066.

LINSKY, A. S., STRAUS, M. A., & COLBY, J. P., JR. (1985). Stressful events, stressful condition and alcohol problems in the United States: A partial test of Coles' theory. *Journal of Studies on Alcohol, 46*, 72–80.

LIPOWSKI, Z. J. (1987). Delirium (acute confusional states). *Journal of the American Medical Association, 258*, 1789–1792.

LIPSIUS, S. H. (1987). Prescribing sensate focus without proscribing intercourse. *Journal of Sex and Marital Therapy, 13*, 106–116.

LITZ, B. T., & KEANE, T. M. (1989). Information processing in anxiety disorders: Application to the understanding of posttraumatic stress disorder. *Clinical Psychology Review, 9*, 243–257.

LLEWELYN, S. P. (1988). Psychological therapy as viewed by clients and therapists. *British Journal of Clinical Psychology, 27*, 223–237.

LOBATO, D. (1983). Siblings of handicapped children: A review. *Journal of Autism, 13*, 347–364.

LOCKE, S. E., KRAUS, L., HURST, M. W., HEISEL, J. S., & WILLIAMS, R. M. (1984). Life change stress, psychiatric symptoms, and natural killer cell-activity. *Psychosomatic Medicine, 46*, 441–453.

LOEBER, R. R. (1990). Development and risk factors of juvenile antisocial behavior and delinquency. *Clinical Psychology Review, 10*, 1–41.

LOEBER, R. R., LAHEY, B. B., & THOMAS, J. C. (1991). Diagnostic conundrum of oppositional defiant disorder and conduct disorder. *Journal of Abnormal Psychology, 100*, 379–390.

LOO, R. (1986). Post-shooting stress reactions among police officers. *Journal of Human Stress, 12*, 27–31.

LOVAAS, O. I. (1987). Behavioral treatment and normal educational and intellectual functioning in young autistic children. *Journal of Consulting and Clinical Psychology, 55*, 3–9.

LOVEJOY, M. (1982). Expectations and the recovery process. *Schizophrenia Bulletin, 8*, 605–609.

LOWE, M. (1985). Rapid smoking. In A. S. Bellack & M. Hersen, eds., *Dictionary of behavior therapy techniques*. New York: Pergamon Press.

LUBORSKY, L., CRITS-CHRISTOPH, P., MCLELLAN, T., WOODY, G., PIPER, W., LIBERMAN, B., IMBER, S., & PILKONIS, P. (1986). Do therapists vary much in their success? Findings from four outcome studies. *American Journal of Orthopsychiatry, 56*, 501–512.

LUMRY, A. E., GOTTESMAN, I. I., & TUASON, V. B. (1982). MMPI state dependency during the course of bipolar psychosis. *Psychiatry Research, 7*, 59–67.

MACCOBY, E., & MACCOBY, N. (1954). The interview: A tool of social science. In G. Lindzey, ed., *Handbook of social psychology*. Cambridge, MA: Addison-Wesley, 449–487.

MACDOUGALL, J. M., DEMBROSKI, T. M., & KRANTZ, D. S. (1981). Effects of types of challenge on pressor and heart rate responses in Type A and B women. *Psychophysiology, 18*, 1–9.

MACMILLAN, M. (1986). Souvenir de la Salpetriere: M. le Dr. Freud a Paris, 1885. *Australian Psychologist, 21*, 3–29.

MACTURK, R. H., VIETZE, P. M., MCCARTHY, M. E., MCQUISTAN, S. T., & YARROW, L. J. (1985). The organization of exploratory behavior in Down's syndrome and nondelayed infants. *Child Development, 56*, 573–581.

MAGAZINER, J. (1980). *Density, living alone, age and psychopathology in the urban environment*. Unpublished doctoral dissertation, University of Chicago.

MAHL, G. L. (1968). Gestures and body movements in interviews. In

J. M. Shlien, Ed., *Research in psychotherapy: Proceedings of the third conference*. Washington, DC: American Psychological Association.

MAHONEY, E. R. (1983). *Human sexuality*. New York: McGraw-Hill.

MALAMUTH, N. M. (1981). Rape proclivity among males. *Journal of Social Issues, 37*, 138–157.

MALATESTA, V. J. (1979). Alcohol effects on the orgasmic-ejaculatory response in human males. *Journal of Sex Research, 15*, 101–107.

MALATESTA, V. J., POLLACK, R. H., CROTTY, T. O., & PEACOCK, L. J. (1982). Acute alcohol intoxication and female orgasmic response. *Journal of Sex Research, 18*, 1–16.

MANN, J. J., STANLEY, M., McBRIDE, A., & EWEN, B. S. (1986). Increased serotonin and beta-adrenergic receptor binding in the frontal cortices of suicide victims. *Archives of General Psychiatry, 43*, 954–959.

MANNUZZA, S., KLEIN, R. G., BONAGURA, N., MALLOY, P., GIAMPINO, T. L., & ADDALLI, K. A. (1991). Hyperactive boys almost grown up. *Archives of General Psychiatry, 48*, 77–83.

MANSCHRECK, T., & PETRI, M. (1978). The paranoid syndrome. *Lancet, 2*, 251–253.

MANUCK, S. B., MORRISON, R. L., BELLACK, A. S., & POLEFRONE, J. M. (1985). Behavioral factors in hypertension, cardiovascular responsivity, anger, and social competence. In M. A. Chesney & R. H. Rosenman, eds., *Anger and hostility in cardiovascular and behavioral disorders*. Washington, D.C.: Hemisphere.

MARENGO, J. T., HARROW, M., LANIN-KETTERING, I., & WILSON, A. (1986). Evaluating bizarre-idiosyncratic thinking: A comprehensive index of positive thought disorder. *Schizophrenia Bulletin, 12*, 497–510.

MARKMAN, H. J., FLOYD, F. J., STANLEY, S. M., & STORAASLI, R. D. (1988). Prevention of marital distress: A longitudinal investigation. *Journal of Consulting and Clinical Psychology, 56*, 210–217.

MARKOWITZ, J., BROWN, R., SWEENEY, J., & MANN, J. J. (1987). Reduced length and cost of hospital stay for major depression in patients treated with ECT. *American Journal of Psychiatry, 144*, 1025–1029.

MARKS, I. M. (1978). *Living with fear*. New York: McGraw-Hill.

MARKS, I. M. (1987a). Behavioral aspects of panic disorder. *American Journal of Psychiatry, 144*, 1160–1165.

MARKS, I. M. (1987b). *Fears, phobias, and rituals: Panic, anxiety, and their disorders*. New York: Oxford University Press.

MARLATT, G. A., BAER, J. S., DONOVAN, D. M., & KIVLAHAN, D. R. (1988). Addictive behaviors: Etiology and treatment. In M. R. Rosenzweig & L. W. Porter, eds., *Annual review of psychology*. Palo Alto, CA: Annual Reviews.

MARLATT, G. A., DEMMING, B., & REID, J. B. (1973). Loss of control drinking in alcoholics: An experimental analogue. *Journal of Abnormal Psychology, 81*, 233–241.

MARLATT, G. A., & GORDON, J. R. (1985). *Relapse prevention: Maintenance strategies in the treatment of addictive behaviors*. New York: Guilford.

MARMOR, J. (1980). *Homosexual behavior*. New York: Basic Books.

MARMOT, M. G., & SYME, S. L. (1976). Acculturation and coronary heart disease in Japanese-Americans. *Journal of Epidemiology, 104*, 225–247.

MARSHALL, P. (1989). Attention deficit disorders and allergy: A neurochemical model of relation between illnesses. *Psychological Bulletin, 106*, 434–446.

MARZILLIER, J. S., & BIRCHWOOD, M. J. (1981). Behavioral treatment of cognitive disorders. In L. Michelson, M. Hersen, & S. M. Turner, eds., *Future perspectives on behavior therapy*. New York: Plenum Press.

MASER, J. D., & CLONINGER, C. R., EDS. (1990). *Comorbidity of mood and anxiety disorders*. Washington, DC: American Psychiatric Press.

MASLOW, A. H. (1968). *Toward a psychology of being*, 2nd ed. Princeton, NJ: Van Nostrand.

MASTERS, W. H., & JOHNSON, V. E. (1966). *Human sexual response*. Boston: Little, Brown.

MASTERS, W. H., & JOHNSON, V. E. (1970). *Human sexual inadequacy*. Boston: Little, Brown.

MASTERS, W. H., & JOHNSON, V. E. (1979). *Homosexuality in perspective*. Boston: Little, Brown.

MASTERS, W. H., JOHNSON, V. E., & KOLODNY, R. C. (1985). *Human sexuality*, 2nd ed. Boston: Little, Brown.

MATTHEWS, W. S., BARABAS, G., CUSAK, E., & FERRARI, M. (1986). Social quotients of children with phenylketonuria before and after discon-

tinuation of dietary therapy. *American Journal of Mental Deficiency, 91*, 92–94.

MAY, P. R. A. (1968). *Treatment of schizophrenia: A comparative study of five treatment methods*. New York: Science House.

MAY, P. R. A., TUMA, A. H., & DIXON, W. J. (1981). Schizophrenia: A follow-up study of the results of five forms of treatment. *Archives of General Psychiatry, 38*, 776–784.

McCLELLAND, D. C., ROSS, G., & PATEL, V. (1985). Exam stress and immunoglobulin levels. *Journal of Human Stress, 11*, 52–59.

McGLASHAN, T. H. (1983). The borderline syndrome. *Archives of General Psychiatry, 40*, 1319–1323.

McGLASHAN, T. H. (1986). Schizotypal personality disorder. *Archives of General Psychiatry, 43*, 329–334.

McGLASHAN, T. H. (1988). A selective review of recent North American long-term follow-up studies of schizophrenia. *Schizophrenia Bulletin, 14*, 515–542.

McGUE, M., & GOTTESMAN, I. I. (1989). Genetic linkage in schizophrenia: Perspectives from genetic epidemiology. *Schizophrenia Bulletin, 15*, 453–464.

McGUE, M., GOTTESMAN, I. I., & RAO, D. C. (1985). Resolving genetic models for the transmission of schizophrenia. *Genetic Epidemiology, 21*, 99–110.

McGUFFIN, P., REVELEY, A., & HOLLAND, A. (1982). Identical triplets: Nonidentical psychosis? *British Journal of Psychiatry, 140*, 1–6.

McNALLY, R. J. (1987). Preparedness and phobias: A review. *Psychological Bulletin, 101*, 283–303.

McNALLY, R. J. (1990). Psychological approaches to panic disorder: A review. *Psychological Bulletin, 108*, 403–419.

McNEAL, E. T., & CIMBOLIC, P. (1986). Antidepressants and biochemical theories of depression. *Psychological Bulletin, 99*, 361–374.

McNIEL, D. E., ARKOWITZ, H. S., & PRITCHARD, B. E. (1987). The response of others to face-to-face interaction with depressed patients. *Journal of Abnormal Psychology, 96*, 341–344.

MEDNICK, S. A., CUDECK, R., GRIFFITH, J. J., TALOVIC, S. A., & SCHULSINGER, F. A. (1984). The Danish high-risk project: Recent methods and findings. In N. F. Watt, E. J. Anthony, L. C. Wynne, & J. E. Rolf, eds., *Children at risk for schizophrenia*. New York: Cambridge University Press.

MEDNICK, S. A., MOFFIT, T., POLLACK, V., TALOVIC, S., GABRIELLI, W., & VAN DUSEN, K. T. (1983). "The inheritance of human deviance." In D. Magnusson & V. L. Allen, eds., *Human Development: An interactional perspective*. New York: Academic Press.

MEDNICK, S. A., & SCHULSINGER, F. (1968). Some premorbid characteristics related to breakdown in children with schizophrenic mothers. *Journal of Psychiatric Research, 6*, 267–291.

MEISLER, A. W., & CAREY, M. P. (1990). A critical reevaluation of nocturnal penile tumescence monitoring in the diagnosis of erectile dysfunction. *The Journal of Nervous and Mental Disease, 178*, 78–89.

MELAMED, B. G., & BUSH, J. P. (1986). Parent-child influences during medical procedures. In S. M. Auerbach and A. L. Stolberg, eds., *Crisis intervention within children and families*. Washington, D.C.: Hemisphere.

MELLOR, C. S. (1970). First rank symptoms of schizophrenia. *British Journal of Psychiatry, 177*, 15–23.

MERIKANGAS, K. R. (1990). Comorbidity for anxiety and depression: Review of family and genetic studies. In J. D. Maser and C. R. Cloninger, eds., *Comorbidity of mood and anxiety disorders*. Washington, DC: American Psychiatric Press.

MERIKANGAS, K. R., & WEISSMAN, M. M. (1986). Epidemiology of DSM-III Axis II personality disorders. In A. J. Francis & R. E. Hales, eds., *American Psychiatric Association annual review*, vol. 5. Washington, DC: American Psychiatric Association.

MEYER, J. (1990). Guess who's coming to dinner this time? A study of gay intimate relationships and the support for those relationships. *Journal of Homosexuality, 18*, 59–82.

MEYER, R. (1989). Typologies. In *Treatments of psychiatric disorders* (Vol. 2). Washington, DC: American Psychiatric Association.

MEZZICH, J. E., AHN, C. W., FABREGA, H., JR., & PILKONIS, P. A. (1990). Patterns of psychiatric comorbidity in a large population presenting for care. In J. D. Maser & C. R. Cloninger, eds., *Comorbidity in anxiety and mood disorders*. Washington, DC: American Psychiatric Press.

MILICH, R., & DODGE, K. A. (1984). Social information processing in child psychiatric populations. *Journal of Abnormal Child Psychology, 12*, 471–490.

MILLER, G. E., & PRINZ, R. J. (1990). Enhancement of social learning family interventions for childhood conduct disorders. *Psychological Bulletin, 108*, 291–307.

MILLER, H. L., COOMBS, D. W., LEEPER, J. D., & BARTON, S. N. (1984). An analysis of the effects of suicide prevention facilities on suicide rates in the United States. *American Journal of Public Health, 74*, 340–343.

MILLMAN, R. B. (1986). General principles of diagnosis and treatment. In A. J. Frances and R. E. Hales, eds., *American Psychiatric Association annual review*, vol. 5. Washington, DC: American Psychiatric Press.

MILLON, T. (1986). The avoidant personality. In R. Michels and J. O. Cavenar, Jr., eds., *Psychiatry*, vol. 1. New York: Basic Books.

MINTZ, L. I., LIBERMAN, R. P., LEFF, J., & VAUGHN, C. (1985). *Expressed emotion in families*. New York: Guilford Press.

MINTZ, L. I., LIBERMAN, R. P., MIKLOWITZ, D. J., & MINTZ, J. (1987). Expressed emotion: A call for partnership among relatives, patients, and professionals. *Schizophrenia Bulletin, 13*, 227–235.

MINUCHIN, S., ROSMAN, B., & BAKER, L. (1978). *Psychosomatic families: Anorexia nervosa in context*. Cambridge, MA: Harvard University Press.

MIRSKY, A. F., & BAKAY PRAGNAY, E. (1984). Brainstem mechanisms in the processing of sensory information: Clinical symptoms, animal models and unit analysis. In D. E. Sheer, ed., *Attention: Theory, brain functions and clinical applications*. Hillsdale, NJ: Erlbaum.

MITCHELL, J. E., PYLE, R. L., ECKERT, E. D., HATSUKAMI, D., POMEROY, C., & ZIMMERMAN, R. (1990). A comparison study of antidepressants and structured intensive group psychotherapy in the treatment of bulimia nervosa. *Archives of General Psychiatry, 47*, 149–157.

MIZES, J. S. (1990). Criterion-related validity of the Anorectic Cognitions Questionnaire. *Addictive Behaviors, 15*, 153–163.

MOHR, D. C., & BEUTLER, C. E. (1990). Erectile dysfunction: A review of diagnostic and treatment procedures. *Clinical Psychology Review, 10*, 123–150.

MOLDIN, S., GOTTESMAN, I. I., ERLENMEYER-KIMLING, L., & CORNBLATT, B. A. (1990). Psychometric deviance in offspring at risk for schizophrenia. *Psychiatry Research, 32*, 297–310.

MOLLER, H. J., VON ZERSSEN, D., WERNER-EILERT, K., & WUSCHNER-STOCKHEIM, M. (1982). Outcome in schizophrenic and similar paranoid psychoses. *Schizophrenia Bulletin, 8*, 99–108.

MONAHAN, J. (1981). *Predicting violent behavior: An assessment of clinical techniques*. Beverly Hills: Sage.

MONEY, J. (1984). Food, fitness and vital fluids: Sexual pleasure from graham crackers to Kellogg's cornflakes. *British Journal of Sexual Medicine, 11*, 127–130.

MONEY, J. (1987). Sin, sickness, or status? Homosexual gender identity and psychoneuroendocrinology. *American Psychologist, 42*, 384–399.

MONEY, J., & BOHMER, C. (1980). Prison sexology: Two personal accounts of masturbation, homosexuality, and rape. *Journal of Sex Research, 16*, 258–266.

MONEY, J., & RUSSO, A. J. (1979). Homosexual outcome of discordant gender identity/role in childhood: Longitudinal follow-up. *Journal of Pediatric Psychology, 4*, 29–41.

MONEY, J., & SCHWARTZ, M. (1977). Dating, romantic and nonromantic friendships and sexuality in 17 early-treated adrenogenital females, age 16–25. In P. A. Lee, L. P. Plotnick, A. A. Kowaski, & C. J. Migeon, eds., *Congenital adrenal hyperplasia*. Baltimore: University Park Press.

MONROE, S. M., & DEPUE, R. A. (1991). Life stress and depression. In J. Becker & A. Kleinman, *Psychosocial aspects of depression*, 101–130. Hillsdale, N.J.: Erlbaum.

MOORE, C. (1989). Evaluation of sexual disorders. *Treatment of psychiatric disorders*, vol. 3. Washington, DC: American Psychiatric Association.

MOOS, R. H. (1974). *Family environment scale*. Palo Alto, CA: Consulting Psychologists Press.

MORAN, A. E., FREEDMAN, R. I., & SHARFSTEIN, S. S. (1984). The journey of Sylvia Frumkin: A case study for policymakers. *Hospital and Community Psychiatry, 35*, 887–893.

MORAN, LORD C. M. W. (1966). *Winston Churchill: The struggle for survival, 1940–1965*. Boston: Houghton Mifflin.

MORIHISA, J. M., DUFFY, F. H., & WYATT, R. J. (1983). Brain electrical activity mapping (BEAM) in schizophrenic patients. *Archives of General Psychiatry, 40*, 719–728.

MORRIS, J. (1974). *Conundrum*. New York: Harcourt, Brace, & Jovanovich.

MORRISON, R. L., & WIXTED, J. T. (1989). Social skills training. In A. S. Bellack, ed., *A clinical guide for the treatment of schizophrenia*. New York: Plenum.

MORRISSEY, J. P., & GOLDMAN, H. H. (1986). Care and treatment of the mentally ill in the United States: Historical developments and reforms. *American Association of Political and Social Sciences, 484*, 12–28.

MORTIMER, A. M., LUND, C. E., & MCKENNA, P. J. (1990). The positive:negative dichotomy in schizophrenia. *British Journal of Psychiatry, 157*, 41–49.

MOSHER, L., & GUNDERSON, J. G. (1979). Group, family, milieu, and community support system treatment for schizophrenia. In L. Bellack, ed., *Disorders of the schizophrenic syndrome*. New York: Grune & Stratton.

MOSHER, L. R. (1989). Community residential treatment: Alternatives to hospitalization. In A. S. Bellack, ed., *A clinical guide for the treatment of schizophrenia*. New York: Plenum.

MUESER, K. T., & BERENBAUM, H. (1990). Psychodynamic treatment of schizophrenia: Is there a future? *Psychological Medicine, 20*, 253–262.

MURPHY, E., LINDESAY, J., & GRUNDY, E. (1986). Sixty years of suicide in England and Wales. *Archives of General Psychiatry, 43*, 969–976.

MURPHY, G. E. (1975a). The physician's responsibility for suicide: I. Errors of commission. *Annals of Internal Medicine, 82*, 301–304.

MURPHY, G. E. (1975b). The physician's responsibility for suicide: II. Errors of omission. *Annals of Internal Medicine, 82*, 305–309.

MURPHY, G. E. (1988). Prevention of suicide. In A. J. Frances & R. E. Hales, eds., *Review of psychiatry*, vol. 7. Washington, DC: American Psychiatric Press.

MURPHY, J. M., OLIVIER, D. C., MONSON, R. R., SOBOL, A. M., & LEIGHTON, A. H. (1988). Incidence of depression and anxiety: The Stirling county study. *American Journal of Public Health, 5*, 534–540.

MURPHY, L. B. (1974). Coping, vulnerability, and resilience in childhood. In G. V. Coelho, D. A. Hamburg, & J. E. Adams, eds., *Coping and adaptation*. New York: Basic Books.

MURRAY, H. A. (1943). *Thematic apperception test: Pictures and manual*. Cambridge, MA: Harvard University Press.

MYERS, J. (1988). Drug controls heart/stroke damage. *Alcohol, Drug Abuse, and Mental Health Administration, 14*(9), 1–2.

NAGAYAMA HALL, G. C. (1990). Prediction of sexual aggression. *Clinical Psychology Review, 10*, 229–245.

NAGLER, S., & MIRSKY, A. F. (1985). Introduction: The Israeli high-risk study. *Schizophrenia Bulletin, 11*, 19–29.

NATIONAL ACADEMY OF SCIENCES. (1982). *Marijuana and health*. Washington, DC: National Academy Press.

NATIONAL INSTITUTE OF MENTAL HEALTH. (1990). *Mental health, United States, 1990*. (DHHS Publication No. ADM 90–1708). Washington, DC: US Government Printing Office.

NATIONAL INSTITUTE OF MENTAL HEALTH. (1991). Caring for people with severe mental disorders: A national plan of research to improve services. (DHHS Publication No. ADM 91–1762). Washington, DC: US Government Printing Office.

NEEDLES, D. J., & ABRAMSON, L. Y. (1990). Positive life events, attributional style, and hopefulness: Testing a model of recovery from depression. *Journal of Abnormal Psychology, 99*, 156–165.

NEIMEYER, G. J., & NEIMEYER, R. A. (1985). Relational trajectories: A personal construct contribution. *Journal of Social and Personal Relationships, 2*, 325–349.

NEMIAH, J. C. (1985a). Obsessive-compulsive disorder (obsessive-compulsive neurosis). In H. I. Kaplan & B. J. Sadock, eds., *Comprehensive textbook of psychiatry*, 4th ed. Baltimore, MD: Williams & Wilkins.

NEMIAH, J. C. (1985b). Phobic disorders (phobic neuroses). In H. I. Kaplan and B. J. Sadock, eds., *Comprehensive textbook of psychiatry*, 4th ed. Baltimore, MD: Williams and Wilkins.

NEMIAH, J. C. (1988). Psychoneurotic disorders. In A. M. Nicholi, ed., *The new Harvard guide to modern psychiatry*, 2nd ed. Cambridge, MA: Harvard University Press.

NEMIAH, J. C., & UHDE, T. W. (1989). Phobic disorders. In H. I. Kaplan & B. J. Sadock, eds., *Comprehensive textbook of psychiatry*, 5th ed. Baltimore: Williams & Wilkins.

NEUGEBAUER, R. (1979). Medieval and early modern theories of mental illness. *Archives of General Psychiatry, 36,* 477–483.

NEUWISSEN, I., & OVER, R. (1991). Multidimensionality of the content of female sexual fantasy. *Behavior Research and Therapy, 29,* 179–189.

NEWLIN, D. B., & THOMSON, J. B. (1990). Alcohol challenge with sons of alcoholics: A critical review and analysis. *Psychological Bulletin, 108,* 383–402.

NICHOLS, P. L. (1984). Familial mental retardation. *Behavior Genetics, 14,* 161–170.

NIETZEL, M. T., & HIMELIEN, M. J. (1986). Prevention of crime and delinquency. In B. A. Edelstein and L. Michelson, eds., *Handbook of Prevention*. New York: Plenum.

NOLEN-HOEKSEMA, S. (1987). Sex differences in unipolar depression: Evidence and theory. *Psychological Bulletin, 101,* 259–282.

NOSHPITZ, J. D., & CODDINGTON, R. D., EDS. (1990). *Stressors and the adjustment disorders*. New York: John Wiley.

NUECHTERLEIN, K. H. (1983). Signal detection in vigilance tasks and behavioral attributes among offspring of schizophrenic mothers and among hyperactive children. *Journal of Abnormal Psychology, 92,* 4–28.

NUECHTERLEIN, K. H., & DAWSON, M. E. (1984). Information processing and attentional functioning in the developmental course of schizophrenic disorders. *Schizophrenia Bulletin, 10,* 160–203.

OATLEY, K., & BOLTON, W. (1985). A social-cognitive theory of depression in reaction to life events. *Psychological Review, 92,* 372–388.

OCHBERG, F. M., ED. (1988). *Post-traumatic therapy and victims of violence*. New York: Brunner/Mazel.

O'CONNELL, R. A. (1986). Psychosocial factors in a model of manic-depressive disease. *Integrative Psychiatry, 4,* 150–154.

O'CONNOR, G. (1976). *Home is a good place: A national perspective of community residential facilities for developmentally disabled persons*. Washington, D.C.: American Association on Mental Deficiency.

O'DONOGHUE, E. G. (1914). *The story of Bethlehem Hospital from its foundation in 1247*. London: T. Fisher.

OGDEN, J. A. H. (1947). *The Kingdom of the Lost*. London: Bodley Head.

OKOLO, C., & GUSKIN, S. (1984). Community attitudes toward community placement of mentally retarded persons. *International Review of Research in Mental Retardation, 12,* 25–66.

OLDS, D. C., & HENDERSON, C. R. (1989). The prevention of maltreatment. In D. Cicchetti & V. Carlson, eds., *Child maltreatment: Theory and research on the causes and consequences of child abuse and neglect*. New York: Cambridge University Press.

O'LEARY, A. (1990). Stress, emotion, and human immune function. *Psychological Bulletin, 108,* 363–382.

O'LEARY, K. D., & WILSON, G. T. (1987). *Behavior therapy: Application and outcome*. Englewood Cliffs, NJ: Prentice-Hall.

O'NEAL, J. M. (1984). First person account: Finding myself and loving it. *Schizophrenia Bulletin, 10,* 109–110.

OTHMER, E., & OTHMER, S. C. (1989). *The clinical interview: Using DSM-III-R*. Washington, DC: American Psychiatric Press.

OTTAVIANI, R., & BECK, A. T., (1987). Cognitive aspects of panic disorders. *Journal of Anxiety Disorders, 1,* 15–28.

PAINTER, S. L. (1986). Research on the prevalence of child sexual abuse: New directions. *Canadian Journal of Behavioral Science, 18,* 323–339.

PARKES, C. M. (1986). *Bereavement: Studies of grief in adult life*. Madison, CO: International Universities Press.

PARNAS, J., SCHULSINGER, F., SCHULSINGER, H., MEDNICK, S. A., & TEASDALE, T. W. (1982). Behavioral precursors of schizophrenic spectrum: A prospective study. *Archives of General Psychiatry, 39,* 658–664.

PATTERSON, D. G., & O'GORMAN, E. C. (1989). Sexual anxiety in sexual dysfunction. *British Journal of Psychiatry, 155,* 374–378.

PATTERSON, G. R. (1982). *Coercive family processes*. Eugene, OR: Castilia Press.

PAUL, G. L. (1969). Chronic mental patient: Current status-future directions. *Psychological Bulletin, 71,* 81–93.

PAUL, G. L., & LENTZ, R. J. (1977). *Psychosocial treatment of chronic mental patients: Milieu versus social-learning programs*. Cambridge, MA: Harvard University Press.

PAUL, S. M. (1985). Toward the integration of neuroscience and psychiatry. In H. A. Pincus & H. Pardes, eds., *The integration of neuroscience and psychiatry*. Washington, D.C.: American Psychiatric Press, 39–52.

PAYKEL, E. S. (1991) Depression in women. *British Journal of Psychiatry, 158,* 22–29.

PAYKEL, E. S. (1979). Recent life events in the development of the depressive disorders. In R. A. Depue, ed., *The psychobiology of the depressive disorders: Implications for the effects of stress*. New York: Academic Press.

PENNEBAKER, J. W., COLDER, M., & SHARP, L. K. (1990). Accelerating the coping process. *Journal of Personality and Social Psychology, 58,* 528–537.

PERLS, F. S. (1969). *Gestalt therapy verbatim*. Lafayette, CA; Real People Press.

PERRIS, C. (1987). Toward an integrative theory of depression focusing on the concept of vulnerability. *Integrative Psychiatry, 5,* 27–39.

PERRY, D. G., PERRY, L. C., & BOLDIZAR, J. P. (1990). Learning of aggression. In M. Lewis & S. M. Miller, eds., *Handbook of developmental psychopathology*. New York: Plenum.

PERSAD, E. (1990). Electroconvulsive therapy in depression. *Canadian Journal of Psychiatry, 35,* 175–182.

PERSKY, V. W., KEMPTHORNE-RAWSON, J., & SHEKELLE, R. B. (1987). Personality and risk of cancer: 20-year follow-up of the Western Electric Study. *Psychosomatic Medicine, 49,* 435–449.

PETERSON, C., & SELIGMAN, M. E. P. (1984). Causal explanations as a risk factor for depression: Theory and evidence. *Psychological Review, 91,* 347–374.

PFEFFER, C. R., CONTE, H. R., JERRETT, I., & PLUTCHIK, R. (1980). Suicide behavior in latency age children. *Journal of the American Academy of Child Psychology, 19,* 703–710.

PFOHL, B. (1991). Histrionic personality disorder: A review of available data and recommendations for DSM-IV. *Journal of Personality Disorders, 5,* 150–166.

PFOHL, B., & ANDREASEN, N. C. (1986). Schizophrenia: Diagnosis and classification. In R. E. Hales & A. J. Frances, eds., *American Psychiatric Association annual review*, vol. 6. Washington, DC: American Psychiatric Press.

PHILLIPS, D. P. (1983). The impact of mass media on U.S. homicides. *American Sociological Review, 48,* 560–568.

PHILLIPS, D. P., & CARSTENSEN, L. S. (1986). Clustering of teenage suicides after television news stories about suicide. *New England Journal of Medicine, 315,* 685–689.

PHILLIPS, D. P., & PAIGHT, D. J. (1987). The impact of televised movies about suicide. *New England Journal of Medicine, 317,* 809–811.

PIERCE, G. R. (1990). *Predicting perceptions of social support: An experimental study of behavioral, personality, relationship, and situational variables*. Unpublished doctoral dissertation, University of Washington, Seattle.

PIERCE, G. R., SARASON, I. G., & SARASON, B. R. (1991). General and relationship-based perceptions of social support: Are two constructs better than one? *Journal of Personality and Social Psychology, 61,* 1028–1039.

PIERCEY, B. P. (1985). First person account: Making the best of it. *Schizophrenia Bulletin, 11,* 155–157.

PILLARD, R. C., & WEINRICH, J. D. (1986). Evidence of familial nature of male homosexuality. *Archives of General Psychiatry, 43,* 808–812.

PINEL, P. (1969). *Traite' medico-philosophique sur l'alienation mentale*, 2nd ed. Paris: Brossen, 1809; as quoted in W. Riese, 1968, *The legacy of Philippe Pinel*. New York: Springer.

PIVEN, J., BERTHIER, M. L., STARKSTEIN, S. E., NEHME, E., PEARLSON, G., & FOLSTEIN, S. (1990). Magnetic resonance imaging evidence for a defect of cerebral cortical development in autism. *American Journal of Psychiatry, 147,* 734–739.

PLAKUN, E. M., BURKHARDT, P. E., & MULLER, A. P. (1985). Fourteen-year follow-up of borderline and schizotypal personality disorders. *Comprehensive Psychiatry, 26,* 448–455.

PLISZKA, S. R. (1987). Tricyclic antidepressants in the treatment of children with attention deficit disorder. *Journal of the American Academy of Child and Adolescent Psychiatry, 26,* 127–132.

PLOMIN, R. (1990). The role of inheritance in behavior. *Science, 248,* 183–188.

PLUMB, M. M., & HOLLAND, J. (1977). Comparative studies of psychological function in patients with advanced cancer. I. Self-reported depressive symptoms. *Psychosomatic Medicine, 39,* 264–276.

POGUE-GEILE, M. F., & HARROW, M. (1985). Negative symptoms in schizophrenia: Their longitudinal course and prognostic importance. *Schizophrenia Bulletin, 11,* 427–439.

POGUE-GEILE, M. F., & KESHAVAN, M. (1991). Negative symptomatology in schizophrenia: Syndrome and subtype status. In J. F. Gredin & R. Tandon, eds., *Negative schizophrenic symptoms: Pathophysiology and clinical implications.* Washington, DC: American Psychiatric Press.

POGUE-GEILE, M. F., & ZUBIN, J. (1988). Negative symptomatology in schizophrenia: A conceptual and empirical review. *International Journal of Mental Health, 16,* 3–45.

POLACK, P., KIRBY, M., & DIETCHMAN, W. (1979). Treating acutely psychiatric patients in private homes. In H. R. Lamb, ed., *New directions for mental health services—Alternatives to acute hospitalization,* vol. 1. San Francisco: Jossey-Bass.

POLICH, J. M., & ARMOR, D. J. (1980). *The course of alcoholism: Four years after treatment.* Santa Monica, CA: Rand.

POLITAN, P., & FIEVE, R. R. (1971). Patient rejection of lithium carbonate prophylaxis. *Journal of the American Medical Association, 218,* 864–866.

POMEROY, W. B. (1972). *Kinsey and the Institute for Sex Research.* New York: Harper & Row.

POPE, H. G., JR., IONESCU-PIOGGIA, M., AIZLEY, H. G., & VARMA, D. K. (1990). Drug use and life style among college undergraduates in 1989: A comparison with 1969 and 1978. *American Journal of Psychiatry, 147,* 998–1001.

POPE, H. G., JR., JONAS, J. M., HUDSON, J., COHEN, B. M., & GUNDERSON, J. G. (1983). The validity of DSM-III borderline personality disorder. *Archives of General Psychiatry, 40,* 1319–1323.

PRENTKY, R. A., & KNIGHT, R. A. (1991). Identifying critical dimensions for discriminating among rapists. *Journal of Consulting and Clinical Psychology, 59,* 643–661.

PRESLY, A. S., GRUBB, A. B., & SEMPLE, D. (1982). Predictors of successful rehabilitation in long-term patients. *Acta Psychiatric Scandinavica, 66,* 83–88.

PRINCE, V. C. (1967). *The transvestite and his wife.* Los Angeles: Argyle Books.

PRIOR, M. R., & McGILLVRAY, J. (1980). The performance of autistic children on three learning set tasks. *Journal of Child Psychology and Psychiatry, 21,* 313–324.

PURCELL, K., BRADY, K., SCHAL, H., MUSER, J., MOLK, L., GORDON, N., & MEANS, J. (1969). The effect on asthma in children of experimental separation from the family. *Psychosomatic Medicine, 31,* 144–164.

PUTNAM, F. W. (1991). Dissociative phenomena. In A. Tasman & S. M. Goldfinger, eds., *Review of Psychiatry,* vol. 10. Washington, DC: American Psychiatric Press.

RABKIN, J. G. (1979). Criminal behavior of discharged mental patients: A critical appraisal of the research. *Psychological Bulletin, 86,* 1–27.

RACHMAN, S. J., & deSILVA, P. (1978). Abnormal and normal obsessions. *Behavioral Research and Therapy, 16,* 223–248.

RACHMAN, S. J., & HODGSON, R. J. (1980). *Obsessions and compulsions.* Englewood Cliffs, NJ: Prentice-Hall.

RAGLAND, D. R., & BRAND, R. J. (1988). Type A behavior and mortality from coronary heart disease. *New England Journal of Medicine, 318,* 65–69.

RAHE, R. H., KARSON, S., HOWARD, N. S., RUBIN, R. T., & POLAND, R. E. (1990). Psychological and physiological assessments on American hostages freed from captivity in Iran. *Psychosomatic Medicine, 52,* 1–16.

RAMEY, C. T., & HASKINS, R. (1981). The modification of intelligence through early experience. *Intelligence, 5,* 43–57.

RAPAPORT, K., & BURKART, B. R. (1984). Personality and attitudinal characteristics of sexually coercive college males. *Journal of Abnormal Psychology, 13,* 216–221.

RAPOPORT, J., ELKINS, R., LANGER, D. H., SCEERY, W., BUCHSBAUM, M. S., GILLIN, J. C., MURPHY, D. L., ZAHN, T. P., LAKE, R., LUDLOW, C., & MENDELSON, W. (1981). Childhood obsessive-compulsive disorder. *American Journal of Psychiatry, 138,* 1545–1554.

RAPOPORT, J. L. (1989). *The boy who couldn't stop washing.* New York: Dutton.

RAPPORT, M. D., & KELLY, K. C. (1991). Psychostimulant effects on learning and cognitive function: Findings and implications for children with attention deficit hyperactivity disorder. *Clinical Psychology Review, 11,* 61–92.

RAZ, S., & RAZ, N. (1990). Structural brain abnormalities in the major psychoses: A quantitative review of the evidence from computer imaging. *Psychological Bulletin, 108,* 93–108.

REICH, J., YATES, W., & NDUAGUBA, M. (1989). Prevalence of DSM-III personality disorders in the community. *Social Psychiatry and Psychiatric Epidemiology, 24,* 12–16.

REICH, W. (1949). (originally published 1933) *Character analysis.* New York: Orgone Institute Press.

REISBERG, B. (1985). Alzheimer's disease updated. *Psychiatric Annals, 15,* 319–322.

REISS, B. F. (1980). Psychological tests in homosexuality. In J. Marmor, ed., *Homosexual behavior.* New York: Basic Books.

REHM, L. P., KASLOW, N. J., & RABIN, A. S. (1987). Cognitive and behavioral targets in a self-control therapy program for depression. *Journal of Consulting and Clinical Psychology, 55,* 60–67.

REID, W. H. (1986). Antisocial personality. In R. Michels & J. O. Cavenar, Jr., eds., *Psychiatry,* vol. 1. New York: Basic Books.

REID, W. H., & BALIS, G. U. (1987). Evaluation of the violent patient. In R. E. Hales & A. J. Frances, eds., *American Psychiatric Association Annual Review,* vol. 6. Washington, D.C.: American Psychiatric Press.

REID, W. H., DOOR, D., WALKER, J. L., & BONNER, J. W. (1986). *Unmasking the psychopath: Antisocial personality and related symptoms.* New York: Norton.

REKERS, G. A. (1977). Assessment and treatment of childhood gender problems. In B. B. Lahey & A. E. Kazdin, eds., *Advances in clinical child psychology,* vol. 1. New York: Plenum.

REMAFEDI, G. (1985). Adolescent homosexuality: Issues for pediatricians. *Clinical Pediatrics, 9,* 481–485.

REMAFEDI, G. (1987a). Male homosexuality: The adolescent perspective. *Pediatrics, 79,* 326–330.

REMAFEDI, G. (1987b). Adolescent homosexuality: Psychosocial and medical implications. *Pediatrics, 79,* 331–337.

REPUCCI, N. D., & HAUGAARD, J. J. (1989). Prevention of child sexual abuse. *American Psychologist, 44,* 1266–1275.

RESEARCH NEWS. (1987). Brain grafts benefit Parkinson's patients. *Science, 236,* 149.

RESEARCH ON MENTAL ILLNESS AND ADDICTIVE DISORDERS. (1985). *American Journal of Psychiatry, 142* (supplement), 9–41.

REVELEY, A. M. (1985). Genetic counseling for schizophrenia. *British Journal of Psychiatry, 147,* 107–112.

REYNOLDS, G. P. (1989). Beyond the dopamine hypothesis: The neurochemical pathology of schizophrenia. *British Journal of Psychiatry, 155,* 305–316.

RICE, J., REICH, T., ANDREASEN, N. C., ENDICOTT, J., VanEERDEWEGH, M., FISHMAN, R., HIRSCHFELD, R. M. A., & KLERMAN, G. L. (1987). The familial transmission of bipolar illness. *Archives of General Psychiatry, 44,* 441–447.

RICHELSON, E. (1990). Antidepressants and brain neurochemistry. *Mayo Clinic Proceedings, 65,* 1227–1236.

RICHMANN, N., STEVENSON, J., & GRAHAM, P. J. (1982). *Preschool to school: A behavioral study.* London: Academic Press.

RIE, H., & RIE, E., EDS. (1980). *Handbook of minimal brain dysfunctions: A critical view.* New York: Wiley.

RIESENBERG, D. (1987). Treating a societal malignancy—rape. *Journal of the American Medical Association, 257,* 726–727.

RIST, M. C. (1990). The shadow children. *American Schoolboard Journal,* January 19–24.

RITVO, E. R., JORDE, L. B., MASON-BROTHERS, A., FREEMAN, B. J., PINGREE, C., JONES, M. B., McMAHON, W. M., PETERSEN, P. B., JENSON, W. R., & MO, A. (1989). The UCLA-University of Utah epidemiologic survey of autism: Recurrence risk estimates and genetic counseling. *American Journal of Psychiatry, 146,* 1032–1036.

ROACH, M. (1983). Another name for madness. *New York Times Magazine*, Jan. 16, 22–31.

ROBERTSON, H. A. (1979). Benzodiazepine receptors in "emotional" and "nonemotional" mice: Comparison of four strains. *European Journal of Pharmacology, 56,* 163.

ROBINS, C. J. (1988). Attributions and depression: Why is the literature so inconsistent. *Journal of Personality and Social Psychology, 54,* 847–852.

ROBINS, L. N. (1991). Conduct disorder. *Journal of Child Psychology and Psychiatry, 32,* 193–212.

ROBINS, L. N., HELZER, J. E., CROGHAN, J., & RATCLIFF, K. S. (1981). National Institute of Mental Health Diagnostic Interview Schedule. *Archives of General Psychiatry, 38,* 381–389.

ROBINS, L. N., & PRICE, R. K. (1991). Adult disorders predicted by childhood conduct problems: Results from the NIMH Epidemiological Catchment Area Project. *Psychiatry, 54,* 116–132.

ROBINS, L. N., & REGIER, D. A. (1991). *Psychiatric disorders in America: The epidemiological catchment area.* New York: The Free Press.

ROBINSON, L. A., BERMAN, J. S., & NEIMEYER, R. A. (1990). Psychotherapy for the treatment of depression: A comprehensive view of controlled outcome research. *Psychological Bulletin, 108,* 30–49.

ROCK, C. L., & YAGER, J. (1987). Nutrition and eating disorders: A primer for clinicians. *International Journal of Eating Disorders, 6,* 267–280.

ROGENTINE, G. N., VANKAMMEN, D. P., FOX, B. H., DOGHERTY, J. P., ROSENBLATT, J. E., BOYD, S. C., & BUNNEY, W. E., JR. (1979). Psychological factors in the prognosis of malignant melanoma: A prospective study. *Psychosomatic Medicine, 41,* 647–655.

ROGERS, C. R. (1951). *Client-centered therapy.* Boston: Houghton-Mifflin.

ROGERS, C. R. (1959). A theory of therapy, personality, and interpersonal relationships as developed in the client-centered framework. In S. Koch, ed., *Psychology: A study of a science,* vol. 3. New York: McGraw-Hill.

ROGERS, C. R. (1980). *A way of being.* Boston: Houghton-Mifflin.

ROGLER, L. H., & HOLLINGSHEAD, A. B. (1965). *Trapped: Families and schizophrenia.* New York: John Wiley.

ROMER, D., & HELLER, T. (1983). Social adaptation of mentally retarded adults in community settings: A social-ecological approach. *Applied Research in Mental Retardation, 4,* 303–314.

RORER, L. G. (1989*a*). Rational-emotive theory: I. An integrated psychological and philosophical basis. *Cognitive Therapy and Research, 13,* 475–492.

RORER, L. G. (1989*b*). Rational-emotive theory: II. Explication and evaluation. *Cognitive Therapy and Research, 13,* 531–548.

RORSCHACH, H. (1942). *Psychodiagnostic: Methodik and ergebnisse eines wahrnehmungs-dianostichen experiments,* 2nd ed. (P. Lemkau & B. Kronenberg, trans.). Berne and Berlin: Huber, 1932; republished: New York: Grune & Stratton.

RORSMAN, B., GRASBECK, A., HAGNELL, O., LANKE, J., OHMAN, R., OJESJO, L., & OTTERBECK, L. (1990). A prospective study of first-incidence depression: The Lundby study, 1957–1972. *British Journal of Psychiatry, 156,* 336–342.

ROSENBAUM, A., & O'LEARY, K. D. (1981). Marital violence: Characteristics of abusive couples. *Journal of Consulting and Clinical Psychology, 49,* 63–71.

ROSENBAUM, L. A., & PAULLY, G. S. (1987). Primate models of separation-induced depression. *Psychiatric Clinics of North America, 10,* 437–447.

ROSENHAN, D. L. (1973). On being sane in insane places. *Science, 179,* 250–257.

ROSENMAN, R. H., BRAND, R. J., JENKINS, C. D., FRIEDMAN, M., STRAUS, R., & WURM, M. (1975). Coronary heart disease in the Western Collaborative Group Study. *Journal of the American Medical Association, 233,* 872–877.

ROSENSTEIN, M. J., STEADMAN, H. J., MILAZZO-SAYRE, L. J., MACASKILL, R. C., & MANDERSCHEID, R. W. (1986). Characteristics of admissions to the inpatient services of state and county mental hospitals, United States, 1980. *Mental Health Statistical Note.* No. 177 (U.S. National Institute of Mental Health). Washington, D.C.: U.S. Government Printing Office.

ROSENTHAL, D., ED. (1963). *The Genain quadruplets: A case study and theoretical analysis of heredity and environment in schizophrenia.* New York: Basic Books.

ROSENTHAL, D., WENDER, P. H., KETY, S. S., SCHULSINGER, F., WELNER, J., & OSTERGAARD, L. (1968). Schizophrenics' offspring reared in adoptive homes. In D. Rosenthal & S. S. Kety, eds., *The transmission of schizophrenia.* Oxford: Pergamon Press.

ROSENTHAL, D., WENDER, P. H., KETY, S. S., SCHULSINGER, F., WELNER, J., & REIDER, R. (1975). Parent-child relationships and psychopathological disorder in the child. *Archives of General Psychiatry, 32,* 466–476.

ROSENTHAL, N. E., JACOBSEN, F. M., SACK, D. A., ARENDT, J., JAMES, S. P., PARRY, B. L., & WEHR, T. A. (1988). Atenolol in seasonal affective disorder. *American Journal of Psychiatry, 145,* 52–56.

ROSENTHAL, R. (1991). *Meta-analytical procedures for social research* (2nd ed.). Beverly Hills, CA: Sage.

ROSIE, J. S. (1987). Partial hospitalization: A review of recent literature. *Hospital and Community Psychiatry, 38,* 1291–1299.

ROSS, D. M., & ROSS, S. A. (1982). *Hyperactivity: Research, theory, and action.* New York: John Wiley.

ROSS, H. L., & GLASER, E. M. (1973). Making it out of the ghetto. *Professional Psychology, 4,* 347–356.

ROSSI, P. H. (1989). *Down and out in America.* Chicago: University of Chicago Press.

ROSVOLD, H. E., MIRSKY, A. F., SARASON, I. G., BRANSOME, E. D., & BECK, L. H. (1956). A continuous performance test of brain damage. *Journal of Consulting Psychology, 20,* 343–350.

ROTHENBERG, A. (1990). Adolescence and eating disorder: The obsessive–compulsive syndrome. *Psychiatric Clinics of North America, 13,* 469–488.

ROY, A. (1986). Depression, attempted suicide, and suicide in patients with chronic schizophrenia. *Psychiatric Clinics of North America, 9,* 193–206.

ROY, A., & LINNOILA, M. (1986). Alcoholism and suicide. In R. Maris, ed., *Biology of Suicide,* pp. 162–191. New York: Guilford Press.

ROY-BYRNE, P. P., POST, R. M., UHDE, T. W., PORCU, T., & DAVIS, D. (1985). The longitudinal course of recurrent affective illness: Life chart data from research patients at the NIMH. *Acta Psychiatrica Scandinavica Supplementum, 71,* 3–34.

RUBENS, R. L., & LAPIDUS, L. B. (1978). Schizophrenic patterns of arousal and stimulus barrier functioning. *Journal of Abnormal Psychology, 87,* 199–211.

RUBERMAN, J. W., WEINBLATT, E., GOLDBERG, J. D., & CHAUDHARY, B. S. (1984). Psychological influences on mortality after myocardial infarction. *New England Journal of Medicine, 311,* 552–559.

RUCH, L. O., GARTRELL, J. W., AMEDEO, S. R., & COYNE, B. J. (1991). The Sexual Assault Symptom Scale: Measuring self-reported sexual assault trauma in the emergency room. *Psychological Assessment, 3,* 3–8.

RUND, B. R. (1990). Fully recovered schizophrenics: A retrospective study of some premorbid and treatment factors. *Psychiatry, 53,* 127–139.

RUSSELL, D. E. H. (1984). The prevalence and seriousness of incestuous abuse: Step fathers vs. biological fathers. *Child Abuse and Neglect, 8,* 15–22.

RUTTER, D. R. (1985). Language in schizophrenia: The structure of monologues and conversations. *British Journal of Psychiatry, 146,* 399–404.

RUTTER, M. (1986). Depressive feelings, cognitions, and disorders: A research postscript. In M. Rutter, ed., *Depression in young people.* New York: Guilford Press.

RUTTER, M., COX, A., TYUPLING, C., BERGER, M., & YULE, W. (1975). Attainment and adjustment in two geographical areas: I. The prevalence of psychiatric disorder. *British Journal of Psychiatry, 126,* 493–509.

RUTTER, M., & GARMEZY, N. (1983). Developmental psychopathology. In P. Mussen, ed., *Handbook of child psychology,* vol. 4. New York: John Wiley.

RUTTER, M., & GILLER, H. (1984). *Juvenile delinquency: Trends and perspectives.* Harmondsworth, England: Penguin.

RUTTER, M., GRAHAM, P., & YULE, W. (1970). A neuropsychiatric study in childhood. *Clinics in Developmental Medicine,* Nos. 35/36. London: Heinemann.

RUTTER, M., & HERSOV, L. (1985). *Child and adolescent psychiatry: Modern approaches.* Oxford, England: Blackwell Scientific Publications.

RUTTER, M., & SHAFFER, D. (1980). DSM-III: A step forward or back in terms of the classification of child psychiatric disorders. *Journal of the American Academy of Child Psychiatry, 19,* 371–394.

RUTTER, M., TIZARD, I., & WHITMORE, K., EDS. (1981). (originally published in 1970) *Education, health and behavior.* Huntington, NY: Krieger.

SACKHEIM, H. A., PRUDIC, J., & DEVANAND, D. P. (1990). Treatment of medication-resistant depression with electroconvulsive therapy. In A. Tasman, S. M. Goldfinger, & C. A. Kaufmann, eds., *Review of psychiatry,* vol. 9. Washington, DC: American Psychiatric Press.

SACKHEIM, H. A., & WEGNER, A. Z. (1986). Attributional patterns in depression and euthymia. *Archives of General Psychiatry, 43,* 553–560.

SADOCK, V. A. (1989). Normal human sexuality and sexual disorders. In H. I. Kaplan & B. J. Sadock, eds., *Comprehensive textbook of psychiatry,* 5th ed. Baltimore: Williams & Wilkins.

SADOCK, V. A. (1989). Rape, spouse abuse, and incest. In H. I. Kaplan & B. J. Sadock, eds., *Comprehensive textbook of psychiatry,* 5th ed. Baltimore: Williams & Wilkins.

SAGHIR, M. T., & ROBINS, E. (1973). *Male and female homosexuality: A comprehensive investigation.* Baltimore: Williams & Wilkins.

SALTER, A. C., RICHARDSON, C. M., & KAIRYS, S. W. (1985). Caring for abused preschoolers. *Child Welfare, 64,* 343–356.

SANDERSON, W. C., & BARLOW, D. H. (1990). A description of patients diagnosed with DSM-III-R generalized anxiety disorder. *The Journal of Nervous and Mental Disease, 178,* 588–591.

SANDLER, J., & JOFFEE, W. G. (1965). Notes on childhood depression. *International Journal of Psychoanalysis, 46,* 80–96.

SANDLER, J., with A. FREUD. (1985). *The analysis of defense: The ego and the mechanisms of defense revisited.* New York: International Universities Press.

SANTAYANA, G. (1905–1906). *The life of reason.* New York: Scribner.

SARASON, B. R., SARASON, I. G., HACKER, T. A., & BASHAM, R. B. (1985). Concomitants of social support: Social skills, physical attractiveness, and gender. *Journal of Personality and Social Psychology, 49,* 469–480.

SARASON, I. G. (1979). Three lacunae of cognitive therapy. *Cognitive Therapy and Research, 3,* 223–235.

SARASON, I. G., JOHNSON, J. M., & SIEGEL, J. M. (1978). Assessing the impact of life stress: Development of the Life Experiences Survey. *Journal of Consulting and Clinical Psychology, 46,* 932–946.

SARASON, I. G., LEVINE, H. M., BASHAM, R. B., & SARASON, B. R. (1983). Assessing social support: The Social Support Questionnaire. *Journal of Personality and Social Psychology, 44,* 127–139.

SARASON, I. G., & SARASON, B. R. (1981). Teaching cognitive and social skills to high school students. *Journal of Consulting and Clinical Psychology, 49,* 908–919.

SARASON, I. G., & SARASON, B. R., EDS. (1985). *Social support: Theory, research and applications.* Dordrecht, The Netherlands: Martinus Nijhof.

SARASON, I. G., SARASON, B. R., & PIERCE, G. R. (1990). Social support: The search for theory. *Journal of Social and Clinical Psychology, 9,* 133–147.

SARASON, I. G., SARASON, B. R., POTTER, E. H. III, & ANTONI, M. H. (1985). Life events, social support, and illness. *Psychosomatic Medicine, 47,* 156–163.

SARASON, I. G., & STOOPS, R. (1978). Test anxiety and the passage of time. *Journal of Consulting and Clinical Psychology, 46,* 102–109.

SASS, L. A. (1987). Introspection, schizophrenia, and the fragmentation of self. *Representations, 19,* 1–34.

SAUL, R. A., STEVENSON, R. I., SIMENSEN, R. J., WILKES, G., ALEXANDER, W., & TAYLOR, H. (1982). Fragile X syndrome in South Carolina. *Journal of the South Carolina Medical Association, 78,* 475–477.

SAVIN-WILLIAMS, R. C. (1990). *Gay and lesbian youth: Expressions of identity.* New York: Hemisphere.

SCARR, S. (1981). *Race, social class and individual differences in IQ.* Hillsdale, NJ: Erlbaum.

SCHACHT, T. E., & STRUPP, H. H. (1985). Evaluation of psychotherapy. In H. I. Kaplan & B. J. Sadock, eds. *Comprehensive textbook of psychiatry,* 4th ed., vol. 2. Baltimore: Williams & Wilkins.

SCHACHTER, S. (1982). Recidivism and self-care of smoking and obesity. *American Psychologist, 37,* 436–444.

SCHAFER, R. (1948). *Clinical application of psychological tests.* New York: International Universities Press.

SCHAIE, K. W. (1983). The Seattle longitudinal study: A 21-year exploration of psychometric intelligence in adulthood. In K. W. Schaie, ed., *Longitudinal studies of adult psychological development.* New York: Guilford Press.

SCHAIE, K. W. (1989). The hazards of cognitive aging. *The Gerontological Society of America, 29,* 484–493.

SCHALLING, D. (1978). Psychopathy-related personality variables and the psychophysiology of socialization. In R. D. Hare & D. Schalling, eds., *Psychopathic behavior: Approaches to research.* Chichester, England: John Wiley.

SCHILDKRAUT, J. J. (1965). The catecholamine hypothesis of affective disorders: A review of supporting evidence. *American Journal of Psychiatry, 122,* 509–522.

SCHILLING, R. F., & SCHINKE, S. P. (1984). Maltreatment and mental retardation. In J. M. Berg, ed., *Perspectives and progress in mental retardation,* vol. 1. Baltimore, MD: University Park Press.

SCHLALOCK, R. L., & LILLEY, M. A. (1986). Placement from community-based mental retardation programs: How well do clients do after 8 to 10 years. *American Journal of Mental Deficiency, 90,* 669–676.

SCHLESINGER, H. J., MUMFORD, E., GLASS, G. V., PATRICK, C., & SHARFSTEIN, S. (1983). Mental health treatment and medical care utilization in a fee-for-service system: Outpatient mental health treatment following the onset of a chronic disease. *American Journal of Public Health, 73,* 422–429.

SCHLESSER, M. A., & ALTSHULER, K. Z. (1983). The genetics of affective disorder: Data, theory, and clinical applications. *Hospital and Community Psychiatry, 34,* 415–422.

SCHNALL, P. L., PIEPER, C., SCHWARTZ, J. E., KARASEK, R. A., SCHLUSSEL, Y., DEVEREUX, R. B., GANAU, A., ALDERMAN, M., WARREN, K., & PICKERING, T. G. (1990). The relationship between "job strain," workplace diastolic blood pressure, and left ventricular mass index. *Journal of the American Medical Association, 263,* 1929–1972.

SCHNEIDERMAN, N., WEISS, S. M., & KAUFMANN, P. G., EDS. (1989). *Handbook of research methods in cardiovascular behavioral medicine.* New York: Plenum Press.

SCHOENMAN, T. J. (1984). The mentally ill witch in text books of abnormal psychology: Current status and implications of a fallacy. *Professional Psychiatry, 15,* 299–314.

SCHOTTE, D. E., & STUNKARD, A. J. (1987). Bulimia vs. bulimic behaviors on a college campus. *Journal of the American Medical Association, 258,* 1213–1215.

SCHUCHTER, S. R., & SISSOK, S. (1984). Psychological reactions to the PSA crash. *International Journal of Psychiatry in Medicine, 14,* 293–301.

SCHUCKIT, M. A. (1987). Biological vulnerability to alcoholism. *Journal of Consulting and Clinical Psychology, 55,* 307–309.

SCHWARTZ, S. (1982). Is there a schizophrenic language? *The Behavioral and Brain Sciences, 4,* 579–588.

SCHWEINHART, L. J., & WEIKART, D. P. (1980). *Young children grow up.* Ypsilanti, MI: High/Scope.

SCIENCE REPORTS: NATIONAL INSTITUTE OF MENTAL HEALTH. (1981). *Treating and assessing the chronically mentally ill.* Rockville, MD: U.S. Dept of Health and Human Services.

SEARL, S., JR. (1978). Stages of parent reaction to the birth of a handicapped child. *Exceptional Parent,* (April), 23–27.

SECHEHAYE, M. (1951). *Autobiography of a schizophrenic girl.* New York: Grune & Stratton.

SEDVALL, G., FARDE, L., PERSSON, A., & WIESEL, F. A. (1986). Imaging of neurotransmitter receptors in the living human brain. *Archives of General Psychiatry, 43(10),* 995–1005.

SELIGMAN, M. E. P. (1974). Depression and learned helplessness. In R. J. Friedman & M. M. Katz, eds., *The psychology of depression: Contemporary theory and research.* Washington, DC: V. H. Winston.

SELIGMAN, M. E. P. (1975). *Helplessness: On depression, development, and death.* San Francisco: W. H. Freeman.

SELYE, H. (1976). *The stress of life,* rev. ed. New York: McGraw-Hill.

SHAFFER, J. W., GRAVES, P. L., SWANK, R. T., & PEARSON, T. A. (1987). Clustering of personality traits in youth and the subsequent development of cancer among physicians. *Journal of Behavioral Medicine, 10,* 441–447.

SHAPIRO, D. (1965). *Neurotic styles.* New York: Basic Books.

SHAW, C. R., ED. (1930). *The jack roller.* Chicago: University of Chicago Press.

SHEA, S. C. (1988). *Psychiatric interviewing: The art of understanding.* Philadelphia: Saunders.

SHEAR, M. K., & FYER, M. R. (1988). Biological and psychopathologic findings in panic disorder. In A. J. Frances & R. E. Hales, eds., *Review of psychiatry*, vol. 7. Washington, DC: American Psychiatric Press.

SHEEHAN, S. 1982. *Is there no place on earth for me?* Boston: Houghton Mifflin.

SHEKELLE, R. B., RAYNOR, W. J., OSTFELD, A. M., GARRON, D. C., BIELIAUSKAS, L. A., LIU, S. C., MALIZA, C., & OGLESBY, P. (1981). Psychological depression and 17-year risk of death from cancer. *Psychosomatic Medicine, 43,* 117–125.

SHENGXIAN L., & PHILLIPS, M. R. (1990). Witch doctors and mental illness in Mainland China: A preliminary study. *American Journal of Psychiatry, 147,* 221–224.

SHERMAN, B. (1985). The new realities of "date rape." *New York Times,* Oct. 23, 17.

SHIFFMAN, S. (1982). Relapse following smoking cessation: A situational analysis. *Journal of Consulting and Clinical Psychology, 50,* 71–86.

SHNEIDMAN, E. S. (1980). *Voices of death.* New York: Harper & Row.

SHOHAM-SALOMON, V., AVNER, R., & NEEMAN, R. (1989). You're changed if you do and changed if you don't: Mechanisms underlying paradoxical interventions. *Journal of Consulting and Clinical Psychology, 57,* 590–598.

SHORE, E. R. (1989). What I learned about community psychology from my bout with cancer. *The Community Psychologist, 23,* 25.

SHUMAKER, S. A., & HILL, D. R. (1991). Gender differences in social support and physical health. *Health Psychology, 10,* 102–111.

SHURE, M. B., & SPIVACK, G. (1982). Interpersonal problem-solving in young children: A cognitive approach to prevention. *American Journal of Community Psychology, 10,* 341–356.

SHURE, M. B., & SPIVACK, G. (1987). Competence-building as an approach to prevention of dysfunction: The ICPS model. In J. A. Steinberg & M. M. Silverman, eds., *Preventing mental disorders: A research perspective.* Rockville, MD: National Institute of Mental Health.

SIBLERUD, R. L. (1989). The relationship between mercury from dental amalgam and mental health. *American Journal of Psychotherapy, 43,* 575–587.

SIEGEL, J. M. (1985). The measurement of anger as a multidimensional construct. In M. A. Chesney & R. H. Rosenman, eds., *Anger and hostility in cardiovascular and behavioral disorders.* Washington, DC: Hemisphere.

SIEGEL, S., HINSON, R. E., & KRANK, M. D. (1981). Morphine-induced attenuation of morphine tolerance. *Science, 212,* 1533–1534.

SIEVER, L. J., BERNSTEIN, D. P., & SILVERMAN, J. M. (1991). Schizotypal personality disorder: A review of its current status. *Journal of Personality Disorders, 5,* 178–193.

SIEVER, L. J., & COURSEY, R. D. (1985). Biological markers for schizophrenia and the biological high risk approach. *Journal of Nervous and Mental Disease, 173,* 4–16.

SIEVER, L. J., & DAVIS, K. L. (1985). Overview: Toward a dysregulation hypothesis of depression. *American Journal of Psychiatry, 142,* 1017–1031.

SIEVER, L. J., & KENDLER, K. S. (1986). Schizoid/schizotypal/paranoid personality disorders. In R. Michels and J. O. Cavenar, Jr., eds., *Psychiatry*, vol. 1. New York: Basic Books.

SILVER, J. M., HALES, R. E., & YUDOFSKY, S. C. (1990). Psychiatric consultation to neurology. In A. Tasman, S. M. Goldfinger, & C. A. Kauffmann, eds., *Review of psychiatry*, vol. 9. Washington, DC: American Psychiatric Press.

SILVERSTEIN, M. L., & HARROW, M. (1981). Schneiderian first-rank symptoms in schizophrenia. *Archives of General Psychiatry, 38,* 288–293.

SIMMONS, K. (1987). Adolescent suicide: Second leading death cause. *Journal of the American Medical Association, 257,* 3329–3330.

SKINNER, B. F. (1959). A case history in scientific method. In S. Koch, ed., *Psychology: A study of a science*, vol. 2. New York: McGraw-Hill.

SKLAR, L. S., & ANISMAN, H. (1981). Stress and cancer. *Psychological Bulletin, 89,* 369–406.

SKODOL, A. E. (1989). *Problems in differential diagnosis.* Washington, DC: American Psychiatric Press.

SKULTANS, V. (1979). *English madness.* London: Routledge & Kegan Paul.

SLOANE, R. B., STAPLES, F. R., WHIPPLE, K., & CRISTOL, A. H. (1977). Patients' attitudes toward behavior therapy and psychotherapy. *American Journal of Psychiatry, 134*(2), 134–137.

SLOANE, R. B., STAPLES, F. R., YORKSTON, N. J., WHIPPLE, K., & CRISTOL, A. H. (1975). *Short-term analytically oriented psychotherapy versus behavior therapy.* Cambridge, MA: Harvard University Press.

SMALL, G. W., & NICHOLI, A. M. (1982). Mass hysteria among school children. *Archives of General Psychiatry, 39,* 89–90.

SMITH, D. W., & WILSON, A. A. (1973). *A child with Down's syndrome (monogolism).* Philadelphia: Saunders.

SMITH, E. M., NORTH, C. S., McCOOL, R. E., & SHEA, J. M. (1990). Acute postdisaster psychiatric disorders: Identification of persons at risk. *American Journal of Psychiatry, 147,* 202–206.

SMITH, M. L., GLASS, G. V., & MILLER, T. I. (1980). *The benefits of psychotherapy.* Baltimore: Johns Hopkins University Press.

SMITH, R. N. (1982). *Dewey and his times.* New York: Simon & Schuster.

SMITH, T. W. (1982). Irrational beliefs on the cause and treatment of emotional distress: A critical review of the rational-emotive model. *Clinical Psychology Review, 2,* 505–522.

SOKOL, L., BECK, A. T., GREENBERG, R. L., WRIGHT, F. D., & BERCHICK, R. J. (1989). Cognitive therapy of panic disorder: A nonpharmacological alternative. *The Journal of Nervous and Mental Disease, 177,* 711–716.

SOLOVAY, M. R., SHENTON, M. E., & HOLZMAN, P. S. (1987). Comparative studies of thought disorders. *Archives of General Psychiatry, 44,* 13–20.

SOUTHGATE, M. T. (1990). The cover. *Journal of American Psychology, 264,* 2847.

SPANOS, N. P. (1978). Witchcraft in histories of psychiatry: A critical analysis and an alternative conceptualization. *Psychological Bulletin, 85,* 417–439.

SPIEGEL, D., BLOOM, J. R., KRAEMER, H. C., & GOTTHEIL, E. (1989). Effect of psychosocial treatment on survival of patients with metastatic breast cancer. *The Lancet,* October 14, 888–891.

SPIEGEL, D., & WISSLER, T. (1986). Family environment as a predictor of psychiatric rehospitalization. *American Journal of Psychiatry, 143,* 56–60.

SPIRITO, A., BROWN, L., OVERHOLSER, J., & FRITZ, G. (1989). Attempted suicide in adolescence: A review and critique of the literature. *Clinical Psychology Review, 9,* 335–363.

SPITZER, R. L., GIBBON, M., SKODOL, A. E., WILLIAMS, J. B. W., & FIRST, M. G. (1989). *DSM-III-R casebook.* Washington, DC: American Psychiatric Press.

SPITZER, R. L., SKODOL, A. E., GIBBON, M., & WILLIAMS, J. B. W. (1981). *DSM-III casebook.* Washington, DC: American Psychiatric Association.

SPITZER, R. L., SKODOL, A. E., GIBBON, M., & WILLIAMS, J. B. W. (1983). *Psychopathology: A casebook.* New York: McGraw-Hill.

SPIVACK, G., PLATT, J. J., & SHURE, M. B. (1976). *The problem-solving approach to adjustment.* San Francisco: Jossey-Bass.

SPRING, B., LEMON, M., WEINSTEIN, L., & HASKELL, A. (1989). Distractibility in schizophrenia: State and trait aspects. *British Journal of Psychiatry, 155,* 63–68.

SROLE, L., LANGER, T. S., MICHAEL, S. T., KIRKPATRICK, P., OPLER, M. K., & RENNIE, T. A. C. (1962). *Mental health in the metropolis: The Midtown Manhattan study*, rev. ed. New York: New York University Press.

STABENAU, J. R., & POLLIN, W. (1967). Early characteristics of monozygotic twins discordant for schizophrenia. *Archives of General Psychiatry, 17,* 723–734.

STATTIN, H., & MAGNUSSON, D. (1989). The role of early aggressive behavior in the frequency, seriousness, and types of later crime. *Journal of Consulting and Clinical Psychology, 57,* 710–718.

STEIN, M., SCHLEIFER, S. J., & KELLER, S. E. (1987). Psychoimmunology in clinical psychiatry. In R. E. Hales & A. J. Frances, eds., *American Psychiatric Association annual review*, vol. 6. Washington, DC: American Psychiatric Press.

STEINER, M. (1989). The neurochemistry of mood. *Psychiatric Journal of the University of Ottawa, 14,* 342–342.

STERN, S. L., RUSH, A. J., & MENDELS, J. (1980). Toward a rational pharmacotherapy of depression. *American Journal of Psychiatry, 137,* 545–552.

STILLION, J. M., McDOWELL, E. E., & MAY, J. H. (1989). *Suicide across the life span—Premature exits.* New York: Hemisphere.

STOFFELMAYR, B. E., DILLAVOU, D., & HUNTER, J. E. (1983). Premorbid functioning and outcome in schizophrenia: A cumulative analysis. *Journal of Consulting and Clinical Psychology, 51,* 338–352.

STONE, M. H. (1980). *The borderline syndromes.* New York: McGraw-Hill.

STONE, M. H. (1986). Borderline personality disorder. In R. Michels and J. O. Cavenar, Jr., eds., *Psychiatry,* vol. 1. New York: Basic Books.

STONE, M. H., STONE, D. K. & HURT, S. W. (1987). The natural history of borderline patients treated by intensive hospitalization. *Psychiatric Clinics of North America, 10,* 185–206.

STORR, A. (1980). *The art of psychotherapy.* New York: Methuen.

STORR, A. (1988). Churchill: The man. In A. Storr, ed., *Churchill's black dog, Kafka's mice, and other phenomena of the human mind.* New York: Grove Press.

STOUDEMIRE, A., FRANK, R., HEDEMARK, N., KAMLET, M., & BLAZER, D. (1986). The economic burden of depression. *General Hospital Psychiatry, 8,* 387–394.

STREISSGUTH, A. P., AASE, J. M., CLARREN, S. K., RANDELS, S. P., LaDUE, R. A., & SMITH, D. F. (1991). Fetal alcohol syndrome in adolescents and adults. *Journal of the American Medical Association, 265,* 1961–1967.

STROBER, M., & CARLSON, G. A. (1982). Bipolar illness in adolescents with major depression: Clinical, genetic and psychopharmacologic predictors in a three- to four-year prospective follow-up investigation. *Archives of General Psychiatry, 39,* 545–555.

STROEBE, W., & STROEBE, M. S. (1987). *Bereavement and health: The psychological and physical consequences of partner loss.* Cambridge, England: Cambridge University Press.

STRUNK, R. C., MRAZEK, D. A., FUHRMANN, A. S. W., & LaBRECQUE, J. F. (1985). Physiologic and psychological characteristics associated with deaths due to asthma in childhood: A case-controlled study. *Journal of the American Medical Association, 254,* 1193–1198.

STRUPP, H. H. (1989). Psychotherapy: Can the practitioner learn from the researcher? *American Psychologist, 44,* 717–724.

STRUPP, H. H., & HADLEY, S. W. (1979). Specific versus nonspecific factors in psychotherapy: A controlled study of outcome. *Archives of General Psychiatry, 36,* 1125–1136.

STUBBS, E. G., RITVO, E. R., & MASON-BROTHERS, A. (1985). Autism and shared parental HLA antigens. *Journal of Child Psychiatry, 24,* 182–185.

SUDDATH, R. L., CHRISTISON, G. W., TORREY, E. F., CASANOVA, M. F., & WEINBERGER, D. R. (1990). Anatomical abnormalities in the brains of monozygotic twins discordant for schizophrenia. *New England Journal of Medicine, 322,* 789–794.

SUELZE, M., & KEENAN, V. (1981). Changes in family support networks over the life cycle of mentally retarded persons. *American Journal of Mental Deficiency, 86,* 267–274.

SUOMI, S. J. (1983). Models of depression in primates. *Psychological Medicine, 13,* 465–468.

SUOMI, S. J., & HARLOW, H. F. (1972). Social rehabilitation of isolation-reared monkeys. *Developmental Psychology, 6,* 487–496.

SUOMI, S. J., & HARLOW, H. F. (1978). Early experience and social development in Rhesus monkeys. In M. E. Lamb, ed., *Social and personality development.* New York: Holt, Rinehart and Winston.

SURREY, J., SWETT, C., JR., MICHAELS, A., & LEVIN, S. (1990). Reported history of physical and sexual abuse and severity of symptomatology in women psychiatric outpatients. *American Journal of Orthopsychiatry, 60,* 412–417.

SUTHERLAND, A. J., & RODIN, G. M. (1990). Factitious disorders in a general hospital setting: Clinical features and a review of the literature. *Psychosomatics, 31,* 392–399.

SUTHERLAND, S. (1977). *Breakdown.* London: Granada.

SWANSON, J. W., HOLZER, C. E., III, GANJU, V. K., & JONO, R. T. (1990). Violence and psychiatric disorder in the community: Evidence from the epidemiologic catchment area surveys. *Hospital and Community Psychiatry, 41,* 761–770.

SWEDO, S. E., RAPOPORT, J. L., LEONARD, H., LENANE, M., & CHESLOW, D. (1989). Obsessive–compulsive disorder in children and adolescents. *Archives of General Psychiatry, 46,* 335–341.

SWETT, C., JR., SURREY, J., & COHEN, C. (1990). Sexual and physical abuse histories and psychiatric symptoms among male psychiatric outpatients. *American Journal of Psychiatry, 147,* 632–636.

SZASZ, T. S. (1970). *Ideology and insanity: Essays on the psychiatric dehumanization of man.* Garden City, NY: Anchor Books.

TALBOTT, J. A. (1985). Medical humanism: A personal odyssey. *Psychiatric News, 2,* 31.

TARGUM, S. D. (1984). Persistent neuroendocrine dysregulation in major depressive disorder: A marker for early relapse. *Biological Psychiatry, 19,* 305–310.

TARVER-BEHRING, S., BARKLEY, R. A., & KARLSSON, J. (1985). The mother-child interactions of hyperactive boys and their normal siblings. *American Journal of Orthopsychiatry, 55,* 202–208.

TAYLOR, J. R., & CARROLL, J. L. (1987). Current issues in electroconvulsive therapy. *Psychological Reports, 60,* 747–758.

TAYLOR, S. E. (1991). *Health psychology.* New York: McGraw-Hill.

TAYLOR, S. E., WOOD, J. V., & LICHTMAN, R. R. (1983). It could be worse: Selective evaluation as a response to victimization. *Journal of Social Issues, 39,* 19–40.

TERKELSEN, M. D., & GROSSER, R. C. (1990). Estimating clozapine's cost to the nation. *Hospital and Community Psychiatry, 41,* 863–869.

TERMAN, L. M., & MERRILL, M. A. (1937). *Measuring intelligence.* Boston: Houghton Mifflin.

TERMAN, L. M., & MERRILL, M. A. (1960). *Stanford-Binet Intelligence Scale: Manual for the 3rd revision, Form-M.* Boston: Houghton Mifflin.

TERMAN, L. M., & MERRILL, M. A. (1973). *Stanford-Binet Intelligence Scale: 1972 norms edition.* Boston: Houghton Mifflin.

TERMAN, M., QUITKIN, F. M., TERMAN, J. S., STEWART, J. W., & McGRATH, P. J. (1987). The timing of phototherapy: Effects on clinical response and the melatonin cycle. *Psychopharmacology Bulletin, 23,* 354–357.

TERR, L. C. (1991). Childhood traumas: An outline and overview. *American Journal of Psychiatry, 148,* 10–20.

THELMAR, E. (1932). *The maniac: A realistic study of madness from a maniac's point of view,* 2nd ed. London: C. A. Watts.

THOMAS, C. B., & DUSZYNCKI, K. R. (1974). Closeness to parents and the family: Constellation in a prospective study of five disease states—Suicide, mental illness, malignant tumor, hypertension and coronary heart disease. *Johns Hopkins Medical Journal, 134,* 251–270.

THOMPSON, J. W., & BLAINE, J. D. (1987). Use of ECT in the United States in 1975 and 1980. *American Journal of Psychiatry, 144,* 557–562.

THOMPSON, T. L., II. (1982). Headache. In H. I. Kaplan & B. J. Sadock, eds., *Comprehensive Textbook on Psychiatry,* 4th ed., vol. 2. Baltimore, MD: Williams & Wilkins.

THORESEN, C. E., FRIEDMAN, M., GILL, J. K., & ULMER, D. K. (1982). The recurrent coronary prevention project: Some preliminary findings. *Acta Medica Scandinavica, 68,* 172–192.

TIEN, A. Y., & ANTHONY, J. C. (1990). Epidemiological analysis of alcohol and drug use as risk factors for psychotic experiences. *The Journal of Nervous and Mental Disease, 178,* 473–480.

TIENARI, P., LAHTI, I., SORRI, A., NAARALA, M., MORING, J., KALEVA, M., WAHLBERG, K. E., & WYNNE, L. C. (1990). Adopted-away offspring of schizophrenics and controls: The Finnish adoptive family study of schizophrenia. In L. Robins & M. Rutter, eds., *Straight and devious pathways from childhood to adulthood.* New York: Cambridge University Press.

TIENARI, P., SORRI, A., LAHTI, I., NAARALA, M., WAHLBERG, K. E., MORING, J., POHJOLA, J., & WYNNE, L. C. (1987). Genetic and psychosocial factors in schizophrenia: The Finnish adoptive family study. *Schizophrenia Bulletin, 13,* 477–484.

TISCHLER, G., ED. (1987). *Diagnosis and classification in psychiatry: A critical appraisal of DSM-III.* New York: Cambridge University Press.

TOLSTRUP, K., BRINCH, M., ISAGER, T., NIELSEN, S., NYSTRUP, J., SEVERIN, B., & OLESEN, N. S. 1985. Long-term outcome of 151 cases of anorexia nervosa. *Acta Scandinavica Psychiatrica, 71,* 380–387.

TOMB, D. A., & CHRISTENSEN, D. D. (1987). *Case studies in psychiatry for the house officer.* Baltimore: Williams & Wilkins.

TONER, B. B., GARFINKEL, P. E., & GARDNER, D. M. (1986). Long-term follow-up of anorexia nervosa. *Psychosomatic Medicine, 48,* 520–529.

TOOLAN, J. M. (1981). Depression and suicide in children: An overview. *American Journal of Psychotherapy, 35,* 311–322.

TORGERSEN, S. (1979). The nature and origin of common phobic fears. *British Journal of Psychiatry, 134,* 343–351.

TORREY, E. F., & BOWLER, A. (1990). Geographical distribution of insanity in America: Evidence for an urban factor. *Schizophrenia Bulletin, 16,* 591–604.

TSAI, L. Y. (1987). Pre-, peri-, and neonatal factors in autism. In E. Shopler & G. B. Mesibov, eds., *Neurobiological issues in autism.* New York: Plenum.

TSUANG, M. T., & VANDERMAY, R. (1980). *Genes and the Mind.* Oxford, England: Oxford University Press.

TSUANG, M. T., WOOLSON, R. F., & FLEMING, J. A. (1979). Long-term outcome of major psychoses: I. Schizophrenia and affective disorders compared with psychiatrically symptom-free surgical conditions. *Archives of General Psychiatry, 39,* 1295–1301.

TURK, D. C., & SALOVEY, P. (1985). Cognitive structures, cognitive processes, and cognitive-behavior modification: II. Judgments and inferences of the clinician. *Cognitive Therapy and Research, 9,* 19–33.

TURNER, S. M., BEIDEL, D. C., & COSTELLO, A. (1987). Psychopathology in the offspring of anxiety disorders patients. *Journal of Consulting and Clinical Psychology, 55,* 229–235.

TURNER, S. M., BEIDEL, D. C., DARCU, C. V., & KEYS, D. J. (1986). Psychopathology of social phobia and comparison to avoidant personality disorder. *Journal of Abnormal Psychology, 95,* 389–394.

UHDE, T. W., BOULENGER, J. P., ROY-BYRNE, P., GERACI, M. F., VITONE, B. J., & POST, R. M. (1985). Longitudinal course of panic disorder: Clinical and biological considerations. *Progress in Neuropsychopharmacology and Biological Psychiatry, 9,* 39–51.

U.S. DEPARTMENT OF HEALTH AND HUMAN SERVICES. (1988). *Health promotion and disease-prevention: United States, 1985.* Vital and Health Statistics, National Health Survey, Series 10, Number 183. Hyattsville, MD: U.S. Government Printing Office.

U.S. DEPARTMENT OF HEALTH AND HUMAN SERVICES. (1981). *Schizophrenia, is there an answer?* Rockville, MD: U.S. Dept. of Health & Human Services.

U.S. DEPARTMENT OF HEALTH, EDUCATION, AND WELFARE, PUBLIC HEALTH SERVICE. (1979). *Smoking and health: A report of the Surgeon General.* (DHEW Publication No. PHS 79-50066). Washington, DC: U.S. Government Printing Office.

VACHON, L. (1989). Respiratory disorders. In H. I. Kaplan & B. J. Sadock, eds., *Comprehensive textbook of psychiatry,* 5th ed. Baltimore: Williams & Wilkins.

VAILLANT, G. E. (1973). A 20-year follow-up of New York narcotic addicts. *Archives of General Psychiatry, 29,* 237–241.

VAILLANT, G. E. (1976). History of male psychological health: V. The relation of choice of ego mechanisms of defense to adult adjustment. *Archives of General Psychiatry, 33,* 535–545.

VAILLANT, G. E. (1984). The disadvantages of DSM-III outweigh its advantages. *American Journal of Psychiatry, 14,* 542–545.

VAILLANT, G. E., & MILOFSKY, E. S. (1982). Natural history of male alcoholism: IV. Paths to recovery. *Archives of General Psychiatry, 39,* 127–133.

VALONE, K., GOLDSTEIN, M. J., & NORTON, J. P. (1984). Parental expressed emotion and psychophysiological reactivity in an adolescent sample at risk for schizophrenia spectrum disorders. *Journal of Abnormal Psychology, 93,* 448–457.

VALONE, K., NORTON, J. P., GOLDSTEIN, M. J., & DOANE, J. A. (1983). Parental expressed emotion and affective style in an adolescent sample at risk for schizophrenia spectrum disorders. *Journal of Abnormal Psychology, 92,* 399–407.

VARNHAGEN, C. K., DAS, J. P., & VARNHAGEN, S. (1987). Auditory and visual memory span: Cognitive processing by TMR individuals with Down's syndrome or other etiologies. *American Journal of Mental Deficiency, 91,* 398–405.

VAUGHN, C. E., & LEFF, J. P. (1976). The influence of family and social factors on the course of psychiatric illness. *British Journal of Psychiatry, 129,* 125–137.

VAUGHN, C. E., SNYDER, K. S., JONES, S., FREEMAN, W. B., & FALLOON, I. R. H. (1984). Family factors in schizophrenic relapse. *Archives of General Psychiatry, 41,* 1169–1177.

VENTULANI, J., STAWARZ, R. J., DINGELL, J. V., & SULZER, F. (1976). A possible common mechanism of action of antidepressant treatments: Reduction in the sensitivity of the noradrenergic cyclic AMP generating system in the rat limbic forebrain. *Nauyn Schmiedebergs Archives of Pharmacology, 293,* 109–114.

VERONEN, L. J., & KILPATRICK, D. G. (1983). Stress innoculation training as a treatment for rape victims' fears. In D. Meichenbaum and M. Jaremko, eds., *Stress Reduction and Prevention.* New York: Plenum.

VIDEKA-SHERMAN, L., & LIEBERMAN, M. (1985). The effects of self-help and psychotherapy intervention on child loss: The limits of recovery. *American Journal of Orthopsychiatry, 55,* 70–82.

VINOGRADOV, S., DISHOTSKY, N. I., DOTY, A. K., & TINKLENBERG, J. R. (1988). Patterns of behavior in adolescent rape. *American Journal of Orthopsychiatry, 58,* 179–187.

VINOGRADOV, S., & YALOM, I. D. (1990). Self-disclosure in group psychotherapy. In G. Stricker & M. Fisher, eds., *Self-disclosure in the therapeutic relationship.* New York: Plenum.

VIRKKUNEN, M. (1983). Insulin secretion during the glucose tolerance test in antisocial personality. *British Journal of Psychiatry, 142,* 598–604.

VOLKMAR, F. R., & COHEN, D. J. (1985). The experience of infantile autism: A first-person account by Tony W. *Journal of Autism and Developmental Disorders, 15,* 47–54.

VOLLHARDT, L. T. (1991). Psychoneuroimmunology: A literature review. *American Journal of Orthopsychiatry, 61,* 35–47.

VOLVAKA, J. (1990). Aggression, electroencephalography, and evoked potentials: A critical review. *Neuropsychiatry, Neuropsychology, and Behavioral Neurology, 3,* 249–259.

VON KORFF, M. R., NESTADT, G., ROMANOSKI, A., ANTHONY, J., EATON, W., MERCHANT, A., CHAHAL, R., KRAMER, M., FOLSTEIN, M., & GROENBERG, E. (1985). Prevalence of treated and untreated DSM-III schizophrenia. *The Journal of Nervous and Mental Disease, 173,* 577–581.

VONNEGUT, M. (1975). *The Eden express.* New York: Bantam Books.

WALDER, L. O., COHEN, S. L., & DASTON, P. G. (1967). *Teaching parents and others principles of behavior control for modifying the behavior of children.* Report to U.S. Office of Education, Washington, D.C.

WALKER, J. I., & BRODIE, H. K. H. (1985). Paranoid disorders. In I. H. Kaplan and B. J. Sadock, eds., *Comprehensive textbook of psychiatry,* 4th ed. Baltimore: Williams & Wilkins.

WALKER, L. E. (1984). *The battered woman syndrome.* New York: Springer.

WALLACE, B. C. (1991). *Crack cocaine.* New York: Brunner/Mazel.

WALLACE, C. J. (1984). Community and interpersonal functioning in the course of schizophrenic disorders. *Schizophrenia Bulletin, 10,* 233–257.

WARD, S. K., CHAPMAN, K., COHN, E., WHITE, S., & WILLIAMS, K. (1991). Acquaintance rape and the college social scene. *Family Relations, 40,* 65–71.

WATSON, J. B. (1925). *Behaviorism.* New York: Norton.

WATT, N. F., ED. (1984). *Children at risk for schizophrenia: A longitudinal perspective.* New York: Cambridge University Press.

WECHSLER, D. (1955). *Manual for the Wechsler Adult Intelligence Scale.* New York: Psychological Corporation.

WECHSLER, D. (1958). *The measurement and appraisal of adult intelligence,* 4th ed. Baltimore: Williams & Wilkins.

WEEKE, A. (1979). Causes of death in manic-depressives. In M. Schou and E. Stromgren, eds., *Origin, prevention and treatment of affective disorders.* London: Academic Press.

WEHR, T. A., GOODWIN, F. K., & WIRZ-JUSTICE, A. (1982). Forty-eight hour sleep–wake cycles in manic-depressive illness. *Archives of General Psychiatry, 39,* 559–565.

WEHR, T. A., & SACK, D. A. (1987). Sleep disruption: A treatment for depression and a cause of mania. *Psychiatric Annals, 17,* 654–663.

WEHR, T. A., SACK, D. A., ROSENTHAL, N. E., & GOODWIN, F. K. (1987). Sleep and biological rhythms in bipolar illness. In R. E. Hales and A. J. Frances, eds., *American Psychiatric Association Annual Review,* vol. 6. Washington, D.C.: American Psychiatric Press.

WEHR, T. A., & WERTZ-JUSTICE, A. (1982). Circadian rhythm mechanisms in affective illness and in antidepressant drug action. *Pharmacopsychiatry, 15,* 31–39.

WEINBERG, T. S. (1978). Sadism and masochism: Sociological perspectives. *Bulletin of the American Academy of Psychiatry and Law, 6,* 284–295.

WEINBERG, T. S., & FALK, G. (1980). The social organization of sadism and masochism. *Deviant Behavior, 1,* 379–393.

WEINBERG, T. S., WILLIAMS, C. J., & MOSER, C. (1984). The social constituents of sadomasochism. *Social Problems, 31*, 379–389.

WEINBERGER, D. R. (1984). Computed tomography (CT) findings in schizophrenia: Speculation on the meaning of it all. *Journal of Psychiatric Research, 18*, 477–490.

WEINER, D. B. (1979). The apprenticeship of Philippe Pinel: A new document, "Observations of Citizen Pussin on the Insane." *American Journal of Psychiatry, 136*, 1128–1134.

WEINER, H., CANCRO, R., LEHMANN, H. E., & FRAZIER, S. H. (1989). Psychopharmacologic treatments. In *Treatments of psychiatric disorders: A task force report of the American Psychiatric Association.* Washington, DC: American Psychiatric Association.

WEINER, R. D., ROGERS, H. J., DAVIDSON, J. R. T. et al. (1988). Effects of stimulus parameters on cognitive side effects. In S. Malitz and H. A. Sackeim, eds., Electroconvulsive therapy: Clinical and basic research issues. *Annals of the New York Academy of Sciences, 462*, 315–325.

WEISS, R. D., & MIRIN, S. M. (1987). *Cocaine,* Washington, DC: American Psychiatric Press.

WEISSMAN, M. M. (1987) Epidemiology of depression: Frequency, risk groups, and risk factors. In *Perspectives on depressive disorders.* Rockville, MD: National Institute of Mental Health.

WEISSMAN, M. M. (1990). Panic and generalized anxiety: Are they separate disorders? *Journal of Psychiatric Research, 24*, 157–162.

WEISSMAN, M. M., BRUCE, M. L., LEAF, P. J., FLORIO, L. P., & HOLZER, (1990). Affective disorders. In L. N. Robins and D. A. Regier, eds., *Psychiatric disorders in America.* New York: Free Press.

WEISSMAN, M. M., GAMMON, G. D., JOHN, K., MERIKANGAS, R., WARNER, V., PRUSOFF, B., & SHOLOMSKAS, D. (1987). Children of depressed parents: Increased psychopathology and early onset of major depression. *Archives of General Psychiatry, 44*, 847–853.

WEISSMAN, M. M., GERSHON, E. S., KIDD, K. K., PRUSSOF, B. A., LECKMAN, J. F., DIBBLE, E., HAMOVIT, J., THOMPSON, W. D., PAULS, D. L., & GUROFF, J. J. (1984). Psychiatric disorder in the relatives of probands with affective disorders. *Archives of General Psychiatry, 41*, 13–21.

WEISSMAN, M. M., WICKRAMARATNE, P., MERIKANGAS, K. R., LECKMAN, J. F., PRUSOFF, B. A., CARUSO, K. A., KIDD, K. K., & GAMMON, G. D. (1984). Onset of major depression in early adulthood. *Archives of General Psychiatry, 41*, 1136–1143.

WEISZ, J., YEATES, K., & ZIGLER, E. (1982). Piagetian evidence and the developmental-difference controversy. In E. Zigler & B. Balla, eds., *Mental retardation: The developmental difference controversy.* Hillsdale, NJ: Erlbaum.

WEISZ, J. R., WEISS, B., WASSERMAN, A. A., & RINTOUL, B. (1987). Control-related beliefs and depression among clinic-referred children and adolescents. *Journal of Abnormal Psychology, 96*, 58–63.

WEITZENHOFFER, A. M. (1989). *The practice of hypnotism.* New York: Wiley.

WENDER, P. H., ROSENTHAL, D., KETY, S. S., SCHULSINGER, F., & WELNER, J. (1974). Cross-fostering: A research strategy for clarifying the role of genetic and experiential factors in the etiology of schizophrenia. *Archives of General Psychiatry, 30*, 121–128.

WERDEGAR, D., SOKOLOW, M., PERLOFF, D. B., RIESS, F., HARRIS, R. E., SINGER, T., & BLACKBURN, H. W., JR. (1967). Portable recording of blood pressure: A new approach to assessments of the severity and prognosis of hypertension. *Transactions of the Association of Life Insurance Medical Directors of America, 51*, 93–173.

WERNER, E. E., & SMITH, R. S. (1982). *Vulnerable but invincible: A study of resilient children.* New York: McGraw-Hill.

WESSON, D. R., & SMITH, D. E. (1977). *Barbiturates: Their use, misuse, and abuse.* New York: Human Services Press.

WEST, J. B. 1984. Human physiology at extreme altitudes on Mt. Everest, *Science, 223*, 784–788.

WESTEFELD, J. S., & FURR, S. R. (1987). Suicide and depression among college students. *Professional Psychology: Research and Practice, 18*, 119–123.

WEWERS, M. E., & LOWE, N. K. (1990). A critical review of visual analogue scales in the measurement of clinical phenomena. *Research in Nursing and Health, 13*(4), 227–236.

WEXLER, N. S., GUSELLA, J. F., CONNEALLY, P. M., & HOUSMAN, D. (1985). Huntington's disease and the new genetics: A preview of the future for psychiatric disorders. In H. A. Pincus & H. Pardes, eds., *The integration of neuroscience and psychiatry.* Washington, DC: American Psychiatric Press.

WHALEN, C. K. (1989). Attention deficit and hyperactivity disorders. In T. H. Ollendick & M. Hersen, eds., *Handbook of Child Psychopathology,* 2nd ed. New York: Plenum.

WHALEN, C. K., HENKER, B., & HINSHAW, S. P. (1985). Cognitive-behavioral therapies for hyperactive children: Premises, problems and prospects. *Journal of Abnormal Child Psychology, 13*, 391–410.

WHITEHEAD, W. E., BLACKWELL, B., & ROBINSON, A. (1978). Effects of diazepam on phobic avoidance behavior and phobic anxiety. *Biological Psychiatry, 13*, 59–64.

WIDIGER, T. A. (1991). DSM-IV reviews of the personality disorders: Introduction to special series. *Journal of Personality Disorders, 5*, 122–134.

WIDIGER, T. A., FRANCES, A., & TRULL, T. J. (1987). A psychometric analysis of the social-interpersonal and cognitive perceptual items for the schizotypal personality disorder. *Archives of General Psychiatry, 44*, 741–745.

WIDOM, C. S. (1978). A methodology for studying noninstitutionalized psychopaths. In R. D. Hare & D. A. Schalling, eds., *Psychopathic behavior: Approaches to research.* Chichester, England: John Wiley.

WIENER-LEVY, D., & EXNER, J. E., JR. (1981). The Rorschach comprehensive system: An overview. In P. McReynolds, ed., *Advances in psychological assessment,* vol. 5. San Francisco: Jossey-Bass.

WIKLER, L. M. (1986). Periodic stresses of families of older mentally retarded children: An exploratory study. *American Journal of Mental Deficiency, 90*, 703–706.

WIKLER, L. M., WASOW, M., & HATFIELD, E. (1981). Chronic sorrow revisited. *American Journal of Orthopsychiatry, 51*, 63–70.

WILLE, R. (1981). Ten year follow-up of a representative sample of London heroin addicts: Clinic attendance, abstinence, and mortality. *British Journal of Addiction, 76*, 259–266.

WILLIAMSON, D. A. (1990). *Assessment of eating disorders: Obesity, anorexia, and bulimia nervosa.* New York: Pergamon.

WILSON, G. T. (1987). Cognitive studies in alcoholism. *Journal of Consulting and Clinical Psychology, 55*, 325–331.

WINSON, J. (1985). *Brain and psyche: The biology of the unconscious.* New York: Anchor Press.

WISE, T. N. (1985). Fetishism—etiology and treatment: A review from multiple perspectives. *Comprehensive Psychiatry, 26*, 249–257.

WITTROCK, W. C., BEATTY, J., BOGEN, J. E., GAZZANIGA, M. S., JERISON, H. J., KRASHEN, S. D., NEBES, R. D., & TEY-LER, T. J. (1977). *The human brain.* Englewood Cliffs, N.J.: Prentice Hall.

WOLF, L., & GOLDBERG, B. (1986). Autistic children group: An eight to twenty-four year follow-up study. *Canadian Journal of Psychiatry, 31*, 550–556.

WOLF, S. (1969). Psychosocial factors in myocardial infarction and sudden death. *Circulation, 39*(4), 74–83.

WOLFE, D. A., SANDLER, J., & KAUFMAN, K. (1981). Competency-based parent training program for child abusers. *Journal of Consulting and Clinical Psychology, 49*, 633–640.

WOLKIN, A., JAEGER, J., BRODIE, J. D., WOLF, A. P., FOWLER, J., ROTROSEN, J., GOMEZ-MONT, F., & CANCRO, R. (1985). Persistence of cerebral metabolic abnormalities in chronic schizophrenia as determined by positron emission tomography. *American Journal of Psychiatry, 142*, 564–571.

WOLPE, J., & RACHMAN, S. J. (1960). Psychoanalytic "evidence": A critique based on Freud's case of Little Hans. *Journal of Nervous and Mental Disease, 131*, 135–147.

WOODY, G. E., McLELLAN, A. T., LUBORSKY, L., & O'BRIEN, C. P. (1986). Psychotherapy for substance abuse. *Psychiatric Clinics of North America, 9*, 547–562.

WOOLF, L. (1964). *Beginning again: An autobiography of the years 1911 to 1918.* New York: Harcourt.

WOOLF, V. (1978). *The letters of Virginia Woolf* (N. Nicholson and J. Trautman, eds.). New York: Harcourt.

WORTMAN, C. B. (1983). Coping with victimization: Conclusions and implications for future research. *Journal of Social Issues, 39*, 195–221.

WORTMAN, C. B. (1987). Coping with irrevocable loss. In G. R. Vanden Bos & B. K. Bryant, eds., *Cataclysms, crises, and catastrophes: Psychology in action.* Washington, DC: American Psychological Association.

Wu, J. C., & Bunney, W. E. (1990). The biological basis of an antidepressant response to sleep deprivation and relapse: Review and hypothesis. *American Journal of Psychiatry, 147,* 14–21.

Wulff, S. B. (1985). The symbolic and object play of children with autism: A review. *Journal of Autism and Developmental Disorders, 15,* 139–147.

Wynne, L. C. (1975). Adjustment reaction of adult life. In A. M. Freedman, H. I. Kaplan, & B. J. Sadock, eds., *Contemporary textbook of psychiatry,* vol. 2, 2nd ed. Baltimore: Williams and Wilkins.

Wynne, L. C., Cole, R. E., & Perkins, P. (1987). University of Rochester Child and Family Study: Risk research in progress. *Schizophrenia Bulletin, 13,* 463–476.

Wynne, L. C., Singer, M. T., Bartko, J. J., & Tookey, M. L. (1977). Schizophrenics and their families: Research on parental communication. In J. M. Tanner, ed., *Developments in psychiatric research.* London: Hodder and Stoughton, 254–286.

Young, T. Y., Lawson, G. W., & Gacono, C. B. (1987). Clinical aspects of phencyclidine (PCP). *The International Journal of the Addictions, 22,* 1–15.

Yuwiler, A., Geller, E., & Ritvo, E. (1985). Biochemical studies on autism. In A. Lajtha, ed., *Handbook of Neurochemistry,* vol. 10. New York: Plenum.

Zalewski, C., & Archer, R. P. (1991). Assessment of borderline personality disorder: A review of MMPI and Rorschach findings. *Journal of Nervous and Mental Disease, 179,* 338–345.

Zametkin, A. J., Nordahl, T. E., Gross, M., King, A. C., Semple, W. E., Rumsey, J., Hamburger, S., & Cohen, R. M. (1990). Cerebral glucose metabolism in adults with hyperactivity of childhood onset. *The New England Journal of Medicine, 323,* 1361–1366.

Zanarini, M. C., Gunderson, J. G., Marino, M. F., Schwartz, E. O., & Frankenburg, F. (1988). DSM-III disorders in the families of borderline patients. *Journal of Personality Disorders, 2,* 292–302.

Zetlin, A. G., & Turner, J. L. (1985). Transition from adolescence to adulthood: Perspectives of mentally retarded individuals and their families. *American Journal of Mental Deficiency, 89,* 570–579.

Zigler, E., Bulla, D., & Hodapp, R. (1984). On the definition and classification of mental retardation. *American Journal of Mental Deficiency, 89,* 215–230.

Zigler, E., & Hodapp, R. M. (1991). Behavioral functioning in individuals with mental retardation. *Annual Review of Psychology, 42,* 29–50.

Zigler, E., & Levine, J. (1983). Hallucinations vs. delusions: A developmental approach. *Journal of Nervous and Mental Disorder, 171,* 141–146.

Zubin, J., Magaziner, J., & Steinhauer, S. R. (1983). The metamorphosis of schizophrenia: From chronicity to vulnerability. *Psychological Medicine, 13,* 551–571.

Zubin, J., & Spring, B. (1977). Vulnerability—a new view of schizophrenia. *Journal of Abnormal Psychology, 86,* 103–126.

Zubin, J., Steinhauer, S. R., Day, R., & van Kammen, D. P. (1985). Schizophrenia at the crossroads: A blueprint for the 80s. *Comprehensive Psychiatry, 26,* 217–240.

Photo References

Chapter 1: 3 Brian Masck/The Muskegon Chronicle. 12 (a) Charlyn Zlotnik/Woodfin Camp & Associates; (b) Spencer Grant/Monkmeyer Press; (c) Bernard Gotfryd/Woodfin Camp & Associates. 19 AP/Wide World Photos. 23 University of Wisconsin, Harlow Primate Laboratory.

Chapter 2: 32 Karl Muller/Woodfin Camp & Associates. 33 (top) Courtesy of American Museum of Natural History, photo by T. Bierwert; (bottom) National Museum of Natural History, Smithsonian Institute. 35 The Bettmann Archive. 36 (top) The Bettmann Archive; (bottom) Karales/Peter Arnold. 37 The Bettmann Archive. 38 Denver Art Museum, Samuel H. Kress Foundation Collection. 39 (top) Historical Pictures Service; (bottom) Scala/Art Resource. 40 National Library of Medicine. 41 (top) Victoria and Albert Museum, London. With permission of Bethlehem Royal Hospital, Kent; (bottom) The Bettmann Archive. 42 Wellcome Institute Library, London. 43 Cornell University Hospital. 44 (top) Cornell University Library; (bottom) Katherine Drake, *Lunatic's Ball* (1848). The Royal College of Psychiatrists, London. 45 Colonial Williamsburg Photograph. 46 (top) The Bettmann Archive; (bottom) The Bettmann Archive. 47 National Mental Health Association. 48 Peter Arnold, Inc. 50 Andre Brouillet, *Charcot at Salpetiere* (1887). National Library of Medicine. 51 Mary Evans/Sigmund Freud Copyrights.

Chapter 3: 58 Sinclair Stammers/Science Photo Library, Science Source/Photo Researchers. 59 Bob Sacha. 61 (bottom) Alexander Tsiaras/Science Source/Photo Researchers. 65 Philippe Plailly/Science Photo Library, Science Source/Photo Researchers. 66 Slide courtesy of Dr. M.E. Raichle from research based upon "Positron Emission Tomographic Studies of the Cortical Anatomy of Single Word Processing" by Petersen, S.E., Fox, P.T., Posner, M.I., Mintun, M.A., Raichle, M.E. *Nature,* Vol. 331, pp. 585–589. 1988. 69 The Bettmann Archive. 78 Courtesy of B.F. Skinner. 80 (a) R. Kopstein/Monkmeyer Press; (b) Erika Stone/Photo Researchers. 82 Courtesy of Albert Bandura. 84 Carl Rogers Memorial Library.

Chapter 4: 106 Lew Merrim/Monkmeyer Press. 107 American Guidance Service, Inc. 113 (top-a) Hans Huber, Medical Publisher, Bern; (top-b) Ken Karp. 114 Harvard University Press. 116 (a) Cary Wolinsky/Stock, Boston; (b) The Image Works. 117 David E. Dempster. 119 Courtesy of Spacelabs.

Chapter 5: 127 (a) J. Patrick Forden/Sygma; (b) David E. Dempster; (c) Alan Dorow/Actuality, Inc. 129 Hank Morgan, Science Source/Photo Researchers. 135 UPI/Bettmann Newsphotos. 137 Bill Cramer/*The New York Times.* 139 Rhoda Sidney. 146 Mark Constantini/*San Francisco Examiner.* 148 AP/Wide World Photos.

Chapter 6: 156 Phil Huber/*The New York Times.* 159 AP/Wide World Photos. 162 Reprinted from *Psychology Today* Magazine, Copyright © 1985, American Psychological Association. 165 Les Mahon/Monkmeyer Press. 166 Charles Gupton/Stock, Boston. 169 (top) Chris Hackett/The Image Bank; (bottom) Alvis Upitis/The Image Bank.

Chapter 7: 191 UPI/Bettmann Newsphotos. 192 Robert Goldstein/Photo Researchers. 210 Ted Fitzgerald.

Chapter 8: 221 W. Keith McManus. 222 Bettye Lane/Photo Researchers. 223 Tom McHugh/Photo Researchers. 229 Trustees of the British Museum. 232 (a) Courtesy of Jerry Bauer; (b) Henry Grossman, *People Weekly* © 1974, Time, Inc. 235 (top) *The Seattle Post Intelligencer;* (bottom) Mariette Pathy Allen/VISIONS/E.P. Dutton. 238 Alon Reininger, Contact Press/Woodfin Camp & Associates. 240 Reprinted by permission of the publisher, from *Autoerotic Fatalities* by Robert R. Hazelwood, Park Elliott Dietz, and Ann Wolbert Burgess. Lexington Books, D.C. Heath and Company, Copyright © 1963, D.C. Heath and Company. 241 AP/Wide World Photos. 243 Laimute Druskis. 245 Copyright 1985 Hylands Anatomical Dolls, Inc., Torrance, CA.

Chapter 9: 254 DPI/Uniphoto. 258 Dagmar Fabriculus/Uniphoto. 259 Chuck Pulin/Star File. 266 Tim Kelly/Liaison. 275 Laimute Druskis.

Chapter 10: 289 Collection of the Whitney Museum of American Art, NY. Photo by Geoffrey Clements. 292 (bottom) University of California, L.A. 298 The American Mental Health Fund/Ad Council. 305 (a) New York Public Library; (b) The Bettmann Archive. 310 (a) The Bettmann Archive; (b) UPI/Bettmann; (c) AP/Wide World Photos. 312 Drs. Mazziotta, Phelps, et al., UCLA School of Medicine. 317 The Bettmann Archive.

Chapter 11: 327 UPI/Bettmann Newsphotos. 329 (top) Irene Springer; (bottom) UPI/Bettmann Newsphotos. 336 UPI/Bettmann Newsphotos.

Chapter 12: 363 Daniel R. Weinberger, M.D., NIMH, from *New England Journal of Medicine,* March 23, 1990 and from *Journal of NIH Research,* April 1990, Vol. 2, p. 67. 364 (a) National Institutes of Health; (b and c) Courtesy of Monte S. Buchsbaum, M.D., University of California, Irvine. From *Schizophrenia Bulletin,* 16:377–387, 1990. 365 Karolinska Institute, Sweden. 375 (top) Courtesy of Monte S. Buschsbaum, University of California, Irvine; (bottom) Courtesy of Monte S. Buschsbaum, University of California, Irvine. 377 (top) Courtesy of Monte S. Buschsbaum, University of California, Irvine; (bottom) Courtesy of Monte S. Buschsbaum, University of California, Irvine.

Chapter 13: 383 (left) Jim Berry/*The Seattle Times;* (right) Jim Berry/*The Seattle Times.* 385 Grandma Moses: *The Daughter's Homecoming.* Copyright © 1989, Grandma Moses Properties Co., New York and The Lauren Rogers Museum of Art, Laurel, MS. 389 Abigail Heyman. 391 (a) *Journal of American Medical Association,* November 20, 1987. 393 Lynn Johnson/

Black Star. 395 (top) SIU Biomedical Communications, Science Source/Photo Researchers; (bottom) Peter Arnold, Inc. 398 © Steve Uzzell. 401 AP/Wide World Photos. 402 *New York Daily News* Photo.

Chapter 14: 415 David E. Dempster. 416 (a) Paul Mozell/Stock, Boston; (b) Michael Weisbrot/Stock, Boston. 420 We thank Dr. Henri Begleiter, Neurodynamics Laboratory, SUNY for the use of his data. 422 Ad Council/National Council on Alcoholism, Inc. 423 Mary Levin, University Photography, University of Washington. 424 Sybil Shackman/Monkmeyer Press. 430 (top) John Moran/*New York Times* Pictures.

Chapter 15: 454 Bill Binzen/Photo Researchers. 462 Keith Meyers/*New York Times* Pictures. 465 Peter Vandermark/Stock, Boston. 468 George Goodwin/Monkmeyer Press. 475 © 1989 Sarah Leen/Matrix. 479 Michael Heron/Woodfin Camp & Associates.

Chapter 16: 488 (left) Peter Haley/*Morning News Tribune;* (right) Tom Reese/*Seattle Times.* 491 Allan Grant. 501 (left) National Institutes of Health; (right) City of Hope Medical Center. 502 (top) Paul Hosefros/*New York Times* Pictures;

(bottom) National Down Syndrome Society. 506 *PsychologyToday* Magazine. 509 (top) Alan Carey/The Image Works; (bottom) David M. Grossman/Photo Researchers. 511 AP/Wide World Photos.

Chapter 17: 520 David E. Dempster. 527 David E. Dempster. 528 J.P. Laffont/Sygma. 530 Bob Daemmrich/The Image Works. 532 Bob Daemmrich/Stock, Boston. 539 (a) Freda Leinwand/Monkmeyer Press; (b) Dr. Rose K. Gantner; (c) Katie Deits/FPG. 545 AP/Wide World.

Chapter 18: 551 Bohdan Hrynewych/Southern Light. 552 Jimi Lott/*Seattle Times.* 554 (a) Comstock; (b) F. Paolini/Sygma; (c) Jacques Chenet/Woodfin Camp & Associates. 556 Alan Carey/The Image Works. 561 (a) Bob Daemmrich/The Image Works; (b) Renate Hiller/Monkmeyer Press. 562 Paule Epstein. 566 Bob Daemmrich/Stock, Boston. 567 David E. Dempster. 568 George Rizer, AP/Wide World Photos. 572 Mary Levin, University Photography, University of Washington. 573 Jim Estrin/*New York Times* Pictures. 576 Cole Porter/*Seattle Times.* 578 UPI/Bettmann Newsphotos. 583 James Wilson/Woodfin Camp & Associates.

Name Index

A

Aase, J.M., 506
Abbey, A., 137
Abel, G., 246
Abikoff, H., 458
Abraham, K., 274, 297
Abrams, D.B., 22–23, 25
Abrams, S., 120, 121
Abramson, L.Y., 299, 304, 306
Achenbach, T.M., 471
Adamson, J., 97
Addalli, K.A., 456
Adler, A., 74
Adler, G., 263
Agard, J.A., 508
Ageton, S., 138
Agras, W.S., 201
Ahn, C.W., 181
Aiken, T.W., 555
Aizley, H.G., 431
Akesson, H.O., 498, 507
Akhtar, S., 254, 255
Akiskal, H.S., 289
Albert, M.S., 392
Alderman, M., 201
Alford, B.A., 179
Allan, M.J., 313
Allen, R.A., 201
Alliger, R.J., 363
Allman, C.J., 313
Alloy, L.B., 304
Alphs, L.D., 343
Altman, D., 220
Altmann, M.W., 208
Altshuler, K.Z., 312
Alvarez, A., 314
Ambelas, A., 308
Ambrosini, P.J., 471
Amedeo, S.R., 136
Ameli, R., 366
Amish, P.A., 453
Anastasi, A., 113
Anderson, C., 226
Anderson, C.M., 373
Anderson, D.J., 160
Anderson, E.A., 131
Anderson, N.B., 199
Andolphi, M., 481
Andreasen, N.C., 4, 179, 308, 309, 313,
 327, 335, 361, 363, 370, 507, 541
Andrews, G., 537
Angelo, C., 481
Angst, J., 334
Anisman, H., 202
Anonymous, 168, 339
Anthony, J.C., 418
Anton, M.T., 404
Antoni, M.H., 132
Appelbaum, P.S., 580
Arendt, J., 313
Arieti, S., 297
Arizmendi, T.G., 101

Arkowitz, H.S., 131, 299
Armor, D.J., 424
Arnold, L.E., 22
Aronow, E., 114
Aronson, T.A., 308
Asaad, G., 330
Ashikaga, T., 341, 342
Avner, R., 526
Awad, A.G., 343
Axline, V.M., 479
Ayllon, T., 480

B

Babigan, H.M., 473
Badgley, R.F., 242
Baer, J.S., 413
Bakay Pragay, E., 367
Baker, L., 474, 476
Balis, G.U., 10, 271
Bandura, A., 82, 465, 525
Barabas, G., 499
Bard, M., 566
Barden, H.S., 499
Barefoot, J.C., 199
Barkley, R.A., 456
Barkley, R.J., 456
Barlow, D.H., 144, 158, 175, 181, 230,
 236, 237
Baron, M., 309, 337, 357
Barrett, D., 558
Barrowclough, C., 373
Barsky, A.J., 208
Bartak, L., 490
Bartko, J.J., 335
Barton, R., 306
Barton, S.N., 567
Bartrop, R.W., 67
Basham, R.B., 132
Bass, D., 463
Bassett, A.S., 357
Bateman, A.W., 136
Bauer, R.B., 399
Baumeister, R.F., 317
Bays, K., 464
Becher, J., 246
Beck, A.T., 83, 160, 178, 179, 270, 275,
 300, 301, 302, 303, 317, 471, 518,
 523, 535
Beck, J.G., 230
Beck, L.H., 367
Becker, J., 298
Becker, R.E., 300
Beeghly, M., 500
Beers, C., 47
Beidel, D.C., 179
Beiser, M., 570
Bell, A.P., 217, 219, 221
Bell, C.R., III, 510
Bell, N.W., 15
Bell, Q., 313
Bellack, A.S., 199, 200, 348

Belmaker, R.H., 309
Bemporad, J.R., 297, 298
Bender, L., 105
Benierakis, C., 309
Bennett, P., 202
Benson, D.F., 149
Benson, H., 201
Bentler, P.M., 236
Bentley, W., 500
Benton, M.K., 344
Berchick, R.J., 523
Berenbaum, H., 343
Berg, C.J., 467
Berg, R., 418
Berger, M., 511
Bergin, A.E., 534, 550
Berke, J., 441
Berman, J.S., 307, 481
Bernstein, D.P., 257
Berrettini, W.H., 289
Berry, P., 501
Berthier, M.L., 489
Best, J.A., 553
Beutler, C.E., 225
Beutler, L.E., 101, 131
Bibring, E., 297
Bieber, I., 219
Bieber, T.B., 219
Biederman, J., 457
Bieliauskas, L.A., 202
Black, D.W., 179, 313, 507, 541
Blackburn, H.W., Jr., 120
Blackwell, B., 180
Blader, J.C., 244
Blanchard, E.B., 175
Bland, R.C., 340
Blazer, D., 158
Bleck, D.S., 570
Bleuler, E., 328
Bloch, S., 418
Bloedau, L., 454
Bloom, B., 550
Bloom, J.R., 202
Blose, I., 418
Bodkin, A., 260
Bohman, M., 268, 419
Bohmfalk, G.C., 140, 141
Boldizar, J.P., 556
Bolton, W., 87
Bonagura, N., 456
Bond, L.A., 564
Booth-Butterfield, M., 118
Borbely, A.A., 293
Boulenger, J.P., 159
Bourdon, K., 164
Bousha, D.M., 452, 453
Bowers, K.S., 75
Bowers, M.B., Jr., 336
Bowlby, J., 297, 468
Bowler, A., 9
Boxer, A.M., 220
Boyd, J.H., 164
Boyd, S.C., 202
Boyle, M.H., 469

Bradley, S.J., 231
Brady, K., 204
Braff, D.L., 366
Brand, R.J., 195, 197, 199
Bransome, E.D., 367
Braun, B.G., 147
Breakey, W.R., 572
Breier, A., 180
Brenner, M.H., 134
Brent, D.A., 313
Breslow, N., 239
Breznitz, S., 129
Brier, A., 335, 341, 342
Brier, N., 511
Brinch, M., 475
Brodie, H.K.H., 164, 339, 391, 439
Brody, J.E., 240
Brooks, G.W., 341, 342
Brown, B., 200
Brown, G., 301
Brown, K.S., 553
Brown, L., 471
Brown, R., 295
Brown, R.I., 501
Brown, W.T., 500
Browne, A., 245
Brownell, K.D., 236, 237
Bruce, M.L., 282, 284, 286
Brynjolfsson, J., 357
Buchanan, A., 507
Buchanan, R.W., 365
Buchsbaum, M.S., 376, 467
Buell, J.C., 199
Buffett, W., 572
Buie, D., 263
Bukstel, L.H., 243
Bulla, D., 507
Bunney, W.E., Jr., 202, 293
Burgess, A.W., 239, 240
Burkart, B.R., 137
Burkhardt, P.E., 265
Burns, B.J., 164
Burns, T., 473
Burnside, J.W., 207
Burt, M., 572
Bush, J.P., 465
Butcher, J.N., 110
Butler, G., 179

C

Cahill, C., 246
Caldwell, C.B., 324
Caldwell, R., 550
Cameron, N., 147
Campbell, S.S., 293
Cancro, R., 288, 343
Cannon, T.D., 365, 366
Canton, C.L.M., 572
Caparulo, B.K., 494
Carey, M.P., 225
Carlson, G.A., 455
Carlson, V., 557
Carone, B.J., 343
Carpenter, W.T., Jr., 335, 343, 365
Carrol, J.L., 294
Carrol, K., 477
Carroll, B.J., 291
Carroll, D., 202
Caruso, K.A., 289
Casanova, M.F., 363

Casey, R.J., 481
Caspi, A., 20, 21
Cassem, N.H., 129
Castelloe, P., 487
Castells, S., 500
Catalan, J., 224
Caumartin, S.M., 221
Cautela, J.R., 527
Cavalli-Sforza, L.L., 357
Celis, W., 430
Cerny, J.A., 175, 181
Chalkley, A.J., 235
Chambers, W.J., 471
Chandler, C.L., 564
Chaplain, W., 306
Chapman, K., 137
Charcot, J.M., 49, 50, 52
Charney, D.S., 291
Chaudhary, B.S., 194
Cheifetz, P., 309
Cherlin & Others (1991), 561
Cheslow, D., 467
Chesney, M.A., 200
Chess, S., 128, 470, 505
Chown, M.J., 392
Christensen, D.D., 288
Christensen, H., 537
Christison, G.W., 363
Chuang, H.T., 221
Cicchetti, D., 500, 557
Clark, D., 317
Clark, D.C., 308
Clark, K.A., 566
Clarke, A.D.D., 507
Clarke, A.M., 507
Clarkin, J.F., 264, 345
Clarren, S.K., 506
Clayton, P.J., 143, 308
Cloninger, C.R., 181, 268, 419
Coble, P.A., 293
Coddington, R.D., 134
Coffey, C.E., 542
Coffman, J., 418
Cohen, B.M., 263, 324
Cohen, C., 246
Cohen, D.J., 493, 494
Cohen, D.S., 496
Cohen, G., 363
Cohen, I.L., 500
Cohen, L.H., 134
Cohen, M.E., 208
Cohen, R.A., 328
Cohen, S.L., 563
Cohler, B.J., 220
Cohn, E., 137
Colby, J.P., Jr., 423
Colder, M., 203
Cole, N., 226, 227, 230
Cole, R.E., 361
Coleman, E., 223
Colligan, R.C., 475
Compas, B.E., 564
Comstock, G.W., 143
Conaway, L., 452
Conger, J.J., 139
Conneally, P.M., 399
Conroy, J., 509
Conte, H.R., 471
Conte, J.R., 244
Cook, N.R., 392
Coombs, D.W., 567
Coppel, D.B., 431
Cornblatt, B.A., 368
Corson, E.O., 22

Coryell, W., 317
Costello, A., 179
Courchesne, E., 366, 490
Coursey, R.D., 368
Cowen, E.L., 564, 566
Cox, A., 511
Cox, B.J., 418
Cox, C., 467
Cox, M., 490
Coyle, J.T., 394
Coyne, B.J., 136
Coyne, J.C., 299
Crago, M., 101
Craig, E.M., 509
Craske, M.G., 175, 181
Cressler, D.L., 570
Crisp, A.H., 473
Cristol, A.H., 536
Crits-Christoph, P., 537
Croghan, J., 103
Crosby, D., 376
Crow, T.J., 334
Crowe, M.J., 230
Crowe, R.R., 160
Cummings, E.M., 86
Cunningham-Rathner, J., 246
Curtis, D., 357
Cusak, E., 499
Custance, J., 308
Czeisler, C.A., 293

D

Dahlstrom, W.G., 199
Dain, H.J., 219
Daruna, J.H., 203
Das, J.P., 501
Daston, P.G., 563
D'avernas, J.R., 553
Davidson, J.R.T., 295
Davies, M., 471
Davis, G.E., 244
Davis, H., 454
Davis, J.A., 220
Davis, K., 390, 394, 403
Davis, R.M., 444
Davison, H., 545
Dawson, G., 487, 489, 490
Day, A., 224
De La Selva, A., 373
De Nike, L.D., 163
de Ruiter, C., 181
De Silva, P., 171
Degroot, J., 454
Deitz, P.E., 239
DeLisi, L.E., 357
DeLong, M.R., 394
Deluty, R.H., 315, 316
Dembroski, T.M., 199
Deming, U.E., 333
Demming, B., 422
Demos, J.P., 37
Denckla, M., 467
Depue, R.A., 304
DeRubeis, R.J., 302
Deutsch, A., 48
Devanand, D.P., 295
Devereux, R.B., 201
Devine, E., 361
Devins, G.M., 221
Deykin, E.Y., 489, 490

Dibble, E., 285, 290
Dickey, B., 572
Dickson, L.R., 396
Didion, J., 191
Dietchman, W., 346
Dimsdale, J.E., 199
DiNardo, P.A., 175
Dince, P.R., 219
Dingell, J.V., 291
Dishotsky, N.I., 244
Doane, J.A., 374
Docter, R.F., 236
Dodge, K.A., 463
Dogherty, J.P., 202
Dohrenwend, B.P., 85
Dollard, J., 81, 174
Doman, J., 293
Donovan, D.M., 413
Dorian, B., 203
Dorris, M., 506
Dorwart, R.A., 545
Doty, A.K., 244
Drellich, M.G., 219
Drews, F.R., 200
Drumer, D., 309
Dryfoos, J.G., 553, 565
Duffy, F.H., 365
Dunne-Maxim, K., 569
Dunner, D.L., 308
Du Paul, G.J., 456
Dworkin, R.H., 335
Dyck, M.J., 306
Dyer, J., 335
Dykman, B.M., 299

E

Easton, K., 148
Eaton, W.W., 167
Eaves, L.J., 179, 353
Eberhardy, F., 485
Eckardt, M.J., 418
Eckert, E.D., 478
Egeland, B., 454
Egeland, J.A., 309
Ehrhardt, J.C., 363
Eichenwald, K., 405
Eidelson, J.L., 301
Eisenson, J., 406
Eisler, R.M., 555
Elder, A.H., Jr., 20, 21
Eldred, S.H., 15
Eliot, R.S., 199
Elkins, R., 466, 467
Ellenberger, H.F., 50, 51
Ellis, A., 83, 522
Elmadjian, E., 187
Emery, G., 83, 178, 301, 303
Emmelkamp, P.M.G., 175, 176
Endicott, J., 309, 416
Endler, N.S., 281, 296, 301, 302
Engel, G.L., 187
Engelmann, F., 309
Epps, J., 463
Epstein, A.P., 234
Epstein, S., 545
Erdelyi, M., 75
Erickson, M.F., 454
Erikson, E.H., 74
Erlenmeyer-Kimling, L., 367, 368
Ernst, D., 306
Eron, L.D., 21, 134

Evans, D.E., 392
Evans, L., 239
Evans, M.D., 302
Exner, J.E., Jr., 114
Eysenck, H.J., 202, 239, 534
Eysenck, S.B.G., 239

F

Fabrega, H., Jr, 181
Fairweather, G.W., 570
Falk, G., 238
Falloon, I.R.H., 371
Faraone, S.V., 309, 357
Farber, S.L., 353
Farber, S.S., 86
Farde, L., 365
Farmer, A., 104
Farmer, A.E., 353
Fava, M., 295
Fawcett, J., 308, 317
Fein, D., 500
Feinleib, M., 198
Felner, R.D., 86
Ferinande, R.J., 475
Ferrari, M., 499
Fieve, R.R., 313
Fine, H., 558
Finkelhor, D., 244, 245
Fiore, M.C., 444
Firlik, A.D., 392
First, M.G., 249, 256, 273, 458
Fisch, G.S., 500
Fischer, G.J., 137
Fischer, P.J., 572
Fishman, R., 309
Flament, M.F., 467
Flay, B.R., 553
Fleming, J.A., 340
Fleming, J.E., 469
Florio, L.P., 282, 284, 286
Floyd, F.J., 551
Folks, D.G., 208
Folstein, S., 489
Ford, C.V., 208
Forth, A.E., 268
Fox, B.H., 202
Fox, M.M., 473
Frances, A., 256
Frances, R.J., 161, 253, 261, 412
Frank, E., 226
Frankenburg, F., 263
Franks, C., 491
Franks, L., 412
Frazier, S.H., 343
Freedman, B.J., 331
Freedman, R.I., 324, 571
Freeman, A., 83, 131, 179, 270, 275, 303, 535
Freeman, B.J., 490
Freeman, W.B., 371
Freud, S., 49, 52, 81, 216, 242, 297
Friedman, C., 335
Friedman, M., 195, 197, 199, 200
Friedrich, W.N., 496
Frith, U., 489
Fritz, G., 471
Fromm, K., 431
Fromuth, M.E., 245
Fudge, H., 470
Fuhrmann, A.S.W., 204
Funkenstein, H.H., 392

Furr, S.R., 314, 315
Fyer, A.J., 168
Fyer, M.R., 162

G

Gabbard, G.O., 250
Gadpaille, W.J., 219, 222
Gammon, G.D., 289
Ganau, A., 201
Ganju, V.K., 11
Garbarino, J., 451
Garber, H.L., 507
Gardner, D.M., 475
Garfield, S.L., 534
Garfinkel, B.D., 455
Garfinkel, P.E., 203, 474, 475, 477
Garmezy, N., 361, 454, 490
Garron, D.C., 202
Garssen, P., 181
Gartrell, J.W., 136
Garver, D.L., 362
Garvey, M.J., 302
Gath, D., 175
Gatzanis, S., 6
Gawin, F.H., 437
Gearing, M.L., 243
Gebhard, P.H., 217
Gelardo, M.S., 452
Gelder, M., 175
Gelfand, D., 470
George, L.D., 158
George, M., 308
Gerace, M.F., 159
Gershon, E.S., 285, 289, 290
Geyer, M.A., 366
Giampino, T.L., 456
Gibbon, M., 249, 256, 260, 267, 273, 284, 287, 458
Gibbons, A., 219
Gibbons, F.X., 511
Gibbons, R., 317
Gibbs, E.L., 385
Gibbs, F.A., 385
Gibson, D., 501
Gill, J.J., 199, 200
Gill, M.J., 221
Gillan, P., 230
Gilliam, T.C., 357
Gillin, J.C., 293, 467
Giovino, G.A., 444
Gist, R., 134, 135, 136
Gittelman, R., 168
Gittelman-Klein, R., 458
Giuffra, L.A., 357
Glaser, E.M., 565
Glaser, R., 186, 203
Glass, G.V., 538
Goffman, E., 86
Gold, G., 328
Goldberg, B., 492
Goldberg, J.D., 194
Goldberg, J.F., 313
Goldbloom, D.S., 474, 477
Golden, J.C., 418
Golden, K.M., 32
Goldin, L.R., 289
Goldman, H.H., 44
Goldman, P., 555
Goldstein, C.E., 313
Goldstein, M.J., 371, 374, 458
Goldstein, S., 458

Goldston, D., 469
Golombok, S., 230
Goodwin, D.W., 419
Goodwin, F.K., 292, 307, 311, 312, 313, 314
Goodyer, I., 6
Gordon, J.R., 425, 427
Gordon, N., 204
Gosselin, C., 237, 238, 239
Gotlib, I.H., 299
Gottesman, I.I., 87, 308, 324, 352, 353, 357, 358, 361, 362, 373
Gottheil, E., 202
Gottlieb, A., 445
Gottlieb, J., 508
Gottschalk, L.A., 205
Graham, J.R., 110
Graham, P., 511
Graham, P.J., 464
Grand, H.J., 219
Grandin, T., 485, 493, 494
Grant, B., 416
Grasbeck, A., 282, 284
Graver, B., 418
Graves, P.L., 202
Green, E., 192
Green, R., 218, 231
Greenberg, J., 195
Greenberg, R.L., 523
Greenfeld, J.A., 496
Greenwald, D.P., 373
Greenwald, S., 160
Grenell, M.M., 456
Grillon, C., 366
Grilly, D., 437
Grinker, R., 305
Grochocinski, V.J., 293
Groeneweg, G., 501
Gross, A., 500
Gross, M., 457
Grosser, R.C., 343
Grossman, L.S., 313
Groth, A.N., 240
Grove, W.M., 302, 327
Grubb, A.B., 344
Gruenberg, A.M., 356
Grundlack, R.H., 219
Grundy, E., 471
Guare, J., 564
Gudeman, J.E., 572
Guevremont, D.C., 456
Guillen, T., 576
Gullick, E.L., 206
Gullone, E., 464
Gunderson, J.G., 260, 261, 262, 263, 264, 265, 347
Gurland, B.J., 333
Gurling, H.M.D., 357
Guroff, J.J., 285, 290
Gusella, J.F., 399
Guskin, S., 509

H

Haaga, D.A., 199
Haaga, D.F., 306
Hackett, T.P., 129
Hadley, S.W., 538
Hadzi-Pavlovic, D., 537
Hagerman, R.J., 500
Hagnell, O., 282, 284, 313

Haier, R.J., 376
Hales, R.E., 385, 386, 400
Hall, G.C., 244
Halmi, K.A., 474
Hamborger, R., 309
Hamilton, E., 304
Hamilton, M., 283, 384
Hammersmith, S.F., 217, 219, 221
Hammond, L.K., 316
Hamovit, J., 285, 290
Hansen, D.J., 452
Hanson, D.M., 500
Harbert, T.L., 206
Harding, C.M., 341, 342
Hare, R.D., 268
Harford, T.C., 418
Harlow, H.F., 22–23
Harrington, R., 470
Harris, R.E., 120
Harrow, M., 313, 327, 334, 343
Hart, C., 488
Hartsough, C.S., 457
Harvey, W., 193
Hasin, D.S., 416
Haskell, A., 367
Haskins, R., 507
Hassibi, M., 470
Hatfield, E., 495
Hatsukami, D., 478
Hattie, J.A., 582
Hatziandreu, E.J., 444
Haugaard, J.J., 245
Hauri, P., 65
Hawton, K., 224
Hay, D.P., 541
Hay, L.K., 541
Hayden, M.R., 399
Hayes, S.C., 236, 237
Haynes, S.G., 198
Hazelwood, R.R., 239, 240
Hazlett, B., 432
Heath, A., 179, 353
Hebert, L.E., 392
Hecht, H., 181
Hedeker, D., 317
Heinrichs, D.W., 343
Heller, T., 510
Hellman, S., 572
Helmer, D.C., 199
Helsing, K.J., 143
Helzer, J.E., 103, 104, 145
Henderson, C., 559
Henderson, S., 284
Heninger, G.R., 291
Henker, B., 456, 457, 458
Hennekens, C.H., 392
Hennell, T., 330
Herdt, G.H., 220
Hermann, B.P., 404
Hern, K.L., 457
Hernton, C., 441
Herold, E.S., 217
Hersen, M., 206
Hersov, L., 451
Hess, C.M., 509
Hesselink, J.R., 490
Heston, L.L., 389, 390, 396
Hetherington, E.M., 561
Hightower, A.D., 564
Hilgard, E., 147
Hill, D.R., 284
Hill, J., 470
Himelien, M.J., 558
Hinshaw, S.P., 456, 457, 458

Hinz, L.D., 476
Hirsch, M., 471
Hirschfeld, R.M.A., 273, 292, 309
Hobson, R.P., 489
Hodapp, R., 507, 508
Hodges, W., 550
Hodgson, R.J., 171
Hoenig, J., 334
Hofer, M.A., 143
Hoffman, A., 439
Hoffman, R.E., 370
Hogarty, G.E., 373
Holden, C., 283, 307
Holland, A., 59
Holland, J., 202
Hollon, S.D., 302, 307
Holzer, C.E., III, 11, 282, 284, 286
Holzman, P.S., 368, 369
Hooley, J.M., 372, 373
Hoover, C., 545
Horne, J., 577
Horowitz, L.M., 299
Horowitz, M.J., 145, 519
Horvath, T.B., 390, 394, 403
Horwitz, A.V., 12
Hotaling, G., 244
Houghton, J.F., 2–4
Housman, D., 399
Houston, B.K., 199
Howell, C.T., 471
Hoyt, M.F., 519
Hudson, J., 263
Hughes, D., 158
Hunsley, J., 221
Hurlburt, R.T., 330
Hurt, S.W., 264, 265
Hutton, H.E., 473
Hyde, J.S., 241, 242
Hynd, G.W., 457

I

Iacono, W.G., 368
Iacuone, R., 464
Iannotti, R.J., 86
Imber, S., 537
Ionescu-Pioggia, M., 441
Isager, T., 475

J

Jack-roller, 269
Jackson, A.W., 500
Jacob, R.G., 201
Jacobs, S., 284
Jacobsen, F.M., 313
Jacobson, B., 356
Jaffe, J.H., 433, 435, 443
James, S.P., 313
Jamison, K.R., 307, 310, 311, 313, 314
Jarrett, D.B., 293
Javna, C.D., 373
Jaynes, J., 331
Jellinek, E.M., 419
Jemmott, J.B., III, 203
Jenkins, C.D., 195, 197
Jenkins, E.C., 500
Jenkins, J.H., 373
Jensen, A.R., 507

Jensen, P.S., 454
Jenson, W.R., 490
Jernigan, T.L., 490
Jerrett, I., 471
Joffee, W.G., 297
Johnson, J., 160, 181
Johnson, J.M., 134
Johnson, V.E., 219, 223, 225, 226, 227
Jonas, J.M., 263
Jones, D.J., 473
Jones, J.C., 144
Jones, M.B., 490
Jones, M.C., 421
Jones, S., 371
Jono, R.T., 11
Jorde, L.B., 490
Jorgensen, E.C., 453
Joseph, J.G., 221
Judd, L.L., 4
Julien, R.M., 437
Jung, C., 74
Justice, B., 203

K

Kaelber, C.T., 418
Kahn, J., 299
Kairys, S.W., 452
Kaleva, M., 359, 360
Kalin, N.H., 324
Kamp, J., 475
Kannel, T.W.B., 198
Kaplan, H.S., 229, 300
Karasek, R.A., 201
Karlsson, J., 456
Karno, M.N., 373
Katz, S., 458
Kaufman, A.S., 106, 107
Kaufman, K., 559
Kaufman, M.J., 508
Kaufman, N.L., 107
Kaufmann, C.A., 357
Kay, S.R., 335
Kazdin, A.E., 463, 481
Keane, T.M., 157
Keck, P.E., Jr., 342
Keenan, V., 495
Kegan, R.G., 269
Keith, S.J., 324
Keller, M.B., 286
Keller, S.E., 67
Kellner, R., 193, 207
Kelly, G.A., 82, 522
Kelly, K.C., 457
Kempthorne-Rawson, J., 202
Kendall, P.C., 112, 463
Kendell, R.E., 332
Kendler, K.S., 179, 253, 255, 337, 353,
 356
Kennedy, J.L., 357
Kennedy, S., 186, 203
Kenyon, K., 316
Kernberg, O.F., 264
Kersell, M.W., 553
Keshavan, M., 324
Kessel, R., 499
Kessler, R.C., 221
Kety, S.S., 355, 356, 361
Keyl, P.M., 167
Kidd, J.R., 357
Kidd, K.K., 285, 289, 290

Kiecolt-Glaser, J.K., 186, 203
Kilmann, P.R., 243
Kiloh, L.G., 67
Kilpatrick, D.G., 138
Kim, K., 284
King, N.J., 464
Kinsey, A.C., 217
Kipper, D.A., 151
Kirby, M., 346
Kirkpatrick, B., 365
Kirscht, J.P., 221
Kivlahan, D.R., 413
Kleber, H.D., 434, 436
Klein, D., 458
Klein, D.F., 161, 168
Klein, R.G., 456, 466
Klerman, G.L., 160, 181, 285, 309,
 537
Klosko, J.S., 175, 181
Kluft, R.P., 148, 149, 150
Knauer, R.S., 293
Knight, R.A., 244
Knopp, W., 22
Knowles, P.A.L., 79
Koby, E., 467
Koenig, W.G.R., 368
Kog, E., 474
Kohut, H., 75
Kolata, G., 461, 501
Kolb, L.D., 164, 391, 439
Kolko, D.J., 313
Kolodny, R.C., 223, 225, 226, 227
Kolvin, I., 6
Konner, M., 218
Korlin, D., 234
Kornblith, S.J., 373
Koshner, S., 309
Koss, M.P., 137
Kosten, T.R., 434, 436
Kovacs, M., 469, 471
Kraaimaat, F., 181
Kraemer, H.C., 201, 202
Kraepelin, E., 49, 332, 366
Krakowski, A.J., 250
Kramer, J.J., 561
Kramer, M., 572
Krantz, D.S., 199
Kranz, S., 471
Kremen, W., 309
Kremer, M.W., 219
Krieg, C., 181
Kringlen, E., 196
Kupfer, D.J., 293
Kuriansky, J.B., 333

L

LaBrecque, J.F., 204
Lacks, P., 105
LaDue, R.A., 506
Laffal, J., 328
LaGreca, A.M., 510
Lahey, B.B., 460
Lahti, I., 359, 360
Laing, R.D., 332
Lake, R., 467
Lamb, F., 569
Lambert, M.J., 534, 550
Lambert, N.M., 457
Langer, D.H., 467

Langley, J., 239
Lanin-Kettering, I., 327
Lanke, J., 282, 284, 313
Lanquetot, R., 354, 581
LaRoche, C., 309
Lasky, E., 474
Last, C.G., 466
Latib, A., 509
Lazarus, A.A., 227
Lazarus, L., 67
Leaf, P.J., 11, 282, 284, 286
Lear, M.W., 209
Lebowitz, B.D., 395
Leckman, J.F., 285, 289, 290
Leeper, J.D., 567
Leff, J.P., 345, 371, 372, 373
Lehmann, H.E., 343
Lehner, T., 357
Lehrer, P.M., 190
Leitenberg, H., 244
Lemon, M., 367
Lenane, M., 467
Lennox, W.G., 385
Lentz, R.J., 544
Lenzenweger, M.F., 335
Leon, G.R., 474, 475, 476, 477
Leonard, H., 467
Leslie, A.M., 489
Lester, E.P., 309
Lesyna, K., 316
Levar, I., 85
LeVay, S., 218
Levine, H.M., 132
Levine, J., 330
Levine, R.V., 195
Levine, S.B., 231
Levy, R.F., 233
Lewin, R., 399
Lewine, R.R.J., 361
Lewinsohn, P.M., 306
Lewis, D., 308
Liberman, B., 537
Lichtman, R.R., 138
Lieberman, M., 583
Light, E., 395
Lilienfeld, S.O., 457
Liljefors, I., 196
Lindemalm, G., 234
Lindenmayer, J.P., 335
Lindesay, J., 471
Linehan, M.M., 263, 264, 265, 317
Lingjaerde, O., 292
Link, B.G., 85
Linn, M.V., 347
Linnoila, M., 317
Linsky, A.S., 423
Lipowski, Z.J., 388
Lipsius, S.H., 227
Lipsky, A., 466
Litz, B.T., 157
Liv, S.C., 202
Llewelyn, S.P., 246, 534
Lobato, D., 496
Locke, B.Z., 164
Locke, S.E., 203
Loeber, R.R., 460
Longabaugh, R., 15
Loosen, P.T., 307
Lopez, S., 373
Lovaas, O.I., 491, 492
Lovejoy, M., 329
Lowe, N.K., 112
Lubin, B., 134, 135, 136
Luborsky, L., 436, 537

Lucas, A.R., 475
Lucia, M., 195
Luckhurst, E., 67
Ludlow, C., 467
Lumry, A.E., 308
Lund, C.E., 335
Lynch, K., 195

M

Mac Askill, R.C., 12
Maccoby, E., 100
Maccoby, N., 100
MacDougall, J.M., 199
MacMahon, B., 489, 490
Macmillan, M., 51
MacTurk, R.H., 501
Madonia, M.J., 373
Magaziner, J., 359, 375
Magnusson, D., 464
Mahl, G.L., 101
Mahoney, E.R., 137
Maliza, C., 202
Malloy, P., 456
Mandel, B., 309
Manderscheid, R.W., 12
Mankoo, B.J., 357
Mann, J.J., 295
Mannuzza, S., 456
Manschreck, T., 339
Manuck, S.B., 199, 200
Marengo, J.T., 327
Margalittal, M.P.H., 221
Marino, M.F., 263
Markman, H.J., 551
Markowitz, J., 295
Marks, I.M., 160, 165, 166, 168, 172, 175
Marlatt, G.A., 413, 422, 427, 431, 445
Marmar, C.R., 519
Marmor, J., 220
Marmot, M.G., 195
Marrache, M., 309
Marshall, R.M., 457
Marshall, W.C., 244
Martin, C.E., 217
Martin, N.G., 179, 353
Maser, J.D., 181
Mason-Brothers, A., 490, 500
Masters, W.H., 219, 223, 225, 226, 227
Mastri, A.R., 396
Matherne, P.M., 206
Mattes, J., 458
Matthews, G., 293
Matthews, W.S., 499
Mattick, R., 537
May, J.H., 471
Maynard, H., 570
Mayou, R., 175
McCarthy, M.E., 501
McCarver, R.B., 509
McClelland, D.C., 203
McConaughy, S.H., 471
McCool, R.E., 145
McDowell, E.E., 471
McEvoy, L., 145
McEvoy, L.T., 104
McGillivray, J., 489
McGlashan, T.H., 257, 340, 341
McGrath, P.J., 312
McGue, M., 357
McGuffin, P., 59, 353

McKenna, P.J., 335
McLeer, S., 463
McLellan, A.T., 436
McLellan, T., 537
McMahon, W.M., 490
McNally, R.J., 164, 175
McNiel, D.E., 299
McQuistan, S.T., 501
Means, J., 204
Mednick, S.A., 365, 366, 369
Meichenbaum, D., 75
Meisler, A.W., 225
Melamed, B.G., 465
Melancon, S.M., 330
Mellor, C.S., 333, 334
Meltzer, H.Y., 313
Mendelson, W., 467
Menghi, P., 481
Menlove, F.L., 465
Merikangas, K.R., 181, 250, 289
Metalsky, G.I., 304
Meyer, J., 215
Meyer, R., 418
Mezzich, J.E., 181
Milich, R., 463
Millazo-Sayre, L.J., 12
Miller, B.L., 149
Miller, G.E., 463
Miller, H.L., 567
Miller, N., 81, 174
Miller, S.I., 412
Miller, T.I., 538
Millman, R.B., 414
Millon, T., 252
Milofsky, E.S., 429
Mintz, J., 373
Minuchin, S., 474, 476
Mirin, S.M., 436
Mirsky, A.F., 367
Mischel, W., 306
Mitchell, J.E., 478
Miyake, K., 195
Mizes, J.S., 474
Mo, A., 490
Mohr, D.C., 225
Mohs, R.C., 390, 394, 403
Moises, H.W., 357
Molk, L., 204
Money, J., 218, 219, 220, 231
Monroe, S.M., 304
Monson, R.R., 282
Moore, C., 224
Moore-Ede, M.C., 293
Moos, A., 471
Moos, R.H., 118
Moran, A.E., 324, 571
Moran, Lord C.M.W., 311
Morgan, J.E., 203
Morihisa, J.M., 365
Moring, J., 359, 360
Morris, J., 232
Morrison, R.L., 199, 200, 344
Morrissey, J.P., 44
Mortimer, A.M., 335
Moser, C., 237
Mosher, L., 345, 347
Mrazek, D.A., 204
Mueser, K.T., 343
Muller, A.P., 265
Murphy, A.I., 190
Murphy, D.L., 467
Murphy, E., 471
Murphy, G.E., 314, 568
Murphy, J.M., 282

Murray, H.A., 114
Muser, J., 204
Myers, J., 440
Myers, J.K., 11

N

Naarala, M., 359, 360
Naveh, G., 85
Nduaguba, M., 250
Needles, D.J., 306
Neeman, R., 526
Nehme, E., 489
Neimeyer, R.A., 307
Nemiah, J.C., 149, 163
Nestadt, G., 572
Neugebauer, R., 38
Neuwissen, I., 229
Newcomb, P.A., 444
Newlin, D.B., 420
Newman, M., 309
Nicholi, A.M., 211
Nichols, P.L., 498
Nicolo-Corigliano, A., 481
Nielsen, S., 475
Niemeyer, G.J., 83
Nietzel, M.T., 558
Nordahl, T.E., 457
North, C.S., 145
Norton, J.P., 374
Noshpitz, J.D., 134
Novotny, T.E., 444
Nowling, J.B., 199
Noyes, R., Jr., 160
Nuechterlein, K.H., 367
Nystrup, J., 475

O

O'Brien, C.P., 436
O'Connor, G., 510
O'Donoghue, E.G., 38
O'Leary, A., 202
O'Leary, K.D., 524, 560
O'Neal, J.M., 322
Oatley, K., 87
Offord, D.R., 469
Ogden, J.A.H., 331
Oglesby, P., 202
Ohman, R., 282, 284
Ojesjo, L., 282, 284, 313
Okolo, C., 509
Olds, D.C., 559
Olesen, N.S., 475
Oliver, J.F., 507
Olivier, D.C., 282
Ollendick, T.H., 464
Ollier, K., 464
Orne, H., 340
Oros, C.J., 137
Orr, W.C., 65
Ostergaard, L., 355
Ostfeld, A.M., 202
Ostrow, D.G., 221
Othmer, E., 100, 256, 259
Othmer, S.C., 100, 256, 259
Ottaviani, R., 160
Otterbeck, L., 282, 284
Ouellette, R., 160

Over, R., 229
Overholser J., 471
Owen, W., 474

P

Paez, P., 471
Painter, S.L., 244
Pakstis, A.J., 357
Parker, E.S., 418
Parkes, C.M., 143
Parnas, J., 365, 366, 369
Parry, B.L., 313
Patel, V., 203
Patterson, G.R., 563
Paul, G.L., 544
Paul, S.M., 180
Paully, G.S., 22
Pauls, D.L., 285, 290
Paykel, E.S., 284
Pearlson, G., 489
Pearson, C., 246
Pearson, T.A., 202
Pennebaker, J.W., 203
Penny, R., 67
Perkins, P., 361
Perloff, D.B., 120
Perls, F.S., 522
Perper, J.A., 313
Perry, D.G., 556
Perry, L.C., 556
Persad, E., 295
Persky, V.W., 202
Persson, A., 365
Peters, R., 570
Petersen, P.B., 490
Peterson, B.L., 199
Peterson, R.A., 134
Petri, M., 339
Petursson, H., 357
Pfeffer, C.R., 471
Pfohl, B., 258
Phelan, P.W., 474, 476
Phillips, D.P., 19, 316
Phillips, M.R., 33
Pickar, D., 335
Pickering, T.G., 201
Pickles, A., 470
Pieper, C., 201
Pierce, G.R., 118, 132
Pierce, J.P., 444
Piercey, B.P., 323
Pilkonis, P.A., 181, 537
Pinel, P., 44
Pingree, C., 490
Piper, W., 537
Piven, J., 489
Plakun, E.M., 265
Platt, J.J., 552
Pliszka, S.R., 458
Plochg, I., 175, 176
Plomin, R., 60
Plumb, M.M., 202
Plutchik, R., 471
Pogue-Geile, M.F., 324, 334
Polack, P., 346
Polatin, P., 313
Polefrone, J.M., 199, 200
Polich, J.M., 428
Pollack, E., 458
Pollin, W., 353
Pomeroy, C., 478

Pomeroy, W.B., 217
Pope, H.G., Jr., 263, 342, 441
Possl, J., 181
Post, R.M., 159
Potter, E.H., III, 132
Powell, G.E., 235
Powell, L.H., 200
Prentky, R.A., 244
Presly, A.S., 344
Press, G.A., 490
Price, D.L.C., 394
Price, L.H., 291
Price, R.K., 461
Price, V.A., 200
Primavera, J., 86
Prince, C., 236
Prince, V.C., 236
Prinz, R.J., 463
Prior, M.R., 487, 489
Pritchard, B.E., 299
Prudic, J., 295
Prusoff, B.A., 285, 289, 290
Prutsman, T.D., 79
Puig-Antich, J., 471
Purcell, K., 204
Purtell, J.J., 208
Putnam, F.W., 146
Pyle, R.L., 478

Q

Quitkin, F.M., 312

R

Rabkin, J.G., 575
Rachman, S.J., 171
Rae, D.S., 164, 324
Ragland, D.R., 199
Rahe, R.H., 196
Ramey, C.T., 507
Randels, S.P., 506
Ranseen, J.D., 396
Rao, D.C., 357
Rapaport, K., 137
Rapoport, J.L., 169, 466, 467
Rapport, M.D., 457
Ratcliff, K.S., 103
Rayner, J., 335
Raynor, W.J., 202
Raz, N., 362
Raz, S., 362
Read, T., 357
Reber, M., 463
Reed, D.E., 208
Regier, D.A., 10, 11, 158, 160, 164, 165,
 173, 266, 286, 324, 418
Reich, J., 250
Reich, T., 309
Reich, W., 274
Reid, J.B., 422
Reid, W.H., 10, 269, 271
Reider, R., 355
Reisberg, B., 392
Reiss, B.F., 220
Reiss, D.J., 373
Rekers, G.A., 213
Remafedi, G., 218
Repucci, N.D., 245

Reveley, A., 59
Reveno, W.S., 399
Reynolds, G.P., 364
Reznikoff, M., 114
Rice, J., 309
Richardson, C.M., 452
Richelson, E., 290, 295
Richmann, N., 464
Rie, E., 457
Rie, H., 457
Riesenberg, D., 136, 243
Riess, F., 120
Rifkin, A.H., 219
Rijken, H., 181
Rintoul, B., 471
Risch, N., 309, 337, 357
Riskind, J.H., 301
Rist, M.C., 437
Ritvo, E.R., 490, 500
Roach, M., 394, 395
Robins, E., 208, 218, 220
Robins, L.N., 10, 11, 103, 104, 145, 158,
 160, 164, 165, 173, 266, 286, 418,
 460, 461
Robinson, A., 180
Robinson, L.A., 307
Rock, C.L., 474
Rodgers, M., 480
Rodin, G.M., 209
Rogentine, G.N., 202
Rogers, C.R., 84, 306
Rogers, H.J., 295, 582
Rohrbeck, C.T., 453
Romanoski, A.J., 572
Romer, D., 510
Ronan, K.R., 463
Ronningstam, E., 260
Rorer, L.G., 523
Rorsman, B., 282, 284, 313
Rosenbaum, A., 560
Rosenbaum, H., 399
Rosenblatt, J.E., 202
Rosenblum, L.A., 22
Rosenman, R.H., 195, 197, 200
Rosenstein, M.J., 12
Rosenthal, D., 355, 356, 361, 376
Rosenthal, L.S., 418
Rosenthal, N.E., 313
Rosenthal, R., 538
Rosie, J.S., 544
Rosman, B., 474, 476
Ross, A., 572
Ross, D.M., 456
Ross, G., 203
Ross, H.L., 565
Ross, S.A., 456
Rossi, P.H., 572
Rosvold, H.E., 367
Rounsaville, B.J., 434, 436
Roy, A., 317, 324
Royall, R.M., 572
Roy-Byrne, P., 159
Rubenstein, D., 226
Ruberman, J.W., 194
Ruch, L.O., 136
Rund, B.R., 337
Rush, A.J., 301, 303
Russell, D.E.H., 245
Russo, A.J., 218
Ruttenberg, B.A., 500
Rutter, M., 97, 285, 327, 450, 454, 469,
 470, 489, 490, 511, 557
Ryan, K.B., 553
Ryback, R.S., 418

S

Sabalis, R.F., 243
Sack, D.A., 312, 313
Sackeim, H.A., 295, 306
Sacks, M.H., 335
Sadock, V.A., 255, 560
Saghir, M.T., 218, 220
Salmoiraghi, G.C., 418
Salter, A.C., 452
Sandberg, D.P., 168
Sanders, D.H., 570
Sanderson, W.C., 158
Sandler, J., 297, 559
Sanford, E.E., 452
Santana, F., 373
Santayana, G., 31
Sarason, B.R., 118, 132, 564
Sarason, I.G., 81, 117, 118, 132, 134, 367, 564
Sass, L.A., 331
Saul, R.A., 500
Savin-Williams, R.C., 220
Sceery, W., 467
Schafer, R., 114, 115
Schaie, K.W., 384, 385
Schal, H., 204
Schalling, D., 269
Scheftner, W., 308, 317
Scherr, P.A., 392
Schilling, R.F., 510
Schinke, S.P., 510
Schleifer, S.J., 67
Schlesinger, M., 545
Schlesser, M.A., 312
Schlussel, Y., 201
Schmaling, K., 298
Schnall, P.L., 201
Schneider, M.S., 201
Schoenman, T.J., 37
Schotte, D.E., 477
Schreiber, J.L., 335
Schroeder, H.E., 344
Schuckit, M.A., 419
Schuett, V.E., 499
Schulsinger, F., 355, 356, 361, 369
Schuster, S., 464
Schwartz, E.O., 263
Schwartz, J.E., 201
Schwartz, M., 219
Schwartz, S., 328
Schweinhart, L.J., 463
Scott, F.M., 451
Scovern, A.W., 243
Searl, S., Jr., 495
Sechehaye, M., 328
Sedvall, G., 365
Seligman, M.E.P., 304
Selye, H., 186
Semmel, M.I., 508
Semple, D., 344
Severin, B., 475
Shaffer, D., 97
Shaffer, J.W., 202
Shapiro, A.P., 201
Shapiro, B., 330
Shapiro, D., 258, 274
Sharfstein, S.S., 324, 571
Sharp, L.K., 203
Sharpley, C.F., 582
Shaw, B., 301, 303
Shaw, C.R., 269
Shaywitz, B.A., 494

Shea, J.M., 145
Shea, M.T., 273
Shea, S.C., 270
Shear, M.K., 162
Sheehan, S., 570
Sheiner, R., 309
Shekelle, R.B., 202
Shelton, R.C., 307
Shengxian, L., 33
Shenton, M.E., 368
Sherman, B., 137, 138
Sherman, L.J., 15
Sherrington, R.P., 357
Shibur, L.D., 309
Shiffman, S., 445
Shoham-Salomon, V., 526
Shore, E., 186
Shore, J.H., 570
Shrout, P.E., 85
Shuchter, S.R., 136
Shukla, S., 308
Shumaker, S.A., 284
Shure, M.B., 551, 552
Siegel, J.M., 134, 200
Siegel, T., 463
Siegler, I.C., 199
Siever, L.J., 253, 255, 257, 368, 390, 394, 403
Signer, S.F., 149
Sigvardsson, S., 268, 419
Silver, J.M., 385, 386, 400
Silverman, J.M., 257
Silverstein, M.L., 334
Simmons, K., 471
Simon, K.M., 131
Singer, T., 120
Sjogren, B., 357
Skinner, B.F., 15, 78, 154
Sklar, L.S., 202
Skodol, A.E., 85, 170, 249, 256, 260, 267, 273, 284, 287, 458
Skultans, V., 51
Sloane, R.B., 536
Small, G.W., 211
Smith, D., 480
Smith, D.E., 432
Smith, D.F., 506
Smith, D.W., 504
Smith, E.M., 145
Smith, M.L., 538
Smith, R.N., 2
Smith, R.S., 126
Smith, T., 220
Smith, T.W., 83
Snodgrass, J., 269
Snyder, K.S., 371
Sokol, L., 523
Sokolow, M., 120
Solavoy, M.R., 368
Sorri, A., 359, 360
Spanos, N.P., 37
Spiegel, D., 202, 373
Spirito, A., 471
Spitzer, R.L., 249, 256, 260, 267, 273, 284, 287, 458
Spitznagel, E.L., 104
Spivack, G., 551, 552
Spring, B., 359, 367
Stabenau, J.R., 353
Stanley, S.M., 551
Staples, F.R., 536
Starkstein, S.E., 489
Stattin, H., 464
Stawarz, R.J., 291

Steadman, H.J., 12
Steer, R.A., 301
Stein, M., 67
Steiner, M., 293
Steinhauer, S.R., 359
Stern, S.L.,
Stevens, C., 399
Stevenson, J., 464
Stewart, J.W., 312
Stillion, J.M., 471
Stine, O.C., 572
Stokes, P., 474
Stolzman, R.K., 104
Stone, D.K., 265
Stone, M.H., 262, 263, 265
Stone, W.L., 510
Stoops, R., 117
Stopek, S., 370
Storaasli, R.D., 551
Storr, A., 258, 311, 535
Straus, M.A., 423
Straus, R., 195, 197
Strauss, J.S., 335, 341, 342
Streissguth, A.P., 506
Stroebe, M.S., 143
Stroebe, W., 143
Strunk, R.C., 204
Strupp, H.H., 534, 538
Stubbs, E.G., 490
Stueve, A., 85
Stumphauzer, J.S., 555
Stunkard, A.J., 477
Suddath, R.L., 363
Suelzle, M., 495
Sulzer, F., 291
Suomi, S.J., 22–23
Surawicz, T.S., 444
Surrey, J., 246
Sutherland, A.J., 209
Swank, R.T., 202
Swanson, J.W., 11
Swayze, V.W., II, 363
Swedo, S.E., 467
Sweeney, J., 295
Swett, C., Jr., 246
Syme, S.L., 195, 199
Szelo, M., 143

T

Tabrizi, M.A., 471
Talbott, J.A., 130
Tarrier, N., 373
Tarver-Behring, S., 456
Tatum, E., 570
Taylor, J.O., 392
Taylor, J.R., 294
Taylor, O.B., 201
Taylor, S.E., 138, 187, 193
Teasdale, T.W., 369
Tellis, C., 373
Terkelsen, M.D., 343
Terman, J.S., 312
Terman, M., 312
Terr, L.C., 451
Thelmar, E., 326, 331
Thomas, A., 470
Thomas, C., 463
Thomas, J.C., 460
Thompson, J.W., 164
Thompson, T.L., 190
Thompson, W.D., 285, 290

Thomson, J.B., 420
Thoresen, C.E., 199, 200
Tiber, N., 163
Tien, A.Y., 418
Tienari, P., 359, 360
Tiller, J., 168
Tinklenberg, J.R., 244
Tischler, G.L., 11
Tizard, I., 469
Tolstrup, K., 475
Tomb, D.A., 288
Tommaso, E., 309
Toner, B.B., 475
Toolan, J.M., 472
Torgersen, S., 163
Torrey, E.F., 9, 363
Trull, T.J., 256
Tsai, L.Y., 490
Tsuang, M.T., 309, 340, 367
Tuason, V.B., 302, 308
Turner, J.L., 511
Turner, S.M., 179
Twentyman, C.T., 452, 453

U

Uddenberg, N., 234
Uhde, T.W., 159, 163
Ulmer, D.K., 199, 200
Ulrich, R.F., 293
Usher, M., 299
Ussery, T., 454

V

Vachon, L., 204
Vaillant, G.E., 97, 276, 429, 435
Valone, K., 374
Vandereycken, W., 474
van der Helm, M., 175, 176
van Schaik, A., 181
Vanderveen, E., 418
Van Zanten, B., 175, 176
Vanderzwagg, R., 404
Vaneerdewegh, M., 309
VanKammen, D.P., 202
Varma, D.K., 431
Varnhagen, C.K., 501
Varnhagen, S., 501
Vasile, R.G., 298
Vaughn, C.E., 371, 372, 373
Vavak, C.R., 199
Veldman, D.J., 508
Veloz, E.V., 555
Ventulani, J., 291
Vermilyea, B.B., 175
Vermilyea, J., 175
Veronen, L.J., 138
Videka-Sherman, L., 583
Vietze, P.M., 501
Vinogradov, S., 529
Virkkunen, M., 268
Virogradov, S., 244
Vitone, B.J., 159
Voeller, K.K., 457
Volkmar, F.R., 493
Vollhardt, L.T., 203
Volvaka, J., 268
Von Knorring, A.L., 268
von Zerssen, D., 181

W

Wahlberg, K.E., 359, 360
Walder, L.O., 563
Waldman, I.D., 457
Walker, J.I., 339
Walker, L.E., 245
Wallace, B.C., 438
Wallace, C.J., 374
Wallerstein, J.S., 560
Ward, S.K., 137
Warren, K., 201
Warren, K.R., 418
Wasow, M., 495
Wasserman, A.A., 471
Waterhouse, L., 500
Watson, J.B., 75
Watt, N.F., 362
Way, L., 217
Wechsler, D., 106
Wegner, A.Z., 306
Wehr, T.A., 312, 313
Weikart, D.P., 463
Weinberg, M.S., 217, 219, 221, 237, 238
Weinberger, D.R., 363
Weinblatt, E., 194
Weiner, D.B., 43
Weiner, H., 343
Weiner, R.D., 295, 542
Weinstein, L., 367
Weise, R., 273, 367
Weishaar, M., 523
Weiss, B., 471
Weiss, R.D., 436
Weissberg, R.P., 564
Weissman, M.M., 11, 158, 160, 181, 250, 282, 284, 285, 286, 289, 290
Weisz, J.R., 471
Weitzenhoffer, A.M., 520
Weitzman, G.D., 293
Weller, E.B., 455
Welner, J., 355, 356
Wender, P.H., 355, 356, 361
Werdegar, D., 120
Werner, E.E., 126
Wesson, D.R., 432
Westefeld, J.S., 314, 315
Westermeyer, J.F., 343
Wethington, E., 335
Wetterberg, L., 357
Wewers, M.E., 112
Wexler, N.S., 399
Whalen, C.K., 455, 456, 457, 458
Whipple, K., 536
White, J., 389, 390
White, S., 137
Whitehead, W.E., 180
Whitman, S., 404
Whitmore, K., 469
Wickramaratne, P., 289
Widiger, T.A., 253, 256, 261
Widom, C.S., 268
Wiener-Levy, D., 114
Wiesel, F.A., 365
Wikler, L.M., 495
Wilbur, C.B., 219
Wilcox, L.E., 112
Wille, R., 435
Williams, C.J., 237
Williams, D.A., 555
Williams, J.B.W., 249, 256, 260, 267, 273, 284, 287, 458

Williams, K., 137
Williams, R.B., Jr., 199
Williamson, D.A., 474, 476
Wilson, A., 327
Wilson, A.A., 504
Wilson, G., 237, 238, 239
Wilson, G.T., 22–23, 25, 524
Wilturner, L.T., 496
Wing, R., 201
Winson, J., 75
Wirz-Justice, A.A., 312
Wise, T.N., 235
Wissler, T., 373
Wittchen, H., 181
Wixted, J.T., 344
Wolf, L., 492
Wolf, S., 195
Wolfe, D.A., 559
Wolf-Schein, E.G., 500
Wood, J.V., 138
Woody, G., 537
Woody, G.E., 436
Woolf, L., 310
Woolf, V., 310
Woolson, R.F., 340
Wortman, C.B., 138, 143, 221
Wright, F.D., 179, 523
Wu, J.C., 293
Wulff, S.B., 489
Wurm, M., 195, 197
Wyatt, R.J., 365
Wyler, A.R., 404
Wynne, L.C., 359, 360, 361

X

Xenakis, S.N., 519

Y

Yager, J., 474
Yalom, I.D., 529
Yarrow, L.J., 501
Yates, W., 250
Yates, W.R., 313
Yorkston, N.J., 536
Young-Courchesne, N., 490
Yudofsky, S.C., 385, 386, 400
Yuh, W.T.C., 363
Yule, W., 511

Z

Zahn, T.P., 467
Zahn-Waxler, C., 86
Zametkin, A.J., 457
Zanarini, M.C., 261, 263, 264, 265
Zanna, M.P., 553
Zelenak, J.P., 313
Zetlin, A.G., 511
Ziebell, S., 363
Zigler, E., 330, 507, 508
Zimmerman, J.C., 293
Zimmerman, R., 478
Zisook, S., 136
Zubin, J., 334, 341, 359
Zucker, K.A., 231

Subject Index

A

Abnormal behavior, 1–6
 clinical contacts for, 7–9
 and coping, 6–7
 definition of, 2–6
 epidemiology of, 9–12
 help for, 12–14
 historical views of, 31–53
 and maladaptation, 5–6
 psychological and organic views, 48–87
 research on, 14–27
 stigma of, 4–5, 27
 and stress, 6–7
 vulnerability for, 6–7
Abraham, Karl, 297
Abstinence-violation effect, 427, 447
Abuse:
 of alcohol, 414
 of barbiturates, 432–433
 parental, 263, 558
Acceptance:
 in client–therapist relationship, 151
 in therapy, 153, 533
Accidents:
 and alcohol, 415, 417
 and stress, 135, 152
Acetylcholine, 294, 394
Acrophobia, 164
Activity scheduling, 302
Adaptation, 5, 27–28
Adaptive behavior:
 in aging, 140
 defense mechanisms, 72
 failure of, 56
Addiction:
 heroin, 537
 in newborns, 437
 opioid, 434–435
Addictive disorders, 411–447
 addictive behavior and, 412–414
 alcohol, 414–431
 amphetamines, 438
 barbiturates, 432–433
 cocaine, 436–438
 marijuana, 440–443
 nicotine, 443–446
 opioids, 433–436
 psychedelics, 438–440
 tranquilizers, 432–433
Addington v. Texas, 579
ADHD, *see* Attention-deficit hyperactivity disorder
Adjustment, 5
 in homosexuality, 246
 and sexual abuse, 245
 and sexual reassignment surgery, 232
 in transsexuals, 232
Adjustment disorders, 96, 126, 141–143, 152
 diagnostic overlap in, 181
Adler, Alfred, 74

Adolescence:
 changes in, 139–140
 conduct disorder in, 458–464
 depression in, 468–472
 disorders of, 95, 449–481
 eating disorders in, 472–478
 periods of, 139
 problems of retarded individuals in, 511
 sexual preference in, 218
Adolescent therapy, 478–481
Adoption studies, 378
 of schizophrenia, 354–356, 359
Adrenal cortex, 64
Adrenal corticosteroids, 64
Adrenal gland, 63
Adrenocorticotrophic hormone, 64
Affect:
 in autism, 489–490
 flattened, 325, 334–335
 inappropriate, 264
 instability of, 264
 in schizophrenia, 325
Affective disorders, *see* Mood disorders
Aftercare center, community response to, 575
Aftercare programs, 572
Age:
 and brain disorders, 383
 and depression, 318
 and disorder, 10
 and suicide risk, 314, 315
Age of Reason, 40–42
Aggression:
 in abusive parents, 453
 in childhood, 459
 and family relationships, 556
 in social interaction, 463
Aging:
 adaptation to, 140
 changes in, 140
 and intelligence, 384
 normal, 384–385
 and paranoid thinking, 338
 successful, 385
Agoraphobia, 164, 166–168, 182
AIDS, 221, 222, 218
 and sexual behavior, 217
AIDS dementia complex, 396, 408
Alcohol, 22–23, 414–431, 442, 446
 and rape, 137
 and retardation, 506
Alcohol abuse, 446
 in borderline personality, 265
 and homelessness, 572
 prevention of, 429
Alcoholics Anonymous, 426, 428, 447, 583
Alcoholism, 416–417, 419, 446
 in brain disorder, 409
 and high risk offspring, 557
 Korsakoff's syndrome in, 400
 pellagra in, 400
Alcohol poisoning, 430
Alcohol use:
 guidelines for, 431

 and health, 417, 418, 446
Alcohol use disorders, 181
Alphafetoprotein test, 505, 512
Alpha waves, 376
 in antisocial personality disorder, 269
Alprazolam, 180, 183
Alzheimer's disease, 389, 391–396, 408, 502
 depression in, 283
American Law Institute, 577, 586
American Psychiatric Association, 94, 130, 221
American Psychological Association, 221
Amish group, 309
Amnesia, 145, 147, 148, 152
 and brain trauma, 401
Amnestic syndrome, 396, 397, 408
Amniocentesis, 438, 442, 447, 504, 512
Amphetamines:
 and catecholamines, 364
 effects of, 22
 and paranoid symptoms, 364
Anal stage, 70
Anatomy of Melancholy, 40, 52
Androgen, 218–219
Anencephaly, 505
Anger:
 of Alzheimer caretakers, 395
 in antisocial personality disorder, 267
 in borderline personality, 261
 and grief, 143
 in schizophrenia, 330
 and suicide, 319, 471
 in victims, 145
Anger scale, of MMPI, 110
Animal research, 22
Anomalies, chromosomal, 58
Anorexia nervosa, 472, 482
Anorgasmia, 226, 230, 246
Anterograde amnesia, 397
Anti-anxiety drugs, 180, 542, 547
 for treatment of stress, 151
Antidepressant drugs, 183, 294, 296, 302, 307, 343, 406, 542, 547
 for anxiety, 180–181
 for bulimia, 477
 for children, 472
 effectiveness of, 537
 lethality of, 314
 and neurotransmitters, 291
 for panic attacks, 168
 for personality disorders, 277
 second generation, 294
 for stress, 151
Antigens, 67
 in autism, 490
Antimanic drugs, 542, 547
Antipsychotic drugs, 330, 537, 542, 547
 and amphetamine, 438
 biological changes with, 363
 for delusional disorder, 339
 for personality disorders, 277
 and schizophrenia, 342, 344, 349, 365, 371, 373

Antipsychotic drugs (cont.).
 and thought disorder, 369
Antisocial behavior, 20, 461, 462–463
Antisocial personality, 251–252
Antisocial personality disorder, 263, 265–
 271, 278
 and conduct disorder, 459
 and hyperactivity, 457
Anxiety, 84, 88, 156–157, 182
 in Alzheimer's disease, 393
 in antisocial personality disorder, 269
 in borderline personality, 262
 and bulimia, 477
 and childhood abuse, 452
 chronic, 157
 and grief, 143
 management of, 179
 after natural disaster, 145–146
 physiological changes from, 151
 in psychoanalytic theory, 72
 in rape victims, 136
 and realistic preview, 131
 in schizophrenia, 332
 and sexual dysfunction, 225–226
 and sexual problems, 229–230
 and stressful events, 134
 and suicide risk, 314
 symptom overlap with depression, 180–
 181
 symptoms of, 157
Anxiety attacks, 158
Anxiety disorder, 96, 155–183
 in anorexia nervosa, 475
 behavioral perspective on, 174–176
 biological perspective on, 179–181
 in childhood, 450, 464–468, 482
 cognitive perspective on, 176–179
 diagnostic overlap in, 181
 generalized, 158
 obsessive-compulsive disorder, 168–173
 panic disorder, 158–162
 phobias, 162–168
 psychodynamic perspective on, 173–
 174
 treatment of, 173–181
Apathy:
 in frontal lobe disorders, 386
 in organic personality syndrome, 397
Aphasia 406
Aristotle 35
Arousal:
 and coping, 131
 of stress, 134–140
Asphyxia:
 autoerotic, 239–240, 247
 and retardation, 506
Assault reactions, 136
Assertive behavior, 471
Assertiveness training, 527–528, 546
 for anorexia nervosa, 475
 for personality disorders, 280
Assessment, 19–20, 28, 99–121
 of behavior, 115–117
 of bodily changes, 119–121
 of brain damage, 408
 of childhood depression, 471
 and diagnosis, 93
 of intelligence, 104–109
 interview as, 99–104
 of personality, 110–115
 of relationships, 118–119
 of stressful life events, 134
 of thought, 117–118
Assortative mating, 352–353, 378

Attachment and borderline personality
 disorder, 263
Attention:
 and childhood abuse, 452
 in hyperactivity, 455
 impaired, 334
 in schizophrenia, 331–332, 349, 366–
 368, 378
Attention-deficit hyperactivity disorder, 454,
 481–482
Attraction, 218
Attribution, 304
 in depression, 304–305, 318
 in hyperactivity, 458
Auditory memory in Down syndrome, 501
Aura, 404
Authentic behavior, 85
Autism, 511
 parent-therapists for, 562–563
Autistic disorder, 485–494
Autistic thinking in schizophrenia, 328, 349
Autoerotic asphyxia, 239–240, 247
Autoerotic practices, 239–240, 247
Automatic thoughts, 523
 in anxiety disorder, 179
Autonomic nervous system, 60, 87
 in schizophrenia, 365–366
 voluntary regulation of, 151
Autonomic reactivity, 158
Autoreceptors, 290
Autosomes, 500, 512
Aversion therapy, 241
 for paraphilia, 242
 for transvestism, 236
Aversive conditioning, 426
 and alcohol, 447
Avoidance, 77
Avoidant personality, 251–252
Avoidant personality disorder, 271–272,
 278
Axis I, 94, 251, 252, 257, 278, 461
Axis II, 94, 96, 250, 251–254, 277
Axis III, 94
Axis IV, 94
Axis V, 95
Axon, 60, 61

B

Balanced placebo design, 423
Bandura, Albert, 79, 82–83
Baquet, 42
Barbiturates, 432–433, 442, 447
Baseline observations, 116, 121
BEAM, see Brain electrical activity mapping
Beck, Aaron, 83
Bedlam, see Bethlehem Hospital
Beers, Clifford, 46–47
Behavior:
 in depression, 298
 disruptive, 454–458
 and nervous system, 62–64
 objective study of, 14–16
 and retardation level, 495
Behavioral assessment, 115–117, 121–122
Behavioral change:
 and brain tumor, 402
 in grief, 143
Behavioral checklists, 306
Behavioral excesses, 334

Behavioral observation, 28, 115, 116
 in testing, 108–109
Behavioral perspective, 57, 75–80
 on alcohol treatment, 426–427
 on alcohol use, 421–422, 446
 on anxiety disorders, 174–176, 182
 borderline personality disorder, 264–265
 on brain disorders, 407
 of depression, 298–300, 318
 on gender identity disorder, 231
 on homosexuality, 219
 marital therapy, 531
 on paraphilia, 242
 of phobia, 465
 on separation anxiety, 468
 on smoking, 445
 on suicide, 316
 on transvestism, 236, 237
Behavioral problems in children, 449–483
Behavioral rehearsal, 527
 in assertiveness training, 527–528
Behavioral responses to stress, 134
Behavioral rituals and amphetamines, 22
Behavioral techniques:
 for bulimia, 477
 for panic attacks, 168
 for personality disorders, 280
Behavioral therapy, 182, 523–524, 536,
 546
 for anxiety disorders, 174–176
 for autism, 490–492
 for children, 471, 480, 483
 effectiveness of, 537
 for exhibitionism, 241
 for hyperactivity, 553
 for orgasmic dysfunction, 228
 for personality disorders, 277
 for schizophrenia, 343–344, 345, 349
 for sexual dysfunction, 246
Behavior change experiment, 25–26, 28
Behavior deficits, 334
Behavior disorders of retarded individuals,
 510
Behavior genetics, 59, 88
Behavior modification, 546
 for autistic children, 490–492, 512
 by parents, 478, 562–563
Behavior ratings, 112
Behavior Rating Scale for Children, 112
Behavior therapists and hypnosis, 520
Benzodiazepines, 183, 433, 542, see also
 Antianxiety drugs
 for anxiety disorders, 180
Bereavement, 142–143, 152
Beta amyloid, 394
Beta waves, 61, 365
Bethlehem Hospital, 41
Bibring, Edward, 297
Bicetre, 43
Binet, Alfred, 105
Binet tests, 105–106, 121
Binge eating, see Bulimia nervosa
Binge-purge cycle, 476–477
Biochemical factors:
 in depression, 289–291
 in schizophrenia, 363–365, 378
Biofeedback, 121, 122, 524, 546
 for epilepsy, 405
Biological factors:
 in mental illness, 51
 in retardation, 494
 and sexual preference, 218
Biological markers of risk for schizophrenia,
 367

Biological perspective, 56–68, 88
 on alcohol, 418–421, 425, 446
 on antisocial personality disorder, 268
 on anxiety disorders, 179–181, 183
 on autism, 489
 on borderline personality disorder, 264,
 265
 on depression, 289–297, 318
 on hallucinations, 330
 on homosexuality, 219
 on mental retardation, 498
 on paraphilia, 242
 on transvestism, 236
Biological rhythms, 293
Biological therapies, 540–543
 for depression, 296
 for schizophrenia, 342–343
Bipolar disorder, 282, 285, 289, 296, 307–
 313, 318, 319, see also Mood
 disorder
 causes of, 309, 312
 and creativity, 310–311
 first-rank symptoms, 334
 manic episodes in, 308–309
 treatment of, 312–313
Bipolar II, 282, 308, 319
Birth cohort and depression, 284
Bisexuality, 216, 223–224, 246
 and sadomasochism, 239
Bizarre behavior, 325
 in schizotypal personality disorder, 256
Bleuler, Eugen, 332–333
Blood antibodies in autism, 490
Blood pressure, changes in, 119, 120
Bodily assessment, 119–121, 122
Bodily responses to stress, 134, 141
Body-mind distinction, 57
Bonaparte, Napoleon, 311
Booster sessions, 427
Borderline personality disorder, 260–265,
 278
 depression in, 283
 and suicide, 315
Borderline schizophrenia, 337
Bottom-up studies, 470
Bowlby, John, 297
Brain, 60–61, 382, see also Central nervous
 system
 alcohol effects on, 417
Brain abnormalities:
 and multiple personality, 149
 in schizophrenia, 362–363, 378
Brain atrophy, 396
Brain damage:
 assessment of, 385–387
 results of, 383
Brain degeneration, 384, 408
Brain deterioration, see also Dementia
 and paranoid thinking, 338
Brain disorders, 382–409
 assessment of, 385–387
 causes of, 397–406
 characteristics of, 387–391
 dementia in, 389–397
 integrative approach to, 406–407
 interactional perspective on, 382–385
Brain electrical activity mapping (BEAM),
 365–366, 378
Brain function:
 and mental illness, 49
 psychodynamic perspective on, 75
Brain imaging, 66, 292–294, 386–387,
 408
 and autism, 512

techniques of, 121
Brain impairment, tests of, 386
Brain metabolism, 312
 in bipolar disorder, 312
 delirium and, 388
 in schizophrenia, 363
Brain reward system, 63
Brain trauma, 400–402
Brain tumors, 400–402
Brain waves in antisocial personality
 disorder, 268–269
Breuer, Joseph, 69
Broad Street pump, 10
Brown v. Board of Education, 508, 513
Bulimia, 103, 472, 475, 482
 in borderline personality, 261
Bulimic anorexia, 474, 482
Burton, Robert, 40

C

Caesar, Julius, 402
Caffeine, 442
Case studies, 18–19, 28
Catatonic schizophrenia, 335, 349
Catecholamines, 290, 318, 364
Categorical model of classification, 277
Central nervous system, 60, 88, see also
 Brain
 and aging, 140
 alcohol and, 414, 446
 dysfunction of, 407
 and retardation, 507
Central tendency, measures of, 26, 29
Cerebellum:
 and alcohol, 414
 in autism, 489–490
Cerebral cortex, 60–61
Cerebral ventricles, 362, 378
Cerebrovascular accidents, 406, 409
Change, stages of, 445
Charcot, Jean Martin, 49–50, 52
Checking rituals, 171
Chemical change and paranoid thinking,
 338
Child abuse, 20, 452–453, 454, 557–560,
 585
 and retardation, 507
Childcare training, 552
Childhood disorders, 95, 449–483
 and adult disorders, 450
 anxiety disorders, 464–468
 attention deficit hyperactivity disorder,
 454–458
 conduct disorder, 458–464
 depression, 468–472
 eating disorders, 472–478
 therapy for, 478–481
Childhood experience and depression, 297
Childhood trauma, 481
Child neglect, 452–453
Child rearing techniques, 74
Children:
 eating disorders, 472
 institutionalization, 581
 rights of, 581
 suicide risk in, 314
 treatment of, 44–45
Chorionic villus sampling, 505, 512
Chromosomal abnormality, 512
Chromosomal anomalies, 58
Chromosome breaks, 443

Chromosome mutation, 500
Chromosome number 4, 398, 409
Chromosome number 19, 394
Chromosome number 23, 309
Chromosomes, 58, 88, 309
Chronic care model for schizophrenia, 347
Chronic mental illness, 570, 575
Churchill, Winston, 311
Circadian rhythms, 293
Civil commitment, 576, 579, 585
Civil rights and mental illness, 13, 35
Classical conditioning, 77–78, 88
 and alcohol treatment, 426
 behavior modification through, 523
 after rape, 136, 138
 in therapy, 182
Classification, 91–99, 121
 advantages and disadvantages, 92–93
 categorical model in, 277
 major categories of, 95–96
 of mental retardation, 496–498
 multiaxial approach to, 94–95, 96–98
 of personality disorders, 277, 280
 research on, 98–99
Classification system, characteristics of, 94
Claustrophobia, 164
Cleaning rituals, 171
Client centered therapy, 520, 546
Client factors:
 in clinical judgement, 99
 in therapy, 540
Clinical contact, reasons for, 28
Clinical interview, 99
Clinical judgement in diagnosis, 98–99
Clinical psychologist, 13
Clinical scales of MMPI, 111
Clinical trials, 543, 547
Clomipramine, 180
Clonidine, 435
Close relationships, 118
Clozapine, 343, 365
Cocaine, 436–438, 441, 442, 447
Cocaine Anonymous, 438
Cognitions, 117
 and depression, 300, 301, 305, 317
Cognitive abilities and alcohol, 418
Cognitive appraisals in alcohol use, 422
Cognitive assessment, 122, see also
 Intelligence testing
Cognitive behavioral approach to relapse
 prevention, 427–429
Cognitive behavioral group therapy, 547
Cognitive behavior therapy, 176–177, 183,
 302, 318, 546
 of anxiety disorder, 179
 and attention-deficit hyperactivity
 disorder, 482
Cognitive changes in frontal lobe disorders,
 386
Cognitive coping, 555
Cognitive deficits:
 in autism, 487, 489
 in fetal alcohol syndrome, 506
Cognitive development:
 in Down syndrome, 501
 in retardation, 494
Cognitive distortion model of depression,
 301–303, 305, 318
Cognitive distortion theory, 306
Cognitive function:
 in organic brain syndrome, 387
 in paresis, 399
Cognitive interference, 117
Cognitive Interference Questionaire, 117

Cognitive modification, 151, 153
Cognitive perspective, 57, 81–83, 88–89
 on alcoholism, 422–423
 on alcohol treatment, 427–429
 alcohol use and, 446
 on antisocial personality disorder, 269
 on anxiety disorders, 176–179, 183
 borderline personality disorder, 264
 on brain disorders, 407
 couples therapy, 531
 on depression, 301–303, 318
 on hallucinations, 330
 on sexual difficulty, 228
 on smoking, 445
 and suicide, 317
Cognitive processing in autism, 512
Cognitive psychotherapy, 546
Cognitive rehearsal, 176, 178, 183, 461
 and coping, 131
Cognitive restructuring, 177, 183
Cognitive skills training, 131
Cognitive social learning theory, 81
Cognitive therapy, 522–523
 for anorexia nervosa, 476
 for anxiety disorders, 177–179
 for childhood depression, 471–472
 for children, 480, 483
 for depression, 302–303, 307
 for panic disorder, 175
 for personality disorders, 280
Cognitive triad, 301, 318
Cognitive-behavior therapy, 524–528
Cohort membership and suicide, 471
College students:
 alcohol use by, 429, 430–431
 bulimia in, 477
 drug use surveys of, 441
 suicide risk, 314
Commitment, 575–581, 585
 protection from, 579
Communication:
 in autistic disorder, 486
 in schizophrenia, 328
 in sexual disorder, 227
Communication deviance, 371, 379
Communication skills training, 551
Community:
 prevention in, 585
 treatment in, 570–575
Community agencies as prevention forces, 565, 585
Community based care, 13
 and schizophrenia, 347
Community clinics for drug-dependence, 435
Community living programs for retarded individuals, 508–510
Community mental health services, 572
Community perspective, 57, 85–86, 90, 582
 on alcohol treatment, 425–426
 in alcohol use, 423
 on drug abuse, 435
 on schizophrenia, 374–375
 on smoking, 444
Community problems from maladaptive behavior, 9
Community programs:
 for alcohol abuse, 447
 problems with, 570–571
Community psychology, 90, 581–584, 586
Community strategies for alcohol use prevention, 429
Community support, 566

Comorbidity, 181, 183, 418
Compeer, 584
Competency, 576, 585
Competency focused prevention, 550, 585
Compulsion, 170, 182
 in children, 466
Compulsive personality, 274
Compulsive ritual, 170, 171, 172, 182
Compulsivity, 250
Computer Electroencephalographic Tomography scans (CET), 376
Computerized tomography, 57, 66, 386–387, 408
 of AIDS dementia complex, 396
 of alcoholics, 417
Concordance, 59
 for schizophrenia, 353
Concussion, 400, 409
Conditioned stimulus, 77
Conduct disorder, 6, 265, 458–461, 463–464
 in childhood, 450
 and hyperactivity, 456–457
Conduct disturbance and stress, 142
Confabulation, 390, 397, 408
Conflicts and mental illness, 49
Confounding, 26, 29
Congenital factors in retardation, 498, 512
Consciousness, altered state of, 520
Constitutional factors in retardation, 498, 512
Continuity of care, 570–571
Continuous Performance Test, 367–368, 379
Control, loss of, 135, 331
Control group in therapy research, 540, 541
Controlled drinking, 427, 428–429
Control scales of MMPI, 110
Contusions, brain, 400
Coping:
 with alcohol, 421–422
 and bereavement, 142–143
 cognitive skills training for, 131
 in depression, 298
 failure of, 56
 with peer pressure, 555
 posttraumatic, 145
 in self-help groups, 583
 techniques of, 131–132
Coping skills, 6–7, 12, 27, 28, 87, 121, 126–133, 140, 150, 152
 in alcohol treatment, 427
 for anorexia nervosa, 474–475
 for bulimia, 477
Coping strategy for Alzheimer's disease, 393
Coping style:
 for child depression, 471
 passive-aggressive, 276
Correlation, 20
Correlational studies, 19, 28
Correlation coefficient, 26
Cortex in autism, 489
Corticotrophin-releasing factor, 64
Cortisol in depression, 291–292
Counseling for spouse abuse, 560
Countertransference, 518–519, 546
Couples therapy, see also Marital therapy
 for sexual dysfunction, 228, 229–230
Covert modeling, 527, 546
Covert sensitization:
 and alcohol, 427, 447
 for paraphilia, 242
 for transvestism, 236

Crack babies, 437
Crack cocaine, 436–437, 447
Creativity:
 and bipolar disorder, 313, 319
 and mania, 310–311
Crime prevention training for police, 566
Criminal behavior, 267
Criminal commitment, 575, 576, 585
Crisis centers, 585
Crisis intervention in schizophrenia, 344
Criteria factors in clinical judgement, 99
Criticism and schizophrenia, 373
Cromwell, Oliver, 311
Cross-cultural view of homosexuality, 220, 246
Cross-dressing, 234, 235, 236, 247, see also Transvestism
Cross-fostering study, 356
Cross-sectional studies, 21
 high risk, 361
Cruikshank, George, 43, 44, 52
CT scan, see Computerized tomography
Cullen, William, 41–42
Cultural factors:
 in alcohol use, 423
 and expressed emotion, 373
 in suicide, 315
Cyclothymia, 282, 308, 319
Cytomegalovirus, 505, 512

D

Dangerousness, 8, 9, 579
Date rape, 136, 137
Day-care facilities for schizophrenia, 345, 346, 347
Day hospitalization, 349, 544, 571, 585
Decision-making in diagnosis, 98
Defense mechanisms, 72–74, 88
 and anxiety disorder, 174
 in obsessive-compulsive disorder, 182
Defensiveness scale of MMPI, 110, 111
Deinstitutionalization, 13, 28, 35, 48, 545, 547, 572, 574, 575, 585
 and community support, 570
 of retarded, 509, 513
 and schizophrenia, 347
Delinquency, 265, 553, see also Juvenile delinquency
 aggression in, 461
 and conduct disorder, 461
 and parental behavior, 557
Delirium, 387–389, 408
Delirium tremens, 388–389, 408
Delta waves, 61, 365
Delusional disorder, 95, 336
Delusions, 325, 326, 338
 and first-rank symptoms, 333
 in Huntington's disease, 398
 in paranoid schizophrenia, 336
Demand characteristics, 27, 29
Dementia, 389–397, 408
 causes of, 391–397
 in Down syndrome, 502
Dementia paralytica, see General paresis
Dementia praecox, 49, 52, 332, 335, 349
Dendrites, 60, 61
Denial, 73, 126
 as coping mechanism, 128–129
 and posttraumatic disorder, 144–145
 in stress, 141

symptoms of, 145
type of, 129
Deoxyribonucleic acid, 58–59, 88, 357
Dependence:
　on alcohol, 414–417, 424
　in borderline personality, 260–261
　physiological, 413, 414, 446
　psychological, 413, 414
Dependent personality, 251–252
Dependent personality disorder, 272–274, 278
Dependent variable, 17, 21–22, 28, 110, 533
Depersonalization, 147, 149–150, 152
　in borderline personality, 261
Depressant drugs, 442
Depression, 283–307, 318, see also Mood disorder
　in adolescents, 482
　from alcohol withdrawal, 424
　in Alzheimer's disease, 393
　in anorexia nervosa, 475
　behavioral perspective on, 298–300
　biological perspective on, 289–297
　in borderline personality, 262
　and bulimia, 476, 477
　in childhood, 450, 464, 468–472, 482
　cognitive perspective on, 300–306
　and cognitive therapy, 523
　in college students, 314
　delusional content in, 326
　compared to dementia, 390
　and drug withdrawal, 283
　early views, 40–41, 52
　in elderly, 140, 384
　humanistic-existential perspective on, 306
　in Huntington's disease, 398
　interactional approach, 87
　interactional perspective on, 307
　maternal, 470
　and opioid use, 434
　in panic disorder, 160
　psychodynamic perspective on, 297–298
　psychological theories of depression, 306–307
　psychosis in, 288
　after rape, 136
　in schizophrenia, 335
　separation and, 22–23
　and stressful events, 134, 142
　symptom overlap with anxiety, 180–181
　theories of, 289–307, 283–284, 318
　underdiagnosis of, 314
Depressive disorder, 285–286, 318, see also Mood disorders
　in childhood, 468–472
Description as a research method, 14–16
Descriptive statistics, 18, 26, 28–29
Desensitization, 546
　for epilepsy, 405
Desensitization hypothesis, 291, 318
Determinism, 76
Detoxification, 424, 446
　from opioids, 435
Developmental disorders, 96, 485–511
　autistic disorder, 485–494
　Axis II, 94
　mental retardation, 494–511
Developmental problems, 449–483
Deviance, perspectives on, 51–52
Deviant behavior, 5–6, 96
　and discrimination, 4–5
Dexamethasone suppression test (DST), 291–292

Dexedrine, 457, 482
Dextroamphetamine, 457
Diabetes and retardation, 505
Diagnosis, 92, 121
　of Alzheimer's disease, 395–396
　DSM Axis I, 94
　multiple, 181
　of panic disorder, 161
　process of, 100
　unreliability in, 93
Diagnostic and Statistical Manual of Mental Disorders, 94–98, 121, 272, 276, 277, 278, 309, 335, 356
　evaluation of multiaxial approach of, 96–98
Diagnostic and Statistical Manual of Mental Disorders-III, 94, 96, 97
Diagnostic and Statistical Manual of Mental Disorders-III-R, 94, 96, 97
Diagnostic and Statistical Manual of Mental Disorders-IV, 94, 96, 97, 122, 221
Diagnostic assessment of children, 481
Diagnostic categories, 95–96
　in DSM Axis I, 121
　in DSM Axis II, 121
　and violence, 11
Diagnostic criteria for schizophrenia, 333, 348–349
Diagnostic interview, 99
　with children, 451
Diagnostic Interview for Narcissism (DIN), 260
Diagnostic Interview Schedule (DIS), 103–104, 121
Diagnostic overlap, 181
Diathesis-stress model, 359, 378
Diazepam, 180
Diet:
　and hyperactivity, 457
　and phenylketonuria, 499
Diethyltryptamine, 438
Dieting in anorexia nervosa, 474
Dilantin, 405
Dimensional model of classification, 277
Dimethyl tryptamine, 438
DIS, see Diagnostic Interview Schedule
Disaster, reactions to, 136
Discrimination against mental illness, 4
Disease model of alcoholism, 426
Disorganized schizophrenia, 335
Disorientation, 393
Displacement, 73
Dissociation, 146
Dissociative disorders, 96, 126, 141, 146–150, 152
　diagnostic overlap in, 181
Disulfram, 425
Divorce, 550
　and child outcome, 561
　child preparation for, 561
　and depression, 284
　and immune system, 67
Dix, Dorothea, 45–46, 52
Dizygotic twins, 59
DNA, see deoxyribonucleic acid
Dollard, John, 81–82
Dominant genes, 512
Dopamine, 290, 318, 399
　and alcohol, 422
　and amphetamine, 364, 438
　in anorexia nervosa, 475
　and antipsychotic drugs, 365
　and cocaine use, 436
　and hallucinations, 330

　in hyperactivity, 457
　and vulnerability to schizophrenia, 361
Dopamine hypothesis, 363–364, 378
Dopamine receptors, 365
Dostoyevsky, Fyodor, 402
Double-blind method, 23, 543
Down syndrome, 58, 500–504, 512
Dreams, 152
　Freud's view of, 72
　and natural disaster, 145–146
　in posttraumatic disorder, 144
Drug abuse:
　in borderline personality, 262
　and homelessness, 572
Drug overdose in borderline personality, 262
Drug research, 542–543
Drugs:
　and paranoid thinking, 338
　and retardation, 505–506
Drug therapy, 537, 542–543
　for anxiety disorders, 179–181
　for depression, 307
　for hyperactivity, 458
　for schizophrenia, 343
Drug use:
　and conduct disorder, 460
　and genetic vulnerability, 361
　and hyperactivity, 457
　and suicide, 317, 471
　trends in, 441
Drug withdrawal and depression, 283
DSM, see Diagnostic and Statistical Manual
DTs, see Delirium tremens
Ductless glands, 63–64
Dynorphin, 433, 447
Dysfunction, 387
Dysfunctional thinking in depression, 302–303
Dyspareunia, 226
Dysphoric mood, 285
Dysthymia, 282, 286–287, 318

E

Early detection programs, 563–564
Early education programs, 551–552
Eating disorders:
　anorexia, 472, 482
　bulimia, 103, 472, 474, 475, 482
　in childhood, 450, 472
ECA study, see Epidemiological Catchment Area Study
Eccentric behavior, 257
Echolalia, 511
Economic cost of schizophrenia, 324
ECT, see Electroconvulsive therapy
Education about mental illness, 575
Education for All Handicapped Children Act, 508, 513
EEG, see Electroencephalogram
Ego, 70, 71, 74, 88, 150
Ego boundary, loss of, 330
Ego strength, 517
Electrical activity, brain, 366
Electrical skin conductance and expressed emotion, 374
Electrocardiograph, 365
Electroconvulsive therapy (ECT), 293, 295–297, 318, 537, 540–542, 547
Electroencephalogram, 60–61, 62
Electroencephalograph, 365
Ellis, Albert, 83, 177, 216, 522

Ellis, Havelock, 216
Emotion:
 inappropriate, 330
 in schizophrenia, 330
Emotional changes in adolescence, 139
Emotional numbing, 152
Emotional support as coping, 131
Emotions, 63
 exaggerated expression of, 259
Encounter groups and vulnerability, 361
Endocrine system, 63–64, 88
 in depression, 291–292
Endorphin, 63, 433, 447
Endorphin therapy for drug addiction,
 433
Enkephalin, 433, 447
Enlightenment, the, 40–42
Enthusiasm effect, 533, 547
Environment:
 and adult outcome, 564
 in anxiety disorders, 179
 and illness, 10
 role of, 60, 183
 and schizophrenia outcome, 342–348
 in schizophrenic disorder, 333
Epidemiological Catchment Area study,
 282–283, 307, 324
 and dysthymia, 286
Epidemiological study, 282
 of maladaptive behavior, 9–12, 28
Epilepsy, 34, 61, 402–406, 409
 and autism, 489, 512
Erectile dysfunction, 224, 230, 246
Erikson, Erik, 74
Escape responses, 77
Ethics in research, 29
Evaluation of therapy, 532–540
Exhibitionism, 241, 247
Existential perspective, 90
Existential therapies, 520, 546
Exit events and suicide, 317
Exorcism, 31–32, 52
Expectancy effect, 29
 in alcohol use, 422–423
Experiment in research, 22–23
Experimental studies, 21–26, 28
Exposure in social learning, 79
Exposure orientation to opioid use, 434–
 435, 447
Exposure therapy, 182, 526, 536, 546
 for anxiety disorders, 174–176
 for compulsive rituals, 176
 for obsessive-compulsive behavior, 174–
 175
 for phobia, 165, 174–175
Exposure training, 179
Expressed emotion, 371–373, 379
Expression, genetic, 356
Extinction, 76, 77, 546
 of anxiety, 175
 of fear response, 151
 of rape anxiety, 136, 138
Eye movements, smooth pursuit, 368
Eye tracking, 368, 379
Eysenck Personality Questionnaire, 239

F

F scale of MMPI, 110, 111
Factitious disorders, 96
Fading, 546

Family:
 adjustment to retardation, 495–496
 in anorexia nervosa, 474
 in child therapy, 451
 effect of Alzheimer's disease on, 390–
 391, 394–396
 effects of, 118
 as prevention site, 556–563, 585
 stress from, 370–371
Family communication in schizophrenia,
 371
Family dynamics, 529–531
Family education:
 and relapse prevention, 373
 in schizophrenia, 345, 346, 349
Family environment:
 and schizophrenia, 370–374, 375, 379
 and vulnerability, 360
Family Environment Scale, 118–119
Family stress:
 of epilepsy, 405
 and retarded child, 495
Family studies in schizophrenia, 352
Family system, 480, 531
 and alcoholism, 426
 and cocaine use, 438
Family therapy, 151, 153, 480, 483, 529–
 531, 547, 555
 and alcohol, 426, 447
 for anorexia nervosa, 474–475
 for personality disorders, 277, 280
 for retardation, 511
 in separation anxiety, 468
Family violence, prevention of, 566
Fantasies:
 Freud's view of, 72
 homosexual, 218
 in pedophilia, 242
 sadistic, 240
 sexual, 239
 in sexual behavior, 229
Fear, 22, 526
 of abandonment, 262
 in childhood, 464, 482
 compared to anxiety, 157
 compared to phobia, 162
 of illness, 161
 in panic disorder, 158–159
 paranoid, 257
 after rape, 136
Fetal alcohol syndrome, 418, 446, 506, 512
Fetishism, 234–235, 239, 247
Field trials for DSM, 96–97
First-rank symptoms, 333–334, 340, 349
Fixation, 70
Fixed-role therapy, 83, 90, 522, 546
Flashbacks, 152, 412
 from LSD use, 439–440
Flooding, 175, 183, 546
Fluoxetine, 295, 343
Folk healers, 32
Follow-up study, 21
 of hyperactivity, 456–457
 of opioid treatment, 436
Forgetting in Alzheimer's disease, 392
Foster home, 509, 513
Four A's in schizophrenia, 333
Fragile X syndrome, 500, 512
Free association, 72, 517, 546
Freud, Sigmund, 49–52, 81, 216, 297
Frontal lobe, 365
 and alcohol, 414
 tumors of, 402
Frustration tolerance, modeling for, 527

Fugue state, 147–148, 152
Full Scale IQ, 106, 109, 121
Functioning level, 95

G

GABA, 290, 409
Galen, 35
Gall, Franz Joseph, 41
Galton, Francis, 104
Galvanic skin response, 121
Gamma aminobutyric acid, see GABA
Gay activism, 218
Gay lifestyle, 217
Genain quadruplets, 375–377
Gender identity, 247
Gender identity disorder, 230–231
 in adults, 231–234
 of childhood, 231, 247
Gender nonconformity in childhood, 219–
 220
Gene locations in schizophrenia, 357
Generalized anxiety in childhood, 464
Generalized anxiety disorder, 156–158,
 161, 182
 compared to panic disorder, 160
General paresis, 399, 409
Genes, 58, 499
 mapping of, 58
Genetic basis:
 of Alzheimer's disease, 394
 Huntington's disease, 398–399
Genetic counseling, 357–359, 378
Genetic disorders, 499
Genetic factors, 58–60
 and alcoholism, 419–420, 446
 in anxiety disorders, 179, 183
 in autism, 490
 in epilepsy, 406
 and hyperactivity, 457
 in Pick's disease, 396
 in retardation, 494
 in schizophrenia, 337, 351, 356–359,
 375, 376, 378
Genetic heterogeneity, 357
Genetic liability, 357
Genetic risk for schizophrenia, 371,
 375
Genetic specificity, 378
 in schizophrenia, 353
Genetic testing, 398
Genital stage, 70
Genome, 58
George III, 41
Gestalt therapy, 521–522, 546
Gheel, Belgium, 36
Gilmore, Gary, 266–267
Gonadal glands, 63
Grand mal seizures, 403, 409
Grief, 142–143, 152
 and depression, 283
 process of, 143
 psychotherapy for, 143
Griesinger, Wilhelm, 49, 52
Group homes:
 for retarded, 509, 513
 for schizophrenia, 345
Group hysteria, 36
Group therapy, 528, 537, 546–547
 for Alzheimer caretakers, 395
 for anorexia nervosa, 474–475
 for bulimia, 477

for child abusers, 558
cognitive-behavioral, 529
for drug users, 440
for personality disorders, 280
in psychodrama, 532
GSR, *see* Galvanic skin response
Guided mastery, 176, 183
Guided rehearsal, 526, 546
Guilt, 283
and grief, 143
lack of, 266
in posttraumatic disorder, 144–145
and suicide, 319
of survivors, 135–136

H

Half-way houses, 51, 570, 572–573,
585
community response to, 575
for schizophrenia, 345
Hallucinations, 325, 328–330, 376
amphetamine use and, 438
and first-rank symptoms, 333
in Huntington's disease, 398
and psychedelic drug use, 438
from psychoactive substance use, 412
in schizophrenia, 332, 349
Hallucinogens, 447, *see also* Psychedelics
Halo effect, 112–113
Hamlet, 40
Hara-kiri, 316
Harvey, William, 40
Hashish, 440, 447
Headache, 190–193
in stress, 141
Head injury, 397
and epilepsy, 402
Health and alcohol, 417
Hearing loss and paranoid thinking, 338–
339
Hebephrenic schizophrenia, 335
Heinroth, Johann Christian, 49, 52
Helplessness, 306
Heredity:
and alcohol, 419–420
in Alzheimer's disease, 394
of anxiety disorders, 179
in autism, 490
of bipolar disorder, 309, 319
in childhood depression, 470, 482
of depression, 289
in epilepsy, 403
in Huntington's disease, 398–399
in mental retardation, 498, 499–500
role of, 60
of schizophrenia, 353
Heroin, 434, 435, 442, 447, 537
Herpes simplex, 512
and retardation, 505
Heterocyclics, 294, 318
Heterosexuality and sadomasochism, 239
Hierarchy, stimulus, 151
Hierarchy of needs, 90
High risk, *see* Vulnerability
High risk children, programs for, 507–
508
High risk parents, training for, 558–560
High risk studies of schizophrenia, 361–
362
Hippocampus in Down syndrome, 502
Hippocratic oath, 34

History of abnormal psychology, 31–53
Histrionic personality, 251–252
Histrionic personality disorder, 257–259,
263, 278
HIV, *see* Human immunodeficiency virus
Homelessness, 572–573
Homer, 34
Homicide, 19
Homosexual behavior, 217
Homosexuality, 215, 217–218, 246
attitudes toward, 220
and sadomasochism, 239
sexual problems in, 222
Hone, William, 43, 52
Hopelessness, 304, 306
Hopelessness depression, 304, 318
Hormones, 63–64
and brain growth, 218
and depression, 291–292
nicotine effects on, 444
sexual, 218
and sleep cycle, 65
Hospitalization:
antipsychotic drugs and, 344
psychiatric, 45, 48, 543–545, 585
stress of, 128–130
Hostility, 518
in Alzheimer's disease, 393
and suicide, 317
Hotline for smokers, 445
Huarte, Juan, 37–38, 52
Human immunodeficiency virus, 221, 222,
396
and sexual behavior, 217
Humanistic-existential perspective, 57, 83–
85, 90, 306
of depression, 318
Humanistic perspective, 90, 306
Humanistic therapies, 520, 546
Humor as coping, 131
Humors, four, 35, 52
Huntington's disease, 398–399, 409
Hyperactivity, 454, *see also* Attention-deficit
hyperactivity disorder
animal research and, 22
and conduct disorder, 461
family therapy for, 480
in retarded, 510
in schizophrenia, 331
Hypertension and retardation, 505
Hypervigilance, 177
in generalized anxiety disorder, 157,
158
in posttraumatic disorder, 145
Hypnosis, 52, 69, 520
Hypomania:
and creativity, 313
episodes of, 308
Hypothalamus, 63, 64, 366
in anorexia nervosa, 474–475
and sexual preference, 218
Hypothesis, 17
Hypothesis testing, 25, 28
Hypothetical constructs, 81
Hysteria, 49, 52, 69

I

ICD-10, *see* International Classification of
Diseases
Id, 70, 71, 88, 150
Ideal self, 306, 318

Identification:
with the aggressor, 73
in social learning, 79
Identity:
concepts in borderline personality, 262
disturbance of, 264
Illness, delusions of, 339
Illusions, bodily, 257
Imipramine, 180, 182, 537
for hyperactivity, 458
for panic attacks, 160, 162
Immune system:
and alcohol, 417
and loss, 66–67
Immunological processes, 66–67
Implicit learning, 80–81
Implosive therapy, 175, 183, 526, 546
Impulse control, 96
Impulsivity:
in antisocial personality disorder, 267
in borderline personality, 261
in hyperactivity, 455
in schizophrenia, 376
Inauthentic behavior, 85
Incest, 245–256, 247
Incidence, 10–12, 28
of depression, 284
of stroke, 406
Incompetent person, 576
Inconsistency and aggressive behavior, 557
Increased-stress theory, 375, 379
Indecisiveness in obsessive-compulsive
personality disorder, 274
Independent variables, 17, 21, 28, 110
Index case, 351, 378
Individual psychodynamic therapy, 537
Indolamine, 290, 318
Infections:
and brain disorder, 398–399
and retardation, 505
Inferential statistics, 18, 26, 28–29
Informational preview and stress, 131
Information-processing approach to
depression, 307
Information seeking as coping, 131
Informed consent, 581, 586
Insanity, 576, 585
ancient Greek view, 34
Insanity defense, 577, 578
Insight, 546
in therapy, 534
Insomnia in delirium, 387
Institute for Sex Research, 221
Institutionalization, 575–581
Intellectual functioning in bipolar disorder,
308
Intellectualization, 73
Intelligence:
in aging, 384
in autism, 492–493, 512
and childhood abuse, 452
in Down syndrome, 501
and fetal alcohol syndrome, 506
and phenylketonuria, 499
Intelligence quotient (IQ), 105, 121
Intelligence tests, 104–109, 121
interpretation of, 109
Intensive care partial hospitalization, 347
Interaction, staff-patient, 15
Interactional approach, 86–87, 90
Interactional orientation, 447
Interactional perspective:
on alcohol use, 423–424
on brain function, 382–385

Interactional perspective (*cont.*):
 on drug use, 413
 interactional perspective on depression, 307, 319
 on opioid use, 434
 on transsexualism, 234
Interfering thoughts:
 in anxiety disorder, 168–173, 177
 and sexual arousal, 230–234
Internalizing disorders, 464–472
 in children, 482
Internal reinforcement, 82
International Classification of Diseases, 95
Interpersonal psychotherapy, 298
Interpersonal relationships:
 in borderline personality, 261
 in schizophrenia, 331, 349
 stress from, 370–371
 in therapy, 538, 547
Interpretation in therapy, 519
Intervening variables, 81
Intervention sites, 585
Interview, 121
 as assessment, 99–104
 content of, 100–101
 techniques of, 216–217
Interviewer, task of, 101–103
Intoxication, 412
 alcohol, 415
 barbiturate, 432–433
 and delirium, 388
 in drug withdrawal, 388
Intravenous drug use, 433
Introspection, 517
Intrusive thinking, 145, *see also* Interfering thoughts
In vivo desensitization, 546
In vivo exposure, 175, 183, 526
IQ, *see* Intelligence quotient
Irrational thinking, 48, 52
Isolation, 174, 182

J

Jackson, Hughlings, 402
Janet, Pierre, 51, 52
Jellinek, E.M., 419
Job-related skills training, 552
Job training for retarded individuals, 509–510
Jones v. United States, 577
Jung, Carl, 74
Juvenile delinquency, 461, 553–556, 585

K

K-ABC, *see* Kaufman Assessment Battery for Children
Kanner, Leo, 487
Kaplan approach to sexual therapy, 229–230
Kappa statistic, 98
Karyotype, 58
Kaufman Assessment Battery for Children, 106–108, 121
Kelly, George, 82–83, 522
Kiddie SADS, *see* Schedule for Affective Disorders and Schizophrenia
Kinsey, Alfred, 216–217

Kinsey Report, 217
Klein, Melanie, 75
Kohut, Heinz, 75
Korsakoff's syndrome, 400, 409
Kraepelin, Emil, 49, 332, 366
K scale, *see* Defensiveness scale,

L

Labeling, 86, 90
 problems of, 92–93
La belle indifference, 49
Lacerations, brain, 400, 409
Language:
 in autistic disorder, 486, 489
 in Down syndrome, 501
 in schizophrenia, 369–370, 379
Language delay in retardation, 494
Latency period, 70
L-dopa, 64, 307, 399, 409
Learned helplessness, 304, 305
Learning:
 in Down syndrome, 501
 in hyperactivity, 456
Legal criteria for treatment, 575–581
Legal decisions for slow learners, 508
Legal incompetence, 585
Legal problems:
 and behavior, 9
 and clinical contact, 28
Lesbianism, 217, 219, 222
Level of significance, 29
Libido, 70, 88
Lie scale of MMPI, 110, 111
Life events, 6, 87
 and anxiety disorder, 158
 in schizophrenia, 370–371
 and stress, 130
 and suicide, 317
Life stress and separation anxiety, 468
Lifestyle differences and sexual orientation, 222
Life transitions, 20–21
 stress in, 152
Lifetime prevalence, 11
Light and depression, 312–313
Limbic system, 63
Lincoln, Abraham, 305
Lithium, 277, 294, 295, 309, 313, 319, 542, *see also* Antimanic drugs
Live modeling, 527, 546
Locus, gene, 58
Longitudinal studies, 20–21
 of alcohol abuse, 429
 of childhood depression, 469–470
 of high risk children, 361
 of intellectual function, 384
 of schizophrenia, 335
 of sexual identity, 231
 of sexual preference, 218
Long-term studies of schizophrenia, 339–342, 349
Loosening of associations, 349
Loss, 297
 and depression, 284
 in existential perspective, 306
 and grief, 283
 and illness, 66–67
 of motivation, 325
 and suicide, 317
 worry concerning, 272
LSD, 439–440, 441, 442, 447

Lymphocytes, 67
Lysergic acid diethyltrypatamine, 439

M

Magical powers and abnormal behavior, 31–33
Magical thinking, 257
 in schizophrenia, 325
Magnetic resonance imaging (MRI), 66, 386–387, 408, 489
Magnetism, animal, 42
Mainstreaming, of retarded individuals, 508, 513
Major depression, 282
Major depressive episode, 287–288, 318
Maladaptive behavior, 5–6, 27–28
 causes of, 382
 cognitive factors in, 177
 and disease, 67
 effect on family, 12
 genetic factors in, 58–60
 perspectives on, 55–89
 and social support, 132
 theories of, 55–89
Maladaptive thought, changing of, 151
Maladjustment, 6, 450
Malleus Maleficarum, 37, 39, 52
Mania, 285, 307, 312, 319
 characteristics of, 323
 delusional content in, 326
 drug related, 307
Manic-depressive disorder, *see* Bipolar disorder
Manic-depressive psychosis, 49, 52
Manic episode, 307, 308–309, 319
Manic state and cocaine use, 437
Manipulation:
 in borderline personality, 260–261
 in histrionic personality disorder, 258
MAO inhibitors, 295, 296, 318, 542, *see also* Antidepressant drugs
 and mania, 313
 for personality disorders, 277
Marijuana, 440–441, 442, 443, 447
Marital counseling, 560
Marital relationships and depression, 299
Marital status and depression, 284
Marital therapy, 529–531, 547
 communication skills training in, 551
Marker:
 of depression risk, 291
 genetic, 309
 for Huntington's disease, 398
 of schizophrenia risk, 361–370, 378
Masochism, 237–239, 247
Masters and Johnson approach, 227–228
Mastery ratings, 303
Masturbation and mental illness, 51
Maternal age and Down syndrome, 503
Maternal depression, 482
Mean, 26, 29
Measurement, psychophysiological, 365
Median, 26, 29
Mediators, thoughts as, 87
Meditation, 525–526
Medulla and alcohol, 414
Memories, Freud's view of, 72
Memory:
 in Alzheimer's disease, 392
 in autism, 489
 of early events, 450–451

Memory loss, temporary, 96
Mental age, 105
Mental Health, National Committee for, 47
Mental health and alcohol use, 418
Mental health services, 571–575
 in community, 570
Mental health specialists, 13–14, 28
Mental Hygiene, National Committee for, 47
Mental illness:
 causes of, 4–5
 in childhood, 451, 454
 in homeless, 572
 views of, 4–5
Mental retardation, 96, 494–511, 512
 and alcohol use, 418
 and autism, 487
 diagnostic overlap in, 181
Mental status evaluation, 100
Mental status examination, 386, 408
Mesmer, Franz Anton, 41–42
Meta-analysis, 538, 547
Metabolic changes and mania, 308
Metabolic disorder, 499
Metabolic dysfunction, 482
Metabolism and hyperactivity, 457
Methadone, 435, 447, 537
Method factors in clinical judgement, 99
Methylphenidate, 457
Meyer, Adolf, 333
Midbrain in autism, 489
Middle Ages, views of mental illness, 35–39
Milieu therapy:
 for antisocial personality disorder, 271
 for schizophrenia, 345, 349
Military combat and stress, 135, 152
Miller, Neal, 81–82
Mind, 57
 seat of, 34
Mind-body distinction, 57
Minnesota Multiphasic Personality Inventory, 110–111, 121
Minority groups, 11
Minuchin, Salvadore, 476
Mitochondria, 291
MMPI, see Minnesota Multiphasic Personality Inventory
MMPI-2, see Minnesota Multiphasic Personality Inventory
M'Naghten rule, 576–577, 586
Mode, 26, 29
Modeling, 79, 88, 176, 183, 526–528
 in alcohol use, 421–422
 in assertiveness training, 527–528
 cognitive aspects of, 176
 as prevention, 564
 in sex therapy, 228
Monoamine neurotransmitters, 289–290, 318
Monoamine oxidase (MAO), 290
Monoamine oxidase inhibitors, 294
Monogenic models, 356, 378
Monozygotic twins, 59
Mood disorder, 6, 96, 280–319
 in anorexia nervosa, 475
 behavioral perspective on, 298–300
 biological perspective on, 289–297
 bipolar disorder, 307–313
 and borderline personality, 263
 cognitive perspective on, 300–306
 depression, 283–285

depressive disorder, 285–286
diagnostic overlap in, 181
dysthymia, 286–287
humanistic-existential perspective on, 306
interactional perspective on, 307
major depression, 287–288
psychodynamic perspective on, 297–298
psychological theories of depression, 306–307
and suicide, 313–317
Moral development in antisocial personality disorder, 269
Moral treatment, 44
Moreno, Jacob, 532
Morphine, 433, 442, 447
Mosaicism, 502, 512
Mother-child interaction in hyperactivity disorder, 456
Motivation, 63
 in schizophrenia, 331, 349
Motor behavior in schizophrenia, 331
MRI, see Magnetic resonance imaging
Multiaxial classification, 94–98, 121
Multifactorial polygenic models, 356, 378
Multi-infarct dementia, 396, 408
Multiple personality, 147, 148, 152
Muscular relaxation, 525
Musical therapy, 36
Mutation, 498, 512

N

Naloxone, 433
Naltrexone, 435, 447
Narcissistic personality, 251–252
Narcissistic personality disorder, 259–260, 278
Narcotics, 434, 447
Narcotics Anonymous, 438
Narrow criteria for schizophrenia, 340
Natural disasters and stress, 135, 152
Natural fool, 38, 52
Negative events:
 and depression, 304
 and suicide, 317
Negative reinforcement, 76, 88
Negative symptoms, 325, 334, 349, 365
 and antipsychotic drugs, 365
 and ventricle enlargement, 363
Negative thoughts in depression, 301
Negative transference, 518
Nervous system, 60–64
 alcohol effects on, 420–421
Neuroanatomy, 64
Neurochemicals in Alzheimer's disease, 394
Neurochemistry, 64
 and antisocial personality disorder, 268
Neuroendocrinology, 64
Neurology, 386, 408
Neuron, 60, 61, 290
Neuropathology, 64
Neuropharmacology, 64
Neuropsychology, 64, 386
Neuroscience, 64, 66, 88, 291
Neurosis, 157, see also Anxiety disorders
Neurotransmitters, 60, 61
 in antisocial personality disorder, 268
 and brain disorder, 399
 and cocaine, 437
 and depression, 289–291
 function of, 291

and hyperactivity, 22, 457
 in Parkinson's disease, 399
 in schizophrenia, 363–365
 in sleep, 65
Nicotine, 442, 443–446, 447
Nicotine gum, 445
Nocturnal penile tumescence, 225
Noncompliance in medication, 343
Nontranssexual gender identity disorder, 231, 234, 247
Norepinephrine, 290, 318
 and alcohol, 422
 and amphetamine, 364
 in hyperactivity, 457
Null hypothesis, 29
Nutritional deficiencies and brain disorder, 400

O

Object relations, 75, 88
Obscene calls, 241, 247
Observation:
 as research method, 14–16
 and theory, 17
Observational data, 16–17
Observational learning, 79
Obsession, 170, 182
 in children, 466
Obsessional thought, 170–171, 172–173
Obsessive-compulsive disorder, 156, 157, 168–173, 182
 in children, 466–467, 482
 compared to phobias, 172
Obsessive-compulsive personality, 251–252
Obsessive-compulsive personality disorder, 274–275, 278
O'Connor v. Donaldson, 580
Oedipus complex, 216
Operant conditioning, 78, 88, 523
 for epilepsy, 405
Opiate receptors, 63
Opioid, 433, 442, 447
Opioid addiction, 434–435
Opioid receptor system, 433
Opium, 442
Oppositional defiant disorder, 460, 482
Oral-dependent personality, 421, 446
Oral-genital sexual behavior, 217
Oral stage, 70
Organic affective syndrome, 397
Organic anxiety syndrome, 397, 408
Organic brain disorders, diagnostic overlap in, 181
Organic brain syndrome, 387, 408
 characteristics of, 323
Organic delusional syndrome, 397, 408
Organic deterioration in schizophrenia, 332
Organic hallucinosis, 397, 408
Organic mental disorders, characteristics of, 387–397
Organic personality syndrome, 397, 408
Organismic view, 34–35, 52
Outcome in schizophrenia, 335, 337–342, 349
Outcome measures in therapy research, 534–536
Outreach program for homeless persons, 573
Overanxious disorder, 465–466, 482
Oxygen deprivation and delirium, 388

P

Pain, endorphins and, 433
Pancreas, 63
Panic attacks, 159, 182
 and agoraphobia, 167
 and cognitive therapy, 523
 features of, 159
 treatment for, 167–168
Panic disorder, 103, 156, 157, 158–162,
 see also Panic attacks
 symptoms, of 160
 treatment of, 178
Panic in stress, 141
Panic states:
 and crack cocaine use, 436
 treatment of, 151
Paracelsus, 37, 52
Paradoxical intention, 526, 546
Paranoia, amphetamine use and, 438
Paranoid delusions, 338–339
Paranoid disorder, 181, 337, see also Delu-
 sional disorder
 delusional content in, 326
 diagnostic overlap in, 181
Paranoid ideas, 257
Paranoid personality, 251–252, 338
 and schizophrenic spectrum, 353
Paranoid personality disorder, 253–254,
 257, 278, 337, 338
Paranoid schizophrenia, 335, 338, 349, 353
Paranoid thinking, 338
 in borderline personality, 261
 in elderly, 140
 in organic personality syndrome, 397
Paraphilia, 234–243, 247
Paraprofessionals, 582, 586
Parasuicide, 315, 319
 in mood disorder, 313
Parasympathetic nervous system, 295
Parens patriae, 579, 586
Parent, as point of intervention, 507
Parental adjustment, effect on children,
 557
Parental affective style, 373–374, 379
Parental conflict and child outcome, 560–
 561
Parenting skills training, 558
Parents Anonymous, 558
Parents as therapists, 561–563
Parkinson's disease, 64, 399, 409
Partial hospitalization, 349, 544
 and schizophrenia, 346, 347
Participant modeling, 176
Passive-aggressive personality, 251–252
Passive-aggressive personality disorder,
 275–276, 278
Past experiences and depression, 297–298
Patient rights, 580–591
Pavlov, Ivan, 77
PCP, 440, 442
Pedophilia, 242, 244, 245–246, 247
Peeping Tom, see Voyeurism
Peer pressure, 555
 and marijuana, 443
Pellagra, 400, 409
Penetrance, gene, 58–59, 356
Pennsylvania Hospital, 45
Perception:
 of aggression, 463
 and LSD use, 439
 and marijuana, 443
 and personality, 114

Perceptual distortions in schizophrenia, 330
Perfectionism, 275
 in obsessive-compulsive personality
 disorder, 274
Performance and stress, 142
Performance anxiety, 246
 and sexual dysfunction, 225–226
Performance IQ, 106, 109, 121
Peripheral nervous system, 60, 88
Perls, Fritz, 521–522
Permissiveness and aggressive behavior,
 556
Persecution, delusions of, 339
Personal constructs, 82, 83, 90, 522
Personal crises, 136–138
Personality:
 and alcoholism, 421
 assessment of, 110–115
 and brain disorders, 383
 Freud's theories of, 69–70
 and maturation timing, 454
Personality assessment, 110–115, 121
 ambiguous stimuli in, 113–115
 personality inventories, 110–111
 rating scales, 111–113
Personality change:
 and brain tumor, 402
 in frontal lobe disorders, 386
Personality disorders, 96, 250–279
 antisocial, 265–271
 avoidant, 271–272
 borderline, 260–265
 classification of, 251–253, 277
 dependent, 272–274
 DSM Axis II, 94
 histrionic, 257–259
 narcissistic, 259–260
 obsessive-compulsive, 274–275
 paranoid, 253–254
 passive aggressive, 275–276
 schizoid, 254–255
 schizotypal, 255–257
 and suicide, 471
 treatment of, 276–277
Personality factors and suicide, 317
Personality inventories, 110–111, 121
Persons non compos mentis, 38, 52
Perspectives on abnormal behavior, 55–89
 behavioral, 75–81
 biological, 57–68
 cognitive, 81–83
 community, 85–86
 humanistic-existential, 83–85
 interactional, 86–87
 psychodynamic, 68–75
 psychological, 7
Pervasive developmental disorders, 96
Petit mal seizures, 403, 409
PET scan, see Positron emission tomography
Phallic psychosexual stage, 70
Phencyclidine, 440, 447
Phenobarbitol, 405
Phenothiazines, 542, see also Antipsychotic
 drugs
Phenylketonuria, 499, 512, 553
Phobias, 162–168, 182, 526
 animal, 464–465
 categories of, 163
 in childhood, 450, 464, 482
 compared to obsessive-compulsive
 disorders, 172
 control of, 163
 psychodynamic view of, 173–174
 social, 464–465

Phobic disorder, 156, 157, see also Phobias
Phototherapy, 312–313, 319
Phrenology, 41, 52
Physical condition and brain disorders, 383
Physical symptoms, 96
 of anxiety, 157
 and grief, 143
Physiognomy, 41, 52
Physiological changes:
 in anorexia nervosa, 474–475
 in anxiety, 24
 in grief, 143
 during sexual responses, 222
 in stress, 134–136
Pica, 472
Pick's disease, 396, 408
Pinel, Philippe, 42–43
Pitt, William, 402
Pituitary gland, 63–64
Placebo, 23, 541, 543, 547
Plaques:
 in Alzheimer's disease, 392
 in Down syndrome, 502
Plato, 34–35
Play therapy, 478, 479, 483
Pleasure principle, 71, 81
Poets, mania in, 310–311
Polygenic models, 356, 378
Polygraph, 119, 120
Population genetics, 59
Positive reinforcer, 76
Positive symptoms, 325, 334–335, 349,
 365
Positive transference, 518
Positron emission tomography (PET), 57,
 65, 291, 292, 312, 365, 386–387,
 408
 of Alzheimer's disease, 395–396
 and hallucinations, 330
 in schizophrenia, 363, 364, 376
Posttraumatic disorders, 126, 141, 143–
 146, 152
Posttraumatic psychosis, 400, 409
Posttraumatic stress disorder, 145–146,
 152
Postvention, 317
Poverty of content in schizophrenia, 328,
 349
Preconscious, 71, 88
Predictability and stress, 135
Premarital counseling, 553, 560
Prematurity and retardation, 506
Prenatal factors in retardation, 494, 505–
 506, 512
Preschool enrichment programs, 85
Presenile dementia, 389, 392, 408
Presynaptic terminal, 291
Prevalence, 10–12, 28
 anorexia nervosa, 474
 childhood depression, 469
 childhood mental disorders, 451, 454
 conduct disorder, 461
 depression, 284–285, 286
 epilepsy, 403
 manic episode, 307
 of mood disorder, 282
 Parkinson's disease, 399
 personality disorders, 250–254
 schizophrenia, 324
 suicide, 314, 471
Prevention, 549–584
 Adler's view, 74
 of alcohol abuse, 429
 community programs, 565–575

and community psychology, 85
of conduct disorder, 461, 482
family intervention, 556–563
formula for, 584
legal aspects of, 575–581, 585
levels of, 552–556
of phenylketonuria, 499
of retardation, 507–508
and risk factors, 10–12
self-help groups and, 582–584
sites of, 556–569, 585
school programs, 563–565
society's role in, 581–584
types of, 546–586
Prevention programs:
 for alcohol abuse, 447
 for stress from divorce, 550
Prevention techniques for sexual assault,
 138
Primary appraisal, 126, 152
Primary degenerative dementia, 390, 408
Primary prevention, 552, 585
 for juvenile delinquency, 553–554
 in school programs, 564
Primary process thinking, 71, 75
Probability, 26
Problem drinking, see Alcohol abuse
Problem solving coping, 131
Problem solving in depression, 299, 300
Problem solving skills:
 in alcohol treatment, 427
 for children, 552
 for mothers, 552
Process research, 547
 in psychotherapy, 534
Prognosis in schizophrenia, 322, 335
Project Help, 573
Projection, 73
Projective techniques, 113–115, 121
Prototypal approach, 253
Prozac, see Fluoxetine 343
Psilocybin, 438
Psychedelics, 438, 442, 447
Psychiatric nurse, 13
Psychiatric social worker, 13
Psychiatrist, 13
Psychic determinism, 69, 88
Psychoactive drugs, 67
 for personality disorders, 280
Psychoactive substance dependence
 disorders, 412, 446
Psychoactive substances, 412, 446
Psychoactive substance use disorders, 95
Psychoanalysis, 69–75, 72, 88, 517, 545
 contemporary approaches, 74–75
 technique factors in, 538
Psychoanalytic theory, evaluation of, 75
Psychodrama, 531–532, 547
Psychodynamic perspective, 52, 57, 67–75,
 88, 318, 524
 alcoholism, 421
 alcohol treatment, 426
 anxiety disorders, 173–174, 182
 borderline personality disorder, 264
 brain disorders, 407
 depression, 297–298
 group therapy, 529
 hallucinations, 330
 homosexuality, 219
 marital therapy, 531
 paraphilia, 242
 phobia, 465
 schizophrenia, 376
 separation anxiety, 468

sexual problems, 229–230
 suicide, 317
 transvestism, 236
Psychodynamic therapy, 517, 536
 bulimia, 477
 childhood depression, 471
 depression, 297–298
 exhibitionism, 241
 personality disorders, 277, 280
 schizophrenia, 343, 349
 sexual dysfunction, 247
Psychogenic amnesia, see Amnesia
Psychogenic fugue, see Fugue
Psychological adjustment and sexual
 preference, 220–221
Psychological conflict and phobia, 173
Psychological dependence, 424
Psychological disorders and aging, 140
Psychological perspective on autism, 487,
 489
Psychological problems of retarded
 individuals, 510–511, 513
Psychological responses and stressful events,
 134
Psychological theories:
 of depression, 319
 of suicide, 316
Psychological therapy:
 for depression, 307
 effectiveness, 537
 research on, 532–540
Psychology of personal constructs, 546
Psychomotor epilepsy, 403, 409
Psychomotor retardation, 335
Psychoneuroimmunology, 66–67, 88
Psychophysiological disorders, 96, 186–205
 allergies, 203–204
 cancer, 202–203
 cardiovascular disorders, 193–202
 gastrointestinal disorders, 204–205
 headaches, 190–193
 immune system and, 203
Psychophysiological measurement, 365
Psychophysiological responses, 365
 in schizophrenia, 365–366
Psychosexual development, 70, 216
 stages of, 70, 74
Psychosis, 95, 96, 323, 348, 409
 amphetamine use and, 438
 childhood, 487, 512
 and cocaine use, 436
 delusions in, 326
 and high risk offspring, 557
 in retarded individuals, 510
 posttraumatic, 400
Psychosocial factors in retardation, 494,
 495, 507–510, 512, 513
Psychosocial stages, 74
Psychosocial stressors, 94
Psychosocial theory, 88
Psychosomatic disorders, 525
Psychotherapist, tasks of, 516
Psychotherapy, 84, see also Cognitive
 therapy, Existential therapies,
 Humanistic therapy, Psychodynamic
 therapy, Psychological therapy
 alcohol problems, 426, 447
 anorexia nervosa, 474–475
 antisocial personality disorder, 269–270
 brief, 537
 cocaine use, 438
 delusional disorder, 339
 depression, 302
 epilepsy, 405

obsessive-compulsive personality disorder,
 275
 retarded individuals, 511, 513
Psychotherapy research, meta-analysis and,
 538
Psychotic behavior, causes of, 323
Psychotic depression, characteristics of, 323
PTSD, see Posttraumatic stress disorder
Public opinion poll, 21
Punishment, 76, 88
Purging, 474, 477
Pussin, Jean-Baptiste, 43

Q

Quality of Relationships Inventory, 118–
 119
Questionnaires compared to interviews, 217

R

Racial difference in alcohol metabolism, 421
Rape, 136, 243–244, 247, 462–463
 and posttraumatic stress disorder, 145
 stress from, 152
Rape relief centers, 138
Rapid eye movement (REM) sleep, 293
 in depression, 293
 and penile erection, 225
Rapport in interview, 100
Rating scales, 111–113, 121
 for behavior, 112
Rational emotive therapy, 83, 90, 177,
 522–523, 546
Rational thinking, 48, 52
Reaction formation, 73, 174, 182
Reaction time in schizophrenia, 366
Reactive psychosis, 323
Reactivity, 26–27, 29
Realism in depression, 305
Reappraisal as coping, 131
Receptors:
 for anti-anxiety drugs, 180
 for neurotransmitters, 291
Reference, ideas of, 257
Reform movement, 52
 England, 43, 44
 France, 42–43
 United States, 45–47
Regression, 70, 73
Rehabilitation model for schizophrenia,
 347, 348
Rehabilitation of offenders, 553
Reinforcement, 76, 78, 88
 by alcohol, 421
 in behavior therapy, 523
 of problem behaviors, 116
 schedule of, 78–79
 of sex appropriate behavior, 231
Rejection:
 and aggressive behavior, 557
 fear of, 271
Relapse and expressed emotion, 373
Relapse prevention:
 in alcohol treatment, 427
 programs for, 427–428
Relational assessment, 118–119, 122
Relationship, therapeutic, 150, 517, 518,
 536, 540
Relationship patterns and homosexuality,
 221–222

Relationships:
 for delinquency prevention, 555
 and depression, 297, 298
 homosexual, 246
 and hyperactivity, 456
 as social support, 152
 and stress, 141
 and suicide, 314
 unstable, 264
Relationship survival and rape, 136
Relaxation training, 151, 153, 525, 546
 and bulimia, 477
 for epilepsy, 405
 in sex therapy, 228
Reliability, 15
 of diagnosis, 93, 98, 253
Religious preoccupation, 3, 8
Remissions, spontaneous, 534
REM sleep, see Rapid eye movement sleep
Renaissance views of mental illness, 39–40
Rennie v. Klein, 580
Report writing, 108–109
Repression, 72, 75, 88
Research:
 ethical aspect of, 27, 29
 methods of, 18–27
 steps in, 17–18
Resocialization, 544, 572
Response prevention, 176
Retarded ejaculation, 226
Retrograde amnesia, 397
Risk:
 for Alzheimer's disease, 392
 for bipolar disorder, 309
 genetic, 358
 of schizophrenia, 352
Risk-benefit analysis in therapy choice,
 542–543
Risk factors, 10, 11, 28
 for childhood mental illness, 454, 481
 for depression, 284–285, 289, 318
Ritalin, 457
 in attention-deficit hyperactivity disorder,
 482
Rituals:
 in children, 466
 in obsessive behavior, 177
 in obsessive-compulsives, 168, 170, 171
Rogers, Carl, 84–85, 521
Role models and delinquency, 553
Role play, 79–80, 88, 302, 523, 524, 532
 in separation anxiety, 468
 for treatment of depression, 299, 300
Roles, multiple, 306
Roosevelt, Theodore, 311
Rorschach inkblots, 113–114, 121
Rubella virus and retardation, 505
Rumination disorder of infancy, 472
Rumination in obsessive-compulsive
 behavior, 169
Rush, Benjamin, 45, 52

S

SAD, see Seasonal affective disorder
Sadism, 237–239, 247
Sadomasochism, 239
Safe sex practices, 222
Saint Augustine, 36–37, 52
Salpetriere, 43
Sampling in research, 27
Scanning techniques, 292–294

and autism, 489–490
and brain assessment, 362, 386
detection of genetic defects by, 504
Schedule for Affective Disorders and
 Schizophrenia, 471
Schemata, 81, 89, 302
Schizoaffective disorder, 325, 337, 349
 and schizophrenic spectrum, 353
Schizoid personality, 251–252
Schizoid personality disorder, 254–255,
 257, 278
Schizophrenia, 95, 181, 321–361, see also
 Schizophrenic disorders
 aftercare for, 570
 and borderline personality, 263
 causes of, 351–361
 characteristics of, 323
 childhood, 450, 487, 512
 chronic, 322
 and crack cocaine use, 436
 delusional content in, 326
 depression in, 283
 diagnostic overlap in, 181
 interactional approach, 87
 post-discharge care, 553
 rate of, 9
 risk in schizotypal disorder, 257
 social skills and, 26
Schizophrenias, the, 332–333, 349
Schizophrenic disorders, 321–348, 351–
 377, see also Schizophrenia
 attributes of, 362–370
 characteristics, 325–332
 community role in, 375
 diagnostic criteria for, 324–325
 family relationships and, 370–374
 genetic factors in, 351–359
 high risk studies of, 361–362
 historical view, 332–335
 impact of, 322–324
 long term studies of, 337–342
 markers of, 361–362
 outcome indicators of, 337–342
 treatment of, 342–348
 types of, 335–337
 vulnerability for, 359–361
Schizophrenic episodes, recovery from, 322
Schizophrenic spectrum disorder, 337, 349,
 353, 356
 thought disorder in, 369
Schizophreniform disorder, 325, 349
Schizotypal personality disorder, 255–257,
 263, 278, 325, 337, 349
 and schizophrenic spectrum, 353
Schneider, Kurt, 333, 340
School as prevention site, 585
School dropout, 564–565
School programs as prevention, 507–508
 for delinquency prevention, 554
Scoring profile on MMPI, 111
Seasonal affective disorder (SAD), 312
 and depression, 319
Seattle Longitudinal Study, 384
Seclusiveness, 271, 334
Seconal, 432
Secondary appraisal, 126, 152
Secondary prevention, 553, 585
 children, 563–564
Secondary process thinking, 71
Second generation antidepressants, 318
Second rank symptoms, 334, 349
Seizures, epileptic, 409
Self:
 boundaries of, 330–331, 349

in depression, 297
development of, 260
sense of, 263
Self-actualization, 83–84
Self-care skills in schizophrenia, 344
Self-concept in depression, 306
Self-destructive behaviors in borderline
 personality, 261
Self-determination, 84
Self-disclosure, 528
Self-efficacy, 81, 525
Self-esteem:
 in depression, 318
 and job performance, 564
 in narcissistic personality disorder, 260
 of retarded, 511
Self-evaluation, negative, 301–303
Self-help groups, 582–583, 586
Self-help techniques for social phobia, 166
Self-image, 84, 90
Self-monitoring, 15–16
 and bulimia, 477
Self-mutilation, 262
Self-observation, 15–16, 28
Self-perception in depersonalization, 149
Self-psychology, 75, 88
Self-references in depression, 300
Self-regulation, 82, 90
Self-schemata, 81
Self-stimulation, 491
Senile dementia, 389, 408
Senile disorders, 384
Sensate focus, 227, 246
Sensitivity to alcohol, 421
Sensitivity training and vulnerability, 361
Sensitization, see Systematic desensitization
Sensory deprivation, 388
Sentence completion technique, 115
Separation anxiety, 467
 and agoraphobia, 168
 in childhood, 464
Separation anxiety disorder in children,
 467–468, 482
Serotonin, 290, 318
 and ECT, 295
Serotonin receptors and antipsychotic drugs,
 365
Sex differences:
 adolescent disorders, 454
 alcohol effects, 446
 alcohol metabolism, 421
 anorexia nervosa, 473
 childhood depression, 469
 childhood disorders, 454
 depression, 284, 285
 mental disorders, 9, 11
 mood disorders, 318
Sex offenders, 247
Sex therapy, 226–230
 effectiveness of, 230
Sexual abuse, 535
 child, 242, 243–245
Sexual arousal:
 inhibition of, 224
 interfering thoughts and, 230–234
 in paraphilia, 234
Sexual behavior, 215–245, 246
 bisexuality, 223–224
 changing views of, 216
 dysfunction in, 224–230
 and gender identity disorder, 230–234
 homosexuality, 217–222
 paraphilias, 234–243
 sexual victimization, 243–246

surveys of, 216–217, 246
Sexual disorder, 96, 246, *see also* Sexual dysfunction
Sexual dysfunction, 224–230, 246
 after rape, 136, 138
 types of, 224
Sexual excitement, inhibition of, 224, 246
Sexuality in psychoanalytic theory, 70
Sexual offender, 243
Sexual orientation, development and, 219–220
Sexual practices, surveys of, 216–217
Sexual preference, 219, 246
 development of, 218–220
 and psychological adjustment, 220–221
Sexual-reassignment surgery, 232–235
Sexual response:
 homosexual, 246
 and sexual orientation, 222
Sexual-retraining techniques, 227
Sexual self-identification, 218
Sexual victimization of children, 244
Shakespeare, William, 40
Shaman, 32, 33, 52
Shaping, 78
 in behavior therapy, 523
Sheltered workshops for retarded individuals, 510, 513
Ship of fools, 43
Side effects:
 of antidepressants, 296
 of drug treatment, 542
 of ECT, 295
 of MAO inhibitors, 295
 of tricyclics, 180, 294–295
Significance, level of, 26
Simple phobias, 164–165, 182
Situation-focused prevention, 550, 585
Skills for coping, 131
Skinner, B.F., 78, 174
Sleep, 61, 293, *see also* Rapid eye movement sleep
 antidepressant effects of, 312
 in posttraumatic disorder, 144
 and stress, 142
Sleep deprivation:
 and delirium, 388
 and depression, 293, 312
 and mania, 312
 and vulnerability, 361
Sleep disorder, 95
Sleep disturbance:
 and depression, 293
 and mania, 319
Sleep patterns, 65
 in elderly, 140
Sleep problems:
 in depression, 287
 in dysthymia, 287
 treatment for, 65
Sleep stages, 65
Smoking, 447
 and health, 444
Smoking cessation programs, 444
Smooth pursuit eye movements, 379
Social anxiety, 257
 and alcohol, 22–23
Social behavior in neglected children, 453
Social causation theory, 85, 374
Social facilitation, 79
Social integration and suicide, 317, *see also* Social network, Social support
Social intervention, 151, 153

Social isolation, 254
 in schizophrenia, 325
Socialization and sexual orientation, 219
Social learning, 528
 for fears, 465
 and hospital treatment, 544
Social learning theory, 79–81, 88
Social network 87, *see also* Social integration, Social support
 and outcome, 342
 and retarded individuals, 510
Social phobia, 164, 165–166, 182, 272
 and panic disorder, 181
Social roles, 86, 90, 299
Social selection theory, 374–375, 379
Social services for schizophrenia, 348
Social skills, 26
 in autistic disorder, 486, 489
 in child therapy, 471
 in depression, 299, 305
 and prevention, 463
 in schizoid personality, 254
 in schizophrenia, 331
 in schizotypal personality disorder, 256
 school programs for, 508
 and social support, 133
Social skills training, 537
 for depression, 299–300, 318
 as prevention, 564
 for retardation, 510, 511, 513
 for schizophrenia, 344, 349
Social support, 85, 132–133, 152, 582, *see also* Social integration, Social network
 and alcohol, 447
 in alcoholism rehabilitation, 426
 and brain disorders, 383
 and depression, 284
 after hospitalization, 570
 and illness, 12
 and retarded individuals, 510
 in treatment process, 150
Social Support Questionnaire, 132–133
Social ties, 132
Social withdrawal, 20–21, 257
 in schizophrenia, 331
Socioeconomic status:
 and schizophrenia, 374–375
 and stressful life events, 134
Sociological theories of suicide, 316
Socratic method, 34, 35
Sodium lactate, 162
Somatic symptoms disorders, 6
Somatic system, 60
Somatic therapies, 13
Somatoform disorders, 96, 205–208
 conversion disorders, 208
 hypochondriasis, 206–207
 psychogenic pain disorder, 205–206
 somatization disorders, 207–208
Sonogram, 504
Soto family, 398
Special-education classes, 508
Specific developmental disorders, 96
Spectrum concept, 378
 of schizophrenia, 353
Speech:
 in autism, 490
 bizarre, 369
 poverty of, 334
 in schizophrenia, 326–328, 334, 369–370
Spina bifida, 505

Spinoza, Baruch, 40
Splitting, 75, 264
Spouse abuse, 560, 585
Squeeze technique, 228
Stages of change, 447
Stages of development, 74
Standard deviation, 26
Standardized interview, *see* Structured interview
Stanford-Binet scales, 105
State hospitals, 12
Stereotypy, 22
Stigma of mental illness, 4–5
Stimulant drugs, 442
 amphetamine, 438
 cocaine, 436
Stimulant medication and hyperactivity, 22, 457
Stimulus-response, 76
STP, 447
Stress, 6–7, 27, 28, 56, 121, 125–152
 and adjustment disorder, 141–143
 of Alzheimer caretakers, 394
 in anorexia nervosa, 475
 arousal of, 134–140
 and brain disorders, 383
 and bulimia, 477
 clinical reactions to, 140–150
 cognitive modification for, 152
 coping, 131–132
 and delirium, 388
 and depression, 284, 298, 304
 and dissociative disorders, 146–150
 in divorce, 550, 561
 extreme, 136
 from life transitions, 138–140
 long-term effects of, 135–136
 and mania, 308
 medication for, 152
 modeling for, 527
 and paranoid thinking, 338
 posttraumatic, 143–146
 reactions to, 152
 relaxation treatment for, 152
 responses to, 140
 and schizophrenia, 359–361, 373
 from schizophrenic parent, 353
 and seizures, 404
 situational, 134–146, 152
 social intervention for, 152
 social support and, 132–133
 supportive therapy for, 151–152
 systematic desensitization for, 152
 treatment of, 150–151
 vulnerability to, 126–130, 359
Stress coping in borderline personality, 262
Stress disorders, 140–150
Stress management for family members, 373
Stressor, 64
Stress response and personality, 136
Stroke, 406, 409
Structured interview, 100, 103
 with parents, 471
Sublimation, 73
Substance abuse disorders, 412, 446
Substance dependence, 413, 446
Suicidal behavior in borderline personality, 261
Suicide, 181, 295, 313–317
 in adolescence, 470–471
 and antisocial personality disorder, 268
 and bipolar disorder, 310–311, 313, 319
 in borderline personality, 265
 causes of, 313–317, 319

Suicide (*cont.*).
in childhood, 470–471
in childhood depression, 482
in depression, 296, 319
and divorce, 550
impact on others, 316, 317
public acceptance of, 315–316
risk for, 567, 568
in schizophrenia, 324
and sexual orientation, 218
in unipolar disorder, 313
Suicide postvention, 569, 585
Suicide prevention, 566–568, 585
Suicide threats in borderline personality, 262
Sullivan, Harry Stack, 333
Superego, 70, 71, 75, 88
in depression, 297
Supernatural and mental illness, 41
Support, therapist, 535
Supportive therapy, 153
and cocaine use, 438
for stress-related problems, 150–151
Support programs, 85
for Alzheimer caretakers, 395
for divorced individuals, 550
Support seeking in depression, 298
Surrogate parent model, 346, 349
Survey research, 216–217, 282
Survivor stress, 316, 317
Suspiciousness, 257
in Alzheimer's disease, 393
and stress, 142
Symbolic modeling, 465, 482, 527, 546
Symptom disorders, 251
Synapse, 60, 61, 290
Syndrome, 387, 408
Syphilis, 399, 409
and retardation, 505
Systematic desensitization, 151, 153, 175, 182, 526, 546
for personality disorders, 280
in sex therapy, 228

T

Tardive dyskinesia, 342, 343, 349
TAT, *see* Thematic Apperception Test
Tay-Sachs disease, 499, 512
Technique factors:
in interview, 100
in therapy, 538, 539–540, 547
Teenage mothers, training for, 552
Temperament, 126, 128, 152
Temporal lobes:
in epilepsy, 405
in schizophrenia, 363
Tertiary prevention, 553, 585
THC, *see* Marijuana
Thematic Apperception Test, 114–115, 121, 371
Theoretical perspectives, *see* Perspectives on abnormal behavior
Theory:
in abnormal psychology, 56–57
role of, 17, 28
Therapeutic approaches:
integration of, 532
for schizophrenia, 349
Therapeutic interview, 99
Therapies, 516–547
comparison of, 536–538, 547

evaluation of, 21, 519, 536–540
Therapist, role of, 536–537
Therapist factors, 539, 540
Therapy, *see also* Treatment, specific types of therapy
for adolescents, 477–481, 483
for anorexia, 475–477
for autism, 490–492, 512
for bulimia, 477–478
for children, 477–481, 482–483
for depression, 294–297
effectiveness of, 538
in Down syndrome, 500
informed consent in, 581
research methods for, 519
for schizophrenia, 342–348
Therapy methods, 515–545
behavioral, 523–524
biological, 540–543
cognitive behavioral, 524–528
group, 528–532
and hospitalization, 543–545
marital therapy, 529–531
psychotherapy, 516–523
research on, 532–540
Therapy outcome, 539
for children, 481, 483
Theta waves, 61
Thought content in panic attacks, 160, 161
Thought disorder, 326–328, 368–369, 379
Thought disorder index, 368, 369
Thought sampling, 117
Thought stopping, 178, 183
Threat to others, 3, 8
Thyroid gland, 63
Time-out procedure, 492
Time sampling, 15
Tissue implantations, 399
Token economy, 524, 546
Tolerance:
to amphetamines, 447
for cocaine, 437
drug, 413, 432, 446
Top-down studies, 470
Training programs:
for anxiety management, 179
for retarded, 510
Tranquilizers, 432–433, 433, 442, 447
for anxiety disorders, 180, 183
lethality of, 314
for stress, 151
Transactions, family, 531
Transference, 518–519, 546
Transitions, life, 138–140
Translocation, 502, 512
Transsexualism, 231–234, 235–237, 239, 247
Traumatic events, 135, 145
and amnesia, 147
and behavior, 70
in childhood, 451
emotional support for, 145
and multiple personality, 148–149
and posttraumatic disorder, 143–144
reactions to, 136
Traumatic neurosis, 400, 409
Traumatic paralysis, 50
Treatment, *see also* Behavioral therapy, Biological therapy, Cognitive therapy, Existential therapy, Psychodynamic therapy, Psychological therapy
for alcohol use, 424–429

of Alzheimer's disease, 395–396
of antisocial personality disorder, 269–271
of anxiety disorder, 177
of bipolar disorder, 313, 319
of borderline personality disorder, 264
of brain disorder, 407
of bulimia, 477–478
of childhood depression, 471
for childhood mental illness, 454
for cocaine dependence, 438
of conduct disorder, 461
of dissociative disorders, 150
effectiveness of, 580
of epilepsy, 405
family focus in, 585
of fear, 465
legal aspects of, 575–581, 585
for opioid dependence, 435
of personality disorders, 276–277, 278–279
for psychedelic abuse, 440
rates of, 9–10
reasons for, 7–9
right to discontinue, 581
safety of, 580
of schizophrenia, 324, 342–348
of sexual dysfunction, 226–230
for smoking cessation, 444
of stress, 152
of stress-related problems, 150
Treatment facilities, 28
types of, 12–13
Treatment of Depression Collaborative Research Program, 307–313
Trephination, 33–34, 52
Tricyclic drugs, 183, 294–295, 318, 542, *see also* Antidepressant drugs
for children, 472
and mania, 313
for treatment of anxiety, 180–181
Trisomy 13, 500
Trisomy 18, 500
Trisomy 21, *see* Down syndrome
Tuberous sclerosis, 499, 512
Tumor, 397
Twins:
autism in, 489, 490
depression in, 289
schizophrenia in, 352, 353–354, 363
studies of, 378
ventricle size, 363
Two-headed, 32
Tyramine, 295

U

Ultrasound scan, 504, 512
Unconditional positive regard, 522, 546
Unconditioned response, 77
Unconscious, 40, 71, 88
Unconscious mental processes and phobia, 173
Unconscious thought, 147
Undoing, 174, 182
Unemployment, effects of, 134
Unhappiness, 8, 28
Unipolar disorder, 285, 309, 318, *see also* Mood disorder, depression

V

Vaginismus, 226
Validity of diagnosis, 98
Validity scales of MMPI, 110, 111
Valium, 180, 183, 433
Variability, measures of, 26
Verbal IQ, 106, 121
Verbal Score, 109
Vesicles, 290
Vicarious learning, 79, 528
Victimization:
 experiences of, 138
 and posttraumatic stress disorder, 145
 by rape, 137
 sexual, 243–246
 strategies for recovery from, 138
 stress from, 152
Vietnam veterans, 145
Violent behavior:
 contributors to, 10, 11
 and mass media, 19
Visual analogue scale, 112
Vitamin deficiency in brain disorder, 400,
 409
Volunteers, support from, 584
Voodoo, 32
Voyeurism, 240–241, 247

Vulnerability, 6–7, 27, 28, 56, 86–87,
 121, 126–133, 152, 582
 to alcohol, 424
 to brain disorders, 382–384, 408
 and coping, 132
 in dissociative disorder, 150
 and family environment, 360
 markers of, 366
 to schizophrenia, 222, 337, 356, 359–
 361, 365, 371

W

WAIS-R, *see* Weschler Adult Intelligence
 Scale
Wakefulness, 65
Wandering in Alzheimer's disease, 393
Watson, John B., 75–76
Waxy flexibility, 336
Weight change and depression, 287, 318
Weschler Adult Intelligence Scale, 106,
 121
Weschler Intelligence Scale for Children,
 106, 121
Weschler Preschool and Primary Scale of
 Intelligence, 106, 121
Weschler tests, 106, 121

Weyer, Johann, 39–40
WISC, *see* Weschler Intelligence Scale for
 Children
Witchcraft and mental illness, 37, 38
Witches' Hammer, 37
Withdrawal, 145, 412, 446
 alcohol, 424
 drug, 413
 nicotine, 444
 social, 142
Women, role of, 51
Woolf, Virginia, 313
Word association test, 115
WPPSI, *see* Weschler Preschool and Primary
 Scale of Intelligence
Wyatt v. Stickney, 580

X

X chromosome, 499

Y

Y chromosome, 500

Diagnosis: A Mirror of Changes in Thinking About Disordered Behavior

Concepts of abnormality are not static. They change over time as knowledge accumulates and the dominant theoretical perspectives change. These differences in how we think about disordered behaviors, their causes, symptoms, and possible outcomes have an impact on the way the disorders are classified or grouped together. The changes in the American Psychiatric Association's <u>Diagnostic and Statistical Manual of Mental Disorders</u> (DSM) mirror changes that have occurred since the first DSM was published in 1952. DSM-I and DSM-II sought diagnosis on the basis of causes of disorders. DSM-III, DSM III-R, and DSM-IV have focused attention primarily on describing the various disorders, many of whose causes are as yet unknown.

A Brief History of the <u>Diagnostic and Statistical Manual of Mental Disorders</u> (DSM)

DSM Version	Date Published	Classification Focus
DSM-I DSM-II	1952 1968	Both of these classifications emphasized the person's unconscious processes (defense mechanisms, psychodynamics, anxiety, residues of childhood trauma) and reflected a psychodynamic perspective.
DSM-III	1980	Instead of a theoretical focus, this revision emphasized descriptions of behavior. It used a multiaxial approach in classifying a person's behavior, current level of functioning, past and present stress, and social support.
DSM-III-R	1987	Continued the multiaxial approach modified to increase diagnostic reliability and to provide standardized clinical diagnostic criteria.
DSM-IV	1994	A fine tuning of DSM-III-R with increased emphasis on user friendliness.

Not only has the DSM changed, but its coverage (the number and types of disordered behaviors it includes) has also changed dramatically. DSM-I and DSM-II dealt with only a limited array of disorders. DSM-III, DSM-III-R, and DSM-IV have each included a progressively broader coverage.

The Change in DSM Coverage from 1952 to 1994

DSM-I

Acute Brain Disorders
Chronic Brain Disorders
Mental Deficiency
Psychotic Disorders
Psychophysiological Disorders
Neurotic Disorders
Personality Disorders
Acute (transient) Disorders

DSM-IV

Childhood Disorders (including infancy and adolescence)
Cognitive impairment disorders
Substance related disorders
Schizophrenia and other psychotic disorders
Mood disorders
Anxiety disorders
Somatoform disorders
Factitious disorders
Dissociative disorders
Sexual disorders
Gender identity disorders
Sleep disorders
Eating disorders
Impulse control disorders
Adjustment disorders
Personality disorders